GUIDE TO

DISTANCE

LEARNING

PROGRAMS

2001

www.petersons.com

UNIVERSITY CONTINUING EDUCATION ASSOCIATION

Published in cooperation with the
University Continuing Education Association

PETERSON'S
★
THOMSON LEARNING ™

Australia • Canada • Mexico • Singapore • Spain • United Kingdom • United States

PETERSON'S

THOMSON LEARNING

About Peterson's

Founded in 1966, Peterson's, a division of Thomson Learning, is the nation's largest and most respected provider of lifelong learning online resources, software, reference guides, and books. The Education Supersite^{SM} at petersons.com—the Web's most heavily traveled education resource—has searchable databases and interactive tools for contacting U.S.-accredited institutions and programs. CollegeQuest^{SM} (CollegeQuest.com) offers a complete solution for every step of the college decision-making process. GradAdvantage^{TM} (GradAdvantage.org), developed with Educational Testing Service, is the only electronic admissions service capable of sending official graduate test score reports with a candidate's online application. Peterson's serves more than 55 million education consumers annually.

Thomson Learning is among the world's leading providers of lifelong learning, serving the needs of individuals, learning institutions, and corporations with products and services for both traditional classrooms and for online learning. For more information about the products and services offered by Thomson Learning, please visit www.thomsonlearning.com. Headquartered in Stamford, Connecticut, with offices worldwide, Thomson Learning is part of The Thomson Corporation (www.thomson.com), a leading e-information and solutions company in the business, professional, and education marketplaces. The Corporation's common shares are listed on the Toronto and London stock exchanges.

For more information, contact Peterson's, 2000 Lenox Drive, Lawrenceville, NJ 08648; 800-338-3282; or find us on the World Wide Web at: www.petersons.com/about

ISBN 0-7689-0403-X

Printed in the United States of America

10 9 8 7 6 5 4 3 2 1   02 01

TABLE OF CONTENTS

EDITORIAL ADVISORY BOARD

FOREWORD

by Kay Kohl

Executive Director, University Continuing Education Association

New communications technologies have extended the boundaries of teaching and learning. Colleges and universities are providing education to ever larger and more distant student constituencies. The World Wide Web offers students access to vast information resources and serves as a medium for connecting faculty members and students. By the end of 2000, approximately 72 million American adults—more than 35 percent of the population—are expected to be online. It has taken less than seven years for 30 percent of Americans to embrace the Internet, whereas it took thirteen years for PCs, seventeen for televisions, and thirty-eight for telephones. With online learning, a student need not be in a classroom in order to interact with other students and hear a professor's lecture. In fact, some students may find it easier to learn certain subjects, such as mathematics or foreign languages, by using self-paced, computerized instructional modules. Technology has expanded the higher education alternatives, and this has occurred at the very time that job opportunities and earnings for college-educated workers are growing.

Continuous learning is essential to remaining employable in today's knowledge economy. For the time-pressed working man or woman juggling multiple responsibilities, convenience tends to be a major consideration. Distance education makes it possible to pursue needed learning without regard for time or place. Often, electronic instruction provides an individual with equal or more individualized instruction than in a traditional classroom course. Moreover, pursuing learning through electronic modes tends to enhance a person's capacity to utilize technology and draw upon Web resources.

This edition of *Peterson's Distance Learning* brings together in a single volume an abundant selection of instructional programs that are available electronically from individual colleges, universities, and consortia of higher education institutions. The rapid growth of electronic higher education is evidenced by the fact that this guide lists programs of more than 1,000 accredited North American institutions. When the University Continuing Education Association, in partnership with Peterson's, prepared the first edition of this publication seven years ago, there were fewer than 100 institutional listings.

Peterson's Distance Learning constitutes a valuable resource for any individual or employer interested in accessing electronic learning opportunities offered by accredited colleges and universities. The programs described in this guide rely on diverse distance education technologies and together present a wide array of degree and certificate opportunities. All of the higher education institutions highlighted herein are committed to utilizing communication technologies to help students transcend significant time and geographical barriers and to supporting new approaches to teaching and learning.

Founded in 1915, the University Continuing Education Association represents some 440 accredited colleges and universities, public and private, dedicated to providing degree and nondegree instruction at the prebaccalaureate and postbaccalaureate levels to students of all ages. The association is based in Washington, DC. For more information, visit http://www.nucea.edu.

STUDENT PROFILE

Joel Karlin

Personal: Age 42, married, with two children, ages 3 and 7

Home: Fayetteville, New York

College: Kansas State University

Courses Taken: Graduate courses in agribusiness

Joel is the owner of an agricultural brokerage and risk-management firm in New York. He is taking courses from Kansas State University for a master's degree in agribusiness. He has a Bachelor of Arts degree in economics.

"Taking courses from a distance is a cost-effective way for people to gain skills as they progress through their careers. In agriculture-related fields, where competition is difficult and the number of jobs has been in decline, it is especially important to find ways of providing people with managerial and technical skills.

"The program I am involved with at Kansas State University exposes students to finance, accounting, quantitative methods, and trade from an agricultural business perspective. The program attracts students from all over the world. The faculty is committed, and the material is useful to me in my business.

"The courses are taught in modules on the Web and also given on CD-ROM. Most classes have a chat room, and there is an electronic 'white board' students can use to calculate and display mathematical charting and graphing problems. There are plenty of opportunities for phone and e-mail contact among students and between students and faculty.

"I was living in Kansas when I began this program at Kansas State University and subsequently moved to New York. I have found that I am no less able to participate in this program living in New York."

WHAT YOU NEED TO KNOW ABOUT
DISTANCE LEARNING—

What, Exactly, Is Distance Learning?

Distance learning is the delivery of educational programs to off-site students through the use of technologies such as the Internet, cable or satellite television, videotapes and audiotapes, fax, computer conferencing, videoconferencing, and other means of electronic delivery.

What Does This Mean to You?

It may mean that now you can find the resources of your state's top four-year university right next door at your local community college.

It may mean that you can walk down the hall at your workplace and spend your lunch hour taking a course with like-minded colleagues seeking career advancement.

It may mean that you can connect to your professor's e-mail with your home computer modem, exchange messages, and turn in a ten-page "paper" electronically.

It may mean that you will use your personal computer to locate library references and information.

Distance learning expands the reach of the classroom by using various technologies to deliver university resources to off-campus sites, transmit college courses into the work place, and enable students to view class lectures in the comfort of their homes.

Where and How Can I Take Distance Learning Courses?

The proliferation of new, cheaper telecommunications technologies and the demand for broader access to educational resources have prompted the development of diverse educational networks. Many states have established electronic distance learning systems to advance the delivery of instruction to schools, postsecondary institutions, and state government agencies. Colleges and universities are forming consortia to provide education to far-flung student constituencies. Professions such as law, medicine, and accounting as well as other knowledge-based industries are utilizing telecommunications networks for the transmission of customized higher education programs to working professionals, technicians, and managers.

This guide lists course offerings from accredited colleges and universities, including:

- *Credit courses.* In general, if these credit courses are completed successfully, they may be applied towards a degree.
- *Noncredit courses and courses offered for professional certification.* These programs can help you acquire specialized knowledge in a concentrated, time-efficient manner and stay on top of the latest developments in your field. They provide a flexible way for you to prepare for a new career or study for professional licensure and certification. Many of these university programs are created in cooperation with professional and trade associations so that

courses are based on real-life workforce needs and the practical skills learned are immediately applicable in the field.

What Does Distance Learning Offer?
Professional Certification

Certificate programs often focus on employment specializations, such as hazardous waste management or electronic publishing, and can be helpful to those seeking to advance or change careers. Also, many states mandate continuing education for professionals such as teachers, nursing home administrators, or accountants. Distance learning offers a convenient way for many individuals to meet professional certification requirements. Health care, engineering, and education are just a few of the many professions that take advantage of distance learning to help their professionals maintain certification.

Many colleges offer a sequence of distance learning courses in a specific field of a profession. For instance, within the engineering profession, certificate programs in *Computer Integrated Manufacturing, Systems Engineering, Test & Evaluation,* and *Waste Management* are among those offered via distance learning.

Business offerings include distance learning certification in *Information Technology* and *Health Services Management.*

Within the field of education, you'll find distance learning certificate programs in areas such as *Early Reading Instruction, Special Education for Learning Handicapped,* and *Teaching English to Speakers of Other Languages.*

Degree Programs

This book outlines opportunities for individuals to earn degrees at a distance at the associate, baccalaureate, and graduate levels. Two-year community college students are now able to earn baccalaureate degrees—without relocating—by transferring to distance learning programs offered by four-year universities. Corporations are forming partnerships with universities to bring college courses to the workplace and encourage employees to continue their education. Distance learning is especially popular among working adults who want to earn their degree part-time while continuing to work full-time. Although on-campus residencies are sometimes required for certain distance learning degree programs, they generally can be completed while employees are on short-term leave or vacation.

Continuing Education Units (CEUs)

If you choose to take a course on a noncredit basis, you may be able to earn Continuing Education Units (CEUs). The CEU system is a nationally recognized system to provide a standardized measure for accumulating, transferring, and recognizing participation in continuing education programs. One CEU is defined as 10 contact hours of participation in an organized continuing education experience under responsible sponsorship, capable direction, and qualified instruction. Some institutions in this book allow you to take distance education courses on a continuing education credit or noncredit course basis.

Who Is Learning at a Distance?

Most students who enroll in distance education courses are 25 years of age or older and employed. Many have previous college experience. More than half are women. As a group, distance learners are highly motivated. Their course-completion rate exceeds that of students enrolled in traditional on-campus courses. The successful distance learner is by definition a committed student. The individual must have the discipline to establish a regular study schedule each week and adhere to it without having to be reminded by an instructor or classmates to meet deadlines.

A wide range of employers—businesses, hospitals, government offices, military installations—which find it difficult to release employees for on-campus study, are discovering that it is a good investment to bring the classroom to the workplace. According to a survey conducted by the International Foundation of Employee Benefits Plans, employees rank continuing education as a more important benefit than child care, flextime, or family leave.

Distance Learning Blurs Geographic Boundaries

Access to distance learning is expanding. Although some courses still may be limited to certain states or regional areas, many programs are available to students nationwide and internationally. The geographic boundaries are blurring. To illustrate, the University of Wisconsin–Stout is now collaborating with universities in the United Kingdom and Germany to deliver a two-year hospitality, tourism, and management master's degree program online. Stout's partners include Oxford Brookes University, which offers one of the U.K.'s premier programs in hospitality and tourism, and Nottingham Trent University, which has an M.B.A. program as well as a close working relationship with a major international hospitality company. In Germany, Stout's partner is Paderborn University, which has an expertise in business technology.

The University of Maryland University College (UMUC) and the Carl von Ossietzky University in Oldenburg, Germany, have partnered to develop an online master's degree program in distance education. The 36-credit-hour program offers an international perspective of the field and is designed for education and training professionals. In addition, UMUC offers several different online management and technical master's degree and certificate programs to students around the world.

Embry Riddle Aeronautical University is just one of an increasing number of higher education institutions that deliver degree programs to students anywhere in the world. Embry Riddle offers two specialized undergraduate degrees and a master's degree in aeronautical sciences to students at a distance. The University utilizes a combination of video, CD-ROM, and printed materials, plus the Web for faculty-student and student-to-student communications.

Pennsylvania State University distributes online degree and professional certificate programs internationally through its World Campus. Its online certificate programs—in such fields as geographic information systems, turf grass management, chemical dependency counseling, and architectural lighting design—span a wide range of disciplines. These programs provide learning opportunities for individuals involved in or aspiring to enter specialized occupations that are in high demand internationally.

These are just a few examples of how the world of distance learning is reshaping itself and expanding the breadth of educational opportunities around the globe.

Is Distance Learning Right for Me?
Limitations

You should be aware that some distance learning courses are limited to certain geographical areas and/or times of offering. Others may have some on-campus requirements. Please read the listings of your preferred college or university carefully so that you are aware of any limitations before you enroll.

Consider the Instructional Environment

Some programs may connect students electronically to a live, real-time classroom setting. Other institutions offer students in remote areas the opportunity for periodic face-to-face interaction. In an asynchronous instructional environment, however, students typically interact with one another and the professor through computer conference and e-mail. The level of student-to-instructor and student-to-student interaction is a critical consideration for anyone involved in distance education.

Do You Have the Tools Required to Access Distance Learning?

Colleges and universities use multiple technologies for distance education. Some courses require a VCR and television set. Others require access to a computer and modem. If you do not own a computer with the proper specifications, you may be able to use one where you work. All distance learning programs rely on telephone connections for some services.

Stay Current

The distance learning field is constantly changing. You should contact the sponsoring institutions for the most recent information on any given course or subject area. In many cases, courses are added to or deleted from a given curriculum between printings of this guide.

How Does "Distance Learning" Differ from "Independent Study?"

Independent study in the form of correspondence study is sometimes called distance learning. But while correspondence study has been offered by colleges and universities for more than 100 years, distance learning today is *not* the same educational experience as independent study. While correspondence or "independent" study requires no attendance on campus and no "real-time" interaction with professor or classmates, distance learning may require class participation via technology and short trips to the home campus or a satellite site. Off-site students may be required to work at the same pace as on-campus students. (If you decide that independent study is a better option for you, consult *UCEA/Peterson's The Independent Study Catalog*, a guide to 10,000 correspondence courses offered by accredited colleges and universities.)

Why Is It Important to Take Distance Learning Courses from a Regionally Accredited College or University?

Taking a course from an institution accredited by one of the six U.S. regional accrediting associations[1] is an assurance of quality in terms of the curriculum and the instruction you will receive. Many employers will pay the tuition for an employee to complete a course that seems likely to improve job performance. Most organizations will insist,

ASSESSING QUALITY IN DISTANCE EDUCATION

Your work environment may help you decide which technology to choose for distance education. Even though you may be personally more comfortable with a videocassette course, you may decide it is important to take a course via online computer modem because your employer's strategic plan involves conducting research on the Internet. Likewise, many self-described "computer-phobic" school librarians are now proud holders of certificates and master's degrees in library computer science which they earned through distance education programs.

Whether the program is offered in a synchronous or asynchronous learning mode is an important consideration. Although conference calls, online chat groups, and two-way video hook-ups provide opportunities for class interaction, they may not be available for all courses or for every assignment. It is important to know what you value most in a learning experience and select a course that is delivered by technologies that match your personal preferences.

Inform yourself about testing, evaluation, and assessment systems. It is important to ascertain before registering for a course whether such activities occur on campus or are also available close to home.

What are the qualifications of the faculty? What is the student-faculty ratio and is it important to the subject matter? For online courses that are very time intensive, it's probably best to have no more than 25 students in a class. For lecture classes, a much higher ratio may be acceptable. Find out who your classmates will be and how much peer-to-peer interaction you realistically expect to have with them—and through which media? What are the supporting student services? What library resources are available to you and how much lead time must you allow? Before signing up, you might ask to talk to other distance learning students who have already completed similar courses or degree programs.

however, that an employee relying on employer-provided tuition assistance pursue studies at an accredited college or university. Another important consideration is whether the institution is nonprofit or proprietary, because credits from the latter may not be acknowledged by the former. For that matter, it is always wise to check with an academic adviser at the institution to which you intend to transfer the credits before enrolling in a course. This guide includes institutions whose distance learning programs have obtained accreditation by either a regional accrediting association or, in special circumstances, accreditation by another recognized body as noted in the institution's listing.

The Accrediting Council for Independent Colleges and Schools recommends that students ask an accredited institution to provide the following information: (1) the level of student/teacher interaction, (2) the objectives of the program, (3) the success rate of graduates, (4) the completion rate, and (5) how many graduates are placed in their fields of training.

TRENDS IN DISTANCE EDUCATION OFFERINGS

According to research conducted by International Data Corporation (IDC) and published in a report entitled *Online Distance Learning in Higher Education, 1998–2000*:

- The number of college students enrolled in distance learning courses will reach 2.2 million in 2002, up from 710,000 in 1998
- By 2002, 85 percent of two-year colleges will be offering distance learning courses, up from 58 percent in 1998
- Eighty-four percent of four-year colleges will be offering distance learning courses in 2002, up from 62 percent in 1998
- By 2002, the number of students taking distance learning courses will represent 15 percent of all higher education students, up from 5 percent in 1998

According to Sau Ching Lau, senior analyst for IDC's Education Markets Research program, "The Internet is the catalyst attracting more schools and students to distance learning than ever before." Over the past two years, the Internet has completely changed the distance learning landscape—scope, content, and delivery are now dramatically different, while distance learning courses are more widely available. More details may be found on IDC's Web site (http://www.idc.com).

Dun and Bradstreet's Market Data Retrieval Division conducts an annual review of the use of technology in U.S. colleges and universities. The 1999–2000 report revealed that the number of colleges and universities offering distance degree programs doubled in a single year. (This information was based on a 44 percent response rate from 4,284 accredited two- and four-year institutions.) Seventy-two percent of the 1,238 colleges that answered a question on distance education reported that they were offering a distance learning program; 34 percent were offering an accredited degree. Education, business, and social science all remained predominant areas of distance study, a trend that has remained unchanged from the previous year. In the most recent survey, many more disciplines showed a growing use of distance learning. Among these are computer science, allied health, and general studies. More information may be found on the Internet at http://www.schooldata.com.

---

[1] *The six U.S. regional accrediting associations are: the New England Association of Schools and Colleges, Middle States Association of Colleges and Schools, North Central Association of Colleges and Schools, Northwest Association of Schools and Colleges, Southern Association of Colleges and Schools, and Western Association of Schools and Colleges. In addition to the accreditation of UCEA institutions by these bodies, approval by state educational agencies is conferred separately on some distance education courses.*

STUDENT PROFILE

Kathi Lyle

Personal: Age 46, married, with three children

Home: Rowlett, Texas

College: Indiana University

Courses Taken: Geology, speech, astronomy, art

Kathi has completed her Associate of General Studies degree and has begun work in the Bachelor of General Studies degree program.

"Were there not educational opportunities other than the traditional, I would not have been able to finish my education. I have experienced a much greater level of learning at IU than through many on-campus courses. Distance education works well for many adults who can't be on campus and need alternatives.

"We baby boomers are seeking out educational experiences and degree options that do not tie us to a desk in the classroom. Distance learning is empowering for women returning to school—especially women with families to raise. This experience has boosted my confidence.

"You have to begin the journey somewhere. I love to learn—I want to be informed and educated. Distance learning allows me to do just that, without having to spend time away from my job and family."

WHAT IS A DISTANCE LEARNING CONSORTIUM?

Distance learning consortia are associations or partnerships of higher education institutions that have agreed to cooperate in providing online education. All such consortia provide students with access to online courses and information about the programs at member institutions. The size of an online learning consortium can vary greatly, as can its character in terms of the types of institutions it includes (public and/or private) and the location of member institutions (single state or multistate). When one considers that online learning consortia are a relatively new development, it is striking to find such a variety of consortia and so many differences in the formal arrangements governing them.

The extent of cooperation among consortium members can be as little as an agreement to list member institutions' online courses and program information on a common Web site, as in the case of the Southern Regional Electronic Campus (SREC), to a system where courses offered by several colleges and universities are pooled together to constitute a new degree-granting institution, as in the case of the National Technological University (NTU). There are also multistate consortia of private liberal arts colleges, as well as a variety of statewide consortia incorporating public or public and private institutions.

It is important for students to remember that a distance learning consortium is generally not an independent organization to which the student applies. Although there are exceptions to this, as in the case of NTU (discussed below under Specialized Consortia), students normally apply directly to at least one school in the consortium as a means of accessing the resources of other member institutions. It is safest to regard consortia as an arrangement whereby several institutions pool their resources in order to offer students a wider selection of courses.

Types of Distance Learning Consortia

It is difficult to create a reliable guide for students regarding different types of distance learning consortia because they are a new development. The specific policies and procedures of consortia are still evolving. Five different types of distance learning consortia are listed below, with at least one example of each and a brief description of some of their activities. A listing of distance learning consortia can be found at the end of this article.

Multistate Consortia

Multistate consortia include higher education institutions from more than one state. Such consortia may involve a mix of both public and private institutions or be exclusively one or the other.

The Southern Regional Education Board (SREB) recently launched the Southern Regional Electronic Campus (SREC) (http://www.srec.sreb.org), including courses from 244 colleges and universities in sixteen states. From the SREC Web site, students are able to identify programs and courses that are available electronically. It is possible to search by college or university, discipline, level, and state for more detailed information, including course descriptions and how the programs and courses are delivered. Students can connect directly

to the college or university to learn about registration, enrollment, and costs. SREC attempts to guarantee a standard of quality in the courses it lists by reviewing them and does not list courses in their first year of instruction. All SREC students have access to the University of Georgia library system, and the Electronic Campus is enhancing its student services distribution by using a new Web site known as WAYS IN (http://www.waysin.org). WAYS IN offers a full array of online services. Students may apply for admission, register for classes, get information about and apply for financial aid, make payments, and purchase textbooks.

The SREC system is administratively decentralized. The acceptance of transfer credits and the use of credits for program requirements are determined by the college or university to which the credits are being transferred. Likewise, all institutions set their own levels for in-state and out-of-state tuition, maintain individual student records, and determine policy in regard to access to student services. A student taking three classes from three different institutions might have to be admitted to all three, pay three different tuition rates and contact all three institutions for his or her academic records.

In early 2000, Western Governors University (WGU) (http://www.wgu.edu) and SUNY Empire State College (http://www.esc.edu/) announced an alliance that allows students who graduate with a WGU competency-based associate degree to transfer into credit-based bachelor's degree programs at Empire State. SUNY Empire State awards credit for demonstrated previous learning, whereby students may apply to receive credit for learning and competencies gained prior to enrollment. Credit is awarded after the student has undergone an assessment of prior learning. Students may earn more than half of their bachelor's degree credits in this way. This system is particularly attractive to students who have been in the workforce for several years learning on the job without pursuing formal course work.

Statewide Consortia of Public and Private Higher Education Institutions

Statewide consortia are composed of higher education institutions within a single state. Like multistate consortia, they may include both public and private institutions or one type exclusively.

Statewide virtual universities are also increasingly common. One example is the Kentucky Commonwealth Virtual University (KCVU) (http://www.nku.edu/~kycvu/). Fifty colleges and universities currently participate in the KCVU system, each charging its own tuition rates for in-state and out-of-state students. The KCVU consists of three primary components: 1) a clearinghouse for distance learning opportunities, primarily in certificate and degree programs; 2) competency-based credentialing; and 3) a single point of access to statewide student, library, and academic support services.

The KCVU is a statewide consortium that includes both public and private institutions. Community colleges and technical colleges are also included. KCVU has a highly developed system for providing student services. Students may go online to fill out a common form to apply to all fifty member institutions. Student records are kept by individual institutions, and KCVU maintains students' complete records from all institutions. Library services are also centralized. Once admitted to the KCVU system, students have access to every library book in the system and online access to the full text of 5,000 journals. If a student wishes to check out a book, it is sent to the nearest public library where the student may pick it up free of charge. If there is no library nearby, the book is sent by courier to the student's home or office.

Statewide Consortia of Public Institutions of Higher Education

One of the most common types of statewide consortia is that which involves a public university system. For example, the University of Texas (UT) has established a statewide consortium of fifteen public institutions in the UT system. After a student is admitted to a home institution, he or she may fill out a short form that serves to expedite admission to the other system schools for the purpose of taking courses through the UT TeleCampus (http://www.uol.com/telecampus/).

Several other states are operating or developing consortia, including Illinois, Tennessee, South Dakota, Oklahoma, Ohio, Michigan, New Jersey, and Oregon. All have arrangements in place whereby students can take transferable credits online from more than one institution and apply them to a single degree at their home institution.

Consortia of Peer Institutions of Higher Education

Groups of peer institutions sometimes find they have a common orientation or complementary strengths such that students might benefit from a consortial arrangement.

The Jesuit Distance Education Network (JesuitNET) of the Association of Jesuit Colleges and Universities (AJCU) seeks to expand the array of learning options for students on its campuses. JesuitNET is a collaborative effort of twenty-four American Jesuit colleges and universities in nineteen states. Administrators hope to develop a system whereby a student enrolled at any member institution is able to take fully transferable online courses at any other member institution. Tuition rates are set by individual colleges and universities. Through its Web site (http://www.JesuitNET.edu), JesuitNET promotes these schools' online degree and certificate programs, as well as individual courses.

Another more recent private college and university consortium uses a team-teaching approach to deliver courses to students on multiple campuses. Thirteen institutions in the Associated Colleges of the South have created a virtual classics department (http://www.sunoikisis.org). In this case, students all must log on at the same time in order to tune in to an online audio broadcast of a lecture. (This is in contrast to the more common asynchronous model, in which there is no time when students and professors must be engaged in the course simultaneously.) During the lecture, students may pose questions and make comments in a live chat room. Classes are team taught in the sense that professors from several campuses may take responsibility for course material and log on together with the students.

Specialized Consortia

National Technological University (NTU) is one of the oldest technology-based consortia. As a global university, NTU (http://www.ntu.edu) has arranged for the online delivery of advanced technical education and training with more than fifty colleges and universities across the country. Its participants include thirteen of *U.S. News & World Report*'s top twenty-five graduate engineering programs. Currently, more than 1,200 courses are available through NTU's participating universities, providing fourteen master's degree programs. An unusual aspect of the NTU consortium is that the consortium itself grants degrees. Degree programs consist of courses that are developed by multiple NTU higher education institutions.

NTU primarily provides technical training to its clients' employees. These clients typically purchase equipment necessary to receive the course, such as equipment to receive live satellite transmissions. Although students who are not employed by an NTU client company may take courses, they must pay an extra fee to have tapes or CD-ROMs of courses sent to them.

National Technological University has also partnered with PBS to create the Business and Technology Network, a series of more than seventy-five engineering programs per year that are delivered directly to organizations via satellite. NTU uses a variety of technologies to deliver its courses, including satellite, the Internet, and CD-ROM.

Questions to Ask About Consortia

Consortia offer a broader variety of courses than can normally be found on a single campus; however, a consortium may not serve every student's needs. There is also variety among consortia in how registration, student record maintenance, library services, advising services, and other matters are handled. Students should be sure that any consortium they are considering is able to meet their needs in these areas. Therefore, it is important to ask several questions before enrolling in courses offered through a consortium.

- Will credits transfer inside and outside the consortium? Transfer policies vary among consortium members. Each consortium has its own set of rules regarding credit transfer, and most leave it to the discretion of individual institutions.
- Is there a difference in tuition charges among the consortium's members? Often, consortium members do not coordinate their tuition prices. This means that a student may not pay the same tuition at other institutions as he or she would at the home institution.
- Is there a face-to-face component to any instruction offered by the consortium? Some consortium members may require attendance on campus at some point during an academic program, particularly for those seeking a degree or certificate.
- Is there a residency requirement associated with a course or program? Look closely at consortia and institutional policies regarding residency. Institutions often maintain out-of-state tuition rates for students taking online courses while living in another state.
- Can I register and access my records online? Where are my records kept? Some consortia keep centralized student records for all campuses. In others, students must request records from all institutions where they have taken classes.
- What is the quality of library services? Find out if there is a system in place for ordering library books and if there is an extra cost for delivery. Check to see if you have access to the libraries of all consortium members as well as online access to journals.
- Are technical support services available either through the consortia or individual institutions? Technical support for online students varies among consortia.
- Is financial aid available for online students? Does the consortium or the individual institution provide financial aid services?
- What kind of academic advising services are available, and who provides them?
- What systems are in place to facilitate interaction between students and professors in online classes?

- How much access to faculty members do students have via e-mail and fax?
- How many students will a faculty member have in a single online course?

Consortia Listings in This Book

You can read more about the following consortia in this book:

STUDENT PROFILE

Greig Fields

Personal: Age 42, married with three daughters, ages 17, 15, and 13

Home: Upper Marlboro, Maryland

College: University of Maryland University College

Courses Taken: Intensive writing, literature, computer science

Greig holds an associate degree from Prince Georges Community College and is earning credits toward his Bachelor of Science degree. A UMUC academic advising support team is conducting an analysis of computer and managerial skills he has learned on the job to award up to 30 comparable college credits.

Greig is Director of Technical Support and Specialty Sales for the Federal Government at Compaq Computer Corporation where he supervises 70 employees.

"If you don't have a bachelor's degree, you're really dependent on luck for professional success. I was fortunate that, while working at the Naval Research Lab in 1979, I learned the UNIX platform. In the 1980s, when UNIX really took off, I found my computer consulting skills in high demand. Since the lack of a bachelor's degree hasn't hurt me professionally, some of my colleagues wonder why I'm taking the time to earn it now.

"I believe earning a bachelor's degree will be a confidence booster for me personally. I've found that as you get older, few things in life are very objective. Most of the feedback you get at work is subjective. But it's very rewarding to work hard in a course and receive the positive feedback of an A. Also my employer reimburses us for tuition based on our grades.

"One advantage to distance learning courses is that the syllabus for the entire semester is available at a glance on line. I log over 125,000 miles each year in business travel and many times I need to work ahead. From the instructor's Web pages, I have a much better understanding of where the class is headed. Also, with distance learning, I can log on to Web conferences from my computer at work, home, or on the road."

ACADEMIC ADVISING FOR THE DISTANCE LEARNING STUDENT

Can I Earn a Degree?

If you are contemplating entering a degree program or taking a distance learning course to transfer credit to a program you are already in, it is important to take the time to inform yourself about the institution and its offerings in your field of interest *prior* to enrolling. Some institutions have formed partnerships that guarantee transfer of credit. For example, Penn State and the University of Iowa have a distance learning partnership. Students who have earned an Extended-Access Associate Degree in Letters, Arts and Sciences from Penn State are guaranteed admission to UI's Bachelor of Liberal Studies external degree program.

Official information about the institution's programs is best obtained from the admissions office and the academic department offering the course you wish to take. If you are interested in earning academic credit, it is important for you to consult the institution's *academic advising service* before registering. The academic advising department can explain entrance requirements and application procedures. You should be able to register for a class electronically, by telephone, or by mail from your home.

You may find it necessary to develop a portfolio of your past experiences and of your accomplishments that may have resulted in college-level learning. A detailed portfolio, properly assessed by an accredited institution, can help you earn credits toward your degree.

Applying Distance Learning Credits Toward a Traditional Degree

If you are interested in obtaining degree credit for a course, you should ask your academic adviser:

- Will the college of my choice accept the course credit and apply it toward my graduation?

- How many credits by distance learning will be accepted toward graduation?

- Will my institution accept credit for course work transferred from another institution?

- Will credits earned by distance learning be accepted in my area of concentration?

Applying Distance Learning Credits Toward Certification

If you plan to take the course for certification and not for degree purposes, you should ask the certifying agency:

- What are the certification requirements?

- Will the course be acceptable to the relevant certifying agency or professional association?

- How many credits can be earned or how much of the work can be done by distance learning?

What Options Are Available to Me If I Seek to Transfer Credit?

Institutions offer various ways to take their courses and/or earn degree credit. Important considerations here are:

- Is the pass-fail option acceptable to my college or certifying agency?

- Is credit by examination acceptable? (See below.)

- Is credit for experiential (life experience) learning available and acceptable? (See next page.)

- Is the distance degree program that I'm interested in acceptable to other colleges, employers, and certifying agencies?

Earning Credit for What You Know

Ninety-three percent of the nation's higher education institutions award credit for prior learning if students take examinations to assess their knowledge and skills.

- *Credit by Examination.* If you are already knowledgeable in certain areas, rather than completing prerequisites for an individual course or for degree or certificate programs, you may be able to "test out" of a course by taking and passing its final exam. College and university academic advising can also provide you with information on taking standardized Advanced Placement tests. You can receive degree credit for successful scores on the various tests of the College-Level Examination Program (CLEP, Box 6600, Princeton, NJ 08543), the American College Testing Proficiency Examination Program (ACT-PEP, Box 168, Iowa City, IA 52243), or DANTES Standard Subject Tests (DANTES, DSSTs, 6490 Saufley Field Road, Code 20A, Pensacola, FL 32509-5243; 850-452-1063; Web site: http://voled.doded.mil).

Credits for Life Experience, "Portfolio" Development

To apply for possible credit through a college or university for life experience, you should assemble a file or "portfolio" of information about your work and accomplishments (writing samples, awards, taped presentations, copies of speeches) that may have resulted in college-level learning. With academic guidance, you can identify those activities resulting in learning that can be stated as education outcomes or curriculum-relevant "competencies." Your portfolio is then evaluated by an institution's faculty. Information about assessment opportunities for adult learners is available through the Council for Adult and Experiential Learning (CAEL, 55 East Monroe Street, #1930, Chicago, IL 60603; 312-499-2600; Web site: http://www.cael.org).

- *Credit for Work Training.* Since 1974, thousands of employees have been earning college credit for selected educational programs sponsored by businesses, industry, professional associations, labor unions, and government agencies. The American Council on Education's College Credit Recommendation Service (ACE-CCRS, One Dupont Circle, Suite 250, Washington, DC 20036; 202-939-9475; Web site: http://www.acenet.edu) evaluates such programs according to established college-level criteria and recommends college credit for those programs that measure up to these standards.

• *Credit for Military Training.* Your service in the military, specialized training, and occupational experience can potentially earn you college credit. Many military programs have already been evaluated in terms of their equivalency to college credit. The institutions that belong to Servicemembers Opportunities Colleges (SOC) agree to assess student prior learning and accept each other's credits in transfer. (SOC, 1307 New York Avenue, 5th Floor, Washington, DC 20005-4701; 202-667-0079 or 800-368-5622 (ask for *College Degrees Without Classrooms,* flyer #2122); Web site: http://www.soc.aascu.org/).

• *Credit for Volunteering, Working Inside the Home.* You may be able to reap college credit for skills you have learned as a volunteer or working at home. (Accrediting Women's Competencies, T-154, Educational Testing Service, Princeton, NJ 08541, offers information on this.)

STUDY TIPS FOR SUCCESSFUL DISTANCE LEARNING

Tools. Before enrolling in a course, make sure you have access to the tools necessary to complete assignments. Word processing software can help you to organize your work and communicate your thoughts more clearly. If your lessons appear through cable television, you'll want to know how to program your VCR to record the programs to refer back to. Access to a fax machine, computer with adequate hard disk space, and modem for e-mail transmission are "musts" for many classes.

Schedule. Set aside a regularly scheduled time for study. If you have not been involved in academic pursuits recently, you may find that your career, family, hobbies, and social and civic commitments leave little time for studying. To help you fit studying into your schedule, keep a record for a week of how you spend your time, and then decide what you are willing to give up. Schedule your studies for a time when you are mentally fresh and able to devote at least 1 hour to your work. Think of the hour as "reserved time." If you miss too many study periods, revise your schedule.

Where to Study. You will find it easier to focus in an appropriate environment for study. Find a place that is free from distractions. You might consider work—before or after hours and on your lunch hour—a public library, or a separate room in your home.

Reading Skills. You must comprehend and retain what you read for real learning to take place. Reading skills can be developed by concentrating on what you read and by taking frequent pauses to organize and review the material in your mind. At the end of a study session, review everything you have read, making special notes of important points. Reading a computer screen can be hard on your eyes; it may be necessary to download hard copies of reading assignments and communications from your instructor and coworkers.

Communication Skills. It can be intimidating to speak into a microphone in a video or conference call, but your communication skills are an important part of any assignment—on the job, at home, and at school. Distance learning provides the opportunity to enhance these skills. Pay careful attention to instructions and be certain that you understand what is being asked. It often helps to develop a brief outline before responding to questions whether they are submitted in writing, via e-mail, orally, or on video/audio tape. Organization, grammar, and the appropriate style are important whichever medium you choose.

STUDENT PROFILE

Julie Moore

Personal: Age 52, single mother and grandmother, with a teenager at home

Home: Portland, Oregon

College: University of Colorado at Boulder

Courses Taken: Linguistics of American Sign Language, Discourse Analysis of American Sign Language, and Assessment of Second Language Skills

"Julie Moore has been a sign language interpreter for more than 20 years. She teaches interpreting at Portland Community College in Portland, Oregon. Because American Sign Language is a rapidly developing field, she took distance learning courses to update her knowledge."

"For me, the greatest advantage to distance learning was not having to relocate. With one child still in high school and another on his own with a small child, this wasn't a time I wanted to move to another city. I also valued my teaching job, and didn't want to take time off to continue my education. Distance learning allowed me to pursue continuing studies without leaving home. It also allowed me to use the odd moments in my day to keep up with my studies. Distance learning is always open.

"I strongly recommend distance learning. The quality of the courses I took was excellent. As a busy adult, I found that this format made the best use of my time. Although I am not an expert at computers, I didn't experience trouble with the format, and the support offered by the instructor, fellow students, and support people helped me solve any problems. At the outset, I wasn't sure how well I would adapt to using the computer, but I found that I liked it and would happily use distance learning again."

FINDING A PROGRAM THAT IS
RIGHT FOR YOU

Do I Have the Study Skills Required?

You should take the time to evaluate your own approach to work and study before you enroll. Assess how you spend your time and decide, with as much objectivity as possible, how well you think you can fit distance learning in your life.

Although distance learning can provide many advantages in terms of commuting time saved, often students find it to be more rigorous than regular classroom courses. If you can take responsibility for your own education, you will find distance learning rewarding and satisfying. Before enrolling, consider both the advantages and drawbacks of this method of continuing education.

Completing a distance learning course may or may not be easy for you, but the benefits can be significant. In addition to mastering the subject matter, the study skills you develop should enable you to undertake other difficult educational and work-related tasks with heightened confidence.

How Do I Communicate with My Instructor?

Student/faculty exchanges occur using electronic communication (through fax and e-mail). Many institutions offer their distance learning students access to toll-free numbers so students can talk to their professors or teaching assistants without incurring any long-distance charges. Details about these and other types of electronic communication, including any cost to the student, appear in this book as well as in the institution's catalog and/or the course description.

Responses to your instructor's comments on your lessons, requests for clarification of comments, and all other exchanges between you and your instructor will take time. Interaction with your instructor—whether by computer, telephone, or letter—is important, and you must be willing to take the initiative.

How Does It Work?
Enrolling in a Course

Enrolling in a distance learning course may simply involve filling out a registration form, making sure that you have access to the equipment needed, and paying the tuition/fees by check, money order, or credit card. In these cases your applications may be accepted without entrance examinations or proof of prior educational experience.

Other courses may involve educational prerequisites and access to equipment not found in all geographic locations. Usually such limitations are listed in the institution's profile.

After reviewing the course names shown in this guide, you can obtain registration forms and catalogs that will provide more detailed descriptions of the courses. Some institutions offer detailed information about individual courses, such as a course outline, upon request. To obtain these materials, contact the person whose name and address or telephone number appear at the end of each institution's entry in the "Institutions and Courses Offered" section of this guide. If you have access to the Internet and simply wish to review course descriptions, you may be able to peruse an institution's course catalogs electronically by accessing the institution's Web site.

Time Requirements

Some courses allow you to enroll at your convenience and work at your own pace. Others closely adhere to a traditional classroom schedule. Specific policies and time limitations pertaining to withdrawals, refunds, transfers, and renewal periods can be found in the institutional catalog.

Admission to a Degree Program

If you plan to enter a degree program, you should consult the academic advising department of the institution of your choice to learn of entrance requirements and application procedures. You may find it necessary to develop a portfolio of your past experiences and of your accomplishments that may have resulted in college-level learning.

Transferring Credit

If you wish to apply credit for distance learning courses, you should be aware that some institutions may impose certain requirements before they will accept the credit, and some courses or programs may require previous study or experience.

NOTE: If you wish to earn credit for a course and apply it to a degree program, be certain that it meets the requirements of the institution to which you want to transfer the credit, as well as the requirements of your specific program within that institution.

For example, if you want to earn 3 credits from College A's accounting course and apply those credits toward University B's Bachelor of Arts degree, check with University B and its Department of Business before you enroll in the course to ascertain whether the credits will be accepted. Most institutions' catalogs will list both the general admission requirements and the prerequisites for individual courses.

Most institutions limit the number and kinds of credits that they will accept. You can usually transfer credit earned in a distance learning course from one regionally accredited institution to another. As policies and degree requirements of colleges and universities vary markedly, you should consult the appropriate officials at the institution from which you expect to receive a degree to be sure that the credit is transferable. If you pursue course work at an institution that is not regionally accredited, it may be difficult for you to transfer the credit.

Credit for Distance Learning
College Credit

Academic credit is measured in semester or quarter hours. You should consult the institution(s) to which you are transferring credits because some institutions use different systems of conversion or do not accept partial hours of credit.

Enrollment in Credit Courses on a Noncredit Basis

Most universities and colleges accept enrollment in credit courses on a noncredit basis and take special interest in students who are studying for personal satisfaction or career advancement without regard to credit.

Grades and Transcripts for College Courses

Each institution follows its regular grading policies in evaluating the work of distance learning students. When you complete a course, the institution sends a grade report to you. The grade is also recorded at the institution, and a transcript will be sent to any address you designate in a written request, although most institutions charge for additional transcripts. Some institutions use special designations to indicate courses that have been taken by distance learning.

Course Materials

Course materials include a study guide, which is usually provided as part of the initial cost. A course may also require workbooks, procedure manuals, lab kits, videotapes or audiotapes, slides, photographs, or other audiovisual materials, which you must purchase separately. The cost of these items varies from institution to institution. In some cases, you may borrow materials from the institution by paying a deposit that is partially refunded when you return the materials. Audiovisual materials are usually sent with the study guide, and you will be charged as indicated in the institution's catalog. Details about costs for course materials will be listed in the institution's catalog or in the study guide.

Textbooks

In most cases, the cost of textbooks is not included in the course fee. Depending upon the particular institution, you may purchase the required textbooks and other course materials in a number of ways. In general, you have three choices: (1) you can order the books at the time of enrollment and the institution will send them to you along with the study guide; or (2) you can order books from a designated bookstore after receiving the study guide; or (3) you can obtain the books from local sources. For some courses, the study guide also serves as the text.

The cost of textbooks varies widely, depending upon the number and kinds of texts. The institution's catalog or the course study guide will indicate where textbooks can be obtained and how much they will cost. It may also provide information on the selling of your used textbooks.

Fax, E-mail Communication, and Access to Digital Libraries

Learning to navigate the Internet and its World Wide Web may be part of your distance learning experience. Some course learning guides are available over the Internet, and you can register for courses by fax, telephone, or e-mail at many institutions listed in this guide. Course catalogs are also frequently available over commercial services like America Online®.

Some universities have made their online "digital libraries" available to students learning at a distance. Recognizing that some off-campus students do not have access to computer modems, other colleges allow students to call upon the services of a library services facilitator who may conduct searches, photocopy articles, and check out and mail books to students.

Not all schools are equipped to accept lessons via fax or e-mail. Thus, if you want to submit your work electronically, check with the institution regarding its assignment submission policies *before* you enroll. In many situations, institutions will *not* accept exams (which must be administered by an authorized proctor) via fax.

Special Considerations for Students in Other Countries

If you plan to take a distance learning course from overseas, it is important to make sure you will have access to the proper computer equipment and wiring once you are out of the country. It is wise to enroll before you leave the United States, taking your textbooks and course materials with you to avoid both postage and tariff expenses. An institution's catalog will identify policies, costs, and availability for international enrollments.

Handling and Special Fees

Some institutions charge a handling fee to help them defray the cost of processing materials and registration. In addition, rental fees may be charged for special course materials. Special fees are usually charged for course transfers and course extensions and sometimes for enrollment by out-of-state residents.

STUDENT PROFILE

Karen Ugurbil

College: University of California Extension at Berkeley

Courses Taken: e-commerce/business

Karen works for Visa USA on e-commerce strategy initiatives. She has a master's degree in information systems from Florida International University.

"The computing field requires constant learning, which is one of the reasons I enjoy it. I want to expand my skill base into the e-commerce area, as I presently work in new initiative (e-commerce) strategy for Visa. Taking a college course forces me to go deeper into the subject than I would naturally if I were simply reading about the subject on my own. Also, having deadlines for covering specific material helps me stay disciplined. As a technology professional, these classes help me evolve my skill base along with technology changes.

"Distance learning provided a far greater perspective than I would have gained from a course on campus. Because homework assignments are posted on a message board that is visible to all students, I had access to each student's response to every assignment. I also enjoyed the message board because I was able to view my fellow students' comments and perspectives. That was enriching.

"Distance learning allows me to fit a class into my schedule, rather than changing my life to accommodate a class. The flexibility requires one to exhibit more self-discipline, though. These classes are thorough and require a great deal of reading and homework. Students must pace themselves or they'll regret it at the end of the semester!"

WHAT ARE MY FINANCING OPTIONS?

The costs for distance learning programs vary from course to course and from one college or university to another. Each institution sets its own pricing structure. In general, you can expect direct charges for tuition, textbooks, and other necessary course materials and equipment as well as for any postage and handling.

Tuition

Tuition information is included based on pricing and is subject to change. Before enrolling, check the catalog of the institution for its current rates.

Payment Plans

Most institutions require full payment of all charges due at the time of registration. The preferred method of payment is a check or money order. In a few instances, textbooks are paid for separately. Some institutions accept charge cards and offer partial or deferred payment plans. You should consult the institution's catalog to determine payment policies.

Financial Aid

The list below identifies a few possible sources of financial aid, and students who require aid are encouraged to explore all applicable options.

- *Employers.* Many employers provide educational benefits to their employees. These are generally administered through the human resources or benefits department of the organization. If you are a teacher or other public school employee, you may be able to receive reimbursement of fees paid for college credit. Contact the coordinator of staff development within your district for further information.
- *Unions.* Unions often negotiate educational benefits into their contracts. The union's business manager would be the person to provide information.
- *Veterans' and Military Benefits.* Federal veterans' assistance acts have had provisions for financial assistance for college and university study. The amount and type of assistance varies, and it is best to check with a local Veterans Administration office for specific details. If you are an active-duty military service member, including a member of the National Guard and Armed Forces Reserve, you have two options available to you for financial assistance. The first consists of "in-service" benefits through the U.S. Department of Veteran Affairs. The second is "tuition assistance," which comes from the military person's respective service and is administered by DANTES (Defense Activity for Non-Traditional Educational Support). In either case, the Educational Service Officer of your base, post, or ship can provide information. In addition to the federal government's tuition assistance plans, some states have educational benefits for veterans and military personnel. Direct your questions and inquiries to the state veterans or military affairs offices. Information on the U.S. Army's Continuing Education System's Veterans Educational Assistance Program may be found at http://www.perscom.army.mil/tagd/aces/veap.htm.

- *Other Federal Programs.* Although most federal programs providing grants or loans are directed to the resident student, some are applicable to the distance learning student as well. Under certain conditions, for example, Pell Grants may be available to a person studying at a distance. Because eligibility is limited to degree candidates, you should contact the financial aid office of the institution from which you are seeking your degree.

- *Vocational Rehabilitation.* Nearly all states provide financial benefits for the education of persons with some form of handicap. Direct any questions to your state's department of vocational rehabilitation.

- *Institutional Aid.* A small number of colleges and universities have a limited amount of financial aid available for distance learning students. You should carefully examine an institution's catalog for financial aid information or consult its office of financial aid. Unfortunately, as a distance education student, you may find that you have more difficulty qualifying for financial aid than traditional full-time students, depending upon the institution you contact. For free information on qualifying for financial aid, check out the Web site of the National Association of Student Financial Aid Administrators at http://www.nasfaa.org.

- *Banks.* Many private lenders now offer educational loan programs to older, part-time students. Banks typically have information about these programs on their Web sites.

STUDENT PROFILE

Carol Walter

Personal: Married, with three children, ages 16, 15, and 12

Home: Lake Ozark, Missouri

College: University of Missouri Direct: Continuing and Distance Education

Courses Taken: Graduate courses in public health nursing

Carol is a school nurse in a local school district. She has a Bachelor of Science degree in nursing from the University of Missouri–Columbia. She took one online course and is now pursuing a Master of Science degree in nursing, with a clinical specialty in school-health nursing.

"Distance education was the only way I was ever going to get a master's degree. I have wanted to get a master's degree in nursing for twenty years, but with a full-time job and three children, driving to take courses was impossible. Distance learning makes it possible. It is convenient, fun, challenging, and easy to do.

"Distance learning offers the convenience of doing some things for class when you have the time late at night or early in the morning. My kids can be here with me and I'm still in class.

"I intend to have a master's in public health nursing in five years via distance learning—something that would not have been possible without it. I have learned a lot of computer skills that are helpful in other areas of my profession, and it has been easy. The professors are patient and helpful in showing us how to use the computer for distance learning."

STUDENT PROFILE

Ed Messenger

Personal: Age 37, married, with three children, ages 15, 12, and 8

Home: Glenville, West Virginia

College: University of South Carolina

Courses Taken: Graduate courses in library science

Ed is Interim Library Director at Glenville State College in West Virginia and currently is taking courses in a 36-credit Master of Library Science program at the University of South Carolina. He began the program 2½ years ago and has 12 credits to complete before he receives his degree. Ed has taken all of his credits online or via satellite.

"Job opportunities have really opened up to me since I started the Master of Library Science program at the University of South Carolina. I recently accepted the position of Interim Library Director at Glenville State College, and I will be in a good position to apply for the permanent Library Director position when I graduate. Neither of these positions would have been open to me without participating in a professionally accredited program.

"In order to be taken seriously for high-level college or university library positions, you need to have a degree from a program accredited by the American Library Association. In West Virginia, there are no programs with this accreditation, so I had to look elsewhere. I was one of the first people to inquire about participating in this program at USC through distance education and was one of about 80 students enrolled in the second cohort.

"This has really been a great experience for me. The instructors and staff in Columbia, South Carolina, bent over backwards to make us feel welcome. Once every semester, there is a required hands-on component. The professors come up from Columbia to do this with the West Virginia students. They really make us feel like a part of the main campus."

GLOSSARY

Academic year: The yearly period used by colleges and universities to measure a full year of academic study, typically commencing in early autumn and ending in late summer.

Analog communication: A communication format in which information is transmitted by modulating a continuous signal, such as a radio wave. See also **digital communication.**

Associate degree: A degree awarded upon the successful completion of a prebaccalaureate level program, usually consisting of two years of full-time study at the college level.

Asynchronous communication: Two-way communication in which the parties cannot send and receive simultaneously. Examples include electronic mail and voice mail systems.

Asynchronous digital subscriber lines (ADSL): See **DSL.**

Audioconference: Electronic meeting in which participants in different locations using telephones or speakerphones are linked together to communicate interactively in real-time.

Baccalaureate: A degree conferred upon completion of a four-year course of study at the undergraduate level.

Bachelor's degree: A degree awarded upon the successful completion of a baccalaureate-level program, consisting of four years of full-time study at the college level.

Bandwidth: The width of frequencies required to transmit a communications signal without undue distortion. The more information a signal contains, the more bandwidth it will need to be transmitted. Video, animation, and sound require many times more bandwidth than e-mail.

Bit (binary digit): The smallest unit of information a computer can use. A bit is represented as a 0 or a 1 (also known as "off" or "on"). A group of eight bits is called a byte. Bits are often used to measure the speed of digital transmission systems.

Bitnet: An academic and research computer e-mail network—now used primarily in Europe.

Broadband: High bandwidth communications, such as real-time video and conferencing, that require high-speed data networks for delivery to users.

Browser: A software package that interprets HTML or XML code to produce World Wide Web graphics, animation, and sound on a computer. Browsers such as Netscape® and Internet Explorer® are used both for World Wide Web content and for university or corporate Intranet content.

Bulletin board service: A computer service that allows remote users to access a central "host" computer to read or post electronic messages.

Cable: Optical fiber, coaxial, or twisted pair (telephone) cable connects communications components together. Microwave transmission is sometimes used as an alternative over long distances or rugged terrain.

Certificate: An educational credential awarded upon completion of a structured curriculum, typically including several courses but lasting for a period of less than that required for a degree. Credit awarded upon the completion of a certificate program is generally applicable to degree credit.

CLEP: Acronym for College-Level Examination Program, administered by The College Board, that tests students' general knowledge and subject mastery in order to award college-level credit for non-collegiate learning.

Closed-circuit television: A system using coaxial cable, microwave transmissions, or telephone lines to allow audio and visual interaction within a small network of connected sites located within a limited geographic area.

College: A postsecondary-level institution that offers programs of study leading to an associate's, bachelor's, master's, doctoral, or professional degree. Colleges may be either two- or four-year institutions.

Compact disc (CD): The compact disc, originally developed by Philips Corporation in the Netherlands, is an optical storage medium for computers. It allows large quantities of data, text, and image files to be stored on a single compact disc. Read Only (ROM) types are used for computer applications, movies, photos, and audio recordings. Writeable and rewriteable discs are used for data backups and archiving. See also **Digital Versatile Discs.**

Compressed video: Process by which video images are captured and transmitted/stored more efficiently and at lower cost than traditional broadcast video, with the result that the video information can be sent via phone lines or stored on a compact disc.

Computer conference (online discussion): Computer-facilitated e-mail communication among members of a group, where all messages are seen by all participants. See also **"listserv."**

Computer teleconferencing: Real-time, computer mediated interaction with others in different locations, usually involving simultaneous video and audio streaming so that participants can see and hear each other as in a live meeting.

Continuing Education Unit (CEU): The CEU system is a nationally recognized system to provide a standardized measure for accumulating, transferring, and recognizing participation in continuing education programs. One CEU is defined as 10 contact hours of participation in an organized continuing education experience under responsible sponsorship, capable direction, and qualified instruction.

Continuing higher education: Programs or courses offered by colleges and universities at the pre- or post-baccalaureate levels to students with at least a high school diploma or its equivalent attending on a less-than-full-time basis. Study can be for credit or noncredit, degree or non-degree, certificate or some other generally recognized educational credential.

Correspondence study: Individual or self-guided study by mail from a college or university by which credit is typically granted through written assignments and proctored examinations. More often referred to as "Independent Study."

Credit: A unit of value assigned by colleges or universities upon the successful completion of courses. Credits measure the academic quality of a course in relation to a program of study and measure the progress toward a specified degree program.

Digital communications: A communications format used with both electronic and light-based systems that transmit audio, video, and data as bits (1's and 0's) of information (see Bit). Digital signals require much less bandwidth than analog signals.

Digital subscriber lines (DSL): A new technology that enables ordinary telephone lines to transmit high-speed broadband content. Asynchronous DSL lines (ADSL) cannot send and receive simultaneously.

Digital Versatile Discs (DVDs): DVDs are a new type of compact disc with greatly increased storage capacity. Like CDs, they come in both ROM and writeable formats.

Distance education: The delivery of educational programs to off-site students using one or more technologies such as cable television, videotapes, audiotapes, fax, the Internet and other delivery media.

Doctoral degree: The highest degree awarded upon demonstrated mastery of a subject, including the ability to perform scholarly research. Generally, a master's degree serves as a prerequisite to obtaining a doctorate.

Downlink: An antenna, usually shaped like a dish, that receives signals from a satellite. Different models are designed for digital Internet traffic, or analog television signals.

Downstream: The direction a signal travels as it moves from the transmitting (origination) site to the receiving sites.

e-Business: An integrated suite of business applications that enables all transactions and business processes to be carried out online.

Educational attainment: The highest level of education obtained or the highest level of school attended.

Electronic graphics pad (or tablet): An electronic device resembling a pad of paper that users draw or write on. Images are converted into digital information that can be used and displayed on a computer.

Electronic mail: More often called e-mail, this term refers to text messages and documents sent over telephone lines, cable or satellite, to a receiving computer.

Enrollment: Total number of students officially participating in a given program or institution at a particular time.

Experiential learning: Portfolio of skills and life experiences that may be converted to academic credit by colleges and universities, either by examination or evaluation.

Facsimile machine (fax): A telecopying device that electronically transmits written or graphic material over telephone lines to produce "hard copy" at a remote location.

Fiber optics: Hair-thin, flexible glass filaments that use light signals to transmit audio, video, and data signals. Signals can be sent in either analog or digital format. Fiber optic cable has a much higher capacity than traditional copper or coaxial cable and is not as subject to interference and noise.

First-professional degree: A degree awarded upon the successful completion of program of study for which a bachelor's degree is normally the prerequisite, and which prepares a student for a specific profession.

Freeze frame: One method of transmitting still images over standard telephone lines. A single image is transmitted every 8 to 30 seconds. Also referred to as slow scan.

Frequency: The number of times per second an electromagnetic wave completes a cycle. A single hertz (Hz) is equivalent to one cycle per second.

Full-motion video: A standard video signal that can be transmitted by a variety of means, including television broadcast, microwave, fiber optics, and satellite. **Compressed video** enables full-motion signals to be stored and transmitted more economically.

Full-time enrollment: The number of students enrolled in higher education courses whose total credit-load usually equal at least 75 percent of the normal full-time load specified by the institution.

GED: Acronym for General Educational Development program, or academic instruction to prepare an individual to obtain a high school equivalency diploma.

Graduate: An individual who has successfully completed a specified educational program.

Headend: In a distribution network or cable system, the headend is the central transmission point from which content is distributed to subscribers.

Higher education institution: An institution legally authorized to offer programs at the two- or four-year level for credit and offering degrees. A university is a four-year institution offering degree programs beyond the baccalaureate level. A college may be an institution at the two- or four-year level.

Home page: The first page or welcome page within a "Web site." See also **World Wide Web** and **URL**.

Hyperlinks (also known as Hot Links): URLs or e-mail addresses with built-in programming that takes you to the site when its address is clicked. Hyperlinks usually appear as underlined text in Web pages, but may also consist of icons or image maps.

Hypertext Markup Language (HTML): The code in which World Wide Web pages and interactive CDs are written. Browsers such as Netscape® and Internet Explorer use HTML or its newer cousin XML to produce graphics, text, and animation.

Integrated Services Digital Network (ISDN): An end-to-end digital network that allows users to send voice, data, and video signal over the same line simultaneously. This is increasingly being replaced by DSL.

The Internet: The global computer "network of networks." Initially developed by the U.S. government for defense purposes, the Internet became a common communication medium in homes and schools in the early 1990s with the advent of commercial Internet Service Providers (such as America Online and CompuServ®) and the World Wide Web (see also **World Wide Web**). Today electronic mail (e-mail) and Web content (text, graphics, and sound) account for most of the traffic on the Internet. Colleges, universities, and increasingly, libraries and schools, often provide Internet access for students either for free or at nominal cost. In addition, many students now connect to the Internet at home, using a computer and modem, or cable connection, combined with the free Internet browser software provided by Netscape® and Microsoft.

Intranet: A Local Area Network (LAN), such as a university computer system, which uses Web graphics as an internal communications medium.

"Listserv" (Internet mailing list): Originally developed by Eric Thomas of L-Soft International as the successor to Bitnet, "listservs," or Internet mailing list servers, have become the dominant vehicle of academic and research discussion in the United States and much of the rest of the world. They enable all participants in a discussion to simultaneously view each other's e-mail messages. Public discussions are known as "newsgroups."

Local Area Network (LAN): A private computer network, usually limited to a building or group of buildings, such as a university or corporate network. It may contain Web-type content and be referred to as an "Intranet."

Master's degree: A degree awarded upon the successful completion of a program of study beyond the baccalaureate level, typically requiring one or two years of full-time study.

Microwave: High-frequency radio waves used for point-to-point and omnidirectional communication of audio, data, and video signals. Microwave frequencies require direct line-of-sight to operate; obstructions such as trees or buildings distort the signal.

Modem: A device that converts digital signals for transmission over telephone voice lines. Most home users need modems for Internet access to e-mail and online services. Schools and colleges commonly use much faster leased data lines known as DSLs, T1, T2, and T3 lines—in order of speed.

Part-time enrollment: The number of students enrolled in higher education courses whose total credit-load is less than 75 percent of the full-time load as specified by the institution.

Portfolio: A file comprising information about an individual's work and accomplishments such as writing samples, awards, taped presentations, copies of speeches etc. that may have resulted in college-level learning. An academic advisor evaluates the activities to identify curriculum-relevant "competencies." See also **Experiential learning.**

Postbaccalaureate enrollment: The number of graduate-level and first-professional students enrolled in higher education courses leading to advanced degrees.

Postsecondary education: Courses or programs of study offered to students who have completed high school degrees or the equivalent. These include programs of an academic, vocational, or continuing education nature.

Real-time or synchronous communication: Two-way simultaneous communication, as opposed to asynchronous.

Satellite television: Programming beamed to a satellite orbiting the earth, then retrieved by one or more ground-based satellite dishes. The satellite dish broadcasting the program is called an "uplink," and the receiving dish is called a "downlink."

Search engines: Interactive directories which enable Internet users to search the Web for information on any chosen topic.

Teleconferencing: A general term for any conferencing system using telecommunications links to connect remote sites. There are many types of teleconferencing including videoconferencing, computer conferencing, and audio conferencing.

Telecourse: A course students can take from home, in which they listen to lectures distributed via broadcast or cable television and study accompanying print materials.

Touch screen: A computer screen that allows data to be entered by using a specialized pen to write on the screen or by making direct physical contact with the computer screen.

Undergraduate students: Students matriculated at a higher education institution who are working toward baccalaureate or associate's degrees.

Universal Resource Locator (URL): The address of a World Wide Web home page or site. Educational URLs often end in an "edu;" commercial sites usually end in "com" or "net." Most nonprofit organizations' URLs end in "org."

University: A four-year institution of higher education offering degrees at the baccalaureate, master's, doctoral, or first-professional levels.

Uplink: A satellite dish that transmits signals up to a satellite.

Upstream: The direction a signal travels as it moves from a receive site back to the site of the original transmission. Used especially in two-way cable television systems.

Videoconferencing: May refer to one-way video and two-way audio transmission conducted via satellite; that is, audience members can see and hear the instructors, who can hear but not see them. Two-way videoconferencing links two or more locations by two-way video camera equipment and allows the instructor and participants to see each other simultaneously.

Wide Area Network (WAN): A network composed of Internet connections.

World Wide Web: A graphical interface for the Internet that permits real-time video, sound, and sophisticated graphics to be transmitted to the user. A broad and growing number of institutions (and individuals) are creating Web sites as a source of public information and as an opportunity to market products and services to Internet users.

HOW TO USE THIS GUIDE

> **NOTE** If you have not already done so, please refer to the preceding pages for valuable insights on: *What You Need to Know about Distance Learning; Academic Advising for the Distance Learner; Finding a Program that is Right for You;* and the answer to the question: *What are My Financing Options?*

What's Inside

Institution profiles Here you'll find more than 1000 institutions offering postsecondary education at a distance. For each institution, specific degree and certificate programs are described, followed by a list of subjects for which individual courses are offered (undergraduate, graduate, and noncredit). Profiles also provide a general overview of each institution and offer key information on:

In-Depth Descriptions Additional details on distance learning offerings are provided by participating institutions and consortia. Each two-page entry provides details on delivery media, programs of study, special programs, credit options, faculty, students, admission, tuition and fees, financial aid, and applying.

Student Profiles Get the inside scoop on distance learning from those who have experienced it first hand. Real-life students share their experience, offer advice, and relate how distance learning has worked for them.

eCollege.com Information eCollege.com has the connection to online courses and degree programs at colleges and universities across the U.S. eCollege.com partners with schools, from leading universities to local community colleges, to provide students with a high-quality education via the Internet. Whether you are looking to accelerate your current course schedule or obtain a degree entirely on line, eCollege.com allows you to use the power of the Internet to study any time, from any location. Because the eCollege Help Desk is available via telephone or e-mail 24 hours a day, seven days a week, you will never have to worry about technical problems interfering with your work. For more information, you can visit the eCollege.com Web site (http://www.eCollege.com/scholarships).

Finding What You Want

If you simply want to get a sense of the variety of programs being offered in distance learning, you may want to just browse through the **Institutional Profiles** page by page.

If you are interested in locating a certificate or degree program in a specific field of study, refer to the **Certificate and Degree Programs Index.** Here you'll find institutions offering everything from Accounting to Theological & Ministerial Studies. There are more than 100 areas in all.

If it is individual courses you're looking for, the **Individual Courses Index** will guide you to institutions offering credit and noncredit courses at either the undergraduate or graduate level.

The **Geographic Index** lets you find programs that are offered by institutions that are located near you. Keep in mind that, most institution's offerings are available nationally, and sometimes internationally. See individual listings for details.

How Colleges Get Into the Guide

This book profiles more than 1000 institutions of higher education currently offering courses or entire programs at a distance. To be included, all U.S. institutions must have full accreditation or candidate-for-accreditation (preaccreditation) status granted by an institutional or specialized accrediting body recognized by the U.S. Department of Education or the Council for Higher Education Accreditation.[1] Canadian institutions must be chartered and authorized to grant degrees by the provincial government, be affiliated with a chartered institution, or be accredited by a recognized U.S. accrediting body.

In the research for this guide, the following definition of "distance learning" was used: a planned teaching/learning experience in which teacher and students are separated by physical distance, and use any of a wide spectrum of media. This definition is based on the one developed by the University of Wisconsin Extension.

Research Procedures

The information provided in these profiles was collected during the spring and summer of 2000 by way of a survey sent to colleges and universities. All data included in this edition have been submitted by officials at the schools themselves. All usable information received in time for publication has been included. The omission of any particular item from an index or profile listing signifies that the item is either not applicable to that institution or that data were not available. Although Peterson's has every reason to believe that the information presented in this guide is accurate, students should check with each college or university to verify such figures as tuition and fees, which may have changed since the publication of this volume.

Profiles

Institution profiles appear in alphabetical order in this guide.

Institutional information

The sections here describe overall characteristics of an institution and its distance learning offerings.

General information This section lists key facts and figures about the institution, including when it was founded, the type of accreditation it has, the number of students enrolled in distance learning and the number of course titles offered at a distance.

Course delivery sites This section lists the locations where distance learning students receive instruction: home, work, military bases, other colleges, off-campus centers, high schools, hospitals, or other locations.

---

[1] *The six U.S. regional accrediting associations are: the New England Association of Schools and Colleges, Middle States Association of Colleges and Schools, North Central Association of Colleges and Schools, Northwest Association of Schools and Colleges, Southern Association of Colleges and Schools, and Western Association of Schools and Colleges. In addition to the accreditation of UCEA institutions by these bodies, approval by state educational agencies is conferred separately on some distance education courses.*

Media This section describes the kinds of media used to deliver the courses and for student-teacher interaction. The following media are listed: television (broadcast or cable), videocassettes, videoconferencing (a two-way video connection via satellite, fiber optics, or other connection), interactive television, audiocassettes, audioconferencing (a two-way audio connection via telephone or other means), computer software, CD-ROM, computer conferencing, World Wide Web, e-mail, print, telephone, and fax.

The lists of course delivery sites and media represent a summary of all options of all courses at the institution. Availability at particular sites and use of specific media will vary from course to course; contact the institution for details.

Geographic service area/Restrictions This section outlines any geographical or other restrictions that may affect eligibility to enroll in the institution's distance learning courses. Many of the institutions listed in the guide serve only a local or in-state audience. Be sure to check this section before contacting a school.

Services This section lists the kinds of student services that are available at a distance through computer, phone, fax, or other means. These include library services, access to the campus computer network, e-mail services, tutoring, career placement assistance, bookstore, and academic advising.

Credit-earning options This section lists alternative means of earning college credit that are available to distance learning students at the institution. Among the possibilities are transfer from another college, standardized exams (such as CLEP or PEP), institutionally-developed exams, portfolio assessment, and military and business training programs evaluated by American Council on Education.

Typical costs This section lists the tuition and mandatory fees for distance learning courses—undergraduate, graduate, and noncredit—based on 1999–2000 tuition figures. Where costs differ based on where a student resides, the different figures for in-district, in-state, and out-of-state students are given. This section also indicates whether institutionally-administered financial aid can be applied to courses or programs completed at a distance.

Registration The following means of registering for classes are listed here: mail, fax, phone, e-mail, World Wide Web, and in person.

Contact This section lists the person or office to contact for more information about the institution's distance learning courses.

Degree and Certificate Programs

This part of the profile describes each program leading to a degree or certificate that can be completed entirely at a distance. Programs are grouped by the level of award: associates degrees, baccalaureate degrees, graduate degrees, undergraduate certificates, and graduate certificates.

General information This section identifies the degree awarded, the subjects in which it can be earned, the number of students enrolled in the program, and the number of degrees awarded in the last academic year.

Geographic service area/Restrictions Some distance learning degree or certificate programs have enrollment requirements that differ from other programs at the same institution. If this is the case, the specific service area and enrollment restrictions will be indicated here. Otherwise, refer to the similar sections of the institution profile for information.

Application requirements This section lists what is required when applying to the program. This might include standardized exam scores, high school or college transcripts, letters of recommendation, and application fees.

Completion requirements This section describes the course requirements for the program. The total number of credits or courses is indicated. This section also lists any on-campus requirements for the program. These are usually in the form of brief orientations, weekend seminars, or short summer residencies.

Program contact If there are particular persons or offices to contact about specific programs, they are listed here. Otherwise, contact the person or office given in the institution profile. As a result of Peterson's partnership with eCollege.com, institutions that are members of eCollege.com are identified by a graphic that is located at the end of this section. This graphic includes a Web address (http://www.eCollege.com/scholarships) that students can use to find exciting and up-to-date information about eCollege.com and its member institutions, Peterson's partnership with eCollege-.com, and how to make education via distance learning more accessible and affordable.

Individual Course Subject Areas

This part of the profile lists the general subject areas in which the institution offers individual courses at a distance. Subjects are divided into those offered for undergraduate credit, for graduate credit, and noncredit. (Note that this is not a listing of course titles; you will need to contact the institution for a detailed list of courses offered.) In addition, *Peterson's Independent Study Catalog* also contains lists of distance learning courses.

ABILENE CHRISTIAN UNIVERSITY

Abilene, Texas

Instructional Technology
www.acu.edu/cte/facequip/dlr.html

Abilene Christian University, founded in 1906, is an independent, nonprofit, comprehensive institution affiliated with the Church of Christ. It is accredited by the Southern Association of Colleges and Schools. In 1999–2000, it offered 6 courses at a distance. In fall 1999, there were 8 students enrolled in distance learning courses.

Course delivery sites Courses are delivered to your home, Texas A&M University (College Station), Western Texas College (Snyder), 1 off-campus center in Irving.

Media Courses are delivered via television, videotapes, videoconferencing, computer software, World Wide Web, e-mail. Students and teachers may meet in person or interact via videoconferencing, audioconferencing, mail, telephone, fax, e-mail, World Wide Web. The following equipment may be required: computer, modem, Internet access, e-mail.

Restrictions Programs are available worldwide. Enrollment is open to anyone.

Services Distance learners have access to library services, the campus computer network, e-mail services, academic advising, tutoring, bookstore at a distance.

Credit-earning options Students may transfer credits from another institution or may earn credits through examinations, portfolio assessment.

Typical costs Costs may vary. Financial aid is available to distance learners.

Registration Students may register by telephone, in person.

Contact K. B. Massingill, Director of the Center for Teaching Excellence, Abilene Christian University, ACU Box 29201, Abilene, TX 79699-9201. *Telephone:* 915-674-2833. *Fax:* 915-674-2834. *E-mail:* massingill@cte.acu.edu.

DEGREES AND AWARDS

Undergraduate Certificate(s) Applied Studies (some on-campus requirements)

COURSE SUBJECT AREAS OFFERED OUTSIDE OF DEGREE PROGRAMS

Graduate: Philosophy and religion
Noncredit: Philosophy and religion

ACADIA UNIVERSITY

Wolfville, Nova Scotia, Canada

Division of Continuing and Distance Education
conted.acadiau.ca

Acadia University, founded in 1838, is a province-supported, comprehensive institution. It is accredited by the Association of Theological Schools in the United States and Canada. It first offered distance learning courses in 1968. In 1999–2000, it offered 100 courses at a distance. In fall 1999, there were 1,100 students enrolled in distance learning courses.

Course delivery sites Courses are delivered to your home, your workplace, military bases, 20 off-campus centers.

Media Courses are delivered via videotapes, videoconferencing, audiotapes, computer software, CD-ROM, computer conferencing, World Wide Web, print. Students and teachers may meet in person or interact via videoconferencing, audioconferencing, mail, telephone, fax, e-mail, World Wide Web. The following equipment may be required: e-mail.

Restrictions Programs are available worldwide. Enrollment is open to anyone.

Services Distance learners have access to library services, the campus computer network, e-mail services, academic advising, career placement assistance, bookstore at a distance.

Credit-earning options Students may transfer credits from another institution or may earn credits through examinations.

Typical costs Undergraduate tuition for 3 credit hours is $452.50. Graduate tuition is $506 for 3 credit hours. Mandatory fees are $80 for 3 credit hours and $25 admission fee for new applicants. *Noncredit courses:* Can$300 per course.

Registration Students may register by mail, fax, telephone, e-mail, World Wide Web, in person.

Contact Continuing Education, Acadia University, 42 University Avenue, Wolfville, NS B0P 1X0 Canada. *Telephone:* 902-585-1434. *Fax:* 902-585-1068. *E-mail:* continuing.education@acadiau.ca.

DEGREES AND AWARDS

Undergraduate Certificate(s) Business Administration (certain restrictions apply), Computer Science

COURSE SUBJECT AREAS OFFERED OUTSIDE OF DEGREE PROGRAMS

Undergraduate: Art history and criticism; business; classical languages and literatures; computer and information sciences; education; English language and literature; European languages and literatures; history; home economics and family studies; mathematics; philosophy and religion; physical sciences; psychology; social sciences
Graduate: Education

ADAMS STATE COLLEGE

Alamosa, Colorado

Division of Extended Studies
www.adams.edu/exstudies/index.html

Adams State College, founded in 1921, is a state-supported, comprehensive institution. It is accredited by the North Central Association of Colleges and Schools. It first offered distance learning courses in 1988. In 1999–2000, it offered 50 courses at a distance. In fall 1999, there were 200 students enrolled in distance learning courses.

Course delivery sites Courses are delivered to your home.

Media Courses are delivered via television, videotapes, World Wide Web, e-mail, print. Students and teachers may interact via mail, telephone, fax, e-mail.

Restrictions Programs are available worldwide. Enrollment is open to anyone.

Services Distance learners have access to library services, bookstore at a distance.

Typical costs *Undergraduate:* Tuition of $80 per semester hour. *Graduate:* Tuition of $100 per semester hour. Costs may vary.

Registration Students may register by mail, fax, telephone, in person.

Contact Alberta Coolbaugh, Director, Adams State College, Division of Extended Studies, Alamosa, CO 81102. *Telephone:* 719-587-7671. *Fax:* 719-587-7974. *E-mail:* ascextend@adams.edu.

DEGREES AND AWARDS

Distance programs offered do not lead to a degree or other formal award.

COURSE SUBJECT AREAS OFFERED OUTSIDE OF DEGREE PROGRAMS

Undergraduate: Accounting; business administration and management; business communications; business law; developmental and child psychology; economics; English composition; environmental science; finance; health and physical education/fitness; history; management information systems; mathematics; psychology; radio and television broadcasting; sociology; statistics

Graduate: Biology; health and physical education/fitness; psychology; teacher education

Special note

Adams State College (ASC) is a coeducational, state-supported, comprehensive liberal arts college that awards degrees at the associate, baccalaureate, and master's levels and provides high-quality education with a personal touch. More than 30 areas of study, preprofessional programs, and guaranteed transfer programs are available through 4 undergraduate schools—Business; Education and Graduate Studies; Science, Mathematics, and Technology; and the Arts and Letters. A diverse population of 2,500 students, with a student-faculty ratio of 18:1, provides quality and value that has endured for three quarters of a century. ASC was recently named one of the 100 best college buys in the U.S. by a publication that rates America's colleges and universities. ASC is located in south-central Colorado in Alamosa. ASC Extended Studies is part of the Colorado Statewide Extended Campus. More than 13,000 students enroll for more than 300 sections of contract courses per semester, more than 40 independent study courses, and Internet and Web-based courses. More than 1,300 professionals have provided instruction for Extended Studies. These professionals are educational entrepreneurs that represent private and public institutions and form a strategic network of talent and experience. ASC Extended Studies aligns resources to deliver information and instruction globally, as if there were no barriers "connecting the DOTS" (Delivery of Transparent Systems). For more information, students should call 800-548-6679 (toll-free) or visit the Web site at http://www.adams.edu.

ADELPHI UNIVERSITY

Garden City, New York

Distance Education Program
www.adelphi.edu

Adelphi University, founded in 1896, is an independent, nonprofit university. It is accredited by the Middle States Association of Colleges and Schools. It first offered distance learning courses in 1998. In 1999–2000, it offered 30 courses at a distance. In fall 1999, there were 125 students enrolled in distance learning courses.

Course delivery sites Courses are delivered to your workplace.

Media Courses are delivered via videoconferencing. Students and teachers may interact via videoconferencing, telephone, fax.

Restrictions Programs are available nationwide. Enrollment is restricted to individuals meeting certain criteria.

Services Distance learners have access to library services, e-mail services, academic advising, tutoring, career placement assistance, bookstore at a distance.

Credit-earning options Students may transfer credits from another institution.

Typical costs *Undergraduate:* Tuition of $450 per credit. *Graduate:* Tuition of $500 per credit.

Registration Students may register by mail, fax, telephone, in person.

Contact Ursula Forte, Assistant Coordinator, Adelphi University, School of Management and Business/Room 327, 1 South Avenue, Garden City, NY 11530. *Telephone:* 516-877-3315. *Fax:* 516-877-4571. *E-mail:* forte@adelphi.edu.

DEGREES AND AWARDS

BBA Management (certain restrictions apply)
MBA Management (certain restrictions apply)

COURSE SUBJECT AREAS OFFERED OUTSIDE OF DEGREE PROGRAMS

Undergraduate: Accounting; business administration and management; finance; marketing
Graduate: Accounting; business administration and management; finance; marketing

ALABAMA AGRICULTURAL AND MECHANICAL UNIVERSITY

Normal, Alabama
www.aamu.edu/

Alabama Agricultural and Mechanical University, founded in 1875, is a state-supported university. It is accredited by the Southern Association of Colleges and Schools. In 1999–2000, it offered 6 courses at a distance. In fall 1999, there were 49 students enrolled in distance learning courses.

Course delivery sites Courses are delivered to your home, your workplace, military bases, 7 off-campus centers in Birmingham, Greenville, Scottsboro.

Media Courses are delivered via television, interactive television, computer software, e-mail, print. Students and teachers may meet in person or interact via telephone, e-mail, interactive television, World Wide Web. The following equipment may be required: television, videocassette player, computer, Internet access, e-mail.

Restrictions Programs are available to in-state students only. Enrollment is restricted to individuals meeting certain criteria.

Services Distance learners have access to library services, e-mail services, academic advising at a distance.

Credit-earning options Students may transfer credits from another institution or may earn credits through examinations, military training.

Typical costs *Undergraduate:* Tuition of $1166 per semester. *Graduate:* Tuition of $1166 per semester. Financial aid is available to distance learners.

Registration Students may register by telephone, in person.

Contact Dr. Thomas McAlpine, Director, Extended Studies, Alabama Agricultural and Mechanical University, PO Box 579, Normal, AL 35762. *Telephone:* 256-851-4864.

DEGREES AND AWARDS

Distance programs offered do not lead to a degree or other formal award.

COURSE SUBJECT AREAS OFFERED OUTSIDE OF DEGREE PROGRAMS

Graduate: Biology; computer and information sciences; home economics and family studies

ALAMANCE COMMUNITY COLLEGE

Graham, North Carolina

Alamance Community College, founded in 1959, is a state-supported, two-year college. It is accredited by the Southern Association of Colleges and Schools. In 1999–2000, it offered 20 courses at a distance. In fall 1999, there were 30 students enrolled in distance learning courses.

Course delivery sites Courses are delivered to your home, your workplace, military bases.

Media Courses are delivered via videotapes, computer software, World Wide Web, e-mail. Students and teachers may meet in person or interact via mail, telephone, e-mail. The following equipment may be required: television, videocassette player, computer, modem, Internet access, e-mail.
Restrictions Programs are available to local area students. Enrollment is open to anyone.
Services Distance learners have access to library services, e-mail services at a distance.
Credit-earning options Students may transfer credits from another institution or may earn credits through examinations, military training.
Typical costs Tuition of $26.75 per credit for local area residents. Tuition of $26.75 per credit for in-state residents. Tuition of $169.75 per credit for out-of-state residents. Mandatory fees are between $5 and $15. Financial aid is available to distance learners.
Registration Students may register by telephone, in person.
Contact Ms. Laura Gorham, Director, Learning Resource Center, Alamance Community College, PO Box 8000, Graham, NC 27253. *Telephone:* 336-506-4186.

DEGREES AND AWARDS

Distance programs offered do not lead to a degree or other formal award.

COURSE SUBJECT AREAS OFFERED OUTSIDE OF DEGREE PROGRAMS

Undergraduate: Anatomy; business administration and management; hospitality services management; management; mathematics; technical writing

ALASKA PACIFIC UNIVERSITY

Anchorage, Alaska
Rural Alaska Native Adult (RANA) Program
www.alaskapacific.edu/

Alaska Pacific University, founded in 1959, is an independent, nonprofit, comprehensive institution. It is accredited by the Northwest Association of Schools and Colleges. In 1999–2000, it offered 18 courses at a distance. In fall 1999, there were 20 students enrolled in distance learning courses.
Course delivery sites Courses are delivered to your home, your workplace.
Media Courses are delivered via computer software, CD-ROM, computer conferencing, World Wide Web, e-mail, print. Students and teachers may meet in person or interact via audioconferencing, telephone, e-mail, World Wide Web. The following equipment may be required: computer, modem, Internet access, e-mail.
Restrictions Programs are available statewide but lower 48 states and Canada are also possible. Enrollment is restricted to individuals meeting certain criteria.
Services Distance learners have access to library services, the campus computer network, e-mail services, academic advising, tutoring, career placement assistance, bookstore at a distance.
Credit-earning options Students may transfer credits from another institution or may earn credits through examinations, portfolio assessment, military training.
Typical costs Tuition of $285 per credit hour plus mandatory fees of $25 per semester. *Noncredit courses:* $100 per course. Financial aid is available to distance learners.
Registration Students may register by mail, fax, e-mail, World Wide Web, in person.
Contact Dr. Gary Smith, Director, RANA Program, Alaska Pacific University, 4101 University Drive, Anchorage, AK 99508. *Telephone:* 907-564-8222. *Fax:* 907-562-4276. *E-mail:* gsmith@alaskapacific.edu.

DEGREES AND AWARDS

BA Accounting (some on-campus requirements), Business Administration (some on-campus requirements), Human Services (some on-campus requirements), Teacher Education (K-8) (some on-campus requirements)
MBA Management (some on-campus requirements)

COURSE SUBJECT AREAS OFFERED OUTSIDE OF DEGREE PROGRAMS

Undergraduate: Accounting; business; business administration and management; finance; human resources management; social work; teacher education
Graduate: Business administration and management

ALCORN STATE UNIVERSITY

Alcorn State, Mississippi
Office of Academic Technologies
www.alcorn.edu

Alcorn State University, founded in 1871, is a state-supported, comprehensive institution. It is accredited by the Southern Association of Colleges and Schools. It first offered distance learning courses in 1997.
Contact Alcorn State University, 1000 ASU Drive, Alcorn State, MS 39096-7500. *Telephone:* 601-877-6100.
See full description on page 676.

ALLEGANY COLLEGE OF MARYLAND

Cumberland, Maryland
Institute for Professional Development and Extended Learning
www.ac.cc.md.us

Allegany College of Maryland, founded in 1961, is a state and locally supported, two-year college. It is accredited by the Middle States Association of Colleges and Schools. It first offered distance learning courses in 1995. In 1999–2000, it offered 40 courses at a distance. In fall 1999, there were 298 students enrolled in distance learning courses.
Course delivery sites Courses are delivered to your home, your workplace, high schools, any of 16 Maryland community colleges, 2 off-campus centers in Everett (PA), Somerset (PA).
Media Courses are delivered via television, videotapes, videoconferencing, interactive television, computer software, computer conferencing, World Wide Web, e-mail, print. Students and teachers may meet in person or interact via videoconferencing, mail, telephone, fax, e-mail, interactive television, World Wide Web. The following equipment may be required: television, videocassette player, computer, modem, Internet access, e-mail.
Restrictions Programs are available generally to Western Maryland, south central Pennsylvania, northeastern West Virginia and northwestern Virginia. Enrollment is open to anyone.
Services Distance learners have access to library services, academic advising, career placement assistance at a distance.
Credit-earning options Students may transfer credits from another institution or may earn credits through examinations.
Typical costs Tuition of $83 per credit hour plus mandatory fees of $90 per semester for local area residents. Tuition of $165 per credit hour plus mandatory fees of $90 per semester for in-state residents. Tuition of $249 per credit hour plus mandatory fees of $90 per semester for out-of-state residents. Cost for a noncredit course is $100 for 10 hours. Costs may vary. Financial aid is available to distance learners.
Registration Students may register by mail, fax, telephone, in person.

Contact Ms. Jane Paulson, Director of Distance Education, Allegany College of Maryland, 12401 Willbrook Road, SE, Cumberland, MD 21502. *Telephone:* 301-784-5121. *Fax:* 301-784-5025. *E-mail:* jpaulson@mail.ac.cc.md.us.

DEGREES AND AWARDS

Distance programs offered do not lead to a degree or other formal award.

COURSE SUBJECT AREAS OFFERED OUTSIDE OF DEGREE PROGRAMS

Undergraduate: Accounting; administrative and secretarial services; business; business administration and management; computer and information sciences; criminal justice; developmental and child psychology; economics; English composition; English language and literature; history; journalism; liberal arts, general studies, and humanities; library and information studies; mathematics; philosophy and religion; political science; psychology; sociology
Noncredit: Administrative and secretarial services; business; business administration and management; computer and information sciences; insurance; professional studies

ALLEN COLLEGE

Waterloo, Iowa
www.allencollege.edu/

Allen College, founded in 1989, is an independent, nonprofit, comprehensive institution. It is accredited by the North Central Association of Colleges and Schools. In 1999–2000, it offered 4 courses at a distance.
Course delivery sites Courses are delivered to your workplace, high schools, 3 off-campus centers.
Media Courses are delivered via interactive television, e-mail, print. Students and teachers may meet in person or interact via videoconferencing, mail, telephone, fax, e-mail, interactive television. The following equipment may be required: Internet access.
Restrictions Programs are available to in-state students only. Enrollment is restricted to individuals meeting certain criteria.
Services Distance learners have access to library services, academic advising at a distance.
Credit-earning options Students may transfer credits from another institution or may earn credits through examinations, portfolio assessment.
Typical costs Tuition of $254 per credit hour.
Registration Students may register by mail, fax, telephone, in person.
Contact Vickie Barth, MSN, RN, Coordinator, Distance Education, Allen College, 1825 Logan Avenue, Waterloo, IA 50703. *Telephone:* 319-235-3553. *Fax:* 319-235-5280. *E-mail:* admin@sbtek.net.

DEGREES AND AWARDS

BSN Nursing (certain restrictions apply)

AMERICAN ACADEMY OF NUTRITION, COLLEGE OF NUTRITION

Knoxville, Tennessee
American Academy of Nutrition, College of Nutrition
www.nutritioneducation.com

American Academy of Nutrition, College of Nutrition, founded in 1984, is a proprietary, two-year college. It is accredited by the Distance Education and Training Council. It first offered distance learning courses in 1985. In 1999–2000, it offered 23 courses at a distance. In fall 1999, there were 420 students enrolled in distance learning courses.
Course delivery sites Courses are delivered to your home.
Media Courses are delivered via videotapes, audiotapes, World Wide Web, e-mail, print. Students and teachers may interact via mail, telephone, fax, e-mail, World Wide Web. The following equipment may be required: television, videocassette player, Internet access.
Restrictions Programs are available worldwide. Enrollment is restricted to individuals meeting certain criteria.
Services Distance learners have access to e-mail services at a distance.
Credit-earning options Students may transfer credits from another institution.
Typical costs Tuition of $100 per credit. *Noncredit courses:* $345 per course. Costs may vary.
Registration Students may register by mail, fax, e-mail, World Wide Web.
Contact Kathy Witt, Student Services, American Academy of Nutrition, College of Nutrition, 1204 Kenesaw Avenue, Knoxville, TN 37919. *Telephone:* 423-524-8079. *Fax:* 473-524-8339. *E-mail:* aantn@aol.com.

DEGREES AND AWARDS

AS Nutrition

COURSE SUBJECT AREAS OFFERED OUTSIDE OF DEGREE PROGRAMS

Undergraduate: Anatomy; biology; business administration and management; chemistry; chemistry, organic; communications; developmental and child psychology; English language and literature; environmental health; foods and nutrition studies; health and physical education/fitness; marketing; physiology; psychology

AMERICAN COLLEGE

Bryn Mawr, Pennsylvania
www.amercoll.edu

American College, founded in 1927, is an independent, nonprofit, graduate institution. It is accredited by the Middle States Association of Colleges and Schools. It first offered distance learning courses in 1927. In 1999–2000, it offered 40 courses at a distance. In fall 1999, there were 18,500 students enrolled in distance learning courses.
Course delivery sites Courses are delivered to your home.
Media Courses are delivered via videotapes, videoconferencing, audiotapes, computer software, CD-ROM, World Wide Web, print. Students and teachers may meet in person or interact via videoconferencing, audioconferencing, mail, telephone, fax, e-mail. The following equipment may be required: computer, Internet access, e-mail.
Restrictions Courses can be tested on worldwide basis, but are based on U.S. law. Enrollment is open to anyone.
Services Distance learners have access to library services, academic advising, bookstore at a distance.
Credit-earning options Students may transfer credits from another institution or may earn credits through examinations.
Typical costs Tuition of $525 per course.
Registration Students may register by mail, fax, telephone, World Wide Web, in person.
Contact Office of Student Services, American College, 270 South Bryn Mawr Avenue, Bryn Mawr, PA 19010. *Telephone:* 888-AMERCOL. *Fax:* 610-526-1465. *E-mail:* studentservices@amercoll.edu.

DEGREES AND AWARDS

Undergraduate Certificate(s) Financial Planning, Financial Planning and Insurance, Leadership and Management (some on-campus requirements), Registered Employee Benefits Consultant, Registered Health Underwriter

Graduate Certificate(s) Advanced Management, Asset Management, Business Succession Planning, Estate Planning and Taxation
MSFS Financial Planning (some on-campus requirements), Financial Services (some on-campus requirements)

COURSE SUBJECT AREAS OFFERED OUTSIDE OF DEGREE PROGRAMS

Undergraduate: Business; business administration and management; finance; human resources management; insurance; investments and securities
Graduate: Business; business administration and management; finance; human resources management; insurance; investments and securities

AMERICAN COLLEGE OF PREHOSPITAL MEDICINE

Navarre, Florida
www.acpm.edu

American College of Prehospital Medicine, founded in 1991, is a proprietary, four-year college. It is accredited by the Distance Education and Training Council. It first offered distance learning courses in 1991. In 1999–2000, it offered 150 courses at a distance. In fall 1999, there were 115 students enrolled in distance learning courses.
Course delivery sites Courses are delivered to your home.
Media Courses are delivered via videotapes, audiotapes, computer software, CD-ROM, e-mail, print. Students and teachers may interact via mail, telephone, fax, e-mail. The following equipment may be required: computer, modem.
Restrictions Programs are available worldwide. Enrollment is restricted to individuals meeting certain criteria.
Services Distance learners have access to library services, e-mail services, academic advising, tutoring, bookstore at a distance.
Credit-earning options Students may transfer credits from another institution or may earn credits through examinations, portfolio assessment, military training, business training.
Typical costs Tuition of $250 per semester hour. Financial aid is available to distance learners.
Registration Students may register by mail, fax.
Contact Dr. Richard A. Clinchy III, Chairman/CEO, American College of Prehospital Medicine, 7552 Navarre Parkway, Suite 1, Navarre, FL 32566-7312. *Telephone:* 800-735-2276. *Fax:* 800-350-3870. *E-mail:* admit@acpm.edu.

DEGREES AND AWARDS

AA Emergency Medical Services
BA Emergency Medical Services

COURSE SUBJECT AREAS OFFERED OUTSIDE OF DEGREE PROGRAMS

Undergraduate: Biology; information sciences and systems; mathematics; music; psychology

AMERICAN INSTITUTE FOR COMPUTER SCIENCES

Birmingham, Alabama
www.aics.edu

American Institute for Computer Sciences, founded in 1988, is a proprietary, comprehensive institution. It is accredited by the Distance Educa-
tion and Training Council. In 1999–2000, it offered 72 courses at a distance. In fall 1999, there were 5,000 students enrolled in distance learning courses.
Course delivery sites Courses are delivered to your home, your workplace.
Media Courses are delivered via computer software, CD-ROM, computer conferencing, World Wide Web, e-mail, print. Students and teachers may interact via mail, telephone, fax, e-mail, World Wide Web. The following equipment may be required: computer, modem, Internet access.
Restrictions Programs are available worldwide. Enrollment is restricted to individuals meeting certain criteria.
Services Distance learners have access to library services, the campus computer network, e-mail services, academic advising, tutoring at a distance.
Credit-earning options Students may transfer credits from another institution or may earn credits through portfolio assessment.
Typical costs *Undergraduate:* Tuition of $90 per credit hour. *Graduate:* Tuition of $120 per credit hour.
Registration Students may register by mail, fax, telephone, e-mail, World Wide Web.
Contact Natalie Nixon, Director of Admissions, American Institute for Computer Sciences, Office of Admissions, Suite 207, 2101 Magnolia Avenue, Birmingham, AL 35205. *Telephone:* 800-729-AICS. *Fax:* 205-328-2229. *E-mail:* admiss@aics.edu.

DEGREES AND AWARDS

BS Computer Science (certain restrictions apply), Information Systems (certain restrictions apply)
MS Computer Science (certain restrictions apply)

COURSE SUBJECT AREAS OFFERED OUTSIDE OF DEGREE PROGRAMS

Undergraduate: Algebra; American (U.S.) history; biology; business administration and management; business law; computer programming; database management; English composition; information sciences and systems; management information systems; marketing; psychology; technical writing
Graduate: Computer programming; database management
See full description on page 460.

AMERICAN INSTITUTE FOR PARALEGAL STUDIES, INC.

Oakbrook Terrace, Illinois
Distance Education
www.aips.com

In 1999–2000, it offered 12 courses at a distance. In fall 1999, there were 175 students enrolled in distance learning courses.
Course delivery sites Courses are delivered to your home, your workplace, military bases.
Media Courses are delivered via computer software, computer conferencing, World Wide Web, e-mail, print. Students and teachers may meet in person or interact via mail, telephone, fax, e-mail, World Wide Web. The following equipment may be required: computer, modem, Internet access, e-mail.
Restrictions Programs are available nationwide. Enrollment is restricted to individuals meeting certain criteria.
Services Distance learners have access to library services, e-mail services, academic advising, career placement assistance, bookstore at a distance.
Credit-earning options Students may transfer credits from another institution or may earn credits through military training, business training.

American Institute for Paralegal Studies, Inc.

Typical costs Tuition of $208.12 per credit hour plus mandatory fees of $590 per degree program. Financial aid is available to distance learners.
Registration Students may register by mail, fax, telephone, e-mail, World Wide Web, in person.
Contact Dorene Fink, Admissions Representative, American Institute for Paralegal Studies, Inc., 17 West 705 Butterfield Road, Oakbrook Terrace, IL 60181. *Telephone:* 800-553-2420 Ext. 118. *Fax:* 630-916-6694. *E-mail:* info@aips.com.

DEGREES AND AWARDS

Undergraduate Certificate(s) Paralegal Studies (certain restrictions apply)

COURSE SUBJECT AREAS OFFERED OUTSIDE OF DEGREE PROGRAMS

Undergraduate: Paralegal/legal assistant
See full description on page 462.

AMERICAN MILITARY UNIVERSITY

Manassas Park, Virginia
www.amunet.edu

American Military University, founded in 1991, is a proprietary, comprehensive institution. It is accredited by the Distance Education and Training Council. It first offered distance learning courses in 1993. In 1999–2000, it offered 250 courses at a distance. In fall 1999, there were 750 students enrolled in distance learning courses.
Course delivery sites Courses are delivered to your home, your workplace, military bases.
Media Courses are delivered via videotapes, computer software, computer conferencing, World Wide Web, e-mail, print. Students and teachers may interact via mail, telephone, fax, e-mail, World Wide Web. The following equipment may be required: computer, modem, Internet access, e-mail.
Restrictions Programs are available worldwide. Enrollment is open to anyone.
Services Distance learners have access to library services, the campus computer network, e-mail services, academic advising, bookstore at a distance.
Credit-earning options Students may transfer credits from another institution or may earn credits through examinations, portfolio assessment, military training, business training.
Typical costs *Undergraduate:* Tuition of $750 per course. *Graduate:* Tuition of $750 per course. Financial aid is available to distance learners.
Registration Students may register by mail, fax, telephone, e-mail, World Wide Web, in person.
Contact Nan Lamb, Executive Administrator, American Military University, Student Service Center, 9104-P Manassas Drive, Manassas Park, VA 20111. *Telephone:* 703-330-5398 Ext. 111. *Fax:* 703-330-5109. *E-mail:* amuinfo@amunet.edu.

DEGREES AND AWARDS

AA Military Studies
BA Management, Marketing, Military History, Military Management, Intelligence Studies
BACJ Criminal Justice
MA Military History, Military Management, Intelligence Studies, Military Studies
MAM Management

COURSE SUBJECT AREAS OFFERED OUTSIDE OF DEGREE PROGRAMS

Undergraduate: Business administration and management; criminal justice; history; marketing; military studies
Graduate: Area, ethnic, and cultural studies; business administration and management; history; military studies

Special note

American Military University (AMU) is a private, licensed, and accredited institution offering a curriculum of more than 480 courses in 16 areas of study that lead to associate, bachelor's, and Master of Arts degrees. AMU courses are developed and taught by a distinguished faculty of more than 125 doctoral scholars who are experienced in delivering distance learning courses through AMU's Electronic Campus. AMU offers an AA degree in general studies; BA degrees in military history, intelligence studies, criminal justice, military management, management, and marketing; and MA degrees in air, land, navel, or unconventional warfare; Civil War studies; intelligence; defense management; management; and transportation management. In addition, graduate students may pursue certificate programs in 20 related specialties. AMU accepts up to 75 percent of degree requirements through transfer credits from other accredited institutions and through training and experience credit recommendations of the American Council on Education (ACE). AMU's student body of 2,500 students represents all 50 states and more than 30 other countries. Although 75 percent of AMU's students are from the U.S. Armed Forces, the rest represent a wide range of professions, including education, law enforcement, government, private industry, and the intelligence community. AMU is licensed by the State Council for Higher Education in Virginia (SCHEV) and is accredited by the Distance Education and Training Council. AMU is a Servicemembers Opportunity College and is recognized by the federal government and most corporations for tuition assistance and VA benefits. AMU offers undergraduate financial assistance through merit scholarships and provides all undergraduate textbooks through book grants.

AMERICAN RIVER COLLEGE

Sacramento, California

Distance Education
www.arc.losrios.cc.ca.us/learnres/distance.html

American River College, founded in 1955, is a district-supported, two-year college. It is accredited by the Western Association of Schools and Colleges, Inc. It first offered distance learning courses in 1975. In 1999–2000, it offered 35 courses at a distance. In fall 1999, there were 366 students enrolled in distance learning courses.
Course delivery sites Courses are delivered to your home.
Media Courses are delivered via television, videotapes, computer software, CD-ROM, World Wide Web, e-mail, print. Students and teachers may meet in person or interact via e-mail, World Wide Web. The following equipment may be required: television, computer, modem, Internet access, e-mail.
Restrictions Programs are available mostly on the local level with some enrollments from out of the area. Enrollment is restricted to individuals meeting certain criteria.
Services Distance learners have access to library services, e-mail services, tutoring at a distance.
Credit-earning options Students may transfer credits from another institution or may earn credits through examinations.
Typical costs Tuition of $11 per unit for in-state residents. Tuition of $145 per unit for out-of-state residents. Costs may vary. Financial aid is available to distance learners.

Registration Students may register by mail, telephone, in person.
Contact Debby Ondricka, Administrative Assistant, American River College, 4700 College Oak Drive, Sacramento, CA 95841. *Telephone:* 916-484-8456. *Fax:* 916-484-8018. *E-mail:* ondricd@arc.losrios.cc.ca.us.

DEGREES AND AWARDS

Undergraduate Certificate(s) Computer Information Science (certain restrictions apply; service area differs from that of the overall institution; some on-campus requirements)

COURSE SUBJECT AREAS OFFERED OUTSIDE OF DEGREE PROGRAMS

Undergraduate: Biology; business administration and management; computer and information sciences; English composition; health and physical education/fitness; library and information studies; marketing

ANDERSON UNIVERSITY

Anderson, Indiana
auonline.anderson.edu

Anderson University, founded in 1917, is an independent, religious, comprehensive institution affiliated with the Church of God. It is accredited by the Association of Theological Schools in the United States and Canada, North Central Association of Colleges and Schools. It first offered distance learning courses in 1999. In 1999–2000, it offered 3 courses at a distance.
Course delivery sites Courses are delivered to your home, your workplace.
Media Courses are delivered via videotapes, audiotapes, computer software, computer conferencing, World Wide Web, e-mail. Students and teachers may meet in person or interact via audioconferencing, mail, telephone, e-mail, World Wide Web. The following equipment may be required: computer, modem, Internet access, e-mail.
Restrictions Programs are available worldwide. Enrollment is restricted to individuals meeting certain criteria.
Services Distance learners have access to library services, the campus computer network, e-mail services, academic advising, bookstore at a distance.
Credit-earning options Students may transfer credits from another institution.
Typical costs *Undergraduate:* Tuition of $265 per credit. *Graduate:* Tuition of $321 per credit. Financial aid is available to distance learners.
Registration Students may register by World Wide Web, in person.
Contact Dr. John Aukerman, Liaison to eCollege.com, Anderson University, Anderson School of Theology, 1100 East 5th Street, Anderson, IN 46012-3495. *Telephone:* 765-641-4530. *Fax:* 801-912-6395. *E-mail:* auk@anderson.edu.

eCollege.com *www.ecollege.com/scholarships*

DEGREES AND AWARDS

Distance programs offered do not lead to a degree or other formal award.

COURSE SUBJECT AREAS OFFERED OUTSIDE OF DEGREE PROGRAMS

Graduate: Theological studies
See full description on page 540.

ANDREWS UNIVERSITY

Berrien Springs, Michigan
www.andrews.edu

Andrews University, founded in 1874, is an independent, religious university. It is accredited by the Association of Theological Schools in the United States and Canada, North Central Association of Colleges and Schools. In 1999–2000, it offered 22 courses at a distance. In fall 1999, there were 44 students enrolled in distance learning courses.
Course delivery sites Courses are delivered to your home, your workplace.
Media Courses are delivered via videotapes, audiotapes, computer conferencing, print. Students and teachers may meet in person or interact via mail, telephone, fax, e-mail.
Restrictions Programs are available worldwide. Enrollment is restricted to individuals meeting certain criteria.
Services Distance learners have access to library services, the campus computer network, e-mail services, academic advising at a distance.
Credit-earning options Students may transfer credits from another institution or may earn credits through examinations, military training.
Typical costs Tuition of $175 per semester hour. There is a $60 mandatory processing fee.
Registration Students may register by mail, fax, telephone, e-mail, in person.
Contact Susan Zork, Coordinator of HSI Distance Education, Andrews University, Nethery Hall, Berrien Springs, MI 49104-0070. *Telephone:* 800-471-6210. *Fax:* 616-471-6236. *E-mail:* au-hsi@andrews.edu.

DEGREES AND AWARDS

AA Liberal Arts, General Studies, Humanities
BA Liberal Arts, General Studies, Humanities, Theological Studies
BS Liberal Arts, General Studies, Humanities

COURSE SUBJECT AREAS OFFERED OUTSIDE OF DEGREE PROGRAMS

Undergraduate: Algebra; American literature; American studies; area, ethnic, and cultural studies; astronomy and astrophysics; communications; developmental and child psychology; English composition; English language and literature; foods and nutrition studies; French language and literature; geography; Greek language and literature; history; interdisciplinary studies; liberal arts, general studies, and humanities; music; political science; religious studies; social psychology; sociology; statistics; theological studies
Graduate: Education; nursing; theological studies

ANNE ARUNDEL COMMUNITY COLLEGE

Arnold, Maryland
Distance Learning Center
www.aacc.cc.md.us/diseduc

Anne Arundel Community College, founded in 1961, is a state and locally supported, two-year college. It is accredited by the Middle States Association of Colleges and Schools. It first offered distance learning courses in 1981. In 1999–2000, it offered 71 courses at a distance. In fall 1999, there were 1,650 students enrolled in distance learning courses.
Course delivery sites Courses are delivered to your home, your workplace, military bases, high schools.
Media Courses are delivered via television, videotapes, videoconferencing, interactive television, computer software, World Wide Web. Students and teachers may meet in person or interact via videoconferencing, audioconferencing, mail, telephone, fax, e-mail, interactive television, World

Wide Web. The following equipment may be required: television, video-cassette player, computer, modem, Internet access, e-mail.

Restrictions Programs are available to in-state students only. Enrollment is open to anyone.

Services Distance learners have access to library services, academic advising, bookstore at a distance.

Credit-earning options Students may transfer credits from another institution or may earn credits through examinations, military training, business training.

Typical costs Tuition of $58 per credit hour for local area residents. Tuition of $108 per credit hour for in-state residents. Tuition of $202 per credit hour for out-of-state residents. Financial aid is available to distance learners.

Registration Students may register by mail, fax, telephone, in person.

Contact Mary Barnes, Coordinator, Anne Arundel Community College, Distance Learning, Arnold, MD 21012-1895. *Telephone:* 410-541-2731. *Fax:* 410-541-2691. *E-mail:* mabarnes@mail.aacc.cc.md.us.

DEGREES AND AWARDS

AA General Studies (some on-campus requirements)
AAS Business Management (some on-campus requirements)
AS Business Administration (some on-campus requirements)

COURSE SUBJECT AREAS OFFERED OUTSIDE OF DEGREE PROGRAMS

Undergraduate: Abnormal psychology; accounting; algebra; American (U.S.) history; anthropology; architecture; astronomy and astrophysics; biology; business; business administration and management; business communications; business law; calculus; chemistry; computer and information sciences; computer programming; creative writing; database management; developmental and child psychology; economics; engineering; English composition; English literature; European languages and literatures; finance; fine arts; geography; health and physical education/fitness; history; home economics and family studies; hospitality services management; human resources management; information sciences and systems; liberal arts, general studies, and humanities; marketing; mathematics; music; oceanography; paralegal/legal assistant; philosophy and religion; physical sciences; political science; psychology; social psychology; sociology; statistics; teacher education

See full description on page 676.

AQUINAS COLLEGE

Grand Rapids, Michigan

Learning and Technology
www.aquinas.edu/webslingers

Aquinas College, founded in 1886, is an independent, religious, comprehensive institution. It is accredited by the North Central Association of Colleges and Schools. In 1999–2000, it offered 14 courses at a distance. In fall 1999, there were 95 students enrolled in distance learning courses.

Course delivery sites Courses are delivered to your home, your workplace, high schools.

Media Courses are delivered via television, interactive television, computer software, computer conferencing, World Wide Web, e-mail, print. Students and teachers may meet in person or interact via videoconferencing, audioconferencing, mail, telephone, fax, e-mail, interactive television, World Wide Web. The following equipment may be required: computer, modem, Internet access, e-mail.

Restrictions Programs are available to in-state students only. Enrollment is open to anyone.

Services Distance learners have access to library services, bookstore at a distance.

Credit-earning options Students may earn credits through examinations, portfolio assessment.

Typical costs *Undergraduate:* Tuition of $7017 per semester. *Graduate:* Tuition of $320 per credit. Costs may vary. Financial aid is available to distance learners.

Registration Students may register by mail, fax, telephone, e-mail, in person.

Contact Kim Kenward, Director of Learning and Technology, Aquinas College, 1607 Robinson Road South East, Grand Rapids, MI 49506-1799. *Telephone:* 616-459-8281 Ext. 3970. *Fax:* 616-732-4534. *E-mail:* kenwakim@aquinas.edu.

DEGREES AND AWARDS

Distance programs offered do not lead to a degree or other formal award.

COURSE SUBJECT AREAS OFFERED OUTSIDE OF DEGREE PROGRAMS

Undergraduate: Art history and criticism; business administration and management; computer and information sciences; creative writing; instructional media; liberal arts, general studies, and humanities; sociology
Graduate: Business administration and management; instructional media

ARIZONA STATE UNIVERSITY

Tempe, Arizona

Distance Learning Technology
www.dlt.asu.edu

Arizona State University, founded in 1885, is a state-supported university. It is accredited by the North Central Association of Colleges and Schools. It first offered distance learning courses in 1955. In 1999–2000, it offered 140 courses at a distance. In fall 1999, there were 1,758 students enrolled in distance learning courses.

Course delivery sites Courses are delivered to your home, your workplace, military bases, high schools, Arizona State University East (Mesa), Arizona State University West (Phoenix), Northern Arizona University (Flagstaff), Paradise Valley Community College (Phoenix), Phoenix College (Phoenix), Scottsdale Community College (Scottsdale), South Mountain Community College (Phoenix), University of Arizona (Tucson), 1 off-campus center in Phoenix.

Media Courses are delivered via television, videotapes, interactive television, computer software, CD-ROM, World Wide Web, e-mail, print. Students and teachers may meet in person or interact via videoconferencing, mail, telephone, fax, e-mail, interactive television, World Wide Web. The following equipment may be required: television, videocassette player, computer, modem, Internet access, e-mail.

Restrictions Programs are available worldwide. Enrollment is open to anyone.

Services Distance learners have access to library services, e-mail services, academic advising, tutoring, career placement assistance, bookstore at a distance.

Credit-earning options Students may transfer credits from another institution or may earn credits through examinations.

Typical costs *Undergraduate:* Tuition of $115 per credit hour for in-state residents. Tuition of $389 per credit hour for out-of-state residents. *Graduate:* Tuition of $115 per credit hour for in-state residents. Tuition of $389 per credit hour for out-of-state residents. Costs may vary. Financial aid is available to distance learners.

Registration Students may register by mail, fax, telephone, in person.

Contact Brent Woodhouse, Distance Learning Technology, Arizona State University, PO Box 870501, Tempe, AZ 85287-0501. *Telephone:* 480-965-6738. *Fax:* 480-965-1371. *E-mail:* distance@asu.edu.

DEGREES AND AWARDS

BA History (certain restrictions apply; some on-campus requirements)
ME Engineering
MSE Electrical Engineering (service area differs from that of the overall institution; some on-campus requirements)

COURSE SUBJECT AREAS OFFERED OUTSIDE OF DEGREE PROGRAMS

Undergraduate: Accounting; advertising; aerospace, aeronautical engineering; algebra; architecture; area, ethnic, and cultural studies; art history and criticism; biology; botany; business administration and management; business communications; business law; chemical engineering; civil engineering; communications; computer and information sciences; computer programming; developmental and child psychology; drama and theater; educational psychology; electrical engineering; engineering; engineering-related technologies; engineering/industrial management; English language and literature; environmental engineering; fine arts; geography; health and physical education/fitness; history; home economics and family studies; horticulture; industrial engineering; journalism; Latin language and literature; law and legal studies; liberal arts, general studies, and humanities; library and information studies; marketing; mass media; mechanical engineering; medieval/renaissance studies; nursing; philosophy and religion; physiology; plant sciences; political science; psychology; Spanish language and literature; special education; technical writing; women's studies; zoology
Graduate: Aerospace, aeronautical engineering; architecture; art history and criticism; chemical engineering; civil engineering; computer and information sciences; computer programming; construction; curriculum and instruction; education administration; educational psychology; electrical engineering; electronics; engineering; engineering-related technologies; engineering/industrial management; English language and literature; environmental engineering; health professions and related sciences; history; industrial engineering; instructional media; international business; Latin language and literature; liberal arts, general studies, and humanities; mathematics; mechanical engineering; medieval/renaissance studies; nursing; physical sciences; physics; public health; teacher education
Noncredit: Engineering

ARIZONA WESTERN COLLEGE

Yuma, Arizona
www.awc.cc.az.us/

Arizona Western College, founded in 1962, is a state and locally supported, two-year college. It is accredited by the North Central Association of Colleges and Schools. In 1999–2000, it offered 43 courses at a distance.
Course delivery sites Courses are delivered to your home, your workplace, military bases, 3 off-campus centers in La Paz, San Luis, Yuma.
Media Courses are delivered via television, videoconferencing, interactive television, World Wide Web. Students and teachers may interact via videoconferencing, telephone, fax, e-mail, interactive television. The following equipment may be required: television, computer, modem, Internet access.
Restrictions Programs are available to local area students. Enrollment is restricted to individuals meeting certain criteria.
Services Distance learners have access to library services, the campus computer network, e-mail services, bookstore at a distance.
Typical costs Contact school for information. Costs may vary. Financial aid is available to distance learners.
Registration Students may register by telephone, in person.
Contact Carol Thomas, Administrative Secretary, Division of Modern Languages and Off-Campus Services, Arizona Western College, PO Box 929, Yuma, AZ 85366. *Telephone:* 520-344-7524. *Fax:* 520-344-7730. *E-mail:* aw_thomas@awc.cc.az.us.

DEGREES AND AWARDS

Distance programs offered do not lead to a degree or other formal award.

COURSE SUBJECT AREAS OFFERED OUTSIDE OF DEGREE PROGRAMS

Graduate: Accounting; algebra; anthropology; area, ethnic, and cultural studies; business; child care and development; education; education administration; English as a second language (ESL); English language and literature; history; individual and family development studies; information sciences and systems; marketing; mathematics; philosophy and religion; protective services; psychology; social sciences; speech

ARKANSAS STATE UNIVERSITY

State University, Arkansas
Center for Regional Programs
www.astate.edu/

Arkansas State University, founded in 1909, is a state-supported, comprehensive institution. It is accredited by the North Central Association of Colleges and Schools. In 1999–2000, it offered 91 courses at a distance. In fall 1999, there were 519 students enrolled in distance learning courses.
Course delivery sites Courses are delivered to Arkansas State University, Mountain Home (Mountain Home), Arkansas State University–Beebe (Beebe), 6 off-campus centers in Beebe, Blytheville, Forrest City, Fort Smith, Mountain Home, West Memphis.
Media Courses are delivered via television, videoconferencing, interactive television, World Wide Web, print. Students and teachers may meet in person or interact via videoconferencing, interactive television.
Restrictions Programs are available to in-state students only. Enrollment is restricted to individuals meeting certain criteria.
Credit-earning options Students may transfer credits from another institution.
Typical costs *Undergraduate:* Tuition of $124 per credit plus mandatory fees of $19 per credit for in-state residents. Tuition of $277 per credit plus mandatory fees of $19 per credit for out-of-state residents. *Graduate:* Tuition of $141 per credit plus mandatory fees of $19 per credit for in-state residents. Tuition of $328 per credit plus mandatory fees of $19 per credit for out-of-state residents. *Noncredit courses:* $143 per course. Financial aid is available to distance learners.
Registration Students may register by telephone, World Wide Web, in person.
Contact Dr. Jerry Linnstaedter, Associate Vice President for Academic Affairs, Arkansas State University, PO Box 179, State University, AR 72467. *Telephone:* 870-972-2030. *Fax:* 870-972-2036.

DEGREES AND AWARDS

Distance programs offered do not lead to a degree or other formal award.

COURSE SUBJECT AREAS OFFERED OUTSIDE OF DEGREE PROGRAMS

Undergraduate: Agriculture; business; education; health professions and related sciences; visual and performing arts
Graduate: Agriculture; education; health professions and related sciences

ARKANSAS TECH UNIVERSITY

Russellville, Arkansas

Virtual Learning Center
www.atu.edu

Arkansas Tech University, founded in 1909, is a state-supported, comprehensive institution. It is accredited by the North Central Association of Colleges and Schools. It first offered distance learning courses in 1996.
Contact Arkansas Tech University, Russellville, AR 72801-2222. *Telephone:* 501-968-0389. *Fax:* 501-964-0522.

See full description on page 676.

ARLINGTON BAPTIST COLLEGE

Arlington, Texas

Distance Education Department

Arlington Baptist College, founded in 1939, is an independent, religious, four-year college. It is accredited by the Accrediting Association of Bible Colleges. In 1999–2000, it offered 15 courses at a distance. In fall 1999, there were 19 students enrolled in distance learning courses.
Course delivery sites Courses are delivered to your home.
Media Courses are delivered via print. Students and teachers may meet in person or interact via mail, telephone, fax, e-mail. The following equipment may be required: computer.
Restrictions Programs are available nationwide. Enrollment is restricted to individuals meeting certain criteria.
Services Distance learners have access to academic advising, bookstore at a distance.
Credit-earning options Students may transfer credits from another institution.
Typical costs Tuition of $240 per course. Registration fee is $25. *Noncredit courses:* $200 per course. Financial aid is available to distance learners.
Registration Students may register by mail, telephone, in person.
Contact Carl E. Johnson, Director of Distance Education, Arlington Baptist College, 3001 West Division, Arlington, TX 76012. *Telephone:* 817-461-8741. *Fax:* 817-274-1138.

DEGREES AND AWARDS

BS Bible (certain restrictions apply)

COURSE SUBJECT AREAS OFFERED OUTSIDE OF DEGREE PROGRAMS

Undergraduate: Bible studies
Noncredit: Bible studies

ARMSTRONG ATLANTIC STATE UNIVERSITY

Savannah, Georgia

Academic Off-Campus Programs
www.armstrong.edu

Armstrong Atlantic State University, founded in 1935, is a state-supported, comprehensive institution. It is accredited by the Southern Association of Colleges and Schools. In 1999–2000, it offered 45 courses at a distance. In fall 1999, there were 500 students enrolled in distance learning courses.

Course delivery sites Courses are delivered to your home, military bases, Coastal Georgia Community College (Brunswick), East Georgia College (Swainsboro), Medical College of Georgia (Augusta), Savannah State University (Savannah), 3 off-campus centers in Camden Center, Fort Stewart, Hunter Army Airfield.
Media Courses are delivered via interactive television, World Wide Web. Students and teachers may meet in person or interact via videoconferencing, mail, telephone, fax, e-mail, interactive television, World Wide Web. The following equipment may be required: Internet access.
Restrictions Programs are available to in-state students only. Enrollment is restricted to individuals meeting certain criteria.
Services Distance learners have access to library services, e-mail services, bookstore at a distance.
Credit-earning options Students may transfer credits from another institution or may earn credits through examinations.
Typical costs *Undergraduate:* Tuition of $1050 per semester for in-state residents. Tuition of $3800 per semester for out-of-state residents. *Graduate:* Tuition of $1250 per semester for in-state residents. Tuition of $4500 per semester for out-of-state residents. Costs may vary. Financial aid is available to distance learners.
Registration Students may register by telephone, World Wide Web, in person.
Contact Dr. Keith Martin, Assistant Dean, Academic Off-Campus Programs, Armstrong Atlantic State University, 11935 Abercorn Street, Savannah, GA 31419-1997. *Telephone:* 912-921-5989. *Fax:* 912-961-3047. *E-mail:* martinke@mail.armstrong.edu.

DEGREES AND AWARDS

BEd Education (certain restrictions apply)
BS Dental Hygiene (certain restrictions apply)
BSN Nursing (certain restrictions apply)
MEd Education (certain restrictions apply)
MHSA Health Services Administration (certain restrictions apply)

See full description on page 676.

ASSEMBLIES OF GOD THEOLOGICAL SEMINARY

Springfield, Missouri

Office of Continuing Education
www.agts.edu

Assemblies of God Theological Seminary, founded in 1972, is an independent, religious, graduate institution affiliated with the Assemblies of God. It is accredited by the Association of Theological Schools in the United States and Canada, North Central Association of Colleges and Schools. It first offered distance learning courses in 1980. In 1999–2000, it offered 38 courses at a distance. In fall 1999, there were 62 students enrolled in distance learning courses.
Course delivery sites Courses are delivered to your home, North Central University (Minneapolis, MN), Northwest College (Kirkland, WA), Southeastern College of the Assemblies of God (Lakeland, FL), Valley Forge Christian College (Phoenixville, PA), Vanguard University of Southern California (Costa Mesa, CA).
Media Courses are delivered via videotapes, audiotapes, CD-ROM, print. Students and teachers may meet in person or interact via mail, telephone, fax, e-mail. The following equipment may be required: television, videocassette player, computer, modem, Internet access, e-mail.
Restrictions Programs are available worldwide. Enrollment is open to anyone.
Services Distance learners have access to library services, e-mail services, academic advising, tutoring, career placement assistance, bookstore at a distance.

Credit-earning options Students may transfer credits from another institution or may earn credits through examinations.

Typical costs Tuition of $255 per credit.

Registration Students may register by mail, fax, telephone, e-mail, World Wide Web, in person.

Contact Randy C. Walls, Coordinator, Assemblies of God Theological Seminary, Office of Continuing Education, 1435 North Glenstone Avenue, Springfield, MO 65802. *Telephone:* 800-467-2487 Ext. 1046. *Fax:* 417-268-1009. *E-mail:* rwalls@agseminary.edu.

DEGREES AND AWARDS

MA Christian Ministries (some on-campus requirements)
MDiv Divinity (some on-campus requirements)

COURSE SUBJECT AREAS OFFERED OUTSIDE OF DEGREE PROGRAMS

Graduate: Area, ethnic, and cultural studies; business administration and management; classical languages and literatures; communications; education; English language and literature; history; liberal arts, general studies, and humanities; music; philosophy and religion; psychology; theological studies

Noncredit: Area, ethnic, and cultural studies; business administration and management; classical languages and literatures; communications; education; English language and literature; history; liberal arts, general studies, and humanities; music; philosophy and religion; psychology; theological studies

ATHABASCA UNIVERSITY

Athabasca, Alberta, Canada
www.athabascau.ca

Athabasca University, founded in 1970, is a province-supported, comprehensive institution. It is accredited by the provincial charter. It first offered distance learning courses in 1972. In 1999–2000, it offered 443 courses at a distance. In fall 1999, there were 16,081 students enrolled in distance learning courses.

Course delivery sites Courses are delivered to your home, your workplace, Grant MacEwan Community College (Edmonton).

Media Courses are delivered via television, videotapes, videoconferencing, audiotapes, computer software, CD-ROM, World Wide Web, e-mail, print. Students and teachers may meet in person or interact via mail, telephone, fax, e-mail. The following equipment may be required: television, videocassette player, computer, modem, Internet access, e-mail.

Restrictions Programs are available worldwide. Enrollment is open to anyone.

Services Distance learners have access to library services, the campus computer network, e-mail services, academic advising, tutoring, bookstore at a distance.

Credit-earning options Students may transfer credits from another institution or may earn credits through examinations, business training.

Typical costs Undergraduate in-province tuition is $404 per 3 credit course. Out-of-province tuition is $464 per 3 credit course. Undergraduate non Canadian tuition is $604 per 3 credit course. Application fee is $50. For graduate tuition please call Center for Innovative Management at 800-561-4660 for further information. Financial aid is available to distance learners.

Registration Students may register by mail, fax, telephone, e-mail, World Wide Web, in person.

Contact Information Centre, Athabasca University, 1 University Drive, Athabasca, AB T9S 3A3 Canada. *Telephone:* 800-788-9041. *Fax:* 780-675-6174. *E-mail:* auinfo@athabascau.ca.

DEGREES AND AWARDS

Undergraduate Certificate(s) Accounting (certain restrictions apply), Administration (certain restrictions apply), Advanced Accounting (certain restrictions apply), Career Development, French, Health Development Administration (some on-campus requirements), Home Health Nursing, Humanities, Information Systems, Labor Relations (certain restrictions apply), Labor Studies (certain restrictions apply), Liberal Arts, Public Administration (certain restrictions apply), Social Sciences

BA Administration, Humanities, Liberal Arts, Social Sciences
BAdmin Health Administration, Management, Organization
BAdmin-PD Health Administration, Management, Organization
BComm Commerce
BGS General Studies
BGS-PD Administrative Studies, General Studies, Humanities, Science, Social Studies
BN Nursing
BPA Communications (service area differs from that of the overall institution; some on-campus requirements), Criminal Justice (service area differs from that of the overall institution; some on-campus requirements)
BSc Computer and Information Systems, Science
BSc-PD Computer and Information Systems
Graduate Certificate(s) English Language Studies (certain restrictions apply), Management
MBA Business Administration (some on-campus requirements)
MDE Distance Education

COURSE SUBJECT AREAS OFFERED OUTSIDE OF DEGREE PROGRAMS

Undergraduate: Accounting; area, ethnic, and cultural studies; astronomy and astrophysics; biological and life sciences; biology; botany; business; business administration and management; chemistry; communications; computer and information sciences; conservation and natural resources; creative writing; developmental and child psychology; economics; educational psychology; English as a second language (ESL); English composition; English language and literature; European languages and literatures; geology; health professions and related sciences; history; law and legal studies; liberal arts, general studies, and humanities; mathematics; nursing; philosophy and religion; physical sciences; physics; political science; psychology; public administration and services; social psychology; social sciences; sociology

Graduate: Accounting; business administration and management; developmental and child psychology; health professions and related sciences; nursing

ATHENS AREA TECHNICAL INSTITUTE

Athens, Georgia

Athens Area Technical Institute, founded in 1958, is a state-supported, two-year college. It is accredited by the Southern Association of Colleges and Schools. In 1999–2000, it offered 50 courses at a distance. In fall 1999, there were 200 students enrolled in distance learning courses.

Course delivery sites Courses are delivered to your home, your workplace, military bases, high schools, Carroll Technical Institute (Carrollton), Savannah Technical Institute (Savannah), 3 off-campus centers in Elberton, Greensboro, Monroe.

Media Courses are delivered via television, videoconferencing, interactive television, computer software, CD-ROM, World Wide Web, e-mail, print. Students and teachers may meet in person or interact via videoconferencing, audioconferencing, mail, fax, e-mail, interactive television, World Wide Web. The following equipment may be required: computer, Internet access, e-mail.

Restrictions Programs are available to in-state students only. Enrollment is open to anyone.

Services Distance learners have access to library services, e-mail services, academic advising, career placement assistance, bookstore at a distance.

Credit-earning options Students may transfer credits from another institution or may earn credits through examinations.

Typical costs Tuition of $21 per credit hour plus mandatory fees of $36 per quarter for in-state residents. Tuition of $42 per credit hour plus mandatory fees of $36 per quarter for out-of-state residents. Financial aid is available to distance learners.

Registration Students may register by World Wide Web, in person.

Contact Jennifer Williams, Computer Services Specialist, Athens Area Technical Institute, 800 US 29 North, Athens, GA 30601-1500. *Telephone:* 706-355-5018. *Fax:* 706-355-5018. *E-mail:* jennifer@admin1. athens.tec.ga.us.

DEGREES AND AWARDS

Distance programs offered do not lead to a degree or other formal award.

COURSE SUBJECT AREAS OFFERED OUTSIDE OF DEGREE PROGRAMS

Undergraduate: Accounting; administrative and secretarial services; biological and life sciences; business; child care and development; computer and information sciences; electronics; health professions and related sciences; law and legal studies; marketing; nursing; physical therapy

See full description on page 676.

ATLANTIC CAPE COMMUNITY COLLEGE

Mays Landing, New Jersey

Academic Computing and Distance Education
www.atlantic.edu

Atlantic Cape Community College, founded in 1966, is a county-supported, two-year college. It is accredited by the Middle States Association of Colleges and Schools. It first offered distance learning courses in 1984. In 1999–2000, it offered 50 courses at a distance. In fall 1999, there were 450 students enrolled in distance learning courses.

Course delivery sites Courses are delivered to your home, your workplace, high schools, 1 off-campus center in Atlantic City.

Media Courses are delivered via television, videoconferencing, CD-ROM, computer conferencing, World Wide Web, e-mail, print. Students and teachers may meet in person or interact via videoconferencing, mail, telephone, fax, e-mail, World Wide Web. The following equipment may be required: computer, modem, Internet access.

Restrictions Programs are available worldwide. Enrollment is restricted to individuals meeting certain criteria.

Services Distance learners have access to library services, academic advising, tutoring, bookstore at a distance.

Credit-earning options Students may transfer credits from another institution or may earn credits through examinations, portfolio assessment, military training, business training.

Typical costs Tuition of $80 per credit. Financial aid is available to distance learners.

Registration Students may register by mail, fax, telephone, World Wide Web, in person.

Contact Dr. Mary B. Wall, Dean, Atlantic Cape Community College, Academic Computing and Distance Education, 5100 Black Horse Pike, Mays Landing, NJ 08330. *Telephone:* 609-343-4987. *Fax:* 609-343-5122. *E-mail:* wall@atlantic.edu.

DEGREES AND AWARDS

AA History, Liberal Arts, Social Science

AS Business Administration, General Studies

COURSE SUBJECT AREAS OFFERED OUTSIDE OF DEGREE PROGRAMS

Undergraduate: Accounting; algebra; anthropology; art history and criticism; biology; business; business administration and management; business communications; business law; computer programming; counseling psychology; criminal justice; criminology; developmental and child psychology; English as a second language (ESL); English composition; English language and literature; European languages and literatures; health and physical education/fitness; history; hospitality services management; human resources management; information sciences and systems; liberal arts, general studies, and humanities; marketing; music; nursing; oceanography; social psychology; sociology; statistics

Special note

Atlantic Cape Community College (ACCC), a public, 2-year, accredited institution in Mays Landing, New Jersey, offers 40 degree programs and 25 certificate programs to nearly 5,000 students. The College primarily draws its students from Atlantic and Cape May Counties and maintains extension centers in Atlantic City and Rio Grande in Cape May County. ACCC is a leader in educational technology and offers 7 associate degrees through distance education. The programs are offered through online classes that are available via the Internet or as a combination of online and television courses. The degree programs available are the Associate of Science in general studies, the Associate of Arts in liberal arts, the Associate of Arts in history, the Associate of Science in business administration, the Associate in Science in computer information systems, the Associate in Arts in psychology, and the Associate in Arts in social science. ACCC currently offers more than 60 online courses. Students use a computer with a connection to an Internet Service Provider (ISP). Via e-mail, bulletin boards, and the World Wide Web, students and faculty members gather together in a true classroom without walls. Students should have a Mac or windows-based computer with a 28.8 or higher modem, connection to an ISP, and some knowledge of downloading and installing software. Students must be independent learners who can manage time effectively. ACCC uses conferencing software to help faculty members and students communicate with one another. Online classes cost $80 per credit for all students. There are no additional fees. For more information about ACCC's online courses, students should contact the Admissions Office by telephone at 609-343-5000 or via e-mail at pionegro@atlantic.edu or visit the College's Web site at http://www.atlantic.edu/studinfo/online/online.html.

See full description on page 600.

ATLANTIC INTERNATIONAL UNIVERSITY

Miami, Florida

www.aiu.edu

Atlantic International University is an independent university. In 1999–2000, it offered 70 courses at a distance. In fall 1999, there were 279 students enrolled in distance learning courses.

Course delivery sites Courses are delivered to your home, your workplace.

Media Courses are delivered via World Wide Web, e-mail, print. Students and teachers may meet in person or interact via audioconferencing, mail, telephone, fax, e-mail, World Wide Web.

Restrictions Programs are available worldwide. Enrollment is open to anyone.

Services Distance learners have access to library services, e-mail services, academic advising, career placement assistance at a distance.

Credit-earning options Students may transfer credits from another institution or may earn credits through examinations, portfolio assessment, business training.

Typical costs Tuition for US and Canadian students is $2900 for the Bachelor's degree, $3700 for the Master's degree and $4350 for the Doctorate degree. Tuition for international students is $4500 for the Bachelor's degree, $5000 for the Master's degree, and $5400 for the Doctorate degree. Graduation fee is $150. Enrollment fee is $200 (deducted from tuition). Financial aid is available to distance learners.

Registration Students may register by mail, fax, telephone, e-mail, World Wide Web, in person.

Contact Esther Poler, Admissions Director, Atlantic International University, Admissions Department, 13205 Northeast 16th Avenue, North Miami, FL 33161. *Telephone:* 800-993-0066. *Fax:* 305-981-7943. *E-mail:* esther@aiu.edu.

DEGREES AND AWARDS

BA Architecture, Art History, Communication, Criminal Justice, English, Fine Arts, International Affairs, Legal Studies, Literature and Language, Philosophy, Political Science, Psychology, Public Administration, Sociology, Theology

BS Biology, Chemical Engineering, Chemistry, Civil Engineering, Computer Science, Electrical Engineering, Geography, Geology, Health Science, Industrial Engineering, Informational Science, Math, Mechanical Engineering, Physics, Telecommunications

MA Architecture, Art History, Communication, Criminal Justice, English, Fine Arts, International Affairs, Legal Studies, Literature and languages, Philosophy, Political Science, Psychology, Public Administration, Sociology, Theology

MS Biology, Chemical Engineering, Chemistry, Civil Engineering, Computer Science, Electrical Engineering (some on-campus requirements), Geography, Geology, Health Science, Industrial Engineering, Informational Science, Math, Medical Engineering, Physics, Telecommunications

DSc Biology, Chemical Engineering, Chemistry, Civil Engineering, Computer Science, Education, Electrical Engineering, Geography, Geology, Health Science, Industrial Engineering, Informational Science, Math, Mechanical Engineering, Physics, Telecommunication

PhD Architecture, Art History, Communication, Criminal Justice, English, Fine Arts, International Affairs, Legal Studies, Literature and Languages, Philosophy, Political Science, Psychology, Public Administration, Sociology, Theology

---

Special note

Atlantic International University has embarked on a new and promising mission—to lead its students toward self-discovery and the attainment of their academic and professional goals. It is the goal of AIU to revitalize this important maxim of modern education within the realm of distance learning. Founded as a career preparatory institute, the school has achieved its objective through a nontraditional curriculum, an emphasis on serving students, and a commitment to educational excellence. The University is composed of 3 distinct schools: the School of Business and Economics, the School of Social and Human Studies, and the School of Science and Engineering. These schools offer more than 36 college degree programs and additional programs, designed by and for the student, entirely through distance learning. AIU believes that today's students need flexibility in higher education and shouldn't have to conform to academic archetypes or take unnecessary prerequisites. The students are encouraged to develop a program within a specialty of their choice. Students must have previous experience in their discipline and be capable of learning independently in order to be admitted to the University. Atlantic International University provides continuous support for its students through academic advising and counseling services. Students are assigned an academic adviser who is knowledgeable in the relevant discipline to guide them through their required subjects and prepare them for the challenging requirements

of seminars and research papers. Atlantic International University remains confident and optimistic about the direction of education. Its goal is to help each student achieve his or her goals and assist them in making the economic transitions ahead.

ATLANTIC UNION COLLEGE

South Lancaster, Massachusetts

Adult Degree Program
www.atlanticuc.edu

Atlantic Union College, founded in 1882, is an independent, religious, comprehensive institution. It is accredited by the New England Association of Schools and Colleges. It first offered distance learning courses in 1972. In fall 1999, there were 101 students enrolled in distance learning courses.

Course delivery sites Courses are delivered to your home.

Media Courses are delivered via videotapes, e-mail, print. Students and teachers may interact via mail, telephone, fax, e-mail.

Restrictions Programs are available worldwide. Enrollment is restricted to individuals meeting certain criteria.

Services Distance learners have access to library services, e-mail services, academic advising, bookstore at a distance.

Credit-earning options Students may transfer credits from another institution or may earn credits through examinations, portfolio assessment, military training, business training.

Typical costs *Undergraduate:* Tuition of $3640 per term. *Graduate:* Tuition of $4070 per term.

Registration Students may register by in person.

Contact Anne Gustafson, Associate Director, Atlantic Union College, PO Box 1000, South Lancaster, MA 01561. *Telephone:* 978-368-2300. *Fax:* 978-368-2514. *E-mail:* adp@atlanticuc.edu.

DEGREES AND AWARDS

BA Art (some on-campus requirements), Business Administration (some on-campus requirements), Communications (some on-campus requirements), English (certain restrictions apply; some on-campus requirements), General Science (some on-campus requirements), General Studies (some on-campus requirements), History (some on-campus requirements), Humanities (some on-campus requirements), Modern Languages (some on-campus requirements), Religion (some on-campus requirements), Social Sciences (some on-campus requirements), Theology (some on-campus requirements), Women's Studies (some on-campus requirements)

BS Art (some on-campus requirements), Behavioral Sciences (some on-campus requirements), Computer Science (some on-campus requirements), Early Childhood Education (some on-campus requirements), Elementary Education (some on-campus requirements), Human Movement (some on-campus requirements), Interior Design (some on-campus requirements), Personal Ministries (some on-campus requirements), Psychology (some on-campus requirements)

ATLANTIC UNIVERSITY

Virginia Beach, Virginia
www.atlanticuniv.edu

Atlantic University, founded in 1930, is an independent, nonprofit, graduate institution. It is accredited by the Distance Education and Training Council. It first offered distance learning courses in 1985. In 1999–2000, it offered 47 courses at a distance. In fall 1999, there were 200 students enrolled in distance learning courses.

Course delivery sites Courses are delivered to your home.

Media Courses are delivered via videotapes, audiotapes, print. Students and teachers may interact via mail, telephone, e-mail. The following equipment may be required: television, videocassette player, computer.

Restrictions Programs are available worldwide. Enrollment is restricted to individuals meeting certain criteria.

Services Distance learners have access to library services, e-mail services, academic advising at a distance.

Credit-earning options Students may transfer credits from another institution.

Typical costs Tuition of $510 per course. *Noncredit courses:* $510 per course.

Registration Students may register by mail, fax, telephone, in person.

Contact Gregory Deming, Director of Admissions, Atlantic University, Building 3300, Suite 100, 397 Little Neck Road, Virginia Beach, VA 23452. *Telephone:* 800-428-1512. *Fax:* 757-631-8096. *E-mail:* info@atlanticuniv.edu.

DEGREES AND AWARDS

MA Transpersonal Studies (certain restrictions apply; some on-campus requirements)

COURSE SUBJECT AREAS OFFERED OUTSIDE OF DEGREE PROGRAMS

Graduate: Anthropology; art history and criticism; Bible studies; creative writing; ethics; fine arts; health professions and related sciences; philosophy and religion; psychology; religious studies; theological studies; visual and performing arts; women's studies

Noncredit: Anthropology; art history and criticism; Bible studies; creative writing; ethics; fine arts; health professions and related sciences; philosophy and religion; psychology; religious studies; theological studies; visual and performing arts; women's studies

AUBURN UNIVERSITY

Auburn University, Alabama

Distance Learning/Outreach Technology
www.auburn.edu/outreach/dl

Auburn University, founded in 1856, is a state-supported university. It is accredited by the Southern Association of Colleges and Schools. It first offered distance learning courses in 1976. In 1999–2000, it offered 219 courses at a distance. In fall 1999, there were 1,789 students enrolled in distance learning courses.

Course delivery sites Courses are delivered to your home, your workplace, military bases.

Media Courses are delivered via videotapes, videoconferencing, interactive television, audiotapes, computer software, CD-ROM, World Wide Web, e-mail, print. Students and teachers may meet in person or interact via videoconferencing, audioconferencing, mail, telephone, fax, e-mail, interactive television, World Wide Web. The following equipment may be required: television, videocassette player, computer, modem, Internet access, e-mail.

Restrictions Programs are available nationwide. Enrollment is restricted to individuals meeting certain criteria.

Services Distance learners have access to library services, the campus computer network, e-mail services, academic advising, career placement assistance, bookstore at a distance.

Credit-earning options Students may transfer credits from another institution.

Typical costs *Undergraduate:* Tuition of $260 per course plus mandatory fees of $21 per course. *Graduate:* Tuition of $195 per course. *Noncredit courses:* $425 per course. Costs may vary. Financial aid is available to distance learners.

Registration Students may register by mail, fax, telephone, e-mail, World Wide Web, in person.

Contact Ernestine Morris-Stinson, Coordinator, Student Services, Auburn University, 204 Mell Hall, Auburn University, AL 36849-5611. *Telephone:* 334-844-3114. *Fax:* 334-844-4731. *E-mail:* ernestin@uce.auburn.edu.

DEGREES AND AWARDS

Undergraduate Certificate(s) Dietary Management (certain restrictions apply)

MAE Aerospace Engineering (certain restrictions apply; some on-campus requirements)

MBA Business Administration (certain restrictions apply; some on-campus requirements)

MCE Chemical Engineering (certain restrictions apply; some on-campus requirements), Civil Engineering (certain restrictions apply; some on-campus requirements)

MCSE Computer Science and Engineering (certain restrictions apply; some on-campus requirements)

MISE Industrial and Systems Engineering (certain restrictions apply; some on-campus requirements)

MME Materials Engineering (certain restrictions apply; some on-campus requirements), Mechanical Engineering (certain restrictions apply; some on-campus requirements)

MS Aerospace Engineering (certain restrictions apply; some on-campus requirements), Chemical Engineering (certain restrictions apply; some on-campus requirements), Civil Engineering (certain restrictions apply; some on-campus requirements), Computer Science and Engineering (certain restrictions apply; some on-campus requirements), Hotel and Restaurant Management (some on-campus requirements), Industrial and Systems Engineering (certain restrictions apply; some on-campus requirements), Materials Engineering (certain restrictions apply; some on-campus requirements), Mechanical Engineering (certain restrictions apply; some on-campus requirements)

COURSE SUBJECT AREAS OFFERED OUTSIDE OF DEGREE PROGRAMS

Undergraduate: Adult education; biological and life sciences; biology; communications; criminal justice; developmental and child psychology; economics; entomology; film studies; foods and nutrition studies; geography; health and physical education/fitness; horticulture; hospitality services management; mathematics; political science; social sciences

Graduate: Adult education; business administration and management; engineering

See full descriptions on pages 464 and 676.

AUSTIN COMMUNITY COLLEGE

Austin, Texas

Open Campus
www.austin.cc.tx.us/

Austin Community College, founded in 1972, is a district-supported, two-year college. It is accredited by the Southern Association of Colleges and Schools. It first offered distance learning courses in 1979. In 1999–2000, it offered 166 courses at a distance. In fall 1999, there were 2,700 students enrolled in distance learning courses.

Course delivery sites Courses are delivered to your home, your workplace, high schools, 7 off-campus centers in Bastrop, Buda, Fredericksburg, Georgetown, Marble Falls, Round Rock, San Marcos.

Media Courses are delivered via television, videotapes, videoconferencing, interactive television, computer software, CD-ROM, computer conferencing, World Wide Web, e-mail, print. Students and teachers may meet in person or interact via videoconferencing, audioconferencing, mail,

telephone, fax, e-mail, interactive television, World Wide Web. The following equipment may be required: television, videocassette player, computer, modem, Internet access, e-mail.
Restrictions Programs are available worldwide. Enrollment is restricted to individuals meeting certain criteria.
Services Distance learners have access to library services, the campus computer network, e-mail services, academic advising, bookstore at a distance.
Credit-earning options Students may transfer credits from another institution or may earn credits through examinations, portfolio assessment, military training.
Typical costs Tuition of $72 per course plus mandatory fees of $70 per course for local area residents. Tuition of $183 per course plus mandatory fees of $70 per course for in-state residents. Tuition of $417 per course plus mandatory fees of $70 per course for out-of-state residents. Costs may vary. Financial aid is available to distance learners.
Registration Students may register by mail, telephone, in person.
Contact Student Hotline Open Campus, Austin Community College, 7748 Highway 290 West, Austin, TX 78736-3290. *Telephone:* 512-223-8028. *Fax:* 512-223-8988.

DEGREES AND AWARDS

Undergraduate Certificate(s) Vocational Nursing (certain restrictions apply; service area differs from that of the overall institution; some on-campus requirements)

COURSE SUBJECT AREAS OFFERED OUTSIDE OF DEGREE PROGRAMS

Undergraduate: Accounting; administrative and secretarial services; American literature; anthropology; area, ethnic, and cultural studies; art history and criticism; biology; botany; business; business administration and management; business law; computer and information sciences; computer programming; developmental and child psychology; economics; engineering-related technologies; English composition; English language and literature; European languages and literatures; finance; fine arts; French language and literature; geography; geology; health and physical education/fitness; history; human resources management; journalism; marketing; nursing; philosophy and religion; political science; social psychology; social work; sociology; Spanish language and literature; technical writing

AZUSA PACIFIC UNIVERSITY

Azusa, California
online.apu.edu

Azusa Pacific University, founded in 1899, is an independent, religious, comprehensive institution. It is accredited by the Association of Theological Schools in the United States and Canada, Western Association of Schools and Colleges, Inc. It first offered distance learning courses in 1999. In 1999–2000, it offered 5 courses at a distance.
Course delivery sites Courses are delivered to your home, your workplace, military bases, high schools.
Media Courses are delivered via World Wide Web, e-mail. Students and teachers may interact via telephone, e-mail, World Wide Web. The following equipment may be required: computer, Internet access, e-mail.
Restrictions Programs are available to in-state students only. Enrollment is restricted to individuals meeting certain criteria.
Services Distance learners have access to library services, e-mail services, academic advising, bookstore at a distance.
Credit-earning options Students may transfer credits from another institution or may earn credits through portfolio assessment.
Typical costs *Undergraduate:* Tuition of $365 per unit. *Graduate:* Tuition of $365 per unit. Costs may vary. Financial aid is available to distance learners.

Registration Students may register by mail, telephone, e-mail, World Wide Web, in person.
Contact Dr. Bruce Simmerok, Director of Distance Education, Azusa Pacific University, 901 East Alosta Avenue, Azusa, CA 91702-7000. *E-mail:* bsimmerok@apu.edu.

DEGREES AND AWARDS

Distance programs offered do not lead to a degree or other formal award.

COURSE SUBJECT AREAS OFFERED OUTSIDE OF DEGREE PROGRAMS

Undergraduate: Computer and information sciences; history; theological studies
Graduate: Database management; education; teacher education; theological studies

BAKER COLLEGE-CENTER FOR GRADUATE STUDIES

Flint, Michigan
Baker College Online
online.baker.edu

Baker College-Center for Graduate Studies, founded in 1911, is an independent, nonprofit, four-year college. It is accredited by the North Central Association of Colleges and Schools. It first offered distance learning courses in 1994. In 1999–2000, it offered 265 courses at a distance. In fall 1999, there were 3,200 students enrolled in distance learning courses.
Course delivery sites Courses are delivered to your home, your workplace, military bases.
Media Courses are delivered via computer software, computer conferencing, World Wide Web, e-mail, print. Students and teachers may interact via telephone, fax, e-mail, World Wide Web. The following equipment may be required: computer, modem, Internet access, e-mail.
Restrictions Programs are available worldwide. Enrollment is restricted to individuals meeting certain criteria.
Services Distance learners have access to library services, the campus computer network, e-mail services, academic advising, tutoring, career placement assistance, bookstore at a distance.
Credit-earning options Students may transfer credits from another institution or may earn credits through examinations, portfolio assessment, military training, business training.
Typical costs *Undergraduate:* Tuition of $145 per quarter hour. *Graduate:* Tuition of $220 per quarter hour. *Noncredit courses:* $300 per course. Financial aid is available to distance learners.
Registration Students may register by mail, fax, e-mail, World Wide Web, in person.
Contact Chuck Gurden, Director of Graduate and Online Admissions, Baker College-Center for Graduate Studies, Baker College Online, 1050 West Bristol Road, Flint, MI 48507. *Telephone:* 810-766-4390. *Fax:* 810-766-4399. *E-mail:* gurden_c@corpfl.baker.edu.

DEGREES AND AWARDS

ABA Business Administration (some on-campus requirements)
BBA Business Administration (certain restrictions apply)
MBA Business Administration (some on-campus requirements)

COURSE SUBJECT AREAS OFFERED OUTSIDE OF DEGREE PROGRAMS

Undergraduate: Accounting; business; business administration and management; computer and information sciences; health professions and related sciences; human resources management

Graduate: Accounting; administrative and secretarial services; business; business administration and management; computer and information sciences; finance; health professions and related sciences; human resources management; international business; marketing

Noncredit: Investments and securities

See full description on page 466.

BAKERSFIELD COLLEGE

Bakersfield, California

Distance Learning
www.bc.cc.ca.us

Bakersfield College, founded in 1913, is a state and locally supported, two-year college. It is accredited by the Western Association of Schools and Colleges, Inc. In 1999–2000, it offered 34 courses at a distance. In fall 1999, there were 2,062 students enrolled in distance learning courses.

Course delivery sites Courses are delivered to your home, your workplace, high schools.

Media Courses are delivered via World Wide Web. Students and teachers may meet in person or interact via mail, telephone, fax, e-mail, World Wide Web. The following equipment may be required: computer, Internet access, e-mail.

Restrictions Programs are available worldwide. Enrollment is open to anyone.

Services Distance learners have access to library services, academic advising, tutoring, career placement assistance, bookstore at a distance.

Typical costs Tuition of $11 per unit plus mandatory fees of $16 per semester for in-state residents. Tuition of $122 per unit plus mandatory fees of $16 per semester for out-of-state residents. Costs may vary. Financial aid is available to distance learners.

Registration Students may register by telephone, World Wide Web, in person.

Contact Kathleen Loomis-Tubbesing, Distance Learning Coordinator, Bakersfield College, 1801 Panorama Drive, Bakersfield, CA 93305. *Telephone:* 661-395-4694. *Fax:* 661-395-4690. *E-mail:* kloomis@bc.cc.ca.us.

DEGREES AND AWARDS

Distance programs offered do not lead to a degree or other formal award.

COURSE SUBJECT AREAS OFFERED OUTSIDE OF DEGREE PROGRAMS

Undergraduate: Accounting; astronomy and astrophysics; child care and development; computer and information sciences; English composition; environmental engineering; finance; fire science; geology; mathematics

BALL STATE UNIVERSITY

Muncie, Indiana

School of Continuing Education and Public Service
www.bsu.edu/distance

Ball State University, founded in 1918, is a state-supported university. It is accredited by the North Central Association of Colleges and Schools. It first offered distance learning courses in 1984. In 1999–2000, it offered 110 courses at a distance. In fall 1999, there were 301 students enrolled in distance learning courses.

Course delivery sites Courses are delivered to your home, your workplace, high schools, 2 off-campus centers in Indianapolis, Westfield.

Media Courses are delivered via television, videotapes, videoconferencing, interactive television, World Wide Web, e-mail, print. Students and teachers may interact via videoconferencing, mail, telephone, fax, e-mail, interactive television, World Wide Web. The following equipment may be required: computer, Internet access, e-mail.

Restrictions Televised courses are limited to within Indiana, while Internet courses are available worldwide. The Bachelor of Science in nursing and the Masters of Science in Nursing programs are available nationwide, and courses are available via the Internet. Enrollment is restricted to individuals meeting certain criteria.

Services Distance learners have access to library services, the campus computer network, e-mail services, academic advising, career placement assistance, bookstore at a distance.

Credit-earning options Students may transfer credits from another institution or may earn credits through examinations, military training, business training.

Typical costs *Undergraduate:* Tuition of $135 per credit hour. *Graduate:* Tuition of $141 per credit hour. Financial aid is available to distance learners.

Registration Students may register by mail, fax, telephone, e-mail, World Wide Web, in person.

Contact Kathryn McCartney, Director, Off-Campus Academic Support Services, Ball State University, School of Continuing Education and Public Service, Muncie, IN 47306. *Telephone:* 800-872-0369. *Fax:* 765-285-7161. *E-mail:* kmccartn@bsu.edu.

DEGREES AND AWARDS

AA General Arts (service area differs from that of the overall institution)
AS Business Administration (service area differs from that of the overall institution)
BSN Nursing (service area differs from that of the overall institution)
MA Executive Development (service area differs from that of the overall institution; some on-campus requirements)
MAE Educational Administration and Supervision (service area differs from that of the overall institution; some on-campus requirements), Elementary Education (service area differs from that of the overall institution; some on-campus requirements), Special Education (service area differs from that of the overall institution; some on-campus requirements)
MBA Business Administration (service area differs from that of the overall institution)
MS Computer Science (certain restrictions apply; service area differs from that of the overall institution)
MSN Nursing

COURSE SUBJECT AREAS OFFERED OUTSIDE OF DEGREE PROGRAMS

Undergraduate: Accounting; administrative and secretarial services; advertising; area, ethnic, and cultural studies; astronomy and astrophysics; biological and life sciences; biology; business; business administration and management; economics; educational psychology; English composition; English language and literature; health and physical education/fitness;

health professions and related sciences; home economics and family studies; journalism; liberal arts, general studies, and humanities; mathematics; nursing; philosophy and religion; physical sciences
Graduate: Accounting; administrative and secretarial services; advertising; business; business administration and management; computer and information sciences; economics; education; education administration; educational psychology; human resources management; journalism; nursing; special education; teacher education
See full description on page 540.

BARCLAY COLLEGE

Haviland, Kansas
Home College Program
www.barclaycollege.edu

Barclay College, founded in 1917, is an independent, religious, four-year college affiliated with the Society of Friends. It is accredited by the Accrediting Association of Bible Colleges. It first offered distance learning courses in 1993. In 1999–2000, it offered 40 courses at a distance. In fall 1999, there were 45 students enrolled in distance learning courses.
Course delivery sites Courses are delivered to your home.
Media Courses are delivered via videotapes, print. Students and teachers may meet in person or interact via mail, telephone, fax, e-mail. The following equipment may be required: television, videocassette player.
Restrictions Programs are available nationwide. Enrollment is open to anyone.
Services Distance learners have access to library services, the campus computer network, e-mail services, academic advising at a distance.
Credit-earning options Students may transfer credits from another institution or may earn credits through examinations, portfolio assessment, military training, business training.
Typical costs Tuition of $300 per course plus mandatory fees of $38 per course.
Registration Students may register by mail, fax, telephone, e-mail, in person.
Contact Glenn Leppert, Home College Program Director, Barclay College, PO Box 288, Haviland, KS 67059. *Telephone:* 316-862-5252. *Fax:* 316-862-5403. *E-mail:* barclaycollege@havilandtelco.com.

DEGREES AND AWARDS

Distance programs offered do not lead to a degree or other formal award.

COURSE SUBJECT AREAS OFFERED OUTSIDE OF DEGREE PROGRAMS

Undergraduate: Bible studies; English composition; English language and literature; physical sciences; psychology; religious studies; sociology; theological studies

BARTON COUNTY COMMUNITY COLLEGE

Great Bend, Kansas
BARTONline
www.bartonline.org

Barton County Community College, founded in 1969, is a state and locally supported, two-year college. It is accredited by the North Central Association of Colleges and Schools. It first offered distance learning courses in 1999. In 1999–2000, it offered 35 courses at a distance. In fall 1999, there were 40 students enrolled in distance learning courses.

Course delivery sites Courses are delivered to your home, your workplace, military bases, high schools.
Media Courses are delivered via videotapes, CD-ROM, World Wide Web, e-mail, print. Students and teachers may meet in person or interact via mail, telephone, fax, e-mail, World Wide Web. The following equipment may be required: computer, modem, Internet access, e-mail.
Restrictions Programs are available nationwide. Enrollment is restricted to individuals meeting certain criteria.
Services Distance learners have access to library services, the campus computer network, e-mail services, academic advising, tutoring, career placement assistance, bookstore at a distance.
Credit-earning options Students may transfer credits from another institution or may earn credits through examinations, military training.
Typical costs Tuition of $125 per credit hour. Financial aid is available to distance learners.
Registration Students may register by mail, fax, telephone, World Wide Web, in person.
Contact Matt Gotschall, Director, Outreach Learning Services, Barton County Community College, 245 Northeast 30 Road, Great Bend, KS 67530. *Telephone:* 316-792-9204. *Fax:* 316-786-1168. *E-mail:* gotschallm@barton.cc.ks.us.

eCollege.com *www.ecollege.com/scholarships*

DEGREES AND AWARDS

Undergraduate Certificate(s) Dietary Management (certain restrictions apply), Hazardous Materials (certain restrictions apply), Pension Administration
AGS General Studies

COURSE SUBJECT AREAS OFFERED OUTSIDE OF DEGREE PROGRAMS

Undergraduate: Accounting; biological and life sciences; business; business administration and management; business communications; English language and literature; foods and nutrition studies; history; human resources management; management information systems; mathematics; philosophy and religion; physical sciences; psychology; social sciences
See full descriptions on pages 468 and 520.

BEAUFORT COUNTY COMMUNITY COLLEGE

Washington, North Carolina
Distance Education Center
www.beaufort.cc.nc.us

Beaufort County Community College, founded in 1967, is a state-supported, two-year college. It is accredited by the Southern Association of Colleges and Schools. It first offered distance learning courses in 1995. In 1999–2000, it offered 17 courses at a distance. In fall 1999, there were 264 students enrolled in distance learning courses.
Course delivery sites Courses are delivered to your home, high schools.
Media Courses are delivered via television, videotapes, interactive television, CD-ROM, World Wide Web, e-mail. Students and teachers may meet in person or interact via mail, telephone, fax, e-mail, interactive television, World Wide Web. The following equipment may be required: television, videocassette player, computer, modem, Internet access, e-mail.
Restrictions Programs are available to in-state students only. Enrollment is open to anyone.
Services Distance learners have access to library services, the campus computer network, academic advising, tutoring, career placement assistance, bookstore at a distance.

Credit-earning options Students may transfer credits from another institution.

Typical costs Tuition of $280 per semester plus mandatory fees of $9 per semester for in-state residents. Tuition of $2282 per semester plus mandatory fees of $9 per semester for out-of-state residents. *Noncredit courses:* $55 per course. Financial aid is available to distance learners.

Registration Students may register by fax, in person.

Contact Penny Sermons, Director of Learning Resources Center, Beaufort County Community College, PO Box 1069, Washington, NC 27889. *Telephone:* 252-946-6194 Ext. 243. *Fax:* 252-946-9575. *E-mail:* pennys@email.beaufort.cc.nc.us.

DEGREES AND AWARDS

Distance programs offered do not lead to a degree or other formal award.

COURSE SUBJECT AREAS OFFERED OUTSIDE OF DEGREE PROGRAMS

Undergraduate: Accounting; history; mathematics; political science; social psychology; sociology

See full description on page 676.

BELLEVUE COMMUNITY COLLEGE

Bellevue, Washington

Telecommunications Program–Distance Learning Department
distance-ed.bcc.ctc.edu

Bellevue Community College, founded in 1966, is a state-supported, two-year college. It is accredited by the Northwest Association of Schools and Colleges. It first offered distance learning courses in 1980. In 1999–2000, it offered 104 courses at a distance. In fall 1999, there were 1,665 students enrolled in distance learning courses.

Course delivery sites Courses are delivered to your home, your workplace, high schools.

Media Courses are delivered via television, videotapes, videoconferencing, interactive television, World Wide Web, e-mail, print. Students and teachers may meet in person or interact via videoconferencing, mail, telephone, fax, e-mail, interactive television, World Wide Web. The following equipment may be required: television, videocassette player, computer, modem, Internet access, e-mail.

Restrictions Programs are available worldwide. Enrollment is open to anyone.

Services Distance learners have access to library services, the campus computer network, e-mail services, academic advising, tutoring, bookstore at a distance.

Credit-earning options Students may transfer credits from another institution or may earn credits through examinations.

Typical costs Tuition of $54.30 per credit plus mandatory fees of $20 per course. Financial aid is available to distance learners.

Registration Students may register by mail, fax, telephone, e-mail, World Wide Web, in person.

Contact Thornton Perry, Director of Distance Learning, Bellevue Community College, 3000 Landerholm Circle, South East, Bellevue, WA 98007-6484. *Telephone:* 425-641-2438. *Fax:* 425-562-6187. *E-mail:* tperry@bcc.ctc.edu.

DEGREES AND AWARDS

Undergraduate Certificate(s) Business Software Specialist, Web Authoring

AA General Studies (some on-campus requirements), Web Authoring

AAB Business

AAS Transfer Degree

COURSE SUBJECT AREAS OFFERED OUTSIDE OF DEGREE PROGRAMS

Undergraduate: Abnormal psychology; accounting; administrative and secretarial services; algebra; American literature; American studies; anthropology; archaeology; art history and criticism; astronomy and astrophysics; biology; business administration and management; business law; chemistry; comparative literature; computer and information sciences; computer programming; conservation and natural resources; continuing education; creative writing; database management; economics; English composition; English language and literature; English literature; environmental science; European history; film studies; geography; geology; history; history of science and technology; information sciences and systems; international relations; management information systems; mass media; mathematics; oceanography; political science; psychology; sociology; statistics; technical writing; telecommunications

BELLEVUE UNIVERSITY

Bellevue, Nebraska

Center for Distributed Learning
www.bellevue.edu

Bellevue University, founded in 1965, is an independent, nonprofit, comprehensive institution. It is accredited by the North Central Association of Colleges and Schools. It first offered distance learning courses in 1985. In 1999–2000, it offered 50 courses at a distance. In fall 1999, there were 100 students enrolled in distance learning courses.

Course delivery sites Courses are delivered to your home, your workplace, military bases, Thongsook University (Bangkok, Thailand), 6 off-campus centers in Columbus, Grand Island, Lincoln, Atlantic (IA), Red Oak (IA), Sioux City (IA).

Media Courses are delivered via videotapes, computer software, CD-ROM, computer conferencing, World Wide Web, e-mail, print. Students and teachers may interact via audioconferencing, mail, telephone, fax, e-mail, World Wide Web. The following equipment may be required: computer, Internet access, e-mail.

Restrictions Programs are available worldwide. Enrollment is open to anyone.

Services Distance learners have access to library services, the campus computer network, e-mail services, academic advising, tutoring, career placement assistance, bookstore at a distance.

Credit-earning options Students may transfer credits from another institution or may earn credits through examinations, portfolio assessment, military training, business training.

Typical costs *Undergraduate:* Tuition of $250 per semester hour plus mandatory fees of $150 per degree program. *Graduate:* Tuition of $275 per semester hour plus mandatory fees of $150 per degree program. Costs may vary. Financial aid is available to distance learners.

Registration Students may register by mail, fax, telephone, e-mail, World Wide Web, in person.

Contact Kathy Consbruck, Admissions Counselor, Bellevue University. *Telephone:* 402-293-2000. *Fax:* 402-293-2020. *E-mail:* bellevue-u@scholars.bellevue.edu.

DEGREES AND AWARDS

BA Leadership (certain restrictions apply)

BS Business Information Systems (certain restrictions apply), Criminal Justice Administration (certain restrictions apply), E-Business (certain restrictions apply), Global Business Management (certain restrictions apply), Management (certain restrictions apply), Management Information Systems (certain restrictions apply), Management of Human Resources (certain restrictions apply)

MA Leadership (certain restrictions apply)
MBA Business Administration (certain restrictions apply)

COURSE SUBJECT AREAS OFFERED OUTSIDE OF DEGREE PROGRAMS

Undergraduate: Communications; education; English language and literature; history; information sciences and systems; philosophy and religion; social sciences
Graduate: Information sciences and systems

BENTLEY COLLEGE

Waltham, Massachusetts
Center for Tax and Personal Financial Planning
cyber.bentley.edu/

Bentley College, founded in 1917, is an independent, nonprofit, comprehensive institution. It is accredited by the New England Association of Schools and Colleges. In 1999–2000, it offered 7 courses at a distance. In fall 1999, there were 7 students enrolled in distance learning courses.
Course delivery sites Courses are delivered to your home, your workplace, 2 off-campus centers in Boston, Worcester.
Media Courses are delivered via videoconferencing, computer software, World Wide Web. Students and teachers may interact via videoconferencing, telephone, e-mail, World Wide Web. The following equipment may be required: computer, Internet access, e-mail.
Restrictions Videoconferencing programs are currently available on the regional level. Enrollment is restricted to individuals meeting certain criteria.
Services Distance learners have access to library services, the campus computer network, e-mail services, academic advising, bookstore at a distance.
Typical costs Tuition of $2135 per course.
Registration Students may register by telephone.
Contact William P. Wiggins, Director, Graduate Tax Program, Bentley College, Morison Hall, Room 272, Waltham, MA 02452-4705. *Telephone:* 781-891-2249. *Fax:* 781-891-3169. *E-mail:* wwiggins@bentley.edu.

DEGREES AND AWARDS

Graduate Certificate(s) Taxation (certain restrictions apply)
MS Taxation (certain restrictions apply)
See full description on page 470.

BERGEN COMMUNITY COLLEGE

Paramus, New Jersey
Center for Distance Learning
www.bergen.cc.nj.us

Bergen Community College, founded in 1965, is a county-supported, two-year college. It is accredited by the Middle States Association of Colleges and Schools. It first offered distance learning courses in 1974. In 1999–2000, it offered 60 courses at a distance. In fall 1999, there were 450 students enrolled in distance learning courses.
Course delivery sites Courses are delivered to your home, your workplace, high schools, New Jersey Virtual Community Colleges Consortium (Trenton), Ramapo College of New Jersey (Mahwah), Sussex County Community College (Newton).
Media Courses are delivered via television, videotapes, interactive television, computer software, CD-ROM, World Wide Web, e-mail. Students

and teachers may meet in person or interact via mail, telephone, fax, e-mail, interactive television, World Wide Web. The following equipment may be required: television, videocassette player, computer, modem, Internet access, e-mail.
Restrictions Programs are available to in-state students only. Enrollment is open to anyone.
Services Distance learners have access to library services, the campus computer network, e-mail services, academic advising, tutoring, career placement assistance, bookstore at a distance.
Credit-earning options Students may earn credits through examinations, military training, business training.
Typical costs Tuition of $80 per credit for local area residents. Tuition of $80 per credit for in-state residents. Tuition of $80 per credit for out-of-state residents. Costs may vary. Financial aid is available to distance learners.
Registration Students may register by mail, fax, telephone, e-mail, World Wide Web, in person.
Contact Dr. Mark Kassop, Distance Learning Coordinator, Bergen Community College, 400 Paramus Road, Paramus, NJ 07652. *Telephone:* 201-447-9232. *Fax:* 201-612-8225. *E-mail:* mkassop@bergen.cc.nj.us.

DEGREES AND AWARDS

AA General Curriculum, Philosophy, Social Sciences, Sociology
AS Business Administration, Business Administration and Management, Business Administration and Marketing, Education

COURSE SUBJECT AREAS OFFERED OUTSIDE OF DEGREE PROGRAMS

Undergraduate: Accounting; American (U.S.) history; American literature; animal sciences; biology; business administration and management; chemistry; developmental and child psychology; drama and theater; economics; English composition; European history; finance; health and physical education/fitness; history; information sciences and systems; mass media; mathematics; philosophy and religion; political science; psychology; public relations; religious studies; sociology; teacher education
See full description on page 600.

BERKELEY COLLEGE

West Paterson, New Jersey
www.berkeleycollege.edu/

Berkeley College, founded in 1931, is a proprietary, two-year college. It is accredited by the Middle States Association of Colleges and Schools.
Course delivery sites Courses are delivered to your home.
Media Courses are delivered via World Wide Web, e-mail. Students and teachers may interact via e-mail. The following equipment may be required: computer, modem, Internet access, e-mail.
Restrictions Programs are available to local area students. Enrollment is restricted to individuals meeting certain criteria.
Services Distance learners have access to library services, the campus computer network, e-mail services at a distance.
Credit-earning options Students may transfer credits from another institution or may earn credits through examinations, portfolio assessment, military training, business training.
Typical costs Tuition of $310 per credit plus mandatory fees of $60 per quarter.
Contact Berkeley College. *Telephone:* 973-278-5400. *Fax:* 973-278-9141. *E-mail:* info@berkeleycollege.edu.

DEGREES AND AWARDS

AAS Business Administration (some on-campus requirements)

COURSE SUBJECT AREAS OFFERED OUTSIDE OF DEGREE PROGRAMS

Undergraduate: Business; business administration and management; international business

BERKSHIRE COMMUNITY COLLEGE

Pittsfield, Massachusetts
cc.berkshire.org/

Berkshire Community College, founded in 1960, is a state-supported, two-year college. It is accredited by the New England Association of Schools and Colleges. In 1999–2000, it offered 3 courses at a distance. In fall 1999, there were 30 students enrolled in distance learning courses.
Course delivery sites Courses are delivered to your home.
Media Courses are delivered via television, videotapes, computer software, computer conferencing. Students and teachers may meet in person or interact via mail, telephone, fax, e-mail, interactive television. The following equipment may be required: television, videocassette player.
Restrictions Programs are available to local area students. Enrollment is open to anyone.
Services Distance learners have access to library services at a distance.
Credit-earning options Students may transfer credits from another institution.
Typical costs Tuition of $43.50 per credit plus mandatory fees of $55 per credit for local area residents. Tuition of $29 per credit plus mandatory fees of $55 per credit for in-state residents. Tuition of $230 per credit plus mandatory fees of $55 per credit for out-of-state residents. Financial aid is available to distance learners.
Registration Students may register by mail, fax, telephone, in person.
Contact Janet R. Kroboth, Assistant Dean of Academic Affairs-Business Division, Berkshire Community College, 1350 West Street, Pittsfield, MA 01201-5786. *Telephone:* 413-499-4660 Ext. 271. *Fax:* 413-447-7840. *E-mail:* jkroboth@cc.berkshire.org.

DEGREES AND AWARDS

Distance programs offered do not lead to a degree or other formal award.

COURSE SUBJECT AREAS OFFERED OUTSIDE OF DEGREE PROGRAMS

Undergraduate: Business administration and management; business law; economics; fire science; sociology
Noncredit: Education

BETHANY COLLEGE OF THE ASSEMBLIES OF GOD

Scotts Valley, California

External Degree Program
www.bethany.edu/

Bethany College of the Assemblies of God, founded in 1919, is an independent, religious, comprehensive institution affiliated with the Assemblies of God. It is accredited by the Western Association of Schools and Colleges, Inc. In 1999–2000, it offered 100 courses at a distance. In fall 1999, there were 120 students enrolled in distance learning courses.
Course delivery sites Courses are delivered to your home, your workplace, off-campus center(s) in Sacramento.
Media Courses are delivered via videotapes, audiotapes, computer software, CD-ROM, World Wide Web, e-mail, print. Students and teachers may meet in person or interact via audioconferencing, mail, telephone,

fax, e-mail. The following equipment may be required: television, videocassette player, computer, modem, Internet access, e-mail.
Restrictions Programs are available nationwide. Enrollment is restricted to individuals meeting certain criteria.
Services Distance learners have access to library services, e-mail services, academic advising, bookstore at a distance.
Credit-earning options Students may transfer credits from another institution or may earn credits through examinations, portfolio assessment, military training, business training.
Typical costs Tuition of $310 per unit. Financial aid is available to distance learners.
Registration Students may register by mail, fax, e-mail, in person.
Contact Wade Saari, Director, External Degree Program, Bethany College of the Assemblies of God, 800 Bethany Drive, Scotts Valley, CA 95066. *Telephone:* 831-438-3800 Ext. 1404. *Fax:* 831-439-9983.

DEGREES AND AWARDS

BA Addiction Studies (service area differs from that of the overall institution), Applied Professional Studies (some on-campus requirements), Biblical and Theological Studies (some on-campus requirements), Business (some on-campus requirements), Child Development and Education (some on-campus requirements), Church Leadership (some on-campus requirements), English (some on-campus requirements), Psychology (some on-campus requirements), Social Science (some on-campus requirements)

COURSE SUBJECT AREAS OFFERED OUTSIDE OF DEGREE PROGRAMS

Undergraduate: Anthropology; biological and life sciences; business administration and management; child care and development; communications; English language and literature; history; interdisciplinary studies; liberal arts, general studies, and humanities; philosophy and religion; physical sciences; psychology; social sciences; substance abuse counseling; theological studies

Special note
Bethany College's External Degree Program offers more than 100 courses each semester that lead to a dozen BA degrees. The External Degree Program provides the same course content as the on-campus program. Bethany College is regionally accredited and offers its students an excellent education. The External Degree Program has helped more than 200 students complete their BA degrees since 1992. Students come to the campus for an initial orientation and return to the campus each semester for a progress review. During these visits, they register for classes, arrange for financial aid, and meet with professors. Course work is completed at the student's home or office, with weekly contact with professors via e-mail or telephone. Students must have access to a computer (Pentium II/233 or Apple G3 or better) with an active e-mail account and access to the World Wide Web. Some courses are completely Web-based, while others use a combination of electronic and hard copy faxing to complete the course work. Students have access to the Bethany College library and the ability to register, order textbooks, and contact administration on line. For further information, students should call 831-438-3800 Ext. 1404 or e-mail edp@bethany.edu.

BETHEL SEMINARY

St. Paul, Minnesota

In Ministry Programs
www.bethel.edu

Bethel Seminary, founded in 1871, is an independent, religious, graduate institution affiliated with the Baptist General Conference. It is accredited by the Association of Theological Schools in the United States and Canada, North Central Association of Colleges and Schools. It first offered distance learning courses in 1994. In 1999–2000, it offered 26 courses at a distance. In fall 1999, there were 92 students enrolled in distance learning courses.

Course delivery sites Courses are delivered to your home, your workplace, military bases, 1 off-campus center in San Diego (CA).

Media Courses are delivered via videotapes, videoconferencing, audiotapes, World Wide Web, e-mail, print. Students and teachers may meet in person or interact via videoconferencing, audioconferencing, mail, telephone, fax, e-mail, World Wide Web. The following equipment may be required: television, videocassette player, computer, modem, Internet access, e-mail.

Restrictions Programs are available nationwide. Enrollment is open to anyone.

Services Distance learners have access to library services, academic advising, career placement assistance at a distance.

Credit-earning options Students may transfer credits from another institution.

Typical costs Tuition of $150.50 per quarter credit. Financial aid is available to distance learners.

Registration Students may register by mail, fax, e-mail, World Wide Web, in person.

Contact Morris Anderson, Director of Admissions and Financial Aid, Bethel Seminary, 3949 Bethel Drive, St. Paul, MN 55112. *Telephone:* 651-638-6288. *Fax:* 651-638-6002. *E-mail:* bsem-admit@bethel.edu.

DEGREES AND AWARDS

MA Children and Family Ministry (some on-campus requirements), Transformational Leadership (some on-campus requirements)
MDiv Divinity and Ministry (some on-campus requirements)

BEVILL STATE COMMUNITY COLLEGE

Sumiton, Alabama

Distance Learning
www.bevillst.cc.al.us

Bevill State Community College, founded in 1969, is a state-supported, two-year college. It is accredited by the Southern Association of Colleges and Schools. It first offered distance learning courses in 1998.

Contact Bevill State Community College, PO Box 800, Sumiton, AL 35148. *Telephone:* 205-648-3271.

See full description on page 676.

BLACKHAWK TECHNICAL COLLEGE

Janesville, Wisconsin
www.blackhawk.tec.wi.us/

Blackhawk Technical College, founded in 1968, is a district-supported, two-year college. It is accredited by the North Central Association of Colleges and Schools. In 1999–2000, it offered 2 courses at a distance. In fall 1999, there were 20 students enrolled in distance learning courses.

Course delivery sites Courses are delivered to your home, your workplace, 2 off-campus centers in Janesville, Monroe.

Media Courses are delivered via videotapes, videoconferencing, interactive television, computer software, print. Students and teachers may interact via mail, telephone, fax. The following equipment may be required: computer, Internet access.

Restrictions Programs are available worldwide. Enrollment is open to anyone.

Services Distance learners have access to library services, academic advising, bookstore at a distance.

Credit-earning options Students may transfer credits from another institution or may earn credits through examinations, portfolio assessment, military training, business training.

Typical costs Tuition of $59.25 per credit plus mandatory fees of $5.50 per credit. *Noncredit courses:* $40 per course. Financial aid is available to distance learners.

Registration Students may register by mail, fax, e-mail, World Wide Web, in person.

Contact Connie Richards, Registration Supervisor, Blackhawk Technical College. *Telephone:* 608-757-7654. *Fax:* 608-743-4407. *E-mail:* crichard@mail.blackhawk.tec.wi.us.

DEGREES AND AWARDS

Distance programs offered do not lead to a degree or other formal award.

COURSE SUBJECT AREAS OFFERED OUTSIDE OF DEGREE PROGRAMS

Undergraduate: Business; communications; health professions and related sciences; mathematics; psychology

BLACK HILLS STATE UNIVERSITY

Spearfish, South Dakota

Extended Services and Instructional Technology
www.bhsu.edu

Black Hills State University, founded in 1883, is a state-supported, comprehensive institution. It is accredited by the North Central Association of Colleges and Schools. It first offered distance learning courses in 1994. In 1999–2000, it offered 14 courses at a distance. In fall 1999, there were 117 students enrolled in distance learning courses.

Course delivery sites Courses are delivered to your home, military bases, high schools, South Dakota School of Mines and Technology (Rapid City).

Media Courses are delivered via television, videotapes, World Wide Web. Students and teachers may interact via videoconferencing, mail, telephone, e-mail.

Restrictions Programs are available worldwide. Enrollment is restricted to individuals meeting certain criteria.

Services Distance learners have access to library services, bookstore at a distance.

Credit-earning options Students may transfer credits from another institution or may earn credits through examinations, military training.

Typical costs *Undergraduate:* Tuition of $125 per credit. *Graduate:* Tuition of $161 per credit. Costs may vary. Financial aid is available to distance learners.

Registration Students may register by mail, fax, telephone, e-mail, World Wide Web, in person.

Contact Verla Fish, Coordinator, Extended Services, Black Hills State University, 1200 University, USB #9508, Spearfish, SD 57799-9508. *Telephone:* 605-642-6771. *Fax:* 605-642-6031. *E-mail:* vfish@mystic.bhsu.edu.

DEGREES AND AWARDS

Distance programs offered do not lead to a degree or other formal award.

COURSE SUBJECT AREAS OFFERED OUTSIDE OF DEGREE PROGRAMS

Undergraduate: Accounting; conservation and natural resources; developmental and child psychology; drama and theater; education; English language and literature; genetics; teacher education

Graduate: Developmental and child psychology; education; English language and literature; teacher education

BLINN COLLEGE

Brenham, Texas

Distance Education Center
www.blinncol.edu

Blinn College, founded in 1883, is a state and locally supported, two-year college. It is accredited by the Southern Association of Colleges and Schools. It first offered distance learning courses in 1996. In 1999–2000, it offered 29 courses at a distance. In fall 1999, there were 1,050 students enrolled in distance learning courses.

Course delivery sites Courses are delivered to your home, your workplace, high schools.

Media Courses are delivered via television, videotapes, videoconferencing, World Wide Web. Students and teachers may meet in person or interact via videoconferencing, mail, telephone, fax, e-mail. The following equipment may be required: television, videocassette player, computer, Internet access.

Restrictions Programs are available to local area students. Enrollment is open to anyone.

Services Distance learners have access to library services, tutoring, bookstore at a distance.

Credit-earning options Students may transfer credits from another institution or may earn credits through examinations, military training.

Typical costs Tuition of $60 per course plus mandatory fees of $100 per course for local area residents. Tuition of $60 per course plus mandatory fees of $100 per course for in-state residents. Tuition of $500 per course plus mandatory fees of $136 per course for out-of-state residents. Costs may vary. Financial aid is available to distance learners.

Registration Students may register by World Wide Web, in person.

Contact Candace Schaefer, Coordinator of Distance Learning, Blinn College, Distance Education, PO Box 6030, Bryan, TX 77802. *Telephone:* 979-821-0403. *Fax:* 979-821-0229. *E-mail:* cschaefer@acmail.blinncol.edu.

DEGREES AND AWARDS

Distance programs offered do not lead to a degree or other formal award.

COURSE SUBJECT AREAS OFFERED OUTSIDE OF DEGREE PROGRAMS

Undergraduate: Accounting; administrative and secretarial services; algebra; anthropology; art history and criticism; biology; business; business law; calculus; child care and development; criminal justice; economics; English language and literature; geography; history; philosophy and religion; political science; psychology; sociology; technical writing

BLOOMFIELD COLLEGE

Bloomfield, New Jersey
www.bloomfield.edu/

Bloomfield College, founded in 1868, is an independent, religious, four-year college affiliated with the Presbyterian Church (U.S.A.). It is accredited by the Middle States Association of Colleges and Schools. In 1999–2000, it offered 1 course at a distance.

Course delivery sites Courses are delivered to your home, your workplace.

Media Courses are delivered via television, videoconferencing, interactive television, computer software, computer conferencing, World Wide Web, e-mail. Students and teachers may interact via videoconferencing, telephone, fax, e-mail, interactive television, World Wide Web. The following equipment may be required: computer, modem, Internet access, e-mail.

Restrictions Programs are available to in-state students only. Enrollment is restricted to individuals meeting certain criteria.

Services Distance learners have access to the campus computer network, e-mail services at a distance.

Typical costs Tuition of $1040 per course plus mandatory fees of $25 per semester. Financial aid is available to distance learners.

Registration Students may register by in person.

Contact Ms. Martie LaBare, Dean of Academic Affairs, Bloomfield College, Bloomfield, NJ 07003. *Telephone:* 973-748-9000 Ext. 326. *Fax:* 973-743-3998.

DEGREES AND AWARDS

Distance programs offered do not lead to a degree or other formal award.

COURSE SUBJECT AREAS OFFERED OUTSIDE OF DEGREE PROGRAMS

Undergraduate: Marketing

BLUE RIDGE COMMUNITY COLLEGE

Weyers Cave, Virginia

Distance Learning Office
www.br.cc.va.us

Blue Ridge Community College, founded in 1967, is a state-supported, two-year college. It is accredited by the Southern Association of Colleges and Schools. In 1999–2000, it offered 20 courses at a distance. In fall 1999, there were 200 students enrolled in distance learning courses.

Course delivery sites Courses are delivered to your home, high schools, Tidewater Community College (Norfolk).

Media Courses are delivered via television, interactive television, World Wide Web. Students and teachers may meet in person or interact via mail, telephone, e-mail, interactive television, World Wide Web. The following equipment may be required: Internet access, e-mail.

Restrictions Programs are available to in-state students only. Enrollment is open to anyone.

Services Distance learners have access to library services, the campus computer network, e-mail services, academic advising, bookstore at a distance.

Credit-earning options Students may transfer credits from another institution or may earn credits through examinations.

Typical costs Tuition of $37.12 per credit hour plus mandatory fees of $3.20 per credit hour for local area residents. Tuition of $37.12 per credit hour plus mandatory fees of $3.20 per credit hour for in-state residents. Tuition of $164.80 per credit hour plus mandatory fees of $3.20 per credit hour for out-of-state residents.

Registration Students may register by telephone, e-mail, in person.

Contact Greg Cook, Institutional Technologist, Blue Ridge Community College, PO Box 80, Weyers Cave, VA 24486. *Telephone:* 540-234-9261. *Fax:* 540-234-9600. *E-mail:* brcookg@br.cc.va.us.

DEGREES AND AWARDS

AAS Veterinary Technology (certain restrictions apply; some on-campus requirements)

COURSE SUBJECT AREAS OFFERED OUTSIDE OF DEGREE PROGRAMS

Undergraduate: American (U.S.) history; American literature; animal sciences; business administration and management; electronics; English composition; health and physical education/fitness; history; information sciences and systems; nursing; psychology; Spanish language and literature
See full description on page 676.

BOISE STATE UNIVERSITY

Boise, Idaho

Division of Continuing Education
www.boisestate.edu/conted

Boise State University, founded in 1932, is a state-supported, comprehensive institution. It is accredited by the Northwest Association of Schools and Colleges. It first offered distance learning courses in 1987. In 1999–2000, it offered 110 courses at a distance. In fall 1999, there were 1,041 students enrolled in distance learning courses.
Course delivery sites Courses are delivered to your home, your workplace, military bases, high schools, College of Southern Idaho (Twin Falls), Idaho State University (Pocatello), University of Idaho (Moscow), 21 off-campus centers in Boise, Caldwell, Council, Emmett, Homedale, Melba, Mountain Home, Nampa, Parma, Pocatello, Twin Falls, Weiser.
Media Courses are delivered via television, videotapes, videoconferencing, interactive television, computer software, CD-ROM, computer conferencing, World Wide Web, e-mail, print. Students and teachers may meet in person or interact via videoconferencing, audioconferencing, mail, telephone, fax, e-mail, interactive television, World Wide Web. The following equipment may be required: television, videocassette player, computer, modem, Internet access, e-mail.
Restrictions Programs are available worldwide. Enrollment is open to anyone.
Services Distance learners have access to library services, the campus computer network, e-mail services, academic advising, bookstore at a distance.
Credit-earning options Students may transfer credits from another institution or may earn credits through examinations, military training.
Typical costs *Undergraduate:* Tuition of $0 per semester credit plus mandatory fees of $1322 per semester credit for in-state residents. Tuition of $2940 per semester credit plus mandatory fees of $1322 per semester credit for out-of-state residents. *Graduate:* Tuition of $0 per semester credit plus mandatory fees of $1608 per semester credit for in-state residents. Tuition of $2940 per semester credit plus mandatory fees of $1608 per semester credit for out-of-state residents. Some distance classes have substantial additional fees. Costs may vary. Financial aid is available to distance learners.
Registration Students may register by mail, fax, telephone, e-mail, in person.
Contact Janet Atkinson, Director, Distance Education and Corporate Relations, Boise State University, Division of Continuing Education, 1910 University Drive, Boise, ID 83725. *Telephone:* 208-426-1709. *Fax:* 208-426-3467. *E-mail:* jatkinso@boisestate.edu.

DEGREES AND AWARDS

Undergraduate Certificate(s) Educational Technology (certain restrictions apply)
MS Instructional and Performance Technology (certain restrictions apply)

COURSE SUBJECT AREAS OFFERED OUTSIDE OF DEGREE PROGRAMS

Undergraduate: Accounting; astronomy and astrophysics; business; business administration and management; business communications; communications; computer and information sciences; curriculum and instruction; developmental and child psychology; drama and theater; electrical engineering; engineering; English language and literature; foods and nutrition studies; geography; geology; health professions and related sciences; history; human resources management; information sciences and systems; marketing; mathematics; nursing; philosophy and religion; physical sciences; political science; social sciences; sociology; Spanish language and literature; special education; teacher education; visual and performing arts
Graduate: Instructional media; special education; teacher education

BOROUGH OF MANHATTAN COMMUNITY COLLEGE OF THE CITY UNIVERSITY OF NEW YORK

New York, New York

Office of Academic Affairs
www.bmcc.cuny.edu/

Borough of Manhattan Community College of the City University of New York, founded in 1963, is a state and locally supported, two-year college. It is accredited by the Middle States Association of Colleges and Schools. In 1999–2000, it offered 3 courses at a distance.
Course delivery sites Courses are delivered to high schools, City University of New York System (New York), Sistema Universitario Ana G. Mendez Central Office (Rio Piedras, PR), The University of Texas at Brownsville (Brownsville, TX), University of Puerto Rico, Río Piedras (San Juan, PR), 2 off-campus centers in New York.
Media Courses are delivered via television, videoconferencing, interactive television, World Wide Web. Students and teachers may meet in person or interact via videoconferencing, interactive television, World Wide Web. The following equipment may be required: Internet access.
Restrictions Individual programs participate in initiatives with HETS in Latin America and NYC Board of Education locally. Enrollment is open to anyone.
Services Distance learners have access to library services, career placement assistance at a distance.
Credit-earning options Students may transfer credits from another institution.
Typical costs Tuition of $1250 per semester plus mandatory fees of $44.85 per semester for in-state residents. Tuition of $1538 per semester plus mandatory fees of $44.85 per semester for out-of-state residents. *Noncredit courses:* $300 per course. Financial aid is available to distance learners.
Registration Students may register by in person.
Contact Dr. Erwin Wong, Dean of Curriculum and Instruction, Borough of Manhattan Community College of the City University of New York, 199 Chambers Street, New York, NY 10007. *Telephone:* 212-346-8827. *Fax:* 212-346-8816. *E-mail:* ewong@bmcc.cuny.edu.

DEGREES AND AWARDS

Undergraduate Certificate(s) Computer Operations/Networking (certain restrictions apply; service area differs from that of the overall institution)

COURSE SUBJECT AREAS OFFERED OUTSIDE OF DEGREE PROGRAMS

Noncredit: Information sciences and systems

BOSSIER PARISH COMMUNITY COLLEGE

Bossier City, Louisiana

BPCC Distance Learning Program/Institutional Advancement
www.bpcc.cc.la.us

Bossier Parish Community College, founded in 1967, is a state-supported, two-year college. It is accredited by the Southern Association of Colleges and Schools. It first offered distance learning courses in 1993. In 1999–2000, it offered 42 courses at a distance. In fall 1999, there were 545 students enrolled in distance learning courses.

Course delivery sites Courses are delivered to your home, military bases, high schools, Delgado Community College (New Orleans), Grambling State University (Grambling), Louisiana State University at Eunice (Eunice), 4 off-campus centers in Bossier, Minden, Shreveport, Springhill.

Media Courses are delivered via television, videotapes, videoconferencing, interactive television, computer software, CD-ROM, World Wide Web, e-mail, print. Students and teachers may meet in person or interact via videoconferencing, audioconferencing, mail, telephone, fax, e-mail, interactive television, World Wide Web. The following equipment may be required: television, videocassette player, computer, modem, Internet access, e-mail.

Restrictions Telecourses are available locally, satellite campuses are local, and Internet and compressed video courses are available statewide. Enrollment is open to anyone.

Services Distance learners have access to library services, the campus computer network, e-mail services, academic advising, tutoring, career placement assistance, bookstore at a distance.

Credit-earning options Students may transfer credits from another institution or may earn credits through examinations.

Typical costs Tuition of $230 per course plus mandatory fees of $25 per course for in-state residents. Tuition of $390 per course plus mandatory fees of $25 per course for out-of-state residents. Costs may vary. Financial aid is available to distance learners.

Registration Students may register by mail, in person.

Contact Kathleen Gay, Director of Educational Technology, Bossier Parish Community College, 2719 Airline Drive, Bossier City, LA 71111. *Telephone:* 318-741-7391. *Fax:* 318-741-7393. *E-mail:* kgay@bpcc.cc.la. us.

DEGREES AND AWARDS

Distance programs offered do not lead to a degree or other formal award.

COURSE SUBJECT AREAS OFFERED OUTSIDE OF DEGREE PROGRAMS

Undergraduate: Abnormal psychology; algebra; American (U.S.) history; art history and criticism; biological and life sciences; business administration and management; chemistry; computer and information sciences; developmental and child psychology; English composition; European history; fire science; health and physical education/fitness; health professions and related sciences; psychology; sociology; telecommunications

Noncredit: Education; English language and literature; mathematics

See full description on page 676.

BOSTON UNIVERSITY

Boston, Massachusetts

Department of Manufacturing Engineering
www.bu.edu/mfg/icv

Boston University, founded in 1839, is an independent, nonprofit university. It is accredited by the Association of Theological Schools in the United States and Canada, New England Association of Schools and Colleges. It first offered distance learning courses in 1989. In 1999–2000, it offered 10 courses at a distance. In fall 1999, there were 60 students enrolled in distance learning courses.

Course delivery sites Courses are delivered to your workplace, 1 off-campus center in Tyngsboro.

Media Courses are delivered via videoconferencing. Students and teachers may interact via videoconferencing, audioconferencing, mail, telephone, fax, e-mail, World Wide Web.

Restrictions Programs are available nationwide. Enrollment is restricted to individuals meeting certain criteria.

Services Distance learners have access to e-mail services, academic advising, tutoring, bookstore at a distance.

Credit-earning options Students may transfer credits from another institution.

Typical costs Tuition of $772 per credit plus mandatory fees of $40 per semester. Cost for a noncredit course is $772 per credit.

Registration Students may register by mail, fax, in person.

Contact Elizabeth Spencer-Dawes, Distance Learning Administrator, Boston University, Department of Manufacturing Engineering, Boston, MA 02215. *Telephone:* 617-353-2943. *Fax:* 617-353-5548. *E-mail:* icv@ bu.edu.

DEGREES AND AWARDS

MS Manufacturing Engineering (certain restrictions apply; service area differs from that of the overall institution)

COURSE SUBJECT AREAS OFFERED OUTSIDE OF DEGREE PROGRAMS

Graduate: Engineering; engineering/industrial management; industrial engineering

See full description on page 472.

BRADLEY UNIVERSITY

Peoria, Illinois

Division of Continuing Education and Professional Development
www.bradley.edu/bucepd/

Bradley University, founded in 1897, is an independent, nonprofit, comprehensive institution. It is accredited by the North Central Association of Colleges and Schools. It first offered distance learning courses in 1985. In 1999–2000, it offered 67 courses at a distance. In fall 1999, there were 50 students enrolled in distance learning courses.

Course delivery sites Courses are delivered to your home, your workplace.

Media Courses are delivered via videotapes, videoconferencing, World Wide Web. Students and teachers may meet in person or interact via videoconferencing, audioconferencing, mail, telephone, fax, e-mail, World Wide Web. The following equipment may be required: television, videocassette player, computer, modem, Internet access, e-mail.

Restrictions Programs are available worldwide. Enrollment is restricted to individuals meeting certain criteria.

Services Distance learners have access to library services, the campus computer network, e-mail services, academic advising, bookstore at a distance.

Credit-earning options Students may transfer credits from another institution or may earn credits through examinations.

Typical costs *Undergraduate:* Tuition of $489 per semester hour. *Graduate:* Tuition of $489 per semester hour plus mandatory fees of $175 per course. Financial aid is available to distance learners.

Registration Students may register by mail, fax, telephone, in person.

Contact Susan Manley, Program Director, Bradley University, 1501 West Bradley Avenue, Peoria, IL 61625. *Telephone:* 309-677-2820. *Fax:* 309-677-3321. *E-mail:* susank@bradley.edu.

DEGREES AND AWARDS

MSEE Electrical Engineering (certain restrictions apply; service area differs from that of the overall institution; some on-campus requirements)
MSME Mechanical Engineering (service area differs from that of the overall institution; some on-campus requirements)

COURSE SUBJECT AREAS OFFERED OUTSIDE OF DEGREE PROGRAMS

Undergraduate: Commercial art; communications; computer and information sciences; drama and theater; electrical engineering; English language and literature; history; mathematics; psychology
Graduate: Education; electrical engineering; mechanical engineering; nursing

BRENAU UNIVERSITY

Gainesville, Georgia

Department of Distance Learning
www.brenau.edu/dlearning

Brenau University, founded in 1878, is an independent, nonprofit, comprehensive institution. It is accredited by the Southern Association of Colleges and Schools. In 1999–2000, it offered 28 courses at a distance. In fall 1999, there were 42 students enrolled in distance learning courses.

Course delivery sites Courses are delivered to your home, your workplace, military bases, Athens Area Technical Institute (Athens), 3 off-campus centers in Atlanta, Augusta, St. Mary's.

Media Courses are delivered via CD-ROM, World Wide Web, e-mail. Students and teachers may interact via mail, telephone, fax, e-mail, World Wide Web. The following equipment may be required: computer, Internet access.

Restrictions Programs are available worldwide. Enrollment is open to anyone.

Services Distance learners have access to library services, the campus computer network, e-mail services, academic advising, career placement assistance, bookstore at a distance.

Credit-earning options Students may transfer credits from another institution or may earn credits through examinations, military training.

Typical costs *Undergraduate:* Tuition of $325 per semester hour. *Graduate:* Tuition of $325 per semester hour. Financial aid is available to distance learners.

Registration Students may register by mail, fax, World Wide Web, in person.

Contact Kathy Cobb, Brenau University Office of Admissions, Brenau University, One Centennial Circle, Gainesville, GA 30501. *Telephone:* 770-534-6162. *Fax:* 770-538-4701. *E-mail:* kcobb@lib.brenau.edu.

DEGREES AND AWARDS

BN Nursing
MBA Business Administration

COURSE SUBJECT AREAS OFFERED OUTSIDE OF DEGREE PROGRAMS

Undergraduate: Accounting; American literature; business administration and management; child care and development; drama and theater; earth science; education; history; nursing; organizational behavior studies; political science; Spanish language and literature; statistics
Graduate: Accounting; business administration and management; child care and development; education; ethics; finance; marketing; organizational behavior studies; statistics

See full description on page 676.

BREVARD COMMUNITY COLLEGE

Cocoa, Florida

Distance Learning
www.brevard.cc.fl.us

Brevard Community College, founded in 1960, is a state-supported, two-year college. It is accredited by the Southern Association of Colleges and Schools. It first offered distance learning courses in 1974. In 1999–2000, it offered 72 courses at a distance. In fall 1999, there were 750 students enrolled in distance learning courses.

Course delivery sites Courses are delivered to your home, your workplace, military bases, high schools.

Media Courses are delivered via television, videotapes, computer software, World Wide Web, e-mail, print. Students and teachers may interact via mail, telephone, fax, e-mail, interactive television, World Wide Web. The following equipment may be required: television, videocassette player, computer, modem, Internet access, e-mail.

Restrictions Programs are available nationwide. Enrollment is open to anyone.

Services Distance learners have access to library services, e-mail services, academic advising, tutoring, career placement assistance at a distance.

Credit-earning options Students may transfer credits from another institution or may earn credits through examinations, portfolio assessment, military training, business training.

Typical costs Tuition of $50 per credit hour for in-state residents. Tuition of $188 per credit hour for out-of-state residents. Financial aid is available to distance learners.

Registration Students may register by mail, telephone, World Wide Web, in person.

Contact Paige Mecouch, Admissions Department, Brevard Community College, 1519 Clearlake Road, Cocoa, FL 32922. *Telephone:* 321-632-1111 Ext. 63703. *Fax:* 321-634-3752. *E-mail:* mecouchp@brevard.cc.fl.us.

DEGREES AND AWARDS

AA General Studies
AS Legal Studies

COURSE SUBJECT AREAS OFFERED OUTSIDE OF DEGREE PROGRAMS

Undergraduate: Accounting; administrative and secretarial services; advertising; area, ethnic, and cultural studies; Asian languages and literatures; astronomy and astrophysics; biological and life sciences; biology; business; business administration and management; chemical engineering; computer and information sciences; developmental and child psychology; economics; electrical engineering; English language and literature; geology; health and physical education/fitness; history; home economics and family studies; hospitality services management; journalism; law and legal studies; liberal arts, general studies, and humanities; mathematics; music; philosophy and religion; political science; social psychology; sociology

See full description on page 676.

BRIDGEWATER STATE COLLEGE

Bridgewater, Massachusetts

Distance Learning and Technology Programs
www.bridgew.edu

Bridgewater State College, founded in 1840, is a state-supported, comprehensive institution. It is accredited by the New England Association of Schools and Colleges. In 1999–2000, it offered 23 courses at a distance. In fall 1999, there were 94 students enrolled in distance learning courses.

Course delivery sites Courses are delivered to your home, your workplace, military bases, high schools, Cape Cod Community College (West Barnstable).

Media Courses are delivered via videotapes, videoconferencing, interactive television, computer software, World Wide Web, e-mail, print. Students and teachers may meet in person or interact via videoconferencing, mail, telephone, fax, e-mail, interactive television, World Wide Web. The following equipment may be required: television, videocassette player, computer, modem, Internet access, e-mail.

Restrictions Programs are available to local area students. Enrollment is open to anyone.

Services Distance learners have access to library services, the campus computer network, e-mail services, academic advising, career placement assistance, bookstore at a distance.

Credit-earning options Students may transfer credits from another institution.

Typical costs *Undergraduate:* Tuition of $43 per credit plus mandatory fees of $66.15 per credit for in-state residents. Tuition of $293.75 per credit plus mandatory fees of $66.15 per credit for out-of-state residents. *Graduate:* Tuition of $69.75 per credit plus mandatory fees of $66.15 per credit for in-state residents. Tuition of $293.75 per credit plus mandatory fees of $66.15 per credit for out-of-state residents. *Noncredit courses:* $150 per course. Financial aid is available to distance learners.

Registration Students may register by mail, fax, telephone, e-mail, World Wide Web, in person.

Contact Mary Fuller, Director of Distance Learning and Technology Programs, Bridgewater State College, Moakley Center, 100 Burrill Avenue, Bridgewater, MA 02325. *Telephone:* 508-531-6145. *Fax:* 508-531-6121. *E-mail:* mfuller@bridgew.edu.

DEGREES AND AWARDS

Distance programs offered do not lead to a degree or other formal award.

COURSE SUBJECT AREAS OFFERED OUTSIDE OF DEGREE PROGRAMS

Undergraduate: Anthropology; business administration and management; business communications; communications; geography; Japanese language and literature; sociology; special education
Graduate: Business administration and management; education administration; special education

BRIERCREST BIBLE COLLEGE

Caronport, Saskatchewan, Canada

Briercrest Distance Learning
www.briercrest.ca/

Briercrest Bible College, founded in 1935, is an independent, religious, four-year college. It is accredited by the Accrediting Association of Bible Colleges. In 1999–2000, it offered 70 courses at a distance. In fall 1999, there were 160 students enrolled in distance learning courses.

Course delivery sites Courses are delivered to your home.

Media Courses are delivered via videotapes, audiotapes, computer conferencing, World Wide Web, e-mail, print. Students and teachers may meet in person or interact via mail, telephone, fax, e-mail, World Wide Web. The following equipment may be required: computer, modem, Internet access, e-mail.

Restrictions Programs are available worldwide. Enrollment is open to anyone.

Services Distance learners have access to library services, e-mail services, academic advising, tutoring, career placement assistance, bookstore at a distance.

Credit-earning options Students may transfer credits from another institution or may earn credits through portfolio assessment.

Typical costs *Undergraduate:* Tuition of $315 per course. *Graduate:* Tuition of $390 per course. Financial aid is available to distance learners.

Registration Students may register by mail, fax, telephone, e-mail, in person.

Contact Paul Wilder, Enrollment Services Coordinator, Briercrest Bible College, 510 College Drive, Caronport, SK S0H 0S0 Canada. *Telephone:* 800-667-5199. *Fax:* 800-667-2329. *E-mail:* distanceinfo@briercrest.ca.

DEGREES AND AWARDS

Undergraduate Certificate(s) Bible (certain restrictions apply)
ABS Christian Studies (certain restrictions apply)
BA Christian Studies (certain restrictions apply)

COURSE SUBJECT AREAS OFFERED OUTSIDE OF DEGREE PROGRAMS

Undergraduate: Bible studies; English as a second language (ESL); English literature; Greek language and literature; Hebrew language and literature; religious studies
Graduate: Bible studies; Hebrew language and literature; religious studies

BRIGHAM YOUNG UNIVERSITY

Provo, Utah

Independent Study
www.byu.edu/online/

Brigham Young University, founded in 1875, is an independent, religious university affiliated with the Church of Jesus Christ of Latter-day Saints. It is accredited by the Northwest Association of Schools and Colleges. It first offered distance learning courses in 1921. In 1999–2000, it offered 500 courses at a distance.

Course delivery sites Courses are delivered to your home, your workplace, military bases, high schools, Brigham Young University–Hawaii Campus (Laie, HI), Ricks College (Rexburg, ID).

Media Courses are delivered via computer software, CD-ROM, World Wide Web, print. Students and teachers may interact via mail, telephone, fax, e-mail, World Wide Web. The following equipment may be required: computer, Internet access, e-mail.

Restrictions Programs are available worldwide. Enrollment is open to anyone.

Services Distance learners have access to library services, e-mail services, bookstore at a distance.

Typical costs Tuition of $90 per credit. *Noncredit courses: $20 per course.*

Registration Students may register by mail, fax, telephone, e-mail, World Wide Web, in person.

Contact Steve Brimley, Instructional Designer/Webmaster, Brigham Young University, 206 Harmon Continuing Education Building, Provo, UT 84602. *Telephone:* 801-378-8479. *Fax:* 801-378-5817. *E-mail:* steve_brimley@byu.edu.

DEGREES AND AWARDS

Distance programs offered do not lead to a degree or other formal award.

COURSE SUBJECT AREAS OFFERED OUTSIDE OF DEGREE PROGRAMS

Undergraduate: Abnormal psychology; accounting; algebra; American (U.S.) history; American literature; animal sciences; anthropology; art history and criticism; astronomy and astrophysics; Bible studies; biological and life sciences; biology; botany; business; calculus; chemistry; civil engineering; communications; community health services; creative writing; curriculum and instruction; developmental and child psychology; drama and theater; economics; education; educational psychology; engineering; English composition; English language and literature; English literature; European history; European languages and literatures; film studies; finance; fine arts; geography; German language and literature; health and physical education/fitness; health professions and related sciences; Hebrew language and literature; history; home economics and family studies; logic; marketing; mass media; mathematics; microbiology; music; organizational behavior studies; philosophy and religion; physical sciences; physics; political science; psychology; social sciences; sociology; Spanish language and literature; statistics; technical writing

Noncredit: English language and literature; finance; health and physical education/fitness; history; music

See full description on page 474.

BRISTOL COMMUNITY COLLEGE

Fall River, Massachusetts

Distance Learning
www.dl.mass.edu/dl/index.html

Bristol Community College, founded in 1965, is a state-supported, two-year college. It is accredited by the New England Association of Schools and Colleges. It first offered distance learning courses in 1990. In 1999–2000, it offered 18 courses at a distance. In fall 1999, there were 181 students enrolled in distance learning courses.

Course delivery sites Courses are delivered to your home, high schools, Cape Cod Community College (West Barnstable), off-campus center(s) in Attleboro, New Bedford.

Media Courses are delivered via television, videoconferencing, interactive television, World Wide Web, e-mail. Students and teachers may interact via videoconferencing, e-mail, interactive television, World Wide Web. The following equipment may be required: television, computer, modem, Internet access, e-mail.

Restrictions Programs are available to local area students. Enrollment is open to anyone.

Services Distance learners have access to library services, academic advising at a distance.

Credit-earning options Students may transfer credits from another institution or may earn credits through examinations, military training, business training.

Typical costs Tuition of $27 per credit plus mandatory fees of $42 per credit for in-state residents. Tuition of $230 per credit plus mandatory fees of $42 per credit for out-of-state residents. Financial aid is available to distance learners.

Registration Students may register by mail, fax, telephone, World Wide Web, in person.

Contact Candy M. Center, Director, Bristol Community College, 777 Elsbree Street, Fall River, MA 02720. *Telephone:* 508-678-2811. *Fax:* 508-676-7146. *E-mail:* ccenter@bristol.mass.edu.

DEGREES AND AWARDS

Distance programs offered do not lead to a degree or other formal award.

COURSE SUBJECT AREAS OFFERED OUTSIDE OF DEGREE PROGRAMS

Undergraduate: Abnormal psychology; algebra; business administration and management; calculus; chemistry; computer programming; design; engineering; English composition; environmental science; European history; geography; information sciences and systems; psychology; public health; social sciences; sociology; statistics; technical writing

---

BROOKDALE COMMUNITY COLLEGE

Lincroft, New Jersey

Division of Telecommunication Technologies
www.brookdale.cc.nj.us/staff/telecomm

Brookdale Community College, founded in 1967, is a county-supported, two-year college. It is accredited by the Middle States Association of Colleges and Schools. It first offered distance learning courses in 1974. In 1999–2000, it offered 33 courses at a distance. In fall 1999, there were 460 students enrolled in distance learning courses.

Course delivery sites Courses are delivered to your home, your workplace, military bases, high schools, 4 off-campus centers in Asbury Park, Freehold, Keansburg (Bayshore), Long Branch.

Media Courses are delivered via television, videotapes, videoconferencing, interactive television, audiotapes, computer software, CD-ROM, World Wide Web, e-mail. Students and teachers may meet in person or interact via videoconferencing, mail, telephone, fax, e-mail, interactive television, World Wide Web. The following equipment may be required: television, videocassette player, computer, Internet access, e-mail.

Restrictions Telecourses are available statewide, online courses are available nationwide. Enrollment is open to anyone.

Services Distance learners have access to library services, the campus computer network, e-mail services, academic advising, tutoring, bookstore at a distance.

Credit-earning options Students may transfer credits from another institution or may earn credits through examinations, portfolio assessment, military training, business training.

Typical costs Tuition of $75 per credit plus mandatory fees of $15 per credit for local area residents. Tuition of $150 per credit plus mandatory fees of $15 per credit for in-state residents. Tuition for Online courses is $80 with no fees. Financial aid is available to distance learners.

Registration Students may register by mail, in person.

Contact Dr. Louis Pullano, Director, Brookdale Community College, Division of Telecommunication Technologies, 765 Newman Springs Road, Lincroft, NJ 07738. *Telephone:* 732-224-2491. *Fax:* 732-224-2060. *E-mail:* lpullano@brookdale.cc.nj.us.

DEGREES AND AWARDS

AA Business Administration (some on-campus requirements), Liberal Arts (some on-campus requirements), Social Sciences

COURSE SUBJECT AREAS OFFERED OUTSIDE OF DEGREE PROGRAMS

Undergraduate: Anthropology; biology; business; business administration and management; creative writing; developmental and child psychology; drama and theater; economics; electronics; English composition; English language and literature; ethics; European languages and literatures; health and physical education/fitness; history; liberal arts, general studies, and humanities; marketing; music; social psychology; sociology
See full description on page 600.

BROOME COMMUNITY COLLEGE

Binghamton, New York
www.sunybroome.edu

Broome Community College, founded in 1946, is a state and locally supported, two-year college. It is accredited by the Middle States Association of Colleges and Schools. In 1999–2000, it offered 36 courses at a distance. In fall 1999, there were 400 students enrolled in distance learning courses.
Course delivery sites Courses are delivered to your home.
Media Courses are delivered via World Wide Web. Students and teachers may interact via World Wide Web. The following equipment may be required: computer, modem, Internet access, e-mail.
Restrictions Programs are available worldwide. Enrollment is open to anyone.
Services Distance learners have access to library services, e-mail services, academic advising at a distance.
Credit-earning options Students may transfer credits from another institution.
Typical costs Tuition of $98 per credit for in-state residents. Tuition of $198 per credit for out-of-state residents. There is a non-matriculated flat fee of $20. Financial aid is available to distance learners.
Registration Students may register by mail, World Wide Web, in person.
Contact Will Corprew, Registrar, Broome Community College, PO Box 1017, Binghamton, NY 13902. *Telephone:* 607-778-5027. *E-mail:* corprew_w@sunybroome.edu.

DEGREES AND AWARDS

AS Engineering Science (certain restrictions apply; some on-campus requirements)

BROWARD COMMUNITY COLLEGE

Fort Lauderdale, Florida
Instructional Technology
www.broward.cc.fl.us

Broward Community College, founded in 1960, is a state-supported, two-year college. It is accredited by the Southern Association of Colleges and Schools. It first offered distance learning courses in 1978. In 1999–2000, it offered 55 courses at a distance. In fall 1999, there were 1,086 students enrolled in distance learning courses.
Course delivery sites Courses are delivered to your home, Edison Community College (Fort Myers), Palm Beach Community College (Lake Worth).
Media Courses are delivered via television, videotapes, videoconferencing, audiotapes, CD-ROM, World Wide Web, e-mail, print. Students and teachers may meet in person or interact via mail, telephone, fax, e-mail, World Wide Web. The following equipment may be required: computer, Internet access, e-mail.

Restrictions Programs are available to local area students. Enrollment is restricted to individuals meeting certain criteria.
Services Distance learners have access to library services, the campus computer network, e-mail services, academic advising, tutoring, career placement assistance at a distance.
Credit-earning options Students may transfer credits from another institution or may earn credits through examinations, portfolio assessment, military training.
Typical costs Tuition of $44 per credit for in-state residents. Tuition of $163 per credit for out-of-state residents. Financial aid is available to distance learners.
Registration Students may register by telephone, World Wide Web, in person.
Contact Sharon Parker, Director of Extended Learning Services, Broward Community College, 3501 Southwest Davie Road, Davie, FL 33314. *Telephone:* 954-475-6567. *Fax:* 954-475-6959. *E-mail:* sparker@broward.cc.fl.us.

DEGREES AND AWARDS

Distance programs offered do not lead to a degree or other formal award.

COURSE SUBJECT AREAS OFFERED OUTSIDE OF DEGREE PROGRAMS

Undergraduate: Accounting; algebra; American (U.S.) history; anthropology; astronomy and astrophysics; biology; business administration and management; business law; computer and information sciences; developmental and child psychology; economics; English composition; English language and literature; ethics; European history; geography; geology; health and physical education/fitness; health professions and related sciences; marketing; music; nursing; philosophy and religion; political science; sociology; Spanish language and literature; statistics

---

Special note
Broward Community College (BCC) was founded in 1960 and serves students who reside in southeastern Florida. BCC offers AA degrees that feature 62 different majors, AS degrees that feature 50 different majors, and 32 different certificate programs. Substantial portions of these degree and certificate programs can be completed through flexible distributed or distance learning courses that are offered through BCC's Open College Program. An AS degree with concentrations in nursing for paramedics transitioning to RN, LPN transitioning to RN, and RRT transitioning to RN can be earned entirely on line, excluding clinical course work, which must be completed at a local site. Through BCC's Experiential Learning Program and CLEP programs, students may also be able to earn credit for college-level knowledge and competencies that they have acquired outside the classroom. BCC's Open College Program began in 1978. In 2000, more than 50 different courses that represent a wide range of subject areas were available through the Open College Program. Open College courses use audiotapes, videotapes, television broadcasts, and/or the Internet to deliver course content. These courses require few on-campus meetings and are ideal for self-disciplined and self-motivated students who prefer not to attend traditional classes. Students can complete up to 95 percent of an AA degree through video-based telecourses at Broward Community College. Academic credit and the content of Open College courses are equivalent to traditional classroom-based courses. For more information about distributed and distance learning courses at Broward Community College, students should contact the Extended Learning Services Department at 954-475-6564, send an e-mail to sparker@broward.cc.fl.us, or visit the Web site at http://www.broward.cc.fl.us/.

BRUNSWICK COMMUNITY COLLEGE

Supply, North Carolina
www.brunswick.cc.nc.us

Brunswick Community College, founded in 1979, is a state-supported, two-year college. It is accredited by the Southern Association of Colleges and Schools.

Course delivery sites Courses are delivered to your home, 2 off-campus centers in Leland, Southport.

Media Courses are delivered via television, videotapes, interactive television, World Wide Web, e-mail. Students and teachers may meet in person or interact via mail, telephone, fax, e-mail, interactive television, World Wide Web. The following equipment may be required: television, videocassette player, computer, modem, Internet access, e-mail.

Restrictions Programs are available worldwide. Enrollment is restricted to individuals meeting certain criteria.

Services Distance learners have access to library services, academic advising at a distance.

Credit-earning options Students may transfer credits from another institution.

Typical costs Tuition of $26.75 per credit hour for in-state residents. Tuition of $169.75 per credit hour for out-of-state residents. *Noncredit courses:* $65 per course. Financial aid is available to distance learners.

Registration Students may register by mail, fax, telephone, in person.

Contact Ann Harrison, Director of Distance Learning, Brunswick Community College, PO Box 30, Supply, NC 28462. *Telephone:* 910-755-7303. *E-mail:* harrisona@mail.brunswick.cc.nc.us.

DEGREES AND AWARDS

Distance programs offered do not lead to a degree or other formal award.

COURSE SUBJECT AREAS OFFERED OUTSIDE OF DEGREE PROGRAMS

Undergraduate: Business; communications; economics; English language and literature; fine arts; history; mathematics; philosophy and religion

BRYANT AND STRATTON BUSINESS INSTITUTE

Buffalo, New York
Online
www.bryantstratton.edu/main/onlinepage.htm

Bryant and Stratton Business Institute, founded in 1854, is a proprietary, two-year college. It is accredited by the Accrediting Council for Independent Colleges and Schools. In 1999–2000, it offered 20 courses at a distance. In fall 1999, there were 115 students enrolled in distance learning courses.

Course delivery sites Courses are delivered to your home, your workplace, military bases, high schools.

Media Courses are delivered via computer software, CD-ROM, computer conferencing, World Wide Web, e-mail. Students and teachers may interact via e-mail, World Wide Web. The following equipment may be required: computer, modem, Internet access, e-mail.

Restrictions Programs are available worldwide. Enrollment is restricted to individuals meeting certain criteria.

Services Distance learners have access to library services, academic advising, tutoring, career placement assistance, bookstore at a distance.

Credit-earning options Students may transfer credits from another institution.

Typical costs Tuition of $282 per credit. Application fee is $25. Costs may vary. Financial aid is available to distance learners.

Registration Students may register by mail, fax, telephone, e-mail, in person.

Contact Lenore Falletta, Online Admissions, Bryant and Stratton Business Institute, Bryant and Stratton Online, 40 North Street, Buffalo, NY 14202. *Telephone:* 716-884-8000 Ext. 299. *Fax:* 716-884-4057. *E-mail:* oline@bryantstratton.edu.

DEGREES AND AWARDS

AOS Business (certain restrictions apply), Information Technology (certain restrictions apply)

COURSE SUBJECT AREAS OFFERED OUTSIDE OF DEGREE PROGRAMS

Undergraduate: Business; computer and information sciences; English composition; mathematics

Noncredit: Business; computer and information sciences; English composition; mathematics

BUCKS COUNTY COMMUNITY COLLEGE

Newtown, Pennsylvania
Distance Learning Office
www.bucks.edu/distance

Bucks County Community College, founded in 1964, is a county-supported, two-year college. It is accredited by the Middle States Association of Colleges and Schools. It first offered distance learning courses in 1994. In 1999–2000, it offered 120 courses at a distance. In fall 1999, there were 1,000 students enrolled in distance learning courses.

Course delivery sites Courses are delivered to your home, your workplace, military bases.

Media Courses are delivered via television, videotapes, videoconferencing, audiotapes, computer software, CD-ROM, computer conferencing, World Wide Web, e-mail, print. Students and teachers may meet in person or interact via videoconferencing, audioconferencing, mail, telephone, fax, e-mail, World Wide Web. The following equipment may be required: television, videocassette player, computer, Internet access, e-mail.

Restrictions Programs are available nationwide. Enrollment is open to anyone.

Services Distance learners have access to library services, the campus computer network, e-mail services, academic advising, tutoring, career placement assistance, bookstore at a distance.

Credit-earning options Students may transfer credits from another institution or may earn credits through examinations, portfolio assessment, military training, business training.

Typical costs Tuition of $71 per credit plus mandatory fees of $25 per semester for local area residents. Tuition of $142 per credit plus mandatory fees of $35 per semester for in-state residents. Tuition of $213 per credit plus mandatory fees of $45 per semester for out-of-state residents. Financial aid is available to distance learners.

Registration Students may register by mail, fax, telephone, World Wide Web, in person.

Contact Georglyn Davidson, Distance Learning Coordinator, Bucks County Community College, 434 Swamp Road, Newton, PA 18940. *Telephone:* 215-968-8052. *Fax:* 215-968-8148. *E-mail:* learning@bucks.edu.

DEGREES AND AWARDS

Undergraduate Certificate(s) Business Studies, Microsoft Office
AA Business Administration, Liberal Arts, Management, Marketing

COURSE SUBJECT AREAS OFFERED OUTSIDE OF DEGREE PROGRAMS

Undergraduate: Abnormal psychology; accounting; administrative and secretarial services; advertising; algebra; American (U.S.) history; American literature; art history and criticism; astronomy and astrophysics; biology; business; business administration and management; business law; chemistry; computer and information sciences; database management; developmental and child psychology; economics; education; English composition; English language and literature; English literature; ethics; European history; foods and nutrition studies; health and physical education/fitness; history; human resources management; law and legal studies; liberal arts, general studies, and humanities; marketing; mathematics; music; philosophy and religion; physical sciences; physics; political science; psychology; social psychology; sociology; Spanish language and literature; statistics; teacher education; women's studies

BUENA VISTA UNIVERSITY

Storm Lake, Iowa

Centers
www.bvu.edu/

Buena Vista University, founded in 1891, is an independent, religious, comprehensive institution affiliated with the Presbyterian Church (U.S.A.). It is accredited by the North Central Association of Colleges and Schools. It first offered distance learning courses in 1975. In 1999–2000, it offered 200 courses at a distance. In fall 1999, there were 2,060 students enrolled in distance learning courses.

Course delivery sites Courses are delivered to 17 off-campus centers in Cherokee, Council Bluffs, Creston, Denison, Emmetsburg, Estherville, Fort Dodge, Iowa Falls, Jefferson, Lemars, Marshalltown, Mason City, Osceola, Ottumwa, Red Oak, Spencer, Spirit Lake.

Media Courses are delivered via interactive television. Students and teachers may meet in person or interact via telephone, fax, e-mail, interactive television.

Restrictions Programs are available to in-state students only. Enrollment is open to anyone.

Services Distance learners have access to library services, the campus computer network, e-mail services, academic advising, career placement assistance at a distance.

Credit-earning options Students may transfer credits from another institution or may earn credits through examinations, military training, business training.

Typical costs *Undergraduate:* Tuition of $183 per credit hour. *Graduate:* Tuition of $190 per credit hour. Financial aid is available to distance learners.

Registration Students may register by mail, fax, telephone, e-mail, in person.

Contact Dr. John Phillips, Associate Vice President for External Programs and Marketing, Buena Vista University, 610 West Fourth Street, Storm Lake, IA 50588. *Telephone:* 712-749-2250. *Fax:* 712-749-1470. *E-mail:* centers@bvu.edu.

DEGREES AND AWARDS

BA Business (some on-campus requirements), Education (some on-campus requirements), Social Sciences (some on-campus requirements)
MSEd Educational Administration (service area differs from that of the overall institution; some on-campus requirements), Guidance Counseling (school) (service area differs from that of the overall institution; some on-campus requirements), Teaching Effectiveness (service area differs from that of the overall institution; some on-campus requirements)

COURSE SUBJECT AREAS OFFERED OUTSIDE OF DEGREE PROGRAMS

Undergraduate: Accounting; business administration and management; community services; computer and information sciences; criminal justice; education; English language and literature; finance; history; human resources management; information sciences and systems; management information systems; political science; psychology; social sciences; sociology; special education; teacher education
Graduate: Curriculum and instruction; education; education administration; student counseling

Special note
Founded in 1891, Buena Vista University (BVU) is a leading New American College, preparing students for successful careers as well as leadership and service in their communities. With 1,399 undergraduate and graduate students on its main campus in Storm Lake and an additional 2,060 students at 17 branch sites throughout Iowa, BVU offers a balance between traditional learning and innovative experiential learning opportunities that require the practical application of knowledge. This fall, Buena Vista University's eBVyou program equips its nearly 1,400 full-time students and faculty members on the main campus with wireless Gateway notebook computers linked by a Lucent wireless network, creating the nation's first wireless notebook campus that provides students with anytime, anywhere access to the Internet and University resources. Since 1975, BVU centers have made it possible for thousands of graduates to secure better jobs, achieve promotions, find personal satisfaction, continue their education, and pursue new opportunities in Iowa. BVU is working with area communities and community colleges to provide opportunities to a growing number of students each year. Eighty-two percent of BVU center graduates remain in the state. They are making Iowa communities safer and more livable and improving the state's economic outlook by helping Iowa be more attractive to industry. As BVU's graduates are growing, changing, and learning, and so is BVU. BVU is adding more sites, developing more programs, and bringing more possibilities within reach. For more information about Buena Vista University, students should contact Dr. John Phillips, Associate Vice President for External Programs and Marketing at 712-749-2250 or 800-383-2821 Ext. 2247 (toll-free) or via e-mail at centers@bvu.edu or the Web site at http://www.bvu.edu/centers.

BURLINGTON COLLEGE

Burlington, Vermont

Independent Degree Program (IDP)
www.burlcol.edu

Burlington College, founded in 1972, is an independent, nonprofit, four-year college. It is accredited by the New England Association of Schools and Colleges. In fall 1999, there were 60 students enrolled in distance learning courses.

Course delivery sites Courses are delivered to your home.
Media Courses are delivered via videotapes, computer conferencing, World Wide Web, e-mail, print. Students and teachers may meet in person or interact via mail, telephone, fax, e-mail. The following equipment may be required: computer, modem, Internet access, e-mail.
Restrictions Programs are available worldwide. Enrollment is restricted to individuals meeting certain criteria.
Services Distance learners have access to library services, the campus computer network, e-mail services, academic advising, tutoring, career placement assistance at a distance.

Credit-earning options Students may transfer credits from another institution or may earn credits through examinations, portfolio assessment, military training, business training.

Typical costs Tuition of $3400 per semester. Part-time tuition per semester is $2000. Mandatory fees include $50 application fee and $75 graduation fee. Financial aid is available to distance learners.

Registration Students may register by mail, fax, telephone, e-mail, in person.

Contact Cathleen Sullivan, Assistant Director of Admissions, Burlington College. *Telephone:* 800-862-9616. *Fax:* 802-660-4331. *E-mail:* admissions@burlcol.edu.

DEGREES AND AWARDS

AA General Education (some on-campus requirements)

BA Cinema Studies and Film Production (some on-campus requirements), Human Services (some on-campus requirements), Humanities (some on-campus requirements), Individualized Majors (some on-campus requirements), Psychology (some on-campus requirements), Transpersonal Psychology (some on-campus requirements), Writing and Literature (some on-campus requirements)

COURSE SUBJECT AREAS OFFERED OUTSIDE OF DEGREE PROGRAMS

Undergraduate: Archaeology; area, ethnic, and cultural studies; biological and life sciences; business administration and management; communications; economics; education; educational psychology; English language and literature; environmental science; film studies; fine arts; history; liberal arts, general studies, and humanities; philosophy and religion; psychology; public administration and services; social sciences; visual and performing arts; women's studies

BURLINGTON COUNTY COLLEGE

Pemberton, New Jersey

Distance Learning Office
www.bcc.edu

Burlington County College, founded in 1966, is a county-supported, two-year college. It is accredited by the Middle States Association of Colleges and Schools. It first offered distance learning courses in 1978. In 1999–2000, it offered 69 courses at a distance. In fall 1999, there were 965 students enrolled in distance learning courses.

Course delivery sites Courses are delivered to your home, your workplace, military bases.

Media Courses are delivered via television, videotapes, audiotapes, computer software, World Wide Web, e-mail, print. Students and teachers may meet in person or interact via mail, telephone, fax, e-mail, World Wide Web. The following equipment may be required: television, videocassette player, computer, modem, Internet access, e-mail.

Restrictions Programs are available worldwide. Enrollment is open to anyone.

Services Distance learners have access to library services, the campus computer network, e-mail services, bookstore at a distance.

Credit-earning options Students may transfer credits from another institution or may earn credits through examinations.

Typical costs Tuition of $208.50 per course plus mandatory fees of $25 per course for local area residents. Tuition of $253.50 per course plus mandatory fees of $25 per course for in-state residents. Tuition of $448.50 per course plus mandatory fees of $25 per course for out-of-state residents. Financial aid is available to distance learners.

Registration Students may register by mail, fax, telephone, in person.

Contact Sue Espenshade, Coordinator of Distance Learning, Burlington County College, Office of Distance Learning, Route 530, Pemberton, NJ 08068. *Telephone:* 609-894-9311 Ext. 7790. *Fax:* 609-894-4189. *E-mail:* sespensh@bcc.edu.

DEGREES AND AWARDS

AA Liberal Arts and Sciences

AS Business Management

COURSE SUBJECT AREAS OFFERED OUTSIDE OF DEGREE PROGRAMS

Undergraduate: American (U.S.) history; anthropology; art history and criticism; astronomy and astrophysics; biological and life sciences; biology; business; chemistry; child care and development; clothing/apparel and textile studies; comparative literature; computer and information sciences; conservation and natural resources; developmental and child psychology; ecology; economics; English composition; European history; film studies; French language and literature; geology; history; home economics and family studies; marketing; music; political science; psychology; sociology; Spanish language and literature; statistics

Special note
Burlington County College (BCC) has been a leader in distance education since 1978. Last fall, 969 of its 6,000 for-credit students were enrolled in at least 1 distance learning course. The average BCC student is 28 years of age. The College's nontraditional programming overcomes obstacles of time and place for busy adults who seek college degrees, career training/retraining, and/or personal enrichment. This fall, 24 of BCC's 69 for-credit distance learning courses are offered on line. These courses add new flexibility for students who seek 2 distance degrees that were previously offered solely via telecourse through the nationally acclaimed Public Broadcasting System's (PBS) *Going the Distance* program. Last spring, BCC added 65 online noncredit courses. These courses provide 24-hour, "anytime, anywhere" learning opportunities for students who seek personal or career growth in sought-after computer hardware, software, and networking applications; business communications; and business math. BCC is the only Microsoft Authorized Academic Training Program (AATP) in Burlington County. BCC's membership in 3 distance learning consortiums greatly expands the alternative learning opportunities for BCC students. BCC President Dr. Robert Messina chairs the board of the Consortium of Distance Education (CODE). This association of 30 colleges in New York, New Jersey, Pennsylvania, and Delaware helps BCC stay abreast of programming trends via regular contact with national producers and member providers of distance learning courses. The New Jersey Virtual Community College Consortium (NJVCCC, http://www.njvccc.cc.nj.us), launched in fall 1999, offers BCC students access to the shared distance learning resources among the state's 19 community colleges for one standardized tuition rate. The New Jersey Virtual University (http://www.njvu.org), created by New Jersey Governor Christine Whitman in 1998, provides students with a user-friendly index of credit and noncredit courses and certificate and degree programs offered by 42 participating colleges and universities in New Jersey.

See full description on page 600.

Oroville, California
Media and Distance Learning Center
www.bctv.net/distance/

Butte College, founded in 1966, is a district-supported, two-year college. It is accredited by the Western Association of Schools and Colleges, Inc. It first offered distance learning courses in 1975. In 1999–2000, it offered 46 courses at a distance. In fall 1999, there were 1,400 students enrolled in distance learning courses.

Course delivery sites Courses are delivered to your home, 4 off-campus centers in Chico, Gridley, Paradise, Willows.

Media Courses are delivered via television, videoconferencing, World Wide Web. Students and teachers may interact via videoconferencing, mail, telephone, fax, e-mail, World Wide Web. The following equipment may be required: television, videocassette player, computer, modem, Internet access, e-mail.

Restrictions Programs are available to local area students. Enrollment is open to anyone.

Services Distance learners have access to library services, the campus computer network, e-mail services, academic advising, tutoring, career placement assistance at a distance.

Credit-earning options Students may transfer credits from another institution or may earn credits through examinations.

Typical costs Tuition of $13 per unit plus mandatory fees of $72 per semester for in-state residents. Tuition of $138 per unit plus mandatory fees of $72 per semester for out-of-state residents. Financial aid is available to distance learners.

Registration Students may register by telephone, in person.

Contact Jack Lemley, Media and Distance Learning Director, Butte College. *Telephone:* 530-895-2344. *Fax:* 530-895-2380. *E-mail:* lemleyja@butte.cc.ca.us.

DEGREES AND AWARDS

Distance programs offered do not lead to a degree or other formal award.

COURSE SUBJECT AREAS OFFERED OUTSIDE OF DEGREE PROGRAMS

Undergraduate: Agriculture; area, ethnic, and cultural studies; astronomy and astrophysics; biological and life sciences; biology; business administration and management; developmental and child psychology; English as a second language (ESL); English composition; European languages and literatures; fine arts; health and physical education/fitness; history; home economics and family studies; liberal arts, general studies, and humanities; mathematics; philosophy and religion; political science; protective services; radio and television broadcasting; social psychology; social sciences

CABRILLO COLLEGE

Aptos, California
Instruction, Transfer and Distance Education
www.cabrillo.cc.ca.us

Cabrillo College, founded in 1959, is a district-supported, two-year college. It is accredited by the Western Association of Schools and Colleges, Inc. It first offered distance learning courses in 1994. In 1999–2000, it offered 21 courses at a distance. In fall 1999, there were 690 students enrolled in distance learning courses.

Course delivery sites Courses are delivered to your home, high schools, 1 off-campus center in Watsonville.

Media Courses are delivered via television, videotapes, interactive television, audiotapes, computer software, World Wide Web, e-mail, print. Students and teachers may meet in person or interact via mail, telephone, fax, e-mail, interactive television, World Wide Web. The following equipment may be required: television, videocassette player, computer, Internet access, e-mail.

Restrictions Telecourses and interactive television are available to local students only, and Internet courses are available worldwide. Enrollment is restricted to individuals meeting certain criteria.

Services Distance learners have access to library services, e-mail services, career placement assistance, bookstore at a distance.

Credit-earning options Students may transfer credits from another institution or may earn credits through examinations.

Typical costs Tuition of $12 per credit for in-state residents. Tuition of $125 per credit for out-of-state residents. Financial aid is available to distance learners.

Registration Students may register by mail, telephone, in person.

Contact David Warren, Faculty Project Lead for Distance Education, Cabrillo College, 6500 Soquel Drive, Aptos, CA 95003. *Telephone:* 831-479-6270. *Fax:* 831-479-5721. *E-mail:* dwarren@cabrillo.cc.ca.us.

DEGREES AND AWARDS

Distance programs offered do not lead to a degree or other formal award.

COURSE SUBJECT AREAS OFFERED OUTSIDE OF DEGREE PROGRAMS

Undergraduate: Accounting; administrative and secretarial services; anthropology; business law; child care and development; English as a second language (ESL); film studies; geography; health professions and related sciences; political science; psychology; Spanish language and literature

CABRINI COLLEGE

Radnor, Pennsylvania
Graduate and Professional Studies Division
www.cabrini.edu/

Cabrini College, founded in 1957, is an independent, religious, comprehensive institution. It is accredited by the Middle States Association of Colleges and Schools. In 1999–2000, it offered 7 courses at a distance.

Course delivery sites Courses are delivered to your home, your workplace, military bases, high schools, other colleges.

Media Courses are delivered via computer software, World Wide Web, e-mail. Students and teachers may interact via mail, telephone, e-mail, World Wide Web. The following equipment may be required: computer, modem, Internet access, e-mail.

Restrictions Programs are available worldwide. Enrollment is restricted to individuals meeting certain criteria.

Services Distance learners have access to e-mail services, academic advising, bookstore at a distance.

Typical costs *Undergraduate:* Tuition of $290 per semester credit. *Graduate:* Tuition of $350 per semester credit. Mandatory fees include $120 technology fee (waived for initial online course only) and $45 registration fee. Cost for a noncredit course is two thirds that of for credit tuition.

Registration Students may register by mail, fax, telephone, e-mail, World Wide Web, in person.

Contact Beth Carey, Director of Marketing/Recruitment, Cabrini College, 610 King of Prussia Road, Radnor, PA 19087-3698. *Telephone:* 610-902-8500. *Fax:* 610-902-8522. *E-mail:* bcarey@cabrini.edu.

DEGREES AND AWARDS

Distance programs offered do not lead to a degree or other formal award.

COURSE SUBJECT AREAS OFFERED OUTSIDE OF DEGREE PROGRAMS

Undergraduate: American (U.S.) history; curriculum and instruction; information sciences and systems; special education
Graduate: Curriculum and instruction; education administration

CALDWELL COLLEGE

Caldwell, New Jersey

Center for Continuing Education

Caldwell College, founded in 1939, is an independent, religious, comprehensive institution. It is accredited by the Middle States Association of Colleges and Schools. It first offered distance learning courses in 1979. In 1999–2000, it offered 210 courses at a distance. In fall 1999, there were 500 students enrolled in distance learning courses.
Course delivery sites Courses are delivered to your home.
Media Courses are delivered via videotapes, audiotapes, computer software, computer conferencing, e-mail, print. Students and teachers may interact via mail, telephone, fax, e-mail.
Restrictions Programs are available worldwide. Enrollment is restricted to individuals meeting certain criteria.
Services Distance learners have access to library services, the campus computer network, e-mail services, academic advising, tutoring, career placement assistance, bookstore at a distance.
Credit-earning options Students may transfer credits from another institution or may earn credits through examinations, portfolio assessment, military training, business training.
Typical costs Tuition of $319 per credit. Financial aid is available to distance learners.
Registration Students may register by mail, fax, e-mail, World Wide Web, in person.
Contact Mr. Jack Albalah, Adult Admissions, Caldwell College, 9 Ryerson Avenue, Caldwell, NJ 07006. *Telephone:* 973-618-3285. *Fax:* 973-618-3660. *E-mail:* jalbalah@caldwell.edu.

DEGREES AND AWARDS

BA Communication Arts (some on-campus requirements), Criminal Justice (some on-campus requirements), English (some on-campus requirements), Foreign Language (some on-campus requirements), History (some on-campus requirements), Political Science (some on-campus requirements), Psychology (some on-campus requirements), Religious Studies (some on-campus requirements), Sociology (some on-campus requirements)
BS Accounting (some on-campus requirements), Business (some on-campus requirements), Computer Information Systems (some on-campus requirements), International Business (some on-campus requirements), Management (some on-campus requirements), Marketing (some on-campus requirements)

COURSE SUBJECT AREAS OFFERED OUTSIDE OF DEGREE PROGRAMS

Undergraduate: Business; communications; computer and information sciences; English language and literature; European languages and literatures; history; mathematics; philosophy and religion; protective services; psychology; social sciences; visual and performing arts

See full description on page 476.

CALDWELL COMMUNITY COLLEGE AND TECHNICAL INSTITUTE

Hudson, North Carolina

Caldwell Community College and Technical Institute, founded in 1964, is a state-supported, two-year college. It is accredited by the Southern Association of Colleges and Schools. It first offered distance learning courses in 1989.
Contact Caldwell Community College and Technical Institute, 2855 Hickory Boulevard, Hudson, NC 28638-2397. *Telephone:* 828-726-2200. *Fax:* 828-726-2490.

See full description on page 676.

CALHOUN COMMUNITY COLLEGE

Decatur, Alabama

Distance Education
www.calhoun.cc.al.us

Calhoun Community College, founded in 1965, is a state-supported, two-year college. It is accredited by the Southern Association of Colleges and Schools. It first offered distance learning courses in 1992. In 1999–2000, it offered 52 courses at a distance. In fall 1999, there were 444 students enrolled in distance learning courses.
Course delivery sites Courses are delivered to your home, your workplace, military bases, high schools, 1 off-campus center in Huntsville.
Media Courses are delivered via videotapes, audiotapes, computer software, CD-ROM, World Wide Web, e-mail. Students and teachers may meet in person or interact via mail, telephone, fax, e-mail, World Wide Web. The following equipment may be required: television, videocassette player, computer, Internet access, e-mail.
Restrictions Programs are primarily available to in-district students. Enrollment is open to anyone.
Services Distance learners have access to library services, e-mail services, bookstore at a distance.
Credit-earning options Students may transfer credits from another institution or may earn credits through examinations, military training.
Typical costs Tuition of $56 per credit for in-state residents. Tuition of $104 per credit for out-of-state residents. There is a $4 technology fee per credit. Costs may vary. Financial aid is available to distance learners.
Registration Students may register by mail, telephone, in person.
Contact Dr. Carmen Blalock, Distance Education Coordinator, Calhoun Community College, PO Box 2216, Decatur, AL 35609-2216. *Telephone:* 256-306-2755. *Fax:* 256-306-2507. *E-mail:* ctb@calhoun.cc.al.us.

DEGREES AND AWARDS

Distance programs offered do not lead to a degree or other formal award.

COURSE SUBJECT AREAS OFFERED OUTSIDE OF DEGREE PROGRAMS

Undergraduate: Area, ethnic, and cultural studies; business; business administration and management; computer and information sciences; design; English composition; English language and literature; environmental science; European languages and literatures; fine arts; health and physical education/fitness; history; human resources management; law and legal studies; mathematics; music; philosophy and religion; psychology; social sciences; sociology; statistics; visual and performing arts

See full description on page 676.

CALIFORNIA COLLEGE FOR HEALTH SCIENCES

National City, California
www.cchs.edu/

California College for Health Sciences, founded in 1978, is a proprietary, comprehensive institution. It is accredited by the Accrediting Commission for Career Schools and Colleges of Technology, Distance Education and Training Council. It first offered distance learning courses in 1978. In 1999–2000, it offered 100 courses at a distance. In fall 1999, there were 1,200 students enrolled in distance learning courses.

Course delivery sites Courses are delivered to your home, your workplace, military bases.

Media Courses are delivered via audiotapes, print. Students and teachers may interact via mail, telephone, fax, e-mail. The following equipment may be required: e-mail.

Restrictions Programs are available worldwide. Enrollment is open to anyone.

Services Distance learners have access to academic advising, tutoring, bookstore at a distance.

Credit-earning options Students may transfer credits from another institution or may earn credits through examinations, portfolio assessment, military training, business training.

Typical costs *Undergraduate:* Tuition of $100 per credit plus mandatory fees of $35 per course. *Graduate:* Tuition of $100 per credit plus mandatory fees of $35 per course.

Registration Students may register by mail, fax, telephone, e-mail, in person.

Contact Marita Gubbe, Director of Admissions, California College for Health Sciences, 222 West 24th Street, National City, CA 91950. *Telephone:* 619-477-4800. *Fax:* 619-477-4360. *E-mail:* mgubbe@cchs. edu.

DEGREES AND AWARDS

AS Allied Health (certain restrictions apply), Early Childhood Education, EEG Technology (certain restrictions apply), Medical Transcription, Respiratory Therapy (certain restrictions apply)
BS Health Science/Management, Health Services/Respiratory Care
MBA Business
MS Business, Health Care Administration (certain restrictions apply), Health Services/Community Health (certain restrictions apply), Health Services/Wellness Promotion (certain restrictions apply), Public Health (certain restrictions apply)

COURSE SUBJECT AREAS OFFERED OUTSIDE OF DEGREE PROGRAMS

Undergraduate: Accounting; business; business administration and management; chemistry; computer and information sciences; education administration; English composition; finance; health professions and related sciences; human resources management; law and legal studies; marketing; mathematics; microbiology; physics; social psychology; teacher education
Graduate: Accounting; business; business administration and management; finance; health professions and related sciences; human resources management; law and legal studies; public administration and services; social psychology

Special note

Established in 1978, California College for Health Sciences (CCHS) offers proven, accredited distance education programs designed for working health-care professionals. CCHS offers master's, bachelor's, and associate degree and certificate programs, with all learning materials delivered directly to the student. CCHS programs provide a combination of academically sound instruction with unparalleled convenience. All programs are developed by recognized leaders in their fields and require no on-campus attendance. Students choose when and where they wish to study, without having to worry about registration lines, parking, or the other problems associated with on-campus classes. Although CCHS students study on their own time, they can rely on the support of faculty and student advisers, who can be contacted by telephone, fax, e-mail, or mail. CCHS is licensed as a degree-granting institution by the State of California's Bureau for Private Postsecondary and Vocational Education (BPPVE). CCHS is nationally accredited by the Accrediting Commission of the Distance Education and Training Council (DETC), which is listed by the U.S. Department of Education as a nationally recognized accrediting agency. California College for Health Sciences is a Harcourt Higher Learning Company, based in National City, California. For more information, students should contact CCHS (telephone: 800-774-7616 (toll-free); fax: 619-477-4360) or visit the Web site (http://www.chs.edu).

CALIFORNIA INSTITUTE OF INTEGRAL STUDIES

San Francisco, California
Transformative Learning and Change
www.ciis.edu

California Institute of Integral Studies, founded in 1968, is an independent, nonprofit, upper-level institution. It is accredited by the Western Association of Schools and Colleges, Inc. It first offered distance learning courses in 1993. In 1999–2000, it offered 20 courses at a distance. In fall 1999, there were 115 students enrolled in distance learning courses.

Course delivery sites Courses are delivered to your home.

Media Courses are delivered via World Wide Web, e-mail. Students and teachers may interact via mail, telephone, e-mail. The following equipment may be required: computer, modem, Internet access, e-mail.

Restrictions Programs are available worldwide. Enrollment is open to anyone.

Services Distance learners have access to library services, the campus computer network, e-mail services, academic advising, tutoring, bookstore at a distance.

Credit-earning options Students may transfer credits from another institution.

Typical costs Full-time master's-level tuition is $9650 per year. Full-time doctorate tuition is $12,500 per year. Mandatory fees are $86 per semester. Financial aid is available to distance learners.

Registration Students may register by mail, fax.

Contact Inquiry Office, California Institute of Integral Studies, 1453 Mission Street, San Francisco, CA 94103. *Telephone:* 415-575-6100. *Fax:* 415-575-1264. *E-mail:* info@ciis.edu.

DEGREES AND AWARDS

MA Cultural Anthropology and Social Transformation (some on-campus requirements)
PhD Humanities-Transformative Learning and Change

COURSE SUBJECT AREAS OFFERED OUTSIDE OF DEGREE PROGRAMS

Graduate: Adult education; anthropology; Asian studies; ecology; educational research; information sciences and systems; interdisciplinary studies; organizational behavior studies; religious studies; social psychology; sociology; women's studies
Noncredit: Adult education; anthropology; Asian studies; ecology; information sciences and systems; interdisciplinary studies; organizational behavior studies; religious studies; social psychology; sociology; women's studies

CALIFORNIA NATIONAL UNIVERSITY FOR ADVANCED STUDIES

North Hills, California
www.cnuas.edu/

California National University for Advanced Studies, founded in 1993, is an independent, comprehensive institution. It is accredited by the Distance Education and Training Council. In 1999–2000, it offered 470 courses at a distance. In fall 1999, there were 202 students enrolled in distance learning courses.

Course delivery sites Courses are delivered to your home, your workplace, military bases.

Media Courses are delivered via videotapes, audiotapes, computer software, CD-ROM, computer conferencing, World Wide Web, e-mail, print. Students and teachers may interact via mail, telephone, fax, e-mail, World Wide Web. The following equipment may be required: computer, modem, Internet access, e-mail.

Restrictions Programs are available worldwide. Enrollment is open to anyone.

Services Distance learners have access to library services, the campus computer network, e-mail services, academic advising, tutoring, bookstore at a distance.

Credit-earning options Students may transfer credits from another institution or may earn credits through examinations.

Typical costs *Undergraduate:* Tuition of $235 per unit for local area residents. Tuition of $235 per unit for in-state residents. Tuition of $255 per unit for out-of-state residents. *Graduate:* Tuition of $255 per unit for local area residents. Tuition of $255 per unit for in-state residents. Tuition of $305 per unit for out-of-state residents. Application fee is $50. Registration fee is $150. Financial aid is available to distance learners.

Registration Students may register by mail, fax, e-mail, World Wide Web, in person.

Contact Jeanne Cunneff, Admissions Representative, California National University for Advanced Studies, 16093 Parthenia Street, North Hills, CA 91343. *Telephone:* 800-782-2422. *Fax:* 818-830-2418. *E-mail:* jeanne@mail.cnuas.edu.

DEGREES AND AWARDS

Undergraduate Certificate(s) Human Resource Management Practice (certain restrictions apply)
AIS Human Resource Management (certain restrictions apply)
BS Business Administration, Computer Science, Engineering, Quality Assurance Science
MBA Business Administration
MS Engineering (certain restrictions apply)

COURSE SUBJECT AREAS OFFERED OUTSIDE OF DEGREE PROGRAMS

Undergraduate: Accounting; algebra; American (U.S.) history; American literature; business administration and management; business communications; business law; calculus; chemistry, organic; chemistry, physical; computer programming; database management; electrical engineering; English composition; environmental engineering; finance; human resources management; information sciences and systems; international business; liberal arts, general studies, and humanities; management information systems; marketing; mathematics; mechanical engineering; organizational behavior studies; physics; statistics
Graduate: Accounting; business administration and management; business communications; business law; computer programming; database management; electrical engineering; environmental engineering; finance; human resources management; information sciences and systems; international business; management information systems; marketing; mathematics; mechanical engineering; organizational behavior studies; statistics

CALIFORNIA STATE UNIVERSITY, CHICO

Chico, California
Center for Regional and Continuing Education
rce.csuchico.edu

California State University, Chico, founded in 1887, is a state-supported, comprehensive institution. It is accredited by the Western Association of Schools and Colleges, Inc. It first offered distance learning courses in 1974. In 1999–2000, it offered 70 courses at a distance. In fall 1999, there were 700 students enrolled in distance learning courses.

Course delivery sites Courses are delivered to your home, your workplace, military bases.

Media Courses are delivered via videotapes, videoconferencing, computer software, computer conferencing, World Wide Web. Students and teachers may interact via mail, telephone, fax, e-mail, World Wide Web. The following equipment may be required: computer, modem, Internet access, e-mail.

Restrictions Programs are available nationwide. Enrollment is open to anyone.

Services Distance learners have access to library services, academic advising, career placement assistance, bookstore at a distance.

Credit-earning options Students may transfer credits from another institution or may earn credits through examinations, portfolio assessment.

Typical costs Tuition for distance learning courses vary from $997 per semester to $1600 per course depending on the degree program. Please contact CSU, Chico for current fees. Costs may vary. Financial aid is available to distance learners.

Registration Students may register by mail, fax, telephone, in person.
Contact Jeffrey S. Layne, Telecommunications Specialist, California State University, Chico, Center for Regional and Continuing Education, Chico, CA 95929-0250. *Telephone:* 530-898-6105. *Fax:* 530-898-4020. *E-mail:* jlayne@csuchico.edu.

DEGREES AND AWARDS

BA Jewish Studies (service area differs from that of the overall institution), Liberal Studies (some on-campus requirements), Political Science, Social Sciences, Sociology
BSN Nursing (service area differs from that of the overall institution)
MA Psychology/Organizational Psychology (service area differs from that of the overall institution)
MS Computer Science (certain restrictions apply)
MSIS Telecommunications (some on-campus requirements)

COURSE SUBJECT AREAS OFFERED OUTSIDE OF DEGREE PROGRAMS

Undergraduate: Computer and information sciences; Jewish studies; liberal arts, general studies, and humanities; nursing; political science; social sciences; sociology
Graduate: Computer and information sciences; psychology; telecommunications
Noncredit: Computer and information sciences

CALIFORNIA STATE UNIVERSITY, DOMINGUEZ HILLS

Carson, California
Distance Learning
www.csudh.edu/dominguezonline

California State University, Dominguez Hills, founded in 1960, is a state-supported, comprehensive institution. It is accredited by the Western Association of Schools and Colleges, Inc. It first offered distance learning courses in 1975. In 1999–2000, it offered 120 courses at a distance. In fall 1999, there were 2,000 students enrolled in distance learning courses.

Course delivery sites Courses are delivered to your home, your workplace, military bases, high schools.

Media Courses are delivered via television, videotapes, videoconferencing, interactive television, computer software, World Wide Web, e-mail, print. Students and teachers may meet in person or interact via videoconferencing, audioconferencing, mail, telephone, fax, e-mail, interactive television, World Wide Web. The following equipment may be required: television, computer, modem, Internet access, e-mail.

Restrictions Programs are available worldwide. Enrollment is restricted to individuals meeting certain criteria.

Services Distance learners have access to library services, the campus computer network, e-mail services, academic advising, tutoring, career placement assistance, bookstore at a distance.

Credit-earning options Students may transfer credits from another institution or may earn credits through examinations, business training.

Typical costs *Undergraduate:* Tuition of $170 per semester hour. *Graduate:* Tuition of $170 per semester hour. Costs may vary. Financial aid is available to distance learners.

Registration Students may register by mail, fax, telephone, e-mail, World Wide Web, in person.

Contact Extended Education Registration Office, California State University, Dominguez Hills, 1000 East Victoria Street, Carson, CA 90747. *Telephone:* 877-GO-HILLS. *Fax:* 310-516-3971. *E-mail:* eereg@csudh. edu.

DEGREES AND AWARDS

Undergraduate Certificate(s) Assertive Technology, Purchasing, Quality Assurance, Supply Chain Management
BS Nursing
MA Humanities, Negotiation and Conflict Management
MBA Business Administration
MS Nursing, Quality Assurance

COURSE SUBJECT AREAS OFFERED OUTSIDE OF DEGREE PROGRAMS

Undergraduate: Liberal arts, general studies, and humanities; nursing; teacher education
Graduate: Business administration and management; liberal arts, general studies, and humanities; nursing; teacher education

See full description on page 478.

CALIFORNIA STATE UNIVERSITY, FRESNO

Fresno, California

Academic Innovation Center
www.csufresno.edu/aic/distance.html

California State University, Fresno, founded in 1911, is a state-supported, comprehensive institution. It is accredited by the Western Association of Schools and Colleges, Inc. In 1999–2000, it offered 37 courses at a distance. In fall 1999, there were 768 students enrolled in distance learning courses.

Course delivery sites Courses are delivered to California State University, Bakersfield (Bakersfield), College of the Sequoias (Visalia), West Hills Community College (Coalinga).

Media Courses are delivered via television, videoconferencing, World Wide Web, e-mail, print. Students and teachers may meet in person or

interact via mail, telephone, e-mail, interactive television, World Wide Web. The following equipment may be required: computer, modem, Internet access, e-mail.

Restrictions Programs are available to local area students. Enrollment is open to anyone.

Services Distance learners have access to library services, the campus computer network, e-mail services, bookstore at a distance.

Credit-earning options Students may transfer credits from another institution or may earn credits through examinations, military training.

Typical costs Undergraduate tuition for 0-6 units is $578; for 7 or more units tuition is $878. Graduate tuition for 0-6 units is $602; for 7 or more units tuition is $917. Financial aid is available to distance learners.

Registration Students may register by mail, telephone, in person.

Contact Ray Freeman, Administrative Coordinator, California State University, Fresno, 2225 East San Ramon Avenue, Fresno, CA 93740-0121. *Telephone:* 559-278-5766. *Fax:* 559-278-7026. *E-mail:* ray_freeman@csufresno.edu.

DEGREES AND AWARDS

BA Liberal Studies (certain restrictions apply)

COURSE SUBJECT AREAS OFFERED OUTSIDE OF DEGREE PROGRAMS

Undergraduate: Area, ethnic, and cultural studies; biology; business administration and management; developmental and child psychology; economics; education; education administration; English as a second language (ESL); English language and literature; European languages and literatures; liberal arts, general studies, and humanities; music; nursing; psychology; social psychology; social sciences; teacher education; visual and performing arts
Graduate: Education; teacher education

CALIFORNIA STATE UNIVERSITY, FULLERTON

Fullerton, California

Distributed/Distance Learning Program
www.takethelead.fullerton.edu

California State University, Fullerton, founded in 1957, is a state-supported, comprehensive institution. It is accredited by the Western Association of Schools and Colleges, Inc. In 1999–2000, it offered 38 courses at a distance. In fall 1999, there were 500 students enrolled in distance learning courses.

Course delivery sites Courses are delivered to your home, your workplace, military bases, California State University (Long Beach), University of California System (Oakland), 4 off-campus centers in Anaheim, Corona, El Segundo, Long Beach.

Media Courses are delivered via television, videoconferencing, interactive television, World Wide Web. Students and teachers may meet in person or interact via videoconferencing, telephone, fax, e-mail, interactive television, World Wide Web. The following equipment may be required: television, videocassette player, computer, modem, Internet access, e-mail.

Restrictions Programs are available nationwide. Enrollment is restricted to individuals meeting certain criteria.

Services Distance learners have access to library services, the campus computer network, e-mail services, academic advising, tutoring, career placement assistance, bookstore at a distance.

Credit-earning options Students may transfer credits from another institution or may earn credits through examinations.

Typical costs *Undergraduate:* Tuition of $246 per unit for out-of-state residents. *Graduate:* Tuition of $246 per unit for out-of-state residents. Undergraduate tuition per semester for in-district or in-state students is $714 for 6 or more units; graduate in-district or in-state tuition is

$943.50. Mandatory fees are $190.50 per semester for all students. Typical cost for a noncredit course is $100 to $450. Financial aid is available to distance learners.

Registration Students may register by mail, fax, telephone, in person.

Contact Admissions, California State University, Fullerton, PO Box 34080, Fullerton, CA 92834-9480. *Telephone:* 714-773-2300. *Fax:* 714-773-2341.

DEGREES AND AWARDS

BSN Nursing
MSEE Electrical Engineering (service area differs from that of the overall institution; some on-campus requirements)

COURSE SUBJECT AREAS OFFERED OUTSIDE OF DEGREE PROGRAMS

Undergraduate: Communications; design; education administration; electrical engineering; health and physical education/fitness; history; liberal arts, general studies, and humanities; library and information studies; nursing; religious studies; statistics
Graduate: Accounting; advertising; business; business administration and management; electrical engineering

CALIFORNIA STATE UNIVERSITY, LONG BEACH

Long Beach, California

University College and Extension Services
www.uces.csulb.edu

California State University, Long Beach, founded in 1949, is a state-supported, comprehensive institution. It is accredited by the Western Association of Schools and Colleges, Inc. It first offered distance learning courses in 1988. In 1999–2000, it offered 15 courses at a distance. In fall 1999, there were 235 students enrolled in distance learning courses.

Course delivery sites Courses are delivered to your home, your workplace, California State University Channel Islands, California State University, Bakersfield (Bakersfield), California State University, Chico (Chico), Humboldt State University (Arcata), 7 off-campus centers in Bakersfield, Burlingame, Hayward, Orange County, San Jose, Sunnyvale, Tracy.

Media Courses are delivered via television, videotapes, videoconferencing, computer software, World Wide Web, print. Students and teachers may meet in person or interact via videoconferencing, audioconferencing, mail, telephone, fax, e-mail, interactive television, World Wide Web. The following equipment may be required: television, videocassette player, computer, modem, Internet access.

Restrictions Programs are available to in-state students only. Enrollment is restricted to individuals meeting certain criteria.

Services Distance learners have access to library services, the campus computer network, e-mail services, academic advising, bookstore at a distance.

Credit-earning options Students may transfer credits from another institution or may earn credits through portfolio assessment, military training, business training.

Typical costs *Undergraduate:* Tuition of $175 per unit. *Graduate:* Tuition of $200 per unit. *Noncredit courses:* $545 per course. Financial aid is available to distance learners.

Registration Students may register by mail, fax, telephone, in person.

Contact Lynn E. Henricks, Director of Distance Learning, California State University, Long Beach, 6300 State University Drive, Suite 104, Long Beach, CA 90815. *Telephone:* 562-985-8455. *Fax:* 562-985-8449. *E-mail:* ideas@uces.csulb.edu.

DEGREES AND AWARDS

BA Vocational Education
MSW Social Work

COURSE SUBJECT AREAS OFFERED OUTSIDE OF DEGREE PROGRAMS

Undergraduate: Educational psychology; finance; home economics and family studies
Graduate: Educational psychology; social work

CALIFORNIA STATE UNIVERSITY, LOS ANGELES

Los Angeles, California

Continuing Education
www.calstatela.edu/cont_ed

California State University, Los Angeles, founded in 1947, is a state-supported, comprehensive institution. It is accredited by the Western Association of Schools and Colleges, Inc. It first offered distance learning courses in 1987. In 1999–2000, it offered 10 courses at a distance. In fall 1999, there were 84 students enrolled in distance learning courses.

Course delivery sites Courses are delivered to your home, your workplace.

Media Courses are delivered via World Wide Web. Students and teachers may meet in person or interact via mail, telephone, fax, e-mail. The following equipment may be required: computer, e-mail.

Restrictions Programs are available nationwide. Enrollment is restricted to individuals meeting certain criteria.

Services Distance learners have access to library services, the campus computer network, e-mail services, academic advising, bookstore at a distance.

Credit-earning options Students may earn credits through examinations.

Typical costs Graduate tuition is $500 for 4 units. Costs may vary.

Registration Students may register by mail, fax, telephone, in person.

Contact Alice Marie Gutierrez, Coordinator, California State University, Los Angeles, 5151 State University Drive, Los Angeles, CA 90032-8619. *Telephone:* 323-343-4916. *Fax:* 323-343-4954. *E-mail:* agutier@cslanet.calstatela.edu.

DEGREES AND AWARDS

Undergraduate Certificate(s) Business Management

COURSE SUBJECT AREAS OFFERED OUTSIDE OF DEGREE PROGRAMS

Undergraduate: Teacher education
Graduate: Accounting; business administration and management; finance; marketing

CALIFORNIA STATE UNIVERSITY, NORTHRIDGE

Northridge, California

Educational Technologies and Distance Learning
www.csun.edu/exl/distance

California State University, Northridge, founded in 1958, is a state-supported, comprehensive institution. It is accredited by the Western Association of Schools and Colleges, Inc. It first offered distance learning courses in 1982. In 1999–2000, it offered 40 courses at a distance. In fall 1999, there were 75 students enrolled in distance learning courses.

Course delivery sites Courses are delivered to your home, your workplace, military bases, Antelope Valley College (Lancaster), 5 off-campus centers in China Lake, Edwards, El Segundo, Lancaster, Woodland Hills.

Media Courses are delivered via television, videotapes, computer software, World Wide Web, e-mail, print. Students and teachers may interact via videoconferencing, audioconferencing, mail, telephone, fax, e-mail. The following equipment may be required: computer, modem, Internet access, e-mail.

Restrictions Programs are available to in-state students only. Enrollment is restricted to individuals meeting certain criteria.

Services Distance learners have access to library services, the campus computer network, e-mail services, academic advising, bookstore at a distance.

Credit-earning options Students may transfer credits from another institution or may earn credits through examinations, portfolio assessment.

Typical costs *Noncredit courses:* $300 per course. Costs may vary. Financial aid is available to distance learners.

Registration Students may register by mail, fax, telephone, World Wide Web, in person.

Contact Sheri Kaufman, Project Coordinator, California State University, Northridge, 18111 Nordhoff Street, Northridge, CA 91330-8324. *Telephone:* 818-677-2355. *Fax:* 818-677-2316. *E-mail:* sheri.kaufmann@ csun.edu.

DEGREES AND AWARDS

BS Engineering Management (service area differs from that of the overall institution)
MS Electrical Engineering (service area differs from that of the overall institution), Speech Pathology (service area differs from that of the overall institution)

COURSE SUBJECT AREAS OFFERED OUTSIDE OF DEGREE PROGRAMS

Undergraduate: Electrical engineering
Graduate: Electrical engineering; engineering/industrial management

CALIFORNIA STATE UNIVERSITY, SAN MARCOS

San Marcos, California
Extended Studies
www.csusm.edu/es

California State University, San Marcos, founded in 1990, is a state-supported, comprehensive institution. It is accredited by the Western Association of Schools and Colleges, Inc. It first offered distance learning courses in 1997. In 1999–2000, it offered 15 courses at a distance. In fall 1999, there were 60 students enrolled in distance learning courses.

Course delivery sites Courses are delivered to your home, your workplace, military bases, high schools.

Media Courses are delivered via computer software, World Wide Web, e-mail. Students and teachers may interact via e-mail, World Wide Web. The following equipment may be required: computer, modem, Internet access, e-mail.

Restrictions Programs are available nationwide. Enrollment is open to anyone.

Services Distance learners have access to library services, e-mail services, academic advising, bookstore at a distance.

Typical costs Tuition of $105 per credit. *Noncredit courses:* $500 per course. Costs may vary.

Registration Students may register by mail, fax, telephone, e-mail, World Wide Web, in person.

Contact Bryana Robey, Registration Specialist, California State University, San Marcos, Extended Studies, San Marcos, CA 92096. *Telephone:* 800-500-9377. *Fax:* 760-750-3138. *E-mail:* es@csusm.edu.

DEGREES AND AWARDS

Undergraduate Certificate(s) Construction Supervision (service area differs from that of the overall institution), Paralegal Studies (service area differs from that of the overall institution)

COURSE SUBJECT AREAS OFFERED OUTSIDE OF DEGREE PROGRAMS

Undergraduate: Sociology; teacher education
Graduate: Teacher education
Noncredit: Construction; law and legal studies

CALVARY BIBLE COLLEGE AND THEOLOGICAL SEMINARY

Kansas City, Missouri
Non-Traditional Studies
www.calvary.edu/

Calvary Bible College and Theological Seminary, founded in 1932, is an independent, religious, comprehensive institution. It is accredited by the Accrediting Association of Bible Colleges. In 1999–2000, it offered 15 courses at a distance. In fall 1999, there were 100 students enrolled in distance learning courses.

Course delivery sites Courses are delivered to your home.

Media Courses are delivered via audiotapes, e-mail, print. Students and teachers may meet in person or interact via mail, telephone, fax, e-mail. The following equipment may be required: computer, modem, Internet access, e-mail.

Restrictions Programs are available worldwide. Enrollment is restricted to individuals meeting certain criteria.

Services Distance learners have access to library services, e-mail services, academic advising, career placement assistance, bookstore at a distance.

Credit-earning options Students may transfer credits from another institution or may earn credits through examinations, military training, business training.

Typical costs *Undergraduate:* Tuition of $170 per credit hour plus mandatory fees of $16 per credit hour. *Graduate:* Tuition of $175 per credit hour plus mandatory fees of $19 per credit hour. Cost for noncredit course is $50 per credit hour. Financial aid is available to distance learners.

Registration Students may register by mail, fax, telephone, e-mail, World Wide Web, in person.

Contact Mike Piburn, Director of Admissions, Calvary Bible College and Theological Seminary, 15800 Calvary Road, Kansas City, MO 64147. *Telephone:* 800-326-3960. *Fax:* 816-331-4474. *E-mail:* diradm@ calvary.edu.

DEGREES AND AWARDS

Distance programs offered do not lead to a degree or other formal award.

COURSE SUBJECT AREAS OFFERED OUTSIDE OF DEGREE PROGRAMS

Undergraduate: Bible studies; theological studies

CAMDEN COUNTY COLLEGE

Blackwood, New Jersey

Extended Educational Services
www.camdencc.edu/

Camden County College, founded in 1967, is a state and locally supported, two-year college. It is accredited by the Middle States Association of Colleges and Schools. It first offered distance learning courses in 1995. **Contact** Camden County College, PO Box 200, Blackwood, NJ 08012-0200. *Telephone:* 609-227-7200.

See full description on page 600.

CAMPBELLSVILLE UNIVERSITY

Campbellsville, Kentucky
www.campbellsvil.edu

Campbellsville University, founded in 1906, is an independent, religious, comprehensive institution affiliated with the Kentucky Baptist Convention. It is accredited by the Southern Association of Colleges and Schools. It first offered distance learning courses in 1999. In 1999–2000, it offered 3 courses at a distance.
Course delivery sites Courses are delivered to your home, your workplace.
Media Courses are delivered via interactive television, World Wide Web, e-mail, print. Students and teachers may meet in person or interact via mail, telephone, fax, e-mail, World Wide Web. The following equipment may be required: television, computer, modem, Internet access, e-mail.
Restrictions Programs are available worldwide. Enrollment is restricted to individuals meeting certain criteria.
Services Distance learners have access to library services, the campus computer network, e-mail services, academic advising, bookstore at a distance.
Typical costs *Undergraduate:* Tuition of $336 per credit hour plus mandatory fees of $120 per semester. *Graduate:* Tuition of $336 per credit hour plus mandatory fees of $120 per semester. Financial aid is available to distance learners.
Registration Students may register by mail, World Wide Web, in person.
Contact Dr. Frank Cheatham, Vice President for Academic Affairs, Campbellsville University, 1 University Drive, Campbellsville, KY 42718-2799. *Telephone:* 270-789-5231. *Fax:* 270-789-5550. *E-mail:* frank@campbellsvil.edu.

eCollege *www.ecollege.com/scholarships*
.com

DEGREES AND AWARDS

Distance programs offered do not lead to a degree or other formal award.

COURSE SUBJECT AREAS OFFERED OUTSIDE OF DEGREE PROGRAMS

Undergraduate: Business administration and management
Graduate: Cognitive psychology; educational research; religious studies

CAPE COD COMMUNITY COLLEGE

West Barnstable, Massachusetts

Distance Learning
www.capecod.mass.edu/distancelearning

Cape Cod Community College, founded in 1961, is a state-supported, two-year college. It is accredited by the New England Association of Schools and Colleges. It first offered distance learning courses in 1993. In 1999–2000, it offered 24 courses at a distance. In fall 1999, there were 300 students enrolled in distance learning courses.
Course delivery sites Courses are delivered to your home, military bases.
Media Courses are delivered via videotapes, videoconferencing, World Wide Web, e-mail. Students and teachers may meet in person or interact via videoconferencing, mail, telephone, fax, e-mail, World Wide Web. The following equipment may be required: television, videocassette player, computer, Internet access, e-mail.
Restrictions Programs are available worldwide. Enrollment is open to anyone.
Services Distance learners have access to library services, e-mail services, bookstore at a distance.
Credit-earning options Students may transfer credits from another institution or may earn credits through examinations.
Typical costs Tuition of $125 per course plus mandatory fees of $145 per course. Financial aid is available to distance learners.
Registration Students may register by mail, fax, telephone, in person.
Contact Dale Suffridge, Director of Distance Learning, Cape Cod Community College, 2240 Iyanough Road, West Barnstable, MA 02668. *Telephone:* 508-375-4040. *Fax:* 508-375-4041. *E-mail:* dsuffrid@capecod.mass.edu.

DEGREES AND AWARDS

Distance programs offered do not lead to a degree or other formal award.

COURSE SUBJECT AREAS OFFERED OUTSIDE OF DEGREE PROGRAMS

Undergraduate: Business administration and management; English composition; English language and literature; fine arts; health professions and related sciences; history; mathematics; nursing; psychology; social psychology; sociology

CAPE FEAR COMMUNITY COLLEGE

Wilmington, North Carolina

Cape Fear Community College, founded in 1959, is a state-supported, two-year college. It is accredited by the Southern Association of Colleges and Schools. In 1999–2000, it offered 28 courses at a distance. In fall 1999, there were 230 students enrolled in distance learning courses.
Course delivery sites Courses are delivered to your home.
Media Courses are delivered via television, videotapes, computer software, CD-ROM, World Wide Web, e-mail. Students and teachers may meet in person or interact via mail, telephone, fax, e-mail. The following equipment may be required: television, computer, modem, Internet access, e-mail.
Restrictions Programs are available to local area students. Enrollment is open to anyone.
Services Distance learners have access to e-mail services at a distance.
Credit-earning options Students may transfer credits from another institution or may earn credits through examinations, military training.

Typical costs Tuition of $26.75 per semester hour for local area residents. Tuition of $26.75 per semester hour for in-state residents. Tuition of $169.75 per semester hour for out-of-state residents. Financial aid is available to distance learners.

Registration Students may register by in person.

Contact Orangel Daniels, Dean of Arts and Sciences, Cape Fear Community College, 411 North Front Street, Wilmington, NC 28401. *Telephone:* 910-251-5629. *E-mail:* odaniels@capefear.cc.nc.us.

DEGREES AND AWARDS

Distance programs offered do not lead to a degree or other formal award.

COURSE SUBJECT AREAS OFFERED OUTSIDE OF DEGREE PROGRAMS

Undergraduate: Business law; computer and information sciences; English composition; fine arts; history; management; marketing; psychology; speech

CAPELLA UNIVERSITY

Minneapolis, Minnesota
www.capellauniversity.edu

Capella University, founded in 1993, is a proprietary, graduate institution. It is accredited by the North Central Association of Colleges and Schools. It first offered distance learning courses in 1993. In 1999–2000, it offered 300 courses at a distance. In fall 1999, there were 1,300 students enrolled in distance learning courses.

Course delivery sites Courses are delivered to your home, your workplace.

Media Courses are delivered via World Wide Web, e-mail, print. Students and teachers may interact via mail, telephone, fax, e-mail, World Wide Web. The following equipment may be required: computer, modem, Internet access, e-mail.

Restrictions Programs are available worldwide. Enrollment is restricted to individuals meeting certain criteria.

Services Distance learners have access to library services, e-mail services, academic advising, tutoring, bookstore at a distance.

Credit-earning options Students may transfer credits from another institution.

Typical costs Tuition of $2875 per quarter. Costs may vary. Financial aid is available to distance learners.

Registration Students may register by mail, fax, e-mail, World Wide Web.

Contact Erik Hallberg, Admissions Specialist, Capella University, 330 Second Avenue South, Suite 550, Minneapolis, MN 55401. *Telephone:* 888-CAPELLA. *Fax:* 612-339-8022. *E-mail:* info@capella.edu.

DEGREES AND AWARDS

BS Information Technology
MBA Business Administration
MS Education (some on-campus requirements), Human Services (some on-campus requirements), Organization and Management (some on-campus requirements), Psychology (some on-campus requirements)
PhD Education (some on-campus requirements), Human Services (some on-campus requirements), Organization and Management (some on-campus requirements), Psychology (some on-campus requirements)

COURSE SUBJECT AREAS OFFERED OUTSIDE OF DEGREE PROGRAMS

Undergraduate: Information sciences and systems
Graduate: Abnormal psychology; accounting; adult education; area, ethnic, and cultural studies; business; business administration and management; business communications; cognitive psychology; continuing education; counseling psychology; curriculum and instruction; developmental and child psychology; education; education administration; educational psychology; educational research; health professions and related sciences; human resources management; industrial psychology; information sciences and systems; international business; international relations; labor relations/studies; marketing; organizational behavior studies; philosophy and religion; political science; psychology; school psychology; social psychology; social work; sociology; special education; student counseling

---

Special note
Founded in 1993, Capella University is an accredited distance learning university that is dedicated to helping professionals integrate advanced study into their personal and professional lives. Capella has approximately 1,400 students who come from 50 states and 12 countries. Capella University offers graduate degree programs, certificates, and continuing education in professional development, business, education, human services, and psychology. Average completion time is 3 months for individual courses, 18 months to 2 years for a master's degree, and 3 to 4 years for a doctoral degree. Capella University is accredited by the North Central Association of Colleges and Schools. Online courses, which last about 12 weeks, have 10 to 20 learners per course and an established beginning and end date. There are assigned course materials, case exercises, and learner participation in weekly group discussions about key topics. Every learner is assigned a faculty mentor who guides them through the course completion and research phases of graduate study. The online campus gives instant access to library services through a cooperative arrangement with the University of Alabama in Huntsville. The Cybrary offers convenient links to outstanding resources on the Internet, specialized library databases, reference assistance, and document delivery. Graduate business education is a significant investment. Capella University's tuition is comparable to other leading business schools. Financial aid and several low-cost national student loan alternatives are available. Students may complete an admissions application on line at http://www.capellauniversity.edu or speak with an Enrollment Services counselor by calling 800-987-1133 (toll-free).

CAPITAL COMMUNITY COLLEGE

Hartford, Connecticut
Distance Learning Class
webster.commnet.edu/

Capital Community College, founded in 1946, is a state-supported, two-year college. It is accredited by the New England Association of Schools and Colleges. In 1999–2000, it offered 5 courses at a distance. In fall 1999, there were 38 students enrolled in distance learning courses.

Course delivery sites Courses are delivered to your home.

Media Courses are delivered via World Wide Web. Students and teachers may meet in person or interact via e-mail. The following equipment may be required: computer, modem.

Restrictions Programs are available to in-state students only. Enrollment is open to anyone.

Services Distance learners have access to library services, the campus computer network, e-mail services, academic advising, bookstore at a distance.

Credit-earning options Students may earn credits through examinations.

Typical costs Costs may vary. Financial aid is available to distance learners.

Registration Students may register by fax, e-mail.

Contact Enrollment Services, Capital Community College, 61 Woodland Street, Hartford, CT 06105. *Telephone:* 860-520-7828. *Fax:* 860-520-7906.

DEGREES AND AWARDS

Distance programs offered do not lead to a degree or other formal award.

COURSE SUBJECT AREAS OFFERED OUTSIDE OF DEGREE PROGRAMS

Undergraduate: Computer and information sciences; creative writing; Spanish language and literature

CAPITOL COLLEGE

Laurel, Maryland
www.capitol-college.edu

Capitol College, founded in 1964, is an independent, nonprofit, comprehensive institution. It is accredited by the Middle States Association of Colleges and Schools. It first offered distance learning courses in 1995. In 1999–2000, it offered 25 courses at a distance. In fall 1999, there were 75 students enrolled in distance learning courses.
Course delivery sites Courses are delivered to your home, your workplace, military bases.
Media Courses are delivered via videoconferencing, computer software, CD-ROM, computer conferencing, World Wide Web, e-mail. Students and teachers may interact via videoconferencing, e-mail, World Wide Web. The following equipment may be required: computer, modem, Internet access, e-mail.
Restrictions Programs are available nationwide. Enrollment is open to anyone.
Services Distance learners have access to e-mail services, academic advising, tutoring, career placement assistance, bookstore at a distance.
Credit-earning options Students may transfer credits from another institution or may earn credits through examinations, military training.
Typical costs *Undergraduate:* Tuition of $447 per credit. *Graduate:* Tuition of $390 per credit. Financial aid is available to distance learners.
Registration Students may register by mail, fax, e-mail, World Wide Web, in person.
Contact Anthony G. Miller, Director of Admissions, Capitol College, 11301 Springfield Road, Laurel, MD 20708. *Telephone:* 301-953-3200. *Fax:* 301-953-1442. *E-mail:* admissions@capitol-college.edu.

DEGREES AND AWARDS

BS Management of Information Technology, Software Internet Applications
MS Electronic Commerce Management, Information and Telecommunication Systems Management, Information Sciences and Systems (certain restrictions apply; service area differs from that of the overall institution)

COURSE SUBJECT AREAS OFFERED OUTSIDE OF DEGREE PROGRAMS

Undergraduate: Information sciences and systems
Graduate: Engineering-related technologies; information sciences and systems; management information systems

CARDINAL STRITCH UNIVERSITY

Milwaukee, Wisconsin
College of Education

Cardinal Stritch University, founded in 1937, is an independent, religious, comprehensive institution. It is accredited by the North Central Association of Colleges and Schools. It first offered distance learning courses in 1998. In 1999–2000, it offered 36 courses at a distance. In fall 1999, there were 912 students enrolled in distance learning courses.
Course delivery sites Courses are delivered to your home, your workplace.
Media Courses are delivered via television, videotapes, computer software, computer conferencing, World Wide Web, e-mail. Students and teachers may interact via mail, telephone, fax, e-mail, World Wide Web. The following equipment may be required: television, videocassette player, computer, modem, Internet access, e-mail.
Restrictions Programs are available nationwide. Enrollment is restricted to individuals meeting certain criteria.
Services Distance learners have access to library services, the campus computer network, e-mail services, academic advising, career placement assistance at a distance.
Credit-earning options Students may transfer credits from another institution or may earn credits through examinations, portfolio assessment, military training, business training.
Typical costs Undergraduate tuition is $320 per credit, mandatory fees are $25 per term. Graduate tuition ranges between $117 and $335 per credit, mandatory fees are up to $25 per term. Costs may vary. Financial aid is available to distance learners.
Registration Students may register by mail, fax, telephone, e-mail, in person.
Contact Cynthia A. Marino, Director of Outreach, Cardinal Stritch University. *Telephone:* 414-410-4359. *Fax:* 414-410-4347. *E-mail:* cmarino@acs.stritch.edu.

DEGREES AND AWARDS

BS Education (certain restrictions apply)
MAE Education
MEd Education (certain restrictions apply)
EdD Education (certain restrictions apply)
 Management (certain restrictions apply), Management

COURSE SUBJECT AREAS OFFERED OUTSIDE OF DEGREE PROGRAMS

Undergraduate: Business
Graduate: Business

CARLETON UNIVERSITY

Ottawa, Ontario, Canada
Instructional Television
www.carleton.ca/itv/

Carleton University, founded in 1942, is a province-supported university. It is accredited by the provincial charter. It first offered distance learning courses in 1978. In 1999–2000, it offered 54 courses at a distance. In fall 1999, there were 4,500 students enrolled in distance learning courses.
Course delivery sites Courses are delivered to your home.
Media Courses are delivered via television, videotapes, World Wide Web, e-mail. Students and teachers may meet in person or interact via mail, telephone, fax, e-mail. The following equipment may be required: television, videocassette player, computer, Internet access.

Restrictions Programs are available throughout continental North America. Enrollment is restricted to individuals meeting certain criteria.
Services Distance learners have access to library services, e-mail services, academic advising, tutoring, bookstore at a distance.
Credit-earning options Students may transfer credits from another institution or may earn credits through examinations.
Typical costs Tuition of Can$826 per course. Costs may vary. Financial aid is available to distance learners.
Registration Students may register by telephone.
Contact Beverlae Buckland, Manager, Instructional Student Services, Carleton University, Room 303, Robertson Hall, 1125 Colonel By Drive, Ottawa, ON K1S 5B6 Canada. *Telephone:* 613-520-4055. *Fax:* 613-520-4456. *E-mail:* beverlae_buckland@carleton.ca.

DEGREES AND AWARDS

Distance programs offered do not lead to a degree or other formal award.

COURSE SUBJECT AREAS OFFERED OUTSIDE OF DEGREE PROGRAMS

Undergraduate: Abnormal psychology; accounting; anthropology; architecture; astronomy and astrophysics; biology; Canadian studies; chemistry; civil engineering; cognitive psychology; comparative literature; developmental and child psychology; earth science; economics; English literature; ethics; finance; geography; geology; law and legal studies; philosophy and religion; physics; political science; psychology; public administration and services; religious studies; social psychology; social sciences; social work; sociology

CARLOW COLLEGE

Pittsburgh, Pennsylvania
www.carlow.edu

Carlow College, founded in 1929, is an independent, religious, comprehensive institution. It is accredited by the Middle States Association of Colleges and Schools. In 1999–2000, it offered 5 courses at a distance. In fall 1999, there were 25 students enrolled in distance learning courses.
Course delivery sites Courses are delivered to your home.
Media Courses are delivered via videoconferencing, CD-ROM, World Wide Web, e-mail, print. Students and teachers may meet in person or interact via mail, telephone, fax, e-mail, World Wide Web. The following equipment may be required: computer, modem, Internet access, e-mail.
Restrictions Programs are available to local area students. Enrollment is restricted to individuals meeting certain criteria.
Services Distance learners have access to library services, the campus computer network, e-mail services, academic advising, bookstore at a distance.
Credit-earning options Students may transfer credits from another institution.
Typical costs Tuition of $411 per credit. Financial aid is available to distance learners.
Registration Students may register by mail, fax, World Wide Web, in person.
Contact Mary Lou Bost, Chairperson, Carlow College, 3333 Fifth Avenue, Pittsburgh, PA 15213. *Telephone:* 412-578-6115. *Fax:* 412-578-6114. *E-mail:* mlbost@carlow.edu.

DEGREES AND AWARDS

Undergraduate Certificate(s) Nursing Case Management (some on-campus requirements)
Graduate Certificate(s) Home Health Advanced Practice (some on-campus requirements)
MSN Home Health Advanced Practice (some on-campus requirements), Nursing Case Management/Leadership (some on-campus requirements)

COURSE SUBJECT AREAS OFFERED OUTSIDE OF DEGREE PROGRAMS

Graduate: Nursing

CARNEGIE MELLON UNIVERSITY

Pittsburgh, Pennsylvania
Software Engineering @ Carnegie Mellon, Information Resource Management, MSIA
www.cmu.edu/home/education/education_distance.html

Carnegie Mellon University, founded in 1900, is an independent, non-profit university. It is accredited by the Middle States Association of Colleges and Schools. It first offered distance learning courses in 1996. In fall 1999, there were 210 students enrolled in distance learning courses.
Course delivery sites Courses are delivered to your home, your workplace, Columbia University (New York, NY).
Media Courses are delivered via television, videotapes, videoconferencing, interactive television, computer software, CD-ROM, computer conferencing, World Wide Web, e-mail, print. Students and teachers may meet in person or interact via videoconferencing, audioconferencing, mail, telephone, fax, e-mail, interactive television, World Wide Web. The following equipment may be required: television, videocassette player, computer, modem, Internet access, e-mail.
Restrictions Programs are available nationwide. Enrollment is restricted to individuals meeting certain criteria.
Services Distance learners have access to library services, the campus computer network, e-mail services, academic advising, tutoring, career placement assistance, bookstore at a distance.
Credit-earning options Students may transfer credits from another institution.
Typical costs Graduate tuition for Software Engineering @ Carnegie Mellon is $3888 per course. Tuition for Information Resource Management is $2640 per course. Tuition for the MSIA is $290 per credit. Cost for the noncredit course in Software Engineering @ Carnegie Mellon is $2200 per course. Financial aid is available to distance learners.
Registration Students may register by mail, fax, telephone, e-mail, World Wide Web, in person.
Contact John T. Grasso, Director of Strategic Development/Distance Education, Carnegie Mellon University, 5000 Forbes Avenue, Pittsburgh, PA 15213. *Telephone:* 412-268-1695. *Fax:* 412-268-5569.

DEGREES AND AWARDS

Undergraduate Certificate(s) Information Resource Management (service area differs from that of the overall institution; some on-campus requirements), Software Engineering (some on-campus requirements)
MS Industrial Administration (certain restrictions apply; some on-campus requirements)
MSE Software Engineering (some on-campus requirements)

COURSE SUBJECT AREAS OFFERED OUTSIDE OF DEGREE PROGRAMS

Graduate: Business; computer and information sciences; finance
See full description on page 480.

CARTERET COMMUNITY COLLEGE

Morehead City, North Carolina
gofish.carteret.cc.nc.us/

Carteret Community College, founded in 1963, is a state-supported, two-year college. It is accredited by the Southern Association of Colleges and Schools.

Contact Carteret Community College, 3505 Arendell Street, Morehead City, NC 28557-2989. *Telephone:* 252-247-6000. *Fax:* 252-247-2514.

See full description on page 676.

CATAWBA VALLEY COMMUNITY COLLEGE

Hickory, North Carolina

Telecommunications Department
www.cvcc.cc.nc.us/specserv/lrc/DISTLEAR.HTM

Catawba Valley Community College, founded in 1960, is a state and locally supported, two-year college. It is accredited by the Southern Association of Colleges and Schools. It first offered distance learning courses in 1983. In 1999–2000, it offered 26 courses at a distance. In fall 1999, there were 300 students enrolled in distance learning courses.

Course delivery sites Courses are delivered to your home, your workplace, high schools.

Media Courses are delivered via television, videotapes, interactive television, computer software, World Wide Web. Students and teachers may meet in person or interact via mail, telephone, fax, e-mail, interactive television. The following equipment may be required: videocassette player, computer, Internet access, e-mail.

Restrictions Programs are available worldwide. Enrollment is open to anyone.

Services Distance learners have access to library services, the campus computer network, academic advising, tutoring, career placement assistance, bookstore at a distance.

Credit-earning options Students may transfer credits from another institution or may earn credits through examinations.

Typical costs Tuition of $80.25 per course for in-state residents. Tuition of $509.25 per course for out-of-state residents. Costs may vary. Financial aid is available to distance learners.

Registration Students may register by in person.

Contact Dr. Linda Lutz, Dean, Education Support Services, Catawba Valley Community College, Distance Education, Hickory, NC 28602. *Telephone:* 828-327-7000 Ext. 4130. *Fax:* 828-324-5130. *E-mail:* llutz@linus.cvcc.cc.nc.us.

DEGREES AND AWARDS

Undergraduate Certificate(s) Business Administration (service area differs from that of the overall institution; some on-campus requirements), Health Care Management Technology (service area differs from that of the overall institution; some on-campus requirements)

COURSE SUBJECT AREAS OFFERED OUTSIDE OF DEGREE PROGRAMS

Undergraduate: Advertising; business; business administration and management; creative writing; developmental and child psychology; economics; English composition; English language and literature; health professions and related sciences; history; mathematics; philosophy and religion; social psychology; sociology; teacher education

See full description on page 676.

CAYUGA COUNTY COMMUNITY COLLEGE

Auburn, New York
www.cayuga-cc.edu/

Cayuga County Community College, founded in 1953, is a state and locally supported, two-year college. It is accredited by the Middle States Association of Colleges and Schools. In 1999–2000, it offered 10 courses at a distance. In fall 1999, there were 50 students enrolled in distance learning courses.

Course delivery sites Courses are delivered to your home, your workplace, military bases, high schools.

Media Courses are delivered via videoconferencing, interactive television, World Wide Web. Students and teachers may meet in person or interact via videoconferencing, mail, telephone, fax, e-mail, interactive television, World Wide Web. The following equipment may be required: computer, modem, Internet access, e-mail.

Restrictions Programs are available nationwide. Enrollment is open to anyone.

Services Distance learners have access to the campus computer network, academic advising, career placement assistance at a distance.

Credit-earning options Students may earn credits through examinations, portfolio assessment.

Typical costs Tuition of $90 per credit. Financial aid is available to distance learners.

Registration Students may register by mail, fax, telephone, in person.

Contact Heidi Nightengale, Coordinator, Evening and Special Programs, Cayuga County Community College, 197 Franklin Street, Auburn, NY 13021. *Telephone:* 315-255-1743 Ext. 457. *Fax:* 315-255-2117. *E-mail:* nightengale@cayuga-cc.edu.

DEGREES AND AWARDS

AA Business Administration, Liberal Arts and Sciences
AS Business Administration, Liberal Arts and Sciences
BA Community and Human Services
BS Business Management and Economics, Community and Human Services

COURSE SUBJECT AREAS OFFERED OUTSIDE OF DEGREE PROGRAMS

Undergraduate: Business; English language and literature; psychology

CEDARVILLE UNIVERSITY

Cedarville, Ohio

Cedarville University, founded in 1887, is an independent, religious, comprehensive institution. It is accredited by the North Central Association of Colleges and Schools. In 1999–2000, it offered 7 courses at a distance. In fall 1999, there were 100 students enrolled in distance learning courses.

Course delivery sites Courses are delivered to your home, your workplace.

Media Courses are delivered via videoconferencing, World Wide Web, e-mail. Students and teachers may interact via videoconferencing, fax, e-mail, World Wide Web. The following equipment may be required: television, videocassette player, computer, Internet access, e-mail.

Restrictions Programs are available to local area students. Enrollment is restricted to individuals meeting certain criteria.

Services Distance learners have access to e-mail services, career placement assistance at a distance.

Credit-earning options Students may transfer credits from another institution or may earn credits through examinations.

Cedarville University

Typical costs Tuition of $220 per quarter hour. Financial aid is available to distance learners.

Registration Students may register by mail, in person.

Contact Chuck Allport, Assistant to the Academic Vice President, Cedarville University, PO Box 601, Cedarville, OH 45314. *Telephone:* 937-766-7681. *Fax:* 937-766-3217. *E-mail:* allportc@cedarville.edu.

> eCollege.com   *www.ecollege.com/scholarships*

DEGREES AND AWARDS

Distance programs offered do not lead to a degree or other formal award.

COURSE SUBJECT AREAS OFFERED OUTSIDE OF DEGREE PROGRAMS

Undergraduate: Bible studies; biology; comparative literature; English composition; teacher education; technical writing

CENTRAL ALABAMA COMMUNITY COLLEGE

Alexander City, Alabama

Central Alabama Community College, founded in 1965, is a state-supported, two-year college. It is accredited by the Southern Association of Colleges and Schools.

Contact Central Alabama Community College, PO Box 699, Alexander City, AL 35011-0699. *Telephone:* 256-234-6346. *Fax:* 256-234-0384.

See full description on page 676.

CENTRAL ARIZONA COLLEGE

Coolidge, Arizona
Instructional Technology
www.cac.cc.az.us

Central Arizona College, founded in 1961, is a county-supported, two-year college. It is accredited by the North Central Association of Colleges and Schools. It first offered distance learning courses in 1994. In 1999–2000, it offered 70 courses at a distance. In fall 1999, there were 1,800 students enrolled in distance learning courses.

Course delivery sites Courses are delivered to your home, your workplace, military bases, high schools, 3 off-campus centers in Apache Junction, Casa Grande, Winkelman.

Media Courses are delivered via videotapes, videoconferencing, interactive television, audiotapes, computer software, CD-ROM, World Wide Web, e-mail, print. Students and teachers may meet in person or interact via videoconferencing, audioconferencing, mail, telephone, fax, e-mail, interactive television, World Wide Web. The following equipment may be required: computer, modem, Internet access, e-mail.

Restrictions Programs are available worldwide. Enrollment is open to anyone.

Services Distance learners have access to library services, the campus computer network, e-mail services, academic advising, tutoring, career placement assistance, bookstore at a distance.

Credit-earning options Students may transfer credits from another institution or may earn credits through examinations, portfolio assessment.

Typical costs Tuition of $32 per credit plus mandatory fees of $7 per semester for local area residents. Tuition of $32 per credit plus mandatory fees of $7 per semester for in-state residents. Tuition of $62 per credit plus

mandatory fees of $7 per semester for out-of-state residents. Online courses cost $40 per credit hour. Costs may vary. Financial aid is available to distance learners.

Registration Students may register by mail, telephone, in person.

Contact Registrar's Office, Central Arizona College, 8470 North Overfield Road, Coolidge, AZ 85228. *Telephone:* 800-237-9814. *Fax:* 520-426-4234. *E-mail:* sandra_todd@python.cac.cc.az.us.

DEGREES AND AWARDS

Undergraduate Certificate(s) Child Nutrition (service area differs from that of the overall institution), Community Nutrition Worker (service area differs from that of the overall institution), Dietary Management (service area differs from that of the overall institution), Early Childhood Education (service area differs from that of the overall institution)

AAS Culinary Arts (service area differs from that of the overall institution), Dietetic Technician (service area differs from that of the overall institution), Early Childhood Education (service area differs from that of the overall institution)

COURSE SUBJECT AREAS OFFERED OUTSIDE OF DEGREE PROGRAMS

Undergraduate: Algebra; American (U.S.) history; American literature; anatomy; anthropology; area, ethnic, and cultural studies; art history and criticism; biological and life sciences; business; business law; chemistry; child care and development; communications; education; English composition; foods and nutrition studies; health professions and related sciences; mathematics; music; protective services; psychology; sociology; Spanish language and literature; visual and performing arts

CENTRAL BAPTIST THEOLOGICAL SEMINARY

Kansas City, Kansas
Long Distance Learning
www.cbts.edu

Central Baptist Theological Seminary, founded in 1901, is an independent, religious, graduate institution. It is accredited by the Association of Theological Schools in the United States and Canada, North Central Association of Colleges and Schools. It first offered distance learning courses in 1989. In 1999–2000, it offered 2 courses at a distance. In fall 1999, there were 16 students enrolled in distance learning courses.

Course delivery sites Courses are delivered to your home.

Media Courses are delivered via videotapes. Students and teachers may interact via videoconferencing, audioconferencing, telephone. The following equipment may be required: television, videocassette player.

Restrictions Programs are available worldwide. Enrollment is open to anyone.

Credit-earning options Students may transfer credits from another institution.

Typical costs Tuition of $180 per credit hour plus mandatory fees of $45 per semester.

Registration Students may register by in person.

Contact Bill Hill, Director of Student Life and Enrollment Services, Central Baptist Theological Seminary. *Telephone:* 913-371-5313. *Fax:* 913-371-8110. *E-mail:* central@cbts.edu.

DEGREES AND AWARDS

Undergraduate Certificate(s) Theological Studies (some on-campus requirements)

MARS Theological Studies (some on-campus requirements)

MDiv Theological Studies (some on-campus requirements)

COURSE SUBJECT AREAS OFFERED OUTSIDE OF DEGREE PROGRAMS

Graduate: Theological studies
Noncredit: Theological studies

CENTRAL COMMUNITY COLLEGE–GRAND ISLAND CAMPUS

Grand Island, Nebraska
www.cccneb.edu

Central Community College–Grand Island Campus, founded in 1976, is a state and locally supported, two-year college. It is accredited by the North Central Association of Colleges and Schools. It first offered distance learning courses in 1992. In 1999–2000, it offered 48 courses at a distance. In fall 1999, there were 746 students enrolled in distance learning courses.

Course delivery sites Courses are delivered to your home, your workplace.

Media Courses are delivered via television, videotapes, videoconferencing, interactive television, audiotapes, computer software, World Wide Web, e-mail, print. Students and teachers may interact via videoconferencing, audioconferencing, mail, telephone, fax, e-mail, interactive television.

Restrictions Programs are available worldwide. Enrollment is open to anyone.

Services Distance learners have access to library services, academic advising, career placement assistance at a distance.

Credit-earning options Students may transfer credits from another institution or may earn credits through portfolio assessment, military training, business training.

Typical costs Tuition of $46 per credit hour plus mandatory fees of $4 per credit hour for in-state residents. Tuition of $53 per credit hour plus mandatory fees of $4 per credit hour for out-of-state residents. Financial aid is available to distance learners.

Registration Students may register by in person.

Contact Vicki Harvey, Associate Dean for Community Education, Central Community College–Grand Island Campus, PO Box 4903, Grand Island, NE 68802-4903. *Telephone:* 308-389-6440. *Fax:* 308-389-6398. *E-mail:* hargced@cccadm.cccneb.edu.

DEGREES AND AWARDS

Undergraduate Certificate(s) Accounting, Basic Electronics (some on-campus requirements), Business Administration, Criminal Justice, Health Information Management, Industrial Technology (some on-campus requirements), Information Systems (service area differs from that of the overall institution), Paralegal Studies
AA General Studies
AAS Accounting, Business Administration, Information Services (some on-campus requirements)

COURSE SUBJECT AREAS OFFERED OUTSIDE OF DEGREE PROGRAMS

Undergraduate: Accounting; administrative and secretarial services; advertising; agriculture; area, ethnic, and cultural studies; astronomy and astrophysics; business; business administration and management; communications; computer and information sciences; creative writing; developmental and child psychology; economics; English composition; English language and literature; geology; history; industrial engineering; law and legal studies; liberal arts, general studies, and humanities; mathematics; nursing; social psychology; sociology; Spanish language and literature

CENTRAL FLORIDA COMMUNITY COLLEGE

Ocala, Florida
Distance Learning
www.cfcc.cc.fl.us

Central Florida Community College, founded in 1957, is a state and locally supported, two-year college. It is accredited by the Southern Association of Colleges and Schools. It first offered distance learning courses in 1979.

Contact Central Florida Community College, PO Box 1388, Ocala, FL 34478-1388. *Telephone:* 352-854-2322. *Fax:* 352-237-3747.

See full description on page 676.

CENTRALIA COLLEGE

Centralia, Washington
Distance Learning
www.centralia.ctc.edu/~vfreund/DistLearning/distlearning.html

Centralia College, founded in 1925, is a state-supported, two-year college. It is accredited by the Northwest Association of Schools and Colleges. In 1999–2000, it offered 60 courses at a distance. In fall 1999, there were 370 students enrolled in distance learning courses.

Course delivery sites Courses are delivered to your home, high schools, off-campus center(s) in Morton, Shelton, Tenino.

Media Courses are delivered via videotapes, videoconferencing, audiotapes, World Wide Web, e-mail, print. Students and teachers may meet in person or interact via mail, telephone, fax, e-mail. The following equipment may be required: television, videocassette player, computer, modem, Internet access, e-mail.

Restrictions Programs are available worldwide. Enrollment is open to anyone.

Services Distance learners have access to library services, the campus computer network, e-mail services, academic advising, tutoring, career placement assistance, bookstore at a distance.

Credit-earning options Students may transfer credits from another institution.

Typical costs Tuition of $52.80 per credit for in-state residents. Tuition of $64.80 per credit for out-of-state residents. Tuition for international students is $207.80 per credit. Mandatory fees for all students include $11.85 program fee per class, $5 activity fee per quarter, and $4 student use fee per credit up to 10 credits. *Noncredit courses:* $50 per course. Costs may vary. Financial aid is available to distance learners.

Registration Students may register by mail, in person.

Contact Vic Freund, Director of Distance Learning, Centralia College, 600 West Locust, Centralia, WA 98531. *Telephone:* 360-736-9391. *Fax:* 360-330-7502. *E-mail:* vfreund@centralia.ctc.edu.

DEGREES AND AWARDS

Distance programs offered do not lead to a degree or other formal award.

COURSE SUBJECT AREAS OFFERED OUTSIDE OF DEGREE PROGRAMS

Undergraduate: Accounting; administrative and secretarial services; algebra; American literature; American studies; anthropology; astronomy and astrophysics; biology; business administration and management; business law; calculus; chemistry; earth science; English composition; European history; foods and nutrition studies; geology; health and physical education/ fitness; library and information studies; mathematics; meteorology; ocean-

ography; philosophy and religion; political science; psychology; real estate; sociology; statistics; teacher education
Noncredit: Computer and information sciences

CENTRAL METHODIST COLLEGE

Fayette, Missouri
www.cmc.edu

Central Methodist College, founded in 1854, is an independent, religious, comprehensive institution. It is accredited by the North Central Association of Colleges and Schools. It first offered distance learning courses in 1993. In 1999–2000, it offered 16 courses at a distance. In fall 1999, there were 100 students enrolled in distance learning courses.
Course delivery sites Courses are delivered to high schools, East Central College (Union), Mineral Area College (Park Hills).
Media Courses are delivered via videoconferencing, interactive television, World Wide Web. Students and teachers may interact via videoconferencing, audioconferencing, mail, telephone, fax, e-mail, interactive television, World Wide Web.
Restrictions Programs are available to in-state students only. Enrollment is open to anyone.
Services Distance learners have access to library services, academic advising, tutoring, career placement assistance at a distance.
Credit-earning options Students may transfer credits from another institution or may earn credits through examinations.
Typical costs *Undergraduate:* Tuition of $125 per credit hour. *Graduate:* Tuition of $185 per credit hour. Costs may vary. Financial aid is available to distance learners.
Registration Students may register by mail, fax, e-mail, in person.
Contact Ann Oberhaus, Director of Continuing Studies, Central Methodist College, 411 Central Methodist Square, Fayette, MO 65248. *Telephone:* 660-248-6290. *Fax:* 660-248-2622. *E-mail:* aoberhaus@cmc.edu.

DEGREES AND AWARDS

Distance programs offered do not lead to a degree or other formal award.

COURSE SUBJECT AREAS OFFERED OUTSIDE OF DEGREE PROGRAMS

Undergraduate: Algebra; American (U.S.) history; anatomy; biology; calculus; chemistry; education administration; educational psychology; nursing; physiology; statistics; teacher education
Graduate: Education administration; educational psychology; educational research; teacher education

CENTRAL MICHIGAN UNIVERSITY

Mount Pleasant, Michigan
Distance/Distributed Learning
www.ddl.cmich.edu

Central Michigan University, founded in 1892, is a state-supported university. It is accredited by the North Central Association of Colleges and Schools. It first offered distance learning courses in 1970. In 1999–2000, it offered 80 courses at a distance. In fall 1999, there were 1,490 students enrolled in distance learning courses.
Course delivery sites Courses are delivered to your home, your workplace, military bases.

Media Courses are delivered via television, videotapes, audiotapes, computer software, computer conferencing, World Wide Web, e-mail, print. Students and teachers may meet in person or interact via mail, telephone, fax, e-mail, World Wide Web.
Restrictions Programs are available worldwide. Enrollment is open to anyone.
Services Distance learners have access to library services, e-mail services, academic advising, bookstore at a distance.
Credit-earning options Students may transfer credits from another institution or may earn credits through examinations, portfolio assessment, military training, business training.
Typical costs *Undergraduate:* Tuition of $165 per credit hour. *Graduate:* Tuition of $220 per credit hour. Application fee is $50. Costs may vary. Financial aid is available to distance learners.
Registration Students may register by telephone.
Contact Connie Detwiler, Distance/Distributed Learning, Central Michigan University, College of Extended Learning, Mt. Pleasant, MI 48859. *Telephone:* 800-950-1144 Ext. 3505. *Fax:* 517-774-1822. *E-mail:* celinfo@mail.cel.cmich.edu.

DEGREES AND AWARDS

BAA Health Administration
BS Business Administration, Community Development
MSA General Administration
AuD Audiology

COURSE SUBJECT AREAS OFFERED OUTSIDE OF DEGREE PROGRAMS

Undergraduate: Accounting; astronomy and astrophysics; business; business administration and management; communications; community health services; economics; English language and literature; environmental health; finance; foods and nutrition studies; genetics; geography; health professions and related sciences; health services administration; home economics and family studies; human resources management; individual and family development studies; industrial psychology; information sciences and systems; international business; journalism; marketing; mathematics; mental health services; music; organizational behavior studies; philosophy and religion; physics; political science; psychology; public administration and services; public health; public relations; religious studies; social psychology; sociology; Spanish language and literature; statistics; substance abuse counseling; women's studies
Graduate: Administrative and secretarial services; business administration and management; genetics; health professions and related sciences; marketing; organizational behavior studies; substance abuse counseling
See full description on page 482.

CENTRAL MISSOURI STATE UNIVERSITY

Warrensburg, Missouri
Extended Campus–Distance Learning
www.cmsu.edu/extcamp

Central Missouri State University, founded in 1871, is a state-supported, comprehensive institution. It is accredited by the North Central Association of Colleges and Schools. It first offered distance learning courses in 1993. In 1999–2000, it offered 50 courses at a distance. In fall 1999, there were 450 students enrolled in distance learning courses.
Course delivery sites Courses are delivered to your home, your workplace, high schools, Missouri Southern State College (Joplin), Missouri Western State College (St. Joseph), 21 off-campus centers in Appleton City, Blue Springs, Calhoun, Camdenton, Centerview, Chilhowee, Clinton, Columbia, Concordia, Excelsior Springs, Holden, Kingsville, Kirksville,

Central Piedmont Community College

Mexico, Nevada, Park Hill, Pleasant Hill, Poplar Bluff, Portageville, Reeds Spring, Rolla, Warrensburg, Windsor.

Media Courses are delivered via television, videotapes, videoconferencing, interactive television, World Wide Web, e-mail. Students and teachers may meet in person or interact via videoconferencing, mail, telephone, fax, e-mail, interactive television, World Wide Web. The following equipment may be required: computer, modem, Internet access, e-mail.

Restrictions Programs are available to in-state students only. Enrollment is open to anyone.

Services Distance learners have access to library services, the campus computer network, e-mail services, academic advising, career placement assistance, bookstore at a distance.

Credit-earning options Students may transfer credits from another institution or may earn credits through examinations.

Typical costs *Undergraduate:* Tuition of $129 per credit hour. *Graduate:* Tuition of $199 per credit hour. Costs may vary. Financial aid is available to distance learners.

Registration Students may register by mail, fax, telephone, World Wide Web, in person.

Contact Debbie Bassore, Assistant Director for Distance Learning, Central Missouri State University, 403 Humphreys, Warrensburg, MO 64093. *Telephone:* 660-543-8480. *Fax:* 660-543-8333. *E-mail:* bassore@cmsu1.cmsu.edu.

DEGREES AND AWARDS

MS Criminal Justice (service area differs from that of the overall institution), Occupational Safety Management (service area differs from that of the overall institution)

PhD Technology Management (certain restrictions apply; service area differs from that of the overall institution; some on-campus requirements)

COURSE SUBJECT AREAS OFFERED OUTSIDE OF DEGREE PROGRAMS

Undergraduate: Child care and development; communications; computer and information sciences; criminal justice; curriculum and instruction; education administration; electrical engineering; engineering/industrial management; English as a second language (ESL); foods and nutrition studies; health and physical education/fitness; individual and family development studies; instructional media; liberal arts, general studies, and humanities; library and information studies; mass media; mathematics; nursing; special education; teacher education; telecommunications

Graduate: Corrections; criminal justice; curriculum and instruction; education administration; engineering/industrial management; English as a second language (ESL); health and physical education/fitness; instructional media; mass media; special education; statistics; teacher education; telecommunications

Noncredit: Education administration; instructional media; special education; teacher education; telecommunications

See full description on page 484.

CENTRAL OREGON COMMUNITY COLLEGE

Bend, Oregon

Open Campus Distance Learning Program
www.cocc.edu/opencampus

Central Oregon Community College, founded in 1949, is a district-supported, two-year college. It is accredited by the Northwest Association of Schools and Colleges. In 1999–2000, it offered 41 courses at a distance.

Course delivery sites Courses are delivered to your home, 7 off-campus centers in La Pine, Madras, North Lake, Prineville, Redmond, Sisters, Warm Springs.

Media Courses are delivered via television, interactive television, computer conferencing, World Wide Web, e-mail. Students and teachers may meet in person or interact via mail, telephone, fax, e-mail, interactive television, World Wide Web. The following equipment may be required: computer, Internet access.

Restrictions Programs are available to in-state students only. Enrollment is open to anyone.

Services Distance learners have access to library services, the campus computer network, e-mail services, tutoring, bookstore at a distance.

Credit-earning options Students may transfer credits from another institution or may earn credits through examinations, military training.

Typical costs Tuition of $39 per quarter plus mandatory fees of $1.50 per quarter for local area residents. Tuition of $50 per credit hour plus mandatory fees of $1.50 per credit for in-state residents. Tuition of $140 per credit hour plus mandatory fees of $1.50 per hour for out-of-state residents. For detailed tuition information please check our website: www.cocc.edu/admissions/admissions/tuition.htm. *Noncredit courses:* $50 per course. Costs may vary. Financial aid is available to distance learners.

Registration Students may register by telephone, World Wide Web, in person.

Contact Vickery Viles, Distance Learning Coordinator, Central Oregon Community College, 2600 Northwest College Way, Bend, OR 97701. *Telephone:* 541-383-7258. *Fax:* 541-383-7503. *E-mail:* vviles@cocc.edu.

DEGREES AND AWARDS

AA Liberal Arts (some on-campus requirements)

COURSE SUBJECT AREAS OFFERED OUTSIDE OF DEGREE PROGRAMS

Undergraduate: Algebra; American (U.S.) history; business; business administration and management; chemistry; communications; criminal justice; early childhood education; education; English composition; food service; geology; health and physical education/fitness; information sciences and systems; library and information studies; marketing

CENTRAL PIEDMONT COMMUNITY COLLEGE

Charlotte, North Carolina

College Without Walls
cww.cpcc.cc.nc.us

Central Piedmont Community College, founded in 1963, is a state and locally supported, two-year college. It is accredited by the Southern Association of Colleges and Schools. It first offered distance learning courses in 1977. In 1999–2000, it offered 41 courses at a distance. In fall 1999, there were 967 students enrolled in distance learning courses.

Course delivery sites Courses are delivered to your home, your workplace, high schools, North Carolina Community College System (Raleigh), 3 off-campus centers in Charlotte, Huntersville, Matthews.

Media Courses are delivered via television, videotapes, videoconferencing, interactive television, computer software, World Wide Web, e-mail. Students and teachers may meet in person or interact via mail, telephone, fax, e-mail, interactive television, World Wide Web. The following equipment may be required: television, videocassette player, computer, Internet access, e-mail.

Restrictions Programs are available nationwide. Enrollment is open to anyone.

Services Distance learners have access to library services, e-mail services, bookstore at a distance.

Credit-earning options Students may transfer credits from another institution.

Typical costs Tuition of $20 per credit hour for in-state residents. Tuition of $163 per credit hour for out-of-state residents. Costs may vary. Financial aid is available to distance learners.

Peterson's Guide to Distance Learning Programs

Registration Students may register by mail, telephone, in person.
Contact Virginia Williams, Retention Specialist, Central Piedmont Community College, College Without Walls/Distance Learning Support Center, PO Box 35009, Charlotte, NC 28235. *Telephone:* 704-330-6883. *Fax:* 704-330-6597. *E-mail:* virginia_williams@cpcc.cc.nc.us.

DEGREES AND AWARDS

AA College Transfer Degree (some on-campus requirements)

COURSE SUBJECT AREAS OFFERED OUTSIDE OF DEGREE PROGRAMS

Undergraduate: Abnormal psychology; accounting; administrative and secretarial services; algebra; American literature; anthropology; astronomy and astrophysics; biology; business; business administration and management; business law; calculus; communications; computer and information sciences; developmental and child psychology; economics; English composition; English language and literature; geography; health and physical education/fitness; health professions and related sciences; history; liberal arts, general studies, and humanities; philosophy and religion; political science; psychology; social sciences; sociology; statistics

See full description on page 676.

CENTRAL TEXAS COLLEGE

Killeen, Texas

Distance Education and Educational Technology Division
www.ctcd.cc.tx.us/disted.htm

Central Texas College, founded in 1967, is a state and locally supported, two-year college. It is accredited by the Southern Association of Colleges and Schools. It first offered distance learning courses in 1972. In 1999–2000, it offered 59 courses at a distance. In fall 1999, there were 600 students enrolled in distance learning courses.
Course delivery sites Courses are delivered to your home, your workplace, military bases, high schools, Virtual Colleges of Texas Partners, 3 off-campus centers in Continental Campus, Europe Campus, Pacific Far East Campus.
Media Courses are delivered via television, videotapes, videoconferencing, audiotapes, computer software, CD-ROM, World Wide Web, e-mail. Students and teachers may meet in person or interact via videoconferencing, mail, telephone, fax, e-mail, World Wide Web. The following equipment may be required: television, videocassette player, computer, Internet access, e-mail.
Restrictions Programs are available worldwide. Enrollment is open to anyone.
Services Distance learners have access to library services, academic advising, career placement assistance, bookstore at a distance.
Credit-earning options Students may transfer credits from another institution or may earn credits through examinations, portfolio assessment, military training, business training.
Typical costs Tuition of $60 per course plus mandatory fees of $8 per semester hour for local area residents. Tuition of $60 per course plus mandatory fees of $13 per semester hour for in-state residents. Tuition of $250 per course plus mandatory fees of $8 per semester hour for out-of-state residents. *Noncredit courses:* $30 per course. Costs may vary. Financial aid is available to distance learners.
Registration Students may register by mail, telephone, e-mail, World Wide Web, in person.
Contact Bill Alexander, Dean, Guidance and Counseling, Central Texas College, PO Box 1800, Killeen, TX 76540. *Telephone:* 254-526-1226. *Fax:* 254-526-1481. *E-mail:* distlrnl@ctcd.cc.tx.us.

DEGREES AND AWARDS

AGS General Studies

COURSE SUBJECT AREAS OFFERED OUTSIDE OF DEGREE PROGRAMS

Undergraduate: Abnormal psychology; accounting; administrative and secretarial services; algebra; American (U.S.) history; anthropology; art history and criticism; astronomy and astrophysics; biology; business administration and management; business law; child care and development; communications; computer and information sciences; criminal justice; database management; economics; English composition; fine arts; hospitality services management; human resources management; individual and family development studies; information sciences and systems; mental health services; political science; psychology; real estate; sociology; substance abuse counseling

See full descriptions on pages 486 and 676.

CENTRAL VIRGINIA COMMUNITY COLLEGE

Lynchburg, Virginia

Learning Resources

Central Virginia Community College, founded in 1966, is a state-supported, two-year college. It is accredited by the Southern Association of Colleges and Schools. It first offered distance learning courses in 1984. In 1999–2000, it offered 25 courses at a distance. In fall 1999, there were 306 students enrolled in distance learning courses.
Course delivery sites Courses are delivered to your home.
Media Courses are delivered via videotapes, videoconferencing, audiotapes, World Wide Web, e-mail, print. Students and teachers may meet in person or interact via videoconferencing, mail, telephone, fax, e-mail, World Wide Web. The following equipment may be required: computer, modem, Internet access, e-mail.
Restrictions Programs are available to in-state students only. Enrollment is open to anyone.
Services Distance learners have access to library services, the campus computer network, academic advising at a distance.
Credit-earning options Students may transfer credits from another institution or may earn credits through examinations.
Typical costs Tuition of $46.65 per credit hour for in-state residents. Tuition of $156 per credit hour for out-of-state residents. Financial aid is available to distance learners.
Registration Students may register by telephone, in person.
Contact Susan S. Beasley, Audiovisual Supervisor, Central Virginia Community College, 3506 Wards Road, Lynchburg, VA 24502. *Telephone:* 804-832-7742. *Fax:* 804-386-4531. *E-mail:* beasleys@cv.cc.va.us.

DEGREES AND AWARDS

AAS Medical Laboratory Technology (certain restrictions apply; some on-campus requirements)

COURSE SUBJECT AREAS OFFERED OUTSIDE OF DEGREE PROGRAMS

Undergraduate: Biology; business; business administration and management; developmental and child psychology; economics; health and physical education/fitness; marketing; mathematics; sociology

See full description on page 676.

CENTRAL WASHINGTON UNIVERSITY

Ellensburg, Washington

Center for Learning Technologies
www.cwu.edu

Central Washington University, founded in 1891, is a state-supported, comprehensive institution. It is accredited by the Northwest Association of Schools and Colleges. It first offered distance learning courses in 1995.

Course delivery sites Courses are delivered to your home, your workplace, Big Bend Community College (Moses Lake), Pierce College (Lakewood), Wenatchee Valley College (Wenatchee), Yakima Valley Community College (Yakima), 2 off-campus centers in Lynnwood, Seattle.

Media Courses are delivered via television, videoconferencing, interactive television, computer software, World Wide Web, e-mail, print. Students and teachers may interact via videoconferencing, mail, telephone, fax, e-mail, interactive television, World Wide Web. The following equipment may be required: videocassette player, computer, modem, Internet access, e-mail.

Restrictions Programs are available to in-state students only. Enrollment is open to anyone.

Services Distance learners have access to library services, the campus computer network, e-mail services, academic advising, tutoring, career placement assistance at a distance.

Credit-earning options Students may transfer credits from another institution or may earn credits through examinations, military training.

Typical costs *Undergraduate:* Tuition of $874 per quarter plus mandatory fees of $60 per quarter for in-state residents. Tuition of $3105 per quarter plus mandatory fees of $60 per quarter for out-of-state residents. *Graduate:* Tuition of $1347 per quarter plus mandatory fees of $60 per quarter for in-state residents. Tuition of $4097 per quarter plus mandatory fees of $60 per quarter for out-of-state residents. Costs may vary. Financial aid is available to distance learners.

Registration Students may register by mail, telephone, World Wide Web, in person.

Contact Academic Advising Office, Central Washington University, 400 East Eighth Street, Mitchell Hall, First Floor, Ellensburg, WA 98926. *Telephone:* 509-963-3001. *Fax:* 509-963-1590.

DEGREES AND AWARDS

Undergraduate Certificate(s) Teacher Education (some on-campus requirements)

BA Early Childhood Education (some on-campus requirements), Elementary Education (some on-campus requirements), Law and Justice (some on-campus requirements), Special Education (some on-campus requirements), Teacher Education (some on-campus requirements)

BS Accounting (some on-campus requirements), Business Administration (some on-campus requirements), Business Education (some on-campus requirements), Chemical Dependency (some on-campus requirements), Community Health (some on-campus requirements), Electronic Engineering Technician (some on-campus requirements)

MS Organizational Development (some on-campus requirements)

COURSE SUBJECT AREAS OFFERED OUTSIDE OF DEGREE PROGRAMS

Undergraduate: Anthropology; business; business administration and management; chemistry, organic; creative writing; developmental and child psychology; economics; education; engineering; engineering-related technologies; English composition; English language and literature; finance; health professions and related sciences; human resources management; Latin language and literature; marketing; special education; teacher education

CENTURY COMMUNITY AND TECHNICAL COLLEGE

White Bear Lake, Minnesota

Continuing Education and Customized Training
www.century.cc.mn.us/cect/

Century Community and Technical College, founded in 1970, is a state-supported, two-year college. It is accredited by the North Central Association of Colleges and Schools. It first offered distance learning courses in 1982. In 1999–2000, it offered 20 courses at a distance. In fall 1999, there were 300 students enrolled in distance learning courses.

Course delivery sites Courses are delivered to your home, your workplace.

Media Courses are delivered via computer software, CD-ROM, World Wide Web, print. Students and teachers may interact via mail, telephone, fax, e-mail, World Wide Web. The following equipment may be required: computer, modem, Internet access, e-mail.

Restrictions Programs are available worldwide. Enrollment is open to anyone.

Services Distance learners have access to academic advising, tutoring at a distance.

Typical costs Tuition ranges from $50 to $245 per unit. Costs may vary.

Registration Students may register by mail, fax, telephone, in person.

Contact Lynette Podritz, Distance Learning Department-Customized Training, Century Community and Technical College, 3300 Century Avenue North, White Bear Lake, MN 55110. *Telephone:* 651-779-3904. *Fax:* 651-779-5802. *E-mail:* l.podritz@cctc.cc.mn.us.

DEGREES AND AWARDS

Distance programs offered do not lead to a degree or other formal award.

COURSE SUBJECT AREAS OFFERED OUTSIDE OF DEGREE PROGRAMS

Undergraduate: Business; engineering-related technologies; health professions and related sciences; horticulture
Noncredit: Accounting; anatomy; electronics

CERRITOS COLLEGE

Norwalk, California

Distance Education Program
www.cerritos.edu/de

Cerritos College, founded in 1956, is a state and locally supported, two-year college. It is accredited by the Western Association of Schools and Colleges, Inc. It first offered distance learning courses in 1985. In 1999–2000, it offered 35 courses at a distance. In fall 1999, there were 2,000 students enrolled in distance learning courses.

Course delivery sites Courses are delivered to your home, your workplace, high schools.

Media Courses are delivered via television, videotapes, videoconferencing, computer software, computer conferencing, World Wide Web, e-mail, print. Students and teachers may meet in person or interact via videoconferencing, mail, telephone, fax, e-mail, World Wide Web. The following equipment may be required: television, videocassette player, computer, modem, Internet access, e-mail.

Restrictions Programs are available worldwide. Enrollment is open to anyone.

Services Distance learners have access to library services, the campus computer network, e-mail services, academic advising, bookstore at a distance.

Credit-earning options Students may transfer credits from another institution or may earn credits through examinations.

Typical costs Tuition of $11 per unit plus mandatory fees of $20 per semester for local area residents. Tuition of $11 per unit for in-state residents. Tuition of $125 per unit for out-of-state residents. Financial aid is available to distance learners.

Registration Students may register by mail, fax, telephone, in person.

Contact Leslie Nanasy, Program Assistant, Distance Education, Cerritos College, 11110 Alondra Boulevard, Norwalk, CA 90650. *Telephone:* 562-860-2451 Ext. 2837. *Fax:* 562-467-5091. *E-mail:* lnanasy@cerritos.edu.

DEGREES AND AWARDS

Distance programs offered do not lead to a degree or other formal award.

COURSE SUBJECT AREAS OFFERED OUTSIDE OF DEGREE PROGRAMS

Undergraduate: American (U.S.) history; American literature; anthropology; business administration and management; business communications; business law; computer programming; curriculum and instruction; English composition; English literature; health and physical education/fitness; information sciences and systems; instructional media; journalism; management information systems; philosophy and religion; political science; radio and television broadcasting; sociology; teacher education; telecommunications; visual and performing arts

CERRO COSO COMMUNITY COLLEGE

Ridgecrest, California

Cerro Coso Online

www.cc.cc.ca.us/

Cerro Coso Community College, founded in 1973, is a state-supported, two-year college. It is accredited by the Western Association of Schools and Colleges, Inc. In 1999–2000, it offered 70 courses at a distance. In fall 1999, there were 1,100 students enrolled in distance learning courses.

Course delivery sites Courses are delivered to your home, your workplace, military bases, high schools.

Media Courses are delivered via World Wide Web. Students and teachers may interact via mail, telephone, fax, e-mail, World Wide Web. The following equipment may be required: computer, Internet access, e-mail.

Restrictions Programs are available worldwide. Enrollment is open to anyone.

Services Distance learners have access to library services, academic advising, tutoring, career placement assistance, bookstore at a distance.

Credit-earning options Students may transfer credits from another institution.

Typical costs Tuition of $13 per credit for in-state residents. Tuition of $144 per credit for out-of-state residents. Financial aid is available to distance learners.

Registration Students may register by telephone, World Wide Web, in person.

Contact Matt Hightower, Director, Cerro Coso Community College, PO Box 1865, Mammoth Lakes, CA 93546. *Telephone:* 760-934-2796 Ext. 228. *Fax:* 760-934-6019. *E-mail:* mhightow@cc.cc.ca.us.

DEGREES AND AWARDS

AA Business General, Comparative Literature, English, History, Humanities, Liberal Arts, Social Sciences

AS Administration of Justice, Business Administration, Business Management, Computer Information Systems, Economics

COURSE SUBJECT AREAS OFFERED OUTSIDE OF DEGREE PROGRAMS

Undergraduate: Accounting; American (U.S.) history; American literature; astronomy and astrophysics; biology; business administration and management; business communications; business law; child care and development; comparative literature; computer programming; corrections; criminal justice; criminology; economics; English composition; English literature; human resources management; information sciences and systems; instructional media; labor relations/studies; liberal arts, general studies, and humanities; management information systems; marketing; music; organizational behavior studies; philosophy and religion; political science; professional studies; public health; sociology; Spanish language and literature; statistics; teacher education; technical writing; telecommunications

Special note

Cerro Coso (CC) Online currently offers courses leading to 12 different associate degrees that may be completed completely on line, with no campus attendance requirements. In addition, CC Online delivers complete online student services, including counseling, admission, registration, financial aid, and library services. Cerro Coso offers a Practical Certificate in Online Teaching for faculty members interested in teaching online courses. The Practical Certificate in Online Teaching offers a unique opportunity to learn about online teaching in a practical, hands-on environment. The entire certificate can be completed in a typical semester. Unique to this certificate is the generation of a portfolio. This portfolio is created in the first course and developed as students progress through their course work. All courses are taught by experienced online instructors and presented in a consistent environment. Access to the Internet and a Windows or Macintosh computer with at least 100Mhz and multimedia capabilities is required for participation in the program. This program is specifically designed to assist faculty members in the development and delivery of online courses or course content. Cerro Coso Community College is a Service Member Opportunity College. For more information, students should visit the College's Web site (http://www.cc.cc.ca.us/cconline) or call 888-537-6932 (toll-free).

CHADRON STATE COLLEGE

Chadron, Nebraska

Regional Programs

www.csc.edu/

Chadron State College, founded in 1911, is a state-supported, comprehensive institution. It is accredited by the North Central Association of Colleges and Schools. It first offered distance learning courses in 1991. In 1999–2000, it offered 80 courses at a distance. In fall 1999, there were 400 students enrolled in distance learning courses.

Course delivery sites Courses are delivered to your home, Casper College (Casper, WY), Mid-Plains Community College (North Platte), Western Nebraska Community College (Scottsbluff), 2 off-campus centers in Alliance.

Media Courses are delivered via videotapes, interactive television, computer software, World Wide Web, e-mail, print. Students and teachers may meet in person or interact via videoconferencing, audioconferencing, mail, telephone, fax, e-mail, interactive television, World Wide Web. The following equipment may be required: computer, Internet access.

Restrictions Programs are available statewide, except for interactive television courses which are limited to Western Nebraska only. Enrollment is open to anyone.

Services Distance learners have access to library services, the campus computer network, e-mail services, academic advising, career placement assistance, bookstore at a distance.

Credit-earning options Students may transfer credits from another institution or may earn credits through examinations, portfolio assessment, military training.

Typical costs *Undergraduate:* Tuition of $62.50 per credit plus mandatory fees of $13 per credit for in-state residents. Tuition of $133 per credit plus mandatory fees of $13 per credit for out-of-state residents. *Graduate:* Tuition of $101.25 per credit plus mandatory fees of $13 per credit for in-state residents. Tuition of $156.50 per credit plus mandatory fees of $13 per credit for out-of-state residents. Costs may vary. Financial aid is available to distance learners.

Registration Students may register by mail, telephone, in person.

Contact Annette Langford, Coordinator, Chadron State College, Distance Learning, 1000 Main Street, Chadron, NE 69363. *Telephone:* 308-432-6211. *Fax:* 308-432-6274. *E-mail:* alangford@csc.edu.

DEGREES AND AWARDS

MBA Business Administration

COURSE SUBJECT AREAS OFFERED OUTSIDE OF DEGREE PROGRAMS

Undergraduate: Accounting; administrative and secretarial services; agriculture; area, ethnic, and cultural studies; business; business administration and management; creative writing; developmental and child psychology; economics; education administration; educational psychology; English language and literature; health and physical education/fitness; history; home economics and family studies; human resources management; law and legal studies; liberal arts, general studies, and humanities; mathematics; philosophy and religion; political science; psychology; social work; sociology; special education; teacher education

Graduate: Accounting; administrative and secretarial services; business; business administration and management; creative writing; education administration; English language and literature; human resources management; teacher education

See full description on page 822.

CHAMINADE UNIVERSITY OF HONOLULU

Honolulu, Hawaii
www.chaminade.edu/

Chaminade University of Honolulu, founded in 1955, is an independent, religious, comprehensive institution. It is accredited by the Western Association of Schools and Colleges, Inc.

Course delivery sites Courses are delivered to your home, your workplace, military bases.

Media Courses are delivered via computer conferencing, World Wide Web, e-mail. Students and teachers may meet in person or interact via e-mail, World Wide Web. The following equipment may be required: computer, modem, Internet access, e-mail.

Restrictions Programs are available to local area students. Enrollment is restricted to individuals meeting certain criteria.

Services Distance learners have access to the campus computer network, e-mail services, academic advising at a distance.

Typical costs *Undergraduate:* Tuition of $5800 per semester plus mandatory fees of $50 per semester. *Graduate:* Tuition of $310 per credit. Financial aid is available to distance learners.

Registration Students may register by World Wide Web, in person.

Contact Contact each program separately, Chaminade University of Honolulu.

DEGREES AND AWARDS

Distance programs offered do not lead to a degree or other formal award.

COURSE SUBJECT AREAS OFFERED OUTSIDE OF DEGREE PROGRAMS

Undergraduate: Abnormal psychology; anthropology; business; communications; developmental and child psychology; English composition; English literature; ethics; finance; human resources management; logic; psychology; religious studies

CHAMPLAIN COLLEGE

Burlington, Vermont
Champlain College Online
www.champlain.edu

Champlain College, founded in 1878, is an independent, nonprofit, four-year college. It is accredited by the New England Association of Schools and Colleges. It first offered distance learning courses in 1993. In 1999–2000, it offered 70 courses at a distance. In fall 1999, there were 585 students enrolled in distance learning courses.

Course delivery sites Courses are delivered to your home, your workplace, military bases.

Media Courses are delivered via computer software, World Wide Web, e-mail. Students and teachers may meet in person or interact via mail, telephone, fax, e-mail, World Wide Web. The following equipment may be required: computer, modem, Internet access, e-mail.

Restrictions Programs are available worldwide. Enrollment is open to anyone.

Services Distance learners have access to library services, the campus computer network, e-mail services, academic advising, tutoring, career placement assistance, bookstore at a distance.

Credit-earning options Students may transfer credits from another institution or may earn credits through examinations, portfolio assessment, military training, business training.

Typical costs Tuition of $318 per credit. Financial aid is available to distance learners.

Registration Students may register by mail, fax, telephone, e-mail, World Wide Web, in person.

Contact Colleen Long, Program Coordinator, Champlain College, Champlain College Online, 163 South Willard Street, Burlington, VT 05401. *Telephone:* 802-865-6449. *Fax:* 802-865-6447. *E-mail:* online@champlain.edu.

DEGREES AND AWARDS

Undergraduate Certificate(s) Accounting, Business, Computer Programming, Hotel and Restaurant Management, Management, Telecommunications, Website Development and Management

AS Accounting, Business, Computer Programming, Hotel and Restaurant Management, Management, Telecommunications, Web Site Development and Management

BS Business, Computer Information Systems, Professional Studies

COURSE SUBJECT AREAS OFFERED OUTSIDE OF DEGREE PROGRAMS

Undergraduate: Accounting; advertising; business; business administration and management; computer and information sciences; economics; English composition; English language and literature; history; hospitality services management; human resources management; law and legal studies; liberal arts, general studies, and humanities; marketing; mathematics; philosophy and religion; political science; psychology; sociology; statistics; telecommunications

See full description on page 488.

CHARLES STEWART MOTT COMMUNITY COLLEGE

Flint, Michigan
Distance Learning Office
www.mcc.edu

Charles Stewart Mott Community College, founded in 1923, is a district-supported, two-year college. It is accredited by the North Central Association of Colleges and Schools. It first offered distance learning courses in 1981. In 1999–2000, it offered 65 courses at a distance. In fall 1999, there were 1,087 students enrolled in distance learning courses.

Course delivery sites Courses are delivered to your home, your workplace.

Media Courses are delivered via videotapes, CD-ROM, World Wide Web, print. Students and teachers may interact via videoconferencing, mail, telephone, fax, e-mail, World Wide Web. The following equipment may be required: television, videocassette player, computer, modem.

Restrictions Programs are available worldwide. Enrollment is open to anyone.

Services Distance learners have access to library services, academic advising, tutoring, career placement assistance, bookstore at a distance.

Credit-earning options Students may transfer credits from another institution or may earn credits through examinations.

Typical costs Tuition of $450 per course plus mandatory fees of $35 per semester. Financial aid is available to distance learners.

Registration Students may register by mail, fax, in person.

Contact Lori France, Distance Learning Coordinator, Charles Stewart Mott Community College, College in the Workplace, CM 2124, 1401 East Court Street, Flint, MI 48503. *Telephone:* 800-398-2715. *Fax:* 810-762-0282. *E-mail:* lfrance@edtech.mcc.edu.

DEGREES AND AWARDS

AA Liberal Arts
AAS Computer Occupations Technology, General Business
AGS General Studies
AS Science

COURSE SUBJECT AREAS OFFERED OUTSIDE OF DEGREE PROGRAMS

Undergraduate: Administrative and secretarial services; advertising; American literature; anthropology; area, ethnic, and cultural studies; art history and criticism; biology; business; business administration and management; chemistry; computer and information sciences; developmental and child psychology; economics; engineering-related technologies; English composition; English language and literature; geology; history; liberal arts, general studies, and humanities; mathematics; music; political science; psychology; sociology; technical writing

CHARTER OAK STATE COLLEGE

New Britain, Connecticut
www.cosc.edu

Charter Oak State College, founded in 1973, is a state-supported, four-year college. It is accredited by the New England Association of Schools and Colleges. It first offered distance learning courses in 1992. In 1999–2000, it offered 20 courses at a distance. In fall 1999, there were 166 students enrolled in distance learning courses.

Course delivery sites Courses are delivered to your home, your workplace.

Media Courses are delivered via videotapes, audiotapes, CD-ROM, World Wide Web, e-mail, print. Students and teachers may interact via mail, telephone, fax, e-mail. The following equipment may be required: television, videocassette player, computer, modem, Internet access, e-mail.

Restrictions Programs are available worldwide. Enrollment is open to anyone.

Services Distance learners have access to academic advising, bookstore at a distance.

Credit-earning options Students may transfer credits from another institution or may earn credits through examinations, portfolio assessment, military training, business training.

Typical costs Undergraduate in-state tuition per credit is $68 for video-based courses and $102 for online courses. Undergraduate out-of-state tuition per credit is $99 per video-based courses and $135 for online courses. Mandatory fees are 15 per term. Costs may vary. Financial aid is available to distance learners.

Registration Students may register by mail, fax, telephone, e-mail, in person.

Contact Susan Israel, Assistant Director of Academic Programs, Charter Oak State College, 55 Paul J. Manafort Drive, New Britain, CT 06053-2142. *Telephone:* 860-832-3800. *Fax:* 860-832-3999. *E-mail:* sisrael@mail.cosc.edu.

DEGREES AND AWARDS

AA General Studies
AS General Studies
BA General Studies (certain restrictions apply)
BS General Studies (certain restrictions apply)

COURSE SUBJECT AREAS OFFERED OUTSIDE OF DEGREE PROGRAMS

Undergraduate: Anthropology; art history and criticism; astronomy and astrophysics; biology; business administration and management; economics; English language and literature; history; liberal arts, general studies, and humanities; mass media; mathematics; philosophy and religion; psychology; sociology

See full description on page 490.

CHATTANOOGA STATE TECHNICAL COMMUNITY COLLEGE

Chattanooga, Tennessee
Distance Learning Program
www.chattanoogastate.org

Chattanooga State Technical Community College, founded in 1965, is a state-supported, two-year college. It is accredited by the Southern Association of Colleges and Schools. It first offered distance learning courses in 1985. In 1999–2000, it offered 100 courses at a distance. In fall 1999, there were 1,800 students enrolled in distance learning courses.

Course delivery sites Courses are delivered to your home, your workplace, military bases, Bryan College (Dayton), Milligan College (Milligan College), Southern Adventist University (Collegedale), University of Tennessee at Chattanooga (Chattanooga), 2 off-campus centers in Dayton, Kimball.

Media Courses are delivered via television, videotapes, audiotapes, computer software, CD-ROM, computer conferencing, World Wide Web, e-mail, print. Students and teachers may interact via videoconferencing, mail, telephone, fax, e-mail, World Wide Web. The following equipment may be required: television, videocassette player, computer, modem, Internet access, e-mail.

Restrictions Programs are available nationwide. Enrollment is restricted to individuals meeting certain criteria.

Services Distance learners have access to library services, e-mail services, academic advising, tutoring, career placement assistance, bookstore at a distance.

Credit-earning options Students may transfer credits from another institution or may earn credits through examinations, portfolio assessment, military training.

Typical costs Tuition of $75 per semester hour plus mandatory fees of $22 per semester hour for in-state residents. Tuition of $198 per semester hour plus mandatory fees of $22 per semester hour for out-of-state residents. Costs may vary. Financial aid is available to distance learners.

Registration Students may register by mail, fax, telephone, e-mail, in person.

Contact Richard Seehaus, Dean, Chattanooga State Technical Community College, Distance Education, Amnicola Highway, Chattanooga, TN 37406-1097. *Telephone:* 423-697-4408. *Fax:* 423-697-4479. *E-mail:* seehaus@cstcc.cc.tn.us.

DEGREES AND AWARDS

Undergraduate Certificate(s) Forestry, Medical Transcription (some on-campus requirements)

AAS Emergency Medical Care Concentrations (certain restrictions apply; service area differs from that of the overall institution), Emergency Service Administration (certain restrictions apply; service area differs from that of the overall institution), Engineering Technology (certain restrictions apply; service area differs from that of the overall institution; some on-campus requirements), Fire Science Technology (certain restrictions apply; service area differs from that of the overall institution), Maintenance Technology (certain restrictions apply; service area differs from that of the overall institution; some on-campus requirements)

COURSE SUBJECT AREAS OFFERED OUTSIDE OF DEGREE PROGRAMS

Undergraduate: Accounting; advertising; biological and life sciences; business; business administration and management; computer and information sciences; creative writing; developmental and child psychology; economics; education; educational psychology; electrical engineering; English composition; English language and literature; fine arts; fire science; forestry; history; journalism; liberal arts, general studies, and humanities; mathematics; music; philosophy and religion; political science; protective services; psychology; radio and television broadcasting; social psychology; social work; sociology; teacher education

See full description on page 676.

CHESTNUT HILL COLLEGE

Philadelphia, Pennsylvania

Graduate Division
www.chc.edu

Chestnut Hill College, founded in 1924, is an independent, religious, comprehensive institution. It is accredited by the Middle States Association of Colleges and Schools. It first offered distance learning courses in 1995. In 1999–2000, it offered 30 courses at a distance. In fall 1999, there were 85 students enrolled in distance learning courses.

Course delivery sites Courses are delivered to your home.

Media Courses are delivered via computer software, World Wide Web, e-mail, print. Students and teachers may meet in person or interact via mail, telephone, fax, e-mail, World Wide Web. The following equipment may be required: computer, modem, Internet access, e-mail.

Restrictions Programs are available to local area students. Enrollment is restricted to individuals meeting certain criteria.

Services Distance learners have access to library services, e-mail services, academic advising, bookstore at a distance.

Credit-earning options Students may transfer credits from another institution or may earn credits through examinations, portfolio assessment.

Typical costs Tuition of $355 per credit plus mandatory fees of $25 per semester. Financial aid is available to distance learners.

Registration Students may register by mail, fax, telephone, in person.

Contact Dr. Louis Mayock, SND, Chair, Chestnut Hill College, Department of Applied Technology, 9601 Germantown Avenue, Philadelphia, PA 19118-2693. *Telephone:* 215-248-7186. *Fax:* 215-248-7155. *E-mail:* lmayock@chc.edu.

DEGREES AND AWARDS

MS Applied Technology (some on-campus requirements)

COURSE SUBJECT AREAS OFFERED OUTSIDE OF DEGREE PROGRAMS

Graduate: Communications; computer and information sciences; computer programming; curriculum and instruction; instructional media; teacher education; telecommunications

CHIPPEWA VALLEY TECHNICAL COLLEGE

Eau Claire, Wisconsin

CVTC Virtual Campus
www.chippewa.tec.wi.us/vcampus/

Chippewa Valley Technical College, founded in 1912, is a district-supported, two-year college. It is accredited by the North Central Association of Colleges and Schools. It first offered distance learning courses in 1990. In 1999–2000, it offered 353 courses at a distance. In fall 1999, there were 455 students enrolled in distance learning courses.

Course delivery sites Courses are delivered to your home, your workplace, high schools, 6 off-campus centers in Alma, Chippewa Falls, Eau Claire, Menomonie, Neillsville, River Falls.

Media Courses are delivered via television, videotapes, videoconferencing, interactive television, computer software, CD-ROM, computer conferencing, World Wide Web, e-mail, print. Students and teachers may meet in person or interact via videoconferencing, mail, telephone, fax, e-mail, interactive television, World Wide Web. The following equipment may be required: television, videocassette player, computer, modem, Internet access, e-mail.

Restrictions Programs are available worldwide. Enrollment is open to anyone.

Services Distance learners have access to library services, academic advising, career placement assistance, bookstore at a distance.

Credit-earning options Students may transfer credits from another institution or may earn credits through examinations, portfolio assessment.

Typical costs Tuition of $59.25 per credit plus mandatory fees of $3.50 per course. Financial aid is available to distance learners.

Registration Students may register by mail, fax, telephone, in person.

Contact Ron Doering, Dean, Instructional Design, Chippewa Valley Technical College, 620 West Clairemont Avenue, Eau Claire, WI 54701. *Telephone:* 715-833-6338. *Fax:* 715-833-6470. *E-mail:* rdoering@chippewa.tec.wi.us.

DEGREES AND AWARDS

Undergraduate Certificate(s) Records and Information Management

COURSE SUBJECT AREAS OFFERED OUTSIDE OF DEGREE PROGRAMS

Undergraduate: Accounting; administrative and secretarial services; biology; business; business administration and management; chemistry; computer and information sciences; creative writing; criminal justice;

developmental and child psychology; economics; English composition; health professions and related sciences; law and legal studies; mathematics; nursing; psychology; sociology
Noncredit: Biology; chemistry; computer and information sciences

CHRISTOPHER NEWPORT UNIVERSITY

Newport News, Virginia
CNU Online
www.cnuonline.cnu.edu

Christopher Newport University, founded in 1960, is a state-supported, comprehensive institution. It is accredited by the Southern Association of Colleges and Schools. It first offered distance learning courses in 1993. In 1999–2000, it offered 50 courses at a distance. In fall 1999, there were 700 students enrolled in distance learning courses.
Course delivery sites Courses are delivered to your home, your workplace, military bases, high schools.
Media Courses are delivered via videotapes, videoconferencing, computer software, CD-ROM, World Wide Web, e-mail, print. Students and teachers may interact via mail, telephone, fax, e-mail, World Wide Web. The following equipment may be required: computer, modem, Internet access.
Restrictions Programs are available worldwide. Enrollment is open to anyone.
Services Distance learners have access to library services, the campus computer network, e-mail services, tutoring, bookstore at a distance.
Credit-earning options Students may transfer credits from another institution or may earn credits through examinations, portfolio assessment, military training, business training.
Typical costs *Undergraduate:* Tuition of $126 per credit hour plus mandatory fees of $20 per semester for in-state residents. Tuition of $366 per credit hour plus mandatory fees of $20 per semester for out-of-state residents. *Graduate:* Tuition of $146 per credit hour for in-state residents. Tuition of $377 per credit hour for out-of-state residents. Costs may vary. Financial aid is available to distance learners.
Registration Students may register by mail, fax, telephone, in person.
Contact Catherine Doyle, Director, CNU Online, Christopher Newport University, Smith Libran, Christopher Newport V., Newport News, VA 23606. *Telephone:* 757-594-7130. *Fax:* 757-594-7717. *E-mail:* doyle@cnu.edu.

DEGREES AND AWARDS

BA Philosophy and Religious Studies
BS Governmental Administration
MPSL Public Safety Leadership (some on-campus requirements)

COURSE SUBJECT AREAS OFFERED OUTSIDE OF DEGREE PROGRAMS

Undergraduate: Business administration and management; business law; community services; corrections; criminal justice; economics; English composition; English language and literature; English literature; philosophy and religion; physics; political science; public policy analysis; sociology; Spanish language and literature; statistics
Graduate: Public policy analysis
See full description on page 676.

CINCINNATI BIBLE COLLEGE AND SEMINARY

Cincinnati, Ohio
Correspondence Department
www.cincybible.edu

Cincinnati Bible College and Seminary, founded in 1924, is an independent, religious, comprehensive institution affiliated with the Church of Christ. It is accredited by the Accrediting Association of Bible Colleges, North Central Association of Colleges and Schools. It first offered distance learning courses in 1980. In 1999–2000, it offered 8 courses at a distance. In fall 1999, there were 16 students enrolled in distance learning courses.
Course delivery sites Courses are delivered to your home.
Media Courses are delivered via videotapes, CD-ROM, print. Students and teachers may meet in person or interact via mail, telephone, fax, e-mail, World Wide Web.
Restrictions Programs are available worldwide. Enrollment is open to anyone.
Services Distance learners have access to library services, e-mail services, academic advising, bookstore at a distance.
Credit-earning options Students may transfer credits from another institution.
Typical costs *Undergraduate:* Tuition of $187 per credit hour. *Graduate:* Tuition of $195 per credit hour.
Registration Students may register by mail, fax, telephone, e-mail, in person.
Contact Sharon J. Borntrager, Administrative Assistant to the Vice President for Academic Affairs, Cincinnati Bible College and Seminary, 2700 Glenway Avenue, Cincinnati, OH 45204-3200. *Telephone:* 513-244-8100. *Fax:* 513-244-8140. *E-mail:* sharon.borntrager@cincybible.edu.

DEGREES AND AWARDS

Distance programs offered do not lead to a degree or other formal award.

COURSE SUBJECT AREAS OFFERED OUTSIDE OF DEGREE PROGRAMS

Undergraduate: Bible studies; history; philosophy and religion; theological studies
Graduate: History

CITRUS COLLEGE

Glendora, California
Distance Education
www.citruscollege.com/ACE/ace.htm

Citrus College, founded in 1915, is a state and locally supported, two-year college. It is accredited by the Western Association of Schools and Colleges, Inc. It first offered distance learning courses in 1996. In 1999–2000, it offered 50 courses at a distance. In fall 1999, there were 1,100 students enrolled in distance learning courses.
Course delivery sites Courses are delivered to your home, your workplace, military bases, high schools, off-campus center(s).
Media Courses are delivered via computer software, CD-ROM, World Wide Web, e-mail, print. Students and teachers may meet in person or interact via audioconferencing, mail, telephone, fax, e-mail, World Wide Web. The following equipment may be required: television, videocassette player, computer, modem, Internet access, e-mail.
Restrictions Programs are available worldwide. Enrollment is open to anyone.

Services Distance learners have access to library services, academic advising, tutoring, career placement assistance at a distance.

Credit-earning options Students may transfer credits from another institution.

Typical costs Tuition of $15 per unit for in-state residents. Tuition of $125 per unit for out-of-state residents. Costs may vary. Financial aid is available to distance learners.

Registration Students may register by mail, fax, telephone, in person.

Contact Dr. Bruce Solheim, Distance Education Coordinator, Citrus College, 1000 West Foothill Boulevard, Glendora, VA 91740-1899. *Telephone:* 626-914-8831. *Fax:* 626-852-8080. *E-mail:* online@citrus.cc.ca.us.

DEGREES AND AWARDS

AA Liberal Arts

COURSE SUBJECT AREAS OFFERED OUTSIDE OF DEGREE PROGRAMS

Undergraduate: Algebra; anthropology; art history and criticism; biology; developmental and child psychology; economics; English as a second language (ESL); English language and literature; history; mathematics; music; nursing; political science; psychology; sociology; statistics; technical writing

CITY COLLEGE OF SAN FRANCISCO

San Francisco, California

Telecourses

www.ccsf.cc.ca.us/online

City College of San Francisco, founded in 1935, is a state and locally supported, two-year college. It is accredited by the Western Association of Schools and Colleges, Inc. It first offered distance learning courses in 1988. In 1999–2000, it offered 44 courses at a distance. In fall 1999, there were 1,100 students enrolled in distance learning courses.

Course delivery sites Courses are delivered to your home.

Media Courses are delivered via television, videotapes. Students and teachers may meet in person or interact via mail, telephone, e-mail. The following equipment may be required: television, videocassette player.

Restrictions Programs are available to local area students. Enrollment is open to anyone.

Services Distance learners have access to library services, the campus computer network, academic advising, tutoring, career placement assistance, bookstore at a distance.

Credit-earning options Students may transfer credits from another institution or may earn credits through examinations.

Typical costs Tuition of $11 per unit. Financial aid is available to distance learners.

Registration Students may register by mail, telephone, in person.

Contact Phillip Brown, Telecourse Coordinator, City College of San Francisco, 50 Phelan Avenue, San Francisco, CA 94112. *Telephone:* 415-239-3885. *Fax:* 415-239-3694. *E-mail:* pkbrown@telis.org.

DEGREES AND AWARDS

Distance programs offered do not lead to a degree or other formal award.

COURSE SUBJECT AREAS OFFERED OUTSIDE OF DEGREE PROGRAMS

Undergraduate: Anthropology; area, ethnic, and cultural studies; art history and criticism; astronomy and astrophysics; business; business administration and management; chemistry; drama and theater; ecology; English language and literature; film studies; French language and litera-

ture; health and physical education/fitness; history; liberal arts, general studies, and humanities; music; photography; physics; social psychology

CITY COLLEGES OF CHICAGO, HAROLD WASHINGTON COLLEGE

Chicago, Illinois

Center for Open Learning

www.ccc.edu

City Colleges of Chicago, Harold Washington College, founded in 1962, is a state and locally supported, two-year college. It is accredited by the North Central Association of Colleges and Schools. It first offered distance learning courses in 1956. In 1999–2000, it offered 52 courses at a distance. In fall 1999, there were 2,858 students enrolled in distance learning courses.

Course delivery sites Courses are delivered to your home, military bases, City Colleges of Chicago, Harry S Truman College (Chicago), City Colleges of Chicago, Kennedy-King College (Chicago), City Colleges of Chicago, Malcolm X College (Chicago), City Colleges of Chicago, Olive-Harvey College (Chicago), City Colleges of Chicago, Richard J. Daley College (Chicago), City Colleges of Chicago, Wilbur Wright College (Chicago).

Media Courses are delivered via television, videotapes, videoconferencing, World Wide Web. Students and teachers may meet in person or interact via mail, telephone, fax, e-mail, World Wide Web. The following equipment may be required: television, videocassette player, computer, modem, Internet access, e-mail.

Restrictions Programs are available to local area students. Enrollment is restricted to individuals meeting certain criteria.

Services Distance learners have access to library services, the campus computer network at a distance.

Credit-earning options Students may earn credits through examinations, portfolio assessment, military training.

Typical costs Tuition of $47.50 per credit hour for local area residents. Tuition of $140.36 per credit hour for in-state residents. Tuition of $210.45 per credit hour for out-of-state residents. There is a $30 mandatory technology fee; typical cost for noncredit course ranges between $25 and $168. Financial aid is available to distance learners.

Registration Students may register by telephone, in person.

Contact Pamela C. Lattimore, Assistant Dean, City Colleges of Chicago, Harold Washington College, Center for Open Learning, 30 East Lake Street, Chicago, IL 60601. *Telephone:* 312-553-5980. *Fax:* 312-553-5987. *E-mail:* plattimore@ccc.edu.

DEGREES AND AWARDS

Distance programs offered do not lead to a degree or other formal award.

COURSE SUBJECT AREAS OFFERED OUTSIDE OF DEGREE PROGRAMS

Undergraduate: Accounting; algebra; Asian languages and literatures; astronomy and astrophysics; business administration and management; chemistry; classical languages and literatures; creative writing; developmental and child psychology; economics; English composition; English language and literature; European languages and literatures; fine arts; foods and nutrition studies; geology; health and physical education/fitness; history; physics; political science; social work; sociology; statistics

CITY UNIVERSITY

Bellevue, Washington

Distance Learning Operations
www.cityu.edu

City University, founded in 1973, is an independent, nonprofit, upper-level institution. It is accredited by the Northwest Association of Schools and Colleges. It first offered distance learning courses in 1985. In 1999–2000, it offered 302 courses at a distance. In fall 1999, there were 7,000 students enrolled in distance learning courses.

Course delivery sites Courses are delivered to your home, your workplace.

Media Courses are delivered via videotapes, computer software, computer conferencing, World Wide Web, e-mail. Students and teachers may interact via mail, telephone, fax, e-mail, World Wide Web.

Restrictions Programs are available worldwide. Enrollment is open to anyone.

Services Distance learners have access to library services, e-mail services, academic advising, career placement assistance, bookstore at a distance.

Credit-earning options Students may transfer credits from another institution or may earn credits through examinations, portfolio assessment, military training, business training.

Typical costs *Undergraduate:* Tuition of $165 per credit. *Graduate:* Tuition of $294 per credit.

Registration Students may register by mail, fax, telephone, e-mail, World Wide Web, in person.

Contact Distance Learning Advisor, City University, Office of Admissions and Student Affairs, 919 Southwest Grady Way, 2nd Floor, Renton, WA 98055. *Telephone:* 800-426-5596. *Fax:* 425-277-2437. *E-mail:* info@cityu.edu.

DEGREES AND AWARDS

Undergraduate Certificate(s) Accounting, Computer Programming, Cultural Diversity in Business, Internetworking, Network/Telecommunications, Networking Technologies, Paralegal Studies

AS General Studies, International Management, Management, Medical Laboratory Technology, Medical Office and Laboratory Technology, Paralegal Studies

BA General Studies, International Studies, Management, Marketing, Mass Communications and Journalism, Multi-Sciences, Philosophy, Political Science, Psychology, Sociology

BS Accounting, Business Administration, Computer Systems, General Studies, Law Enforcement Administration, Management Specialty, Marketing

Graduate Certificate(s) Business Policy Management, Criminal Justice, Educational Leadership, Financial Management, Information Systems, Management, Managerial Leadership, Marketing, Networking Technologies, Personal Financial Planning, Principal Certification, Project Management, Public Administration, Special Education

MA Management

MBA Business Administration, Financial Management, Individualized Studies, Information Systems, International Banking, Managerial Leadership, Marketing, Personal Financial Planning

MEd Curriculum and Instruction, Education Leadership and Principal Certification, Educational Technology, English as a Second Language Instructional Methods, Guidance and Counseling, Reading and Literacy, Special Education

MIT Teaching (service area differs from that of the overall institution)

MPA Criminal Justice, Public Administration

MS Computer Systems, Project Management

COURSE SUBJECT AREAS OFFERED OUTSIDE OF DEGREE PROGRAMS

Undergraduate: Accounting; business; business administration and management; computer and information sciences; criminal justice; environmental science; international business; journalism; liberal arts, general studies, and humanities; management information systems; marketing; philosophy and religion; physical sciences; political science; protective services; psychology; social sciences; sociology

Graduate: Business; business administration and management; computer and information sciences; criminal justice; curriculum and instruction; education; English as a second language (ESL); finance; instructional media; management information systems; mental health services; organizational behavior studies; protective services; public administration and services; special education; student counseling; telecommunications

See full descriptions on pages 492 and 822.

CLACKAMAS COMMUNITY COLLEGE

Oregon City, Oregon

Learning Resources
dl.clackamas.cc.or.us

Clackamas Community College, founded in 1966, is a district-supported, two-year college. It is accredited by the Northwest Association of Schools and Colleges. It first offered distance learning courses in 1980. In 1999–2000, it offered 43 courses at a distance. In fall 1999, there were 240 students enrolled in distance learning courses.

Course delivery sites Courses are delivered to your home, your workplace, high schools, Chemeketa Community College (Salem), Southwestern Oregon Community College (Coos Bay), 3 off-campus centers in Milwaukie, Wilsonville.

Media Courses are delivered via television, videotapes, interactive television, computer software, CD-ROM, computer conferencing, World Wide Web, e-mail, print. Students and teachers may meet in person or interact via mail, telephone, fax, e-mail, interactive television, World Wide Web. The following equipment may be required: television, computer, modem, Internet access, e-mail.

Restrictions Programs are available nationwide. Enrollment is restricted to individuals meeting certain criteria.

Services Distance learners have access to library services, the campus computer network, e-mail services, academic advising, tutoring, bookstore at a distance.

Credit-earning options Students may transfer credits from another institution or may earn credits through examinations, portfolio assessment, military training, business training.

Typical costs Tuition of $35 per credit plus mandatory fees of $2 per credit for in-state residents. Tuition of $123 per credit plus mandatory fees of $2 per credit for out-of-state residents. There is a $30 Distance Learning fee per course. Costs may vary. Financial aid is available to distance learners.

Registration Students may register by mail, fax, telephone, e-mail, in person.

Contact Cynthia R. Andrews, Director, Clackamas Community College, Learning Resource Center, 19600 South Molalla Avenue, Oregon City, OR 97045. *Telephone:* 503-657-6958 Ext. 2417. *Fax:* 503-655-8925. *E-mail:* cyndia@clackamas.cc.or.us.

DEGREES AND AWARDS

Distance programs offered do not lead to a degree or other formal award.

COURSE SUBJECT AREAS OFFERED OUTSIDE OF DEGREE PROGRAMS

Undergraduate: Adult education; American (U.S.) history; anthropology; area, ethnic, and cultural studies; biology; business; business administration and management; chemistry; child care and development; computer and information sciences; criminal justice; English as a second language (ESL); European history; health and physical education/fitness; history; home economics and family studies; journalism; mathematics; psychology; sociology; theological studies

CLARION UNIVERSITY OF PENNSYLVANIA

Clarion, Pennsylvania
Extended Studies and Distance Learning Department
www.clarion.edu/

Clarion University of Pennsylvania, founded in 1867, is a state-supported, comprehensive institution. It is accredited by the Middle States Association of Colleges and Schools. In 1999–2000, it offered 33 courses at a distance. In fall 1999, there were 120 students enrolled in distance learning courses.

Course delivery sites Courses are delivered to high schools, California University of Pennsylvania (California), Dixon University Center (Harrisburg), Lock Haven University of Pennsylvania (Lock Haven), Slippery Rock University of Pennsylvania (Slippery Rock), 4 off-campus centers in Coudersport, Oil City, Pittsburgh, St. Mary's.

Media Courses are delivered via videoconferencing, interactive television, computer software, CD-ROM, World Wide Web, e-mail, print. Students and teachers may meet in person or interact via videoconferencing, audioconferencing, mail, telephone, fax, e-mail, interactive television, World Wide Web. The following equipment may be required: computer, modem, Internet access, e-mail.

Restrictions Programs are available to in-state students only. Enrollment is open to anyone.

Services Distance learners have access to library services, the campus computer network, e-mail services, bookstore at a distance.

Credit-earning options Students may transfer credits from another institution or may earn credits through examinations, portfolio assessment.

Typical costs *Undergraduate:* Tuition of $150 per credit for in-state residents. Tuition of $226 per credit for out-of-state residents. *Graduate:* Tuition of $210 per credit for in-state residents. Tuition of $367 per credit for out-of-state residents. Financial aid is available to distance learners.

Registration Students may register by mail, telephone, in person.

Contact Angel Muschweck, Assistant to Director/Extended Studies and Distance Learning, Clarion University of Pennsylvania, 1801 West First Street, Oil City, PA 16301. *Telephone:* 814-676-6591 Ext. 279. *Fax:* 814-677-2056. *E-mail:* cmuschweck@clarion.edu.

DEGREES AND AWARDS

Distance programs offered do not lead to a degree or other formal award.

COURSE SUBJECT AREAS OFFERED OUTSIDE OF DEGREE PROGRAMS

Undergraduate: Biology; communications; German language and literature; nursing; sociology; statistics
Graduate: German language and literature; library and information studies; nursing

CLARK COLLEGE

Vancouver, Washington
www.clark.edu

Clark College, founded in 1933, is a state-supported, two-year college. It is accredited by the Northwest Association of Schools and Colleges. It first offered distance learning courses in 1982. In 1999–2000, it offered 31 courses at a distance. In fall 1999, there were 391 students enrolled in distance learning courses.

Course delivery sites Courses are delivered to your home, your workplace, Centralia College (Centralia), Highline Community College (Des Moines).

Media Courses are delivered via television, videotapes, interactive television, audiotapes, World Wide Web, e-mail. Students and teachers may meet in person or interact via mail, telephone, fax, e-mail, interactive television, World Wide Web. The following equipment may be required: television, videocassette player, computer, modem, Internet access, e-mail.

Restrictions Programs are available to in-state students only. Enrollment is open to anyone.

Services Distance learners have access to library services, the campus computer network, e-mail services, academic advising, career placement assistance, bookstore at a distance.

Credit-earning options Students may transfer credits from another institution or may earn credits through examinations.

Typical costs Tuition of $56.55 per credit for in-state residents. Tuition of $211 per credit for out-of-state residents. Financial aid is available to distance learners.

Registration Students may register by mail, telephone, in person.

Contact Susan Wolff, Associate Dean of Instruction, Clark College, 1800 East McLoughlin Boulevard, Vancouver, WA 98663. *Telephone:* 360-992-2314. *Fax:* 360-992-2870. *E-mail:* swolff@clark.edu.

DEGREES AND AWARDS

Distance programs offered do not lead to a degree or other formal award.

COURSE SUBJECT AREAS OFFERED OUTSIDE OF DEGREE PROGRAMS

Undergraduate: Biological and life sciences; business; business administration and management; chemistry; creative writing; developmental and child psychology; economics; electronics; English language and literature; European languages and literatures; film studies; finance; health and physical education/fitness; marketing; mathematics; psychology; technical writing

CLARKE COLLEGE

Dubuque, Iowa
www.clarke.edu/

Clarke College, founded in 1843, is an independent, religious, comprehensive institution. It is accredited by the North Central Association of Colleges and Schools. In 1999–2000, it offered 2 courses at a distance.

Course delivery sites Courses are delivered to your home, Mount St. Clare College (Clinton).

Media Courses are delivered via videoconferencing, World Wide Web. Students and teachers may meet in person or interact via e-mail, World Wide Web. The following equipment may be required: computer, modem, Internet access, e-mail.

Restrictions Programs are available to in-state students only. Enrollment is open to anyone.

Services Distance learners have access to library services, the campus computer network, e-mail services, academic advising, bookstore at a distance.

Credit-earning options Students may transfer credits from another institution or may earn credits through examinations, portfolio assessment.

Typical costs *Undergraduate:* Tuition of $945 per course plus mandatory fees of $15 per course. *Graduate:* Tuition of $1020 per course plus mandatory fees of $15 per course. Financial aid is available to distance learners.

Registration Students may register by mail, fax, telephone, e-mail, in person.
Contact Sr. Margaret Feldner, Department Chair, Education, Clarke College, 1550 Clarke Drive, Dubuque, IA 52001. *Telephone:* 319-588-6300. *Fax:* 319-588-6789. *E-mail:* mfeldner@clarke.edu.

DEGREES AND AWARDS

Distance programs offered do not lead to a degree or other formal award.

COURSE SUBJECT AREAS OFFERED OUTSIDE OF DEGREE PROGRAMS

Undergraduate: Nursing
Graduate: Instructional media

CLARKSON COLLEGE

Omaha, Nebraska
Office of Distance Education
www.clarksoncollege.edu

Clarkson College, founded in 1888, is an independent, religious, comprehensive institution affiliated with the Episcopal Church. It is accredited by the North Central Association of Colleges and Schools. It first offered distance learning courses in 1986. In 1999–2000, it offered 100 courses at a distance. In fall 1999, there were 200 students enrolled in distance learning courses.
Course delivery sites Courses are delivered to your home.
Media Courses are delivered via videotapes, audiotapes, computer software, CD-ROM, World Wide Web, e-mail, print. Students and teachers may meet in person or interact via audioconferencing, mail, telephone, fax, e-mail, World Wide Web. The following equipment may be required: television, videocassette player, computer, modem, Internet access, e-mail.
Restrictions Programs are available nationwide. Enrollment is restricted to individuals meeting certain criteria.
Services Distance learners have access to library services, academic advising, tutoring, career placement assistance, bookstore at a distance.
Credit-earning options Students may transfer credits from another institution or may earn credits through examinations, portfolio assessment, military training, business training.
Typical costs *Undergraduate:* Tuition of $289 per credit hour plus mandatory fees of $17 per credit hour. *Graduate:* Tuition of $334 per credit hour plus mandatory fees of $17 per credit hour. Cost for a noncredit course is the same as a credit course. Financial aid is available to distance learners.
Registration Students may register by mail, fax, telephone, e-mail, in person.
Contact Admissions, Clarkson College, 101 South 42nd Street, Omaha, NE 68131. *Telephone:* 800-647-5500. *Fax:* 402-552-6019. *E-mail:* admissions@clarksoncollege.edu.

DEGREES AND AWARDS

BS Business Administration, Medical Imaging
BSN Nursing
Graduate Certificate(s) Family Nurse Practitioner (service area differs from that of the overall institution; some on-campus requirements)
MSN Nursing (service area differs from that of the overall institution; some on-campus requirements)

COURSE SUBJECT AREAS OFFERED OUTSIDE OF DEGREE PROGRAMS

Undergraduate: Accounting; business administration and management; developmental and child psychology; economics; English composition; English language and literature; fine arts; health professions and related sciences; history; liberal arts, general studies, and humanities; mathematics; nursing; philosophy and religion; political science; social psychology; sociology
Graduate: Business administration and management; health professions and related sciences; mathematics; nursing
See full description on page 494.

CLARK STATE COMMUNITY COLLEGE

Springfield, Ohio
Alternative Methods of Instructional Delivery
www.clark.cc.oh.us

Clark State Community College, founded in 1962, is a state-supported, two-year college. It is accredited by the North Central Association of Colleges and Schools. It first offered distance learning courses in 1996. In 1999–2000, it offered 15 courses at a distance. In fall 1999, there were 201 students enrolled in distance learning courses.
Course delivery sites Courses are delivered to your home.
Media Courses are delivered via television, videotapes, World Wide Web, e-mail, print. Students and teachers may interact via mail, telephone, fax, e-mail, World Wide Web. The following equipment may be required: television, videocassette player, computer, modem, Internet access, e-mail.
Restrictions Programs are available worldwide. Enrollment is open to anyone.
Services Distance learners have access to library services, the campus computer network, e-mail services, academic advising, tutoring, career placement assistance at a distance.
Credit-earning options Students may transfer credits from another institution or may earn credits through examinations, portfolio assessment, military training.
Typical costs Tuition of $57 per quarter hour for in-state residents. Tuition of $106 per quarter hour for out-of-state residents. Financial aid is available to distance learners.
Registration Students may register by mail, in person.
Contact Todd Jones, Director, Admissions, Clark State Community College, PO Box 570, Springfield, OH 45501-0570. *Telephone:* 937-328-6028. *Fax:* 937-328-3853. *E-mail:* jonest@clark.cc.oh.us.

DEGREES AND AWARDS

Distance programs offered do not lead to a degree or other formal award.

COURSE SUBJECT AREAS OFFERED OUTSIDE OF DEGREE PROGRAMS

Undergraduate: Abnormal psychology; American (U.S.) history; art history and criticism; comparative literature; creative writing; English composition; health professions and related sciences; nursing; plant sciences; Spanish language and literature

CLATSOP COMMUNITY COLLEGE

Astoria, Oregon

Clatsop Community College, founded in 1958, is a county-supported, two-year college. It is accredited by the Northwest Association of Schools and Colleges. It first offered distance learning courses in 1986. In 1999–2000, it offered 71 courses at a distance. In fall 1999, there were 62 students enrolled in distance learning courses.
Course delivery sites Courses are delivered to your home, 1 off-campus center in Seaside.

Media Courses are delivered via television, videotapes, computer conferencing, World Wide Web. Students and teachers may meet in person or interact via mail, telephone, fax, e-mail. The following equipment may be required: television, videocassette player, computer, modem, Internet access, e-mail.

Restrictions Programs are available in Oregon and its bordering states. Enrollment is open to anyone.

Services Distance learners have access to library services at a distance.

Credit-earning options Students may transfer credits from another institution or may earn credits through examinations, portfolio assessment.

Typical costs Tuition of $38 per credit plus mandatory fees of $40 per course. Financial aid is available to distance learners.

Registration Students may register by mail, telephone, in person.

Contact Kirsten Horning, Telecommunications Specialist, Clatsop Community College, 1680 Lexington, Astoria, OR 97103. *Telephone:* 503-338-2341. *Fax:* 503-338-2387. *E-mail:* khorning@clatsop.cc.or.us.

DEGREES AND AWARDS

Distance programs offered do not lead to a degree or other formal award.

COURSE SUBJECT AREAS OFFERED OUTSIDE OF DEGREE PROGRAMS

Undergraduate: Algebra; business; computer and information sciences; economics; English composition; English language and literature; geography; health and physical education/fitness; history; home economics and family studies; psychology; religious studies; sociology

CLAYTON COLLEGE & STATE UNIVERSITY

Morrow, Georgia

Office of Distance Learning
distancelearning.clayton.edu

Clayton College & State University, founded in 1969, is a state-supported, four-year college. It is accredited by the Southern Association of Colleges and Schools. It first offered distance learning courses in 1995. In 1999–2000, it offered 85 courses at a distance. In fall 1999, there were 1,400 students enrolled in distance learning courses.

Course delivery sites Courses are delivered to your home, your workplace, military bases.

Media Courses are delivered via television, videotapes, videoconferencing, audiotapes, computer software, CD-ROM, computer conferencing, World Wide Web, e-mail. Students and teachers may meet in person or interact via videoconferencing, mail, telephone, e-mail, World Wide Web. The following equipment may be required: television, videocassette player, computer, modem, Internet access, e-mail.

Restrictions Programs are available nationwide. Enrollment is open to anyone.

Services Distance learners have access to library services, the campus computer network, e-mail services, academic advising, bookstore at a distance.

Credit-earning options Students may transfer credits from another institution or may earn credits through examinations.

Typical costs Tuition of $1051 per semester plus mandatory fees of $300 per semester for in-state residents. Tuition of $3763 per semester plus mandatory fees of $300 per semester for out-of-state residents. *Noncredit courses:* $100 per course. Costs may vary. Financial aid is available to distance learners.

Registration Students may register by World Wide Web, in person.

Contact Dr. C. Blaine Carpenter, Academic Director of Distance Learning, Clayton College & State University, 5900 North Lee Street, Morrow, GA 30260-0285. *Telephone:* 770-961-3634. *Fax:* 770-961-3630. *E-mail:* blainecarpenter@mail.clayton.edu.

DEGREES AND AWARDS

AA Integrative Studies (some on-campus requirements)
AS Integrative Studies (some on-campus requirements)
BA Integrative Studies (some on-campus requirements)
BS Integrative Studies (some on-campus requirements)

COURSE SUBJECT AREAS OFFERED OUTSIDE OF DEGREE PROGRAMS

Undergraduate: Accounting; administrative and secretarial services; algebra; biological and life sciences; computer and information sciences; computer programming; English language and literature; genetics; history; human resources management; information sciences and systems; interdisciplinary studies; paralegal/legal assistant; philosophy and religion; physical sciences; political science; protective services; public administration and services

See full description on page 676.

CLEARY COLLEGE

Howell, Michigan

Center for Distance Learning
www.cleary.edu

Cleary College, founded in 1883, is an independent, nonprofit, comprehensive institution. It is accredited by the North Central Association of Colleges and Schools. It first offered distance learning courses in 1995. In 1999–2000, it offered 60 courses at a distance. In fall 1999, there were 350 students enrolled in distance learning courses.

Course delivery sites Courses are delivered to your home.

Media Courses are delivered via computer conferencing, World Wide Web, e-mail, print. Students and teachers may interact via mail, telephone, fax, e-mail, World Wide Web. The following equipment may be required: computer, modem, Internet access, e-mail.

Restrictions Programs are available to local area students. Enrollment is open to anyone.

Services Distance learners have access to library services, the campus computer network, e-mail services, tutoring at a distance.

Credit-earning options Students may transfer credits from another institution or may earn credits through examinations, portfolio assessment, military training, business training.

Typical costs Tuition of $169 per credit hour. *Noncredit courses:* $100 per course. Costs may vary. Financial aid is available to distance learners.

Registration Students may register by telephone, in person.

Contact Carrie Bonofiglio, Admissions Office, Cleary College, 3750 Cleary Drive, Howell, MI 48843. *Telephone:* 517-548-3670. *Fax:* 517-548-2170. *E-mail:* cbonfiglio@cleary.edu.

DEGREES AND AWARDS

ABA Accounting, Health Services, Human Resources, Management, Management Information Technology (some on-campus requirements), Marketing, Quality Assurance
AD General Business
BBA Accounting (some on-campus requirements), Health Services (some on-campus requirements), Human Resources (some on-campus requirements), Management (some on-campus requirements), Management Information Technology (some on-campus requirements), Marketing (some on-campus requirements), Quality (some on-campus requirements)

COURSE SUBJECT AREAS OFFERED OUTSIDE OF DEGREE PROGRAMS

Undergraduate: Administrative and secretarial services; business; business administration and management; computer and information sciences; human resources management; law and legal studies; liberal arts, general studies, and humanities

CLEMSON UNIVERSITY

Clemson, South Carolina

Office of Off-Campus, Distance, and Continuing Education
www.clemson.edu/odce

Clemson University, founded in 1889, is a state-supported university. It is accredited by the Southern Association of Colleges and Schools. It first offered distance learning courses in 1984. In 1999–2000, it offered 300 courses at a distance. In fall 1999, there were 1,500 students enrolled in distance learning courses.

Course delivery sites Courses are delivered to your home, your workplace, high schools, Lander University (Greenwood), Trident Technical College (Charleston), 1 off-campus center in Greenville.

Media Courses are delivered via television, videotapes, videoconferencing, computer software, CD-ROM, computer conferencing, World Wide Web, e-mail, print. Students and teachers may meet in person or interact via videoconferencing, audioconferencing, mail, telephone, fax, e-mail, World Wide Web. The following equipment may be required: television, videocassette player, computer, Internet access, e-mail.

Restrictions Programs are available nationwide. Enrollment is restricted to individuals meeting certain criteria.

Services Distance learners have access to library services, the campus computer network, e-mail services, academic advising, bookstore at a distance.

Credit-earning options Students may transfer credits from another institution.

Typical costs *Undergraduate:* Tuition of $175 per credit for in-state residents. Tuition of $425 per credit for out-of-state residents. *Graduate:* Tuition of $195 per credit for in-state residents. Tuition of $490 per credit for out-of-state residents. Costs may vary. Financial aid is available to distance learners.

Registration Students may register by telephone, World Wide Web, in person.

Contact Dr. Barbara Hoskins, Assistant Vice Provost, ODCE, Clemson University, PO Box 912, Clemson, SC 29633-0912. *Telephone:* 888-253-6766. *Fax:* 864-656-3997. *E-mail:* barbara@clemson.edu.

DEGREES AND AWARDS

RN to BSN Nursing (service area differs from that of the overall institution)
MCSM Construction Science and Management
MHRD Human Resource Development
MSEE Electrical Engineering
MSN Nursing (service area differs from that of the overall institution)

COURSE SUBJECT AREAS OFFERED OUTSIDE OF DEGREE PROGRAMS

Undergraduate: Forestry; nursing
Graduate: Construction; education; electrical engineering; entomology; health services administration; human resources management; nursing; political science

See full description on page 676.

CLEVELAND COLLEGE OF JEWISH STUDIES

Beachwood, Ohio
www.ccjs.edu/page6.html

Cleveland College of Jewish Studies, founded in 1963, is an independent, nonprofit, comprehensive institution. It is accredited by the North Central Association of Colleges and Schools. In 1999–2000, it offered 9 courses at a distance. In fall 1999, there were 36 students enrolled in distance learning courses.

Course delivery sites Courses are delivered to 3 off-campus centers in Dallas (TX), Houston (TX), Kansas City (MO).

Media Courses are delivered via videoconferencing. Students and teachers may meet in person or interact via videoconferencing, mail, telephone, e-mail.

Restrictions Programs are available nationwide. Enrollment is open to anyone.

Services Distance learners have access to library services, academic advising at a distance.

Credit-earning options Students may transfer credits from another institution or may earn credits through examinations.

Typical costs *Undergraduate:* Tuition of $1750 per semester. *Graduate:* Tuition of $1750 per semester. *Noncredit courses:* $225 per course.

Registration Students may register by mail, fax, telephone, e-mail, World Wide Web, in person.

Contact Sylvia Abrams, Dean, Cleveland College of Jewish Studies, 26500 Shaker Boulevard, Beachwood, OH 44122. *Telephone:* 216-464-4050 Ext. 114. *Fax:* 216-464-5827. *E-mail:* sfabrams@ccjs.edu.

DEGREES AND AWARDS

MJS Education Administration, Hebrew language and literature, Jewish Studies

COURSE SUBJECT AREAS OFFERED OUTSIDE OF DEGREE PROGRAMS

Undergraduate: Education administration; Hebrew language and literature; Jewish studies
Graduate: Education administration; Hebrew language and literature; Jewish studies
Noncredit: Education administration; Hebrew language and literature; Jewish studies

CLEVELAND COMMUNITY COLLEGE

Shelby, North Carolina

Distance Learning Program

Cleveland Community College, founded in 1965, is a state-supported, two-year college. It is accredited by the Southern Association of Colleges and Schools.

Contact Cleveland Community College, 137 South Post Road, Shelby, NC 28152. *Telephone:* 704-484-4000.

See full description on page 676.

CLEVELAND INSTITUTE OF ELECTRONICS

Cleveland, Ohio
www.cie-wc.edu

Cleveland Institute of Electronics, founded in 1934, is a proprietary, two-year college. It is accredited by the Distance Education and Training

Council. In 1999–2000, it offered 55 courses at a distance. In fall 1999, there were 4,500 students enrolled in distance learning courses.

Course delivery sites Courses are delivered to your home, your workplace, military bases.

Media Courses are delivered via print. Students and teachers may meet in person or interact via mail, telephone, fax, e-mail, World Wide Web. The following equipment may be required: television, videocassette player, computer, modem, Internet access, e-mail.

Restrictions Programs are available worldwide. Enrollment is open to anyone.

Services Distance learners have access to e-mail services, academic advising, tutoring, bookstore at a distance.

Credit-earning options Students may transfer credits from another institution or may earn credits through examinations, portfolio assessment, military training, business training.

Typical costs Tuition of $1495 per term. *Noncredit courses:* $200 per course. Costs may vary. Financial aid is available to distance learners.

Registration Students may register by mail, fax, telephone, e-mail, World Wide Web, in person.

Contact Scott Katzenmeyer, Guidance Counselor Director, Cleveland Institute of Electronics, 1776 East 17th Street, Cleveland, OH 44114. *Telephone:* 800-243-6446. *Fax:* 216-781-0331. *E-mail:* info@cie-wc.edu.

DEGREES AND AWARDS

AAS Electronics Engineering Technology (certain restrictions apply)

COURSE SUBJECT AREAS OFFERED OUTSIDE OF DEGREE PROGRAMS

Undergraduate: Computer programming; electronics

CLEVELAND STATE COMMUNITY COLLEGE

Cleveland, Tennessee
Instructional Computer Technology Center of Emphasis
www.clscc.cc.tn.us

Cleveland State Community College, founded in 1967, is a state-supported, two-year college. It is accredited by the Southern Association of Colleges and Schools. In 1999–2000, it offered 19 courses at a distance. In fall 1999, there were 1,822 students enrolled in distance learning courses.

Course delivery sites Courses are delivered to your home, 1 off-campus center in Vonore.

Media Courses are delivered via television, videotapes, videoconferencing, audiotapes, World Wide Web, e-mail, print. Students and teachers may meet in person or interact via videoconferencing, mail, telephone, fax, e-mail. The following equipment may be required: computer, modem, Internet access, e-mail.

Restrictions Programs are available to local area students. Enrollment is open to anyone.

Services Distance learners have access to library services, the campus computer network, e-mail services, academic advising, career placement assistance at a distance.

Credit-earning options Students may transfer credits from another institution or may earn credits through examinations.

Typical costs Tuition of $53 per credit hour for local area residents. Tuition of $157 per credit hour for out-of-state residents. Mandatory fees include a flat-rate fee of $8 plus $4 per credit hour. Financial aid is available to distance learners.

Registration Students may register by telephone, in person.

Contact Deborah McLachlan, Assistant to the Executive Vice President, Cleveland State Community College, PO Box 3570, Cleveland, TN 37320-3570. *Telephone:* 423-478-6244. *Fax:* 423-478-6255. *E-mail:* dmclachlan@clscc.cc.tn.us.

DEGREES AND AWARDS

Distance programs offered do not lead to a degree or other formal award.

COURSE SUBJECT AREAS OFFERED OUTSIDE OF DEGREE PROGRAMS

Undergraduate: Accounting; American (U.S.) history; biology; business; chemistry; computer and information sciences; English composition; mathematics; paralegal/legal assistant; philosophy and religion; statistics

See full description on page 676.

CLEVELAND STATE UNIVERSITY

Cleveland, Ohio
Off-Campus Academic Programs
www.csuohio.edu

Cleveland State University, founded in 1964, is a state-supported university. It is accredited by the North Central Association of Colleges and Schools. It first offered distance learning courses in 1994. In 1999–2000, it offered 70 courses at a distance. In fall 1999, there were 250 students enrolled in distance learning courses.

Course delivery sites Courses are delivered to your home, your workplace, high schools, Cuyahoga Community College, Metropolitan Campus (Cleveland), Lakeland Community College (Kirtland), Lorain County Community College (Elyria), University of Akron (Akron), 2 off-campus centers in Cleveland, Strongsville.

Media Courses are delivered via television, videotapes, videoconferencing, interactive television, audiotapes, computer software, CD-ROM, computer conferencing, World Wide Web, e-mail, print. Students and teachers may meet in person or interact via videoconferencing, audioconferencing, mail, telephone, fax, e-mail, interactive television, World Wide Web. The following equipment may be required: television, videocassette player, computer, modem, Internet access, e-mail.

Restrictions Programs are available worldwide. Enrollment is open to anyone.

Services Distance learners have access to library services, the campus computer network, e-mail services, academic advising, tutoring, career placement assistance, bookstore at a distance.

Credit-earning options Students may transfer credits from another institution or may earn credits through examinations.

Typical costs *Undergraduate:* Tuition of $161 per semester hour for in-state residents. Tuition of $317 per semester hour for out-of-state residents. *Graduate:* Tuition of $215 per semester hour for in-state residents. Tuition of $425 per semester hour for out-of-state residents. Average cost for noncredit course is $175. Financial aid is available to distance learners.

Registration Students may register by mail, fax, telephone, e-mail, in person.

Contact Dr. M. Judith Crocker, Director, Off-Campus Academic Programs, Cleveland State University, 1860 East 22nd Street, Route 1209, Cleveland, OH 44114. *Telephone:* 216-687-5322. *Fax:* 216-687-9290. *E-mail:* j.crocker@csuohio.edu.

DEGREES AND AWARDS

Graduate Certificate(s) Adult Learning and Development (service area differs from that of the overall institution; some on-campus requirements), Bioethics (service area differs from that of the overall institution)

MS Health Science (service area differs from that of the overall institution; some on-campus requirements)

MSW Social Work (some on-campus requirements)

COURSE SUBJECT AREAS OFFERED OUTSIDE OF DEGREE PROGRAMS

Undergraduate: Computer and information sciences; English language and literature; ethics; European history; European languages and literatures; geology; health professions and related sciences; philosophy and religion; public administration and services; sign language; social work; women's studies

Graduate: Adult education; curriculum and instruction; education; electrical engineering; ethics; European languages and literatures; health professions and related sciences; industrial engineering; philosophy and religion; public administration and services; social work

COASTAL CAROLINA COMMUNITY COLLEGE

Jacksonville, North Carolina
www.coastalcarolina.org

Coastal Carolina Community College, founded in 1964, is a state and locally supported, two-year college. It is accredited by the Southern Association of Colleges and Schools. In fall 1999, there were 26 students enrolled in distance learning courses.

Course delivery sites Courses are delivered to your home, your workplace, military bases, high schools.

Media Courses are delivered via World Wide Web, e-mail. Students and teachers may meet in person or interact via mail, fax, e-mail, World Wide Web. The following equipment may be required: computer, Internet access, e-mail.

Restrictions Programs are available to in-state students only. Enrollment is restricted to individuals meeting certain criteria.

Services Distance learners have access to library services, academic advising, tutoring, career placement assistance, bookstore at a distance.

Credit-earning options Students may transfer credits from another institution or may earn credits through examinations, military training.

Typical costs Tuition of $26.75 per credit hour for in-state residents. Tuition of $169.75 per credit hour for out-of-state residents. Financial aid is available to distance learners.

Registration Students may register by in person.

Contact Michael R. Dodge, Dean of Information Resources, Coastal Carolina Community College, 444 Western Boulevard, Jacksonville, NC 28546. *Telephone:* 910-938-6148. *Fax:* 910-455-7027. *E-mail:* dodgem@coastal.cc.nc.us.

DEGREES AND AWARDS

Distance programs offered do not lead to a degree or other formal award.

COURSE SUBJECT AREAS OFFERED OUTSIDE OF DEGREE PROGRAMS

Undergraduate: Computer and information sciences; fire services administration

Noncredit: Fire services administration

COASTLINE COMMUNITY COLLEGE

Fountain Valley, California
Distance Learning Department
pelican.ccc.cccd.edu/~dl/

Coastline Community College, founded in 1976, is a state and locally supported, two-year college. It is accredited by the Western Association of Schools and Colleges, Inc. It first offered distance learning courses in 1976. In 1999–2000, it offered 70 courses at a distance. In fall 1999, there were 4,500 students enrolled in distance learning courses.

Course delivery sites Courses are delivered to your home, your workplace, military bases, high schools, California State University (Long Beach), 3 off-campus centers in Dominguez Hills, Fountain Valley, Garden Grove.

Media Courses are delivered via television, videotapes, videoconferencing, interactive television, audiotapes, computer software, CD-ROM, World Wide Web, e-mail, print. Students and teachers may meet in person or interact via videoconferencing, audioconferencing, mail, telephone, fax, e-mail, interactive television, World Wide Web. The following equipment may be required: television, videocassette player, computer, modem, Internet access, e-mail.

Restrictions Programs are available worldwide. Enrollment is open to anyone.

Services Distance learners have access to library services, academic advising, career placement assistance, bookstore at a distance.

Credit-earning options Students may transfer credits from another institution or may earn credits through examinations.

Typical costs *Undergraduate:* Tuition of $11 per unit plus mandatory fees of $10 per semester for local area residents. Tuition of $11 per unit plus mandatory fees of $10 per semester for in-state residents. Tuition of $136 per unit plus mandatory fees of $10 per semester for out-of-state residents. *Graduate:* Tuition of $11 per unit plus mandatory fees of $10 per semester for in-state residents. Tuition of $136 per unit plus mandatory fees of $10 per semester for out-of-state residents. Costs may vary. Financial aid is available to distance learners.

Registration Students may register by mail, telephone, in person.

Contact Distance Learning Department/General Information Line, Coastline Community College, 11460 Warner Avenue, Fountain Valley, CA 92708. *Telephone:* 714-241-6216. *Fax:* 714-241-6287. *E-mail:* dl@mail.ccc.cccd.edu.

DEGREES AND AWARDS

Undergraduate Certificate(s) Cognitive Retraining (some on-campus requirements)

AA Accounting (some on-campus requirements), Business (some on-campus requirements), Fine and Applied Arts (some on-campus requirements), Humanities (some on-campus requirements)

COURSE SUBJECT AREAS OFFERED OUTSIDE OF DEGREE PROGRAMS

Undergraduate: Algebra; American (U.S.) history; anatomy; anthropology; area, ethnic, and cultural studies; astronomy and astrophysics; biological and life sciences; biology; business; business administration and management; chemistry; communications; computer and information sciences; developmental and child psychology; ecology; economics; education; English composition; English language and literature; ethics; European languages and literatures; French language and literature; geology; health and physical education/fitness; history; human resources management; information sciences and systems; law and legal studies; liberal arts, general studies, and humanities; logic; mass media; mathematics; music; oceanography; paralegal/legal assistant; philosophy and religion; physical sciences; political science; psychology; social sciences; sociology; Spanish language and literature; statistics; visual and performing arts

Noncredit: Algebra; American (U.S.) history; anatomy; anthropology; area, ethnic, and cultural studies; astronomy and astrophysics; biological and life sciences; biology; business; business administration and management; chemistry; communications; computer and information sciences; developmental and child psychology; ecology; economics; education; English composition; English language and literature; ethics; European languages and literatures; French language and literature; geology; health and physical education/fitness; history; human resources management; information sciences and systems; law and legal studies; liberal arts, general studies, and humanities; logic; mass media; mathematics; music;

oceanography; paralegal/legal assistant; philosophy and religion; physical sciences; political science; psychology; social sciences; sociology; Spanish language and literature; statistics; visual and performing arts

COCHISE COLLEGE

Douglas, Arizona

Online Campus

www.cochise.cc.az.us

Cochise College, founded in 1962, is a state and locally supported, two-year college. It is accredited by the North Central Association of Colleges and Schools. In 1999–2000, it offered 35 courses at a distance. In fall 1999, there were 350 students enrolled in distance learning courses.

Course delivery sites Courses are delivered to your home, your workplace, military bases.

Media Courses are delivered via computer software, computer conferencing, World Wide Web, e-mail. Students and teachers may interact via mail, telephone, e-mail, World Wide Web. The following equipment may be required: computer, modem, Internet access, e-mail.

Restrictions Programs are available worldwide. Enrollment is open to anyone.

Services Distance learners have access to library services, e-mail services, academic advising, bookstore at a distance.

Typical costs Tuition of $52 per credit.

Registration Students may register by World Wide Web, in person.

Contact Bill Akins, Director, Online Campus, Cochise College, 901 North Colombo, Sierra Vista, AZ 85635. *Telephone:* 520-515-5429. *Fax:* 520-515-5406. *E-mail:* mrbill@cochise.cc.az.us.

DEGREES AND AWARDS

Undergraduate Certificate(s) International Business, Unix System Administrator

COURSE SUBJECT AREAS OFFERED OUTSIDE OF DEGREE PROGRAMS

Undergraduate: Accounting; algebra; American literature; biology; business administration and management; calculus; computer programming; criminal justice; economics; English composition; information sciences and systems; liberal arts, general studies, and humanities; philosophy and religion; political science; psychology; social psychology; sociology; teacher education; technical writing

COLLEGE FOR FINANCIAL PLANNING

Greenwood Village, Colorado

www.fp.edu

College for Financial Planning, founded in 1972, is a proprietary, graduate institution. It is accredited by the Distance Education and Training Council, North Central Association of Colleges and Schools. It first offered distance learning courses in 1972. In 1999–2000, it offered 29 courses at a distance. In fall 1999, there were 22,500 students enrolled in distance learning courses.

Course delivery sites Courses are delivered to your home, your workplace, military bases.

Media Courses are delivered via computer software, computer conferencing, World Wide Web, e-mail, print. Students and teachers may interact via mail, telephone, fax, e-mail, World Wide Web. The following equipment may be required: computer, modem, Internet access, e-mail.

Restrictions Programs are available worldwide. Enrollment is open to anyone.

Services Distance learners have access to library services, e-mail services, academic advising, tutoring at a distance.

Credit-earning options Students may transfer credits from another institution or may earn credits through examinations, business training.

Typical costs Tuition of $600 per course.

Registration Students may register by mail, fax, telephone, e-mail, World Wide Web, in person.

Contact Student Services Center, College for Financial Planning, 6161 South Syracuse Way, Greenwood Village, CO 80111. *Telephone:* 800-237-9990. *Fax:* 303-220-5146. *E-mail:* ssc@fp.edu.

DEGREES AND AWARDS

MS Personal Financial Planning

COURSE SUBJECT AREAS OFFERED OUTSIDE OF DEGREE PROGRAMS

Undergraduate: Investments and securities
Graduate: Accounting; finance; investments and securities

COLLEGE FOR LIFELONG LEARNING, UNIVERSITY SYSTEM OF NEW HAMPSHIRE

Concord, New Hampshire

www.cll.edu/services/oic.htm

College for Lifelong Learning, University System of New Hampshire, founded in 1972, is a state and locally supported, four-year college. It is accredited by the New England Association of Schools and Colleges. In 1999–2000, it offered 20 courses at a distance.

Course delivery sites Courses are delivered to your home, your workplace.

Media Courses are delivered via computer software, CD-ROM, computer conferencing, World Wide Web. Students and teachers may meet in person or interact via mail, e-mail, World Wide Web. The following equipment may be required: computer, Internet access.

Restrictions Programs are available to in-state students only. Enrollment is open to anyone.

Services Distance learners have access to library services, bookstore at a distance.

Credit-earning options Students may transfer credits from another institution or may earn credits through examinations, portfolio assessment, military training, business training.

Typical costs Tuition of $161 per credit for in-state residents. Tuition of $179 per credit for out-of-state residents. Mandatory fees include $20 registration fee and $20 materials fee. Financial aid is available to distance learners.

Registration Students may register by mail, fax, telephone, in person.

Contact Pamela Woods, Program Support Assistant, College for Lifelong Learning, University System of New Hampshire, Educational Technology and Computing, 175 Ammon Drive, Unit 1, Manchester, NH 03103-3311. *Telephone:* 603-669-7997. *Fax:* 603-627-5103. *E-mail:* oic.cll@unh.edu.

DEGREES AND AWARDS

Distance programs offered do not lead to a degree or other formal award.

COURSE SUBJECT AREAS OFFERED OUTSIDE OF DEGREE PROGRAMS

Undergraduate: Adult education; business administration and management; computer and information sciences; criminal justice; health services administration; human resources management; investments and securities; liberal arts, general studies, and humanities; management information systems; psychology; social sciences

COLLEGE OF AERONAUTICS

Flushing, New York

Distance Education Department
www.aero.edu/

College of Aeronautics, founded in 1932, is an independent, nonprofit, four-year college. It is accredited by the Middle States Association of Colleges and Schools. In 1999–2000, it offered 30 courses at a distance. In fall 1999, there were 65 students enrolled in distance learning courses.

Course delivery sites Courses are delivered to your home, your workplace.

Media Courses are delivered via videotapes, videoconferencing, interactive television. Students and teachers may interact via videoconferencing, fax, e-mail. The following equipment may be required: television, videocassette player, computer, modem, Internet access, e-mail.

Restrictions Programs are available nationwide. Enrollment is restricted to individuals meeting certain criteria.

Services Distance learners have access to e-mail services, academic advising, tutoring, career placement assistance, bookstore at a distance.

Credit-earning options Students may transfer credits from another institution or may earn credits through examinations.

Typical costs Tuition of $285 per credit hour for local area residents. Tuition of $385 per credit hour for out-of-state residents. There is a mandatory fee of $125 for seminars and labs. Costs may vary. Financial aid is available to distance learners.

Registration Students may register by mail, fax, in person.

Contact Ray Axmacher, Director of Distance Education, College of Aeronautics, LaGuardia Airport, 86-01 23rd Avenue, Flushing, NY 11369. *Telephone:* 917-495-3893. *Fax:* 718-396-4413. *E-mail:* rayax@aero.edu.

DEGREES AND AWARDS

AAS Aviation Maintenance (certain restrictions apply)
BS Aviation Maintenance (certain restrictions apply; some on-campus requirements)
BST Maintenance Management (certain restrictions apply)

COURSE SUBJECT AREAS OFFERED OUTSIDE OF DEGREE PROGRAMS

Undergraduate: Aerospace, aeronautical engineering; business administration and management; economics; English language and literature; history; mathematics; meteorology; organizational behavior studies; physics; technical writing

COLLEGE OF ALBEMARLE

Elizabeth City, North Carolina

Distance Education
www.albemarle.cc.nc.us/courses

College of Albemarle, founded in 1960, is a state-supported, two-year college. It is accredited by the Southern Association of Colleges and Schools. It first offered distance learning courses in 1993. In 1999–2000, it offered 32 courses at a distance. In fall 1999, there were 287 students enrolled in distance learning courses.

Course delivery sites Courses are delivered to your home, your workplace, high schools, 2 off-campus centers in Edenton, Manteo.

Media Courses are delivered via television, videotapes, videoconferencing, computer software, computer conferencing, World Wide Web, e-mail, print. Students and teachers may meet in person or interact via videoconferencing, audioconferencing, mail, telephone, fax, e-mail, World Wide Web. The following equipment may be required: television, videocassette player, computer, modem, Internet access, e-mail.

Restrictions Programs are available to seven area counties (College's service area). Enrollment is open to anyone.

Services Distance learners have access to library services, the campus computer network, e-mail services, academic advising, tutoring, career placement assistance, bookstore at a distance.

Credit-earning options Students may transfer credits from another institution or may earn credits through examinations.

Typical costs Tuition of $26.75 per semester credit plus mandatory fees of $14 per semester for in-state residents. Tuition of $169.75 per semester credit plus mandatory fees of $14 per semester for out-of-state residents. *Noncredit courses:* $55 per course. Costs may vary. Financial aid is available to distance learners.

Registration Students may register by in person.

Contact Jeff Zeigler, Distance Education Coordinator, College of Albemarle, PO Box 2327, Elizabeth City, NC 27906-2327. *Telephone:* 252-335-0821 Ext. 2313. *Fax:* 252-337-6710. *E-mail:* jzeigler@albemarle.cc.nc.us.

DEGREES AND AWARDS

Distance programs offered do not lead to a degree or other formal award.

COURSE SUBJECT AREAS OFFERED OUTSIDE OF DEGREE PROGRAMS

Undergraduate: Accounting; advertising; algebra; art history and criticism; aviation; business administration and management; business communications; business law; creative writing; criminal justice; early childhood education; economics; European history; information sciences and systems; international relations; marketing; recreation and leisure studies; social psychology; sociology; technical writing

See full description on page 676.

COLLEGE OF DUPAGE

Glen Ellyn, Illinois

Alternative Learning Division
www.cod.edu/cil/

College of DuPage, founded in 1967, is a state and locally supported, two-year college. It is accredited by the North Central Association of Colleges and Schools. It first offered distance learning courses in 1980. In 1999–2000, it offered 170 courses at a distance. In fall 1999, there were 5,000 students enrolled in distance learning courses.

Course delivery sites Courses are delivered to your home, your workplace, 4 off-campus centers in Glendale Heights, Lombard, Naperville, Westmont.

Media Courses are delivered via television, videotapes, videoconferencing, interactive television, audiotapes, computer software, CD-ROM, computer conferencing, World Wide Web, e-mail, print. Students and teachers may meet in person or interact via videoconferencing, mail, telephone, fax, e-mail, interactive television, World Wide Web. The following equipment may be required: television, computer, modem, Internet access, e-mail.

Restrictions Program availability depends upon the course delivery format used. Enrollment is open to anyone.

Services Distance learners have access to library services, e-mail services, academic advising, career placement assistance, bookstore at a distance.

Credit-earning options Students may transfer credits from another institution or may earn credits through examinations.

Typical costs Tuition of $32 per quarter credit plus mandatory fees of $30 per course for local area residents. Tuition of $108 per quarter credit

for in-state residents. Tuition of $149 per quarter credit for out-of-state residents. Cost for noncredit course varies from $40 to $200. Financial aid is available to distance learners.
Registration Students may register by mail, fax, telephone, World Wide Web, in person.
Contact Ron Schiesz, Counselor, Alternative Learning Program, College of DuPage, Center for Independent Learning, 425 22nd Street, Glen Ellyn, IL 60137-6599. *Telephone:* 630-942-2130 Ext. 3326. *Fax:* 630-942-3749. *E-mail:* schiesz@cdnet.cod.edu.

DEGREES AND AWARDS

Undergraduate Certificate(s) Marketing/Supervision (service area differs from that of the overall institution; some on-campus requirements)
AA Liberal Arts (some on-campus requirements)

COURSE SUBJECT AREAS OFFERED OUTSIDE OF DEGREE PROGRAMS

Undergraduate: Accounting; administrative and secretarial services; American (U.S.) history; anthropology; area, ethnic, and cultural studies; biological and life sciences; biology; business; business administration and management; chemistry; child care and development; computer and information sciences; database management; developmental and child psychology; earth science; economics; education; educational psychology; English as a second language (ESL); English composition; English language and literature; European languages and literatures; geology; history; information sciences and systems; liberal arts, general studies, and humanities; mathematics; music; philosophy and religion; physical sciences; physics; political science; psychology; social psychology; social sciences; sociology; Spanish language and literature; teacher education

COLLEGE OF MOUNT ST. JOSEPH

Cincinnati, Ohio
www.msj.edu/

College of Mount St. Joseph, founded in 1920, is an independent, religious, comprehensive institution. It is accredited by the North Central Association of Colleges and Schools. In 1999–2000, it offered 6 courses at a distance.
Course delivery sites Courses are delivered to your home, your workplace, military bases, high schools.
Media Courses are delivered via videotapes, computer software, CD-ROM, computer conferencing, World Wide Web, e-mail. Students and teachers may meet in person or interact via audioconferencing, telephone, e-mail, World Wide Web. The following equipment may be required: computer, Internet access.
Restrictions Programs are available worldwide. Enrollment is open to anyone.
Services Distance learners have access to library services, the campus computer network, e-mail services, career placement assistance, bookstore at a distance.
Credit-earning options Students may transfer credits from another institution or may earn credits through portfolio assessment.
Typical costs Tuition of $333 per credit hour. Costs may vary. Financial aid is available to distance learners.
Registration Students may register by fax, World Wide Web, in person.
Contact Jerry Hamburg, Instructional Designer, College of Mount St. Joseph, 5701 Delhi Road, Cincinnati, OH 45233. *Telephone:* 513-244-4589. *Fax:* 513-244-4222. *E-mail:* jerry_hamburg@mail.msj.edu.

DEGREES AND AWARDS

Undergraduate Certificate(s) Paralegal Studies (certain restrictions apply; some on-campus requirements)

COURSE SUBJECT AREAS OFFERED OUTSIDE OF DEGREE PROGRAMS

Undergraduate: Biology; gerontology; paralegal/legal assistant; religious studies; social psychology
See full description on page 496.

COLLEGE OF ST. SCHOLASTICA

Duluth, Minnesota
Graduate Studies
www.css.edu

College of St. Scholastica, founded in 1912, is an independent, religious, comprehensive institution affiliated with the Roman Catholic Church. It is accredited by the North Central Association of Colleges and Schools. It first offered distance learning courses in 1986. In 1999–2000, it offered 30 courses at a distance. In fall 1999, there were 250 students enrolled in distance learning courses.
Course delivery sites Courses are delivered to your home.
Media Courses are delivered via television, videotapes, audiotapes, World Wide Web, print. Students and teachers may interact via videoconferencing, mail, telephone, fax, e-mail, World Wide Web. The following equipment may be required: television, videocassette player, computer, Internet access, e-mail.
Restrictions Programs are available worldwide. Enrollment is open to anyone.
Services Distance learners have access to library services, the campus computer network, e-mail services, academic advising, bookstore at a distance.
Credit-earning options Students may transfer credits from another institution or may earn credits through portfolio assessment, military training.
Typical costs *Undergraduate:* Tuition of $482 per semester hour. *Graduate:* Tuition of $250 per semester hour. Costs may vary. Financial aid is available to distance learners.
Registration Students may register by mail, fax, in person.
Contact Admissions, College of St. Scholastica, 1200 Kenwood Avenue, Duluth, MN 55811. *Telephone:* 218-723-6046. *Fax:* 218-723-5991. *E-mail:* admiss@css.edu.

DEGREES AND AWARDS

MEd Curriculum and Instruction (some on-campus requirements)

COURSE SUBJECT AREAS OFFERED OUTSIDE OF DEGREE PROGRAMS

Undergraduate: Abnormal psychology; biological and life sciences; business administration and management; communications; psychology; sociology
Graduate: Biological and life sciences; business administration and management; curriculum and instruction; education; instructional media
Noncredit: Nursing

COLLEGE OF SOUTHERN MARYLAND

La Plata, Maryland
Distance Learning Department
www.charles.cc.md.us

College of Southern Maryland, founded in 1958, is a state and locally supported, two-year college. It is accredited by the Middle States Association of Colleges and Schools. It first offered distance learning courses in 1985. In 1999–2000, it offered 51 courses at a distance. In fall 1999, there were 685 students enrolled in distance learning courses.

Course delivery sites Courses are delivered to your home, your workplace, military bases, Anne Arundel Community College (Arnold), Chesapeake College (Wye Mills), Montgomery College–Rockville Campus (Rockville).

Media Courses are delivered via television, videotapes, videoconferencing, interactive television, CD-ROM, World Wide Web, e-mail, print. Students and teachers may meet in person or interact via videoconferencing, mail, telephone, fax, e-mail, interactive television, World Wide Web. The following equipment may be required: television, videocassette player, computer, modem, Internet access, e-mail.

Restrictions Programs are available to in-state students only. Enrollment is open to anyone.

Services Distance learners have access to library services, the campus computer network, e-mail services, academic advising, career placement assistance, bookstore at a distance.

Credit-earning options Students may transfer credits from another institution or may earn credits through portfolio assessment, military training, business training.

Typical costs Tuition of $70 per credit hour plus mandatory fees of $14 per credit for local area residents. Tuition of $140 per credit hour plus mandatory fees of $28 per credit for in-state residents. Tuition of $210 per credit hour plus mandatory fees of $42 per credit for out-of-state residents. Financial aid is available to distance learners.

Registration Students may register by mail, fax, telephone, in person.

Contact Paul Toscano, Distance Learning Coordinator, College of Southern Maryland, 8730 Mitchell Road, PO Box 910, La Plata, MD 20646-0910. *Telephone:* 301-934-2251. *Fax:* 301-934-7699. *E-mail:* pault@charles.cc.md.us.

DEGREES AND AWARDS

AA General Studies (some on-campus requirements)

COURSE SUBJECT AREAS OFFERED OUTSIDE OF DEGREE PROGRAMS

Undergraduate: Abnormal psychology; accounting; administrative and secretarial services; American (U.S.) history; art history and criticism; astronomy and astrophysics; biology; business administration and management; business law; calculus; computer and information sciences; computer programming; creative writing; developmental and child psychology; economics; education; electrical engineering; English composition; English language and literature; ethics; European history; European languages and literatures; film studies; fine arts; French language and literature; geology; health and physical education/fitness; history; international business; journalism; liberal arts, general studies, and humanities; logic; marketing; mathematics; nursing; oceanography; philosophy and religion; physical therapy; political science; psychology; sociology; Spanish language and literature; statistics; teacher education; technical writing

See full description on page 676.

COLLEGE OF THE MAINLAND

Texas City, Texas

College of the Mainland, founded in 1967, is a state and locally supported, two-year college. It is accredited by the Southern Association of Colleges and Schools. It first offered distance learning courses in 1996.

Course delivery sites Courses are delivered to your home, Galveston College (Galveston).

Media Courses are delivered via television, videotapes, e-mail. Students and teachers may meet in person or interact via telephone, e-mail. The following equipment may be required: television, computer, Internet access, e-mail.

Restrictions Programs are available to local area students. Enrollment is open to anyone.

Services Distance learners have access to library services, the campus computer network, academic advising, career placement assistance, bookstore at a distance.

Credit-earning options Students may transfer credits from another institution or may earn credits through examinations, military training, business training.

Typical costs Undergraduate tuition per three credit-hours is $113.75 in-district, $212 in-state, and $306 out-of-state. Financial aid is available to distance learners.

Registration Students may register by telephone, in person.

Contact Alexander Pratt, Associate Dean, College of the Mainland, 1200 Amburn Road, Texas City, TX 77591-2499. *Telephone:* 409-938-1211 Ext. 435. *E-mail:* apratt@mail.mainland.cc.tx.us.

DEGREES AND AWARDS

Distance programs offered do not lead to a degree or other formal award.

COURSE SUBJECT AREAS OFFERED OUTSIDE OF DEGREE PROGRAMS

Undergraduate: English composition; history; political science

COLLEGE OF THE REDWOODS

Eureka, California
www.redwoods.cc.ca.us

College of the Redwoods, founded in 1964, is a state and locally supported, two-year college. It is accredited by the Western Association of Schools and Colleges, Inc. In 1999–2000, it offered 15 courses at a distance. In fall 1999, there were 359 students enrolled in distance learning courses.

Course delivery sites Courses are delivered to your home, 2 off-campus centers in Crescent City, Fort Bragg.

Media Courses are delivered via television, videotapes, videoconferencing, World Wide Web, e-mail. Students and teachers may interact via videoconferencing, mail, telephone, fax, e-mail, World Wide Web. The following equipment may be required: television, Internet access.

Restrictions Programs are available to local area students. Enrollment is restricted to individuals meeting certain criteria.

Services Distance learners have access to library services, academic advising, bookstore at a distance.

Typical costs Tuition of $11 per unit for local area residents. Tuition of $11 per unit for in-state residents. Tuition of $144 per unit for out-of-state residents. Financial aid is available to distance learners.

Registration Students may register by mail, telephone, in person.

Contact Dr. Jeff Bobbitt, Vice President for Academic Affairs, College of the Redwoods, 7351 Tompkins Hill Road, Eureka, CA 95501. *Telephone:* 707-476-4174. *Fax:* 707-476-4400. *E-mail:* jeff-bobbitt@eureka.redwoods.cc.ca.us.

DEGREES AND AWARDS

Distance programs offered do not lead to a degree or other formal award.

COURSE SUBJECT AREAS OFFERED OUTSIDE OF DEGREE PROGRAMS

Undergraduate: Algebra; calculus; geology; health professions and related sciences; psychology; statistics

COLLEGE OF THE SISKIYOUS

Weed, California

Distance Learning
www.siskiyous.edu/

College of the Siskiyous, founded in 1957, is a state and locally supported, two-year college. It is accredited by the Western Association of Schools and Colleges, Inc. In 1999–2000, it offered 23 courses at a distance. In fall 1999, there were 161 students enrolled in distance learning courses.
Course delivery sites Courses are delivered to your home, your workplace, military bases, high schools.
Media Courses are delivered via videoconferencing, computer software, CD-ROM, computer conferencing, World Wide Web, e-mail, print. Students and teachers may meet in person or interact via videoconferencing, mail, telephone, fax, e-mail, World Wide Web. The following equipment may be required: computer, modem, Internet access, e-mail.
Restrictions Programs are available mainly on a local level, with some statewide participation. Enrollment is open to anyone.
Services Distance learners have access to library services, tutoring, bookstore at a distance.
Credit-earning options Students may transfer credits from another institution.
Typical costs Tuition of $11 per credit hour for in-state residents. Tuition of $141 per credit hour for out-of-state residents. Financial aid is available to distance learners.
Registration Students may register by mail, fax, in person.
Contact Nancy Shepard, Telecommunications Specialist/Distance Learning Coordinator, College of the Siskiyous, 800 College Avenue, Weed, CA 96094. *Telephone:* 530-938-5520. *Fax:* 530-938-5228. *E-mail:* shepard@siskiyous.edu.

DEGREES AND AWARDS

Distance programs offered do not lead to a degree or other formal award.

COURSE SUBJECT AREAS OFFERED OUTSIDE OF DEGREE PROGRAMS

Undergraduate: Business; computer and information sciences; engineering-related technologies; English language and literature; health professions and related sciences; history; psychology; recreation and leisure studies

COLLEGE OF THE SOUTHWEST

Hobbs, New Mexico

College of the Southwest, founded in 1962, is an independent, nonprofit, comprehensive institution. It is accredited by the North Central Association of Colleges and Schools. It first offered distance learning courses in 1994. In 1999–2000, it offered 40 courses at a distance. In fall 1999, there were 52 students enrolled in distance learning courses.
Course delivery sites Courses are delivered to 1 off-campus center in Carlsbad.
Media Courses are delivered via television. Students and teachers may interact via videoconferencing.
Restrictions Programs are available to local area students. Enrollment is open to anyone.

Services Distance learners have access to library services at a distance.
Credit-earning options Students may transfer credits from another institution or may earn credits through examinations, portfolio assessment, military training.
Typical costs *Undergraduate:* Tuition of $143 per semester hour. *Graduate:* Tuition of $150 per semester hour. Costs may vary. Financial aid is available to distance learners.
Registration Students may register by in person.
Contact Glenna Ohaver, Director of Educational Services, College of the Southwest, 6610 Lovington Highway, Hobbs, NM 88240. *Telephone:* 505-392-6561. *Fax:* 505-392-6006.

DEGREES AND AWARDS

MSE Curriculum and Instruction (some on-campus requirements), Educational Administration and Counseling (some on-campus requirements)

COURSE SUBJECT AREAS OFFERED OUTSIDE OF DEGREE PROGRAMS

Undergraduate: Accounting; advertising; area, ethnic, and cultural studies; biology; botany; business; business administration and management; conservation and natural resources; creative writing; developmental and child psychology; economics; education administration; educational psychology; English as a second language (ESL); English composition; English language and literature; fine arts; health and physical education/fitness; history; human resources management; industrial psychology; liberal arts, general studies, and humanities; mathematics; philosophy and religion; political science; social psychology; sociology; special education; teacher education; zoology
Graduate: Education administration; educational psychology

COLLEGE OF WEST VIRGINIA

Beckley, West Virginia

School of Academic Enrichment and Lifelong Learning (SAELL)
www.cwv.edu/saell

College of West Virginia, founded in 1933, is an independent, nonprofit, comprehensive institution. It is accredited by the North Central Association of Colleges and Schools. It first offered distance learning courses in 1992. In 1999–2000, it offered 200 courses at a distance. In fall 1999, there were 508 students enrolled in distance learning courses.
Course delivery sites Courses are delivered to your home, your workplace, military bases.
Media Courses are delivered via videotapes, audiotapes, computer software, CD-ROM, World Wide Web, e-mail, print. Students and teachers may meet in person or interact via mail, telephone, fax, e-mail, World Wide Web.
Restrictions Programs are available worldwide. Enrollment is open to anyone.
Services Distance learners have access to library services, the campus computer network, e-mail services, academic advising, tutoring, career placement assistance, bookstore at a distance.
Credit-earning options Students may transfer credits from another institution or may earn credits through examinations, portfolio assessment, military training, business training.
Typical costs Tuition of $135 per credit hour plus mandatory fees of $25 per credit hour. Financial aid is available to distance learners.
Registration Students may register by mail, fax, telephone, e-mail, World Wide Web, in person.
Contact Karen Carter-Harvey, Assistant Registrar, College of West Virginia, PO Box AG, Beckley, WV 25802-2830. *Telephone:* 304-253-7351 Ext. 1366. *Fax:* 304-256-0917. *E-mail:* saell@cwv.edu.

DEGREES AND AWARDS

Undergraduate Certificate(s) Aviation Technology (certain restrictions apply), Diagnostic Medical Sonography, General Business Management, Office Technology, Travel and Tourism

AA Elementary Teacher Preparation, General Studies, Primary Teacher Preparation, Secondary Teacher Preparation

AS Accounting, Aviation Technology (certain restrictions apply), Business Administration, Business Law, Computer Information Systems, Environmental Studies, General Business, General Studies, Management, Office Management, Secretarial Science, Travel

BS Accounting, Business Administration, Business Law, Computer Information Systems, Criminal Justice, Environmental Studies, General Business, Health Care Management, Interdisciplinary Studies, Legal Studies, Management, Office Management

RN to BSN RN to BSN (certain restrictions apply)

COURSE SUBJECT AREAS OFFERED OUTSIDE OF DEGREE PROGRAMS

Undergraduate: Abnormal psychology; accounting; administrative and secretarial services; advertising; algebra; American (U.S.) history; anatomy; art history and criticism; astronomy and astrophysics; biochemistry; biological and life sciences; biology; business; business administration and management; business law; calculus; chemistry; chemistry, organic; communications; computer and information sciences; corrections; criminal justice; database management; developmental and child psychology; earth science; ecology; economics; English composition; English language and literature; English literature; environmental health; environmental science; ethics; European history; family and marriage counseling; finance; fine arts; geography; geology; health professions and related sciences; health services administration; history; hospitality services management; human resources management; insurance; interdisciplinary studies; international business; labor relations/studies; law and legal studies; liberal arts, general studies, and humanities; logic; management information systems; marketing; mathematics; meteorology; microbiology; music; nursing; organizational behavior studies; philosophy and religion; physical sciences; physics; physiology; political science; psychology; public policy analysis; social psychology; social sciences; social work; sociology; statistics; technical writing

COLORADO CHRISTIAN UNIVERSITY

Lakewood, Colorado
Academic Technologies Group
online.ccu.edu

Colorado Christian University, founded in 1914, is an independent, religious, comprehensive institution. It is accredited by the North Central Association of Colleges and Schools. It first offered distance learning courses in 1999. In 1999–2000, it offered 6 courses at a distance.

Course delivery sites Courses are delivered to your home, your workplace, military bases, off-campus center(s) in Colorado Springs, Fort Collins, Grand Junction, Morrison.

Media Courses are delivered via computer software, CD-ROM, computer conferencing, World Wide Web, e-mail, print. Students and teachers may meet in person or interact via audioconferencing, mail, telephone, fax, e-mail, World Wide Web. The following equipment may be required: computer, modem, Internet access, e-mail.

Restrictions Programs are available worldwide. Enrollment is restricted to individuals meeting certain criteria.

Services Distance learners have access to library services, the campus computer network, e-mail services, academic advising, career placement assistance, bookstore at a distance.

Credit-earning options Students may transfer credits from another institution or may earn credits through portfolio assessment.

Typical costs *Undergraduate:* Mandatory fees of $40 per semester hour. *Graduate:* Mandatory fees of $40 per semester hour. Undergraduate tuition ranges between $225 to $415 per semester hour. Graduate tuition ranges between $250 and $550 per semester hour. Costs may vary. Financial aid is available to distance learners.

Registration Students may register by mail, fax, telephone, e-mail, in person.

Contact Jan Coombs, Technical Assistant, Colorado Christian University, 180 South Garrison Street, Lakewood, CO 80226. *Telephone:* 303-963-3382. *Fax:* 303-963-3381. *E-mail:* ccuonline@ccu.edu.

---

eCollege.com   *www.ecollege.com/scholarships*

DEGREES AND AWARDS

Distance programs offered do not lead to a degree or other formal award.

COURSE SUBJECT AREAS OFFERED OUTSIDE OF DEGREE PROGRAMS

Undergraduate: Business administration and management; curriculum and instruction; English language and literature; European languages and literatures; history; information sciences and systems; mathematics; psychology

Graduate: Accounting; business administration and management; curriculum and instruction; information sciences and systems; marketing

COLORADO ELECTRONIC COMMUNITY COLLEGE

Aurora, Colorado
www.cccoes.edu

Colorado Electronic Community College is a state-supported, 2-year college. It first offered distance learning courses in 1995. In 1999–2000, it offered 300 courses at a distance. In fall 1999, there were 1,200 students enrolled in distance learning courses.

Course delivery sites Courses are delivered to your home, your workplace, military bases.

Media Courses are delivered via videotapes, audiotapes, computer software, World Wide Web, e-mail, print. Students and teachers may interact via videoconferencing, audioconferencing, mail, telephone, fax, e-mail, World Wide Web. The following equipment may be required: television, videocassette player, computer, modem, Internet access, e-mail.

Restrictions Programs are available worldwide. Enrollment is open to anyone.

Services Distance learners have access to library services, e-mail services, academic advising, tutoring, bookstore at a distance.

Credit-earning options Students may transfer credits from another institution or may earn credits through examinations, portfolio assessment, military training, business training.

Typical costs Tuition of $115 per credit hour plus mandatory fees of $70 per course. Costs may vary. Financial aid is available to distance learners.

Registration Students may register by mail, fax, telephone, e-mail, World Wide Web, in person.

Contact John Schmahl, Director of Student Services, Colorado Electronic Community College, 8880 East 10th Place, Building 967, Denver, CO 80230. *Telephone:* 303-365-8807. *Fax:* 303-365-7616. *E-mail:* john.schmahl@heat.cccoes.edu.

DEGREES AND AWARDS

AA Gerontology (certain restrictions apply), Liberal Arts (certain restrictions apply), Public Administration (certain restrictions apply)

AAS Business (certain restrictions apply), Construction Electrician (certain restrictions apply)

COURSE SUBJECT AREAS OFFERED OUTSIDE OF DEGREE PROGRAMS

Undergraduate: Agriculture; algebra; anthropology; astronomy and astrophysics; biological and life sciences; business; child care and development; communications; computer and information sciences; developmental and child psychology; engineering-related technologies; English composition; English language and literature; ethics; geography; geology; history; history of science and technology; mass media; music; physics; psychology; public administration and services; sociology; statistics

See full descriptions on pages 498 and 822.

COLORADO MOUNTAIN COLLEGE DISTRICT

Glenwood Springs, Colorado
Educational Technology/Academic Services
www.coloradomtn.edu

Colorado Mountain College District is a district-supported, system. It is accredited by the North Central Association of Colleges and Schools. It first offered distance learning courses in 1985. In 1999–2000, it offered 76 courses at a distance. In fall 1999, there were 702 students enrolled in distance learning courses.

Course delivery sites Courses are delivered to your home, your workplace, high schools, 13 off-campus centers in Aspen, Breckenridge, Buena Vista, Carbondale, Eagle, Glenwood Springs, Leadville, Rifle, Salida, Silverthorne, Spring Valley, Steamboat Springs, Vail.

Media Courses are delivered via videotapes, videoconferencing, computer software, CD-ROM, World Wide Web, print. Students and teachers may meet in person or interact via videoconferencing, audioconferencing, mail, telephone, fax, e-mail, World Wide Web. The following equipment may be required: television, videocassette player, computer, modem, Internet access, e-mail.

Restrictions Programs are available worldwide. Enrollment is open to anyone.

Services Distance learners have access to library services, the campus computer network, e-mail services, academic advising, tutoring, career placement assistance, bookstore at a distance.

Credit-earning options Students may transfer credits from another institution or may earn credits through examinations, portfolio assessment, military training, business training.

Typical costs Tuition of $46 per semester hour plus mandatory fees of $70 per semester for local area residents. Tuition of $77 per semester hour plus mandatory fees of $70 per semester for in-state residents. Tuition of $215 per semester hour plus mandatory fees of $70 per semester for out-of-state residents. Costs may vary. Financial aid is available to distance learners.

Registration Students may register by mail, fax, telephone, in person.

Contact Prof. Robert J. McGill, Director of Educational Technology, Colorado Mountain College District, 831 Grand Avenue, Glenwood Springs, CO 81601. *Telephone:* 970-947-8345. *Fax:* 970-947-8307. *E-mail:* bmcgill@coloradomtn.edu.

DEGREES AND AWARDS

Distance programs offered do not lead to a degree or other formal award.

COURSE SUBJECT AREAS OFFERED OUTSIDE OF DEGREE PROGRAMS

Undergraduate: Abnormal psychology; accounting; algebra; American literature; anthropology; archaeology; area, ethnic, and cultural studies; art history and criticism; biology; business administration and management; business communications; business law; calculus; chemistry; child care and development; creative writing; criminal justice; developmental and child psychology; drama and theater; earth science; economics; electronics; English as a second language (ESL); English composition; English language and literature; ethics; fine arts; foods and nutrition studies; geography; health and physical education/fitness; history; journalism; liberal arts, general studies, and humanities; marketing; mathematics; philosophy and religion; physics; political science; social psychology; sociology; Spanish language and literature; statistics; teacher education; visual and performing arts

COLORADO STATE UNIVERSITY

Fort Collins, Colorado
Division of Educational Outreach
www.csu2learn.colostate.edu

Colorado State University, founded in 1870, is a state-supported university. It is accredited by the North Central Association of Colleges and Schools. It first offered distance learning courses in 1967. In 1999–2000, it offered 136 courses at a distance. In fall 1999, there were 900 students enrolled in distance learning courses.

Course delivery sites Courses are delivered to your home, your workplace, military bases, 2 off-campus centers in Denver, Fort Collins.

Media Courses are delivered via television, videotapes, videoconferencing, audiotapes, computer software, World Wide Web, print. Students and teachers may meet in person or interact via videoconferencing, mail, telephone, fax, e-mail. The following equipment may be required: television, videocassette player, computer, modem, Internet access, e-mail.

Restrictions Programs are available nationwide. Enrollment is open to anyone.

Services Distance learners have access to library services, the campus computer network, e-mail services, academic advising, bookstore at a distance.

Credit-earning options Students may transfer credits from another institution or may earn credits through examinations.

Typical costs Undergraduate tuition ranges between $150 and $225 per credit hour. Graduate tuition is $416 per credit hour. Financial aid is available to distance learners.

Registration Students may register by mail, fax, telephone, in person.

Contact Student Support Staff, Colorado State University, Division of Educational Outreach, Spruce Hall, Fort Collins, CO 80523-1040. *Telephone:* 877-491-5288. *Fax:* 970-491-7885. *E-mail:* info@learn. colostate.edu.

DEGREES AND AWARDS

Undergraduate Certificate(s) Gerontology, Natural Resources and the Environment

BS Fire Science Management and Training (service area differs from that of the overall institution)

Graduate Certificate(s) Postsecondary Teaching

MAgrSc Agricultural Sciences (service area differs from that of the overall institution)

MBA Business Administration (service area differs from that of the overall institution)

MEd Education (Human Resource Development) (service area differs from that of the overall institution)

MS Bioresources and Agricultural Engineering, Chemical Engineering (service area differs from that of the overall institution), Civil Engineering

Colorado State University

(service area differs from that of the overall institution), Computer Science (service area differs from that of the overall institution), Electrical Engineering (service area differs from that of the overall institution), Environmental Engineering (service area differs from that of the overall institution), Industrial Engineering (service area differs from that of the overall institution), Management (service area differs from that of the overall institution), Mechanical Engineering (service area differs from that of the overall institution), Statistics (service area differs from that of the overall institution), Systems Engineering (service area differs from that of the overall institution)

PhD Electrical Engineering (service area differs from that of the overall institution), Industrial Engineering (service area differs from that of the overall institution), Mechanical Engineering (service area differs from that of the overall institution), Systems Engineering (service area differs from that of the overall institution)

COURSE SUBJECT AREAS OFFERED OUTSIDE OF DEGREE PROGRAMS

Undergraduate: Abnormal psychology; agriculture; animal sciences; child care and development; cognitive psychology; conservation and natural resources; developmental and child psychology; economics; educational psychology; foods and nutrition studies; gerontology; history; home economics and family studies; individual and family development studies; philosophy and religion; plant sciences; psychology; sociology

Graduate: Accounting; agriculture; business; business administration and management; chemical engineering; civil engineering; computer and information sciences; conservation and natural resources; electrical engineering; engineering mechanics; engineering/industrial management; environmental engineering; finance; human resources management; industrial engineering; marketing; mathematics; mechanical engineering; teacher education

See full descriptions on pages 500 and 592.

COLUMBIA BASIN COLLEGE

Pasco, Washington
www.cbc2.org

Columbia Basin College, founded in 1955, is a state-supported, two-year college. It is accredited by the Northwest Association of Schools and Colleges. It first offered distance learning courses in 1985. In 1999–2000, it offered 25 courses at a distance. In fall 1999, there were 400 students enrolled in distance learning courses.

Course delivery sites Courses are delivered to your home, your workplace.

Media Courses are delivered via videotapes, CD-ROM, World Wide Web, e-mail, print. Students and teachers may meet in person or interact via mail, telephone, fax, e-mail, World Wide Web. The following equipment may be required: computer, modem, Internet access, e-mail.

Restrictions Programs are available to local area students. Enrollment is open to anyone.

Services Distance learners have access to library services, the campus computer network, e-mail services, academic advising, tutoring, career placement assistance at a distance.

Credit-earning options Students may transfer credits from another institution or may earn credits through examinations.

Typical costs Tuition of $1450 per year plus mandatory fees of $25 per quarter. Financial aid is available to distance learners.

Registration Students may register by mail, fax, telephone, e-mail, World Wide Web, in person.

Contact Deborah Meadows, Dean for Business/Social Science, Columbia Basin College, 2600 North 20th Avenue, Pasco, WA 99301. *Telephone:* 509-547-0511 Ext. 2373. *Fax:* 509-546-0401. *E-mail:* dmeadows@ctc.edu.

DEGREES AND AWARDS

Distance programs offered do not lead to a degree or other formal award.

COURSE SUBJECT AREAS OFFERED OUTSIDE OF DEGREE PROGRAMS

Undergraduate: Abnormal psychology; accounting; algebra; anthropology; art history and criticism; creative writing; English composition; English language and literature; film studies; psychology; sociology; technical writing

COLUMBIA COLLEGE

Columbia, South Carolina
Evening College
www.columbiacollegesc.edu

Columbia College, founded in 1854, is an independent, religious, comprehensive institution. It is accredited by the Southern Association of Colleges and Schools. It first offered distance learning courses in 1999. In 1999–2000, it offered 7 courses at a distance. In fall 1999, there were 33 students enrolled in distance learning courses.

Course delivery sites Courses are delivered to your home, your workplace.

Media Courses are delivered via World Wide Web, e-mail. Students and teachers may meet in person or interact via mail, telephone, fax, e-mail, World Wide Web. The following equipment may be required: computer, modem, Internet access, e-mail.

Restrictions Programs are available to local area students. Enrollment is open to anyone.

Services Distance learners have access to library services, e-mail services, academic advising, career placement assistance, bookstore at a distance.

Credit-earning options Students may transfer credits from another institution or may earn credits through examinations, portfolio assessment.

Typical costs Tuition of $385 per credit. Financial aid is available to distance learners.

Registration Students may register by mail, fax, World Wide Web, in person.

Contact Dr. Anne M. McCulloch, Dean of the Evening College and External Programs, Columbia College, 1301 Columbia College Drive, Columbia, SC 29203. *Telephone:* 803-786-3788. *Fax:* 803-786-3393. *E-mail:* amcculloch@colacoll.edu.

DEGREES AND AWARDS

Distance programs offered do not lead to a degree or other formal award.

COURSE SUBJECT AREAS OFFERED OUTSIDE OF DEGREE PROGRAMS

Undergraduate: Art history and criticism; Bible studies; business; health and physical education/fitness; history; women's studies

See full description on page 676.

COLUMBIA INTERNATIONAL UNIVERSITY

Columbia, South Carolina
Columbia Extension
www.ciuextension.com

Columbia International University, founded in 1923, is an independent, religious, comprehensive institution. It is accredited by the Accrediting Association of Bible Colleges, Association of Theological Schools in the United States and Canada, Southern Association of Colleges and Schools. It first offered distance learning courses in 1978. In 1999–2000, it offered 52 courses at a distance. In fall 1999, there were 600 students enrolled in distance learning courses.

Course delivery sites Courses are delivered to your home, 2 off-campus centers in St. Pawley's Island, Korntal, Afghanistan.

Media Courses are delivered via videotapes, audiotapes, print. Students and teachers may meet in person or interact via mail, telephone, fax, e-mail.

Restrictions Programs are available worldwide. Enrollment is restricted to individuals meeting certain criteria.

Services Distance learners have access to library services, academic advising, bookstore at a distance.

Credit-earning options Students may transfer credits from another institution or may earn credits through examinations, portfolio assessment.

Typical costs *Undergraduate:* Tuition of $125 per semester hour. *Graduate:* Tuition of $165 per semester hour.

Registration Students may register by mail, fax, telephone, e-mail, World Wide Web, in person.

Contact Director of Admissions, Columbia International University, PO Box 3122, Columbia, SC 29230-3122. *Telephone:* 800-777-2227 Ext. 3024. *Fax:* 803-786-4209. *E-mail:* yesciu@ciu.edu.

DEGREES AND AWARDS

BA General Studies (some on-campus requirements)

Graduate Certificate(s) Biblical Studies

MA Counseling (some on-campus requirements), Intercultural Studies (some on-campus requirements), Leadership for Evangelism and Discipleship (some on-campus requirements), Muslim Studies (some on-campus requirements), Teaching English as a Foreign Language/Intercultural Studies (some on-campus requirements)

MABS Bible (some on-campus requirements), New Testament (some on-campus requirements), Old Testament (some on-campus requirements)

MAR General Theological Studies (some on-campus requirements)

MAT Teaching (some on-campus requirements)

MDiv Divinity (some on-campus requirements)

MEd Christian Education (some on-campus requirements), Education (some on-campus requirements)

DMin Ministry (some on-campus requirements)

COURSE SUBJECT AREAS OFFERED OUTSIDE OF DEGREE PROGRAMS

Undergraduate: Bible studies; theological studies

Graduate: Anthropology; Bible studies; educational psychology; Greek language and literature; history; theological studies

Noncredit: Anthropology; Bible studies; educational psychology; Greek language and literature; history; theological studies

COLUMBIA STATE COMMUNITY COLLEGE

Columbia, Tennessee
Extended Services

Columbia State Community College, founded in 1966, is a state-supported, two-year college. It is accredited by the Southern Association of Colleges and Schools. It first offered distance learning courses in 1994. In 1999–2000, it offered 28 courses at a distance. In fall 1999, there were 600 students enrolled in distance learning courses.

Course delivery sites Courses are delivered to your home, your workplace, Middle Tennessee State University (Murfreesboro), 5 off-campus centers in Clifton, Franklin, Lawrenceburg, Lewisburg, Waverly.

Media Courses are delivered via videotapes, videoconferencing, interactive television, audiotapes, computer software, World Wide Web, print. Students and teachers may interact via videoconferencing, mail, telephone, fax, e-mail. The following equipment may be required: television, videocassette player, computer, modem, Internet access, e-mail.

Restrictions Programs are available to in-state students only. Enrollment is open to anyone.

Services Distance learners have access to library services, the campus computer network, e-mail services at a distance.

Credit-earning options Students may transfer credits from another institution or may earn credits through examinations, military training.

Typical costs Tuition of $599 per semester plus mandatory fees of $58 per semester for in-state residents. Tuition of $2451 per semester plus mandatory fees of $58 per semester for out-of-state residents. Financial aid is available to distance learners.

Registration Students may register by telephone, in person.

Contact Mike Shuler, Dean of Extended Services, Columbia State Community College. *Telephone:* 931-540-2750. *Fax:* 931-540-2796.

DEGREES AND AWARDS

Distance programs offered do not lead to a degree or other formal award.

COURSE SUBJECT AREAS OFFERED OUTSIDE OF DEGREE PROGRAMS

Undergraduate: Accounting; administrative and secretarial services; business; business administration and management; communications; criminal justice; economics; English composition; health and physical education/fitness; liberal arts, general studies, and humanities; mathematics; nursing; philosophy and religion; psychology

COLUMBIA UNIVERSITY

New York, New York
Columbia Video Network
www.cvn.columbia.edu

Columbia University, founded in 1754, is an independent, nonprofit university. It is accredited by the Middle States Association of Colleges and Schools. It first offered distance learning courses in 1986. In 1999–2000, it offered 120 courses at a distance. In fall 1999, there were 310 students enrolled in distance learning courses.

Course delivery sites Courses are delivered to your home, your workplace, National Technological University (Fort Collins, CO).

Media Courses are delivered via videotapes, videoconferencing, computer software, computer conferencing, World Wide Web. Students and teachers may meet in person or interact via telephone, fax, e-mail, World Wide Web. The following equipment may be required: television, videocassette player, computer, modem, Internet access, e-mail.

Columbia University

Restrictions Programs are available worldwide. Enrollment is open to anyone.
Services Distance learners have access to library services, the campus computer network, e-mail services, academic advising, bookstore at a distance.
Credit-earning options Students may transfer credits from another institution.
Typical costs Tuition of $951 per credit. *Noncredit courses:* $530 per course. Financial aid is available to distance learners.
Registration Students may register by mail, fax, telephone, e-mail, World Wide Web, in person.
Contact Kamal Hasan Basri, Associate Director, Columbia University, Columbia Video Network, 540 Mudd Building, MC 4719, 500 West 120th Street, New York, NY 10027. *Telephone:* 212-854-6447. *Fax:* 212-854-2325. *E-mail:* cvn@cvn.columbia.edu.

DEGREES AND AWARDS

Graduate Certificate(s) Computer Science, Engineering
MS Computer Science, Engineering
PD Computer Science, Engineering

COURSE SUBJECT AREAS OFFERED OUTSIDE OF DEGREE PROGRAMS

Graduate: Business; computer and information sciences; computer programming; database management; electrical engineering; engineering; engineering/industrial management; environmental engineering; industrial engineering; information sciences and systems; journalism; mechanical engineering
Noncredit: Business; computer and information sciences; computer programming; database management; electrical engineering; engineering; engineering/industrial management; environmental engineering; industrial engineering; information sciences and systems; journalism; mechanical engineering
See full description on page 502.

See full description on page 502.

COLUMBUS STATE COMMUNITY COLLEGE

Columbus, Ohio
Global Campus
global.cscc.edu

Columbus State Community College, founded in 1963, is a state-supported, two-year college. It is accredited by the North Central Association of Colleges and Schools. It first offered distance learning courses in 1980. In 1999–2000, it offered 90 courses at a distance. In fall 1999, there were 1,500 students enrolled in distance learning courses.
Course delivery sites Courses are delivered to your home, your workplace, 7 off-campus centers in Bolton Field, Dublin, Gahanna, Groveport, Marysville, Westerville.
Media Courses are delivered via television, videotapes, videoconferencing, audiotapes, computer software, CD-ROM, computer conferencing, World Wide Web, e-mail. Students and teachers may interact via videoconferencing, mail, telephone, fax, e-mail, World Wide Web. The following equipment may be required: television, videocassette player, computer, modem, Internet access, e-mail.
Restrictions Programs are available worldwide. Enrollment is open to anyone.
Services Distance learners have access to library services, the campus computer network, e-mail services, academic advising, bookstore at a distance.
Credit-earning options Students may transfer credits from another institution or may earn credits through portfolio assessment.

Typical costs Tuition of $59 per credit plus mandatory fees of $20 per course for in-state residents. Tuition of $130 per credit plus mandatory fees of $20 per course for out-of-state residents. Financial aid is available to distance learners.
Registration Students may register by mail, telephone, World Wide Web, in person.
Contact Tom Erney, Director, Instructional Services, Columbus State Community College. *Telephone:* 614-287-2532. *Fax:* 614-287-5123. *E-mail:* terney@cscc.edu.

DEGREES AND AWARDS

AA General Studies
AAS Business Management

COURSE SUBJECT AREAS OFFERED OUTSIDE OF DEGREE PROGRAMS

Undergraduate: Accounting; American literature; business administration and management; business communications; business law; computer and information sciences; design; economics; English composition; English literature; finance; French language and literature; human resources management; marketing; mathematics; organizational behavior studies; psychology; Spanish language and literature; technical writing

COLUMBUS STATE UNIVERSITY

Columbus, Georgia
Instructional Technology Services
www.colstate.edu

Columbus State University, founded in 1958, is a state-supported, comprehensive institution. It is accredited by the Southern Association of Colleges and Schools. It first offered distance learning courses in 1991. In 1999–2000, it offered 58 courses at a distance.
Course delivery sites Courses are delivered to your home, your workplace, Georgia Southwestern State University (Americus), 3 off-campus centers in Americus, Griffin, Thomaston.
Media Courses are delivered via interactive television, World Wide Web. Students and teachers may meet in person or interact via videoconferencing, mail, telephone, fax, e-mail, World Wide Web. The following equipment may be required: computer, Internet access.
Restrictions Programs involving two-way interactive television courses are limited to in-state students, while web-based courses are available worldwide. Enrollment is restricted to individuals meeting certain criteria.
Services Distance learners have access to library services, the campus computer network, e-mail services, academic advising, bookstore at a distance.
Credit-earning options Students may transfer credits from another institution or may earn credits through examinations.
Typical costs *Undergraduate:* Tuition of $118 per hour for in-state residents. Tuition of $414 per hour for out-of-state residents. *Graduate:* Tuition of $203 per hour for in-state residents. Tuition of $475 per hour for out-of-state residents. Costs may vary. Financial aid is available to distance learners.
Registration Students may register by mail, telephone, in person.
Contact Timothy Daniels, Distance Learning Coordinator, Columbus State University, Instructional Technology Services, 4225 University Avenue, Columbus, GA 31907. *Telephone:* 706-569-3456. *Fax:* 706-568-2459. *E-mail:* daniels_timothy@colstate.edu.

DEGREES AND AWARDS

MS Applied Computer Science (service area differs from that of the overall institution)

COURSE SUBJECT AREAS OFFERED OUTSIDE OF DEGREE PROGRAMS

Undergraduate: Computer programming; curriculum and instruction; teacher education

Graduate: Computer programming; counseling psychology; curriculum and instruction; education administration; educational psychology; teacher education

Noncredit: Real estate

See full description on page 676.

COMMUNITY COLLEGE OF BALTIMORE COUNTY

Catonsville, Maryland

Office of Distance/Extended Learning
www.ccbc.cc.md.us

Community College of Baltimore County, founded in 1957, is a county-supported, two-year college. It is accredited by the Middle States Association of Colleges and Schools. In 1999–2000, it offered 110 courses at a distance. In fall 1999, there were 800 students enrolled in distance learning courses.

Course delivery sites Courses are delivered to your home, your workplace, military bases, high schools, Anna Arundel Community College (Arnold), Baltimore City Community College (Baltimore), Carroll Community College (Westminster), Community College of Baltimore County–Essex Campus (Baltimore), Howard Community College (Columbia), The Community College of Baltimore County–Catonsville Campus (Catonsville), The Community College of Baltimore County–Dundalk Campus (Baltimore), 6 off-campus centers in Baltimore.

Media Courses are delivered via television, videotapes, videoconferencing, interactive television, audiotapes, computer software, CD-ROM, computer conferencing, World Wide Web, e-mail, print. Students and teachers may meet in person or interact via videoconferencing, mail, telephone, fax, e-mail, interactive television, World Wide Web. The following equipment may be required: television, computer, modem, Internet access, e-mail.

Restrictions Programs are available worldwide. Enrollment is open to anyone.

Services Distance learners have access to library services, academic advising, tutoring, bookstore at a distance.

Credit-earning options Students may transfer credits from another institution or may earn credits through examinations, portfolio assessment, military training, business training.

Typical costs Tuition of $65 per credit plus mandatory fees of $10 per credit for local area residents. Tuition of $110 per credit plus mandatory fees of $10 per credit for in-state residents. Tuition of $170 per credit plus mandatory fees of $10 per credit for out-of-state residents. Costs may vary. Financial aid is available to distance learners.

Registration Students may register by mail, fax, telephone, in person.

Contact Aviva Adir, Senior Director, Community College of Baltimore County, Office of Distance/Extended Learning, 800 South Rolling Road, Catonsville, MD 21228. *Telephone:* 410-455-4540. *Fax:* 410-455-6106. *E-mail:* aadir@ccbc.cc.md.us.

DEGREES AND AWARDS

AA Business Administration, General Studies

COURSE SUBJECT AREAS OFFERED OUTSIDE OF DEGREE PROGRAMS

Undergraduate: Area, ethnic, and cultural studies; astronomy and astrophysics; business; business administration and management; communications; creative writing; English language and literature; English literature; European languages and literatures; French language and literature; geology; health and physical education/fitness; history; law and legal studies; liberal arts, general studies, and humanities; marketing; oceanography; philosophy and religion; political science; sociology; Spanish language and literature

---

COMMUNITY COLLEGE OF RHODE ISLAND

Warwick, Rhode Island

Instructional Technology and Distance Education

Community College of Rhode Island, founded in 1964, is a state-supported, two-year college. It is accredited by the New England Association of Schools and Colleges. It first offered distance learning courses in 1982. In 1999–2000, it offered 63 courses at a distance. In fall 1999, there were 820 students enrolled in distance learning courses.

Course delivery sites Courses are delivered to your home.

Media Courses are delivered via television, videotapes. Students and teachers may meet in person or interact via mail, telephone, e-mail. The following equipment may be required: television.

Restrictions Programs are available to in-state students only. Enrollment is restricted to individuals meeting certain criteria.

Services Distance learners have access to e-mail services at a distance.

Credit-earning options Students may transfer credits from another institution or may earn credits through examinations, portfolio assessment, military training, business training.

Typical costs Tuition of $75 per credit plus mandatory fees of $4 per credit for in-state residents. Tuition of $224 per credit plus mandatory fees of $4 per credit for out-of-state residents. Students pay an additional $21 per semester in fees. *Noncredit courses:* $220 per course. Financial aid is available to distance learners.

Registration Students may register by mail, telephone, in person.

Contact Philip J. Sisson, Assistant Dean of Academic Affairs, Community College of Rhode Island, Academic Affairs Office, Providence Campus, One Hilton Street, Providence, RI 02905. *Telephone:* 401-455-6113. *Fax:* 401-455-5190. *E-mail:* pssison@ccri.cc.ri.us.

DEGREES AND AWARDS

Distance programs offered do not lead to a degree or other formal award.

COURSE SUBJECT AREAS OFFERED OUTSIDE OF DEGREE PROGRAMS

Undergraduate: Biological and life sciences; business administration and management; classical languages and literatures; developmental and child psychology; economics; English composition; English language and literature; health and physical education/fitness; history; law and legal studies; liberal arts, general studies, and humanities; mathematics; philosophy and religion; political science; psychology; sociology

COMMUNITY HOSPITAL OF ROANOKE VALLEY–COLLEGE OF HEALTH SCIENCES

Roanoke, Virginia
www.chs.edu

Community Hospital of Roanoke Valley–College of Health Sciences, founded in 1982, is an independent, nonprofit, four-year college. It is accredited by the Southern Association of Colleges and Schools. In 1999–2000, it offered 15 courses at a distance. In fall 1999, there were 80 students enrolled in distance learning courses.

Course delivery sites Courses are delivered to your home, your workplace.

Media Courses are delivered via videotapes, CD-ROM, World Wide Web, e-mail, print. Students and teachers may meet in person or interact via mail, telephone, e-mail, World Wide Web.

Restrictions Programs are available worldwide. Enrollment is restricted to individuals meeting certain criteria.

Services Distance learners have access to library services, e-mail services, academic advising at a distance.

Credit-earning options Students may transfer credits from another institution or may earn credits through examinations.

Typical costs Tuition of $190 per credit hour for in-state residents. Costs may vary. Financial aid is available to distance learners.

Registration Students may register by mail, in person.

Contact Bridget Franklin, Director of Distance Learning, Community Hospital of Roanoke Valley–College of Health Sciences, PO Box 13186, Roanoke, VA 24031. *Telephone:* 540-985-4046. *Fax:* 540-985-9773. *E-mail:* bfranklin@health.chs.edu.

DEGREES AND AWARDS

Distance programs offered do not lead to a degree or other formal award.

COURSE SUBJECT AREAS OFFERED OUTSIDE OF DEGREE PROGRAMS

Undergraduate: Anatomy; biology; English language and literature; health professions and related sciences; interdisciplinary studies; philosophy and religion; psychology; sociology; statistics

CONCORDIA COLLEGE

Bronxville, New York

CUENET (Concordia University Education Network)
www.concordia-ny.edu

Concordia College, founded in 1881, is an independent, religious, four-year college. It is accredited by the Middle States Association of Colleges and Schools. It first offered distance learning courses in 1995. In 1999–2000, it offered 6 courses at a distance. In fall 1999, there were 40 students enrolled in distance learning courses.

Course delivery sites Courses are delivered to high schools, Concordia College (Ann Arbor, MI).

Media Courses are delivered via videoconferencing, interactive television. Students and teachers may interact via videoconferencing, mail, telephone, fax, e-mail, interactive television.

Restrictions Programs are available nationwide. Enrollment is restricted to individuals meeting certain criteria.

Services Distance learners have access to library services, e-mail services at a distance.

Typical costs Tuition of $388 per credit. *Noncredit courses:* $90 per course. Costs may vary.

Registration Students may register by mail, in person.

Contact Mark Blanco, Registrar, Concordia College, 171 White Plains Road, Bronxville, NY 10708. *Telephone:* 914-337-9300 Ext. 2103. *Fax:* 914-395-4500. *E-mail:* meb@concordia-ny.edu.

DEGREES AND AWARDS

Distance programs offered do not lead to a degree or other formal award.

COURSE SUBJECT AREAS OFFERED OUTSIDE OF DEGREE PROGRAMS

Undergraduate: Business communications; philosophy and religion; psychology

CONCORDIA COLLEGE

Ann Arbor, Michigan

Concordia College, founded in 1963, is an independent, religious, four-year college affiliated with the Lutheran Church–Missouri Synod. It is accredited by the North Central Association of Colleges and Schools. It first offered distance learning courses in 1996. In 1999–2000, it offered 4 courses at a distance. In fall 1999, there were 31 students enrolled in distance learning courses.

Course delivery sites Courses are delivered to high schools, Concordia College (Selma, AL), Concordia College (Bronxville, NY), Concordia College (Ann Arbor), Concordia University (Seward, NE), Concordia University (River Forest, IL), Concordia University (Portland, OR), Concordia University (Irvine, CA), Concordia University at Austin (Austin, TX), Concordia University at St. Paul (St. Paul, MN), Concordia University Wisconsin (Mequon, WI).

Media Courses are delivered via videoconferencing, interactive television, World Wide Web. Students and teachers may interact via videoconferencing, telephone, e-mail, interactive television. The following equipment may be required: computer, Internet access, e-mail.

Restrictions Programs are available nationwide. Enrollment is open to anyone.

Services Distance learners have access to library services, the campus computer network, e-mail services, academic advising, tutoring, career placement assistance, bookstore at a distance.

Credit-earning options Students may transfer credits from another institution or may earn credits through examinations.

Typical costs Tuition of $420 per credit hour. Financial aid is available to distance learners.

Registration Students may register by mail, fax, telephone, in person.

Contact Prof. Richard Buesing, Director, AV Services, Concordia College, 4090 Geddes Road, Ann Arbor, MI 48105. *Telephone:* 734-995-7354. *Fax:* 734-995-7405. *E-mail:* buesir@ccaa.edu.

DEGREES AND AWARDS

Distance programs offered do not lead to a degree or other formal award.

COURSE SUBJECT AREAS OFFERED OUTSIDE OF DEGREE PROGRAMS

Undergraduate: American (U.S.) history; chemistry, organic; psychology; religious studies; teacher education

CONCORDIA UNIVERSITY AT ST. PAUL

St. Paul, Minnesota
School of Human Services
www.csp.edu/hspd

Concordia University at St. Paul, founded in 1893, is an independent, religious, comprehensive institution affiliated with the Lutheran Church–Missouri Synod. It is accredited by the North Central Association of Colleges and Schools. It first offered distance learning courses in 1997. In 1999–2000, it offered 125 courses at a distance. In fall 1999, there were 170 students enrolled in distance learning courses.
Course delivery sites Courses are delivered to your home, your workplace, military bases.
Media Courses are delivered via videotapes, audiotapes, computer conferencing, World Wide Web, e-mail, print. Students and teachers may meet in person or interact via videoconferencing, mail, telephone, fax, e-mail, World Wide Web. The following equipment may be required: television, videocassette player, computer, modem, Internet access, e-mail.
Restrictions Programs are available worldwide. Enrollment is restricted to individuals meeting certain criteria.
Services Distance learners have access to library services, the campus computer network, e-mail services, academic advising, tutoring, bookstore at a distance.
Credit-earning options Students may transfer credits from another institution or may earn credits through examinations, portfolio assessment, military training, business training.
Typical costs *Undergraduate:* Tuition of $205 per credit. *Graduate:* Tuition of $240 per credit. *Noncredit courses:* $125 per course. Financial aid is available to distance learners.
Registration Students may register by mail, fax, telephone, e-mail, World Wide Web, in person.
Contact Polly Prendergast, Program Representative, Concordia University at St. Paul, 275 Syndicate Street North, St. Paul, MN 55104. *Telephone:* 800-211-3370. *Fax:* 651-603-6144. *E-mail:* gradstudies@csp.edu.

DEGREES AND AWARDS

BA Child Development (some on-campus requirements), Human Services (some on-campus requirements), School Age Care (some on-campus requirements), Youth Development (some on-campus requirements)
BACJ Criminal Justice (some on-campus requirements)
MAE Early Childhood (some on-campus requirements), Parish Education (some on-campus requirements), School-Age Care (some on-campus requirements), Youth Development (some on-campus requirements)

COURSE SUBJECT AREAS OFFERED OUTSIDE OF DEGREE PROGRAMS

Undergraduate: Child care and development; computer and information sciences; developmental and child psychology; English composition; fine arts; sociology

CONCORDIA UNIVERSITY WISCONSIN

Mequon, Wisconsin
Continuing Education Division/Distance Education
www.cuw.edu

Concordia University Wisconsin, founded in 1881, is an independent, religious, comprehensive institution affiliated with the Lutheran Church–Missouri Synod. It is accredited by the North Central Association of Colleges and Schools. It first offered distance learning courses in 1992. In 1999–2000, it offered 15 courses at a distance. In fall 1999, there were 300 students enrolled in distance learning courses.
Course delivery sites Courses are delivered to your home.
Media Courses are delivered via videotapes, audiotapes. Students and teachers may interact via mail, telephone, fax, e-mail. The following equipment may be required: television, videocassette player.
Restrictions Programs are available worldwide. Enrollment is open to anyone.
Services Distance learners have access to library services, e-mail services, academic advising, bookstore at a distance.
Credit-earning options Students may transfer credits from another institution.
Typical costs Tuition of $645 per course. Financial aid is available to distance learners.
Registration Students may register by mail, fax, telephone, in person.
Contact Sarah Weaver, Coordinator for Distance Learning, Concordia University Wisconsin, 12800 North Lake Shore Drive, Mequon, WI 53097. *Telephone:* 262-243-4400. *Fax:* 262-243-4459. *E-mail:* sarah.weaver@cuw.edu.

DEGREES AND AWARDS

MBA Business Administration
MS Curriculum and Instruction, Education Administration, Education Counseling, Reading
MSN Nursing

COURSE SUBJECT AREAS OFFERED OUTSIDE OF DEGREE PROGRAMS

Undergraduate: Abnormal psychology; anthropology; area, ethnic, and cultural studies; art history and criticism; chemistry; earth science; English composition; English language and literature; European history; European languages and literatures; geography; history; liberal arts, general studies, and humanities; philosophy and religion; religious studies; Spanish language and literature
Graduate: Area, ethnic, and cultural studies; business administration and management; chemistry; curriculum and instruction; education; English composition; English language and literature; European languages and literatures; history; liberal arts, general studies, and humanities; nursing; philosophy and religion; student counseling

CONNECTICUT STATE UNIVERSITY SYSTEM

Hartford, Connecticut
OnlineCSU
onlinecsu.ctstateu.edu

Connecticut State University System is a state-supported, system. It is accredited by the New England Association of Schools and Colleges. It first offered distance learning courses in 1998. In 1999–2000, it offered 118 courses at a distance. In fall 1999, there were 377 students enrolled in distance learning courses.
Course delivery sites Courses are delivered to your home, your workplace, military bases, high schools.
Media Courses are delivered via World Wide Web, e-mail. Students and teachers may meet in person or interact via mail, telephone, fax, e-mail, World Wide Web. The following equipment may be required: computer, modem, Internet access, e-mail.
Restrictions Programs are available worldwide. Enrollment is open to anyone.
Services Distance learners have access to library services, the campus computer network, e-mail services, academic advising, tutoring, bookstore at a distance.

Typical costs *Undergraduate:* Tuition of $190 per credit plus mandatory fees of $25 per course. *Graduate:* Tuition of $190 per credit plus mandatory fees of $25 per course. Costs may vary. Financial aid is available to distance learners.

Registration Students may register by World Wide Web.

Contact Amy Feest, Public Relations Director, Connecticut State University System, 39 Woodland Street, Hartford, CT 16105. *Telephone:* 860-493-0021. *Fax:* 860-493-0120. *E-mail:* feesta@sysoff.ctstateu.edu.

---

eCollege.com   *www.ecollege.com/scholarships*

DEGREES AND AWARDS

MLS Library Science

COURSE SUBJECT AREAS OFFERED OUTSIDE OF DEGREE PROGRAMS

Undergraduate: Accounting; American literature; anthropology; Asian studies; computer programming; continuing education; curriculum and instruction; database management; drama and theater; education administration; educational research; English composition; health and physical education/fitness; history; information sciences and systems; instructional media; law and legal studies; liberal arts, general studies, and humanities; library and information studies; management information systems; marketing; mechanical engineering; nursing; organizational behavior studies; philosophy and religion; psychology; social sciences; sociology; statistics; teacher education

Graduate: Accounting; American literature; anthropology; Asian studies; computer programming; continuing education; curriculum and instruction; database management; drama and theater; education administration; educational research; English composition; health and physical education/fitness; history; information sciences and systems; instructional media; law and legal studies; liberal arts, general studies, and humanities; library and information studies; management information systems; marketing; mechanical engineering; nursing; organizational behavior studies; philosophy and religion; psychology; social sciences; sociology; statistics; teacher education

See full description on page 504.

CONNORS STATE COLLEGE

Warner, Oklahoma
Academics and Technology
www.connors.cc.ok.us

Connors State College, founded in 1908, is a state-supported, two-year college. It is accredited by the North Central Association of Colleges and Schools. It first offered distance learning courses in 1997. In 1999–2000, it offered 22 courses at a distance. In fall 1999, there were 200 students enrolled in distance learning courses.

Course delivery sites Courses are delivered to Carl Albert State College (Poteau), Eastern Oklahoma State College (Wilburton), Murray State College (Tishomingo), 1 off-campus center in Muskogee.

Media Courses are delivered via videotapes, videoconferencing, interactive television, computer software, World Wide Web, e-mail. Students and teachers may interact via videoconferencing, mail, telephone, fax, e-mail, World Wide Web. The following equipment may be required: computer, modem, Internet access, e-mail.

Restrictions Programs are available to in-state students only. Enrollment is open to anyone.

Services Distance learners have access to library services, bookstore at a distance.

Credit-earning options Students may transfer credits from another institution or may earn credits through examinations.

Typical costs Tuition of $42.75 per hour for in-state residents. Tuition of $108.75 per hour for out-of-state residents. Costs may vary. Financial aid is available to distance learners.

Registration Students may register by mail, in person.

Contact Dr. Jo Lynn Autry Digranes, Vice President for Academics and Technology, Connors State College, RR 1, Box 1000, Warner, OK 74469. *Telephone:* 918-463-2931. *Fax:* 918-463-2233. *E-mail:* jdigranes@connors.cc.ok.us.

DEGREES AND AWARDS

Distance programs offered do not lead to a degree or other formal award.

COURSE SUBJECT AREAS OFFERED OUTSIDE OF DEGREE PROGRAMS

Undergraduate: Agricultural economics; animal sciences; art history and criticism; business; criminal justice; geography; mathematics; physical sciences; political science; psychology; sociology; Spanish language and literature

---

COPIAH-LINCOLN COMMUNITY COLLEGE

Wesson, Mississippi
www.colin.cc.ms.us/

Copiah-Lincoln Community College, founded in 1928, is a state and locally supported, two-year college. It is accredited by the Southern Association of Colleges and Schools. It first offered distance learning courses in 1995. In 1999–2000, it offered 8 courses at a distance. In fall 1999, there were 125 students enrolled in distance learning courses.

Course delivery sites Courses are delivered to your home, your workplace, Jackson State University (Jackson), Mississippi State University (Mississippi State), University of Mississippi Medical Center (Jackson).

Media Courses are delivered via television, videotapes, videoconferencing, computer software, World Wide Web, e-mail, print. Students and teachers may meet in person or interact via videoconferencing, mail, telephone, fax, e-mail, World Wide Web. The following equipment may be required: computer, modem, Internet access, e-mail.

Restrictions Programs are available to in-state students only. Enrollment is open to anyone.

Services Distance learners have access to library services, the campus computer network, e-mail services, academic advising at a distance.

Credit-earning options Students may transfer credits from another institution or may earn credits through examinations, military training, business training.

Typical costs Tuition of $500 per semester for local area residents. Tuition of $500 per semester for in-state residents. Tuition of $1220 per semester for out-of-state residents. *Noncredit courses:* $45 per course. Costs may vary. Financial aid is available to distance learners.

Registration Students may register by mail, fax, telephone, in person.

Contact Paul Johnson, Dean, Copiah-Lincoln Community College, Wesson, MS 39191. *Telephone:* 601-643-8306. *Fax:* 601-643-8213. *E-mail:* paul.johnson@colin.cc.ms.us.

DEGREES AND AWARDS

Distance programs offered do not lead to a degree or other formal award.

COURSE SUBJECT AREAS OFFERED OUTSIDE OF DEGREE PROGRAMS

Undergraduate: Algebra; biology; communications; computer and information sciences; English composition; English language and literature; music; Spanish language and literature

COPPIN STATE COLLEGE

Baltimore, Maryland

Office of Academic Affairs/Masters of Education in Curriculum and Instruction Via Distance Learning

Coppin State College, founded in 1900, is a state-supported, comprehensive institution. It is accredited by the Middle States Association of Colleges and Schools. It first offered distance learning courses in 1998. In fall 1999, there were 107 students enrolled in distance learning courses.
Course delivery sites Courses are delivered to your home, your workplace, high schools, 1 off-campus center in Aberdeen.
Media Courses are delivered via videotapes, interactive television, World Wide Web, e-mail, print. Students and teachers may meet in person or interact via mail, telephone, fax, e-mail, interactive television. The following equipment may be required: television, videocassette player, computer, Internet access, e-mail.
Restrictions Programs are available in most states in the southeast region. Enrollment is restricted to individuals meeting certain criteria.
Services Distance learners have access to library services, academic advising, career placement assistance at a distance.
Credit-earning options Students may transfer credits from another institution or may earn credits through examinations.
Typical costs Tuition for the Masters of Education in Curriculum and Instruction via Distance Learning is $149 per credit. Financial aid is available to distance learners.
Registration Students may register by mail, fax, in person.
Contact Dr. Richard Rembold, Associate Vice President for Academic Affairs, Coppin State College, 2500 West North Avenue, Baltimore, MD 21216-3698. *Telephone:* 410-383-5953. *Fax:* 410-383-1221. *E-mail:* rrembold@coppin.edu.

DEGREES AND AWARDS

BS Special Education (certain restrictions apply)
MEd Curriculum and Instruction, Special Education (certain restrictions apply)

COURSE SUBJECT AREAS OFFERED OUTSIDE OF DEGREE PROGRAMS

Undergraduate: Special education
Graduate: Curriculum and instruction; special education

CORNING COMMUNITY COLLEGE

Corning, New York

Open Learning Program
www.corning-cc.edu

Corning Community College, founded in 1956, is a state and locally supported, two-year college. It is accredited by the Middle States Association of Colleges and Schools. It first offered distance learning courses in 1996. In 1999–2000, it offered 24 courses at a distance. In fall 1999, there were 210 students enrolled in distance learning courses.

Course delivery sites Courses are delivered to your home, your workplace, high schools, 9 off-campus centers in Addison, Arkport, Avoca, BOCES-Coopers Center, BOCES-Wildwood, Canaseraga, Hammondsport, Plattsburgh.
Media Courses are delivered via television, videoconferencing, World Wide Web. Students and teachers may interact via videoconferencing, e-mail, interactive television, World Wide Web. The following equipment may be required: computer, Internet access.
Restrictions Interactive video programs are available over a closed network only in the local area. Enrollment is open to anyone.
Services Distance learners have access to library services, e-mail services, career placement assistance at a distance.
Credit-earning options Students may transfer credits from another institution or may earn credits through examinations, portfolio assessment, military training.
Typical costs Tuition of $105 per credit for in-state residents. Tuition of $315 per credit for out-of-state residents. Financial aid is available to distance learners.
Registration Students may register by telephone, in person.
Contact Office of Registration and Records, Corning Community College, 1 Academic Drive, Corning, NY 14830. *Telephone:* 607-962-9230.

DEGREES AND AWARDS

Distance programs offered do not lead to a degree or other formal award.

COURSE SUBJECT AREAS OFFERED OUTSIDE OF DEGREE PROGRAMS

Undergraduate: Accounting; business administration and management; classical languages and literatures; English composition; English language and literature; health and physical education/fitness; journalism; liberal arts, general studies, and humanities; mathematics; psychology; social sciences

COSSATOT TECHNICAL COLLEGE

DeQueen, Arkansas

Division of Distance Education
cossatot.ctc.tec.ar.us

Cossatot Technical College is a state-supported, two-year college. It is accredited by the North Central Association of Colleges and Schools. It first offered distance learning courses in 1996. In 1999–2000, it offered 50 courses at a distance. In fall 1999, there were 260 students enrolled in distance learning courses.
Course delivery sites Courses are delivered to your home, your workplace, military bases, high schools, 2 off-campus centers in Ashdown, Nashville.
Media Courses are delivered via television, videotapes, audiotapes, computer software, CD-ROM, computer conferencing, World Wide Web, e-mail, print. Students and teachers may meet in person or interact via mail, telephone, fax, e-mail, World Wide Web. The following equipment may be required: television, videocassette player, computer, modem, Internet access, e-mail.
Restrictions Programs are available worldwide. Enrollment is restricted to individuals meeting certain criteria.
Services Distance learners have access to library services, the campus computer network, e-mail services, academic advising, tutoring, career placement assistance, bookstore at a distance.
Credit-earning options Students may transfer credits from another institution or may earn credits through examinations, portfolio assessment, military training, business training.
Typical costs Tuition of $40 per semester hour plus mandatory fees of $37 per term for in-state residents. Tuition of $120 per semester hour plus

mandatory fees of $37 per term for out-of-state residents. Costs may vary. Financial aid is available to distance learners.

Registration Students may register by mail, fax, telephone, e-mail, World Wide Web, in person.

Contact Donald W. Park, Director, Cossatot Technical College, PO Box 960, DeQueen, AR 71832. *Telephone:* 870-584-4471. *Fax:* 870-642-3320. *E-mail:* dpark@cossatot.ctc.tec.ar.us.

DEGREES AND AWARDS

AD General Studies

COURSE SUBJECT AREAS OFFERED OUTSIDE OF DEGREE PROGRAMS

Undergraduate: Algebra; American (U.S.) history; art history and criticism; business administration and management; business communications; business law; child care and development; community health services; comparative literature; computer programming; database management; developmental and child psychology; ecology; economics; English composition; English language and literature; environmental science; European history; finance; fine arts; foods and nutrition studies; geography; health and physical education/fitness; human resources management; information sciences and systems; international business; international relations; investments and securities; journalism; management information systems; marketing; music; philosophy and religion; physical sciences; psychology; sociology; Spanish language and literature; statistics

See full description on page 676.

COUNTY COLLEGE OF MORRIS

Randolph, New Jersey

Professional Programs and Distance Education
www.ccm.edu

County College of Morris, founded in 1966, is a county-supported, two-year college. It is accredited by the Middle States Association of Colleges and Schools. It first offered distance learning courses in 1979. In 1999–2000, it offered 42 courses at a distance. In fall 1999, there were 445 students enrolled in distance learning courses.

Course delivery sites Courses are delivered to your home, your workplace, military bases, high schools, 3 off-campus centers in Boonton, Morristown, Parsippany.

Media Courses are delivered via television, videotapes, interactive television, audiotapes, World Wide Web, e-mail. Students and teachers may meet in person or interact via mail, telephone, fax, e-mail. The following equipment may be required: television, videocassette player, computer, Internet access, e-mail.

Restrictions Programs are available to local area students. Enrollment is open to anyone.

Services Distance learners have access to library services, the campus computer network, e-mail services, bookstore at a distance.

Credit-earning options Students may transfer credits from another institution or may earn credits through examinations.

Typical costs Tuition of $67 per credit plus mandatory fees of $10 per credit for local area residents. Tuition of $134 per credit plus mandatory fees of $10 per credit for in-state residents. Tuition of $184 per credit plus mandatory fees of $10 per credit for out-of-state residents. Costs may vary. Financial aid is available to distance learners.

Registration Students may register by mail, fax, telephone, in person.

Contact Mary Ann McGowan, Coordinator of Distance Learning, County College of Morris. *Telephone:* 973-328-5184. *Fax:* 973-328-5082. *E-mail:* mcgowan@ccm.edu.

DEGREES AND AWARDS

AA Humanities (some on-campus requirements)

COURSE SUBJECT AREAS OFFERED OUTSIDE OF DEGREE PROGRAMS

Undergraduate: Business administration and management; chemistry; developmental and child psychology; economics; English composition; health and physical education/fitness; history; music; political science; sociology

See full description on page 600.

COVENANT THEOLOGICAL SEMINARY

St. Louis, Missouri

External Studies Office
www.covenantseminary.edu

Covenant Theological Seminary, founded in 1956, is an independent, religious, graduate institution. It is accredited by the Association of Theological Schools in the United States and Canada, North Central Association of Colleges and Schools. It first offered distance learning courses in 1988. In 1999–2000, it offered 18 courses at a distance. In fall 1999, there were 212 students enrolled in distance learning courses.

Course delivery sites Courses are delivered to your home, your workplace, 15 off-campus centers in Artesia (CA), Atlanta (GA), Chattanooga (TN), Houston (TX), Lincoln (NE), Memphis (TN), Miami (FL), Nashville (TN), Tucson (AZ).

Media Courses are delivered via videotapes, audiotapes, print. Students and teachers may interact via audioconferencing, mail, telephone, fax, e-mail. The following equipment may be required: television, videocassette player.

Restrictions Programs are available worldwide. Enrollment is restricted to individuals meeting certain criteria.

Services Distance learners have access to library services, e-mail services, academic advising, tutoring, bookstore at a distance.

Credit-earning options Students may transfer credits from another institution or may earn credits through examinations.

Typical costs Tuition of $155 per credit. Cost for noncredit course is $85 per unit hour. Costs may vary. Financial aid is available to distance learners.

Registration Students may register by mail, fax, telephone, e-mail, in person.

Contact Lois M. Gilchrist, Director of Seminary Extension Training, Covenant Theological Seminary, 12330 Conway Road, St. Louis, MO 63141. *Telephone:* 800-264-8064. *Fax:* 314-434-4819. *E-mail:* admissions@covenantseminary.edu.

DEGREES AND AWARDS

Graduate Certificate(s) Theology (certain restrictions apply)
MA Theology (certain restrictions apply; service area differs from that of the overall institution)

COURSE SUBJECT AREAS OFFERED OUTSIDE OF DEGREE PROGRAMS

Graduate: Communications; philosophy and religion; theological studies
Noncredit: Communications; philosophy and religion; theological studies

CRAVEN COMMUNITY COLLEGE

New Bern, North Carolina
www.craven.cc.nc.us/

Craven Community College, founded in 1965, is a state-supported, two-year college. It is accredited by the Southern Association of Colleges and Schools.

Contact Craven Community College, 800 College Court, New Bern, NC 28562-4984. *Telephone:* 252-638-4131. *Fax:* 252-638-4649.

See full description on page 676.

CROWN COLLEGE

St. Bonifacius, Minnesota
Crown Adult Programs
www.crown.edu

Crown College, founded in 1916, is an independent, religious, comprehensive institution affiliated with The Christian and Missionary Alliance. It is accredited by the Accrediting Association of Bible Colleges, North Central Association of Colleges and Schools. It first offered distance learning courses in 1999. In 1999–2000, it offered 10 courses at a distance.

Course delivery sites Courses are delivered to your home.

Media Courses are delivered via videotapes, computer software, CD-ROM, computer conferencing, World Wide Web, e-mail, print. Students and teachers may meet in person or interact via mail, telephone, fax, e-mail, World Wide Web. The following equipment may be required: television, videocassette player, computer, modem, Internet access, e-mail.

Restrictions Programs are available worldwide. Enrollment is restricted to individuals meeting certain criteria.

Services Distance learners have access to library services, the campus computer network, e-mail services, academic advising, bookstore at a distance.

Credit-earning options Students may transfer credits from another institution or may earn credits through examinations, portfolio assessment, military training, business training.

Typical costs *Undergraduate:* Tuition of $273 per semester credit. *Graduate:* Tuition of $195 per semester credit. Financial aid is available to distance learners.

Registration Students may register by mail, fax, telephone, e-mail, World Wide Web, in person.

Contact Crown Adult Programs, Crown College, 6425 County 30, St. Bonifacius, MN 55375. *Telephone:* 612-446-4300. *Fax:* 612-446-4149. *E-mail:* cap@crown.edu.

eCollege.com *www.ecollege.com/scholarships*

DEGREES AND AWARDS

BS Christian Ministry (certain restrictions apply)
MA Church Leadership (certain restrictions apply; some on-campus requirements), Ethnomusicology (certain restrictions apply; some on-campus requirements), Missiology (certain restrictions apply; some on-campus requirements)

COURSE SUBJECT AREAS OFFERED OUTSIDE OF DEGREE PROGRAMS

Undergraduate: Bible studies; philosophy and religion; religious studies; theological studies

Graduate: Bible studies; philosophy and religion; religious studies; theological studies

CTS UNIVERSITY, INC.

Phoenix, Arizona
www.ctsunetworld.com

In 1999–2000, it offered 45 courses at a distance. In fall 1999, there were 200 students enrolled in distance learning courses.

Course delivery sites Courses are delivered to your home, your workplace, military bases.

Media Courses are delivered via videoconferencing, computer software, CD-ROM, computer conferencing, World Wide Web, e-mail, print. Students and teachers may interact via videoconferencing, audioconferencing, mail, e-mail, interactive television, World Wide Web. The following equipment may be required: computer, modem, Internet access, e-mail.

Restrictions Programs are available worldwide. Enrollment is open to anyone.

Services Distance learners have access to library services, the campus computer network, e-mail services, academic advising, tutoring, bookstore at a distance.

Credit-earning options Students may transfer credits from another institution or may earn credits through examinations.

Typical costs Tuition ranges from $299 to $999 per course for undergraduate, graduate and professional students.

Registration Students may register by mail, fax, telephone, e-mail, World Wide Web, in person.

Contact Dr. Charles Shively, Vice President and Chief Learning Officer, CTS University, Inc., 777 East Missouri Avenue, Suite 200, Phoenix, AZ 85014. *Telephone:* 602-287-7700. *Fax:* 602-274-0797. *E-mail:* charles. shively@ctssw.com.

eCollege.com *www.ecollege.com/scholarships*

DEGREES AND AWARDS

Undergraduate Certificate(s) Computer and Information Sciences, Computer Programming, Database Management, Information Sciences and Systems
AA Computer and Information Sciences, Computer Programming, Database Management, Information Sciences and Systems

COURSE SUBJECT AREAS OFFERED OUTSIDE OF DEGREE PROGRAMS

Undergraduate: Computer and information sciences; computer programming; database management; education; information sciences and systems; management information systems; teacher education
Noncredit: Business; business administration and management; business communications; computer and information sciences; computer programming; database management; education; human resources management; information sciences and systems; management information systems; teacher education

CULINARY INSTITUTE OF AMERICA·

Hyde Park, New York
CIA Self Study Programs
www.ciachef.edu

Culinary Institute of America, founded in 1946, is an independent, nonprofit, four-year college. It is accredited by the Accrediting Commission for Career Schools and Colleges of Technology, Middle States Association of Colleges and Schools (candidate). In 1999–2000, it offered 6 courses at a distance.

Course delivery sites Courses are delivered to your home, your workplace.

Media Courses are delivered via videotapes, print. Students and teachers may interact via mail, fax, e-mail. The following equipment may be required: television, videocassette player, computer, Internet access.

Restrictions Programs are available worldwide. Enrollment is restricted to individuals meeting certain criteria.

Services Distance learners have access to e-mail services at a distance.

Typical costs Tuition ranges between $200 and $600 per course. *Noncredit courses:* $525 per course. Costs may vary.

Registration Students may register by mail, fax, telephone, e-mail, in person.

Contact Continuing Education Department, Culinary Institute of America, Customer Service Representative, 433 Albany Post Road, Hide Park, NY 12538. *Telephone:* 800-888-7850. *Fax:* 914-451-1066.

DEGREES AND AWARDS

Distance programs offered do not lead to a degree or other formal award.

COURSE SUBJECT AREAS OFFERED OUTSIDE OF DEGREE PROGRAMS

Noncredit: Food products operations; foods and nutrition studies; management

CUMBERLAND COUNTY COLLEGE

Vineland, New Jersey

Multimedia and Distance Learning Services
www.cccnj.net

Cumberland County College, founded in 1963, is a state and locally supported, two-year college. It is accredited by the Middle States Association of Colleges and Schools. It first offered distance learning courses in 1990. In 1999–2000, it offered 30 courses at a distance. In fall 1999, there were 250 students enrolled in distance learning courses.

Course delivery sites Courses are delivered to your home, your workplace.

Media Courses are delivered via television, videotapes, videoconferencing, World Wide Web. Students and teachers may meet in person or interact via mail, telephone, fax, e-mail, World Wide Web. The following equipment may be required: television, videocassette player, computer, modem, Internet access, e-mail.

Restrictions Programs are available to local area students. Enrollment is open to anyone.

Services Distance learners have access to library services, e-mail services at a distance.

Credit-earning options Students may transfer credits from another institution or may earn credits through examinations.

Typical costs Tuition of $67 per credit plus mandatory fees of $25 per course for local area residents. Tuition of $140 per credit plus mandatory fees of $25 per course for in-state residents. Financial aid is available to distance learners.

Registration Students may register by mail, telephone, in person.

Contact Amar Madineni, Assistant Dean of Instruction, Cumberland County College, PO Box 517, College Drive, Vineland, NJ 08362. *Telephone:* 856-691-8600 Ext. 341. *Fax:* 856-691-9489. *E-mail:* amar@cccnj.net.

DEGREES AND AWARDS

Distance programs offered do not lead to a degree or other formal award.

COURSE SUBJECT AREAS OFFERED OUTSIDE OF DEGREE PROGRAMS

Undergraduate: Abnormal psychology; adult education; anthropology; biology; business administration and management; computer programming; creative writing; economics; English composition; English language and literature; history; hospitality services management; human resources management; information sciences and systems; mass media; mathematics; music; philosophy and religion; psychology; sociology

CUMBERLAND UNIVERSITY

Lebanon, Tennessee

Master of Arts in Education
www.masters4teachers.net

Cumberland University, founded in 1842, is an independent, nonprofit, comprehensive institution. It is accredited by the Southern Association of Colleges and Schools. It first offered distance learning courses in 1999. In 1999–2000, it offered 6 courses at a distance. In fall 1999, there were 60 students enrolled in distance learning courses.

Course delivery sites Courses are delivered to your home.

Media Courses are delivered via videotapes, e-mail, print. Students and teachers may interact via mail, telephone, fax, e-mail. The following equipment may be required: television, videocassette player, computer.

Restrictions Programs are available to in-state students only. Enrollment is open to anyone.

Services Distance learners have access to library services at a distance.

Typical costs Tuition of $199 per semester hour plus mandatory fees of $70 per course. Financial aid is available to distance learners.

Registration Students may register by mail, fax, in person.

Contact Deborah Gardner, Program Coordinator, Cumberland University, One Cumberland Square, Lebanon, TN 37087-3554. *Telephone:* 800-467-0562 Ext. 1217. *Fax:* 877-217-5284. *E-mail:* dgardner@cumberland.edu.

DEGREES AND AWARDS

MEd Education (some on-campus requirements)

COURSE SUBJECT AREAS OFFERED OUTSIDE OF DEGREE PROGRAMS

Graduate: Teacher education

CUYAHOGA COMMUNITY COLLEGE, METROPOLITAN CAMPUS

Cleveland, Ohio

Distance Learning Center
dlc.tri-c.cc.oh.us

Cuyahoga Community College, Metropolitan Campus, founded in 1963, is a state and locally supported, two-year college. It is accredited by the North Central Association of Colleges and Schools. It first offered distance learning courses in 1973. In 1999–2000, it offered 80 courses at a distance. In fall 1999, there were 2,248 students enrolled in distance learning courses.

Course delivery sites Courses are delivered to your home, your workplace, high schools.

Media Courses are delivered via television, videotapes, videoconferencing, interactive television, audiotapes, computer software, computer conferencing, World Wide Web, e-mail, print. Students and teachers may meet in person or interact via videoconferencing, mail, telephone, fax, e-mail, interactive television, World Wide Web. The following equipment may be required: television, videocassette player, computer, modem, Internet access, e-mail.
Restrictions Programs are available to local area students. Enrollment is restricted to individuals meeting certain criteria.
Services Distance learners have access to library services, the campus computer network, e-mail services, bookstore at a distance.
Credit-earning options Students may transfer credits from another institution.
Typical costs Tuition of $61.50 per credit for local area residents. Tuition of $81.65 per credit for in-state residents. Tuition of $163 per credit for out-of-state residents. *Noncredit courses:* $65 per course. Costs may vary. Financial aid is available to distance learners.
Registration Students may register by telephone, World Wide Web, in person.
Contact Cindy Potteiger, Operations Coordinator, Distance Learning, Cuyahoga Community College, Metropolitan Campus, 2900 Community College Avenue, Cleveland, OH 44115. *Telephone:* 216-987-4257. *Fax:* 216-987-4101. *E-mail:* cindy.potteiger@tri-c.cc.oh.us.

DEGREES AND AWARDS

AA Liberal Arts (some on-campus requirements)

COURSE SUBJECT AREAS OFFERED OUTSIDE OF DEGREE PROGRAMS

Undergraduate: Accounting; African-American studies; anthropology; archaeology; area, ethnic, and cultural studies; business administration and management; computer and information sciences; developmental and child psychology; economics; English composition; European languages and literatures; film studies; foods and nutrition studies; health and physical education/fitness; history; journalism; liberal arts, general studies, and humanities; library and information studies; marketing; mathematics; philosophy and religion; social psychology; sociology; women's studies

CUYAMACA COLLEGE

El Cajon, California
Telecourse Program
www.cuyamaca.net

Cuyamaca College, founded in 1978, is a state-supported, two-year college. It is accredited by the Western Association of Schools and Colleges, Inc. It first offered distance learning courses in 1985. In 1999–2000, it offered 28 courses at a distance. In fall 1999, there were 375 students enrolled in distance learning courses.
Course delivery sites Courses are delivered to your home.
Media Courses are delivered via television, videotapes. Students and teachers may meet in person or interact via telephone, e-mail. The following equipment may be required: television.
Restrictions Televised courses are available in San Diego County only. Enrollment is open to anyone.
Credit-earning options Students may earn credits through business training.
Typical costs Tuition of $11 per unit plus mandatory fees of $10 per semester for in-state residents. Tuition of $125 per unit plus mandatory fees of $10 per semester for out-of-state residents. Financial aid is available to distance learners.
Registration Students may register by telephone, in person.

Contact Nancy Asbury, Administrative Secretary, Cuyamaca College, Telecourse Program, El Cajon, CA 92019-4304. *Telephone:* 619-660-4401. *Fax:* 619-660-4493.

DEGREES AND AWARDS

Distance programs offered do not lead to a degree or other formal award.

COURSE SUBJECT AREAS OFFERED OUTSIDE OF DEGREE PROGRAMS

Undergraduate: Astronomy and astrophysics; business administration and management; developmental and child psychology; economics; English language and literature; geology; history; liberal arts, general studies, and humanities; political science; sociology

DAKOTA STATE UNIVERSITY

Madison, South Dakota
Office of Distance Education
www.courses.dsu.edu/disted/

Dakota State University, founded in 1881, is a state-supported, comprehensive institution. It is accredited by the North Central Association of Colleges and Schools. It first offered distance learning courses in 1990. In 1999–2000, it offered 30 courses at a distance. In fall 1999, there were 525 students enrolled in distance learning courses.
Course delivery sites Courses are delivered to your home, your workplace, military bases, high schools.
Media Courses are delivered via videoconferencing, computer software, World Wide Web, e-mail. Students and teachers may meet in person or interact via videoconferencing, mail, telephone, fax, e-mail, World Wide Web. The following equipment may be required: computer, modem, Internet access, e-mail.
Restrictions Programs are available worldwide. Enrollment is open to anyone.
Services Distance learners have access to library services, the campus computer network, e-mail services, academic advising, tutoring, career placement assistance, bookstore at a distance.
Credit-earning options Students may transfer credits from another institution or may earn credits through examinations, portfolio assessment, military training.
Typical costs *Undergraduate:* Tuition of $132.20 per credit hour. *Graduate:* Tuition of $169.95 per credit hour.
Registration Students may register by mail, fax, telephone, e-mail, World Wide Web, in person.
Contact Deb Gearhart, Director of Distance Education, Dakota State University, 201A Mundt Library, Madison, SD 57042-1799. *Telephone:* 800-641-4309. *Fax:* 605-256-5208. *E-mail:* dsuinfo@pluto.dsu.edu.

DEGREES AND AWARDS

BS Health Information Administration Degree Completion Program (certain restrictions apply)

COURSE SUBJECT AREAS OFFERED OUTSIDE OF DEGREE PROGRAMS

Undergraduate: Business; computer and information sciences; English composition; English language and literature; health services administration; mathematics; music; psychology; teacher education

Dakota State University

Graduate: Teacher education

Special note
DSU Online at Dakota State University offers more than 30 courses for online programs every academic year. DSU delivers courses for 3 programs as well as general education courses. The programs at DSU include the High School Fast Track Program, where high school students can get a jump start on college and earn high school credit at the same time. The Health Information Administration is a degree-completion program where those who have an associate degree can complete their bachelor's degree. All but 2 courses are delivered at a distance for the master's degree in computer education and technology. The courses on DSU Online are Web-based, with the course work, assignments, class discussion, and in many cases, quizzes and exams conducted on line or by e-mail. The Office of Distance Education provides services to distance students. Distance students have access to the library, bookstore, and other offices of the University. Students must have access to a 486 or higher computer with Internet connection and e-mail. Programming courses come with a text that includes a compiler to load on the student's computer. Other individual course requirements are listed on the Web site. For more information on DSU Online, students should visit the Web site at http://www.courses.dsu.edu/disted, send an e-mail to dsuinfo@pluto.dsu.edu, or call 800-641-4309 (toll-free).

DALHOUSIE UNIVERSITY

Halifax, Nova Scotia, Canada
Office of Instructional Development and Technology
www.dal.ca

Dalhousie University, founded in 1818, is a province-supported university. It is accredited by the provincial charter.
Course delivery sites Courses are delivered to your home, your workplace, military bases, other colleges, off-campus center(s) in Yarmouth.
Media Courses are delivered via videotapes, videoconferencing, audiotapes, computer software, computer conferencing, World Wide Web, e-mail, print. Students and teachers may interact via videoconferencing, audioconferencing, mail, telephone, fax, e-mail, World Wide Web. The following equipment may be required: computer, modem, Internet access, e-mail.
Restrictions Programs are available worldwide. Enrollment is open to anyone.
Services Distance learners have access to library services, the campus computer network, e-mail services at a distance.
Credit-earning options Students may transfer credits from another institution or may earn credits through examinations.
Typical costs Undergraduate tuition ranges between $400 and $800 per course. Graduate tuition ranges between $445 and $725 per course. Mandatory fees are $100 per course. Financial aid is available to distance learners.
Registration Students may register by mail, fax, telephone, e-mail, in person.
Contact Registrar's Office, Dalhousie University, Halifax, NS B3H 4H6 Canada. *Telephone:* 902-494-2450. *Fax:* 902-494-1630. *E-mail:* admissions@dal.ca.

DEGREES AND AWARDS

Undergraduate Certificate(s) Disability Services Management, Emergency Health Services Management
BN Nursing (some on-campus requirements)
MBA Financial Services (certain restrictions apply; some on-campus requirements)
MN Nursing (some on-campus requirements)

MSW Social Work (some on-campus requirements)

COURSE SUBJECT AREAS OFFERED OUTSIDE OF DEGREE PROGRAMS

Undergraduate: Anatomy; nursing; occupational therapy; physiology; public administration and services; social work
Graduate: Accounting; business administration and management; finance; health and medical administrative services; international business; marketing; nursing; social work
Noncredit: Information sciences and systems

DALLAS BAPTIST UNIVERSITY

Dallas, Texas
Dallas Baptist University Online (DBU Online)
www.dbuonline.org

Dallas Baptist University, founded in 1965, is an independent, religious, comprehensive institution affiliated with the Baptist Church. It is accredited by the Southern Association of Colleges and Schools. It first offered distance learning courses in 1997. In 1999–2000, it offered 24 courses at a distance. In fall 1999, there were 490 students enrolled in distance learning courses.
Course delivery sites Courses are delivered to your home, your workplace, 14 off-campus centers in Arkansas, Florida, Georgia, Kansas, Louisiana, Oklahoma.
Media Courses are delivered via videotapes, videoconferencing, interactive television, audiotapes, World Wide Web, e-mail, print. Students and teachers may meet in person or interact via videoconferencing, mail, telephone, fax, e-mail, interactive television, World Wide Web. The following equipment may be required: television, videocassette player, computer, modem, Internet access, e-mail.
Restrictions Programs are available worldwide. Enrollment is restricted to individuals meeting certain criteria.
Services Distance learners have access to library services, e-mail services, academic advising, tutoring, career placement assistance, bookstore at a distance.
Credit-earning options Students may transfer credits from another institution or may earn credits through examinations, portfolio assessment, military training, business training.
Typical costs *Undergraduate:* Tuition of $330 per credit hour. *Graduate:* Tuition of $338 per credit hour. Costs may vary. Financial aid is available to distance learners.
Registration Students may register by mail, fax, World Wide Web, in person.
Contact Sandee Smith, Acting Student Coordinator, Dallas Baptist University. *Telephone:* 800-460-8188. *Fax:* 214-333-5373. *E-mail:* online@dbu.edu.

DEGREES AND AWARDS

BAS Business Administration (certain restrictions apply)
MBA Management (certain restrictions apply)

COURSE SUBJECT AREAS OFFERED OUTSIDE OF DEGREE PROGRAMS

Undergraduate: Algebra; American (U.S.) history; Bible studies; business; business administration and management; computer and information sciences; English composition; English literature; sociology
Graduate: Business administration and management

See full description on page 506.

DALLAS COUNTY COMMUNITY COLLEGE DISTRICT

Dallas, Texas

LeCroy Center for Educational Telecommunications-Dallas Distance Education
telecollege.dcccd.edu

Dallas County Community College District is a district-supported system. It is accredited by the Southern Association of Colleges and Schools. It first offered distance learning courses in 1972. In 1999–2000, it offered 100 courses at a distance.

Course delivery sites Courses are delivered to your home, your workplace, military bases.

Media Courses are delivered via television, videotapes, computer software, CD-ROM, World Wide Web, e-mail, print. Students and teachers may interact via videoconferencing, audioconferencing, mail, telephone, fax, e-mail, World Wide Web. The following equipment may be required: television, videocassette player, computer, Internet access.

Restrictions Programs are available worldwide. Enrollment is restricted to individuals meeting certain criteria.

Services Distance learners have access to library services, e-mail services, academic advising, career placement assistance, bookstore at a distance.

Credit-earning options Students may transfer credits from another institution or may earn credits through examinations, portfolio assessment, military training, business training.

Typical costs Tuition of $69 per course plus mandatory fees of $15 per course for local area residents. Tuition of $129 per course plus mandatory fees of $15 per course for in-state residents. Tuition of $219 per course plus mandatory fees of $170 per course for out-of-state residents. Costs may vary. Financial aid is available to distance learners.

Registration Students may register by mail, fax, telephone, World Wide Web, in person.

Contact Distance Learning Hotline, Dallas County Community College District, LeCroy Center, Dallas, TX 75243. *Telephone:* 888-468-4268. *Fax:* 972-669-6409.

DEGREES AND AWARDS

AA Liberal Arts and General Studies (certain restrictions apply)
AS General Studies (certain restrictions apply)

COURSE SUBJECT AREAS OFFERED OUTSIDE OF DEGREE PROGRAMS

Undergraduate: Accounting; administrative and secretarial services; algebra; astronomy and astrophysics; biology; business administration and management; business communications; computer programming; creative writing; developmental and child psychology; economics; electronics; English as a second language (ESL); English composition; European languages and literatures; foods and nutrition studies; health and physical education/fitness; history; information sciences and systems; liberal arts, general studies, and humanities; marketing; mathematics; music; philosophy and religion; political science; sociology

See full descriptions on pages 508, 676, and 822.

DALLAS THEOLOGICAL SEMINARY

Dallas, Texas

External Studies Department
www.dts.edu

Dallas Theological Seminary, founded in 1924, is an independent, nonprofit, graduate institution. It is accredited by the Association of Theological Schools in the United States and Canada, Southern Association of Colleges and Schools. It first offered distance learning courses in 1987. In 1999–2000, it offered 25 courses at a distance. In fall 1999, there were 32 students enrolled in distance learning courses.

Course delivery sites Courses are delivered to your home, 6 off-campus centers in Austin, Houston, San Antonio, Atlanta (GA), Chattanooga (TN), Tampa (FL).

Media Courses are delivered via audiotapes, print. Students and teachers may meet in person or interact via mail, telephone, fax, e-mail.

Restrictions Programs are available worldwide. Enrollment is open to anyone.

Services Distance learners have access to library services, the campus computer network, e-mail services, academic advising, tutoring, bookstore at a distance.

Credit-earning options Students may transfer credits from another institution or may earn credits through examinations.

Typical costs Tuition of $280 per semester hour. *Noncredit courses:* $320 per course. Costs may vary.

Registration Students may register by mail, fax, telephone, e-mail, in person.

Contact Ben Scott, Director of External Studies, Dallas Theological Seminary, 3909 Swiss Avenue, Dallas, TX 75204. *Telephone:* 214-841-3757. *Fax:* 214-841-3532. *E-mail:* external_studies@dts.edu.

DEGREES AND AWARDS

Distance programs offered do not lead to a degree or other formal award.

COURSE SUBJECT AREAS OFFERED OUTSIDE OF DEGREE PROGRAMS

Graduate: Education administration; philosophy and religion; religious studies; theological studies
Noncredit: Education administration; philosophy and religion; religious studies; theological studies

DANVILLE AREA COMMUNITY COLLEGE

Danville, Illinois

Distance Learning Department
www.dacc.cc.il.us

Danville Area Community College, founded in 1946, is a state and locally supported, two-year college. It is accredited by the North Central Association of Colleges and Schools. It first offered distance learning courses in 1994. In 1999–2000, it offered 28 courses at a distance. In fall 1999, there were 167 students enrolled in distance learning courses.

Course delivery sites Courses are delivered to your home, your workplace, high schools, Lakeview College of Nursing (Danville), 5 off-campus centers in Bismarck, Danville, Georgetown, Hoopeston, Votec.

Media Courses are delivered via television, videotapes, videoconferencing, interactive television, computer software, computer conferencing, World Wide Web, e-mail, print. Students and teachers may meet in person or interact via videoconferencing, mail, telephone, fax, e-mail, interactive television, World Wide Web. The following equipment may be required: television, videocassette player, computer, Internet access.

Restrictions Programs are available to in-state students only. Enrollment is open to anyone.

Services Distance learners have access to library services, the campus computer network, e-mail services, academic advising, tutoring, career placement assistance, bookstore at a distance.

Credit-earning options Students may transfer credits from another institution or may earn credits through portfolio assessment, military training.

Typical costs *Undergraduate:* Tuition of $44 per credit plus mandatory fees of $40 per course. *Graduate:* Tuition of $44 per credit plus mandatory fees of $40 per course. Costs may vary. Financial aid is available to distance learners.

Registration Students may register by mail, fax, telephone, e-mail, World Wide Web, in person.

Contact Jon Spors, Director, Danville Area Community College, Instructional Media, 2000 East Main Street, Danville, IL 61832. *Telephone:* 217-443-8577. *Fax:* 217-443-3178. *E-mail:* jspors@dacc.cc.il.us.

DEGREES AND AWARDS

Distance programs offered do not lead to a degree or other formal award.

COURSE SUBJECT AREAS OFFERED OUTSIDE OF DEGREE PROGRAMS

Undergraduate: Accounting; biological and life sciences; English composition; English language and literature; history; human resources management; liberal arts, general studies, and humanities; mathematics; philosophy and religion; political science; psychology; social sciences

DANVILLE COMMUNITY COLLEGE

Danville, Virginia

Learning Resource Center
www.dc.cc.va.us

Danville Community College, founded in 1967, is a state-supported, two-year college. It is accredited by the Southern Association of Colleges and Schools. It first offered distance learning courses in 1990. In 1999–2000, it offered 6 courses at a distance. In fall 1999, there were 78 students enrolled in distance learning courses.

Course delivery sites Courses are delivered to your home, high schools, Virginia Community College System (Richmond), 2 off-campus centers in Danville, South Boston.

Media Courses are delivered via television, videotapes, videoconferencing, interactive television, e-mail. Students and teachers may meet in person or interact via videoconferencing, mail, telephone, fax, e-mail, interactive television. The following equipment may be required: television, computer, Internet access, e-mail.

Restrictions Programs are available worldwide. Enrollment is open to anyone.

Services Distance learners have access to library services, e-mail services, academic advising, bookstore at a distance.

Credit-earning options Students may transfer credits from another institution or may earn credits through portfolio assessment.

Typical costs Tuition of $38.62 per credit hour plus mandatory fees of $1.50 per credit hour for local area residents. Tuition of $38.62 per credit hour plus mandatory fees of $1.50 per credit hour for in-state residents. Tuition of $166.32 per credit hour plus mandatory fees of $1.50 per credit hour for out-of-state residents. Cost for noncredit course is $160 for 3 credit hours. Financial aid is available to distance learners.

Registration Students may register by mail, telephone, in person.

Contact Dr. Betty Jo Foster, Dean of Instruction, Danville Community College. *Telephone:* 804-797-8410. *Fax:* 804-797-8415. *E-mail:* bfoster@dc.cc.va.us.

DEGREES AND AWARDS

Distance programs offered do not lead to a degree or other formal award.

COURSE SUBJECT AREAS OFFERED OUTSIDE OF DEGREE PROGRAMS

Undergraduate: Accounting; business; business administration and management; English composition; health and physical education/fitness; marketing; mathematics; music

DARTON COLLEGE

Albany, Georgia

Office of Distance Learning
www.dartnet.peachnet.edu

Darton College, founded in 1965, is a state-supported, two-year college. It is accredited by the Southern Association of Colleges and Schools. It first offered distance learning courses in 1993. In 1999–2000, it offered 30 courses at a distance. In fall 1999, there were 350 students enrolled in distance learning courses.

Course delivery sites Courses are delivered to your home, your workplace, military bases, Abraham Baldwin Agricultural College (Tifton), Middle Georgia College (Cochran), South Georgia College (Douglas), Waycross College (Waycross), 6 off-campus centers in Camilla, Leesburg, Sylvester.

Media Courses are delivered via television, videotapes, videoconferencing, World Wide Web, e-mail, print. Students and teachers may interact via videoconferencing, audioconferencing, mail, telephone, fax, e-mail, World Wide Web.

Restrictions Programs are available nationwide. Enrollment is open to anyone.

Services Distance learners have access to library services, the campus computer network, e-mail services, academic advising, tutoring, career placement assistance at a distance.

Credit-earning options Students may transfer credits from another institution or may earn credits through examinations.

Typical costs Tuition of $52 per semester hour for in-state residents. Tuition of $155 per semester hour for out-of-state residents. *Noncredit courses:* $156 per course. Costs may vary. Financial aid is available to distance learners.

Registration Students may register by telephone, World Wide Web, in person.

Contact Kathy Bishop, Coordinator, Darton College. *Telephone:* 912-430-6838. *Fax:* 912-430-6910. *E-mail:* bishopk@mail.dartnet.peachnet.edu.

DEGREES AND AWARDS

Distance programs offered do not lead to a degree or other formal award.

COURSE SUBJECT AREAS OFFERED OUTSIDE OF DEGREE PROGRAMS

Undergraduate: Asian languages and literatures; English composition; English language and literature; European languages and literatures; fine arts; health professions and related sciences; industrial engineering; mathematics; music; political science; visual and performing arts

Noncredit: Classical languages and literatures

See full description on page 676.

DAVENPORT COLLEGE OF BUSINESS, KALAMAZOO CAMPUS

Kalamazoo, Michigan
www.davenport.edu/

Davenport College of Business, Kalamazoo Campus, founded in 1866, is an independent, nonprofit, four-year college. It is accredited by the Accrediting Bureau of Health Education Schools, North Central Association of Colleges and Schools. In 1999–2000, it offered 100 courses at a distance. In fall 1999, there were 150 students enrolled in distance learning courses.

Course delivery sites Courses are delivered to your home.

Media Courses are delivered via World Wide Web. Students and teachers may meet in person or interact via mail, telephone, fax, e-mail.

Restrictions Programs are available nationwide. Enrollment is restricted to individuals meeting certain criteria.

Services Distance learners have access to e-mail services at a distance.

Typical costs Tuition of $196 per credit plus mandatory fees of $25 per term. Financial aid is available to distance learners.

Registration Students may register by mail, fax, telephone, e-mail, in person.

Contact Ligita Samsons, Director of Student Services, Davenport College of Business, Kalamazoo Campus, 4123 West Main, Kalamazoo, MI 49006. *Telephone:* 616-382-2835. *Fax:* 616-382-3541. *E-mail:* kzlsamsons@davenport.edu.

DEGREES AND AWARDS

Distance programs offered do not lead to a degree or other formal award.

COURSE SUBJECT AREAS OFFERED OUTSIDE OF DEGREE PROGRAMS

Undergraduate: Accounting; administrative and secretarial services; business administration and management; computer programming; database management; English language and literature; health professions and related sciences; information sciences and systems; paralegal/legal assistant

See full description on page 510.

DAVENPORT EDUCATIONAL SYSTEM, INC.

Grand Rapids, Michigan
Learning Network
www.davenport.edu

Davenport Educational System, Inc. system. It is accredited by the North Central Association of Colleges and Schools. It first offered distance learning courses in 1995.

Contact Davenport Educational System, Inc., 415 East Fulton Street, Grand Rapids, MI 49503.

See full description on page 510.

DAVID LIPSCOMB UNIVERSITY

Nashville, Tennessee
www.lipscombonline.net

David Lipscomb University, founded in 1891, is an independent, religious, comprehensive institution affiliated with the Church of Christ. It is accredited by the Southern Association of Colleges and Schools. In 1999–2000, it offered 7 courses at a distance.

Course delivery sites Courses are delivered to your home.

Media Courses are delivered via World Wide Web. Students and teachers may interact via telephone, e-mail, World Wide Web. The following equipment may be required: computer, modem, Internet access, e-mail.

Restrictions Programs are available nationwide. Enrollment is restricted to individuals meeting certain criteria.

Services Distance learners have access to library services, e-mail services, academic advising, career placement assistance, bookstore at a distance.

Credit-earning options Students may transfer credits from another institution or may earn credits through examinations, military training, business training.

Typical costs *Undergraduate:* Tuition of $311.50 per semester hour. *Graduate:* Tuition of $363 per semester hour. Financial aid is available to distance learners.

Registration Students may register by mail, fax, telephone, e-mail, World Wide Web, in person.

Contact Mr. Al Austelle, Director of the Center for Instructional Technology, David Lipscomb University, 3901 Granny White Pike, Nashville, TN 37204-3951. *Telephone:* 615-279-5703. *Fax:* 615-279-6052. *E-mail:* al.austelle@lipscomb.edu.

DEGREES AND AWARDS

Distance programs offered do not lead to a degree or other formal award.

COURSE SUBJECT AREAS OFFERED OUTSIDE OF DEGREE PROGRAMS

Undergraduate: American (U.S.) history; chemistry; conservation and natural resources; education; English language and literature; film studies; history; public relations; teacher education

Graduate: Bible studies; human resources management; special education; theological studies

DAVID N. MYERS COLLEGE

Cleveland, Ohio
Myers Online Center
www.dnmyers.edu

David N. Myers College, founded in 1848, is an independent, nonprofit, four-year college. It is accredited by the North Central Association of Colleges and Schools. It first offered distance learning courses in 1995. In 1999–2000, it offered 21 courses at a distance. In fall 1999, there were 85 students enrolled in distance learning courses.

Course delivery sites Courses are delivered to your home, your workplace.

Media Courses are delivered via computer software, CD-ROM, computer conferencing, World Wide Web, e-mail, print. Students and teachers may meet in person or interact via mail, telephone, fax, e-mail, World Wide Web. The following equipment may be required: computer, modem, Internet access, e-mail.

Restrictions Programs are available worldwide. Enrollment is open to anyone.

Services Distance learners have access to library services, the campus computer network, e-mail services at a distance.

Credit-earning options Students may transfer credits from another institution or may earn credits through examinations, portfolio assessment, military training, business training.

Typical costs Tuition of $282 per semester hour. Financial aid is available to distance learners.

Registration Students may register by fax, telephone, e-mail, in person.

Contact Charles Dull, Director, Division of Adult Learning, David N. Myers College, 112 Prospect Avenue, Cleveland, OH 44115. *Telephone:* 216-523-3853. *Fax:* 216-523-3808. *E-mail:* cdull@dnmyers.edu.

DEGREES AND AWARDS

Undergraduate Certificate(s) Human Resource Management
BS Business Administration, Human Resource Management

COURSE SUBJECT AREAS OFFERED OUTSIDE OF DEGREE PROGRAMS

Undergraduate: Accounting; business; business administration and management; communications; English composition; English language and literature
Graduate: Business administration and management

DAWSON COMMUNITY COLLEGE

Glendive, Montana

Academic Services

www.dawson.cc.mt.us

Dawson Community College, founded in 1940, is a state and locally supported, two-year college. It is accredited by the Northwest Association of Schools and Colleges. It first offered distance learning courses in 1990. In 1999–2000, it offered 80 courses at a distance. In fall 1999, there were 166 students enrolled in distance learning courses.

Course delivery sites Courses are delivered to high schools, Miles Community College (Miles City), Montana State University–Billings (Billings), 11 off-campus centers in Baker, Circle, Ekalaka, Glendive, Lambert, Miles City, Plevna, Richey, Savage, Sidney, Terry.

Media Courses are delivered via interactive television. Students and teachers may interact via videoconferencing, mail, telephone, fax, e-mail, interactive television. The following equipment may be required: television, videocassette player, computer.

Restrictions Programs are available to in-state students only. Enrollment is restricted to individuals meeting certain criteria.

Services Distance learners have access to library services, e-mail services, academic advising, tutoring, career placement assistance, bookstore at a distance.

Credit-earning options Students may transfer credits from another institution or may earn credits through examinations, portfolio assessment, military training, business training.

Typical costs Tuition of $30 per credit plus mandatory fees of $27 per credit for local area residents. Tuition of $51.50 per credit plus mandatory fees of $27 per credit for in-state residents. Tuition of $152 per credit plus mandatory fees of $27 per credit for out-of-state residents. Costs may vary. Financial aid is available to distance learners.

Registration Students may register by mail, in person.

Contact John Myers, Admissions, Dawson Community College. *Telephone:* 406-377-3396. *Fax:* 406-377-8132. *E-mail:* diane_d@dawson.cc.mt.us.

DEGREES AND AWARDS

AAS Human Services (service area differs from that of the overall institution)
AS Business Management (service area differs from that of the overall institution)

COURSE SUBJECT AREAS OFFERED OUTSIDE OF DEGREE PROGRAMS

Undergraduate: Administrative and secretarial services; agriculture; biology; business; business administration and management; creative writing; developmental and child psychology; economics; English composition; English language and literature; fine arts; health and physical education/fitness; history; liberal arts, general studies, and humanities; mathematics; sociology; teacher education
Noncredit: Agriculture

DE ANZA COLLEGE

Cupertino, California

Distance Learning Center

distance.deanza.fhda.edu/

De Anza College, founded in 1967, is a state and locally supported, two-year college. It is accredited by the Western Association of Schools and Colleges, Inc. It first offered distance learning courses in 1974. In 1999–2000, it offered 69 courses at a distance. In fall 1999, there were 3,119 students enrolled in distance learning courses.

Course delivery sites Courses are delivered to your home, your workplace.

Media Courses are delivered via television, videotapes, interactive television, audiotapes, computer software, CD-ROM, World Wide Web, e-mail, print. Students and teachers may meet in person or interact via mail, telephone, fax, e-mail, interactive television, World Wide Web. The following equipment may be required: television, videocassette player, Internet access, e-mail.

Restrictions Programs are available to local area students. Enrollment is open to anyone.

Services Distance learners have access to library services, the campus computer network, e-mail services, bookstore at a distance.

Credit-earning options Students may transfer credits from another institution or may earn credits through examinations.

Typical costs Tuition of $9 per unit plus mandatory fees of $31 per quarter for in-state residents. Tuition of $85 per unit plus mandatory fees of $31 per quarter for out-of-state residents. Costs may vary. Financial aid is available to distance learners.

Registration Students may register by mail, telephone, World Wide Web, in person.

Contact Distance Learning Center, De Anza College, 21250 Stevens Creek Boulevard, Cupertino, CA 95014. *Telephone:* 408-864-8969. *Fax:* 408-864-8245. *E-mail:* information@dadistance.fhda.edu.

DEGREES AND AWARDS

Undergraduate Certificate(s) Business Administration (some on-campus requirements)
AA Liberal Arts (some on-campus requirements)

COURSE SUBJECT AREAS OFFERED OUTSIDE OF DEGREE PROGRAMS

Undergraduate: Abnormal psychology; accounting; African-American studies; algebra; American (U.S.) history; anthropology; area, ethnic, and cultural studies; Asian studies; biological and life sciences; biology; business; business administration and management; business law; computer and information sciences; conservation and natural resources; design; developmental and child psychology; economics; education; English composition; English language and literature; fine arts; foods and nutrition studies; health and physical education/fitness; health professions and related sciences; information sciences and systems; journalism; liberal arts, general studies, and humanities; library and information studies; marketing; mass media; mathematics; music; nursing; philosophy and religion;

political science; psychology; religious studies; social psychology; social sciences; sociology; statistics; technical writing; telecommunications

DEFIANCE COLLEGE

Defiance, Ohio
Design for Leadership
www.defiance.edu/

Defiance College, founded in 1850, is an independent, religious, comprehensive institution affiliated with the United Church of Christ. It is accredited by the North Central Association of Colleges and Schools. In 1999–2000, it offered 25 courses at a distance. In fall 1999, there were 12 students enrolled in distance learning courses.

Course delivery sites Courses are delivered to your home.

Media Courses are delivered via computer software, computer conferencing, World Wide Web, e-mail, print. Students and teachers may meet in person or interact via mail, telephone, fax, e-mail, World Wide Web. The following equipment may be required: computer, modem, Internet access, e-mail.

Restrictions Programs are available worldwide. Enrollment is open to anyone.

Services Distance learners have access to the campus computer network, e-mail services, academic advising, career placement assistance at a distance.

Credit-earning options Students may transfer credits from another institution or may earn credits through examinations, portfolio assessment.

Typical costs Tuition of $132 per credit. Costs may vary.

Registration Students may register by mail, fax, telephone, e-mail, World Wide Web, in person.

Contact Dr. Keith Chism, Director, Defiance College, 701 North Clinton Street, Defiance, OH 43512. *Telephone:* 419-783-2338. *Fax:* 419-784-0426. *E-mail:* kchism@defiance.edu.

DEGREES AND AWARDS

Undergraduate Certificate(s) Christian Education
BS Christian Education (some on-campus requirements)

COURSE SUBJECT AREAS OFFERED OUTSIDE OF DEGREE PROGRAMS

Undergraduate: Philosophy and religion; religious studies

DELAWARE TECHNICAL & COMMUNITY COLLEGE, JACK F. OWENS CAMPUS

Georgetown, Delaware
www.dtcc.edu/dl

Delaware Technical & Community College, Jack F. Owens Campus, founded in 1967, is a state-supported, two-year college. It is accredited by the Middle States Association of Colleges and Schools. It first offered distance learning courses in 1994. In 1999–2000, it offered 44 courses at a distance. In fall 1999, there were 198 students enrolled in distance learning courses.

Course delivery sites Courses are delivered to your home.

Media Courses are delivered via television, videotapes, interactive television, CD-ROM, World Wide Web, e-mail. Students and teachers may meet in person or interact via telephone, e-mail, interactive television, World Wide Web. The following equipment may be required: television, videocassette player, computer, Internet access, e-mail.

Restrictions Programs are available worldwide. Enrollment is open to anyone.

Services Distance learners have access to library services, e-mail services, academic advising, bookstore at a distance.

Credit-earning options Students may transfer credits from another institution or may earn credits through examinations, military training.

Typical costs Tuition of $60 per credit hour plus mandatory fees of $52.50 per course for in-state residents. Tuition of $150 per credit hour plus mandatory fees of $52.50 per course for out-of-state residents. Financial aid is available to distance learners.

Registration Students may register by mail, fax, telephone, World Wide Web, in person.

Contact Dr. Ileana Smith, Assistant to the Campus Director, Delaware Technical & Community College, Jack F. Owens Campus, PO Box 660, Route 18, Georgetown, DE 19947. *Telephone:* 302-855-1600. *Fax:* 302-855-5982. *E-mail:* ismith@outland.dtcc.edu.

DEGREES AND AWARDS

Distance programs offered do not lead to a degree or other formal award.

COURSE SUBJECT AREAS OFFERED OUTSIDE OF DEGREE PROGRAMS

Undergraduate: American (U.S.) history; biology; business; business administration and management; chemistry; education; English language and literature; journalism; marketing; psychology; sociology; Spanish language and literature

DELAWARE TECHNICAL & COMMUNITY COLLEGE, STANTON/WILMINGTON CAMPUS

Newark, Delaware
Distance Learning Programs and Outreach
www.dtcc.edu

Delaware Technical & Community College, Stanton/Wilmington Campus, founded in 1968, is a state-supported, two-year college. It is accredited by the Middle States Association of Colleges and Schools. It first offered distance learning courses in 1980. In 1999–2000, it offered 22 courses at a distance. In fall 1999, there were 401 students enrolled in distance learning courses.

Course delivery sites Courses are delivered to your home, your workplace.

Media Courses are delivered via television, videotapes, videoconferencing, e-mail, print. Students and teachers may interact via videoconferencing, mail, telephone, fax, e-mail. The following equipment may be required: television, videocassette player, e-mail.

Restrictions Programs are available worldwide. Enrollment is open to anyone.

Services Distance learners have access to library services, the campus computer network, e-mail services, academic advising, tutoring, career placement assistance at a distance.

Credit-earning options Students may transfer credits from another institution or may earn credits through examinations, portfolio assessment, military training, business training.

Typical costs Tuition of $60 per credit hour plus mandatory fees of $30 per semester for in-state residents. Tuition of $150 per credit hour plus mandatory fees of $30 per semester for out-of-state residents. $210-$480. Financial aid is available to distance learners.

Registration Students may register by mail, fax, telephone, in person.

Contact Charles Poplos, Distance Learning Outreach Coordinator, Delaware Technical & Community College, Stanton/Wilmington Campus, 400 Stanton-Christiana Road, Newark, DE 19713. *Telephone:* 302-454-3192. *Fax:* 302-453-3025. *E-mail:* dlearn@hopi.dtcc.edu.

DEGREES AND AWARDS

Distance programs offered do not lead to a degree or other formal award.

COURSE SUBJECT AREAS OFFERED OUTSIDE OF DEGREE PROGRAMS

Undergraduate: Abnormal psychology; advertising; African-American studies; algebra; American (U.S.) history; American literature; business administration and management; business law; calculus; chemistry; child care and development; developmental and child psychology; economics; English composition; English language and literature; health professions and related sciences; home economics and family studies; journalism; marketing; mathematics; political science; psychology; social psychology; sociology; statistics; technical writing

See full description on page 676.

DELGADO COMMUNITY COLLEGE

New Orleans, Louisiana
Community Campus
www.dcc.edu

Delgado Community College, founded in 1921, is a state-supported, two-year college. It is accredited by the Southern Association of Colleges and Schools. It first offered distance learning courses in 1989.

Contact Delgado Community College, 501 City Park Avenue, New Orleans, LA 70119-4399. *Telephone:* 504-483-4114.

See full description on page 676.

DEL MAR COLLEGE

Corpus Christi, Texas
www.delmar.edu/

Del Mar College, founded in 1935, is a state and locally supported, two-year college. It is accredited by the Southern Association of Colleges and Schools. In 1999–2000, it offered 109 courses at a distance. In fall 1999, there were 789 students enrolled in distance learning courses.

Course delivery sites Courses are delivered to your home, your workplace, military bases, high schools, Victoria College (Victoria).

Media Courses are delivered via television, videotapes, videoconferencing, audiotapes, computer software, World Wide Web, e-mail. Students and teachers may meet in person or interact via videoconferencing, mail, telephone, fax, e-mail, World Wide Web. The following equipment may be required: television, videocassette player, computer, modem, Internet access, e-mail.

Restrictions Programs are available to local area students. Enrollment is open to anyone.

Services Distance learners have access to library services, academic advising, career placement assistance at a distance.

Credit-earning options Students may transfer credits from another institution or may earn credits through examinations, portfolio assessment.

Typical costs Undergraduate, in-district tuition per 3 semester hours is $57, in-state is $85, and out-of-state is $200. Mandatory fees are $50 per three semester hours. Financial aid is available to distance learners.

Registration Students may register by mail, telephone, World Wide Web, in person.

Contact Don Tyler, Assistant Dean, Distance Learning, Del Mar College, 101 Baldwin, Corpus Christi, TX 78404. *Telephone:* 361-698-1312. *Fax:* 361-698-1981. *E-mail:* dtyler@delmar.edu.

DEGREES AND AWARDS

Distance programs offered do not lead to a degree or other formal award.

COURSE SUBJECT AREAS OFFERED OUTSIDE OF DEGREE PROGRAMS

Undergraduate: American (U.S.) history; American literature; biology; business administration and management; chemistry, organic; computer and information sciences; economics; English composition; information sciences and systems; marketing; music; nursing; political science; psychology; real estate; sociology; Spanish language and literature; technical writing

DELTA COLLEGE

University Center, Michigan
Distance Learning Office and Telelearning
www.delta.edu/~telelrn

Delta College, founded in 1961, is a district-supported, two-year college. It is accredited by the North Central Association of Colleges and Schools. It first offered distance learning courses in 1982. In 1999–2000, it offered 40 courses at a distance. In fall 1999, there were 800 students enrolled in distance learning courses.

Course delivery sites Courses are delivered to your home, your workplace, high schools, Grand Valley State University (Allendale), 2 off-campus centers in Bay City, Midland.

Media Courses are delivered via television, videotapes, videoconferencing, audiotapes, World Wide Web, e-mail, print. Students and teachers may meet in person or interact via videoconferencing, mail, telephone, fax, e-mail, World Wide Web. The following equipment may be required: television, videocassette player, computer, modem, Internet access, e-mail.

Restrictions Programs are available worldwide. Enrollment is open to anyone.

Services Distance learners have access to library services, the campus computer network, e-mail services, academic advising, tutoring, career placement assistance, bookstore at a distance.

Credit-earning options Students may transfer credits from another institution or may earn credits through examinations, portfolio assessment, military training, business training.

Typical costs Tuition of $58 per credit hour for local area residents. Tuition of $79 per credit hour for in-state residents. Tuition of $113 per credit hour for out-of-state residents. Mandatory fees range between $3.50 and $82.50 per course. Financial aid is available to distance learners.

Registration Students may register by telephone, in person.

Contact Chris Curtis, Coordinator of Distance Learning, Delta College, 1961 Delta Road, Office A-62, University Center, MI 48710-0002. *Telephone:* 517-686-9088. *Fax:* 517-686-8736. *E-mail:* clcurtis@alpha.delta.edu.

DEGREES AND AWARDS

AA General Studies (some on-campus requirements)

COURSE SUBJECT AREAS OFFERED OUTSIDE OF DEGREE PROGRAMS

Undergraduate: Abnormal psychology; algebra; American (U.S.) history; American literature; biology; business; business administration and management; business communications; business law; calculus; chemistry; developmental and child psychology; e-commerce; economics; English composition; ethics; health and physical education/fitness; history; information sciences and systems; liberal arts, general studies, and humanities; marketing; microbiology; philosophy and religion; political science; psychology; sociology; Spanish language and literature; statistics; teacher education; technical writing

DELTA STATE UNIVERSITY

Cleveland, Mississippi

Division of Continuing Education and Distance Learning

Delta State University, founded in 1924, is a state-supported, comprehensive institution. It is accredited by the Southern Association of Colleges and Schools. It first offered distance learning courses in 1993.

Contact Delta State University, Highway 8 West, Cleveland, MS 38733-0001. *Telephone:* 662-846-3000. *Fax:* 662-846-4016.

See full description on page 676.

DENVER SEMINARY

Denver, Colorado
www.densem.edu

Denver Seminary, founded in 1950, is an independent, religious, graduate institution. It is accredited by the Association of Theological Schools in the United States and Canada, North Central Association of Colleges and Schools. It first offered distance learning courses in 1988. In 1999–2000, it offered 12 courses at a distance. In fall 1999, there were 30 students enrolled in distance learning courses.

Course delivery sites Courses are delivered to your home, 1 off-campus center in Colorado Springs.

Media Courses are delivered via videotapes, audiotapes, e-mail, print. Students and teachers may meet in person or interact via mail, telephone, fax, e-mail. The following equipment may be required: computer, modem, Internet access, e-mail.

Restrictions Programs are available worldwide. Enrollment is restricted to individuals meeting certain criteria.

Services Distance learners have access to library services, e-mail services, academic advising, tutoring, career placement assistance, bookstore at a distance.

Credit-earning options Students may transfer credits from another institution or may earn credits through examinations, portfolio assessment.

Typical costs Tuition of $305 per semester hour for local area residents. Tuition of $200 per semester hour for out-of-state residents. Costs may vary.

Registration Students may register by mail, fax, telephone, in person.

Contact William W. Klein, Associate Dean, Denver Seminary, PO Box 100000, Denver, CO 80250. *Telephone:* 303-761-2482 Ext. 1241. *Fax:* 303-761-8060. *E-mail:* bill.klein@densem.edu.

DEGREES AND AWARDS

Distance programs offered do not lead to a degree or other formal award.

COURSE SUBJECT AREAS OFFERED OUTSIDE OF DEGREE PROGRAMS

Graduate: Bible studies; counseling psychology; education administration; ethics; history; philosophy and religion; psychology; theological studies

Noncredit: Bible studies; counseling psychology; education administration; ethics; history; philosophy and religion; psychology; theological studies

DES MOINES AREA COMMUNITY COLLEGE

Ankeny, Iowa

Distance Learning/Continuing Education
www.dmacc.cc.ia.us

Des Moines Area Community College, founded in 1966, is a state and locally supported, two-year college. It is accredited by the North Central Association of Colleges and Schools. It first offered distance learning courses in 1970. In 1999–2000, it offered 40 courses at a distance.

Course delivery sites Courses are delivered to your home, high schools, 4 off-campus centers in Boone, Carroll, Des Moines, Newton.

Media Courses are delivered via television, videotapes, videoconferencing, interactive television, audiotapes, computer software, World Wide Web, e-mail. Students and teachers may meet in person or interact via videoconferencing, audioconferencing, mail, telephone, fax, e-mail, interactive television. The following equipment may be required: television, computer, Internet access.

Restrictions Some telecourses are offered statewide through PBS; some are offered regionally through cable, and interactive video courses are offered locally. Enrollment is restricted to individuals meeting certain criteria.

Services Distance learners have access to library services, e-mail services, academic advising, career placement assistance, bookstore at a distance.

Credit-earning options Students may transfer credits from another institution or may earn credits through examinations.

Typical costs Tuition of $51 per credit hour plus mandatory fees of $6.40 per credit hour for in-state residents. Tuition of $118.80 per credit hour plus mandatory fees of $6.40 per credit hour for out-of-state residents. Costs may vary. Financial aid is available to distance learners.

Registration Students may register by mail, fax, telephone, World Wide Web, in person.

Contact Winston Black, Director, Distance Learning, Des Moines Area Community College, 2006 South Ankeny Boulevard, Ankeny, IA 50021. *Telephone:* 515-964-6546. *Fax:* 515-965-6002. *E-mail:* jwblack@dmacc.cc.ia.us.

DEGREES AND AWARDS

Distance programs offered do not lead to a degree or other formal award.

COURSE SUBJECT AREAS OFFERED OUTSIDE OF DEGREE PROGRAMS

Undergraduate: Accounting; administrative and secretarial services; area, ethnic, and cultural studies; biology; business administration and management; computer and information sciences; developmental and child psychology; economics; English composition; English language and literature; health professions and related sciences; history; home economics and family studies; liberal arts, general studies, and humanities; mathematics; music; nursing; political science; psychology; sociology; teacher education

Noncredit: Health professions and related sciences; home economics and family studies

DRAKE UNIVERSITY

Des Moines, Iowa

Distance Learning Program

Drake University, founded in 1881, is an independent, nonprofit university. It is accredited by the North Central Association of Colleges and Schools. It first offered distance learning courses in 1991. In 1999–2000, it offered 50 courses at a distance. In fall 1999, there were 1,200 students enrolled in distance learning courses.

Course delivery sites Courses are delivered to your workplace, military bases, high schools, North Iowa Area Community College (Mason City).

Media Courses are delivered via television, videoconferencing, computer software, computer conferencing, World Wide Web, e-mail, print. Students and teachers may meet in person or interact via mail, telephone, fax, e-mail, interactive television, World Wide Web. The following equipment may be required: computer, modem, Internet access, e-mail.

Restrictions ICN at specified sites only; Web courses nationwide. Enrollment is open to anyone.

Services Distance learners have access to library services, the campus computer network, academic advising, career placement assistance, bookstore at a distance.

Credit-earning options Students may transfer credits from another institution.

Typical costs *Undergraduate:* Tuition of $230 per credit hour. *Graduate:* Tuition of $260 per credit hour. MBA Program tuition is $340 per credit hour. Financial aid is available to distance learners.

Registration Students may register by mail, fax, telephone, e-mail, in person.

Contact Dr. Michael Cheney, Associate Provost, Drake University, 2507 University Avenue, Des Moines, IA 50311. *Telephone:* 515-271-3751. *Fax:* 515-271-3016. *E-mail:* michael.cheney@drake.edu.

DEGREES AND AWARDS

MBA Business Administration (certain restrictions apply; service area differs from that of the overall institution)

MSE Adult Education (service area differs from that of the overall institution; some on-campus requirements)

COURSE SUBJECT AREAS OFFERED OUTSIDE OF DEGREE PROGRAMS

Undergraduate: Adult education; advertising; algebra; American literature; American studies; biochemistry; biology; business administration and management; calculus; community health services; creative writing; curriculum and instruction; English language and literature; English literature; foods and nutrition studies; health professions and related sciences; history; human resources management; industrial psychology; information sciences and systems; international relations; journalism; management information systems; marketing; mathematics; mental health services; organizational behavior studies; political science; psychology; social psychology; technical writing; women's studies

Graduate: Accounting; administrative and secretarial services; adult education; business; business administration and management; education; education administration; educational psychology; English literature; human resources management; industrial psychology; information sciences and systems; special education; teacher education

Special note

Distance education at Drake University includes an array of Web-based courses. These online courses, available on the World Wide Web, are designed so that students can complete a course without having to attend class at a fixed time or place. During summer 2000, more than 50 courses were offered for both undergraduate and graduate credit. All courses are transferable as college credit. Two new programs were developed for summer 2000—12 courses suitable for advanced high school students and/or students about to enter college and a cross-discipline program for students who want to become professional pharmacists. Students must register on line for Web-based courses at http://www.multimedia.drake.edu/summer/. Additional information about Web-based courses is also available at http://www.drake.edu/provost/summer/. Experienced Drake faculty members teach every online course. Students rank Drake's distance education courses on the Web as highly satisfactory, particularly because of the convenience, quality of instruction, variety of courses, and interactivity of the courses. Drake's Web-based program also provides access to on-campus library sources, advising, information about ordering books on line, and discussion forums. This learner-centered course delivery system is best suited to those who know how to work independently, are self-starters and self-motivated, and are well-organized and know how to manage their time. Since Drake began offering Web-based courses in 1997, the program has grown to serve registrants throughout the United States and several other countries. For more information on the Web-based program, students should contact the Director of Summer Programming at 800-44-DRAKE Ext. 2000 (toll-free) or e-mail summer.sessions@drake.edu.

DREXEL UNIVERSITY

Philadelphia, Pennsylvania

Lifelong Learning
www.drexel.edu/distance

Drexel University, founded in 1891, is an independent, nonprofit university. It is accredited by the Middle States Association of Colleges and Schools. It first offered distance learning courses in 1994. In 1999–2000, it offered 18 courses at a distance. In fall 1999, there were 319 students enrolled in distance learning courses.

Course delivery sites Courses are delivered to your home, your workplace, military bases.

Media Courses are delivered via computer software, World Wide Web, e-mail, print. Students and teachers may interact via mail, telephone, fax, e-mail, World Wide Web. The following equipment may be required: computer, modem, Internet access, e-mail.

Restrictions Programs are available worldwide. Enrollment is restricted to individuals meeting certain criteria.

Services Distance learners have access to library services, the campus computer network, e-mail services, academic advising, career placement assistance, bookstore at a distance.

Credit-earning options Students may transfer credits from another institution.

Typical costs Tuition of $1750 per course plus mandatory fees of $70 per quarter. Cost for the Competitive Intelligence non-degree course is $2275. Costs may vary.

Registration Students may register by World Wide Web.

Contact Timothy Perkins, Vice President, Drexel University, 3141 Chestnut Street, 1-102, Philadelphia, PA 19104. *Telephone:* 215-895-1093. *Fax:* 215-895-1056. *E-mail:* tperkins@drexel.edu.

eCollege.com *www.ecollege.com/scholarships*

DEGREES AND AWARDS

MBA Business Administration (some on-campus requirements)

MS Engineering Management (some on-campus requirements), Information Systems

COURSE SUBJECT AREAS OFFERED OUTSIDE OF DEGREE PROGRAMS

Graduate: Business administration and management; engineering/industrial management; information sciences and systems
Noncredit: Information sciences and systems
See full description on page 512.

DUKE UNIVERSITY

Durham, North Carolina

Executive MBA Programs
www.fuqua.duke.edu

Duke University, founded in 1838, is an independent, religious university affiliated with the United Methodist Church. It is accredited by the Association of Theological Schools in the United States and Canada, Southern Association of Colleges and Schools. It first offered distance learning courses in 1996. In 1999–2000, it offered 31 courses at a distance. In fall 1999, there were 257 students enrolled in distance learning courses.
Course delivery sites Courses are delivered to your home, your workplace, Fuqua School of Business Europe (Frankfurt, Afghanistan), other residencies in Europe, Asia and South America (Frankfurt, Afghanistan).
Media Courses are delivered via computer software, CD-ROM, computer conferencing, World Wide Web, e-mail, print. Students and teachers may meet in person or interact via telephone, fax, e-mail, World Wide Web. The following equipment may be required: computer, Internet access, e-mail.
Restrictions Programs are available worldwide. Enrollment is restricted to individuals meeting certain criteria.
Services Distance learners have access to library services, the campus computer network, e-mail services, academic advising, tutoring at a distance.
Typical costs Tuition for Duke MBA-Cross Continent is $67500 per degree program. Tuition for Duke MBA-Global Executive is $89700 per degree program.
Registration Students may register by telephone, e-mail.
Contact Karen Courtney, Director of Recruiting and Admissions, Duke University, The Fuqua School of Business, 1 Towerview Drive, Durham, NC 27708. *Telephone:* 919-660-7804. *Fax:* 919-660-8044. *E-mail:* kcourtney@mail.duke.edu.

DEGREES AND AWARDS

MBA General Management (some on-campus requirements)

COURSE SUBJECT AREAS OFFERED OUTSIDE OF DEGREE PROGRAMS

Graduate: Accounting; business; business administration and management; economics; finance; international business; marketing; organizational behavior studies; statistics
See full description on page 514.

DUQUESNE UNIVERSITY

Pittsburgh, Pennsylvania

Center for Distance Learning
www.duq.edu/distancelearning

Duquesne University, founded in 1878, is an independent, religious university. It is accredited by the Middle States Association of Colleges and Schools. It first offered distance learning courses in 1996. In 1999–2000, it offered 34 courses at a distance. In fall 1999, there were 392 students enrolled in distance learning courses.
Course delivery sites Courses are delivered to your home, your workplace, high schools, 1 off-campus center in Harrisburg.
Media Courses are delivered via videoconferencing, computer software, CD-ROM, computer conferencing, World Wide Web, e-mail, print. Students and teachers may meet in person or interact via videoconferencing, mail, telephone, fax, e-mail, World Wide Web. The following equipment may be required: computer, modem, Internet access.
Restrictions Programs are available worldwide. Enrollment is open to anyone.
Services Distance learners have access to library services, the campus computer network, e-mail services, academic advising, career placement assistance, bookstore at a distance.
Credit-earning options Students may transfer credits from another institution or may earn credits through examinations, portfolio assessment, military training.
Typical costs *Undergraduate:* Tuition of $485 per credit plus mandatory fees of $46 per credit. *Graduate:* Tuition of $507 per credit plus mandatory fees of $46 per credit. Financial aid is available to distance learners.
Registration Students may register by mail, fax, telephone, e-mail, World Wide Web, in person.
Contact Cynthia Golden, Executive Director, CTS, Duquesne University, Rockwell Hall, 600 Forbes Avenue, Pittsburgh, PA 15206. *Telephone:* 412-396-6200. *Fax:* 412-396-5144. *E-mail:* golden@duq.edu.

DEGREES AND AWARDS

BS Nursing (service area differs from that of the overall institution)
MBA Business Administration
MLLS Liberal Arts
PharmD Pharmacy
PhD Nursing (some on-campus requirements)

COURSE SUBJECT AREAS OFFERED OUTSIDE OF DEGREE PROGRAMS

Undergraduate: Art history and criticism; business; communications; computer and information sciences; education; educational psychology; educational research; English language and literature; environmental science; ethics; fine arts; health professions and related sciences; music; nursing; philosophy and religion
Graduate: Business; communications; curriculum and instruction; education; educational research; environmental science; ethics; music; nursing; pharmacy; public policy analysis; theological studies
Noncredit: Business
See full description on page 516.

DURHAM TECHNICAL COMMUNITY COLLEGE

Durham, North Carolina
www.dtcc.cc.nc.us/

Durham Technical Community College, founded in 1961, is a state-supported, two-year college. It is accredited by the Southern Association of Colleges and Schools.

Contact Durham Technical Community College, 1637 Lawson Street, Durham, NC 27703-5023. *Telephone:* 919-686-3300.

See full description on page 676.

DUTCHESS COMMUNITY COLLEGE

Poughkeepsie, New York
www.sunydutchess.edu

Dutchess Community College, founded in 1957, is a state and locally supported, two-year college. It is accredited by the Middle States Association of Colleges and Schools. It first offered distance learning courses in 1977. In 1999–2000, it offered 17 courses at a distance. In fall 1999, there were 250 students enrolled in distance learning courses.

Course delivery sites Courses are delivered to your home, your workplace, high schools, 1 off-campus center in Wappingers Falls.

Media Courses are delivered via television, videotapes, interactive television, computer software, World Wide Web, e-mail, print. Students and teachers may meet in person or interact via mail, telephone, fax, e-mail, interactive television, World Wide Web. The following equipment may be required: television, videocassette player, computer, modem, Internet access, e-mail.

Restrictions Programs are available to in-state students only. Enrollment is open to anyone.

Services Distance learners have access to library services, the campus computer network, e-mail services, bookstore at a distance.

Credit-earning options Students may transfer credits from another institution or may earn credits through examinations, portfolio assessment, military training.

Typical costs Tuition of $89 per credit plus mandatory fees of $11 per semester for in-state residents. Tuition of $178 per credit plus mandatory fees of $11 per semester for out-of-state residents. Costs may vary. Financial aid is available to distance learners.

Registration Students may register by mail, fax, telephone, e-mail, World Wide Web, in person.

Contact Deborah Weibman, Registrar, Dutchess Community College, 53 Pendell Road, Poughkeepsie, NY 12601. *Telephone:* 914-431-8099. *Fax:* 914-431-8983. *E-mail:* weibman@sunydutchess.edu.

DEGREES AND AWARDS

Distance programs offered do not lead to a degree or other formal award.

COURSE SUBJECT AREAS OFFERED OUTSIDE OF DEGREE PROGRAMS

Undergraduate: Algebra; business administration and management; business law; criminal justice; developmental and child psychology; economics; English composition; English language and literature; genetics; human resources management; physical sciences; psychology; Spanish language and literature; statistics; teacher education

D'YOUVILLE COLLEGE

Buffalo, New York
Distance Learning
www.dyc.edu

D'Youville College, founded in 1908, is an independent, nonprofit, comprehensive institution. It is accredited by the Middle States Association of Colleges and Schools. In 1999–2000, it offered 23 courses at a distance. In fall 1999, there were 165 students enrolled in distance learning courses.

Course delivery sites Courses are delivered to your home, your workplace.

Media Courses are delivered via computer software, computer conferencing, World Wide Web, e-mail, print. Students and teachers may meet in person or interact via mail, telephone, fax, e-mail, World Wide Web. The following equipment may be required: computer, Internet access, e-mail.

Restrictions Programs are available worldwide. Enrollment is restricted to individuals meeting certain criteria.

Services Distance learners have access to library services, the campus computer network, e-mail services, academic advising, bookstore at a distance.

Credit-earning options Students may transfer credits from another institution or may earn credits through examinations.

Typical costs *Undergraduate:* Tuition of $300 per credit plus mandatory fees of $150 per semester. *Graduate:* Tuition of $377 per credit plus mandatory fees of $150 per semester. Financial aid is available to distance learners.

Registration Students may register by mail, fax, in person.

Contact Dr. John Murphy, Director of Information Technology, D'Youville College, 320 Porter Avenue, Buffalo, NY 14201. *Telephone:* 716-881-8147. *Fax:* 716-881-7790. *E-mail:* murphyj@dyc.edu.

DEGREES AND AWARDS

Distance programs offered do not lead to a degree or other formal award.

COURSE SUBJECT AREAS OFFERED OUTSIDE OF DEGREE PROGRAMS

Undergraduate: Abnormal psychology; American (U.S.) history; American literature; business administration and management; comparative literature; economics; English literature; human resources management; political science

Graduate: Health services administration; international business; special education; statistics; teacher education

EAST CAROLINA UNIVERSITY

Greenville, North Carolina
Division of Continuing Studies
www.dcs.ecu.edu

East Carolina University, founded in 1907, is a state-supported university. It is accredited by the Southern Association of Colleges and Schools. It first offered distance learning courses in 1954. In 1999–2000, it offered 310 courses at a distance. In fall 1999, there were 870 students enrolled in distance learning courses.

Course delivery sites Courses are delivered to your home, your workplace, military bases, high schools.

Media Courses are delivered via videoconferencing, interactive television, computer software, CD-ROM, computer conferencing, World Wide Web, e-mail. Students and teachers may interact via videoconferencing, audioconferencing, telephone, fax, e-mail, interactive television, World Wide Web. The following equipment may be required: computer, modem, Internet access, e-mail.

Restrictions Internet courses available worldwide, television courses limited to in-state. Enrollment is restricted to individuals meeting certain criteria.

Services Distance learners have access to library services, e-mail services, academic advising, career placement assistance, bookstore at a distance.

Credit-earning options Students may transfer credits from another institution or may earn credits through examinations.

Typical costs *Undergraduate:* Tuition of $34 per semester hour plus mandatory fees of $2 per semester hour for in-state residents. Tuition of $120 per semester hour plus mandatory fees of $3 per semester hour for out-of-state residents. *Graduate:* Tuition of $50 per semester hour plus mandatory fees of $3 per semester hour for in-state residents. Tuition of $120 per semester hour plus mandatory fees of $3 per semester hour for out-of-state residents. Costs may vary. Financial aid is available to distance learners.

Registration Students may register by mail, fax, telephone, e-mail, World Wide Web, in person.

Contact Jennifer Baysden, Distance Education Program Coordinator, East Carolina University, Erwin Building, Room 205, Greenville, NC 27871. *Telephone:* 800-398-9275. *Fax:* 919-328-4350. *E-mail:* baysdenj@mail.ecu.edu.

DEGREES AND AWARDS

BS Hospitality Management (some on-campus requirements), Industrial Technology (certain restrictions apply)
BSBE Information Technologies (certain restrictions apply)
Graduate Certificate(s) Computer Network Professional, Tele-Learning, Virtual Reality in Education and Training, Website Developer
MAE Distance Learning/Instructional Technology (some on-campus requirements)
MLS Library Science
MS Digital Communication Technology (certain restrictions apply), Industrial Technology (certain restrictions apply), Manufacturing (certain restrictions apply), Nutrition (some on-campus requirements), Occupational Safety (certain restrictions apply), Speech Language and Auditory Pathology

COURSE SUBJECT AREAS OFFERED OUTSIDE OF DEGREE PROGRAMS

Undergraduate: Engineering-related technologies; engineering/industrial management; ethics; finance; fine arts; health professions and related sciences; hospitality services management; information sciences and systems; instructional media; liberal arts, general studies, and humanities; nursing; psychology; statistics; telecommunications
Graduate: Adult education; criminal justice; education; engineering-related technologies; engineering/industrial management; fine arts; foods and nutrition studies; health professions and related sciences; hospitality services management; instructional media; library and information studies; nursing; social work; special education; teacher education; technical writing; telecommunications

See full descriptions on pages 518 and 676.

EASTERN CONNECTICUT STATE UNIVERSITY

Willimantic, Connecticut

OnlineCSU
www.onlinecsu.ctstateu.edu

Eastern Connecticut State University, founded in 1889, is a state-supported, comprehensive institution. It is accredited by the New England Association of Schools and Colleges. In 1999–2000, it offered 30 courses at a distance.

Course delivery sites Courses are delivered to your home, your workplace, military bases.

Media Courses are delivered via World Wide Web. The following equipment may be required: computer, Internet access, e-mail.

Restrictions Programs are available to in-state students only. Enrollment is open to anyone.

Services Distance learners have access to library services, the campus computer network, e-mail services, academic advising, tutoring, bookstore at a distance.

Credit-earning options Students may transfer credits from another institution or may earn credits through examinations, portfolio assessment, military training.

Typical costs *Undergraduate:* Tuition of $215 per credit hour plus mandatory fees of $30 per course. *Graduate:* Tuition of $250 per credit hour plus mandatory fees of $30 per course. Financial aid is available to distance learners.

Registration Students may register by mail, telephone, e-mail, World Wide Web, in person.

Contact Registrar's Office, Eastern Connecticut State University. *Telephone:* 860-465-5386. *Fax:* 860-465-4382.

DEGREES AND AWARDS

Distance programs offered do not lead to a degree or other formal award.

COURSE SUBJECT AREAS OFFERED OUTSIDE OF DEGREE PROGRAMS

Undergraduate: Accounting; anthropology; calculus; database management; education; ethics; health professions and related sciences; library and information studies; mathematics; nursing; psychology; statistics; visual and performing arts
Graduate: Chemistry; database management; education; health professions and related sciences; library and information studies; social work

See full descriptions on pages 504.

EASTERN ILLINOIS UNIVERSITY

Charleston, Illinois

School of Adult and Continuing Education
www.eiu.edu/~adulted

Eastern Illinois University, founded in 1895, is a state-supported, comprehensive institution. It is accredited by the North Central Association of Colleges and Schools. It first offered distance learning courses in 1994. In 1999–2000, it offered 10 courses at a distance. In fall 1999, there were 100 students enrolled in distance learning courses.

Course delivery sites Courses are delivered to your home, your workplace, Danville Area Community College (Danville), Lake Land College (Mattoon), Parkland College (Champaign), Richland Community College (Decatur).

Media Courses are delivered via television, computer software, World Wide Web. Students and teachers may interact via videoconferencing, mail, telephone, fax, e-mail. The following equipment may be required: computer, Internet access, e-mail.

Restrictions Programs are available worldwide. Enrollment is open to anyone.

Services Distance learners have access to library services, the campus computer network, e-mail services, academic advising, tutoring, career placement assistance at a distance.

Credit-earning options Students may transfer credits from another institution or may earn credits through examinations, portfolio assessment, military training, business training.

Typical costs *Undergraduate:* Tuition of $94 per credit plus mandatory fees of $26.25 per credit for in-state residents. Tuition of $281.75 per

credit plus mandatory fees of $26.25 per credit for out-of-state residents. *Graduate:* Tuition of $99 per credit plus mandatory fees of $26.25 per credit for in-state residents. Tuition of $297 per credit plus mandatory fees of $26.25 per credit for out-of-state residents. *Noncredit courses:* $150 per course. Costs may vary. Financial aid is available to distance learners.
Registration Students may register by telephone.
Contact Dr. Kaye Woodward, Director, Board of Trustees BA Program, Eastern Illinois University, 600 Lincoln Avenue, Charleston, IL 61920. *Telephone:* 217-581-5618. *Fax:* 217-581-6697. *E-mail:* bogba@www.eiu.edu.

DEGREES AND AWARDS

BA Liberal Arts (certain restrictions apply)

COURSE SUBJECT AREAS OFFERED OUTSIDE OF DEGREE PROGRAMS

Undergraduate: Business administration and management; home economics and family studies; human resources management; physical sciences
Graduate: Business administration and management; home economics and family studies; human resources management; teacher education
Noncredit: Business administration and management

EASTERN KENTUCKY UNIVERSITY

Richmond, Kentucky
Division of Extended Programs
www.eku.edu

Eastern Kentucky University, founded in 1906, is a state-supported, comprehensive institution. It is accredited by the Southern Association of Colleges and Schools. It first offered distance learning courses in 1941. In 1999–2000, it offered 160 courses at a distance. In fall 1999, there were 1,500 students enrolled in distance learning courses.
Course delivery sites Courses are delivered to your home, high schools, Morehead State University (Morehead), 3 off-campus centers in Corbin, Danville, Manchester.
Media Courses are delivered via television, videotapes, videoconferencing, interactive television, audiotapes, computer conferencing, World Wide Web, e-mail, print. Students and teachers may interact via mail, telephone, e-mail, interactive television. The following equipment may be required: television, computer, Internet access.
Restrictions Programs are available worldwide. Enrollment is open to anyone.
Services Distance learners have access to library services, the campus computer network, e-mail services at a distance.
Credit-earning options Students may transfer credits from another institution or may earn credits through examinations.
Typical costs *Undergraduate:* Tuition of $100 per credit for in-state residents. Tuition of $268 per credit for out-of-state residents. *Graduate:* Tuition of $145 per credit for in-state residents. Tuition of $391 per credit for out-of-state residents. *Noncredit courses:* $140 per course. Financial aid is available to distance learners.
Registration Students may register by mail, telephone, in person.
Contact Kenneth R. Nelson, Director, Eastern Kentucky University, Box 27-A, Richmond, KY 40475. *Telephone:* 606-622-2001. *Fax:* 606-622-1177. *E-mail:* sosnelso@acs.eku.edu.

DEGREES AND AWARDS

Distance programs offered do not lead to a degree or other formal award.

COURSE SUBJECT AREAS OFFERED OUTSIDE OF DEGREE PROGRAMS

Undergraduate: Algebra; American (U.S.) history; anthropology; art history and criticism; biology; botany; business administration and management; comparative literature; corrections; criminal justice; curriculum and instruction; economics; educational psychology; English composition; English literature; ethics; family and marriage counseling; foods and nutrition studies; geography; German language and literature; health and physical education/fitness; information sciences and systems; marketing; mass media; music; political science; psychology; radio and television broadcasting; real estate; religious studies; sign language; sociology; Spanish language and literature; special education; teacher education
Graduate: Curriculum and instruction; education administration; educational psychology; library and information studies; nursing; student counseling
See full descriptions on pages 556 and 676.

EASTERN MAINE TECHNICAL COLLEGE

Bangor, Maine
Outreach Services
www.emtc.org

Eastern Maine Technical College, founded in 1966, is a state-supported, two-year college. It is accredited by the New England Association of Schools and Colleges. It first offered distance learning courses in 1991. In 1999–2000, it offered 2 courses at a distance. In fall 1999, there were 50 students enrolled in distance learning courses.
Course delivery sites Courses are delivered to your home, your workplace, military bases, high schools, University of Maine System (Bangor), 3 off-campus centers in Belfast, East Millinochet, Ellsworth.
Media Courses are delivered via videoconferencing, interactive television, computer software, World Wide Web, e-mail, print. Students and teachers may meet in person or interact via videoconferencing, audioconferencing, mail, telephone, fax, e-mail, interactive television, World Wide Web. The following equipment may be required: Internet access, e-mail.
Restrictions Programs are available to in-state students only. Enrollment is open to anyone.
Services Distance learners have access to library services, e-mail services, academic advising, tutoring, career placement assistance, bookstore at a distance.
Credit-earning options Students may transfer credits from another institution or may earn credits through examinations, portfolio assessment, military training, business training.
Typical costs Tuition of $68 per credit plus mandatory fees of $9 per credit. Costs may vary. Financial aid is available to distance learners.
Registration Students may register by mail, fax, telephone, in person.
Contact Beth Mahoney, Dean of Outreach Services, Eastern Maine Technical College, One Industrial Drive, East Millinochet, ME 04430. *Telephone:* 207-746-5741. *Fax:* 207-746-9389. *E-mail:* mahoney@maine.edu.

DEGREES AND AWARDS

Distance programs offered do not lead to a degree or other formal award.

COURSE SUBJECT AREAS OFFERED OUTSIDE OF DEGREE PROGRAMS

Undergraduate: Child care and development; computer and information sciences; electricians technology; English composition; hospitality services management

EASTERN MENNONITE UNIVERSITY

Harrisonburg, Virginia

Eastern Mennonite Seminary
www.emu.edu/dist_lrn/index.html

Eastern Mennonite University, founded in 1917, is an independent, religious, comprehensive institution. It is accredited by the Association of Theological Schools in the United States and Canada, Southern Association of Colleges and Schools. It first offered distance learning courses in 1997. In 1999–2000, it offered 3 courses at a distance.

Course delivery sites Courses are delivered to your home, your workplace.

Media Courses are delivered via World Wide Web, e-mail, print. Students and teachers may interact via mail, telephone, fax, e-mail, World Wide Web. The following equipment may be required: computer, modem, Internet access, e-mail.

Restrictions Programs are available worldwide. Enrollment is restricted to individuals meeting certain criteria.

Services Distance learners have access to library services, the campus computer network, e-mail services, bookstore at a distance.

Credit-earning options Students may transfer credits from another institution.

Typical costs Tuition of $278 per credit.

Registration Students may register by mail, fax, World Wide Web, in person.

Contact Don Yoder, Director of Admissions, Seminary and Graduate Programs, Eastern Mennonite University, 1200 Park Road, Harrisonburg, VA 22802-2462. *Telephone:* 540-432-4257. *Fax:* 540-432-4444. *E-mail:* yoderda@emu.edu.

DEGREES AND AWARDS

Undergraduate Certificate(s) Theological Studies (certain restrictions apply)

COURSE SUBJECT AREAS OFFERED OUTSIDE OF DEGREE PROGRAMS

Graduate: Bible studies; religious studies; theological studies

EASTERN MICHIGAN UNIVERSITY

Ypsilanti, Michigan

Distance Education
emuonline.edu/

Eastern Michigan University, founded in 1849, is a state-supported, comprehensive institution. It is accredited by the North Central Association of Colleges and Schools. In 1999–2000, it offered 60 courses at a distance. In fall 1999, there were 500 students enrolled in distance learning courses.

Course delivery sites Courses are delivered to your home, your workplace, high schools, Northwestern Michigan College (Traverse City), Washtenaw Community College (Ann Arbor), 5 off-campus centers in Flint, Jackson, Livonia, Monroe, Traverse City.

Media Courses are delivered via television, videotapes, interactive television, audiotapes, computer software, CD-ROM, computer conferencing, World Wide Web, e-mail, print. Students and teachers may meet in person or interact via audioconferencing, mail, telephone, fax, e-mail, interactive television, World Wide Web. The following equipment may be required: television, videocassette player, computer, modem, Internet access, e-mail.

Restrictions Programs are available worldwide. Enrollment is open to anyone.

Services Distance learners have access to library services, the campus computer network, e-mail services, academic advising, career placement assistance, bookstore at a distance.

Credit-earning options Students may transfer credits from another institution or may earn credits through examinations, portfolio assessment, military training, business training.

Typical costs *Undergraduate:* Tuition of $115 per credit hour plus mandatory fees of $58 per credit hour. *Graduate:* Tuition of $220 per credit hour plus mandatory fees of $58 per credit hour. Costs may vary. Financial aid is available to distance learners.

Registration Students may register by mail, fax, telephone, e-mail, World Wide Web, in person.

Contact Kathy Randles, Director of Distance Education, Eastern Michigan University, 611 West Cross Street, Ypsilanti, MI 48197. *Telephone:* 734-487-1081. *Fax:* 734-487-6695. *E-mail:* distance.education@emich.edu.

eCollege.com *www.ecollege.com/scholarships*

DEGREES AND AWARDS

Distance programs offered do not lead to a degree or other formal award.

COURSE SUBJECT AREAS OFFERED OUTSIDE OF DEGREE PROGRAMS

Undergraduate: African-American studies; American (U.S.) history; American literature; business administration and management; business communications; business law; computer and information sciences; drama and theater; English composition; English literature; French language and literature; genetics; interior design; investments and securities; mathematics; military studies; music; nursing; philosophy and religion; psychology; sociology; women's studies

Graduate: African-American studies; business administration and management; business law; education administration; gerontology; special education; teacher education

EASTERN NAZARENE COLLEGE

Quincy, Massachusetts

ENConline
enconline.org

Eastern Nazarene College, founded in 1918, is an independent, religious, comprehensive institution affiliated with the Church of the Nazarene. It is accredited by the New England Association of Schools and Colleges. It first offered distance learning courses in 1999. In 1999–2000, it offered 7 courses at a distance.

Course delivery sites Courses are delivered to your home.

Media Courses are delivered via videotapes, audiotapes, computer software, computer conferencing, World Wide Web, e-mail, print. Students and teachers may interact via mail, telephone, fax, e-mail, World Wide Web. The following equipment may be required: television, videocassette player, computer, modem, Internet access, e-mail.

Restrictions Programs are available to Mid-Atlantic and New England states. Enrollment is restricted to individuals meeting certain criteria.

Services Distance learners have access to library services, bookstore at a distance.

Typical costs *Undergraduate:* Tuition of $230 per credit hour. *Graduate:* Tuition of $330 per credit hour. Tuition for Pastoral Education is $150 per credit hour. Fees for Online courses are $40 per credit hour.

Registration Students may register by mail, fax, World Wide Web, in person.

Contact Fred Cawthorne, Director of Distance Learning, Eastern Nazarene College, 23 East Elm Avenue, Quincy, MA 02170. *Telephone:* 617-745-3531. *Fax:* 617-745-3937. *E-mail:* cawthorf@enc.edu.

eCollege.com *www.ecollege.com/scholarships*

DEGREES AND AWARDS

Distance programs offered do not lead to a degree or other formal award.

COURSE SUBJECT AREAS OFFERED OUTSIDE OF DEGREE PROGRAMS

Undergraduate: American (U.S.) history; religious studies
Graduate: Educational psychology; English as a second language (ESL)
Noncredit: Religious studies

EASTERN OKLAHOMA STATE COLLEGE

Wilburton, Oklahoma

Eastern Oklahoma State College, founded in 1908, is a state-supported, two-year college. It is accredited by the North Central Association of Colleges and Schools. It first offered distance learning courses in 1992. In 1999–2000, it offered 16 courses at a distance. In fall 1999, there were 88 students enrolled in distance learning courses.
Course delivery sites Courses are delivered to your home, high schools, 2 off-campus centers in Idabel, McAlester.
Media Courses are delivered via television, interactive television, World Wide Web. Students and teachers may interact via fax, e-mail, interactive television, World Wide Web. The following equipment may be required: computer, Internet access, e-mail.
Restrictions Programs are available nationwide. Enrollment is open to anyone.
Services Distance learners have access to library services, the campus computer network, e-mail services at a distance.
Credit-earning options Students may transfer credits from another institution or may earn credits through examinations.
Typical costs Tuition of $47.50 per credit hour. Financial aid is available to distance learners.
Registration Students may register by in person.
Contact Eddie Woods, Registrar, Eastern Oklahoma State College, 1301 West Main Street, Wilburton, OK 74578. *Telephone:* 918-465-2361 Ext. 210. *Fax:* 918-465-2431. *E-mail:* ewoods@eosc.cc.ok.us.

DEGREES AND AWARDS

Distance programs offered do not lead to a degree or other formal award.

COURSE SUBJECT AREAS OFFERED OUTSIDE OF DEGREE PROGRAMS

Undergraduate: Algebra; American (U.S.) history; criminology; English composition; English literature; horticulture; human resources management; nursing; political science; social psychology; statistics

EASTERN OREGON UNIVERSITY

La Grande, Oregon
Division of Distance Education
www.eou.edu/dde

Eastern Oregon University, founded in 1929, is a state-supported, comprehensive institution. It is accredited by the Northwest Association of Schools and Colleges. It first offered distance learning courses in 1978. In 1999–2000, it offered 300 courses at a distance. In fall 1999, there were 800 students enrolled in distance learning courses.
Course delivery sites Courses are delivered to your home, your workplace, military bases, Blue Mountain Community College (Pendleton), Central Oregon Community College (Bend), Southwestern Oregon Community College (Coos Bay), Treasure Valley Community College (Ontario), 9 off-campus centers in Baker City, Bend, Burns, Coos Bay, Enterprise, John Day, Ontario, Pendleton, Portland.
Media Courses are delivered via television, videotapes, videoconferencing, audiotapes, computer software, World Wide Web, e-mail, print. Students and teachers may interact via videoconferencing, audioconferencing, mail, telephone, e-mail, World Wide Web. The following equipment may be required: television, videocassette player, computer, modem, Internet access, e-mail.
Restrictions Programs are available in North America and to armed services personnel abroad. Enrollment is open to anyone.
Services Distance learners have access to library services, e-mail services, academic advising, career placement assistance, bookstore at a distance.
Credit-earning options Students may transfer credits from another institution or may earn credits through examinations, portfolio assessment, military training, business training.
Typical costs *Undergraduate:* Tuition of $85 per credit. *Graduate:* Tuition of $132 per credit. Financial aid is available to distance learners.
Registration Students may register by mail, fax, e-mail, World Wide Web, in person.
Contact Dr. Joseph Hart, Director, Distance Learning, Eastern Oregon University, Division of Distance Education, Zabel Hall #232, One University Boulevard, La Grande, OR 97850-2899. *Telephone:* 541-962-3378. *Fax:* 541-962-3627. *E-mail:* dde@eou.edu.

eCollege.com *www.ecollege.com/scholarships*

DEGREES AND AWARDS

BS Business Administration, Business and Economics, Fire Services Administration (some on-campus requirements), Liberal Studies, Philosophy, Politics and Economics, Physical Education/Health

COURSE SUBJECT AREAS OFFERED OUTSIDE OF DEGREE PROGRAMS

Undergraduate: Accounting; administrative and secretarial services; agriculture; area, ethnic, and cultural studies; biological and life sciences; business; business administration and management; computer and information sciences; education; English language and literature; health and physical education/fitness; human resources management; journalism; liberal arts, general studies, and humanities; mathematics; nursing; philosophy and religion; physical sciences; psychology; social sciences; teacher education; visual and performing arts
Graduate: Education

Special note
Founded in 1929, Eastern Oregon University is a state-supported, comprehensive institution. Eastern is accredited by the Northwest Association of Schools and Colleges. The Division of Distance Education is the distance learning arm of the institution, with a long

history of experience delivering both courses and degrees (the first courses were offered in 1978). In 2000–01, Eastern offers more than 300 courses at a distance and 6 different BA/BS distance degree programs: the multidisciplinary liberal studies degree; the philosophy, politics, and economics degree; the business/economics degree; the business administration degree; the physical education and health degree; and the fire services administration degree. Distance learning courses are offered in a variety of modalities (Web, computer conferencing, correspondence, weekend college) to accommodate the requirements of each degree program. All students are required to have e-mail access and Web-browsing capabilities. More than 1,100 students are currently enrolled in the distance learning degree programs. The courses and degrees are available to students in the United States and Canada and to armed services personnel abroad. Eastern does not charge extra out-of-state tuition. Most of the courses are taught by the same faculty members who teach on-campus courses; the distance learning degrees are the same as those available on campus. Degree-seeking students receive close advising support and have access to full library services at a distance. The admission requirements for students entering the distance learning degree programs are the same as those for on-campus programs; Eastern is not an open admission university. Students may take up to 8 quarter course units per term without being admitted. Specific information about enrollment is available at the online class registration site (http://webster.eou.edu. For more information about courses or degree programs, students should send an e-mail to dde@eou.edu or visit the Division of Distance Education Web site (http://www.eou.edu/dde) and fill out an online inquiry form.

See full description on page 822.

EASTERN SHORE COMMUNITY COLLEGE

Melfa, Virginia
Academic Division
www.es.cc.va.us

Eastern Shore Community College, founded in 1971, is a state-supported, two-year college. It is accredited by the Southern Association of Colleges and Schools. In 1999–2000, it offered 8 courses at a distance. In fall 1999, there were 40 students enrolled in distance learning courses.
Course delivery sites Courses are delivered to your home.
Media Courses are delivered via interactive television, computer software, CD-ROM, e-mail. Students and teachers may meet in person or interact via videoconferencing, telephone, fax, e-mail. The following equipment may be required: computer, e-mail.
Restrictions Programs are available to local area students. Enrollment is open to anyone.
Services Distance learners have access to library services, e-mail services, academic advising at a distance.
Typical costs Tuition of $37 per credit plus mandatory fees of $3 per credit for local area residents. Tuition of $37 per credit for in-state residents. Tuition of $165 per credit plus mandatory fees of $3 per credit for out-of-state residents. Financial aid is available to distance learners.
Registration Students may register by mail, in person.
Contact Mary Kay Mulligan, Director of the Academic Division, Eastern Shore Community College, 29300 Lankford Highway, Melfa, VA 23410. *Telephone:* 757-787-5948. *Fax:* 757-787-5984. *E-mail:* esmullm@es.cc.va.us.

DEGREES AND AWARDS

Distance programs offered do not lead to a degree or other formal award.

COURSE SUBJECT AREAS OFFERED OUTSIDE OF DEGREE PROGRAMS

Undergraduate: Business; computer and information sciences; German language and literature; mathematics; music

EASTERN WYOMING COLLEGE

Torrington, Wyoming
Outreach
ewcweb.ewc.whecn.edu

Eastern Wyoming College, founded in 1948, is a state and locally supported, two-year college. It is accredited by the North Central Association of Colleges and Schools. It first offered distance learning courses in 1990. In 1999–2000, it offered 1 course at a distance. In fall 1999, there were 20 students enrolled in distance learning courses.
Course delivery sites Courses are delivered to your home, 12 off-campus centers in Chugwater, Douglas, Glendo, Glenrock, Guernsey, Hulett, Lusk, Moorcroft, Newcastle, Sundance, Upton, Whesland.
Media Courses are delivered via television, videotapes, World Wide Web, e-mail. Students and teachers may meet in person or interact via mail, telephone, fax, e-mail. The following equipment may be required: television, videocassette player, computer, Internet access, e-mail.
Restrictions Programs are available to in-state students only. Enrollment is open to anyone.
Services Distance learners have access to library services, the campus computer network, e-mail services, academic advising, tutoring, career placement assistance, bookstore at a distance.
Credit-earning options Students may transfer credits from another institution or may earn credits through examinations, military training.
Typical costs Tuition of $42 per credit hour plus mandatory fees of $15 per credit hour. Costs may vary. Financial aid is available to distance learners.
Registration Students may register by mail, fax, telephone, e-mail, in person.
Contact Dee Ludwig, Associate Dean of Instruction, Eastern Wyoming College, 3200 West C Street, Torrington, WY 82240. *Telephone:* 307-532-8221. *Fax:* 307-532-8222. *E-mail:* dludwig@ewc1.ewc.whecn.edu.

DEGREES AND AWARDS

Distance programs offered do not lead to a degree or other formal award.

COURSE SUBJECT AREAS OFFERED OUTSIDE OF DEGREE PROGRAMS

Undergraduate: Area, ethnic, and cultural studies; business; business administration and management; economics; fine arts; history; human resources management; information sciences and systems; law and legal studies; liberal arts, general studies, and humanities; philosophy and religion; political science; psychology; sociology

EAST GEORGIA COLLEGE

Swainsboro, Georgia

East Georgia College, founded in 1973, is a state-supported, two-year college. It is accredited by the Southern Association of Colleges and Schools. It first offered distance learning courses in 1997.
Contact East Georgia College, 131 College Circle, Swainsboro, GA 30401-2699. *Telephone:* 912-289-2000.
See full description on page 676.

EAST TENNESSEE STATE UNIVERSITY

Johnson City, Tennessee
Office of Distance Education
de.etsu.edu/

East Tennessee State University, founded in 1911, is a state-supported university. It is accredited by the Southern Association of Colleges and Schools. It first offered distance learning courses in 1991. In 1999–2000, it offered 75 courses at a distance. In fall 1999, there were 1,408 students enrolled in distance learning courses.

Course delivery sites Courses are delivered to your home, your workplace, Pellissippi State Technical Community College (Knoxville), 3 off-campus centers in Bristol, Greeneville, Kingsport.

Media Courses are delivered via television, videotapes, videoconferencing, interactive television, computer software, computer conferencing, World Wide Web. Students and teachers may meet in person or interact via videoconferencing, telephone, e-mail, interactive television, World Wide Web. The following equipment may be required: television, videocassette player, computer, modem, Internet access, e-mail.

Restrictions Programs are available to in-state students only. Enrollment is open to anyone.

Services Distance learners have access to library services, e-mail services, academic advising, tutoring, career placement assistance, bookstore at a distance.

Credit-earning options Students may transfer credits from another institution or may earn credits through examinations, portfolio assessment, military training.

Typical costs *Undergraduate:* Tuition of $90 per credit plus mandatory fees of $10 per credit for in-state residents. Tuition of $224 per credit for out-of-state residents. *Graduate:* Tuition of $137 per credit plus mandatory fees of $10 per credit for in-state residents. Tuition of $224 per credit for out-of-state residents. Financial aid is available to distance learners.

Registration Students may register by telephone, e-mail, World Wide Web, in person.

Contact Dr. Darcey Cuffman, Programming Coordinator, East Tennessee State University, Box 70427, Johnson City, TN 37614. *Telephone:* 423-439-6809. *Fax:* 423-439-8564. *E-mail:* cuffmand@etsu.edu.

DEGREES AND AWARDS

MBA Business Administration (service area differs from that of the overall institution)

COURSE SUBJECT AREAS OFFERED OUTSIDE OF DEGREE PROGRAMS

Undergraduate: Business administration and management; chemistry; developmental and child psychology; economics; educational psychology; English language and literature; geology; history; home economics and family studies; liberal arts, general studies, and humanities; mathematics; nursing; protective services; public health; special education

Graduate: Business administration and management; economics; educational psychology; teacher education

See full description on page 676.

ECKERD COLLEGE

St. Petersburg, Florida
Extended Campus Program
www.eckerd.edu/

Eckerd College, founded in 1958, is an independent, religious, four-year college. It is accredited by the Southern Association of Colleges and Schools. In 1999–2000, it offered 90 courses at a distance. In fall 1999, there were 90 students enrolled in distance learning courses.

Course delivery sites Courses are delivered to your home, your workplace, military bases, 3 off-campus centers in Sarasota, Seminole, Tampa.

Media Courses are delivered via World Wide Web, e-mail, print. Students and teachers may interact via mail, telephone, fax, e-mail. The following equipment may be required: computer, modem, Internet access, e-mail.

Restrictions Programs are available nationwide. Enrollment is open to anyone.

Services Distance learners have access to library services, the campus computer network, e-mail services, academic advising, tutoring, career placement assistance, bookstore at a distance.

Credit-earning options Students may transfer credits from another institution or may earn credits through examinations, portfolio assessment, military training, business training.

Typical costs Tuition of $655 per course. There is a $160 admission fee. Financial aid is available to distance learners.

Registration Students may register by mail, fax, telephone, in person.

Contact Alina M. Freedman, Coordinator of Directed Studies, Eckerd College, 4200 54th Avenue South, St. Petersburg, FL 33711. *Telephone:* 800-234-4735. *Fax:* 727-864-8422. *E-mail:* freedmam@eckerd.edu.

DEGREES AND AWARDS

BA Business Management, Human Development, Organizational Studies

EDGECOMBE COMMUNITY COLLEGE

Tarboro, North Carolina

Edgecombe Community College, founded in 1968, is a state and locally supported, two-year college. It is accredited by the Southern Association of Colleges and Schools.

Contact Edgecombe Community College, 2009 West Wilson Street, Tarboro, NC 27886-9399. *Telephone:* 252-823-5166. *Fax:* 252-823-6817.

See full description on page 676.

EDISON COMMUNITY COLLEGE

Fort Myers, Florida
Distance Learning
edison.edu

Edison Community College, founded in 1962, is a state and locally supported, two-year college. It is accredited by the Southern Association of Colleges and Schools. It first offered distance learning courses in 1993. In 1999–2000, it offered 25 courses at a distance. In fall 1999, there were 1,200 students enrolled in distance learning courses.

Course delivery sites Courses are delivered to your home, Broward Community College (Fort Lauderdale), 3 off-campus centers in La Belle, Naples, Punta Gorda.

Media Courses are delivered via videotapes, videoconferencing, interactive television, audiotapes, CD-ROM, World Wide Web, e-mail, print. Students and teachers may meet in person or interact via videoconferencing, mail, telephone, fax, e-mail, World Wide Web. The following equipment may be required: television, videocassette player, computer, Internet access, e-mail.

Restrictions Programs are available to local area students. Enrollment is open to anyone.

Services Distance learners have access to library services, academic advising, career placement assistance, bookstore at a distance.

Credit-earning options Students may transfer credits from another institution or may earn credits through examinations.

Typical costs Tuition of $38 per credit hour for local area residents. Tuition of $142 per credit hour for in-state residents. *Noncredit courses:* $30 per course. Financial aid is available to distance learners.

Registration Students may register by mail, telephone, e-mail, World Wide Web, in person.

Contact Estrella Iglesias, District Director, Learning Resources, Edison Community College, PO Box 60210, Fort Myers, FL 33910. *Telephone:* 941-489-9455. *Fax:* 941-489-9095. *E-mail:* eiglesia@edison.edu.

DEGREES AND AWARDS

AA Liberal Arts (service area differs from that of the overall institution)

COURSE SUBJECT AREAS OFFERED OUTSIDE OF DEGREE PROGRAMS

Undergraduate: Area, ethnic, and cultural studies; astronomy and astrophysics; business; business administration and management; chemistry; communications; developmental and child psychology; economics; educational psychology; English composition; English language and literature; European languages and literatures; geology; health and physical education/fitness; history; liberal arts, general studies, and humanities; mathematics; political science; psychology; sociology; statistics

Special note
Edison Community College celebrates 39 years of service to southwest Florida this year. Edison serves a 5-county district, with campus locations in Lee, Collier, and Charlotte Counties and services in Hendry and Glades Counties. Since the first students were admitted to Edison in fall 1962, the College has enrolled more than 150,000 students in credit courses. The College is accredited by the Southern Association of Colleges and Schools. It first offered distance learning courses in 1993. In 1998–99, it offered 65 courses at a distance. Distance learning courses are offered via video-based telecourse, Internet, and compressed video technologies and meet transfer, degree, and certificate requirements. Telecourse materials are available for check out through the Learning Resource Centers at each campus location and through Hendry/Glades services. Students must have a VCR to view VHS tapes. Students may earn a complete Associate of Arts (AA) degree through Edison's telecourse offerings. Online courses are conducted on the Internet. To participate in Web-based courses, students must have access to a computer that runs Windows 95 or Windows NT or a 60 megahertz 603 CPU Macintosh with OS 7.05 or later, an Internet connection, and Netscape Navigator 4.0 or Internet Explorer 4.0 or higher. Students who plan to enroll in distance learning courses must follow the same admission procedures as other students. Students should visit the College's Web site (http://www.edison.edu) for a schedule of classes, an application, and enrollment information.

EDISON STATE COMMUNITY COLLEGE

Piqua, Ohio
www.edison.cc.oh.us

Edison State Community College, founded in 1973, is a state-supported, two-year college. It is accredited by the North Central Association of Colleges and Schools. It first offered distance learning courses in 1987. In 1999–2000, it offered 47 courses at a distance. In fall 1999, there were 503 students enrolled in distance learning courses.

Course delivery sites Courses are delivered to your home, your workplace, military bases, high schools, 1 off-campus center in Greenville.

Media Courses are delivered via videotapes, videoconferencing, computer software, CD-ROM, World Wide Web, e-mail, print. Students and teachers may meet in person or interact via videoconferencing, mail, telephone, fax, e-mail, World Wide Web. The following equipment may be required: television, videocassette player, computer, modem, Internet access, e-mail.

Restrictions Programs are available worldwide. Enrollment is open to anyone.

Services Distance learners have access to library services, the campus computer network, e-mail services, academic advising, tutoring, bookstore at a distance.

Credit-earning options Students may transfer credits from another institution or may earn credits through examinations, portfolio assessment, military training, business training.

Typical costs Tuition of $81 per semester credit for in-state residents. Tuition of $162 per semester credit for out-of-state residents. Costs may vary. Financial aid is available to distance learners.

Registration Students may register by mail, fax, telephone, e-mail, in person.

Contact Beth Culbertson, Admissions Office, Edison State Community College. *Telephone:* 937-778-8600 Ext. 317. *Fax:* 937-778-1920. *E-mail:* info@edison.cc.oh.us.

DEGREES AND AWARDS

Distance programs offered do not lead to a degree or other formal award.

COURSE SUBJECT AREAS OFFERED OUTSIDE OF DEGREE PROGRAMS

Undergraduate: Accounting; archaeology; art history and criticism; biological and life sciences; biology; business; business administration and management; business communications; cell biology; communications; computer and information sciences; drama and theater; ecology; economics; English composition; English language and literature; English literature; ethics; French language and literature; human resources management; liberal arts, general studies, and humanities; marketing; nursing; philosophy and religion; psychology; social sciences; sociology; Spanish language and literature; technical writing

EDUKAN

Great Bend, Kansas
EduKan
www.edukan.org

EduKan, founded in 1999, is a state-supported, two-year college. It first offered distance learning courses in 1999. In 1999–2000, it offered 65 courses at a distance. In fall 1999, there were 54 students enrolled in distance learning courses.

Course delivery sites Courses are delivered to your home, your workplace, military bases, high schools, Barton County Community College (Great Bend), Colby Community College (Colby), Dodge City Community College (Dodge City), Garden City Community College (Garden City), Pratt Community College and Area Vocational School (Pratt), Seward County Community College (Liberal).

Media Courses are delivered via videotapes, CD-ROM, World Wide Web, e-mail, print. Students and teachers may meet in person or interact via mail, telephone, fax, e-mail, World Wide Web. The following equipment may be required: computer, modem, Internet access, e-mail.

Restrictions Programs are available worldwide. Enrollment is open to anyone.

Services Distance learners have access to library services, e-mail services, academic advising, tutoring, career placement assistance, bookstore at a distance.

Credit-earning options Students may transfer credits from another institution or may earn credits through examinations, military training, business training.
Typical costs Tuition of $115 per credit hour. Financial aid is available to distance learners.
Registration Students may register by World Wide Web.
Contact Matt Gotschall, Executive Director, EduKan, 245 Northeast 30th Road, Great Bend, KS 67530. *Telephone:* 316-792-9204. *Fax:* 316-786-1168. *E-mail:* gotschallm@barton.cc.ks.us.

eCollege.com *www.ecollege.com/scholarships*

DEGREES AND AWARDS

AGS General Studies (some on-campus requirements)

COURSE SUBJECT AREAS OFFERED OUTSIDE OF DEGREE PROGRAMS

Undergraduate: Biological and life sciences; business; English language and literature; history; mathematics; philosophy and religion; physical sciences; psychology; social sciences; visual and performing arts
See full description on page 520.

EL CAMINO COLLEGE

Torrance, California
Distance Education
www.elcamino.cc.ca.us

El Camino College, founded in 1947, is a state-supported, two-year college. It is accredited by the Western Association of Schools and Colleges, Inc. In 1999–2000, it offered 15 courses at a distance. In fall 1999, there were 800 students enrolled in distance learning courses.
Course delivery sites Courses are delivered to your home, your workplace.
Media Courses are delivered via television, videotapes, World Wide Web, e-mail. Students and teachers may meet in person or interact via telephone, e-mail. The following equipment may be required: television, computer, modem, Internet access, e-mail.
Restrictions Programs are available to local area students. Enrollment is open to anyone.
Services Distance learners have access to library services, tutoring at a distance.
Credit-earning options Students may transfer credits from another institution.
Typical costs Mandatory fees of $11 per unit for in-state residents. Mandatory fees of $11 per unit for in-state residents. Mandatory fees of $136 per unit for out-of-state residents. Financial aid is available to distance learners.
Registration Students may register by in person.
Contact Joanie Shannon, Program Coordinator, El Camino College, Distance Education, 16007 Crenshaw Boulevard, Torrance, CA 90506. *Telephone:* 310-660-6453. *Fax:* 310-660-3513. *E-mail:* jshannon@elcamino.cc.ca.us.

DEGREES AND AWARDS

Distance programs offered do not lead to a degree or other formal award.

COURSE SUBJECT AREAS OFFERED OUTSIDE OF DEGREE PROGRAMS

Undergraduate: American (U.S.) history; anthropology; astronomy and astrophysics; child care and development; English as a second language (ESL); English language and literature; ethics; geology; health and physical education/fitness; liberal arts, general studies, and humanities; logic; music; political science; psychology; real estate; sociology

ELIZABETH CITY STATE UNIVERSITY

Elizabeth City, North Carolina

Elizabeth City State University, founded in 1891, is a state-supported, four-year college. It is accredited by the Southern Association of Colleges and Schools.
Contact Elizabeth City State University, 1704 Weeksville Road, Elizabeth City, NC 27909-7806. *Telephone:* 252-335-3400. *Fax:* 252-335-3731.
See full description on page 676.

ELIZABETHTOWN COLLEGE

Elizabethtown, Pennsylvania
Center for Continuing Education and Distance Learning
courses.etown.edu

Elizabethtown College, founded in 1899, is an independent, religious, four-year college affiliated with the Church of the Brethren. It is accredited by the Middle States Association of Colleges and Schools. In 1999–2000, it offered 5 courses at a distance. In fall 1999, there were 50 students enrolled in distance learning courses.
Course delivery sites Courses are delivered to your home, your workplace, military bases, other colleges.
Media Courses are delivered via videoconferencing, computer software, computer conferencing, World Wide Web, e-mail. Students and teachers may meet in person or interact via videoconferencing, mail, telephone, fax, e-mail, World Wide Web. The following equipment may be required: computer, modem, Internet access, e-mail.
Restrictions Programs are available worldwide. Enrollment is restricted to individuals meeting certain criteria.
Services Distance learners have access to library services, the campus computer network, academic advising, tutoring at a distance.
Credit-earning options Students may transfer credits from another institution or may earn credits through examinations, portfolio assessment, military training, business training.
Typical costs Tuition of $225 per credit plus mandatory fees of $100 per course. Costs may vary. Financial aid is available to distance learners.
Registration Students may register by mail, fax, telephone, e-mail, in person.
Contact Dr. John Kokolus, Dean of Continuing Education and Distance Learning, Elizabethtown College, One Alpha Drive, Elizabethtown, PA 17022-2298. *Telephone:* 800-877-2694. *Fax:* 717-361-1466. *E-mail:* kokolusj@etown.edu.

DEGREES AND AWARDS

Undergraduate Certificate(s) Accounting
BPS Business Administration, Communications, Computer Engineering, Criminal Justice, Early Childhood Education, Human Services, Industrial Engineering, Public Administration

ELIZABETHTOWN COMMUNITY COLLEGE

Elizabethtown, Kentucky

Distance Learning Program
www.elizabethtowncc.com

Elizabethtown Community College, founded in 1964, is a state-supported, two-year college. It is accredited by the Southern Association of Colleges and Schools. It first offered distance learning courses in 1985. In 1999–2000, it offered 25 courses at a distance. In fall 1999, there were 130 students enrolled in distance learning courses.
Course delivery sites Courses are delivered to your home, military bases, high schools, 1 off-campus center in Fort Knox.
Media Courses are delivered via television, videotapes, videoconferencing, interactive television, CD-ROM, World Wide Web, e-mail. Students and teachers may meet in person or interact via videoconferencing, mail, telephone, fax, e-mail, interactive television, World Wide Web. The following equipment may be required: computer, modem, Internet access, e-mail.
Restrictions Programs are available worldwide. Enrollment is open to anyone.
Services Distance learners have access to library services, academic advising, bookstore at a distance.
Credit-earning options Students may transfer credits from another institution or may earn credits through examinations, military training.
Typical costs Tuition of $46 per credit hour plus mandatory fees of $4 per credit hour for in-state residents. Tuition of $138 per credit hour plus mandatory fees of $4 per credit hour for out-of-state residents. Costs may vary. Financial aid is available to distance learners.
Registration Students may register by World Wide Web, in person.
Contact Dr. Jon Burke, Dean of Student Affairs, Elizabethtown Community College, 600 College Street Road, Elizabethtown, KY 42701. *Telephone:* 270-769-2371. *Fax:* 270-769-0736. *E-mail:* jon.burke@kctcs.net.

DEGREES AND AWARDS

Distance programs offered do not lead to a degree or other formal award.

COURSE SUBJECT AREAS OFFERED OUTSIDE OF DEGREE PROGRAMS

Undergraduate: American (U.S.) history; art history and criticism; business administration and management; drama and theater; European history; fire science; German language and literature; liberal arts, general studies, and humanities; nursing; psychology; social psychology; sociology; Spanish language and literature
See full description on page 556.

EL PASO COMMUNITY COLLEGE

El Paso, Texas

Distance Education Network

El Paso Community College, founded in 1969, is a county-supported, two-year college. It is accredited by the Southern Association of Colleges and Schools. It first offered distance learning courses in 1983. In 1999–2000, it offered 40 courses at a distance. In fall 1999, there were 1,000 students enrolled in distance learning courses.
Course delivery sites Courses are delivered to your home, your workplace, military bases, high schools, 6 off-campus centers in El Paso.
Media Courses are delivered via television, videoconferencing, World Wide Web. Students and teachers may meet in person or interact via mail, telephone, fax, e-mail, World Wide Web. The following equipment may be required: television, videocassette player, computer, modem, Internet access, e-mail.
Restrictions Televised courses are available to students within the broadcast area; videoconferencing and Internet courses are available statewide. Enrollment is open to anyone.
Services Distance learners have access to the campus computer network, e-mail services at a distance.
Credit-earning options Students may transfer credits from another institution or may earn credits through examinations, portfolio assessment.
Typical costs Tuition is $269 for six hours for in-state students and $324 for six hours for out-of-state students. Costs may vary. Financial aid is available to distance learners.
Registration Students may register by mail, telephone, in person.
Contact Jenny Giron, Associate Vice President, El Paso Community College, Instructional Services, PO Box 20500, El Paso, TX 79908. *Telephone:* 915-831-2348. *Fax:* 915-831-2363. *E-mail:* jennyg@epcc.edu.

DEGREES AND AWARDS

eCollege.com *www.ecollege.com/scholarships*

Distance programs offered do not lead to a degree or other formal award.

COURSE SUBJECT AREAS OFFERED OUTSIDE OF DEGREE PROGRAMS

Undergraduate: Accounting; American (U.S.) history; anthropology; business administration and management; business communications; child care and development; economics; English as a second language (ESL); English composition; environmental science; fire science; geology; health professions and related sciences; human resources management; marketing; mass media; music; political science; psychology; sociology; Spanish language and literature
Noncredit: Spanish language and literature

EMBRY-RIDDLE AERONAUTICAL UNIVERSITY

Daytona Beach, Florida

Department of Distance Learning
www.db.erau.edu

Embry-Riddle Aeronautical University, founded in 1926, is an independent, nonprofit, comprehensive institution. It is accredited by the Southern Association of Colleges and Schools. In 1999–2000, it offered 75 courses at a distance. In fall 1999, there were 2,535 students enrolled in distance learning courses.
Course delivery sites Courses are delivered to your home, your workplace, military bases, 110 off-campus centers in Fort Lauderdale, Fort Walton, Jacksonville, Miami, Orlando, Panama City, Pensacola, Space Coast (Cocoa), Tampa, Abilene (TX), Alamagordo (NM), Albequerque (NM), Altus (OK), Anchorage (AK), Atlanta (GA), Atlantic City (NJ), Aviano, Italy, Barstow (CA), Beaufort (SC), Biloxi (MS), Brunswick (ME), Charleston (SC), Cheyenne (WY), Cincinnati (OH), Clovis (NM), Colorado Springs (Ft. Carson) (CO), Columbus (GA), Columbus (MS), Corpus Christi (TX), Dayton (OH), Del Rio (TX), East Mesa (Phoenix) (AZ), Edwards AFB (CA), Enid (OK), Enterprise (AL), Everett (WA), Fairbanks (AK), Fairfield (CA), Fallon (NV), Fayetteville (NC), Fort Worth (TX), Ft. Campbell (KE), Ft. Eustis (VA), Ft. Knox (KE), Giebelstadt, Germany, Gielenkirchen, Germany, Goldsboro (NC), Grand Forks (ND), Great Falls (MT), Hanau, Germany, Heidelberg, Germany, Honolulu (HI), Houston (TX), Illesheim, Germany, Indianapolis (IN), Kailua (HI), Katterbach, Germany, Kingsville (TX), Lakenheath, England,

Langley AFB (VA), Las Vegas (NV), Lemoore (CA), Little Rock ANGB (AR), Long Beach/Los Angeles (CA), Luke (Phoenix) (AZ), Macon (GA), Malilani (HI), Marysville/Yuba City (CA), McGuire AFB(Philadelphia Area) (NJ), Memphis (TN), Mildenhall, England, Minneapolis (MN), Minot (ND), Mobile (AL), Mountain Home (ID), Norfolk (VA), Oakland (CA), Oceanside (CA), Ogden/Salt Lake City (UT), Oklahoma City (OK), Omaha (NE), Palmdale (CA), Patuxent River (MD), Ramstein, Germany, Rapid City (SD), Riverside (CA), Rota, Spain, Sacramento (CA), San Antonio (TX), San Diego (CA), San Jose (CA), Savannah (GA), Seattle (WA), Selfridge ANG (Detroit) (MI), Shreveport (LA), Sigonella, Sicily, Sky Harbor Airport (Phoenix) (AZ), Spangdahlem, Germany, Spokane (WA), Sumter (SC), Tacoma (WA), Tucson (AZ), Valdosta (GA), Ventura (CA), Vicenza, Italy, Washington (DC), Whidbey Island (WA), Wichita (KA), Wiesbaden, Germany.

Media Courses are delivered via videotapes, computer software, computer conferencing, World Wide Web, print. Students and teachers may meet in person or interact via mail, telephone, fax, e-mail, World Wide Web. The following equipment may be required: videocassette player, computer, Internet access, e-mail.

Restrictions Programs are available worldwide. Enrollment is restricted to individuals meeting certain criteria.

Services Distance learners have access to library services, academic advising, career placement assistance, bookstore at a distance.

Credit-earning options Students may transfer credits from another institution or may earn credits through examinations, portfolio assessment, military training.

Typical costs *Undergraduate:* Tuition of $145 per credit. *Graduate:* Tuition of $306 per credit. Financial aid is available to distance learners.

Registration Students may register by mail, fax, telephone, e-mail, in person.

Contact Terry Whittum, Director, Distance Learning Enrollment Office, Embry-Riddle Aeronautical University, 600 South Clyde Morris Boulevard, Daytona Beach, FL 32114. *Telephone:* 904-226-6397. *Fax:* 904-226-7627. *E-mail:* whittumt@db.erau.edu.

DEGREES AND AWARDS

BS Management of Technical Operations (certain restrictions apply), Professional Aeronautics (certain restrictions apply)
MAS Aeronautical Science (certain restrictions apply)

COURSE SUBJECT AREAS OFFERED OUTSIDE OF DEGREE PROGRAMS

Undergraduate: Aviation; business; English composition; mathematics; technical writing
Graduate: Aviation; business
See full description on page 522.

EMBRY-RIDDLE AERONAUTICAL UNIVERSITY, EXTENDED CAMPUS

Daytona Beach, Florida

Center for Distance Learning
www.erau.edu

Embry-Riddle Aeronautical University, Extended Campus, founded in 1970, is an independent, nonprofit, comprehensive institution. It is accredited by the Southern Association of Colleges and Schools. It first offered distance learning courses in 1980. In 1999–2000, it offered 60 courses at a distance. In fall 1999, there were 1,012 students enrolled in distance learning courses.

Course delivery sites Courses are delivered to your home, your workplace, military bases.

Media Courses are delivered via videotapes, audiotapes, World Wide Web, print. Students and teachers may interact via mail, telephone, fax, e-mail, World Wide Web. The following equipment may be required: television, videocassette player, computer, Internet access.

Restrictions Programs are available worldwide. Enrollment is restricted to individuals meeting certain criteria.

Services Distance learners have access to library services, academic advising, career placement assistance at a distance.

Credit-earning options Students may transfer credits from another institution or may earn credits through examinations, portfolio assessment, military training.

Typical costs *Undergraduate:* Tuition of $141 per credit hour. *Graduate:* Tuition of $297 per credit hour.

Registration Students may register by mail, fax, telephone, e-mail, in person.

Contact John Holub, Applications Processor, Embry-Riddle Aeronautical University, Extended Campus, Center for Distance Learning, 600 South Clyde Morris Boulevard, Daytona Beach, FL 32114-3900. *Telephone:* 904-226-6363. *Fax:* 904-226-7627. *E-mail:* holubj@cts.db.erau.edu.

DEGREES AND AWARDS

AS Aviation Business Administration, Professional Aeronautics
BS Management of Technical Operations, Professional Aeronautics
MAS Aeronautical Science (certain restrictions apply)

COURSE SUBJECT AREAS OFFERED OUTSIDE OF DEGREE PROGRAMS

Undergraduate: Accounting; business; business administration and management; business law; calculus; computer and information sciences; economics; English composition; English language and literature; finance; human resources management; marketing; mathematics; organizational behavior studies; physics; psychology; statistics; technical writing
Graduate: Business administration and management; computer and information sciences; labor relations/studies; management information systems

EMPORIA STATE UNIVERSITY

Emporia, Kansas

Office of Lifelong Learning
lifelong.emporia.edu

Emporia State University, founded in 1863, is a state-supported, comprehensive institution. It is accredited by the North Central Association of Colleges and Schools. It first offered distance learning courses in 1970. In 1999–2000, it offered 83 courses at a distance. In fall 1999, there were 912 students enrolled in distance learning courses.

Course delivery sites Courses are delivered to your home, your workplace.

Media Courses are delivered via computer software, computer conferencing, World Wide Web, e-mail, print. Students and teachers may interact via audioconferencing, mail, telephone, fax, e-mail, World Wide Web. The following equipment may be required: computer, modem, Internet access, e-mail.

Restrictions Programs are available nationwide. Enrollment is open to anyone.

Services Distance learners have access to library services, the campus computer network, e-mail services, academic advising, career placement assistance, bookstore at a distance.

Credit-earning options Students may transfer credits from another institution or may earn credits through examinations, military training.

Typical costs *Undergraduate:* Tuition of $84 per credit hour. *Graduate:* Tuition of $114 per credit hour. Financial aid is available to distance learners.

Registration Students may register by mail, fax, telephone, World Wide Web, in person.

Contact Office of Lifelong Learning, Emporia State University, 1200 Commercial Street, Emporia, KS 66801-5087. *Telephone:* 316-341-5385. *Fax:* 316-341-5744. *E-mail:* lifelong@emporia.edu.

DEGREES AND AWARDS

BGS Integrated Studies (certain restrictions apply)
MS Physical Education (certain restrictions apply)

COURSE SUBJECT AREAS OFFERED OUTSIDE OF DEGREE PROGRAMS

Undergraduate: Education; geology; health and physical education/fitness; information sciences and systems; library and information studies
Graduate: Education; geology; health and physical education/fitness; library and information studies

ERIE COMMUNITY COLLEGE, NORTH CAMPUS

Williamsville, New York
www.sunyerie.edu/

Erie Community College, North Campus, founded in 1946, is a state and locally supported, two-year college. It is accredited by the Middle States Association of Colleges and Schools. In 1999–2000, it offered 60 courses at a distance. In fall 1999, there were 600 students enrolled in distance learning courses.

Course delivery sites Courses are delivered to your home, your workplace.

Media Courses are delivered via videotapes, interactive television, computer software, World Wide Web. Students and teachers may meet in person or interact via mail, telephone, e-mail, interactive television. The following equipment may be required: television, videocassette player, computer, modem, Internet access, e-mail.

Restrictions Programs are available nationwide. Enrollment is open to anyone.

Services Distance learners have access to library services, the campus computer network, e-mail services, career placement assistance at a distance.

Credit-earning options Students may earn credits through examinations.

Typical costs Undergraduate in-county tuition is $1237 per semester. In-state tuition is $2475 per semester. Out-of-state tuition is $2475 per semester. Mandatory fees are $90 per semester. Some offsite locations offer discounts on courses at that location. Cost for a noncredit course varies. Costs may vary. Financial aid is available to distance learners.

Registration Students may register by fax, telephone, e-mail, in person.

Contact John Birks, Media Coordinator, Distance Learning, Erie Community College, North Campus, 6205 Main Street, Williamsville, NY 14221. *Telephone:* 716-851-1282. *Fax:* 716-851-1266. *E-mail:* birks@ecc.edu.

DEGREES AND AWARDS

Distance programs offered do not lead to a degree or other formal award.

COURSE SUBJECT AREAS OFFERED OUTSIDE OF DEGREE PROGRAMS

Undergraduate: Biology; business; chemistry; English language and literature; liberal arts, general studies, and humanities; mathematics; physical sciences; physics; social sciences

ESSEX COUNTY COLLEGE

Newark, New Jersey

Essex County College, founded in 1966, is a county-supported, two-year college. It is accredited by the Middle States Association of Colleges and Schools.

Contact Essex County College, 303 University Avenue, Newark, NJ 07102-1798. *Telephone:* 973-877-3000. *Fax:* 973-623-6449.

See full description on page 600.

EUGENE BIBLE COLLEGE

Eugene, Oregon
External Studies Department
www.ebc.edu/external.htm

Eugene Bible College, founded in 1925, is an independent, religious, four-year college affiliated with the Open Bible Standard Churches. It is accredited by the Accrediting Association of Bible Colleges. In 1999–2000, it offered 58 courses at a distance. In fall 1999, there were 55 students enrolled in distance learning courses.

Course delivery sites Courses are delivered to your home, your workplace, military bases, high schools.

Media Courses are delivered via audiotapes, print. Students and teachers may meet in person or interact via mail, telephone, fax, e-mail.

Restrictions Programs are available worldwide. Enrollment is open to anyone.

Services Distance learners have access to e-mail services, academic advising at a distance.

Credit-earning options Students may transfer credits from another institution.

Typical costs Tuition of $50 per quarter hour. There is a one-time registration fee of $25. *Noncredit courses:* $100 per course. Costs may vary.

Registration Students may register by mail, fax, telephone, e-mail, in person.

Contact Dave Sinclair, Director of External Studies, Eugene Bible College, 2155 Bailey Hill Road, Eugene, OR 97405. *Telephone:* 541-485-1780 Ext. 115. *Fax:* 541-343-5801. *E-mail:* distance-ed@ebc.edu.

DEGREES AND AWARDS

Undergraduate Certificate(s) Bible Studies
BA Biblical Studies Completion Program (certain restrictions apply; some on-campus requirements), Christian Counseling Completion Program (certain restrictions apply; some on-campus requirements), Missionary Studies Completion Program (certain restrictions apply; some on-campus requirements), Pastoral Studies Completion Program (certain restrictions apply; some on-campus requirements), Youth Ministry Completion Program (certain restrictions apply; some on-campus requirements)
BRE Christian Education Completion Program (certain restrictions apply; some on-campus requirements)
BS Biblical Studies Completion Program (certain restrictions apply; some on-campus requirements), Christian Counseling Completion Program (certain restrictions apply; some on-campus requirements), Missionary Studies Completion Program (certain restrictions apply; some on-campus requirements), Pastoral Studies Completion Program (certain restrictions apply; some on-campus requirements), Youth Ministry Completion Program (certain restrictions apply; some on-campus requirements)
BSM Sacred Music Completion Program (certain restrictions apply; some on-campus requirements)

COURSE SUBJECT AREAS OFFERED OUTSIDE OF DEGREE PROGRAMS

Undergraduate: Bible studies; education; religious studies; speech; theological studies
Noncredit: Bible studies; education; religious studies; speech; theological studies

---

EVERETT COMMUNITY COLLEGE

Everett, Washington

Library/Media/Arts and Distance Learning
www.evcc.ctc.edu

Everett Community College, founded in 1941, is a state-supported, two-year college. It is accredited by the Northwest Association of Schools and Colleges.
Course delivery sites Courses are delivered to your home.
Media Courses are delivered via videotapes, audiotapes, computer conferencing, World Wide Web, e-mail, print. Students and teachers may meet in person or interact via mail, telephone, e-mail, World Wide Web. The following equipment may be required: television, videocassette player, computer, modem, Internet access, e-mail.
Restrictions Programs are available to local area students. Enrollment is open to anyone.
Services Distance learners have access to library services, bookstore at a distance.
Credit-earning options Students may transfer credits from another institution or may earn credits through examinations.
Typical costs Tuition of $52.60 per credit for local area residents. Tuition of $52.60 per credit for in-state residents. Tuition of $207.60 per credit for out-of-state residents. Financial aid is available to distance learners.
Registration Students may register by telephone, in person.
Contact Sharon Stier, Administrative Assistant, Everett Community College, Department of Distance Learning, 2000 Tower Street, Everet, WA 98201. *Telephone:* 425-388-9501. *Fax:* 425-388-9144. *E-mail:* distance@evcc.ctc.edu.

DEGREES AND AWARDS

AAS Arts and Science (certain restrictions apply; some on-campus requirements)
AFA Fine Arts (certain restrictions apply; some on-campus requirements)
AGS General Studies (certain restrictions apply; some on-campus requirements)
ATA Technical Arts (certain restrictions apply; some on-campus requirements)

COURSE SUBJECT AREAS OFFERED OUTSIDE OF DEGREE PROGRAMS

Undergraduate: Anthropology; art history and criticism; business; computer and information sciences; earth science; English language and literature; French language and literature; history; library and information studies; music; psychology; sociology; Spanish language and literature

---

EVERGLADES COLLEGE

Ft. Lauderdale, Florida
www.evergladescollege.edu

Everglades College is a proprietary, four-year college. It is accredited by the Accrediting Commission of Career Schools and Colleges of Technology. In 1999–2000, it offered 40 courses at a distance. In fall 1999, there were 20 students enrolled in distance learning courses.

Course delivery sites Courses are delivered to your home, your workplace, military bases, high schools.
Media Courses are delivered via computer software, CD-ROM, computer conferencing, World Wide Web, e-mail, print. Students and teachers may interact via mail, telephone, fax, e-mail, World Wide Web. The following equipment may be required: videocassette player, computer, modem, Internet access, e-mail.
Restrictions Programs are available worldwide. Enrollment is restricted to individuals meeting certain criteria.
Services Distance learners have access to library services, the campus computer network, academic advising, career placement assistance, bookstore at a distance.
Credit-earning options Students may transfer credits from another institution.
Typical costs Tuition of $338 per credit hour. Financial aid is available to distance learners.
Registration Students may register by mail, fax, telephone, e-mail, World Wide Web, in person.
Contact Gary Markowitz, Campus Director, Everglades College, 1500 Northwest 49th Street, Suite 600, Fort Lauderdale, FL 33309. *Telephone:* 954-772-2655. *Fax:* 954-772-2695. *E-mail:* garym@evergladescollege.edu.

DEGREES AND AWARDS

AS Aviation Management (some on-campus requirements), Professional Aviation (service area differs from that of the overall institution)
BS Applied Management, Aviation Management (some on-campus requirements), Business Administration, e-Commerce, Information Technology, Professional Aviation

See full description on page 524.

EVERGREEN VALLEY COLLEGE

San Jose, California

Distance Education Program
www.evc.edu/distance_education/index.html

Evergreen Valley College, founded in 1975, is a state and locally supported, two-year college. It is accredited by the Western Association of Schools and Colleges, Inc. It first offered distance learning courses in 1981. In 1999–2000, it offered 12 courses at a distance. In fall 1999, there were 592 students enrolled in distance learning courses.
Course delivery sites Courses are delivered to your home, your workplace, military bases, high schools.
Media Courses are delivered via television, videotapes, audiotapes, computer software, e-mail. Students and teachers may meet in person or interact via mail, telephone, fax, e-mail, World Wide Web. The following equipment may be required: television, computer, Internet access.
Restrictions Programs are available to in-state students only. Enrollment is restricted to individuals meeting certain criteria.
Services Distance learners have access to e-mail services at a distance.
Credit-earning options Students may transfer credits from another institution or may earn credits through examinations, business training.
Typical costs Tuition of $11 per credit for in-state residents. Tuition of $137 per credit for out-of-state residents. Costs may vary.
Registration Students may register by telephone, in person.
Contact Jan Tomisaka, Program Specialist, Evergreen Valley College, 3095 Yerba Buena Road, San Jose, CA 95135-1598. *Telephone:* 408-270-6422. *Fax:* 408-532-1858. *E-mail:* jan.tomisaka@sjeccd.cc.ca.us.

DEGREES AND AWARDS

Distance programs offered do not lead to a degree or other formal award.

COURSE SUBJECT AREAS OFFERED OUTSIDE OF DEGREE PROGRAMS

Undergraduate: Accounting; astronomy and astrophysics; business administration and management; computer and information sciences; European languages and literatures; history; political science; social psychology; sociology; Spanish language and literature

FAIRLEIGH DICKINSON UNIVERSITY, THE NEW COLLEGE OF GENERAL AND CONTINUING STUDIES

Teaneck, New Jersey

Office of Educational Technology
www.fdu.edu

Fairleigh Dickinson University, The New College of General and Continuing Studies, founded in 1942, is an independent, nonprofit, comprehensive institution. It is accredited by the Middle States Association of Colleges and Schools. It first offered distance learning courses in 1990. In 1999–2000, it offered 20 courses at a distance.
Course delivery sites Courses are delivered to your home, your workplace, high schools, Sussex County Community College (Newton).
Media Courses are delivered via videotapes, videoconferencing, interactive television, computer software, computer conferencing, World Wide Web, e-mail, print. Students and teachers may meet in person or interact via videoconferencing, mail, telephone, fax, e-mail, interactive television, World Wide Web.
Restrictions Interactive television is offered statewide; Web courses are available worldwide. Enrollment is restricted to individuals meeting certain criteria.
Services Distance learners have access to library services, e-mail services, academic advising, career placement assistance, bookstore at a distance.
Credit-earning options Students may earn credits through examinations, portfolio assessment.
Typical costs *Undergraduate:* Tuition of $478 per credit. *Graduate:* Tuition of $550 per credit. Costs may vary. Financial aid is available to distance learners.
Registration Students may register by mail, fax, telephone, in person.
Contact Ellen Spaldo, Director of Educational Technology, Fairleigh Dickinson University, The New College of General and Continuing Studies, Office of Educational Technology, 1000 River Road, H328A, Teaneck, NJ 07666. *Telephone:* 201-692-7155. *Fax:* 201-692-7273. *E-mail:* spaldo@fdu.edu.

> **eCollege**.com *www.ecollege.com/scholarships*

DEGREES AND AWARDS

Graduate Certificate(s) Education (service area differs from that of the overall institution), English as a Second Language (service area differs from that of the overall institution), Information Systems (certain restrictions apply; service area differs from that of the overall institution; some on-campus requirements)
MS Electrical Engineering (service area differs from that of the overall institution)

COURSE SUBJECT AREAS OFFERED OUTSIDE OF DEGREE PROGRAMS

Undergraduate: Biology; economics; English composition; English language and literature; history; logic; marketing
Graduate: Accounting; business; communications; computer and information sciences; electrical engineering; information sciences and systems; psychology; teacher education

FAIRMONT STATE COLLEGE

Fairmont, West Virginia

Fairmont State College, founded in 1865, is a state-supported, four-year college. It is accredited by the North Central Association of Colleges and Schools.
Contact Fairmont State College, 1201 Locust Avenue, Fairmont, WV 26554. *Telephone:* 304-367-4000. *Fax:* 304-367-4789.
See full description on page 676.

FASHION INSTITUTE OF TECHNOLOGY

New York, New York

Fashion Institute of Technology, founded in 1944, is a state and locally supported, comprehensive institution. It is accredited by the Middle States Association of Colleges and Schools. In 1999–2000, it offered 25 courses at a distance. In fall 1999, there were 160 students enrolled in distance learning courses.
Course delivery sites Courses are delivered to your home.
Media Courses are delivered via computer software, World Wide Web, e-mail. Students and teachers may interact via e-mail, World Wide Web. The following equipment may be required: computer, modem, Internet access, e-mail.
Restrictions Programs are available nationwide. Enrollment is restricted to individuals meeting certain criteria.
Services Distance learners have access to library services at a distance.
Typical costs *Undergraduate:* Tuition of $125 per credit for local area residents. Tuition of $125 per credit for in-state residents. Tuition of $310 per credit for out-of-state residents. *Graduate:* Tuition of $125 per credit for local area residents. Tuition of $310 per credit for in-state residents. Tuition of $460 per credit for out-of-state residents. Financial aid is available to distance learners.
Registration Students may register by mail, World Wide Web, in person.
Contact Prof. Helena Glass, Fashion Institute of Technology, 27th Street and 7th Avenue, New York, NY 10001. *Telephone:* 212-217-7683.

DEGREES AND AWARDS

AAS Fashion Merchandising Management

COURSE SUBJECT AREAS OFFERED OUTSIDE OF DEGREE PROGRAMS

Undergraduate: Advertising; business; business law; clothing/apparel and textile studies; English as a second language (ESL); management information systems; marketing; photography
See full description on page 526.

FAYETTEVILLE TECHNICAL COMMUNITY COLLEGE

Fayetteville, North Carolina

Virtual Campus
www.faytech.cc.nc.us

Fayetteville Technical Community College, founded in 1961, is a state-supported, two-year college. It is accredited by the Southern Association of Colleges and Schools. It first offered distance learning courses in 1980.

In 1999–2000, it offered 45 courses at a distance. In fall 1999, there were 950 students enrolled in distance learning courses.

Course delivery sites Courses are delivered to your home, your workplace, military bases.

Media Courses are delivered via television, videotapes, videoconferencing, World Wide Web, e-mail. Students and teachers may meet in person or interact via videoconferencing, mail, telephone, fax, e-mail, World Wide Web. The following equipment may be required: television, videocassette player, computer, modem, Internet access, e-mail.

Restrictions Programs are available worldwide. Enrollment is open to anyone.

Services Distance learners have access to library services, academic advising, tutoring, career placement assistance, bookstore at a distance.

Credit-earning options Students may transfer credits from another institution or may earn credits through examinations, military training.

Typical costs Tuition of $27.50 per credit hour plus mandatory fees of $9.25 per semester for in-state residents. Tuition of $169.75 per credit hour plus mandatory fees of $9.25 per semester for out-of-state residents. *Noncredit courses:* $35 per course. Financial aid is available to distance learners.

Registration Students may register by mail, fax, telephone, e-mail, in person.

Contact Bobby J. Ervin, Dean of Business Programs, Fayetteville Technical Community College, PO Box 35236, Fayetteville, NC 28303. *Telephone:* 910-678-8466. *Fax:* 910-678-8445. *E-mail:* ervinb@ftccmail. faytech.cc.nc.us.

DEGREES AND AWARDS

AA Liberal Arts and General Studies (service area differs from that of the overall institution)
AD Business Administration (service area differs from that of the overall institution), Funeral Service Education (service area differs from that of the overall institution; some on-campus requirements)

COURSE SUBJECT AREAS OFFERED OUTSIDE OF DEGREE PROGRAMS

Undergraduate: Accounting; business; child care and development; computer and information sciences; criminology; economics; English language and literature; funeral service education; history; marketing; mathematics; music; political science; psychology; religious studies; sociology

See full description on page 676.

FERRIS STATE UNIVERSITY

Big Rapids, Michigan
www.ferris.edu

Ferris State University, founded in 1884, is a state-supported, comprehensive institution. It is accredited by the North Central Association of Colleges and Schools. In 1999–2000, it offered 50 courses at a distance. In fall 1999, there were 500 students enrolled in distance learning courses.

Course delivery sites Courses are delivered to your home, your workplace, other colleges, 5 off-campus centers in Dowagiac/Niles, Flint, Grand Rapids, Muskegon, Traverse City.

Media Courses are delivered via videotapes, interactive television, CD-ROM, World Wide Web, e-mail, print. Students and teachers may meet in person or interact via mail, telephone, fax, e-mail, interactive television, World Wide Web. The following equipment may be required: computer, Internet access, e-mail.

Restrictions Programs are predominately available local and statewide; specified courses are available nationwide and worldwide. Enrollment is restricted to individuals meeting certain criteria.

Services Distance learners have access to library services, the campus computer network, e-mail services, academic advising, career placement assistance, bookstore at a distance.

Credit-earning options Students may transfer credits from another institution or may earn credits through examinations, portfolio assessment, military training.

Typical costs *Undergraduate:* Tuition of $172 per credit hour plus mandatory fees of $38.50 per semester for local area residents. Tuition of $172 per credit hour plus mandatory fees of $38.50 per semester for in-state residents. Tuition of $366 per credit hour plus mandatory fees of $38.50 per semester for out-of-state residents. *Graduate:* Tuition of $230 per credit hour plus mandatory fees of $38.50 per semester for local area residents. Tuition of $230 per credit hour plus mandatory fees of $38.50 per semester for in-state residents. Tuition of $470 per credit hour plus mandatory fees of $38.50 per semester for out-of-state residents. Costs may vary. Financial aid is available to distance learners.

Registration Students may register by mail, fax, telephone, e-mail, World Wide Web, in person.

Contact Office of Admissions, Ferris State University, 420 Oak Street, PRK-101, Big Rapids, MI 49307-2020. *Telephone:* 616-592-2100. *Fax:* 616-592-3944. *E-mail:* admissions@titan.ferris.edu.

DEGREES AND AWARDS

Distance programs offered do not lead to a degree or other formal award.

COURSE SUBJECT AREAS OFFERED OUTSIDE OF DEGREE PROGRAMS

Undergraduate: Computer and information sciences; computer programming
Graduate: Computer and information sciences; computer programming

FIELDING INSTITUTE

Santa Barbara, California
www.fielding.edu

Fielding Institute, founded in 1974, is an independent, nonprofit, graduate institution. It is accredited by the Western Association of Schools and Colleges, Inc. It first offered distance learning courses in 1974. In fall 1999, there were 1,300 students enrolled in distance learning courses.

Course delivery sites Courses are delivered to your home, your workplace.

Media Courses are delivered via computer software, World Wide Web, e-mail, print. Students and teachers may interact via audioconferencing, mail, telephone, fax, e-mail, World Wide Web. The following equipment may be required: computer, modem, Internet access, e-mail.

Restrictions Programs are available worldwide. Enrollment is restricted to individuals meeting certain criteria.

Services Distance learners have access to library services, the campus computer network, e-mail services, academic advising, tutoring at a distance.

Typical costs Tuition of $12,750 per year. Costs may vary. Financial aid is available to distance learners.

Contact Sylvia Williams, Director, Enrollment Management Services, Fielding Institute, 2112 Santa Barbara Street, Santa Barbara, CA 93105. *Telephone:* 805-687-1099 Ext. 4006. *Fax:* 805-687-9793. *E-mail:* sawilliams@fielding.edu.

DEGREES AND AWARDS

Graduate Certificate(s) Neuropsychology (certain restrictions apply; service area differs from that of the overall institution; some on-campus requirements)
MA Organizational Design and Effectiveness (some on-campus requirements)

EdD Educational Leadership and Change (certain restrictions apply; service area differs from that of the overall institution; some on-campus requirements)

PhD Clinical Psychology (service area differs from that of the overall institution; some on-campus requirements), Human and Organizational Development (some on-campus requirements)

COURSE SUBJECT AREAS OFFERED OUTSIDE OF DEGREE PROGRAMS

Graduate: Education administration; organizational behavior studies; psychology

FINGER LAKES COMMUNITY COLLEGE

Canandaigua, New York
www.fingerlakes.edu

Finger Lakes Community College, founded in 1965, is a state and locally supported, two-year college. It is accredited by the Middle States Association of Colleges and Schools. In 1999–2000, it offered 13 courses at a distance. In fall 1999, there were 76 students enrolled in distance learning courses.

Course delivery sites Courses are delivered to your home, your workplace, military bases, high schools, State University of New York College at Brockport (Brockport).

Media Courses are delivered via television, videotapes, videoconferencing, CD-ROM, World Wide Web, e-mail. Students and teachers may meet in person or interact via videoconferencing, mail, telephone, fax, e-mail, World Wide Web. The following equipment may be required: television, videocassette player, computer, modem, Internet access, e-mail.

Restrictions Programs are available to in-state students only. Enrollment is open to anyone.

Services Distance learners have access to library services, e-mail services, academic advising at a distance.

Credit-earning options Students may transfer credits from another institution or may earn credits through examinations, military training, business training.

Typical costs Tuition of $87 per credit hour plus mandatory fees of $3 per credit hour for in-state residents. Tuition of $174 per credit hour plus mandatory fees of $3 per credit hour for out-of-state residents. Cost for noncredit course ranges from $40 to $150. Financial aid is available to distance learners.

Registration Students may register by mail, fax, in person.

Contact Nancy Purdy, Associate Dean of Instruction, Finger Lakes Community College, 4355 Lakeshore Drive, Canandaigua, NY 14424. *Telephone:* 716-394-3500 Ext. 290. *Fax:* 716-394-5005. *E-mail:* purdynh@ mail.fingerlakes.edu.

DEGREES AND AWARDS

Distance programs offered do not lead to a degree or other formal award.

COURSE SUBJECT AREAS OFFERED OUTSIDE OF DEGREE PROGRAMS

Undergraduate: Biology; business administration and management; business communications; economics; ethics; law and legal studies; marketing; physics; sociology; technical writing

FITCHBURG STATE COLLEGE

Fitchburg, Massachusetts
Office of Graduate and Continuing Education
www.fsc.edu

Fitchburg State College, founded in 1894, is a state-supported, comprehensive institution. It is accredited by the New England Association of Schools and Colleges. It first offered distance learning courses in 1989. In 1999–2000, it offered 20 courses at a distance. In fall 1999, there were 41 students enrolled in distance learning courses.

Course delivery sites Courses are delivered to your home, your workplace, 1 off-campus center in South Hampton, Bermuda.

Media Courses are delivered via television, computer software, World Wide Web. Students and teachers may interact via mail, telephone, fax, e-mail, World Wide Web. The following equipment may be required: television, computer, modem, Internet access, e-mail.

Restrictions Programs are available worldwide. Enrollment is restricted to individuals meeting certain criteria.

Services Distance learners have access to library services, the campus computer network, e-mail services, academic advising, tutoring at a distance.

Credit-earning options Students may transfer credits from another institution or may earn credits through examinations, portfolio assessment, military training.

Typical costs *Undergraduate:* Tuition of $110 per semester hour plus mandatory fees of $7 per credit. *Graduate:* Tuition of $140 per semester hour plus mandatory fees of $7 per credit. Other mandatory fees include $10 application fee and $55 per semester registration fee. Financial aid is available to distance learners.

Registration Students may register by mail, fax, telephone, e-mail, World Wide Web, in person.

Contact Kathy Radley, Coordinator of Extended Instruction Programs, Fitchburg State College, 160 Pearl Street, Fitchburg, MA 01420. *Telephone:* 978-665-3181. *Fax:* 978-665-3658. *E-mail:* gce@fsc.edu.

DEGREES AND AWARDS

MEd Elementary Education (service area differs from that of the overall institution), Secondary Education (service area differs from that of the overall institution)

COURSE SUBJECT AREAS OFFERED OUTSIDE OF DEGREE PROGRAMS

Undergraduate: Biology; business administration and management; developmental and child psychology; economics; geology; history; liberal arts, general studies, and humanities; sociology
Graduate: Business administration and management; teacher education

FLATHEAD VALLEY COMMUNITY COLLEGE

Kalispell, Montana
Education Services

Flathead Valley Community College, founded in 1967, is a state and locally supported, two-year college. It is accredited by the Northwest Association of Schools and Colleges. In 1999–2000, it offered 1 course at a distance. In fall 1999, there were 24 students enrolled in distance learning courses.

Course delivery sites Courses are delivered to your home, your workplace.

Media Courses are delivered via television, audiotapes, World Wide Web. Students and teachers may meet in person or interact via telephone. The following equipment may be required: television, videocassette player.

Restrictions Programs are available to local area students. Enrollment is open to anyone.

Services Distance learners have access to e-mail services at a distance.

Credit-earning options Students may transfer credits from another institution or may earn credits through examinations, portfolio assessment, military training, business training.

Typical costs Tuition of $41 per credit plus mandatory fees of $22.35 per credit for local area residents. Tuition of $67 per credit plus mandatory fees of $22.35 per credit for in-state residents. Tuition of $169 per credit plus mandatory fees of $22.35 per credit for out-of-state residents. *Noncredit courses:* $64 per course. Costs may vary. Financial aid is available to distance learners.

Registration Students may register by mail, fax, telephone, in person.

Contact Faith Hodges, Director of Institutional Research and Planning, Flathead Valley Community College, 777 Grandview Drive, Kalispell, MT 59901. *Telephone:* 406-756-3812. *Fax:* 406-756-3815. *E-mail:* fhodges@mail.fvcc.cc.mt.us.

DEGREES AND AWARDS

Distance programs offered do not lead to a degree or other formal award.

COURSE SUBJECT AREAS OFFERED OUTSIDE OF DEGREE PROGRAMS

Undergraduate: Area, ethnic, and cultural studies; astronomy and astrophysics; English language and literature; geography

FLORENCE-DARLINGTON TECHNICAL COLLEGE

Florence, South Carolina

Learning Resources Division
www.flo.tec.sc.us

Florence-Darlington Technical College, founded in 1963, is a state-supported, two-year college. It is accredited by the Southern Association of Colleges and Schools. It first offered distance learning courses in 1985. In 1999–2000, it offered 42 courses at a distance. In fall 1999, there were 250 students enrolled in distance learning courses.

Course delivery sites Courses are delivered to your home, your workplace, military bases, high schools, Chesterfield-Marlboro Technical College (Cheraw), Denmark Technical College (Denmark), Horry-Georgetown Technical College (Conway), Orangeburg-Calhoun Technical College (Orangeburg), Technical College of the Lowcountry (Beaufort), Williamsburg Technical College (Kingstree), York Technical College (Rock Hill), 2 off-campus centers in Hartsville, Lake City.

Media Courses are delivered via television, videotapes, videoconferencing, interactive television, audiotapes, computer software, CD-ROM, computer conferencing, World Wide Web, e-mail, print. Students and teachers may meet in person or interact via videoconferencing, audioconferencing, mail, telephone, fax, e-mail, interactive television, World Wide Web. The following equipment may be required: computer, modem, Internet access, e-mail.

Restrictions Programs are available worldwide. Enrollment is open to anyone.

Services Distance learners have access to library services, e-mail services, academic advising, tutoring, career placement assistance, bookstore at a distance.

Credit-earning options Students may transfer credits from another institution or may earn credits through examinations.

Typical costs Tuition of $54.50 per credit for local area residents. Tuition of $60.50 per credit for in-state residents. Tuition of $128 per credit for out-of-state residents. Costs may vary. Financial aid is available to distance learners.

Registration Students may register by mail, fax, telephone, e-mail, World Wide Web, in person.

Contact Jane Lucas, Administration Specialist, Florence-Darlington Technical College. *Telephone:* 843-661-8133. *Fax:* 843-661-8217. *E-mail:* lucasj@flo.tec.sc.us.

DEGREES AND AWARDS

AA Liberal Arts
AD Business, Criminal Justice

COURSE SUBJECT AREAS OFFERED OUTSIDE OF DEGREE PROGRAMS

Undergraduate: Business; business administration and management; criminal justice; developmental and child psychology; educational psychology; English composition; English language and literature; mathematics; psychology; sociology; teacher education

See full description on page 676.

FLORIDA ATLANTIC UNIVERSITY

Boca Raton, Florida

University Resource Management
www.fau.edu

Florida Atlantic University, founded in 1961, is a state-supported university. It is accredited by the Southern Association of Colleges and Schools. It first offered distance learning courses in 1965.

Contact Florida Atlantic University, 777 Glades Road, PO Box 3091, Boca Raton, FL 33431-0991. *Telephone:* 561-297-3000.

See full description on page 676.

FLORIDA BAPTIST THEOLOGICAL COLLEGE

Graceville, Florida

Division of Distance Learning
www.fbtc.edu

Florida Baptist Theological College, founded in 1943, is an independent, religious, four-year college. It is accredited by the Southern Association of Colleges and Schools. It first offered distance learning courses in 1997. In 1999–2000, it offered 10 courses at a distance. In fall 1999, there were 20 students enrolled in distance learning courses.

Course delivery sites Courses are delivered to your home, 3 off-campus centers in Jacksonville, Lakeland, Miami.

Media Courses are delivered via videoconferencing, interactive television, computer software, computer conferencing, e-mail, print. Students and teachers may meet in person or interact via videoconferencing, mail, telephone, fax, e-mail, interactive television, World Wide Web. The following equipment may be required: television, videocassette player, computer, modem, Internet access, e-mail.

Restrictions Programs are available worldwide. Enrollment is restricted to individuals meeting certain criteria.

Services Distance learners have access to library services, e-mail services, academic advising, career placement assistance, bookstore at a distance.

Credit-earning options Students may transfer credits from another institution or may earn credits through examinations, military training.

Typical costs Tuition of $480 per course. Costs may vary. Financial aid is available to distance learners.

Registration Students may register by World Wide Web, in person.

Contact Jerry E. Oswalt, Vice President, Academic Affairs, Florida Baptist Theological College, 5400 College Drive, Graceville, FL 32440. *Telephone:* 850-263-3261 Ext. 412. *Fax:* 850-263-7506. *E-mail:* jeoswalt@fbtc.edu.

eCollege.com   *www.ecollege.com/scholarships*

DEGREES AND AWARDS

BS Biblical Studies

COURSE SUBJECT AREAS OFFERED OUTSIDE OF DEGREE PROGRAMS

Undergraduate: Bible studies; counseling psychology; theological studies
Noncredit: Bible studies; counseling psychology; theological studies

FLORIDA COMMUNITY COLLEGE AT JACKSONVILLE

Jacksonville, Florida
Open Campus
www.distancelearning.org

Florida Community College at Jacksonville, founded in 1963, is a state-supported, two-year college. It is accredited by the Southern Association of Colleges and Schools. In 1999–2000, it offered 64 courses at a distance.
Course delivery sites Courses are delivered to your home, your workplace, military bases.
Media Courses are delivered via television, videotapes, computer software, CD-ROM, computer conferencing, World Wide Web, e-mail. Students and teachers may meet in person or interact via mail, telephone, fax, e-mail, World Wide Web. The following equipment may be required: television, videocassette player, computer, modem, Internet access, e-mail.
Restrictions Programs are available to in-state students only. Enrollment is open to anyone.
Services Distance learners have access to library services, e-mail services, academic advising, bookstore at a distance.
Credit-earning options Students may transfer credits from another institution or may earn credits through examinations, military training.
Typical costs Tuition of $47.10 per credit hour plus mandatory fees of $10 per course for in-state residents. Tuition of $174.40 per credit hour plus mandatory fees of $10 per course for out-of-state residents. Costs may vary. Financial aid is available to distance learners.
Registration Students may register by telephone, in person.
Contact Lynne S. Crosby, Distance Learning Coordinator, Florida Community College at Jacksonville, Open Campus, 101 West State Street, Jacksonville, FL 32202. *Telephone:* 904-633-8116. *Fax:* 904-633-8435. *E-mail:* lcrosby@fccj.org.

DEGREES AND AWARDS

Distance programs offered do not lead to a degree or other formal award.

COURSE SUBJECT AREAS OFFERED OUTSIDE OF DEGREE PROGRAMS

Undergraduate: Accounting; administrative and secretarial services; algebra; American (U.S.) history; anatomy; anthropology; biological and life sciences; biology; business; business administration and management; business law; chemistry; communications; computer and information sciences; computer programming; developmental and child psychology; earth science; economics; English composition; English language and literature; European history; European languages and literatures; finance; French language and literature; geography; geology; health and physical education/fitness; health professions and related sciences; history; instructional media; Latin American studies; liberal arts, general studies, and humanities; marketing; mathematics; philosophy and religion; political science; psychology; religious studies; sociology

FLORIDA GULF COAST UNIVERSITY

Fort Myers, Florida
Enrollment Services
www.fgcu.edu

Florida Gulf Coast University, founded in 1991, is a state-supported, comprehensive institution. It is accredited by the Southern Association of Colleges and Schools (candidate). It first offered distance learning courses in 1997. In 1999–2000, it offered 63 courses at a distance. In fall 1999, there were 731 students enrolled in distance learning courses.
Course delivery sites Courses are delivered to your home.
Media Courses are delivered via television, videotapes, videoconferencing, World Wide Web, e-mail. Students and teachers may meet in person or interact via videoconferencing, audioconferencing, mail, telephone, e-mail, World Wide Web. The following equipment may be required: television, videocassette player, computer, modem, Internet access, e-mail.
Restrictions Programs are available worldwide. Enrollment is open to anyone.
Services Distance learners have access to library services, the campus computer network, e-mail services, academic advising, tutoring, career placement assistance, bookstore at a distance.
Credit-earning options Students may transfer credits from another institution.
Typical costs *Undergraduate:* Tuition of $69.68 per credit hour plus mandatory fees of $23 per semester for in-state residents. Tuition of $314.29 per credit hour plus mandatory fees of $23 per semester for out-of-state residents. *Graduate:* Tuition of $146.13 per credit hour plus mandatory fees of $23 per semester for in-state residents. Tuition of $524.91 per credit hour plus mandatory fees of $23 per semester for out-of-state residents. Costs may vary. Financial aid is available to distance learners.
Registration Students may register by telephone, World Wide Web, in person.
Contact Admissions Counselor, Florida Gulf Coast University, 10501 FGCU Boulevard, Fort Myers, FL 33965-6565. *Telephone:* 941-590-7878. *Fax:* 941-590-7894. *E-mail:* advising@fgcu.edu.

DEGREES AND AWARDS

BA Education (certain restrictions apply; some on-campus requirements)
BS Criminal Justice, Education (certain restrictions apply), Health Services Administration (certain restrictions apply)
Graduate Certificate(s) English for Speakers of Other Languages (certain restrictions apply; some on-campus requirements)
MA Curriculum and Instruction (certain restrictions apply; some on-campus requirements)
MBA Business Administration (some on-campus requirements)
MEd Curriculum and Instruction (certain restrictions apply; some on-campus requirements)
MPA Public Administration
MS Health Professions Education (certain restrictions apply), Health Services Administration (certain restrictions apply)

COURSE SUBJECT AREAS OFFERED OUTSIDE OF DEGREE PROGRAMS

Undergraduate: Criminal justice; English as a second language (ESL); health professions and related sciences

Florida Gulf Coast University

Graduate: Business; English as a second language (ESL); health professions and related sciences; instructional media; public administration and services

See full descriptions on pages 528 and 676.

FLORIDA INTERNATIONAL UNIVERSITY

Miami, Florida

Office of Distance Learning
www.outreach.fiu.edu/distance.htm

Florida International University, founded in 1965, is a state-supported university. It is accredited by the Southern Association of Colleges and Schools. It first offered distance learning courses in 1995. In 1999–2000, it offered 165 courses at a distance. In fall 1999, there were 993 students enrolled in distance learning courses.

Course delivery sites Courses are delivered to your home, your workplace, military bases, high schools, DCT (Luzern, Switzerland), St. Petersburg Junior College (St. Petersburg), University of Florida (Gainesville), off-campus center(s) in Miami.

Media Courses are delivered via television, videotapes, videoconferencing, World Wide Web, e-mail. Students and teachers may meet in person or interact via videoconferencing, telephone, e-mail, World Wide Web. The following equipment may be required: television, videocassette player, computer, modem, Internet access, e-mail.

Restrictions Programs are available to in-state students only. Enrollment is open to anyone.

Services Distance learners have access to library services, the campus computer network, e-mail services, tutoring, career placement assistance, bookstore at a distance.

Credit-earning options Students may transfer credits from another institution.

Typical costs *Undergraduate:* Tuition of $72.14 per credit plus mandatory fees of $60 per semester for in-state residents. Tuition of $144.96 per credit plus mandatory fees of $60 per semester for out-of-state residents. *Graduate:* Tuition of $305 per credit plus mandatory fees of $60 per semester for in-state residents. Tuition of $505 per credit plus mandatory fees of $60 per semester for out-of-state residents. Costs may vary. Financial aid is available to distance learners.

Registration Students may register by mail, telephone, World Wide Web, in person.

Contact Jeffrey Miller, Director of Distance Learning, Florida International University, 3000 North East 151 Street—KCC 324, North Miami, FL 33181. *Telephone:* 305-919-5357. *Fax:* 305-919-5484. *E-mail:* miller@fiu.edu.

DEGREES AND AWARDS

Undergraduate Certificate(s) Gerontology
MS Computer Engineering (service area differs from that of the overall institution; some on-campus requirements), Construction Management (service area differs from that of the overall institution), Electrical Engineering (service area differs from that of the overall institution; some on-campus requirements)

COURSE SUBJECT AREAS OFFERED OUTSIDE OF DEGREE PROGRAMS

Undergraduate: Accounting; adult education; criminology; geology; hospitality services management; Middle Eastern languages and literatures; oceanography; technical writing

Graduate: Accounting; chemistry, analytical; civil engineering; electrical engineering; engineering/industrial management; finance; gerontology; hospitality services management; international business; journalism; mechanical engineering

See full description on page 676.

FLORIDA KEYS COMMUNITY COLLEGE

Key West, Florida

Learning Resource Center
www.firn.edu/fkcc/library

Florida Keys Community College, founded in 1965, is a state-supported, two-year college. It is accredited by the Southern Association of Colleges and Schools. In 1999–2000, it offered 16 courses at a distance. In fall 1999, there were 167 students enrolled in distance learning courses.

Course delivery sites Courses are delivered to your home.

Media Courses are delivered via television, videotapes. Students and teachers may meet in person or interact via telephone, e-mail. The following equipment may be required: television, videocassette player.

Restrictions Programs are available to local area students. Enrollment is open to anyone.

Services Distance learners have access to library services at a distance.

Credit-earning options Students may transfer credits from another institution or may earn credits through examinations.

Typical costs Tuition of $48.17 per unit for in-state residents. Tuition of $180.28 per unit for out-of-state residents. There is a $25 mandatory fee. Financial aid is available to distance learners.

Registration Students may register by telephone, in person.

Contact Cynthia Lawson, Assistant Librarian, Florida Keys Community College, Learning Resource Center, 5901 College Road, Key West, FL 33040. *Telephone:* 305-296-9081 Ext. 210. *Fax:* 305-292-5162. *E-mail:* lawson-c@popmail.firn.edu.

DEGREES AND AWARDS

Distance programs offered do not lead to a degree or other formal award.

COURSE SUBJECT AREAS OFFERED OUTSIDE OF DEGREE PROGRAMS

Undergraduate: Anthropology; art history and criticism; astronomy and astrophysics; business administration and management; film studies; health and physical education/fitness; library and information studies; marketing; psychology; religious studies; sociology

FLORIDA STATE UNIVERSITY

Tallahassee, Florida

Office for Distributed and Distance Learning
www.fsu.edu/~distance

Florida State University, founded in 1857, is a state-supported university. It is accredited by the Southern Association of Colleges and Schools. It first offered distance learning courses in 1987. In 1999–2000, it offered 42 courses at a distance. In fall 1999, there were 600 students enrolled in distance learning courses.

Course delivery sites Courses are delivered to your home.

Media Courses are delivered via videotapes, videoconferencing, interactive television, audiotapes, computer software, CD-ROM, computer conferencing, World Wide Web, e-mail, print. Students and teachers may meet in person or interact via videoconferencing, audioconferencing, mail, telephone, fax, e-mail, interactive television, World Wide Web. The following equipment may be required: television, videocassette player, computer, modem, Internet access, e-mail.

Restrictions Programs are available worldwide. Enrollment is restricted to individuals meeting certain criteria.

Services Distance learners have access to library services, the campus computer network, e-mail services, academic advising, tutoring, career placement assistance, bookstore at a distance.

Credit-earning options Students may transfer credits from another institution or may earn credits through examinations.

Typical costs Contact the school for information. Costs may vary. Financial aid is available to distance learners.

Registration Students may register by mail, fax, telephone, e-mail, World Wide Web, in person.

Contact Ms. Carol Abel, Student Services Coordinator, Florida State University, 3500 C University Center, Tallahassee, FL 32306-2550. *Telephone:* 877-357-8283. *Fax:* 850-644-5803. *E-mail:* cable@oddl.fsu.edu.

DEGREES AND AWARDS

BS Computer and Information Sciences, Information Studies, Interdisciplinary Social Science

BSN Nursing (service area differs from that of the overall institution; some on-campus requirements)

MS Criminology/Criminal Justice, Instructional Systems, Mechanical Engineering

COURSE SUBJECT AREAS OFFERED OUTSIDE OF DEGREE PROGRAMS

Undergraduate: Child care and development; computer and information sciences; criminology; geology; liberal arts, general studies, and humanities; music; nursing; social sciences; special education

Graduate: Business administration and management; chemical engineering; civil engineering; criminal justice; education administration; electrical engineering; industrial engineering; instructional media; library and information studies; mechanical engineering; social work; teacher education

Noncredit: Business administration and management; child care and development; special education

Special note

Florida State University's (FSU) distance learning programs allow students to earn a bachelor's or master's degree part-time and with no on-campus requirements. These programs are recognized for providing the same first-rate education as their on-campus counterparts. Distance learning students follow a regular semester schedule. Communication among class participants is enhanced through the use of e-mail, threaded discussion, and live chat. Student support, both technical and course related, is personalized and always available. State-of-the-art tools and techniques are used to ensure that students become active members of a collaborative, online learning community. Florida State University has earned worldwide recognition as a leading distance learning provider by developing and implementing innovative program features that meet student's needs. FSU offers entire degree-completion programs. Students enter with an AA degree and graduate with a bachelor's degree or enter with a bachelor's degree and graduate with a master's degree. FSU designs courses specifically for learning at a distance. Course activities and materials enable students to learn at a time and place of their choosing. Every course promotes frequent interaction with instructional staff members. FSU has virtually eliminated the distance in distance learning. In many undergraduate programs, course mentors support distance students through classes and help them collaborate with fellow students. FSU partners with state community colleges to provide students with local resources. Regional community colleges support local students through library access, proctored testing, and program awareness. FSU is leading the way in educa-

tional technology. FSU is ranked among the top 20 most wired universities in the nation and was again named the most wired university in Florida by *Yahoo! Internet Life.*

See full description on page 676.

FLOYD COLLEGE

Rome, Georgia

Extended Learning
www.fc.peachnet.edu

Floyd College, founded in 1970, is a state-supported, two-year college. It is accredited by the Southern Association of Colleges and Schools. It first offered distance learning courses in 1977. In 1999–2000, it offered 30 courses at a distance. In fall 1999, there were 275 students enrolled in distance learning courses.

Course delivery sites Courses are delivered to your home, your workplace, high schools, other colleges, 3 off-campus centers in Acworth, Cartersville, Waco.

Media Courses are delivered via television, videotapes, videoconferencing, computer software, CD-ROM, computer conferencing, World Wide Web, e-mail, print. Students and teachers may meet in person or interact via videoconferencing, audioconferencing, mail, telephone, fax, e-mail, World Wide Web. The following equipment may be required: television, videocassette player, computer, Internet access, e-mail.

Restrictions Programs are available worldwide. Enrollment is restricted to individuals meeting certain criteria.

Services Distance learners have access to library services, the campus computer network, e-mail services, academic advising, tutoring, career placement assistance, bookstore at a distance.

Credit-earning options Students may transfer credits from another institution or may earn credits through examinations.

Typical costs Tuition of $52 per credit hour for local area residents. Tuition of $52 per semester hour plus mandatory fees of $342 per semester for in-state residents. Tuition of $155 per semester hour plus mandatory fees of $342 per semester for out-of-state residents. Costs may vary. Financial aid is available to distance learners.

Registration Students may register by mail, telephone, World Wide Web, in person.

Contact Carla Patterson, Director of Extended Learning, Floyd College, PO Box 1864, Rome, GA 30162. *Telephone:* 706-802-5300. *Fax:* 706-802-5997. *E-mail:* carla_patterson@fc.peachnet.edu.

DEGREES AND AWARDS

Distance programs offered do not lead to a degree or other formal award.

COURSE SUBJECT AREAS OFFERED OUTSIDE OF DEGREE PROGRAMS

Undergraduate: Algebra; American (U.S.) history; American literature; anatomy; calculus; chemistry; comparative literature; corrections; criminal justice; developmental and child psychology; economics; English composition; English literature; European history; foods and nutrition studies; geology; health and physical education/fitness; nursing; physiology; political science; sign language; sociology

FOOTHILL COLLEGE

Los Altos Hills, California

Foothill Global Access

www.foothill.fhda.edu

Foothill College, founded in 1958, is a state and locally supported, two-year college. It is accredited by the Western Association of Schools and Colleges, Inc. It first offered distance learning courses in 1970. In 1999–2000, it offered 62 courses at a distance. In fall 1999, there were 1,500 students enrolled in distance learning courses.

Course delivery sites Courses are delivered to your home, your workplace, military bases, 1 off-campus center in Mountainview.

Media Courses are delivered via television, videotapes, videoconferencing, audiotapes, computer software, CD-ROM, computer conferencing, World Wide Web, e-mail, print. Students and teachers may meet in person or interact via audioconferencing, mail, telephone, fax, e-mail, World Wide Web. The following equipment may be required: television, videocassette player, computer, modem, Internet access, e-mail.

Restrictions Programs are available worldwide. Enrollment is open to anyone.

Services Distance learners have access to library services, the campus computer network, e-mail services, academic advising, bookstore at a distance.

Credit-earning options Students may transfer credits from another institution or may earn credits through military training, business training.

Typical costs Tuition of $7 per unit for in-state residents. Tuition of $85 per unit for out-of-state residents. Financial aid is available to distance learners.

Registration Students may register by mail, telephone, World Wide Web, in person.

Contact Art Turmelle, Coordinator, Distance Learning Program, Foothill College, 12345 El Monte Road, Los Altos Hills, CA 94022. *Telephone:* 650-949-7614. *Fax:* 650-949-7123. *E-mail:* turmelle@fhda.edu.

DEGREES AND AWARDS

AA General Studies/Social Science

COURSE SUBJECT AREAS OFFERED OUTSIDE OF DEGREE PROGRAMS

Undergraduate: Area, ethnic, and cultural studies; art history and criticism; business; communications; computer and information sciences; drama and theater; economics; education; English language and literature; European languages and literatures; film studies; health and physical education/fitness; health professions and related sciences; history; library and information studies; mathematics; music; philosophy and religion; physical sciences; psychology; radio and television broadcasting; social sciences; sociology; visual and performing arts

FORSYTH TECHNICAL COMMUNITY COLLEGE

Winston-Salem, North Carolina

Distance Learning

www.forsyth.tec.nc.us

Forsyth Technical Community College, founded in 1964, is a state-supported, two-year college. It is accredited by the Southern Association of Colleges and Schools. It first offered distance learning courses in 1992. In 1999–2000, it offered 34 courses at a distance. In fall 1999, there were 450 students enrolled in distance learning courses.

Course delivery sites Courses are delivered to your home, your workplace, military bases, high schools, 2 off-campus centers in Kernersville, Winston-Salem.

Media Courses are delivered via television, videotapes, videoconferencing, interactive television, audiotapes, computer software, CD-ROM, computer conferencing, World Wide Web, e-mail, print. Students and teachers may meet in person or interact via videoconferencing, audioconferencing, mail, telephone, fax, e-mail, interactive television, World Wide Web. The following equipment may be required: television, videocassette player, computer, Internet access, e-mail.

Restrictions Programs are available to local area students. Enrollment is open to anyone.

Services Distance learners have access to library services, the campus computer network, e-mail services, academic advising, tutoring, career placement assistance at a distance.

Credit-earning options Students may transfer credits from another institution or may earn credits through examinations, portfolio assessment.

Typical costs Tuition of $20 per semester hour plus mandatory fees of $20 per course for in-state residents. Tuition of $163 per semester hour plus mandatory fees of $20 per course for out-of-state residents. *Noncredit courses:* $55 per course. Costs may vary. Financial aid is available to distance learners.

Registration Students may register by mail, fax, telephone, in person.

Contact Dr. Bill Randall, Director of Distance Learning, Forsyth Technical Community College. *Telephone:* 336-723-0371 Ext. 7311. *Fax:* 336-761-2598. *E-mail:* brandall@forsyth.cc.ns.us.

DEGREES AND AWARDS

AD Business Administration

COURSE SUBJECT AREAS OFFERED OUTSIDE OF DEGREE PROGRAMS

Undergraduate: Accounting; American literature; anthropology; area, ethnic, and cultural studies; business administration and management; business law; child care and development; computer programming; continuing education; database management; economics; electronics; English literature; finance; information sciences and systems; marketing; sociology

Noncredit: Algebra; American (U.S.) history; anatomy; English composition; management information systems; women's studies

See full description on page 676.

FORT HAYS STATE UNIVERSITY

Hays, Kansas

Virtual College

www.fhsu.edu/virtual_college

Fort Hays State University, founded in 1902, is a state-supported, comprehensive institution. It is accredited by the North Central Association of Colleges and Schools. It first offered distance learning courses in 1987. In 1999–2000, it offered 200 courses at a distance. In fall 1999, there were 1,800 students enrolled in distance learning courses.

Course delivery sites Courses are delivered to your home, your workplace, military bases, high schools, Colby Community College (Colby), Dodge City Community College (Dodge City), Garden City Community College (Garden City), Pratt Community College and Area Vocational School (Pratt), Seward County Community College (Liberal).

Media Courses are delivered via television, videotapes, videoconferencing, interactive television, audiotapes, computer software, CD-ROM, computer conferencing, World Wide Web, e-mail, print. Students and teachers may meet in person or interact via videoconferencing, audioconferencing, mail, telephone, fax, e-mail, interactive television, World Wide Web. The following equipment may be required: television, videocassette player, computer, modem, Internet access, e-mail.

Restrictions Programs are available worldwide. Enrollment is restricted to individuals meeting certain criteria.

Services Distance learners have access to library services, the campus computer network, e-mail services, academic advising, tutoring, career placement assistance, bookstore at a distance.

Credit-earning options Students may transfer credits from another institution or may earn credits through examinations, portfolio assessment, military training, business training.

Typical costs *Undergraduate:* Tuition of $75 per credit. *Graduate:* Tuition of $102 per credit. Costs may vary. Financial aid is available to distance learners.

Registration Students may register by mail, fax, telephone, World Wide Web, in person.

Contact Cynthia Elliott, Dean, Fort Hays State University, Virtual College, 600 Park Street, Hays, KS 67601. *Telephone:* 785-628-4291. *Fax:* 785-628-4037. *E-mail:* v_college@tiger.fhsu.edu.

DEGREES AND AWARDS

BGS General Studies
BS Elementary Education (service area differs from that of the overall institution)
BSN Nursing (service area differs from that of the overall institution)
MLS Liberal Studies

COURSE SUBJECT AREAS OFFERED OUTSIDE OF DEGREE PROGRAMS

Undergraduate: Accounting; area, ethnic, and cultural studies; biology; business administration and management; chemistry; chemistry, organic; continuing education; criminal justice; developmental and child psychology; economics; education administration; educational psychology; English as a second language (ESL); English language and literature; geology; history; instructional media; law and legal studies; library and information studies; mathematics; nursing; oceanography; philosophy and religion; physics; political science; public administration and services; public health; social work; sociology; special education; teacher education; telecommunications

Graduate: Biology; business administration and management; chemistry; continuing education; criminal justice; developmental and child psychology; education administration; educational psychology; English as a second language (ESL); English language and literature; history; instructional media; library and information studies; mathematics; nursing; oceanography; philosophy and religion; physics; political science; public administration and services; public health; social work; sociology; special education; teacher education

FRANCISCAN UNIVERSITY OF STEUBENVILLE

Steubenville, Ohio

Distance Learning
www2.franuniv.edu/disted/

Franciscan University of Steubenville, founded in 1946, is an independent, religious, comprehensive institution. It is accredited by the North Central Association of Colleges and Schools. It first offered distance learning courses in 1995. In 1999–2000, it offered 13 courses at a distance. In fall 1999, there were 228 students enrolled in distance learning courses.

Course delivery sites Courses are delivered to your home.
Media Courses are delivered via audiotapes. Students and teachers may interact via mail, telephone, fax, e-mail.

Restrictions Programs are available worldwide. Enrollment is open to anyone.

Services Distance learners have access to library services, e-mail services, academic advising, career placement assistance, bookstore at a distance.

Credit-earning options Students may transfer credits from another institution.

Typical costs *Undergraduate:* Tuition of $525 per course plus mandatory fees of $75 per course. *Graduate:* Tuition of $525 per course plus mandatory fees of $75 per course. *Noncredit courses:* $150 per course. Financial aid is available to distance learners.

Registration Students may register by mail, fax, in person.

Contact Lorrie Campana, Administrative Clerk, Franciscan University of Steubenville, 1235 University Boulevard, Steubenville, OH 43952. *Telephone:* 740-283-6517. *Fax:* 740-284-7037. *E-mail:* distance@franuniv. edu.

DEGREES AND AWARDS

MA Theology (certain restrictions apply; some on-campus requirements)

COURSE SUBJECT AREAS OFFERED OUTSIDE OF DEGREE PROGRAMS

Undergraduate: Philosophy and religion; theological studies
Graduate: Theological studies
Noncredit: Philosophy and religion; theological studies

FRANKLIN PIERCE LAW CENTER

Concord, New Hampshire

Education Law Institute
www.fplc.edu

Franklin Pierce Law Center, founded in 1973, is an independent, nonprofit, graduate institution. It is accredited by the American Bar Association. It first offered distance learning courses in 1997. In 1999–2000, it offered 6 courses at a distance. In fall 1999, there were 23 students enrolled in distance learning courses.

Course delivery sites Courses are delivered to your home, your workplace.

Media Courses are delivered via videoconferencing, computer conferencing, World Wide Web, e-mail, print. Students and teachers may meet in person or interact via mail, telephone, fax, e-mail, World Wide Web. The following equipment may be required: computer, modem, Internet access, e-mail.

Restrictions Programs are available nationwide. Enrollment is open to anyone.

Services Distance learners have access to library services, the campus computer network, e-mail services, academic advising, bookstore at a distance.

Credit-earning options Students may transfer credits from another institution or may earn credits through examinations.

Typical costs *Undergraduate:* Tuition of $375 per credit plus mandatory fees of $120 per course. *Graduate:* Tuition of $375 per credit plus mandatory fees of $120 per course. Financial aid is available to distance learners.

Registration Students may register by mail, fax, telephone, e-mail, in person.

Contact Sarah E. Redfield, Professor, Franklin Pierce Law Center, 2 White Street, Concord, NH 03301. *Telephone:* 603-228-1541. *Fax:* 603-228-1074. *E-mail:* sredfield@fplc.edu.

DEGREES AND AWARDS

Graduate Certificate(s) Education Law (some on-campus requirements)
MEL Education Law (some on-campus requirements)

COURSE SUBJECT AREAS OFFERED OUTSIDE OF DEGREE PROGRAMS

Graduate: Education; law and legal studies

FRANKLIN UNIVERSITY

Columbus, Ohio
www.franklin.edu

Franklin University, founded in 1902, is an independent, nonprofit, comprehensive institution. It is accredited by the North Central Association of Colleges and Schools. It first offered distance learning courses in 1996. In 1999–2000, it offered 60 courses at a distance. In fall 1999, there were 540 students enrolled in distance learning courses.
Course delivery sites Courses are delivered to your home, your workplace.
Media Courses are delivered via World Wide Web, e-mail, print. Students and teachers may interact via audioconferencing, mail, telephone, fax, e-mail, World Wide Web. The following equipment may be required: computer, Internet access, e-mail.
Restrictions Programs are available worldwide. Enrollment is open to anyone.
Services Distance learners have access to library services, e-mail services, academic advising, tutoring, bookstore at a distance.
Credit-earning options Students may transfer credits from another institution or may earn credits through examinations, portfolio assessment, military training.
Typical costs Tuition of $212 per credit hour plus mandatory fees of $25 per trimester. Costs may vary. Financial aid is available to distance learners.
Registration Students may register by mail, fax, telephone, e-mail, World Wide Web, in person.
Contact Assistant Director of Student Services, Franklin University, 201 South Grant Avenue, Columbus, OH 43215. *Telephone:* 614-341-6256. *Fax:* 614-224-8027. *E-mail:* info@franklin.edu.

DEGREES AND AWARDS

Distance programs offered do not lead to a degree or other formal award.

COURSE SUBJECT AREAS OFFERED OUTSIDE OF DEGREE PROGRAMS

Undergraduate: Accounting; business administration and management; computer and information sciences; English language and literature; health services administration; liberal arts, general studies, and humanities; management information systems; mathematics; physical sciences

See full description on page 530.

FRANK PHILLIPS COLLEGE

Borger, Texas

Frank Phillips College, founded in 1948, is a state and locally supported, two-year college. It is accredited by the Southern Association of Colleges and Schools. In 1999–2000, it offered 20 courses at a distance.
Course delivery sites Courses are delivered to your home, high schools.

Media Courses are delivered via television, videotapes, videoconferencing. Students and teachers may meet in person or interact via videoconferencing, e-mail. The following equipment may be required: television, videocassette player.
Restrictions Programs are available to local area students. Enrollment is open to anyone.
Services Distance learners have access to academic advising at a distance.
Credit-earning options Students may transfer credits from another institution or may earn credits through examinations.
Typical costs Tuition of $25 per credit hour plus mandatory fees of $10 per credit hour for local area residents. Tuition of $25 per credit hour plus mandatory fees of $10 per credit hour for in-state residents. Tuition of $30 per credit hour plus mandatory fees of $10 per credit hour for out-of-state residents. Costs may vary. Financial aid is available to distance learners.
Registration Students may register by mail, in person.
Contact Preston Haddan, Director of Continuing Education, Frank Phillips College, 1301 Roosevelt, Borger, TX 79007. *Telephone:* 800-687-2056 Ext. 775. *Fax:* 806-274-9834. *E-mail:* phaddan@fpc.cc.tx.us.

DEGREES AND AWARDS

Distance programs offered do not lead to a degree or other formal award.

COURSE SUBJECT AREAS OFFERED OUTSIDE OF DEGREE PROGRAMS

Undergraduate: Algebra; American (U.S.) history; business; developmental and child psychology; English composition; marketing; mathematics; physics

FRESNO PACIFIC UNIVERSITY

Fresno, California
Fresno Pacific Graduate School
fresnopacific.org

Fresno Pacific University, founded in 1944, is an independent, religious, comprehensive institution affiliated with the Mennonite Brethren Church. It is accredited by the Western Association of Schools and Colleges, Inc. It first offered distance learning courses in 1999. In 1999–2000, it offered 5 courses at a distance. In fall 1999, there were 30 students enrolled in distance learning courses.
Course delivery sites Courses are delivered to your home, your workplace.
Media Courses are delivered via World Wide Web, e-mail. Students and teachers may meet in person or interact via mail, telephone, fax, e-mail, World Wide Web. The following equipment may be required: computer, modem, Internet access, e-mail.
Restrictions Programs are available to in-state students only. Enrollment is restricted to individuals meeting certain criteria.
Services Distance learners have access to library services, the campus computer network, e-mail services, bookstore at a distance.
Credit-earning options Students may transfer credits from another institution or may earn credits through examinations, business training.
Typical costs Tuition of $290 per credit plus mandatory fees of $40 per credit. Costs may vary. Financial aid is available to distance learners.
Registration Students may register by mail, fax, e-mail, in person.
Contact Jacqueline M. Chavanu, Director of Graduate Marketing, Fresno Pacific University, Fresno Pacific Graduate School, 1717 South Chestnut Avenue, Fresno, CA 93702. *Telephone:* 559-453-3618. *Fax:* 559-453-2001. *E-mail:* jchavanu@fresno.edu.

DEGREES AND AWARDS

Distance programs offered do not lead to a degree or other formal award.

COURSE SUBJECT AREAS OFFERED OUTSIDE OF DEGREE PROGRAMS

Graduate: Education; finance; human resources management; law and legal studies; management information systems

FRONT RANGE COMMUNITY COLLEGE

Westminster, Colorado

Distance Learning Office
frcc.cc.co.us

Front Range Community College, founded in 1968, is a state-supported, two-year college. It is accredited by the North Central Association of Colleges and Schools. It first offered distance learning courses in 1986. In 1999–2000, it offered 75 courses at a distance. In fall 1999, there were 750 students enrolled in distance learning courses.

Course delivery sites Courses are delivered to your home, your workplace.

Media Courses are delivered via television, videotapes, videoconferencing, audiotapes, computer software, World Wide Web, e-mail, print. Students and teachers may meet in person or interact via videoconferencing, audioconferencing, mail, telephone, fax, e-mail, World Wide Web. The following equipment may be required: television, videocassette player, computer, modem, Internet access, e-mail.

Restrictions Programs are available to in-state students only. Enrollment is open to anyone.

Services Distance learners have access to library services, academic advising at a distance.

Credit-earning options Students may transfer credits from another institution or may earn credits through examinations, portfolio assessment, military training, business training.

Typical costs Tuition of $58 per credit hour for in-state residents. Tuition of $277.50 per credit hour for out-of-state residents.

Registration Students may register by mail, telephone, World Wide Web, in person.

Contact Gertrude Dathe, Distance Learning Administrator, Front Range Community College, 3645 West 112th Avenue, Westminster, CO 80030. *Telephone:* 303-404-5554. *Fax:* 303-404-5156. *E-mail:* gertrude@cccs.cccoes.edu.

DEGREES AND AWARDS

AA Liberal Arts

COURSE SUBJECT AREAS OFFERED OUTSIDE OF DEGREE PROGRAMS

Undergraduate: Art history and criticism; biology; business administration and management; chemistry; computer and information sciences; English composition; English language and literature; geography; geology; history; liberal arts, general studies, and humanities; library and information studies; mathematics; philosophy and religion; physics; political science; psychology; sociology; teacher education

FROSTBURG STATE UNIVERSITY

Frostburg, Maryland

Frostburg State University, founded in 1898, is a state-supported, comprehensive institution. It is accredited by the Middle States Association of Colleges and Schools. It first offered distance learning courses in 1995. In 1999–2000, it offered 7 courses at a distance. In fall 1999, there were 86 students enrolled in distance learning courses.

Course delivery sites Courses are delivered to Allegany College of Maryland (Cumberland), Garrett Community College (McHenry), 1 off-campus center in Hagerstown.

Media Courses are delivered via television, videotapes, videoconferencing, interactive television, computer software, World Wide Web, e-mail. Students and teachers may meet in person or interact via videoconferencing, audioconferencing, mail, telephone, fax, e-mail, interactive television, World Wide Web.

Restrictions Programs are available to in-state students only. Enrollment is restricted to individuals meeting certain criteria.

Services Distance learners have access to library services, e-mail services, academic advising at a distance.

Credit-earning options Students may transfer credits from another institution or may earn credits through examinations.

Typical costs *Undergraduate:* Tuition of $134 per credit hour plus mandatory fees of $31 per credit hour for in-state residents. Tuition of $236 per credit hour plus mandatory fees of $31 per credit hour for out-of-state residents. *Graduate:* Tuition of $174 per credit hour plus mandatory fees of $31 per credit hour for in-state residents. Tuition of $202 per credit hour plus mandatory fees of $31 per credit hour for out-of-state residents. Financial aid is available to distance learners.

Registration Students may register by mail, fax, telephone, in person.

Contact Dr. John Bowman, Associate Provost, Frostburg State University, Frostburg, MD 21532. *Telephone:* 301-687-4211. *E-mail:* jbowman@frostburg.edu.

DEGREES AND AWARDS

Distance programs offered do not lead to a degree or other formal award.

COURSE SUBJECT AREAS OFFERED OUTSIDE OF DEGREE PROGRAMS

Undergraduate: Accounting; criminal justice; criminology; curriculum and instruction; political science; social psychology; social work; sociology; technical writing

Graduate: Accounting; business administration and management; curriculum and instruction; education administration; educational research; marketing; social psychology; social work; teacher education

See full description on page 676.

FULLER THEOLOGICAL SEMINARY

Pasadena, California

Office of Distance Learning
www.fuller.edu

Fuller Theological Seminary, founded in 1947, is an independent, religious, graduate institution. It is accredited by the Association of Theological Schools in the United States and Canada, Western Association of Schools and Colleges, Inc. It first offered distance learning courses in 1975. In 1999–2000, it offered 30 courses at a distance. In fall 1999, there were 150 students enrolled in distance learning courses.

Course delivery sites Courses are delivered to your home.

Media Courses are delivered via videotapes, audiotapes, World Wide Web, e-mail, print. Students and teachers may interact via mail, telephone, fax, e-mail, World Wide Web. The following equipment may be required: television, videocassette player, computer, Internet access, e-mail.

Restrictions Programs are available worldwide. Enrollment is open to anyone.

Services Distance learners have access to library services, e-mail services, academic advising, bookstore at a distance.

Credit-earning options Students may transfer credits from another institution.

Typical costs Tuition of $200 per unit. Costs may vary.

Registration Students may register by mail, fax, telephone, World Wide Web, in person.

Contact Program Coordinator, Fuller Theological Seminary, Office of Distance Learning, 135 North Oakland Avenue, Pasadena, CA 91182. *Telephone:* 800-999-9578 Ext. 5266. *Fax:* 626-304-3740. *E-mail:* idl-info@dept.fuller.edu.

---

eCollege.com *www.ecollege.com/scholarships*

DEGREES AND AWARDS

Undergraduate Certificate(s) Christian Studies

COURSE SUBJECT AREAS OFFERED OUTSIDE OF DEGREE PROGRAMS

Graduate: Anthropology; Bible studies; religious studies

See full description on page 532.

FULLERTON COLLEGE

Fullerton, California

Distance Education–Media Production Center
www.fullcoll.edu

Fullerton College, founded in 1913, is a state and locally supported, two-year college. It is accredited by the Western Association of Schools and Colleges, Inc. It first offered distance learning courses in 1984. In 1999–2000, it offered 22 courses at a distance. In fall 1999, there were 700 students enrolled in distance learning courses.

Course delivery sites Courses are delivered to your home, your workplace, military bases, Cypress College (Cypress).

Media Courses are delivered via television, videotapes, World Wide Web, e-mail, print. Students and teachers may meet in person or interact via mail, telephone, fax, e-mail, World Wide Web. The following equipment may be required: television, videocassette player, computer, modem, Internet access, e-mail.

Restrictions Programs are available to local area students. Enrollment is open to anyone.

Services Distance learners have access to library services, the campus computer network, e-mail services, bookstore at a distance.

Credit-earning options Students may transfer credits from another institution.

Typical costs Tuition of $11 per unit plus mandatory fees of $11 per semester for local area residents. Tuition of $11 per unit plus mandatory fees of $11 per semester for in-state residents. Tuition of $125 per unit plus mandatory fees of $11 per semester for out-of-state residents. Financial aid is available to distance learners.

Registration Students may register by mail, telephone, in person.

Contact Jay Goldstein, Coordinator, Fullerton College, Distance Education, 321 East Fullerton, Fullerton, CA 92632. *Telephone:* 714-992-7487. *Fax:* 714-879-3972. *E-mail:* goldsteinj@hotmail.com.

DEGREES AND AWARDS

Distance programs offered do not lead to a degree or other formal award.

COURSE SUBJECT AREAS OFFERED OUTSIDE OF DEGREE PROGRAMS

Undergraduate: American (U.S.) history; biology; business; database management; developmental and child psychology; English as a second language (ESL); film studies; foods and nutrition studies; geography; geology; health and physical education/fitness; history; oceanography; political science; psychology; social sciences

---

GADSDEN STATE COMMUNITY COLLEGE

Gadsden, Alabama

Distance Learning

Gadsden State Community College, founded in 1985, is a state-supported, two-year college. It is accredited by the Southern Association of Colleges and Schools. It first offered distance learning courses in 1978.

Contact Gadsden State Community College, PO Box 227, Gadsden, AL 35902-0227. *Telephone:* 256-549-8200. *Fax:* 256-549-8444.

See full description on page 676.

GALLAUDET UNIVERSITY

Washington, District of Columbia

Extension and Online Programs
academic.gallaudet.edu/cce/extonline.nsf

Gallaudet University, founded in 1864, is an independent, nonprofit university. It is accredited by the Middle States Association of Colleges and Schools. In 1999–2000, it offered 9 courses at a distance. In fall 1999, there were 12 students enrolled in distance learning courses.

Course delivery sites Courses are delivered to your home, your workplace.

Media Courses are delivered via World Wide Web. Students and teachers may interact via e-mail. The following equipment may be required: computer, Internet access, e-mail.

Restrictions Programs are available nationwide. Enrollment is restricted to individuals meeting certain criteria.

Services Distance learners have access to library services, e-mail services at a distance.

Typical costs *Undergraduate:* Tuition of $343.50 per credit plus mandatory fees of $10 per course. *Graduate:* Tuition of $420 per credit plus mandatory fees of $10 per semester. *Noncredit courses:* $200 per course. Financial aid is available to distance learners.

Registration Students may register by mail, fax.

Contact Jackie Mann, Coordinator of Extension and Online Programs, Gallaudet University, 800 Florida Avenue North East, Washington, DC 20015. *Telephone:* 202-651-6054. *Fax:* 202-651-6074. *E-mail:* extension.online@gallaudet.edu.

DEGREES AND AWARDS

Undergraduate Certificate(s) Integrating Technology Into the Classroom

COURSE SUBJECT AREAS OFFERED OUTSIDE OF DEGREE PROGRAMS

Graduate: Social work; special education; teacher education

GANNON UNIVERSITY

Erie, Pennsylvania

Center for Adult Learning

www.gannon.edu

Gannon University, founded in 1925, is an independent, religious, comprehensive institution. It is accredited by the Middle States Association of Colleges and Schools. It first offered distance learning courses in 1976. In 1999–2000, it offered 21 courses at a distance. In fall 1999, there were 71 students enrolled in distance learning courses.

Course delivery sites Courses are delivered to your home.

Media Courses are delivered via World Wide Web, print. Students and teachers may interact via mail, telephone, fax, e-mail. The following equipment may be required: computer, Internet access.

Restrictions Programs are available worldwide. Enrollment is open to anyone.

Services Distance learners have access to library services, e-mail services, academic advising, tutoring, career placement assistance at a distance.

Credit-earning options Students may transfer credits from another institution or may earn credits through examinations.

Typical costs Tuition of $405 per credit. Graduate tuition ranges between $270 and $425 per credit. Financial aid is available to distance learners.

Registration Students may register by mail, fax, telephone, e-mail, in person.

Contact Debra Meszaros, Assistant Director, Center for Adult Learning, Gannon University, University Square, Erie, PA 16541. *Telephone:* 814-871-7458. *Fax:* 814-871-5827. *E-mail:* openu@cluster.gannon.edu.

DEGREES AND AWARDS

Distance programs offered do not lead to a degree or other formal award.

COURSE SUBJECT AREAS OFFERED OUTSIDE OF DEGREE PROGRAMS

Undergraduate: Business administration and management; business communications; economics; English composition; history; law and legal studies; marketing; music; philosophy and religion; psychology

Graduate: Business administration and management

GARLAND COUNTY COMMUNITY COLLEGE

Hot Springs, Arkansas

Distance Education

Garland County Community College, founded in 1973, is a state and locally supported, two-year college. It is accredited by the North Central Association of Colleges and Schools. It first offered distance learning courses in 1985. In 1999–2000, it offered 8 courses at a distance. In fall 1999, there were 90 students enrolled in distance learning courses.

Course delivery sites Courses are delivered to your home.

Media Courses are delivered via television. Students and teachers may interact via mail, telephone, fax, e-mail.

Restrictions Courses are available to students within television transmission area only. Enrollment is open to anyone.

Services Distance learners have access to library services, academic advising, tutoring, career placement assistance at a distance.

Credit-earning options Students may transfer credits from another institution or may earn credits through military training.

Typical costs Tuition of $37 per credit hour plus mandatory fees of $20 per course for local area residents. Tuition of $46 per credit hour plus mandatory fees of $20 per course for in-state residents. Tuition of $115

per credit hour plus mandatory fees of $20 per course for out-of-state residents. Costs may vary. Financial aid is available to distance learners.

Registration Students may register by in person.

Contact Dr. Alan Hoffman, Vice President for Instruction, Garland County Community College, 101 College Drive, Hot Springs, AR 71913. *Telephone:* 501-760-4202. *Fax:* 501-760-4100. *E-mail:* ahoffman@admin.gccc.cc.ar.us.

DEGREES AND AWARDS

ALS Liberal Studies (certain restrictions apply; service area differs from that of the overall institution; some on-campus requirements)

COURSE SUBJECT AREAS OFFERED OUTSIDE OF DEGREE PROGRAMS

Undergraduate: Accounting; administrative and secretarial services; astronomy and astrophysics; biology; botany; business; business administration and management; chemistry; computer and information sciences; conservation and natural resources; creative writing; design; developmental and child psychology; economics; English composition; English language and literature; European languages and literatures; fine arts; geology; health and physical education/fitness; health professions and related sciences; history; journalism; liberal arts, general studies, and humanities; mathematics; microbiology; music; nursing; philosophy and religion; physics; political science; protective services; public health; sociology; teacher education; zoology

Noncredit: Hospitality services management; human resources management

GATEWAY COMMUNITY COLLEGE

New Haven, Connecticut

www.gwctc.commnet.edu

Gateway Community College, founded in 1992, is a state-supported, two-year college. It is accredited by the New England Association of Schools and Colleges. In 1999–2000, it offered 1 course at a distance.

Course delivery sites Courses are delivered to your home, your workplace.

Media Courses are delivered via computer software, computer conferencing, World Wide Web, e-mail. Students and teachers may meet in person or interact via mail, telephone, fax, e-mail, World Wide Web. The following equipment may be required: computer, modem, Internet access, e-mail.

Restrictions Programs are available worldwide. Enrollment is open to anyone.

Services Distance learners have access to library services at a distance.

Typical costs Tuition of $67 per credit plus mandatory fees of $42 per credit for in-state residents. Tuition of $218 per credit plus mandatory fees of $42 per credit for out-of-state residents.

Registration Students may register by mail, fax, in person.

Contact Cathy Surface, Director of Admissions and Counseling, Gateway Community College, 60 Sargent Drive, New Haven, CT 06511. *Telephone:* 203-789-7043. *E-mail:* gw_surface@commnet.edu.

DEGREES AND AWARDS

Distance programs offered do not lead to a degree or other formal award.

COURSE SUBJECT AREAS OFFERED OUTSIDE OF DEGREE PROGRAMS

Undergraduate: Political science

GENESEE COMMUNITY COLLEGE

Batavia, New York

Information Technology and Distance Learning
www.sunygenesee.cc.ny.us

Genesee Community College, founded in 1966, is a state and locally supported, two-year college. It is accredited by the Middle States Association of Colleges and Schools. It first offered distance learning courses in 1988. In 1999–2000, it offered 35 courses at a distance. In fall 1999, there were 550 students enrolled in distance learning courses.

Course delivery sites Courses are delivered to your home, your workplace, high schools, 4 off-campus centers in Albion, Arcade, Lakeville, Warsaw.

Media Courses are delivered via television, videotapes, videoconferencing, interactive television, audiotapes, computer software, CD-ROM, computer conferencing, World Wide Web, e-mail, print. Students and teachers may meet in person or interact via videoconferencing, audioconferencing, mail, telephone, fax, e-mail, interactive television, World Wide Web. The following equipment may be required: television, videocassette player, computer, Internet access, e-mail.

Restrictions Programs are available in a four-county service area; Internet-based courses are available statewide. Enrollment is open to anyone.

Services Distance learners have access to library services, the campus computer network, e-mail services, academic advising, tutoring, bookstore at a distance.

Credit-earning options Students may transfer credits from another institution or may earn credits through examinations, military training.

Typical costs Tuition of $97 per semester credit for in-state residents. Tuition of $106 per semester credit for out-of-state residents. Mandatory fees range between $10 and $25 per course. Financial aid is available to distance learners.

Registration Students may register by mail, fax, in person.

Contact Robert G. Knipe, Dean, Genesee Community College, 1 College Road, Batavia, NY 14020-9704. *Telephone:* 716-343-0055 Ext. 6595. *Fax:* 716-343-0433. *E-mail:* rgknipe@sunygenesee.cc.ny.us.

DEGREES AND AWARDS

Distance programs offered do not lead to a degree or other formal award.

COURSE SUBJECT AREAS OFFERED OUTSIDE OF DEGREE PROGRAMS

Undergraduate: Abnormal psychology; accounting; administrative and secretarial services; algebra; anthropology; art history and criticism; biology; business; business administration and management; creative writing; developmental and child psychology; economics; English composition; English language and literature; European history; film studies; gerontology; health and physical education/fitness; history; law and legal studies; liberal arts, general studies, and humanities; marketing; mass media; music; political science; psychology; sociology; special education; technical writing; women's studies

GEORGE WASHINGTON UNIVERSITY

Washington, District of Columbia
www.gwu.edu/~distance

George Washington University, founded in 1821, is an independent, nonprofit university. It is accredited by the Middle States Association of Colleges and Schools. It first offered distance learning courses in 1983. In 1999–2000, it offered 76 courses at a distance. In fall 1999, there were 1,000 students enrolled in distance learning courses.

Course delivery sites Courses are delivered to your home, your workplace, military bases, Hebrew University of Jerusalem (Jerusalem, Israel), Jerusalem University (Jerusalem, Israel).

Media Courses are delivered via television, videotapes, videoconferencing, CD-ROM, World Wide Web, e-mail, print. Students and teachers may meet in person or interact via videoconferencing, mail, telephone, fax, e-mail, World Wide Web. The following equipment may be required: television, videocassette player, computer, modem, Internet access, e-mail.

Restrictions Programs are available worldwide. Enrollment is open to anyone.

Services Distance learners have access to library services, the campus computer network, e-mail services, academic advising, bookstore at a distance.

Credit-earning options Students may transfer credits from another institution.

Typical costs Contact the school for information. Costs may vary. Financial aid is available to distance learners.

Registration Students may register by mail, fax, telephone, e-mail, World Wide Web, in person.

Contact Arlene Polinsky, Manager, Special Services, George Washington University, GW Television, 801 22nd Street, North West, Suite 350, Washington, DC 20052. *Telephone:* 202-994-1692. *Fax:* 202-994-5048. *E-mail:* polinsky@gwu.edu.

DEGREES AND AWARDS

Undergraduate Certificate(s) Event Management, International Public Health-Community Oriented Primary Care Option (some on-campus requirements), Records Management

BSHS Clinical Health Sciences (certain restrictions apply), Clinical Management and Leadership (certain restrictions apply), Clinical Research Administration (certain restrictions apply), Emergency Health Services (certain restrictions apply)

MA Educational Technology Leadership

MS Health Science (certain restrictions apply), Project Management (some on-campus requirements)

COURSE SUBJECT AREAS OFFERED OUTSIDE OF DEGREE PROGRAMS

Undergraduate: Health professions and related sciences
Graduate: Business; education; health professions and related sciences
Noncredit: Business; education

Special note
The School of Public Health and Health Services (SPHHS) offers 18-credit-hour graduate certificate options that may be taken entirely by distance education and may be transferred upon acceptance to the MPH program. Options include public health generalist, health services, and health information systems. The public health generalist option includes all core course work required for an MPH degree by the Council on Education for Public Health. The new health services option is scheduled to begin in January 2001. The health information systems program also includes an optional on-campus, 2-week session in late June. Additional course work in long-term care is expected to be offered in summer 2001. Courses will be designed to meet the educational requirements in most states to sit for the examination to become a licensed nursing home administrator. Course work is generally Web based and includes CD-ROM material prepared by the SPHHS. Students may complete a certificate program in 1 to 2 years. Applicants must have earned a bachelor's degree. Applicants who have earned a GPA of 3.0 (on a 4.0 scale) for their bachelor's degree or have earned a previous graduate degree are not required to submit standardized test scores. Students may be eligible for the GW Loan program and a limited number of partial scholarships. The SPHHS is fully accredited by CEPH. For more information, students should call 202-994-2160, send an

e-mail to sphhsinfo@gwumc.edu, or visit the Web site at http://www.gwumc.edu/sphhs.

GEORGIA INSTITUTE OF TECHNOLOGY

Atlanta, Georgia
Center for Distance Learning
www.conted.gatech.edu/distance

Georgia Institute of Technology, founded in 1885, is a state-supported university. It is accredited by the Southern Association of Colleges and Schools. It first offered distance learning courses in 1977. In 1999–2000, it offered 115 courses at a distance. In fall 1999, there were 400 students enrolled in distance learning courses.

Course delivery sites Courses are delivered to your home, your workplace, military bases.

Media Courses are delivered via television, videotapes, videoconferencing, CD-ROM, World Wide Web. Students and teachers may meet in person or interact via videoconferencing, mail, telephone, fax, e-mail, World Wide Web. The following equipment may be required: television, videocassette player, computer, modem, Internet access, e-mail.

Restrictions Programs are available worldwide. Enrollment is open to anyone.

Services Distance learners have access to library services, the campus computer network, e-mail services, academic advising, career placement assistance, bookstore at a distance.

Credit-earning options Students may transfer credits from another institution or may earn credits through examinations.

Typical costs Tuition of $510 per credit. *Noncredit courses:* $1500 per course.

Registration Students may register by mail, fax, telephone, e-mail, World Wide Web, in person.

Contact Joe Boland, Director, Georgia Institute of Technology, Center for Distance Learning, 613 Cherry Street, Atlanta, GA 30332-0385. *Telephone:* 404-894-8572. *Fax:* 404-385-0322. *E-mail:* joe.boland@conted.gatech.edu.

DEGREES AND AWARDS

MS Electrical Engineering, Environmental Engineering, Health Physics, Industrial and Systems Engineering, Mechanical Engineering

COURSE SUBJECT AREAS OFFERED OUTSIDE OF DEGREE PROGRAMS

Graduate: Aerospace, aeronautical engineering; biology; civil engineering; electrical engineering; environmental engineering; industrial engineering; mathematics; mechanical engineering; physics

Noncredit: Aerospace, aeronautical engineering; biology; civil engineering; electrical engineering; environmental engineering; industrial engineering; mathematics; mechanical engineering; physics

See full descriptions on pages 534 and 676.

GEORGIA PERIMETER COLLEGE

Decatur, Georgia
Center for Distance Learning
www.gpc.peachnet.edu/~dl

Georgia Perimeter College, founded in 1964, is a state-supported, two-year college. It is accredited by the Southern Association of Colleges and Schools. It first offered distance learning courses in 1981. In 1999–2000,

it offered 60 courses at a distance. In fall 1999, there were 750 students enrolled in distance learning courses.

Course delivery sites Courses are delivered to your home, your workplace, 5 off-campus centers in Clarkston, Conyers, Decatur, Dunwoody, Lawrenceville.

Media Courses are delivered via television, videotapes, videoconferencing, audiotapes, computer software, CD-ROM, computer conferencing, World Wide Web, e-mail, print. Students and teachers may meet in person or interact via videoconferencing, mail, telephone, fax, e-mail, World Wide Web. The following equipment may be required: television, videocassette player, computer, modem, Internet access, e-mail.

Restrictions Courses are available to students in metropolitan Atlanta and surrounding areas. Enrollment is open to anyone.

Services Distance learners have access to library services, the campus computer network, e-mail services, bookstore at a distance.

Credit-earning options Students may transfer credits from another institution.

Typical costs Tuition of $52 per credit hour for in-state residents. Tuition of $207 per credit hour for out-of-state residents. There is a mandatory technology fee of $38 for all students. Costs may vary. Financial aid is available to distance learners.

Registration Students may register by mail, fax, telephone, in person.

Contact Robert A. Harrell, Director of Distance Learning, Georgia Perimeter College, 555 North Indian Creek Drive, Clarkston, GA 30021-2396. *Telephone:* 404-294-3490. *Fax:* 404-294-3492. *E-mail:* rharrell@gpc.peachnet.edu.

DEGREES AND AWARDS

Distance programs offered do not lead to a degree or other formal award.

COURSE SUBJECT AREAS OFFERED OUTSIDE OF DEGREE PROGRAMS

Undergraduate: Developmental and child psychology; economics; European languages and literatures; health and physical education/fitness; health professions and related sciences; history; liberal arts, general studies, and humanities; political science; sign language; sociology

See full description on page 676.

GEORGIA SOUTHERN UNIVERSITY

Statesboro, Georgia
Distance Learning Center
www2.gasou.edu/distance_learning/index.html

Georgia Southern University, founded in 1906, is a state-supported, comprehensive institution. It is accredited by the Southern Association of Colleges and Schools. It first offered distance learning courses in 1992. In 1999–2000, it offered 119 courses at a distance. In fall 1999, there were 512 students enrolled in distance learning courses.

Course delivery sites Courses are delivered to your home, your workplace, military bases, high schools, other colleges, 2 off-campus centers in Brunswick, Savannah.

Media Courses are delivered via videotapes, videoconferencing, interactive television, CD-ROM, computer conferencing, World Wide Web, e-mail, print. Students and teachers may meet in person or interact via videoconferencing, audioconferencing, mail, telephone, fax, e-mail, interactive television, World Wide Web. The following equipment may be required: computer, Internet access, e-mail.

Restrictions GSAMS Network Video Teleconferences are available in state; Internet courses are available worldwide. Enrollment is restricted to individuals meeting certain criteria.

Services Distance learners have access to library services, the campus computer network, e-mail services, bookstore at a distance.
Credit-earning options Students may transfer credits from another institution or may earn credits through examinations, military training.
Typical costs *Undergraduate:* Tuition of $1216 per semester for in-state residents. Tuition of $3928 per semester for out-of-state residents. *Graduate:* Tuition of $1397 per semester for in-state residents. Tuition of $4652 per semester for out-of-state residents. Costs may vary. Financial aid is available to distance learners.
Registration Students may register by mail, in person.
Contact Peggy Smith, Administrative Secretary, Georgia Southern University. *Telephone:* 912-881-0882. *Fax:* 912-871-1424. *E-mail:* pegsmith@gasou.edu.

DEGREES AND AWARDS

BBA Business Administration
MBA Business Administration (certain restrictions apply)
MPA Public Administration (certain restrictions apply)

COURSE SUBJECT AREAS OFFERED OUTSIDE OF DEGREE PROGRAMS

Undergraduate: Accounting; astronomy and astrophysics; business; business administration and management; economics; engineering mechanics; English composition; European languages and literatures; geology; history; mathematics; nursing; physics; political science; sociology; special education
Graduate: Accounting; business; business administration and management; curriculum and instruction; economics; education administration; educational research; geology; instructional media; law and legal studies; mathematics; nursing; political science; sociology; special education; teacher education
Noncredit: European languages and literatures; home economics and family studies; mathematics

See full description on page 676.

GEORGIA SOUTHWESTERN STATE UNIVERSITY

Americus, Georgia

Instructional Technology Center
www.gsw.edu/~itc/

Georgia Southwestern State University, founded in 1906, is a state-supported, comprehensive institution. It is accredited by the Southern Association of Colleges and Schools. It first offered distance learning courses in 1994. In 1999–2000, it offered 34 courses at a distance. In fall 1999, there were 183 students enrolled in distance learning courses.
Course delivery sites Courses are delivered to your home, your workplace, military bases, high schools, Abraham Baldwin Agricultural College (Tifton), Darton College (Albany), Middle Georgia College (Cochran), 2 off-campus centers.
Media Courses are delivered via videotapes, videoconferencing, computer software, CD-ROM, World Wide Web, e-mail, print. Students and teachers may meet in person or interact via videoconferencing, mail, telephone, fax, e-mail, World Wide Web. The following equipment may be required: computer, modem, Internet access, e-mail.
Restrictions Programs are available to in-state students only. Enrollment is restricted to individuals meeting certain criteria.
Services Distance learners have access to library services, the campus computer network, e-mail services, academic advising, bookstore at a distance.
Credit-earning options Students may earn credits through examinations.

Typical costs *Undergraduate:* Tuition of $76 per semester hour for in-state residents. Tuition of $302 per semester hour for out-of-state residents. *Graduate:* Tuition of $91 per semester hour for in-state residents. Tuition of $363 per semester hour for out-of-state residents. Costs may vary. Financial aid is available to distance learners.
Registration Students may register by mail, fax, telephone, e-mail, World Wide Web, in person.
Contact Dr. Jho-Ju Tu, Instructional Technology Center, Georgia Southwestern State University, 800 Wheatley Street, Americus, GA 31709. *Telephone:* 912-931-2140. *Fax:* 912-931-2928. *E-mail:* tu@canes.gsw.edu.

DEGREES AND AWARDS

Distance programs offered do not lead to a degree or other formal award.

COURSE SUBJECT AREAS OFFERED OUTSIDE OF DEGREE PROGRAMS

Undergraduate: Computer and information sciences; education
Graduate: Accounting; business; business administration and management; curriculum and instruction; education; education administration; educational psychology; educational research; marketing
See full description on page 676.

GEORGIA STATE UNIVERSITY

Atlanta, Georgia

Division of Distance and Distributed Learning
www.gsu.edu

Georgia State University, founded in 1913, is a state-supported university. It is accredited by the Southern Association of Colleges and Schools. In 1999–2000, it offered 40 courses at a distance. In fall 1999, there were 341 students enrolled in distance learning courses.
Course delivery sites Courses are delivered to your home, high schools, 360 off-campus centers.
Media Courses are delivered via videotapes, videoconferencing, interactive television, computer software, CD-ROM, World Wide Web, e-mail, print. Students and teachers may interact via videoconferencing, fax, e-mail, interactive television, World Wide Web. The following equipment may be required: television, videocassette player, computer, modem, Internet access, e-mail.
Restrictions Programs are available to in-state students only. Enrollment is restricted to individuals meeting certain criteria.
Services Distance learners have access to library services, the campus computer network, e-mail services, academic advising, bookstore at a distance.
Credit-earning options Students may transfer credits from another institution.
Typical costs *Undergraduate:* Tuition of $101 per credit for in-state residents. Tuition of $403 per credit for out-of-state residents. *Graduate:* Tuition of $121 per credit for in-state residents. Tuition of $483 per credit for out-of-state residents. Costs may vary. Financial aid is available to distance learners.
Registration Students may register by mail, fax, telephone, World Wide Web.
Contact Jacquelynn Sharpe, Instructional Services Coordinator, Georgia State University, PO Box 4044, Atlanta, GA 30302-4044. *Telephone:* 404-651-3483. *Fax:* 404-651-3452. *E-mail:* dcejws@langate.gsu.edu.

DEGREES AND AWARDS

Distance programs offered do not lead to a degree or other formal award.

COURSE SUBJECT AREAS OFFERED OUTSIDE OF DEGREE PROGRAMS

Undergraduate: Business; physical sciences
Graduate: Business; education
Noncredit: Health professions and related sciences
See full description on page 676.

GLENDALE COMMUNITY COLLEGE

Glendale, California
Letters, Arts, and Sciences
www.glendale.cc.ca.us

Glendale Community College, founded in 1927, is a state and locally supported, two-year college. It is accredited by the Western Association of Schools and Colleges, Inc. It first offered distance learning courses in 1980. In 1999–2000, it offered 9 courses at a distance. In fall 1999, there were 376 students enrolled in distance learning courses.
Course delivery sites Courses are delivered to your home.
Media Courses are delivered via television, videotapes, audiotapes, World Wide Web, print. Students and teachers may meet in person or interact via mail, telephone, fax, e-mail, World Wide Web. The following equipment may be required: television, videocassette player, computer, modem, Internet access, e-mail.
Restrictions Programs are available worldwide. Enrollment is open to anyone.
Services Distance learners have access to library services at a distance.
Credit-earning options Students may transfer credits from another institution.
Typical costs Tuition of $11 per credit plus mandatory fees of $30 per semester for in-state residents. Tuition of $120 per credit plus mandatory fees of $30 per semester for out-of-state residents. Financial aid is available to distance learners.
Registration Students may register by mail, telephone, in person.
Contact Dr. Veloris Lang, Dean, Glendale Community College, Letters, Arts and Sciences, 1500 North Verdugo Road, Glendale, CA 91208. *Telephone:* 818-240-1000 Ext. 5150. *Fax:* 818-551-5228. *E-mail:* vlang@glendale.cc.ca.us.

DEGREES AND AWARDS

Distance programs offered do not lead to a degree or other formal award.

COURSE SUBJECT AREAS OFFERED OUTSIDE OF DEGREE PROGRAMS

Undergraduate: Business administration and management; child care and development; computer and information sciences; developmental and child psychology; English as a second language (ESL); geology; history; liberal arts, general studies, and humanities; political science; psychology; real estate; sociology

GLOBAL UNIVERSITY OF THE ASSEMBLIES OF GOD

Springfield, Missouri
www.globaluniversity.edu

Global University of the Assemblies of God, founded in 1948, is an independent, religious, comprehensive institution affiliated with the Assemblies of God. It is accredited by the Distance Education and Training Council. It first offered distance learning courses in 1948. In 1999–2000, it offered 110 courses at a distance. In fall 1999, there were 7,681 students enrolled in distance learning courses.
Course delivery sites Courses are delivered to your home.
Media Courses are delivered via videoconferencing, World Wide Web, e-mail, print. Students and teachers may meet in person or interact via videoconferencing, audioconferencing, mail, telephone, fax, e-mail, World Wide Web. The following equipment may be required: computer, modem, Internet access, e-mail.
Restrictions Programs are available worldwide. Enrollment is open to anyone.
Services Distance learners have access to library services, the campus computer network, e-mail services, academic advising, bookstore at a distance.
Credit-earning options Students may transfer credits from another institution or may earn credits through examinations, portfolio assessment, military training, business training.
Typical costs *Undergraduate:* Tuition of $75 per credit hour. *Graduate:* Tuition of $139 per credit hour. Other fees include: $35 application fee and approximately $90 for textbooks per course. Costs may vary.
Registration Students may register by mail, fax, telephone, e-mail, World Wide Web, in person.
Contact Student Affairs, Global University of the Assemblies of God, 1211 South Glenstone Avenue, Springfield, MO 65804. *Telephone:* 800-443-1083. *Fax:* 417-862-5318. *E-mail:* sgs@globaluniversity.edu.

DEGREES AND AWARDS

AA Bible and Theology, Missions, Religious Education
BA Bible and Theology, Missions, Religious Education
MA Bible and Theology, Leadership-Christian, Missions, Religious Education

COURSE SUBJECT AREAS OFFERED OUTSIDE OF DEGREE PROGRAMS

Undergraduate: Bible studies; philosophy and religion; religious studies; theological studies
Graduate: Bible studies; education; philosophy and religion; religious studies; theological studies
Noncredit: Bible studies; philosophy and religion; religious studies; theological studies

Special note
Berean University of the Assemblies of God has 5 decades of experience in distance education. Present enrollment is approximately 12,000 adults of varying ages and denominations. The mission of Berean University is to provide accredited distance education for ministers and laypersons, based on a Christian worldview, utilizing current technologies to facilitate the evangelization of the world, the nurture of the church, and the well-being and improvement of society. The University anticipates tremendous growth in educational technology. Some courses are already offered on line. Students now have 24-hour access to the voice-mail boxes of their own student services representatives. This new phone system will eventually offer students access to their own records and a convenient way to take tests and receive scores. The University has a presence on the Internet (http://www.berean.edu) where students and prospective students can send in prayer requests, listen to chapel messages, send e-mail messages to Berean employees, access free online Bible reference materials, link up with a study partner or mentor, and much more. The Web page is regularly updated. Local groups who desire to study together may register as a Berean Study Center. These groups should contact the school to receive a free copy of the *Study Center Guidelines* for establishing an authorized study group or to ask any questions about Berean's study programs. Berean University is committed to providing convenient, high-quality distance education for students who must sandwich their studies

between their families and their jobs or for anyone who desires to increase his or her biblical knowledge.

GLOUCESTER COUNTY COLLEGE

Sewell, New Jersey

Gloucester County College, founded in 1967, is a county-supported, two-year college. It is accredited by the Middle States Association of Colleges and Schools.
Contact Gloucester County College, 1400 Tanyard Road, Sewell, NJ 08080. *Telephone:* 609-468-5000. *Fax:* 609-468-8498.

See full description on page 600.

GODDARD COLLEGE

Plainfield, Vermont
Distance Learning Programs
www.goddard.edu

Goddard College, founded in 1938, is an independent, nonprofit, comprehensive institution. It is accredited by the New England Association of Schools and Colleges. It first offered distance learning courses in 1963. In fall 1999, there were 360 students enrolled in distance learning courses.
Course delivery sites Courses are delivered to your home.
Media Courses are delivered via computer conferencing. Students and teachers may meet in person or interact via mail, telephone, fax, e-mail.
Restrictions Programs are available worldwide. Enrollment is open to anyone.
Services Distance learners have access to library services, the campus computer network, academic advising at a distance.
Credit-earning options Students may transfer credits from another institution or may earn credits through portfolio assessment.
Typical costs *Undergraduate:* Tuition of $4125 per semester. *Graduate:* Tuition of $4815 per semester. For Master of Fine Arts degree, tuition is $4912 per semester. Costs may vary. Financial aid is available to distance learners.
Registration Students may register by in person.
Contact Ellen W. Codling, Admissions, Goddard College, 123 Pitkin Road, Plainfield, VT 05667. *Telephone:* 800-468-4888. *Fax:* 802-454-1029. *E-mail:* admissions@earth.goddard.edu.

DEGREES AND AWARDS

BA Health Arts (certain restrictions apply; some on-campus requirements), Individualized Studies (certain restrictions apply; some on-campus requirements), Liberal Arts (certain restrictions apply; some on-campus requirements), Social Ecology (certain restrictions apply; some on-campus requirements)
MA Health Arts (certain restrictions apply; some on-campus requirements), Individualized Study in the Liberal Arts (certain restrictions apply; some on-campus requirements), Psychology and Counseling (certain restrictions apply; some on-campus requirements), Social Ecology (some on-campus requirements), Teacher Education (certain restrictions apply; some on-campus requirements)
MFA Creative Writing (certain restrictions apply; some on-campus requirements), Interdisciplinary Arts (certain restrictions apply; some on-campus requirements)

COURSE SUBJECT AREAS OFFERED OUTSIDE OF DEGREE PROGRAMS

Undergraduate: Abnormal psychology; anthropology; area, ethnic, and cultural studies; art history and criticism; conservation and natural resources; counseling psychology; curriculum and instruction; developmental and child psychology; drama and theater; education; English language and literature; fine arts; foods and nutrition studies; health professions and related sciences; history; individual and family development studies; interdisciplinary studies; liberal arts, general studies, and humanities; music; philosophy and religion; photography; psychology; social sciences; teacher education; visual and performing arts
Graduate: Abnormal psychology; anthropology; area, ethnic, and cultural studies; art history and criticism; conservation and natural resources; counseling psychology; curriculum and instruction; developmental and child psychology; drama and theater; education; English language and literature; fine arts; foods and nutrition studies; health professions and related sciences; history; individual and family development studies; interdisciplinary studies; liberal arts, general studies, and humanities; music; philosophy and religion; photography; psychology; social sciences; teacher education; visual and performing arts

See full description on page 536.

GOGEBIC COMMUNITY COLLEGE

Ironwood, Michigan
www.gogebic.cc.mi.us

Gogebic Community College, founded in 1932, is a state and locally supported, two-year college. It is accredited by the North Central Association of Colleges and Schools. In 1999–2000, it offered 16 courses at a distance. In fall 1999, there were 94 students enrolled in distance learning courses.
Course delivery sites Courses are delivered to your home, high schools, 4 off-campus centers in Hancock, Iron River, L'Anse, Ontonagon.
Media Courses are delivered via television, videotapes, interactive television, World Wide Web. Students and teachers may meet in person or interact via videoconferencing, mail, fax, e-mail, interactive television. The following equipment may be required: television, computer, Internet access, e-mail.
Restrictions Programs are available worldwide. Enrollment is restricted to individuals meeting certain criteria.
Services Distance learners have access to library services, e-mail services, academic advising, bookstore at a distance.
Credit-earning options Students may transfer credits from another institution or may earn credits through examinations.
Typical costs Tuition of $45 per credit plus mandatory fees of $220 per semester for local area residents. Tuition of $62 per credit plus mandatory fees of $220 per semester for in-state residents. Tuition of $87 per credit plus mandatory fees of $220 per semester for out-of-state residents. Financial aid is available to distance learners.
Registration Students may register by mail, fax, telephone, World Wide Web, in person.
Contact Admissions Office, Gogebic Community College, East 4946 Jackson Road, Ironwood, MI 49938. *Telephone:* 906-932-4231 Ext. 306. *Fax:* 906-932-2339. *E-mail:* jeannew@admit1.gogebic.cc.mi.us.

DEGREES AND AWARDS

Distance programs offered do not lead to a degree or other formal award.

COURSE SUBJECT AREAS OFFERED OUTSIDE OF DEGREE PROGRAMS

Undergraduate: Accounting; business communications; ecology; English composition; English language and literature; history; journalism; philosophy and religion; political science; psychology; sociology

GOLDEN GATE UNIVERSITY

San Francisco, California
Cyber Campus
cybercampus.ggu.edu

Golden Gate University, founded in 1853, is an independent, nonprofit university. It is accredited by the Western Association of Schools and Colleges, Inc. It first offered distance learning courses in 1997. In 1999–2000, it offered 270 courses at a distance. In fall 1999, there were 900 students enrolled in distance learning courses.

Course delivery sites Courses are delivered to your home, your workplace, military bases.

Media Courses are delivered via World Wide Web, e-mail. Students and teachers may meet in person or interact via mail, telephone, fax, e-mail, World Wide Web. The following equipment may be required: computer, modem, Internet access, e-mail.

Restrictions Programs are available worldwide. Enrollment is open to anyone.

Services Distance learners have access to library services, e-mail services, academic advising, career placement assistance, bookstore at a distance.

Credit-earning options Students may transfer credits from another institution or may earn credits through examinations.

Typical costs Undergraduate tuition is $1104 per course. Graduate tuition ranges between $1136 and $1650 depending on course. Costs may vary. Financial aid is available to distance learners.

Registration Students may register by mail, fax, World Wide Web, in person.

Contact Alan Roper, Senior Program Administrator, Golden Gate University, 536 Mission Street, San Francisco, CA 94105. *Telephone:* 415-442-7060. *Fax:* 415-227-4502. *E-mail:* cybercampus@ggu.edu.

DEGREES AND AWARDS

Undergraduate Certificate(s) Finance, Technology Management
BPA Public Administration
Graduate Certificate(s) Accounting, Arts Administration, Finance, Healthcare Administration, Personal Financial Planning, Taxation
EMPA Public Administration
MHA Health Care Administration
MS Finance, Taxation, Telecommunications Management

COURSE SUBJECT AREAS OFFERED OUTSIDE OF DEGREE PROGRAMS

Undergraduate: Accounting; business administration and management; communications; computer and information sciences; English composition; English language and literature; finance; hospitality services management; management information systems; mathematics
Graduate: Accounting; business administration and management; communications; computer and information sciences; economics; English composition; English language and literature; finance; health services administration; hospitality services management; management information systems; marketing; public administration and services; telecommunications

GONZAGA UNIVERSITY

Spokane, Washington
School of Professional Studies
www.gonzaga.edu/professionalstudies/

Gonzaga University, founded in 1887, is an independent, religious, comprehensive institution. It is accredited by the Association of Theological Schools in the United States and Canada (candidate), Northwest

Association of Schools and Colleges. In fall 1999, there were 220 students enrolled in distance learning courses.

Course delivery sites Courses are delivered to your home, your workplace, Lewis-Clark State College (Lewiston, ID).

Media Courses are delivered via videotapes, videoconferencing, computer software. Students and teachers may meet in person or interact via videoconferencing, audioconferencing, mail, telephone, fax, e-mail, World Wide Web. The following equipment may be required: television, videocassette player, computer, Internet access, e-mail.

Restrictions Programs are available nationwide. Enrollment is restricted to individuals meeting certain criteria.

Services Distance learners have access to library services, the campus computer network, e-mail services, academic advising, bookstore at a distance.

Credit-earning options Students may transfer credits from another institution or may earn credits through examinations.

Typical costs *Undergraduate:* Tuition of $480 per credit. *Graduate:* Tuition of $425 per credit. Financial aid is available to distance learners.

Registration Students may register by fax, telephone, World Wide Web, in person.

Contact Mary McFarland, Dean, Gonzaga University, School of Professional Studies, Spokane, WA 99258. *Telephone:* 509-323-3544. *Fax:* 509-323-5987. *E-mail:* mcfarlandm@gu.gonzaga.edu.

DEGREES AND AWARDS

BSN Nursing (certain restrictions apply; some on-campus requirements)
MA Organizational Leadership
MSN Nursing (certain restrictions apply; some on-campus requirements)

COURSE SUBJECT AREAS OFFERED OUTSIDE OF DEGREE PROGRAMS

Undergraduate: Ethics; logic; nursing; religious studies
Graduate: Ethics; logic; nursing; organizational behavior studies; religious studies

GOUCHER COLLEGE

Baltimore, Maryland
Center for Graduate and Continuing Studies
www.goucher.edu

Goucher College, founded in 1885, is an independent, nonprofit, comprehensive institution. It is accredited by the Middle States Association of Colleges and Schools. It first offered distance learning courses in 1995. In 1999–2000, it offered 18 courses at a distance. In fall 1999, there were 55 students enrolled in distance learning courses.

Course delivery sites Courses are delivered to your home.

Media Courses are delivered via computer conferencing, World Wide Web, e-mail, print. Students and teachers may interact via mail, telephone, fax, e-mail, World Wide Web. The following equipment may be required: computer, modem, Internet access, e-mail.

Restrictions Courses are available to U.S. and Canadian students only. Enrollment is open to anyone.

Services Distance learners have access to library services, the campus computer network, e-mail services, academic advising, bookstore at a distance.

Credit-earning options Students may transfer credits from another institution.

Typical costs Tuition of $510 per credit. *Noncredit courses:* $385 per course. Financial aid is available to distance learners.

Registration Students may register by mail, fax, telephone, in person.

Contact Debbie Culbertson, Executive Director, Goucher College, Center for Graduate and Continuing Studies, 1021 Dulaney Valley Road, Baltimore, MD 21204. *Telephone:* 410-337-6200. *Fax:* 410-337-6085. *E-mail:* center@goucher.edu.

DEGREES AND AWARDS

MA Historic Preservation (service area differs from that of the overall institution; some on-campus requirements), Women, Aging and Public Policy (service area differs from that of the overall institution; some on-campus requirements)
MAAA Arts Administration (service area differs from that of the overall institution; some on-campus requirements)
MFA Creative Nonfiction (service area differs from that of the overall institution; some on-campus requirements)

COURSE SUBJECT AREAS OFFERED OUTSIDE OF DEGREE PROGRAMS

Graduate: Area, ethnic, and cultural studies; creative writing; history; visual and performing arts

GOVERNORS STATE UNIVERSITY

University Park, Illinois
Center for Extended Learning and Communications Services
www.govst.edu

Governors State University, founded in 1969, is a state-supported, upper-level institution. It is accredited by the North Central Association of Colleges and Schools. It first offered distance learning courses in 1981. In 1999–2000, it offered 52 courses at a distance. In fall 1999, there were 1,221 students enrolled in distance learning courses.
Course delivery sites Courses are delivered to your home, your workplace.
Media Courses are delivered via television, videotapes, interactive television, audiotapes, computer software, World Wide Web, e-mail, print. Students and teachers may interact via audioconferencing, mail, telephone, fax, e-mail, interactive television. The following equipment may be required: television, videocassette player, computer, modem, Internet access, e-mail.
Restrictions Programs are available worldwide. Enrollment is restricted to individuals meeting certain criteria.
Services Distance learners have access to academic advising at a distance.
Credit-earning options Students may transfer credits from another institution or may earn credits through examinations, portfolio assessment, military training.
Typical costs *Undergraduate:* Tuition of $92 per credit plus mandatory fees of $10 per credit. *Graduate:* Tuition of $98 per credit plus mandatory fees of $10 per credit. *Noncredit courses:* $306 per course. Financial aid is available to distance learners.
Registration Students may register by mail, fax, in person.
Contact Veronica Williams, Director, Governors State University. *Telephone:* 708-534-3143. *Fax:* 708-534-8458. *E-mail:* v-willia@govst.edu.

DEGREES AND AWARDS

BA Individualized Studies

COURSE SUBJECT AREAS OFFERED OUTSIDE OF DEGREE PROGRAMS

Undergraduate: Anthropology; art history and criticism; biological and life sciences; business; business administration and management; communications; developmental and child psychology; economics; English composition; English language and literature; geography; history; liberal arts,

general studies, and humanities; marketing; music; philosophy and religion; psychology; public health; social work; sociology; special education; teacher education
Graduate: Anthropology; art history and criticism; developmental and child psychology; English language and literature; history; liberal arts, general studies, and humanities; music; psychology; public health; social work; sociology; special education

GRACELAND COLLEGE

Lamoni, Iowa
Distance Learning
www.graceland.edu

Graceland College, founded in 1895, is an independent, religious, comprehensive institution. It is accredited by the North Central Association of Colleges and Schools. It first offered distance learning courses in 1988. In 1999–2000, it offered 130 courses at a distance. In fall 1999, there were 400 students enrolled in distance learning courses.
Course delivery sites Courses are delivered to your home, high schools, American Institute of Business (Des Moines), Indian Hills Community College (Ottumwa), North Central Missouri College (Trenton, MO), Southwestern Community College (Creston), 3 off-campus centers in Centerville, Des Moines, Trenton (MO).
Media Courses are delivered via videotapes, videoconferencing, interactive television, computer software, CD-ROM, World Wide Web, e-mail, print. Students and teachers may meet in person or interact via videoconferencing, mail, telephone, fax, e-mail, interactive television.
Restrictions Partnership is available within the local area only; ACE courses are offered statewide; Outreach is worldwide. Enrollment is restricted to individuals meeting certain criteria.
Services Distance learners have access to library services, the campus computer network, e-mail services, academic advising, bookstore at a distance.
Credit-earning options Students may transfer credits from another institution or may earn credits through examinations, portfolio assessment, military training, business training.
Typical costs Tuition of $170 per semester hour. Costs may vary. Financial aid is available to distance learners.
Registration Students may register by mail, fax, telephone, e-mail, in person.
Contact Karen Robb, Office of Continuing Education and Distance Learning/Site Coordinator, Graceland College, 700 College Avenue, Lamoni, IA 50140. *Telephone:* 515-784-5309. *Fax:* 515-784-5405. *E-mail:* robb@graceland.edu.

DEGREES AND AWARDS

BA Accounting (service area differs from that of the overall institution; some on-campus requirements), Business Administration (service area differs from that of the overall institution; some on-campus requirements), Elementary Education (service area differs from that of the overall institution; some on-campus requirements), Information Technology (service area differs from that of the overall institution; some on-campus requirements), Sociology (service area differs from that of the overall institution; some on-campus requirements)
BSN Professional Nursing (service area differs from that of the overall institution; some on-campus requirements)
MEd Education (certain restrictions apply; service area differs from that of the overall institution)
MSN Clinical Nurse Specialist—Family Nursing (service area differs from that of the overall institution; some on-campus requirements), Family Nurse Practitioner (service area differs from that of the overall institution; some on-campus requirements), Health Care Administration (service area differs from that of the overall institution; some on-campus requirements)

COURSE SUBJECT AREAS OFFERED OUTSIDE OF DEGREE PROGRAMS

Undergraduate: Accounting; American (U.S.) history; biology; business administration and management; chemistry; computer and information sciences; computer programming; criminal justice; curriculum and instruction; database management; developmental and child psychology; drama and theater; economics; educational psychology; English composition; English language and literature; finance; fine arts; health and physical education/fitness; health professions and related sciences; history; human resources management; industrial psychology; information sciences and systems; liberal arts, general studies, and humanities; marketing; mathematics; microbiology; music; nursing; philosophy and religion; psychology; school psychology; sociology; special education
Graduate: Educational psychology; nursing; school psychology

GRACE UNIVERSITY

Omaha, Nebraska
Grace University i-Studies
209.35.213.122

Grace University, founded in 1943, is an independent, religious, comprehensive institution. It is accredited by the Accrediting Association of Bible Colleges, North Central Association of Colleges and Schools. In 1999–2000, it offered 10 courses at a distance. In fall 1999, there were 100 students enrolled in distance learning courses.
Course delivery sites Courses are delivered to your home, military bases, high schools.
Media Courses are delivered via World Wide Web, e-mail, print. Students and teachers may meet in person or interact via mail, telephone, fax, e-mail, World Wide Web. The following equipment may be required: computer, modem, Internet access, e-mail.
Restrictions Programs are available nationwide. Enrollment is restricted to individuals meeting certain criteria.
Services Distance learners have access to library services, bookstore at a distance.
Credit-earning options Students may transfer credits from another institution or may earn credits through examinations.
Typical costs Tuition of $248 per credit. There is a $25 one-time application fee. *Noncredit courses:* $124 per course. Financial aid is available to distance learners.
Registration Students may register by mail, fax, telephone, e-mail, World Wide Web, in person.
Contact Terri Dingfield, Director, Grace University Admissions, Grace University, 1311 South 9th Street, Omaha, NE 68108. *Telephone:* 402-449-2831. *Fax:* 402-341-9587. *E-mail:* guterri@graceu.edu.

DEGREES AND AWARDS

Distance programs offered do not lead to a degree or other formal award.

COURSE SUBJECT AREAS OFFERED OUTSIDE OF DEGREE PROGRAMS

Undergraduate: Bible studies; counseling psychology; history; liberal arts, general studies, and humanities
Noncredit: Bible studies; counseling psychology; history; liberal arts, general studies, and humanities

GRAMBLING STATE UNIVERSITY

Grambling, Louisiana
Grambling State University Distance Learning
www.gram.edu

Grambling State University, founded in 1901, is a state-supported, comprehensive institution. It is accredited by the Southern Association of Colleges and Schools. It first offered distance learning courses in 1991. In 1999–2000, it offered 5 courses at a distance. In fall 1999, there were 25 students enrolled in distance learning courses.
Course delivery sites Courses are delivered to your home.
Media Courses are delivered via television, videoconferencing. Students and teachers may meet in person or interact via videoconferencing, mail, telephone, e-mail. The following equipment may be required: television, videocassette player, computer, modem, e-mail.
Restrictions Programs are available nationwide. Enrollment is restricted to individuals meeting certain criteria.
Services Distance learners have access to library services, e-mail services, academic advising, tutoring, career placement assistance, bookstore at a distance.
Credit-earning options Students may earn credits through examinations.
Typical costs Tuition for both undergraduates and graduates is $487.50 for 1-3 credits. There is a mandatory distance learning fee of $35. Costs may vary. Financial aid is available to distance learners.
Registration Students may register by fax, telephone, in person.
Contact Carolyn Wilson, Secretary, Grambling State University, 100 Main Street, Grambling, LA 71245. *Telephone:* 318-274-6412. *Fax:* 318-274-3761. *E-mail:* ctwilson@alphao.gram.edu.

DEGREES AND AWARDS

Distance programs offered do not lead to a degree or other formal award.

COURSE SUBJECT AREAS OFFERED OUTSIDE OF DEGREE PROGRAMS

Graduate: Education; education administration
See full description on page 676.

GRAND CANYON UNIVERSITY

Phoenix, Arizona
College of Education
www.grand-canyon.edu

Grand Canyon University, founded in 1949, is an independent, religious, comprehensive institution. It is accredited by the North Central Association of Colleges and Schools. It first offered distance learning courses in 1990. In 1999–2000, it offered 30 courses at a distance. In fall 1999, there were 1,473 students enrolled in distance learning courses.
Course delivery sites Courses are delivered to your home.
Media Courses are delivered via videotapes, e-mail. Students and teachers may interact via mail, telephone, fax, e-mail. The following equipment may be required: television, videocassette player.
Restrictions Courses are available to students in Arizona and contiguous states only. Enrollment is restricted to individuals meeting certain criteria.
Services Distance learners have access to library services, e-mail services, academic advising, career placement assistance at a distance.
Credit-earning options Students may transfer credits from another institution.

Typical costs Tuition of $205 per semester hour plus mandatory fees of $70 per course. Costs may vary. Financial aid is available to distance learners.

Registration Students may register by mail, fax, in person.

Contact Dr. Ron Graham, Director for Distance Learning, Grand Canyon University, College of Education, 3300 West Camelback Road, Phoenix, AZ 85017. *Telephone:* 800-600-5019 Ext. 2900. *Fax:* 602-589-2010. *E-mail:* rgraham@grand-canyon.edu.

DEGREES AND AWARDS

MAT Teaching (certain restrictions apply; service area differs from that of the overall institution)

COURSE SUBJECT AREAS OFFERED OUTSIDE OF DEGREE PROGRAMS

Graduate: Teacher education

GRAND RAPIDS BAPTIST SEMINARY

Grand Rapids, Michigan

Grand Rapids Baptist Seminary, founded in 1945, is an independent, religious, graduate institution affiliated with the General Association of Regular Baptist Churches. It is accredited by the North Central Association of Colleges and Schools. It first offered distance learning courses in 1969. In 1999–2000, it offered 40 courses at a distance. In fall 1999, there were 62 students enrolled in distance learning courses.

Course delivery sites Courses are delivered to your home.

Media Courses are delivered via audiotapes, print. Students and teachers may interact via mail, telephone, fax, e-mail.

Restrictions Programs are available worldwide. Enrollment is restricted to individuals meeting certain criteria.

Services Distance learners have access to library services, e-mail services, academic advising, career placement assistance, bookstore at a distance.

Credit-earning options Students may transfer credits from another institution or may earn credits through examinations.

Typical costs Tuition of $277 per credit.

Registration Students may register by mail, fax, in person.

Contact John F. VerBerkmoes, Assistant Dean for Academic Services, Grand Rapids Baptist Seminary, 1001 East Beltline, North East, Grand Rapids, MI 49505. *Telephone:* 616-222-1422. *Fax:* 616-222-1414. *E-mail:* j.verberkmoes@cornerstone.edu.

DEGREES AND AWARDS

MRE Christian Education (certain restrictions apply; some on-campus requirements), Christian School Administration (certain restrictions apply; some on-campus requirements), Missions (certain restrictions apply; some on-campus requirements), Pastoral Studies (certain restrictions apply; some on-campus requirements)

COURSE SUBJECT AREAS OFFERED OUTSIDE OF DEGREE PROGRAMS

Graduate: Education administration; philosophy and religion; theological studies

GRAND VALLEY STATE UNIVERSITY

Allendale, Michigan

Division of Continuing Education
www4.gvsu.edu/dist_ed/DE.htm

Grand Valley State University, founded in 1960, is a state-supported, comprehensive institution. It is accredited by the North Central Association of Colleges and Schools. It first offered distance learning courses in 1973. In 1999–2000, it offered 60 courses at a distance. In fall 1999, there were 1,100 students enrolled in distance learning courses.

Course delivery sites Courses are delivered to Lake Superior State University (Sault Sainte Marie), Montcalm Community College (Sidney), Muskegon Community College (Muskegon), North Central Michigan College (Petoskey), Northwestern Michigan College (Traverse City), West Shore Community College (Scottville), 1 off-campus center in Holland.

Media Courses are delivered via television, videotapes, videoconferencing, interactive television, computer conferencing, World Wide Web, e-mail, print. Students and teachers may meet in person or interact via videoconferencing, audioconferencing, mail, telephone, fax, e-mail, interactive television, World Wide Web.

Restrictions Programs are available in select locations in western Michigan. Enrollment is open to anyone.

Services Distance learners have access to library services, e-mail services, academic advising, tutoring, bookstore at a distance.

Credit-earning options Students may transfer credits from another institution or may earn credits through examinations, military training, business training.

Typical costs Undergraduate tuition ranges between $179 and $390 per credit. Graduate tuition ranges between $187 and $390 per credit. Financial aid is available to distance learners.

Registration Students may register by mail, telephone, World Wide Web, in person.

Contact Sandy Becker, Secretary of Distance Education, Grand Valley State University, 301 West Fulton, Eberhard Center, Grand Rapids, MI 49504. *Telephone:* 616-771-6616. *Fax:* 616-771-6642. *E-mail:* beckers@gvsu.edu.

DEGREES AND AWARDS

Distance programs offered do not lead to a degree or other formal award.

COURSE SUBJECT AREAS OFFERED OUTSIDE OF DEGREE PROGRAMS

Undergraduate: Accounting; area, ethnic, and cultural studies; Asian languages and literatures; business; business administration and management; economics; education administration; educational psychology; engineering/industrial management; history; hospitality services management; liberal arts, general studies, and humanities; mathematics; nursing; political science; protective services; public administration and services; social psychology; social work; sociology; special education; teacher education

Graduate: Accounting; area, ethnic, and cultural studies; business; business administration and management; economics; education administration; educational psychology; engineering/industrial management; history; hospitality services management; liberal arts, general studies, and humanities; mathematics; nursing; political science; protective services; public administration and services; social psychology; social work; sociology; special education; teacher education

GRAND VIEW COLLEGE

Des Moines, Iowa
Camp Dodge Campus
www.gvc.edu/

Grand View College, founded in 1896, is an independent, religious, four-year college affiliated with the Evangelical Lutheran Church in America. It is accredited by the North Central Association of Colleges and Schools. In 1999–2000, it offered 6 courses at a distance. In fall 1999, there were 25 students enrolled in distance learning courses.
Course delivery sites Courses are delivered to military bases.
Media Courses are delivered via interactive television. Students and teachers may interact via mail, fax, e-mail, interactive television. The following equipment may be required: television, e-mail.
Restrictions Programs are available to in-state students only. Enrollment is open to anyone.
Services Distance learners have access to the campus computer network, e-mail services, academic advising, career placement assistance, bookstore at a distance.
Credit-earning options Students may transfer credits from another institution or may earn credits through examinations, military training.
Typical costs Tuition of $175 per credit. *Noncredit courses:* $175 per course. Financial aid is available to distance learners.
Registration Students may register by mail, fax, telephone, e-mail, in person.
Contact Sharon Timm, Director, Camp Dodge Campus, Grand View College, 1200 Grandview Avenue, Des Moines, IA 50316. *Telephone:* 515-252-4546. *Fax:* 515-263-2974. *E-mail:* stimm@gvc.edu.

DEGREES AND AWARDS

BA Organizational and Technical Studies (certain restrictions apply)
BSN Nursing Completion Program (certain restrictions apply)

COURSE SUBJECT AREAS OFFERED OUTSIDE OF DEGREE PROGRAMS

Undergraduate: Business administration and management; liberal arts, general studies, and humanities; nursing

GRANTHAM COLLEGE OF ENGINEERING

Slidell, Louisiana
www.grantham.edu

Grantham College of Engineering, founded in 1951, is a proprietary, four-year college. It is accredited by the Distance Education and Training Council. It first offered distance learning courses in 1961. In 1999–2000, it offered 70 courses at a distance. In fall 1999, there were 780 students enrolled in distance learning courses.
Course delivery sites Courses are delivered to your home, military bases.
Media Courses are delivered via computer software, CD-ROM, World Wide Web, e-mail, print. Students and teachers may meet in person or interact via mail, fax, e-mail, World Wide Web. The following equipment may be required: computer, modem, Internet access, e-mail.
Restrictions Programs are available worldwide. Enrollment is restricted to individuals meeting certain criteria.
Services Distance learners have access to library services, e-mail services, academic advising at a distance.
Credit-earning options Students may transfer credits from another institution or may earn credits through military training, business training.
Typical costs Tuition of $2600 per semester.

Registration Students may register by mail, fax, telephone, e-mail, World Wide Web, in person.
Contact Maria Adcock, Student Services, Grantham College of Engineering, PO Box 5700, Slidell, LA 70469-5700. *Telephone:* 504-649-4191. *Fax:* 504-649-4183. *E-mail:* madcock@grantham.edu.

DEGREES AND AWARDS

AS Computer Science (certain restrictions apply), Electronics Engineering Technology (certain restrictions apply)
BS Computer Science (certain restrictions apply), Electronics Engineering Technology (certain restrictions apply)

COURSE SUBJECT AREAS OFFERED OUTSIDE OF DEGREE PROGRAMS

Undergraduate: Algebra; business administration and management; calculus; chemistry; computer and information sciences; computer programming; database management; economics; electrical engineering; electronics; engineering; engineering-related technologies; English composition; information sciences and systems; mathematics; physics; psychology; technical writing

GRAYSON COUNTY COLLEGE

Denison, Texas
Center for Distance Learning
www.grayson.edu/distance/courselist/DLindex.html

Grayson County College, founded in 1964, is a state and locally supported, two-year college. It is accredited by the Southern Association of Colleges and Schools. It first offered distance learning courses in 1990. In 1999–2000, it offered 30 courses at a distance. In fall 1999, there were 400 students enrolled in distance learning courses.
Course delivery sites Courses are delivered to your home.
Media Courses are delivered via television, World Wide Web. Students and teachers may interact via mail, telephone, e-mail. The following equipment may be required: computer, Internet access.
Restrictions Programs are available worldwide. Enrollment is open to anyone.
Services Distance learners have access to library services at a distance.
Typical costs Tuition of $144 per course. Students pay $33 per hour for Internet courses. Costs may vary. Financial aid is available to distance learners.
Registration Students may register by mail, e-mail, World Wide Web, in person.
Contact Gary F. Paikowski, Dean of Information Technology, Grayson County College, 6101 Grayson Drive, Denison, TX 75020. *Telephone:* 903-463-8707. *Fax:* 903-465-4123. *E-mail:* paikowski@grayson.edu.

DEGREES AND AWARDS

Distance programs offered do not lead to a degree or other formal award.

COURSE SUBJECT AREAS OFFERED OUTSIDE OF DEGREE PROGRAMS

Undergraduate: American Government and Politics; business; computer and information sciences; database management; developmental and child psychology; economics; English language and literature; geology; health professions and related sciences; social sciences; sociology; Spanish language and literature

See full description on page 676.

GREAT BASIN COLLEGE

Elko, Nevada
www.gbcnv.edu

Great Basin College, founded in 1967, is a state-supported, primarily two-year college. It is accredited by the Northwest Association of Schools and Colleges. It first offered distance learning courses in 1968. In 1999–2000, it offered 50 courses at a distance. In fall 1999, there were 500 students enrolled in distance learning courses.

Course delivery sites Courses are delivered to your home, your workplace, high schools, 5 off-campus centers in Battle Mountain, Ely, Eureka, Wells, Winnemucca.

Media Courses are delivered via videotapes, videoconferencing, interactive television, audiotapes, computer software, World Wide Web, e-mail, print. Students and teachers may meet in person or interact via videoconferencing, mail, telephone, fax, e-mail, interactive television, World Wide Web. The following equipment may be required: television, videocassette player, computer, modem, Internet access, e-mail.

Restrictions Programs are primarily available in the college service area. Enrollment is open to anyone.

Services Distance learners have access to library services, the campus computer network, e-mail services, academic advising, tutoring, bookstore at a distance.

Credit-earning options Students may transfer credits from another institution or may earn credits through examinations.

Typical costs Tuition for 100 to 200 level courses per semester credit is $45 for undergraduate in-state and in-district students, and $61.50 for out-of-state. Tuition for level 300 to 400 courses is $56.50 for in-state and in-district and $105.75 for out-of-state students. Financial aid is available to distance learners.

Registration Students may register by mail, fax, telephone, World Wide Web, in person.

Contact Dr. Garry Heberer, Executive Director for Off Campus Programs, Great Basin College. *Telephone:* 775-753-2213. *Fax:* 775-753-2160. *E-mail:* garry@gbcnv.edu.

DEGREES AND AWARDS

Distance programs offered do not lead to a degree or other formal award.

COURSE SUBJECT AREAS OFFERED OUTSIDE OF DEGREE PROGRAMS

Undergraduate: Algebra; biological and life sciences; business; chemistry; computer and information sciences; economics; engineering-related technologies; English composition; environmental health; geography; home economics and family studies; political science; protective services; psychology; religious studies; social sciences; sociology; teacher education

GREEN RIVER COMMUNITY COLLEGE

Auburn, Washington
Distance Learning
www.grcc.ctc.edu

Green River Community College, founded in 1965, is a state-supported, two-year college. It is accredited by the Northwest Association of Schools and Colleges. In 1999–2000, it offered 33 courses at a distance. In fall 1999, there were 800 students enrolled in distance learning courses.

Course delivery sites Courses are delivered to your home, your workplace, military bases, high schools.

Media Courses are delivered via television, videotapes, videoconferencing, interactive television, World Wide Web, e-mail, print. Students and teachers may meet in person or interact via videoconferencing, audioconferencing, mail, telephone, fax, e-mail, interactive television. The following equipment may be required: television, videocassette player, computer, modem, Internet access, e-mail.

Restrictions Programs are available worldwide. Enrollment is restricted to individuals meeting certain criteria.

Services Distance learners have access to library services, career placement assistance, bookstore at a distance.

Credit-earning options Students may transfer credits from another institution or may earn credits through military training, business training.

Typical costs Tuition of $300 per course plus mandatory fees of $30 per course. $60-$140 per course range for noncredit courses. Costs may vary. Financial aid is available to distance learners.

Registration Students may register by mail, fax, telephone, e-mail, World Wide Web, in person.

Contact Paul Allen, Director of Distance Learning, Green River Community College, 12401 Southeast 320th Street, Auburn, WA 98092. *Telephone:* 253-288-3354. *E-mail:* pallen@grcc.ctc.edu.

DEGREES AND AWARDS

AA General Studies

COURSE SUBJECT AREAS OFFERED OUTSIDE OF DEGREE PROGRAMS

Undergraduate: Business; education; English composition; health and physical education/fitness; history; liberal arts, general studies, and humanities; mathematics; psychology; social sciences

GREENVILLE TECHNICAL COLLEGE

Greenville, South Carolina
Distance Learning
www.greenvilletech.com

Greenville Technical College, founded in 1962, is a state-supported, two-year college. It is accredited by the Southern Association of Colleges and Schools. It first offered distance learning courses in 1991. In 1999–2000, it offered 49 courses at a distance. In fall 1999, there were 839 students enrolled in distance learning courses.

Course delivery sites Courses are delivered to your home, your workplace, Anderson College (Anderson), Chesterfield-Marlboro Technical College (Cheraw), 3 off-campus centers in Bereu, Greer, Simpsonville.

Media Courses are delivered via television, videotapes, videoconferencing, audiotapes, World Wide Web. Students and teachers may meet in person or interact via mail, telephone, fax, e-mail. The following equipment may be required: television, videocassette player, computer, Internet access.

Restrictions Programs are available worldwide. Enrollment is open to anyone.

Services Distance learners have access to library services, academic advising, bookstore at a distance.

Credit-earning options Students may transfer credits from another institution or may earn credits through examinations, military training, business training.

Typical costs Tuition of $53 per credit hour plus mandatory fees of $15 per semester for local area residents. Tuition of $57 per credit hour plus mandatory fees of $15 per semester for in-state residents. Tuition of $134 per credit hour plus mandatory fees of $15 per semester for out-of-state residents. Financial aid is available to distance learners.

Registration Students may register by mail, fax, telephone, World Wide Web, in person.

Contact Stan Bagwell, Associate Dean for College on TV, Greenville Technical College, PO Box 5616, Greenville, SC 29606-5616. *Telephone:* 864-250-8164. *Fax:* 864-250-8085. *E-mail:* bagweljsb@gvltec.edu.

DEGREES AND AWARDS

AA Liberal Arts (some on-campus requirements)

COURSE SUBJECT AREAS OFFERED OUTSIDE OF DEGREE PROGRAMS

Undergraduate: Accounting; administrative and secretarial services; art history and criticism; astronomy and astrophysics; biology; business administration and management; business law; computer and information sciences; developmental and child psychology; economics; English composition; English language and literature; history; liberal arts, general studies, and humanities; mathematics; philosophy and religion; protective services; social psychology; sociology; Spanish language and literature

See full description on page 676.

GRIGGS UNIVERSITY

Silver Spring, Maryland

HSI/Griggs University

Griggs University, founded in 1990, is an independent, religious, four-year college. It is accredited by the Distance Education and Training Council. It first offered distance learning courses in 1909. In 1999–2000, it offered 103 courses at a distance. In fall 1999, there were 400 students enrolled in distance learning courses.

Course delivery sites Courses are delivered to your home.

Media Courses are delivered via videotapes, audiotapes, e-mail, print. Students and teachers may interact via mail, telephone, fax, e-mail.

Restrictions Programs are available worldwide. Enrollment is open to anyone.

Services Distance learners have access to library services, e-mail services, academic advising, bookstore at a distance.

Credit-earning options Students may transfer credits from another institution or may earn credits through examinations, portfolio assessment, military training, business training.

Typical costs Tuition of $170 per semester hour. There is a $60 mandatory enrollment fee.

Registration Students may register by mail, fax, in person.

Contact Dorothy M. Bascom, Director of Admissions/Registrar, Griggs University, PO Box 4437, Silver Spring, MD 20914-4437. *Telephone:* 301-680-6579. *Fax:* 301-680-6526. *E-mail:* dbascom@griggs.edu.

DEGREES AND AWARDS

AA Personal Ministries
BS Church Business Management, Religious Education
Religion, Theological Studies

COURSE SUBJECT AREAS OFFERED OUTSIDE OF DEGREE PROGRAMS

Undergraduate: Biology; business; communications; education; English language and literature; European languages and literatures; fine arts; foods and nutrition studies; geography; mathematics; political science; psychology; sociology; theological studies

HALIFAX COMMUNITY COLLEGE

Weldon, North Carolina

Distance Learning
www.hcc.cc.nc.us

Halifax Community College, founded in 1967, is a state and locally supported, two-year college. It is accredited by the Southern Association of Colleges and Schools. It first offered distance learning courses in 1999. In 1999–2000, it offered 9 courses at a distance. In fall 1999, there were 114 students enrolled in distance learning courses.

Course delivery sites Courses are delivered to your home, your workplace, military bases, high schools.

Media Courses are delivered via television, videotapes, videoconferencing, World Wide Web, print. Students and teachers may meet in person or interact via videoconferencing, mail, telephone, fax, e-mail, World Wide Web. The following equipment may be required: television, videocassette player, computer, modem, Internet access, e-mail.

Restrictions Programs are available worldwide. Enrollment is restricted to individuals meeting certain criteria.

Services Distance learners have access to library services, e-mail services, academic advising, bookstore at a distance.

Typical costs Tuition of $27 per semester hour for in-state residents. Tuition of $170 per semester hour for out-of-state residents. There is a $40 video course deposit for all students. *Noncredit courses:* $50 per course.

Registration Students may register by mail, fax, telephone, e-mail, World Wide Web, in person.

Contact Joan G. Gilstrap, Director of Distance Learning, Halifax Community College, PO Drawer 809, Weldon, NC 27890. *Telephone:* 252-536-7299. *Fax:* 252-536-4144. *E-mail:* gilstrapj@halifax.hcc.cc.nc.us.

DEGREES AND AWARDS

Distance programs offered do not lead to a degree or other formal award.

COURSE SUBJECT AREAS OFFERED OUTSIDE OF DEGREE PROGRAMS

Undergraduate: American literature; communications; design; economics; English language and literature; information sciences and systems; religious studies

See full description on page 676.

HAMILTON COLLEGE

Cedar Rapids, Iowa

Center for Distance Education
www.hamiltonia.edu/hconline

Hamilton College, founded in 1900, is a proprietary, two-year college. It is accredited by the Accrediting Council for Independent Colleges and Schools, North Central Association of Colleges and Schools. In 1999–2000, it offered 200 courses at a distance. In fall 1999, there were 1,200 students enrolled in distance learning courses.

Course delivery sites Courses are delivered to your home, your workplace, military bases, high schools.

Media Courses are delivered via computer software, CD-ROM, computer conferencing, World Wide Web. Students and teachers may interact via audioconferencing, mail, e-mail, World Wide Web. The following equipment may be required: computer, modem, Internet access, e-mail.

Restrictions Programs are available worldwide. Enrollment is open to anyone.

Services Distance learners have access to library services, academic advising, career placement assistance, bookstore at a distance.

Credit-earning options Students may transfer credits from another institution or may earn credits through examinations, portfolio assessment, military training, business training.

Typical costs Tuition of $3000 per term. Financial aid is available to distance learners.

Registration Students may register by mail, fax, telephone, e-mail, World Wide Web, in person.

Contact Cathy Bradley, Enrollment Advisor, Hamilton College, 1801 East Kimberly Road, Suite 2, Davenport, IA 52807. *Telephone:* 800-817-8272. *Fax:* 319-441-2441. *E-mail:* bradleca@questcollege.com.

DEGREES AND AWARDS

Undergraduate Certificate(s) Medical Transcription
AS Applied Management, Interdisciplinary Studies

HARCOURT LEARNING DIRECT

Scranton, Pennsylvania
Center for Degree Studies
www.harcourt-learning.com

Harcourt Learning Direct, founded in 1975, is a proprietary, two-year college. It is accredited by the Distance Education and Training Council. It first offered distance learning courses in 1975. In 1999–2000, it offered 11 courses at a distance.

Course delivery sites Courses are delivered to your home.

Media Courses are delivered via computer software, e-mail, print. Students and teachers may interact via mail, telephone, fax, e-mail. The following equipment may be required: computer.

Restrictions Programs are available worldwide. Enrollment is restricted to individuals meeting certain criteria.

Services Distance learners have access to e-mail services, academic advising, tutoring at a distance.

Credit-earning options Students may transfer credits from another institution or may earn credits through military training, business training.

Typical costs Undergraduate tuition ranges between $3156 and $4266 per program. Costs may vary.

Registration Students may register by mail, fax, telephone, World Wide Web.

Contact HLD Enrollment Center, Harcourt Learning Direct, 925 Oak Street, Scranton, PA 18515. *Telephone:* 800-233-4191.

DEGREES AND AWARDS

ASB Accounting, Applied Computer Science, Business Management, Business Management with Finance Option, Business Management with Marketing Option, Hospitality Management
AST Civil Engineering Technology (some on-campus requirements), Electrical Engineering Technology (some on-campus requirements), Electronics Technology (some on-campus requirements), Industrial Engineering Technology (some on-campus requirements), Mechanical Engineering Technology (some on-campus requirements)

COURSE SUBJECT AREAS OFFERED OUTSIDE OF DEGREE PROGRAMS

Undergraduate: Accounting; business administration and management; civil engineering; electrical engineering; electronics; finance; hospitality services management; industrial engineering; information sciences and systems; marketing; mechanical engineering

HARRISBURG AREA COMMUNITY COLLEGE

Harrisburg, Pennsylvania
Distance Education Office
www.hacc.edu

Harrisburg Area Community College, founded in 1964, is a state and locally supported, two-year college. It is accredited by the Middle States Association of Colleges and Schools. It first offered distance learning courses in 1987. In 1999–2000, it offered 55 courses at a distance. In fall 1999, there were 800 students enrolled in distance learning courses.

Course delivery sites Courses are delivered to your home, your workplace, military bases, high schools.

Media Courses are delivered via videotapes, videoconferencing, interactive television, audiotapes, computer software, CD-ROM, World Wide Web, e-mail, print. Students and teachers may meet in person or interact via videoconferencing, mail, telephone, fax, e-mail, World Wide Web. The following equipment may be required: television, videocassette player, computer, modem, Internet access, e-mail.

Restrictions Programs are available worldwide. Enrollment is open to anyone.

Services Distance learners have access to library services, the campus computer network, e-mail services at a distance.

Credit-earning options Students may transfer credits from another institution or may earn credits through examinations, portfolio assessment.

Typical costs Tuition of $64 per credit hour plus mandatory fees of $5 per credit hour for local area residents. Tuition of $127 per credit hour plus mandatory fees of $7 per credit hour for in-state residents. Tuition of $191 per credit hour plus mandatory fees of $5 per credit hour for out-of-state residents. *Noncredit courses:* $50 per course. Costs may vary. Financial aid is available to distance learners.

Registration Students may register by mail, fax, telephone, in person.

Contact Elaine Stoneroad, Distance Education Manager, Harrisburg Area Community College, One HACC Drive, Harrisburg, PA 17110. *Telephone:* 717-780-2541. *Fax:* 717-780-3250.

DEGREES AND AWARDS

Distance programs offered do not lead to a degree or other formal award.

COURSE SUBJECT AREAS OFFERED OUTSIDE OF DEGREE PROGRAMS

Undergraduate: Biological and life sciences; business; child care and development; computer and information sciences; conservation and natural resources; English language and literature; health and physical education/fitness; history; law and legal studies; liberal arts, general studies, and humanities; mathematics; philosophy and religion; physical sciences; psychology; social sciences

HARVARD UNIVERSITY

Cambridge, Massachusetts
Division of Continuing Education–Harvard Extension School
extension.dce.harvard.edu/

Harvard University, founded in 1636, is an independent, nonprofit university. It is accredited by the Association of Theological Schools in the United States and Canada, New England Association of Schools and Colleges. It first offered distance learning courses in 1996. In 1999–2000, it offered 7 courses at a distance. In fall 1999, there were 25 students enrolled in distance learning courses.

Course delivery sites Courses are delivered to your home, your workplace.

Media Courses are delivered via videoconferencing, World Wide Web. Students and teachers may interact via videoconferencing, telephone, e-mail. The following equipment may be required: computer, Internet access, e-mail.

Restrictions Programs are available worldwide. Enrollment is open to anyone.

Services Distance learners have access to e-mail services, tutoring at a distance.

Typical costs *Undergraduate:* Tuition of $1200 per course. *Graduate:* Tuition of $1250 per course. *Noncredit courses:* $950 per course. Costs may vary.

Registration Students may register by mail, fax, World Wide Web, in person.

Contact Leonard Evenchik, Director of Distance and Innovative Learning, Harvard University. *Telephone:* 617-496-6021. *Fax:* 617-495-9176. *E-mail:* evenchik@fas.harvard.edu.

DEGREES AND AWARDS

MLA Information Technology (service area differs from that of the overall institution)

COURSE SUBJECT AREAS OFFERED OUTSIDE OF DEGREE PROGRAMS

Graduate: Computer programming; information sciences and systems
Noncredit: Computer programming; information sciences and systems

HAWKEYE COMMUNITY COLLEGE

Waterloo, Iowa

Department of Academic Telecommunications
www.hawkeye.cc.ia.us

Hawkeye Community College, founded in 1967, is a state and locally supported, two-year college. It is accredited by the North Central Association of Colleges and Schools. It first offered distance learning courses in 1993. In 1999–2000, it offered 55 courses at a distance. In fall 1999, there were 345 students enrolled in distance learning courses.

Course delivery sites Courses are delivered to your home, your workplace, military bases, high schools, 28 off-campus centers in Allison, Black Hawk County, Bremer County, Buchanan County, Butler County, Cedar Falls, Grundy Center, Grundy County, Independence, Nashua, Waterloo, Waverly.

Media Courses are delivered via television, videotapes, videoconferencing, interactive television, World Wide Web. Students and teachers may interact via videoconferencing, telephone, fax, e-mail, interactive television, World Wide Web. The following equipment may be required: television, videocassette player, computer, modem, Internet access, e-mail.

Restrictions Programs are available worldwide. Enrollment is open to anyone.

Services Distance learners have access to library services, the campus computer network, academic advising, career placement assistance, bookstore at a distance.

Credit-earning options Students may transfer credits from another institution or may earn credits through examinations, portfolio assessment, military training.

Typical costs Tuition of $68 per credit hour plus mandatory fees of $9 per credit hour for in-state residents. Tuition of $136 per credit hour plus mandatory fees of $9 per credit hour for out-of-state residents. *Noncredit courses:* $85 per course. Financial aid is available to distance learners.

Registration Students may register by mail, fax, telephone, e-mail, in person.

Contact Roger Rezabek, Director of Distance Learning, Hawkeye Community College, 1501 East Orange Road, Waterloo, IA 50704. *Telephone:* 319-296-4017. *Fax:* 319-296-4018. *E-mail:* rrezabek@hawkeye.cc.ia.us.

DEGREES AND AWARDS

AA Arts and Sciences, Business Management, Liberal Arts
AS Arts and Sciences

COURSE SUBJECT AREAS OFFERED OUTSIDE OF DEGREE PROGRAMS

Undergraduate: Agriculture; biological and life sciences; business administration and management; education; English composition; liberal arts, general studies, and humanities; mathematics; psychology; social sciences

HEBREW COLLEGE

Brookline, Massachusetts
www.hebrewcollege.edu/online/

Hebrew College, founded in 1921, is an independent, religious, comprehensive institution. It is accredited by the New England Association of Schools and Colleges. In 1999–2000, it offered 8 courses at a distance. In fall 1999, there were 50 students enrolled in distance learning courses.

Course delivery sites Courses are delivered to your home, your workplace.

Media Courses are delivered via computer conferencing, World Wide Web, e-mail, print. Students and teachers may meet in person or interact via mail, telephone, e-mail, World Wide Web. The following equipment may be required: computer, modem, Internet access, e-mail.

Restrictions Programs are available worldwide. Enrollment is restricted to individuals meeting certain criteria.

Services Distance learners have access to library services, the campus computer network, e-mail services, academic advising, career placement assistance at a distance.

Credit-earning options Students may transfer credits from another institution.

Typical costs *Undergraduate:* Tuition of $750 per course. *Graduate:* Tuition of $1000 per course. *Noncredit courses:* $190 per course. Financial aid is available to distance learners.

Registration Students may register by mail, fax, telephone, e-mail, World Wide Web, in person.

Contact Nathan Ehrlich, Director, Center for Information Technology, Hebrew College, 43 Hawes Street, Brookline, MA 02446. *Telephone:* 617-278-4929. *Fax:* 617-264-9264. *E-mail:* nathan@hebrewcollege.edu.

DEGREES AND AWARDS

Undergraduate Certificate(s) Jewish Studies

COURSE SUBJECT AREAS OFFERED OUTSIDE OF DEGREE PROGRAMS

Undergraduate: Bible studies; creative writing; education; history; Jewish studies; philosophy and religion; theological studies
Graduate: Bible studies; creative writing; education; history; Jewish studies; philosophy and religion; theological studies
Noncredit: Bible studies; creative writing; education; history; Jewish studies; philosophy and religion; theological studies

HENDERSON COMMUNITY COLLEGE

Henderson, Kentucky
www.hencc.uky.edu

Henderson Community College, founded in 1963, is a state-supported, two-year college. It is accredited by the Southern Association of Colleges and Schools. It first offered distance learning courses in 1985.

Contact Henderson Community College, 2660 South Green Street, Henderson, KY 42420-4623. *Telephone:* 270-827-1867.

See full description on page 556.

HENDERSON STATE UNIVERSITY

Arkadelphia, Arkansas
www.hsu.edu

Henderson State University, founded in 1890, is a state-supported, comprehensive institution. It is accredited by the North Central Association of Colleges and Schools. In 1999–2000, it offered 4 courses at a distance. In fall 1999, there were 40 students enrolled in distance learning courses.

Course delivery sites Courses are delivered to 3 off-campus centers in Gillam, Hope, Monticello.

Media Courses are delivered via interactive television. Students and teachers may meet in person or interact via mail, telephone, fax, e-mail, interactive television, World Wide Web.

Restrictions Programs are available to local area students. Enrollment is restricted to individuals meeting certain criteria.

Services Distance learners have access to library services, the campus computer network, e-mail services, academic advising, career placement assistance, bookstore at a distance.

Credit-earning options Students may transfer credits from another institution or may earn credits through examinations, portfolio assessment.

Typical costs *Undergraduate:* Tuition of $105 per hour plus mandatory fees of $5 per course. *Graduate:* Tuition of $136 per hour plus mandatory fees of $5 per course. Financial aid is available to distance learners.

Registration Students may register by mail, fax, telephone, e-mail, World Wide Web, in person.

Contact Dr. Ana Caldwell, Director, Off Campus Programs, Henderson State University, PO Box 7602, Arkadelphia, AR 71923. *Telephone:* 870-230-5369. *Fax:* 870-230-5459. *E-mail:* caldwea@hsu.edu.

DEGREES AND AWARDS

MSE Education (certain restrictions apply; some on-campus requirements)

COURSE SUBJECT AREAS OFFERED OUTSIDE OF DEGREE PROGRAMS

Graduate: Education administration
Noncredit: Education administration

HERIOT-WATT UNIVERSITY

Edinburgh, United Kingdom
Edinburgh Business School
www.ebs.hw.ac.uk

Heriot-Watt University, founded in 1821, is a public university. It first offered distance learning courses in 1990. In 1999–2000, it offered 22 courses at a distance. In fall 1999, there were 8,000 students enrolled in distance learning courses.

Course delivery sites Courses are delivered to your home.

Media Courses are delivered via e-mail, print. Students and teachers may interact via mail, fax, e-mail.

Restrictions Programs are available worldwide. Enrollment is open to anyone.

Services Distance learners have access to library services, the campus computer network at a distance.

Credit-earning options Students may transfer credits from another institution.

Typical costs Tuition of $995 per course. There is a $110 mandatory exam fee.

Registration Students may register by mail, fax, telephone, in person.

Contact Financial Times Knowledge, Inc., Heriot-Watt University, Two World Trade Center, Suite 1700, New York, NY 10048. *E-mail:* info@hwmba.net.

DEGREES AND AWARDS

MBA Business Administration

COURSE SUBJECT AREAS OFFERED OUTSIDE OF DEGREE PROGRAMS

Graduate: Accounting; business; economics; finance; human resources management; international business; management information systems; marketing; mathematics; organizational behavior studies

See full description on page 538.

HERKIMER COUNTY COMMUNITY COLLEGE

Herkimer, New York
Internet Academy
www.hccc.ntcnet.com/ia

Herkimer County Community College, founded in 1966, is a state and locally supported, two-year college. It is accredited by the Middle States Association of Colleges and Schools. In 1999–2000, it offered 60 courses at a distance. In fall 1999, there were 350 students enrolled in distance learning courses.

Course delivery sites Courses are delivered to your home, your workplace, military bases, high schools, 1 off-campus center in Old Forge.

Media Courses are delivered via videoconferencing, World Wide Web, e-mail. Students and teachers may meet in person or interact via videoconferencing, mail, telephone, fax, e-mail, World Wide Web. The following equipment may be required: computer, modem, Internet access, e-mail.

Restrictions Programs are available to in-state students only. Enrollment is open to anyone.

Services Distance learners have access to library services, the campus computer network, e-mail services, academic advising, tutoring, career placement assistance, bookstore at a distance.

Credit-earning options Students may transfer credits from another institution or may earn credits through examinations, military training, business training.

Typical costs Tuition of $80 per credit for local area residents. Tuition of $80 per credit for in-state residents. Tuition of $145 per credit for out-of-state residents. Financial aid is available to distance learners.

Registration Students may register by mail, fax, telephone, e-mail, World Wide Web, in person.

Contact Prof. William Pelz, Coordinator, Internet Academy, Herkimer County Community College, 100 Reservoir Road, Herkimer, NY 13350. *Telephone:* 315-866-0300 Ext. 211. *Fax:* 315-866-7253. *E-mail:* pelzwm@hccc.suny.edu.

DEGREES AND AWARDS

AA General Studies
AAS Accounting, Business Administration, Criminal Justice, Travel and Tourism
AS Business Administration, Criminal Justice, Economic Crime

COURSE SUBJECT AREAS OFFERED OUTSIDE OF DEGREE PROGRAMS

Undergraduate: Accounting; business administration and management; criminal justice; hospitality services management; liberal arts, general studies, and humanities

HIBBING COMMUNITY COLLEGE

Hibbing, Minnesota
www.hcc.mnscu.edu

Hibbing Community College, founded in 1916, is a state-supported, two-year college. It is accredited by the North Central Association of Colleges and Schools.

Course delivery sites Courses are delivered to Itasca Community College (Grand Rapids), Rainy River Community College (International Falls).

Media Courses are delivered via television, videotapes, videoconferencing, interactive television, audiotapes, computer software, World Wide Web, e-mail, print. Students and teachers may interact via videoconferencing, audioconferencing, mail, telephone, fax, e-mail, interactive television.

Restrictions Programs are available worldwide. Enrollment is open to anyone.

Services Distance learners have access to library services, e-mail services, academic advising, career placement assistance at a distance.

Credit-earning options Students may transfer credits from another institution or may earn credits through examinations, military training.

Typical costs Tuition of $67.55 per credit plus mandatory fees of $10.15 per credit for in-state residents. Tuition of $131.20 per credit plus mandatory fees of $10.15 per credit for out-of-state residents. Costs may vary. Financial aid is available to distance learners.

Registration Students may register by mail, fax, telephone, in person.

Contact James Antilla, Director of Instructional Technology, Hibbing Community College, 1515 East 25th Street, Hibbing, MN 55746-3300. *Telephone:* 218-262-7250. *Fax:* 218-262-7222. *E-mail:* j.antilla@hcc.mnscu.edu.

DEGREES AND AWARDS

Distance programs offered do not lead to a degree or other formal award.

COURSE SUBJECT AREAS OFFERED OUTSIDE OF DEGREE PROGRAMS

Undergraduate: Anthropology; astronomy and astrophysics; business; chemistry; engineering; English language and literature; geology; liberal arts, general studies, and humanities; philosophy and religion; physics; political science; psychology; social sciences; sociology; visual and performing arts

HIGHLAND COMMUNITY COLLEGE

Freeport, Illinois
highland.userworld.com/telecour

Highland Community College, founded in 1962, is a state and locally supported, two-year college. It is accredited by the North Central Association of Colleges and Schools. It first offered distance learning courses in 1983. In 1999–2000, it offered 13 courses at a distance. In fall 1999, there were 148 students enrolled in distance learning courses.

Course delivery sites Courses are delivered to your home, Black Hawk College (Moline), Western Illinois University (Macomb).

Media Courses are delivered via television, videotapes, videoconferencing, interactive television, audiotapes, print. Students and teachers may meet in person or interact via videoconferencing, mail, telephone, fax, e-mail, interactive television, World Wide Web. The following equipment may be required: television, videocassette player, computer, modem, Internet access, e-mail.

Restrictions Programs are available to in-state students only. Enrollment is open to anyone.

Services Distance learners have access to library services, the campus computer network, e-mail services, academic advising, tutoring, career placement assistance, bookstore at a distance.

Credit-earning options Students may transfer credits from another institution or may earn credits through examinations.

Typical costs Tuition of $43 per credit plus mandatory fees of $25 per course. Financial aid is available to distance learners.

Registration Students may register by mail, telephone, in person.

Contact Eric Welch, Dean of Learning Resources, Highland Community College, 2998 West Pearl City Road, Freeport, IL 61032-9341. *Telephone:* 815-599-3457. *Fax:* 815-235-1366. *E-mail:* ewelch@admin.highland.cc.il.us.

DEGREES AND AWARDS

Distance programs offered do not lead to a degree or other formal award.

COURSE SUBJECT AREAS OFFERED OUTSIDE OF DEGREE PROGRAMS

Undergraduate: Accounting; African-American studies; algebra; American (U.S.) history; biology; criminal justice; nursing; photography; psychology; teacher education

HILL COLLEGE OF THE HILL JUNIOR COLLEGE DISTRICT

Hillsboro, Texas
www.hill-college.cc.tx.us

Hill College of the Hill Junior College District, founded in 1923, is a district-supported, two-year college. It is accredited by the Southern Association of Colleges and Schools. In 1999–2000, it offered 20 courses at a distance. In fall 1999, there were 58 students enrolled in distance learning courses.

Course delivery sites Courses are delivered to your home, your workplace, high schools.

Media Courses are delivered via television, videotapes, videoconferencing, interactive television, audiotapes, computer software, CD-ROM, World Wide Web, e-mail, print. Students and teachers may meet in person or interact via videoconferencing, audioconferencing, mail, telephone, fax, e-mail, interactive television, World Wide Web. The following equipment may be required: computer, modem, Internet access, e-mail.

Restrictions Programs are available to local area students. Enrollment is restricted to individuals meeting certain criteria.

Services Distance learners have access to library services, the campus computer network, e-mail services, academic advising, tutoring, career placement assistance, bookstore at a distance.

Credit-earning options Students may transfer credits from another institution or may earn credits through examinations, military training.

Typical costs Financial aid is available to distance learners.

Registration Students may register by in person.

Contact Sandy Marek, Director of Admissions, Hill College of the Hill Junior College District, PO Box 619, Hillsboro, TX 76645. *Telephone:* 254-582-2555. *Fax:* 254-582-7591. *E-mail:* smarek@hill-college.cc.tx.us.

DEGREES AND AWARDS

Undergraduate Certificate(s) Management (service area differs from that of the overall institution; some on-campus requirements)

COURSE SUBJECT AREAS OFFERED OUTSIDE OF DEGREE PROGRAMS

Undergraduate: Algebra; business administration and management; calculus; English composition; marketing

HILLSBOROUGH COMMUNITY COLLEGE

Tampa, Florida

Distance Learning Office
www.hcc.cc.fl.us/DistanceLearning

Hillsborough Community College, founded in 1968, is a state-supported, two-year college. It is accredited by the Southern Association of Colleges and Schools. It first offered distance learning courses in 1971. In 1999–2000, it offered 40 courses at a distance. In fall 1999, there were 800 students enrolled in distance learning courses.

Course delivery sites Courses are delivered to your home, your workplace, military bases.

Media Courses are delivered via television, videotapes, videoconferencing, interactive television, computer software, World Wide Web, e-mail, print. Students and teachers may interact via videoconferencing, audioconferencing, mail, telephone, fax, e-mail, interactive television. The following equipment may be required: television, videocassette player, computer, modem, Internet access, e-mail.

Restrictions Programs are available to local area students. Enrollment is open to anyone.

Services Distance learners have access to library services, academic advising, tutoring, career placement assistance at a distance.

Credit-earning options Students may transfer credits from another institution or may earn credits through examinations.

Typical costs Tuition of $48 per credit for in-state residents. Tuition of $177.61 per credit for out-of-state residents. Application fee is $20. Financial aid is available to distance learners.

Registration Students may register by telephone, in person.

Contact Michael Comins, Director, Hillsborough Community College, Distance Learning, PO Box 31127, BACA 207-E, Tampa, FL 33631-3127. *Telephone:* 813-253-7017. *Fax:* 813-253-7196. *E-mail:* cominsm@mail.firn.edu.

DEGREES AND AWARDS

Distance programs offered do not lead to a degree or other formal award.

COURSE SUBJECT AREAS OFFERED OUTSIDE OF DEGREE PROGRAMS

Undergraduate: Astronomy and astrophysics; biology; business; business administration and management; chemistry; computer and information sciences; developmental and child psychology; economics; English composition; finance; geology; health and physical education/fitness; history; liberal arts, general studies, and humanities; marketing; mathematics; political science; psychology; sociology

HILLSDALE FREE WILL BAPTIST COLLEGE

Moore, Oklahoma

Department of External Studies

Hillsdale Free Will Baptist College, founded in 1959, is an independent, religious, four-year college. It is accredited by the Transnational Association of Christian Colleges and Schools. It first offered distance learning courses in 1975. In 1999–2000, it offered 27 courses at a distance. In fall 1999, there were 27 students enrolled in distance learning courses.

Course delivery sites Courses are delivered to your home, your workplace.

Media Courses are delivered via audiotapes, computer software, computer conferencing, e-mail, print. Students and teachers may meet in person or interact via mail, telephone, fax.

Restrictions Programs are available nationwide. Enrollment is open to anyone.

Services Distance learners have access to e-mail services, academic advising, tutoring, bookstore at a distance.

Credit-earning options Students may transfer credits from another institution or may earn credits through examinations, military training.

Typical costs Tuition of $65 per credit hour. Students pay a $10 matriculation fee. *Noncredit courses:* $10.95 per course. Financial aid is available to distance learners.

Registration Students may register by mail, fax, in person.

Contact Edwin L. Wade, Director of External Studies, Hillsdale Free Will Baptist College, PO Box 7208, Moore, OK 73163-1208. *Telephone:* 405-912-9000. *Fax:* 405-912-9050. *E-mail:* xstudies@hc.edu.

DEGREES AND AWARDS

Undergraduate Certificate(s) Bible

COURSE SUBJECT AREAS OFFERED OUTSIDE OF DEGREE PROGRAMS

Undergraduate: Bible studies; education; English composition; Greek language and literature; religious studies
Noncredit: Bible studies

HINDS COMMUNITY COLLEGE

Raymond, Mississippi

Office of Distance Learning

Hinds Community College, founded in 1917, is a state and locally supported, two-year college. It is accredited by the Southern Association of Colleges and Schools. In 1999–2000, it offered 14 courses at a distance. In fall 1999, there were 230 students enrolled in distance learning courses.

Course delivery sites Courses are delivered to your home, military bases, East Central Community College (Decatur), Mississippi Gulf Coast Community College (Perkinston).

Media Courses are delivered via television, videotapes, videoconferencing, computer software, World Wide Web, e-mail, print. Students and teachers may meet in person or interact via videoconferencing, mail, telephone, fax, e-mail, interactive television, World Wide Web. The following equipment may be required: television, videocassette player, computer, modem, Internet access, e-mail.

Restrictions Courses are available on the local and statewide level. Enrollment is open to anyone.

Services Distance learners have access to library services, academic advising, tutoring, career placement assistance, bookstore at a distance.

Credit-earning options Students may transfer credits from another institution or may earn credits through examinations.

Typical costs Tuition of $55 per semester hour. Registration fee is $40. Financial aid is available to distance learners.

Registration Students may register by in person.

Contact Curtis Kynerd, Dean of Distance Learning, Hinds Community College, DMB 1166, Raymond, MS 39154. *Telephone:* 601-857-3624. *Fax:* 601-857-3607. *E-mail:* crkynerd@hinds.cc.ms.us.

DEGREES AND AWARDS

AA Fire Science Technology

COURSE SUBJECT AREAS OFFERED OUTSIDE OF DEGREE PROGRAMS

Undergraduate: American (U.S.) history; American Government and Politics; chemistry; computer and information sciences; English composition; European history; psychology; sociology

---

HOBE SOUND BIBLE COLLEGE

Hobe Sound, Florida

Department of External Studies

Hobe Sound Bible College, founded in 1960, is an independent, religious, four-year college. It is accredited by the Accrediting Association of Bible Colleges. In 1999–2000, it offered 22 courses at a distance. In fall 1999, there were 26 students enrolled in distance learning courses.

Course delivery sites Courses are delivered to your home, high schools, God's Bible School and College (Cincinnati, OH).

Media Courses are delivered via videotapes, audiotapes, print. Students and teachers may meet in person or interact via mail, telephone, fax. The following equipment may be required: videocassette player, Internet access.

Restrictions Programs are available worldwide. Enrollment is open to anyone.

Services Distance learners have access to academic advising, tutoring, bookstore at a distance.

Credit-earning options Students may transfer credits from another institution or may earn credits through portfolio assessment.

Typical costs Undergraduate tuition is $255 for three credit hours. Financial aid is available to distance learners.

Registration Students may register by mail, fax, telephone, e-mail, in person.

Contact John W. Basham, Dean of External Studies, Hobe Sound Bible College, PO Box 1065, Hobe Sound, FL 33475. *Telephone:* 561-546-5534 Ext. 1014. *Fax:* 561-545-1422.

DEGREES AND AWARDS

AA Life Grow (certain restrictions apply)

COURSE SUBJECT AREAS OFFERED OUTSIDE OF DEGREE PROGRAMS

Undergraduate: Education; English language and literature; mathematics; philosophy and religion; psychology; social sciences; theological studies

---

HOLMES COMMUNITY COLLEGE

Goodman, Mississippi

Distance Learning
www.holmes.cc.ms.us

Holmes Community College, founded in 1928, is a state and locally supported, two-year college. It is accredited by the Southern Association of Colleges and Schools. In 1999–2000, it offered 12 courses at a distance. In fall 1999, there were 80 students enrolled in distance learning courses.

Course delivery sites Courses are delivered to your home, 2 off-campus centers in Grenada, Ridgeland.

Media Courses are delivered via television, videoconferencing, interactive television, computer software, World Wide Web, e-mail. Students and teachers may meet in person or interact via videoconferencing, e-mail, interactive television, World Wide Web. The following equipment may be required: computer, modem, Internet access, e-mail.

Restrictions Programs are available to in-state students only. Enrollment is open to anyone.

Services Distance learners have access to library services, the campus computer network, career placement assistance at a distance.

Typical costs Tuition of $50 per credit hour. Financial aid is available to distance learners.

Registration Students may register by in person.

Contact Dr. Kevin R. Martin, Coordinator of Instructional Technology, Holmes Community College, PO Box 369, Goodman, MS 39079. *Telephone:* 662-472-9033. *Fax:* 662-472-9155. *E-mail:* kmartin@holmes. cc.ms.us.

DEGREES AND AWARDS

Distance programs offered do not lead to a degree or other formal award.

COURSE SUBJECT AREAS OFFERED OUTSIDE OF DEGREE PROGRAMS

Undergraduate: Computer and information sciences; history; mathematics; physics; psychology; real estate; sociology; Spanish language and literature

---

HOLY NAMES COLLEGE

Oakland, California

Nursing Department

Holy Names College, founded in 1868, is an independent, religious, comprehensive institution. It is accredited by the Western Association of Schools and Colleges, Inc. It first offered distance learning courses in 1995. In 1999–2000, it offered 6 courses at a distance. In fall 1999, there were 165 students enrolled in distance learning courses.

Course delivery sites Courses are delivered to your workplace, 12 off-campus centers in Bellflower, Fontana, Fresno, Los Angeles, Martinez, Oakland, Panorama City, Sacramento, San Diego, San Francisco, Santa Teresa, Walnut Creek.

Media Courses are delivered via videoconferencing, interactive television, computer software, CD-ROM, e-mail, print. Students and teachers may meet in person or interact via videoconferencing, mail, telephone, fax, e-mail. The following equipment may be required: computer, Internet access.

Restrictions Programs are available to in-state students only. Enrollment is open to anyone.

Services Distance learners have access to library services, e-mail services, academic advising, tutoring, career placement assistance, bookstore at a distance.

Credit-earning options Students may transfer credits from another institution or may earn credits through examinations, portfolio assessment, military training, business training.

Typical costs Tuition of $250 per unit. Financial aid is available to distance learners.

Registration Students may register by mail, fax, telephone, in person.

Contact Dr. Charles Beauchamp, Director, Nursing Department, Holy Names College, 3500 Mountain Boulevard, Oakland, CA 94619. *Telephone:* 510-436-1127. *Fax:* 510-436-1376.

DEGREES AND AWARDS

BSN Nursing Studies

HONOLULU COMMUNITY COLLEGE

Honolulu, Hawaii

Outreach Office

www.hcc.hawaii.edu/distlearn

Honolulu Community College, founded in 1920, is a state-supported, two-year college. It is accredited by the Western Association of Schools and Colleges, Inc. It first offered distance learning courses in 1991. In 1999–2000, it offered 13 courses at a distance. In fall 1999, there were 229 students enrolled in distance learning courses.

Course delivery sites Courses are delivered to your home, your workplace, military bases, high schools, University of Hawaii System (Honolulu).

Media Courses are delivered via television, World Wide Web, print. Students and teachers may meet in person or interact via mail, telephone, fax, e-mail, World Wide Web. The following equipment may be required: television, computer, modem, Internet access, e-mail.

Restrictions Cable courses are available statewide; online courses are available worldwide. Enrollment is open to anyone.

Services Distance learners have access to library services, the campus computer network, e-mail services, academic advising, career placement assistance, bookstore at a distance.

Credit-earning options Students may transfer credits from another institution or may earn credits through examinations.

Typical costs Tuition of $43 per credit plus mandatory fees of $20 per course for in-state residents. Costs may vary. Financial aid is available to distance learners.

Registration Students may register by mail, fax, World Wide Web, in person.

Contact Sherrie Rupert, Coordinator, Distance Learning, Honolulu Community College, 874 Dillingham Boulevard, Honolulu, HI 96817. *Telephone:* 808-845-9151. *Fax:* 808-845-3767. *E-mail:* srupert@hcc.hawaii.edu.

DEGREES AND AWARDS

AA Arts (some on-campus requirements)

COURSE SUBJECT AREAS OFFERED OUTSIDE OF DEGREE PROGRAMS

Undergraduate: Anthropology; astronomy and astrophysics; computer and information sciences; engineering; English as a second language (ESL); English composition; English language and literature; fire science; foods and nutrition studies; geology; history; physical sciences; political science; psychology

HOPE INTERNATIONAL UNIVERSITY

Fullerton, California

Distance Learning Department

Hope International University, founded in 1928, is an independent, religious, comprehensive institution affiliated with the Christian Churches and Churches of Christ. It is accredited by the Western Association of Schools and Colleges, Inc. In 1999–2000, it offered 50 courses at a distance. In fall 1999, there were 110 students enrolled in distance learning courses.

Course delivery sites Courses are delivered to your home.

Media Courses are delivered via videotapes, World Wide Web, e-mail, print. Students and teachers may meet in person or interact via telephone, fax, e-mail. The following equipment may be required: television, videocassette player, computer, modem, Internet access, e-mail.

Restrictions Programs are available worldwide. Enrollment is open to anyone.

Services Distance learners have access to library services, academic advising, career placement assistance, bookstore at a distance.

Credit-earning options Students may transfer credits from another institution or may earn credits through portfolio assessment.

Typical costs *Undergraduate:* Tuition of $900 per course. *Graduate:* Tuition of $900 per course. Financial aid is available to distance learners.

Registration Students may register by mail, fax, telephone, e-mail, World Wide Web, in person.

Contact Distance Learning Department, Hope International University, 2500 East Nutwood Avenue, Fullerton, CA 92831. *Telephone:* 714-879-3901 Ext. 1228. *E-mail:* palexander@hiu.edu.

eCollege.com *www.ecollege.com/scholarships*

DEGREES AND AWARDS

Distance programs offered do not lead to a degree or other formal award.

COURSE SUBJECT AREAS OFFERED OUTSIDE OF DEGREE PROGRAMS

Undergraduate: Bible studies; family and marriage counseling; history
Graduate: Bible studies; family and marriage counseling

HOPKINSVILLE COMMUNITY COLLEGE

Hopkinsville, Kentucky

Hopkinsville Community College, founded in 1965, is a state-supported, two-year college. It is accredited by the Southern Association of Colleges and Schools. In 1999–2000, it offered 5 courses at a distance. In fall 1999, there were 65 students enrolled in distance learning courses.

Course delivery sites Courses are delivered to your home, your workplace, military bases, 2 off-campus centers in Cadiz, Elkton, Ft. Campbell, Princeton.

Media Courses are delivered via television, interactive television, World Wide Web. Students and teachers may meet in person or interact via mail, telephone, e-mail, World Wide Web. The following equipment may be required: television, videocassette player, computer, modem, Internet access, e-mail.

Restrictions Courses are available primarily on the local level, with some statewide participation. Enrollment is open to anyone.

Services Distance learners have access to library services, e-mail services at a distance.

Credit-earning options Students may transfer credits from another institution or may earn credits through examinations, military training.
Typical costs Tuition of $46 per credit hour plus mandatory fees of $6 per credit hour for in-state residents. Tuition of $138 per credit hour plus mandatory fees of $6 per credit hour for out-of-state residents.
Registration Students may register by e-mail, World Wide Web, in person.
Contact Academic Office, Hopkinsville Community College, Hopkinsville, KY 42240. *Telephone:* 270-886-3921 Ext. 6104. *Fax:* 270-885-5755. *E-mail:* debbie.owens@kctcs.net.

DEGREES AND AWARDS

Distance programs offered do not lead to a degree or other formal award.

COURSE SUBJECT AREAS OFFERED OUTSIDE OF DEGREE PROGRAMS

Undergraduate: American (U.S.) history; astronomy and astrophysics; chemistry; foods and nutrition studies; psychology; sociology
See full description on page 556.

HORRY-GEORGETOWN TECHNICAL COLLEGE

Conway, South Carolina
Department of Distance Learning
www.hor.tec.sc.us/distance

Horry-Georgetown Technical College, founded in 1965, is a state and locally supported, two-year college. It is accredited by the Southern Association of Colleges and Schools. It first offered distance learning courses in 1995. In 1999–2000, it offered 35 courses at a distance. In fall 1999, there were 400 students enrolled in distance learning courses.
Course delivery sites Courses are delivered to your home, your workplace, high schools, Chesterfield-Marlboro Technical College (Cheraw), York Technical College (Rock Hill).
Media Courses are delivered via videotapes, videoconferencing, World Wide Web. Students and teachers may meet in person or interact via videoconferencing, mail, telephone, fax, e-mail, World Wide Web. The following equipment may be required: television, videocassette player, computer, Internet access, e-mail.
Restrictions Programs are available to in-state students only. Enrollment is restricted to individuals meeting certain criteria.
Services Distance learners have access to library services, bookstore at a distance.
Credit-earning options Students may transfer credits from another institution or may earn credits through examinations.
Typical costs Tuition of $600 per semester for local area residents. Tuition of $660 per semester for in-state residents. Tuition of $1431 per semester for out-of-state residents. There is a $15 application fee. Financial aid is available to distance learners.
Registration Students may register by in person.
Contact Ahmed Abdelsalam, Distance Learning Technician, Horry-Georgetown Technical College, PO Box 261966, Conway, SC 29528-6066. *Telephone:* 843-349-5311. *Fax:* 843-349-7554. *E-mail:* abdelsalama@hor.tec.sc.us.

DEGREES AND AWARDS

Distance programs offered do not lead to a degree or other formal award.

COURSE SUBJECT AREAS OFFERED OUTSIDE OF DEGREE PROGRAMS

Undergraduate: Algebra; astronomy and astrophysics; business; business administration and management; calculus; English composition; mathematics; political science; psychology
See full description on page 676.

HOUSATONIC COMMUNITY COLLEGE

Bridgeport, Connecticut
www.hcc.commnet.edu

Housatonic Community College, founded in 1965, is a state-supported, two-year college. It is accredited by the New England Association of Schools and Colleges. In 1999–2000, it offered 6 courses at a distance. In fall 1999, there were 30 students enrolled in distance learning courses.
Course delivery sites Courses are delivered to your home, your workplace, military bases, high schools, other colleges.
Media Courses are delivered via audiotapes, computer software, CD-ROM, World Wide Web, e-mail, print. Students and teachers may meet in person or interact via mail, telephone, fax, e-mail, World Wide Web. The following equipment may be required: computer, modem, Internet access, e-mail.
Restrictions Programs are available worldwide. Enrollment is open to anyone.
Services Distance learners have access to library services, academic advising, career placement assistance, bookstore at a distance.
Credit-earning options Students may transfer credits from another institution or may earn credits through examinations, portfolio assessment.
Typical costs Tuition of $67 per credit. Mandatory fees are $42 for 1-4 credits.
Registration Students may register by mail, fax, in person.
Contact Ruth K. McDonald, Dean of Learning, Housatonic Community College, 900 Lafayette Boulevard, Bridgeport, CT 06604. *Telephone:* 203-332-5061. *Fax:* 203-332-5247. *E-mail:* ho_macdonald@commnet.edu.

DEGREES AND AWARDS

Distance programs offered do not lead to a degree or other formal award.

COURSE SUBJECT AREAS OFFERED OUTSIDE OF DEGREE PROGRAMS

Undergraduate: Finance; Latin language and literature; psychology

HOUSTON COMMUNITY COLLEGE SYSTEM

Houston, Texas
Distance Education Department
www.distance.hccs.cc.tx.us

Houston Community College System, founded in 1971, is a state and locally supported, two-year college. It is accredited by the Southern Association of Colleges and Schools. It first offered distance learning courses in 1985. In 1999–2000, it offered 59 courses at a distance. In fall 1999, there were 1,300 students enrolled in distance learning courses.
Course delivery sites Courses are delivered to your home, your workplace, military bases, high schools.
Media Courses are delivered via television, videotapes, audiotapes, computer software, CD-ROM, computer conferencing, World Wide Web,

e-mail, print. Students and teachers may meet in person or interact via mail, telephone, fax, e-mail, World Wide Web. The following equipment may be required: television, videocassette player, computer, modem, Internet access, e-mail.

Restrictions Programs are available worldwide. Enrollment is open to anyone.

Services Distance learners have access to academic advising, bookstore at a distance.

Credit-earning options Students may transfer credits from another institution or may earn credits through examinations.

Typical costs Tuition of $107 per course plus mandatory fees of $24 per course for local area residents. Tuition of $179 per course plus mandatory fees of $24 per course for in-state residents. Tuition of $366 per course plus mandatory fees of $24 per course for out-of-state residents. Costs may vary. Financial aid is available to distance learners.

Registration Students may register by mail, fax, telephone, in person.

Contact Pat Barden, Distance Education Associate, Houston Community College System, 4310 Dunlavy, Houston, TX 77006. *Telephone:* 713-718-5276. *Fax:* 713-718-5388. *E-mail:* barden_p@hccs.cc.tx.us.

DEGREES AND AWARDS

Distance programs offered do not lead to a degree or other formal award.

COURSE SUBJECT AREAS OFFERED OUTSIDE OF DEGREE PROGRAMS

Undergraduate: Accounting; algebra; American (U.S.) history; anthropology; art history and criticism; astronomy and astrophysics; business; business administration and management; business law; chemistry; child care and development; computer and information sciences; computer programming; criminal justice; developmental and child psychology; earth science; economics; engineering; English composition; English language and literature; environmental science; European history; geography; geology; health and physical education/fitness; information sciences and systems; liberal arts, general studies, and humanities; management information systems; marketing; mental health services; philosophy and religion; photography; political science; psychology; real estate; social sciences; sociology; Spanish language and literature; technical writing

HOWARD COMMUNITY COLLEGE

Columbia, Maryland
Learning Centers Division
www.howardcc.edu

Howard Community College, founded in 1966, is a state and locally supported, two-year college. It is accredited by the Middle States Association of Colleges and Schools. It first offered distance learning courses in 1995. In 1999–2000, it offered 100 courses at a distance. In fall 1999, there were 1,000 students enrolled in distance learning courses.

Course delivery sites Courses are delivered to your home, high schools, Anne Arundel Community College (Arnold), Harford Community College (Bel Air), Prince George's Community College (Largo), University of Baltimore (Baltimore).

Media Courses are delivered via television, interactive television, computer software, World Wide Web, e-mail. Students and teachers may meet in person or interact via telephone, e-mail, interactive television. The following equipment may be required: television, videocassette player, computer, Internet access, e-mail.

Restrictions Programs are available worldwide. Enrollment is open to anyone.

Services Distance learners have access to library services, the campus computer network, e-mail services, academic advising, tutoring, bookstore at a distance.

Credit-earning options Students may transfer credits from another institution or may earn credits through examinations, portfolio assessment, military training.

Typical costs Tuition of $81 per credit for local area residents. Tuition of $152 per credit for in-state residents. Tuition of $220 per credit for out-of-state residents. *Noncredit courses:* $125 per course. Costs may vary. Financial aid is available to distance learners.

Registration Students may register by mail, telephone, e-mail, in person.

Contact Barbara Greenfeld, Director of Admissions, Howard Community College, 10901 Little Patuxent Parkway, Columbia, MD 21044. *Telephone:* 410-772-4856. *Fax:* 410-715-2426. *E-mail:* bgreenfeld@ howardcc.edu.

DEGREES AND AWARDS

AA General Studies

COURSE SUBJECT AREAS OFFERED OUTSIDE OF DEGREE PROGRAMS

Undergraduate: Accounting; architecture; area, ethnic, and cultural studies; biological and life sciences; computer and information sciences; economics; engineering; engineering-related technologies; English composition; English language and literature; European languages and literatures; health professions and related sciences; history; human resources management; law and legal studies; liberal arts, general studies, and humanities; mathematics; music; psychology; social sciences
Noncredit: Business

HUDSON COUNTY COMMUNITY COLLEGE

Jersey City, New Jersey

Hudson County Community College, founded in 1974, is a state and locally supported, two-year college. It is accredited by the Middle States Association of Colleges and Schools.

Contact Hudson County Community College, 25 Journal Square, Jersey City, NJ 07306. *Telephone:* 201-656-2020. *Fax:* 201-714-2136.

See full description on page 600.

HUSSON COLLEGE

Bangor, Maine
RNBSN Online Program
www.husson.edu/classroom

Husson College, founded in 1898, is an independent, nonprofit, comprehensive institution. It is accredited by the New England Association of Schools and Colleges. In 1999–2000, it offered 11 courses at a distance. In fall 1999, there were 13 students enrolled in distance learning courses.

Course delivery sites Courses are delivered to your home.

Media Courses are delivered via computer conferencing, World Wide Web, e-mail. Students and teachers may interact via mail, telephone, fax, e-mail. The following equipment may be required: computer, modem, Internet access, e-mail.

Restrictions Programs are available worldwide. Enrollment is restricted to individuals meeting certain criteria.

Services Distance learners have access to library services, academic advising, bookstore at a distance.

Credit-earning options Students may transfer credits from another institution or may earn credits through examinations, military training.

Typical costs Tuition of $307 per credit hour. Costs may vary. Financial aid is available to distance learners.

Registration Students may register by mail, fax, telephone, e-mail.

Contact Mimi Padgett, Director of RN Studies, Husson College, One College Circle, Bangor, ME 04401. *Telephone:* 207-941-7079. *Fax:* 207-941-7883. *E-mail:* padgettm@husson.edu.

DEGREES AND AWARDS

BSN Nursing (certain restrictions apply)

COURSE SUBJECT AREAS OFFERED OUTSIDE OF DEGREE PROGRAMS

Undergraduate: Abnormal psychology; communications; English composition; English literature; ethics; liberal arts, general studies, and humanities; nursing; philosophy and religion; physiology; statistics

HUTCHINSON COMMUNITY COLLEGE AND AREA VOCATIONAL SCHOOL

Hutchinson, Kansas

Instructional Technology
www.hutchcc.edu/academics

Hutchinson Community College and Area Vocational School, founded in 1928, is a state and locally supported, two-year college. It is accredited by the North Central Association of Colleges and Schools. In 1999–2000, it offered 46 courses at a distance. In fall 1999, there were 250 students enrolled in distance learning courses.
Course delivery sites Courses are delivered to your home, your workplace, high schools.
Media Courses are delivered via television, videotapes, interactive television, audiotapes, computer software, CD-ROM, World Wide Web, e-mail, print. Students and teachers may meet in person or interact via mail, telephone, fax, e-mail, interactive television. The following equipment may be required: television, videocassette player, computer, Internet access, e-mail.
Restrictions Programs are available to in-state students only. Enrollment is restricted to individuals meeting certain criteria.
Services Distance learners have access to library services, the campus computer network, e-mail services, academic advising, bookstore at a distance.
Credit-earning options Students may transfer credits from another institution.
Typical costs Tuition of $34 per credit hour plus mandatory fees of $5 per credit hour for local area residents. Tuition of $34 per credit hour plus mandatory fees of $5 per credit hour for in-state residents. Tuition of $87 per credit hour plus mandatory fees of $11 per credit hour for out-of-state residents. Financial aid is available to distance learners.
Registration Students may register by mail, fax, telephone, e-mail, World Wide Web, in person.
Contact Janice Hilyard, Director, Hutchinson Community College and Area Vocational School, 1300 North Plum, Hutchinson, KS 67501. *Telephone:* 316-665-8145. *Fax:* 316-728-8146. *E-mail:* hilyardj@hutchcc.edu.

DEGREES AND AWARDS

Distance programs offered do not lead to a degree or other formal award.

COURSE SUBJECT AREAS OFFERED OUTSIDE OF DEGREE PROGRAMS

Undergraduate: Abnormal psychology; algebra; American (U.S.) history; anthropology; business administration and management; computer and information sciences; developmental and child psychology; ecology; English language and literature; ethics; foods and nutrition studies; French language and literature; geography; German language and litera-

ture; health services administration; political science; psychology; religious studies; sociology; Spanish language and literature; visual and performing arts

ILLINOIS EASTERN COMMUNITY COLLEGES, WABASH VALLEY COLLEGE

Mount Carmel, Illinois
www.iecc.cc.il.us

Illinois Eastern Community Colleges, Wabash Valley College, founded in 1960, is a state and locally supported, two-year college. It is accredited by the North Central Association of Colleges and Schools. In 1999–2000, it offered 25 courses at a distance. In fall 1999, there were 80 students enrolled in distance learning courses.
Course delivery sites Courses are delivered to your home, Illinois Eastern Community Colleges, Frontier Community College (Fairfield), Illinois Eastern Community Colleges, Lincoln Trail College (Robinson), Illinois Eastern Community Colleges, Olney Central College (Olney).
Media Courses are delivered via television, videotapes, videoconferencing, interactive television, audiotapes, computer software, CD-ROM, computer conferencing, World Wide Web, e-mail, print. Students and teachers may interact via videoconferencing, mail, telephone, fax, e-mail, interactive television, World Wide Web. The following equipment may be required: computer, Internet access, e-mail.
Restrictions Programs are available to in-state students only. Enrollment is open to anyone.
Services Distance learners have access to library services, the campus computer network, e-mail services, academic advising, tutoring, career placement assistance, bookstore at a distance.
Credit-earning options Students may transfer credits from another institution or may earn credits through examinations.
Typical costs Tuition of $40 per credit hour for local area residents. Tuition of $132.28 per credit hour for in-state residents. Tuition of $167.99 per credit hour for out-of-state residents. *Noncredit courses:* $50 per course. Financial aid is available to distance learners.
Registration Students may register by mail, fax, telephone, e-mail, World Wide Web, in person.
Contact Mrs. Diana Spear, Assistant Dean for Student Services, Illinois Eastern Community Colleges, Wabash Valley College, Wabash Valley College, 2200 College Drive, Mount Carmel, IL 62863. *Telephone:* 618-262-8641. *Fax:* 618-262-5614. *E-mail:* speard@iecc.cc.il.us.

DEGREES AND AWARDS

Distance programs offered do not lead to a degree or other formal award.

COURSE SUBJECT AREAS OFFERED OUTSIDE OF DEGREE PROGRAMS

Undergraduate: Algebra; art history and criticism; continuing education; developmental and child psychology; journalism; radio and television broadcasting; sign language; statistics

ILLINOIS INSTITUTE OF TECHNOLOGY

Chicago, Illinois

Distance Learning Technologies
www.dlt.iit.edu

Illinois Institute of Technology, founded in 1890, is an independent, nonprofit university. It is accredited by the North Central Association of Colleges and Schools. It first offered distance learning courses in 1976. In

1999–2000, it offered 251 courses at a distance. In fall 1999, there were 902 students enrolled in distance learning courses.

Course delivery sites Courses are delivered to your home, your workplace, high schools, Calumet College of Saint Joseph (Whiting, IN), College of Lake County (Grayslake), Elmhurst College (Elmhurst), Governors State University (University Park), Joliet Junior College (Joliet), Moraine Valley Community College (Palos Hills), Morton College (Cicero), Oakton Community College (Des Plaines), Prairie State College (Chicago Heights), South Suburban College (South Holland), Triton College (River Grove), William Rainey Harper College (Palatine), 4 off-campus centers in Arlington Heights, Mundelein, Schaumburg, Bangalore, India.

Media Courses are delivered via television, videotapes, videoconferencing, World Wide Web. Students and teachers may interact via videoconferencing, telephone, fax, e-mail, World Wide Web. The following equipment may be required: television, computer, modem, Internet access, e-mail.

Restrictions Programs are available to local area students. Enrollment is restricted to individuals meeting certain criteria.

Services Distance learners have access to library services, the campus computer network, e-mail services, academic advising, career placement assistance, bookstore at a distance.

Credit-earning options Students may transfer credits from another institution.

Typical costs *Undergraduate:* Tuition of $550 per credit. *Graduate:* Tuition of $590 per credit.

Registration Students may register by mail, fax, World Wide Web, in person.

Contact Holli Pryor-Harris, Director, Client Services, Illinois Institute of Technology, Office of Academic Affairs, Graduate College, 3300 South Federal, Room 110A, Chicago, IL 60616-3793. *Telephone:* 312-567-3167. *Fax:* 312-567-7140. *E-mail:* holli.pryorharris@iit.edu.

DEGREES AND AWARDS

Graduate Certificate(s) Advanced Electronics (some on-campus requirements), Chemistry (service area differs from that of the overall institution; some on-campus requirements), Computer Engineering (some on-campus requirements), Computer Networking and Telecommunications (some on-campus requirements), Construction Management (some on-campus requirements), Control Systems (some on-campus requirements), Electricity Markets (some on-campus requirements), Hazardous Waste Engineering (some on-campus requirements), Indoor Air Quality (some on-campus requirements), Intelligent Information Systems (some on-campus requirements), Internet (some on-campus requirements), Particle Processing (some on-campus requirements), Pharmaceutical Processing (some on-campus requirements), Polymer Operations Management (some on-campus requirements), Power Engineering (some on-campus requirements), Signal Processing (some on-campus requirements), Software Engineering (some on-campus requirements), Water and Wastewater Treatment (some on-campus requirements), Wireless Communications (some on-campus requirements)

MCE Chemical Engineering (some on-campus requirements)

MChem Chemistry (service area differs from that of the overall institution)

MHP Health Physics (some on-campus requirements)

MMAE Mechanical and Aerospace Engineering (some on-campus requirements)

MS Chemical Engineering (some on-campus requirements), Chemistry (some on-campus requirements), Computer Science (service area differs from that of the overall institution; some on-campus requirements), Electrical and Computer Engineering (some on-campus requirements), Electrical Engineering (some on-campus requirements), Electricity Markets (some on-campus requirements), Environmental Engineering (some on-campus requirements), Geotechnical Engineering (some on-campus requirements), Manufacturing Engineering (some on-campus requirements), Mechanical and Aerospace Engineering (some on-campus requirements), Metallurgical and Materials Engineering (some on-campus requirements), Public Works (some on-campus requirements), Structural

Engineering (some on-campus requirements), Telecommunications and Software Engineering (service area differs from that of the overall institution), Transportation Engineering (some on-campus requirements)

COURSE SUBJECT AREAS OFFERED OUTSIDE OF DEGREE PROGRAMS

Undergraduate: Aerospace, aeronautical engineering; biological and life sciences; civil engineering; computer and information sciences; computer programming; construction; database management; electrical engineering; engineering; engineering mechanics; information sciences and systems; mathematics; mechanical engineering; physics

Graduate: Aerospace, aeronautical engineering; biological and life sciences; chemical engineering; chemistry; chemistry, analytical; chemistry, inorganic; chemistry, organic; civil engineering; computer and information sciences; computer programming; construction; database management; electrical engineering; engineering; environmental engineering; industrial engineering; information sciences and systems; mathematics; mechanical engineering; physics

ILLINOIS STATE UNIVERSITY

Normal, Illinois

Extended University
www.exu.ilstu.edu

Illinois State University, founded in 1857, is a state-supported university. It is accredited by the North Central Association of Colleges and Schools. It first offered distance learning courses in 1994. In 1999–2000, it offered 25 courses at a distance. In fall 1999, there were 124 students enrolled in distance learning courses.

Course delivery sites Courses are delivered to your home, your workplace, Illinois Central College (East Peoria), Illinois Valley Community College (Oglesby), 1 off-campus center in Quad Cities Graduate Center.

Media Courses are delivered via interactive television, World Wide Web, e-mail, print. Students and teachers may meet in person or interact via videoconferencing, mail, telephone, fax, e-mail, interactive television, World Wide Web. The following equipment may be required: television, computer, modem, Internet access, e-mail.

Restrictions Programs are available to in-state students only. Enrollment is open to anyone.

Services Distance learners have access to library services, the campus computer network, e-mail services, academic advising, bookstore at a distance.

Credit-earning options Students may earn credits through examinations.

Typical costs *Undergraduate:* Tuition of $104.25 per credit hour plus mandatory fees of $30 per credit hour. *Graduate:* Tuition of $105.25 per credit hour plus mandatory fees of $30 per credit hour. Financial aid is available to distance learners.

Registration Students may register by telephone, World Wide Web.

Contact Dr. Galen Crow, Executive Director, Extended University, Illinois State University, Campus Box 4090, Normal, IL 61790. *Telephone:* 309-438-5288. *Fax:* 309-438-5069. *E-mail:* gbcrow@ilstu.edu.

DEGREES AND AWARDS

Undergraduate Certificate(s) Education Superintendence (certain restrictions apply), Visual Impairment and Blindness (certain restrictions apply)

COURSE SUBJECT AREAS OFFERED OUTSIDE OF DEGREE PROGRAMS

Undergraduate: American literature; economics; education administration; health professions and related sciences; political science; Spanish language and literature; visual and performing arts

Graduate: American literature; curriculum and instruction; education administration; recreation and leisure studies; Spanish language and literature; special education

INDEPENDENCE COMMUNITY COLLEGE

Independence, Kansas

Center for Distance Learning
www.indy.cc.ks.us

Independence Community College, founded in 1925, is a state-supported, two-year college. It is accredited by the North Central Association of Colleges and Schools. It first offered distance learning courses in 1998. In 1999–2000, it offered 4 courses at a distance. In fall 1999, there were 25 students enrolled in distance learning courses.

Course delivery sites Courses are delivered to your home, your workplace.

Media Courses are delivered via videotapes, computer software, CD-ROM, World Wide Web, e-mail, print. Students and teachers may meet in person or interact via audioconferencing, mail, telephone, e-mail, World Wide Web. The following equipment may be required: computer, Internet access, e-mail.

Restrictions Programs are available to local area students. Enrollment is open to anyone.

Services Distance learners have access to library services, academic advising, bookstore at a distance.

Credit-earning options Students may transfer credits from another institution or may earn credits through examinations.

Typical costs Tuition of $25 per credit hour plus mandatory fees of $12 per credit hour for in-state residents. Tuition of $62 per credit hour plus mandatory fees of $12 per credit hour for out-of-state residents. Financial aid is available to distance learners.

Registration Students may register by mail, fax, telephone, e-mail, World Wide Web, in person.

Contact Joy Pierson, Instructor, Independence Community College, East College and Brookside Drive, Independence, KS 67301. *Telephone:* 316-331-4100 Ext. 4290. *Fax:* 316-331-5344. *E-mail:* jpierson@indy.cc. ks.us.

DEGREES AND AWARDS

Distance programs offered do not lead to a degree or other formal award.

COURSE SUBJECT AREAS OFFERED OUTSIDE OF DEGREE PROGRAMS

Undergraduate: Computer and information sciences; computer programming; English composition; English literature; technical writing

INDIANA INSTITUTE OF TECHNOLOGY

Fort Wayne, Indiana

Independent Study
www.indtech.edu

Indiana Institute of Technology, founded in 1930, is an independent, nonprofit, comprehensive institution. It is accredited by the North Central Association of Colleges and Schools. In 1999–2000, it offered 71 courses at a distance. In fall 1999, there were 255 students enrolled in distance learning courses.

Course delivery sites Courses are delivered to your home.

Media Courses are delivered via print. Students and teachers may meet in person or interact via mail, telephone, fax, e-mail.

Restrictions Programs are available worldwide. Enrollment is open to anyone.

Services Distance learners have access to e-mail services, academic advising, career placement assistance at a distance.

Credit-earning options Students may transfer credits from another institution or may earn credits through examinations, portfolio assessment, military training, business training.

Typical costs Tuition of $199 per credit hour. Financial aid is available to distance learners.

Registration Students may register by mail, fax, telephone, e-mail, World Wide Web, in person.

Contact Teresa Merryman, Admissions Counselor, Indiana Institute of Technology, 1600 East Washington Boulevard, Fort Wayne, IN 46803. *Telephone:* 888-666-TECH Ext. 2261. *Fax:* 219-422-1518. *E-mail:* merryman@indtech.edu.

DEGREES AND AWARDS

AS Business Administration
BS Business Administration

COURSE SUBJECT AREAS OFFERED OUTSIDE OF DEGREE PROGRAMS

Undergraduate: Abnormal psychology; accounting; business; business administration and management; business law; English language and literature; human resources management; insurance; international business; labor relations/studies; liberal arts, general studies, and humanities; management information systems; marketing; mathematics; organizational behavior studies; philosophy and religion; psychology; sociology

INDIANA STATE UNIVERSITY

Terre Haute, Indiana

Division of Lifelong Learning
web.indstate.edu/distance

Indiana State University, founded in 1865, is a state-supported university. It is accredited by the North Central Association of Colleges and Schools. It first offered distance learning courses in 1969. In 1999–2000, it offered 300 courses at a distance. In fall 1999, there were 1,010 students enrolled in distance learning courses.

Course delivery sites Courses are delivered to your home, your workplace, military bases, high schools, Ivy Tech State College System (Indianapolis), University of Southern Indiana (Evansville), Vincennes University (Vincennes), 300 off-campus centers.

Media Courses are delivered via television, videotapes, videoconferencing, interactive television, World Wide Web, e-mail, print. Students and teachers may interact via videoconferencing, mail, telephone, fax, e-mail, interactive television, World Wide Web. The following equipment may be required: television, videocassette player, computer, modem, Internet access, e-mail.

Restrictions Most courses are limited to in-state students only; Internet courses are available worldwide. Enrollment is open to anyone.

Services Distance learners have access to library services, the campus computer network, e-mail services, academic advising, career placement assistance, bookstore at a distance.

Credit-earning options Students may transfer credits from another institution.

Typical costs *Undergraduate:* Tuition of $123 per credit hour. *Graduate:* Tuition of $148 per credit hour. Financial aid is available to distance learners.

Registration Students may register by mail, telephone, in person.

Contact Harry K. Barnes, Director, Office of Student Services, Indiana State University, Division of Lifelong Learning, Erickson Hall, Room

Indiana State University

210-211, Terre Haute, IN 47809. *Telephone:* 888-237-8080. *Fax:* 812-237-8540. *E-mail:* studentservices@indstate.edu.

DEGREES AND AWARDS

Undergraduate Certificate(s) Corrections (service area differs from that of the overall institution), Law Enforcement (service area differs from that of the overall institution), Private Security (service area differs from that of the overall institution)

AS General Aviation Flight Technology (service area differs from that of the overall institution)

BS Business Administration (certain restrictions apply; service area differs from that of the overall institution), Criminology (certain restrictions apply; service area differs from that of the overall institution), Electronics Technology (certain restrictions apply; service area differs from that of the overall institution; some on-campus requirements), General Industrial Technology (certain restrictions apply; service area differs from that of the overall institution; some on-campus requirements), Human Resource Development (service area differs from that of the overall institution; some on-campus requirements), Industrial Supervision (certain restrictions apply; service area differs from that of the overall institution; some on-campus requirements), Insurance (certain restrictions apply; service area differs from that of the overall institution), Nursing (certain restrictions apply; service area differs from that of the overall institution; some on-campus requirements), Vocational Trade-Industrial-Technical Area Major (certain restrictions apply; service area differs from that of the overall institution)

Graduate Certificate(s) Driver Education (service area differs from that of the overall institution; some on-campus requirements), Educational Administration (service area differs from that of the overall institution; some on-campus requirements), Public Administration (service area differs from that of the overall institution), School Administration (service area differs from that of the overall institution; some on-campus requirements)

MA Criminology (service area differs from that of the overall institution), Nursing (service area differs from that of the overall institution), Student Affairs Administration (service area differs from that of the overall institution; some on-campus requirements)

MS Criminology (service area differs from that of the overall institution), Human Resource Development (service area differs from that of the overall institution; some on-campus requirements), Nursing (service area differs from that of the overall institution; some on-campus requirements), Occupational Safety Management (service area differs from that of the overall institution; some on-campus requirements), Student Affairs Administration (service area differs from that of the overall institution; some on-campus requirements)

PhD Technology Management (service area differs from that of the overall institution; some on-campus requirements)

COURSE SUBJECT AREAS OFFERED OUTSIDE OF DEGREE PROGRAMS

Undergraduate: Abnormal psychology; algebra; biological and life sciences; calculus; cognitive psychology; community health services; criminology; curriculum and instruction; economics; engineering-related technologies; English language and literature; fine arts; geography; health and physical education/fitness; health professions and related sciences; history; human resources management; instructional media; insurance; international business; journalism; nursing; political science; psychology; sociology; statistics

Graduate: Biological and life sciences; criminology; curriculum and instruction; education administration; educational psychology; engineering-related technologies; health professions and related sciences; human

resources management; instructional media; nursing; public administration and services; student counseling

Special note
The DegreeLink Program offers eligible individuals an opportunity to transfer college credit to Indiana State University and complete selected Bachelor of Science degrees via distance education. Individuals who have completed designated degrees from Ivy Tech State College and Vincennes University may transfer credit as a 2-year block into one or more DegreeLink programs. In addition, individuals who have earned credits or an associate degree from any accredited collegiate institution are eligible for and encouraged to transfer credit on a course-by-course basis and complete a Bachelor of Science degree via distance technologies. Baccalaureate degree-completion programs offered include business administration, criminology, electronics technology, general industrial technology, human resource development, industrial supervision, insurance, nursing, and vocational trade-industrial-technical. In addition, 3 new programs are tentatively scheduled for distance delivery beginning fall 2000, including community health, instrumentation and control technology, and mechanical technology. A unique feature of the DegreeLink Program is a statewide network of area learning centers that offer free access to Internet-connected computers and student services coordinators who provide one-on-one assistance to in-state and out-of-state students and all individuals interested in DegreeLink. Degree-completion courses are offered primarily via the Internet, text-based correspondence, videotape, and live televised courses that are accessible at more than 300 receiving sites in Indiana. Most DegreeLink programs can be completed via distance education within Indiana. Selected DegreeLink programs are accessible globally via the Internet. For more information, students should call the Office of Student Services—Lifelong Learning at 888-237-8080 (toll-free) or visit the Web site at http://web.indstate.edu/degreelink.

See full descriptions on pages 540 and 542.

INDIANA UNIVERSITY OF PENNSYLVANIA

Indiana, Pennsylvania
School of Continuing Education
www.iup.edu/contin/

Indiana University of Pennsylvania, founded in 1875, is a state-supported university. It is accredited by the Middle States Association of Colleges and Schools. In 1999–2000, it offered 3 courses at a distance. In fall 1999, there were 10 students enrolled in distance learning courses.

Course delivery sites Courses are delivered to your home, your workplace, military bases, high schools.

Media Courses are delivered via computer software, CD-ROM, computer conferencing, World Wide Web, e-mail, print. Students and teachers may meet in person or interact via mail, telephone, fax, e-mail, World Wide Web. The following equipment may be required: computer, modem, Internet access, e-mail.

Restrictions Programs are available worldwide. Enrollment is open to anyone.

Services Distance learners have access to library services, the campus computer network, e-mail services, career placement assistance, bookstore at a distance.

Credit-earning options Students may transfer credits from another institution or may earn credits through examinations.

Typical costs *Undergraduate:* Tuition of $150 per credit for local area residents. Tuition of $150 per credit for in-state residents. Tuition of $153 per credit for out-of-state residents. *Graduate:* Tuition of $210 per credit for local area residents. Tuition of $210 per credit for in-state residents. Tuition of $214 per credit for out-of-state residents. Financial aid is available to distance learners.

Registration Students may register by mail, fax, telephone, in person.

Contact Ms. K. Wijekumar, Director, Distance Education Development, Indiana University of Pennsylvania, 100 Keith Hall, 390 Pratt Drive, Indiana, PA 15705-1092. *Telephone:* 800-845-0131. *Fax:* 724-357-7597. *E-mail:* ce-ocp@grove.iup.edu.

DEGREES AND AWARDS

Undergraduate Certificate(s) Safety Sciences (certain restrictions apply)

COURSE SUBJECT AREAS OFFERED OUTSIDE OF DEGREE PROGRAMS

Undergraduate: Criminal justice; foods and nutrition studies; geology; mathematics; political science

Graduate: Interdisciplinary studies; physics

INDIANA UNIVERSITY SYSTEM

Bloomington, Indiana

Office of Distributed Education
www.indiana.edu/~iude

Indiana University System is a state-supported, system. It is accredited by the North Central Association of Colleges and Schools. It first offered distance learning courses in 1912. In 1999–2000, it offered 583 courses at a distance. In fall 1999, there were 20,186 students enrolled in distance learning courses.

Course delivery sites Courses are delivered to your home, your workplace, military bases, high schools.

Media Courses are delivered via television, videotapes, videoconferencing, interactive television, audiotapes, computer software, CD-ROM, computer conferencing, World Wide Web, e-mail, print. Students and teachers may meet in person or interact via videoconferencing, audioconferencing, mail, telephone, fax, e-mail, interactive television, World Wide Web.

Restrictions Programs are available worldwide. Enrollment is open to anyone.

Services Distance learners have access to library services, the campus computer network, e-mail services, academic advising, career placement assistance, bookstore at a distance.

Credit-earning options Students may transfer credits from another institution or may earn credits through examinations, portfolio assessment, military training.

Typical costs Undergraduate tuition ranges between $94 and $114 per credit hour. Graduate tuition varies depending on courses taken. *Noncredit courses:* $150 per course. Costs may vary. Financial aid is available to distance learners.

Registration Students may register by mail, fax, telephone, e-mail, World Wide Web, in person.

Contact Carol Kegeris, Administrative Assistant, Indiana University System, Office of Distributed Education, 902 West New York Street, ES 2129, Indianapolis, IN 46202-5157. *Telephone:* 317-278-4833. *Fax:* 317-274-4513. *E-mail:* ckegeris@iupui.edu.

DEGREES AND AWARDS

Undergraduate Certificate(s) Distance Education (certain restrictions apply; service area differs from that of the overall institution), Information Technology, Labor Studies

AGS General Studies (certain restrictions apply)

AS Histotechnology (certain restrictions apply; service area differs from that of the overall institution)

ASLS Labor Studies

BGS General Studies (certain restrictions apply)

BSLS Labor Studies

MBA Business Administration (service area differs from that of the overall institution)

MS Adult Education (service area differs from that of the overall institution), Nursing (service area differs from that of the overall institution; some on-campus requirements), Therapeutic Recreation (service area differs from that of the overall institution)

MSE Language Education

COURSE SUBJECT AREAS OFFERED OUTSIDE OF DEGREE PROGRAMS

Undergraduate: Accounting; African-American studies; algebra; American studies; anatomy; anthropology; area, ethnic, and cultural studies; art history and criticism; astronomy and astrophysics; biological and life sciences; biology; business; business administration and management; chemistry; classical languages and literatures; communications; computer and information sciences; conservation and natural resources; creative writing; developmental and child psychology; economics; education; English composition; English language and literature; English literature; ethics; European languages and literatures; fine arts; French language and literature; geology; health and physical education/fitness; health professions and related sciences; history; home economics and family studies; hospitality services management; human resources management; international business; Japanese language and literature; journalism; labor relations/studies; liberal arts, general studies, and humanities; logic; mathematics; music; nursing; philosophy and religion; physical sciences; physics; political science; protective services; psychology; public administration and services; public health; social psychology; social sciences; sociology; Spanish language and literature; teacher education; visual and performing arts

Graduate: Adult education; area, ethnic, and cultural studies; curriculum and instruction; education administration; educational psychology; educational research; electrical engineering; environmental science; fine arts; health and physical education/fitness; health professions and related sciences; instructional media; journalism; library and information studies; nursing; public administration and services; special education; teacher education

Noncredit: English language and literature; European languages and literatures; health and physical education/fitness; home economics and family studies; labor relations/studies; liberal arts, general studies, and humanities; mathematics; physical sciences; visual and performing arts

See full description on page 540.

INDIANA WESLEYAN UNIVERSITY

Marion, Indiana

Distance Education Department
www.indwes.edu/aps

Indiana Wesleyan University, founded in 1920, is an independent, religious, comprehensive institution. It is accredited by the North Central Association of Colleges and Schools. It first offered distance learning courses in 1992. In 1999–2000, it offered 29 courses at a distance. In fall 1999, there were 461 students enrolled in distance learning courses.

Course delivery sites Courses are delivered to your home, your workplace.

Media Courses are delivered via videotapes, computer conferencing, World Wide Web, e-mail. Students and teachers may interact via mail, telephone, fax, e-mail. The following equipment may be required: television, videocassette player, computer, Internet access.

Restrictions Programs are available worldwide. Enrollment is restricted to individuals meeting certain criteria.

Services Distance learners have access to library services, academic advising at a distance.

Credit-earning options Students may transfer credits from another institution or may earn credits through examinations, portfolio assessment, military training, business training.

Typical costs *Undergraduate:* Tuition of $200 per credit hour. *Graduate:* Tuition of $345 per course. Financial aid is available to distance learners.

Registration Students may register by mail, fax.

Contact Emily Prows, Adult Education Services, Indiana Wesleyan University, 4301 South Washington Street, Marion, IN 46953. *Telephone:* 765-677-2385. *Fax:* 765-677-2380. *E-mail:* eprows@indwes.edu.

DEGREES AND AWARDS

MBA Business Administration (certain restrictions apply; some on-campus requirements)

COURSE SUBJECT AREAS OFFERED OUTSIDE OF DEGREE PROGRAMS

Undergraduate: Bible studies; earth science; English composition; ethics; individual and family development studies; information sciences and systems; liberal arts, general studies, and humanities

Graduate: Teacher education

See full description on page 544.

INDIAN RIVER COMMUNITY COLLEGE

Fort Pierce, Florida

Distance Learning
www.ircc.cc.fl.us

Indian River Community College, founded in 1960, is a state-supported, two-year college. It is accredited by the Southern Association of Colleges and Schools. In 1999–2000, it offered 55 courses at a distance. In fall 1999, there were 700 students enrolled in distance learning courses.

Course delivery sites Courses are delivered to your home, your workplace.

Media Courses are delivered via television, videotapes, interactive television, computer software, World Wide Web, e-mail. Students and teachers may meet in person or interact via telephone, fax, e-mail, interactive television, World Wide Web. The following equipment may be required: television, videocassette player, computer, modem, Internet access, e-mail.

Restrictions Programs are available to in-state students only. Enrollment is open to anyone.

Services Distance learners have access to library services, the campus computer network, e-mail services, academic advising, bookstore at a distance.

Credit-earning options Students may transfer credits from another institution or may earn credits through military training, business training.

Typical costs Tuition of $46 per credit for local area residents. Tuition of $46 per credit for in-state residents. Tuition of $172 per credit for out-of-state residents. Financial aid is available to distance learners.

Registration Students may register by telephone, World Wide Web.

Contact Susan Archer, Chairperson of Instructional Advisement, Indian River Community College, 3209 Virginia Avenue, Fort Pierce, FL 34981. *Telephone:* 561-462-4746. *Fax:* 561-462-4699. *E-mail:* marcher@ircc.cc.fl.us.

DEGREES AND AWARDS

AA 2 Year Transfer Degree-General Studies
AS 2 Year Terminal Degree-General Studies, Library Technical Assistant

---

COURSE SUBJECT AREAS OFFERED OUTSIDE OF DEGREE PROGRAMS

Undergraduate: Accounting; algebra; American (U.S.) history; anthropology; art history and criticism; astronomy and astrophysics; biology; business administration and management; chemistry; computer and information sciences; computer programming; education; English language and literature; European history; foods and nutrition studies; French language and literature; geography; health and physical education/fitness; oceanography; philosophy and religion; psychology; real estate; social sciences; sociology; Spanish language and literature; statistics; teacher education

See full description on page 676.

INSTITUTE OF TRANSPERSONAL PSYCHOLOGY

Palo Alto, California

Global Program
www.itp.edu

Institute of Transpersonal Psychology, founded in 1975, is an independent, nonprofit, graduate institution. It is accredited by the Western Association of Schools and Colleges, Inc. It first offered distance learning courses in 1985. In 1999–2000, it offered 35 courses at a distance. In fall 1999, there were 120 students enrolled in distance learning courses.

Course delivery sites Courses are delivered to your home.

Media Courses are delivered via audiotapes, computer conferencing, World Wide Web, e-mail, print. Students and teachers may meet in person or interact via mail, telephone, fax, e-mail, World Wide Web. The following equipment may be required: computer, modem, Internet access, e-mail.

Restrictions Programs are available worldwide. Enrollment is open to anyone.

Services Distance learners have access to library services, e-mail services, academic advising, tutoring, bookstore at a distance.

Credit-earning options Students may transfer credits from another institution.

Typical costs Tuition of $878 per course. *Noncredit courses:* $520 per course. Financial aid is available to distance learners.

Registration Students may register by mail, fax, telephone, e-mail, World Wide Web, in person.

Contact Edith Parker, Admissions, Institute of Transpersonal Psychology, 744 San Antonio Road, Palto Alto, CA 94303. *Telephone:* 650-493-4430. *Fax:* 650-493-6835. *E-mail:* itpinfo@itp.edu.

DEGREES AND AWARDS

Graduate Certificate(s) Creative Expression (some on-campus requirements), Transpersonal Studies (some on-campus requirements), Wellness-Body Mind Consciousness (some on-campus requirements)

MA Transpersonal Studies (some on-campus requirements)

MTP Transpersonal Psychology (some on-campus requirements)

COURSE SUBJECT AREAS OFFERED OUTSIDE OF DEGREE PROGRAMS

Graduate: Philosophy and religion; psychology
Noncredit: Philosophy and religion; psychology

INSTITUTO TECNOLÓGICO Y DE ESTUDIOS SUPERIORES DE MONTERREY, CAMPUS MONTERREY

Monterrey, Mexico
Virtual University
www.ruv.itesm.mx

Instituto Tecnológico y de Estudios Superiores de Monterrey, Campus Monterrey, founded in 1943, is an independent, nonprofit university. It is accredited by the Southern Association of Colleges and Schools. In 1999–2000, it offered 260 courses at a distance. In fall 1999, there were 38,338 students enrolled in distance learning courses.

Course delivery sites Courses are delivered to your home, your workplace, high schools, Corp. Universidad de Ibague (Ibague, Colombia), Corp. Universidad Technologico de Bolivar (Cartagena, Colombia), Fundacion Universidad de Popayan (Popayan, Colombia), Suramericana de Seguros (Medellin, Colombia), Universida San Ignacio de Loyola (Lima) (Lima, Peru), Universida Simon Rodriguez (La Urbina) (Caracas, Venezuela), Universidad Autonoma de Bucaramanga (Bucaramanga, Colombia), Universidad Autonoma de Manizales (Manizales, Colombia), Universidad Autonoma de Occidente (Cali, Colombia), Universidad de Pamplona (Pamplona, Colombia), Universidad Federico Santa Maria, Concepcion (Concepcion, Mexico), Universidad Federico Santa Maria, Talcahuano (Talcahuano, Mexico), Universidad Federico Santa Maria, Valparaiso (Valparaiso, Mexico), Universidad Interamericana de Costa Rica (San Jose, Afghanistan), Universidad Simon Rodriguez (Barcelona, Venezuela), Universidad Simon Rodriguez (Barquisimeto, Venezuela), Universidad Simon Rodriguez (Valencia, Venezuela), Universidad Simon Rodriguez (Palo Verde) (Caracas, Venezuela), Universidad Tecnologia Centroamericana (Tegucigalpa) (Tegucigalpa, Honduras), Universidad Tecnologica Centroamericana (San Pedro Sula) (San Pedro, Honduras), 69 off-campus centers in Aguascalientes, Mexico, Altamira, Mexico, Bogota, Colombia, Campeche, Mexico, Cd. Cuauhtemoc, Mexico, Cd. Victoria, Mexico, Celaya, Mexico, Chihuahua, Mexico, Chuao, Venezuela, Ciudad Juarez, Mexico, Colima, Mexico, Cordoba, Mexico, Cuernavaca, Mexico, Culiacan, Mexico, Delicias, Mexico, Durango, Mexico, Estado de Mexico, Mexico, Fresnillo, Mexico, Guayaquil, Ecuador, Guaymas, Mexico, Hermosillo, Mexico, Hidalgo de Parral, Mexico, Irapueto, Mexico, La Paz, Mexico, Leon, Mexico, Lima, Peru, Los Cabos, Mexico, Malipu, Chile, Mazatlan, Mexico, Mexicali, Mexico, Mexico City, Mexico, Monclova, Mexico, Monterrey, Mexico, Morelia, Mexico, Navojoa, Mexico, Nogales, Mexico, Obregon, Mexico, Pachuca, Mexico, Panama, Panama, Piedras Negras, Mexico, Queretaro, Mexico, Quito, Ecuador, Reynosa, Mexico, Saltillo, Mexico, San Luis Potosi, Mexico, Tapachula, Mexico, Tijuana, Mexico, Tlaxcala, Mexico, Toluca, Mexico, Torreon, Mexico, Tuxtla Gutierrez, Mexico, Veracruz, Mexico, Villahermosa, Mexico, Zacatecas, Mexico, Zapopen, Mexico.

Media Courses are delivered via television, videotapes, videoconferencing, interactive television, audiotapes, computer software, CD-ROM, computer conferencing, World Wide Web, e-mail, print. Students and teachers may meet in person or interact via videoconferencing, audioconferencing, mail, telephone, fax, e-mail, interactive television, World Wide Web. The following equipment may be required: computer, modem, Internet access, e-mail.

Restrictions Programs are available worldwide. Enrollment is restricted to individuals meeting certain criteria.

Services Distance learners have access to library services, the campus computer network, e-mail services, academic advising, tutoring at a distance.

Credit-earning options Students may transfer credits from another institution or may earn credits through examinations.

Typical costs Undergraduate tuition for online courses is $464 per course. Graduate tuition is $756 per course. Costs may vary.

Registration Students may register by mail, fax, telephone, e-mail, World Wide Web, in person.
Contact Aracely Rodriguez, Admissions Coordinator, Instituto Tecnológico y de Estudios Superiores de Monterrey, Campus Monterrey, Avenue Eugenio Garza Sada 2501 Sur, Edificio Talleres II, Monterrey Mexico. *Telephone:* 528-3-284320 Ext. 6542. *Fax:* 528-3-284321. *E-mail:* arodrigu@campus.ruv.itesm.mx.

DEGREES AND AWARDS

Undergraduate Certificate(s) Administration for Government Officials, Administration for Institutional Education, Educational Innovation Technology, Entrepreneurship for Social Development (not-for-profit institutions for the social, economic, cultural and environmental development of Latin America), Library and Information Science
EdM Education (with areas of specialization) (certain restrictions apply)
MBA Business Administration (certain restrictions apply), Finance (certain restrictions apply), Marketing (certain restrictions apply)
MEdTech Administration in Educational Technology (certain restrictions apply), Education Technology (certain restrictions apply)
MIMLA International Management (certain restrictions apply)
MIT Teaching in the Humanities (certain restrictions apply)
MLIS Library and Information Science (certain restrictions apply)
MS Administration for Institutional Education (certain restrictions apply), Architecture (certain restrictions apply), Computer Science (certain restrictions apply), E-commerce (certain restrictions apply), Environmental Systems (certain restrictions apply), Quality and Production Systems (certain restrictions apply)
MSIS Information Technology (certain restrictions apply)
MTEL Telecommunications (certain restrictions apply)
PhD Educational Innovation and Technology (certain restrictions apply)

COURSE SUBJECT AREAS OFFERED OUTSIDE OF DEGREE PROGRAMS

Undergraduate: Business administration and management; finance; industrial engineering; information sciences and systems; international business; marketing; telecommunications
Graduate: Education administration; information sciences and systems; library and information studies
Noncredit: Adult education; business administration and management; business communications; community services; continuing education; curriculum and instruction; educational psychology; English as a second language (ESL); finance; human resources management; information sciences and systems; international business; organizational behavior studies; public policy analysis; public relations; teacher education

See full description on page 546.

INTER AMERICAN UNIVERSITY OF PUERTO RICO, SAN GERMÁN CAMPUS

San Germán, Puerto Rico
www.sg.inter.edu

Inter American University of Puerto Rico, San Germán Campus, founded in 1912, is an independent, nonprofit, comprehensive institution. It is accredited by the Middle States Association of Colleges and Schools. In 1999–2000, it offered 5 courses at a distance. In fall 1999, there were 30 students enrolled in distance learning courses.
Course delivery sites Courses are delivered to your home, your workplace.
Media Courses are delivered via videoconferencing, computer software, CD-ROM, World Wide Web, e-mail. Students and teachers may meet in

person or interact via videoconferencing, mail, telephone, fax, e-mail, World Wide Web. The following equipment may be required: computer, modem, Internet access, e-mail.

Restrictions Programs are available to local area students. Enrollment is restricted to individuals meeting certain criteria.

Services Distance learners have access to library services, the campus computer network, e-mail services at a distance.

Credit-earning options Students may transfer credits from another institution or may earn credits through examinations, portfolio assessment.

Typical costs *Undergraduate:* Tuition of $115 per credit. *Graduate:* Tuition of $155 per credit. Financial aid is available to distance learners.

Registration Students may register by mail, World Wide Web, in person.

Contact Prof. Waldemar Velez, Acting Director of Graduate Programs, Inter American University of Puerto Rico, San Germán Campus, PO Box 5100, San Germán, PR 00683. *Telephone:* 787-264-1912 Ext. 7357. *Fax:* 787-892-6350. *E-mail:* wvelez@sg.inter.edu.

DEGREES AND AWARDS

Distance programs offered do not lead to a degree or other formal award.

COURSE SUBJECT AREAS OFFERED OUTSIDE OF DEGREE PROGRAMS

Graduate: Business administration and management; education; library and information studies

IOWA STATE UNIVERSITY OF SCIENCE AND TECHNOLOGY

Ames, Iowa

Extended and Continuing Education
www.lifelearner.iastate.edu/

Iowa State University of Science and Technology, founded in 1858, is a state-supported university. It is accredited by the North Central Association of Colleges and Schools. It first offered distance learning courses in 1969. In 1999–2000, it offered 185 courses at a distance. In fall 1999, there were 693 students enrolled in distance learning courses.

Course delivery sites Courses are delivered to your home, your workplace, military bases, high schools, Iowa Area Community Colleges System, 15 colleges across the state.

Media Courses are delivered via videotapes, videoconferencing, interactive television, CD-ROM, World Wide Web. Students and teachers may meet in person or interact via mail, telephone, fax, e-mail, interactive television. The following equipment may be required: television, videocassette player, computer, modem, Internet access, e-mail.

Restrictions Programs are available nationwide. Enrollment is open to anyone.

Services Distance learners have access to library services, the campus computer network, e-mail services, academic advising, career placement assistance, bookstore at a distance.

Credit-earning options Students may transfer credits from another institution or may earn credits through examinations.

Typical costs *Undergraduate:* Tuition of $122 per credit. *Graduate:* Tuition of $192 per credit. *Noncredit courses:* $385 per course. Costs may vary. Financial aid is available to distance learners.

Registration Students may register by mail, fax, telephone, World Wide Web, in person.

Contact Lynette Spicer, Communication Specialist, Iowa State University of Science and Technology, 102 Scheman, Ames, IA 50011-1112. *Telephone:* 515-294-1327. *Fax:* 515-294-6146. *E-mail:* lspicer@iastate.edu.

DEGREES AND AWARDS

BS Professional Agriculture
ME Systems Engineering (some on-campus requirements)
MS Agriculture, Agronomy, Computer Engineering (some on-campus requirements), Electrical Engineering (some on-campus requirements), Mechanical Engineering (some on-campus requirements), Microbiology, Statistics (some on-campus requirements)

COURSE SUBJECT AREAS OFFERED OUTSIDE OF DEGREE PROGRAMS

Undergraduate: Agricultural economics; agriculture; animal sciences; biochemistry; biology; economics; electrical engineering; engineering mechanics; entomology; genetics; meteorology; microbiology; zoology
Graduate: Aerospace, aeronautical engineering; agricultural economics; agriculture; animal sciences; biochemistry; civil engineering; electrical engineering; engineering/industrial management; genetics; industrial engineering; mechanical engineering; meteorology; microbiology; statistics

IOWA WESLEYAN COLLEGE

Mount Pleasant, Iowa

Office of Continuing Education
www.iwc.edu

Iowa Wesleyan College, founded in 1842, is an independent, religious, four-year college. It is accredited by the North Central Association of Colleges and Schools. It first offered distance learning courses in 1989. In 1999–2000, it offered 9 courses at a distance. In fall 1999, there were 30 students enrolled in distance learning courses.

Course delivery sites Courses are delivered to your home, your workplace, high schools, Indian Hills Community College (Ottumwa), Muscatine Community College (Muscatine), Southeastern Community College, North Campus (West Burlington), Southwestern Community College (Creston).

Media Courses are delivered via television, interactive television. Students and teachers may meet in person or interact via mail, telephone, fax, e-mail, interactive television. The following equipment may be required: television, videocassette player, computer, modem.

Restrictions Programs are available to in-state students only. Enrollment is open to anyone.

Services Distance learners have access to library services, e-mail services, academic advising, career placement assistance, bookstore at a distance.

Credit-earning options Students may transfer credits from another institution or may earn credits through examinations, portfolio assessment, military training.

Typical costs *Undergraduate:* Tuition of $200 per credit hour. *Graduate:* Tuition of $200 per credit hour. Costs may vary. Financial aid is available to distance learners.

Registration Students may register by mail, fax, telephone, e-mail, in person.

Contact David C. File, Assistant Vice President of Non-Traditional Programming, Iowa Wesleyan College, 601 North Main Street, Mount Pleasant, IA 52641-1398. *Telephone:* 319-385-6247. *Fax:* 319-385-6296. *E-mail:* conted@iwc.edu.

DEGREES AND AWARDS

Distance programs offered do not lead to a degree or other formal award.

COURSE SUBJECT AREAS OFFERED OUTSIDE OF DEGREE PROGRAMS

Undergraduate: Business administration and management; fine arts; health and physical education/fitness; mathematics; psychology; sociology

IOWA WESTERN COMMUNITY COLLEGE

Council Bluffs, Iowa
iwcc.cc.ia.us

Iowa Western Community College, founded in 1966, is a district-supported, two-year college. It is accredited by the North Central Association of Colleges and Schools. It first offered distance learning courses in 1983. In 1999–2000, it offered 30 courses at a distance. In fall 1999, there were 150 students enrolled in distance learning courses.

Course delivery sites Courses are delivered to your home, your workplace, high schools, 4 off-campus centers in Atlantic, Clarinda, Harlan, Shenandoah.

Media Courses are delivered via television, videotapes, interactive television, e-mail. Students and teachers may meet in person or interact via mail, telephone, fax, e-mail, World Wide Web. The following equipment may be required: Internet access, e-mail.

Restrictions Courses are available to students in the state of Iowa or within the Midwest only. Enrollment is restricted to individuals meeting certain criteria.

Services Distance learners have access to library services, academic advising, career placement assistance at a distance.

Credit-earning options Students may transfer credits from another institution or may earn credits through examinations, portfolio assessment, military training.

Typical costs Tuition of $67 per credit hour plus mandatory fees of $8 per credit hour for in-state residents. Tuition of $100.50 per credit hour plus mandatory fees of $8 per credit hour for out-of-state residents. Financial aid is available to distance learners.

Registration Students may register by mail, telephone, in person.

Contact Dr. Bob Franzese, Dean, Iowa Western Community College, School of Arts and Sciences, Box 4-C, Council Bluffs, IA 51502. *Telephone:* 712-325-3257. *Fax:* 712-325-3717. *E-mail:* bfranzes@iwcc.cc.ia.us.

DEGREES AND AWARDS

AA General Studies (service area differs from that of the overall institution; some on-campus requirements)

COURSE SUBJECT AREAS OFFERED OUTSIDE OF DEGREE PROGRAMS

Undergraduate: Accounting; biology; chemistry; English language and literature; fine arts; geology; history; law and legal studies; liberal arts, general studies, and humanities; mathematics; microbiology; nursing; philosophy and religion; political science; public health; social work; sociology

ISIM UNIVERSITY

Denver, Colorado
www.isimu.edu

ISIM University, founded in 1987, is an independent, nonprofit, graduate institution. It is accredited by the Distance Education and Training Council. It first offered distance learning courses in 1992. In 1999–2000, it offered 22 courses at a distance. In fall 1999, there were 100 students enrolled in distance learning courses.

Course delivery sites Courses are delivered to your home, your workplace, military bases.

Media Courses are delivered via computer software, World Wide Web, e-mail, print. Students and teachers may interact via mail, telephone, fax, e-mail, World Wide Web. The following equipment may be required: computer, modem, Internet access, e-mail.

Restrictions Programs are available worldwide. Enrollment is open to anyone.

Services Distance learners have access to e-mail services, academic advising at a distance.

Credit-earning options Students may transfer credits from another institution or may earn credits through examinations, portfolio assessment.

Typical costs Tuition of $415 per credit.

Registration Students may register by mail, fax, e-mail.

Contact Robin Thompson, Admissions Representative, ISIM University, 501 South Cherry Street, Suite 350, Denver, CO 80246. *Telephone:* 303-333-4224. *Fax:* 303-336-1144. *E-mail:* admissions@isimu.edu.

DEGREES AND AWARDS

MBA Business Administration
MS Information Management

COURSE SUBJECT AREAS OFFERED OUTSIDE OF DEGREE PROGRAMS

Graduate: Accounting; business; business administration and management; computer and information sciences; human resources management

IVY TECH STATE COLLEGE–CENTRAL INDIANA

Indianapolis, Indiana
www.ivy.tec.in.us/indianapolis/disted/index.html

Ivy Tech State College–Central Indiana, founded in 1963, is a state-supported, two-year college. It is accredited by the North Central Association of Colleges and Schools. In 1999–2000, it offered 12 courses at a distance. In fall 1999, there were 96 students enrolled in distance learning courses.

Course delivery sites Courses are delivered to your home, your workplace, high schools.

Media Courses are delivered via television, videoconferencing, World Wide Web, e-mail. Students and teachers may meet in person or interact via videoconferencing, mail, telephone, fax, e-mail, World Wide Web. The following equipment may be required: computer, Internet access, e-mail.

Restrictions Programs are available to local area students. Enrollment is open to anyone.

Services Distance learners have access to library services, academic advising, career placement assistance at a distance.

Credit-earning options Students may transfer credits from another institution.

Typical costs Tuition of $66.20 per credit hour. Financial aid is available to distance learners.

Registration Students may register by mail, fax, telephone, in person.

Contact Susan Mannan, Distance Education Coordinator, Ivy Tech State College–Central Indiana, PO Box 1763, Indianapolis, IN 46206. *Telephone:* 317-921-4916. *Fax:* 317-921-4355. *E-mail:* smannan@ivy.tec.in.us.

DEGREES AND AWARDS

Undergraduate Certificate(s) Child Development
AAS Child Development

COURSE SUBJECT AREAS OFFERED OUTSIDE OF DEGREE PROGRAMS

Undergraduate: Administrative and secretarial services; fire science; health professions and related sciences; hospitality services management; law and legal studies

See full description on page 540.

IVY TECH STATE COLLEGE–COLUMBUS

Columbus, Indiana
www.ivy.tec.in.us/columbus/disted.html

Ivy Tech State College–Columbus, founded in 1963, is a state-supported, two-year college. It is accredited by the North Central Association of Colleges and Schools. In 1999–2000, it offered 17 courses at a distance. In fall 1999, there were 109 students enrolled in distance learning courses.

Course delivery sites Courses are delivered to your home, your workplace, high schools.

Media Courses are delivered via television, videoconferencing, World Wide Web, e-mail. Students and teachers may meet in person or interact via videoconferencing, audioconferencing, mail, telephone, fax, e-mail. The following equipment may be required: computer, Internet access, e-mail.

Restrictions Programs are available to local area students. Enrollment is open to anyone.

Services Distance learners have access to library services, academic advising, career placement assistance at a distance.

Credit-earning options Students may transfer credits from another institution.

Typical costs Tuition of $66.20 per credit hour. Financial aid is available to distance learners.

Registration Students may register by mail, fax, telephone, in person.

Contact Karen Nissen, Manager of Learning Resource Center, Ivy Tech State College–Columbus, 4475 Central Avenue, Columbus, IN 47203-1868. *Telephone:* 812-372-9925. *Fax:* 812-372-0311. *E-mail:* knissen@ivy.tec.in.us.

DEGREES AND AWARDS

Undergraduate Certificate(s) Child Development
AAS Child Development

COURSE SUBJECT AREAS OFFERED OUTSIDE OF DEGREE PROGRAMS

Undergraduate: Accounting; administrative and secretarial services; business administration and management; computer and information sciences; design; mathematics

See full description on page 540.

IVY TECH STATE COLLEGE–EASTCENTRAL

Muncie, Indiana
www.ivy.tec.in.us/muncie

Ivy Tech State College–Eastcentral, founded in 1968, is a state-supported, two-year college. It is accredited by the North Central Association of Colleges and Schools. In 1999–2000, it offered 36 courses at a distance. In fall 1999, there were 239 students enrolled in distance learning courses.

Course delivery sites Courses are delivered to your home, your workplace, high schools.

Media Courses are delivered via television, videoconferencing, World Wide Web, e-mail. Students and teachers may meet in person or interact via videoconferencing, mail, telephone, fax, e-mail, World Wide Web. The following equipment may be required: computer, Internet access, e-mail.

Restrictions Programs are available to local area students. Enrollment is open to anyone.

Services Distance learners have access to library services, academic advising, career placement assistance at a distance.

Credit-earning options Students may transfer credits from another institution.

Typical costs Tuition of $66.20 per credit hour. Financial aid is available to distance learners.

Registration Students may register by mail, fax, telephone, in person.

Contact Beth Dewees, Learning Resource Center Coordinator, Ivy Tech State College–Eastcentral, 4301 South Cowan Road, Muncie, IN 47302-9448. *Telephone:* 765-289-2291. *Fax:* 765-289-2291. *E-mail:* bdewees@ivy.tec.in.us.

DEGREES AND AWARDS

Undergraduate Certificate(s) Child Development
AAS Child Development

COURSE SUBJECT AREAS OFFERED OUTSIDE OF DEGREE PROGRAMS

Undergraduate: Administrative and secretarial services; art history and criticism; business administration and management; child care and development; computer and information sciences; design; electronics; health professions and related sciences; law and legal studies; marketing; mathematics; philosophy and religion

See full description on page 540.

IVY TECH STATE COLLEGE–KOKOMO

Kokomo, Indiana
www.ivy.tec.in.us/Kokomo/Distance_Ed/distance_ed.htm

Ivy Tech State College–Kokomo, founded in 1968, is a state-supported, two-year college. It is accredited by the North Central Association of Colleges and Schools. In 1999–2000, it offered 10 courses at a distance. In fall 1999, there were 93 students enrolled in distance learning courses.

Course delivery sites Courses are delivered to your home, your workplace, high schools.

Media Courses are delivered via television, videoconferencing, World Wide Web, e-mail. Students and teachers may meet in person or interact via videoconferencing, mail, telephone, fax, e-mail, World Wide Web. The following equipment may be required: computer, Internet access, e-mail.

Restrictions Programs are available to local area students. Enrollment is open to anyone.

Services Distance learners have access to library services, academic advising, career placement assistance at a distance.

Credit-earning options Students may transfer credits from another institution.

Typical costs Tuition of $66.20 per credit hour. Financial aid is available to distance learners.

Registration Students may register by mail, fax, telephone, in person.

Contact Kathryn Ross, Distance Education Coordinator, Ivy Tech State College–Kokomo, 1815 East Morgan Street, Kokomo, IN 46903-1373. *Telephone:* 765-459-0561. *Fax:* 765-454-5111. *E-mail:* kross@ivy.tec.in.us.

DEGREES AND AWARDS

Undergraduate Certificate(s) Child Development
AAS Child Development

COURSE SUBJECT AREAS OFFERED OUTSIDE OF DEGREE PROGRAMS

Undergraduate: Accounting; American (U.S.) history; computer and information sciences; engineering-related technologies; English composition

See full description on page 540.

IVY TECH STATE COLLEGE–NORTH CENTRAL

South Bend, Indiana

Instructional Technology
www.ivy.tec.in.us/SouthBend/distance_ed/DE.HTM

Ivy Tech State College–North Central, founded in 1968, is a state-supported, two-year college. It is accredited by the North Central Association of Colleges and Schools. It first offered distance learning courses in 1989. In 1999–2000, it offered 25 courses at a distance. In fall 1999, there were 286 students enrolled in distance learning courses.
Course delivery sites Courses are delivered to your home, your workplace, high schools, Indiana State University (Terre Haute).
Media Courses are delivered via television, videotapes, videoconferencing, computer conferencing, World Wide Web, e-mail. Students and teachers may interact via videoconferencing, audioconferencing, mail, telephone, fax, e-mail, World Wide Web. The following equipment may be required: computer, Internet access.
Restrictions Programs are available to in-state students only. Enrollment is open to anyone.
Services Distance learners have access to library services, the campus computer network, e-mail services, academic advising, career placement assistance, bookstore at a distance.
Credit-earning options Students may transfer credits from another institution or may earn credits through examinations, portfolio assessment, military training.
Typical costs Tuition of $66.20 per credit hour. Costs may vary. Financial aid is available to distance learners.
Registration Students may register by mail, fax, telephone, in person.
Contact Elaine Bennington, Instructional Technology Manager, Ivy Tech State College–North Central, 1534 West Sample Street, South Bend, IN 46619. *Telephone:* 219-289-7001 Ext. 334. *Fax:* 219-236-7178. *E-mail:* ebenning@ivy.tec.in.us.

DEGREES AND AWARDS

Undergraduate Certificate(s) Accounting (some on-campus requirements), Child Development, Design Technology (CAD) (some on-campus requirements), Paralegal Studies (some on-campus requirements), Pharmacy Technician (some on-campus requirements)
AAS Child Development

COURSE SUBJECT AREAS OFFERED OUTSIDE OF DEGREE PROGRAMS

Undergraduate: Accounting; administrative and secretarial services; advertising; biology; business administration and management; economics; engineering-related technologies; English composition; health professions and related sciences; hospitality services management; insurance; law and legal studies; nursing; psychology; sociology

See full description on page 540.

IVY TECH STATE COLLEGE–NORTHWEST

Gary, Indiana
gar.ivy.tec.in.us/Online_Classes/online_classes.html

Ivy Tech State College–Northwest, founded in 1963, is a state-supported, two-year college. It is accredited by the North Central Association of Colleges and Schools. In 1999–2000, it offered 53 courses at a distance. In fall 1999, there were 85 students enrolled in distance learning courses.
Course delivery sites Courses are delivered to your home, your workplace, high schools.
Media Courses are delivered via television, videoconferencing, World Wide Web, e-mail. Students and teachers may meet in person or interact via videoconferencing, mail, telephone, fax, e-mail, World Wide Web. The following equipment may be required: computer, Internet access, e-mail.
Restrictions Programs are available to local area students. Enrollment is open to anyone.
Services Distance learners have access to library services, academic advising, career placement assistance at a distance.
Credit-earning options Students may transfer credits from another institution.
Typical costs Tuition of $66.20 per credit hour. Financial aid is available to distance learners.
Registration Students may register by mail, fax, telephone, in person.
Contact Francine Conard, Ivy Tech State College–Northwest, 1440 East 35th Avenue, Gary, IN 46409-1499. *Telephone:* 219-981-1111. *Fax:* 219-981-4415. *E-mail:* fconard@ivy.tec.in.us.

DEGREES AND AWARDS

Undergraduate Certificate(s) Child Development
AAS Child Development

COURSE SUBJECT AREAS OFFERED OUTSIDE OF DEGREE PROGRAMS

Undergraduate: Accounting; administrative and secretarial services; business administration and management; computer and information sciences; economics; English composition; environmental science; fire science; health professions and related sciences; hospitality services management; marketing; mathematics; nursing; physical sciences; psychology; sociology

See full description on page 540.

IVY TECH STATE COLLEGE–SOUTHCENTRAL

Sellersburg, Indiana
www.ivy.tec.in.us/sellersburg

Ivy Tech State College–Southcentral, founded in 1968, is a state-supported, two-year college. It is accredited by the North Central Association of Colleges and Schools. In 1999–2000, it offered 7 courses at a distance. In fall 1999, there were 17 students enrolled in distance learning courses.
Course delivery sites Courses are delivered to your home, your workplace, high schools.
Media Courses are delivered via World Wide Web, e-mail. Students and teachers may meet in person or interact via mail, telephone, fax, e-mail, World Wide Web. The following equipment may be required: computer, Internet access, e-mail.
Restrictions Programs are available to local area students. Enrollment is open to anyone.
Services Distance learners have access to library services, academic advising, career placement assistance at a distance.

Credit-earning options Students may transfer credits from another institution.

Typical costs Tuition of $66.20 per credit hour. Financial aid is available to distance learners.

Registration Students may register by mail, fax, telephone, in person.

Contact Cherry Kay Smith, Director of Instructional Technology, Ivy Tech State College–Southcentral, 8204 Highway 311, Sellersburg, IN 47172-1897. *Telephone:* 812-246-3301. *Fax:* 812-246-9905. *E-mail:* csmith@ivy.tec.in.us.

DEGREES AND AWARDS

Undergraduate Certificate(s) Child Development Child Development
AAS Child Development

COURSE SUBJECT AREAS OFFERED OUTSIDE OF DEGREE PROGRAMS

Undergraduate: Business administration and management; electronics; health professions and related sciences

See full description on page 540.

IVY TECH STATE COLLEGE–SOUTHEAST

Madison, Indiana
www.ivy.tec.in.us/Madison/disted.htm

Ivy Tech State College–Southeast, founded in 1963, is a state-supported, two-year college. It is accredited by the North Central Association of Colleges and Schools. In 1999–2000, it offered 6 courses at a distance. In fall 1999, there were 52 students enrolled in distance learning courses.

Course delivery sites Courses are delivered to your home, your workplace, high schools.

Media Courses are delivered via television, videoconferencing, World Wide Web, e-mail. Students and teachers may meet in person or interact via videoconferencing, mail, telephone, fax, e-mail, World Wide Web. The following equipment may be required: computer, Internet access, e-mail.

Restrictions Programs are available to local area students. Enrollment is open to anyone.

Services Distance learners have access to library services, academic advising, career placement assistance at a distance.

Credit-earning options Students may transfer credits from another institution.

Typical costs Tuition of $66.20 per credit hour. Financial aid is available to distance learners.

Registration Students may register by mail, fax, telephone, in person.

Contact Margaret Seifert, Coordinator of Libraries and Distance Education, Ivy Tech State College–Southeast, 590 Ivy Tech Drive, Madison, IN 47250-1881. *Telephone:* 800-403-2190 Ext. 4106. *Fax:* 812-265-2579. *E-mail:* mseifert@ivy.tec.in.us.

DEGREES AND AWARDS

Undergraduate Certificate(s) Child Development
AAS Child Development

COURSE SUBJECT AREAS OFFERED OUTSIDE OF DEGREE PROGRAMS

Undergraduate: Administrative and secretarial services; anatomy; business administration and management

See full description on page 540.

IVY TECH STATE COLLEGE–SOUTHWEST

Evansville, Indiana
fc1.ivytech12.cc.in.us/

Ivy Tech State College–Southwest, founded in 1963, is a state-supported, two-year college. It is accredited by the North Central Association of Colleges and Schools. In 1999–2000, it offered 19 courses at a distance. In fall 1999, there were 107 students enrolled in distance learning courses.

Course delivery sites Courses are delivered to your home, your workplace, high schools.

Media Courses are delivered via television, videoconferencing, World Wide Web, e-mail. Students and teachers may meet in person or interact via videoconferencing, mail, telephone, fax, e-mail, World Wide Web. The following equipment may be required: computer, Internet access, e-mail.

Restrictions Programs are available to local area students. Enrollment is open to anyone.

Services Distance learners have access to library services, academic advising, career placement assistance at a distance.

Credit-earning options Students may transfer credits from another institution.

Typical costs Tuition of $66.20 per credit hour. Financial aid is available to distance learners.

Registration Students may register by mail, fax, telephone, in person.

Contact Steve Combs, Ivy Tech State College–Southwest, 3501 First Avenue, Evansville, IN 47710. *Telephone:* 812-426-2865. *Fax:* 812-429-9814. *E-mail:* scombs@ivy.tec.in.us.

DEGREES AND AWARDS

Undergraduate Certificate(s) Child Development
AAS Child Development

COURSE SUBJECT AREAS OFFERED OUTSIDE OF DEGREE PROGRAMS

Undergraduate: Accounting; administrative and secretarial services; business administration and management; computer and information sciences; design; health professions and related sciences; mathematics

See full description on page 540.

IVY TECH STATE COLLEGE–WABASH VALLEY

Terre Haute, Indiana
www.ivytech7.cc.in.us/distance-education/

Ivy Tech State College–Wabash Valley, founded in 1966, is a state-supported, two-year college. It is accredited by the North Central Association of Colleges and Schools. It first offered distance learning courses in 1996. In 1999–2000, it offered 80 courses at a distance. In fall 1999, there were 850 students enrolled in distance learning courses.

Course delivery sites Courses are delivered to your home, your workplace, military bases.

Media Courses are delivered via videoconferencing, World Wide Web, e-mail, print. Students and teachers may interact via videoconferencing, mail, e-mail, World Wide Web. The following equipment may be required: computer, modem, Internet access, e-mail.

Restrictions Programs are available worldwide. Enrollment is open to anyone.

Services Distance learners have access to library services, academic advising, tutoring, career placement assistance, bookstore at a distance.

Credit-earning options Students may transfer credits from another institution or may earn credits through examinations, portfolio assessment, military training, business training.
Typical costs Tuition of $66.20 per credit. Financial aid is available to distance learners.
Registration Students may register by mail, e-mail, World Wide Web, in person.
Contact Don Arney, Instructional Affairs Chair, Ivy Tech State College–Wabash Valley, Information and Instructional Technology, 7999 US Highway 41, South, Terre Haute, IN 47802. *Telephone:* 812-299-1121. *Fax:* 812-299-8770. *E-mail:* darney@ivy.tec.in.us.

DEGREES AND AWARDS

AAS Accounting, Drafting and Design Technology
AS Business Management–Hospitality

COURSE SUBJECT AREAS OFFERED OUTSIDE OF DEGREE PROGRAMS

Undergraduate: Accounting; administrative and secretarial services; business; business administration and management; computer and information sciences; design; economics; English composition; health services administration; liberal arts, general studies, and humanities; mathematics; mental health services; physics; social psychology; sociology
See full description on page 540.

IVY TECH STATE COLLEGE–WHITEWATER

Richmond, Indiana
www.ivy.tec.in.us/Richmond/Programs/DistanceEducation

Ivy Tech State College–Whitewater, founded in 1963, is a state-supported, two-year college. It is accredited by the North Central Association of Colleges and Schools. In 1999–2000, it offered 25 courses at a distance. In fall 1999, there were 171 students enrolled in distance learning courses.
Course delivery sites Courses are delivered to your home, your workplace, high schools.
Media Courses are delivered via World Wide Web, e-mail. Students and teachers may meet in person or interact via videoconferencing, mail, telephone, fax, e-mail, World Wide Web. The following equipment may be required: computer, Internet access, e-mail.
Restrictions Programs are available to local area students. Enrollment is open to anyone.
Services Distance learners have access to library services, academic advising, career placement assistance at a distance.
Credit-earning options Students may transfer credits from another institution.
Typical costs Tuition of $66.20 per credit hour. Financial aid is available to distance learners.
Registration Students may register by mail, fax, telephone, in person.
Contact Kara Monroe, Instructional Technology Manager, Ivy Tech State College–Whitewater, 2325 Chester Boulevard, Richmond, IN 47374-1298. *Telephone:* 765-966-2656 Ext. 358. *Fax:* 765-962-8741. *E-mail:* kmonroe@ivy.tec.in.us.

DEGREES AND AWARDS

Undergraduate Certificate(s) Child Development
AAS Child Development

COURSE SUBJECT AREAS OFFERED OUTSIDE OF DEGREE PROGRAMS

Undergraduate: Accounting; American (U.S.) history; business administration and management; child care and development; computer and

information sciences; English composition; health professions and related sciences; mathematics; physical sciences; psychology
See full description on page 540.

JACKSONVILLE STATE UNIVERSITY

Jacksonville, Alabama
Instructional Services Unit
jsucc.jsu.edu/depart/distance

Jacksonville State University, founded in 1883, is a state-supported, comprehensive institution. It is accredited by the Southern Association of Colleges and Schools. It first offered distance learning courses in 1994. In 1999–2000, it offered 20 courses at a distance. In fall 1999, there were 538 students enrolled in distance learning courses.
Course delivery sites Courses are delivered to your home, high schools, Gadsden State Community College (Gadsden), Northeast Alabama Community College (Rainsville), Snead State Community College (Boaz), 7 off-campus centers in Guntersville, Oxford, Pell City, Wintersboro, Cartersville (GA), Rome (GA).
Media Courses are delivered via television, videotapes, videoconferencing, World Wide Web. Students and teachers may meet in person or interact via videoconferencing, mail, telephone, e-mail. The following equipment may be required: television, videocassette player, computer, modem, Internet access, e-mail.
Restrictions Programs are available nationwide. Enrollment is open to anyone.
Services Distance learners have access to library services, the campus computer network, e-mail services at a distance.
Credit-earning options Students may transfer credits from another institution or may earn credits through examinations, portfolio assessment, military training.
Typical costs *Undergraduate:* Tuition of $168 per hour for local area residents. Tuition of $168 per hour for in-state residents. Tuition of $204 per hour for out-of-state residents. *Graduate:* Tuition of $122 per hour for local area residents. Tuition of $122 per hour for in-state residents. Tuition of $244 per hour for out-of-state residents. Costs may vary. Financial aid is available to distance learners.
Registration Students may register by telephone, World Wide Web, in person.
Contact Dr. Franklin L. King, Director, Jacksonville State University, Room 101, Ramona Wood Building, 700 Pelham Road, North, Jacksonville, AL 36285-1602. *Telephone:* 256-782-5616. *Fax:* 256-782-5959. *E-mail:* fking@jsucc.jsu.edu.

DEGREES AND AWARDS

MPA Emergency Management

COURSE SUBJECT AREAS OFFERED OUTSIDE OF DEGREE PROGRAMS

Undergraduate: Anthropology; business administration and management; computer and information sciences; developmental and child psychology; English language and literature; geology; health and physical education/fitness; history; mathematics; political science; sociology; special education
Graduate: Education administration; educational psychology; public administration and services; teacher education
See full description on page 676.

JAMES MADISON UNIVERSITY

Harrisonburg, Virginia

Distance Learning Center, Office of Continuing Education
www.jmu.edu

James Madison University, founded in 1908, is a state-supported, comprehensive institution. It is accredited by the Southern Association of Colleges and Schools. It first offered distance learning courses in 1996. In 1999–2000, it offered 2 courses at a distance. In fall 1999, there were 8 students enrolled in distance learning courses.

Course delivery sites Courses are delivered to your home, your workplace, military bases.

Media Courses are delivered via videoconferencing, World Wide Web, e-mail, print. Students and teachers may meet in person or interact via videoconferencing, mail, telephone, fax, e-mail, World Wide Web. The following equipment may be required: computer, Internet access, e-mail.

Restrictions Programs are available nationwide. Enrollment is restricted to individuals meeting certain criteria.

Services Distance learners have access to library services, e-mail services, academic advising, career placement assistance at a distance.

Credit-earning options Students may transfer credits from another institution or may earn credits through examinations, portfolio assessment, military training, business training.

Typical costs *Undergraduate:* Tuition of $1966 per semester for in-state residents. Tuition of $4766 per semester for out-of-state residents. *Graduate:* Tuition of $135 per credit hour for in-state residents. Tuition of $415 per credit hour for out-of-state residents. Costs may vary. Financial aid is available to distance learners.

Registration Students may register by telephone, World Wide Web, in person.

Contact Instructional Technology Services Coordinator, James Madison University, MSC 2502, Harrisonburg, VA 22807. *Telephone:* 540-568-8115. *Fax:* 540-568-7860. *E-mail:* continuing-ed@jmu.edu.

DEGREES AND AWARDS

Distance programs offered do not lead to a degree or other formal award.

COURSE SUBJECT AREAS OFFERED OUTSIDE OF DEGREE PROGRAMS

Undergraduate: Adult education; communications; philosophy and religion
Graduate: Communications
See full description on page 676.

JAMES SPRUNT COMMUNITY COLLEGE

Kenansville, North Carolina

James Sprunt Community College Distance Learning
www.sprunt.com

James Sprunt Community College, founded in 1964, is a state-supported, two-year college. It is accredited by the Southern Association of Colleges and Schools. In 1999–2000, it offered 8 courses at a distance. In fall 1999, there were 107 students enrolled in distance learning courses.

Course delivery sites Courses are delivered to your home, your workplace, high schools, Any Community College in North Carolina.

Media Courses are delivered via television, videotapes, videoconferencing, interactive television, audiotapes, computer software, World Wide Web, e-mail, print. Students and teachers may meet in person or interact via videoconferencing, audioconferencing, mail, telephone, fax, e-mail, World Wide Web. The following equipment may be required: television, videocassette player, computer, modem, Internet access, e-mail.

Restrictions Programs are available nationwide. Enrollment is restricted to individuals meeting certain criteria.

Services Distance learners have access to library services, academic advising, bookstore at a distance.

Credit-earning options Students may transfer credits from another institution or may earn credits through examinations.

Typical costs *Undergraduate:* Tuition of $481 per semester plus mandatory fees of $553 per semester for in-state residents. Tuition of $4116 per semester plus mandatory fees of $553 per semester for out-of-state residents. *Graduate:* Tuition of $459 per semester plus mandatory fees of $508 per semester for in-state residents. Tuition of $4094 per semester plus mandatory fees of $508 per semester for out-of-state residents. Undergraduate in-state tuition for the associate degree is $280 per semester, out-of-state tuition is $2282. Mandatory fees are $14 per semester. Costs may vary. Financial aid is available to distance learners.

Registration Students may register by mail, World Wide Web, in person.

Contact Heather Lanier, Distance Learning Coordinator, James Sprunt Community College, PO Box 398, Kenansville, NC 28349. *Telephone:* 910-296-1334. *Fax:* 910-296-0731. *E-mail:* hlanier@jscc.cc.nc.us.

DEGREES AND AWARDS

Distance programs offered do not lead to a degree or other formal award.

COURSE SUBJECT AREAS OFFERED OUTSIDE OF DEGREE PROGRAMS

Undergraduate: American literature; animal sciences; history; nursing
Graduate: Education

JAMESTOWN COMMUNITY COLLEGE

Jamestown, New York

Distance Education
www.sunyjcc.edu/

Jamestown Community College, founded in 1950, is a state and locally supported, two-year college. It is accredited by the Middle States Association of Colleges and Schools. It first offered distance learning courses in 1995. In 1999–2000, it offered 13 courses at a distance. In fall 1999, there were 145 students enrolled in distance learning courses.

Course delivery sites Courses are delivered to your home, your workplace, high schools, 3 off-campus centers in Dunkirk, Olean, Warren (PA).

Media Courses are delivered via videoconferencing, World Wide Web. Students and teachers may interact via videoconferencing, mail, telephone, fax, e-mail, World Wide Web. The following equipment may be required: computer, Internet access.

Restrictions Programs are available worldwide. Enrollment is open to anyone.

Services Distance learners have access to library services, the campus computer network, e-mail services at a distance.

Typical costs Tuition of $88 per credit hour for in-state residents. Tuition of $154 per credit hour for out-of-state residents. *Noncredit courses:* $40 per course. Financial aid is available to distance learners.

Registration Students may register by mail, in person.

Contact Admissions Office, Jamestown Community College, 525 Falconer Street, Jamestown, NY 14702-0020. *Telephone:* 716-665-5220 Ext. 239. *Fax:* 716-664-9592.

DEGREES AND AWARDS

Distance programs offered do not lead to a degree or other formal award.

COURSE SUBJECT AREAS OFFERED OUTSIDE OF DEGREE PROGRAMS

Undergraduate: Accounting; astronomy and astrophysics; business administration and management; chemistry; computer and information sciences; database management; fine arts; human resources management; music; philosophy and religion; physics; sociology

JEFFERSON COMMUNITY COLLEGE

Watertown, New York

Division of Continuing Education

Jefferson Community College, founded in 1961, is a state and locally supported, two-year college. It is accredited by the Middle States Association of Colleges and Schools. It first offered distance learning courses in 1995. In 1999–2000, it offered 10 courses at a distance. In fall 1999, there were 100 students enrolled in distance learning courses.

Course delivery sites Courses are delivered to your home, high schools.

Media Courses are delivered via television, videoconferencing. Students and teachers may meet in person or interact via videoconferencing, mail, telephone, fax, e-mail. The following equipment may be required: television, videocassette player.

Restrictions Programs are available to local area students. Enrollment is open to anyone.

Services Distance learners have access to library services, e-mail services, academic advising, tutoring at a distance.

Credit-earning options Students may transfer credits from another institution or may earn credits through examinations, military training.

Typical costs Tuition of $91 per credit hour. Costs may vary. Financial aid is available to distance learners.

Registration Students may register by mail, in person.

Contact Barry Jennison, Associate Dean for Continuing Education, Jefferson Community College, Coffeen Street, Watertown, NY 13601. *Telephone:* 315-786-2238. *Fax:* 315-786-2391.

DEGREES AND AWARDS

Distance programs offered do not lead to a degree or other formal award.

COURSE SUBJECT AREAS OFFERED OUTSIDE OF DEGREE PROGRAMS

Undergraduate: Business administration and management; calculus; child care and development; computer programming; economics; political science; psychology; sociology

Noncredit: Human resources management

See full description on page 556.

JEFFERSON STATE COMMUNITY COLLEGE

Birmingham, Alabama

Instructional Technology Services

www.jscc.cc.al.us

Jefferson State Community College, founded in 1965, is a state-supported, two-year college. It is accredited by the Southern Association of Colleges and Schools. It first offered distance learning courses in 1978.

Contact Jefferson State Community College, 2601 Carson Road, Birmingham, AL 35215-3098. *Telephone:* 205-853-1200. *Fax:* 205-856-8547.

See full description on page 676.

JOHNS HOPKINS UNIVERSITY

Baltimore, Maryland

Hopkins ITS

www.jhu.edu/www/library

Johns Hopkins University, founded in 1876, is an independent, nonprofit university. It is accredited by the Middle States Association of Colleges and Schools. It first offered distance learning courses in 1998. In 1999–2000, it offered 13 courses at a distance. In fall 1999, there were 300 students enrolled in distance learning courses.

Course delivery sites Courses are delivered to your home, your workplace, 5 off-campus centers in Baltimore, Columbia, Laurel, Rockville, St. Mary's County.

Media Courses are delivered via videotapes, videoconferencing, interactive television, computer software, CD-ROM, computer conferencing, World Wide Web, e-mail, print. Students and teachers may meet in person or interact via videoconferencing, mail, telephone, fax, e-mail, interactive television, World Wide Web. The following equipment may be required: computer, modem, Internet access, e-mail.

Restrictions Geographical restrictions are dependent upon the area of study. Enrollment is open to anyone.

Services Distance learners have access to library services, the campus computer network, e-mail services, academic advising, tutoring, bookstore at a distance.

Credit-earning options Students may transfer credits from another institution or may earn credits through examinations.

Typical costs *Undergraduate:* Tuition of $473 per credit. *Graduate:* Tuition of $473 per credit. Costs may vary. Financial aid is available to distance learners.

Registration Students may register by mail, fax, telephone, e-mail, in person.

Contact Lee Watkins, Director, Johns Hopkins University. *Telephone:* 410-516-5418. *Fax:* 410-516-4575. *E-mail:* lee.watkins@jhu.edu.

eCollege.com *www.ecollege.com/scholarships*

DEGREES AND AWARDS

Graduate Certificate(s) Healthcare Services Administration (service area differs from that of the overall institution)

MPH Health (service area differs from that of the overall institution; some on-campus requirements), Public Health (service area differs from that of the overall institution; some on-campus requirements)

COURSE SUBJECT AREAS OFFERED OUTSIDE OF DEGREE PROGRAMS

Graduate: Business administration and management; community health services; computer and information sciences; electrical engineering; engineering; environmental engineering; environmental health; health professions and related sciences; health services administration; information sciences and systems; mechanical engineering; public health; statistics

JOHNSON BIBLE COLLEGE

Knoxville, Tennessee
Distance Learning Office

Johnson Bible College, founded in 1893, is an independent, religious, comprehensive institution affiliated with the Christian Churches and Churches of Christ. It is accredited by the Accrediting Association of Bible Colleges, Southern Association of Colleges and Schools. It first offered distance learning courses in 1988. In 1999–2000, it offered 16 courses at a distance. In fall 1999, there were 50 students enrolled in distance learning courses.

Course delivery sites Courses are delivered to your home.

Media Courses are delivered via videotapes, audiotapes, print. Students and teachers may interact via mail, telephone, fax, e-mail. The following equipment may be required: television, videocassette player.

Restrictions Programs are available worldwide. Enrollment is open to anyone.

Services Distance learners have access to library services, academic advising at a distance.

Credit-earning options Students may transfer credits from another institution.

Typical costs Tuition of $150 per credit hour.

Registration Students may register by mail, fax, telephone, e-mail, in person.

Contact John C. Ketchen, Director of Distance Learning, Johnson Bible College, Box 777031, Knoxville, TN 37998. *Telephone:* 865-251-2254. *Fax:* 865-251-2285. *E-mail:* jketchen@jbc.edu.

DEGREES AND AWARDS

MA New Testament (some on-campus requirements)

COURSE SUBJECT AREAS OFFERED OUTSIDE OF DEGREE PROGRAMS

Graduate: Theological studies

JOHNSON COUNTY COMMUNITY COLLEGE

Overland Park, Kansas

Johnson County Community College, founded in 1967, is a state and locally supported, two-year college. It is accredited by the North Central Association of Colleges and Schools. It first offered distance learning courses in 1975. In 1999–2000, it offered 72 courses at a distance. In fall 1999, there were 1,400 students enrolled in distance learning courses.

Course delivery sites Courses are delivered to your home.

Media Courses are delivered via television, videotapes, videoconferencing, interactive television, CD-ROM, computer conferencing, World Wide Web, e-mail, print. Students and teachers may meet in person or interact via videoconferencing, mail, telephone, fax, e-mail, interactive television, World Wide Web. The following equipment may be required: television, videocassette player, computer, modem, Internet access, e-mail.

Restrictions Programs are available worldwide. Enrollment is open to anyone.

Services Distance learners have access to library services, the campus computer network, e-mail services at a distance.

Credit-earning options Students may transfer credits from another institution or may earn credits through examinations, portfolio assessment, military training.

Typical costs Tuition of $48 per credit hour for local area residents. Tuition of $53 per credit hour for in-state residents. Tuition of $124 per credit hour for out-of-state residents. Financial aid is available to distance learners.

Registration Students may register by telephone, World Wide Web, in person.

Contact Mel Cunningham, Associate Dean of Instruction, Johnson County Community College, Library, 12345 College Boulevard, Overland Park, KS 66210. *Telephone:* 913-469-8500 Ext. 3882. *Fax:* 913-469-4417. *E-mail:* mcunning@johnco.cc.ks.us.

DEGREES AND AWARDS

AA Arts and Humanities
AGS General Studies

COURSE SUBJECT AREAS OFFERED OUTSIDE OF DEGREE PROGRAMS

Undergraduate: Accounting; American (U.S.) history; anthropology; astronomy and astrophysics; biology; business; chemistry; computer and information sciences; computer programming; criminal justice; database management; economics; engineering-related technologies; English composition; environmental science; geology; health and physical education/fitness; law and legal studies; liberal arts, general studies, and humanities; library and information studies; marketing; mathematics; oceanography; paralegal/legal assistant; philosophy and religion; psychology; sociology

JOHNSON STATE COLLEGE

Johnson, Vermont
External Degree Program
online.jsc.vsc.edu

Johnson State College, founded in 1828, is a state-supported, comprehensive institution. It is accredited by the New England Association of Schools and Colleges. In 1999–2000, it offered 10 courses at a distance. In fall 1999, there were 50 students enrolled in distance learning courses.

Course delivery sites Courses are delivered to your home, your workplace, 12 off-campus centers.

Media Courses are delivered via interactive television, audiotapes, computer conferencing, World Wide Web, e-mail, print. Students and teachers may interact via mail, telephone, fax, e-mail, interactive television, World Wide Web. The following equipment may be required: computer, modem, Internet access, e-mail.

Restrictions Programs are available mainly statewide. Enrollment is open to anyone.

Services Distance learners have access to library services, academic advising, bookstore at a distance.

Credit-earning options Students may transfer credits from another institution or may earn credits through portfolio assessment, military training, business training.

Typical costs Tuition of $171 per credit for in-state residents. Tuition of $401 per credit for out-of-state residents. There is a $5 continuing education fee per 3 credits. Financial aid is available to distance learners.

Registration Students may register by mail, fax, telephone, e-mail, in person.

Contact External Degree Office, Johnson State College, Johnson, VT 05656. *Telephone:* 802-635-1290. *Fax:* 802-635-1381. *E-mail:* osgoodr@badger.jsc.vsc.edu.

DEGREES AND AWARDS

Distance programs offered do not lead to a degree or other formal award.

COURSE SUBJECT AREAS OFFERED OUTSIDE OF DEGREE PROGRAMS

Undergraduate: American (U.S.) history; American literature; English literature; European history; finance; information sciences and systems; liberal arts, general studies, and humanities; marketing

JOHN WOOD COMMUNITY COLLEGE

Quincy, Illinois
Instructional Technology and Telecommunications
www.jwcc.edu

John Wood Community College, founded in 1974, is a district-supported, two-year college. It is accredited by the North Central Association of Colleges and Schools. It first offered distance learning courses in 1987. In 1999–2000, it offered 40 courses at a distance. In fall 1999, there were 200 students enrolled in distance learning courses.

Course delivery sites Courses are delivered to high schools, Spoon River College (Canton), 3 off-campus centers in Mount Sterling, Perry, Pittsfield.

Media Courses are delivered via videotapes, videoconferencing, audiotapes, computer software, CD-ROM, World Wide Web, print. Students and teachers may interact via videoconferencing, telephone, fax, e-mail.

Restrictions Programs are available regionally. Enrollment is restricted to individuals meeting certain criteria.

Services Distance learners have access to library services, academic advising, tutoring, career placement assistance, bookstore at a distance.

Credit-earning options Students may transfer credits from another institution or may earn credits through examinations, portfolio assessment, military training.

Typical costs Tuition of $52 per credit hour. *Noncredit courses:* $20 per course. Financial aid is available to distance learners.

Registration Students may register by mail, telephone, in person.

Contact Mark McNett, Admissions, John Wood Community College, 150 South 48th Street, Quincy, IL 62301. *Telephone:* 217-224-6500. *Fax:* 217-224-4339. *E-mail:* mcnett@jwcc.edu.

DEGREES AND AWARDS

Distance programs offered do not lead to a degree or other formal award.

COURSE SUBJECT AREAS OFFERED OUTSIDE OF DEGREE PROGRAMS

Undergraduate: Abnormal psychology; American (U.S.) history; American literature; anatomy; archaeology; art history and criticism; astronomy and astrophysics; biological and life sciences; business administration and management; business law; child care and development; corrections; criminal justice; developmental and child psychology; economics; education administration; educational psychology; English literature; ethics; European languages and literatures; industrial psychology; instructional media; liberal arts, general studies, and humanities; mathematics; music; political science; religious studies; social psychology; social sciences; sociology; teacher education

Noncredit: Insurance

See full description on page 708.

JONES INTERNATIONAL UNIVERSITY

Englewood, Colorado
www.jonesinternational.edu

Jones International University, founded in 1995, is an independent, nonprofit, upper-level institution. It is accredited by the North Central Association of Colleges and Schools. It first offered distance learning courses in 1995. In 1999–2000, it offered 35 courses at a distance.

Course delivery sites Courses are delivered to your home, your workplace, military bases.

Media Courses are delivered via television, videotapes, audiotapes, World Wide Web, e-mail. Students and teachers may interact via mail, telephone, fax, e-mail, World Wide Web. The following equipment may be required: computer, modem, Internet access, e-mail.

Restrictions Programs are available worldwide. Enrollment is open to anyone.

Services Distance learners have access to library services, the campus computer network, e-mail services, academic advising, bookstore at a distance.

Credit-earning options Students may transfer credits from another institution or may earn credits through examinations, portfolio assessment.

Typical costs *Undergraduate:* Tuition of $600 per course plus mandatory fees of $25 per course. *Graduate:* Tuition of $725 per course plus mandatory fees of $25 per course.

Registration Students may register by mail, fax, telephone, e-mail, World Wide Web, in person.

Contact Student Recruitment Center, Jones International University, 9697 East Mineral Avenue, Englewood, CO 80112. *Telephone:* 800-811-5663. *Fax:* 303-784-8547. *E-mail:* info@international.edu.

DEGREES AND AWARDS

BA Business Communication
MA Business Communication
MBA Business Administration

COURSE SUBJECT AREAS OFFERED OUTSIDE OF DEGREE PROGRAMS

Undergraduate: Business communications
Graduate: Business administration and management; business communications

See full description on page 548.

J. SARGEANT REYNOLDS COMMUNITY COLLEGE

Richmond, Virginia
Division of Instructional Technologies and Distance Education
www.jsr.cc.va.us/cpd/cpd_09.htm

J. Sargeant Reynolds Community College, founded in 1972, is a state-supported, two-year college. It is accredited by the Southern Association of Colleges and Schools. It first offered distance learning courses in 1982.

Contact J. Sargeant Reynolds Community College, PO Box 85622, Richmond, VA 23285-5622. *Telephone:* 804-371-3000. *Fax:* 804-371-3650.

See full description on page 676.

JUDSON COLLEGE

Elgin, Illinois
Division of Continuing Education
www.judsononline.org

Judson College, founded in 1963, is an independent, religious, four-year college. It is accredited by the North Central Association of Colleges and Schools. In 1999–2000, it offered 23 courses at a distance. In fall 1999, there were 80 students enrolled in distance learning courses.

Course delivery sites Courses are delivered to your home, your workplace, military bases, high schools.

Media Courses are delivered via videoconferencing, interactive television, computer software, CD-ROM, World Wide Web. Students and teachers may meet in person or interact via videoconferencing, mail, telephone, fax, e-mail, interactive television, World Wide Web. The following equipment may be required: computer, modem, Internet access, e-mail.

Restrictions Programs are available worldwide. Enrollment is restricted to individuals meeting certain criteria.

Services Distance learners have access to library services, academic advising, bookstore at a distance.

Credit-earning options Students may transfer credits from another institution or may earn credits through examinations, portfolio assessment.

Typical costs Tuition of $250 per credit. Financial aid is available to distance learners.

Registration Students may register by mail, fax, telephone, in person.

Contact Sherri Deck, Customized Learning/Online Advisor, Judson College, 1151 North State Street, Elgin, IL 60123. *Telephone:* 847-695-2500 Ext. 2227. *Fax:* 847-695-4880. *E-mail:* sdeck@judson-il.edu.

DEGREES AND AWARDS

BA Human Resource Management, Human Services, Management and Leadership, Management Criminal Justice, Management Information Systems

COURSE SUBJECT AREAS OFFERED OUTSIDE OF DEGREE PROGRAMS

Undergraduate: Algebra; astronomy and astrophysics; Bible studies; calculus; computer and information sciences; database management; ecology; English language and literature; mathematics; technical writing; theological studies

JUDSON COLLEGE

Marion, Alabama

Adult Studies Program

Judson College, founded in 1838, is an independent, religious, four-year college. It is accredited by the Southern Association of Colleges and Schools. It first offered distance learning courses in 1976. In 1999–2000, it offered 30 courses at a distance. In fall 1999, there were 65 students enrolled in distance learning courses.

Course delivery sites Courses are delivered to your home.

Media Courses are delivered via videotapes, audiotapes, computer software, CD-ROM, World Wide Web, e-mail, print. Students and teachers may meet in person or interact via mail, telephone, fax, e-mail, World Wide Web. The following equipment may be required: television, videocassette player, computer, modem, Internet access, e-mail.

Restrictions Programs are available nationwide. Enrollment is restricted to individuals meeting certain criteria.

Services Distance learners have access to library services, the campus computer network, e-mail services, academic advising, career placement assistance, bookstore at a distance.

Credit-earning options Students may transfer credits from another institution or may earn credits through examinations, portfolio assessment, military training, business training.

Typical costs Tuition of $216 per semester hour. Financial aid is available to distance learners.

Registration Students may register by mail, fax, in person.

Contact W. Mark Tew, Vice President, Judson College. *Telephone:* 800-447-9472 Ext. 169. *Fax:* 334-683-5158. *E-mail:* adultstudies@future.judson.edu.

DEGREES AND AWARDS

BA Business, Criminal Justice, English, History, Ministry Studies, Music (certain restrictions apply), Psychology, Religious Studies, Technical Communications and Journalism
BMin Ministry Studies
BS Business, Criminal Justice, Psychology

COURSE SUBJECT AREAS OFFERED OUTSIDE OF DEGREE PROGRAMS

Undergraduate: Biochemistry; biology; business; computer and information sciences; creative writing; educational psychology; English composition; English language and literature; fine arts; history; journalism; music; philosophy and religion; political science; psychology; sociology; technical writing; theological studies; women's studies

See full description on page 550.

KANSAS CITY KANSAS COMMUNITY COLLEGE

Kansas City, Kansas

Distance Education
www.kckcc.cc.ks.us

Kansas City Kansas Community College, founded in 1923, is a state and locally supported, two-year college. It is accredited by the North Central Association of Colleges and Schools. In 1999–2000, it offered 79 courses at a distance. In fall 1999, there were 866 students enrolled in distance learning courses.

Course delivery sites Courses are delivered to your home, your workplace, military bases.

Media Courses are delivered via television, videotapes, audiotapes, computer software, CD-ROM, World Wide Web, e-mail, print. Students and teachers may meet in person or interact via videoconferencing, mail, telephone, fax, e-mail, World Wide Web. The following equipment may be required: television, videocassette player, computer, Internet access, e-mail.

Restrictions Programs are available worldwide. Enrollment is open to anyone.

Services Distance learners have access to library services, the campus computer network, e-mail services, academic advising, tutoring, career placement assistance, bookstore at a distance.

Typical costs Tuition of $41 per hour plus mandatory fees of $20 per course for in-state residents. Tuition of $111 per hour plus mandatory fees of $20 per course for out-of-state residents. Financial aid is available to distance learners.

Registration Students may register by mail, fax, telephone, e-mail, World Wide Web, in person.

Contact Lori Trumbo, Dean of Business and Continuing Education, Kansas City Kansas Community College, 7250 State Avenue, Kansas City, KS 66112. *Telephone:* 913-596-9669. *Fax:* 913-596-9663. *E-mail:* ltrumbo@toto.net.

DEGREES AND AWARDS

Distance programs offered do not lead to a degree or other formal award.

COURSE SUBJECT AREAS OFFERED OUTSIDE OF DEGREE PROGRAMS

Undergraduate: Algebra; American (U.S.) history; anthropology; archaeology; business; business communications; chemistry; child care and development; computer and information sciences; economics; English composition; English language and literature; fire science; foods and nutrition studies; health and physical education/fitness; health professions and related sciences; home economics and family studies; human resources management; law and legal studies; liberal arts, general studies, and humanities; marketing; mathematics; philosophy and religion; psychology; recreation and leisure studies; social sciences; sociology; Spanish language and literature; substance abuse counseling

KANSAS STATE UNIVERSITY

Manhattan, Kansas

Division of Continuing Education, Academic Services
www.dce.ksu.edu

Kansas State University, founded in 1863, is a state-supported university. It is accredited by the North Central Association of Colleges and Schools. It first offered distance learning courses in 1919. In 1999–2000, it offered 187 courses at a distance. In fall 1999, there were 1,102 students enrolled in distance learning courses.

Course delivery sites Courses are delivered to your home, your workplace, military bases.

Media Courses are delivered via videotapes, videoconferencing, audiotapes, computer software, CD-ROM, computer conferencing, World Wide Web, e-mail, print. Students and teachers may interact via videoconferencing, audioconferencing, mail, telephone, fax, e-mail, World Wide Web. The following equipment may be required: television, videocassette player, computer, modem, Internet access, e-mail.

Restrictions Programs are available worldwide. Enrollment is restricted to individuals meeting certain criteria.

Services Distance learners have access to library services, the campus computer network, e-mail services, academic advising, career placement assistance, bookstore at a distance.

Credit-earning options Students may transfer credits from another institution or may earn credits through examinations, portfolio assessment, military training.

Typical costs *Undergraduate:* Tuition of $92 per semester hour plus mandatory fees of $8 per course. *Graduate:* Tuition of $135 per semester hour plus mandatory fees of $8 per course. Costs may vary. Financial aid is available to distance learners.

Registration Students may register by mail, fax, telephone, World Wide Web, in person.

Contact Academic Services, College Court Building, Kansas State University, Division of Continuing Education, 218 College Court, Manhattan, KS 66506. *Telephone:* 800-622-2KSU. *Fax:* 785-532-5637. *E-mail:* academic/services@dce.ksu.edu.

DEGREES AND AWARDS

Undergraduate Certificate(s) Food Science

BS Animal Science and Industry (certain restrictions apply; service area differs from that of the overall institution), Dietetics (certain restrictions apply; service area differs from that of the overall institution), Food Science and Industry (certain restrictions apply; service area differs from that of the overall institution), General Business (certain restrictions apply; service area differs from that of the overall institution), Interdisciplinary Social Sciences (certain restrictions apply; service area differs from that of the overall institution)

MS Agribusiness (some on-campus requirements), Chemical Engineering (service area differs from that of the overall institution), Civil Engineering (service area differs from that of the overall institution), Electrical Engineering (service area differs from that of the overall institution), Engineering Management (service area differs from that of the overall institution), Industrial/Organizational Psychology (some on-campus requirements), Software Engineering (service area differs from that of the overall institution)

COURSE SUBJECT AREAS OFFERED OUTSIDE OF DEGREE PROGRAMS

Undergraduate: Accounting; agriculture; American (U.S.) history; animal sciences; area, ethnic, and cultural studies; biochemistry; business administration and management; child care and development; computer and information sciences; film studies; finance; foods and nutrition studies; geology; history; home economics and family studies; horticulture; individual and family development studies; labor relations/studies; management information systems; marketing; music; organizational behavior studies; plant sciences; political science; psychology; sociology; statistics; women's studies

Graduate: Agriculture; animal sciences; area, ethnic, and cultural studies; biochemistry; business administration and management; chemical engineering; child care and development; civil engineering; computer and information sciences; educational psychology; electrical engineering; engineering/industrial management; film studies; foods and nutrition studies; home economics and family studies; horticulture; individual and family development studies; industrial engineering; information sciences and systems; labor relations/studies; plant sciences; psychology; sociology; statistics; women's studies

Noncredit: Accounting; agriculture; American (U.S.) history; animal sciences; area, ethnic, and cultural studies; biochemistry; business administration and management; chemical engineering; child care and development; civil engineering; computer and information sciences; electrical engineering; film studies; finance; foods and nutrition studies; geology; history; home economics and family studies; horticulture; individual and family development studies; industrial engineering; labor relations/studies; management information systems; marketing; music; organizational behavior studies; psychology; sociology; statistics; women's studies

See full descriptions on pages 552 and 592.

KAPIOLANI COMMUNITY COLLEGE

Honolulu, Hawaii

KCC Distance Learning
www.kcc.hawaii.edu/academics/distance/index.htm

Kapiolani Community College, founded in 1957, is a state-supported, two-year college. It is accredited by the Western Association of Schools and Colleges, Inc. In 1999–2000, it offered 20 courses at a distance. In fall 1999, there were 450 students enrolled in distance learning courses.

Course delivery sites Courses are delivered to your home, your workplace, military bases, Hawaii Community College (Hilo).

Media Courses are delivered via television, interactive television, computer software, CD-ROM, computer conferencing, World Wide Web, e-mail, print. Students and teachers may meet in person or interact via audioconferencing, mail, telephone, fax, e-mail, interactive television, World Wide Web. The following equipment may be required: television, computer, modem, Internet access, e-mail.

Restrictions Programs are available to in-state students only. Enrollment is restricted to individuals meeting certain criteria.

Services Distance learners have access to library services, the campus computer network, e-mail services, academic advising, career placement assistance, bookstore at a distance.

Typical costs Tuition of $43 per unit. There is a $12 mandatory activity fee. Financial aid is available to distance learners.

Registration Students may register by mail, in person.

Contact Kelli Goya, Distance Learning Coordinator, Kapiolani Community College, 4303 Diamond Head Road, Honolulu, HI 96816. *Telephone:* 808-734-9711. *Fax:* 808-734-9287. *E-mail:* kgoya@hawaii.edu.

DEGREES AND AWARDS

Undergraduate Certificate(s) Medical Assisting (certain restrictions apply; some on-campus requirements)

COURSE SUBJECT AREAS OFFERED OUTSIDE OF DEGREE PROGRAMS

Undergraduate: Anthropology; biology; earth science; English literature; French language and literature; geography; health professions and related sciences; Japanese language and literature; journalism; liberal arts, general studies, and humanities; psychology; Spanish language and literature

KAPLAN COLLEGE

Boca Raton, Florida

Distance Education
www.kaplancollege.edu

Kaplan College, founded in 1976, is a proprietary, primarily two-year college. It is accredited by the Distance Education and Training Council. In 1999–2000, it offered 100 courses at a distance. In fall 1999, there were 6,500 students enrolled in distance learning courses.

Course delivery sites Courses are delivered to your home, your workplace, military bases.

Media Courses are delivered via World Wide Web, e-mail, print. Students and teachers may interact via mail, telephone, fax, e-mail, World Wide Web.

Restrictions Programs are available worldwide. Enrollment is open to anyone.

Services Distance learners have access to library services, e-mail services, academic advising, tutoring, bookstore at a distance.

Credit-earning options Students may transfer credits from another institution or may earn credits through examinations, portfolio assessment, military training, business training.

Typical costs Tuition varies per program, ranging from $2995 for the complete Paralegal Diploma Program to $19995 for the complete Bachelor of Science in Criminal Justice, including textbooks. Costs may vary.

Registration Students may register by mail, fax, telephone, e-mail, World Wide Web, in person.

Contact Linda Lee, Director of Admissions, Kaplan College, 1801 Clint Moore Road, Suite 215, Boca Raton, FL 33487. *Telephone:* 800-669-2555. *Fax:* 561-988-2223. *E-mail:* info@kaplancollege.com.

DEGREES AND AWARDS

BS Criminal Justice, Paralegal Studies

COURSE SUBJECT AREAS OFFERED OUTSIDE OF DEGREE PROGRAMS

Undergraduate: Criminal justice; law and legal studies; paralegal/legal assistant

Special note
Kaplan College, founded in 1976, is a distance education institution offering diplomas, certificates, and degrees. Kaplan College and Concord University School of Law, the nation's first online law school, comprise the distance education division of Kaplan, Inc., a wholly owned subsidiary of the Washington Post Company. Kaplan College is licensed by the State of Florida Board of Independent Colleges and Universities and Board of Nonpublic Career Education and is accredited by the Accrediting Commission of the Distance Education and Training Council. Kaplan College currently consists of 3 academic divisions—the School of Paralegal Studies, the School of Criminal Justice, and the School of Legal Nurse Consulting. Applicants may request an evaluation of their past academic, life, and work experi-

ence for the purpose of advanced placement in the degree programs. This evaluation is conducted free of charge and based upon its outcome, applicants may be awarded both academic and tuition credit. The all-inclusive tuition, which includes all textbooks and materials for the degree programs prior to any appropriate reductions for transfer credit, is as follows: paralegal specialized associate degree, $7500; legal nurse consultant paralegal specialized associate degree, $7500; Bachelor of Science degree program in paralegal studies, $15,995; criminal justice specialized associate degree, $8995; and Bachelor of Science degree program in criminal justice, $19,995. Kaplan College provides flexible financing options and is approved by the U.S. Department of Defense/DANTES for all programs and by the U.S. Department of Veterans Affairs for several programs. For more information, students should contact Admissions at 800-669-2555 (toll-free), send an e-mail to info@kaplancollege.com, or visit the Web site at http://www.kaplancollege.edu.

KAUAI COMMUNITY COLLEGE

Lihue, Hawaii

University Center-Kauai
www.kauaicc.hawaii.edu

Kauai Community College, founded in 1965, is a state-supported, two-year college. It is accredited by the Western Association of Schools and Colleges, Inc. In 1999–2000, it offered 6 courses at a distance. In fall 1999, there were 35 students enrolled in distance learning courses.

Course delivery sites Courses are delivered to your home, high schools.

Media Courses are delivered via television, interactive television, World Wide Web, e-mail, print. Students and teachers may meet in person or interact via mail, telephone, fax, e-mail, interactive television, World Wide Web. The following equipment may be required: television, videocassette player, computer, modem, Internet access, e-mail.

Restrictions Programs are available to in-state students only. Enrollment is restricted to individuals meeting certain criteria.

Services Distance learners have access to library services, the campus computer network, e-mail services, academic advising, career placement assistance, bookstore at a distance.

Credit-earning options Students may transfer credits from another institution or may earn credits through examinations, military training.

Typical costs *Undergraduate:* Tuition of $43 per unit for in-state residents. Tuition of $242 per unit for out-of-state residents. *Graduate:* Tuition of $168 per unit for in-state residents. Tuition of $415 per unit for out-of-state residents. Costs may vary. Financial aid is available to distance learners.

Registration Students may register by in person.

Contact Helen Sina, Director, University Center, Kauai Community College, 3-1901 Kaumualii Highway, Lihue, HI 96766. *Telephone:* 808-245-8336. *Fax:* 808-245-8232. *E-mail:* hsina@mail.kauaicc.hawaii.edu.

DEGREES AND AWARDS

Distance programs offered do not lead to a degree or other formal award.

COURSE SUBJECT AREAS OFFERED OUTSIDE OF DEGREE PROGRAMS

Undergraduate: English composition; information sciences and systems; nursing

KEISER COLLEGE

Fort Lauderdale, Florida
www.keisercollege.org

Keiser College, founded in 1977, is a proprietary, two-year college. It is accredited by the Accrediting Bureau of Health Education Schools, Southern Association of Colleges and Schools. It first offered distance learning courses in 1999. In 1999–2000, it offered 20 courses at a distance. In fall 1999, there were 200 students enrolled in distance learning courses.

Course delivery sites Courses are delivered to your home, your workplace, military bases, high schools.

Media Courses are delivered via computer software, CD-ROM, computer conferencing, World Wide Web, e-mail, print. Students and teachers may interact via telephone, fax, e-mail, World Wide Web. The following equipment may be required: computer, modem, Internet access, e-mail.

Restrictions Programs are available worldwide. Enrollment is restricted to individuals meeting certain criteria.

Services Distance learners have access to library services, academic advising, career placement assistance, bookstore at a distance.

Credit-earning options Students may transfer credits from another institution.

Typical costs Tuition of $333 per credit hour. Financial aid is available to distance learners.

Registration Students may register by mail, fax, telephone, e-mail, World Wide Web, in person.

Contact Ms. Diana McCown, Online Admissions Counselor, Keiser College, 1500 Northwest 49th Street, Fort Lauderdale, FL 33309. *Telephone:* 800-749-4456. *Fax:* 954-351-4043. *E-mail:* dianam@keisercollege.cc.fl.us.

eCollege.com *www.ecollege.com/scholarships*

DEGREES AND AWARDS

AA Business (some on-campus requirements)

AS Allied Health (some on-campus requirements), Computer Science and Technology (some on-campus requirements), Culinary Arts (some on-campus requirements), Travel and Hospitality (some on-campus requirements)

COURSE SUBJECT AREAS OFFERED OUTSIDE OF DEGREE PROGRAMS

Undergraduate: Biological and life sciences; communications; computer and information sciences; conservation and natural resources; English language and literature; mathematics; physical sciences; psychology; social sciences

See full description on page 554.

KELLER GRADUATE SCHOOL OF MANAGEMENT

Oakbrook Terrace, Illinois
Online Educational Center
www.online.keller.edu

Keller Graduate School of Management, founded in 1973, is a proprietary, graduate institution. It is accredited by the North Central Association of Colleges and Schools. It first offered distance learning courses in 1997. In 1999–2000, it offered 60 courses at a distance. In fall 1999, there were 700 students enrolled in distance learning courses.

Course delivery sites Courses are delivered to your home, your workplace.

Media Courses are delivered via videotapes, computer software, CD-ROM, computer conferencing, World Wide Web, e-mail, print. Students and teachers may interact via mail, telephone, fax, e-mail, World Wide Web. The following equipment may be required: computer, modem, Internet access, e-mail.

Restrictions Programs are available worldwide. Enrollment is restricted to individuals meeting certain criteria.

Services Distance learners have access to library services, e-mail services, academic advising, tutoring, career placement assistance, bookstore at a distance.

Credit-earning options Students may transfer credits from another institution or may earn credits through examinations, military training, business training.

Typical costs Tuition of $1440 per course. Financial aid is available to distance learners.

Registration Students may register by mail, fax, telephone, e-mail, World Wide Web, in person.

Contact Michelle Alford, Center Director, Keller Graduate School of Management, One Tower Lane, 11th Floor, Oakbrook Terrace, IL 60181-4624. *Telephone:* 630-574-1960 Ext. 4094. *Fax:* 630-574-1973. *E-mail:* malford@keller.edu.

eCollege.com *www.ecollege.com/scholarships*

DEGREES AND AWARDS

AIS Information Systems (certain restrictions apply)

MBA Business Administration (certain restrictions apply)

MPA Project Management (certain restrictions apply)

MPH Human Resources (certain restrictions apply)

MS Accounting/Finance (certain restrictions apply), Telecommunications (certain restrictions apply)

COURSE SUBJECT AREAS OFFERED OUTSIDE OF DEGREE PROGRAMS

Graduate: Accounting; business administration and management; finance; health services administration; human resources management; information sciences and systems; international business; marketing; telecommunications

KELLOGG COMMUNITY COLLEGE

Battle Creek, Michigan
Distributed Learning
www.kellogg.cc.mi.us

Kellogg Community College, founded in 1956, is a state and locally supported, two-year college. It is accredited by the North Central Association of Colleges and Schools. It first offered distance learning courses in 1990. In 1999–2000, it offered 50 courses at a distance. In fall 1999, there were 539 students enrolled in distance learning courses.

Course delivery sites Courses are delivered to your home, your workplace, high schools, Olivet College (Olivet), 2 off-campus centers in Coldwater, Hastings.

Media Courses are delivered via television, videotapes, interactive television, computer software, CD-ROM, World Wide Web, e-mail, print. Students and teachers may meet in person or interact via mail, telephone, fax, e-mail, interactive television, World Wide Web. The following equipment may be required: television, videocassette player, computer, modem, Internet access, e-mail.

Kellogg Community College

Restrictions Programs are available to local area students. Enrollment is open to anyone.

Services Distance learners have access to library services, the campus computer network, e-mail services, academic advising, tutoring, career placement assistance, bookstore at a distance.

Credit-earning options Students may transfer credits from another institution or may earn credits through examinations, portfolio assessment, military training, business training.

Typical costs Tuition of $53.50 per credit hour plus mandatory fees of $5 per credit hour for local area residents. Tuition of $85.75 per credit hour plus mandatory fees of $5 per credit hour for in-state residents. Tuition of $131.25 per credit hour plus mandatory fees of $5 per credit hour for out-of-state residents. Costs may vary. Financial aid is available to distance learners.

Registration Students may register by mail, fax, telephone, e-mail, World Wide Web, in person.

Contact Linda Blekking, Secretary, Learning Resources and Distributed Learning, Kellogg Community College, 450 North Avenue, Battle Creek, MI 49017. *Telephone:* 616-965-3931. *Fax:* 616-965-4133. *E-mail:* benanzere@kellogg.cc.mi.us.

DEGREES AND AWARDS

Distance programs offered do not lead to a degree or other formal award.

COURSE SUBJECT AREAS OFFERED OUTSIDE OF DEGREE PROGRAMS

Undergraduate: Accounting; advertising; American (U.S.) history; American literature; anthropology; area, ethnic, and cultural studies; business; business administration and management; business communications; business law; calculus; chemistry; communications; comparative literature; creative writing; criminal justice; economics; electronics; environmental science; ethics; European history; health and medical administrative services; history; information sciences and systems; international business; law and legal studies; liberal arts, general studies, and humanities; marketing; mass media; mathematics; political science; psychology; social sciences; sociology; Spanish language and literature; teacher education

KENT STATE UNIVERSITY

Kent, Ohio

Learning Technology Services
www.dl.kent.edu

Kent State University, founded in 1910, is a state-supported university. It is accredited by the North Central Association of Colleges and Schools. In 1999–2000, it offered 108 courses at a distance. In fall 1999, there were 1,348 students enrolled in distance learning courses.

Course delivery sites Courses are delivered to your home, your workplace, high schools, Kent State University, Ashtabula Campus (Ashtabula), Kent State University, East Liverpool Campus (East Liverpool), Kent State University, Geauga Campus (Burton), Kent State University, Salem Campus (Salem), Kent State University, Stark Campus (Canton), Kent State University, Trumbull Campus (Warren), Kent State University, Tuscarawas Campus (New Philadelphia), 5 off-campus centers in Athens, Bowling Green, Cincinnati, Cleveland, Lorain.

Media Courses are delivered via videotapes, videoconferencing, interactive television, computer software, computer conferencing, World Wide Web. Students and teachers may meet in person or interact via videoconferencing, audioconferencing, mail, telephone, fax, e-mail, World Wide Web. The following equipment may be required: videocassette player, computer, modem, Internet access, e-mail.

Restrictions Programs are available nationwide. Enrollment is restricted to individuals meeting certain criteria.

Services Distance learners have access to library services, the campus computer network, e-mail services, academic advising, bookstore at a distance.

Credit-earning options Students may transfer credits from another institution or may earn credits through examinations.

Typical costs *Undergraduate:* Tuition of $228 per semester hour for in-state residents. Tuition of $451 per semester hour for out-of-state residents. *Graduate:* Tuition of $242.50 per semester hour for in-state residents. Tuition of $465.50 per semester hour for out-of-state residents. Regional campus undergraduate tuition is $144 per semester hour, graduate tuition is $242.50 per semester hour. Costs may vary. Financial aid is available to distance learners.

Registration Students may register by telephone, World Wide Web, in person.

Contact Judy Hirschman, Associate Dean, Kent State University, Learning Technology Services, Moulton Hall, Kent, OH 44242. *Telephone:* 330-672-9842 Ext. 40. *Fax:* 330-672-9876. *E-mail:* judy@dl.kent.edu.

DEGREES AND AWARDS

Undergraduate Certificate(s) Computer Programming
BA Management (certain restrictions apply)
BSN Nursing (certain restrictions apply)
MA Technology (certain restrictions apply)

COURSE SUBJECT AREAS OFFERED OUTSIDE OF DEGREE PROGRAMS

Undergraduate: Accounting; algebra; biology; business administration and management; chemistry; conservation and natural resources; criminal justice; drama and theater; economics; engineering-related technologies; English language and literature; finance; journalism; liberal arts, general studies, and humanities; marketing; nursing; philosophy and religion; physics; political science; psychology; sociology
Graduate: Engineering-related technologies; instructional media; international business; library and information studies; nursing; public health; special education

KENTUCKY STATE UNIVERSITY

Frankfort, Kentucky

KSU Distance Learning
www.kysu.edu

Kentucky State University, founded in 1886, is a state-related, comprehensive institution. It is accredited by the Southern Association of Colleges and Schools. It first offered distance learning courses in 1997. In 1999–2000, it offered 9 courses at a distance. In fall 1999, there were 196 students enrolled in distance learning courses.

Course delivery sites Courses are delivered to your home, high schools, 1 off-campus center in Shelbyville.

Media Courses are delivered via videotapes, videoconferencing, computer software, CD-ROM, World Wide Web, e-mail. Students and teachers may meet in person or interact via videoconferencing, fax, e-mail, interactive television. The following equipment may be required: television.

Restrictions Programs are available to local area students. Enrollment is open to anyone.

Services Distance learners have access to library services, e-mail services, academic advising at a distance.

Credit-earning options Students may transfer credits from another institution.

Typical costs *Undergraduate:* Tuition of $91 per unit plus mandatory fees of $20 per course for in-state residents. Tuition of $260 per unit plus mandatory fees of $20 per course for out-of-state residents. *Graduate:* Tuition of $130 per unit plus mandatory fees of $20 per course for in-state residents. Tuition of $377 per unit plus mandatory fees of $20 per course for out-of-state residents. Costs may vary. Financial aid is available to distance learners.

Registration Students may register by mail, fax, telephone, e-mail, in person.

Contact Tod Porter, Videoconferencing Coordinator, Kentucky State University, 400 East Main, ASB 526, Frankfort, KY 40601. *Telephone:* 502-564-7980. *Fax:* 502-564-7928. *E-mail:* tporter@gwmail.kysu.edu.

DEGREES AND AWARDS

Distance programs offered do not lead to a degree or other formal award.

COURSE SUBJECT AREAS OFFERED OUTSIDE OF DEGREE PROGRAMS

Undergraduate: Accounting; algebra; American literature; criminal justice; English composition; psychology

See full description on page 556.

KETTERING UNIVERSITY

Flint, Michigan

Office of Graduate Studies
www.kettering.edu/official/acad/grad

Kettering University, founded in 1919, is an independent, nonprofit, comprehensive institution. It is accredited by the North Central Association of Colleges and Schools. It first offered distance learning courses in 1982. In 1999–2000, it offered 33 courses at a distance. In fall 1999, there were 901 students enrolled in distance learning courses.

Course delivery sites Courses are delivered to your workplace.

Media Courses are delivered via videotapes. Students and teachers may meet in person or interact via mail, telephone, fax, e-mail. The following equipment may be required: computer, Internet access.

Restrictions Programs are available nationwide. Enrollment is open to anyone.

Services Distance learners have access to library services, academic advising at a distance.

Credit-earning options Students may transfer credits from another institution or may earn credits through examinations.

Typical costs Tuition of $1281 per course plus mandatory fees of $45 per course.

Registration Students may register by mail, fax, telephone, e-mail, in person.

Contact Betty Bedore, Coordinator, Graduate Publications, Kettering University, 1700 West Third Avenue, Flint, MI 48504. *Telephone:* 810-762-7494. *Fax:* 810-762-9935. *E-mail:* bbedore@kettering.edu.

DEGREES AND AWARDS

MS Engineering (certain restrictions apply), Manufacturing Management (certain restrictions apply), Operations Management (certain restrictions apply)

COURSE SUBJECT AREAS OFFERED OUTSIDE OF DEGREE PROGRAMS

Graduate: Accounting; business administration and management; finance; human resources management; industrial engineering; international business; management information systems; marketing; mechanical engineering

See full description on page 558.

KING'S COLLEGE

Wilkes-Barre, Pennsylvania

Distance Learning Program
www.kings.edu/dstlrng

King's College, founded in 1946, is an independent, religious, comprehensive institution. It is accredited by the Middle States Association of Colleges and Schools. It first offered distance learning courses in 1997. In 1999–2000, it offered 8 courses at a distance. In fall 1999, there were 45 students enrolled in distance learning courses.

Course delivery sites Courses are delivered to high schools.

Media Courses are delivered via videoconferencing, World Wide Web. Students and teachers may meet in person or interact via videoconferencing, mail, telephone, fax, e-mail. The following equipment may be required: computer, Internet access.

Restrictions Programs are available in Pennsylvania, New Jersey, New York, Connecticut, and Maryland. Enrollment is restricted to individuals meeting certain criteria.

Services Distance learners have access to library services, academic advising, bookstore at a distance.

Typical costs Tuition of $100 per course.

Registration Students may register by mail, fax, telephone, in person.

Contact Bill Keating, Director of Distance Learning, King's College, 133 North River Street, Wilkes-Barre, PA 18711. *Telephone:* 570-208-5960. *Fax:* 570-208-5961. *E-mail:* wpkeatin@rs01.kings.edu.

DEGREES AND AWARDS

Distance programs offered do not lead to a degree or other formal award.

COURSE SUBJECT AREAS OFFERED OUTSIDE OF DEGREE PROGRAMS

Undergraduate: American (U.S.) history; communications; creative writing; critical thinking; economics; English language and literature; European languages and literatures; psychology; sociology

KINGWOOD COLLEGE

Kingwood, Texas

Distance Education
wwwkc.nhmccd.edu/programs/cybercol/distance.htm

Kingwood College, founded in 1984, is a state and locally supported, two-year college. It is accredited by the Southern Association of Colleges and Schools. It first offered distance learning courses in 1990. In 1999–2000, it offered 70 courses at a distance. In fall 1999, there were 900 students enrolled in distance learning courses.

Course delivery sites Courses are delivered to your home, your workplace, military bases, high schools.

Media Courses are delivered via television, videotapes, interactive television, audiotapes, computer software, CD-ROM, World Wide Web, e-mail, print. Students and teachers may meet in person or interact via mail, telephone, fax, e-mail, interactive television, World Wide Web. The following equipment may be required: television, videocassette player, computer, Internet access, e-mail.

Restrictions Programs are available worldwide. Enrollment is restricted to individuals meeting certain criteria.

Services Distance learners have access to library services, the campus computer network, e-mail services, academic advising, tutoring, career placement assistance, bookstore at a distance.

Credit-earning options Students may transfer credits from another institution or may earn credits through examinations.

Typical costs Tuition of $22 per credit hour plus mandatory fees of $4 per credit hour for local area residents. Tuition of $57 per credit hour plus mandatory fees of $4 per credit hour for in-state residents. Tuition of $67 per credit hour plus mandatory fees of $4 per credit hour for out-of-state residents. *Noncredit courses:* $79 per course. Costs may vary. Financial aid is available to distance learners.

Registration Students may register by mail, fax, telephone, in person.

Contact Peggy Whitley, Director of Teaching, Learning, and Distance Education, Kingwood College, 2000 Kingwood Drive, Kingwood, TX 77339. *Telephone:* 281-312-1493. *Fax:* 281-312-1456. *E-mail:* pwhitley@ nhmccd.edu.

DEGREES AND AWARDS

Undergraduate Certificate(s) Technology
AA Liberal Arts

COURSE SUBJECT AREAS OFFERED OUTSIDE OF DEGREE PROGRAMS

Undergraduate: Accounting; administrative and secretarial services; American (U.S.) history; computer programming; database management; drama and theater; economics; English composition; health and physical education/fitness; information sciences and systems; political science; psychology; Spanish language and literature

KIRKSVILLE COLLEGE OF OSTEOPATHIC MEDICINE

Kirksville, Missouri
School of Health Management
www.shm.kcom.edu

Kirksville College of Osteopathic Medicine, founded in 1892, is an independent, nonprofit, graduate institution. It is accredited by the North Central Association of Colleges and Schools. It first offered distance learning courses in 1994. In 1999–2000, it offered 3 courses at a distance. In fall 1999, there were 35 students enrolled in distance learning courses.

Course delivery sites Courses are delivered to your home, your workplace, military bases, high schools.

Media Courses are delivered via videoconferencing, computer software, computer conferencing, World Wide Web, e-mail. Students and teachers may meet in person or interact via mail, telephone, e-mail, World Wide Web. The following equipment may be required: computer, modem, Internet access, e-mail.

Restrictions Programs are available worldwide. Enrollment is open to anyone.

Services Distance learners have access to library services, e-mail services, academic advising, bookstore at a distance.

Credit-earning options Students may transfer credits from another institution.

Typical costs Tuition of $1050 per course. Mandatory fees include $50 registration fee and $50 technology fee per course. Cost of noncredit courses is 50% of regular tuition. Financial aid is available to distance learners.

Registration Students may register by mail, fax, World Wide Web, in person.

Contact Dr. D. Kent Mulford, Dean, Kirksville College of Osteopathic Medicine, 210A South Osteopathy, Kirksville, MO 63501. *Telephone:* 660-626-2820. *Fax:* 660-626-2826. *E-mail:* hmgp@kcom.edu.

DEGREES AND AWARDS

MGH Master of Geriatric Health (certain restrictions apply)
MHA Master of Health Administration (certain restrictions apply)
MPH Master of Public Health (certain restrictions apply)

COURSE SUBJECT AREAS OFFERED OUTSIDE OF DEGREE PROGRAMS

Graduate: Gerontology; health services administration; public health
See full description on page 560.

LAC COURTE OREILLES OJIBWA COMMUNITY COLLEGE

Hayward, Wisconsin
www.lco-college.edu

Lac Courte Oreilles Ojibwa Community College, founded in 1982, is a federally supported, two-year college. It is accredited by the North Central Association of Colleges and Schools. In fall 1999, there were 11 students enrolled in distance learning courses.

Course delivery sites Courses are delivered to high schools.

Media Courses are delivered via interactive television. Students and teachers may interact via telephone, fax, interactive television. The following equipment may be required: television.

Restrictions Programs are available to local area students. Enrollment is open to anyone.

Typical costs Tuition of $90 per credit. Financial aid is available to distance learners.

Registration Students may register by in person.

Contact Dan Gretz, Academic Dean, Lac Courte Oreilles Ojibwa Community College, 13466 West Trepania Road, Hayward, WI 54843. *Telephone:* 715-634-4790 Ext. 138. *Fax:* 715-634-5049. *E-mail:* djgretz@ lco-college.edu.

DEGREES AND AWARDS

Distance programs offered do not lead to a degree or other formal award.

COURSE SUBJECT AREAS OFFERED OUTSIDE OF DEGREE PROGRAMS

Undergraduate: Earth science

LACKAWANNA JUNIOR COLLEGE

Scranton, Pennsylvania
Distance Learning Center
www.ljc.edu/dlc.html

Lackawanna Junior College, founded in 1894, is an independent, nonprofit, two-year college. It is accredited by the Middle States Association of Colleges and Schools. It first offered distance learning courses in 1994. In 1999–2000, it offered 9 courses at a distance. In fall 1999, there were 50 students enrolled in distance learning courses.

Course delivery sites Courses are delivered to 5 off-campus centers in Carbondale, Hazleton, Honesdale, Towanda, Troy.

Media Courses are delivered via videoconferencing. Students and teachers may interact via videoconferencing, mail, telephone, fax.

Restrictions Programs are available to in-state students only. Enrollment is open to anyone.

Services Distance learners have access to the campus computer network, academic advising, tutoring, career placement assistance at a distance.

Credit-earning options Students may transfer credits from another institution or may earn credits through examinations, military training.

Typical costs Tuition of $240 per credit. *Noncredit courses:* $175 per course. Financial aid is available to distance learners.

Registration Students may register by in person.

Contact Griffith R. Lewis, Registrar, Lackawanna Junior College, Distance Learning Operations, 501 Vine Street, Scranton, PA 18509. *Telephone:* 570-961-7840. *Fax:* 570-961-7858. *E-mail:* lewisg@ljc.edu.

DEGREES AND AWARDS

Distance programs offered do not lead to a degree or other formal award.

COURSE SUBJECT AREAS OFFERED OUTSIDE OF DEGREE PROGRAMS

Undergraduate: Business administration and management; economics; English composition; history; liberal arts, general studies, and humanities; mathematics; philosophy and religion; psychology; sociology
Noncredit: English composition; mathematics

LAFAYETTE COLLEGE

Easton, Pennsylvania
www.lafayette.edu

Lafayette College, founded in 1826, is an independent, religious, four-year college affiliated with the Presbyterian Church (U.S.A.). It is accredited by the Middle States Association of Colleges and Schools. It first offered distance learning courses in 1995. In 1999–2000, it offered 2 courses at a distance. In fall 1999, there were 21 students enrolled in distance learning courses.

Course delivery sites Courses are delivered to Albright College (Reading), Vesalius College (Brussels, Belgium).

Media Courses are delivered via videoconferencing, CD-ROM, computer conferencing, World Wide Web, e-mail, print. Students and teachers may meet in person or interact via videoconferencing, mail, telephone, fax, e-mail, World Wide Web. The following equipment may be required: computer, modem, Internet access, e-mail.

Restrictions Programs are available worldwide. Enrollment is restricted to individuals meeting certain criteria.

Services Distance learners have access to library services, the campus computer network, e-mail services, academic advising, career placement assistance, bookstore at a distance.

Credit-earning options Students may transfer credits from another institution or may earn credits through examinations.

Typical costs Tuition of $22,929 per year. Financial aid is available to distance learners.

Registration Students may register by mail, fax, in person.

Contact Patricia A. Facciponti, Instructional Technologist, Lafayette College, 214 Skillman Library, Easton, PA 18042. *Telephone:* 610-330-5632. *Fax:* 610-252-0370. *E-mail:* faccipop@lafayette.edu.

DEGREES AND AWARDS

Distance programs offered do not lead to a degree or other formal award.

COURSE SUBJECT AREAS OFFERED OUTSIDE OF DEGREE PROGRAMS

Undergraduate: Anthropology; engineering; French language and literature; German language and literature; history; political science; social sciences; sociology; theological studies; women's studies

LAKEHEAD UNIVERSITY

Thunder Bay, Ontario, Canada
Department of Part-Time Studies and Distance Education
www.lakeheadu.ca/~disedwww

Lakehead University, founded in 1965, is a province-supported, comprehensive institution. It is accredited by the provincial charter. It first offered distance learning courses in 1987. In 1999–2000, it offered 28 courses at a distance. In fall 1999, there were 600 students enrolled in distance learning courses.

Course delivery sites Courses are delivered to your home, your workplace.

Media Courses are delivered via television, videotapes, videoconferencing, audiotapes, computer software, CD-ROM, computer conferencing, World Wide Web, e-mail, print. Students and teachers may meet in person or interact via videoconferencing, audioconferencing, mail, telephone, fax, e-mail, World Wide Web. The following equipment may be required: television, videocassette player, computer, modem, Internet access, e-mail.

Restrictions Programs are available worldwide. Enrollment is restricted to individuals meeting certain criteria.

Services Distance learners have access to library services, the campus computer network, e-mail services, academic advising, tutoring, career placement assistance, bookstore at a distance.

Credit-earning options Students may transfer credits from another institution or may earn credits through examinations.

Typical costs Undergraduate tuition per full credit course is $760 for in-district and in-state students, $1580 for out-of-state students. Graduate tuition per full credit course is $1784 in-district and in-state, $3360 out-of-state. Half-credit courses are $380 for undergraduates and $892 for graduate students. Fees vary according to program depending on use of manuals, texts, and video/audio materials. *Noncredit courses:* Can$1000 per course. Costs may vary. Financial aid is available to distance learners.

Registration Students may register by mail, fax, telephone, e-mail, World Wide Web, in person.

Contact Part-Time Studies and Distance Education, Lakehead University, Regional Centre 0009, 955 Oliver Road, Thunder Bay, ON P7B 5E1 Canada. *Telephone:* 807-346-7730. *Fax:* 807-343-8008. *E-mail:* parttime@lakeheadu.ca.

DEGREES AND AWARDS

Undergraduate Certificate(s) Environmental Assessment
BA General Studies
BSN Nursing (service area differs from that of the overall institution)
BSW Social Work
MF Forestry (some on-campus requirements)

COURSE SUBJECT AREAS OFFERED OUTSIDE OF DEGREE PROGRAMS

Undergraduate: Abnormal psychology; biology; chemistry; cognitive psychology; conservation and natural resources; developmental and child psychology; economics; history; liberal arts, general studies, and humanities; mathematics; microbiology; nursing; philosophy and religion; political science; psychology; social psychology; sociology; teacher education
Graduate: Education administration; forestry; special education

See full description on page 562.

LAKELAND COLLEGE

Sheboygan, Wisconsin
Lakeland Online
www.lakeland.edu/online

Lakeland College, founded in 1862, is an independent, religious, comprehensive institution affiliated with the United Church of Christ. It is accredited by the North Central Association of Colleges and Schools.

Course delivery sites Courses are delivered to your home.

Media Courses are delivered via World Wide Web, e-mail. Students and teachers may interact via e-mail, World Wide Web. The following equipment may be required: computer, Internet access, e-mail.

Restrictions Programs are available worldwide. Enrollment is open to anyone.

Services Distance learners have access to academic advising, bookstore at a distance.

Credit-earning options Students may transfer credits from another institution or may earn credits through military training.

Typical costs *Undergraduate:* Tuition of $685 per course. *Graduate:* Tuition of $750 per course.

Registration Students may register by mail, fax, World Wide Web, in person.

Contact Carol Butzen, Adult Education Counselor, Lakeland College, PO Box 358, Sheboygan, WI 53082-0359. *Telephone:* 920-565-1293. *Fax:* 920-565-1341. *E-mail:* butzencl@lakeland.edu.

DEGREES AND AWARDS

BA Accounting, Business Administration, Computer Science, Marketing

COURSE SUBJECT AREAS OFFERED OUTSIDE OF DEGREE PROGRAMS

Undergraduate: Accounting; business administration and management; computer and information sciences; marketing

Graduate: Business administration and management

See full description on page 564.

LAKE LAND COLLEGE

Mattoon, Illinois
Continuing Education Department
www.lakeland.cc.il.us

Lake Land College, founded in 1966, is a state and locally supported, two-year college. It is accredited by the North Central Association of Colleges and Schools. It first offered distance learning courses in 1994. In 1999–2000, it offered 25 courses at a distance. In fall 1999, there were 484 students enrolled in distance learning courses.

Course delivery sites Courses are delivered to 8 off-campus centers in Arthur, Effingham, Lovington, Mattoon, Pana, Shelbyville, Stew-Stras, Windsor.

Media Courses are delivered via television, videoconferencing, interactive television, computer software, e-mail. Students and teachers may meet in person or interact via mail, telephone, e-mail, interactive television, World Wide Web. The following equipment may be required: computer, Internet access.

Restrictions Programs are available to in-state students only. Enrollment is open to anyone.

Services Distance learners have access to library services, the campus computer network, e-mail services, academic advising, tutoring, career placement assistance, bookstore at a distance.

Credit-earning options Students may transfer credits from another institution or may earn credits through examinations, portfolio assessment, military training.

Typical costs Tuition of $41 per credit hour plus mandatory fees of $8.50 per credit hour for local area residents. Tuition of $106 per credit hour plus mandatory fees of $8.50 per credit hour for in-state residents. Tuition of $226 per credit hour plus mandatory fees of $8.50 per credit hour for out-of-state residents. Financial aid is available to distance learners.

Registration Students may register by mail, fax, telephone, e-mail, World Wide Web, in person.

Contact Cheryl Yount, Associate Dean of Continuing Education, Lake Land College, 5001 Lake Land Boulevard, Mattoon, IL 61938. *Telephone:* 217-234-5450. *Fax:* 217-234-5400. *E-mail:* cyount@lakeland.cc.il.us.

DEGREES AND AWARDS

Distance programs offered do not lead to a degree or other formal award.

COURSE SUBJECT AREAS OFFERED OUTSIDE OF DEGREE PROGRAMS

Undergraduate: Accounting; algebra; American (U.S.) history; American literature; anthropology; business; business administration and management; business law; chemistry; computer and information sciences; criminal justice; economics; English composition; ethics; health and physical education/fitness; history; international business; logic; marketing; psychology; social psychology; sociology; statistics; substance abuse counseling

LAKELAND COMMUNITY COLLEGE

Kirtland, Ohio
Instructional Technology
www.lakeland.cc.oh.us

Lakeland Community College, founded in 1967, is a state and locally supported, two-year college. It is accredited by the North Central Association of Colleges and Schools. It first offered distance learning courses in 1980. In 1999–2000, it offered 65 courses at a distance. In fall 1999, there were 260 students enrolled in distance learning courses.

Course delivery sites Courses are delivered to your home, your workplace, 1 off-campus center in Madison.

Media Courses are delivered via television, videotapes, videoconferencing, CD-ROM, computer conferencing, World Wide Web. Students and teachers may meet in person or interact via videoconferencing, mail, telephone, fax, e-mail, World Wide Web. The following equipment may be required: television, videocassette player, computer, modem, Internet access, e-mail.

Restrictions Programs are available to local area students. Enrollment is open to anyone.

Services Distance learners have access to library services, the campus computer network, e-mail services, academic advising, tutoring, career placement assistance, bookstore at a distance.

Credit-earning options Students may transfer credits from another institution or may earn credits through examinations, portfolio assessment, military training.

Typical costs Tuition of $44.20 per credit hour plus mandatory fees of $20 per course for local area residents. Tuition of $54.20 per credit hour plus mandatory fees of $20 per course for in-state residents. Tuition of $115.75 per credit hour plus mandatory fees of $20 per course for out-of-state residents. *Noncredit courses:* $40 per course. Financial aid is available to distance learners.

Registration Students may register by mail, fax, telephone, e-mail, World Wide Web, in person.

Contact William Ryan, Vice President for Technology, Lakeland Community College, 7700 Clocktower Drive, Kirtland, OH 44094-5198. *Telephone:* 440-953-7127. *Fax:* 440-953-9710. *E-mail:* wjryan@lakeland.cc.oh.us.

DEGREES AND AWARDS

Distance programs offered do not lead to a degree or other formal award.

COURSE SUBJECT AREAS OFFERED OUTSIDE OF DEGREE PROGRAMS

Undergraduate: Art history and criticism; biology; business administration and management; economics; geography; health and physical education/fitness; marketing; political science; sociology; statistics

LAKESHORE TECHNICAL COLLEGE

Cleveland, Wisconsin
Center for Working Adults
www.ltc.tec.wi.us

Lakeshore Technical College, founded in 1967, is a state and locally supported, two-year college. It is accredited by the North Central Association of Colleges and Schools. It first offered distance learning courses in 1985.

Course delivery sites Courses are delivered to your home, your workplace, Waukesha County Technical College (Pewaukee), 2 off-campus centers in Manitowoc, Sheboygan.

Media Courses are delivered via television, videotapes, videoconferencing, interactive television, audiotapes, CD-ROM, World Wide Web, print. Students and teachers may meet in person or interact via videoconferencing, mail, telephone, fax, e-mail, interactive television. The following equipment may be required: television, videocassette player, computer, Internet access.

Restrictions Some courses are available locally, and some are available statewide. Enrollment is open to anyone.

Services Distance learners have access to e-mail services, academic advising, bookstore at a distance.

Credit-earning options Students may transfer credits from another institution or may earn credits through examinations, portfolio assessment.

Typical costs Tuition of $59 per credit for local area residents. Tuition of $395 per credit for out-of-state residents. Costs may vary. Financial aid is available to distance learners.

Registration Students may register by mail, telephone, in person.

Contact Darlene Jaeger, Lakeshore Technical College. *Telephone:* 800-443-2129. *Fax:* 920-693-3561. *E-mail:* daja@ltc.tec.wi.us.

DEGREES AND AWARDS

Undergraduate Certificate(s) Certified Nursing Assistant (service area differs from that of the overall institution), Family Child Care, Medical Assisting (service area differs from that of the overall institution), Pharmacy Technology (service area differs from that of the overall institution), School Age Child Care

AA Court and Conference Reporting, Paralegal Studies

AAS Health Physics (service area differs from that of the overall institution), Individualized Technical Studies (service area differs from that of the overall institution)

COURSE SUBJECT AREAS OFFERED OUTSIDE OF DEGREE PROGRAMS

Undergraduate: Business; business administration and management; communications; educational psychology; English composition; English language and literature; health professions and related sciences; home economics and family studies; law and legal studies; liberal arts, general studies, and humanities; mathematics; psychology; social sciences; sociology

LAKE SUPERIOR STATE UNIVERSITY

Sault Sainte Marie, Michigan
Continuing Education
www.lssu.edu/conted

Lake Superior State University, founded in 1946, is a state-supported, comprehensive institution. It is accredited by the North Central Association of Colleges and Schools. It first offered distance learning courses in 1986. In 1999–2000, it offered 5 courses at a distance. In fall 1999, there were 52 students enrolled in distance learning courses.

Course delivery sites Courses are delivered to your home, Alpena Community College (Alpena), Bay de Noc Community College (Escanaba), North Central Michigan College (Petoskey), Northwestern Michigan College (Traverse City).

Media Courses are delivered via videotapes, interactive television, World Wide Web. Students and teachers may meet in person or interact via mail, telephone, fax, e-mail, interactive television. The following equipment may be required: television, videocassette player, computer, modem, Internet access, e-mail.

Restrictions Courses are available in the upper peninsula and northern lower peninsula of Michigan. Enrollment is restricted to individuals meeting certain criteria.

Services Distance learners have access to library services, the campus computer network, e-mail services, academic advising, career placement assistance, bookstore at a distance.

Credit-earning options Students may transfer credits from another institution or may earn credits through examinations, military training.

Typical costs *Undergraduate:* Tuition of $159.90 per credit hour plus mandatory fees of $4 per credit for in-state residents. Tuition of $314.25 per credit hour plus mandatory fees of $4 per credit for out-of-state residents. *Graduate:* Tuition of $180.35 per credit hour plus mandatory fees of $4 per credit for in-state residents. Tuition of $180.35 per credit hour plus mandatory fees of $4 per credit for out-of-state residents. Costs may vary. Financial aid is available to distance learners.

Registration Students may register by mail, fax, telephone, e-mail, in person.

Contact Susan K. Camp, Director of Continuing Education, Lake Superior State University, 650 West Easterday, Sault Sainte Marie, MI 49783. *Telephone:* 906-635-2802. *Fax:* 906-635-2762. *E-mail:* scamp@lakers.lssu.edu.

DEGREES AND AWARDS

BS Accounting, Business Administration, Criminal Justice, Engineering Management, Nursing

COURSE SUBJECT AREAS OFFERED OUTSIDE OF DEGREE PROGRAMS

Undergraduate: Accounting; business administration and management; criminal justice; engineering/industrial management; nursing

LAKE WASHINGTON TECHNICAL COLLEGE

Kirkland, Washington
Continuing Education
www.lwtc.ctc.edu

Lake Washington Technical College, founded in 1949, is a district-supported, two-year college. It is accredited by the Northwest Association of Schools and Colleges. In 1999–2000, it offered 13 courses at a distance. In fall 1999, there were 74 students enrolled in distance learning courses.

Course delivery sites Courses are delivered to your home, your workplace, military bases.

Media Courses are delivered via CD-ROM, World Wide Web. Students and teachers may meet in person or interact via e-mail, World Wide Web. The following equipment may be required: computer, modem, Internet access, e-mail.

Restrictions Programs are available to in-state students only. Enrollment is open to anyone.

Services Distance learners have access to library services, the campus computer network, e-mail services, academic advising, career placement assistance, bookstore at a distance.

Credit-earning options Students may transfer credits from another institution.

Typical costs Tuition of $44 per credit. *Noncredit courses:* $45 per course. Costs may vary. Financial aid is available to distance learners.

Registration Students may register by mail, fax, telephone, in person.

Contact Michael Miller, Advisor, Student Services, Lake Washington Technical College, 11605-132nd Avenue North East, Kirkland, WA 98034. *Telephone:* 425-739-8100 Ext. 500. *Fax:* 425-739-8298. *E-mail:* michael.miller@lwtc.ctc.edu.

DEGREES AND AWARDS

Distance programs offered do not lead to a degree or other formal award.

COURSE SUBJECT AREAS OFFERED OUTSIDE OF DEGREE PROGRAMS

Undergraduate: Chemistry; child care and development; computer programming; English composition; information sciences and systems; mathematics; psychology; real estate

LAMAR STATE COLLEGE–ORANGE

Orange, Texas

www.orange.lamar.edu

Lamar State College–Orange, founded in 1969, is a state-supported, two-year college. It is accredited by the Southern Association of Colleges and Schools. In 1999–2000, it offered 6 courses at a distance. In fall 1999, there were 50 students enrolled in distance learning courses.

Course delivery sites Courses are delivered to your home, high schools, Lamar State College–Port Arthur (Port Arthur).

Media Courses are delivered via television, videotapes, interactive television, computer software, World Wide Web, e-mail, print. Students and teachers may meet in person or interact via videoconferencing, mail, telephone, fax, e-mail, interactive television, World Wide Web. The following equipment may be required: television, videocassette player, computer, modem, Internet access, e-mail.

Restrictions Programs are available worldwide. Enrollment is restricted to individuals meeting certain criteria.

Services Distance learners have access to library services, the campus computer network, e-mail services, academic advising, bookstore at a distance.

Credit-earning options Students may transfer credits from another institution or may earn credits through military training.

Typical costs Tuition of $341 per course for local area residents. Tuition of $341 per course for in-state residents. Tuition of $891 per course for out-of-state residents. Costs may vary. Financial aid is available to distance learners.

Registration Students may register by mail, fax, telephone, e-mail, World Wide Web, in person.

Contact Dr. Sheila Williams, Vice President for Academic Affairs, Lamar State College–Orange, 410 Front Street, Orange, TX 77630. *Telephone:* 409-882-3336. *Fax:* 409-882-5027. *E-mail:* willisa@lub002.lamar.edu.

DEGREES AND AWARDS

Distance programs offered do not lead to a degree or other formal award.

COURSE SUBJECT AREAS OFFERED OUTSIDE OF DEGREE PROGRAMS

Undergraduate: Computer programming; English composition; nursing; political science

LAMAR STATE COLLEGE–PORT ARTHUR

Port Arthur, Texas

Academic Division

lupa02.lamar.edu

Lamar State College–Port Arthur, founded in 1909, is a state-supported, two-year college. It is accredited by the Southern Association of Colleges and Schools. It first offered distance learning courses in 1996. In 1999–2000, it offered 10 courses at a distance. In fall 1999, there were 100 students enrolled in distance learning courses.

Course delivery sites Courses are delivered to your home, your workplace, high schools.

Media Courses are delivered via television, videotapes, interactive television, World Wide Web. Students and teachers may meet in person or interact via mail, telephone, fax, e-mail, interactive television. The following equipment may be required: television, videocassette player, computer, Internet access, e-mail.

Restrictions Programs are available to local area students. Enrollment is open to anyone.

Services Distance learners have access to library services, the campus computer network, e-mail services at a distance.

Credit-earning options Students may transfer credits from another institution or may earn credits through examinations.

Typical costs Tuition of $138 per semester hour plus mandatory fees of $46 per semester hour for in-state residents. Tuition of $272 per semester hour plus mandatory fees of $46 per semester hour for out-of-state residents. *Noncredit courses:* $49 per course. Costs may vary. Financial aid is available to distance learners.

Registration Students may register by mail, telephone, World Wide Web, in person.

Contact Dr. Charles Gongre, Dean, Academic Programs, Lamar State College–Port Arthur, PO Box 310, Port Arthur, TX 77641. *Telephone:* 409-984-6229. *Fax:* 409-984-6000. *E-mail:* charles.gongre@lamarpa.edu.

DEGREES AND AWARDS

Distance programs offered do not lead to a degree or other formal award.

COURSE SUBJECT AREAS OFFERED OUTSIDE OF DEGREE PROGRAMS

Undergraduate: American (U.S.) history; art history and criticism; business administration and management; computer and information sciences; English composition; foods and nutrition studies; political science; psychology; sociology; technical writing
Noncredit: Computer and information sciences

LAMAR UNIVERSITY

Beaumont, Texas
Division of Continuing Education
www.lamar.edu/students

Lamar University, founded in 1923, is a state-supported university. It is accredited by the Southern Association of Colleges and Schools. It first offered distance learning courses in 1994. In 1999–2000, it offered 50 courses at a distance. In fall 1999, there were 1,000 students enrolled in distance learning courses.

Course delivery sites Courses are delivered to your home, high schools, Lamar State College–Orange (Orange), 4 off-campus centers in Buna, Jasper, Silsbee, Vidor.

Media Courses are delivered via television, videotapes, videoconferencing, interactive television, World Wide Web. Students and teachers may meet in person or interact via videoconferencing, mail, telephone, fax, e-mail, interactive television, World Wide Web. The following equipment may be required: television, videocassette player, computer, modem, Internet access, e-mail.

Restrictions Programs are available to local area students. Enrollment is open to anyone.

Services Distance learners have access to library services, e-mail services, academic advising, tutoring, career placement assistance at a distance.

Credit-earning options Students may transfer credits from another institution or may earn credits through examinations, portfolio assessment, military training, business training.

Typical costs *Undergraduate:* Tuition of $192 per course plus mandatory fees of $75 per course for in-state residents. Tuition of $834 per course plus mandatory fees of $75 per course for out-of-state residents. *Graduate:* Tuition of $192 per course plus mandatory fees of $75 per course for in-state residents. Tuition of $834 per course plus mandatory fees of $75 per course for out-of-state residents. *Noncredit courses:* $100 per course. Financial aid is available to distance learners.

Registration Students may register by mail, telephone, World Wide Web, in person.

Contact Janice Trammell, Executive Director, Lamar University, Division of Continuing Education, PO Box 10008, Beaumont, TX 77710. *Telephone:* 409-880-8209. *Fax:* 409-880-8683. *E-mail:* trammjd@lub002. lamar.edu.

eCollege.com *www.ecollege.com/scholarships*

DEGREES AND AWARDS

Distance programs offered do not lead to a degree or other formal award.

COURSE SUBJECT AREAS OFFERED OUTSIDE OF DEGREE PROGRAMS

Undergraduate: Business; communications; economics; education administration; educational psychology; English composition; English language and literature; fine arts; history; home economics and family studies; liberal arts, general studies, and humanities; political science; psychology; sociology; special education; teacher education
Graduate: Education administration; educational psychology; home economics and family studies; special education; teacher education

LANSING COMMUNITY COLLEGE

Lansing, Michigan
Virtual College
vcollege.lansing.cc.mi.us

Lansing Community College, founded in 1957, is a state and locally supported, two-year college. It is accredited by the North Central Association of Colleges and Schools. It first offered distance learning courses in 1979. In 1999–2000, it offered 51 courses at a distance. In fall 1999, there were 522 students enrolled in distance learning courses.

Course delivery sites Courses are delivered to your home, your workplace, military bases, high schools, 1 off-campus center in Howell.

Media Courses are delivered via television, videotapes, interactive television, computer software, CD-ROM, computer conferencing, World Wide Web, e-mail, print. Students and teachers may meet in person or interact via videoconferencing, mail, telephone, fax, e-mail, interactive television, World Wide Web. The following equipment may be required: television, videocassette player, computer, modem, Internet access, e-mail.

Restrictions Programs are available worldwide. Enrollment is restricted to individuals meeting certain criteria.

Services Distance learners have access to library services, the campus computer network, e-mail services, academic advising, tutoring, career placement assistance, bookstore at a distance.

Credit-earning options Students may transfer credits from another institution or may earn credits through examinations, portfolio assessment, military training, business training.

Typical costs Tuition of $49 per semester credit plus mandatory fees of $20 per semester for local area residents. Tuition of $78 per semester credit plus mandatory fees of $20 per semester for in-state residents. Tuition of $107 per semester credit plus mandatory fees of $20 per semester for out-of-state residents. Financial aid is available to distance learners.

Registration Students may register by mail, fax, telephone, e-mail, World Wide Web, in person.

Contact Chuck Parker, Director of Distance Learning Educational Initiatives, Lansing Community College, 8270 RCH, PO Box 40010, Lansing, MI 48901-7210. *Telephone:* 517-483-9940. *Fax:* 517-483-9750. *E-mail:* cparker@lansing.cc.mi.us.

DEGREES AND AWARDS

AD Business (certain restrictions apply)

COURSE SUBJECT AREAS OFFERED OUTSIDE OF DEGREE PROGRAMS

Undergraduate: Accounting; algebra; astronomy and astrophysics; business administration and management; business law; chemistry; computer and information sciences; computer programming; creative writing; criminal justice; drama and theater; earth science; economics; English composition; information sciences and systems; mathematics; philosophy and religion; political science; social psychology; sociology; technical writing

LARAMIE COUNTY COMMUNITY COLLEGE

Cheyenne, Wyoming
www.lcc.whecn.edu/comm_outreach

Laramie County Community College, founded in 1968, is a county-supported, two-year college. It is accredited by the North Central Association of Colleges and Schools. It first offered distance learning courses in 1981. In 1999–2000, it offered 32 courses at a distance. In fall 1999, there were 339 students enrolled in distance learning courses.

Course delivery sites Courses are delivered to your home, your workplace, military bases, 2 off-campus centers in Laramie, Pine Bluffs.

Media Courses are delivered via television, videotapes, videoconferencing, audiotapes, World Wide Web. Students and teachers may interact via videoconferencing, mail, telephone, fax, e-mail. The following equipment may be required: television, videocassette player, computer, Internet access, e-mail.

Restrictions Programs are available worldwide. Enrollment is open to anyone.

Services Distance learners have access to library services, e-mail services, bookstore at a distance.

Credit-earning options Students may transfer credits from another institution or may earn credits through examinations, military training.

Typical costs Tuition of $526 per semester plus mandatory fees of $106 per semester for in-state residents. Tuition of $1578 per semester plus mandatory fees of $106 per semester for out-of-state residents. Costs may vary. Financial aid is available to distance learners.

Registration Students may register by mail, telephone, in person.

Contact Admissions Office, Laramie County Community College. *Telephone:* 307-778-1212. *Fax:* 307-778-1350. *E-mail:* cfearney@lccc.cc.wy.us.

DEGREES AND AWARDS

Distance programs offered do not lead to a degree or other formal award.

COURSE SUBJECT AREAS OFFERED OUTSIDE OF DEGREE PROGRAMS

Undergraduate: American (U.S.) history; American studies; anthropology; astronomy and astrophysics; biology; business; business administration and management; business law; calculus; communications; comparative literature; computer and information sciences; criminal justice; developmental and child psychology; economics; English composition; geography; geology; individual and family development studies; law and legal studies; liberal arts, general studies, and humanities; philosophy and religion; political science; psychology; sign language; teacher education

LAWSON STATE COMMUNITY COLLEGE

Birmingham, Alabama
Distance Education
www.ls.cc.al.us

Lawson State Community College, founded in 1949, is a state-supported, two-year college. It is accredited by the Southern Association of Colleges and Schools. It first offered distance learning courses in 1995. In 1999–2000, it offered 25 courses at a distance. In fall 1999, there were 400 students enrolled in distance learning courses.

Course delivery sites Courses are delivered to your home, your workplace.

Media Courses are delivered via videoconferencing, computer conferencing, World Wide Web, e-mail. Students and teachers may meet in person or interact via videoconferencing, mail, telephone, fax, e-mail, World Wide Web. The following equipment may be required: computer, Internet access, e-mail.

Restrictions Programs are available to in-state students only. Enrollment is open to anyone.

Services Distance learners have access to the campus computer network, e-mail services, bookstore at a distance.

Credit-earning options Students may transfer credits from another institution or may earn credits through examinations, portfolio assessment, military training, business training.

Typical costs Contact the school for information. Financial aid is available to distance learners.

Registration Students may register by mail, in person.

Contact Henry Nance, Director, Lawson State Community College, 3060 Wilson Road, SW, Birmingham, AL 35221. *Telephone:* 205-929-6427. *Fax:* 205-929-6428. *E-mail:* hnance@cougar.ls.cc.al.us.

DEGREES AND AWARDS

Distance programs offered do not lead to a degree or other formal award.

COURSE SUBJECT AREAS OFFERED OUTSIDE OF DEGREE PROGRAMS

Undergraduate: Accounting; biology; business administration and management; developmental and child psychology; educational psychology; history; industrial psychology; political science; radio and television broadcasting; social psychology; social work; sociology

See full description on page 676.

LEHIGH CARBON COMMUNITY COLLEGE

Schnecksville, Pennsylvania
Office of Distance Learning
www.lccc.edu

Lehigh Carbon Community College, founded in 1967, is a state and locally supported, two-year college. It is accredited by the Middle States Association of Colleges and Schools. It first offered distance learning courses in 1991. In 1999–2000, it offered 46 courses at a distance. In fall 1999, there were 186 students enrolled in distance learning courses.

Course delivery sites Courses are delivered to your home, your workplace, high schools, Kutztown University of Pennsylvania (Kutztown), Northampton County Area Community College (Bethlehem), 3 off-campus centers in Allentown, Nesquehoning.

Media Courses are delivered via television, videotapes, videoconferencing, computer software, CD-ROM, World Wide Web, e-mail. Students and teachers may meet in person or interact via videoconferencing, mail, telephone, fax, e-mail, World Wide Web. The following equipment may be required: television, videocassette player, computer, modem, Internet access, e-mail.

Restrictions Programs are available nationwide. Enrollment is open to anyone.

Services Distance learners have access to library services, e-mail services, academic advising, bookstore at a distance.

Credit-earning options Students may transfer credits from another institution or may earn credits through examinations, portfolio assessment, military training.

Typical costs Tuition of $189 per course plus mandatory fees of $45 per course for local area residents. Tuition of $378 per course plus mandatory fees of $45 per course for in-state residents. Tuition of $567 per course plus mandatory fees of $45 per course for out-of-state residents. Costs may vary. Financial aid is available to distance learners.

Registration Students may register by mail, fax, telephone, e-mail, in person.

Contact Judith Horvath, Director, Lehigh Carbon Community College. *Telephone:* 610-799-1591. *Fax:* 610-799-1526. *E-mail:* mhorvath@ptd.net.

DEGREES AND AWARDS

AA Teacher Education
AAS Business Administration and Management

COURSE SUBJECT AREAS OFFERED OUTSIDE OF DEGREE PROGRAMS

Undergraduate: Accounting; administrative and secretarial services; American (U.S.) history; art history and criticism; astronomy and astrophysics; biology; business administration and management; business communications; business law; communications; economics; English composition; finance; French language and literature; geography; geology; gerontology; health and physical education/fitness; history; home economics and family studies; human resources management; information sciences and systems; journalism; law and legal studies; liberal arts, general studies, and humanities; marketing; mathematics; nursing; political science; psychology; sociology; Spanish language and literature; statistics; teacher education; visual and performing arts

LEHIGH UNIVERSITY

Bethlehem, Pennsylvania

Office of Distance Education

www.distance.lehigh.edu

Lehigh University, founded in 1865, is an independent, nonprofit university. It is accredited by the Middle States Association of Colleges and Schools. It first offered distance learning courses in 1992. In 1999–2000, it offered 60 courses at a distance. In fall 1999, there were 441 students enrolled in distance learning courses.

Course delivery sites Courses are delivered to your home, your workplace.

Media Courses are delivered via television, videoconferencing, World Wide Web. Students and teachers may meet in person or interact via videoconferencing, mail, telephone, fax, e-mail, World Wide Web. The following equipment may be required: television, videocassette player, computer, modem, Internet access, e-mail.

Restrictions Programs are available nationwide. Enrollment is open to anyone.

Services Distance learners have access to library services, the campus computer network, e-mail services, academic advising, bookstore at a distance.

Credit-earning options Students may transfer credits from another institution or may earn credits through examinations.

Typical costs Tuition of $575 per credit hour. *Noncredit courses:* $575 per course.

Registration Students may register by mail, fax, in person.

Contact Peg Kercsmar, Manager, Lehigh University, Distance Education, 205 Johnson Hall, 36 University Drive, Bethlehem, PA 18015. *Telephone:* 610-758-5794. *Fax:* 610-758-6269. *E-mail:* mak5@lehigh.edu.

DEGREES AND AWARDS

MBA Business Administration (some on-campus requirements)
MEng Chemical Engineering
MS Chemistry, Environmental Engineering, Molecular Biology, Pharmaceutical Chemistry, Polymer Science and Engineering, Quality Engineering

COURSE SUBJECT AREAS OFFERED OUTSIDE OF DEGREE PROGRAMS

Graduate: Biology; business; chemical engineering; chemistry; engineering-related technologies
Noncredit: Biology; business; chemical engineering; chemistry; engineering-related technologies

Special note

To enable working professionals to pursue graduate and continuing education at work, Lehigh University's Educational Satellite Network (LESN) carries live, on-campus classes that are broadcast by satellite to students at multiple corporate sites. Companies partner with Lehigh to offer their employees the opportunity to earn master's degrees in chemistry, chemical engineering, environmental engineering, molecular biology, pharmaceutical chemistry, polymer science and engineering, quality engineering, and business administration (MBA). Students interested in Lehigh's credit and noncredit programs must get their companies involved as participating client sites in order to receive LESN broadcasts. Students express high satisfaction with Lehigh's distance education programs, particularly the convenience, quality of instruction, and the University's responsiveness to distance students. With emphasis on interactivity, students are expected to view the courses live (videotape back-up is available for those who may miss a class due to business or personal travel), interact with the instructors, and complete all assignments on time. As a result, when completing a credit program, distance students receive the same degree as on-campus students. Lehigh's new LESN-Online now offers distance education programming via the Internet by using video streaming technology. Selected courses in business, science, and engineering (credit and noncredit) are available for anytime, anywhere student access using a home or office computer. Students should contact the Distance Education Office for specific information on LESN-Online. Since Lehigh began offering distance education in 1992, LESN has grown to serve more than 800 students at more than 35 corporate sites, including 3M, Air Products, Allied Signal, AstraZeneca, Aventis, Aventis Pasteur, Bayer, BetzDearborn Laboratories, Bristol Myers Squibb, Buckman Laboratories, Cytec Industries, Dupont Pharmaceuticals, Fox Chase Cancer Center, GlaxoWellcome, Hercules, Johnson & Johnson, Lonza, Mack Trucks, Merck & Company, Ortho McNeil Pharmaceuticals, Parke Davis, Robert Wood Johnson, Rohm & Haas, SmithKline Pharmaceuticals, TVA, and Warner Lambert.

LENOIR COMMUNITY COLLEGE

Kinston, North Carolina

Distance Learning Services

www.lenoir.cc.nc.us

Lenoir Community College, founded in 1960, is a state-supported, two-year college. It is accredited by the Southern Association of Colleges and Schools. In 1999–2000, it offered 60 courses at a distance. In fall 1999, there were 358 students enrolled in distance learning courses.

Course delivery sites Courses are delivered to your home, your workplace, high schools, Catawba Valley Community College (Hickory).

Media Courses are delivered via videotapes, interactive television, computer software, CD-ROM, World Wide Web, e-mail. Students and teachers may meet in person or interact via mail, telephone, fax, e-mail, interactive television, World Wide Web. The following equipment may be required: television, videocassette player, computer, Internet access, e-mail.

Restrictions Programs are available to in-state students only. Enrollment is open to anyone.

Services Distance learners have access to library services, academic advising at a distance.

Typical costs Tuition of $28 per credit hour for in-state residents. Tuition of $169.75 per credit hour for out-of-state residents. *Noncredit courses:* $35 per course. Costs may vary. Financial aid is available to distance learners.

Registration Students may register by telephone, e-mail, in person.

Contact Duane Leith, Coordinator of Distance Education, Lenoir Community College, PO Box 188, Kinston, NC 28502-0188. *Telephone:* 252-527-6223 Ext. 500. *Fax:* 252-527-7205. *E-mail:* dal500@email.lenoir.cc.nc.us.

DEGREES AND AWARDS

AAS Court Reporting and Captioning (service area differs from that of the overall institution)

COURSE SUBJECT AREAS OFFERED OUTSIDE OF DEGREE PROGRAMS

Undergraduate: Art history and criticism; business; child care and development; computer and information sciences; English language and literature; European languages and literatures; foods and nutrition studies; health professions and related sciences; history; psychology; telecommunications

See full description on page 676.

LESLEY COLLEGE

Cambridge, Massachusetts
www.lesley.edu

Lesley College, founded in 1909, is an independent, nonprofit, comprehensive institution. It is accredited by the New England Association of Schools and Colleges. It first offered distance learning courses in 1996. In 1999–2000, it offered 12 courses at a distance. In fall 1999, there were 250 students enrolled in distance learning courses.
Course delivery sites Courses are delivered to your home, your workplace.
Media Courses are delivered via videotapes, videoconferencing, computer software, CD-ROM, computer conferencing, World Wide Web, e-mail, print. Students and teachers may interact via audioconferencing, mail, telephone, fax, e-mail, World Wide Web. The following equipment may be required: videocassette player, computer, modem, Internet access, e-mail.
Restrictions Programs are available worldwide. Enrollment is restricted to individuals meeting certain criteria.
Services Distance learners have access to library services, the campus computer network, e-mail services, academic advising at a distance.
Credit-earning options Students may transfer credits from another institution.
Typical costs Tuition of $300 per credit. Mandatory fees range between $30 and $60 for materials. Financial aid is available to distance learners.
Registration Students may register by mail, fax, telephone, in person.
Contact Maureen Yoder, Director, Online Technology and Education Program, Lesley College, 29 Everett Street, Cambridge, MA 02138. *Telephone:* 617-349-8421. *Fax:* 617-349-8169. *E-mail:* myoder@mail. lesley.edu.

DEGREES AND AWARDS

MEd Technology in Education

COURSE SUBJECT AREAS OFFERED OUTSIDE OF DEGREE PROGRAMS

Graduate: Business administration and management; curriculum and instruction; education

See full description on page 566.

LETOURNEAU UNIVERSITY

Longview, Texas
Graduate and Adult Continuing Studies
www.letourneauonline.net

LeTourneau University, founded in 1946, is an independent, religious, comprehensive institution. It is accredited by the Southern Association of Colleges and Schools. In 1999–2000, it offered 6 courses at a distance. In fall 1999, there were 20 students enrolled in distance learning courses.
Course delivery sites Courses are delivered to your home, your workplace.
Media Courses are delivered via videoconferencing, computer software, CD-ROM, computer conferencing, World Wide Web, e-mail, print. Students and teachers may meet in person or interact via videoconferencing, mail, telephone, fax, e-mail, World Wide Web. The following equipment may be required: computer, Internet access, e-mail.
Restrictions Programs are available worldwide. Enrollment is open to anyone.
Services Distance learners have access to library services, bookstore at a distance.
Typical costs Tuition of $245 per credit hour. Financial aid is available to distance learners.
Registration Students may register by mail, fax, in person.
Contact Julian Cowart, Director of Curriculum and Classroom Technology, LeTourneau University. *Telephone:* 903-233-3250. *Fax:* 903-233-3227. *E-mail:* cowartj@letu.edu.

DEGREES AND AWARDS

Distance programs offered do not lead to a degree or other formal award.

COURSE SUBJECT AREAS OFFERED OUTSIDE OF DEGREE PROGRAMS

Undergraduate: Biological and life sciences; business; communications; computer and information sciences; English language and literature; health and physical education/fitness; history; philosophy and religion; psychology; theological studies

LEWIS AND CLARK COMMUNITY COLLEGE

Godfrey, Illinois

Lewis and Clark Community College, founded in 1970, is a district-supported, two-year college. It is accredited by the North Central Association of Colleges and Schools. In 1999–2000, it offered 45 courses at a distance.
Course delivery sites Courses are delivered to your home, your workplace, high schools, 4 off-campus centers in Carlinville, East Alton, Edwardsville, Jerseyville.
Media Courses are delivered via videotapes, computer software, computer conferencing, World Wide Web, e-mail, print. Students and teachers may meet in person or interact via mail, telephone, fax, e-mail, World Wide Web. The following equipment may be required: television, videocassette player, computer, modem, Internet access, e-mail.
Restrictions Programs are available to in-state students only. Enrollment is open to anyone.
Services Distance learners have access to library services, the campus computer network, academic advising, career placement assistance, bookstore at a distance.
Credit-earning options Students may transfer credits from another institution.

Typical costs Tuition of $47 per credit hour plus mandatory fees of $6 per semester for local area residents. Tuition of $80 per credit hour for in-state residents. Tuition of $80 per credit hour for out-of-state residents.
Registration Students may register by mail, fax, telephone, in person.
Contact Mary Hales, Director, Technology Enhanced Learning, Lewis and Clark Community College, 5800 Godfrey Road, Godfrey, IL 62035. *Telephone:* 618-468-2610. *Fax:* 618-466-1294. *E-mail:* mhales@lc.cc.il.us.

DEGREES AND AWARDS

Distance programs offered do not lead to a degree or other formal award.

COURSE SUBJECT AREAS OFFERED OUTSIDE OF DEGREE PROGRAMS

Undergraduate: Accounting; administrative and secretarial services; American (U.S.) history; art history and criticism; biology; business administration and management; child care and development; community health services; criminal justice; developmental and child psychology; gerontology; hospitality services management; information sciences and systems; library and information studies; marketing; political science

LIBERTY UNIVERSITY

Lynchburg, Virginia
External Degree Program
www.liberty.edu

Liberty University, founded in 1971, is an independent, religious, comprehensive institution. It is accredited by the Southern Association of Colleges and Schools, Transnational Association of Christian Colleges and Schools. It first offered distance learning courses in 1985. In 1999–2000, it offered 146 courses at a distance. In fall 1999, there were 1,369 students enrolled in distance learning courses.
Course delivery sites Courses are delivered to your home, your workplace, military bases.
Media Courses are delivered via videotapes, World Wide Web. Students and teachers may meet in person or interact via mail, telephone, fax, e-mail, World Wide Web. The following equipment may be required: television, videocassette player, computer, Internet access.
Restrictions Programs are available worldwide. Enrollment is open to anyone.
Services Distance learners have access to library services, the campus computer network, e-mail services, academic advising, tutoring, career placement assistance, bookstore at a distance.
Credit-earning options Students may transfer credits from another institution or may earn credits through examinations, portfolio assessment, military training, business training.
Typical costs *Undergraduate:* Tuition of $115 per credit. *Graduate:* Tuition of $200 per credit. Financial aid is available to distance learners.
Registration Students may register by mail, fax, telephone, e-mail, World Wide Web, in person.
Contact Dr. Rick Rasberry, Director of Academic Support Services (EDP), Liberty University, 1971 University Boulevard, Lynchburg, VA 24502. *Telephone:* 800-424-9595. *Fax:* 800-628-7977. *E-mail:* rlrasber@liberty.edu.

DEGREES AND AWARDS

AA General Studies (some on-campus requirements), Religion (some on-campus requirements)
BS Business (some on-campus requirements), Multidisciplinary Studies (some on-campus requirements), Psychology (some on-campus requirements), Religion (some on-campus requirements)
MA Counseling (some on-campus requirements)

MAR Religion (some on-campus requirements)
MBA Business Administration (some on-campus requirements)
MDiv Divinity (some on-campus requirements)
MEd Education (some on-campus requirements)
EdD Education (some on-campus requirements)

COURSE SUBJECT AREAS OFFERED OUTSIDE OF DEGREE PROGRAMS

Undergraduate: Accounting; business administration and management; liberal arts, general studies, and humanities; marketing; psychology; religious studies
Graduate: Business administration and management; counseling psychology; education administration; philosophy and religion; religious studies; special education; student counseling; teacher education
See full description on page 568.

LIFE BIBLE COLLEGE

San Dimas, California
School of Correspondence Studies
www.lifebible.edu

LIFE Bible College, founded in 1923, is an independent, religious, four-year college affiliated with the International Church of the Foursquare Gospel. It is accredited by the Accrediting Association of Bible Colleges. It first offered distance learning courses in 1924. In 1999–2000, it offered 20 courses at a distance. In fall 1999, there were 1,000 students enrolled in distance learning courses.
Course delivery sites Courses are delivered to your home.
Media Courses are delivered via print. Students and teachers may meet in person or interact via mail, telephone, fax, e-mail.
Restrictions Programs are available worldwide. Enrollment is restricted to individuals meeting certain criteria.
Services Distance learners have access to library services, the campus computer network, e-mail services, academic advising, career placement assistance at a distance.
Credit-earning options Students may transfer credits from another institution.
Typical costs Tuition of $65 per credit. Costs may vary. Financial aid is available to distance learners.
Registration Students may register by mail, fax, telephone, e-mail, in person.
Contact Brian Tomhave, Director, LIFE Bible College. *Telephone:* 909-599-5433. *Fax:* 909-599-6690. *E-mail:* correspo@lifebible.edu.

DEGREES AND AWARDS

AA Biblical Studies (certain restrictions apply)

COURSE SUBJECT AREAS OFFERED OUTSIDE OF DEGREE PROGRAMS

Undergraduate: Bible studies; classical languages and literatures; communications; ethics; history; physical sciences; religious studies

LINCOLN CHRISTIAN COLLEGE

Lincoln, Illinois
Distance Learning
www.lccs.edu

Lincoln Christian College, founded in 1944, is an independent, religious, four-year college affiliated with the Christian Churches and Churches of

Christ. It is accredited by the Accrediting Association of Bible Colleges, North Central Association of Colleges and Schools. It first offered distance learning courses in 1993. In 1999–2000, it offered 26 courses at a distance. In fall 1999, there were 150 students enrolled in distance learning courses.

Course delivery sites Courses are delivered to your home.

Media Courses are delivered via videotapes, World Wide Web. Students and teachers may meet in person or interact via mail, telephone, fax, e-mail, World Wide Web. The following equipment may be required: television, videocassette player, computer, Internet access, e-mail.

Restrictions Programs are available worldwide. Enrollment is open to anyone.

Services Distance learners have access to library services, academic advising, tutoring, bookstore at a distance.

Credit-earning options Students may transfer credits from another institution or may earn credits through military training.

Typical costs *Undergraduate:* Tuition of $182 per credit hour. *Graduate:* Tuition of $205 per credit hour. *Noncredit courses:* $50 per course. Financial aid is available to distance learners.

Registration Students may register by mail, fax, in person.

Contact Tom Sowers, Director, Lincoln Christian College, Video Correspondence, 100 Campus View Drive, Lincoln, IL 62656. *Telephone:* 217-732-3168. *Fax:* 217-732-1821. *E-mail:* dl@lccs.edu.

DEGREES AND AWARDS

Undergraduate Certificate(s) Theological Studies

COURSE SUBJECT AREAS OFFERED OUTSIDE OF DEGREE PROGRAMS

Undergraduate: Adult education; Greek language and literature; Hebrew language and literature; management information systems; theological studies

Graduate: Counseling psychology; Greek language and literature; Hebrew language and literature; theological studies

Noncredit: Adult education; counseling psychology; Greek language and literature; Hebrew language and literature; management information systems; theological studies

LINN-BENTON COMMUNITY COLLEGE

Albany, Oregon
Media Services
cf.lbcc.cc.or.us/disted/

Linn-Benton Community College, founded in 1966, is a state and locally supported, two-year college. It is accredited by the Northwest Association of Schools and Colleges. In 1999–2000, it offered 83 courses at a distance. In fall 1999, there were 250 students enrolled in distance learning courses.

Course delivery sites Courses are delivered to your home, your workplace, off-campus center(s) in Corvallis, Lebanon, Sweet Home.

Media Courses are delivered via television, videotapes, videoconferencing, interactive television, computer software, CD-ROM, computer conferencing, World Wide Web, e-mail, print. Students and teachers may meet in person or interact via videoconferencing, audioconferencing, mail, telephone, fax, e-mail, interactive television, World Wide Web. The following equipment may be required: television, videocassette player, computer, modem, Internet access, e-mail.

Restrictions Programs are available to local area students. Enrollment is restricted to individuals meeting certain criteria.

Services Distance learners have access to library services, e-mail services, academic advising, bookstore at a distance.

Typical costs Undergraduate in-state tuition is $514.50 for fifteen or more credits plus a $1 per credit technology fee. Out-of-state tuition is $1819.50 for fifteen or more credits plus a $1 per credit technology fee.

Registration Students may register by mail, fax, telephone, in person.

Contact Paul Snyder, Department Chair, Distance Learning and Media Services, Linn-Benton Community College, 6500 Southwest Pacific Boulevard, Albany, OR 97321. *Telephone:* 541-917-4643. *Fax:* 541-917-4659. *E-mail:* snyderp@gw.lbcc.cc.or.us.

DEGREES AND AWARDS

Distance programs offered do not lead to a degree or other formal award.

COURSE SUBJECT AREAS OFFERED OUTSIDE OF DEGREE PROGRAMS

Undergraduate: American literature; biology; business administration and management; calculus; comparative literature; computer programming; creative writing; criminology; English as a second language (ESL); English composition; English literature; film studies; health and physical education/fitness; health professions and related sciences; hospitality services management; journalism; marketing; mass media; physics; technical writing

LOMA LINDA UNIVERSITY

Loma Linda, California
www.llu.edu/llu/

Loma Linda University, founded in 1905, is an independent, religious university. It is accredited by the Western Association of Schools and Colleges, Inc. It first offered distance learning courses in 1996. In 1999–2000, it offered 26 courses at a distance. In fall 1999, there were 20 students enrolled in distance learning courses.

Course delivery sites Courses are delivered to your workplace, Fresno City College (Fresno), Oakwood College (Huntsville, AL), 1 off-campus center in Glendale.

Media Courses are delivered via videotapes, videoconferencing, interactive television, computer software, CD-ROM, World Wide Web, e-mail, print. Students and teachers may meet in person or interact via videoconferencing, audioconferencing, mail, telephone, fax, e-mail, World Wide Web. The following equipment may be required: television, videocassette player, computer, modem, Internet access, e-mail.

Restrictions Programs are available nationwide. Enrollment is restricted to individuals meeting certain criteria.

Services Distance learners have access to library services, academic advising, tutoring, career placement assistance at a distance.

Credit-earning options Students may transfer credits from another institution or may earn credits through examinations, portfolio assessment, military training.

Typical costs Tuition of $315 per unit. Financial aid is available to distance learners.

Registration Students may register by mail, fax, telephone, World Wide Web, in person.

Contact Marvalee Hoffman, Assistant to the Vice President for Academic Affairs, Loma Linda University. *Telephone:* 909-558-4542. *Fax:* 909-558-0242. *E-mail:* mhoffman@univ.llu.edu.

DEGREES AND AWARDS

AA Basic Sciences (service area differs from that of the overall institution; some on-campus requirements), Humanities (service area differs from that of the overall institution; some on-campus requirements)

AS Health Science (service area differs from that of the overall institution; some on-campus requirements)

BS Health Information Administration (service area differs from that of the overall institution)

COURSE SUBJECT AREAS OFFERED OUTSIDE OF DEGREE PROGRAMS

Undergraduate: Biological and life sciences; health professions and related sciences; social work

LONG ISLAND UNIVERSITY, BROOKLYN CAMPUS

Brooklyn, New York
School of Continuing Studies
www.liu.edu

Long Island University, Brooklyn Campus, founded in 1926, is an independent, nonprofit, comprehensive institution. It is accredited by the Middle States Association of Colleges and Schools. It first offered distance learning courses in 1998. In 1999–2000, it offered 5 courses at a distance. In fall 1999, there were 6 students enrolled in distance learning courses.

Course delivery sites Courses are delivered to your home, your workplace, military bases, high schools.

Media Courses are delivered via computer conferencing, World Wide Web, e-mail, print. Students and teachers may interact via mail, telephone, fax, e-mail, World Wide Web. The following equipment may be required: computer, modem, Internet access, e-mail.

Restrictions Programs are available worldwide. Enrollment is open to anyone.

Services Distance learners have access to e-mail services, academic advising at a distance.

Typical costs Please contact school for information. *Noncredit courses:* $375 per course.

Registration Students may register by mail, fax, telephone, in person.

Contact Dr. Ronald White, Dean of Continuing Education, Long Island University, Brooklyn Campus, University Plaza, Room 101, Brooklyn, NY 11201. *Telephone:* 718-488-1010. *Fax:* 718-488-1367. *E-mail:* ronald.white@liu.edu.

DEGREES AND AWARDS

Distance programs offered do not lead to a degree or other formal award.

COURSE SUBJECT AREAS OFFERED OUTSIDE OF DEGREE PROGRAMS

Noncredit: Business communications; health services administration; human resources management; law and legal studies; social work; student counseling

LONGVIEW COMMUNITY COLLEGE

Lee's Summit, Missouri
Program for Adult College Education (PACE)

Longview Community College, founded in 1969, is a state and locally supported, two-year college. It is accredited by the North Central Association of Colleges and Schools. It first offered distance learning courses in 1992. In 1999–2000, it offered 50 courses at a distance. In fall 1999, there were 951 students enrolled in distance learning courses.

Course delivery sites Courses are delivered to your home, your workplace, University of Missouri–Kansas City (Kansas City), 6 off-campus centers in Belton, Blue Springs, Harrisonville, Independence, Kansas City, Raytown.

Media Courses are delivered via television, videotapes, interactive television, World Wide Web. Students and teachers may meet in person or interact via mail, telephone, fax, interactive television. The following equipment may be required: television, Internet access.

Restrictions Programs are available to local area students. Enrollment is open to anyone.

Services Distance learners have access to library services, the campus computer network, e-mail services, academic advising, bookstore at a distance.

Credit-earning options Students may transfer credits from another institution or may earn credits through examinations.

Typical costs Tuition of $51 per credit hour for local area residents. Tuition of $87 per credit hour for out-of-state residents. Costs may vary. Financial aid is available to distance learners.

Registration Students may register by mail, fax, telephone, in person.

Contact Tamara Miller, PACE Outreach Coordinator, Longview Community College, 500 Southwest Longview Road, Lee's Summit, MO 64063. *Telephone:* 816-672-2369. *Fax:* 816-672-2426.

DEGREES AND AWARDS

AA General Studies (some on-campus requirements), Liberal Arts (some on-campus requirements)

COURSE SUBJECT AREAS OFFERED OUTSIDE OF DEGREE PROGRAMS

Undergraduate: Biology; computer and information sciences; computer programming; database management; economics; English composition; English language and literature; history; information sciences and systems; liberal arts, general studies, and humanities; mathematics; philosophy and religion; physical sciences; psychology; social work; sociology

LORAIN COUNTY COMMUNITY COLLEGE

Elyria, Ohio
Instructional Television
www.lorainccc.edu

Lorain County Community College, founded in 1963, is a state and locally supported, two-year college. It is accredited by the North Central Association of Colleges and Schools. It first offered distance learning courses in 1990. In 1999–2000, it offered 69 courses at a distance. In fall 1999, there were 615 students enrolled in distance learning courses.

Course delivery sites Courses are delivered to your home, your workplace, high schools, Bowling Green State University–Firelands College (Huron), off-campus center(s) in High School Sites.

Media Courses are delivered via television, videotapes, videoconferencing, interactive television, World Wide Web, e-mail, print. Students and teachers may meet in person or interact via videoconferencing, audioconferencing, mail, telephone, fax, e-mail, interactive television, World Wide Web. The following equipment may be required: television, videocassette player, computer, modem, Internet access, e-mail.

Restrictions Programs are available worldwide. Enrollment is open to anyone.

Services Distance learners have access to library services, e-mail services, academic advising, career placement assistance, bookstore at a distance.

Credit-earning options Students may transfer credits from another institution or may earn credits through examinations, portfolio assessment, military training, business training.

Typical costs Tuition of $76.35 per credit for local area residents. Tuition of $92.10 per credit for in-state residents. Tuition of $187.35 per credit for out-of-state residents. Financial aid is available to distance learners.

Registration Students may register by mail, fax, telephone, e-mail, World Wide Web, in person.

Contact David Weiser, Director, Lorain County Community College, 1005 North Abbe Road, Elyria, OH 44035. *Telephone:* 800-995-5222 Ext. 7573. *Fax:* 216-365-6519. *E-mail:* dweiser@lorainccc.edu.

DEGREES AND AWARDS

Distance programs offered do not lead to a degree or other formal award.

COURSE SUBJECT AREAS OFFERED OUTSIDE OF DEGREE PROGRAMS

Undergraduate: Accounting; Asian languages and literatures; business administration and management; creative writing; English as a second language (ESL); English composition; English language and literature; history; liberal arts, general studies, and humanities; mathematics; music; philosophy and religion; physics; psychology; social psychology; sociology; teacher education

LOS ANGELES HARBOR COLLEGE

Wilmington, California
Distance Education Programs
www.lahc.cc.ca.us

Los Angeles Harbor College, founded in 1949, is a state and locally supported, two-year college. It is accredited by the Western Association of Schools and Colleges, Inc. It first offered distance learning courses in 1996. In 1999–2000, it offered 6 courses at a distance. In fall 1999, there were 302 students enrolled in distance learning courses.

Course delivery sites Courses are delivered to your home, your workplace, military bases, high schools.

Media Courses are delivered via videoconferencing, World Wide Web, e-mail. Students and teachers may meet in person or interact via mail, telephone, fax, e-mail, World Wide Web. The following equipment may be required: computer, modem, Internet access, e-mail.

Restrictions Programs are available to local area students. Enrollment is open to anyone.

Services Distance learners have access to library services, the campus computer network, e-mail services, academic advising, tutoring, career placement assistance, bookstore at a distance.

Credit-earning options Students may earn credits through examinations.

Typical costs Mandatory fees of $11 per unit for in-state residents. Mandatory fees of $11 per unit for in-state residents. Mandatory fees of $128 per unit for out-of-state residents. *Noncredit courses:* $75 per course. Financial aid is available to distance learners.

Registration Students may register by mail, telephone, e-mail, World Wide Web, in person.

Contact Bonnie Easley, Coordinator, Distance Education Program, Los Angeles Harbor College, 1111 Figueroa Place, Wilmington, CA 90744. *Telephone:* 310-522-8469. *Fax:* 310-834-1882. *E-mail:* easleyb@laccd. edu.

DEGREES AND AWARDS

Distance programs offered do not lead to a degree or other formal award.

COURSE SUBJECT AREAS OFFERED OUTSIDE OF DEGREE PROGRAMS

Undergraduate: Accounting; economics; English composition; information sciences and systems; political science; teacher education

LOS ANGELES MISSION COLLEGE

Sylmar, California
www.lamission.cc.ca.us

Los Angeles Mission College, founded in 1974, is a state and locally supported, two-year college. It is accredited by the Western Association of Schools and Colleges, Inc. In 1999–2000, it offered 5 courses at a distance. In fall 1999, there were 72 students enrolled in distance learning courses.

Course delivery sites Courses are delivered to your home, your workplace, military bases, high schools.

Media Courses are delivered via computer software, World Wide Web, e-mail, print. Students and teachers may meet in person or interact via mail, telephone, fax, e-mail, World Wide Web. The following equipment may be required: computer, modem, Internet access, e-mail.

Restrictions Programs are available to local area students. Enrollment is open to anyone.

Services Distance learners have access to the campus computer network, e-mail services at a distance.

Credit-earning options Students may transfer credits from another institution or may earn credits through examinations, military training.

Typical costs Tuition of $12 per unit plus mandatory fees of $12 per unit for local area residents. Tuition of $12 per unit plus mandatory fees of $12 per unit for in-state residents. Tuition of $128 per unit plus mandatory fees of $12 per unit for out-of-state residents. Cost for a noncredit course is $12 per unit. Financial aid is available to distance learners.

Registration Students may register by mail, telephone, World Wide Web, in person.

Contact Dr. Daniel A. Castro, Vice President, Academic Affairs, Los Angeles Mission College, 13356 Eldridge Avenue, Sylmar, CA 91342-3245. *Telephone:* 818-364-7635. *Fax:* 818-364-7755. *E-mail:* daniel_a._ castro@laccd.cc.ca.us.

DEGREES AND AWARDS

Undergraduate Certificate(s) General Studies (certain restrictions apply; some on-campus requirements)

AA Arts (certain restrictions apply; some on-campus requirements)

AS Science (certain restrictions apply; some on-campus requirements)

COURSE SUBJECT AREAS OFFERED OUTSIDE OF DEGREE PROGRAMS

Undergraduate: Astronomy and astrophysics; business administration and management; English composition; hospitality services management; individual and family development studies; philosophy and religion

LOS ANGELES PIERCE COLLEGE

Woodland Hills, California
www.lapc.cc.ca.us

Los Angeles Pierce College, founded in 1947, is a state and locally supported, two-year college. It is accredited by the Western Association of Schools and Colleges, Inc. It first offered distance learning courses in 1997. In 1999–2000, it offered 6 courses at a distance. In fall 1999, there were 48 students enrolled in distance learning courses.

Course delivery sites Courses are delivered to your home, California Polytechnic State University, San Luis Obispo (San Luis Obispo), California State Polytechnic University, Pomona (Pomona).

Media Courses are delivered via television, videoconferencing, interactive television, e-mail. Students and teachers may meet in person or interact via videoconferencing, mail, fax, e-mail, interactive television, World Wide Web. The following equipment may be required: television, computer, Internet access, e-mail.

Restrictions Programs are available to local area students. Enrollment is open to anyone.

Services Distance learners have access to the campus computer network, e-mail services, academic advising at a distance.

Credit-earning options Students may transfer credits from another institution or may earn credits through examinations.

Typical costs Tuition of $12 per unit for in-state residents. Tuition of $140 per unit for out-of-state residents. Costs may vary.

Registration Students may register by mail, telephone, World Wide Web, in person.

Contact Carlos Martinez, Dean of Academic Affairs, Los Angeles Pierce College, 6201 Winnetka Avenue, Woodland Hills, CA 91371. *Telephone:* 818-710-4224. *Fax:* 818-710-9844. *E-mail:* martinc@laccd.cc.ca.us.

DEGREES AND AWARDS

Distance programs offered do not lead to a degree or other formal award.

COURSE SUBJECT AREAS OFFERED OUTSIDE OF DEGREE PROGRAMS

Undergraduate: Animal sciences; chemistry; conservation and natural resources

LOUISIANA STATE UNIVERSITY AND AGRICULTURAL AND MECHANICAL COLLEGE

Baton Rouge, Louisiana

Division of Instructional Support and Development
de.disd.lsu.edu

Louisiana State University and Agricultural and Mechanical College, founded in 1860, is a state-supported university. It is accredited by the Southern Association of Colleges and Schools. It first offered distance learning courses in 1984. In 1999–2000, it offered 45 courses at a distance. In fall 1999, there were 456 students enrolled in distance learning courses.

Course delivery sites Courses are delivered to your home, your workplace, military bases, high schools, Louisiana State University System (Baton Rouge).

Media Courses are delivered via television, videotapes, videoconferencing, interactive television, computer software, CD-ROM, computer conferencing, World Wide Web, e-mail, print. Students and teachers may meet in person or interact via videoconferencing, audioconferencing, mail, telephone, fax, e-mail, interactive television, World Wide Web. The following equipment may be required: television, videocassette player, computer, modem, Internet access, e-mail.

Restrictions Programs are available to in-state students only. Enrollment is open to anyone.

Services Distance learners have access to library services, the campus computer network, e-mail services, academic advising, career placement assistance, bookstore at a distance.

Credit-earning options Students may transfer credits from another institution or may earn credits through examinations.

Typical costs *Undergraduate:* Tuition of $285 per course. *Graduate:* Tuition of $285 per course. Costs may vary. Financial aid is available to distance learners.

Registration Students may register by mail, telephone, World Wide Web, in person.

Contact Tammy E. Adams, Director, Instructional Telecommunications, Louisiana State University and Agricultural and Mechanical College, 118 Himes Hall, Baton Rouge, LA 70803. *Telephone:* 225-388-1135. *Fax:* 225-388-5789. *E-mail:* tadams3@lsu.edu.

DEGREES AND AWARDS

MS Library and Information Sciences (service area differs from that of the overall institution)

COURSE SUBJECT AREAS OFFERED OUTSIDE OF DEGREE PROGRAMS

Undergraduate: Business administration and management; communications; engineering; English language and literature; history; home economics and family studies; political science; psychology; sociology

Graduate: Agriculture; business administration and management; home economics and family studies; library and information studies; teacher education

See full description on page 676.

LOUISIANA STATE UNIVERSITY AT ALEXANDRIA

Alexandria, Louisiana

Distance Education

Louisiana State University at Alexandria, founded in 1960, is a state-supported, two-year college. It is accredited by the Southern Association of Colleges and Schools. In 1999–2000, it offered 25 courses at a distance. In fall 1999, there were 180 students enrolled in distance learning courses.

Course delivery sites Courses are delivered to your home, your workplace, military bases, Louisiana State University at Eunice (Eunice), Louisiana State University in Shreveport (Shreveport), Northwestern State University of Louisiana (Natchitoches), off-campus center(s) in Alexandria.

Media Courses are delivered via television, videotapes, videoconferencing, interactive television, CD-ROM, World Wide Web, e-mail, print. Students and teachers may meet in person or interact via videoconferencing, mail, telephone, fax, e-mail, interactive television, World Wide Web. The following equipment may be required: television, Internet access, e-mail.

Restrictions Programs are available to in-state students only. Enrollment is open to anyone.

Services Distance learners have access to library services, bookstore at a distance.

Credit-earning options Students may transfer credits from another institution.

Typical costs Tuition of $43 per semester hour. Mandatory fees include $20 application fee, $57 registration and other fees. Financial aid is available to distance learners.

Registration Students may register by telephone, in person.

Contact Teresa Seymour, Associate Director, Continuing Education and Technology, Louisiana State University at Alexandria, 8100 Highway 71 South, Alexandria, LA 71302. *Telephone:* 318-473-6566. *Fax:* 318-473-6575. *E-mail:* tseymour@lsuamail.lsua.edu.

DEGREES AND AWARDS

Distance programs offered do not lead to a degree or other formal award.

COURSE SUBJECT AREAS OFFERED OUTSIDE OF DEGREE PROGRAMS

Undergraduate: Anthropology; business administration and management; calculus; chemistry; civil engineering; criminology; finance; social psychology; sociology; Spanish language and literature; technical writing

Noncredit: Finance

See full description on page 676.

LOUISIANA STATE UNIVERSITY AT EUNICE

Eunice, Louisiana
Continuing Education
www.lsue.edu

Louisiana State University at Eunice, founded in 1967, is a state-supported, two-year college. It is accredited by the Southern Association of Colleges and Schools. It first offered distance learning courses in 1996. In 1999–2000, it offered 20 courses at a distance. In fall 1999, there were 100 students enrolled in distance learning courses.

Course delivery sites Courses are delivered to your home, your workplace, Louisiana State University and Agricultural and Mechanical College (Baton Rouge), Louisiana State University at Alexandria (Alexandria), Louisiana State University Health Sciences Center (New Orleans).

Media Courses are delivered via television, videoconferencing. Students and teachers may meet in person or interact via videoconferencing, mail, telephone, fax, e-mail.

Restrictions Programs are available to in-state students only. Enrollment is open to anyone.

Services Distance learners have access to library services, the campus computer network, e-mail services, academic advising at a distance.

Credit-earning options Students may transfer credits from another institution or may earn credits through examinations, military training.

Typical costs Tuition of $48.50 per credit for local area residents. Tuition of $48.50 per credit for in-state residents. Tuition of $158.50 per credit for out-of-state residents. Application fee is $10. *Noncredit courses:* $50 per course. Financial aid is available to distance learners.

Registration Students may register by mail, fax, telephone, e-mail, in person.

Contact Steven Bays, Continuing Education Department, Louisiana State University at Eunice, PO Box 1129, Eunice, LA 70535. *Telephone:* 318-550-1390. *Fax:* 318-550-1393. *E-mail:* sbays@lsue.edu.

DEGREES AND AWARDS

Distance programs offered do not lead to a degree or other formal award.

COURSE SUBJECT AREAS OFFERED OUTSIDE OF DEGREE PROGRAMS

Undergraduate: Adult education; animal sciences; European languages and literatures; fire science; French language and literature; health professions and related sciences; horticulture; physical sciences; physics; psychology; sociology
Graduate: Adult education; library and information studies; special education

See full description on page 676.

LOUISIANA STATE UNIVERSITY IN SHREVEPORT

Shreveport, Louisiana
Division of Continuing Education and Public Service
www.lsus.edu/

Louisiana State University in Shreveport, founded in 1965, is a state-supported, comprehensive institution. It is accredited by the Southern Association of Colleges and Schools. It first offered distance learning courses in 1995.

Contact Louisiana State University in Shreveport, 1 University Place, Shreveport, LA 71115-2399. *Telephone:* 318-797-5000. *Fax:* 318-797-5286.

See full description on page 676.

LOUISIANA STATE UNIVERSITY SYSTEM

Baton Rouge, Louisiana
Independent Study
www.is.lsu.edu

Louisiana State University System is a state-supported, system. It is accredited by the Southern Association of Colleges and Schools. It first offered distance learning courses in 1924. In 1999–2000, it offered 164 courses at a distance. In fall 1999, there were 2,300 students enrolled in distance learning courses.

Course delivery sites Courses are delivered to your home.

Media Courses are delivered via World Wide Web, print. Students and teachers may interact via mail, telephone, fax, e-mail, World Wide Web.

Restrictions Programs are available worldwide. Enrollment is open to anyone.

Services Distance learners have access to library services, e-mail services, bookstore at a distance.

Typical costs *Undergraduate:* Tuition of $60 per semester hour plus mandatory fees of $10 per course. *Graduate:* Tuition of $60 per semester hour plus mandatory fees of $10 per course. Costs may vary.

Registration Students may register by mail, fax, World Wide Web, in person.

Contact College Services, Louisiana State University System, Independent Study, 106 East Pleasant Hall, Baton Rouge, LA 70803. *Telephone:* 800-234-5046. *Fax:* 225-388-3920. *E-mail:* iservices@doce.lsu.edu.

DEGREES AND AWARDS

MS Library and Information Sciences (service area differs from that of the overall institution)

COURSE SUBJECT AREAS OFFERED OUTSIDE OF DEGREE PROGRAMS

Undergraduate: Accounting; administrative and secretarial services; adult education; algebra; American (U.S.) history; American literature; anatomy; animal sciences; anthropology; astronomy and astrophysics; biology; business; business administration and management; business law; calculus; chemistry; community health services; comparative literature; criminology; curriculum and instruction; developmental and child psychology; drama and theater; economics; education; engineering; English composition; English language and literature; English literature; environmental health; environmental science; European history; European languages and literatures; finance; fire science; foods and nutrition studies; French language and literature; geography; geology; German language and literature; human resources management; information sciences and systems; instructional media; journalism; labor relations/studies; Latin language and literature; library and information studies; logic; management information systems; marketing; mathematics; mechanical engineering; music; organizational behavior studies; philosophy and religion; physics; physiology; political science; psychology; real estate; religious studies; school psychology; sociology; Spanish language and literature; statistics; teacher education; technical writing; women's studies

LOUISIANA TECH UNIVERSITY

Ruston, Louisiana

Center for Instructional Technology and Distance Learning
www.latech.edu

Louisiana Tech University, founded in 1894, is a state-supported university. It is accredited by the Southern Association of Colleges and Schools. In 1999–2000, it offered 44 courses at a distance. In fall 1999, there were 212 students enrolled in distance learning courses.

Course delivery sites Courses are delivered to your home, high schools, Louisiana State University in Shreveport (Shreveport), University of Louisiana at Lafayette (Lafayette), University of Louisiana at Monroe (Monroe), 2 off-campus centers in Minden, Shreveport, Technology Transfer.

Media Courses are delivered via videotapes, videoconferencing, interactive television, computer conferencing, e-mail, print. Students and teachers may meet in person or interact via videoconferencing, mail, telephone, fax, e-mail, interactive television. The following equipment may be required: computer, modem, Internet access, e-mail.

Restrictions Programs are available to in-state students only. Enrollment is restricted to individuals meeting certain criteria.

Services Distance learners have access to library services, the campus computer network, e-mail services, academic advising, bookstore at a distance.

Credit-earning options Students may transfer credits from another institution or may earn credits through examinations.

Typical costs Graduate and undergraduate tuition is $222 per 1-3 hours. *Noncredit courses:* $100 per course. Costs may vary. Financial aid is available to distance learners.

Registration Students may register by mail, fax, telephone, e-mail, in person.

Contact David R. Cargill, Director, Center for Instructional Technology and Distance Learning, Louisiana Tech University, PO Box 10408, Ruston, LA 71272. *Telephone:* 318-257-2912. *Fax:* 318-257-2731. *E-mail:* david@latech.edu.

DEGREES AND AWARDS

Distance programs offered do not lead to a degree or other formal award.

COURSE SUBJECT AREAS OFFERED OUTSIDE OF DEGREE PROGRAMS

Undergraduate: Architecture; biological and life sciences; health and physical education/fitness; journalism; technical writing
Graduate: Curriculum and instruction; engineering; health and physical education/fitness; history
See full description on page 676.

LOYOLA UNIVERSITY CHICAGO

Chicago, Illinois

Mundelein College
online.luc.edu

Loyola University Chicago, founded in 1870, is an independent, religious university. It is accredited by the Association of Theological Schools in the United States and Canada (candidate), North Central Association of Colleges and Schools. It first offered distance learning courses in 1999.
Course delivery sites Courses are delivered to your home, your workplace, military bases, high schools.

Media Courses are delivered via computer software, computer conferencing, World Wide Web, e-mail. Students and teachers may interact via e-mail, World Wide Web. The following equipment may be required: computer, modem, Internet access, e-mail.

Restrictions Programs are available worldwide. Enrollment is open to anyone.

Services Distance learners have access to library services, academic advising, tutoring, bookstore at a distance.

Typical costs Tuition of $360 per credit hour.

Registration Students may register by telephone, e-mail, World Wide Web.

Contact Hilary Ward Schnadt, Associate Dean, Loyola University Chicago, Mundelein College, 6525 North Sheridan Road, Skyscraper 204, Chicago, IL 60626. *Telephone:* 773-508-8004. *Fax:* 773-508-8008. *E-mail:* hschnad@luc.edu.

eCollege.com *www.ecollege.com/scholarships*

DEGREES AND AWARDS

Undergraduate Certificate(s) Java Programming, Networks: Telecommunications, Java Programming: Database Applications, Java Programming: Web Design, Object-Oriented Software Development: Design Patterns

COURSE SUBJECT AREAS OFFERED OUTSIDE OF DEGREE PROGRAMS

Undergraduate: Computer and information sciences
See full description on page 570.

LOYOLA UNIVERSITY NEW ORLEANS

New Orleans, Louisiana

Off-Campus Learning Program

Loyola University New Orleans, founded in 1912, is an independent, religious, comprehensive institution. It is accredited by the Southern Association of Colleges and Schools. It first offered distance learning courses in 1990.

Course delivery sites Courses are delivered to your workplace, 1 off-campus center in Baton Rouge.

Media Courses are delivered via videotapes. Students and teachers may interact via mail, telephone, fax, e-mail. The following equipment may be required: television, videocassette player.

Restrictions Programs are available to in-state students only. Enrollment is restricted to individuals meeting certain criteria.

Services Distance learners have access to library services, e-mail services, academic advising, tutoring, career placement assistance, bookstore at a distance.

Credit-earning options Students may transfer credits from another institution or may earn credits through examinations, portfolio assessment, military training, business training.

Typical costs Tuition of $207 per credit. Costs may vary. Financial aid is available to distance learners.

Registration Students may register by mail, telephone.

Contact Kristel Scheuermann, Off Campus Learning Program Coordinator, Loyola University New Orleans, 6363 St. Charles Avenue, New Orleans, LA 70118. *Telephone:* 504-865-3250. *Fax:* 504-865-3883. *E-mail:* scheuer@loyno.edu.

DEGREES AND AWARDS

BCJ Criminal Justice (certain restrictions apply; some on-campus requirements)

BSN Nursing (certain restrictions apply; some on-campus requirements)

COURSE SUBJECT AREAS OFFERED OUTSIDE OF DEGREE PROGRAMS

Undergraduate: Criminal justice; English composition; fine arts; liberal arts, general studies, and humanities; music; nursing; sociology; statistics; theological studies

See full description on page 676.

LUZERNE COUNTY COMMUNITY COLLEGE

Nanticoke, Pennsylvania
Telecollege

Luzerne County Community College, founded in 1966, is a county-supported, two-year college. It is accredited by the Middle States Association of Colleges and Schools. It first offered distance learning courses in 1981. In 1999–2000, it offered 52 courses at a distance. In fall 1999, there were 600 students enrolled in distance learning courses.
Course delivery sites Courses are delivered to your home, your workplace.
Media Courses are delivered via television, videotapes, videoconferencing, interactive television, CD-ROM, World Wide Web, e-mail, print. Students and teachers may meet in person or interact via videoconferencing, mail, telephone, fax, e-mail, interactive television, World Wide Web. The following equipment may be required: television, videocassette player, computer, modem, Internet access, e-mail.
Restrictions Programs are available to in-state students only. Enrollment is open to anyone.
Services Distance learners have access to library services, e-mail services, academic advising, bookstore at a distance.
Credit-earning options Students may transfer credits from another institution or may earn credits through examinations, portfolio assessment, military training, business training.
Typical costs Tuition of $159 per course for in-state residents. Tuition of $477 per course for out-of-state residents. Students pay $79 in fees. Costs may vary. Financial aid is available to distance learners.
Registration Students may register by mail, fax, telephone, in person.
Contact Karen Droms, Instructional Technologist, Luzerne County Community College, 1333 South Prospect Street, Nanticoke, PA 18634. *Telephone:* 570-740-0326. *Fax:* 570-740-0526.

DEGREES AND AWARDS

AS General Studies (some on-campus requirements)

COURSE SUBJECT AREAS OFFERED OUTSIDE OF DEGREE PROGRAMS

Undergraduate: Advertising; astronomy and astrophysics; business administration and management; conservation and natural resources; developmental and child psychology; economics; English composition; English language and literature; European languages and literatures; fine arts; geology; health and physical education/fitness; history; home economics and family studies; information sciences and systems; journalism; law and legal studies; mathematics; philosophy and religion; political science; sociology

LYNN UNIVERSITY

Boca Raton, Florida
The Institute for Distance Learning
www.lynn.edu/academics/distance

Lynn University, founded in 1962, is an independent, nonprofit, comprehensive institution. It is accredited by the Southern Association of Colleges and Schools. In 1999–2000, it offered 40 courses at a distance. In fall 1999, there were 220 students enrolled in distance learning courses.
Course delivery sites Courses are delivered to your home, your workplace, military bases.
Media Courses are delivered via videoconferencing, World Wide Web. Students and teachers may meet in person or interact via videoconferencing, audioconferencing, mail, telephone, fax, e-mail, World Wide Web. The following equipment may be required: computer, modem, Internet access, e-mail.
Restrictions Programs are available worldwide. Enrollment is restricted to individuals meeting certain criteria.
Services Distance learners have access to library services, the campus computer network, e-mail services, academic advising, career placement assistance, bookstore at a distance.
Credit-earning options Students may transfer credits from another institution or may earn credits through examinations, portfolio assessment, military training, business training.
Typical costs *Undergraduate:* Tuition of $220 per credit plus mandatory fees of $80 per term. *Graduate:* Tuition of $425 per credit plus mandatory fees of $80 per term. Tuition for Doctoral courses is $525 per credit. *Noncredit courses:* $495 per course. Costs may vary. Financial aid is available to distance learners.
Registration Students may register by mail, fax, telephone, e-mail, in person.
Contact Mary L. Tebes, Executive Director, Lynn University, 3601 North Military Trail, Boca Raton, FL 33431. *Telephone:* 561-237-7803. *Fax:* 561-237-7799. *E-mail:* mtebes@lynn.edu.

DEGREES AND AWARDS

BPS Bachelor of Professional Studies (certain restrictions apply)

COURSE SUBJECT AREAS OFFERED OUTSIDE OF DEGREE PROGRAMS

Undergraduate: American (U.S.) history; art history and criticism; business administration and management; business communications; computer and information sciences; curriculum and instruction; education; education administration; educational psychology; English language and literature; environmental science; health professions and related sciences; hospitality services management; human resources management; international business; management information systems; mathematics; psychology; special education; teacher education
Graduate: Business administration and management; criminal justice; curriculum and instruction; education; education administration; educational research; health professions and related sciences; hospitality services management; international business; special education; teacher education
Noncredit: Human resources management

See full description on page 572.

MACON STATE COLLEGE

Macon, Georgia
Office of Distance Learning
www.maconstate.edu/webcourses.asp

Macon State College, founded in 1968, is a state-supported, four-year college. It is accredited by the Southern Association of Colleges and Schools. In 1999–2000, it offered 13 courses at a distance. In fall 1999, there were 97 students enrolled in distance learning courses.

Course delivery sites Courses are delivered to your home, your work-place, Georgia Perimeter College (Decatur), off-campus center(s) in Warner Robins.

Media Courses are delivered via television, videotapes, videoconferencing, interactive television, computer software, CD-ROM, computer conferencing, World Wide Web, e-mail, print. Students and teachers may meet in person or interact via videoconferencing, mail, telephone, fax, e-mail, interactive television, World Wide Web. The following equipment may be required: television, videocassette player, computer, modem, Internet access, e-mail.

Restrictions Programs are available to in-state students only. Enrollment is open to anyone.

Services Distance learners have access to library services, the campus computer network, e-mail services at a distance.

Credit-earning options Students may transfer credits from another institution or may earn credits through examinations.

Typical costs Tuition is $52 per semester hour for lower division undergraduate in-state and $155 out-of-state. For upper division undergraduate in-state it is $76 per semester hour and $226 out-of-state. Mandatory fees are $44 per semester. Costs may vary. Financial aid is available to distance learners.

Registration Students may register by World Wide Web, in person.

Contact Wanda M. Eanes, Director of Technology Support Services, Macon State College, 100 College Station Drive, Macon, GA 31206. *Telephone:* 912-471-2823. *Fax:* 912-471-2896. *E-mail:* weanes@mail.maconstate.edu.

DEGREES AND AWARDS

Distance programs offered do not lead to a degree or other formal award.

COURSE SUBJECT AREAS OFFERED OUTSIDE OF DEGREE PROGRAMS

Undergraduate: Accounting; database management; English composition; health professions and related sciences; information sciences and systems
Noncredit: Adult education

MACON TECHNICAL INSTITUTE

Macon, Georgia
www.macontech.org/online/

Macon Technical Institute, founded in 1966, is a state-supported, two-year college. It is accredited by the Council on Occupational Education, Southern Association of Colleges and Schools. In 1999–2000, it offered 45 courses at a distance. In fall 1999, there were 50 students enrolled in distance learning courses.

Course delivery sites Courses are delivered to your home, your work-place, 1 off-campus center in Milledgeville.

Media Courses are delivered via television, computer software, World Wide Web, e-mail. Students and teachers may meet in person or interact

via mail, telephone, fax, e-mail, interactive television, World Wide Web. The following equipment may be required: computer, modem, Internet access, e-mail.

Restrictions Programs are available worldwide. Enrollment is open to anyone.

Services Distance learners have access to library services, the campus computer network, e-mail services, academic advising, career placement assistance, bookstore at a distance.

Credit-earning options Students may transfer credits from another institution or may earn credits through examinations.

Typical costs Tuition of $23 per credit hour plus mandatory fees of $35 per quarter. Financial aid is available to distance learners.

Registration Students may register by e-mail, World Wide Web, in person.

Contact Glenn Deibert, Director of Curriculum, Macon Technical Institute, 3300 Macon Tech Drive, Macon, GA 31206. *Telephone:* 912-757-3430. *Fax:* 912-757-3534. *E-mail:* gdeibert@macontech.org.

DEGREES AND AWARDS

Undergraduate Certificate(s) AutoCAD Operator, Certified Construction Worker, CISCO Specialist, Computer Software Application Specialist, Insurance Specialist, Microsoft User Specialist, Residential Drawing Technician

COURSE SUBJECT AREAS OFFERED OUTSIDE OF DEGREE PROGRAMS

Undergraduate: Algebra; computer programming; construction; engineering-related technologies

MADISON AREA TECHNICAL COLLEGE

Madison, Wisconsin
Instructional Media/Distance Education Department
www.madison.tec.wi.us

Madison Area Technical College, founded in 1911, is a district-supported, two-year college. It is accredited by the North Central Association of Colleges and Schools. It first offered distance learning courses in 1994. In 1999–2000, it offered 65 courses at a distance. In fall 1999, there were 1,200 students enrolled in distance learning courses.

Course delivery sites Courses are delivered to your home, your work-place, high schools, 17 off-campus centers in Mauston, Pardeeville, Spring Green, Sun Prairie.

Media Courses are delivered via videotapes, interactive television, audiotapes, computer software, CD-ROM, World Wide Web. Students and teachers may meet in person or interact via videoconferencing, mail, telephone, fax, e-mail, interactive television, World Wide Web. The following equipment may be required: television, videocassette player, computer, modem, Internet access, e-mail.

Restrictions Programs are available to local area students. Enrollment is restricted to individuals meeting certain criteria.

Services Distance learners have access to library services, bookstore at a distance.

Credit-earning options Students may transfer credits from another institution or may earn credits through examinations, portfolio assessment, military training, business training.

Typical costs Tuition of $87 per credit plus mandatory fees of $4 per credit for in-state residents. Tuition of $373 per credit plus mandatory fees of $4 per credit for out-of-state residents. Costs may vary. Financial aid is available to distance learners.

Registration Students may register by mail, telephone, in person.

Madison Area Technical College

Contact Paul Meske, Instructional Media/Distance Education Specialist, Madison Area Technical College, 3550 Anderson Street, Madison, WI 53704. *Telephone:* 608-246-6050. *Fax:* 608-246-6287. *E-mail:* meske@madison.tec.wi.us.

DEGREES AND AWARDS

Undergraduate Certificate(s) Quality Management (service area differs from that of the overall institution)
AD Accounting

COURSE SUBJECT AREAS OFFERED OUTSIDE OF DEGREE PROGRAMS

Undergraduate: Accounting; African-American studies; algebra; American (U.S.) history; American literature; anthropology; business; business administration and management; business law; economics; English as a second language (ESL); English composition; English language and literature; English literature; European languages and literatures; home economics and family studies; liberal arts, general studies, and humanities; marketing; nursing; psychology; real estate; sociology; statistics; women's studies
Noncredit: Business administration and management

MADISONVILLE COMMUNITY COLLEGE

Madisonville, Kentucky

Madisonville Community College, founded in 1968, is a state-supported, two-year college. It is accredited by the Southern Association of Colleges and Schools. In 1999–2000, it offered 17 courses at a distance. In fall 1999, there were 144 students enrolled in distance learning courses.
Course delivery sites Courses are delivered to your home.
Media Courses are delivered via television, videotapes, interactive television, World Wide Web. Students and teachers may interact via videoconferencing, mail, telephone, fax, e-mail, interactive television. The following equipment may be required: television, videocassette player, computer, Internet access.
Restrictions Internet courses are available worldwide; telecourses and ITV courses are available locally. Enrollment is restricted to individuals meeting certain criteria.
Services Distance learners have access to library services, e-mail services, academic advising, career placement assistance at a distance.
Typical costs Tuition of $46 per credit hour plus mandatory fees of $4 per credit hour for in-state residents. Tuition of $138 per credit hour plus mandatory fees of $4 per credit hour for out-of-state residents. Costs may vary. Financial aid is available to distance learners.
Registration Students may register by mail, in person.
Contact Cherry Berges, Director of Library Services, Madisonville Community College, 2000 College Drive, Madisonville, KY 42431. *Telephone:* 502-821-2250 Ext. 2251. *Fax:* 502-825-8553. *E-mail:* madclber@ukcc.uky.edu.

DEGREES AND AWARDS

Distance programs offered do not lead to a degree or other formal award.

COURSE SUBJECT AREAS OFFERED OUTSIDE OF DEGREE PROGRAMS

Undergraduate: Biology; business administration and management; creative writing; economics; English language and literature; history; liberal arts, general studies, and humanities; political science; psychology; sociology

See full description on page 556.

MADONNA UNIVERSITY

Livonia, Michigan
College of Continuing and Professional Studies
www.munet.edu

Madonna University, founded in 1947, is an independent, religious, comprehensive institution. It is accredited by the North Central Association of Colleges and Schools. It first offered distance learning courses in 1983. In 1999–2000, it offered 56 courses at a distance. In fall 1999, there were 273 students enrolled in distance learning courses.
Course delivery sites Courses are delivered to your home, your workplace, Schoolcraft College (Livonia), 2 off-campus centers in Gaylord, Indian River.
Media Courses are delivered via television, videotapes, videoconferencing, interactive television, audiotapes, computer software, computer conferencing, World Wide Web, e-mail, print. Students and teachers may meet in person or interact via videoconferencing, audioconferencing, mail, telephone, fax, e-mail, interactive television, World Wide Web. The following equipment may be required: television, videocassette player, computer, modem, Internet access, e-mail.
Restrictions Some programs are available to in-state students only. Enrollment is open to anyone.
Services Distance learners have access to library services, the campus computer network, e-mail services, academic advising, tutoring, career placement assistance, bookstore at a distance.
Credit-earning options Students may transfer credits from another institution or may earn credits through examinations, portfolio assessment, military training, business training.
Typical costs *Undergraduate:* Tuition of $217 per semester hour plus mandatory fees of $50 per semester. *Graduate:* Tuition of $272 per semester hour plus mandatory fees of $50 per semester. Costs may vary. Financial aid is available to distance learners.
Registration Students may register by mail, fax, telephone, e-mail, in person.
Contact Dr. James Novak, Dean, Madonna University, College of Continuing and Professional Studies, 36600 Schoolcraft Road, Livonia, MI 48150. *Telephone:* 734-432-5731. *Fax:* 734-432-5364. *E-mail:* novak@smtp.munet.edu.

DEGREES AND AWARDS

BGS General Studies (certain restrictions apply; service area differs from that of the overall institution; some on-campus requirements)
BSBA Business Administration and Management (service area differs from that of the overall institution; some on-campus requirements)
BSW Social Work (certain restrictions apply; service area differs from that of the overall institution)
MSBA Leadership Studies (certain restrictions apply; service area differs from that of the overall institution; some on-campus requirements), Leadership Studies–Healthcare (certain restrictions apply; service area differs from that of the overall institution; some on-campus requirements), Medical and Dental Practice Administration (certain restrictions apply; service area differs from that of the overall institution; some on-campus requirements)

COURSE SUBJECT AREAS OFFERED OUTSIDE OF DEGREE PROGRAMS

Undergraduate: Business; conservation and natural resources; foods and nutrition studies; gerontology; liberal arts, general studies, and humanities; religious studies; social sciences; social work; substance abuse counseling
Graduate: Business

MAHARISHI UNIVERSITY OF MANAGEMENT

Fairfield, Iowa

Distance MBA Program
mum.edu/SBPA/distance

Maharishi University of Management, founded in 1971, is an independent, nonprofit university. It is accredited by the North Central Association of Colleges and Schools. It first offered distance learning courses in 1995. In 1999–2000, it offered 15 courses at a distance. In fall 1999, there were 200 students enrolled in distance learning courses.

Course delivery sites Courses are delivered to your home.

Media Courses are delivered via videotapes, computer conferencing, print. Students and teachers may interact via telephone, e-mail, World Wide Web. The following equipment may be required: television, videocassette player, computer, Internet access, e-mail.

Restrictions Programs are available worldwide. Enrollment is open to anyone.

Services Distance learners have access to library services, e-mail services, academic advising, bookstore at a distance.

Credit-earning options Students may transfer credits from another institution or may earn credits through examinations, portfolio assessment.

Typical costs Tuition of $3100 per semester. Financial aid is available to distance learners.

Registration Students may register by mail.

Contact Michael Matzkin, Director, Distance MBA Programs, Maharishi University of Management, 1000 North Fourth Street, Fairfield, IA 52557. *Telephone:* 515-472-1128. *Fax:* 515-472-1128. *E-mail:* distance@mum.edu.

DEGREES AND AWARDS

MBA Business Administration

COURSE SUBJECT AREAS OFFERED OUTSIDE OF DEGREE PROGRAMS

Graduate: Accounting; business administration and management; finance; human resources management; international business; investments and securities; management information systems; marketing

Noncredit: Accounting; business administration and management; finance; human resources management; international business; investments and securities; management information systems; marketing

MALONE COLLEGE

Canton, Ohio

Malone College Online Learning
malone-online.org

Malone College, founded in 1892, is an independent, religious, comprehensive institution affiliated with the Evangelical Friends Church–Eastern Region. It is accredited by the North Central Association of Colleges and Schools. It first offered distance learning courses in 1999. In 1999–2000, it offered 9 courses at a distance.

Course delivery sites Courses are delivered to your home, your workplace, military bases, high schools.

Media Courses are delivered via World Wide Web. Students and teachers may interact via mail, telephone, fax, e-mail, World Wide Web. The following equipment may be required: computer, modem, Internet access, e-mail.

Restrictions Programs are available worldwide. Enrollment is restricted to individuals meeting certain criteria.

Services Distance learners have access to library services, the campus computer network, e-mail services, academic advising, bookstore at a distance.

Credit-earning options Students may transfer credits from another institution or may earn credits through examinations, portfolio assessment, military training, business training.

Typical costs Tuition of $340 per semester credit. Financial aid is available to distance learners.

Registration Students may register by e-mail, World Wide Web, in person.

Contact Deborah Craven, Department Assistant, Malone College, 515 25th Street North West, Canton, OH 44709. *Telephone:* 330-471-8242. *Fax:* 330-471-8478. *E-mail:* onlineinquiry@malone.edu.

eCollege.com *www.ecollege.com/scholarships*

DEGREES AND AWARDS

Distance programs offered do not lead to a degree or other formal award.

COURSE SUBJECT AREAS OFFERED OUTSIDE OF DEGREE PROGRAMS

Undergraduate: Business administration and management; business communications; communications; comparative literature; fine arts; health and physical education/fitness; political science

MANATEE COMMUNITY COLLEGE

Bradenton, Florida

Distance Education
www.mcc.cc.fl.us

Manatee Community College, founded in 1957, is a state-supported, two-year college. It is accredited by the Southern Association of Colleges and Schools. It first offered distance learning courses in 1990. In 1999–2000, it offered 49 courses at a distance.

Course delivery sites Courses are delivered to your home.

Media Courses are delivered via television, videotapes, videoconferencing, interactive television, audiotapes, computer software, World Wide Web, e-mail, print. Students and teachers may meet in person or interact via videoconferencing, audioconferencing, mail, telephone, fax, e-mail, World Wide Web. The following equipment may be required: television, videocassette player, computer, Internet access.

Restrictions Programs are available in Sarasota and Manatee Counties. Enrollment is open to anyone.

Services Distance learners have access to the campus computer network, e-mail services at a distance.

Credit-earning options Students may transfer credits from another institution or may earn credits through examinations, portfolio assessment.

Typical costs Tuition of $135 per course for in-state residents. Tuition of $492 per course for out-of-state residents. There is a mandatory fee of $25. Costs may vary. Financial aid is available to distance learners.

Registration Students may register by mail, fax, telephone, World Wide Web, in person.

Contact Dr. John Rosen, Vice President for Academic Affairs, Manatee Community College, PO Box 1849, Bradenton, FL 34206. *Telephone:* 941-755-4200. *Fax:* 941-727-6077.

DEGREES AND AWARDS

Distance programs offered do not lead to a degree or other formal award.

COURSE SUBJECT AREAS OFFERED OUTSIDE OF DEGREE PROGRAMS

Undergraduate: Accounting; algebra; American (U.S.) history; anatomy; art history and criticism; biology; business administration and management; calculus; chemistry; child care and development; Chinese language and literature; design; developmental and child psychology; economics; English composition; English language and literature; ethics; health and physical education/fitness; history; information sciences and systems; instructional media; liberal arts, general studies, and humanities; logic; management information systems; marketing; meteorology; microbiology; paralegal/legal assistant; political science; psychology; religious studies; sociology; statistics; teacher education

MANCHESTER COMMUNITY COLLEGE

Manchester, Connecticut

Manchester Community College, founded in 1963, is a state-supported, two-year college. It is accredited by the New England Association of Schools and Colleges. It first offered distance learning courses in 1989. In 1999–2000, it offered 16 courses at a distance. In fall 1999, there were 125 students enrolled in distance learning courses.

Course delivery sites Courses are delivered to your home, your workplace, high schools.

Media Courses are delivered via television, World Wide Web. Students and teachers may meet in person or interact via mail, telephone, fax, e-mail. The following equipment may be required: television, computer, modem, Internet access, e-mail.

Restrictions Programs are available to in-state students only. Enrollment is open to anyone.

Services Distance learners have access to library services at a distance.

Credit-earning options Students may transfer credits from another institution or may earn credits through examinations, military training.

Typical costs Tuition of $67 per credit plus mandatory fees of $42 per credit for in-state residents. Tuition of $218 per credit plus mandatory fees of $42 per credit for out-of-state residents. Financial aid is available to distance learners.

Registration Students may register by mail, fax, in person.

Contact Randy Fournier, Director of Distance Learning, Manchester Community College, Great Path, MS #3, Manchester, CT 06045-1046. *Telephone:* 860-647-6227. *Fax:* 860-647-6238. *E-mail:* maxrsf@commnet. edu.

DEGREES AND AWARDS

Distance programs offered do not lead to a degree or other formal award.

COURSE SUBJECT AREAS OFFERED OUTSIDE OF DEGREE PROGRAMS

Undergraduate: American (U.S.) history; criminology; English composition; English literature; geography; Japanese language and literature; occupational therapy

MANOR COLLEGE

Jenkintown, Pennsylvania
www.manor.edu

Manor College, founded in 1947, is an independent, religious, two-year college. It is accredited by the Middle States Association of Colleges and Schools. It first offered distance learning courses in 1998. In 1999–2000, it offered 10 courses at a distance. In fall 1999, there were 63 students enrolled in distance learning courses.

Course delivery sites Courses are delivered to your home, Holy Cross College (Notre Dame, IN), Presentation College (Aberdeen, SD).

Media Courses are delivered via videoconferencing, interactive television, computer conferencing, World Wide Web, e-mail. Students and teachers may meet in person or interact via videoconferencing, telephone, e-mail, interactive television, World Wide Web. The following equipment may be required: television, videocassette player, computer, modem, Internet access, e-mail.

Restrictions Programs are available nationwide. Enrollment is open to anyone.

Services Distance learners have access to library services, the campus computer network, e-mail services at a distance.

Credit-earning options Students may transfer credits from another institution or may earn credits through examinations, portfolio assessment, military training.

Typical costs Basic undergraduate tuition is $195 per credit. Allied Health tuition is $290 per credit. Mandatory fees for 1 to 11 credits is between $15 and $25. Full-time general fee is $150. Costs may vary. Financial aid is available to distance learners.

Registration Students may register by mail, fax, in person.

Contact Chris Whaumbush, Director, Part-Time Admissions and Professional Development, Manor College, 700 Fox Chase Road, Jenkintown, PA 19046. *Telephone:* 215-884-2218. *Fax:* 215-576-6564. *E-mail:* ptadmiss@manor.edu.

DEGREES AND AWARDS

Distance programs offered do not lead to a degree or other formal award.

COURSE SUBJECT AREAS OFFERED OUTSIDE OF DEGREE PROGRAMS

Undergraduate: Animal sciences; business administration and management; business law; English composition; marketing; religious studies

MANSFIELD UNIVERSITY OF PENNSYLVANIA

Mansfield, Pennsylvania
Center for Lifelong Learning
www.mnsfld.edu

Mansfield University of Pennsylvania, founded in 1857, is a state-supported, comprehensive institution. It is accredited by the Middle States Association of Colleges and Schools. It first offered distance learning courses in 1995. In 1999–2000, it offered 25 courses at a distance. In fall 1999, there were 100 students enrolled in distance learning courses.

Course delivery sites Courses are delivered to your home, high schools, off-campus center(s) in (NY).

Media Courses are delivered via videotapes, videoconferencing, computer software, CD-ROM, World Wide Web, e-mail, print. Students and teachers may interact via videoconferencing, telephone, fax, e-mail, World Wide Web. The following equipment may be required: computer, modem, Internet access, e-mail.

Restrictions Programs are available nationwide. Enrollment is restricted to individuals meeting certain criteria.

Services Distance learners have access to library services, e-mail services, academic advising, tutoring, bookstore at a distance.

Credit-earning options Students may transfer credits from another institution or may earn credits through examinations.

Typical costs *Undergraduate:* Tuition of $150 per credit plus mandatory fees of $15 per credit for in-state residents. Tuition of $377 per credit plus mandatory fees of $15 per credit for out-of-state residents. *Graduate:* Tuition of $210 per credit plus mandatory fees of $20 per credit for

in-state residents. Tuition of $367 per credit plus mandatory fees of $20 per credit for out-of-state residents. Costs may vary. Financial aid is available to distance learners.
Registration Students may register by mail, fax, telephone, in person.
Contact Karen Norton, Director of Credit Programs, Mansfield University of Pennsylvania, 211 Doane Center, Mansfield, PA 16933. *Telephone:* 717-662-4244. *Fax:* 717-662-4120. *E-mail:* knorton@mnsfld.edu.

DEGREES AND AWARDS

AS Criminal Justice (service area differs from that of the overall institution)
MEd Education
MS School Library and Information Technologies (certain restrictions apply; service area differs from that of the overall institution)

COURSE SUBJECT AREAS OFFERED OUTSIDE OF DEGREE PROGRAMS

Undergraduate: Anatomy; business administration and management; Canadian studies; communications; community health services; criminal justice; criminology; English language and literature; geology; nursing; philosophy and religion; psychology
Graduate: Curriculum and instruction; geology; library and information studies; psychology; special education

MARIAN COLLEGE OF FOND DU LAC

Fond du Lac, Wisconsin
www.mariancollege.edu

Marian College of Fond du Lac, founded in 1936, is an independent, religious, comprehensive institution. It is accredited by the North Central Association of Colleges and Schools. In 1999–2000, it offered 2 courses at a distance. In fall 1999, there were 27 students enrolled in distance learning courses.
Course delivery sites Courses are delivered to your home, high schools.
Media Courses are delivered via television, videoconferencing, interactive television, computer software, computer conferencing, World Wide Web, e-mail. Students and teachers may meet in person or interact via videoconferencing, e-mail, interactive television, World Wide Web. The following equipment may be required: television, computer, modem, Internet access, e-mail.
Restrictions Programs are available on a regional level. Enrollment is open to anyone.
Services Distance learners have access to library services, the campus computer network, e-mail services, academic advising, tutoring, career placement assistance, bookstore at a distance.
Credit-earning options Students may transfer credits from another institution.
Typical costs Tuition of $255 per credit. Application fee is $15. Financial aid is available to distance learners.
Registration Students may register by mail, in person.
Contact Dr. Gary Boelhower, Assistant Dean Academic Affairs, Marian College of Fond du Lac, 45 South National Avenue, Fond du Lac, WI 54935. *Telephone:* 920-923-8796. *Fax:* 920-923-7154. *E-mail:* gboelhower@mariancollege.edu.

DEGREES AND AWARDS

Distance programs offered do not lead to a degree or other formal award.

COURSE SUBJECT AREAS OFFERED OUTSIDE OF DEGREE PROGRAMS

Undergraduate: Education; social sciences

MARIST COLLEGE

Poughkeepsie, New York
School of Management
www.marist.edu/graduate/

Marist College, founded in 1929, is an independent, nonprofit, comprehensive institution. It is accredited by the Middle States Association of Colleges and Schools. In 1999–2000, it offered 10 courses at a distance. In fall 1999, there were 80 students enrolled in distance learning courses.
Course delivery sites Courses are delivered to your home, your workplace.
Media Courses are delivered via World Wide Web. Students and teachers may meet in person or interact via telephone, e-mail, World Wide Web. The following equipment may be required: computer, modem, Internet access.
Restrictions Programs are available worldwide. Enrollment is restricted to individuals meeting certain criteria.
Services Distance learners have access to library services, the campus computer network, e-mail services, academic advising, career placement assistance, bookstore at a distance.
Credit-earning options Students may transfer credits from another institution.
Typical costs Tuition of $436 per credit. Costs may vary. Financial aid is available to distance learners.
Registration Students may register by mail, telephone, in person.
Contact Jean Theobald, Graduate Academic Advisor, Marist College, Graduate and Continuing Education, Poughkeepsie, NY 12601. *Telephone:* 888-877-7900. *Fax:* 914-575-3166. *E-mail:* jean.theobald@marist.edu.

DEGREES AND AWARDS

MBA Business Administration (certain restrictions apply)
MPA Public Administration (certain restrictions apply)
See full description on page 574.

MARSHALL UNIVERSITY

Huntington, West Virginia
School of Extended Education
www.marshall.edu

Marshall University, founded in 1837, is a state-supported, comprehensive institution. It is accredited by the North Central Association of Colleges and Schools. It first offered distance learning courses in 1986. In 1999–2000, it offered 132 courses at a distance. In fall 1999, there were 929 students enrolled in distance learning courses.
Course delivery sites Courses are delivered to high schools, 6 off-campus centers in Beckley, Bluefield, Hurricane, Logan and Williamson, Point Pleasant, South Charleston.
Media Courses are delivered via television, videotapes, videoconferencing, interactive television, computer software, CD-ROM, World Wide Web, e-mail. Students and teachers may meet in person or interact via videoconferencing, audioconferencing, mail, telephone, fax, e-mail, interactive television, World Wide Web. The following equipment may be required: television, videocassette player, computer, Internet access, e-mail.
Restrictions Programs are available to in-state students only. Enrollment is open to anyone.
Services Distance learners have access to library services, e-mail services, career placement assistance, bookstore at a distance.

Credit-earning options Students may transfer credits from another institution or may earn credits through examinations, portfolio assessment.

Typical costs *Undergraduate:* Tuition of $186 per hour for local area residents. Tuition of $102 per hour for in-state residents. Tuition of $271.50 per hour for out-of-state residents. *Graduate:* Tuition of $267 per hour for local area residents. Tuition of $136.75 per hour for in-state residents. Tuition of $396.50 per hour for out-of-state residents. Costs may vary. Financial aid is available to distance learners.

Registration Students may register by mail, telephone, World Wide Web, in person.

Contact Crystal Stewart, Office Manager, Marshall University. *Telephone:* 304-696-3150. *Fax:* 304-696-2973. *E-mail:* stewar14@marshall.edu.

DEGREES AND AWARDS

Distance programs offered do not lead to a degree or other formal award.

COURSE SUBJECT AREAS OFFERED OUTSIDE OF DEGREE PROGRAMS

Undergraduate: Accounting; administrative and secretarial services; anthropology; area, ethnic, and cultural studies; business; business administration and management; computer and information sciences; criminology; developmental and child psychology; economics; education administration; educational psychology; fine arts; geography; geology; health professions and related sciences; history; home economics and family studies; journalism; law and legal studies; liberal arts, general studies, and humanities; management information systems; marketing; mathematics; nursing; philosophy and religion; psychology; real estate; social work; sociology; special education; teacher education

Graduate: Accounting; area, ethnic, and cultural studies; business; business administration and management; education administration; educational psychology; history; liberal arts, general studies, and humanities; nursing; social work; sociology; special education; teacher education

See full description on page 676.

MARTIN COMMUNITY COLLEGE

Williamston, North Carolina
www.martin.cc.nc.us

Martin Community College, founded in 1968, is a state-supported, two-year college. It is accredited by the Southern Association of Colleges and Schools. In 1999–2000, it offered 12 courses at a distance. In fall 1999, there were 76 students enrolled in distance learning courses.

Course delivery sites Courses are delivered to your home, high schools, off-campus center(s) in Windsor.

Media Courses are delivered via television, videotapes, World Wide Web. Students and teachers may meet in person or interact via e-mail, interactive television, World Wide Web. The following equipment may be required: television, videocassette player, computer, modem, Internet access, e-mail.

Restrictions Programs are available to local area students. Enrollment is open to anyone.

Credit-earning options Students may transfer credits from another institution or may earn credits through examinations.

Typical costs Tuition of $26.75 per credit plus mandatory fees of $1.50 per credit for in-state residents. Tuition of $169.75 per credit plus mandatory fees of $1.50 per credit for out-of-state residents.

Registration Students may register by in person.

Contact Rob Goldberg, Admissions Counselor, Martin Community College, 1161 Kehukee Park Road, Williamston, NC 27892. *Telephone:* 252-792-1521. *Fax:* 252-792-0826. *E-mail:* rgoldberg@martin.cc.nc.us.

DEGREES AND AWARDS

Distance programs offered do not lead to a degree or other formal award.

COURSE SUBJECT AREAS OFFERED OUTSIDE OF DEGREE PROGRAMS

Undergraduate: Business; business administration and management; communications; education; electronics; English language and literature; information sciences and systems; psychology; sociology

MARY BALDWIN COLLEGE

Staunton, Virginia
Adult Degree Program
www.mbc.edu/adp

Mary Baldwin College, founded in 1842, is an independent, religious, comprehensive institution affiliated with the Presbyterian Church (U.S.A.). It is accredited by the Southern Association of Colleges and Schools. In 1999–2000, it offered 75 courses at a distance. In fall 1999, there were 1,250 students enrolled in distance learning courses.

Course delivery sites Courses are delivered to your home, your workplace, 4 off-campus centers in Charlottesville, Richmond, Roanoke, Weyers Cave.

Media Courses are delivered via computer software, World Wide Web, e-mail, print. Students and teachers may meet in person or interact via mail, telephone, fax, e-mail, World Wide Web. The following equipment may be required: computer, Internet access, e-mail.

Restrictions Programs are available to in-state students only. Enrollment is restricted to individuals meeting certain criteria.

Services Distance learners have access to library services, e-mail services, academic advising, career placement assistance, bookstore at a distance.

Credit-earning options Students may transfer credits from another institution or may earn credits through examinations, portfolio assessment, military training.

Typical costs Tuition of $290 per semester hour. Mandatory fees include $25 application fee, $70 graduation fee, and $30 orientation fee. Financial aid is available to distance learners.

Registration Students may register by mail, fax, World Wide Web, in person.

Contact Ms. Debby Camden, ADP Recruiting Coordinator, Mary Baldwin College, ADP House, Staunton, VA 24401. *Telephone:* 540-887-7003. *Fax:* 540-887-7265. *E-mail:* adp@mbc.edu.

DEGREES AND AWARDS

BA Art (some on-campus requirements), Biology (some on-campus requirements), Business Administration, Chemistry, Communications, Economics, English, Health Care Administration (some on-campus requirements), History, Marketing Communications, Mathematics (some on-campus requirements), Music, Philosophy/Religion, Political Science, Sociology, Theatre (some on-campus requirements)
BS Biology, Business Administration, Chemistry, Mathematics

MARYGROVE COLLEGE

Detroit, Michigan
Master in the Art of Teaching Program
www.marygrove.edu

Marygrove College, founded in 1905, is an independent, religious, comprehensive institution. It is accredited by the North Central Association of Colleges and Schools. It first offered distance learning courses in 1989. In 1999–2000, it offered 10 courses at a distance. In fall 1999, there were 3,850 students enrolled in distance learning courses.

Course delivery sites Courses are delivered to your home, your workplace.

Media Courses are delivered via videotapes, print. Students and teachers may interact via mail, telephone, fax, e-mail, World Wide Web. The following equipment may be required: television, videocassette player, Internet access, e-mail.

Restrictions Courses are available to students in Pennsylvania, Ohio, New Jersey, and Michigan only. Enrollment is restricted to individuals meeting certain criteria.

Services Distance learners have access to library services, academic advising at a distance.

Credit-earning options Students may transfer credits from another institution or may earn credits through portfolio assessment.

Typical costs Tuition of $237 per credit hour plus mandatory fees of $95 per course. Financial aid is available to distance learners.

Registration Students may register by mail, fax, telephone.

Contact Dr. Eunice Jordan, Director, Marygrove College, Master in the Art of Teaching Program, Detroit, MI 48221. *Telephone:* 313-927-1507. *Fax:* 313-927-1530. *E-mail:* ejordan@marygrove.edu.

DEGREES AND AWARDS

MAT Teacher Education

COURSE SUBJECT AREAS OFFERED OUTSIDE OF DEGREE PROGRAMS

Graduate: Teacher education

Special note

Marygrove College, located in Detroit, is accredited by the North Central Association of Colleges and Schools and has more than 3,000 graduate and undergraduate students. The College has an established reputation for teacher preparation and is approved by the Michigan Department of Education. Marygrove's distance learning Master of Arts in Teaching (MAT) degree program is available to all K–12 educators who desire to become better teachers. The program uses an innovative, student-centered learning model that allows the learner to participate at his or her own convenience. A few of the features of this noteworthy, multimedia MAT program include learning the latest practical classroom strategies applicable to today's children from nationally known experts; seeing master teachers model the practical strategies in actual classrooms with real students; regular contact by telephone, e-mail, fax, or optional in-person visits with Marygrove's faculty mentors (mentors are available for feedback, consultation, advice, and guidance as students progress through the program); and working collaboratively with a peer study team. Marygrove College offers the MAT degree program in Ohio, Michigan, New Jersey, and Pennsylvania. The entire program can be completed in approximately 5 semesters and is designed for working educators wishing to become high-performing teachers and/or seeking career advancement. For more information on the MAT program, students should call 800–339–0736 (toll-free) and ask for Maureen or visit the Web site at http://www.masters4teachers.net.

MARYLAND INSTITUTE, COLLEGE OF ART

Baltimore, Maryland
MICA Online
www.mica.edu/cs/contents_main.html

Maryland Institute, College of Art, founded in 1826, is an independent, nonprofit, comprehensive institution. It is accredited by the Middle States Association of Colleges and Schools. It first offered distance learning courses in 1997. In 1999–2000, it offered 3 courses at a distance. In fall 1999, there were 75 students enrolled in distance learning courses.

Course delivery sites Courses are delivered to your home, your workplace.

Media Courses are delivered via computer software, computer conferencing, World Wide Web, e-mail, print. Students and teachers may meet in person or interact via fax, e-mail, World Wide Web. The following equipment may be required: computer, modem, Internet access, e-mail.

Restrictions Programs are available worldwide. Enrollment is open to anyone.

Services Distance learners have access to library services, the campus computer network, academic advising at a distance.

Credit-earning options Students may earn credits through portfolio assessment.

Typical costs Tuition of $220 per credit. Registration fee is $20. *Noncredit courses:* $325 per course. Costs may vary.

Registration Students may register by mail, fax, telephone, in person.

Contact Claudia Jenkins, Continuing Studies Registrar, Maryland Institute, College of Art, Office of Continuing Studies, Baltimore, MD 21217. *Telephone:* 410-225-2217. *Fax:* 410-225-2229. *E-mail:* cs@mica.edu.

DEGREES AND AWARDS

Undergraduate Certificate(s) Digital Imagining and Web Design (service area differs from that of the overall institution)

COURSE SUBJECT AREAS OFFERED OUTSIDE OF DEGREE PROGRAMS

Undergraduate: Commercial art; design; fine arts
Noncredit: Commercial art; design; fine arts

MARYLHURST UNIVERSITY

Marylhurst, Oregon
Department of Web-based Learning
www.marylhurst.edu

Marylhurst University, founded in 1893, is an independent, religious, comprehensive institution. It is accredited by the Northwest Association of Schools and Colleges. It first offered distance learning courses in 1996. In 1999–2000, it offered 75 courses at a distance. In fall 1999, there were 190 students enrolled in distance learning courses.

Course delivery sites Courses are delivered to your home, your workplace.

Media Courses are delivered via computer software, computer conferencing, World Wide Web, e-mail, print. Students and teachers may meet in person or interact via mail, telephone, fax, e-mail, World Wide Web. The following equipment may be required: computer, modem, Internet access.

Restrictions Programs are available worldwide. Enrollment is restricted to individuals meeting certain criteria.

Services Distance learners have access to library services, academic advising, tutoring, bookstore at a distance.

Credit-earning options Students may transfer credits from another institution or may earn credits through portfolio assessment.

Marylhurst University

Typical costs *Undergraduate:* Tuition of $235 per credit hour plus mandatory fees of $17 per quarter. *Graduate:* Tuition of $276 per credit hour plus mandatory fees of $17 per quarter. Other fees include $4 per credit up to $48. Costs may vary. Financial aid is available to distance learners.

Registration Students may register by mail, fax, telephone, e-mail, World Wide Web, in person.

Contact Web-based Learning Office, Marylhurst University, 17600 Pacific Highway, PO Box 261, Marylhurst, OR 97036. *Telephone:* 800-634-9982 Ext. 6319. *E-mail:* learning@marylhurst.edu.

DEGREES AND AWARDS

BA Organizational Communications
BS Management

COURSE SUBJECT AREAS OFFERED OUTSIDE OF DEGREE PROGRAMS

Undergraduate: Algebra; American (U.S.) history; American literature; American studies; anthropology; biology; business administration and management; business communications; communications; comparative literature; creative writing; economics; educational psychology; English composition; English literature; ethics; film studies; finance; Jewish studies; library and information studies; logic; marketing; political science; psychology; religious studies; statistics; theological studies

Graduate: Business administration and management; business communications; ethics; finance; marketing; statistics; theological studies

See full descriptions on pages 576 and 882.

MARYWOOD UNIVERSITY

Scranton, Pennsylvania

Office of Distance Education
www.marywood.edu

Marywood University, founded in 1915, is an independent, religious, comprehensive institution. It is accredited by the Middle States Association of Colleges and Schools. It first offered distance learning courses in 1975. In 1999–2000, it offered 60 courses at a distance. In fall 1999, there were 126 students enrolled in distance learning courses.

Course delivery sites Courses are delivered to your home, your workplace, military bases, other colleges.

Media Courses are delivered via videotapes, e-mail, print. Students and teachers may meet in person or interact via mail, telephone, fax, e-mail.

Restrictions Programs are available worldwide. Enrollment is restricted to individuals meeting certain criteria.

Services Distance learners have access to library services, the campus computer network, e-mail services, academic advising, career placement assistance, bookstore at a distance.

Credit-earning options Students may transfer credits from another institution or may earn credits through examinations, portfolio assessment, military training, business training.

Typical costs Tuition of $281 per credit. Financial aid is available to distance learners.

Registration Students may register by mail, fax, in person.

Contact Cheryll Gen, Coordinator for Student Enrollment and Retention, Marywood University. *Telephone:* 800-836-6940. *Fax:* 570-961-4751. *E-mail:* disted_adm@ac.marywood.edu.

DEGREES AND AWARDS

Undergraduate Certificate(s) Comprehensive Business Skills, Office Administration, Professional Communications

BS Accounting (certain restrictions apply; some on-campus requirements), Business Administration (certain restrictions apply; some on-campus requirements)

COURSE SUBJECT AREAS OFFERED OUTSIDE OF DEGREE PROGRAMS

Undergraduate: Accounting; advertising; algebra; American literature; art history and criticism; business administration and management; business communications; business law; communications; earth science; English composition; English language and literature; ethics; finance; French language and literature; health and physical education/fitness; human resources management; international business; investments and securities; management information systems; marketing; philosophy and religion; public relations; religious studies; sociology; Spanish language and literature; statistics

Special note

Marywood's Off Campus Degree Program is a flexible system of education designed to meet the needs of industrious adults. It was designed in the mid-1970s to make a Marywood education accessible to those who otherwise may not be able to complete their higher education goals due to professional, personal, or family responsibilities. Through individualized guided study, students learn in their own personal surroundings, free of classroom sessions and traditional semester schedules. They study at a pace consistent with their own goals and available time. Many experience the flavor and spirit of the Marywood community through conveniently scheduled residencies on campus. Marywood University is accredited by the Middle States Association of Colleges and Schools. This agency is responsible for reviewing and approving the major colleges and universities in New York, Pennsylvania, New Jersey, Maryland, and Delaware. This prestigious accreditation is recognized by prominent colleges and universities throughout the U.S. and abroad. Marywood University, located in Scranton, Pennsylvania, is an independent, comprehensive Catholic university owned and sponsored by the Congregation of the Sisters, Servants of the Immaculate Heart of Mary. It is collaboratively staffed by lay and religious personnel. Its mission is the education of men and women of all ages in undergraduate, graduate, and continuing education programs. The University serves a wide range of students, both nationally and internationally, while maintaining a concern for the education of women, culturally diverse persons, and first-generation students. Committed to spiritual, ethical, and religious values and a tradition of service, Marywood provides a framework that enables students both to develop fully as persons and to master the professional and leadership skills necessary for meeting human needs on regional and global levels.

MASSACHUSETTS INSTITUTE OF TECHNOLOGY

Cambridge, Massachusetts

Center for Advanced Educational Services (CAES)
www-caes.mit.edu

Massachusetts Institute of Technology, founded in 1861, is an independent, nonprofit university. It is accredited by the New England Association of Schools and Colleges. It first offered distance learning courses in 1996. In 1999–2000, it offered 12 courses at a distance. In fall 1999, there were 250 students enrolled in distance learning courses.

Course delivery sites Courses are delivered to your home, your workplace, military bases.

Media Courses are delivered via television, videotapes, videoconferencing, computer software, CD-ROM, computer conferencing, World Wide Web, e-mail, print. Students and teachers may meet in person or interact via videoconferencing, mail, telephone, fax, e-mail, World Wide Web. The following equipment may be required: computer, modem, Internet access, e-mail.

Restrictions Programs are available worldwide. Enrollment is restricted to individuals meeting certain criteria.

Services Distance learners have access to library services, the campus computer network, e-mail services, academic advising, tutoring at a distance.

Credit-earning options Students may earn credits through examinations.

Typical costs Costs may vary by subject and program. Costs may vary.

Registration Students may register by mail, fax, telephone, e-mail, World Wide Web, in person.

Contact Diane Molino-Fox, Marketing Assistant, Massachusetts Institute of Technology, Center for Advanced Educational Services, 77 Massachusetts Avenue, Cambridge, MA 02139. *Telephone:* 617-253-6128. *Fax:* 617-258-8831. *E-mail:* caes-asp@mit.edu.

DEGREES AND AWARDS

Distance programs offered do not lead to a degree or other formal award.

COURSE SUBJECT AREAS OFFERED OUTSIDE OF DEGREE PROGRAMS

Graduate: Business administration and management
Noncredit: Business; information sciences and systems

Special note

MIT's System Design and Management (SDM) program is a fast-paced, 2-year, graduate-level distance learning program that educates future technical leaders in architecting, engineering, and designing complex products and systems. By integrating advanced studies in engineering and management sciences, SDM prepares early and mid-career executives to be the technically grounded senior leaders of their enterprises, offering them the opportunity to participate in a lifelong partnership with a community of change agents around the world. SDM curriculum includes class work, research, and opportunities to lead and learn through on-the-job application and at-a-distance collaboration with classmates. The program provides a solid background in systems thinking, system design and architecture, engineering, management, global teamwork, and change management. SDM's 24-month distance learning option has both on- and off-campus components. Designed to blend the best of traditional campus education with cutting-edge distance learning technologies, it offers geographically dispersed students a comprehensive career- and family-compatible program that maintains the integrity, high academic standards, and individual engagement of MIT's in-residence programs. Students spend 1 term on campus and, while in a distance mode, attend live, interactive courses via videoconferencing at their work sites. Distance students return to campus for 1-week sessions each term and participate in an international business trip during their second year. An intensive, 13-month on-campus option is also available. The program awards a master's degree in engineering and management from MIT's School of Engineering and the Sloan School of Management. All students complete a project-oriented thesis that involves applying knowledge gained through SDM to a company-related challenge. For more information, students should visit SDM's Web site at http://sdm.mit.edu.

See full description on page 578.

Spruce Pine, North Carolina

Learning Resources Center
www.mayland.cc.nc.us

Mayland Community College, founded in 1971, is a state and locally supported, two-year college. It is accredited by the Southern Association of Colleges and Schools. It first offered distance learning courses in 1990. In 1999–2000, it offered 15 courses at a distance. In fall 1999, there were 161 students enrolled in distance learning courses.

Course delivery sites Courses are delivered to your home, Mayland Community College (Burnsville), Mayland Community College (Newland), 2 off-campus centers in Burnsville, Newland.

Media Courses are delivered via videotapes, videoconferencing, interactive television, World Wide Web. Students and teachers may meet in person or interact via videoconferencing, mail, telephone, fax, e-mail, interactive television, World Wide Web. The following equipment may be required: television, videocassette player, computer, modem, Internet access, e-mail.

Restrictions Programs are available worldwide. Enrollment is open to anyone.

Services Distance learners have access to library services, e-mail services, academic advising, career placement assistance at a distance.

Credit-earning options Students may transfer credits from another institution or may earn credits through examinations.

Typical costs Tuition of $20 per hour plus mandatory fees of $28 per year for in-state residents. Tuition of $163 per hour plus mandatory fees of $28 per year for out-of-state residents. Financial aid is available to distance learners.

Registration Students may register by telephone, in person.

Contact Dr. Rick Garrett, Vice President of Instructional Services, Mayland Community College, 200 Mayland Tech Drive, Spruce Pine, NC 28777. *Telephone:* 828-765-7351. *Fax:* 828-765-2327.

DEGREES AND AWARDS

Distance programs offered do not lead to a degree or other formal award.

COURSE SUBJECT AREAS OFFERED OUTSIDE OF DEGREE PROGRAMS

Undergraduate: Administrative and secretarial services; art history and criticism; Bible studies; business; business administration and management; English composition; film studies; history; horticulture; information sciences and systems; technical writing

See full description on page 676.

Maysville, Kentucky
www.maycc.kctcs.net/dl/dlhomepage.htm

Maysville Community College, founded in 1967, is a state-supported, two-year college. It is accredited by the Southern Association of Colleges and Schools. In 1999–2000, it offered 22 courses at a distance. In fall 1999, there were 160 students enrolled in distance learning courses.

Course delivery sites Courses are delivered to your home, 1 off-campus center in Cynthiiana.

Media Courses are delivered via television, videotapes, videoconferencing, interactive television, computer software, CD-ROM, computer conferencing, World Wide Web, e-mail, print. Students and teachers may meet in person or interact via videoconferencing, mail, telephone, fax, e-mail, interactive television, World Wide Web. The following equipment may be required: television, computer, Internet access, e-mail.

Restrictions Programs are available to in-state students only. Enrollment is open to anyone.

Services Distance learners have access to library services, the campus computer network, academic advising, career placement assistance, bookstore at a distance.

Credit-earning options Students may transfer credits from another institution or may earn credits through examinations.

Typical costs Tuition of $52 per semester plus mandatory fees of $4 per credit hour for local area residents. Tuition of $52 per credit hour plus mandatory fees of $4 per credit hour for in-state residents. Tuition of $156 per credit hour plus mandatory fees of $4 per credit hour for out-of-state residents. Financial aid is available to distance learners.

Registration Students may register by mail, fax, telephone, e-mail, in person.

Contact Barbara Campbell, Assistant Dean, Maysville Community College, 1755 US 68, Maysville, KY 41056. *Telephone:* 606-759-7141 Ext. 116. *Fax:* 606-759-9601. *E-mail:* barbara.campbell@kctcs.net.

DEGREES AND AWARDS

AA Business

COURSE SUBJECT AREAS OFFERED OUTSIDE OF DEGREE PROGRAMS

Undergraduate: Administrative and secretarial services; American (U.S.) history; astronomy and astrophysics; economics; English literature; environmental science; European history; finance; genetics; geography; information sciences and systems; physics; real estate; religious studies; sociology

See full description on page 556.

MAYVILLE STATE UNIVERSITY

Mayville, North Dakota

Enrollment Services Office
www.masu.nodak.edu

Mayville State University, founded in 1889, is a state-supported, four-year college. It is accredited by the North Central Association of Colleges and Schools. In 1999–2000, it offered 8 courses at a distance. In fall 1999, there were 96 students enrolled in distance learning courses.

Course delivery sites Courses are delivered to your home, high schools.

Media Courses are delivered via interactive television, World Wide Web, e-mail. Students and teachers may meet in person or interact via mail, e-mail, interactive television, World Wide Web. The following equipment may be required: computer, modem, Internet access.

Restrictions Programs are available to in-state students only. Enrollment is restricted to individuals meeting certain criteria.

Services Distance learners have access to library services, the campus computer network, e-mail services at a distance.

Credit-earning options Students may transfer credits from another institution or may earn credits through examinations.

Typical costs Tuition of $79.42 per semester credit plus mandatory fees of $50 per semester credit for in-state residents. Tuition of $212 per semester credit plus mandatory fees of $50 per semester credit for out-of-state residents. Financial aid is available to distance learners.

Registration Students may register by mail, in person.

Contact Brian Larsen, Director of Enrollment Services, Mayville State University, 330 3rd Street North East, Mayville, ND 58257. *Telephone:* 701-786-4842. *Fax:* 701-786-4748. *E-mail:* admit@mail.masu.nodak. edu.

DEGREES AND AWARDS

Distance programs offered do not lead to a degree or other formal award.

COURSE SUBJECT AREAS OFFERED OUTSIDE OF DEGREE PROGRAMS

Undergraduate: Algebra; business; library and information studies

MCDOWELL TECHNICAL COMMUNITY COLLEGE

Marion, North Carolina

Educational Programs

McDowell Technical Community College, founded in 1964, is a state-supported, two-year college. It is accredited by the Southern Association of Colleges and Schools. It first offered distance learning courses in 1992. In 1999–2000, it offered 18 courses at a distance. In fall 1999, there were 50 students enrolled in distance learning courses.

Course delivery sites Courses are delivered to your home, Brunswick Community College (Supply), 1 off-campus center in Marion.

Media Courses are delivered via television, videotapes, videoconferencing, interactive television, e-mail. Students and teachers may interact via mail, telephone, fax, e-mail, interactive television. The following equipment may be required: television, videocassette player, computer.

Restrictions Programs are available to in-state students only. Enrollment is open to anyone.

Services Distance learners have access to library services, academic advising, tutoring, career placement assistance at a distance.

Credit-earning options Students may transfer credits from another institution or may earn credits through examinations.

Typical costs Tuition of $20 per semester hour. Financial aid is available to distance learners.

Registration Students may register by in person.

Contact Donald G. Ford, Director of Evening Programs, McDowell Technical Community College, Route 1, Box 170, Marion, NC 28752. *Telephone:* 828-652-6021. *Fax:* 828-652-1014. *E-mail:* dongford@yahoo. com.

DEGREES AND AWARDS

Undergraduate Certificate(s) Computer Programming (certain restrictions apply; service area differs from that of the overall institution; some on-campus requirements)

AAS Marketing (certain restrictions apply; service area differs from that of the overall institution; some on-campus requirements)

COURSE SUBJECT AREAS OFFERED OUTSIDE OF DEGREE PROGRAMS

Undergraduate: Abnormal psychology; business; business administration and management; finance; history; social psychology; sociology

MCGILL UNIVERSITY

Montréal, Québec, Canada

Distance Education/Faculty of Education
www.education.mcgill.ca/distance

McGill University, founded in 1821, is an independent, nonprofit university. It is accredited by the Association of Theological Schools in the United States and Canada. It first offered distance learning courses in

1938. In 1999–2000, it offered 60 courses at a distance. In fall 1999, there were 300 students enrolled in distance learning courses.

Course delivery sites Courses are delivered to your home, your workplace.

Media Courses are delivered via videotapes, audiotapes, computer conferencing, World Wide Web, print. Students and teachers may interact via mail, telephone, fax, e-mail, World Wide Web. The following equipment may be required: television, videocassette player, computer, Internet access, e-mail.

Restrictions Programs are available worldwide. Enrollment is restricted to individuals meeting certain criteria.

Services Distance learners have access to the campus computer network, e-mail services, academic advising, tutoring at a distance.

Credit-earning options Students may transfer credits from another institution.

Typical costs *Undergraduate:* Tuition of $320 per course for in-state residents. Tuition of $494 per course for out-of-state residents. *Graduate:* Tuition of $582 per course for in-state residents. Tuition of $660 per course for out-of-state residents. Costs may vary.

Registration Students may register by mail, fax, in person.

Contact Boyd White, Director, Distance Education, McGill University. *Telephone:* 514-398-3457. *Fax:* 514-398-2182. *E-mail:* distance@education.mcgill.ca.

DEGREES AND AWARDS

Undergraduate Certificate(s) Educational Technology
Graduate Certificate(s) Teaching English as a Second Language
MSc Occupational Health (certain restrictions apply; service area differs from that of the overall institution; some on-campus requirements)

COURSE SUBJECT AREAS OFFERED OUTSIDE OF DEGREE PROGRAMS

Undergraduate: Curriculum and instruction; education; instructional media; special education; teacher education
Graduate: Health professions and related sciences

MCGREGOR SCHOOL OF ANTIOCH UNIVERSITY

Yellow Springs, Ohio
Individualized Master of Arts
www.mcgregor.edu

McGregor School of Antioch University, founded in 1988, is an independent, nonprofit, upper-level institution. It is accredited by the North Central Association of Colleges and Schools. It first offered distance learning courses in 1988. In fall 1999, there were 293 students enrolled in distance learning courses.

Course delivery sites Courses are delivered to your home, your workplace.

Media Courses are delivered via World Wide Web, e-mail, print. Students and teachers may meet in person or interact via mail, telephone, fax, e-mail. The following equipment may be required: computer, modem, Internet access, e-mail.

Restrictions Programs are available worldwide. Enrollment is open to anyone.

Services Distance learners have access to the campus computer network, e-mail services, academic advising, bookstore at a distance.

Credit-earning options Students may transfer credits from another institution or may earn credits through portfolio assessment.

Typical costs Tuition ranges between $2000 and $2500 per quarter. Costs may vary. Financial aid is available to distance learners.

Registration Students may register by mail, in person.

Contact Ruth M. Paige, Admissions Officer, McGregor School of Antioch University, 800 Livermore Street, Yellow Springs, OH 45387. *Telephone:* 937-767-6325. *Fax:* 937-767-6461. *E-mail:* admiss@mcgregor.edu.

DEGREES AND AWARDS

MA Conflict Resolution (some on-campus requirements), Individualized Studies (some on-campus requirements), Intercultural Relations (some on-campus requirements)

MCP HAHNEMANN UNIVERSITY

Philadelphia, Pennsylvania
Lifelong Learning
www.drexel.edu/distance/

MCP Hahnemann University, founded in 1848, is an independent, nonprofit university. It is accredited by the Middle States Association of Colleges and Schools. It first offered distance learning courses in 1995. In 1999–2000, it offered 20 courses at a distance. In fall 1999, there were 80 students enrolled in distance learning courses.

Course delivery sites Courses are delivered to your home, 1 off-campus center in Pittsburgh.

Media Courses are delivered via videotapes, computer software, computer conferencing, World Wide Web, e-mail, print. Students and teachers may interact via mail, telephone, fax, e-mail, World Wide Web. The following equipment may be required: videocassette player, computer, modem, Internet access, e-mail.

Restrictions Programs are available worldwide. Enrollment is restricted to individuals meeting certain criteria.

Services Distance learners have access to library services, the campus computer network, e-mail services, academic advising, career placement assistance, bookstore at a distance.

Credit-earning options Students may transfer credits from another institution or may earn credits through examinations, portfolio assessment.

Typical costs *Undergraduate:* Tuition of $460 per credit. *Graduate:* Tuition of $655 per credit. Graduate and undergraduate fees are $62.50 for 6 or more credits per semester or $32.50 for 5 or less credits. Costs may vary. Financial aid is available to distance learners.

Registration Students may register by mail, fax, telephone, e-mail, World Wide Web, in person.

Contact Timothy Perkins, Vice President, MCP Hahnemann University, Drexel University, 3141 Chestnut Street, 1-102, Philadelphia, PA 19104. *Telephone:* 215-895-1093. *Fax:* 215-895-1056. *E-mail:* tperkins@drexel.edu.

DEGREES AND AWARDS

MSN Women's Care Nurse Practitioner (certain restrictions apply)

COURSE SUBJECT AREAS OFFERED OUTSIDE OF DEGREE PROGRAMS

Undergraduate: Ethics; nursing; statistics
Graduate: Nursing

MEDICAL COLLEGE OF WISCONSIN

Milwaukee, Wisconsin
Master of Public Health Degree Programs
www.mcw.edu

Medical College of Wisconsin, founded in 1913, is an independent, nonprofit, graduate institution. It is accredited by the North Central

Association of Colleges and Schools. It first offered distance learning courses in 1986. In 1999–2000, it offered 34 courses at a distance. In fall 1999, there were 251 students enrolled in distance learning courses.

Course delivery sites Courses are delivered to your home, your workplace.

Media Courses are delivered via computer software, World Wide Web, e-mail, print. Students and teachers may meet in person or interact via mail, telephone, fax, e-mail, World Wide Web. The following equipment may be required: computer, modem, Internet access.

Restrictions Programs are available in the U.S. and Canada. Enrollment is restricted to individuals meeting certain criteria.

Services Distance learners have access to library services, e-mail services, academic advising, career placement assistance, bookstore at a distance.

Credit-earning options Students may transfer credits from another institution.

Typical costs Tuition of $555 per credit. Costs may vary.

Registration Students may register by mail, in person.

Contact Kevin D. Brown, Associate Director, MPH Degree Programs, Medical College of Wisconsin, Department of Preventive Medicine, 8701 Watertown Plank Road, Milwaukee, WI 53226. *Telephone:* 414-456-4510. *Fax:* 414-456-6547. *E-mail:* mph@mcw.edu.

DEGREES AND AWARDS

MPH General Preventative Medicine (certain restrictions apply; some on-campus requirements), Health Services Administration (certain restrictions apply; some on-campus requirements), Occupational Medicine (certain restrictions apply; some on-campus requirements)

COURSE SUBJECT AREAS OFFERED OUTSIDE OF DEGREE PROGRAMS

Graduate: Accounting; biological and life sciences; business administration and management; environmental health; finance; health professions and related sciences; health services administration; industrial psychology; organizational behavior studies; public health

MEDICAL UNIVERSITY OF SOUTH CAROLINA

Charleston, South Carolina

Distance Education

Medical University of South Carolina, founded in 1824, is a state-supported, upper-level institution. It is accredited by the Southern Association of Colleges and Schools.

Contact Medical University of South Carolina, 171 Ashley Avenue, Charleston, SC 29425-0002. *Telephone:* 843-792-2300. *Fax:* 843-792-3764.

See full description on page 676.

MEMORIAL UNIVERSITY OF NEWFOUNDLAND

St. John's, Newfoundland, Canada

School of Continuing Education
www.ce.mun.ca

Memorial University of Newfoundland, founded in 1925, is a province-supported university. It is accredited by the provincial charter. It first offered distance learning courses in 1969. In 1999–2000, it offered 180 courses at a distance. In fall 1999, there were 2,800 students enrolled in distance learning courses.

Course delivery sites Courses are delivered to your home, your workplace, high schools, College of the North Atlantic, off-campus center(s).

Media Courses are delivered via videotapes, audiotapes, computer software, CD-ROM, computer conferencing, World Wide Web, e-mail, print. Students and teachers may interact via audioconferencing, mail, telephone, fax, e-mail, World Wide Web. The following equipment may be required: television, videocassette player, computer, modem, Internet access, e-mail.

Restrictions Programs are available nationwide. Enrollment is restricted to individuals meeting certain criteria.

Services Distance learners have access to library services, the campus computer network, e-mail services, academic advising, career placement assistance, bookstore at a distance.

Credit-earning options Students may transfer credits from another institution or may earn credits through examinations.

Typical costs Canadian residents pay $110 per credit hour and $12 per credit hour in fees. Non-Canadian students pay $220 per credit hour plus $24 per credit hour in fees. *Noncredit courses:* Can$155 per course. Costs may vary.

Registration Students may register by telephone, World Wide Web.

Contact V. Edison, Customer Services Coordinator, Memorial University of Newfoundland, School of Continuing Education, St. John's, NF A1B 3X8 Canada. *Telephone:* 709-737-3084. *Fax:* 709-737-4070. *E-mail:* cstudies@morgan.ucs.mun.ca.

DEGREES AND AWARDS

Undergraduate Certificate(s) Business Administration, Career Development, Criminology (certain restrictions apply), Library Studies, Municipal Administration (certain restrictions apply), Newfoundland Studies, Public Administration (certain restrictions apply), Records and Information Management, Telelearning and Rural School Teaching
BBA Business Administration
BComm Commerce (General)
BN Nursing (Post-Basic RN)
BSW Social Work (as a 2nd degree)
BT Technology

COURSE SUBJECT AREAS OFFERED OUTSIDE OF DEGREE PROGRAMS

Undergraduate: Accounting; administrative and secretarial services; area, ethnic, and cultural studies; biological and life sciences; biology; business; business administration and management; Canadian studies; computer and information sciences; conservation and natural resources; developmental and child psychology; economics; education; education administration; educational psychology; English composition; English language and literature; history; human resources management; industrial psychology; law and legal studies; liberal arts, general studies, and humanities; library and information studies; mathematics; nursing; philosophy and religion; political science; psychology; public administration and services; social psychology; social sciences; social work; sociology; special education; teacher education; women's studies
Graduate: Education
Noncredit: European languages and literatures; protective services

MERCER COUNTY COMMUNITY COLLEGE

Trenton, New Jersey

Mercer County Community College, founded in 1966, is a state and locally supported, two-year college. It is accredited by the Middle States Association of Colleges and Schools.

Contact Mercer County Community College, 1200 Old Trenton Road, PO Box B, Trenton, NJ 08690-1004. *Telephone:* 609-586-4800. *Fax:* 609-586-6944.

See full description on page 600.

MERCER UNIVERSITY

Macon, Georgia
Office of Distance Learning
www.emercer.com

Mercer University, founded in 1833, is an independent, religious, comprehensive institution. It is accredited by the Southern Association of Colleges and Schools. In 1999–2000, it offered 30 courses at a distance.

Course delivery sites Courses are delivered to your home, your workplace, military bases.

Media Courses are delivered via CD-ROM, World Wide Web, e-mail. Students and teachers may interact via e-mail. The following equipment may be required: computer, modem, Internet access.

Restrictions Programs are available worldwide. Enrollment is open to anyone.

Services Distance learners have access to e-mail services at a distance.

Typical costs Tuition ranges from $200 to $400 per course.

Registration Students may register by fax, telephone, e-mail, World Wide Web.

Contact Elizabeth Simonetti Horner, Director, Distance Learning, Mercer University, 3001 Mercer University Drive, Atlanta, GA 30341. *Telephone:* 770-986-3187. *Fax:* 770-986-3102. *E-mail:* horner_e@mercer.edu.

DEGREES AND AWARDS

Undergraduate Certificate(s) General Studies

COURSE SUBJECT AREAS OFFERED OUTSIDE OF DEGREE PROGRAMS

Noncredit: Accounting; art history and criticism; Bible studies; business; engineering; environmental engineering; finance; gerontology; health professions and related sciences; history; law and legal studies; organizational behavior studies; philosophy and religion; recreation and leisure studies; religious studies; theological studies; visual and performing arts

See full description on page 580.

MERCY COLLEGE

Dobbs Ferry, New York
MerLIN
merlin.mercynet.edu

Mercy College, founded in 1951, is an independent, nonprofit, comprehensive institution. It is accredited by the Middle States Association of Colleges and Schools. It first offered distance learning courses in 1992. In 1999–2000, it offered 200 courses at a distance. In fall 1999, there were 90 students enrolled in distance learning courses.

Course delivery sites Courses are delivered to your home, your workplace.

Media Courses are delivered via computer software, computer conferencing, World Wide Web, e-mail. Students and teachers may interact via e-mail, World Wide Web. The following equipment may be required: computer, modem, Internet access, e-mail.

Restrictions Programs are available worldwide. Enrollment is open to anyone.

Services Distance learners have access to library services, academic advising, tutoring, career placement assistance, bookstore at a distance.

Credit-earning options Students may transfer credits from another institution or may earn credits through examinations, portfolio assessment, military training, business training.

Typical costs Tuition of $345 per credit. Graduate tuition for the MS in Banking is $525 per credit. Tuition for all other degrees is $435 per credit. Costs may vary. Financial aid is available to distance learners.

Registration Students may register by mail, fax, telephone, e-mail, World Wide Web, in person.

Contact Loretta Donovan, Director of Distance Learning, Mercy College, 555 Broadway, Dobbs Ferry, NY 10522. *Telephone:* 914-674-7527. *Fax:* 914-674-7518. *E-mail:* ldonovan@merlin.mercynet.edu.

DEGREES AND AWARDS

AA Liberal Arts and Sciences
AS Liberal Arts and Sciences
BA Psychology
BS Business Administration, Computer Science, Psychology
MBA Business Administration
MPA Health Sciences
MS Banking, Direct Marketing, Internet Business Systems

COURSE SUBJECT AREAS OFFERED OUTSIDE OF DEGREE PROGRAMS

Undergraduate: Abnormal psychology; accounting; algebra; American (U.S.) history; art history and criticism; biology; business; business administration and management; business law; comparative literature; computer and information sciences; criminal justice; developmental and child psychology; economics; English composition; English literature; environmental science; European history; finance; history; international business; international relations; liberal arts, general studies, and humanities; management information systems; marketing; mathematics; music; philosophy and religion; political science; psychology; social psychology; sociology; statistics

Graduate: Business; business administration and management; computer and information sciences; English composition; English literature; European history; management information systems; marketing; psychology

See full description on page 582.

METROPOLITAN COMMUNITY COLLEGE

Omaha, Nebraska
Student and Instructional Services
www.mccneb.edu

Metropolitan Community College, founded in 1974, is a state and locally supported, two-year college. It is accredited by the North Central Association of Colleges and Schools. It first offered distance learning courses in 1985. In 1999–2000, it offered 55 courses at a distance. In fall 1999, there were 1,400 students enrolled in distance learning courses.

Course delivery sites Courses are delivered to your home, your workplace, military bases.

Media Courses are delivered via television, videotapes, audiotapes, computer software, CD-ROM, World Wide Web, e-mail, print. Students and teachers may interact via mail, telephone, fax, e-mail, World Wide Web. The following equipment may be required: television, videocassette player, computer, modem, Internet access, e-mail.

Restrictions Programs are available worldwide. Enrollment is open to anyone.

Services Distance learners have access to library services, e-mail services, academic advising, career placement assistance, bookstore at a distance.

Credit-earning options Students may transfer credits from another institution or may earn credits through examinations, portfolio assessment, military training, business training.

Typical costs Tuition of $26.50 per credit plus mandatory fees of $2 per credit for in-state residents. Tuition of $33 per credit plus mandatory fees of $2 per credit for out-of-state residents. Financial aid is available to distance learners.

Registration Students may register by telephone, World Wide Web, in person.

Contact Arlene Jordan, Director of Enrollment Management, Metropolitan Community College. *Telephone:* 402-457-2418. *Fax:* 402-457-2564. *E-mail:* ajordan@metropo.mccneb.edu.

DEGREES AND AWARDS

AA Liberal Arts
AAS Professional Studies

COURSE SUBJECT AREAS OFFERED OUTSIDE OF DEGREE PROGRAMS

Undergraduate: Accounting; art history and criticism; biology; business administration and management; English composition; film studies; finance; French language and literature; liberal arts, general studies, and humanities; mathematics; music; philosophy and religion; physical sciences; political science; psychology; sociology; Spanish language and literature

METROPOLITAN COMMUNITY COLLEGES

Kansas City, Missouri

Distance Education Services
distance.kcmetro.cc.mo.us/disted.tpl

Metropolitan Community Colleges, founded in 1969, is a state and locally supported, two-year college. It is accredited by the North Central Association of Colleges and Schools. In 1999–2000, it offered 91 courses at a distance. In fall 1999, there were 720 students enrolled in distance learning courses.

Course delivery sites Courses are delivered to your home, your workplace.

Media Courses are delivered via television, videotapes, videoconferencing, interactive television, computer software, CD-ROM, computer conferencing, World Wide Web, e-mail, print. Students and teachers may meet in person or interact via videoconferencing, audioconferencing, mail, telephone, fax, e-mail, interactive television, World Wide Web. The following equipment may be required: television, videocassette player, computer, modem, Internet access, e-mail.

Restrictions Programs are available to in-state students only. Enrollment is restricted to individuals meeting certain criteria.

Services Distance learners have access to e-mail services, academic advising at a distance.

Credit-earning options Students may transfer credits from another institution or may earn credits through examinations.

Typical costs Tuition of $51 per credit hour plus mandatory fees of $10 per credit hour for local area residents. Tuition of $87 per credit hour plus mandatory fees of $10 per credit hour for in-state residents. Tuition of $122 per credit hour plus mandatory fees of $10 per credit hour for out-of-state residents. Financial aid is available to distance learners.

Registration Students may register by mail, fax, telephone, e-mail, World Wide Web, in person.

Contact Distance Education Services Office #123, Metropolitan Community Colleges, Penn Valley Community College, 3201 Southwest Trafficway, Kansas City, MO 64111. *Telephone:* 816-759-4490. *Fax:* 816-759-4673. *E-mail:* lvadvising@kcmetro.cc.mo.us.

DEGREES AND AWARDS

Distance programs offered do not lead to a degree or other formal award.

COURSE SUBJECT AREAS OFFERED OUTSIDE OF DEGREE PROGRAMS

Undergraduate: Accounting; algebra; biology; business; business administration and management; business law; chemistry; child care and development; computer and information sciences; computer programming; database management; engineering; English composition; fire science; information sciences and systems; marketing; physical therapy; psychology; sociology; statistics

METROPOLITAN STATE UNIVERSITY

St. Paul, Minnesota
www.metrostate.edu

Metropolitan State University, founded in 1971, is a state-supported, comprehensive institution. It is accredited by the North Central Association of Colleges and Schools. It first offered distance learning courses in 1994. In 1999–2000, it offered 205 courses at a distance. In fall 1999, there were 390 students enrolled in distance learning courses.

Course delivery sites Courses are delivered to your home, your workplace.

Media Courses are delivered via television, videoconferencing, interactive television, World Wide Web. Students and teachers may meet in person or interact via videoconferencing, audioconferencing, mail, telephone, fax, e-mail, interactive television. The following equipment may be required: computer, Internet access.

Restrictions Programs are available to in-state students only. Enrollment is open to anyone.

Services Distance learners have access to library services, the campus computer network, e-mail services, academic advising at a distance.

Credit-earning options Students may transfer credits from another institution or may earn credits through examinations, portfolio assessment, military training, business training.

Typical costs *Undergraduate:* Tuition of $88.20 per credit plus mandatory fees of $6.33 per credit for in-state residents. Tuition of $194.94 per credit plus mandatory fees of $6.33 per credit for out-of-state residents. *Graduate:* Tuition of $133.30 per credit plus mandatory fees of $6.33 per credit for in-state residents. Tuition of $211.20 per credit plus mandatory fees of $6.33 per credit for out-of-state residents. Financial aid is available to distance learners.

Registration Students may register by mail, fax, telephone, World Wide Web, in person.

Contact Cindy Herring, Registrar, Metropolitan State University, 700 East Seventh Street, St. Paul, MN 55106. *Telephone:* 651-772-7770. *Fax:* 651-772-7519. *E-mail:* cindy.herring@metrostate.edu.

DEGREES AND AWARDS

Distance programs offered do not lead to a degree or other formal award.

COURSE SUBJECT AREAS OFFERED OUTSIDE OF DEGREE PROGRAMS

Undergraduate: Accounting; anthropology; area, ethnic, and cultural studies; biology; business administration and management; business law; communications; computer and information sciences; drama and theater; economics; English composition; English language and literature; finance; French language and literature; history; human resources management; international business; library and information studies; management information systems; marketing; mass media; mathematics; music; philosophy and religion; physics; political science; protective services; psychology; public administration and services; religious studies; social sciences; sociology; statistics; women's studies

Graduate: Area, ethnic, and cultural studies; business administration and management; English language and literature; management information systems; marketing; mathematics; nursing; protective services

MIAMI-DADE COMMUNITY COLLEGE

Miami, Florida
Virtual College
www.mdcc.edu/vcollege/

Miami-Dade Community College, founded in 1960, is a state and locally supported, two-year college. It is accredited by the Southern Association of Colleges and Schools. In 1999–2000, it offered 30 courses at a distance. In fall 1999, there were 600 students enrolled in distance learning courses.
Course delivery sites Courses are delivered to your home, your workplace, military bases.
Media Courses are delivered via videotapes, videoconferencing, audiotapes, CD-ROM, World Wide Web. Students and teachers may meet in person or interact via videoconferencing, mail, telephone, fax, e-mail, World Wide Web. The following equipment may be required: computer, Internet access, e-mail.
Restrictions Programs are available to local area students. Enrollment is open to anyone.
Services Distance learners have access to library services, academic advising, bookstore at a distance.
Credit-earning options Students may transfer credits from another institution or may earn credits through examinations, portfolio assessment, military training, business training.
Typical costs Tuition of $49.65 per credit for in-state residents. Tuition of $173.40 per credit for out-of-state residents. Costs may vary. Financial aid is available to distance learners.
Registration Students may register by mail, telephone, in person.
Contact Lloyd Hollingsworth, Virtual College Webmaster/Technical Support, Miami-Dade Community College, 950 Northwest 20th Street, Miami, FL 33127-4693. *Telephone:* 305-237-4222. *Fax:* 305-237-4081. *E-mail:* lholling@mdcc.edu.

DEGREES AND AWARDS

AA Liberal Arts (service area differs from that of the overall institution; some on-campus requirements)
AS Liberal Science (service area differs from that of the overall institution; some on-campus requirements)

COURSE SUBJECT AREAS OFFERED OUTSIDE OF DEGREE PROGRAMS

Undergraduate: Algebra; business communications; English as a second language (ESL); English composition; environmental science; health services administration; marketing; music; nursing; oceanography; political science; psychology; social sciences; visual and performing arts
See full descriptions on pages 584 and 676.

MICHIGAN STATE UNIVERSITY

East Lansing, Michigan
.
www.msu.edu/unit/outreach

Michigan State University, founded in 1855, is a state-supported university. It is accredited by the American Academy for Liberal Education, North Central Association of Colleges and Schools. It first offered distance learning courses in 1992. In 1999–2000, it offered 110 courses at a distance. In fall 1999, there were 2,015 students enrolled in distance learning courses.
Course delivery sites Courses are delivered to your home, your workplace, high schools, Northwestern Michigan College (Traverse City), 6 off-campus centers in Birmingham, Grand Rapids, Kalamazoo, Marquette, Midland, Traverse City.
Media Courses are delivered via interactive television, World Wide Web. Students and teachers may meet in person or interact via videoconferencing, audioconferencing, mail, telephone, fax, e-mail, interactive television, World Wide Web. The following equipment may be required: computer, modem, Internet access.
Restrictions Programs are available worldwide. Enrollment is restricted to individuals meeting certain criteria.
Services Distance learners have access to library services, the campus computer network, academic advising, career placement assistance, bookstore at a distance.
Credit-earning options Students may transfer credits from another institution.
Typical costs *Undergraduate:* Tuition of $164 per credit plus mandatory fees of $293 per semester for in-state residents. Tuition of $408.25 per credit plus mandatory fees of $293 per semester for out-of-state residents. *Graduate:* Tuition of $229.25 per credit plus mandatory fees of $293 per semester for in-state residents. Tuition of $463.50 per credit plus mandatory fees of $293 per semester for out-of-state residents. Cost for noncredit course ranges from $300 to $450. Costs may vary. Financial aid is available to distance learners.
Registration Students may register by mail, fax, telephone, World Wide Web, in person.
Contact Dr. Barbara Fails, Director, Outreach Instructional Programs, Michigan State University, 51 Kellogg Center, East Lansing, MI 48824. *Telephone:* 517-353-0791. *Fax:* 517-432-1327. *E-mail:* fails@msu.edu.

DEGREES AND AWARDS

Undergraduate Certificate(s) Computer-Aided Design (CAD) Technologies, Nursing (service area differs from that of the overall institution), Social Work (service area differs from that of the overall institution; some on-campus requirements), Watershed Management
Graduate Certificate(s) Facility Management
MS Beam Physics (some on-campus requirements), Criminal Justice (some on-campus requirements)
MSN Nursing (service area differs from that of the overall institution)
PhD Beam Physics (some on-campus requirements)

COURSE SUBJECT AREAS OFFERED OUTSIDE OF DEGREE PROGRAMS

Undergraduate: Agricultural economics; agriculture; anthropology; biological and life sciences; chemical engineering; computer and information sciences; educational psychology; geography; horticulture; individual and family development studies; interior design; nursing; physics; social sciences; telecommunications
Graduate: Adult education; advertising; biological and life sciences; chemistry; communications; computer and information sciences; conservation and natural resources; criminal justice; education administration; foods and nutrition studies; health professions and related sciences; home economics and family studies; individual and family development studies; interior design; nursing; organizational behavior studies; physics; social work; telecommunications
Noncredit: Economics; education; international business; mathematics; teacher education
See full description on page 586.

MICHIGAN TECHNOLOGICAL UNIVERSITY

Houghton, Michigan

Extended University Programs
www.admin.mtu.edu/eup

Michigan Technological University, founded in 1885, is a state-supported university. It is accredited by the North Central Association of Colleges and Schools. It first offered distance learning courses in 1984. In 1999–2000, it offered 36 courses at a distance. In fall 1999, there were 166 students enrolled in distance learning courses.

Course delivery sites Courses are delivered to your workplace, military bases.

Media Courses are delivered via videotapes, videoconferencing, World Wide Web, e-mail, print. Students and teachers may meet in person or interact via videoconferencing, mail, telephone, fax, e-mail. The following equipment may be required: television, videocassette player, computer, Internet access, e-mail.

Restrictions Courses are available regionally in the upper Midwest. Enrollment is restricted to individuals meeting certain criteria.

Services Distance learners have access to library services, the campus computer network, e-mail services, academic advising, career placement assistance, bookstore at a distance.

Credit-earning options Students may transfer credits from another institution or may earn credits through examinations, portfolio assessment.

Typical costs Mandatory fees of $600 per credit. Undergraduate mandatory fees range between $175 and $280 per credit. Note: Michigan Technological University is switching to the semester system; however, course fees have not yet been established. Costs may vary. Financial aid is available to distance learners.

Registration Students may register by mail, fax, in person.

Contact Lynn Artman, Program Manager, Student Services, Michigan Technological University, Extended University Programs, 1400 Townsend Drive, Houghton, MI 49931. *Telephone:* 800-405-4678. *Fax:* 906-487-2463. *E-mail:* laartman@mtu.edu.

DEGREES AND AWARDS

BS Engineering (certain restrictions apply), Surveying (certain restrictions apply; some on-campus requirements)
MS Electrical Engineering (certain restrictions apply; some on-campus requirements), Mechanical Engineering (certain restrictions apply; some on-campus requirements)
PhD Mechanical Engineering (certain restrictions apply; some on-campus requirements)

COURSE SUBJECT AREAS OFFERED OUTSIDE OF DEGREE PROGRAMS

Undergraduate: Business; business administration and management; engineering mechanics; geology; mechanical engineering; surveying
Graduate: Electrical engineering; mechanical engineering
Noncredit: Business; business administration and management; engineering mechanics; geology; mechanical engineering

MID-AMERICA BIBLE COLLEGE

Oklahoma City, Oklahoma

DELTIC
www.mabc.edu

Mid-America Bible College, founded in 1953, is an independent, religious, four-year college affiliated with the Church of God. It is accredited by the Accrediting Association of Bible Colleges, North Central Associa-

tion of Colleges and Schools. In 1999–2000, it offered 3 courses at a distance. In fall 1999, there were 25 students enrolled in distance learning courses.

Course delivery sites Courses are delivered to your home, your workplace, military bases, high schools.

Media Courses are delivered via television, interactive television, World Wide Web. Students and teachers may meet in person or interact via mail, telephone, fax, e-mail, interactive television, World Wide Web. The following equipment may be required: television, computer, modem, Internet access.

Restrictions Programs are available worldwide. Enrollment is restricted to individuals meeting certain criteria.

Services Distance learners have access to academic advising at a distance.

Credit-earning options Students may transfer credits from another institution.

Typical costs Tuition of $219 per hour plus mandatory fees of $215 per semester. Cost for a noncredit course is $25 per semester hour. Financial aid is available to distance learners.

Registration Students may register by mail, fax, telephone, e-mail, in person.

Contact Deanne Mowry, Recruiter, Mid-America Bible College, 3500 South West 119th Street, Oklahoma City, OK 73170-4504. *Telephone:* 405-691-3800. *Fax:* 405-692-3165. *E-mail:* dmowry@mabc.edu.

DEGREES AND AWARDS

AA Pastoral Ministry/Specialized Ministry
BA Pastoral Ministry/Specialized Ministry
BS Pastoral Ministry/Specialized Ministry

COURSE SUBJECT AREAS OFFERED OUTSIDE OF DEGREE PROGRAMS

Undergraduate: American Government and Politics; Bible studies; business; communications; economics; education; elementary education; English language and literature; geography; health and physical education/fitness; history; mathematics; music; philosophy and religion; physical sciences; psychology; sociology; Spanish language and literature; theological studies

MIDDLESEX COUNTY COLLEGE

Edison, New Jersey

Academic Services and Urban Centers

Middlesex County College, founded in 1964, is a county-supported, two-year college. It is accredited by the Middle States Association of Colleges and Schools. In 1999–2000, it offered 6 courses at a distance.

Course delivery sites Courses are delivered to your home, your workplace, military bases.

Media Courses are delivered via World Wide Web, e-mail, print. Students and teachers may interact via telephone, e-mail, World Wide Web. The following equipment may be required: computer, modem, Internet access, e-mail.

Restrictions Programs are available to in-state students only. Enrollment is restricted to individuals meeting certain criteria.

Credit-earning options Students may transfer credits from another institution or may earn credits through examinations, military training, business training.

Typical costs Undergraduate tuition for Middlesex county residents is $81 per credit. Mandatory fees vary by course. Financial aid is available to distance learners.

Registration Students may register by mail, fax, in person.

Contact Beverly Buono, Administrative Assistant, Middlesex County College, Division of Academic Services and Urban Centers, Chambers

Hall, 2600 Woodbridge Avenue, Edison, NJ 08818-3050. *Telephone:* 732-906-2509. *Fax:* 732-906-7785. *E-mail:* beverly_buono@middlesex. cc.nj.us.

DEGREES AND AWARDS

Distance programs offered do not lead to a degree or other formal award.

COURSE SUBJECT AREAS OFFERED OUTSIDE OF DEGREE PROGRAMS

Undergraduate: Algebra; calculus; English composition
See full description on page 600.

MIDDLE TENNESSEE STATE UNIVERSITY

Murfreesboro, Tennessee
Division of Continuing Studies
www.mtsu.edu/~contstud

Middle Tennessee State University, founded in 1911, is a state-supported university. It is accredited by the Southern Association of Colleges and Schools. It first offered distance learning courses in 1994. In 1999–2000, it offered 60 courses at a distance. In fall 1999, there were 395 students enrolled in distance learning courses.
Course delivery sites Courses are delivered to your home, your workplace, high schools, Columbia State Community College (Columbia), Motlow State Community College (Lynchburg).
Media Courses are delivered via television, videoconferencing, interactive television, audiotapes, World Wide Web, print. Students and teachers may interact via videoconferencing, mail, telephone, fax, e-mail. The following equipment may be required: television, videocassette player, computer, Internet access, e-mail.
Restrictions Programs are available worldwide. Enrollment is open to anyone.
Services Distance learners have access to library services, e-mail services, academic advising, bookstore at a distance.
Credit-earning options Students may transfer credits from another institution or may earn credits through examinations, portfolio assessment, military training.
Typical costs *Undergraduate:* Tuition of $85 per credit plus mandatory fees of $40 per semester for in-state residents. Tuition of $296 per credit plus mandatory fees of $40 per semester for out-of-state residents. *Graduate:* Tuition of $129 per credit plus mandatory fees of $40 per semester for in-state residents. Tuition of $340 per credit plus mandatory fees of $40 per semester for out-of-state residents. Costs may vary. Financial aid is available to distance learners.
Registration Students may register by mail, telephone, World Wide Web, in person.
Contact Dianna Zeh, Director, Academic Outreach and Distance Learning, Middle Tennessee State University, Division of Continuing Studies, 1301 East Main Street, Cope 113, Murfreesboro, TN 37132. *Telephone:* 615-898-5611. *Fax:* 615-904-8108. *E-mail:* dzeh@mtsu.edu.

DEGREES AND AWARDS

MS Mathematics (service area differs from that of the overall institution)

COURSE SUBJECT AREAS OFFERED OUTSIDE OF DEGREE PROGRAMS

Undergraduate: Accounting; business; business administration and management; economics; education administration; English language and literature; health and physical education/fitness; law and legal studies; liberal arts, general studies, and humanities; mathematics; special education; teacher education
Graduate: Business; business administration and management; economics; education administration; law and legal studies; liberal arts, general studies, and humanities; mathematics; special education; teacher education

Special note
Middle Tennessee State University (MTSU) now offers accredited classes through a variety of technologies for students who may not be able to come to the campus. Compressed video courses are instructed at one site and simultaneously sent to distant sites. Students and instructors can see one another on television monitors and talk to one another using microphones. Telecourses are offered via cable television or videotape. Students consult with instructors during telephone office hours or through e-mail. Students can view course segments on the MTSU cable channel or the local PBS affiliate or at the McWherter Learning Resources Center at MTSU. Students are required to attend an orientation, a midterm exam, and a final exam on campus. Correspondence courses involve individual instruction of a student by an instructor. Typically, students study at home. Interaction between correspondence course faculty members and students consists of written assignments, testing, and assistance via such media as print/written word, telephone, fax, and e-mail. After registration, students receive a packet in the mail from the correspondence course coordinator that contains information about assignments and directions for completing and submitting them. Online courses are taught primarily over the Internet through e-mail, newsgroups, distribution lists, and the World Wide Web. These various distance learning programs are closing the gap between students and the campus.

See full description on page 676.

MIDLAND COLLEGE

Midland, Texas
Distance Learning Program
www.midland.cc.tx.us

Midland College, founded in 1969, is a state and locally supported, two-year college. It is accredited by the Southern Association of Colleges and Schools. It first offered distance learning courses in 1996. In 1999–2000, it offered 24 courses at a distance. In fall 1999, there were 179 students enrolled in distance learning courses.
Course delivery sites Courses are delivered to your home, high schools, Howard College (Big Spring), Odessa College (Odessa), University of Texas of the Permian Basin (Odessa), 6 off-campus centers in Big Lake, Fort Stockton, Greenwood, Iraan, Ozona, Rankin.
Media Courses are delivered via videoconferencing, interactive television, computer software, World Wide Web, e-mail. Students and teachers may meet in person or interact via videoconferencing, mail, telephone, fax, e-mail, interactive television. The following equipment may be required: computer, modem, Internet access, e-mail.
Restrictions Programs are available worldwide. Enrollment is open to anyone.
Services Distance learners have access to library services, the campus computer network, e-mail services, academic advising, tutoring, career placement assistance, bookstore at a distance.
Credit-earning options Students may transfer credits from another institution or may earn credits through examinations, portfolio assessment, military training, business training.

Typical costs Tuition of $368 per semester for local area residents. Tuition of $392 per semester for in-state residents. Tuition of $464 per semester for out-of-state residents. Costs may vary. Financial aid is available to distance learners.

Registration Students may register by mail, fax, telephone, in person.

Contact Camille C. Duchesne, Dean, Midland College, 3600 North Garfield, Midland, TX 79705. *Telephone:* 915-685-4516. *Fax:* 915-685-4776. *E-mail:* cduchesne@midland.cc.tx.us.

DEGREES AND AWARDS

Distance programs offered do not lead to a degree or other formal award.

COURSE SUBJECT AREAS OFFERED OUTSIDE OF DEGREE PROGRAMS

Undergraduate: Accounting; administrative and secretarial services; algebra; American (U.S.) history; American literature; business; business administration and management; business communications; business law; calculus; computer and information sciences; computer programming; continuing education; criminal justice; database management; developmental and child psychology; economics; English composition; English literature; ethics; gerontology; history; information sciences and systems; mathematics; music; political science; psychology; social psychology; sociology; Spanish language and literature; statistics

MID-PLAINS COMMUNITY COLLEGE AREA

North Platte, Nebraska

Distance Learning

Mid-Plains Community College Area is a district-supported, two-year college. It is accredited by the North Central Association of Colleges and Schools. In 1999–2000, it offered 49 courses at a distance. In fall 1999, there were 282 students enrolled in distance learning courses.

Course delivery sites Courses are delivered to your home, high schools.

Media Courses are delivered via television, videotapes, interactive television, audiotapes, World Wide Web, e-mail, print. Students and teachers may meet in person or interact via mail, telephone, fax, e-mail, interactive television, World Wide Web. The following equipment may be required: television, videocassette player, computer, Internet access, e-mail.

Restrictions Programs are available to local area students. Enrollment is open to anyone.

Services Distance learners have access to e-mail services, academic advising, career placement assistance, bookstore at a distance.

Credit-earning options Students may transfer credits from another institution or may earn credits through examinations.

Typical costs Tuition of $40 per credit hour plus mandatory fees of $3 per credit hour for in-state residents. Tuition of $45 per credit hour plus mandatory fees of $3 per credit hour for out-of-state residents. Financial aid is available to distance learners.

Registration Students may register by mail, fax, in person.

Contact Judi Haney, Dean of Community Services/Distance Learning, Mid-Plains Community College Area, 1205 East 3rd, McCook, NE 69001. *Telephone:* 308-345-6303 Ext. 225. *Fax:* 308-345-5744. *E-mail:* jhaney@mcc.mccook.cc.ne.us.

DEGREES AND AWARDS

Distance programs offered do not lead to a degree or other formal award.

COURSE SUBJECT AREAS OFFERED OUTSIDE OF DEGREE PROGRAMS

Undergraduate: Adult education; area, ethnic, and cultural studies; biological and life sciences; business; computer and information sciences; English language and literature; health and physical education/fitness; history; mathematics; philosophy and religion; psychology; social sciences; sociology

MIDWESTERN STATE UNIVERSITY

Wichita Falls, Texas

Midwestern State University, founded in 1922, is a state-supported, comprehensive institution. It is accredited by the Southern Association of Colleges and Schools. It first offered distance learning courses in 1987. In fall 1999, there were 250 students enrolled in distance learning courses.

Course delivery sites Courses are delivered to your home, your workplace, high schools, The Texas A&M University System (College Station), University of Texas at Arlington (Arlington), Vernon Regional Junior College (Vernon), off-campus center(s).

Media Courses are delivered via television, videotapes, videoconferencing, interactive television, World Wide Web, print. Students and teachers may meet in person or interact via videoconferencing, audioconferencing, mail, telephone, fax, e-mail, interactive television, World Wide Web. The following equipment may be required: television, videocassette player, computer, modem, Internet access, e-mail.

Restrictions Programs are available nationwide. Enrollment is open to anyone.

Services Distance learners have access to library services, the campus computer network, e-mail services, academic advising, tutoring, career placement assistance, bookstore at a distance.

Credit-earning options Students may transfer credits from another institution or may earn credits through examinations, portfolio assessment.

Typical costs *Undergraduate:* Tuition of $34 per credit hour plus mandatory fees of $912 per year for in-state residents. Tuition of $248 per credit hour plus mandatory fees of $912 per year for out-of-state residents. *Graduate:* Tuition of $44 per credit hour plus mandatory fees of $912 per year for in-state residents. Tuition of $258 per credit hour plus mandatory fees of $912 per year for out-of-state residents. *Noncredit courses:* $34 per course. Financial aid is available to distance learners.

Registration Students may register by mail, telephone, in person.

Contact Pamela Morgan, Director of Distance Education, Midwestern State University, 3410 Taft Boulevard, Wichita Falls, TX 76308-2099. *Telephone:* 940-397-4785. *Fax:* 940-397-4861. *E-mail:* pam.cope@nexus.mwsu.edu.

DEGREES AND AWARDS

Distance programs offered do not lead to a degree or other formal award.

COURSE SUBJECT AREAS OFFERED OUTSIDE OF DEGREE PROGRAMS

Undergraduate: Business administration and management; developmental and child psychology; economics; English language and literature; finance; health professions and related sciences; history; marketing; nursing; political science; social sciences; sociology

Graduate: Business administration and management; business law; chemistry; educational psychology; finance; health professions and related sciences; marketing; mathematics; physics; teacher education

See full description on page 676.

MILLERSVILLE UNIVERSITY OF PENNSYLVANIA

Millersville, Pennsylvania
Virtual University
www.millersv.edu/

Millersville University of Pennsylvania, founded in 1855, is a state-supported, comprehensive institution. It is accredited by the Middle States Association of Colleges and Schools. In 1999–2000, it offered 3 courses at a distance. In fall 1999, there were 15 students enrolled in distance learning courses.

Course delivery sites Courses are delivered to your home, your workplace, military bases, high schools, 1 off-campus center in Harrisburg.

Media Courses are delivered via videotapes, videoconferencing, audiotapes, computer software, CD-ROM, World Wide Web, e-mail, print. Students and teachers may meet in person or interact via videoconferencing, mail, telephone, fax, e-mail, World Wide Web. The following equipment may be required: videocassette player, computer, modem, Internet access, e-mail.

Restrictions Programs are available to in-state students only. Enrollment is open to anyone.

Services Distance learners have access to library services, the campus computer network, e-mail services, academic advising, career placement assistance at a distance.

Credit-earning options Students may transfer credits from another institution or may earn credits through examinations.

Typical costs *Undergraduate:* Tuition of $150 per credit plus mandatory fees of $41 per credit. *Graduate:* Tuition of $210 per credit plus mandatory fees of $41 per credit. Financial aid is available to distance learners.

Registration Students may register by mail, telephone, in person.

Contact Barbara Hunsberger, Virtual University Advocate, Millersville University of Pennsylvania, PO Box 1002, Millersville, PA 17551-0302. *Telephone:* 717-872-3605. *Fax:* 717-871-2075. *E-mail:* barbara.hunsberger@millersv.edu.

DEGREES AND AWARDS

Distance programs offered do not lead to a degree or other formal award.

COURSE SUBJECT AREAS OFFERED OUTSIDE OF DEGREE PROGRAMS

Undergraduate: Nursing
Graduate: Teacher education

MILWAUKEE SCHOOL OF ENGINEERING

Milwaukee, Wisconsin
MSOE-TV
www.msoe.edu

Milwaukee School of Engineering, founded in 1903, is an independent, nonprofit, comprehensive institution. It is accredited by the North Central Association of Colleges and Schools. It first offered distance learning courses in 1989. In 1999–2000, it offered 5 courses at a distance. In fall 1999, there were 25 students enrolled in distance learning courses.

Course delivery sites Courses are delivered to your home, your workplace.

Media Courses are delivered via videotapes, World Wide Web, e-mail. Students and teachers may meet in person or interact via audioconferencing, mail, telephone, fax, e-mail, World Wide Web. The following equipment may be required: television, videocassette player, computer, modem.

Restrictions Courses for credit are restricted to in-state students only. Enrollment is open to anyone.

Services Distance learners have access to library services, the campus computer network, e-mail services, academic advising, career placement assistance, bookstore at a distance.

Credit-earning options Students may transfer credits from another institution.

Typical costs *Undergraduate:* Tuition of $345 per credit. *Graduate:* Tuition of $420 per credit. *Noncredit courses:* $795 per course. Costs may vary. Financial aid is available to distance learners.

Registration Students may register by mail, fax, telephone, e-mail, in person.

Contact Paul Borens, Interim Director of Admission, Milwaukee School of Engineering, Enrollment Management, 1025 North Broadway, Milwaukee, WI 53202-3109. *Telephone:* 414-277-7481. *Fax:* 414-277-7475. *E-mail:* explore@msoe.edu.

DEGREES AND AWARDS

Distance programs offered do not lead to a degree or other formal award.

COURSE SUBJECT AREAS OFFERED OUTSIDE OF DEGREE PROGRAMS

Graduate: Accounting; business administration and management; business communications; finance; international business; marketing; organizational behavior studies
Noncredit: Accounting; business administration and management; business communications; finance; international business; marketing; organizational behavior studies

MINNESOTA WEST COMMUNITY AND TECHNICAL COLLEGE

Worthington, Minnesota
Distributed Education and Technology
www.mnwest.mnscu.edu

Minnesota West Community and Technical College is a state-supported, system. In 1999–2000, it offered 39 courses at a distance. In fall 1999, there were 320 students enrolled in distance learning courses.

Course delivery sites Courses are delivered to your home, your workplace, military bases, high schools, Minnesota West Community and Technical College–Canby Campus (Canby), Minnesota West Community and Technical College–Granite Falls Campus (Granite Falls), Minnesota West Community and Technical College–Jackson Campus (Jackson), Minnesota West Community and Technical College–Pipestone Campus (Pipestone), off-campus center(s) in Marshall.

Media Courses are delivered via television, interactive television, CD-ROM, World Wide Web, e-mail. Students and teachers may meet in person or interact via videoconferencing, mail, telephone, fax, e-mail, interactive television, World Wide Web. The following equipment may be required: computer, modem, Internet access, e-mail.

Restrictions Programs are available to local area students. Enrollment is open to anyone.

Services Distance learners have access to library services, the campus computer network, e-mail services, academic advising, bookstore at a distance.

Credit-earning options Students may transfer credits from another institution or may earn credits through examinations, portfolio assessment, military training.

Typical costs Tuition of $78 per semester hour. Financial aid is available to distance learners.

Registration Students may register by mail, fax, telephone, e-mail, World Wide Web, in person.

Contact Gary L. Phelps, Associate Vice President for Distributed Learning and Technology, Minnesota West Community and Technical College,

Minnesota West Community and Technical College

1450 Collegeway, Worthington, MN 56187. *Telephone:* 507-372-2687. *Fax:* 507-372-3454. *E-mail:* gphelps@wr.mnwest.mnscu.edu.

DEGREES AND AWARDS

AA Liberal Arts

COURSE SUBJECT AREAS OFFERED OUTSIDE OF DEGREE PROGRAMS

Undergraduate: Area, ethnic, and cultural studies; biology; computer and information sciences; conservation and natural resources; developmental and child psychology; economics; English composition; English language and literature; European languages and literatures; fine arts; fire protection; health and physical education/fitness; history; liberal arts, general studies, and humanities; mathematics; music; philosophy and religion; physics; political science; psychology; sociology; visual and performing arts

Special note

Minnesota West is a cutting-edge, Web-based learning institution. With 5 campuses located in a 300-mile circumference, faculty members have a rich history of teaching with technology. For 12 years, they have been perfecting their teaching-with-technology skills through interactive television and have matured to a level of delivering total and complete Web-interactive teaching. Online students learn and are supported as though they were in face-to-face settings—a direct result of Minnesota West's commitment to designing highly interactive courses rather than independent study packets. Courses include accounting, computerized Ag accounting concepts, physical education, sheep production, and sociology. Tuition for all online courses is $72.25 per credit. In partnership with the Minnesota State College and University System, Minnesota West is developing an online product and process for communicating with and engaging technical program industry leaders and craft professionals. The outcome is increased learning effectiveness. Students are assured that their courses are current and relevant. More importantly, they can forge online relationships with company personnel during their training. All course work is conducted electronically. Students need access to a computer (at least a 486-class CPU or Quadra) and to the World Wide Web (via Netscape 2.0, Microsoft Internet Explorer 4.0, or later browser versions). Minnesota West operates a telephone help-desk and provides technical support electronically. For more information, students should visit the College's Web site (http://www.mnwest.mnscu.edu) or they can contact the school at 800-657-3966 Ext. 2685 (toll-free) or siverson@wr.mnwest.mnscu.edu.

MINOT STATE UNIVERSITY

Minot, North Dakota

Continuing Education
www.misu.nodak.edu/conted/

Minot State University, founded in 1913, is a state-supported, comprehensive institution. It is accredited by the North Central Association of Colleges and Schools. It first offered distance learning courses in 1991. In 1999–2000, it offered 208 courses at a distance. In fall 1999, there were 298 students enrolled in distance learning courses.
Course delivery sites Courses are delivered to your home, your workplace, military bases, high schools.
Media Courses are delivered via television, interactive television, computer software, World Wide Web, e-mail, print. Students and teachers may meet in person or interact via mail, telephone, fax, e-mail, interactive television, World Wide Web. The following equipment may be required: computer, modem, Internet access, e-mail.

Restrictions Programs are available worldwide. Enrollment is open to anyone.
Services Distance learners have access to library services, e-mail services, academic advising, tutoring, career placement assistance, bookstore at a distance.
Credit-earning options Students may transfer credits from another institution or may earn credits through examinations, military training.
Typical costs *Undergraduate:* Tuition of $100 per semester hour. *Graduate:* Tuition of $125 per semester hour. Tuition for online courses is $139 per semester hour for undergraduate students, and $161 for graduate students. Costs may vary. Financial aid is available to distance learners.
Registration Students may register by mail, fax, telephone, e-mail, World Wide Web, in person.
Contact Teresa Loftesnes, Director of Continuing Education, Minot State University, 500 University Avenue West, Minot, ND 58707. *Telephone:* 701-858-3062. *Fax:* 701-858-4343. *E-mail:* loftesne@misu.nodak.edu.

DEGREES AND AWARDS

Distance programs offered do not lead to a degree or other formal award.

COURSE SUBJECT AREAS OFFERED OUTSIDE OF DEGREE PROGRAMS

Undergraduate: Accounting; advertising; area, ethnic, and cultural studies; business; business administration and management; creative writing; English composition; English language and literature; history; human resources management; mathematics; philosophy and religion; sociology; teacher education
Graduate: Business; teacher education

MISSISSIPPI COUNTY COMMUNITY COLLEGE

Blytheville, Arkansas

MCCC Compressed Video Network

Mississippi County Community College, founded in 1975, is a state-supported, two-year college. It is accredited by the North Central Association of Colleges and Schools. In 1999–2000, it offered 6 courses at a distance.
Course delivery sites Courses are delivered to 2 off-campus centers in Leachville, Osceola.
Media Courses are delivered via videotapes, interactive television, print. Students and teachers may meet in person or interact via mail, telephone, fax, e-mail, interactive television.
Restrictions Programs are available to local area students. Enrollment is open to anyone.
Services Distance learners have access to bookstore at a distance.
Credit-earning options Students may earn credits through examinations.
Typical costs Tuition of $47 per hour for local area residents. Tuition of $97 per hour for out-of-state residents. Costs may vary. Financial aid is available to distance learners.
Registration Students may register by in person.
Contact James Odom, Distance Learning Coordinator, Mississippi County Community College, PO Box 1109, Blytheville, AR 72316. *Telephone:* 870-762-1020. *Fax:* 870-780-6114. *E-mail:* jodom@mccc.cc.ar.us.

DEGREES AND AWARDS

Distance programs offered do not lead to a degree or other formal award.

COURSE SUBJECT AREAS OFFERED OUTSIDE OF DEGREE PROGRAMS

Undergraduate: Algebra; chemistry; developmental and child psychology; English language and literature; human resources management; management

MISSISSIPPI STATE UNIVERSITY

Mississippi State, Mississippi

Division of Continuing Education
distance.ce.msstate.edu

Mississippi State University, founded in 1878, is a state-supported university. It is accredited by the Southern Association of Colleges and Schools. It first offered distance learning courses in 1989. In 1999–2000, it offered 76 courses at a distance. In fall 1999, there were 810 students enrolled in distance learning courses.

Course delivery sites Courses are delivered to your home, military bases, high schools.

Media Courses are delivered via videotapes, videoconferencing, interactive television, computer software, computer conferencing, World Wide Web, e-mail, print. Students and teachers may interact via videoconferencing, audioconferencing, mail, telephone, fax, e-mail. The following equipment may be required: television, videocassette player, computer, Internet access, e-mail.

Restrictions Programs are available worldwide. Enrollment is open to anyone.

Services Distance learners have access to library services, the campus computer network, e-mail services, academic advising, bookstore at a distance.

Credit-earning options Students may transfer credits from another institution or may earn credits through examinations.

Typical costs *Undergraduate:* Tuition of $377 per course. *Graduate:* Tuition of $503 per course. Costs may vary. Financial aid is available to distance learners.

Registration Students may register by mail, fax, telephone, e-mail, in person.

Contact Susan Brown, Information Specialist Coordinator, Mississippi State University. *Telephone:* 662-325-2655. *Fax:* 662-325-8666. *E-mail:* sbrown@ce.msstate.edu.

DEGREES AND AWARDS

Undergraduate Certificate(s) Broadcast Meteorology (some on-campus requirements), Computer Applications

BS Geoscience, Broadcast Meteorology (some on-campus requirements), Operational Meteorology

Graduate Certificate(s) Vocational-Technical Licensure (service area differs from that of the overall institution)

MS Chemical Engineering (service area differs from that of the overall institution; some on-campus requirements), Civil Engineering (service area differs from that of the overall institution; some on-campus requirements), Counselor Education (service area differs from that of the overall institution; some on-campus requirements), Electrical and Computer Engineering (service area differs from that of the overall institution; some on-campus requirements), Geoscience (certain restrictions apply), Industrial Engineering (service area differs from that of the overall institution; some on-campus requirements), Mechanical Engineering (service area differs from that of the overall institution; some on-campus requirements), Physical Education, Systems Management (service area differs from that of the overall institution)

PhD Chemical Engineering (service area differs from that of the overall institution; some on-campus requirements), Civil Engineering (service area differs from that of the overall institution; some on-campus requirements), Electrical and Computer Engineering (service area differs from

that of the overall institution; some on-campus requirements), Industrial Engineering (service area differs from that of the overall institution; some on-campus requirements), Mechanical Engineering (service area differs from that of the overall institution; some on-campus requirements)

COURSE SUBJECT AREAS OFFERED OUTSIDE OF DEGREE PROGRAMS

Undergraduate: Meteorology; philosophy and religion
Graduate: Agriculture; business administration and management; chemical engineering; civil engineering; computer and information sciences; educational psychology; electrical engineering; engineering mechanics; engineering/industrial management; environmental engineering; health and physical education/fitness; home economics and family studies; industrial engineering; instructional media; mathematics; mechanical engineering; teacher education

Special note

Mississippi State University was founded as a land-grant institution in 1878 to meet the needs of the people, institutions, and organizations of the state and nation through undergraduate and graduate education. Mississippi State University enrolls more than 15,000 students on the main campus, branch campus, and off-campus centers and through distance learning. Mississippi State University is a Doctoral I university and is placed among the top 100 universities in the nation to receive federal research support. The University is fully accredited by the Southern Association of Colleges and Schools. The Division of Continuing Education is an academic service arm of the University and is committed to meeting the academic needs of nontraditional students who are not able to attend classes on campus due to geographic location and/or career and personal commitments. With expertise in advanced telecommunication technology and its application in education, the Division of Continuing Education continues to be a leader in distance learning by utilizing the following delivery mediums: the Internet, videotapes, and the Mississippi Interactive Video Network (MIVN), which is a two-way, interactive audio/video network with 150 sites. The division coordinates 7 programs that are offered though the MIVN—the Vocational Teacher Licensure Program; the Master of Science in counselor education, elementary education, early childhood development, and educational leadership of science in interdisciplinary studies; and courses leading to the Master of Instructional Technology. A Master of Science in physical education and health that is offered via videotape began in 1998. A certificate in computer applications is offered over the Internet and includes 12 semester hours of classes.

See full descriptions on pages 592 and 676.

MISSISSIPPI UNIVERSITY FOR WOMEN

Columbus, Mississippi

Continuing Education
www.muw.edu

Mississippi University for Women, founded in 1884, is a state-supported, comprehensive institution. It is accredited by the Southern Association of Colleges and Schools. It first offered distance learning courses in 1994.

Contact Mississippi University for Women, Box W-1600, Columbus, MS 39701-9998. *Telephone:* 662-329-4750. *Fax:* 662-329-7297.

See full description on page 676.

MISSOURI SOUTHERN STATE COLLEGE

Joplin, Missouri
Continuing Education

Missouri Southern State College, founded in 1937, is a state-supported, four-year college. It is accredited by the North Central Association of Colleges and Schools. It first offered distance learning courses in 1986. In 1999–2000, it offered 27 courses at a distance. In fall 1999, there were 350 students enrolled in distance learning courses.

Course delivery sites Courses are delivered to your home, your workplace, high schools, Crowder College (Neosho), 2 off-campus centers in Lamar, Monett.

Media Courses are delivered via television, videotapes, videoconferencing, interactive television, computer software, computer conferencing, World Wide Web, e-mail. Students and teachers may meet in person or interact via videoconferencing, audioconferencing, mail, telephone, fax, e-mail, interactive television, World Wide Web. The following equipment may be required: television, videocassette player, computer, modem, Internet access, e-mail.

Restrictions Program covers a four-state region within Missouri, Kansas, Oklahoma, and Arkansas. Enrollment is open to anyone.

Services Distance learners have access to library services, e-mail services, academic advising, tutoring, career placement assistance, bookstore at a distance.

Credit-earning options Students may transfer credits from another institution or may earn credits through examinations, portfolio assessment, military training.

Typical costs Tuition of $76 per semester hour plus mandatory fees of $40 per semester for in-state residents. Tuition of $140 per semester hour plus mandatory fees of $40 per semester for out-of-state residents. *Noncredit courses:* $50 per course. Costs may vary. Financial aid is available to distance learners.

Registration Students may register by mail, fax, telephone, World Wide Web.

Contact Dr. Jerry Williams, Director of Continuing Education, Missouri Southern State College, 3950 East Newman Road, Joplin, MO 64801. *Telephone:* 417-625-9387. *Fax:* 417-625-3024. *E-mail:* williams-r@mail.mssc.edu.

DEGREES AND AWARDS

AA General Studies (some on-campus requirements)

COURSE SUBJECT AREAS OFFERED OUTSIDE OF DEGREE PROGRAMS

Undergraduate: Accounting; biological and life sciences; biology; botany; business; business administration and management; communications; computer and information sciences; developmental and child psychology; economics; English language and literature; fine arts; geology; health professions and related sciences; history; home economics and family studies; human resources management; law and legal studies; mass media; nursing; physical sciences; political science; psychology; public administration and services; radio and television broadcasting; social psychology; social sciences; sociology; visual and performing arts

MISSOURI WESTERN STATE COLLEGE

St. Joseph, Missouri
Division of Continuing Education
www.mwsc.edu

Missouri Western State College, founded in 1915, is a state-supported, four-year college. It is accredited by the North Central Association of Colleges and Schools. It first offered distance learning courses in 1987. In 1999–2000, it offered 16 courses at a distance. In fall 1999, there were 57 students enrolled in distance learning courses.

Course delivery sites Courses are delivered to your home, your workplace, high schools, North Central Missouri College (Trenton), Northwest Missouri State University (Maryville).

Media Courses are delivered via television, videotapes, videoconferencing, computer software, World Wide Web, e-mail. Students and teachers may meet in person or interact via videoconferencing, mail, telephone, fax, e-mail. The following equipment may be required: television, videocassette player, computer, modem.

Restrictions Video-based courses are available to regional students only. Enrollment is open to anyone.

Services Distance learners have access to library services, the campus computer network, e-mail services, academic advising at a distance.

Credit-earning options Students may transfer credits from another institution or may earn credits through examinations, military training.

Typical costs Tuition of $96 per credit plus mandatory fees of $12 per credit. *Noncredit courses:* $265 per course. Financial aid is available to distance learners.

Registration Students may register by mail, fax, in person.

Contact Dr. Edwin L. Gorsky, Dean of Continuing Education and Special Programs, Missouri Western State College, 4525 Downs Drive, MC 105, St. Joseph, MO 64507. *Telephone:* 816-271-4100. *Fax:* 816-271-5922. *E-mail:* gorsky@mwsc.edu.

DEGREES AND AWARDS

Distance programs offered do not lead to a degree or other formal award.

COURSE SUBJECT AREAS OFFERED OUTSIDE OF DEGREE PROGRAMS

Undergraduate: American (U.S.) history; anthropology; biology; chemistry; comparative literature; computer programming; criminology; developmental and child psychology; English composition; English literature; finance; fire science; music; nursing; physics; protective services; sociology

MITCHELL COMMUNITY COLLEGE

Statesville, North Carolina
Distance Learning Technology

Mitchell Community College, founded in 1852, is a state-supported, two-year college. It is accredited by the Southern Association of Colleges and Schools. In 1999–2000, it offered 5 courses at a distance. In fall 1999, there were 24 students enrolled in distance learning courses.

Course delivery sites Courses are delivered to your home.

Media Courses are delivered via videotapes. The following equipment may be required: television, videocassette player.

Restrictions Programs are available to local area students. Enrollment is open to anyone.

Services Distance learners have access to e-mail services at a distance.

Credit-earning options Students may transfer credits from another institution or may earn credits through examinations.

Typical costs Tuition of $26.75 per credit hour plus mandatory fees of $20 per course for local area residents. Tuition of $26.75 per credit hour plus mandatory fees of $20 per course for in-state residents. Tuition of $169.75 per credit hour plus mandatory fees of $20 per course for out-of-state residents.

Registration Students may register by in person.

Contact Gordon Knight, Coordinator, Distance Learning, Mitchell Community College, 500 West Broad Street, Statesville, NC 28677. *Telephone:* 704-878-3253. *Fax:* 704-878-4271. *E-mail:* gknight@mitchell.cc.nc.us.

DEGREES AND AWARDS

Distance programs offered do not lead to a degree or other formal award.

COURSE SUBJECT AREAS OFFERED OUTSIDE OF DEGREE PROGRAMS

Undergraduate: Business administration and management; psychology; sociology

MODESTO JUNIOR COLLEGE

Modesto, California

Instruction
virtual.yosemite.cc.ca.us/

Modesto Junior College, founded in 1921, is a state and locally supported, two-year college. It is accredited by the Western Association of Schools and Colleges, Inc. It first offered distance learning courses in 1984. In 1999–2000, it offered 30 courses at a distance. In fall 1999, there were 1,825 students enrolled in distance learning courses.

Course delivery sites Courses are delivered to your home, your workplace, high schools.

Media Courses are delivered via television, videotapes, videoconferencing, audiotapes, computer software, CD-ROM, computer conferencing, World Wide Web, e-mail, print. Students and teachers may meet in person or interact via mail, telephone, fax, e-mail, World Wide Web. The following equipment may be required: television, computer, modem, Internet access, e-mail.

Restrictions Televised courses are available in the local area only; Internet courses are available worldwide. Enrollment is open to anyone.

Services Distance learners have access to library services, academic advising, career placement assistance, bookstore at a distance.

Credit-earning options Students may transfer credits from another institution.

Typical costs Tuition of $12 per credit plus mandatory fees of $11 per semester for in-state residents. Tuition of $121 per credit plus mandatory fees of $11 per semester for out-of-state residents. Financial aid is available to distance learners.

Registration Students may register by telephone, in person.

Contact Lucy Muñoz, Administrative Secretary, Modesto Junior College, MJC Distance Education, 435 College, Modesto, CA 95350. *Telephone:* 209-575-6235. *Fax:* 209-575-6669. *E-mail:* munozl@yosemite. cc.ca.us.

DEGREES AND AWARDS

Distance programs offered do not lead to a degree or other formal award.

COURSE SUBJECT AREAS OFFERED OUTSIDE OF DEGREE PROGRAMS

Undergraduate: Accounting; African-American studies; agriculture; area, ethnic, and cultural studies; business administration and management; chemistry; communications; community health services; computer and information sciences; English composition; ethics; geology; health and physical education/fitness; health professions and related sciences; history; home economics and family studies; horticulture; mathematics; philosophy and religion; political science; psychology; sociology; Spanish language and literature; statistics

MOHAWK VALLEY COMMUNITY COLLEGE

Utica, New York

Educational Technology
www.mvcc.edu/edtech/distance_learning.htm

Mohawk Valley Community College, founded in 1946, is a state and locally supported, two-year college. It is accredited by the Middle States Association of Colleges and Schools. It first offered distance learning courses in 1991. In 1999–2000, it offered 30 courses at a distance. In fall 1999, there were 90 students enrolled in distance learning courses.

Course delivery sites Courses are delivered to your home, high schools, State University of New York College at Cortland (Cortland), State University of New York College at Oneonta (Oneonta), 8 off-campus centers in Clinton, New Hartford, Oriskany, Sauquoit, Utica, Waterville, Westmoreland.

Media Courses are delivered via videoconferencing, interactive television, World Wide Web, e-mail. Students and teachers may interact via videoconferencing, e-mail, interactive television, World Wide Web. The following equipment may be required: computer, Internet access, e-mail.

Restrictions Programs are available worldwide. Enrollment is open to anyone.

Services Distance learners have access to library services, the campus computer network, e-mail services, academic advising, tutoring, career placement assistance at a distance.

Credit-earning options Students may transfer credits from another institution or may earn credits through examinations.

Typical costs Tuition of $1250 per semester for local area residents. Tuition of $2500 per semester for in-state residents. Tuition of $2500 per semester for out-of-state residents. *Noncredit courses:* $25 per course. Financial aid is available to distance learners.

Registration Students may register by mail, telephone, World Wide Web, in person.

Contact Michael Sprague, Coordinator of Distance Learning, Mohawk Valley Community College, 1101 Sherman Drive, Utica, NY 13501-5394. *Telephone:* 315-792-5316. *Fax:* 315-792-5666. *E-mail:* msprague@ www.mvcc.edu.

DEGREES AND AWARDS

AAS Graphic Design

COURSE SUBJECT AREAS OFFERED OUTSIDE OF DEGREE PROGRAMS

Undergraduate: Accounting; commercial art; computer and information sciences; design; developmental and child psychology; educational psychology; English language and literature; ethics; European history; health professions and related sciences; mathematics; photography; social work; sociology; special education; teacher education

MONTANA STATE UNIVERSITY–BILLINGS

Billings, Montana
www.msubillings.edu

Montana State University–Billings, founded in 1927, is a state-supported, comprehensive institution. It is accredited by the Northwest Association of Schools and Colleges. In 1999–2000, it offered 70 courses at a distance. In fall 1999, there were 153 students enrolled in distance learning courses.

Course delivery sites Courses are delivered to your home, your workplace, military bases, high schools.

Media Courses are delivered via World Wide Web, e-mail, print. Students and teachers may interact via e-mail, World Wide Web. The following equipment may be required: computer, modem, Internet access, e-mail.

Restrictions Programs are available worldwide. Enrollment is restricted to individuals meeting certain criteria.

Services Distance learners have access to library services, e-mail services, academic advising, career placement assistance, bookstore at a distance.

Credit-earning options Students may transfer credits from another institution or may earn credits through examinations.

Typical costs *Undergraduate:* Tuition of $390.25 per course plus mandatory fees of $36 per credit for in-state residents. Tuition of $962.95 per course plus mandatory fees of $36 per credit for out-of-state residents. *Graduate:* Tuition of $439.21 per course plus mandatory fees of $36 per credit for in-state residents. Tuition of $1011.91 per course plus mandatory fees of $36 per credit for out-of-state residents. Costs may vary. Financial aid is available to distance learners.

Registration Students may register by World Wide Web.

Contact Kirk Lacy, MSU-B Online Coordinator, Montana State University–Billings, Apsaruke Hall 116, College of Professional Studies and Lifelong Learning, Billings, MT 59101. *Telephone:* 800-708-0068. *Fax:* 406-657-2254. *E-mail:* inquiry@msubonline.org.

eCollege.com *www.ecollege.com/scholarships*

DEGREES AND AWARDS

BA Communication/Organizational Communications
BS Liberal Studies with Concentration in Management and Communication
MS Information Processing and Communications (certain restrictions apply)

COURSE SUBJECT AREAS OFFERED OUTSIDE OF DEGREE PROGRAMS

Undergraduate: Accounting; art history and criticism; biology; business; business administration and management; chemistry; communications; curriculum and instruction; drama and theater; economics; education; English composition; history; industrial psychology; marketing; mathematics; organizational behavior studies; special education; teacher education

Graduate: Curriculum and instruction; education; health services administration; special education; teacher education

See full description on page 588.

MONTANA STATE UNIVERSITY–BOZEMAN

Bozeman, Montana

The Burns Telecommunications Center/Extended Studies
btc.montana.edu/distance/

Montana State University–Bozeman, founded in 1893, is a state-supported university. It is accredited by the Northwest Association of Schools and Colleges. It first offered distance learning courses in 1992. In 1999–2000, it offered 85 courses at a distance. In fall 1999, there were 300 students enrolled in distance learning courses.

Course delivery sites Courses are delivered to your home, your workplace.

Media Courses are delivered via television, videotapes, videoconferencing, computer software, CD-ROM, computer conferencing, World Wide Web, e-mail, print. Students and teachers may meet in person or interact via videoconferencing, audioconferencing, mail, telephone, fax, e-mail,

World Wide Web. The following equipment may be required: television, computer, modem, Internet access, e-mail.

Restrictions Availability varies by program. Enrollment is restricted to individuals meeting certain criteria.

Services Distance learners have access to library services, the campus computer network, academic advising, bookstore at a distance.

Credit-earning options Students may transfer credits from another institution or may earn credits through examinations, military training, business training.

Typical costs *Undergraduate:* Tuition of $166.70 per semester hour for local area residents. Tuition of $215.55 per semester hour for in-state residents. Tuition of $406.25 per semester hour for out-of-state residents. *Graduate:* Tuition of $184.85 per semester hour for local area residents. Tuition of $424.40 per semester hour for out-of-state residents. Costs may vary. Financial aid is available to distance learners.

Registration Students may register by mail, fax, telephone, e-mail, World Wide Web, in person.

Contact Kelly Boyce, Program Manager, Montana State University–Bozeman, Burns Telecommunications Center, Bozeman, MT 59717. *Telephone:* 406-994-6812. *Fax:* 406-994-7856. *E-mail:* kboyce@montana. edu.

DEGREES AND AWARDS

MN Nursing (service area differs from that of the overall institution; some on-campus requirements)
MS Mathematics (service area differs from that of the overall institution; some on-campus requirements), Science Education Education (service area differs from that of the overall institution; some on-campus requirements)
MSE Education (service area differs from that of the overall institution; some on-campus requirements)

COURSE SUBJECT AREAS OFFERED OUTSIDE OF DEGREE PROGRAMS

Undergraduate: Computer and information sciences; education; English language and literature; plant sciences
Graduate: Biology; chemistry; civil engineering; earth science; education; geology; health and physical education/fitness; mathematics; mechanical engineering; microbiology; nursing; physics; plant sciences; social psychology; teacher education
Noncredit: Electrical engineering

See full description on page 822.

MONTANA STATE UNIVERSITY–GREAT FALLS COLLEGE OF TECHNOLOGY

Great Falls, Montana

Outreach Department
www.msugf.edu/outreach

Montana State University—Great Falls College of Technology, founded in 1969, is a state-supported, two-year college. It is accredited by the Northwest Association of Schools and Colleges. In 1999–2000, it offered 18 courses at a distance. In fall 1999, there were 135 students enrolled in distance learning courses.

Course delivery sites Courses are delivered to your home, off-campus center(s) in Bozeman.

Media Courses are delivered via interactive television, computer conferencing, World Wide Web. Students and teachers may meet in person or interact via mail, telephone, fax, e-mail, World Wide Web. The following equipment may be required: computer, modem, Internet access.

Restrictions Programs are available to in-state students only. Enrollment is open to anyone.

Services Distance learners have access to library services, e-mail services, academic advising at a distance.
Credit-earning options Students may transfer credits from another institution.
Typical costs Undergraduate in-district tuition is $285.50 per three semester credits. Financial aid is available to distance learners.
Registration Students may register by mail, fax, e-mail, World Wide Web, in person.
Contact Karen Vosen, Distance Learning Technician, Montana State University—Great Falls College of Technology, PO Box 6010, Great Falls, MT 59406-6010. *Telephone:* 800-446-2698. *Fax:* 406-771-4317. *E-mail:* kvosen@msugf.edu.

DEGREES AND AWARDS

Distance programs offered do not lead to a degree or other formal award.

COURSE SUBJECT AREAS OFFERED OUTSIDE OF DEGREE PROGRAMS

Undergraduate: Biology; business administration and management; community health services; comparative literature; English composition; information sciences and systems; international business; physical sciences; psychology; sociology; technical writing

MONTGOMERY COLLEGE

Takoma Park, Maryland
Office of Distance Learning
www.montgomerycollege.com/departments/distlrng

Montgomery College, founded in 1946, is a state and locally supported, two-year college. It is accredited by the Middle States Association of Colleges and Schools. In 1999–2000, it offered 50 courses at a distance. In fall 1999, there were 500 students enrolled in distance learning courses.
Course delivery sites Courses are delivered to your home, your workplace, MECT Consortium 16 Community Colleges in Maryland.
Media Courses are delivered via television, videotapes, videoconferencing, computer software, CD-ROM, computer conferencing, World Wide Web. Students and teachers may meet in person or interact via videoconferencing, mail, telephone, fax, e-mail, World Wide Web. The following equipment may be required: television, videocassette player, computer, modem, Internet access, e-mail.
Restrictions Programs are available to local area students. Enrollment is restricted to individuals meeting certain criteria.
Services Distance learners have access to library services, bookstore at a distance.
Credit-earning options Students may transfer credits from another institution or may earn credits through examinations, portfolio assessment.
Typical costs Tuition of $71 per credit for local area residents. Tuition of $148 per credit for in-state residents. Tuition of $193 per credit for out-of-state residents. Mandatory fees range from $51 to $119 for up to three credits. Cost for a noncredit course ranges between $49 and $99. Costs may vary. Financial aid is available to distance learners.
Registration Students may register by mail, fax, telephone, World Wide Web, in person.
Contact Buddy Muse, Senior Program Director for Distance Learning, Montgomery College, 7600 Takoma Avenue, Takoma Park, MD 20912. *Telephone:* 301-650-1552. *Fax:* 301-650-1550. *E-mail:* bmuse@mc.cc.md.us.

DEGREES AND AWARDS

Distance programs offered do not lead to a degree or other formal award.

COURSE SUBJECT AREAS OFFERED OUTSIDE OF DEGREE PROGRAMS

Undergraduate: Abnormal psychology; accounting; American (U.S.) history; astronomy and astrophysics; biology; business administration and management; business law; chemistry; computer and information sciences; computer programming; creative writing; database management; economics; finance; information sciences and systems; paralegal/legal assistant; philosophy and religion; psychology; sociology; Spanish language and literature; statistics; technical writing

MONTGOMERY COUNTY COMMUNITY COLLEGE

Blue Bell, Pennsylvania
Learning Resources Unit
www.mc3.edu

Montgomery County Community College, founded in 1964, is a county-supported, two-year college. It is accredited by the Middle States Association of Colleges and Schools. It first offered distance learning courses in 1992. In 1999–2000, it offered 50 courses at a distance. In fall 1999, there were 500 students enrolled in distance learning courses.
Course delivery sites Courses are delivered to your home, your workplace, high schools.
Media Courses are delivered via television, videotapes, videoconferencing, computer software, computer conferencing, World Wide Web, e-mail. Students and teachers may meet in person or interact via mail, telephone, fax, e-mail, World Wide Web. The following equipment may be required: television, videocassette player, computer, Internet access, e-mail.
Restrictions Programs are available nationwide. Enrollment is open to anyone.
Services Distance learners have access to library services, the campus computer network, e-mail services, academic advising, tutoring, career placement assistance, bookstore at a distance.
Credit-earning options Students may transfer credits from another institution or may earn credits through examinations, portfolio assessment.
Typical costs Tuition of $72 per credit plus mandatory fees of $6 per credit for local area residents. Tuition of $144 per credit plus mandatory fees of $11 per credit for in-state residents. Tuition of $216 per credit plus mandatory fees of $16 per credit for out-of-state residents. Financial aid is available to distance learners.
Registration Students may register by mail, fax, telephone, World Wide Web, in person.
Contact Dr. Bradley M. Gottfried, Dean of Academic Affairs, Montgomery County Community College, 340 DeKalb Pike, Blue Bell, PA 19422. *Telephone:* 215-641-6430. *Fax:* 215-619-7161. *E-mail:* bgottfri@mc3.edu.

DEGREES AND AWARDS

AGS Liberal Studies

COURSE SUBJECT AREAS OFFERED OUTSIDE OF DEGREE PROGRAMS

Undergraduate: Abnormal psychology; accounting; anthropology; biology; business administration and management; computer and information sciences; criminology; developmental and child psychology; economics; engineering-related technologies; English composition; English literature; geology; health and physical education/fitness; health professions and related sciences; history; liberal arts, general studies, and humanities; nursing; philosophy and religion; political science; psychology; social psychology; social sciences; sociology; Spanish language and literature; statistics

MOODY BIBLE INSTITUTE

Chicago, Illinois

Moody Bible Institute External Studies Division
www.moody.edu

Moody Bible Institute, founded in 1886, is an independent, religious, comprehensive institution. It is accredited by the Accrediting Association of Bible Colleges, North Central Association of Colleges and Schools. It first offered distance learning courses in 1901. In 1999–2000, it offered 86 courses at a distance.

Course delivery sites Courses are delivered to your home.

Media Courses are delivered via print. Students and teachers may meet in person or interact via mail, telephone.

Restrictions Programs are available worldwide. Enrollment is restricted to individuals meeting certain criteria.

Services Distance learners have access to library services, the campus computer network, academic advising, career placement assistance, bookstore at a distance.

Credit-earning options Students may transfer credits from another institution or may earn credits through examinations.

Typical costs Tuition of $120 per semester hour. *Noncredit courses:* $30 per course.

Registration Students may register by mail, fax, telephone, in person.

Contact Independent Studies Customer Service, Moody Bible Institute, 820 North LaSalle Boulevard, Chicago, IL 60610. *Telephone:* 800-955-1123. *Fax:* 312-329-2081. *E-mail:* xstudies@moody.edu.

DEGREES AND AWARDS

Undergraduate Certificate(s) Biblical Studies (certain restrictions apply)
ABS Biblical Studies (certain restrictions apply)
BS Biblical Studies (certain restrictions apply)

COURSE SUBJECT AREAS OFFERED OUTSIDE OF DEGREE PROGRAMS

Undergraduate: Bible studies; classical languages and literatures; educational psychology; English language and literature; history; philosophy and religion; religious studies; theological studies
Noncredit: Bible studies; philosophy and religion; religious studies; theological studies

MORAINE VALLEY COMMUNITY COLLEGE

Palos Hills, Illinois

Academic Services and Learning Technologies
www.mv.cc.il.us

Moraine Valley Community College, founded in 1967, is a state and locally supported, two-year college. It is accredited by the North Central Association of Colleges and Schools. It first offered distance learning courses in 1976. In 1999–2000, it offered 28 courses at a distance. In fall 1999, there were 630 students enrolled in distance learning courses.

Course delivery sites Courses are delivered to your home, your workplace, Joliet Junior College (Joliet), Kankakee Community College (Kankakee), Prairie State College (Chicago Heights), South Suburban College (South Holland), 4 off-campus centers in Blue Island, Evergreen Park, Tinley Park.

Media Courses are delivered via videotapes, videoconferencing, interactive television, computer conferencing, World Wide Web, e-mail, print. Students and teachers may meet in person or interact via videoconferencing, mail, telephone, fax, e-mail, interactive television, World Wide Web. The following equipment may be required: television, videocassette player, computer, modem, Internet access, e-mail.

Restrictions Programs are available worldwide. Enrollment is open to anyone.

Services Distance learners have access to library services, e-mail services, academic advising, tutoring, career placement assistance, bookstore at a distance.

Credit-earning options Students may transfer credits from another institution or may earn credits through examinations.

Typical costs Tuition of $44 per credit hour for local area residents. Tuition of $189 per credit hour for in-state residents. Tuition of $220 per credit hour for out-of-state residents. Tuition is for 1999-2000. Mandatory fees are $5 per credit hour. Financial aid is available to distance learners.

Registration Students may register by mail, telephone, World Wide Web, in person.

Contact Rod Seaney, Director, Alternative Learning, Moraine Valley Community College, 10900 South 88th Avenue, Palos Hills, IL 60465. *Telephone:* 708-974-5288. *Fax:* 708-974-1184. *E-mail:* seaney@moraine.cc.il.us.

DEGREES AND AWARDS

Distance programs offered do not lead to a degree or other formal award.

COURSE SUBJECT AREAS OFFERED OUTSIDE OF DEGREE PROGRAMS

Undergraduate: Abnormal psychology; astronomy and astrophysics; business; business law; design; developmental and child psychology; economics; engineering; English language and literature; film studies; French language and literature; geography; health professions and related sciences; history; horticulture; law and legal studies; philosophy and religion; physics; psychology; sociology

MOREHEAD STATE UNIVERSITY

Morehead, Kentucky

Office of Distance Learning
www.morehead-st.edu/units/distance

Morehead State University, founded in 1922, is a state-supported, comprehensive institution. It is accredited by the Southern Association of Colleges and Schools. It first offered distance learning courses in 1995. In 1999–2000, it offered 80 courses at a distance. In fall 1999, there were 622 students enrolled in distance learning courses.

Course delivery sites Courses are delivered to your home, your workplace, high schools, Berea College (Berea), Eastern Kentucky University (Richmond), Murray State University (Murray), Northern Kentucky University (Highland Heights), University of Kentucky (Lexington), University of Louisville (Louisville), Western Kentucky University (Bowling Green), 4 off-campus centers in Ashland, Jackson, Prestonsburg, West Liberty.

Media Courses are delivered via videotapes, videoconferencing, audiotapes, computer software, World Wide Web, e-mail, print. Students and teachers may meet in person or interact via videoconferencing, mail, telephone, fax, e-mail. The following equipment may be required: computer, Internet access, e-mail.

Restrictions Programs are available worldwide. Enrollment is open to anyone.

Services Distance learners have access to library services, the campus computer network, e-mail services, academic advising, tutoring, career placement assistance at a distance.

Credit-earning options Students may transfer credits from another institution or may earn credits through examinations.

Typical costs *Undergraduate:* Tuition of $102 per credit for local area residents. Tuition of $102 per credit for in-state residents. Tuition of $270

per credit for out-of-state residents. *Graduate:* Tuition of $147 per credit for local area residents. Tuition of $147 per credit for in-state residents. Tuition of $394 per credit for out-of-state residents. There is a $30 per credit mandatory Internet fee for Internet courses only. Costs may vary. Financial aid is available to distance learners.
Registration Students may register by mail, World Wide Web, in person.
Contact Tim Young, Director, Morehead State University, Distance Learning, 408 Ginger Hall, Morehead, KY 40351. *Telephone:* 606-783-2082. *Fax:* 606-783-5052.

DEGREES AND AWARDS

BBA Business Administration
MBA Business Administration (certain restrictions apply; some on-campus requirements)

COURSE SUBJECT AREAS OFFERED OUTSIDE OF DEGREE PROGRAMS

Undergraduate: Accounting; administrative and secretarial services; area, ethnic, and cultural studies; business; business administration and management; computer and information sciences; education; education administration; English composition; English language and literature; health and physical education/fitness; mathematics; nursing; public health; special education; teacher education
Graduate: Accounting; administrative and secretarial services; business; business administration and management; computer and information sciences; education; education administration; English composition; nursing; public health; special education; teacher education
See full description on page 676.

MOTLOW STATE COMMUNITY COLLEGE

Lynchburg, Tennessee
Academic Affairs
www.mscc.cc.tn.us

Motlow State Community College, founded in 1969, is a state-supported, two-year college. It is accredited by the Southern Association of Colleges and Schools. It first offered distance learning courses in 1996. In 1999–2000, it offered 7 courses at a distance. In fall 1999, there were 130 students enrolled in distance learning courses.
Course delivery sites Courses are delivered to your home, your workplace, military bases, 3 off-campus centers in Fayetteville, McMinnville, Shelbyville.
Media Courses are delivered via videotapes, videoconferencing, computer software, World Wide Web. Students and teachers may meet in person or interact via videoconferencing, telephone, e-mail, World Wide Web. The following equipment may be required: videocassette player, computer, modem, Internet access, e-mail.
Restrictions Programs are available to local area students. Enrollment is restricted to individuals meeting certain criteria.
Services Distance learners have access to the campus computer network, e-mail services, academic advising, career placement assistance at a distance.
Credit-earning options Students may transfer credits from another institution or may earn credits through examinations.
Typical costs Tuition of $0 per credit hour for in-state residents. Tuition of $157 per course plus mandatory fees of $53 per course for out-of-state residents. Varies depending on course, average is approximately $100. Costs may vary. Financial aid is available to distance learners.
Registration Students may register by mail, telephone, World Wide Web, in person.

Contact Dr. Art Walker, Vice President for Academic Affairs, Motlow State Community College, PO Box 8500, Lynchburg, TN 37352-8500. *Telephone:* 931-393-1696. *Fax:* 931-393-1681. *E-mail:* awalker@mscc.cc.tn.us.

DEGREES AND AWARDS

Distance programs offered do not lead to a degree or other formal award.

COURSE SUBJECT AREAS OFFERED OUTSIDE OF DEGREE PROGRAMS

Undergraduate: Business administration and management; chemistry; economics; information sciences and systems; mathematics; nursing
Noncredit: Business administration and management; chemistry; economics; information sciences and systems; mathematics; nursing
See full description on page 676.

MOUNTAIN EMPIRE COMMUNITY COLLEGE

Big Stone Gap, Virginia
Office of Continuing and Distance Education
www.me.cc.va.us/coned.htm

Mountain Empire Community College, founded in 1972, is a state-supported, two-year college. It is accredited by the Southern Association of Colleges and Schools. It first offered distance learning courses in 1979. In 1999–2000, it offered 50 courses at a distance. In fall 1999, there were 538 students enrolled in distance learning courses.
Course delivery sites Courses are delivered to your home, your workplace, high schools, All 23 Virginia Community Colleges, 3 off-campus centers in Gate City, Pennington Gap, St. Paul.
Media Courses are delivered via television, videotapes, videoconferencing, interactive television, audiotapes, computer software, CD-ROM, World Wide Web, e-mail, print. Students and teachers may meet in person or interact via videoconferencing, mail, telephone, fax, e-mail, interactive television, World Wide Web. The following equipment may be required: television, videocassette player, computer, modem, Internet access, e-mail.
Restrictions Programs are available nationwide. Enrollment is open to anyone.
Services Distance learners have access to library services, the campus computer network, e-mail services, academic advising, tutoring, career placement assistance, bookstore at a distance.
Credit-earning options Students may transfer credits from another institution or may earn credits through examinations.
Typical costs Tuition of $41.62 per credit hour for in-state residents. Tuition of $169.32 per credit hour for out-of-state residents. Financial aid is available to distance learners.
Registration Students may register by mail, fax, telephone, e-mail, World Wide Web, in person.
Contact Susan Kennedy, Coordinator of Distance Education, Mountain Empire Community College, US Route 23, South, PO Drawer 700, Big Stone Gap, VA 24219. *Telephone:* 540-523-2400 Ext. 284. *Fax:* 540-523-8297. *E-mail:* skennedy@me.cc.va.us.

DEGREES AND AWARDS

AAS Business Administration (some on-campus requirements), Education (some on-campus requirements), General Studies (some on-campus requirements), Liberal Arts (some on-campus requirements), Water/Wastewater Specialization

COURSE SUBJECT AREAS OFFERED OUTSIDE OF DEGREE PROGRAMS

Undergraduate: Accounting; American (U.S.) history; art history and criticism; astronomy and astrophysics; biology; business; business law; child care and development; communications; computer and information sciences; developmental and child psychology; economics; English composition; English language and literature; environmental science; health and physical education/fitness; health professions and related sciences; marketing; mathematics; meteorology; music; philosophy and religion; psychology; sociology; Spanish language and literature

See full description on page 676.

MOUNT ALLISON UNIVERSITY

Sackville, New Brunswick, Canada

Continuing and Distance Education

Mount Allison University, founded in 1839, is a province-supported, comprehensive institution. It is accredited by the provincial charter. It first offered distance learning courses in 1965. In 1999–2000, it offered 40 courses at a distance. In fall 1999, there were 400 students enrolled in distance learning courses.

Course delivery sites Courses are delivered to your home, your workplace, military bases, high schools, 2 off-campus centers in Miramichi, Moncton.

Media Courses are delivered via audiotapes, computer software, CD-ROM, World Wide Web, e-mail, print. Students and teachers may meet in person or interact via audioconferencing, mail, telephone, fax, e-mail. The following equipment may be required: computer, e-mail.

Restrictions Programs are available nationwide. Enrollment is restricted to individuals meeting certain criteria.

Services Distance learners have access to library services, the campus computer network, e-mail services, academic advising, bookstore at a distance.

Credit-earning options Students may transfer credits from another institution.

Typical costs Tuition for undergraduate Canadian students is Can$422 per course. For Non-Canadian students it is Can$844 per course. Financial aid is available to distance learners.

Registration Students may register by mail, fax, telephone, e-mail, in person.

Contact Marilyn McCullough, Director, Mount Allison University, 65 York Street, Sackville, NB E4L 1E4 Canada. *Telephone:* 506-364-2266. *Fax:* 506-364-2272. *E-mail:* mmccullough@mta.ca.

DEGREES AND AWARDS

BA English, History

COURSE SUBJECT AREAS OFFERED OUTSIDE OF DEGREE PROGRAMS

Undergraduate: American (U.S.) history; American literature; area, ethnic, and cultural studies; Asian studies; biological and life sciences; calculus; comparative literature; computer programming; English literature; European history; geography; history; information sciences and systems; mathematics; philosophy and religion; political science; psychology; religious studies; statistics

MOUNT SAINT VINCENT UNIVERSITY

Halifax, Nova Scotia, Canada

Distance University Education via Technology (DUET)
www.msvu.ca/distance

Mount Saint Vincent University, founded in 1873, is a province-supported, comprehensive institution. It is accredited by the provincial charter. It first offered distance learning courses in 1980. In 1999–2000, it offered 100 courses at a distance. In fall 1999, there were 1,500 students enrolled in distance learning courses.

Course delivery sites Courses are delivered to your home, your workplace.

Media Courses are delivered via television, videotapes, videoconferencing, interactive television, computer software, CD-ROM, World Wide Web, e-mail, print. Students and teachers may meet in person or interact via audioconferencing, mail, telephone, fax, e-mail, interactive television. The following equipment may be required: television, videocassette player, computer.

Restrictions Programs are available worldwide. Enrollment is open to anyone.

Services Distance learners have access to library services, the campus computer network, e-mail services, academic advising, tutoring at a distance.

Credit-earning options Students may transfer credits from another institution or may earn credits through examinations, portfolio assessment.

Typical costs *Undergraduate:* Tuition of $405.50 per course. *Graduate:* Tuition of $837 per course. Financial aid is available to distance learners.

Registration Students may register by mail, fax, telephone, e-mail, World Wide Web, in person.

Contact Mary Hart-Baker, DUET Secretary, Mount Saint Vincent University, 166 Bedford Highway, Halifax, NS B3M 2J6 Canada. *Telephone:* 902-457-6437. *Fax:* 902-457-6455. *E-mail:* mary.hart-baker@msvu.ca.

DEGREES AND AWARDS

Undergraduate Certificate(s) Business Administration, French, Gerontology, Information Technology Management

BA Liberal Arts and General Studies

BBA Business Administration

BTHM Tourism and Hospitality Management

MEd Education

COURSE SUBJECT AREAS OFFERED OUTSIDE OF DEGREE PROGRAMS

Undergraduate: Accounting; administrative and secretarial services; advertising; business; business administration and management; computer programming; economics; English language and literature; European languages and literatures; French language and literature; gerontology; history; home economics and family studies; hospitality services management; human resources management; information sciences and systems; liberal arts, general studies, and humanities; mathematics; philosophy and religion; political science; psychology; religious studies; social sciences; sociology; teacher education; theological studies; women's studies

Graduate: Adult education; teacher education

Noncredit: Theological studies

MT. SAN ANTONIO COLLEGE

Walnut, California
Distance Learning
vclass.mtsac.edu/distance/

Mt. San Antonio College, founded in 1946, is a district-supported, two-year college. It is accredited by the Western Association of Schools and Colleges, Inc. It first offered distance learning courses in 1993. In 1999–2000, it offered 30 courses at a distance. In fall 1999, there were 700 students enrolled in distance learning courses.

Course delivery sites Courses are delivered to your home.

Media Courses are delivered via television, videotapes, audiotapes, computer software, World Wide Web, e-mail, print. Students and teachers may meet in person or interact via mail, telephone, fax, e-mail, World Wide Web. The following equipment may be required: television, videocassette player, computer, Internet access, e-mail.

Restrictions Programs are available to local area students. Enrollment is open to anyone.

Services Distance learners have access to library services, the campus computer network, e-mail services, academic advising at a distance.

Credit-earning options Students may transfer credits from another institution or may earn credits through military training.

Typical costs Tuition of $12 per unit for in-state residents. Tuition of $114 per unit for out-of-state residents. Financial aid is available to distance learners.

Registration Students may register by mail, fax, telephone, World Wide Web, in person.

Contact Kerry C. Stern, Dean, Mt. San Antonio College, Learning Resources, 1100 North Grand Avenue, Walnut, CA 91789. *Telephone:* 909-594-5611 Ext. 5658. *Fax:* 909-468-3992. *E-mail:* kstern@mtsac. edu.

DEGREES AND AWARDS

Distance programs offered do not lead to a degree or other formal award.

COURSE SUBJECT AREAS OFFERED OUTSIDE OF DEGREE PROGRAMS

Undergraduate: Accounting; anthropology; area, ethnic, and cultural studies; astronomy and astrophysics; business administration and management; business law; creative writing; English as a second language (ESL); English composition; home economics and family studies; hospitality services management; information sciences and systems; journalism; philosophy and religion; psychology; sociology

MT. SAN JACINTO COLLEGE

San Jacinto, California

Mt. San Jacinto College, founded in 1963, is a state and locally supported, two-year college. It is accredited by the Western Association of Schools and Colleges, Inc. In 1999–2000, it offered 11 courses at a distance. In fall 1999, there were 350 students enrolled in distance learning courses.

Course delivery sites Courses are delivered to your home.

Media Courses are delivered via videotapes, videoconferencing. Students and teachers may meet in person or interact via videoconferencing, mail, telephone, e-mail. The following equipment may be required: television, videocassette player.

Restrictions Programs are available to local area students. Enrollment is open to anyone.

Credit-earning options Students may transfer credits from another institution.

Typical costs *Undergraduate:* Tuition of $11 per semester for local area residents. Tuition of $11 per semester for in-state residents. Tuition of $137 per semester for out-of-state residents. *Graduate:* Tuition of $11 per semester for local area residents. Tuition of $11 per semester for in-state residents. Tuition of $137 per semester for out-of-state residents. Financial aid is available to distance learners.

Registration Students may register by mail, fax, telephone, in person.

Contact John Norman, Distance Education Coordinator, Mt. San Jacinto College, 1499 North State Street, San Jacinto, CA 92583. *Telephone:* 909-487-6752. *Fax:* 909-487-1903. *E-mail:* jnorman@msjc.cc.ca.us.

DEGREES AND AWARDS

Distance programs offered do not lead to a degree or other formal award.

COURSE SUBJECT AREAS OFFERED OUTSIDE OF DEGREE PROGRAMS

Undergraduate: American (U.S.) history; anthropology; child care and development; computer and information sciences; environmental science; foods and nutrition studies; geology; health and physical education/fitness; political science; psychology; sociology

MOUNT VERNON NAZARENE COLLEGE

Mount Vernon, Ohio
EXCELL
online.mvnc.edu

Mount Vernon Nazarene College, founded in 1964, is an independent, religious, comprehensive institution. It is accredited by the North Central Association of Colleges and Schools. It first offered distance learning courses in 1999. In 1999–2000, it offered 6 courses at a distance. In fall 1999, there were 54 students enrolled in distance learning courses.

Course delivery sites Courses are delivered to your home.

Media Courses are delivered via computer conferencing, World Wide Web, e-mail. Students and teachers may meet in person or interact via mail, telephone, fax, e-mail, World Wide Web. The following equipment may be required: computer, modem, Internet access, e-mail.

Restrictions Programs are available regionally. Enrollment is open to anyone.

Services Distance learners have access to library services, e-mail services, academic advising, bookstore at a distance.

Credit-earning options Students may transfer credits from another institution.

Typical costs Tuition of $300 per credit. Costs may vary. Financial aid is available to distance learners.

Registration Students may register by mail, fax, telephone, e-mail, World Wide Web, in person.

Contact Jeffrey P. Lineman, Distance Learning Coordinator, Mount Vernon Nazarene College, 2000 Polaris Parkway, Suite 130, Columbus, OH 43240. *Telephone:* 800-839-2355. *Fax:* 614-888-5675. *E-mail:* jlineman@mvnc.edu.

DEGREES AND AWARDS

Distance programs offered do not lead to a degree or other formal award.

COURSE SUBJECT AREAS OFFERED OUTSIDE OF DEGREE PROGRAMS

Undergraduate: American (U.S.) history; English language and literature; management information systems; mathematics; sociology; theological studies

MOUNT WACHUSETT COMMUNITY COLLEGE

Gardner, Massachusetts

Division of Continuing Education
www.mwcc.mass.edu

Mount Wachusett Community College, founded in 1963, is a state-supported, two-year college. It is accredited by the New England Association of Schools and Colleges. It first offered distance learning courses in 1994. In 1999–2000, it offered 25 courses at a distance. In fall 1999, there were 205 students enrolled in distance learning courses.

Course delivery sites Courses are delivered to your home, your workplace, military bases, Fitchburg State College (Fitchburg), 1 off-campus center in Leominster.

Media Courses are delivered via television, videotapes, videoconferencing, computer software, CD-ROM, computer conferencing, World Wide Web, e-mail. Students and teachers may interact via audioconferencing, mail, telephone, fax, e-mail, World Wide Web. The following equipment may be required: television, videocassette player, computer, modem, Internet access, e-mail.

Restrictions Programs are available worldwide. Enrollment is open to anyone.

Services Distance learners have access to library services, academic advising, tutoring, career placement assistance at a distance.

Credit-earning options Students may transfer credits from another institution or may earn credits through examinations, portfolio assessment, military training.

Typical costs Tuition of $29 per credit plus mandatory fees of $57 per credit. *Noncredit courses:* $305 per course. Costs may vary. Financial aid is available to distance learners.

Registration Students may register by mail, fax, telephone, e-mail, World Wide Web, in person.

Contact Stuart Shuman, Dean of Continuing Education, Mount Wachusett Community College, 444 Green Street, Gardner, MA 01440. *Telephone:* 508-632-6600 Ext. 309. *Fax:* 508-632-6155. *E-mail:* s_shuman@mwcc.mass.edu.

DEGREES AND AWARDS

AA Business Administration
AS Business Administration, Criminal Justices

COURSE SUBJECT AREAS OFFERED OUTSIDE OF DEGREE PROGRAMS

Undergraduate: Abnormal psychology; advertising; algebra; American (U.S.) history; anthropology; biology; calculus; computer programming; criminology; economics; English composition; European history; family and marriage counseling; foods and nutrition studies; gerontology; human resources management; marketing; mass media; mathematics; music; psychology; sociology

MURRAY STATE UNIVERSITY

Murray, Kentucky

Continuing Education
www.murraystate.edu

Murray State University, founded in 1922, is a state-supported, comprehensive institution. It is accredited by the Southern Association of Colleges and Schools. It first offered distance learning courses in 1987.
Contact Murray State University, PO Box 9, Murray, KY 42071-0009. *Telephone:* 270-762-3011. *Fax:* 270-762-3050.

See full descriptions on pages 556 and 676.

NAROPA UNIVERSITY

Boulder, Colorado

Outreach Office
ecampus.naropa.edu

Naropa University, founded in 1974, is an independent, nonprofit, comprehensive institution. It is accredited by the North Central Association of Colleges and Schools. It first offered distance learning courses in 1999. In 1999–2000, it offered 27 courses at a distance.

Course delivery sites Courses are delivered to your home, your workplace.

Media Courses are delivered via World Wide Web. Students and teachers may interact via telephone, e-mail, World Wide Web. The following equipment may be required: computer, modem, Internet access, e-mail.

Restrictions Programs are available worldwide. Enrollment is restricted to individuals meeting certain criteria.

Services Distance learners have access to library services, e-mail services, academic advising, bookstore at a distance.

Typical costs *Undergraduate:* Tuition of $451 per credit plus mandatory fees of $40 per credit. *Graduate:* Tuition of $451 per credit plus mandatory fees of $40 per credit. Costs may vary.

Registration Students may register by World Wide Web.
Contact Brian Van Way, Director, Distance Learning, Naropa University. *Telephone:* 800-772-6951. *E-mail:* inquiry@ecampus.naropa.edu.

| **eCollege**.com | *www.ecollege.com/scholarships* |

DEGREES AND AWARDS

Distance programs offered do not lead to a degree or other formal award.

COURSE SUBJECT AREAS OFFERED OUTSIDE OF DEGREE PROGRAMS

Undergraduate: Conservation and natural resources; English language and literature; gerontology; philosophy and religion; psychology
Graduate: Conservation and natural resources; English language and literature; gerontology; philosophy and religion; psychology

NASSAU COMMUNITY COLLEGE

Garden City, New York
College of the Air
www.sunynassau.edu

Nassau Community College, founded in 1959, is a state and locally supported, two-year college. It is accredited by the Middle States Association of Colleges and Schools. It first offered distance learning courses in 1991. In 1999–2000, it offered 43 courses at a distance. In fall 1999, there were 800 students enrolled in distance learning courses.

Course delivery sites Courses are delivered to your home.

Media Courses are delivered via television, videotapes, audiotapes, computer software, World Wide Web, e-mail, print. Students and teachers may meet in person or interact via audioconferencing, mail, telephone, fax, e-mail. The following equipment may be required: television, videocassette player.

Restrictions Courses are available to regional area students; special administration may also be arranged. Enrollment is open to anyone.

Services Distance learners have access to library services, academic advising, bookstore at a distance.

Credit-earning options Students may transfer credits from another institution or may earn credits through examinations, portfolio assessment.

Typical costs Tuition of $90 per credit plus mandatory fees of $6 per credit for local area residents. Tuition of $180 per credit plus mandatory fees of $6 per credit for in-state residents. Tuition of $180 per credit plus mandatory fees of $6 per credit for out-of-state residents. Costs may vary.

Registration Students may register by mail, fax, telephone, e-mail, in person.

Contact Arthur L. Friedman, Professor and Coordinator, Nassau Community College, College of the Air, One Education Drive, Garden City, NY 11530-6793. *Telephone:* 516-572-7883. *Fax:* 516-572-0690. *E-mail:* friedma@sunynassau.edu.

DEGREES AND AWARDS

Distance programs offered do not lead to a degree or other formal award.

COURSE SUBJECT AREAS OFFERED OUTSIDE OF DEGREE PROGRAMS

Undergraduate: Abnormal psychology; accounting; algebra; anthropology; area, ethnic, and cultural studies; Asian languages and literatures; astronomy and astrophysics; business; business administration and management; business law; communications; developmental and child psychology; economics; English language and literature; European languages and literatures; fine arts; French language and literature; health and physical education/fitness; history; Italian language and literature; law and legal studies; liberal arts, general studies, and humanities; marketing; mass media; mathematics; meteorology; music; psychology; sociology; Spanish language and literature; statistics
Noncredit: Mathematics

NATIONAL AMERICAN UNIVERSITY

Rapid City, South Dakota
NAU online
www.nationalcollege.edu/

National American University, founded in 1941, is a proprietary, four-year college. It is accredited by the North Central Association of Colleges and Schools. It first offered distance learning courses in 1997. In 1999–2000, it offered 32 courses at a distance. In fall 1999, there were 300 students enrolled in distance learning courses.

Course delivery sites Courses are delivered to your home, your workplace, military bases, high schools, off-campus center(s) in Ellsworth Air Force Base, Rapid City, Sioux Falls, Albuquerque (NM), Colorado Springs (CO), Denver (CO), Kansas City (MO), Mall of America (MN), Rio Rancho (NM), St. Paul (MN).

Media Courses are delivered via World Wide Web. Students and teachers may interact via mail, telephone, fax, e-mail, World Wide Web. The following equipment may be required: computer, modem, Internet access, e-mail.

Restrictions Programs are available worldwide. Enrollment is restricted to individuals meeting certain criteria.

Services Distance learners have access to library services, the campus computer network, e-mail services, academic advising, tutoring, career placement assistance, bookstore at a distance.

Credit-earning options Students may transfer credits from another institution or may earn credits through examinations, portfolio assessment, military training, business training.

Typical costs Tuition of $200 per credit. One-time mandatory fees are $25 application fee and $50 matriculation fee. Financial aid is available to distance learners.

Registration Students may register by World Wide Web.

Contact Blake Faulkner, Vice President for Administration, National American University. *Telephone:* 800-843-8892 Ext. 4933. *Fax:* 605-394-4871. *E-mail:* bfaulkner@national.edu.

DEGREES AND AWARDS

BS Applied Management (certain restrictions apply), Business Administration (certain restrictions apply), Information Systems (certain restrictions apply)

COURSE SUBJECT AREAS OFFERED OUTSIDE OF DEGREE PROGRAMS

Undergraduate: Business; computer and information sciences; statistics
See full description on page 590.

NATIONAL TECHNOLOGICAL UNIVERSITY

Fort Collins, Colorado
www.ntu.edu

National Technological University, founded in 1984, is an independent, nonprofit, graduate institution. It is accredited by the North Central Association of Colleges and Schools. It first offered distance learning courses in 1984. In 1999–2000, it offered 500 courses at a distance. In fall 1999, there were 1,234 students enrolled in distance learning courses.

Course delivery sites Courses are delivered to your home, your workplace, military bases.

Media Courses are delivered via television, videotapes, World Wide Web, print. Students and teachers may interact via videoconferencing, audioconferencing, mail, telephone, fax, e-mail. The following equipment may be required: television, videocassette player, computer, e-mail.

Restrictions Programs are available worldwide. Enrollment is restricted to individuals meeting certain criteria.

Services Distance learners have access to academic advising, bookstore at a distance.

Credit-earning options Students may transfer credits from another institution.

Typical costs Tuition of $263 per credit plus mandatory fees of $362 per credit. *Noncredit courses:* $525 per course. Costs may vary.

Registration Students may register by mail, fax, World Wide Web.

Contact Jeanne Breiner, Director of Admissions and Records, National Technological University, 700 Centre Avenue, Fort Collins, CO 80526. *Telephone:* 970-495-6408. *Fax:* 970-498-0601. *E-mail:* jeanne@mail.ntu. edu.

DEGREES AND AWARDS

Graduate Certificate(s) Chemical Engineering (certain restrictions apply), Computer Engineering (certain restrictions apply), Computer Science (certain restrictions apply), Electrical Engineering (certain restrictions apply), Engineering Management (certain restrictions apply), Hazardous Waste Management (certain restrictions apply), Health Physics (certain restrictions apply), Manufacturing Systems Engineering (certain restrictions apply), Materials Science and Engineering (certain restrictions apply), Software Engineering (certain restrictions apply), Technical Japanese (certain restrictions apply), Transportation Systems Engineering (certain restrictions apply)

IMBA Business Administration (certain restrictions apply)

MS Chemical Engineering (certain restrictions apply), Computer Engineering (certain restrictions apply), Computer Science (certain restrictions apply), Electrical Engineering (certain restrictions apply), Engineering Management (certain restrictions apply; some on-campus requirements), Hazardous Waste Management (certain restrictions apply), Health Physics (certain restrictions apply), Management of Technology (certain restrictions apply; some on-campus requirements), Manufacturing Systems Engineering (certain restrictions apply), Materials Science and Engineering (certain restrictions apply), Software Engineering (certain restrictions apply), Transportation Systems Engineering (certain restrictions apply)

COURSE SUBJECT AREAS OFFERED OUTSIDE OF DEGREE PROGRAMS

Graduate: Accounting; aerospace, aeronautical engineering; chemical engineering; chemistry; civil engineering; computer and information sciences; computer programming; database management; economics; electrical engineering; engineering mechanics; engineering-related technologies; engineering/industrial management; environmental engineering; industrial engineering; information sciences and systems; international business; Japanese language and literature; mathematics; mechanical engineering; physics; telecommunications

Noncredit: Aerospace, aeronautical engineering; business; business administration and management; chemical engineering; chemistry; civil engineering; computer and information sciences; computer programming; database management; economics; electrical engineering; engineering mechanics; engineering-related technologies; engineering/industrial management; environmental engineering; human resources management; industrial engineering; information sciences and systems; Japanese language and literature; management information systems; mathematics; mechanical engineering; physics; telecommunications

NATIONAL UNIVERSITY

La Jolla, California
NU Online
www.nu.edu

National University, founded in 1971, is an independent, nonprofit, comprehensive institution. It is accredited by the Western Association of Schools and Colleges, Inc. It first offered distance learning courses in 1994. In 1999–2000, it offered 60 courses at a distance. In fall 1999, there were 256 students enrolled in distance learning courses.

Course delivery sites Courses are delivered to your home, your workplace, military bases.

Media Courses are delivered via videoconferencing, computer software, CD-ROM, computer conferencing, World Wide Web, e-mail, print.

Students and teachers may meet in person or interact via mail, telephone, fax, e-mail, World Wide Web. The following equipment may be required: computer, modem, Internet access, e-mail.

Restrictions Programs are available worldwide. Enrollment is restricted to individuals meeting certain criteria.

Services Distance learners have access to library services, the campus computer network, e-mail services, academic advising, bookstore at a distance.

Credit-earning options Students may transfer credits from another institution or may earn credits through examinations, military training.

Typical costs *Undergraduate:* Tuition of $165 per quarter credit. *Graduate:* Tuition of $185 per quarter credit. Costs may vary. Financial aid is available to distance learners.

Registration Students may register by mail, fax, telephone, e-mail, World Wide Web, in person.

Contact Brian Jensen, Admissions Advisor, National University, 11255 North Torrey Pines Road, La Jolla, CA 92037. *Telephone:* 858-642-8211. *Fax:* 858-642-8709. *E-mail:* advising@online.nu.edu.

eCollege.com *www.ecollege.com/scholarships*

DEGREES AND AWARDS

BACJ Criminal Justice

BBA Business Administration

BS Nursing (service area differs from that of the overall institution)

Graduate Certificate(s) Preliminary and Professional Clear Multiple and Single Subject with CLAD and BCLAD Emphasis (service area differs from that of the overall institution; some on-campus requirements), Preliminary Level 1 Education Specialist: Mild/Moderate Disabilities with Concurrent CLD/BCLAD (service area differs from that of the overall institution; some on-campus requirements), Professional Tier I Administrative Services (certain restrictions apply; service area differs from that of the overall institution; some on-campus requirements), Professional Tier II Administrative Services (certain restrictions apply; service area differs from that of the overall institution; some on-campus requirements), Pupil Personnel Services Credential School Counseling (service area differs from that of the overall institution; some on-campus requirements), Pupil Personnel Services Credential School Psychology (service area differs from that of the overall institution; some on-campus requirements)

GMBA Business Administration, Global Studies

MAE Teaching

MEd Educational Technology

MS Electronic Commerce, Instructional Technology, Nursing (service area differs from that of the overall institution)

COURSE SUBJECT AREAS OFFERED OUTSIDE OF DEGREE PROGRAMS

Undergraduate: Business; criminal justice; criminal justice and corrections; liberal arts, general studies, and humanities; nursing

Graduate: Business; education; education administration; educational psychology; instructional media; nursing; special education; teacher education

NEBRASKA METHODIST COLLEGE OF NURSING AND ALLIED HEALTH

Omaha, Nebraska
www.methodistcollege.edu

Nebraska Methodist College of Nursing and Allied Health, founded in 1891, is an independent, religious, comprehensive institution affiliated with the United Methodist Church. It is accredited by the North Central

Association of Colleges and Schools. In 1999–2000, it offered 2 courses at a distance. In fall 1999, there were 12 students enrolled in distance learning courses.

Course delivery sites Courses are delivered to your home, your workplace, 1 off-campus center in Des Moines (IA).

Media Courses are delivered via videoconferencing, CD-ROM, World Wide Web, e-mail, print. Students and teachers may meet in person or interact via videoconferencing, audioconferencing, mail, telephone, fax, e-mail, interactive television, World Wide Web. The following equipment may be required: computer, modem, Internet access, e-mail.

Restrictions Programs are available nationwide. Enrollment is open to anyone.

Services Distance learners have access to library services, the campus computer network, e-mail services, academic advising, tutoring, career placement assistance, bookstore at a distance.

Credit-earning options Students may transfer credits from another institution or may earn credits through examinations, portfolio assessment, military training.

Typical costs *Undergraduate:* Tuition of $272 per credit plus mandatory fees of $18 per credit. *Graduate:* Tuition of $350 per credit plus mandatory fees of $20 per credit. Financial aid is available to distance learners.

Registration Students may register by mail, fax, telephone, e-mail, in person.

Contact Dr. Bill Lambrecht, Educational Technologist, Nebraska Methodist College of Nursing and Allied Health, 8501 West Dodge Road, Omaha, NE 68114. *Telephone:* 402-354-6174. *Fax:* 402-354-8893. *E-mail:* blambre@methodistcollege.edu.

DEGREES AND AWARDS

AIS Health Promotion and Worksite Wellness (some on-campus requirements)

COURSE SUBJECT AREAS OFFERED OUTSIDE OF DEGREE PROGRAMS

Undergraduate: Biological and life sciences
Graduate: Health professions and related sciences

NEUMANN COLLEGE

Aston, Pennsylvania

eCollege.com

www.neumannonline.org

Neumann College, founded in 1965, is an independent, religious, comprehensive institution. It is accredited by the Middle States Association of Colleges and Schools. It first offered distance learning courses in 1998. In 1999–2000, it offered 8 courses at a distance. In fall 1999, there were 50 students enrolled in distance learning courses.

Course delivery sites Courses are delivered to your home, your workplace.

Media Courses are delivered via television, videotapes, videoconferencing, computer conferencing, World Wide Web, e-mail. Students and teachers may meet in person or interact via videoconferencing, mail, telephone, fax, e-mail, World Wide Web. The following equipment may be required: television, computer, modem, Internet access, e-mail.

Restrictions Programs are available worldwide. Enrollment is open to anyone.

Services Distance learners have access to library services, e-mail services, academic advising, tutoring, career placement assistance, bookstore at a distance.

Credit-earning options Students may transfer credits from another institution or may earn credits through examinations, portfolio assessment, military training, business training.

Typical costs *Undergraduate:* Tuition of $360 per credit. *Graduate:* Tuition of $450 per credit. Costs may vary. Financial aid is available to distance learners.

Registration Students may register by mail, fax, telephone, World Wide Web, in person.

Contact Scott Bogard, Executive Director of Admissions and Financial Aid, Neumann College, One Neumann Drive, Aston, PA 19014-1298. *Telephone:* 610-558-5616. *Fax:* 610-558-5652. *E-mail:* neumann@neumann.edu.

eCollege.com   *www.ecollege.com/scholarships*

DEGREES AND AWARDS

AA Liberal Studies (certain restrictions apply)

COURSE SUBJECT AREAS OFFERED OUTSIDE OF DEGREE PROGRAMS

Undergraduate: Computer and information sciences; English language and literature; finance; marketing; philosophy and religion; political science; psychology; sociology; visual and performing arts
Graduate: Education; nursing; physical therapy; theological studies
See full description on page 594.

NEWBERRY COLLEGE

Newberry, South Carolina
www.newberry.edu

Newberry College, founded in 1856, is an independent, religious, four-year college. It is accredited by the Southern Association of Colleges and Schools. In 1999–2000, it offered 1 course at a distance.

Course delivery sites Courses are delivered to your home.

Media Courses are delivered via World Wide Web. Students and teachers may interact via telephone, e-mail, World Wide Web. The following equipment may be required: computer, modem, Internet access, e-mail.

Restrictions Programs are available worldwide. Enrollment is open to anyone.

Services Distance learners have access to library services, the campus computer network, e-mail services, academic advising, tutoring, career placement assistance, bookstore at a distance.

Credit-earning options Students may transfer credits from another institution or may earn credits through examinations, portfolio assessment, military training, business training.

Typical costs Tuition of $185 per credit hour.

Registration Students may register by mail, fax, telephone, e-mail, in person.

Contact Jonathan Reece, Director of Admissions, Newberry College, 2100 College Street, Newberry, SC 29108. *Telephone:* 800-845-4955. *Fax:* 803-321-5138. *E-mail:* jreece@newberry.edu.

DEGREES AND AWARDS

Distance programs offered do not lead to a degree or other formal award.

COURSE SUBJECT AREAS OFFERED OUTSIDE OF DEGREE PROGRAMS

Undergraduate: Philosophy and religion; psychology
See full description on page 676.

NEWGRADUATE SCHOOLS

Muncie, Indiana

newGraduate School of e-Commerce/School of Architecture
www.newgraduate.org

newGraduate Schools, founded in 1998, is a proprietary, graduate institution. In 1999–2000, it offered 60 courses at a distance.

Course delivery sites Courses are delivered to your home, your workplace, military bases.

Media Courses are delivered via World Wide Web, e-mail. Students and teachers may interact via e-mail, World Wide Web. The following equipment may be required: computer, Internet access, e-mail.

Restrictions Programs are available worldwide. Enrollment is open to anyone.

Services Distance learners have access to e-mail services, academic advising, bookstore at a distance.

Credit-earning options Students may transfer credits from another institution or may earn credits through military training, business training.

Typical costs Tuition of $148 per credit hour.

Registration Students may register by World Wide Web.

Contact Martha Heil, Director of Admissions, newGraduate Schools, 2900 West Jackson Street, Building 202, Muncie, IN 47304. *Telephone:* 765-286-5613. *E-mail:* admissions@newgraduate.org.

DEGREES AND AWARDS

Undergraduate Certificate(s) Continuing Education System Registered Provider, e-Commerce

MArch Architecture (certain restrictions apply)

MBA e-Commerce (certain restrictions apply)

COURSE SUBJECT AREAS OFFERED OUTSIDE OF DEGREE PROGRAMS

Graduate: Architecture; business administration and management; business law; commercial art; computer and information sciences; computer programming; database management; design; ecology; environmental engineering; environmental science; ethics; finance; instructional media; management information systems; marketing; organizational behavior studies; public policy analysis

NEW HAMPSHIRE COLLEGE

Manchester, New Hampshire

Distance Education Program
de.nhc.edu

New Hampshire College, founded in 1932, is an independent, nonprofit, comprehensive institution. It is accredited by the New England Association of Schools and Colleges. It first offered distance learning courses in 1996. In 1999–2000, it offered 110 courses at a distance. In fall 1999, there were 800 students enrolled in distance learning courses.

Course delivery sites Courses are delivered to your home, your workplace, military bases, high schools.

Media Courses are delivered via computer software, computer conferencing, World Wide Web, e-mail, print. Students and teachers may interact via e-mail, World Wide Web. The following equipment may be required: computer, modem, Internet access.

Restrictions Programs are available worldwide. Enrollment is open to anyone.

Services Distance learners have access to library services, e-mail services, academic advising, career placement assistance, bookstore at a distance.

Credit-earning options Students may transfer credits from another institution or may earn credits through examinations, portfolio assessment, military training, business training.

Typical costs *Undergraduate:* Tuition of $567 per course. *Graduate:* Tuition of $999 per course. Financial aid is available to distance learners.

Registration Students may register by mail, fax, telephone, e-mail, World Wide Web, in person.

Contact H. Alan Goodman, Director of Distance Education, New Hampshire College. *Telephone:* 603-645-9766. *Fax:* 603-645-9706. *E-mail:* depinfo@minerva.nhc.edu.

DEGREES AND AWARDS

Undergraduate Certificate(s) Accounting, Business Administration, Computer Information Systems, Health Administration, Human Resources Management

MBA Business Administration

COURSE SUBJECT AREAS OFFERED OUTSIDE OF DEGREE PROGRAMS

Undergraduate: Abnormal psychology; accounting; advertising; business; business administration and management; business law; computer and information sciences; computer programming; creative writing; developmental and child psychology; economics; English composition; English language and literature; English literature; finance; history; human resources management; international business; liberal arts, general studies, and humanities; marketing; mathematics; organizational behavior studies; philosophy and religion; political science; psychology; sociology; statistics

Graduate: Accounting; advertising; business; business administration and management; computer and information sciences; economics; finance; international business; marketing; organizational behavior studies; statistics

Special note

New Hampshire College is a leader in the development of educational programs and services that maintain pace with the changing demands and needs of students and society. Its primary goal is to provide an educational basis for students that enhances their ability to be successful in a global economy. The College was founded in 1932 and is regionally, nationally, and professionally accredited. The College has 3 undergraduate divisions (business, liberal arts, and hospitality) and a graduate school of business that offers master's and PhD programs. The traditional day school is located in Manchester, New Hampshire, with weekend and evening classes offered through the Continuing Education program in Manchester, Nashua, Salem, Laconia, and Portsmouth, New Hampshire; Brunswick, Maine; and Roosevelt Roads, Puerto Rico. The College began to offer its traditional accredited courses via distance education in 1996. The program has grown continually over the past 5 years and now offers more than 100 undergraduate courses. In September 2000, it began offering classes leading to an MBA. All classes are 100 percent Internet-based and are designed to support the needs of a busy, highly mobile, and geographically diverse student population. Students participate in a dynamic and collaborative online educational environment that keeps students and faculty members actively involved in the learning process. The College enrolls a diverse population that is well represented by a wide range of ages, backgrounds, and ethnic origins. The College takes pride in offering an environment that fosters mutual respect and understanding of others as an integral component of its globally oriented educational purpose. Students and faculty members may participate from any location, at any time, as long as they have a PC/Mac computer system and an Internet service provider. Students are invited to visit the Web site (http://de.nhc.edu), call (603-645-9766), or e-mail (depinfo@minerva.nhc.edu) for further information.

See full description on page 596.

NEW HAMPSHIRE COMMUNITY TECHNICAL COLLEGE, NASHUA/CLAREMONT

Nashua, New Hampshire

Division of Continuing Education and Distance Learning
192.233.241.4/gtd/welcome.html

New Hampshire Community Technical College, Nashua/Claremont, founded in 1967, is a state-supported, two-year college. It is accredited by the New England Association of Schools and Colleges. In 1999–2000, it offered 9 courses at a distance. In fall 1999, there were 35 students enrolled in distance learning courses.

Course delivery sites Courses are delivered to your home, your workplace.

Media Courses are delivered via television, videotapes. Students and teachers may meet in person or interact via mail, telephone, fax, e-mail. The following equipment may be required: television, videocassette player.

Restrictions Programs are available in New Hampshire and Vermont. Enrollment is open to anyone.

Services Distance learners have access to library services, e-mail services, academic advising, bookstore at a distance.

Credit-earning options Students may transfer credits from another institution or may earn credits through examinations.

Typical costs Tuition of $110 per credit plus mandatory fees of $3 per credit. Cost for noncredit course is between $80 and $200. Financial aid is available to distance learners.

Registration Students may register by mail, fax, telephone, e-mail, in person.

Contact Charles W. Kusselow, Director of Continuing Education, New Hampshire Community Technical College, Nashua/Claremont, 1 College Drive, Claremont, NH 03743. *Telephone:* 603-542-7744 Ext. 2269. *Fax:* 603-543-1844. *E-mail:* ckusselow@tec.nh.us.

DEGREES AND AWARDS

AA Arts

COURSE SUBJECT AREAS OFFERED OUTSIDE OF DEGREE PROGRAMS

Undergraduate: Anthropology; art history and criticism; economics; history; philosophy and religion; psychology; sociology

NEW JERSEY CITY UNIVERSITY

Jersey City, New Jersey

Continuing Education
conted4.njcu.edu/weblearning

New Jersey City University, founded in 1927, is a state-supported, comprehensive institution. It is accredited by the Middle States Association of Colleges and Schools. It first offered distance learning courses in 1997. In 1999–2000, it offered 30 courses at a distance. In fall 1999, there were 126 students enrolled in distance learning courses.

Course delivery sites Courses are delivered to your home, your workplace, military bases, high schools.

Media Courses are delivered via World Wide Web. Students and teachers may interact via telephone, e-mail, World Wide Web. The following equipment may be required: computer, modem, Internet access, e-mail.

Restrictions Programs are available worldwide. Enrollment is restricted to individuals meeting certain criteria.

Services Distance learners have access to library services, the campus computer network, e-mail services, academic advising, bookstore at a distance.

Credit-earning options Students may transfer credits from another institution or may earn credits through examinations.

Typical costs Tuition of $675 per course. Financial aid is available to distance learners.

Registration Students may register by mail, fax, World Wide Web, in person.

Contact Marie A. Fosello, Director of Special Programs, New Jersey City University, Continuing Education Department, 2039 Kennedy Boulevard, Jersey City, NJ 07305-1597. *Telephone:* 201-200-3449. *Fax:* 201-200-2188. *E-mail:* conted@njcu.edu.

DEGREES AND AWARDS

Distance programs offered do not lead to a degree or other formal award.

COURSE SUBJECT AREAS OFFERED OUTSIDE OF DEGREE PROGRAMS

Graduate: Accounting; business administration and management; education; health professions and related sciences
Noncredit: Computer and information sciences

NEW JERSEY INSTITUTE OF TECHNOLOGY

Newark, New Jersey

Continuing Professional Education
www.njit.edu/dl

New Jersey Institute of Technology, founded in 1881, is a state-supported university. It is accredited by the Middle States Association of Colleges and Schools. It first offered distance learning courses in 1985. In 1999–2000, it offered 120 courses at a distance. In fall 1999, there were 825 students enrolled in distance learning courses.

Course delivery sites Courses are delivered to your home, your workplace, military bases.

Media Courses are delivered via television, videotapes, interactive television, computer software, CD-ROM, computer conferencing, World Wide Web, e-mail, print. Students and teachers may meet in person or interact via mail, telephone, fax, e-mail, interactive television. The following equipment may be required: television, videocassette player, computer, modem, Internet access, e-mail.

Restrictions Programs are available worldwide. Enrollment is open to anyone.

Services Distance learners have access to library services, the campus computer network, e-mail services, academic advising, career placement assistance, bookstore at a distance.

Credit-earning options Students may transfer credits from another institution or may earn credits through examinations.

Typical costs *Undergraduate:* Tuition of $206 per credit plus mandatory fees of $265 per semester for in-state residents. *Graduate:* Tuition of $388 per credit plus mandatory fees of $280 per semester for in-state residents. Costs may vary. Financial aid is available to distance learners.

Registration Students may register by mail, fax, e-mail, World Wide Web, in person.

Contact Anthony Jackson, Director, Extended Learning Delivery, New Jersey Institute of Technology, 323 Martin Luther King Boulevard, Newark, NJ 07102-1948. *Telephone:* 973-596-6093. *Fax:* 973-596-3255. *E-mail:* tonyj@adm.njit.edu.

DEGREES AND AWARDS

Undergraduate Certificate(s) Electronic Media Design (certain restrictions apply), Object-Oriented Design (certain restrictions apply), Practice of Technical Communications (certain restrictions apply)
BA Information Systems (certain restrictions apply)
BS Computer Science (certain restrictions apply)

Graduate Certificate(s) Programming Environment Tools (certain restrictions apply), Project Management (certain restrictions apply), Telecommunications Networking (certain restrictions apply)
MS Information Systems (certain restrictions apply)

COURSE SUBJECT AREAS OFFERED OUTSIDE OF DEGREE PROGRAMS

Undergraduate: Business administration and management; chemistry; computer and information sciences; conservation and natural resources; economics; electrical engineering; engineering-related technologies; English language and literature; human resources management; liberal arts, general studies, and humanities; mathematics; physics; social psychology
Graduate: Business; business administration and management; chemical engineering; civil engineering; computer and information sciences; conservation and natural resources; economics; electrical engineering; engineering/industrial management; environmental engineering; health professions and related sciences; human resources management; industrial engineering; journalism; law and legal studies; library and information studies; physics
See full description on page 598.

NEWMAN UNIVERSITY

Wichita, Kansas
Distance Learning
www.newmanu.edu

Newman University, founded in 1933, is an independent, religious, comprehensive institution. It is accredited by the North Central Association of Colleges and Schools. It first offered distance learning courses in 1987. In 1999–2000, it offered 25 courses at a distance. In fall 1999, there were 250 students enrolled in distance learning courses.
Course delivery sites Courses are delivered to your home, your workplace, military bases, high schools, 10 off-campus centers in Dodge City, Garden City, Great Bend, Hugoton, Hutchinson, Liberel, Merienthal, Pratt, Spearville, Oklahoma City (OK).
Media Courses are delivered via videotapes, interactive television, World Wide Web, print. Students and teachers may meet in person or interact via mail, telephone, e-mail, interactive television, World Wide Web. The following equipment may be required: computer, modem, Internet access, e-mail.
Restrictions Programs are available to in-state students only. Enrollment is restricted to individuals meeting certain criteria.
Services Distance learners have access to library services, e-mail services, academic advising, career placement assistance, bookstore at a distance.
Credit-earning options Students may transfer credits from another institution or may earn credits through examinations, portfolio assessment.
Typical costs *Undergraduate:* Tuition of $299 per hour plus mandatory fees of $5 per hour. *Graduate:* Tuition of $257 per hour plus mandatory fees of $5 per hour. Costs may vary. Financial aid is available to distance learners.
Registration Students may register by mail, in person.
Contact Norman Correll, Director, Distance Learning, Newman University. *Telephone:* 316-942-4291 Ext. 222. *Fax:* 316-942-4483. *E-mail:* cornelln@newmanu.edu.

DEGREES AND AWARDS

BS Contemporary Business Management

COURSE SUBJECT AREAS OFFERED OUTSIDE OF DEGREE PROGRAMS

Undergraduate: Religious studies

NEW MEXICO INSTITUTE OF MINING AND TECHNOLOGY

Socorro, New Mexico
Distance Education Department
www.nmt.edu/

New Mexico Institute of Mining and Technology, founded in 1889, is a state-supported university. It is accredited by the North Central Association of Colleges and Schools. In fall 1999, there were 70 students enrolled in distance learning courses.
Course delivery sites Courses are delivered to your workplace, high schools, Arizona State University (Tempe, AZ), New Mexico State University (Las Cruces), University of New Mexico (Albuquerque).
Media Courses are delivered via television, videotapes, videoconferencing, interactive television. Students and teachers may meet in person or interact via telephone, e-mail, interactive television. The following equipment may be required: television.
Restrictions Programs are available statewide with occasional service to other states. Enrollment is restricted to individuals meeting certain criteria.
Credit-earning options Students may transfer credits from another institution.
Typical costs Special student tuition is $67 per credit hour for undergraduates and $94 per credit hour for graduates. For degree seeking students tuition is $800 for 12-18 credit hours for undergraduates, $846 for 9-12 credit hours for graduates. Mandatory fees vary. Costs may vary. Financial aid is available to distance learners.
Registration Students may register by in person.
Contact Claire Fenton, Director of Distance Education, New Mexico Institute of Mining and Technology, 801 Leroy Place, Socorro, NM 87801-4796. *Telephone:* 505-835-5690. *Fax:* 505-835-5899. *E-mail:* cfenton@admin.nmt.edu.

DEGREES AND AWARDS

BS Waste Management (certain restrictions apply; some on-campus requirements)
MS Science Teaching (certain restrictions apply; some on-campus requirements), Waste Management (certain restrictions apply; some on-campus requirements)

COURSE SUBJECT AREAS OFFERED OUTSIDE OF DEGREE PROGRAMS

Undergraduate: Biology; chemical engineering; environmental engineering
Graduate: Chemical engineering; environmental engineering; teacher education

NEW MEXICO STATE UNIVERSITY

Las Cruces, New Mexico
Office of Distance Education
www.nmsu.edu/~distance/

New Mexico State University, founded in 1888, is a state-supported university. It is accredited by the North Central Association of Colleges and Schools. It first offered distance learning courses in 1989. In

1999–2000, it offered 20 courses at a distance. In fall 1999, there were 300 students enrolled in distance learning courses.

Course delivery sites Courses are delivered to your workplace, military bases, New Mexico State University–Alamogordo (Alamogordo), New Mexico State University–Carlsbad (Carlsbad), New Mexico State University–Grants (Grants), San Juan College (Farmington).

Media Courses are delivered via television, videotapes, videoconferencing. Students and teachers may meet in person or interact via videoconferencing, telephone, fax, e-mail.

Restrictions Programs are available to in-state students only. Enrollment is restricted to individuals meeting certain criteria.

Services Distance learners have access to the campus computer network, e-mail services, academic advising at a distance.

Credit-earning options Students may transfer credits from another institution or may earn credits through examinations, military training.

Typical costs *Undergraduate:* Tuition of $125 per credit. *Graduate:* Tuition of $125 per credit. Financial aid is available to distance learners.

Registration Students may register by mail, fax, telephone, e-mail, World Wide Web, in person.

Contact Lynford L. Ames, Director of Distance Education, New Mexico State University, Box 3WEC, Las Cruces, NM 88003. *Telephone:* 505-646-5837. *Fax:* 505-646-2044. *E-mail:* lames@nmsu.edu.

DEGREES AND AWARDS

BBA General Business (service area differs from that of the overall institution)

MS Engineering (service area differs from that of the overall institution)

COURSE SUBJECT AREAS OFFERED OUTSIDE OF DEGREE PROGRAMS

Undergraduate: Accounting; business; business administration and management; human resources management

Graduate: Accounting; business; business administration and management; chemical engineering; civil engineering; electrical engineering; engineering/industrial management; environmental engineering; human resources management; industrial engineering; public health

NEW ORLEANS BAPTIST THEOLOGICAL SEMINARY

New Orleans, Louisiana

NOBTS Virtual Campus/NOBTS Extension Center System
online.nobts.edu/

New Orleans Baptist Theological Seminary, founded in 1917, is an independent, religious, comprehensive institution. It is accredited by the Association of Theological Schools in the United States and Canada, Southern Association of Colleges and Schools. In 1999–2000, it offered 40 courses at a distance. In fall 1999, there were 1,000 students enrolled in distance learning courses.

Course delivery sites Courses are delivered to your home, 16 off-campus centers in Alexandria, Baton Rouge, Lake Charles, Shreveport, Albany (GA), Birmingham (AL), Cleveland (TN), Decatur (GA), Graceville (FL), Huntsville (AL), Jackson (MS), Jacksonville (FL), Madison (MS), Miami (FL), Orlando (FL), Tampa (FL).

Media Courses are delivered via interactive television, computer conferencing, World Wide Web, e-mail. Students and teachers may meet in person or interact via mail, telephone, fax, e-mail, interactive television, World Wide Web. The following equipment may be required: computer, modem, Internet access, e-mail.

Restrictions Programs are available worldwide. Enrollment is restricted to individuals meeting certain criteria.

Services Distance learners have access to library services, the campus computer network, e-mail services, academic advising, career placement assistance at a distance.

Credit-earning options Students may transfer credits from another institution or may earn credits through examinations, military training, business training.

Typical costs *Undergraduate:* Tuition of $95 per credit. *Graduate:* Tuition of $130 per credit. Costs may vary. Financial aid is available to distance learners.

Registration Students may register by mail, fax, e-mail, World Wide Web, in person.

Contact Dr. Jimmy Dukes, New Orleans Baptist Theological Seminary, Extension Center, 862 Columbia Drive, Decatur, GA 30030. *Telephone:* 800-514-1175. *Fax:* 404-284-1187. *E-mail:* jdukes@nobts.edu.

eCollege.com *www.ecollege.com/scholarships*

DEGREES AND AWARDS

ABS Biblical Studies (certain restrictions apply; some on-campus requirements)

BMin Divinity (certain restrictions apply; some on-campus requirements)

MAR Divinity (certain restrictions apply; some on-campus requirements)

COURSE SUBJECT AREAS OFFERED OUTSIDE OF DEGREE PROGRAMS

Undergraduate: Bible studies
Graduate: Bible studies
Noncredit: Bible studies

NEW SCHOOL UNIVERSITY

New York, New York
www.dialnsa.edu

New School University, founded in 1919, is an independent, nonprofit university. It is accredited by the Middle States Association of Colleges and Schools. It first offered distance learning courses in 1994. In 1999–2000, it offered 300 courses at a distance. In fall 1999, there were 787 students enrolled in distance learning courses.

Course delivery sites Courses are delivered to your home, your workplace, military bases, other colleges.

Media Courses are delivered via videoconferencing, World Wide Web. Students and teachers may meet in person or interact via videoconferencing, mail, telephone, fax, e-mail, World Wide Web. The following equipment may be required: computer, Internet access.

Restrictions Programs are available worldwide. Enrollment is open to anyone.

Services Distance learners have access to library services, academic advising, career placement assistance, bookstore at a distance.

Credit-earning options Students may transfer credits from another institution or may earn credits through portfolio assessment.

Typical costs *Undergraduate:* Tuition of $558 per credit plus mandatory fees of $108 per semester. *Graduate:* Tuition of $686 per credit plus mandatory fees of $108 per semester. Financial aid is available to distance learners.

Registration Students may register by mail, fax, telephone, e-mail, World Wide Web, in person.

Contact Gerianne Brosati, Associate Dean, Admissions and Student Services, New School University, 66 West 12th Street, New York, NY 10011. *Telephone:* 212-229-5630. *Fax:* 212-989-3887. *E-mail:* nsadmissions@newschool.edu.

DEGREES AND AWARDS

BA Liberal Arts
MA Media Studies

COURSE SUBJECT AREAS OFFERED OUTSIDE OF DEGREE PROGRAMS

Undergraduate: Accounting; area, ethnic, and cultural studies; Asian languages and literatures; astronomy and astrophysics; business; business administration and management; classical languages and literatures; communications; computer and information sciences; creative writing; design; developmental and child psychology; economics; English as a second language (ESL); English composition; English language and literature; European languages and literatures; fine arts; geology; health and physical education/fitness; history; human resources management; industrial psychology; journalism; liberal arts, general studies, and humanities; mathematics; Middle Eastern languages and literatures; music; philosophy and religion; physics; political science; social psychology; social sciences; sociology; teacher education
Graduate: Communications; creative writing; English as a second language (ESL); history; human resources management; teacher education
Noncredit: Accounting; area, ethnic, and cultural studies; Asian languages and literatures; astronomy and astrophysics; business; business administration and management; classical languages and literatures; communications; computer and information sciences; creative writing; design; developmental and child psychology; economics; English as a second language (ESL); English composition; English language and literature; European languages and literatures; fine arts; geology; health and physical education/fitness; history; human resources management; industrial psychology; journalism; liberal arts, general studies, and humanities; mathematics; Middle Eastern languages and literatures; music; philosophy and religion; physics; political science; social psychology; social sciences; sociology; teacher education

See full description on page 602.

NEW YORK INSTITUTE OF TECHNOLOGY

Old Westbury, New York

Online Campus
www.nyit.edu/olc

New York Institute of Technology, founded in 1955, is an independent, nonprofit, comprehensive institution. It is accredited by the Middle States Association of Colleges and Schools. It first offered distance learning courses in 1985. In 1999–2000, it offered 225 courses at a distance. In fall 1999, there were 1,177 students enrolled in distance learning courses.
Course delivery sites Courses are delivered to your home, your workplace, military bases, high schools.
Media Courses are delivered via videoconferencing, computer conferencing, World Wide Web, e-mail. Students and teachers may meet in person or interact via videoconferencing, audioconferencing, mail, telephone, fax, e-mail, interactive television, World Wide Web. The following equipment may be required: computer, modem, Internet access, e-mail.
Restrictions Programs are available worldwide. Enrollment is open to anyone.
Services Distance learners have access to library services, the campus computer network, e-mail services, academic advising, tutoring, career placement assistance, bookstore at a distance.
Credit-earning options Students may transfer credits from another institution or may earn credits through examinations, portfolio assessment, military training, business training.
Typical costs *Undergraduate:* Tuition of $370 per credit. *Graduate:* Tuition of $450 per credit. Costs may vary. Financial aid is available to distance learners.

Registration Students may register by mail, fax, telephone, e-mail, World Wide Web, in person.
Contact Katie Lyons, Admissions and Recruitment, New York Institute of Technology, OnLine Campus, Central Islip, NY 11722-9029. *Telephone:* 800-222-NYIT. *Fax:* 516-348-0299. *E-mail:* mlehmann@nyit.edu.

DEGREES AND AWARDS

BA Interdisciplinary Studies
BPS Hospitality Management, Interdisciplinary Studies
BS Business Administration, Community Mental Health, Criminal Justice, Interdisciplinary Studies, Psychology, Sociology, Telecommunications Management
MBA Business
MS Energy Management

COURSE SUBJECT AREAS OFFERED OUTSIDE OF DEGREE PROGRAMS

Undergraduate: Accounting; anthropology; biological and life sciences; business; business administration and management; communications; computer and information sciences; counseling psychology; criminal justice; criminology; economics; English composition; English language and literature; ethics; finance; foods and nutrition studies; history; hospitality services management; human resources management; industrial engineering; interior design; liberal arts, general studies, and humanities; marketing; mathematics; mechanical engineering; philosophy and religion; physical sciences; political science; psychology; public administration and services; social psychology; social work; sociology; statistics; teacher education; technical writing; telecommunications
Graduate: Business administration and management; computer and information sciences; counseling psychology; educational research; instructional media; marketing; teacher education

NEW YORK UNIVERSITY

New York, New York

The School of Continuing and Professional Studies
www.scps.nyu.edu

New York University, founded in 1831, is an independent, nonprofit university. It is accredited by the Middle States Association of Colleges and Schools. It first offered distance learning courses in 1992. In 1999–2000, it offered 50 courses at a distance. In fall 1999, there were 327 students enrolled in distance learning courses.
Course delivery sites Courses are delivered to your home.
Media Courses are delivered via interactive television, computer software, World Wide Web, e-mail. Students and teachers may interact via telephone, fax, e-mail, World Wide Web. The following equipment may be required: computer, modem, Internet access.
Restrictions Programs are available worldwide. Enrollment is open to anyone.
Services Distance learners have access to library services, the campus computer network, e-mail services, academic advising, tutoring, career placement assistance, bookstore at a distance.
Credit-earning options Students may transfer credits from another institution.
Typical costs *Undergraduate:* Tuition of $709 per credit. *Graduate:* Tuition of $610 per credit. Costs may vary. Financial aid is available to distance learners.
Registration Students may register by mail, fax, telephone, e-mail, World Wide Web, in person.
Contact Joseph Kornoski, Educational Advisement Coordinator, New York University. *Telephone:* 212-998-7088. *Fax:* 212-995-4675. *E-mail:* advice.scps@nyu.edu.

DEGREES AND AWARDS

Graduate Certificate(s) Information Technology
MS Management and Systems

COURSE SUBJECT AREAS OFFERED OUTSIDE OF DEGREE PROGRAMS

Undergraduate: Accounting; computer and information sciences; English language and literature; finance; health professions and related sciences; Latin American studies; organizational behavior studies; psychology; social sciences; sociology
Graduate: Business; computer and information sciences; management information systems
Noncredit: Business administration and management; business communications; computer programming; creative writing; hospitality services management; information sciences and systems; international relations; labor relations/studies; law and legal studies; mental health services; real estate; recreation and leisure studies; Spanish language and literature
See full description on page 604.

NIPISSING UNIVERSITY

North Bay, Ontario, Canada

Center for Continuing Business Education
www.unipissing.ca

Nipissing University, founded in 1992, is a province-supported, comprehensive institution. It is accredited by the provincial charter. In 1999–2000, it offered 19 courses at a distance. In fall 1999, there were 90 students enrolled in distance learning courses.
Course delivery sites Courses are delivered to your home, your workplace.
Media Courses are delivered via computer software, e-mail, print. Students and teachers may meet in person or interact via audioconferencing, mail, telephone, fax, e-mail. The following equipment may be required: computer, e-mail.
Restrictions Programs are available worldwide. Enrollment is restricted to individuals meeting certain criteria.
Services Distance learners have access to library services, e-mail services, academic advising at a distance.
Credit-earning options Students may transfer credits from another institution or may earn credits through examinations, portfolio assessment.
Typical costs Tuition of Can$570 per course plus mandatory fees of Can$26 per course for in-state residents. Tuition of Can$570 per course plus mandatory fees of Can$116 per course for out-of-state residents. Costs may vary.
Registration Students may register by mail, fax, telephone, e-mail, in person.
Contact Cindy Forth, Program Coordinator, Nipissing University, 100 College Drive, Box 5002, North Bay, ON P1B 8L7 Canada. *Telephone:* 705-474-3461 Ext. 4219. *Fax:* 705-475-0264. *E-mail:* cindyf@unipissing. ca.

DEGREES AND AWARDS

Undergraduate Certificate(s) Financial Services (certain restrictions apply; service area differs from that of the overall institution)
BComm Financial Services (certain restrictions apply)

NORTHAMPTON COUNTY AREA COMMUNITY COLLEGE

Bethlehem, Pennsylvania

Distance Learning
www.northampton.edu

Northampton County Area Community College, founded in 1967, is a state and locally supported, two-year college. It is accredited by the Middle States Association of Colleges and Schools. It first offered distance learning courses in 1974. In 1999–2000, it offered 99 courses at a distance. In fall 1999, there were 669 students enrolled in distance learning courses.
Course delivery sites Courses are delivered to your home, Lehigh Carbon Community College (Schnecksville), 1 off-campus center in Tannersville.
Media Courses are delivered via television, videotapes, videoconferencing, audiotapes, computer software, computer conferencing, World Wide Web, print. Students and teachers may meet in person or interact via videoconferencing, mail, telephone, fax, e-mail, World Wide Web. The following equipment may be required: television, videocassette player, computer, Internet access, e-mail.
Restrictions Tele-Web courses available within broadcasting range, and Internet courses are available worldwide. Enrollment is open to anyone.
Services Distance learners have access to library services, academic advising, tutoring, career placement assistance, bookstore at a distance.
Credit-earning options Students may transfer credits from another institution or may earn credits through examinations.
Typical costs Tuition of $81 per credit for local area residents. Tuition of $167 per credit for in-state residents. Tuition of $254 per credit for out-of-state residents. Students pay a $25 application fee. Costs may vary. Financial aid is available to distance learners.
Registration Students may register by mail, fax, telephone, in person.
Contact Admissions Office, Northampton County Area Community College, 3835 Green Pond Road, Bethlehem, PA 18020. *Telephone:* 610-861-4100. *Fax:* 610-861-5551.

DEGREES AND AWARDS

Undergraduate Certificate(s) Home-based Early Childhood Education (service area differs from that of the overall institution), Library Technical Assistant (service area differs from that of the overall institution)
AA Business Administration (service area differs from that of the overall institution), General Studies (service area differs from that of the overall institution)

COURSE SUBJECT AREAS OFFERED OUTSIDE OF DEGREE PROGRAMS

Undergraduate: Business administration and management; education; engineering; liberal arts, general studies, and humanities; library and information studies; social sciences

---

NORTH ARKANSAS COLLEGE

Harrison, Arkansas

Articulated Programs and Distance Learning
pioneer.northark.cc.ar.us/

North Arkansas College, founded in 1974, is a state and locally supported, two-year college. It is accredited by the North Central Association of Colleges and Schools. It first offered distance learning courses in 1988. In 1999–2000, it offered 7 courses at a distance. In fall 1999, there were 140 students enrolled in distance learning courses.

Course delivery sites Courses are delivered to your home, your workplace, high schools, Arkansas State University (State University), 12 off-campus centers in Alpena, Bergman, Berryville, Green Forest, Harrison, Lead Hill, Marshall, Mount Judea, Omaha, Valley Springs, Yellville.

Media Courses are delivered via television, interactive television, computer software, computer conferencing, World Wide Web, e-mail. Students and teachers may meet in person or interact via mail, telephone, fax, e-mail, interactive television, World Wide Web. The following equipment may be required: television, computer, modem, Internet access, e-mail.

Restrictions Programs are available to in-state students only. Enrollment is open to anyone.

Services Distance learners have access to the campus computer network, e-mail services, academic advising at a distance.

Credit-earning options Students may transfer credits from another institution or may earn credits through examinations, military training, business training.

Typical costs Tuition of $39 per credit hour for local area residents. Tuition of $49 per credit hour for in-state residents. Tuition of $99 per credit hour for out-of-state residents. *Noncredit courses:* $25 per course. Costs may vary. Financial aid is available to distance learners.

Registration Students may register by in person.

Contact Mr. James A. Robb, Coordinator of Articulated Programs and Distance Learning, North Arkansas College, 1515 Pioneer Drive, Harrison, AR 72601. *Telephone:* 870-391-3345. *Fax:* 870-391-3250. *E-mail:* jrobb@northark.cc.ar.us.

DEGREES AND AWARDS

Distance programs offered do not lead to a degree or other formal award.

COURSE SUBJECT AREAS OFFERED OUTSIDE OF DEGREE PROGRAMS

Undergraduate: Art history and criticism; computer and information sciences; English composition; health and physical education/fitness; history; mathematics; philosophy and religion; political science; psychology; technical writing

NORTH CAROLINA AGRICULTURAL AND TECHNICAL STATE UNIVERSITY

Greensboro, North Carolina

Distance Learning Initiative Office
www.ncatonline.org

North Carolina Agricultural and Technical State University, founded in 1891, is a state-supported university. It is accredited by the Southern Association of Colleges and Schools. It first offered distance learning courses in 1998. In 1999–2000, it offered 10 courses at a distance. In fall 1999, there were 83 students enrolled in distance learning courses.

Course delivery sites Courses are delivered to your home, your workplace, military bases, high schools, Gaston College (Dallas), Stanly Community College (Albemarle).

Media Courses are delivered via interactive television, World Wide Web, e-mail, print. Students and teachers may meet in person or interact via mail, telephone, fax, e-mail, interactive television, World Wide Web. The following equipment may be required: television, videocassette player, computer, Internet access, e-mail.

Restrictions Programs are available to in-state students only. Enrollment is restricted to individuals meeting certain criteria.

Services Distance learners have access to library services, the campus computer network, e-mail services, academic advising, tutoring, career placement assistance, bookstore at a distance.

Credit-earning options Students may transfer credits from another institution or may earn credits through examinations.

Typical costs *Undergraduate:* Tuition of $31 per credit hour plus mandatory fees of $4 per credit hour for in-state residents. Tuition of $276 per credit hour plus mandatory fees of $4 per credit hour for out-of-state residents. *Graduate:* Tuition of $45 per credit hour plus mandatory fees of $6 per credit hour for in-state residents. Tuition of $401 per credit hour plus mandatory fees of $6 per credit hour for out-of-state residents. Costs may vary. Financial aid is available to distance learners.

Registration Students may register by mail, fax, telephone, e-mail, World Wide Web, in person.

Contact Dr. Marcy Dingle Johnson, Director, Distance Learning, North Carolina Agricultural and Technical State University, Office of Continuing Studies and Distance Learning, 1601 East Market Street, Greensboro, NC 27411-1117. *Telephone:* 336-334-7607. *Fax:* 336-334-7081. *E-mail:* marcyj@ncat.edu.

eCollege.com   *www.ecollege.com/scholarships*

DEGREES AND AWARDS

MS Adult Education, Engineering (certain restrictions apply), Physical Education, Technology Education

COURSE SUBJECT AREAS OFFERED OUTSIDE OF DEGREE PROGRAMS

Undergraduate: Education; engineering-related technologies
Graduate: Education; engineering-related technologies
See full description on page 606.

NORTH CAROLINA STATE UNIVERSITY

Raleigh, North Carolina

Distance Education
www.ncsu.edu/cont_ed/dec.htm

North Carolina State University, founded in 1887, is a state-supported university. It is accredited by the Southern Association of Colleges and Schools. It first offered distance learning courses in 1976. In 1999–2000, it offered 400 courses at a distance. In fall 1999, there were 1,321 students enrolled in distance learning courses.

Course delivery sites Courses are delivered to your home, your workplace, military bases, high schools, off-campus center(s) in Asheville.

Media Courses are delivered via television, videotapes, videoconferencing, interactive television, computer software, CD-ROM, computer conferencing, World Wide Web, e-mail, print. Students and teachers may meet in person or interact via videoconferencing, audioconferencing, mail, telephone, fax, e-mail, interactive television, World Wide Web. The following equipment may be required: television, videocassette player, computer, Internet access, e-mail.

Restrictions Programs are available worldwide. Enrollment is open to anyone.

Services Distance learners have access to library services, the campus computer network, e-mail services, academic advising, career placement assistance, bookstore at a distance.

Credit-earning options Students may earn credits through examinations.

Typical costs *Undergraduate:* Tuition of $50 per credit hour plus mandatory fees of $10 per credit hour for in-state residents. Tuition of $100 per credit hour plus mandatory fees of $10 per credit hour for out-of-state residents. *Graduate:* Tuition of $72 per credit hour plus mandatory fees of $14 per credit hour for in-state residents. Tuition of $144 per credit hour plus mandatory fees of $14 per credit hour for out-of-state residents. Costs may vary. Financial aid is available to distance learners.

Registration Students may register by mail, fax, telephone, e-mail, World Wide Web, in person.
Contact Michael Yoakam, Director, North Carolina State University. *Telephone:* 919-515-9323. *Fax:* 919-515-5778. *E-mail:* michael_yoakam@ncsu.edu.

DEGREES AND AWARDS

BSET Engineering-Mechatronics
Graduate Certificate(s) Textile Manufacturing (service area differs from that of the overall institution), Training and Development (service area differs from that of the overall institution)
MA Word and Paper Science
ME Engineering (service area differs from that of the overall institution)
MEd Education-School Administration
MT Textiles (service area differs from that of the overall institution; some on-campus requirements)
EdD Education-Adult and Community College
PhD Marine Science

COURSE SUBJECT AREAS OFFERED OUTSIDE OF DEGREE PROGRAMS

Undergraduate: Accounting; agriculture; area, ethnic, and cultural studies; biological and life sciences; biology; botany; business; business law; chemistry; classical languages and literatures; communications; computer and information sciences; creative writing; economics; English as a second language (ESL); English composition; English language and literature; European languages and literatures; genetics; health and physical education/fitness; history; liberal arts, general studies, and humanities; logic; mathematics; microbiology; music; oceanography; philosophy and religion; physical sciences; physics; political science; psychology; radio and television broadcasting; social sciences; sociology; visual and performing arts
Graduate: Aerospace, aeronautical engineering; chemical engineering; civil engineering; developmental and child psychology; education; education administration; educational psychology; electrical engineering; engineering engineering mechanics; engineering-related technologies; engineering/industrial management; environmental engineering; human resources management; industrial engineering; mechanical engineering; political science; public administration and services; teacher education

See full description on page 676.

See full description on page 676.

NORTH CENTRAL STATE COLLEGE

Mansfield, Ohio
www.ncstate.tec.oh.us

North Central State College, founded in 1961, is a state-supported, two-year college. It is accredited by the North Central Association of Colleges and Schools. It first offered distance learning courses in 1994. In 1999–2000, it offered 8 courses at a distance. In fall 1999, there were 250 students enrolled in distance learning courses.
Course delivery sites Courses are delivered to your home.
Media Courses are delivered via videotapes. Students and teachers may interact via mail, telephone, World Wide Web. The following equipment may be required: television, videocassette player.
Restrictions Programs are available to in-state students only. Enrollment is restricted to individuals meeting certain criteria.
Services Distance learners have access to library services, bookstore at a distance.
Credit-earning options Students may transfer credits from another institution or may earn credits through examinations, portfolio assessment, military training, business training.
Typical costs Tuition of $56 per credit hour. Cost for noncredit course ranges from $150 to $200. Financial aid is available to distance learners.

Registration Students may register by mail, in person.
Contact Daniel Kraska, Distance Learning Coordinator, North Central State College, Department of Business, Mansfield, OH 44901. *Telephone:* 419-755-4801. *Fax:* 419-755-4750. *E-mail:* dkraska@ncstate.tec.oh.us.

DEGREES AND AWARDS

Distance programs offered do not lead to a degree or other formal award.

COURSE SUBJECT AREAS OFFERED OUTSIDE OF DEGREE PROGRAMS

Undergraduate: Business; business administration and management; health professions and related sciences; human resources management; international business; liberal arts, general studies, and humanities

NORTHCENTRAL TECHNICAL COLLEGE

Wausau, Wisconsin
Learning Resources
www.northcentral.tec.wi.us

Northcentral Technical College, founded in 1912, is a district-supported, two-year college. It is accredited by the North Central Association of Colleges and Schools. It first offered distance learning courses in 1986. In 1999–2000, it offered 381 courses at a distance.
Course delivery sites Courses are delivered to your home, your workplace, high schools, Blackhawk Technical College (Janesville), Chippewa Valley Technical College (Eau Claire), Fox Valley Technical College (Appleton), Gateway Technical College (Kenosha), Lakeshore Technical College (Cleveland), Madison Area Technical College (Madison), Mid-State Technical College (Wisconsin Rapids), Milwaukee Area Technical College (Milwaukee), Moraine Park Technical College (Fond du Lac), Nicolet Area Technical College (Rhinelander), Northeast Wisconsin Technical College (Green Bay), Southwest Wisconsin Technical College (Fennimore), Western Wisconsin Technical College (La Crosse), Wisconsin Indianhead Technical College, Superior Campus (Superior), 15 off-campus centers in Abbotsford, Antigo, Athens, Edgar, Granton, Keshena, Loyal, Medford, Merrill, Mosinee, Phillips, Spencer, Stratford, Wittenberg.
Media Courses are delivered via television, videotapes, videoconferencing, interactive television, computer conferencing, World Wide Web, e-mail, print. Students and teachers may interact via videoconferencing, audioconferencing, mail, telephone, fax, e-mail, interactive television, World Wide Web. The following equipment may be required: television, videocassette player, computer, modem, Internet access, e-mail.
Restrictions Programs are available to in-state students only. Enrollment is open to anyone.
Services Distance learners have access to library services, the campus computer network, e-mail services, academic advising, career placement assistance, bookstore at a distance.
Credit-earning options Students may transfer credits from another institution or may earn credits through examinations, portfolio assessment, military training, business training.
Typical costs Tuition of $59.25 per credit. Financial aid is available to distance learners.
Registration Students may register by mail, telephone, in person.
Contact Barbara Cummings, Team Leader, Northcentral Technical College, Learning Resources, 1000 Campus Drive, Wausau, WI 54401-1899. *Telephone:* 715-675-3331 Ext. 4056. *Fax:* 715-675-9776. *E-mail:* cummings@northcentral.tec.wi.us.

DEGREES AND AWARDS

Undergraduate Certificate(s) Legal Nurse (certain restrictions apply; service area differs from that of the overall institution)

AD Accounting (service area differs from that of the overall institution), Computer Informational Systems (service area differs from that of the overall institution), Criminal Justice (service area differs from that of the overall institution; some on-campus requirements), Dental Hygiene (service area differs from that of the overall institution; some on-campus requirements), Educational Interpreter Technician (some on-campus requirements), Healthcare Business Application (service area differs from that of the overall institution), Microcomputer Application Specialist (service area differs from that of the overall institution), Nursing (service area differs from that of the overall institution; some on-campus requirements), Supervisory Management (service area differs from that of the overall institution)

COURSE SUBJECT AREAS OFFERED OUTSIDE OF DEGREE PROGRAMS

Undergraduate: Accounting; administrative and secretarial services; agriculture; business; chemistry; developmental and child psychology; economics; health professions and related sciences; home economics and family studies; human resources management; industrial engineering; law and legal studies; mathematics; nursing; protective services; social psychology; sociology

NORTH CENTRAL TEXAS COLLEGE

Gainesville, Texas
www.nctc.cc.tx.us

North Central Texas College, founded in 1924, is a county-supported, two-year college. It is accredited by the Southern Association of Colleges and Schools. It first offered distance learning courses in 1992. In 1999–2000, it offered 7 courses at a distance. In fall 1999, there were 200 students enrolled in distance learning courses.

Course delivery sites Courses are delivered to your home, your workplace.

Media Courses are delivered via television, computer conferencing. Students and teachers may meet in person or interact via mail, telephone, fax, e-mail. The following equipment may be required: television, modem, Internet access, e-mail.

Restrictions Programs are available to local area students. Enrollment is open to anyone.

Services Distance learners have access to library services, e-mail services, academic advising, tutoring, career placement assistance at a distance.

Credit-earning options Students may transfer credits from another institution or may earn credits through examinations, military training.

Typical costs Tuition of $18 per hour plus mandatory fees of $58 per course for in-state residents. Tuition of $42 per hour plus mandatory fees of $83 per course for out-of-state residents. Costs may vary. Financial aid is available to distance learners.

Registration Students may register by in person.

Contact Dr. Eddie C. Hadlock, Dean of Arts and Sciences, North Central Texas College, 1525 West California, Gainesville, TX 76240. *Telephone:* 940-668-4234. *Fax:* 940-668-4258. *E-mail:* ehadlock@nctc. cc.tx.us.

DEGREES AND AWARDS

AA General Education General Education

AAS Business Management, Criminal Justice, Industrial Management, Nursing

AS General Education

COURSE SUBJECT AREAS OFFERED OUTSIDE OF DEGREE PROGRAMS

Undergraduate: Computer and information sciences; criminal justice; economics; English language and literature; history; political science; psychology; sociology

NORTH CENTRAL UNIVERSITY

Prescott, Arizona
ncu.edu

North Central University is an independent university. It is accredited by the North Central Association of Colleges and Schools. In 1999–2000, it offered 285 courses at a distance. In fall 1999, there were 200 students enrolled in distance learning courses.

Course delivery sites Courses are delivered to your home, your workplace.

Media Courses are delivered via videotapes, videoconferencing, audiotapes, computer software, CD-ROM, computer conferencing, World Wide Web, e-mail, print. Students and teachers may meet in person or interact via videoconferencing, audioconferencing, mail, telephone, fax, e-mail, World Wide Web. The following equipment may be required: computer, modem, Internet access, e-mail.

Restrictions Programs are available worldwide. Enrollment is restricted to individuals meeting certain criteria.

Services Distance learners have access to library services, the campus computer network, e-mail services, academic advising, bookstore at a distance.

Credit-earning options Students may transfer credits from another institution or may earn credits through examinations.

Typical costs *Undergraduate:* Tuition of $110 per unit. *Graduate:* Tuition of $120 per unit. There is a mandatory dissertation fee of $900 for PhD degrees only.

Registration Students may register by mail, fax, telephone, e-mail, World Wide Web, in person.

Contact Martha Monroe, Chair of Learner Affairs, North Central University, 505 West Whipple Street, Prescott, AZ 86301. *Telephone:* 888-327-2877. *Fax:* 520-541-7817. *E-mail:* mmonroe@ncu.edu.

DEGREES AND AWARDS

BA Psychology (some on-campus requirements)

BBA Business Administration (some on-campus requirements)

MA Psychology (certain restrictions apply; some on-campus requirements)

MBA Business Administration (certain restrictions apply; some on-campus requirements)

PhD Business Administration (certain restrictions apply; some on-campus requirements), Psychology (certain restrictions apply; some on-campus requirements)

COURSE SUBJECT AREAS OFFERED OUTSIDE OF DEGREE PROGRAMS

Undergraduate: Astronomy and astrophysics; business; computer and information sciences; economics; English language and literature; foods and nutrition studies; geology; health professions and related sciences; history; liberal arts, general studies, and humanities; library and information studies; mathematics; psychology; visual and performing arts

Graduate: Business; computer and information sciences; economics; engineering/industrial management; ethics; health services administration; psychology; public administration and services

See full description on page 608.

NORTH COUNTRY COMMUNITY COLLEGE

Saranac Lake, New York
www.nccc.edu

North Country Community College, founded in 1967, is a state and locally supported, two-year college. It is accredited by the Middle States Association of Colleges and Schools. In 1999–2000, it offered 24 courses at a distance. In fall 1999, there were 120 students enrolled in distance learning courses.

Course delivery sites Courses are delivered to your home.

Media Courses are delivered via World Wide Web, e-mail. Students and teachers may meet in person or interact via mail, telephone, fax, e-mail, World Wide Web. The following equipment may be required: computer, modem, Internet access, e-mail.

Restrictions Programs are available within two counties only. Enrollment is open to anyone.

Services Distance learners have access to e-mail services at a distance.

Credit-earning options Students may transfer credits from another institution or may earn credits through military training.

Typical costs Tuition of $85 per credit plus mandatory fees of $74 per course for local area residents. Tuition of $85 per credit plus mandatory fees of $74 per course for in-state residents. Tuition of $170 per credit plus mandatory fees of $74 per course for out-of-state residents. Financial aid is available to distance learners.

Registration Students may register by mail, fax, telephone, e-mail, World Wide Web, in person.

Contact Dr. Douglas R. Wilmes, Dean of Academic Affairs, North Country Community College, 20 Winona Avenue, PO Box 89, Saranac Lake, NY 12983-0089. *Telephone:* 518-891-2915 Ext. 203. *Fax:* 518-891-5029. *E-mail:* acdean@nccc.edu.

DEGREES AND AWARDS

Undergraduate Certificate(s) Community Residence Aide (some on-campus requirements), Office Technology (some on-campus requirements), Practical Nursing (certain restrictions apply; some on-campus requirements)

AA Liberal Arts and Science Humanities/Social Science (some on-campus requirements)

AAS Business Administration (some on-campus requirements), Business: Office Technology (some on-campus requirements), Community Mental Health Assistant (some on-campus requirements), Criminal Justice (some on-campus requirements), Massage Therapy (certain restrictions apply; some on-campus requirements), Nursing (ADN/RN) (certain restrictions apply; some on-campus requirements), Radiological Technology (certain restrictions apply; some on-campus requirements), Retail Business Management (some on-campus requirements)

AS Business Administration (some on-campus requirements), Liberal Arts and Science Mathematics and Science (some on-campus requirements), Recreation Facility Management (some on-campus requirements), Wilderness Recreation Management (some on-campus requirements)

COURSE SUBJECT AREAS OFFERED OUTSIDE OF DEGREE PROGRAMS

Undergraduate: Anthropology; art history and criticism; business administration and management; business communications; computer and information sciences; developmental and child psychology; earth science; English composition; English language and literature; environmental science; geography; health and physical education/fitness; marketing; meteorology

NORTH DAKOTA STATE COLLEGE OF SCIENCE

Wahpeton, North Dakota
www.ndscs.nodak.edu

North Dakota State College of Science, founded in 1903, is a state-supported, two-year college. It is accredited by the North Central Association of Colleges and Schools. It first offered distance learning courses in 1968. In 1999–2000, it offered 137 courses at a distance. In fall 1999, there were 1,061 students enrolled in distance learning courses.

Course delivery sites Courses are delivered to your home, your workplace, Bismarck State College (Bismarck).

Media Courses are delivered via television, videotapes, videoconferencing, interactive television, print. Students and teachers may interact via videoconferencing, mail, telephone, fax, e-mail, interactive television. The following equipment may be required: computer.

Restrictions Programs are available regionally. Enrollment is restricted to individuals meeting certain criteria.

Services Distance learners have access to library services, e-mail services, academic advising, career placement assistance, bookstore at a distance.

Credit-earning options Students may transfer credits from another institution or may earn credits through examinations.

Typical costs Tuition of $74 per credit for in-state residents. Tuition of $100 per credit for out-of-state residents. Costs may vary. Financial aid is available to distance learners.

Registration Students may register by mail, fax, telephone, in person.

Contact Steve Krohn, Coordinator, North Dakota State College of Science, 800 North 6th Street, Wahpeton, ND 58076-0002. *Telephone:* 701-671-2626. *Fax:* 701-671-2674. *E-mail:* krohn@plains.nodak.edu.

DEGREES AND AWARDS

AS Practical Nursing (certain restrictions apply; service area differs from that of the overall institution; some on-campus requirements)

COURSE SUBJECT AREAS OFFERED OUTSIDE OF DEGREE PROGRAMS

Undergraduate: Biological and life sciences; business; chemistry; developmental and child psychology; electronics; English composition; foods and nutrition studies; liberal arts, general studies, and humanities; mental health services; microbiology; nursing; philosophy and religion; sociology

NORTH DAKOTA STATE UNIVERSITY

Fargo, North Dakota
www.ndsu.edu

North Dakota State University, founded in 1890, is a state-supported university. It is accredited by the North Central Association of Colleges and Schools. It first offered distance learning courses in 1974. In 1999–2000, it offered 20 courses at a distance.

Course delivery sites Courses are delivered to your home, your workplace, military bases, high schools, North Dakota University System (Bismarck).

Media Courses are delivered via television, videotapes, videoconferencing, interactive television, audiotapes, computer software, CD-ROM, World Wide Web, e-mail, print. Students and teachers may meet in person or interact via videoconferencing, audioconferencing, mail, telephone, fax, e-mail, interactive television, World Wide Web. The following equipment may be required: television, videocassette player, computer, modem, Internet access, e-mail.

Restrictions Programs are available worldwide. Enrollment is restricted to individuals meeting certain criteria.

Services Distance learners have access to library services, the campus computer network, e-mail services, career placement assistance, bookstore at a distance.

Credit-earning options Students may transfer credits from another institution or may earn credits through examinations, portfolio assessment, military training, business training.

Typical costs *Undergraduate:* Tuition of $120 per credit plus mandatory fees of $17 per credit for in-state residents. Tuition of $293 per credit plus mandatory fees of $17 per credit for out-of-state residents. *Graduate:* Tuition of $129 per credit plus mandatory fees of $17 per credit for in-state residents. Tuition of $316 per credit plus mandatory fees of $17 per credit for out-of-state residents. Costs may vary. Financial aid is available to distance learners.

Registration Students may register by mail, fax, telephone, e-mail, World Wide Web, in person.

Contact Richard Chenoweth, Special Assistant to the Vice President for Academic Affairs, North Dakota State University, PO Box 5014, Fargo, ND 58105-5014. *Telephone:* 701-231-7106. *Fax:* 701-231-1013. *E-mail:* rchenowe@prairie.nodak.edu.

eCollege.com *www.ecollege.com/scholarships*

DEGREES AND AWARDS

MBA Business Administration (service area differs from that of the overall institution)

MS Transportation Program (service area differs from that of the overall institution; some on-campus requirements)

COURSE SUBJECT AREAS OFFERED OUTSIDE OF DEGREE PROGRAMS

Undergraduate: Accounting; aerospace, aeronautical engineering; child care and development; communications; computer and information sciences; continuing education; criminal justice; developmental and child psychology; electrical engineering; home economics and family studies; mathematics; statistics

Graduate: Accounting; agriculture; business administration and management; child care and development; civil engineering; computer and information sciences; continuing education; criminal justice; education; education administration; electrical engineering; home economics and family studies

See full description on page 822.

NORTHEASTERN STATE UNIVERSITY

Tahlequah, Oklahoma

Center for Academic Technology and Distance Learning
www.nsuok.edu

Northeastern State University, founded in 1846, is a state-supported, comprehensive institution. It is accredited by the North Central Association of Colleges and Schools. In 1999–2000, it offered 34 courses at a distance. In fall 1999, there were 545 students enrolled in distance learning courses.

Course delivery sites Courses are delivered to your home, Carl Albert State College (Poteau), Rogers State University (Claremore).

Media Courses are delivered via videotapes, videoconferencing, interactive television, audiotapes, World Wide Web, print. Students and teachers may meet in person or interact via videoconferencing, audioconferencing, mail, telephone, fax, e-mail, interactive television, World Wide Web. The following equipment may be required: videocassette player, computer, modem, Internet access, e-mail.

Restrictions Programs are available to in-state students only. Enrollment is open to anyone.

Services Distance learners have access to library services, the campus computer network, e-mail services, academic advising, tutoring, bookstore at a distance.

Credit-earning options Students may transfer credits from another institution or may earn credits through examinations, portfolio assessment.

Typical costs *Undergraduate:* Tuition of $50 per semester hour plus mandatory fees of $13.15 per semester for local area residents. Tuition of $50 per semester hour plus mandatory fees of $13.15 per semester for in-state residents. Tuition of $66 per semester hour plus mandatory fees of $13.15 per semester for out-of-state residents. *Graduate:* Tuition of $143 per semester hour plus mandatory fees of $13.15 per semester for local area residents. Tuition of $143 per semester hour plus mandatory fees of $13.15 per semester for in-state residents. Tuition of $175 per semester hour plus mandatory fees of $13.15 per semester for out-of-state residents. Financial aid is available to distance learners.

Registration Students may register by telephone, in person.

Contact Dr. Donna Wood, Coordinator of Distance Learning, Northeastern State University, 600 North Grand Avenue, Net 416, Tahlequah, OK 74464. *Telephone:* 918-456-5511 Ext. 5859. *Fax:* 918-458-2061. *E-mail:* wooddg@nsuok.edu.

DEGREES AND AWARDS

BBA Business Administration
BSN Nursing (certain restrictions apply)

COURSE SUBJECT AREAS OFFERED OUTSIDE OF DEGREE PROGRAMS

Undergraduate: Business administration and management; nursing
See full description on page 676.

NORTHEASTERN UNIVERSITY

Boston, Massachusetts

Network Northeastern
www.neu.edu/network-nu

Northeastern University, founded in 1898, is an independent, nonprofit university. It is accredited by the New England Association of Schools and Colleges. It first offered distance learning courses in 1983. In 1999–2000, it offered 200 courses at a distance. In fall 1999, there were 2,000 students enrolled in distance learning courses.

Course delivery sites Courses are delivered to your home, your workplace, military bases, 2 off-campus centers in Burlington, Dedham.

Media Courses are delivered via television, videotapes, videoconferencing, computer software, computer conferencing, World Wide Web, e-mail. Students and teachers may interact via videoconferencing, mail, telephone, fax, e-mail, World Wide Web. The following equipment may be required: television, videocassette player, computer, modem, Internet access, e-mail.

Restrictions Programs are available worldwide. Enrollment is restricted to individuals meeting certain criteria.

Services Distance learners have access to the campus computer network, e-mail services, academic advising, career placement assistance, bookstore at a distance.

Credit-earning options Students may transfer credits from another institution.

Typical costs *Undergraduate:* Tuition of $880 per course. *Graduate:* Tuition of $1940 per course. Costs may vary. Financial aid is available to distance learners.

Registration Students may register by mail, fax, telephone, e-mail, World Wide Web, in person.

Contact Linda Alosso, Assistant Director, Northeastern University, 360 Huntington Avenue, 328 CP, Boston, MA 02115. *Telephone:* 617-373-5620. *Fax:* 617-373-5625. *E-mail:* lalosso@lynx.neu.edu.

DEGREES AND AWARDS

Undergraduate Certificate(s) C++/Unix Programming
MSEE Electrical and Computer Engineering
MSIS Information Systems

COURSE SUBJECT AREAS OFFERED OUTSIDE OF DEGREE PROGRAMS

Undergraduate: Algebra; calculus; computer programming; engineering-related technologies; technical writing
Graduate: Computer and information sciences; electrical engineering; engineering/industrial management; industrial engineering; mechanical engineering
Noncredit: Computer programming
See full description on page 610.

NORTHEAST STATE TECHNICAL COMMUNITY COLLEGE

Blountville, Tennessee
Evening and Distance Education
www.nstcc.cc.tn.us

Northeast State Technical Community College, founded in 1966, is a state-supported, two-year college. It is accredited by the Southern Association of Colleges and Schools. In 1999–2000, it offered 27 courses at a distance. In fall 1999, there were 450 students enrolled in distance learning courses.
Course delivery sites Courses are delivered to your home, 2 off-campus centers in Elizabethton, Kingsport.
Media Courses are delivered via videotapes, computer software, World Wide Web, e-mail, print. Students and teachers may meet in person or interact via mail, telephone, fax, e-mail, World Wide Web. The following equipment may be required: television, videocassette player, computer, modem, Internet access, e-mail.
Restrictions Programs are available to local area students. Enrollment is restricted to individuals meeting certain criteria.
Services Distance learners have access to library services, the campus computer network, e-mail services, academic advising, career placement assistance, bookstore at a distance.
Credit-earning options Students may transfer credits from another institution or may earn credits through examinations, military training, business training.
Typical costs Full-time undergraduate tuition in-state is $599; out-of-state is $2393. Mandatory fees are $60. *Noncredit courses:* $90 per course. Financial aid is available to distance learners.
Registration Students may register by mail, fax, telephone, in person.
Contact Dr. James C. Lefler, Dean, Evening and Distance Education, Northeast State Technical Community College, PO Box 246, Blountville, TN 37617. *Telephone:* 423-323-0221. *Fax:* 423-323-0224. *E-mail:* jclefler@nstcc.cc.tn.us.

DEGREES AND AWARDS

Distance programs offered do not lead to a degree or other formal award.

COURSE SUBJECT AREAS OFFERED OUTSIDE OF DEGREE PROGRAMS

Undergraduate: American (U.S.) history; American literature; astronomy and astrophysics; biology; business administration and management; business communications; business law; child care and development; English composition; family and marriage counseling; finance; health and physical education/fitness; liberal arts, general studies, and humanities; marketing; mathematics; psychology; social sciences; Spanish language and literature; teacher education; technical writing; visual and performing arts

NORTHEAST TEXAS COMMUNITY COLLEGE

Mount Pleasant, Texas
www.ntcc.cc.tx.us

Northeast Texas Community College, founded in 1985, is a state and locally supported, two-year college. It is accredited by the Southern Association of Colleges and Schools. In 1999–2000, it offered 6 courses at a distance. In fall 1999, there were 1,952 students enrolled in distance learning courses.
Course delivery sites Courses are delivered to your home, your workplace, military bases, high schools, 1 off-campus center in Naplez.
Media Courses are delivered via interactive television, computer software, World Wide Web, e-mail. Students and teachers may meet in person or interact via videoconferencing, e-mail, World Wide Web. The following equipment may be required: computer, modem, Internet access, e-mail.
Restrictions Programs are available to local area students. Enrollment is open to anyone.
Services Distance learners have access to library services, e-mail services, academic advising, bookstore at a distance.
Credit-earning options Students may transfer credits from another institution.
Typical costs Tuition of $51 per credit for local area residents. Tuition of $61 per credit for in-state residents. Tuition of $226 per credit for out-of-state residents. Costs may vary. Financial aid is available to distance learners.
Registration Students may register by in person.
Contact Michael Dennehy, Director of Distance Education, Northeast Texas Community College, PO Box 1307, Mount Pleasant, TX 75456. *Telephone:* 903-572-9630. *Fax:* 903-572-6712. *E-mail:* mdennehy@ntcc.cc.tx.us.

DEGREES AND AWARDS

Distance programs offered do not lead to a degree or other formal award.

COURSE SUBJECT AREAS OFFERED OUTSIDE OF DEGREE PROGRAMS

Undergraduate: Computer and information sciences; economics; English composition; English literature; geology; music; political science; psychology

NORTHEAST WISCONSIN TECHNICAL COLLEGE

Green Bay, Wisconsin
Distance Learning
www.nwtc.tec.wi.us/

Northeast Wisconsin Technical College, founded in 1913, is a state and locally supported, two-year college. It is accredited by the North Central

Association of Colleges and Schools. It first offered distance learning courses in 1981. In 1999–2000, it offered 198 courses at a distance. In fall 1999, there were 1,700 students enrolled in distance learning courses.

Course delivery sites Courses are delivered to your home, your workplace, high schools, Northeast Wisconsin Technical Institute (Sturgeon Bay), St. Norbert College (De Pere), University of Wisconsin–Oshkosh (Oshkosh), 54 off-campus centers.

Media Courses are delivered via television, videotapes, videoconferencing, interactive television, computer software, computer conferencing, World Wide Web, e-mail, print. Students and teachers may meet in person or interact via videoconferencing, audioconferencing, mail, telephone, fax, e-mail, interactive television, World Wide Web. The following equipment may be required: television, videocassette player, computer, modem, Internet access, e-mail.

Restrictions Programs are available nationwide. Enrollment is restricted to individuals meeting certain criteria.

Services Distance learners have access to library services, e-mail services, academic advising, career placement assistance, bookstore at a distance.

Credit-earning options Students may transfer credits from another institution or may earn credits through examinations, portfolio assessment, military training, business training.

Typical costs Tuition of $64.75 per credit. *Noncredit courses:* $15 per course. Financial aid is available to distance learners.

Registration Students may register by mail, fax, telephone, in person.

Contact Anne Kamps, Distance Learning Coordinator, Northeast Wisconsin Technical College. *Telephone:* 920-498-6367. *Fax:* 920-498-6378. *E-mail:* akamps@nwtc.tec.wi.us.

DEGREES AND AWARDS

AD Corrections, Hospitality and Tourism Management Hospitality and Tourism Management (service area differs from that of the overall institution)

COURSE SUBJECT AREAS OFFERED OUTSIDE OF DEGREE PROGRAMS

Undergraduate: Abnormal psychology; accounting; advertising; agriculture; anatomy; animal sciences; business; business administration and management; business law; child care and development; cognitive psychology; communications; corrections; criminal justice; criminology; economics; educational psychology; English language and literature; finance; fire science; foods and nutrition studies; health professions and related sciences; hospitality services management; international business; law and legal studies; marketing; mathematics; protective services; psychology; sociology; Spanish language and literature; veterinary science

Noncredit: Insurance; real estate

NORTHERN ARIZONA UNIVERSITY

Flagstaff, Arizona

NAU Statewide Campus and NAU Worldwide Campus
www.nau.edu/statewide

Northern Arizona University, founded in 1899, is a state-supported university. It is accredited by the North Central Association of Colleges and Schools. In 1999–2000, it offered 290 courses at a distance. In fall 1999, there were 3,000 students enrolled in distance learning courses.

Course delivery sites Courses are delivered to your home, your workplace, high schools, Arizona Community Colleges, 30 off-campus centers.

Media Courses are delivered via television, videotapes, interactive television, computer software, computer conferencing, World Wide Web. Students and teachers may meet in person or interact via mail, telephone, fax, e-mail, interactive television, World Wide Web. The following equipment may be required: television, videocassette player, computer, modem, Internet access, e-mail.

Restrictions Programs are available nationwide. Enrollment is restricted to individuals meeting certain criteria.

Services Distance learners have access to library services, the campus computer network, e-mail services, academic advising, tutoring, career placement assistance, bookstore at a distance.

Credit-earning options Students may transfer credits from another institution or may earn credits through examinations.

Typical costs *Undergraduate:* Tuition of $115 per credit hour for in-state residents. Tuition of $179 per credit hour for out-of-state residents. *Graduate:* Tuition of $115 per credit hour for in-state residents. Tuition of $179 per credit hour for out-of-state residents. Mandatory fees are $6 for one to six credits. Financial aid is available to distance learners.

Registration Students may register by mail, fax, World Wide Web, in person.

Contact Janet Carlson, NAU Statewide Campus, Northern Arizona University, PO Box 04117, Flagstaff, AZ 86011. *Telephone:* 800-426-8315. *Fax:* 520-523-1169. *E-mail:* janet.carlson@nau.edu.

DEGREES AND AWARDS

BAS Health Promotion (certain restrictions apply)

BN Liberal Studies (certain restrictions apply)

BS Dental Hygiene Completion Program (certain restrictions apply), Hotel and Restaurant Management (certain restrictions apply), Nursing (certain restrictions apply)

ME Engineering (certain restrictions apply)

MEd Educational Technology (certain restrictions apply)

COURSE SUBJECT AREAS OFFERED OUTSIDE OF DEGREE PROGRAMS

Undergraduate: Accounting; advertising; African-American studies; anthropology; area, ethnic, and cultural studies; art history and criticism; biological and life sciences; business; business administration and management; communications; computer and information sciences; criminal justice; curriculum and instruction; design; developmental and child psychology; drama and theater; education; educational psychology; English language and literature; environmental engineering; environmental science; film studies; fine arts; health professions and related sciences; history; hospitality services management; interior design; liberal arts, general studies, and humanities; marketing; music; nursing; philosophy and religion; political science; psychology; social psychology; social sciences; social work; sociology; teacher education; visual and performing arts

Graduate: Business administration and management; curriculum and instruction; economics; education; education administration; educational psychology; educational research; engineering; English language and literature; health professions and related sciences; liberal arts, general studies, and humanities; nursing; physical therapy; political science; public administration and services; social sciences; student counseling; teacher education

NORTHERN ESSEX COMMUNITY COLLEGE

Haverhill, Massachusetts

Business, International Programs and Non-Traditional Learning

Northern Essex Community College, founded in 1960, is a state-supported, two-year college. It is accredited by the New England Association of Schools and Colleges. It first offered distance learning courses in 1979. In 1999–2000, it offered 24 courses at a distance. In fall 1999, there were 158 students enrolled in distance learning courses.

Course delivery sites Courses are delivered to your home, high schools, Bunker Hill Community College (Boston), Framingham State College

(Framingham), Middlesex Community College (Bedford), North Shore Community College (Danvers), University of Massachusetts Lowell (Lowell).

Media Courses are delivered via television, videotapes, videoconferencing, computer software, CD-ROM, computer conferencing, World Wide Web, e-mail, print. Students and teachers may meet in person or interact via videoconferencing, mail, telephone, fax, e-mail, World Wide Web. The following equipment may be required: television, computer, Internet access, e-mail.

Restrictions Programs are available predominantly in Massachusetts and southern New Hampshire. Enrollment is open to anyone.

Services Distance learners have access to library services, the campus computer network, e-mail services at a distance.

Credit-earning options Students may transfer credits from another institution or may earn credits through examinations, portfolio assessment, military training, business training.

Typical costs Tuition of $74 per credit for local area residents. Tuition of $81 per credit for in-state residents. Tuition of $98 per credit for out-of-state residents. *Noncredit courses:* $90 per course. Financial aid is available to distance learners.

Registration Students may register by mail, fax, telephone, in person.

Contact Diane Sweeney, Administrative Assistant, Northern Essex Community College. *Telephone:* 978-556-3321. *Fax:* 978-556-3775. *E-mail:* dsweeney@necc.mass.edu.

DEGREES AND AWARDS

Distance programs offered do not lead to a degree or other formal award.

COURSE SUBJECT AREAS OFFERED OUTSIDE OF DEGREE PROGRAMS

Undergraduate: Administrative and secretarial services; American literature; anthropology; business; business administration and management; business communications; computer and information sciences; earth science; English composition; English language and literature; health services administration; Japanese language and literature; liberal arts, general studies, and humanities; psychology; social sciences

NORTHERN ILLINOIS UNIVERSITY

De Kalb, Illinois

Division of Continuing Education
www.online.niu.edu

Northern Illinois University, founded in 1895, is a state-supported university. It is accredited by the North Central Association of Colleges and Schools. It first offered distance learning courses in 1995. In 1999–2000, it offered 40 courses at a distance. In fall 1999, there were 382 students enrolled in distance learning courses.

Course delivery sites Courses are delivered to College of DuPage (Glen Ellyn), Elgin Community College (Elgin), off-campus center(s) in Elgin, Hoffman Estates, Naperville, Oak Brook, Rock Island, Rockford.

Media Courses are delivered via videoconferencing, interactive television. Students and teachers may meet in person or interact via videoconferencing, audioconferencing, mail, telephone, fax, e-mail, interactive television, World Wide Web.

Restrictions Programs are available regionally to northern Illinois. Enrollment is restricted to individuals meeting certain criteria.

Services Distance learners have access to library services, the campus computer network, e-mail services, academic advising, bookstore at a distance.

Credit-earning options Students may transfer credits from another institution.

Typical costs *Undergraduate:* Tuition of $118 per semester hour plus mandatory fees of $35 per semester hour. *Graduate:* Tuition of $130 per semester hour plus mandatory fees of $35 per semester hour. Costs may vary. Financial aid is available to distance learners.

Registration Students may register by mail, telephone, in person.

Contact Caroline Harmison, Distance Education Coordinator, Northern Illinois University, Division of Continuing Education, DeKalb, IL 60115-2860. *Telephone:* 815-753-0727. *Fax:* 815-753-6900. *E-mail:* charmison@niu.edu.

eCollege.com *www.ecollege.com/scholarships*

DEGREES AND AWARDS

Distance programs offered do not lead to a degree or other formal award.

COURSE SUBJECT AREAS OFFERED OUTSIDE OF DEGREE PROGRAMS

Undergraduate: Engineering-related technologies
Graduate: Accounting; adult education; business administration and management; continuing education; curriculum and instruction; electrical engineering; engineering-related technologies; English composition; finance; human resources management; instructional media; management information systems; marketing; mechanical engineering; nursing; public policy analysis

NORTHERN KENTUCKY UNIVERSITY

Highland Heights, Kentucky

Credit Continuing Education and Distance Learning
www.nku.edu/~dist_learn

Northern Kentucky University, founded in 1968, is a state-supported, comprehensive institution. It is accredited by the Southern Association of Colleges and Schools. It first offered distance learning courses in 1983. In 1999–2000, it offered 32 courses at a distance. In fall 1999, there were 300 students enrolled in distance learning courses.

Course delivery sites Courses are delivered to your home, your workplace, high schools, Kentucky Commonwealth Virtual University (Frankfort).

Media Courses are delivered via television, interactive television, World Wide Web, e-mail. Students and teachers may meet in person or interact via videoconferencing, mail, telephone, fax, e-mail, World Wide Web. The following equipment may be required: television, computer, Internet access.

Restrictions Programs are available to local area students. Enrollment is restricted to individuals meeting certain criteria.

Services Distance learners have access to library services, the campus computer network, e-mail services, academic advising, bookstore at a distance.

Credit-earning options Students may transfer credits from another institution or may earn credits through examinations, portfolio assessment, military training.

Typical costs *Undergraduate:* Tuition of $89 per credit hour plus mandatory fees of $12 per credit hour for in-state residents. Tuition of $257 per credit hour plus mandatory fees of $12 per credit hour for out-of-state residents. *Graduate:* Tuition of $128 per credit hour plus mandatory fees of $12 per credit hour for in-state residents. Tuition of $374 per credit hour plus mandatory fees of $12 per credit hour for out-of-state residents. Financial aid is available to distance learners.

Registration Students may register by in person.

Contact Barbara Hedges, Interim Director, Northern Kentucky University, Credit Continuing Education and Distance Learning, Highland Heights, KY 41099-5700. *Telephone:* 606-572-5601. *Fax:* 606-572-5174. *E-mail:* hedgesb@nku.edu.

DEGREES AND AWARDS

Distance programs offered do not lead to a degree or other formal award.

COURSE SUBJECT AREAS OFFERED OUTSIDE OF DEGREE PROGRAMS

Undergraduate: Anthropology; archaeology; business administration and management; communications; geography; history; journalism; liberal arts, general studies, and humanities; music; nursing; political science; psychology; public administration and services; social work; sociology; teacher education

Graduate: Business administration and management; nursing; political science; public administration and services; social work; teacher education

See full description on page 556.

NORTHERN MICHIGAN UNIVERSITY

Marquette, Michigan

Continuing Education
www.nmu.edu/ce

Northern Michigan University, founded in 1899, is a state-supported, comprehensive institution. It is accredited by the North Central Association of Colleges and Schools. It first offered distance learning courses in 1995. In 1999–2000, it offered 111 courses at a distance. In fall 1999, there were 697 students enrolled in distance learning courses.

Course delivery sites Courses are delivered to your home, your workplace, military bases, high schools, Bay de Noc Community College (Escanaba), Gogebic Community College (Ironwood), 3 off-campus centers in Escanaba, Iron Mountain/ Kingsford, Ironwood.

Media Courses are delivered via videotapes, interactive television, computer software, CD-ROM, World Wide Web, e-mail, print. Students and teachers may meet in person or interact via mail, telephone, fax, e-mail, interactive television, World Wide Web. The following equipment may be required: computer, modem, Internet access, e-mail.

Restrictions Programs are available to in-state students only. Enrollment is open to anyone.

Services Distance learners have access to library services, the campus computer network, e-mail services, academic advising, career placement assistance, bookstore at a distance.

Credit-earning options Students may transfer credits from another institution or may earn credits through examinations, military training.

Typical costs *Undergraduate:* Tuition of $135 per credit. *Graduate:* Tuition of $165 per credit. Financial aid is available to distance learners.

Registration Students may register by mail, fax, telephone, e-mail, World Wide Web, in person.

Contact Joe Holman, Distance Education Specialist, Northern Michigan University, 1401 Presque Isle Avenue, Marquette, MI 49855. *Telephone:* 906-227-1683. *Fax:* 906-227-2108. *E-mail:* jholman@nmu.edu.

DEGREES AND AWARDS

BACJ Criminal Justice (service area differs from that of the overall institution; some on-campus requirements)

BBA Management (service area differs from that of the overall institution; some on-campus requirements)

BEd Elementary Education (service area differs from that of the overall institution; some on-campus requirements)

BS Social Science

BSW Social Work (service area differs from that of the overall institution)
MN Nursing
MPA Public Administration

COURSE SUBJECT AREAS OFFERED OUTSIDE OF DEGREE PROGRAMS

Undergraduate: Accounting; business; business administration and management; conservation and natural resources; criminal justice; economics; education; English composition; English language and literature; geography; history of science and technology; marketing; mathematics; nursing; social sciences; sociology

Graduate: Education; nursing; political science; teacher education

NORTHERN STATE UNIVERSITY

Aberdeen, South Dakota

Continuing Education
www.northern.edu

Northern State University, founded in 1901, is a state-supported, comprehensive institution. It is accredited by the North Central Association of Colleges and Schools. In 1999–2000, it offered 32 courses at a distance. In fall 1999, there were 51 students enrolled in distance learning courses.

Course delivery sites Courses are delivered to your home, your workplace.

Media Courses are delivered via videotapes, videoconferencing, World Wide Web, print. Students and teachers may meet in person or interact via mail, telephone, fax, e-mail. The following equipment may be required: computer.

Restrictions Programs are available worldwide. Enrollment is open to anyone.

Services Distance learners have access to library services, e-mail services, tutoring, bookstore at a distance.

Typical costs Tuition of $125.45 per credit. Costs may vary. Financial aid is available to distance learners.

Registration Students may register by mail, fax, telephone, e-mail, in person.

Contact Peggy Hallstrom, Continuing Education, Northern State University. *Telephone:* 605-626-2568. *Fax:* 605-626-2542. *E-mail:* hallstrp@northern.edu.

DEGREES AND AWARDS

Distance programs offered do not lead to a degree or other formal award.

COURSE SUBJECT AREAS OFFERED OUTSIDE OF DEGREE PROGRAMS

Undergraduate: Algebra; biology; business administration and management; calculus; computer and information sciences; educational psychology; English composition; history; library and information studies; political science; sociology

NORTHERN VIRGINIA COMMUNITY COLLEGE

Annandale, Virginia

Extended Learning Institute
eli.nv.cc.va.us/

Northern Virginia Community College, founded in 1965, is a state-supported, two-year college. It is accredited by the Southern Association of Colleges and Schools. It first offered distance learning courses in 1975.

In 1999–2000, it offered 148 courses at a distance. In fall 1999, there were 3,515 students enrolled in distance learning courses.

Course delivery sites Courses are delivered to your home, your workplace, military bases, Blue Ridge Community College (Weyers Cave), Dabney S. Lancaster Community College (Clifton Forge), Lord Fairfax Community College (Middletown), Mountain Empire Community College (Big Stone Gap), Piedmont Virginia Community College (Charlottesville), Rappahannock Community College (Glenns).

Media Courses are delivered via television, videotapes, videoconferencing, audiotapes, computer software, CD-ROM, computer conferencing, World Wide Web, e-mail, print. Students and teachers may meet in person or interact via audioconferencing, mail, telephone, fax, e-mail, World Wide Web. The following equipment may be required: television, videocassette player, computer, Internet access.

Restrictions Programs are available nationwide. Enrollment is open to anyone.

Services Distance learners have access to library services, the campus computer network, e-mail services, academic advising, tutoring, bookstore at a distance.

Credit-earning options Students may transfer credits from another institution or may earn credits through examinations, portfolio assessment, military training, business training.

Typical costs Tuition of $37 per credit plus mandatory fees of $2 per credit for in-state residents. Tuition of $165 per credit plus mandatory fees of $2 per credit for out-of-state residents. Financial aid is available to distance learners.

Registration Students may register by mail, fax, telephone, in person.

Contact Admissions and Records, Northern Virginia Community College, Extended Learning Institute, Annandale, VA 22003-3796. *Telephone:* 703-323-3368. *Fax:* 703-323-3392. *E-mail:* nvtownj@nv.cc.va.us.

DEGREES AND AWARDS

Undergraduate Certificate(s) Health Information Technology (service area differs from that of the overall institution; some on-campus requirements)

AA Liberal Arts (service area differs from that of the overall institution; some on-campus requirements)

AAS Business Management (service area differs from that of the overall institution; some on-campus requirements), Business Management, Public Management Specialization (service area differs from that of the overall institution; some on-campus requirements), Information Systems Technology (service area differs from that of the overall institution; some on-campus requirements)

AS Business Administration (service area differs from that of the overall institution; some on-campus requirements), Engineering (service area differs from that of the overall institution; some on-campus requirements), General Studies (service area differs from that of the overall institution; some on-campus requirements)

COURSE SUBJECT AREAS OFFERED OUTSIDE OF DEGREE PROGRAMS

Undergraduate: Abnormal psychology; accounting; administrative and secretarial services; advertising; algebra; American (U.S.) history; American literature; art history and criticism; biology; business; business administration and management; business law; calculus; chemistry; comparative literature; computer and information sciences; computer programming; creative writing; criminal justice; criminology; database management; developmental and child psychology; drama and theater; economics; education; engineering; English composition; English language and literature; English literature; ethics; film studies; finance; fine arts; French language and literature; geography; health and physical education/fitness; health professions and related sciences; history; human resources management; information sciences and systems; instructional media; journalism; liberal arts, general studies, and humanities; logic; management information systems; marketing; mathematics; mechanical engineering; organizational behavior studies; philosophy and religion; physics; political science;

psychology; public administration and services; sociology; Spanish language and literature; statistics; technical writing

See full description on page 676.

See full description on page 676.

NORTH FLORIDA COMMUNITY COLLEGE

Madison, Florida

North Florida Community College, founded in 1958, is a state-supported, two-year college. It is accredited by the Southern Association of Colleges and Schools.

Contact North Florida Community College, 1000 Turner Davis Drive, Madison, FL 32340-1602. *Telephone:* 850-973-2288. *Fax:* 850-973-1696.

See full description on page 676.

NORTH GEORGIA COLLEGE & STATE UNIVERSITY

Dahlonega, Georgia

Office of Distance Education
www.ngcsu.edu

North Georgia College & State University, founded in 1873, is a state-supported, comprehensive institution. It is accredited by the Southern Association of Colleges and Schools. It first offered distance learning courses in 1995. In 1999–2000, it offered 8 courses at a distance. In fall 1999, there were 150 students enrolled in distance learning courses.

Course delivery sites Courses are delivered to your home, high schools, Gainesville College (Gainesville).

Media Courses are delivered via television, videotapes, videoconferencing, interactive television, World Wide Web, e-mail, print. Students and teachers may meet in person or interact via videoconferencing, mail, telephone, fax, e-mail, interactive television, World Wide Web. The following equipment may be required: television, videocassette player, computer, modem, Internet access, e-mail.

Restrictions Courses are available to students in northeast Georgia only. Enrollment is open to anyone.

Services Distance learners have access to library services, the campus computer network, e-mail services, academic advising, tutoring at a distance.

Credit-earning options Students may transfer credits from another institution or may earn credits through examinations.

Typical costs *Undergraduate:* Tuition of $840 per semester plus mandatory fees of $186 per term for in-state residents. Tuition of $2231 per semester for out-of-state residents. *Graduate:* Tuition of $926 per semester plus mandatory fees of $129 per term for in-state residents. Tuition of $2460 per semester for out-of-state residents. *Noncredit courses:* $40 per course. Costs may vary. Financial aid is available to distance learners.

Registration Students may register by mail, World Wide Web, in person.

Contact Tom McCracken, Distance Learning Coordinator, North Georgia College & State University. *Telephone:* 706-864-1844. *Fax:* 706-864-1886. *E-mail:* tmccracken@ngcsu.edu.

DEGREES AND AWARDS

Distance programs offered do not lead to a degree or other formal award.

COURSE SUBJECT AREAS OFFERED OUTSIDE OF DEGREE PROGRAMS

Undergraduate: Education administration; educational psychology; educational research; health professions and related sciences; nursing; public policy analysis; special education; teacher education
Graduate: Education administration; educational psychology; educational research; public administration and services; public policy analysis; special education; statistics

NORTH HARRIS COLLEGE

Houston, Texas

The Center for Technology and Distance Learning
nhmccd.edu

North Harris College, founded in 1972, is a state and locally supported, two-year college. It is accredited by the Southern Association of Colleges and Schools. It first offered distance learning courses in 1993. In 1999–2000, it offered 97 courses at a distance. In fall 1999, there were 3,425 students enrolled in distance learning courses.
Course delivery sites Courses are delivered to your home, your workplace, high schools, off-campus center(s) in Conroe, Cy-Fair, Houston, Humble, Tomball.
Media Courses are delivered via television, videotapes, videoconferencing, interactive television, audiotapes, computer software, World Wide Web, e-mail, print. Students and teachers may interact via videoconferencing, audioconferencing, mail, telephone, fax, e-mail, interactive television, World Wide Web. The following equipment may be required: television, videocassette player, computer, modem, Internet access, e-mail.
Restrictions Programs are available regionally and statewide through the Virtual College of Texas. Enrollment is restricted to individuals meeting certain criteria.
Services Distance learners have access to library services, the campus computer network, e-mail services, bookstore at a distance.
Credit-earning options Students may transfer credits from another institution or may earn credits through examinations, military training.
Typical costs Tuition of $41 per credit hour for local area residents. Tuition of $76 per credit hour for in-state residents. Tuition of $216 per credit hour for out-of-state residents. *Noncredit courses:* $50 per course. Costs may vary. Financial aid is available to distance learners.
Registration Students may register by telephone, in person.
Contact D. Ryan Carstens, District Director of Distance Learning and Instructional Technology, North Harris College, 3232 College Park Drive, Highway 242, The Woodlands, TX 77384. *Telephone:* 409-273-7655. *Fax:* 409-273-7653. *E-mail:* ryan.carstens@nhmccd.edu.

DEGREES AND AWARDS

AA Business Administration (certain restrictions apply; service area differs from that of the overall institution), Liberal Arts (certain restrictions apply; service area differs from that of the overall institution), Social Sciences (certain restrictions apply; service area differs from that of the overall institution)

COURSE SUBJECT AREAS OFFERED OUTSIDE OF DEGREE PROGRAMS

Undergraduate: Accounting; administrative and secretarial services; biology; business administration and management; communications; computer and information sciences; developmental and child psychology; economics; English composition; English language and literature; European languages and literatures; health and physical education/fitness; history; journalism; liberal arts, general studies, and humanities; mathematics; political science; social psychology; sociology

NORTH IOWA AREA COMMUNITY COLLEGE

Mason City, Iowa

Evening Credit Division
www.niacc.cc.ia.us

North Iowa Area Community College, founded in 1918, is a state and locally supported, two-year college. It is accredited by the North Central Association of Colleges and Schools. It first offered distance learning courses in 1993. In 1999–2000, it offered 45 courses at a distance. In fall 1999, there were 27 students enrolled in distance learning courses.
Course delivery sites Courses are delivered to your home, your workplace, high schools, off-campus center(s) in Belmond, Britt, Charles City, Corwith, Forest City, Garner, Greene, Hampton, Lake Mills, Latimer, Mason City, Northwood, Osage, Rockford, Rockwell, Sheffield, St. Ansgar.
Media Courses are delivered via television, videotapes, videoconferencing, interactive television, World Wide Web, e-mail. Students and teachers may interact via videoconferencing, mail, telephone, fax, e-mail, interactive television, World Wide Web. The following equipment may be required: television, videocassette player, computer, Internet access.
Restrictions Programs are available nationwide. Enrollment is open to anyone.
Services Distance learners have access to library services, the campus computer network, e-mail services, bookstore at a distance.
Credit-earning options Students may transfer credits from another institution or may earn credits through examinations, portfolio assessment, military training.
Typical costs Tuition of $62 per semester hour plus mandatory fees of $17 per semester hour. *Noncredit courses:* $200 per course. Financial aid is available to distance learners.
Registration Students may register by mail, World Wide Web, in person.
Contact Don Kamps, Evening Dean, North Iowa Area Community College, 500 College Drive, Mason City, IA 50401. *Telephone:* 515-422-4326. *Fax:* 515-423-1711. *E-mail:* kampsdon@niacc.cc.ia.us.

DEGREES AND AWARDS

Distance programs offered do not lead to a degree or other formal award.

COURSE SUBJECT AREAS OFFERED OUTSIDE OF DEGREE PROGRAMS

Undergraduate: Anthropology; business; business administration and management; chemistry; communications; developmental and child psychology; economics; English language and literature; geography; history; law and legal studies; mathematics; music; philosophy and religion; political science; sociology

NORTH SEATTLE COMMUNITY COLLEGE

Seattle, Washington

Distance Learning Office
www.virtualcollege.org

North Seattle Community College, founded in 1970, is a state-supported, two-year college. It is accredited by the Northwest Association of Schools and Colleges. It first offered distance learning courses in 1994. In 1999–2000, it offered 77 courses at a distance. In fall 1999, there were 410 students enrolled in distance learning courses.
Course delivery sites Courses are delivered to your home, your workplace, high schools, Seattle Central Community College (Seattle), South Seattle Community College (Seattle).

Media Courses are delivered via television, videotapes, videoconferencing, interactive television, audiotapes, computer software, CD-ROM, World Wide Web, e-mail, print. Students and teachers may meet in person or interact via mail, telephone, fax, e-mail, interactive television, World Wide Web. The following equipment may be required: television, video-cassette player, computer, modem, Internet access, e-mail.

Restrictions Programs are available worldwide. Enrollment is open to anyone.

Services Distance learners have access to library services, e-mail services, academic advising, tutoring, bookstore at a distance.

Credit-earning options Students may transfer credits from another institution or may earn credits through examinations.

Typical costs Tuition of $52.60 per credit plus mandatory fees of $27.75 per course for in-state residents. Tuition of $207.60 per credit plus mandatory fees of $27.75 per course for out-of-state residents. *Noncredit courses:* $90 per course. Costs may vary. Financial aid is available to distance learners.

Registration Students may register by mail, telephone, World Wide Web, in person.

Contact Dr. Tom Braziunas, Distance Learning Manager, North Seattle Community College, 9600 College Way North, Seattle, WA 98103. *Telephone:* 206-527-3619. *Fax:* 206-527-3748. *E-mail:* tbraziun@sccd.ctc.edu.

DEGREES AND AWARDS

Distance programs offered do not lead to a degree or other formal award.

COURSE SUBJECT AREAS OFFERED OUTSIDE OF DEGREE PROGRAMS

Undergraduate: Accounting; algebra; anthropology; area, ethnic, and cultural studies; Asian languages and literatures; astronomy and astrophysics; biological and life sciences; business; business administration and management; chemistry; child care and development; computer programming; economics; English as a second language (ESL); English composition; environmental health; European languages and literatures; foods and nutrition studies; geology; health and physical education/fitness; international business; liberal arts, general studies, and humanities; library and information studies; mass media; political science; psychology; real estate; sociology

NORTHWEST ARKANSAS COMMUNITY COLLEGE

Bentonville, Arkansas

Northwest Arkansas Distance Learning
labs.nwacc.cc.ar.us/disted/

NorthWest Arkansas Community College, founded in 1989, is a state and locally supported, two-year college. It is accredited by the North Central Association of Colleges and Schools. It first offered distance learning courses in 1997. In 1999–2000, it offered 15 courses at a distance. In fall 1999, there were 95 students enrolled in distance learning courses.

Course delivery sites Courses are delivered to your home, your workplace, high schools, University of Arkansas (Fayetteville), off-campus center(s) in Lincoln, Springdale.

Media Courses are delivered via television, videotapes, videoconferencing, World Wide Web, print. Students and teachers may meet in person or interact via videoconferencing, mail, telephone, fax, e-mail, World Wide Web. The following equipment may be required: television, videocassette player, computer, modem, Internet access, e-mail.

Restrictions Courses are available regionally depending upon class and student. Enrollment is open to anyone.

Services Distance learners have access to e-mail services at a distance.

Credit-earning options Students may transfer credits from another institution or may earn credits through examinations, military training, business training.

Typical costs Tuition of $42 per credit hour plus mandatory fees of $22 per course for local area residents. Tuition of $84 per credit hour plus mandatory fees of $22 per course for in-state residents. Tuition of $105 per credit hour plus mandatory fees of $22 per course for out-of-state residents. Financial aid is available to distance learners.

Registration Students may register by mail, telephone, in person.

Contact Clint Brooks, Distance Learning Coordinator, NorthWest Arkansas Community College. *Telephone:* 501-619-4382. *Fax:* 501-519-4383. *E-mail:* cbrooks@nwacc.cc.ar.us.

DEGREES AND AWARDS

Distance programs offered do not lead to a degree or other formal award.

COURSE SUBJECT AREAS OFFERED OUTSIDE OF DEGREE PROGRAMS

Undergraduate: Business communications; chemistry; computer programming; database management; English language and literature; fine arts; information sciences and systems; psychology; sociology
Noncredit: Algebra

NORTHWEST BAPTIST THEOLOGICAL COLLEGE

Langley, British Columbia, Canada

Northwest Baptist Theological College, founded in 1934, is an independent, religious, four-year college. It is accredited by the Accrediting Association of Bible Colleges. In 1999–2000, it offered 15 courses at a distance. In fall 1999, there were 10 students enrolled in distance learning courses.

Course delivery sites Courses are delivered to your home.

Media Courses are delivered via audiotapes, print. Students and teachers may meet in person or interact via mail, telephone, fax, e-mail. The following equipment may be required: computer, e-mail.

Restrictions Programs are available usually only in Canada and the U.S. Enrollment is open to anyone.

Services Distance learners have access to e-mail services, academic advising, tutoring, bookstore at a distance.

Credit-earning options Students may transfer credits from another institution.

Typical costs Tuition of Can$95 per credit plus mandatory fees of Can$100 per course.

Registration Students may register by mail, telephone, in person.

Contact Carole Davis, Academic Administrative Assistant, Northwest Baptist Theological College, PO Box 790, Langley, BC V3A 8B8 Canada. *Telephone:* 604-888-3310. *Fax:* 604-888-3354. *E-mail:* davis@nbtc.bc.ca.

DEGREES AND AWARDS

Distance programs offered do not lead to a degree or other formal award.

COURSE SUBJECT AREAS OFFERED OUTSIDE OF DEGREE PROGRAMS

Undergraduate: Bible studies; theological studies

NORTHWEST CHRISTIAN COLLEGE

Eugene, Oregon

www.nwcconline.org

Northwest Christian College, founded in 1895, is an independent, religious, comprehensive institution. It is accredited by the Northwest Association of Schools and Colleges. In 1999–2000, it offered 7 courses at a distance.

Course delivery sites Courses are delivered to your home.

Media Courses are delivered via World Wide Web, e-mail, print. Students and teachers may interact via mail, e-mail, World Wide Web. The following equipment may be required: videocassette player, computer, Internet access, e-mail.

Restrictions Programs are available to in-state students only. Enrollment is open to anyone.

Services Distance learners have access to library services, the campus computer network, academic advising at a distance.

Credit-earning options Students may transfer credits from another institution or may earn credits through examinations, portfolio assessment, business training.

Typical costs *Undergraduate:* Tuition of $286 per unit. *Graduate:* Tuition of $336 per unit. Mandatory fees for all students are $100 per 3 units. *Noncredit courses:* $200 per course. Financial aid is available to distance learners.

Registration Students may register by mail, fax, telephone, e-mail, World Wide Web, in person.

Contact Dr. Gerald C. Tiffin, Provost, Northwest Christian College, 828 East 11th Avenue, Eugene, OR 97401. *Telephone:* 541-684-7214. *Fax:* 541-684-7323. *E-mail:* gary@nwcc.edu.

eCollege.com *www.ecollege.com/scholarships*

DEGREES AND AWARDS

Distance programs offered do not lead to a degree or other formal award.

COURSE SUBJECT AREAS OFFERED OUTSIDE OF DEGREE PROGRAMS

Undergraduate: Bible studies; communications; statistics; teacher education

NORTHWESTERN BUSINESS COLLEGE

Chicago, Illinois

Institute of Technology

itechinstitute.com

Northwestern Business College, founded in 1902, is a proprietary, two-year college. It is accredited by the Accrediting Council for Independent Colleges and Schools, North Central Association of Colleges and Schools. It first offered distance learning courses in 1999. In 1999–2000, it offered 10 courses at a distance. In fall 1999, there were 4 students enrolled in distance learning courses.

Course delivery sites Courses are delivered to your home, your workplace.

Media Courses are delivered via World Wide Web. Students and teachers may meet in person or interact via audioconferencing, mail, telephone, fax, e-mail, World Wide Web. The following equipment may be required: computer, modem, Internet access, e-mail.

Restrictions Programs are available worldwide. Enrollment is restricted to individuals meeting certain criteria.

Services Distance learners have access to bookstore at a distance.

Credit-earning options Students may earn credits through examinations.

Typical costs Tuition of $995 per course. Costs may vary. Financial aid is available to distance learners.

Registration Students may register by mail, fax, telephone, e-mail, World Wide Web, in person.

Contact Julie Giuliani, Director of Distance Education, Northwestern Business College, 4849 North Milwaukee Avenue, Chicago, IL 60630. *Telephone:* 773-736-3580. *Fax:* 773-736-9860. *E-mail:* giuliani@ itechinstitute.com.

eCollege.com *www.ecollege.com/scholarships*

DEGREES AND AWARDS

Undergraduate Certificate(s) Microsoft Certified Systems Engineer (certain restrictions apply)

COURSE SUBJECT AREAS OFFERED OUTSIDE OF DEGREE PROGRAMS

Undergraduate: Information sciences and systems
Graduate: Information sciences and systems
Noncredit: Information sciences and systems

NORTHWESTERN COLLEGE

Lima, Ohio

Division of Distance Learning

www.nc.edu

Northwestern College, founded in 1920, is an independent, nonprofit, primarily two-year college. It is accredited by the North Central Association of Colleges and Schools. It first offered distance learning courses in 1993. In 1999–2000, it offered 165 courses at a distance. In fall 1999, there were 173 students enrolled in distance learning courses.

Course delivery sites Courses are delivered to your home, your workplace.

Media Courses are delivered via videoconferencing, World Wide Web, e-mail, print. Students and teachers may meet in person or interact via videoconferencing, mail, telephone, fax, e-mail. The following equipment may be required: computer, modem, Internet access, e-mail.

Restrictions Programs are available worldwide. Enrollment is restricted to individuals meeting certain criteria.

Services Distance learners have access to library services, e-mail services, academic advising, career placement assistance, bookstore at a distance.

Credit-earning options Students may transfer credits from another institution or may earn credits through examinations, portfolio assessment, military training, business training.

Typical costs Tuition of $154 per credit. Costs may vary. Financial aid is available to distance learners.

Registration Students may register by mail, fax, telephone, e-mail, World Wide Web, in person.

Contact Rick Morrison, Director of Admissions, Northwestern College, 1441 North Cable Road, Lima, OH 45805. *Telephone:* 419-227-3141. *Fax:* 419-229-6926. *E-mail:* info@nc.edu.

DEGREES AND AWARDS

AAB Accounting, Agribusiness, Automotive Management, Business Administration, Information Systems Technology, Legal Assisting, Marketing, Marketing, Management and Technology, Medical Assistant Technology, Secretarial (Administrative, Legal, Medical), Travel Management, Word Processing-Administrative Support

COURSE SUBJECT AREAS OFFERED OUTSIDE OF DEGREE PROGRAMS

Undergraduate: Accounting; administrative and secretarial services; advertising; agricultural economics; algebra; American (U.S.) history; business; business administration and management; business law; computer and information sciences; economics; English composition; English language and literature; ethics; geography; health professions and related sciences; history; human resources management; international business; liberal arts, general studies, and humanities; marketing; mathematics; physical sciences; political science; psychology; sociology; statistics

See full description on page 822.

NORTHWESTERN COLLEGE

St. Paul, Minnesota
Center for Distance Education
www.distance.nwc.edu

Northwestern College, founded in 1902, is an independent, religious, four-year college. It is accredited by the North Central Association of Colleges and Schools. It first offered distance learning courses in 1994. In 1999–2000, it offered 26 courses at a distance. In fall 1999, there were 375 students enrolled in distance learning courses.

Course delivery sites Courses are delivered to your home.

Media Courses are delivered via videotapes, audiotapes, CD-ROM, World Wide Web, print. Students and teachers may meet in person or interact via mail, telephone, fax, e-mail, World Wide Web. The following equipment may be required: television, videocassette player, computer, Internet access.

Restrictions Programs are available worldwide. Enrollment is open to anyone.

Services Distance learners have access to library services, academic advising, tutoring, career placement assistance, bookstore at a distance.

Credit-earning options Students may transfer credits from another institution or may earn credits through examinations, portfolio assessment, military training.

Typical costs Tuition of $180 per semester credit plus mandatory fees of $60 per course. *Noncredit courses:* $100 per course. Financial aid is available to distance learners.

Registration Students may register by mail, fax, telephone, e-mail, World Wide Web, in person.

Contact Betty Piper, Student Relations Coordinator, Northwestern College, Center for Distance Education, 3003 Snelling Avenue, North, St. Paul, MN 55113. *Telephone:* 651-631-5494. *Fax:* 651-631-5133. *E-mail:* bap@nwc.edu.

DEGREES AND AWARDS

Undergraduate Certificate(s) Bible
BA Intercultural Ministries

COURSE SUBJECT AREAS OFFERED OUTSIDE OF DEGREE PROGRAMS

Undergraduate: Algebra; archaeology; area, ethnic, and cultural studies; astronomy and astrophysics; Bible studies; chemistry; education; Greek language and literature; history; mathematics; philosophy and religion; psychology; theological studies

---

NORTHWESTERN MICHIGAN COLLEGE

Traverse City, Michigan
Distance Education Services
www.nmc.edu/~flo/

Northwestern Michigan College, founded in 1951, is a state and locally supported, two-year college. It is accredited by the North Central Association of Colleges and Schools. It first offered distance learning courses in 1982. In 1999–2000, it offered 41 courses at a distance. In fall 1999, there were 600 students enrolled in distance learning courses.

Course delivery sites Courses are delivered to your home, your workplace, high schools, 1 off-campus center in Cadillac.

Media Courses are delivered via television, videoconferencing, interactive television, computer software, computer conferencing, World Wide Web, e-mail. Students and teachers may meet in person or interact via videoconferencing, audioconferencing, mail, telephone, fax, e-mail, interactive television, World Wide Web. The following equipment may be required: television, videocassette player, computer, modem, Internet access, e-mail.

Restrictions Programs are available to in-state students only. Enrollment is open to anyone.

Services Distance learners have access to library services, the campus computer network, e-mail services, academic advising, career placement assistance at a distance.

Credit-earning options Students may transfer credits from another institution or may earn credits through examinations, portfolio assessment.

Typical costs Tuition of $54.75 per contact hour for local area residents. Tuition of $90.50 per contact hour for in-state residents. Tuition of $101.75 per contact hour for out-of-state residents. Financial aid is available to distance learners.

Registration Students may register by telephone, in person.

Contact Ronda Edwards, Director, Northwestern Michigan College, Media Services, Traverse City, MI 49686. *Telephone:* 231-922-1075. *Fax:* 231-922-1080. *E-mail:* redwards@nmc.edu.

DEGREES AND AWARDS

Distance programs offered do not lead to a degree or other formal award.

COURSE SUBJECT AREAS OFFERED OUTSIDE OF DEGREE PROGRAMS

Undergraduate: Accounting; American (U.S.) history; anthropology; biology; business; business administration and management; calculus; child care and development; computer and information sciences; creative writing; developmental and child psychology; English composition; English language and literature; European history; European languages and literatures; health professions and related sciences; history; Japanese language and literature; law and legal studies; liberal arts, general studies, and humanities; nursing; political science; psychology; social work; sociology; visual and performing arts

---

NORTHWESTERN STATE UNIVERSITY OF LOUISIANA

Natchitoches, Louisiana
www.nsula.edu

Northwestern State University of Louisiana, founded in 1884, is a state-supported, comprehensive institution. It is accredited by the Southern Association of Colleges and Schools. It first offered distance learning courses in 1990.

Contact Northwestern State University of Louisiana, 350 Sam Sibley Drive, Natchitoches, LA 71497. *Telephone:* 318-357-6361.

See full description on page 676.

NORTHWESTERN TECHNICAL INSTITUTE

Rock Springs, Georgia
www.northwestern.tec.ga.us/

Northwestern Technical Institute, founded in 1966, is a state-supported, two-year college. It is accredited by the Southern Association of Colleges and Schools. In 1999–2000, it offered 30 courses at a distance. In fall 1999, there were 128 students enrolled in distance learning courses.

Course delivery sites Courses are delivered to your home, your workplace.

Media Courses are delivered via computer software, computer conferencing, e-mail. Students and teachers may interact via e-mail. The following equipment may be required: computer, Internet access, e-mail.

Restrictions Programs are available to in-state students only. Enrollment is restricted to individuals meeting certain criteria.

Services Distance learners have access to library services, e-mail services, academic advising, career placement assistance at a distance.

Typical costs Tuition of $23 per credit plus mandatory fees of $35 per quarter for local area residents. Tuition of $23 per credit plus mandatory fees of $35 per quarter for in-state residents. Tuition of $46 per credit plus mandatory fees of $35 per quarter for out-of-state residents. Financial aid is available to distance learners.

Registration Students may register by mail, fax, telephone, e-mail, World Wide Web, in person.

Contact Laura Mathis, Technical Assistance Specialist, Northwestern Technical Institute, Georgia Virtual Technical Institute, 265 Bicentennial Trail, Rock Spring, GA 30739. *Telephone:* 706-764-3673. *Fax:* 706-764-3734. *E-mail:* lmathis@northwestern.tec.ga.us.

DEGREES AND AWARDS

Undergraduate Certificate(s) Medical Coding, Microsoft Officer User Specialist

COURSE SUBJECT AREAS OFFERED OUTSIDE OF DEGREE PROGRAMS

Undergraduate: Anatomy; database management; engineering-related technologies; fine arts; information sciences and systems; mathematics; psychology; technical writing

---

NORTHWEST MISSOURI STATE UNIVERSITY

Maryville, Missouri
Center for Information Technology in Education
www.northwestonline.org

Northwest Missouri State University, founded in 1905, is a state-supported, comprehensive institution. It is accredited by the North Central Association of Colleges and Schools. It first offered distance learning courses in 1999. In 1999–2000, it offered 15 courses at a distance. In fall 1999, there were 200 students enrolled in distance learning courses.

Course delivery sites Courses are delivered to your home, your workplace.

Media Courses are delivered via CD-ROM, World Wide Web, e-mail, print. Students and teachers may meet in person or interact via mail, telephone, e-mail, World Wide Web. The following equipment may be required: computer, modem, Internet access, e-mail.

Restrictions Programs are available nationwide. Enrollment is restricted to individuals meeting certain criteria.

Services Distance learners have access to library services, the campus computer network, e-mail services, academic advising, career placement assistance, bookstore at a distance.

Credit-earning options Students may transfer credits from another institution.

Typical costs *Undergraduate:* Tuition of $180 per credit plus mandatory fees of $4 per credit. *Graduate:* Tuition of $225 per credit plus mandatory fees of $4 per credit. Financial aid is available to distance learners.

Registration Students may register by mail, World Wide Web, in person.

Contact Admissions, Northwest Missouri State University, 800 University Drive, Maryville, MO 64468. *Telephone:* 800-633-1175. *Fax:* 660-562-1121. *E-mail:* admissions@northwestonline.org.

> **eCollege**.com *www.ecollege.com/scholarships*

DEGREES AND AWARDS

BS Accounting, Business Management

COURSE SUBJECT AREAS OFFERED OUTSIDE OF DEGREE PROGRAMS

Undergraduate: Accounting; administrative and secretarial services; American (U.S.) history; area, ethnic, and cultural studies; business administration and management; drama and theater; earth science; geography; music; philosophy and religion

---

NORTHWEST TECHNICAL COLLEGE

Bemidji, Minnesota
Distance Education
www.ntc-online.com/distance

Northwest Technical College, founded in 1993, is a state-supported, two-year college. It is accredited by the North Central Association of Colleges and Schools. In 1999–2000, it offered 40 courses at a distance. In fall 1999, there were 200 students enrolled in distance learning courses.

Course delivery sites Courses are delivered to your home, your workplace, military bases, high schools.

Media Courses are delivered via videotapes, audiotapes, computer software, CD-ROM, computer conferencing, World Wide Web, e-mail, print. Students and teachers may meet in person or interact via mail, telephone, fax, e-mail, World Wide Web. The following equipment may be required: television, videocassette player, computer, modem, Internet access, e-mail.

Restrictions Programs are available to in-state students only. Enrollment is open to anyone.

Services Distance learners have access to library services, academic advising, tutoring, career placement assistance, bookstore at a distance.

Credit-earning options Students may transfer credits from another institution or may earn credits through examinations.

Typical costs Tuition of $73.40 per credit plus mandatory fees of $22 per credit for in-state residents. Tuition of $146.80 per credit plus mandatory fees of $22 per credit for out-of-state residents. Costs may vary. Financial aid is available to distance learners.

Registration Students may register by mail, fax, e-mail, World Wide Web, in person.

Contact Linda Cordell, Administrative Assistant, Northwest Technical College, PO Box 309, Perham, MN. *Telephone:* 218-347-6200. *Fax:* 218-347-6210. *E-mail:* linda.cordell@mail.ntc.mnscu.edu.

DEGREES AND AWARDS

Undergraduate Certificate(s) Medical Transcription

AAS Accounting, Computer Technology (some on-campus requirements), License in Practical Nursing (certain restrictions apply)

COURSE SUBJECT AREAS OFFERED OUTSIDE OF DEGREE PROGRAMS

Undergraduate: Accounting; computer and information sciences; health professions and related sciences; library and information studies; nursing

NORTHWOOD UNIVERSITY

Midland, Michigan
University College
www.northwoodonline.org

Northwood University, founded in 1959, is an independent, nonprofit, comprehensive institution. It is accredited by the North Central Association of Colleges and Schools. It first offered distance learning courses in 1965. In 1999–2000, it offered 67 courses at a distance. In fall 1999, there were 263 students enrolled in distance learning courses.

Course delivery sites Courses are delivered to your home, your workplace, military bases, other colleges, 25 off-campus centers in Flint, Grand Rapids, Lansing, Livonia, Midland, Selfridge Ang. Base, Southgate, Troy, Warren, Anderson (IN), Carlsbad (NM), Cedar Hill (TX), Chicago (IL), Columbus (IN), Evansville (IN), Fort Worth (TX), Georgetown (KE), Indianapolis (IN), Lafayette (IN), Louisville (KY), Marion (IN), New Orleans (LA), Tampa (FL), Terre Haute (IN), West Palm Beach (FL).

Media Courses are delivered via World Wide Web, print. Students and teachers may meet in person or interact via mail, telephone, fax, e-mail, World Wide Web. The following equipment may be required: computer, Internet access, e-mail.

Restrictions Programs are available worldwide. Enrollment is open to anyone.

Services Distance learners have access to library services, e-mail services, academic advising, career placement assistance, bookstore at a distance.

Credit-earning options Students may transfer credits from another institution or may earn credits through examinations, portfolio assessment, military training, business training.

Typical costs Undergraduate tuition ranges between $70 and $240 per credit hour. Costs may vary.

Registration Students may register by mail, fax, telephone, e-mail, World Wide Web, in person.

Contact Dr. Kevin G. Fegan, Dean, University College, Northwood University, 4000 Whiting Drive, Midland, MI 48640. *Telephone:* 800-445-5873. *Fax:* 517-837-4457. *E-mail:* fegan@northwood.edu.

---

eCollege.com   *www.ecollege.com/scholarships*

DEGREES AND AWARDS

BBA Management (some on-campus requirements)

COURSE SUBJECT AREAS OFFERED OUTSIDE OF DEGREE PROGRAMS

Undergraduate: Business administration and management

NORWICH UNIVERSITY

Northfield, Vermont
New College / Vermont College Graduate Program Online
www.norwich.edu/vermontcollege

Norwich University, founded in 1819, is an independent, nonprofit, comprehensive institution. It is accredited by the New England Association of Schools and Colleges. It first offered distance learning courses in 1977. In fall 1999, there were 25 students enrolled in distance learning courses.

Course delivery sites Courses are delivered to your home.

Media Courses are delivered via computer software, computer conferencing, World Wide Web, e-mail, print. Students and teachers may meet in person or interact via mail, telephone, fax, e-mail, World Wide Web. The following equipment may be required: computer, modem, Internet access.

Restrictions Programs are available worldwide. Enrollment is open to anyone.

Services Distance learners have access to library services, the campus computer network, e-mail services, academic advising, tutoring, career placement assistance at a distance.

Credit-earning options Students may transfer credits from another institution or may earn credits through examinations.

Typical costs Tuition of $4500 per semester. Financial aid is available to distance learners.

Registration Students may register by mail, in person.

Contact Matt Jason, New College Counselor, Norwich University, Vermont College Admissions, Montpelier, VT 05602. *Telephone:* 802-828-8707. *Fax:* 802-828-8855. *E-mail:* mjason@norwich.edu.

DEGREES AND AWARDS

BA Liberal Arts (some on-campus requirements)
Graduate Certificate(s) Graduate Study (some on-campus requirements)
MA Art Therapy (some on-campus requirements), Liberal Arts (some on-campus requirements)
MEd Education (some on-campus requirements)
MFA Visual Art (some on-campus requirements), Writing (some on-campus requirements)

COURSE SUBJECT AREAS OFFERED OUTSIDE OF DEGREE PROGRAMS

Undergraduate: Area, ethnic, and cultural studies; art history and criticism; business; communications; conservation and natural resources; education; English language and literature; history; home economics and family studies; interdisciplinary studies; law and legal studies; liberal arts, general studies, and humanities; library and information studies; military studies; philosophy and religion; psychology; public administration and services; recreation and leisure studies; social sciences; theological studies

Graduate: Area, ethnic, and cultural studies; art history and criticism; business; communications; conservation and natural resources; education; English language and literature; history; home economics and family studies; interdisciplinary studies; law and legal studies; liberal arts, general studies, and humanities; library and information studies; military studies; philosophy and religion; psychology; public administration and services; recreation and leisure studies; social sciences; theological studies

See full description on page 612.

NOVA SOUTHEASTERN UNIVERSITY

Fort Lauderdale, Florida
School of Computer and Information Sciences
www.scis.nova.edu

Nova Southeastern University, founded in 1964, is an independent, nonprofit university. It is accredited by the Southern Association of Colleges and Schools. It first offered distance learning courses in 1984. In 1999–2000, it offered 120 courses at a distance. In fall 1999, there were 900 students enrolled in distance learning courses.

Course delivery sites Courses are delivered to your home.

Media Courses are delivered via computer software, World Wide Web, e-mail. Students and teachers may meet in person or interact via audioconferencing, mail, telephone, fax, e-mail, World Wide Web. The following equipment may be required: computer, modem, Internet access.

Restrictions Programs are available worldwide. Enrollment is open to anyone.

Services Distance learners have access to library services, the campus computer network, e-mail services, academic advising, career placement assistance, bookstore at a distance.

Credit-earning options Students may transfer credits from another institution.

Typical costs Tuition for the Master's degree is $370 per credit; $415 per credit for the Doctoral degree. Financial aid is available to distance learners.

Registration Students may register by mail, in person.

Contact Sharon Brown, Director of Marketing, Nova Southeastern University, School of Computer and Information Sciences, 6100 Griffin Road, Fort Lauderdale, FL 33314-4416. *Telephone:* 800-986-2247. *Fax:* 954-262-3915. *E-mail:* scisinfo@scis.nova.edu.

DEGREES AND AWARDS

MS Computer Information Systems, Computer Science, Computing Technology in Education, Management Information Systems

EdD Computing Technology in Education (some on-campus requirements)

PhD Computer Information Systems (some on-campus requirements), Computer Science (some on-campus requirements), Computing Technology in Education (some on-campus requirements), Information Sciences (some on-campus requirements), Information Systems (some on-campus requirements)

COURSE SUBJECT AREAS OFFERED OUTSIDE OF DEGREE PROGRAMS

Graduate: Computer and information sciences

See full descriptions on pages 614 and 676.

NYACK COLLEGE

Nyack, New York
nyackcollege.org

Nyack College, founded in 1882, is an independent, religious, four-year college affiliated with The Christian and Missionary Alliance. It is accredited by the Middle States Association of Colleges and Schools. It first offered distance learning courses in 1999. In 1999–2000, it offered 7 courses at a distance. In fall 1999, there were 60 students enrolled in distance learning courses.

Course delivery sites Courses are delivered to your home, your workplace, military bases.

Media Courses are delivered via World Wide Web. Students and teachers may interact via mail, telephone, fax, e-mail, World Wide Web. The following equipment may be required: computer, modem, Internet access, e-mail.

Restrictions Programs are available to local area students. Enrollment is open to anyone.

Services Distance learners have access to library services, e-mail services, academic advising, career placement assistance, bookstore at a distance.

Credit-earning options Students may transfer credits from another institution.

Typical costs Tuition of $480 per credit. Costs may vary.

Registration Students may register by World Wide Web, in person.

Contact Dr. Ronald W. Ruegsegger, Vice President/Dean of the College, Nyack College, 1 South Boulevard, Nyack, NY 10960. *Telephone:* 914-358-1710 Ext. 726. *Fax:* 914-353-6429. *E-mail:* ruegsegr@nyack.edu.

eCollege.com   *www.ecollege.com/scholarships*

DEGREES AND AWARDS

Distance programs offered do not lead to a degree or other formal award.

COURSE SUBJECT AREAS OFFERED OUTSIDE OF DEGREE PROGRAMS

Undergraduate: Adult education; business; history; philosophy and religion; physics; teacher education

Graduate: Bible studies

OAKLAND COMMUNITY COLLEGE

Bloomfield Hills, Michigan
www.occ.cc.mi.us

Oakland Community College, founded in 1964, is a state and locally supported, two-year college. It is accredited by the North Central Association of Colleges and Schools. In 1999–2000, it offered 5 courses at a distance. In fall 1999, there were 108 students enrolled in distance learning courses.

Course delivery sites Courses are delivered to your home, your workplace.

Media Courses are delivered via television, videotapes, World Wide Web. Students and teachers may interact via mail, telephone, e-mail. The following equipment may be required: television, videocassette player, computer, Internet access.

Restrictions Programs are available worldwide. Enrollment is open to anyone.

Services Distance learners have access to library services at a distance.

Credit-earning options Students may transfer credits from another institution.

Typical costs Tuition of $47.70 per credit plus mandatory fees of $35 per semester for local area residents. Tuition of $80.70 per credit plus mandatory fees of $35 per semester for in-state residents. Tuition of $113.20 per credit plus mandatory fees of $35 per semester for out-of-state residents. Costs may vary. Financial aid is available to distance learners.

Registration Students may register by telephone, in person.

Contact Jonathan Campbell, Dean of Enrollment Services, Oakland Community College, 2480 Opdyke Road, Bloomfield Hills, MI 48304-2266. *Telephone:* 248-540-1881. *Fax:* 248-540-1508. *E-mail:* jccampbe@occ.cc.mi.us.

DEGREES AND AWARDS

Distance programs offered do not lead to a degree or other formal award.

COURSE SUBJECT AREAS OFFERED OUTSIDE OF DEGREE PROGRAMS

Undergraduate: Business administration and management; English language and literature; history; political science; psychology; social sciences

OCEAN COUNTY COLLEGE

Toms River, New Jersey

Ocean County College, founded in 1964, is a county-supported, two-year college. It is accredited by the Middle States Association of Colleges and Schools.

Contact Ocean County College, College Drive, PO Box 2001, Toms River, NJ 08754-2001. *Telephone:* 732-255-0400.

See full description on page 600.

OHIO NORTHERN UNIVERSITY

Ada, Ohio
Raabe College of Pharmacy
www.onu.edu/pharmacy/ntpd/

Ohio Northern University, founded in 1871, is an independent, religious, comprehensive institution. It is accredited by the North Central Association of Colleges and Schools. In 1999–2000, it offered 54 courses at a distance. In fall 1999, there were 70 students enrolled in distance learning courses.

Course delivery sites Courses are delivered to your home, your workplace, military bases.

Media Courses are delivered via computer software, computer conferencing, World Wide Web, print. Students and teachers may interact via fax, e-mail, World Wide Web. The following equipment may be required: computer, modem, Internet access, e-mail.

Restrictions Programs are available worldwide. Enrollment is restricted to individuals meeting certain criteria.

Services Distance learners have access to library services, the campus computer network, e-mail services, academic advising, tutoring, career placement assistance, bookstore at a distance.

Credit-earning options Students may transfer credits from another institution or may earn credits through examinations, portfolio assessment.

Typical costs Tuition of $405 per credit.

Registration Students may register by mail, fax, telephone, e-mail, World Wide Web, in person.

Contact Dr. Bob McCurdy, Assistant Dean/Director of Pharmacy Student Services, Ohio Northern University, Raabe College of Pharmacy, Ada, OH 45810. *Telephone:* 419-772-2659. *Fax:* 419-772-1917. *E-mail:* r-mccurdy@onu.edu.

DEGREES AND AWARDS

Undergraduate Certificate(s) Pharmacy Continuing Education (certain restrictions apply)

PharmD Pharmacy (certain restrictions apply; some on-campus requirements)

OHIO STATE UNIVERSITY–MANSFIELD CAMPUS

Mansfield, Ohio
www.mansfield.ohio-state.edu

Ohio State University–Mansfield Campus, founded in 1958, is a state-supported, four-year college. It is accredited by the North Central Association of Colleges and Schools. It first offered distance learning courses in 1995. In 1999–2000, it offered 13 courses at a distance. In fall 1999, there were 50 students enrolled in distance learning courses.

Course delivery sites Courses are delivered to The Ohio State University (Columbus), The Ohio State University at Lima (Lima), The Ohio State University at Marion (Marion), The Ohio State University–Newark Campus (Newark).

Media Courses are delivered via videotapes, videoconferencing, computer software, World Wide Web, e-mail. Students and teachers may interact via videoconferencing, mail, telephone, fax, e-mail.

Restrictions Programs are available to in-state students only. Enrollment is restricted to individuals meeting certain criteria.

Services Distance learners have access to library services, the campus computer network, e-mail services, academic advising, tutoring, career placement assistance at a distance.

Credit-earning options Students may transfer credits from another institution or may earn credits through examinations.

Typical costs *Undergraduate:* Tuition of $490 per course for in-state residents. Tuition of $1594 per course for out-of-state residents. *Graduate:* Tuition of $657 per course for in-state residents. Tuition of $1471 per course for out-of-state residents. *Noncredit courses:* $150 per course. Costs may vary. Financial aid is available to distance learners.

Registration Students may register by mail, telephone, in person.

Contact Frederick C. Dahlstrand, Associate Dean, Ohio State University–Mansfield Campus, 1680 University Drive, Mansfield, OH 44906. *Telephone:* 419-755-4222. *Fax:* 419-755-4241. *E-mail:* dahlstrand.1@osu.edu.

DEGREES AND AWARDS

Distance programs offered do not lead to a degree or other formal award.

COURSE SUBJECT AREAS OFFERED OUTSIDE OF DEGREE PROGRAMS

Undergraduate: Business communications; English composition; English literature; human resources management; Japanese language and literature; social work; teacher education; technical writing

Graduate: Social work; teacher education

OHIO UNIVERSITY

Athens, Ohio
Independent Study
www.ohiou.edu/independent/

Ohio University, founded in 1804, is a state-supported university. It is accredited by the North Central Association of Colleges and Schools. It first offered distance learning courses in 1924. In 1999–2000, it offered 300 courses at a distance. In fall 1999, there were 3,975 students enrolled in distance learning courses.

Course delivery sites Courses are delivered to your home.

Media Courses are delivered via videotapes, audiotapes, CD-ROM, World Wide Web, print. Students and teachers may interact via mail, fax, e-mail.

Restrictions Programs are available worldwide. Enrollment is open to anyone.

Services Distance learners have access to library services, e-mail services, academic advising, bookstore at a distance.

Credit-earning options Students may transfer credits from another institution or may earn credits through examinations, portfolio assessment, military training, business training.

Typical costs Tuition of $75 per credit. Costs may vary.

Registration Students may register by mail, fax, World Wide Web, in person.

Contact Independent Study, Ohio University, 302 Tupper Hall, Athens, OH 45701. *Telephone:* 800-444-2910. *Fax:* 740-593-2901. *E-mail:* independent.study@ohio.edu.

DEGREES AND AWARDS

AA Arts and Humanities, Social Sciences
AIS Individualized Studies
AS Mathematics, Natural Science
BSS Specialized Studies

COURSE SUBJECT AREAS OFFERED OUTSIDE OF DEGREE PROGRAMS

Undergraduate: Accounting; anthropology; astronomy and astrophysics; biology; business; business administration and management; chemistry; creative writing; developmental and child psychology; economics; educational psychology; engineering-related technologies; English composition; English language and literature; European languages and literatures; geography; health and physical education/fitness; health professions and related sciences; history; home economics and family studies; journalism; liberal arts, general studies, and humanities; mathematics; music; philosophy and religion; physics; political science; protective services; social psychology; sociology; women's studies

See full description on page 616.

OHIO UNIVERSITY–SOUTHERN CAMPUS

Ironton, Ohio
Ohio University Learning Network
www.tcom.ohiou.edu/oln

Ohio University–Southern Campus, founded in 1956, is a state-supported, primarily two-year college. It is accredited by the North Central Association of Colleges and Schools. It first offered distance learning courses in 1983. In 1999–2000, it offered 80 courses at a distance. In fall 1999, there were 610 students enrolled in distance learning courses.

Course delivery sites Courses are delivered to your home, your workplace, 5 off-campus centers in Chillicothe, Ironton, Lancaster, St. Clairsville, Zanesville.

Media Courses are delivered via television, videotapes, videoconferencing, interactive television, World Wide Web. Students and teachers may interact via videoconferencing, telephone, fax, e-mail, interactive television. The following equipment may be required: television, e-mail.

Restrictions Programs are available worldwide. Enrollment is open to anyone.

Services Distance learners have access to library services, the campus computer network, e-mail services, academic advising, tutoring, career placement assistance at a distance.

Credit-earning options Students may transfer credits from another institution or may earn credits through examinations, portfolio assessment, military training, business training.

Typical costs *Undergraduate:* Tuition of $4326 per year for in-state residents. Tuition of $9090 per year for out-of-state residents. *Graduate:*

Tuition of $1630 per quarter for in-state residents. Tuition of $3128 per quarter for out-of-state residents. Financial aid is available to distance learners.

Registration Students may register by mail, telephone, in person.

Contact Teri Combs, Distance Learning Coordinator, Ohio University–Southern Campus. *Telephone:* 740-593-0241. *Fax:* 740-593-9679.

DEGREES AND AWARDS

MBA Business (certain restrictions apply; some on-campus requirements)

COURSE SUBJECT AREAS OFFERED OUTSIDE OF DEGREE PROGRAMS

Undergraduate: Accounting; business; business administration and management; classical languages and literatures; economics; education administration; educational psychology; English language and literature; French language and literature; history; human resources management; journalism; liberal arts, general studies, and humanities; mathematics; music; nursing; radio and television broadcasting; Spanish language and literature; special education; teacher education

Graduate: Business administration and management

Noncredit: Engineering/industrial management; environmental engineering

OHLONE COLLEGE

Fremont, California
Learning Resources and Instructional Technology Division
www.ohlone.cc.ca.us

Ohlone College, founded in 1967, is a state and locally supported, two-year college. It is accredited by the Western Association of Schools and Colleges, Inc. It first offered distance learning courses in 1973. In 1999–2000, it offered 21 courses at a distance. In fall 1999, there were 526 students enrolled in distance learning courses.

Course delivery sites Courses are delivered to your home, your workplace, military bases, 1 off-campus center in Newark.

Media Courses are delivered via television, videotapes, videoconferencing, audiotapes, World Wide Web, e-mail, print. Students and teachers may meet in person or interact via videoconferencing, mail, telephone, fax, e-mail, World Wide Web. The following equipment may be required: television, computer, modem, Internet access, e-mail.

Restrictions Programs are available to local area students. Enrollment is open to anyone.

Services Distance learners have access to library services, e-mail services, academic advising, tutoring, career placement assistance at a distance.

Credit-earning options Students may transfer credits from another institution or may earn credits through examinations.

Typical costs Tuition of $12 per unit for in-state residents. Tuition of $120 per unit for out-of-state residents.

Registration Students may register by mail, fax, telephone, World Wide Web, in person.

Contact Dr. Shirley S. Peck, Dean, Ohlone College, Learning Resources and Instructional Technology Division, 43600 Mission Boulevard, Fremont, CA 94539-5884. *Telephone:* 510-659-6166. *Fax:* 510-659-6265. *E-mail:* speck@ohlone.cc.ca.us.

DEGREES AND AWARDS

Distance programs offered do not lead to a degree or other formal award.

COURSE SUBJECT AREAS OFFERED OUTSIDE OF DEGREE PROGRAMS

Undergraduate: Anthropology; astronomy and astrophysics; business administration and management; computer and information sciences;

computer programming; English as a second language (ESL); English composition; European languages and literatures; fine arts; foods and nutrition studies; geography; gerontology; health and physical education/fitness; library and information studies; mass media; photography; physical therapy; political science

OKALOOSA-WALTON COMMUNITY COLLEGE

Niceville, Florida

Distance Learning

www.owcc.cc.fl.us/departs/distance/index.html

Okaloosa-Walton Community College, founded in 1963, is a state and locally supported, two-year college. It is accredited by the Southern Association of Colleges and Schools. In 1999–2000, it offered 55 courses at a distance. In fall 1999, there were 1,200 students enrolled in distance learning courses.

Course delivery sites Courses are delivered to your home, your workplace.

Media Courses are delivered via television, interactive television, audiotapes, World Wide Web, e-mail, print. Students and teachers may meet in person or interact via mail, telephone, fax, e-mail, interactive television, World Wide Web. The following equipment may be required: television, videocassette player, computer, modem, Internet access, e-mail.

Restrictions Programs are available to local area students. Enrollment is open to anyone.

Services Distance learners have access to library services, the campus computer network, academic advising, tutoring, career placement assistance at a distance.

Credit-earning options Students may transfer credits from another institution.

Typical costs Tuition of $39.95 per credit for in-state residents. Tuition of $152 per credit for out-of-state residents. Lab fee is between $12 and $30 per course. *Noncredit courses:* $39.95 per course. Costs may vary. Financial aid is available to distance learners.

Registration Students may register by in person.

Contact Wanda Edwards, Okaloosa-Walton Community College, 1170 Martin Luther King Jr. Boulevard, Fort Walton Beach, FL 32547. *Telephone:* 850-863-0701. *Fax:* 850-863-6560. *E-mail:* edwardsw@owcc.net.

DEGREES AND AWARDS

Distance programs offered do not lead to a degree or other formal award.

COURSE SUBJECT AREAS OFFERED OUTSIDE OF DEGREE PROGRAMS

Undergraduate: Abnormal psychology; accounting; advertising; American (U.S.) history; American literature; anatomy; biology; business law; child care and development; corrections; creative writing; criminal justice; developmental and child psychology; earth science; economics; educational psychology; English composition; fine arts; foods and nutrition studies; health and physical education/fitness; health professions and related sciences; hospitality services management; information sciences and systems; library and information studies; marketing; organizational behavior studies; political science; social psychology; sociology

OKLAHOMA CITY COMMUNITY COLLEGE

Oklahoma City, Oklahoma

Distance Education

www.okc.cc.ok.us/distanced

Oklahoma City Community College, founded in 1969, is a state-supported, two-year college. It is accredited by the North Central Association of Colleges and Schools. It first offered distance learning courses in 1971. In 1999–2000, it offered 45 courses at a distance. In fall 1999, there were 1,000 students enrolled in distance learning courses.

Course delivery sites Courses are delivered to your home, your workplace, high schools.

Media Courses are delivered via television, videotapes, videoconferencing, interactive television, audiotapes, computer software, CD-ROM, computer conferencing, World Wide Web, e-mail, print. Students and teachers may meet in person or interact via videoconferencing, mail, telephone, fax, e-mail, interactive television, World Wide Web. The following equipment may be required: television, videocassette player, computer, modem, Internet access, e-mail.

Restrictions Programs are available to local area students. Enrollment is open to anyone.

Services Distance learners have access to library services, the campus computer network, e-mail services, bookstore at a distance.

Credit-earning options Students may transfer credits from another institution or may earn credits through examinations.

Typical costs Tuition of $31.50 per credit hour plus mandatory fees of $20 per credit hour for in-state residents. Tuition of $99 per credit hour plus mandatory fees of $14.10 per credit hour for out-of-state residents. Costs may vary. Financial aid is available to distance learners.

Registration Students may register by mail, fax, telephone, World Wide Web, in person.

Contact Glenda Prince, Coordinator for Distance Education, Oklahoma City Community College, 7777 South May Avenue, Oklahoma City, OK 73159. *Telephone:* 405-682-7574. *Fax:* 405-685-8399. *E-mail:* gprince@okc.cc.ok.us.

DEGREES AND AWARDS

AS Diversified Studies

COURSE SUBJECT AREAS OFFERED OUTSIDE OF DEGREE PROGRAMS

Undergraduate: Astronomy and astrophysics; biological and life sciences; biology; business; business administration and management; business communications; business law; computer and information sciences; developmental and child psychology; economics; English composition; English language and literature; geology; history; liberal arts, general studies, and humanities; mathematics; philosophy and religion; physical sciences; physics; political science; psychology; social sciences; sociology; technical writing; visual and performing arts

See full description on page 676.

OKLAHOMA CITY UNIVERSITY

Oklahoma City, Oklahoma

Prior Learning and University Studies (PLUS)

www.okcu.edu/plus

Oklahoma City University, founded in 1904, is an independent, religious, comprehensive institution. It is accredited by the North Central Association of Colleges and Schools. It first offered distance learning courses in

1976. In 1999–2000, it offered 30 courses at a distance. In fall 1999, there were 280 students enrolled in distance learning courses.

Course delivery sites Courses are delivered to your home, 1 off-campus center in Tulsa.

Media Courses are delivered via print. Students and teachers may interact via mail, telephone, fax, e-mail.

Restrictions Programs are available nationwide. Enrollment is open to anyone.

Services Distance learners have access to library services, e-mail services, academic advising, bookstore at a distance.

Credit-earning options Students may transfer credits from another institution or may earn credits through examinations, portfolio assessment, military training, business training.

Typical costs Tuition of $158 per credit plus mandatory fees of $45 per term. Undergraduate tuition is approximately $200 per credit. Mandatory fees range between $50 and $100. Costs may vary. Financial aid is available to distance learners.

Registration Students may register by mail, in person.

Contact Stacy Messinger, Admissions Counselor/Recruiter, Oklahoma City University, 2501 North Blackwelder, Oklahoma City, OK 73106. *Telephone:* 405-521-5265. *E-mail:* plus@frodo.okcu.edu.

DEGREES AND AWARDS

BA Business (some on-campus requirements), Liberal Arts (some on-campus requirements)
BS Technical Management (some on-campus requirements)

COURSE SUBJECT AREAS OFFERED OUTSIDE OF DEGREE PROGRAMS

Undergraduate: American (U.S.) history; area, ethnic, and cultural studies; business communications; environmental health; film studies; finance; liberal arts, general studies, and humanities; social psychology

OKLAHOMA STATE UNIVERSITY

Stillwater, Oklahoma

Distance Learning
www.okstate.edu/outreach

Oklahoma State University, founded in 1890, is a state-supported university. It is accredited by the North Central Association of Colleges and Schools. It first offered distance learning courses in 1921. In 1999–2000, it offered 330 courses at a distance. In fall 1999, there were 4,700 students enrolled in distance learning courses.

Course delivery sites Courses are delivered to your home, your workplace, military bases, Oklahoma State University, Oklahoma City (Oklahoma City), Rose State College (Midwest City), off-campus center(s) in Oklahoma City, Tulsa.

Media Courses are delivered via television, videotapes, videoconferencing, interactive television, audiotapes, computer software, CD-ROM, World Wide Web, e-mail, print. Students and teachers may meet in person or interact via videoconferencing, audioconferencing, mail, telephone, fax, e-mail, interactive television, World Wide Web. The following equipment may be required: television, videocassette player, computer, modem, Internet access, e-mail.

Restrictions Programs are available worldwide. Enrollment is restricted to individuals meeting certain criteria.

Services Distance learners have access to library services, the campus computer network, e-mail services, academic advising, tutoring, career placement assistance at a distance.

Credit-earning options Students may transfer credits from another institution or may earn credits through examinations, military training, business training.

Typical costs *Undergraduate:* Tuition of $90 per semester hour for in-state residents. *Graduate:* Tuition of $190 per semester hour for in-state residents. Tuition of $350 per semester hour for out-of-state residents. Costs may vary. Financial aid is available to distance learners.

Registration Students may register by mail, fax, telephone, e-mail, World Wide Web, in person.

Contact Bill Cooper, Interim Director, Distance Learning, Oklahoma State University, University Extension, International and Economic Development (UEIED), 470 Student Union, Stillwater, OK 74078. *Telephone:* 405-744-6700. *Fax:* 405-744-7793. *E-mail:* bcoop@okstate.edu.

DEGREES AND AWARDS

BS Electrical Engineering Technology (service area differs from that of the overall institution)
MBA Business Administration (service area differs from that of the overall institution)
MS Biosystems Engineering (service area differs from that of the overall institution), Computer Science (service area differs from that of the overall institution; some on-campus requirements), Control Systems Engineering (certain restrictions apply; service area differs from that of the overall institution), Electrical Engineering (certain restrictions apply; service area differs from that of the overall institution), Engineering Technology Management (certain restrictions apply; service area differs from that of the overall institution), Environmental Science/Management (service area differs from that of the overall institution; some on-campus requirements), Fire and Emergency Management Administration, Telecommunications Management (service area differs from that of the overall institution; some on-campus requirements)

COURSE SUBJECT AREAS OFFERED OUTSIDE OF DEGREE PROGRAMS

Undergraduate: Accounting; agricultural economics; agriculture; algebra; American (U.S.) history; animal sciences; area, ethnic, and cultural studies; business communications; business law; calculus; chemical engineering; computer programming; creative writing; developmental and child psychology; economics; educational psychology; electronics; engineering-related technologies; English composition; European languages and literatures; finance; fire science; French language and literature; geography; geology; German language and literature; health and physical education/fitness; history; home economics and family studies; journalism; law and legal studies; liberal arts, general studies, and humanities; management information systems; marketing; mathematics; meteorology; organizational behavior studies; philosophy and religion; political science; psychology; sociology; Spanish language and literature; statistics; teacher education; technical writing; visual and performing arts

Graduate: Agriculture; business; business administration and management; chemical engineering; communications; computer and information sciences; education administration; electrical engineering; environmental engineering; fire science; health professions and related sciences; industrial engineering; mechanical engineering; radio and television broadcasting; telecommunications

Noncredit: Community health services; continuing education; real estate

See full descriptions on pages 592, 676, and 822.

OLD DOMINION UNIVERSITY

Norfolk, Virginia

Office of Distance Learning and Extended Education
web.odu.edu/webroot/FrontEnd.nsf/pages/distlrn

Old Dominion University, founded in 1930, is a state-supported university. It is accredited by the Southern Association of Colleges and Schools.

It first offered distance learning courses in 1984. In 1999–2000, it offered 229 courses at a distance. In fall 1999, there were 3,945 students enrolled in distance learning courses.

Course delivery sites Courses are delivered to your home, your workplace, military bases, Blue Ridge Community College (Weyers Cave), Central Virginia Community College (Lynchburg), Dabney S. Lancaster Community College (Clifton Forge), Danville Community College (Danville), Eastern Shore Community College (Melfa), Germanna Community College (Locust Grove), John Tyler Community College (Chester), J. Sargeant Reynolds Community College (Richmond), Lord Fairfax Community College (Middletown), Mountain Empire Community College (Big Stone Gap), New River Community College (Dublin), Northern Virginia Community College (Annandale), Patrick Henry Community College (Martinsville), Paul D. Camp Community College (Franklin), Piedmont Virginia Community College (Charlottesville), Rappahannock Community College (Glenns), Southside Virginia Community College (Alberta), Southwest Virginia Community College (Richlands), Tidewater Community College (Norfolk), Virginia Highlands Community College (Abingdon), Virginia Western Community College (Roanoke), Wytheville Community College (Wytheville), Yavapai College (Prescott, AZ), 3 off-campus centers in Hampton, Portsmouth, Virginia Beach.

Media Courses are delivered via videotapes, videoconferencing, computer software, World Wide Web. Students and teachers may interact via videoconferencing, mail, telephone, fax, e-mail, World Wide Web.

Restrictions Teletechnet has primarily in-state sites; some programs are available at sites in other states. Enrollment is restricted to individuals meeting certain criteria.

Services Distance learners have access to library services, the campus computer network, e-mail services, academic advising, tutoring, career placement assistance, bookstore at a distance.

Credit-earning options Students may transfer credits from another institution or may earn credits through examinations, portfolio assessment, military training.

Typical costs Undergraduate in-state tuition ranges between $105 and $122 per credit, out-of-state is between $336 and $375. Graduate in-state tuition is $185 per credit, out-of-state ranges between $426 and $491. Mandatory fees are $8 per semester. Financial aid is available to distance learners.

Registration Students may register by telephone, World Wide Web, in person.

Contact Dr. Jeanie Kline, Director of Distance Learning Operations, Old Dominion University, Gornto Teletechnet Center, Norfolk, VA 23529. *Telephone:* 757-683-3163. *Fax:* 757-683-5492. *E-mail:* jkline@odu.edu.

DEGREES AND AWARDS

BA Criminal Justice
BS Computer Science (certain restrictions apply), Criminal Justice, Education-Pre K Through 6 (certain restrictions apply), Human Services Counseling, Interdisciplinary Studies, Occupational and Technical Studies, Professional Communications
BSBA Business Administration
BSET Civil Engineering Technology (some on-campus requirements), Electrical Engineering Technology (some on-campus requirements), Mechanical Engineering Technology (some on-campus requirements)
BSHS Health Science
BSN Nursing
MBA Business Administration
ME Environmental Engineering (some on-campus requirements)
MEM Engineering Management (some on-campus requirements)
MS Education-Pre K Through 6 (certain restrictions apply), Occupational and Technical Studies, Special Education
MSN Family Nurse Practitioner (some on-campus requirements)
MTX Taxation

COURSE SUBJECT AREAS OFFERED OUTSIDE OF DEGREE PROGRAMS

Undergraduate: Accounting; business; business administration and management; communications; computer and information sciences; engineering-related technologies; English language and literature; finance; health professions and related sciences; history; human resources management; industrial psychology; journalism; management information systems; marketing; mathematics; music; nursing; political science; public health; social psychology; sociology

Graduate: Accounting; aerospace, aeronautical engineering; business; business administration and management; civil engineering; computer and information sciences; education; electrical engineering; engineering/industrial management; environmental engineering; finance; management information systems; marketing; mechanical engineering; nursing; special education; teacher education

See full descriptions on pages 618 and 676.

OLIVET NAZARENE UNIVERSITY

Bourbonnais, Illinois
School of Graduate and Adult Studies
www.olivet.edu

Olivet Nazarene University, founded in 1907, is an independent, religious, comprehensive institution affiliated with the Church of the Nazarene. It is accredited by the North Central Association of Colleges and Schools. It first offered distance learning courses in 1997. In 1999–2000, it offered 25 courses at a distance. In fall 1999, there were 502 students enrolled in distance learning courses.

Course delivery sites Courses are delivered to your home, your workplace, high schools.

Media Courses are delivered via videotapes, e-mail, print. Students and teachers may interact via mail, telephone, fax, e-mail. The following equipment may be required: television, videocassette player, computer, modem, Internet access, e-mail.

Restrictions Master's of Education program is available in Wisconsin and Indiana; graduate level, stand-alone education courses are available in Illinois only. Enrollment is restricted to individuals meeting certain criteria.

Services Distance learners have access to academic advising, bookstore at a distance.

Credit-earning options Students may transfer credits from another institution.

Typical costs Tuition of $221 per credit hour plus mandatory fees of $100 per degree program. Costs may vary. Financial aid is available to distance learners.

Registration Students may register by mail, fax, in person.

Contact Amber Mead, Program Specialist, Olivet Nazarene University. *Telephone:* 800-576-5157. *Fax:* 815-939-5390. *E-mail:* amead@olivet.edu.

DEGREES AND AWARDS

MEd Education (certain restrictions apply)

COURSE SUBJECT AREAS OFFERED OUTSIDE OF DEGREE PROGRAMS

Graduate: Curriculum and instruction

OPEN LEARNING AGENCY

Burnaby, British Columbia, Canada

Career and College Prep./College Courses and Programs/ B.C. Open University Courses and Programs
www.ola.bc.ca

Open Learning Agency, founded in 1978, is a province-supported, comprehensive institution. It is accredited by the provincial charter. In 1999–2000, it offered 300 courses at a distance.

Course delivery sites Courses are delivered to your home, your workplace, Simon Fraser University (Burnaby), University of British Columbia (Vancouver), off-campus center(s).

Media Courses are delivered via television, videotapes, videoconferencing, audiotapes, computer software, computer conferencing, World Wide Web, e-mail, print. Students and teachers may interact via audioconferencing, mail, telephone, fax, e-mail, World Wide Web. The following equipment may be required: television, videocassette player, computer, modem, Internet access, e-mail.

Restrictions Programs are available nationwide. Enrollment is restricted to individuals meeting certain criteria.

Services Distance learners have access to library services, the campus computer network, e-mail services, academic advising, tutoring at a distance.

Credit-earning options Students may transfer credits from another institution or may earn credits through examinations, portfolio assessment.

Typical costs Tuition ranges from $50 to $64 per credit depending on the course. Adult Basic Education is $50 per course, from which permanent BC residents are exempt. Costs may vary. Financial aid is available to distance learners.

Registration Students may register by mail, fax, telephone, e-mail, World Wide Web, in person.

Contact Student Services, Open Learning Agency, 4355 Mathissi Place, Burnaby, BC V5G 4S8 Canada. *Telephone:* 604-431-3300. *Fax:* 604-431-3444. *E-mail:* student@ola.bc.ca.

DEGREES AND AWARDS

AA General Program
BA Design, Fine Art, Music, Music Therapy
BBA Business Administration
BGS General Studies
BHS Physiotherapy, Psychiatric Nursing, Respiratory Therapy
BS General Program
BSN Nursing

COURSE SUBJECT AREAS OFFERED OUTSIDE OF DEGREE PROGRAMS

Undergraduate: Abnormal psychology; accounting; anthropology; archaeology; biology; business communications; business law; cell biology; chemistry; chemistry, organic; communications; computer and information sciences; criminology; developmental and child psychology; ecology; economics; education; English language and literature; ethics; European languages and literatures; finance; forestry; genetics; geography; geology; health services administration; history; home economics and family studies; liberal arts, general studies, and humanities; logic; management information systems; marketing; mathematics; microbiology; music; oceanography; organizational behavior studies; physics; political science; social psychology; sociology

OREGON HEALTH SCIENCES UNIVERSITY

Portland, Oregon

School of Nursing
www.ohsu.edu

Oregon Health Sciences University, founded in 1974, is a state-related, upper-level institution. It is accredited by the Northwest Association of Schools and Colleges. It first offered distance learning courses in 1992. In 1999–2000, it offered 13 courses at a distance. In fall 1999, there were 200 students enrolled in distance learning courses.

Course delivery sites Courses are delivered to your home, your workplace, Chemeketa Community College (Salem), Lane Community College (Eugene), Linn-Benton Community College (Albany), 2 off-campus centers in Eastern Oregon, OIT, Southern Oregon.

Media Courses are delivered via television, videotapes, videoconferencing, computer conferencing, e-mail, print. Students and teachers may meet in person or interact via videoconferencing, mail, telephone, fax, e-mail, interactive television. The following equipment may be required: television, videocassette player, computer, modem, Internet access, e-mail.

Restrictions Programs are available to in-state students only. Enrollment is restricted to individuals meeting certain criteria.

Services Distance learners have access to library services, the campus computer network, e-mail services, academic advising, tutoring, career placement assistance at a distance.

Credit-earning options Students may transfer credits from another institution or may earn credits through examinations, portfolio assessment.

Typical costs *Undergraduate:* Tuition of $3912 per year plus mandatory fees of $868.50 per year for local area residents. Tuition of $3912 per year plus mandatory fees of $868.50 per year for in-state residents. Tuition of $9780 per year plus mandatory fees of $868.50 per year for out-of-state residents. *Graduate:* Tuition of $6399 per year plus mandatory fees of $868.50 per year for local area residents. Tuition of $6399 per year plus mandatory fees of $868.50 per year for in-state residents. Tuition of $10,617 per year plus mandatory fees of $868.50 per year for out-of-state residents. Costs may vary. Financial aid is available to distance learners.

Registration Students may register by mail, World Wide Web, in person.

Contact Karen Thomas, Associate Dean, Oregon Health Sciences University. *Telephone:* 503-494-7725. *Fax:* 503-494-4350. *E-mail:* proginfo@ohsu.edu.

---

eCollege.com   *www.ecollege.com/scholarships*

DEGREES AND AWARDS

BSN Nursing

COURSE SUBJECT AREAS OFFERED OUTSIDE OF DEGREE PROGRAMS

Undergraduate: Nursing
Graduate: Nursing

OREGON STATE UNIVERSITY

Corvallis, Oregon

Distance and Continuing Education
statewide.orst.edu

Oregon State University, founded in 1868, is a state-supported university. It is accredited by the Northwest Association of Schools and Colleges. It first offered distance learning courses in 1986. In 1999–2000, it offered 150 courses at a distance. In fall 1999, there were 1,000 students enrolled in distance learning courses.

Course delivery sites Courses are delivered to your home, your workplace, military bases, high schools, Central Oregon Community College (Bend), Chemeketa Community College (Salem), Coast Community College (Newport), Columbia Gorge Community College (The Dalles), Eastern Oregon University (La Grande), Portland State University (Portland), Southern Oregon University (Ashland), Southwestern Oregon Community College (Coos Bay), 2 off-campus centers in Beaverton, Bend.

Media Courses are delivered via television, videotapes, videoconferencing, interactive television, computer conferencing, World Wide Web, e-mail, print. Students and teachers may meet in person or interact via videoconferencing, audioconferencing, mail, telephone, fax, e-mail, interactive television, World Wide Web. The following equipment may be required: videocassette player, computer, modem, Internet access, e-mail.

Restrictions Programs are available worldwide. Enrollment is open to anyone.

Services Distance learners have access to library services, e-mail services, academic advising, tutoring, career placement assistance, bookstore at a distance.

Credit-earning options Students may transfer credits from another institution.

Typical costs *Undergraduate:* Tuition of $125 per quarter credit. *Graduate:* Tuition of $240 per quarter credit. Costs may vary. Financial aid is available to distance learners.

Registration Students may register by telephone, World Wide Web.

Contact Student Services, Oregon State University, Distance and Continuing Education, 4943 The Valley Library, Corvallis, OR 97331-4504. *Telephone:* 541-737-2676. *Fax:* 541-737-2734. *E-mail:* ostateu@orst.edu.

DEGREES AND AWARDS

BA Liberal Studies (service area differs from that of the overall institution)
BS Environmental Sciences, General Agriculture, Liberal Studies (service area differs from that of the overall institution), Natural Resources
MS Nutrition and Food Management

COURSE SUBJECT AREAS OFFERED OUTSIDE OF DEGREE PROGRAMS

Undergraduate: Abnormal psychology; adult education; agricultural economics; agriculture; algebra; American (U.S.) history; American literature; anthropology; area, ethnic, and cultural studies; Asian studies; biological and life sciences; biology; botany; calculus; chemistry; child care and development; Chinese language and literature; communications; computer and information sciences; conservation and natural resources; creative writing; developmental and child psychology; ecology; economics; education; English composition; English language and literature; English literature; environmental science; ethics; European history; foods and nutrition studies; forestry; geology; health services administration; history of science and technology; individual and family development studies; interdisciplinary studies; liberal arts, general studies, and humanities; mathematics; meteorology; oceanography; philosophy and religion; physical sciences; political science; psychology; public health; sociology; Spanish language and literature; statistics; teacher education; technical writing; visual and performing arts; women's studies
Graduate: Adult education; agricultural economics; agriculture; anthropology; child care and development; civil engineering; computer and information sciences; conservation and natural resources; education; electrical engineering; engineering-related technologies; foods and nutrition studies; health services administration; individual and family development studies; mechanical engineering; political science; public health; teacher education; technical writing

See full description on page 620.

OTTAWA UNIVERSITY

Ottawa, Kansas
Kansas City Campus
www.ottawa.edu

Ottawa University, founded in 1865, is an independent, religious, comprehensive institution. It is accredited by the North Central Association of Colleges and Schools. It first offered distance learning courses in 1976. In 1999–2000, it offered 20 courses at a distance. In fall 1999, there were 254 students enrolled in distance learning courses.

Course delivery sites Courses are delivered to your home.

Media Courses are delivered via videotapes, computer software, computer conferencing, World Wide Web, e-mail, print. Students and teachers may meet in person or interact via mail, telephone, fax, e-mail, World Wide Web. The following equipment may be required: computer, modem, Internet access.

Restrictions Programs are available nationwide. Enrollment is restricted to individuals meeting certain criteria.

Services Distance learners have access to library services, e-mail services, academic advising, tutoring, bookstore at a distance.

Credit-earning options Students may transfer credits from another institution or may earn credits through examinations, portfolio assessment, military training, business training.

Typical costs *Undergraduate:* Tuition of $182 per hour. *Graduate:* Tuition of $267 per hour.

Registration Students may register by in person.

Contact Karen Adams, Director of Admissions, Ottawa University, 10865 Grandview, Overland Park, KS 66210. *Telephone:* 913-451-1431. *Fax:* 913-451-0806. *E-mail:* adamsk@ottawa.edu.

DEGREES AND AWARDS

BA Management of Health Services (service area differs from that of the overall institution; some on-campus requirements)
MA Human Resources (service area differs from that of the overall institution; some on-campus requirements)

COURSE SUBJECT AREAS OFFERED OUTSIDE OF DEGREE PROGRAMS

Undergraduate: Health services administration
Graduate: Human resources management

OUACHITA TECHNICAL COLLEGE

Malvern, Arkansas
www.otc.tec.ar.us

Ouachita Technical College, founded in 1972, is a state-supported, two-year college. It is accredited by the North Central Association of Colleges and Schools. In 1999–2000, it offered 15 courses at a distance. In fall 1999, there were 70 students enrolled in distance learning courses.

Course delivery sites Courses are delivered to your home, your workplace.

Media Courses are delivered via World Wide Web. Students and teachers may interact via World Wide Web. The following equipment may be required: computer, Internet access, e-mail.

Restrictions Programs are available nationwide. Enrollment is restricted to individuals meeting certain criteria.

Services Distance learners have access to library services, academic advising, tutoring, career placement assistance, bookstore at a distance.

Credit-earning options Students may transfer credits from another institution or may earn credits through examinations.

Typical costs Tuition of $38 per credit plus mandatory fees of $5 per credit.

Registration Students may register by mail, telephone, e-mail, in person.

Contact Dr. Susan Azbell, Vice President and Provost, Ouachita Technical College, PO Box 816, Malvern, AR 72104. *Telephone:* 501-332-3658. *Fax:* 501-337-9382. *E-mail:* susan@otcweb.org.

DEGREES AND AWARDS

Distance programs offered do not lead to a degree or other formal award.

COURSE SUBJECT AREAS OFFERED OUTSIDE OF DEGREE PROGRAMS

Undergraduate: Administrative and secretarial services; computer and information sciences; earth science; English language and literature; environmental science; information sciences and systems; labor relations/studies; philosophy and religion; psychology; sociology

OWENS COMMUNITY COLLEGE

Toledo, Ohio

Center for Development and Training
www.owens.cc.oh.us/Academic/Distance_Education

Owens Community College, founded in 1966, is a state-supported, two-year college. It is accredited by the North Central Association of Colleges and Schools. It first offered distance learning courses in 1993. In 1999–2000, it offered 46 courses at a distance. In fall 1999, there were 850 students enrolled in distance learning courses.

Course delivery sites Courses are delivered to your home, your workplace.

Media Courses are delivered via television, videotapes, videoconferencing, audiotapes, CD-ROM, World Wide Web, e-mail, print. Students and teachers may meet in person or interact via videoconferencing, audioconferencing, mail, telephone, fax, e-mail, interactive television, World Wide Web. The following equipment may be required: television, videocassette player, computer, modem, Internet access, e-mail.

Restrictions Programs are available worldwide. Enrollment is open to anyone.

Services Distance learners have access to library services, e-mail services, academic advising, tutoring, career placement assistance, bookstore at a distance.

Credit-earning options Students may transfer credits from another institution or may earn credits through examinations, portfolio assessment, military training, business training.

Typical costs Tuition of $79 per credit for in-state residents. Tuition of $148 per credit for out-of-state residents. Costs may vary. Financial aid is available to distance learners.

Registration Students may register by mail, fax, telephone, in person.

Contact Dr. Ron Skulas, Alternative Learning Coordinator, Owens Community College, PO Box 10000, AVCC 152, Toledo, OH 43699-1947. *Telephone:* 419-661-7061. *Fax:* 419-661-7801. *E-mail:* rskulas@owens.cc.oh.us.

DEGREES AND AWARDS

Undergraduate Certificate(s) Supervision

COURSE SUBJECT AREAS OFFERED OUTSIDE OF DEGREE PROGRAMS

Undergraduate: Accounting; American (U.S.) history; American literature; business; business administration and management; business law; computer and information sciences; conservation and natural resources; criminal justice; developmental and child psychology; English composition; environmental engineering; environmental science; European lan-

guages and literatures; fire science; health and physical education/fitness; industrial psychology; liberal arts, general studies, and humanities; marketing; mathematics; organizational behavior studies; psychology; sociology; statistics

PACIFIC GRADUATE SCHOOL OF PSYCHOLOGY

Palo Alto, California

Master's Degree (M.S.) in Psychology
www.pgsp.edu/njdistance.htm

Pacific Graduate School of Psychology, founded in 1975, is an independent, nonprofit, graduate institution. It is accredited by the Western Association of Schools and Colleges, Inc. In 1999–2000, it offered 6 courses at a distance.

Course delivery sites Courses are delivered to your home.

Media Courses are delivered via videotapes, World Wide Web, e-mail, print. Students and teachers may interact via e-mail, World Wide Web. The following equipment may be required: computer, modem, Internet access, e-mail.

Restrictions Programs are available worldwide. Enrollment is restricted to individuals meeting certain criteria.

Services Distance learners have access to library services, e-mail services at a distance.

Typical costs Tuition of $588 per unit. There is a $90 mandatory technology fee per course.

Registration Students may register by mail, fax, telephone, e-mail.

Contact Dr. William Froming, Faculty Chair, Pacific Graduate School of Psychology, 940 East Meadow Drive, Palo Alto, CA 94303. *Telephone:* 650-843-3530. *Fax:* 650-856-6734. *E-mail:* w.froming@pgsp.edu.

DEGREES AND AWARDS

MS Psychology (certain restrictions apply; some on-campus requirements)

PACIFIC OAKS COLLEGE

Pasadena, California

Distance Learning
www.pacificoaks.edu

Pacific Oaks College, founded in 1945, is an independent, nonprofit, upper-level institution. It is accredited by the Western Association of Schools and Colleges, Inc. It first offered distance learning courses in 1996. In 1999–2000, it offered 30 courses at a distance. In fall 1999, there were 140 students enrolled in distance learning courses.

Course delivery sites Courses are delivered to your home.

Media Courses are delivered via e-mail. Students and teachers may interact via e-mail. The following equipment may be required: computer, modem.

Restrictions Programs are available worldwide. Enrollment is restricted to individuals meeting certain criteria.

Services Distance learners have access to library services, e-mail services, academic advising, bookstore at a distance.

Credit-earning options Students may transfer credits from another institution or may earn credits through examinations, portfolio assessment.

Typical costs *Undergraduate:* Tuition of $500 per unit plus mandatory fees of $30 per semester. *Graduate:* Tuition of $500 per unit plus mandatory fees of $30 per semester. Financial aid is available to distance learners.

Registration Students may register by mail, fax, e-mail, in person.

Contact Admissions Office, Pacific Oaks College, 5 Westmoreland Place, Pasadena, CA 91103. *Telephone:* 800-684-0900. *Fax:* 626-577-6144. *E-mail:* admissions@pacificoaks.edu.

DEGREES AND AWARDS

BA Human Development (service area differs from that of the overall institution; some on-campus requirements)
MA Human Development (some on-campus requirements)
PGC Early Childhood Education, Human Development

PADUCAH COMMUNITY COLLEGE

Paducah, Kentucky

Paducah Community College, founded in 1932, is a state-supported, two-year college. It is accredited by the Southern Association of Colleges and Schools.
Contact Paducah Community College, PO Box 7380, Paducah, KY 42002-7380. *Telephone:* 502-554-9200.

See full descriptions on pages 556 and 676.

PALM BEACH COMMUNITY COLLEGE

Lake Worth, Florida

Palm Beach Community College, founded in 1933, is a state-supported, two-year college. It is accredited by the Southern Association of Colleges and Schools.
Contact Palm Beach Community College, 4200 Congress Avenue, Lake Worth, FL 33461-4796. *Telephone:* 561-967-7222.

See full description on page 676.

PALOMAR COLLEGE

San Marcos, California
Educational Television
etv.palomar.edu

Palomar College, founded in 1946, is a state and locally supported, two-year college. It is accredited by the Western Association of Schools and Colleges, Inc. It first offered distance learning courses in 1978. In 1999–2000, it offered 59 courses at a distance. In fall 1999, there were 1,756 students enrolled in distance learning courses.
Course delivery sites Courses are delivered to your home, military bases, 6 off-campus centers in Borrego Springs, Camp Pendleton, Escondido, Fallbrook, Mount Carmel, Poway.
Media Courses are delivered via television, videotapes, videoconferencing, computer software, World Wide Web, e-mail, print. Students and teachers may meet in person or interact via videoconferencing, mail, telephone, fax, e-mail, World Wide Web. The following equipment may be required: television, videocassette player, computer, modem, Internet access, e-mail.
Restrictions Programs are available to local area students. Enrollment is open to anyone.
Services Distance learners have access to library services, e-mail services, academic advising, career placement assistance at a distance.
Credit-earning options Students may transfer credits from another institution or may earn credits through examinations.
Typical costs Tuition of $11 per credit plus mandatory fees of $11 per semester for in-state residents. Tuition of $136 per credit plus mandatory

fees of $11 per semester for out-of-state residents. Costs may vary. Financial aid is available to distance learners.
Registration Students may register by telephone, World Wide Web.
Contact Sherilyn Hargraves, ETV Manager, Palomar College, P31, 1140 West Mission Road, San Marcos, CA 92069. *Telephone:* 760-744-1150 Ext. 2431. *Fax:* 760-761-3519. *E-mail:* etvoffice@palomar.edu.

DEGREES AND AWARDS

Undergraduate Certificate(s) Microsoft Office User Specialist (MOUS) (some on-campus requirements)

COURSE SUBJECT AREAS OFFERED OUTSIDE OF DEGREE PROGRAMS

Undergraduate: Abnormal psychology; accounting; anthropology; area, ethnic, and cultural studies; biology; business; business administration and management; business law; computer and information sciences; creative writing; criminal justice; developmental and child psychology; electronics; English as a second language (ESL); finance; health and physical education/fitness; home economics and family studies; instructional media; law and legal studies; liberal arts, general studies, and humanities; logic; mass media; music; psychology; sign language; sociology; Spanish language and literature; student counseling; visual and performing arts

PARKLAND COLLEGE

Champaign, Illinois
Distance Education
online.parkland.cc.il.us

Parkland College, founded in 1967, is a district-supported, two-year college. It is accredited by the North Central Association of Colleges and Schools. It first offered distance learning courses in 1988. In 1999–2000, it offered 51 courses at a distance. In fall 1999, there were 750 students enrolled in distance learning courses.
Course delivery sites Courses are delivered to your home, high schools, 12 off-campus centers in Fisher, Gibson City, Heritage, Le Roy, Mahonut, Monticello, Paxton, Prairie Central, Rantoul, Tri-Point, Tuscola, Villagrove.
Media Courses are delivered via television, videotapes, videoconferencing, interactive television, computer software, World Wide Web, e-mail, print. Students and teachers may meet in person or interact via videoconferencing, mail, telephone, fax, e-mail, interactive television, World Wide Web. The following equipment may be required: television, videocassette player, computer, Internet access, e-mail.
Restrictions Programs are available worldwide. Enrollment is open to anyone.
Services Distance learners have access to library services, the campus computer network, e-mail services, academic advising, bookstore at a distance.
Credit-earning options Students may transfer credits from another institution or may earn credits through examinations.
Typical costs Tuition of $51 per credit for local area residents. Tuition of $91 per credit for in-state residents. Tuition of $91 per credit for out-of-state residents. Costs may vary. Financial aid is available to distance learners.
Registration Students may register by mail, fax, telephone, in person.
Contact Haiti Eastin, Program Coordinator, Parkland College, 2400 West Bradley Aevnue, Champaign, IL 61821. *Telephone:* 217-353-2342. *Fax:* 217-353-2241. *E-mail:* heastin@parkland.cc.il.us.

DEGREES AND AWARDS

AA Mass Communication: Advertising/Public Relations (certain restrictions apply), Mass Communications (Journalism) (certain restrictions apply), Psychology (certain restrictions apply)

AAS Business Management (certain restrictions apply)
AGS General Studies (certain restrictions apply)
AS Business Administration (certain restrictions apply), Business Education (certain restrictions apply)

COURSE SUBJECT AREAS OFFERED OUTSIDE OF DEGREE PROGRAMS

Undergraduate: Abnormal psychology; accounting; algebra; American (U.S.) history; anatomy; anthropology; area, ethnic, and cultural studies; art history and criticism; biological and life sciences; biology; business; business administration and management; business law; calculus; chemistry; computer programming; continuing education; developmental and child psychology; drama and theater; earth science; economics; English composition; fine arts; foods and nutrition studies; health and physical education/fitness; history; information sciences and systems; journalism; law and legal studies; marketing; mass media; mathematics; music; nursing; philosophy and religion; political science; psychology; social psychology; sociology; statistics; theological studies

PARK UNIVERSITY

Parkville, Missouri
School for Extended Learning
www.park.edu

Park University, founded in 1875, is an independent, religious, comprehensive institution affiliated with the Reorganized Church of Jesus Christ of Latter Day Saints. It is accredited by the North Central Association of Colleges and Schools. It first offered distance learning courses in 1996. In 1999–2000, it offered 62 courses at a distance. In fall 1999, there were 1,152 students enrolled in distance learning courses.
Course delivery sites Courses are delivered to your home, your workplace, military bases.
Media Courses are delivered via videoconferencing, CD-ROM, World Wide Web. Students and teachers may interact via videoconferencing, audioconferencing, e-mail, World Wide Web. The following equipment may be required: computer, Internet access, e-mail.
Restrictions Programs are available worldwide. Enrollment is open to anyone.
Services Distance learners have access to library services, bookstore at a distance.
Credit-earning options Students may transfer credits from another institution or may earn credits through examinations, military training.
Typical costs Tuition of $169 per semester hour. Costs may vary. Financial aid is available to distance learners.
Registration Students may register by mail, fax, e-mail, World Wide Web, in person.
Contact Beverly Gauper, Administrator, Park University, 8700 Northwest River Park Drive, Parkville, MO 64152. *Telephone:* 877-505-1059. *E-mail:* bevg@mail.park.edu.

DEGREES AND AWARDS

BS Criminal Justice Administration (some on-campus requirements), Management (some on-campus requirements), Management/Computer Information Systems (some on-campus requirements)

COURSE SUBJECT AREAS OFFERED OUTSIDE OF DEGREE PROGRAMS

Undergraduate: American (U.S.) history; biology; business administration and management; business law; chemistry; computer programming; creative writing; criminal justice; database management; economics; ethics; finance; geography; geology; health services administration; human resources management; information sciences and systems; journalism;

labor relations/studies; marketing; organizational behavior studies; psychology; public administration and services; social psychology; statistics; technical writing
Graduate: Theological studies
See full description on page 622.

PASSAIC COUNTY COMMUNITY COLLEGE

Paterson, New Jersey

Passaic County Community College, founded in 1968, is a county-supported, two-year college. It is accredited by the Middle States Association of Colleges and Schools. In fall 1999, there were 78 students enrolled in distance learning courses.
Course delivery sites Courses are delivered to your home, your workplace, military bases, high schools, Passaic County Vocational Tech (Wayne), Sussex County Community College (Newton), 3 off-campus centers in Bergen, Passaic, Sussex.
Media Courses are delivered via interactive television, World Wide Web. Students and teachers may meet in person or interact via telephone, fax, e-mail, interactive television, World Wide Web. The following equipment may be required: computer, modem, Internet access, e-mail.
Restrictions Programs are available to in-state students only. Enrollment is open to anyone.
Services Distance learners have access to library services, tutoring at a distance.
Credit-earning options Students may transfer credits from another institution or may earn credits through examinations, portfolio assessment, military training, business training.
Typical costs Tuition ranges $63.50 and $80 per credit. Financial aid is available to distance learners.
Registration Students may register by mail, fax, telephone, in person.
Contact Brian Lewis, Dean of Admissions and Enrollment Management, Passaic County Community College, One College Boulevard, Paterson, NJ 07505. *Telephone:* 973-684-6304. *Fax:* 973-684-6778. *E-mail:* blewis@pccc.cc.nj.us.

DEGREES AND AWARDS

Distance programs offered do not lead to a degree or other formal award.

COURSE SUBJECT AREAS OFFERED OUTSIDE OF DEGREE PROGRAMS

Undergraduate: Communications; health professions and related sciences; nursing; political science; statistics
See full description on page 600.

PATRICK HENRY COMMUNITY COLLEGE

Martinsville, Virginia
Learning Resource Center
www.ph.cc.va.us

Patrick Henry Community College, founded in 1962, is a state-supported, two-year college. It is accredited by the Southern Association of Colleges and Schools. It first offered distance learning courses in 1981. In 1999–2000, it offered 45 courses at a distance. In fall 1999, there were 464 students enrolled in distance learning courses.

Course delivery sites Courses are delivered to your home, your workplace, Virginia Community College System (Richmond), 3 off-campus centers in Franklin County, Martinsville, Patrick County.

Media Courses are delivered via television, videotapes, videoconferencing, computer software, CD-ROM, computer conferencing, World Wide Web, e-mail, print. Students and teachers may meet in person or interact via videoconferencing, audioconferencing, mail, telephone, fax, e-mail, World Wide Web. The following equipment may be required: television, videocassette player, computer, modem, Internet access, e-mail.

Restrictions Programs are available nationwide. Enrollment is restricted to individuals meeting certain criteria.

Services Distance learners have access to library services, the campus computer network, e-mail services, academic advising, tutoring, bookstore at a distance.

Credit-earning options Students may transfer credits from another institution or may earn credits through examinations.

Typical costs Tuition of $37.12 per credit for in-state residents. Tuition of $164.82 per credit plus mandatory fees of $1.50 per credit for out-of-state residents. There is a mandatory fee of $5 per student. Financial aid is available to distance learners.

Registration Students may register by mail, in person.

Contact Carolyn R. Byrd, Director, Instructional Support Services, Patrick Henry Community College, PO Box 5311, Martinsville, VA 24115. *Telephone:* 540-656-0211. *Fax:* 540-656-0327. *E-mail:* phbyrdc@ph.cc.va.us.

DEGREES AND AWARDS

Distance programs offered do not lead to a degree or other formal award.

COURSE SUBJECT AREAS OFFERED OUTSIDE OF DEGREE PROGRAMS

Undergraduate: American (U.S.) history; art history and criticism; cognitive psychology; database management; developmental and child psychology; economics; English composition; health and physical education/fitness; information sciences and systems; nursing; sociology
See full description on page 676.

PEIRCE COLLEGE

Philadelphia, Pennsylvania
Peirce College Non-Traditional Education
www.peirce.edu

Peirce College, founded in 1865, is an independent, nonprofit, four-year college. It is accredited by the Middle States Association of Colleges and Schools. In 1999–2000, it offered 10 courses at a distance. In fall 1999, there were 100 students enrolled in distance learning courses.

Course delivery sites Courses are delivered to your home, your workplace, military bases, high schools.

Media Courses are delivered via television, videotapes, videoconferencing, CD-ROM, World Wide Web, e-mail, print. Students and teachers may meet in person or interact via videoconferencing, audioconferencing, mail, telephone, fax, e-mail. The following equipment may be required: television, videocassette player, computer, modem, Internet access, e-mail.

Restrictions Programs are available nationwide. Enrollment is open to anyone.

Services Distance learners have access to library services, e-mail services, academic advising, tutoring, career placement assistance, bookstore at a distance.

Credit-earning options Students may transfer credits from another institution or may earn credits through examinations, portfolio assessment, military training, business training.

Typical costs Tuition of $266 per credit. There is a mandatory fee of $60 per six credits. Financial aid is available to distance learners.

Registration Students may register by in person.

Contact Kevin Lamb, Manager, Peirce College, 1420 Pine Street, Philadelphia, PA 19102. *Telephone:* 215-545-6400. *Fax:* 215-546-5996. *E-mail:* kdlamb@peirce.edu.

DEGREES AND AWARDS

AS Business Administration, Information Technology Management
BS Business Administration, Information Technology Management

COURSE SUBJECT AREAS OFFERED OUTSIDE OF DEGREE PROGRAMS

Undergraduate: Business administration and management; business law; computer and information sciences; economics; liberal arts, general studies, and humanities; marketing; mathematics; psychology; sociology

PELLISSIPPI STATE TECHNICAL COMMUNITY COLLEGE

Knoxville, Tennessee
Educational Technology Services
www.pstcc.cc.tn.us/ets/

Pellissippi State Technical Community College, founded in 1974, is a state-supported, two-year college. It is accredited by the Southern Association of Colleges and Schools. It first offered distance learning courses in 1991. In 1999–2000, it offered 70 courses at a distance. In fall 1999, there were 850 students enrolled in distance learning courses.

Course delivery sites Courses are delivered to your home, your workplace, military bases, 2 off-campus centers in Alcoa, Knoxville.

Media Courses are delivered via videotapes, videoconferencing, interactive television, CD-ROM, World Wide Web. Students and teachers may meet in person or interact via videoconferencing, mail, telephone, fax, e-mail, interactive television, World Wide Web. The following equipment may be required: television, videocassette player, computer, modem, Internet access, e-mail.

Restrictions Programs are available to in-state students only. Enrollment is open to anyone.

Services Distance learners have access to library services, the campus computer network, e-mail services, academic advising, career placement assistance, bookstore at a distance.

Credit-earning options Students may transfer credits from another institution or may earn credits through examinations, portfolio assessment, military training.

Typical costs Tuition of $71 per credit for in-state residents. Tuition of $219 per credit for out-of-state residents. Costs may vary. Financial aid is available to distance learners.

Registration Students may register by telephone, World Wide Web, in person.

Contact Dr. Lana Doncaster, Director of Educational Technology Services, Pellissippi State Technical Community College, 10915 Hardin Valley Road, Knoxville, TN 37933. *Telephone:* 423-694-6593. *Fax:* 423-539-7068. *E-mail:* ldoncaster@pstcc.cc.tn.us.

DEGREES AND AWARDS

Distance programs offered do not lead to a degree or other formal award.

COURSE SUBJECT AREAS OFFERED OUTSIDE OF DEGREE PROGRAMS

Undergraduate: Accounting; administrative and secretarial services; biology; business administration and management; calculus; economics; English composition; environmental engineering; marketing; statistics
See full description on page 676.

PENNSYLVANIA COLLEGE OF TECHNOLOGY

Williamsport, Pennsylvania
www.pct.edu

Pennsylvania College of Technology, founded in 1965, is a state-related, primarily two-year college. It is accredited by the Middle States Association of Colleges and Schools. In 1999–2000, it offered 40 courses at a distance. In fall 1999, there were 183 students enrolled in distance learning courses.
Course delivery sites Courses are delivered to your home, your workplace, Harcum College (Bryn Mawr), Harrisburg Area Community College (Harrisburg), Montgomery County Community College (Blue Bell).
Media Courses are delivered via videotapes, videoconferencing, audiotapes, computer software, CD-ROM, computer conferencing, World Wide Web, e-mail, print. Students and teachers may meet in person or interact via videoconferencing, mail, telephone, fax, e-mail, World Wide Web. The following equipment may be required: television, videocassette player, computer, modem, Internet access, e-mail.
Restrictions Programs are available nationwide. Enrollment is restricted to individuals meeting certain criteria.
Services Distance learners have access to library services, the campus computer network, e-mail services, bookstore at a distance.
Credit-earning options Students may transfer credits from another institution.
Typical costs Tuition of $236.20 per credit for in-state residents. Tuition of $278.80 per credit for out-of-state residents. Costs may vary. Financial aid is available to distance learners.
Registration Students may register by fax, telephone, e-mail, in person.
Contact Vicki Paulina, Coordinator of Curriculum Development, Pennsylvania College of Technology, One College Avenue, Williamsport, PA 17701. *Telephone:* 570-326-3761 Ext. 7628. *Fax:* 570-321-5559. *E-mail:* vpaulina@pct.edu.

DEGREES AND AWARDS

BS Applied Health Studies (certain restrictions apply), Automotive Technology (certain restrictions apply), Dental Hygiene (certain restrictions apply), Technology Management (certain restrictions apply)

COURSE SUBJECT AREAS OFFERED OUTSIDE OF DEGREE PROGRAMS

Undergraduate: Accounting; art history and criticism; biology; business administration and management; ethics; finance; health and physical education/fitness; health professions and related sciences; history of science and technology; human resources management; international business; liberal arts, general studies, and humanities; marketing; organizational behavior studies; statistics

PENNSYLVANIA STATE UNIVERSITY UNIVERSITY PARK CAMPUS

University Park, Pennsylvania
Department of Distance Education/World Campus
www.outreach.psu.edu/de

Pennsylvania State University University Park Campus, founded in 1855, is a state-related university. It is accredited by the Middle States Association of Colleges and Schools. It first offered distance learning courses in 1892. In 1999–2000, it offered 450 courses at a distance. In fall 1999, there were 12,500 students enrolled in distance learning courses.
Course delivery sites Courses are delivered to your home, your workplace, military bases.
Media Courses are delivered via television, videotapes, videoconferencing, audiotapes, computer software, CD-ROM, World Wide Web, e-mail, print. Students and teachers may interact via videoconferencing, audioconferencing, mail, telephone, fax, e-mail, World Wide Web. The following equipment may be required: television, videocassette player, computer, Internet access, e-mail.
Restrictions Programs are available worldwide. Enrollment is open to anyone.
Services Distance learners have access to library services, the campus computer network, e-mail services, academic advising, bookstore at a distance.
Credit-earning options Students may transfer credits from another institution or may earn credits through examinations, military training, business training.
Typical costs Tuition ranges from $130 to $240 per credit depending on the course. There is a $30 mandatory fee per course. *Noncredit courses:* $150 per course. Costs may vary.
Registration Students may register by mail, fax, telephone, e-mail, World Wide Web, in person.
Contact Advising Office, Pennsylvania State University University Park Campus, Department of Distance Education/The World Campus, 207 Mitchell Building, University Park, PA 16802. *Telephone:* 800-252-3592. *Fax:* 814-865-3290. *E-mail:* psude@cde.psu.edu.

DEGREES AND AWARDS

Undergraduate Certificate(s) Adult Development and Aging Services, Advanced Business Management, Basic Supervisory Leadership, Business Management, Children, Youth and Family Services, Counselor Education-Chemical Dependency, Customer Relationship Management, Dietary Manager, Dietetics and Aging, Educational Technology Integration, General Business, Geographic Information Systems, Human Resources, Legal Issues for Business Professionals, Legal Issues for Those Dealing with the Elderly, Logistics and Supply Chain Management, Marketing Management, Noise Control Engineering, Paralegal Program, Retail Management, Small Business Management, Turfgrass Management, Webmaster, Writing Social Commentary
AA Letters, Arts, and Sciences Letters, Arts and Sciences
AS Business Administration, Dietetic Food Systems Management, Hotel, Restaurant, and Institutional Management, Human Development and Family Studies
BA Letters, Arts, and Sciences
MEd Adult Education
MEng Acoustical Engineering (certain restrictions apply; some on-campus requirements)

COURSE SUBJECT AREAS OFFERED OUTSIDE OF DEGREE PROGRAMS

Undergraduate: Accounting; adult education; algebra; American (U.S.) history; animal sciences; anthropology; architecture; art history and criticism; biological and life sciences; biology; business administration and management; business communications; business law; calculus; chemistry; chemistry, organic; cognitive psychology; comparative literature; creative writing; criminal justice; curriculum and instruction; developmental and child psychology; earth science; economics; education administration; educational psychology; electrical engineering; engineering; engineering mechanics; English composition; English language and literature; environmental science; ethics; European languages and literatures; finance; fine arts; foods and nutrition studies; French language and literature; genetics; geography; geology; German language and literature; gerontology; health and physical education/fitness; health professions and related sciences; health services administration; history; history of science and technology; hospitality services management; human resources management; individual and family development studies; instructional media; investments and securities; journalism; labor relations/studies; law and legal studies; liberal arts, general studies, and humanities; management information systems; marketing; mathematics; mechanical engineering; music; organizational behavior studies; philosophy and religion; physical sciences; physiology; political science; psychology; religious studies; Spanish language and literature; statistics; substance abuse counseling

Graduate: Adult education; architecture; curriculum and instruction; education administration; electrical engineering; engineering; instructional media; substance abuse counseling; teacher education

Noncredit: Acoustics; agricultural economics; animal sciences; business administration and management; business communications; engineering; engineering-related technologies; English composition; health professions and related sciences; horticulture; law and legal studies; paralegal/legal assistant; plant sciences

See full description on page 624.

PENSACOLA JUNIOR COLLEGE

Pensacola, Florida

Distance Learning Department
www.pjc.cc.fl.us

Pensacola Junior College, founded in 1948, is a state-supported, two-year college. It is accredited by the Southern Association of Colleges and Schools. It first offered distance learning courses in 1977. In 1999–2000, it offered 30 courses at a distance. In fall 1999, there were 780 students enrolled in distance learning courses.

Course delivery sites Courses are delivered to your home.

Media Courses are delivered via television, videotapes, videoconferencing, World Wide Web. Students and teachers may interact via mail, telephone, e-mail. The following equipment may be required: television, videocassette player, computer, modem, Internet access, e-mail.

Restrictions Programs are available to local area students. Enrollment is open to anyone.

Services Distance learners have access to library services, academic advising, tutoring, career placement assistance at a distance.

Credit-earning options Students may transfer credits from another institution or may earn credits through examinations, portfolio assessment, military training, business training.

Typical costs Tuition of $145.50 per course plus mandatory fees of $20 per course for in-state residents. Tuition of $534.75 per course plus mandatory fees of $20 per course for out-of-state residents. Financial aid is available to distance learners.

Registration Students may register by mail, in person.

Contact Dr. Bill Waters, Director, Pensacola Junior College. *Telephone:* 850-484-1238. *Fax:* 850-484-1838. *E-mail:* bwaters@pjc.cc.fl.us.

DEGREES AND AWARDS

Distance programs offered do not lead to a degree or other formal award.

COURSE SUBJECT AREAS OFFERED OUTSIDE OF DEGREE PROGRAMS

Undergraduate: Astronomy and astrophysics; business; business administration and management; developmental and child psychology; economics; geology; history; home economics and family studies; liberal arts, general studies, and humanities; mathematics; social psychology; sociology

PERALTA COMMUNITY COLLEGE DISTRICT

Oakland, California
www.peralta.cc.ca.us/tvcourse

Peralta Community College District is a state and locally supported, system. It is accredited by the Western Association of Schools and Colleges, Inc. In 1999–2000, it offered 30 courses at a distance. In fall 1999, there were 1,000 students enrolled in distance learning courses.

Course delivery sites Courses are delivered to your home.

Media Courses are delivered via television, videotapes, audiotapes, computer software, CD-ROM, World Wide Web, e-mail, print. Students and teachers may meet in person or interact via mail, telephone, e-mail. The following equipment may be required: television, videocassette player, computer, modem, Internet access, e-mail.

Restrictions Programs are available to local area students. Enrollment is open to anyone.

Typical costs Tuition of $11 per unit for in-state residents. Tuition of $151 per unit for out-of-state residents. Financial aid is available to distance learners.

Contact Joseph Rhone, Peralta Community College District. *Telephone:* 510-466-7366. *Fax:* 510-466-7394. *E-mail:* josephin@peralta.cc.ca.us.

DEGREES AND AWARDS

AA General Curriculum

COURSE SUBJECT AREAS OFFERED OUTSIDE OF DEGREE PROGRAMS

Undergraduate: Anthropology; biology; business; business administration and management; computer and information sciences; developmental and child psychology; European languages and literatures; health and physical education/fitness; history; liberal arts, general studies, and humanities; music; political science; psychology; sociology

PIEDMONT COLLEGE

Demorest, Georgia

Office of Academic Affairs
www.piedmont.edu

Piedmont College, founded in 1897, is an independent, religious, comprehensive institution affiliated with the Congregational Christian Church. It is accredited by the Southern Association of Colleges and Schools. It first offered distance learning courses in 1994. In 1999–2000, it offered 20 courses at a distance. In fall 1999, there were 100 students enrolled in distance learning courses.

Course delivery sites Courses are delivered to your home, high schools, 1 off-campus center in Athens.

Media Courses are delivered via videoconferencing, computer software, computer conferencing, World Wide Web, e-mail. Students and teachers may meet in person or interact via videoconferencing, telephone, fax, e-mail, World Wide Web. The following equipment may be required: computer, modem, Internet access, e-mail.

Restrictions Programs are available to local area students. Enrollment is open to anyone.

Services Distance learners have access to library services, the campus computer network, e-mail services, academic advising, tutoring, career placement assistance, bookstore at a distance.

Credit-earning options Students may transfer credits from another institution or may earn credits through examinations, portfolio assessment, military training, business training.

Typical costs *Undergraduate:* Tuition of $342 per semester hour. *Graduate:* Tuition of $160 per semester hour. Costs may vary. Financial aid is available to distance learners.

Registration Students may register by mail, fax, telephone, e-mail, in person.

Contact Dr. James Mellichamp, Vice President of Academic Affairs, Piedmont College, PO Box 10, Demorest, GA 30535. *Telephone:* 706-776-0110. *Fax:* 706-776-2811. *E-mail:* jmellichamp@piedmont.edu.

DEGREES AND AWARDS

Distance programs offered do not lead to a degree or other formal award.

COURSE SUBJECT AREAS OFFERED OUTSIDE OF DEGREE PROGRAMS

Undergraduate: Asian languages and literatures; communications; economics; English composition; European languages and literatures; history; mathematics; sociology

See full description on page 676.

PIEDMONT TECHNICAL COLLEGE

Greenwood, South Carolina

Instructional Technology Division

www.piedmont.tec.sc.us/dl/

Piedmont Technical College, founded in 1966, is a state-supported, two-year college. It is accredited by the Southern Association of Colleges and Schools. It first offered distance learning courses in 1995. In 1999–2000, it offered 120 courses at a distance. In fall 1999, there were 1,000 students enrolled in distance learning courses.

Course delivery sites Courses are delivered to your home, your workplace, high schools, Lander University (Greenwood), 6 off-campus centers in Abbeville, Edgefield, Laurens, McCormick, Newberry, Saluda.

Media Courses are delivered via television, videotapes, videoconferencing, interactive television, World Wide Web. Students and teachers may meet in person or interact via videoconferencing, mail, telephone, fax, e-mail, interactive television, World Wide Web. The following equipment may be required: television, videocassette player, computer, modem, Internet access, e-mail.

Restrictions Programs are available nationwide. Enrollment is open to anyone.

Services Distance learners have access to library services, the campus computer network, e-mail services, academic advising, tutoring, career placement assistance, bookstore at a distance.

Credit-earning options Students may transfer credits from another institution or may earn credits through examinations.

Typical costs Tuition of $50 per credit hour plus mandatory fees of $15 per term for local area residents. Tuition of $70 per credit hour plus mandatory fees of $15 per term for in-state residents. Tuition of $85 per credit hour plus mandatory fees of $15 per term for out-of-state residents. Costs may vary. Financial aid is available to distance learners.

Registration Students may register by mail, fax, telephone, e-mail, World Wide Web, in person.

Contact Dr. Daniel D. Koenig, Assistant Vice President for Instructional Technology, Piedmont Technical College, PO Drawer 1467, 620 North

---

Emerald Road, Greenwood, SC 29648. *Telephone:* 864-941-8446. *Fax:* 864-941-8703. *E-mail:* koenig_d@piedmont.tec.sc.us.

DEGREES AND AWARDS

AA Liberal Arts

COURSE SUBJECT AREAS OFFERED OUTSIDE OF DEGREE PROGRAMS

Undergraduate: Abnormal psychology; algebra; American (U.S.) history; American literature; anatomy; art history and criticism; astronomy and astrophysics; biology; business administration and management; business law; calculus; chemistry; criminal justice; economics; electrical engineering; electronics; English composition; English literature; ethics; European history; foods and nutrition studies; horticulture; political science; psychology; public administration and services; sociology; Spanish language and literature; statistics

See full description on page 676.

PIERCE COLLEGE

Lakewood, Washington

Continuing Education

www.pierce.ctc.edu

Pierce College, founded in 1967, is a state-supported, two-year college. It is accredited by the Northwest Association of Schools and Colleges. It first offered distance learning courses in 1982. In 1999–2000, it offered 30 courses at a distance. In fall 1999, there were 150 students enrolled in distance learning courses.

Course delivery sites Courses are delivered to your home.

Media Courses are delivered via television, videotapes, audiotapes, World Wide Web, e-mail, print. Students and teachers may interact via mail, telephone, fax, e-mail, World Wide Web. The following equipment may be required: television, videocassette player, computer, Internet access.

Restrictions Programs are available worldwide. Enrollment is open to anyone.

Services Distance learners have access to academic advising, bookstore at a distance.

Credit-earning options Students may transfer credits from another institution.

Typical costs Tuition of $57.30 per credit hour for in-state residents. Tuition of $69.30 per credit hour for out-of-state residents. *Noncredit courses:* $258.50 per course. Costs may vary. Financial aid is available to distance learners.

Registration Students may register by mail, fax, telephone, in person.

Contact Martha Makaneole, Programs Assistant, Pierce College, 9401 Farwest Drive, South West, Lakewood, WA 98498. *Telephone:* 253-964-6244. *Fax:* 253-964-6299. *E-mail:* mmakaneo@pierce.etc.edu.

DEGREES AND AWARDS

AAS General Studies (some on-campus requirements)

COURSE SUBJECT AREAS OFFERED OUTSIDE OF DEGREE PROGRAMS

Undergraduate: Abnormal psychology; anthropology; biology; developmental and child psychology; earth science; English composition; English language and literature; English literature; ethics; French language and literature; geology; health and physical education/fitness; psychology

PIKES PEAK COMMUNITY COLLEGE

Colorado Springs, Colorado
Learning Technologies/Distance Education
www.ppcc.cccoes.edu

Pikes Peak Community College, founded in 1968, is a state-supported, two-year college. It is accredited by the North Central Association of Colleges and Schools. It first offered distance learning courses in 1978. In 1999–2000, it offered 90 courses at a distance. In fall 1999, there were 900 students enrolled in distance learning courses.

Course delivery sites Courses are delivered to your home, your workplace, military bases.

Media Courses are delivered via television, videotapes, videoconferencing, interactive television, World Wide Web, e-mail, print. Students and teachers may meet in person or interact via videoconferencing, mail, telephone, fax, e-mail, interactive television, World Wide Web. The following equipment may be required: television, computer, Internet access.

Restrictions Internet courses are available worldwide while ITV courses require access to one or more of Colorado Springs' cable companies. Enrollment is open to anyone.

Services Distance learners have access to library services, academic advising, tutoring at a distance.

Credit-earning options Students may transfer credits from another institution or may earn credits through examinations, portfolio assessment, military training, business training.

Typical costs Tuition of $56 per credit hour plus mandatory fees of $35 per course for in-state residents. Tuition of $266 per credit hour plus mandatory fees of $35 per course for out-of-state residents. Students who take distance classes only pay no fees. Some courses are subject to class fees. Financial aid is available to distance learners.

Registration Students may register by telephone, World Wide Web, in person.

Contact Julie Witherow, Director of Distance Education, Pikes Peak Community College, 5675 South Academy Boulevard, Colorado Springs, CO 80906-5498. *Telephone:* 719-540-7539. *Fax:* 719-540-7532. *E-mail:* witherow@ppcc.cccoes.edu.

DEGREES AND AWARDS

AAS Fire Science Technology (service area differs from that of the overall institution)

COURSE SUBJECT AREAS OFFERED OUTSIDE OF DEGREE PROGRAMS

Undergraduate: Accounting; administrative and secretarial services; business; business administration and management; chemistry; communications; computer and information sciences; conservation and natural resources; geology; history; hospitality services management; human resources management; library and information studies; mathematics; philosophy and religion; radio and television broadcasting; social psychology; sociology

Noncredit: Accounting; administrative and secretarial services; business; business administration and management; chemistry; communications; computer and information sciences; conservation and natural resources; geology; history; hospitality services management; human resources management; library and information studies; mathematics; philosophy and religion; radio and television broadcasting; social psychology; sociology

PITT COMMUNITY COLLEGE

Greenville, North Carolina
Distance Education Department
www.pitt.cc.nc.us

Pitt Community College, founded in 1961, is a state and locally supported, two-year college. It is accredited by the Southern Association of Colleges and Schools. It first offered distance learning courses in 1995. In 1999–2000, it offered 95 courses at a distance. In fall 1999, there were 600 students enrolled in distance learning courses.

Course delivery sites Courses are delivered to your home, your workplace, military bases, Brunswick Community College (Supply), Edgecombe Community College (Tarboro), Elizabeth City State University (Elizabeth City), Fayetteville State University (Fayetteville), Halifax Community College (Weldon), James Sprunt Community College (Kenansville), Southeastern Community College (Whiteville), Southwestern Community College (Sylva).

Media Courses are delivered via television, videotapes, videoconferencing, interactive television, computer software, CD-ROM, computer conferencing, World Wide Web, e-mail, print. Students and teachers may meet in person or interact via videoconferencing, audioconferencing, mail, telephone, fax, e-mail, interactive television, World Wide Web. The following equipment may be required: television, videocassette player, computer, modem, Internet access, e-mail.

Restrictions Programs are available nationwide. Enrollment is open to anyone.

Services Distance learners have access to library services, the campus computer network, e-mail services, academic advising, career placement assistance, bookstore at a distance.

Credit-earning options Students may transfer credits from another institution or may earn credits through examinations, portfolio assessment.

Typical costs Tuition of $26.75 per credit for in-state residents. Tuition of $169.75 per credit for out-of-state residents. There is a mandatory fee of $11.50 per 1-5 credits. Costs may vary. Financial aid is available to distance learners.

Registration Students may register by mail, fax, telephone, e-mail, World Wide Web, in person.

Contact Elaine Seeman, Director of Distance Learning, Pitt Community College. *Telephone:* 252-321-4608. *Fax:* 252-321-4401. *E-mail:* eseeman@pcc.pitt.cc.nc.us.

DEGREES AND AWARDS

AA Business Administration
AAS Health Information Technology, Information Systems

COURSE SUBJECT AREAS OFFERED OUTSIDE OF DEGREE PROGRAMS

Undergraduate: Accounting; administrative and secretarial services; advertising; American literature; biochemistry; biology; business; business administration and management; business communications; business law; computer and information sciences; computer programming; corrections; criminal justice; database management; economics; English composition; health professions and related sciences; information sciences and systems; international business; logic; marketing; sociology; substance abuse counseling; technical writing

Noncredit: Business; business administration and management; business communications; computer and information sciences; computer programming; continuing education; creative writing; economics; finance; information sciences and systems

See full description on page 676.

PLATTSBURGH STATE UNIVERSITY OF NEW YORK

Plattsburgh, New York

Distance Learning Office

www.plattsburgh.edu

Plattsburgh State University of New York, founded in 1889, is a state-supported, comprehensive institution. It is accredited by the Middle States Association of Colleges and Schools. It first offered distance learning courses in 1992. In 1999–2000, it offered 21 courses at a distance. In fall 1999, there were 210 students enrolled in distance learning courses.

Course delivery sites Courses are delivered to your home, high schools, Adirondack Community College (Queensbury), Cayuga County Community College (Auburn), Fulton-Montgomery Community College (Johnstown), Jefferson Community College (Watertown), State University of New York College at Potsdam (Potsdam).

Media Courses are delivered via videotapes, videoconferencing, World Wide Web, e-mail. Students and teachers may interact via videoconferencing, mail, telephone, fax, e-mail, World Wide Web.

Restrictions Programs are available to in-state students only. Enrollment is restricted to individuals meeting certain criteria.

Services Distance learners have access to library services, e-mail services, academic advising, tutoring, bookstore at a distance.

Credit-earning options Students may transfer credits from another institution or may earn credits through examinations.

Typical costs *Undergraduate:* Tuition of $137 per credit hour plus mandatory fees of $8.85 per credit hour for in-state residents. Tuition of $346 per credit hour plus mandatory fees of $8.85 per credit hour for out-of-state residents. *Graduate:* Tuition of $213 per credit hour plus mandatory fees of $8.85 per credit hour for in-state residents. Tuition of $351 per credit hour plus mandatory fees of $8.85 per credit hour for out-of-state residents. Financial aid is available to distance learners.

Registration Students may register by mail, telephone, in person.

Contact Mrs. Cheryl Marshall, Coordinator, Distance Learning Office, Plattsburgh State University of New York, 101 Broad Street, Sibley Hall 418 A, Plattsburgh, NY 12901. *Telephone:* 518-564-4234. *Fax:* 518-564-4236. *E-mail:* cheryl.marshall@plattsburgh.edu.

DEGREES AND AWARDS

BS Nursing

COURSE SUBJECT AREAS OFFERED OUTSIDE OF DEGREE PROGRAMS

Undergraduate: Nursing
Graduate: Education administration

PORTLAND COMMUNITY COLLEGE

Portland, Oregon

Distance Learning Department

www.distance.pcc.edu

Portland Community College, founded in 1961, is a state and locally supported, two-year college. It is accredited by the Northwest Association of Schools and Colleges. It first offered distance learning courses in 1981. In 1999–2000, it offered 200 courses at a distance. In fall 1999, there were 3,200 students enrolled in distance learning courses.

Course delivery sites Courses are delivered to your home, your workplace.

Media Courses are delivered via television, videotapes, videoconferencing, interactive television, audiotapes, CD-ROM, computer conferencing, World Wide Web, e-mail. Students and teachers may meet in person or interact via videoconferencing, audioconferencing, mail, telephone, fax, e-mail, interactive television, World Wide Web. The following equipment may be required: television, videocassette player, computer, modem, Internet access, e-mail.

Restrictions Programs are available to in-state students only. Enrollment is restricted to individuals meeting certain criteria.

Services Distance learners have access to library services, academic advising, bookstore at a distance.

Credit-earning options Students may transfer credits from another institution or may earn credits through examinations, portfolio assessment, military training, business training.

Typical costs Tuition of $38 per credit for in-state residents. Tuition of $140 per credit for out-of-state residents. There is a $16 mandatory fee per class. *Noncredit courses:* $100 per course. Financial aid is available to distance learners.

Registration Students may register by mail, fax, telephone, e-mail, World Wide Web, in person.

Contact Barbara Baker, Distance Learning Support, Portland Community College. *Telephone:* 503-977-4730. *Fax:* 503-977-4858. *E-mail:* bbaker@pcc.edu.

DEGREES AND AWARDS

Undergraduate Certificate(s) Medical Assisting (service area differs from that of the overall institution; some on-campus requirements)
AAOT General Studies

COURSE SUBJECT AREAS OFFERED OUTSIDE OF DEGREE PROGRAMS

Undergraduate: Abnormal psychology; accounting; algebra; American (U.S.) history; American literature; astronomy and astrophysics; biology; business; business administration and management; business communications; business law; chemistry; computer and information sciences; computer programming; creative writing; developmental and child psychology; earth science; ecology; economics; English composition; English language and literature; fine arts; fire science; geography; health and physical education/fitness; history; law and legal studies; liberal arts, general studies, and humanities; marketing; mathematics; music; oceanography; philosophy and religion; political science; psychology; real estate; sociology; statistics

Noncredit: Administrative and secretarial services; business administration and management; health professions and related sciences; human resources management

PORTLAND STATE UNIVERSITY

Portland, Oregon

Distance Learning

extended.pdx.edu

Portland State University, founded in 1946, is a state-supported university. It is accredited by the Northwest Association of Schools and Colleges. It first offered distance learning courses in 1907. In 1999–2000, it offered 100 courses at a distance. In fall 1999, there were 3,500 students enrolled in distance learning courses.

Course delivery sites Courses are delivered to your home, your workplace, military bases, high schools.

Media Courses are delivered via television, videotapes, videoconferencing, interactive television, CD-ROM, computer conferencing, World Wide Web, e-mail, print. Students and teachers may interact via videoconferencing, mail, telephone, fax, e-mail, interactive television, World Wide Web. The following equipment may be required: television, videocassette player, computer, modem, Internet access, e-mail.

Restrictions Graduate programs are limited to within Oregon, while Independent Study courses are available worldwide. Enrollment is open to anyone.

Services Distance learners have access to library services, bookstore at a distance.

Credit-earning options Students may earn credits through examinations.

Typical costs *Undergraduate:* Tuition of $75 per quarter credit plus mandatory fees of $15 per unit. *Graduate:* Tuition of $250 per quarter credit. *Noncredit courses:* $150 per course. Costs may vary. Financial aid is available to distance learners.

Registration Students may register by mail, fax, telephone, e-mail, World Wide Web, in person.

Contact Thomas Luba, Director of Distance Learning, Portland State University. *Telephone:* 800-547-8887. *Fax:* 503-725-4840. *E-mail:* lubat@pdx.edu.

DEGREES AND AWARDS

MBA Business Administration (service area differs from that of the overall institution; some on-campus requirements)

COURSE SUBJECT AREAS OFFERED OUTSIDE OF DEGREE PROGRAMS

Undergraduate: Accounting; algebra; anthropology; area, ethnic, and cultural studies; biology; business; business administration and management; calculus; creative writing; developmental and child psychology; economics; English composition; English language and literature; European languages and literatures; fine arts; geography; geology; history; liberal arts, general studies, and humanities; mathematics; philosophy and religion; sociology; statistics
Graduate: Business

PRAIRIE BIBLE COLLEGE

Three Hills, Alberta, Canada
Prairie Distance Education
www.pbi.ab.ca

Prairie Bible College, founded in 1922, is an independent, religious, four-year college. It is accredited by the Accrediting Association of Bible Colleges. It first offered distance learning courses in 1950. In 1999–2000, it offered 90 courses at a distance. In fall 1999, there were 625 students enrolled in distance learning courses.

Course delivery sites Courses are delivered to your home, your workplace.

Media Courses are delivered via videotapes, audiotapes, computer software, CD-ROM, computer conferencing, World Wide Web, e-mail, print. Students and teachers may meet in person or interact via mail, telephone, fax, e-mail, World Wide Web. The following equipment may be required: computer, Internet access.

Restrictions Programs are available worldwide. Enrollment is open to anyone.

Services Distance learners have access to library services, e-mail services, academic advising, tutoring, bookstore at a distance.

Credit-earning options Students may transfer credits from another institution or may earn credits through examinations, portfolio assessment.

Typical costs *Undergraduate:* Tuition of $119 per credit hour. *Graduate:* Tuition of $139 per credit hour.

Registration Students may register by mail, fax, telephone, e-mail, World Wide Web, in person.

Contact Dr. Arnold L. Stauffer, Associate Dean, Prairie Bible College, Box 4000, Prairie Distance Education, Three Hills, AB T0M 2N0 Canada. *Telephone:* 403-443-3036. *Fax:* 403-443-3099. *E-mail:* distance.ed@pbi.ab.ca.

DEGREES AND AWARDS

Undergraduate Certificate(s) Bible and Theology (certain restrictions apply)
AARS Bible and Theology (certain restrictions apply)
BMin Bible and Theology (certain restrictions apply), Ministry (certain restrictions apply)
Graduate Certificate(s) Bible and Theology (certain restrictions apply)

COURSE SUBJECT AREAS OFFERED OUTSIDE OF DEGREE PROGRAMS

Undergraduate: Anthropology; Bible studies; counseling psychology; English composition; ethics; European history; fine arts; Greek language and literature; history; music; philosophy and religion; religious studies; teacher education; theological studies
Graduate: American (U.S.) history; anthropology; Bible studies; business administration and management; Greek language and literature; history; religious studies; theological studies

PRAIRIE STATE COLLEGE

Chicago Heights, Illinois
Learning Resources Center
www.prairie.cc.il.us

Prairie State College, founded in 1958, is a state and locally supported, two-year college. It is accredited by the North Central Association of Colleges and Schools. It first offered distance learning courses in 1981. In 1999–2000, it offered 25 courses at a distance. In fall 1999, there were 350 students enrolled in distance learning courses.

Course delivery sites Courses are delivered to your home, high schools, 1 off-campus center in Matteson.

Media Courses are delivered via television, videotapes, videoconferencing, computer conferencing, World Wide Web. Students and teachers may interact via videoconferencing, mail, telephone, fax, e-mail, World Wide Web. The following equipment may be required: television, videocassette player, computer, modem, Internet access, e-mail.

Restrictions Programs are available to local area students. Enrollment is open to anyone.

Services Distance learners have access to library services at a distance.

Credit-earning options Students may transfer credits from another institution or may earn credits through examinations, portfolio assessment, military training.

Typical costs Tuition of $51 per credit hour plus mandatory fees of $9 per credit hour for local area residents. Tuition of $163 per credit hour plus mandatory fees of $9 per credit hour for in-state residents. Tuition of $198 per credit hour plus mandatory fees of $9 per credit hour for out-of-state residents. Costs may vary. Financial aid is available to distance learners.

Registration Students may register by mail, fax, telephone, in person.

Contact Carol Cleator, Director of Admissions, Prairie State College, 202 South Halsted Street, Chicago Heights, IL 60411. *Telephone:* 708-709-3513. *Fax:* 708-755-2587. *E-mail:* ccleator@prairie.cc.il.us.

DEGREES AND AWARDS

Distance programs offered do not lead to a degree or other formal award.

COURSE SUBJECT AREAS OFFERED OUTSIDE OF DEGREE PROGRAMS

Undergraduate: Accounting; astronomy and astrophysics; business administration and management; economics; English composition; English language and literature; health professions and related sciences; history; interior design; political science; psychology; sociology

PRAIRIE VIEW A&M UNIVERSITY

Prairie View, Texas
College of Nursing
www.pvamu.edu

Prairie View A&M University, founded in 1878, is a state-supported, comprehensive institution. It is accredited by the Southern Association of Colleges and Schools. In 1999–2000, it offered 6 courses at a distance. In fall 1999, there were 26 students enrolled in distance learning courses.
Course delivery sites Courses are delivered to The University Center of North Harris Montgomery Community College District (The Woodlands).
Media Courses are delivered via videoconferencing. Students and teachers may meet in person or interact via videoconferencing, fax, e-mail.
Restrictions Programs are available to local area students. Enrollment is restricted to individuals meeting certain criteria.
Services Distance learners have access to library services, e-mail services at a distance.
Typical costs Undergraduate in-state tuition is $120 for 3 semester hours, out-of-state tuition is $762. Mandatory fees are $296 for 3 semester hours. Costs may vary. Financial aid is available to distance learners.
Registration Students may register by in person.
Contact Dr. Lillian Bernard, Interim Dean, College of Nursing, Prairie View A&M University, 6436 Fannin, Houston, TX 77030. *Telephone:* 713-797-7009. *Fax:* 713-797-7013. *E-mail:* lillian_bernard@pvamu.edu.

DEGREES AND AWARDS

BS Nursing (certain restrictions apply; some on-campus requirements)

PRESENTATION COLLEGE

Aberdeen, South Dakota
www.presentation.edu

Presentation College, founded in 1951, is an independent, religious, four-year college. It is accredited by the North Central Association of Colleges and Schools.
Course delivery sites Courses are delivered to your home, high schools, 1 off-campus center in Eagle Bluff.
Media Courses are delivered via videoconferencing, computer conferencing, World Wide Web, e-mail. Students and teachers may meet in person or interact via videoconferencing, mail, telephone, fax, e-mail.
Restrictions Programs are available to in-state students only. Enrollment is open to anyone.
Services Distance learners have access to library services, academic advising, tutoring, bookstore at a distance.
Credit-earning options Students may transfer credits from another institution or may earn credits through examinations, portfolio assessment.
Typical costs Financial aid is available to distance learners.
Registration Students may register by mail, in person.
Contact Registrar's Office, Presentation College, 1500 North Main Street, Aberdeen, SD 57401. *Telephone:* 605-229-8424. *Fax:* 605-229-8332.

DEGREES AND AWARDS

Distance programs offered do not lead to a degree or other formal award.

COURSE SUBJECT AREAS OFFERED OUTSIDE OF DEGREE PROGRAMS

Undergraduate: Algebra; English composition; English literature; foods and nutrition studies; psychology; sign language; sociology; statistics

PRINCE GEORGE'S COMMUNITY COLLEGE

Largo, Maryland
Distance Learning
pgweb.pg.cc.md.us/pgweb/pgdocs/distlern/index.htm

Prince George's Community College, founded in 1958, is a county-supported, two-year college. It is accredited by the Middle States Association of Colleges and Schools. It first offered distance learning courses in 1976. In 1999–2000, it offered 50 courses at a distance. In fall 1999, there were 1,000 students enrolled in distance learning courses.
Course delivery sites Courses are delivered to your home, your workplace, military bases, high schools.
Media Courses are delivered via television, videotapes, videoconferencing, interactive television, audiotapes, computer software, CD-ROM, computer conferencing, World Wide Web, e-mail, print. Students and teachers may meet in person or interact via videoconferencing, mail, telephone, fax, e-mail, interactive television, World Wide Web. The following equipment may be required: television, videocassette player, computer, modem, Internet access, e-mail.
Restrictions Telecourses are generally available in the local area only, but most other courses are available worldwide. Enrollment is open to anyone.
Services Distance learners have access to the campus computer network, e-mail services, academic advising, career placement assistance, bookstore at a distance.
Credit-earning options Students may transfer credits from another institution or may earn credits through examinations, portfolio assessment.
Typical costs Tuition of $76 per credit plus mandatory fees of $20 per hour for local area residents. Tuition of $140 per credit plus mandatory fees of $20 per hour for in-state residents. Tuition of $222 per credit plus mandatory fees of $20 per hour for out-of-state residents. Students pay a $20 registration fee and a $15, $20 or $25 instructional service fee (per credit) based upon course level. Costs may vary. Financial aid is available to distance learners.
Registration Students may register by telephone, in person.
Contact Chris Barbee, Program Assistant, Prince George's Community College, 301 Largo Road, K212, Largo, MD 20774. *Telephone:* 301-322-0781. *Fax:* 301-386-7502. *E-mail:* barbeecx@pg.cc.md.us.

DEGREES AND AWARDS

Undergraduate Certificate(s) General Management (service area differs from that of the overall institution; some on-campus requirements)
AA Business Management (service area differs from that of the overall institution; some on-campus requirements), General Studies (service area differs from that of the overall institution; some on-campus requirements)

COURSE SUBJECT AREAS OFFERED OUTSIDE OF DEGREE PROGRAMS

Undergraduate: Accounting; anthropology; area, ethnic, and cultural studies; astronomy and astrophysics; biology; business administration and management; computer and information sciences; criminal justice; developmental and child psychology; economics; English composition; English language and literature; geology; health and physical education/fitness;

history; human resources management; liberal arts, general studies, and humanities; marketing; mathematics; philosophy and religion; political science; radio and television broadcasting; social psychology; sociology
Noncredit: Business; business administration and management; computer and information sciences; continuing education; developmental and child psychology; economics; English composition; English language and literature; health and physical education/fitness; history; insurance; marketing; mathematics; philosophy and religion; political science; real estate; social psychology; sociology; substance abuse counseling; teacher education

PRINCETON THEOLOGICAL SEMINARY

Princeton, New Jersey
Center of Continuing Education
www.ptsem.edu/ce

Princeton Theological Seminary, founded in 1812, is an independent, religious, graduate institution. It is accredited by the Association of Theological Schools in the United States and Canada, Middle States Association of Colleges and Schools. It first offered distance learning courses in 1998. In 1999–2000, it offered 3 courses at a distance. In fall 1999, there were 10 students enrolled in distance learning courses.
Course delivery sites Courses are delivered to your home, your workplace.
Media Courses are delivered via computer conferencing, World Wide Web, e-mail, print. Students and teachers may interact via e-mail, World Wide Web. The following equipment may be required: computer, modem, Internet access, e-mail.
Restrictions Programs are available worldwide. Enrollment is restricted to individuals meeting certain criteria.
Services Distance learners have access to library services, e-mail services at a distance.
Typical costs Contact school for information. *Noncredit courses:* $100 per course.
Registration Students may register by mail, fax, telephone, in person.
Contact David H. Wall, Program Coordinator, Princeton Theological Seminary, Center of Continuing Education, 20 Library Place, Princeton, NJ 08540. *Telephone:* 609-497-7990. *Fax:* 609-497-0709. *E-mail:* david.wall@ptsem.edu.

DEGREES AND AWARDS

Distance programs offered do not lead to a degree or other formal award.

COURSE SUBJECT AREAS OFFERED OUTSIDE OF DEGREE PROGRAMS

Noncredit: Bible studies; religious studies; theological studies

PROFESSIONAL DEVELOPMENT EUROPE LIMITED

Chertsey, United Kingdom
www.mba-degree.com

Professional Development Europe Limited is a proprietary, graduate institution. In 1999–2000, it offered 2 courses at a distance.
Course delivery sites Courses are delivered to your home.
Media Courses are delivered via computer software, CD-ROM, e-mail, print. Students and teachers may interact via telephone, fax, e-mail. The following equipment may be required: computer, modem, Internet access, e-mail.
Restrictions Programs are available worldwide. Enrollment is restricted to individuals meeting certain criteria.

Services Distance learners have access to academic advising, tutoring, bookstore at a distance.
Credit-earning options Students may transfer credits from another institution.
Typical costs Tuition of $800 per unit.
Registration Students may register by e-mail.
Contact Alan Cain, Director, Management Education, Professional Development Europe Limited, Flaxman House, Gogmore Lane, Chertsey KT16 9JS. *Telephone:* 193-2 577-087. *Fax:* 193-2 577-089. *E-mail:* enquiries@pde.org.uk.

DEGREES AND AWARDS

MBA Business Administration (certain restrictions apply; some on-campus requirements), Technology Management (certain restrictions apply; some on-campus requirements)
See full description on page 626.

PROVIDENCE COLLEGE AND THEOLOGICAL SEMINARY

Otterburne, Manitoba, Canada
Department of Continuing Education
www.providence.mb.ca

Providence College and Theological Seminary, founded in 1925, is an independent, religious, comprehensive institution. It is accredited by the Accrediting Association of Bible Colleges, Association of Theological Schools in the United States and Canada.
Course delivery sites Courses are delivered to your home, off-campus center(s) in Winnipeg, Calgary (AB), Moncton (NB).
Media Courses are delivered via videotapes, audiotapes, computer software, print. Students and teachers may meet in person or interact via mail, telephone, fax, e-mail, World Wide Web.
Restrictions Programs are available nationwide. Enrollment is open to anyone.
Services Distance learners have access to library services, the campus computer network, academic advising, tutoring, career placement assistance, bookstore at a distance.
Credit-earning options Students may transfer credits from another institution or may earn credits through examinations.
Typical costs *Undergraduate:* Tuition of $157 per credit hour. *Graduate:* Tuition of $157 per credit hour. Financial aid is available to distance learners.
Registration Students may register by mail, fax, telephone, e-mail, in person.
Contact Brian D. Hamilton, Director of Continuing Education, Providence College and Theological Seminary, Otterburne, MB R0A 1G0 Canada. *Telephone:* 204-433-7488. *Fax:* 204-433-7158. *E-mail:* bhamilton@providence.mb.ca.

DEGREES AND AWARDS

BA Aviation (some on-campus requirements), Business Administration (some on-campus requirements), Educational Studies (some on-campus requirements), Humanities (some on-campus requirements), Intercultural Studies (some on-campus requirements), Music (some on-campus requirements), Social Science (some on-campus requirements), Theology (some on-campus requirements)
BFA Drama (some on-campus requirements), Music (some on-campus requirements), Performing Arts (some on-campus requirements)
MA Counseling and Psychology (some on-campus requirements), Educational Ministries (some on-campus requirements), Global Christian Studies (some on-campus requirements), Research (some on-campus

requirements), Student Development (some on-campus requirements), TESOL/TTESOL (some on-campus requirements), Worship (some on-campus requirements)
MDiv Divinity (some on-campus requirements)
DMin Ministry Studies (some on-campus requirements)

COURSE SUBJECT AREAS OFFERED OUTSIDE OF DEGREE PROGRAMS

Undergraduate: Adult education; Bible studies; drama and theater; English as a second language (ESL); family and marriage counseling; music; theological studies
Graduate: Abnormal psychology; adult education; Bible studies; counseling psychology; English as a second language (ESL); family and marriage counseling; theological studies
Noncredit: Abnormal psychology; adult education; Bible studies; counseling psychology; drama and theater; English as a second language (ESL); family and marriage counseling; music; theological studies

PUEBLO COMMUNITY COLLEGE

Pueblo, Colorado
Educational Technology and Telecommunications
www.pcc.cccoes.edu

Pueblo Community College, founded in 1933, is a state-supported, two-year college. It is accredited by the North Central Association of Colleges and Schools. It first offered distance learning courses in 1993. In 1999–2000, it offered 90 courses at a distance. In fall 1999, there were 375 students enrolled in distance learning courses.
Course delivery sites Courses are delivered to your home, high schools, 2 off-campus centers in Canon City, Cortez.
Media Courses are delivered via television, videotapes, videoconferencing, interactive television, audiotapes, World Wide Web, e-mail. Students and teachers may meet in person or interact via videoconferencing, mail, telephone, fax, e-mail, interactive television, World Wide Web. The following equipment may be required: television, videocassette player, computer, modem, Internet access, e-mail.
Restrictions Programs are available to in-state students only. Enrollment is open to anyone.
Services Distance learners have access to library services, e-mail services, academic advising, tutoring, bookstore at a distance.
Credit-earning options Students may transfer credits from another institution or may earn credits through examinations, portfolio assessment, military training, business training.
Typical costs Tuition of $73.15 per credit plus mandatory fees of $7.85 per credit for in-state residents. Tuition of $283.65 per credit plus mandatory fees of $7.85 per credit for out-of-state residents. Costs may vary. Financial aid is available to distance learners.
Registration Students may register by mail, fax, telephone, in person.
Contact Paula McPheeters, Distance Learning Specialist, Pueblo Community College, Distance Learning Office, 900 West Orman Avenue, Pueblo, CO 81004-1499. *Telephone:* 719-549-3343. *Fax:* 719-549-3453. *E-mail:* mcpheeters@pcc.cccoes.edu.

DEGREES AND AWARDS

Distance programs offered do not lead to a degree or other formal award.

COURSE SUBJECT AREAS OFFERED OUTSIDE OF DEGREE PROGRAMS

Undergraduate: Accounting; astronomy and astrophysics; biological and life sciences; business administration and management; chemistry; computer and information sciences; economics; English composition; English language and literature; European languages and literatures; foods and nutrition studies; geology; journalism; law and legal studies; mathematics; psychology; sociology; visual and performing arts

PURDUE UNIVERSITY

West Lafayette, Indiana
Distributed Learning Services
www.cll.purdue.edu/dls

Purdue University, founded in 1869, is a state-supported university. It is accredited by the North Central Association of Colleges and Schools. It first offered distance learning courses in 1965. In 1999–2000, it offered 84 courses at a distance. In fall 1999, there were 1,091 students enrolled in distance learning courses.
Course delivery sites Courses are delivered to your home, your workplace, high schools, 300 off-campus centers.
Media Courses are delivered via television, videotapes, videoconferencing, interactive television, computer software, World Wide Web, print. Students and teachers may meet in person or interact via videoconferencing, audioconferencing, mail, telephone, fax, e-mail, interactive television, World Wide Web. The following equipment may be required: television, videocassette player, computer, modem, Internet access, e-mail.
Restrictions Programs are available worldwide. Enrollment is restricted to individuals meeting certain criteria.
Services Distance learners have access to library services, the campus computer network, e-mail services, academic advising, career placement assistance at a distance.
Credit-earning options Students may transfer credits from another institution.
Typical costs Fees vary depending upon which school the student is enrolled in. Please contact the individual schools for information. Costs may vary.
Registration Students may register by mail, World Wide Web, in person.
Contact Joetta Burrous, Director, Purdue University, Distributed Learning Services, 1586 Stewart Center, Room 117, West Lafayette, IN 47907-1586. *Telephone:* 800-359-2968. *Fax:* 765-496-6384. *E-mail:* jburrous@purdue.edu.

DEGREES AND AWARDS

Undergraduate Certificate(s) Digital Signal Processing, Pharmacy
AD Veterinary Technology
EMBA Agribusiness Management
EMS Business
MS Industrial Engineering
MSCE Civil Engineering
MSE Engineering
MSEE Electrical and Computer Engineering
MSME Mechanical Engineering

COURSE SUBJECT AREAS OFFERED OUTSIDE OF DEGREE PROGRAMS

Undergraduate: Health professions and related sciences; hospitality services management; veterinary science
Graduate: Business administration and management; engineering; visual and performing arts
Noncredit: Agriculture; engineering; pharmacy
See full descriptions on pages 540 and 628.

PURDUE UNIVERSITY

West Lafayette, Indiana

Krannert Executive Education Programs
www2.mgmt.purdue.edu

Purdue University, founded in 1869, is a state-supported university. It is accredited by the North Central Association of Colleges and Schools. In 1999–2000, it offered 28 courses at a distance. In fall 1999, there were 243 students enrolled in distance learning courses.

Course delivery sites Courses are delivered to your home, your workplace, Budapest University of Economic Sciences (Budapest, Hungary), Tias Business School, Tilburg University (Tilburg, Netherlands).

Media Courses are delivered via videotapes, videoconferencing, audiotapes, computer software, CD-ROM, computer conferencing, World Wide Web, e-mail, print. Students and teachers may meet in person or interact via videoconferencing, mail, telephone, fax, e-mail, World Wide Web. The following equipment may be required: computer, modem, Internet access, e-mail.

Restrictions Programs are available worldwide. Enrollment is open to anyone.

Services Distance learners have access to library services, the campus computer network, e-mail services, academic advising, tutoring at a distance.

Typical costs Tuition of $14,000 per course. Financial aid is available to distance learners.

Registration Students may register by mail, fax, telephone, e-mail, World Wide Web, in person.

Contact Erika Steuterman, Associate Director, Purdue University, 1310 Krannert Center, Suite 208, West Lafayette, IN 47907-1310. *Telephone:* 765-494-7700. *Fax:* 765-494-0862. *E-mail:* keepinfo@mgmt.purdue.edu.

DEGREES AND AWARDS

MSM General Management (certain restrictions apply; some on-campus requirements)

See full descriptions on pages 540 and 630.

PURDUE UNIVERSITY NORTH CENTRAL

Westville, Indiana

Math/Physics
www.purduenc.edu

Purdue University North Central, founded in 1967, is a state-supported, comprehensive institution. It is accredited by the North Central Association of Colleges and Schools. In 1999–2000, it offered 1 course at a distance. In fall 1999, there were 5 students enrolled in distance learning courses.

Course delivery sites Courses are delivered to your home.

Media Courses are delivered via computer software, World Wide Web, e-mail. Students and teachers may meet in person or interact via mail, e-mail, World Wide Web. The following equipment may be required: computer, modem, Internet access, e-mail.

Restrictions Programs are available nationwide. Enrollment is restricted to individuals meeting certain criteria.

Services Distance learners have access to library services, the campus computer network, e-mail services, academic advising, tutoring, career placement assistance, bookstore at a distance.

Typical costs Tuition of $135 per credit hour. Costs may vary. Financial aid is available to distance learners.

Registration Students may register by mail, fax, telephone, e-mail, World Wide Web, in person.

Contact Joyce E. Stumpe, Director, Learning Center, Purdue University North Central, 1401 South US 421, Westville, IN 46391. *Telephone:* 219-785-5439. *Fax:* 219-785-5470. *E-mail:* jes@purduenc.edu.

DEGREES AND AWARDS

Distance programs offered do not lead to a degree or other formal award.

COURSE SUBJECT AREAS OFFERED OUTSIDE OF DEGREE PROGRAMS

Undergraduate: Statistics
See full description on page 540.

QUEEN'S UNIVERSITY AT KINGSTON

Kingston, Ontario, Canada

Continuing and Distance Studies
www.queensu.ca/cds

Queen's University at Kingston, founded in 1841, is a province-supported university. It is accredited by the Association of Theological Schools in the United States and Canada. It first offered distance learning courses in 1889. In 1999–2000, it offered 60 courses at a distance. In fall 1999, there were 2,548 students enrolled in distance learning courses.

Course delivery sites Courses are delivered to your home.

Media Courses are delivered via videotapes, audiotapes, computer software, CD-ROM, computer conferencing, World Wide Web, e-mail, print. Students and teachers may meet in person or interact via mail, telephone, fax, e-mail, World Wide Web. The following equipment may be required: computer, Internet access.

Restrictions Programs are available worldwide. Enrollment is restricted to individuals meeting certain criteria.

Services Distance learners have access to library services, the campus computer network, e-mail services, academic advising, tutoring, career placement assistance, bookstore at a distance.

Credit-earning options Students may transfer credits from another institution.

Typical costs Canadian undergraduates pay $794 per full course, international undergraduates pay $2060 per full course. Financial aid is available to distance learners.

Registration Students may register by mail, fax, e-mail, World Wide Web, in person.

Contact Reception, Queen's University at Kingston, Continuing and Distance Studies, F1 Mackintosh-Corry Hall, Kingston, ON K7L 3N6 Canada. *Telephone:* 613-533-2471. *Fax:* 613-533-6805. *E-mail:* cds@post.queensu.ca.

DEGREES AND AWARDS

BA English, German, History, Political Science, Psychology, Women's Studies

COURSE SUBJECT AREAS OFFERED OUTSIDE OF DEGREE PROGRAMS

Undergraduate: Biological and life sciences; drama and theater; economics; English composition; English language and literature; French language and literature; geography; German language and literature; history; microbiology; philosophy and religion; political science; psychology; religious studies; sociology; Spanish language and literature; statistics; women's studies

QUEST COLLEGE

Davenport, Iowa

Quest College Online
questcollege.com/online

Quest College, founded in 1937, is a proprietary, two-year college. It is accredited by the Accrediting Council for Independent Colleges and Schools, North Central Association of Colleges and Schools.

Course delivery sites Courses are delivered to your home, your workplace, military bases, high schools.

Media Courses are delivered via CD-ROM, World Wide Web. Students and teachers may interact via audioconferencing, telephone, e-mail, World Wide Web. The following equipment may be required: computer, modem, Internet access, e-mail.

Restrictions Programs are available worldwide. Enrollment is restricted to individuals meeting certain criteria.

Services Distance learners have access to library services, academic advising, career placement assistance, bookstore at a distance.

Credit-earning options Students may transfer credits from another institution or may earn credits through examinations, portfolio assessment, military training, business training.

Typical costs Tuition of $3000 per course. Financial aid is available to distance learners.

Registration Students may register by mail, fax, telephone, e-mail, World Wide Web, in person.

Contact Jeffrey Gettleman, Quest College, 1801 East Kimberly Road, Suite 2, Davenport, IA 52807. *Telephone:* 800-817-8272 Ext. 145. *E-mail:* jgettleman@questcollege.com.

DEGREES AND AWARDS

Undergraduate Certificate(s) Microsoft Database Administrator, Microsoft Solution Developer, Microsoft Systems Engineer

See full description on page 632.

QUINCY COLLEGE

Quincy, Massachusetts

Continuing Education

Quincy College, founded in 1958, is a city-supported, two-year college. It is accredited by the New England Association of Schools and Colleges. It first offered distance learning courses in 1995.

Course delivery sites Courses are delivered to your home.

Media Courses are delivered via television, print.

Restrictions Programs are available to in-state students only. Enrollment is open to anyone.

Services Distance learners have access to academic advising, career placement assistance at a distance.

Credit-earning options Students may transfer credits from another institution or may earn credits through examinations, portfolio assessment, military training, business training.

Typical costs Tuition of $96 per unit. Financial aid is available to distance learners.

Registration Students may register by mail, fax, telephone, in person.

Contact Bob Baker, Executive Director, Quincy College, Institutional Advancement, 34 Coddington Street, Quincy, MA 02169. *Telephone:* 617-984-1662. *Fax:* 617-984-1669.

DEGREES AND AWARDS

Distance programs offered do not lead to a degree or other formal award.

COURSE SUBJECT AREAS OFFERED OUTSIDE OF DEGREE PROGRAMS

Undergraduate: Area, ethnic, and cultural studies; biological and life sciences; biology; business; business administration and management; communications; developmental and child psychology; journalism; liberal arts, general studies, and humanities; philosophy and religion; psychology; social psychology; social sciences; sociology

RANDOLPH COMMUNITY COLLEGE

Asheboro, North Carolina

Virtual Campus
www.virtualrandolph.org

Randolph Community College, founded in 1962, is a state-supported, two-year college. It is accredited by the Southern Association of Colleges and Schools. It first offered distance learning courses in 1987. In 1999–2000, it offered 26 courses at a distance. In fall 1999, there were 180 students enrolled in distance learning courses.

Course delivery sites Courses are delivered to your home.

Media Courses are delivered via television, videotapes, computer software, CD-ROM, World Wide Web, e-mail, print. Students and teachers may meet in person or interact via mail, telephone, fax, e-mail, World Wide Web. The following equipment may be required: television, videocassette player, computer, Internet access, e-mail.

Restrictions Programs are available to local area students. Enrollment is open to anyone.

Services Distance learners have access to library services, e-mail services, academic advising, career placement assistance, bookstore at a distance.

Credit-earning options Students may transfer credits from another institution or may earn credits through examinations.

Typical costs Tuition of $27 per credit hour plus mandatory fees of $1.25 per credit hour for in-state residents. Tuition of $168 per credit hour plus mandatory fees of $1.25 per credit hour for out-of-state residents. *Noncredit courses:* $55 per course. Costs may vary. Financial aid is available to distance learners.

Registration Students may register by in person.

Contact Celia Hurley, Director of Teaching Excellence/Distance Education, Randolph Community College, PO Box 1009, 629 Industrial Park Avenue, Asheboro, NC 27203. *Telephone:* 336-633-0299. *Fax:* 336-629-4695. *E-mail:* cthurley@randolph.cc.nc.us.

DEGREES AND AWARDS

Distance programs offered do not lead to a degree or other formal award.

COURSE SUBJECT AREAS OFFERED OUTSIDE OF DEGREE PROGRAMS

Undergraduate: Accounting; business administration and management; business law; cognitive psychology; economics; English composition; ethics; European history; film studies; finance; marketing; music; political science; religious studies; sociology

See full description on page 676.

RAPPAHANNOCK COMMUNITY COLLEGE

Glenns, Virginia

Flexible Learning Opportunities (FLO)

www.rcc.cc.va.us/public/distance_ed/flo/index.htm

Rappahannock Community College, founded in 1970, is a state-related, two-year college. It is accredited by the Southern Association of Colleges and Schools. In 1999–2000, it offered 50 courses at a distance. In fall 1999, there were 552 students enrolled in distance learning courses.

Course delivery sites Courses are delivered to your home, your workplace, military bases.

Media Courses are delivered via videotapes, audiotapes, computer software, CD-ROM, computer conferencing, World Wide Web, e-mail, print. Students and teachers may meet in person or interact via audioconferencing, mail, telephone, fax, e-mail, interactive television, World Wide Web. The following equipment may be required: television, videocassette player, computer, modem, Internet access, e-mail.

Restrictions Programs are available to local area students. Enrollment is open to anyone.

Services Distance learners have access to library services, e-mail services at a distance.

Typical costs Tuition of $37.12 per credit plus mandatory fees of $2.25 per credit for in-state residents. Tuition of $164.82 per credit plus mandatory fees of $2.25 per credit for out-of-state residents. *Noncredit courses:* $75.50 per course. Financial aid is available to distance learners.

Registration Students may register by in person.

Contact Leslie S. Smith, Director, Technology and Distance Education, Rappahannock Community College, 52 Campus Drive, Warsaw, VA 22572. *Telephone:* 804-333-6781. *Fax:* 804-333-0106. *E-mail:* lsmith@rcc.cc.va.us.

DEGREES AND AWARDS

AAS Liberal Arts and Sciences

COURSE SUBJECT AREAS OFFERED OUTSIDE OF DEGREE PROGRAMS

Undergraduate: Accounting; American literature; art history and criticism; biology; business administration and management; business communications; business law; community health services; criminal justice; economics; English composition; health and physical education/fitness; history; mathematics; psychology; religious studies; sociology

RARITAN VALLEY COMMUNITY COLLEGE

Somerville, New Jersey

Virtual Campus

www.raritanval.edu/distlearn/index.html

Raritan Valley Community College, founded in 1965, is a county-supported, two-year college. It is accredited by the Middle States Association of Colleges and Schools. In 1999–2000, it offered 24 courses at a distance. In fall 1999, there were 110 students enrolled in distance learning courses.

Course delivery sites Courses are delivered to your home, your workplace, New Jersey Virtual Community Colleges Consortium (Trenton).

Media Courses are delivered via television, videotapes, interactive television, computer software, CD-ROM, World Wide Web, e-mail, print. Students and teachers may meet in person or interact via mail, telephone, e-mail, interactive television, World Wide Web. The following equipment may be required: television, videocassette player, computer, modem, Internet access, e-mail.

Restrictions Programs are available to in-state students only. Enrollment is open to anyone.

Services Distance learners have access to library services, the campus computer network, e-mail services, academic advising, career placement assistance, bookstore at a distance.

Credit-earning options Students may transfer credits from another institution or may earn credits through examinations.

Typical costs Tuition of $62 per credit plus mandatory fees of $53 per semester for local area residents. Tuition of $124 per credit plus mandatory fees of $53 per semester for in-state residents. Tuition of $124 per credit plus mandatory fees of $53 per semester for out-of-state residents. Students taking courses through the New Jersey Virtual Community College Consortium pay $80 per credit and no fees. Financial aid is available to distance learners.

Registration Students may register by mail, fax, World Wide Web, in person.

Contact Chuck Chulvick, Vice President of Learning Services, Raritan Valley Community College, PO Box 3300, Somerville, NJ 08876. *Telephone:* 908-526-1200 Ext. 8409. *Fax:* 908-526-0255. *E-mail:* cchulvic@raritanval.edu.

DEGREES AND AWARDS

Distance programs offered do not lead to a degree or other formal award.

COURSE SUBJECT AREAS OFFERED OUTSIDE OF DEGREE PROGRAMS

Undergraduate: Anthropology; calculus; computer and information sciences; criminal justice; English language and literature; film studies; law and legal studies; marketing; social sciences

See full description on page 600.

REDLANDS COMMUNITY COLLEGE

El Reno, Oklahoma

www.redlands.cc.ok.us

Redlands Community College, founded in 1938, is a state-supported, two-year college. It is accredited by the North Central Association of Colleges and Schools. It first offered distance learning courses in 1985. In 1999–2000, it offered 17 courses at a distance. In fall 1999, there were 305 students enrolled in distance learning courses.

Course delivery sites Courses are delivered to your home, your workplace, military bases, high schools.

Media Courses are delivered via television, videotapes, videoconferencing, interactive television, audiotapes, computer software, CD-ROM, computer conferencing, World Wide Web, e-mail, print. Students and teachers may meet in person or interact via videoconferencing, mail, telephone, fax, e-mail, interactive television, World Wide Web. The following equipment may be required: television, computer, modem, Internet access, e-mail.

Restrictions Programs are available worldwide. Enrollment is open to anyone.

Services Distance learners have access to library services, e-mail services, academic advising, bookstore at a distance.

Credit-earning options Students may transfer credits from another institution or may earn credits through examinations, portfolio assessment, military training, business training.

Typical costs Tuition of $35 per credit hour plus mandatory fees of $25 per credit hour for in-state residents. Tuition of $35 per credit hour plus mandatory fees of $105 per credit hour for out-of-state residents. Costs may vary. Financial aid is available to distance learners.

Registration Students may register by mail, telephone, World Wide Web, in person.
Contact Dr. Donna A. Payne, Director, American Academy for Distance Education and Training, Redlands Community College. *Telephone:* 405-262-2552. *Fax:* 405-422-1229. *E-mail:* payned@redlands.cc.ok.us.

DEGREES AND AWARDS

Distance programs offered do not lead to a degree or other formal award.

COURSE SUBJECT AREAS OFFERED OUTSIDE OF DEGREE PROGRAMS

Undergraduate: Agriculture; Bible studies; biological and life sciences; business; business administration and management; computer and information sciences; creative writing; criminology; developmental and child psychology; economics; English composition; English language and literature; environmental science; health and physical education/fitness; health professions and related sciences; history; home economics and family studies; law and legal studies; liberal arts, general studies, and humanities; mathematics; philosophy and religion; physical sciences; political science; protective services; social work; sociology; Spanish language and literature; technical writing
Noncredit: Biological and life sciences; computer and information sciences; health professions and related sciences; protective services

---

RED ROCKS COMMUNITY COLLEGE

Lakewood, Colorado
Instruction
www.rrcc.cccoes.edu

Red Rocks Community College, founded in 1969, is a state-supported, two-year college. It is accredited by the North Central Association of Colleges and Schools. It first offered distance learning courses in 1980. In 1999–2000, it offered 55 courses at a distance. In fall 1999, there were 700 students enrolled in distance learning courses.
Course delivery sites Courses are delivered to your home, your workplace, high schools, 2 off-campus centers in Arvada, Conifer.
Media Courses are delivered via television, videoconferencing, interactive television, computer software, CD-ROM, computer conferencing, World Wide Web, e-mail, print. Students and teachers may meet in person or interact via videoconferencing, mail, telephone, fax, e-mail, interactive television, World Wide Web. The following equipment may be required: television, videocassette player, computer, Internet access, e-mail.
Restrictions Programs are available worldwide. Enrollment is open to anyone.
Services Distance learners have access to library services, academic advising, tutoring, career placement assistance at a distance.
Credit-earning options Students may transfer credits from another institution or may earn credits through examinations, portfolio assessment, military training, business training.
Typical costs Tuition of $200 per course plus mandatory fees of $40 per course. Costs may vary. Financial aid is available to distance learners.
Registration Students may register by mail, fax, telephone, e-mail, World Wide Web, in person.
Contact Diane Hegeman, Associate Vice President, Red Rocks Community College, 13300 West 6th Avenue, Box 11, Lakewood, CO 80228-1255. *Telephone:* 303-914-6704. *Fax:* 303-989-6285. *E-mail:* diane.hegeman@rrcc.cccoes.edu.

DEGREES AND AWARDS

AAS Business

COURSE SUBJECT AREAS OFFERED OUTSIDE OF DEGREE PROGRAMS

Undergraduate: Accounting; art history and criticism; biological and life sciences; business; business administration and management; communications; computer and information sciences; developmental and child psychology; economics; education; English as a second language (ESL); English composition; English language and literature; geography; geology; health and physical education/fitness; health professions and related sciences; history; liberal arts, general studies, and humanities; mathematics; music; philosophy and religion; political science; protective services; psychology; social psychology; social sciences; sociology; teacher education

---

REFORMED THEOLOGICAL SEMINARY

Oviedo, Florida
Virtual Campus
www.rtsvirtual.org

Reformed Theological Seminary, founded in 1989, is an independent, religious, graduate institution. It is accredited by the Association of Theological Schools in the United States and Canada, Southern Association of Colleges and Schools. It first offered distance learning courses in 1991. In 1999–2000, it offered 40 courses at a distance. In fall 1999, there were 236 students enrolled in distance learning courses.
Course delivery sites Courses are delivered to your home, your workplace, military bases, 3 off-campus centers in Atlanta (GA), Detroit (MI), Memphis (TN).
Media Courses are delivered via videoconferencing, audiotapes, computer software, CD-ROM, World Wide Web, e-mail, print. Students and teachers may interact via videoconferencing, mail, telephone, fax, e-mail, World Wide Web. The following equipment may be required: Internet access.
Restrictions Programs are available worldwide. Enrollment is open to anyone.
Services Distance learners have access to library services, e-mail services, academic advising, bookstore at a distance.
Credit-earning options Students may transfer credits from another institution.
Typical costs Tuition of $220 per credit hour. *Noncredit courses:* $80 per course. Financial aid is available to distance learners.
Registration Students may register by mail, fax, telephone, e-mail, World Wide Web, in person.
Contact Walt DeHart, Director of Marketing, Reformed Theological Seminary, 2101 Carmel Road, Virtual Campus, Charlotte, NC 28226. *Telephone:* 800-227-2013 Ext. 232. *Fax:* 704-366-9295. *E-mail:* wdehart@rts.edu.

DEGREES AND AWARDS

Undergraduate Certificate(s) General Studies
Graduate Certificate(s) Biblical Studies (some on-campus requirements), Church History (some on-campus requirements), Missions (some on-campus requirements), Theological Studies (some on-campus requirements)
MAR Religion (some on-campus requirements)

COURSE SUBJECT AREAS OFFERED OUTSIDE OF DEGREE PROGRAMS

Graduate: Bible studies; Greek language and literature; theological studies
Noncredit: Bible studies; theological studies

REGENTS COLLEGE

Learning Services
www.regents.edu

Regents College, founded in 1970, is an independent, nonprofit, comprehensive institution. It is accredited by the Middle States Association of Colleges and Schools. It first offered distance learning courses in 1970. In 1999–2000, it offered 40 courses at a distance. In fall 1999, there were 17,443 students enrolled in distance learning courses.

Course delivery sites Courses are delivered to your home, your workplace, military bases.

Media Courses are delivered via videotapes, audiotapes, computer software, CD-ROM, computer conferencing, World Wide Web, e-mail, print. Students and teachers may interact via audioconferencing, telephone, e-mail, World Wide Web. The following equipment may be required: computer, Internet access.

Restrictions Programs are available worldwide. Enrollment is open to anyone.

Services Distance learners have access to library services, e-mail services, academic advising, tutoring, career placement assistance, bookstore at a distance.

Credit-earning options Students may transfer credits from another institution or may earn credits through examinations, portfolio assessment, military training, business training.

Typical costs Tuition of $275 per credit. Contact the school for information. Costs may vary. Financial aid is available to distance learners.

Registration Students may register by mail, fax, telephone, in person.

Contact Admissions Office, Regents College, 7 Columbia Circle, Albany, NY 12203. *Telephone:* 888-647-2388. *Fax:* 518-464-8777. *E-mail:* admissions@regents.edu.

DEGREES AND AWARDS

Undergraduate Certificate(s) Health Care Informatics
AA Liberal Arts
AAS Administrative/Management Studies, Aviation Studies, Nursing (certain restrictions apply), Technical Studies
AOS Aviation
AS Business, Computer Software, Electronics Technology, Liberal Arts, Nuclear Technology, Nursing (certain restrictions apply), Technology
BA Liberal Arts, Liberal Studies
BS Accounting, Computer Information Systems, Computer Software, Computer Technology, Electronics Technology, Finance, General Business, International Business, Liberal Arts, Liberal Studies, Management Information Systems, Management of Human Resources, Marketing, Nuclear Technology, Operations Management, Technology
BSN Nursing (certain restrictions apply)
MA Liberal Studies
MS Nursing (certain restrictions apply)

COURSE SUBJECT AREAS OFFERED OUTSIDE OF DEGREE PROGRAMS

Undergraduate: Abnormal psychology; biological and life sciences; business; business administration and management; developmental and child psychology; English composition; gerontology; history; human resources management; liberal arts, general studies, and humanities; nursing; philosophy and religion; physiology; political science; psychology; sociology; statistics; teacher education
Graduate: Liberal arts, general studies, and humanities; nursing

REGENT UNIVERSITY

Distance Education
www.regent.edu

Regent University, founded in 1977, is an independent, nonprofit, graduate institution. It is accredited by the Association of Theological Schools in the United States and Canada, Southern Association of Colleges and Schools. It first offered distance learning courses in 1991. In fall 1999, there were 953 students enrolled in distance learning courses.

Course delivery sites Courses are delivered to your home, your workplace, military bases.

Media Courses are delivered via videotapes, videoconferencing, audiotapes, computer software, CD-ROM, computer conferencing, World Wide Web, e-mail, print. Students and teachers may meet in person or interact via audioconferencing, mail, telephone, fax, e-mail, World Wide Web. The following equipment may be required: computer, modem, Internet access, e-mail.

Restrictions Programs are available worldwide. Enrollment is restricted to individuals meeting certain criteria.

Services Distance learners have access to library services, e-mail services, academic advising, tutoring, career placement assistance, bookstore at a distance.

Credit-earning options Students may transfer credits from another institution.

Typical costs Tuition of $418 per credit. Costs may vary. Financial aid is available to distance learners.

Registration Students may register by telephone, World Wide Web, in person.

Contact Central Enrollment, Regent University. *Telephone:* 800-373-5504. *Fax:* 757-226-4388. *E-mail:* admissions@regent.edu.

DEGREES AND AWARDS

EMBA Business Administration (certain restrictions apply)
LLM International Taxation (certain restrictions apply)
MA Communication Studies (certain restrictions apply; some on-campus requirements), Organizational Leadership (certain restrictions apply), Political Management (certain restrictions apply; some on-campus requirements), Public Policy (certain restrictions apply; some on-campus requirements)
MAOM Organizational Management (certain restrictions apply)
MBA Business Administration (certain restrictions apply; some on-campus requirements)
MEd Educational Leadership (certain restrictions apply; service area differs from that of the overall institution)
MIM Management (certain restrictions apply)
MPA Public Administration (certain restrictions apply; some on-campus requirements)
PhD Communications (certain restrictions apply; some on-campus requirements), Organizational Leadership (certain restrictions apply; some on-campus requirements)

COURSE SUBJECT AREAS OFFERED OUTSIDE OF DEGREE PROGRAMS

Graduate: Bible studies; business; business administration and management; communications; education administration; finance; international business; law and legal studies; marketing; organizational behavior studies; public administration and services; public policy analysis; special education

Special note

Regent University is a pioneer in online/distance learning and currently offers 17 graduate degrees through the Worldwide Campus. Regent ranks in the upper one third of all colleges and universities in its use of technology in learning. In addition to this distinction, Regent embraces the Judeo-Christian tradition and enjoys a highly ecumenical environment. With faith as the foundation of its mission, Regent prepares leaders to make a positive impact upon American society and the world. Unique among universities, Regent offers predominantly graduate-level study in 8 professional fields—business, communication, divinity, education, government, law, organization leadership, and psychology/counseling (not currently available in a distance format). In addition to the home campus in Virginia Beach, Virginia, Regent offers graduate degrees on site in northern Virginia/Washington, D.C. The Bachelor's Degree Completion program is offered through the Graduate Center in Alexandria, Virginia, and in Virginia Beach. Professionals who wish to develop leadership skills while continuing to work or to maintain responsibilities at home are encouraged to apply.

See full description on page 634.

REGIS UNIVERSITY

Denver, Colorado

School for Professional Studies and Distance Learning
www.regis.edu

Regis University, founded in 1877, is an independent, religious, comprehensive institution. It is accredited by the North Central Association of Colleges and Schools. It first offered distance learning courses in 1992. In 1999–2000, it offered 75 courses at a distance. In fall 1999, there were 1,600 students enrolled in distance learning courses.

Course delivery sites Courses are delivered to your home, your workplace, military bases.

Media Courses are delivered via videotapes, audiotapes, computer software, World Wide Web, e-mail, print. Students and teachers may meet in person or interact via mail, telephone, fax, e-mail, World Wide Web. The following equipment may be required: television, videocassette player, computer, modem, Internet access, e-mail.

Restrictions Programs are available worldwide. Enrollment is restricted to individuals meeting certain criteria.

Services Distance learners have access to library services, academic advising, career placement assistance, bookstore at a distance.

Credit-earning options Students may transfer credits from another institution or may earn credits through examinations, portfolio assessment, military training, business training.

Typical costs *Undergraduate:* Tuition of $223 per credit. *Graduate:* Tuition of $290 per credit. Costs may vary. Financial aid is available to distance learners.

Registration Students may register by mail, fax, telephone, e-mail, World Wide Web, in person.

Contact Admissions Representative, Regis University, 3333 Regis Boulevard, Denver, CO 80221. *Telephone:* 800-967-3237. *Fax:* 303-964-5539. *E-mail:* mualc@regis.edu.

DEGREES AND AWARDS

BA Guided Independent Studies
BSBA Business Administration
BSN RN to BSN
Graduate Certificate(s) Education, Liberal Studies
EMBA Business Administration
MALS Guided Independent Study: Early Childhood Education/License and Certification, Guided Independent Study: Early Childhood Special Education/License and Certification, Guided Independent Study: Elementary Education/License and Certification, Guided Independent Study: English as a Second Language/License and Certification, Guided Independent Study: Licensed Professional Counseling/License and Certifica-
tion, Guided Independent Study: Middle School Education/License and Certification, Guided Independent Study: Secondary Education/License and Certification, Guided Independent Study: Special Education Moderate Needs/License and Certification
MNM Non Profit Management
MSCIS Computer Information Systems
PEMBA Physicians Business Administration

COURSE SUBJECT AREAS OFFERED OUTSIDE OF DEGREE PROGRAMS

Undergraduate: Accounting; business; business administration and management; computer and information sciences; economics; ethics; finance; health professions and related sciences; human resources management; liberal arts, general studies, and humanities; marketing; organizational behavior studies; philosophy and religion; psychology; social sciences; sociology; statistics; teacher education; technical writing

Graduate: Accounting; adult education; anthropology; business; business administration and management; communications; computer and information sciences; counseling psychology; curriculum and instruction; database management; economics; educational research; ethics; finance; health professions and related sciences; history; human resources management; international business; law and legal studies; liberal arts, general studies, and humanities; management; management information systems; marketing; nursing; organizational behavior studies; psychology; public policy analysis; social sciences; special education; teacher education

See full descriptions on pages 722 and 822.

REND LAKE COLLEGE

Ina, Illinois

Learning Resource Center
www.rlc.cc.il.us

Rend Lake College, founded in 1967, is a state-supported, two-year college. It is accredited by the North Central Association of Colleges and Schools. It first offered distance learning courses in 1995. In 1999–2000, it offered 23 courses at a distance. In fall 1999, there were 305 students enrolled in distance learning courses.

Course delivery sites Courses are delivered to your home, high schools, 6 off-campus centers in Benton, Mount Vernon, Pinckneyville, Sesser, Thompsonville, Wayne City.

Media Courses are delivered via videotapes, videoconferencing, interactive television, World Wide Web, print. Students and teachers may meet in person or interact via videoconferencing, audioconferencing, mail, telephone, fax, e-mail, interactive television, World Wide Web. The following equipment may be required: television, videocassette player, computer, modem, Internet access, e-mail.

Restrictions Programs are available to local area students. Enrollment is open to anyone.

Services Distance learners have access to e-mail services, academic advising, career placement assistance at a distance.

Credit-earning options Students may transfer credits from another institution or may earn credits through examinations.

Typical costs Tuition of $40 per credit hour for local area residents. Tuition of $88 per credit hour for in-state residents. Tuition of $88 per credit hour for out-of-state residents. *Noncredit courses:* $30 per course. Costs may vary. Financial aid is available to distance learners.

Registration Students may register by mail, fax, in person.

Contact Andrea Witthoft, Director of Learning Resources and Instructional Technology, Rend Lake College, Learning Resource Center, Ina, IL 62846. *Telephone:* 618-437-5321 Ext. 277. *Fax:* 618-437-5598. *E-mail:* witthoft@rlc.cc.il.us.

DEGREES AND AWARDS
Distance programs offered do not lead to a degree or other formal award.

COURSE SUBJECT AREAS OFFERED OUTSIDE OF DEGREE PROGRAMS

Undergraduate: Anthropology; astronomy and astrophysics; botany; economics; English language and literature; fine arts; foods and nutrition studies; health and physical education/fitness; horticulture; Latin American studies; liberal arts, general studies, and humanities; microbiology; philosophy and religion; psychology

RENSSELAER POLYTECHNIC INSTITUTE

Troy, New York

Office of Professional and Distance Education
www.rsvp.rpi.edu

Rensselaer Polytechnic Institute, founded in 1824, is an independent, nonprofit university. It is accredited by the Middle States Association of Colleges and Schools. It first offered distance learning courses in 1987. In 1999–2000, it offered 75 courses at a distance. In fall 1999, there were 1,000 students enrolled in distance learning courses.
Course delivery sites Courses are delivered to your home, your workplace, military bases, 1 off-campus center in Springfield (VA).
Media Courses are delivered via television, videotapes, videoconferencing, CD-ROM, computer conferencing, World Wide Web. Students and teachers may meet in person or interact via videoconferencing, audioconferencing, mail, telephone, fax, e-mail, interactive television, World Wide Web. The following equipment may be required: television, videocassette player, computer, modem, Internet access, e-mail.
Restrictions Programs are available worldwide. Enrollment is restricted to individuals meeting certain criteria.
Services Distance learners have access to library services, the campus computer network, e-mail services, academic advising, career placement assistance, bookstore at a distance.
Credit-earning options Students may transfer credits from another institution.
Typical costs *Undergraduate:* Tuition of $700 per credit hour. *Graduate:* Tuition of $700 per credit hour. *Noncredit courses:* $1000 per course. Costs may vary.
Registration Students may register by mail, fax, telephone.
Contact Peter A. Miller, Associate Director, Marketing, Rensselaer Polytechnic Institute, Center for Industrial Innovation, Suite 4011, 110 8th Street, Troy, NY 12180. *Telephone:* 518-276-8351. *Fax:* 518-276-8026. *E-mail:* rsvp@rpi.edu.

DEGREES AND AWARDS

Graduate Certificate(s) Bioinformatics (certain restrictions apply; some on-campus requirements), Computer Graphics and Data Visualization (certain restrictions apply), Computer Networks (certain restrictions apply), Computer Science (certain restrictions apply), Database Systems Design (certain restrictions apply), Electric Power Engineering (certain restrictions apply), Graphical User Interfaces (certain restrictions apply), Human-Computer Interaction (certain restrictions apply), Management and Technology (certain restrictions apply), Manufacturing Systems Engineering (certain restrictions apply), Microelectronics Manufacturing Engineering (certain restrictions apply), Microelectronics Technology and Design (certain restrictions apply), Quality and Reliability (certain restrictions apply), Service Systems (certain restrictions apply), Software Engineering (certain restrictions apply)
MBA Management and Technology (certain restrictions apply)
ME Computer and Systems Engineering (certain restrictions apply), Electric Power Engineering (certain restrictions apply), Electrical Engi-

neering (certain restrictions apply), Mechanical Engineering (certain restrictions apply), Quality and Reliability (certain restrictions apply), Service Systems (certain restrictions apply)
MS Computer Science (certain restrictions apply), Electric Power Engineering (certain restrictions apply), Electrical Engineering (certain restrictions apply), Engineering Science (certain restrictions apply), Industrial and Management Engineering (certain restrictions apply), Information Technology (certain restrictions apply), Management (certain restrictions apply), Manufacturing Systems Engineering (certain restrictions apply), Mechanical Engineering (certain restrictions apply), Microelectronics Manufacturing Engineering (certain restrictions apply), Technical Communications (certain restrictions apply)

COURSE SUBJECT AREAS OFFERED OUTSIDE OF DEGREE PROGRAMS

Graduate: Accounting; business administration and management; business communications; chemistry; civil engineering; communications; computer and information sciences; computer programming; database management; design; electrical engineering; electronics; engineering/industrial management; finance; human resources management; industrial engineering; information sciences and systems; instructional media; international business; management information systems; marketing; mechanical engineering; organizational behavior studies; statistics; technical writing; telecommunications
Noncredit: Accounting; business communications; chemistry; civil engineering; communications; computer and information sciences; computer programming; database management; design; electronics; finance; information sciences and systems; instructional media; international business; management information systems; marketing; organizational behavior studies; statistics; technical writing; telecommunications

See full description on page 636.

RICHARD STOCKTON COLLEGE OF NEW JERSEY

Pomona, New Jersey

Office of Distance Education
loki.stockton.edu/~learning/dist.html

Richard Stockton College of New Jersey, founded in 1969, is a state-supported, comprehensive institution. It is accredited by the Middle States Association of Colleges and Schools. It first offered distance learning courses in 1996. In 1999–2000, it offered 28 courses at a distance. In fall 1999, there were 396 students enrolled in distance learning courses.
Course delivery sites Courses are delivered to your home, your workplace, Burlington County College (Pemberton).
Media Courses are delivered via television, videotapes, interactive television, audiotapes, computer conferencing, World Wide Web, e-mail, print. Students and teachers may meet in person or interact via mail, telephone, fax, e-mail, interactive television. The following equipment may be required: television, videocassette player, computer, modem, Internet access, e-mail.
Restrictions Programs are available nationwide. Enrollment is restricted to individuals meeting certain criteria.
Services Distance learners have access to library services, the campus computer network, e-mail services at a distance.
Credit-earning options Students may transfer credits from another institution or may earn credits through examinations.
Typical costs Tuition of $410 per course plus mandatory fees of $190 per course for in-state residents. Tuition of $664 per course plus mandatory fees of $190 per course for out-of-state residents. *Noncredit courses:* $100 per course. Costs may vary. Financial aid is available to distance learners.

Registration Students may register by mail, fax, World Wide Web, in person.

Contact Scott B. Greenberg, Assistant Dean of Lifelong Learning, Richard Stockton College of New Jersey, Office of Lifelong Learning, Pomona, NJ 08240. *Telephone:* 609-652-4227. *Fax:* 609-748-5528. *E-mail:* scott.greenberg@stockton.edu.

DEGREES AND AWARDS

Distance programs offered do not lead to a degree or other formal award.

COURSE SUBJECT AREAS OFFERED OUTSIDE OF DEGREE PROGRAMS

Undergraduate: Area, ethnic, and cultural studies; business; business administration and management; chemistry; communications; comparative literature; conservation and natural resources; criminology; English composition; English language and literature; fine arts; health professions and related sciences; individual and family development studies; liberal arts, general studies, and humanities; marketing; mass media; mathematics; philosophy and religion; photography; physical sciences; political science; psychology; social sciences; sociology; visual and performing arts; women's studies
Noncredit: Area, ethnic, and cultural studies; business; computer and information sciences; education; liberal arts, general studies, and humanities; teacher education

RICHLAND COMMUNITY COLLEGE

Decatur, Illinois

Lifelong Learning Division
www.richland.cc.il.us

Richland Community College, founded in 1971, is a district-supported, two-year college. It is accredited by the North Central Association of Colleges and Schools. It first offered distance learning courses in 1994. In 1999–2000, it offered 15 courses at a distance. In fall 1999, there were 359 students enrolled in distance learning courses.
Course delivery sites Courses are delivered to high schools, Danville Area Community College (Danville), Lake Land College (Mattoon), Parkland College (Champaign), 9 off-campus centers in Clinton, Decatur Public Library, Illiopolis, Macon, Mount Zion, Moweaqua, Niantic, Warrensburg.
Media Courses are delivered via television, videoconferencing, World Wide Web. Students and teachers may meet in person or interact via videoconferencing, e-mail, interactive television, World Wide Web. The following equipment may be required: computer, modem, Internet access, e-mail.
Restrictions Programs are available to local area students. Enrollment is open to anyone.
Services Distance learners have access to library services, academic advising at a distance.
Credit-earning options Students may transfer credits from another institution or may earn credits through examinations, portfolio assessment.
Typical costs Tuition of $47 per credit for local area residents. Tuition of $143 per credit for in-state residents. Tuition of $237 per credit for out-of-state residents. *Noncredit courses:* $70 per course. Costs may vary. Financial aid is available to distance learners.
Registration Students may register by mail, fax, telephone, e-mail, World Wide Web, in person.
Contact Cathy Sebok, Extension Coordinator, Richland Community College, One College Park, Decatur, IL 62521. *Telephone:* 217-875-7200 Ext. 558. *Fax:* 217-875-6964. *E-mail:* csebok@richland.cc.il.us.

DEGREES AND AWARDS

Distance programs offered do not lead to a degree or other formal award.

COURSE SUBJECT AREAS OFFERED OUTSIDE OF DEGREE PROGRAMS

Undergraduate: Accounting; algebra; art history and criticism; creative writing; developmental and child psychology; economics; English composition; English language and literature; European history; history; liberal arts, general studies, and humanities; social psychology; sociology
Noncredit: European languages and literatures

RIO SALADO COLLEGE

Tempe, Arizona

Distance Learning
www.rio.maricopa.edu

Rio Salado College, founded in 1978, is a state and locally supported, two-year college. It is accredited by the North Central Association of Colleges and Schools. It first offered distance learning courses in 1979. In 1999–2000, it offered 330 courses at a distance. In fall 1999, there were 9,000 students enrolled in distance learning courses.
Course delivery sites Courses are delivered to your home, your workplace, military bases, high schools, 4 off-campus centers in Glendale, Mesa, Phoenix, Sun City.
Media Courses are delivered via videotapes, audiotapes, computer software, CD-ROM, computer conferencing, World Wide Web, e-mail, print. Students and teachers may meet in person or interact via audioconferencing, mail, telephone, fax, e-mail, World Wide Web. The following equipment may be required: television, videocassette player, computer, modem, Internet access, e-mail.
Restrictions Programs are available worldwide. Enrollment is open to anyone.
Services Distance learners have access to library services, the campus computer network, e-mail services, academic advising, tutoring, career placement assistance, bookstore at a distance.
Credit-earning options Students may transfer credits from another institution or may earn credits through examinations, military training, business training.
Typical costs Tuition of $125 per credit hour plus mandatory fees of $5 per semester. Financial aid is available to distance learners.
Registration Students may register by mail, fax, telephone, World Wide Web, in person.
Contact Kisha Brock, Student Services, Rio Salado College, 2323 West 14th Street, Tempe, AZ 85281. *Telephone:* 480-717-8540. *E-mail:* kisha.brock@riomail.maricopa.edu.

DEGREES AND AWARDS

AA General Studies
AAS Computer Usage and Technology, Water/Wastewater Management
AGS General Studies

COURSE SUBJECT AREAS OFFERED OUTSIDE OF DEGREE PROGRAMS

Undergraduate: Accounting; algebra; American (U.S.) history; American literature; anthropology; art history and criticism; astronomy and astrophysics; biology; business; business administration and management; calculus; chemistry; communications; computer and information sciences; computer programming; counseling psychology; creative writing; drama and theater; economics; education; English composition; English language and literature; English literature; foods and nutrition studies; geography; geology; health professions and related sciences; history;

information sciences and systems; liberal arts, general studies, and humanities; marketing; mathematics; philosophy and religion; political science; psychology; sociology; Spanish language and literature; teacher education

Special note

With Rio's "26 Starts" schedule, students have the opportunity to begin distance learning classes 26 times throughout the year. The longest a student has to wait to begin most classes is 2 weeks. Students have 13 weeks to complete the course; however, some instructors and courses allow students to work ahead and complete the course in less time than required. A course calendar provides the specific dates for submitting assignments and taking exams. Credit classes offered through "26 Starts" include academic subjects such as accounting, business, English, math, computers, and Spanish. Several hundred course sections in 29 different subjects are now offered every other week through "26 Starts." Delivery modes include print-based, mixed media (audiocassette and/or videocassette, teleconference, computer), and Internet. As with all distance learning classes, in-person testing is required for the midterm and final exams. For out-of-country or out-of-state students, the College will work with a proctor for the in-person testing. More information is available by visiting Rio's Web site at http://www.rio.maricopa.edu/ or by calling the College's Student Services Department at 480-517-8540.

See full descriptions on pages 638 and 822.

RIVERLAND COMMUNITY COLLEGE

Austin, Minnesota
www.riverland.cc.mn.us

Riverland Community College, founded in 1940, is a state-supported, two-year college. It is accredited by the North Central Association of Colleges and Schools. It first offered distance learning courses in 1978. In 1999–2000, it offered 26 courses at a distance. In fall 1999, there were 210 students enrolled in distance learning courses.

Course delivery sites Courses are delivered to Rochester Community and Technical College (Rochester), 5 off-campus centers in Albert Lea, Cleveland, Owatonna, St. Clair, St. Peter.

Media Courses are delivered via television, videotapes, audiotapes. Students and teachers may interact via videoconferencing, mail, telephone, fax, e-mail.

Restrictions Programs are available to local area students. Enrollment is restricted to individuals meeting certain criteria.

Services Distance learners have access to library services, e-mail services at a distance.

Credit-earning options Students may transfer credits from another institution or may earn credits through examinations.

Typical costs Tuition of $67 per credit plus mandatory fees of $8 per credit. Financial aid is available to distance learners.

Registration Students may register by mail, fax, telephone, in person.

Contact Carolyn Meier, ITV Coordinator, Riverland Community College, 1600 8th Avenue, North West, Austin, MN 55912. *Telephone:* 507-433-0534. *Fax:* 507-433-0515. *E-mail:* meierca@au.cc.mn.us.

DEGREES AND AWARDS

Distance programs offered do not lead to a degree or other formal award.

COURSE SUBJECT AREAS OFFERED OUTSIDE OF DEGREE PROGRAMS

Undergraduate: American (U.S.) history; developmental and child psychology; English composition; European languages and literatures; home economics and family studies; information sciences and systems; social psychology; sociology

Noncredit: Business administration and management; law and legal studies

RIVERSIDE COMMUNITY COLLEGE

Riverside, California
Open Campus
www.opencampus.com

Riverside Community College, founded in 1916, is a state and locally supported, two-year college. It is accredited by the Western Association of Schools and Colleges, Inc. In 1999–2000, it offered 25 courses at a distance. In fall 1999, there were 1,000 students enrolled in distance learning courses.

Course delivery sites Courses are delivered to your home, your workplace, military bases, high schools.

Media Courses are delivered via television, videotapes, videoconferencing, audiotapes, computer software, CD-ROM, computer conferencing, World Wide Web, e-mail, print. Students and teachers may meet in person or interact via mail, telephone, fax, e-mail, World Wide Web. The following equipment may be required: television, computer, modem, Internet access, e-mail.

Restrictions Programs are available worldwide. Enrollment is open to anyone.

Services Distance learners have access to library services, academic advising, bookstore at a distance.

Credit-earning options Students may transfer credits from another institution.

Typical costs Tuition of $11 per unit for in-state residents. Tuition of $118 per unit plus mandatory fees of $12 per unit for out-of-state residents. *Noncredit courses:* $59 per course. Costs may vary. Financial aid is available to distance learners.

Registration Students may register by mail, fax, telephone, in person.

Contact Dr. Anthony E. Beebe, Dean, Open Campus, Riverside Community College, 4800 Magnolia Avenue, Riverside, CA 92506. *Telephone:* 909-222-8094. *Fax:* 909-222-8877.

DEGREES AND AWARDS

Distance programs offered do not lead to a degree or other formal award.

COURSE SUBJECT AREAS OFFERED OUTSIDE OF DEGREE PROGRAMS

Undergraduate: Astronomy and astrophysics; business administration and management; classical languages and literatures; economics; geography; health and physical education/fitness; history; home economics and family studies; law and legal studies; mathematics; oceanography; political science; social psychology; sociology; student counseling; teacher education

ROANE STATE COMMUNITY COLLEGE

Harriman, Tennessee

Adult Learning and Program Development
www.rscc.cc.tn.us/noncredit/distance.html

Roane State Community College, founded in 1971, is a state-supported, two-year college. It is accredited by the Southern Association of Colleges and Schools. It first offered distance learning courses in 1991. In 1999–2000, it offered 75 courses at a distance.

Course delivery sites Courses are delivered to your home, your workplace, East Tennessee State University (Johnson City), University of Tennessee at Chattanooga (Chattanooga), 6 off-campus centers in Crossville, Huntsville, Knoxville, LaFollette, Lenoir City, Oak Ridge.

Media Courses are delivered via videotapes, interactive television, audiotapes, CD-ROM, World Wide Web, e-mail, print. Students and teachers may meet in person or interact via audioconferencing, mail, telephone, fax, e-mail, interactive television, World Wide Web. The following equipment may be required: television, videocassette player, computer, modem, Internet access, e-mail.

Restrictions Programs are available worldwide. Enrollment is open to anyone.

Services Distance learners have access to library services, the campus computer network, e-mail services, academic advising, career placement assistance, bookstore at a distance.

Credit-earning options Students may transfer credits from another institution or may earn credits through examinations, portfolio assessment, military training, business training.

Typical costs Tuition of $53 per credit hour for in-state residents. Tuition of $210 per credit hour for out-of-state residents. Mandatory fees are $6 per credit hour with maximum of $50. Costs may vary. Financial aid is available to distance learners.

Registration Students may register by telephone, World Wide Web, in person.

Contact Joni Allison, Director, Roane State Community College, 276 Patton Lane, Harriman, TN 37748. *Telephone:* 865-882-4602. *Fax:* 865-882-4683. *E-mail:* allison_jk@rscc.cc.tn.us.

DEGREES AND AWARDS

Distance programs offered do not lead to a degree or other formal award.

COURSE SUBJECT AREAS OFFERED OUTSIDE OF DEGREE PROGRAMS

Undergraduate: Abnormal psychology; administrative and secretarial services; algebra; American (U.S.) history; American literature; anatomy; anthropology; art history and criticism; biology; business; business administration and management; business communications; business law; calculus; chemistry, organic; chemistry, physical; computer and information sciences; developmental and child psychology; economics; education; engineering; English composition; English literature; ethics; European history; finance; financial management and services; foods and nutrition studies; geology; health and physical education/fitness; law and legal studies; liberal arts, general studies, and humanities; marketing; mass media; mathematics; music; organizational behavior studies; philosophy and religion; psychology; religious studies; social sciences; sociology; statistics; technical writing

See full description on page 676.

ROBERT MORRIS COLLEGE

Chicago, Illinois

University Center
www.rmcil.edu

Robert Morris College, founded in 1913, is an independent, nonprofit, four-year college. It is accredited by the North Central Association of Colleges and Schools. It first offered distance learning courses in 1999. In 1999–2000, it offered 20 courses at a distance. In fall 1999, there were 40 students enrolled in distance learning courses.

Course delivery sites Courses are delivered to your home, your workplace.

Media Courses are delivered via videotapes, videoconferencing, CD-ROM, e-mail. Students and teachers may meet in person or interact via telephone, fax, e-mail. The following equipment may be required: computer, modem, Internet access, e-mail.

Restrictions Programs are available to in-state students only. Enrollment is restricted to individuals meeting certain criteria.

Services Distance learners have access to library services, e-mail services at a distance.

Credit-earning options Students may transfer credits from another institution or may earn credits through examinations, portfolio assessment.

Typical costs Undergraduate tuition is $3650 per quarter. Tuition for the Certificate Program is $5000. Financial aid is available to distance learners.

Registration Students may register by e-mail, in person.

Contact Candace Goodwin, Executive Director, Robert Morris College, 401 South State Street, Chicago, IL 60605. *Telephone:* 312-935-4433. *Fax:* 312-935-4440. *E-mail:* cgoodwin@smtp.rmcil.edu.

eCollege.com *www.ecollege.com/scholarships*

DEGREES AND AWARDS

Undergraduate Certificate(s) Business Management (certain restrictions apply; some on-campus requirements)

COURSE SUBJECT AREAS OFFERED OUTSIDE OF DEGREE PROGRAMS

Undergraduate: Accounting; art history and criticism; business administration and management; computer and information sciences; ethics; finance; human resources management; management information systems; marketing; organizational behavior studies; psychology

ROBERT MORRIS COLLEGE

Moon Township, Pennsylvania

Department of Enrollment Management
www.rmconline.org

Robert Morris College, founded in 1921, is an independent, nonprofit, comprehensive institution. It is accredited by the Middle States Association of Colleges and Schools. It first offered distance learning courses in 1999. In 1999–2000, it offered 15 courses at a distance. In fall 1999, there were 35 students enrolled in distance learning courses.

Course delivery sites Courses are delivered to your home, your workplace, military bases.

Media Courses are delivered via computer software, CD-ROM, World Wide Web, e-mail, print. Students and teachers may meet in person or interact via mail, telephone, fax, e-mail, World Wide Web. The following equipment may be required: computer, modem, Internet access, e-mail.

Restrictions Programs are available to local area students. Enrollment is restricted to individuals meeting certain criteria.

Services Distance learners have access to library services, the campus computer network, e-mail services, academic advising, tutoring, career placement assistance, bookstore at a distance.

Credit-earning options Students may transfer credits from another institution or may earn credits through examinations, military training, business training.

Typical costs *Undergraduate:* Tuition of $894 per course plus mandatory fees of $60 per course. *Graduate:* Tuition of $375 per credit plus mandatory fees of $20 per credit. Financial aid is available to distance learners.

Registration Students may register by mail, fax, telephone, e-mail, World Wide Web, in person.

Contact Darcy B. Tannehill, Dean, Pittsburgh Center, Robert Morris College, 600 Fifth Avenue, Pittsburgh, PA 15219. *Telephone:* 412-227-6472. *Fax:* 412-281-5539. *E-mail:* tannehil@robert-morris.edu.

---

eCollege.com *www.ecollege.com/scholarships*

DEGREES AND AWARDS

BSBA Accounting (some on-campus requirements), Information Systems (some on-campus requirements), Management (some on-campus requirements)

COURSE SUBJECT AREAS OFFERED OUTSIDE OF DEGREE PROGRAMS

Undergraduate: Accounting; business administration and management; business law; economics; English composition; English literature; finance; management information systems; marketing; psychology

See full description on page 640.

ROCHESTER COLLEGE

Rochester Hills, Michigan

College of Extended Learning
www.rc.edu/CEL/

Rochester College, founded in 1959, is an independent, religious, four-year college affiliated with the Church of Christ. It is accredited by the North Central Association of Colleges and Schools. In 1999–2000, it offered 6 courses at a distance. In fall 1999, there were 45 students enrolled in distance learning courses.

Course delivery sites Courses are delivered to your home, your workplace, Macomb Community College (Warren).

Media Courses are delivered via computer software, computer conferencing, World Wide Web, e-mail, print. Students and teachers may meet in person or interact via mail, telephone, fax, e-mail, World Wide Web. The following equipment may be required: computer, modem, Internet access, e-mail.

Restrictions Programs are available nationwide. Enrollment is restricted to individuals meeting certain criteria.

Services Distance learners have access to e-mail services, academic advising at a distance.

Credit-earning options Students may transfer credits from another institution or may earn credits through examinations, portfolio assessment, military training, business training.

Typical costs Tuition of $175 per credit hour. Financial aid is available to distance learners.

Registration Students may register by mail, fax, in person.

Contact Angela Hazel, Associate Dean, Rochester College, College of Extended Learning, 800 West Avon Road, Rochester Hills, MI 48307. *Telephone:* 248-218-2223. *Fax:* 248-218-2235. *E-mail:* ahazel@rc.edu.

DEGREES AND AWARDS

AA Arts (certain restrictions apply; service area differs from that of the overall institution; some on-campus requirements)

BBA Management (certain restrictions apply; service area differs from that of the overall institution; some on-campus requirements), Management/Criminal Justice (certain restrictions apply; service area differs from that of the overall institution; some on-campus requirements)

BRE Professional Ministry (certain restrictions apply; service area differs from that of the overall institution; some on-campus requirements)

BS Business Communications (certain restrictions apply; service area differs from that of the overall institution; some on-campus requirements), Counseling Psychology (certain restrictions apply; service area differs from that of the overall institution; some on-campus requirements), Early Childhood Education (certain restrictions apply; service area differs from that of the overall institution; some on-campus requirements)

COURSE SUBJECT AREAS OFFERED OUTSIDE OF DEGREE PROGRAMS

Undergraduate: American literature; ethics; psychology; religious studies

---

ROCHESTER COMMUNITY AND TECHNICAL COLLEGE

Rochester, Minnesota
www.roch.edu

Rochester Community and Technical College, founded in 1915, is a state-supported, two-year college. It is accredited by the North Central Association of Colleges and Schools.

Course delivery sites Courses are delivered to your home, your workplace.

Media Courses are delivered via television, videotapes, interactive television, audiotapes, computer software, CD-ROM, World Wide Web, e-mail, print. Students and teachers may meet in person or interact via mail, telephone, fax, e-mail, interactive television, World Wide Web. The following equipment may be required: computer, modem, Internet access, e-mail.

Restrictions Programs are available nationwide. Enrollment is restricted to individuals meeting certain criteria.

Services Distance learners have access to library services, the campus computer network, e-mail services, academic advising at a distance.

Credit-earning options Students may transfer credits from another institution or may earn credits through examinations.

Typical costs Tuition of $71.50 per credit plus mandatory fees of $8.50 per credit for local area residents. Tuition of $71.50 per credit plus mandatory fees of $8.50 per credit for in-state residents. Tuition of $143 per credit plus mandatory fees of $8.50 per credit for out-of-state residents. Financial aid is available to distance learners.

Registration Students may register by mail, telephone, World Wide Web, in person.

Contact Counseling Center, Rochester Community and Technical College, 851 30th Avenue South East, Rochester, MN 55904. *Telephone:* 507-285-7260.

DEGREES AND AWARDS

Undergraduate Certificate(s) Digital Arts: Computer Graphics

COURSE SUBJECT AREAS OFFERED OUTSIDE OF DEGREE PROGRAMS

Undergraduate: Accounting; administrative and secretarial services; biology; design; English composition; liberal arts, general studies, and humanities

ROCHESTER INSTITUTE OF TECHNOLOGY

Rochester, New York

Offices of Part-Time and Graduate Enrollment Services
distancelearning.rit.edu

Rochester Institute of Technology, founded in 1829, is an independent, nonprofit, comprehensive institution. It is accredited by the Middle States Association of Colleges and Schools. It first offered distance learning courses in 1979. In 1999–2000, it offered 170 courses at a distance. In fall 1999, there were 1,600 students enrolled in distance learning courses.

Course delivery sites Courses are delivered to your home, your workplace, military bases, high schools.

Media Courses are delivered via television, videotapes, videoconferencing, audiotapes, computer software, CD-ROM, computer conferencing, World Wide Web, e-mail, print. Students and teachers may interact via videoconferencing, audioconferencing, mail, telephone, fax, e-mail, World Wide Web. The following equipment may be required: television, videocassette player, computer, modem, Internet access.

Restrictions Programs are available worldwide. Enrollment is open to anyone.

Services Distance learners have access to library services, the campus computer network, e-mail services, academic advising, career placement assistance, bookstore at a distance.

Credit-earning options Students may transfer credits from another institution or may earn credits through examinations, portfolio assessment, military training, business training.

Typical costs Tuition of $546 per credit. Undergraduate tuition ranges between $249 per credit for lower division courses and $273 per credit for upper division courses. Financial aid is available to distance learners.

Registration Students may register by mail, fax, telephone, e-mail, World Wide Web, in person.

Contact Office of Part-Time and Graduate Enrollment Services, Rochester Institute of Technology, Bausch and Lomb Center, 58 Lomb Memorial Drive, Rochester, NY 14534. *Telephone:* 800-CALL-RIT. *Fax:* 716-475-7164. *E-mail:* opes@rit.edu.

DEGREES AND AWARDS

Undergraduate Certificate(s) Basic Quality Management, Data Communications, Digital Imaging and Publishing, Emergency Management, Environmental Management and Technology, Environmental Management Science, Health Systems Administration, Telecommunications Network Management, Voice Communications

BS Applied Arts and Science, Electrical and Mechanical Engineering Technology (certain restrictions apply; some on-campus requirements), Environmental Management, Telecommunications

Graduate Certificate(s) Integrated Health Systems, Health Systems Finance, Statistical Quality, Technical Communications

MS Applied Statistical Quality, Cross Disciplinary Professional Studies, Environmental Health and Safety Management, Health Systems Administration, Information Technology, Software Development and Management

COURSE SUBJECT AREAS OFFERED OUTSIDE OF DEGREE PROGRAMS

Undergraduate: Accounting; area, ethnic, and cultural studies; business; business administration and management; chemistry; communications; computer and information sciences; conservation and natural resources; economics; electrical engineering; engineering; engineering mechanics; engineering-related technologies; engineering/industrial management; English composition; English language and literature; environmental science; geology; health and physical education/fitness; health professions and related sciences; history; information sciences and systems; liberal arts, general studies, and humanities; mathematics; mechanical engineering; philosophy and religion; physical sciences; political science; psychology; public health; social sciences; sociology; telecommunications

Graduate: Business; business administration and management; chemistry; computer and information sciences; conservation and natural resources; electrical engineering; health professions and related sciences; information sciences and systems; mathematics; public health; telecommunications

See full description on page 642.

ROCKLAND COMMUNITY COLLEGE

Suffern, New York

Distance Learning Department

Rockland Community College, founded in 1959, is a state and locally supported, two-year college. It is accredited by the Middle States Association of Colleges and Schools. It first offered distance learning courses in 1985. In 1999–2000, it offered 40 courses at a distance. In fall 1999, there were 600 students enrolled in distance learning courses.

Course delivery sites Courses are delivered to your home, military bases, high schools, 1 off-campus center in Spring Valley.

Media Courses are delivered via television, videotapes, audiotapes, computer software, computer conferencing, World Wide Web, e-mail, print. Students and teachers may meet in person or interact via mail, telephone, e-mail, World Wide Web. The following equipment may be required: television, videocassette player, Internet access.

Restrictions Programs are available nationwide. Enrollment is restricted to individuals meeting certain criteria.

Services Distance learners have access to library services, the campus computer network, e-mail services, academic advising, career placement assistance, bookstore at a distance.

Credit-earning options Students may transfer credits from another institution or may earn credits through examinations.

Typical costs Tuition of $97 per credit plus mandatory fees of $20 per course for in-state residents. Tuition of $243 per credit for out-of-state residents. Financial aid is available to distance learners.

Registration Students may register by mail, telephone, in person.

Contact Lynne Koplik, Distance Learning Supervisor, Rockland Community College, 145 College Road, Room 4104, Suffern, NY 10901. *Telephone:* 914-574-4780. *Fax:* 914-356-5811. *E-mail:* lkoplik@sunyrockland.edu.

DEGREES AND AWARDS

AA Liberal Arts and Sciences (certain restrictions apply; some on-campus requirements)

COURSE SUBJECT AREAS OFFERED OUTSIDE OF DEGREE PROGRAMS

Undergraduate: Abnormal psychology; area, ethnic, and cultural studies; art history and criticism; astronomy and astrophysics; business; business administration and management; developmental and child psychology; economics; English composition; English language and literature; fine arts; geography; health and physical education/fitness; history; liberal arts, general studies, and humanities; mathematics; philosophy and religion; political science; sociology

ROGERS STATE UNIVERSITY

Claremore, Oklahoma
RSU Online
rsuonline.edu

Rogers State University, founded in 1909, is a state-supported, two-year college. It is accredited by the North Central Association of Colleges and Schools. It first offered distance learning courses in 1989. In 1999–2000, it offered 92 courses at a distance. In fall 1999, there were 928 students enrolled in distance learning courses.

Course delivery sites Courses are delivered to your home, your workplace, military bases, high schools, Northeastern State University (Tahlequah), 2 off-campus centers in Bartlesville, Pryor.

Media Courses are delivered via television, videotapes, interactive television, audiotapes, computer software, CD-ROM, World Wide Web, e-mail, print. Students and teachers may meet in person or interact via mail, telephone, fax, e-mail, interactive television, World Wide Web. The following equipment may be required: television, videocassette player, computer, modem, Internet access, e-mail.

Restrictions Programs are available worldwide. Enrollment is restricted to individuals meeting certain criteria.

Services Distance learners have access to library services, e-mail services, academic advising, career placement assistance, bookstore at a distance.

Credit-earning options Students may transfer credits from another institution or may earn credits through examinations, military training, business training.

Typical costs Tuition of $50 per credit hour plus mandatory fees of $53.53 per credit hour for in-state residents. Tuition of $143 per credit hour plus mandatory fees of $53.53 per credit hour for out-of-state residents. Costs may vary. Financial aid is available to distance learners.

Registration Students may register by mail, fax, telephone, e-mail, World Wide Web.

Contact Kevin Cook, Online Marketing, Rogers State University, 1701 West Will Rogers Boulevard, Claremore, OK 74017. *Telephone:* 918-343-7548. *Fax:* 918-343-7595. *E-mail:* kcook@rsu.edu.

eCollege.com *www.ecollege.com/scholarships*

DEGREES AND AWARDS

AA Business Administration (certain restrictions apply), Liberal Arts (certain restrictions apply)
AAS Applied Technology (certain restrictions apply)
AS Computer Science (certain restrictions apply)
BA Liberal Arts (certain restrictions apply)
BS Information Technology (certain restrictions apply)
BT Applied Technology (certain restrictions apply)

COURSE SUBJECT AREAS OFFERED OUTSIDE OF DEGREE PROGRAMS

Undergraduate: Area, ethnic, and cultural studies; biological and life sciences; business; communications; computer and information sciences; conservation and natural resources; English language and literature; European languages and literatures; history; law and legal studies; mathematics; philosophy and religion; physical sciences; psychology; social sciences; visual and performing arts

See full descriptions on pages 644 and 676.

ROGER WILLIAMS UNIVERSITY

Bristol, Rhode Island
Open Program
www.rwu.edu

Roger Williams University, founded in 1956, is an independent, nonprofit, comprehensive institution. It is accredited by the New England Association of Schools and Colleges. It first offered distance learning courses in 1974. In 1999–2000, it offered 95 courses at a distance. In fall 1999, there were 100 students enrolled in distance learning courses.

Course delivery sites Courses are delivered to your home, your workplace, military bases.

Media Courses are delivered via videotapes, audiotapes, computer software, computer conferencing, World Wide Web, e-mail, print. Students and teachers may meet in person or interact via audioconferencing, mail, telephone, fax, e-mail, World Wide Web. The following equipment may be required: computer, Internet access, e-mail.

Restrictions Programs are available worldwide. Enrollment is restricted to individuals meeting certain criteria.

Services Distance learners have access to library services, the campus computer network, e-mail services, academic advising, career placement assistance, bookstore at a distance.

Credit-earning options Students may transfer credits from another institution or may earn credits through examinations, portfolio assessment, military training, business training.

Typical costs Tuition ranges between $230 to $400 per credit depending on the type of course. Costs may vary. Financial aid is available to distance learners.

Registration Students may register by mail, fax, telephone, e-mail, World Wide Web, in person.

Contact Mary Dionisopoulos, Administrative Assistant, Roger Williams University, One Old Ferry Road, Bristol, RI 02809. *Telephone:* 401-254-3530. *Fax:* 401-254-3560. *E-mail:* jws@alpha.rwu.edu.

eCollege.com *www.ecollege.com/scholarships*

DEGREES AND AWARDS

BS Business Management, Criminal Justice, Industrial Technology, Public Administration

COURSE SUBJECT AREAS OFFERED OUTSIDE OF DEGREE PROGRAMS

Undergraduate: Accounting; anthropology; biology; business administration and management; business law; communications; computer and information sciences; criminology; engineering-related technologies; engineering/industrial management; English language and literature; history of science and technology; human resources management; insurance; investments and securities; logic; marketing; political science; protective services; psychology; public administration and services; sociology

See full description on page 646.

ROOSEVELT UNIVERSITY

Chicago, Illinois
External Studies Program
www.roosevelt.edu/distance-learning

Roosevelt University, founded in 1945, is an independent, nonprofit, comprehensive institution. It is accredited by the North Central Association of Colleges and Schools. It first offered distance learning courses in 1974. In 1999–2000, it offered 90 courses at a distance. In fall 1999, there were 400 students enrolled in distance learning courses.

Course delivery sites Courses are delivered to your home, your workplace, military bases.

Media Courses are delivered via World Wide Web, e-mail, print. Students and teachers may meet in person or interact via mail, telephone, fax, e-mail, World Wide Web. The following equipment may be required: Internet access, e-mail.

Restrictions Programs are available to local area students. Enrollment is restricted to individuals meeting certain criteria.

Services Distance learners have access to library services, e-mail services, academic advising, tutoring, career placement assistance, bookstore at a distance.

Credit-earning options Students may transfer credits from another institution or may earn credits through examinations, portfolio assessment.

Typical costs Tuition of $429 per credit. Financial aid is available to distance learners.

Registration Students may register by mail, e-mail, in person.

Contact Admissions Office, Roosevelt University, 430 South Michigan, Room 104, Chicago, IL 60605. *Telephone:* 312-341-3515. *Fax:* 312-341-3523. *E-mail:* dessim@admrs6k.roosevelt.edu.

DEGREES AND AWARDS

Distance programs offered do not lead to a degree or other formal award.

COURSE SUBJECT AREAS OFFERED OUTSIDE OF DEGREE PROGRAMS

Undergraduate: Accounting; American (U.S.) history; business; business administration and management; business communications; business information and data processing services; business law; computer and information sciences; computer programming; database management; economics; English composition; finance; geography; history; hospitality services management; physical sciences; social psychology; social sciences

ROSE STATE COLLEGE

Midwest City, Oklahoma
Academic Affairs
www.rose.cc.ok.us/index1.htm

Rose State College, founded in 1968, is a state and locally supported, two-year college. It is accredited by the North Central Association of Colleges and Schools. It first offered distance learning courses in 1972.

Contact Rose State College, 6420 Southeast 15th Street, Midwest City, OK 73110-2799. *Telephone:* 405-733-7311. *Fax:* 405-736-0339.

See full description on page 676.

ROWAN-CABARRUS COMMUNITY COLLEGE

Salisbury, North Carolina

Rowan-Cabarrus Community College, founded in 1963, is a state-supported, two-year college. It is accredited by the Southern Association of Colleges and Schools.

Contact Rowan-Cabarrus Community College, PO Box 1595, Salisbury, NC 28145-1595. *Telephone:* 704-637-0760. *Fax:* 704-633-6804.

See full description on page 676.

ROYAL MILITARY COLLEGE OF CANADA

Kingston, Ontario, Canada
Office of Continuing Studies
www.rmc.ca

Royal Military College of Canada, founded in 1876, is a federally supported, comprehensive institution. It is accredited by the provincial charter. In 1999–2000, it offered 100 courses at a distance. In fall 1999, there were 1,000 students enrolled in distance learning courses.

Course delivery sites Courses are delivered to your home, your workplace, military bases, 17 off-campus centers.

Media Courses are delivered via videotapes, videoconferencing, audiotapes, CD-ROM, World Wide Web, e-mail, print. Students and teachers may meet in person or interact via videoconferencing, mail, telephone, fax, e-mail, World Wide Web. The following equipment may be required: e-mail.

Restrictions Programs are available worldwide. Enrollment is restricted to individuals meeting certain criteria.

Services Distance learners have access to e-mail services, academic advising, tutoring, bookstore at a distance.

Credit-earning options Students may transfer credits from another institution or may earn credits through military training.

Typical costs Undergraduate tuition is $125 per semester course and graduate tuition is $250 per semester course.

Registration Students may register by mail, fax, e-mail, in person.

Contact Counselors, Office of Continuing Studies, Royal Military College of Canada, CFP0 17000, Station Forces, Kingston, ON K7K 7B4 Canada. *Telephone:* 800-352-8979. *Fax:* 613-541-6706. *E-mail:* warstudy@rmc.ca.

DEGREES AND AWARDS

BA Military Arts and Science (certain restrictions apply)
MA Military Arts and Science (certain restrictions apply)
MAM Defense Management (certain restrictions apply)

COURSE SUBJECT AREAS OFFERED OUTSIDE OF DEGREE PROGRAMS

Undergraduate: Accounting; business administration and management; calculus; chemistry; comparative literature; English literature; ethics; history; human resources management; marketing; organizational behavior studies; physics; psychology; statistics

Graduate: Business administration and management; comparative literature; ethics; finance; history; human resources management; management information systems; psychology

ROYAL ROADS UNIVERSITY

Victoria, British Columbia, Canada
www.royalroads.ca

Royal Roads University, founded in 1996, is a province-supported, upper-level institution. It is accredited by the provincial charter. In 1999–2000, it offered 30 courses at a distance. In fall 1999, there were 600 students enrolled in distance learning courses.

Course delivery sites Courses are delivered to your home, your workplace, military bases.

Media Courses are delivered via CD-ROM, computer conferencing, World Wide Web, e-mail, print. Students and teachers may interact via mail, telephone, fax, e-mail, World Wide Web. The following equipment may be required: computer, modem, Internet access, e-mail.

Restrictions Programs are available worldwide. Enrollment is restricted to individuals meeting certain criteria.

Services Distance learners have access to library services, the campus computer network, e-mail services, career placement assistance, bookstore at a distance.

Credit-earning options Students may transfer credits from another institution or may earn credits through examinations, portfolio assessment.

Typical costs Tuition for Canadian students ranges between $275 and $400. International student tuition ranges between $550 and $600. Mandatory fees are $140 per year. Costs may vary. Financial aid is available to distance learners.

Registration Students may register by mail, fax, e-mail, in person.

Contact Learner Services and Registrar's Office, Royal Roads University, 2025 Sooke Road, Victoria, BC V9B 5Y2 Canada. *Telephone:* 800-788-8028. *Fax:* 250-391-2522. *E-mail:* rruregistrar@royalroads.ca.

DEGREES AND AWARDS

MA Conflict Analysis and Management (certain restrictions apply; some on-campus requirements), Environment and Management (certain restrictions apply; some on-campus requirements), Leadership and Training (certain restrictions apply; some on-campus requirements)

MBA Digital Technologies Management (certain restrictions apply; some on-campus requirements), Executive Management (certain restrictions apply; some on-campus requirements), Human Resources Management (certain restrictions apply; some on-campus requirements), Public Relations and Communication Management (certain restrictions apply; some on-campus requirements)

MSc Environment and Management (certain restrictions apply; some on-campus requirements)

COURSE SUBJECT AREAS OFFERED OUTSIDE OF DEGREE PROGRAMS

Graduate: Adult education; business; business administration and management; business communications; community services; environmental science; health services administration; human resources management; international relations; management information systems; public policy analysis; public relations

---

RUTGERS, THE STATE UNIVERSITY OF NEW JERSEY, NEW BRUNSWICK

New Brunswick, New Jersey

Office of Vice President for Continuous Education and Outreach
ce1766.rutgers.edu

Rutgers, The State University of New Jersey, New Brunswick, founded in 1766, is a state-supported university. It is accredited by the Middle States Association of Colleges and Schools. It first offered distance learning courses in 1995. In 1999–2000, it offered 17 courses at a distance. In fall 1999, there were 350 students enrolled in distance learning courses.

Course delivery sites Courses are delivered to your home, your workplace, military bases, high schools, Atlantic Cape Community College (Mays Landing), Brookdale Community College (Lincroft), 1 off-campus center in Freehold.

Media Courses are delivered via television, videoconferencing, computer software, World Wide Web, e-mail, print. Students and teachers may meet in person or interact via videoconferencing, mail, telephone, fax, e-mail. The following equipment may be required: computer, modem, Internet access, e-mail.

Restrictions Programs are available worldwide. Enrollment is open to anyone.

Services Distance learners have access to library services, the campus computer network, e-mail services, academic advising, tutoring, career placement assistance, bookstore at a distance.

Credit-earning options Students may transfer credits from another institution or may earn credits through examinations, portfolio assessment.

Typical costs *Undergraduate:* Tuition of $158 per credit plus mandatory fees of $1182 per year for in-state residents. Tuition of $316 per credit plus mandatory fees of $1182 per year for out-of-state residents. *Graduate:* Tuition of $278 per credit plus mandatory fees of $1048 per year for in-state residents. Tuition of $412.30 per credit plus mandatory fees of $1048 per year for out-of-state residents. Cost for a noncredit course varies between $100 and $2000. Costs may vary. Financial aid is available to distance learners.

Registration Students may register by mail, fax, telephone, in person.

Contact Dr. Raphael J. Caprio, Vice President, Continuous Education and Outreach, Rutgers, The State University of New Jersey, New Brunswick, 83 Somerset Street, College Avenue Campus, New Brunswick, NJ 08903. *Telephone:* 732-932-5935. *Fax:* 732-932-9225. *E-mail:* caprio@andromeda.rutgers.edu.

---

eCollege.com   *www.ecollege.com/scholarships*

DEGREES AND AWARDS

Distance programs offered do not lead to a degree or other formal award.

COURSE SUBJECT AREAS OFFERED OUTSIDE OF DEGREE PROGRAMS

Undergraduate: Chinese language and literature; economics; education administration; electrical engineering; German language and literature; history; human resources management; Italian language and literature; liberal arts, general studies, and humanities; library and information studies; mathematics; nursing; organizational behavior studies; philosophy and religion; religious studies; sociology; teacher education

Graduate: Education administration; electrical engineering; human resources management; instructional media; library and information studies; microbiology; nursing; organizational behavior studies; teacher education

Noncredit: Electrical engineering; human resources management; instructional media; liberal arts, general studies, and humanities; nursing; organizational behavior studies; religious studies; teacher education

See full description on page 648.

RYERSON POLYTECHNIC UNIVERSITY

Toronto, Ontario, Canada

Distance Education
www.ryerson.ca/ce/

Ryerson Polytechnic University, founded in 1948, is a province-supported, four-year college. It is accredited by the provincial charter. It first offered distance learning courses in 1970. In 1999–2000, it offered 63 courses at a distance. In fall 1999, there were 687 students enrolled in distance learning courses.

Course delivery sites Courses are delivered to your home, your workplace.

Media Courses are delivered via audiotapes, computer software, CD-ROM, computer conferencing, World Wide Web, e-mail, print. Students and teachers may meet in person or interact via audioconferencing, mail, telephone, fax, e-mail, World Wide Web. The following equipment may be required: computer, modem, Internet access.

Restrictions Programs are available worldwide. Enrollment is restricted to individuals meeting certain criteria.

Services Distance learners have access to library services, the campus computer network, e-mail services, academic advising, tutoring at a distance.

Credit-earning options Students may transfer credits from another institution or may earn credits through examinations.

Typical costs Tuition of Can$420 per course. *Noncredit courses:* Can$420 per course. Costs may vary.

Registration Students may register by mail, fax, telephone, in person.

Contact Program Assistant, Distance Education, Ryerson Polytechnic University, Continuing Education Division, 350 Victoria Street, Toronto, ON M5B 2K3 Canada. *Telephone:* 416-979-5135. *Fax:* 416-979-5148. *E-mail:* de@acs.ryerson.ca.

DEGREES AND AWARDS

Undergraduate Certificate(s) Fundraising Management, Gerontology, Non-profit Sector Management, Occupational Health and Safety, Public Administration

Graduate Certificate(s) BIA Insolvency Counselor's Qualification (service area differs from that of the overall institution)

COURSE SUBJECT AREAS OFFERED OUTSIDE OF DEGREE PROGRAMS

Undergraduate: Business; business administration and management; Canadian studies; communications; economics; English language and literature; environmental health; gerontology; history; home economics and family studies; human resources management; liberal arts, general studies, and humanities; political science; psychology; public administration and services; sociology

Noncredit: Business; business administration and management; human resources management

---

SACRAMENTO CITY COLLEGE

Sacramento, California

Courses by Television

Sacramento City College, founded in 1916, is a state and locally supported, two-year college. It is accredited by the Western Association of Schools and Colleges, Inc. It first offered distance learning courses in 1986. In 1999–2000, it offered 24 courses at a distance. In fall 1999, there were 725 students enrolled in distance learning courses.

Course delivery sites Courses are delivered to your home.

Media Courses are delivered via television, videotapes. Students and teachers may meet in person or interact via mail, telephone, fax, e-mail. The following equipment may be required: television, videocassette player.

Restrictions Programs are available to local area students. Enrollment is open to anyone.

Services Distance learners have access to library services at a distance.

Credit-earning options Students may transfer credits from another institution.

Typical costs Tuition of $11 per unit for in-state residents. Tuition of $134 per unit for out-of-state residents. Financial aid is available to distance learners.

Registration Students may register by mail, telephone, in person.

Contact Jeanne Feeney, Student Coordinator of Distance Education, Sacramento City College, Learning Resources, Sacramento, CA 95822. *Telephone:* 916-558-2361. *E-mail:* feeneyj@exi.scc.losrios.cc.ca.us.

DEGREES AND AWARDS

Distance programs offered do not lead to a degree or other formal award.

COURSE SUBJECT AREAS OFFERED OUTSIDE OF DEGREE PROGRAMS

Undergraduate: Anthropology; area, ethnic, and cultural studies; business; business administration and management; English language and literature; European languages and literatures; geography; gerontology; health and physical education/fitness; history; music; philosophy and religion; psychology; sociology

---

SACRED HEART UNIVERSITY

Fairfield, Connecticut

University College

www.sacredheart.edu/acad/ucollege/

Sacred Heart University, founded in 1963, is an independent, religious, comprehensive institution. It is accredited by the New England Association of Schools and Colleges. It first offered distance learning courses in 1997. In 1999–2000, it offered 11 courses at a distance. In fall 1999, there were 35 students enrolled in distance learning courses.

Course delivery sites Courses are delivered to your home, your workplace.

Media Courses are delivered via videoconferencing, World Wide Web, e-mail. Students and teachers may meet in person or interact via mail, telephone, fax, e-mail, World Wide Web. The following equipment may be required: computer, modem, Internet access, e-mail.

Restrictions Programs are available worldwide. Enrollment is open to anyone.

Services Distance learners have access to library services, the campus computer network, e-mail services, academic advising, career placement assistance, bookstore at a distance.

Credit-earning options Students may transfer credits from another institution or may earn credits through examinations, portfolio assessment, military training, business training.

Typical costs *Undergraduate:* Tuition of $305 per credit plus mandatory fees of $58 per semester. *Graduate:* Tuition of $345 per credit plus mandatory fees of $83 per semester. Financial aid is available to distance learners.

Registration Students may register by mail, fax, World Wide Web, in person.

Contact Edward Donato, Associate Dean, University College, Sacred Heart University, 5151 Park Avenue, Fairfield, CT 06432. *Telephone:* 203-371-7836. *Fax:* 203-365-7500. *E-mail:* donatoe@sacredheart.edu.

DEGREES AND AWARDS

BSN Nursing (certain restrictions apply; some on-campus requirements)

COURSE SUBJECT AREAS OFFERED OUTSIDE OF DEGREE PROGRAMS

Undergraduate: Business administration and management; business law; comparative literature; criminal justice; English composition; finance; international business; marketing; mathematics; nursing; organizational behavior studies

Graduate: Teacher education

Noncredit: Teacher education

Special note

Sacred Heart University's dynamic link to adult and corporate communities, University College, brings Sacred Heart's resources and programs to the adult learner through 5 regional campus locations in Danbury, Derby, Fairfield, Shelton, and Stamford, Connecticut; on site at local corporations; or through distance learning. Founded in 1963, Sacred Heart was created to embody a new direction within American Catholic higher education, led and staffed by laity and independent and locally oriented. As the University grew, the vision and mission expanded, producing a high-quality institution that now serves a regional, national, and international purpose. University College has maintained the founding premise of the University by continuing to serve the needs of adults in their quest for knowledge; personal, professional, and spiritual growth; and continuous learning. The University offers its distance learning courses on a semester-based calendar. Most courses are delivered asynchronously, so students can schedule their own "work time." Small class size ensures personal attention in the Web-based courses. Sacred Heart employs Jones Knowledge.Com as its partner in delivering online courses. This partnership provides students with redundant hardware systems, 24 hour support, and state-of-the-art software. Sacred Heart offers undergraduate distance learning courses in disciplines such as business administration and management, business law, comparative literature, English composition, history, international business, mathematics, media studies, nursing, and sports marketing. It also offers a complete degree program for registered nurses who wish to complete a Bachelor of Science in Nursing. The RN-to-BSN program, which is accredited by the National League for Nursing, requires 57 credits in nursing; 30 credits may be awarded for previous nursing work, and as many as 90 credits may be transferable from an accredited academic program. A graduate certificate in educational technology for certified teachers, consisting of 4 Web-based courses, is also available. All MBA prerequisites are available on line, as is the Sports Business University, a partnership to provide relevant business education to the sports industry. A graduate-level program in elder care and an undergraduate certificate in leadership studies will be available next academic year. For further information, students should contact Edward Donato, Associate Dean, University College at 203-371-7836 or at donatoe@sacred heart.edu.

SADDLEBACK COLLEGE

Mission Viejo, California
Advanced Technology and Applied Science
www.saddleback.cc.ca.us

Saddleback College, founded in 1967, is a state and locally supported, two-year college. It is accredited by the Western Association of Schools and Colleges, Inc. It first offered distance learning courses in 1975. In 1999–2000, it offered 45 courses at a distance. In fall 1999, there were 1,160 students enrolled in distance learning courses.
Course delivery sites Courses are delivered to your home.
Media Courses are delivered via television, videotapes, audiotapes, computer software, CD-ROM, World Wide Web, e-mail. Students and teachers may meet in person or interact via mail, telephone, fax, e-mail. The following equipment may be required: television, computer, modem, Internet access, e-mail.
Restrictions Programs are available to local area students. Enrollment is open to anyone.
Services Distance learners have access to library services, the campus computer network, e-mail services, academic advising, bookstore at a distance.
Credit-earning options Students may transfer credits from another institution or may earn credits through examinations, portfolio assessment.
Typical costs *Undergraduate:* Tuition of $11 per unit for in-state residents. Tuition of $125 per unit for out-of-state residents. *Graduate:* Tuition of $11 per unit for in-state residents. Tuition of $125 per unit for out-of-state residents. Financial aid is available to distance learners.
Registration Students may register by mail, telephone, World Wide Web, in person.

Contact Sheri L. Nelson, Senior Administrative Assistant, Saddleback College, Saddleback College Library 218, 28000 Marguerite Parkway, Mission Viejo, CA 92692. *Telephone:* 949-582-4515. *Fax:* 949-582-4753. *E-mail:* snelson@saddleback.cc.ca.us.

DEGREES AND AWARDS

Distance programs offered do not lead to a degree or other formal award.

COURSE SUBJECT AREAS OFFERED OUTSIDE OF DEGREE PROGRAMS

Undergraduate: Accounting; American (U.S.) history; anthropology; business administration and management; business law; child care and development; computer and information sciences; creative writing; health and physical education/fitness; individual and family development studies; marketing; music; oceanography; political science; psychology; real estate; sociology

ST. AMBROSE UNIVERSITY

Davenport, Iowa
web.sau.edu/accel/

St. Ambrose University, founded in 1882, is an independent, religious, comprehensive institution. It is accredited by the North Central Association of Colleges and Schools. In 1999–2000, it offered 3 courses at a distance. In fall 1999, there were 29 students enrolled in distance learning courses.
Course delivery sites Courses are delivered to your home, your workplace, military bases.
Media Courses are delivered via interactive television. Students and teachers may interact via interactive television.
Restrictions Iowa, Illinois, and South Dakota. Enrollment is open to anyone.
Typical costs *Undergraduate:* Tuition of $432 per credit. *Graduate:* Tuition of $432 per credit. Undergraduate tuition for the accelerated program is $295 per credit (5-8 week courses).
Contact Dr. Hope Gardina, Dean of Adult Education and Professional Development, St. Ambrose University, St. Ambrose Continuing Studies and Conference Center, 1950 East 54th Street, Davenport, IA 52807. *Telephone:* 888-222-3578 Ext. 205. *Fax:* 319-441-9470. *E-mail:* hgardina@ saunix.sau.edu.

DEGREES AND AWARDS

Distance programs offered do not lead to a degree or other formal award.

COURSE SUBJECT AREAS OFFERED OUTSIDE OF DEGREE PROGRAMS

Undergraduate: Business administration and management; mass media; religious studies; teacher education
Graduate: Business administration and management; occupational therapy; physical therapy; special education; statistics

SAINT CHARLES COUNTY COMMUNITY COLLEGE

St. Peters, Missouri

Distance Learning

www.stchas.edu/academics/distance/dlmain.htm

Saint Charles County Community College, founded in 1986, is a state-supported, two-year college. It is accredited by the North Central Association of Colleges and Schools. In 1999–2000, it offered 25 courses at a distance. In fall 1999, there were 850 students enrolled in distance learning courses.

Course delivery sites Courses are delivered to your home, your workplace, 3 off-campus centers in Eolia, Montgomery City, South Callaway.

Media Courses are delivered via television, videotapes, interactive television, World Wide Web. Students and teachers may meet in person or interact via mail, telephone, fax, e-mail, interactive television. The following equipment may be required: television, videocassette player, computer, modem, Internet access.

Restrictions Programs available within a 5-county region. Enrollment is open to anyone.

Services Distance learners have access to library services, academic advising, tutoring, bookstore at a distance.

Credit-earning options Students may transfer credits from another institution.

Typical costs Tuition of $43 per credit hour plus mandatory fees of $5 per credit hour for local area residents. Tuition of $63 per credit hour plus mandatory fees of $5 per credit hour for in-state residents. Tuition of $97 per credit hour plus mandatory fees of $5 per credit hour for out-of-state residents. Financial aid is available to distance learners.

Registration Students may register by mail, fax, in person.

Contact Joan Clarke, Dean of Learning Resources, Saint Charles County Community College, 4601 Mid Rivers Mall Drive, St. Peters, MO 63376. *Telephone:* 636-922-8512. *Fax:* 636-922-8433. *E-mail:* jclarke@chuck.stchas.edu.

DEGREES AND AWARDS

Distance programs offered do not lead to a degree or other formal award.

COURSE SUBJECT AREAS OFFERED OUTSIDE OF DEGREE PROGRAMS

Undergraduate: Algebra; American (U.S.) history; anthropology; art history and criticism; biology; business; chemistry; communications; criminal justice; developmental and child psychology; English composition; film studies; health and physical education/fitness; mathematics; music; political science; psychology; sociology

Graduate: Algebra; American (U.S.) history; anthropology; art history and criticism; biology; business; chemistry; communications; criminal justice; developmental and child psychology; English composition; film studies; health and physical education/fitness; mathematics; music; political science; psychology; sociology

ST. CLOUD STATE UNIVERSITY

St. Cloud, Minnesota

Center for Continuing Studies

condor.stcloudstate.edu/~ccs/

St. Cloud State University, founded in 1869, is a state-supported, comprehensive institution. It is accredited by the North Central Association of Colleges and Schools. It first offered distance learning courses in

1975. In 1999–2000, it offered 120 courses at a distance. In fall 1999, there were 1,000 students enrolled in distance learning courses.

Course delivery sites Courses are delivered to your home, your workplace, high schools.

Media Courses are delivered via television, interactive television, computer software, e-mail, print. Students and teachers may meet in person or interact via mail, telephone, fax, e-mail, interactive television, World Wide Web. The following equipment may be required: computer, modem, Internet access, e-mail.

Restrictions Programs are available to in-state students only. Enrollment is restricted to individuals meeting certain criteria.

Services Distance learners have access to e-mail services, bookstore at a distance.

Credit-earning options Students may transfer credits from another institution or may earn credits through examinations, military training.

Typical costs *Undergraduate:* Tuition of $104.83 per credit. *Graduate:* Tuition of $151 per credit. Costs may vary. Financial aid is available to distance learners.

Registration Students may register by mail, fax, telephone, in person.

Contact Sue Handley, Secretary, Center for Continuing Studies, St. Cloud State University, 720 Fourth Avenue, South, St. Cloud, MN 56301-4498. *Telephone:* 320-255-3081. *Fax:* 320-654-5041. *E-mail:* shandley@stcloudstate.edu.

DEGREES AND AWARDS

AA Liberal Arts (certain restrictions apply; some on-campus requirements)

AES Self Designed Studies (certain restrictions apply; some on-campus requirements)

BES Applied Psychology (certain restrictions apply; some on-campus requirements), Marketing (certain restrictions apply; some on-campus requirements), Self Designed (certain restrictions apply; some on-campus requirements), Speech Communication (certain restrictions apply; some on-campus requirements)

MEd Educational Administration (certain restrictions apply; some on-campus requirements)

COURSE SUBJECT AREAS OFFERED OUTSIDE OF DEGREE PROGRAMS

Undergraduate: Anthropology; biology; chemistry; criminal justice; economics; English language and literature; environmental science; fine arts; history; philosophy and religion; psychology; social sciences; sociology; speech

Graduate: Education administration; English as a second language (ESL); individual and family development studies; information sciences and systems; mass media; mathematics

ST. EDWARD'S UNIVERSITY

Austin, Texas

New College

St. Edward's University, founded in 1885, is an independent, religious, comprehensive institution. It is accredited by the Southern Association of Colleges and Schools. In 1999–2000, it offered 10 courses at a distance. In fall 1999, there were 65 students enrolled in distance learning courses.

Course delivery sites Courses are delivered to your home, your workplace.

Media Courses are delivered via World Wide Web, e-mail, print. Students and teachers may meet in person or interact via mail, telephone, e-mail, World Wide Web. The following equipment may be required: computer, modem, Internet access, e-mail.

Restrictions Programs are available to in-state students only. Enrollment is open to anyone.

Services Distance learners have access to library services, the campus computer network, e-mail services, academic advising, tutoring, career placement assistance, bookstore at a distance.

Credit-earning options Students may transfer credits from another institution or may earn credits through examinations, portfolio assessment, military training, business training.

Typical costs Tuition of $381 per credit. Application fee is $21. Financial aid is available to distance learners.

Registration Students may register by mail, fax, telephone, e-mail, World Wide Web, in person.

Contact Dr. H. Ramsey Fowler, Dean, St. Edward's University, New College at St. Edward's, 3001 South Congress Avenue, Austin, TX 78704-6489. *Telephone:* 512-448-8701. *Fax:* 512-448-8767. *E-mail:* ramseyf@admin.stedwards.edu.

DEGREES AND AWARDS

Distance programs offered do not lead to a degree or other formal award.

COURSE SUBJECT AREAS OFFERED OUTSIDE OF DEGREE PROGRAMS

Undergraduate: Anthropology; business communications; economics; English composition; English literature; ethics; European history; geography

SAINT FRANCIS COLLEGE

Loretto, Pennsylvania
Academic Affairs
www.sfcpa.edu

Saint Francis College, founded in 1847, is an independent, religious, comprehensive institution. It is accredited by the Middle States Association of Colleges and Schools. It first offered distance learning courses in 1994. In 1999–2000, it offered 12 courses at a distance. In fall 1999, there were 50 students enrolled in distance learning courses.

Course delivery sites Courses are delivered to your home, your workplace, military bases.

Media Courses are delivered via videotapes, videoconferencing, computer software, CD-ROM, computer conferencing, World Wide Web, e-mail, print. Students and teachers may meet in person or interact via videoconferencing, audioconferencing, mail, telephone, fax, e-mail, World Wide Web. The following equipment may be required: computer, modem, Internet access, e-mail.

Restrictions Programs are available worldwide. Enrollment is open to anyone.

Services Distance learners have access to library services, the campus computer network, e-mail services, academic advising, tutoring, career placement assistance at a distance.

Credit-earning options Students may transfer credits from another institution or may earn credits through examinations, military training, business training.

Typical costs Tuition of $495 per credit hour plus mandatory fees of $45 per semester. Financial aid is available to distance learners.

Registration Students may register by mail, fax, telephone, e-mail, in person.

Contact Dr. William Duryea, Director, Saint Francis College, MMS Program, Sullivan Hall, Loretto, PA 15940. *Telephone:* 814-472-3130. *Fax:* 814-472-3137. *E-mail:* wduryea@sfcpa.edu.

DEGREES AND AWARDS

MMS Health Science (Physician Assistant)

ST. FRANCIS XAVIER UNIVERSITY

Antigonish, Nova Scotia, Canada
Continuing Education
www.stfx.ca/

St. Francis Xavier University, founded in 1853, is an independent, religious, comprehensive institution. It is accredited by the provincial charter. In 1999–2000, it offered 30 courses at a distance. In fall 1999, there were 700 students enrolled in distance learning courses.

Course delivery sites Courses are delivered to your home, your workplace.

Media Courses are delivered via CD-ROM, computer conferencing, World Wide Web, print. Students and teachers may meet in person or interact via telephone, fax, e-mail, World Wide Web. The following equipment may be required: computer, Internet access, e-mail.

Restrictions Programs are available nationwide. Enrollment is open to anyone.

Services Distance learners have access to library services, e-mail services, academic advising, tutoring, bookstore at a distance.

Credit-earning options Students may transfer credits from another institution.

Typical costs Tuition for Canadian students is $450 for half a year or 3 credits; tuition for U.S. students is $550 for half a year or 3 credits. *Noncredit courses:* $450 per course. Costs may vary.

Registration Students may register by mail, fax, telephone, e-mail, in person.

Contact Coleen Jones, Secretary, St. Francis Xavier University, Continuing Education, Antigonish, NS B2G 2W5 Canada. *Telephone:* 902-867-3906. *Fax:* 902-867-5154. *E-mail:* cjones@stfx.ca.

DEGREES AND AWARDS

BSc Nursing (certain restrictions apply)
Graduate Certificate(s) Catholic Ministry (certain restrictions apply), Real Property Appraisal and Assessment

COURSE SUBJECT AREAS OFFERED OUTSIDE OF DEGREE PROGRAMS

Undergraduate: Health professions and related sciences; real estate; theological studies

ST. JOHNS RIVER COMMUNITY COLLEGE

Palatka, Florida
Continuing Education
www.sjrcc.cc.fl.us

St. Johns River Community College, founded in 1958, is a state-supported, two-year college. It is accredited by the Southern Association of Colleges and Schools. It first offered distance learning courses in 1996. In 1999–2000, it offered 27 courses at a distance. In fall 1999, there were 131 students enrolled in distance learning courses.

Course delivery sites Courses are delivered to your home, your workplace.

Media Courses are delivered via television, computer software, World Wide Web. Students and teachers may interact via mail, telephone, fax, e-mail. The following equipment may be required: television, computer, modem, Internet access.

Restrictions Courses are available to in-district students only. Enrollment is open to anyone.

Services Distance learners have access to library services, academic advising, career placement assistance at a distance.

Credit-earning options Students may transfer credits from another institution or may earn credits through examinations, military training.
Typical costs Tuition of $44 per credit hour for in-state residents. Tuition of $166 per credit hour for out-of-state residents. Financial aid is available to distance learners.
Registration Students may register by in person.
Contact Dr. John T. Skelton, Director, Continuing Education and Distance Learning, St. Johns River Community College, 5001 St. Johns Avenue, Palatka, FL 32177. *Telephone:* 904-312-4211. *Fax:* 904-312-4292. *E-mail:* skelton_j@popmail.firn.edu.

DEGREES AND AWARDS

Distance programs offered do not lead to a degree or other formal award.

COURSE SUBJECT AREAS OFFERED OUTSIDE OF DEGREE PROGRAMS

Undergraduate: Astronomy and astrophysics; business; business administration and management; communications; computer and information sciences; developmental and child psychology; economics; English composition; English language and literature; history; human resources management; liberal arts, general studies, and humanities; mathematics; political science; sociology
See full description on page 676.

ST. JOHN'S UNIVERSITY

Jamaica, New York
www.stjohns.edu

St. John's University, founded in 1870, is an independent, religious university affiliated with the Roman Catholic Church. It is accredited by the Middle States Association of Colleges and Schools. In 1999–2000, it offered 23 courses at a distance.
Course delivery sites Courses are delivered to your home, your workplace, military bases, high schools.
Media Courses are delivered via videoconferencing, computer software, CD-ROM, computer conferencing, World Wide Web, e-mail, print. Students and teachers may meet in person or interact via videoconferencing, audioconferencing, mail, telephone, fax, e-mail, World Wide Web. The following equipment may be required: computer, modem, Internet access, e-mail.
Restrictions Programs are available worldwide. Enrollment is restricted to individuals meeting certain criteria.
Services Distance learners have access to library services, the campus computer network, e-mail services, academic advising, tutoring, career placement assistance, bookstore at a distance.
Credit-earning options Students may transfer credits from another institution or may earn credits through examinations, portfolio assessment, military training, business training.
Typical costs *Undergraduate:* Tuition of $466 per credit plus mandatory fees of $70 per semester. *Graduate:* Tuition of $600 per credit plus mandatory fees of $75 per semester. Costs may vary. Financial aid is available to distance learners.
Registration Students may register by telephone, World Wide Web, in person.
Contact SJU Online, St. John's University, 8000 Utopia Parkway, Jamaica, NY 11439. *Telephone:* 888-9STJOHNS. *E-mail:* sjuonline@stjohns.edu.

DEGREES AND AWARDS

Distance programs offered do not lead to a degree or other formal award.

COURSE SUBJECT AREAS OFFERED OUTSIDE OF DEGREE PROGRAMS

Undergraduate: Business administration and management; economics; English composition; paralegal/legal assistant
Graduate: Business administration and management; economics; finance

SAINT JOSEPH'S COLLEGE

Standish, Maine
Division of Continuing and Professional Studies
www.sjcme.edu/cps

Saint Joseph's College, founded in 1912, is an independent, religious, comprehensive institution affiliated with the Roman Catholic Church. It is accredited by the New England Association of Schools and Colleges. It first offered distance learning courses in 1976. In 1999–2000, it offered 185 courses at a distance. In fall 1999, there were 4,000 students enrolled in distance learning courses.
Course delivery sites Courses are delivered to your home.
Media Courses are delivered via videotapes, audiotapes, computer software, CD-ROM, computer conferencing, World Wide Web, e-mail, print. Students and teachers may meet in person or interact via mail, telephone, fax, e-mail, World Wide Web. The following equipment may be required: computer.
Restrictions Programs are available worldwide. Enrollment is open to anyone.
Services Distance learners have access to library services, e-mail services, academic advising, tutoring, career placement assistance, bookstore at a distance.
Credit-earning options Students may transfer credits from another institution or may earn credits through examinations, portfolio assessment, military training.
Typical costs *Undergraduate:* Tuition of $195 per credit. *Graduate:* Tuition of $235 per credit. Costs may vary. Financial aid is available to distance learners.
Registration Students may register by mail, fax, telephone, e-mail, in person.
Contact Admissions Office, Saint Joseph's College, 278 White's Bridge Road, Department 840, Standish, ME 04084-5263. *Telephone:* 800-752-4723. *Fax:* 207-892-7480. *E-mail:* admiss@sjcme.edu.

DEGREES AND AWARDS

Undergraduate Certificate(s) American Studies, Business Administration, Christian Tradition, Health Care Management, Long-term Care Administration, Professional Studies
ASM Business Administration (some on-campus requirements)
BACJ Criminal Justice (some on-campus requirements)
BLS American Studies (some on-campus requirements), Christian Tradition (some on-campus requirements)
BS Health Care Administration (some on-campus requirements), Long-Term Care Administration (some on-campus requirements)
BSBA Business Administration (some on-campus requirements)
BSN Nursing (service area differs from that of the overall institution; some on-campus requirements)
BSPA Professional Arts (some on-campus requirements)
BSRC Respiratory Care (some on-campus requirements)
BSRS Radiological Sciences (some on-campus requirements)
Graduate Certificate(s) Health Care Finance (certain restrictions apply), Medical and Dental Practice Administration (certain restrictions apply), Secondary Education
MAPS Pastoral Studies (some on-campus requirements)
MHSA Health Services Administration (some on-campus requirements)
MS Nursing (some on-campus requirements)
MSEd Education (some on-campus requirements)

COURSE SUBJECT AREAS OFFERED OUTSIDE OF DEGREE PROGRAMS

Undergraduate: Accounting; business; business administration and management; developmental and child psychology; economics; education administration; educational psychology; English composition; English language and literature; fine arts; health professions and related sciences; history; human resources management; industrial psychology; law and legal studies; liberal arts, general studies, and humanities; mathematics; music; nursing; philosophy and religion; public health; social psychology; sociology

Graduate: Accounting; economics; education administration; health professions and related sciences; human resources management; law and legal studies; nursing

See full description on page 650.

SAINT LEO UNIVERSITY

Saint Leo, Florida
Center for Distance Learning
www.saintleo.edu

Saint Leo University, founded in 1889, is an independent, religious, comprehensive institution. It is accredited by the Southern Association of Colleges and Schools. It first offered distance learning courses in 1996. In 1999–2000, it offered 30 courses at a distance. In fall 1999, there were 950 students enrolled in distance learning courses.

Course delivery sites Courses are delivered to your home, your workplace, military bases, 22 off-campus centers.

Media Courses are delivered via videotapes, videoconferencing, computer software, CD-ROM, computer conferencing, World Wide Web, e-mail. Students and teachers may meet in person or interact via audioconferencing, mail, telephone, fax, e-mail, World Wide Web. The following equipment may be required: computer, modem, Internet access, e-mail.

Restrictions Programs are available mainly in the southeast U.S. Enrollment is open to anyone.

Services Distance learners have access to library services, the campus computer network, e-mail services, academic advising, bookstore at a distance.

Credit-earning options Students may transfer credits from another institution or may earn credits through examinations, military training, business training.

Typical costs *Undergraduate:* Tuition of $156 per semester hour plus mandatory fees of $20 per semester hour. *Graduate:* Tuition of $250 per semester hour plus mandatory fees of $20 per semester hour. Costs may vary. Financial aid is available to distance learners.

Registration Students may register by mail, fax, telephone, in person.

Contact Terry Redman, Director of Educational Technology, Saint Leo University. *Telephone:* 352-588-8206. *Fax:* 352-588-8207. *E-mail:* terry.redman@saintleo.edu.

DEGREES AND AWARDS

BA Business Administration

COURSE SUBJECT AREAS OFFERED OUTSIDE OF DEGREE PROGRAMS

Undergraduate: Accounting; business administration and management; business communications; computer and information sciences; philosophy and religion; statistics

Special note
Saint Leo University, a leader in adult education since 1974, offers several options in obtaining an accredited degree on line. Saint Leo University's complete online programs include bachelor's degrees in accounting, business administration (management), and computer information systems, which are available through the Center for Online Learning. Alternative delivery classes are delivered on line through the School of Continuing Education's Distance Learning System to supplement site-based programs that are offered at the regional campuses. A wide array of courses is available in such subjects as computer information systems, management, philosophy, and psychology. New course content is added every semester, and students should call or visit the Web site (http://video.saintleo.edu) for complete information. The distance learning courses are delivered by a variety of methods, including Web-based synchronous and asynchronous techniques, electronic mail, computer conferencing, and video teleconferencing. The majority of the courses permit the learner to complete the courses at home, provided that they have access to a properly equipped computer and telephone connections. The online programs are designed to permit adult learners to complete their degrees without on-campus residential requirements. The online course system provides the ability to register for courses, receive student services, and complete instruction on line. This flexible program is ideal for working professionals who desire to complete a bachelor's degree but cannot afford to do so by placing their careers on hold.

See full description on page 722.

ST. LOUIS COMMUNITY COLLEGE SYSTEM

St. Louis, Missouri
Telelearning Services
www.stlcc.cc.mo.us

St. Louis Community College System is a public, system. It is accredited by the North Central Association of Colleges and Schools. In 1999–2000, it offered 71 courses at a distance. In fall 1999, there were 3,145 students enrolled in distance learning courses.

Course delivery sites Courses are delivered to your home, your workplace, high schools, Mineral Area College (Park Hills, MS), Saint Charles County Community College (St. Peters, MS), University of Missouri-Rolla (Rolla, MS).

Media Courses are delivered via television, videotapes, videoconferencing, interactive television, audiotapes, computer software, CD-ROM, computer conferencing, World Wide Web, e-mail, print. Students and teachers may meet in person or interact via videoconferencing, audioconferencing, mail, telephone, fax, e-mail, interactive television, World Wide Web. The following equipment may be required: television, videocassette player, computer, modem, Internet access, e-mail.

Restrictions Courses are available to students in the St. Louis Metropolitan area (Eastern Missouri and Western Illinois). Enrollment is open to anyone.

Services Distance learners have access to library services, the campus computer network, e-mail services, academic advising, tutoring, career placement assistance, bookstore at a distance.

Credit-earning options Students may transfer credits from another institution or may earn credits through examinations, military training, business training.

Typical costs Tuition of $42 per credit for local area residents. Tuition of $53 per credit for in-state residents. Tuition of $67 per credit for out-of-state residents. There is a $30 mandatory fee for telecourses only. Costs may vary. Financial aid is available to distance learners.

Registration Students may register by mail, World Wide Web, in person.

Contact Dan Bain, Director Telelearning Services, St. Louis Community College System, 300 South Broadway, St. Louis, MO 63102-2810. *Telephone:* 314-539-5056. *Fax:* 314-539-5005. *E-mail:* dbain@stlcc.cc. mo.us.

DEGREES AND AWARDS

Distance programs offered do not lead to a degree or other formal award.

COURSE SUBJECT AREAS OFFERED OUTSIDE OF DEGREE PROGRAMS

Undergraduate: Accounting; administrative and secretarial services; American (U.S.) history; anthropology; archaeology; art history and criticism; biology; business; business administration and management; computer and information sciences; developmental and child psychology; earth science; economics; English as a second language (ESL); English composition; European languages and literatures; fine arts; fire services administration; health and physical education/fitness; health professions and related sciences; investments and securities; liberal arts, general studies, and humanities; marketing; mathematics; occupational therapy; physical therapy; physics; physiology; political science; psychology; social sciences; sociology; substance abuse counseling; visual and performing arts

Noncredit: Fire services administration

SAINT LOUIS UNIVERSITY

St. Louis, Missouri
School of Nursing
nursing.slu.edu

Saint Louis University, founded in 1818, is an independent, religious university. It is accredited by the North Central Association of Colleges and Schools. It first offered distance learning courses in 1997. In 1999–2000, it offered 13 courses at a distance. In fall 1999, there were 75 students enrolled in distance learning courses.

Course delivery sites Courses are delivered to your home, your workplace, military bases.

Media Courses are delivered via videotapes, computer software, computer conferencing, World Wide Web, e-mail, print. Students and teachers may interact via telephone, e-mail, World Wide Web. The following equipment may be required: computer, modem, Internet access, e-mail.

Restrictions Programs are available worldwide. Enrollment is restricted to individuals meeting certain criteria.

Services Distance learners have access to library services, e-mail services, academic advising, bookstore at a distance.

Credit-earning options Students may transfer credits from another institution or may earn credits through examinations, portfolio assessment.

Typical costs *Undergraduate:* Tuition of $335 per credit hour plus mandatory fees of $20 per credit hour. *Graduate:* Tuition of $542 per credit hour plus mandatory fees of $20 per credit hour. Financial aid is available to distance learners.

Registration Students may register by mail, fax, telephone, e-mail, World Wide Web.

Contact Elaine Dempsey, Director of Marketing and Recruitment, Saint Louis University, Saint Louis University School of Nursing, 3525 Caroline, St. Louis, MO 63104-1099. *Telephone:* 314-577-8993. *Fax:* 314-577-8949. *E-mail:* slunurse@slu.edu.

DEGREES AND AWARDS

BSN Nursing-RN-BSN Completion (certain restrictions apply)
Graduate Certificate(s) Nursing (some on-campus requirements)
MSN Nursing (some on-campus requirements)
MSN(R) Nursing (some on-campus requirements)

COURSE SUBJECT AREAS OFFERED OUTSIDE OF DEGREE PROGRAMS

Undergraduate: Nursing
Graduate: Nursing

Special note
Saint Louis University School of Nursing is a leader in nursing distance education. It was the first nursing school to offer complete master's degree programs in nursing online through the World Wide Web. The School also offers its own online BSN-completion program for RNs. Currently, M.S.N., M.S.N. (research), and post-master's certificate programs are available on line for the adult, family, gerontological, and pediatric nurse practitioner tracks and for the adult and gerontological clinical nurse specialist tracks. Students complete all course work for the degree program through distance education. The online tracks are designed to follow the same curriculum and program objectives that are required of on-campus students. Faculty members work with students to help select clinical sites and preceptors that are compatible with the student's and the program's objectives. To participate, students must be comfortable using PC hardware and software and should have an e-mail account and be proficient in accessing the World Wide Web. Students enrolled in the online programs have access to the University's main and health sciences libraries and resources via the Internet. On campus, the School offers several BSN programs; master's programs in adult nursing (CNS, NP), family and community health nursing (PHNS, NP), gerontological nursing (CNS, NP), informatics (informatics nurse), nursing of children (CNS, NP), perinatal nursing (CNS), and psychiatric–mental health nursing (CNS); and a doctoral program in nursing. Saint Louis University is accredited by the North Central Association of Colleges and Secondary Schools. The master's programs in nursing are accredited by the National League for Nursing Council for Baccalaureate and Higher Degree Programs.

SAINT MARY-OF-THE-WOODS COLLEGE

Saint Mary-of-the-Woods, Indiana
Women's External Degree Program
www.smwc.edu

Saint Mary-of-the-Woods College, founded in 1840, is an independent, religious, comprehensive institution. It is accredited by the North Central Association of Colleges and Schools. It first offered distance learning courses in 1973. In 1999–2000, it offered 250 courses at a distance. In fall 1999, there were 1,300 students enrolled in distance learning courses.

Course delivery sites Courses are delivered to your home.

Media Courses are delivered via videotapes, audiotapes, computer software, CD-ROM, computer conferencing, World Wide Web, e-mail, print. Students and teachers may meet in person or interact via mail, telephone, fax, e-mail.

Restrictions Programs are available nationwide. Enrollment is restricted to individuals meeting certain criteria.

Services Distance learners have access to library services, e-mail services, academic advising, career placement assistance, bookstore at a distance.

Credit-earning options Students may transfer credits from another institution or may earn credits through examinations, portfolio assessment, military training, business training.

Typical costs *Undergraduate:* Tuition of $277 per semester hour. *Graduate:* Tuition of $315 per semester hour. Financial aid is available to distance learners.

Registration Students may register by mail, in person.

Contact Gwen Hagemeyer, WED Admission Director, Saint Mary-of-the-Woods College, Saint Mary-of-the-Woods, IN 47876. *Telephone:* 812-535-5186. *Fax:* 812-535-5215. *E-mail:* wedadms@smwc.edu.

DEGREES AND AWARDS

Undergraduate Certificate(s) Gerontology (some on-campus requirements), Paralegal Studies (some on-campus requirements), Pastoral Theology (some on-campus requirements), Theology (some on-campus requirements)

AA Humanities (some on-campus requirements), Paralegal Studies (some on-campus requirements)

AS Early Childhood Education (certain restrictions apply; service area differs from that of the overall institution), General Business (some on-campus requirements), Gerontology (some on-campus requirements)

BA English (some on-campus requirements), History and Political Studies (some on-campus requirements), Humanities (some on-campus requirements), Journalism (some on-campus requirements), Mathematics (some on-campus requirements), Paralegal Studies (some on-campus requirements), Professional Writing (some on-campus requirements), Theology (some on-campus requirements)

BS Accounting (some on-campus requirements), Business Administration (some on-campus requirements), Computer Information Systems (some on-campus requirements), Digital Media Communication (some on-campus requirements), Early Childhood Education (some on-campus requirements), Elementary Education (service area differs from that of the overall institution; some on-campus requirements), Gerontology (some on-campus requirements), Human Resource Management (some on-campus requirements), Human Services (some on-campus requirements), Kindergarten–Primary Education (service area differs from that of the overall institution; some on-campus requirements), Marketing (some on-campus requirements), Occupational Therapy Applications (some on-campus requirements), Psychology (some on-campus requirements), Special Education (service area differs from that of the overall institution; some on-campus requirements)

Graduate Certificate(s) Legal Nurse (certain restrictions apply; some on-campus requirements)

MA Art Therapy (some on-campus requirements), Earth Literacy (service area differs from that of the overall institution; some on-campus requirements), Music Therapy (some on-campus requirements), Pastoral Theology (service area differs from that of the overall institution; some on-campus requirements)

See full descriptions on pages 540 and 652.

ST. MARY'S UNIVERSITY OF SAN ANTONIO

San Antonio, Texas
Graduate School

St. Mary's University of San Antonio, founded in 1852, is an independent, religious, comprehensive institution. It is accredited by the Southern Association of Colleges and Schools. In 1999–2000, it offered 84 courses at a distance. In fall 1999, there were 185 students enrolled in distance learning courses.

Course delivery sites Courses are delivered to your workplace, military bases, off-campus center(s) in Corpus Christi, Kileen, Laredo, San Antonio, Insbruck, Australia, London, Afghanistan.

Media Courses are delivered via videoconferencing. Students and teachers may meet in person or interact via videoconferencing, mail, fax, e-mail, World Wide Web.

Restrictions Programs are available to in-state students only. Enrollment is open to anyone.

Services Distance learners have access to library services, the campus computer network, e-mail services, academic advising, career placement assistance, bookstore at a distance.

Credit-earning options Students may transfer credits from another institution or may earn credits through examinations, military training, business training.

Typical costs *Undergraduate:* Tuition of $377 per hour for local area residents. Tuition of $377 per hour for in-state residents. Tuition of $377 per hour for out-of-state residents. *Graduate:* Tuition of $427 per hour for local area residents. Tuition of $427 per hour for in-state residents. Tuition of $427 per hour for out-of-state residents. *Noncredit courses:* $142 per course. Financial aid is available to distance learners.

Registration Students may register by telephone, e-mail, in person.

Contact Please contact the Director for the specific graduate program, St. Mary's University of San Antonio.

DEGREES AND AWARDS

Graduate Certificate(s) Catholic School Leadership, Theology

MA Catholic School Leadership, Community Counseling, International Relations, Pastoral Ministry, Theology

MBA Business Administration

MPA Public Administration

MS Computer Information Systems, Engineering Systems Management

COURSE SUBJECT AREAS OFFERED OUTSIDE OF DEGREE PROGRAMS

Undergraduate: Theological studies

Graduate: Business administration and management; counseling psychology; education administration; engineering/industrial management; information sciences and systems; international relations; public administration and services; theological studies

ST. NORBERT COLLEGE

De Pere, Wisconsin
Master of Science in Education
www.snc.edu/mse

St. Norbert College, founded in 1898, is an independent, religious, comprehensive institution. It is accredited by the North Central Association of Colleges and Schools.

Course delivery sites Courses are delivered to Triton Distance learning consortium.

Media Courses are delivered via interactive television. Students and teachers may interact via interactive television.

Restrictions Programs are available to in-state students only. Enrollment is restricted to individuals meeting certain criteria.

Services Distance learners have access to library services, the campus computer network, e-mail services, academic advising, bookstore at a distance.

Credit-earning options Students may transfer credits from another institution.

Typical costs Tuition of $6800 per degree program. Financial aid is available to distance learners.

Registration Students may register by mail, fax, in person.

St. Norbert College

Contact Yvonne Murname, Director, Master of Science in Education, St. Norbert College, 100 Grant Street, DePere, WI 54115. *Telephone:* 920-403-4044. *Fax:* 920-403-4086. *E-mail:* mse@mail.snc.edu.

DEGREES AND AWARDS

MS Education (certain restrictions apply; some on-campus requirements)

ST. PETERSBURG JUNIOR COLLEGE

St. Petersburg, Florida

Electronic Campus
seminole.spjc.edu/ecampus

St. Petersburg Junior College, founded in 1927, is a state and locally supported, two-year college. It is accredited by the Southern Association of Colleges and Schools. It first offered distance learning courses in 1970. In 1999–2000, it offered 80 courses at a distance. In fall 1999, there were 3,000 students enrolled in distance learning courses.
Course delivery sites Courses are delivered to your home, your workplace, military bases, high schools.
Media Courses are delivered via television, videotapes, videoconferencing, audiotapes, computer software, World Wide Web, e-mail, print. Students and teachers may meet in person or interact via videoconferencing, audioconferencing, mail, telephone, fax, e-mail, World Wide Web. The following equipment may be required: television, videocassette player, computer, Internet access, e-mail.
Restrictions Programs are available worldwide. Enrollment is open to anyone.
Services Distance learners have access to library services, e-mail services, academic advising, tutoring, bookstore at a distance.
Credit-earning options Students may transfer credits from another institution or may earn credits through examinations.
Typical costs Tuition of $50.38 per credit hour for in-state residents. Tuition of $186.34 per credit hour for out-of-state residents. Mandatory fees are between $10 and $20 per course. Financial aid is available to distance learners.
Registration Students may register by mail, telephone, World Wide Web, in person.
Contact Lynda Womer, Program Director, St. Petersburg Junior College, SPJC Seminole Campus, PO Box 13489, St. Petersburg, FL 33733. *Telephone:* 727-394-6116. *Fax:* 727-394-6124. *E-mail:* womerl@spjc.edu.

DEGREES AND AWARDS

AS Veterinary Technology (certain restrictions apply; some on-campus requirements)

COURSE SUBJECT AREAS OFFERED OUTSIDE OF DEGREE PROGRAMS

Undergraduate: Accounting; algebra; American (U.S.) history; American literature; anatomy; anthropology; art history and criticism; astronomy and astrophysics; biology; business; business administration and management; business communications; chemistry; child care and development; computer and information sciences; corrections; creative writing; criminal justice; criminology; developmental and child psychology; earth science; economics; education; English composition; English literature; ethics; European history; European languages and literatures; family and marriage counseling; finance; fire science; fire services administration; French language and literature; geology; health and physical education/fitness; history; journalism; law and legal studies; liberal arts, general studies, and humanities; marketing; mathematics; meteorology; microbiology; ocean-

ography; political science; religious studies; social psychology; sociology; Spanish language and literature; statistics; teacher education; technical writing

See full description on page 676.

SAINT PETER'S COLLEGE

Jersey City, New Jersey

Institute for the Advancement of Urban Education
www.spc.edu

Saint Peter's College, founded in 1872, is an independent, religious, comprehensive institution. It is accredited by the Middle States Association of Colleges and Schools. It first offered distance learning courses in 1992. In 1999–2000, it offered 8 courses at a distance. In fall 1999, there were 35 students enrolled in distance learning courses.
Course delivery sites Courses are delivered to your workplace, high schools.
Media Courses are delivered via videotapes, videoconferencing, interactive television, e-mail. Students and teachers may interact via audioconferencing, mail, telephone, fax, e-mail, interactive television. The following equipment may be required: television, videocassette player, computer, modem, e-mail.
Restrictions Programs are available to in-state students only. Enrollment is restricted to individuals meeting certain criteria.
Services Distance learners have access to library services, the campus computer network, e-mail services, academic advising, bookstore at a distance.
Credit-earning options Students may earn credits through examinations, portfolio assessment.
Typical costs *Undergraduate:* Tuition of $200 per course. *Graduate:* Tuition of $450 per course. Costs may vary. Financial aid is available to distance learners.
Registration Students may register by mail, fax, telephone, e-mail, in person.
Contact Dr. David S. Surrey, Director, Saint Peter's College, 2641 Kennedy Boulevard, Jersey City, NJ 07306-5997. *Telephone:* 201-915-9329. *Fax:* 201-432-4997. *E-mail:* surrey_d@spcvxa.spc.edu.

DEGREES AND AWARDS

Distance programs offered do not lead to a degree or other formal award.

COURSE SUBJECT AREAS OFFERED OUTSIDE OF DEGREE PROGRAMS

Undergraduate: American (U.S.) history; comparative literature; political science; sociology
Graduate: Business administration and management; business communications; curriculum and instruction; education administration; teacher education

Special note

Saint Peter's College currently offers distance learning graduate education courses through videotape as well as selected graduate and undergraduate courses via ITV (interactive television). During the 2000–01 academic year, the College intends to offer designated graduate and undergraduate Web-based courses. Graduate education students can work at their own pace on any of the nine 3-credit courses that were developed with the direct participation of and within the context of the expressed needs of K–12 teachers, school administrators, college faculty members, and students. These courses can be applied toward a Saint Peter's Master of Arts in Education with a concentration in urban education as well as toward other degrees and certificates at Saint Peter's or most other graduate education programs. The concentration in urban education, with a careful choice of electives, leads to eligibility for Supervisor of Instruction. The courses are offered at a significant discount. The College also offers selected graduate education courses at a discount via its ATV facilities. The courses can be used as electives in other concentrations at the College. Advanced high school seniors and juniors can take advantage of the ITV rooms in their schools to join introductory 3-credit college classes. The classes are acceptable to virtually any college in the nation. For more information, students should contact the Institute for the Advancement of Urban Education at 201-915-9329 or via e-mail at iauedept@spcvxa.spc.edu or visit the Web site at http://www.spc.edu/iaue.

SALEM COMMUNITY COLLEGE

Carneys Point, New Jersey

Salem Community College, founded in 1972, is a county-supported, two-year college. It is accredited by the Middle States Association of Colleges and Schools.

Contact Salem Community College, 460 Hollywood Avenue, Carneys Point, NJ 08069-2799. *Telephone:* 609-299-2100. *Fax:* 609-299-9193.

See full description on page 600.

SALT LAKE COMMUNITY COLLEGE

Salt Lake City, Utah

Division of Continuing Education
ecampus.slcc.edu

Salt Lake Community College, founded in 1948, is a state-supported, two-year college. It is accredited by the Northwest Association of Schools and Colleges. It first offered distance learning courses in 1991. In 1999–2000, it offered 52 courses at a distance. In fall 1999, there were 1,413 students enrolled in distance learning courses.

Course delivery sites Courses are delivered to your home, your workplace, military bases, high schools, 5 off-campus centers in Salt Lake City, Tooele.

Media Courses are delivered via television, videotapes, videoconferencing, audiotapes, computer software, CD-ROM, World Wide Web, e-mail, print. Students and teachers may interact via videoconferencing, audioconferencing, mail, telephone, fax, e-mail, World Wide Web. The following equipment may be required: television, videocassette player, computer, modem, Internet access, e-mail.

Restrictions Programs are available worldwide. Enrollment is open to anyone.

Services Distance learners have access to library services, the campus computer network, e-mail services, academic advising, tutoring, bookstore at a distance.

Credit-earning options Students may transfer credits from another institution or may earn credits through examinations, military training.

Typical costs Tuition of $139 per credit hour for in-state residents. Tuition of $351 per credit hour for out-of-state residents. *Noncredit courses:* $75 per course. Costs may vary. Financial aid is available to distance learners.

Registration Students may register by mail, fax, telephone, World Wide Web, in person.

Contact Shanna Schaefermeyer, Director of Distance Education, Salt Lake Community College, 4600 South Redwood Road, Salt Lake City, UT 84130. *Telephone:* 801-957-4064. *Fax:* 801-957-4609. *E-mail:* schaefsh@slcc.edu.

DEGREES AND AWARDS

Undergraduate Certificate(s) Railroad Operations
AS Business Transfer, General Studies Transfer

COURSE SUBJECT AREAS OFFERED OUTSIDE OF DEGREE PROGRAMS

Undergraduate: Accounting; American (U.S.) history; astronomy and astrophysics; biology; business; business administration and management; business communications; communications; computer and information sciences; criminal justice; economics; English composition; environmental science; fine arts; health and physical education/fitness; liberal arts, general studies, and humanities; library and information studies; mathematics; physics; sociology; technical writing; telecommunications

SALVE REGINA UNIVERSITY

Newport, Rhode Island

Extension Study
www.salve.edu

Salve Regina University, founded in 1934, is an independent, religious, comprehensive institution. It is accredited by the New England Association of Schools and Colleges. It first offered distance learning courses in 1985. In 1999–2000, it offered 60 courses at a distance. In fall 1999, there were 301 students enrolled in distance learning courses.

Course delivery sites Courses are delivered to your home, high schools, 1 off-campus center in Providence.

Media Courses are delivered via videotapes, World Wide Web, e-mail, print. Students and teachers may meet in person or interact via mail, telephone, fax, e-mail, World Wide Web.

Restrictions Programs are available worldwide. Enrollment is open to anyone.

Services Distance learners have access to library services, e-mail services, academic advising, career placement assistance, bookstore at a distance.

Credit-earning options Students may transfer credits from another institution or may earn credits through examinations, portfolio assessment, military training, business training.

Typical costs *Undergraduate:* Tuition of $150 per credit for in-state residents. Tuition of $175 per credit for out-of-state residents. *Graduate:* Tuition of $900 per course for in-state residents. Tuition of $900 per course for out-of-state residents. Financial aid is available to distance learners.

Registration Students may register by mail, fax, telephone, e-mail, World Wide Web, in person.

Contact Debra R. Mitchell, Associate Director, Salve Regina University, Extension Study, 100 Ochre Point Avenue, Newport, RI 02840. *Telephone:* 800-637-0002. *Fax:* 401-849-0702. *E-mail:* sruexten@salve.edu.

DEGREES AND AWARDS

Undergraduate Certificate(s) Management, Management and Correctional Administration
BA Liberal Studies (some on-campus requirements)
BS Business (some on-campus requirements)
MA Human Development (some on-campus requirements), International Relations (some on-campus requirements)
MBA Business Administration (some on-campus requirements)
MS Management (some on-campus requirements)

COURSE SUBJECT AREAS OFFERED OUTSIDE OF DEGREE PROGRAMS

Undergraduate: American (U.S.) history; American literature; art history and criticism; business; business administration and management; business law; community health services; comparative literature; English language and literature; ethics; finance; gerontology; human resources management; international business; labor relations/studies; liberal arts, general studies, and humanities; marketing; music; nursing; organizational behavior studies; philosophy and religion; protective services; psychology; religious studies; social psychology

Graduate: Accounting; business; business administration and management; business law; cognitive psychology; comparative literature; computer and information sciences; database management; developmental and child psychology; economics; English language and literature; ethics; finance; human resources management; international business; international relations; labor relations/studies; Latin American studies; liberal arts, general studies, and humanities; management information systems; marketing; organizational behavior studies; philosophy and religion; political science; protective services; social psychology

Noncredit: Accounting; American (U.S.) history; American literature; art history and criticism; business; business administration and management; business law; cognitive psychology; community health services; comparative literature; computer and information sciences; database management; developmental and child psychology; economics; English language and literature; ethics; finance; gerontology; human resources management; international business; international relations; labor relations/ studies; Latin American studies; liberal arts, general studies, and humanities; management information systems; marketing; music; nursing; organizational behavior studies; philosophy and religion; political science; protective services; psychology; religious studies; social psychology

See full description on page 654.

SAMFORD UNIVERSITY

Birmingham, Alabama
www.samford.edu/schools/metro.html

Samford University, founded in 1841, is an independent, religious university. It is accredited by the Association of Theological Schools in the United States and Canada, Southern Association of Colleges and Schools.
Contact Samford University, 800 Lakeshore Drive, Birmingham, AL 35229-0002. *Telephone:* 205-726-2011. *Fax:* 205-726-2171.

See full description on page 676.

SAM HOUSTON STATE UNIVERSITY

Huntsville, Texas
Correspondence Course Division
www.shsu.edu/~cor_www

Sam Houston State University, founded in 1879, is a state-supported, comprehensive institution. It is accredited by the Southern Association of Colleges and Schools. In 1999–2000, it offered 73 courses at a distance. In fall 1999, there were 1,700 students enrolled in distance learning courses.
Course delivery sites Courses are delivered to your home, your workplace, military bases.
Media Courses are delivered via World Wide Web, e-mail. Students and teachers may meet in person or interact via mail, fax, e-mail, World Wide Web. The following equipment may be required: computer, Internet access, e-mail.
Restrictions Programs are available worldwide. Enrollment is restricted to individuals meeting certain criteria.
Services Distance learners have access to library services, e-mail services, bookstore at a distance.
Credit-earning options Students may earn credits through examinations.

Typical costs Tuition of $155 per course.
Registration Students may register by mail, World Wide Web, in person.
Contact Gail M. Wright, Correspondence Course Coordinator, Sam Houston State University, PO Box 2536, Huntsville, TX 77341-2536. *Telephone:* 936-294-1003. *Fax:* 936-294-3703. *E-mail:* cor_gmw@shsu. edu.

DEGREES AND AWARDS

Distance programs offered do not lead to a degree or other formal award.

COURSE SUBJECT AREAS OFFERED OUTSIDE OF DEGREE PROGRAMS

Undergraduate: Accounting; agriculture; algebra; American (U.S.) history; American literature; anthropology; business; business administration and management; business law; calculus; chemistry; chemistry, inorganic; chemistry, organic; clothing/apparel and textile studies; creative writing; economics; engineering; English language and literature; English literature; finance; foods and nutrition studies; geography; health and physical education/fitness; history; home economics and family studies; human resources management; individual and family development studies; insurance; marketing; mathematics; philosophy and religion; photography; political science; psychology; sociology; technical writing; visual and performing arts

See full description on page 676.

SAMUEL MERRITT COLLEGE

Oakland, California
Academic Affairs
www.samuelmerritt.edu

Samuel Merritt College, founded in 1909, is an independent, nonprofit, comprehensive institution. It is accredited by the Western Association of Schools and Colleges, Inc.
Course delivery sites Courses are delivered to your home, your workplace, military bases.
Media Courses are delivered via videoconferencing, computer software, computer conferencing, World Wide Web, e-mail. Students and teachers may meet in person or interact via mail, telephone, fax, e-mail, World Wide Web. The following equipment may be required: computer, modem, Internet access, e-mail.
Restrictions Programs are available nationwide. Enrollment is restricted to individuals meeting certain criteria.
Services Distance learners have access to library services, the campus computer network, e-mail services, academic advising, tutoring, career placement assistance, bookstore at a distance.
Credit-earning options Students may transfer credits from another institution or may earn credits through examinations, portfolio assessment.
Typical costs Tuition of $600 per unit. Costs may vary. Financial aid is available to distance learners.
Registration Students may register by mail, fax, World Wide Web, in person.
Contact John Garten-Shumen, Director of Admission, Samuel Merritt College, 370 Hawthorne Avenue, Oakland, CA 94610. *Telephone:* 510-869-6727. *Fax:* 510-869-6525. *E-mail:* jgartens@samuelmerritt.edu.

DEGREES AND AWARDS

MS Nursing (certain restrictions apply)

SAN ANTONIO COLLEGE

San Antonio, Texas

Distance Education

www.accd.edu/sac

San Antonio College, founded in 1925, is a state and locally supported, two-year college. It is accredited by the Southern Association of Colleges and Schools.

Course delivery sites Courses are delivered to your home, your workplace, military bases, high schools, 13 off-campus centers in Kerrville, New Braunfels, Seguin.

Media Courses are delivered via television, videoconferencing, World Wide Web. Students and teachers may meet in person or interact via videoconferencing, telephone, fax, e-mail, interactive television, World Wide Web. The following equipment may be required: television, videocassette player, computer, modem, Internet access, e-mail.

Restrictions Telecourses are available locally; Web courses are available nationally and internationally. Enrollment is open to anyone.

Services Distance learners have access to library services, e-mail services, academic advising, tutoring, career placement assistance, bookstore at a distance.

Credit-earning options Students may transfer credits from another institution or may earn credits through examinations.

Typical costs Tuition of $120 per credit hour plus mandatory fees of $86.50 per credit hour for local area residents. Tuition of $230 per credit hour plus mandatory fees of $86.50 per credit hour for in-state residents. Tuition of $460 per credit hour plus mandatory fees of $86.50 per credit hour for out-of-state residents. Costs may vary.

Registration Students may register by telephone, World Wide Web, in person.

Contact Helen Torres, Director of Distance Education, San Antonio College, 1300 San Pedro Avenue, San Antonio, TX 78212. *Telephone:* 210-733-2045. *Fax:* 210-785-6494. *E-mail:* htorres@accd.edu.

DEGREES AND AWARDS

Distance programs offered do not lead to a degree or other formal award.

COURSE SUBJECT AREAS OFFERED OUTSIDE OF DEGREE PROGRAMS

Undergraduate: Abnormal psychology; astronomy and astrophysics; biology; business; business administration and management; communications; computer and information sciences; criminal justice; developmental and child psychology; English composition; European languages and literatures; family and marriage counseling; fine arts; foods and nutrition studies; geography; geology; history; law and legal studies; microbiology; nursing; political science; psychology; sociology; Spanish language and literature

SANDHILLS COMMUNITY COLLEGE

Pinehurst, North Carolina

Division of Curriculum Education

198.85.71.34/login

Sandhills Community College, founded in 1963, is a state and locally supported, two-year college. It is accredited by the Southern Association of Colleges and Schools. It first offered distance learning courses in 1982. In 1999–2000, it offered 12 courses at a distance. In fall 1999, there were 100 students enrolled in distance learning courses.

Course delivery sites Courses are delivered to your home, your workplace, military bases.

Media Courses are delivered via television, videotapes, audiotapes, computer software, World Wide Web, e-mail. Students and teachers may meet in person or interact via telephone, e-mail, World Wide Web. The following equipment may be required: television, videocassette player, computer, Internet access.

Restrictions Programs are available regionally. Enrollment is restricted to individuals meeting certain criteria.

Credit-earning options Students may transfer credits from another institution or may earn credits through examinations, portfolio assessment, military training, business training.

Typical costs Tuition of $27 per credit hour plus mandatory fees of $14 per semester for in-state residents. Tuition of $170 per credit hour plus mandatory fees of $14 per semester for out-of-state residents. Financial aid is available to distance learners.

Registration Students may register by mail, e-mail, World Wide Web, in person.

Contact Ricky Hodges, Director of Recruitment, Sandhills Community College, 2200 Airport Road, Pinehurst, NC 28374. *Telephone:* 910-695-3734. *Fax:* 910-695-1823.

DEGREES AND AWARDS

AA Arts
AAS Applied Science
AFA Fine Arts
AS Science

COURSE SUBJECT AREAS OFFERED OUTSIDE OF DEGREE PROGRAMS

Undergraduate: English composition; English literature; film studies; fine arts; history; nursing; psychology; sociology

SAN DIEGO CITY COLLEGE

San Diego, California

Office of Distance Education

www.sdccd.net/

San Diego City College, founded in 1914, is a state and locally supported, two-year college. It is accredited by the Western Association of Schools and Colleges, Inc. It first offered distance learning courses in 1994. In 1999–2000, it offered 42 courses at a distance. In fall 1999, there were 723 students enrolled in distance learning courses.

Course delivery sites Courses are delivered to your home, your workplace, military bases, San Diego Mesa College (San Diego), San Diego Miramar College (San Diego).

Media Courses are delivered via television, videotapes, videoconferencing, interactive television, World Wide Web, print. Students and teachers may meet in person or interact via videoconferencing, mail, telephone, e-mail, interactive television, World Wide Web. The following equipment may be required: computer, Internet access.

Restrictions Programs are available to local area students. Enrollment is restricted to individuals meeting certain criteria.

Services Distance learners have access to library services, e-mail services, academic advising, career placement assistance, bookstore at a distance.

Credit-earning options Students may transfer credits from another institution or may earn credits through examinations, military training, business training.

Typical costs Tuition of $11 per unit for in-state residents. Tuition of $118 per unit for out-of-state residents. There is an $11 mandatory health fee. Costs may vary. Financial aid is available to distance learners.

Registration Students may register by mail, fax, telephone, in person.

Contact Curtis J. McCarty, Faculty Coordinator, San Diego City College, Distance Education, San Diego, CA 92101-4787. *Telephone:* 619-230-2534. *Fax:* 619-230-2063. *E-mail:* cmccarty@sdccd.cc.ca.us.

DEGREES AND AWARDS

Distance programs offered do not lead to a degree or other formal award.

COURSE SUBJECT AREAS OFFERED OUTSIDE OF DEGREE PROGRAMS

Undergraduate: Anthropology; astronomy and astrophysics; business; business administration and management; business law; child care and development; classical languages and literatures; computer and information sciences; economics; geography; geology; health professions and related sciences; history; liberal arts, general studies, and humanities; photography; psychology; radio and television broadcasting

SAN DIEGO STATE UNIVERSITY

San Diego, California
Academic Affairs
www.sdsu.edu/dl

San Diego State University, founded in 1897, is a state-supported university. It is accredited by the Western Association of Schools and Colleges, Inc. It first offered distance learning courses in 1984. In 1999–2000, it offered 26 courses at a distance. In fall 1999, there were 973 students enrolled in distance learning courses.

Course delivery sites Courses are delivered to your home, your workplace.

Media Courses are delivered via television, videotapes, videoconferencing, interactive television, computer software, World Wide Web, e-mail. Students and teachers may meet in person or interact via videoconferencing, mail, telephone, fax, e-mail, interactive television, World Wide Web. The following equipment may be required: computer, modem, Internet access, e-mail.

Restrictions Programs are available worldwide. Enrollment is restricted to individuals meeting certain criteria.

Services Distance learners have access to library services, e-mail services, bookstore at a distance.

Credit-earning options Students may earn credits through examinations.

Typical costs *Undergraduate:* Tuition of $130 per credit. *Graduate:* Tuition of $250 per credit. Costs may vary.

Registration Students may register by mail, fax, telephone, World Wide Web, in person.

Contact Treacy Lau, Principal Coordinator for Distributed Learning, San Diego State University, Office of the Associate Vice President for Academic Affairs, 5500 Campanile Drive, San Diego, CA 92182-8010. *Telephone:* 619-594-0508. *Fax:* 619-594-7443. *E-mail:* tlau@mail.sdsu.edu.

DEGREES AND AWARDS

Undergraduate Certificate(s) Education Technology
MA Rehabilitation Science Counseling (certain restrictions apply; service area differs from that of the overall institution; some on-campus requirements)

COURSE SUBJECT AREAS OFFERED OUTSIDE OF DEGREE PROGRAMS

Undergraduate: American (U.S.) history; art history and criticism; biological and life sciences; computer and information sciences; continuing education; education; education administration; health and physical education/fitness; instructional media; Jewish studies; music; physiology; political science; teacher education
Graduate: Continuing education; education; education administration; instructional media; teacher education

SAN FRANCISCO STATE UNIVERSITY

San Francisco, California
Multimedia Studies Program
www.sfsuonline.org

San Francisco State University, founded in 1899, is a state-supported, comprehensive institution. It is accredited by the Western Association of Schools and Colleges, Inc. It first offered distance learning courses in 1999. In 1999–2000, it offered 10 courses at a distance.

Course delivery sites Courses are delivered to your home, your workplace, military bases, high schools.

Media Courses are delivered via World Wide Web, e-mail. Students and teachers may interact via e-mail, World Wide Web. The following equipment may be required: computer, modem, Internet access, e-mail.

Restrictions Programs are available worldwide. Enrollment is open to anyone.

Services Distance learners have access to bookstore at a distance.

Credit-earning options Students may earn credits through examinations.

Typical costs *Undergraduate:* Tuition of $540 per course. *Graduate:* Tuition of $540 per course. *Noncredit courses:* $540 per course. Costs may vary.

Registration Students may register by World Wide Web, in person.

Contact Leslie Todd, Operations Coordinator, San Francisco State University, 425 Market Street, Second Floor, San Fransisco, CA 94105. *Telephone:* 415-405-7767. *Fax:* 415-405-7760. *E-mail:* ltodd@sfsu.edu.

eCollege.com *www.ecollege.com/scholarships*

DEGREES AND AWARDS

Distance programs offered do not lead to a degree or other formal award.

COURSE SUBJECT AREAS OFFERED OUTSIDE OF DEGREE PROGRAMS

Undergraduate: Information sciences and systems
Noncredit: Continuing education; visual and performing arts
See full description on page 656.

SAN JACINTO COLLEGE DISTRICT

Pasadena, Texas
Distance Learning
www.sjcd.cc.tx.us/distlearn/index.htm

San Jacinto College District is a state and locally supported, system. It is accredited by the Southern Association of Colleges and Schools. In 1999–2000, it offered 25 courses at a distance. In fall 1999, there were 920 students enrolled in distance learning courses.

Course delivery sites Courses are delivered to your home.

Media Courses are delivered via videotapes, World Wide Web. Students and teachers may meet in person or interact via audioconferencing, mail, telephone, fax, e-mail, World Wide Web. The following equipment may be required: television, videocassette player, computer, modem, Internet access, e-mail.

Restrictions Programs are available to local area students. Enrollment is open to anyone.

Services Distance learners have access to library services at a distance.

Credit-earning options Students may transfer credits from another institution or may earn credits through examinations.

Typical costs Tuition of $16 per hour plus mandatory fees of $35 per credit hour for local area residents. Tuition of $16 per hour plus mandatory fees of $49 per credit hour for in-state residents. Tuition of $60 per hour plus mandatory fees of $35 per credit hour for out-of-state residents. Costs may vary. Financial aid is available to distance learners.

Registration Students may register by telephone, in person.

Contact Niki Harris, Distance Learning Director, San Jacinto College District, 4624 Fairmont Parkway, Pasadena, TX 77504. *Telephone:* 281-998-6338. *Fax:* 281-998-6130. *E-mail:* nharris@sjcd.cc.tx.us.

DEGREES AND AWARDS

Distance programs offered do not lead to a degree or other formal award.

COURSE SUBJECT AREAS OFFERED OUTSIDE OF DEGREE PROGRAMS

Undergraduate: Accounting; algebra; American (U.S.) history; business administration and management; child care and development; computer programming; English composition; health services administration; information sciences and systems; journalism; marketing; political science; school psychology; sociology; technical writing

SAN JOAQUIN DELTA COLLEGE

Stockton, California

Instructional Development
www.deltaonline.org

San Joaquin Delta College, founded in 1935, is a district-supported, two-year college. It is accredited by the Western Association of Schools and Colleges, Inc. It first offered distance learning courses in 1976. In 1999–2000, it offered 32 courses at a distance. In fall 1999, there were 869 students enrolled in distance learning courses.

Course delivery sites Courses are delivered to your home, 4 off-campus centers in Jackson, Manteca, San Andreas, Tracy.

Media Courses are delivered via television, videotapes, videoconferencing, interactive television, World Wide Web. Students and teachers may meet in person or interact via videoconferencing, mail, telephone, fax, e-mail, interactive television, World Wide Web. The following equipment may be required: television, videocassette player, computer, modem, Internet access, e-mail.

Restrictions Programs are available worldwide. Enrollment is open to anyone.

Services Distance learners have access to library services, e-mail services, academic advising, tutoring, career placement assistance, bookstore at a distance.

Credit-earning options Students may transfer credits from another institution or may earn credits through examinations.

Typical costs Mandatory fees of $11 per unit for in-state residents. Tuition of $125 per unit plus mandatory fees of $11 per unit for out-of-state residents. There is an additional fee of $307 per Internet course for graduate students. Costs may vary. Financial aid is available to distance learners.

Registration Students may register by telephone, World Wide Web, in person.

Contact Kathryn Campbell, Dean of Instruction for Instructional Development and Regional Education, San Joaquin Delta College, 5151 Pacific Avenue, Stockton, CA 95207. *Telephone:* 209-954-5039. *Fax:* 209-954-5600. *E-mail:* kcampbell@sjdccd.cc.ca.us.

DEGREES AND AWARDS

Distance programs offered do not lead to a degree or other formal award.

COURSE SUBJECT AREAS OFFERED OUTSIDE OF DEGREE PROGRAMS

Undergraduate: Accounting; advertising; algebra; business; business administration and management; business law; child care and development; computer and information sciences; English composition; health professions and related sciences; home economics and family studies; interior design; liberal arts, general studies, and humanities; marketing; nursing; psychology; sociology

See full description on page 658.

SAN JOSE STATE UNIVERSITY

San Jose, California

Technology Education Network
www.sjsu.edu/academic.html

San Jose State University, founded in 1857, is a state-supported, comprehensive institution. It is accredited by the Western Association of Schools and Colleges, Inc. It first offered distance learning courses in 1985. In 1999–2000, it offered 60 courses at a distance. In fall 1999, there were 300 students enrolled in distance learning courses.

Course delivery sites Courses are delivered to your workplace, Cabrillo College (Aptos), Gavilan College (Gilroy).

Media Courses are delivered via television, videotapes, videoconferencing, interactive television, computer software, World Wide Web, e-mail. Students and teachers may interact via videoconferencing, mail, telephone, fax, e-mail. The following equipment may be required: television, videocassette player, computer, Internet access, e-mail.

Restrictions Programs are available to in-state students only. Enrollment is restricted to individuals meeting certain criteria.

Services Distance learners have access to library services, the campus computer network, e-mail services, academic advising, bookstore at a distance.

Credit-earning options Students may transfer credits from another institution or may earn credits through examinations.

Typical costs Undergraduate tuition for 1 to 6 units is $630.50; for 6.1 units or more it is $930.50. Graduate tuition is $654.50 for 1 to 6 units and $969.50 for 6.1 units or more. Mandatory non-resident fee is $246 per unit. Financial aid is available to distance learners.

Registration Students may register by mail, fax, telephone, in person.

Contact Linda Elvin, Program Assistant, San Jose State University, Technology Education Network, San Jose, CA 95192-0169. *Telephone:* 408-924-2636. *Fax:* 408-924-2881. *E-mail:* lelvin@sjsu.edu.

DEGREES AND AWARDS

Undergraduate Certificate(s) Instructional Design (certain restrictions apply; service area differs from that of the overall institution)

Graduate Certificate(s) Library and Information Sciences (certain restrictions apply; some on-campus requirements), Transportation Management (certain restrictions apply; service area differs from that of the overall institution)

MLIS Library and Information Sciences (certain restrictions apply; some on-campus requirements)

MS Nursing (some on-campus requirements), Occupational Therapy (service area differs from that of the overall institution; some on-campus requirements)

MSTM Transportation Management (certain restrictions apply; service area differs from that of the overall institution)

COURSE SUBJECT AREAS OFFERED OUTSIDE OF DEGREE PROGRAMS

Undergraduate: Continuing education; developmental and child psychology; ethics; geography; geology; liberal arts, general studies, and humanities; nursing; philosophy and religion; political science; sociology; special education; teacher education

Graduate: Library and information studies; special education; teacher education

SAN JUAN COLLEGE

Farmington, New Mexico

Distance Education
www.sjc.cc.nm.us

San Juan College, founded in 1958, is a county-supported, two-year college. It is accredited by the North Central Association of Colleges and Schools. It first offered distance learning courses in 1996. In 1999–2000, it offered 11 courses at a distance. In fall 1999, there were 372 students enrolled in distance learning courses.

Course delivery sites Courses are delivered to your home, your workplace, high schools, 3 off-campus centers in Aztec, Bloomfield, Kirtland.

Media Courses are delivered via television, videotapes, videoconferencing, World Wide Web. Students and teachers may interact via videoconferencing, mail, telephone, fax, e-mail. The following equipment may be required: television, videocassette player, computer, Internet access, e-mail.

Restrictions Programs are available to local area students. Enrollment is open to anyone.

Services Distance learners have access to library services, academic advising, tutoring, career placement assistance at a distance.

Credit-earning options Students may transfer credits from another institution or may earn credits through examinations, portfolio assessment, military training.

Typical costs Tuition of $15 per semester hour. Costs may vary. Financial aid is available to distance learners.

Registration Students may register by telephone, in person.

Contact Mike McDonald, Coordinator of Media Services, San Juan College. *Telephone:* 505-599-0295. *Fax:* 505-599-0385. *E-mail:* mcdonald@sjc.cc.nm.us.

DEGREES AND AWARDS

Distance programs offered do not lead to a degree or other formal award.

COURSE SUBJECT AREAS OFFERED OUTSIDE OF DEGREE PROGRAMS

Undergraduate: Algebra; American literature; business; child care and development; economics; marketing; mathematics; music; nursing; psychology; social sciences

SANTA ANA COLLEGE

Santa Ana, California

Distance Education Office
www.rancho.cc.ca.us/disted/

Santa Ana College, founded in 1915, is a state-supported, two-year college. It is accredited by the Western Association of Schools and Colleges, Inc. In 1999–2000, it offered 24 courses at a distance.

Course delivery sites Courses are delivered to your home, your workplace, military bases.

Media Courses are delivered via television, videotapes, videoconferencing, audiotapes, computer software, CD-ROM, World Wide Web, e-mail, print. Students and teachers may meet in person or interact via mail, telephone, fax, e-mail. The following equipment may be required: television, videocassette player, computer, modem, Internet access, e-mail.

Restrictions Programs are available nationwide. Enrollment is restricted to individuals meeting certain criteria.

Services Distance learners have access to library services, academic advising at a distance.

Credit-earning options Students may transfer credits from another institution.

Typical costs Tuition of $11 per unit plus mandatory fees of $7.50 per unit for local area residents. Tuition of $11 per unit plus mandatory fees of $7.50 per unit for in-state residents. Tuition of $133 per unit plus mandatory fees of $7.50 per unit for out-of-state residents. Financial aid is available to distance learners.

Registration Students may register by mail, telephone, in person.

Contact Jacque O'Lea, Distance Education Coordinator, Santa Ana College, 1530 Seventeenth Street, Santa Ana, CA 92706. *Telephone:* 714-564-6725. *Fax:* 714-647-0761. *E-mail:* oleaj@mail.rsccd.org.

DEGREES AND AWARDS

Distance programs offered do not lead to a degree or other formal award.

COURSE SUBJECT AREAS OFFERED OUTSIDE OF DEGREE PROGRAMS

Undergraduate: Anthropology; astronomy and astrophysics; biology; business administration and management; foods and nutrition studies; geology; individual and family development studies; information sciences and systems; marketing; philosophy and religion; psychology; real estate; sociology; visual and performing arts

SANTA BARBARA CITY COLLEGE

Santa Barbara, California

Online College
online.sbcc.net

Santa Barbara City College, founded in 1908, is a state and locally supported, two-year college. It is accredited by the Western Association of Schools and Colleges, Inc. In 1999–2000, it offered 26 courses at a distance. In fall 1999, there were 900 students enrolled in distance learning courses.

Course delivery sites Courses are delivered to your home, your workplace, high schools.

Media Courses are delivered via CD-ROM, World Wide Web. Students and teachers may meet in person or interact via mail, telephone, fax, e-mail, World Wide Web. The following equipment may be required: computer, modem, Internet access, e-mail.

Restrictions Programs are available worldwide. Enrollment is open to anyone.

Services Distance learners have access to library services, e-mail services, bookstore at a distance.

Typical costs Tuition of $11 per unit for local area residents. Tuition of $11 per unit for in-state residents. Tuition of $125 per unit for out-of-state residents. Undergraduate international tuition is $140 per unit. Financial aid is available to distance learners.

Registration Students may register by mail, e-mail, World Wide Web, in person.

Contact Pablo Buckelew, Dean, Online College, Santa Barbara City College, 721 Cliff Drive, Santa Barbara, CA 93109. *Telephone:* 805-965-0581 Ext. 2541. *Fax:* 805-963-7222. *E-mail:* buckelew@sbcc.net.

DEGREES AND AWARDS

Undergraduate Certificate(s) Health Information Technology, Home Health Care for RNs and LUNs
AS Health Information Technology

COURSE SUBJECT AREAS OFFERED OUTSIDE OF DEGREE PROGRAMS

Undergraduate: Biology; community health services; computer and information sciences; education; health services administration; nursing; psychology; Spanish language and literature

SANTA MONICA COLLEGE

Santa Monica, California

Distance Education Department
www.smconline.org

Santa Monica College, founded in 1929, is a state and locally supported, two-year college. It is accredited by the Western Association of Schools and Colleges, Inc. It first offered distance learning courses in 1997. In 1999–2000, it offered 24 courses at a distance. In fall 1999, there were 500 students enrolled in distance learning courses.
Course delivery sites Courses are delivered to your home, your workplace.
Media Courses are delivered via television, videotapes, videoconferencing, interactive television, computer conferencing, World Wide Web, e-mail. Students and teachers may interact via mail, telephone, e-mail, World Wide Web. The following equipment may be required: computer, modem, Internet access, e-mail.
Restrictions Programs are available worldwide. Enrollment is open to anyone.
Services Distance learners have access to library services, academic advising, tutoring, bookstore at a distance.
Credit-earning options Students may earn credits through examinations, portfolio assessment.
Typical costs Tuition of $11 per credit plus mandatory fees of $29 per semester for local area residents. Tuition of $125 per credit plus mandatory fees of $29 per semester for out-of-state residents. Costs may vary. Financial aid is available to distance learners.
Registration Students may register by mail, World Wide Web, in person.
Contact Winniphred Stone, Associate Dean of Distance Education, Santa Monica College, 1900 Pico Boulevard, Santa Monica, CA 90405. *Telephone:* 310-434-3761. *Fax:* 310-434-3769. *E-mail:* stone_winniphred@smc.edu.

eCollege.com *www.ecollege.com/scholarships*

DEGREES AND AWARDS

Distance programs offered do not lead to a degree or other formal award.

COURSE SUBJECT AREAS OFFERED OUTSIDE OF DEGREE PROGRAMS

Undergraduate: Accounting; art history and criticism; biology; business; chemistry; computer and information sciences; design; economics; English as a second language (ESL); English composition; English language and literature; film studies; music; philosophy and religion; political science; sociology

See full description on page 660.

SAUK VALLEY COMMUNITY COLLEGE

Dixon, Illinois
www.svcc.edu

Sauk Valley Community College, founded in 1965, is a district-supported, two-year college. It is accredited by the North Central Association of Colleges and Schools. It first offered distance learning courses in 1993. In 1999–2000, it offered 21 courses at a distance. In fall 1999, there were 153 students enrolled in distance learning courses.
Course delivery sites Courses are delivered to your home, your workplace, high schools, Carl Sandburg College (Galesburg), John Wood Community College (Quincy), Spoon River College (Canton).
Media Courses are delivered via television, videoconferencing, computer software, computer conferencing, World Wide Web, e-mail. Students and teachers may meet in person or interact via videoconferencing, mail, telephone, fax, e-mail, World Wide Web. The following equipment may be required: television, videocassette player, computer, modem, Internet access, e-mail.
Restrictions Programs are available worldwide. Enrollment is open to anyone.
Services Distance learners have access to library services, e-mail services, academic advising, bookstore at a distance.
Credit-earning options Students may transfer credits from another institution or may earn credits through examinations, portfolio assessment, military training, business training.
Typical costs Tuition of $46 per credit hour for local area residents. Tuition of $170 per credit hour for in-state residents. Tuition of $220 per credit hour for out-of-state residents. Internet courses are $46 per credit in state and $78 per credit out of state. Costs may vary. Financial aid is available to distance learners.
Registration Students may register by mail, telephone, e-mail, World Wide Web, in person.
Contact Alan Pfeifer, Director of Academic Computing, Sauk Valley Community College, 173 Illinois Route 2, Dixon, IL 61021. *Telephone:* 815-288-5511 Ext. 218. *Fax:* 815-288-5958. *E-mail:* pfeifer@svcc.edu.

DEGREES AND AWARDS

AAS Criminal Justice

COURSE SUBJECT AREAS OFFERED OUTSIDE OF DEGREE PROGRAMS

Undergraduate: Accounting; American (U.S.) history; biology; business; calculus; criminal justice; English composition; international business; psychology; sociology; visual and performing arts

SAYBROOK GRADUATE SCHOOL

San Francisco, California
www.saybrook.edu

Saybrook Graduate School, founded in 1970, is an independent, nonprofit, graduate institution. It is accredited by the Western Association of Schools and Colleges, Inc. In 1999–2000, it offered 94 courses at a distance. In fall 1999, there were 435 students enrolled in distance learning courses.
Course delivery sites Courses are delivered to your home.
Media Courses are delivered via World Wide Web, e-mail, print. Students and teachers may meet in person or interact via mail, telephone, fax, e-mail, World Wide Web. The following equipment may be required: computer, modem, Internet access, e-mail.
Restrictions Programs are available worldwide. Enrollment is open to anyone.

Services Distance learners have access to library services, the campus computer network, academic advising, tutoring, bookstore at a distance.
Credit-earning options Students may transfer credits from another institution.
Typical costs Tuition of $13,125 per year. Financial aid is available to distance learners.
Registration Students may register by mail, fax, e-mail, in person.
Contact Mindy Myers, Vice President for Admissions and Recruitment, Saybrook Graduate School, 450 Pacific, Third Floor, San Francisco, CA 94133. *Telephone:* 800-825-4480 Ext. 117. *Fax:* 415-433-9271. *E-mail:* mmyers@saybrook.edu.

DEGREES AND AWARDS

MA Human Science, Organizational Systems Inquiry, Psychology
PhD Human Science, Organizational Systems Inquiry, Psychology

COURSE SUBJECT AREAS OFFERED OUTSIDE OF DEGREE PROGRAMS

Graduate: Abnormal psychology; cognitive psychology; community health services; community services; counseling psychology; developmental and child psychology; ethics; humanistic psychology; management information systems; organizational behavior studies; psychology; public policy analysis; social psychology
See full description on page 662.

SCOTTSDALE COMMUNITY COLLEGE

Scottsdale, Arizona
www.sc.maricopa.edu

Scottsdale Community College, founded in 1969, is a state and locally supported, two-year college. It is accredited by the North Central Association of Colleges and Schools. It first offered distance learning courses in 1994. In 1999–2000, it offered 7 courses at a distance. In fall 1999, there were 175 students enrolled in distance learning courses.
Course delivery sites Courses are delivered to your home, high schools, 1 off-campus center in Scottsdale Airpark.
Media Courses are delivered via television, World Wide Web, e-mail. Students and teachers may meet in person or interact via mail, telephone, fax, e-mail. The following equipment may be required: television, computer, modem, Internet access, e-mail.
Restrictions Programs are available to in-state students only. Enrollment is open to anyone.
Services Distance learners have access to library services, the campus computer network, e-mail services, academic advising, career placement assistance at a distance.
Credit-earning options Students may transfer credits from another institution or may earn credits through examinations, portfolio assessment, military training.
Typical costs Tuition of $40 per credit hour. *Noncredit courses:* $111 per course. Financial aid is available to distance learners.
Registration Students may register by mail, fax, in person.
Contact John Silvester, Senior Associate Dean of Instruction, Scottsdale Community College. *Telephone:* 480-423-6390. *Fax:* 480-423-6066. *E-mail:* john.silvester@scmail.maricopa.edu.

DEGREES AND AWARDS

AAS Business Management (some on-campus requirements)

COURSE SUBJECT AREAS OFFERED OUTSIDE OF DEGREE PROGRAMS

Undergraduate: Business; computer and information sciences; creative writing; music

SEABURY-WESTERN THEOLOGICAL SEMINARY

Evanston, Illinois
www.swts.nwu.edu

Seabury-Western Theological Seminary, founded in 1933, is an independent, religious, graduate institution. It is accredited by the Association of Theological Schools in the United States and Canada, North Central Association of Colleges and Schools. It first offered distance learning courses in 1995. In 1999–2000, it offered 1 course at a distance.
Course delivery sites Courses are delivered to your home.
Media Courses are delivered via World Wide Web, e-mail. Students and teachers may interact via e-mail. The following equipment may be required: computer, modem, Internet access, e-mail.
Restrictions Programs are available worldwide. Enrollment is open to anyone.
Typical costs Tuition of $1150 per course. *Noncredit courses:* $350 per course.
Registration Students may register by mail, fax, telephone, e-mail, World Wide Web, in person.
Contact Rev. Meredith Woods Potter, Director of Academic Affairs, Seabury-Western Theological Seminary, 2122 Sheridan Road, Evanston, IL 60201. *Telephone:* 847-328-9300. *Fax:* 847-328-9624. *E-mail:* swts@nwu.edu.

DEGREES AND AWARDS

Distance programs offered do not lead to a degree or other formal award.

COURSE SUBJECT AREAS OFFERED OUTSIDE OF DEGREE PROGRAMS

Graduate: Theological studies
Noncredit: Theological studies

SEATTLE CENTRAL COMMUNITY COLLEGE

Seattle, Washington
Distance Learning Program
www.distantlearning.net

Seattle Central Community College, founded in 1966, is a state-supported, two-year college. It is accredited by the Northwest Association of Schools and Colleges. It first offered distance learning courses in 1990. In 1999–2000, it offered 50 courses at a distance. In fall 1999, there were 494 students enrolled in distance learning courses.
Course delivery sites Courses are delivered to your home, your workplace, military bases.
Media Courses are delivered via television, videotapes, audiotapes, World Wide Web, e-mail, print. Students and teachers may interact via mail, telephone, fax, e-mail. The following equipment may be required: television, videocassette player, computer, modem, Internet access, e-mail.
Restrictions Programs are available worldwide. Enrollment is open to anyone.
Services Distance learners have access to the campus computer network, e-mail services, academic advising, bookstore at a distance.
Credit-earning options Students may transfer credits from another institution or may earn credits through examinations.
Typical costs Undergraduate in-state tuition for 10 to 18 credits is $526. Out-of-state tuition ranges between $323 and $370 per five credit class. Mandatory fees range between $30 and $65 depending on type of class. Costs may vary. Financial aid is available to distance learners.
Registration Students may register by mail, fax, telephone, e-mail, World Wide Web, in person.

Contact Queenie L. Baker, Director, Seattle Central Community College, 1701 Broadway, BE1144, Seattle, WA 98122-2400. *Telephone:* 800-510-1724. *Fax:* 206-287-5562. *E-mail:* qbaker@sccd.ctc.edu.

DEGREES AND AWARDS

Undergraduate Certificate(s) Teaching English as a Second Language (service area differs from that of the overall institution; some on-campus requirements)
AA Liberal Arts

COURSE SUBJECT AREAS OFFERED OUTSIDE OF DEGREE PROGRAMS

Undergraduate: Abnormal psychology; accounting; algebra; American literature; American studies; anthropology; Asian studies; astronomy and astrophysics; biology; business administration and management; chemistry; child care and development; computer and information sciences; developmental and child psychology; economics; English as a second language (ESL); English composition; English language and literature; English literature; environmental science; ethics; film studies; foods and nutrition studies; geography; journalism; logic; mass media; medieval/renaissance studies; music; oceanography; psychology; sociology; Spanish language and literature; statistics

Special note
Since its founding in 1967, Seattle Central Community College has developed into a school with a national reputation for innovative educational programs. Located in Seattle, Washington, Seattle Central is one of the largest colleges in the state, with an enrollment of 10,000 students. The College is unique among the state's community colleges for its ethnic and cultural diversity. Each year, more students from Seattle Central go on to 4-year institutions than from any other community college in the state. If the ultimate goal is a 4-year degree, the Associate of Arts (AA) degree via distance learning provides freshman- and sophomore-level classes recognized by most universities. For those not sure about college, distance learning may help them decide. Students can enroll via distance learning in an individual course that interests them or helps improve their knowledge and skills and earn credit toward an AA degree, or they can earn a certificate in a specific technical area. There are several reasons why distance learning may work for students, including those with a work or home schedule conflict, disability or homebound situation, lifestyle preferences, traffic gridlock, or a residence too far from a college. It can also be a good match with the student's learning style or simply more convenient. Seattle Central's distance learning program offers courses in a variety of formats, including correspondence courses, telecourses, videocassette courses, and online courses. For more information, students should contact the Distance Learning Program at 800-510-1724 (toll-free) or by e-mail (dislrn@sccd.ctc.edu) or visit the home page (http://www.distantlearning.net).

SEMINOLE COMMUNITY COLLEGE

Sanford, Florida
Distance Learning Department
www.seminole.cc.fl.us/dl

Seminole Community College, founded in 1966, is a state and locally supported, two-year college. It is accredited by the Southern Association of Colleges and Schools. In 1999–2000, it offered 130 courses at a distance. In fall 1999, there were 400 students enrolled in distance learning courses.
Course delivery sites Courses are delivered to your home, your workplace, military bases, high schools, 1 off-campus center in Altamonte.

Media Courses are delivered via videotapes, videoconferencing, interactive television, computer software, CD-ROM, computer conferencing, World Wide Web, e-mail, print. Students and teachers may meet in person or interact via videoconferencing, mail, telephone, fax, e-mail, interactive television, World Wide Web. The following equipment may be required: television, videocassette player, computer, modem, Internet access, e-mail.
Restrictions Programs are available worldwide. Enrollment is open to anyone.
Services Distance learners have access to library services, the campus computer network, e-mail services, academic advising, career placement assistance, bookstore at a distance.
Credit-earning options Students may transfer credits from another institution or may earn credits through examinations.
Typical costs Tuition of $136 per course for local area residents. Tuition of $136 per course for in-state residents. Tuition of $172 per course for out-of-state residents. There is an additional $30 fee per lab. *Noncredit courses:* $136 per course. Costs may vary. Financial aid is available to distance learners.
Registration Students may register by mail, fax, telephone, World Wide Web, in person.
Contact Lillie Gibson, Distance Learning Departmental Secretary, Seminole Community College, 100 Weldon Boulevard, Sanford, FL 32773. *Telephone:* 407-328-2424. *Fax:* 407-328-2233. *E-mail:* gibsonl@mail.seminole.cc.fl.us.

DEGREES AND AWARDS

Distance programs offered do not lead to a degree or other formal award.

COURSE SUBJECT AREAS OFFERED OUTSIDE OF DEGREE PROGRAMS

Undergraduate: Administrative and secretarial services; American (U.S.) history; anthropology; art history and criticism; business administration and management; business communications; computer programming; criminal justice; database management; economics; English composition; family and marriage counseling; fire science; geology; health and physical education/fitness; information sciences and systems; library and information studies; music; nursing; oceanography; psychology; sociology; teacher education; technical writing

See full description on page 676.

SETON HALL UNIVERSITY

South Orange, New Jersey
SetonWorldWide
www.setonworldwide.net

Seton Hall University, founded in 1856, is an independent, religious university. It is accredited by the Association of Theological Schools in the United States and Canada, Middle States Association of Colleges and Schools. It first offered distance learning courses in 1998. In 1999–2000, it offered 12 courses at a distance. In fall 1999, there were 100 students enrolled in distance learning courses.
Course delivery sites Courses are delivered to your home, your workplace, military bases.
Media Courses are delivered via videotapes, videoconferencing, audiotapes, computer software, CD-ROM, computer conferencing, World Wide Web, e-mail, print. Students and teachers may meet in person or interact via mail, telephone, fax, e-mail, World Wide Web. The following equipment may be required: computer, modem, Internet access, e-mail.
Restrictions Programs are available worldwide. Enrollment is open to anyone.

Services Distance learners have access to library services, e-mail services, academic advising at a distance.

Typical costs Graduate tuition ranges between $24500 and $31500 per degree program. Financial aid is available to distance learners.

Registration Students may register by World Wide Web.

Contact Dr. Philip DiSalvio, Director, Seton Hall University, Kozlowski Hall, 400 South Orange Avenue, South Orange, NJ 07079. *Telephone:* 888-SETONWW. *Fax:* 973-761-9086. *E-mail:* setonworldwide@shu.edu.

eCollege.com *www.ecollege.com/scholarships*

DEGREES AND AWARDS

Graduate Certificate(s) Theological Studies (some on-campus requirements)

MA Counseling Psychology (certain restrictions apply; some on-campus requirements), Educational Administration (some on-campus requirements), Educational Administration and Supervision (some on-campus requirements), Executive Communication (some on-campus requirements), Protective Services (some on-campus requirements)

MS Business (some on-campus requirements)

COURSE SUBJECT AREAS OFFERED OUTSIDE OF DEGREE PROGRAMS

Graduate: Accounting; business; business communications; communications; community health services; counseling psychology; education; education administration; health professions and related sciences; health services administration; human resources management; mental health services; special education; teacher education; theological studies

See full description on page 664.

SETON HILL COLLEGE

Greensburg, Pennsylvania

Academic Affairs

Seton Hill College, founded in 1883, is an independent, religious, comprehensive institution. It is accredited by the Middle States Association of Colleges and Schools. In 1999–2000, it offered 2 courses at a distance. In fall 1999, there were 20 students enrolled in distance learning courses.

Course delivery sites Courses are delivered to your home, your workplace.

Media Courses are delivered via World Wide Web, e-mail. Students and teachers may meet in person or interact via mail, telephone, fax, e-mail, World Wide Web. The following equipment may be required: computer, modem, Internet access, e-mail.

Restrictions Programs are available to local area students. Enrollment is open to anyone.

Services Distance learners have access to library services, the campus computer network, e-mail services, bookstore at a distance.

Credit-earning options Students may transfer credits from another institution or may earn credits through examinations, military training.

Typical costs *Undergraduate:* Tuition of $360 per credit. *Graduate:* Tuition of $360 per credit. Costs may vary. Financial aid is available to distance learners.

Registration Students may register by mail, fax, in person.

Contact Mary Kay Cooper, Director, Adult and Graduate Studies, Seton Hill College, Box 510, Seton Hill Drive, Greensburg, PA 15601. *Telephone:* 724-838-4209. *Fax:* 724-830-1294. *E-mail:* mcooper@setonhill.edu.

DEGREES AND AWARDS

Distance programs offered do not lead to a degree or other formal award.

COURSE SUBJECT AREAS OFFERED OUTSIDE OF DEGREE PROGRAMS

Undergraduate: European history

SHASTA BIBLE COLLEGE

Redding, California

Individualized Distance Learning
www.shasta.edu

Shasta Bible College, founded in 1971, is an independent, religious, four-year college. It is accredited by the Transnational Association of Christian Colleges and Schools. In 1999–2000, it offered 10 courses at a distance. In fall 1999, there was one student enrolled in distance learning courses.

Course delivery sites Courses are delivered to your home, your workplace.

Media Courses are delivered via e-mail. Students and teachers may meet in person or interact via mail, telephone, fax, e-mail.

Restrictions Programs are available worldwide. Enrollment is restricted to individuals meeting certain criteria.

Services Distance learners have access to e-mail services, academic advising, career placement assistance at a distance.

Credit-earning options Students may transfer credits from another institution or may earn credits through examinations, portfolio assessment.

Typical costs *Undergraduate:* Tuition of $155 per unit. *Graduate:* Tuition of $155 per unit.

Registration Students may register by mail, in person.

Contact George Gunn, Dean of Admissions, Shasta Bible College, 2980 Hartnell Avenue, Redding, CA 96002. *Telephone:* 530-221-4275. *Fax:* 530-221-6929. *E-mail:* ggunn@shasta.edu.

DEGREES AND AWARDS

Undergraduate Certificate(s) Bible and Theology (certain restrictions apply; some on-campus requirements)

AA Bible and Theology (certain restrictions apply; some on-campus requirements), Early Childhood Education (certain restrictions apply; some on-campus requirements)

BS Bible and Theology (certain restrictions apply; some on-campus requirements)

COURSE SUBJECT AREAS OFFERED OUTSIDE OF DEGREE PROGRAMS

Undergraduate: Teacher education; theological studies

Noncredit: Teacher education; theological studies

SHAWNEE COMMUNITY COLLEGE

Ullin, Illinois

Learning Resources
www.shawnee.cc.il.us/

Shawnee Community College, founded in 1967, is a state and locally supported, two-year college. It is accredited by the North Central Association of Colleges and Schools. It first offered distance learning courses in 1994. In 1999–2000, it offered 60 courses at a distance. In fall 1999, there were 560 students enrolled in distance learning courses.

Course delivery sites Courses are delivered to your home, your workplace, high schools, Southeastern Illinois College (Harrisburg), 9 off-campus centers in Anna, Cairo, Goreville, Joppa, Metropolis, Vienna.
Media Courses are delivered via videotapes, interactive television, CD-ROM, World Wide Web. Students and teachers may meet in person or interact via videoconferencing, mail, telephone, fax, e-mail, interactive television. The following equipment may be required: television, videocassette player, Internet access.
Restrictions Interactive video courses are available primarily to in-state students; telecourses are available to students in Illinois, Kentucky, and Missouri only. Enrollment is open to anyone.
Services Distance learners have access to library services, e-mail services, academic advising at a distance.
Credit-earning options Students may transfer credits from another institution or may earn credits through examinations.
Typical costs Tuition of $38 per credit hour for local area residents. Tuition of $117 per credit hour for in-state residents. Tuition of $234 per credit hour for out-of-state residents. Financial aid is available to distance learners.
Registration Students may register by mail, fax, World Wide Web, in person.
Contact Russ Stoup, Distance Learning Coordinator, Shawnee Community College, 8364 Shawnee College Road, Ullin, IL 62992. *Telephone:* 618-634-2242 Ext. 276. *Fax:* 618-634-9711.

DEGREES AND AWARDS

Distance programs offered do not lead to a degree or other formal award.

COURSE SUBJECT AREAS OFFERED OUTSIDE OF DEGREE PROGRAMS

Undergraduate: Abnormal psychology; accounting; American literature; anthropology; biology; business administration and management; business law; computer and information sciences; developmental and child psychology; economics; engineering/industrial management; English composition; geology; health professions and related sciences; liberal arts, general studies, and humanities; mathematics; nursing; sociology; zoology

SHAWNEE STATE UNIVERSITY

Portsmouth, Ohio

Nursing Department

Shawnee State University, founded in 1986, is a state-supported, four-year college. It is accredited by the North Central Association of Colleges and Schools. In 1999–2000, it offered 9 courses at a distance. In fall 1999, there were 37 students enrolled in distance learning courses.
Course delivery sites Courses are delivered to your home, high schools.
Media Courses are delivered via computer software, CD-ROM, computer conferencing, World Wide Web, e-mail. Students and teachers may meet in person or interact via mail, telephone, fax, e-mail, World Wide Web. The following equipment may be required: computer, modem, Internet access, e-mail.
Restrictions Programs are available to local area students. Enrollment is restricted to individuals meeting certain criteria.
Services Distance learners have access to library services, the campus computer network, e-mail services at a distance.
Credit-earning options Students may transfer credits from another institution or may earn credits through examinations, military training, business training.
Typical costs Tuition of $915 per quarter plus mandatory fees of $183 per quarter for in-state residents. Tuition of $1716 per quarter plus mandatory fees of $183 per quarter for out-of-state residents. Financial aid is available to distance learners.
Registration Students may register by telephone, in person.

Contact Mary Ann Lubno, Chair, Nursing Department, Shawnee State University, Health Sciences Building, 940 Second Street, Portsmouth, OH 45662. *Telephone:* 740-355-2249. *E-mail:* mlubno@shawnee.edu.

DEGREES AND AWARDS

BSN Nursing Nursing (certain restrictions apply; some on-campus requirements)

COURSE SUBJECT AREAS OFFERED OUTSIDE OF DEGREE PROGRAMS

Undergraduate: Nursing

SHENANDOAH UNIVERSITY

Winchester, Virginia

Division of Continuing Education
www.su.edu

Shenandoah University, founded in 1875, is an independent, religious, comprehensive institution. It is accredited by the Southern Association of Colleges and Schools. It first offered distance learning courses in 1988. In 1999–2000, it offered 17 courses at a distance. In fall 1999, there were 400 students enrolled in distance learning courses.
Course delivery sites Courses are delivered to your home, your workplace, 1 off-campus center in Winchester.
Media Courses are delivered via television, videoconferencing, e-mail. Students and teachers may interact via mail, telephone, e-mail, World Wide Web. The following equipment may be required: television, videocassette player.
Restrictions Programs are available nationwide. Enrollment is open to anyone.
Services Distance learners have access to library services, the campus computer network, e-mail services at a distance.
Credit-earning options Students may transfer credits from another institution or may earn credits through examinations.
Typical costs Tuition of $345 per course.
Registration Students may register by mail, fax, telephone, World Wide Web, in person.
Contact Dr. R.J. Good, Associate Director, Shenandoah University. *Telephone:* 540-665-4643. *Fax:* 540-665-3496. *E-mail:* rgood@su.edu.

DEGREES AND AWARDS

PharmD Non-Traditional Pharmacy (certain restrictions apply)

COURSE SUBJECT AREAS OFFERED OUTSIDE OF DEGREE PROGRAMS

Graduate: Aerospace, aeronautical engineering; chemical engineering; civil engineering; electrical engineering; engineering mechanics; engineering/industrial management; environmental engineering; industrial engineering; mathematics; mechanical engineering; teacher education

SHERIDAN COLLEGE

Sheridan, Wyoming
www.sc.whecn.edu

Sheridan College, founded in 1948, is a state and locally supported, two-year college. It is accredited by the North Central Association of Colleges and Schools. In 1999–2000, it offered 14 courses at a distance. In fall 1999, there were 84 students enrolled in distance learning courses.
Course delivery sites Courses are delivered to your home, 1 off-campus center in Gillette.

Media Courses are delivered via interactive television, World Wide Web. Students and teachers may interact via telephone, e-mail, interactive television, World Wide Web. The following equipment may be required: computer, modem, Internet access, e-mail.

Restrictions Programs are available to in-state students only. Enrollment is open to anyone.

Services Distance learners have access to the campus computer network, e-mail services, bookstore at a distance.

Credit-earning options Students may transfer credits from another institution or may earn credits through examinations, portfolio assessment.

Typical costs Tuition of $46 per credit hour plus mandatory fees of $12 per credit hour for local area residents. Tuition of $46 per credit hour plus mandatory fees of $12 per credit hour for in-state residents. Tuition of $138 per credit hour plus mandatory fees of $12 per credit hour for out-of-state residents. Financial aid is available to distance learners.

Registration Students may register by telephone, in person.

Contact Mark Englert, Dean of Arts and Sciences, Sheridan College, PO Box 1500, Sheridan, WY 82801. *Telephone:* 307-674-6446 Ext. 6135. *Fax:* 307-674-4293. *E-mail:* menglert@radar.sc.whecn.edu.

DEGREES AND AWARDS

Distance programs offered do not lead to a degree or other formal award.

COURSE SUBJECT AREAS OFFERED OUTSIDE OF DEGREE PROGRAMS

Undergraduate: Business administration and management; creative writing; ecology; English composition; English literature; instructional media; liberal arts, general studies, and humanities; marketing; railroad operations; Spanish language and literature

SHIPPENSBURG UNIVERSITY OF PENNSYLVANIA

Shippensburg, Pennsylvania

Extended Studies

vu.sshe.edu

Shippensburg University of Pennsylvania, founded in 1871, is a state-supported, comprehensive institution. It is accredited by the Middle States Association of Colleges and Schools. In 1999–2000, it offered 21 courses at a distance. In fall 1999, there were 133 students enrolled in distance learning courses.

Course delivery sites Courses are delivered to your home, your workplace, high schools, Millersville University of Pennsylvania (Millersville), West Chester University of Pennsylvania (West Chester), 1 off-campus center in Dixon.

Media Courses are delivered via videoconferencing, World Wide Web. Students and teachers may meet in person or interact via videoconferencing, telephone, fax, e-mail, World Wide Web. The following equipment may be required: computer, modem, Internet access, e-mail.

Restrictions Programs are available to in-state students only. Enrollment is restricted to individuals meeting certain criteria.

Services Distance learners have access to library services, academic advising, career placement assistance at a distance.

Credit-earning options Students may transfer credits from another institution or may earn credits through examinations.

Typical costs *Undergraduate:* Tuition of $150 per credit plus mandatory fees of $15 per credit for local area residents. Tuition of $150 per credit plus mandatory fees of $15 per credit for in-state residents. Tuition of $153 per credit plus mandatory fees of $15 per credit for out-of-state residents. *Graduate:* Tuition of $210 per credit plus mandatory fees of $21 per credit for local area residents. Tuition of $210 per credit plus

mandatory fees of $21 per credit for in-state residents. Tuition of $214.20 per credit plus mandatory fees of $21 per credit for out-of-state residents. Financial aid is available to distance learners.

Registration Students may register by mail, fax, e-mail, in person.

Contact Dr. Kathleen M. Howley, Dean of Extended Studies, Shippensburg University of Pennsylvania, 1871 Old Main Drive, Horton Hall 111, Shippensburg, PA 17257-2299. *Telephone:* 717-477-1348. *Fax:* 717-477-4050. *E-mail:* kmhowl@wharf.ship.edu.

DEGREES AND AWARDS

Distance programs offered do not lead to a degree or other formal award.

COURSE SUBJECT AREAS OFFERED OUTSIDE OF DEGREE PROGRAMS

Undergraduate: Economics; English composition; English language and literature; finance; mathematics; philosophy and religion; physics; psychology

Graduate: Economics; educational research; English composition; English language and literature; English literature; finance; information sciences and systems; journalism; mathematics; philosophy and religion; physics; psychology; student counseling; teacher education

SIERRA COLLEGE

Rocklin, California

Distance Learning Department

lrc.sierra.cc.ca.us/dl

Sierra College, founded in 1936, is a state-supported, two-year college. It is accredited by the Western Association of Schools and Colleges, Inc. It first offered distance learning courses in 1986. In 1999–2000, it offered 33 courses at a distance. In fall 1999, there were 950 students enrolled in distance learning courses.

Course delivery sites Courses are delivered to your home, your workplace, high schools, 2 off-campus centers in Grass Valley, Nevada City.

Media Courses are delivered via television. Students and teachers may meet in person or interact via mail, telephone, fax, e-mail, interactive television. The following equipment may be required: television.

Restrictions Programs are available to local area students. Enrollment is open to anyone.

Services Distance learners have access to library services, the campus computer network, e-mail services, academic advising, tutoring at a distance.

Credit-earning options Students may earn credits through examinations.

Typical costs Tuition of $11 per unit for in-state residents. Tuition of $125 per unit for out-of-state residents. Financial aid is available to distance learners.

Registration Students may register by mail, telephone, World Wide Web, in person.

Contact Suzanne Davenport, LRC Coordinator-Distance Learning, Sierra College, 5000 Rocklin Road, Rocklin, CA 95678. *Telephone:* 916-789-2638. *Fax:* 916-789-2992. *E-mail:* sdavenport@scmail.sierra.cc.ca.us.

DEGREES AND AWARDS

Distance programs offered do not lead to a degree or other formal award.

COURSE SUBJECT AREAS OFFERED OUTSIDE OF DEGREE PROGRAMS

Undergraduate: Algebra; business administration and management; computer programming; criminal justice; developmental and child psychology; drama and theater; English composition; English language and literature; ethics; fine arts; geography; history; information sciences and systems; liberal arts, general studies, and humanities; mathematics; microbiology; music; political science; public policy analysis; social psychology; sociology; statistics

SIMPSON COLLEGE

Indianola, Iowa
Division of Adult Learning
www.simpson.edu

Simpson College, founded in 1860, is an independent, religious, four-year college. It is accredited by the North Central Association of Colleges and Schools. It first offered distance learning courses in 1996. In 1999–2000, it offered 9 courses at a distance.
Course delivery sites Courses are delivered to your home, your workplace, off-campus center(s) in West Des Moines.
Media Courses are delivered via World Wide Web, e-mail. Students and teachers may meet in person or interact via mail, telephone, fax, e-mail. The following equipment may be required: computer, modem, Internet access, e-mail.
Restrictions Programs are available in central Iowa. Enrollment is restricted to individuals meeting certain criteria.
Services Distance learners have access to library services, the campus computer network, e-mail services, academic advising, tutoring, bookstore at a distance.
Credit-earning options Students may transfer credits from another institution or may earn credits through examinations, portfolio assessment, military training, business training.
Typical costs Tuition of $195 per credit. *Noncredit courses:* $300 per course. Financial aid is available to distance learners.
Registration Students may register by mail, fax, telephone, e-mail, World Wide Web, in person.
Contact Walter Pearson, Director, Simpson College, 701 North C Street, Indianola, IA 50125. *Telephone:* 515-961-1615. *Fax:* 515-961-1498. *E-mail:* adultlrn@simpson.edu.

eCollege.com *www.ecollege.com/scholarships*

DEGREES AND AWARDS

Distance programs offered do not lead to a degree or other formal award.

COURSE SUBJECT AREAS OFFERED OUTSIDE OF DEGREE PROGRAMS

Undergraduate: Business administration and management; communications; criminal justice

SINCLAIR COMMUNITY COLLEGE

Dayton, Ohio
Distance Learning Division
www.sinclair.edu/distance

Sinclair Community College, founded in 1887, is a state and locally supported, two-year college. It is accredited by the North Central Association of Colleges and Schools. It first offered distance learning courses in 1979. In 1999–2000, it offered 150 courses at a distance. In fall 1999, there were 4,600 students enrolled in distance learning courses.
Course delivery sites Courses are delivered to your home, your workplace, military bases, high schools, 11 off-campus centers in Bellbrook, Camden, Centerville, Clayton, Dayton, Fairborn, Huber Heights, Kettering, Miamisburg, Trotwood, Vandalia.
Media Courses are delivered via television, videotapes, videoconferencing, interactive television, audiotapes, CD-ROM, World Wide Web, print. Students and teachers may meet in person or interact via videoconferencing, mail, telephone, fax, e-mail, interactive television, World Wide Web. The following equipment may be required: television, videocassette player, computer, modem, Internet access, e-mail.
Restrictions Programs are available worldwide. Enrollment is open to anyone.
Services Distance learners have access to library services, e-mail services, academic advising, tutoring, career placement assistance, bookstore at a distance.
Credit-earning options Students may transfer credits from another institution or may earn credits through examinations, portfolio assessment, military training, business training.
Typical costs Tuition of $29.45 per credit hour for local area residents. Tuition of $48.45 per credit hour for in-state residents. Tuition of $81.45 per credit hour for out-of-state residents. Financial aid is available to distance learners.
Registration Students may register by mail, fax, telephone, e-mail, World Wide Web, in person.
Contact Linda PaHud, Coordinator of Distance Learning Services, Sinclair Community College, 444 West Third Street, Dayton, OH 45402. *Telephone:* 937-512-2694. *Fax:* 937-512-2891. *E-mail:* lpahud@sinclair.edu.

DEGREES AND AWARDS

AA Liberal Arts
AS Business Administration

COURSE SUBJECT AREAS OFFERED OUTSIDE OF DEGREE PROGRAMS

Undergraduate: Abnormal psychology; accounting; administrative and secretarial services; algebra; American (U.S.) history; anthropology; area, ethnic, and cultural studies; art history and criticism; astronomy and astrophysics; biological and life sciences; business; business administration and management; business communications; business law; chemistry; communications; computer and information sciences; creative writing; developmental and child psychology; economics; electrical engineering; English composition; English literature; fine arts; health and physical education/fitness; health professions and related sciences; health services administration; history; law and legal studies; liberal arts, general studies, and humanities; marketing; mathematics; music; organizational behavior studies; philosophy and religion; photography; physics; protective services; psychology; social sciences; sociology; Spanish language and literature

See full description on page 666.

SKIDMORE COLLEGE

Saratoga Springs, New York
University Without Walls
www.skidmore.edu

Skidmore College, founded in 1903, is an independent, nonprofit, comprehensive institution. It is accredited by the Middle States Association of Colleges and Schools. It first offered distance learning courses in 1971. In 1999–2000, it offered 210 courses at a distance. In fall 1999, there were 250 students enrolled in distance learning courses.
Course delivery sites Courses are delivered to your home.

Media Courses are delivered via World Wide Web, e-mail, print. Students and teachers may interact via mail, telephone, fax, e-mail, World Wide Web. The following equipment may be required: computer, Internet access.

Restrictions Programs are available worldwide. Enrollment is restricted to individuals meeting certain criteria.

Services Distance learners have access to academic advising at a distance.

Credit-earning options Students may transfer credits from another institution or may earn credits through examinations, portfolio assessment, military training, business training.

Typical costs Tuition of $475 per course plus mandatory fees of $2800 per year. Financial aid is available to distance learners.

Registration Students may register by mail, fax, e-mail, World Wide Web, in person.

Contact Cornel Reinhart, Director, Skidmore College, University Without Walls, Saratoga Springs, NY 12866. *Telephone:* 518-580-5450. *Fax:* 518-580-5449. *E-mail:* uww@skidmore.edu.

DEGREES AND AWARDS

BA Individualized Studies (some on-campus requirements)

COURSE SUBJECT AREAS OFFERED OUTSIDE OF DEGREE PROGRAMS

Undergraduate: Accounting; area, ethnic, and cultural studies; biology; botany; business; business administration and management; chemistry; classical languages and literatures; communications; computer and information sciences; creative writing; criminal justice; developmental and child psychology; economics; education; English composition; English language and literature; environmental health; European languages and literatures; fine arts; French language and literature; geography; geology; health professions and related sciences; history; human resources management; interdisciplinary studies; international relations; journalism; liberal arts, general studies, and humanities; mathematics; microbiology; philosophy and religion; physical sciences; physics; political science; psychology; public administration and services; social sciences; social work; sociology; theological studies; visual and performing arts; zoology

See full description on page 668.

SNOW COLLEGE

Ephraim, Utah

Snow College Outreach Education
www.snow.edu/

Snow College, founded in 1888, is a state-supported, two-year college. It is accredited by the Northwest Association of Schools and Colleges. In 1999–2000, it offered 35 courses at a distance. In fall 1999, there were 150 students enrolled in distance learning courses.

Course delivery sites Courses are delivered to your home, high schools, 1 off-campus center in Richfield.

Media Courses are delivered via videotapes, interactive television, World Wide Web, e-mail, print. Students and teachers may meet in person or interact via mail, telephone, fax, e-mail, interactive television, World Wide Web. The following equipment may be required: television, videocassette player, computer, e-mail.

Restrictions Programs are available to in-state students only. Enrollment is open to anyone.

Services Distance learners have access to library services, the campus computer network, e-mail services, academic advising, bookstore at a distance.

Credit-earning options Students may transfer credits from another institution or may earn credits through examinations, military training.

Typical costs Undergraduate tuition is $153 for 2 credit-hours fees $27.50, $199 for 3-credit hours, fees $40.50 and $245 for 4 credit-hours, fees $54. *Noncredit courses:* $65 per course.

Registration Students may register by mail, fax, telephone, World Wide Web, in person.

Contact Wendy Christensen, Continuing Education Coordinator, Snow College, 150 East College Avenue, Ephraim, UT 84627. *Telephone:* 435-283-7320. *Fax:* 435-283-7329. *E-mail:* wendy.christensen@snow.edu.

DEGREES AND AWARDS

AS Criminology/Criminal Justice

COURSE SUBJECT AREAS OFFERED OUTSIDE OF DEGREE PROGRAMS

Undergraduate: Accounting; adult education; anthropology; art history and criticism; biology; botany; business administration and management; calculus; continuing education; criminology; drama and theater; English literature; ethics; finance; foods and nutrition studies; geography; history; human resources management; individual and family development studies; microbiology; social psychology; sociology

Noncredit: Adult education; continuing education

SOMERSET COMMUNITY COLLEGE

Somerset, Kentucky

Office of Distance Learning
www.somcc.uky.edu/

Somerset Community College, founded in 1965, is a state-supported, two-year college. It is accredited by the Southern Association of Colleges and Schools. In 1999–2000, it offered 28 courses at a distance. In fall 1999, there were 408 students enrolled in distance learning courses.

Course delivery sites Courses are delivered to your home, your workplace, military bases, Eastern Kentucky University (Richmond), 2 off-campus centers in London, Whitley City.

Media Courses are delivered via television, videotapes, interactive television, computer software, World Wide Web, e-mail. Students and teachers may meet in person or interact via mail, telephone, fax, e-mail, interactive television, World Wide Web. The following equipment may be required: television, videocassette player, computer, modem, Internet access, e-mail.

Restrictions Programs are available to in-state students only. Enrollment is open to anyone.

Services Distance learners have access to library services, the campus computer network, e-mail services, tutoring at a distance.

Credit-earning options Students may transfer credits from another institution or may earn credits through examinations, military training, business training.

Typical costs Undergraduate in state tuition is $144 for 3 credit-hours. Out-of-state tuition is $432 for 3 credit-hours. Mandatory fees are $20 per class. Financial aid is available to distance learners.

Registration Students may register by mail, in person.

Contact Linda Bourne, Director of Distance Learning, Somerset Community College, 808 Monticello Street, Somerset, KY 42501. *Telephone:* 606-679-8501. *Fax:* 606-677-6992. *E-mail:* linda.bourne@kctcs.net.

DEGREES AND AWARDS

Distance programs offered do not lead to a degree or other formal award.

COURSE SUBJECT AREAS OFFERED OUTSIDE OF DEGREE PROGRAMS

Undergraduate: Computer and information sciences; information sciences and systems

SONOMA STATE UNIVERSITY

Rohnert Park, California
Liberal Studies Degree Completion Program
www.sonoma.edu/exed/lsdcp

Sonoma State University, founded in 1960, is a state-supported, comprehensive institution. It is accredited by the Western Association of Schools and Colleges, Inc. It first offered distance learning courses in 1996. In 1999–2000, it offered 4 courses at a distance. In fall 1999, there were 43 students enrolled in distance learning courses.

Course delivery sites Courses are delivered to your home, your workplace.

Media Courses are delivered via computer conferencing, World Wide Web, e-mail. Students and teachers may meet in person or interact via mail, telephone, fax, e-mail, World Wide Web. The following equipment may be required: computer, modem, Internet access, e-mail.

Restrictions Programs are available to in-state students only. Enrollment is restricted to individuals meeting certain criteria.

Services Distance learners have access to library services, academic advising, bookstore at a distance.

Credit-earning options Students may transfer credits from another institution or may earn credits through examinations, portfolio assessment.

Typical costs Tuition of $2800 per semester. Financial aid is available to distance learners.

Registration Students may register by mail, fax, telephone, in person.

Contact Beth Warner, Administrative Coordinator, Sonoma State University, SSU Extended Education, Rohnert Park, CA 94928. *Telephone:* 707-664-3977. *Fax:* 707-664-2613. *E-mail:* beth.warner@sonoma.edu.

DEGREES AND AWARDS

BA Liberal Studies (some on-campus requirements)

SOUTH DAKOTA STATE UNIVERSITY

Brookings, South Dakota
Instructional Technologies Center
www.sdstate.edu/witc/http/itc1.html

South Dakota State University, founded in 1881, is a state-supported university. It is accredited by the North Central Association of Colleges and Schools. In 1999–2000, it offered 85 courses at a distance. In fall 1999, there were 606 students enrolled in distance learning courses.

Course delivery sites Courses are delivered to your home, your workplace, military bases, high schools, Northern State University (Aberdeen), South Dakota School of Mines and Technology (Rapid City), University of South Dakota (Vermillion), 1 off-campus center in Sioux Falls.

Media Courses are delivered via television, videotapes, videoconferencing, interactive television, computer software, CD-ROM, World Wide Web, e-mail. Students and teachers may meet in person or interact via videoconferencing, mail, telephone, fax, e-mail, interactive television, World Wide Web. The following equipment may be required: television, videocassette player, computer, modem, Internet access, e-mail.

Restrictions Programs are available nationwide. Enrollment is restricted to individuals meeting certain criteria.

Services Distance learners have access to library services, the campus computer network, e-mail services, academic advising, career placement assistance, bookstore at a distance.

Credit-earning options Students may transfer credits from another institution or may earn credits through examinations.

Typical costs *Undergraduate:* Tuition of $125.45 per credit. *Graduate:* Tuition of $161.25 per credit. Costs may vary. Financial aid is available to distance learners.

Registration Students may register by mail, fax, telephone, e-mail, World Wide Web, in person.

Contact JoAnn Sckerl, Coordinator of Outreach Programming, South Dakota State University, 315 Administration Building, Brookings, SD 57007. *Telephone:* 605-688-4431. *E-mail:* joann_sckerl@sdstate.edu.

DEGREES AND AWARDS

Distance programs offered do not lead to a degree or other formal award.

COURSE SUBJECT AREAS OFFERED OUTSIDE OF DEGREE PROGRAMS

Undergraduate: Agriculture; biological and life sciences; business; communications; computer and information sciences; education; engineering; English language and literature; European languages and literatures; health and physical education/fitness; health professions and related sciences; history; home economics and family studies; mathematics; physical sciences; psychology; social sciences

Graduate: Business; education; engineering; health professions and related sciences; home economics and family studies; mathematics; social sciences

SOUTHEAST COMMUNITY COLLEGE, BEATRICE CAMPUS

Beatrice, Nebraska

Southeast Community College, Beatrice Campus, founded in 1976, is a district-supported, two-year college. It is accredited by the North Central Association of Colleges and Schools. It first offered distance learning courses in 1996. In 1999–2000, it offered 10 courses at a distance. In fall 1999, there were 75 students enrolled in distance learning courses.

Course delivery sites Courses are delivered to your home, your workplace, high schools.

Media Courses are delivered via television, videotapes, videoconferencing, interactive television, computer software, World Wide Web. Students and teachers may meet in person or interact via mail, telephone, fax, e-mail, interactive television, World Wide Web.

Restrictions Programs are available worldwide. Enrollment is open to anyone.

Services Distance learners have access to library services, e-mail services, academic advising, career placement assistance, bookstore at a distance.

Credit-earning options Students may transfer credits from another institution.

Typical costs Tuition of $42.75 per credit plus mandatory fees of $3.50 per credit for in-state residents. Tuition of $50.25 per credit plus mandatory fees of $3.50 per credit for out-of-state residents. Costs may vary. Financial aid is available to distance learners.

Registration Students may register by mail, fax, telephone, e-mail, in person.

Contact Neal Henning, Distance Learning Coordinator, Southeast Community College, Beatrice Campus, Route 2, Box 35A, Beatrice, NE 68310. *Telephone:* 402-228-3488 Ext. 326. *Fax:* 402-228-2218. *E-mail:* nlhennin@sccm.cc.ne.us.

DEGREES AND AWARDS

AAS Business Administration

COURSE SUBJECT AREAS OFFERED OUTSIDE OF DEGREE PROGRAMS

Undergraduate: Accounting; business administration and management; education administration; English composition; European languages and literatures; health professions and related sciences; nursing; social psychology; special education; teacher education

SOUTHEAST COMMUNITY COLLEGE, LINCOLN CAMPUS

Lincoln, Nebraska
Academic Education

Southeast Community College, Lincoln Campus, founded in 1973, is a district-supported, two-year college. It is accredited by the North Central Association of Colleges and Schools. It first offered distance learning courses in 1994. In 1999–2000, it offered 25 courses at a distance. In fall 1999, there were 800 students enrolled in distance learning courses.

Course delivery sites Courses are delivered to your home, your workplace, high schools, Central Community College–Grand Island Campus (Grand Island), Mid-Plains Community College (North Platte), Northeast Community College (Norfolk), 24 off-campus centers.

Media Courses are delivered via television, videotapes, videoconferencing, interactive television, computer software, computer conferencing, e-mail. Students and teachers may meet in person or interact via videoconferencing, telephone, e-mail, interactive television. The following equipment may be required: television, videocassette player, computer, Internet access, e-mail.

Restrictions Programs are available to in-state students only. Enrollment is open to anyone.

Services Distance learners have access to library services, academic advising, career placement assistance, bookstore at a distance.

Credit-earning options Students may transfer credits from another institution or may earn credits through examinations, military training.

Typical costs Tuition of $28.50 per quarter credit plus mandatory fees of $1 per quarter credit. Costs may vary. Financial aid is available to distance learners.

Registration Students may register by mail, fax, in person.

Contact Randy Hiatt, Director of Distance Education, Southeast Community College, Lincoln Campus, 8800 "O" Street, Lincoln, NE 68520. *Telephone:* 402-437-2705. *Fax:* 402-437-2497. *E-mail:* ru.hiatt@sccm.cc.ne.us.

DEGREES AND AWARDS

AAS Surgical Technology (certain restrictions apply)
AS Radiological Technology (certain restrictions apply)

COURSE SUBJECT AREAS OFFERED OUTSIDE OF DEGREE PROGRAMS

Undergraduate: Accounting; agriculture; American (U.S.) history; anthropology; archaeology; area, ethnic, and cultural studies; business administration and management; business law; child care and development; communications; continuing education; earth science; economics; English composition; English language and literature; ethics; European history; foods and nutrition studies; geography; geology; health professions and related sciences; mathematics; psychology; sociology; Spanish language and literature

SOUTHEASTERN COMMUNITY COLLEGE, NORTH CAMPUS

West Burlington, Iowa
Distance Learning
www.secc.cc.ia.us

Southeastern Community College, North Campus, founded in 1968, is a state and locally supported, two-year college. It is accredited by the North Central Association of Colleges and Schools. It first offered distance learning courses in 1982. In 1999–2000, it offered 12 courses at a distance. In fall 1999, there were 175 students enrolled in distance learning courses.

Course delivery sites Courses are delivered to your home, your workplace, high schools, Southeastern Community College, South Campus (Keokuk), off-campus center(s) in Fort Madison, Mt. Pleasant.

Media Courses are delivered via television, videoconferencing, interactive television, print. Students and teachers may meet in person or interact via videoconferencing, mail, telephone, fax, e-mail, interactive television. The following equipment may be required: television, videocassette player, computer, e-mail.

Restrictions Programs are available to in-state students only. Enrollment is restricted to individuals meeting certain criteria.

Services Distance learners have access to library services, e-mail services, academic advising, bookstore at a distance.

Credit-earning options Students may transfer credits from another institution or may earn credits through examinations.

Typical costs Tuition of $65 per credit hour for in-state residents. Tuition of $89.75 per credit hour for out-of-state residents. Financial aid is available to distance learners.

Registration Students may register by mail, telephone, in person.

Contact Chuck Chrisman, Admissions Office, Southeastern Community College, North Campus. *Telephone:* 319-752-2731. *Fax:* 319-752-4957. *E-mail:* cchrisman@secc.cc.ia.us.

eCollege.com   *www.ecollege.com/scholarships*

DEGREES AND AWARDS

Distance programs offered do not lead to a degree or other formal award.

COURSE SUBJECT AREAS OFFERED OUTSIDE OF DEGREE PROGRAMS

Undergraduate: Biology; business administration and management; European languages and literatures; liberal arts, general studies, and humanities; political science; psychology; social work
Noncredit: Business; business administration and management

SOUTHEASTERN ILLINOIS COLLEGE

Harrisburg, Illinois
Distance Learning
www.sic.cc.il.us/virtual.htm

Southeastern Illinois College, founded in 1960, is a state-supported, two-year college. It is accredited by the North Central Association of Colleges and Schools. It first offered distance learning courses in 1988. In 1999–2000, it offered 20 courses at a distance. In fall 1999, there were 150 students enrolled in distance learning courses.

Course delivery sites Courses are delivered to your home, high schools, 1 off-campus center in Carmi.

Media Courses are delivered via television, videotapes, interactive television, World Wide Web. Students and teachers may meet in person or interact via videoconferencing, mail, telephone, fax, e-mail, interactive television, World Wide Web. The following equipment may be required: television, videocassette player, computer, modem, Internet access, e-mail.

Restrictions Programs are available to local area students. Enrollment is open to anyone.

Services Distance learners have access to library services, the campus computer network, e-mail services, academic advising, bookstore at a distance.

Credit-earning options Students may transfer credits from another institution.

Typical costs Tuition of $36 per credit hour plus mandatory fees of $10 per course for local area residents. Tuition of $165 per credit hour plus mandatory fees of $10 per course for in-state residents. Tuition of $215 per credit hour plus mandatory fees of $10 per course for out-of-state residents. Financial aid is available to distance learners.

Registration Students may register by mail, fax, World Wide Web, in person.

Contact Mr. Gary Jones, Media Specialist, Southeastern Illinois College, 3575 College Road, Harrisburg, IL 62946. *Telephone:* 618-252-6376 Ext. 2265. *Fax:* 618-252-2713. *E-mail:* gjones@sic.cc.il.us.

DEGREES AND AWARDS

Distance programs offered do not lead to a degree or other formal award.

COURSE SUBJECT AREAS OFFERED OUTSIDE OF DEGREE PROGRAMS

Undergraduate: Business; educational psychology; English language and literature; health professions and related sciences; history; home economics and family studies; mathematics; philosophy and religion; political science; psychology

SOUTHEASTERN LOUISIANA UNIVERSITY

Hammond, Louisiana

Continuing Education
www.selu.edu/Academics/ContEd/

Southeastern Louisiana University, founded in 1925, is a state-supported, comprehensive institution. It is accredited by the Southern Association of Colleges and Schools. It first offered distance learning courses in 1982. In 1999–2000, it offered 19 courses at a distance. In fall 1999, there were 260 students enrolled in distance learning courses.

Course delivery sites Courses are delivered to your home, your workplace, Grambling State University (Grambling), Louisiana State University and Agricultural and Mechanical College (Baton Rouge), Louisiana State University in Shreveport (Shreveport), Louisiana Tech University (Ruston), McNeese State University (Lake Charles), Nicholls State University (Thibodaux), Northwestern State University of Louisiana (Natchitoches), Southern University and Agricultural and Mechanical College (Baton Rouge), University of Louisiana at Monroe (Monroe), 2 off-campus centers in Baton Rouge, St. Tammany.

Media Courses are delivered via television, videotapes, videoconferencing, computer software, computer conferencing, World Wide Web, e-mail. Students and teachers may interact via videoconferencing, mail, telephone, fax, e-mail, World Wide Web. The following equipment may be required: television, videocassette player, computer, modem, Internet access, e-mail.

Restrictions Programs are available regionally. Enrollment is open to anyone.

Services Distance learners have access to library services, the campus computer network, e-mail services, academic advising, tutoring, career placement assistance, bookstore at a distance.

Credit-earning options Students may transfer credits from another institution or may earn credits through examinations.

Typical costs *Undergraduate:* Tuition of $1075 per semester for in-state residents. Tuition of $3223 per semester for out-of-state residents. *Graduate:* Tuition of $1041 per semester for in-state residents. Tuition of $2657 per semester for out-of-state residents. Tuition per 3 credit hours is $300.50 for undergraduates and graduates. Financial aid is available to distance learners.

Registration Students may register by mail, telephone, World Wide Web, in person.

Contact Dr. Gerald Guidroz, Dean, Southeastern Louisiana University, Continuing Education, SLU10858, Hammond, LA 70402. *Telephone:* 504-549-2301. *Fax:* 504-549-5078. *E-mail:* gguidroz@selu.edu.

DEGREES AND AWARDS

Distance programs offered do not lead to a degree or other formal award.

COURSE SUBJECT AREAS OFFERED OUTSIDE OF DEGREE PROGRAMS

Undergraduate: Biology; business administration and management; chemistry; developmental and child psychology; English language and literature; finance; French language and literature; health and physical education/fitness; history; library and information studies; marketing; mathematics; nursing; psychology; sociology; special education
Graduate: Education; special education

See full description on page 676.

SOUTHEASTERN OKLAHOMA STATE UNIVERSITY

Durant, Oklahoma

Telecommunications

Southeastern Oklahoma State University, founded in 1909, is a state-supported, comprehensive institution. It is accredited by the North Central Association of Colleges and Schools. In 1999–2000, it offered 37 courses at a distance. In fall 1999, there were 156 students enrolled in distance learning courses.

Course delivery sites Courses are delivered to high schools, 3 off-campus centers in Ardmore, Idabel, McAlestar.

Media Courses are delivered via interactive television, World Wide Web, e-mail. Students and teachers may meet in person or interact via mail, telephone, fax, e-mail, interactive television. The following equipment may be required: Internet access, e-mail.

Restrictions Programs are available to local area students. Enrollment is open to anyone.

Services Distance learners have access to library services, the campus computer network, e-mail services, academic advising, bookstore at a distance.

Credit-earning options Students may transfer credits from another institution or may earn credits through examinations, portfolio assessment, military training, business training.

Typical costs *Undergraduate:* Tuition of $71 per credit hour plus mandatory fees of $7.50 per semester for in-state residents. Tuition of $158 per credit hour plus mandatory fees of $7.50 per semester for out-of-state residents. *Graduate:* Tuition of $91 per credit hour plus mandatory fees of $7.50 per semester for in-state residents. Tuition of $192 per credit hour plus mandatory fees of $7.50 per semester for out-of-state residents. Costs may vary. Financial aid is available to distance learners.

Registration Students may register by telephone, in person.

Contact Jesse O. Snowden, Vice President for Academic Affairs, Southeastern Oklahoma State University, PO Box 4137, Durant, OK 74701-0609. *Telephone:* 580-745-2200. *Fax:* 580-745-7474. *E-mail:* jsnowden@sosu.edu.

DEGREES AND AWARDS

Distance programs offered do not lead to a degree or other formal award.

COURSE SUBJECT AREAS OFFERED OUTSIDE OF DEGREE PROGRAMS

Undergraduate: Cognitive psychology; communications; criminal justice; curriculum and instruction; European history; finance; health and physical education/fitness; information sciences and systems; management information systems; mathematics

Graduate: Business administration and management; curriculum and instruction; education administration; management information systems

SOUTHERN ARKANSAS UNIVERSITY TECH

Camden, Arkansas

Business and Industry Productivity Center
www.sautech.edu

Southern Arkansas University Tech, founded in 1968, is a state-supported, two-year college. It is accredited by the North Central Association of Colleges and Schools. It first offered distance learning courses in 1995. In 1999–2000, it offered 5 courses at a distance. In fall 1999, there were 42 students enrolled in distance learning courses.

Course delivery sites Courses are delivered to your home, your workplace, military bases, high schools.

Media Courses are delivered via World Wide Web. Students and teachers may meet in person or interact via telephone, fax, e-mail. The following equipment may be required: computer, Internet access, e-mail.

Restrictions Programs are available worldwide. Enrollment is open to anyone.

Services Distance learners have access to library services, the campus computer network, e-mail services, bookstore at a distance.

Credit-earning options Students may transfer credits from another institution or may earn credits through examinations, portfolio assessment, military training, business training.

Typical costs Tuition of $35 per credit plus mandatory fees of $12 per credit. Financial aid is available to distance learners.

Registration Students may register by mail, fax, in person.

Contact Judy Blevins, Dean of General/Business Education, Southern Arkansas University Tech, SAU Tech Station, Camden, AR 71701. *Telephone:* 870-574-4541. *Fax:* 870-574-4477. *E-mail:* jblevins@sautech.edu.

DEGREES AND AWARDS

Distance programs offered do not lead to a degree or other formal award.

COURSE SUBJECT AREAS OFFERED OUTSIDE OF DEGREE PROGRAMS

Undergraduate: Algebra; biological and life sciences; business administration and management; computer and information sciences; English language and literature; history; philosophy and religion; physical sciences; psychology

See full description on page 676.

SOUTHERN CALIFORNIA UNIVERSITY FOR PROFESSIONAL STUDIES

Santa Ana, California
www.scups.edu

Southern California University for Professional Studies, founded in 1978, is a proprietary university. In 1999–2000, it offered 275 courses at a distance. In fall 1999, there were 1,100 students enrolled in distance learning courses.

Course delivery sites Courses are delivered to your home, your workplace.

Media Courses are delivered via e-mail, print. Students and teachers may meet in person or interact via mail, telephone, fax, e-mail. The following equipment may be required: computer, modem, Internet access, e-mail.

Restrictions Programs are available worldwide. Enrollment is open to anyone.

Services Distance learners have access to library services, academic advising at a distance.

Credit-earning options Students may transfer credits from another institution or may earn credits through military training, business training.

Typical costs *Undergraduate:* Tuition of $140 per semester. *Graduate:* Tuition of $155 per semester. Application fee is $100.

Registration Students may register by mail, fax, telephone, e-mail.

Contact Admission Department, Southern California University for Professional Studies, 1840 East 17th Street, Santa Ana, CA 92705-8605. *Telephone:* 800-477-2254. *Fax:* 714-480-0834. *E-mail:* enroll@scups.edu.

DEGREES AND AWARDS

AA Criminal Justice, Liberal Studies, Paralegal Studies
AAB Business Administration
BA Criminal Justice, Liberal Studies, Psychology
BBA Business Administration
BS Law
LLM Law-Taxation
MA Psychology
MBA Business Administration
MS Law, Management of Engineering and Technology
DBA Business Administration
PhD Business, Management of Engineering and Technology, Psychology
PsyD Psychology
ScD Management of Engineering and Technology
JD Law

COURSE SUBJECT AREAS OFFERED OUTSIDE OF DEGREE PROGRAMS

Undergraduate: Business administration and management; law and legal studies; psychology

Graduate: Business administration and management; law and legal studies; psychology

See full description on page 670.

SOUTHERN CHRISTIAN UNIVERSITY

Montgomery, Alabama

Extended Learning Program
www.southernchristian.edu

Southern Christian University, founded in 1967, is an independent, religious, comprehensive institution affiliated with the Church of Christ. It is accredited by the Southern Association of Colleges and Schools. It first offered distance learning courses in 1993. In 1999–2000, it offered 200 courses at a distance. In fall 1999, there were 207 students enrolled in distance learning courses.

Course delivery sites Courses are delivered to your home, your workplace, military bases.

Media Courses are delivered via videotapes, World Wide Web. Students and teachers may interact via mail, telephone, fax, e-mail. The following equipment may be required: television, computer, modem, Internet access, e-mail.

Restrictions Programs are available worldwide. Enrollment is open to anyone.

Services Distance learners have access to library services, e-mail services, academic advising, career placement assistance at a distance.

Credit-earning options Students may transfer credits from another institution or may earn credits through examinations, portfolio assessment, military training.

Typical costs *Noncredit courses:* $150 per course. Costs may vary. Financial aid is available to distance learners.
Registration Students may register by mail, fax, telephone, e-mail, World Wide Web, in person.
Contact Rick Johnson, Admissions Officer, Southern Christian University, 1200 Taylor Road, Montgomery, AL 36117-3553. *Telephone:* 800-351-4040 Ext. 213. *Fax:* 334-387-3878. *E-mail:* rickjohnson@southernchristian.edu.

DEGREES AND AWARDS

BA Biblical Studies
BS Biblical Studies, Human Development, Liberal Studies, Management Communication
MA Biblical Studies
MDiv Biblical Studies, Counseling
MS Biblical Studies, Counseling, Organizational Leadership
DMin Counseling, Ministry

COURSE SUBJECT AREAS OFFERED OUTSIDE OF DEGREE PROGRAMS

Undergraduate: Counseling psychology; liberal arts, general studies, and humanities; organizational behavior studies; philosophy and religion; theological studies
Graduate: Counseling psychology; liberal arts, general studies, and humanities; organizational behavior studies; philosophy and religion; theological studies
Noncredit: Counseling psychology; liberal arts, general studies, and humanities; organizational behavior studies; philosophy and religion; theological studies
See full descriptions on pages 672 and 676.

SOUTHERN CONNECTICUT STATE UNIVERSITY

New Haven, Connecticut
School of Extended Learning
www.southernct.edu

Southern Connecticut State University, founded in 1893, is a state-supported, comprehensive institution. It is accredited by the New England Association of Schools and Colleges. In 1999–2000, it offered 60 courses at a distance. In fall 1999, there were 300 students enrolled in distance learning courses.
Course delivery sites Courses are delivered to your home, your workplace.
Media Courses are delivered via World Wide Web. Students and teachers may interact via e-mail, World Wide Web. The following equipment may be required: computer, modem, Internet access, e-mail.
Restrictions Programs are available worldwide. Enrollment is open to anyone.
Services Distance learners have access to library services, the campus computer network, e-mail services, academic advising, tutoring, career placement assistance, bookstore at a distance.
Credit-earning options Students may transfer credits from another institution or may earn credits through examinations.
Typical costs *Undergraduate:* Tuition of $215 per credit plus mandatory fees of $30 per course. *Graduate:* Tuition of $250 per credit plus mandatory fees of $30 per course. Costs may vary. Financial aid is available to distance learners.
Registration Students may register by World Wide Web.
Contact Chuck Munster, Assistant Dean, Southern Connecticut State University, 501 Crescent Street, New Haven, CT 06515. *Telephone:* 203-392-6194. *Fax:* 203-392-5252. *E-mail:* munster@southernct.edu.

DEGREES AND AWARDS
MLS Library Science

COURSE SUBJECT AREAS OFFERED OUTSIDE OF DEGREE PROGRAMS

Undergraduate: Accounting; drama and theater; nursing
Graduate: Computer and information sciences; library and information studies; nursing
See full description on page 504.

SOUTHERN ILLINOIS UNIVERSITY CARBONDALE

Carbondale, Illinois
Library Affairs
www.lib.siu.edu/dlearn

Southern Illinois University Carbondale, founded in 1869, is a state-supported university. It is accredited by the North Central Association of Colleges and Schools. It first offered distance learning courses in 1994. In 1999–2000, it offered 12 courses at a distance. In fall 1999, there were 18 students enrolled in distance learning courses.
Course delivery sites Courses are delivered to your workplace, high schools, John A. Logan College (Carterville), Kaskaskia College (Centralia), Lewis and Clark Community College (Godfrey), Metropolitan Community College (East St. Louis), Rend Lake College (Ina), Shawnee Community College (Ullin), Southeastern Illinois College (Harrisburg), Southern Illinois University Edwardsville (Edwardsville), Southwestern Illinois College (Belleville).
Media Courses are delivered via videotapes, videoconferencing, World Wide Web, e-mail, print. Students and teachers may meet in person or interact via videoconferencing, mail, telephone, fax, e-mail, World Wide Web.
Restrictions Courses are available to students in the Southern Illinois region only. Enrollment is restricted to individuals meeting certain criteria.
Services Distance learners have access to library services, the campus computer network, e-mail services, academic advising, tutoring, career placement assistance at a distance.
Credit-earning options Students may transfer credits from another institution or may earn credits through examinations, portfolio assessment, military training, business training.
Typical costs *Undergraduate:* Tuition of $100.35 per semester credit. *Graduate:* Tuition of $121 per semester credit. Financial aid is available to distance learners.
Registration Students may register by mail, fax, in person.
Contact Heidi Greer, Distance Learning Coordinator, Southern Illinois University Carbondale, Morris Library, Carbondale, IL 62901-6632. *Telephone:* 618-453-1018. *Fax:* 618-453-3010. *E-mail:* hgreer@lib.siu.edu.

DEGREES AND AWARDS
BS Electrical Engineering (some on-campus requirements)

COURSE SUBJECT AREAS OFFERED OUTSIDE OF DEGREE PROGRAMS

Undergraduate: Agricultural economics; anatomy; electrical engineering; information sciences and systems; law and legal studies
Graduate: Adult education; electrical engineering; health services administration; social work; special education

SOUTHERN ILLINOIS UNIVERSITY EDWARDSVILLE

Edwardsville, Illinois

Office of Continuing Education
www.siue.edu

Southern Illinois University Edwardsville, founded in 1957, is a state-supported, comprehensive institution. It is accredited by the North Central Association of Colleges and Schools. It first offered distance learning courses in 1994. In 1999–2000, it offered 12 courses at a distance. In fall 1999, there were 36 students enrolled in distance learning courses.

Course delivery sites Courses are delivered to Illinois Eastern Community Colleges, Olney Central College (Olney), Illinois Eastern Community Colleges, Wabash Valley College (Mount Carmel).

Media Courses are delivered via videoconferencing, interactive television. Students and teachers may meet in person or interact via videoconferencing, mail, telephone, fax, e-mail, interactive television. The following equipment may be required: e-mail.

Restrictions Courses are available to regional area students only. Enrollment is restricted to individuals meeting certain criteria.

Services Distance learners have access to library services, the campus computer network, e-mail services, academic advising, tutoring, career placement assistance, bookstore at a distance.

Credit-earning options Students may transfer credits from another institution or may earn credits through examinations.

Typical costs *Undergraduate:* Tuition of $89 per semester hour plus mandatory fees of $72 per course for in-state residents. Tuition of $179 per semester hour plus mandatory fees of $72 per course for out-of-state residents. *Graduate:* Tuition of $101 per semester hour plus mandatory fees of $72 per course for in-state residents. Tuition of $202 per semester hour plus mandatory fees of $72 per course for out-of-state residents. Costs may vary. Financial aid is available to distance learners.

Registration Students may register by mail, fax, telephone, e-mail, in person.

Contact Christa Oxford, Director, Southern Illinois University Edwardsville, Admission and Records, Campus Box 1047, Edwardsville, IL 62026-1047. *Telephone:* 618-650-2080. *Fax:* 618-650-2081. *E-mail:* coxford@siue.edu.

DEGREES AND AWARDS

BSN Nursing

SOUTHERN METHODIST UNIVERSITY

Dallas, Texas

School of Engineering and Applied Science–Distance Learning
www.seas.smu.edu

Southern Methodist University, founded in 1911, is an independent, religious university affiliated with the United Methodist Church. It is accredited by the Association of Theological Schools in the United States and Canada, Southern Association of Colleges and Schools. It first offered distance learning courses in 1962. In 1999–2000, it offered 180 courses at a distance. In fall 1999, there were 700 students enrolled in distance learning courses.

Course delivery sites Courses are delivered to your home, your workplace, military bases.

Media Courses are delivered via television, videotapes, videoconferencing, e-mail. Students and teachers may interact via mail, telephone, fax, e-mail, World Wide Web. The following equipment may be required: television, videocassette player, Internet access.

Restrictions Programs are available worldwide. Enrollment is restricted to individuals meeting certain criteria.

Services Distance learners have access to library services, the campus computer network, academic advising, career placement assistance, bookstore at a distance.

Credit-earning options Students may transfer credits from another institution.

Typical costs Tuition of $700 per credit hour. Financial aid is available to distance learners.

Registration Students may register by mail, fax, in person.

Contact Stephanie Dye, Associate Director, Distance Education, Southern Methodist University, PO Box 750335, Dallas, TX 75275-0335. *Telephone:* 800-601-4040. *Fax:* 214-768-3778. *E-mail:* sdye@seas.smu.edu.

DEGREES AND AWARDS

MS Computer Science, Electrical Engineering, Engineering Management, Hazardous and Waste Materials Management, Manufacturing Systems Management, Mechanical Engineering, Software Engineering, Systems Engineering, Telecommunications

COURSE SUBJECT AREAS OFFERED OUTSIDE OF DEGREE PROGRAMS

Graduate: Computer and information sciences; electrical engineering; engineering; engineering-related technologies; engineering/industrial management; environmental engineering; mechanical engineering; telecommunications

See full description on page 674.

SOUTHERN OREGON UNIVERSITY

Ashland, Oregon

Extended Campus Programs
www.sou.edu

Southern Oregon University, founded in 1926, is a state-supported, comprehensive institution. It is accredited by the Northwest Association of Schools and Colleges. It first offered distance learning courses in 1992. In 1999–2000, it offered 25 courses at a distance. In fall 1999, there were 150 students enrolled in distance learning courses.

Course delivery sites Courses are delivered to your home, your workplace, Oregon Institute of Technology (Klamath Falls), Rogue Community College (Grants Pass), Southwestern Oregon Community College (Coos Bay), Umpqua Community College (Roseburg), 3 off-campus centers in Gold Beach, Lakeview, Medford.

Media Courses are delivered via television, videotapes, interactive television, computer software, CD-ROM, computer conferencing, World Wide Web, e-mail, print. Students and teachers may meet in person or interact via videoconferencing, mail, telephone, fax, e-mail, interactive television, World Wide Web. The following equipment may be required: computer, modem, Internet access, e-mail.

Restrictions Courses are available to regional area students only. Enrollment is restricted to individuals meeting certain criteria.

Services Distance learners have access to library services, the campus computer network, e-mail services, academic advising, career placement assistance, bookstore at a distance.

Credit-earning options Students may transfer credits from another institution or may earn credits through examinations.

Typical costs *Undergraduate:* Tuition of $264 per course. *Graduate:* Tuition of $540 per course. Costs may vary. Financial aid is available to distance learners.

Registration Students may register by mail, fax, telephone, e-mail, World Wide Web, in person.

Contact Pat Bentley, Director, Southern Oregon University, Regional Academic Programs/Distance Learning, 1250 Siskiyou Boulevard, Ashland, OR 97520. *Telephone:* 541-552-6902. *Fax:* 541-552-6047.

DEGREES AND AWARDS

AGS Special Education (certain restrictions apply; some on-campus requirements)

Graduate Certificate(s) Early Childhood Education (certain restrictions apply; some on-campus requirements)

MS Early Childhood Education (certain restrictions apply; some on-campus requirements), Management (service area differs from that of the overall institution; some on-campus requirements), Secondary Education (certain restrictions apply; some on-campus requirements), Special Education (certain restrictions apply; some on-campus requirements)

COURSE SUBJECT AREAS OFFERED OUTSIDE OF DEGREE PROGRAMS

Undergraduate: Business; criminology
Graduate: Business; education; special education; teacher education

SOUTHERN POLYTECHNIC STATE UNIVERSITY

Marietta, Georgia
www2.spsu.edu/ois/

Southern Polytechnic State University, founded in 1948, is a state-supported, comprehensive institution. It is accredited by the Southern Association of Colleges and Schools. It first offered distance learning courses in 1995. In 1999–2000, it offered 25 courses at a distance.

Course delivery sites Courses are delivered to your home, your workplace, Darton College (Albany), off-campus center(s).

Media Courses are delivered via videoconferencing, World Wide Web, e-mail. Students and teachers may meet in person or interact via videoconferencing, mail, telephone, fax, e-mail, World Wide Web. The following equipment may be required: computer, Internet access, e-mail.

Restrictions Programs are available worldwide. Enrollment is open to anyone.

Services Distance learners have access to library services, the campus computer network, e-mail services, academic advising, career placement assistance at a distance.

Credit-earning options Students may transfer credits from another institution or may earn credits through examinations, military training, business training.

Typical costs Undergraduate in-state tuition is $391, out-of-state is $1064 for 3 credit-hours. Graduate in-state tuition is $436, out-of-state is $1252 for 3 credit-hours. Costs may vary. Financial aid is available to distance learners.

Registration Students may register by mail, telephone, in person.

Contact Dawn Ramsey, Director, Extended University, Southern Polytechnic State University, 1100 South Marietta Parkway, Marietta, GA 30060. *Telephone:* 770-528-5531. *Fax:* 770-528-7490. *E-mail:* dramsey@spsu.edu.

DEGREES AND AWARDS

BS Industrial Distribution (service area differs from that of the overall institution)

MS Computer Science (service area differs from that of the overall institution), Quality Assurance (some on-campus requirements), Technical Communications (service area differs from that of the overall institution)

COURSE SUBJECT AREAS OFFERED OUTSIDE OF DEGREE PROGRAMS

Undergraduate: Civil engineering; industrial engineering
Graduate: Computer and information sciences; computer programming; industrial engineering; information sciences and systems
See full description on page 676.

SOUTHERN UNIVERSITY AND AGRICULTURAL AND MECHANICAL COLLEGE

Baton Rouge, Louisiana
Continuing Distance Education
www.subr.edu

Southern University and Agricultural and Mechanical College, founded in 1880, is a state-supported, comprehensive institution. It is accredited by the Southern Association of Colleges and Schools. In 1999–2000, it offered 14 courses at a distance. In fall 1999, there were 178 students enrolled in distance learning courses.

Course delivery sites Courses are delivered to your home.

Media Courses are delivered via videoconferencing, World Wide Web, e-mail, print. Students and teachers may meet in person or interact via videoconferencing, mail, telephone, fax, e-mail, World Wide Web. The following equipment may be required: computer, modem, Internet access, e-mail.

Restrictions Programs are available to in-state students only. Enrollment is restricted to individuals meeting certain criteria.

Services Distance learners have access to library services, e-mail services, academic advising at a distance.

Credit-earning options Students may transfer credits from another institution.

Registration Students may register by mail, fax, telephone, in person.

Contact Hilton J. LaSalle, III, Distance Education Coordinator, Southern University and Agricultural and Mechanical College, PO Box 9772, Baton Rouge, LA 70813. *Telephone:* 225-771-2613. *Fax:* 225-771-2654. *E-mail:* hiltonl307@sus.edu.

DEGREES AND AWARDS

Distance programs offered do not lead to a degree or other formal award.

COURSE SUBJECT AREAS OFFERED OUTSIDE OF DEGREE PROGRAMS

Undergraduate: Biological and life sciences; database management; special education
Graduate: Nursing; special education
See full description on page 676.

SOUTHERN UTAH UNIVERSITY

Cedar City, Utah
Division of Continuing Education
www.suu.edu/webpages/contedu/distance/inserv.html

Southern Utah University, founded in 1897, is a state-supported, comprehensive institution. It is accredited by the Northwest Association of Schools and Colleges. It first offered distance learning courses in 1993. In 1999–2000, it offered 23 courses at a distance. In fall 1999, there were 300 students enrolled in distance learning courses.

Course delivery sites Courses are delivered to your home, your workplace, military bases, high schools, Dixie State College of Utah (St. George), 80 off-campus centers.

Media Courses are delivered via videoconferencing, World Wide Web, e-mail, print. Students and teachers may meet in person or interact via videoconferencing, mail, telephone, fax, e-mail, interactive television, World Wide Web.

Restrictions Televised courses are available to in-state students only; Web-based courses are available worldwide. Enrollment is open to anyone.

Services Distance learners have access to library services, e-mail services, academic advising, career placement assistance at a distance.

Credit-earning options Students may transfer credits from another institution or may earn credits through examinations.

Typical costs *Undergraduate:* Tuition of $78 per credit. *Graduate:* Tuition of $96 per credit. Financial aid is available to distance learners.

Registration Students may register by mail, fax, telephone, World Wide Web, in person.

Contact Susan Durfee, Education Network Coordinator, Southern Utah University, 351 West Center Street, Cedar City, UT 84720-2498. *Telephone:* 435-586-7850. *Fax:* 435-865-8087. *E-mail:* durfee@suu.edu.

DEGREES AND AWARDS

BA Business Administration (service area differs from that of the overall institution)

COURSE SUBJECT AREAS OFFERED OUTSIDE OF DEGREE PROGRAMS

Undergraduate: Administrative and secretarial services; business; computer and information sciences; education administration; English composition; English language and literature; fine arts; history; human resources management; liberal arts, general studies, and humanities; library and information studies; music; political science; teacher education

Graduate: Teacher education

SOUTHERN VERMONT COLLEGE

Bennington, Vermont
Distance Learning
www.svc.edu

Southern Vermont College, founded in 1926, is an independent, nonprofit, four-year college. It is accredited by the New England Association of Schools and Colleges. It first offered distance learning courses in 1996. In 1999–2000, it offered 7 courses at a distance. In fall 1999, there were 30 students enrolled in distance learning courses.

Course delivery sites Courses are delivered to your home, your workplace, military bases.

Media Courses are delivered via television, videotapes, audiotapes, computer software, e-mail, print. Students and teachers may interact via audioconferencing, mail, telephone, fax, e-mail. The following equipment may be required: computer, Internet access, e-mail.

Restrictions Programs are available to local area students. Enrollment is open to anyone.

Services Distance learners have access to the campus computer network, e-mail services, career placement assistance, bookstore at a distance.

Credit-earning options Students may transfer credits from another institution or may earn credits through examinations, portfolio assessment, military training, business training.

Typical costs Tuition of $265 per credit. *Noncredit courses:* $265 per course. Costs may vary. Financial aid is available to distance learners.

Registration Students may register by mail, fax, telephone, e-mail, in person.

Contact Bobbi Gabrenya, Director of Admissions, Southern Vermont College, 982 Mansion Drive, Bennington, VT 05201. *Telephone:* 800-378-2782. *Fax:* 802-447-4695. *E-mail:* admis@svc.edu.

DEGREES AND AWARDS

Distance programs offered do not lead to a degree or other formal award.

COURSE SUBJECT AREAS OFFERED OUTSIDE OF DEGREE PROGRAMS

Undergraduate: Accounting; creative writing; information sciences and systems; liberal arts, general studies, and humanities; nursing

SOUTH FLORIDA COMMUNITY COLLEGE

Avon Park, Florida

South Florida Community College, founded in 1965, is a state-supported, two-year college. It is accredited by the Southern Association of Colleges and Schools. It first offered distance learning courses in 1985. In 1999–2000, it offered 30 courses at a distance. In fall 1999, there were 375 students enrolled in distance learning courses.

Course delivery sites Courses are delivered to your home, your workplace, 3 off-campus centers in Arcadia, Lake Placid, Wauchula.

Media Courses are delivered via television, videotapes, interactive television, World Wide Web. Students and teachers may meet in person or interact via videoconferencing, audioconferencing, mail, telephone, fax, e-mail, interactive television. The following equipment may be required: television, videocassette player, computer, modem, Internet access, e-mail.

Restrictions Programs are available to local area students. Enrollment is open to anyone.

Services Distance learners have access to library services, academic advising, career placement assistance, bookstore at a distance.

Credit-earning options Students may transfer credits from another institution or may earn credits through examinations, portfolio assessment.

Typical costs Tuition of $126 per course plus mandatory fees of $20 per course for in-state residents. Tuition of $449.97 per course plus mandatory fees of $20 per course for out-of-state residents. Financial aid is available to distance learners.

Registration Students may register by mail, telephone, in person.

Contact Dr. David Sconyers, Dean, School of Arts and Sciences, South Florida Community College, Arts and Sciences, 600 West College Drive, Avon Park, FL 33825-9356. *Telephone:* 863-784-7329. *Fax:* 863-453-2365. *E-mail:* sconda3951@sfcc.cc.fl.us.

DEGREES AND AWARDS

BS Elementary Education (some on-campus requirements)

COURSE SUBJECT AREAS OFFERED OUTSIDE OF DEGREE PROGRAMS

Undergraduate: Astronomy and astrophysics; biology; business administration and management; chemistry; developmental and child psychology; economics; English language and literature; geography; geology; history; law and legal studies; physical sciences; political science; sociology

SOUTH PUGET SOUND COMMUNITY COLLEGE

Olympia, Washington

South Puget Sound Community College, founded in 1970, is a state-supported, two-year college. It is accredited by the Northwest Association of Schools and Colleges. It first offered distance learning courses in 1983.

In 1999–2000, it offered 3 courses at a distance. In fall 1999, there were 105 students enrolled in distance learning courses.

Course delivery sites Courses are delivered to your home, your workplace.

Media Courses are delivered via television, videotapes, videoconferencing, interactive television, World Wide Web. Students and teachers may meet in person or interact via mail, telephone, fax, e-mail, interactive television, World Wide Web. The following equipment may be required: television, videocassette player, computer, modem, Internet access, e-mail.

Restrictions Programs are available to local area students. Enrollment is open to anyone.

Services Distance learners have access to library services, academic advising, tutoring, career placement assistance at a distance.

Credit-earning options Students may transfer credits from another institution or may earn credits through examinations, portfolio assessment, military training, business training.

Typical costs Tuition of $48 per credit plus mandatory fees of $40 per course. Costs may vary. Financial aid is available to distance learners.

Registration Students may register by telephone, World Wide Web, in person.

Contact Russell Rose, Director, South Puget Sound Community College, Library and Media Center, 2011 Mottman Road, Southwest, Olympia, WA 98512. *Telephone:* 360-754-7711 Ext. 258. *Fax:* 360-664-0780. *E-mail:* rrose@spscc.ctc.edu.

DEGREES AND AWARDS

Distance programs offered do not lead to a degree or other formal award.

COURSE SUBJECT AREAS OFFERED OUTSIDE OF DEGREE PROGRAMS

Undergraduate: Anthropology; astronomy and astrophysics; early childhood education; history; mathematics; technical writing; theological studies

SOUTHWESTERN ADVENTIST UNIVERSITY

Keene, Texas

Adult Degree Program
www.swau.edu

Southwestern Adventist University, founded in 1894, is an independent, religious, comprehensive institution. It is accredited by the Southern Association of Colleges and Schools. It first offered distance learning courses in 1978. In 1999–2000, it offered 270 courses at a distance. In fall 1999, there were 260 students enrolled in distance learning courses.

Course delivery sites Courses are delivered to your home.

Media Courses are delivered via videotapes. Students and teachers may interact via mail, telephone, fax, e-mail. The following equipment may be required: television, videocassette player.

Restrictions Programs are available worldwide. Enrollment is open to anyone.

Services Distance learners have access to library services, the campus computer network, e-mail services, academic advising at a distance.

Credit-earning options Students may transfer credits from another institution or may earn credits through examinations, portfolio assessment, military training, business training.

Typical costs Tuition of $299 per hour. Students pay a $100 one-time seminar fee. Financial aid is available to distance learners.

Registration Students may register by mail, fax, telephone, e-mail, in person.

Contact Dr. Larry Philbeck, Director, Southwestern Adventist University, Adult Degree Program, PO Box 567, Keene, TX 76059. *Telephone:* 800-433-2240. *Fax:* 817-556-4742. *E-mail:* adpsec@swau.edu.

DEGREES AND AWARDS

AS Computer Information Systems (some on-campus requirements), Office Technology (some on-campus requirements)

BA Business Administration (some on-campus requirements), Computer Information Systems (some on-campus requirements), English (some on-campus requirements), History (some on-campus requirements), International Affairs (some on-campus requirements), Journalism (some on-campus requirements), Mathematics (some on-campus requirements), Religion (some on-campus requirements), Social Sciences (some on-campus requirements), Theology (some on-campus requirements)

BS Broadcasting (some on-campus requirements), Business Management (some on-campus requirements), Computer Information Systems (some on-campus requirements), Computer Science (some on-campus requirements), Corporate Communications (some on-campus requirements), Criminal Justice (certain restrictions apply; some on-campus requirements), Elementary Education (some on-campus requirements), History (some on-campus requirements), Journalism (some on-campus requirements), Mathematics (some on-campus requirements), Nursing (certain restrictions apply; some on-campus requirements), Office Administration (some on-campus requirements), Office Systems Administration (some on-campus requirements), Psychology (some on-campus requirements), Social Sciences (some on-campus requirements)

SOUTHWESTERN ASSEMBLIES OF GOD UNIVERSITY

Waxahachie, Texas

School of Distance Education
www.sagu.edu/sde

Southwestern Assemblies of God University, founded in 1927, is an independent, religious, comprehensive institution affiliated with the Assemblies of God. It is accredited by the Accrediting Association of Bible Colleges, Southern Association of Colleges and Schools. It first offered distance learning courses in 1983. In 1999–2000, it offered 150 courses at a distance. In fall 1999, there were 360 students enrolled in distance learning courses.

Course delivery sites Courses are delivered to your home.

Media Courses are delivered via videotapes, audiotapes, computer software, CD-ROM, World Wide Web, e-mail, print. Students and teachers may meet in person or interact via mail, telephone, fax, e-mail, World Wide Web. The following equipment may be required: videocassette player, computer, modem, Internet access, e-mail.

Restrictions Programs are available worldwide. Enrollment is restricted to individuals meeting certain criteria.

Services Distance learners have access to library services, the campus computer network, e-mail services, academic advising, career placement assistance, bookstore at a distance.

Credit-earning options Students may transfer credits from another institution or may earn credits through examinations, portfolio assessment, military training, business training.

Typical costs *Undergraduate:* Tuition of $190 per credit. *Graduate:* Tuition of $190 per credit. Costs may vary. Financial aid is available to distance learners.

Registration Students may register by mail, fax, telephone, e-mail, World Wide Web, in person.

Contact Greg Smith, Enrollment Counselor, Southwestern Assemblies of God University. *Telephone:* 972-937-4010. *Fax:* 972-923-0488. *E-mail:* info@sagu.edu.

DEGREES AND AWARDS

BA Business (certain restrictions apply; some on-campus requirements), Church Ministries (certain restrictions apply; some on-campus require-

ments), Education (certain restrictions apply; some on-campus requirements), Professional Studies (certain restrictions apply; some on-campus requirements)
BS Business (certain restrictions apply; some on-campus requirements), Church Ministries (certain restrictions apply; some on-campus requirements), Education (certain restrictions apply; some on-campus requirements), Professional Studies (certain restrictions apply; some on-campus requirements)

COURSE SUBJECT AREAS OFFERED OUTSIDE OF DEGREE PROGRAMS

Undergraduate: Accounting; area, ethnic, and cultural studies; Bible studies; biological and life sciences; biology; business; business administration and management; communications; computer and information sciences; counseling psychology; creative writing; developmental and child psychology; education; educational psychology; English composition; English language and literature; fine arts; health and physical education/fitness; history; human resources management; mathematics; music; philosophy and religion; physical sciences; psychology; social psychology; social sciences; sociology; teacher education; theological studies
Graduate: Education; education administration; theological studies

SOUTHWESTERN BAPTIST THEOLOGICAL SEMINARY

Fort Worth, Texas

Department of Continuing Education
www.swbts.edu

Southwestern Baptist Theological Seminary, founded in 1908, is an independent, religious, graduate institution. It is accredited by the Association of Theological Schools in the United States and Canada, Southern Association of Colleges and Schools. It first offered distance learning courses in 1993. In 1999–2000, it offered 7 courses at a distance. In fall 1999, there were 40 students enrolled in distance learning courses.
Course delivery sites Courses are delivered to your home, 5 off-campus centers in Houston, Marshall, San Antonio, Little Rock (AK), Shawnee (OK).
Media Courses are delivered via videoconferencing, computer conferencing, World Wide Web, e-mail. Students and teachers may interact via videoconferencing, mail, telephone, fax, e-mail, World Wide Web. The following equipment may be required: computer, Internet access, e-mail.
Restrictions Programs are available nationwide. Enrollment is restricted to individuals meeting certain criteria.
Services Distance learners have access to library services, the campus computer network, e-mail services, academic advising at a distance.
Credit-earning options Students may transfer credits from another institution or may earn credits through examinations, portfolio assessment.
Typical costs *Undergraduate:* Tuition of $110 per semester hour plus mandatory fees of $50 per semester. *Graduate:* Tuition of $110 per semester hour plus mandatory fees of $50 per semester. *Noncredit courses:* $125 per course. Costs may vary. Financial aid is available to distance learners.
Registration Students may register by mail, telephone, in person.
Contact Gary Waller, Director of Distance Learning, Southwestern Baptist Theological Seminary, PO Box 22487, Fort Worth, TX 76122. *Telephone:* 817-923-1921 Ext. 3510. *Fax:* 817-921-8763. *E-mail:* gww@swbts.edu.

DEGREES AND AWARDS

MA Christian School Education (some on-campus requirements)
MACE Christian Education (some on-campus requirements)

MDiv Divinity (some on-campus requirements)

COURSE SUBJECT AREAS OFFERED OUTSIDE OF DEGREE PROGRAMS

Undergraduate: Philosophy and religion; theological studies
Graduate: Philosophy and religion; theological studies
Noncredit: Philosophy and religion; theological studies

SOUTHWESTERN COMMUNITY COLLEGE

Creston, Iowa
www.swcc.cc.ia.us

Southwestern Community College, founded in 1966, is a state-supported, two-year college. It is accredited by the North Central Association of Colleges and Schools. It first offered distance learning courses in 1985. In 1999–2000, it offered 52 courses at a distance. In fall 1999, there were 360 students enrolled in distance learning courses.
Course delivery sites Courses are delivered to your home, high schools, 2 off-campus centers in Osceola, Red Oak.
Media Courses are delivered via television, videotapes, interactive television, World Wide Web, e-mail. Students and teachers may meet in person or interact via mail, telephone, e-mail, interactive television, World Wide Web. The following equipment may be required: television, videocassette player, computer, Internet access, e-mail.
Restrictions Programs are available in an eight-county region. Enrollment is open to anyone.
Services Distance learners have access to e-mail services, academic advising, career placement assistance, bookstore at a distance.
Credit-earning options Students may transfer credits from another institution or may earn credits through examinations.
Typical costs Tuition of $71 per credit hour plus mandatory fees of $20 per course. Costs may vary.
Registration Students may register by mail, telephone, in person.
Contact Tom Brotherton, Director of Arts and Sciences, Southwestern Community College, 1501 West Townline, Creston, IA 50801. *Telephone:* 515-782-7081. *Fax:* 515-782-3312. *E-mail:* brotherton@swcc.cc.ia.us.

DEGREES AND AWARDS

Distance programs offered do not lead to a degree or other formal award.

COURSE SUBJECT AREAS OFFERED OUTSIDE OF DEGREE PROGRAMS

Undergraduate: Accounting; algebra; American literature; American studies; anatomy; art history and criticism; biology; business administration and management; chemistry; economics; English composition; environmental science; ethics; geography; history; journalism; music; psychology; sociology

SOUTHWESTERN MICHIGAN COLLEGE

Dowagiac, Michigan

Instructional Division
www.smc.cc.mi.us

Southwestern Michigan College, founded in 1964, is a state and locally supported, two-year college. It is accredited by the North Central Association of Colleges and Schools. It first offered distance learning courses in 1991. In 1999–2000, it offered 14 courses at a distance. In fall 1999, there were 77 students enrolled in distance learning courses.
Course delivery sites Courses are delivered to your home, 1 off-campus center in Lawrence.

Media Courses are delivered via television, videotapes, videoconferencing, interactive television, World Wide Web. Students and teachers may interact via mail, telephone, fax, e-mail, interactive television. The following equipment may be required: television, videocassette player.

Restrictions Programs are available nationwide. Enrollment is open to anyone.

Services Distance learners have access to library services, the campus computer network, e-mail services at a distance.

Credit-earning options Students may transfer credits from another institution or may earn credits through examinations, military training.

Typical costs Tuition of $47 per credit hour plus mandatory fees of $9 per credit hour for local area residents. Tuition of $52.50 per credit hour plus mandatory fees of $9 per credit hour for in-state residents. Tuition of $70.50 per credit hour plus mandatory fees of $9 per credit hour for out-of-state residents. Financial aid is available to distance learners.

Registration Students may register by mail, telephone, in person.

Contact Dr. Ilene Sheffer, Vice President for Community Services and Development, Southwestern Michigan College, 58900 Cherry Grove Road, Dowagiac, MI 49047. *Telephone:* 616-782-1369. *Fax:* 616-782-8414. *E-mail:* isheffer@smc.cc.mi.us.

DEGREES AND AWARDS

Distance programs offered do not lead to a degree or other formal award.

COURSE SUBJECT AREAS OFFERED OUTSIDE OF DEGREE PROGRAMS

Undergraduate: Accounting; business; business administration and management; communications; computer and information sciences; education; European languages and literatures; film studies; health and physical education/fitness; health professions and related sciences; liberal arts, general studies, and humanities; mathematics; political science; psychology; social psychology; social sciences; sociology

SOUTHWEST MISSOURI STATE UNIVERSITY

Springfield, Missouri

College of Continuing Education and The Extended University
ce.smsu.edu/outreach

Southwest Missouri State University, founded in 1905, is a state-supported, comprehensive institution. It is accredited by the North Central Association of Colleges and Schools. It first offered distance learning courses in 1974. In 1999–2000, it offered 130 courses at a distance. In fall 1999, there were 743 students enrolled in distance learning courses.

Course delivery sites Courses are delivered to your home, your workplace, high schools, Crowder College (Neosho), Missouri Southern State College (Joplin), Southwest Missouri State University Research Campus (Mountain Grove), Southwest Missouri State University–West Plains (West Plains), 2 off-campus centers in Lebanon, Nevada.

Media Courses are delivered via television, videotapes, videoconferencing, interactive television, audiotapes, computer software, World Wide Web, e-mail, print. Students and teachers may meet in person or interact via videoconferencing, audioconferencing, mail, telephone, fax, e-mail, interactive television, World Wide Web. The following equipment may be required: television, videocassette player, computer, modem, Internet access, e-mail.

Restrictions Programs are available worldwide. Enrollment is open to anyone.

Services Distance learners have access to library services, the campus computer network, e-mail services, academic advising, bookstore at a distance.

Credit-earning options Students may transfer credits from another institution or may earn credits through examinations, military training, business training.

Typical costs *Undergraduate:* Tuition of $101 per credit. *Graduate:* Tuition of $115 per credit. Costs may vary. Financial aid is available to distance learners.

Registration Students may register by mail, fax, in person.

Contact Diana Garland, Associate Director, Academic Outreach, Southwest Missouri State University, Academic Outreach, Springfield, MO 65804. *Telephone:* 417-836-4128. *Fax:* 417-836-6016. *E-mail:* dianagarland@mail.smsu.edu.

DEGREES AND AWARDS

BS Elementary Education (service area differs from that of the overall institution)

MBA Business Administration (service area differs from that of the overall institution)

MS Administrative Studies, Computer Information Systems (some on-campus requirements), Elementary Education (service area differs from that of the overall institution)

COURSE SUBJECT AREAS OFFERED OUTSIDE OF DEGREE PROGRAMS

Undergraduate: Accounting; agriculture; American (U.S.) history; anthropology; astronomy and astrophysics; biology; business administration and management; calculus; chemistry; child care and development; classical languages and literatures; communications; computer and information sciences; design; economics; English language and literature; European languages and literatures; film studies; finance; foods and nutrition studies; individual and family development studies; marketing; music; nursing; philosophy and religion; physics; political science; psychology; social work; sociology; Spanish language and literature; substance abuse counseling; teacher education; visual and performing arts

Graduate: Accounting; business administration and management; communications; computer and information sciences; curriculum and instruction; economics; education administration; educational research; finance; marketing; philosophy and religion; physics; plant sciences; political science; psychology; social work; special education; teacher education

Noncredit: Community health services; substance abuse counseling

SOUTHWEST MISSOURI STATE UNIVERSITY–WEST PLAINS

West Plains, Missouri

College of Business Administration
www.mscis.smsu.edu

Southwest Missouri State University–West Plains, founded in 1963, is a state-supported, two-year college. It is accredited by the North Central Association of Colleges and Schools. In 1999–2000, it offered 12 courses at a distance. In fall 1999, there were 40 students enrolled in distance learning courses.

Course delivery sites Courses are delivered to your home, your workplace.

Media Courses are delivered via computer software, computer conferencing, World Wide Web, e-mail, print. Students and teachers may meet in person or interact via mail, telephone, fax, e-mail, World Wide Web. The following equipment may be required: computer, modem, Internet access, e-mail.

Restrictions Programs are available worldwide. Enrollment is restricted to individuals meeting certain criteria.

Services Distance learners have access to library services, the campus computer network, e-mail services, academic advising, career placement assistance, bookstore at a distance.

Credit-earning options Students may transfer credits from another institution.

Typical costs Tuition of $3105 per semester. Financial aid is available to distance learners.

Contact Dr. David Meinert, Director, MSCIS Program, Southwest Missouri State University–West Plains, CIS Department, 901 South National Avenue, Springfield, MO 65804. *Telephone:* 417-836-4178. *Fax:* 417-836-6907. *E-mail:* mscis@mail.smsu.edu.

DEGREES AND AWARDS

MS Computer Information Systems (certain restrictions apply; some on-campus requirements)

SOUTHWEST TEXAS STATE UNIVERSITY

San Marcos, Texas

Correspondence and Extension Studies
www.ideal.swt.edu/correspondence

Southwest Texas State University, founded in 1899, is a state-supported, comprehensive institution. It is accredited by the Southern Association of Colleges and Schools. It first offered distance learning courses in 1953. In 1999–2000, it offered 60 courses at a distance. In fall 1999, there were 2,000 students enrolled in distance learning courses.

Course delivery sites Courses are delivered to your home, your workplace, military bases.

Media Courses are delivered via videotapes, audiotapes, World Wide Web, e-mail, print. Students and teachers may interact via mail, telephone, fax, e-mail. The following equipment may be required: television, videocassette player, computer, Internet access, e-mail.

Restrictions Programs are available worldwide. Enrollment is restricted to individuals meeting certain criteria.

Services Distance learners have access to e-mail services, bookstore at a distance.

Typical costs *Undergraduate:* Tuition of $57 per unit. *Graduate:* Tuition of $95 per unit.

Registration Students may register by mail, fax, telephone, in person.

Contact James P. Andrews, Director, Southwest Texas State University, Office of Correspondence and Extension Studies, 302 ASB North, 601 University Drive, San Marcos, TX 78666. *Telephone:* 512-245-2322. *Fax:* 512-245-8934. *E-mail:* ja09@swt.edu.

DEGREES AND AWARDS

Distance programs offered do not lead to a degree or other formal award.

COURSE SUBJECT AREAS OFFERED OUTSIDE OF DEGREE PROGRAMS

Undergraduate: Art history and criticism; biology; criminal justice; education; English language and literature; fine arts; geography; health services administration; history; mathematics; philosophy and religion; political science; psychology; sociology; Spanish language and literature **Graduate:** Geography; mathematics

Special note
The century-old Southwest Texas State University (SWT) is a state-supported university that was considered by *Money* magazine in 1998 as one of the top 10 educational values in the United States. With nearly 50 years of experience in distributed learning, the distance education program at SWT was developed to provide up-to-date service to all students. Most courses are available in print-based instruction, with some courses containing audiotape and videotape components. Entering the millennium, SWT provides more Internet-delivered courses, including new courses in graduate-level geography, which are also available in a print-based format. The program does not exclude students who do not have access to all technologies, which has made the program popular on a worldwide basis. Courses typically cost $171 per 3-credit-hour course ($57 per credit hour) for undergraduate credit and $285 per 3-credit-hour course ($95 per credit hour) for graduate credit. Students outside the U.S. should add $50 per course for overseas postage. Courses are written and instructed by departmentally approved SWT instructors. Students have 12 months to complete a course and may apply for a 6-month extension. All applications from Texas residents are reviewed for compliance with TASP regulations. Students may apply directly to the Office of Correspondence and Extension Studies. For current course listings, students should visit the Web site (http://www.ideal.swt.edu/correspondence) or call 512-245-2322 for a catalog.

SOUTHWEST VIRGINIA COMMUNITY COLLEGE

Richlands, Virginia

Audiovisual and Distance Education Services

Southwest Virginia Community College, founded in 1968, is a state-supported, two-year college. It is accredited by the Southern Association of Colleges and Schools. It first offered distance learning courses in 1991. In 1999–2000, it offered 32 courses at a distance. In fall 1999, there were 625 students enrolled in distance learning courses.

Course delivery sites Courses are delivered to your home, your workplace, military bases, high schools, Virginia Community College System (Richmond).

Media Courses are delivered via television, videotapes, videoconferencing, interactive television, audiotapes, computer software, computer conferencing, World Wide Web, print. Students and teachers may meet in person or interact via videoconferencing, audioconferencing, mail, telephone, fax, e-mail, interactive television, World Wide Web. The following equipment may be required: television, videocassette player, computer, modem, Internet access, e-mail.

Restrictions Programs are available worldwide. Enrollment is open to anyone.

Services Distance learners have access to library services, the campus computer network, e-mail services, academic advising, tutoring, career placement assistance, bookstore at a distance.

Credit-earning options Students may transfer credits from another institution or may earn credits through examinations, portfolio assessment, military training.

Typical costs Tuition of $37.12 per credit plus mandatory fees of $2.50 per course for in-state residents. Tuition of $164.82 per credit plus mandatory fees of $2.50 per course for out-of-state residents. Costs may vary. Financial aid is available to distance learners.

Registration Students may register by mail, fax, telephone, World Wide Web, in person.

Contact Sylvia Dye, Program Support Technician, Southwest Virginia Community College, PO Box SVCC, Richlands, VA 24641. *Telephone:* 540-964-7279. *Fax:* 540-964-7581. *E-mail:* sylvia-dye@sw.cc.va.us.

DEGREES AND AWARDS

Undergraduate Certificate(s) Network and Internet Administration **AS** General Studies

COURSE SUBJECT AREAS OFFERED OUTSIDE OF DEGREE PROGRAMS

Undergraduate: American (U.S.) history; business; business administration and management; calculus; creative writing; developmental and child psychology; economics; educational psychology; English composition;

English literature; health professions and related sciences; library and information studies; philosophy and religion; sociology; Spanish language and literature; special education; statistics

See full description on page 676.

SPERTUS INSTITUTE OF JEWISH STUDIES

Chicago, Illinois
www.spertus.edu

Spertus Institute of Jewish Studies, founded in 1925, is an independent, nonprofit, graduate institution. It is accredited by the North Central Association of Colleges and Schools. It first offered distance learning courses in 1995. In 1999–2000, it offered 20 courses at a distance. In fall 1999, there were 145 students enrolled in distance learning courses.

Course delivery sites Courses are delivered to your home.

Media Courses are delivered via videotapes, audiotapes, print. Students and teachers may meet in person or interact via mail, telephone, fax, e-mail. The following equipment may be required: television, videocassette player.

Restrictions Programs are available worldwide. Enrollment is open to anyone.

Services Distance learners have access to library services, e-mail services, academic advising at a distance.

Credit-earning options Students may transfer credits from another institution or may earn credits through examinations.

Typical costs Tuition of $600 per course plus mandatory fees of $25 per course. Costs may vary. Financial aid is available to distance learners.

Registration Students may register by mail, fax, telephone, e-mail, in person.

Contact Lisa Burnstein, Director of Student Services, Spertus Institute of Jewish Studies, 618 South Michigan Avenue, Chicago, IL 60605. *Telephone:* 888-322-1769. *Fax:* 312-922-6406. *E-mail:* college@spertus.edu.

DEGREES AND AWARDS

MSJS Jewish Studies (some on-campus requirements)
DJS Jewish Studies (some on-campus requirements)

COURSE SUBJECT AREAS OFFERED OUTSIDE OF DEGREE PROGRAMS

Graduate: Area, ethnic, and cultural studies; Jewish studies

Special note
Accredited by the North Central Association of Colleges and Schools, Spertus currently offers 4 degree programs on a distance learning basis: the Master of Science in Jewish Studies (MSJS), the Master of Science in Jewish Education (MSJE), the Doctor of Jewish Studies (DJS), and the Doctor of Science in Jewish Studies (DSJS). The MSJS and the MSJE are designed for students with an accredited undergraduate degree and a desire to enrich their Jewish education or acquire a professional credential in Jewish education or Jewish communal service. The MSJS and MSJE programs are identical, except that students in the MSJE must choose a concentration area in Jewish education. Courses are delivered in a variety of ways, including distance learning packages, intensive seminars, and independent study. The programs progress at the learner's individual rate. Distance learners are encouraged to spend a minimum of 6 days per year at Spertus's Chicago campus for intensive course work. Fifty quarter hours are required for the degrees. Tuition is currently $200 per quarter hour. Scholarships, in the form of partial tuition remission, are available. The DJS is designed for in-service Jewish clergy, educators, and communal service workers who are interested in and committed to building upon and enhancing previ-

ously acquired Judaica knowledge and professional skills and who desire to make a cutting-edge contribution to their respective fields. Admission to the DJS program is highly selective. Eighteen courses are required for the degree: 7 reading courses, 7 intensive seminars, and 4 courses toward the completion of a Project Demonstrating Excellence. The DSJS program has been designed primarily for students who already hold a master's degree in Jewish studies and who want to explore how the wisdom of the Jewish past—as embodied in its sacred and significant texts and in the diverse historical experiences of the Jewish people—can be utilized to address the perplexities and problems of Jewish life in the present—both communal and individual. The DSJS program requires 18 courses, including 7 core courses; 3 text courses; 5 courses on issues, problems, methodologies, and major intellectual or historical figures in Jewish history; and 3 research and writing courses related to a final project. (In some cases, additional prerequisite courses may also be required.) Tuition for both the DJS and DSJS programs is currently $250 per quarter hour. For more information, students should visit Spertus's Web site (http://www.spertus.edu) or should contact the Office of the Registrar: 888–322–1769 (toll-free); fax: 312–922–6406; e-mail: college@spertus.edu.

SPOON RIVER COLLEGE

Canton, Illinois
www.spoonrivercollege.net

Spoon River College, founded in 1959, is a state-supported, two-year college. It is accredited by the North Central Association of Colleges and Schools. In 1999–2000, it offered 15 courses at a distance. In fall 1999, there were 200 students enrolled in distance learning courses.

Course delivery sites Courses are delivered to your home, high schools, off-campus center(s) in Havana, Macomb, Rushville.

Media Courses are delivered via interactive television, World Wide Web. Students and teachers may meet in person or interact via mail, telephone, fax, e-mail, interactive television, World Wide Web. The following equipment may be required: computer, modem, Internet access, e-mail.

Restrictions Programs are available to in-state students only. Enrollment is open to anyone.

Services Distance learners have access to library services, academic advising, bookstore at a distance.

Credit-earning options Students may transfer credits from another institution or may earn credits through examinations.

Typical costs Tuition for 30 credit hours is $1410 in-district; $4620 in-state; $8258 out-of-state. Mandatory fees for 30 credit hours are $210. *Noncredit courses:* $60 per course.

Registration Students may register by telephone, in person.

Contact Sharon Wrenn, Dean of Student Services, Spoon River College, 23235 North County 22, Canton, IL 61455. *Telephone:* 309-649-6305. *Fax:* 309-649-6235. *E-mail:* swrenn@src.cc.il.us.

DEGREES AND AWARDS

Distance programs offered do not lead to a degree or other formal award.

COURSE SUBJECT AREAS OFFERED OUTSIDE OF DEGREE PROGRAMS

Undergraduate: American literature; biology; economics; education; English composition; health and physical education/fitness; philosophy and religion; psychology; sociology; visual and performing arts

SPRING ARBOR COLLEGE

Spring Arbor, Michigan
arboronline.org

Spring Arbor College, founded in 1873, is an independent, religious, comprehensive institution. It is accredited by the North Central Association of Colleges and Schools. It first offered distance learning courses in 1998. In 1999–2000, it offered 45 courses at a distance. In fall 1999, there were 32 students enrolled in distance learning courses.

Course delivery sites Courses are delivered to your home, your workplace, 2 off-campus centers in Alpena, Gaylord.

Media Courses are delivered via television, videotapes, interactive television, World Wide Web, e-mail, print. Students and teachers may interact via mail, telephone, fax, e-mail, interactive television, World Wide Web. The following equipment may be required: computer, modem, Internet access, e-mail.

Restrictions Programs are available worldwide. Enrollment is open to anyone.

Services Distance learners have access to library services, e-mail services, academic advising, bookstore at a distance.

Credit-earning options Students may transfer credits from another institution or may earn credits through examinations, portfolio assessment.

Typical costs *Undergraduate:* Tuition of $175 per credit. *Graduate:* Tuition of $225 per credit. Costs may vary. Financial aid is available to distance learners.

Registration Students may register by mail, fax, telephone, e-mail, World Wide Web, in person.

Contact Dr. John Nemecek, Assistant Dean, School of Adult Studies, Spring Arbor College, 106 East Main Street, Spring Arbor, MI 49283. *Telephone:* 517-750-6351. *Fax:* 517-750-6602. *E-mail:* jnemecek@arbor.edu.

eCollege.com www.ecollege.com/scholarships

DEGREES AND AWARDS

Distance programs offered do not lead to a degree or other formal award.

COURSE SUBJECT AREAS OFFERED OUTSIDE OF DEGREE PROGRAMS

Undergraduate: Bible studies; business; business communications; communications; computer and information sciences; creative writing; English composition; fine arts; marketing; philosophy and religion; psychology; sociology

Graduate: Business; business communications; international business; marketing

See full description on page 678.

SPRINGFIELD TECHNICAL COMMUNITY COLLEGE

Springfield, Massachusetts
Academic Affairs
www.stcc.mass.edu

Springfield Technical Community College, founded in 1967, is a state-supported, two-year college. It is accredited by the New England Associa-tion of Schools and Colleges. In 1999–2000, it offered 16 courses at a distance. In fall 1999, there were 230 students enrolled in distance learning courses.

Course delivery sites Courses are delivered to your home, your workplace, military bases.

Media Courses are delivered via videotapes, CD-ROM, World Wide Web, e-mail. Students and teachers may meet in person or interact via mail, e-mail, World Wide Web. The following equipment may be required: computer, modem, Internet access, e-mail.

Restrictions Programs are available nationwide. Enrollment is open to anyone.

Services Distance learners have access to library services, e-mail services, academic advising at a distance.

Credit-earning options Students may transfer credits from another institution.

Typical costs Tuition of $57 per credit plus mandatory fees of $17 per credit.

Registration Students may register by mail, fax, telephone, in person.

Contact Debbie Bellucci, Chair, Distance Education Committee, Springfield Technical Community College, One Armory Square, Springfield, MA 01105. *Telephone:* 413-755-4487. *Fax:* 413-739-0298. *E-mail:* dbellucci@stcc.mass.edu.

DEGREES AND AWARDS

Distance programs offered do not lead to a degree or other formal award.

COURSE SUBJECT AREAS OFFERED OUTSIDE OF DEGREE PROGRAMS

Undergraduate: Biological and life sciences; business; computer and information sciences; engineering; English language and literature; mathematics; psychology; social sciences

STANFORD UNIVERSITY

Stanford, California
Stanford Center for Professional Development
scpd.stanford.edu

Stanford University, founded in 1891, is an independent, nonprofit university. It is accredited by the Western Association of Schools and Colleges, Inc. It first offered distance learning courses in 1969. In 1999–2000, it offered 255 courses at a distance. In fall 1999, there were 1,500 students enrolled in distance learning courses.

Course delivery sites Courses are delivered to your home, your workplace.

Media Courses are delivered via television, videotapes, videoconferencing, interactive television, computer conferencing, World Wide Web, print. Students and teachers may interact via videoconferencing, audioconferencing, mail, telephone, fax, e-mail, interactive television, World Wide Web. The following equipment may be required: computer, Internet access, e-mail.

Restrictions Programs are available worldwide. Enrollment is restricted to individuals meeting certain criteria.

Services Distance learners have access to the campus computer network, e-mail services, bookstore at a distance.

Credit-earning options Students may transfer credits from another institution.

Typical costs Tuition of $995 per unit. Degree students pay $995 per unit and non-degree students pay $426 per unit.

Registration Students may register by mail, fax, in person.

Contact Frank Schroeder, SITN Customer Relations, Stanford University, 496 Lomita Hall, Room 401, Stanford, CA 94305-4036. *Telephone:* 650-725-6950. *Fax:* 650-725-2868. *E-mail:* frankschroeder@stanford.edu.

DEGREES AND AWARDS

MS Management Science and Engineering (certain restrictions apply)
MSIE Aerospace Engineering (certain restrictions apply), Computer Science (certain restrictions apply), Electrical Engineering (certain restrictions apply), Materials Science and Engineering (certain restrictions apply), Mechanical Engineering (certain restrictions apply)

COURSE SUBJECT AREAS OFFERED OUTSIDE OF DEGREE PROGRAMS

Graduate: Aerospace, aeronautical engineering; biological and life sciences; computer and information sciences; electrical engineering; engineering/industrial management; industrial engineering; mechanical engineering
Noncredit: Aerospace, aeronautical engineering; biological and life sciences; computer and information sciences; electrical engineering; engineering/industrial management; industrial engineering; mechanical engineering
See full description on page 680.

STANLY COMMUNITY COLLEGE

Albemarle, North Carolina

Stanly Community College, founded in 1971, is a state-supported, two-year college. It is accredited by the Southern Association of Colleges and Schools. It first offered distance learning courses in 1990.
Course delivery sites Courses are delivered to your home, your workplace, military bases.
Media Courses are delivered via television, videotapes, audiotapes, computer software, CD-ROM, World Wide Web, e-mail. Students and teachers may meet in person or interact via mail, telephone, fax, e-mail. The following equipment may be required: television, videocassette player, computer, Internet access, e-mail.
Restrictions Programs are available nationwide. Enrollment is open to anyone.
Services Distance learners have access to library services, the campus computer network, e-mail services, academic advising, tutoring, career placement assistance, bookstore at a distance.
Credit-earning options Students may transfer credits from another institution or may earn credits through examinations.
Typical costs Tuition of $20 per credit plus mandatory fees of $1 per credit for in-state residents. Tuition of $107.50 per credit plus mandatory fees of $11 per credit for out-of-state residents. Costs may vary. Financial aid is available to distance learners.
Registration Students may register by mail, fax, telephone, in person.
Contact Barbara Wiggins, Director of Evening and Weekend College, Stanly Community College. *Telephone:* 704-991-0266. *Fax:* 704-982-0819. *E-mail:* wigginbo@stanly.cc.nc.us.

DEGREES AND AWARDS

Distance programs offered do not lead to a degree or other formal award.

COURSE SUBJECT AREAS OFFERED OUTSIDE OF DEGREE PROGRAMS

Undergraduate: Abnormal psychology; accounting; business administration and management; criminal justice; developmental and child psychology; English composition; English literature; health and physical education/

fitness; history; liberal arts, general studies, and humanities; marketing; mathematics; philosophy and religion; psychology; sociology; technical writing
See full description on page 676.

STATE UNIVERSITY OF NEW YORK AT BUFFALO

Buffalo, New York

Millard Fillmore College Distance Learning Office
www.mfc.buffalo.edu

State University of New York at Buffalo, founded in 1846, is a state-supported university. It is accredited by the Middle States Association of Colleges and Schools. It first offered distance learning courses in 1994. In 1999–2000, it offered 88 courses at a distance. In fall 1999, there were 522 students enrolled in distance learning courses.
Course delivery sites Courses are delivered to your home, your workplace, military bases, high schools, Jamestown Community College (Jamestown), Stanford University (Stanford, CA), 1 off-campus center in Corning.
Media Courses are delivered via television, videotapes, videoconferencing, interactive television, CD-ROM, computer conferencing, World Wide Web, e-mail, print. Students and teachers may meet in person or interact via mail, telephone, fax, e-mail, interactive television, World Wide Web. The following equipment may be required: television, videocassette player, computer, modem, Internet access, e-mail.
Restrictions Programs are available to in-state students only. Enrollment is open to anyone.
Services Distance learners have access to library services, the campus computer network, e-mail services, academic advising, career placement assistance, bookstore at a distance.
Credit-earning options Students may transfer credits from another institution or may earn credits through examinations, portfolio assessment.
Typical costs *Undergraduate:* Tuition of $137 per credit hour plus mandatory fees of $35.25 per credit hour for in-state residents. Tuition of $346 per credit hour plus mandatory fees of $43.35 per credit hour for out-of-state residents. *Graduate:* Tuition of $213 per credit hour plus mandatory fees of $59.10 per credit hour for in-state residents. Tuition of $351 per credit hour plus mandatory fees of $59.10 per credit hour for out-of-state residents. Costs may vary. Financial aid is available to distance learners.
Registration Students may register by mail, telephone, World Wide Web, in person.
Contact Dr. George Lopos, Dean, State University of New York at Buffalo, Millard Fillmore College, 128 Parker Hall, Buffalo, NY 14214-3007. *Telephone:* 716-829-3131. *Fax:* 716-829-2475. *E-mail:* mfc-inquire@buffalo.edu.

DEGREES AND AWARDS

Undergraduate Certificate(s) Civil Engineering (service area differs from that of the overall institution), Computing and Network Management (service area differs from that of the overall institution), Environmental Engineering (service area differs from that of the overall institution), Structural Engineering (service area differs from that of the overall institution)
Graduate Certificate(s) Electrical and Computer Engineering–Controls, Communications and Software (service area differs from that of the overall institution), Electrical and Computer Engineering–Microelectronics (service area differs from that of the overall institution), Mechanical and Aerospace Engineering–Computer-Aided Design (service area differs from that of the overall institution)

ME Civil Engineering (service area differs from that of the overall institution), Electrical and Computer Engineering–Controls, Communications and Software (service area differs from that of the overall institution), Electrical and Computer Engineering–Microelectronics (service area differs from that of the overall institution), Environmental Engineering (service area differs from that of the overall institution), Industrial Engineering–Manufacturing and Production Engineering (service area differs from that of the overall institution), Mechanical and Aerospace Engineering–Computer-Aided Design (service area differs from that of the overall institution), Structural Engineering (service area differs from that of the overall institution)

MS Electrical and Computer Engineering–Controls, Communications and Software (service area differs from that of the overall institution), Electrical and Computer Engineering–Microelectronics (service area differs from that of the overall institution), Mechanical and Aerospace Engineering–Computer-Aided Design (service area differs from that of the overall institution)

COURSE SUBJECT AREAS OFFERED OUTSIDE OF DEGREE PROGRAMS

Undergraduate: Computer and information sciences; English composition; film studies; health and physical education/fitness; health professions and related sciences; nursing; psychology

Graduate: Aerospace, aeronautical engineering; civil engineering; education; education administration; electrical engineering; engineering mechanics; engineering/industrial management; environmental engineering; industrial engineering; library and information studies; mechanical engineering; nursing; social work; teacher education

Noncredit: Computer and information sciences; education; education administration; nursing; special education; teacher education

STATE UNIVERSITY OF NEW YORK AT FARMINGDALE

Farmingdale, New York

State University of New York at Farmingdale, founded in 1912, is a state-supported, four-year college. It is accredited by the Middle States Association of Colleges and Schools. It first offered distance learning courses in 1989. In 1999–2000, it offered 4 courses at a distance. In fall 1999, there were 40 students enrolled in distance learning courses.

Course delivery sites Courses are delivered to your home, your workplace.

Media Courses are delivered via television, videoconferencing, computer software, e-mail, print. Students and teachers may interact via mail, telephone, fax, e-mail. The following equipment may be required: computer, Internet access, e-mail.

Restrictions Programs are available worldwide. Enrollment is open to anyone.

Services Distance learners have access to the campus computer network, e-mail services at a distance.

Typical costs Tuition of $128 per credit plus mandatory fees of $11.10 per credit for in-state residents. Tuition of $346 per credit plus mandatory fees of $11.10 per credit for out-of-state residents. Costs may vary. Financial aid is available to distance learners.

Registration Students may register by mail, fax, World Wide Web, in person.

Contact Admissions Office, State University of New York at Farmingdale, Memorial Hall, Farmingdale, NY 11735. *Telephone:* 516-420-2200. *Fax:* 516-420-2633.

DEGREES AND AWARDS

Distance programs offered do not lead to a degree or other formal award.

COURSE SUBJECT AREAS OFFERED OUTSIDE OF DEGREE PROGRAMS

Undergraduate: Business; engineering-related technologies; physics

STATE UNIVERSITY OF NEW YORK AT NEW PALTZ

New Paltz, New York

Center for Continuing and Professional Education
www.newpaltz.edu/continuing_ed/

State University of New York at New Paltz, founded in 1828, is a state-supported, comprehensive institution. It is accredited by the Middle States Association of Colleges and Schools. It first offered distance learning courses in 1995. In 1999–2000, it offered 22 courses at a distance. In fall 1999, there were 153 students enrolled in distance learning courses.

Course delivery sites Courses are delivered to your home, your workplace, military bases, high schools, Adirondack Community College (Queensbury), 1 off-campus center in Middletown.

Media Courses are delivered via videotapes, videoconferencing, computer conferencing, World Wide Web, e-mail. Students and teachers may interact via videoconferencing, telephone, e-mail, World Wide Web. The following equipment may be required: computer, Internet access.

Restrictions Programs are available worldwide. Enrollment is open to anyone.

Services Distance learners have access to library services, the campus computer network, e-mail services, bookstore at a distance.

Credit-earning options Students may transfer credits from another institution or may earn credits through examinations, portfolio assessment, military training, business training.

Typical costs *Undergraduate:* Tuition of $137 per credit for in-state residents. Tuition of $346 per credit for out-of-state residents. *Graduate:* Tuition of $213 per credit for in-state residents. Tuition of $351 per credit for out-of-state residents. There is a mandatory fee of $85 per 3 credit course. Costs may vary. Financial aid is available to distance learners.

Registration Students may register by mail, fax, telephone, in person.

Contact Helise Winters, Extension and Distance Learning Coordinator, State University of New York at New Paltz, Continuing and Professional Education, New Paltz, NY 12561-2443. *Telephone:* 914-257-2904. *Fax:* 914-257-2899. *E-mail:* edl@newpaltz.edu.

DEGREES AND AWARDS

Distance programs offered do not lead to a degree or other formal award.

COURSE SUBJECT AREAS OFFERED OUTSIDE OF DEGREE PROGRAMS

Undergraduate: Anthropology; astronomy and astrophysics; communications; design; English composition; political science; psychology; sociology

Graduate: Teacher education

STATE UNIVERSITY OF NEW YORK AT OSWEGO

Oswego, New York

Office of Distance Learning
www.oswego.edu/

State University of New York at Oswego, founded in 1861, is a state-supported, comprehensive institution. It is accredited by the Middle

States Association of Colleges and Schools. It first offered distance learning courses in 1995. In 1999–2000, it offered 12 courses at a distance. In fall 1999, there were 85 students enrolled in distance learning courses.

Course delivery sites Courses are delivered to your home, your workplace, military bases, high schools, State University of New York Upstate Medical University (Syracuse), 1 off-campus center in Phoenix.

Media Courses are delivered via computer software, computer conferencing, World Wide Web, e-mail. Students and teachers may interact via mail, telephone, fax, e-mail, World Wide Web. The following equipment may be required: computer, Internet access, e-mail.

Restrictions Programs are available worldwide. Enrollment is open to anyone.

Services Distance learners have access to library services, the campus computer network, e-mail services, academic advising, tutoring, career placement assistance, bookstore at a distance.

Credit-earning options Students may transfer credits from another institution or may earn credits through examinations.

Typical costs *Undergraduate:* Tuition of $137 per credit hour plus mandatory fees of $12 per credit hour for in-state residents. Tuition of $346 per credit hour plus mandatory fees of $12 per credit hour for out-of-state residents. *Graduate:* Tuition of $213 per credit hour plus mandatory fees of $5 per credit hour for in-state residents. Tuition of $351 per credit hour plus mandatory fees of $5 per credit hour for out-of-state residents. Financial aid is available to distance learners.

Registration Students may register by mail, fax, telephone, e-mail, World Wide Web, in person.

Contact Yvonne A. Petrella, Director of Continuing Education, State University of New York at Oswego. *Telephone:* 315-341-2270. *Fax:* 315-341-3078. *E-mail:* ced@oswego.edu.

DEGREES AND AWARDS

Distance programs offered do not lead to a degree or other formal award.

COURSE SUBJECT AREAS OFFERED OUTSIDE OF DEGREE PROGRAMS

Undergraduate: Cognitive psychology; computer programming; economics; European history; geology; mass media; radio and television broadcasting; Russian language and literature; statistics; teacher education

Graduate: Abnormal psychology; business administration and management; education administration

STATE UNIVERSITY OF NEW YORK AT STONY BROOK

Stony Brook, New York

Electronic Extension Program
www.sunysb.edu/spd/electric.htm

State University of New York at Stony Brook, founded in 1957, is a state-supported university. It is accredited by the Middle States Association of Colleges and Schools. It first offered distance learning courses in 1996. In 1999–2000, it offered 48 courses at a distance. In fall 1999, there were 240 students enrolled in distance learning courses.

Course delivery sites Courses are delivered to your home, your workplace.

Media Courses are delivered via computer conferencing, World Wide Web, e-mail, print. Students and teachers may interact via mail, telephone, fax, e-mail, World Wide Web. The following equipment may be required: computer, modem, Internet access, e-mail.

Restrictions Programs are available to in-state students only. Enrollment is restricted to individuals meeting certain criteria.

Services Distance learners have access to library services, the campus computer network, e-mail services, academic advising, bookstore at a distance.

Credit-earning options Students may transfer credits from another institution.

Typical costs Tuition of $213 per credit plus mandatory fees of $85 per semester. Costs may vary. Financial aid is available to distance learners.

Registration Students may register by mail, telephone, in person.

Contact Patricia Baker, Director, State University of New York at Stony Brook, School of Professional Development, Stony Brook, NY 11794-4310. *Telephone:* 631-632-9484. *Fax:* 631-632-9046. *E-mail:* pbaker@ccmail.sunysb.edu.

DEGREES AND AWARDS

Distance programs offered do not lead to a degree or other formal award.

COURSE SUBJECT AREAS OFFERED OUTSIDE OF DEGREE PROGRAMS

Graduate: Adult education; continuing education; education; teacher education

STATE UNIVERSITY OF NEW YORK COLLEGE AT CORTLAND

Cortland, New York

State University of New York College at Cortland, founded in 1868, is a state-supported, comprehensive institution. It is accredited by the Middle States Association of Colleges and Schools. In 1999–2000, it offered 20 courses at a distance. In fall 1999, there were 89 students enrolled in distance learning courses.

Course delivery sites Courses are delivered to your home, your workplace, Corning Community College (Corning), Mohawk Valley Community College (Utica), State University of New York College at Brockport (Brockport), State University of New York College at Geneseo (Geneseo), State University of New York College of Environmental Science and Forestry (Syracuse), off-campus center(s) in Rome.

Media Courses are delivered via television, videotapes, videoconferencing, interactive television, computer software, computer conferencing, World Wide Web, e-mail, print. Students and teachers may meet in person or interact via mail, telephone, fax, e-mail. The following equipment may be required: computer, modem, Internet access.

Restrictions Programs are available to in-state students only. Enrollment is open to anyone.

Services Distance learners have access to e-mail services at a distance.

Typical costs Costs may vary. Financial aid is available to distance learners.

Registration Students may register by in person.

Contact Paula Warnken, Associate Vice President for Information Resources, State University of New York College at Cortland, PO Box 2000, Miller Building, Cortland, NY 13045. *Telephone:* 607-753-5942. *Fax:* 607-753-5985.

DEGREES AND AWARDS

Distance programs offered do not lead to a degree or other formal award.

COURSE SUBJECT AREAS OFFERED OUTSIDE OF DEGREE PROGRAMS

Undergraduate: Communications; education; English language and literature; health and physical education/fitness; health professions and related sciences; Middle Eastern languages and literatures; music; philosophy and religion; political science; psychology; sociology

Graduate: Education

STATE UNIVERSITY OF NEW YORK COLLEGE AT FREDONIA

Fredonia, New York

Office of Lifelong Learning/SUNY Learning Network
sln.suny.edu

State University of New York College at Fredonia, founded in 1826, is a state-supported, comprehensive institution. It is accredited by the Middle States Association of Colleges and Schools. In 1999–2000, it offered 11 courses at a distance. In fall 1999, there were 50 students enrolled in distance learning courses.

Course delivery sites Courses are delivered to your home, Jamestown Community College (Jamestown).

Media Courses are delivered via television, interactive television, computer software, computer conferencing, e-mail, print. Students and teachers may meet in person or interact via mail, telephone, fax, e-mail, interactive television. The following equipment may be required: computer, modem, Internet access.

Restrictions Programs are available nationwide. Enrollment is open to anyone.

Services Distance learners have access to academic advising, tutoring, bookstore at a distance.

Credit-earning options Students may transfer credits from another institution or may earn credits through portfolio assessment, military training, business training.

Typical costs *Undergraduate:* Tuition of $187 per credit plus mandatory fees of $32.10 per credit for local area residents. Tuition of $187 per credit plus mandatory fees of $32.10 per credit for in-state residents. Tuition of $346 per credit plus mandatory fees of $32.10 per credit for out-of-state residents. *Graduate:* Tuition of $213 per credit plus mandatory fees of $32.10 per credit for local area residents. Tuition of $213 per credit plus mandatory fees of $32.10 per credit for in-state residents. Tuition of $351 per credit plus mandatory fees of $32.10 per credit for out-of-state residents. Cost for a noncredit course ranges between $75 and $125. Costs may vary. Financial aid is available to distance learners.

Registration Students may register by mail, fax, telephone, e-mail, in person.

Contact Richard Goodman, Director, State University of New York College at Fredonia, Office of Lifelong Learning, Lograsso Hall, Fredonia, NY 14063. *Telephone:* 716-673-3177. *Fax:* 716-673-3175. *E-mail:* goodman@fredonia.edu.

DEGREES AND AWARDS

Distance programs offered do not lead to a degree or other formal award.

COURSE SUBJECT AREAS OFFERED OUTSIDE OF DEGREE PROGRAMS

Undergraduate: Business administration and management; computer and information sciences

STATE UNIVERSITY OF NEW YORK COLLEGE AT ONEONTA

Oneonta, New York

Academic Support Services

State University of New York College at Oneonta, founded in 1889, is a state-supported, comprehensive institution. It is accredited by the Middle States Association of Colleges and Schools. In 1999–2000, it offered 4 courses at a distance. In fall 1999, there were 150 students enrolled in distance learning courses.

Course delivery sites Courses are delivered to your home, high schools, Herkimer County Community College (Herkimer).

Media Courses are delivered via videoconferencing, computer software, computer conferencing, World Wide Web. Students and teachers may meet in person or interact via videoconferencing, mail, telephone, fax, e-mail, World Wide Web. The following equipment may be required: computer, Internet access.

Restrictions Programs are available to in-state students only. Enrollment is open to anyone.

Services Distance learners have access to library services, the campus computer network, e-mail services, tutoring, bookstore at a distance.

Credit-earning options Students may transfer credits from another institution or may earn credits through examinations, portfolio assessment, military training, business training.

Typical costs Tuition of $137 per credit plus mandatory fees of $16.85 per credit for local area residents. Tuition of $137 per credit plus mandatory fees of $16.85 per credit for in-state residents. Tuition of $346 per credit plus mandatory fees of $16.85 per credit for out-of-state residents. Cost of a noncredit course is the same as for credit courses. Financial aid is available to distance learners.

Registration Students may register by mail, fax, World Wide Web, in person.

Contact Dr. Marguerite Culver, Interim Dean, Division of Academic Support Services, State University of New York College at Oneonta, 135 Netzer Administration Building, Oneonta, NY 13820. *Telephone:* 607-436-2548. *Fax:* 607-436-3084. *E-mail:* jamiesmm@oneonta.edu.

DEGREES AND AWARDS

Distance programs offered do not lead to a degree or other formal award.

COURSE SUBJECT AREAS OFFERED OUTSIDE OF DEGREE PROGRAMS

Undergraduate: Abnormal psychology; anthropology; business administration and management; sociology
Noncredit: Abnormal psychology; anthropology; business administration and management; sociology

STATE UNIVERSITY OF NEW YORK COLLEGE OF AGRICULTURE AND TECHNOLOGY AT MORRISVILLE

Morrisville, New York
www.morrisville.edu

State University of New York College of Agriculture and Technology at Morrisville, founded in 1908, is a state-supported, primarily two-year college. It is accredited by the Middle States Association of Colleges and Schools. In 1999–2000, it offered 49 courses at a distance. In fall 1999, there were 426 students enrolled in distance learning courses.

Course delivery sites Courses are delivered to your home, your workplace, military bases, State University of New York College of Technology at Delhi (Delhi).

Media Courses are delivered via World Wide Web. Students and teachers may interact via World Wide Web. The following equipment may be required: computer, Internet access.

Restrictions Programs are available worldwide. Enrollment is open to anyone.

Services Distance learners have access to library services, the campus computer network, e-mail services, bookstore at a distance.

Typical costs Tuition of $99 per credit plus mandatory fees of $0.85 per credit.

Registration Students may register by mail, fax, telephone, e-mail, World Wide Web, in person.

Contact Chris Cring, Distance Learning Coordinator, State University of New York College of Agriculture and Technology at Morrisville, PO Box 901, Morrisville, NY 13408. *Telephone:* 315-684-6080. *E-mail:* cringca@morrisville.edu.

DEGREES AND AWARDS

Distance programs offered do not lead to a degree or other formal award.

COURSE SUBJECT AREAS OFFERED OUTSIDE OF DEGREE PROGRAMS

Undergraduate: Accounting; business; computer programming; English language and literature; mathematics

STATE UNIVERSITY OF NEW YORK COLLEGE OF TECHNOLOGY AT ALFRED

Alfred, New York

State University of New York College of Technology at Alfred, founded in 1908, is a state-supported, primarily two-year college. It is accredited by the Middle States Association of Colleges and Schools. In 1999–2000, it offered 8 courses at a distance. In fall 1999, there were 22 students enrolled in distance learning courses.

Course delivery sites Courses are delivered to your home.

Media Courses are delivered via World Wide Web, e-mail, print. Students and teachers may meet in person or interact via mail, telephone, fax, e-mail, World Wide Web. The following equipment may be required: computer, modem, Internet access, e-mail.

Restrictions Programs are available worldwide. Enrollment is open to anyone.

Services Distance learners have access to library services, the campus computer network, e-mail services, academic advising, tutoring, career placement assistance, bookstore at a distance.

Credit-earning options Students may transfer credits from another institution or may earn credits through examinations.

Typical costs Tuition of $128 per credit plus mandatory fees of $5.35 per credit. Financial aid is available to distance learners.

Registration Students may register by mail, fax, telephone, e-mail, in person.

Contact Delores Ackerman, Secretary, State University of New York College of Technology at Alfred, Alfred State College, 10 Upper College Drive, Alfred, NY 14802-1196. *Telephone:* 607-587-4544. *Fax:* 607-587-3295. *E-mail:* ackermdd@alfredtech.edu.

DEGREES AND AWARDS

Undergraduate Certificate(s) Cancer Registry Management (certain restrictions apply)

COURSE SUBJECT AREAS OFFERED OUTSIDE OF DEGREE PROGRAMS

Undergraduate: Business; health professions and related sciences

STATE UNIVERSITY OF NEW YORK COLLEGE OF TECHNOLOGY AT CANTON

Canton, New York
Academic Affairs
www.canton.edu

State University of New York College of Technology at Canton, founded in 1906, is a state-supported, four-year college. It is accredited by the Middle States Association of Colleges and Schools. In 1999–2000, it offered 16 courses at a distance. In fall 1999, there were 205 students enrolled in distance learning courses.

Course delivery sites Courses are delivered to your home, high schools, State University of New York College of Agriculture and Technology at Cobleskill (Cobleskill), State University of New York College of Agriculture and Technology at Morrisville (Morrisville), State University of New York College of Technology at Alfred (Alfred), State University of New York College of Technology at Delhi (Delhi).

Media Courses are delivered via videoconferencing, computer software, World Wide Web, e-mail. Students and teachers may interact via videoconferencing, mail, telephone, fax, e-mail, World Wide Web. The following equipment may be required: computer, Internet access, e-mail.

Restrictions Program availability may be dependent upon the form of the distance learning class, whether online or interactive video. Enrollment is restricted to individuals meeting certain criteria.

Services Distance learners have access to library services, e-mail services, bookstore at a distance.

Credit-earning options Students may transfer credits from another institution or may earn credits through examinations.

Typical costs Tuition of $99 per credit plus mandatory fees of $5 per credit.

Registration Students may register by mail, fax, World Wide Web, in person.

Contact Barbara Porter, Registrar, State University of New York College of Technology at Canton, Canton, NY 13617. *Telephone:* 315-386-7647. *Fax:* 315-379-3819. *E-mail:* porter@canton.edu.

DEGREES AND AWARDS

Distance programs offered do not lead to a degree or other formal award.

COURSE SUBJECT AREAS OFFERED OUTSIDE OF DEGREE PROGRAMS

Undergraduate: Animal sciences; business administration and management; earth science; insurance; law and legal studies

STATE UNIVERSITY OF NEW YORK COLLEGE OF TECHNOLOGY AT DELHI

Delhi, New York
www.delhi.edu

State University of New York College of Technology at Delhi, founded in 1913, is a state-supported, primarily two-year college. It is accredited by the Middle States Association of Colleges and Schools. In 1999–2000, it offered 20 courses at a distance. In fall 1999, there were 177 students enrolled in distance learning courses.

Course delivery sites Courses are delivered to your home, Mohawk Valley Community College (Utica), State University of New York College of Agriculture and Technology at Cobleskill (Cobleskill), State University of New York College of Agriculture and Technology at Morrisville (Morrisville), State University of New York College of Technology at

Alfred (Alfred), State University of New York College of Technology at Canton (Canton), 1 off-campus center in Stamford.

Media Courses are delivered via television, interactive television, World Wide Web, e-mail, print. Students and teachers may interact via mail, telephone, e-mail, interactive television, World Wide Web. The following equipment may be required: Internet access.

Restrictions Programs are available to in-state students only. Enrollment is open to anyone.

Services Distance learners have access to library services, e-mail services, bookstore at a distance.

Credit-earning options Students may transfer credits from another institution or may earn credits through examinations, military training.

Typical costs Tuition of $128 per credit hour plus mandatory fees of $19 per credit hour for in-state residents. Tuition of $346 per credit hour plus mandatory fees of $19 per credit hour for out-of-state residents. Financial aid is available to distance learners.

Registration Students may register by in person.

Contact Registrar, State University of New York College of Technology at Delhi, 124 Bush Hall, Delhi College, Delhi, NY 13753. *Telephone:* 607-746-4560. *Fax:* 607-746-4569.

DEGREES AND AWARDS

Distance programs offered do not lead to a degree or other formal award.

COURSE SUBJECT AREAS OFFERED OUTSIDE OF DEGREE PROGRAMS

Undergraduate: Accounting; animal sciences; business administration and management; criminal justice; engineering; English language and literature; foods and nutrition studies; information sciences and systems; psychology

STATE UNIVERSITY OF NEW YORK EMPIRE STATE COLLEGE

Saratoga Springs, New York

Center for Distance Learning
www.esc.edu

State University of New York Empire State College, founded in 1971, is a state-supported, comprehensive institution. It is accredited by the Middle States Association of Colleges and Schools. It first offered distance learning courses in 1982. In 1999–2000, it offered 243 courses at a distance. In fall 1999, there were 4,000 students enrolled in distance learning courses.

Course delivery sites Courses are delivered to your home, your workplace, military bases.

Media Courses are delivered via videotapes, audiotapes, computer software, computer conferencing, World Wide Web, e-mail, print. Students and teachers may interact via mail, telephone, fax, e-mail, World Wide Web. The following equipment may be required: television, videocassette player, computer, modem, Internet access, e-mail.

Restrictions Programs are available worldwide. Enrollment is open to anyone.

Services Distance learners have access to library services, the campus computer network, e-mail services, academic advising, tutoring, bookstore at a distance.

Credit-earning options Students may transfer credits from another institution or may earn credits through examinations, portfolio assessment, military training, business training.

Typical costs Tuition of $113 per credit plus mandatory fees of $1 per credit. Cost for noncredit courses is $520 for matriculated students and $591 for non-matriculated students. Financial aid is available to distance learners.

Registration Students may register by mail, fax, telephone, e-mail, World Wide Web, in person.

Contact Dr. Margaret Craft, Assistant Director, Academic Program Development, State University of New York Empire State College, Center for Distance Learning, 3 Union Avenue, Saratoga Springs, NY 12866. *Telephone:* 800-847-3000. *Fax:* 518-587-2660. *E-mail:* cdl@esc.edu.

DEGREES AND AWARDS

AA Business, Management and Economics, Community and Human Services, Cultural Studies, Educational Studies, Historical Studies, Human Development, Interdisciplinary Studies, Labor Studies, Science, Math and Technology, Special Theory, Social Structure and Change, The Arts
AS Business, Management and Economics, Community and Human Services, Cultural Studies, Educational Studies, Historical Studies, Human Development, Interdisciplinary Studies, Labor Studies, Science, Math and Technology, Social Theory, Social Structure and Change, The Arts
BA Business, Management and Economics, Community and Human Services, Cultural Studies, Educational Studies, Historical Studies, Human Development, Interdisciplinary Studies, Labor Studies, Science, Math and Technology, Social Theory, Social Structure and Change, The Arts
BPS Business, Management and Economics, Community and Human Services
BS Business, Management and Economics, Community and Human Services, Cultural Studies, Educational Studies, Historical Studies, Human Development, Interdisciplinary Studies, Labor Studies, Science, Math and Technology, Social Theory, Social Structure and Change, The Arts

COURSE SUBJECT AREAS OFFERED OUTSIDE OF DEGREE PROGRAMS

Undergraduate: Abnormal psychology; accounting; administrative and secretarial services; algebra; American (U.S.) history; area, ethnic, and cultural studies; biology; business; business administration and management; business communications; business law; calculus; child care and development; communications; community health services; computer and information sciences; counseling psychology; criminal justice; economics; English composition; English language and literature; finance; fire services administration; health professions and related sciences; history; home economics and family studies; human resources management; individual and family development studies; information sciences and systems; international business; labor relations/studies; liberal arts, general studies, and humanities; management information systems; mathematics; organizational behavior studies; philosophy and religion; political science; public administration and services; religious studies; social psychology; social sciences; sociology; statistics; telecommunications

See full description on page 682.

STATE UNIVERSITY OF NEW YORK INSTITUTE OF TECHNOLOGY AT UTICA/ROME

Utica, New York

SUNY Learning Network
sln.suny.edu

State University of New York Institute of Technology at Utica/Rome, founded in 1966, is a state-supported, upper-level institution. It is accredited by the Middle States Association of Colleges and Schools. In 1999–2000, it offered 233 courses at a distance. In fall 1999, there were 158 students enrolled in distance learning courses.

Course delivery sites Courses are delivered to your home, your workplace.

Media Courses are delivered via computer software, CD-ROM, World Wide Web, e-mail, print. Students and teachers may meet in person or

interact via mail, telephone, fax, e-mail, World Wide Web. The following equipment may be required: computer, modem, Internet access, e-mail.
Restrictions Programs are available worldwide. Enrollment is restricted to individuals meeting certain criteria.
Services Distance learners have access to library services, the campus computer network, e-mail services, academic advising, tutoring, career placement assistance, bookstore at a distance.
Credit-earning options Students may transfer credits from another institution or may earn credits through examinations, military training, business training.
Typical costs *Undergraduate:* Tuition of $137 per credit plus mandatory fees of $16.95 per credit for in-state residents. Tuition of $346 per credit plus mandatory fees of $16.95 per credit for out-of-state residents. *Graduate:* Tuition of $213 per credit plus mandatory fees of $12.95 per credit for in-state residents. Tuition of $351 per credit plus mandatory fees of $12.95 per credit for out-of-state residents. Cost for noncredit course ranges from $59 to $185 per course. Financial aid is available to distance learners.
Registration Students may register by telephone, World Wide Web, in person.
Contact Diane Palen, Registrar, State University of New York Institute of Technology at Utica/Rome, PO Box 3050, Utica, NY 13504-3050. *Telephone:* 315-792-7265. *Fax:* 315-792-7802. *E-mail:* sdpc1@sunyit.edu.

DEGREES AND AWARDS

MS Accountancy (certain restrictions apply)

COURSE SUBJECT AREAS OFFERED OUTSIDE OF DEGREE PROGRAMS

Undergraduate: Accounting; health professions and related sciences; nursing
Graduate: Accounting; business; health professions and related sciences; nursing
Noncredit: Computer and information sciences
See full description on page 684.

STATE UNIVERSITY OF WEST GEORGIA

Carrollton, Georgia
Special Programs
www.westga.edu

State University of West Georgia, founded in 1933, is a state-supported, comprehensive institution. It is accredited by the Southern Association of Colleges and Schools. It first offered distance learning courses in 1995. In 1999–2000, it offered 100 courses at a distance. In fall 1999, there were 1,000 students enrolled in distance learning courses.
Course delivery sites Courses are delivered to your home, your workplace, high schools, Dalton State College (Dalton), Floyd College (Rome), 1 off-campus center in Newnan.
Media Courses are delivered via videoconferencing, interactive television, computer software, computer conferencing, World Wide Web, e-mail, print. Students and teachers may interact via videoconferencing, mail, telephone, fax, e-mail. The following equipment may be required: computer, modem, Internet access, e-mail.
Restrictions Most courses are limited to in-state students only. Enrollment is open to anyone.
Services Distance learners have access to library services, the campus computer network, e-mail services, career placement assistance, bookstore at a distance.
Credit-earning options Students may transfer credits from another institution or may earn credits through examinations.

Typical costs *Undergraduate:* Tuition of $865 per semester for in-state residents. Tuition of $2610 per semester for out-of-state residents. *Graduate:* Tuition of $1000 per semester for in-state residents. Tuition of $3000 per semester for out-of-state residents. Costs may vary. Financial aid is available to distance learners.
Registration Students may register by mail, telephone, World Wide Web, in person.
Contact Melanie Clay, Distance Education Administrator, State University of West Georgia, Honors House, Carrollton, GA 30118 United States of America. *Telephone:* 770-836-4647. *Fax:* 770-836-4666. *E-mail:* melaniec@westga.edu.

DEGREES AND AWARDS

MEd Educational Leadership, Media and Technology

COURSE SUBJECT AREAS OFFERED OUTSIDE OF DEGREE PROGRAMS

Undergraduate: Accounting; administrative and secretarial services; algebra; American (U.S.) history; American literature; art history and criticism; business administration and management; business law; calculus; computer and information sciences; creative writing; drama and theater; economics; education; education administration; educational psychology; English as a second language (ESL); English composition; English language and literature; English literature; European history; history; management information systems; marketing; mass media; mathematics; music; nursing; philosophy and religion; political science; psychology; public administration and services; real estate; social sciences; sociology; special education; student counseling; teacher education
Graduate: Accounting; American (U.S.) history; American literature; business administration and management; education; education administration; educational psychology; educational research; English language and literature; English literature; European history; history; instructional media; psychology; public administration and services; real estate; special education; student counseling; teacher education
See full description on page 676.

STEPHENS COLLEGE

Columbia, Missouri
School of Graduate and Continuing Education
www.stephens.edu

Stephens College, founded in 1833, is an independent, nonprofit, comprehensive institution. It is accredited by the North Central Association of Colleges and Schools. It first offered distance learning courses in 1971. In 1999–2000, it offered 100 courses at a distance. In fall 1999, there were 250 students enrolled in distance learning courses.
Course delivery sites Courses are delivered to your home, your workplace.
Media Courses are delivered via World Wide Web, e-mail, print. Students and teachers may meet in person or interact via mail, telephone, fax, e-mail, World Wide Web. The following equipment may be required: computer, Internet access, e-mail.
Restrictions Programs are available worldwide. Enrollment is open to anyone.
Services Distance learners have access to library services, e-mail services, academic advising, bookstore at a distance.
Credit-earning options Students may transfer credits from another institution or may earn credits through examinations, portfolio assessment, military training, business training.
Typical costs *Undergraduate:* Tuition of $500 per course for local area residents. Tuition of $500 per course for in-state residents. Tuition of $650 per course for out-of-state residents. *Graduate:* Tuition of $690 per course

for in-state residents. Tuition of $690 per course for out-of-state residents. Application fee is $50. Costs may vary.

Registration Students may register by mail, fax, telephone, e-mail, in person.

Contact Rachelle A. Freese, Marketing Coordinator, Stephens College. *Telephone:* 800-388-7579. *Fax:* 573-876-7248. *E-mail:* sce@stephens. edu.

DEGREES AND AWARDS

BA Business Administration (some on-campus requirements), English (some on-campus requirements), Law, Philosophy and Rhetoric (some on-campus requirements), Psychology (some on-campus requirements)
BS Education (service area differs from that of the overall institution; some on-campus requirements), Health Care (some on-campus requirements), Health Information Management (some on-campus requirements)
Graduate Certificate(s) Health Information Management (some on-campus requirements)
MBA Business Administration (certain restrictions apply; some on-campus requirements), Clinical Information Systems Management (certain restrictions apply; some on-campus requirements), Entrepreneurship Management (certain restrictions apply; some on-campus requirements)

COURSE SUBJECT AREAS OFFERED OUTSIDE OF DEGREE PROGRAMS

Undergraduate: Abnormal psychology; accounting; advertising; American (U.S.) history; American literature; American studies; anatomy; Asian studies; Bible studies; business; business administration and management; business law; chemistry; cognitive psychology; computer and information sciences; counseling psychology; creative writing; developmental and child psychology; earth science; economics; education; educational psychology; English language and literature; English literature; ethics; finance; Hebrew language and literature; history; human resources management; information sciences and systems; international business; investments and securities; Japanese language and literature; Latin American studies; logic; marketing; organizational behavior studies; philosophy and religion; physiology; psychology; religious studies; school psychology; social psychology; social sciences; statistics; student counseling; teacher education; technical writing
Graduate: Accounting; business; business administration and management; business law; computer and information sciences; economics; finance; human resources management; information sciences and systems; marketing; statistics

See full description on page 686.

STEVENS INSTITUTE OF TECHNOLOGY

Hoboken, New Jersey
The Graduate School
www.webcampus.stevens.edu

Stevens Institute of Technology, founded in 1870, is an independent, nonprofit university. It is accredited by the Middle States Association of Colleges and Schools. It first offered distance learning courses in 1993. In 1999–2000, it offered 100 courses at a distance. In fall 1999, there were 150 students enrolled in distance learning courses.
Course delivery sites Courses are delivered to your workplace, Brookdale Community College (Lincroft), William Paterson University of New Jersey (Wayne).
Media Courses are delivered via videoconferencing, interactive television, computer software, World Wide Web, e-mail. Students and teachers may meet in person or interact via videoconferencing, mail, telephone,

fax, e-mail, interactive television, World Wide Web. The following equipment may be required: computer, Internet access.
Restrictions Programs are available worldwide. Enrollment is restricted to individuals meeting certain criteria.
Services Distance learners have access to library services, the campus computer network, e-mail services, academic advising, tutoring, career placement assistance, bookstore at a distance.
Credit-earning options Students may transfer credits from another institution or may earn credits through examinations.
Typical costs Mandatory fees of $80 per semester. Graduate tuition for management courses is $605 per credit, $726 per credit for engineering and science courses. Application fee is $50. *Noncredit courses:* $500 per course. Financial aid is available to distance learners.
Registration Students may register by mail, fax, telephone, e-mail, World Wide Web, in person.
Contact Robert Ubell, Director Web-Distance Learning, Stevens Institute of Technology, Castle Point on Hudson, Hoboken, NJ 07030. *Telephone:* 800-496-4935. *Fax:* 201-216-8044. *E-mail:* webcampus@ stevens-tech.edu.

DEGREES AND AWARDS

Graduate Certificate(s) Computer Science, Concurrent Engineering, Project Management, Technology Applications in Science, Technology Management, Telecommunications Management, Wireless Communications
MA Project Management
ME Concurrent Engineering (certain restrictions apply)
MS Computer Science (certain restrictions apply), Management (certain restrictions apply), Telecommunications Management, Wireless Communications

COURSE SUBJECT AREAS OFFERED OUTSIDE OF DEGREE PROGRAMS

Graduate: Business; business administration and management; computer and information sciences; education; engineering; management; management information systems; telecommunications

See full description on page 688.

STRAYER UNIVERSITY

Washington, District of Columbia
Strayer Online
www.strayer.edu

Strayer University, founded in 1892, is a proprietary, comprehensive institution. It is accredited by the Middle States Association of Colleges and Schools. It first offered distance learning courses in 1996. In 1999–2000, it offered 70 courses at a distance. In fall 1999, there were 876 students enrolled in distance learning courses.
Course delivery sites Courses are delivered to your home, your workplace, military bases.
Media Courses are delivered via computer software, World Wide Web. Students and teachers may meet in person or interact via audioconferencing, telephone, e-mail, World Wide Web. The following equipment may be required: computer, modem, Internet access, e-mail.
Restrictions Programs are available worldwide. Enrollment is restricted to individuals meeting certain criteria.
Services Distance learners have access to library services, the campus computer network, e-mail services, academic advising, career placement assistance, bookstore at a distance.
Credit-earning options Students may transfer credits from another institution or may earn credits through examinations, portfolio assessment, military training, business training.

Typical costs *Undergraduate:* Tuition of $200 per credit. *Graduate:* Tuition of $270 per credit. *Noncredit courses:* $900 per course. Costs may vary. Financial aid is available to distance learners.

Registration Students may register by telephone, World Wide Web, in person.

Contact Allen Durgin, Strayer University Distance Learning Center, Strayer University, PO Box 487, Newington, VA 22122. *Telephone:* 888-360-1588. *Fax:* 703-339-1852. *E-mail:* axd@strayer.edu.

DEGREES AND AWARDS

Undergraduate Certificate(s) Computer Information Systems
AA Accounting, Business Administration, Computer Information Systems, Economics, General Studies, Marketing
BS Accounting, Business Administration, Computer Information Systems, Computer Networking, Economics, International Business
MS Accounting, Business Administration, Information Systems

COURSE SUBJECT AREAS OFFERED OUTSIDE OF DEGREE PROGRAMS

Undergraduate: Accounting; algebra; area, ethnic, and cultural studies; art history and criticism; business administration and management; business law; calculus; computer and information sciences; computer programming; database management; economics; English composition; ethics; finance; human resources management; information sciences and systems; international business; logic; management information systems; marketing; organizational behavior studies; philosophy and religion; political science; psychology; sociology; statistics; technical writing
Graduate: Accounting; business administration and management; business communications; computer and information sciences; computer programming; database management; economics; finance; information sciences and systems; marketing; organizational behavior studies; statistics

See full description on page 690.

SUFFOLK COUNTY COMMUNITY COLLEGE

Selden, New York

Office of Academic and Campus Affairs
www.sunysuffolk.edu/

Suffolk County Community College, founded in 1959, is a state and locally supported, two-year college. It is accredited by the Middle States Association of Colleges and Schools. It first offered distance learning courses in 1989. In 1999–2000, it offered 50 courses at a distance. In fall 1999, there were 500 students enrolled in distance learning courses.

Course delivery sites Courses are delivered to your home, your workplace, State University of New York System (Albany).

Media Courses are delivered via television, videotapes, interactive television, World Wide Web. Students and teachers may meet in person or interact via mail, telephone, fax, e-mail, interactive television, World Wide Web. The following equipment may be required: television, videocassette player, computer, modem, Internet access, e-mail.

Restrictions Programs are available to local area students. Enrollment is open to anyone.

Services Distance learners have access to library services, the campus computer network, e-mail services at a distance.

Credit-earning options Students may transfer credits from another institution.

Typical costs Tuition of $94 per credit plus mandatory fees of $40 per course for in-state residents. Tuition of $118 per credit plus mandatory fees of $40 per course for out-of-state residents. *Noncredit courses:* $70 per course. Costs may vary.

Registration Students may register by telephone, in person.

Contact Dr. Sandra Susman Palmer, Coordinator of Distance Education/Academic Chair, Department of Fine Arts, Suffolk County Community College, 533 College Road, Selden, NY 11784. *Telephone:* 631-451-4352. *Fax:* 631-451-4631. *E-mail:* susmans@sunysuffolk.edu.

DEGREES AND AWARDS

Distance programs offered do not lead to a degree or other formal award.

COURSE SUBJECT AREAS OFFERED OUTSIDE OF DEGREE PROGRAMS

Undergraduate: Abnormal psychology; accounting; algebra; American (U.S.) history; art history and criticism; Asian studies; business; business administration and management; business law; calculus; communications; creative writing; developmental and child psychology; earth science; economics; English composition; English language and literature; ethics; European history; foods and nutrition studies; geology; health and physical education/fitness; liberal arts, general studies, and humanities; marketing; radio and television broadcasting; sociology; women's studies

---

SUFFOLK UNIVERSITY

Boston, Massachusetts

Suffolk eMBA
www.suffolkemba.org

Suffolk University, founded in 1906, is an independent, nonprofit, comprehensive institution. It is accredited by the New England Association of Schools and Colleges. It first offered distance learning courses in 1999.

Course delivery sites Courses are delivered to your home, your workplace.

Media Courses are delivered via computer software, CD-ROM, computer conferencing, World Wide Web, e-mail. Students and teachers may interact via audioconferencing, mail, telephone, fax, e-mail, World Wide Web. The following equipment may be required: computer, modem, Internet access, e-mail.

Restrictions Programs are available worldwide. Enrollment is restricted to individuals meeting certain criteria.

Services Distance learners have access to library services, the campus computer network, e-mail services, academic advising, tutoring, career placement assistance, bookstore at a distance.

Credit-earning options Students may transfer credits from another institution.

Typical costs Tuition of $1845 per course plus mandatory fees of $120 per course. Financial aid is available to distance learners.

Registration Students may register by mail, fax, e-mail, World Wide Web, in person.

Contact Mawdudur Rahman, Director, Suffolk University, 8 Ashburton Place, Boston, MA 02108. *Telephone:* 617-573-8372. *Fax:* 617-723-0139. *E-mail:* mrahman@suffolk.edu.

eCollege.com *www.ecollege.com/scholarships*

DEGREES AND AWARDS

MBA Business Administration

COURSE SUBJECT AREAS OFFERED OUTSIDE OF DEGREE PROGRAMS

Graduate: Accounting; administrative and secretarial services; business administration and management; business communications; finance;

human resources management; international business; investments and securities; management information systems; marketing; organizational behavior studies

See full description on page 692.

SURRY COMMUNITY COLLEGE

Dobson, North Carolina
www.surry.cc.nc.us

Surry Community College, founded in 1965, is a state-supported, two-year college. It is accredited by the Southern Association of Colleges and Schools. In 1999–2000, it offered 20 courses at a distance. In fall 1999, there were 300 students enrolled in distance learning courses.
Course delivery sites Courses are delivered to your home, high schools.
Media Courses are delivered via television, videotapes, World Wide Web, e-mail, print. Students and teachers may meet in person or interact via videoconferencing, mail, telephone, fax, e-mail, World Wide Web. The following equipment may be required: television, videocassette player, computer, modem, Internet access, e-mail.
Restrictions Programs are available to in-state students only. Enrollment is open to anyone.
Services Distance learners have access to library services, academic advising, tutoring at a distance.
Credit-earning options Students may transfer credits from another institution or may earn credits through examinations, military training, business training.
Typical costs Tuition of $26.75 per credit hour for in-state residents. Tuition of $169.75 per credit hour for out-of-state residents. Financial aid is available to distance learners.
Registration Students may register by mail, fax, telephone, e-mail, in person.
Contact Tony Searcy, Counselor, Surry Community College, PO Box 304, Dobson, NC 27017. *Telephone:* 336-386-8121. *Fax:* 336-386-4262.

DEGREES AND AWARDS

Distance programs offered do not lead to a degree or other formal award.

COURSE SUBJECT AREAS OFFERED OUTSIDE OF DEGREE PROGRAMS

Undergraduate: Biology; business administration and management; business law; chemistry, inorganic; child care and development; English composition; history; horticulture; psychology; sociology

SUSSEX COUNTY COMMUNITY COLLEGE

Newton, New Jersey
Academic Affairs
sussex.cc.nj.us

Sussex County Community College, founded in 1981, is a state and locally supported, two-year college. It is accredited by the Middle States Association of Colleges and Schools. It first offered distance learning courses in 1990. In 1999–2000, it offered 18 courses at a distance. In fall 1999, there were 125 students enrolled in distance learning courses.
Course delivery sites Courses are delivered to your home, high schools, community colleges throughout New Jersey.
Media Courses are delivered via television, videotapes, interactive television, World Wide Web. Students and teachers may meet in person or interact via videoconferencing, mail, telephone, fax, e-mail, interactive television, World Wide Web. The following equipment may be required: television, videocassette player, computer, modem, Internet access, e-mail.
Restrictions Programs are available worldwide. Enrollment is open to anyone.
Services Distance learners have access to library services, the campus computer network, e-mail services, academic advising, bookstore at a distance.
Credit-earning options Students may transfer credits from another institution or may earn credits through examinations, portfolio assessment, military training, business training.
Typical costs Tuition of $68 per credit plus mandatory fees of $9 per credit for local area residents. Tuition of $136 per credit plus mandatory fees of $9 per credit for in-state residents. Tuition of $204 per credit plus mandatory fees of $9 per credit for out-of-state residents. Costs may vary. Financial aid is available to distance learners.
Registration Students may register by mail, e-mail, World Wide Web, in person.
Contact Dr. Thomas A. Isekenegbe, Associate Dean of Academic Affairs, Sussex County Community College, 1 College Hill, Newton, NJ 07860. *Telephone:* 973-300-2136. *Fax:* 973-300-2277. *E-mail:* thomasi@sussex.cc.nj.us.

DEGREES AND AWARDS

Undergraduate Certificate(s) Legal Studies (service area differs from that of the overall institution)

COURSE SUBJECT AREAS OFFERED OUTSIDE OF DEGREE PROGRAMS

Undergraduate: Astronomy and astrophysics; business administration and management; database management; English composition; history; information sciences and systems; journalism; social psychology

See full description on page 600.

SYRACUSE UNIVERSITY

Syracuse, New York
Division of Continuing Education
www.suce.syr.edu

Syracuse University, founded in 1870, is an independent, nonprofit university. It is accredited by the Middle States Association of Colleges and Schools. It first offered distance learning courses in 1966. In 1999–2000, it offered 100 courses at a distance. In fall 1999, there were 1,000 students enrolled in distance learning courses.
Course delivery sites Courses are delivered to your home.
Media Courses are delivered via computer software, World Wide Web, e-mail, print. Students and teachers may meet in person or interact via mail, telephone, fax, e-mail, World Wide Web. The following equipment may be required: computer, modem, Internet access, e-mail.
Restrictions Programs are available worldwide. Enrollment is open to anyone.
Services Distance learners have access to library services, the campus computer network, e-mail services, academic advising, career placement assistance, bookstore at a distance.
Credit-earning options Students may transfer credits from another institution or may earn credits through examinations, portfolio assessment, military training, business training.
Typical costs *Undergraduate:* Tuition of $371 per credit. *Graduate:* Tuition of $613 per credit. Cost for noncredit course ranges from $250-$350. Financial aid is available to distance learners.
Registration Students may register by mail, in person.
Contact Robert M. Colley, Director, Marketing Communications and Distance Education, Syracuse University, Independent Study Degree

Programs, 700 University Avenue, Syracuse, NY 13244-2530. *Telephone:* 800-442-0501. *Fax:* 315-443-4174. *E-mail:* suisdp@uc.syr.edu.

DEGREES AND AWARDS

Undergraduate Certificate(s) Library Science (some on-campus requirements)
AA Liberal Arts (some on-campus requirements)
BA Liberal Studies (some on-campus requirements)
MA Advertising Design (certain restrictions apply; some on-campus requirements), Illustration (certain restrictions apply; some on-campus requirements)
MBA Business Administration (some on-campus requirements)
MS Communications Management (some on-campus requirements), Engineering Management (some on-campus requirements), Information Resource Management (some on-campus requirements), Nursing (certain restrictions apply; some on-campus requirements), Telecommunications Network Management (some on-campus requirements)
MSS Social Sciences (some on-campus requirements)

COURSE SUBJECT AREAS OFFERED OUTSIDE OF DEGREE PROGRAMS

Undergraduate: Accounting; anthropology; area, ethnic, and cultural studies; biology; business; business administration and management; business communications; calculus; comparative literature; developmental and child psychology; earth science; economics; English composition; English language and literature; ethics; fine arts; foods and nutrition studies; genetics; geology; history; hospitality services management; international relations; liberal arts, general studies, and humanities; logic; mathematics; philosophy and religion; physics; political science; social psychology; sociology; statistics
Graduate: Accounting; anthropology; business; economics; engineering/industrial management; history; international relations; political science; social sciences; statistics

See full description on page 694.

TACOMA COMMUNITY COLLEGE

Tacoma, Washington
Sciences Division
www.tacoma.ctc.edu/inst_dept/distancelearning/

Tacoma Community College, founded in 1965, is a state-supported, two-year college. It is accredited by the Northwest Association of Schools and Colleges. It first offered distance learning courses in 1980. In 1999–2000, it offered 88 courses at a distance. In fall 1999, there were 140 students enrolled in distance learning courses.
Course delivery sites Courses are delivered to your home, your workplace, military bases, high schools, 2 off-campus centers in Gig Harbor, Tacoma.
Media Courses are delivered via television, videotapes, videoconferencing, interactive television, computer software, computer conferencing, World Wide Web, e-mail, print. Students and teachers may meet in person or interact via videoconferencing, audioconferencing, mail, telephone, fax, e-mail, interactive television, World Wide Web. The following equipment may be required: television, videocassette player, computer, modem, Internet access, e-mail.
Restrictions Programs are available worldwide. Enrollment is open to anyone.
Services Distance learners have access to library services, the campus computer network, e-mail services, bookstore at a distance.
Credit-earning options Students may transfer credits from another institution or may earn credits through examinations, military training.

Typical costs Tuition of $258 per course plus mandatory fees of $40 per course for in-state residents. Tuition of $999 per course plus mandatory fees of $40 per course for out-of-state residents. Financial aid is available to distance learners.
Registration Students may register by mail, fax, telephone, World Wide Web, in person.
Contact Teresita Hartwell, Associate Dean for Distance Learning, Tacoma Community College, 6501 South 19th Street, Tacoma, WA 98466. *Telephone:* 253-566-6005. *Fax:* 253-566-5398. *E-mail:* thartwel@tcc.tacoma.ctc.edu.

DEGREES AND AWARDS

Distance programs offered do not lead to a degree or other formal award.

COURSE SUBJECT AREAS OFFERED OUTSIDE OF DEGREE PROGRAMS

Undergraduate: Abnormal psychology; anthropology; biology; English language and literature; European languages and literatures; geography; geology; history; liberal arts, general studies, and humanities; philosophy and religion; psychology; social psychology; sociology

---

TALLAHASSEE COMMUNITY COLLEGE

Tallahassee, Florida
Extended Studies Division

Tallahassee Community College, founded in 1966, is a state and locally supported, two-year college. It is accredited by the Southern Association of Colleges and Schools. It first offered distance learning courses in 1985.
Contact Tallahassee Community College, 444 Appleyard Drive, Tallahassee, FL 32304-2895. *Telephone:* 850-488-9200. *Fax:* 850-921-0563.

See full description on page 676.

TARRANT COUNTY COLLEGE DISTRICT

Fort Worth, Texas
Center for Distance Learning
dl.tccd.net

Tarrant County College District, founded in 1967, is a county-supported, two-year college. It is accredited by the Southern Association of Colleges and Schools. It first offered distance learning courses in 1973. In 1999–2000, it offered 100 courses at a distance. In fall 1999, there were 4,000 students enrolled in distance learning courses.
Course delivery sites Courses are delivered to your home, your workplace, military bases, high schools.
Media Courses are delivered via television, videotapes, audiotapes, computer software, computer conferencing, World Wide Web, e-mail, print. Students and teachers may meet in person or interact via mail, telephone, fax, e-mail. The following equipment may be required: television, videocassette player, computer, Internet access, e-mail.
Restrictions Programs are available worldwide. Enrollment is open to anyone.
Services Distance learners have access to library services, e-mail services at a distance.
Credit-earning options Students may transfer credits from another institution or may earn credits through examinations, military training.
Typical costs Tuition of $26 per semester hour plus mandatory fees of $8 per semester hour for local area residents. Tuition of $38 per semester hour plus mandatory fees of $10 per semester hour for in-state residents.

Tuition of $140 per semester hour for out-of-state residents. Minimum tuition for in-county residents is $100 per semester. Costs may vary. Financial aid is available to distance learners.

Registration Students may register by telephone, World Wide Web, in person.

Contact Kevin Eason, Assistant Director of Distance Learning, Tarrant County College District, 5301 Campus Drive, Fort Worth, TX 76119. *Telephone:* 817-515-4430. *Fax:* 817-515-4400. *E-mail:* keason@tcjc.cc.tx. us.

DEGREES AND AWARDS

AA General Studies (some on-campus requirements)

COURSE SUBJECT AREAS OFFERED OUTSIDE OF DEGREE PROGRAMS

Undergraduate: Accounting; astronomy and astrophysics; biological and life sciences; biology; business; business administration and management; computer and information sciences; creative writing; developmental and child psychology; economics; engineering mechanics; English composition; English language and literature; fine arts; geology; health and physical education/fitness; history; home economics and family studies; liberal arts, general studies, and humanities; mathematics; mechanical engineering; music; philosophy and religion; physical sciences; political science; social psychology; sociology

TAYLOR UNIVERSITY, WORLD WIDE CAMPUS

Fort Wayne, Indiana
World Wide Campus
wwcampus.tayloru.edu

Taylor University, World Wide Campus, founded in 1938, is an independent, religious, two-year college. It is accredited by the North Central Association of Colleges and Schools. In 1999–2000, it offered 75 courses at a distance. In fall 1999, there were 1,247 students enrolled in distance learning courses.

Course delivery sites Courses are delivered to your home, your workplace, military bases, high schools.

Media Courses are delivered via videotapes, audiotapes, computer software, CD-ROM, print. Students and teachers may interact via mail, telephone, e-mail, World Wide Web.

Restrictions Programs are available worldwide. Enrollment is open to anyone.

Services Distance learners have access to library services, e-mail services, academic advising, tutoring, career placement assistance, bookstore at a distance.

Credit-earning options Students may transfer credits from another institution or may earn credits through examinations.

Typical costs Undergraduate tuition ranges between $119 and $169 per credit. Typical cost for a non credit course ranges between $169 and $219 per course. Costs may vary. Financial aid is available to distance learners.

Registration Students may register by mail, fax, telephone, e-mail, World Wide Web, in person.

Contact Kevin Mahaffy, Enrollment Manager, Taylor University, World Wide Campus, Taylor University World Wide Campus, 1025 West Rudisill Boulevard, Fort Wayne, IN 46807-2197. *Telephone:* 800-845-3149. *Fax:* 219-744-8796. *E-mail:* wwcampus@tayloru.edu.

DEGREES AND AWARDS

Undergraduate Certificate(s) Christian Workers, Justice and Ministry (some on-campus requirements)
AA Biblical Studies, General Studies, Justice Administration (some on-campus requirements), Liberal Arts

COURSE SUBJECT AREAS OFFERED OUTSIDE OF DEGREE PROGRAMS

Undergraduate: Abnormal psychology; American (U.S.) history; American literature; anthropology; Bible studies; biology; communications; computer and information sciences; corrections; counseling psychology; criminal justice; educational psychology; English composition; English literature; fine arts; geography; Greek language and literature; health and physical education/fitness; Hebrew language and literature; history; interdisciplinary studies; journalism; logic; mathematics; music; philosophy and religion; physical sciences; psychology; religious studies; social sciences; social work; theological studies

See full descriptions on pages 540 and 696.

TECHNICAL COLLEGE OF THE LOWCOUNTRY

Beaufort, South Carolina
www.tcl-tec-sc-us.org/

Technical College of the Lowcountry, founded in 1972, is a state-supported, two-year college. It is accredited by the Southern Association of Colleges and Schools. It first offered distance learning courses in 1996. In 1999–2000, it offered 70 courses at a distance. In fall 1999, there were 500 students enrolled in distance learning courses.

Course delivery sites Courses are delivered to your home, your workplace, military bases, high schools, 1,500 off-campus centers.

Media Courses are delivered via television, videotapes, World Wide Web. Students and teachers may interact via videoconferencing, mail, telephone, fax, World Wide Web. The following equipment may be required: television, videocassette player, computer, modem, Internet access, e-mail.

Restrictions Programs are available in state for video courses, worldwide for internet courses. Enrollment is open to anyone.

Services Distance learners have access to library services, e-mail services, academic advising, tutoring, career placement assistance at a distance.

Credit-earning options Students may transfer credits from another institution or may earn credits through examinations, portfolio assessment, military training.

Typical costs Tuition of $48 per credit hour for in-state residents. Tuition of $155 per credit hour for out-of-state residents. There is a $10 mandatory registration fee. Cost for a noncredit course varies depending on the course selected. Financial aid is available to distance learners.

Registration Students may register by mail, in person.

Contact Fred Seitz, Director, Technical College of the Lowcountry, Curriculum Development, PO Box 1288, Beaufort, SC 29901. *Telephone:* 843-525-8204. *Fax:* 843-525-8330. *E-mail:* fseitz@tcl.tec.sc.us.

DEGREES AND AWARDS

Distance programs offered do not lead to a degree or other formal award.

COURSE SUBJECT AREAS OFFERED OUTSIDE OF DEGREE PROGRAMS

Undergraduate: Administrative and secretarial services; business administration and management; English composition; English language and literature; environmental science; history; law and legal studies; liberal arts, general studies, and humanities; mathematics; political science; protective services; psychology

TEMPLE BAPTIST SEMINARY

Chattanooga, Tennessee

Distance Education
www.templebaptistseminary.edu

Temple Baptist Seminary, founded in 1948, is an independent, religious, graduate institution. It is accredited by the Transnational Association of Christian Colleges and Schools (candidate). It first offered distance learning courses in 1993. In 1999–2000, it offered 53 courses at a distance. In fall 1999, there were 18 students enrolled in distance learning courses.

Course delivery sites Courses are delivered to your home.

Media Courses are delivered via videotapes, audiotapes, print. Students and teachers may meet in person or interact via mail, telephone, fax, e-mail. The following equipment may be required: television, videocassette player.

Restrictions Programs are available worldwide. Enrollment is open to anyone.

Services Distance learners have access to library services, e-mail services, academic advising, tutoring, career placement assistance, bookstore at a distance.

Credit-earning options Students may transfer credits from another institution or may earn credits through examinations, military training.

Typical costs Tuition of $150 per semester hour plus mandatory fees of $25 per course. Additional fees include $80 for audiotapes and $130 for videotapes.

Registration Students may register by mail, fax, e-mail, in person.

Contact Carlos Casteel, Enrollment Counselor, Temple Baptist Seminary, 1815 Union Avenue, Chattanooga, TN 37404. *Telephone:* 423-493-4221. *Fax:* 423-493-4471. *E-mail:* tbsinfo@templebaptistseminary.edu.

DEGREES AND AWARDS

Undergraduate Certificate(s) Biblical Studies (certain restrictions apply)
MABS Biblical Studies (certain restrictions apply; some on-campus requirements)
MM Church Ministries (certain restrictions apply)
MRE Religious Education (certain restrictions apply; some on-campus requirements)
DMin Ministry Studies (certain restrictions apply; some on-campus requirements)

COURSE SUBJECT AREAS OFFERED OUTSIDE OF DEGREE PROGRAMS

Graduate: Bible studies; counseling psychology; ethics; philosophy and religion; religious studies; teacher education; theological studies
Noncredit: Bible studies; counseling psychology; ethics; philosophy and religion; religious studies; teacher education; theological studies

TEMPLE UNIVERSITY

Philadelphia, Pennsylvania

Online Learning Program
oll.temple.edu/oll

Temple University, founded in 1884, is a state-related university. It is accredited by the Middle States Association of Colleges and Schools. In 1999–2000, it offered 70 courses at a distance. In fall 1999, there were 800 students enrolled in distance learning courses.

Course delivery sites Courses are delivered to your home, your workplace, military bases, off-campus center(s) in Ambler, Fort Washington, Harrisburg.

Media Courses are delivered via videoconferencing, computer software, CD-ROM, computer conferencing, World Wide Web, e-mail. Students and teachers may meet in person or interact via videoconferencing, mail, telephone, fax, e-mail, World Wide Web. The following equipment may be required: computer, modem, Internet access, e-mail.

Restrictions Programs are available worldwide. Enrollment is restricted to individuals meeting certain criteria.

Services Distance learners have access to library services, the campus computer network, e-mail services, academic advising, career placement assistance, bookstore at a distance.

Typical costs *Undergraduate:* Tuition of $234 per credit hour for local area residents. Tuition of $234 per credit hour for in-state residents. Tuition of $368 per credit hour for out-of-state residents. *Graduate:* Tuition of $335 per credit hour for local area residents. Tuition of $335 per credit hour for in-state residents. Tuition of $461 per credit hour for out-of-state residents. There is a $17 mandatory fee for 1-4 credit hours. Costs may vary. Financial aid is available to distance learners.

Registration Students may register by mail, fax, telephone, e-mail, World Wide Web, in person.

Contact Dr. Catherine C. Schifter, Associate Professor and Director of Academic Technology, Temple University, 665 Ritter Annex (004-00), Philadelphia, PA 19122. *Telephone:* 215-204-3943. *Fax:* 215-204-2666. *E-mail:* dist-ed@blue.temple.edu.

DEGREES AND AWARDS

BS Organizational Studies (certain restrictions apply; some on-campus requirements)
MBA e-Commerce (certain restrictions apply; some on-campus requirements)

COURSE SUBJECT AREAS OFFERED OUTSIDE OF DEGREE PROGRAMS

Undergraduate: American studies; curriculum and instruction; educational research; engineering; English language and literature; geology; history; instructional media; journalism; mass media; mathematics; nursing; physics; psychology; radio and television broadcasting; special education; telecommunications; women's studies
Graduate: Accounting; English language and literature; finance; information sciences and systems; marketing; mass media; occupational therapy; physical therapy; radio and television broadcasting; special education; telecommunications

TENNESSEE TECHNOLOGICAL UNIVERSITY

Cookeville, Tennessee

Extended Education
www.tntech.edu/www/acad/extend/

Tennessee Technological University, founded in 1915, is a state-supported university. It is accredited by the Southern Association of Colleges and Schools. It first offered distance learning courses in 1985. In 1999–2000, it offered 21 courses at a distance. In fall 1999, there were 217 students enrolled in distance learning courses.

Course delivery sites Courses are delivered to your home, your workplace, high schools, Austin Peay State University (Clarksville), Cleveland State Community College (Cleveland), Motlow State Community College (Lynchburg), Roane State Community College (Harriman), Volunteer State Community College (Gallatin), 9 off-campus centers in Byrdstown, Celina, Clarkrange, Gainesboro, Hermitage Springs, Jamestown, Livingston, McMinnville, Red Boiling Springs.

Media Courses are delivered via television, videotapes, videoconferencing, interactive television, computer software, CD-ROM, World Wide Web. Students and teachers may meet in person or interact via videoconferencing, mail, telephone, fax, e-mail, interactive television, World Wide Web. The following equipment may be required: television, videocassette player, computer, Internet access, e-mail.

Restrictions Programs are available in bordering states. Enrollment is open to anyone.

Services Distance learners have access to library services, the campus computer network, e-mail services, academic advising, career placement assistance, bookstore at a distance.

Credit-earning options Students may transfer credits from another institution or may earn credits through examinations.

Typical costs *Undergraduate:* Tuition of $1010 per semester plus mandatory fees of $185 per semester for in-state residents. Tuition of $2558 per semester plus mandatory fees of $185 per semester for out-of-state residents. *Graduate:* Tuition of $1356 per semester plus mandatory fees of $185 per semester for in-state residents. Tuition of $2558 per semester plus mandatory fees of $185 per semester for out-of-state residents. *Noncredit courses:* $65 per course. Costs may vary. Financial aid is available to distance learners.

Registration Students may register by mail, fax, telephone, World Wide Web, in person.

Contact Susan A. Elkins, Director of Extended Education, Tennessee Technological University, Extended Education, Box 5073, Cookeville, TN 38505. *Telephone:* 931-372-3394. *Fax:* 931-372-3499. *E-mail:* selkins@ tntech.edu.

DEGREES AND AWARDS

Distance programs offered do not lead to a degree or other formal award.

COURSE SUBJECT AREAS OFFERED OUTSIDE OF DEGREE PROGRAMS

Undergraduate: Accounting; curriculum and instruction; English language and literature; philosophy and religion; sociology; teacher education

Graduate: Accounting; curriculum and instruction; education administration; educational psychology; educational research; English language and literature; teacher education

Noncredit: Algebra; chemistry; industrial engineering; public health

See full description on page 676.

TENNESSEE TEMPLE UNIVERSITY

Chattanooga, Tennessee

School of External Studies
www.tntemple.edu

Tennessee Temple University, founded in 1946, is an independent, religious, comprehensive institution. It is accredited by the Accrediting Association of Bible Colleges. It first offered distance learning courses in 1988. In 1999–2000, it offered 70 courses at a distance. In fall 1999, there were 300 students enrolled in distance learning courses.

Course delivery sites Courses are delivered to your home, your workplace.

Media Courses are delivered via videotapes, audiotapes, print. Students and teachers may meet in person or interact via mail, telephone, fax, e-mail.

Restrictions Programs are available worldwide. Enrollment is open to anyone.

Services Distance learners have access to library services, e-mail services, academic advising, tutoring, bookstore at a distance.

Credit-earning options Students may transfer credits from another institution or may earn credits through examinations, military training, business training.

Typical costs Tuition of $75 per credit hour plus mandatory fees of $100 per course. Costs may vary. Financial aid is available to distance learners.

Registration Students may register by mail, fax, telephone, e-mail, World Wide Web, in person.

Contact Dr. William K. Henry, Dean, School of External Studies, Tennessee Temple University, 1815 Union Avenue, Chattanooga, TN 37404. *Telephone:* 423-493-4288. *Fax:* 423-493-4444. *E-mail:* 76554. 125@compuserve.com.

DEGREES AND AWARDS

AA Biblical Studies (certain restrictions apply; some on-campus requirements)
AS Biblical Studies (certain restrictions apply)
BS Biblical Studies (certain restrictions apply)

COURSE SUBJECT AREAS OFFERED OUTSIDE OF DEGREE PROGRAMS

Undergraduate: Biology; creative writing; developmental and child psychology; economics; educational psychology; English composition; English language and literature; family and marriage counseling; history; home economics and family studies; liberal arts, general studies, and humanities; mathematics; Middle Eastern languages and literatures; philosophy and religion; political science; psychology; social sciences; sociology; theological studies

Special note
Tennessee Temple University (TTU) was founded with the intent to provide a strong academic education integrated within the framework of the Bible, which TTU believes is the only source of ultimate truth. In line with this founding purpose, the TTU School of External Studies offers an Associate of Science and a Bachelor of Science degree in biblical studies. The course requirements provide an outstanding theological basis for every student's education, which becomes the cement that holds all of the other building blocks of education together into a unified body of knowledge and wisdom. The courses are offered to anyone from the United States or around the world. TTU works with missionaries on varied schedules. Students also find that TTU's prices fit well into most budgets. Students who have scheduling conflicts at home or work, are disabled or homebound, or are geographically too far away from a college campus and want an outstanding, biblically based, and integrated academic education should call TTU at 800-553-4050 (toll-free) or send an e-mail to ttuinfo@tntenmple.edu.

TERRA STATE COMMUNITY COLLEGE

Fremont, Ohio

Educational Catalyst Center
www.terra.cc.oh.us/

Terra State Community College, founded in 1968, is a state-supported, two-year college. It is accredited by the North Central Association of Colleges and Schools. It first offered distance learning courses in 1996. In 1999–2000, it offered 22 courses at a distance. In fall 1999, there were 167 students enrolled in distance learning courses.

Course delivery sites Courses are delivered to your home, your workplace, high schools.

Media Courses are delivered via videotapes, videoconferencing, audiotapes, computer software, CD-ROM, World Wide Web, e-mail, print. Students and teachers may meet in person or interact via videoconferencing, mail, telephone, fax, e-mail, World Wide Web. The following equipment may be required: television, videocassette player, computer, Internet access, e-mail.

Restrictions Programs are available worldwide, but to date all Distance Education students have resided in Ohio. Enrollment is open to anyone.
Services Distance learners have access to library services, e-mail services at a distance.
Credit-earning options Students may transfer credits from another institution or may earn credits through examinations, portfolio assessment, military training.
Typical costs Tuition of $51 per credit for in-state residents. Tuition of $131 per credit for out-of-state residents. Students pay from $10-$25 per course in mandatory fees. Financial aid is available to distance learners.
Registration Students may register by mail, fax, telephone, World Wide Web, in person.
Contact Theresa L. Eishen, Coordinator, Terra State Community College, 2830 Napoleon Road, Fremont, OH 43420-9670. *Telephone:* 419-334-8400 Ext. 321. *Fax:* 419-334-3667. *E-mail:* teishen@terra.cc.oh.us.

DEGREES AND AWARDS

Distance programs offered do not lead to a degree or other formal award.

COURSE SUBJECT AREAS OFFERED OUTSIDE OF DEGREE PROGRAMS

Undergraduate: Accounting; algebra; business administration and management; computer and information sciences; economics; education; English composition; French language and literature; industrial engineering; liberal arts, general studies, and humanities; mathematics; psychology; sociology; technical writing

TEXAS A&M UNIVERSITY–COMMERCE

Commerce, Texas

Instructional Technology
www.tamu-commerce.edu/ntep

Texas A&M University–Commerce, founded in 1889, is a state-supported university. It is accredited by the Southern Association of Colleges and Schools. It first offered distance learning courses in 1993. In 1999–2000, it offered 80 courses at a distance. In fall 1999, there were 750 students enrolled in distance learning courses.
Course delivery sites Courses are delivered to your home, your workplace, military bases, high schools, Grayson County College (Denison), Northeast Texas Community College (Mount Pleasant), Paris Junior College (Paris), Trinity Valley Community College (Athens), 11 off-campus centers in Alba-Golden, Dallas, Gilmer, Gladewater, Greenville, Harmony, Mesquite, Mount Vernon, Ore City, Rains(Emory), Yantis.
Media Courses are delivered via videotapes, videoconferencing, interactive television, CD-ROM, World Wide Web, e-mail, print. Students and teachers may meet in person or interact via videoconferencing, audioconferencing, mail, telephone, fax, e-mail, interactive television, World Wide Web. The following equipment may be required: television, videocassette player, computer, modem, Internet access, e-mail.
Restrictions Web-based courses are available on a worldwide level. Enrollment is open to anyone.
Services Distance learners have access to library services, the campus computer network, e-mail services, academic advising, career placement assistance, bookstore at a distance.
Credit-earning options Students may transfer credits from another institution or may earn credits through examinations, military training, business training.
Typical costs *Undergraduate:* Tuition of $300 per course for in-state residents. Tuition of $900 per course for out-of-state residents. *Graduate:* Tuition of $400 per course for in-state residents. Tuition of $960 per course for out-of-state residents. *Noncredit courses:* $100 per course. Costs may vary. Financial aid is available to distance learners.

Registration Students may register by mail, fax, telephone, World Wide Web, in person.
Contact Mary W. Hendrix, Director, Instructional Technology and Distance Education, Texas A&M University–Commerce, PO Box 3011, Commerce, TX 75429. *Telephone:* 903-886-5511. *Fax:* 903-886-5991. *E-mail:* mary_hendrix@tamu-commerce.edu.

DEGREES AND AWARDS

MBA Business Administration

COURSE SUBJECT AREAS OFFERED OUTSIDE OF DEGREE PROGRAMS

Undergraduate: Cognitive psychology; creative writing; developmental and child psychology; economics; education; education administration; educational psychology; English composition; history; journalism; library and information studies; physics; political science; radio and television broadcasting; social work; sociology; special education; teacher education
Graduate: Accounting; business; chemistry; cognitive psychology; education administration; educational psychology; engineering/industrial management; English literature; finance; human resources management; library and information studies; marketing; physics; radio and television broadcasting; special education; teacher education
Noncredit: Education administration; educational psychology; health professions and related sciences; library and information studies; nursing; public health; special education; teacher education

TEXAS A&M UNIVERSITY–KINGSVILLE

Kingsville, Texas

Center for Distance Learning and Continuing Education
www.tamuk.edu/

Texas A&M University–Kingsville, founded in 1925, is a state-supported university. It is accredited by the Southern Association of Colleges and Schools. In 1999–2000, it offered 15 courses at a distance. In fall 1999, there were 561 students enrolled in distance learning courses.
Course delivery sites Courses are delivered to your home, your workplace, military bases, high schools, Tarleton State University (Stephenville), Texas A&M University (College Station), West Texas A&M University (Canyon), 3 off-campus centers in Alice, Falfurrias, Pleasanton.
Media Courses are delivered via television, videoconferencing, interactive television, computer software, computer conferencing, World Wide Web, e-mail, print. Students and teachers may meet in person or interact via videoconferencing, mail, telephone, fax, e-mail, interactive television, World Wide Web. The following equipment may be required: computer, modem, Internet access, e-mail.
Restrictions Programs are available to in-state students only. Enrollment is open to anyone.
Services Distance learners have access to library services, the campus computer network, e-mail services, academic advising, career placement assistance, bookstore at a distance.
Credit-earning options Students may transfer credits from another institution or may earn credits through examinations.
Typical costs *Undergraduate:* Tuition of $120 per credit hour plus mandatory fees of $89 per credit hour for local area residents. Tuition of $120 per credit hour plus mandatory fees of $89 per credit hour for in-state residents. Tuition of $254 per credit hour plus mandatory fees of $89 per credit hour for out-of-state residents. *Graduate:* Tuition of $120 per credit hour plus mandatory fees of $89 per credit hour for local area residents. Tuition of $120 per credit hour plus mandatory fees of $89 per credit hour for in-state residents. Tuition of $254 per credit hour plus mandatory fees of $89 per credit hour for out-of-state residents. Cost for a noncredit course is the same as for credit courses plus an additional $60. Costs may vary. Financial aid is available to distance learners.

Registration Students may register by mail, fax, telephone, e-mail, in person.
Contact Dr. Tadeo Reyna, Distance Learning Director, Texas A&M University–Kingsville, MSC 147, Kingsville, TX 78363. *Telephone:* 361-593-2861. *Fax:* 361-593-2859. *E-mail:* t-reyna@tamuk.edu.

DEGREES AND AWARDS

MA Educational Administration, Supervision

TEXAS A&M UNIVERSITY–TEXARKANA

Texarkana, Texas
www.tamut.edu

Texas A&M University–Texarkana, founded in 1971, is a state-supported, upper-level institution. It is accredited by the Southern Association of Colleges and Schools. In 1999–2000, it offered 20 courses at a distance.
Course delivery sites Courses are delivered to your home, Northeast Texas Community College (Mount Pleasant), 1 off-campus center in Jefferson.
Media Courses are delivered via interactive television, World Wide Web. Students and teachers may interact via mail, fax, e-mail, interactive television, World Wide Web. The following equipment may be required: computer, modem, Internet access, e-mail.
Restrictions Programs are available to in-state students only. Enrollment is open to anyone.
Services Distance learners have access to academic advising, career placement assistance at a distance.
Credit-earning options Students may transfer credits from another institution or may earn credits through portfolio assessment, military training, business training.
Typical costs Financial aid is available to distance learners.
Registration Students may register by mail, fax, e-mail, World Wide Web, in person.
Contact Mrs. Patricia Black, Director of Admissions and Registrar, Texas A&M University–Texarkana, PO Box 5518, Texarkana, TX 75503-6518. *Telephone:* 903-223-3069. *Fax:* 903-223-3140. *E-mail:* pat.black@tamut.edu.

DEGREES AND AWARDS

Distance programs offered do not lead to a degree or other formal award.

COURSE SUBJECT AREAS OFFERED OUTSIDE OF DEGREE PROGRAMS

Undergraduate: Business administration and management; business communications; English literature; marketing; teacher education; technical writing
Graduate: English literature

TEXAS CHRISTIAN UNIVERSITY

Fort Worth, Texas
TCUglobalcenter
www.tcuglobal.edu

Texas Christian University, founded in 1873, is an independent, religious university affiliated with the Christian Church (Disciples of Christ). It is accredited by the Association of Theological Schools in the United States and Canada, Southern Association of Colleges and Schools. It first offered distance learning courses in 1999. In 1999–2000, it offered 12 courses at a distance. In fall 1999, there were 8 students enrolled in distance learning courses.

Course delivery sites Courses are delivered to your home, your workplace, military bases.
Media Courses are delivered via computer software, computer conferencing, World Wide Web, e-mail. Students and teachers may interact via mail, telephone, e-mail, World Wide Web. The following equipment may be required: computer, modem, Internet access, e-mail.
Restrictions Programs are available worldwide. Enrollment is restricted to individuals meeting certain criteria.
Services Distance learners have access to library services, the campus computer network, e-mail services, academic advising, bookstore at a distance.
Typical costs Tuition of $385 per credit plus mandatory fees of $150 per course. Costs may vary. Financial aid is available to distance learners.
Registration Students may register by mail, e-mail, World Wide Web, in person.
Contact Dr. H. Kirk Downey, Associate Provost, Texas Christian University, 13600 Heritage Parkway, Suite 100, Fort Worth, TX 76177. *Telephone:* 817-257-7525. *Fax:* 817-257-7564. *E-mail:* k.downey@tcu.edu.

eCollege.com *www.ecollege.com/scholarships*

DEGREES AND AWARDS

MLA Liberal Arts
MS Nursing

COURSE SUBJECT AREAS OFFERED OUTSIDE OF DEGREE PROGRAMS

Undergraduate: American (U.S.) history; art history and criticism; biology; business; drama and theater; education; English language and literature; geology; mathematics; nursing; political science; psychology
See full description on page 698.

TEXAS STATE TECHNICAL COLLEGE

Sweetwater, Texas
www.tstc.edu

Texas State Technical College, founded in 1970, is a state-supported, two-year college. It is accredited by the Southern Association of Colleges and Schools. In 1999–2000, it offered 93 courses at a distance. In fall 1999, there were 150 students enrolled in distance learning courses.
Course delivery sites Courses are delivered to military bases, high schools, Northern New Mexico Community College (Española, NM), TSTC Brownwood Community College (Brownwoods, Afghanistan), Vernon Regional Junior College (Vernon), 7 off-campus centers in Abilene, Breckenridge, El Paso.
Media Courses are delivered via videoconferencing, interactive television, World Wide Web. Students and teachers may meet in person or interact via audioconferencing, mail, telephone, fax, e-mail, interactive television. The following equipment may be required: computer, Internet access.
Restrictions Programs are available to in-state students only. Enrollment is restricted to individuals meeting certain criteria.
Services Distance learners have access to library services, the campus computer network, e-mail services, academic advising, career placement assistance, bookstore at a distance.
Credit-earning options Students may transfer credits from another institution or may earn credits through examinations, military training.
Typical costs Tuition of $28 per credit hour plus mandatory fees of $45 per credit hour for local area residents. Tuition of $28 per credit hour plus mandatory fees of $45 per credit hour for in-state residents. Tuition of $90

per credit hour plus mandatory fees of $45 per credit hour for out-of-state residents. *Noncredit courses:* $100 per course.

Registration Students may register by mail, fax, telephone, in person.

Contact Ken Woods, Director of Distance Learning, Texas State Technical College, 300 College Drive, Sweetwater, TX 79556. *Telephone:* 915-235-7326. *Fax:* 915-235-7309. *E-mail:* ken.woods@sweetwater.tstc.edu.

DEGREES AND AWARDS

Distance programs offered do not lead to a degree or other formal award.

COURSE SUBJECT AREAS OFFERED OUTSIDE OF DEGREE PROGRAMS

Undergraduate: Algebra; chemistry; computer and information sciences; computer programming; database management; engineering; information sciences and systems; mathematics; nursing; psychology; technical writing

TEXAS STATE TECHNICAL COLLEGE–HARLINGEN

Harlingen, Texas

Distance Learning
www.harlingen.tstc.edu

Texas State Technical College–Harlingen, founded in 1967, is a state-supported, two-year college. It is accredited by the Southern Association of Colleges and Schools. In 1999–2000, it offered 5 courses at a distance. In fall 1999, there were 134 students enrolled in distance learning courses.

Course delivery sites Courses are delivered to your home, high schools.

Media Courses are delivered via videoconferencing, interactive television, computer software, CD-ROM, computer conferencing, World Wide Web, e-mail, print. Students and teachers may meet in person or interact via videoconferencing, mail, fax, e-mail, interactive television, World Wide Web. The following equipment may be required: computer, modem, Internet access, e-mail.

Restrictions Programs are available to local area students. Enrollment is open to anyone.

Services Distance learners have access to library services, the campus computer network, e-mail services, academic advising at a distance.

Credit-earning options Students may transfer credits from another institution or may earn credits through military training.

Typical costs Tuition of $24 per credit hour plus mandatory fees of $42.25 per credit hour for local area residents. Tuition of $24 per credit hour plus mandatory fees of $42.25 per credit hour for in-state residents. Tuition of $90 per credit hour plus mandatory fees of $42.25 per credit hour for out-of-state residents. Cost for a noncredit course is $2 per contact hour depending on course. Financial aid is available to distance learners.

Registration Students may register by in person.

Contact Robert Serrano, Director, Distance Learning, Texas State Technical College–Harlingen, 1901 North Loop 499, Harlingen, TX 78550-3697. *Telephone:* 956-364-4950. *Fax:* 956-364-5154. *E-mail:* robert.serrano@harlingen.tstc.edu.

DEGREES AND AWARDS

Distance programs offered do not lead to a degree or other formal award.

COURSE SUBJECT AREAS OFFERED OUTSIDE OF DEGREE PROGRAMS

Undergraduate: American Government and Politics; anatomy; computer and information sciences; economics; instructional media; physiology; sociology

TEXAS TECH UNIVERSITY

Lubbock, Texas

Extended Studies
www.dce.ttu.edu

Texas Tech University, founded in 1923, is a state-supported university. It is accredited by the Southern Association of Colleges and Schools. It first offered distance learning courses in 1927. In 1999–2000, it offered 91 courses at a distance. In fall 1999, there were 3,066 students enrolled in distance learning courses.

Course delivery sites Courses are delivered to your home, your workplace, military bases, Abilene Christian University (Abilene), Amarillo College (Amarillo), Angelo State University (San Angelo), Northern New Mexico Community College (Española, NM), South Plains College (Levelland), Texas State Technical College (Sweetwater), Texas State Technical College–Waco Campus (Waco), University of Houston (Houston), University of Texas at Tyler (Tyler), Vernon Regional Junior College (Vernon), West Texas A&M University (Canyon), 1 off-campus center in Junction Campus.

Media Courses are delivered via videotapes, videoconferencing, audiotapes, computer software, computer conferencing, World Wide Web, e-mail, print. Students and teachers may interact via videoconferencing, audioconferencing, mail, telephone, fax, e-mail, World Wide Web. The following equipment may be required: television, videocassette player, computer, modem, Internet access, e-mail.

Restrictions Programs are available worldwide. Enrollment is open to anyone.

Services Distance learners have access to library services, the campus computer network, e-mail services, academic advising, tutoring, bookstore at a distance.

Credit-earning options Students may transfer credits from another institution.

Typical costs *Undergraduate:* Tuition of $63 per hour plus mandatory fees of $25 per course. *Graduate:* Tuition of $63 per hour plus mandatory fees of $25 per course. *Noncredit courses:* $180 per course. Costs may vary. Financial aid is available to distance learners.

Registration Students may register by mail, fax, telephone, e-mail, World Wide Web, in person.

Contact Ariel Fernández, Distance Learning College Advisor, Texas Tech University, Extended Studies, 6901 Quaker Avenue, Lubbock, TX 79413. *Telephone:* 806-742-7200 Ext. 249. *Fax:* 806-742-7222. *E-mail:* distlearn@ttu.edu.

DEGREES AND AWARDS

BBA Business Administration
BGS General Studies

COURSE SUBJECT AREAS OFFERED OUTSIDE OF DEGREE PROGRAMS

Undergraduate: Accounting; agricultural economics; agriculture; algebra; American (U.S.) history; American literature; anthropology; botany; business administration and management; business law; calculus; computer and information sciences; creative writing; developmental and child psychology; economics; educational psychology; engineering; English composition; English language and literature; English literature; ethics; European history; finance; foods and nutrition studies; history; individual and family development studies; information sciences and systems; instructional media; journalism; liberal arts, general studies, and humanities; marketing; mathematics; music; philosophy and religion; plant sciences; political science; public relations; radio and television broadcasting; social psychology; sociology; Spanish language and literature; teacher education; technical writing; telecommunications

Graduate: Computer programming; curriculum and instruction; database management; educational psychology; engineering; instructional media

Noncredit: Agricultural economics; algebra; American (U.S.) history; American literature; anthropology; architecture; business; business law; calculus; engineering; English literature; ethics; European history; finance; foods and nutrition studies; individual and family development studies; information sciences and systems; instructional media; marketing; plant sciences; public relations; real estate; Spanish language and literature; teacher education; technical writing; telecommunications

See full descriptions on pages 700 and 822.

TEXAS WESLEYAN UNIVERSITY

Fort Worth, Texas

Distance Learning Master of Education Degree Program
www.txwesleyan.edu

Texas Wesleyan University, founded in 1890, is an independent, religious, comprehensive institution. It is accredited by the Southern Association of Colleges and Schools. It first offered distance learning courses in 1996. In 1999–2000, it offered 25 courses at a distance. In fall 1999, there were 100 students enrolled in distance learning courses.

Course delivery sites Courses are delivered to your home, your workplace.

Media Courses are delivered via videotapes, audiotapes, e-mail, print. Students and teachers may meet in person or interact via audioconferencing, mail, telephone, fax, e-mail. The following equipment may be required: videocassette player.

Restrictions Courses are mainly statewide with limited activity outside of Texas. Enrollment is open to anyone.

Services Distance learners have access to library services, e-mail services, academic advising, tutoring, career placement assistance at a distance.

Credit-earning options Students may transfer credits from another institution.

Typical costs Tuition of $200 per credit hour plus mandatory fees of $75 per course. Financial aid is available to distance learners.

Registration Students may register by mail, fax, telephone, e-mail, in person.

Contact Dr. Joy Edwards, Program Director, Texas Wesleyan University, 1201 Wesleyan Street, Fort Worth, TX 76105-1536. *Telephone:* 800-604-6088. *Fax:* 817-531-4204. *E-mail:* edwardsj@txwes.edu.

DEGREES AND AWARDS

MEd Education

TEXAS WOMAN'S UNIVERSITY

Denton, Texas
www.dl.twu.edu

Texas Woman's University, founded in 1901, is a state-supported university. It is accredited by the Southern Association of Colleges and Schools. It first offered distance learning courses in 1994.

Contact Texas Woman's University, Denton, TX 76204. *Telephone:* 940-898-2000. *Fax:* 940-898-3198.

See full description on page 676.

THE COMMUNITY COLLEGE OF BALTIMORE COUNTY–CATONSVILLE CAMPUS

Catonsville, Maryland

Educational Communications and Technology (ECT)
www.cat.cc.md.us/ect

The Community College of Baltimore County–Catonsville Campus, founded in 1957, is a county-supported, two-year college. It is accredited by the Middle States Association of Colleges and Schools. It first offered distance learning courses in 1972.

Contact The Community College of Baltimore County–Catonsville Campus, 800 South Rolling Road, Catonsville, MD 21228-5381. *Telephone:* 410-455-6050. *Fax:* 410-719-6546.

See full description on page 676.

THOMAS EDISON STATE COLLEGE

Trenton, New Jersey

DIAL–Distance and Independent Adult Learning
www.tesc.edu

Thomas Edison State College, founded in 1972, is a state-supported, comprehensive institution. It is accredited by the Middle States Association of Colleges and Schools. It first offered distance learning courses in 1972. In 1999–2000, it offered 141 courses at a distance.

Course delivery sites Courses are delivered to your home, your workplace, military bases.

Media Courses are delivered via videotapes, audiotapes, computer software, World Wide Web, e-mail, print. Students and teachers may interact via mail, telephone, fax, e-mail. The following equipment may be required: television, videocassette player, computer, Internet access, e-mail.

Restrictions Programs are available worldwide. Enrollment is open to anyone.

Services Distance learners have access to the campus computer network, e-mail services, academic advising, bookstore at a distance.

Credit-earning options Students may transfer credits from another institution or may earn credits through examinations, portfolio assessment, military training, business training.

Typical costs *Undergraduate:* Tuition of $72 per credit plus mandatory fees of $640 per year for in-state residents. Tuition of $107 per credit plus mandatory fees of $1095 per year for out-of-state residents. *Graduate:* Tuition of $298 per credit for in-state residents. Tuition of $298 per credit for out-of-state residents. Undergraduate students may also chose the Comprehensive Tuition Plan which includes unlimited tests, portfolios, and courses for $2400 in-state, or $3400 out-of-state. Financial aid is available to distance learners.

Registration Students may register by mail, fax, telephone, e-mail, World Wide Web, in person.

Contact Gordon Holly, Director of Admissions, Thomas Edison State College, Office of Admissions, 101 West State Street, Trenton, NJ 08608-1176. *Telephone:* 609-984-1150. *Fax:* 609-984-8447. *E-mail:* info@tesc.edu.

eCollege.com *www.ecollege.com/scholarships*

DEGREES AND AWARDS

AA Arts
ASAST Computer Science Technology Computer Science Technology
ASM Finance, General Management, Human Resource Management, Marketing, Small Business Management/Entrepreneurship

ASNSM Computer Science
BA Communications, History, Humanities, Liberal Studies, Natural Sciences/Mathematics, Psychology, Social Sciences/History
BS Mental Health and Rehabilitative Services
BSBA General Management, Human Resources Management, Marketing
MSM Management Management (some on-campus requirements)

COURSE SUBJECT AREAS OFFERED OUTSIDE OF DEGREE PROGRAMS

Undergraduate: Accounting; African-American studies; American (U.S.) history; anthropology; archaeology; art history and criticism; Asian studies; astronomy and astrophysics; biology; business; business communications; business law; chemistry; computer and information sciences; developmental and child psychology; earth science; electronics; English composition; English language and literature; environmental science; ethics; European languages and literatures; family and marriage counseling; film studies; finance; geology; history; liberal arts, general studies, and humanities; marketing; medieval/renaissance studies; organizational behavior studies; philosophy and religion; photography; physics; religious studies; social psychology; sociology; Spanish language and literature; women's studies
Graduate: Business administration and management

See full description on page 702.

THOMAS NELSON COMMUNITY COLLEGE

Hampton, Virginia
Instructional Services
www.tncc.cc.va.us

Thomas Nelson Community College, founded in 1968, is a state-supported, two-year college. It is accredited by the Southern Association of Colleges and Schools. It first offered distance learning courses in 1983. In 1999–2000, it offered 35 courses at a distance. In fall 1999, there were 425 students enrolled in distance learning courses.
Course delivery sites Courses are delivered to your home.
Media Courses are delivered via television, videotapes, computer software, World Wide Web. Students and teachers may meet in person or interact via mail, telephone, fax, e-mail, interactive television, World Wide Web. The following equipment may be required: computer, Internet access.
Restrictions Programs are available to local area students. Enrollment is open to anyone.
Services Distance learners have access to library services, e-mail services, tutoring, bookstore at a distance.
Credit-earning options Students may transfer credits from another institution or may earn credits through examinations, military training, business training.
Typical costs Tuition of $37.12 per credit plus mandatory fees of $1.50 per credit for in-state residents. Tuition of $169 per credit plus mandatory fees of $1.50 per credit for out-of-state residents. Financial aid is available to distance learners.
Registration Students may register by in person.
Contact Michael Bruno, Director, Instructional Services, Thomas Nelson Community College, 161C John Jefferson Square, Williamsburg, VA 23185. *Telephone:* 757-253-4300. *Fax:* 757-253-4335. *E-mail:* brunom@tncc.cc.va.us.

DEGREES AND AWARDS

Distance programs offered do not lead to a degree or other formal award.

COURSE SUBJECT AREAS OFFERED OUTSIDE OF DEGREE PROGRAMS

Undergraduate: Computer and information sciences; history; information sciences and systems; mathematics; public health; social psychology; sociology

TIDEWATER COMMUNITY COLLEGE

Norfolk, Virginia
www.tc.cc.va.us/dl

Tidewater Community College, founded in 1968, is a state-supported, two-year college. It is accredited by the Southern Association of Colleges and Schools. It first offered distance learning courses in 1975. In 1999–2000, it offered 32 courses at a distance. In fall 1999, there were 1,092 students enrolled in distance learning courses.
Course delivery sites Courses are delivered to your home, your workplace, military bases.
Media Courses are delivered via television, videotapes, videoconferencing, interactive television, computer software, CD-ROM, computer conferencing, World Wide Web, e-mail. Students and teachers may meet in person or interact via audioconferencing, mail, telephone, fax, e-mail, interactive television, World Wide Web. The following equipment may be required: television, computer, modem, Internet access, e-mail.
Restrictions Web courses and interactive television courses are available worldwide. Enrollment is open to anyone.
Services Distance learners have access to library services, e-mail services, academic advising, tutoring, career placement assistance at a distance.
Credit-earning options Students may transfer credits from another institution or may earn credits through examinations, portfolio assessment, military training.
Typical costs Tuition of $37 per credit hour plus mandatory fees of $7 per credit hour for in-state residents. Tuition of $165 per credit hour plus mandatory fees of $7 per credit hour for out-of-state residents. Costs may vary. Financial aid is available to distance learners.
Registration Students may register by mail, telephone, in person.
Contact Felicia Jones, Coordinator, Distance Learning, Tidewater Community College, 1700 College Crescent, Virginia Beach, VA 23456. *Telephone:* 757-822-7271. *Fax:* 757-427-1338. *E-mail:* tcjonef@tc.cc.va.us.

DEGREES AND AWARDS

Distance programs offered do not lead to a degree or other formal award.

COURSE SUBJECT AREAS OFFERED OUTSIDE OF DEGREE PROGRAMS

Undergraduate: Accounting; astronomy and astrophysics; economics; English composition; health professions and related sciences; history; liberal arts, general studies, and humanities; political science; psychology; sociology

TIFFIN UNIVERSITY

Tiffin, Ohio
School of Off-Campus Learning
tiffin-global.org

Tiffin University, founded in 1888, is an independent, nonprofit, comprehensive institution. It is accredited by the North Central Association of Colleges and Schools.

Course delivery sites Courses are delivered to your home, your workplace, military bases.

Media Courses are delivered via World Wide Web. Students and teachers may meet in person or interact via mail, telephone, fax, e-mail, interactive television, World Wide Web. The following equipment may be required: computer, modem, Internet access, e-mail.

Restrictions Programs are available worldwide. Enrollment is restricted to individuals meeting certain criteria.

Services Distance learners have access to library services, e-mail services, academic advising, career placement assistance, bookstore at a distance.

Credit-earning options Students may transfer credits from another institution.

Typical costs Tuition of $825 per course. Financial aid is available to distance learners.

Registration Students may register by mail, fax, telephone, e-mail, World Wide Web, in person.

Contact Dr. Charles R. Christensen, Coordinator for Online Education, Tiffin University, 155 Miami Street, Tiffin, OH 44883-2161. *Telephone:* 419-448-3268. *Fax:* 419-448-3268. *E-mail:* christensenc@tiffin.edu.

eCollege www.ecollege.com/scholarships
.com

DEGREES AND AWARDS

MBA Business Administration (certain restrictions apply; some on-campus requirements)

TOMPKINS CORTLAND COMMUNITY COLLEGE

Dryden, New York

Instructional and Learning Resources

Tompkins Cortland Community College, founded in 1968, is a state and locally supported, two-year college. It is accredited by the Middle States Association of Colleges and Schools. It first offered distance learning courses in 1997. In fall 1999, there were 200 students enrolled in distance learning courses.

Course delivery sites Courses are delivered to your home, your workplace, 2 off-campus centers in Cortland, Ithaca.

Media Courses are delivered via World Wide Web. Students and teachers may interact via e-mail, World Wide Web. The following equipment may be required: computer, modem, Internet access.

Restrictions Programs are available worldwide. Enrollment is open to anyone.

Services Distance learners have access to library services, academic advising, tutoring, career placement assistance, bookstore at a distance.

Credit-earning options Students may transfer credits from another institution or may earn credits through military training.

Typical costs Tuition of $100 per credit for in-state residents. Tuition of $200 per credit for out-of-state residents. *Noncredit courses:* $99 per course. Financial aid is available to distance learners.

Registration Students may register by mail, fax, in person.

Contact Bob Yavits, Instructional Software Specialist, Tompkins Cortland Community College, 170 North Street, PO Box 139, Dryden, NY 13053-0139. *Telephone:* 607-844-8211 Ext. 4357. *Fax:* 607-844-9665. *E-mail:* yavitsr@sunytccc.edu.

DEGREES AND AWARDS

AD Chemical Dependency Studies Counseling (service area differs from that of the overall institution), Hotel and Restaurant Management, Paralegal Studies

COURSE SUBJECT AREAS OFFERED OUTSIDE OF DEGREE PROGRAMS

Undergraduate: Accounting; business administration and management; business communications; business law; communications; criminal justice; criminology; English composition; hospitality services management; information sciences and systems; international business; law and legal studies; marketing; psychology; social psychology; social sciences; sociology; substance abuse counseling; technical writing

See full description on page 704.

TOURO INTERNATIONAL UNIVERSITY

Los Alamitos, California
www.tourou.edu

Touro International University is an independent, nonprofit, comprehensive institution. It is accredited by the Middle States Association of Colleges and Schools. In 1999–2000, it offered 40 courses at a distance. In fall 1999, there were 350 students enrolled in distance learning courses.

Course delivery sites Courses are delivered to your home, your workplace, military bases, high schools.

Media Courses are delivered via videoconferencing, interactive television, computer software, CD-ROM, computer conferencing, World Wide Web, e-mail. Students and teachers may meet in person or interact via videoconferencing, mail, telephone, fax, e-mail, World Wide Web. The following equipment may be required: computer, modem, Internet access.

Restrictions Programs are available worldwide. Enrollment is open to anyone.

Services Distance learners have access to library services, the campus computer network, e-mail services, academic advising at a distance.

Credit-earning options Students may transfer credits from another institution.

Typical costs *Undergraduate:* Tuition of $400 per unit. *Graduate:* Tuition of $500 per unit. Tuition for the PhD degree is $600 per unit. Financial aid is available to distance learners.

Registration Students may register by mail, fax, telephone, e-mail, World Wide Web, in person.

Contact Wei Ren, Registrar, Touro International University, 10542 Calle Lee, Suite 102, Los Alamitos, CA 90720. *Telephone:* 714-816-0366. *Fax:* 714-816-0367. *E-mail:* info@touiou.edu.

DEGREES AND AWARDS

Undergraduate Certificate(s) e-Commerce

BA e-Commerce, Finance, Information Technology, Internal Auditing, International Business, Tourism and Hospitality Management

BHS Health Education, Healthcare Management, Professional Degree Completion

BS e-Commerce, Finance, Information Technology, Internal Auditing, International Business, Tourism and Hospitality Management

MBA e-Commerce, Information Technology Management, International Business

MSHA Forensic Examination, Healthcare Management, International Health

PhD Business Administration, Health Sciences

COURSE SUBJECT AREAS OFFERED OUTSIDE OF DEGREE PROGRAMS

Undergraduate: Accounting; business; business administration and management; business communications; environmental health; finance; health services administration; hospitality services management; international business; marketing; occupational therapy

Graduate: Accounting; business; business administration and management; community health services; finance; health services administration; international business; marketing; occupational therapy; organizational behavior studies; physical therapy
Noncredit: Business
See full description on page 706.

TRIDENT TECHNICAL COLLEGE

Charleston, South Carolina

Trident Technical College, founded in 1964, is a state and locally supported, two-year college. It is accredited by the Southern Association of Colleges and Schools.
Contact Trident Technical College, PO Box 118067, Charleston, SC 29423-8067. *Telephone:* 843-574-6111. *Fax:* 843-574-6109.
See full description on page 676.

TRINITY COLLEGE OF VERMONT

Burlington, Vermont

Program in Community Mental Health (PCMH)
www.trinityvt.edu/apcmh

Trinity College of Vermont, founded in 1925, is an independent, religious, comprehensive institution. It is accredited by the New England Association of Schools and Colleges. It first offered distance learning courses in 1995. In 1999–2000, it offered 20 courses at a distance. In fall 1999, there were 100 students enrolled in distance learning courses.
Course delivery sites Courses are delivered to 5 off-campus centers in Burlington, Anchorage (AK), Baltimore (MD), Milwaukee (WI), Providence (RI).
Media Courses are delivered via World Wide Web, e-mail, print. Students and teachers may meet in person or interact via mail, telephone, fax, e-mail, World Wide Web. The following equipment may be required: computer, Internet access, e-mail.
Restrictions Programs are available in a large (multi-state) geographical area surrounding local learning sites, and some courses are available worldwide through the Internet. Enrollment is restricted to individuals meeting certain criteria.
Services Distance learners have access to library services, the campus computer network, e-mail services, academic advising, career placement assistance, bookstore at a distance.
Credit-earning options Students may transfer credits from another institution.
Typical costs Tuition of $240 per credit for local area residents. Tuition of $285 per credit for in-state residents. Costs may vary. Financial aid is available to distance learners.
Registration Students may register by mail, fax, in person.
Contact Susan Maslack, Site Development Coordinator, Trinity College of Vermont, Program in Community Mental Health, 208 Colchester Avenue, Burlington, VT 05401. *Telephone:* 802-846-7306. *Fax:* 802-846-7004. *E-mail:* smaslack@trinityvt.edu.

> **eCollege**.com   *www.ecollege.com/scholarships*

DEGREES AND AWARDS

Graduate Certificate(s) Community Mental Health (service area differs from that of the overall institution)

MS Community Mental Health (service area differs from that of the overall institution)

COURSE SUBJECT AREAS OFFERED OUTSIDE OF DEGREE PROGRAMS

Graduate: Community health services; mental health services; substance abuse counseling

---

TRINITY INTERNATIONAL UNIVERSITY

Deerfield, Illinois

Division of Open Studies
www.tiu.edu

Trinity International University, founded in 1897, is an independent, religious university affiliated with the Evangelical Free Church of America. It is accredited by the Association of Theological Schools in the United States and Canada, North Central Association of Colleges and Schools. It first offered distance learning courses in 1979. In 1999–2000, it offered 38 courses at a distance. In fall 1999, there were 61 students enrolled in distance learning courses.
Course delivery sites Courses are delivered to your home.
Media Courses are delivered via videotapes, audiotapes, print. Students and teachers may meet in person or interact via mail, telephone, e-mail.
Restrictions Programs are available worldwide. Enrollment is open to anyone.
Services Distance learners have access to library services, academic advising, bookstore at a distance.
Credit-earning options Students may transfer credits from another institution or may earn credits through examinations.
Typical costs Tuition of $243 per semester hour.
Registration Students may register by mail, fax, telephone, e-mail, in person.
Contact Division of Open Studies, Trinity International University, 2065 Half Day Road, Deerfield, IL 60015. *Telephone:* 800-588-7705. *Fax:* 847-317-6509. *E-mail:* extension@tiu.edu.

DEGREES AND AWARDS

Distance programs offered do not lead to a degree or other formal award.

COURSE SUBJECT AREAS OFFERED OUTSIDE OF DEGREE PROGRAMS

Graduate: Theological studies

TRITON COLLEGE

River Grove, Illinois

Alternative Learning at Triton
www.triton.cc.il.us/

Triton College, founded in 1964, is a state-supported, two-year college. It is accredited by the North Central Association of Colleges and Schools. It first offered distance learning courses in 1979. In 1999–2000, it offered 57 courses at a distance. In fall 1999, there were 900 students enrolled in distance learning courses.
Course delivery sites Courses are delivered to your home, your workplace.
Media Courses are delivered via television, videotapes, videoconferencing, computer software, World Wide Web, e-mail. Students and teachers may meet in person or interact via videoconferencing, mail, telephone, fax,

e-mail, World Wide Web. The following equipment may be required: television, videocassette player, computer, modem, Internet access, e-mail.
Restrictions Telecourses are available to local students only; Internet courses are available nationwide. Enrollment is open to anyone.
Services Distance learners have access to library services, e-mail services, career placement assistance, bookstore at a distance.
Credit-earning options Students may transfer credits from another institution or may earn credits through examinations, portfolio assessment, military training.
Typical costs Tuition of $43 per credit hour plus mandatory fees of $3.50 per credit hour for local area residents. Tuition of $128.25 per credit hour plus mandatory fees of $3.50 per credit hour for in-state residents. Tuition of $197.31 per credit hour plus mandatory fees of $3.50 per credit hour for out-of-state residents. *Noncredit courses:* $50 per course. Costs may vary. Financial aid is available to distance learners.
Registration Students may register by mail, telephone, World Wide Web, in person.
Contact Gail Fuller, Director of Admissions and Records, Triton College, 2000 Fifth Avenue, River Grove, IL 60171. *Telephone:* 708-456-0300 Ext. 3397. *Fax:* 708-583-3121.

DEGREES AND AWARDS

Distance programs offered do not lead to a degree or other formal award.

COURSE SUBJECT AREAS OFFERED OUTSIDE OF DEGREE PROGRAMS

Undergraduate: Abnormal psychology; accounting; American (U.S.) history; anthropology; art history and criticism; biology; business administration and management; business law; comparative literature; design; developmental and child psychology; drama and theater; economics; educational psychology; electronics; English composition; English language and literature; ethics; health and physical education/fitness; Latin American studies; marketing; mathematics; music; philosophy and religion; political science; psychology; religious studies; social psychology; sociology; Spanish language and literature; statistics
Noncredit: Computer and information sciences

TROY STATE UNIVERSITY

Troy, Alabama

Distance Learning Center
tsulearn.net

Troy State University, founded in 1887, is a state-supported, comprehensive institution. It is accredited by the Southern Association of Colleges and Schools. It first offered distance learning courses in 1993. In 1999–2000, it offered 37 courses at a distance. In fall 1999, there were 212 students enrolled in distance learning courses.
Course delivery sites Courses are delivered to your home, your workplace, military bases, high schools, Troy State University Dothan (Dothan), Troy State University Montgomery (Montgomery).
Media Courses are delivered via television, videotapes, videoconferencing, interactive television, audiotapes, computer software, CD-ROM, computer conferencing, World Wide Web, e-mail, print. Students and teachers may meet in person or interact via videoconferencing, audioconferencing, mail, telephone, fax, e-mail, interactive television, World Wide Web. The following equipment may be required: computer, Internet access, e-mail.
Restrictions Programs are available at TSU sites in Alabama, while Web courses are available worldwide. Enrollment is restricted to individuals meeting certain criteria.

Services Distance learners have access to library services, the campus computer network, e-mail services, academic advising, bookstore at a distance.
Credit-earning options Students may transfer credits from another institution or may earn credits through examinations, portfolio assessment, military training, business training.
Typical costs *Undergraduate:* Tuition of $170 per credit hour. *Graduate:* Tuition of $250 per credit hour. Costs may vary. Financial aid is available to distance learners.
Registration Students may register by mail, fax, World Wide Web, in person.
Contact Student Services, Troy State University, 304 Wallace Hall, Troy, AL 36082. *Telephone:* 334-670-5672. *Fax:* 334-670-5679. *E-mail:* tsulearn@trojan.troyst.edu.

DEGREES AND AWARDS

AA Business, General Education
BAS Resource Management
EMBA Business Administration (certain restrictions apply)
MS Human Resource Management, International Relations, Public Administration
MS/CJA Criminal Justice

COURSE SUBJECT AREAS OFFERED OUTSIDE OF DEGREE PROGRAMS

Undergraduate: Accounting; astronomy and astrophysics; foods and nutrition studies; nursing; physics
Graduate: Business administration and management; educational psychology; educational research; instructional media; nursing
Noncredit: Continuing education
See full descriptions on pages 676 and 710.

TROY STATE UNIVERSITY DOTHAN

Dothan, Alabama

Information Services/Distance Learning
www.tsud.edu/distance

Troy State University Dothan, founded in 1961, is a state-supported, comprehensive institution. It is accredited by the Southern Association of Colleges and Schools. It first offered distance learning courses in 1991. In 1999–2000, it offered 30 courses at a distance. In fall 1999, there were 300 students enrolled in distance learning courses.
Course delivery sites Courses are delivered to your home, your workplace, military bases, Troy State University (Troy).
Media Courses are delivered via television, videotapes, videoconferencing, interactive television, computer conferencing, World Wide Web, e-mail, print. Students and teachers may interact via videoconferencing, mail, telephone, fax, e-mail, interactive television, World Wide Web. The following equipment may be required: television, videocassette player, computer, Internet access, e-mail.
Restrictions Programs are available to local area students. Enrollment is restricted to individuals meeting certain criteria.
Services Distance learners have access to library services at a distance.
Credit-earning options Students may transfer credits from another institution or may earn credits through military training, business training.
Typical costs *Undergraduate:* Tuition of $1380 per semester for local area residents. Tuition of $2820 per semester for in-state residents. Tuition of $2820 per semester for out-of-state residents. *Graduate:* Tuition of $120 per semester hour for local area residents. Tuition of $120 per semester hour for in-state residents. Tuition of $240 per semester hour for

out-of-state residents. Mandatory fees for all students are $3 per semester hour with a $36 maximum. Financial aid is available to distance learners.
Registration Students may register by in person.
Contact Sallie J. Johnson, Associate Director for Distance Learning, Troy State University Dothan. *Telephone:* 334-983-6556 Ext. 326. *Fax:* 334-983-6322. *E-mail:* sjohnson@tsud.edu.

DEGREES AND AWARDS

Distance programs offered do not lead to a degree or other formal award.

COURSE SUBJECT AREAS OFFERED OUTSIDE OF DEGREE PROGRAMS

Undergraduate: Business; business administration and management; database management; economics; English composition; ethics; geology; health and physical education/fitness; history; information sciences and systems; political science; psychology; sociology

TROY STATE UNIVERSITY MONTGOMERY

Montgomery, Alabama
External Degree Program
www.tsum.edu/dl/edp

Troy State University Montgomery, founded in 1965, is a state-supported, comprehensive institution. It is accredited by the Southern Association of Colleges and Schools. It first offered distance learning courses in 1987. In 1999–2000, it offered 100 courses at a distance. In fall 1999, there were 1,100 students enrolled in distance learning courses.
Course delivery sites Courses are delivered to your home, your workplace, military bases.
Media Courses are delivered via television, World Wide Web, e-mail, print. Students and teachers may meet in person or interact via mail, telephone, fax, e-mail. The following equipment may be required: television, computer, Internet access, e-mail.
Restrictions Programs are available worldwide. Enrollment is open to anyone.
Services Distance learners have access to library services, e-mail services, academic advising, tutoring, bookstore at a distance.
Credit-earning options Students may transfer credits from another institution or may earn credits through examinations, portfolio assessment, military training.
Typical costs Tuition of $315 per course for in-state residents. Tuition of $435 per course for out-of-state residents.
Registration Students may register by mail, fax, telephone, e-mail, in person.
Contact Ms. Angela Barrow, Secretary, Distance Learning, Troy State University Montgomery. *Telephone:* 334-241-9553. *Fax:* 334-241-5465. *E-mail:* edp@tsum.edu.

DEGREES AND AWARDS

AS Business Administration, General Education, History, Political Science, Psychology, Social Sciences
BA Business Administration (some on-campus requirements), English (some on-campus requirements), History (some on-campus requirements), Political Science (some on-campus requirements), Professional Studies (some on-campus requirements), Psychology (some on-campus requirements), Social Sciences (some on-campus requirements)
BS Business Administration (some on-campus requirements), English (some on-campus requirements), History (some on-campus requirements), Political Science (some on-campus requirements), Professional Studies (some on-campus requirements), Psychology (some on-campus requirements), Social Sciences (some on-campus requirements)

COURSE SUBJECT AREAS OFFERED OUTSIDE OF DEGREE PROGRAMS

Undergraduate: Accounting; astronomy and astrophysics; biological and life sciences; biology; business; business administration and management; business law; chemistry; child care and development; developmental and child psychology; economics; English composition; English language and literature; European languages and literatures; finance; history; human resources management; liberal arts, general studies, and humanities; marketing; mathematics; organizational behavior studies; philosophy and religion; political science; psychology; social sciences; sociology; Spanish language and literature
See full description on page 676.

TUFTS UNIVERSITY

Medford, Massachusetts
The Fletcher School
fletcher.tufts.edu/gmap/

Tufts University, founded in 1852, is an independent, nonprofit university. It is accredited by the New England Association of Schools and Colleges. In 1999–2000, it offered 8 courses at a distance.
Course delivery sites Courses are delivered to your home, your workplace.
Media Courses are delivered via computer software, CD-ROM, World Wide Web, e-mail, print. Students and teachers may meet in person or interact via e-mail, World Wide Web. The following equipment may be required: computer, Internet access, e-mail.
Restrictions Programs are available worldwide. Enrollment is restricted to individuals meeting certain criteria.
Services Distance learners have access to library services, the campus computer network, e-mail services, academic advising at a distance.
Typical costs Tuition of $42,500 per degree program. Financial aid is available to distance learners.
Registration Students may register by in person.
Contact Marjean Knokey, Manager of Admissions, Tufts University, The Fletcher School of Law and Diplomacy, 160 Packard Avenue, Medford, MA 02155. *Telephone:* 617-627-4524. *Fax:* 617-627-3005. *E-mail:* fletcher_gmap@tufts.edu.

DEGREES AND AWARDS

MA International Affairs (certain restrictions apply; service area differs from that of the overall institution; some on-campus requirements)
See full description on page 712.

TULANE UNIVERSITY

New Orleans, Louisiana
University College
www.tulane.edu/~uc

Tulane University, founded in 1834, is an independent, nonprofit university. It is accredited by the Southern Association of Colleges and Schools. In 1999–2000, it offered 3 courses at a distance. In fall 1999, there were 50 students enrolled in distance learning courses.
Course delivery sites Courses are delivered to your home, your workplace, military bases.

Media Courses are delivered via World Wide Web, e-mail. Students and teachers may meet in person or interact via mail, telephone, e-mail, World Wide Web. The following equipment may be required: computer, modem, Internet access, e-mail.

Restrictions Programs are available worldwide. Enrollment is open to anyone.

Services Distance learners have access to library services, the campus computer network, e-mail services, academic advising, bookstore at a distance.

Credit-earning options Students may transfer credits from another institution.

Typical costs Tuition of $195 per credit plus mandatory fees of $60 per semester. Financial aid is available to distance learners.

Registration Students may register by mail, fax, telephone, in person.

Contact Julia Houston, Director of Media Arts, Tulane University, University College, New Orleans, LA 70118. *Telephone:* 504-862-8000 Ext. 1672. *Fax:* 504-865-5562. *E-mail:* jhousto@mailhost.tcs.tulane.edu.

DEGREES AND AWARDS

Distance programs offered do not lead to a degree or other formal award.

COURSE SUBJECT AREAS OFFERED OUTSIDE OF DEGREE PROGRAMS

Undergraduate: Computer and information sciences; English composition

See full description on page 676.

TULSA COMMUNITY COLLEGE

Tulsa, Oklahoma

Distance Learning Office
www.tulsa.cc.ok.us/dl

Tulsa Community College, founded in 1968, is a state-supported, two-year college. It is accredited by the North Central Association of Colleges and Schools. It first offered distance learning courses in 1979. In 1999–2000, it offered 96 courses at a distance. In fall 1999, there were 1,000 students enrolled in distance learning courses.

Course delivery sites Courses are delivered to your home, your workplace.

Media Courses are delivered via television, videotapes, videoconferencing, interactive television, computer software, CD-ROM, computer conferencing, World Wide Web, e-mail, print. Students and teachers may meet in person or interact via videoconferencing, mail, telephone, fax, e-mail, interactive television, World Wide Web. The following equipment may be required: television, computer, modem, Internet access, e-mail.

Restrictions Programs are available to local area students. Enrollment is open to anyone.

Services Distance learners have access to library services, academic advising, tutoring, career placement assistance at a distance.

Credit-earning options Students may transfer credits from another institution or may earn credits through examinations, military training.

Typical costs Tuition of $43 per credit hour for in-state residents. Tuition of $108.25 per credit hour for out-of-state residents. Costs may vary. Financial aid is available to distance learners.

Registration Students may register by telephone, in person.

Contact Randy Dominguez, Director of Distance Learning, Tulsa Community College, 909 South Boston Avenue, Tulsa, OK 74119-2095. *Telephone:* 918-595-7143. *Fax:* 918-595-7306. *E-mail:* rdomingu@tulsa.cc.ok.us.

DEGREES AND AWARDS

AA Liberal Arts (some on-campus requirements)

COURSE SUBJECT AREAS OFFERED OUTSIDE OF DEGREE PROGRAMS

Undergraduate: Accounting; area, ethnic, and cultural studies; astronomy and astrophysics; business; business administration and management; computer and information sciences; conservation and natural resources; developmental and child psychology; economics; English composition; English language and literature; European languages and literatures; geology; liberal arts, general studies, and humanities; mathematics; political science; social psychology; sociology

See full description on page 676.

TYLER JUNIOR COLLEGE

Tyler, Texas

Learning Resources
www.tyler.cc.tx.us

Tyler Junior College, founded in 1926, is a state and locally supported, two-year college. It is accredited by the Southern Association of Colleges and Schools. It first offered distance learning courses in 1969. In 1999–2000, it offered 45 courses at a distance. In fall 1999, there were 1,100 students enrolled in distance learning courses.

Course delivery sites Courses are delivered to your home, your workplace, high schools, Virtual College of Texas.

Media Courses are delivered via television, videotapes, videoconferencing, interactive television, audiotapes, computer software, CD-ROM, computer conferencing, World Wide Web, e-mail. Students and teachers may meet in person or interact via videoconferencing, mail, telephone, fax, e-mail, interactive television, World Wide Web. The following equipment may be required: television, videocassette player, computer, modem, Internet access, e-mail.

Restrictions Programs are available nationwide. Enrollment is restricted to individuals meeting certain criteria.

Services Distance learners have access to library services, e-mail services, academic advising, tutoring, career placement assistance at a distance.

Credit-earning options Students may transfer credits from another institution or may earn credits through examinations.

Typical costs Undergraduate in-district tuition is $103 for three hours, in-state is $148, and out-of-state is $303. Costs may vary. Financial aid is available to distance learners.

Registration Students may register by telephone, in person.

Contact Janna Chancey, Recruiter, Tyler Junior College, PO Box 9020, Tyler, TX 75711. *Telephone:* 903-510-2396. *Fax:* 903-510-2634. *E-mail:* jcha@tjc.tyler.cc.tx.us.

DEGREES AND AWARDS

Distance programs offered do not lead to a degree or other formal award.

COURSE SUBJECT AREAS OFFERED OUTSIDE OF DEGREE PROGRAMS

Undergraduate: Accounting; algebra; American (U.S.) history; American literature; anatomy; art history and criticism; astronomy and astrophysics; biology; business; business administration and management; business communications; business law; chemistry; comparative literature; computer and information sciences; computer programming; creative writing; database management; design; economics; English composition; English language and literature; English literature; environmental science; health professions and related sciences; history; information sciences and systems; liberal arts, general studies, and humanities; music; paralegal/legal assistant; political science; psychology; sign language; sociology; Spanish language and literature

ULSTER COUNTY COMMUNITY COLLEGE

Stone Ridge, New York
SUNY at Ulster Online Degree Program
www.ulster.cc.ny.us

Ulster County Community College, founded in 1961, is a state and locally supported, two-year college. It is accredited by the Middle States Association of Colleges and Schools. It first offered distance learning courses in 1983. In 1999–2000, it offered 300 courses at a distance. In fall 1999, there were 2,000 students enrolled in distance learning courses.
Course delivery sites Courses are delivered to your home, your workplace, military bases, State University of New York System (Albany), 1 off-campus center in Kingston.
Media Courses are delivered via videotapes, computer software, World Wide Web, e-mail, print. Students and teachers may interact via audioconferencing, telephone, e-mail, interactive television, World Wide Web. The following equipment may be required: computer, modem, Internet access, e-mail.
Restrictions Programs are available worldwide. Enrollment is open to anyone.
Services Distance learners have access to e-mail services, academic advising, career placement assistance, bookstore at a distance.
Credit-earning options Students may transfer credits from another institution or may earn credits through examinations, portfolio assessment, military training, business training.
Typical costs Tuition of $87 per unit for in-state residents. Tuition of $174 per unit for out-of-state residents. Costs may vary. Financial aid is available to distance learners.
Registration Students may register by mail, fax, telephone, e-mail, World Wide Web, in person.
Contact Susan Weatherly, Admissions Recruiter, Ulster County Community College, Stone Ridge, NY 12484. *Telephone:* 800-724-0833 Ext. 5018. *Fax:* 914-687-5090. *E-mail:* weathers@sunyulster.edu.

DEGREES AND AWARDS

AS Liberal Arts

COURSE SUBJECT AREAS OFFERED OUTSIDE OF DEGREE PROGRAMS

Undergraduate: Biological and life sciences; business; computer and information sciences; European languages and literatures; Latin American studies; library and information studies; mathematics; social sciences; Spanish language and literature
See full description on page 714.

UMPQUA COMMUNITY COLLEGE

Roseburg, Oregon
Media Services Department

Umpqua Community College, founded in 1964, is a state and locally supported, two-year college. It is accredited by the Northwest Association of Schools and Colleges. It first offered distance learning courses in 1980. In 1999–2000, it offered 40 courses at a distance. In fall 1999, there were 20 students enrolled in distance learning courses.

Course delivery sites Courses are delivered to your home, your workplace.
Media Courses are delivered via television, videotapes, World Wide Web, print. Students and teachers may meet in person or interact via mail, telephone, e-mail, World Wide Web. The following equipment may be required: television, videocassette player, computer, Internet access, e-mail.
Restrictions Programs are available to local area students. Enrollment is open to anyone.
Services Distance learners have access to library services, bookstore at a distance.
Credit-earning options Students may transfer credits from another institution or may earn credits through examinations, military training, business training.
Typical costs Tuition of $37 per credit for in-state residents. Tuition of $105 per credit for out-of-state residents. Costs may vary. Financial aid is available to distance learners.
Registration Students may register by mail, in person.
Contact Christopher Bingham, Director of Media Services, Umpqua Community College, 1140 College Road, Roseburg, OR 97470. *Telephone:* 541-440-4717. *Fax:* 541-440-4665. *E-mail:* binghac@umpqua.cc.or.us.

DEGREES AND AWARDS

Distance programs offered do not lead to a degree or other formal award.

COURSE SUBJECT AREAS OFFERED OUTSIDE OF DEGREE PROGRAMS

Undergraduate: Archaeology; astronomy and astrophysics; biological and life sciences; business; business administration and management; computer and information sciences; English language and literature; geology; health professions and related sciences; liberal arts, general studies, and humanities; library and information studies; mathematics; music; oceanography; social sciences; sociology

UNION COUNTY COLLEGE

Cranford, New Jersey

Union County College, founded in 1933, is a state and locally supported, two-year college. It is accredited by the Middle States Association of Colleges and Schools.
Contact Union County College, 1033 Springfield Avenue, Cranford, NJ 07016-1528. *Telephone:* 908-709-7000. *Fax:* 908-709-0527.
See full description on page 600.

UNION INSTITUTE

Cincinnati, Ohio
Center for Distance Learning/Graduate College
www.tui.edu

Union Institute, founded in 1969, is an independent, nonprofit university. It is accredited by the North Central Association of Colleges and Schools. It first offered distance learning courses in 1971. In 1999–2000, it offered 180 courses at a distance. In fall 1999, there were 1,288 students enrolled in distance learning courses.
Course delivery sites Courses are delivered to your home.
Media Courses are delivered via World Wide Web, e-mail, print. Students and teachers may meet in person or interact via mail, telephone, fax, e-mail, World Wide Web. The following equipment may be required: computer, modem, Internet access, e-mail.

Restrictions Programs are available worldwide. Enrollment is restricted to individuals meeting certain criteria.

Services Distance learners have access to library services, the campus computer network, e-mail services, academic advising, bookstore at a distance.

Credit-earning options Students may transfer credits from another institution or may earn credits through examinations, portfolio assessment, military training, business training.

Typical costs *Undergraduate:* Tuition of $262 per semester hour. *Graduate:* Tuition of $4300 per semester. Financial aid is available to distance learners.

Registration Students may register by mail, fax, e-mail, World Wide Web, in person.

Contact Mr. Michael Robertson, Associate Registrar for Graduate College, Union Institute, 440 East McMillan Street, Cincinnati, OH 45206. *Telephone:* 800-486-3116. *Fax:* 513-861-3218. *E-mail:* admissions@tui. edu.

DEGREES AND AWARDS

BA Liberal Arts and Sciences (certain restrictions apply; some on-campus requirements)
BS Liberal Arts and Sciences (certain restrictions apply; some on-campus requirements)
PhD Interdisciplinary Studies (some on-campus requirements)

COURSE SUBJECT AREAS OFFERED OUTSIDE OF DEGREE PROGRAMS

Undergraduate: Biological and life sciences; business; communications; computer and information sciences; criminal justice; education; health professions and related sciences; history; liberal arts, general studies, and humanities; mathematics; physical sciences; psychology; public administration and services; social sciences

Graduate: Education; interdisciplinary studies; organizational behavior studies; psychology; public administration and services

See full description on page 716.

UNION UNIVERSITY

Jackson, Tennessee

Union University, founded in 1823, is an independent, religious, comprehensive institution. It is accredited by the Southern Association of Colleges and Schools. In 1999–2000, it offered 10 courses at a distance.

Course delivery sites Courses are delivered to your home, your workplace.

Media Courses are delivered via World Wide Web, e-mail. Students and teachers may meet in person or interact via telephone, fax, e-mail. The following equipment may be required: computer, Internet access, e-mail.

Restrictions Programs are available worldwide. Enrollment is open to anyone.

Services Distance learners have access to library services, bookstore at a distance.

Credit-earning options Students may transfer credits from another institution or may earn credits through examinations, portfolio assessment, military training, business training.

Typical costs *Undergraduate:* Tuition of $405 per semester hour. *Graduate:* Tuition of $320 per semester hour.

Registration Students may register by mail, fax, telephone, e-mail, World Wide Web, in person.

Contact Dr. Wayne Day, Assistant Director of Research, Union University, 1050 Union University Drive, Jackson, TN 38305. *Telephone:* 800-338-6466. *E-mail:* wday@uu.edu.

eCollege.com *www.ecollege.com/scholarships*

DEGREES AND AWARDS

Distance programs offered do not lead to a degree or other formal award.

COURSE SUBJECT AREAS OFFERED OUTSIDE OF DEGREE PROGRAMS

Undergraduate: Physical sciences; psychology; sociology; theological studies
Graduate: Education

UNITED STATES INTERNATIONAL UNIVERSITY

San Diego, California
www.usiuonline.net

United States International University, founded in 1952, is an independent, nonprofit university. It is accredited by the Western Association of Schools and Colleges, Inc. In 1999–2000, it offered 8 courses at a distance. In fall 1999, there were 30 students enrolled in distance learning courses.

Course delivery sites Courses are delivered to your home, your workplace, military bases.

Media Courses are delivered via computer software, computer conferencing, World Wide Web, e-mail, print. Students and teachers may meet in person or interact via mail, telephone, fax, e-mail, World Wide Web. The following equipment may be required: computer, modem, Internet access, e-mail.

Restrictions Programs are available worldwide. Enrollment is restricted to individuals meeting certain criteria.

Services Distance learners have access to library services, the campus computer network, e-mail services, academic advising, career placement assistance, bookstore at a distance.

Credit-earning options Students may transfer credits from another institution.

Typical costs Tuition of $265 per credit. Mandatory fees are $250 per class. Costs may vary. Financial aid is available to distance learners.

Registration Students may register by mail, fax, e-mail, World Wide Web, in person.

Contact Sandra Temores, Academic Adviser, Department of Education, United States International University, 10455 Pomerado Road, San Diego, CA 92131. *Telephone:* 858-635-4507. *Fax:* 858-635-4714. *E-mail:* stemores@usiu.edu.

eCollege.com *www.ecollege.com/scholarships*

DEGREES AND AWARDS

MA Education Technology and Learning (certain restrictions apply)

COURSE SUBJECT AREAS OFFERED OUTSIDE OF DEGREE PROGRAMS

Graduate: Business administration and management; education
See full description on page 718.

UNITED STATES OPEN UNIVERSITY

Wilmington, Delaware
www.open.edu

United States Open University, founded in 1999, is an independent, nonprofit, comprehensive institution. It is accredited by the Middle States Association of Colleges and Schools (candidate). In 1999–2000, it offered 21 courses at a distance. In fall 1999, there were 69 students enrolled in distance learning courses.

Course delivery sites Courses are delivered to your home, your workplace.

Media Courses are delivered via videotapes, audiotapes, computer software, CD-ROM, computer conferencing, World Wide Web, e-mail, print. Students and teachers may interact via telephone, e-mail, World Wide Web. The following equipment may be required: television, videocassette player, computer, modem, Internet access, e-mail.

Restrictions Programs are available nationwide. Enrollment is restricted to individuals meeting certain criteria.

Services Distance learners have access to library services, e-mail services, academic advising, tutoring, bookstore at a distance.

Credit-earning options Students may transfer credits from another institution.

Typical costs *Undergraduate:* Tuition of $200 per credit. *Graduate:* Tuition of $300 per credit. Application fee is $50 for both graduate and undergraduate students.

Registration Students may register by mail, fax, e-mail, World Wide Web.

Contact Pamela Hinden, Director of Enrollment and Student Services, United States Open University, 6 Denny Road, Suite 301, Wilmington, DE 19809. *Telephone:* 800-232-7705. *Fax:* 302-765-9503. *E-mail:* p.s.hinden@open.edu.

DEGREES AND AWARDS

BA Business (certain restrictions apply), English (certain restrictions apply), Humanities (certain restrictions apply), International Studies (certain restrictions apply), Liberal Arts (certain restrictions apply), Social Sciences (certain restrictions apply)

BS Computing (certain restrictions apply), Information Technology (certain restrictions apply)

MBA Business (certain restrictions apply)

MS Computing (certain restrictions apply)

COURSE SUBJECT AREAS OFFERED OUTSIDE OF DEGREE PROGRAMS

Undergraduate: Area, ethnic, and cultural studies; business; computer and information sciences; English language and literature; information sciences and systems; liberal arts, general studies, and humanities; social sciences

Graduate: Business; computer and information sciences

UNITED STATES SPORTS ACADEMY

Daphne, Alabama
Continuing Education and Distance Learning
www.sport.ussa.edu

United States Sports Academy, founded in 1972, is an independent, nonprofit, graduate institution. It is accredited by the Southern Association of Colleges and Schools. It first offered distance learning courses in 1993. In 1999–2000, it offered 56 courses at a distance. In fall 1999, there were 570 students enrolled in distance learning courses.

Course delivery sites Courses are delivered to your home, your workplace, military bases, United States Merchant Marine Academy (Kings Point, NY), University of Dallas (Irving, TX), 5 off-campus centers in Charleston (SC), Columbia (SC), Long Island (NY), San Diego (CA).

Media Courses are delivered via audiotapes, World Wide Web, e-mail, print. Students and teachers may interact via mail, telephone, fax, e-mail. The following equipment may be required: e-mail.

Restrictions Programs are available worldwide. Enrollment is open to anyone.

Services Distance learners have access to library services, the campus computer network, academic advising, tutoring, career placement assistance, bookstore at a distance.

Credit-earning options Students may transfer credits from another institution or may earn credits through military training.

Typical costs Tuition of $350 per semester hour. *Noncredit courses:* $350 per course. Financial aid is available to distance learners.

Registration Students may register by mail, fax, telephone, e-mail, World Wide Web, in person.

Contact Molly Martinson, Admissions Office, United States Sports Academy. *Telephone:* 800-223-2527. *Fax:* 334-625-1035. *E-mail:* admissions@usa-sport.ussa.edu.

DEGREES AND AWARDS

MSS Sports Coaching (some on-campus requirements), Sports Management (some on-campus requirements), Sports Medicine (some on-campus requirements)

COURSE SUBJECT AREAS OFFERED OUTSIDE OF DEGREE PROGRAMS

Graduate: Business; business administration and management; education administration; health and physical education/fitness; health professions and related sciences; human resources management; journalism; law and legal studies; public administration and services; social psychology; social sciences

Noncredit: Business; business administration and management; education administration; health and physical education/fitness; health professions and related sciences; human resources management; journalism; law and legal studies; public administration and services; social psychology; social sciences

See full descriptions on pages 676 and 720.

UNIVERSITÉ DE MONTRÉAL

Montréal, Québec, Canada
Facultè de L'èducation Permanente, Formation à Distance
www.fep.umontreal.ca

Université de Montréal, founded in 1920, is an independent, nonprofit university. It is accredited by the provincial charter. In 1999–2000, it offered 33 courses at a distance.

Course delivery sites Courses are delivered to your home.

Media Courses are delivered via television, videotapes, audiotapes, computer software, CD-ROM, World Wide Web, e-mail, print. Students and teachers may meet in person or interact via telephone, World Wide Web. The following equipment may be required: television, videocassette player, computer.

Restrictions Programs are available nationwide. Enrollment is restricted to individuals meeting certain criteria.

Services Distance learners have access to library services, e-mail services, tutoring at a distance.

Credit-earning options Students may earn credits through examinations.

Typical costs Undergraduate tuition for Canadians who are Quebec residents is $91.31 per credit hour. Tuition for Canadian non-residents is $150.31 per credit hour. Tuition for foreigners is $311.31 per credit hour. Costs may vary.

Registration Students may register by mail, fax, telephone, e-mail, World Wide Web, in person.

Contact Faculté de L'èducation Permanente, Université de Montréal, C.P. 6128 Succursale Centre-ville, Montrèal, QC H3C 3J7 Canada. *Telephone:* 800-363-8876. *E-mail:* distance@umontreal.ca.

DEGREES AND AWARDS

Undergraduate Certificate(s) Gerontology (certain restrictions apply)

COURSE SUBJECT AREAS OFFERED OUTSIDE OF DEGREE PROGRAMS

Graduate: Architecture; community health services; criminology; French language and literature; gerontology; mass media; public relations
Noncredit: French language and literature

UNIVERSITÉ LAVAL

Sainte-Foy, Québec, Canada

Continuing Education Division (Direction Générale de la Formation Continue)
www.ulaval.ca/dgfc

Université Laval, founded in 1852, is an independent, nonprofit university. It is accredited by the provincial charter. It first offered distance learning courses in 1984. In 1999–2000, it offered 130 courses at a distance. In fall 1999, there were 7,000 students enrolled in distance learning courses.

Course delivery sites Courses are delivered to your home, your workplace.

Media Courses are delivered via television, videotapes, audiotapes, computer software, CD-ROM, World Wide Web, print. Students and teachers may interact via videoconferencing, mail, telephone, fax, e-mail, World Wide Web. The following equipment may be required: television, videocassette player, computer, modem, Internet access, e-mail.

Restrictions Programs are available worldwide. Enrollment is open to anyone.

Services Distance learners have access to library services, e-mail services, academic advising, tutoring, bookstore at a distance.

Credit-earning options Students may transfer credits from another institution or may earn credits through examinations, portfolio assessment.

Typical costs *Undergraduate:* Tuition of Can$55.60 per credit plus mandatory fees of Can$6.25 per credit for in-state residents. Tuition of Can$114.60 per credit plus mandatory fees of Can$6.25 per credit for out-of-state residents. *Graduate:* Tuition of Can$55.60 per credit plus mandatory fees of Can$6.25 per credit for in-state residents. Tuition of Can$114.60 per credit plus mandatory fees of Can$6.25 per credit for out-of-state residents. Costs may vary.

Registration Students may register by mail, fax, telephone, in person.

Contact Monsieur Serge Dion, Communications Director, Université Laval. *Telephone:* 418-656-3202. *Fax:* 418-656-5538. *E-mail:* dgfc@dgfc.ulaval.ca.

DEGREES AND AWARDS

Undergraduate Certificate(s) Business Administration and Management, Computer Science, Food Distribution, Food Safety, Personal Financial Planning

COURSE SUBJECT AREAS OFFERED OUTSIDE OF DEGREE PROGRAMS

Undergraduate: Accounting; adult education; advertising; anthropology; business administration and management; business law; Canadian studies; cell biology; cognitive psychology; communications; computer and information sciences; computer programming; database management; economics; education administration; film studies; finance; foods and nutrition studies; French language and literature; geography; geology; German language and literature; gerontology; health services administration; human resources management; journalism; marketing; microbiology; philosophy and religion; psychology; public health; real estate; sociology; theological studies
Graduate: Business administration and management; marketing

UNIVERSITY ALLIANCE

Tampa, Florida
www.universityalliance.com

University Alliance is an independent, comprehensive institution. In 1999–2000, it offered 62 courses at a distance. In fall 1999, there were 3,000 students enrolled in distance learning courses.

Course delivery sites Courses are delivered to your home, your workplace, military bases.

Media Courses are delivered via videotapes, World Wide Web, e-mail. Students and teachers may interact via telephone, fax, e-mail, World Wide Web. The following equipment may be required: computer, Internet access, e-mail.

Restrictions Programs are available worldwide. Enrollment is restricted to individuals meeting certain criteria.

Services Distance learners have access to academic advising at a distance.

Credit-earning options Students may transfer credits from another institution.

Typical costs *Undergraduate:* Tuition of $295 per credit. *Graduate:* Tuition of $360 per credit. Undergraduate application fee is $35. Graduate application fee is $75. Financial aid is available to distance learners.

Registration Students may register by mail, fax, telephone, e-mail.

Contact Lisa Lambert, Assistant Director Student Services, University Alliance, 9417 Princess Palm Avenue, Tampa, FL 33619. *Telephone:* 877-334-7377. *Fax:* 888-879-3255. *E-mail:* info@universityalliance.com.

DEGREES AND AWARDS

BA Accounting, Business Administration, Business Administration and Accounting, Business Administration and Management
BS Computer Information Systems
See full description on page 722.

UNIVERSITY COLLEGE OF CAPE BRETON

Sydney, Nova Scotia, Canada
www.uccb.ns.ca/distance/

University College of Cape Breton, founded in 1974, is a province-supported, comprehensive institution. It is accredited by the provincial charter. In 1999–2000, it offered 58 courses at a distance. In fall 1999, there were 202 students enrolled in distance learning courses.

Course delivery sites Courses are delivered to your home.

Media Courses are delivered via CD-ROM, World Wide Web, e-mail, print. Students and teachers may meet in person or interact via audioconferencing, mail, telephone, fax, e-mail, World Wide Web. The following equipment may be required: computer, modem, Internet access, e-mail.

Restrictions Programs are available worldwide. Enrollment is open to anyone.
Services Distance learners have access to library services, the campus computer network, e-mail services, academic advising, tutoring, career placement assistance, bookstore at a distance.
Credit-earning options Students may transfer credits from another institution or may earn credits through examinations, portfolio assessment, military training, business training.
Typical costs Undergraduate tuition is Can$431.50 per 3 credit course and Can$813 per 6 credit course. Mandatory fee is Can$73. *Noncredit courses:* Can$431.50 per course. Financial aid is available to distance learners.
Registration Students may register by mail, fax, telephone, e-mail, World Wide Web, in person.
Contact Joanne Pyke, Coordinator, Distance Education, University College of Cape Breton, PO Box 5300, Sydney, NS B1P 6L2 Canada. *Telephone:* 902-563-1806. *Fax:* 902-563-1449. *E-mail:* jpyke@uccb.ns.ca.

DEGREES AND AWARDS

Undergraduate Certificate(s) Public Administration
BA Community Studies
BES Environmental Science
Graduate Certificate(s) Education Counseling (certain restrictions apply; service area differs from that of the overall institution; some on-campus requirements), Education Curriculum (certain restrictions apply; service area differs from that of the overall institution; some on-campus requirements), Education Technology

COURSE SUBJECT AREAS OFFERED OUTSIDE OF DEGREE PROGRAMS

Undergraduate: Accounting; creative writing; developmental and child psychology; economics; environmental engineering; environmental health; human resources management; international business; marketing; philosophy and religion; political science; social psychology; statistics
Graduate: Education

UNIVERSITY COLLEGE OF THE FRASER VALLEY

Abbotsford, British Columbia, Canada
UCFV Online
www.ucfv.bc.ca/online

University College of the Fraser Valley, founded in 1974, is a province-supported, four-year college. It is accredited by the provincial charter. In 1999–2000, it offered 12 courses at a distance.
Course delivery sites Courses are delivered to your home.
Media Courses are delivered via World Wide Web, e-mail. Students and teachers may interact via e-mail, World Wide Web. The following equipment may be required: computer, modem, Internet access, e-mail.
Restrictions Programs are available worldwide. Enrollment is open to anyone.
Services Distance learners have access to library services, e-mail services, academic advising, tutoring at a distance.
Credit-earning options Students may transfer credits from another institution or may earn credits through examinations, portfolio assessment.
Typical costs Tuition of $40 per credit plus mandatory fees of $2.50 per credit. Cost for a noncredit course ranges between $100 and $200. Financial aid is available to distance learners.
Registration Students may register by mail, fax, telephone, in person.

Contact Patrick O'Brien, Manager, UCFV Online, University College of the Fraser Valley, 33844 King Road, Abbotsford, BC V25 7M9 Canada. *Telephone:* 604-853-7441 Ext. 4382. *E-mail:* obrien@ucfv.bc.ca.

eCollege.com *www.ecollege.com/scholarships*

DEGREES AND AWARDS

Distance programs offered do not lead to a degree or other formal award.

COURSE SUBJECT AREAS OFFERED OUTSIDE OF DEGREE PROGRAMS

Undergraduate: Adult education; business; communications; English as a second language (ESL); ethics; health professions and related sciences; information sciences and systems; library and information studies; mass media; philosophy and religion; religious studies; social work

UNIVERSITY OF AKRON

Akron, Ohio
www.uakron.edu/distance

University of Akron, founded in 1870, is a state-supported university. It is accredited by the North Central Association of Colleges and Schools. It first offered distance learning courses in 1994. In 1999–2000, it offered 32 courses at a distance. In fall 1999, there were 160 students enrolled in distance learning courses.
Course delivery sites Courses are delivered to your home, high schools, Cleveland State University (Cleveland), Shawnee State University (Portsmouth), Stark State College of Technology (Canton), 10 off-campus centers in Barberton, Brunswick, Lodi, Medina, Orrville, Sullivan, Wadsworth.
Media Courses are delivered via videoconferencing, World Wide Web. Students and teachers may interact via videoconferencing, telephone, fax, e-mail. The following equipment may be required: computer, modem, Internet access, e-mail.
Restrictions Web courses are worldwide; video-conferencing courses are restricted regionally. Enrollment is restricted to individuals meeting certain criteria.
Services Distance learners have access to library services, the campus computer network, e-mail services, academic advising, bookstore at a distance.
Credit-earning options Students may transfer credits from another institution.
Typical costs *Undergraduate:* Tuition of $157 per credit for in-state residents. Tuition of $363 per credit for out-of-state residents. *Graduate:* Tuition of $189 per credit for in-state residents. Tuition of $353 per credit for out-of-state residents. Financial aid is available to distance learners.
Registration Students may register by mail, fax, telephone, e-mail, in person.
Contact Dr. Lynne Pachnowski, Distance Learning Coordinator, University of Akron, Zook Hall 130, Akron, OH 44326. *Telephone:* 330-972-7115. *Fax:* 330-972-5636. *E-mail:* lmp@uakron.edu.

DEGREES AND AWARDS

MS Education (certain restrictions apply; service area differs from that of the overall institution), Nursing (certain restrictions apply; service area differs from that of the overall institution), Social Work (certain restrictions apply; service area differs from that of the overall institution; some on-campus requirements)

COURSE SUBJECT AREAS OFFERED OUTSIDE OF DEGREE PROGRAMS

Undergraduate: Business administration and management; communications; economics; English composition; geography; German language and literature; Japanese language and literature; mathematics; political science; sociology

Graduate: Business administration and management; education; mathematics; nursing; political science; social work

UNIVERSITY OF ALABAMA

Tuscaloosa, Alabama

College of Continuing Studies
bama.disted.ua.edu

University of Alabama, founded in 1831, is a state-supported university. It is accredited by the Southern Association of Colleges and Schools. It first offered distance learning courses in 1991. In 1999–2000, it offered 300 courses at a distance. In fall 1999, there were 3,500 students enrolled in distance learning courses.

Course delivery sites Courses are delivered to your home, your workplace, military bases, other colleges, 3 off-campus centers in Dothan, Gadsden, Selma.

Media Courses are delivered via videotapes, videoconferencing, World Wide Web, e-mail, print. Students and teachers may interact via videoconferencing, mail, telephone, fax, e-mail.

Restrictions Programs are available worldwide. Enrollment is open to anyone.

Services Distance learners have access to library services, the campus computer network, e-mail services, academic advising, bookstore at a distance.

Credit-earning options Students may transfer credits from another institution.

Typical costs *Undergraduate:* Tuition of $165 per semester hour plus mandatory fees of $25 per semester. *Graduate:* Tuition of $165 per semester hour plus mandatory fees of $25 per semester. Costs may vary. Financial aid is available to distance learners.

Registration Students may register by mail, fax, telephone, e-mail, in person.

Contact Carroll Tingle, Director, University of Alabama, Distance Education, Box 870388, Tuscaloosa, AL 35487-0388. *Telephone:* 205-348-9278. *Fax:* 205-348-0249. *E-mail:* ctingle@ccs.ua.edu.

DEGREES AND AWARDS

MS Engineering, Environmental Engineering
MSAE Aerospace Engineering
MSCE Civil Engineering
MSE Engineering Management
MSEE Electrical Engineering
MSME Mechanical Engineering

COURSE SUBJECT AREAS OFFERED OUTSIDE OF DEGREE PROGRAMS

Undergraduate: Business; business administration and management; computer and information sciences; history; home economics and family studies; liberal arts, general studies, and humanities; mathematics; mechanical engineering; nursing

Graduate: Accounting; advertising; aerospace, aeronautical engineering; business administration and management; chemical engineering; civil engineering; computer and information sciences; education administration; electrical engineering; engineering mechanics; environmental engineering; health and physical education/fitness; health professions and related sciences; history; human resources management; industrial engineering; law and legal studies; liberal arts, general studies, and humanities; library and information studies; mathematics

See full descriptions on pages 592, 676, and 724.

UNIVERSITY OF ALABAMA AT BIRMINGHAM

Birmingham, Alabama

Academic Programs and Policy; IITS
www.uab.edu/conted

University of Alabama at Birmingham, founded in 1969, is a state-supported university. It is accredited by the Southern Association of Colleges and Schools. It first offered distance learning courses in 1991. In 1999–2000, it offered 5 courses at a distance. In fall 1999, there were 5 students enrolled in distance learning courses.

Course delivery sites Courses are delivered to Auburn University (Auburn University), The University of Alabama in Huntsville (Huntsville), University of Alabama (Tuscaloosa).

Media Courses are delivered via videoconferencing, World Wide Web, print. Students and teachers may meet in person or interact via videoconferencing, mail, fax, e-mail, World Wide Web. The following equipment may be required: computer, modem, Internet access, e-mail.

Restrictions Programs are available to in-state students only. Enrollment is restricted to individuals meeting certain criteria.

Services Distance learners have access to library services, the campus computer network, e-mail services at a distance.

Credit-earning options Students may transfer credits from another institution or may earn credits through examinations, portfolio assessment, military training, business training.

Typical costs *Undergraduate:* Tuition of $91 per credit hour plus mandatory fees of $8 per credit hour for in-state residents. Tuition of $182 per credit hour plus mandatory fees of $8 per credit hour for out-of-state residents. *Graduate:* Tuition of $104 per credit hour plus mandatory fees of $8 per credit hour for in-state residents. Tuition of $208 per credit hour plus mandatory fees of $8 per credit hour for out-of-state residents. *Noncredit courses:* $120 per course. Financial aid is available to distance learners.

Registration Students may register by telephone, World Wide Web, in person.

Contact Brenda Harbison, Coordinator, University of Alabama at Birmingham, 924 19th Street South, UAB Station, Birmingham, AL 35294. *Telephone:* 205-934-8167. *Fax:* 205-934-8251. *E-mail:* harbison@uab.edu.

DEGREES AND AWARDS

Distance programs offered do not lead to a degree or other formal award.

COURSE SUBJECT AREAS OFFERED OUTSIDE OF DEGREE PROGRAMS

Undergraduate: Civil engineering

Graduate: Advertising; civil engineering; engineering; health professions and related sciences; journalism; nursing

See full description on page 676.

UNIVERSITY OF ALASKA FAIRBANKS

Fairbanks, Alaska

Center for Distance Education and Independent Learning
www.dist-ed.uaf.edu

University of Alaska Fairbanks, founded in 1917, is a state-supported university. It is accredited by the Northwest Association of Schools and Colleges. It first offered distance learning courses in 1970. In 1999–2000, it offered 200 courses at a distance. In fall 1999, there were 2,385 students enrolled in distance learning courses.

Course delivery sites Courses are delivered to your home, 20 off-campus centers in Anchorage, Barrow, Bethel, Dillingham, Fort Yukon, Galena, Homer, Juneau, Kenai, Ketchikan, Kodiak, Kotzebue, McGrath, Nenana, Nome, Palmer, Sitka, Tok, Unalaska, Valdez.

Media Courses are delivered via videotapes, audiotapes, computer software, CD-ROM, computer conferencing, World Wide Web, e-mail, print. Students and teachers may interact via audioconferencing, mail, telephone, fax, e-mail, World Wide Web.

Restrictions Programs are available worldwide. Enrollment is restricted to individuals meeting certain criteria.

Services Distance learners have access to library services, the campus computer network, e-mail services, academic advising, tutoring, career placement assistance, bookstore at a distance.

Credit-earning options Students may transfer credits from another institution or may earn credits through examinations, portfolio assessment, military training, business training.

Typical costs *Undergraduate:* Tuition of $77 per credit plus mandatory fees of $20 per course. *Graduate:* Tuition of $172 per credit plus mandatory fees of $20 per course. Financial aid is available to distance learners.

Registration Students may register by mail, fax, telephone, e-mail, World Wide Web, in person.

Contact Carone Sturm, Director, University of Alaska Fairbanks, Center for Distance Education, PO Box 756700, Fairbanks, AK 99775. *Telephone:* 907-474-5353. *Fax:* 907-474-5402. *E-mail:* distance@uaf.edu.

DEGREES AND AWARDS

Undergraduate Certificate(s) Community Health (service area differs from that of the overall institution; some on-campus requirements), Early Childhood Development (service area differs from that of the overall institution), Microcomputer Support Specialist (service area differs from that of the overall institution)

AA General Studies (service area differs from that of the overall institution)

AAS Community Health (service area differs from that of the overall institution; some on-campus requirements), Early Childhood Development (service area differs from that of the overall institution), Human Services Technology (service area differs from that of the overall institution), Microcomputer Support Specialist (service area differs from that of the overall institution)

BA Rural Development (service area differs from that of the overall institution), Social Work (service area differs from that of the overall institution)

COURSE SUBJECT AREAS OFFERED OUTSIDE OF DEGREE PROGRAMS

Undergraduate: Abnormal psychology; accounting; administrative and secretarial services; advertising; algebra; anthropology; area, ethnic, and cultural studies; art history and criticism; biological and life sciences; biology; business; business administration and management; calculus; chemistry; child care and development; classical languages and literatures; communications; computer and information sciences; creative writing; economics; education; education administration; educational psychology; English composition; English language and literature; ethics; film studies; geography; geology; Greek language and literature; health and physical education/fitness; history; journalism; Latin language and literature; liberal arts, general studies, and humanities; library and information studies; mathematics; music; philosophy and religion; physical sciences; physics; political science; psychology; real estate; social sciences; social work; sociology; special education; statistics; teacher education; technical writing; women's studies

Graduate: Education administration; educational psychology; teacher education

See full descriptions on pages 726 and 822.

UNIVERSITY OF ALASKA SOUTHEAST

Juneau, Alaska

Distance Learning at UAS

University of Alaska Southeast, founded in 1972, is a state-supported, comprehensive institution. It is accredited by the Northwest Association of Schools and Colleges. It first offered distance learning courses in 1986. In 1999–2000, it offered 85 courses at a distance. In fall 1999, there were 709 students enrolled in distance learning courses.

Course delivery sites Courses are delivered to your home, military bases, high schools, University of Arkansas Community College at Batesville (Batesville, AR), University of Arkansas Community College at Hope (Hope, AR), Yukon College (Whitehorse, Canada).

Media Courses are delivered via television, videotapes, interactive television, audiotapes, computer software, CD-ROM, computer conferencing, World Wide Web, e-mail, print. Students and teachers may meet in person or interact via audioconferencing, mail, telephone, fax, e-mail, interactive television, World Wide Web. The following equipment may be required: television, videocassette player, computer, Internet access, e-mail.

Restrictions Programs are available to in-state students only. Enrollment is open to anyone.

Services Distance learners have access to library services, the campus computer network, e-mail services, academic advising, tutoring, career placement assistance, bookstore at a distance.

Credit-earning options Students may transfer credits from another institution or may earn credits through examinations, military training.

Typical costs *Undergraduate:* Tuition of $87 per credit plus mandatory fees of $75 per course for in-state residents. Tuition of $261 per credit plus mandatory fees of $75 per course for out-of-state residents. *Graduate:* Tuition of $172 per credit plus mandatory fees of $75 per course for in-state residents. Tuition of $516 per credit plus mandatory fees of $75 per course for out-of-state residents. Costs may vary. Financial aid is available to distance learners.

Registration Students may register by mail, fax, telephone, in person.

Contact Shirley Grubb, Assistant to the Dean of Faculty, University of Alaska Southeast, 11120 Glacier Highway, Juneau, AK 99801. *Telephone:* 907-465-6353. *Fax:* 907-465-6549. *E-mail:* distance.ed@uas.alaska.edu.

DEGREES AND AWARDS

BBA Business Administration

BLA Liberal Arts (certain restrictions apply)

Graduate Certificate(s) Early Childhood Education (certain restrictions apply; service area differs from that of the overall institution; some on-campus requirements), Educational Technology (some on-campus requirements), Elementary Education (certain restrictions apply)

MEd Education (certain restrictions apply; some on-campus requirements)

MPA Public Administration

COURSE SUBJECT AREAS OFFERED OUTSIDE OF DEGREE PROGRAMS

Undergraduate: Biology; business administration and management; business law; computer and information sciences; curriculum and instruction; finance; human resources management; international business; management information systems; marketing; organizational behavior studies; teacher education

Graduate: Continuing education; curriculum and instruction; public administration and services; public policy analysis

Noncredit: Continuing education

See full description on page 822.

UNIVERSITY OF ALASKA SOUTHEAST, KETCHIKAN CAMPUS

Ketchikan, Alaska
www.ketch.alaska.edu

University of Alaska Southeast, Ketchikan Campus, founded in 1954, is a state and locally supported, two-year college. It is accredited by the Northwest Association of Schools and Colleges. In 1999–2000, it offered 11 courses at a distance. In fall 1999, there were 100 students enrolled in distance learning courses.

Course delivery sites Courses are delivered to your home, high schools.

Media Courses are delivered via videotapes, computer software, CD-ROM, computer conferencing, World Wide Web, e-mail, print. Students and teachers may meet in person or interact via audioconferencing, mail, telephone, fax, e-mail, World Wide Web. The following equipment may be required: videocassette player, computer, Internet access, e-mail.

Restrictions Programs are available to in-state students only. Enrollment is open to anyone.

Services Distance learners have access to library services, the campus computer network, e-mail services, academic advising, bookstore at a distance.

Credit-earning options Students may transfer credits from another institution or may earn credits through examinations, military training.

Typical costs Tuition of $87 per credit plus mandatory fees of $40 per course for in-state residents. Tuition of $261 per credit plus mandatory fees of $40 per course for out-of-state residents. Financial aid is available to distance learners.

Registration Students may register by mail, fax, telephone, in person.

Contact Dawn Montgomery, Learning Center Coordinator, University of Alaska Southeast, Ketchikan Campus, 2600 Seventh Avenue, Ketchikan, AK 99901. *Telephone:* 907-228-4524. *Fax:* 907-228-4542. *E-mail:* dawn. montgomery@uas.alaska.edu.

DEGREES AND AWARDS

Distance programs offered do not lead to a degree or other formal award.

COURSE SUBJECT AREAS OFFERED OUTSIDE OF DEGREE PROGRAMS

Undergraduate: Accounting; American (U.S.) history; anthropology; art history and criticism; European history; information sciences and systems

UNIVERSITY OF ALASKA SOUTHEAST, SITKA CAMPUS

Sitka, Alaska
www.jun.alaska.edu/uas/sitka/index.html

University of Alaska Southeast, Sitka Campus, founded in 1962, is a state-supported, two-year college. It is accredited by the Northwest Association of Schools and Colleges. It first offered distance learning courses in 1986. In 1999–2000, it offered 150 courses at a distance. In fall 1999, there were 700 students enrolled in distance learning courses.

Course delivery sites Courses are delivered to your home, your workplace, military bases, high schools.

Media Courses are delivered via television, videotapes, audiotapes, computer software, CD-ROM, computer conferencing, World Wide Web, e-mail, print. Students and teachers may interact via audioconferencing, mail, telephone, fax, e-mail, World Wide Web. The following equipment may be required: television, videocassette player.

Restrictions Programs are primarily available to in-state students. Enrollment is open to anyone.

Services Distance learners have access to library services, e-mail services, academic advising, tutoring, bookstore at a distance.

Credit-earning options Students may transfer credits from another institution or may earn credits through examinations, military training.

Typical costs *Undergraduate:* Tuition of $75 per credit plus mandatory fees of $45 per course. *Graduate:* Tuition of $167 per credit plus mandatory fees of $80 per course. Undergraduates pay $75 per credit for lower-level courses and $84 per credit for 300 level or higher courses. *Noncredit courses:* $35 per course. Financial aid is available to distance learners.

Registration Students may register by mail, fax, telephone, e-mail, in person.

Contact Denise Blankenship, Coordinator, University of Alaska Southeast, Sitka Campus, Distance Education, 1332 Seward Avenue, Sitka, AK 99835. *Telephone:* 907-747-6653. *Fax:* 907-747-3552. *E-mail:* tndmb@ uas.alaska.edu.

DEGREES AND AWARDS

Undergraduate Certificate(s) Administrative Office Support (service area differs from that of the overall institution), Desktop Publishing and Graphics (service area differs from that of the overall institution), Environmental Technology (service area differs from that of the overall institution), Medical Office Specialist (service area differs from that of the overall institution), Microcomputer Support Specialist (service area differs from that of the overall institution), Networking Essentials (service area differs from that of the overall institution), Web Publishing (service area differs from that of the overall institution)

AAS Computer Information Office Systems (service area differs from that of the overall institution), Early Childhood Education (service area differs from that of the overall institution), Environmental Technology (service area differs from that of the overall institution), Health Information Management, Human Services Technology (service area differs from that of the overall institution), Microcomputer Support Specialist (service area differs from that of the overall institution)

Graduate Certificate(s) Computer Applications (service area differs from that of the overall institution), Elementary Education (service area differs from that of the overall institution)

COURSE SUBJECT AREAS OFFERED OUTSIDE OF DEGREE PROGRAMS

Undergraduate: Accounting; administrative and secretarial services; area, ethnic, and cultural studies; biological and life sciences; biology; business; business administration and management; chemistry; communications; computer and information sciences; creative writing; developmental and child psychology; education; English composition; English language and literature; environmental science; geology; health professions and related sciences; history; journalism; law and legal studies; liberal arts, general studies, and humanities; mathematics; philosophy and religion; physical sciences; psychology; social psychology; social sciences; sociology; teacher education

See full description on page 822.

See full description on page 822.

UNIVERSITY OF ARIZONA

Tucson, Arizona

Extended University, Distance Learning Program
www.eu.arizona.edu/dist/

University of Arizona, founded in 1885, is a state-supported university. It is accredited by the North Central Association of Colleges and Schools. It first offered distance learning courses in 1972. In 1999–2000, it offered 220 courses at a distance. In fall 1999, there were 900 students enrolled in distance learning courses.

Course delivery sites Courses are delivered to your home, your workplace, military bases, National Technological University (Fort Collins, CO).

Media Courses are delivered via television, videotapes, videoconferencing, computer software, CD-ROM, computer conferencing, World Wide Web, e-mail, print. Students and teachers may interact via videoconferencing, audioconferencing, mail, telephone, fax, e-mail, World Wide Web. The following equipment may be required: television, videocassette player, computer, modem, Internet access, e-mail.

Restrictions Programs are available nationwide. Enrollment is open to anyone.

Services Distance learners have access to library services, the campus computer network, e-mail services, academic advising, career placement assistance, bookstore at a distance.

Credit-earning options Students may transfer credits from another institution.

Typical costs Contact the school for information. Costs may vary.

Registration Students may register by mail, fax, telephone, e-mail, in person.

Contact Pam Shack, Program Coordinator, Distance Learning, University of Arizona, Distance Learning, Extended University, University Services Building, Room 302, Tucson, AZ 85721-0158. *Telephone:* 520-626-4573. *Fax:* 520-621-3269. *E-mail:* pshack@u.arizona.edu.

DEGREES AND AWARDS

Graduate Certificate(s) Reliability and Quality Engineering (certain restrictions apply)
MEng Engineering (certain restrictions apply)

COURSE SUBJECT AREAS OFFERED OUTSIDE OF DEGREE PROGRAMS

Undergraduate: Abnormal psychology; accounting; African-American studies; agriculture; algebra; American (U.S.) history; American studies; anatomy; anthropology; area, ethnic, and cultural studies; calculus; cell biology; chemistry; civil engineering; cognitive psychology; community health services; conservation and natural resources; corrections; criminology; developmental and child psychology; entomology; European history; French language and literature; geography; German language and literature; health professions and related sciences; home economics and family studies; industrial engineering; industrial psychology; international relations; Jewish studies; mathematics; meteorology; physics; plant sciences; political science; professional studies; psychology; religious studies; Russian language and literature; social psychology; sociology; statistics
Graduate: Aerospace, aeronautical engineering; chemical engineering; civil engineering; electrical engineering; engineering; engineering mechan-

ics; engineering/industrial management; industrial engineering; library and information studies; mechanical engineering; physics; public health

Special note
Students can update their technical skills and gain new perspectives on their fields through the distance learning classes at the University of Arizona. Courses are taught by top faculty members and incorporate the latest research and technological developments. Students can choose the distance learning courses and formats that best meet their needs. The University offers classes via videotape, the NTU network, and the Internet. The University offers a wide range of technical courses in areas such as aerospace and mechanical engineering, electrical and computer engineering, optical sciences, reliability and quality engineering, and systems and industrial engineering. The Tri-University Master of Engineering degree, administered jointly by the University of Arizona, Arizona State University, and Northern Arizona University, is designed by faculty members from all 3 universities with input from industry professionals to meet the individual educational needs of practicing engineers. New this year is the Professional Graduate Certificate in Systems Engineering, a program of the University of Arizona College of Engineering and Mines, which is available totally at a distance. Students learn how to ensure that a system satisfies its requirements throughout the entire system life cycle, from cradle to grave, to increase a system's probability of success, reduce the risk of failure, and reduce total life-cycle cost. The University's online master's degree program in information resources and library science offers Internet-based courses. Other Web-based courses will join the lineup in the months ahead. Students should visit the University's Web site at http://www.eu.arizona.edu/~dist/ or students can call 520-626-2079 or 800-478-9508 (toll-free) or e-mail distance@u.arizona.edu for further details.

UNIVERSITY OF ARKANSAS

Fayetteville, Arkansas

Division for Continuing Education
www.uacted.uark.edu

University of Arkansas, founded in 1871, is a state-supported university. It is accredited by the North Central Association of Colleges and Schools. In 1999–2000, it offered 33 courses at a distance. In fall 1999, there were 338 students enrolled in distance learning courses.

Course delivery sites Courses are delivered to your home, your workplace, military bases, high schools, North Arkansas College (Harrison), Pulaski Technical College (North Little Rock), University of Arkansas at Pine Bluff (Pine Bluff), University of Arkansas Community College at Hope (Hope), Westark College (Fort Smith), off-campus center(s) in Batesville, Helena, Springdale.

Media Courses are delivered via videoconferencing, print. Students and teachers may meet in person or interact via videoconferencing, mail, telephone, fax, e-mail.

Restrictions Programs are available statewide only; correspondence courses are offered worldwide. Enrollment is open to anyone.

Services Distance learners have access to library services, e-mail services, academic advising, career placement assistance, bookstore at a distance.

Credit-earning options Students may transfer credits from another institution or may earn credits through portfolio assessment.

Typical costs *Undergraduate:* Tuition of $125 per semester hour for in-state residents. Tuition of $125 per semester hour for out-of-state residents. *Graduate:* Tuition of $202 per semester hour for in-state residents. Tuition of $445 per semester hour for out-of-state residents. Costs may vary.

Registration Students may register by mail, fax, in person.

University of Arkansas

Contact Gary McHenry, Director, University of Arkansas, Office of Credit Studies, 2 East Center Street, Fayetteville, AR 72701. *Telephone:* 501-575-3648. *Fax:* 501-575-7232. *E-mail:* garyn@postbox.uark.edu.

DEGREES AND AWARDS

BS Human Resource Development (service area differs from that of the overall institution)

COURSE SUBJECT AREAS OFFERED OUTSIDE OF DEGREE PROGRAMS

Undergraduate: Abnormal psychology; algebra; American (U.S.) history; animal sciences; business administration and management; business law; calculus; communications; criminal justice; criminology; curriculum and instruction; developmental and child psychology; drama and theater; education; educational psychology; English composition; English literature; environmental science; ethics; fine arts; foods and nutrition studies; French language and literature; geography; geology; German language and literature; health and physical education/fitness; industrial psychology; journalism; Latin language and literature; logic; microbiology; political science; school psychology; social work; sociology; Spanish language and literature; zoology
Graduate: Education

See full description on page 676.

UNIVERSITY OF ARKANSAS AT LITTLE ROCK

Little Rock, Arkansas

Department of Computing Services

University of Arkansas at Little Rock, founded in 1927, is a state-supported university. It is accredited by the North Central Association of Colleges and Schools. It first offered distance learning courses in 1994.
Contact University of Arkansas at Little Rock, 2801 South University Avenue, Little Rock, AR 72204-1099. *Telephone:* 501-569-3000. *Fax:* 501-569-8915.

See full description on page 676.

UNIVERSITY OF BALTIMORE

Baltimore, Maryland

UBOnline
www.ubalt.edu

University of Baltimore, founded in 1925, is a state-supported, upper-level institution. It is accredited by the Middle States Association of Colleges and Schools. It first offered distance learning courses in 1994. In 1999–2000, it offered 180 courses at a distance. In fall 1999, there were 500 students enrolled in distance learning courses.
Course delivery sites Courses are delivered to your home, your workplace, Community College of Baltimore County–Essex Campus (Baltimore), Frostburg State University (Frostburg), Hagerstown Community College (Hagerstown), Harford Community College (Bel Air), Howard Community College (Columbia), The Community College of Baltimore County–Catonsville Campus (Catonsville), 7 off-campus centers in Aberdeen, Baltimore, Columbia, Gaithersburg, Hunt Valley, Owings Mills, Shady Grove.
Media Courses are delivered via videotapes, interactive television, World Wide Web. Students and teachers may meet in person or interact via mail, telephone, fax, e-mail, interactive television, World Wide Web. The

following equipment may be required: television, videocassette player, computer, modem, Internet access, e-mail.
Restrictions Interactive video classes are available statewide; World Wide Web courses are available worldwide. Enrollment is open to anyone.
Services Distance learners have access to library services, the campus computer network, e-mail services, academic advising, tutoring, career placement assistance, bookstore at a distance.
Credit-earning options Students may transfer credits from another institution or may earn credits through examinations, military training.
Typical costs *Undergraduate:* Tuition of $163 per credit plus mandatory fees of $20 per credit for in-state residents. Tuition of $454 per credit plus mandatory fees of $20 per credit for out-of-state residents. *Graduate:* Tuition of $264 per credit plus mandatory fees of $20 per credit for in-state residents. Tuition of $393 per credit plus mandatory fees of $20 per credit for out-of-state residents. Costs may vary. Financial aid is available to distance learners.
Registration Students may register by mail, fax, telephone, in person.
Contact Julia Pitman, Associate Director of Admissions, University of Baltimore, 1420 North Charles Street, Baltimore, MD 21201. *Telephone:* 877-APPLYUB. *Fax:* 410-837-4793. *E-mail:* admissions@ubmail.ubalt.edu.

DEGREES AND AWARDS

BS Corporate Communication (some on-campus requirements), Criminal Justice
MBA Business Administration (service area differs from that of the overall institution)

COURSE SUBJECT AREAS OFFERED OUTSIDE OF DEGREE PROGRAMS

Undergraduate: American literature; area, ethnic, and cultural studies; communications; creative writing; criminology; history; political science
Graduate: Accounting; business; business administration and management; computer and information sciences; counseling psychology; marketing; public administration and services

See full descriptions on pages 676 and 728.

UNIVERSITY OF BRIDGEPORT

Bridgeport, Connecticut

Office of Distance Education
www.bridgeport.edu

University of Bridgeport, founded in 1927, is an independent, nonprofit, comprehensive institution. It is accredited by the New England Association of Schools and Colleges. It first offered distance learning courses in 1997. In 1999–2000, it offered 12 courses at a distance. In fall 1999, there were 65 students enrolled in distance learning courses.
Course delivery sites Courses are delivered to your home, your workplace, military bases.
Media Courses are delivered via videotapes, audiotapes, computer software, computer conferencing, World Wide Web, e-mail, print. Students and teachers may meet in person or interact via mail, telephone, fax, e-mail, World Wide Web. The following equipment may be required: computer, modem, Internet access, e-mail.
Restrictions Programs are available worldwide. Enrollment is open to anyone.
Services Distance learners have access to library services, academic advising, tutoring, career placement assistance, bookstore at a distance.
Credit-earning options Students may transfer credits from another institution.

Typical costs Tuition of $370 per credit plus mandatory fees of $50 per semester. *Noncredit courses:* $120 per course. Costs may vary. Financial aid is available to distance learners.

Registration Students may register by mail, fax, telephone, e-mail, World Wide Web, in person.

Contact Michael J. Giampaoli, Coordinator for Distance Education, University of Bridgeport, 303 University Avenue, Bridgeport, CT 06601. *Telephone:* 203-576-4851. *Fax:* 203-576-4852. *E-mail:* ubonline@bridgeport.edu.

DEGREES AND AWARDS

MS Human Nutrition (some on-campus requirements)

COURSE SUBJECT AREAS OFFERED OUTSIDE OF DEGREE PROGRAMS

Undergraduate: Computer programming; law and legal studies; political science

Graduate: Computer programming; finance; health professions and related sciences

See full description on page 730.

UNIVERSITY OF BRITISH COLUMBIA

Vancouver, British Columbia, Canada

Distance Education and Technology
det.cstudies.ubc.ca

University of British Columbia, founded in 1915, is a province-supported university. It is accredited by the provincial charter. It first offered distance learning courses in 1949. In 1999–2000, it offered 118 courses at a distance. In fall 1999, there were 4,000 students enrolled in distance learning courses.

Course delivery sites Courses are delivered to your home, your workplace, Open Learning Agency (Burnaby).

Media Courses are delivered via television, videotapes, videoconferencing, audiotapes, computer software, CD-ROM, World Wide Web, e-mail, print. Students and teachers may interact via videoconferencing, audioconferencing, mail, telephone, fax, e-mail, World Wide Web.

Restrictions Programs are available worldwide. Enrollment is restricted to individuals meeting certain criteria.

Services Distance learners have access to library services, the campus computer network, e-mail services, academic advising, tutoring, bookstore at a distance.

Credit-earning options Students may transfer credits from another institution or may earn credits through examinations, portfolio assessment.

Typical costs *Undergraduate:* Tuition of $75 per credit. *Graduate:* Tuition of $194 per credit. Costs may vary. Financial aid is available to distance learners.

Registration Students may register by mail, fax, telephone, e-mail, World Wide Web, in person.

Contact Heather Francis, Manager of New Business Development, University of British Columbia, 2329 West Mall, Room 1170, University Services Building, Vancouver, BC V6T 1Z4 Canada. *Telephone:* 604-822-6565. *Fax:* 604-822-8636. *E-mail:* heather.francis@ubc.ca.

DEGREES AND AWARDS

Graduate Certificate(s) Education

COURSE SUBJECT AREAS OFFERED OUTSIDE OF DEGREE PROGRAMS

Undergraduate: Agricultural economics; agriculture; animal sciences; astronomy and astrophysics; Canadian studies; civil engineering; computer and information sciences; education; English language and literature; film studies; foods and nutrition studies; forestry; French language and literature; geology; German language and literature; history; medieval/renaissance studies; music; nursing; oceanography; philosophy and religion; physical sciences; plant sciences; psychology; social sciences; women's studies

Graduate: Education

Special note

The Distance Education & Technology (DE&T) division of Continuing Studies develops and delivers programs, courses, and learning materials for individual and institutional clients who require cost-effective, quality education delivered in flexible formats. Established as the Department of University Extensions at UBC in 1949, the division continues to collaborate with twelve UBC faculties plus Continuing Studies program areas to produce distance education services and courses to serve local, national, and international clients. UBC currently offers 118 courses via distance technology, including print-based materials, audio, video, CD-ROM, and World Wide Web and other Internet services. In addition, DE&T at UBC is now developing more than 25 new courses annually, many with an online component. DE&T's inventory consists of degree-credit, noncredit, certificate, and diploma courses. For a complete list of courses and projects, students should visit the Web site at http://det.cstudies.ubc.ca or call 604-822-6565 or 800-754-1811 (toll-free in British Columbia and Yukon) for a printed catalogue and registration requirements. Those who are interested in DE&T's consultation and collaboration services, course development, training, research, or technological expertise should visit the DE&T Web site at http://det.cstudies.ubc.ca or the Director's Web site at http://bates.cstudies.ubc.ca. Dr. Tony Bates, Director of DE&T, is a founding member of the British Open University, has authored 6 books on distance education, and has consulted for UNESCO, the World Bank, and other institutions in more than 30 countries. Along with a staff of 20 people, Dr. Bates has initiated several partnership franchises with organizations offering distance education around the world.

UNIVERSITY OF CALGARY

Calgary, Alberta, Canada

Distance and Distributed Learning
www.ucalgary.ca/uofc/departments/ddlc/

University of Calgary, founded in 1945, is a province-supported university. It is accredited by the provincial charter. It first offered distance learning courses in 1977. In 1999–2000, it offered 100 courses at a distance. In fall 1999, there were 700 students enrolled in distance learning courses.

Course delivery sites Courses are delivered to your home, your workplace, military bases, high schools, other colleges, 95 off-campus centers.

Media Courses are delivered via television, videoconferencing, computer software, CD-ROM, computer conferencing, World Wide Web, e-mail. Students and teachers may meet in person or interact via videoconferencing, audioconferencing, mail, telephone, fax, e-mail. The following equipment may be required: computer, modem, Internet access, e-mail.

Restrictions Programs are available nationwide. Enrollment is restricted to individuals meeting certain criteria.

Services Distance learners have access to library services, the campus computer network, e-mail services, academic advising, tutoring, career placement assistance, bookstore at a distance.

Credit-earning options Students may transfer credits from another institution or may earn credits through examinations.

Typical costs *Undergraduate:* Tuition of $365 per course plus mandatory fees of $26 per course. *Graduate:* Tuition of $481 per course plus mandatory fees of $59 per course. *Noncredit courses:* $200 per course. Costs may vary.

Registration Students may register by mail, fax, telephone, in person.

Contact Irena Kirek, Director, University of Calgary, 546 Bi Sci Building, 2500 University Drive North West, Calgary, AB T2N 1N4 Canada. *Telephone:* 403-220-7346. *Fax:* 403-297-2999. *E-mail:* ikirek@ucalgary.ca.

DEGREES AND AWARDS

Undergraduate Certificate(s) Teacher Assistant (service area differs from that of the overall institution)

BCR Community Rehabilitation (service area differs from that of the overall institution)

BN Nursing (service area differs from that of the overall institution)

MCE Continuing Education (some on-campus requirements)

MEd Adult, Community and Higher Education (service area differs from that of the overall institution; some on-campus requirements), Educational Leadership, Educational Technology, English as a Second Language, Teaching and Learning

COURSE SUBJECT AREAS OFFERED OUTSIDE OF DEGREE PROGRAMS

Undergraduate: Biological and life sciences; biology; chemistry; civil engineering; economics; education; education administration; electrical engineering; English composition; history; liberal arts, general studies, and humanities; nursing; philosophy and religion; physics; political science; sociology; special education; teacher education

Graduate: Chemistry; computer and information sciences; education; education administration; electrical engineering; social work; special education; teacher education

Noncredit: Conservation and natural resources; continuing education; education

UNIVERSITY OF CALIFORNIA, BERKELEY

Berkeley, California

Center for Media and Independent Learning
learn.berkeley.edu

University of California, Berkeley, founded in 1868, is a state-supported university. It is accredited by the Western Association of Schools and Colleges, Inc. It first offered distance learning courses in 1998. In 1999–2000, it offered 200 courses at a distance. In fall 1999, there were 3,500 students enrolled in distance learning courses.

Course delivery sites Courses are delivered to your home, your workplace.

Media Courses are delivered via videotapes, computer software, CD-ROM, World Wide Web, e-mail, print. Students and teachers may interact via mail, fax, e-mail, World Wide Web. The following equipment may be required: computer, modem, Internet access, e-mail.

Restrictions Programs are available worldwide. Enrollment is open to anyone.

Services Distance learners have access to bookstore at a distance.

Credit-earning options Students may earn credits through business training.

Typical costs Tuition of $485 per course. Students pay an additional $50 online resource fee.

Registration Students may register by mail, fax, telephone, e-mail, World Wide Web, in person.

Contact Student Services, University of California, Berkeley, UC Extension Center—Center for Media and Independent Learning, 2000 Center Street, Suite 400, Berkeley, CA 94704. *Telephone:* 510-642-4124. *Fax:* 510-643-9271. *E-mail:* askcmil@uclink4.berkeley.edu.

DEGREES AND AWARDS

Graduate Certificate(s) Business Administration, Computer Information Systems, Direct Marketing Methods, e-Commerce, Hazardous Materials Management, Integrated Marketing Communications, Marketing, Project Management, Telecommunications Fundamentals

COURSE SUBJECT AREAS OFFERED OUTSIDE OF DEGREE PROGRAMS

Undergraduate: Accounting; advertising; American (U.S.) history; American literature; American studies; anthropology; area, ethnic, and cultural studies; biological and life sciences; biology; botany; business; business administration and management; business communications; chemistry; Chinese language and literature; civil engineering; communications; computer programming; conservation and natural resources; creative writing; database management; design; developmental and child psychology; economics; electrical engineering; English as a second language (ESL); English composition; English language and literature; film studies; finance; fine arts; French language and literature; geology; health professions and related sciences; history; human resources management; information sciences and systems; international business; Italian language and literature; library and information studies; management information systems; marketing; mathematics; music; philosophy and religion; physics; political science; psychology; public relations; religious studies; social psychology; sociology; Spanish language and literature; teacher education; technical writing; telecommunications; women's studies

UNIVERSITY OF CALIFORNIA, DAVIS

Davis, California

University Extension
universityextension.ucdavis.edu

University of California, Davis, founded in 1905, is a state-supported university. It is accredited by the Western Association of Schools and Colleges, Inc. It first offered distance learning courses in 1987. In 1999–2000, it offered 13 courses at a distance. In fall 1999, there were 182 students enrolled in distance learning courses.

Course delivery sites Courses are delivered to your home, your workplace, 1 off-campus center in Sacramento.

Media Courses are delivered via television, videotapes, videoconferencing, computer software, CD-ROM, World Wide Web, e-mail, print. Students and teachers may interact via videoconferencing, mail, telephone, fax, e-mail, World Wide Web. The following equipment may be required: television, videocassette player, computer, modem, Internet access, e-mail.

Restrictions Programs are available worldwide. Enrollment is open to anyone.

Services Distance learners have access to e-mail services, academic advising, tutoring at a distance.

Typical costs Tuition of $645 per course. Costs may vary.

Registration Students may register by mail, fax, telephone, e-mail, World Wide Web, in person.

Contact Student Services, University of California, Davis, University Extension, 1333 Research Park Drive, Davis, CA 95616. *Telephone:* 800-752-0881. *Fax:* 530-757-8558. *E-mail:* questions@unexmail.ucdavis.edu.

DEGREES AND AWARDS

Distance programs offered do not lead to a degree or other formal award.

COURSE SUBJECT AREAS OFFERED OUTSIDE OF DEGREE PROGRAMS

Undergraduate: Business administration and management; computer and information sciences; computer programming; database management; environmental science; foods and nutrition studies

UNIVERSITY OF CALIFORNIA EXTENSION

Berkeley, California

Center for Media and Independent Learning
learn.berkeley.edu

University of California Extension is a state-related university extension. It first offered distance learning courses in 1913. In 1999–2000, it offered 200 courses at a distance. In fall 1999, there were 3,500 students enrolled in distance learning courses.

Course delivery sites Courses are delivered to your home, your workplace.

Media Courses are delivered via audiotapes, computer software, computer conferencing, World Wide Web, print. Students and teachers may interact via mail, telephone, fax, e-mail, World Wide Web. The following equipment may be required: computer, modem, Internet access, e-mail.

Restrictions Programs are available worldwide. Enrollment is open to anyone.

Services Distance learners have access to bookstore at a distance.

Typical costs Tuition of $485 per course. *Noncredit courses:* $385 per course.

Registration Students may register by mail, fax, telephone, e-mail, World Wide Web, in person.

Contact Student Services, University of California Extension, Center for Media and Independent Learning, Berkeley, CA 94704. *Telephone:* 510-642-4124. *Fax:* 510-643-9271. *E-mail:* askcmil@uclink4.berkeley.edu.

DEGREES AND AWARDS

Graduate Certificate(s) Business Administration, Computer Information Systems, Direct Marketing Methods, e-Commerce, Hazardous Materials Management, Integrated Marketing Communications, Marketing, Project Management, Telecommunications Fundamentals

COURSE SUBJECT AREAS OFFERED OUTSIDE OF DEGREE PROGRAMS

Undergraduate: Accounting; administrative and secretarial services; advertising; American (U.S.) history; American literature; American studies; anthropology; area, ethnic, and cultural studies; Asian languages and literatures; astronomy and astrophysics; biological and life sciences; biology; botany; business; business administration and management; business communications; chemistry; Chinese language and literature; civil engineering; communications; computer and information sciences; computer programming; conservation and natural resources; creative writing; database management; design; developmental and child psychology; economics; electrical engineering; English as a second language (ESL); English composition; English language and literature; English literature; film studies; finance; fine arts; French language and literature; geology; health professions and related sciences; history; human resources management; information sciences and systems; international business; Italian language and literature; library and information studies; management information systems; marketing; mathematics; music; philosophy and religion; physics; political science; psychology; public health; public

relations; real estate; religious studies; social psychology; sociology; Spanish language and literature; teacher education; technical writing; telecommunications; women's studies

Noncredit: Creative writing; English composition; English language and literature; health professions and related sciences

See full description on page 732.

UNIVERSITY OF CALIFORNIA, IRVINE

Irvine, California

University Extension
www.unex.uci.edu/

University of California, Irvine, founded in 1965, is a state-supported university. It is accredited by the Western Association of Schools and Colleges, Inc. It first offered distance learning courses in 1994. In 1999–2000, it offered 20 courses at a distance. In fall 1999, there were 45 students enrolled in distance learning courses.

Course delivery sites Courses are delivered to your home, your workplace, military bases.

Media Courses are delivered via computer software, World Wide Web, e-mail. Students and teachers may interact via telephone, fax, e-mail, World Wide Web. The following equipment may be required: computer, modem, Internet access, e-mail.

Restrictions Programs are available nationwide. Enrollment is open to anyone.

Typical costs Please contact school for information. Financial aid is available to distance learners.

Registration Students may register by mail, fax, telephone, World Wide Web, in person.

Contact Student Services, University of California, Irvine, PO Box 6050, Irvine, CA 92616-6050. *Telephone:* 949-824-1010. *Fax:* 949-824-2090.

DEGREES AND AWARDS

Distance programs offered do not lead to a degree or other formal award.

COURSE SUBJECT AREAS OFFERED OUTSIDE OF DEGREE PROGRAMS

Noncredit: Computer programming

UNIVERSITY OF CALIFORNIA, LOS ANGELES

Los Angeles, California

University Extension
www.unex.ucla.edu

University of California, Los Angeles, founded in 1919, is a state-supported university. It is accredited by the Western Association of Schools and Colleges, Inc. In 1999–2000, it offered 250 courses at a distance. In fall 1999, there were 2,000 students enrolled in distance learning courses.

Course delivery sites Courses are delivered to your home, your workplace, military bases, high schools.

Media Courses are delivered via videoconferencing, computer software, computer conferencing, World Wide Web, e-mail. Students and teachers may interact via videoconferencing, mail, fax, e-mail, World Wide Web. The following equipment may be required: computer, modem, Internet access.

Restrictions Programs are available worldwide. Enrollment is open to anyone.

Services Distance learners have access to e-mail services, academic advising, tutoring, bookstore at a distance.

Credit-earning options Students may transfer credits from another institution or may earn credits through examinations, portfolio assessment.

Typical costs Tuition of $475 per course. Costs may vary. Financial aid is available to distance learners.

Registration Students may register by mail, fax, telephone, e-mail, World Wide Web, in person.

Contact Dr. Kathleen McGuire, Manager, Distance Learning Programs, University of California, Los Angeles, 10995 Le Conte Avenue, Suite 639, Los Angeles, CA 90024. *Telephone:* 310-206-1576. *Fax:* 310-206-5006. *E-mail:* dstlrng@unex.ucla.edu.

DEGREES AND AWARDS

Undergraduate Certificate(s) College Counseling Program (service area differs from that of the overall institution), Cross-Cultural Language and Academic Development (CLAD) Program (service area differs from that of the overall institution), General Business Studies (service area differs from that of the overall institution), General Business Systems Concentration in Accounting (service area differs from that of the overall institution), General Business Systems Concentration in Human Resources Management (service area differs from that of the overall institution), General Business Systems Concentration in Personal Financial Planning (service area differs from that of the overall institution), General Business Systems Concentration in Technical Communications (service area differs from that of the overall institution), Online Teaching Program (service area differs from that of the overall institution), Teaching English to Speakers of Other Languages (TESOL) Program (service area differs from that of the overall institution)

Graduate Certificate(s) Applications Programming (service area differs from that of the overall institution), Personal Financial Planning (service area differs from that of the overall institution), Teaching English as a Foreign Language (TEFL) Program (service area differs from that of the overall institution)

COURSE SUBJECT AREAS OFFERED OUTSIDE OF DEGREE PROGRAMS

Graduate: American (U.S.) history; archaeology; business; business administration and management; business communications; computer and information sciences; computer programming; counseling psychology; creative writing; design; economics; education; ethics; European languages and literatures; film studies; finance; health and physical education/fitness; human resources management; information sciences and systems; instructional media; international business; investments and securities; journalism; liberal arts, general studies, and humanities; management information systems; marketing; mathematics; philosophy and religion; psychology; public relations; social sciences; Spanish language and literature; student counseling; technical writing; visual and performing arts

See full description on page 734.

UNIVERSITY OF CALIFORNIA, RIVERSIDE

Riverside, California

University Extension

www.unex.ucr.edu

University of California, Riverside, founded in 1954, is a state-supported university. It is accredited by the Western Association of Schools and Colleges, Inc.

Course delivery sites Courses are delivered to your home, your workplace, military bases, high schools, 1 off-campus center in Temecula.

Media Courses are delivered via videoconferencing, computer software, World Wide Web, e-mail, print. Students and teachers may meet in person or interact via audioconferencing, mail, telephone, fax, e-mail, World Wide Web. The following equipment may be required: computer, modem, Internet access, e-mail.

Restrictions Programs are available worldwide. Enrollment is open to anyone.

Services Distance learners have access to academic advising, bookstore at a distance.

Credit-earning options Students may earn credits through examinations.

Typical costs *Undergraduate:* Tuition of $290 per course. *Graduate:* Tuition of $290 per course.

Registration Students may register by mail, fax, telephone, e-mail, in person.

Contact Eric Tompkins, Distance Learning Coordinator, University of California, Riverside, 1200 University Avenue, Riverside, CA 92507. *Telephone:* 909-787-4105 Ext. 1741. *Fax:* 909-787-7273. *E-mail:* etompkins@ucr.ucx.edu.

DEGREES AND AWARDS

Graduate Certificate(s) Marketing Management in a Global Environment (certain restrictions apply; service area differs from that of the overall institution)

COURSE SUBJECT AREAS OFFERED OUTSIDE OF DEGREE PROGRAMS

Undergraduate: Education; education administration; English as a second language (ESL); environmental science; plant sciences

Graduate: Education; education administration; English as a second language (ESL); environmental science; plant sciences

UNIVERSITY OF CALIFORNIA, SANTA CRUZ

Santa Cruz, California

Media Services

media.ucsc.edu

University of California, Santa Cruz, founded in 1965, is a state-supported university. It is accredited by the Western Association of Schools and Colleges, Inc. It first offered distance learning courses in 1995.

Course delivery sites Courses are delivered to University of California, Davis (Davis), off-campus center(s) in Cupertino.

Media Courses are delivered via videoconferencing. Students and teachers may meet in person or interact via videoconferencing, mail, telephone, fax, e-mail.

Restrictions Programs are available to in-state students only. Enrollment is restricted to individuals meeting certain criteria.

Services Distance learners have access to library services, academic advising, tutoring, career placement assistance at a distance.

Typical costs *Undergraduate:* Tuition of $2896 per quarter plus mandatory fees of $1459.60 per quarter for in-state residents. Tuition of $9385 per quarter plus mandatory fees of $190 per quarter for out-of-state residents. *Graduate:* Tuition of $3086 per quarter plus mandatory fees of $1082 per quarter for in-state residents. Tuition of $9384 per quarter for out-of-state residents. Tuition for in-state graduate and undergraduate students is $605 per 3 units. Financial aid is available to distance learners.

Contact Chris Laxton, Presentations Manager, University of California, Santa Cruz, Media Services, Santa Cruz, CA 95064. *Telephone:* 831-459-3105. *Fax:* 831-459-3953. *E-mail:* claxton@cats.ucsc.edu.

DEGREES AND AWARDS

Undergraduate Certificate(s) Network Management (service area differs from that of the overall institution), Semiconductor Engineering (service area differs from that of the overall institution), Systems Administration (service area differs from that of the overall institution), Web Systems Engineering (service area differs from that of the overall institution)
MCE Computer Engineering (service area differs from that of the overall institution)

COURSE SUBJECT AREAS OFFERED OUTSIDE OF DEGREE PROGRAMS

Undergraduate: Computer and information sciences; economics; history; liberal arts, general studies, and humanities; political science
Graduate: Computer and information sciences; economics; history; liberal arts, general studies, and humanities; political science

UNIVERSITY OF CENTRAL ARKANSAS

Conway, Arkansas
Division of Continuing Education
www.uca.edu/conted

University of Central Arkansas, founded in 1907, is a state-supported, comprehensive institution. It is accredited by the North Central Association of Colleges and Schools. It first offered distance learning courses in 1929. In 1999–2000, it offered 120 courses at a distance. In fall 1999, there were 2,500 students enrolled in distance learning courses.
Course delivery sites Courses are delivered to your home, your workplace, military bases, Mid-South Community College (West Memphis), Mississippi County Community College (Blytheville), University of Arkansas at Monticello (Monticello), off-campus center(s).
Media Courses are delivered via interactive television, computer software, World Wide Web, e-mail, print. Students and teachers may interact via mail, e-mail, interactive television, World Wide Web. The following equipment may be required: computer, modem, Internet access, e-mail.
Restrictions Programs are available worldwide. Enrollment is restricted to individuals meeting certain criteria.
Services Distance learners have access to library services, e-mail services, academic advising, bookstore at a distance.
Credit-earning options Students may earn credits through examinations.
Typical costs *Undergraduate:* Tuition of $115 per semester hour plus mandatory fees of $30 per semester hour for in-state residents. Tuition of $226 per semester hour plus mandatory fees of $30 per semester hour for out-of-state residents. *Graduate:* Tuition of $143.50 per semester hour plus mandatory fees of $30 per semester hour for in-state residents. Tuition of $296.50 per semester hour plus mandatory fees of $30 per semester hour for out-of-state residents. Tuition for guided study is $70 per semester hour with a $30 per course mandatory fee. Costs may vary. Financial aid is available to distance learners.
Registration Students may register by mail, fax, in person.
Contact Rebecca Rodgers, Secretary, Compressed Video/Internet, University of Central Arkansas, 201 Donaghey Avenue, Conway, AR 72035-5003. *Telephone:* 501-450-5372. *Fax:* 501-450-5277. *E-mail:* rebeccar@ecom.uca.edu.

DEGREES AND AWARDS

Distance programs offered do not lead to a degree or other formal award.

COURSE SUBJECT AREAS OFFERED OUTSIDE OF DEGREE PROGRAMS

Undergraduate: Business; creative writing; economics; education; English language and literature; finance; geography; German language and literature; health and physical education/fitness; history; home economics and family studies; marketing; mathematics; philosophy and religion; physical sciences; political science; psychology; social sciences; special education
Graduate: Curriculum and instruction; education; geography; occupational therapy; physical therapy; special education
See full description on page 736.

UNIVERSITY OF CENTRAL FLORIDA

Orlando, Florida
Center for Distributed Learning
distrib.ucf.edu

University of Central Florida, founded in 1963, is a state-supported university. It is accredited by the Southern Association of Colleges and Schools. In 1999–2000, it offered 251 courses at a distance. In fall 1999, there were 1,800 students enrolled in distance learning courses.
Course delivery sites Courses are delivered to your home, your workplace, military bases, Florida Gulf Coast University (Fort Myers), 3 off-campus centers in Cocoa, Daytona Beach, Downtown Academic Center, Palm Bay, South Orlando Campus.
Media Courses are delivered via videotapes, interactive television, computer software, CD-ROM, computer conferencing, World Wide Web, e-mail, print. Students and teachers may meet in person or interact via mail, telephone, fax, e-mail, interactive television, World Wide Web. The following equipment may be required: computer, modem, Internet access.
Restrictions Programs are available to in-state students only. Enrollment is restricted to individuals meeting certain criteria.
Services Distance learners have access to library services, the campus computer network, e-mail services, academic advising, bookstore at a distance.
Credit-earning options Students may transfer credits from another institution or may earn credits through examinations, portfolio assessment, military training.
Typical costs *Undergraduate:* Tuition of $73.40 per semester for in-state residents. Tuition of $306.35 per semester for out-of-state residents. *Graduate:* Tuition of $146.22 per credit for in-state residents. Tuition of $506.95 per credit for out-of-state residents. Application fee is $20. Costs may vary. Financial aid is available to distance learners.
Registration Students may register by telephone, World Wide Web, in person.
Contact Dr. Steven E. Sorg, Assistant Vice President and Director Center for Distributed Learning, University of Central Florida, 12424 Research Parkway, Suite 264, Orlando, FL 32826-3269. *Telephone:* 407-207-4910. *Fax:* 407-207-4911. *E-mail:* distrib@mail.ucf.edu.

DEGREES AND AWARDS

BA Liberal Studies (service area differs from that of the overall institution; some on-campus requirements)
BS Education (service area differs from that of the overall institution; some on-campus requirements), Liberal Studies (service area differs from that of the overall institution; some on-campus requirements)
BSET Engineering Technology (service area differs from that of the overall institution)
BSN Nursing (some on-campus requirements)
RN to BSN Nursing
MChem Forensic Chemistry (certain restrictions apply; service area differs from that of the overall institution)

COURSE SUBJECT AREAS OFFERED OUTSIDE OF DEGREE PROGRAMS

Undergraduate: Business administration and management; computer and information sciences; economics; education; electrical engineering; engineering; engineering-related technologies; English language and literature; health services administration; hospitality services management; industrial engineering; law and legal studies; mechanical engineering; nursing; philosophy and religion; political science; psychology; public administration and services; radio and television broadcasting; social sciences; sociology; special education; statistics; visual and performing arts
Graduate: Chemistry; civil engineering; education; electrical engineering; health services administration; industrial engineering; mathematics; mechanical engineering; psychology; statistics

See full descriptions on pages 676 and 738.

COURSE SUBJECT AREAS OFFERED OUTSIDE OF DEGREE PROGRAMS

Undergraduate: Art history and criticism; computer programming; counseling psychology; criminal justice; education; education administration; English as a second language (ESL); English composition; European languages and literatures; health and physical education/fitness; instructional media; law and legal studies; management information systems; marketing; student counseling; teacher education; visual and performing arts; women's studies
Graduate: Art history and criticism; counseling psychology; criminal justice; education; education administration; educational psychology; law and legal studies; student counseling; teacher education; visual and performing arts

See full description on page 676.

UNIVERSITY OF CENTRAL OKLAHOMA

Edmond, Oklahoma

Distance Learning Technologies
www.ucok.edu/cyber

University of Central Oklahoma, founded in 1890, is a state-supported, comprehensive institution. It is accredited by the North Central Association of Colleges and Schools. It first offered distance learning courses in 1993. In 1999–2000, it offered 30 courses at a distance. In fall 1999, there were 150 students enrolled in distance learning courses.

Course delivery sites Courses are delivered to your home, your workplace, military bases, high schools, Rose State College (Midwest City), Southwestern Oklahoma State University (Weatherford), Tulsa Community College (Tulsa).

Media Courses are delivered via television, videoconferencing, interactive television, computer software, computer conferencing, World Wide Web, e-mail, print. Students and teachers may meet in person or interact via videoconferencing, mail, telephone, fax, e-mail, interactive television, World Wide Web. The following equipment may be required: computer, modem, Internet access, e-mail.

Restrictions Programs are available worldwide. Enrollment is open to anyone.

Services Distance learners have access to library services, the campus computer network, e-mail services, academic advising, tutoring, career placement assistance, bookstore at a distance.

Credit-earning options Students may transfer credits from another institution.

Typical costs *Undergraduate:* Tuition of $50 per credit hour plus mandatory fees of $14.20 per credit hour for in-state residents. Tuition of $93 per credit hour plus mandatory fees of $64 per credit hour for out-of-state residents. *Graduate:* Tuition of $66 per credit hour plus mandatory fees of $14.20 per credit hour for in-state residents. Tuition of $109 per credit hour plus mandatory fees of $80.20 per credit hour for out-of-state residents. Costs may vary. Financial aid is available to distance learners.

Registration Students may register by telephone, in person.

Contact Sandra Thomas, Assistant to the Chief Technology Officer, University of Central Oklahoma, Information Technology Consulting, 100 North University Drive, Box 188, Edmond, OK 73034-5209. *Telephone:* 405-974-2690. *Fax:* 405-974-3899. *E-mail:* sthomas@ucok.edu.

DEGREES AND AWARDS

Distance programs offered do not lead to a degree or other formal award.

UNIVERSITY OF CHARLESTON

Charleston, West Virginia

Off-Campus Programs
www.uchaswv.edu

University of Charleston, founded in 1888, is an independent, nonprofit, comprehensive institution. It is accredited by the North Central Association of Colleges and Schools. It first offered distance learning courses in 1982. In 1999–2000, it offered 4 courses at a distance. In fall 1999, there were 30 students enrolled in distance learning courses.

Course delivery sites Courses are delivered to your home, your workplace, military bases.

Media Courses are delivered via computer software, World Wide Web, e-mail, print. Students and teachers may meet in person or interact via mail, telephone, fax, e-mail, World Wide Web. The following equipment may be required: computer, modem, Internet access, e-mail.

Restrictions Programs are available worldwide. Enrollment is open to anyone.

Services Distance learners have access to library services, the campus computer network, e-mail services, academic advising at a distance.

Credit-earning options Students may transfer credits from another institution or may earn credits through examinations, portfolio assessment, military training, business training.

Typical costs Tuition of $265 per credit. Costs may vary.

Registration Students may register by mail, fax, telephone, e-mail, World Wide Web, in person.

Contact Connie Young, Registrar, University of Charleston. *Telephone:* 304-357-4737. *Fax:* 304-357-4769. *E-mail:* cyoung@uchaswv.edu.

DEGREES AND AWARDS

Distance programs offered do not lead to a degree or other formal award.

COURSE SUBJECT AREAS OFFERED OUTSIDE OF DEGREE PROGRAMS

Undergraduate: Business; computer and information sciences; English language and literature; health and physical education/fitness
Noncredit: Business; computer and information sciences; English language and literature

UNIVERSITY OF CINCINNATI

Cincinnati, Ohio

College of Evening and Continuing Education (CECE)
www.uc.edu/cece

University of Cincinnati, founded in 1819, is a state-supported university. It is accredited by the North Central Association of Colleges and Schools. It first offered distance learning courses in 1976. In 1999–2000, it offered 55 courses at a distance.

Course delivery sites Courses are delivered to your home, high schools, Central Ohio Technical College (Newark), Columbus State Community College (Columbus), Lima Technical College (Lima), Terra State Community College (Fremont), 1 off-campus center in Warren County.

Media Courses are delivered via television, videotapes, videoconferencing, interactive television, computer software, World Wide Web, e-mail, print. Students and teachers may meet in person or interact via videoconferencing, audioconferencing, mail, telephone, fax, e-mail, interactive television, World Wide Web. The following equipment may be required: television, videocassette player, computer, modem, Internet access.

Restrictions Fire Science courses are offered nationwide; video conference courses are offered statewide; telecourses are offered locally. Enrollment is open to anyone.

Services Distance learners have access to library services, the campus computer network, e-mail services, academic advising, bookstore at a distance.

Credit-earning options Students may transfer credits from another institution or may earn credits through examinations, portfolio assessment.

Typical costs *Undergraduate:* Tuition of $139 per credit for in-state residents. Tuition of $358 per credit for out-of-state residents. *Graduate:* Tuition of $196 per credit for in-state residents. Tuition of $369 per credit for out-of-state residents. *Noncredit courses:* $35 per course. Costs may vary. Financial aid is available to distance learners.

Registration Students may register by mail, fax, telephone, World Wide Web, in person.

Contact Melody Clark, Director, Special Projects, University of Cincinnati, College of Evening and Continuing Education, PO Box 210019, Cincinnati, OH 45221-0019. *Telephone:* 513-556-9154. *Fax:* 513-556-6380. *E-mail:* melody.clark@uc.edu.

DEGREES AND AWARDS

BS Fire Science Administration (service area differs from that of the overall institution)

COURSE SUBJECT AREAS OFFERED OUTSIDE OF DEGREE PROGRAMS

Undergraduate: Business; business administration and management; criminal justice; economics; ethics; fire science; history; logic; nursing; sociology; substance abuse counseling; women's studies
Graduate: Nursing

UNIVERSITY OF CINCINNATI RAYMOND WALTERS COLLEGE

Cincinnati, Ohio

Outreach and Continuing Education
www.rwc.uc.edu/admins/oce/oce.html

University of Cincinnati Raymond Walters College, founded in 1967, is a state-supported, two-year college. It is accredited by the North Central Association of Colleges and Schools. It first offered distance learning

courses in 1995. In 1999–2000, it offered 20 courses at a distance. In fall 1999, there were 150 students enrolled in distance learning courses.

Course delivery sites Courses are delivered to your home, your workplace.

Media Courses are delivered via videotapes, computer software, CD-ROM, World Wide Web, e-mail, print. Students and teachers may meet in person or interact via mail, telephone, fax, e-mail, World Wide Web. The following equipment may be required: television, videocassette player, computer, modem, Internet access, e-mail.

Restrictions Programs are available to local area students. Enrollment is open to anyone.

Services Distance learners have access to library services, the campus computer network, e-mail services at a distance.

Credit-earning options Students may transfer credits from another institution or may earn credits through examinations, military training, business training.

Typical costs *Undergraduate:* Tuition of $99 per credit plus mandatory fees of $115 per quarter for in-state residents. Tuition of $250 per credit plus mandatory fees of $115 per quarter for out-of-state residents. *Graduate:* Tuition of $185 per credit for in-state residents. Tuition of $350 per credit for out-of-state residents. Varies. Financial aid is available to distance learners.

Registration Students may register by mail, fax, telephone, in person.

Contact Dr. Susan Kemper, Assistant Dean, University of Cincinnati Raymond Walters College, 9555 Plainfield Road, Cincinnati, OH 45236-1096. *Telephone:* 513-745-5776. *Fax:* 513-745-8315. *E-mail:* susan.kemper@uc.edu.

DEGREES AND AWARDS

Distance programs offered do not lead to a degree or other formal award.

COURSE SUBJECT AREAS OFFERED OUTSIDE OF DEGREE PROGRAMS

Undergraduate: Biological and life sciences; business; business communications; communications; English composition; English language and literature; health professions and related sciences; human resources management; sociology

UNIVERSITY OF COLORADO AT BOULDER

Boulder, Colorado

Center for Advanced Training in Engineering and Computer Science (CATECS)
www.colorado.edu/CATECS

University of Colorado at Boulder, founded in 1876, is a state-supported university. It is accredited by the North Central Association of Colleges and Schools. It first offered distance learning courses in 1983. In 1999–2000, it offered 150 courses at a distance. In fall 1999, there were 550 students enrolled in distance learning courses.

Course delivery sites Courses are delivered to your home, your workplace, military bases, other colleges, 2 off-campus centers in Broomfield, Littleton.

Media Courses are delivered via television, videotapes, videoconferencing, World Wide Web. Students and teachers may meet in person or interact via videoconferencing, mail, telephone, fax, e-mail, World Wide Web. The following equipment may be required: television, videocassette player, computer, Internet access, e-mail.

Restrictions Programs are available worldwide. Enrollment is open to anyone.

Services Distance learners have access to the campus computer network, e-mail services, academic advising, bookstore at a distance.

Credit-earning options Students may transfer credits from another institution.

Typical costs Tuition of $1200 per course. *Noncredit courses:* $1200 per course. Financial aid is available to distance learners.

Registration Students may register by mail, fax, in person.

Contact Vincent P. Micucci, Director, University of Colorado at Boulder, CATECS, Campus Box 435, Boulder, CO 80309. *Telephone:* 303-492-6048. *Fax:* 303-492-5987. *E-mail:* micucciv@spot.colorado.edu.

DEGREES AND AWARDS

ME Aerospace Engineering (some on-campus requirements), Computer Science (some on-campus requirements), Electrical and Computer Engineering (some on-campus requirements), Engineering Management (some on-campus requirements), Telecommunications (some on-campus requirements)

MS Aerospace Engineering, Electrical and Computer Engineering (some on-campus requirements), Mechanical Engineering (some on-campus requirements), Telecommunications (some on-campus requirements)

COURSE SUBJECT AREAS OFFERED OUTSIDE OF DEGREE PROGRAMS

Graduate: Aerospace, aeronautical engineering; civil engineering; computer and information sciences; electrical engineering; engineering-related technologies; engineering/industrial management; environmental engineering; mechanical engineering; telecommunications

Noncredit: Aerospace, aeronautical engineering; civil engineering; computer and information sciences; electrical engineering; engineering-related technologies; engineering/industrial management; environmental engineering; mechanical engineering; telecommunications

See full description on page 822.

UNIVERSITY OF COLORADO AT COLORADO SPRINGS

Colorado Springs, Colorado
CU-NET
www.uccs.edu

University of Colorado at Colorado Springs, founded in 1965, is a state-supported, comprehensive institution. It is accredited by the North Central Association of Colleges and Schools. It first offered distance learning courses in 1987. In 1999–2000, it offered 3 courses at a distance. In fall 1999, there were 100 students enrolled in distance learning courses.

Course delivery sites Courses are delivered to your home, your workplace, military bases.

Media Courses are delivered via television, videotapes, computer software, World Wide Web, e-mail, print. Students and teachers may meet in person or interact via mail, telephone, fax, e-mail. The following equipment may be required: television, videocassette player.

Restrictions Programs, other than certificate and M.B.A., are limited to the local broadcast area. Enrollment is open to anyone.

Services Distance learners have access to library services, the campus computer network, e-mail services, academic advising, career placement assistance, bookstore at a distance.

Credit-earning options Students may transfer credits from another institution.

Typical costs *Undergraduate:* Tuition of $99 per credit. *Graduate:* Tuition of $350 per course. Contact school for mandatory fee information. Costs may vary.

Registration Students may register by mail, fax, telephone, in person.

Contact The JEC College Connection, University of Colorado at Colorado Springs, 9697 East Mineral Avenue, Englewood, CO 80112. *Telephone:* 800-777-MIND.

DEGREES AND AWARDS

Undergraduate Certificate(s) Early Reading Instruction (service area differs from that of the overall institution)

MBA Business Administration (service area differs from that of the overall institution)

COURSE SUBJECT AREAS OFFERED OUTSIDE OF DEGREE PROGRAMS

Undergraduate: Liberal arts, general studies, and humanities

Graduate: Business administration and management; teacher education

UNIVERSITY OF COLORADO AT DENVER

Denver, Colorado
CU Online
cuonline.edu

University of Colorado at Denver, founded in 1912, is a state-supported university. It is accredited by the North Central Association of Colleges and Schools. It first offered distance learning courses in 1996. In 1999–2000, it offered 85 courses at a distance. In fall 1999, there were 550 students enrolled in distance learning courses.

Course delivery sites Courses are delivered to your home, your workplace, military bases, high schools.

Media Courses are delivered via computer software, World Wide Web, e-mail. Students and teachers may meet in person or interact via mail, telephone, fax, e-mail, World Wide Web. The following equipment may be required: computer, modem, Internet access, e-mail.

Restrictions Programs are available worldwide. Enrollment is restricted to individuals meeting certain criteria.

Services Distance learners have access to library services, academic advising, bookstore at a distance.

Credit-earning options Students may transfer credits from another institution or may earn credits through examinations, military training.

Typical costs *Undergraduate:* Tuition of $126 per credit hour plus mandatory fees of $100 per course for in-state residents. Tuition of $183 per credit hour plus mandatory fees of $100 per course for out-of-state residents. *Graduate:* Tuition of $185 per credit hour plus mandatory fees of $100 per course for in-state residents. Tuition of $277 per credit hour plus mandatory fees of $100 per course for out-of-state residents. Costs may vary. Financial aid is available to distance learners.

Registration Students may register by World Wide Web.

Contact Patty Godbey, Program Manager, CU Online, University of Colorado at Denver. *Telephone:* 303-556-6505. *Fax:* 303-556-6530. *E-mail:* inquiry@cuonline.edu.

DEGREES AND AWARDS

BA Sociology (certain restrictions apply)
MBA Business Administration (certain restrictions apply)
MEM Engineering Management (certain restrictions apply)
MEng Geographic Information Systems (GIS)

COURSE SUBJECT AREAS OFFERED OUTSIDE OF DEGREE PROGRAMS

Undergraduate: American (U.S.) history; American literature; anthropology; area, ethnic, and cultural studies; biology; calculus; cell biology; civil engineering; communications; computer programming; creative writing; drama and theater; economics; engineering; English composition; English literature; ethics; film studies; fine arts; genetics; history; industrial psychology; Latin language and literature; liberal arts, general studies, and humanities; logic; mathematics; mechanical engineering; music; philosophy and religion; physics; political science; psychology; public relations; social psychology; social sciences; sociology; statistics; technical writing

Graduate: Anthropology; architecture; business; business administration and management; computer programming; engineering; engineering/industrial management; information sciences and systems; liberal arts, general studies, and humanities; management information systems; political science; social sciences; sociology

See full descriptions on pages 740 and 822.

UNIVERSITY OF CONNECTICUT

Storrs, Connecticut

University Center for Instructional Media and Technology
www.uconn.edu/

University of Connecticut, founded in 1881, is a state-supported university. It is accredited by the New England Association of Schools and Colleges. In 1999–2000, it offered 34 courses at a distance. In fall 1999, there were 2,500 students enrolled in distance learning courses.

Course delivery sites Courses are delivered to your home, your workplace, University of Connecticut.

Media Courses are delivered via television, videoconferencing, interactive television, computer software, World Wide Web, e-mail. Students and teachers may meet in person or interact via videoconferencing, mail, telephone, fax, e-mail, interactive television, World Wide Web. The following equipment may be required: television, videocassette player, computer, modem, Internet access, e-mail.

Restrictions Programs are available worldwide. Enrollment is open to anyone.

Services Distance learners have access to library services, the campus computer network, e-mail services, academic advising, tutoring, career placement assistance, bookstore at a distance.

Credit-earning options Students may earn credits through examinations, portfolio assessment.

Typical costs *Undergraduate:* Tuition of $2141 per semester plus mandatory fees of $479 per semester. *Graduate:* Tuition of $4100 per semester. Financial aid is available to distance learners.

Registration Students may register by mail, fax, telephone, e-mail, World Wide Web, in person.

Contact Richard L. Gorham, Director, University of Connecticut, 249 Glenbrook Road, UCONN U-2001, Storrs, CT 06269-2001. *Telephone:* 860-486-2530. *Fax:* 860-486-1766. *E-mail:* dgorham@uconnvm.uconn.edu.

DEGREES AND AWARDS

Distance programs offered do not lead to a degree or other formal award.

COURSE SUBJECT AREAS OFFERED OUTSIDE OF DEGREE PROGRAMS

Undergraduate: Animal sciences; biology; business communications; chemical engineering; environmental science; health professions and related sciences; information sciences and systems; liberal arts, general studies, and humanities; management information systems; mass media; radio and television broadcasting; sociology

Graduate: Chemical engineering; curriculum and instruction; educational psychology; environmental science; health professions and related sciences; liberal arts, general studies, and humanities; management information systems

UNIVERSITY OF DALLAS

Irving, Texas

Graduate School of Management, Center for Distance Learning
gsm.udallas.edu

University of Dallas, founded in 1955, is an independent, religious university. It is accredited by the American Academy for Liberal Education, Southern Association of Colleges and Schools. It first offered distance learning courses in 1970. In 1999–2000, it offered 25 courses at a distance. In fall 1999, there were 300 students enrolled in distance learning courses.

Course delivery sites Courses are delivered to your home, your workplace, military bases, 3 off-campus centers in Fort Worth, Plano, Richardson.

Media Courses are delivered via television, videotapes, videoconferencing, interactive television, computer software, World Wide Web, e-mail, print. Students and teachers may meet in person or interact via videoconferencing, audioconferencing, mail, telephone, fax, e-mail, interactive television, World Wide Web. The following equipment may be required: television, videocassette player, computer, modem, Internet access, e-mail.

Restrictions Programs are available worldwide. Enrollment is restricted to individuals meeting certain criteria.

Services Distance learners have access to library services, e-mail services, academic advising, tutoring, bookstore at a distance.

Credit-earning options Students may transfer credits from another institution or may earn credits through examinations.

Typical costs Tuition of $1173 per course. Financial aid is available to distance learners.

Registration Students may register by mail, fax, e-mail, World Wide Web, in person.

Contact Kate Potwarka, Distance Learning Marketing Coordinator, University of Dallas, 1845 East Northgate Drive, Irving, TX 75062-4736. *Telephone:* 800-832-5622. *Fax:* 972-721-4009. *E-mail:* cfdl@gsm.udallas.edu.

DEGREES AND AWARDS

Graduate Certificate(s) e-Commerce Management, Health Services Management, Information Technology, Sports Management, Telecommunications Management

MBA e-Commerce Management, Health Services Management, Information Technology, Sports Management, Telecommunications Management

MMGT e-Commerce Management, Health Services Management, Information Technology, Sports Management, Telecommunications Management

COURSE SUBJECT AREAS OFFERED OUTSIDE OF DEGREE PROGRAMS

Graduate: Accounting; business; business administration and management; engineering/industrial management; finance; health professions and related sciences; health services administration; human resources management; insurance; international business; investments and securities; management information systems; marketing; organizational behavior studies; telecommunications

See full description on page 742.

UNIVERSITY OF DAYTON

Dayton, Ohio

Continuing Education
www.udayton.edu/~cont_ed

University of Dayton, founded in 1850, is an independent, religious university. It is accredited by the North Central Association of Colleges and Schools.

Course delivery sites Courses are delivered to your home.

Media Courses are delivered via television, videotapes, videoconferencing, print. Students and teachers may meet in person or interact via mail, telephone, fax, e-mail. The following equipment may be required: television, videocassette player, computer, modem, Internet access, e-mail.

Restrictions Programs are available to in-state students only. Enrollment is restricted to individuals meeting certain criteria.

Services Distance learners have access to library services, the campus computer network, e-mail services, career placement assistance at a distance.

Credit-earning options Students may transfer credits from another institution.

Typical costs Tuition of $501 per semester hour. Financial aid is available to distance learners.

Registration Students may register by mail, fax, telephone, e-mail, World Wide Web, in person.

Contact Gina Newlin, Special Programs and Continuing Education, University of Dayton, 300 College Park Drive, Dayton, OH 45469-0800. *Telephone:* 937-229-2605.

DEGREES AND AWARDS

Distance programs offered do not lead to a degree or other formal award.

COURSE SUBJECT AREAS OFFERED OUTSIDE OF DEGREE PROGRAMS

Undergraduate: Engineering; philosophy and religion
Noncredit: Philosophy and religion

UNIVERSITY OF DELAWARE

Newark, Delaware

Division of Continuing and Distance Education
www.udel.edu/ce/index.html

University of Delaware, founded in 1743, is a state-related university. It is accredited by the Middle States Association of Colleges and Schools. It first offered distance learning courses in 1988. In 1999–2000, it offered 200 courses at a distance. In fall 1999, there were 593 students enrolled in distance learning courses.

Course delivery sites Courses are delivered to your home, your workplace, military bases, Atlantic Cape Community College (Mays Landing, NJ), Bucks County Community College (Newtown, PA), Cumberland County College (Vineland, NJ), Harcum College (Bryn Mawr, PA), Helene Fuld School of Nursing (Blackwood, NJ), Luzerne County Community College (Nanticoke, PA), Mercer County Community College (Trenton, NJ), Northampton County Area Community College (Bethlehem, PA).

Media Courses are delivered via videotapes, interactive television, World Wide Web, print. Students and teachers may meet in person or interact via videoconferencing, mail, telephone, fax, e-mail, World Wide Web. The following equipment may be required: television, videocassette player, computer, modem, Internet access, e-mail.

Restrictions Programs are available nationwide. Enrollment is open to anyone.

Services Distance learners have access to library services, the campus computer network, e-mail services, academic advising, career placement assistance, bookstore at a distance.

Credit-earning options Students may transfer credits from another institution or may earn credits through examinations.

Typical costs *Undergraduate:* Tuition of $183 per credit plus mandatory fees of $90 per course for in-state residents. Tuition of $531 per credit plus mandatory fees of $90 per course for out-of-state residents. *Graduate:* Tuition of $243 per credit plus mandatory fees of $90 per course for in-state residents. Tuition of $708 per credit plus mandatory fees of $90 per course for out-of-state residents. Costs may vary. Financial aid is available to distance learners.

Registration Students may register by mail, fax, telephone, in person.

Contact Mary Pritchard, Director, University of Delaware, UD Online, Newark, DE 19716. *Telephone:* 302-831-6442. *Fax:* 302-831-3292. *E-mail:* maryvp@udel.edu.

DEGREES AND AWARDS

BS Hotel, Restaurant, and Institutional Management (service area differs from that of the overall institution; some on-campus requirements), Nursing (service area differs from that of the overall institution; some on-campus requirements)

COURSE SUBJECT AREAS OFFERED OUTSIDE OF DEGREE PROGRAMS

Undergraduate: Agriculture; algebra; American (U.S.) history; area, ethnic, and cultural studies; biology; business administration and management; calculus; chemical engineering; chemistry; child care and development; classical languages and literatures; communications; developmental and child psychology; economics; educational psychology; electrical engineering; engineering-related technologies; English composition; English language and literature; ethics; foods and nutrition studies; home economics and family studies; hospitality services management; human resources management; individual and family development studies; instructional media; liberal arts, general studies, and humanities; marketing; mathematics; mechanical engineering; microbiology; nursing; organizational behavior studies; philosophy and religion; political science; religious studies; sociology; teacher education

Graduate: Aerospace, aeronautical engineering; biology; chemical engineering; civil engineering; education administration; educational psychology; electrical engineering; engineering mechanics; environmental engineering; instructional media; mechanical engineering; nursing; political science; teacher education

Noncredit: Chemical engineering; electrical engineering; engineering mechanics; English composition; environmental engineering; fine arts; microbiology; nursing; protective services

See full descriptions on pages 676 and 744.

UNIVERSITY OF DENVER

Denver, Colorado

University College
www.universitycollege.du.edu/online/overview.html

University of Denver, founded in 1864, is an independent, nonprofit university. It is accredited by the North Central Association of Colleges and Schools. It first offered distance learning courses in 1996. In 1999–2000, it offered 101 courses at a distance. In fall 1999, there were 156 students enrolled in distance learning courses.

Course delivery sites Courses are delivered to your home, your workplace, military bases.

Media Courses are delivered via World Wide Web, e-mail, print. Students and teachers may interact via audioconferencing, mail, telephone, fax, e-mail, World Wide Web. The following equipment may be required: computer, modem, Internet access, e-mail.

Restrictions Programs are available worldwide. Enrollment is open to anyone.

Services Distance learners have access to library services, the campus computer network, e-mail services, academic advising, career placement assistance, bookstore at a distance.

Credit-earning options Students may transfer credits from another institution or may earn credits through business training.

Typical costs Tuition of $310 per quarter hour plus mandatory fees of $4 per quarter hour. Costs may vary. Financial aid is available to distance learners.

Registration Students may register by mail, fax, telephone, in person.

Contact Cynthia M. De Larber, Director of Marketing, University of Denver, 2211 South Josephine Street, Denver, CO 80210. *Telephone:* 303-871-3074. *Fax:* 303-871-3070. *E-mail:* cdelarbe@du.edu.

DEGREES AND AWARDS

Graduate Certificate(s) American Indian Studies, Business Environmental Management, Ecotourism Management Ecotourism Management, Environmental Health and Safety Management, Environmental Management, Environmental Regulatory Compliance, Geographic Information Systems, Management of Hazardous Materials, Natural Resource Management, Network Analysis and Design, Telecommunications

MCIS Computer Information Systems

MEPM Environmental Policy and Management

MTEL Telecommunications

COURSE SUBJECT AREAS OFFERED OUTSIDE OF DEGREE PROGRAMS

Undergraduate: American studies

Graduate: American studies; biological and life sciences; communications; computer and information sciences; conservation and natural resources; creative writing; information sciences and systems; physical sciences; technical writing; telecommunications

UNIVERSITY OF FINDLAY

Findlay, Ohio

Global Campus

www.gcampus.org

University of Findlay, founded in 1882, is an independent, religious, comprehensive institution affiliated with the Church of God. It is accredited by the North Central Association of Colleges and Schools. In 1999–2000, it offered 76 courses at a distance. In fall 1999, there were 318 students enrolled in distance learning courses.

Course delivery sites Courses are delivered to your home, your workplace, high schools, 1 off-campus center in Zanesville.

Media Courses are delivered via videotapes, videoconferencing, CD-ROM, computer conferencing, World Wide Web, print. Students and teachers may meet in person or interact via videoconferencing, mail, telephone, fax, e-mail, World Wide Web. The following equipment may be required: television, videocassette player, computer, modem, Internet access, e-mail.

Restrictions Programs are available worldwide. Enrollment is open to anyone.

Services Distance learners have access to library services, the campus computer network, e-mail services, academic advising, career placement assistance, bookstore at a distance.

Credit-earning options Students may transfer credits from another institution or may earn credits through examinations, portfolio assessment, military training, business training.

Typical costs Undergraduate tuition ranges between $203 and $328 per credit. Graduate tuition ranges between $215 and $340 per credit. Typical cost for a noncredit course is between $75 and $125. Costs may vary. Financial aid is available to distance learners.

Registration Students may register by mail, fax, telephone, e-mail, World Wide Web, in person.

Contact Doris Salis, Dean, Adult and Continuing Education, University of Findlay, 1000 North Main Street, Findlay, OH 45840. *Telephone:* 800-558-9060. *Fax:* 419-424-4822. *E-mail:* salis@mail.findlay.edu.

DEGREES AND AWARDS

BS Business Management (certain restrictions apply), Environmental Management (certain restrictions apply; some on-campus requirements)

MS Business Administration (certain restrictions apply), Environmental Management (certain restrictions apply; some on-campus requirements)

COURSE SUBJECT AREAS OFFERED OUTSIDE OF DEGREE PROGRAMS

Undergraduate: Accounting; Asian languages and literatures; business law; chemistry, organic; English composition; environmental science; fine arts; health and medical administrative services; marketing; mathematics; organizational behavior studies; paralegal/legal assistant; religious studies; social sciences; substance abuse counseling; technical writing

Graduate: Accounting; environmental science; health and medical administrative services; health services administration; human resources management; instructional media; marketing; organizational behavior studies; substance abuse counseling; teacher education

Noncredit: Continuing education; environmental science; health and medical administrative services; teacher education

See full description on page 746.

UNIVERSITY OF FLORIDA

Gainesville, Florida

Florida Campus Direct

nersp.nerdc.ufl.edu/~oirweb/fcd/

University of Florida, founded in 1853, is a state-supported university. It is accredited by the Southern Association of Colleges and Schools. It first offered distance learning courses in 1919. In 1999–2000, it offered 284 courses at a distance. In fall 1999, there were 4,600 students enrolled in distance learning courses.

Course delivery sites Courses are delivered to your home, your workplace, military bases, 8 off-campus centers in Fort Lauderdale, Immokalee, Jacksonville, Orlando, Tampa.

Media Courses are delivered via videotapes, videoconferencing, computer software, CD-ROM, World Wide Web, e-mail, print. Students and teachers may meet in person or interact via videoconferencing, audioconferencing, mail, telephone, fax, e-mail, World Wide Web. The following equipment may be required: computer, modem, e-mail.

Restrictions Programs are available worldwide. Enrollment is open to anyone.

Services Distance learners have access to library services, the campus computer network, e-mail services, academic advising, bookstore at a distance.

Credit-earning options Students may transfer credits from another institution or may earn credits through examinations.

Typical costs *Undergraduate:* Tuition of $64 per credit for in-state residents. Tuition of $129 per credit for out-of-state residents. *Graduate:* Tuition of $261 per credit for in-state residents. Tuition of $434 per credit for out-of-state residents. Costs may vary. Financial aid is available to distance learners.

Registration Students may register by mail, World Wide Web, in person.

University of Florida

Contact Dr. Sue M. Legg, Director, Office of Instructional Resources, University of Florida, 1012 Turlington Hall, Gainesville, FL 32611-7345. *Telephone:* 352-392-0365. *Fax:* 352-392-7065. *E-mail:* smlegg@nersp. nerdc.ufl.edu.

DEGREES AND AWARDS

Graduate Certificate(s) Forensic Toxicology
EMHA Health Services Administration (service area differs from that of the overall institution; some on-campus requirements)
MAg Agricultural Education (certain restrictions apply; service area differs from that of the overall institution; some on-campus requirements), Communications (certain restrictions apply; service area differs from that of the overall institution; some on-campus requirements), Food and Resource Economics (certain restrictions apply; service area differs from that of the overall institution; some on-campus requirements)
MBA Business Administration (some on-campus requirements)
MS Electrical Engineering (some on-campus requirements)
AuD Audiology (service area differs from that of the overall institution)
PharmD Pharmacy (certain restrictions apply; service area differs from that of the overall institution)

COURSE SUBJECT AREAS OFFERED OUTSIDE OF DEGREE PROGRAMS

Undergraduate: Agriculture; algebra; biology; chemistry; computer and information sciences; engineering; English as a second language (ESL); English composition; horticulture; plant sciences; political science; teacher education
Graduate: Nursing
See full description on page 676.

UNIVERSITY OF GREAT FALLS

Great Falls, Montana

Center for Distance Learning
www.ugf.edu/

University of Great Falls, founded in 1932, is an independent, religious, comprehensive institution. It is accredited by the Northwest Association of Schools and Colleges.
Course delivery sites Courses are delivered to your home, your workplace, Blackfeet Community College (Browning), Brooks Campus of Medicine Hat (Brooks, AB), Casper College (Casper, WY), Central Wyoming College (Riverton, WY), Dawson Community College (Glendive), Dull Knife Memorial College (Lame Deer), Eastern Wyoming College (Torrington, WY), Flathead Valley Community College (Kalispell), Fort Belknap College (Harlem), Grant MacEwan Community College (Edmonton, AB), Laramie County Community College (Cheyenne, WY), Lethbridge Community College (Lethbridge, AB), Medicine Hat College (Medicine Hat, AB), Miles Community College (Miles City), Northern Wyoming Community College (Sheridan, WY), Northwest College (Powell, WY), Stone Child College (Box Elder), Western Wyoming Community College (Rock Springs, WY), 15 off-campus centers in Anaconda, Conrad, Cut Bank, Glasgow, Helena, Lewistown, Libby, Livingston, Shelby, Thompson Falls, Wolf Point, Chewelah (WA), Colville (WA), Evanston (WY), Gillette (WY).
Media Courses are delivered via videotapes, videoconferencing, audiotapes, computer software, CD-ROM, World Wide Web, e-mail, print. Students and teachers may interact via telephone, World Wide Web. The following equipment may be required: television, videocassette player, computer, Internet access.
Restrictions Programs are available worldwide. Enrollment is open to anyone.

Services Distance learners have access to library services, academic advising at a distance.
Credit-earning options Students may transfer credits from another institution or may earn credits through examinations, portfolio assessment, military training, business training.
Typical costs Tuition of $280 per credit hour. Costs may vary. Financial aid is available to distance learners.
Registration Students may register by mail, fax, telephone, e-mail, World Wide Web, in person.
Contact Dr. Coburn Currier, Dean of Distance Learning, University of Great Falls, 1301 20th Street, South, Great Falls, MT 59405. *Telephone:* 406-791-5321. *Fax:* 406-791-5394. *E-mail:* ccurrier@ugf.edu.

DEGREES AND AWARDS

AA Business Administration, Chemical Dependency Counseling, Criminal Justice, Human Services, Microcomputer Management, Paralegal Studies
AS Business Administration/Accounting, Chemical Dependency Counseling, Human Services, Microcomputer Management, Paralegal Studies
BA Business Administration/Management, Computer Science, Counseling Psychology (some on-campus requirements), Criminal Justice, Health Care Administration, Human Services, Microcomputer Management, Paralegal Studies, Religious Studies, Sociology
BS Business Administration/Marketing, Computer Science, Counseling Psychology (some on-campus requirements), Criminal Justice, Health Care Administration, Human Services, Microcomputer Management, Paralegal Studies, Religious Studies, Sociology

COURSE SUBJECT AREAS OFFERED OUTSIDE OF DEGREE PROGRAMS

Undergraduate: Accounting; area, ethnic, and cultural studies; astronomy and astrophysics; biological and life sciences; biology; botany; business; business administration and management; chemistry; communications; computer and information sciences; creative writing; developmental and child psychology; economics; education; education administration; educational psychology; English as a second language (ESL); English composition; English language and literature; geology; health and physical education/fitness; health professions and related sciences; history; law and legal studies; liberal arts, general studies, and humanities; mathematics; philosophy and religion; physical sciences; physics; political science; protective services; psychology; public administration and services; social psychology; social sciences; social work; sociology; special education; teacher education; theological studies; visual and performing arts
Graduate: Computer and information sciences

UNIVERSITY OF GUAM

Mangilao, Guam

Center for Continuing Education and Outreach Programs
www.uog.edu/cceop/links.html

University of Guam, founded in 1952, is a territory-supported, comprehensive institution. It is accredited by the Western Association of Schools and Colleges, Inc. In 1999–2000, it offered 5 courses at a distance. In fall 1999, there were 55 students enrolled in distance learning courses.
Course delivery sites Courses are delivered to your home, your workplace, military bases, high schools.
Media Courses are delivered via television, videotapes, videoconferencing, interactive television, audiotapes, computer software, CD-ROM, computer conferencing, World Wide Web, e-mail, print. Students and teachers may meet in person or interact via videoconferencing, audioconferencing, mail, telephone, fax, e-mail, interactive television. The following equipment may be required: television, videocassette player, computer, modem, Internet access, e-mail.

Restrictions Programs are available on a Regional level. Enrollment is open to anyone.
Services Distance learners have access to library services, the campus computer network, e-mail services at a distance.
Credit-earning options Students may transfer credits from another institution or may earn credits through examinations, portfolio assessment.
Typical costs Tuition is variable and increases every fall semester. Costs may vary.
Registration Students may register by mail, fax, telephone, e-mail, World Wide Web, in person.
Contact Bruce Best, Telecommunications and Distance Education Operation Manager/Research Associate, University of Guam, University of Guam Station, Mangilao, GU 96923. *Telephone:* 671-735-2620. *Fax:* 671-734-8377. *E-mail:* bbest@uog9.uog.edu.

DEGREES AND AWARDS

BSN Nursing (some on-campus requirements)

COURSE SUBJECT AREAS OFFERED OUTSIDE OF DEGREE PROGRAMS

Undergraduate: History; nursing; teacher education
Noncredit: History

UNIVERSITY OF HAWAII AT MANOA

Honolulu, Hawaii
Outreach College
www.aln.hawaii.edu

University of Hawaii at Manoa, founded in 1907, is a state-supported university. It is accredited by the Western Association of Schools and Colleges, Inc.
Course delivery sites Courses are delivered to your home, your workplace, military bases.
Media Courses are delivered via computer software, CD-ROM, computer conferencing, World Wide Web, e-mail, print. Students and teachers may interact via telephone, fax, e-mail, World Wide Web. The following equipment may be required: computer, modem, Internet access, e-mail.
Restrictions Programs are available nationwide. Enrollment is restricted to individuals meeting certain criteria.
Services Distance learners have access to library services, the campus computer network, e-mail services, academic advising, career placement assistance, bookstore at a distance.
Credit-earning options Students may earn credits through examinations.
Typical costs *Undergraduate:* Tuition of $126 per semester credit. *Graduate:* Tuition of $168 per semester credit.
Registration Students may register by mail, fax, telephone, e-mail, World Wide Web, in person.
Contact Jaishree Odin, Interim Assistant Dean, University of Hawaii at Manoa, 2530 Dole Street, Sakamaki C-403, Honolulu, HI 96822. *Telephone:* 808-956-8547. *Fax:* 808-956-3364. *E-mail:* jodin@outreach.hawaii.edu.

DEGREES AND AWARDS

Undergraduate Certificate(s) Database Management (certain restrictions apply)
BA Information and Computer Sciences (certain restrictions apply; some on-campus requirements), Liberal Studies (certain restrictions apply; some on-campus requirements)
MS Information and Computer Sciences (certain restrictions apply)

COURSE SUBJECT AREAS OFFERED OUTSIDE OF DEGREE PROGRAMS

Undergraduate: Communications; database management; information sciences and systems; political science; sociology
Graduate: Information sciences and systems; political science
See full description on page 822.

UNIVERSITY OF HOUSTON

Houston, Texas
Division of Distance and Continuing Education
www.uh.edu/uhdistance

University of Houston, founded in 1927, is a state-supported university. It is accredited by the Southern Association of Colleges and Schools. It first offered distance learning courses in 1984. In 1999–2000, it offered 200 courses at a distance. In fall 1999, there were 2,500 students enrolled in distance learning courses.
Course delivery sites Courses are delivered to your home, your workplace, Alvin Community College (Alvin), Brazosport College (Lake Jackson), College of the Mainland (Texas City), Galveston College (Galveston), Lee College (Baytown), North Harris-Montgomery College District (Houston), San Jacinto College District (Pasadena), Wharton County Junior College (Wharton), 4 off-campus centers in Houston, Katy, Sugar Land, The Woodlands.
Media Courses are delivered via television, videotapes, videoconferencing, interactive television, World Wide Web, print. Students and teachers may meet in person or interact via videoconferencing, mail, telephone, fax, e-mail, interactive television, World Wide Web. The following equipment may be required: television, videocassette player, computer, modem, Internet access, e-mail.
Restrictions Programs are available nationwide. Enrollment is open to anyone.
Services Distance learners have access to library services, the campus computer network, e-mail services, academic advising, tutoring, career placement assistance, bookstore at a distance.
Credit-earning options Students may transfer credits from another institution or may earn credits through examinations.
Typical costs *Undergraduate:* Tuition of $388 per course plus mandatory fees of $50 per course for in-state residents. Tuition of $1030 per course plus mandatory fees of $50 per course for out-of-state residents. *Graduate:* Tuition of $484 per course plus mandatory fees of $50 per semester for in-state residents. Tuition of $1090 per course plus mandatory fees of $50 per semester for out-of-state residents. Other mandatory fees include a $140 per course off campus and electronic course fee assessed for only the first two off-campus courses for which the student registers. Financial aid is available to distance learners.
Registration Students may register by telephone, in person.
Contact Distance Education Advisor, University of Houston, 4242 South Mason Road, Katy, TX 77450. *Telephone:* 281-395-2800. *Fax:* 281-395-2629. *E-mail:* deadvisor@uh.edu.

DEGREES AND AWARDS

BA English, History, Psychology
BS Hotel and Restaurant Management (some on-campus requirements), Psychology
BST Computer Drafting Design (service area differs from that of the overall institution; some on-campus requirements), Industrial Supervision (service area differs from that of the overall institution; some on-campus requirements)
MEE Electrical Engineering (service area differs from that of the overall institution)
MHM Hospitality Management (some on-campus requirements)

MIE Engineering Management (service area differs from that of the overall institution)
MS Computer Science (service area differs from that of the overall institution)
MSOT Training and Development (service area differs from that of the overall institution; some on-campus requirements)

COURSE SUBJECT AREAS OFFERED OUTSIDE OF DEGREE PROGRAMS

Undergraduate: American literature; anthropology; communications; computer and information sciences; creative writing; developmental and child psychology; educational psychology; engineering-related technologies; English language and literature; European languages and literatures; film studies; geology; German language and literature; history; hospitality services management; liberal arts, general studies, and humanities; mathematics; political science; psychology; public health; social psychology; sociology; Spanish language and literature; visual and performing arts
Graduate: Business; business administration and management; computer and information sciences; curriculum and instruction; economics; education; education administration; educational psychology; electrical engineering; European languages and literatures; hospitality services management; industrial engineering; social work; Spanish language and literature

See full descriptions on pages 676 and 748.

UNIVERSITY OF HOUSTON–CLEAR LAKE

Houston, Texas
Distance and Extended Education
www.cl.uh.edu

University of Houston–Clear Lake, founded in 1974, is a state-supported, upper-level institution. It is accredited by the Southern Association of Colleges and Schools. It first offered distance learning courses in 1995. In 1999–2000, it offered 36 courses at a distance. In fall 1999, there were 91 students enrolled in distance learning courses.
Course delivery sites Courses are delivered to your home, your workplace, other colleges, 1 off-campus center in Fort Bend.
Media Courses are delivered via videotapes, videoconferencing, interactive television, computer software, computer conferencing, World Wide Web, e-mail. Students and teachers may meet in person or interact via videoconferencing, mail, telephone, fax, e-mail, interactive television, World Wide Web. The following equipment may be required: television, videocassette player, computer, modem, Internet access, e-mail.
Restrictions Programs will offered on the national and international levels with the advent of Web courses. Enrollment is restricted to individuals meeting certain criteria.
Services Distance learners have access to library services, e-mail services, academic advising, tutoring, bookstore at a distance.
Credit-earning options Students may transfer credits from another institution.
Typical costs *Undergraduate:* Tuition of $38 per credit hour plus mandatory fees of $15 per credit hour for in-state residents. *Graduate:* Tuition of $76 per credit hour plus mandatory fees of $15 per credit hour for in-state residents. Tuition of $255 per credit hour plus mandatory fees of $100 per course for out-of-state residents. Students also pay $43 per semester in various other fees. Costs may vary. Financial aid is available to distance learners.
Registration Students may register by mail, telephone, World Wide Web.

Contact Laurel Dodds, Director, Distance and Extended Education, University of Houston–Clear Lake, 2700 Bay Area Boulevard, Houston, TX 77058-1098. *Telephone:* 281-283-3026. *Fax:* 281-283-2119. *E-mail:* dodds@cl.uh.edu.

DEGREES AND AWARDS

MS Software Engineering (certain restrictions apply; service area differs from that of the overall institution)

COURSE SUBJECT AREAS OFFERED OUTSIDE OF DEGREE PROGRAMS

Undergraduate: English composition
Graduate: Abnormal psychology; computer and information sciences; educational psychology; educational research; engineering; health services administration; instructional media; teacher education

UNIVERSITY OF HOUSTON–DOWNTOWN

Houston, Texas

University of Houston–Downtown, founded in 1974, is a state-supported, four-year college. It is accredited by the Southern Association of Colleges and Schools. In 1999–2000, it offered 25 courses at a distance. In fall 1999, there were 616 students enrolled in distance learning courses.
Course delivery sites Courses are delivered to your home, your workplace, San Jacinto College District (Pasadena), off-campus center(s) in Sugar Land, Woodlands.
Media Courses are delivered via videotapes, interactive television, CD-ROM, World Wide Web, e-mail, print. Students and teachers may meet in person or interact via audioconferencing, mail, telephone, fax, e-mail, interactive television, World Wide Web. The following equipment may be required: television, videocassette player, computer, modem, Internet access, e-mail.
Restrictions Programs are available to local area students. Enrollment is restricted to individuals meeting certain criteria.
Services Distance learners have access to library services, the campus computer network, e-mail services, academic advising, tutoring, career placement assistance, bookstore at a distance.
Credit-earning options Students may transfer credits from another institution or may earn credits through examinations, military training.
Typical costs Tuition of $120 per credit hour for local area residents. Tuition of $120 per credit hour for in-state residents. Tuition of $254 per credit hour for out-of-state residents. Costs may vary. Financial aid is available to distance learners.
Registration Students may register by telephone, in person.
Contact Dr. George Hampton, Assistant Vice President for Academic Affairs, University of Houston–Downtown, One Main Street, Houston, TX 77002. *Telephone:* 713-221-8000. *Fax:* 713-221-8922.

DEGREES AND AWARDS

Distance programs offered do not lead to a degree or other formal award.

COURSE SUBJECT AREAS OFFERED OUTSIDE OF DEGREE PROGRAMS

Undergraduate: Abnormal psychology; accounting; administrative and secretarial services; American (U.S.) history; business administration and management; business law; cognitive psychology; computer programming; creative writing; criminal justice; database management; developmental and child psychology; English literature; finance; gerontology; industrial psychology; international business; liberal arts, general studies, and humanities; management information systems; marketing; music; philosophy and religion; sociology; statistics; teacher education
Graduate: Criminal justice

UNIVERSITY OF HOUSTON–VICTORIA

Victoria, Texas
www.vic.uh.edu

University of Houston–Victoria, founded in 1973, is a state-supported, upper-level institution. It is accredited by the Southern Association of Colleges and Schools. In 1999–2000, it offered 60 courses at a distance. In fall 1999, there were 235 students enrolled in distance learning courses.

Course delivery sites Courses are delivered to your home, 1 off-campus center in Sugar Land.

Media Courses are delivered via interactive television, World Wide Web. Students and teachers may meet in person or interact via mail, telephone, fax, e-mail, interactive television. The following equipment may be required: computer, modem, Internet access, e-mail.

Restrictions Programs are available to local area students. Enrollment is restricted to individuals meeting certain criteria.

Services Distance learners have access to library services, the campus computer network, e-mail services, academic advising at a distance.

Credit-earning options Students may transfer credits from another institution or may earn credits through examinations.

Typical costs *Undergraduate:* Tuition of $38 per semester credit plus mandatory fees of $46 per semester credit for in-state residents. Tuition of $254 per semester credit plus mandatory fees of $46 per semester credit for out-of-state residents. *Graduate:* Tuition of $67 per semester credit plus mandatory fees of $46 per semester credit for in-state residents. Tuition of $254 per semester credit plus mandatory fees of $46 per semester credit for out-of-state residents. Financial aid is available to distance learners.

Registration Students may register by telephone.

Contact Registrar's Office, University of Houston–Victoria, 2506 East Red River, Victoria, TX 77901. *Telephone:* 361-576-3151.

DEGREES AND AWARDS

BS Computer Science (certain restrictions apply; some on-campus requirements), Mathematics (certain restrictions apply; some on-campus requirements)

MBA Business (certain restrictions apply)

MEd Education (certain restrictions apply; some on-campus requirements)

COURSE SUBJECT AREAS OFFERED OUTSIDE OF DEGREE PROGRAMS

Undergraduate: Business; computer and information sciences; education; English composition; history; mathematics

Graduate: Business; computer and information sciences; education; history

UNIVERSITY OF IDAHO

Moscow, Idaho

Engineering Outreach
www.uidaho.edu/evo

University of Idaho, founded in 1889, is a state-supported university. It is accredited by the Northwest Association of Schools and Colleges. It first offered distance learning courses in 1976. In 1999–2000, it offered 175 courses at a distance. In fall 1999, there were 400 students enrolled in distance learning courses.

Course delivery sites Courses are delivered to your home, your workplace, military bases, 3 off-campus centers in Boise, Coeur d'Alene, Idaho Falls.

Media Courses are delivered via videotapes, videoconferencing, interactive television, computer conferencing, World Wide Web, e-mail, print. Students and teachers may meet in person or interact via videoconferencing, mail, telephone, fax, e-mail, World Wide Web. The following equipment may be required: television, videocassette player, computer, Internet access, e-mail.

Restrictions Programs are available worldwide. Enrollment is open to anyone.

Services Distance learners have access to library services, the campus computer network, e-mail services, academic advising, career placement assistance, bookstore at a distance.

Credit-earning options Students may transfer credits from another institution or may earn credits through examinations.

Typical costs *Undergraduate:* Tuition of $324 per credit. *Graduate:* Tuition of $351 per credit. Costs may vary. Financial aid is available to distance learners.

Registration Students may register by mail, fax, telephone, e-mail, in person.

Contact Diane Bancke, Engineering Outreach, University of Idaho, PO Box 441014, Moscow, ID 83844-1014. *Telephone:* 800-824-2889. *Fax:* 208-885-6165. *E-mail:* outreach@uidaho.edu.

DEGREES AND AWARDS

Undergraduate Certificate(s) Computer Science, Education, Electrical Engineering

MAT Teaching Mathematics (some on-campus requirements)

ME Engineering Management (some on-campus requirements), Mechanical Engineering (some on-campus requirements)

MEngr Biological and Agricultural Engineering (some on-campus requirements), Civil Engineering (some on-campus requirements), Computer Engineering (some on-campus requirements), Electrical Engineering (some on-campus requirements), Geological Engineering (some on-campus requirements)

MS Biological and Agricultural Engineering (some on-campus requirements), Civil Engineering (some on-campus requirements), Computer Engineering (some on-campus requirements), Computer Science (some on-campus requirements), Electrical Engineering (some on-campus requirements), Geological Engineering (some on-campus requirements), Metallurgical Engineering (some on-campus requirements), Mining Engineering (some on-campus requirements), Psychology (some on-campus requirements)

PhD Computer Science (some on-campus requirements), Electrical Engineering (some on-campus requirements)

COURSE SUBJECT AREAS OFFERED OUTSIDE OF DEGREE PROGRAMS

Undergraduate: Agriculture; algebra; biology; calculus; chemical engineering; civil engineering; computer and information sciences; earth science; education; electrical engineering; engineering; engineering/industrial management; geography; geology; mathematics; mechanical engineering; psychology; statistics; teacher education

Graduate: Agriculture; algebra; calculus; chemical engineering; civil engineering; computer and information sciences; education; electrical engineering; engineering; engineering/industrial management; ethics; geology; mathematics; mechanical engineering; psychology; teacher education

See full descriptions on pages 750 and 822.

UNIVERSITY OF ILLINOIS AT CHICAGO

Chicago, Illinois

Office of Continuing Education and Public Service/Office of External Education
www.oceps.uic.edu

University of Illinois at Chicago, founded in 1946, is a state-supported university. It is accredited by the North Central Association of Colleges and Schools. In 1999–2000, it offered 50 courses at a distance. In fall 1999, there were 634 students enrolled in distance learning courses.

Course delivery sites Courses are delivered to your home, your workplace.

Media Courses are delivered via computer software, CD-ROM, computer conferencing, World Wide Web, e-mail, print. Students and teachers may meet in person or interact via e-mail, World Wide Web. The following equipment may be required: computer, Internet access, e-mail.

Restrictions Programs are available worldwide. Enrollment is restricted to individuals meeting certain criteria.

Services Distance learners have access to library services, the campus computer network, e-mail services, academic advising, career placement assistance, bookstore at a distance.

Credit-earning options Students may transfer credits from another institution.

Typical costs Contact the school for information. Costs may vary by specific program of study, number of credits taken, and course delivery options. Costs may vary. Financial aid is available to distance learners.

Registration Students may register by mail, fax, telephone, e-mail, in person.

Contact Justine L. McCormick, Senior Program Coordinator, University of Illinois at Chicago, Office of Continuing Education and Public Service (MC 165), 322 South Green Street, Suite 202, Chicago, IL 60607. *Telephone:* 312-996-2470. *Fax:* 312-996-8026. *E-mail:* justinem@uic.edu.

DEGREES AND AWARDS

Undergraduate Certificate(s) Designing and Implementing an Anticoagulation Clinic (certain restrictions apply), Health Information Management (certain restrictions apply; some on-campus requirements), School Nurse Development Program (certain restrictions apply; some on-campus requirements)

Graduate Certificate(s) Advanced Practice Nurse (certain restrictions apply; some on-campus requirements)

MEngr Engineering (certain restrictions apply)

MHPE Health Professions Education (certain restrictions apply)

PharmD Continuation Curriculum Option Pathway to the Doctor/Pharmacy (certain restrictions apply; some on-campus requirements)

COURSE SUBJECT AREAS OFFERED OUTSIDE OF DEGREE PROGRAMS

Undergraduate: Nursing
Graduate: Community health services; electrical engineering; environmental health; health professions and related sciences; health services administration; nursing; pharmacy; public health
Noncredit: Pharmacy

UNIVERSITY OF ILLINOIS AT SPRINGFIELD

Springfield, Illinois

Office of Technology Enhanced Learning (OTEL)
online.uis.edu

University of Illinois at Springfield, founded in 1969, is a state-supported, upper-level institution. It is accredited by the North Central Association of Colleges and Schools. It first offered distance learning courses in 1984. In 1999–2000, it offered 40 courses at a distance. In fall 1999, there were 467 students enrolled in distance learning courses.

Course delivery sites Courses are delivered to your home, other colleges.

Media Courses are delivered via television, videotapes, videoconferencing, interactive television, computer software, CD-ROM, computer conferencing, World Wide Web, e-mail. Students and teachers may meet in person or interact via videoconferencing, audioconferencing, mail, telephone, fax, e-mail, interactive television, World Wide Web. The following equipment may be required: computer, Internet access, e-mail.

Restrictions Programs are available nationwide. Enrollment is open to anyone.

Services Distance learners have access to library services, the campus computer network, e-mail services, academic advising, career placement assistance, bookstore at a distance.

Credit-earning options Students may transfer credits from another institution.

Typical costs *Undergraduate:* Tuition of $93 per credit hour plus mandatory fees of $15 per credit hour for in-state residents. Tuition of $279 per credit hour plus mandatory fees of $15 per credit hour for out-of-state residents. *Graduate:* Tuition of $104.50 per credit hour plus mandatory fees of $15 per credit hour for in-state residents. Tuition of $313.50 per credit hour plus mandatory fees of $15 per credit hour for out-of-state residents. Students pay $78 in fees. Financial aid is available to distance learners.

Registration Students may register by telephone, in person.

Contact Ray Schroeder, Director, University of Illinois at Springfield, Office of Technology Enhanced Learning (OTEL), HSB 316, PO Box 19243, Springfield, IL 62794-9243. *Telephone:* 217-206-7317. *Fax:* 217-206-6162. *E-mail:* schroeder.ray@uis.edu.

DEGREES AND AWARDS

BLS Liberal Studies
MEd Education
MS Management Information Systems

COURSE SUBJECT AREAS OFFERED OUTSIDE OF DEGREE PROGRAMS

Undergraduate: Accounting; biological and life sciences; computer and information sciences; English language and literature; history; mathematics; nursing; philosophy and religion; teacher education; women's studies
Graduate: Accounting; business administration and management; computer and information sciences; history; management information systems; teacher education; women's studies

See full description on page 752.

UNIVERSITY OF ILLINOIS AT URBANA–CHAMPAIGN

Urbana, Illinois

Academic Outreach
www.outreach.uiuc.edu

University of Illinois at Urbana–Champaign, founded in 1867, is a state-supported university. It is accredited by the North Central Association of Colleges and Schools. It first offered distance learning courses in 1925. In 1999–2000, it offered 175 courses at a distance. In fall 1999, there were 2,500 students enrolled in distance learning courses.

Course delivery sites Courses are delivered to your home, your workplace, high schools, 5 off-campus centers in Oak Brook, Peoria, Quad Cities (Moline), Rockford, Springfield.

Media Courses are delivered via videotapes, videoconferencing, audiotapes, computer conferencing, World Wide Web, e-mail, print. Students and teachers may meet in person or interact via videoconferencing, audioconferencing, mail, telephone, fax, e-mail, World Wide Web. The following equipment may be required: computer, Internet access.

Restrictions Primarily a statewide program, though a few programs can be national or worldwide. Enrollment is restricted to individuals meeting certain criteria.

Services Distance learners have access to library services, the campus computer network, e-mail services, academic advising, career placement assistance, bookstore at a distance.

Credit-earning options Students may transfer credits from another institution.

Typical costs Tuition varies. Contact school for information. Mandatory fees for undergraduate and graduate students are $30 per credit hour. *Noncredit courses:* $120 per course. Costs may vary.

Registration Students may register by mail, fax, World Wide Web, in person.

Contact Faye Lesht, Assistant Head, Academic Outreach, University of Illinois at Urbana–Champaign. *Telephone:* 217-333-1320. *Fax:* 217-244-8481. *E-mail:* f-lesht@uiuc.edu.

DEGREES AND AWARDS

EdM Education (certain restrictions apply; service area differs from that of the overall institution; some on-campus requirements)

MS Computer Science (service area differs from that of the overall institution), Electrical Engineering (service area differs from that of the overall institution), General Engineering (service area differs from that of the overall institution), Library and Information Sciences (service area differs from that of the overall institution; some on-campus requirements), Mechanical Engineering (service area differs from that of the overall institution), Theoretical and Applied Mechanics (service area differs from that of the overall institution)

COURSE SUBJECT AREAS OFFERED OUTSIDE OF DEGREE PROGRAMS

Undergraduate: Abnormal psychology; accounting; advertising; agricultural economics; American (U.S.) history; American literature; anthropology; Asian studies; business administration and management; business communications; cognitive psychology; community health services; comparative literature; developmental and child psychology; economics; educational psychology; electrical engineering; engineering mechanics; English composition; English literature; European history; film studies; French language and literature; geography; German language and literature; health services administration; industrial psychology; international relations; Latin language and literature; marketing; mathematics; mechanical engineering; political science; public health; Russian language and literature; social psychology; sociology; Spanish language and literature; technical writing

Graduate: Computer and information sciences; curriculum and instruction; electrical engineering; engineering mechanics; library and information studies; mathematics; mechanical engineering

Special note

University of Illinois at Urbana-Champaign offers a variety of distance learning courses at the undergraduate and graduate levels as well as master's degree programs. More than 130 undergraduate courses are available in a correspondence format. Enrollments are accepted at any time. Some courses use e-mail for submission of work. The NetMath program provides a number of tutored undergraduate math courses via the Internet. Several graduate degree programs are delivered using the Internet, with a few also offered via videotape. These include master's degree programs in library and information sciences, curriculum and instruction, human resource education, electrical engineering, general engineering, mechanical engineering, theoretical and applied mechanics, and computer science. Admission to degree programs is competitive. Combined on-campus and online programs are being developed in the fields of veterinary medicine and agricultural education. Internet-based graduate course sequences include a series of courses in French translation. Distance learning degree programs are identical to the campus program and are taught primarily by regular campus faculty members. Library and other support services are provided. Internet courses are generally available nationally and, in some cases, internationally. Videoconferencing courses are offered at various locations, primarily in Illinois. Information about offerings can be obtained from Academic Outreach. To be eligible for student loans, distance learners must be officially admitted to a degree program at the University and enrolled at least part-time. Organizations interested in contractual courses or programs for their constituencies should contact Academic Outreach. For more information, students should visit the Web site at http://www.outreach.uiuc.edu or contact Academic Outreach at 800-252-1360 Ext. 33061 (toll-free).

UNIVERSITY OF INDIANAPOLIS

Indianapolis, Indiana

Center for Technology and Learning
ctl.uindy.edu

University of Indianapolis, founded in 1902, is an independent, religious, comprehensive institution affiliated with the United Methodist Church. It is accredited by the North Central Association of Colleges and Schools.

Contact University of Indianapolis, 1400 East Hanna Avenue, Indianapolis, IN 46227-3697. *Telephone:* 317-788-3368. *Fax:* 317-788-3300.

See full description on page 540.

UNIVERSITY OF IOWA

Iowa City, Iowa

Center for Credit Programs
www.uiowa.edu/~ccp/

University of Iowa, founded in 1847, is a state-supported university. It is accredited by the North Central Association of Colleges and Schools. It first offered distance learning courses in 1916. In 1999–2000, it offered 220 courses at a distance. In fall 1999, there were 3,000 students enrolled in distance learning courses.

Course delivery sites Courses are delivered to your home, your workplace, 8 off-campus centers in Cedar Rapids, Council Bluffs, Davenport, Fort Dodge, Mason City, Newton, Sioux City, Spencer.

Media Courses are delivered via television, videotapes, videoconferencing, interactive television, audiotapes, computer software, CD-ROM, computer conferencing, World Wide Web, e-mail, print. Students and teachers may meet in person or interact via videoconferencing, mail, telephone, fax, e-mail, interactive television, World Wide Web. The following equipment may be required: television, videocassette player, computer, modem, Internet access, e-mail.

Restrictions Interactive video programs are available to in-state students only; Guided Correspondence Study available nationwide. Enrollment is open to anyone.

Services Distance learners have access to library services, the campus computer network, e-mail services, academic advising, bookstore at a distance.

Credit-earning options Students may transfer credits from another institution or may earn credits through examinations.

Typical costs *Undergraduate:* Tuition of $113 per semester hour. *Graduate:* Tuition of $176 per semester hour. Graduate and undergraduate tuition for Guided Correspondence Study is $88 per semester hour. Costs may vary. Financial aid is available to distance learners.

Registration Students may register by mail, fax, telephone, e-mail, World Wide Web, in person.

Contact Center for Credit Programs, University of Iowa, 116 International Center, Iowa City, IA 52242. *Telephone:* 319-335-2575. *Fax:* 319-335-2740. *E-mail:* credit-programs@uiowa.edu.

DEGREES AND AWARDS

BLS Liberal Studies
RN to BSN Nursing (completion) (certain restrictions apply)
MS Computer Science (certain restrictions apply)
MSEE Electrical Engineering (certain restrictions apply)
MSN Nursing (certain restrictions apply; some on-campus requirements)
PharmD Pharmacy (certain restrictions apply)

COURSE SUBJECT AREAS OFFERED OUTSIDE OF DEGREE PROGRAMS

Undergraduate: African-American studies; algebra; American (U.S.) history; American studies; anthropology; archaeology; Asian studies; astronomy and astrophysics; business; calculus; criminology; earth science; economics; education; English language and literature; environmental health; European history; French language and literature; geography; geology; German language and literature; gerontology; journalism; Latin language and literature; nursing; political science; psychology; religious studies; social work; sociology; Spanish language and literature; statistics; visual and performing arts; women's studies
Graduate: African-American studies; algebra; American (U.S.) history; anthropology; archaeology; Asian studies; astronomy and astrophysics; business; calculus; computer and information sciences; criminology; earth science; economics; education; engineering; English language and literature; environmental health; European history; geography; geology; gerontology; journalism; nursing; political science; psychology; religious studies; social work; sociology; statistics; visual and performing arts; women's studies

See full description on page 754.

See full description on page 754.

UNIVERSITY OF KANSAS

Lawrence, Kansas

Academic Outreach Programs
www.kuce.org

University of Kansas, founded in 1866, is a state-supported university. It is accredited by the North Central Association of Colleges and Schools. It first offered distance learning courses in 1891. In 1999–2000, it offered 150 courses at a distance. In fall 1999, there were 2,300 students enrolled in distance learning courses.

Course delivery sites Courses are delivered to your home, your workplace, military bases, high schools.

Media Courses are delivered via videotapes, audiotapes, computer software, CD-ROM, World Wide Web, e-mail, print. Students and teachers may meet in person or interact via mail, telephone, fax, e-mail, World Wide Web. The following equipment may be required: television, videocassette player, computer, modem, Internet access, e-mail.

Restrictions Programs are available worldwide. Enrollment is open to anyone.

Services Distance learners have access to library services, the campus computer network, e-mail services, academic advising, bookstore at a distance.

Typical costs *Undergraduate:* Tuition of $92 per credit plus mandatory fees of $47 per course. *Graduate:* Tuition of $134 per credit plus mandatory fees of $47 per course. Costs may vary. Financial aid is available to distance learners.

Registration Students may register by mail, fax, e-mail, World Wide Web, in person.

Contact Jean Redeker, Manager, Student Services, University of Kansas, Independent Study, Lawrence, KS 66047-1625. *Telephone:* 913-864-9193. *Fax:* 913-864-7895. *E-mail:* enroll@ukans.edu.

DEGREES AND AWARDS

Distance programs offered do not lead to a degree or other formal award.

COURSE SUBJECT AREAS OFFERED OUTSIDE OF DEGREE PROGRAMS

Undergraduate: Area, ethnic, and cultural studies; biology; classical languages and literatures; conservation and natural resources; creative writing; developmental and child psychology; economics; education administration; educational psychology; English composition; English language and literature; film studies; French language and literature; geology; German language and literature; health and physical education/fitness; history; home economics and family studies; journalism; liberal arts, general studies, and humanities; mathematics; music; philosophy and religion; physiology; political science; public administration and services; public health; radio and television broadcasting; social psychology; social work; sociology; Spanish language and literature; special education; teacher education; technical writing; theological studies
Graduate: Area, ethnic, and cultural studies; developmental and child psychology; education administration; health and physical education/fitness; history; liberal arts, general studies, and humanities; public health; special education; teacher education
Noncredit: Area, ethnic, and cultural studies; biology; classical languages and literatures; conservation and natural resources; creative writing; developmental and child psychology; economics; education administration; educational psychology; English composition; English language and literature; film studies; French language and literature; geology; German language and literature; health and physical education/fitness; history; home economics and family studies; journalism; liberal arts, general studies, and humanities; mathematics; music; philosophy and religion; physiology; political science; public administration and services; public health; radio and television broadcasting; social psychology; social work; sociology; Spanish language and literature; special education; teacher education; technical writing; theological studies

UNIVERSITY OF KENTUCKY

Lexington, Kentucky

Distance Learning Programs
www.uky.edu

University of Kentucky, founded in 1865, is a state-supported university. It is accredited by the Southern Association of Colleges and Schools. It first offered distance learning courses in 1974.

Contact University of Kentucky, Lexington, KY 40506-0032. *Telephone:* 606-257-9000.

See full description on page 676.

See full description on page 676.

UNIVERSITY OF LA VERNE

La Verne, California
Distance Learning Center
www.ulv.edu/dlc/dlc.html

University of La Verne, founded in 1891, is an independent, nonprofit university. It is accredited by the Western Association of Schools and Colleges, Inc. In 1999–2000, it offered 23 courses at a distance. In fall 1999, there were 87 students enrolled in distance learning courses.

Course delivery sites Courses are delivered to your home, your workplace.

Media Courses are delivered via videotapes, audiotapes, computer software, computer conferencing, World Wide Web, e-mail, print. Students and teachers may meet in person or interact via mail, telephone, fax, e-mail, World Wide Web. The following equipment may be required: computer, Internet access, e-mail.

Restrictions Programs are available to in-state students only. Enrollment is restricted to individuals meeting certain criteria.

Services Distance learners have access to library services, the campus computer network, e-mail services, career placement assistance, bookstore at a distance.

Credit-earning options Students may transfer credits from another institution or may earn credits through examinations, portfolio assessment, military training.

Typical costs *Undergraduate:* Tuition of $310 per unit plus mandatory fees of $10 per unit. *Graduate:* Tuition of $245 per unit plus mandatory fees of $10 per unit. *Noncredit courses:* $240 per course. Costs may vary. Financial aid is available to distance learners.

Registration Students may register by mail, fax, telephone, e-mail, World Wide Web, in person.

Contact Alene Harrison, Registrar, Distance Learning, University of La Verne, 1950 3rd Street, La Verne, CA 91750. *Telephone:* 909-985-0944 Ext. 5301. *Fax:* 909-981-8695. *E-mail:* harrisoa@ulv.edu.

DEGREES AND AWARDS

Distance programs offered do not lead to a degree or other formal award.

COURSE SUBJECT AREAS OFFERED OUTSIDE OF DEGREE PROGRAMS

Undergraduate: Biology; chemistry; developmental and child psychology; ethics; history; liberal arts, general studies, and humanities; political science; public policy analysis; statistics
Graduate: Business administration and management
Noncredit: Continuing education

UNIVERSITY OF LEICESTER

Leicester, United Kingdom
The Center for Labor Market Studies
www.clms.le.ac.uk

University of Leicester, founded in 1921, is a public university. It first offered distance learning courses in 1991. In 1999–2000, it offered 4 courses at a distance. In fall 1999, there were 600 students enrolled in distance learning courses.

Course delivery sites Courses are delivered to your home, off-campus center(s) in New York (NY).

Media Courses are delivered via computer conferencing, World Wide Web, print. Students and teachers may meet in person or interact via mail, telephone, fax, e-mail, World Wide Web.

Restrictions Programs are available worldwide. Enrollment is restricted to individuals meeting certain criteria.

Services Distance learners have access to library services, the campus computer network, academic advising, tutoring at a distance.

Typical costs *Undergraduate:* Tuition of $3295 per year. *Graduate:* Tuition of $2475 per semester.

Registration Students may register by mail, fax, telephone, in person.

Contact Jessie Curtis, Student Services, University of Leicester, FT Knowledge, Inc., Two World Trade Center, Suite 1700, New York, NY 10048. *Telephone:* 212-390-5092. *Fax:* 212-844-8469. *E-mail:* info@ leicester.net.

DEGREES AND AWARDS

Graduate Certificate(s) Human Resource Management, Training and Development
MSc Training and Performance Management

See full description on page 756.

UNIVERSITY OF LOUISIANA AT MONROE

Monroe, Louisiana
Continuing Education and Distance Education
www.nlu.edu/nludl.html

University of Louisiana at Monroe, founded in 1931, is a state-supported, comprehensive institution. It is accredited by the Southern Association of Colleges and Schools. It first offered distance learning courses in 1983.

Contact University of Louisiana at Monroe, Monroe, LA 71209-0001. *Telephone:* 318-342-1000. *Fax:* 318-342-1049.

See full description on page 676.

UNIVERSITY OF LOUISVILLE

Louisville, Kentucky
Department of Special Education
www.louisville.edu/edu/edsp/distance/

University of Louisville, founded in 1798, is a state-supported university. It is accredited by the Southern Association of Colleges and Schools. It first offered distance learning courses in 1992. In 1999–2000, it offered 40 courses at a distance. In fall 1999, there were 150 students enrolled in distance learning courses.

Course delivery sites Courses are delivered to your home, your workplace, military bases.

Media Courses are delivered via television, videotapes, videoconferencing, computer software, computer conferencing, World Wide Web, e-mail, print. Students and teachers may interact via audioconferencing, mail, telephone, fax, e-mail, World Wide Web. The following equipment may be required: computer, Internet access, e-mail.

Restrictions Programs are available worldwide. Enrollment is restricted to individuals meeting certain criteria.

Services Distance learners have access to library services, academic advising, tutoring, bookstore at a distance.

Credit-earning options Students may transfer credits from another institution or may earn credits through examinations, portfolio assessment.

Typical costs Tuition of $209.50 per credit for in-state residents. Tuition of $571.50 per credit for out-of-state residents. Financial aid is available to distance learners.

Registration Students may register by mail, fax, telephone, e-mail, World Wide Web, in person.

Contact Denzil Edge, Director, Distance Education, University of Louisville, School of Education, EDU 158, Louisville, KY 40292. *Telephone:* 502-852-6421. *Fax:* 502-852-1419. *E-mail:* denzil.edge@louisville.edu.

DEGREES AND AWARDS

MEd Moderate/Severe Disabilities, Orientation and Mobility (some on-campus requirements), Special Education, Visual Impairment (some on-campus requirements)

COURSE SUBJECT AREAS OFFERED OUTSIDE OF DEGREE PROGRAMS

Graduate: Social work; special education

Special note
University of Louisville, Department of Special Education, located in Louisville, Kentucky, is an accredited college (National Council for Accreditation of Teacher Education) that offers teacher certification and master's degrees in special education with an emphasis on visual impairment, autism, assistive technology, orientation and mobility, and moderate/severe disabilities. The Distance Education Program of the Department of Special Education is entering its 8th year of operations and now provides 45 courses through advanced technologies, including interactive television, compressed video, videostreaming, and the World Wide Web. As the University is committed to offering distance education students the same high-quality services and support as on-campus students enjoy, students have continuous access to library services, professors, and colleagues via listserv connections and e-mail. Based on the need for teacher preparation in the area of visual impairment, the Department of Special Education has created a new delivery system that combines summer institutes, conducted in collaboration with the Kentucky School for the Blind, and distance education courses during the fall and spring. Students participating in programs with a concentration in autism or assistive technology can complete their course of study through distance education courses. All programs are available to students nationally and internationally. For the academic year 2000–01, the tuition rate for non-Kentucky residents is $556.50 per credit hour. Many states offer financial aid for students in the field of special education. Additional information may be obtained by visiting the Department of Special Education's Web site (http://www.louisville.edu/edu/edsp) or by contacting Dr. Denzil Edge at 502-852-6421 or toll-free at 800-334-8635 Ext. 6421 or via e-mail (denzil.edge@louisville.edu).

See full descriptions on pages 556 and 676.

UNIVERSITY OF MAINE

Orono, Maine

Continuing Education Division
www.ume.maine.edu/~ced/ced

University of Maine, founded in 1865, is a state-supported university. It is accredited by the New England Association of Schools and Colleges. It first offered distance learning courses in 1989. In 1999–2000, it offered 144 courses at a distance. In fall 1999, there were 1,000 students enrolled in distance learning courses.

Course delivery sites Courses are delivered to your home, your workplace, high schools, 10 off-campus centers.

Media Courses are delivered via television, videotapes, videoconferencing, interactive television, computer software, computer conferencing, World Wide Web, e-mail. Students and teachers may interact via videoconferencing, audioconferencing, mail, telephone, fax, e-mail, interactive television, World Wide Web. The following equipment may be required: computer, Internet access.

Restrictions Programs are available worldwide. Enrollment is open to anyone.

Services Distance learners have access to library services, the campus computer network, e-mail services, academic advising, tutoring, career placement assistance at a distance.

Credit-earning options Students may transfer credits from another institution or may earn credits through examinations, portfolio assessment, military training, business training.

Typical costs *Undergraduate:* Tuition of $132 per credit hour plus mandatory fees of $45 per credit. *Graduate:* Tuition of $198 per credit hour plus mandatory fees of $45 per credit. Financial aid is available to distance learners.

Registration Students may register by mail, fax, telephone, e-mail, World Wide Web, in person.

Contact James F. Toner, Associate Director, University of Maine, Continuing Education Division and Summer Session, 5713 Chadbourne Hall, Orono, ME 04469-5713. *Telephone:* 207-581-3142. *Fax:* 207-581-3141. *E-mail:* jtoner@maine.maine.edu.

DEGREES AND AWARDS

Undergraduate Certificate(s) Education, Electric Power Systems
BUS University Studies (certain restrictions apply)

COURSE SUBJECT AREAS OFFERED OUTSIDE OF DEGREE PROGRAMS

Undergraduate: Accounting; American literature; animal sciences; area, ethnic, and cultural studies; Asian studies; biology; business; civil engineering; creative writing; developmental and child psychology; educational psychology; electrical engineering; English as a second language (ESL); English composition; English language and literature; English literature; environmental health; European languages and literatures; health professions and related sciences; history; home economics and family studies; horticulture; interdisciplinary studies; law and legal studies; liberal arts, general studies, and humanities; mathematics; mechanical engineering; music; nursing; philosophy and religion; political science; psychology; social psychology; sociology; special education; surveying; teacher education; technical writing; women's studies

Graduate: Area, ethnic, and cultural studies; civil engineering; education administration; electrical engineering; English language and literature; liberal arts, general studies, and humanities; mechanical engineering; special education; teacher education

Noncredit: Electrical engineering

UNIVERSITY OF MAINE AT FORT KENT

Fort Kent, Maine

External Programs
www.umfk.maine.edu

University of Maine at Fort Kent, founded in 1878, is a state-supported, four-year college. It is accredited by the New England Association of Schools and Colleges. It first offered distance learning courses in 1989. In 1999–2000, it offered 10 courses at a distance. In fall 1999, there were 141 students enrolled in distance learning courses.

Course delivery sites Courses are delivered to your home, your workplace, high schools, The University of Maine at Augusta (Augusta), University of Maine at Machias (Machias), University of Maine at Presque

Isle (Presque Isle), 9 off-campus centers in Brunswick, Calais, East Millinocket, Ellsworth, Houlton, Rumford-Mexico, Saco, Sanford, Thomaston.
Media Courses are delivered via television, videotapes, videoconferencing, World Wide Web, e-mail. Students and teachers may meet in person or interact via videoconferencing, audioconferencing, mail, telephone, fax, e-mail. The following equipment may be required: television, videocassette player, computer, Internet access.
Restrictions Programs are mostly offered statewide, but World Wide Web courses are available worldwide. Enrollment is open to anyone.
Services Distance learners have access to library services, e-mail services, academic advising, tutoring, career placement assistance, bookstore at a distance.
Credit-earning options Students may transfer credits from another institution or may earn credits through examinations, portfolio assessment, military training.
Typical costs *Undergraduate:* Tuition of $103 per credit hour plus mandatory fees of $10 per credit hour for in-state residents. Tuition of $252 per credit hour plus mandatory fees of $10 per credit hour for out-of-state residents. *Graduate:* Tuition of $198 per credit hour plus mandatory fees of $10 per credit hour for in-state residents. Tuition of $562 per credit hour plus mandatory fees of $10 per credit hour for out-of-state residents. Costs may vary. Financial aid is available to distance learners.
Registration Students may register by mail, fax, telephone, e-mail, in person.
Contact Sharon Johnson, Dean of Information Services, University of Maine at Fort Kent, 25 Pleasant Street, Fort Kent, ME 04743. *Telephone:* 207-834-7522. *Fax:* 207-834-7518. *E-mail:* sharonj@maine.maine.edu.

DEGREES AND AWARDS

BA Behavioral Science
BSN Nursing (service area differs from that of the overall institution)

COURSE SUBJECT AREAS OFFERED OUTSIDE OF DEGREE PROGRAMS

Undergraduate: Accounting; area, ethnic, and cultural studies; business; business administration and management; computer programming; developmental and child psychology; economics; educational psychology; English composition; English language and literature; European languages and literatures; history; liberal arts, general studies, and humanities; mathematics; nursing; political science; social psychology; sociology

UNIVERSITY OF MAINE AT MACHIAS

Machias, Maine

Tri-Campus Consortium
www.umm.maine.edu/BEX

University of Maine at Machias, founded in 1909, is a state-supported, four-year college. It is accredited by the New England Association of Schools and Colleges. It first offered distance learning courses in 1996. In 1999–2000, it offered 11 courses at a distance. In fall 1999, there were 185 students enrolled in distance learning courses.
Course delivery sites Courses are delivered to your home, your workplace, military bases.
Media Courses are delivered via interactive television, computer conferencing, World Wide Web, e-mail. Students and teachers may interact via audioconferencing, mail, telephone, fax, e-mail, interactive television, World Wide Web. The following equipment may be required: computer, modem, Internet access, e-mail.
Restrictions Programs are available worldwide. Enrollment is restricted to individuals meeting certain criteria.

Services Distance learners have access to library services, the campus computer network, e-mail services, academic advising, bookstore at a distance.
Credit-earning options Students may transfer credits from another institution or may earn credits through portfolio assessment.
Typical costs Undergraduate tuition ranges between $103 and $132 per credit hour depending on the campus which originates the course. There is a mandatory fee of $5 per credit hour. This applies to students matriculated in web-based programs taking web-based courses. Financial aid is available to distance learners.
Registration Students may register by mail, fax, telephone, e-mail.
Contact Bonnie Cook, Program Assistant, University of Maine at Machias, 9 O'Brien Avenue, Machias, ME 04654-1397. *Telephone:* 207-255-1374. *Fax:* 207-255-1376. *E-mail:* bcook@acad.umm.maine.edu.

DEGREES AND AWARDS

BA Behavioral Sciences

COURSE SUBJECT AREAS OFFERED OUTSIDE OF DEGREE PROGRAMS

Undergraduate: Economics; English language and literature; geography; history; music; physical sciences; psychology; social sciences

UNIVERSITY OF MANAGEMENT AND TECHNOLOGY

Arlington, Virginia
www.umtweb.edu

University of Management and Technology, founded in 1998, is a proprietary, graduate institution. In 1999–2000, it offered 10 courses at a distance. In fall 1999, there were 25 students enrolled in distance learning courses.
Course delivery sites Courses are delivered to your home, your workplace, military bases.
Media Courses are delivered via television, videotapes, audiotapes, computer software, CD-ROM, computer conferencing, World Wide Web, e-mail, print. Students and teachers may meet in person or interact via mail, telephone, fax, e-mail, World Wide Web. The following equipment may be required: computer, modem, Internet access, e-mail.
Restrictions Programs are available worldwide. Enrollment is open to anyone.
Services Distance learners have access to library services, academic advising, tutoring, career placement assistance, bookstore at a distance.
Credit-earning options Students may transfer credits from another institution or may earn credits through examinations, portfolio assessment.
Typical costs Tuition of $390 per course. Registration fee is $30. Application fee is $30. *Noncredit courses:* $390 per course. Financial aid is available to distance learners.
Registration Students may register by mail, fax, telephone, e-mail, World Wide Web, in person.
Contact Carolyn A. Ruff, Director of Enrollment, University of Management and Technology, 1925 North Lynn Street, Suite 306, Arlington, VA 22209. *Telephone:* 703-516-0035. *Fax:* 703-516-9896. *E-mail:* info@umtweb.edu.

DEGREES AND AWARDS

MBA Business Administration
MS Management
PhD Management

COURSE SUBJECT AREAS OFFERED OUTSIDE OF DEGREE PROGRAMS

Graduate: Accounting; business; business administration and management; business communications; finance; international business; management information systems; marketing; organizational behavior studies
Noncredit: Accounting; business; business administration and management; business communications; finance; international business; management information systems; marketing; organizational behavior studies

Special note

The University of Management and Technology (UMT) offers its Master of Science in management and MBA programs through distance education. The MS in management program has 4 tracks (majors): project management, telecommunications management, public sector management, and general management. UMT is a leader in the area of project management education, and Dean J. Davidson Frame is one of the world's leading authorities in project management. He has written 6 books and trained more than 20,000 managers worldwide. The distance program delivers a high-quality master's program directly to students using the latest information technologies. Instruction in the distance learning program is carried out primarily over the Internet and uses a combination of media, including textbooks, written materials, CDs, teleconferencing, and e-mail. Distance learning students cover the same content as on-campus students. Interaction with faculty members and fellow students is further enhanced through regular telephone calls and other contacts. The distance courses are taught by the same professors who teach on-campus courses. UMT offers 4 semesters per year. There are no deadlines for application; admissions are done on a rolling basis. Tuition typically costs $390 per credit hour; there are also a $30 registration fee per semester and a one-time application fee of $30. Scholarships are also available. For more information, students should write to Carolyn Ruff, Director of Enrollment, University of Management and Technology, 1925 North Lynn Street, Third Floor, Arlington, Virginia 22209. Students can also contact UMT via telephone (703-516-0035), fax (703-516-0985), or e-mail (info@umtweb.edu), or they can visit UMT's Web site at http://www.umtweb.edu.

UNIVERSITY OF MANITOBA

Winnipeg, Manitoba, Canada

Distance Education Program
www.umanitoba.ca/coned/de

University of Manitoba, founded in 1877, is a province-supported university. It is accredited by the provincial charter. It first offered distance learning courses in 1975. In 1999–2000, it offered 135 courses at a distance. In fall 1999, there were 3,000 students enrolled in distance learning courses.
Course delivery sites Courses are delivered to your home, your workplace, military bases, high schools, 14 off-campus centers in Boissevain, Brandon, Carman, Dauphin, Eriksdale, Flin Flon, Gimli, Portage la Prairie, Russell, Swan River, The Pas, Thompson, Winkler.
Media Courses are delivered via videotapes, audiotapes, computer software, CD-ROM, computer conferencing, World Wide Web, e-mail, print. Students and teachers may interact via audioconferencing, mail, telephone, fax, e-mail, World Wide Web. The following equipment may be required: television, videocassette player, computer, modem, Internet access, e-mail.
Restrictions Programs are available worldwide. Enrollment is restricted to individuals meeting certain criteria.

Services Distance learners have access to library services, the campus computer network, e-mail services, academic advising, bookstore at a distance.
Credit-earning options Students may transfer credits from another institution or may earn credits through examinations, military training.
Typical costs Undergraduate tuition is $360 for 3 credit hours, $480 for four credit hours, and $721 for 6 credit hours. *Noncredit courses:* Can$350 per course. Financial aid is available to distance learners.
Registration Students may register by mail, fax, telephone, in person.
Contact Student Services, University of Manitoba, Room 188, Continuing Education Complex, Winnipeg, MB R3T 2N2 Canada. *Telephone:* 204-474-8012. *Fax:* 204-474-7661. *E-mail:* stusvcs_ced@umanitoba.ca.

DEGREES AND AWARDS

BA General Studies
BPRN Nursing (certain restrictions apply)
BSW Social Work (certain restrictions apply; service area differs from that of the overall institution)
Graduate Certificate(s) Education (certain restrictions apply; service area differs from that of the overall institution)

COURSE SUBJECT AREAS OFFERED OUTSIDE OF DEGREE PROGRAMS

Undergraduate: Abnormal psychology; adult education; algebra; American (U.S.) history; anthropology; biology; calculus; computer and information sciences; earth science; economics; educational psychology; English literature; ethics; French language and literature; geography; history; information sciences and systems; logic; microbiology; nursing; philosophy and religion; political science; psychology; recreation and leisure studies; religious studies; social psychology; social work; sociology; Spanish language and literature; statistics
Graduate: Education administration
Noncredit: Horticulture

UNIVERSITY OF MARYLAND, BALTIMORE COUNTY

Baltimore, Maryland

UMBC Continuing Education
www.umbc.edu

University of Maryland, Baltimore County, founded in 1963, is a state-supported university. It is accredited by the Middle States Association of Colleges and Schools. It first offered distance learning courses in 1990. In 1999–2000, it offered 20 courses at a distance. In fall 1999, there were 250 students enrolled in distance learning courses.
Course delivery sites Courses are delivered to your home, your workplace, military bases, 2 off-campus centers in Baltimore, Shady Grove.
Media Courses are delivered via television, videotapes, videoconferencing, interactive television, audiotapes, computer software, CD-ROM, computer conferencing, World Wide Web, e-mail, print. Students and teachers may interact via videoconferencing, audioconferencing, mail, telephone, fax, e-mail, interactive television, World Wide Web. The following equipment may be required: television, videocassette player, computer, modem, Internet access, e-mail.
Restrictions Programs are available worldwide. Enrollment is open to anyone.
Services Distance learners have access to library services, the campus computer network, e-mail services, academic advising, bookstore at a distance.
Credit-earning options Students may transfer credits from another institution or may earn credits through portfolio assessment.
Typical costs *Undergraduate:* Tuition of $170 per credit plus mandatory fees of $45 per semester for in-state residents. Tuition of $353 per credit

plus mandatory fees of $45 per semester for out-of-state residents. *Graduate:* Tuition of $268 per credit plus mandatory fees of $40 per semester for in-state residents. Tuition of $470 per credit plus mandatory fees of $40 per semester for out-of-state residents. Costs may vary. Financial aid is available to distance learners.

Registration Students may register by telephone, World Wide Web.

Contact Donna Taylor, Associate Vice Provost, University of Maryland, Baltimore County, 1000 Hilltop Circle, Baltimore, MD 21250. *Telephone:* 410-455-2797. *Fax:* 410-455-1115. *E-mail:* connect@umbc.edu.

DEGREES AND AWARDS

Undergraduate Certificate(s) Industrial Systems Development
MS Emergency Health Services

COURSE SUBJECT AREAS OFFERED OUTSIDE OF DEGREE PROGRAMS

Undergraduate: Health professions and related sciences; mechanical engineering
Graduate: Education; engineering/industrial management; fire services administration; health professions and related sciences; information sciences and systems; mechanical engineering

See full description on page 676.

UNIVERSITY OF MARYLAND UNIVERSITY COLLEGE

College Park, Maryland

Office of Distance Education and Lifelong Learning
www.umuc.edu/distance

University of Maryland University College, founded in 1947, is a state-supported, comprehensive institution. It is accredited by the Middle States Association of Colleges and Schools. It first offered distance learning courses in 1972. In 1999–2000, it offered 388 courses at a distance. In fall 1999, there were 8,834 students enrolled in distance learning courses.

Course delivery sites Courses are delivered to your home, your workplace, military bases, 4 off-campus centers in Annapolis, Frederick, Rockville, Waldorf.

Media Courses are delivered via television, videotapes, videoconferencing, interactive television, audiotapes, computer software, computer conferencing, World Wide Web, print. Students and teachers may interact via videoconferencing, mail, telephone, fax, e-mail, interactive television, World Wide Web. The following equipment may be required: computer, Internet access, e-mail.

Restrictions Programs are available worldwide. Enrollment is open to anyone.

Services Distance learners have access to library services, the campus computer network, e-mail services, academic advising, tutoring, bookstore at a distance.

Credit-earning options Students may transfer credits from another institution or may earn credits through examinations, portfolio assessment, military training, business training.

Typical costs *Undergraduate:* Tuition of $184 per credit for in-state residents. Tuition of $236 per credit for out-of-state residents. *Graduate:* Tuition of $281 per credit for in-state residents. Tuition of $382 per credit for out-of-state residents. *Noncredit courses:* $225 per course. Costs may vary. Financial aid is available to distance learners.

Registration Students may register by mail, fax, telephone, e-mail, World Wide Web, in person.

Contact Undergraduate Enrollment Team, University of Maryland University College, Undergraduate Student Services, College Park, MD 20742-1636. *Telephone:* 800-888-UMUC. *Fax:* 301-985-7364. *E-mail:* umucinfo@nova.umuc.edu.

DEGREES AND AWARDS

BA Behavioral and Social Sciences (service area differs from that of the overall institution), Communication Studies (service area differs from that of the overall institution), Computer and Information Sciences (service area differs from that of the overall institution), Fire Science (service area differs from that of the overall institution), Humanities (service area differs from that of the overall institution), Management (service area differs from that of the overall institution), Paralegal Studies (service area differs from that of the overall institution), Technology Management (service area differs from that of the overall institution)
BS Liberal Studies
MIM International Management
MS Computer Systems Management (certain restrictions apply), Environmental Management, Management (certain restrictions apply), Technology Management (certain restrictions apply)

COURSE SUBJECT AREAS OFFERED OUTSIDE OF DEGREE PROGRAMS

Undergraduate: Accounting; biology; business; business administration and management; communications; computer and information sciences; criminal justice; economics; English composition; English language and literature; fire science; French language and literature; history; human resources management; journalism; law and legal studies; liberal arts, general studies, and humanities; management information systems; mathematics; microbiology; physical sciences; political science; psychology; social sciences; sociology; Spanish language and literature
Graduate: Business administration and management; computer and information sciences; environmental science; finance; information sciences and systems; international business; management information systems; marketing; telecommunications

See full descriptions on pages 592, 676, and 758.

UNIVERSITY OF MASSACHUSETTS AMHERST

Amherst, Massachusetts

Division of Continuing Education and Video Instructional Program
www.umass.edu/contined

University of Massachusetts Amherst, founded in 1863, is a state-supported university. It is accredited by the New England Association of Schools and Colleges. It first offered distance learning courses in 1974. In 1999–2000, it offered 120 courses at a distance. In fall 1999, there were 479 students enrolled in distance learning courses.

Course delivery sites Courses are delivered to your home, your workplace, military bases.

Media Courses are delivered via television, videotapes, videoconferencing, World Wide Web. Students and teachers may interact via videoconferencing, mail, telephone, fax, e-mail, World Wide Web. The following equipment may be required: television, videocassette player, computer, modem, Internet access, e-mail.

Restrictions Programs are available nationwide. Enrollment is restricted to individuals meeting certain criteria.

Services Distance learners have access to library services, the campus computer network, e-mail services, academic advising, career placement assistance, bookstore at a distance.

Credit-earning options Students may transfer credits from another institution.

University of Massachusetts Amherst

Typical costs Undergraduate tuition is $175 per credit. Graduate tuition ranges between $200 and $600 per credit. Registration fee is $20. Cost for a noncredit course ranges between $150 and $500. Costs may vary. Financial aid is available to distance learners.

Registration Students may register by mail, fax, telephone, World Wide Web, in person.

Contact Kevin Aiken, Director, Division of Continuing Education, University of Massachusetts Amherst, Box 31650, Amherst, MA 01003-1650. *Telephone:* 412-545-2111. *Fax:* 415-545-3351. *E-mail:* kaiken@admin.umass.edu.

eCollege.com   *www.ecollege.com/scholarships*

DEGREES AND AWARDS

Undergraduate Certificate(s) Arts Management
MBA Business Administration (certain restrictions apply)
MCSE Computer Science (certain restrictions apply; service area differs from that of the overall institution)
MPH Public Health (certain restrictions apply)
MS Electrical and Computer Engineering (certain restrictions apply; service area differs from that of the overall institution), Engineering Management (certain restrictions apply; service area differs from that of the overall institution), Nursing (certain restrictions apply)

COURSE SUBJECT AREAS OFFERED OUTSIDE OF DEGREE PROGRAMS

Undergraduate: Accounting; computer and information sciences; conservation and natural resources; electrical engineering; foods and nutrition studies; hospitality services management; marketing; mathematics; psychology

Graduate: Accounting; business administration and management; chemical engineering; community health services; computer and information sciences; electrical engineering; engineering/industrial management; environmental health; industrial engineering; mathematics; mechanical engineering; nursing; public health

Noncredit: Chemical engineering; computer and information sciences; electrical engineering; engineering-related technologies; engineering/industrial management; industrial engineering; mathematics; mechanical engineering

See full description on page 760.

UNIVERSITY OF MASSACHUSETTS LOWELL

Lowell, Massachusetts

Continuing Studies and Corporate Education
www.continuinged.uml.edu

University of Massachusetts Lowell, founded in 1894, is a state-supported university. It is accredited by the New England Association of Schools and Colleges. It first offered distance learning courses in 1995. In 1999–2000, it offered 100 courses at a distance. In fall 1999, there were 600 students enrolled in distance learning courses.

Course delivery sites Courses are delivered to your home, your workplace, military bases, high schools, Bunker Hill Community College (Boston), University of Massachusetts Amherst (Amherst), University of Massachusetts Boston (Boston), University of Massachusetts Dartmouth (North Dartmouth).

Media Courses are delivered via television, videoconferencing, interactive television, computer conferencing, World Wide Web, e-mail. Students and teachers may interact via telephone, fax, e-mail, interactive television, World Wide Web. The following equipment may be required: computer, modem, Internet access, e-mail.

Restrictions Programs are available worldwide. Enrollment is open to anyone.

Services Distance learners have access to library services, the campus computer network, e-mail services, academic advising, tutoring, career placement assistance, bookstore at a distance.

Credit-earning options Students may transfer credits from another institution or may earn credits through examinations, military training, business training.

Typical costs Tuition of $200 per credit. Financial aid is available to distance learners.

Registration Students may register by mail, fax, telephone, in person.

Contact Steven Tello, Assistant Director of Distance Learning, University of Massachusetts Lowell, One University Avenue, Lowell, MA 01854-2881. *Telephone:* 978-934-2467. *Fax:* 978-934-4064. *E-mail:* cybered@uml.edu.

DEGREES AND AWARDS

Undergraduate Certificate(s) Fundamentals of Information Technology, Intranet Development, Plastics Engineering Technology (service area differs from that of the overall institution; some on-campus requirements), Unix Certificate (Information Systems Program)
AS Information Systems
BS Information Systems

COURSE SUBJECT AREAS OFFERED OUTSIDE OF DEGREE PROGRAMS

Undergraduate: Business administration and management; computer and information sciences; continuing education; economics; engineering-related technologies; English composition; health professions and related sciences; history; journalism; liberal arts, general studies, and humanities; mathematics; psychology; sociology; technical writing

See full description on page 762.

UNIVERSITY OF MEMPHIS

Memphis, Tennessee

Extended Programs
www.extended.memphis.edu

University of Memphis, founded in 1912, is a state-supported university. It is accredited by the Southern Association of Colleges and Schools. It first offered distance learning courses in 1985. In 1999–2000, it offered 50 courses at a distance. In fall 1999, there were 583 students enrolled in distance learning courses.

Course delivery sites Courses are delivered to your home, your workplace, military bases, Dyersburg State Community College (Dyersburg), Jackson State Community College (Jackson), 3 off-campus centers in Collierville, Jackson, Millington.

Media Courses are delivered via television, videotapes, videoconferencing, interactive television, World Wide Web, e-mail. Students and teachers may meet in person or interact via mail, telephone, fax, e-mail, World Wide Web. The following equipment may be required: television, videocassette player, computer, modem, Internet access, e-mail.

Restrictions Programs are available worldwide. Enrollment is restricted to individuals meeting certain criteria.

Services Distance learners have access to library services, the campus computer network, e-mail services, academic advising at a distance.

Credit-earning options Students may transfer credits from another institution or may earn credits through examinations, portfolio assessment, military training.

Typical costs *Undergraduate:* Tuition of $130 per credit hour plus mandatory fees of $6 per credit hour for in-state residents. Tuition of $360 per credit hour plus mandatory fees of $6 per credit hour for out-of-state residents. *Graduate:* Tuition of $172 per credit hour plus mandatory fees of $6 per credit hour for in-state residents. Tuition of $402 per credit hour plus mandatory fees of $6 per credit hour for out-of-state residents. Costs may vary. Financial aid is available to distance learners.

Registration Students may register by mail, telephone, World Wide Web, in person.

Contact Sheila Owens, Distance Learning Coordinator, University of Memphis, Administration 376, Memphis, TN 38152. *Telephone:* 901-678-3807. *Fax:* 901-678-5112. *E-mail:* sowens@memphis.edu.

DEGREES AND AWARDS

MA Journalism

COURSE SUBJECT AREAS OFFERED OUTSIDE OF DEGREE PROGRAMS

Undergraduate: Area, ethnic, and cultural studies; biological and life sciences; English language and literature; fire services administration; foods and nutrition studies; geology; health and physical education/fitness; mathematics; nursing; social sciences; visual and performing arts
Graduate: English language and literature; journalism

Special note
Practicing professionals in print and electronic journalism, advertising, and public relations will find the University of Memphis's online master's degree program in journalism highly attractive. This fully accredited program is delivered via the Internet to students around the world. The degree requires 30 to 36 semester hours—30 hours, including a 6-hour thesis; 33 hours, including a 3-hour professional project; or 36 hours of course work. Three-semester-hour courses are offered and begin each September, January, and June. Students who take a full course load each semester can complete the degree program in 18 months, although most students choose to take fewer courses per semester. Students complete a 12-hour core curriculum (law, theory, research, and administration) and then select from a broad range of electives. Students may review these courses at http://umvirtual.memphis.edu/masscomm. More information concerning the University and the Department of Journalism can be found at http://www.memphis.edu. Students can apply for admission to the program at http://www.people.memphis.edu/~gradsch/adminfo.html. Candidates for admission to the program are expected to have completed undergraduate degrees with a grade point average of 3.0 on a 4.0 scale and attained scores of 480 or better on the verbal portion and 420 or better on the quantitative portion of the Graduate Record Examinations or a score of 40 on the Miller Analogies Test. Students may take up to 9 hours if they have not yet taken either test. For more information, students should contact Rick Fischer, Coordinator of the Online Program (rfischer@memphis.edu) or Dr. David Arant, Journalism Graduate Studies Coordinator (darant@memphis.edu).

See full description on page 676.

UNIVERSITY OF MICHIGAN

Ann Arbor, Michigan
Media Union
www.ummu.umich.edu

University of Michigan, founded in 1817, is a state-supported university. It is accredited by the North Central Association of Colleges and Schools.

It first offered distance learning courses in 1969. In 1999–2000, it offered 50 courses at a distance. In fall 1999, there were 750 students enrolled in distance learning courses.

Course delivery sites Courses are delivered to your workplace, off-campus center(s) in Grand Rapids, McComb.

Media Courses are delivered via videotapes, videoconferencing, audiotapes, World Wide Web, e-mail. Students and teachers may meet in person or interact via videoconferencing, audioconferencing, mail, telephone, fax, e-mail, World Wide Web. The following equipment may be required: television, videocassette player, computer, Internet access, e-mail.

Restrictions Programs are available worldwide. Enrollment is restricted to individuals meeting certain criteria.

Services Distance learners have access to library services, the campus computer network, e-mail services, academic advising, tutoring at a distance.

Credit-earning options Students may transfer credits from another institution.

Typical costs Tuition of $915 per credit hour.

Registration Students may register by mail, World Wide Web, in person.

Contact Glenda Radine, Assistant Director, University of Michigan, Media Union, Bonisteel Boulevard, Room 2161, Ann Arbor, MI 48109-2094. *Telephone:* 734-764-5319. *Fax:* 734-936-3107. *E-mail:* gradine@umich.edu.

DEGREES AND AWARDS

MEng Automotive Engineering (certain restrictions apply), Manufacturing Engineering (certain restrictions apply)

COURSE SUBJECT AREAS OFFERED OUTSIDE OF DEGREE PROGRAMS

Graduate: Engineering

UNIVERSITY OF MICHIGAN–FLINT

Flint, Michigan
Distance Learning Program
umflintonline.org

University of Michigan–Flint, founded in 1956, is a state-supported, comprehensive institution. It is accredited by the North Central Association of Colleges and Schools. In 1999–2000, it offered 12 courses at a distance. In fall 1999, there were 160 students enrolled in distance learning courses.

Course delivery sites Courses are delivered to your home, your workplace, military bases, high schools, other colleges.

Media Courses are delivered via interactive television, computer software, World Wide Web, e-mail. Students and teachers may meet in person or interact via mail, telephone, e-mail, interactive television, World Wide Web. The following equipment may be required: computer, Internet access.

Restrictions Programs are available worldwide. Enrollment is open to anyone.

Services Distance learners have access to library services, the campus computer network, e-mail services, academic advising, tutoring, bookstore at a distance.

Typical costs Undergraduate in-state tuition is $503 per 3 credits, out-of-state is $1397. Graduate in-state or out-of-state tuition is $1052 per 3 credits. Mandatory fees for both undergraduate and graduate students are $197.50 per semester. Costs may vary. Financial aid is available to distance learners.

Registration Students may register by mail, fax, World Wide Web, in person.

Contact Dr. Vahid Lotfi, Executive Director of Information Technology Services, University of Michigan–Flint, 207 MSB, Flint, MI 48502. *Telephone:* 810-762-3123. *Fax:* 810-766-6805. *E-mail:* vahid@umich. edu.

---

eCollege.com *www.ecollege.com/scholarships*

DEGREES AND AWARDS

Distance programs offered do not lead to a degree or other formal award.

COURSE SUBJECT AREAS OFFERED OUTSIDE OF DEGREE PROGRAMS

Undergraduate: African-American studies; business administration and management; health professions and related sciences; marketing; nursing; social work
Graduate: African-American studies; business administration and management; health professions and related sciences; marketing; nursing; social work

---

UNIVERSITY OF MINNESOTA, CROOKSTON

Crookston, Minnesota
Office of Continuing Education
www.crk.umn.edu/index.htm

University of Minnesota, Crookston, founded in 1966, is a state-supported, four-year college. It is accredited by the North Central Association of Colleges and Schools. It first offered distance learning courses in 1990. In 1999–2000, it offered 84 courses at a distance. In fall 1999, there were 150 students enrolled in distance learning courses.
Course delivery sites Courses are delivered to your home, your workplace, high schools, Northwest Technical College (Bemidji).
Media Courses are delivered via videotapes, videoconferencing, interactive television, computer software, CD-ROM, computer conferencing, World Wide Web, e-mail, print. Students and teachers may meet in person or interact via videoconferencing, mail, telephone, fax, e-mail, interactive television, World Wide Web. The following equipment may be required: computer, Internet access, e-mail.
Restrictions Programs are available worldwide. Enrollment is open to anyone.
Services Distance learners have access to library services, the campus computer network, e-mail services, academic advising, career placement assistance, bookstore at a distance.
Credit-earning options Students may transfer credits from another institution or may earn credits through examinations.
Typical costs Tuition of $120 per semester. Costs may vary. Financial aid is available to distance learners.
Registration Students may register by mail, fax, telephone, e-mail, World Wide Web, in person.
Contact Douglas Knowlton, Vice Chancellor for Academic Affairs, University of Minnesota, Crookston. *Telephone:* 218-281-8340. *Fax:* 218-281-8050. *E-mail:* dknowlto@mail.crk.umn.edu.

DEGREES AND AWARDS

Undergraduate Certificate(s) Hotel, Restaurant, and Institutional Management (some on-campus requirements)
BS Applied Health (service area differs from that of the overall institution)

COURSE SUBJECT AREAS OFFERED OUTSIDE OF DEGREE PROGRAMS

Undergraduate: Agriculture; algebra; biology; business; business administration and management; computer and information sciences; continuing education; English composition; foods and nutrition studies; health services administration; hospitality services management; management information systems; marketing; mathematics; microbiology; psychology; technical writing

---

UNIVERSITY OF MINNESOTA, MORRIS

Morris, Minnesota
College of Continuing Education-GenEdWeb Program
genedweb.mrs.umn.edu

University of Minnesota, Morris, founded in 1959, is a state-supported, four-year college. It is accredited by the North Central Association of Colleges and Schools. In 1999–2000, it offered 5 courses at a distance. In fall 1999, there were 8 students enrolled in distance learning courses.
Course delivery sites Courses are delivered to your home, your workplace, high schools.
Media Courses are delivered via World Wide Web. Students and teachers may interact via mail, telephone, e-mail, World Wide Web. The following equipment may be required: computer, modem, Internet access, e-mail.
Restrictions Programs are available worldwide. Enrollment is open to anyone.
Services Distance learners have access to library services, the campus computer network, e-mail services, academic advising, bookstore at a distance.
Credit-earning options Students may transfer credits from another institution or may earn credits through examinations, portfolio assessment.
Typical costs Tuition of $159.25 per credit. Financial aid is available to distance learners.
Registration Students may register by mail, fax, telephone, e-mail, World Wide Web, in person.
Contact Karen Johnson, Program Associate, University of Minnesota, Morris, College of Continuing Education-Morris, 231 Community Services Building, Morris, MN 56267. *Telephone:* 800-842-0030. *Fax:* 320-589-1661. *E-mail:* genedweb@mrs.umn.edu.

DEGREES AND AWARDS

Distance programs offered do not lead to a degree or other formal award.

COURSE SUBJECT AREAS OFFERED OUTSIDE OF DEGREE PROGRAMS

Undergraduate: English composition; political science; statistics; teacher education

---

UNIVERSITY OF MINNESOTA, TWIN CITIES CAMPUS

Minneapolis, Minnesota
Independent and Distance Learning
www.idl.umn.edu/

University of Minnesota, Twin Cities Campus, founded in 1851, is a state-supported university. It is accredited by the North Central Association of Colleges and Schools. It first offered distance learning courses in 1909. In 1999–2000, it offered 150 courses at a distance. In fall 1999, there were 1,500 students enrolled in distance learning courses.

Course delivery sites Courses are delivered to your home.
Media Courses are delivered via videotapes, audiotapes, computer software, World Wide Web, print. Students and teachers may interact via mail, e-mail, World Wide Web. The following equipment may be required: television, videocassette player, computer, Internet access, e-mail.
Restrictions Programs are available worldwide. Enrollment is open to anyone.
Services Distance learners have access to library services, e-mail services, academic advising, bookstore at a distance.
Credit-earning options Students may transfer credits from another institution.
Typical costs *Undergraduate:* Tuition of $155 per semester credit plus mandatory fees of $50 per course. *Graduate:* Tuition of $201 per semester credit plus mandatory fees of $50 per course. Costs may vary. Financial aid is available to distance learners.
Registration Students may register by mail, fax, World Wide Web.
Contact Receptionist, University of Minnesota, Twin Cities Campus, Student Support Services, College of Continuing Education, 101 Wesbrook Hall, 77 Pleasant Street, South East, Minneapolis, MN 55455. *Telephone:* 800-234-6564. *Fax:* 612-625-1511. *E-mail:* ceeadv@mail.cce.umn.edu.

DEGREES AND AWARDS

Distance programs offered do not lead to a degree or other formal award.

COURSE SUBJECT AREAS OFFERED OUTSIDE OF DEGREE PROGRAMS

Undergraduate: Abnormal psychology; accounting; algebra; American (U.S.) history; American literature; American studies; anthropology; area, ethnic, and cultural studies; art history and criticism; astronomy and astrophysics; biological and life sciences; biology; business; business administration and management; calculus; chemistry; child care and development; classical languages and literatures; computer and information sciences; conservation and natural resources; counseling psychology; creative writing; developmental and child psychology; ecology; economics; educational psychology; English composition; English language and literature; English literature; ethics; European history; European languages and literatures; finance; foods and nutrition studies; French language and literature; genetics; geography; geology; German language and literature; history; home economics and family studies; individual and family development studies; journalism; Latin language and literature; liberal arts, general studies, and humanities; logic; management information systems; marketing; mathematics; music; nursing; occupational therapy; philosophy and religion; physics; plant sciences; political science; psychology; public health; Russian language and literature; social work; Spanish language and literature; statistics; technical writing; visual and performing arts; women's studies
Noncredit: Social sciences

See full description on page 764.

See full description on page 764.

UNIVERSITY OF MISSISSIPPI

University, Mississippi

Office of Distance Learning
sunset.backbone.olemiss.edu/depts/continuing_studies

University of Mississippi, founded in 1844, is a state-supported university. It is accredited by the Southern Association of Colleges and Schools. It first offered distance learning courses in 1995.
Contact University of Mississippi, University, MS 38677-9702. *Telephone:* 662-232-7211. *Fax:* 662-232-5869.

See full description on page 676.

UNIVERSITY OF MISSOURI-COLUMBIA

Columbia, Missouri

MU Direct: Continuing and Distance Education
mudirect.missouri.edu

University of Missouri-Columbia, founded in 1839, is a state-supported university. It is accredited by the North Central Association of Colleges and Schools. In 1999–2000, it offered 180 courses at a distance. In fall 1999, there were 1,014 students enrolled in distance learning courses.
Course delivery sites Courses are delivered to your home, your workplace, military bases, University of Missouri–Kansas City (Kansas City), University of Missouri–St. Louis (St. Louis), 6 off-campus centers in Branson, Brookfield, Camdenton, Mexico, Milan, Mount Vernon.
Media Courses are delivered via videotapes, interactive television, computer software, World Wide Web, print. Students and teachers may interact via mail, telephone, fax, e-mail, interactive television, World Wide Web. The following equipment may be required: computer, Internet access.
Restrictions Programs are available worldwide. Enrollment is restricted to individuals meeting certain criteria.
Services Distance learners have access to library services, the campus computer network, e-mail services, academic advising, bookstore at a distance.
Credit-earning options Students may transfer credits from another institution.
Typical costs *Undergraduate:* Tuition of $136.80 per credit hour plus mandatory fees of $8.60 per credit hour. *Graduate:* Tuition of $173.20 per credit hour plus mandatory fees of $8.60 per credit hour. Cost for a noncredit course ranges between $40 and $500. Financial aid is available to distance learners.
Registration Students may register by mail, fax, telephone, World Wide Web, in person.
Contact Anna Ragland, Administrative Assistant, University of Missouri-Columbia, MU Direct: Continuing and Distance Education, 109 Whitten Hall, Columbia, MO 65211. *Telephone:* 800-545-2604. *Fax:* 573-884-5371. *E-mail:* mudirect@missouri.edu.

DEGREES AND AWARDS

Undergraduate Certificate(s) Computed Tomography (certain restrictions apply), Labor Studies (certain restrictions apply; service area differs from that of the overall institution; some on-campus requirements), Magnetic Resonance Imaging (certain restrictions apply)
BHS Radiography (certain restrictions apply), Respiratory Therapy (certain restrictions apply)
BSN Nursing RN Bachelor's Completion Program (certain restrictions apply; service area differs from that of the overall institution; some on-campus requirements)
MEd Educational Technology (certain restrictions apply)
MHA Health Sciences Management (certain restrictions apply; service area differs from that of the overall institution; some on-campus requirements)
MSN Nursing-Mental Health (certain restrictions apply), Nursing-Midwifery (certain restrictions apply; some on-campus requirements), Nursing-Pediatrics (certain restrictions apply), Nursing-Public Health/School Health (certain restrictions apply)

COURSE SUBJECT AREAS OFFERED OUTSIDE OF DEGREE PROGRAMS

Undergraduate: Agriculture; curriculum and instruction; education; educational psychology; health professions and related sciences; horticulture; labor relations/studies; nursing; occupational therapy; philosophy and religion; real estate; sociology
Graduate: Agriculture; curriculum and instruction; education; education administration; educational psychology; educational research; envi-

ronmental engineering; health professions and related sciences; health services administration; horticulture; labor relations/studies; library and information studies; mental health services; nursing; philosophy and religion; public health; real estate; special education

Noncredit: Environmental health; health professions and related sciences; horticulture; labor relations/studies; real estate

Special note

Building on its long history of bringing individual distance education courses to students around the world, the University of Missouri–Columbia offers distance degrees and interactive online courses through MU Direct: Continuing and Distance Education. The courses, usually conducted within the time frame of one semester, allow students to interact with faculty members and classmates while "attending" class virtually at their convenience—anytime, day or night. Cited in several publications as one of the nation's best values in higher education, the University of Missouri–Columbia is one of only 31 public universities selected for membership in the Association of American Universities. Graduate degrees are available in several health-care fields, including 3 nursing specialty areas and health administration. Some programs require on-campus class work. A bachelor's completion program for registered nurses is offered in selected Missouri cities via interactive television. The popular master's degree in educational technology can be completed entirely at a distance, and any course may be taken individually by educators who are interested in enhancing their use of technology in the classroom. Certificate programs are offered in computerized tomography and magnetic resonance imaging. Two unique courses leading to national certification in rural real estate appraisal may be taken on either a credit or noncredit basis. New programs and courses will be added throughout the year. MU Direct's new Web site (http://MUdirect.missouri.edu) offers the most current options as well as online advising and access to registration, library services, textbook purchasing, and other academic resources. Questions also are welcome via e-mail at mudirect@missouri.edu or at 800-545-2604 (toll-free).

UNIVERSITY OF MISSOURI–COLUMBIA

Columbia, Missouri

Center for Distance and Independent Study
cdis.missouri.edu

University of Missouri–Columbia, founded in 1839, is a state-supported university. It is accredited by the North Central Association of Colleges and Schools. It first offered distance learning courses in 1911. In 1999–2000, it offered 160 courses at a distance. In fall 1999, there were 4,000 students enrolled in distance learning courses.

Course delivery sites Courses are delivered to your home, your workplace, military bases, high schools.

Media Courses are delivered via videotapes, audiotapes, World Wide Web, print. Students and teachers may interact via mail, e-mail, World Wide Web. The following equipment may be required: computer, Internet access.

Restrictions Programs are available worldwide. Enrollment is open to anyone.

Services Distance learners have access to library services, e-mail services, academic advising, bookstore at a distance.

Typical costs *Undergraduate:* Tuition of $136.80 per credit hour plus mandatory fees of $10 per course. *Graduate:* Tuition of $173.20 per credit hour plus mandatory fees of $10 per course.

Registration Students may register by mail, fax, telephone, World Wide Web, in person.

Contact Terrie Nagel, Student Services Advisor, University of Missouri–Columbia, 136 Clark Hall, Columbia, MO 65211-4200. *Telephone:* 800-858-6413. *Fax:* 573-882-6808. *E-mail:* cdis@missouri.edu.

DEGREES AND AWARDS

Distance programs offered do not lead to a degree or other formal award.

COURSE SUBJECT AREAS OFFERED OUTSIDE OF DEGREE PROGRAMS

Undergraduate: Abnormal psychology; accounting; African-American studies; agriculture; algebra; animal sciences; anthropology; area, ethnic, and cultural studies; astronomy and astrophysics; biological and life sciences; biology; business; business administration and management; business law; calculus; classical languages and literatures; comparative literature; computer and information sciences; corrections; creative writing; criminal justice; curriculum and instruction; developmental and child psychology; economics; education; educational psychology; educational research; engineering; engineering mechanics; English composition; English language and literature; entomology; ethics; European languages and literatures; finance; French language and literature; geography; geology; German language and literature; health and physical education/fitness; health professions and related sciences; health services administration; history; home economics and family studies; horticulture; law and legal studies; liberal arts, general studies, and humanities; logic; marketing; mathematics; meteorology; philosophy and religion; physical sciences; physics; political science; protective services; psychology; Russian language and literature; social psychology; sociology; Spanish language and literature; statistics; technical writing; theological studies; women's studies

Graduate: Agriculture; animal sciences; astronomy and astrophysics; biological and life sciences; business; business administration and management; classical languages and literatures; criminal justice; curriculum and instruction; economics; education; education administration; educational psychology; educational research; English language and literature; geology; health professions and related sciences; history; home economics and family studies; human resources management; law and legal studies; marketing; mathematics; organizational behavior studies; physics; plant sciences; political science; protective services; psychology; sociology; special education; teacher education

Noncredit: Protective services

See full description on page 766.

UNIVERSITY OF MISSOURI–KANSAS CITY

Kansas City, Missouri

Interactive Video Network

University of Missouri–Kansas City, founded in 1929, is a state-supported university. It is accredited by the North Central Association of Colleges and Schools. It first offered distance learning courses in 1986. In 1999–2000, it offered 40 courses at a distance. In fall 1999, there were 550 students enrolled in distance learning courses.

Course delivery sites Courses are delivered to your home, your workplace, 15 off-campus centers.

Media Courses are delivered via television, videotapes, videoconferencing, computer software, computer conferencing, print. Students and teachers may meet in person or interact via videoconferencing, telephone, fax, e-mail, interactive television, World Wide Web. The following equipment may be required: television, videocassette player, computer.

Restrictions Programs are available to in-state students only. Enrollment is open to anyone.

Services Distance learners have access to library services, the campus computer network, academic advising, tutoring at a distance.

Credit-earning options Students may transfer credits from another institution or may earn credits through examinations, military training.

Typical costs Contact the school for information.

Registration Students may register by mail, fax, telephone, in person.

Contact Janet Carnett, Supervisor, University of Missouri–Kansas City, 301 Fine Arts Building, 5100 Rockhill Road, Kansas City, MO 64110-2499. *Telephone:* 816-235-1096. *Fax:* 816-235-1170. *E-mail:* carnettj@umkc.edu.

DEGREES AND AWARDS

Distance programs offered do not lead to a degree or other formal award.

COURSE SUBJECT AREAS OFFERED OUTSIDE OF DEGREE PROGRAMS

Undergraduate: Accounting; business; computer and information sciences; creative writing; economics; English composition; English language and literature; history; home economics and family studies; liberal arts, general studies, and humanities; mathematics; nursing; philosophy and religion; physics; social psychology; social work; sociology

Graduate: Civil engineering; computer and information sciences; electrical engineering; engineering/industrial management; English composition; industrial engineering; mechanical engineering; nursing; sociology

UNIVERSITY OF MISSOURI–ROLLA

Rolla, Missouri

Engineering Management Department
www.umr.edu/~emgt

University of Missouri–Rolla, founded in 1870, is a state-supported university. It is accredited by the North Central Association of Colleges and Schools. In 1999–2000, it offered 12 courses at a distance. In fall 1999, there were 100 students enrolled in distance learning courses.

Course delivery sites Courses are delivered to your home, your workplace, military bases, Central Missouri State University (Warrensburg), Northwest Missouri State University (Maryville), Southeast Missouri State University (Cape Girardeau), Southwest Missouri State University (Springfield), Truman State University (Kirksville), 10 off-campus centers in Camdenton, Kirksville, Mexico, Nevada, Park Hills, Poplar Bluff, Portageville, Reeds Spring, St. Joseph, St. Louis.

Media Courses are delivered via television, videotapes, interactive television, CD-ROM, World Wide Web, e-mail. Students and teachers may interact via videoconferencing, mail, telephone, fax, e-mail, interactive television, World Wide Web. The following equipment may be required: videocassette player, computer, modem, Internet access, e-mail.

Restrictions Programs are available nationwide. Enrollment is restricted to individuals meeting certain criteria.

Services Distance learners have access to e-mail services, academic advising, career placement assistance, bookstore at a distance.

Credit-earning options Students may transfer credits from another institution.

Typical costs Graduate tuition ranges between $450 and $1000 per credit hour. Costs may vary. Financial aid is available to distance learners.

Registration Students may register by mail, fax, telephone, e-mail, in person.

Contact Krista Chambers, Teleconference Program Specialist, University of Missouri–Rolla, Engineering Management Department, Room 223 Engineering Management Building, Rolla, MO 65409. *Telephone:* 573-341-4990. *Fax:* 573-341-6990. *E-mail:* krista@umr.edu.

DEGREES AND AWARDS

MS Engineering Management (certain restrictions apply; service area differs from that of the overall institution), Systems Engineering (certain restrictions apply)

COURSE SUBJECT AREAS OFFERED OUTSIDE OF DEGREE PROGRAMS

Graduate: Accounting; business administration and management; engineering; engineering/industrial management; finance; industrial engineering; marketing

UNIVERSITY OF MISSOURI–ST. LOUIS

St. Louis, Missouri

Video Instructional Program
www.umsl.edu/services/itc/itc.htm

University of Missouri–St. Louis, founded in 1963, is a state-supported university. It is accredited by the North Central Association of Colleges and Schools. It first offered distance learning courses in 1988. In 1999–2000, it offered 17 courses at a distance. In fall 1999, there were 377 students enrolled in distance learning courses.

Course delivery sites Courses are delivered to your home, your workplace, East Central College (Union), Jefferson College (Hillsboro), Mineral Area College (Park Hills), Saint Charles County Community College (St. Peters).

Media Courses are delivered via television, videotapes, videoconferencing, computer software, computer conferencing, World Wide Web. Students and teachers may meet in person or interact via videoconferencing, mail, telephone, fax, e-mail. The following equipment may be required: television, videocassette player, computer, modem, Internet access, e-mail.

Restrictions Programs are available nationwide. Enrollment is open to anyone.

Services Distance learners have access to library services, the campus computer network, e-mail services, academic advising, tutoring, career placement assistance at a distance.

Typical costs *Undergraduate:* Tuition of $136.80 per credit hour for in-state residents. Tuition of $409.10 per credit hour for out-of-state residents. *Graduate:* Tuition of $173.20 per credit hour for in-state residents. Tuition of $521 per credit hour for out-of-state residents. Costs may vary. Financial aid is available to distance learners.

Registration Students may register by mail, fax, telephone, World Wide Web, in person.

Contact Tealjoy Stephens, Program Coordinator, University of Missouri–St. Louis, Video Instructional Program, 113 Lucas Hall, St. Louis, MO 63121. *Telephone:* 314-516-6171. *Fax:* 314-516-5294. *E-mail:* tjstephens@umsl.edu.

DEGREES AND AWARDS

BN Nursing

MBA Business Administration (some on-campus requirements), Nursing

COURSE SUBJECT AREAS OFFERED OUTSIDE OF DEGREE PROGRAMS

Undergraduate: Area, ethnic, and cultural studies; developmental and child psychology; education administration; fine arts; history; nursing; philosophy and religion; radio and television broadcasting; teacher education

Graduate: Business administration and management; nursing

UNIVERSITY OF MONTANA–MISSOULA

Missoula, Montana
Continuing Education
www.umt.edu/ccesp/

University of Montana–Missoula, founded in 1893, is a state-supported university. It is accredited by the Northwest Association of Schools and Colleges. It first offered distance learning courses in 1989. In 1999–2000, it offered 81 courses at a distance. In fall 1999, there were 250 students enrolled in distance learning courses.

Course delivery sites Courses are delivered to your home, your workplace, military bases, high schools, College of Technology of The University of Montana–Missoula (Missoula), Flathead Valley Community College (Kalispell), Helena College of Technology of The University of Montana (Helena), Montana State University–Billings (Billings), Montana State University–Bozeman (Bozeman), Montana State University—Great Falls College of Technology (Great Falls), Montana Tech of The University of Montana (Butte), Western Montana College of University of Montana (Dillon).

Media Courses are delivered via videotapes, interactive television, computer software, computer conferencing, World Wide Web, e-mail, print. Students and teachers may meet in person or interact via mail, telephone, fax, e-mail, interactive television, World Wide Web. The following equipment may be required: computer, modem, Internet access, e-mail.

Restrictions Programs are available predominately in the western United States and Canada, while some are available worldwide. Enrollment is restricted to individuals meeting certain criteria.

Services Distance learners have access to library services, the campus computer network, e-mail services, academic advising, tutoring, career placement assistance, bookstore at a distance.

Credit-earning options Students may transfer credits from another institution or may earn credits through examinations.

Typical costs *Undergraduate:* Tuition of $142 per credit plus mandatory fees of $35 per credit for local area residents. Tuition of $142 per credit plus mandatory fees of $35 per credit for in-state residents. Tuition of $340 per credit plus mandatory fees of $35 per credit for out-of-state residents. *Graduate:* Tuition of $142 per credit plus mandatory fees of $35 per credit for local area residents. Tuition of $142 per credit plus mandatory fees of $35 per credit for in-state residents. Tuition of $340 per credit plus mandatory fees of $35 per credit for out-of-state residents. *Noncredit courses:* $495 per course. Costs may vary. Financial aid is available to distance learners.

Registration Students may register by mail, fax, telephone, e-mail, World Wide Web, in person.

Contact Division Manager, External Graduate Programs, University of Montana–Missoula, Continuing Education, Missoula, MT 59812. *Telephone:* 406-243-6431. *Fax:* 406-243-2047. *E-mail:* acobb@selway.umt.edu.

---

eCollege.com *www.ecollege.com/scholarships*

DEGREES AND AWARDS

Graduate Certificate(s) Library Media (certain restrictions apply)
EdM Education (certain restrictions apply; some on-campus requirements)
MBA Business Administration (certain restrictions apply; some on-campus requirements)
MEd Curriculum Studies (certain restrictions apply; some on-campus requirements), School Counseling (certain restrictions apply; some on-campus requirements)
MEM Engineering Management (certain restrictions apply; some on-campus requirements)

EdD Educational Leadership (certain restrictions apply; some on-campus requirements)
PharmD Pharmacy (certain restrictions apply; some on-campus requirements)

COURSE SUBJECT AREAS OFFERED OUTSIDE OF DEGREE PROGRAMS

Undergraduate: Creative writing; curriculum and instruction; engineering-related technologies; forestry; instructional media
Graduate: Accounting; business administration and management; curriculum and instruction; education administration; engineering-related technologies; finance; health professions and related sciences; instructional media; political science; student counseling; teacher education

UNIVERSITY OF NEBRASKA–LINCOLN

Lincoln, Nebraska
Division of Continuing Studies
www.unl.edu/conted

University of Nebraska–Lincoln, founded in 1869, is a state-supported university. It is accredited by the North Central Association of Colleges and Schools. It first offered distance learning courses in 1909. In 1999–2000, it offered 141 courses at a distance. In fall 1999, there were 1,300 students enrolled in distance learning courses.

Course delivery sites Courses are delivered to your home, your workplace, military bases, high schools, 5 off-campus centers in Grand Island, Norfolk, North Platte, Scottsbluff, Sioux City (IA).

Media Courses are delivered via television, videotapes, videoconferencing, interactive television, audiotapes, computer software, CD-ROM, computer conferencing, World Wide Web, e-mail, print. Students and teachers may meet in person or interact via videoconferencing, audioconferencing, mail, telephone, fax, e-mail, interactive television, World Wide Web. The following equipment may be required: television, videocassette player, computer, modem, Internet access, e-mail.

Restrictions Programs are available worldwide. Enrollment is open to anyone.

Services Distance learners have access to library services, the campus computer network, e-mail services, academic advising, bookstore at a distance.

Credit-earning options Students may transfer credits from another institution or may earn credits through examinations.

Typical costs *Undergraduate:* Tuition of $99 per credit plus mandatory fees of $23 per course. *Graduate:* Tuition of $115.50 per credit plus mandatory fees of $85 per course. Other mandatory fees include $15 enrollment fee per semester and $5 technology fee per credit hour. Costs may vary. Financial aid is available to distance learners.

Registration Students may register by mail, fax, telephone, e-mail, World Wide Web, in person.

Contact Marie A. Barber, Assistant Director, University of Nebraska–Lincoln, 332 C NCCE, Department of Distance Education, Lincoln, NE 68583-9800. *Telephone:* 402-472-4354. *Fax:* 402-472-4317. *E-mail:* mbarber2@unl.edu.

DEGREES AND AWARDS

Undergraduate Certificate(s) Educational Technology
MA Journalism
MBA Business Administration
MEd Education
MS Entomology, Human Resources and Family Sciences, Industrial and Management Systems Engineering, Manufacturing Systems Engineering, Textiles, Clothing and Design

EdD Administration, Curriculum, and Instruction (certain restrictions apply; some on-campus requirements), Educational Leadership in Higher Education (some on-campus requirements)

COURSE SUBJECT AREAS OFFERED OUTSIDE OF DEGREE PROGRAMS

Undergraduate: Accounting; agricultural economics; agriculture; algebra; American (U.S.) history; American literature; American studies; area, ethnic, and cultural studies; art history and criticism; Asian studies; biological and life sciences; biology; business; business administration and management; calculus; chemistry; civil engineering; classical languages and literatures; communications; conservation and natural resources; curriculum and instruction; developmental and child psychology; ecology; economics; education; engineering; English composition; English language and literature; English literature; European history; European languages and literatures; finance; foods and nutrition studies; geography; geology; health and physical education/fitness; history; home economics and family studies; horticulture; human resources management; insurance; international business; international relations; journalism; Latin American studies; liberal arts, general studies, and humanities; logic; marketing; mathematics; medieval/renaissance studies; nursing; organizational behavior studies; philosophy and religion; physical sciences; physics; plant sciences; political science; psychology; public administration and services; radio and television broadcasting; real estate; religious studies; social psychology; social sciences; sociology; Spanish language and literature; statistics; teacher education; technical writing; visual and performing arts
Graduate: Accounting; advertising; business administration and management; civil engineering; computer and information sciences; curriculum and instruction; education administration; educational psychology; electrical engineering; engineering/industrial management; foods and nutrition studies; home economics and family studies; human resources management; industrial engineering; international business; international relations; journalism; music; statistics; teacher education
Noncredit: Agriculture; algebra; architecture; conservation and natural resources; engineering/industrial management; industrial engineering
See full description on page 822.

UNIVERSITY OF NEBRASKA MEDICAL CENTER

Omaha, Nebraska

CON Rural Nursing Education/CON Graduate Program
www.unmc.edu/nursing

University of Nebraska Medical Center, founded in 1869, is a state-supported, upper-level institution. It is accredited by the North Central Association of Colleges and Schools. In 1999–2000, it offered 25 courses at a distance. In fall 1999, there were 125 students enrolled in distance learning courses.
Course delivery sites Courses are delivered to your home, Mid-Plains Community College (North Platte), Northeast Community College (Norfolk), South Dakota State University (Brookings, SD), 5 off-campus centers in Grand Island, Lincoln, Norfolk, North Platte, Scottsbluff.
Media Courses are delivered via television, videotapes, videoconferencing, interactive television, audiotapes, computer software, CD-ROM, computer conferencing, World Wide Web, e-mail, print. Students and teachers may meet in person or interact via videoconferencing, audioconferencing, mail, telephone, fax, e-mail, interactive television, World Wide Web. The following equipment may be required: television, videocassette player, computer, modem, Internet access, e-mail.
Restrictions Programs are available nationwide. Enrollment is open to anyone.

Services Distance learners have access to library services, the campus computer network, e-mail services, academic advising, bookstore at a distance.
Credit-earning options Students may transfer credits from another institution or may earn credits through examinations.
Typical costs *Undergraduate:* Tuition of $111 per credit plus mandatory fees of $25 per semester for local area residents. Tuition of $111 per credit plus mandatory fees of $25 per semester for in-state residents. Tuition of $297 per credit plus mandatory fees of $25 per semester for out-of-state residents. *Graduate:* Tuition of $126 per credit plus mandatory fees of $25 per semester for local area residents. Tuition of $126 per credit plus mandatory fees of $25 per semester for in-state residents. Tuition of $320 per credit plus mandatory fees of $25 per semester for out-of-state residents. Costs may vary. Financial aid is available to distance learners.
Registration Students may register by mail, fax, in person.
Contact Larry P. Hewitt, Director of Student Services, University of Nebraska Medical Center, College of Nursing, 985330 Nebraska Medical Center, Omaha, NE 68198-5330. *Telephone:* 402-559-4110. *Fax:* 402-559-6379. *E-mail:* lhewitt@unmc.edu.

DEGREES AND AWARDS

BSN Nursing (service area differs from that of the overall institution; some on-campus requirements)
MSN Nursing (some on-campus requirements)
PhD Nursing (some on-campus requirements)

COURSE SUBJECT AREAS OFFERED OUTSIDE OF DEGREE PROGRAMS

Undergraduate: Nursing
Graduate: Nursing

UNIVERSITY OF NEVADA, LAS VEGAS

Las Vegas, Nevada

Distance Education
www.nscee.edu/unlv/infotech/Distance_Education/

University of Nevada, Las Vegas, founded in 1957, is a state-supported university. It is accredited by the Northwest Association of Schools and Colleges. It first offered distance learning courses in 1986. In 1999–2000, it offered 40 courses at a distance. In fall 1999, there were 270 students enrolled in distance learning courses.
Course delivery sites Courses are delivered to your home, your workplace, military bases, high schools.
Media Courses are delivered via television, videotapes, videoconferencing, interactive television, World Wide Web, e-mail, print. Students and teachers may meet in person or interact via videoconferencing, audioconferencing, mail, telephone, fax, e-mail, interactive television, World Wide Web. The following equipment may be required: television, videocassette player, computer, Internet access.
Restrictions Compressed video courses are available to in-state students only, while some courses are available nationwide. Enrollment is open to anyone.
Services Distance learners have access to library services, the campus computer network, e-mail services, academic advising, bookstore at a distance.
Credit-earning options Students may transfer credits from another institution or may earn credits through examinations, military training.
Typical costs *Undergraduate:* Tuition of $71.50 per credit plus mandatory fees of $5 per credit for in-state residents. Tuition of $149.50 per credit plus mandatory fees of $5 per credit for out-of-state residents. *Graduate:* Tuition of $93 per credit plus mandatory fees of $8 per credit

for in-state residents. Tuition of $190 per credit plus mandatory fees of $8 per credit for out-of-state residents. Costs may vary. Financial aid is available to distance learners.

Registration Students may register by mail, fax, telephone, e-mail, in person.

Contact Charlotte Farr, Director, University of Nevada, Las Vegas, 4505 Maryland Parkway, Las Vegas, NV 89154-1038. *Telephone:* 702-895-0707. *Fax:* 702-895-3850. *E-mail:* distanceed@ccmail.nevada.edu.

DEGREES AND AWARDS

Distance programs offered do not lead to a degree or other formal award.

COURSE SUBJECT AREAS OFFERED OUTSIDE OF DEGREE PROGRAMS

Undergraduate: Conservation and natural resources; developmental and child psychology; English as a second language (ESL); hospitality services management; nursing; special education; teacher education

Graduate: Education administration; special education; teacher education

Special note

The University of Nevada, Las Vegas (UNLV) offers a series of courses in 2 areas of interest to the hospitality industry: casino management and hotel administration. These classes, using mostly videotape augmented by Internet and/or telephone, may be taken by any adult anywhere. While all of the courses count in the undergraduate program at UNLV, they also may be useful for individuals in the industry who want to acquire competency in particular areas without enrolling in a degree program. If there is enough interest, UNLV may aggregate these courses into a certificate program in the future. Courses developed so far include Introduction to the Casino, which provides an overview of the casino, it economics, and its interface with the hotel; Gaming Device Management, which reviews the casino slot department and route operation management procedures, the history of equipment development, future outlook, and career opportunities; Gaming Regulations and Control, which focuses on the history, purpose, politics, methods, and limitations of governmental regulations and control of legal gambling; Introduction to the Hospitality Industry, which focuses on the history, likely direction, and dynamics of the hospitality industry from the perspective of the global economy; and Lodging Operations, which reviews front-office procedures from reservations through checkout, including the night audit and property management system. For more information, students should contact Distance Education, UNLV (telephone: 702-895-0334; e-mail: distanceed@ccmail.nevada.edu).

UNIVERSITY OF NEVADA, RENO

Reno, Nevada

Independent Study and Division of Continuing Education
www.dce.unr.edu/istudy

University of Nevada, Reno, founded in 1874, is a state-supported university. It is accredited by the Northwest Association of Schools and Colleges. It first offered distance learning courses in 1945. In 1999–2000, it offered 110 courses at a distance. In fall 1999, there were 2,500 students enrolled in distance learning courses.

Course delivery sites Courses are delivered to your home, your workplace, military bases.

Media Courses are delivered via videotapes, audiotapes, computer software, World Wide Web, e-mail, print. Students and teachers may interact

via mail, fax, e-mail, World Wide Web. The following equipment may be required: television, videocassette player, computer, modem, Internet access, e-mail.

Restrictions Programs are available worldwide. Enrollment is open to anyone.

Services Distance learners have access to library services, the campus computer network, e-mail services, academic advising, bookstore at a distance.

Typical costs *Undergraduate:* Tuition of $81 per semester credit plus mandatory fees of $10 per semester credit. *Graduate:* Tuition of $103 per semester credit plus mandatory fees of $10 per semester credit.

Registration Students may register by mail, fax, telephone, e-mail, World Wide Web, in person.

Contact Kerri Garcia, Director, University of Nevada, Reno, Independent Study 050, Reno, NV 89557. *Telephone:* 775-784-4652. *Fax:* 775-784-1280. *E-mail:* istudy@scs.unr.edu.

DEGREES AND AWARDS

Distance programs offered do not lead to a degree or other formal award.

COURSE SUBJECT AREAS OFFERED OUTSIDE OF DEGREE PROGRAMS

Undergraduate: Abnormal psychology; accounting; advertising; American (U.S.) history; American studies; anthropology; area, ethnic, and cultural studies; business; business administration and management; criminal justice; developmental and child psychology; earth science; economics; education; English language and literature; European history; French language and literature; geography; German language and literature; gerontology; health professions and related sciences; history; hospitality services management; investments and securities; Italian language and literature; journalism; liberal arts, general studies, and humanities; marketing; mathematics; music; political science; psychology; sociology; Spanish language and literature; teacher education

Graduate: Area, ethnic, and cultural studies; education; gerontology; teacher education

Noncredit: Business communications

See full description on page 768.

UNIVERSITY OF NEW BRUNSWICK

Fredericton, New Brunswick, Canada

Department of Extension and Summer Session
www.unb.ca/coned

University of New Brunswick, founded in 1785, is a province-supported university. It is accredited by the provincial charter. It first offered distance learning courses in 1970. In 1999–2000, it offered 209 courses at a distance. In fall 1999, there were 805 students enrolled in distance learning courses.

Course delivery sites Courses are delivered to your home, your workplace, high schools.

Media Courses are delivered via television, videotapes, videoconferencing, audiotapes, computer software, CD-ROM, World Wide Web, e-mail, print. Students and teachers may meet in person or interact via mail, telephone, fax, e-mail. The following equipment may be required: television, videocassette player, computer, Internet access, e-mail.

Restrictions Web-based courses are available worldwide, other courses limited to New Brunswick province. Enrollment is restricted to individuals meeting certain criteria.

Services Distance learners have access to library services, the campus computer network, e-mail services, academic advising, bookstore at a distance.

Credit-earning options Students may transfer credits from another institution or may earn credits through examinations, portfolio assessment.

Typical costs *Undergraduate:* Tuition of $343 per course plus mandatory fees of $8 per course. *Graduate:* Tuition of $615 per term plus mandatory fees of $15 per year. Financial aid is available to distance learners.

Registration Students may register by mail, fax, telephone, e-mail, World Wide Web, in person.

Contact Ian Allen, Program Director, University of New Brunswick, Distance Education and Off-Campus Service, PO Box 4400, Fredericton, NB E3B 5A3 Canada. *Telephone:* 506-453-4854. *Fax:* 506-453-3572. *E-mail:* iallen@unb.ca.

DEGREES AND AWARDS

Undergraduate Certificate(s) Adult Education (certain restrictions apply; some on-campus requirements)
BEd Adult Education (certain restrictions apply; some on-campus requirements)
BN Nursing (certain restrictions apply; some on-campus requirements)
MEd Adult Education (certain restrictions apply; some on-campus requirements)
MN Nursing (certain restrictions apply; some on-campus requirements)

COURSE SUBJECT AREAS OFFERED OUTSIDE OF DEGREE PROGRAMS

Undergraduate: Accounting; adult education; biology; business; business administration and management; civil engineering; economics; education administration; educational psychology; electrical engineering; engineering; English language and literature; history; human resources management; microbiology; nursing; organizational behavior studies; political science; psychology; sociology; special education; statistics; teacher education
Graduate: Adult education; education administration; educational psychology; nursing; special education; teacher education

UNIVERSITY OF NEW ENGLAND

Biddeford, Maine
Master of Science in Education Program
www.une.edu/msed

University of New England, founded in 1831, is an independent, non-profit, comprehensive institution. It is accredited by the New England Association of Schools and Colleges. It first offered distance learning courses in 1991. In 1999–2000, it offered 13 courses at a distance. In fall 1999, there were 500 students enrolled in distance learning courses.

Course delivery sites Courses are delivered to your home, your workplace.

Media Courses are delivered via videotapes, print. Students and teachers may interact via mail, telephone, fax, e-mail. The following equipment may be required: television, videocassette player, Internet access, e-mail.

Restrictions Programs are available primarily to teachers in New York, New England, and abroad. Enrollment is restricted to individuals meeting certain criteria.

Services Distance learners have access to library services, academic advising, career placement assistance at a distance.

Credit-earning options Students may transfer credits from another institution.

Typical costs Tuition of $235 per credit plus mandatory fees of $70 per course. Financial aid is available to distance learners.

Registration Students may register by mail, fax, telephone, e-mail, in person.

Contact Dr. Robert Knapp, Director, University of New England, Master of Science in Education Program, 716 Stevens Avenue, Portland, ME 04103. *Telephone:* 800-339-0155. *Fax:* 207-878-2434. *E-mail:* msed@mailbox.une.edu.

eCollege.com *www.ecollege.com/scholarships*

DEGREES AND AWARDS

MSEd Education (certain restrictions apply)

COURSE SUBJECT AREAS OFFERED OUTSIDE OF DEGREE PROGRAMS

Graduate: Teacher education
See full description on page 770.

UNIVERSITY OF NEW HAMPSHIRE

Durham, New Hampshire
Instructional Technology Center
www.learn.unh.edu

University of New Hampshire, founded in 1866, is a state-supported university. It is accredited by the New England Association of Schools and Colleges. It first offered distance learning courses in 1980. In 1999–2000, it offered 6 courses at a distance. In fall 1999, there were 34 students enrolled in distance learning courses.

Course delivery sites Courses are delivered to your home, your workplace, 1 off-campus center in Manchester.

Media Courses are delivered via videotapes, videoconferencing, interactive television, computer software, World Wide Web, print. Students and teachers may meet in person or interact via videoconferencing, audioconferencing, mail, telephone, fax, e-mail, interactive television, World Wide Web. The following equipment may be required: television, videocassette player, computer, modem, Internet access, e-mail.

Restrictions Programs are available to in-state students only. Enrollment is open to anyone.

Services Distance learners have access to library services, the campus computer network, e-mail services, academic advising, bookstore at a distance.

Credit-earning options Students may transfer credits from another institution or may earn credits through examinations.

Typical costs *Undergraduate:* Tuition of $178 per credit plus mandatory fees of $15 per semester for in-state residents. Tuition of $196 per credit plus mandatory fees of $15 per semester for out-of-state residents. *Graduate:* Tuition of $206 per credit plus mandatory fees of $15 per semester for in-state residents. Tuition of $227 per credit plus mandatory fees of $15 per semester for out-of-state residents. *Noncredit courses:* $135 per course. Costs may vary.

Registration Students may register by mail, fax, telephone, e-mail, World Wide Web, in person.

Contact William F. Murphy, Dean, University of New Hampshire, Division of Continuing Education, 6 Garrison Avenue, Durham, NH 03824. *Telephone:* 603-862-1938. *Fax:* 603-862-1113. *E-mail:* wfm@christa.unh.edu.

DEGREES AND AWARDS

MS Computer Science (some on-campus requirements), Engineering (some on-campus requirements)

COURSE SUBJECT AREAS OFFERED OUTSIDE OF DEGREE PROGRAMS

Undergraduate: Business administration and management
Graduate: Engineering; information sciences and systems
Noncredit: Business; foods and nutrition studies; public health; teacher education

UNIVERSITY OF NEW MEXICO

Albuquerque, New Mexico

Distance Education Center
mts.unm.edu

University of New Mexico, founded in 1889, is a state-supported university. It is accredited by the North Central Association of Colleges and Schools. In 1999–2000, it offered 130 courses at a distance. In fall 1999, there were 600 students enrolled in distance learning courses.

Course delivery sites Courses are delivered to your home, your workplace, high schools, New Mexico Institute of Mining and Technology (Socorro), Northern New Mexico Community College (Española), San Juan College (Farmington), off-campus center(s) in Espanola, Gallup, Los Alamos, Los Lunes, Santa Fe, Taos.

Media Courses are delivered via television, videotapes, videoconferencing, interactive television, audiotapes, computer conferencing, World Wide Web. Students and teachers may meet in person or interact via videoconferencing, audioconferencing, mail, telephone, fax, e-mail, interactive television, World Wide Web. The following equipment may be required: television, computer, modem, Internet access.

Restrictions Programs are available in New Mexico, Colorado, and Wyoming. Enrollment is open to anyone.

Services Distance learners have access to library services, the campus computer network, e-mail services, academic advising, bookstore at a distance.

Credit-earning options Students may transfer credits from another institution or may earn credits through examinations, military training, business training.

Typical costs *Undergraduate:* Tuition of $101 per credit hour for in-state residents. *Graduate:* Tuition of $112 per credit hour for in-state residents. Contact the school for out-of-state tuition. Costs may vary. Financial aid is available to distance learners.

Registration Students may register by mail, telephone, World Wide Web, in person.

Contact Lisa Thomas, Distance Education Coordinator, University of New Mexico, Woodward Hall, Albuquerque, NM 87131. *Telephone:* 505-277-8821. *Fax:* 505-277-6908. *E-mail:* lthomas@unm.edu.

DEGREES AND AWARDS

BN Nursing
BS Speech and Hearing Science
MA Educational Administration (certain restrictions apply; some on-campus requirements)
MPA Public Administration

COURSE SUBJECT AREAS OFFERED OUTSIDE OF DEGREE PROGRAMS

Undergraduate: Anthropology; chemical engineering; civil engineering; electrical engineering; English literature; health professions and related sciences; mechanical engineering; nursing; special education; technical writing; telecommunications
Graduate: Chemical engineering; civil engineering; education administration; electrical engineering; English literature; mechanical engineering; public policy analysis; special education; technical writing; telecommunications

UNIVERSITY OF NEW ORLEANS

New Orleans, Louisiana

UNO Metropolitan College
www.uno.edu

University of New Orleans, founded in 1958, is a state-supported university. It is accredited by the Southern Association of Colleges and Schools. It first offered distance learning courses in 1985. In 1999–2000, it offered 20 courses at a distance. In fall 1999, there were 500 students enrolled in distance learning courses.

Course delivery sites Courses are delivered to your home, your workplace, military bases, high schools, Louisiana State University and Agricultural and Mechanical College (Baton Rouge), Louisiana State University at Alexandria (Alexandria), Louisiana State University at Eunice (Eunice), Louisiana State University in Shreveport (Shreveport), 2 off-campus centers in Marerro, Slidell.

Media Courses are delivered via television, videotapes, videoconferencing, interactive television, computer software, World Wide Web, e-mail, print. Students and teachers may meet in person or interact via videoconferencing, mail, telephone, fax, e-mail, interactive television, World Wide Web. The following equipment may be required: television, videocassette player, computer, modem, Internet access, e-mail.

Restrictions Programs are available nationwide. Enrollment is open to anyone.

Services Distance learners have access to library services, the campus computer network, e-mail services, academic advising at a distance.

Credit-earning options Students may transfer credits from another institution or may earn credits through examinations.

Typical costs *Undergraduate:* Tuition of $435 per course. *Graduate:* Tuition of $435 per course. Costs may vary.

Registration Students may register by mail, fax, telephone, in person.

Contact Carl E. Drichta, Associate Dean and Director, University of New Orleans, Metropolitan College, New Orleans, LA 70148. *Telephone:* 504-280-7100. *Fax:* 504-280-7317. *E-mail:* edrichta@uno.edu.

DEGREES AND AWARDS

Distance programs offered do not lead to a degree or other formal award.

COURSE SUBJECT AREAS OFFERED OUTSIDE OF DEGREE PROGRAMS

Undergraduate: Adult education; developmental and child psychology; English language and literature; finance; geology; health and physical education/fitness; history; liberal arts, general studies, and humanities; political science; public administration and services; real estate; special education; teacher education
Graduate: Adult education; library and information studies; public administration and services; special education; teacher education

See full descriptions on pages 592 and 676.

UNIVERSITY OF NORTH ALABAMA

Florence, Alabama

Educational Technology Services/Distance Learning
distance.una.edu

University of North Alabama, founded in 1830, is a state-supported, comprehensive institution. It is accredited by the Southern Association of Colleges and Schools. It first offered distance learning courses in 1997. In

1999–2000, it offered 40 courses at a distance. In fall 1999, there were 613 students enrolled in distance learning courses.

Course delivery sites Courses are delivered to your home, your workplace, military bases, high schools, The University of Alabama in Huntsville (Huntsville).

Media Courses are delivered via videotapes, videoconferencing, audiotapes, World Wide Web, e-mail. Students and teachers may meet in person or interact via videoconferencing, mail, telephone, fax, e-mail, World Wide Web. The following equipment may be required: television, videocassette player, computer, modem, Internet access, e-mail.

Restrictions Programs are available worldwide. Enrollment is open to anyone.

Services Distance learners have access to library services, e-mail services, academic advising, career placement assistance, bookstore at a distance.

Credit-earning options Students may transfer credits from another institution or may earn credits through examinations.

Typical costs *Undergraduate:* Tuition of $89 per credit hour plus mandatory fees of $30 per course for in-state residents. Tuition of $178 per credit hour plus mandatory fees of $30 per course for out-of-state residents. *Graduate:* Tuition of $102 per credit hour plus mandatory fees of $30 per course for in-state residents. Tuition of $204 per credit hour plus mandatory fees of $30 per course for out-of-state residents. Costs may vary. Financial aid is available to distance learners.

Registration Students may register by telephone, in person.

Contact Brenda J. Hill, Coordinator of Distance Learning, University of North Alabama, Box 5005, Florence, AL 35632-0001. *Telephone:* 256-765-4651. *Fax:* 256-765-4863. *E-mail:* bhill@unanov.una.edu.

DEGREES AND AWARDS

Graduate Certificate(s) Geography (service area differs from that of the overall institution; some on-campus requirements)

EMBA Business Administration (service area differs from that of the overall institution; some on-campus requirements)

COURSE SUBJECT AREAS OFFERED OUTSIDE OF DEGREE PROGRAMS

Undergraduate: American (U.S.) history; American studies; business; computer and information sciences; economics; education; English composition; English language and literature; geography; gerontology; history; marketing; nursing; political science; sociology

Graduate: American studies; business; English language and literature

See full description on page 676.

UNIVERSITY OF NORTH CAROLINA AT CHAPEL HILL

Chapel Hill, North Carolina

Division of Continuing Education
www.fridaycenter.unc.edu

University of North Carolina at Chapel Hill, founded in 1789, is a state-supported university. It is accredited by the Southern Association of Colleges and Schools. It first offered distance learning courses in 1913. In 1999–2000, it offered 150 courses at a distance. In fall 1999, there were 2,800 students enrolled in distance learning courses.

Course delivery sites Courses are delivered to your home, your workplace.

Media Courses are delivered via videotapes, World Wide Web, print. Students and teachers may interact via mail, telephone, fax, e-mail, World Wide Web. The following equipment may be required: computer, Internet access, e-mail.

Restrictions Programs are available worldwide. Enrollment is open to anyone.

Services Distance learners have access to academic advising, bookstore at a distance.

Credit-earning options Students may transfer credits from another institution or may earn credits through examinations.

Typical costs Tuition of $156 per course for in-state residents. Tuition of $390 per course for out-of-state residents. Costs may vary.

Registration Students may register by mail, fax, in person.

Contact Student Services and Advising, University of North Carolina at Chapel Hill, CB# 1020 The Friday Center, Chapel Hill, NC 27599-1020. *Telephone:* 919-962-1134. *Fax:* 919-962-5549. *E-mail:* stuserv@unc.edu.

DEGREES AND AWARDS

Distance programs offered do not lead to a degree or other formal award.

COURSE SUBJECT AREAS OFFERED OUTSIDE OF DEGREE PROGRAMS

Undergraduate: Accounting; African-American studies; algebra; American (U.S.) history; American literature; American studies; anthropology; art history and criticism; biology; business communications; calculus; chemistry; communications; computer and information sciences; creative writing; drama and theater; economics; education; English as a second language (ESL); English composition; English literature; environmental science; ethics; European history; foods and nutrition studies; French language and literature; geography; health services administration; history; hospitality services management; Italian language and literature; journalism; Latin language and literature; liberal arts, general studies, and humanities; library and information studies; logic; mathematics; music; oceanography; philosophy and religion; physics; political science; psychology; recreation and leisure studies; religious studies; Russian language and literature; sociology; Spanish language and literature; statistics

Noncredit: Nursing

See full description on page 676.

UNIVERSITY OF NORTH CAROLINA AT CHARLOTTE

Charlotte, North Carolina

Continuing Education, Extension and Summer Programs
www.uncc.edu/conteduc

University of North Carolina at Charlotte, founded in 1946, is a state-supported university. It is accredited by the Southern Association of Colleges and Schools. It first offered distance learning courses in 1985. In 1999–2000, it offered 9 courses at a distance. In fall 1999, there were 132 students enrolled in distance learning courses.

Course delivery sites Courses are delivered to your home, your workplace.

Media Courses are delivered via television, videotapes, videoconferencing, interactive television, audiotapes, computer software, CD-ROM, computer conferencing, World Wide Web, e-mail, print. Students and teachers may meet in person or interact via videoconferencing, audioconferencing, mail, telephone, fax, e-mail, World Wide Web. The following equipment may be required: television, videocassette player, computer, modem, Internet access, e-mail.

Restrictions Programs are available nationwide. Enrollment is restricted to individuals meeting certain criteria.

Services Distance learners have access to library services, the campus computer network, e-mail services, academic advising, tutoring, career placement assistance at a distance.

Credit-earning options Students may transfer credits from another institution or may earn credits through examinations.

Typical costs *Undergraduate:* Tuition of $32.50 per credit plus mandatory fees of $3 per credit for in-state residents. Tuition of $278 per credit plus mandatory fees of $3 per credit for out-of-state residents. *Graduate:* Tuition of $48 per credit plus mandatory fees of $4.25 per credit for in-state residents. Tuition of $404.50 per credit plus mandatory fees of $4.25 per credit for out-of-state residents. Costs may vary. Financial aid is available to distance learners.

Registration Students may register by mail, fax, telephone, e-mail, in person.

Contact Mary Faye Englebert, Program Coordinator, University of North Carolina at Charlotte. *Telephone:* 704-547-4594. *Fax:* 704-547-3158. *E-mail:* mfengleb@email.uncc.edu.

DEGREES AND AWARDS

BSET Engineering Technology (some on-campus requirements), Fire Science (some on-campus requirements)

COURSE SUBJECT AREAS OFFERED OUTSIDE OF DEGREE PROGRAMS

Undergraduate: Electronics; fire science

UNIVERSITY OF NORTH CAROLINA AT GREENSBORO

Greensboro, North Carolina

Division of Continual Learning and Summer Session
www.uncg.edu/cex

University of North Carolina at Greensboro, founded in 1891, is a state-supported university. It is accredited by the Southern Association of Colleges and Schools. It first offered distance learning courses in 1972. In 1999–2000, it offered 35 courses at a distance. In fall 1999, there were 210 students enrolled in distance learning courses.

Course delivery sites Courses are delivered to your home, your workplace, high schools, The University of North Carolina at Asheville (Asheville), University of North Carolina at Charlotte (Charlotte).

Media Courses are delivered via videotapes, videoconferencing, audiotapes, computer software, CD-ROM, World Wide Web, e-mail, print. Students and teachers may meet in person or interact via videoconferencing, mail, telephone, fax, e-mail, World Wide Web. The following equipment may be required: television, videocassette player, computer, modem, Internet access, e-mail.

Restrictions Courses are available to regional area students only, selected courses are available state- and nation-wide. Enrollment is restricted to individuals meeting certain criteria.

Services Distance learners have access to library services, e-mail services, academic advising, bookstore at a distance.

Credit-earning options Students may transfer credits from another institution or may earn credits through examinations.

Typical costs *Undergraduate:* Tuition of $37 per semester hour plus mandatory fees of $5 per semester hour for in-state residents. *Graduate:* Tuition of $54 per semester hour plus mandatory fees of $5 per semester hour for in-state residents. Undergraduate out-of-state tuition ranges between $110 and $322 per semester hour. Graduate out-of-state tuition ranges between $150 and $469 per semester hour. Graduate and undergraduate mandatory fees are $5 per semester hour. Costs may vary. Financial aid is available to distance learners.

Registration Students may register by mail, fax, telephone, e-mail, World Wide Web, in person.

Contact William H. Taylor, Director of Distance Learning and Professional Development, University of North Carolina at Greensboro, Division of Continual Learning and Summer Session, 202 Forney Building, UNCG, PO Box 26170, Greensboro, NC 27402-6170. *Telephone:* 336-334-5414. *Fax:* 336-334-5628.

eCollege.com *www.ecollege.com/scholarships*

DEGREES AND AWARDS

MA Speech Pathology and Audiology (certain restrictions apply; service area differs from that of the overall institution; some on-campus requirements)

MLIS Library and Information Studies (service area differs from that of the overall institution; some on-campus requirements)

COURSE SUBJECT AREAS OFFERED OUTSIDE OF DEGREE PROGRAMS

Undergraduate: American (U.S.) history; astronomy and astrophysics; biology; business administration and management; child care and development; community health services; liberal arts, general studies, and humanities; nursing; Russian language and literature; Spanish language and literature; visual and performing arts

Graduate: Curriculum and instruction; education administration; English as a second language (ESL); French language and literature; German language and literature; Latin language and literature; liberal arts, general studies, and humanities; library and information studies; nursing; Russian language and literature; Spanish language and literature; special education; visual and performing arts

See full description on page 676.

UNIVERSITY OF NORTH CAROLINA AT PEMBROKE

Pembroke, North Carolina

Distance Learning Video Facility
www.uncp.edu/dl

University of North Carolina at Pembroke, founded in 1887, is a state-supported, comprehensive institution. It is accredited by the Southern Association of Colleges and Schools. In 1999–2000, it offered 6 courses at a distance. In fall 1999, there were 35 students enrolled in distance learning courses.

Course delivery sites Courses are delivered to your home, high schools, Richmond Community College (Hamlet), Sandhills Community College (Pinehurst), Southeastern Community College (Whiteville).

Media Courses are delivered via interactive television, World Wide Web, e-mail. Students and teachers may meet in person or interact via e-mail, interactive television, World Wide Web. The following equipment may be required: computer, modem, Internet access, e-mail.

Restrictions Programs are available to in-state students only. Enrollment is restricted to individuals meeting certain criteria.

Services Distance learners have access to library services, the campus computer network, e-mail services, academic advising, bookstore at a distance.

Typical costs *Undergraduate:* Tuition of $105 per course plus mandatory fees of $6 per course. *Graduate:* Tuition of $150 per course plus mandatory fees of $6 per course. Financial aid is available to distance learners.

Registration Students may register by in person.

Contact Reggie Oxendine, Manager Distance Learning Video Facility, University of North Carolina at Pembroke, PO Box 1510, Pembroke, NC 28372. *Telephone:* 910-521-6563. *Fax:* 910-521-6564. *E-mail:* reggie. oxendine@uncp.edu.

DEGREES AND AWARDS

MBA Business Administration (some on-campus requirements)

COURSE SUBJECT AREAS OFFERED OUTSIDE OF DEGREE PROGRAMS

Undergraduate: American studies; business administration and management; education; nursing
Graduate: Business administration and management

UNIVERSITY OF NORTH CAROLINA AT WILMINGTON

Wilmington, North Carolina

Division for Public Service and Extended Education
www.uncwil.edu/dpsee

University of North Carolina at Wilmington, founded in 1947, is a state-supported, comprehensive institution. It is accredited by the Southern Association of Colleges and Schools. It first offered distance learning courses in 1992. In 1999–2000, it offered 58 courses at a distance. In fall 1999, there were 300 students enrolled in distance learning courses.
Course delivery sites Courses are delivered to your home, your workplace, military bases, high schools, Bladen Community College (Dublin), Brunswick Community College (Supply), Coastal Carolina Community College (Jacksonville), James Sprunt Community College (Kenansville), Sampson Community College (Clinton), Southeastern Community College (Whiteville).
Media Courses are delivered via videotapes, videoconferencing, interactive television, computer software, World Wide Web, e-mail, print. Students and teachers may meet in person or interact via videoconferencing, telephone, fax, e-mail, interactive television, World Wide Web. The following equipment may be required: computer, Internet access, e-mail.
Restrictions Programs are available worldwide. Enrollment is restricted to individuals meeting certain criteria.
Services Distance learners have access to library services, the campus computer network, e-mail services, academic advising, career placement assistance, bookstore at a distance.
Credit-earning options Students may transfer credits from another institution or may earn credits through examinations.
Typical costs *Undergraduate:* Tuition of $32 per credit hour plus mandatory fees of $6 per credit hour for in-state residents. Tuition of $276 per credit hour plus mandatory fees of $6 per credit hour for out-of-state residents. *Graduate:* Tuition of $49 per credit hour plus mandatory fees of $9 per credit hour for in-state residents. Tuition of $401 per credit hour plus mandatory fees of $9 per credit hour for out-of-state residents. *Noncredit courses:* $69 per course. Costs may vary. Financial aid is available to distance learners.
Registration Students may register by telephone, World Wide Web.
Contact Dr. Jim Edmundson, Director of Extension, University of North Carolina at Wilmington, Division for Public Service and Extended Education, 601 South College Road, Wilmington, NC 28412. *Telephone:* 910-962-3192. *Fax:* 910-962-3990. *E-mail:* edmundsonj@uncwil.edu.

DEGREES AND AWARDS

Distance programs offered do not lead to a degree or other formal award.

COURSE SUBJECT AREAS OFFERED OUTSIDE OF DEGREE PROGRAMS

Undergraduate: Business administration and management; criminology; curriculum and instruction; educational psychology; educational

research; English as a second language (ESL); English literature; information sciences and systems; Japanese language and literature; nursing; sociology; teacher education
Graduate: Education administration; educational research
See full description on page 676.

UNIVERSITY OF NORTH DAKOTA

Grand Forks, North Dakota

Division of Continuing Education
www.conted.und.edu

University of North Dakota, founded in 1883, is a state-supported university. It is accredited by the North Central Association of Colleges and Schools. It first offered distance learning courses in 1910. In 1999–2000, it offered 705 courses at a distance. In fall 1999, there were 6,000 students enrolled in distance learning courses.
Course delivery sites Courses are delivered to your home, your workplace, military bases, high schools, Lake Region State College (Devils Lake), Williston State College (Williston), 1 off-campus center in Bismarck.
Media Courses are delivered via videotapes, videoconferencing, interactive television, audiotapes, computer software, CD-ROM, computer conferencing, World Wide Web, e-mail, print. Students and teachers may meet in person or interact via videoconferencing, audioconferencing, mail, telephone, fax, e-mail, interactive television, World Wide Web. The following equipment may be required: television, videocassette player, computer, modem, Internet access, e-mail.
Restrictions Programs are available worldwide. Enrollment is restricted to individuals meeting certain criteria.
Services Distance learners have access to library services, the campus computer network, e-mail services, academic advising, bookstore at a distance.
Credit-earning options Students may transfer credits from another institution or may earn credits through examinations, portfolio assessment.
Typical costs *Undergraduate:* Tuition of $1338.50 per semester plus mandatory fees of $238 per semester for in-state residents. Tuition of $3205.50 per semester plus mandatory fees of $238 per semester for out-of-state residents. *Graduate:* Tuition of $1443.50 per semester plus mandatory fees of $238 per semester for in-state residents. Tuition of $2055 per semester plus mandatory fees of $238 per semester for out-of-state residents. Costs may vary. Financial aid is available to distance learners.
Registration Students may register by mail, fax, telephone, e-mail, World Wide Web, in person.
Contact Lynette Krenelka, Program Director, University of North Dakota, Extended Degree Programs, Box 9021, Grand Forks, ND 58202-9021. *Telephone:* 877-450-1842. *Fax:* 701-777-4282. *E-mail:* lynette_krenelka@mail.und.nodak.edu.

DEGREES AND AWARDS

MS Rural Health Nursing (service area differs from that of the overall institution; some on-campus requirements), Space Studies (certain restrictions apply; service area differs from that of the overall institution; some on-campus requirements)

COURSE SUBJECT AREAS OFFERED OUTSIDE OF DEGREE PROGRAMS

Undergraduate: Accounting; biological and life sciences; business; business administration and management; chemical engineering; civil engineering; electrical engineering; engineering mechanics; industrial psychology; liberal arts, general studies, and humanities; mathematics;

mechanical engineering; music; nursing; philosophy and religion; physical sciences; physics; political science; psychology; public administration and services; social sciences; social work; teacher education; visual and performing arts

Graduate: Business administration and management; education administration; health professions and related sciences; nursing; physical sciences; political science; public administration and services; social work; special education; teacher education

Noncredit: Public health

UNIVERSITY OF NORTHERN COLORADO

Greeley, Colorado
Office of Extended Studies
uconline.edu

University of Northern Colorado, founded in 1890, is a state-supported university. It is accredited by the North Central Association of Colleges and Schools. It first offered distance learning courses in 1906. In 1999–2000, it offered 70 courses at a distance. In fall 1999, there were 300 students enrolled in distance learning courses.

Course delivery sites Courses are delivered to your home, your workplace, military bases, 5 off-campus centers in Colorado Springs, Denver.

Media Courses are delivered via videotapes, audiotapes, computer software, e-mail, print. Students and teachers may meet in person or interact via mail, telephone, fax, e-mail. The following equipment may be required: videocassette player, computer, e-mail.

Restrictions Programs are available worldwide. Enrollment is open to anyone.

Services Distance learners have access to library services, academic advising, bookstore at a distance.

Credit-earning options Students may transfer credits from another institution or may earn credits through examinations.

Typical costs *Undergraduate:* Tuition of $90 per credit. *Graduate:* Tuition of $90 per credit. Contact the school for information.

Registration Students may register by mail, fax, telephone, e-mail, in person.

Contact Susan Pelis, Student Service Manager, University of Northern Colorado, Office of Extended Studies, 130 Candelaria Hall, Greely, CO 80639. *Telephone:* 970-351-2944. *Fax:* 970-351-2519. *E-mail:* askus@cce.univnorthco.edu.

DEGREES AND AWARDS

Distance programs offered do not lead to a degree or other formal award.

COURSE SUBJECT AREAS OFFERED OUTSIDE OF DEGREE PROGRAMS

Undergraduate: Biology; community health services; economics; foods and nutrition studies; geography; gerontology; health professions and related sciences; mathematics; nursing; special education

Graduate: Law and legal studies; teacher education

UNIVERSITY OF NORTHERN IOWA

Cedar Falls, Iowa
Division of Continuing Education
www.uni.edu/contined/gcs

University of Northern Iowa, founded in 1876, is a state-supported, comprehensive institution. It is accredited by the North Central Association of Colleges and Schools. It first offered distance learning courses in 1920. In 1999–2000, it offered 80 courses at a distance. In fall 1999, there were 700 students enrolled in distance learning courses.

Course delivery sites Courses are delivered to your home, your workplace, military bases, high schools.

Media Courses are delivered via interactive television, World Wide Web, print. Students and teachers may meet in person or interact via videoconferencing, mail, telephone, fax, e-mail, interactive television, World Wide Web. The following equipment may be required: computer, Internet access.

Restrictions Courses offered via the fiber optics network (ICN) are available to in-state students only. Courses offered through the Web or correspondence study are available worldwide. Enrollment is restricted to individuals meeting certain criteria.

Services Distance learners have access to library services, academic advising, bookstore at a distance.

Credit-earning options Students may transfer credits from another institution or may earn credits through examinations, military training.

Typical costs *Undergraduate:* Tuition of $117 per credit hour. *Graduate:* Tuition of $184 per credit hour. Costs may vary.

Registration Students may register by mail, fax, World Wide Web, in person.

Contact Kent Johnson, Associate Director, University of Northern Iowa, Credit Programs, 124 SHC, Cedar Falls, IA 50614-0223. *Telephone:* 319-273-5970. *Fax:* 319-273-2872. *E-mail:* kent.johnson@uni.edu.

DEGREES AND AWARDS

BLS Liberal Studies (certain restrictions apply)

COURSE SUBJECT AREAS OFFERED OUTSIDE OF DEGREE PROGRAMS

Undergraduate: Accounting; area, ethnic, and cultural studies; communications; criminology; developmental and child psychology; economics; education; educational psychology; English language and literature; health and physical education/fitness; health professions and related sciences; history; home economics and family studies; international relations; liberal arts, general studies, and humanities; marketing; mathematics; music; philosophy and religion; political science; psychology; public health; social psychology; social sciences; social work; sociology; teacher education

Graduate: Area, ethnic, and cultural studies; communications; criminology; developmental and child psychology; education; educational psychology; English language and literature; history; philosophy and religion; social work; sociology; teacher education

UNIVERSITY OF NORTH FLORIDA

Jacksonville, Florida
www.unf.edu

University of North Florida, founded in 1965, is a state-supported, comprehensive institution. It is accredited by the Southern Association of Colleges and Schools. It first offered distance learning courses in 1983.

Contact University of North Florida, 4567 St. Johns Bluff Road South, Jacksonville, FL 32224-2645. *Telephone:* 904-620-1000. *Fax:* 904-620-1040.

See full description on page 676.

UNIVERSITY OF NORTH TEXAS

Denton, Texas
Center for Distributed Learning
www.courses.unt.edu

University of North Texas, founded in 1890, is a state-supported university. It is accredited by the Southern Association of Colleges and Schools. It first offered distance learning courses in 1993. In 1999–2000, it offered 75 courses at a distance. In fall 1999, there were 914 students enrolled in distance learning courses.

Course delivery sites Courses are delivered to your home, your workplace, military bases, high schools, Abilene Christian University (Abilene), Midwestern State University (Wichita Falls), St. Cloud State University (St. Cloud, MN), South Plains College (Levelland), Stephen F. Austin State University (Nacogdoches), Texas A&M University–Texarkana (Texarkana), Texas State Technical College–Waco Campus (Waco), Texas Tech University Health Sciences Center (Lubbock), University of Houston (Houston), University of Texas–Pan American (Edinburg), 4 off-campus centers in Dallas.

Media Courses are delivered via videotapes, videoconferencing, interactive television, computer software, CD-ROM, computer conferencing, World Wide Web, e-mail. Students and teachers may meet in person or interact via videoconferencing, audioconferencing, mail, telephone, fax, e-mail, interactive television, World Wide Web. The following equipment may be required: computer, modem, Internet access, e-mail.

Restrictions Programs are available nationwide. Enrollment is open to anyone.

Services Distance learners have access to library services, the campus computer network, e-mail services, academic advising, career placement assistance, bookstore at a distance.

Credit-earning options Students may transfer credits from another institution or may earn credits through examinations, military training, business training.

Typical costs *Undergraduate:* Tuition of $72 per credit hour plus mandatory fees of $74 per semester for in-state residents. Tuition of $288 per credit hour plus mandatory fees of $74 per semester for out-of-state residents. *Graduate:* Tuition of $98 per credit hour plus mandatory fees of $287 per semester for in-state residents. Tuition of $314 per credit hour plus mandatory fees of $287 per semester for out-of-state residents. Costs may vary. Financial aid is available to distance learners.

Registration Students may register by telephone, World Wide Web, in person.

Contact Kathy Krejci, Distributed Learning Information Specialist, University of North Texas, PO Box 310889, Denton, TX 76203-0889. *Telephone:* 940-565-2947. *Fax:* 940-389-7819. *E-mail:* kkrejci@unt.edu.

DEGREES AND AWARDS

Undergraduate Certificate(s) Library and Information Sciences (service area differs from that of the overall institution; some on-campus requirements)

Graduate Certificate(s) Applied Gerontology (service area differs from that of the overall institution; some on-campus requirements)

MS Applied Gerontology (service area differs from that of the overall institution; some on-campus requirements), Information Sciences (service area differs from that of the overall institution), Library Science (service area differs from that of the overall institution), Merchandising (certain restrictions apply; service area differs from that of the overall

institution; some on-campus requirements), Technological Studies (service area differs from that of the overall institution; some on-campus requirements)

COURSE SUBJECT AREAS OFFERED OUTSIDE OF DEGREE PROGRAMS

Undergraduate: Anthropology; art history and criticism; computer and information sciences; criminal justice; electronics; gerontology; health and physical education/fitness; history of science and technology; hospitality services management; instructional media; library and information studies; marketing; music; psychology; technical writing

Graduate: Community services; computer programming; criminal justice; curriculum and instruction; education; education administration; educational psychology; electronics; engineering; environmental health; environmental science; gerontology; hospitality services management; instructional media; library and information studies; marketing; mechanical engineering; psychology; special education; teacher education

See full description on page 676.

UNIVERSITY OF NOTRE DAME

Notre Dame, Indiana
Executive Education
www.nd.edu/~execprog

University of Notre Dame, founded in 1842, is an independent, religious university. It is accredited by the Association of Theological Schools in the United States and Canada, North Central Association of Colleges and Schools. It first offered distance learning courses in 1995. In 1999–2000, it offered 19 courses at a distance. In fall 1999, there were 160 students enrolled in distance learning courses.

Course delivery sites Courses are delivered to 6 off-campus centers in Indianapolis, Chicago (IL), Green Bay (WI), Hoffman Estates (IL), Nashville (TN), Toledo (OH).

Media Courses are delivered via videoconferencing, World Wide Web. Students and teachers may meet in person or interact via videoconferencing, audioconferencing, mail, telephone, fax, e-mail, World Wide Web.

Restrictions Programs are available nationwide. Enrollment is open to anyone.

Services Distance learners have access to library services, the campus computer network, e-mail services, bookstore at a distance.

Typical costs Tuition for the EMBA program is $27580 per year. Tuition for proprietary corporate sponsored programs is based on total program fees. Costs may vary. Financial aid is available to distance learners.

Registration Students may register by mail, fax, telephone, e-mail, in person.

Contact Arnie Ludwig, Assistant Dean, University of Notre Dame, 126 Mendoza College of Business, Notre Dame, IN 46556. *Telephone:* 800-631-3622. *E-mail:* arnie.f.ludwig.1@nd.edu.

DEGREES AND AWARDS

Undergraduate Certificate(s) Executive Management (some on-campus requirements), Finance and Accounting (service area differs from that of the overall institution)

EMBA Business Administration (some on-campus requirements)

COURSE SUBJECT AREAS OFFERED OUTSIDE OF DEGREE PROGRAMS

Graduate: Accounting; business; business administration and management; business communications; finance; international business; investments and securities; management information systems; marketing; organizational behavior studies

Special note

Executive education at Notre Dame focuses primarily on EMBA, tailored degree curriculums, and customized nondegree programs. The first steps with any program are development of solid and results-oriented learning objectives and selection of expert facilitation. The design team then applies appropriate technology to both leverage the learning and add convenience to geographically distributed participants. The team operates 3 distance education systems, which consist of 2 advanced technology classrooms and 1 videoconference (vc) room that is dedicated to smaller learning events and meetings. The 2 main classrooms utilize the latest vc and wide-area computer network technologies to optimize learning for both campus and noncampus students at multiple locations. The latest programs combine the best of traditional face-to-face facilitation, videoconferencing, and Web technologies. The delivery objectives of these programs have 3 dimensions: to use technology to enhance learning opportunities for participants, to minimize the potential distractors or constraints that are inherent to some distance education methodologies, and to reduce or eliminate extensive travel by the participants as a result of a convenience of programming. Successful completion of these objectives is achieved with a system that incorporates use of multiple distance learning technologies. The University of Notre Dame continues to make significant investments in distance learning technology to enhance learning and to reach globally dispersed participants. For example, even the technology of the USDLA award-winning facilities has been completely redesigned or replaced to meet the changing needs of distance education students. Participants and sponsors alike are not only consistently impressed with the technology resources but, more importantly, with the team's ability to leverage the technology for improved results.

See full description on page 540.

Services Distance learners have access to library services, e-mail services, academic advising, bookstore at a distance.

Credit-earning options Students may transfer credits from another institution or may earn credits through examinations, military training, business training.

Typical costs Contact the school for information. Costs may vary. Financial aid is available to distance learners.

Registration Students may register by mail, fax, telephone, e-mail, in person.

Contact Larry Hayes, Information Assistant, University of Oklahoma, 1700 Asp Avenue, Norman, OK 73072. *Telephone:* 800-522-0772 Ext. 4414. *Fax:* 405-325-7196. *E-mail:* lhayes@ou.edu.

DEGREES AND AWARDS

Distance programs offered do not lead to a degree or other formal award.

COURSE SUBJECT AREAS OFFERED OUTSIDE OF DEGREE PROGRAMS

Undergraduate: American (U.S.) history; anthropology; archaeology; area, ethnic, and cultural studies; Asian studies; astronomy and astrophysics; business administration and management; chemistry; Chinese language and literature; classical languages and literatures; drama and theater; economics; education; engineering; English language and literature; ethics; European languages and literatures; finance; fine arts; French language and literature; geography; geology; German language and literature; Greek language and literature; health and physical education/fitness; history; Japanese language and literature; journalism; Latin language and literature; library and information studies; management; marketing; mathematics; music; political science; psychology; Russian language and literature; social psychology; sociology; Spanish language and literature

Graduate: Accounting; economics; education administration; electronics; English language and literature; finance; information sciences and systems; library and information studies; management information systems; marketing; political science; social psychology

Noncredit: English language and literature; finance; fine arts; information sciences and systems; journalism; library and information studies; management information systems; marketing; mathematics; social psychology

See full descriptions on pages 676 and 772.

UNIVERSITY OF OKLAHOMA

Norman, Oklahoma

College of Continuing Education
www.occe.ou.edu

University of Oklahoma, founded in 1890, is a state-supported university. It is accredited by the North Central Association of Colleges and Schools. It first offered distance learning courses in 1913. In 1999–2000, it offered 175 courses at a distance. In fall 1999, there were 5,300 students enrolled in distance learning courses.

Course delivery sites Courses are delivered to your home, your workplace, military bases.

Media Courses are delivered via television, videotapes, videoconferencing, interactive television, audiotapes, computer software, CD-ROM, computer conferencing, World Wide Web, e-mail, print. Students and teachers may meet in person or interact via videoconferencing, audioconferencing, mail, telephone, fax, e-mail, interactive television, World Wide Web. The following equipment may be required: television, videocassette player, computer, modem, Internet access, e-mail.

Restrictions Programs are available worldwide. Enrollment is restricted to individuals meeting certain criteria.

UNIVERSITY OF OREGON

Eugene, Oregon

Distance Education
de.uoregon.edu

University of Oregon, founded in 1872, is a state-supported university. It is accredited by the Northwest Association of Schools and Colleges. It first offered distance learning courses in 1992. In 1999–2000, it offered 21 courses at a distance. In fall 1999, there were 298 students enrolled in distance learning courses.

Course delivery sites Courses are delivered to your home, your workplace, military bases.

Media Courses are delivered via videoconferencing, computer conferencing, World Wide Web, e-mail, print. Students and teachers may meet in person or interact via videoconferencing, mail, e-mail, World Wide Web. The following equipment may be required: computer, modem, Internet access, e-mail.

Restrictions Programs are available nationwide. Enrollment is open to anyone.

Services Distance learners have access to library services, e-mail services, academic advising, bookstore at a distance.

Credit-earning options Students may transfer credits from another institution.

Typical costs Tuition of $415 per course. *Noncredit courses:* $415 per course. Costs may vary. Financial aid is available to distance learners.

Registration Students may register by telephone, World Wide Web, in person.

Contact Sandra Gladney, Program Coordinator, University of Oregon, 1277 University of Oregon, Eugene, OR 97403-1277. *Telephone:* 800-824-2714. *Fax:* 541-346-3545. *E-mail:* dasst@continue.uoregon.edu.

eCollege.com *www.ecollege.com/scholarships*

DEGREES AND AWARDS

MS Applied Information Management (certain restrictions apply)

COURSE SUBJECT AREAS OFFERED OUTSIDE OF DEGREE PROGRAMS

Undergraduate: Astronomy and astrophysics; economics; English language and literature; geology; liberal arts, general studies, and humanities; oceanography; physics; political science
Graduate: Interdisciplinary studies; management information systems

UNIVERSITY OF PENNSYLVANIA

Philadelphia, Pennsylvania

Distance Education
www.upenn.edu/schools_prog/distance.html

University of Pennsylvania, founded in 1740, is an independent, non-profit university. It is accredited by the Middle States Association of Colleges and Schools. It first offered distance learning courses in 1994. In 1999–2000, it offered 50 courses at a distance. In fall 1999, there were 1,000 students enrolled in distance learning courses.
Course delivery sites Courses are delivered to your home, your workplace, military bases, high schools.
Media Courses are delivered via computer software, World Wide Web, print. Students and teachers may interact via e-mail, World Wide Web. The following equipment may be required: computer, modem, Internet access, e-mail.
Restrictions Programs are available worldwide. Enrollment is restricted to individuals meeting certain criteria.
Services Distance learners have access to library services, academic advising, bookstore at a distance.
Typical costs Please contact individual program coordinators for cost and financial aid information. Costs may vary.
Registration Students may register by mail, fax, telephone, e-mail, World Wide Web, in person.
Contact University of Pennsylvania. *Telephone:* 215-898-1783. *E-mail:* dl@isc.upenn.edu.

eCollege.com *www.ecollege.com/scholarships*

DEGREES AND AWARDS

Undergraduate Certificate(s) Business (certain restrictions apply)
Graduate Certificate(s) Nurse Midwifery (certain restrictions apply)
MSN Nurse Midwifery (certain restrictions apply; service area differs from that of the overall institution; some on-campus requirements)

COURSE SUBJECT AREAS OFFERED OUTSIDE OF DEGREE PROGRAMS

Undergraduate: Calculus; economics; English literature; geology; physics; psychology; sociology; theological studies
Noncredit: Calculus; dental services; economics; English literature; finance; geology; human resources management; investments and securities; management information systems; marketing; mathematics; organizational behavior studies; physics; psychology; social work; sociology; theological studies; veterinary science

See full description on page 774.

UNIVERSITY OF PHOENIX

Phoenix, Arizona

University of Phoenix Online
www.uophx.edu/online

University of Phoenix, founded in 1976, is a proprietary, comprehensive institution. It is accredited by the North Central Association of Colleges and Schools. It first offered distance learning courses in 1989. In 1999–2000, it offered 120 courses at a distance. In fall 1999, there were 13,000 students enrolled in distance learning courses.
Course delivery sites Courses are delivered to your home, your workplace, military bases.
Media Courses are delivered via computer software, computer conferencing, World Wide Web, e-mail. Students and teachers may interact via mail, telephone, e-mail, World Wide Web. The following equipment may be required: computer, modem, Internet access, e-mail.
Restrictions Programs are available worldwide. Enrollment is open to anyone.
Services Distance learners have access to library services, the campus computer network, e-mail services, academic advising, bookstore at a distance.
Credit-earning options Students may transfer credits from another institution or may earn credits through examinations, portfolio assessment, business training.
Typical costs *Undergraduate:* Tuition of $390 per credit hour. *Graduate:* Tuition of $485 per credit hour. Costs may vary. Financial aid is available to distance learners.
Registration Students may register by mail, telephone, in person.
Contact Enrollment Department, University of Phoenix, 3157 East Elwood Street, Phoenix, AZ 85034. *Telephone:* 800-742-4742. *Fax:* 602-894-2152. *E-mail:* online@apollogrp.edu.

DEGREES AND AWARDS

BS Business Administration, Business and Management, Business and Project Management, Business Information Systems, Marketing, Nursing
MA Education, Organizational Management
MBA Business Administration, Global Management, Technology Management
MS Computer Information Systems, Nursing

COURSE SUBJECT AREAS OFFERED OUTSIDE OF DEGREE PROGRAMS

Undergraduate: Accounting; business; business administration and management; communications; computer and information sciences; human resources management; marketing; mathematics; nursing
Graduate: Accounting; business; business administration and management; communications; computer and information sciences; economics;

education administration; human resources management; international business; management information systems; marketing; nursing; organizational behavior studies

See full description on page 776.

UNIVERSITY OF PITTSBURGH

Pittsburgh, Pennsylvania

Center for Instructional Development and Distance Education

www.pitt.edu/~ciddeweb

University of Pittsburgh, founded in 1787, is a state-related university. It is accredited by the Middle States Association of Colleges and Schools. It first offered distance learning courses in 1972. In 1999–2000, it offered 150 courses at a distance. In fall 1999, there were 1,000 students enrolled in distance learning courses.

Course delivery sites Courses are delivered to your home, University of Pittsburgh at Bradford (Bradford), University of Pittsburgh at Johnstown (Johnstown), 4 off-campus centers in Bradford, Greensburg, Johnstown, Titusville.

Media Courses are delivered via videotapes, videoconferencing, interactive television, computer software, computer conferencing, World Wide Web, print. Students and teachers may meet in person or interact via videoconferencing, mail, telephone, fax, e-mail, interactive television, World Wide Web.

Restrictions Programs are available to in-state students only. Enrollment is restricted to individuals meeting certain criteria.

Services Distance learners have access to library services, the campus computer network, e-mail services, academic advising, tutoring, career placement assistance, bookstore at a distance.

Credit-earning options Students may transfer credits from another institution or may earn credits through examinations.

Typical costs Tuition of $212 per credit plus mandatory fees of $103 per term for in-state residents. Tuition of $459 per credit for out-of-state residents. Costs may vary. Financial aid is available to distance learners.

Registration Students may register by mail, in person.

Contact Andrea Abt, Coordinator, Student and Faculty Support Services, University of Pittsburgh, 616 Masonic Temple, 4227 Fifth Avenue, Pittsburgh, PA 15260. *Telephone:* 412-624-7206. *Fax:* 412-624-7213. *E-mail:* aabt@pitt.edu.

DEGREES AND AWARDS

BA Humanities (some on-campus requirements), Social Sciences (some on-campus requirements)

MBA Business Administration (service area differs from that of the overall institution; some on-campus requirements)

MEd Elementary Education (service area differs from that of the overall institution)

COURSE SUBJECT AREAS OFFERED OUTSIDE OF DEGREE PROGRAMS

Undergraduate: Anthropology; astronomy and astrophysics; communications; economics; educational psychology; English composition; English literature; history; information sciences and systems; law and legal studies; liberal arts, general studies, and humanities; logic; mathematics; philosophy and religion; political science; protective services; psychology; public administration and services; social sciences; statistics; visual and performing arts

Graduate: Business administration and management; curriculum and instruction; nursing; teacher education

---

UNIVERSITY OF REGINA

Regina, Saskatchewan, Canada

Off-Campus Degree Credit Division

www.uregina.ca/extension/index.html

University of Regina, founded in 1974, is a province-supported university. In 1999–2000, it offered 20 courses at a distance. In fall 1999, there were 500 students enrolled in distance learning courses.

Course delivery sites Courses are delivered to your home, 12 off-campus centers.

Media Courses are delivered via television, computer conferencing, World Wide Web. Students and teachers may interact via videoconferencing, interactive television, World Wide Web. The following equipment may be required: computer, Internet access.

Restrictions Programs are available to in-state students only. Enrollment is restricted to individuals meeting certain criteria.

Typical costs Tuition of Can$281 per course.

Contact Brian Campbell, Head, Off-Campus Degree Credit Division, University of Regina, Regina, SK S4S 0A2 Canada. *Telephone:* 306-585-5803. *Fax:* 306-585-5779. *E-mail:* offcamp@uregina.ca.

DEGREES AND AWARDS

Distance programs offered do not lead to a degree or other formal award.

COURSE SUBJECT AREAS OFFERED OUTSIDE OF DEGREE PROGRAMS

Undergraduate: Geography; mathematics

UNIVERSITY OF RICHMOND

University of Richmond, Virginia

School of Continuing Studies

www.richmond.edu/

University of Richmond, founded in 1830, is an independent, nonprofit, comprehensive institution. It is accredited by the Southern Association of Colleges and Schools. In 1999–2000, it offered 6 courses at a distance.

Course delivery sites Courses are delivered to your home, your workplace.

Media Courses are delivered via computer conferencing, World Wide Web, e-mail, print. Students and teachers may interact via e-mail, World Wide Web. The following equipment may be required: computer, Internet access, e-mail.

Restrictions Programs are available worldwide. Enrollment is open to anyone.

Services Distance learners have access to library services, academic advising at a distance.

Credit-earning options Students may transfer credits from another institution or may earn credits through military training, business training.

Typical costs Tuition of $206 per credit plus mandatory fees of $5 per semester. *Noncredit courses:* $120 per course.

Registration Students may register by mail, World Wide Web, in person.

Contact Walter G. Green, III, Assistant Professor of Emergency Services Management, University of Richmond, School of Continuing Studies, Richmond, VA 23173. *Telephone:* 804-287-1246. *Fax:* 804-289-8138. *E-mail:* wgreen@richmond.edu.

DEGREES AND AWARDS

Undergraduate Certificate(s) Crisis Management (certain restrictions apply)

COURSE SUBJECT AREAS OFFERED OUTSIDE OF DEGREE PROGRAMS

Undergraduate: Protective services; public administration and services

UNIVERSITY OF ST. AUGUSTINE FOR HEALTH SCIENCES

St. Augustine, Florida
Division of Advanced Studies
www.usa.edu

University of St. Augustine for Health Sciences, founded in 1978, is a proprietary, graduate institution. It is accredited by the Distance Education and Training Council. It first offered distance learning courses in 1979. In 1999–2000, it offered 40 courses at a distance. In fall 1999, there were 380 students enrolled in distance learning courses.

Course delivery sites Courses are delivered to your home, your workplace.

Media Courses are delivered via videotapes, audiotapes, CD-ROM, computer conferencing, World Wide Web, e-mail, print. Students and teachers may meet in person or interact via mail, telephone, fax, e-mail, World Wide Web. The following equipment may be required: television, videocassette player, computer, modem, Internet access, e-mail.

Restrictions Programs are available worldwide. Enrollment is open to anyone.

Services Distance learners have access to library services, e-mail services, academic advising, tutoring, bookstore at a distance.

Credit-earning options Students may transfer credits from another institution or may earn credits through examinations, portfolio assessment.

Typical costs Tuition of $350 per credit hour. *Noncredit courses:* $500 per course. Costs may vary. Financial aid is available to distance learners.

Registration Students may register by mail, fax, telephone, e-mail, World Wide Web, in person.

Contact Dr. Richard Jensen, Director of Advanced Studies, University of St. Augustine for Health Sciences. *Telephone:* 904-826-0084 Ext. 262. *Fax:* 904-826-0085. *E-mail:* info@usa.edu.

DEGREES AND AWARDS

MHA Health Sciences (some on-campus requirements)
MSPT Physical Therapy (some on-campus requirements)

COURSE SUBJECT AREAS OFFERED OUTSIDE OF DEGREE PROGRAMS

Graduate: Gerontology; health professions and related sciences; occupational therapy; physical therapy

UNIVERSITY OF ST. FRANCIS

Joliet, Illinois
www.stfrancis.edu

University of St. Francis, founded in 1920, is an independent, religious, comprehensive institution. It is accredited by the North Central Association of Colleges and Schools. It first offered distance learning courses in 1995. In 1999–2000, it offered 24 courses at a distance. In fall 1999, there were 360 students enrolled in distance learning courses.

Course delivery sites Courses are delivered to your home, your workplace.

Media Courses are delivered via videoconferencing, interactive television, World Wide Web, e-mail. Students and teachers may interact via videoconferencing, fax, e-mail, interactive television, World Wide Web. The following equipment may be required: computer, modem, Internet access, e-mail.

Restrictions Programs are available nationwide. Enrollment is open to anyone.

Services Distance learners have access to library services, the campus computer network, e-mail services, academic advising, career placement assistance, bookstore at a distance.

Credit-earning options Students may transfer credits from another institution or may earn credits through examinations, portfolio assessment, military training.

Typical costs *Undergraduate:* Tuition of $370 per hour. *Graduate:* Tuition of $400 per hour. Costs may vary. Financial aid is available to distance learners.

Registration Students may register by mail, fax, telephone, e-mail, World Wide Web, in person.

Contact Charles M. Beutel, Registrar, University of St. Francis, 500 North Wilcox Street, Joliet, IL 60435. *Telephone:* 815-740-3391. *Fax:* 815-740-5084. *E-mail:* cbeutel@stfrancis.edu.

DEGREES AND AWARDS

BS Health Arts, Professional Arts
MBA Business

COURSE SUBJECT AREAS OFFERED OUTSIDE OF DEGREE PROGRAMS

Undergraduate: Business administration and management; health professions and related sciences; nursing
Graduate: Business administration and management; health services administration

UNIVERSITY OF ST. THOMAS

St. Paul, Minnesota
www.iss.stthomas.edu

University of St. Thomas, founded in 1885, is an independent, religious university. It is accredited by the Association of Theological Schools in the United States and Canada, North Central Association of Colleges and Schools. It first offered distance learning courses in 1994. In 1999–2000, it offered 12 courses at a distance. In fall 1999, there were 70 students enrolled in distance learning courses.

Course delivery sites Courses are delivered to your home, your workplace, high schools, other colleges, 2 off-campus centers in Chaska, Owatonna.

Media Courses are delivered via videoconferencing, World Wide Web, e-mail. Students and teachers may interact via videoconferencing, telephone, fax, e-mail, World Wide Web. The following equipment may be required: computer, modem, Internet access, e-mail.

Restrictions Programs are available worldwide. Enrollment is open to anyone.

Services Distance learners have access to library services, e-mail services, bookstore at a distance.

Credit-earning options Students may transfer credits from another institution or may earn credits through examinations.

Typical costs *Undergraduate:* Tuition of $1400 per semester. *Graduate:* Tuition of $1671 per semester. Costs may vary.

Registration Students may register by mail, fax, telephone, World Wide Web, in person.

Contact Robert Rehn, Director, University of St. Thomas, 2115 Summit Avenue, St. Paul, MN 55105. *Telephone:* 612-962-6800. *Fax:* 612-962-6816. *E-mail:* rarehn@stthomas.edu.

DEGREES AND AWARDS

MBA Health Service (certain restrictions apply)

COURSE SUBJECT AREAS OFFERED OUTSIDE OF DEGREE PROGRAMS

Undergraduate: Classical languages and literatures; sociology
Graduate: Accounting; business; business administration and management; computer and information sciences; engineering; health services administration; law and legal studies; social work
Noncredit: Computer and information sciences

UNIVERSITY OF SAN FRANCISCO

San Francisco, California
College of Professional Studies
www.cps.usfca.edu

University of San Francisco, founded in 1855, is an independent, religious university. It is accredited by the Western Association of Schools and Colleges, Inc. In 1999–2000, it offered 6 courses at a distance. In fall 1999, there were 6 students enrolled in distance learning courses.
Course delivery sites Courses are delivered to your home, your workplace.
Media Courses are delivered via computer conferencing, World Wide Web. Students and teachers may interact via World Wide Web. The following equipment may be required: computer, Internet access.
Restrictions Programs are available to in-state students only. Enrollment is open to anyone.
Services Distance learners have access to library services, the campus computer network, e-mail services, bookstore at a distance.
Typical costs Undergraduate tuition ranges between $568 and $588 per unit. Financial aid is available to distance learners.
Registration Students may register by mail, fax.
Contact Admissions, College of Professional Studies, University of San Francisco, 2130 Fulton Street, San Francisco, CA 94117. *Telephone:* 415-422-6000.

DEGREES AND AWARDS

Distance programs offered do not lead to a degree or other formal award.

COURSE SUBJECT AREAS OFFERED OUTSIDE OF DEGREE PROGRAMS

Undergraduate: Religious studies; telecommunications

UNIVERSITY OF SARASOTA

Sarasota, Florida
Enrollment Management
www.sarasota.edu

University of Sarasota, founded in 1974, is an independent, nonprofit university. It is accredited by the Southern Association of Colleges and Schools. It first offered distance learning courses in 1993. In 1999–2000, it offered 160 courses at a distance. In fall 1999, there were 1,605 students enrolled in distance learning courses.
Course delivery sites Courses are delivered to your home, your workplace.
Media Courses are delivered via computer conferencing, World Wide Web, e-mail, print. Students and teachers may interact via audioconferencing, mail, telephone, fax, e-mail. The following equipment may be required: computer, Internet access.
Restrictions Programs are available worldwide. Enrollment is open to anyone.

Services Distance learners have access to library services, the campus computer network, e-mail services, academic advising, bookstore at a distance.
Credit-earning options Students may transfer credits from another institution.
Typical costs Tuition of $397 per semester hour plus mandatory fees of $10 per credit. Financial aid is available to distance learners.
Registration Students may register by mail, fax, telephone, e-mail, World Wide Web, in person.
Contact Linda Volz, Admissions Representative, University of Sarasota. *Telephone:* 800-331-5995 Ext. 222. *Fax:* 941-379-9464. *E-mail:* univsar@compuserve.com.

DEGREES AND AWARDS

Undergraduate Certificate(s) Business Areas
BSBA Business Administration (some on-campus requirements)
MAED Education (some on-campus requirements)
MBA Business Administration (some on-campus requirements)
DBA Accounting (some on-campus requirements), Information Systems (some on-campus requirements), International Business (some on-campus requirements), Management (some on-campus requirements), Marketing (some on-campus requirements)
EdD Counseling Psychology (some on-campus requirements), Higher Education Administration (some on-campus requirements), Pastoral Community Counseling (some on-campus requirements)

COURSE SUBJECT AREAS OFFERED OUTSIDE OF DEGREE PROGRAMS

Graduate: Business administration and management; counseling psychology; curriculum and instruction; education administration; finance; health services administration; human resources management; international business; management information systems; marketing; special education; student counseling

UNIVERSITY OF SASKATCHEWAN

Saskatoon, Saskatchewan, Canada
Extension Credit Studies
www.extension.usask.ca

University of Saskatchewan, founded in 1907, is a province-supported university. It is accredited by the provincial charter. It first offered distance learning courses in 1920. In 1999–2000, it offered 110 courses at a distance. In fall 1999, there were 1,200 students enrolled in distance learning courses.
Course delivery sites Courses are delivered to your home, your workplace, 56 off-campus centers.
Media Courses are delivered via television, videotapes, audiotapes, computer software, CD-ROM, computer conferencing, World Wide Web, e-mail, print. Students and teachers may interact via videoconferencing, audioconferencing, mail, telephone, fax, e-mail. The following equipment may be required: television, videocassette player, computer, modem, Internet access, e-mail.
Restrictions Programs are available worldwide. Enrollment is open to anyone.
Services Distance learners have access to library services, the campus computer network, e-mail services, academic advising, tutoring, bookstore at a distance.
Credit-earning options Students may transfer credits from another institution or may earn credits through examinations, portfolio assessment.
Typical costs Tuition of $100 per credit. Costs may vary. Financial aid is available to distance learners.
Registration Students may register by mail, telephone, in person.

Contact Parminder Soor, Secretary, Extension Credit Studies, University of Saskatchewan, Room 326, Kirk Hall, 117 Science Place, Saskatoon, SK S7N 5C8 Canada. *Telephone:* 306-966-5563. *Fax:* 306-966-5590. *E-mail:* extcred@usask.ca.

DEGREES AND AWARDS

Undergraduate Certificate(s) Adult and Continuing Education, Agriculture (service area differs from that of the overall institution), Prairie Horticulture, Teaching English as a Second Language

COURSE SUBJECT AREAS OFFERED OUTSIDE OF DEGREE PROGRAMS

Undergraduate: Adult education; anthropology; area, ethnic, and cultural studies; computer and information sciences; continuing education; economics; English language and literature; geography; geology; history; liberal arts, general studies, and humanities; mathematics; music; nursing; philosophy and religion; psychology; teacher education

UNIVERSITY OF SCIENCE AND ARTS OF OKLAHOMA

Chickasha, Oklahoma

University of Science and Arts of Oklahoma, founded in 1908, is a state-supported, four-year college. It is accredited by the North Central Association of Colleges and Schools. In 1999–2000, it offered 1 course at a distance.

Course delivery sites Courses are delivered to high schools.

Media Courses are delivered via videoconferencing, World Wide Web. Students and teachers may interact via videoconferencing. The following equipment may be required: Internet access.

Restrictions Programs are available to local area students. Enrollment is restricted to individuals meeting certain criteria.

Services Distance learners have access to library services, e-mail services at a distance.

Credit-earning options Students may transfer credits from another institution or may earn credits through examinations.

Typical costs Tuition of $49 per credit hour plus mandatory fees of $5 per credit hour for local area residents. Tuition of $49 per credit hour plus mandatory fees of $5 per credit hour for in-state residents. Tuition of $133 per credit hour plus mandatory fees of $5 per credit hour for out-of-state residents. Financial aid is available to distance learners.

Registration Students may register by in person.

Contact Mr. Joe Evans, Director of Admissions/Registrar, University of Science and Arts of Oklahoma, Box 82345, Chickasha, OK 73018-0001. *Telephone:* 405-574-1204. *Fax:* 405-574-1220. *E-mail:* jwevans@usao. edu.

DEGREES AND AWARDS

Distance programs offered do not lead to a degree or other formal award.

COURSE SUBJECT AREAS OFFERED OUTSIDE OF DEGREE PROGRAMS

Undergraduate: Algebra

UNIVERSITY OF SOUTH ALABAMA

Mobile, Alabama
USA Online
usaonline.southalabama.edu

University of South Alabama, founded in 1963, is a state-supported university. It is accredited by the Southern Association of Colleges and Schools. It first offered distance learning courses in 1999. In 1999–2000, it offered 12 courses at a distance.

Course delivery sites Courses are delivered to your home, your workplace, military bases, high schools.

Media Courses are delivered via computer software, CD-ROM, computer conferencing, World Wide Web, e-mail, print. Students and teachers may meet in person or interact via videoconferencing, mail, telephone, fax, e-mail, World Wide Web. The following equipment may be required: computer, modem, Internet access, e-mail.

Restrictions Programs are available worldwide. Enrollment is open to anyone.

Services Distance learners have access to library services, academic advising, career placement assistance, bookstore at a distance.

Credit-earning options Students may transfer credits from another institution or may earn credits through examinations, portfolio assessment.

Typical costs *Undergraduate:* Tuition of $438 per course. *Graduate:* Tuition of $515 per course. Students pay an additional $33 registration fee. Costs may vary. Financial aid is available to distance learners.

Registration Students may register by telephone, World Wide Web, in person.

Contact Dr. Thomas L. Chilton, Associate Dean of Education, University of South Alabama, 75 North University Boulevard—UCOM 3600, Mobile, AL 36688-0002. *Telephone:* 334-380-2738. *Fax:* 334-380-2748. *E-mail:* tchilton@usamail.usouthal.edu.

eCollege.com   *www.ecollege.com/scholarships*

DEGREES AND AWARDS

BSN Nursing
Graduate Certificate(s) Educational Administration
MEd Special Education (Gifted)
MS Instructional Design and Development

COURSE SUBJECT AREAS OFFERED OUTSIDE OF DEGREE PROGRAMS

Undergraduate: Business administration and management; nursing
Graduate: Business administration and management; education administration; educational psychology; educational research; electrical engineering; engineering/industrial management; finance; instructional media; nursing; special education; teacher education

See full description on page 778.

UNIVERSITY OF SOUTH CAROLINA

Columbia, South Carolina
Department of Distance Education and Instructional Support
www.sc.edu/deis

University of South Carolina, founded in 1801, is a state-supported university. It is accredited by the Southern Association of Colleges and

Schools. It first offered distance learning courses in 1969. In 1999–2000, it offered 280 courses at a distance. In fall 1999, there were 3,700 students enrolled in distance learning courses.

Course delivery sites Courses are delivered to your home, your workplace, military bases, high schools, University of South Carolina System (Columbia), 16 off-campus centers.

Media Courses are delivered via television, videotapes, videoconferencing, interactive television, audiotapes, CD-ROM, World Wide Web, e-mail, print. Students and teachers may meet in person or interact via videoconferencing, mail, telephone, fax, e-mail, interactive television, World Wide Web. The following equipment may be required: television, videocassette player, computer, modem, Internet access, e-mail.

Restrictions Programs are available statewide or by special agreement. Enrollment is open to anyone.

Services Distance learners have access to library services, the campus computer network, e-mail services, academic advising, tutoring, career placement assistance, bookstore at a distance.

Credit-earning options Students may transfer credits from another institution or may earn credits through examinations.

Typical costs *Undergraduate:* Tuition of $172 per credit hour plus mandatory fees of $4 per credit hour for in-state residents. Tuition of $442 per credit hour plus mandatory fees of $4 per credit hour for out-of-state residents. *Graduate:* Tuition of $202 per credit hour plus mandatory fees of $4 per credit hour for in-state residents. Tuition of $428 per credit hour plus mandatory fees of $4 per credit hour for out-of-state residents. The above fees apply to Telecommunications program only. For the Independent Learning program the tuition fee is $85 per credit hour. Costs may vary. Financial aid is available to distance learners.

Registration Students may register by mail, fax, telephone, World Wide Web, in person.

Contact Student Services Area, University of South Carolina, Department of Distance Education and Instructional Support, 915 Gregg Street, Columbia, SC 29208. *Telephone:* 800-922-2577. *Fax:* 803-777-6264. *E-mail:* question@gwm.sc.edu.

DEGREES AND AWARDS

MBA Business Administration (some on-campus requirements)

ME Chemical Engineering (some on-campus requirements), Civil and Environmental Engineering (some on-campus requirements), Computer Engineering (some on-campus requirements), Electrical Engineering (some on-campus requirements), Mechanical Engineering (some on-campus requirements)

MLIS Library and Information Sciences (some on-campus requirements)

MS Chemical Engineering (some on-campus requirements), Civil and Environmental Engineering (some on-campus requirements), Computer Engineering (some on-campus requirements), Electrical Engineering (some on-campus requirements), Mechanical Engineering (some on-campus requirements)

PhD Chemical Engineering (some on-campus requirements), Computer Engineering (some on-campus requirements), Electrical Engineering (some on-campus requirements), Mechanical Engineering (some on-campus requirements)

COURSE SUBJECT AREAS OFFERED OUTSIDE OF DEGREE PROGRAMS

Undergraduate: Accounting; astronomy and astrophysics; business; business administration and management; economics; education; engineering; English language and literature; history; hospitality services management; human resources management; journalism; liberal arts, general studies, and humanities; nursing; physics; public health; social work

Graduate: Accounting; astronomy and astrophysics; business; business administration and management; computer and information sciences; education; education administration; engineering; English language and literature; health professions and related sciences; history; hospitality services management; human resources management; journalism; library

and information studies; nursing; physics; public administration and services; public health; social work; teacher education

See full descriptions on pages 592 and 676.

UNIVERSITY OF SOUTH CAROLINA SPARTANBURG

Spartanburg, South Carolina

University of South Carolina Spartanburg, founded in 1967, is a state-supported, comprehensive institution. It is accredited by the Southern Association of Colleges and Schools.

Contact University of South Carolina Spartanburg, 800 University Way, Spartanburg, SC 29303-4999. *Telephone:* 864-503-5000. *Fax:* 864-503-5201.

See full description on page 676.

UNIVERSITY OF SOUTH DAKOTA

Vermillion, South Dakota

State-Wide Educational Services
www.usd.edu/swes

University of South Dakota, founded in 1862, is a state-supported university. It is accredited by the North Central Association of Colleges and Schools. It first offered distance learning courses in 1967. In 1999–2000, it offered 334 courses at a distance. In fall 1999, there were 925 students enrolled in distance learning courses.

Course delivery sites Courses are delivered to your home, your workplace, military bases, high schools, Morningside College (Sioux City, IA), Southeast Technical Institute (Sioux Falls), Western Iowa Tech Community College (Sioux City, IA), 5 off-campus centers in Aberdeen, Pierre, Rapid City, Sioux Falls, Sioux City (IA).

Media Courses are delivered via television, videotapes, videoconferencing, interactive television, audiotapes, World Wide Web, e-mail, print. Students and teachers may interact via videoconferencing, mail, telephone, fax, e-mail, interactive television, World Wide Web. The following equipment may be required: television, Internet access.

Restrictions Programs are available worldwide. Enrollment is open to anyone.

Services Distance learners have access to library services, the campus computer network, e-mail services at a distance.

Credit-earning options Students may transfer credits from another institution or may earn credits through examinations, portfolio assessment.

Typical costs *Undergraduate:* Tuition of $125 per credit. *Graduate:* Tuition of $161 per credit. Financial aid is available to distance learners.

Registration Students may register by mail, fax, telephone, World Wide Web, in person.

Contact State-Wide Educational Services, University of South Dakota, 414 East Clark Street, Vermillion, SD 57069. *Telephone:* 800-233-7937. *Fax:* 605-677-6118. *E-mail:* swes@usd.edu.

DEGREES AND AWARDS

AA General Studies

COURSE SUBJECT AREAS OFFERED OUTSIDE OF DEGREE PROGRAMS

Undergraduate: Abnormal psychology; algebra; American literature; anatomy; anthropology; area, ethnic, and cultural studies; art history and criticism; astronomy and astrophysics; biology; business administration and management; calculus; computer and information sciences; corrections; criminal justice; criminology; developmental and child psychology; drama and theater; economics; educational psychology; English composition; English language and literature; English literature; European languages and literatures; film studies; geography; health and physical education/fitness; history; human resources management; liberal arts, general studies, and humanities; library and information studies; mass media; mathematics; nursing; philosophy and religion; political science; school psychology; sociology; Spanish language and literature; statistics; teacher education; technical writing

Graduate: Accounting; biology; business; business administration and management; community health services; education administration; health professions and related sciences; human resources management; philosophy and religion; sociology; special education; teacher education

Noncredit: Real estate

UNIVERSITY OF SOUTHERN CALIFORNIA

Los Angeles, California
Center for Scholarly Technology (CST)
www.usc.edu

University of Southern California, founded in 1880, is an independent, nonprofit university. It is accredited by the Western Association of Schools and Colleges, Inc. It first offered distance learning courses in 1972. In 1999–2000, it offered 150 courses at a distance. In fall 1999, there were 800 students enrolled in distance learning courses.

Course delivery sites Courses are delivered to your home, your workplace, 3 off-campus centers in Orange County, Sacramento, Washington (DC).

Media Courses are delivered via television, videotapes, videoconferencing, audiotapes, CD-ROM, computer conferencing, World Wide Web, e-mail, print. Students and teachers may meet in person or interact via videoconferencing, audioconferencing, mail, telephone, fax, e-mail, World Wide Web. The following equipment may be required: computer, Internet access.

Restrictions Programs are available nationwide. Enrollment is restricted to individuals meeting certain criteria.

Services Distance learners have access to library services, the campus computer network, e-mail services, academic advising, tutoring, career placement assistance at a distance.

Credit-earning options Students may transfer credits from another institution.

Typical costs *Undergraduate:* Tuition of $748 per credit. *Graduate:* Tuition of $748 per credit. Costs may vary. Financial aid is available to distance learners.

Registration Students may register by telephone, in person.

Contact Central Admissions, University of Southern California, 700 Childs Way—SAS 210, Los Angeles, CA 90089-0911. *Telephone:* 213-740-6753. *Fax:* 213-740-8826.

DEGREES AND AWARDS

MS Computer Engineering (certain restrictions apply; service area differs from that of the overall institution; some on-campus requirements), Computer Science (certain restrictions apply; service area differs from that of the overall institution; some on-campus requirements), Gerontology (certain restrictions apply; some on-campus requirements)

MSEE Electrical Engineering (certain restrictions apply; service area differs from that of the overall institution; some on-campus requirements)

COURSE SUBJECT AREAS OFFERED OUTSIDE OF DEGREE PROGRAMS

Graduate: Aerospace, aeronautical engineering; computer and information sciences; electrical engineering; engineering/industrial management; gerontology; industrial engineering; mechanical engineering
Noncredit: Aerospace, aeronautical engineering; business administration and management; computer and information sciences; electrical engineering; engineering/industrial management; gerontology; health professions and related sciences; industrial engineering; mechanical engineering

UNIVERSITY OF SOUTHERN COLORADO

Pueblo, Colorado
Division of Continuing Education
www.uscolo.edu/coned

University of Southern Colorado, founded in 1933, is a state-supported, comprehensive institution. It is accredited by the North Central Association of Colleges and Schools. It first offered distance learning courses in 1987. In 1999–2000, it offered 110 courses at a distance. In fall 1999, there were 500 students enrolled in distance learning courses.

Course delivery sites Courses are delivered to your home, your workplace, military bases, off-campus center(s) in Colorado Springs, Altus Air Force Base (OK), McGuire Air Force Base (NJ).

Media Courses are delivered via television, videotapes, CD-ROM, World Wide Web, e-mail, print. Students and teachers may meet in person or interact via mail, telephone, fax, e-mail. The following equipment may be required: television, videocassette player, computer, Internet access.

Restrictions Programs are available worldwide. Enrollment is open to anyone.

Services Distance learners have access to library services, e-mail services, academic advising, career placement assistance, bookstore at a distance.

Credit-earning options Students may transfer credits from another institution or may earn credits through examinations, portfolio assessment, military training, business training.

Typical costs *Undergraduate:* Tuition of $75 per credit. *Graduate:* Tuition of $85 per credit. *Noncredit courses:* $395 per course. Costs may vary.

Registration Students may register by mail, fax, telephone, e-mail, World Wide Web, in person.

Contact Lara L. Van Buskirk, Assistant Program Manager, University of Southern Colorado, Division of Continuing Education, Pueblo, CO 81001-4901. *Telephone:* 877-USC-WOLF. *Fax:* 719-549-2438. *E-mail:* coned@uscolo.edu.

DEGREES AND AWARDS

Undergraduate Certificate(s) Paralegal Studies
BS Social Sciences

COURSE SUBJECT AREAS OFFERED OUTSIDE OF DEGREE PROGRAMS

Undergraduate: Area, ethnic, and cultural studies; art history and criticism; biology; business administration and management; chemistry; conservation and natural resources; economics; English language and literature; family and marriage counseling; geography; geology; history; marketing; nursing; political science; social psychology; social work; sociology; substance abuse counseling; teacher education
Graduate: Family and marriage counseling; teacher education

See full description on page 780.

UNIVERSITY OF SOUTHERN INDIANA

Evansville, Indiana

Distance Education Programming
www.usi.edu/distance

University of Southern Indiana, founded in 1965, is a state-supported, comprehensive institution. It is accredited by the North Central Association of Colleges and Schools. It first offered distance learning courses in 1994. In 1999–2000, it offered 69 courses at a distance. In fall 1999, there were 649 students enrolled in distance learning courses.

Course delivery sites Courses are delivered to your home, your workplace, military bases, high schools, off-campus center(s).

Media Courses are delivered via television, videotapes, videoconferencing, interactive television, audiotapes, computer software, CD-ROM, computer conferencing, World Wide Web, e-mail, print. Students and teachers may meet in person or interact via videoconferencing, audioconferencing, mail, telephone, fax, e-mail, interactive television, World Wide Web. The following equipment may be required: television, videocassette player, computer, Internet access, e-mail.

Restrictions Programs are available to in-state students only. Enrollment is open to anyone.

Services Distance learners have access to library services, e-mail services, academic advising, bookstore at a distance.

Credit-earning options Students may transfer credits from another institution or may earn credits through examinations, military training.

Typical costs *Undergraduate:* Tuition of $92.25 per credit hour for in-state residents. Tuition of $226 per credit hour plus mandatory fees of $25 per semester hour for out-of-state residents. *Graduate:* Tuition of $135.75 per credit hour for in-state residents. Tuition of $272.75 per credit hour plus mandatory fees of $25 per semester hour for out-of-state residents. There is a $25 one-time, nonrefundable application fee for all students. Costs may vary. Financial aid is available to distance learners.

Registration Students may register by mail, fax, telephone, World Wide Web, in person.

Contact Dr. Saxon Reasons, Programming Manager, Instructional Technology Services, University of Southern Indiana, 8600 University Boulevard, Evansville, IN 47712. *Telephone:* 800-813-4238. *Fax:* 812-465-7131. *E-mail:* saxrea@usi.edu.

DEGREES AND AWARDS

AS Communications

BS Health Professions and Related Sciences (service area differs from that of the overall institution; some on-campus requirements)

BSN Nursing (service area differs from that of the overall institution; some on-campus requirements)

COURSE SUBJECT AREAS OFFERED OUTSIDE OF DEGREE PROGRAMS

Undergraduate: Abnormal psychology; advertising; American literature; biological and life sciences; business; communications; computer and information sciences; English literature; environmental science; fine arts; health professions and related sciences; journalism; law and legal studies; liberal arts, general studies, and humanities; mass media; nursing; political science; psychology; public health; public relations; radio and television broadcasting; special education

Graduate: Nursing; teacher education

See full description on page 540.

UNIVERSITY OF SOUTHERN MAINE

Portland, Maine

USU Distance Learning Program
usm.maine.edu/eap/distanceeducation/

University of Southern Maine, founded in 1878, is a state-supported, comprehensive institution. It is accredited by the New England Association of Schools and Colleges. In 1999–2000, it offered 43 courses at a distance. In fall 1999, there were 500 students enrolled in distance learning courses.

Course delivery sites Courses are delivered to your home, your workplace, military bases, high schools, 3 off-campus centers in Brunswick, Saco, Sanford.

Media Courses are delivered via television, videotapes, videoconferencing, interactive television, computer software, computer conferencing, World Wide Web, e-mail, print. Students and teachers may interact via videoconferencing, mail, telephone, fax, e-mail, interactive television, World Wide Web. The following equipment may be required: television, videocassette player, computer, Internet access, e-mail.

Restrictions Programs are available nationwide. Enrollment is restricted to individuals meeting certain criteria.

Services Distance learners have access to library services, the campus computer network, e-mail services, academic advising, bookstore at a distance.

Credit-earning options Students may earn credits through examinations.

Typical costs *Undergraduate:* Tuition of $124 per credit. *Graduate:* Tuition of $186 per credit. Financial aid is available to distance learners.

Registration Students may register by mail, fax, telephone, e-mail, in person.

Contact Ann E. Clarey, Coordinator of Distance Education and Off Campus Programs, University of Southern Maine, PO Box 9300, Portland, ME 04104-9300. *Telephone:* 207-780-4077. *Fax:* 207-780-5307. *E-mail:* clarey@usm.maine.edu.

DEGREES AND AWARDS

RN to BSN RN to BSN (certain restrictions apply; some on-campus requirements)

Graduate Certificate(s) Community Planning and Development (certain restrictions apply; some on-campus requirements), Health Policy and Management (certain restrictions apply), Non-Profit Management (certain restrictions apply)

MHA Health Policy and Management (certain restrictions apply; some on-campus requirements)

MHSA Accelerated Program for Certified Advance Practice Nurses (certain restrictions apply; some on-campus requirements)

MPA Public Policy and Management (certain restrictions apply; some on-campus requirements)

MS Rehabilitation Counseling (certain restrictions apply)

COURSE SUBJECT AREAS OFFERED OUTSIDE OF DEGREE PROGRAMS

Undergraduate: Abnormal psychology; American (U.S.) history; calculus; communications; computer and information sciences; conservation and natural resources; curriculum and instruction; environmental science; finance; health professions and related sciences; industrial engineering; psychology; sociology

Graduate: Gerontology; health professions and related sciences; special education

UNIVERSITY OF SOUTHERN MISSISSIPPI

Hattiesburg, Mississippi

Department of Continuing Education and Distance Learning
www-dept.usm.edu/~cice/ce/index.html

University of Southern Mississippi, founded in 1910, is a state-supported university. It is accredited by the Southern Association of Colleges and Schools. It first offered distance learning courses in 1913. In 1999–2000, it offered 245 courses at a distance. In fall 1999, there were 3,000 students enrolled in distance learning courses.

Course delivery sites Courses are delivered to your home, your workplace, military bases, high schools, 3 off-campus centers in Gulf Park, Jackson County, Stennis Space Center.

Media Courses are delivered via television, videotapes, videoconferencing, interactive television, computer software, CD-ROM, World Wide Web, e-mail, print. Students and teachers may interact via videoconferencing, mail, telephone, fax, e-mail, interactive television, World Wide Web. The following equipment may be required: television, videocassette player, computer, modem, Internet access, e-mail.

Restrictions Programs are available worldwide. Enrollment is open to anyone.

Services Distance learners have access to library services, the campus computer network, e-mail services, career placement assistance, bookstore at a distance.

Credit-earning options Students may transfer credits from another institution or may earn credits through examinations, military training.

Typical costs *Undergraduate:* Tuition of $210 per course plus mandatory fees of $15 per course. *Graduate:* Tuition of $285 per course plus mandatory fees of $15 per course. Online courses are $330 per course for undergraduates and $426 per course for graduates. *Noncredit courses:* $85 per course. Costs may vary. Financial aid is available to distance learners.

Registration Students may register by mail, fax, telephone, e-mail, World Wide Web, in person.

Contact Sue Pace, Director, University of Southern Mississippi, Continuing Education and Distance Learning, Box 5055, Hattiesburg, MS 39406-5055. *Telephone:* 601-266-4210. *Fax:* 601-266-5839. *E-mail:* sue.pace@usm.edu.

DEGREES AND AWARDS

Distance programs offered do not lead to a degree or other formal award.

COURSE SUBJECT AREAS OFFERED OUTSIDE OF DEGREE PROGRAMS

Undergraduate: Accounting; algebra; anthropology; Bible studies; biology; business administration and management; calculus; communications; community health services; creative writing; criminal justice; economics; electrical engineering; electronics; English language and literature; ethics; foods and nutrition studies; genetics; geography; gerontology; health and physical education/fitness; history; logic; management information systems; marketing; mathematics; philosophy and religion; real estate; sociology; special education; technical writing; zoology

Graduate: Gerontology; hospitality services management; special education; statistics; telecommunications; visual and performing arts

See full description on page 676.

UNIVERSITY OF SOUTH FLORIDA

Tampa, Florida

Educational Outreach
www.usf.edu/

University of South Florida, founded in 1956, is a state-supported university. It is accredited by the Southern Association of Colleges and Schools. It first offered distance learning courses in 1983. In 1999–2000, it offered 275 courses at a distance. In fall 1999, there were 3,800 students enrolled in distance learning courses.

Course delivery sites Courses are delivered to your home, your workplace, military bases, high schools, Pasco-Hernando Community College (New Port Richey), St. Petersburg Junior College (St. Petersburg), 70 off-campus centers in Tampa, Atlanta (GA), Ft. Collins (CO), Venezue.

Media Courses are delivered via television, videotapes, videoconferencing, interactive television, audiotapes, computer software, CD-ROM, computer conferencing, World Wide Web, e-mail. Students and teachers may meet in person or interact via videoconferencing, audioconferencing, mail, telephone, fax, e-mail, interactive television, World Wide Web. The following equipment may be required: television, videocassette player, computer, modem, Internet access, e-mail.

Restrictions Programs are available worldwide. Enrollment is restricted to individuals meeting certain criteria.

Services Distance learners have access to library services, the campus computer network, e-mail services, academic advising, career placement assistance, bookstore at a distance.

Credit-earning options Students may transfer credits from another institution.

Typical costs *Undergraduate:* Tuition of $70.15 per semester hour for in-state residents. Tuition of $303.10 per semester hour for out-of-state residents. *Graduate:* Tuition of $142.97 per semester hour for in-state residents. Tuition of $503.70 per semester hour for out-of-state residents.

Registration Students may register by mail, telephone, World Wide Web.

Contact Dr. Barbara Emil, Dean, University of South Florida, Educational Outreach, 4202 East Fowler Avenue, SVC 1072, Tampa, FL 33620. *Telephone:* 813-974-7984. *Fax:* 813-974-7272. *E-mail:* bemil@admin.usf.edu.

DEGREES AND AWARDS

BSN Nursing (service area differs from that of the overall institution; some on-campus requirements)
MPH Public Health (service area differs from that of the overall institution; some on-campus requirements)
MSE Engineering (certain restrictions apply; service area differs from that of the overall institution)

COURSE SUBJECT AREAS OFFERED OUTSIDE OF DEGREE PROGRAMS

Undergraduate: American (U.S.) history; American literature; American studies; anthropology; archaeology; area, ethnic, and cultural studies; art history and criticism; biology; business administration and management; chemistry; communications; computer and information sciences; creative writing; criminology; drama and theater; economics; educational psychology; educational research; electrical engineering; English composition; English language and literature; English literature; ethics; European languages and literatures; fine arts; geography; geology; history; industrial engineering; instructional media; interdisciplinary studies; liberal arts, general studies, and humanities; mathematics; music; nursing; oceanography; political science; religious studies; sociology; Spanish language and literature; teacher education; women's studies

Graduate: Area, ethnic, and cultural studies; business; business administration and management; chemical engineering; civil engineering; computer and information sciences; education administration; educational research; electrical engineering; engineering/industrial management; environmental engineering; fine arts; geology; gerontology; human resources management; industrial engineering; instructional media; library and information studies; mechanical engineering; nursing; political science; public administration and services; public health; public policy analysis; social work; special education; teacher education

See full descriptions on pages 676 and 782.

UNIVERSITY OF TENNESSEE

Knoxville, Tennessee

Department of Distance Education and Independent Study
www.outreach.utk.edu/deis

University of Tennessee, founded in 1794, is a state-supported university. It is accredited by the Southern Association of Colleges and Schools. It first offered distance learning courses in 1923. In 1999–2000, it offered 155 courses at a distance. In fall 1999, there were 2,750 students enrolled in distance learning courses.

Course delivery sites Courses are delivered to your home, your workplace, military bases, high schools, University of Tennessee at Martin (Martin), University of Virginia (Charlottesville, VA), off-campus center(s) in Kingsport, Nashville.

Media Courses are delivered via videotapes, videoconferencing, interactive television, audiotapes, computer software, CD-ROM, computer conferencing, World Wide Web, e-mail, print. Students and teachers may meet in person or interact via videoconferencing, audioconferencing, mail, telephone, fax, e-mail, interactive television, World Wide Web. The following equipment may be required: television, videocassette player, computer, modem, Internet access, e-mail.

Restrictions Programs are available worldwide. Enrollment is restricted to individuals meeting certain criteria.

Services Distance learners have access to library services, the campus computer network, e-mail services, academic advising, career placement assistance, bookstore at a distance.

Credit-earning options Students may transfer credits from another institution or may earn credits through examinations.

Typical costs *Undergraduate:* Tuition of $109 per semester hour plus mandatory fees of $22 per semester hour for in-state residents. Tuition of $362 per semester hour plus mandatory fees of $22 per semester hour for out-of-state residents. *Graduate:* Tuition of $184 per semester hour plus mandatory fees of $22 per credit hour for in-state residents. Tuition of $522 per semester hour plus mandatory fees of $22 per semester hour for out-of-state residents. Cost for a noncredit course is $20 per contact hour. Costs may vary. Financial aid is available to distance learners.

Registration Students may register by mail, fax, telephone, World Wide Web, in person.

Contact Assistant Director, Learner Services, University of Tennessee, Distance Education Call Center, 1534 White Avenue Building, Knoxville, TN 37986-1525. *Telephone:* 800-325-8857. *Fax:* 423-974-6629. *E-mail:* disteducation@utk.edu.

DEGREES AND AWARDS

Graduate Certificate(s) Applied Statistics (certain restrictions apply), Internet Mastery (certain restrictions apply)
EMBA Business Administration (certain restrictions apply; service area differs from that of the overall institution; some on-campus requirements)
MBA Business Administration (certain restrictions apply; service area differs from that of the overall institution; some on-campus requirements)
MS Industrial Engineering
MSIS Information Sciences (certain restrictions apply)

COURSE SUBJECT AREAS OFFERED OUTSIDE OF DEGREE PROGRAMS

Undergraduate: Abnormal psychology; accounting; agricultural economics; algebra; American (U.S.) history; American literature; anthropology; astronomy and astrophysics; business administration and management; calculus; chemistry; child care and development; cognitive psychology; conservation and natural resources; creative writing; criminal justice; criminology; curriculum and instruction; developmental and child psychology; economics; English composition; English language and literature; English literature; ethics; European history; foods and nutrition studies; forestry; French language and literature; geography; German language and literature; gerontology; history; individual and family development studies; international relations; Italian language and literature; physics; political science; psychology; religious studies; social psychology; sociology; Spanish language and literature; special education; statistics; teacher education; technical writing

Graduate: Agricultural economics; chemical engineering; civil engineering; communications; computer and information sciences; database management; electrical engineering; engineering mechanics; engineering/industrial management; environmental engineering; forestry; human resources management; industrial engineering; information sciences and systems; journalism; library and information studies; mechanical engineering; public relations; statistics; veterinary science

Noncredit: Algebra; computer and information sciences; computer programming; creative writing; database management; developmental and child psychology; e-commerce; European history; individual and family development studies; information sciences and systems; marketing

See full descriptions on pages 676 and 784.

UNIVERSITY OF TENNESSEE AT CHATTANOOGA

Chattanooga, Tennessee

UTC Continuing Education
www.utc.edu

University of Tennessee at Chattanooga, founded in 1886, is a state-supported, comprehensive institution. It is accredited by the Southern Association of Colleges and Schools. In 1999–2000, it offered 38 courses at a distance. In fall 1999, there were 188 students enrolled in distance learning courses.

Course delivery sites Courses are delivered to your home, your workplace, high schools, Cleveland State Community College (Cleveland), Roane State Community College (Harriman), University of Tennessee (Knoxville).

Media Courses are delivered via television, interactive television, World Wide Web. Students and teachers may meet in person or interact via mail, telephone, fax, e-mail, interactive television, World Wide Web. The following equipment may be required: Internet access, e-mail.

Restrictions Programs are available regionally. Enrollment is restricted to individuals meeting certain criteria.

Services Distance learners have access to library services, the campus computer network, e-mail services, academic advising, bookstore at a distance.

Credit-earning options Students may transfer credits from another institution or may earn credits through examinations, portfolio assessment.

Typical costs *Undergraduate:* Mandatory fees of $115 per hour for in-state residents. Tuition of $204 per hour plus mandatory fees of $115 per hour for out-of-state residents. *Graduate:* Mandatory fees of $183 per hour for in-state residents. Tuition of $251 per hour plus mandatory fees of $183 per hour for out-of-state residents. Financial aid is available to distance learners.

Registration Students may register by mail, fax, telephone, e-mail, World Wide Web, in person.

Contact Tonya Pace, Distance Learning Manager, University of Tennessee at Chattanooga, 615 McCallie Avenue, 119 Race Hall, Chattanooga, TN 37403. *Telephone:* 423-755-5305. *Fax:* 423-266-5549. *E-mail:* tonyapace@utc.edu.

DEGREES AND AWARDS

Graduate Certificate(s) Educational Specialist
EMBA Business Administration
MEd Elementary Education
MS Criminal Justice

COURSE SUBJECT AREAS OFFERED OUTSIDE OF DEGREE PROGRAMS

Undergraduate: Criminal justice
Graduate: Business administration and management; criminal justice; education; elementary education

See full description on page 786.

UNIVERSITY OF TENNESSEE AT MARTIN

Martin, Tennessee

Office of Extended Campus and Continuing Education
www.utm.edu

University of Tennessee at Martin, founded in 1900, is a state-supported, comprehensive institution. It is accredited by the Southern Association of Colleges and Schools. It first offered distance learning courses in 1992. In 1999–2000, it offered 22 courses at a distance. In fall 1999, there were 114 students enrolled in distance learning courses.

Course delivery sites Courses are delivered to your home, your workplace, 2 off-campus centers in Jackson, Oak Ridge.

Media Courses are delivered via videotapes, audiotapes, computer software, CD-ROM, World Wide Web, e-mail, print. Students and teachers may meet in person or interact via mail, telephone, fax, e-mail, interactive television, World Wide Web. The following equipment may be required: computer, Internet access.

Restrictions Programs are available to in-state students only. Enrollment is restricted to individuals meeting certain criteria.

Services Distance learners have access to library services, e-mail services, academic advising, career placement assistance, bookstore at a distance.

Credit-earning options Students may transfer credits from another institution or may earn credits through examinations.

Typical costs *Undergraduate:* Tuition of $91 per credit plus mandatory fees of $21 per credit for in-state residents. Tuition of $220 per credit plus mandatory fees of $112 per credit for out-of-state residents. *Graduate:* Tuition of $159 per credit plus mandatory fees of $28 per credit for in-state residents. Tuition of $293 per credit plus mandatory fees of $187 per credit for out-of-state residents. Costs may vary. Financial aid is available to distance learners.

Registration Students may register by mail, fax, telephone, e-mail, World Wide Web, in person.

Contact Katy Crapo, Coordinator, University of Tennessee at Martin, 110 Gooch Hall, Martin, TN 38238-5050. *Telephone:* 901-587-7080. *Fax:* 901-587-7984. *E-mail:* kcrapo@utm.edu.

DEGREES AND AWARDS

MBA Business Administration
MSE Education (service area differs from that of the overall institution)

COURSE SUBJECT AREAS OFFERED OUTSIDE OF DEGREE PROGRAMS

Undergraduate: Accounting; business; business administration and management; education administration; fine arts; special education; teacher education
Graduate: Accounting; business; business administration and management; education administration; special education; teacher education

See full descriptions on pages 676 and 786.

UNIVERSITY OF TENNESSEE SPACE INSTITUTE

Tullahoma, Tennessee

Distance and Continuing Education
www.utsi.edu

University of Tennessee Space Institute is a state-supported, graduate institution. It is accredited by the Southern Association of Colleges and Schools. It first offered distance learning courses in 1982. In 1999–2000, it offered 31 courses at a distance. In fall 1999, there were 157 students enrolled in distance learning courses.

Course delivery sites Courses are delivered to your home, your workplace, military bases, other colleges, 9 off-campus centers in Jackson, Kingsport, Nashville, Oak Ridge, China Lake (CA), Eglin Air Force Base (FL), Fort Rucker (AL), Medley (AB), Pax River (MD).

Media Courses are delivered via videotapes, videoconferencing, interactive television. Students and teachers may interact via videoconferencing, audioconferencing, mail, telephone, fax, e-mail, World Wide Web. The following equipment may be required: television, videocassette player, computer.

Restrictions Programs are available worldwide. Enrollment is open to anyone.

Services Distance learners have access to library services, e-mail services, academic advising, tutoring, career placement assistance, bookstore at a distance.

Credit-earning options Students may transfer credits from another institution or may earn credits through examinations.

Typical costs Tuition of $652 per semester for in-state residents. Tuition of $1666 per semester for out-of-state residents. Costs may vary. Financial aid is available to distance learners.

Registration Students may register by mail, fax, telephone, e-mail, in person.

Contact Dr. Max Hailey, Chairman and Associate Professor, University of Tennessee Space Institute, 411 B.H. Geothert Parkqay, Tullahoma, TN 37388-9700. *Telephone:* 931-393-7293. *Fax:* 931-393-7201. *E-mail:* mhailey@utsi.edu.

DEGREES AND AWARDS

MS Aviation Systems (some on-campus requirements), Industrial Engineering (some on-campus requirements)

COURSE SUBJECT AREAS OFFERED OUTSIDE OF DEGREE PROGRAMS

Graduate: Aerospace, aeronautical engineering; computer and information sciences; engineering-related technologies; engineering/industrial management; industrial engineering; mathematics; mechanical engineering

See full description on page 676.

UNIVERSITY OF TEXAS AT ARLINGTON

Arlington, Texas

Center for Distance Education
distance.uta.edu

University of Texas at Arlington, founded in 1895, is a state-supported university. It is accredited by the Southern Association of Colleges and Schools. It first offered distance learning courses in 1973. In 1999–2000, it offered 63 courses at a distance. In fall 1999, there were 765 students enrolled in distance learning courses.

Course delivery sites Courses are delivered to your home, your workplace, military bases, high schools, off-campus center(s) in Unversity Center Dallas.

Media Courses are delivered via television, videotapes, videoconferencing, interactive television, computer software, CD-ROM, computer conferencing, World Wide Web, e-mail, print. Students and teachers may meet in person or interact via videoconferencing, audioconferencing, mail, telephone, fax, e-mail, interactive television, World Wide Web. The following equipment may be required: television, videocassette player, computer, modem, Internet access, e-mail.

Restrictions Programs are available worldwide. Enrollment is restricted to individuals meeting certain criteria.

Services Distance learners have access to library services, the campus computer network, e-mail services, academic advising, tutoring, career placement assistance, bookstore at a distance.

Credit-earning options Students may transfer credits from another institution or may earn credits through examinations.

Typical costs Contact the school for information. Costs may vary. Financial aid is available to distance learners.

Registration Students may register by mail, fax, telephone, World Wide Web, in person.

Contact Dr. Pete Smith, Director, Distance Education, University of Texas at Arlington, Center for Distance Education, PO Box 19027, Arlington, TX 76019. *Telephone:* 817-272-5727. *Fax:* 817-272-5728. *E-mail:* info@distance.uta.edu.

DEGREES AND AWARDS

BSN Nursing
MEng Aerospace Engineering, Computer Science and Engineering, Electrical Engineering, Engineering Mechanics, Industrial Engineering, Materials Sciences and Engineering, Mechanical Engineering

COURSE SUBJECT AREAS OFFERED OUTSIDE OF DEGREE PROGRAMS

Undergraduate: Biology; English composition; English literature; geology; nursing; political science
Graduate: Aerospace, aeronautical engineering; civil engineering; curriculum and instruction; electrical engineering; engineering mechanics; environmental engineering; finance; industrial engineering; mechanical engineering; public administration and services

Special note
The University of Texas at Arlington (UTA) is a Carnegie Doctoral I institution with a nationwide reputation for the design and delivery of Internet-based classes. High-quality courses and programs and first-rate student support services cause more than 90 percent of UTA distance learners to express high levels of satisfaction. UTA provides both Internet-based certificate and degree programs through the University of Texas System TeleCampus. Programs include the MBA Online and master's degrees in electrical engineering and computer science. For educators, UTA offers the unique opportunity to complete graduate course work in reading, which leads to the English as a Second Language (ESL) Endorsement. This endorsement prepares them to teach children from all cultural and language backgrounds and is required for those teachers in the state of Texas who are working with students in grades K–12 whose first language is not English. UTA also offers an online Master of Education in reading with a Reading Specialist Certificate (grades 1–12) and an ESL Endorsement (grades 1–12). For further information, students should visit UTA's Web site at http://distance.uta.edu or call the Center for Distance Education at 888-UTA-DIST (toll-free).

UNIVERSITY OF TEXAS AT AUSTIN

Austin, Texas

Continuing and Extended Education
www.utexas.edu/cee/dec

University of Texas at Austin, founded in 1883, is a state-supported university. It is accredited by the Southern Association of Colleges and Schools. It first offered distance learning courses in 1909. In 1999–2000, it offered 607 courses at a distance. In fall 1999, there were 9,957 students enrolled in distance learning courses.

Course delivery sites Courses are delivered to your home, your workplace, military bases, high schools, University of Texas System (Austin).

Media Courses are delivered via videotapes, videoconferencing, audiotapes, computer software, CD-ROM, World Wide Web, e-mail, print. Students and teachers may meet in person or interact via videoconferencing, audioconferencing, mail, telephone, fax, e-mail, World Wide Web. The following equipment may be required: videocassette player, computer, modem, Internet access, e-mail.

Restrictions Programs are available worldwide. Enrollment is open to anyone.

Services Distance learners have access to the campus computer network, e-mail services, academic advising, bookstore at a distance.

Credit-earning options Students may earn credits through examinations.

Typical costs Tuition of $83 per credit plus mandatory fees of $20 per course.

Registration Students may register by mail, fax, telephone, e-mail, World Wide Web, in person.

Contact Olga Garza, Supervisor of Student Services, University of Texas at Austin, UT Austin Continuing and Extended Education Distance Education Center, PO Box 7700, Austin, TX 78713-7700. *Telephone:* 888-BE-A-GRAD. *Fax:* 512-475-7933. *E-mail:* dec@www.utexas.edu.

DEGREES AND AWARDS

Distance programs offered do not lead to a degree or other formal award.

COURSE SUBJECT AREAS OFFERED OUTSIDE OF DEGREE PROGRAMS

Undergraduate: Abnormal psychology; adult education; algebra; American (U.S.) history; American Government and Politics; American literature; anthropology; art history and criticism; astronomy and astrophysics; business; calculus; cognitive psychology; communications; creative writing; developmental and child psychology; economics; educational psychology; English composition; English literature; ethics; European history; film studies; foods and nutrition studies; French language and literature; geography; German language and literature; health and physical education/fitness; international relations; Latin language and literature; logic; music; nursing; physics; political science; public health; religious studies; social psychology; sociology; Spanish language and literature; statistics; technical writing; women's studies; zoology

See full description on page 788.

UNIVERSITY OF TEXAS AT DALLAS

Richardson, Texas

Global MBA Online
som.utdallas.edu/globalmba

University of Texas at Dallas, founded in 1969, is a state-supported university. It is accredited by the Southern Association of Colleges and Schools. In 1999–2000, it offered 11 courses at a distance. In fall 1999, there were 50 students enrolled in distance learning courses.

Course delivery sites Courses are delivered to your home, your workplace, military bases.

Media Courses are delivered via CD-ROM, World Wide Web, print. Students and teachers may interact via telephone, e-mail, World Wide Web. The following equipment may be required: computer, modem, Internet access, e-mail.

Restrictions Programs are available worldwide. Enrollment is restricted to individuals meeting certain criteria.

Services Distance learners have access to library services, e-mail services, academic advising, bookstore at a distance.

Credit-earning options Students may transfer credits from another institution or may earn credits through examinations.

Typical costs Tuition of $660 per course for in-state residents. Tuition of $1300 per course for out-of-state residents. Costs may vary. Financial aid is available to distance learners.

Registration Students may register by telephone, World Wide Web, in person.

Contact George Barnes, Director, Global MBA Online, University of Texas at Dallas, PO Box 830688, J051, Richardson, TX 75083. *Telephone:* 972-883-2783. *Fax:* 972-883-2799. *E-mail:* gbarnes@utdallas.edu.

DEGREES AND AWARDS

MBA Business Administration (certain restrictions apply)
See full description on page 790.

UNIVERSITY OF TEXAS AT DALLAS

Richardson, Texas

MIMS Global Leadership Executive Program
www.utdallas.edu/mims

University of Texas at Dallas, founded in 1969, is a state-supported university. It is accredited by the Southern Association of Colleges and Schools. In 1999–2000, it offered 20 courses at a distance. In fall 1999, there were 70 students enrolled in distance learning courses.

Course delivery sites Courses are delivered to your home.

Media Courses are delivered via CD-ROM, World Wide Web, e-mail, print. Students and teachers may interact via audioconferencing, telephone, e-mail, World Wide Web. The following equipment may be required: computer, modem, Internet access.

Restrictions Programs are available worldwide. Enrollment is open to anyone.

Services Distance learners have access to library services, e-mail services at a distance.

Credit-earning options Students may transfer credits from another institution.

Typical costs Total cost for the MBA program is $33,000. Total cost for the MA program is $27,500. Financial aid is available to distance learners.

Registration Students may register by mail, fax, telephone, e-mail, World Wide Web, in person.

Contact Dr. Stephen Guisinger, MIMS Program Director, University of Texas at Dallas. *Telephone:* 972-883-6467. *E-mail:* steveg@utdallas.edu.

DEGREES AND AWARDS

MA International Management Studies
MBA Global Leadership
See full description on page 792.

UNIVERSITY OF TEXAS AT EL PASO

El Paso, Texas

Office of Technology Planning and Distance Learning
www.utep.edu

University of Texas at El Paso, founded in 1913, is a state-supported university. It is accredited by the Southern Association of Colleges and Schools. It first offered distance learning courses in 1994. In 1999–2000, it offered 15 courses at a distance. In fall 1999, there were 175 students enrolled in distance learning courses.

Course delivery sites Courses are delivered to your home, your workplace, military bases, high schools, El Paso Community College (El Paso), The University of Texas at Brownsville (Brownsville), Universidad Autonoma de Cuidad Juarez (Chihuahua, Mexico), University of Texas at Arlington (Arlington), University of Texas at Dallas (Richardson), University of Texas at San Antonio (San Antonio), University of Texas–Pan American (Edinburg), University of Texas System (Austin).

Media Courses are delivered via videoconferencing, CD-ROM, computer conferencing, World Wide Web, e-mail. Students and teachers may meet in person or interact via videoconferencing, audioconferencing, mail, telephone, fax, e-mail, World Wide Web. The following equipment may be required: computer, modem, Internet access, e-mail.

Restrictions Programs are available through the University of Texas telecampus, to the El Paso border region, and to military personnel and their dependents at Fort Bliss. Enrollment is restricted to individuals meeting certain criteria.

Services Distance learners have access to library services, the campus computer network, e-mail services, academic advising, tutoring, bookstore at a distance.

Credit-earning options Students may transfer credits from another institution or may earn credits through examinations, portfolio assessment.

Typical costs *Undergraduate:* Tuition of $650 per course for local area residents. Tuition of $650 per course for in-state residents. Tuition of $1200 per course for out-of-state residents. *Graduate:* Tuition of $680 per course for local area residents. Tuition of $680 per course for in-state residents. Tuition of $1600 per course for out-of-state residents. For mandatory fees consult our website. *Noncredit courses:* $300 per course. Costs may vary. Financial aid is available to distance learners.

Registration Students may register by mail, fax, telephone, e-mail, World Wide Web, in person.

Contact Dr. Henry T. Ingle, Associate Vice President for Academic Affairs, University of Texas at El Paso. *Telephone:* 915-747-8901. *Fax:* 915-747-8610. *E-mail:* htingle@utep.edu.

DEGREES AND AWARDS

MBA Business Administration (service area differs from that of the overall institution)
MEdTech Educational Technology (service area differs from that of the overall institution)

COURSE SUBJECT AREAS OFFERED OUTSIDE OF DEGREE PROGRAMS

Undergraduate: Area, ethnic, and cultural studies; communications; English as a second language (ESL); political science; teacher education; telecommunications

Graduate: Area, ethnic, and cultural studies; biological and life sciences; business administration and management; communications; education; English as a second language (ESL); environmental engineering; environmental science; health professions and related sciences; management information systems; political science; teacher education; telecommunications

Noncredit: Area, ethnic, and cultural studies; telecommunications

See full description on page 676.

UNIVERSITY OF TEXAS AT SAN ANTONIO

San Antonio, Texas

Distance Learning Center
dlc.utsa.edu

University of Texas at San Antonio, founded in 1969, is a state-supported, comprehensive institution. It is accredited by the Southern Association of Colleges and Schools. It first offered distance learning courses in 1993. In 1999–2000, it offered 29 courses at a distance. In fall 1999, there were 297 students enrolled in distance learning courses.

Course delivery sites Courses are delivered to your workplace, St. Philip's College (San Antonio), The University of Texas at Brownsville (Brownsville), University of Texas at El Paso (El Paso), University of Texas–Pan American (Edinburg).

Media Courses are delivered via television, videoconferencing, World Wide Web, print. Students and teachers may interact via videoconferencing, mail, telephone, fax, e-mail, World Wide Web. The following equipment may be required: computer, modem, Internet access, e-mail.

Restrictions Courses are available to students enrolled at participating institutions only. Enrollment is open to anyone.

Services Distance learners have access to library services, the campus computer network, e-mail services, academic advising, career placement assistance, bookstore at a distance.

Credit-earning options Students may transfer credits from another institution or may earn credits through examinations, portfolio assessment.

Typical costs *Undergraduate:* Tuition of $1080 per semester plus mandatory fees of $431 per semester for in-state residents. Tuition of $4320 per semester plus mandatory fees of $431 per semester for out-of-state residents. *Graduate:* Tuition of $990 per semester plus mandatory fees of $357 per semester for in-state residents. Tuition of $2934 per semester plus mandatory fees of $357 per semester for out-of-state residents. Costs may vary. Financial aid is available to distance learners.

Registration Students may register by telephone, World Wide Web, in person.

Contact Bill Angrove, Director of the Distance Learning Center, University of Texas at San Antonio, 6900 North Loop 1604 W, San Antonio, TX 78249-0617. *Telephone:* 210-458-5855. *Fax:* 210-458-7378. *E-mail:* bangrove@utsa.edu.

DEGREES AND AWARDS

MS Management of Technology (certain restrictions apply)

COURSE SUBJECT AREAS OFFERED OUTSIDE OF DEGREE PROGRAMS

Undergraduate: Accounting; business; business administration and management; business law; civil engineering; communications; engineering; English language and literature; information sciences and systems; management information systems; marketing; Spanish language and literature

UNIVERSITY OF TEXAS AT TYLER

Tyler, Texas

Interactive Television
www.uttyl.edu

University of Texas at Tyler, founded in 1971, is a state-supported, comprehensive institution. It is accredited by the Southern Association of Colleges and Schools. It first offered distance learning courses in 1991. In 1999–2000, it offered 70 courses at a distance. In fall 1999, there were 254 students enrolled in distance learning courses.

Course delivery sites Courses are delivered to your home, Navarro College (Corsicana), Trinity Valley Community College (Athens), 3 off-campus centers in Longview, Mexia, Palestine.

Media Courses are delivered via television, World Wide Web. Students and teachers may interact via videoconferencing, mail, telephone, fax, e-mail.

Restrictions Programs are available to local area students. Enrollment is open to anyone.

Services Distance learners have access to library services, the campus computer network, e-mail services, academic advising, career placement assistance at a distance.

Credit-earning options Students may transfer credits from another institution or may earn credits through examinations.

Typical costs *Undergraduate:* Tuition of $38 per credit plus mandatory fees of $64 per credit for in-state residents. Tuition of $250 per credit plus mandatory fees of $64 per credit for out-of-state residents. *Graduate:* Tuition of $38 per credit plus mandatory fees of $64 per credit for in-state residents. Tuition of $250 per credit plus mandatory fees of $64 per credit for out-of-state residents. Costs may vary. Financial aid is available to distance learners.

Registration Students may register by telephone, in person.

Contact Pam Morrow, Information Specialist, University of Texas at Tyler. *Telephone:* 903-566-7205. *Fax:* 903-566-8368.

DEGREES AND AWARDS

BSN Nursing (certain restrictions apply)

COURSE SUBJECT AREAS OFFERED OUTSIDE OF DEGREE PROGRAMS

Undergraduate: Accounting; area, ethnic, and cultural studies; biology; business administration and management; communications; economics; education administration; English language and literature; health and physical education/fitness; history; liberal arts, general studies, and humanities; mathematics; nursing; political science; protective services; sociology; special education; teacher education

Graduate: Accounting; area, ethnic, and cultural studies; business administration and management; communications; education administration; electrical engineering; engineering/industrial management; English language and literature; health and physical education/fitness; history; liberal arts, general studies, and humanities; mathematics; mechanical engineering; nursing; protective services; public administration and services; special education; teacher education

See full description on page 676.

UNIVERSITY OF TEXAS MEDICAL BRANCH AT GALVESTON

Galveston, Texas
www2.utmb.edu/gme/

University of Texas Medical Branch at Galveston, founded in 1891, is a state-supported, upper-level institution. It is accredited by the Southern Association of Colleges and Schools.

Contact Mr. Richard L. Lewis, University Registrar, University of Texas Medical Branch at Galveston, Office of the Registrar, 1.212 Ashbel Smith Building, Route 1305, Galveston, TX 77555-1305. *Telephone:* 409-772-1215. *Fax:* 409-772-5056. *E-mail:* rllewis@utmb.edu.

DEGREES AND AWARDS

Distance programs offered do not lead to a degree or other formal award.

UNIVERSITY OF TEXAS OF THE PERMIAN BASIN

Odessa, Texas

REACH Program Center
www.utpb.edu/reach/

University of Texas of the Permian Basin, founded in 1969, is a state-supported, comprehensive institution. It is accredited by the Southern Association of Colleges and Schools. It first offered distance learning courses in 1996. In 1999–2000, it offered 40 courses at a distance. In fall 1999, there were 300 students enrolled in distance learning courses.

Course delivery sites Courses are delivered to your home, your workplace, high schools, Angelo State University (San Angelo), Howard College (Big Spring), Midland College (Midland), Odessa College (Odessa), Sul Ross State University (Alpine), University of Texas System (Austin), off-campus center(s) in Fort Stockton, Iraan, Pecos, Presidio.

Media Courses are delivered via television, videoconferencing, interactive television, computer conferencing, World Wide Web, e-mail. Students and teachers may interact via videoconferencing, telephone, fax, e-mail, interactive television, World Wide Web. The following equipment may be required: computer, modem, Internet access, e-mail.

Restrictions Programs are available to in-state students only. Enrollment is restricted to individuals meeting certain criteria.

Services Distance learners have access to library services, the campus computer network, e-mail services, academic advising at a distance.

Credit-earning options Students may transfer credits from another institution or may earn credits through examinations.

Typical costs *Undergraduate:* Tuition of $63 per hour plus mandatory fees of $90 per hour for in-state residents. Tuition of $279 per hour plus mandatory fees of $90 per hour for out-of-state residents. *Graduate:* Tuition of $81 per hour plus mandatory fees of $90 per hour for in-state residents. Tuition of $283 per hour plus mandatory fees of $90 per hour for out-of-state residents. Financial aid is available to distance learners.

Registration Students may register by mail, fax, e-mail, in person.

Contact Carrie Vasquez, Administrative Secretary, University of Texas of the Permian Basin. *Telephone:* 915-552-2870. *Fax:* 915-522-2871. *E-mail:* vasquez_c@utpb.edu.

DEGREES AND AWARDS

MBA Business Administration (service area differs from that of the overall institution)
MS/CJA Criminal Justice (service area differs from that of the overall institution)

COURSE SUBJECT AREAS OFFERED OUTSIDE OF DEGREE PROGRAMS

Undergraduate: Art history and criticism; business; communications; computer and information sciences; curriculum and instruction; drama and theater; English as a second language (ESL); English language and literature; fine arts; health and physical education/fitness; logic; mathematics; political science; psychology; sociology; statistics; visual and performing arts

Graduate: American (U.S.) history; business; criminal justice; criminology; curriculum and instruction; education administration; educational research; English as a second language (ESL); health and physical education/fitness

UNIVERSITY OF TEXAS–PAN AMERICAN

Edinburg, Texas

Center for Distance Learning and Teaching Excellence
www.panam.edu/cdl

University of Texas–Pan American, founded in 1927, is a state-supported, comprehensive institution. It is accredited by the Southern Association of Colleges and Schools.

Course delivery sites Courses are delivered to your home, your workplace, high schools, The University of Texas at Brownsville (Brownsville), University of Texas at San Antonio (San Antonio), University of Texas of the Permian Basin (Odessa), off-campus center(s) in Hidalgo.

Media Courses are delivered via videoconferencing, interactive television, computer software, CD-ROM, computer conferencing, World Wide Web, e-mail, print. Students and teachers may interact via videoconferencing, mail, telephone, fax, e-mail, interactive television, World Wide Web. The following equipment may be required: computer, modem, Internet access, e-mail.

Restrictions Programs are available to local area students. Enrollment is restricted to individuals meeting certain criteria.

Services Distance learners have access to library services, the campus computer network, e-mail services, career placement assistance at a distance.

Credit-earning options Students may transfer credits from another institution.

Typical costs *Undergraduate:* Tuition of $188 per course plus mandatory fees of $95.75 per course for in-state residents. Tuition of $830 per course plus mandatory fees of $95.75 per course for out-of-state residents. *Graduate:* Tuition of $248 per course plus mandatory fees of $95.75 per course for in-state residents. Tuition of $890 per course plus mandatory fees of $95.75 per course for out-of-state residents. Students pay an additional fee for interactive television courses delivered to a University of Texas System campus. Costs may vary. Financial aid is available to distance learners.

Registration Students may register by telephone, World Wide Web, in person.

Contact Dr. Wendy Lawrence-Fowler, Director, Center for Distance Learning, University of Texas–Pan American, ABS 2.124, 1201 West University Drive, Edinburg, TX 78539. *Telephone:* 956-381-2894. *Fax:* 956-318-5276. *E-mail:* wfowler@panam.edu.

DEGREES AND AWARDS

MBA Business Administration (certain restrictions apply)

COURSE SUBJECT AREAS OFFERED OUTSIDE OF DEGREE PROGRAMS

Undergraduate: Accounting; algebra; American (U.S.) history; business communications; computer and information sciences; music

University of Texas–Pan American

Graduate: Computer and information sciences; criminology; education administration; educational psychology; English as a second language (ESL)

Noncredit: Adult education; continuing education; interdisciplinary studies; professional studies

See full description on page 794.

UNIVERSITY OF TEXAS SYSTEM

Austin, Texas

UT TeleCampus

www.telecampus.utsystem.edu

University of Texas System is a state-supported, system. It is accredited by the Southern Association of Colleges and Schools. In 1999–2000, it offered 50 courses at a distance.

Course delivery sites Courses are delivered to your home, your workplace.

Media Courses are delivered via computer software, CD-ROM, computer conferencing, World Wide Web, e-mail, print. Students and teachers may interact via telephone, fax, e-mail, World Wide Web. The following equipment may be required: computer, modem, Internet access, e-mail.

Restrictions Programs are available worldwide. Enrollment is restricted to individuals meeting certain criteria.

Services Distance learners have access to library services, the campus computer network, e-mail services, academic advising, tutoring, career placement assistance, bookstore at a distance.

Credit-earning options Students may transfer credits from another institution or may earn credits through examinations.

Typical costs Tuition and fees may vary by campus or specific program of study. Generally, graduate level courses are $580 per 3-hour credit course in-state. Undergraduate in-state tuition typically ranges from $250 to $350 per 3-hour credit course. Costs may vary. Financial aid is available to distance learners.

Registration Students may register by mail, fax, telephone, e-mail, World Wide Web, in person.

Contact Darcy W. Hardy, Director, University of Texas System, UT TeleCampus, 201 West Seventh Street, Austin, TX 78701. *Telephone:* 888-TEXAS-16. *Fax:* 512-499-4715. *E-mail:* telecampus@utsystem.edu.

DEGREES AND AWARDS

Undergraduate Certificate(s) Reading Specialist
Graduate Certificate(s) English as a Second Language (ESL), Telecommunications and Engineering
MBA General Management
MEd Educational Technology, Health and Kinesiology, Reading
MS Computer Science, Computer Science and Engineering, Electrical Engineering, Kinesiology

COURSE SUBJECT AREAS OFFERED OUTSIDE OF DEGREE PROGRAMS

Undergraduate: Algebra; American (U.S.) history; American literature; art history and criticism; biology; chemistry; economics; English composition; English literature; history; mathematics; music; political science; psychology; sociology

Graduate: Accounting; business; business administration and management; business communications; business law; communications; computer and information sciences; curriculum and instruction; education; educational research; electrical engineering; electronics; engineering; engineering-related technologies; English as a second language (ESL); English language and literature; finance; health and physical education/fitness; health professions and related sciences; human resources management; information sciences and systems; instructional media; international business; management information systems; marketing; physiology; statistics; teacher education; telecommunications

UNIVERSITY OF THE INCARNATE WORD

San Antonio, Texas

Universe Online

www.uiw.edu/online

University of the Incarnate Word, founded in 1881, is an independent, religious, comprehensive institution. It is accredited by the Southern Association of Colleges and Schools. In 1999–2000, it offered 72 courses at a distance. In fall 1999, there were 150 students enrolled in distance learning courses.

Course delivery sites Courses are delivered to your home, your workplace, military bases.

Media Courses are delivered via computer software, computer conferencing, World Wide Web, e-mail. Students and teachers may interact via telephone, fax, e-mail, World Wide Web. The following equipment may be required: computer, Internet access.

Restrictions Programs are available worldwide. Enrollment is open to anyone.

Services Distance learners have access to library services, e-mail services, academic advising, tutoring, career placement assistance, bookstore at a distance.

Credit-earning options Students may transfer credits from another institution or may earn credits through examinations.

Typical costs *Undergraduate:* Tuition of $390 per credit. *Graduate:* Tuition of $420 per credit. Transcript fee is $30. Financial aid is available to distance learners.

Registration Students may register by mail, fax, telephone, e-mail, World Wide Web, in person.

Contact Dr. Cindi Wilson Porter, Assistant Vice President Extended Academic Programs/Director, Universe Online, University of the Incarnate Word, 4301 Broadway, CPO #324, San Antonio, TX 78209. *Telephone:* 877-827-2702. *Fax:* 210-829-2756. *E-mail:* virtual@universe.uiwtx.edu.

DEGREES AND AWARDS

BA Organizations and Development
BBA Accounting, Information Systems, International Business, Management, Marketing
BS Computer Science

COURSE SUBJECT AREAS OFFERED OUTSIDE OF DEGREE PROGRAMS

Undergraduate: Accounting; American literature; biology; business administration and management; business law; chemistry; computer programming; database management; economics; English composition; English literature; history; human resources management; information sciences and systems; international business; international relations; labor relations/studies; marketing; mathematics; organizational behavior studies; philosophy and religion; political science; sociology; Spanish language and literature

See full description on page 796.

UNIVERSITY OF THE PACIFIC

Stockton, California

Center for Professional and Continuing Education
www1.uop.edu/cpce

University of the Pacific, founded in 1851, is an independent, nonprofit university. It is accredited by the Western Association of Schools and Colleges, Inc. In 1999–2000, it offered 10 courses at a distance.

Course delivery sites Courses are delivered to your home, your workplace.

Media Courses are delivered via videoconferencing, computer software, e-mail, print. Students and teachers may meet in person or interact via mail, telephone, fax, e-mail. The following equipment may be required: computer, Internet access, e-mail.

Restrictions Programs are available nationwide. Enrollment is restricted to individuals meeting certain criteria.

Services Distance learners have access to library services, academic advising at a distance.

Typical costs *Undergraduate:* Tuition of $100 per unit. *Graduate:* Tuition of $100 per unit.

Registration Students may register by mail, fax, telephone, e-mail, World Wide Web, in person.

Contact Barbara Shaw, Assistant Provost, University of the Pacific, 3601 Pacific Avenue, Stockton, CA 95211-0197. *Telephone:* 209-946-2424. *Fax:* 209-946-3916. *E-mail:* bshaw@uop.edu.

DEGREES AND AWARDS

Distance programs offered do not lead to a degree or other formal award.

COURSE SUBJECT AREAS OFFERED OUTSIDE OF DEGREE PROGRAMS

Graduate: Teacher education

UNIVERSITY OF TOLEDO

Toledo, Ohio

Division of Distance Learning
www.ucollege.utoledo.edu/dislrn.htm

University of Toledo, founded in 1872, is a state-supported university. It is accredited by the North Central Association of Colleges and Schools. It first offered distance learning courses in 1996. In 1999–2000, it offered 70 courses at a distance. In fall 1999, there were 1,200 students enrolled in distance learning courses.

Course delivery sites Courses are delivered to your home, your workplace, military bases, high schools.

Media Courses are delivered via television, videotapes, videoconferencing, interactive television, computer software, CD-ROM, computer conferencing, World Wide Web, e-mail, print. Students and teachers may meet in person or interact via videoconferencing, audioconferencing, mail, telephone, fax, e-mail, interactive television, World Wide Web. The following equipment may be required: television, videocassette player, computer, modem, Internet access, e-mail.

Restrictions Programs are available worldwide. Enrollment is open to anyone.

Services Distance learners have access to library services, the campus computer network, e-mail services, academic advising, tutoring, career placement assistance, bookstore at a distance.

Credit-earning options Students may transfer credits from another institution or may earn credits through examinations, portfolio assessment, military training, business training.

Typical costs *Undergraduate:* Tuition of $150.46 per credit hour for in-state residents. Tuition of $415.86 per credit hour for out-of-state residents. *Graduate:* Tuition of $228.45 per credit hour for in-state residents. Tuition of $533.90 per credit hour for out-of-state residents. *Noncredit courses:* $300 per course. Costs may vary. Financial aid is available to distance learners.

Registration Students may register by mail, fax, telephone, e-mail, World Wide Web, in person.

Contact Rick Kruzel, Interim Technical Coordinator, University of Toledo, Division of Distance Learning, Toledo, OH 43604-1005. *Telephone:* 419-321-5130. *Fax:* 419-321-5147. *E-mail:* rkruzel@utnet.utoledo.edu.

DEGREES AND AWARDS

Distance programs offered do not lead to a degree or other formal award.

COURSE SUBJECT AREAS OFFERED OUTSIDE OF DEGREE PROGRAMS

Undergraduate: Business administration and management; communications; comparative literature; computer and information sciences; developmental and child psychology; economics; education; engineering; ethics; foods and nutrition studies; health professions and related sciences; history; human resources management; law and legal studies; logic; mass media; philosophy and religion; physics; political science; psychology; sociology; statistics; women's studies

Graduate: Education; history; law and legal studies; philosophy and religion; political science; psychology; special education

Noncredit: Continuing education

Special note

The University of Toledo (UT) established University College (UC) in June 1995 to meet its outreach and lifelong learning mission. University College performs the University's outreach to geographically dispersed students, businesses, organizations, and other colleges and universities. UC's Divisions of Continuing Education, Contract Education, Distance Learning, Individualized and Special Programs (including 2+2 programs), and Organization Development work together to promote long-term, proactive partnerships with business, industry, and UT's global community. The College serves as the advocate for lifelong learning at the University of Toledo. The Division of Distance Learning connects UT and educational opportunities wherever they may exist. This is accomplished by responding to market needs and synergistically joining the instructional design of learner-centered course work with innovative uses of technology and teacher preparation for global instruction. Distance learning courses are taught via videotapes, compressed video using ISDN lines, UT's Virtual Campus, coax cable technology, and CD-ROM. Student-faculty interaction is accomplished through face-to-face or compressed video meetings, telephone, or e-mail or via chat room discussions on the Internet. The University of Toledo is a nationally recognized, comprehensive public university with a broad range of undergraduate and graduate programs that serve more than 20,000 students from all 50 states and 98 countries. Seven colleges award undergraduate degrees: Arts and Sciences, Business Administration, Education, Engineering, Health and Human Services, and University College. Advanced degrees are offered through the Graduate School and the College of Law. Courses may be offered through University College via distance learning from any of the colleges. The Division of Distance Learning is administered by Karen Rhoda, PhD, Interim Director of the Division of Distance Learning. Students should contact the division (telephone: 419–321–5130; fax: 419–321–5147; e-mail: rkruzel@utnet.utoledo.edu) for an inventory of current offerings, or students can have their company, school, or agency representative call to discuss how distance learning can meet the educational needs of their organization. Students should visit the World Wide Web at http://www.ucollege.utoledo.edu/dislrn.htm.

UNIVERSITY OF TORONTO

Toronto, Ontario, Canada
School of Continuing Studies
www.continuallyuoft.utoronto.ca

University of Toronto, founded in 1827, is a province-supported university. It is accredited by the Association of Theological Schools in the United States and Canada. It first offered distance learning courses in 1945. In 1999–2000, it offered 79 courses at a distance. In fall 1999, there were 4,400 students enrolled in distance learning courses.

Course delivery sites Courses are delivered to your home, your workplace.

Media Courses are delivered via videotapes, audiotapes, World Wide Web, e-mail, print. Students and teachers may meet in person or interact via mail, telephone, fax, e-mail, World Wide Web. The following equipment may be required: computer, Internet access.

Restrictions Programs are available worldwide. Enrollment is restricted to individuals meeting certain criteria.

Services Distance learners have access to library services, e-mail services, academic advising, tutoring, bookstore at a distance.

Typical costs *Undergraduate:* Tuition of $495 per course plus mandatory fees of $12 per course. *Graduate:* Tuition of $495 per course plus mandatory fees of $12 per course. *Noncredit courses:* $442 per course. Costs may vary.

Registration Students may register by mail, fax, telephone, World Wide Web, in person.

Contact Margaret White, Program Assistant, University of Toronto, Business, Professional and Entrepreneurial Studies, 158 St. George Street, Toronto, ON M5S 2V8 Canada. *Telephone:* 416-978-7687. *Fax:* 416-978-5673. *E-mail:* dlp@scs.utoronto.ca.

DEGREES AND AWARDS

Undergraduate Certificate(s) Business, Cantonese, French, German, Italian, Korean, Mandarin, Spanish

COURSE SUBJECT AREAS OFFERED OUTSIDE OF DEGREE PROGRAMS

Noncredit: Accounting; business; business administration and management; business communications; business law; Chinese language and literature; finance; French language and literature; German language and literature; human resources management; insurance; Italian language and literature; marketing; organizational behavior studies; Spanish language and literature

UNIVERSITY OF UTAH

Salt Lake City, Utah
Distance Education
instudy.utah.edu

University of Utah, founded in 1850, is a state-supported university. It is accredited by the Northwest Association of Schools and Colleges. It first offered distance learning courses in 1916. In 1999–2000, it offered 102 courses at a distance. In fall 1999, there were 2,028 students enrolled in distance learning courses.

Course delivery sites Courses are delivered to your home, your workplace, military bases, high schools.

Media Courses are delivered via television, videotapes, audiotapes, computer software, CD-ROM, World Wide Web, e-mail, print. Students and teachers may meet in person or interact via mail, telephone, fax, e-mail, World Wide Web.

Restrictions Programs are available worldwide. Enrollment is open to anyone.

Services Distance learners have access to library services, the campus computer network, academic advising, bookstore at a distance.

Credit-earning options Students may transfer credits from another institution.

Typical costs Tuition of $85 per semester hour plus mandatory fees of $15 per semester. Costs may vary.

Registration Students may register by mail, fax, telephone, e-mail, World Wide Web, in person.

Contact Roberta Lopez, Program Coordinator, University of Utah, Distance Education, 1901 East South Campus Drive, Salt Lake City, UT 84112-9324. *Telephone:* 800-INSTUDY. *Fax:* 801-581-6267. *E-mail:* rlopez@aoce.utah.edu.

DEGREES AND AWARDS

Distance programs offered do not lead to a degree or other formal award.

COURSE SUBJECT AREAS OFFERED OUTSIDE OF DEGREE PROGRAMS

Undergraduate: Abnormal psychology; algebra; American literature; anthropology; area, ethnic, and cultural studies; art history and criticism; biology; calculus; chemistry; chemistry, organic; cognitive psychology; communications; comparative literature; creative writing; developmental and child psychology; drama and theater; economics; educational psychology; English language and literature; English literature; film studies; fine arts; foods and nutrition studies; geography; gerontology; history; library and information studies; mathematics; meteorology; music; philosophy and religion; physics; physiology; political science; psychology; recreation and leisure studies; sign language; social psychology; special education; statistics; teacher education

See full description on page 798.

UNIVERSITY OF VERMONT

Burlington, Vermont
Distance Learning Network
dmdl.uvm.edu

University of Vermont, founded in 1791, is a state-supported university. It is accredited by the New England Association of Schools and Colleges. It first offered distance learning courses in 1990. In 1999–2000, it offered 50 courses at a distance. In fall 1999, there were 330 students enrolled in distance learning courses.

Course delivery sites Courses are delivered to your workplace, high schools, 3 off-campus centers in Brattleboro, Montpelier, Rutland.

Media Courses are delivered via television, videotapes, videoconferencing, interactive television, CD-ROM, World Wide Web, print. Students and teachers may meet in person or interact via videoconferencing, mail, telephone, fax, e-mail, interactive television, World Wide Web. The following equipment may be required: computer, Internet access, e-mail.

Restrictions Programs are available nationwide. Enrollment is restricted to individuals meeting certain criteria.

Services Distance learners have access to library services, the campus computer network, e-mail services, academic advising, tutoring, career placement assistance, bookstore at a distance.

Credit-earning options Students may transfer credits from another institution or may earn credits through examinations.

Typical costs *Undergraduate:* Tuition of $257 per credit hour. *Graduate:* Tuition of $257 per credit hour. Financial aid is available to distance learners.

Registration Students may register by mail, fax, telephone, e-mail, World Wide Web, in person.

Contact Nicole D. Hathaway, Information Specialist, University of Vermont, 322 South Prospect Street, Burlington, VT 05401. *Telephone:* 802-656-2229. *Fax:* 802-656-0306.

DEGREES AND AWARDS

Undergraduate Certificate(s) Gerontology (certain restrictions apply)
MEd Leadership (certain restrictions apply)

COURSE SUBJECT AREAS OFFERED OUTSIDE OF DEGREE PROGRAMS

Undergraduate: Calculus; education administration; electrical engineering; English language and literature; gerontology; mathematics; nursing; social work; teacher education
Graduate: Gerontology; nursing; public administration and services; social work

UNIVERSITY OF VIRGINIA

Charlottesville, Virginia

Educational Technologies
uvace.virginia.edu

University of Virginia, founded in 1819, is a state-supported university. It is accredited by the Southern Association of Colleges and Schools. It first offered distance learning courses in 1984. In 1999–2000, it offered 38 courses at a distance. In fall 1999, there were 143 students enrolled in distance learning courses.

Course delivery sites Courses are delivered to your workplace, 7 off-campus centers in Abingdon, Charlottesville, Fairfax, Hampton Roads, Lynchburg, Richmond, Roanoke.

Media Courses are delivered via videoconferencing. Students and teachers may interact via videoconferencing, audioconferencing, mail, telephone, fax, e-mail.

Restrictions Programs are available to in-state students only. Enrollment is open to anyone.

Services Distance learners have access to library services, academic advising at a distance.

Credit-earning options Students may transfer credits from another institution.

Typical costs Tuition of $771 per course for in-state residents. Tuition of $1407 per course for out-of-state residents. Costs may vary. Financial aid is available to distance learners.

Registration Students may register by mail, fax, telephone, World Wide Web, in person.

Contact John H. Payne III, Director, University of Virginia, 104 Midmont Lane, Charlottesville, VA 22911. *Telephone:* 804-982-5254. *Fax:* 804-982-5270. *E-mail:* jdp6m@virginia.edu.

eCollege.com *www.ecollege.com/scholarships*

DEGREES AND AWARDS

ME Engineering (service area differs from that of the overall institution)
PhD Engineering (service area differs from that of the overall institution; some on-campus requirements)

COURSE SUBJECT AREAS OFFERED OUTSIDE OF DEGREE PROGRAMS

Graduate: Aerospace, aeronautical engineering; architecture; chemical engineering; civil engineering; electrical engineering; engineering mechanics; engineering/industrial management; health professions and related sciences; mechanical engineering; teacher education
Noncredit: Teacher education

UNIVERSITY OF WASHINGTON

Seattle, Washington

Extension
www.extension.washington.edu

University of Washington, founded in 1861, is a state-supported university. It is accredited by the Northwest Association of Schools and Colleges. It first offered distance learning courses in 1915. In 1999–2000, it offered 130 courses at a distance. In fall 1999, there were 2,600 students enrolled in distance learning courses.

Course delivery sites Courses are delivered to your home, your workplace, military bases.

Media Courses are delivered via television, videotapes, World Wide Web, e-mail, print. Students and teachers may meet in person or interact via audioconferencing, mail, telephone, fax, e-mail, World Wide Web. The following equipment may be required: videocassette player, computer, modem, Internet access, e-mail.

Restrictions Programs are available worldwide. Enrollment is restricted to individuals meeting certain criteria.

Services Distance learners have access to library services, the campus computer network, e-mail services, academic advising, bookstore at a distance.

Credit-earning options Students may transfer credits from another institution or may earn credits through examinations, portfolio assessment.

Typical costs *Undergraduate:* Tuition of $109 per quarter credit plus mandatory fees of $20 per quarter. *Graduate:* Tuition of $252 per quarter credit plus mandatory fees of $20 per quarter. Cost for a noncredit course varies between $415 and $1098.

Registration Students may register by mail, fax, telephone, World Wide Web, in person.

Contact University of Washington Extension, University of Washington, 5001 25th Avenue, North East, Seattle, WA 98105. *Telephone:* 800-543-2320. *Fax:* 206-685-9359. *E-mail:* requests@ese.washington.edu.

DEGREES AND AWARDS

Undergraduate Certificate(s) Basic Internet Programming, C Programming, C++ Programming, Construction Management (service area differs from that of the overall institution; some on-campus requirements), Curriculum Integration in Action, Data Communications (service area differs from that of the overall institution; some on-campus requirements), Data Resource Management, Distance Learning Design and Development (some on-campus requirements), Facility Management, Fiction Writing, Gerontology (service area differs from that of the overall institution; some on-campus requirements), Java Programming, Nonfiction Writing, Project Management (some on-campus requirements), School Library Media Specialist (service area differs from that of the overall institution; some on-campus requirements), Small Business Webmaster, Teaching, Learning, and Technology (service area differs from that of the overall institution; some on-campus requirements), Technical Computing, Writing
BS Aeronautics and Astronautics (certain restrictions apply)
Graduate Certificate(s) Public Health (certain restrictions apply; some on-campus requirements)
MAE Aerospace Engineering (certain restrictions apply)

MEE Electrical Engineering (certain restrictions apply)
MSE Manufacturing Engineering (certain restrictions apply), Materials Science and Engineering (certain restrictions apply)
MSME Mechanical Engineering (certain restrictions apply)
PharmD Pharmacy (certain restrictions apply; service area differs from that of the overall institution)

COURSE SUBJECT AREAS OFFERED OUTSIDE OF DEGREE PROGRAMS

Undergraduate: Accounting; anthropology; area, ethnic, and cultural studies; astronomy and astrophysics; business; chemistry; communications; creative writing; developmental and child psychology; economics; English as a second language (ESL); English composition; English language and literature; European languages and literatures; foods and nutrition studies; French language and literature; geography; geology; gerontology; health professions and related sciences; history; international business; library and information studies; marketing; mathematics; meteorology; music; oceanography; philosophy and religion; political science; psychology; social psychology; sociology; Spanish language and literature; teacher education; technical writing; women's studies
Graduate: Health professions and related sciences; public health; social work
Noncredit: Computer and information sciences; creative writing
See full description on page 800.

UNIVERSITY OF WATERLOO

Waterloo, Ontario, Canada
Distance and Continuing Education
dce.uwaterloo.ca

University of Waterloo, founded in 1957, is a province-supported university. It is accredited by the provincial charter. It first offered distance learning courses in 1968. In 1999–2000, it offered 250 courses at a distance. In fall 1999, there were 3,100 students enrolled in distance learning courses.
Course delivery sites Courses are delivered to your home.
Media Courses are delivered via videotapes, audiotapes, computer software, CD-ROM, computer conferencing, World Wide Web, e-mail, print. Students and teachers may meet in person or interact via mail, telephone, fax, e-mail, World Wide Web. The following equipment may be required: television, videocassette player, computer, modem, Internet access.
Restrictions Undergraduate courses are normally available to students in the U.S. and Canada, but Master of Technology program courses are available on a worldwide basis. Enrollment is restricted to individuals meeting certain criteria.
Services Distance learners have access to library services, the campus computer network, e-mail services, academic advising, tutoring, career placement assistance, bookstore at a distance.
Credit-earning options Students may transfer credits from another institution.
Typical costs Undergraduate tuition is $435 per half-credit course for Canadian citizens or permanent residents. Non-Canadian students pay $1217.40 per half-credit course in most programs. Graduate tuition for Canadian or non-Canadian citizens is $2500 per half-credit course. Cost for noncredit distance courses in Chemistry, Physics, and Mathematics ranges from $125 to $215. Costs may vary. Financial aid is available to distance learners.
Registration Students may register by mail, fax, in person.

Contact Information and Student Services, University of Waterloo, Distance and Continuing Education Office, Waterloo, ON N2L 3G1 Canada. *Telephone:* 519-888-4050. *Fax:* 519-746-6393. *E-mail:* distance@uwaterloo.ca.

DEGREES AND AWARDS

BA Canadian Studies, Classical Studies, Economics, English, French, Geography, History, Humanities, Philosophy, Psychology, Religious Studies, Social Development Studies, Social Sciences, Sociology
BES Geography
BSc General Science
MASc Management Sciences

COURSE SUBJECT AREAS OFFERED OUTSIDE OF DEGREE PROGRAMS

Undergraduate: Abnormal psychology; algebra; American (U.S.) history; American literature; anthropology; astronomy and astrophysics; Bible studies; biochemistry; biology; business administration and management; calculus; Canadian studies; chemistry; chemistry, organic; chemistry, physical; comparative literature; computer programming; corrections; criminology; developmental and child psychology; earth science; ecology; economics; educational psychology; electronics; English composition; English literature; environmental science; ethics; European history; European languages and literatures; film studies; foods and nutrition studies; French language and literature; genetics; geography; geology; German language and literature; gerontology; Greek language and literature; health professions and related sciences; Hebrew language and literature; history; history of science and technology; insurance; investments and securities; Jewish studies; Latin language and literature; logic; mathematics; medieval/renaissance studies; microbiology; organizational behavior studies; philosophy and religion; physical sciences; physics; physiology; plant sciences; psychology; religious studies; Russian language and literature; social psychology; social sciences; social work; sociology; Spanish language and literature; special education; statistics; women's studies
Graduate: Business; business administration and management; engineering/industrial management; industrial engineering; management information systems
Noncredit: Algebra; calculus; chemistry; mathematics; physics

UNIVERSITY OF WEST FLORIDA

Pensacola, Florida
Information Technology Services
nautical.uwf.edu

University of West Florida, founded in 1963, is a state-supported, comprehensive institution. It is accredited by the Southern Association of Colleges and Schools. It first offered distance learning courses in 1988. In 1999–2000, it offered 51 courses at a distance. In fall 1999, there were 655 students enrolled in distance learning courses.
Course delivery sites Courses are delivered to your home, your workplace, military bases, high schools, 1 off-campus center in Fort Walton Beach.
Media Courses are delivered via television, videoconferencing, interactive television, computer software, World Wide Web, e-mail. Students and teachers may meet in person or interact via videoconferencing, audioconferencing, mail, telephone, fax, e-mail, interactive television, World Wide Web. The following equipment may be required: computer, modem, Internet access, e-mail.
Restrictions Programs are available worldwide. Enrollment is open to anyone.
Services Distance learners have access to library services, the campus computer network, e-mail services, academic advising at a distance.

Credit-earning options Students may transfer credits from another institution or may earn credits through examinations, military training.
Typical costs *Undergraduate:* Tuition of $73.45 per credit hour for in-state residents. Tuition of $306.40 per credit hour for out-of-state residents. *Graduate:* Tuition of $146.27 per credit hour for in-state residents. Tuition of $507 per credit hour for out-of-state residents. Costs may vary. Financial aid is available to distance learners.
Registration Students may register by mail, fax, e-mail, World Wide Web, in person.
Contact Ann Dziadon, Registrar, University of West Florida, Building 18, Pensacola, FL 32514. *Telephone:* 850-474-2244. *Fax:* 850-474-3360. *E-mail:* adziadon@uwf.edu.

DEGREES AND AWARDS

Distance programs offered do not lead to a degree or other formal award.

COURSE SUBJECT AREAS OFFERED OUTSIDE OF DEGREE PROGRAMS

Undergraduate: Advertising; algebra; archaeology; business administration and management; communications; computer and information sciences; education; education administration; English language and literature; physics; public administration and services; recreation and leisure studies; teacher education
Graduate: Abnormal psychology; business administration and management; education; education administration; professional studies; recreation and leisure studies; teacher education

See full description on page 676.

UNIVERSITY OF WISCONSIN COLLEGES

Madison, Wisconsin
UWC Online
www.uwcolleges.com

University of Wisconsin Colleges is a state-supported, two-year college. It is accredited by the North Central Association of Colleges and Schools. In 1999–2000, it offered 20 courses at a distance. In fall 1999, there were 230 students enrolled in distance learning courses.
Course delivery sites Courses are delivered to your home, your workplace, military bases, high schools.
Media Courses are delivered via World Wide Web. Students and teachers may interact via e-mail, World Wide Web. The following equipment may be required: computer, modem, Internet access, e-mail.
Restrictions Programs are available worldwide. Enrollment is restricted to individuals meeting certain criteria.
Services Distance learners have access to library services, academic advising, tutoring, bookstore at a distance.
Credit-earning options Students may transfer credits from another institution or may earn credits through military training.
Typical costs Tuition of $130 per credit plus mandatory fees of $50 per course. Financial aid is available to distance learners.
Registration Students may register by mail, World Wide Web.
Contact Elizabeth Owen, Online Student Advisor, University of Wisconsin Colleges, Madinson, WS 53708. *Telephone:* 877-449-1877. *E-mail:* equinnow@uwc.edu.

DEGREES AND AWARDS

AAS Liberal Arts and Sciences

COURSE SUBJECT AREAS OFFERED OUTSIDE OF DEGREE PROGRAMS

Undergraduate: American (U.S.) history; American literature; art history and criticism; communications; earth science; engineering; English composition; English language and literature; European history; geography; history; logic; mathematics; meteorology; music; political science; sociology; statistics

UNIVERSITY OF WISCONSIN EXTENSION

Madison, Wisconsin
Learning Innovations
learn.wisconsin.edu

University of Wisconsin Extension, founded in 1862, is a state-supported, comprehensive institution. It first offered distance learning courses in 1891. In 1999–2000, it offered 500 courses at a distance. In fall 1999, there were 3,650 students enrolled in distance learning courses.
Course delivery sites Courses are delivered to your home, your workplace, military bases.
Media Courses are delivered via television, videotapes, audiotapes, World Wide Web, e-mail, print. Students and teachers may interact via mail, telephone, fax, e-mail, World Wide Web. The following equipment may be required: television, videocassette player, computer, modem, Internet access, e-mail.
Restrictions Programs are available worldwide. Enrollment is open to anyone.
Services Distance learners have access to library services, e-mail services, academic advising at a distance.
Typical costs Tuition of $126 per credit. There is a $50 registration fee. *Noncredit courses:* $125 per course. Costs may vary.
Registration Students may register by mail, fax, telephone, e-mail, World Wide Web, in person.
Contact Student Services Advising Office, University of Wisconsin Extension, University of Wisconsin Learning Innovations, 505 South Rosa Road, Madison, WI 53719. *Telephone:* 800-442-6460. *Fax:* 608-262-4096. *E-mail:* info@learn.uwsa.edu.

DEGREES AND AWARDS

Undergraduate Certificate(s) Business

COURSE SUBJECT AREAS OFFERED OUTSIDE OF DEGREE PROGRAMS

Undergraduate: Abnormal psychology; accounting; African-American studies; agricultural economics; algebra; American (U.S.) history; American literature; anthropology; art history and criticism; astronomy and astrophysics; botany; business; business administration and management; business law; calculus; child care and development; civil engineering; creative writing; criminology; curriculum and instruction; design; economics; education; engineering; English language and literature; English literature; ethics; finance; fine arts; forestry; French language and literature; geography; geology; German language and literature; Greek language and literature; Hebrew language and literature; human resources management; individual and family development studies; Italian language and literature; journalism; Latin language and literature; logic; meteorology; music; public administration and services; Russian language and literature; social sciences; Spanish language and literature; statistics; technical writing; women's studies
Noncredit: Agricultural economics; algebra; art history and criticism; astronomy and astrophysics; business; business administration and management; business law; child care and development; civil engineering; creative writing; design; engineering; English language and literature; English literature; environmental engineering; finance; fine arts; French

language and literature; human resources management; international business; mechanical engineering; music

UNIVERSITY OF WISCONSIN–LA CROSSE

La Crosse, Wisconsin
perth.uwlax.edu/distanceed/

University of Wisconsin–La Crosse, founded in 1909, is a state-supported, comprehensive institution. It is accredited by the North Central Association of Colleges and Schools. It first offered distance learning courses in 1995. In 1999–2000, it offered 8 courses at a distance. In fall 1999, there were 60 students enrolled in distance learning courses.

Course delivery sites Courses are delivered to your workplace, high schools, University of Wisconsin–Eau Claire (Eau Claire), University of Wisconsin–Parkside (Kenosha), University of Wisconsin–Platteville (Platteville), University of Wisconsin–River Falls (River Falls), University of Wisconsin–Stevens Point (Stevens Point), University of Wisconsin–Superior (Superior).

Media Courses are delivered via interactive television, computer software, World Wide Web. Students and teachers may meet in person or interact via mail, telephone, fax, e-mail, interactive television. The following equipment may be required: computer, Internet access, e-mail.

Restrictions Programs are available to in-state students only. Enrollment is restricted to individuals meeting certain criteria.

Services Distance learners have access to library services, e-mail services, academic advising, career placement assistance, bookstore at a distance.

Credit-earning options Students may transfer credits from another institution or may earn credits through examinations, military training.

Typical costs *Undergraduate:* Tuition of $109 per credit plus mandatory fees of $43 per credit for in-state residents. Tuition of $395 per credit plus mandatory fees of $43 per credit for out-of-state residents. *Graduate:* Tuition of $195 per credit plus mandatory fees of $35 per credit for in-state residents. Tuition of $661 per credit plus mandatory fees of $35 per credit for out-of-state residents. Costs may vary. Financial aid is available to distance learners.

Registration Students may register by mail, fax, telephone, e-mail, in person.

Contact Diane Schumacher, University Registrar, University of Wisconsin–La Crosse, 1725 State Street, La Crosse, WI 54601. *Telephone:* 608-785-8953. *Fax:* 608-785-6695. *E-mail:* schumach.dian@uwlax.edu.

DEGREES AND AWARDS

Distance programs offered do not lead to a degree or other formal award.

COURSE SUBJECT AREAS OFFERED OUTSIDE OF DEGREE PROGRAMS

Undergraduate: Accounting; business administration and management; health professions and related sciences; insurance; Russian language and literature; teacher education
Graduate: Business administration and management; economics; finance; teacher education

UNIVERSITY OF WISCONSIN–MADISON

Madison, Wisconsin
www.wisc.edu/provost/collab/online.html

University of Wisconsin–Madison, founded in 1848, is a state-supported university. It is accredited by the North Central Association of Colleges and Schools. It first offered distance learning courses in 1891. In 1999–2000, it offered 50 courses at a distance. In fall 1999, there were 1,600 students enrolled in distance learning courses.

Course delivery sites Courses are delivered to your home, your workplace, University of Wisconsin–Milwaukee (Milwaukee).

Media Courses are delivered via television, videotapes, videoconferencing, CD-ROM, computer conferencing, World Wide Web, e-mail, print. Students and teachers may interact via videoconferencing, audioconferencing, mail, telephone, fax, e-mail, World Wide Web. The following equipment may be required: television, videocassette player, computer, Internet access, e-mail.

Restrictions Programs are available nationwide. Enrollment is open to anyone.

Services Distance learners have access to the campus computer network, e-mail services, academic advising at a distance.

Credit-earning options Students may transfer credits from another institution.

Typical costs *Undergraduate:* Tuition of $155 per credit for in-state residents. Tuition of $544 per credit for out-of-state residents. *Graduate:* Tuition of $310 per credit for in-state residents. Tuition of $1042 per credit for out-of-state residents. Costs may vary. Financial aid is available to distance learners.

Registration Students may register by mail, telephone.

Contact Steven Siehr, Outreach Program Manager, University of Wisconsin–Madison, 352 Bascom Hall, Madison, WI 53706. *Telephone:* 608-262-6765. *Fax:* 608-265-4777. *E-mail:* ssiehr@mail.bascom.wisc.edu.

DEGREES AND AWARDS

Undergraduate Certificate(s) Distance Education
BS Nursing (service area differs from that of the overall institution; some on-campus requirements)
MEngr Professional Practice (certain restrictions apply; service area differs from that of the overall institution; some on-campus requirements), Technical Japanese (service area differs from that of the overall institution)
MS Computer Engineering (service area differs from that of the overall institution; some on-campus requirements), Electrical Engineering (service area differs from that of the overall institution; some on-campus requirements), Mechanical Engineering (service area differs from that of the overall institution; some on-campus requirements)
PharmD Pharmacy (certain restrictions apply; service area differs from that of the overall institution; some on-campus requirements)
PD Engineering (certain restrictions apply; service area differs from that of the overall institution)

COURSE SUBJECT AREAS OFFERED OUTSIDE OF DEGREE PROGRAMS

Undergraduate: Agriculture; American (U.S.) history; child care and development; community services; electrical engineering; geology; mechanical engineering; organizational behavior studies
Graduate: Electrical engineering; health professions and related sciences; mechanical engineering; organizational behavior studies

Special note
University of Wisconsin Learning Innovations (UWLI) was formed by the UW System Board of Regents in October 1997 and has brought together talent and expertise from both the academic and private sectors. As a result, UWLI not only works with the 15 UW institutions to develop full degree and certificate programs on line, but it also serves as a full-service, integrated, e-learning consultation and courseware design enterprise that creates customized training that is focused on measurable learner outcomes. Among UWLI's more novel features are a business model that combines world-class University content with a corporate client's training content, thereby enhancing the educational opportunities of external clients and providing additional distribution channels for UW programs. In addition, UWLI provides course creation and migration that can successfully transform classroom-based training into an accessible, online experience; online learning that is available anywhere in the

world 24 hours a day, 7 days a week; educational advising; comprehensive registration services; course and learner tracking; a virtual bookstore; and e-commerce that allows online payment via a credit card. The combination of a learner-centered model, UW System interinstitutional collaboration, UWLI's distribution strategy, and its "one-stop" learner and faculty support structure set UW Learning Innovations apart from other universities engaged in the delivery of online training and education.

UNIVERSITY OF WISCONSIN–MILWAUKEE

Milwaukee, Wisconsin

Distance Learning and Instructional Support
www.uwm.edu/Dept/DOCE/

University of Wisconsin–Milwaukee, founded in 1956, is a state-supported university. It is accredited by the North Central Association of Colleges and Schools. It first offered distance learning courses in 1972. In 1999–2000, it offered 20 courses at a distance. In fall 1999, there were 110 students enrolled in distance learning courses.

Course delivery sites Courses are delivered to your home, your workplace, high schools, University of Wisconsin–River Falls (River Falls), University of Wisconsin–Rock County (Janesville), University of Wisconsin–Sheboygan (Sheboygan), University of Wisconsin–Washington County (West Bend), University of Wisconsin–Waukesha (Waukesha).

Media Courses are delivered via television, videoconferencing, interactive television, computer software, CD-ROM, computer conferencing, World Wide Web, e-mail. Students and teachers may meet in person or interact via videoconferencing, audioconferencing, mail, telephone, fax, e-mail, interactive television, World Wide Web. The following equipment may be required: television, videocassette player, computer, modem, Internet access, e-mail.

Restrictions Programs are available worldwide. Enrollment is restricted to individuals meeting certain criteria.

Services Distance learners have access to library services, the campus computer network, e-mail services, tutoring, bookstore at a distance.

Credit-earning options Students may transfer credits from another institution or may earn credits through examinations, portfolio assessment.

Typical costs Contact the school for information. Financial aid is available to distance learners.

Registration Students may register by mail, telephone, e-mail, in person.

Contact Susan Simkowski, Distance Learning Coordinator, University of Wisconsin–Milwaukee, 161 West Wisconsin Avenue, #6000, Milwaukee, WI 53203. *Telephone:* 414-227-3223. *Fax:* 414-227-3396. *E-mail:* susansim@uwm.edu.

eCollege .com *www.ecollege.com/scholarships*

DEGREES AND AWARDS

Distance programs offered do not lead to a degree or other formal award.

COURSE SUBJECT AREAS OFFERED OUTSIDE OF DEGREE PROGRAMS

Undergraduate: Accounting; business; business administration and management; communications; economics; education; European languages and literatures; finance; French language and literature; German language and literature; health professions and related sciences; history; human resources management; Japanese language and literature; labor relations/studies; marketing; nursing; occupational therapy; organizational behavior studies; political science; real estate; social work
Graduate: Library and information studies; social work

UNIVERSITY OF WISCONSIN–PLATTEVILLE

Platteville, Wisconsin

Distance Learning Center
www.uwplatt.edu/~disted/

University of Wisconsin–Platteville, founded in 1866, is a state-supported, comprehensive institution. It is accredited by the North Central Association of Colleges and Schools. It first offered distance learning courses in 1979. In 1999–2000, it offered 50 courses at a distance. In fall 1999, there were 350 students enrolled in distance learning courses.

Course delivery sites Courses are delivered to your home, your workplace.

Media Courses are delivered via videotapes, interactive television, audiotapes, computer conferencing, World Wide Web, e-mail, print. Students and teachers may interact via audioconferencing, mail, telephone, fax, e-mail, World Wide Web. The following equipment may be required: computer, modem, Internet access, e-mail.

Restrictions Programs are available worldwide. Enrollment is restricted to individuals meeting certain criteria.

Services Distance learners have access to library services, the campus computer network, e-mail services, academic advising, career placement assistance, bookstore at a distance.

Credit-earning options Students may transfer credits from another institution or may earn credits through examinations, portfolio assessment, military training, business training.

Typical costs *Undergraduate:* Mandatory fees of $5 per credit for in-state residents. Mandatory fees of $5 per credit for out-of-state residents. *Graduate:* Tuition of $468 per credit for in-state residents. Tuition of $608 per credit for out-of-state residents. Undergraduate in-state tuition ranges between $109 and $160 per credit; out-of-state is between $340 and $395 per credit. Costs may vary. Financial aid is available to distance learners.

Registration Students may register by mail, World Wide Web, in person.

Contact Distance Learning Center, University of Wisconsin–Platteville, B12 Karrmann, 1 University Plaza, Platteville, WI 53818-3099. *Telephone:* 800-362-5460. *Fax:* 608-342-1071. *E-mail:* disted@uwplatt.edu.

DEGREES AND AWARDS

Undergraduate Certificate(s) Business (certain restrictions apply), Project Management (certain restrictions apply)
BS Business Administration (certain restrictions apply)
Graduate Certificate(s) Criminal Justice (certain restrictions apply)
MOE Engineering (certain restrictions apply)
MS Criminal Justice (certain restrictions apply), Project Management (certain restrictions apply)

COURSE SUBJECT AREAS OFFERED OUTSIDE OF DEGREE PROGRAMS

Undergraduate: Accounting; business; business administration and management; business communications; civil engineering; economics; finance; geography; human resources management; marketing; mathematics
Graduate: Adult education; business communications; civil engineering; criminal justice; management; mathematics; mechanical engineering; teacher education

UNIVERSITY OF WISCONSIN–RIVER FALLS

River Falls, Wisconsin

Outreach Office
www.uwrf.edu/outreach/

University of Wisconsin–River Falls, founded in 1874, is a state-supported, comprehensive institution. It is accredited by the North

Central Association of Colleges and Schools. It first offered distance learning courses in 1994. In 1999–2000, it offered 10 courses at a distance. In fall 1999, there were 100 students enrolled in distance learning courses.

Course delivery sites Courses are delivered to Lac Courte Oreilles Ojibwa Community College (Hayward), University of Wisconsin–Eau Claire (Eau Claire), University of Wisconsin–La Crosse (La Crosse), University of Wisconsin–Madison (Madison), University of Wisconsin–Platteville (Platteville), University of Wisconsin–Stevens Point (Stevens Point), University of Wisconsin–Stout (Menomonie), University of Wisconsin–Superior (Superior), 24 off-campus centers in Baldwin, Balsam Lake, Barron, Birchwood, Boyceville, Cameron, Clear Lake, Cumberland, Frederic, Grantsburg, Luck, New Richmond, Osceola, Plum City, Prairie Farm, Rice Lake, Shell Lake, Siren, Somerset, Spooner, Spring Valley, St. Croix Falls, Turtle Lake, Webster.

Media Courses are delivered via television, videotapes, videoconferencing, interactive television, computer software, computer conferencing, World Wide Web, e-mail, print. Students and teachers may meet in person or interact via videoconferencing, audioconferencing, mail, telephone, fax, e-mail, interactive television, World Wide Web. The following equipment may be required: computer, Internet access, e-mail.

Restrictions Programs are available to in-state students only. Enrollment is restricted to individuals meeting certain criteria.

Services Distance learners have access to library services, the campus computer network, e-mail services, bookstore at a distance.

Credit-earning options Students may transfer credits from another institution or may earn credits through examinations.

Typical costs *Undergraduate:* Tuition of $109 per credit plus mandatory fees of $45 per course for in-state residents. Tuition of $395 per credit plus mandatory fees of $45 per course for out-of-state residents. *Graduate:* Tuition of $195 per credit plus mandatory fees of $45 per course for in-state residents. Tuition of $660 per credit plus mandatory fees of $45 per course for out-of-state residents. For Minnesota reciprocity students, undergraduate tuition is $110 and graduate tuition is $195. *Noncredit courses:* $40 per course. Costs may vary. Financial aid is available to distance learners.

Registration Students may register by mail, fax, World Wide Web, in person.

Contact Katrina Larsen, CAFES Outreach Program Manager, University of Wisconsin–River Falls, 410 South Third Street, River Falls, WI 54022-5001. *Telephone:* 715-425-3276. *Fax:* 715-425-3785. *E-mail:* katrina.larsen@uwrf.edu.

DEGREES AND AWARDS

Distance programs offered do not lead to a degree or other formal award.

COURSE SUBJECT AREAS OFFERED OUTSIDE OF DEGREE PROGRAMS

Undergraduate: Accounting; agriculture; astronomy and astrophysics; business; business administration and management; communications; conservation and natural resources; drama and theater; education; geology; liberal arts, general studies, and humanities; political science; teacher education

Graduate: Teacher education

Noncredit: Agriculture; business; business administration and management; education; teacher education

---

UNIVERSITY OF WISCONSIN–STEVENS POINT

Stevens Point, Wisconsin

University Telecommunications and Distance Learning Resources
uwsp.edu/extension/Distance_Learning.htm

University of Wisconsin–Stevens Point, founded in 1894, is a state-supported, comprehensive institution. It is accredited by the North Central Association of Colleges and Schools. It first offered distance learning courses in 1985. In 1999–2000, it offered 50 courses at a distance. In fall 1999, there were 260 students enrolled in distance learning courses.

Course delivery sites Courses are delivered to your home, your workplace, high schools, University of Wisconsin System (Madison), Wisconsin Technical College System (Madison).

Media Courses are delivered via television, videoconferencing, interactive television, computer software, computer conferencing, World Wide Web, e-mail, print. Students and teachers may meet in person or interact via videoconferencing, audioconferencing, mail, telephone, fax, e-mail, interactive television, World Wide Web. The following equipment may be required: computer, modem, Internet access, e-mail.

Restrictions Programs are available worldwide. Enrollment is restricted to individuals meeting certain criteria.

Services Distance learners have access to library services, the campus computer network, e-mail services, academic advising, bookstore at a distance.

Credit-earning options Students may transfer credits from another institution.

Typical costs *Undergraduate:* Tuition of $111.75 per credit for in-state residents. Tuition of $165.75 per credit for out-of-state residents. *Graduate:* Tuition of $195 per credit for in-state residents. Tuition of $292.50 per credit for out-of-state residents. Mandatory fees range between $50 and $85 per course. Costs may vary. Financial aid is available to distance learners.

Registration Students may register by mail, in person.

Contact Judi Pitt, Scheduling Coordinator, University of Wisconsin–Stevens Point, 1101 Reserve, Room 110, Stevens Point, WI 54481. *Telephone:* 800-898-9472. *Fax:* 715-346-3998. *E-mail:* jpitt@uwsp.edu.

DEGREES AND AWARDS

Undergraduate Certificate(s) Technology and Leadership (certain restrictions apply)

COURSE SUBJECT AREAS OFFERED OUTSIDE OF DEGREE PROGRAMS

Undergraduate: American (U.S.) history; anthropology; archaeology; art history and criticism; business; child care and development; communications; computer and information sciences; conservation and natural resources; economics; education; health professions and related sciences; instructional media; Japanese language and literature; music; religious studies; Russian language and literature; school psychology; sociology; special education; statistics; teacher education; women's studies

Graduate: Algebra; American (U.S.) history; anthropology; child care and development; communications; computer and information sciences; conservation and natural resources; economics; education; instructional media; special education; statistics; teacher education

Noncredit: Business; conservation and natural resources

UNIVERSITY OF WISCONSIN–STOUT

Menomonie, Wisconsin

Stout Solutions-Continuing Education
oce.uwstout.edu

University of Wisconsin–Stout, founded in 1891, is a state-supported, comprehensive institution. It is accredited by the North Central Association of Colleges and Schools. It first offered distance learning courses in 1980. In 1999–2000, it offered 50 courses at a distance. In fall 1999, there were 400 students enrolled in distance learning courses.

Course delivery sites Courses are delivered to your home, your workplace, military bases, high schools, Fox Valley Technical College (Appleton), Madison Area Technical College (Madison), Milwaukee Area Technical College (Milwaukee), Northcentral Technical College (Wausau), Waukesha County Technical College (Pewaukee), Western Wisconsin Technical College (La Crosse), 3 off-campus centers in Medford, Phillips, Princeton.

Media Courses are delivered via television, videotapes, videoconferencing, interactive television, audiotapes, computer software, CD-ROM, computer conferencing, World Wide Web, e-mail, print. Students and teachers may interact via videoconferencing, audioconferencing, mail, telephone, fax, e-mail, interactive television, World Wide Web. The following equipment may be required: computer, modem, Internet access, e-mail.

Restrictions Availability varies depending on the specific course or program. Enrollment is open to anyone.

Services Distance learners have access to library services, the campus computer network, e-mail services, academic advising, career placement assistance, bookstore at a distance.

Credit-earning options Students may transfer credits from another institution or may earn credits through examinations, military training, business training.

Typical costs *Undergraduate:* Tuition of $124 per credit for in-state residents. Tuition of $175 per credit for out-of-state residents. *Graduate:* Tuition of $208 per credit for in-state residents. Tuition of $260 per credit for out-of-state residents. *Noncredit courses:* $195 per course. Costs may vary. Financial aid is available to distance learners.

Registration Students may register by mail, fax, telephone, e-mail, World Wide Web, in person.

Contact Sandra White, Credit Outreach Program Manager III, University of Wisconsin–Stout, Stout Solutions-Continuing Education, 140 Vocational Rehabilitation Building, Menomonie, WI 54751-0790. *Telephone:* 715-232-2693. *Fax:* 715-232-3385. *E-mail:* whites@uwstout.edu.

DEGREES AND AWARDS

BS Industrial Management
MS Education, Hospitality and Tourism Management (service area differs from that of the overall institution), Training and Development

COURSE SUBJECT AREAS OFFERED OUTSIDE OF DEGREE PROGRAMS

Undergraduate: Developmental and child psychology; education; engineering/industrial management; home economics and family studies; human resources management; physics; psychology; recreation and leisure studies
Graduate: Developmental and child psychology; education; engineering/industrial management; home economics and family studies; human resources management; management; psychology; recreation and leisure studies

See full description on page 802.

UNIVERSITY OF WISCONSIN–WHITEWATER

Whitewater, Wisconsin

Graduate Studies, Continuing Education, and Summer Session
www.uww.edu

University of Wisconsin–Whitewater, founded in 1868, is a state-supported, comprehensive institution. It is accredited by the North Central Association of Colleges and Schools. It first offered distance learning courses in 1986. In 1999–2000, it offered 24 courses at a distance. In fall 1999, there were 182 students enrolled in distance learning courses.

Course delivery sites Courses are delivered to your home, your workplace, 26 off-campus centers.

Media Courses are delivered via television, videoconferencing, interactive television, CD-ROM, World Wide Web, e-mail, print. Students and teachers may meet in person or interact via videoconferencing, audioconferencing, mail, telephone, fax, e-mail, interactive television, World Wide Web. The following equipment may be required: computer, modem, Internet access, e-mail.

Restrictions The majority of offerings are in state only, but Online M.B.A. is available worldwide. Enrollment is open to anyone.

Services Distance learners have access to library services, the campus computer network, e-mail services, academic advising, career placement assistance, bookstore at a distance.

Credit-earning options Students may transfer credits from another institution or may earn credits through examinations, military training.

Typical costs *Undergraduate:* Tuition of $130.30 per semester hour for in-state residents. Tuition of $416.30 per semester hour for out-of-state residents. *Graduate:* Tuition of $218.50 per semester hour for in-state residents. Tuition of $683 per semester hour for out-of-state residents. Graduate Business Fees (online MBA) are $243.50 per semester hour in-state and $708.50 per semester hour out-of-state. Costs may vary. Financial aid is available to distance learners.

Registration Students may register by mail, telephone, in person.

Contact Kathy Gibbs, Distance Education Coordinator, University of Wisconsin–Whitewater, 800 West Main Street, Whitewater, WI 53190. *Telephone:* 414-472-5247. *Fax:* 414-472-5210. *E-mail:* gibbsk@uwwvax.uww.edu.

DEGREES AND AWARDS

MBA Finance (service area differs from that of the overall institution), Human Resource Management (service area differs from that of the overall institution), International Business (service area differs from that of the overall institution), Management (service area differs from that of the overall institution), Marketing (service area differs from that of the overall institution)

COURSE SUBJECT AREAS OFFERED OUTSIDE OF DEGREE PROGRAMS

Undergraduate: Communications; teacher education; women's studies
Graduate: Business administration and management; communications; education administration; teacher education

UNIVERSITY OF WYOMING

Laramie, Wyoming

The Outreach School
ecampus.uwyo.edu

University of Wyoming, founded in 1886, is a state-supported university. It is accredited by the North Central Association of Colleges and Schools.

It first offered distance learning courses in 1954. In 1999–2000, it offered 300 courses at a distance. In fall 1999, there were 2,200 students enrolled in distance learning courses.

Course delivery sites Courses are delivered to your home, your workplace, military bases, 15 off-campus centers in Casper, Cheyenne, Douglas, Evanston, Gillette, Green River, Jackson Hole, Lander, Lusk, Newcastle, Rawlins, Riverton, Rock Springs, Sheridan, Torrington.

Media Courses are delivered via videotapes, videoconferencing, interactive television, computer conferencing, World Wide Web, e-mail, print. Students and teachers may interact via videoconferencing, audioconferencing, mail, telephone, fax, e-mail, interactive television, World Wide Web. The following equipment may be required: television, videocassette player, computer, modem, Internet access, e-mail.

Restrictions Programs are available worldwide. Enrollment is restricted to individuals meeting certain criteria.

Services Distance learners have access to library services, academic advising, tutoring, career placement assistance, bookstore at a distance.

Credit-earning options Students may transfer credits from another institution or may earn credits through examinations, portfolio assessment.

Typical costs *Undergraduate:* Tuition of $90.25 per credit hour plus mandatory fees of $3.50 per credit hour for in-state residents. Tuition of $264 per credit hour plus mandatory fees of $4.50 per credit hour for out-of-state residents. *Graduate:* Tuition of $150.40 per credit hour plus mandatory fees of $4.50 per credit hour for in-state residents. Tuition of $270 per credit hour plus mandatory fees of $4.50 per credit hour for out-of-state residents. Online courses and degrees are at in-state tuition rates plus $40 technology fee per credit hour. Costs may vary. Financial aid is available to distance learners.

Registration Students may register by mail, fax, telephone, e-mail, World Wide Web, in person.

Contact Judith A. Powell, Associate Vice President and Dean, The Outreach School, University of Wyoming, Box 3106, University Station, Laramie, WY 82071. *Telephone:* 307-766-3152. *Fax:* 307-766-3445. *E-mail:* jpowell@uwyo.edu.

DEGREES AND AWARDS

Undergraduate Certificate(s) Land Surveying (service area differs from that of the overall institution)

BA Administration of Justice (service area differs from that of the overall institution), Social Sciences (service area differs from that of the overall institution)

BS Business Administration, Psychology (service area differs from that of the overall institution), Social Sciences (service area differs from that of the overall institution)

BSN Nursing, RN to BSN

MA Special Education (service area differs from that of the overall institution), Teaching and Learning (service area differs from that of the overall institution)

MBA Business Administration

MPA Public Administration (service area differs from that of the overall institution)

MS Adult Learning and Technology, Nursing, Speech Pathology

COURSE SUBJECT AREAS OFFERED OUTSIDE OF DEGREE PROGRAMS

Undergraduate: Accounting; African-American studies; agriculture; anatomy; astronomy and astrophysics; child care and development; civil engineering; communications; conservation and natural resources; criminal justice; economics; education; English composition; English language and literature; foods and nutrition studies; health and physical education/fitness; health professions and related sciences; history; home economics and family studies; labor relations/studies; liberal arts, general studies, and

humanities; nursing; political science; protective services; psychology; real estate; religious studies; social psychology; social sciences; sociology; statistics; surveying; women's studies

Graduate: Accounting; business; business administration and management; curriculum and instruction; education administration; educational psychology; health and physical education/fitness; health professions and related sciences; human resources management; labor relations/studies; nursing; political science; special education; teacher education

See full descriptions on pages 804 and 822.

UNIVERSITY SYSTEM OF GEORGIA

Atlanta, Georgia

University System of Georgia Independent Study
www.gactr.uga.edu/usgis

University System of Georgia is a state-supported, system. It is accredited by the Southern Association of Colleges and Schools. It first offered distance learning courses in 1932. In fall 1999, there were 4,000 students enrolled in distance learning courses.

Course delivery sites Courses are delivered to your home, your workplace.

Media Courses are delivered via videotapes, audiotapes, computer software, World Wide Web, e-mail, print. Students and teachers may interact via mail, telephone, fax, e-mail, World Wide Web. The following equipment may be required: computer, Internet access, e-mail.

Restrictions Programs are available worldwide. Enrollment is restricted to individuals meeting certain criteria.

Services Distance learners have access to library services, bookstore at a distance.

Credit-earning options Students may earn credits through examinations.

Typical costs Tuition of $104 per semester hour. Costs may vary. Financial aid is available to distance learners.

Registration Students may register by mail, fax, World Wide Web, in person.

Contact Melissa Pettigrew, Coordinator of Marketing, Student Recruitment and Outreach, University System of Georgia, Georgia Center, 1197 South Lumpkin Street, Suite 193, Athens, GA 30602-3603. *Telephone:* 800-877-3243. *Fax:* 706-542-9012. *E-mail:* melissa_pettigrew@gactr.uga.edu.

DEGREES AND AWARDS

Undergraduate Certificate(s) Marketing Research (service area differs from that of the overall institution), Towing and Recovery with Light-Duty Equipment (service area differs from that of the overall institution), Turfgrass Management (service area differs from that of the overall institution)

COURSE SUBJECT AREAS OFFERED OUTSIDE OF DEGREE PROGRAMS

Undergraduate: Abnormal psychology; accounting; administrative and secretarial services; advertising; agriculture; algebra; American (U.S.) history; American literature; anthropology; area, ethnic, and cultural studies; art history and criticism; biological and life sciences; biology; business; business administration and management; calculus; classical languages and literatures; communications; conservation and natural resources; developmental and child psychology; ecology; economics; education; educational psychology; English composition; English language and literature; English literature; ethics; European history; European languages and literatures; fine arts; foods and nutrition studies; forestry; French language and literature; geography; geology; German language and literature; health and physical education/fitness; health professions and related sciences; history; home economics and family studies; horticulture; human resources management; individual and family development studies; journalism; Latin language and literature; law and legal studies; liberal arts, general studies, and humanities; logic; marketing; mathematics; organizational behavior studies; philosophy and religion; plant sciences; political science; psychology; public health; religious studies; social psychology; sociology; Spanish language and literature; special education; statistics; teacher education; technical writing; theological studies; visual and performing arts; women's studies

See full description on page 806.

UPPER IOWA UNIVERSITY

Fayette, Iowa
External Degree
www.uiu.edu

Upper Iowa University, founded in 1857, is an independent, nonprofit, comprehensive institution. It is accredited by the North Central Association of Colleges and Schools. It first offered distance learning courses in 1973. In 1999–2000, it offered 75 courses at a distance. In fall 1999, there were 856 students enrolled in distance learning courses.

Course delivery sites Courses are delivered to your home, your workplace, military bases, 11 off-campus centers in Des Moines, Manchester, Waterloo, Fort Leavenworth (KS), Fort Polk (LA), Fort Riley (KS), Janesville (WI), Madison (WI), Prairie du Chien (WI), Wausau (WI), West Allis (WI).

Media Courses are delivered via videotapes, print. Students and teachers may interact via mail, telephone, fax, e-mail. The following equipment may be required: e-mail.

Restrictions Programs are available worldwide. Enrollment is open to anyone.

Services Distance learners have access to library services, e-mail services, academic advising, career placement assistance, bookstore at a distance.

Credit-earning options Students may transfer credits from another institution or may earn credits through examinations, portfolio assessment, military training, business training.

Typical costs Tuition of $155 per semester hour. $80 audit fee per semester hour. Financial aid is available to distance learners.

Registration Students may register by mail, fax, telephone, e-mail, in person.

Contact Barb Schultz, Director of External Degree, Upper Iowa University. *Telephone:* 888-877-3742. *Fax:* 319-425-5353. *E-mail:* extdegree@uiu.edu.

DEGREES AND AWARDS

AA Business, Liberal Arts
BS Accounting, Business, Human Resources Management, Human Services, Management, Marketing, Public Administration, Social Sciences

COURSE SUBJECT AREAS OFFERED OUTSIDE OF DEGREE PROGRAMS

Undergraduate: Abnormal psychology; accounting; American (U.S.) history; art history and criticism; biology; business; business administration and management; business communications; business law; earth science; economics; English composition; English language and literature; history; human resources management; industrial psychology; international business; labor relations/studies; management information systems; marketing; mathematics; physical sciences; psychology; public administration and services; social sciences; sociology; statistics
Noncredit: Abnormal psychology; accounting; American (U.S.) history; art history and criticism; biology; business; business administration and management; business communications; business law; economics; English

composition; English language and literature; history; human resources management; industrial psychology; international business; labor relations/studies; management information systems; marketing; mathematics; physical sciences; psychology; public administration and services; social sciences; sociology; statistics

See full description on page 808.

UTAH STATE UNIVERSITY

Logan, Utah
Independent and Distance Education
www.ext.usu.edu/distance/

Utah State University, founded in 1888, is a state-supported university. It is accredited by the Northwest Association of Schools and Colleges. It first offered distance learning courses in 1984. In 1999–2000, it offered 193 courses at a distance. In fall 1999, there were 3,048 students enrolled in distance learning courses.

Course delivery sites Courses are delivered to your home, high schools, College of Eastern Utah (Price), Colorado Northwestern Community College (Rangely, CO), Dixie State College of Utah (St. George), Snow College (Ephraim), Southern Utah University (Cedar City), Utah Valley State College (Orem), Western Wyoming Community College (Rock Springs, WY), 37 off-campus centers in Bicknell, Blanding, Bluffdale, Brigham City, Cedar City, Delta, Dugway, Emery, Ephraim, Gunnison, Heber, Manila, Moab, Monticello, Ogden, Orem, Price, Randolph, Richfield, Roosevelt, Salt Lake City, St. George, Tooele, Tremonton, Vernal, Wendover, Afton (WY), Beaver (WY), Caliente (NV), Cortez (CO), Evanston (WY), Kemmerer (WY), Rangley (CO), Rock Springs (WY), Wendover (NV).

Media Courses are delivered via television, videoconferencing, computer software, World Wide Web, e-mail, print. Students and teachers may interact via videoconferencing, audioconferencing, mail, telephone, fax, e-mail. The following equipment may be required: computer, Internet access, e-mail.

Restrictions Programs are available nationwide. Enrollment is open to anyone.

Services Distance learners have access to library services, the campus computer network, e-mail services, academic advising, tutoring, career placement assistance, bookstore at a distance.

Credit-earning options Students may transfer credits from another institution or may earn credits through examinations.

Typical costs *Undergraduate:* Tuition of $298 per credit for in-state residents. Tuition of $710 per credit for out-of-state residents. *Graduate:* Tuition of $325 per credit for in-state residents. Tuition of $816 per credit for out-of-state residents. Graduate mandatory fees vary. Cost for a no-credit course varies depending on course. Costs may vary. Financial aid is available to distance learners.

Registration Students may register by mail, fax, in person.
Contact Heather R. Thomas, Distance Learning Coordinator, Utah State University, 3080 Old Main Hill, Logan, UT 84322-3080. *Telephone:* 435-797-2709. *Fax:* 435-797-1399. *E-mail:* hearaa@mdls.usu.edu.

DEGREES AND AWARDS

Undergraduate Certificate(s) Child Development Education, Early Childhood Education, Mild to Moderate Education, School Library Media Specialist
BS Accounting, Agribusiness, Business, Business Administration, Business Information Systems and Education, Computer Science, Psychology
Graduate Certificate(s) Administrative Supervisory Education
MEd Elementary Education, Instructional Technology, Secondary Education

MS Business Information Systems and Education, Computer Science, Human Environments, Rehabilitation Counseling, School Counseling, Technical Writing
MSS Human Resource Management

COURSE SUBJECT AREAS OFFERED OUTSIDE OF DEGREE PROGRAMS

Undergraduate: Accounting; agriculture; astronomy and astrophysics; biology; business; business administration and management; chemistry; computer and information sciences; conservation and natural resources; creative writing; developmental and child psychology; economics; education administration; educational psychology; English composition; English language and literature; European languages and literatures; fine arts; geology; health professions and related sciences; history; home economics and family studies; human resources management; journalism; liberal arts, general studies, and humanities; mathematics; microbiology; philosophy and religion; physics; political science; social psychology; social work; sociology; special education; teacher education
Graduate: Business; computer and information sciences; developmental and child psychology; education administration; English composition; home economics and family studies; human resources management; social psychology; special education; teacher education
Noncredit: Fine arts
See full descriptions on pages 810 and 822.

UTICA COLLEGE OF SYRACUSE UNIVERSITY

Utica, New York

Economic Crime Management/Studies in Gerontology
www.utica.edu

Utica College of Syracuse University, founded in 1946, is an independent, nonprofit, comprehensive institution. It is accredited by the Middle States Association of Colleges and Schools. In 1999–2000, it offered 19 courses at a distance. In fall 1999, there were 46 students enrolled in distance learning courses.
Course delivery sites Courses are delivered to your home, your workplace.
Media Courses are delivered via computer software, computer conferencing, World Wide Web, e-mail. Students and teachers may meet in person or interact via telephone, fax, e-mail, World Wide Web. The following equipment may be required: computer, modem, Internet access, e-mail.
Restrictions Programs are available worldwide. Enrollment is restricted to individuals meeting certain criteria.
Services Distance learners have access to library services, e-mail services, academic advising, tutoring, bookstore at a distance.
Credit-earning options Students may transfer credits from another institution or may earn credits through examinations.
Typical costs Tuition for 'Studies in Gerontology' credit certificate program is $368 pre credit hour plus $60 distance learning fee per course. Tuition for 'Economic Crime Management' graduate program is $612 per credit hour, plus $75 technology fee per semester. Financial aid is available to distance learners.
Registration Students may register by mail, fax, telephone, in person.
Contact Kate Cominsky, Office of Graduate Studies, Utica College of Syracuse University, 1600 Burrstone Road, Utica, NY 13501. *Telephone:* 315-792-3244. *Fax:* 315-792-3002. *E-mail:* ccomins@utica.ucsu.edu.

DEGREES AND AWARDS

Undergraduate Certificate(s) Gerontology
MS Economic Crime Management (certain restrictions apply; some on-campus requirements)

COURSE SUBJECT AREAS OFFERED OUTSIDE OF DEGREE PROGRAMS

Undergraduate: Gerontology
Graduate: Criminology
See full description on page 812.

VALDOSTA STATE UNIVERSITY

Valdosta, Georgia

Division of Public Services
www.valdosta.edu

Valdosta State University, founded in 1906, is a state-supported university. It is accredited by the Southern Association of Colleges and Schools. It first offered distance learning courses in 1992. In 1999–2000, it offered 66 courses at a distance. In fall 1999, there were 450 students enrolled in distance learning courses.
Course delivery sites Courses are delivered to military bases, high schools, Abraham Baldwin Agricultural College (Tifton), Bainbridge College (Bainbridge), South Georgia College (Douglas), Waycross College (Waycross), 2 off-campus centers in Kings Bay Naval Submarine Base, Moody AFB.
Media Courses are delivered via videotapes, videoconferencing, interactive television, World Wide Web, e-mail. Students and teachers may meet in person or interact via videoconferencing, mail, telephone, fax, e-mail, interactive television. The following equipment may be required: computer, modem, Internet access, e-mail.
Restrictions Programs are available to in-state students only. Enrollment is restricted to individuals meeting certain criteria.
Services Distance learners have access to library services, the campus computer network, e-mail services, academic advising, career placement assistance, bookstore at a distance.
Typical costs *Undergraduate:* Tuition of $76 per semester hour for in-state residents. Tuition of $302 per semester hour for out-of-state residents. *Graduate:* Tuition of $91 per semester hour for in-state residents. Tuition of $363 per semester hour for out-of-state residents. Financial aid is available to distance learners.
Registration Students may register by mail, fax, telephone, e-mail, World Wide Web, in person.
Contact Philip D. Allen, Interim Director, Division of Public Services, Valdosta State University. *Telephone:* 912-245-6484. *Fax:* 912-333-5397. *E-mail:* pdallen@valdosta.edu.

eCollege.com *www.ecollege.com/scholarships*

DEGREES AND AWARDS

BA Management (certain restrictions apply; some on-campus requirements)
BSED Education (certain restrictions apply; some on-campus requirements)

COURSE SUBJECT AREAS OFFERED OUTSIDE OF DEGREE PROGRAMS

Undergraduate: Business administration and management; nursing; teacher education
Graduate: Teacher education
See full description on page 676.

VANCE-GRANVILLE COMMUNITY COLLEGE

Henderson, North Carolina
www.vgcc.cc.nc.us

Vance-Granville Community College, founded in 1969, is a state-supported, two-year college. It is accredited by the Southern Association of Colleges and Schools. In 1999–2000, it offered 55 courses at a distance. In fall 1999, there were 136 students enrolled in distance learning courses.

Course delivery sites Courses are delivered to your home.

Media Courses are delivered via television, interactive television, World Wide Web. Students and teachers may meet in person or interact via telephone, e-mail, interactive television. The following equipment may be required: computer, Internet access, e-mail.

Restrictions Programs are available to in-state students only. Enrollment is open to anyone.

Services Distance learners have access to library services at a distance.

Credit-earning options Students may transfer credits from another institution or may earn credits through examinations.

Typical costs Tuition of $26.75 per credit hour for in-state residents. Tuition of $169.75 per credit hour for out-of-state residents. Mandatory fees are $14 for one to eleven credit-hours. Financial aid is available to distance learners.

Registration Students may register by mail, telephone, World Wide Web, in person.

Contact Mr. Ken Lewis, Director of Information Technology, Vance-Granville Community College, PO Box 917, Henderson, NC 27536. *Telephone:* 252-492-2061 Ext. 304. *Fax:* 252-430-0460. *E-mail:* lewis@admin.vgcc.cc.nc.us.

DEGREES AND AWARDS

Distance programs offered do not lead to a degree or other formal award.

COURSE SUBJECT AREAS OFFERED OUTSIDE OF DEGREE PROGRAMS

Undergraduate: American (U.S.) history; biology; business administration and management; European history; marketing; philosophy and religion; psychology; sociology

Noncredit: Computer and information sciences

See full description on page 676.

VERMONT TECHNICAL COLLEGE

Randolph Center, Vermont
www.vtc.vsc.edu

Vermont Technical College, founded in 1866, is a state-supported, primarily two-year college. It is accredited by the New England Association of Schools and Colleges. In 1999–2000, it offered 8 courses at a distance. In fall 1999, there were 50 students enrolled in distance learning courses.

Course delivery sites Courses are delivered to your home, your workplace, high schools.

Media Courses are delivered via interactive television, World Wide Web, e-mail, print. Students and teachers may meet in person or interact via mail, telephone, fax, e-mail, interactive television, World Wide Web. The following equipment may be required: computer, modem, Internet access, e-mail.

Restrictions Programs are available worldwide. Enrollment is restricted to individuals meeting certain criteria.

Services Distance learners have access to library services, the campus computer network, e-mail services, career placement assistance at a distance.

Credit-earning options Students may transfer credits from another institution or may earn credits through examinations, military training.

Typical costs Tuition of $214 per credit plus mandatory fees of $23.50 per credit for in-state residents. Tuition of $432 per credit plus mandatory fees of $23.50 per credit for out-of-state residents. Financial aid is available to distance learners.

Registration Students may register by mail, fax, telephone, e-mail, in person.

Contact Michael Dempsey, Registrar, Vermont Technical College, PO Box 500, Randolph Center, VT 05061. *Telephone:* 802-728-1630. *Fax:* 802-728-1390. *E-mail:* mdempsey@vtc.vsc.edu.

DEGREES AND AWARDS

Distance programs offered do not lead to a degree or other formal award.

COURSE SUBJECT AREAS OFFERED OUTSIDE OF DEGREE PROGRAMS

Undergraduate: Calculus; computer programming; database management; English composition; English literature; history; information sciences and systems; technical writing

VICTOR VALLEY COLLEGE

Victorville, California
vvcconline.com

Victor Valley College, founded in 1961, is a state-supported, two-year college. It is accredited by the Western Association of Schools and Colleges, Inc. In 1999–2000, it offered 20 courses at a distance. In fall 1999, there were 155 students enrolled in distance learning courses.

Course delivery sites Courses are delivered to your home.

Media Courses are delivered via television, videotapes, World Wide Web, e-mail. Students and teachers may meet in person or interact via telephone, e-mail, World Wide Web. The following equipment may be required: television, videocassette player, computer, modem, Internet access, e-mail.

Restrictions Programs are available worldwide. Enrollment is open to anyone.

Services Distance learners have access to library services, tutoring at a distance.

Credit-earning options Students may transfer credits from another institution or may earn credits through examinations, military training.

Typical costs Mandatory fees of $11 per unit for in-state residents. Mandatory fees of $11 per unit for in-state residents. Tuition of $33 per unit for out-of-state residents. Financial aid is available to distance learners.

Registration Students may register by mail, telephone, in person.

Contact Kathleen Moore, Coordinator, Victor Valley College, Instructional Media Services, Victorville, CA 92392. *Telephone:* 760-245-4271 Ext. 424. *Fax:* 760-245-4373. *E-mail:* kmoore@victor.cc.ca.us.

DEGREES AND AWARDS

Distance programs offered do not lead to a degree or other formal award.

COURSE SUBJECT AREAS OFFERED OUTSIDE OF DEGREE PROGRAMS

Undergraduate: Anthropology; biology; business; business administration and management; computer and information sciences; developmental and child psychology; history; philosophy and religion; physical sciences; political science; psychology

VILLANOVA UNIVERSITY

Villanova, Pennsylvania

Division of Par-time Studies/Summer Sessions
www.parttime.villanova.edu

Villanova University, founded in 1842, is an independent, religious, comprehensive institution. It is accredited by the Middle States Association of Colleges and Schools. In 1999–2000, it offered 20 courses at a distance.

Course delivery sites Courses are delivered to your home.

Media Courses are delivered via videotapes, World Wide Web. Students and teachers may interact via telephone, e-mail, World Wide Web. The following equipment may be required: computer, modem, Internet access, e-mail.

Restrictions Programs are available worldwide. Enrollment is restricted to individuals meeting certain criteria.

Services Distance learners have access to the campus computer network, e-mail services, academic advising at a distance.

Credit-earning options Students may transfer credits from another institution.

Typical costs *Undergraduate:* Tuition of $300 per credit hour. *Graduate:* Tuition of $415 per credit hour. Financial aid is available to distance learners.

Registration Students may register by mail, fax, e-mail, World Wide Web, in person.

Contact James R. Johnson, Director, Summer Sessions, Villanova University, Villanova, PA 19085. *Telephone:* 610-519-4300. *Fax:* 610-517-7910.

DEGREES AND AWARDS

Distance programs offered do not lead to a degree or other formal award.

COURSE SUBJECT AREAS OFFERED OUTSIDE OF DEGREE PROGRAMS

Undergraduate: Business; communications; nursing; philosophy and religion; psychology

VINCENNES UNIVERSITY

Vincennes, Indiana

Distance Education/Degree Completion
www.vinu.edu

Vincennes University, founded in 1801, is a state-supported, two-year college. It is accredited by the North Central Association of Colleges and Schools. It first offered distance learning courses in 1989. In 1999–2000, it offered 90 courses at a distance. In fall 1999, there were 527 students enrolled in distance learning courses.

Course delivery sites Courses are delivered to your home, your workplace, military bases, 3 off-campus centers in Elkhart, Indianapolis, Jasper.

Media Courses are delivered via television, videotapes, interactive television, audiotapes, computer software, World Wide Web, e-mail, print. Students and teachers may meet in person or interact via mail, telephone, fax, e-mail, interactive television, World Wide Web. The following equipment may be required: television, videocassette player, computer, modem, Internet access, e-mail.

Restrictions Television-based courses are limited to within the state; other courses are available worldwide. Enrollment is restricted to individuals meeting certain criteria.

Services Distance learners have access to library services, academic advising, career placement assistance, bookstore at a distance.

Credit-earning options Students may transfer credits from another institution or may earn credits through examinations, portfolio assessment, military training.

Typical costs Tuition of $83.35 per credit plus mandatory fees of $20 per course. Financial aid is available to distance learners.

Registration Students may register by mail, fax, telephone, in person.

Contact Vernon E. Houchins, Director, Vincennes University, 1002 North 1st Street, Vincennes, IN 47591. *Telephone:* 812-888-5048. *Fax:* 812-888-2054. *E-mail:* disted@indian.vinu.edu.

DEGREES AND AWARDS

Undergraduate Certificate(s) Community Rehabilitation, General Studies, Office Software Specialist

AAS Behavioral Sciences, Business Studies, General Studies, Law Enforcement Studies, Technology Apprenticeship

AS Behavioral Sciences, Business Administration, Business Studies (service area differs from that of the overall institution), Fire Science (service area differs from that of the overall institution), General Studies (service area differs from that of the overall institution), General Studies Surgical Technology Degree Completion, Health Information Management, Law Enforcement Studies (service area differs from that of the overall institution), Recreation Management-Therapeutic Option (service area differs from that of the overall institution), Surgical Technology (certain restrictions apply; service area differs from that of the overall institution), Technology Apprenticeship (certain restrictions apply; service area differs from that of the overall institution)

COURSE SUBJECT AREAS OFFERED OUTSIDE OF DEGREE PROGRAMS

Undergraduate: Accounting; administrative and secretarial services; American literature; business administration and management; chemistry; computer and information sciences; corrections; creative writing; criminal justice; developmental and child psychology; earth science; economics; English composition; fire science; geology; health and physical education/fitness; health professions and related sciences; history; liberal arts, general studies, and humanities; marketing; mathematics; political science; protective services; psychology; social work; sociology

See full description on page 540.

VIRGINIA COMMONWEALTH UNIVERSITY

Richmond, Virginia

Office of Academic Technology
www.wcb.vcu.edu/

Virginia Commonwealth University, founded in 1838, is a state-supported university. It is accredited by the Southern Association of Colleges and Schools. It first offered distance learning courses in 1988.

Course delivery sites Courses are delivered to your home, your workplace, military bases, off-campus center(s) in Abingdon.

Media Courses are delivered via videoconferencing, computer software, World Wide Web, e-mail. Students and teachers may meet in person or interact via videoconferencing, audioconferencing, mail, telephone, fax, e-mail, World Wide Web. The following equipment may be required: computer, modem, Internet access, e-mail.

Restrictions Programs are available worldwide. Enrollment is open to anyone.

Services Distance learners have access to library services, the campus computer network, e-mail services, bookstore at a distance.

Credit-earning options Students may transfer credits from another institution or may earn credits through examinations.

Typical costs *Undergraduate:* Tuition of $130 per credit hour plus mandatory fees of $2 per credit hour. *Graduate:* Tuition of $218 per credit hour plus mandatory fees of $2 per credit hour. Costs may vary.

Registration Students may register by mail, fax, World Wide Web, in person.

Contact Sonja Moore, Director of Distance Education, Virginia Commonwealth University, Ritter-Hickok House Room 306, 821 West Franklin Street, Richmond, VA 23284-2041. *Telephone:* 804-828-8470. *Fax:* 804-828-8172. *E-mail:* smoore@atlas.vcu.edu.

DEGREES AND AWARDS

MSHA Health Administration (certain restrictions apply; some on-campus requirements)

PhD Health Professions and Related Sciences (service area differs from that of the overall institution; some on-campus requirements)

COURSE SUBJECT AREAS OFFERED OUTSIDE OF DEGREE PROGRAMS

Undergraduate: Business; European languages and literatures; nursing; philosophy and religion

Graduate: Business; criminal justice; European languages and literatures; gerontology; health and physical education/fitness; health services administration; nursing; social work; special education

Noncredit: Business

Special note

The Executive Program is an innovative 22-month course of study that leads to the degree of Master of Science Health Administration (MSHA). The course of study can be completed by individuals residing anywhere and working full-time in health care. It is a distance learning program accomplished mainly over the World Wide Web, with 6 one-week on-campus sessions over a 22-month period of study. The program is designed for self-motivated, experienced professionals who are seeking graduate education in management for continued career advancement. The program is offered by the Department of Health Administration in the School of Allied Health Professions at Virginia Commonwealth University (VCU), on the Medical College of Virginia (MCV) campus in Richmond. To be considered for admission, an applicant must hold a baccalaureate degree from an institution of higher learning recognized by VCU and have at least a 2.75 grade point average (GPA) for all undergraduate work completed. Applicants with less than a 2.75 undergraduate GPA who have exceptional work experience will be considered for admission on provisional status. The applicant must also submit scores on a standardized aptitude test for graduate studies. Applicants holding professional degrees (e.g., MD, DDS, JD, and PharmD) may have testing requirements waived upon petition to the graduate dean. Applicants should have at least 5 years of increasingly responsible work experience. The specific experience profile depends upon an individual's particular profession or occupation. A resume should accurately and completely describe an applicant's accomplishments. No specific prerequisite course work is required for application to the program. Upon acceptance, associates complete independent study modules in 3 areas: microeconomics, accounting, and quantitative analysis. For more information, prospective students can visit the Web site (http://www.had.vcu.edu) or can call 804-828-0719.

See full description on page 676.

VIRGINIA POLYTECHNIC INSTITUTE AND STATE UNIVERSITY

Blacksburg, Virginia

Institute of Distance and Distributed Learning
www.iddl.vt.edu

Virginia Polytechnic Institute and State University, founded in 1872, is a state-supported university. It is accredited by the Southern Association of Colleges and Schools. It first offered distance learning courses in 1983. In 1999–2000, it offered 166 courses at a distance. In fall 1999, there were 2,218 students enrolled in distance learning courses.

Course delivery sites Courses are delivered to your home, your workplace, military bases, high schools, Central Virginia Community College (Lynchburg), Dabney S. Lancaster Community College (Clifton Forge), J. Sargeant Reynolds Community College (Richmond), Mary Washington College (Fredericksburg), Old Dominion University (Norfolk), Shenandoah University (Winchester), University of Virginia (Charlottesville), Virginia Commonwealth University (Richmond), 6 off-campus centers in Abingdon, Falls Church, Hampton, Roanoke, South Boston, Virginia Beach.

Media Courses are delivered via television, videotapes, videoconferencing, interactive television, computer software, CD-ROM, computer conferencing, World Wide Web, e-mail. Students and teachers may meet in person or interact via videoconferencing, audioconferencing, mail, telephone, fax, e-mail, interactive television, World Wide Web. The following equipment may be required: computer, modem, Internet access, e-mail.

Restrictions Interactive videoconferencing courses and programs are available primarily at in-state sites; online courses and programs are available worldwide. Enrollment is open to anyone.

Services Distance learners have access to library services, the campus computer network, e-mail services, academic advising, tutoring, career placement assistance, bookstore at a distance.

Credit-earning options Students may transfer credits from another institution.

Typical costs *Undergraduate:* Tuition of $456.25 per course for in-state residents. Tuition of $1483.75 per course for out-of-state residents. *Graduate:* Tuition of $771 per course for in-state residents. Tuition of $1248 per course for out-of-state residents. Financial aid is available to distance learners.

Registration Students may register by mail, fax, World Wide Web, in person.

Contact Cate Mowrey, Media Relations Specialist, Virginia Polytechnic Institute and State University, Institute for Distance and Distributed Learning, 101 Henderson Hall, Blacksburg, VA 24162. *Telephone:* 540-231-9584. *Fax:* 540-231-2079. *E-mail:* catem@vt.edu.

DEGREES AND AWARDS

MA Health and Physical Education (some on-campus requirements), Health Promotion, Instructional Technology (certain restrictions apply)

MBA Business Administration

MS Aerospace Engineering (certain restrictions apply), Civil Engineering (certain restrictions apply), Computer Engineering (certain restrictions apply), Electrical Engineering (certain restrictions apply), Industrial Engineering (certain restrictions apply), Materials Science and Engineering (certain restrictions apply), Ocean Engineering (certain restrictions apply), Political Science, Systems Engineering (certain restrictions apply)

COURSE SUBJECT AREAS OFFERED OUTSIDE OF DEGREE PROGRAMS

Undergraduate: African-American studies; agriculture; algebra; American (U.S.) history; American literature; architecture; art history and criticism; biology; chemical engineering; chemistry; civil engineering; communications; comparative literature; creative writing; economics; electrical engineering; engineering/industrial management; environmental engineering; finance; geography; health and physical education/fitness; individual and family development studies; industrial engineering; marketing; mechanical engineering; medieval/renaissance studies; microbiology; philosophy and religion; political science; sociology; Spanish language and literature; technical writing; women's studies

Graduate: Accounting; aerospace, aeronautical engineering; architecture; business administration and management; civil engineering; curriculum and instruction; economics; education administration; electrical engineering; engineering/industrial management; environmental engineering; health and physical education/fitness; hospitality services management; individual and family development studies; industrial engineering; information sciences and systems; instructional media; management information systems; mechanical engineering; organizational behavior studies; political science; public administration and services; public policy analysis; Spanish language and literature; statistics; student counseling; teacher education; women's studies

Noncredit: Continuing education

See full descriptions on pages 676 and 814.

VIRGINIA WESTERN COMMUNITY COLLEGE

Roanoke, Virginia

Distance Learning
www.vw.cc.va.us/

Virginia Western Community College, founded in 1966, is a state-supported, two-year college. It is accredited by the Southern Association of Colleges and Schools. In 1999–2000, it offered 20 courses at a distance. In fall 1999, there were 950 students enrolled in distance learning courses.

Course delivery sites Courses are delivered to your home, your workplace, military bases, high schools.

Media Courses are delivered via television, videotapes, interactive television, audiotapes, computer software, computer conferencing, e-mail, print. Students and teachers may meet in person or interact via audioconferencing, mail, telephone, e-mail, interactive television. The following equipment may be required: television, videocassette player, computer, Internet access, e-mail.

Restrictions Programs are available to in-state students only. Enrollment is restricted to individuals meeting certain criteria.

Services Distance learners have access to library services, tutoring, bookstore at a distance.

Typical costs Tuition of $40 per credit hour for in-state residents. Tuition of $170 per credit hour for out-of-state residents. Financial aid is available to distance learners.

Registration Students may register by mail, fax, e-mail, World Wide Web, in person.

Contact Dr. David Hanson, Director of Instructional Services, Virginia Western Community College, PO Box 24038, Roanoke, VA 24038. *Telephone:* 540-857-7942. *Fax:* 540-857-7544. *E-mail:* dhanson@vw.cc.va.us.

DEGREES AND AWARDS

Distance programs offered do not lead to a degree or other formal award.

COURSE SUBJECT AREAS OFFERED OUTSIDE OF DEGREE PROGRAMS

Undergraduate: Abnormal psychology; accounting; American (U.S.) history; American literature; art history and criticism; biology; business; community health services; computer and information sciences; economics; English composition; European history; marketing; mathematics; music; psychology; sociology; statistics

VOLUNTEER STATE COMMUNITY COLLEGE

Gallatin, Tennessee

Distance Learning/College at Home
www.vscc.cc.tn.us

Volunteer State Community College, founded in 1970, is a state-supported, two-year college. It is accredited by the Southern Association of Colleges and Schools. It first offered distance learning courses in 1991. In 1999–2000, it offered 42 courses at a distance. In fall 1999, there were 2,350 students enrolled in distance learning courses.

Course delivery sites Courses are delivered to your home, your workplace, high schools, 2 off-campus centers in Livingston, Nashville.

Media Courses are delivered via videotapes, videoconferencing, interactive television, audiotapes, computer software, CD-ROM, computer conferencing, World Wide Web, e-mail. Students and teachers may meet in person or interact via videoconferencing, audioconferencing, mail, telephone, fax, e-mail, interactive television, World Wide Web. The following equipment may be required: television, videocassette player, computer, modem, Internet access, e-mail.

Restrictions Courses are available to U.S. and Canadian students only. Enrollment is open to anyone.

Services Distance learners have access to library services, the campus computer network, e-mail services, academic advising, tutoring, career placement assistance at a distance.

Credit-earning options Students may transfer credits from another institution or may earn credits through examinations, portfolio assessment, military training, business training.

Typical costs Tuition of $497 per semester for in-state residents. Tuition of $1463 per semester for out-of-state residents. *Noncredit courses:* $100 per course. Financial aid is available to distance learners.

Registration Students may register by mail, fax, telephone, e-mail, World Wide Web, in person.

Contact Nan Matson, College at Home, Volunteer State Community College, 1480 Nashville Pike, Gallatin, TN 37066. *Telephone:* 615-452-8600 Ext. 3409. *Fax:* 615-230-3546. *E-mail:* nmatson@vscc.cc.tn.us.

DEGREES AND AWARDS

Distance programs offered do not lead to a degree or other formal award.

COURSE SUBJECT AREAS OFFERED OUTSIDE OF DEGREE PROGRAMS

Undergraduate: Accounting; administrative and secretarial services; astronomy and astrophysics; business; business administration and management; communications; computer and information sciences; creative writing; economics; educational psychology; English composition; English language and literature; European languages and literatures; fine arts; geology; health and physical education/fitness; health professions and related sciences; history; industrial psychology; liberal arts, general studies, and humanities; library and information studies; marketing; mathematics; music; philosophy and religion; physics; public administration and services; social psychology; social work; sociology

See full description on page 676.

WAKE TECHNICAL COMMUNITY COLLEGE

Raleigh, North Carolina
www.wake.tec.nc.us/dist_ed/index.html

Wake Technical Community College, founded in 1958, is a state and locally supported, two-year college. It is accredited by the Southern

Association of Colleges and Schools. It first offered distance learning courses in 1986. In 1999–2000, it offered 18 courses at a distance. In fall 1999, there were 750 students enrolled in distance learning courses.

Course delivery sites Courses are delivered to your home, your workplace.

Media Courses are delivered via videotapes, computer software, World Wide Web, e-mail. Students and teachers may meet in person or interact via mail, telephone, e-mail, World Wide Web. The following equipment may be required: television, videocassette player, computer, Internet access, e-mail.

Restrictions Programs are available to in-state students only. Enrollment is open to anyone.

Services Distance learners have access to library services, the campus computer network, academic advising, bookstore at a distance.

Credit-earning options Students may transfer credits from another institution or may earn credits through examinations.

Typical costs Tuition of $374.50 per semester plus mandatory fees of $8 per semester for in-state residents. Tuition of $2376.50 per semester plus mandatory fees of $8 per semester for out-of-state residents. Average cost for a noncredit course ranges between $50 and $99. *Noncredit courses:* $35 per course. Financial aid is available to distance learners.

Registration Students may register by mail, telephone, in person.

Contact Janet Hobbs, Dean, Wake Technical Community College. *Telephone:* 919-662-3431. *Fax:* 919-779-3360. *E-mail:* jhhobbs@mail. wake.tec.nc.us.

DEGREES AND AWARDS

Distance programs offered do not lead to a degree or other formal award.

COURSE SUBJECT AREAS OFFERED OUTSIDE OF DEGREE PROGRAMS

Undergraduate: Business; business administration and management; computer and information sciences; computer programming; database management; English composition; history; psychology; social psychology; social sciences

See full description on page 676.

WALDEN UNIVERSITY

Minneapolis, Minnesota
www.waldenu.edu

Walden University is a proprietary, graduate institution. It is accredited by the North Central Association of Colleges and Schools. It first offered distance learning courses in 1970. In 1999–2000, it offered 320 courses at a distance. In fall 1999, there were 1,476 students enrolled in distance learning courses.

Course delivery sites Courses are delivered to your home, your workplace, military bases, 5 off-campus centers in Minneapolis, Bonita Springs (FL), Fort Dix (NJ), Phoenix (AZ), Washington (DC).

Media Courses are delivered via computer conferencing, World Wide Web, e-mail, print. Students and teachers may meet in person or interact via audioconferencing, mail, telephone, fax, e-mail, World Wide Web. The following equipment may be required: computer, modem, Internet access, e-mail.

Restrictions Programs are available worldwide. Enrollment is open to anyone.

Services Distance learners have access to library services, the campus computer network, e-mail services, academic advising, tutoring, bookstore at a distance.

Credit-earning options Students may transfer credits from another institution.

Typical costs Tuition for the Master of Science in education program is $230 per quarter credit. Tuition for the Doctorate and Master of Science in psychology program is $305 per quarter credit. For all other Doctorate degree programs, tuition is $3175 per quarter. Mandatory fees total $1200. *Noncredit courses:* $75 per course. Costs may vary. Financial aid is available to distance learners.

Registration Students may register by mail, e-mail, World Wide Web.

Contact Office of Student Recruitment, Walden University, 24311 Walden Center Drive, Bonita Springs, FL 34134. *Telephone:* 800-444-6795 Ext. 5000. *Fax:* 941-498-4266. *E-mail:* request@waldenu.edu.

DEGREES AND AWARDS

MS Education, Psychology

PhD Applied Management and Decision Sciences (some on-campus requirements), Education (some on-campus requirements), Health Services (some on-campus requirements), Human Services (some on-campus requirements), Professional Psychology (some on-campus requirements)

COURSE SUBJECT AREAS OFFERED OUTSIDE OF DEGREE PROGRAMS

Graduate: Adult education; business; business administration and management; community health services; counseling psychology; criminal justice; developmental and child psychology; education; education administration; educational psychology; finance; gerontology; health professions and related sciences; health services administration; human resources management; industrial psychology; management information systems; psychology; public administration and services; public policy analysis; school psychology; social psychology; social sciences; social work; teacher education

See full description on page 816.

WALLA WALLA COMMUNITY COLLEGE

Walla Walla, Washington
Distance Learning Department
www.wallawalla.cc/dl.html

Walla Walla Community College, founded in 1967, is a state-supported, two-year college. It is accredited by the Northwest Association of Schools and Colleges. In 1999–2000, it offered 51 courses at a distance. In fall 1999, there were 290 students enrolled in distance learning courses.

Course delivery sites Courses are delivered to your home, high schools, Big Bend Community College (Moses Lake), off-campus center(s) in Clarkston.

Media Courses are delivered via videotapes, audiotapes, computer software, CD-ROM, World Wide Web, e-mail, print. Students and teachers may meet in person or interact via mail, telephone, fax, e-mail, World Wide Web. The following equipment may be required: television, videocassette player, computer, modem, Internet access, e-mail.

Restrictions Courses largely available within Washington, Oregon, and Idaho; worldwide for turf management program. Enrollment is open to anyone.

Services Distance learners have access to library services, the campus computer network, e-mail services, academic advising, career placement assistance, bookstore at a distance.

Credit-earning options Students may transfer credits from another institution or may earn credits through examinations.

Typical costs Undergraduate tuition per credit is $56.80 for up to 5 credits; after 5 credits $86.50 per credit. Mandatory fees range between $40 and $75 per quarter. Costs may vary. Financial aid is available to distance learners.

Registration Students may register by mail, fax, telephone, World Wide Web, in person.

Contact Dr. Jim Willis, Director, Distance Learning, Walla Walla Community College, 500 Tausick Way, Walla Walla, WA 99362-9267. *Telephone:* 509-527-4324. *Fax:* 509-527-4480. *E-mail:* jim.willis@po.ww.cc.wa.us.

DEGREES AND AWARDS

AA Transfer Degree (some on-campus requirements)
AAAS Turf Management
AS Transfer Degree (some on-campus requirements)

COURSE SUBJECT AREAS OFFERED OUTSIDE OF DEGREE PROGRAMS

Undergraduate: Agriculture; business; computer and information sciences; English language and literature; European languages and literatures; history; home economics and family studies; liberal arts, general studies, and humanities; mathematics; physical sciences; psychology; social sciences; visual and performing arts

WALSH COLLEGE OF ACCOUNTANCY AND BUSINESS ADMINISTRATION

Troy, Michigan
www.walshcollege.edu

Walsh College of Accountancy and Business Administration, founded in 1922, is an independent, nonprofit, upper-level institution. It is accredited by the North Central Association of Colleges and Schools. In 1999–2000, it offered 20 courses at a distance. In fall 1999, there were 346 students enrolled in distance learning courses.
Course delivery sites Courses are delivered to your home, your workplace.
Media Courses are delivered via World Wide Web, e-mail. Students and teachers may meet in person or interact via e-mail, World Wide Web. The following equipment may be required: computer, modem, Internet access, e-mail.
Restrictions Programs are available worldwide. Enrollment is restricted to individuals meeting certain criteria.
Services Distance learners have access to library services, e-mail services at a distance.
Credit-earning options Students may earn credits through examinations.
Typical costs *Undergraduate:* Tuition of $205 per semester credit. *Graduate:* Tuition of $283 per semester credit. Registration fee is $75. *Noncredit courses:* $680 per course. Financial aid is available to distance learners.
Registration Students may register by mail, fax, World Wide Web, in person.
Contact Diane Zalapi, Director of New Student Recruitment and Admissions, Walsh College of Accountancy and Business Administration, PO Box 7006, Troy, MI 48007-7006. *Telephone:* 248-689-8282. *Fax:* 248-689-0938. *E-mail:* admissions@walshcol.edu.

DEGREES AND AWARDS

Undergraduate Certificate(s) Interactive Marketing (certain restrictions apply)

COURSE SUBJECT AREAS OFFERED OUTSIDE OF DEGREE PROGRAMS

Undergraduate: Marketing
Graduate: Business administration and management; marketing
Noncredit: Marketing

WALTERS STATE COMMUNITY COLLEGE

Morristown, Tennessee
Evening and Distance Education Office
www.wscc.cc.tn.us

Walters State Community College, founded in 1970, is a state-supported, two-year college. It is accredited by the Southern Association of Colleges and Schools. It first offered distance learning courses in 1988. In 1999–2000, it offered 75 courses at a distance. In fall 1999, there were 881 students enrolled in distance learning courses.
Course delivery sites Courses are delivered to your home, your workplace, 3 off-campus centers in Greeneville, New Tazewell, Sevierville.
Media Courses are delivered via television, videotapes, interactive television, World Wide Web, e-mail. Students and teachers may interact via videoconferencing, mail, telephone, fax, e-mail, interactive television, World Wide Web. The following equipment may be required: television, videocassette player, computer, modem, Internet access, e-mail.
Restrictions Programs are available to local area students. Enrollment is restricted to individuals meeting certain criteria.
Services Distance learners have access to library services, the campus computer network, e-mail services, academic advising, tutoring at a distance.
Credit-earning options Students may transfer credits from another institution or may earn credits through examinations, military training.
Typical costs Tuition of $53 per credit hour plus mandatory fees of $13 per semester for in-state residents. Tuition of $210 per credit hour plus mandatory fees of $13 per semester for out-of-state residents. Financial aid is available to distance learners.
Registration Students may register by mail, telephone, in person.
Contact Dave Roberts, Dean, Walters State Community College, 500 South Davy Crockett Parkway, Morristown, TN 37813-6899. *Telephone:* 423-585-6899. *Fax:* 423-585-6853. *E-mail:* dave.roberts@wscc.cc.tn.us.

DEGREES AND AWARDS

Distance programs offered do not lead to a degree or other formal award.

COURSE SUBJECT AREAS OFFERED OUTSIDE OF DEGREE PROGRAMS

Undergraduate: American literature; anthropology; art history and criticism; astronomy and astrophysics; business administration and management; child care and development; creative writing; developmental and child psychology; economics; educational psychology; English composition; English literature; European history; geology; gerontology; history; hospitality services management; human resources management; liberal arts, general studies, and humanities; marketing; mathematics; music; physical therapy; protective services; real estate; social psychology; social work; sociology; Spanish language and literature

WARREN COUNTY COMMUNITY COLLEGE

Washington, New Jersey

Warren County Community College, founded in 1981, is a state and locally supported, two-year college. It is accredited by the Middle States Association of Colleges and Schools.
Contact Warren County Community College, 475 Route 57 West, Washington, NJ 07882-4343. *Telephone:* 908-689-1090.

See full description on page 600.

WASHBURN UNIVERSITY OF TOPEKA

Topeka, Kansas

Division of Continuing Education
www.washburn.edu/PLAN

Washburn University of Topeka, founded in 1865, is a city-supported, comprehensive institution. It is accredited by the North Central Association of Colleges and Schools. In 1999–2000, it offered 40 courses at a distance. In fall 1999, there were 500 students enrolled in distance learning courses.

Course delivery sites Courses are delivered to your home, Johnson County Community College (Overland Park), Kansas City Kansas Community College (Kansas City).

Media Courses are delivered via videotapes, videoconferencing, interactive television, audiotapes, computer software, CD-ROM, World Wide Web, e-mail, print. Students and teachers may interact via videoconferencing, telephone, fax, e-mail, interactive television. The following equipment may be required: television, computer, Internet access.

Restrictions 2+2 programs are available in the Kansas City and Topeka areas and Web courses are available worldwide. Enrollment is restricted to individuals meeting certain criteria.

Services Distance learners have access to library services, the campus computer network, e-mail services, academic advising, tutoring, career placement assistance, bookstore at a distance.

Credit-earning options Students may transfer credits from another institution or may earn credits through examinations, military training.

Typical costs *Undergraduate:* Tuition of $140 per credit hour. *Graduate:* Tuition of $175 per credit hour. Application fee is $20. Costs may vary. Financial aid is available to distance learners.

Registration Students may register by mail, telephone, in person.

Contact Dr. Tim Peterson, Director, Division of Continuing Education, Washburn University of Topeka, 1700 College Avenue, Topeka, KS 66621. *Telephone:* 785-231-1010 Ext. 1399. *Fax:* 785-231-1028. *E-mail:* tim@washburn.edu.

DEGREES AND AWARDS

BA Integrated Studies (some on-campus requirements)
BAS Human Services (some on-campus requirements), Technology Administration (some on-campus requirements)
BS Criminal Justice (some on-campus requirements)

COURSE SUBJECT AREAS OFFERED OUTSIDE OF DEGREE PROGRAMS

Undergraduate: Business; business administration and management; criminology; English language and literature; psychology; public administration and services; social sciences; substance abuse counseling

WASHINGTON & JEFFERSON COLLEGE

Washington, Pennsylvania

Washington & Jefferson College, founded in 1781, is an independent, nonprofit, four-year college. It is accredited by the Middle States Association of Colleges and Schools. It first offered distance learning courses in 1996. In 1999–2000, it offered 2 courses at a distance. In fall 1999, there were 8 students enrolled in distance learning courses.

Course delivery sites Courses are delivered to International University (Moscow, Russia).

Media Courses are delivered via videoconferencing, World Wide Web, e-mail, print. Students and teachers may meet in person or interact via videoconferencing, audioconferencing, mail, telephone, fax, e-mail. The following equipment may be required: computer, modem, Internet access, e-mail.

Restrictions Programs are available worldwide. Enrollment is open to anyone.

Services Distance learners have access to library services, the campus computer network, e-mail services, tutoring at a distance.

Credit-earning options Students may earn credits through examinations.

Typical costs Tuition of $1800 per course. Costs may vary.

Registration Students may register by mail, fax, in person.

Contact Dr. G. Andrew Rembert, Vice President for Academic Affairs/ Dean of the College, Washington & Jefferson College, 60 South Lincoln Street, Washington, PA 15301. *Telephone:* 724-223-6005. *Fax:* 724-223-2657. *E-mail:* grembert@washjeff.edu.

DEGREES AND AWARDS

Distance programs offered do not lead to a degree or other formal award.

COURSE SUBJECT AREAS OFFERED OUTSIDE OF DEGREE PROGRAMS

Undergraduate: Business; education

WASHINGTON STATE UNIVERSITY

Pullman, Washington

Extended Degree Programs
www.eus.wsu.edu/edp/

Washington State University, founded in 1890, is a state-supported university. It is accredited by the Northwest Association of Schools and Colleges. It first offered distance learning courses in 1992. In 1999–2000, it offered 160 courses at a distance. In fall 1999, there were 890 students enrolled in distance learning courses.

Course delivery sites Courses are delivered to your home, military bases.

Media Courses are delivered via videotapes, audiotapes, CD-ROM, World Wide Web, print. Students and teachers may interact via audioconferencing, mail, telephone, fax, e-mail, World Wide Web. The following equipment may be required: television, videocassette player, computer, Internet access.

Restrictions Programs are available worldwide. Enrollment is open to anyone.

Services Distance learners have access to library services, e-mail services, academic advising, tutoring, career placement assistance, bookstore at a distance.

Credit-earning options Students may transfer credits from another institution or may earn credits through examinations, military training.

Typical costs Tuition of $178 per credit for in-state residents. Tuition of $265 per credit for out-of-state residents. Flexible enrollment courses are $120 per credit regardless of where student resides. Costs may vary. Financial aid is available to distance learners.

Registration Students may register by mail, fax, telephone, e-mail, World Wide Web, in person.

Contact Cheri Curtis, Program Coordinator, Extended Degree Programs, Washington State University, 204 Van Doren Hall, PO Box 645220, Pullman, WA 99164-5220. *Telephone:* 800-222-4978. *Fax:* 509-335-0945. *E-mail:* curtisc@wsu.edu.

DEGREES AND AWARDS

BA Business Administration, Criminal Justice, Human Development, Social Sciences
BS General Agriculture

COURSE SUBJECT AREAS OFFERED OUTSIDE OF DEGREE PROGRAMS

Undergraduate: Accounting; American (U.S.) history; American literature; American studies; anthropology; architecture; area, ethnic, and cultural studies; Asian studies; biology; business; business administration and management; business law; child care and development; communications; conservation and natural resources; creative writing; criminal justice; developmental and child psychology; economics; English composition; English language and literature; European history; finance; fine arts; foods and nutrition studies; French language and literature; geology; history; human resources management; individual and family development studies; insurance; international business; investments and securities; liberal arts, general studies, and humanities; marketing; mathematics; philosophy and religion; political science; psychology; real estate; social psychology; social sciences; sociology; Spanish language and literature; statistics; technical writing; women's studies

See full descriptions on pages 592, 818, and 822.

WAUBONSEE COMMUNITY COLLEGE

Sugar Grove, Illinois

Center for Distance Learning
www.wcc.cc.il.us/distancelearning

Waubonsee Community College, founded in 1966, is a district-supported, two-year college. It is accredited by the North Central Association of Colleges and Schools. It first offered distance learning courses in 1988. In 1999–2000, it offered 150 courses at a distance. In fall 1999, there were 820 students enrolled in distance learning courses.

Course delivery sites Courses are delivered to your home, your workplace, high schools.

Media Courses are delivered via television, videotapes, videoconferencing, interactive television, CD-ROM, computer conferencing, World Wide Web. Students and teachers may meet in person or interact via mail, telephone, fax, e-mail, interactive television, World Wide Web. The following equipment may be required: television, videocassette player, computer, modem, Internet access, e-mail.

Restrictions Online courses are available worldwide, while other forms of distance learning courses are available statewide. Enrollment is open to anyone.

Services Distance learners have access to library services, academic advising, tutoring, career placement assistance, bookstore at a distance.

Credit-earning options Students may transfer credits from another institution or may earn credits through examinations.

Typical costs Tuition of $43 per credit hour plus mandatory fees of $30 per semester for in-state residents. Tuition of $104 per credit hour plus mandatory fees of $30 per semester for out-of-state residents. Financial aid is available to distance learners.

Registration Students may register by mail, fax, telephone, World Wide Web, in person.

Contact Christine McGuire, Program Development and Evaluation Specialist, Waubonsee Community College. *Telephone:* 630-466-7900 Ext. 2503. *E-mail:* cmcguire@mail.wcc.cc.il.us.

DEGREES AND AWARDS

Undergraduate Certificate(s) General Studies

COURSE SUBJECT AREAS OFFERED OUTSIDE OF DEGREE PROGRAMS

Undergraduate: Accounting; Asian languages and literatures; biology; business; computer and information sciences; creative writing; criminal justice; developmental and child psychology; economics; engineering; English composition; English language and literature; European languages and literatures; fine arts; health professions and related sciences; history; human resources management; law and legal studies; liberal arts, general studies, and humanities; mathematics; music; philosophy and religion; physical sciences; political science; psychology; recreation and leisure studies; sign language; social psychology; social work; sociology; special education; statistics

WAYLAND BAPTIST UNIVERSITY

Plainview, Texas
www.wbu.edu

Wayland Baptist University, founded in 1908, is an independent, religious, comprehensive institution. It is accredited by the Southern Association of Colleges and Schools. In 1999–2000, it offered 11 courses at a distance.

Course delivery sites Courses are delivered to your home, your workplace.

Media Courses are delivered via World Wide Web, e-mail. Students and teachers may interact via e-mail, World Wide Web. The following equipment may be required: Internet access, e-mail.

Restrictions Programs available within Texas, Arizona, Hawaii, Alaska, and New Mexico. Enrollment is restricted to individuals meeting certain criteria.

Typical costs *Undergraduate:* Tuition of $235 per credit hour. *Graduate:* Tuition of $245 per credit hour. There is a $50 mandatory fee for courses in management information systems. Financial aid is available to distance learners.

Contact Stan DeMerritt, Registrar, Wayland Baptist University, 1900 West 7th Street, CMB #735, Plainview, TX 79072. *Telephone:* 806-296-4706. *Fax:* 806-296-4580.

DEGREES AND AWARDS

Distance programs offered do not lead to a degree or other formal award.

COURSE SUBJECT AREAS OFFERED OUTSIDE OF DEGREE PROGRAMS

Undergraduate: Business administration and management; curriculum and instruction; instructional media; management information systems
Graduate: Management information systems

WAYNE COUNTY COMMUNITY COLLEGE DISTRICT

Detroit, Michigan

Distance Learning

Wayne County Community College District, founded in 1967, is a state and locally supported, two-year college. It is accredited by the North Central Association of Colleges and Schools. It first offered distance learning courses in 1978. In 1999–2000, it offered 74 courses at a distance. In fall 1999, there were 642 students enrolled in distance learning courses.

Course delivery sites Courses are delivered to your home, your workplace.

Media Courses are delivered via television, videotapes, interactive television, computer software, CD-ROM, World Wide Web. Students and teachers may meet in person or interact via mail, telephone, fax, e-mail, interactive television. The following equipment may be required: television, videocassette player, computer, modem, Internet access, e-mail.

Restrictions Programs are available to local area students. Enrollment is open to anyone.

Services Distance learners have access to library services, the campus computer network, e-mail services, bookstore at a distance.

Credit-earning options Students may transfer credits from another institution or may earn credits through examinations, portfolio assessment, military training.

Typical costs Tuition of $54 per credit plus mandatory fees of $2 per credit for local area residents. Tuition of $70 per credit plus mandatory fees of $2 per credit for in-state residents. Tuition of $89 per credit plus mandatory fees of $2 per credit for out-of-state residents. Students pay an additional $25 per semester in fees. Financial aid is available to distance learners.

Registration Students may register by mail, in person.

Contact Deborah Fiedler, District Director, Wayne County Community College District, 801 West Fort Street, Detroit, MI 48226. *Telephone:* 313-496-2602. *Fax:* 313-496-8718. *E-mail:* dfiedler@mail.wccc.edu.

DEGREES AND AWARDS

AA Business (some on-campus requirements)
AGS General Studies (some on-campus requirements)

COURSE SUBJECT AREAS OFFERED OUTSIDE OF DEGREE PROGRAMS

Undergraduate: Accounting; algebra; American (U.S.) history; anthropology; business; business administration and management; business law; computer and information sciences; economics; English composition; English language and literature; finance; geography; geology; health professions and related sciences; history; law and legal studies; liberal arts, general studies, and humanities; marketing; mathematics; philosophy and religion; physical sciences; physiology; political science; psychology; sociology

WAYNE STATE COLLEGE

Wayne, Nebraska

Regional Education and Distance Learning
www.wsc.edu

Wayne State College, founded in 1910, is a state-supported, comprehensive institution. It is accredited by the North Central Association of Colleges and Schools. In 1999–2000, it offered 15 courses at a distance. In fall 1999, there were 50 students enrolled in distance learning courses.

Course delivery sites Courses are delivered to high schools, Chadron State College (Chadron), Peru State College (Peru).

Media Courses are delivered via television, interactive television, World Wide Web, e-mail. Students and teachers may meet in person or interact via videoconferencing, audioconferencing, e-mail, World Wide Web.

Restrictions Program available within Northeast Nebraska. Enrollment is restricted to individuals meeting certain criteria.

Services Distance learners have access to library services, the campus computer network, e-mail services, career placement assistance, bookstore at a distance.

Credit-earning options Students may earn credits through examinations, portfolio assessment.

Typical costs *Undergraduate:* Tuition of $62.50 per credit hour plus mandatory fees of $13 per credit hour for in-state residents. Tuition of $125 per credit hour plus mandatory fees of $13 per credit hour for out-of-state residents. *Graduate:* Tuition of $78.25 per credit hour plus mandatory fees of $13 per credit hour for in-state residents. Tuition of $156.50 per credit hour plus mandatory fees of $13 per credit hour for out-of-state residents. Financial aid is available to distance learners.

Registration Students may register by mail, telephone, e-mail, World Wide Web, in person.

Contact Cena Johnson, Assistant Director of Regional Education, Wayne State College, 1111 Main Street, Wayne, NE 68787. *Telephone:* 402-375-7217. *Fax:* 402-375-7204. *E-mail:* cjohnson@wscgate.wsc.edu.

DEGREES AND AWARDS

Distance programs offered do not lead to a degree or other formal award.

COURSE SUBJECT AREAS OFFERED OUTSIDE OF DEGREE PROGRAMS

Undergraduate: Business
Graduate: Business; education

WEBER STATE UNIVERSITY

Ogden, Utah

Distance Learning and Independent Study
catsis.weber.edu/ce/default.html

Weber State University, founded in 1889, is a state-supported, comprehensive institution. It is accredited by the Northwest Association of Schools and Colleges. It first offered distance learning courses in 1980. In 1999–2000, it offered 320 courses at a distance. In fall 1999, there were 2,055 students enrolled in distance learning courses.

Course delivery sites Courses are delivered to your home, your workplace.

Media Courses are delivered via videotapes, audiotapes, computer software, CD-ROM, World Wide Web, e-mail, print. Students and teachers may meet in person or interact via mail, telephone, fax, e-mail, World Wide Web. The following equipment may be required: computer, modem, Internet access, e-mail.

Restrictions Programs are available worldwide. Enrollment is open to anyone.

Services Distance learners have access to library services, the campus computer network, e-mail services, academic advising, tutoring, career placement assistance, bookstore at a distance.

Credit-earning options Students may transfer credits from another institution or may earn credits through examinations, military training, business training.

Typical costs Tuition of $95 per credit hour. Contact the school for information. Costs may vary. Financial aid is available to distance learners.

Registration Students may register by mail, fax, telephone, e-mail, World Wide Web, in person.

Contact Distance Learning Customer Services, Weber State University, 4005 University Circle, Ogden, UT 84408-4005. *Telephone:* 801-626-6785. *Fax:* 801-626-8035. *E-mail:* dist-learn@weber.edu.

DEGREES AND AWARDS

Undergraduate Certificate(s) Nuclear Medicine, Radiation Therapy, Radiological Sciences
AAS Respiratory Therapy
AS Criminal Justice, General Studies, Respiratory Therapy
BS Advanced Respiratory Therapy, Clinical Laboratory Sciences, Health Administrative Services, Radiological Sciences

COURSE SUBJECT AREAS OFFERED OUTSIDE OF DEGREE PROGRAMS

Undergraduate: Abnormal psychology; accounting; algebra; American (U.S.) history; anthropology; art history and criticism; botany; business; business administration and management; calculus; chemistry; child care and development; cognitive psychology; communications; computer and information sciences; construction; corrections; counseling psychology; creative writing; criminal justice; design; drama and theater; economics; electrical engineering; English composition; English language and literature; English literature; European history; finance; foods and nutrition studies; French language and literature; geography; geology; gerontology; health and physical education/fitness; health professions and related sciences; health services administration; history; home economics and family studies; interior design; management information systems; marketing; mass media; mathematics; meteorology; music; nursing; organizational behavior studies; philosophy and religion; political science; psychology; social psychology; social work; sociology; statistics

See full description on page 820.

WEST CHESTER UNIVERSITY OF PENNSYLVANIA

West Chester, Pennsylvania

The Virtual University
vu.sshe.edu

West Chester University of Pennsylvania, founded in 1871, is a state-supported, comprehensive institution. It is accredited by the Middle States Association of Colleges and Schools. In 1999–2000, it offered 34 courses at a distance.

Course delivery sites Courses are delivered to your home, your workplace, other colleges.

Media Courses are delivered via videoconferencing, interactive television, computer software, computer conferencing, World Wide Web, e-mail. Students and teachers may meet in person or interact via mail, telephone, fax, e-mail, interactive television, World Wide Web. The following equipment may be required: computer, modem, Internet access, e-mail.

Restrictions Programs are available to in-state students only. Enrollment is open to anyone.

Services Distance learners have access to library services, the campus computer network, e-mail services, academic advising, career placement assistance at a distance.

Typical costs *Undergraduate:* Tuition of $150 per credit for local area residents. Tuition of $150 per credit for in-state residents. Tuition of $377 per credit for out-of-state residents. *Graduate:* Tuition of $210 per credit for local area residents. Tuition of $210 per credit for in-state residents. Tuition of $367 per credit for out-of-state residents. Costs may vary.

Registration Students may register by mail, fax, telephone, e-mail, World Wide Web, in person.

Contact Registrar's Office, West Chester University of Pennsylvania, West Chester Avenue, West Chester, PA 19383. *Telephone:* 610-436-3550. *E-mail:* registrar@wcupa.edu.

DEGREES AND AWARDS

MS Communicative Disorders (certain restrictions apply)

COURSE SUBJECT AREAS OFFERED OUTSIDE OF DEGREE PROGRAMS

Undergraduate: Biology; computer programming; mass media; psychology; sociology
Graduate: Communications; English language and literature; health professions and related sciences

WESTERN BAPTIST COLLEGE

Salem, Oregon

Management and Communication Online Program/Family Studies Online Program
www.wbc.edu/prospect/degree

Western Baptist College, founded in 1935, is an independent, religious, four-year college. It is accredited by the Northwest Association of Schools and Colleges. In fall 1999, there were 100 students enrolled in distance learning courses.

Course delivery sites Courses are delivered to your home.

Media Courses are delivered via computer software, computer conferencing, World Wide Web, e-mail, print. Students and teachers may interact via videoconferencing, audioconferencing, mail, telephone, fax, e-mail, World Wide Web. The following equipment may be required: computer, modem, Internet access, e-mail.

Restrictions Programs are available worldwide. Enrollment is restricted to individuals meeting certain criteria.

Services Distance learners have access to library services, the campus computer network, e-mail services, academic advising, bookstore at a distance.

Credit-earning options Students may transfer credits from another institution or may earn credits through examinations, portfolio assessment, military training.

Typical costs Tuition of $11,800 per degree program. There is a $100 class reservation fee. Financial aid is available to distance learners.

Registration Students may register by mail, telephone, e-mail, World Wide Web, in person.

Contact Nancy Martyn, Director, Adult Studies, Western Baptist College, 5000 Deer Park Drive South East, Salem, OR 97301. *Telephone:* 503-375-7585. *Fax:* 503-375-7583. *E-mail:* nmartyn@wbc.edu.

DEGREES AND AWARDS

BA Family Studies (certain restrictions apply; some on-campus requirements), Management and Communication (certain restrictions apply; some on-campus requirements)
BS Family Studies (certain restrictions apply; some on-campus requirements), Management and Communication (certain restrictions apply; some on-campus requirements)

WESTERN CAROLINA UNIVERSITY

Cullowhee, North Carolina

Continuing Education and Summer School
www.wcu.edu/

Western Carolina University, founded in 1889, is a state-supported, comprehensive institution. It is accredited by the Southern Association of Colleges and Schools. It first offered distance learning courses in 1982. In 1999–2000, it offered 12 courses at a distance. In fall 1999, there were 215 students enrolled in distance learning courses.

Course delivery sites Courses are delivered to your home, your workplace, Catawba Valley Community College (Hickory), McDowell Technical Community College (Marion), Tri-County Community College (Murphy), 4 off-campus centers in Franklin, Kingston, Jamaica, Mandeville, Jamaica, Montego Bay, Jamaica.

Media Courses are delivered via videoconferencing, interactive television, computer software, computer conferencing, World Wide Web, e-mail. Students and teachers may meet in person or interact via videoconferencing, telephone, e-mail, interactive television, World Wide Web. The following equipment may be required: computer, modem, Internet access, e-mail.

Restrictions Programs are available worldwide. Enrollment is restricted to individuals meeting certain criteria.

Services Distance learners have access to library services, the campus computer network, e-mail services, academic advising, bookstore at a distance.

Credit-earning options Students may transfer credits from another institution or may earn credits through examinations.

Typical costs *Undergraduate:* Tuition of $32.50 per credit hour plus mandatory fees of $3.50 per credit hour for in-state residents. Tuition of $278 per credit hour plus mandatory fees of $3.50 per credit hour for out-of-state residents. *Graduate:* Tuition of $48.25 per credit hour plus mandatory fees of $5 per credit hour for in-state residents. Tuition of $404.50 per credit hour plus mandatory fees of $5 per credit hour for out-of-state residents.

Registration Students may register by mail, e-mail, World Wide Web, in person.

Contact Oakley Winters, Dean, Continuing Education, Western Carolina University, 138 Outreach Center, Cullowhee, NC 28723. *Telephone:* 828-227-7397. *Fax:* 828-227-7115. *E-mail:* winters@wcu.edu.

DEGREES AND AWARDS

MPM Project Management (certain restrictions apply)

COURSE SUBJECT AREAS OFFERED OUTSIDE OF DEGREE PROGRAMS

Undergraduate: Child care and development; community health services; criminal justice; engineering-related technologies; information sciences and systems; teacher education

Graduate: Business administration and management; education administration; teacher education

See full description on page 676.

WESTERN CONNECTICUT STATE UNIVERSITY

Danbury, Connecticut
Online CSU
www.onlinecsu.ctstateu.edu

Western Connecticut State University, founded in 1903, is a state-supported, comprehensive institution. It is accredited by the New England Association of Schools and Colleges. In 1999–2000, it offered 10 courses at a distance. In fall 1999, there were 26 students enrolled in distance learning courses.

Course delivery sites Courses are delivered to your home.

Media Courses are delivered via World Wide Web. Students and teachers may meet in person or interact via mail, telephone, fax, e-mail, World Wide Web. The following equipment may be required: computer, modem, Internet access, e-mail.

Restrictions Programs are available nationwide. Enrollment is open to anyone.

Services Distance learners have access to library services, the campus computer network, e-mail services, academic advising, career placement assistance, bookstore at a distance.

Credit-earning options Students may transfer credits from another institution or may earn credits through examinations.

Typical costs *Undergraduate:* Tuition of $190 per credit hour plus mandatory fees of $25 per course. *Graduate:* Tuition of $190 per credit hour plus mandatory fees of $25 per course. *Noncredit courses:* $215 per course. Financial aid is available to distance learners.

Registration Students may register by World Wide Web.

Contact Peter Serniak, Director of Continuing Education, Western Connecticut State University, Danbury, CT 06810. *Telephone:* 203-837-8229. *Fax:* 203-837-8338.

DEGREES AND AWARDS

Distance programs offered do not lead to a degree or other formal award.

COURSE SUBJECT AREAS OFFERED OUTSIDE OF DEGREE PROGRAMS

Undergraduate: Area, ethnic, and cultural studies; health professions and related sciences; marketing; nursing; psychology; social sciences; statistics

Graduate: Education

See full description on page 504.

WESTERN GOVERNORS UNIVERSITY

Aurora, Colorado
www.wgu.edu

Western Governors University is an independent, nonprofit, comprehensive institution. In 1999–2000, it offered 950 courses at a distance.

Course delivery sites Courses are delivered to your home, your workplace, military bases, high schools, 40 off-campus centers in affiliated education providers.

Media Courses are delivered via videotapes, videoconferencing, audiotapes, computer software, CD-ROM, computer conferencing, World Wide Web, e-mail, print. Students and teachers may interact via videoconferencing, audioconferencing, mail, telephone, fax, e-mail, World Wide Web. The following equipment may be required: computer, modem, Internet access, e-mail.

Restrictions Programs are available nationwide. Enrollment is open to anyone.

Services Distance learners have access to library services, academic advising, tutoring, bookstore at a distance.

Typical costs *Undergraduate:* Tuition of $3250 per degree program. *Graduate:* Tuition of $3850 per degree program. There is a mandatory $100 application fee for all students. Additional costs for undergraduate students range between $2000 to $3500; for graduate students between $2500 and $3500. Noncredit courses range from $20 to $1000. Costs may vary. Financial aid is available to distance learners.

Registration Students may register by mail, fax, telephone, e-mail, World Wide Web.

Contact Wendy Gregory, Enrollment Manager, Western Governors University, 2040 East Murray Holladay Road, Suite 106, Salt Lake City, UT 84117. *Telephone:* 801-274-3280. *Fax:* 801-274-3305. *E-mail:* info@wgu.edu.

DEGREES AND AWARDS

Undergraduate Certificate(s) Electronics Manufacturing Technology (some on-campus requirements), Network Administration (some on-campus requirements), Software Applications Analysis and Integration (some on-campus requirements)

AA General Education (certain restrictions apply; some on-campus requirements)

AAS Electronics Manufacturing Technology (certain restrictions apply; some on-campus requirements), Network Administration (certain restrictions apply; some on-campus requirements), Software Applications Analysis and Integration (certain restrictions apply; some on-campus requirements)

MA Learning and Technology (certain restrictions apply; some on-campus requirements)

COURSE SUBJECT AREAS OFFERED OUTSIDE OF DEGREE PROGRAMS

Undergraduate: Accounting; algebra; American (U.S.) history; anthropology; art history and criticism; biology; business; business law; calculus;

communications; computer and information sciences; computer programming; creative writing; criminology; database management; developmental and child psychology; earth science; economics; education; electronics; engineering; English composition; English language and literature; environmental engineering; ethics; finance; French language and literature; geology; German language and literature; health services administration; marketing; mass media; microbiology; music; political science; public administration and services; religious studies; sign language; sociology; Spanish language and literature; statistics; substance abuse counseling; telecommunications; visual and performing arts
Graduate: Developmental and child psychology; education; educational research; health and physical education/fitness
Noncredit: Accounting; algebra; communications; computer and information sciences; computer programming; database management; education; marketing; telecommunications

See full description on page 822.

WESTERN ILLINOIS UNIVERSITY

Macomb, Illinois

School of Extended and Continuing Education
www.wiu.edu

Western Illinois University, founded in 1899, is a state-supported, comprehensive institution. It is accredited by the North Central Association of Colleges and Schools. It first offered distance learning courses in 1984. In 1999–2000, it offered 135 courses at a distance. In fall 1999, there were 1,286 students enrolled in distance learning courses.
Course delivery sites Courses are delivered to your home, your workplace, military bases, high schools, Black Hawk College (Moline), Carl Sandburg College (Galesburg), Highland Community College (Freeport), John Wood Community College (Quincy), Sauk Valley Community College (Dixon), Spoon River College (Canton), 2 off-campus centers in Moline, Rock Island.
Media Courses are delivered via television, videotapes, videoconferencing, audiotapes, computer software, CD-ROM, World Wide Web, e-mail, print. Students and teachers may meet in person or interact via videoconferencing, mail, telephone, fax, e-mail, World Wide Web. The following equipment may be required: television, videocassette player, computer, Internet access, e-mail.
Restrictions West Central Illinois for MBA program offered via fiber optic network. Enrollment is restricted to individuals meeting certain criteria.
Services Distance learners have access to library services, the campus computer network, e-mail services, academic advising, career placement assistance, bookstore at a distance.
Credit-earning options Students may transfer credits from another institution or may earn credits through examinations, portfolio assessment, military training, business training.
Typical costs *Undergraduate:* Tuition of $91 per semester hour. *Graduate:* Tuition of $99 per semester hour. Costs may vary. Financial aid is available to distance learners.
Registration Students may register by mail, fax, telephone, e-mail, World Wide Web, in person.
Contact Joyce E. Nielsen, Associate Dean, Western Illinois University, School of Extended and Continuing Education, 5 Horrabin Hall, Macomb, IL 61455. *Telephone:* 309-298-2496. *Fax:* 309-298-2226. *E-mail:* joyce_nielsen@ccmail.wiu.edu.

DEGREES AND AWARDS

BA General Studies (service area differs from that of the overall institution)
Graduate Certificate(s) Instructional Technology (service area differs from that of the overall institution)

MBA Business Administration (service area differs from that of the overall institution)
MS Instructional Technology and Telecommunications (service area differs from that of the overall institution)

COURSE SUBJECT AREAS OFFERED OUTSIDE OF DEGREE PROGRAMS

Undergraduate: Accounting; administrative and secretarial services; agriculture; American (U.S.) history; American literature; area, ethnic, and cultural studies; astronomy and astrophysics; biology; business; business administration and management; computer and information sciences; creative writing; economics; English language and literature; English literature; European languages and literatures; finance; fire science; fire services administration; geography; geology; health and physical education/fitness; history; home economics and family studies; human resources management; international business; liberal arts, general studies, and humanities; management information systems; marketing; microbiology; organizational behavior studies; philosophy and religion; political science; public health; real estate; sociology; Spanish language and literature; special education; teacher education; technical writing; zoology
Graduate: Accounting; administrative and secretarial services; biology; business; business administration and management; creative writing; economics; education administration; finance; instructional media; management information systems; marketing; microbiology; special education; teacher education; telecommunications; zoology

See full description on page 824.

WESTERN MICHIGAN UNIVERSITY

Kalamazoo, Michigan

Department of Distance Education

Western Michigan University, founded in 1903, is a state-supported university. It is accredited by the North Central Association of Colleges and Schools. It first offered distance learning courses in 1906. In 1999–2000, it offered 180 courses at a distance. In fall 1999, there were 1,003 students enrolled in distance learning courses.
Course delivery sites Courses are delivered to your home, your workplace, military bases, Jackson Community College (Jackson), Northwestern Michigan College (Traverse City), Oakland Community College (Bloomfield Hills), 7 off-campus centers in Battle Creek, Grand Rapids, Holland, Lansing, Muskegon, St. Joseph/ Benton Harbor, Traverse City.
Media Courses are delivered via television, videotapes, videoconferencing, interactive television, audiotapes, e-mail, print. Students and teachers may interact via videoconferencing, audioconferencing, mail, telephone, e-mail, interactive television.
Restrictions Programs are primarily available to in-state students; self-instructional courses can be taken worldwide. Enrollment is restricted to individuals meeting certain criteria.
Services Distance learners have access to library services, the campus computer network, e-mail services, academic advising, career placement assistance, bookstore at a distance.
Credit-earning options Students may transfer credits from another institution.
Typical costs Undergraduate tuition is $164 per credit hour. Graduate in-district tuition ranges between $199.62 and $221.22 per credit hour. Costs may vary. Financial aid is available to distance learners.
Registration Students may register by mail, fax, telephone, in person.
Contact Rosemary Nichols, Office Manager, Western Michigan University, Department of Distance Education, Ellsworth A-103, Kalamazoo, MI 49008-5161. *Telephone:* 616-387-4129. *Fax:* 616-387-4226. *E-mail:* rosemary.nicholas@wmich.edu.

DEGREES AND AWARDS

Distance programs offered do not lead to a degree or other formal award.

COURSE SUBJECT AREAS OFFERED OUTSIDE OF DEGREE PROGRAMS

Undergraduate: African-American studies; anthropology; biological and life sciences; chemistry; community health services; computer and information sciences; counseling psychology; economics; education; engineering/industrial management; English language and literature; geography; geology; health and physical education/fitness; history; mathematics; music; occupational therapy; philosophy and religion; political science; psychology; religious studies; social work; sociology

WESTERN MONTANA COLLEGE OF UNIVERSITY OF MONTANA

Dillon, Montana

Division of Outreach
www.wmc.edu/academics/outreach.html

Western Montana College of University of Montana, founded in 1893, is a state-supported, four-year college. It is accredited by the Northwest Association of Schools and Colleges. It first offered distance learning courses in 1989. In 1999–2000, it offered 10 courses at a distance. In fall 1999, there were 47 students enrolled in distance learning courses.

Course delivery sites Courses are delivered to your home, your workplace.

Media Courses are delivered via computer software, World Wide Web, e-mail. Students and teachers may interact via telephone, e-mail, World Wide Web. The following equipment may be required: computer, modem, Internet access, e-mail.

Restrictions Programs are available to in-state students only. Enrollment is open to anyone.

Services Distance learners have access to library services, academic advising, bookstore at a distance.

Credit-earning options Students may transfer credits from another institution.

Typical costs Undergraduate tuition ranges between $80 and $190 per credit. Costs may vary. Financial aid is available to distance learners.

Registration Students may register by mail, telephone, in person.

Contact Vickie Lansing, Program Assistant, Western Montana College of University of Montana, Division of Outreach, 710 South Atlantic Street, Campus Box 114, Dillon, MT 59725-3598. *Telephone:* 406-683-7537. *Fax:* 406-683-7809. *E-mail:* v_lansing@wmc.edu.

DEGREES AND AWARDS

Distance programs offered do not lead to a degree or other formal award.

COURSE SUBJECT AREAS OFFERED OUTSIDE OF DEGREE PROGRAMS

Undergraduate: Computer and information sciences; teacher education
Noncredit: Computer and information sciences; teacher education

WESTERN NEBRASKA COMMUNITY COLLEGE

Scottsbluff, Nebraska

Information Technology
www.wncc.net

Western Nebraska Community College, founded in 1926, is a state and locally supported, two-year college. It is accredited by the North Central Association of Colleges and Schools. It first offered distance learning courses in 1994. In 1999–2000, it offered 47 courses at a distance. In fall 1999, there were 175 students enrolled in distance learning courses.

Course delivery sites Courses are delivered to your home, high schools, Central Community College–Grand Island Campus (Grand Island), Central Community College–Hastings Campus (Hastings), 4 off-campus centers in Alliance, Scottsbluff, Sidney.

Media Courses are delivered via videotapes, videoconferencing, interactive television, audiotapes, computer software, CD-ROM, World Wide Web, e-mail, print. Students and teachers may meet in person or interact via videoconferencing, mail, telephone, fax, e-mail, interactive television, World Wide Web.

Restrictions Programs are available to in-state students only. Enrollment is open to anyone.

Services Distance learners have access to library services, e-mail services, academic advising, tutoring, career placement assistance, bookstore at a distance.

Credit-earning options Students may transfer credits from another institution or may earn credits through examinations, portfolio assessment, military training.

Typical costs Tuition of $41 per credit hour plus mandatory fees of $5 per credit hour for in-state residents. Tuition of $49 per credit hour plus mandatory fees of $5 per credit hour for out-of-state residents. *Noncredit courses:* $33 per course. Financial aid is available to distance learners.

Registration Students may register by mail, telephone, in person.

Contact Dan Doherty, Dean of Instruction, Western Nebraska Community College, 1601 East 27th Street, Scottsbluff, NE 69361. *Telephone:* 308-635-6032. *Fax:* 308-635-6176. *E-mail:* dohertyd@wncc.net.

DEGREES AND AWARDS

Distance programs offered do not lead to a degree or other formal award.

COURSE SUBJECT AREAS OFFERED OUTSIDE OF DEGREE PROGRAMS

Undergraduate: Area, ethnic, and cultural studies; business administration and management; developmental and child psychology; English composition; English language and literature; European languages and literatures; liberal arts, general studies, and humanities; mathematics; nursing; protective services; psychology; sociology

WESTERN NEVADA COMMUNITY COLLEGE

Carson City, Nevada
www.wncc.nevada.edu

Western Nevada Community College, founded in 1971, is a state-supported, two-year college. It is accredited by the Northwest Association of Schools and Colleges. In 1999–2000, it offered 37 courses at a distance. In fall 1999, there were 637 students enrolled in distance learning courses.

Course delivery sites Courses are delivered to your home, your workplace, military bases, high schools, 12 off-campus centers in Carson City, Dayton, Fallon, Fernley, Hawthorne, Lake Tahoe, Lovelock, Minden, Smith, Yerington.

Media Courses are delivered via television, videotapes, videoconferencing, audiotapes, computer software, World Wide Web, e-mail, print. Students and teachers may meet in person or interact via videoconferencing, mail, telephone, fax, e-mail, World Wide Web. The following equipment may be required: television, computer, modem, Internet access, e-mail.
Restrictions Programs are available to in-state students only. Enrollment is open to anyone.
Services Distance learners have access to library services, the campus computer network, e-mail services at a distance.
Typical costs Tuition of $45 per unit. Financial aid is available to distance learners.
Registration Students may register by telephone, World Wide Web, in person.
Contact Walter Lewis, Distance Education Technician, Western Nevada Community College, 160 Campus Way, Fallon, NV 89406. *Telephone:* 775-423-7565. *Fax:* 775-423-8029. *E-mail:* wlewis@wncc.nevada.edu.

DEGREES AND AWARDS

Distance programs offered do not lead to a degree or other formal award.

COURSE SUBJECT AREAS OFFERED OUTSIDE OF DEGREE PROGRAMS

Undergraduate: Accounting; biology; business; chemistry; early childhood education; economics; electrical engineering; English language and literature; geography; individual and family development studies; management; mathematics; mechanical engineering; music; nursing; physics; psychology; sociology; Spanish language and literature

WESTERN OKLAHOMA STATE COLLEGE

Altus, Oklahoma
Information Services
www.western.cc.ok.us

Western Oklahoma State College, founded in 1926, is a state-supported, two-year college. It is accredited by the North Central Association of Colleges and Schools. It first offered distance learning courses in 1976. In 1999–2000, it offered 40 courses at a distance. In fall 1999, there were 100 students enrolled in distance learning courses.
Course delivery sites Courses are delivered to your home, military bases, high schools, Cameron University (Lawton), Southwestern Oklahoma State University (Weatherford).
Media Courses are delivered via videotapes, videoconferencing, print. Students and teachers may interact via videoconferencing, audioconferencing, mail, telephone, fax, e-mail, World Wide Web. The following equipment may be required: television, videocassette player, computer, modem, Internet access, e-mail.
Restrictions Programs are available worldwide. Enrollment is open to anyone.
Services Distance learners have access to library services, bookstore at a distance.
Credit-earning options Students may transfer credits from another institution or may earn credits through examinations, military training.
Typical costs Tuition of $40 per credit hour plus mandatory fees of $20 per credit hour for in-state residents. Tuition of $103 per credit hour plus mandatory fees of $20 per credit hour for out-of-state residents. *Noncredit courses:* $35 per course. Financial aid is available to distance learners.
Registration Students may register by mail, telephone, in person.
Contact Kent Brooks, Dean of Information Service and Distance Education/Chief Technology Officer, Western Oklahoma State College, 2801 North Main, Altus, OK 73521. *Telephone:* 580-477-7764. *Fax:* 580-477-7777. *E-mail:* kent@western.cc.ok.us.

DEGREES AND AWARDS

AA General Studies (certain restrictions apply; service area differs from that of the overall institution)

COURSE SUBJECT AREAS OFFERED OUTSIDE OF DEGREE PROGRAMS

Undergraduate: Biology; botany; business; business administration and management; chemistry; criminal justice; developmental and child psychology; economics; English composition; English language and literature; European languages and literatures; fine arts; geology; health and physical education/fitness; history; liberal arts, general studies, and humanities; mathematics; music; philosophy and religion; political science; psychology; sociology; zoology

WESTERN OREGON UNIVERSITY

Monmouth, Oregon
Division of Extended Programs
www.wou.edu

Western Oregon University, founded in 1856, is a state-supported, comprehensive institution. It is accredited by the Northwest Association of Schools and Colleges. It first offered distance learning courses in 1976. In 1999–2000, it offered 35 courses at a distance.
Course delivery sites Courses are delivered to your home, your workplace, military bases, high schools.
Media Courses are delivered via videotapes, videoconferencing, World Wide Web, print. Students and teachers may interact via videoconferencing, audioconferencing, mail, telephone, fax, e-mail.
Restrictions Programs are available in nine western states: Arkansas, Colorado, Hawaii, Idaho, Montana, Oregon, Utah, Washington, and Wyoming. Enrollment is restricted to individuals meeting certain criteria.
Services Distance learners have access to library services, the campus computer network, e-mail services, academic advising, career placement assistance, bookstore at a distance.
Credit-earning options Students may transfer credits from another institution or may earn credits through examinations, military training.
Typical costs *Undergraduate:* Tuition of $90 per credit hour. *Graduate:* Tuition of $120 per credit hour. Costs may vary. Financial aid is available to distance learners.
Registration Students may register by mail, fax, telephone, in person.
Contact LaRon Tolley, Distance Education Resource/Budget Manager, Western Oregon University. *Telephone:* 503-838-8483. *Fax:* 503-838-8473. *E-mail:* dess@wou.edu.

eCollege.com *www.ecollege.com/scholarships*

DEGREES AND AWARDS

Undergraduate Certificate(s) Fire Services Administration

COURSE SUBJECT AREAS OFFERED OUTSIDE OF DEGREE PROGRAMS

Undergraduate: Business communications; computer and information sciences; psychology; social psychology; social sciences; teacher education
Graduate: Psychology; social sciences; teacher education

WESTERN PIEDMONT COMMUNITY COLLEGE

Morganton, North Carolina

Western Piedmont Community College, founded in 1964, is a state-supported, two-year college. It is accredited by the Southern Association of Colleges and Schools. In 1999–2000, it offered 45 courses at a distance. In fall 1999, there were 2,282 students enrolled in distance learning courses.

Course delivery sites Courses are delivered to your home.

Media Courses are delivered via television, videotapes, World Wide Web, e-mail. Students and teachers may interact via e-mail, World Wide Web. The following equipment may be required: television, videocassette player, computer, Internet access.

Restrictions Programs are available regionally. Enrollment is open to anyone.

Services Distance learners have access to library services, e-mail services at a distance.

Credit-earning options Students may transfer credits from another institution or may earn credits through examinations, portfolio assessment.

Typical costs Tuition of $340 per semester for in-state residents. Tuition of $2376 per semester for out-of-state residents. Financial aid is available to distance learners.

Registration Students may register by telephone, e-mail, in person.

Contact Jane Carswell, Dean of Business Technology Division, Western Piedmont Community College, 1001 Burkemont Avenue, Morganton, NC 28655-4511. *Telephone:* 828-438-6000. *Fax:* 828-438-6015. *E-mail:* j.carswell@wp.cc.nc.us.

DEGREES AND AWARDS

AA Business Administration (some on-campus requirements), Paralegal Studies (some on-campus requirements)

COURSE SUBJECT AREAS OFFERED OUTSIDE OF DEGREE PROGRAMS

Undergraduate: Business; law and legal studies; mathematics

See full description on page 676.

WESTERN WASHINGTON UNIVERSITY

Bellingham, Washington

University Extended Programs
www.ac.wwu.edu/~extended/

Western Washington University, founded in 1893, is a state-supported, comprehensive institution. It is accredited by the Northwest Association of Schools and Colleges. It first offered distance learning courses in 1912. In 1999–2000, it offered 100 courses at a distance. In fall 1999, there were 400 students enrolled in distance learning courses.

Course delivery sites Courses are delivered to your home.

Media Courses are delivered via videotapes, audiotapes, computer software, World Wide Web, e-mail, print. Students and teachers may meet in person or interact via mail, telephone, fax, e-mail.

Restrictions Programs are available worldwide. Enrollment is open to anyone.

Services Distance learners have access to library services, bookstore at a distance.

Credit-earning options Students may transfer credits from another institution.

Typical costs Tuition of $75 per credit plus mandatory fees of $15 per course. *Noncredit courses:* $2450 per course.

Registration Students may register by mail, fax, telephone, in person.

Contact Meredith Gilbert, Independent Learning, Western Washington University, Bellingham, WA 98225-5293. *Telephone:* 360-650-3650. *Fax:* 360-650-6858. *E-mail:* ilearn@cc.wwu.edu.

DEGREES AND AWARDS

Undergraduate Certificate(s) Microsoft Certified System Engineers

BA Human Services (certain restrictions apply; service area differs from that of the overall institution; some on-campus requirements)

COURSE SUBJECT AREAS OFFERED OUTSIDE OF DEGREE PROGRAMS

Undergraduate: Abnormal psychology; algebra; American (U.S.) history; American literature; anthropology; Asian studies; biology; calculus; Canadian studies; creative writing; curriculum and instruction; developmental and child psychology; economics; education administration; English language and literature; English literature; environmental science; European history; French language and literature; Greek language and literature; history; medieval/renaissance studies; music; sociology; statistics; women's studies

Special note

Western Washington University (WWU) is a regional public university that emphasizes high-quality undergraduate education. Distance education offerings are primarily correspondence courses that are taught by University faculty members. Courses are offered by the following departments: anthropology, Canadian studies, classical studies, East Asian studies, economics, education, English, mathematics, music, psychology, sociology, and women studies. These courses are open to all students, providing they meet the prerequisites for the course. Students may enroll at any time. In addition, the College of Education offers professional development for teachers as well as a BA in human services delivered via technology. For more information, students should access Western's Web page at http://www.ac.wwu.edu/~extended.

WESTERN WYOMING COMMUNITY COLLEGE

Rock Springs, Wyoming

Extended Education
www.wwcc.cc.wy.us/distance.htm

Western Wyoming Community College, founded in 1959, is a state and locally supported, two-year college. It is accredited by the North Central Association of Colleges and Schools. In 1999–2000, it offered 39 courses at a distance. In fall 1999, there were 863 students enrolled in distance learning courses.

Course delivery sites Courses are delivered to your home, high schools, 3 off-campus centers in Evanston, Rawlins, Wyoming State Hospital.

Media Courses are delivered via television, videotapes, videoconferencing, interactive television, audiotapes, World Wide Web, e-mail, print. Students and teachers may meet in person or interact via videoconferencing, audioconferencing, mail, telephone, fax, e-mail, World Wide Web. The following equipment may be required: television, videocassette player, computer, modem, Internet access, e-mail.

Restrictions Programs are available regionally within southwest Wyoming. Enrollment is open to anyone.

Services Distance learners have access to library services, academic advising, tutoring, career placement assistance, bookstore at a distance.

Credit-earning options Students may transfer credits from another institution or may earn credits through examinations, military training.

Typical costs Tuition of $53 per credit plus mandatory fees of $18 per course for in-state residents. Tuition of $145 per credit plus mandatory fees of $18 per course for out-of-state residents. Financial aid is available to distance learners.

Registration Students may register by mail, telephone, in person.

Contact David Gutierrez, Director, Extended Education, Western Wyoming Community College, B-644 2500 College Drive, PO Box 428, Rock Springs, WY 82902-0428. *Telephone:* 307-382-1757. *Fax:* 307-382-1812. *E-mail:* dgutierr@wwcc.cc.wy.us.

DEGREES AND AWARDS

Undergraduate Certificate(s) Nursing (certain restrictions apply)
AA Arts

COURSE SUBJECT AREAS OFFERED OUTSIDE OF DEGREE PROGRAMS

Undergraduate: Biological and life sciences; business; communications; computer and information sciences; education; English language and literature; European languages and literatures; health professions and related sciences; history; home economics and family studies; mathematics; philosophy and religion; physical sciences; protective services; psychology; social sciences

WEST HILLS COMMUNITY COLLEGE

Coalinga, California

Learning Resources Division
www.westhills.cc.ca.us/distance_ed

West Hills Community College, founded in 1932, is a state-supported, two-year college. It is accredited by the Western Association of Schools and Colleges, Inc. In 1999–2000, it offered 27 courses at a distance. In fall 1999, there were 280 students enrolled in distance learning courses.

Course delivery sites Courses are delivered to your home, your workplace, military bases, high schools.

Media Courses are delivered via television, videotapes, World Wide Web. Students and teachers may meet in person or interact via mail, telephone, fax, e-mail. The following equipment may be required: television, videocassette player, computer, modem, Internet access, e-mail.

Restrictions Programs are available worldwide. Enrollment is open to anyone.

Services Distance learners have access to library services, tutoring at a distance.

Credit-earning options Students may transfer credits from another institution or may earn credits through examinations, military training.

Typical costs Tuition of $11 per unit for local area residents. Tuition of $11 per unit for in-state residents. Tuition of $121 per unit for out-of-state residents. *Noncredit courses:* $0 per course. Financial aid is available to distance learners.

Registration Students may register by mail, in person.

Contact Lorna Davis, Learning Resources Division Secretary, West Hills Community College, 300 Cherry Lane, Coalinga, CA 93210. *Telephone:* 559-935-0801 Ext. 3353. *Fax:* 559-935-2633. *E-mail:* davisll@whccd.cc.ca.us.

DEGREES AND AWARDS

Distance programs offered do not lead to a degree or other formal award.

COURSE SUBJECT AREAS OFFERED OUTSIDE OF DEGREE PROGRAMS

Undergraduate: Algebra; American (U.S.) history; biology; business administration and management; cognitive psychology; computer programming; corrections; criminal justice; English composition; English

literature; geography; health and physical education/fitness; information sciences and systems; political science

WEST LOS ANGELES COLLEGE

Culver City, California

Distance Learning Center
www.wlac.cc.ca.us/dised

West Los Angeles College, founded in 1969, is a state and locally supported, two-year college. It is accredited by the Western Association of Schools and Colleges, Inc. In 1999–2000, it offered 7 courses at a distance. In fall 1999, there were 14 students enrolled in distance learning courses.

Course delivery sites Courses are delivered to your home, your workplace, high schools.

Media Courses are delivered via videotapes, videoconferencing, audiotapes, computer software, CD-ROM, World Wide Web, e-mail, print. Students and teachers may meet in person or interact via videoconferencing, mail, telephone, fax, e-mail, World Wide Web. The following equipment may be required: computer, modem, Internet access, e-mail.

Restrictions Programs are available worldwide. Enrollment is open to anyone.

Services Distance learners have access to library services, academic advising, tutoring, bookstore at a distance.

Credit-earning options Students may transfer credits from another institution or may earn credits through examinations.

Typical costs Tuition of $11 per unit plus mandatory fees of $12 per semester for local area residents. Tuition of $11 per unit plus mandatory fees of $12 per semester for in-state residents. Tuition of $128 per unit plus mandatory fees of $16 per unit for out-of-state residents. Enrollment fee is $11 per unit, capital improvement fee is $5 per unit. Financial aid is available to distance learners.

Registration Students may register by mail, telephone, e-mail, World Wide Web, in person.

Contact Eric Ichon, Distance Learning Coordinator, West Los Angeles College, 4800 Freshman Drive, Culver City, CA 90230. *Telephone:* 310-287-4305. *Fax:* 310-287-4418. *E-mail:* eric_ichon@laccd.cc.ca.us.

DEGREES AND AWARDS

Distance programs offered do not lead to a degree or other formal award.

COURSE SUBJECT AREAS OFFERED OUTSIDE OF DEGREE PROGRAMS

Undergraduate: Creative writing; English composition; health professions and related sciences; liberal arts, general studies, and humanities; library and information studies; recreation and leisure studies; Spanish language and literature

WESTMORELAND COUNTY COMMUNITY COLLEGE

Youngwood, Pennsylvania

Learning Resources
www.westmoreland.cc.pa.us

Westmoreland County Community College, founded in 1970, is a county-supported, two-year college. It is accredited by the Middle States

Association of Colleges and Schools. It first offered distance learning courses in 1987. In 1999–2000, it offered 45 courses at a distance. In fall 1999, there were 963 students enrolled in distance learning courses.

Course delivery sites Courses are delivered to your home, your workplace, 4 off-campus centers in Latrobe, Lower Burrell, Penn Township, Rostraver Township.

Media Courses are delivered via videotapes, videoconferencing, interactive television, audiotapes, World Wide Web, print. Students and teachers may interact via videoconferencing, telephone, fax, e-mail, interactive television, World Wide Web. The following equipment may be required: computer, Internet access, e-mail.

Restrictions Programs are available worldwide. Enrollment is open to anyone.

Services Distance learners have access to library services, academic advising, tutoring, career placement assistance, bookstore at a distance.

Credit-earning options Students may transfer credits from another institution or may earn credits through examinations, portfolio assessment, military training.

Typical costs Tuition of $48 per credit for local area residents. Tuition of $96 per credit for in-state residents. Tuition of $144 per credit for out-of-state residents. Financial aid is available to distance learners.

Registration Students may register by mail, fax, telephone, in person.

Contact Dr. Mary J. Stubbs, Director, Westmoreland County Community College, Learning Resources/Special Projects, 400 Armbrust Road, Youngwood, PA 15697. *Telephone:* 724-925-4097. *Fax:* 724-925-1150. *E-mail:* stubbsms@wccc.westmoreland.cc.pa.us.

DEGREES AND AWARDS

AAS Business Management

COURSE SUBJECT AREAS OFFERED OUTSIDE OF DEGREE PROGRAMS

Undergraduate: Abnormal psychology; accounting; administrative and secretarial services; art history and criticism; biology; botany; business; business administration and management; business law; computer and information sciences; conservation and natural resources; creative writing; developmental and child psychology; early childhood education; economics; education; educational psychology; electronics; English language and literature; film studies; foods and nutrition studies; geology; health and physical education/fitness; health professions and related sciences; health services administration; history; individual and family development studies; information sciences and systems; law and legal studies; liberal arts, general studies, and humanities; mathematics; mechanical engineering; philosophy and religion; physical sciences; physics; political science; psychology; public relations; sociology; telecommunications

WEST SHORE COMMUNITY COLLEGE

Scottville, Michigan
www.westshore.cc.mi.us/

West Shore Community College, founded in 1967, is a district-supported, two-year college. It is accredited by the North Central Association of Colleges and Schools. In 1999–2000, it offered 13 courses at a distance. In fall 1999, there were 110 students enrolled in distance learning courses.

Course delivery sites Courses are delivered to your home, your workplace, high schools, off-campus center(s) in Onekama.

Media Courses are delivered via videotapes, interactive television, audiotapes, computer software, CD-ROM, World Wide Web, e-mail, print. Students and teachers may meet in person or interact via mail, telephone, fax, e-mail, interactive television, World Wide Web. The following equipment may be required: television, videocassette player, computer, modem, Internet access, e-mail.

Restrictions Programs are available nationwide. Enrollment is open to anyone.

Services Distance learners have access to library services, the campus computer network, e-mail services, academic advising, tutoring, career placement assistance, bookstore at a distance.

Credit-earning options Students may transfer credits from another institution or may earn credits through portfolio assessment.

Typical costs Tuition of $51.50 per credit plus mandatory fees of $35 per semester for local area residents. Tuition of $80 per credit plus mandatory fees of $35 per semester for in-state residents. Tuition of $100 per credit plus mandatory fees of $35 per semester for out-of-state residents. Financial aid is available to distance learners.

Registration Students may register by telephone, in person.

Contact Patti Davidson, Director of Distance Learning and Information Technology, West Shore Community College, 3000 North Stiles Road, Scottville, MI 49454-0277. *Telephone:* 231-845-6211 Ext. 3106. *Fax:* 231-845-0207. *E-mail:* pldavidson@westshore.cc.mi.us.

DEGREES AND AWARDS

Distance programs offered do not lead to a degree or other formal award.

COURSE SUBJECT AREAS OFFERED OUTSIDE OF DEGREE PROGRAMS

Undergraduate: Algebra; biology; business; business administration and management; computer and information sciences; English composition; liberal arts, general studies, and humanities; marketing; physics; psychology; sociology

WEST VALLEY COLLEGE

Saratoga, California
Distance Learning
www.westvalley.edu/wvc/dl/dl.html

West Valley College, founded in 1963, is a state and locally supported, two-year college. It is accredited by the Western Association of Schools and Colleges, Inc. It first offered distance learning courses in 1985. In 1999–2000, it offered 46 courses at a distance. In fall 1999, there were 1,351 students enrolled in distance learning courses.

Course delivery sites Courses are delivered to your home, your workplace, high schools.

Media Courses are delivered via television, videotapes, computer software, CD-ROM, computer conferencing, World Wide Web, e-mail, print. Students and teachers may meet in person or interact via videoconferencing, mail, telephone, fax, e-mail, World Wide Web. The following equipment may be required: television, videocassette player, computer, modem, Internet access, e-mail.

Restrictions Programs are available worldwide. Enrollment is open to anyone.

Services Distance learners have access to library services, the campus computer network, e-mail services, tutoring at a distance.

Credit-earning options Students may transfer credits from another institution or may earn credits through examinations.

Typical costs Tuition of $11 per unit plus mandatory fees of $17 per semester for in-state residents. Tuition of $125 per unit plus mandatory fees of $17 per semester for out-of-state residents. Costs may vary. Financial aid is available to distance learners.

Registration Students may register by mail, fax, telephone, e-mail, World Wide Web, in person.

Contact Steve Peltz, Instructional Technology/Distance Learning Coordinator, West Valley College, 14000 Fruitvale Avenue, Saratoga, CA 95070. *Telephone:* 408-741-2065. *Fax:* 408-741-2134. *E-mail:* steve_peltz@westvalley.edu.

DEGREES AND AWARDS

Distance programs offered do not lead to a degree or other formal award.

COURSE SUBJECT AREAS OFFERED OUTSIDE OF DEGREE PROGRAMS

Undergraduate: American (U.S.) history; anthropology; art history and criticism; astronomy and astrophysics; business administration and management; business law; computer and information sciences; creative writing; design; developmental and child psychology; economics; English composition; film studies; foods and nutrition studies; French language and literature; geology; health and physical education/fitness; health professions and related sciences; individual and family development studies; library and information studies; marketing; oceanography; photography; political science; sociology; Spanish language and literature

WEST VIRGINIA NORTHERN COMMUNITY COLLEGE

Wheeling, West Virginia
www.northern.wvnet.edu

West Virginia Northern Community College, founded in 1972, is a state-supported, two-year college. It is accredited by the North Central Association of Colleges and Schools. It first offered distance learning courses in 1988. In 1999–2000, it offered 12 courses at a distance. In fall 1999, there were 147 students enrolled in distance learning courses.

Course delivery sites Courses are delivered to your home, high schools, 2 off-campus centers in New Martinsville, Weirton.

Media Courses are delivered via television, computer software, computer conferencing, World Wide Web, e-mail. Students and teachers may meet in person or interact via mail, telephone, e-mail, World Wide Web. The following equipment may be required: television, computer, Internet access, e-mail.

Restrictions Programs are available nationwide. Enrollment is open to anyone.

Services Distance learners have access to library services, the campus computer network, e-mail services, bookstore at a distance.

Credit-earning options Students may transfer credits from another institution or may earn credits through examinations, military training, business training.

Typical costs Tuition of $65 per credit for in-state residents. Tuition of $187 per credit for out-of-state residents. Costs may vary. Financial aid is available to distance learners.

Registration Students may register by mail, fax, e-mail, World Wide Web, in person.

Contact Sharon A. Bungard, Dean, Marketing and Institutional Research/ Student Development, West Virginia Northern Community College. *Telephone:* 304-233-5900 Ext. 4261. *Fax:* 304-232-0965. *E-mail:* sbungard@northern.wvnet.edu.

DEGREES AND AWARDS

Distance programs offered do not lead to a degree or other formal award.

COURSE SUBJECT AREAS OFFERED OUTSIDE OF DEGREE PROGRAMS

Undergraduate: Accounting; American (U.S.) history; biology; business administration and management; calculus; economics; English composition; health professions and related sciences; history; information sciences and systems; management information systems; microbiology; nursing; physical sciences; political science; social sciences; sociology

See full description on page 676.

WEST VIRGINIA STATE COLLEGE

Institute, West Virginia
www.wvsc.edu/

West Virginia State College, founded in 1891, is a state-supported, four-year college. It is accredited by the North Central Association of Colleges and Schools.

Contact West Virginia State College, PO Box 1000, Institute, WV 25112-1000. *Telephone:* 304-766-3000. *Fax:* 304-766-4158.

See full description on page 676.

WEST VIRGINIA UNIVERSITY

Morgantown, West Virginia
Extended Learning
www.wvu.edu/~exlearn

West Virginia University, founded in 1867, is a state-supported university. It is accredited by the North Central Association of Colleges and Schools. It first offered distance learning courses in 1972. In 1999–2000, it offered 106 courses at a distance. In fall 1999, there were 1,116 students enrolled in distance learning courses.

Course delivery sites Courses are delivered to your home, your workplace, military bases, high schools, 5 off-campus centers in Clarksburg, Parkersburg, Wheeling.

Media Courses are delivered via television, videotapes, videoconferencing, interactive television, computer software, CD-ROM, computer conferencing, World Wide Web, e-mail, print. Students and teachers may meet in person or interact via videoconferencing, audioconferencing, mail, telephone, fax, e-mail, interactive television, World Wide Web. The following equipment may be required: television, videocassette player, computer, modem, Internet access, e-mail.

Restrictions Programs are available worldwide. Enrollment is open to anyone.

Services Distance learners have access to library services, tutoring at a distance.

Credit-earning options Students may transfer credits from another institution or may earn credits through examinations, portfolio assessment, military training, business training.

Typical costs *Undergraduate:* Tuition of $115 per credit for in-state residents. Tuition of $338 per credit for out-of-state residents. *Graduate:* Tuition of $151 per credit for in-state residents. Tuition of $454 per credit for out-of-state residents. Costs may vary. Financial aid is available to distance learners.

Registration Students may register by mail, fax, telephone, e-mail, in person.

Contact Sue Day-Perroots, Director, West Virginia University, Extended Learning, PO Box 6800, West Everly Street, Morgantown, WV 26506-6800. *Telephone:* 304-293-2852. *Fax:* 304-293-4899. *E-mail:* sdayperr@wvu.edu.

DEGREES AND AWARDS

EMBA Business Administration (certain restrictions apply; service area differs from that of the overall institution)
MA Special Education
MS Software Engineering (certain restrictions apply; service area differs from that of the overall institution)

COURSE SUBJECT AREAS OFFERED OUTSIDE OF DEGREE PROGRAMS

Undergraduate: Astronomy and astrophysics; biology; developmental and child psychology; economics; English composition; English language and literature; history; liberal arts, general studies, and humanities; mathematics; music; nursing; social psychology; sociology
Graduate: Business administration and management; chemical engineering; computer and information sciences; environmental engineering; geology; health and physical education/fitness; nursing; public health; social work; special education
See full description on page 676.

WEST VIRGINIA UNIVERSITY INSTITUTE OF TECHNOLOGY

Montgomery, West Virginia
Extension and Community Service
wvit.wvnet.edu

West Virginia University Institute of Technology, founded in 1895, is a state-supported, comprehensive institution. It is accredited by the North Central Association of Colleges and Schools. It first offered distance learning courses in 1978. In 1999–2000, it offered 5 courses at a distance. In fall 1999, there were 150 students enrolled in distance learning courses.
Course delivery sites Courses are delivered to your home, your workplace, high schools, University of Charleston (Charleston), West Virginia State College (Institute), 2 off-campus centers in Charleston, Oak Hill.
Media Courses are delivered via television, videotapes, videoconferencing, interactive television, computer conferencing, World Wide Web, e-mail. Students and teachers may interact via videoconferencing, mail, telephone, fax, e-mail, interactive television. The following equipment may be required: television, modem, Internet access, e-mail.
Restrictions Programs are available to local area students. Enrollment is open to anyone.
Services Distance learners have access to library services, the campus computer network, e-mail services, academic advising at a distance.
Credit-earning options Students may earn credits through examinations, portfolio assessment, military training, business training.
Typical costs *Undergraduate:* Tuition of $250 per course for in-state residents. Tuition of $550 per course for out-of-state residents. *Graduate:* Tuition of $265 per course for in-state residents. Tuition of $600 per course for out-of-state residents. Costs may vary. Financial aid is available to distance learners.
Registration Students may register by mail, fax, telephone, in person.
Contact Rodney Stewart, Director, West Virginia University Institute of Technology, Vining Library, Montgomery, WV 25136. *Telephone:* 304-442-3200. *Fax:* 304-442-3090. *E-mail:* rstewart@wvutech.edu.

DEGREES AND AWARDS

Distance programs offered do not lead to a degree or other formal award.

COURSE SUBJECT AREAS OFFERED OUTSIDE OF DEGREE PROGRAMS

Undergraduate: Electrical engineering; engineering; English composition; management information systems; nursing
Graduate: Electrical engineering; engineering

WEST VIRGINIA WESLEYAN COLLEGE

Buckhannon, West Virginia
Distance Education Program
www.wvwc.edu

West Virginia Wesleyan College, founded in 1890, is an independent, religious, comprehensive institution affiliated with the United Methodist Church. It is accredited by the North Central Association of Colleges and Schools. It first offered distance learning courses in 1975. In 1999–2000, it offered 50 courses at a distance. In fall 1999, there were 200 students enrolled in distance learning courses.
Course delivery sites Courses are delivered to your home.
Media Courses are delivered via videotapes, audiotapes, computer software, CD-ROM, World Wide Web, e-mail, print. Students and teachers may meet in person or interact via audioconferencing, mail, telephone, fax, e-mail, World Wide Web. The following equipment may be required: television, videocassette player, computer, modem, Internet access, e-mail.
Restrictions Programs are available worldwide. Enrollment is restricted to individuals meeting certain criteria.
Services Distance learners have access to library services, the campus computer network, academic advising, bookstore at a distance.
Credit-earning options Students may transfer credits from another institution or may earn credits through examinations, portfolio assessment, military training.
Typical costs Tuition of $100 per credit hour. Financial aid is available to distance learners.
Registration Students may register by mail, fax, telephone, e-mail, World Wide Web, in person.
Contact Jennifer Bunner, Coordinator of Distance Education, West Virginia Wesleyan College, Distance Education Program, 59 College Avenue, Buckhannon, WV 26201. *Telephone:* 888-340-7574. *Fax:* 304-473-8429. *E-mail:* distanceed@wvwc.edu.

DEGREES AND AWARDS

Undergraduate Certificate(s) Business Principles
BSN Nursing (service area differs from that of the overall institution; some on-campus requirements)

COURSE SUBJECT AREAS OFFERED OUTSIDE OF DEGREE PROGRAMS

Undergraduate: Accounting; African-American studies; algebra; American (U.S.) history; anatomy; area, ethnic, and cultural studies; art history and criticism; biological and life sciences; business administration and management; business communications; computer and information sciences; criminology; developmental and child psychology; English language and literature; European history; fine arts; foods and nutrition studies; geology; health and physical education/fitness; history; liberal arts, general studies, and humanities; marketing; music; nursing; philosophy and religion; physical sciences; physiology; political science; social psychology; sociology; women's studies

WHATCOM COMMUNITY COLLEGE

Bellingham, Washington
www.whatcom.ctc.edu/

Whatcom Community College, founded in 1970, is a state-supported, two-year college. It is accredited by the Northwest Association of Schools and Colleges. It first offered distance learning courses in 1991. In 1999–2000, it offered 20 courses at a distance. In fall 1999, there were 200 students enrolled in distance learning courses.
Course delivery sites Courses are delivered to your home.

Media Courses are delivered via videotapes, computer conferencing, e-mail, print. Students and teachers may meet in person or interact via mail, telephone, e-mail. The following equipment may be required: television, videocassette player, computer, modem, Internet access, e-mail. **Restrictions** Programs are available to in-state students only. Enrollment is open to anyone.
Services Distance learners have access to bookstore at a distance.
Credit-earning options Students may transfer credits from another institution or may earn credits through examinations, portfolio assessment, military training.
Typical costs Tuition of $54 per credit for local area residents. Tuition of $54 per credit for in-state residents. Tuition of $209 per credit for out-of-state residents. Mandatory fees are between $20 and $40 per course. Costs may vary. Financial aid is available to distance learners.
Registration Students may register by World Wide Web, in person.
Contact Stephen Tanzer, Alternative Learning Coordinator, Whatcom Community College, 237 West Kellogg Road, Bellingham, WA 98226. *Telephone:* 360-676-2170. *Fax:* 360-676-2171. *E-mail:* stanzer@whatcom. ctc.edu.

DEGREES AND AWARDS

Distance programs offered do not lead to a degree or other formal award.

COURSE SUBJECT AREAS OFFERED OUTSIDE OF DEGREE PROGRAMS

Undergraduate: Anthropology; astronomy and astrophysics; biology; English composition; English language and literature; geology; history; library and information studies; mathematics; music; psychology; social psychology; social sciences; sociology

WHEATON COLLEGE

Wheaton, Illinois

Distance Learning
www.wheatononline.org

Wheaton College, founded in 1860, is an independent, religious, comprehensive institution. It is accredited by the North Central Association of Colleges and Schools. It first offered distance learning courses in 1972. In 1999–2000, it offered 10 courses at a distance. In fall 1999, there were 85 students enrolled in distance learning courses.
Course delivery sites Courses are delivered to your home, your workplace, military bases.
Media Courses are delivered via audiotapes, computer conferencing, World Wide Web, print. Students and teachers may interact via mail, telephone, fax, e-mail, World Wide Web. The following equipment may be required: computer, modem, Internet access, e-mail.
Restrictions Programs are available worldwide. Enrollment is restricted to individuals meeting certain criteria.
Services Distance learners have access to library services, academic advising, bookstore at a distance.
Typical costs Tuition of $380 per semester. *Noncredit courses:* $200 per course. Costs may vary.
Registration Students may register by mail, fax, telephone, e-mail, World Wide Web, in person.
Contact Douglas Milford, Director, Wheaton College, Distance Learning, Wheaton, IL 60187. *Telephone:* 630-752-5944. *Fax:* 630-752-5935. *E-mail:* distance.learning@wheaton.edu.

eCollege.com *www.ecollege.com/scholarships*

DEGREES AND AWARDS

Graduate Certificate(s) Biblical Studies (certain restrictions apply)

COURSE SUBJECT AREAS OFFERED OUTSIDE OF DEGREE PROGRAMS

Graduate: Bible studies; religious studies; theological studies
Noncredit: Bible studies; theological studies
See full description on page 826.

WICHITA STATE UNIVERSITY

Wichita, Kansas

Media Resources Center
www.twsu.edu/

Wichita State University, founded in 1895, is a state-supported university. It is accredited by the North Central Association of Colleges and Schools. It first offered distance learning courses in 1982. In 1999–2000, it offered 60 courses at a distance. In fall 1999, there were 1,000 students enrolled in distance learning courses.
Course delivery sites Courses are delivered to your home, your workplace, military bases.
Media Courses are delivered via television, videotapes, videoconferencing, World Wide Web, e-mail. Students and teachers may meet in person or interact via videoconferencing, mail, telephone, fax, e-mail, interactive television. The following equipment may be required: television, videocassette player.
Restrictions Programs are available to in-state students only. Enrollment is open to anyone.
Services Distance learners have access to library services, academic advising, tutoring, career placement assistance at a distance.
Credit-earning options Students may transfer credits from another institution or may earn credits through examinations, portfolio assessment.
Typical costs *Undergraduate:* Tuition of $82 per credit hour plus mandatory fees of $12 per credit hour for in-state residents. Tuition of $287 per credit hour plus mandatory fees of $12 per credit hour for out-of-state residents. *Graduate:* Tuition of $112 per credit hour plus mandatory fees of $12 per credit hour for in-state residents. Tuition of $332 per credit hour plus mandatory fees of $12 per credit hour for out-of-state residents. Financial aid is available to distance learners.
Registration Students may register by telephone, in person.
Contact Mary Morriss, Telecourse Coordinator, Wichita State University, 1845 Fairmount, Wichita, KS 67260-0057. *Telephone:* 316-978-3575. *Fax:* 316-978-3560. *E-mail:* morriss@mrc.twsu.edu.

DEGREES AND AWARDS

Distance programs offered do not lead to a degree or other formal award.

COURSE SUBJECT AREAS OFFERED OUTSIDE OF DEGREE PROGRAMS

Undergraduate: Area, ethnic, and cultural studies; astronomy and astrophysics; biology; business; business administration and management; communications; computer and information sciences; economics; English language and literature; fine arts; geology; health professions and related sciences; history; human resources management; liberal arts, general studies, and humanities; music; nursing; physics; sociology
Graduate: Area, ethnic, and cultural studies; biology; business; business administration and management; communications; economics; fine arts; health professions and related sciences; human resources management; nursing

WILFRID LAURIER UNIVERSITY

Waterloo, Ontario, Canada

Office of Part-Time, Distance and Continuing Education
www.wlu.ca/~wwwconte

Wilfrid Laurier University, founded in 1911, is a province-supported, comprehensive institution. It is accredited by the Association of Theological Schools in the United States and Canada. It first offered distance learning courses in 1978. In 1999–2000, it offered 63 courses at a distance. In fall 1999, there were 892 students enrolled in distance learning courses.

Course delivery sites Courses are delivered to your home.

Media Courses are delivered via television, videotapes, videoconferencing, audiotapes, World Wide Web, print. Students and teachers may meet in person or interact via videoconferencing, mail, telephone, fax, e-mail, World Wide Web. The following equipment may be required: television, videocassette player, computer, Internet access.

Restrictions Programs are available worldwide. Enrollment is open to anyone.

Services Distance learners have access to library services, the campus computer network, e-mail services, academic advising, career placement assistance at a distance.

Credit-earning options Students may transfer credits from another institution or may earn credits through examinations.

Typical costs Undergraduate tuition for a full-credit, 72-hour course is $796; for a half-credit, 36-hour course, tuition is $398. *Noncredit courses:* $180 per course. Costs may vary. Financial aid is available to distance learners.

Registration Students may register by mail, fax, in person.

Contact Ms. Joan Hawkins, Administrative Assistant, Wilfrid Laurier University, Office of Part-Time, Distance and Continuing Education, 75 University Avenue West, Waterloo, ON N2L 3C5 Canada. *Telephone:* 519-884-0710 Ext. 4448. *Fax:* 519-884-6063. *E-mail:* 22coned@wlu.ca.

DEGREES AND AWARDS

BA Geography, Sociology

COURSE SUBJECT AREAS OFFERED OUTSIDE OF DEGREE PROGRAMS

Undergraduate: Abnormal psychology; accounting; anthropology; biological and life sciences; biology; business; business administration and management; business law; chemistry; criminology; developmental and child psychology; economics; English language and literature; environmental science; European languages and literatures; fine arts; French language and literature; genetics; geography; geology; German language and literature; history; investments and securities; philosophy and religion; physical sciences; political science; psychology; religious studies; social sciences; social work; sociology

WILKES COMMUNITY COLLEGE

Wilkesboro, North Carolina

Individualized Studies Department
www.wilkes.cc.nc.us

Wilkes Community College, founded in 1965, is a state-supported, two-year college. It is accredited by the Southern Association of Colleges and Schools. It first offered distance learning courses in 1984.

Contact Wilkes Community College, 1328 Collegiate Drive, PO Box 120, Wilkesboro, NC 28697. *Telephone:* 336-838-6100. *Fax:* 336-838-6277.

See full description on page 676.

WILLIAM PATERSON UNIVERSITY OF NEW JERSEY

Wayne, New Jersey

The Center for Continuing Education and Distance Learning (CEDL)
www.wpunj.edu/cedl

William Paterson University of New Jersey, founded in 1855, is a state-supported, comprehensive institution. It is accredited by the Middle States Association of Colleges and Schools. In 1999–2000, it offered 9 courses at a distance. In fall 1999, there were 20 students enrolled in distance learning courses.

Course delivery sites Courses are delivered to your home, your workplace, high schools, County College of Morris (Randolph).

Media Courses are delivered via videotapes, videoconferencing, interactive television, CD-ROM, computer conferencing, World Wide Web, e-mail. Students and teachers may interact via videoconferencing, e-mail, interactive television, World Wide Web. The following equipment may be required: computer, modem, Internet access, e-mail.

Restrictions Programs are available nationwide. Enrollment is open to anyone.

Services Distance learners have access to library services, the campus computer network, e-mail services, academic advising, bookstore at a distance.

Credit-earning options Students may transfer credits from another institution or may earn credits through examinations.

Typical costs *Undergraduate:* Tuition of $451.50 per course for in-state residents. Tuition of $751.50 per course for out-of-state residents. *Graduate:* Tuition of $766.50 per course for in-state residents. Tuition of $1084.50 per course for out-of-state residents. Costs may vary.

Registration Students may register by mail, fax, telephone, in person.

Contact Peter Shapiro, Director of Distance Learning, William Paterson University of New Jersey, CEDL, 358 Hamburg Turnpike, Wayne, NJ 07470. *Telephone:* 973-720-2354. *Fax:* 973-720-2298. *E-mail:* shapirop@wpunj.edu.

DEGREES AND AWARDS

Distance programs offered do not lead to a degree or other formal award.

COURSE SUBJECT AREAS OFFERED OUTSIDE OF DEGREE PROGRAMS

Undergraduate: Accounting; American (U.S.) history; botany; calculus; communications; community health services; curriculum and instruction; English composition; environmental science; European history; marketing; nursing; organizational behavior studies; sociology; theological studies

Graduate: Education; instructional media

Noncredit: Technical writing

WILLIAM RAINEY HARPER COLLEGE

Palatine, Illinois

Learning Resource Center

William Rainey Harper College, founded in 1965, is a state and locally supported, two-year college. It is accredited by the North Central Association of Colleges and Schools. It first offered distance learning courses in 1984. In 1999–2000, it offered 35 courses at a distance. In fall 1999, there were 865 students enrolled in distance learning courses.

Course delivery sites Courses are delivered to your home, your workplace, College of Lake County (Grayslake), Oakton Community College (Des Plaines), 1 off-campus center in Wheeling.

Media Courses are delivered via television, videotapes, videoconferencing, interactive television, computer software, CD-ROM, World Wide Web, e-mail. Students and teachers may meet in person or interact via videoconferencing, mail, telephone, fax, e-mail, interactive television, World Wide Web. The following equipment may be required: television, videocassette player, computer, modem, Internet access, e-mail.

Restrictions Programs are available to in-state students only. Enrollment is restricted to individuals meeting certain criteria.

Services Distance learners have access to library services, the campus computer network, bookstore at a distance.

Credit-earning options Students may transfer credits from another institution or may earn credits through examinations.

Typical costs Tuition of $54 per credit hour plus mandatory fees of $20 per course for local area residents. Tuition of $216.40 per credit hour for in-state residents. Tuition of $263.90 per credit hour for out-of-state residents. Costs may vary. Financial aid is available to distance learners.

Registration Students may register by telephone, World Wide Web, in person.

Contact Fran Hendrickson, Program Assistant, William Rainey Harper College. *Telephone:* 847-925-6586. *Fax:* 847-925-6037. *E-mail:* fhendric@ harper.cc.il.us.

DEGREES AND AWARDS

Distance programs offered do not lead to a degree or other formal award.

COURSE SUBJECT AREAS OFFERED OUTSIDE OF DEGREE PROGRAMS

Undergraduate: Accounting; administrative and secretarial services; astronomy and astrophysics; business; business administration and management; chemistry, physical; computer and information sciences; developmental and child psychology; economics; English composition; geography; health and physical education/fitness; health professions and related sciences; history; hospitality services management; individual and family development studies; law and legal studies; music; philosophy and religion; sociology

WILMINGTON COLLEGE

New Castle, Delaware
www.wilmcoll.edu/

Wilmington College, founded in 1967, is an independent, nonprofit, comprehensive institution. It is accredited by the Middle States Association of Colleges and Schools. In 1999–2000, it offered 16 courses at a distance. In fall 1999, there were 200 students enrolled in distance learning courses.

Course delivery sites Courses are delivered to your home.

Media Courses are delivered via television, videotapes, audiotapes, e-mail, print. Students and teachers may meet in person or interact via mail, telephone, fax, e-mail, World Wide Web. The following equipment may be required: television, videocassette player.

Restrictions Programs available statewide and to surrounding states. Enrollment is open to anyone.

Services Distance learners have access to library services at a distance.

Credit-earning options Students may transfer credits from another institution or may earn credits through examinations, portfolio assessment.

Typical costs *Undergraduate:* Tuition of $208 per credit. *Graduate:* Tuition of $249 per credit. There is a $25 registration fee. Costs may vary. Financial aid is available to distance learners.

Registration Students may register by mail, fax, in person.

Contact Dr. JoAnn Ciuffetelli, Assistant Director of Admissions, Wilmington College, 320 DuPont Highway, New Castle, DE 19720. *Telephone:* 302-328-9407. *Fax:* 302-328-5902.

DEGREES AND AWARDS

Distance programs offered do not lead to a degree or other formal award.

COURSE SUBJECT AREAS OFFERED OUTSIDE OF DEGREE PROGRAMS

Undergraduate: Biological and life sciences; business; business administration and management; psychology; social sciences

Graduate: Business administration and management; education; health professions and related sciences; psychology

WORCESTER POLYTECHNIC INSTITUTE

Worcester, Massachusetts
Advanced Distance Learning Network
www.wpi.edu/Academics/ADLN

Worcester Polytechnic Institute, founded in 1865, is an independent, nonprofit university. It is accredited by the New England Association of Schools and Colleges. It first offered distance learning courses in 1979. In 1999–2000, it offered 25 courses at a distance. In fall 1999, there were 139 students enrolled in distance learning courses.

Course delivery sites Courses are delivered to your home, your workplace.

Media Courses are delivered via videotapes, videoconferencing, computer software, CD-ROM, computer conferencing, World Wide Web, e-mail, print. Students and teachers may interact via videoconferencing, audioconferencing, mail, telephone, fax, e-mail, World Wide Web. The following equipment may be required: television, videocassette player, computer, modem, Internet access, e-mail.

Restrictions Programs are available worldwide. Enrollment is open to anyone.

Services Distance learners have access to library services, the campus computer network, e-mail services, academic advising, career placement assistance, bookstore at a distance.

Credit-earning options Students may transfer credits from another institution.

Typical costs Tuition of $661 per credit hour. Costs may vary. Financial aid is available to distance learners.

Registration Students may register by mail, fax, telephone, e-mail, World Wide Web, in person.

Contact Pennie S. Turgeon, Director, Advanced Distance Learning Network, Worcester Polytechnic Institute, 100 Institute Road, Worcester, MA 01609-2280. *Telephone:* 508-831-5810. *Fax:* 508-831-5881. *E-mail:* adln@wpi.edu.

DEGREES AND AWARDS

Graduate Certificate(s) Civil Engineering, Environmental Engineering, Fire Protection Engineering, Management
MBA Business Administration
MS Civil Engineering, Environmental Engineering, Fire Protection Engineering

COURSE SUBJECT AREAS OFFERED OUTSIDE OF DEGREE PROGRAMS

Graduate: Accounting; business; business administration and management; business communications; civil engineering; economics; engineering; engineering/industrial management; environmental engineering;

finance; fire science; human resources management; industrial engineering; international business; management information systems; marketing; organizational behavior studies

See full description on page 828.

WORCESTER STATE COLLEGE

Worcester, Massachusetts
www.worc.mass.edu/

Worcester State College, founded in 1874, is a state-supported, comprehensive institution. It is accredited by the New England Association of Schools and Colleges. In 1999–2000, it offered 8 courses at a distance. In fall 1999, there were 10 students enrolled in distance learning courses.

Course delivery sites Courses are delivered to your home, your workplace.

Media Courses are delivered via interactive television, World Wide Web. Students and teachers may interact via telephone, e-mail, interactive television, World Wide Web. The following equipment may be required: computer, modem, Internet access, e-mail.

Restrictions Programs are available worldwide. Enrollment is open to anyone.

Services Distance learners have access to library services, the campus computer network, e-mail services, bookstore at a distance.

Credit-earning options Students may transfer credits from another institution or may earn credits through examinations, military training.

Typical costs *Undergraduate:* Tuition of $92 per credit hour plus mandatory fees of $24.50 per credit hour. *Graduate:* Tuition of $107 per credit hour plus mandatory fees of $20 per credit hour. Costs may vary.

Registration Students may register by mail, fax, telephone, e-mail, in person.

Contact William White, Acting Dean, Graduate and Continuing Education, Worcester State College, Sullivan Building S-112A, 486 Chandler Street, Worcester, MA 01602-2597. *Telephone:* 508-929-8811. *Fax:* 508-929-8100. *E-mail:* wwhite@worcester.edu.

DEGREES AND AWARDS

Distance programs offered do not lead to a degree or other formal award.

COURSE SUBJECT AREAS OFFERED OUTSIDE OF DEGREE PROGRAMS

Noncredit: Computer and information sciences

WRIGHT STATE UNIVERSITY

Dayton, Ohio
Center for Teaching and Learning/Distance Learning
www.wright.edu/dl

Wright State University, founded in 1964, is a state-supported university. It is accredited by the North Central Association of Colleges and Schools. It first offered distance learning courses in 1995. In 1999–2000, it offered 50 courses at a distance. In fall 1999, there were 400 students enrolled in distance learning courses.

Course delivery sites Courses are delivered to your home, your workplace, military bases, high schools, The Ohio State University (Columbus), University of Cincinnati (Cincinnati), University of Dayton (Dayton), University of Virginia (Charlottesville, VA).

Media Courses are delivered via videotapes, videoconferencing, computer software, CD-ROM, computer conferencing, World Wide Web, e-mail, print. Students and teachers may meet in person or interact via videoconferencing, mail, telephone, fax, e-mail, World Wide Web. The following equipment may be required: videocassette player, computer, modem, Internet access, e-mail.

Restrictions Programs are available worldwide. Enrollment is open to anyone.

Services Distance learners have access to library services, the campus computer network, e-mail services, academic advising, bookstore at a distance.

Credit-earning options Students may transfer credits from another institution or may earn credits through examinations.

Typical costs *Undergraduate:* Tuition of $134 per credit hour for in-state residents. Tuition of $268 per credit hour for out-of-state residents. *Graduate:* Tuition of $184 per credit hour for in-state residents. Tuition of $368 per credit hour for out-of-state residents. Costs may vary. Financial aid is available to distance learners.

Registration Students may register by mail, telephone, World Wide Web, in person.

Contact Terri Klaus, Associate Director, Center for Teaching and Learning, Distance Learning, Wright State University, 023 Library, 3640 Colonel Glenn Highway, Dayton, OH 45435. *Telephone:* 937-775-4965. *Fax:* 937-775-3152. *E-mail:* terri.klaus@wright.edu.

DEGREES AND AWARDS

BS Nursing (certain restrictions apply)
MS Human Factors Engineering (certain restrictions apply), Rehabilitation Counseling (certain restrictions apply)

COURSE SUBJECT AREAS OFFERED OUTSIDE OF DEGREE PROGRAMS

Undergraduate: Education; electrical engineering; English language and literature; mechanical engineering; nursing; philosophy and religion
Graduate: Economics; engineering; geology; health professions and related sciences; nursing

WYTHEVILLE COMMUNITY COLLEGE

Wytheville, Virginia
www.wc.cc.va.us/

Wytheville Community College, founded in 1967, is a state-supported, two-year college. It is accredited by the Southern Association of Colleges and Schools. It first offered distance learning courses in 1981. In 1999–2000, it offered 30 courses at a distance. In fall 1999, there were 700 students enrolled in distance learning courses.

Course delivery sites Courses are delivered to your home, your workplace, high schools, 2 off-campus centers in Atkins, Galax.

Media Courses are delivered via television, videotapes, videoconferencing, interactive television, audiotapes, computer software, CD-ROM, computer conferencing, World Wide Web, e-mail, print. Students and teachers may meet in person or interact via videoconferencing, mail, telephone, fax, e-mail, interactive television, World Wide Web. The following equipment may be required: television, videocassette player, computer, Internet access, e-mail.

Restrictions Programs are available to in-state students only. Enrollment is open to anyone.

Services Distance learners have access to library services, e-mail services, academic advising, tutoring, bookstore at a distance.

Credit-earning options Students may transfer credits from another institution or may earn credits through examinations, portfolio assessment, military training, business training.

Typical costs Tuition of $37 per credit plus mandatory fees of $1.50 per credit for in-state residents. Tuition of $165 per credit plus mandatory fees of $1.50 per credit for out-of-state residents. *Noncredit courses:* $75 per course. Costs may vary. Financial aid is available to distance learners.

Registration Students may register by mail, fax, in person.

Contact Mr. David Carter-Tod, Instructional Technologist, Wytheville Community College, 1000 East Main Street, Wytheville, VA 24382. *Telephone:* 540-223-4784. *Fax:* 540-223-4778. *E-mail:* wccartd@wc.cc.va.us.

DEGREES AND AWARDS

Undergraduate Certificate(s) Information Systems Technology (service area differs from that of the overall institution)

COURSE SUBJECT AREAS OFFERED OUTSIDE OF DEGREE PROGRAMS

Undergraduate: Accounting; American (U.S.) history; biology; business; business administration and management; computer and information sciences; computer programming; database management; developmental and child psychology; economics; education; electronics; fine arts; health and physical education/fitness; information sciences and systems; marketing; philosophy and religion; political science; social sciences

See full description on page 676.

XAVIER UNIVERSITY OF LOUISIANA

New Orleans, Louisiana
Drexel Center for Extended Learning
www.xula.edu

Xavier University of Louisiana, founded in 1925, is an independent, religious, comprehensive institution. It is accredited by the Southern Association of Colleges and Schools. It first offered distance learning courses in 1989. In 1999–2000, it offered 4 courses at a distance. In fall 1999, there were 40 students enrolled in distance learning courses.
Course delivery sites Courses are delivered to your home, your workplace.
Media Courses are delivered via television, videotapes, videoconferencing, print. Students and teachers may meet in person or interact via telephone. The following equipment may be required: television, videocassette player.
Restrictions Programs are available to local area students. Enrollment is restricted to individuals meeting certain criteria.
Services Distance learners have access to the campus computer network, e-mail services at a distance.
Typical costs Tuition of $375 per credit. Financial aid is available to distance learners.
Registration Students may register by in person.
Contact Charlotte Johnson, Program Director, Xavier University of Louisiana, 7325 Palmetto Street, Box 41 A, New Orleans, LA 70125. *Telephone:* 504-483-7376. *Fax:* 504-485-7915.

DEGREES AND AWARDS

Undergraduate Certificate(s) Marketing (certain restrictions apply)

COURSE SUBJECT AREAS OFFERED OUTSIDE OF DEGREE PROGRAMS

Undergraduate: Area, ethnic, and cultural studies; business; business administration and management; economics; law and legal studies; political science; sociology

YORK COLLEGE OF PENNSYLVANIA

York, Pennsylvania
Special Programs
www.ycp.edu

York College of Pennsylvania, founded in 1787, is an independent, nonprofit, comprehensive institution. It is accredited by the Middle States Association of Colleges and Schools. It first offered distance learning courses in 1981. In 1999–2000, it offered 98 courses at a distance. In fall 1999, there were 315 students enrolled in distance learning courses.
Course delivery sites Courses are delivered to your home, your workplace, 5 off-campus centers in Chambersburg, Hanover, Harrisburg.
Media Courses are delivered via videoconferencing, interactive television, computer software, World Wide Web. Students and teachers may meet in person or interact via videoconferencing, telephone, fax, e-mail, interactive television. The following equipment may be required: Internet access.
Restrictions Programs are available worldwide. Enrollment is open to anyone.
Services Distance learners have access to library services, academic advising, bookstore at a distance.
Credit-earning options Students may transfer credits from another institution or may earn credits through examinations, portfolio assessment.
Typical costs Tuition of $600 per course plus mandatory fees of $76 per semester. Financial aid is available to distance learners.
Registration Students may register by mail, fax, telephone, e-mail, in person.
Contact Leroy M. Keeney, Director, Special Programs, York College of Pennsylvania, 1 Country Club Road, York, PA 17405. *Telephone:* 717-846-7788. *Fax:* 717-849-1607. *E-mail:* lkeeney@ycp.edu.

DEGREES AND AWARDS

BS Nursing

COURSE SUBJECT AREAS OFFERED OUTSIDE OF DEGREE PROGRAMS

Undergraduate: Accounting; business administration and management; business communications; communications; computer programming; database management; finance; information sciences and systems; investments and securities; mathematics; nursing

YORK TECHNICAL COLLEGE

Rock Hill, South Carolina
Distance Learning Department
www.yorktech.com

York Technical College, founded in 1961, is a state-supported, two-year college. It is accredited by the Southern Association of Colleges and Schools. It first offered distance learning courses in 1995. In 1999–2000, it offered 38 courses at a distance. In fall 1999, there were 603 students enrolled in distance learning courses.
Course delivery sites Courses are delivered to your home, your workplace, high schools, 1 off-campus center in Chester.
Media Courses are delivered via television, videotapes, interactive television, computer software, CD-ROM, computer conferencing, World Wide Web, print. Students and teachers may meet in person or interact via videoconferencing, mail, telephone, fax, e-mail, interactive television, World Wide Web. The following equipment may be required: television, videocassette player, computer, Internet access.

Restrictions Programs are available to in-state students only. Enrollment is restricted to individuals meeting certain criteria.
Services Distance learners have access to library services, the campus computer network, e-mail services at a distance.
Credit-earning options Students may transfer credits from another institution or may earn credits through examinations.
Typical costs Tuition of $47 per credit for local area residents. Tuition of $57 per credit for in-state residents. Tuition of $143 per credit for out-of-state residents. Costs may vary. Financial aid is available to distance learners.
Registration Students may register by mail, fax, telephone, e-mail, World Wide Web, in person.
Contact Anita McBride, Department Manager, York Technical College, Distance Learning, 452 South Anderson Road, Rock Hill, SC 29730. *Telephone:* 803-981-7044. *Fax:* 803-981-7193. *E-mail:* mcbride@york.tec.sc.us.

DEGREES AND AWARDS

Distance programs offered do not lead to a degree or other formal award.

COURSE SUBJECT AREAS OFFERED OUTSIDE OF DEGREE PROGRAMS

Undergraduate: Accounting; administrative and secretarial services; business administration and management; developmental and child psychology; electrical engineering; engineering-related technologies; English composition; history; industrial engineering; liberal arts, general studies, and humanities

See full description on page 676.

YUBA COLLEGE

Marysville, California
Learning Resource Center
yubalib.yuba.cc.ca.us

Yuba College, founded in 1927, is a state and locally supported, two-year college. It is accredited by the Western Association of Schools and Colleges, Inc. It first offered distance learning courses in 1975. In 1999–2000, it offered 79 courses at a distance. In fall 1999, there were 893 students enrolled in distance learning courses.

Course delivery sites Courses are delivered to your home, your workplace, military bases, high schools, 5 off-campus centers in Beale Center, Clearlake, Colusa Center, Live Oak Center, Woodland.
Media Courses are delivered via television, videotapes, videoconferencing, interactive television, computer conferencing, World Wide Web, e-mail, print. Students and teachers may meet in person or interact via videoconferencing, mail, telephone, fax, e-mail, interactive television, World Wide Web. The following equipment may be required: television, videocassette player.
Restrictions Programs are available in the Yuba Community College District. Enrollment is restricted to individuals meeting certain criteria.
Services Distance learners have access to library services, e-mail services, academic advising, career placement assistance at a distance.
Credit-earning options Students may transfer credits from another institution or may earn credits through examinations.
Typical costs *Undergraduate:* Tuition of $11 per unit plus mandatory fees of $6 per semester for in-state residents. Tuition of $145 per unit plus mandatory fees of $6 per unit for out-of-state residents. *Graduate:* Tuition of $11 per unit plus mandatory fees of $6 per semester for in-state residents. Tuition of $145 per unit plus mandatory fees of $11 per unit for out-of-state residents. Financial aid is available to distance learners.
Registration Students may register by in person.
Contact Jeanette O'Bryan, Distance Learning/Media Specialist, Yuba College, 2088 North Beale Road, Marysville, CA 95901. *Telephone:* 530-741-6754. *Fax:* 530-741-6824. *E-mail:* jobryan@mail2.yuba.cc.ca.us.

DEGREES AND AWARDS

Distance programs offered do not lead to a degree or other formal award.

COURSE SUBJECT AREAS OFFERED OUTSIDE OF DEGREE PROGRAMS

Undergraduate: Algebra; animal sciences; anthropology; area, ethnic, and cultural studies; astronomy and astrophysics; business administration and management; calculus; child care and development; classical languages and literatures; creative writing; education; electronics; English as a second language (ESL); English language and literature; film studies; fine arts; foods and nutrition studies; health and physical education/fitness; health professions and related sciences; history; home economics and family studies; Japanese language and literature; liberal arts, general studies, and humanities; mass media; nursing; philosophy and religion; physical sciences; political science; radio and television broadcasting; social psychology; Spanish language and literature

IN-DEPTH DESCRIPTIONS

The following two-page descriptions were prepared for this book by the institutions. An institution's absence from this section does not constitute an editorial decision on the part of Peterson's. Rather, it was offered as an open forum for institutions to expand upon the information provided in the previous section of this book. The descriptions are arranged alphabetically by institution name.

The American Institute for Computer Sciences

Distance Learning Programs

Birmingham, Alabama

The American Institute for Computer Sciences (AICS) is a privately owned independent college founded in 1988 to offer computer science and information systems degree programs. AICS provides busy adults with the opportunity to pursue their education at their convenience, in their own homes and offices. AICS is accredited by the Accrediting Commission of the Distance Education and Training Council.

DISTANCE LEARNING PROGRAM

AICS offers Bachelor of Science (B.S.) degrees in computer science and information systems and a Master of Science degree in computer science. All courses are taught via distance, through a combination of college textbooks, course materials, and multimedia tutorials. Students may enroll at anytime, anywhere. AICS does not require on-campus residency or scheduled class attendance, although online chats and lectures take place weekly. Full-time faculty are also available to assist students individually. Approximately 5,000 AICS students are located in over 120 countries.

DELIVERY MEDIA

AICS course delivery uses a mixture of text and technology in all degree programs. College textbooks and AICS' printed course materials are shipped in phases throughout the student's tenure. Online learning includes multimedia tutorials that take students through examples and self-tests of course concepts. These tutorials are also available in CD-ROM format. Additional reference materials and faculty-written tutorials are offered in online course labs, accessed through AICS' virtual campus.

Students interact with faculty during online weekly lectures and chats and individualized tutorial sessions via phone, fax and e-mail. Course assignments and final examinations are required throughout the programs; computer science courses require additional programming assignments. All graded work can be mailed to the school; however, AICS uses online testing and feedback software with many courses, and students may also submit work electronically.

Students must have a computer with Windows 95/98 or NT, a CD-ROM drive, and Internet access. Some IS courses require a sound card.

Programs Of Study All AICS curricula follows guidelines established by leading technology organizations, including the Association for Computing Machinery and the Institute for Electronic and Electrical Engineers. Both B.S. programs require 120-credit hours, with 60 hours in the core curriculum and 60 hours in the major. The core curriculum offers courses in written communications, humanities, behavioral and social sciences, and business.

The B.S. in information systems is designed for students interested in acquiring a broad base knowledge of computer information systems as they are used in modern organizational settings. Students complete a curriculum of required courses that cover the foundations of programming, database administration, networking and IS management. Students then choose one of three IS concentra-

tions: computer programming, electronic business development and management, or networking.

The B.S. in computer science uses C++ as its core language, adopted because it prepares students for real-world programming by teaching the methods for learning new languages. Students complete a series of required courses that cover fundamental programming concepts such as data structures, software engineering, computer architecture and operating systems. Electives include other programming languages and concepts such as Java, Visual Basic, artificial intelligence and database systems.

The M.S. in computer science is designed for students seeking research and development positions in business and industry. The program requires 36 credit hours and offers an in-depth treatment of theoretical foundations and formal methods in computer science, through study of several major concepts: algorithm design, communication networks, database systems, software engineering, compiler design and parallel processing.

STUDENT SERVICES

AICS' virtual campus offers a variety of services, including a Library with hundreds of links and online references; a Career Center with resume tips, job search guidelines, and job postings; a dormitory where students can link to personal and professional Web sites; a Student Center, complete with an online coffeehouse for chats and bulletin board discussions and an online post office; and a Conference Center where students can download music, link to technology seminars and conference notices and more.

CREDIT OPTIONS

Students may receive up to a total of 80 hours credit through a combination of credits transferred from other universities and credit awarded for life and work experience. Of the 80 hours, no more than 20 may be applied to the student's major. Students may receive up to 30 hours for life and work experience, which can be applied toward core curriculum credits. Students must complete a detailed work analysis and submit a resume and applicable documents for evaluation.

FACULTY

AICS has 21 full- and part-time faculty available to assist students through their course programs. Ninety percent of AICS faculty have earned their terminal or advanced degrees.

ADMISSION

Graduation from high school or satisfactory completion of the GED is required for admission into the B.S. programs. A Bachelor's degree in computer science or a related discipline is required for admission into the M.S. program.

TUITION AND FEES

Tuition includes all instruction and books and materials. Tuition for the B.S. programs is $90 per credit hour. Tuition for the M.S. program is $120 per credit hour. Individual courses may be taken for $395 (undergraduate), $515 (graduate). There is no application fee.

FINANCIAL AID

More than half of all AICS students receive financing assistance. AICS offers both interest-free and low-cost finance plans. Students may also gain financing through Sallie Mae Corporation. In addition, over 350 employers have reimbursed their employees who earned an AICS degree.

APPLYING

Students can apply for admission and enroll at any time. Both online and printed applications are available. Admissions advisers work with students by phone and e-mail to design a program most appropriate to their needs. The AICS Admissions Committee evaluates life and work experience documents and transcripts provided by the student and awards transfer credit. The enrollment process can be as short as one week.

CONTACT

AICS
Suite 207
2101 Magnolia Avenue
Birmingham, Alabama 35205
Phone: 205-323-6191
        800-729-2427 (toll-free)
E-mail: admiss@aics.edu
Web site: www.aics.edu

American Institute for Paralegal Studies

Oakbrook Terrace, Illinois

The American Institute for Paralegal Studies, offering certificate programs since 1978, is among the oldest providers of paralegal training in the United States. The Institute has trained paralegals from across the country within its unique, highly interactive learning environment.

The Institute's mission is to teach practical legal skills to working adult professionals in a supportive, flexible, and challenging academic environment. The American Institute for Paralegal Studies has been continuously accredited since 1981. The accrediting agency is the Accrediting Council for Continuing Education and Training (ACCET). ACCET is a national accrediting body recognized by the U.S. Department of Education.

DISTANCE LEARNING PROGRAM

Computer Mediated Distance Learning (CMDL) is a highly structured, highly interactive method of facilitating online courses. CMDL is much like a traditional classroom. The biggest difference is that there are no in-class lectures to attend. The computer network, which is accessed via the Internet, provides the structure for the interaction between paralegal students and faculty members. Easy-to-use computer conferencing software is provided to course registrants. A Web-based interface is also available.

DELIVERY MEDIA

CMDL should not be confused with home study courses, correspondence courses, or independent study courses. CMDL is much more like a traditional classroom. Traditional textbooks are the norm and are usually supplemented with workbooks and online study guides. Just like a traditional classroom, the instructor leads the class, gives reading and homework assignments, provides e-lectures or references for additional reading, and facilitates discussions. Paralegal courses are organized into units, with each unit open from several days to a week. Within each unit,

the instructor assigns reading, exercises, and other homework. Class discussion is an integral part of each unit. The instructor presents an initial question. Students think about and post their initial answers, and the instructor comments, corrects, encourages, and then further develops the discussion. Students quickly learn how to prepare for a discussion question and how best to participate.

Discussion questions are not conducted in real time. While live chat rooms are available for socializing, they are not used for formal class work. Instead, the software organizes the discussions into threaded conferences, which makes it easy to follow the discussion flow. Students can participate any time of the day or night, seven days a week. However, because CMDL classes follow a traditional schedule, it is essential that students keep up with the work. Equipment needs are simple. Students need a PC or Macintosh computer and Internet access. The Institute provides the software to connect to its network.

PROGRAMS OF STUDY

The Institute offers the following courses: American jurisprudence; estates, trusts, and probate; torts and personal injury; business law; family law; criminal law; real estate, transfer, and ownership; litigation, pleadings, and arbitration; legal research and writing; legal writing; bankruptcy; LEXIS workshop; alternative dispute resolution; and employment law.

SPECIAL PROGRAMS

The American Institute for Paralegal Studies is a sponsor of the Consortium for Advanced Legal Education (CALE). CALE is a nonprofit educational organization established for the purpose of providing advanced specialty courses for learning delivery to legal professionals. Its goal is to service the legal education marketplace through strategic alliances among educators, publishers, content providers, associations, organizations, and legal professionals. Paralegal graduates of the Institute are eligible to enroll in CALE courses. To sign up for CALE courses, students should visit the CALE Web site (http://www. cale.org).

STUDENT SERVICES

The goal of placement assistance is to help students understand the array of career options available to paralegal graduates and to offer individualized guidance in making knowledgeable choices based on these career options. This is accomplished by customizing a plan of action for each student who chooses placement assistance. The customized plan of action is developed jointly by the program director and the student. It identifies which areas of law are of particular interest to the student, which avenues need to be explored to pursue a career in one or more of these areas, and which specific strategies should be used to seek a position. Specific job search options are identified, including Internet searches, local placement agencies, temporary legal staffing agencies, professional paralegal associations, local newspaper classifieds, and selected legal publications.

CREDIT OPTIONS

Since 1997, the Institute has maintained an articulation agreement with the University of Phoenix, America's largest private accredited university for working adults. Currently, up to 20 semester credits can be awarded by the University of Phoenix as upper-division credits for American Institute course work.

FACULTY

All American Institute faculty members are licensed attorneys. All are involved extensively in distance education. Faculty members respond to questions quickly, within 24 hours.

Peer-to-peer conferences are also available to facilitate student collaboration.

ADMISSION

Registrants must have an undergraduate degree (associate's, bachelor's, or equivalent credits) or have two years of law related work experience prior to registering for the Institute's program.

TUITION AND FEES

The cost of tuition is $4815. Books cost $590.

FINANCIAL AID

For the convenience of its students, the American Institute works in cooperation with the Sallie Mae Financial Corporation in order to meet the financial needs of its students seeking resources for distance learning

education. The loan amount can include tuition, books, and funds to purchase computer equipment for students' education. Rates as low as Prime + 1 percent produce low monthly payments and an ideal educational loan value. SLM offers terms up to 15 years.

Students also have the option to elect an interest free payment plan by paying tuition in twelve equal installments of $384.58. Students electing this plan can begin the program with a deposit of $200 plus the book fee.

APPLYING

Interested candidates can register for the Institute's paralegal program by printing out and completing the application form, available on the Web at http://www.aips.com/registration. html. Questions should be directed to Course Facilitator John Shaheen at 800-472-9404 (toll-free) or via e-mail (john@aips.com).

CONTACT

American Institute for Paralegal Studies
17W705 Butterfield Road, Suite A
Oakbrook Terrace, Illinois 60181
Telephone: 630-916-6880
       800-553-2420 (toll-free)
Fax: 630-916-6694
World Wide Web: http://www.aips.com

Auburn University

Graduate Outreach Program

Auburn, Alabama

Auburn University was chartered in 1856 as the East Alabama Male College. In 1872, Auburn became a state institution—the first land-grant university in the South to be separate from a state university. Auburn University, selected as one of the nation's top 100 college buys by The Student Guide to America's 100 Best College Buys 1999, is dedicated to serving the state and the nation through instruction, research, and extension. Auburn University is accredited by the Commission on Colleges of the Southern Association of Colleges and Schools.

The campus consists of more than 1,800 acres, with a student body of approximately 21,500. Auburn University, the largest school in the state of Alabama, is located in east-central Alabama. The city of Auburn has a population of about 35,000. Auburn is known for its small-town, friendly atmosphere and is often referred to as "the loveliest village on the Plain."

DISTANCE LEARNING PROGRAM

In response to industry's request, Auburn's College of Engineering began offering courses to off-campus students through the Graduate Outreach Program in 1984. The College of Business made Master of Business Administration (M.B.A.) courses available in 1990. The Graduate Outreach Program allows professionals the opportunity to continue their education while maintaining full-time employment. The program serves more than 400 students in forty states. The M.B.A. program is accredited by AACSB–The International Association for Management Education.

Note for international inquirers: Due to material distribution methods, the current distance learning program service area is limited to the U.S. and Canada and to U.S. military personnel with APO or FPO mailing addresses.

DELIVERY MEDIA

The Graduate Outreach Program makes every effort to ensure that the off-campus students receive the same high-quality education as on-campus students. Live classes are videotaped daily and distributed in standard VHS format. Professors establish telephone office hours and/or e-mail communication so that off-campus students may receive answers to any questions they may have. E-mail accounts are established for the Graduate Outreach Program students. Most faculty members also utilize the Internet to post handouts and class materials.

PROGRAMS OF STUDY

The Graduate Outreach Program offers master's degrees in eight different disciplines in engineering, the Master of Management Information Systems, the Master of Accounting, and the Master of Business Administration degree. The Master of Aerospace Engineering, Chemical Engineering, Civil Engineering, Computer Science and Engineering, Electrical and Computer Engineering, Industrial and Systems Engineering, Materials Engineering, and Mechanical Engineering are all nonthesis programs without residency requirements. Each candidate must pass an on-campus, comprehensive, oral examination covering the program of study to graduate. The examination covers the major and minor subjects, including any research or special projects involved. The Master of Science degree, offered in eight disciplines, requires a formal written thesis and at least one quarter of full-time residence.

In the Master of Business Administration program, students may earn a concentration in either finance, health care administration, human resource management, marketing, operations management, management information systems, or management of technology. The program consists of 36 to 42 semester hours of course work, including a minimum of 15 elective hours. Applicants are required to complete a course in calculus and statistics prior to entering the program. Students with non-business undergraduate degrees may be required to pass foundations exams in economics, finance, marketing, management, and accounting. Incoming students are also advised to have a working knowledge of word processing and spreadsheet software and an elementary understanding of database applications. M.B.A. students must visit the campus for three to five days during their last quarter prior to graduating for on-campus presentations.

Nondegree professional development courses are available for those who need to meet job requirements or professional certification.

SPECIAL PROGRAMS

Career and job placement assistance is available through Auburn University's Career and Student Development Services. Accessibility to the R. B. Draughon Library is also available. A valid Auburn University student identification card is required to check out resources. The Division of University Computing provides University-wide computing and networking services to students. Computer accounts are free of charge to currently enrolled students.

CREDIT OPTIONS

Graduate credit taken in residence at another approved graduate school may be transferred to Auburn University but is not accepted until the student has completed at least 9 hours of work in the Graduate School at Auburn University. No prior commitment is made concerning whether transfer credit will be accepted. A student must earn at least 21 semester hours or half of the total hours required for a master's degree (whichever is greater) at Auburn University. No transfer credit is approved without two official transcripts. No course in which a grade lower than B was earned may be transferred.

FACULTY

The Auburn University faculty consists of more than 1,200 members. Eighty percent of the faculty members hold a doctoral degree, and 88 percent hold a terminal degree in their field.

ADMISSION

An applicant to the Graduate School must hold a bachelor's degree or its equivalent from an accredited college or university. The Graduate Record Examinations (GRE) is required for admission to the College of Engineering, and the Graduate Management Admission Test (GMAT) is required for admission to the M.B.A. program. Admission is based on the grade point average of university-level courses, GRE or GMAT scores, and recommendation letters from instructors and supervisors. Students can be informed by the Graduate Outreach Program on how they can enroll as off-campus students once they are accepted by the Graduate School.

TUITION AND FEES

The Graduate Outreach Program fees are $303 per credit hour for engineering and $341 per credit hour for the M.B.A. program. There is no longer a part-time registration fee. Registration schedules and fee bills are mailed to the student prior to the beginning of each quarter.

FINANCIAL AID

Military personnel who have been accepted into the Graduate School may apply for tuition aid through DANTES at their local education office. Many of the Graduate Outreach Program students receive tuition assistance through their employer's tuition reimbursement plan. The Auburn University Office of Student Financial Aid assists in the awarding of grants, loans, and scholarships for qualified full-time students.

APPLYING

To apply for admission, a prospective student must return a Graduate School application, an M.B.A. application (if applicable), a $25 nonrefundable application fee, three letters of recommendation, GRE or GMAT scores, and two official transcripts of all undergraduate and subsequent course work from the respective institutions. An online application is now available for Graduate School applicants (http://gradweb.duc.auburn.edu/webapp/appfrm_web.mv). This ensures a quicker response in most cases.

CONTACT

James C. Brandt
Student Services
Graduate Outreach Program
202 Ramsay Hall
Auburn University
Auburn, Alabama 36849-5336
Telephone: 888-844-5300 (toll-free)
Fax: 334-844-2519
E-mail: jcbrandt@eng.auburn.edu
Web site: http://www.auburn.edu/gop/

Baker College

Center for Graduate Studies
On-Line College

Flint, Michigan

Baker College, founded in the true American tradition as a small business college in 1888, is a private, nonprofit, accredited, coeducational institution. The College has more than a dozen campuses and branch locations in the Midwest and has a total enrollment of more than 17,000 students. The College is uniquely designed for one purpose: to provide high-quality higher education that enables graduates to be successful throughout their challenging and rewarding careers. The College offers diploma, certificate, and associate, bachelor's, and master's degree programs in the fields of business, technical, and health service fields. Total commitment to the students' employment success in uniquely evident in all aspects of the College's operations.

Baker College is accredited by the Commission on Institutions of Higher Education of the North Central Association of Colleges and Schools. Baker College is an equal opportunity affirmative action institution.

DISTANCE LEARNING PROGRAM

Baker College On-Line offers the convenience of classroom accessibility 24 hours a day, seven days a week, from virtually anywhere in the world. Because students do all classroom work off-line, schedules are flexible. A student goes on line to send and receive completed work and other materials. It is not a self-paced program. Courses begin and end on specific dates, and class work is assigned deadlines.

DELIVERY MEDIA

Students are required to have a computer with the following minimum requirements: a 486 computer system or higher, a 3.5 high-density floppy drive, a 28.8 bps modem (minimum), and a hard drive capacity exceeding the student's current demands by at least 100 megabytes. A CD-ROM and an Internet service provider are required. The virtual classroom is the common meeting area for all students taking classes on line. Communication is accomplished by sending messages back and forth from the student's computer to the classroom computer. Each classroom has a unique name, and only students taking that class have access to the virtual classroom. This ensures privacy for all students.

PROGRAMS OF STUDY

Baker College On-Line offers the delivery of high-quality, respected courses and programs that enable a student to earn an associate, bachelor's, or master's degree at home, on the road, or anywhere in the world.

The Associate of Business Administration degree has been designed specifically for the On-Line College environment, where students have a variety of choices in filling out the degree plan. The curriculum gives students a good background of business facts and knowledge upon which to build or enhance a career in business.

The Bachelor of Business Administration degree is a program designed for the working professional that combines core course work with independent research and experiential credit to provide a contemporary business degree for today's business environment. Each core course contains focused study in the content area accompanied by independent research.

The Master of Business Administration degree program seeks to combine the best of conventional academic training with the best of field-based learning. Most typical business disciplines are represented in the curriculum because the College believes that a successful manager must be conversant with different aspects of running any of today's organizations or companies. Students may also elect to focus their studies in one of the following areas: computer information systems, health-care management, human resource management, industrial management, integrated health care, international business, leadership studies, or marketing.

SPECIAL PROGRAMS

The On-Line College offers undergraduate courses at all levels to support all of the campuses and their program offerings as a convenience for students who may have trouble commuting to a campus. The On-Line College publishes a listing each quarter showing which classes will be offered.

STUDENT SERVICES

Every Baker College student is assigned an e-mail account on the BakerNet system. Through this system, students can communicate with each other and their instructors and with members of the graduate school staff. Students may also use their accounts to access the World Wide Web. They also have access to the Baker

College Library System and FALCON, a consortium of libraries that supports an online catalog database of more than 500,000 holdings. Students also have access to InfoTrac periodical indexing databases, the UMI/ProQuest General Periodicals On-Disc full-article imaging station, Books-in-Print with Reviews, and all available Internet and World Wide Web resources.

Baker College offers a renowned Lifetime Employment Service, with access to thousands of career opportunities and employment databases, to all students. This service can be used for the rest of one's life.

CREDIT OPTIONS

Baker College recognizes the expediency of understandable and universally accepted standards related to transfer of academic credit. The College follows the Michigan Association of Collegiate Registrars and Admissions Officers Official Policies and recognizes the College-Level Examination Program (CLEP) or other standardized tests.

FACULTY

The focus of Baker's faculty is somewhat different from that of traditional universities. Instead of placing an emphasis on empirical research, Baker values practitioner-oriented educa-tion. Faculty members remain continually active in their professions by consulting, conducting seminars, running their own businesses, writing, volunteering in their communities, and working with other organizations. The faculty-student ratio in distance education is 1:11.

ADMISSION

Graduate program candidates must have a bachelor's degree from an accredited institution and a 2.5 or better GPA in their undergraduate work, be able to display appropriate communication skills, submit three letters of reference, submit a current resume, and have completed no less than three years of full-time work. Undergraduates must have graduated from high school, completed a GED, or passed an Ability to Benefit assessment before entering.

TUITION AND FEES

Undergraduate tuition for the 2000–01 school year is $150 per credit hour. Graduate tuition is $230 per credit hour. The cost of books ranges from $200 to $300 per quarter.

FINANCIAL AID

Students who are accepted into Baker College may be considered for several forms of state, federal, and insti-tutional financial aid. Students are requested to complete the Free Application for Federal Student Aid (FAFSA) and return it directly to the College.

APPLYING

Baker College uses a rolling admission process, so there are no deadlines for applications. Students are allowed to begin in any quarter. Once the Admissions Committee receives an application, applicants usually receive a decision in approximately four weeks. Once accepted, students participate in a three-week online orientation. They are not required to visit a campus at any time.

CONTACT

Chuck J. Gurden
Director of On-Line Admissions
Center for Graduate Studies
Baker College
1050 West Bristol Road
Flint, Michigan 48507-5508
Telephone: 810-766-4390
800-469-3165 (toll-free)
Fax: 810-766-4399
E-mail: gurden_c@corpfl.baker.edu
Web site: http://www.baker.edu

Barton County Community College

BARTONline

Great Bend, Kansas

> *Barton County Community College was formed in 1965 and has always worked to fulfill the mission of improving the economic and social being of its students.*

DISTANCE LEARNING PROGRAM

BARTONline was created in March 1999 to provide greater access for students and to provide much-needed course work and student services to current, former, and potential Barton County Community College students. The online campus was created through the assistance of the Colorado-based company eCollege.com.

DELIVERY MEDIA

Students must have access to a computer with Windows 95 or 98 or Mac OS. In addition, a computer with multimedia capability, a modem, a full-service Web browser, audio and video capability, an Internet provider, and an e-mail account is required. Some classes may also require the student to view videos via a television and VCR. BARTONline has partnered with eCollege.com to provide the course delivery system for courses offered via the Internet.

PROGRAM OF STUDY

More than fifty courses are offered in the special fields of business, dietary management, hazardous materials, nutrition, military history, and pension administration. All courses are offered for college credit and can count toward an associate degree. The courses have been developed to provide certification opportunities through the national Dietary Manag-

er's Association and American Society of Pension Actuaries. The program is approved by DANTES, and Barton County Community College is a Servicemember's Opportunity College. Barton is experienced with the special circumstances of military students. Through participation in EduKan.org, Barton County Community College offers students general education courses that can complement the specialized courses on the BARTONline site.

SPECIAL PROGRAMS

These courses are recommended for adult learners who may not be able to take traditional classes due to conflicting schedules, multiple responsibilities, and/or long driving distances. High school students who would like to get a head start on their college education are good candidates as well.

STUDENT SERVICES

BARTONline provides a wide array of services to the student on line. These services include academic advising, career placement assistance, library services, transcript requests, business office services, and bookstore access. The College's goal is to provide any essential campus service via the Internet.

CREDIT OPTIONS

All courses are offered for college credit and count toward Barton

County Community College's graduation requirements. Courses are offered in eight- and sixteen-week cycles of classes, and most courses are 3 credit hours.

FACULTY

All of the faculty members have teaching experience and online training and are respected members of the College and their profession. Military history courses are taught by retired military officers, and dietary management courses are taught by registered dieticians. Most of the other instructors also teach full-time for Barton County Community College.

ADMISSION

Kansas community colleges operate under an open admissions policy. Admission and enrollment forms are combined into one form and outlined on the Web site. Current high school students may get a start in their college education through these courses or receive training for a full- or part-time job. Most students admitted are high school or GED graduates or transfer students. The College is also a Servicemember's Opportunity College and a DANTES member and encourages military student enrollment.

TUITION AND FEES

The cost is the same for all students, at $125 per credit hour, excluding textbooks. The cost is the same, regardless of Kansas residency status.

FINANCIAL AID

Part-time scholarships and other forms of financial aid are available for those who qualify. Application information is available on the Web site.

Federal financial aid forms can also be completed on line. Students may also qualify for veterans aid and military tuition assistance.

APPLYING

Students may apply and learn more about BARTONline via the Web site listed below.

CONTACT

Leigh Cunningham
Bartonline Coordinator
Barton County Community College
245 Northeast 30th Road
Great Bend, Kansas 67530
Telephone: 800-732-6842 (toll-free)
E-mail: cunninghaml@barton.cc.ks.us
Web site: http://www.bartonline.org

Bentley College

Graduate Programs in Taxation

Waltham, Massachusetts

Bentley College is committed to providing the most advanced business education possible. Approximately 4,200 undergraduate, 1,500 graduate and 2,500 executive and professional education students learn in an environment that integrates information technology with a broad business and arts and sciences curriculum. Students gain knowledge, interpersonal skills, and experience for careers in a global economy. Bentley is located in Waltham, Massachusetts, ten miles west of Boston. Founded in 1917, Bentley is accredited by the New England Association of Schools and Colleges and AACSB–The International Association for Management Education.

Academic programs at Bentley combine business and information technology to prepare students for a workplace that is increasingly global, information-rich, and technology-driven. The College offers undergraduate degrees in all major business fields and in the arts and sciences; graduate programs that include specialized master of science degrees and a new two-year Information Age MBA; and a variety of executive and professional education programs designed for working professions.

DISTANCE LEARNING PROGRAM

Building on twenty-five years of national prominence, the graduate tax program at Bentley College offers new opportunities for accounting, financial planning, and tax practitioners through its new distance learning program. Distance education students enjoy the same high-quality learning experience as the students who are taking classes on campus. The course material is identical.

DELIVERY MEDIA

Using specialized software, classes meet in real time over the Internet. This highly collaborative courseware provides live, two-way audio communication among students and faculty members, using a PC microphone and dial-up modem or corporate network. Classes are enhanced with on-screen graphics.

Live videoconferencing is another way to pursue distance learning at Bentley. Several courses taught on campus are simultaneously broadcast to videoconference sites in Boston and Worcester, Massachusetts. Interaction also occurs via e-mail, telephone, and a comprehensive, dynamic course Web site.

PROGRAMS OF STUDY

The Department of Taxation and Personal Financial Planning offers a distance program that can lead to a Master of Science in Taxation or a graduate certificate in taxation. Established in 1974, the Master of Science in Taxation (M.S.T.) program at Bentley College was one of the first programs of its kind in the United States. The M.S.T. offers a unique all-tax learning experience that readies students for leadership in the field of taxation as well as careers as tax advisers, consultants, and executives in private and public firms. The M.S.T. program consists of 10 graduate tax courses, all of which earn three hours of credit. Five of the courses are required and five are electives. Two courses constitutes a full-time load for part-time students.

The graduate certificate in taxation enables students who have earned a bachelor's degree to gain essential knowledge in the foundation of taxation principles. Certificate candidates take all five of the required courses in the M.S.T. program. Course work must be completed in five years.

SPECIAL PROGRAMS

The Elkin B. McCallum Graduate School and the Center for Professional and Executive Education offer a selected number of credit and noncredit courses via the Web and through videoconferencing. Information on these programs is available on the College Web site listed below.

FACULTY

The professors teaching courses through distance education are the same faculty members who teach on campus. Generally, they have earned doctorates and possess professional business experience.

ADMISSION

The GMAT may be waived for applicants who have passed the bar or COA exam, or who have earned a graduate degree in an appropriate business-related area. Detailed information is available on the Web site listed below.

TUITION AND FEES

Students taking synchronous web or videoconferencing classes pay regular campus tuition, which is $2,135 per three-credit course.

FINANCIAL AID

The Office of Graduate Financial Assistance administers need-based financial aid programs and offers non-need-based loans, using a combination of federal and institutional formulas to determine eligibility. Students should contact the Office of Graduate Financial Assistance at 781-891-3168 for information. Copies of the brochure *Financing Your Graduate Education* are available from the Graduate Admission Office and the Office of Graduate Financial Assistance.

APPLYING

Applications may be downloaded from the Web at www.bentley.edu/ graduate. Distance learning students may take up to two courses before being accepted into the M.S.T. or certificate program by completing a special distance learning application. These students must submit a regular application if they later choose to pursue the certificate or M.S.T. degree.

CONTACT

William Wiggins
Associate Professor and Chairperson
Department of Taxation and Personal Financial Planning
Bentley College
175 Forest Street
Waltham, Massachusetts 02452
Telephone: 781-891-2249
E-mail: wwiggins@bentley.edu
Web site: http:\\www.bentley.edu

Boston University

College of Engineering
Department of Manufacturing Engineering

Boston, Massachusetts

Boston University, incorporated in 1869, is an independent, coeducational, nonsectarian university, open to members of all minority groups. Its 22,515 full-time students and 2,559 faculty members make it one of the largest independent universities in the world. The Department of Manufacturing Engineering offers B.S., M.S., and Ph.D. degrees and was the first department in the country with an ABET-accredited B.S. program in manufacturing engineering. Interaction with local industry through research and part-time-study corporate programs has created a focus on state-of-the-art educational and research issues.

DISTANCE LEARNING PROGRAM

The Interactive-Compressed Video (ICV) graduate program in manufacturing engineering, comprised of courses identical to those for the on-campus degree, is designed to satisfy the needs of part-time students in industry. The department is a pioneer in distance learning, graduating its first student with an M.S. degree entirely attained by ICV in 1992.

DELIVERY MEDIA

The department maintains three state-of-the-art PictureTel videoconferencing systems. These systems transmit at speeds ranging from switched 56 to the full-motion video capability of 384 K. PictureTel equipment is compatible with other PictureTel equipment, as well as equipment from other vendors, if those systems meet H.320 standards for video and audio.

PROGRAMS OF STUDY

Courses focus on the technical aspects of design and production. Three concentrations are offered for the master's degree via ICV: manufacturing systems, manufacturing operations management, and process design. While not all of the courses available on campus are offered via ICV, sufficient courses are offered to enable a student to complete all requirements for the M.S. degree in manufacturing engineering, which may be completed in approximately three years.

A limited number of special/nondegree students are admitted each semester. Persons not wishing to pursue a graduate degree may enroll in courses for which they meet prerequisite requirements. Special/nondegree students may apply at any time prior to completing a third course for admission to the degree program. Only three courses taken as a special/nondegree student may be applied to the master's degree.

SPECIAL PROGRAMS

The department encourages all part-time students in industry to visit the campus and become familiar with the resources it can offer. The faculty particularly welcomes the opportunity provided in these visits to develop more significant and lasting relationships with the part-time video students. Matriculated students who wish to visit the campus have access to all facilities, including University libraries and athletic facilities.

Another feature of the program is that each instructor is expected to visit the company at least once during each course offering so that students get to know their instructors firsthand.

Boston University has developed a substantial collaborative relationship with the Fraunhofer Resource Center Massachusetts. A state-of-the-art laboratory supporting this endeavor houses exceptional equipment for work in high-performance machining and rapid prototyping. The Boston University/Fraunhofer collaboration engages manufacturing engineering students and faculty members in programs of contract industrial research directed toward finding practical solutions to actual problems from manufacturing industry customers. Although participation by Fraunhofer personnel in ICV education is limited at present, this interaction is expected to increase.

CREDIT OPTIONS

The master's program in manufacturing engineering consists of 36 credit hours (ordinarily nine courses), of which no fewer than 28 credits must be earned at

Boston University and at least 20 credits are from technically oriented courses. A cumulative grade point average of at least 3.0 (B) is required for all courses taken at Boston University and for all courses offered for the degree.

FACULTY

The Department of Manufacturing Engineering has about 20 full-time faculty members. All are actively engaged in industrial problems through writing, consulting, and research.

ADMISSION

Students accepted into the master's program in manufacturing engineering are expected to have earned a bachelor's degree in engineering. Students with strong mathematics backgrounds and aptitudes, but nonengineering degrees, may also apply.

TUITION AND FEES

Tuition for 2000–2001 is $772 per credit hour. There is an additional registration fee of $40 per semester. Students may pay as individuals and seek reimbursement from their company, or the University can bill the company.

FINANCIAL AID

No departmental financial aid is offered. Students are typically sponsored by their companies.

APPLYING

Students seeking special student status should contact the department. Students seeking admission to the M.S. program should request and complete an application packet.

CONTACT

Elizabeth Spencer-Dawes
Distance Learning Administrator
Department of Manufacturing Engineering
Boston University
15 St. Mary's Street
Boston, Massachusetts 02215
Telephone: 617-353-2943
Fax: 617-353-5548
E-mail: icu@bu.edu
Web site: http://www.bu.edu/mfg/icu

Brigham Young University

Independent Study

Provo, Utah

Brigham Young University (BYU) traces its roots to Utah's rich pioneer heritage. The original school, Brigham Young Academy, was established in 1875, on a little more than 1 acre of land in what is today downtown Provo. At that time, Brigham Young, the second president of the Church of Jesus Christ of Latter-day Saints (LDS), charged that all secular learning at the institution should be fused with teaching from the scriptures. No longer a primary school in a pioneer town, BYU is a world-renowned center of learning that remains true to that original charge from its namesake.

The mission of Brigham Young University—founded, supported, and guided by the Church of Jesus Christ of Latter-day Saints—is to assist individuals in their quest for perfection and eternal life. That assistance should provide a period of intensive learning in a stimulating setting where a commitment to excellence is expected and the full realization of human potential is pursued. All instruction, programs, and services at BYU, including a wide variety of extracurricular experiences, should make their own contribution toward the balanced development of the total person. Such a broadly prepared individual is not only be capable of meeting personal challenge and change but also brings strength to others in the tasks of home and family life, social relationships, civic duty, and service to mankind.

DISTANCE LEARNING PROGRAM

Independent Study serves as an extension of the University by providing quality correspondence courses. There are more than 44,000 enrollments in distance education or a nontraditional education. BYU offers more than 350 college courses and more than 175 high school courses through Independent Study. BYU Independent Study is fully accredited by the Northwest Association of Schools and Colleges and is a member of the National University Continuing Education Association.

DELIVERY MEDIA

Faculty members and students maintain regular contact through mail service, telephone, and e-mail. Fax and UPS Express services are also available if a student is in a rush to submit assignments or to receive grades. Many courses make use of speedback, cassette tapes, fax, and CD-ROM. Many courses may be taken on line (http://coned.byu.edu/is/). Students are also able to enroll and check grades on the Internet, if they have access to a computer.

PROGRAMS OF STUDY

Up to 36 semester hours of work completed through Independent Study can be used toward a bachelor's degree from BYU, and courses are also available for teacher recertification. Individual high school–level courses, an adult diploma program, a transcript program, and noncredit courses for personal development and enrichment are also available.

Certificate programs are offered for organ and family history research. The organ performance program offers six levels designed to provide motivation for an organist to improve his or her skills by working toward specific goals. A certificate of competence is received for each level completed. The certificate program for family his-tory research provides a solid background in fundamental family history research principles coupled with specialized genealogical training in North American or British research. The certificate requires 18 hours of course work. Through the Bachelor of General Studies Department, BYU offers a Bachelor of General Studies (B.G.S.) degree. This degree has a general studies major, with an emphasis in one of eight areas.

SPECIAL PROGRAMS

Brigham Young University's Division of Continuing Education is one of the largest such programs in America. These enrollments are the equivalent of more than 22,000 full-time students. In conjunction with the LDS Church Educational System, the Division provides an extensive schedule of classes, lectures, and seminars—including BYU Campus Education Week, which attracts nearly 30,000 participants. Other learning opportunities include evening classes, conferences, and workshops; independent study; travel study; and youth and family programs. The Division also operates and coordinates programs from centers in Salt Lake City, California, Idaho, and Hawaii.

The purpose of the Division of Continuing Education is to provide educational programs and University services for part-time and off-campus students. These educational opportunities also assist regular daytime students. BYU cooperates with the Continuing Education programs as sponsored by the Church Educational System and its various components. The same University standards required of regular day students apply to those enrolled through the

Division of Continuing Education while they are on campus.

CREDIT OPTIONS

Independent Study courses carry BYU credit, which is awarded on a semester hour basis. The courses are comparable in content and rigor to courses taken on campus. Independent Study does not grant credit by test or for life experience.

FACULTY

There are 352 instructors at BYU Independent Study. Fifty-eight percent of the faculty have doctoral or other terminal academic degrees.

ADMISSION

BYU Independent Study has an open enrollment policy. Enrollment in an Independent Study course does not constitute admission to BYU.

TUITION AND FEES

Tuition for University-level courses is $94 per semester hour, unless otherwise stated. Tuition includes the cost of the course manual for each course. It does not include the cost of textbooks, supplemental course materials, handling fees, airmail fees, or fax fees. High school tuition is $90 per half-unit and $55 per quarter-unit credit.

FINANCIAL AID

Independent Study scholarships and grants-in-aid are awarded three times a year. Awards are made for 1, 2, and 3 University semester hours. Preference is given to applicants who have completed one or more Independent Study courses. The University also considers applicants with a B+ (3.4) or higher grade point average for scholarships first.

APPLYING

Enrollments are accepted by telephone and on line. BYU Independent Study accepts MasterCard, Visa, or Discover. Once enrollment information has been received, the materials ordered for the course are sent. Textbooks are not included in the price of tuition; they may be purchased at the BYU Bookstore.

CONTACT

Registrar
BYU Independent Study
Brigham Young University
206 Harman Building
P.O. Box 21514
Provo, Utah 84606-1514
Telephone: 801-378-8292
          800-914-8931 (toll-free)
Fax: 801-378-5817
E-mail: indstudy@byu.edu
Web site: http://coned.byu.edu/is/

Caldwell College

External Degree Program

Caldwell, New Jersey

Caldwell College is a Catholic, coeducational, four-year liberal arts institution committed to intellectual rigor, individual attention, and the ethical values of the Judeo-Christian academic tradition. Founded in 1939 by the Sisters of St. Dominic, the College is accredited by the Middle States Association of Colleges and Universities, chartered by the State of New Jersey, and registered with the Regents of the University of the State of New York. Located on a 100-acre wooded campus in a quiet suburban community 20 miles from New York City, Caldwell provides a serene and secure environment conducive to study and learning.

Caldwell College offers a 13:1 student-faculty ratio, small classes, and individual attention. Professors know their students by name, challenge them to strive for excellence, and provide the support needed to achieve it. This close relationship between faculty members and students also leads to a spirit of friendship throughout the campus community. Approximately half of the 1,902 men and women enrolled at the College are adults pursuing degrees part-time or obtaining new skills to compete in the changing marketplace. Through the College's Center for Continuing Education, these adults seek personal growth, professional enrichment, and career advancement. All students find the staff ready to provide the personalized academic planning that will help them succeed in their studies and careers.

DISTANCE LEARNING PROGRAM

Caldwell College pioneered the external degree concept in 1979, becoming the first higher education institution in the state of New Jersey to offer students the option of completing their degrees without attending on-campus classes. Caldwell designed the program especially for busy adults whose work or family commitments make it difficult to follow a weekly on-campus academic schedule. Traditional course work is presented in a flexible and convenient format. External Degree students are required to be on campus only for External Degree Saturday at the beginning of each semester. Students pursuing their bachelor's degrees through the External Degree Program use the same textbooks and complete the same course work as their on-campus counterparts.

DELIVERY MEDIA

Students learn with the guidance of an academic mentor and through interaction with the faculty via phone, personal conferences, e-mail, mailing or faxing of assignments, audiocassette, videocassette, and computer technologies.

PROGRAM OF STUDY

The External Degree Program offers seventeen majors. Bachelor of Science degrees are offered in accounting, business administration, computer information systems, international business, marketing, and management. Bachelor of Arts degrees are offered in art (some on-campus work is required for art majors), communication arts, criminal justice, English, history, political science, psychology, religious studies, sociology, and social studies.

Eligibility for a degree requires completion of 122 credits and a GPA of at least 2.0 (C). This includes completing 57 liberal arts and science core curriculum credits, requirements specific to the student's major, and open electives. Students must also complete major courses with a minimum grade of C and satisfy all other departmental requirements. Overall, a minimum of 45 credits must be taken at Caldwell

College, with the last 30 credits of the 122-credit requirement completed at the College before a degree is awarded. Transfer students must complete at least half the total number of credits for a given major at Caldwell College.

Students enrolled in undergraduate or graduate distance education programs at other institutions are permitted to enroll as visiting (nonmatriculated) students in the Caldwell College External Degree Program. Visiting External Degree students may register for courses offered in accounting, business administration, international business, management, and marketing only and must be age 23 or older. Course registration opens three weeks prior to the beginning of each semester. Permission to enroll as a visiting student is granted by the Director of the External Degree Program through the Center for Continuing Education. Visiting students are required to attend new-student orientation and mandatory meetings with instructors on External Degree Saturday to receive course materials. In order to participate in this program, students must submit a completed External Degree Visiting Student Application form with a $10 processing fee to the Center for Continuing Education. Visiting students may register for two courses per semester (four courses per year) and have access to the Caldwell College Library. Tuition costs are the same as those for all other External Degree Program students and are payable at the time of registration.

SPECIAL PROGRAMS

Students majoring in business administration, English, or psychology who have earned at least 60 prior college credits in courses applicable to their major may apply for Accelerated Degree Completion through the External Degree Program. Students admitted to the Accelerated Degree Completion Program can complete their degrees within two years by taking approximately 27 credits per year (9 credits per term) or an equivalent combination of course credits and College Level Examination Program, Prior Learning Assessment, internships, and/or cooperative education credits. Each student is expected to work closely with an academic adviser in developing and following a specific course of study.

STUDENT SERVICES

All of the following services are available to External Degree students. The Jennings Library and the Academic Computing Center are open on evenings and weekends. Students have the ability to access the library's vast database from their home computers. The library's home page also provides links to the Internet and other databases and informational resources. The Career Development Center, Campus Minister, Counseling Office, and Learning Center are also available during the evening by appointment. The college bookstore is open evenings and during External Degree Saturday. The Learning Center assists students in academic skill development for all majors through tutoring.

CREDIT OPTIONS

Credit is given for courses completed at an accredited college or university with a grade of C or above, provided it is appropriate to the curriculum chosen at Caldwell College. Students may transfer no more than 75 credits from a baccalaureate institution or 60 credits from a junior college. Students may earn credits by examination through standardized testing (CLEP, DANTES, OHIO, and TECEP). Credit is also awarded for noncollegiate military or corporate training courses accredited by the American Council on Education. Credits may be earned through the Prior Learning Assessment portfolio development process.

ADMISSION

Students must be 23 years of age or older and must possess a high school

diploma or the GED and have completed at least 12 college credits may matriculate as an External Degree student upon acceptance to the College. Those students with fewer than 12 college credits must complete the following courses to be eligible for the External Degree Program: EN/101 Basic Composition, r EN/111 Literary Types and Themes, PS/111 Re-entry Seminar for Adults, and 1 liberal arts core course. These courses are not available via the distance learning format, but they can be completed at any college.

TUITION AND FEES

Tuition for all students is $337 per credit. The additional cost for books is the responsibility of the student.

FINANCIAL AID

External Degree students are eligible for several of the federal financial aid programs available to full-time students, including Pell Grants and various loans. Approximately 10 percent of External Degree students receive Pell Grants, 70 percent Stafford Loans, 10 percent Caldwell College Grants, and 2 percent Federal Supplemental Educational Opportunity Grants. Tuition Aid Grants are available for full-time External Degree students. Academic advisers of the Center for Continuing Education and the staff of the Financial Aid Office also inform students of special privately funded scholarship opportunities for which they may qualify.

APPLYING

Students wishing to pursue a degree through the External Degree Program must submit the following to the Office of Corporate Education and Adult Undergraduate Admissions: a completed application for adult undergraduate admission; a nonrefundable application fee of $40 made payable to Caldwell College (the student's Social Security number should be included on the memo line); official transcripts from high schools, career schools, or colleges previously at-

tended (GED certification may be submitted in place of a high school transcript); and a photocopy of the student's Social Security card. There is no testing for adults. All application material must be received by the Office of Adult Undergraduate Admissions by the deadline date of each semester, approximately one month prior to the beginning of classes.

Students in the External Degree Program may enroll for a minimum of one and a maximum of five courses per semester, depending on their personal schedules and abilities. The program offers three semesters: fall, spring, and summer. Students are required to be on campus only for the External Degree Saturday at the beginning of each semester. New students attend an orientation program and participate in workshops designed to enhance their college experience. On External Degree Saturday, students meet with their faculty mentor and receive an overview of the course material, faculty evaluation criteria, and dates that assignments are due. Students also attend department meetings and learn about recent developments and career options in their chosen fields of study. Prior to each semester, students consult with their academic advisers for guidance in selecting courses. Academic counseling is available through the semester as a supportive, ongoing service.

CONTACT

Jack Albalah, Director
Corporate and Adult Undergraduate Admissions
Caldwell College
9 Ryerson Avenue
Caldwell, New Jersey 07006
Telephone: 973-618-3285
          888-864-9518 (toll-free)
Fax: 973-618-3660
E-mail: jalbalah@caldwell.edu
Web site: http://www.caldwell.edu

California State University, Dominguez Hills

Division of Extended Education

Carson, California

California State University, Dominguez Hills, is a national leader in distance learning, named by Forbes magazine as one of the top twenty Cyber universities. Founded in 1960, the University is one of twenty-three California State University (CSU) campuses, and it has the largest distance learning program in the CSU system. The University offered its first distance learning degree in 1974, and in 1995 offered the first online master's degree program ever accredited by the Western Association of Schools and Colleges.

CSU Dominguez Hills continues to be in the forefront of distance learning technology and academic excellence, garnering numerous awards, including the Best Distance Learning Teacher from the U.S. Distance Learning Association, a 1999 Omni Intermedia Award, a 1999 Aegis Award, and two Telly Awards.

The CSU Dominguez Hills campus is located in the South Bay Area of Los Angeles and is accredited by the Western Association of Schools and Colleges.

DISTANCE LEARNING PROGRAM

The distance learning unit is part of the Division of Extended Education, whose mission is to extend the resources of the University to better serve the communities of which it is a part. In the fall of 1999, the University had more than 2,000 students enrolled in distance learning programs in all fifty states and more than sixty countries.

DELIVERY MEDIA

All distance learning courses have a Web site, and participants can interact with faculty and staff members via e-mail, telephone, and correspondence. Courses are conducted via live Internet, where students participate in a live, interactive educational environment, including video transmission of the lecture; via asynchronous Internet, where participants log in at their convenience to complete class assignments and engage in discussion groups with their peers; via television, where CSUDH broadcasts 24 hours a day on cable systems throughout Southern California; and via correspondence.

PROGRAMS OF STUDY

Dominguez Hills currently offers four degree and four certificate programs via distance learning. There are no on-campus requirements for any CSUDH distance learning program.

The Master of Arts in the humanities offers a broad interdisciplinary exposure to all of the areas of the humanities—history, literature, philosophy, music, and art, with emphasis on their interrelating effects and influences. The student may specialize in a particular discipline of the humanities or in specific cultural thematic areas that can be traced across all of the humanistic disciplines. The program is conducted via correspondence, and 30 semester units are required for graduation.

Participants in the Master of Science in Quality Assurance (MSQA) receive education in both the technical and administrative foundations of quality assurance, an interdisciplinary profession utilized in management in manufacturing, service, government, and health-care organizations. The MSQA has been developed by experienced and dedicated professionals to ensure course offerings meet the constantly changing requirements for improved organizational competitiveness. All course work for the MSQA is conducted via asynchronous Internet, and it requires 33 units of approved graduate course work.

The Behavioral Science Master's Degree program in Negotiation and Conflict Management teaches participants valuable skills and knowledge that may be applied directly to police work, counseling, human resources management, labor relations, supervision, administration, alternative dispute resolution, arbitration, public policy, social work, teaching, intercultural and community conflicts, corporate contracts, and purchasing. This is a 33-semester-unit graduate program that can be completed in two years. In addition to course work, all students must complete a 3-unit internship during the second year and pass a comprehensive examination at the conclusion of the program. The program is conducted via live, interactive Internet and television broadcast.

The Bachelor of Science completion program in nursing offers an individualized approach to nursing education designed for the self-directed, employed professional. It is one of the largest post-licensure programs in the United States. Graduates are equipped to function as leaders, managers, and resource persons in a variety of health-care settings. Course work for the B.S. in nursing degree is conducted via Web sites, discussion groups, e-mail, and videotape. It requires 124 semester units for graduation.

The Assistive Technology Certificate program prepares individuals to comply with state and federal laws that require that school personnel be prepared to offer a full range of assistive technology services to disabled persons. The online program is useful to educational administrators, teachers, special education teachers, occupational and physical therapists, speech and language specialists, rehabilitation specialists, program specialists, resource specialists, and psychologists.

The Certificate in Production and Inventory Control is conducted entirely online and is designed for those who wish to gain a broad education in the principles of production and inventory control. The program is taught by professionals certified in production and inventory management who are currently employed in the field.

The Certificate Award in Purchasing is designed for those who wish to gain a broad education in the principles of procurement management. Conducted online, the program is also designed to help students prepare for the National Association of Purchasing Managers Certified Purchasing Manager certification exam.

The certificate-completion program in quality assurance allows professionals to gain certification in specialized areas of quality as well as prepare for American Society for Quality Exams. Conducted online, students who successfully complete three master's-level courses and the associated capstone course can earn a certificate of completion in quality management, quality engineering, quality auditing, reliability engineering, or software quality engineering.

SPECIAL PROGRAMS

The Center for Training and Development at CSUDH works closely with the business community to develop custom-designed training programs to help meet the demands of the fast-paced workplace of the new millennium. Programs are delivered via distance learning, on-site, and on the CSUDH campus.

STUDENT SERVICES

Faculty members are available to students via e-mail, telephone, and mail. Student services available at a distance include academic advising, technical support, and online tutoring and access to the library and bookstore.

CREDIT OPTIONS

Depending on the specific program, students may transfer credit earned at other accredited colleges and universities. For more information, students should consult the Web site, listed below.

FACULTY

CSU Dominguez Hills has more than 100 faculty members teaching distance learning courses. Most of these faculty members have doctoral degrees in their chosen fields.

ADMISSION

Admission requirements vary for each program. Students should consult the CSUDH distance learning Web site, listed below, for specific program requirements.

TUITION AND FEES

Tuition and fees vary for each program. Students should consult the CSUDH distance learning Web site, listed below, for specific cost information.

FINANCIAL AID

More than $33 million in financial aid was disbursed to CSUDH students during the 1998–99 school year. Approximately 68 percent of CSUDH students receive some form of financial assistance, and most financial aid programs are available to qualified distance learning students. For further information, students should visit the financial aid Web site at http://www.csudh.edu/fin_aid/default.htm.

APPLYING

Application processes vary for each program, and campus visits are not required for any program. Students should consult the CSUDH distance learning Web site for specific application information.

CONTACT
Extended Education Registration Office
California State University, Dominguez Hills
1000 East Victoria Street
Carson, California 90747
Telephone: 310-243-3741
            877-GO-HILLS (toll-free)
Fax: 310-516-3971
E-mail: eereg@csudh.edu
Web site: http://www.csudh.edu/dominguezonline

Carnegie Mellon University

Distance Learning Programs
Pittsburgh, Pennsylvania

Founded by industrialist Andrew Carnegie as the Carnegie Technical Schools in 1900, Carnegie Mellon University has emerged as one of the nation's top private research institutions. Today, it includes seven colleges—Carnegie Institute of Technology, College of Fine Arts, College of Humanities and Social Sciences, Graduate School of Industrial Administration, H. John Heinz III School of Public Policy and Management, Mellon College of Science, and School of Computer Science—and more than sixty research centers and institutes. Its internationally recognized programs encompass the areas of computer science, engineering, fine arts, liberal arts, public and private management, science, and technology. This Pittsburgh-based university is accredited by the Middle States Association of Colleges and Schools (MSA). The colleges within the University are accredited by various accrediting bodies that are specific to their disciplines.

DISTANCE LEARNING PROGRAM

Students worldwide can benefit from Carnegie Mellon's educational and research resources through a variety of graduate-level certificate and degree programs in management and information technology. Programs include the Certificate in Software Engineering (CSE); Master of Science in Technology–Software Engineering (M.S.I.T.-S.E.) and Master of Software Engineering (M.S.E., corporate-sponsored); Master of Science in Information Technology–Management (M.S.I.T.-I.T.M., corporate-sponsored); the Master of Medical Management (M.M.M.); Flex-Mode (company-sponsored); and Computational Finance.

DELIVERY MEDIA

The latest Web, CD, and teleconferencing technologies are the primary delivery media for Carnegie Mellon's distance learning programs. Faculty members and students interact regularly via e-mail, interactive chat, threaded bulletin boards, and teleconferencing. In the Software Engineering and IT Management programs, videotaped lectures and just-in-time CDs are used to deliver lectures and

libraries of supporting materials. The CDs also contain transcripts and outlines of the lectures, as well as links to support materials such as slide presentations, readings, and Web pages. Further, the technology provides keyword search capabilities.

PROGRAMS OF STUDY

The software engineering certificate and degree programs include the five core courses of the School of Computer Science's Master of Software Engineering program and prepare students to excel as software engineers and project leaders. The Certificate in Software Engineering (CSE) program provides software professionals with continuing education credit in the five core courses. The Master of Science in Information Technology–Software Engineering (M.S.I.T.-S.E.) program provides software professionals with credit for the five course courses as well as four elective courses drawn from the School of Computer Science and an applied practicum project designed to facilitate the integration of the course work. Finally, the Master of Software Engineering (M.S.E.) program is a corporate-sponsored program similar to the M.S.I.T.-S.E. with a software studio component in the place of the practicum. Whereas the

practicum involves individual work, the studio component of the M.S.E. program is a collaborative practical experience in software engineering and requires that the students participating are colocated (hence the need for corporate sponsorship).

The Master of Science in Information Technology–Management (M.S.I.T.-I.T.M.) program offered through the H. J. Heinz III School of Public Policy and Management provides business and information technology professionals with credit for five core information technology courses as well as seven electives in the management and strategic use of information technology. This program is available on campus or at a distance via a corporate partnership.

The Master of Medical Management (M.M.M.) program, also offered through the Heinz School, is open to physicians who have completed a prerequisite program through the American College of Physicians Executives. Through distance learning and on-campus sessions, the M.M.M. program prepares physicians to lead health-care organizations.

Carnegie Mellon's Graduate School of Industrial Administration (GSIA) offers two long-distance programs via interactive video technologies: the company-sponsored Flex-Mode Program (at company locations; see Special Programs) and the Computational Finance Program (Pittsburgh and New York City). Combining the resources of four Carnegie Mellon colleges, the Computational Finance Program lets participants move seamlessly among the fields of computer science, finance, mathematics, and statistics. This lets them gain an understanding of current practices in the financial industry, as well as high-level skills and conceptual framework for career growth.

SPECIAL PROGRAMS

All students in Flex-Mode Program (Master of Industrial Administration courses) offered through Carnegie Mellon's Graduate School of Industrial Administration are company sponsored. This program uses teleconferencing to deliver courses to company locations. The three-year program is just as comprehensive as the school's full-time master's degree track, covering areas such as quantitative managerial decision making, business communication, and the political environment for business leaders.

STUDENT SERVICES

Small class sizes in the various programs enhance the delivery of many student services, such as technical orientations in the use of distance learning technologies, evening and weekend phone access to teaching and technical assistants, and online enrollment. Individualized Web pages for each course offered in the Software Engineering and IT Management programs facilitate access to student services and contact with instructors, courseware specialists, and administrators. Student services information for the GSIA distance learning programs is available through the program-specific Web sites.

CREDIT OPTIONS

In the Software Engineering programs, courses can be taken not-for-credit, for continuing education units (CEU), for-credit, or for credit toward a master's degree. Students taking courses not-for-credit or for continuing education units must retake the course in order to get credit for it. Students taking courses for credit toward

a master's degree must be accepted into the master's degree program. Additional information about the various credit options for the Software Engineering programs is available through the Software Engineering Distance Education Web site. Credit information for the GSIA programs is available through the GSIA program Web site.

FACULTY

Faculty members for the Software Engineering programs are drawn from the School of Computer Science, the Software Engineering Institute, the Master of Software Engineering program, and industry. Information about individual faculty members can be found on the Software Engineering Distance Education Web site. Faculty members for the M.S.I.T.-I.T.M. program are drawn from the Heinz School, the Software Engineering Institute, the School of Computer Science, and the information technology industry. Faculty member information for the GSIA programs is available through their Web sites.

ADMISSION

Students interested in Carnegie Mellon distance learning programs must apply to the appropriate school just as campus-based students do. Admission standards are essentially the same for both types of programs. Program-specific requirements are available through the specific program Web sites.

TUITION AND FEES

While tuition rates vary among programs, the rates for a specific distance learning program and a similar campus-based program are generally the same. Program-specific tuition details are available through the specific program Web site or contact person listed below.

FINANCIAL AID

The amount and type of financial aid varies from program to program. Program-specific financial aid information is available through the specific program Web site or contact person listed below.

APPLYING

Procedures for application, acceptance, and orientation differ for each Carnegie Mellon distance learning program. Students interested in applying for a specific program should request an application through that program's Web site or from the contact person listed below.

CONTACT

Michael Carriger, Associate Director of M.S.E. for Distance Education
Telephone: 412-268-6191
Fax: 412-268-5576
E-mail: dist-ed@cs.cmu.edu
Web site: http://www.distance.cmu.edu/

Karyn Moore, Program Director, M.S.I.T.-I.T.M.
Telephone: 412-268-8465
Fax: 412-268-7036
E-mail: karyn@cmu.edu
Web site: http://www.mism.cmu.edu/

Robert Pearson, Associate Dean, Master of Medical Management Program
Telephone: 412-268-2194
Fax: 412-268-7036
E-mail: bp2v@andrew.cmu.edu

Flex-Mode Program
Web site: http://www.flexmode.gsia.cmu.edu

Computational Finance
Web site: http://www.fastweb.gsia.cmu.edu/MSCF

Central Michigan University

College of Extended Learning
Distance/Distributed Learning

Mount Pleasant, Michigan

Since its founding in 1892, Central Michigan University (CMU) has grown from a small teachers' college into a world class Midwestern university offering more than 150 programs at the bachelor's level and nearly 60 programs at the master's, specialist's, and doctoral level. CMU is accredited by the North Central Association of Colleges and Schools. This accreditation includes all on- and off-campus programs. The College of Extended Learning is an institutional member of the Council for Adult and Experiential Learning; the Adult Education Association; the Alliance: An Association of Alternative Degree Programs for Adults; and the National Association of Institutions in Military Education.

DISTANCE LEARNING PROGRAM

Distance/Distributed Learning is a division of CMU's College of Extended Learning, which serves off-campus students. Distance learning at CMU has its roots in the University's correspondence study program, which was created more than 70 years ago. As CMU's commitment to distance learning grew, the University developed a number of options for students to complete courses outside of the traditional classroom setting.

DELIVERY MEDIA

Students have a choice of delivery systems, including print-based learning packages, World Wide Web courses, and video/televised courses. Courses are offered in a twelve-week format with specific start and end dates.

Learning packages are print-based courses that use textbooks and study guides but can also include audio and videocassettes, CD-ROMs, and use of e-mail and/or Internet chat rooms to enrich the content.

World Wide Web courses use Web technology to involve the student in interactive learning. Students can interact with instructors and others through e-mail chat sessions and mes-

sage forums. Student lecture materials and assignments are all online. Textbooks may be required.

Televised or video courses are available on the Central Michigan University Public Television Network and also on videotape. These courses include a study guide, text, and supplementary materials.

PROGRAMS OF STUDY

Distance/Distributed Learning offers undergraduate degree programs and graduate programs with additional classes being added each term.

Bachelor's degrees are available through the Bachelor of Science with an option in community development and the Bachelor of Science with a major in administration.

The 36-semester-hour Master of Science in Administration degree approaches administration and management from a broader perspective than other graduate-level programs. The M.S.A. features eight concentrations, including general, human resources, health services, hospitality and tourism, international, public, and software engineering administration; and information resource management.

SPECIAL PROGRAMS

The Master of Science in Nutrition and Dietetics is designed to provide

advanced training in human nutritional sciences for new and experienced professionals. The M.S. in Nutrition and Dietetics is available through distance learning courses, although practical internships are still required.

Also available entirely through distance learning is the Au.D. program, created by CMU exclusively for professional audiologists. It is based on a minimum 36 to 40 credit-hour sequence and a comprehensive exam. There is a 12-hour capstone experience in lieu of a formal thesis. The courses are self-paced, and it is possible to complete the program within two years.

STUDENT SERVICES

Central Michigan University's Distance/Distributed Learning offers students many timesaving services. In addition to touch-tone (phone-in) registrations and online admissions, textbook purchases, academic advising, and library resources are available via a toll-free phone call, fax, or the World Wide Web.

Central Michigan University offers library support services tailored to meet the needs of the adult learner. Students can contact CMU's Off Campus Library Services and request reference assistance, book loans, and copies of journal articles. An online catalog of book and periodical holdings as well as subject databases are available.

FACULTY

Faculty members who teach off-campus courses are drawn from the regular CMU faculty, other colleges and universities, government, and business and industry. Faculty members are approved for teaching assignments by the department chairperson on the basis of their academic and professional qualifications. Selection criteria vary from department to department. Additionally, all graduate course approvals are subject to the approval of the Graduate Dean.

ADMISSION

Distance/Distributed Learning courses are part of the regular offerings of Central Michigan University. Students must be admitted to CMU in order to take distance learning courses. The minimum requirement for admission to CMU undergraduate programs is a high school diploma or GED certificate. Students can be awarded up to 60 hours of credit toward the bachelor's degree and up to 10 hours of credit toward the master's degree for relevant work, training, and other life experiences through CMU's Prior Learning Assessment Program.

Graduate applicants must have a baccalaureate or equivalent degree from an institution that has received regional accreditation or recognized standing at the time the student attended.

Audiology applicants must have a graduate degree in audiology with a minimum grade point average of 3.0 in graduate work, and either the ASHA Certificate of Clinical Competence in Audiology or a valid state license to practice audiology. Five years of professional audiological experience beyond the master's degree is also required.

TUITION AND FEES

Tuition for the distance learning program is $173 per credit hour for undergraduate students and $231 per credit hour for graduate students. Tuition for the Audiology Ph.D. program is $236 per credit hour at the government rate or $331 at the nongovernment rate.

Additional fees (per credit hour) include a $50 admission fee, $50 graduation fee, $65 prior learning application fee, and a $40 prior learning assessment fee.

FINANCIAL AID

Financial aid is available to those students who qualify. Students interested in financial aid are encouraged to contact CMU for more information.

APPLYING

Students interested in taking classes through Distance/Distributed Learning are encouraged to apply for regular admission to Central Michigan University. Admission applications can be downloaded from the Web site listed below.

CONTACT

Central Michigan University
Distance/Distributed Learning
College of Extended Learning
Mount Pleasant, Michigan 48859
Telephone: 800-688-4268 (toll-free)
Fax: 517-774-1822
Web site: http:// www.ddl.cmich.edu

Central Missouri State University

Office of Extended Campus–Distance Learning

Warrensburg, Missouri

Founded in 1871, Central Missouri State University is a state university offering approximately 150 areas of study to 11,500 undergraduate and graduate students. In 1996, Central Missouri State University was designated Missouri's lead institution for professional technology, an area long recognized as one of the University's greatest strengths. The new mission has expanded this commitment and means that Central will continue to integrate the latest technologies into every level of its comprehensive liberal arts curriculum. Central is committed to acquiring, disseminating, and utilizing technology to enhance the University's comprehensive educational mission. Central is accredited by the North Central Association of Colleges and Schools.

DISTANCE LEARNING PROGRAM

Central's main Distance Learning Program provides undergraduate- and graduate-level courses through two-way interactive television and Web-based courses. The program currently includes one doctoral degree, one master's degree, and numerous graduate and undergraduate courses. From fall 1994 through spring 2000, Central provided instruction to more than 2,500 graduate, undergraduate, and high school students in a distance learning environment.

Central Missouri State University is a member of Missouri Learners Network, a voluntary, collaborative project among Missouri postsecondary institutions. The Missouri Learners Network was developed to share information, promote educational opportunities, and act as a referral service for students searching for distance educational opportunities.

DELIVERY MEDIA

Central uses a variety of technologies to deliver its distance learning courses. These include two-way, interactive television; broadcast television; and Internet technologies, including video and audio streaming.

Central links to the Missouri Research and Educational Network (MOREnet) statewide backbone, which connects all of Missouri's public higher education institutions and several K–12 schools, to provide Internet-based and interactive television programming. Finally, Central's complement of six 2-way videoconferencing facilities, which are capable of dedicated T-1, ISDN, H.323, T.120, and audio-conferencing, allow Central to provide distance learning content to anywhere in the world.

PROGRAMS OF STUDY

The Master of Science in Criminal Justice is designed for those students who wish to enter or progress in the criminal justice fields of law enforcement, corrections, and juvenile justice or for those who plan to seek positions in leadership, professional specialization, research, or instruction in criminal justice. Completion of the program requires a minimum of 36 credit hours in required and elective courses. Curricula is delivered by interactive television, with certain courses available online.

Course work toward completion of the 32-credit-hour Master of Science in Education degree is available via interactive television. Areas of specialization include curriculum and in-

struction, special education, and education administration. Courses meeting state of Missouri certification requirements for teachers of the severely developmentally disabled follow a rotation schedule and are available throughout the state.

Central is one of a consortium of six higher education institutions that collectively offer the Ph.D. in Technology Management. This degree requires a minimum of 90 hours above an undergraduate degree and includes a dissertation. There is a two-semester residency requirement; the majority of the course work is Internet based.

The Master of Science in Rural Family Nursing offers its degree program in a combination of Internet-based and on-campus instruction. This new degree in nursing is designed to emphasize advanced practice nursing knowledge and skills as well as the application of the research process to clinical phenomena within the context of rural family health. The emphasis areas of nursing informatics and nurse educator studies focus on the dissemination and utilization of technologies to enhance lives.

Beginning in 2001, Central will offer a Master of Science in Library Science and Information Services in a combination of Internet, interactive television, and on-site formats to accommodate the students it serves. The emphasis of the program is the education of school library media specialists. It is the only graduate program in Missouri that exclusively targets education for school librarians.

SPECIAL PROGRAMS

Central's Distance Learning Program builds upon the existing curriculum offerings at Central as well as offerings that address special distance learning needs.

Central's distance learning students are eligible to participate in the same opportunities as on-campus students. These include study tours and internships in many disciplines.

The Office of Career Services reports a 95 percent placement rate for Central graduates within six months of graduation.

STUDENT SERVICES

A toll-free University number, 800-SAY-CMSU, allows access to offices involved with student services: extended campus–distance learning, admissions, academic advising, registrar, financial aid, revenue, accounts receivable, University housing, and the Graduate School. All students enrolled at Central are issued a mainframe Internet account. The HELP Desk is available to Central students needing technical computer assistance. Distance learning students receive individualized course information prior to the start of each semester as well as information regarding University resources available to them. Online library resources are available for distance learning and off-campus students. Access is also available to LUIS, the online card catalog for the James C. Kirkpatrick Library, a new state-of-the-art facility dedicated in March 1999.

CREDIT OPTIONS

The University accepts undergraduate transfer students from other accredited colleges and universities and evaluates their credit on the same bases used for other Central students. Thus, admission requires students to be in good standing and to have a grade point average of C (2.0) or better, computed by Central's methods. Students may be considered on an individual basis if their GPA is less than 2.0. For entering graduate students, Central will accept up to 8 hours of transfer credits in graduate work.

FACULTY

Faculty members at Central exemplify the goals of the institution as they balance personal attention with expertise in their respective fields. Approximately 70 percent of the 443 full-time faculty members hold doctoral degrees. The undergraduate student-faculty ratio is 17:1; the graduate student-faculty ratio is 3:1.

ADMISSION

A rolling admission policy is employed at Central. First-time undergraduate students, students returning after an absence of one or more semesters, and students who desire to enroll as visiting students should contact the Office of Admissions at 660-543-4677 or 800-SAY-CMSU (toll-free).

First-time graduate students taking Extended Campus courses may be admitted either by completing the Graduate School application in person or when calling to enroll in a class. Students must submit official copies of their transcripts to the Graduate School. Graduate students may enroll in up to 6 credit hours before finalizing their admission.

Students currently attending another university may enroll as visiting students. Graduate students who are not seeking a degree may enroll as non-degree-seeking students.

A nonrefundable application fee of $25 is due upon submission of the application. This applies to first-time applications only.

TUITION AND FEES

For 2000–01, graduate tuition is $210 and undergraduate tuition is $137 per credit hour for interactive television courses. For Internet-based courses, graduate tuition is $164 per credit hour, and undergraduate tuition is $127 per credit hour. Doctoral courses are $177 per credit hour.

FINANCIAL AID

Central recognizes a student's continuing need for financial assistance. Federal grant and loan funds are available for eligible students who have been accepted for regular degree programs at Central. Application eligibility information may be obtained by contacting the Office of Financial Aid and Veteran Services at 660-543-4040 or the toll-free number below. Students who are veterans may also be considered for VA educational benefits to help with tuition costs.

The University participates in all federal student financial aid grant, loan, and employment programs. Visiting and non-degree-seeking students are not eligible to receive federal financial aid.

APPLYING

Undergraduate students should contact the Admissions Office at 660-543-4290 or the toll-free number listed below. Graduate students should contact the Graduate School at 660-543-4621 or at the toll-free number.

CONTACT

Debbie Bassore
Assistant Director for Distance
  Learning
Office of Extended Campus
Humphreys 403
Central Missouri State University
Warrensburg, Missouri 64093
Telephone: 660-543-8480
        800-SAY-CMSU (toll-free)
Fax: 660-543-8333
E-mail: bassore@cmsu1.cmsu.edu
Web site:
  http://www.cmsu.edu/extcamp

Central Texas College

Distance Learning Program

Killeen, Texas

In 1965, the citizens of central Texas joined together to authorize the building of a community college that would serve Bell, Coryell, Lampasas, Mills, and seven other central Texas counties as well as Fort Hood and correctional facilities in Gatesville. Central Texas College (CTC) opened its doors with an initial enrollment of 2,068 students in the fall of 1967.

CTC initiated on-site programs on Fort Hood in 1970 and in Europe in 1974. CTC's success at Fort Hood and Europe led to the explosive expansion of CTC's locations across the United States and the Pacific Far East. Today, CTC offers Associate in Science, Associate in Arts, Associate in General Studies, and Associate in Applied Science degrees at the Texas Campus, Continental Campus, Pacific Far East Campus and Navy Campus. CTC enrolls approximately 55,000 students annually and employs nearly 3,193 full-time faculty worldwide.

Central Texas College is accredited by the Commission on Colleges of the Southern Association of Colleges and School to award associate degrees and certificates of completion.

DISTANCE LEARNING PROGRAM

Central Texas College has provided off-campus programs and services for more than thirty years and offered distance learning courses for more than twenty-five years. All CTC programs are accredited by the Southern Association of Colleges and Schools and approved by the Texas Higher Education Coordinating Board.

Since 1995, CTC has been committed to creating the best distance learning program complete with services and support designed specifically for the distance learner. Today, CTC offers distant learners the choice of delivery modes—online, video-based, videoconferencing, or multimedia. Distance learners can choose from more than 45 online courses, 25 telecourses, and a variety of videoconference and multimedia courses. CTC offers distance learning opportunities in criminal justice, business, hospitality, mental health services, nursing, social and behavioral sciences, communications, computer science, and mathematics. Both credit and noncredit courses are available.

CTC distance learning courses are developed by a team comprised of instructional design specialists, faculty members, and instructional technologists. CTC courses are field tested and continuously updated and improved to ensure that every course meets the highest standards of education.

All services available to resident students are available to CTC's distance learners. CTC offers on-site student support through six campuses in Texas, the continental US Pacific–Far East, Europe, and in the Navy. Distance learners can call upon a distance learning counselor to help with full range of student services, including admissions, course selection, enrollment, and financial aid. CTC also provides instructional and technical support to enhance the learning experience.

DELIVERY MEDIA

Central Texas College offers college-level distance learning courses in a variety of instructional formats. Distance learning courses may be telecourses, video conference courses, multimedia courses, or online courses. Students have direct and continuous access to their instructor, opportunities to collaborate with other students, and full access to library and support services. A telecourse uses broadcast television or videotapes to enhance the course with images not easily conveyed in a printed format. Students view simulations, demonstrations, or artifacts to increase understanding of the subject. In a video conference course, the distant learner has two-way audio and two-way video synchronous interaction with the instructor and other students. This delivery system allows for instructor-delivered lectures, in-depth discussions, question/answer sessions, and demonstrations.

Multimedia courses use textbooks, CD-ROMs, computer software, and videotapes, along with curricular materials, to guide the student in learning. Online courses use the Internet as the primary delivery system for instruction. Instructional materials in online courses (guides, syllabi, reading lists, and lecture notes) are posted on the Internet and interactive learning activities and testing are available online. Communication and collaboration among distance learners, instructors, and counselors are accomplished through voice mail, e-mail, or regular mail. Students enrolling in distance learning courses must supply their own equipment.

PROGRAMS OF STUDY

Central Texas College offers an Associate in General Studies degree online with support of credit for testing, evaluated military credit, and transfer credit from regionally accredited institutions. The distance learning curriculum consists of various occupational/vocational courses as well as core curriculum courses. In the spirit of accomplishing CTC's mission, the core curriculum experience will prepare the learner to effectively develop the aptitudes necessary for career success. It is the goal of CTC to graduate well-educated men and women who are articulate, interested in lifelong learning, and capable of becoming creative citizens. The core curriculum design and implementation will also facilitate the transferability of lower division courses between CTC and universities.

STUDENT SERVICES

CTC has a full-time adviser dedicated to distance learning students. A student may also find a complete list of specific Services and Support Offices with points of contact online. A student may get counseling and admissions assistance from a distant learner advisor; download forms and request services from the distance learning web site; obtain expert assistance in financial aid and veterans' services; order books from the bookstore, use the library; get career counseling and placement aid information; and determine if he or she is academically and technically prepared for distance learning.

CREDIT OPTIONS

CTC offers the General Studies degree online. Students may earn credits ranging from 2 to 4 hours for each distance learning course successfully completed. These credits may be used to meet resident credit requirements. Once resident credit has been established, students may use a number of alternative credit sources to meet degree requirements. These sources include transfer credits from regionally accredited institutions, military credit evaluations, Defense Activity for Non-

traditional Education Support (DANTES) courses and subject standardized tests, the College Level Examination Program (CLEP) general and subject examinations, American College Testing (ACT) program, and the college board admissions testing program.

FACULTY

CTC employs over 200 faculty members who provide instruction for the distance learning program. Faculty members in distance learning courses meet the academic and professional preparation criteria of regional accreditation, the standards established by the Texas Higher Education Coordinating Board rules and regulations, and licensure and approval requirements or applicable regulatory boards. Both DANTES and the Servicemembers' Opportunity College have approved CTC as a provider of distance learning courses.

ADMISSION

Central Texas College is a two-year open admissions institution. Before enrolling in distance learning courses, a student should consider course needs, learning styles, and learning preferences. Students physically residing in Texas are obligated by TASP laws. Students not residing in Texas may enroll in most online courses, the exceptions being English and college-level math. Students must provide the appropriate documentation indicating preparedness for those courses. The distance learning semesters are consistent with CTC's Central Campus schedule. Occasionally, 8-week sessions are offered beginning in October and March.

TUITION AND FEES

Tuition costs are the same as those for traditional lecture courses. Resident tuition rates are $20 per credit hour. Non-resident rates are $250 for the first

credit hour and $50 for each additional credit hour. There is also a $50 nonrefundable distance learning fee and $8 per credit hour Technology fee. If a student is registered at a continental CTC site, they will be charged the MOU rate which has been negotiated with that military installation. The Distance Learning fee will also apply. Tuition and fees are subject to change.

FINANCIAL AID

Students desiring financial assistance must file a Free Application for Federal Student Aid (FAFSA); the school code is 004003. Distance learning students will be awarded federal aid in line with Department of Education and College regulations. Student Aid files must be completed prior to semester deadline.

APPLYING

Students may register in person at most local CTC sites. If the student is not located near a CTC site, the application and registration form(s) may be faxed or mailed to the distance learning adviser for processing. Payment must accompany the enrollment information and can be made by credit card, check, or money order. If the student is using Tuition Assistance or DANTES, those forms must also be faxed or mailed.

CONTACT

Diana L. Castillo
Distance Learning Coordinator
Central Texas College
Guidance and Counseling
P.O. Box 1800
Killeen, Texas 76540-1800
Telephone: 254-526-1296
      800-792-3348 Ext. 1296
Fax: 254-526-1481
E-mail: distlrn1@ctcd.cc.tx.us
Web site: http://www.ctcd.cc.tx.us

Champlain College

On-Line Distance Learning Program
Continuing Education Division

Burlington, Vermont

Since 1878, Champlain College has been dedicated to providing education that reflects the realities and needs of the contemporary workplace. It offers professional certificates and two-year and four-year degree programs that are designed to provide sound professional training or updating for careers in today's complex world, as well as to provide broadening education in the humanities and general education. Champlain College is recognized as one of the leading career-building colleges in northern New England, and it has earned the respect of business, technical, and human services professions for its outstanding career-oriented education.

DISTANCE LEARNING PROGRAM

Champlain College is a pioneer in the use of computer technologies in distance learning applications. Champlain College On-Line serves hundreds of students in the United States and internationally. Champlain offers complete degree and professional certificate programs that may be accessed on line at any time of day.

Champlain College is an independent, nonprofit four- and two-year college. It is accredited by the New England Association of Schools and Colleges. It first offered distance learning courses in 1993, with more than seventy courses offered in 1999–2000.

DELIVERY MEDIA

Those who have access to a computer and the World Wide Web can access Champlain College On-Line. Once connected, students find messages posted from the instructor and classmates either in the course forum or in private e-mail. All communication occurs on line and includes discussion comments from classmates, lectures, instructional material, and assignments. The material covered in Champlain College's online classes is the same as in traditional courses.

PROGRAMS OF STUDY

Champlain College offers an extensive array of traditionally delivered, career-oriented four- and two-year degrees. Through its distance learning program, the College offers both Professional Certificates and Associate in Science (A.S.) degrees in accounting, business, computer programming, e-commerce, hotel-restaurant management, international business management, management, telecommunications, and Web site development and management. The College also offers Bachelor in Science (B.S.) degrees in professional studies and in computer information systems, both of which are designed to complement associate degrees in career areas. Professional certificates require successful completion of 16 to 24 credits. Associate degrees require completion of 60 credits, half of which must be taken through Champlain College. The bachelor's degree requires completion of 120 credits, at least 45 of which must be taken through Champlain. Students can also take individual courses on a nonmatriculated basis.

SPECIAL PROGRAMS

The College has several expanding international programs that offer degree programs to students in Israel, Malaysia, and the United Arab Emirates. All of these programs incorporate distance learning into the curriculum.

Corporate partnerships are also available for businesses that are interested in training employees. Since classes are available at anytime, from anywhere the Internet can be accessed, distance learning allows businesses to offer high-quality training programs to employees—even when different shifts, different locations, and even different time zones are involved.

STUDENT SERVICES

Champlain College provides a number of services to adult learners. Distance learners receive academic advising from the Advising and Registration Center and the Career Planning Office, a full range of online library services, and access to the Computer Help Desk and an online bookstore.

CREDIT OPTIONS

Students may transfer credits earned through other accredited postsecondary institutions. Depending on the program selected, students may also transfer credit for life/work experience or credits from approved testing programs. Champlain accepts credit through approved portfolio assessment programs, CLEP, DANTES, and PONSI.

FACULTY

Champlain's strength lies in its faculty. More than 120 full-time and part-time faculty members focus their primary energies on teaching. Faculty members have completed programs of advanced study, and many have doctoral or terminal degrees.

ADMISSION

Admission requirements for degree programs include graduation from a recognized secondary school or possession of a high school equivalency certificate and submission of SAT I or ACT scores. Students who have been out of high school for several years and who may not have taken all of the course work that is required for acceptance to a particular major or who have not taken SAT or ACT tests should speak with an admission counselor or academic adviser about how to apply. Admission to the certificate program requires submission of a high school transcript (or GED) and a current resume. Given the method of instructional delivery, online students should be self-motivated and possess effective reading and writing skills as well as basic computer skills.

TUITION AND FEES

In 2000–01, tuition is $330 per credit; most courses are 3 credits. The application fee is $35. Textbooks may be purchased on line through the bookstore. There are no additional fees.

FINANCIAL AID

Payment and financial aid options depend on personal circumstances and whether students attend full- or part-time. The College participates in several federal financial aid programs, including Federal Pell Grant and Federal Stafford Student Loan, and state loan and grant programs.

APPLYING

Students may enroll for online courses as nonmatriculating students by registering on line or by mail, fax, or telephone. The College reviews applications for degree programs when they are received. A short, online orientation is required for all online students prior to gaining access to their courses.

CONTACT

Colleen Long, Program Coordinator
Champlain College On-Line
Champlain College
163 South Willard Street
Burlington, Vermont 05402
Telephone: 802-865-6449
888-545-3459 (toll-free)
Fax: 802-865-6447
E-mail: online@champlain.edu

Charter Oak State College

New Britain, Connecticut

Charter Oak State College was established in 1973 by the Connecticut Legislature to provide an alternate way for adults to earn a college degree. The College offers associate and bachelor's degrees and is regionally accredited by the New England Association of Schools and Colleges. Charter Oak is a Servicemembers Opportunity College.

Charter Oak's degree program was designed to be especially appealing to people who work full-time and have family and financial responsibilities as well. The program is designed for independent adult learners who have the capacity and motivation to pursue a degree program that provides flexibility in how, where, and when they can earn credits. The Charter Oak program assumes that its students possess a basic understanding of the elements of a degree program and that they will seek guidance as often as necessary to progress satisfactorily with their studies.

Charter Oak teaches no classes. Students earn credits based on faculty evaluation of courses transferred from regionally accredited colleges and universities, noncollegiate sponsored instruction, standardized tests, special assessment, contract learning, and portfolio assessment.

One of the hallmarks of Charter Oak State College is its individualized professional advisement services. Each student is assigned to an academic adviser, who is a specialist in the student's chosen field of study. That adviser is accessible via telephone, fax, or e-mail and works closely with the student to develop a plan of study for completion of the degree program.

ral sciences, and social sciences. Achievement in these areas demonstrates breadth of learning. In addition, students pursuing a baccalaureate degree must complete a concentration, consisting of at least 36 credits, that demonstrates depth of learning.

A concentration plan, in conjunction with an essay, must be submitted to the faculty for approval. Concentrations may be constructed in many areas, including applied arts, art history, the behavioral sciences, business, child study, communication, computer science, engineering studies, fire science technology, human services, individualized studies, languages, liberal studies, literature, music history, the natural sciences, religious studies, the social sciences, and technology studies.

DISTANCE LEARNING PROGRAM

Charter Oak State College offers an external degree program and so, by definition, is a distance learning institution. Students earn their credits "externally" and transfer them into the College; there is no residence requirement. Charter Oak offers more than a dozen distance learning courses each semester. Courses run for a period of sixteen weeks but may be completed in less time with the permission of faculty members.

DELIVERY MEDIA

The College offers a selection of distance learning courses. Some of the courses use videotapes and texts and some are online courses. The courses are facilitated by faculty mentors who are accessible by e-mail, telephone,

and U.S. mail. Students purchase texts at a distance from a designated bookstore and rent videotapes from a mail-order service. A catalog of offerings is available each semester.

PROGRAMS OF STUDY

Charter Oak State College offers four degrees in general studies: Associate of Arts, Associate of Science, Bachelor of Arts, and Bachelor of Science. To earn an associate degree, a student must complete at least 60 credits; a bachelor's degree requires at least 120 credits.

A Charter Oak degree is more than an accumulation of the required number of credits. At least one half of the credits toward a degree must be earned in subjects traditionally included among the liberal arts and sciences: humanities, mathematics, natu-

SPECIAL PROGRAMS

The College has evaluated a number of noncollegiate courses and programs that can be used in Charter Oak degree programs. Many healthcare specialties from hospital-based programs are included, such as medical laboratory technician, nurse practitioner, physician assistant, radiologic technologist, registered nurse, and respiratory therapist or technician. Other evaluations include the Child Development Associate (CDA) credential; the FAA Airman Certificate; Famous Artists School in Westport, Connecticut; Institute of Children's Literature in West Redding, Connecticut; the National Opticianry Competency Examination; the Contact Lens Registry Examination; and several fire certifications, including Fire Marshal, Deputy Fire Marshal, Fire Inspector, Fire Fighter III, Fire Officer I or II, and Fire Service Instructor I or II.

CREDIT OPTIONS

Students can transfer credits from other regionally accredited colleges and universities; age of credits is not a factor in their transferability. There is no limit to the number of credits that can be earned using standardized examinations, prior learning, including ACE-evaluated military credits, ACE and PONSI-evaluated noncollegiate learning, and portfolio assessment.

FACULTY

Full-time faculty members from public and independent institutions of higher education in Connecticut are appointed to serve as consulting examiners at Charter Oak.

ADMISSION

Admission is open to any person 16 years or older, regardless of level of formal education, who is able to demonstrate college-level achievement. To be admitted, a student must have earned 9 college-level credits from acceptable sources of credit.

TUITION AND FEES

All students pay a $45 application fee; Connecticut residents pay a first-year enrollment fee of $457 and nonresidents pay $660. Active-duty servicemembers and their spouses pay a special active-duty military fee for all Charter Oak fees and services that is equivalent to the in-state resident fee. All baccalaureate degree candidates pay a Concentration Proposal Review fee of $250. All students pay a graduation fee of $140. Tuition for video-based courses is $71 per credit for Connecticut residents and $106 per credit for nonresidents; tuition for all online courses is $103 per credit for Connecticut residents and $140 per credit for nonresidents. All students pay a $15 registration fee.

FINANCIAL AID

Financial aid is available in the form of fee waivers and foundation grants, as well as federal financial aid (Title IV) funds. Fee-waiver awards are made available through the College's financial resources and may be applied to the cost for the Enrollment And Records Conversion fee, Concentration Proposal Review fee, Annual Advisement and Records Maintenance fee, Reinstatement fee, and the Graduation fee. The foundation grants are made available through generous contributions from both private and corporate donations. These grants are for enrolled students. Federal aid is also available to those who qualify.

The following fees are eligible for Title IV funds: Enrollment And Records Conversion fee, Concentration Proposal Review fee, Annual Advisement and Records Maintenance fee, and the Reinstatement fee. Federal aid may be applied to the cost associated with tuition for COSC video-based courses, COSC contract learning courses, online and/or onsite courses at any CTDLC consortium member institution. For information, or to receive the appropriate application for aid, please contact the financial aid office. Veterans Administration benefits are also available for eligible students.

APPLYING

Charter Oak reviews applications on a rolling basis; students may enroll anytime during the year.

CONTACT

Admissions Office
Charter Oak State College
55 Paul Manafort Drive
New Britain, Connecticut 06053-2142
Telephone: 860-832-3800
Fax: 860-832-3999
Web site: http://www.cosc.edu

City University

Distance Learning Option
Renton, Washington

City University was founded in 1973 on the philosophy that everyone should have access to quality higher education. The University upholds this philosophy by offering programs that are well designed, cost effective, and convenient. The University's progressive approach to education has fueled its growth from a single classroom in downtown Seattle to the largest private university in the state of Washington. It is a private, nonprofit institution and is accredited by the Northwest Association of Schools and Colleges.

City University's programs cover a variety of academic fields ranging from business management and technology to humanities, social sciences, counseling, and teacher preparation. The majority of faculty members actively work in the fields they teach. The combination of innovative program design and outstanding instruction make City University an exceptional higher learning institution.

DISTANCE LEARNING PROGRAM

In keeping with its mission of providing convenient, accessible education, City University offers most of its degree programs through distance learning (DL). The DL option makes degree programs available through traditional correspondence and electronically, through the World Wide Web. City University serves approximately 4,600 students annually through DL.

DELIVERY MEDIA

City University offers DL and electronic DL programs. Electronic DL students complete course work through the University's online instructional center, using computers and the World Wide Web. DL students communicate with instructors by e-mail or by phone, mail, or fax. Electronic DL students need an e-mail address, a computer with a modem, Internet access, and CD-ROM capacity.

PROGRAMS OF STUDY

City University's undergraduate programs prepare students to compete in today's marketplace. Students may complete an Associate of Science (A.S.), a Bachelor of Science (B.S.), or a Bachelor of Arts (B.A.) degree. Within these degrees, students may pursue one of several areas of study, including business administration, accounting, sociology, management specialty, computer systems, international studies, marketing, philosophy, political science, mass communications, journalism, and e-commerce. Undergraduate courses are 5 credits each; 180 credits are required for completion of a B.S. or B.A. degree.

City University's graduate business and public administration programs prepare management professionals for leadership roles at local, national, and international levels. Students may pursue a graduate certificate or a Master of Business Administration (M.B.A.), with an array of specialties; a Master of Public Administration (M.P.A.); a combined M.B.A./M.P.A.; a Master of Science in either project management or computer systems; or an M.A. in management degree. Most graduate courses are worth 3 credits; total required credits range from 45 to 60. City University also offers programs in education and human services. Students may pursue a Master of Education (M.Ed.) in curriculum and instruction or educational technology, or they may pursue an M.A. degree in counseling psychology. Total required credits for these programs range from 45 to 73.

SPECIAL PROGRAMS

City University has an "open door" admissions policy. Students may begin a distance learning course at the beginning of any month, and there is no application deadline. City University has partnerships with several institutions and organizations worldwide. Through these affiliations, the University offers in-house programs and evaluates prior training for college-level credit.

All of City University's programs are geared for adult students. From its student body to its faculty and staff, City University is a community of professionals. All who are associated with the University understand the needs of adult learners who are seeking quality education that applies to their individual lifestyle.

STUDENT SERVICES

Students may register by touch-tone phone. Academic advising and assistance is available from a distance learning adviser by phone, fax, or e-mail. Students have full access to the library, including an online search service; a reference librarian, via a toll-free phone number; and a mailing service for circulation books and articles.

CREDIT OPTIONS

Undergraduate students may transfer up to 90 approved lower-division and 45 approved upper-division credits from approved institutions for baccalaureate programs. The Prior Learning Assessment Program lets students earn credits through documented experiential learning. Students may receive credit for the CLEP or other standardized tests. Graduate students may transfer up to 12 credits from approved programs.

FACULTY

There are more than 250 faculty members included in the distance learning program, 36 of whom are full-time. More than 25 percent of the full-time faculty members have terminal degrees.

ADMISSION

Undergraduate programs are generally open to applicants over 18 years of age who hold a high school diploma or GED. Admission to graduate programs requires that students hold a baccalaureate degree from an accredited or otherwise recognized institution. Additional requirements apply to education and human services programs. International students whose first language is not English are required to submit a TOEFL score of at least 540 for admission to undergraduate programs and 565 for graduate programs.

TUITION AND FEES

Undergraduate tuition is $173 per credit, and graduate tuition is $309 per credit. The application fee is $75.

FINANCIAL AID

For more information, students should contact the Student Financial Services Department (telephone: 800-426-5596, toll-free).

APPLYING

DL students may enroll on a rolling admissions basis. Students must speak with an academic adviser to complete the initial enrollment. Students should then submit the application form, nonrefundable application fee, and admission documents to the Office of Admissions and Student Affairs. Official transcripts should be sent to the Office of the Registrar.

CONTACT

DL/Online Advisor
Office of Admissions and Student Affairs
City University
919 Southwest Grady Way
Renton, Washington 98055
Fax: 425-277-2437

Office of the Registrar
335 116th Avenue, SE
Bellevue, Washington 98004
Fax: 425-637-9689

Telephone: 425-637-1010
       800-422-4898 (toll-free)
       425-450-4660 (TTY)
Web site: http://www.cityu.edu

Clarkson College

Omaha, Nebraska

Clarkson College is a regionally accredited private institution, with exceptional programs in health-related business, nursing, occupational therapy assistant studies, physical therapist assistant studies, and radiologic technology and medical imaging. The College offers the personal qualities of a small institution and the technological advantages found within a larger educational environment. Founded in 1888, it was the first school of nursing in Nebraska and was approved to grant academic degrees in 1984. Clarkson College is accredited by the Commission on Institutions of Higher Education and the North Central Association of Colleges and Schools.

The mission of Clarkson College is to improve the quality of patient care by offering undergraduate and graduate health science degrees. The College provides high-quality education to prepare competent, thoughtful, ethical, and compassionate health-care professionals for service to individuals, families, and communities.

Clarkson College recognizes that all students do not have the opportunity to give up employment and/or move to a college campus to continue their education. Clarkson offers the opportunity for working adults who live more than 75 miles from campus to complete degree programs through a variety of delivery methods.

DISTANCE LEARNING PROGRAM

The Clarkson College Distance Education Program currently serves about 150 students in thirty states. Since distance education is an outreach of the College's current programs, it is governed by the academic and administrative policies in effect. Distance students follow the same semester schedule, pay the same tuition, and receive the same support services as on-campus students. Distance Education Programs have the same accreditation as on-campus programs.

DELIVERY MEDIA

Clarkson delivers theory course work to students via the Internet, mail, videotape and audiotape, fax transmission, computer e-mail, and telephone conferencing. Clarkson advisers help students to access and use the computer system. Syllabi, textbooks, and study questions are available on line; follow-up calls are made by faculty members. Tests are mailed to proctors in the students' area who monitor test-taking.

Students must have access to a computer with a modem, a fax machine, a VCR, and an audiocassette player. All students are required to have either a telephone answering machine or voice mail and access to the Internet and e-mail.

PROGRAMS OF STUDY

Registered nurses who hold a diploma or associate degree can complete the Bachelor of Science in Nursing (B.S.N.). All courses can be taken by distance education. The B.S.N. requires 128 credit hours. Clarkson's Master of Science in Nursing (M.S.N.), which requires 18 credit hours of core courses plus appropriate credit hours in a selected option, allows nurses to enhance their career mobility. Options include nursing administration (additional 18 credit hours), nursing

education (additional 18 credit hours), and family nurse practitioner (additional 27 credit hours). M.S.N. students are required to come to campus for thesis defense or comprehensive exams. M.S.N.–F.N.P. students must come to campus three times for testing and assessment. Clinicals are completed using qualified preceptors in the student's community. M.S.N.–F.N.P. students who wish to study via distance learning must reside in Nebraska, Iowa, Wyoming, South Dakota, Missouri, Kansas, or Colorado.

The Bachelor of Science in medical imaging is open to ARRT Registered Technologists and/or board-eligible graduates of an associate degree or diploma program in radiography. Students can earn their bachelor's degree (128 credit hours) in medical imaging completely through distance education.

The B.S. in health-related business (128 credit hours) prepares students to assume leadership roles in the health-care industry. The program is available entirely through distance education.

SPECIAL PROGRAMS

There are no special programs offered in distance learning education at Clarkson College.

STUDENT SERVICES

Distance education students have access to many of the same resources as on-campus students. Distance students have regular contact with the Coordinator of Distance Education and Advanced Placement, who serves as a liaison between students and faculty members. The coordinator assists the students in the areas of advisement, registration, and textbook orders, which are accomplished through phone calls, faxes, and e-mail. Distance students' research and informational needs are supported by the College Library Services. Library resources are available via phone, computer, or fax, allowing students the ability to search for articles and books. Distance students have access to the College library loan services. Students also receive a listing of other students enrolled in the same courses for the semester, which facilitates communication with fellow students to discuss course work and share information. Distance students have access to career planning, counseling, and academic skill development services through the Student Success Center.

CREDIT OPTIONS

Students can transfer credits taken at other regionally accredited institutions if the course work is comparable and there is evidence of satisfactory scholarship (at least a C in undergraduate courses and a B for graduate courses). In major course work, up to one third of the total number of credit hours in the major may be transferred. Registered nurses can receive 47 credit hours for their previous nursing education. An ARRT Registered Technologist can receive 44 credit hours for previous radiography education. Students beginning graduate programs may transfer no more than 9 semester credit hours from other institutions. Advanced placement students may take the College-Level Examination Program (CLEP) and/or conduct a portfolio review.

FACULTY

Clarkson College has 37 full-time and 4 part-time faculty members, 27 percent of whom hold doctoral degrees.

ADMISSION

Distance education students are subject to the same admissions requirements as on-campus students. Undergraduate students must have a C+ GPA or higher and an ACT score of 20 or better. Graduate students must have a 3.0 GPA on a 4.0 scale and have completed an appropriate undergraduate degree from an accredited college or university. There are certain program-specific admission requirements.

TUITION AND FEES

Distance students pay the same tuition as on-campus students. For the 1999–2000 academic year, undergraduate tuition is $282 per credit hour and graduate tuition is $324 per credit hour. There is an additional $17 per credit hour in fees. Distance students pay a $75 per semester distance fee.

FINANCIAL AID

Distance students are eligible for many of the financial aid opportunities as on-campus students. Scholarships, grants, and loans are available to meet the individual financial needs of students who qualify.

Scholarships are awarded to outstanding applicants. Students are required to submit the completed Free Application for Federal Student Aid (FAFSA) and the Clarkson College Financial Aid Information Form for eligibility for all forms of aid.

APPLYING

The enrollment policy at Clarkson College allows potential students to apply at any time during the year. A completed application form, accompanied by the $15 application fee, and all official transcripts (high school and previous colleges) should be submitted when seeking admission. Students who have graduated from high school in the past two years must also submit ACT or SAT scores.

CONTACT

Tony Damewood
Director of Enrollment
Clarkson College
101 South 42nd Street
Omaha, Nebraska 68131-2739
Telephone: 402-552-3041
            800-647-5500 (toll-free)
E-mail: admiss@clrkcol.crhsnet.edu
Web site: http://www.clarksoncollege.edu

The College of Mount St. Joseph

Distance Learning Programs

Cincinnati, Ohio

As a private, Catholic, liberal arts college founded in 1920, the College of Mount St. Joseph has a rich history of preparing students for the future. Today, the Mount has more than 2,200 students and offers an outstanding liberal arts curriculum that emphasizes values, integrity, and social responsibility, as well as practical career preparation. Required courses in humanities, science, and the arts are complemented by opportunities for cooperative work experience, specialized professionally oriented courses, development of computer skills through a universal computing requirement, and extracurricular opportunities to give students the broad-based background that is in high demand among employers.

The College is accredited by the North Central Association of Colleges and Schools.

DISTANCE LEARNING PROGRAM

A leader in the field of technology, the College of Mount St. Joseph is committed to providing convenient, accessible, and high-quality education. The Mount's online programs provide a flexible alternative for those wanting to further their education, but for whom attending regularly scheduled classes would be difficult or impossible.

DELIVERY MEDIA

While all courses are taken via distance delivery, distance learning programs require a one-week orientation session at the Mount's campus in Cincinnati, Ohio. During this time, program participants learn the technical skills necessary to succeed in the program, meet their classmates, and become familiar with the College services available to them.

The distance program uses Web-based interactive learning materials, videotapes, and textbooks for "classroom" instruction and provides for student/teacher and student/student interaction through a variety of communication vehicles, includ-ing telephone, voice mail, e-mail, and teleconferences.

PROGRAMS OF STUDY

The Mount offers two certificate programs via distance learning. The Paralegal Studies Certificate Online is a postdegree certificate available to anyone holding either an associate or a bachelor's degree. The Paralegal Studies for Nurses Certificate Online is a postdegree certificate available to RNs holding a Bachelor of Science in Nursing degree. Both programs are approved by the American Bar Association. Both certificates require 33 credit hours. Courses are offered in a structured sequence over a fifteen-month period and begin in January or July. Classes are limited to 20 students.

STUDENT SERVICES

The College of Mount St. Joseph is known for outstanding student support and extends the same services to students learning at a distance. Technical service is available via a toll-free support line from 8 a.m. to 11 p.m. Eastern time. The College library offers many resources in electronic form, including its catalog, journal indexes, journal articles, and reference materials. An electronic reserves system provides distance learners with Web access to articles placed on reserve by their professors. Because access to library resources, including LEXIS, has been built using Web technologies, integration with a predominant Web-based distance program is ensured.

Students also have access to the bookstore, which provides delivery and online ordering. Other student services include advising, financial aid, career counseling and placement, a Wellness Center, and an Academic Performance Center.

FACULTY

The Mount's two distance programs make use of the same faculty as their on-campus counterparts. This includes 1 full-time and 8 part-time faculty members, 8 of whom have doctoral degrees.

ADMISSION

To be admitted to the Paralegal Studies Certificate Online program, a student must have either an associate or a bachelor's degree from an accredited institution.

To be admitted to the Paralegal Studies for Nurses Certificate Online program, a student must be an RN with a Bachelor of Science in Nursing degree from an accredited institution and have had at least 2,000 hours of clinical experience.

CREDIT OPTIONS

There are no credit options for the distance learning programs at the College of Mount St. Joseph.

TUITION AND FEES

The tuition for either online program is $13,000, which includes the use of a laptop computer, the week of residency at the College, and all the support one should expect from a high-quality distance learning program. The application fee is $25.

FINANCIAL AID

There are several financing options, including Stafford loans or interest-free monthly payments. Students should call Student Financial Services at 800-654-9314 Ext. 4418 (toll-free), or 513-244-4418 for more information.

APPLYING

Classes begin in January and July. The application deadline is one month before classes begin. Students should submit the application form, nonrefundable application fee, transcripts, and admission documents to the Office of Admission.

CONTACT

Georgana Taggart, Program Director
College of Mount St. Joseph
5701 Delhi Road
Cincinnati, Ohio 45233
Telephone: 513-244-4952 (Paralegal Studies)
513-244-4531 (Admission Office)
800-654-9314 (toll-free)
Fax: 513-244-4601
E-mail: georgana_taggart@mail.msj.edu
Web site: http://www.msj.edu/paralegal

Colorado Electronic Community College

Denver, Colorado

Colorado Electronic Community College (CECC) was founded in 1995 as a significant innovation of the Colorado Community College and Occupational Education System (CCCOES), a thirteen-college state system. CECC develops and delivers the excellent degree and certificate programs of the system colleges via communication technologies. Students registering with CECC are awarded their degrees/certificates from one of the CCCOES colleges, which are accredited by the North Central Association of Colleges and Schools.

Colorado Electronic Community College was one of the first of its kind to offer a postsecondary degree completely asynchronously. CECC partners with private communications and multimedia companies and its sister colleges to provide unlimited access to its programs. It has articulated its degree program with all of the public four-year colleges in Colorado and several out-of-state colleges.

DISTANCE LEARNING PROGRAM

CECC has served 817 students in forty-eight states as well as Canada, the Caribbean, Brazil, and Sweden. Students can receive the complete Associate of Arts degree and various occupational certificates from their home or office without ever visiting a campus. All student support services are available at a distance as well.

DELIVERY MEDIA

Course work includes print, videotape, audiotape, broadcast, Internet, and CD-ROM materials, depending on the course of study. Students need only a telephone and a VCR to be able to complete an A.A. degree. Presentations, discussions, and study groups with classmates and faculty members occur through a voice-mail system or via electronic mail. Video components may be rented or accessed via cable. Several courses offer sections through the Internet.

PROGRAMS OF STUDY

CECC offers the entire Associate of Arts degree by distance. This degree is awarded by Arapahoe Community College, one of the thirteen CCCOES Colleges, and includes freshman- and sophomore-level general education courses that transfer toward the completion of a baccalaureate degree. The A.A. degree of the Colorado Community Colleges is a low-cost, high-quality, accredited degree that offers variety, flexibility, and a learner-centered curriculum. Every course guide clearly informs students of the potential learning outcomes they can expect from their investment.

The A.A. degree requires 60 hours, 38 hours of core curriculum and 22 hours of general education electives. Fifteen hours must be completed through CECC. Students completing the core curriculum are guaranteed transferability to Colorado four-year colleges.

Colorado Electronic Community College also brokers the degrees and certificates of its thirteen system colleges. It now offers the CCC Online program. CCC Online offers fully accredited associate degrees or certificates completely via the Internet. At a single Web site, students can earn an Associate of Applied Science degree in business, an Associate of Arts degree, or an Associate of Arts degree with emphasis in public administration from any one of the state system community colleges. Additionally, students can earn certificates in computer information systems, emergency management and planning, agribusiness, or gerontology. CECC also offers an advanced farm-ranch management certificate delivered via the Internet through Morgan Community College, an occupational safety and health construction standards certificate via the Internet through Trinidad State Junior College, and a computer programming certificate via the Internet through Aurora Community College. Students can also enroll in a 30-credit–hour Emergency Management Planning certificate that is awarded by Red Rocks Community College. Regardless of the degree-awarding college, students need only reg-

498

ister at one place with the Colorado Electronic Community College.

SPECIAL PROGRAMS

Colorado Electronic Community College has a state-of-the-art, multimillion-dollar digital video and multimedia production and training facility called the Education Technology Training Center located in Denver, Colorado. It provides training to instructional designers and faculty members as well as business and government in the applications of technology to curriculum. Visitors to the center learn how to produce videos, press CD-ROMs, and create multimedia presentations and Internet applications and other technologies for the enhancement of learning and education access. In addition, the center has videoconferencing capabilities with all of the thirteen colleges in Colorado as well as with sites around the globe. Training, production, and communication can be delivered from the Education Technology Training Center to anywhere in the world.

STUDENT SERVICES

CECC is dedicated to the satisfaction and success of its students. CECC provides easy access to the complete array of student enrollment, academic, financial aid, special support, and career counseling services and provides tutoring to distance learning students. Library access is provided through various Internet library resources, interlibrary loan, and by the Colorado Association for Research Libraries.

CREDIT OPTIONS

Transfer credit and prior-learning portfolio development and assessment are offered toward degree/certificate completion. Credit through the College-Level Examination Program (CLEP) and other standardized tests is also available. Students may transfer up to 45 credits of their 60-hour Associate of Arts degree. College staff members understand that school and work experiences add richness to the education environment for participants. Staff members strive to provide credit for students' experiences.

FACULTY

CECC uses full-time (80 percent) and part-time (20 percent) faculty members from its sister colleges. These faculty members have won regional and national awards for teaching skills and have long experience with a student-centered philosophy.

ADMISSION

Colorado community colleges are open-door institutions, admitting anyone 16 years of age or older. A high school diploma or GED is not required for admission.

TUITION AND FEES

Tuition is $120 per credit hour. Student charges may include a $9 registration fee (once per semester), a $30-per-course voice mail fee, a $45-per-course telecourse license (AV videotape license), and a $35-per-course Internet technology fee.

FINANCIAL AID

General financial aid programs are available through Arapahoe Community College and include the Federal Pell Grant, Federal Supplemental Educational Opportunity Grant, Federal Perkins Loan, Federal Stafford Student Loan, and Federal Work-Study Programs. Approximately 20 percent of CECC's students receive financial aid. Last year, CECC students received a total of more than $125,000.

APPLYING

Distance learners can enroll by telephone (800-801-5040, toll-free). Admission and enrollment occur simultaneously as CECC is an open-door college. Because of the asynchronous nature of the course, there is always room in every section of every course.

CONTACT

John Schmahl
Director of College Support Services
Colorado Electronic Community College
9075 Lowry Boulevard
Denver, Colorado 80220
Telephone: 303-365-8888
            800-801-5040 (toll-free)
Fax: 303-365-8822
E-mail: john.schmahl@cecc.cccoes.edu
Web site: http://www.cecc.cccoes.edu

Colorado State University

Division of Educational Outreach

Fort Collins, Colorado

Colorado State University has served the people of Colorado as the state's land-grant university since 1870. Today, the campus in Fort Collins is home to 19,000 students pursuing degrees at all levels in a wide range of subjects in the liberal arts, engineering, business, natural resources, agriculture, and the sciences. The University's instructional outreach activities go far beyond the campus and the state of Colorado.

DISTANCE LEARNING PROGRAM

Colorado State University's distance education courses are designed to begin or to finish a degree, to explore new topics, to enrich life, and to give students an opportunity to develop a level of proficiency in professional development. Approximately 2,500 individuals from all over the country and overseas enrolled in distance education courses from Colorado State University during the 1999–2000 academic year.

DELIVERY MEDIA

Colorado State offers courses in online, print, and video formats. All courses are supported by Colorado State University faculty members. Students may contact course faculty members via telephone, fax, e-mail, or regular mail. Students should call Educational Outreach for contact information for an instructor.

PROGRAMS OF STUDY

Colorado State University's Network for Learning (CSUN) links learners to all of Colorado State's distance options—correspondence courses, telecourses, distance degree programs, online courses, face-to-face programs at satellite locations, and those offering a mix of media.

As an institution, Colorado State has been involved in distance education since 1967 and was one of the first schools to utilize technology in distance education.

Independent Study: Correspondence Study, Telecourses, and Online Courses removes the traditional boundaries of time and location for the distance learner. Through the use of a study guide, textbooks, videotapes, the Internet, and applicable reference materials, students have the opportunity to participate in an individualized mode of instruction offering a high degree of flexibility. Students interested in correspondence courses and telecourses may enroll at any time, set their own pace, and choose the most convenient time and place to study. Online courses are taught according to the regular University semester schedule.

The Distance Degree Program offers working professionals the opportunity to earn credit from Colorado State without coming to campus. It is a semester-based, primarily videotaped program. Whether students are working on their degree or taking courses to stay current in their field, the Distance Degree Program offers the flexibility to pursue educational objectives as work schedules permit.

Courses are available in several disciplines, including agriculture, business, computer science, engineering, fire service, human resource development, and statistics. Distance Degree Program students are located throughout the United States and Canada and at U.S. military APO and FPO addresses. More than 860 motivated people have earned their degrees, and countless others have taken individual courses to enhance their skill base or keep current with the latest technology.

SPECIAL PROGRAMS

Colorado State also provides other distance education opportunities. These courses are open-entry/open-exit, meaning students may register at any time and take from six to twelve months to complete, depending on the course. Many of the courses can be used for specific programs, such as Child Care Administration Certification, the Gerontology Interdisciplinary Studies Program, the Educator's Portfolio Builder, or Seed Analyst Training.

The state of Colorado requires certification of all child-care center directors and substitute directors by the State Department of Social Services. Certification requires both experience working with young children and specific education. Colorado State University is proud to offer courses through distance education that satisfy the educational requirements. Other states may have individual specific educational requirements. Students should contact the appropriate agency in their area for further information.

The Gerontology Interdisciplinary Studies certificate program helps individuals increase their knowledge, skills, and effectiveness in working with older adults. The objectives of the program are congruent with standards and guidelines for gerontology programs advocated by the Association of Gerontology in Higher Education (AGHE), of which Colorado State is an institutional member.

The Educator's Portfolio Builder distance education courses are designed for independent, self-paced learning. Students choose an area of interest and focus; they can mix and match and build the portfolio that meets their individual professional development needs. Courses are designed for practicing teachers, with assignments and activities relevant to teachers and students, and they are all college-credit courses. Instructors are Colorado State University faculty members. They are available to answer questions and give feedback via telephone, fax, e-mail, or regular mail.

An innovative Seed Analyst Training consisting of four distance learning (correspondence) courses has been developed by the National Seed Storage Laboratory and Colorado State University. The courses were prepared over a two-year period by University professors and other experts with the support of the Colorado seed industry. The four courses cover the basics of seed analyst training: 1) Seed Anatomy and Identification, 2) Seed Development and Metabolism, 3) Seed Purity Analysis, and 4) Seed Germination and Viability.

Advising and career counseling services through the University HELP/ Success Center are offered to all persons interested in continuing their learning. There is no fee for academic advising services. Students may schedule an appointment with an academic adviser by calling 970-491-

7095. The Extended University Programs librarian is available to assist students with identifying and accessing library materials. Students should call 970-491-6952 to speak with the librarian.

CREDIT OPTIONS

All credits earned through distance education are recorded on a Colorado State University transcript. Distance education courses are the same as on-campus courses and are accredited by each department. A student currently enrolled in a degree program elsewhere is responsible for checking with the appropriate official at the degree-granting institution to make certain the course will apply.

FACULTY

Distance education faculty members must meet the same high standards any Colorado State University faculty member must meet. Most of the distance faculty members are faculty members within the department granting the course credit. Faculty members are available to answer questions and give feedback via telephone, fax, e-mail, or regular mail.

ADMISSION

Anyone who has the interest, desire, background, and ability may register for distance learning courses. However, if prerequisites are listed for a course, they must be met. Registra-

tion in distance learning courses does not constitute admission to Colorado State University.

TUITION AND FEES

Tuition for the Distance Degree Program for the 2000–01 academic year is $416 per semester credit hour. Tuition for other distance education courses for the 2000–01 academic year varies from $150 to $225 per semester credit hour depending on course instruction level and delivery method.

FINANCIAL AID

Colorado State University courses are approved for the DANTES program. Eligible military personnel should process DANTES applications through their education office. For information regarding veterans' benefits, students should contact the VA office at Colorado State University. With the exception of the Distance Degree Program, distance learning is not a degree-granting program and is therefore not eligible for federal grants. Students are encouraged to seek scholarship aid from organizations and local civic groups that may sponsor such study.

APPLYING

There is no application for distance education. Students should simply register for the course(s) of interest by mail, fax, telephone, or in person and pay the tuition. To complete a degree via the Distance Degree Program, admittance to the University's Graduate School is required.

CONTACT

For more information about these and other distance courses from Colorado State University or for registration information:

Telephone: 970-491-5288
877-491-4336 (toll-free)
Fax: 970-491-7885
E-mail: info@learn.colostate.edu
Web site: http://www.csu2learn.colostate.edu

Columbia University

Columbia Video Network
Fu Foundation School of Engineering and Applied Science

New York, New York

Columbia University's reputation and recognized excellence as a leading research university ensures that all students receive the benefits of instruction by world-class faculty members and information on the most current research findings available. A degree from Columbia University stands out on a resume; more importantly, Columbia graduates stand out on the job. Columbia students are able to apply their mastery of theoretical essentials and newly acquired knowledge of cutting-edge technology to bring creative solutions to their everyday professional work.

DISTANCE LEARNING PROGRAM

Columbia Video Network (CVN) is a premier distance learning program affiliated with Columbia University's Fu Foundation School of Engineering and Applied Science. It brings the prestigious faculty members of Columbia University's school of engineering and applied science to the working professional, providing the opportunity to participate in the same courses, interact with the same instructors, and ultimately earn the same fully accredited Columbia University degree as on-campus students. The key component of CVN is flexibility without compromise to the high-caliber teaching, resources, and standards inherent in the Columbia School of Engineering and Applied Science. Flexible degree requirements and interdepartmental curricula allow programs to be tailored to address the individual needs of practitioners in the field.

DELIVERY MEDIA

CVN strives to be a leader in providing remote students with the most flexible options in course delivery through state-of-the-art technology and extensive support services.

Course lectures are delivered via videocassettes, videoconferencing, and the Internet. Videocassettes, which may not be duplicated, are returned to CVN at the end of the semester.

PROGRAMS OF STUDY

CVN provides Master of Science (M. S.) degree programs in computer science, electrical engineering, engineering and management systems (industrial engineering and operations research), materials science, and mechanical engineering. CVN also offers certificate programs and professional degree programs, as well as professional development seminar courses and courses from Columbia University's Graduate School of Business. Students with a strong engineering background need not matriculate into a degree program before beginning their studies.

The CVN program is flexible and can be completed as early as one year from commencement of the program. However, students planning to graduate from the M.S. degree program must complete all of the requirements within five years. Continuous registration is expected, unless a leave of absence is formally requested. All other degree require-

ments should be fulfilled as outlined on the CVN Web site, as well as in the *CVN Course Book* and the School of Engineering and Applied Science catalog.

SPECIAL PROGRAMS

The nonmatriculated student is assigned the status of Video Special (VS) and may take courses for credit or audit immediately by completing the New Student Information section of the CVN Registration Form. Through CVN, students may later choose to pursue a Master of Science degree or a professional degree. This is also an excellent option for those who simply wish to polish their skills and knowledge and keep up to date with the latest technological advances.

FACULTY

CVN students not only learn from Columbia's distinguished full-time faculty members, but also from many adjunct professors who are also working professionals at the top of their fields. They apply the latest theoretical tools to their own work and pass their knowledge along to their students. CVN provides a nurturing environment where ideas and knowledge are easily shared between student and teacher, ultimately providing Columbia students with a competitive edge in domestic and international business and technology. Once admitted into the degree program, students are assigned a CVN faculty adviser for each department. CVN faculty advisers help shape a program of study to meet the student's needs.

502

ADMISSION

Potential students are invited to submit an application for graduate admission to any one of the CVN degree programs. The Graduate Application requires students to submit GRE scores, two letters of recommendation, official transcripts of all previous undergraduate and graduate studies, a personal/professional statement, a resume, and a signed application form, along with the requisite fee. Students who completed their bachelor's degree in a country where English is not the official language are also required to submit TOEFL exam scores.

APPLYING

Complete information on CVN policies and procedures, course descriptions and syllabi, and contacts at CVN can be found on the CVN Web site. Students can contact the School with any questions.

CONTACT

Columbia Video Network/Columbia University
Fu Foundation School of Engineering and Applied Science
540 Mudd Building
500 West 120th Street
New York, New York 10027
Telephone: 212-854-6447
Fax: 212-854-2325
E-mail: cvn@cvn.columbia.edu
Web site: http://www.cvn.columbia.edu

Online CSU

Connecticut State University
Online Learning Program
Hartford, Connecticut

The Connecticut State University System's (CSU's) four universities are located in urban areas throughout Connecticut: Central Connecticut State University in New Britain, Eastern Connecticut State University in Willimantic, Southern Connecticut State University in New Haven, and Western Connecticut State University in Danbury. A fully accredited university system, CSU is the largest university system in Connecticut, with more than 130,000 alumni and a present enrollment of more than 34,000 students. CSU provides affordable and high-quality active learning opportunities that are geographically and technologically accessible. A CSU education leads to baccalaureate, graduate, and professional degrees and career advancement. CSU designed OnlineCSU to ensure that the education it has traditionally made available in the classroom can now be offered without regard to time, distance, or circumstance.

DISTANCE LEARNING PROGRAM

OnlineCSU is the online classroom of the Connecticut State University System. Offerings include graduate and undergraduate courses. CSU offers courses through OnlineCSU that are approved for credit by the university offering the course and are eligible for credit toward a degree.

DELIVERY MEDIA

OnlineCSU is an asynchronous learning environment; students and teachers do not need to log on at the same time. Faculty members and students share documents and interact regularly through chat rooms, threaded discussions, and e-mail. The equipment requirements for taking an OnlineCSU course are: Windows 95/MacOs 7.5.5 or greater; a Pentium 75 or Power PC or faster processor, with 16 MB or more of RAM and a 28.8-kbps or faster modem; and an Internet service provider.

PROGRAMS OF STUDY

OnlineCSU is now offering its first online degree: a Master in Library Sci-

ence (MLS). This program is offered by Southern Connecticut State University's Department of Library Science and Instructional Technology. Southern's MLS program integrates library science, information science, and instructional technology and offers preparation for carers in various types of libraries, including academic, public, special, and school libraries, and a range of alternative information science occupations. The Master of Library Science degree program is accredited by the American Library Association. The school media specialist concentration is also approved by the Connecticut State Board of Education and offers Connecticut certified teachers the opportunity to obtain cross endorsement as a School Media Specialist through the online program. A minimum of 36 credits, taken as part of a planned program, is required for the Master of Library Science degree. Some specialization alternatives may require additional credits.

Other online degree programs CSU is considering for the future include accounting, business administration, nursing, and education. More information will be posted to the Web site as it becomes available.

SPECIAL PROGRAMS

Online learners are invited to participate in the same programs that are available to on-ground students. CSU's four universities offer a full range of special programs for students, including internships, work-study programs, study-abroad programs, and more. More information can be obtained by linking to the four university Web sites from the OnlineCSU site (listed below).

STUDENT SERVICES

All OnlineCSU students have full access to CSU's online library services, including full-text resources; online bookstores; and a round-the-clock, toll-free help desk. In addition, all of the on-campus student services, such as academic advising, financial aid, and career counseling, are available to OnlineCSU students.

CREDIT OPTIONS

CSU is a fully accredited university system, and the courses that are offered through OnlineCSU are part of the regular curriculum of the four CSU universities. Therefore, these credits should be transferable to other higher education institutions.

FACULTY

Regular CSU faculty members teach all of the courses offered through OnlineCSU. At CSU, the faculty members who develop the course teach the course, whether the course is delivered on ground or on line.

ADMISSION

Students wishing to enroll in the online Master in Library Science (MLS)

504

degree program can do so completely online. Other than the MLS degree, students wishing to matriculate at one of the four CSU universities must apply to the university of choice using the on-campus application process.

TUITION AND FEES

Part-time graduate students pay $250 per credit hour. Part-time undergraduate students pay $215 per credit hour.

All OnlineCSU students pay a $30 online fee for each OnlineCSU course they take.

FINANCIAL AID

Students who receive financial aid may be able to apply all or part of this aid to the OnlineCSU courses.

APPLYING

OnlineCSU courses are open to full- and part-time students, whether or not they matriculated at one of the four CSU universities. Students register for OnlineCSU courses online through the Web site. Registration data is forwarded to the appropriate university for approval. No orientation is required. Students complete a self-rated questionnaire, Is Online Learning For Me, and are asked to consult regularly with their advisers regarding online learning choices.

CONTACT

Robin Worley
Telephone: 860-493-0023
Fax: 860-493-0080
E-mail: worleyr@sysoff.ctstateu.edu
Web site: http://www.OnlineCSU.ctstateu.edu

Dallas Baptist University

Distance Education Program

Dallas, Texas

The purpose of Dallas Baptist University (DBU) is to provide Christ-centered, high-quality higher education in the arts, sciences, and professional studies at both the undergraduate and graduate levels to traditional age and adult students in order to produce servant leaders who have the ability to integrate faith and learning through their respective callings.

Dallas Baptist University celebrated its 100th anniversary in 1998 and in fall 1999 reached a record enrollment of 3,921 students on campus and across a nine-state region.

The adult degree-completion program received national recognition in 1992, and the Master of Business Administration is one of the few M.B.A. programs available on line that has both regional and national accreditation.

All degree programs are accredited by the Southern Association of Colleges and Schools, 1866 Southern Lane, Decatur, Georgia 30033-4097 (telephone: 404-670-4501). The Graduate School of Business M.B.A. program is also accredited by ACBSP.

DISTANCE LEARNING PROGRAM

The Distance Education Program provides students with the same high-quality degree programs, student services support, library access, and technology access as local students receive on the main campus. Multiple technologies served more than 700 distance education students by March 2000. Students may take courses from anywhere in the world.

DELIVERY MEDIA

Internet courses are instructor led from password-protected Web sites with a wide variety of interactions, such as chat rooms and threaded discussion. Students must have appropriate computer equipment, technical skills, and Internet access via a Web browser. The online courses are offered via the eCollege.com system.

Two-way audio/video courses are provided for corporate clients over their videoconferencing networks.

Both undergraduate and graduate business degree programs are available.

Video courses are instructor led using a VHS format.

Audio courses are standard 60-minute cassettes.

PROGRAMS OF STUDY

Dallas Baptist University offers a Bachelor of Business Studies and Bachelor of Arts and Sciences degrees in business administration and management through the College of Adult Education via distance education. Students may earn up to 30 semester credit hours through the successful completion of an academic portfolio. A total of 66 semester hours can be transferred from a regionally accredited two-year college, and an unlimited number of semester hours can be transferred from a regionally accredited four-year institution for students who earned a GPA of 2.0 or above. A minimum of 126 semester hours is required for graduation, with 32 semester hours taken from DBU.

Courses required for the M.B.A. degree are available through distance education. The M.B.A. program consists of a 24-semester-hour core plus a student-selected concentration of 12 semester hours. Some applicants may need to add 3–18 semester hours of foundational courses if their undergraduate degree is not in business. An M.B.A. in management and a new concentration in e-commerce are now available completely online.

The management curriculum is designed to serve the educational needs of business managers and professionals who desire to enhance their management skills or acquire new skills. A variety of courses are provided in strategy, research, quantitative analysis, financial management, marketing, and international business. The e-commerce concentration provides both the business and technical knowledge needed to succeed in the exciting new world of electronic commerce.

DBU welcomes corporations that are interested in providing these degree programs to employees via the Internet or videoconferencing networks. For more information, companies should contact the University.

SPECIAL PROGRAMS

College credit for knowledge gained through life and work experiences is available to adults who have at least four years of full-time work experience. This is accomplished through the College of Adult Education.

Dallas Baptist University's internship program provides students with opportunities to participate in an experimental work environment supervised by a professor and a business professional. The internship offers research, observation, study, and work in an approved organization. An international study program offers students international business knowledge through periodic overseas travel. Up to 6 semester hours of credit may be earned.

Special programs available to distance learners include on-site classes held at corporations in the Dallas/Fort Worth metroplex area and corporate sites in Texas, Oklahoma, Arkansas, Kansas, Georgia, and Florida. Currently, Dallas Baptist University teaches undergraduate and/or graduate classes at twenty-five corporate sites.

STUDENT SERVICES

Distance education students receive the same high-quality degree programs, administrative support, library access, technology access, bookstore services, academic advising, and access to the University Writing Center as local students receive on the main campus. Student computer equipment and computer skills are tested via the Internet prior to admission to the Internet courses. Any technical problems are identified for the student.

CREDIT OPTIONS

For the Bachelor of Business Studies or the Bachelor of Arts and Sciences degrees, students can transfer earned academic credits from accredited two-year colleges, accredited four-year institutions, CLEP examinations, and ACE/PONSI.

For the M.B.A. program, students may transfer up to 6 semester hours of graduate-level courses.

Students can supplement distance education courses with DBU's weekend and miniterm courses.

FACULTY

Courses are taught by the same faculty members who teach on-campus classes to assure high-quality learning. Graduate students do not teach at DBU.

ADMISSION

In addition to the University's standard admission requirements, a brief computer skills assessment is required for Internet courses. For degree-specific requirements, students should contact the University.

TUITION AND FEES

Tuition for 2000–01 undergraduate online courses is $345 per credit hour. Graduate online courses are $355 per credit hour. There is a $40 fee for video courses and a $20 fee for audio courses.

FINANCIAL AID

A variety of federal, state, and private funds may be available for students who meet specific requirements.

For institutional scholarships, students must be in good standing and satisfactorily progressing toward their educational goals. Other eligibility requirements may exist for specific awards.

For federal or state financial assistance, a student must meet the guidelines established by the U.S. Department of Education and the state of Texas.

Students interested in such assistance should contact the Financial Aid Office for more information (telephone: 214-333-5363).

APPLYING

Applicants may apply online at http://www.dbu.edu or by requesting an application packet. Undergraduates must submit an application, official transcripts, and/or GED scores and an essay on why they wish to attend DBU. Applicants to the Graduate School of Business M.B.A. program must submit an application, transcripts, GMAT scores, two references, a resume, and an essay. Students for whom English is a second language must submit a minimum TOEFL score of 550.

CONTACT

Distance Education Program
Dallas Baptist University
3000 Mountain Creek Parkway
Dallas, Texas 75211-9299
Telephone: 214-333-5337
　　　　(undergraduate
　　　　program)
　　　　214-333-5242 (graduate program)
　　　　800-460-8188 (toll-free online
　　　　program)
E-mail: caed@dbu.edu
　　　　(undergraduate
　　　　program)
　　　　graduate@dbu.edu (graduate program)
　　　　online@dbu.edu (online program)
Web site: http://www.dbu.edu
　　　　http://www.dbuonline.org

Dallas Community Colleges

Distance Learning Program

Dallas, Texas

More than 250,000 students have enrolled in the Distance Learning Program of the Dallas Community College (DCC) District since it began in 1972. Currently, approximately 10,000 students enroll in the program each academic year. The Dallas Community Colleges program is a product of the collaboration of seven colleges, all accredited by the Commission on Colleges of the Southern Association of Colleges and Schools to award the associate degree. The program draws its strength from the full-time faculty members of these colleges and from more than twenty-five years of experience in the development and implementation of distance learning courses, which are used by many colleges worldwide.

DISTANCE LEARNING PROGRAM

The Dallas Distance Learning Program provides greater access to educational opportunities for learners in Dallas County and worldwide through the delivery of flexible, cost-effective courses. These courses are offered through a variety of technologies and lead to the Associate of Arts (A.A.) or the Associate of Sciences (A.S.) degree. The Distance Learning Program also provides opportunities for skill development or enhancement in career fields such as business. Dallas also provides a variety of noncredit courses.

DELIVERY MEDIA

Video-based telecourses include a preproduced video series with print materials. Students may lease videos or view them on television (Dallas area only). Class interaction is offered through the telephone, fax, and mail. Students are required to have a TV, VCR, and telephone.

Video-based telecourse PLUS includes the same materials as above with online activities. Minimum requirements to access the sites are Netscape 4.0 or Internet Explorer 4.0.

Online courses are conducted entirely on the Internet. These courses require a computer, an Internet connection, an e-mail account, and Netscape Navigator 4.0 or Internet Explorer 4.0 or higher.

Some courses require additional hardware, software, or telephone resources. Print-based courses include print materials and participation in specialized activities. Courses may require a VCR or telephone.

PROGRAMS OF STUDY

The Associate of Arts and the Associate of Sciences degrees require the completion of 61 credit hours, which includes a 48-credit-hour core plus an additional 13 credit hours of electives. The A.A. and A.S. degrees may be earned in their entirety through the Distance Learning Program of the Dallas Community Colleges.

More than 100 courses are available in a variety of subjects, including business, communications, computer programming, electronics, health, humanities and arts, literature, mathematics, office technology and software, sciences, and social sciences.

Students who plan to transfer to a four-year institution should consult the catalog of that institution to ensure that selected courses will both transfer and apply toward the intended major.

SPECIAL PROGRAMS

Dallas participates in the special open-enrollment Navy College PACE program that reaches ships, submarines, and remote sites of the U.S. Navy. More than 10,000 military personnel have enrolled in courses through Dallas since 1992. Dallas is also a participant in Western Governor's University and Southern Regional Electronic Campus, which offers courses to students in the U.S. and abroad. Dallas Community Colleges also deliver credit and noncredit courses to employees of major corporations based in the north Texas area and beyond.

STUDENT SERVICES

Distance learners have access to admission and enrollment processes as well as library services, including an online search, study skills assistance, and academic advising. There are services that are available through the Web site or by fax, telephone, or mail.

CREDIT OPTIONS

The DCC transfers many passing grade credits from other colleges accredited through one of the U.S. regional associations. The DCC registrar completes course evaluations as needed for degree planning.

Credits earned through credit-by-examination, military experience, and the U.S. Armed Forces Institute are reviewed by the registrar. Credit may be granted if applicable. The DCC requires that at least 25 percent of the credit hours required for graduation be taken by instruction rather than these methods.

FACULTY

Most of the courses in the Distance Learning Program are taught by full-time faculty members who also teach on-campus classes. Each of the more than 100 faculty members holds credentials approved by the Colleges' accrediting agency. To ensure high-quality instruction, the number of students assigned to a faculty member in a distance learning course is limited.

ADMISSION

Students must have a high school diploma or its equivalent, be at least 18 years of age, or receive special approval for admission as outlined in the DCC catalog. Texas students must also fulfill testing requirements as mandated by state law. International students must take the TOEFL.

TUITION AND FEES

Tuition and fees vary with the learner's residence and the number of credit hours. This may range from approximately $84 per 3-credit course for a local Dallas resident to $389 per 3-credit course for an out-of-state student. Other expenses may include tape leasing and the cost of study guides, textbooks, and course-related software.

FINANCIAL AID

Students accepted for enrollment may be considered for several forms of institutional and federal financial aid. Veterans and financial aid recipients should consult an adviser before enrolling in distance learning courses.

APPLYING

Applicants should submit an official application along with appropriate documentation, such as an official high school transcript, GED scores, or official transcripts from previous colleges, and should complete any required assessment procedures. The DCC application is available on line or through the mail.

CONTACT

Distance Learning Program
Dallas Community Colleges
9596 Walnut Street
Dallas, Texas 75243
Telephone: 972-669-6400
   888-468-4268 (toll-free)
   972-669-6410 (for recorded information)
Fax: 972-669-6409
Web site: http://dallas.dcccd.edu

Davenport Educational System, Inc. Learning Network

Davenport College, Detroit College of Business, and Great Lakes College

Grand Rapids, Michigan

By taking online courses through the Learning Network, students are part of the largest independent college system in Michigan, the Davenport Educational System, Inc. Combined, the system's Learning Network offers more than 230 years of educational excellence of Davenport College, Detroit College of Business, and Great Lakes College from any computer. The Learning Network is a consortium dedicated to delivering a wide range of online courses and educational degrees and programs from the three colleges of the Davenport Educational System. These colleges are dedicated to providing superior workforce preparedness degrees. Accredited by the North Central Association of Colleges and Schools (NCA), all three colleges undergo continuous and comprehensive evaluation processes to ensure that the degree programs offered are of consistently high quality.

DISTANCE LEARNING PROGRAM

The Learning Network offers the convenience of classroom accessibility 24 hours a day, seven days a week from virtually anywhere in the world. Online courses are truly interactive. Through group assignments, online research projects, and case study analyses, students collaborate with peers and immediately apply textbook theory to real business situations. The computer is simply a tool through which to communicate. Courses begin and end on specific dates, and class work is assigned deadlines.

DELIVERY MEDIA

Students within the Learning Network are required to have a computer with the following minimum requirements: a Pentium 100-MHz processor or Macintosh Power PC 601 100 MHz or higher with 16 MB of RAM, a 28.8-kbps modem, Windows 95 or newer operating system, Internet access through an Internet service provider including e-mail, Netscape 4.0 or Explorer 5.0 or higher (AOL users should use Netscape), and 640 x 480 monitor resolution. A CD-ROM is strongly recommended.

PROGRAMS OF STUDY

The three colleges of Davenport Educational System, Inc.—Davenport College, Detroit College of Business, and Great Lakes College—through North Central Association of Colleges and Schools, offer complete online degrees through the Learning Network. Currently, the undergraduate online degrees include both bachelor's and associate degrees in the areas of management (including human resource, self-directed, industrial, general, and entrepreneurship) and marketing. The M.B.A. program through Detroit College of Business is also offered completely on line. In addition, Learning Network also offers technical specialties and preparation for certification within the areas of management and marketing, including human resource management, international business, leadership, quality leadership, small-business management, certified manager, marketing manager, and many more.

FACULTY

All faculty members who teach with the Learning Network have at least a master's degree in the area of study and practical work experience. Their combined knowledge of theory and practice enhances the learning environment. All faculty members must complete an instructional design training program to become certified as an online instructor.

ADMISSION

Online course work relies heavily on written communication and problem-solving skills. So that all students can have a successful online experience, applicants are expected to demonstrate these skills prior to entry into a Learning Network course. Students must possess the skills that are necessary to place beyond developmental courses, or they need proof of these skills from previous college transcripts or placement testing. Standardized exams or other measures may be used with the approval of the Learning Network.

TUITION AND FEES

The Learning Network undergraduate tuition rate is $795 per course; master's-level tuition is $895 per course. No additional fees are assessed. Registration schedules and fee bills are mailed to the student prior to the beginning of each session. Courses need to be finalized before the beginning of each session.

FINANCIAL AID

Financial aid, such as grants, loans, and scholarships, is available to all qualified students. Students must first fill out a Free Application for Federal Student Aid (FAFSA) to begin the process. Many students receive tuition assistance through their employer's tuition reimbursement plan.

APPLYING

Students must apply and be admitted to one of the three colleges: Davenport College, Detroit College of Business, or Great Lakes College. There is a $25 application fee associated with admittance to the colleges. Students can complete the Learning Network application on line at the Web site listed below. After students apply and are accepted to the Learning Network, they receive information on specifics about how to activate their courses, purchase books, etc. Students may view a demonstration of the learning environment to familiarize themselves with the course format and to become oriented with the platform before courses begin. Books are purchased through MBS Direct and delivered to students' homes.

CONTACT
Dennis Zoet
Director for Enrollment Services
Learning Network
415 East Fulton Street
Grand Rapids, Michigan 49503
Telephone: 800-203-5323 (toll-free)
Fax: 616-742-2076
E-mail: admissionsln@davenport.edu
Web site: http://www.learningnetwork.davenport.edu

Drexel University

MBA Online

Philadelphia, Pennsylvania

In 1891, near the end of a long and prosperous life, Philadelphia financier Anthony J. Drexel founded the Drexel Institute of Art, Science, and Industry. As society's need for technically proficient leaders grew, so did Mr. Drexel's Institution, first becoming Drexel Institute of Technology in 1936 and then Drexel University in 1970. Today, more than 6,800 undergraduate and 2,800 graduate students attend Drexel's six colleges and three schools. The Bennett S. LeBow College of Business founded its M.B.A. degree program in 1947 and currently has 900 students in the M.B.A., five M.S. programs, and the APC program. Located on 49 acres in Philadelphia's University City neighborhood, Drexel's programs are enhanced by the industrial, commercial, professional, and cultural activities of the nation's fourth-largest metropolitan area.

DISTANCE LEARNING PROGRAM

MBA Online is a Web-based version of the renowned Drexel M.B.A. program. It is fully a part of the graduate program in the College of Business, with the same admissions standards, same faculty, and same degree program. The mission of MBA Online is to serve the needs of graduate students whose schedule or location prevent them from otherwise participating in a high-quality M.B.A. program.

The first year, or foundation level, is an open enrollment program of ten courses. The second year, or advanced year, is a cohort track open by special admission. There are 20 students per cohort. The curriculum of the advanced year is delivered as a "techno-MBA," designed to meet the needs of professionals in technology-related positions. The technology-management focus is derived from a selection of courses from the Management Information Systems (MIS) area, as well as those developed by

the Center for e-Commerce Management. The curriculum uses enterprise-wide business simulations at the beginning and end of the program, as well as a unique case study in the application of Enterprise Resource Planning. It is designed to meet the needs of professionals and managers who wish to enhance their skills in the rapidly emerging technology-oriented marketplace.

Unique features of the program include focus on ERP as a unifying theme; focus on e-commerce as an important framework for the future; technology-management orientation; cutting-edge technology for program delivery, utilizing the strength of simulation experiences; the Business Mentors program, which features a highly placed executive in a mentorship role; and an active advisory board of executives that provides continuous improvement of the program.

DELIVERY MEDIA

The MBA Online program is delivered over the World Wide

Web in the asynchronous mode via the eCollege.com system. Students need a computer, an Internet service provider, and Web navigation software. No other special equipment or software is needed. Since the program is Web based, students have access to their classes from anywhere they can plug into the Web. The MBA Online site carries not only all of the educational materials that the student needs to participate but communications features as well in order to communicate with the instructor, fellow students, advisers, and support services.

PROGRAM OF STUDY

MBA Online comprises two parts: ten required foundation-level M.B.A. classes in an open enrollment program (i.e., any accepted student can register for these courses to meet requirements in the regular "real-time" program or the online program) and sixteen advanced-level M.B.A. classes. Students who qualify and wish to complete the M.B.A. entirely online are admitted to a select group of 20 students, called a cohort, at the advanced level. Cohorts start in September and April of each year. Students complete a sixteen-course sequence with their cohorts over a twenty-one-month period. Students in the advanced-level MBA Online are required to attend three on-campus residencies at the beginning, middle, and end of the program. These residencies are structured as concentrated weekend workshops and include an on-campus course component that continues online throughout the academic quarter. Other than these three residencies, students are not required to come onto campus. At the foundation level, there is no residency requirement.

STUDENT SERVICES

All services available to on-campus students are also available to distance learning students. They are accessible through hot links on the MBA Online Web site. These links include academic advisers, cashier, and bookstore and access to the resources of Drexel's Hagerty Library.

CREDIT OPTIONS

Course credits earned at the undergraduate and graduate levels may be transferred into the program to meet foundation-level requirements. Credit is granted based on academic course work only; no credit is granted on the basis of profes-sional experience. At the foundation level, credit for all eight courses may be transferred from undergraduate programs or other previous study.

FACULTY

There are 85 full-time and 21 part-time faculty members on staff at the LeBow Business College. Ninety-two percent of the full-time faculty members hold a Ph.D. in their fields. Instructors are regular members of the faculty of the LeBow College of Business at Drexel University and meet all of the requirements as faculty members of one of the nation's premier institutions for professional education. Students interact with each of their instructors regularly, and, in most cases, instructors are experienced in teaching the same courses in "real time" on campus. All instructors are committed to their students' success in the course.

ADMISSION

All applicants must have received a bachelor's degree from an accredited college or university. Students must submit a fee, college transcripts, GMAT scores, TOEFL scores for international students, an essay, and letters of recommendation for admission to the advanced level.

TUITION AND FEES

Tuition for the twenty-one-month advanced-level program for the cohort beginning in the academic year 2000 is $31,500. Students should see the Web site for tuition for individual courses in the open enrollment program.

FINANCIAL AID

There is no financial aid specifically for the MBA Online program at this time. Students may contact the graduate financial aid officer, Mr. Robert Forest (rdf22@drexel.edu), for information on applicable federal and state loan and grant programs.

APPLYING

Applications may be made through the MBA Online Web site.

CONTACT

Dr. Thomas Wieckowski
Director of Master's Programs in Business
Bennett S. LeBow College of Business
Drexel University
3141 Chestnut Street
Philadelphia, Pennsylvania 19104
Telephone: 215-895-1791
E-mail: mba@drexel.edu
World Wide Web: http://mbaonline.lebow.drexel.edu

Duke University

The Fuqua School of Business

Durham, North Carolina

Chartered in 1924 and accredited by AACSB–The International Association for Management Education in 1979, Duke University is one of the world's preeminent research and teaching universities. Duke consistently ranks among the top schools in the annual survey of "America's Best Colleges" by U.S. News & World Report. In addition to 6,000 undergraduates from ninety-six countries, Duke is home to 5,000 graduate students studying arts and sciences, business, divinity, engineering, the environment, and law and medicine.

Founded in 1969, Duke University's Fuqua School of Business is an established world leader among M.B.A. and executive education programs. Fuqua ranked seventh in the most recent biennial rankings of the best business schools by Business Week. U.S. News & World Report ranked Fuqua fourth in Executive M.B.A. programs among all schools in 2000. In the summer of 1999, Duke University established the Fuqua School of Business Europe in Frankfurt, Germany. The Fuqua School of Business Europe serves as headquarters for the Duke M.B.A. Cross Continent and Global Executive programs during European residential learning sessions.

DISTANCE LEARNING PROGRAM

The Duke M.B.A. Cross Continent program allows high-potential young managers to earn an internationally focused M.B.A. degree in less than two years, utilizing a format that minimizes the disruption of careers and personal life. Two class sections, each comprised of 40 to 60 students, are enrolled concurrently. One is based on Duke's Durham, North Carolina, campus, and the other in Frankfurt, Germany, at the Fuqua School of Business Europe. Each term includes one week of intensive residential learning, coupled with significant team-oriented distance learning.

The Duke M.B.A. Global Executive program enrolls approximately 90 mid- to senior-level executives from all over the world who wish to earn an internationally focused M.B.A. degree while minimizing the disruption of their careers and personal life. With five separate residencies in North America, Europe, Asia, and South America, the program is designed specifically to capitalize on its unique combination of "place and space." By combining face-to-face residential sessions (place) with Internet-mediated learning (space), the program helps students develop skills in the core functional areas of business, as well as learn how to think and manage globally. Moreover, through frequent interaction with international classmates, Global Executive students are exposed to a wealth of ideas and approaches to each topic studied.

DELIVERY MEDIA

In the course of the twenty-month program, Cross Continent students attend nine weeks of residential sessions (8 one-week learning sessions plus a week of orientation), mostly on their primary campus, with one to three residential sessions on the other campus. The remainder of the program is delivered via an innovative Internet-mediated learning platform. Students complete sixteen courses over 8 ten-week terms.

Global Executive students attend eleven weeks of classroom sessions on four different continents. The program is broken into five academic terms, each of which is preceded by a two-week residency (the first term includes an extra week of orientation). The first and last residencies are held at Fuqua's Durham campus. The other three residential learning sessions take place in Europe, Asia, and South America. The remainder of the Global Executive program is delivered via interactive distance education.

PROGRAMS OF STUDY

In the Duke M.B.A. Cross Continent program, all students take the same courses together in the same sequence, with a heavy emphasis on teamwork. Four of the sixteen courses offered are electives. The courses are designed to build from fundamental business knowledge to functional and strategy courses.

The Duke M.B.A. Global Executive curriculum, delivered by Duke's world-class faculty, offers a rigorous general management education with a focus on global management. Global Executive is also a lock-step program, and courses are designed to build from fundamental business courses to functional and strategy courses.

STUDENT SERVICES

Both the Cross Continent and Global Executive programs provide each student with a laptop computer, portable printer, and all associated software and support. Students are required to secure their own online access through a local Internet service provider. Library services are offered online 24 hours a day, seven days a week. The programs offer extensive technical and operational support.

CREDIT OPTIONS

All credits must be earned in both the Cross Continent (48) and Global Executive (45) programs. No transferred credits are accepted.

FACULTY

Duke's Fuqua School of Business has one faculty body that teaches across all of its M.B.A. degree programs and executive education programs. The School employs 75 full-time, tenure-track and 48 part-time/adjunct faculty members. All of the 123 faculty members hold the Ph.D.

ADMISSION

Applicants to the Duke M.B.A. Cross Continent should have two to eight years of professional work experience, a bachelor's degree or equivalent, company sponsorship, GMAT scores, and TOEFL scores (if applicable). Interviews are strongly recommended but not required.

Applicants to the Duke M.B.A. Global Executive program should have a minimum of ten years of professional experience, an undergraduate degree from an accredited four-year college or university or equivalent, strong quantitative skills, proficient written and verbal English skills, company sponsorship before applying, and TOEFL scores (if applicable). Interviews are strongly recommended but not required

TUITION AND FEES

The Duke M.B.A. Cross Continent program tuition for 2000 is $67,500. The Duke M.B.A. Global Executive program tuition for 2000 is $89,700. The tuition cost for both programs includes all room and board during residential learning sessions, a laptop computer and peripherals, and all books and materials. It does not include travel to and from residencies.

FINANCIAL AID

The Duke M.B.A. Cross Continent and Global Executive programs do not offer financial aid. Eligible students can apply for Federal Stafford or private loans.

APPLYING

Applicants should request application materials from the addresses below.

CONTACT

Karen Courtney, Director of Recruiting and Admissions, Cross Continent
The Fuqua School of Business
1 Towerview Drive
Durham, North Carolina 27708
Telephone: 919-660-7804
Fax: 919-660-8044
E-mail: fuqua-cross-continent@mail.duke.edu
Web site: http://www.fuqua.duke.edu

Lisa Lee, Associate Director of Recruiting and Admissions, Global Executive
The Fuqua School of Business
1 Towerview Drive
Durham, North Carolina 27708
Telephone: 919-660-7804
Fax: 919-660-8044
E-mail: globalexec@fuqua.duke.edu
Web site: http://www.fuqua.duke.edu

Fuqua School of Business Europe
Taunusanlage 21
D-60325 Frankfurt am Main
Germany
Telephone: 49-69-972699-0
Fax: 49-69-972699-99
E-mail: europe@fuqua.duke.edu
Web site: http://www.fuqua.duke.edu

Duquesne University

Distance Learning Programs

Pittsburgh, Pennsylvania

Duquesne University first opened its doors as the Pittsburgh Catholic College of the Holy Ghost in October 1878 with an enrollment of 40 students. Today Duquesne has more than 10,000 students in nine schools, who come from 110 nations and enjoy the University's global environment steeped in Duquesne's unique tradition of education for the mind, the heart, and the soul.

Known for its innovative educational programs for traditional and nontraditional students, Duquesne has been consistently ranked among America's top ten Catholic universities by U.S. News & World Report. *It is rated as very competitive by* Barron's Profiles of American Colleges *and as one of* Barron's 300 Best Buys in College Education. *Duquesne has been listed among the 100 Most Wired Colleges by* Yahoo! Internet Life *magazine for three consecutive years. Duquesne is accredited by the Middle States Association of Colleges and Schools.*

DISTANCE LEARNING PROGRAM

Distance learning opportunities are available in the areas of business, education, leadership, music, nursing, and pharmacy. Students are offered the best in online education and benefit from the same resources as students on campus, with access to Duquesne's library and technology resources. An outstanding faculty and a substantial student support system provide students with the opportunity to take courses from anywhere in the world.

DELIVERY MEDIA

Distance learning courses are led by Duquesne faculty using Blackboard's CourseInfo, WebCT, or FirstClass. Students are able to interact with professors during online office hours or with other classmates using chatrooms or message boards. Courses are also offered via video teleconferencing (VTEL) at the Dixon University Center in Harrisburg, Pennsylvania, or at two locations on the Duquesne campus.

Students are expected to use equipment that meets the University sys-

tem requirements, have access to the Internet through a Web browser, and possess relevant technology skills.

PROGRAMS OF STUDY

Duquesne University offers online graduate programs in a variety of academic areas. New programs are anticipated to be added to the current offerings. A complete list of courses offered each semester can be found at http://www.duq.edu/distancelearning/explore.html. In addition to complete degree programs, the University also offers a number of individual undergraduate and graduate online courses.

The School of Business Administration, new in fall 2000, offers core M.B.A. courses with the option of completing a certificate in e-commerce.

The Division of Continuing Education offers a Master of Arts in leadership and liberal studies program that focuses on self-assessment and development of skills that are crucial to the leader's role, as well as an examination of the world in which today's leaders function.

The School of Education, also new in fall 2000, offers instructional technology certificate programs that give K–12 educators, technology coordinators, higher education faculty members, and corporate business trainers the opportunity to enhance their approach to effectively linking teaching and learning.

The School of Music offers a Master of Music Education that emphasizes national standards, leadership, and advocacy.

The School of Nursing is the only school to offer both undergraduate and graduate online programs for RN to B.S.N., M.S.N., and Ph.D. degrees; post-B.S.N. certificates in RN First Assistant (RNFA) and nursing informatics; and post-master's degree programs in nursing administration, nursing education, family nurse practitioner (FNP), transcultural nursing, and psychiatric–mental health.

The School of Pharmacy offers a nontraditional Doctor of Pharmacy (Pharm.D.) program that is targeted for adult learners and is designed as an accessible and flexible way for working pharmacy practitioners to obtain a Doctor of Pharmacy degree.

SPECIAL PROGRAMS

Designed for adult students, the online Master of Arts in Leadership and Liberal Studies (M.L.L.S.) is designed to enhance leadership capabilities and an understanding of the world in which tomorrow's leaders must function. Online M.L.L.S. students come from a variety of disciplines in the for-profit, nonprofit, and government sectors worldwide. The Master of Arts in Leadership and Liberal Studies is the recipient of the national Distinguished Credit Program

Award by the Association of Continuing Higher Education and the national Outstanding Leadership Program for 1999 award from the Association for Leadership Educators. While the focus of the program is to cultivate the ability to lead at any level, individuals also develop and refine skills in critical thinking, problem solving, motivating and empowering others, communicating effectively and persuasively, and sharing knowledge with a community of like-minded professionals. For more information on this program, students should visit http://coned.duq.edu/mlls/mllsmain.html.

STUDENT SERVICES

Textbooks and other materials are available through mail order from the Duquesne bookstore or online via the Duquesne distance learning Web site (listed below).

Students have continuous support for the duration of their studies. Course monitors are available through online chats, e-mail, or telephone to assist students in troubleshooting connectivity problems or other technically related questions.

CREDIT OPTIONS

Credit transfer and degree completion requirements vary with each individual school and program. Information on program specifications can be found from the list of available programs at the Web site for individual schools and programs (listed below).

FACULTY

While they are leaders in the community and in their professions, Duquesne's dynamic faculty members make students their highest priority. Online classes cover identical curricula and are taught by the same distinguished faculty members as on-campus courses.

ADMISSION

Admissions for the distance education programs are handled separately through each school offering online programs and courses. Admission procedures and requirements can be found at the Web site for individual schools and programs (listed below).

TUITION AND FEES

Tuition and fee schedules vary from school to school. Information can be found by clicking on the appropriate school at the Web site for individual schools and programs (listed below).

FINANCIAL AID

Financial aid opportunities vary according to the program. For more information, students should consult http://www.duq.edu/StudentLife/services/financial/financial.html or the school administering the program.

APPLYING

Application procedures and requirements vary by program. Students should see the admissions section within each program by visiting the Web site for individual schools and programs (listed below).

CONTACT

Distance Learning Programs
Computing and Technology Services
Duquesne University
600 Forbes Avenue
Pittsburgh, Pennsylvania 15282
Telephone: 800-283-3853 (toll-free)
E-mail: virtualcampus@duq.edu
Web site: http://www.duq.edu/distancelearning
      http://www.duq.edu/distancelearning/
        program.html (for individual schools
        and programs)

East Carolina University

Division of Continuing Studies

Greenville, North Carolina

Founded in 1907, East Carolina University (ECU) is the third-largest of the sixteen institutions comprising the University of North Carolina and offers baccalaureate, master's, specialist, and doctoral degrees in the liberal arts and sciences and professional fields, including medicine. Fully accredited by the Southern Association of Colleges and Schools, the University's goal is to give students a rich and distinctive educational experience. ECU made its mark in the adult education arena more than fifty years ago. Today, the Division of Continuing Studies still serves as a gateway to the resources of the University, and adult learners can choose programs that fit both their schedules and their academic goals. East Carolina University is constantly evaluating its distance learning programs to utilize the latest technology and is committed to meeting the evolving needs of the lifelong learner far into the future.

DISTANCE LEARNING PROGRAM

East Carolina University has developed its distance learning programs in direct response to the needs of students. A number of programs are available, and more are under development. ECU provides programs for busy, working adults, and, just as their lives change, the University's distance learning options also must change. The latest offerings can be found on the Division of Continuing Studies Web site (listed below).

DELIVERY MEDIA

East Carolina University delivers programs to students through the following methods: Internet, face-to-face, interactive TV, and mixed media. Web-based courses utilize current audio, video, and real-time technologies such as PowerPoint, chatrooms (synchronous), discussion threads (asynchronous), and RealPlayer.

Internet students need a current computer that is compliant with the program of study they have chosen. Internet students also need Internet service and an e-mail account.

PROGRAMS OF STUDY

Degree programs include the M.S.I.T. in manufacturing, the M.S.I.T. in digital communications technology, and the M.S.O.S. in occupational safety.

The M.S.I.T. in manufacturing program emphasizes the design, management, and control of human and technological systems in manufacturing. The manufacturing concentration provides experiences that would be helpful in the following areas and jobs: plant management, division manager, product line manager, head of production, engineering, and facilities engineering.

The M.S.I.T. in digital communications technology program emphasizes the use of information processing systems to effectively communicate, process information, access data, and solve problems in industry.

The M.S.O.S. in occupational safety program emphasizes the management of safety programs, as well as the technical aspects of industrial safety and health. Occupations that would benefit from the occupational safety curriculum include safety man-

ager, safety director, OSHA compliance officer, safety professional, safety consultant, and environmental health and safety director.

Certificate programs include Website Developer (WD), Computer Network Professional (CNP), Virtual Reality in Education and Training, Tele-Learning, and Professional Communication.

The Website Developer certificate prepares graduates for employment as a Web site planner, developer, and manager. The program provides experience in the planning, creation, and maintenance of commercial Web sites using Microsoft creation tools and network servers. Graduates are prepared to be successful in such jobs as Webmaster, Web designer, and Web administrator. Successful completion of the Website Developer certificate program prepares an individual to sit for an industry-standard professional certificate examination—the Microsoft Site Builder exam.

The Computer Network Professional (CNP) certificate prepares graduates for employment in computer networking. The program provides hardware and software experience in the selection, installation, and management of NT-based Intranet and Internet client/server networking systems. The skills learned in this certificate program enable participants to succeed in such positions as network administrator, data communications manager, communications specialist, and others. Successful completion of the CNP also prepares an individual to sit for the Microsoft Certified Systems Engineer (MCSE) certification exam.

The educational objectives of the Certificate in Virtual Reality in Education and Training are to provide interested persons an opportunity to learn to use basic virtual reality software and to apply that knowledge in educational and training settings. The Certificate in Virtual Reality in Education and Training requires 15 semester hours of graduate-level course work in virtual reality and emphasizes educational and training applications.

The educational objectives of the Certificate in Tele-Learning are to provide interested persons an opportunity to learn the basic principles of distance delivery of classes, to manage distance-delivered classes, and to evaluate their effectiveness. The Certificate in Tele-Learning requires 18 semester hours of graduate-level course work in distance delivery of courses.

Communication professionals work in a rapidly changing environment that requires them to update their abilities throughout their working careers. Both technological and conceptual issues underlie those changes. To help these professionals remain competitive, East Carolina University offers a Certificate in Professional Communication that is designed primarily for professionals who want to improve their communication abilities and learn about significant communication advances. Teachers who design professional communication curricula and corporate trainers who provide on-site communication training can benefit from this program.

SPECIAL PROGRAMS

In addition to the programs detailed above, East Carolina University offers undergraduate programs in cooperation with community colleges in the areas of information technology and industrial technology. Graduate programs that are partially online are available in the areas of library science, special education, and instructional technology. Certification

courses for teachers are also available. A complete listing of distance offerings is available on the Web site.

STUDENT SERVICES

Distance learners at East Carolina University have access to library services, the campus network, e-mail accounts, the bookstore, registration, and academic advising at a distance. Academic advisers are available by phone, e-mail, and fax and in person to assist students with course selection.

CREDIT OPTIONS

Students may be admitted as degree-seeking, nondegree, or visiting students. Nondegree students may apply no more than 9 graduate or 28 undergraduate semester hours to a degree program at East Carolina University. Transfer credit is granted on academic course work within degree-specific limits, and no credit is granted on the basis of professional experience. CLEP course credit may also be available.

FACULTY

ECU's approximately 1,300 full-time faculty members, the majority of whom hold terminal degrees, teach both the on-campus and distance learning courses.

ADMISSION

Admission for students seeking a degree is based on their previous academic record and standardized test scores. Degree-seeking students are required to submit official transcripts of all previous academic work. In addition, graduate students are required to submit letters of recommendation.

TUITION AND FEES

Undergraduate tuition and fees are $36 per semester hour for in-state residents, $123 per semester hour for out-of-state students, and $291 per semester hour for in-state nonresidents. Graduate tuition and fees are $53 per semester hour for in-state residents, $123 per semester hour for out-of-state students, and $424 per semester hour for in-state nonresidents. Tuition is subject to change without notice.

FINANCIAL AID

Distance learning students are eligible to apply for financial aid and are encouraged to contact the Office of Financial Aid at 252-328-6610, faques@mail.ecu.edu, or via the Web at http://www.ecu.edu/financial/ for more information.

APPLYING

Prospective students must submit an application, accompanied by a fee of $40, for admission. Applications can also be obtained online from the Division of Continuing Studies at http://www.dcs.ecu.edu/registration.htm. While most programs accept students year-round, students are urged to apply early. No on-campus orientation is required for distance learning students.

CONTACT

Jennifer Baysden
Division of Continuing Studies
207 Erwin Building
East Carolina University
Greenville, North Carolina
27858-4353
Telephone: 252-328-2658
800-398-9275 (toll-free)
Fax: 252-328-0613
E-mail: baysdenj@mail.ecu.edu
Web site: http://www.dcs.ecu.edu

EduKan Consortium

Great Bend, Kansas

The Western Kansas Community College Virtual Education Consortium (EduKan) brings students a new way of receiving their college courses. In 1999 EduKan launched a series of college courses via the Internet. EduKan consists of the following colleges: Barton County Community College, Colby Community College, Dodge City Community College, Garden City Community College, Pratt Community College, and Seward County Community College.

DISTANCE LEARNING PROGRAM

The Western Kansas Community College Virtual Education Consortium (EduKan) began offering classes via the Internet 1999. Enrollments have increased every semester since that time. Students who enroll in the online program can take course work that leads to an associate degree from one of six participating institutions. The institutions involved include Barton County Community College, in Great Bend; Colby Community College, in Colby; Dodge City Community College, in Dodge City; Garden City Community College, in Garden City; Pratt Community College, in Pratt; and Seward County Community College, in Liberal.

DELIVERY MEDIA

Students must have access to a computer with Windows 95 or 98 or Mac OS. In addition, a computer with multimedia capability, a modem, a full-service Web browser, audio and video capability, an Internet provider, and an e-mail account is required. Some classes may also require the student to view videos via a TV and VCR. EduKan has partnered with eCollege.com to provide their virtual campus and their Internet course system.

PROGRAM OF STUDY

More than forty courses will be offered through EduKan in multisemester formats. These courses include: Fundamentals of Writing, English Composition I and II, Speech I, Intermediate Algebra, College Algebra, Principles of Biology, Physical Science, Introduction to Astronomy, General Psychology, Human Growth and Development, Principles of Macroeconomics, World and Regional Geography, American Government, Native American Culture, Introduction to Sociology, Personal Finance, Human Relations, History and Criticism of Art I, American History Since 1865, World Literature, Introduction to Music, Introduction to Ethics, Introduction to Geology, Accounting I and II, Horse Production, Cultural Anthropology, History and Criticism of Art II, Anatomy & Physiology I and II, Introduction to Business, General Chemistry, Introduction to Computers, Microcomputer Applications, Web Page Design, Principles of Microeconomics, Foundations of Modern Education, Children's Literature, Spanish I and II, Beginning Algebra, and Personal and Community Health. Each course provides a solid foundation that leads to an Associate of General Studies degree, with transferability to four-year colleges and universities.

SPECIAL PROGRAMS

These courses are recommended for adult learners who may not be able to take traditional classes due to conflicting schedules, multiple responsibilities, and/or long driving distances. High school and college students who would like to get a head start on their college education are good candidates as well.

STUDENT SERVICES

EduKan provides a wide array of services to students online. They include academic advising, career placement assistance, library services, transcript request, business office services, bookstore access, and more. The goal is to provide any essential campus service via the Internet.

CREDIT OPTIONS

All courses are offered for college credit and, with the exception of the developmental courses, count toward graduation requirements at any of the institutions. Courses are offered on a semester basis, and most are offered for 3–5 credit hours per course.

FACULTY

All faculty members have teaching experience and online training and are respected members of their institutions. Their complete biographies are listed online. More than 85 percent of the faculty members also teach full-time at the member institutions.

ADMISSION

Kansas community colleges operate under an open admissions policy. Admission and enrollment forms are standardized for all six EduKan schools and are outlined on the EduKan Web site (listed below). Current high school students may get a start in their college education through this process, but most students who are admitted are high school or GED graduates or transfer students. Each college is also a member of the Servicemen's Opportunity College.

TUITION AND FEES

Tuition is $115 per credit hour, excluding textbooks. The cost is the same for all students, regardless of Kansas residency status.

FINANCIAL AID

Financial aid is available through the participating colleges. Some part-time scholarships are available. Federal financial aid can also be completed online.

APPLYING

Students may apply to and learn more about EduKan via the Web site.

CONTACT

Matt Gotschall, Executive Director
245 Northeast 30th Road
Great Bend, Kansas 67530
Telephone: 877-4EDUKAN (toll-free)
E-mail: gotschallm@barton.cc.ks.us
Web site: http://www.edukan.org

Embry-Riddle Aeronautical University

Extended Campus

Daytona Beach, Florida

Embry-Riddle Aeronautical University is an independent, nonsectarian, nonprofit coeducational university with a history dating back to the early days of aviation. The University is accredited by the Commission on Colleges of the Southern Association of Colleges and Schools. Residential campuses in Daytona Beach, Florida, and Prescott, Arizona, provide education in a traditional setting. The Extended Campus network of education centers throughout the United States and Europe and the Distance Learning Program serve civilian and military working adults around the world. Embry-Riddle Aeronautical University has served the public and private sectors of aviation through education for more than seventy years and is the only accredited not-for-profit university in the world totally oriented to aviation/aerospace. Alumni are employed in all facets of civilian and military aviation.

DISTANCE LEARNING PROGRAM

Since 1970, Embry-Riddle has provided educational opportunities for professionals working in civilian and military aviation and aerospace careers. To meet the varied needs of the adult working student, Embry-Riddle established the Extended Campus, which includes the College of Career Education's classroom and distance learning operations.

The Extended Campus maintains a comprehensive system of academic quality control, sustaining the requirements and elements of courses as delivered on the residential campuses. The curricula, academic standards, and academic policies are the same throughout the University and are modified only to accommodate certain requirements resulting from different delivery methods.

The College of Career Education provides working adults with the opportunity to earn undergraduate and graduate degrees through a network of teaching centers spread across the United States and Europe and through distance learning. The College operates more than 130 resident centers and teaching sites in thirty-six

states and five European nations. Resident centers and teaching sites are found at or near major aviation industry installations, both civilian and military. When students are not located near a center or a teaching site, they can enroll in many of the same programs through distance learning. All teaching centers and the distance learning programs are approved for veterans educational benefits. Students receive personalized academic advisement whether they take their classes in the classroom or by distance learning. Classroom instruction is conducted during hours convenient for working students, and distance learning students can work on their studies at any time and at any place that is convenient for them. Degree requirements are completed through a combination of course work, transfer credit, prior learning assessment, or by achieving the University's required scores in standardized national testing programs, such as CLEP or DANTES.

DELIVERY MEDIA

The Distance Learning bachelor's and master's degree courses are delivered via the Internet. Each class is hosted on a private Embry-Riddle

Web site, where students and professors interact by way of a bulletin board–type discussion forum. As a result, students are not required to log on to the Web site at specific times, but they may access their course work at a time most convenient to them. To participate in a Distance Learning class, students need access to a personal computer and the World Wide Web. Students who do not have access to the Web from home via a local Internet Service Provider (ISP) can usually gain access through their local library, military base education center, Embry-Riddle resident center, or other public facility.

PROGRAMS OF STUDY

The Master of Aeronautical Science (M.A.S.) degree with specializations in operations, management, human factors, or safety requires 36 semester hours of course work. The M.A.S. program was designed to enable the aviation/aerospace professional to master the application of modern management concepts, methods, and tools to the challenges of aviation and general business. The special intricacies of aviation are woven into a strong, traditional management foundation and examined in greater detail through the wide variety of electives. M.A.S. core topics (12 credit hours) include air transportation, aircraft and space craft development, human factors in aviation/aerospace, and research methods and statistics. Specialization courses (12 credit hours) provide a strong knowledge base of subject material required. Each of the four courses provides the student with skills needed in the professional arena. Electives and a graduate research project (GRP) (12 credit hours) provide students with the ability to tailor their degrees, adding greater breadth and depth in aviation/aerospace–related intellectual pursuits.

Undergraduate degree offerings include Associate of Science and Bachelor of Science degrees in professional aeronautics and a Bachelor of Science degree in management of technical operations (BSMTO).

The professional aeronautics degree program was conceived and developed especially for individuals who have already established and progressed in an aviation career. The curriculum is designed to build upon the knowledge and skills acquired through training and experience in one of the many aviation occupations. The combination of aviation experience and required and elective courses in aeronautical science, management, computer science, economics, communications, humanities, social science, mathematics, and physical science prepares graduates for career growth and increased responsibility. The Bachelor of Science in professional aeronautics requires 120 credit hours, and the Associate of Science in professional aeronautics requires 60 credit hours.

The Bachelor of Science in management of technical operations degree requires successful completion of 120 credit hours. Designed for the student who possesses some technical expertise either through previous course work, licensing, or experience, this degree provides the student a flexible yet solid business program.

The Associate of Science in aviation business administration degree requires successful completion of 60 credit hours. This degree provides courses in general education and an introduction to business coupled with some business applications.

SPECIAL PROGRAMS

The Division of Continuing Education is the unit of Embry-Riddle Aeronautical University's Extended Campus that offers quality training programs, including seminars, conferences, and workshops. These programs serve domestic and international aviation professionals, evening/weekend credit and non-credit-seeking adult students, and aviation-oriented youth and educators. Specialized training courses at the customer's site and consulting services to the international education and aviation community are also made available on a contract basis. Seminars are offered through distance learning on a variety of topics.

Student Services Students are provided online library access in addition to a library guide that lists local points of reference for research. Each student is assigned to an admission specialist/academic adviser. The adviser assists students in registering for courses that qualify for their degree program and provides administrative support.

CREDIT OPTIONS

Master's degree applicants may transfer up to 12 semester hours of credit into the University. Credit must be from a regionally accredited institution with a grade of B or better and awarded within seven years of application to Embry-Riddle. Courses must be applicable to the M.A.S. degree program.

Undergraduate applicants may transfer credit from regionally accredited institutions with the letter grade of D or better. Advanced standing credit may be awarded for prior learning achieved through postsecondary education, testing, and work or training experience.

FACULTY

The faculty is a blend of traditionally prepared academicians and leaders with significant industry track records. Nearly all faculty members have doctorate or terminal degrees.

ADMISSION

Admission to the master's degree program requires a bachelor's degree from a regionally accredited institution. Admission to the undergraduate programs is unique to each degree.

TUITION AND FEES

Tuition for master's degree courses is $306 per credit hour. Textbook and shipping fees vary from $50 to $125 per course based on textbook prices.

Undergraduate tuition is $145 per credit hour. Other fees vary by course. Each course is 3 semester credit hours.

FINANCIAL AID

Students accepted for enrollment may be considered for several forms of federal financial aid. There are three different federal programs available. Additional information is provided at time of application.

All Embry-Riddle degree programs have been approved by the Department of Veterans' Affairs for enrollment of persons eligible to receive benefits from U.S. Department of Veterans' Affairs (DVA).

APPLYING

Applications must be submitted with appropriate documentation, such as official high school transcripts, GED scores, or official transcripts from previous colleges or universities.

CONTACT

Terry E. Whittum, Director
Linda Dammer, Assistant Director
Distance Learning Enrollment Office
Embry-Riddle Aeronautical University
600 South Clyde Morris Boulevard
Daytona Beach, Florida 32114-3900
Telephone: 800-359-3728 (toll-free)
Fax: 904-226-7627
E-mail: indstudy@cts.db.erau.edu
Web site: http://www.embryriddle.edu

Everglades College

Distance Learning Program

Fort Lauderdale, Florida

Everglades College is a private, four-year, coeducational institution located in Fort Lauderdale, Florida. The college is accredited by the Accrediting Commission of Career Schools and Colleges of Technology (ACCSCT) and licensed by the State Board of Independent Colleges and Universities (SBICU). Everglades College awards an Associate of Science degree in aviation studies and baccalaureate degrees in information technology and business administration. The College is totally designed for the working adult learner by providing a practical, hands-on education in a professional environment with schedules appropriate to the working adult.

DISTANCE LEARNING PROGRAM

Everglades College offers classes online and on campus. Students enrolled in Everglades College's online learning program have easy access to the latest online educational delivery methods. Courses are taken on the Internet, from home, office, or any convenient location at a time that fits a student's schedule.

DELIVERY MEDIA

The online courses are designed by qualified faculty and staff members to create an interesting, interactive learning environment. The virtual classroom is comfortable, and courses can be taken easily by anyone with access to the World Wide Web. Lesson plans, assignments, and class schedules are posted online, while student/teacher interaction and student/student interaction also occur over the Internet. Scheduled discussions, e-mail messages, live chats, streaming video, and group discussions are a few of the opportunities for interaction during online courses.

PROGRAMS OF STUDY

Currently, all courses leading to an A.S. degree in aviation management are offered on line. These include general education courses in English, communications, science, mathematics, and social and behavioral sciences, as well as required core classes. During the 2000–01 academic year, courses leading to bachelor's degrees in business administration and information technology will be added to Everglades College's online course offerings.

SPECIAL PROGRAMS

Online students are enrolled in a free orientation class that provides simple instructions for making the most of the online learning environment. The help desk is available to online students via a toll-free number, twenty-four hours a day, seven days a week. Everglades College explores ongoing community and business partnerships that provide additional learning opportunities for students enrolled online or on campus. Students benefit from affiliations with organizations that offer additional educational resources, such as a statewide network of library consortia. Online students also have access to LIRN, a comprehensive, online library database.

STUDENT SERVICES

Everglades College students have a wide variety of opportunities available both on-campus and online. An extensive placement program is available to current students and graduates that assists them in finding employment in their chosen fields. Registered employers can access student resumes online to help them identify graduates with appropriate skills. The online campus includes application and registration procedures, financial aid information, tuition and fee information, course schedules and descriptions, faculty information, and a chat room. Online students can access academic advising by phone or e-mail.

CREDIT OPTIONS

Students may transfer credits taken at other accredited institutions if the course work is comparable, the faculty has appropriate degrees, and there is evidence of satisfactory scholarship (at least a C). The Dean of Academic Affairs evaluates transcripts and accepts credits on a course-by-course basis.

FACULTY

Online faculty members satisfy the criteria set by the appropriate accrediting agency. Currently, most Everglades College online faculty members are full-time instructors. The program directors, who teach many of the online courses, have doctoral degrees and other faculty members hold master's degrees in their field of study.

ADMISSION

Entrance requirements for admissions to Everglades College include high school completion or GED, as well as an entrance examination or an SAT or ACT score (a minimum score of 800 on the SAT and 17 on the ACT).

TUITION AND FEES

For 1999–2000, tuition for the Everglades College distance learning credit courses was $333 per credit hour.

FINANCIAL AID

Everglades College is approved for federal financial aid programs. Each student who is admitted to Everglades College has a financial aid adviser who determines the student's eligibility for financial aid. Aid is available to students who qualify based on federal guidelines.

APPLYING

Students can apply online when visiting Everglades College's Web site or can contact the admissions department at the telephone number listed below. General information about Everglades College's online education is available via e-mail or by visiting the Web site listed below.

CONTACT

Department of Admissions
Everglades College
1500 NW 49th Street
Fort Lauderdale, Florida 33309
Telephone: 954-772-2655
Fax: 954-772-2695
E-mail: admissions@evergladescollege.edu
Web site: http://www.evergladescollege.edu

Fashion Institute of Technology

On-Line Program

New York, New York

The Fashion Institute of Technology, a State University of New York (SUNY) college of art and design, business and technology, has been educating professionals for careers in the fashion and related fields since 1944. FIT now offers its students thirty-one degree programs in areas of study where industry has made New York City its focal point. Many of them are innovative and one of a kind, such as the country's only two-year program in accessories design and the only bachelor's degree program in home products development and marketing.

FIT is an accredited institutional member of the Middle States Association of Colleges and Schools, the National Association of Schools of Art and Design, and the Foundation for Interior Design Education Research. FIT serves more than 5,700 full-time students and 5,400 part-time students who come from all fifty states and sixty-five countries.

DISTANCE LEARNING PROGRAM

The college's online program serves students by offering a variety of courses as well as a curriculum that can lead to the fashion merchandising management (FMM) one-year A.A.S. degree. Students who already possess a degree from another college or who have earned 30 transferable credits may apply to the one-year FMM program, which is offered entirely online.

The FMM program provides a sound grasp of the practical aspects of the fashion industry, which is essential to building a successful merchandising career. Students take courses in buying, merchandising, retail operations, product development, team management, and wholesale strategies of selling. They learn about the fashion industry at every level and how each segment is affected by both domestic and global influences. Graduates find careers with retail stores, wholesale showrooms, or buying offices.

DELIVERY MEDIA

FIT delivers its courses through the SUNY Learning Network (SLN), an electronic forum where students and professors learn collaboratively via the Internet. Courses may require the use of specific software programs and computer hardware products to complete course requirements. Prior to registering for an online course, students should test their access to the SLN Web site at http://www.sln.suny.edu.

PROGRAMS OF STUDY

FIT's online program currently offers courses leading to the fashion merchandising management one-year A.A.S. degree. These courses include introduction to the fashion industry, merchandise planning and control, fashion merchandising (principles and techniques), advertising and promotion, apparel design and production analysis, textile fundamentals, fashion business practices, consumer motivation in fashion, product development, consumer motivation in fashion, introduction to direct marketing, workshop in fashion merchandising management, import buying, and product development.

Other online offerings include starting a small business, English as a second language, professional proce-dures in commercial photography, photography portfolio development for the World Wide Web, introduction to business law, information systems in business management, and multimedia computing for advertising and marketing communications.

For detailed descriptions of each course, students should visit the FIT Web site at http://www.fitnyc.suny.edu/academic.

SPECIAL PROGRAMS

FIT is developing additional online courses and degree programs. The college plans to add required liberal arts courses providing students with the opportunity to complete the FMM two-year A.A.S. program entirely online. Students should periodically check the FIT Web site for online course updates.

CREDIT OPTIONS

Students may apply up to 30 credits earned through subject examinations (CLEP and Advanced Placement) and transfer credit toward fulfillment of degree requirements at FIT. Students who have completed courses at accredited institutions receive credit for course work similar to courses at FIT and in which a grade of C or better has been achieved. Complete information about obtaining academic credit by evaluation is available from the Registrar's Office at 212-217-7676.

FACULTY

Currently, there are 173 full-time faculty members and approximately 690 part-time faculty members. In addition to their academic backgrounds, all of FIT's faculty members have extensive experience in the diverse industries from which they come. This enables them to bring the immediacy of their continuing professional activity to their teaching.

ADMISSION

All applicants must have a high school diploma or the equivalent and must supply their high school transcript showing average and rank in class. Transfer students must provide official college transcripts. FIT operates on a rolling admission basis.

For additional information on how to apply or obtain specific admissions requirements or to obtain a SUNY application form, applicants should call the FIT Admissions Office at 212-217-7675, send e-mail to fitinfo@fitsuny.edu, or visit the World Wide Web at the address listed below.

TUITION AND FEES

Undergraduate tuition is currently $105 per credit for New York State residents and $255 per credit for all others. In addition, course instructors may require the purchase of textbooks, reference materials, and supplies. Additional fees may apply. For the most updated tuition and fee information, applicants should visit the Web at http://www.sln.suny.edu/sln or at FIT's Web site, listed below.

FINANCIAL AID

Financial aid is available to eligible students and includes PELL, TAP, and Stafford Loans. Applications are available through FIT's Financial Aid Office (telephone: 212-217-7177), local high schools, libraries, and post offices. Additional information regarding financial aid is available at the FIT Web site.

APPLYING

Anyone can register for an online course on a nonmatriculating basis. To matriculate toward the FMM degree program, students must apply through the usual application process. Applicants can apply in one of the following ways: online at the FIT Web site; submission by mail of a downloaded application form; or by filling out the State University of New York application.

For more information, applicants should call the FIT Admissions Office at 212-217-7675, or send e-mail to fitinfo@fitsuny.edu.

CONTACT

Helena Glass
Fashion Institute of Technology
Seventh Avenue at 27th Street
New York, New York 10001
Telephone: 212-217-7683 (online program information)
212-217-7999 (general information)
Fax: 212-217-7481
E-mail: fitonline@fitsuny.edu
Web site: http://www.fitnyc.suny.edu

Florida Gulf Coast University

Distance Learning Programs

Fort Myers, Florida

Florida Gulf Coast University (FGCU) opened its doors to students in August 1997 and is housed on a state-of-the art campus located on the southwest coast of Florida between Fort Myers and Naples. Its primary mission is undergraduate education, providing a broad range of programs in arts and sciences, business, technology, environmental science, education, allied health, and social services. Graduate programs at the master's level are also provided. FGCU was founded as a dual-mode institution to provide a full range of on-campus degree programs and selected degree programs for distance learners. FGCU is fully accredited by the Southern Association of Colleges and Schools (SACS). The University now serves a regional, state, and national audience with these programs. Additional information about the University and its programs may be found on the World Wide Web at http://www.fgcu.edu.

DISTANCE LEARNING PROGRAM

Distance learning at FGCU is an instructional strategy that is central to the University's mission. FGCU is committed to the development of innovative distance learning course designs that utilize a technology-rich learning environment. FGCU's distance-learning students receive personalized attention from faculty members strategically selected to accomplish high-quality instruction and exceptional service.

DELIVERY MEDIA

FGCU supports five methods of distance learning delivery: the Internet, videotape, two-way interactive video, broadcast video, and e-mail. Each course uses one or more of these methods, depending on the intended learning outcomes. All distance-learning courses currently being offered include extensive Web site and e-mail communication. The use of video is incorporated into many, but not all, courses.

PROGRAMS OF STUDY

There are currently four master's and two bachelor's degree programs of-fered by FGCU via distance learning. Brief descriptions of these programs appear below. For full details, students should visit the Web site (http://itech.fgcu.edu/distance) and select Programs and Courses to see course offerings in the current semester.

The Master of Business Administration (M.B.A.) provides a challenging curriculum designed to prepare students for leadership positions in organizations. Leadership, teamwork, information technology, entrepreneurial vision, and global awareness are integrated throughout the program. All courses for this program are available at a distance. For more information, students should visit the Web site at http://www.fgcu.edu/cob/mba.

The Curriculum and Instruction–Educational Technology (M.A./M.Ed.) graduate program at FGCU is designed to provide a theoretical foundation and practical skills. The emphasis is on enabling students to provide leadership in distance learning, provide technical support and education in schools or colleges, and design and implement courses in computer programming, applica-tions, and literacy. This program is offered largely through Internet courses, with two special, on-campus summer institutes. For more information, students should visit the Web site at http://soe.fgcu.edu/soe/programs/CIM.html.

The interdisciplinary Master of Science in Health Science program offers a choice of four concentrations: health professions education, practice, health services administration, and gerontology. The education and practice concentrations are limited to those qualified in a health profession. All courses for this program are available at a distance. For more information, students should visit the Web site at http://www.fgcu.edu/chp/discipline.

The Master of Public Administration (M.P.A.) is an applied degree program that prepares students for successful administrative careers in the public sector. It is designed for students who have significant in-service experience and for students who have little prior work experience in public agencies. All courses for this program are available at a distance. For more information, students should visit the Web site at http://spss.fgcu.edu.

The Bachelor of Science in criminal justice degree program prepares students for careers in criminal justice professions and/or graduate education. The curriculum provides students the opportunity to acquire knowledge of the roles and challenges faced by police, courts, and corrections and their interrelationship within the justice system. All upper-division undergraduate courses for this program are available at a distance to those students who have completed at least 60 hours of undergraduate course work. For more information, students should visit the Web site at http://spss.fgcu.edu.

The interdisciplinary Bachelor of Science in Health Science program is designed to provide career advancement opportunities for entry-level health profession practitioners and individuals who seek careers in health care, such as physical therapy. All of the upper-division undergraduate courses for this program are available at a distance to those students who have completed at least 60 hours of undergraduate course work. For more information, students should visit the Web site at http://www.fgcu.edu/chp/discipline.

SPECIAL PROGRAMS

The English for Speakers of Other Languages (ESOL) endorsement program at FGCU strives to prepare graduate students, teachers, and school personnel to teach and work with limited English proficient students (LEP) and/or English language learners (ELL) in K–12 school environments. This includes teaching ELL/LEP students in mainstream settings and in pullout programs and serving as advocates by sharing the information and knowledge gained with other professionals working with culturally and linguistically diverse student populations. Learning experiences are varied, including on-campus courses at the graduate level and distance delivery. These professional learning experiences are supported by regular interaction among students and professors.

Florida Gulf Coast University is part of a consortium of forty-six universities that participate in the National Technological University (NTU) Satellite Network, serving the needs of engineers, technical professionals, and managers using advanced telecommunications technology. Degrees and certificates are awarded at the master's level to candidates sponsored by corporations or organizations affiliated

with NTU. Students who wish to participate need to confirm NTU sponsorship with employers.

STUDENT SERVICES

Many of the services for students on campus also are available to students at a distance. A spirit of cooperation within Student Services fosters a learning environment that promotes the academic success and personal and career development of students, with an emphasis on leadership skills, community services, and an appreciation for diversity. For more information, students should visit the Web site at http://condor.fgcu.edu.

CREDIT OPTIONS

Credits earned through distance education are recorded on a Florida Gulf Coast University transcript in the same manner as credits earned in on-campus courses. Individuals may enroll as non–degree-seeking or degree seeking students, but there are limits on the amount of credit awarded to non-degree-seeking students that may be transferred to a degree seeking program. Students should contact the Office of the Admissions at OAR@fgcu.edu or 888-889-1095 (toll-free) for additional details and assistance.

FACULTY

Distance education faculty members meet all of the standards set forth by the Southern Association of Colleges and Schools and the State of Florida. All are full-time or adjunct members within the department granting the course credit. They are available to answer questions and provide feedback via telephone, fax, e-mail, or regular mail.

ADMISSION

Admission decisions are based on standards set by the Board of Regents for the State University System of Florida. Criteria for admissions depend on student status: degree seeking or non–degree-seeking, graduate or undergraduate, transferring to FGCU or just beginning college edu-

cation. More information, students should visit the Web site at http://condor.fgcu.edu/ES/ARR/lg_category.htm.

TUITION AND FEES

Current tuition and fees are published on the Web site at http://condor.fgcu.edu/ES. For the 2000–01 academic year, these are $69.68 per credit hour for undergraduate Florida residents, $146.13 for graduate residents, $314.29 for undergraduate nonresidents, and $524.91 for graduate nonresidents.

FINANCIAL AID

The University offers a comprehensive program of financial assistance for traditional and nontraditional students pursuing undergraduate or graduate degrees. The Financial Aid and Scholarships Office is responsible for helping students secure the necessary funds to pursue education. The office is proactive in offering information to enrolled and prospective students about the availability of financial assistance. Students should contact the Financial Aid and Scholarships Office at FASO@fgcu.edu or 941-590-7920.

APPLYING

Students may apply for admission as a degree seeking or non–degree-seeking student via the Web site by completing the University's Application for Admission at http://www.fgcu.edu/online.html. To complete the application, students must include a $20 application fee with their completed and signed residency statement.

CONTACT

Florida Gulf Coast University
10501 FGCU Boulevard South
Fort Myers, Florida 33965-6565
Telephone: 914-590-7878
    888-889-1095 (toll-free)
    941-590-7886 (TTY)
E-mail: oar@fgcu.edu
Web site: http://www.fgcu.edu

Franklin University
Community College Alliance and Online Degree Programs
Columbus, Ohio

Franklin University is an independent, nonprofit institution of higher education and is best characterized by its student-centered philosophy. Annually, more than 6,000 students—the majority of whom work full-time and are more than 32 years of age—pursue programs leading to a bachelor's degree in seventeen undergraduate majors and four master's degree programs. Franklin University has been offering online courses since 1996 and has made the decision to increase its course offerings through distance learning methods. In 1998, the University began the Community College Alliance (CCA) program that provides a four-year degree to community college graduates via the Internet. The University also unveiled six-week Balanced Learning Format courses that allow students to complete eight courses per year, either on line, on-site, or through a combined online/on-site format.

DISTANCE LEARNING PROGRAM

Through educational alliances with more than seventy community colleges in the U.S. and Canada, the Community College Alliance Program (CCA) enables community college graduates to earn a bachelor's degree from Franklin without leaving their community. Students complete their degrees through a combination of on-site courses at the community college and online courses with Franklin. Franklin's Balanced Learning Format allows students to complete a course in just six weeks.

DELIVERY MEDIA

Students in Franklin's online programs can get all the help they need via the Internet. Chat rooms are set up so students can interact with each other and with faculty members. Students enrolled directly through Franklin need access to a multimedia computer, a modem, and to the Internet and the ability to create, send, and receive e-mail. In addition, some instructors may require access to other equipment, such as a fax machine, a VCR, and an audio cassette

player. Students enrolled through the CCA program also must have access to computers and the World Wide Web, either at home, at work, or at their local community college.

PROGRAMS OF STUDY

Students enrolled in the CCA or the six-week Balanced Learning Format can choose from six different Bachelor of Science degree programs. Business administration combines a knowledge of general business practices with analytical ability that is suited to today's problem-solving tasks. Computer science is for students who are interested in applying, designing, and implementing computer systems. Graduates are prepared to seek a wide variety of jobs, including software engineer, systems analyst, and database administrator or to pursue graduate school. Health services administration recognizes the fact that health-care reform is inevitable and that the industry needs leaders with a vision for the future. This major program develops leaders of change in the health-care profession. Management information systems (MIS) graduates are prepared for careers in a variety of areas, including

systems analysis, application development, and computer support. Technical administration is designed to complement the existing skills that are acquired through a two-year technical degree. This major program is for people who want to move into management and leadership roles in their technical organization. The public safety management major prepares public safety professionals to be upwardly mobile in their agencies. Franklin also offers a variety of online courses that can be applied to any of the University's seventeen undergraduate majors.

SPECIAL PROGRAMS

In today's evolving business organizations, employees are being asked to take on many responsibilities that cross functional lines. Often, those employees have no formal training for completing their increased responsibilities. In response to these additional educational demands, Franklin University has developed twenty-six professional certificates for those with or without undergraduate degrees. Each certificate program consists of three or four courses that are designed to enhance the knowledge of the business professional who is interested in personal growth or career or business development.

STUDENT SERVICES

Through Franklin University's student-centered approach, each student is matched with a Student Services Associate (SSA) who, along with the course instructor, becomes an important contact at the University. SSAs serve as an initial, as well as long-term, resource for helping the student with admission and course scheduling until the academic goals are achieved.

CREDIT OPTIONS

Franklin University has a transfer credit policy that is more liberal than most other institutions. More than 75 percent of Franklin students have transferred credit from other colleges and universities. Students also can earn credit outside the classroom through College-Level Examination Program (CLEP), ACT Proficiency Program (ACT-PEP), Franklin University Proficiency Exams (FUPE), or Prior Learning Portfolios.

FACULTY

Franklin faculty members enrich the classroom, both virtual and physical, with special talents and abilities drawn from successful careers in business, industry, government, and social service. Franklin University faculty members are working professionals who bring real-world experience to the classroom.

ADMISSION

Students applying to the CCA program must have an associate's degree or have completed 60 semester credit hours or 90 quarter credit hours to be admitted to the program.

TUITION AND FEES

Tuition for online courses from Franklin University is $212 per credit hour for standard courses and $258 per credit hour for computer science and MIS courses.

FINANCIAL AID

Franklin offers a variety of financial aid options, including a deferred payment plan for students whose employers offer a tuition reimbursement program. Approximately 75 percent of Franklin students receive some type of financial assistance through grants, scholarships, loans, employer tuition reimbursement, and student employment. Franklin University awards nearly 225 scholarships every year to new and current students.

APPLYING

Anyone who is a graduate of an accredited high school or has passed the GED is eligible for admission as a degree-seeking student. Those seeking a bachelor's degree must complete an admission application and forward an official high school transcript or an official GED test score report. To apply transfer credits from another institution, all official transcripts should be forwarded to Franklin University directly from the previous institution(s). However, a student can begin a distance learning course before the transcripts have been received. Students who would like to take courses as non-degree-seeking students do not need to be high school graduates.

CONTACT

Student Services
Franklin University
201 South Grant Avenue
Columbus, Ohio 43215
Telephone: 614-341-6300
877-341-6300 (toll-free)
Fax: 888-625-8678 (toll-free)
E-mail: info@franklin.edu
Web site: http://www.franklin.edu
CCA
Franklin University
201 South Grant Avenue
Columbus, Ohio 43215
Telephone: 888-341-6237 (toll-free)
Fax: 614-341-6366
Web site: http://www.alliance.franklin.edu

Fuller Theological Seminary

Individualized Distance Learning (IDL) and Fuller Online (FOL) Programs

Pasadena, California

eCollege.com   www.ecollege.com/scholarships

Fuller Theological Seminary, which embraces the Schools of Theology, Psychology, and World Mission, is an evangelical, multidenominational, international, and multiethnic graduate institution dedicated to the preparation of men and women for the manifold ministries of Christ and his Church. It is accredited by the Western Association of Schools and Colleges and the Association of Theological Schools. Founded in 1947 by radio evangelist Charles Fuller and pastor-scholar Harold Ockenga, Fuller has grown to be one of the largest evangelical seminaries, with more than 3,000 students from more than sixty-three countries and 100 denominations. Under the authority of Scripture, Fuller seeks to fulfill its commitment to ministry through graduate education, professional development, and spiritual formation while striving for excellence in the service of Jesus Christ under the guidance and power of the Holy Spirit to the glory of the Father.

DISTANCE LEARNING PROGRAM

To help prepare more and better leaders for Christ's Church, Fuller began offering its first distance learning courses in 1975. During 1999–2000, it offered more than twenty courses, which were used by more than 500 students. Called Individualized Distance Learning, these courses can be studied anytime and anyplace. Online courses, called Fuller Online, are offered in ten-week quarters. Fuller's accreditation extends to these distance learning courses, which can be applied to up to one third of the requirements of many Fuller degrees.

DELIVERY MEDIA

Individualized Distance Learning courses are taught through audiocassette lectures and notebooks, which are supplemented by readings and some videos. Students and teachers may interact via mail, telephone, e-mail, and fax. Fuller Online courses require interaction through the World Wide Web.

All online courses are offered via the eCollege.com system.

PROGRAMS OF STUDY

The certificate of Christian studies can be completed entirely through distance learning. It requires the successful completion of six graduate courses of the student's choice. The certificate offers students an opportunity to complete a focused course of study or a sampling of master's-level courses from the Schools of Theology or World Mission. As the program requires less course work than degree programs, the certificate can be completed in a shorter period of time. Because each individual's course of study is personalized, students can achieve a wide range of goals, including training for a specific church or parachurch ministry, for specialized work in missions, or for spiritual and personal enrichment.

Up to one third of the requirements of many Fuller degrees can be completed through distance learning. Stu-

dents can then complete the degree at a Fuller extension site in Washington state, Northern California, Southern California, Arizona, or Colorado or on the main Pasadena campus. Students should check the Web site listed below for the variety of degrees offered and individual degree requirements.

STUDENT SERVICES

A variety of services exists for the distance learning student, including academic advising; online library resources; an e-mail connection to fellow students, TAs, and professors; and technical support for online courses as well as a friendly and helpful distance learning staff.

CREDIT OPTIONS

Most distance learning courses consist of 4 quarter units of credit, which can be applied to a Fuller degree or transferred to other accredited institutions. Students may also transfer eligible credits from another accredited institution to Fuller. Up to one third of the requirements of many Fuller degrees can be completed through distance learning.

FACULTY

Each year, approximately 15–20 full-time faculty members teach distance learning program courses, along with 5–6 fully qualified adjuncts.

ADMISSION

In general, applicants must have a baccalaureate degree or its equivalent from an institution that is accredited by a recognized regional or national accreditation body before they can be admitted to master's degree or certificate programs at Fuller. Students must be admitted before enrolling in distance learning courses. For further admission qualifications, students should check the Seminary's Web site (listed below).

TUITION AND FEES

Typical costs include tuition, at approximately $200 per quarter unit ($800 per 4-quarter-unit course) for the 2000–01 academic year, plus materials for some courses.

FINANCIAL AID

The FOL program offers a special $100 tuition discount for each FOL course. Details can be found on the FOL Web site, listed below. Institutional financial aid is not available for distance IDL courses, but federal student loans may be applied for.

APPLYING

Students may apply on line at the FOL Web site or contact the Distance Learning Office, which provides admission applications and registration information. Students should see the Web site for deadlines. Once admitted, students may register for IDL courses by mail, fax, or phone and, for FOL courses, on line.

CONTACT

Distance Learning Program Coordinator
Fuller Theological Seminary
135 North Oakland Avenue
Pasadena, California 91182
Telephone: 800-999-9578 (toll-free)
Fax: 626-584-5313
E-mail: idl@fuller.edu
Web site: http://www.fuller.edu (click on Distance Learning)
　　　　http://www.fulleronline.org

Georgia Institute of Technology

Center for Distance Learning
Atlanta, Georgia

Founded in 1885, the Georgia Institute of Technology is the Southeast's largest technological institution. Georgia Tech is located on a 330-acre campus near downtown Atlanta—the financial, communications, and cultural hub of the Southeast. The Institute's mission is to be a leader among those few technological universities whose alumni, faculty, students, and staff define, expand, and communicate the frontiers of knowledge and innovation.

U.S. News & World Report consistently lists Georgia Tech among the fifty best universities in the nation. Georgia Tech also makes their list of the top graduate engineering programs in the country. Seven of the engineering options were ranked in the top ten, with several in the top five.

In addition to its high-quality undergraduate and graduate instructional programs, Tech has a world-class research program, with $217 million in new grants and contracts awarded during the 1999 fiscal year. This ranks Tech as the South's largest engineering research university.

DISTANCE LEARNING PROGRAM

Georgia Tech's Center for Distance Learning serves more than 450 distance learning students and is housed within a unit that reports directly to the provost. Georgia Tech is accredited by the Southern Association of Colleges and Schools. Engineering disciplines are accredited by the Accrediting Board for Engineering and Technology, Inc.

DELIVERY MEDIA

Video cameras record instructor presentations and student-instructor interaction during regular Georgia Tech graduate classes. The videotapes and supporting materials are sent to off-campus students, who take courses without having to come to the campus. Selected courses are available at some locations via video-conferencing, satellite, and the Internet. Students enrolled in the program communicate with their Georgia Tech professor by telephone, fax, and/or electronic mail. Students have access to the Georgia Tech Electronic Library and the computer system via a business or home computer and a modem. Access is also provided over the Internet.

PROGRAMS OF STUDY

The Georgia Tech video-based distance delivery program provides high-quality graduate-level courses that can be applied to several master's degree programs. The Master of Science in Electrical and Computer Engineering is offered with options in computer engineering, digital signal processing, power, and telecommunications; all options require 30 hours of course work. The Master of Science (M.S.) and the Master of Science in Environmental Engineering (M.S.Env.E.) degrees are offered with concentrations in water quality, surface and subsurface systems, hazardous and solid waste, and air quality; all programs require 30 hours of course work or the equivalent. The Master of Science in Health Physics/Radiological Engineering degree requires 30 hours of course work. The Master of Science in Industrial Engineering is offered with specializations in automation, produc-

tion and logistics systems, and statistical process control and quality assurance; it requires 30 hours of course work, students must hold an undergraduate degree from an ABET-accredited engineering curriculum. The Master of Science in Mechanical Engineering is offered with specializations in thermal science and mechanical systems; it requires 30 hours of course work.

Specific information on admission and degree requirements can be obtained by calling the academic coordinators for each area. Students should call the contact name for additional information.

SPECIAL PROGRAMS

As of August 1999, Georgia Tech offers the first two in a series of graduate-level credit courses in mechanical engineering (ME) that enable qualified students around the world the earn a Georgia Tech master's degree in ME completely on line. Once all the required courses are developed and offered, Georgia Tech will become the first and only university in the nation to offer a master's degree in ME in an asynchronous mode via the desktop. Also, in the fall semester of 2000, Georgia Tech began offering online graduate courses in electrical engineering that can be applied toward master's degrees in this discipline.

All Georgia Tech online graduate courses use state-of-the-art streaming audio and video technologies synchronized with slides, simulations, and other multimedia and make maximum use of the pedagogical advantages offered by Web-based courseware and instruction. Further information about these new online degree programs is available at the Georgia Tech Center for Distance Learning Web site (http://www.conted.gatech.edu/distance/gatech-online.html).

A Certificate in Manufacturing provides students with the fundamentals in support of education and research in manufacturing. Each student pursuing the certificate develops knowledge and skills in a particular discipline coupled with a general knowledge of the entire manufacturing enterprise and an ability to work well as a member of a team. The certificate emphasizes the philosophy that it is not possible to educate engineers, managers, or scientists in all aspects of manufacturing. Accordingly, the program is structured to broaden and enhance the education of students who are enrolled in traditional academic disciplines. The program encourages students to develop knowledge in multiple disciplines from class work and experiences in multidisciplinary team activities. Thus, the program balances technical depth with a broad exposure and comprehension of the problems (and potential solutions) facing industry in the manufacturing arena. The Certificate in Manufacturing is obtained as part of a graduate degree program (M.S. or Ph.D.) from the Georgia Institute of Technology. Students must complete a graduate degree to obtain the certificate. The certificate program consists of a set of key courses that are fundamental to manufacturing, from the which the students select 12 semester hours or 18 quarter hours. Students are also required to attend seminars.

CREDIT OPTIONS

Students earn credit toward their degree by registering for and completing courses delivered by videotape. Requirements for each course are the same as for on-campus students enrolled in the course. A student may receive transfer credit of up to 6 hours for graduate-level courses (approved by the academic adviser) taken at an accredited institution in the United States or Canada and not used for credit toward another degree.

FACULTY

There are 672 full-time faculty members at Georgia Tech, 93 percent with doctoral degrees. One hundred ten, or 16 percent, teach in the distance learning program.

ADMISSION

Admission requirements vary among the academic disciplines. To apply, individuals should contact the academic adviser or admissions office in the School to which he or she is applying.

TUITION AND FEES

Video enrollment fees for in-state and out-of-state students for the 1999–2000 academic year were $510 per credit hour. Fees are subject to change each year. There are no supplemental fees; however, students must purchase their own textbooks.

FINANCIAL AID

There are no financial aid programs available through Georgia Tech for distance learning students. Most employers have programs that will help students pay the course fees. The Department of Veterans Affairs has approved the Georgia Tech Video Program as independent study. Georgia Tech has a memorandum of understanding with DANTES and with the Air Force.

APPLYING

Application materials can be obtained from the School to which the student is applying. Applicants must submit an Application for Admission, three letters of recommendation, a biographical sketch, two official transcripts of all previous college work, and scores from the Graduate Record Examinations (GRE). Decisions are made by the individuals Schools.

CONTACT

Program Coordinator
Center for Distance Learning
Georgia Institute of Technology
Atlanta, Georgia 30332-0240
Telephone: 404-894-3378
Fax: 404-894-8924
Web site: http://www.conted.gatech.edu/distance/

Goddard College

Distance Learning Programs

Plainfield, Vermont

Goddard College pioneered distance learning and became the first college to offer accredited distance learning programs. Goddard continues to experiment and innovate by employing various styles of learning and learning modes. In addition to the individually designed low-residency B.A., M.A., and M.F.A. programs, the College also has an undergraduate resident program. Goddard was chartered in 1938 and is accredited by NEASC.

Goddard's campus is situated on 250 acres of rolling forest and meadows in rural Vermont. The main campus buildings include the former farm buildings of the historic Martin Estate and two other clusters of buildings, added in the 1960s, that consist of the library, the dormitories, and an arts complex. Plainfield is located in central Vermont, about 10 miles northeast of Montpelier, the state's capital.

DISTANCE LEARNING PROGRAM

The low-residency, student-designed programs enable students to study across the liberal arts at the undergraduate and graduate levels and to pursue several professional graduate programs. The College also offers an M.F.A. in creative writing and an M.F.A. in the interdisciplinary arts in a low-residency mode.

DELIVERY MEDIA

Twice a year, at the outset of each semester, students come to the Vermont campus for an intensive weeklong collaboration with fellow students as well as a faculty mentor to plan their semester's work through detailed study plans that enable them to reach their individual long-term learning goals. Throughout the rest of the semester, students work independently in their own communities, communicating with their mentor every three weeks.

PROGRAMS OF STUDY

Goddard offers the B.A. and the M.A. in individualized study, for which students craft diverse programs across the liberal arts. The areas of interest that studies cover include but are not limited to literature and writing, the performing arts, community organization and development, cultural theory, education, environmental studies, gay and lesbian studies, history, health arts, holistic health systems, women's studies, psychology and counseling, and philosophy.

Also offered are M.A. degrees in psychology/counseling, teacher education, social ecology, and health arts. M.F.A. degrees are offered in creative writing and in interdisciplinary arts.

For the B.A. degree, students must earn a minimum of 120 semester hours of credit. For the M.A. in individualized study, the M.A. in teacher education, the M.A. in social ecology, and the M.A. in health arts, students must earn a minimum of 36 semester hours of credit. For the M.A. in psychology and counseling, students must earn a minimum of 48 semester hours of credit. The M.F.A. degree in creative writing requires a minimum of 48 semester hours of credit, and the M.F.A. in interdisciplinary arts requires a minimum of 60 semester hours of credit.

SPECIAL PROGRAMS

Students in the low-residency programs can make use of study leaves, internships, apprenticeships, and travel-abroad opportunities as well as summer programs with the Institute for Social Ecology in Plainfield. Up to 45 B.A. credits may also be granted for life experience through an assessment of prior learning.

CREDIT OPTIONS

A maximum of 90 semester hours of credit may be transferred at the undergraduate level. Up to 12 transfer credits may be considered at the graduate level. In lieu of tests and grades, Goddard uses a written evaluative system, whereby each semester's work is viewed as successful or not. Each successful undergraduate semester is worth 15 credit hours, while each successful graduate semester is worth 12 credit hours.

FACULTY

Each of Goddard's programs is served by a body of core faculty members plus associate faculty members who are chosen for their general training as well as their individual areas of expertise. The faculty-student ratio is 1:10. Ninety percent of faculty members have terminal degrees in their fields.

ADMISSION

Goddard's admissions policy is inclusive rather than exclusive. Instead of grade point averages and test scores, applicants are judged on their interest, readiness, and willingness to begin study with the College and their apparent potential to complete college-level work. Previous credit must have been gained at accredited schools.

TUITION AND FEES

Tuition for the undergraduate program is $4115 per semester.

M.A. tuition is $4825 per semester, and M.F.A. tuition is $4912 per semester. All fees include the costs of the residencies.

FINANCIAL AID

Financial aid is based on financial need. Eligible undergraduate students may qualify for the Federal Pell Grant as well as various state grants. Guaranteed student loans, based on eligibility, are also available to both graduate and undergraduate students. Last year, more than $1.5 million was awarded in financial aid to Goddard students. Of Goddard's newly enrolled students, 100 percent received financial aid.

APPLYING

Goddard College accepts applications on a rolling basis, and

prospective students must supply required documents. Students applying to the M.F.A. programs must also provide an appropriate portfolio. Application materials can be acquired by contacting Admissions or via the College's Web site (address below).

CONTACT

Ellen W. Codling
Admissions
Goddard College
123 Pitkin Road
Plainfield, Vermont 05667
Telephone: 800-468-4888 (toll-free)
Fax: 802-454-1029
E-mail: admissions@earth.goddard.edu
Web site: http://www.goddard.edu

Heriot-Watt University

Edinburgh Business School

Edinburgh, Scotland

Edinburgh Business School, the graduate school of business of Heriot-Watt University, was created in 1995 by combining the former Heriot-Watt University Business School and the Esmee Fairbairn Research Center. This marked a milestone in Heriot-Watt University's program of postgraduate management education and executive development.

Edinburgh Business School offers a portfolio of M.B.A. programs, each of which leads to the Heriot-Watt University M.B.A. degree. The School also specializes in the design and delivery of tailored executive development programs.

The M.B.A. by Distance Learning was developed to address the career and education needs of adult professionals. Today, it is among the world's most popular M.B.A.s, with more than 8,000 students.

DISTANCE LEARNING PROGRAM

Edinburgh Business School offers a comprehensive M.B.A. program based on materials developed for companies and business schools around the world. In 2001, the M.B.A. program will expand to include specializations in human resources management, portfolio management, and marketing.

DELIVERY MEDIA

Heriot-Watt University was among the first to develop an M.B.A. program by distance learning. The program was launched in 1985, and became available to students outside of the U.K. in 1990. Media include instructional modules, study aids available via the Web site, and instructor-led tutorial sessions either by e-mail or in a classroom setting (depending on the number of students). Six weeks of on-campus study is optional. Student access to the Web site includes features which allow course members to check their exam grades, join discussion groups, or post questions on a bulletin board.

PROGRAMS OF STUDY

The M.B.A. of Edinburgh Business School generally takes 2 to 2½ years to complete, although students have seven years from the date of their first exam to complete the program. Students work at their own pace, taking courses in the order they prefer. The program is completely nonresidential—six weeks of on-campus study is optional.

The M.B.A. provides the business, management, and analytical skills needed in today's fast-paced, international business environment. New M.B.A. specializations offered by Edinburgh Business School will include human resources management, portfolio management, and marketing.

CREDIT OPTIONS

Edinburgh Business School will grant up to two exemptions (in the core curriculum only) based on prior academic studies or a professional qualification. Credit transfers up to a maximum of four applicable to the M.B.A. degree are accepted from recognized institutions. Applications for exemptions must be submitted with

transcripts and/or copies of qualifications to the Director of Studies, EBS, Heriot-Watt University, Riccarton, Edinburgh, EH14 4AS.

FACULTY

As part of the internationally respected British university system, Heriot-Watt is fully accredited by the British government. Designed for distance learners, the M.B.A. of Edinburgh Business School has been welcomed by businesses in the U.S. and Canada because the materials are portable, study is flexible, and the course modules have practical business application.

The M.B.A. is international in scope and designed by teams of leading faculty from business schools around the world. Course authors include professors from Stanford University, INSEAD, London Business School, Tulane University, University of Arkansas, University of Edinburgh, and Heriot-Watt University.

ADMISSION

Enrollment is open and continuous. There are no entrance exams required because the M.B.A. degree is exam-based.

TUITION AND FEES

Tuition per course is $995 (U.S.). The tuition includes study aids and Web access to discussion and study groups. Prices are subject to change.

FINANCIAL AID

Most student receive tuition reimbursement from their employers. Students in Canada can benefit from Canadian student loans and tax credits on tuition (students should contact their local government office for loan forms, or visit the Revenue Canada Web site). Private loans are available to students from private lending comapanies such as Educaid or the International Education Finance Corporation (IEFC). These loans are not guaranteed, but are based on good credit. International students residing in the U.S. are eligible for loans if they have a U.S. resident co-signer with good credit. The IEFC offers a loan program for students in Canada as well. All aspects of finacial aid are between the student and his or her lender.

For more information, students can phone Stafford Loan Information toll-free at 800-4-FED-AID (800-433-3243) or contact the IEFC by phone at 617-696-7840 or by e-mail at iefc@aol. com. Students should also visit the Web sites http://www.educaid.com or http://www.salliemae.com.

APPLYING

Prospective students must request an enrollment form and prospectus from the U.S.-based student services office by phone or e-mail as listed below. All documents should be sent to Heirot-Watt University Student Services at the address listed below.

CONTACT
Heirot-Watt University Student Services
2 World Trade Center
Suite 1700
New York, New York 10048.
Telephone: 212-390-5030
           800-622-9661 (toll-free in U.S. and Canada)
Fax: 212-344-3469
E-mail info@hwmba.net
Web site: http://www.hwmba.edu

Indiana Higher Education Telecommunication System

Indiana Partnership for Statewide Education

Indianapolis, Indiana

Since 1967, Indiana's colleges and universities have cooperatively managed telecommunications networks through IHETS to share resources and disseminate a wide variety of educational opportunities. In 1992, the institutions established the Indiana Partnership for Statewide Education as the vehicle for collaboration in program planning, delivery of student services, needs assessment and promotion, faculty development, and evaluation. The Partnership's goal is to ensure that lifelong learning is available via distance education to Indiana citizens wherever they may live and work. Technology developments mean that many of the same programs are available on campus and around the world. Consortium members are Ball State University, Independent Colleges of Indiana, Indiana State University, Indiana University, Ivy Tech State College, Purdue University, University of Southern Indiana, and Vincennes University.

DISTANCE LEARNING PROGRAM

Each consortium member is fully accredited and responsible for its own programs. Collectively, enrollments on a statewide basis approach 10,000 per year in high school and college credit courses; hundreds of others are served locally or regionally by distance education, and correspondence programs serve thousands of students around the world. The Partnership has adopted the umbrella label "Indiana College Network" to refer to the comprehensive array of degree programs and learning opportunities provided by Indiana's higher education institutions.

DELIVERY MEDIA

Partnership institutions use a variety of delivery methods, including independent study by correspondence, satellite television (one-way video with two-way audio), public or cable television, two-way video, computer disks and CD-ROM, videotape, and the Internet. Some degrees are available entirely via satellite to specially equipped Receive Sites, but most degrees permit students to take course

work in a combination of modes. Most programs with "live" interaction are still available only within Indiana, though more are becoming available at locations throughout the United States and in other countries.

PROGRAMS OF STUDY

Certificate and degree programs are listed with the name of the originating institution: Certificate in Distance Education (Indiana University); Certificate in General Studies (Vincennes University); Certificate in Labor Studies (Indiana University); Certificate in Public Library, Librarian IV and V (Indiana University); Certificate in School Library/Media and Information Technology (Indiana University); Christian Worker Certificate (Taylor University); Technical Certificate in Child Development (Ivy Tech State College); Technical Certificate in Histotechnology (Indiana University); Associate of Applied Science (A.A.S.) in accounting (Ivy Tech State College); A.A.S. in business administration (Ivy Tech State College); A.A.S. in child development (Ivy Tech State College); A.A.S. in design technology (Ivy Tech State College); Associate of Arts (A.A.) in general arts (Ball State University);

Associate of General Studies (Indiana University); Associate of Science (A.S.) in behavioral sciences (Vincennes University); A.S. in business administration (Ball State University); A.S. in business administration (Vincennes University); A.S. in communications (University of Southern Indiana); A.S. in computer technology (Purdue University); A.S. in general aviation flight technology (Indiana State University); A.S. in general studies (Vincennes University); A.S. in histotechnology (Indiana University); A.S. in labor studies (Indiana University); A.S. in law enforcement (Vincennes University); A.S. in social science (Vincennes University); A.S. in veterinary technology; Bachelor of General Studies (Indiana University); Bachelor of Science (B.S.) in electronics technology (Indiana State University); B.S. in general industrial supervision (Indian State University; B.S. in general industrial technology (Indiana State University); B.S. in health services (University of Southern Indiana); B.S. in human resource development (Indiana State University); B.S. in labor studies (Indiana University); B.S. in nursing (Ball State University); B.S. in nursing (University of Southern Indiana); Master of Arts (M.A.) in executive development and public service (Ball State University); Master of Arts in Education (M.A.Ed.) in educational administration and supervision (Ball State University); M.A.Ed. in elementary education (Ball State University); M.A. Ed. in special education (Ball State University); Master of Business Administration (Ball State University); Master of Business Administration (Indiana University); Master of Business Administration (M.B.A.) in agribusiness (Purdue University); Master of Science (M.S.) in adult education (Indiana University); M.S in computer science

(Ball State University); M.S./M.A. in criminology (Indiana State University); Master of Science in Education (M.S.Ed.) in language education (Indiana University); M.S. in electrical engineering (Purdue University); M.S. or M.A. in health and safety (Indiana State University); M.S. in human resource development (Indiana State University); M.S. in industrial engineering (Purdue University); M.S. or Master of Science in Engineering (M.S.E) in interdisciplinary engineering (Purdue University); M.S. in mechanical engineering (Purdue University); M.S. in nursing (Ball State University); M.S. in nursing (Indiana University); M.S. in nursing (Purdue University Calumet); and M.S. in recreation (Indiana University).

Several other programs were nearing authorization at the time of this publication. Information is available in the separate listings for the institutions or via the World Wide Web.

STUDENT SERVICES

All of the partner institutions participate in a library automation network, which makes library catalogs accessible via the Internet. Most professors expect students at a distance to use the Internet for library research and class-related communications. Students are generally expected to obtain Internet access from a local provider, but Learning Centers in Indiana house computers with dial-up access for students unable to obtain affordable service.

CREDIT OPTIONS

The undergraduate degree programs listed here allow some credit to be transferred from other institutions; the amount varies for each program. The Indiana University (IU) general studies degree programs are tailored for adults to permit credit transfer and learning portfolios along with courses to be taken to complete the degree. All other degrees are the same programs as those offered to students on campus; many courses are taken simultaneously by students on and off campus. Graduate degree programs typically allow limited credit transfer.

FACULTY

Faculty members' credentials vary among the institutions, but professors in the university programs are almost exclusively full-time institutional faculty members with terminal degrees.

ADMISSION

Admission requirements are the same as those for on-campus programs, with special flexibility in the IU general studies programs. Older or reentering students are not usually required to take or retake SAT or other standardized tests.

TUITION AND FEES

Fees are highly variable, with a range of $67 to $130 per credit hour for in-state undergraduate students; some institutions charge an additional $25 per credit hour to help cover support-service costs for students at a distance.

FINANCIAL AID

Since most distance education students are independent, employed adults attending college part-time, few receive federal or state financial aid, although it is the personal circumstances rather than the delivery methods that reduce or eliminate benefits. Many students are receiving support from Veterans Administration benefits or from employer tuition reimbursement programs.

APPLYING

Application and acceptance processes are approximately the same for on- and off-campus students, although distant students usually apply through special distance education or program coordinators at the offering institutions rather than through the main college or university admissions office.

CONTACT

Indiana College Network (ICN) Student Services Center
2805 East Tenth Street
Bloomington, Indiana 47408
Telephone: 800-426-8899 (toll-free)
Fax: 812-855-9380

Additional information, including a searchable database of courses and degree programs, is available at the Partnership's Web site: http://www.icn.org.

Indiana State University

Distance Education Program
Terre Haute, Indiana

Indiana State University is a medium-sized, comprehensive university accredited by the North Central Association of Colleges and Schools. Founded in 1865, the University has grown to serve a student population that includes 11,000 students from all 50 states and 82 countries. International students comprise 13 percent of the student population.

Attention to and concern for the individual is reflected in the institution's offerings. Flexible and responsive programs are designed to facilitate student attainment of academic, vocational, and personal goals. Classes are designed to meet the needs of full-time and part-time students. Nondegree study is also available for those seeking personal growth, transferable credit, and enrichment through lifelong learning.

In addition to offering distance programs and courses, the University offers undergraduate and graduate programs in 180 areas of study on the Indiana State University campus in Terre Haute, Indiana.

DISTANCE LEARNING PROGRAM

Indiana State University (ISU) has offered distance programs since 1969. Many programs can be completed entirely via distance education; others require minimal campus visits. Selected distance programs and numerous courses can be completed by out-of-state and international students. Over 1,000 students enroll in ISU distance learning courses each semester.

DELIVERY MEDIA

Courses are offered via the Internet, videotapes, correspondence, and live television accessible at 300 sites in Indiana. Television courses offer live, two-way interaction among students and the instructor. Students enrolled in correspondence courses work independently, interacting with their instructor via written communications. Students in Internet courses and some videotape courses interact via e-mail and Internet chat rooms. Equipment requirements depend on course format, and may include an Internet-connected computer, VCR, and audio cassette player.

PROGRAMS OF STUDY

Students may complete individual undergraduate or graduate courses; each semester over 100 ISU courses are offered via distance education. In addition, eligible students may complete numerous undergraduate and graduate degrees and professional development programs.

Undergraduate degree programs include an Associate of Science in general aviation flight technology and bachelor degree completion programs in business administration, community health, criminology, electronics technology, general industrial technology, human resource development, industrial supervision, instrumentation and control technology, insurance, mechanical technology, nursing, and vocational trade-industrial-technical. Undergraduate nondegree programs include basic and advanced certificate programs in corrections, law enforcement, and private security; an endorsement in driver education; and a certification program in library/media services.

Graduate degree programs include a doctoral program in technology man-agement, and master's programs in criminology, health and safety, human resource development, nursing, and student affairs administration. Graduate nondegree programs include an endorsement in driver education, a licensure program in educational administration, and certification programs in public administration and library/media services.

SPECIAL PROGRAMS

DegreeLink is a bachelor's degree completion program that enables individuals to transfer up to 62 hours to ISU, and complete selected bachelor's degrees via distance education. Students may transfer credit earned from Ivy Tech State College, Vincennes University, or another accredited institution.

The Library/Media Services Certification Program consists of 27 hours of library and media courses leading to an undergraduate minor and certification or graduate certification in library/media services.

The Ph.D. in technology management is offered through the School of Technology in cooperation with a consortium of eight other universities. Course work includes a general technology core, a technical specialization, cognate studies, an internship, and a research core and dissertation.

STUDENT SERVICES

Indiana State University offers distance learners a comprehensive package of services, including academic advisement, a virtual bookstore, library services, technical support, and career counseling. The Office of Student Services–Lifelong Learning offers one-stop assistance to individuals interested in pursuing undergraduate and graduate courses and programs via distance learning.

CREDIT OPTIONS

Students earn credit by registering for and completing semester-based courses offered on campus or via distance learning. In addition, undergraduate students may opt to earn credit via year-based study. Undergraduate students are eligible to transfer up to 64 hours of credit earned from an accredited institution. Selected programs enable undergraduates to earn credit for prior work experience, by examination, and through portfolios. Graduate students are eligible to transfer selected credit; each department determines the number of hours transferable.

FACULTY

Distance courses are developed and taught by ISU's 536 full-time faculty members. Working with instructional designers and media specialists, faculty members transform on-campus courses to distance formats.

ADMISSION

Admission requirements vary by program of study. For information, prospective students should contact the Office of Student Services–Lifelong Learning.

TUITION AND FEES

All distance learners pay Indiana residence fees. Undergraduate tuition is $123 per credit hour; graduate tuition is $148 per credit hour. Tuition is subject to change.

APPLYING

Individuals may obtain undergraduate and graduate applications, information, and assistance by contacting the Office of Student Services–Lifelong Learning.

CONTACT

Harry K. Barnes, Director
Office of Student Services–Lifelong Learning
Indiana State University
Erickson Hall, Room 210–211
Terre Haute, Indiana 47809
Telephone: 888-237-8080 (toll-free)
Fax: 812-237-8540
E-mail: studentservices@indstate.edu
Web site: http://indstate.edu/distance

Indiana Wesleyan University

MBA Online Degree Program

Marion, Indiana

Founded in 1920, Indiana Wesleyan University (IWU) has the largest M.B.A. enrollment of any college or university in Indiana. Since 1985, IWU has offered conveniently accessible associate's, bachelor's, and master's programs to working adult professionals across the state of Indiana. More than 4,000 students participate in these adult and professional studies programs while nearly 2,000 students are enrolled in traditional undergraduate and graduate programs on the main campus. Affiliated with The Wesleyan Church, IWU is a "Christ-centered academic community committed to changing the world by developing students in character, scholarship, and leadership." IWU is accredited by the North Central Association of Colleges and Schools.

DISTANCE LEARNING PROGRAM

IWU offers the MBA Online degree to working adult professionals who must overcome time and geographic barriers in order to obtain an M.B.A. Built upon a successful M.B.A. on-site program and launched in September 1998, the MBA Online Degree Program enrolls more than 100 students. Student-to-student interaction coupled with expert faculty-facilitated learning makes this program ideal for the person who wants to be able to put a theoretical knowledge base to work in actual business situations.

DELIVERY MEDIA

Courses in the MBA Online Degree Program are delivered via the Internet using IWU's state-of-the-art customized interface design. Web page discussion forums, live chats, and whiteboard collaborative software allow for both synchronous and asynchronous interaction between faculty members and students. Completed assignments are typically submitted as e-mail attachments while proctored exams help students to as-

sess their progress. One course is delivered in a three-day, on-site, intensive learning format with opportunities for significant interaction with University experts and corporate executives. Students need a computer, a modem, and Internet access to participate in the program.

PROGRAM OF STUDY

The MBA Online Degree Program comprises a 46-credit lockstep-sequence curriculum which is completed in thirty months. Students take courses one at a time and consecutively, with appropriate holiday breaks included in the calendar. Cohorts (groups of students who move through the program on the same schedule) begin the program approximately every two months. A "capstone" applied management project must be completed successfully as part of the curriculum. Students are required to participate in one 3-day intensive learning experience. Successful progress through the MBA Online program requires maintaining a 3.0 GPA and a minimum grade of C in each course.

STUDENT SERVICES

In addition to the timely delivery of textbooks and other study materials to students, IWU offers off-campus library services to MBA Online participants. Students may request copies of articles and other items by e-mail or a toll-free number. Academic advising is also available. Students also receive friendly, proactive, and personalized technical assistance before the first course in the program with similar help continuing throughout the thirty-month curriculum.

FACULTY

Experienced, well-trained faculty members provide guidance for students as they master the knowledge base and seek to apply what they are learning in their vocational settings. Because of the "practitioner focus" of this M.B.A. program, many of the faculty members are full-time professionals who facilitate learning on a part-time basis. All faculty members hold advanced degrees.

ADMISSION

Students who wish to be admitted to the MBA Online Degree Program must hold a bachelor's degree from a regionally accredited college or university, have a cumulative GPA of at least 2.5 in all previous undergraduate work, and have three years of significant full-time work experience. Students must satisfy prerequisites in math, economics, accounting, and finance. The math prerequisite must be met before a student can begin the M.B.A. core curriculum.

TUITION AND FEES

The total cost of the MBA Online program is $18,990, which includes tuition, books, and fees. The tuition per credit hour is $365 while books cost a total of $1820 for the entire program. Fees (off-campus library services, graduation, etc.) total $380. Hotel and food costs for the two intensive learning experiences are also included in the total cost. An application fee of $20 is required.

FINANCIAL AID

Guaranteed Stafford loans are available for students who need financial assistance. Approximately one-third of MBA Online students access these loans to help pay for their education.

APPLYING

Prospective students are asked to complete an application data form and a narrative statement. Two recommendation forms and official transcripts from all colleges or universities at which the student did undergraduate course work are also required. Admission decisions are usually made within two weeks following the completion of the application file.

CONTACT

Rob Long, Program Manager
Frank Brown, Program Representative
MBA Online
Adult and Professional Studies
Indiana Wesleyan University
4301 South Washington Street
Marion, Indiana 46953-5279
Telephone: 800-621-8667 (toll-free)
Fax: 765-677-2380
E-mail: rlong@indwes.edu
        fbrown@indwes.edu
Web site: http://OnlineMBA.net
        http://www.indwes.edu

Instituto Tecnológico y de Estudios Superiores de Monterrey

Virtual University

Monterrey, Mexico

Leadership—the key to success at the Monterrey Institute of Technology (Monterrey Tech) since 1943 when founded by a group of businessmen led by Eugenio Garza Sada. Their vision was to have a human resources base that stimulated development and growth of industry in Monterrey. The engineering and scientific talent produced at Monterrey Tech has made Monterrey the best city in Latin America for doing business. With a reputation for academic excellence, Monterrey Tech is currently the largest privately run university in all of Latin America and fully accredited in the U.S. by the Southern Association of Colleges and Schools. It consists of thirty campuses in Mexico, a traditional student enrollment of nearly 85,000, and a faculty of approximately 6,000 professors. A presence felt throughout Latin America, Monterrey Tech extends educational services to nine other countries in the region via the Virtual University. Its mission is to educate students to be individuals who are committed to the social, economic, and political development of their communities and who are internationally competitive in their professional fields; and to carry out research and extension services relevant to Mexico's sustainable development.

DISTANCE LEARNING PROGRAM

The Virtual University is an institution of higher education that offers undergraduate, master's, Ph.D., and continuing education programs through innovative educational models and the most advanced telecommunications and computer networking technology. Helping students worldwide to generate their own knowledge and develop their skills, the Virtual University has transformed professor-centered learning into a group learning process, where students learn to learn. The professor designs experiences, exercises, and activities that facilitate group work and encourage students to learn actively. Under the Virtual University's learning model, students acquire useful knowledge as well as the ability to transfer this knowledge to the workplace.

DELIVERY MEDIA

The most advanced Internet, multimedia, satellite, and videoconferencing technologies are utilized by the Virtual University for its many educational programs. This wide variety of technologies allows students extraordinary flexibility to interact globally with faculty members and other students. Among its many applications, the Internet can be used to broadcast live events, perform simulations, hold group discussions and interactive chats, create virtual communities, provide Web sites, and exchange e-mail. Students must, therefore, have access to a computer and the Internet.

PROGRAMS OF STUDY

The Virtual University offers twenty-five degree programs that can be earned entirely at a distance. These comprise three undergraduate and seventeen postgraduate degree programs, including a Ph.D. in innovation and educational technology. Online and virtual degree programs are offered. Virtual degree programs consist of a combination of satellite, Internet video conferencing, and multimedia technology.

Online bachelor's degree programs are offered online in computer administration, humanities, and accounting. Online master's degree programs are offered in business administration, education, and educational technology. Virtual master's degree programs are offered in business administration (with a specialization in e-commerce), e-commerce, finance, marketing, international management for Latin American managers, education (with areas of specialization), humanities, library and information science, administration and educational institutions, educational technology, educational technology management, information technology management, telecommunications management, environmental engineering and planning, architecture, quality and productivity systems, and computer science. A virtual Ph.D. program is offered in innovation and educational technology.

A description of all programs, including details regarding degree requirements, number of credits required, and other features may be found at http://www.ruv.itesm.mx by selecting "Programas Educativos." To consult the online programs exclusively, students should visit the Web site listed in the Contact section.

SPECIAL PROGRAMS

The Virtual University offers a large variety of specialized programs for professionals.

The Virtual University for Executives is an innovative learning system aimed at raising business competitiveness by making Monterrey Tech's educational services available in the workplace. Programming content is distributed among six fields: organizational culture, languages, sustainable development, trade, finance, and productivity.

Customized courses and programs are developed to meet the specific training requirements at a company.

The in-company master's degree program allows companies to establish a receiving site for offering some master's degree programs to key personnel at company facilities.

The Teaching Skills Development Program is designed to prepare teachers at different levels of precollege education to respond to the challenges in contemporary education. By focusing on the areas of active learning, educational models and technology, Monterrey Tech hopes to contribute to a transformation of education in Latin America.

The Public Officials Training Program is administered in partnership with the World Bank to assist Latin American municipal officials with the development of abilities in management of fiscal resources, strategic planning, leadership abilities, quality principles, and values and honesty.

The Training for Leaders of Social Enterprises provides participants with an orientation for guiding and producing successful organizations and projects with the purpose of fostering social development. Continuing Education provides seminars, short courses, and extended programs in various fields.

STUDENT SERVICES

The variety of services available to Virtual University students include keynote conferences (live interactive presentations made by prominent international figures via satellite) a digital library containing the complete text of more than 4,000 newspaper and magazine articles; tutors, with every student in every course having access to tutoring through e-mail and Hypernews; administrative services, providing students with up-to-date information on their individual scholastic status at any given moment via the Internet; and CASA, a student services center that assists students with the logistics of receiving materials and videos, which provides students with general information, and responds to students' complaints, concerns, and needs.

CREDIT OPTIONS

Credits from other universities can be revalidated before beginning a Virtual University program. This involves an approval process by the SEP (Department of Public Education). Completing a course for credit is the only other way credit can be earned through the Virtual University.

FACULTY

Of the 121 faculty members at the Virtual University, 69 percent are full-time and 57 percent have Ph.D.'s. Further faculty member information is available by program and by visiting the individual faculty Web sites.

ADMISSION

Many programs require students to have access to certain computer equipment, the Internet, and sometimes to sites where class sessions are received via satellite. Degree programs require a previous degree in addition to an admissions exam, the GRE, the GMAT, or other standardized test deemed appropriate. Both degree and special program admission details are available by visiting the specific program's Web site, as well as through the contact information listed below.

TUITION AND FEES

Assuming a 10:1 peso to dollar ratio, tuition per class/subject (in U.S. dollars) is $1,208.40 for trimester satellite-based classes, $1,292.40 for semester satellite-based classes, $702 for online graduate classes, and $432 for online undergraduate classes.

Tuition for special programs can be found at the specific program's Web site or by using the contact information listed below.

FINANCIAL AID

Scholarships are available to online students. This information can be found on the Web at http://www.ruv.itesm.mx/programas/mlinea.

APPLYING

Procedures for application, acceptance, and orientation differ among the many Virtual University programs. Students interested in applying for a specific program may request this information through the specific program's Web site or the contact listed below.

CONTACT

Office of the Dean of Communications
Telephone: 528-328-4312
Fax: 528-328-4341
E-mail: jmarcos@campus.ruv.itesm.mx
Admissions Office
Telephone: 528-387-7470
Fax: 528-328-4321
E-mail: arodrigu@campus.ruv.itesm.mx
Web site: http://www.tec.com.mx

Jones International University
Program in Business Communication
Englewood, Colorado

Jones International University™, Ltd. (JIU), the first fully online accredited university, offers courses, certificates, and undergraduate and graduate degree programs. The innovative online programs are an exciting opportunity for adult learners looking to either complete their bachelor's, master's, or M.B.A. degree or explore new fields of interest.

The content-rich, highly focused curriculum is designed by experts drawn from some of the most prestigious universities around the world. Discussions, interactions, lectures, and assignments are all available online whenever and wherever it is most convenient for the student. The level of instruction and interaction between students from around the world is exceptional.

JIU received formal institutional accreditation from the North Central Association of Colleges and Schools (NCA) in March 1999.

DISTANCE LEARNING PROGRAM

Information technology is the driving force in today's marketplace. At JIU, technology is used to provide adult learners the knowledge, confidence, and credentials they need to succeed in their chosen careers. JIU has served more than 1,500 students from forty-two countries. Students use the Internet to access their course material, discussions, and resources.

DELIVERY MEDIA

JIU courses occur entirely over the Internet and take full advantage of the power of the Internet to foster communication and skill acquisition. Students work collaboratively with instructors and classmates and put what they learn online to use in business immediately. This "community of learners" is a highly interactive way to exchange ideas and learn. Using computers and Internet connectivity, students can learn at home, at work, or during travel.

PROGRAMS OF STUDY

The Bachelor of Arts (B.A.) in Business Communication Degree Comple-

tion Program blends theory and practice for the effective management of communication. This program of study focuses on the knowledge and communication skills, which help develop creativity, innovation, entrepreneurship, and leadership.

Master of Arts (M.A.) in business communication students gain valuable skills in human communication, current and emerging communication technologies, and oral and written communication skills. Through this course of study, students learn the tools and expert knowledge that lead to increased workplace productivity, creativity, and leadership.

Through JIU's Master of Business Administration (M.B.A.) Program, students gain a solid grounding in the fundamentals of business and study in depth one of seven high-demand specializations: global enterprise management, e-commerce, healthcare management, entrepreneurship, information technology management, negotiation and conflict management, and project management.

SPECIAL PROGRAMS

Students enroll in any one of twenty-seven certification programs, which are available in fifteen areas of study.

Students may also enroll in single courses and choose to transfer those credits into a certificate or degree program.

STUDENT SERVICES

JIU students purchase textbooks through the online bookstore and use the e-global Library™, a Web-based library, to access reference resources through the Internet and World Wide Web. The Student Advising Center offers academic goals and degree planning and career advising services. JIU offers technical assistance for issues relating to the JIU Web site and online courses 24 hours a day, seven days a week.

CREDIT OPTIONS

Students may transfer credits they have earned at other regionally accredited institutions of higher learning and apply them to their JIU program. Students in the M.A. and M.B.A. programs may transfer up to 9 graduate credits earned at other schools. Students in the B.A. program may transfer up to 90 credit hours. JIU awards a maximum of 15 credit hours for prior learning experience toward the bachelor's degree.

FACULTY

JIU has 4 full-time faculty members and 150 part-time faculty members. Seventy-five percent of the faculty members hold doctorates and 25 percent have master's degrees.

ADMISSION

Students seeking enrollment in JIU's B.A., M.A., or M.B.A. degree programs must submit a completed application package, including a nonrefundable $75 application fee, a JIU application, official transcripts, resume, writing sample, and references.

TUITION AND FEES

Tuition for 3 credit-hour courses at the bachelor level is $600. Master's level courses are $700. M.B.A course tuition is $725. An application fee, one-time registration fee, and technology fee per course also apply.

FINANCIAL AID

JIU students can apply for student loans from Sallie Mae or PLATO. Both loan options are available to individuals who are U.S. citizens, U.S. nationals, or U.S. permanent residents.

Students may be qualified for financial assistance under the Montgomery GI Bill, the Dependents' Educational Assistance Program, and the Veteran's Educational Assistance Program.

JIU also offers scholarship services to graduates of two-year colleges with which it has articulation partnerships. For an updated list of JIU's articulation partners, students should visit the Web site at http://www.getmyba.com/scholarship.

APPLYING

JIU courses begin every month. Students may enroll in individual courses or apply to degree programs at any time. Applicants to degree programs must complete an online application or obtain an application by sending an e-mail request to the address listed below.

CONTACT

Jones International University™, Ltd.
9697 East Mineral Avenue
Englewood, Colorado 80112
Telephone: 303-784-8045
          800-811-5663 (toll-free)
Fax: 303-784-8547
E-mail: info@international.edu
Web site: http://www.jonesinternational.edu

Judson College

Adult Studies Program

Marion, Alabama

As the nation's sixth-oldest women's college, Judson College was founded in 1838 by Baptists in Marion, Alabama, to educate young women in a Christian environment. The independent, liberal arts college was named for Ann Hasseltine Judson, America's first female foreign missionary, and remains affiliated with the Alabama Baptist Convention. Judson College is accredited by the Commission on Colleges of the Southern Association of Colleges and Schools.

DISTANCE LEARNING PROGRAM

The Judson College Adult Studies Program is designed primarily for adult students, women and men, whose circumstances prevent them from attending traditionally offered higher education. Judson College faculty and staff members work with students to design flexible programs of study that fit their individual schedules.

DELIVERY MEDIA

Courses are delivered by means of learning contracts. Faculty members from the Judson College campus design learning objectives for each course. Faculty members select resource material and structure assignments and methods of evaluating learning. They are available for guidance and consultation by phone, mail, and e-mail. Many courses are technology-intensive and all students use technology in the completion of their degree requirements. Access to computer resources is the responsibility of the student.

PROGRAMS OF STUDY

Students can earn a B.A. degree in business administration and management information systems, criminal justice, elementary education, English, history, interdisciplinary major, music (by permission), music educa-

tion (by permission), psychology, religious studies, and secondary education (language arts education and social science education). B.S. degrees are offered in administration and management information systems, criminal justice, interdisciplinary major, psychology, and secondary education (general science education and mathematics education).

Use of an academic library with appropriate college-level resources is essential to the completion of educational goals through the Adult Studies Program. Students in the Perry County area use the Bowling Library located on the Judson campus. Students more removed from the campus should use a library in their area. Students with Internet access may search the Bowling Library holdings through the Alabama Library Catalog (ALICAT) provided by the Alabama Public Library Service. Orientation for use of this service may be received by calling the Adult Studies Program office.

STUDENT SERVICES

Student services that are offered on the Judson campus are available to all students, traditional and nontraditional. Cultural and spiritual events that are sponsored by the College are routinely posted on the Judson College Web site. Students in the vicinity of the campus are encouraged to at-

tend any or all of these events. Other resources of the Student Services Office may be requested by calling or corresponding directly with the office.

CREDIT OPTIONS

Courses in Judson College Adult Studies Program are taken on a credit basis. Transcripts reflecting completed courses may be requested from the College registrar.

FACULTY

All Adult Studies Program courses are taught by the Judson College faculty. All of Judson's faculty members have appropriate credentials, and 75 percent hold terminal degrees in the teaching field.

ADMISSION

Admission to Judson College is available to students of diverse backgrounds, talents, interests, and experiences, whose academic and personal qualities show promise of future success.

TUITION AND FEES

The Adult Studies Program tuition is $225 per credit hour. The College reserves the right to modify its financial policies and to adjust charges for tuition and fees at any time.

FINANCIAL AID

Financial aid programs that are available to Adult Studies Program students include the Federal Pell Grant, Federal Supplemental Educational Opportunity Grant, Federal Perkins

Loan, Federal Stafford Loan, Federal Parent's Loan for Undergraduate Students, and the Alabama Student Grant. Personnel in the Financial Aid Office are available to assist students in applying for aid.

APPLYING

Applicants must have a high school diploma or GED and must complete the Adult Studies Program application form. The College does not admit into any program persons who are incarcerated or who are otherwise legally restricted in their movements. Applications are available by request and from the College Web site.

CONTACT

Adult Studies Program
Judson College
P.O. Box 120
Marion Alabama 36756
Telephone: 334-683-5169
Fax: 334-683-5158
E-mail: adultstudies@future.judson.edu
Web site: http://www.judson.edu

Kansas State University

Division of Continuing Education
Distance Education

Manhattan, Kansas

Kansas State University (KSU or K-State) was founded on February 16, 1863, as a land-grant institution under the Morrill Act. Originally located on the grounds of the old Bluemont Central College, which was chartered in 1858, the University was moved to its present site in 1875.

The 664-acre campus is in Manhattan, 125 miles west of Kansas City, via Interstate 70, in the rolling Flint Hills of northeast Kansas. The Salina campus, 70 miles west of Manhattan, was established through a merger of the former Kansas College of Technology with the University. This was made possible by an enactment of the 1991 Kansas Legislature.

KSU is accredited by the North Central Association of Colleges and Schools (NCA). One of the six universities governed by the Kansas Board of Regents, Kansas State University continues to fulfill its historic educational mission in teaching, research, and public service.

DISTANCE LEARNING PROGRAM

Kansas State University innovatively offers high-quality courses and degree programs to students who are not geographically located near the Manhattan campus. KSU utilizes cutting-edge technologies that enhance the learning environment and extend it far beyond the University's physical boundaries.

Adults across the country want to complete their education, advance their careers, or change their professions. Success requires dedication, self-direction, and perseverance on the part of the student. Distance education offered by K-State provides people with an opportunity to pursue these goals without leaving a current job or family. KSU offers bachelor's degrees and master's degrees at a distance.

DELIVERY MEDIA

K-State offers courses through a variety of delivery methods. Most courses follow regular K-State semester dates. Some courses require minimum computer system requirements.

Kansas State University offers more than 250 courses per semester through distance education. Courses are offered in a variety of subject areas and students can take many of these without enrolling in a degree program.

Delivery methods include use of videotapes and audiotapes, the World Wide Web, listservs, e-mail, discussion rooms, guided study, desktop video, community-based outreach courses, independent study, correspondence coursework with other institutions, military training credit evaluations (based on American Council for Education Guidelines), portfolio/experiential credit assessments, standardized test taking, credit by examination and competency assessments, and petitions for special exams.

PROGRAMS OF STUDY

For more than twenty-five years, K-State has been offering degree completion programs through distance education. The goal of the distance education degree completion programs is to help students complete the last two years of a Bachelor of Science degree. K-State staff is available to help students begin their studies, stay directed, and earn a Bachelor of Science degree.

Requirements include a minimum of 30 KSU hours, with 20 of the last 30 hours earned at K-State. Students may transfer a maximum of 60 credit hours to KSU from a community college. The average student completes a bachelor's degree in two to six years. The student sets the pace.

Bachelor's degree completion programs include animal science and industry, general business, food science and industry, interdisciplinary social science, early childhood education (limited to Kansas), and coursework leading to a degree in dietetics.

Master's degrees are offered at a distance. Master's degree programs include agribusiness, industrial/organizational psychology, electrical engineering, civil engineering, chemical engineering, software engineering, and engineering management.

SPECIAL PROGRAMS

Certificate/endorsement programs are also offered. These programs include a food science certificate program, English as a second language (ESL) endorsement (limited to Kansas), and early childhood education (limited to Kansas).

K-State is a member of Service Members Opportunity College for the SOCAD-2 flexible-degree network. This network guarantees worldwide transfer of credit for military personnel who take courses from participating colleges and universities.

STUDENT SERVICES

Each person in the bachelor's degree completion program receives indi-

---

552

vidual academic advising. A program of study is developed to meet the specific needs of each student. Library services are available to students enrolled in degree completion programs. A K-State library services facilitator helps students access materials in the K-State library. For more information, visit the library Web site at http://www.dce.ksu.edu/dce/as/library/.

The Division of Continuing Education student handbook is available on the Web at www.dce.ksu/edu/dce/division/studenthandbook.html.

The technical support help desk can provide a variety of technical support services once a student is enrolled in a distance education course and has paid the media fee. For information about the help desk visit the Web site at http://online.ksu.edu/support/.

FACULTY

Kansas State University is an accredited institution offering credit courses through distance education. Distance education courses are taught by faculty members who teach K-State on-campus courses.

ADMISSION

Each distance education degree program has specific admission requirements and procedures. Bachelor's degree completion programs require an application fee of $30. Admission information is available for each program at the Web address listed below.

TUITION AND FEES

Course fees are set by the Kansas Board of Regents and vary from year to year. In 2000–01, undergraduate tuition is $100 per credit hour. Graduate tuition is $143 per credit hour. Students pay an additional media fee and other fees.

FINANCIAL AID

Financial aid is available for students in degree programs. Students may be eligible for financial aid for distance education courses if federal requirements are met, they are admitted and enrolled in a degree program in Kansas State University, and enrolled in a minimum of 6 credit hours of Kansas State University coursework. Each student is assigned a financial aid advisor.

The Maurine Allison O'Bannon Scholarship, perpetuating the memory of Maurine Allison O'Bannon at Kansas State University, provides $350 to undergraduate students and $400 to graduate students who are in degree programs at KSU and enrolled in Division of Continuing Education courses.

There is also the Robert F. Sykes Scholarship. The purpose of this scholarship is to honor Robert F. Sykes and to fund a scholarship for a graduate of an accredited college of engineering who is pursuing a graduate degree in civil engineering or engineering management at Kansas State University via distance education. For more information about financial aid, students can access the Web site at http://www.dce.ksu.edu/dce/division/finaid.html.

APPLYING

The application process for each program is varied. For complete information on a specific program, students can access the Web site at the address listed below or contact the Division of Continuing Education at 785-532-5687 or 800-622-2KSU (toll-free) or e-mail: academic-services@dce.ksu.edu.

CONTACT

Division of Continuing Education
Kansas State University
13 College Court Building
Manhattan, Kansas 66506-6002
Telephone: 785-532-5566
        800-432-8222 (toll-free)
Fax: 785-532-5637
E-mail: info@dce.ksu.edu
Web site: http://www.dce.ksu.edu

Keiser College

Online Education Program

Fort Lauderdale, Florida

Keiser College was founded in 1977 with a mission to provide students with high-quality, hands-on education in a caring and professional environment. The College is accredited by the Commission on Colleges of the Southern Association of Colleges and Schools and offers associate degrees in the high-demand business, computer, and health-care fields. Keiser College degrees combine practical technical skills and general academics to provide students with a marketable degree upon graduation.

DISTANCE LEARNING PROGRAM

Students enrolled in Keiser College's distance learning program have the convenience of taking courses online from a regionally accredited college. Students can complete associate degree programs online from home or the office at times that fit their schedules. Keiser College online students benefit from small, interactive classes.

DELIVERY MEDIA

Keiser College faculty and staff members use modern technology to create a stimulating learning environment. Keiser's virtual classrooms are comfortable. Courses are easily accessible by logging onto the Internet. Course information, lectures, assignments, and tests are all online. Students and instructors interact in asynchronous discussions, in live chat rooms, and by e-mail. Students can share documents, review grades, and visit external Web sites. The online courses use the eCollege.com delivery system.

PROGRAMS OF STUDY

Keiser College offers general academic courses and full associate degree programs online. Three-credit, general academic courses in English, communication, science, math, and social and behavioral sciences are available. Keiser offers 60-credit, Associate of Arts degrees in the Business Program, with majors in business administration, paralegal studies, and e-commerce. Each online course lasts three weeks, and four courses can be taken per semester, year round. Keiser's online campus provides a complete list of courses that are offered for each four-week module. Keiser College plans to add additional courses and programs throughout the year. Continuing education courses are also planned.

SPECIAL PROGRAMS

Online students are enrolled in a free orientation class that provides simple instructions for making the most of the online learning environment. The Help Desk is available to online students via a toll-free number, 24 hours per day, seven days per week. Keiser College explores ongoing community and business partnerships that provide additional learning opportunities for students enrolled online or on campus. Keiser students benefit from affiliations with organizations that offer additional educational resources, such as a statewide network of library consortia. Online students also have access to LIRN, a comprehensive, online library database.

STUDENT SERVICES

Online students have access to all of Keiser College's resources, including the bookstore and on-campus libraries. Keiser College provides an extensive placement program to current students and graduates that assists them in finding jobs in their chosen fields. Student resumes are forwarded to employers or can be posted on a secure area of the College's Web site. Students may also find internship opportunities through the Placement Office. The online campus includes application and registration procedures, financial aid information, tuition and fee information, course schedules and descriptions, faculty information, and a chat room. Online students can access academic advising by phone or e-mail.

CREDIT OPTIONS

Students may transfer credits taken at other accredited institutions if the course work is comparable, the faculty members have the appropriate degrees, and there is evidence of satisfactory scholarship. The Dean of Academics evaluates transcripts and accepts credits on a course-by-course basis.

FACULTY

Online faculty members satisfy the criteria set by the Southern Association of Colleges and Schools (SACS), a regional accreditation agency. Most faculty members are full-time Keiser College instructors. Three of the College's instructors have doctoral degrees; the rest have master's degrees in their fields.

ADMISSION

Entrance requirements for admission to Keiser College include a high school degree or GED as well as an entrance examination or SAT I or ACT scores (a minimum score of 800 on the SAT I or 17 on the ACT).

TUITION AND FEES

For 1999–2000, tuition for the Keiser College distance learning credit courses was $333 per credit hour.

FINANCIAL AID

Keiser College is approved for federal government grant and loan programs. When students are admitted, a financial aid adviser confers with them to determine eligibility and the appropriate financial aid award. Financial aid is available based on federal guidelines to those who qualify.

APPLYING

Students can submit applications on line when visiting Keiser College's online campus or can contact the admissions department at the telephone number listed below. General information about Keiser College's online education programs is available via e-mail (admissions@keisercollege.cc.fl.us).

CONTACT
Online Education Admissions Counselor
Admissions Department
Keiser College
1500 Northwest 49th Street
Fort Lauderdale, Florida 33309
Telephone: 800-749-4456 (toll-free)
Fax: 954-351-4043
E-mail: admissions@keisercollege.cc.fl.us
Web site: http://www.keisercollege.org

Kentucky Commonwealth Virtual University

Frankfort, Kentucky

The Kentucky Commonwealth Virtual University (KCVU) is a program of the Kentucky Council on Postsecondary Education. Created by the Kentucky General Assembly in 1997, the virtual University is part of sweeping higher education reforms designed to raise education achievement. KCVU strategically coordinates the anywhere, any time delivery of online courses, degrees, and certificates in a learner-friendly system.

Kentucky's virtual University is in partnership with the state's four-year and two-year public and independent colleges and universities. For the fall 2000 term, the following Kentucky colleges and universities offer courses and/or programs through KCVU: Eastern Kentucky University, Kentucky State University, Lexington Community College, Morehead State University, Murray State University, Northern Kentucky University, University of Kentucky, University of Louisville, and Western Kentucky University. In addition, the colleges within the Kentucky Community and Technical College System participating include: Central Kentucky Technical College, Elizabethtown Community College, Henderson Community College, Hopkinsville Community College, Jefferson Community College, Lees/Hazard Community College, Madisonville Community College, Maysville Community College, Owensboro Community College, Paducah Community College, and Prestonsburg Community College.

DISTANCE LEARNING PROGRAM

KCVU is a student-centered, technology-based system for the delivery of postsecondary education. Created by the Kentucky General Assembly as part of Governor Paul Patton's historic higher education reforms, KCVU addresses the needs of Kentuckians who want to learn longer but, due to barriers such as time and distance, are unable to access traditional, on-campus education. KCVU serves as a clearinghouse for quality distance learning opportunities offered by Kentucky postsecondary education institutions and provides competency based credentialing and a single point of access to student, library, and academic support services.

Given the charge to increase access to and attainment of postsecondary education opportunities, KCVU primarily targets place- and time-bound students, employers, and employees in business, government, and industry, and P-12 students, teachers, and administrators. However, the nature of electronic delivery systems is such that potential users/clients are essentially unlimited and include traditional residential students and students in other states and countries. All are welcome.

All KCVU courses and programs are offered by existing, fully-accredited institutions that will confer the diploma, certificate, or degree. All courses are transferable and taught by Kentucky faculty members.

KCVU has experienced tremendous growth since its inaugural fall 1999 semester, when it offered 30 courses in nine pilot programs and registered 235 students. By the spring 2000 term, registration increased more than 700 percent with more than 150 courses offered in a wide range of program areas.

A survey of students revealed high satisfaction levels of online learning through the virtual university. Students also reported high levels of student-faculty member interaction and student-to-student interaction.

In addition to its role to enhance and encourage lifelong learning for all Kentuckians, KCVU is also an important economic development driver to provide knowledge workers for Kentucky business and industry, and to provide upward mobility opportunities for citizens.

DELIVERY MEDIA

Courses and programs offered through KCVU are delivered through various technologies, but most rely on Web-based, asynchronous video-to-desktop instruction platforms through a high-speed ATM network, the Kentucky Information Highway (KIH) supported in substantial part by the KCVU.

PROGRAMS OF STUDY

KCVU is rapidly gaining popularity among students looking for convenience, value, and quality in their higher education pursuits. To meet the demand for online learning, KCVU is adding several new programs during the 2000–01 academic calendar year. Currently, students can enroll in these certificate or degree programs: Associate in Applied Science (Network and Information System Technology (NIST)), Associate in Arts (Business Transfer Framework), Associate in Arts (Going the Distance: The Next Frontier), Bachelor of Independent Studies, Bachelor of Science in Nursing, Certificate (Office Systems Technology), Library Science, Master of Science (Communication Disorders), and Teacher

Certificate (Special Education: Moderate and Severe Disabilities).

In addition to these programs, KCVU offers more than 150 courses required for and which may be applied to degree programs in a wide variety of disciplines. Subject areas range from general education core courses to specialized science and humanities courses, in addition to online courses leading to a master's of business administration.

STUDENT SERVICES

The KCVU offers a wide range of one-stop services to students, faculty members, and the public. Through the Call Center and Web page, KCVU provides a course catalog and schedule, general advising and referral of students, expedited admission and online registration, an online bookstore, and technical assistance. Also, KCVU provides local testing and assessment, course material delivery to home or workplace, and online library services on a 24/7 basis.

The Kentucky Commonwealth Virtual Library (KCVL) is a fundamental and vital component of KCVU. While associated with KCVU, the virtual library serves all the citizens of Kentucky, whether or not they are KCVU students and faculty members. KCVL services include access to a wide range of electronic databases through a single gateway, inter-library document delivery service, Internet/fax/e-mail transmission of journal articles, a single point of service for technical and reference assistance, and an information literacy tutorial program.

CREDIT OPTIONS

All KCVU courses are fully transferable and may be applied to the student's program degree or skill certification at any of the partnering institutions and, because all courses for academic credit are offered by accredited institutions, should be transferable to other institutions.

FACULTY

Faculty members of the partnering institutions provide instruction for all KCVU courses. KCVU supports faculty development through continuous improvement programs and delivery software and course publishing training.

ADMISSION

All students can apply for admission to an institution through KCVU, but admissions decisions ultimately are made by the respective institutions. KCVU facilitates the process.

TUITION AND FEES

The 1999–2000 tuition for public community colleges was $46 per credit hour for Kentucky residents. The public university rate for residents ranged from $85 to $124 per credit. Nonresident tuition is approximately three times the resident rate. The tuition at independent institutions in Kentucky is approximately 2 to 3 times that of the public institution resident rates.

FINANCIAL AID

Financial aid for KCVU students is governed by the rules of the institutions offering the course or courses. The KCVU Call Center staff assists in this process.

APPLYING

Students may apply for admission through the KCVU with the final admissions decisions made by the institutions providing the courses. Students and prospective students may call the KCVU Call Center toll-free at 877-740-4357 to register for courses by phone or for assistance if needed in the online registration process. Students may also register for classes online at www.kcvu.org.

CONTACT

For more information regarding KCVU and KCVL courses, programs, and services, students should contact:
Kentucky Commonwealth Virtual University
1024 Capital Center Drive, Suite 320
Frankfort, Kentucky 40601
Phone: 877-740-4357 (toll-free) (KCVU Call Center)
Fax: 502-573-0222
E-mail: KCVU@mail.state.ky.us
Web site: www.kcvu.org

Kettering University

Graduate Studies Department

Flint, Michigan

In 1919, the Industrial Fellowship League of Flint sponsored a night school for employees of Flint-area industries. General Motors Corporation agreed to underwrite the school in 1926, and General Motors Institute was born. In 1982, GMI became independent of General Motors when the private corporation "GMI Engineering & Management Institute" was established. In January 1998, GMI changed its name to Kettering University. Kettering continues to maintain a close affiliation with industry, as it has throughout its history.

In the fall of 1982, Kettering began a video-based, distance learning graduate program leading to a Master of Science in Manufacturing Management degree. In 1990, the Master of Science in Engineering degree was initiated.

Kettering's mission is to serve society by preparing leaders to meet the technical and managerial needs of business and industry in both the public and private sectors. World renowned as America's Co-op College, Kettering focuses on practice rather than theory. Continuing the University's long and continuous association with industry and the working student, the Master of Science degrees have a strong orientation toward manufacturing. Kettering is accredited by the Commission on Institutions of Higher Education of the North Central Association of Colleges and Schools.

DISTANCE LEARNING PROGRAM

Offering flexibility and convenience, these programs were developed to fit the needs of working professionals. The educational process consists of the on-campus presentation, off-campus communication of the courses via videotape, telephone contact, and evaluation. The video-based program is offered at host companies where the number of prospective students is sufficient. The video-based distance learning program serves approximately 800 students at host companies throughout the United States, Canada, and Mexico. The program, however, is not a correspondence course. It is a rigorous, bona fide graduate program.

DELIVERY MEDIA

Kettering's distance learning program is video-based and tapes are delivered to established industrial learning centers throughout the United States. Industrial partners at the centers provide video equipment for classes. Students at the centers have telephone, facsimile, and e-mail access to the professors. A regular schedule of telephone communication is established in the first session of each course. For some courses students may need access to a personal computer for homework.

PROGRAMS OF STUDY

Kettering offers a Master of Science in Manufacturing Management (M.S.M.M.) degree requiring 54 credit hours, a Master of Science in Operations Management (M.S.O.M.) degree requiring 48 credit hours, and a Master of Science in Engineering (M.S.Eng.) degree that requires 45 credit hours. Students in the engineering program can specialize in mechanical design, manufacturing systems engineering, or automotive systems.

The University designed the Master of Science programs to be terminal professional degrees for engineers and managers. The programs are particularly attractive to working professionals who want to extend and broaden their related skills. Although designed as terminal degrees, they also provide preparation for study at the doctoral level.

The M.S.M.M. degree is a part-time program designed to be completed in three years. Areas of study include finance and economics, quantitative skills and computer applications, management and administration, and manufacturing engineering. The M.S.O.M. is a new degree program, designed to be completed in two years on a part-time basis. Offered as an interdisciplinary degree program, the M.S.O.M. combines the core areas of business administration with systems and process engineering skills from the engineering disciplines. The M.S.O.M. takes tools and methodologies most often associated with manufacturing and applies them to service industries and non-manufacturing areas of manufacturing businesses. The M.S.Eng. degree can be completed in one year full-time or two years on a part-time basis. There is no thesis required for any of the M.S. programs.

CREDIT OPTIONS

Credits are earned by completing courses; however, students may transfer up to 9 credit hours. Credit may be transferred for grades of B or better upon the recommendation of the candidate's adviser and is granted only for completed graduate study. Credit is not given for experience.

Anyone interested in transfer credit should obtain an application for transfer credit from the Graduate Office.

FACULTY

There are 41 full- and part-time professors teaching in the Graduate Studies program. Ninety-seven percent of the faculty members have doctoral or other terminal academic degrees.

ADMISSION

No one is accepted into the program without a bachelor's degree. A bachelor's degree in engineering is required for the Master of Science in Engineering degree program. Requirements include a minimum 3.0 grade point average in undergraduate work, scores on the GRE, and two supervisor recommendations. The same requirements apply to on-campus and distance learning students.

TUITION AND FEES

In 2000–01, graduate tuition is $1281 per 3-credit course. There is no application fee, but there is a $45 registration fee per course. The same fees apply to out-of-state students.

APPLYING

Kettering accepts applications for fall and winter terms only. The deadline for fall application is July 15 and for winter, November 1.

CONTACT

Betty Bedore
Coordinator, Graduate Publications
Office of Graduate Studies
Kettering University
1700 West Third Avenue
Flint, Michigan 48504-4898
Telephone: 810-762-7494
            888-464-4723 (toll-free)
Fax: 810-762-9935
E-mail: bbedore@kettering.edu
Web site: http://www.gmi.edu/official/acad/grad/

Kirksville College of Osteopathic Medicine

School of Health Management

Kirksville, Missouri

The School of Health Management (SHM) is a division of the Kirksville College of Osteopathic Medicine (KCOM). Founded in 1892, KCOM is a professional and graduate institution that offers the Doctor of Osteopathic Medicine (D.O.), the Master of Public Health (M.P.H.), the Master of Health Administration (M.H.A.), and the Master of Geriatric Health Management (M.G.H.) degrees. Since its beginning a century ago, KCOM has established itself as a leader in osteopathic medical education by providing training and instruction to osteopathic physicians across the country. The College, accredited by the American Osteopathic Association (AOA) and the North Central Association of Colleges and Schools, takes pride in its strong curricula, outstanding faculty, clinical experiences, scientific research, service programs, and regional training programs. The College has 108 full-time faculty members, and the student body consists of more than 500 main campus students. KCOM has developed a school to better prepare leaders in health care for the twenty-first century by offering health management courses and degrees.

DISTANCE LEARNING PROGRAM

The School of Health Management offers the convenience of classroom accessibility 24 hours a day, seven days a week, from virtually anywhere in the world. Online courses are interactive. Through group assignments, case study analyses, and forums (threaded discussions), students collaborate with peers and immediately apply textbook theory to real health management situations. The computer is simply a tool through which to communicate. Courses begin and end on specific dates, and classwork is assigned deadlines; however, students my participate on demand.

Cost-effective courses run for a period of ten weeks but may be completed in less time. The curriculum is designed for students who want to begin or finish a degree, especially busy adults and students whose work or family commitments make it difficult to follow a weekly on-campus academic schedule. SHM is a leader in the use of distance learning applications for master's degrees in public

health, geriatric health, and health administration. The School of Health Management educates and prepares current and future health professionals for management positions in a variety of health-care settings. Its goal is to provide comprehensive and relevant health management instruction through high-quality, innovative, distance education.

DELIVERY MEDIA

Courses are available via the Web and may contain both synchronous and asynchronous modes. Media typically includes multimedia slideshows, other forms of online text, and streaming audio and video to provide students with course materials. These media, combined with document sharing, e-mail, chat rooms, course home pages, and forums (threaded discussions) provide interaction with instructors and between students as needed to facilitate class discussions, group work, case evaluations, simulations, and exercises and to provide feedback. Students are offered all the rewards of classroom learning without ever having to leave their homes or offices. SHM courses employ in-

teractive technology designed for a variety of learning styles, with all courses using an interactive syllabus that describes assignments, discussions, and other information required for a particular course. For specific requirements and course information, students may visit the SHM Web site, listed below.

PROGRAMS OF STUDY

SHM offers the M.P.H., M.H.A., and M.G.H. degrees. The M.P.H. is a 45-credit-hour program designed to prepare graduates who can apply their knowledge, expertise, and experience in specific areas of public health in order to solve public health problems. The degree consists of 27 hours of core curriculum and 18 degree-specific hours.

The M.H.A. is a 54-credit-hour program designed to prepare health-care administrators who are capable of assuming management and leadership positions within a variety of health-care organizations. The degree consists of 27 hours of core curriculum and 27 degree-specific hours.

The M.G.H. is a 45-credit-hour program designed to provide students with the knowledge and skills needed to deal with the needs of older individuals in long-term-care and geriatric settings. The degree consists of 27 hours of core curriculum and 18 degree-specific hours.

Degrees must be completed within seven years, and the program requires students to maintain a 3.0 GPA (on a 4.0 scale) in order to graduate.

STUDENT SERVICES

Full program services are available to SHM students participating in online courses. The Dean of Students, admissions, the Registrar, the Controller, student counseling, financial aid, the library, and other student services may be accessed on line.

CREDIT OPTIONS

SHM accepts transfer credit from accredited institutions. Students can transfer up to three core courses (9 credits) with a grade of B or higher, as long as the courses are appropriate to the chosen program's curriculum.

FACULTY

The faculty consists of professionals who are recognized in their chosen academic fields. It is supplemented with experts in medicine, public health, geriatric management, and hospital administration, who bring their real-world work experiences to the program. Program Directors utilize the distance education model to attract both experienced and new educators to the expanding faculty.

ADMISSION

The program requires a bachelor's degree from a regionally accredited institution; scores from the Graduate Record Examinations (GRE), Graduate Management Admissions Test (GMAT), Medical College Admission Test (MCAT), Dental Admission Test (DAT), or Law School Admission Test (LSAT) (Applicants who possess an advanced and/or terminal degree awarded in the United States from an accredited institution do not need to provide a test score.); a cumulative GPA of 2.5 (on a 4.0 scale); two current letters of recommendation; and an interview, which may be conducted via the Internet, by telephone or other electronic medium, or in person. SHM applicants who are enrolled at the Kirksville College of Osteopathic Medicine have no further admissions requirements besides a bachelor's degree.

TUITION AND FEES

Tuition in SHM for the 2001–02 year is $364 per credit hour. Discounts are available to qualified students. A technology fee of $50 per course per student is also assessed. SHM accepts the following for payment of tuition and fees: U.S. dollars, a student's personal check drawn on a U.S. bank, a money order, an electronic wire transfer (students should contact the Controller's office for procedures at 800-626-5266 Ext. 2022), or a credit card. Tuition fees must accompany the student's registration form two weeks before the start of each quarter. The nonrefundable $50 application fee is due at the time the application is submitted. The application fee does not apply to tuition. A one-time acceptance fee of $100 is due two weeks prior to the start of class for first-time students who plan to enroll in the program but not register for courses. This fee is applied to tuition upon matriculation. Students who are not citizens of the United States are welcomed and encouraged to attend SHM; however, they are not eligible for any U.S. federal financial aid. Therefore, all noncitizen students must pay tuition in full in U.S. dollars by midnight (Eastern Standard/Daylight Time) two weeks prior to the start of each quarter.

FINANCIAL AID

Students must be registered at least half-time to receive financial aid. Half-time is defined as taking 6 credits (two or more courses) each quarter. Students can contact the Financial Assistance Office (telephone: 800-626-5266 Ext. 2529) for further information. Financial aid is available to students who are simultaneously enrolled at KCOM or the Arizona School of Health Sciences (ASHS).

APPLYING

The application deadline for SHM courses is one month prior to the start of each quarter. Completed applications that are submitted before the deadline are given preference, provided all application materials and fees have been received. Students may complete a downloadable application packet from the Web site listed below or request one in writing or call the Admissions Office at the toll-free number listed below.

CONTACT

For more information:
School of Health Management
210A South Osteopathy
Kirksville, Missouri 63501
Telephone: 800-626-5266 Ext. 2820 (toll-free)
E-mail: shminfo@kcom.edu
Web site: http://www.shm.kcom.edu

Send application materials to:
Admissions Office
800 West Jefferson Street
Kirksville, Missouri 63501
Telephone: 800-626-5266 Ext. 2158 (toll-free)
E-mail: shmapp@kcom.edu

Lakehead University

Part-Time Studies and Distance Education

Thunder Bay, Ontario, Canada

Lakehead University is committed to excellence and innovation in undergraduate and graduate teaching, service, research, and other scholarly activity. As part of this commitment, Lakehead is dedicated to a student-centered learning environment by offering a wide range of programs and courses that are designed to meet the needs of its students. Lakehead values its people and the diversity of their ideas, contributions, and achievements. It is dedicated to working with Aboriginal peoples in furthering their educational aspirations. As a global participant, Lakehead University is committed to educating students who are recognized for their leadership, independent critical thinking, and awareness of social and environmental responsibilities.

DISTANCE LEARNING PROGRAM

Through extensive offerings by the Office of Part-Time Studies and Distance Education, the University extends its programming to students regionally, nationally, and internationally. Lakehead offers credit courses for University degrees, diplomas, and certificates with interactive, accessible, and convenient approaches. Through ongoing development, new courses are offered annually.

DELIVERY MEDIA

A variety of modes of delivery are used to enhance distance education courses, including online Web-based instruction, print materials, audioconferencing, videoconferencing, computer conferencing, and simulcast lectures. Lakehead's new Advanced Technology and Academic Centre, a state-of-the-art facility to be completed in 2002, will further enhance advanced technological applications to support "at-a-distance" course delivery.

PROGRAMS OF STUDY

Students may choose from a wide range of programs and courses on-and off-campus. Three programs—the Bachelor of Arts (general program), Bachelor of Science in Nursing for registered nurses, and Certificate in Environmental Assessment—may be completed entirely at a distance.

The Bachelor of Arts program provides latitude in choice of courses within a general framework; courses are designed to acquaint students with a broad range of thought in the liberal arts. Fifteen full courses are required.

The Bachelor of Science in Nursing degree is intended for registered nurses. The program uses multimode delivery methods, including self-directed study, audioconferencing, and computer conferencing, to offer registered nurses the opportunity to obtain a Bachelor of Science in Nursing. Students are encouraged to contact the Office of Admissions and Recruitment for details regarding admission criteria and program requirements.

The objectives of the Certificate Program in Environmental Assessment are to develop an understanding of the basic premises, theories, and practices underlying environmental impact assessment; to create a clear understanding of the Environmental Assessment Act of Ontario and of the federal environmental assessment process; and to develop an understanding of how planning development and resource management decisions are made, particularly in a hinterland context.

Courses pertaining to the following programs are also offered annually: Bachelor of Education (professional development), Master of Education, Joint Doctor of Philosophy in Educational Studies, Master of Forestry, Honours Bachelor of Social Work (one- and four-year programs), and Master of Social Work.

SPECIAL PROGRAMS

Ongoing development of print, online, and online-enhanced courses (i.e., print materials and online tools such as bulletin boards and chat programs) provides for continuing variety in the selection of courses offered. For online courses, a PC with Windows 95/98 or a PowerMac, a connection to the Internet, and either Netscape 4 or above or Internet Explorer 4 or above are required. Online course selection varies. Current courses include Foundations of Curriculum (Education 5210), Educational Administrative Theory (Education 5230), Policy Making in Education (Education 5232), Basic General Science 0261, Introductory Statistics–Quantitative Methods–Kinesiology 3030, Research and the Internet (Library and Information Studies 2051), Introduction to Case Management (Gerontology/Nursing/Women's Studies 3450), Social Psychology (Psychology 2801), Introduction to Psychology (Psychology 1100), Critical Thinking Philosophy (Philosophy 2413), Introduction to Cognitive Psychology (Psychology 2003), Statistical Methods for Behavioural Research (Psychology 2101), and Quantitative Methods for the Health Scientist (Math 0212).

STUDENT SERVICES

To assist students in their studies, Lakehead provides a wide range of student support services, including academic advising, study skills seminars, library services, learning assistance, individual/peer tutoring, career planning, and personal counseling.

CREDIT OPTIONS

When applying for admission with advanced standing, students must provide school records and official transcripts from the institutions attended. For information regarding the transfer of credits, students should call the Office of Admissions and Recruitment at 807-343-8500 (fax: 807-343-8156; e-mail: liaison@lakeheadu.ca).

FACULTY

Lakehead University has 260 faculty members as well as sessional lecturers appointed by academic units. Approximately 30 faculty members and sessional lecturers are appointed annually as instructors of distance education courses.

ADMISSION

Admission to Lakehead University is necessary for registration in distance education courses. Applicants are encouraged to visit Lakehead's Web site for procedures and regulations and contact the Office of Admission and Recruitment regarding specific program requirements.

TUITION AND FEES

The 2000–01 tuition fees for undergraduate degree programs are $782 full-course and $391 half-course for Canadian residents and landed immi-

grants, and $1700 full-course and $850 half-course nonresidents on a student visa. For graduate degree programs, the fees are $1948.80 full-course and $974.40 half-course for Canadian residents and landed immigrants; $3600 full-course and $1800 half-course for nonresidents on a student visa.

FINANCIAL AID

Students are encouraged to contact the Financial Aid Office regarding scholarships, bursaries, and financial assistance programs (telephone: 807-343-8206; e-mail: financial.aid@lakeheadu.ca).

APPLYING

Full descriptions of programs and courses are available on the University's Web site. Application forms for distance education courses may be obtained by contacting the Office of Part-Time Studies and Distance Education or by visiting the Web site.

CONTACT

Lakehead University
Office of Part-Time Studies
    and Distance Education
Regional Centre 0009
955 Oliver Road
Thunder Bay, Ontario P7B 5E1
Canada
Telephone: 807-346-7730
Fax: 807-343-8008
E-mail: parttime@lakeheadu.ca
Web site: http://www.lakeheadu.ca

Lakeland College

Lakeland College Online

Sheboygan, Wisconsin

Lakeland College, an independent four-year liberal arts institution in Sheboygan, Wisconsin, was founded in 1862 to provide higher education opportunities for Wisconsin's new frontiersmen. Lakeland became an early adopter of the distance learning concept when, in 1978, it established its first lifelong learning satellite campus. During the past twenty years, this program has grown to include ten locations throughout Wisconsin. In 1997, continuing its innovation in education, Lakeland became a world leader in online education and one of the few fully accredited colleges and universities nationwide that offer full bachelor's degrees totally online.

Located about 50 miles north of Milwaukee, Lakeland has an enrollment of more than 4,000 students in its on-campus undergraduate and graduate, lifelong learning, international, and electronically delivered online programs. All Lakeland courses and programs are fully accredited by the North Central Association of Colleges and Schools.

DISTANCE LEARNING PROGRAM

Lakeland offers complete bachelor's degrees in five majors. Courses are conducted online from start to finish, including all prerequisites, and are delivered entirely at each student's convenience. The same fully accredited courses and degrees as those offered on-site are available. More than 2,500 students from across the country and overseas register annually.

DELIVERY MEDIA

Through national online educational services provider and leader convene. com, Lakeland College Online uses proprietary, user-friendly software that allows students to participate in an online system orientation and to communicate at their convenience with the College, faculty members, and fellow students. The software is available for Windows 3.1, Windows 95, Windows 98, and Windows NT. Minimum hardware requirements are an IBM or 100 percent–compatible computer with a minimum 386 processor; 8 mb RAM for Windows 3.1 or 12 mb RAM for Windows 95, 98,

or NT; a 30-meg hard drive; and a minimum 9,600-bps modem. Recommended specifications are a Pentium-class computer (100Mhz or higher) with 32 mb RAM for Windows 95, 98, or NT; a 150-meg hard drive; and a 28.8k-bps modem.

PROGRAM OF STUDY

Each online course is 4 credits, and each program of study requires students to complete a minimum of 128 credits. Lakeland accepts many transfer credits from other schools. The business administration major encompasses the coordination, implementation, promotion, supervision, and direction of activities of organizations and individuals. Students who wish to be generalists in business find that this program meets their needs. The accounting program prepares students for positions in business and industry. Graduates who have completed the accounting major and a few additional courses are qualified to sit for the CPA and CMA examinations. The computer science program offers a sound basis for careers in information technology, business applications programming, and sys-

tems analysis. The marketing major explores consumers' needs and desires for products and services and their willingness to pay for them. Students are prepared for a wide variety of tasks in diverse areas. The specialized administration major is available to students who wish to complete a bachelor's degree after having completed an associate degree in certain technical fields.

SPECIAL PROGRAMS

Lakeland is accredited to offer an online bachelor's degree in specialized administration that is available only to students with associate degrees in a technical field.

STUDENT SERVICES

Lakeland College Online students can do all of the following online: apply for admission, register for classes, participate in chat groups, work with a personal admission counselor for academic advising, and access the Lakeland bookstore. Ordering textbooks online is encouraged. Students also have access to career planning and placement services.

CREDIT OPTIONS

Online courses are 4 credits each. Online students may enroll in three courses without being accepted for admission. Students seeking a degree must be accepted for admission. Degree programs have a minimum requirement of 128 credits.

Lakeland accepts credits transferred from most other regionally accredited schools. Credits earned in the online program can be combined with credits earned on campus to complete a degree.

FACULTY

Lakeland College Online courses are taught by both on-campus instructors and adjunct faculty members. Forty-one percent of Lakeland's full-time faculty members have participated in the online program. Of the current faculty members, 67 percent hold terminal academic degrees in their chosen discipline.

ADMISSION

Students must have a high school diploma or its equivalent. They can take three courses before applying for admission. International students must apply for admission before taking classes. Nonnative speakers of English must have a minimum TOEFL score of 500.

TUITION AND FEES

All students pay a $25 application fee. Tuition for all online courses is $725 per 4-credit undergraduate course. This cost includes software. Books and other materials (computer course software or other required resources) are additional.

FINANCIAL AID

Financial aid and/or military benefits are available to any qualifying student who is enrolled part-time (taking at least two courses) or full-time if they have already been accepted to Lakeland.

APPLYING

Applications are available by e-mailing online@lakeland.edu, visiting the College's Web site at http://www.lakeland.edu, or calling toll-free at 888-LAKENET (525-3638). Students are asked to submit their application, nonrefundable application fee, and high school and postsecondary school transcripts. Students are notified of acceptance by mail. System orientation is offered completely online.

CONTACT

Carol Butzen or Katherine Van Sluys
Lakeland College Online
P.O. Box 359
Sheboygan, Wisconsin 53082-0359
Telephone: 888-LAKENET (525-3638, toll-free)
Fax: 920-565-1341
E-mail: online@lakeland.edu
Web site: http://www.lakeland.edu/online

Lesley College

Distance Learning Programs

Cambridge, Massachusetts

Lesley prepares women and men for professional careers in education, human services, management, and the arts. Since 1909, Lesley has been a leader and innovator in educating for professions that put people first. Lesley is accredited by the New England Association of Schools and Colleges.

Lesley offers interdisciplinary and self-designed graduate and undergraduate degree programs in a low or no residency format. Central to Lesley is the conviction that people matter, and that adult students bring knowledge and experience with them that can inform their own study and enrich the Lesley learning community.

The goal of a Lesley education is to empower students with the knowledge, skills, and practical experience they need to succeed as catalysts and leaders in their professions, their own lives, and the world in which they live.

DISTANCE LEARNING PROGRAM

Lesley offers self-designed study options at the graduate and undergraduate level. Students range in age from 24 to over 70 years, and come from all over the world. A pioneer in independent and interdisciplinary study, Lesley has been helping students develop their unique interests into practical, academic degree programs for nearly thirty years. These programs feature brief, intensive residencies in between faculty-guided self-study.

DELIVERY MEDIA

Lesley's nontraditional degree programs combine the best of distance and face-to-face education by providing participation in a learning community, both virtual and actual, and intensive faculty guidance enhanced by technology. During the residency period, students attend workshops, presentations, and small study groups to plan their customized learning contracts. Students then study and work at home, submitting work-in-progress to faculty advisers. Advisers are always available via phone, e-mail, and through personal meeting. There is

no residency requirement for the independent study degree program.

PROGRAMS OF STUDY

Students seeking an undergraduate degree from the Adult Baccalaureate College may combine a wide range of disciplines to shape their own specialization. Sample majors include, but are not limited to, psychology, counseling, human development, writing, women's and gender studies, environmental studies, history, art entrepreneurship, management, holistic health, and expressive therapy. Projects must include research, writing, a substantive biography, and expressive components. The Bachelor of Arts in behavioral science (B.A. B.S.), Bachelor of Arts in liberal studies (B.A.L.S.), and Bachelor of Science (B.S.) may be awarded. Students must complete a total of 128 credits in order to receive a bachelor's degree.

At the Graduate School of Arts and Social Sciences, Lesley's interdisciplinary and individualized programs are designed for those graduate students who want to put their personal stamp on their education. Flexibility of academic specialization is the hallmark

of these programs, and graduate students with unique interests that cross or reach past traditional academic disciplines can craft a personalized study program in consultation with Lesley's renowned faculty. An emphasis on integrating life and professional experiences with academic study informs all of Lesley's graduate programs. Students may earn the Master of Science (M.S.) in ecological teaching and learning, the M.S. in environmental education, the Master of Arts (M.A.) in independent study, the M.A. in interdisciplinary studies, the Master of Education (M.Ed.) in independent study, or the Certificate of Advanced Graduate Study (C.A.G.S.) in independent study.

STUDENT SERVICES

Students in off-campus and independent study programs are given full and complete access to all administrative Student Services functions (Registrar, Bursar, Financial Aid, etc.) In addition, Lesley offers all students access to a variety of library resources including subject databases and other resources via the Internet, instructional materials, and telephone reference services. Lesley negotiates agreements with college and university libraries near national sites for library services to Lesley students. The Career Resource Center provides a wide range of career planning and job services. Students in both graduate and undergraduate programs may communicate with their faculty adviser by phone, mail, e-mail, and in person.

CREDIT OPTIONS

At the undergraduate level, students may transfer up to 96 credits of approved course work. Credits must be from an accredited institution and a letter grade of C (2.0) or better must have been awarded. Undergraduate students may receive a total of 16 credits through the College Level Exam Program (CLEP). The combined total of test credits and transfer credits may not exceed 96 credits. Lesley also recognized the extensive work experience and life skills of its adult students. Accepted degree candidates who document and evaluate past experiences relevant to their course of study may petition to receive a maximum of 48 prior learning assessment credits.

FACULTY

There are 11 full-time faculty members within the interdisciplinary and independent study programs at Lesley College, at both the undergraduate and graduate levels. All possess earned doctorates, and many specialize in adult learning. In addition to full-time faculty, Lesley employs adjunct faculty practitioners who offer real-world experience and specialization in a variety of disciplines. The faculty-student ratio for these programs is less than 7:1, and all students receive personalized attention from a dedicated faculty adviser.

ADMISSION

Admission requirements and procedures vary by program and students are encouraged to identify a potential area of study in advance. Students should visit the Lesley admissions Web site (http://www.lesley.edu/grad_admiss.html) for a detailed description of admissions policies and procedures.

TUITION AND FEES

Undergraduate tuition is $280 per credit for the 2000–01 academic year.

Graduate tuition is $475 per credit for the 2000–01 academic year.

FINANCIAL AID

Financial aid is available to qualified students. To be considered for financial aid, students must complete a Free Application for Federal Student Aid and a Lesley College Financial Aid Request Form. Students should call 800-999-1959 Ext. 8710 for more details, or visit the Lesley financial aid Web site (http://www.lesley.edu/financial.html).

APPLYING

Prospective students may request a bachelor's or master's application from the Office of Graduate and Adult Baccalaureate Admissions by calling 800-999-1959 Ext. 8300, or by downloading an application from the admissions Web site (http://www.lesley.edu/grad_admiss.html).

CONTACT

Adult Baccalaureate College
Olive Silva, Program Advisor
29 Everett Street, Cambridge, MA 02138
Telephone: 800-999-1959 Ext. 8478 (toll-free)
Fax: 617-349-8420
E-mail: IRO@mail.lesley.edu
Web site: http://www.lesley.edu/abc.html
Graduate School of Arts and Social Sciences
Lisa Lombardi, Program Advisor
29 Everett Street, Cambridge, MA 02138
Telephone: 800-999-1959 Ext. 8454 (toll-free)
Fax: 617-349-8124
E-mail: llombard@mail.lesley.edu
Web site: http://www.lesley.edu/gsass.html

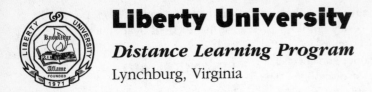

Liberty University

Distance Learning Program

Lynchburg, Virginia

Liberty University (LU) was founded in 1971 as a private, independent, Christian, comprehensive institution. Since then, Liberty has grown to an enrollment of more than 10,000 students through its various undergraduate and graduate divisions, the Liberty Baptist Theological Seminary, the Distance Learning Program, and the Liberty Bible Institute. Liberty University is accredited by the Commission on Colleges of the Southern Association of Colleges and Schools to award associate, bachelor's, master's, and doctoral degrees.

DISTANCE LEARNING PROGRAM

Liberty University offers adult students the opportunity to pursue an accredited college degree at a distance on the associate, bachelor's, master's, and doctoral levels. The University assists students who are pursuing a degree with such services as transcript evaluation, academic advising, and degree planning. Flexible semesters allow course work to begin at the most convenient times for students.

DELIVERY MEDIA

Course lectures are presented on prerecorded VHS videocassettes that students purchase along with the required print materials, such as books, workbooks, and study notes (all class materials are required to complete each class). Testing is monitored by a University-approved proctor. Students in need of class assistance may contact the assigned academic adviser, faculty member, and library services via phone, fax, e-mail, or regular mail.

PROGRAMS OF STUDY

Liberty University's Distance Learning Program offers associate degrees in general studies and religion. Baccalaureate degrees are offered in business (accounting, finance, marketing, and management), multidisciplinary studies, psychology, and religion. Students may pursue a master's degree in professional counseling. A 36-credit-hour traditional program and a 48-credit-hour licensure program are available. Other master's degrees include the Master of Arts in religion, the Master of Divinity, the Master of Business Administration, and the Master of Education (M.Ed.). The M.Ed. programs are approved by the Virginia Department of Education for the licensure of school personnel. The LU School of Education also offers the Doctor of Education (Ed.D.), with an emphasis in educational leadership, through distance learning.

SPECIAL PROGRAMS

Distance learners have access to library services, the campus computer network, e-mail services, academic advising, tutoring, and career placement assistance.

CREDIT OPTIONS

Credit is given for courses completed at an accredited institution, provided the credit is appropriate to the curriculum chosen at Liberty University. Undergraduate students may also earn credit through standardized testing (CLEP, PEP, DANTES, and ICE), advanced placement, portfolio assessment, military training (ACE), and business training.

FACULTY

There are 210 full-time and 55 part-time faculty members at Liberty University. Of the 210 full-time faculty members, 35 work specifically for the Distance Learning Program in either a full-time or part-time capacity. Faculty members who work with the Distance Learning Program hold a master's, doctorate, or other terminal degree in their field of specialty and are specially trained in order to ensure the best-quality education possible for students.

ADMISSION

An application with a $35 nonrefundable fee must be submitted prior to admittance. All official transcripts must be sent to the Office of Admissions to determine acceptance to a degree program and the evaluation of credit.

TUITION AND FEES

For the 2000–01 academic year, tuition for the undergraduate and seminary programs is $115 per semester hour. Military and public service personnel in these programs pay $100 per semester hour. Graduate tuition is $200 per semester hour. Course materials are a separate charge and must be purchased by the student through the University's supplier, MBS Direct (telephone: 800-325-3252, toll-free).

FINANCIAL AID

Liberty offers a full range of state (Virginia Tuition Assistance Grant), federal (Pell Grant), and school-sponsored financial assistance programs for those enrolled as matriculated students. Forms for state and federal aid can be obtained through the University's Web site (address below) or by calling the Office of Admissions. All students who apply for a Federal Stafford Student Loan must submit a Free Application for Federal Student Aid (FAFSA).

APPLYING

Distance Learning students can apply for admission at any time of the year. Correspondence between the student and the University is conducted through the Office of Admissions. The student has 120 days from the enrollment date to complete each class.

CONTACT

Dr. Patricia Thompson, Executive Director for Administrative and Academic Affairs
Distance Learning Program
Liberty University
1971 University Boulevard
Lynchburg, Virginia 24502
Telephone: 800-424-9595 (toll-free)
Fax: 800-628-7977 (toll-free)
E-mail: wcpenn@liberty.edu
Web site: http://www.liberty.edu

Loyola University Chicago

Mundelein College

Chicago, Illinois

Loyola University Chicago is one of the largest of the twenty-eight American Jesuit colleges and universities. Fully accredited by the North Central Association of Colleges and Schools and other relevant accrediting agencies, the University includes the Loyola University Medical Center and four other campuses, three in the Chicago metropolitan area and one in Rome, Italy. Loyola's nine colleges and schools have an enrollment of nearly 14,000 students. Loyola University Chicago emphasizes the Jesuit tradition of developing the intellectual, social, moral, and spiritual aspects of the individual.

DISTANCE LEARNING PROGRAM

Mundelein College and the Department of Mathematical and Computer Sciences are partnering with eCollege.com to provide online, Web-based courses. All courses offered in the Web-based format are the same as courses that are offered on campus and are taught by the regular full-time faculty members. All courses are as interactive and virtual as possible, including threaded discussions, collaborative learning opportunities, video streaming, and faculty member office hours. Students have a complete range of online services, including a bookstore, academic advising, and learning support.

DELIVERY MEDIA

All courses offered are Web based. Communication with faculty members, fellow students, and other academic services is conducted primarily by e-mail. Admissions and registration are Web based. Web-based classes are limited in size in order to promote strong faculty-student interaction. Generally, no more than 25 students are permitted in each course section. All assignments are "handed in" via e-mail.

To participate in the program, students must have a minimum of a Pentium I (or equivalent Macintosh) with modem and access to the Internet. Students should have a basic understanding of how to use e-mail and the Internet.

PROGRAMS OF STUDY

Beginning in fall 1999, the College offers complete certificate programs in computer science—Java Programming and Web Development and Java Programming, Networks, and Telecommunications. The College will soon add another certificate in Java Programming and Database Administration. Students can begin these programs with a minimal understanding of computers and finish with the skills necessary to master the rapid development of computer technologies. Students gain an understanding of Oracle and Microsoft software, Visual Basic, Java, C++, PERL, and Object-Oriented Programming. Students learn Internet programming, client/server applications, data mining, protocols and applications for data and voice communication, and the skills to build interactive Web services as distributed client/server systems.

For more information, students should visit the Web site at http://www.online.luc.edu or send e-mail for more information to online@luc.edu.

CREDIT OPTIONS

All courses are fully accredited and taken for credit. The courses can be transferred to other colleges and universities, or they can be used to complete either the bachelor's degree in computer science or the Bachelor of General and Integrative Studies at Loyola University Chicago. These courses can also be used to provide the prerequisite background to apply for either the master's degrees in computer science or the information systems management at Loyola.

ADMISSION

Applicants for the certificate program must have graduated from high school or have passed the GED. There are no prerequisites or computer competency tests required. Initial course placement is determined from each student's computer background. Students should e-mail their questions about initial course placement to online@luc.edu.

TUITION AND FEES

Tuition for the online courses is currently $1080 per course. Tuition is subject to change. Other general expenses include costs for books and software and vary depending on the course.

APPLYING

Students can apply on line at http://www.luc.edu/schools/mundelein/onlineapp.html. To apply, students need only to complete an application and include a one-time application fee of $25. No transcripts are required to apply for the certificate programs.

Lynn University

Institute for Distance Learning (IDL)

Boca Raton, Florida

Founded in 1962 and located in Boca Raton, Florida, Lynn University is a private coeducational institution whose primary purposes are education; the preservation, discovery, dissemination and creative application of knowledge; and the preparation of its graduates with the academic foundation for life-long learning. Service, scholarly activity that includes research, and ongoing professional development allow the faculty, in conjunction with the entire University community, to fulfill its purposes: facilitating student-centered learning and fostering the intellectual life of the University.

DISTANCE LEARNING PROGRAM

Lynn University continues to deliver its academic programs at both the undergraduate and graduate levels to students who cannot participate in a traditional classroom-based environment at the main campus. The aim of the University is to be a global institution for the twenty-first century, where learners have access to higher learning opportunities independent of time schedules and geographical limitations.

The Institute for Distance Learning (IDL) is designed to facilitate educational opportunities for independent self-directed learners using technology and flexible delivery methods. The design and implementation of the programs recognizes and values prior skills and knowledge that mature global learners bring to the educational experience. In fulfilling its mission, the Institute delivers both credit and noncredit course work at the undergraduate and graduate levels to meet the needs of learners seeking academic work and lifelong learning experiences.

DELIVERY MEDIA

IDL delivers interactive distance learning courses using Internet technology that allows interactions between faculty members and students, students and other students, and students and resources (e.g., books, journals, electronic library services, Internet resources). In addition, videoconferencing facilities are in place, which are used to deliver interactive courses from the main campus to the campus in Old Forge, New York; the campus in Dublin, Ireland; and other sites.

PROGRAMS OF STUDY

The Southern Association of Colleges and Schools (SACS) has approved Lynn University to offer complete distance learning degree programs via the Web. The Bachelor of Professional Studies (B.P.S.) degree, designed for adult learners seeking college credit for prior learning, is available entirely via course work over the Internet. Majors available are business, psychology, and hospitality administration. In addition, numerous undergraduate, graduate, and doctoral courses, as well as noncredit courses, are available via the Web. The course listing is available at http://www.lynn.edu/online.

SPECIAL PROGRAMS

IDL also facilitates a variety of noncredit accelerated courses that can be tailored to address corporate needs. Customized courses on selected topics in business and technology can be delivered via video conferencing or over the Web.

CREDIT OPTIONS

Most online courses are 3 credits each. Courses with labs are 4 credits. Courses offered with less than 3 credits are identified in the catalog. Lynn University accepts transfer credits from most other regionally accredited schools. Credits earned in the online program can be combined with credits earned on campus to complete a degree.

FACULTY

The faculty and staff members of IDL are highly qualified and committed to providing quality instruction and learning opportunities for self-directed learners. Along with excellent academic credentials, the faculty members are primarily practitioners in their fields of expertise, thus providing the theoretical context for the practical applications of the subject matter.

ADMISSION

Admission to the Bachelor of Professional Studies degree program requires five years of post–high school professional work experience. This program is intended for adult learners who have significant skills and knowledge that can be translated into college-level credits. The process involves the participation in a 1-credit portfolio seminar where the development of a portfolio documenting the prior learning is explained and initiated. Students may earn a minimum of 3 credits, and up to 30 credits, through this process.

Individuals participating in any course work via distance learning (for college credit or certificate programs) must demonstrate proficiency in the use of Office 95 (minimum), e-mail composition and file attachments, and downloading and uploading files.

TUITION AND FEES

The application fee for all new students is a one-time nonrefundable $50 fee. The tuition fees and registration fees follow the pricing established for the respective colleges and non-credit programs. For the 2000–01 academic year, the fees are as follows: undergraduate, $220 per credit hour (adult evening division); graduate, $425 per credit hour; doctoral, $535 per credit hour; non-credit, tuition varies with the individual courses. Please check the Web site for further

details. There is a registration fee of $30 at the beginning of each term enrolled; lab fees of $30 to $60, depending on the specific course; and a portfolio administration fee of $75 per credit placed on transcript. More information and specific details regarding fees are available in the catalog.

FINANCIAL AID

Financial Aid is available to any qualified Lynn student. For specific information, students should contact the financial aid office at 561-237-7941.

APPLYING

Students wishing to enroll in undergraduate courses, noncredit courses, or in the Bachelor of Professional Studies degree program apply through the Center for Professional and Continuing Education (CPCE).

The College of Graduate Studies administers graduate and doctoral courses.

Applications may be obtained on the University Web page at http://www.lynn.edu/online or by phone, fax, or e-mail.

CONTACT

Lynn University
The Institute for Distance Learning
3601 North Military Trail
Boca Raton, Florida 33431
Telephone: 561-237-7800
Fax: 561-237-7965
Web site: http://www.lynn.edu

Lynn University
College of Graduate Studies
Telephone: 561-237-7846
Fax: 561-237-7965
Web site: http://www.lynn.edu

Marist College

School of Management

Poughkeepsie, New York

Marist College is an independent, coeducational liberal arts and sciences institution located in Poughkeepsie, New York. Marist began offering graduate programs in 1972 and currently serves some 750 graduate students from all over the world. Marist has been listed among the finest colleges and universities in America by both the Barron's Guide *and* U.S. News & World Report.

Marist is registered by the New York State Education Department, Office of Higher Education and the Professions, and is accredited by the Middle States Association of Colleges and Schools.

DISTANCE LEARNING PROGRAM

Marist College was among the nation's frontrunners in distance learning, offering working adults the unique opportunity to complete challenging graduate programs in business administration or public administration entirely on the Web. Professionals from as far away as Europe, India, and China currently count themselves as members of the Marist College family.

Marist's M.B.A. and M.P.A. programs provide an unsurpassed mix of quality, convenience, and flexibility. Students for whom regularly scheduled on-site classes are difficult may pursue equally challenging graduate course work at their convenience from anywhere in the world.

DELIVERY MEDIA

Cutting-edge instructional technology enables students to interact extensively with their instructors and classmates. Communication is ongoing via e-mail, bulletin boards, group conference rooms, or private chat rooms.

A personal computer with a Pentium 166 processor, 32 megabytes of RAM, a 28.8 modem (56K recommended), and access to the World Wide Web

via MS Explorer, Netscape 4.0, or America Online browser version 4.0 are required for the program. In addition, to insure compatibility in reading attached files and sharing work with other classmates, Microsoft Office 97 is essential throughout the program.

PROGRAMS OF STUDY

Marist's online graduate programs in business administration and public administration are available to students worldwide. Candidates for either program must meet the admissions criteria required by that program and must have completed a baccalaureate degree from an accredited institution. International applicants must submit official TOEFL and TWE scores for admission.

Marist's M.B.A. is designed to cultivate managers who are capable of effective decision-making in today's complex business environment. Emphasis is placed on the management process and the behavioral influences that significantly affect the success of modern organizations. Graduates of the program possess the strategic perspective necessary to identify opportunities and risks in a rapidly changing economic environment. Course requirements consist of a combination of foundation, core, and elective courses designed to de-

velop the professional analytical, communication, and leadership skills needed to keep pace with the competitive demands of a global economy.

Marist's M.P.A. is designed to provide students with the knowledge and skills necessary for effective public sector and not-for-profit program management. The M.P.A. program consists of ten core courses and three sub-field courses in which students do reading, research, and writing. Sub-fields include criminal justice administration, health services administration, human services administration, and nonprofit agency administration.

The curriculum stresses the ethical, legal, and social context of administration. Graduates are proficient in understanding and developing positive organizational behavior and effectively utilizing a full range of management and administrative techniques to solve problems, address issues, and lead important programs.

CREDIT OPTIONS

The M.B.A. program requires a minimum of 30 credit hours, with a maximum of 51 credit hours, for the degree. Up to 21 credits of foundation courses may be waived, based on prior graduate or undergraduate study. Transfer credits are not applicable to foundation course work. Instead, particular foundation requirements are waived on the basis of prior study.

Transfer of credits into the M.B.A. or M.P.A. program requires the prior approval of the program director. Up to 6 graduate credits may be transferred from a regionally accredited graduate program to satisfy graduate core and/or elective requirements. Criteria considered in awarding transfer credit include the grade received (must be B or higher), the level of the course in the program at which it was taken, and the course content. Transfer credit is awarded for core courses only if the course is substantially equivalent to the Marist course requirement.

FACULTY

The Marist College faculty is comprised of highly experienced credentialed educators, many of whom are skilled professionals with practical hands-on experience in corporate, government, not-for-profit, and community settings. Faculty members regularly take part in research, publishing, and consulting and are frequently called upon by various organizations and institutions for their expertise in their given academic areas.

ADMISSION

The M.B.A. and M.P.A. programs are concerned with the interest, aptitude, and capacity of a prospective student as indicated in the applicant's previous academic record, achievement on the Graduate Management Admission Test (GMAT) or Graduate Records Examination (GRE), and past professional achievement and growth. Each applicant's credentials are evaluated on an individual basis. Specific requirements for admission and completion vary by program. At a minimum, all applicants must submit the graduate application, application fee, official transcripts, and current resume. A personal statement is required of M.P.A. candidates. The GMAT/GRE is waived for applicants who already hold a master's degree.

TUITION AND FEES

Tuition for the 2000–01 academic year is $455 per credit, plus a $30 registration fee per semester and a one-time matriculation fee of $30. A $30 nonrefundable application fee is required at application.

FINANCIAL AID

Marist College offers merit-based and need-based financial programs to assist students in meeting the cost of their graduate education. To be eligible, a student must be matriculated in a graduate program and maintain satisfactory academic progress each semester. Awards are made without reference to racial or ethnic origin, sex, age, religion, color, marital status, or disability. The process of applying for aid should begin in early summer for fall admittance and mid-fall for spring admittance.

APPLYING

Student wishing to pursue their M.B.A. or M.P.A. on line should follow the same procedures as campus-based graduate students. All admissions documents should be sent directly to the Office of Graduate Admissions.

CONTACT

Graduate Admissions
School of Graduate and Continuing Education
Marist College
North Road
Poughkeepsie, New York 12601
Telephone: 914-575-3800
     888-877-7900 (toll-free)
Fax: 914-575-3166
E-mail: graduate@marist.edu
Web site: http://www.Marist.edu/graduate

Marylhurst University

Distance Learning Program

Marylhurst, Oregon

The oldest Catholic liberal arts university in Oregon, Marylhurst was established in 1893 by the Sisters of the Holy Names of Jesus and Mary. Marylhurst's founders believed in offering educational choices to people who had few — and that belief forms the cornerstone of its mission today. Marylhurst University is a recognized center of academic excellence offering undergraduate degrees in communication studies, organizational communication, business and management, human studies, humanities, interdisciplinary studies, science, social sciences, religious studies and philosophy, art, interior design, and music. Marylhurst's graduate programs include Master of Business Administration, Master of Arts in art therapy, and Master of Art in interdisciplinary studies. Fully accredited by the Northwest Association of Schools and Colleges (NASC), Marylhurst has been a leader in competency-based education, prior learning assessment, and the delivery of a classic liberal arts education across the Internet.

DISTANCE LEARNING PROGRAM

The Web-based distance learning program offers an opportunity to engage in a collaborative, highly interactive learning experience with flexibility and convenience. Undergraduate and graduate courses are offered, and students may complete general education requirements through online courses. Specific programs, such as the B.A./B.S. degree completion program and the M.B.A. program, are available entirely online.

DELIVERY MEDIA

Students must have access to the Internet and at least a moderate level of comfort working on the World Wide Web to participate in online courses. Marylhurst's online program is designed to allow students without personal computers to use public computing stations such as those found in libraries. The Web-based delivery system incorporates private mail, conferencing, course materials, and other features. Specific courses may require specific software. Textbooks and other tradi-

tional study materials are routinely used with online courses.

PROGRAMS OF STUDY

In addition to offering traditional liberal arts courses that allow students to complete their general education requirements, Marylhurst University offers several programs entirely online.

The B.A./B.S. degree completion program is a competency-based, integrated program that allows students to complete a B.A. in organizational communication or a B.S. in management. Students who have completed at least 90 credits or have an associate degree are eligible for this selective program. The integrated curriculum eliminates redundancy with a comprehensive core curriculum that is common to both degrees. Full-time students take two learning units of 9 credits each per term; the curriculum design supports successful completion of a larger number of credits than usual. By the end of the program, students complete both an academic and a professional portfolio.

SPECIAL PROGRAMS

Through Marylhurst's Prior Learning Assessment (PLA) Program, students' documented life experiences—such as employment, homemaking, company-sponsored or military training, community service and volunteer activities, independent research, and travel study—can be applied toward an undergraduate degree program and are available on line.

Internships with public and private agencies and businesses are required for most undergraduate degrees. The internship orientation and mentoring process may take place on line.

Marylhurst University offers a cooperative program with San Francisco Theological Seminary (SFTS) that offers graduate courses that lead to a doctoral degree from SFTS. Most courses are taught at Marylhurst, with a single summer residency requirement at SFTS.

STUDENT SERVICES

Students who take online courses may access all necessary materials and services available to on-campus students. Remote access to library services, online registration, academic advising, financial aid information, and other services are available through either the general Web site, password-protected sites, e-mail, or telephone.

CREDIT OPTIONS

Students may transfer undergraduate credits from other accredited institutions, subject to approval by the Marylhurst University Credit Evaluator. Credits earned through the College-Level Examination Program (CLEP) or DANTES may also be applied toward a bachelor's degree. Students may earn up to 45 undergraduate credits through the Prior Learning Assessment Program, which may be applied toward a bachelor's degree.

FACULTY

Marylhurst University faculty members are practitioner faculty members who apply their studies in the real world. Eighty-five percent of undergraduate faculty members and 95 percent of graduate faculty members hold doctoral degrees. The remainder hold master's degrees or terminal degrees in their fields.

ADMISSION

Applicants to the University must have a high school degree or its equivalent. The B.A./B.S. degree completion program and all graduate programs are selective admissions programs with specific requirements.

TUITION AND FEES

Tuition for online courses is the same as for on-campus courses: $264 per credit for undergraduate courses and $311 per credit for graduate courses.

FINANCIAL AID

All students are eligible for the standard range of federal aid programs, including Federal Pell Grants and the Federal Work-Study Program. Additional opportunities for aid come from state-sponsored programs and University and private scholarships. In 1999–2000, approximately $4.9 million was awarded to Marylhurst students from these combined sources. Sixty-five percent of Marylhurst students receive financial aid of some kind.

APPLYING

To enroll in classes, online students must complete the admission process. Formal application for undergraduate admission requires high school and college transcripts and a $20 application fee. Graduate school admission requires additional supporting materials, including test scores and a $40 application fee.

CONTACT

Mark Jenkins, Director, Distance Learning and Instructional Technology
Elizabeth Bileu, Associate Faculty, Distance Learning and Instructional Technology
David Plotkin, Web-based Learning and Instructional Technology
Bernadette Howlett, Program Coordinator
Marylhurst University
17600 Pacific Highway (Highway 43)
P.O. Box 261
Marylhurst, Oregon 97036
Telephone: (503) 699-6246
        (800) 634-9982 Ext. 6319 (toll-free)
Fax: (503) 636-9526
E-mail: mjenkins@marylhurst.edu
        bhowlett@marylhurst.edu
Website: http//online.marylhurst.edu

Massachusetts Institute of Technology

Center for Advanced Educational Services (CAES)

Cambridge, Massachusetts

The Massachusetts Institute of Technology (MIT) is one of the world's outstanding universities. MIT is independent, coeducational, and privately endowed. It is organized into five schools that contain twenty-one academic departments, as well as many interdepartmental programs, laboratories, and centers whose work extends beyond traditional departmental boundaries.

The Institute was founded in 1865 by William Barton Rogers. Rogers' philosophy envisioned a new kind of institution relevant to the times and the nation's needs, where students would be educated in the application as well as the acquisition of knowledge. A distinguished natural scientist, Rogers stressed the importance of basic research and believed that professional competence was best fostered by the coupling of teaching and research and attention to real-world problems.

MIT's programs in engineering, the sciences, economics, management, linguistics, architecture, and other areas are internationally recognized, and leaders in industry and government routinely draw on the expertise of MIT faculty members.

DISTANCE LEARNING PROGRAM

The Center for Advanced Educational Services (CAES) offers various undergraduate and graduate educational programs via multimodal distance learning. These programs fall into three categories. The first is the Distributed Classroom. In this model, interactive telecommunications technologies extend an on-campus classroom-based credit course from one location to learners at one or more remote locations. These programs are most often delivered in a synchronous manner. The second category is Strategic Partner Relationships. This model involves the redistribution of MIT content through CAES partnerships with leading universities and organizations around the world.

DELIVERY MEDIA

Off-campus learners use a combination of communication technologies for course delivery, including videoconferencing, satellite broadcast, the Internet, videotapes, e-mail, and fax machines. The design of MIT's distance learning programs recognizes the benefits of student-professor and student-student interaction. Depending upon the specific programs, students may need access to an e-mail account, the Internet, a videotape player, a satellite downlink, and/or a videoconferencing facility. At a minimum, the Web-based portion of the programs requires a Pentium or Power Macintosh computer with a Web browser.

PROGRAMS OF STUDY

Programs that exist through the Center for Advanced Educational Services range from entirely asynchronous independent learning to entirely synchronous group-based learning. At present, there is no degree-granting program offered through CAES; however, some of the courses can be taken for MIT credit that may later be applied toward a degree-granting program. Through Strategic Partner Relationships, participants can take MIT courses that earn credit at their home institutions. Several programs exist within CAES for delivery of distance learning courses, including the Advanced Study Program (ASP), the primary provider for Distributed Classroom learning, and NTU/PBS The Business and Technology Network, the primary provider of Strategic Partner Relationships.

The Advanced Study Program provides lifelong learning opportunities for working professionals to be a part of the MIT experience through a unique partnership with academia. ASP courses delivered via distance learning technologies allow learners to participate at their location instead of coming to the MIT campus. Participants in the off-campus courses benefit through interaction with other learners in different locations by sharing concepts and ideas through real-time videoconferencing, online study groups, and direct e-mail contact with faculty members. Presentation of program content is through real-time videoconferencing or videostreaming over the World Wide Web and is supplemented by print, videotape, and Internet activity.

In addition to programs offered through the Center for Advanced Educational Services, CAES distributes a number of professional development programs through NTU/PBS The Business and Technology Network. More information on these programs can be found at http://www-caes.mit.edu/Programs/distance.html.

CREDIT OPTIONS

Both credit and noncredit courses are offered through CAES. Distance learners participating in the Advanced

Study Program are eligible to receive MIT credit for course work that is successfully completed. In addition, CAES is currently developing a number of distance learning programs that utilize advanced technologies to offer for-credit courses at a distance.

FACULTY

The Center for Advanced Educational Services draws from all faculty members across the Institute. The MIT faculty numbers approximately 1,100, with a total teaching staff of more than 2,000. Most faculty members at MIT teach both graduate and undergraduate students.

ADMISSION

Applicants seeking for-credit courses are admitted based on their official transcripts from the colleges from which they earned their degrees and a record of other graduate work they have completed. A letter of nomination, written by a principal executive in the applicant's organization, confirming approval of their candidacy and the organization's willingness to provide the appropriate support must be included. In addition, a summary of professional experience and a statement indicating the applicant's immediate and ultimate objectives in taking the course are required.

Applicants seeking noncredit courses are accepted based upon their academic training and professional experience. In order to maintain the highest standards, CAES reserves the right to select those applicants whose qualifications and experiences suggest that they will receive the most benefit from a given program.

TUITION AND FEES

Tuition is based on the type of academic credit provided. For-credit courses, delivered live through the Advanced Study Program, carry full MIT tuition for qualified candidates. Academic credit from the Strategic Partner Relationships, with other universities using MIT professors, is based on tuition arrangements established by those institutions.

FINANCIAL AID

There is no financial aid provided for any of the distance learning programs offered through the Center for Advanced Educational Services.

APPLYING

Individuals interested in applying to any of the CAES distance learning programs need to submit an application, along with the required supporting documents.

CONTACT

Diane Molino-Fox
Marketing Assistant
Room 9-335
Center for Advanced Educational Services
Massachusetts Institute of Technology
77 Massachusetts Avenue
Cambridge, Massachusetts 02139-9906
Telephone: 617-253-6128
Fax: 617-258-8831
E-mail: caes-courses@mit.edu
Web site: http://www-caes.mit.edu

Mercer University

Office of Distance Learning
Macon, Georgia

Beginning as a small liberal arts college founded in 1883 by Georgia Baptist leader Jesse Mercer, Mercer University is now the only independent university of its size in the U.S. that combines programs in eight diversified fields of study—liberal arts, pharmacy, medicine, engineering, law, theology, business and economics, and education. The Mercer University system includes six academic campuses as well as the Mercer University Press and the Mercer Engineering Research Center (MERC). U.S. News and World Report has ranked Mercer among the top colleges and universities in the South for ten consecutive years. More than 50,000 alumni live in fifty states and in over seventy countries.

DISTANCE LEARNING PROGRAM

Mercer University's Office of Distance Learning provides corporate training and continuing professional education through eMercer.com. The innovative course development process of eMercer.com involves a senior-level management team of Mercer University faculty members, distinguished faculty members from other leading universities, educational consultants, instructional designers, course developers, multimedia designers, and other expert practitioners dedicated to professional continuing education access and enhancement.

DELIVERY MEDIA

Courses offered by eMercer.com are CD-ROM based and Web-enabled. All course work is delivered by high quality video and audio clips and sophisticated graphics that play from the computer's CD-ROM drive. High-speed Internet connections are not required to take any of eMercer. com's courses. Only when students take the post-module test do they need an Internet connection so that the scores can be sent to the eMercer. com databases. This is the same database that constantly updates and records students' eMercer.com course work and transcripts, and allows students to print their course certificates of completion.

PROGRAMS OF STUDY

eMercer.com provides continuing professional education and training courses to a variety of professionals. Since many professional disciplines require continuing professional education credit for relicensure or recredentialing, courses offered by eMercer.com meet the continuing education needs of corporate and continuing professional training and education. Courses provide continuing professional education credit upon completion; specialized CE credit approved by recognized accrediting and licensing boards for specific disciplines are also available.

Continuing professional development and certificate programs are offered in the following disciplines (new courses are added frequently, so students should visit the eMercer. com Web site for a complete catalogue listing):

Accounting: continuing professional education (CEP) credit for specialty programs in areas such as tax liability, banking, public accounting, IRS practices and procedures, accounts liability, and preparing for a certified audit.

Business: continuing professional courses in employee motivation and business communications.

Engineering: specialized courses in project management and managing highly technical people offer NSPE–approved professional development hours for professional engineers.

Theology: courses in Internet resources for Bible study and servant leadership for managers.

Risk Management: specialty courses in sexual harassment, violence in the workplace, van safety, and asbestos management are available for corporate and professional continuing education and training.

Pharmacy: a certificate program in geriatric pharmacy practice offers 25 hours of ACEP–approved continuing pharmaceutical education credit; a 3-hour short course in biostatistics also provides continuing pharmaceutical education; other certificate programs in cardiovascular diseases, asthma, diabetes, and pain management are available in late 2000.

SPECIAL PROGRAMS

Continuing professional education programs are also offered on the Mercer University campuses; distance learning students are encouraged to visit the Web site http://www.mercer. edu to learn more about campus-based courses in their disciplines.

CREDIT OPTIONS

Upon successful completion of eMercer.com course work, students can print continuing professional education credit awarded for each course is clearly identified in the course catalogue. Courses that provide credit approved by recognized accrediting and licensing boards are clearly marked.

FACULTY

Faculty members who create course work for eMercer.com are experienced faculty members who teach in undergraduate, graduate, and professional programs nationwide.

ADMISSION

Professionals, life-long learners, and corporate employees can register for any of eMercer.com's continuing professional education courses. For complete details, students should visit the Web site listed below.

TUITION AND FEES

Current registration fees are published on the Web site listed below. Registration fees vary by course length and discipline.

FINANCIAL AID

Students are encouraged to check with their professional association or employers for financial aid or tuition assistance programs.

APPLYING

Students can register for courses via the Web site listed below. There is no application form or fee required for eMercer.com courses.

CONTACT

Mercer University
Office of Distance Learning
3001 Mercer University Drive
Atlanta, Georgia 30341
Telephone: 770-986-3455
FAX: 770-986-3102
E-mail: horner_e@mercer.edu
Web site: http://www.eMercer.com

Mercy College

MerLIN Distance Learning Program

Dobbs Ferry, New York

Mercy College is a comprehensive college that offers both undergraduate and graduate degrees. Founded in 1950 by the Sisters of Mercy, the College became independent in 1969. The guiding principles of the College are service to the community through the education of both traditional and nontraditional students, reliance on the liberal arts and sciences as the foundation of education, and dedication to teaching and the advancement of knowledge.

The College provides programs in the liberal arts and sciences as well as career-oriented, preprofessional, and professional degree programs; offers activities and services that enrich students' intellectual, social, personal, and work lives; and serves students with varied backgrounds through innovative learning methodologies and flexible scheduling at multiple locations.

Mercy College is accredited by the Middle States Association of Colleges and Schools and the New York State Board of Regents of the University of the State of New York. Programs in accounting, nursing, paralegal studies, physical and occupational therapy, social work, and veterinary technology have additional accreditations.

DISTANCE LEARNING PROGRAM

MerLIN, the Mercy Long-distance Instructional Network, offers courses without time restrictions, wherever students have access to the Internet. The same high-quality educational experience is available online as in Mercy's traditional courses. There are currently more than 600 students matriculated for degrees or taking individual courses in the program. Each semester more than 100 courses are offered through MerLIN. Courses are convenient but not self-paced. Faculty members have incorporated weekly online discussions and Web-based activities and assignments in their MerLIN courses. Students must be prepared to log in to their courses a minimum of three times per week.

DELIVERY MEDIA

Learning and communication in a MerLIN course takes place in a group environment with other students and the professor. Courses incorporate streaming media for audio and video, hyperlinks, and synchronous chat. Students enrolling in a MerLIN course must have basic computer and Internet skills, including word processing, e-mail, and Web searching. Access to a computer with a modem (at least 28.8 kbs) as well as an Internet service provider is necessary. A sound card and speakers are recommended.

PROGRAMS OF STUDY

The Distance Learning Program offers the Master of Business Administration, Master of Science in banking, Master of Science in direct marketing, Master of Science in Internet business systems, Bachelor of Arts in business administration, Bachelor of Science in computer science, Bachelor of Science in psychology, and Associate of Arts or Associate of Science in liberal studies degrees.

SPECIAL PROGRAMS

College services available to the traditional student are provided to distance learning students, including access to the College's library, computer support, and student advising. Individual and group tutoring is available to students studying via MerLIN. An online bookstore allows students to purchase all textbooks via the Internet.

CREDIT OPTIONS

Mercy College accepts transfer credit from accredited institutions of higher education. In order to have credits accepted in transfer, a student must be matriculated in a degree program, and the credits must be applicable to degree requirements. A maximum of 75 credits may be accepted in transfer from an accredited two-year institution and a maximum of 90 credits from a four-year institution. Up to 18 credits can be earned through CLEP's general examinations. All evaluation of transcripts for the purpose of determining transferable credits is done on an individual basis.

FACULTY

All Distance Learning Program courses are taught by experienced Mercy College faculty members. More than 80 percent of the 75 faculty members teaching in the program have a doctorate or other terminal degree.

ADMISSION

All students are required to have an admission interview. Individual arrangements can be made for telephone interviews. Some applicants may be required to take a placement examination. Individual graduate and undergraduate programs may have additional requirements.

TUITION AND FEES

Undergraduate tuition in 2000–01 is $4250 per semester for 12 to 18 credits and $355 per credit for less than 12 credits. Graduate tuition is $435 per credit for M.B.A., M.S. in direct marketing, and M.S. in Internet business systems programs and $525 per credit for the M.S. in banking program. There is a $35 application fee for both undergraduate and graduate students.

FINANCIAL AID

Financial assistance is available in the form of scholarships, grants, loans, and employment for eligible matriculated students. All students requesting financial assistance are requested to file the Free Application for Federal Student Aid (FAFSA). Mercy College awarded $310,000 in scholarships and $1.5 million in grants to students last year.

APPLYING

Students may complete an application on line or on paper via mail. First-time distance learning students are required to take an online orientation course that covers the basics of how to log in, participate in courses, send and receive messages, and access the online resources.

CONTACT

Joy Colelli, Dean for Admissions
Loretta Donovan, Director of Distance Learning
Mercy College
555 Broadway
Dobbs Ferry, New York 10533
Telephone: 914-674-7527
Fax: 914-674-7382
E-mail: admission@mercynet.edu
Web site: http://merlin.mercynet.edu

Miami-Dade Community College

Virtual Campus Distance Education

Miami, Florida

A multicampus, two-year, state-supported community college with six campuses and numerous outreach centers, Miami-Dade Community College (M-DCC) is nationally recognized as one of the largest and best community colleges in the country. It is governed by a 7-member District Board of Trustees and a college president. Established in 1959, the first M-DCC campus opened in September 1960. M-DCC is accredited by the Commission on Colleges of the Southern Association of Colleges and Schools. The mission of M-DCC is to provide accessible, affordable, and high-quality education by keeping the learner's needs at the center of decision making and working in partnership with its dynamic, multicultural community. M-DCC enrolls the most Hispanic-American students and the second-largest number of African-American students of any college or university in the United States.

DISTANCE LEARNING PROGRAM

M-DCC's Virtual College provides learning opportunities for students with time or employment constraints, physical disabilities, or geographic constraints. Virtual College delivers the same high-quality education found in every M-DCC classroom but uses the Internet and video-conferencing technology to reach the distant learner. Nearly 1,000 students took classes through the seventy-two Virtual College courses offered last year.

DELIVERY MEDIA

Courses are offered synchronously and asynchronously. The synchronous courses use videoconferencing systems that connect all six campuses. Instructors lecture to students at one campus, while students at one or more of the other campuses interact via the videoconferencing system.

Asynchronous courses are primarily online courses that use the Internet to bring courses directly to a student's computer. All students taking asynchronous courses must have access to a computer connected to the Internet, a current version of a graphical browser, and the ability to install provided software.

PROGRAMS OF STUDY

Many new courses are under development, and eventually all courses needed for the Associate of Arts (A. A.) degree will be offered. Currently, nine online courses satisfy the general education requirements for the Associate of Arts and Associate of Science (A.S.) degrees. That is 27 of the 36 general education credits that M-DCC requires for the A.A. degree and 6 of the 15 general education credits required for the A.S. degree. In addition to such general education courses as English composition, psychology, humanities, college algebra, and oceanography, numerous courses in nursing, medical records technology, midwifery, and business are also offered.

SPECIAL PROGRAMS

Continuing education credits in the health-care field are available online. In order to help students find and enroll in high-quality courses, M-DCC's Virtual College is an active participant of the Southern Regional Electronic Campus (SREC), America's Learning Exchange (ALX), and the Florida Community College Distance Learning Consortium (FCCDLC).

STUDENT SERVICES

Students may visit the College's Web site to apply for admission, view final grades, search for open classes, display schedules, and order textbooks online. Registration and tuition payment soon will be available online as well. Currently, students may register and make tuition payments by telephone via STAR Service, a computerized voice-response system.

CREDIT OPTIONS

Transfer credits are accepted from regionally accredited colleges and universities for courses with grades of a D or better. Students participating in credit-by-examination programs, such as the Advanced Placement Program (APP) of the College Board, the College-Level Examination Program (CLEP), the Proficiency Examination Program (PEP), and International Baccalaureate Program (IB), may be granted credit toward an associate degree based on M-DCC–approved course equivalents. Credit may also be granted for validated military training.

FACULTY

All Virtual College courses are taught by M-DCC faculty members who also teach on-campus classes. Currently, more than 25 percent of Virtual College faculty members hold doctoral degrees.

ADMISSION

Students must have a high school diploma or its equivalent. International students who have an education equivalent to that of U.S. secondary schools must meet language standards as stated in the College's catalog. People 18 years of age and older who do not hold a high school diploma or its equivalent may be admitted under nondegree status for up to 15 credits in vocational courses.

TUITION AND FEES

For the 1999–2000 academic year, Florida residents paid $49.65 per credit; out-of-state students paid $173.40 per credit. The cost for full-time (12 credits) resident students was $595.80 per semester, plus approximately $350 for textbooks and supplies. Some courses carry special fees in addition to regular registration fees. Tuition is subject to change.

FINANCIAL AID

Financial aid is available for both college credit and vocational credit programs. The amounts and types of financial aid that a student receives are determined by federal, state, and institutional guidelines and are offered to students in packages that consist of grants, loans, and scholarships. The College also maintains a Veterans Affairs (V.A.) Office to assist veterans and eligible dependents wishing to receive V.A. education benefits.

APPLYING

Students should submit an admission application at the earliest possible date prior to the beginning of the desired term of enrollment. Out-of-state and international applicants must submit the application at least sixty days prior to the beginning of the term of expected enrollment. A nonrefundable $20 application fee is charged for processing a student's first application. Students may submit their applications electronically via the Internet.

CONTACT

Virtual College
Miami-Dade Community College
950 Northwest 20th Street
Miami, Florida 33127-4693
Telephone: 305-237-4285
Fax: 305-237-4081
E-mail: vcollege@mdcc.edu
Web site: http://www.mdcc.edu/vcollege

Michigan State University

East Lansing, Michigan

Michigan State University (MSU), founded in 1855, is a research-intensive, land-grant university, offering more than 200 programs at the bachelor's through doctoral levels. It is one of only fifty-eight members of the prestigious American Association of Universities and is a member of the Big Ten Conference.

The core of MSU's land-grant tradition is the belief that educational opportunities should be available to the widest possible audience. Six guiding principles reflect the land-grant tradition at MSU: access to quality education, active learning, the generation of new knowledge, problem solving, diversity, and making people matter. A recently announced Technology Guarantee ensures students an intensive, quality-based technological experience (with increased interactive instruction) and lifelong access to MSU technology.

The University's outreach mission, involving all fourteen of its colleges, emphasizes the extension of knowledge to serve the needs of individuals, groups, and communities.

DISTANCE LEARNING PROGRAM

MSU serves more than 6,000 off-campus students per year in Michigan and around the world, about half through distance technology. Offerings expand each year. The University is fully accredited by the North Central Association of Colleges and Schools, and individual programs are accredited, where appropriate, by professional associations. MSU's distance education programs are offered by the individual academic departments, not by a centralized continuing education unit.

DELIVERY MEDIA

MSU uses interactive and satellite television (usually viewed at local sites), the Internet, computer conferencing, and e-mail. Access to a computer with a modem is important. Students are in frequent contact with faculty members by e-mail and/or telephone.

PROGRAMS OF STUDY

At numerous sites throughout the state, MSU offers master's-level pro-

grams in advertising, business, child development, community services, criminal justice, educational administration, family studies, nursing, social work, teacher education, and telecommunications and bachelor's programs in interdisciplinary social science and nursing.

The distance learning programs currently available outside Michigan include courses and programs offered via MSU's Virtual University in telecommunications, computing, criminal justice, security management, social work, nursing, physics, human environment and design, information technology, and facility management.

Master's degree programs require a minimum of 30 semester credits (some require more), and bachelor's programs require 120 credits. Students who wish to take courses without or before applying to a degree program may enroll as Lifelong Education students.

SPECIAL PROGRAMS

MSU's off-campus programs are fully equivalent to on-campus programs, follow the same curriculum, have the same entrance and graduation requirements, and charge the same tuition and fees. Courses are almost always taught by the University's regular faculty, not by local adjuncts.

STUDENT SERVICES

All students receive University e-mail accounts and access to the Internet, to MSU and other library catalogs, and to extensive databases. Off-campus students may seek research assistance or request books and articles by telephone, fax, or mail from the MSU libraries.

CREDIT OPTIONS

MSU accepts transfer credit from accredited institutions but does not offer or accept credit through assessment of prior learning. Some College-Level Examination Program (CLEP) and Advanced Placement credits are accepted. For a bachelor's degree, at least 30 semester credits must be earned at MSU; for a master's degree, at least 21 credits of a 30-credit program must be earned at MSU.

FACULTY

MSU has 2,600 faculty members, with 2,000 in the tenure system; about 2,300 are appointed on a full-time basis. Almost all MSU faculty members hold doctoral or other terminal degrees. The regular on-campus faculty members provide 90 percent of the instruction in off-campus programs.

ADMISSION

Distance learners meet the same admission requirements as on-campus students. Admission to undergraduate programs is based on high school grade point average, recent trend of grades, other activities and accomplishments, SAT or ACT scores, and recommendations.

Master's program admission is based on grade point average for the third and fourth years of undergraduate study, other relevant accomplishments, GRE scores, recommendations, and the availability of space in the program.

TUITION AND FEES

Upper-division undergraduate tuition for 1998–99 was $160.25 for Michigan residents and $399 for out-of-state students; graduate tuition was $222.50 for Michigan residents and $450 for out-of-state students. Matriculation and technology fees were $288 for full-time students (5 or more credits) and $238 for part-time students. Lifelong Education students (those not in a degree program) paid $222.50 per credit hour (graduate or undergraduate, resident or nonresident), with no additional fees. There was an additional Engineering Program fee of $237 for full-time status and $131 for part-time status.

FINANCIAL AID

Distance learners are eligible for the same federal and state and University financial aid programs as on-campus students, based on part-time or full-time status. However, graduate assistantships are usually not available to students at a distance because they involve on-campus assigned work hours. One fellowship program is targeted specifically for reentry adult students, the Mildred B. Erickson Fellowship.

APPLYING

Applications are accepted all year. However, some programs only accept new students in the fall semester. In some programs, students must attend an orientation program either on campus or at a local site.

CONTACT

Dr. Barbara Fails
Outreach Instructional Programs
51 Kellogg Center
Michigan State University
East Lansing, Michigan 48824
Telephone: 517-353-0791
Fax: 517-432-1327
Web site: http://www.msu.edu/unit/outreach

Montana State University-Billings

MSU–B Online Program

Billings, Montana

eCollege.com   *www.ecollege.com/scholarships*

> *Established in 1927, Montana State University–Billings provides excellent instructional and learning opportunities in the arts and sciences as well as in its professional programs in business, technology, human services, rehabilitation, and education. MSU–Billings is accredited by the Northwest Association of Schools and Colleges, and its various degree programs, including teacher education, are accredited by other individual organizations. The University offers a wide variety of preprofessional and certification programs and awards degrees at the associate's, bachelor's, and master's levels to over 4000 students annually. For more information on Montana State University–Billings, please visit the University Web site.*

DISTANCE LEARNING PROGRAM

Through the Montana State University–Billings (MSU–B) Online Program established in the fall of 1998, MSU–Billings is pleased to offer students an opportunity to take college courses via the Internet as a way of overcoming barriers of time and place. The program ensures that students can achieve their personal, professional, and academic goals while not having to sacrifice the other things that are important in their lives. The program currently offers over 65 online courses annually (25 each semester and 15 during the summer session) to approximately 1200 students.

DELIVERY MEDIA

All MSU–B online classes are delivered entirely via the Internet using the sophisticated eCollege.com online course delivery system. This system provides for complete course content hosting whereby all readings, assignments, multimedia tutorials, audio and video streaming media, and instructional documents, are provided online. In addition to hosting course content, the delivery system provides access to a variety of cutting-edge online interaction tools including centralized e-mail, internet and course search tools, chat rooms, and threaded discussions, as well as an online journal, calendar, webliography, document sharing, exam manager, and gradebook features. Minimal hardware, software, and Internet connectivity requirements exist for all online classes.

PROGRAMS OF STUDY

Students can select from three online degree programs through MSU–B Online, including the Bachelor of Science in Liberal Studies (B.S.L.S.) with a concentration in management and communication; a Bachelor of Arts (B.A.) degree with an organizational communication Major, and the B.S.L.S. degree completion program.

The B.S.L.S. degree completion program uses the same curriculum as the full four-year B.S.L.S. degree, but allows students to transfer or substitute prior academic coursework into the program while completing the thematic concentration in management and communication. To complete the B.S.L.S. degree or the B.S.L.S. degree completion program, individuals must earn a minimum of 120 credits with a cumulative grade point average of 2.0 or better. In addition, all students must satisfy the General Education requirements at MSU–Billings. MSU–Billings will accept transfer students with completed A.A. or A.S. degrees from other institutions as having fulfilled their MSU–Billings General Education requirements. Sudents must complete a minimum of 30 credits through MSU–Billings, 36 upper division credits, and 30 credits of the management and communications thematic concentration.

The organizational communication degree program shares the same requirements as the B.S.L.S. degree program described above, with the exception of a major core of online organizational communications classes instead of the 30-credit Management and Communication concentration. The degree is designed to educate students entering the fields of business and social service as managers, public relations personnel, trainers, human resource officers, and corporate communication staff. This option is excellent preparation for graduate study in communication or law.

SPECIAL PROGRAMS

Through the MSU–B Online Program, students can complete the B.S.L.S. degree completion program described above, which offers a thematic concentration in management and communication. Additionally, students can complete a variety of courses in General Education Requirements typically required of undergraduate students.

STUDENT SERVICES

MSU–B Online provides online students with access to all student services offered to MSU–Billings on-site students, including admissions, degree planning and advising, financial aid, ordering books and supplies, fee payment, library, twenty-four-hour online course HelpDesk support, and a number of other student support services. In addition, all students enrolling in an online class receive access to an online orientation course that is designed to help students learn how to use the course delivery system and to maximize their success and satisfaction in online learning.

FACULTY

All 30 faculty members who teach classes online for the MSU–B Online Program are full-time faculty of Montana State University–Billings. In addition to teaching their online classes, these faculty members teach equivalent courses in traditional on-site classes. Eighty-six percent of the University's faculty members hold the highest degrees in their fields.

ADMISSION

The requirements for admission to MSU–B are the same as those for individuals taking classes on-site.

TUITION AND FEES

Tuition and fees for online classes are the same as for taking classes on-site with an additional $36 per credit nonrefundable fee that is assessed for all Internet courses. The exact rate of tuition and fees depends upon the number of credits taken and whether the student is a resident or nonresident of Montana.

FINANCIAL AID

Financial aid is awarded to more than 60 percent of the University population—including students taking courses online—in the form of grants, scholarships, tuition waivers, employment, and loans.

APPLYING

All students wishing to enroll in MSU–B Online courses or degree programs should do so by submitting an online application and registration form.

CONTACT

Kirk Lacy
MSU–B Online Coordinator
College of Professional Studies
  and Lifelong Learning
Apsaruke Hall 116
Montana State University–Billings
1500 North 30th Street
Billings, Montana 59101
Telephone: 406-657-2294
  800-708-0068 (toll-free)
Fax: 406-657-2254
E-mail: inquiry@msubonline.org
Web site: http://www.msubonline.
  org
or http://www.msubillings.edu

National American University
Distance Learning Program
Rapid City, South Dakota

Since 1941, National American University (NAU) has been serving the needs of adult students. In keeping with that mission, the University began to offer courses on line in 1996. Since then, National American University has been approved to offer full-degree programs via the online format. National American University's innovative approach to student services emphasizes personal contact and 24-hour service to ensure the success of its students. Highly personalized attention and a full range of student services are available to every online student. Online courses at National American University provide students with a unique learning experience. Through highly interactive classes, students communicate frequently with instructors and classmates from around the world.

DISTANCE LEARNING PROGRAM

Asynchronous courses, bachelor's degree programs, and professional diplomas are available on line through National American University's Distance Learning Program. Online degree programs include applied management, business administration, and information technology. Professional diploma programs include e-commerce, Webmaster studies, and Microsoft network management. National American University is accredited by the Commission on Institutions of Higher Education of the North Central Association of Colleges and Schools.

DELIVERY MEDIA

Utilizing evolving technology, professional instructors provide students with an interactive learning environment that surpasses the boundaries of the traditional classroom. Students accessing courses through the Internet explore sites on the virtual campus, such as the study carrel, the lecture hall, and the student union. Students receive information concerning learning objectives, course content, and assignments to be completed on line. Through asynchronous discussion, students

engage in educational dialogue with instructors and peers at times convenient to their own schedules.

To make the students' online learning experience as successful as possible, National American University recommends the following hardware and software configurations: Pentium processor or equivalent; a RAM of 16 Mb or better; Windows 95, 98, or NT; and an Internet browser. In addition, students need a word processor and access to e-mail.

PROGRAMS OF STUDY

Students may complete individual courses or pursue a bachelor's degree in one of three academic disciplines: applied management, business administration, and information technology. Students can also pursue three professional diplomas: Microsoft network management, e-commerce, and Webmaster studies. Four terms are offered each year, with classes from eight to eleven weeks in length.

SPECIAL PROGRAMS

National American University offers business and corporate clients customized programs in the areas of business and computers.

STUDENT SERVICES

National American University offers a full range of student services for its online students. All online students are enrolled in a free online orientation, which introduces students to National American University's virtual campus. Students may utilize the online library 24 hours a day and may access resources such as ProQuest Direct, FirstSearch, Net Advantage, and Encyclopedia Americana Online.

For the convenience of online students, applications and registrations may also be completed on line. Academic advisers are available to assist applicants with quarterly academic advising and placement. The NAU bookstore offers students the opportunity to purchase textbooks and supplementary materials through the mail. Students who need additional help in their online courses can receive free online tutoring. Financial assistance services are provided through National American University's Financial Aid Office. Technical support is available to distance learning students 24 hours a day. For more information, students are encouraged to visit the catalog on the University's Web site (listed below).

CREDIT OPTIONS

Credits earned at accredited business or technical schools, colleges, or universities may be transferred to National American University depending on comparability of subject matter and the applicability of the credit earned to the student's program. The student must have received a grade of C or better for each of the courses transferred. In addition, a student may obtain up to 50 percent of the required credit hours toward graduation from nontraditional methods, including experiential learning/portfolio credit awarded by National American University, evaluated corporate training certificates, work experience credit, and nontranscripted military training.

National American University also accepts credit earned through national standardized examinations, including the College-Level Examination Program (CLEP), the Defense Activity for Nontraditional Education Supports (DANTES), and the American College Testing Proficiency Examination Program (ACT PEP).

FACULTY

National American University online faculty members are experienced professionals with both appropriate academic credentials and professional experience. All online faculty members receive extensive training in online course facilitation and are required to respond to student inquiries and assignments within 24 hours. The combination of cutting-edge technology and caring, concerned faculty members allows students to achieve more both academically and professionally.

ADMISSION

Graduation from an accredited high school is a requirement for admission. Those who have satisfied graduation requirements through the General Education Development test (GED) are also eligible for admission. In addition, students enrolled in online courses must sign and return a self-directed learner/accountability statement to help ensure that the student understands the nature and requirements of online course work.

TUITION AND FEES

Tuition and fees are due on the first day of each quarter unless advance arrangements are made. A commitment for tuition and fees is made for three academic quarters, subject to the current refund policy. Students may qualify for short-term financial assistance to complete their registration. Tuition for online courses is $200 per credit hour. Select information technology courses have a separate fee schedule.

FINANCIAL AID

Financial aid is available to those who qualify. Financial aid advisers are available to assist students through the process of applying for financial aid. It is suggested that students check with their companies to determine the availability of financial assistance.

APPLYING

On-campus students enrolling in online courses must follow the same procedures (listed in the University catalog) as do other students taking courses on campus. Students enrolling in National American University's online courses must complete an application for admission (available on line), submit an original high school transcript or a certificate of GED and all college transcripts, complete a self-directed learner statement, and submit an application fee of $25.

Students whose native language is not English are required to provide a TOEFL score of at least 500. TOEFL scores should be forwarded directly from ETS and must be less than two years old. For more information on TOEFL, students should contact ETS at 609-921-9000 or at http://www.toefl.org.

International applicants must also complete an admissions application and return it with the $45 application fee and a $100 refundable tuition deposit; obtain official transcripts and diplomas from all high schools, colleges, and universities attended (non-English documents must be accompanied by certified English translations); and pay quarterly tuition and fees (in U.S. dollars) in advance.

CONTACT

Tricia Torpey, Director of Distance Learning Operations
Tyler Faulkner, Admissions Coordinator
Jon Outland, Associate Academic Dean for Distance Learning
Jim Leonard, Director of Technology
Distance Learning Program
National American University
321 Kansas City Street
Rapid City, South Dakota 57701
Telephone: 800-843-8892 Ext. 4933 (toll-free)
Fax: 605-394-4871
E-mail: ptorpey@national.edu
Web site: http://www.national.edu

National Universities Degree Consortium

The National Universities Degree Consortium (NUDC), established in 1991, is a consortium of regionally accredited universities across the United States that offer courses, certificates, and degrees through distance education. NUDC members include Colorado State University, Kansas State University, Mississippi State University, Oklahoma State University, University of Alabama, University of Maryland University College, University of New Orleans, University of South Carolina, and Washington State University.

DISTANCE LEARNING PROGRAM

NUDC was established in response to widespread requests from potential, nontraditional-age students for integrated, external degree programs that are delivered in a flexible, off-campus format and readily available to adults and part-time students. In many cases, these students are one to two years away from completing their undergraduate degrees. The member institutions of the consortium develop and manage the operations of the consortium and ensure high-quality programs with the ultimate goal of providing university-credit courses that lead to external degrees. NUDC serves as a vehicle for the development and promotion of undergraduate courses and programs, graduate degree programs, certificate programs (credit and noncredit), and noncredit courses in a variety of subject areas.

DELIVERY MEDIA

More than 1,000 courses are offered through a variety of distance learning formats. These courses include traditional print-based correspondence courses, online and Internet courses, and courses that include other media components, such as audiotapes, videotapes, computer disks, CD-ROM, e-mail, and more. Many courses feature technology-mediated interaction between students and faculty members. Students are encouraged to contact the offering university to find out the format for the course or courses of choice.

PROGRAMS OF STUDY

Through NUDC, each member of the consortium offers courses through a variety of distance education formats. Some institutions offer external degree completion programs. The NUDC Web site lists the programs offered by each institution.

Bachelor's degrees are available in accounting, administrative sciences, animal sciences and industry, applied sciences, behavioral and social sciences, business and management, communication, communication studies, computer and management information science, computer studies, criminal justice, English, fire science, food science and industry, general business, human development, human services, humanities, interdisciplinary social sciences, management, management studies, natural sciences, paralegal studies, social sciences, and technology and management.

Master's degrees are available in agribusiness, business administration, business management, computer science, computer systems management, engineering (aerospace, biosystems, chemical and bioresource, chemical, civil, control systems, electrical, electrical and computer, environmental, industrial, mechanical, software, and systems and optimization), engineering and technology management, engineering with a concentration in engineering management, engineering management, fire and emergency management administration, general administration, health education/health promotion, health studies, human resource development, industrial/organizational psychology, international management, library science, natural and applied sciences with a specialization in gerontology, statistics, technology management, and telecommunications management.

The Education Specialist degree is available in educational leadership and policy studies.

Doctoral degrees are available in electrical engineering, industrial engineering, and mechanical engineering.

Certificate programs are available in bail bonds management, broadcast meteorology, criminal justice, fire protection technology, food science, operational meteorology, and technical and professional writing.

SPECIAL PROGRAMS

Members of NUDC offer special services such as academic advising and external library resources to their distance students. To learn more about distinctive programs available to students through NUDC member institutions, students should contact the institution of choice directly.

CREDIT OPTIONS

NUDC members have agreed to accept credits from other member institutions toward completion of the external degree programs. A student wishing to complete a degree must verify transfer credits with the degree-granting institution.

FACULTY

Each university member of NUDC is an accredited institution that maintains the highest standards for all faculty members. These standards are reflected in the high quality of instruction offered to the distance learner.

STUDENT PROFILE

The students who are interested in degree completion via distance learning are typical of all distance students. They often are not able to attend courses on a campus during the day due to work or family obligations, geographic location, or other inhibitors. Most distance students are 23 years old or older. For profiles distinctive to a particular university, students should contact the institution directly.

ADMISSION

Degree-seeking students must follow the admission and graduation requirements of the particular institution whose degree they are pursuing. The student may choose from more than 1,000 courses offered by the consortium members to complete the degree program of a particular institution. Formal admission is not required for students not interested in a degree.

TUITION AND FEES

NUDC does not have a tuition and fee standard for participants. Each institution sets tuition and fees according to its own schedule.

FINANCIAL AID

The rules for financial aid vary by program. Students should contact the financial aid office at the institution offering the courses of interest for specific information. Courses taken in a non-degree-granting program may not be eligible for federal grants.

APPLYING

Each NUDC member has its own application requirements and deadlines. Students should contact the institution offering the course or program of interest for specific information.

CONTACT

For more information regarding any NUDC program or course offering, students should contact the offering institution. For general information about the National Universities Degree Consortium or to view the NUDC catalog, students should visit the NUDC Web site at http://www.NUDC.org.

Neumann College

neumannonline.org

Aston, Pennsylvania

Founded and sponsored by the Sisters of St. Francis of Philadelphia, Neumann College is a Catholic, coeducational institution of higher learning in the Franciscan tradition. The educational philosophy is based on the concepts that knowledge, while valuable in itself, is best used in the service of others and that learning is a lifelong process. The College offers undergraduate degrees in a broad variety of subjects, five graduate programs, and accelerated associate and bachelor's degree programs for adults. Faculty members bring to online courses the same commitment to personal attention that they exhibit in the classroom. A recent expansion of programs and services, coupled with the College's commitment to first-rate academic instruction and real-world career preparation, has caused Neumann's popularity to boom in recent years. The College's total enrollment stands at more that 1,625 students.

DISTANCE LEARNING PROGRAM

An implicit part of Neumann College's mission is that it recognizes its responsibility to offer educational programs that anticipate and respond to the changing needs of society. Neumannonline.org is particularly attractive to those students who are motivated self-starters and who enjoy a learning environment with no time constraints or distance barriers. A variety of courses are available each semester at http://www.neumannonline.org.

DELIVERY MEDIA

Neumannonline.org is an integrated system that uses an interactive syllabus. Lectures are a combination of virtual lecture, real audio, and real video. Discussion groups, online chats, and threaded discussions provide collaboration between faculty members and students. E-mail and the message center are vehicles for communication and information. Students are required to have Windows 95, 98, or NT, with a 75-MHz or faster Pentium processor, 32 Mb of RAM or more, a 28.8-kbps or faster modem,

a sound card, speakers, and 4.0 or higher Internet Explorer or Netscape Navigator.

The online courses are offered via the eCollege.com system.

PROGRAMS OF STUDY

Neumann College offers an Associate of Arts degree and majors leading to Bachelor of Arts and Bachelor of Science degrees.

Bachelor of Arts degree candidates may choose a major from the following: communication arts, early childhood/elementary education, English, international studies (dual degree with international business), liberal arts, political science, or psychology.

Bachelor of Science degree candidates may choose a major from the following: accounting, biological science, business administration, computer and information management, environmental studies and education, international business (dual degree with international studies), marketing, nursing, psychology, or sport management.

Neumann College also offers academic programs leading to Master of

Science degrees in education, nursing, pastoral care and counseling, sport management, and physical therapy.

SPECIAL PROGRAMS

Neumann offers an Associate of Arts degree that can be completed entirely online. The program's special 6-credit courses (twice the standard 3-credit value) ensure that students make accelerated progress toward their degree, and online faculty members give students the personal attention they need to succeed. After meeting the Associate of Arts degree requirements, students can earn an accelerated bachelor's degree with just ten additional courses.

STUDENT SERVICES

The mission of the Career Development Office is to promote a values-based approach to career and life planning, with opportunities for career exploration through community service activities, service learning, and internship and cooperative education experiences.

The Computer Center consists of four state-of-the art classrooms/labs and a central administrative office area. Neumann College has a local area network (LAN), which connects academic and Internet computer resources. This network consolidates a number of functions, such as printing, e-mail, and support for the instructional use of computers. Access to the Internet, Web browsing, and Neumann's Web site are also available.

The Learning Assistance Center enables students to meet Neumann's academic standards and successfully attain their personal educational goals. The center assists students with specific direction in the organization and writing of papers and research documentation, provides tutorial assistance, and aids in developing students' study and test-taking skills.

The Neumann College Library plays a crucial role in the learning experience of the student and in the teaching and researching needs of the faculty. The heart of the collection is available on Francis, Neumann College Library's online catalog, which lists the College's more than 76,000 books and more than 52,000 audiovisual materials. Neumann subscribes to approximately 1,700 periodicals, many of which are available online in full-text databases.

CREDIT OPTIONS

The curriculum for the College's academic major is divided into four sections: core requirements, major requirements, allied requirements, and general electives. Traditional students are required to have 43 core credits, with a minimum of 30 credits in the academic major. Allied requirements vary from one major to another, and the general electives are designated courses of study that students may pursue to meet their needs or interests. The number of required general electives is based on the student's academic program.

Neumann College offers various supplemental ways of earning credits. Advanced Placement tests; challenge examinations; ACT, CLEP, and DANTES examinations; directed study; an independent study program; portfolio assessment; study abroad; and summer session courses are the various methods through which a student can earn credits.

FACULTY

The Neumann College faculty consists of 53 full-time faculty members and 112 per-course faculty members, all of whom are dedicated to the intellectual and affective development of the students as well as to portraying the spirit and values of St. Francis of Assisi by developing a sense of responsibility, which fosters and respects diversity.

ADMISSION

Admission to Neumann College is open to all students, regardless of race, religion, creed, or national origin. Distance learners must meet the same requirements as traditional college students. An application for admission to Neumann College can be accessed online at the Web address listed below.

TUITION AND FEES

In 2000–01, part-time undergraduate tuition is $370 per credit. Graduate tuition is $460 per credit for all programs except physical therapy, which is $600 per credit. Various fees included a graduation fee of $80, a portfolio assessment application fee of $80, a liberal studies certificate fee of $25, and a transcript fee of $3. There is a late payment fine of $45 and a returned check penalty of $35.

FINANCIAL AID

Neumann College accepts all financial aid forms. The College, however, recommends the Free Application for Federal Student Aid (FAFSA) because there is no fee required to process this form. More information about financial aid can be obtained by writing to or calling the Office of Admissions and Financial Aid (610-558-5521). The Neumann College Title IV code is 003988.

APPLYING

Students who wish to apply to Neumann College may do so by following instructions found at the Web address listed below, or they may call the admissions office.

CONTACT

Telephone: 610-558-5616
E-mail: inquiry@neumannonline.org
Web site: http://neumannonline.org

New Hampshire College
Distance Education Program
Manchester, New Hampshire

New Hampshire College (NHC), founded in 1932, is a private, accredited, coeducational, professional college. The College has a total enrollment of more than 8,900 in various divisions—undergraduate day, Continuing Education, Distance Education, the Culinary Institute, and the Graduate School of Business. New Hampshire College maintains Continuing Education undergraduate and graduate centers in Laconia, Manchester, Nashua, Portsmouth, and Salem, New Hampshire; Brunswick, Maine; and Roosevelt Roads, Puerto Rico.

New Hampshire College and the Distance Education Program are accredited by the New England Association of School and Colleges. Accreditation by this association indicates that the institution has been carefully evaluated and found to meet the standards agreed upon by qualified educators. The College and the program are also accredited by the Association of Collegiate Business Schools and Programs (ACBSP), the New Hampshire Postsecondary Education Commission, and the New Hampshire State Department of Education for Teacher Certification. New Hampshire College is also approved for the education of veterans and the children of veterans, approved for the rehabilitation training of handicapped students, and listed in the Department of Education's Education Directory, Part 3, Higher Education.

DISTANCE LEARNING PROGRAM

Through means of computer technology, the New Hampshire College Distance Education Program provides an online learning environment that rivals the traditional classroom. The communications options provided by the Internet offer new opportunities for meaningful interaction between faculty members and students and for collaborative learning among students in an asynchronous environment.

Distance education scheduling allows students and faculty members to break the boundaries of time and space that are associated with the traditional classroom. The program provides an environment for flexible learning and teaching where students may interact with experts in their field of study, drawing upon resources from a global environment.

DELIVERY MEDIA

The Distance Education Program offers many advantages to students and faculty members. The classes are limited in size, providing a significant measure of faculty-student interaction not found in more traditional class environments. The average faculty-student ratio is 1:12. Blackboard software (a product of Blackboard, Inc.) is the primary delivery media. While most instructors use Blackboard, some may use other tools such as e-mail, Web pages, and links to other sites that might enhance the learning process.

To participate in distance education through New Hampshire College, the student must have a computer with a modem and access to the Internet. A working knowledge of Internet use and applications is helpful.

PROGRAMS OF STUDY

New Hampshire College provides students with a solid educational foundation and professional training through programs in the Divisions of Business, Liberal Arts, and Hospitality Administration. Degree programs available within the Division of Business include accounting, business administration, business studies, computer information systems, economics/finance, international business, management advisory services, marketing, retailing, sport management, and technical management. Degree programs offered by the Division of Liberal Arts include communication, English language and literature, humanities, psychology, social science, and teacher education (concentrations in business, English, and marketing). Degree programs conferred by the Division of Hospitality Administration include hotel management, restaurant management, and travel and tourism.

Associate of Science degree programs are offered in accounting, business administration, computer information systems, liberal arts, marketing, and retailing/fashion merchandising. All associate degree programs are transferable into bachelor's degree programs. For an overview of undergraduate degree requirements, students should visit the Web site (http://www.nhc.

edu/academic/us/Default.htm). Undergraduate certificates in accounting, human resource management, and computer programming are offered on line. Most of the College's traditional undergraduate courses are offered on line and offer exactly the same credit toward a degree.

The Graduate School of Business offers programs leading to the Master of Science degree in accounting, business education, community economic development, computer information systems, finance, and international business and to the Master of Business Administration degree. The Doctor of Philosophy (Ph.D.) in community economic development and the Doctor of Business Administration (D.B.A.) in international business began in September 1998. Graduate certificates may be earned in any of twelve areas of concentration in conjunction with or independent of a degree. For an overview of graduate degree requirements, students should visit the Web site (http://www.nhc.edu/academic/newgsb/index.htm). The Graduate School also offers course work through the Distance Education Program. For complete information, students should refer to the distance education projected schedule on the Web site (http://de.nhc.edu/corsinfo/classinfo.html).

SPECIAL PROGRAMS

Cooperative education work experiences are available in all academic programs and range from 3 to 12 credits; all students have the option of participating in work experience abroad. An NHC program in which students live and learn in London, England, is available to selected students through arrangements with the Polytechnic of North London.

Through the College's membership in the New Hampshire College and University Council, New Hampshire College students may take advantage of academic facilities and course offerings at eleven other four-year colleges and universities in the consortium.

CREDIT OPTIONS

Students can transfer undergraduate credits earned at other accredited postsecondary institutions to New Hampshire College and can receive undergraduate credit by taking the College-Level Examination Program (CLEP) or other standardized tests. A maximum of 90 credits may be transferred toward a bachelor's degree, and 30 credits may be applied to an associate degree. A maximum of 6 semester hours may be transferred into any of the graduate degree programs.

FACULTY

New Hampshire College faculty members must meet strict educational and background criteria and are considered experts in their fields. Students participating in distance education have the unique opportunity to study with the finest instructors throughout the world.

ADMISSION

Applicants for undergraduate degrees must have graduated from high school or passed the GED test before entering. Admission to the Graduate School requires a bachelor's degree from an accredited institution.

TUITION AND FEES

The tuition for undergraduate distance education courses is $615 per course. Tuition for distance education graduate courses is $1245 per course. Other general ex-

penses include textbooks, which may be ordered on line, and some courses require specific software packages. These fees are subject to change.

FINANCIAL AID

Students accepted for enrollment in a degree or certificate program through New Hampshire College may be considered for several forms of institutional and federal financial aid. The College participates in the Federal Work-Study Program, the Federal Perkins Loan program, and the Federal Supplemental Educational Opportunity Grant program and is an eligible institution under the Federal Stafford Student Loan program and the Federal Pell Grant program.

APPLYING

Distance education students may enroll in undergraduate or graduate classes on a rolling basis. Applicants must submit an application along with appropriate documentation, such as an official high school transcript, GED scores, or official transcripts from previous colleges. There is no application fee. Applicants may register for course work immediately.

CONTACT

Kim Dabilis Byrne, Assistant Director
Distance Education Program
New Hampshire College
2500 North River Road
Manchester, New Hampshire 03106-1045
Telephone: 603-645-9766
Fax: 603-645-9706
E-mail: kbyrne@nhc.edu
Web site: http://de.nhc.edu

New Jersey Institute of Technology

Division of Continuing Professional Education
Distance Learning—Extension Programs

Newark, New Jersey

Founded in 1881, New Jersey Institute of Technology (NJIT) is New Jersey's technological research university. An international leader in scientific and technological education, NJIT educates students to become frontrunners in the global marketplace. The university seeks students who are seriously committed to education and can bring energy, creativity, and a practical outlook to solving today's pressing problems. The degree programs are demanding, rewarding, and highly regarded by employers.

Since publication in 1978 of The Networked Nation: Human Communication via Computers, by NJIT's Professors Murray Turrof and S. Roxanne Hiltz, the university has served as a leader in distance education. With four degree programs and six graduate certificate programs offered completely through distance learning, NJIT course work is made available to students regardless of their geographic location. For the adult professional, in particular, NJIT courses provide the flexibility and convenience needed to fit in with work, family, and community responsibilities. NJIT's customer-service orientation allows each student to receive the personal attention that is required for successful completion of a degree program or certificate.

DISTANCE LEARNING PROGRAM

Via distance learning, NJIT conducts full undergraduate and graduate degree programs, graduate certificates, and individual college courses using today's home electronics to provide the college experience. By virtue of the academic quality, focus, and advanced delivery format, NJIT helps adult men and women cross one bridge to knowledge acquisition leading to gainful employment.

DELIVERY MEDIA

Today's home electronics can be used in a new way to pursue education. Through integration of the personal computer, streaming audio, streaming video, on-line chat, threaded discussion, videocassette recorder (VCR), television, and telephone, the classroom can be a student's home, office, or any place other than the college campus. Each NJIT course consists of two components: a telelecture conducted by NJIT faculty members and an electronic discussion through which students conduct dialogue with a mentor and other classmates at any time of the day or night. The medium of the telelecture is streaming video, streaming audio, or video (furnished as a set of stand-alone, leased videotapes that are shipped to the student's home or office for replaying in sequence).

PROGRAMS OF STUDY

The university offers four complete degree programs via NJIT. The 129-credit Bachelor of Arts in information systems program provides students with a solid foundation in applying the principles of computing and information systems to business and industrial problems and managerial decision making.

The 134-credit Bachelor of Science in computer science program provides students with the most comprehensive treatment of computers, with considerable breadth and depth in computer science topics, the sci-

ences, mathematics, and supporting interdisciplinary studies.

The 36-credit Master of Science in Information Systems (M.S.I.S.) program has been designed to train individuals who can assume responsibility for analyzing and organizing the information needs and resources of an organization and develop systems to respond to those needs.

The 30-credit Master of Science in Engineering Management (M.S.E.M.) program has been designed to develop engineers and other technically trained individuals for leadership roles in technology-based, project-oriented enterprises. It provides individuals with the broad-based knowledge and skills to succeed as managers of organizations and of projects from conceptualization through implementation.

In addition, students who wish to complete individual undergraduate or graduate courses in one or more of a dozen academic disciplines may enroll on a nonmatriculated basis.

SPECIAL PROGRAMS

Through the Division of Continuing Professional Education, the administrative unit in which distance learning program is housed, NJIT offers several graduate-level certificates that are available in their entirety or in part via distance learning techniques, including e-commerce, computer networks, object-oriented design (C++), client/server architecture, project management, practice of technical communications, telecommunications networking, Internet applications development, and information systems design and development. Each certificate, worth 12 graduate credits, can be used as a springboard to advanced degree study at NJIT or elsewhere. Consisting of four courses, each certificate is in a topic area considered by today's corporations to be employable "hot tracks" through the year 2005.

CREDIT OPTIONS

Students may be awarded transfer credit at the time of admission for courses that were completed at other institutions and are equivalent to courses offered by NJIT. A minimum grade of C must be earned in a course in order to receive transfer credit.

FACULTY

Ninety-eight percent of NJIT's full-time faculty members hold the terminal degree in their field.

ADMISSION

Admission policies for the NJIT distance learning programs follow the same admission criteria as do traditionally delivered NJIT academic pro-grams. In general, admission on a nonmatriculated basis to an undergraduate course requires possession of a high school diploma or General Equivalency Degree. Admission as a nonmatriculated student to a graduate course requires possession, at minimum, of an undergraduate degree from an accredited college or university with a grade point average that meets NJIT academic department standards for regular admission as a Master of Science degree candidate. In general, an acceptable grade point average is no lower than a 2.8 on a 4.0 scale.

TUITION AND FEES

In 1999–2000, undergraduate tuition was $206 per credit for New Jersey residents and $424 per credit for nonresidents. Graduate tuition was $388 per credit for New Jersey residents and $534 per credit for nonresidents. Graduate certificate students pay in-state tuition regardless of location. Required supplemental fees, not includ-ing rental of video telelectures, totaled $247 for a 3-credit course taken during the 1999–2000 academic year. Updated tuition and fees can be found online (http://www.njit.edu/cpe).

FINANCIAL AID

NJIT's Office of Financial Aid provides counseling and administers loans, scholarships, and grants to qualified students. Federal and state programs and private, industrial, and university resources are utilized to support the university's financial aid programs.

APPLYING

Students may apply on a nonmatriculated basis by mail, fax, or online (http://www.njit.edu/cpe). To apply for admission on a matriculated basis, students should contact the Office of Admissions at 973-596-3300 or 800-925-6548 (toll-free) to request a degree application or use the online matriculated application form (http://www.njit.edu).

CONTACT

Division of Continuing Professional Education
New Jersey Institute of Technology
University Heights, New Jersey 07102-1948
Telephone: 973-596-3060
Fax: 973-596-3203
Web site: http://www.njit.edu/DL

The New Jersey Virtual Community College Consortium

A Partnership of New Jersey's Nineteen Community Colleges

Trenton, New Jersey

New Jersey's community colleges have formed a consortium to share online courses. The New Jersey Virtual Community College Consortium's (NJVCCC) mission is to increase access to postsecondary education for all New Jerseyans regardless of geographic or time constraints. The NJVCCC was developed as a companion to the New Jersey Virtual University, which was launched in January 1999. The NJVCCC began offering distance learning courses via the Internet in fall 1999. In spring 2000, more than 200 distance learning courses were offered to community college students throughout the state of New Jersey. The NJVCCC is not a separate degree-granting college.

DISTANCE LEARNING PROGRAM

A New Jersey community college serves as either a host for a course, a provider of a course, or both. One college develops or provides the course, while the other colleges subscribe to the course to offer or host it to their students locally.

The NJVCCC provides high-tech college-level courses with the "high-touch" services students have come to expect from their local community colleges, such as tutoring, advisement, and counseling.

The NJVCCC served several hundred students across New Jersey during its first year of operation in 1999–2000.

DELIVERY MEDIA

All NJVCCC courses are offered using the Internet. Students enrolled in NJVCCC courses correspond with professors via e-mail, bulletin boards, and the World Wide Web. Online courses require a computer with a graphical user interface (Mac or Windows), a modem (28.8 kbps or higher), and connection to an Internet service provider (ISP), and students need to know how to download software from the Internet and install and configure software.

PROGRAMS OF STUDY

The NJVCCC does not grant degrees. However, three New Jersey community colleges offer online degrees.

Atlantic Cape Community College (ACCC) in Mays Landing, New Jersey, offers online Associate in Arts degrees in liberal arts, history, and social science. ACCC offers online Associate in Science degrees in general studies and business administration. For more information on ACCC's online degree offerings, students should visit the College's Web site at http://www.atlantic.edu.

Burlington County College (BCC) in Pemberton, New Jersey, offers an online Associate in Science degree in business administration and an online Associate in Arts degree in liberal arts. For more information on BCC's online degree offerings, students should visit the College's Web site at http://www.bcc.edu.

Mercer County Community College (MCCC) in Trenton, New Jersey, offers an online Associate in Applied Science degree in general business and an online Associate in Arts degree in humanities and social sciences. For more information on MCCC's online degree offerings, students should visit the College's Web site at http://www.mccc.edu.

SPECIAL PROGRAMS

All nineteen NJVCCC member community colleges are accredited by the Commission of Higher Education, Middle States Association of Colleges and Schools. All New Jersey community colleges offer credit courses that lead to various associate degrees. Separate from the NJVCCC, many New Jersey community colleges offer other distance learning credit and noncredit courses using television, video, CD-ROM, and radio.

STUDENT SERVICES

Students who take NJVCCC courses are entitled to all services offered by their local community college, such as tutoring, library services, proctored testing, advisement, counseling, registration, and access to computer labs.

CREDIT OPTIONS

Many of the courses offered by the NJVCCC are 3-credit college-level courses. NJVCCC courses can be used to fulfill partial requirements of a degree program at one of New Jersey's community colleges. Degrees earned at community colleges can be used to transfer to four-year institutions, or students can enter the workforce directly.

FACULTY

All of New Jersey's community college faculty members who teach NJVCCC courses are highly skilled instructors with extensive distance learning experience. Many NJVCCC teachers hold doctorates, master's degrees, or other terminal degrees.

ADMISSION

The principal requirement for admission is the applicant's possession of a high school diploma or its equivalent.

TUITION AND FEES

NJVCCC courses cost $80 per credit, with no service fees, for in-state and out-of-state students. The only fee a student may pay is a registration fee.

FINANCIAL AID

Financial aid is available to distance learners who are enrolled as full- or part-time students in degree programs at any of New Jersey's nineteen community colleges. General financial aid programs include state Tuition Aid Grants, Federal Pell Grants, state Educational Opportunity Fund Grants, and the Federal Direct Student Loan Program.

APPLYING

To register for NJVCCC courses, students should visit the Consortium's Web site (listed below). Full registration instructions are provided online.

CONTACT

Jacob C. Farbman
Public Relations Officer
New Jersey Council of County Colleges
330 West State Street
Trenton, New Jersey 08618
Phone: 609-392-3434
Fax: 609-392-8158
E-mail: farbmanj@aol.com
Web site: http://www.njvccc.cc.nj.us (NJVCCC courses
and registration)
http://www.njccc.org (New Jersey community
colleges information)

New School University

Cyberspace Campus (DIAL)

New York, New York

The New School was founded in 1919 as America's first university for adults. Over the years, it has grown into an accredited, degree-granting institution comprising seven divisions (the New School, the Graduate Faculty of Political and Social Science, the Robert J. Milano Graduate School of Management and Urban Policy, Parsons School of Design, Mannes College of Music, Eugene Lang College, and the School of Dramatic Arts). About 40,000 students attend the University annually, bringing a wide variety of cultures, perspectives, aspirations, priorities, interests, and talents. But the New School has never neglected its original mission: it continues to serve the intellectual, cultural, artistic, and professional needs and interests of adult students.

DISTANCE LEARNING PROGRAM

The New School's DIAL program first went on line with seven noncredit courses in 1994. Since then, DIAL has grown into a full cyberspace campus, offering 300 courses each year for credit and noncredit, as well as master's-level courses and bachelor's degrees on line. DIAL courses are sections of the same courses that are taught on the Greenwich Village campus and are created and led by the same distinguished faculty. The New School and its programs, including DIAL, are accredited by the Commission on Higher Education of the Middle States Association of Colleges and Schools and chartered as a university by the Regents of the University of the State of New York.

DELIVERY MEDIA

DIAL courses are offered through interactive computer conferencing via the Internet's World Wide Web facility. Programs are asynchronous and fully interactive, meaning that students receive instruction, ask questions of the instructor and each other, discuss issues, and actively participate in the class, all from home or office. It is recommended that students acquire the highest-speed connection that they can afford (14.4 bps modem minimum) from their Internet Service Providers (ISPs), and guidelines are available for those students who need help in identifying and arranging for service from a local ISP. Students and faculty also need computers (PC or Mac) capable of running one of today's graphical Web browsers (Netscape® recommended).

PROGRAMS OF STUDY

Credit, noncredit, and degree courses are offered in many curriculum areas, including the social sciences, humanities, writing, and communication. The New School's Bachelor of Arts degree in liberal arts is offered through DIAL. Students work closely with an academic adviser (on line) to clarify their educational objectives, assess intellectual strengths and weaknesses, evaluate past academic accomplishments, and then draw on the curriculum available through DIAL to design a program of study reflecting their individual needs and goals. The process of organizing and synthesizing his or her own education is the essential and ongoing responsibility of every New School student. Applicants to the on-line B.A. program must have completed 60 semester credits of course work at an accredited college prior to matriculation. In general, students are required to complete an additional 60 credits to graduate; more information may be obtained by sending e-mail to admissions@dialnsa.edu. In addition to courses offered in fulfillment of B.A. requirements, students may study through DIAL for credits that may be applied to the New School's M.A. in Media Studies and several other graduate degrees.

SPECIAL PROGRAMS

Almost all New School courses, including those offered through DIAL, are available for credit or noncredit registration. About half of the students study each semester not for credit but for personal enrichment or intellectual stimulation. A significant proportion of the remaining half study for general credit, which means that the credit earned is transferable to a degree program elsewhere. The balance of the students in DIAL study for credit to be applied to one of the University's degree programs (predominantly the New School B.A. and M.A. in Media Studies). Through its Institute for Professional Development (IPD), the New School's Distance Learning Program seeks to make courses, certificates, and degree programs available to employees through special arrangements with organizations and other employers; for more information, students may send e-mail to dialexec@dialnsa. edu. All New School distance learning students have access to the full range of facilities on the cyberspace campus, including faculty office hours, library support, an orientation center, and 24-hour technical support (on line and by telephone). There is also a full program of public events, performances, social gatherings—even the New School's unique art collection.

CREDIT OPTIONS

For matriculated students, the academic credits earned upon successful completion of a DIAL course are applied toward degree requirements. Matriculants may earn credit for prior academic and other developmental work; specific information may be obtained by e-mail from advisors@dialnsa.edu. Students who are degree candidates at another college or university or have not yet entered an undergraduate degree program may register for general credit. Students receive academic credit for each course successfully completed. Students at other institutions should make arrangements for transfer of credit at their home institutions prior to registering for New School DIAL courses. Students may also elect to take DIAL courses on a noncredit basis. The University does not maintain a permanent record of noncredit enrollment, although students may request a "Record of Attendance" should verification of enrollment be necessary. Students may send e-mail to advisors@dialnsa.edu for more information or clarification.

FACULTY

Close to 700 of the New School's 1,800 instructors have completed the preparation required to teach on line. In the core curriculum areas (humanities, social sciences, writing, and communication), about 68 percent of New School faculty members have earned the doctorate or other terminal degree in their fields of specialty.

ADMISSION

General requirements for B.A. matriculants are that they have completed 60 semester credits at an accredited college and that they be at least 24 years of age. Specific information can be obtained by sending e-mail to admissions@dialnsa.edu or calling 212-229-5630. Noncredit and general credit students may simply review course offerings and complete registration on line at http://www.dialnsa.edu at any time.

TUITION AND FEES

For the 1999–2000 academic year, matriculated students enrolled in the B.A. program pay $528 per credit; for those enrolled in the M.A. in Media Studies, the cost is $650 per credit. All degree students pay a $100 registration fee per term. General credit students pay $602 per credit for New School courses and $695 per credit for Parsons courses. General credit students pay a $43 registration fee per term. Noncredit tuition varies by course and is listed with each description. Some courses carry additional lab, materials, or other fees; these are also listed with each description. The noncredit registration fee is $10 per term.

FINANCIAL AID

The New School offers a full range of state, federal, and New School–sponsored programs for students enrolled in degree programs, depending on the jurisdiction in which the DIAL student resides. Students at other institutions may be eligible for financial support from those institutions. Applicants must file the FAFSA form; this form may be obtained from the Financial Aid Office. No student should decide against applying to the New School for financial reasons. For specific information and assistance, students may send e-mail to finance@dialnsa.edu or call 212-229-8930.

APPLYING

Distance students may apply for admission to the New School's B.A. program through DIAL by sending an inquiry to admissions@dialnsa.edu. Students may send e-mail or call 212-229-5630 or 800-862-5039 (toll-free) to find out about online "open houses." All new students are required to participate in a weeklong, online orientation program.

CONTACT

Stephen J. Anspacher
Associate Provost for Distance
  Learning
New School for Social Research
68 Fifth Avenue
New York, New York 10011
Telephone: 212-229-5880
Fax: 212-989-2928
E-mail: dialexec@dialnsa.edu
  nsadmissions@newschool.edu
Web site: http://www.dialnsa.edu

New York University

The Virtual College

New York, New York

New York University (NYU) was founded in 1831 to enlarge the scope of higher education to meet the needs of persons aspiring to careers in business, industry, science, and the arts, as well as in law, medicine, and the ministry. Continuing this tradition, NYU's School of Continuing Education and Professional Studies has grown over the past sixty years to become the nation's largest private university-based adult education provider, offering more than 2,000 credit and noncredit courses to more than 60,000 students annually. NYU is a member of the Association of American Universities and is accredited by the Middle States Association of Colleges and Schools.

NYU pioneered distance learning in the 1950s with its Sunrise Semester series, which aired for twenty-five years on national television. In the spirit of Sunrise Semester, NYU introduced the Virtual College in 1992 to expand the spatial and temporal boundaries of learning and respond to the increasing professional education needs of working adults.

As the physical infrastructure of the global economy is changing from concrete and steel to computers and communication, NYU's teleprogram gives practitioners those collaborative and technical skills necessary for working within (as well as on) decentralized and networked workplaces—in effect, a virtual college preparing employees for tomorrow's virtual organizations.

DISTANCE LEARNING PROGRAM

Created to deliver high-quality, interactive instruction directly to students, the Virtual College is the electronic equivalent of a traditional college and provides adult learners with a broad range of course, faculty, library, and administrative services.

Through the Virtual College, students receive instruction, ask questions, conduct analyses, manage projects, and complete assignments at their own convenience and from practically anywhere. The teleprogram network provides an electronic workplace for students and faculty members, allowing them to go from just talking about course projects to actually completing them. The Virtual College course work is conducted from the student's home or office PC; there are no on-campus sessions.

More than 200 students have completed the Virtual College's telecourses. Students range in age from 25 to 50 (with a mean age of 35), and 35 percent are women. Most students are employed as full-time managers or professionals in finance, accounting, and marketing and study on a part-time basis. All students have a bachelor's degree, and 30 percent have advanced degrees, typically an M.B.A.

DELIVERY MEDIA

The Virtual College uses the Internet to provide students and faculty members with an electronic environment for taking courses using networked PCs. The teleprogram delivers to distance learners the same level of dynamic, hands-on instruction that characterizes the best on-campus lectures, seminars, and laboratories. All telecourses employ such advanced technologies as streaming video, online laboratories, and hypertext readings. The Virtual College is a unique distance education program where all instructional materials, including video, simulations, laboratories, and readings, are digital and interactively accessible through one common user interface.

During the Virtual College's telecourses, students and faculty members collaborate on-line to analyze and implement case study management and information systems using advanced applications software packages. By the second or third week of each course, students are divided into small groups to work asynchronously on various phases of business and systems case study projects. Functioning as members of their virtual project teams, students establish guidelines, conduct studies, and manage online project responsibilities. During a typical telecourse, each student creates about 50 discussion, analysis, and assignment documents—a level of participation that would be rare in most on-campus courses.

The Virtual College students must have a Pentium PC; Windows 95, 98, or NT; and a CD-ROM drive.

PROGRAMS OF STUDY

The Virtual College offers two online graduate programs: a 36-credit master's degree in management and systems and a 16-credit graduate certificate in information technology.

The Master of Science in Management and Systems is designed to prepare midcareer audit, systems, and other professionals wishing to assume management responsibilities within audit, systems, or related departments or organizations. The degree requires the completion of 36 credits of graduate education, selected from required business and systems core courses, a group of electives, and a final master's project. Typically, the program can be completed in two to three years of part-time study.

In addition to the Master of Science degree, the Virtual College teleprogram offers an Advanced Professional Certificate (APC) in information technology. This 16-credit graduate program is intended for nontechnical generalists faced with the need to analyze and develop information systems for their own organizations and lead teams working within networked environments.

Candidates for both programs must complete all course requirements with a cumulative grade point average of 3.0 (B). The time limit for completion of all teleprogram requirements is four years for the M.S. and two years for the APC.

SPECIAL PROGRAMS

To accommodate the schedule of today's busy adult student, the Virtual College teleprogram is offered in an "education-on-demand" format. Once students are admitted to the program, they can register for telecourses anytime and have from four to fourteen weeks to complete each one. Telecourses utilize software agents to track, prompt, and record student progress through the courses. Each on-demand telecourse consists of multiple sessions that contain video, tutorial, laboratory, and reading modules.

While students largely work independently on these courses, faculty members are available to answer questions, evaluate assignments and examinations, and provide advisement via computer conferencing, electronic mail, and even desktop videoconferencing. Throughout each telecourse, the intelligent network identifies and supports groups of students to collaborate on assignments. Faculty member–led projects are offered on a scheduled basis throughout the year.

CREDIT OPTIONS

Up to 8 transfer credits may be approved toward the 36-credit requirement for the M.S. degree. All transfer credit must be from graduate-level course work completed at accredited institutions with a grade of 3.0 (B) or better. No transfer credit may be approved toward the 16-credit requirement for the APC.

FACULTY

There are eight full-time and part-time faculty members dedicated to the Virtual College teleprogram. All Virtual College faculty members have doctoral or other terminal academic degrees.

ADMISSION

Admission to the Virtual College M.S. and APC teleprograms is open to all qualified applicants holding a bachelor's degree or higher from an accredited undergraduate or graduate institution. Factors considered in evaluating applications include academic achievement in previous degree course work, scores on the GMAT or GRE exam (M.S. only), TOEFL scores (for international students), the nature and extent of previous work experience, a personal essay, and two letters of recommendation (M.S. only). In addition, each candidate must possess good business writing skills as the teleprograms require extensive electronic text communications for all course discussions, analyses, and projects.

TUITION AND FEES

In 2000–01, graduate tuition is $783 for the first credit and $665 for each additional credit. There are no additional charges for teleprogram software, electronic readings, or network connections.

FINANCIAL AID

Financial assistance in the form of Federal Perkins Loans or Federal Stafford Student Loans is available through the Higher Education Assistance Corporation in New York State and in New Jersey. About 15 percent of M.S. and APC students receive student loans.

APPLYING

New York University reviews applications in the date order of receipt of all materials. Students are not required to attend any on-campus orientation sessions.

CONTACT

Annie Stanton
Associate Director
The Virtual College
New York University
48 Cooper Square
New York, New York 10003
Telephone: 212-998-7193
Fax: 212-995-3550
E-mail: scps.virtualms@nyu.edu
Web site: http://www.scps.nyu.edu/virtualms

North Carolina Agricultural and Technical State University

Center for Distance Learning

Greensboro, North Carolina

North Carolina Agricultural and Technical State University (NC A&T), a public, comprehensive, land-grant university, is accredited by the Commission on Colleges of the Southern Association of Colleges and Schools to award bachelor's, master's, and doctoral degrees. The University offers degree programs in technology, education, agriculture, and arts and sciences at the bachelor's and master's levels; in nursing and business at the bachelor's level only; and in electrical and mechanical engineering at the doctoral level. The University was established by an act of the General Assembly of North Carolina in 1891 as an agricultural and mechanical college and became a constituent institution of the University of North Carolina system in 1972. The mission statement of the University reads in part, "to . . . develop innovative instructional programs that will meet the needs of a diverse student body and the expectation of the various professions . . . to develop and maintain undergraduate and graduate programs of high academic quality and excellence."

DISTANCE LEARNING PROGRAM

Distance learning at NC A&T, administered in close cooperation with the academic departments, enables students to access courses and degree programs of the University at convenient sites and times. More than 200 people are currently taking classes on-site and via interactive video and Internet instruction.

DELIVERY MEDIA

As of fall 1999, courses are delivered on- and off-campus using two methods of delivery. Asynchronous delivery allows students to determine their own times for instruction. This form of instruction includes such methods as e-mail, listserves, and online discussion boards. Synchronous instruction requires the participation of all students at a set time. Methods include computer conferencing, streaming video, and other forms of interactive video. Students and instructors also interact via group chat-room sessions and individual sessions. Courses at NC A&T are currently offered via interactive video and require interactive video classrooms on- and off-campus. Classes are also offered at a distance through on-site instruction.

PROGRAMS OF STUDY

The programs offered entirely at a distance include Master of Science (M.S.) degree programs in architectural/facilities engineering, physical education, adult education, and technological education. Architectural/facilities engineering courses are currently being offered via interactive video and on-site instruction. The student may complete one of three program options—the thesis option (30 semester hours), the project option (33 semester hours), or the course option (36 semester hours).

In physical education, the M.S. degree/G license–teaching/administration option, a 33-semester-hour-program, is offered via on-site and interactive video instruction. Students must take the 12-semester-hour physical education required core, 9 semester hours in the area of interest, 6 semester hours in education, and 6 semester hours of electives.

Adult education courses are offered via interactive video and on-site instruction; Internet courses are being developed. The program of study consists of a professional core curriculum of 21 semester hours, with a minimum of 15 semester hours in a research or practice concentration. The concentration entails graduate research and cognate studies in an adult education specialty (thesis option) or an adult education practice concentration (nonthesis option). Practice concentrations are currently designed in community education, counseling, higher education, human resource development, and instructional technology.

Technological education courses are offered via the Internet and on site. The program requires at least 30 semester hours of graduate-level courses, which include a 12-semester-hour concentration in technology or vocational/industrial education courses, leading to the G license in technology education or trade and industrial education or to vocational education director.

SPECIAL PROGRAMS

The Center for Distance Learning provides the opportunity for students taking courses online to work towards degrees in six programs. These programs include master's degrees in computer science, adult education, instructional technology, health and physical education, and reading education. Although these programs are still in the planing stages, students may take the available online courses and apply them towards their current degree program. Another program in the planning stages is a bachelor's degree in occupational safety and health.

STUDENT SERVICES

Library services are available to distance learners through the eCollege site. Library orientation and bibliographic resources are posted at this site to help students locate materials for research. Students may access various library holdings through this site.

Academic advising information offers online students the same resources found on campus. Advisement for distance learners is conducted via the Internet, e-mail, regular mail, telephone, and interactive video.

CREDIT OPTIONS

The University allows 6 transfer credits (semester hours) from another accredited graduate program toward graduate degrees and up to 80 semester hours in transfer toward undergraduate degrees. Credit may be earned by examination for any undergraduate course for which a suitable examination has been adopted or prepared by the academic department. Credit may also be granted for the successful completion of standardized tests under the College Level Examination Program (CLEP) for specific approved courses.

FACULTY

Twenty-eight full-time and 8 part-time faculty members teach in the distance learning programs. All of the full-time faculty members hold terminal degrees.

ADMISSION

Distance learners must meet the on-campus admissions requirements of the programs to which they are applying. Non–degree-seeking students may enroll in off-campus credit courses without formal admission; degree-seeking students may earn 9 semester hours off campus prior to admission.

TUITION AND FEES

In-state undergraduate students pay $33 per semester hour plus an educational technology fee of $6 per semester hour, for a total of $39 per semester hour. For out-of-state undergraduate students, tuition is $279 per semester hour plus an educational technology fee of $7.75 per semester hour, for a total of $286.75 per semester hour.

In-state graduate students pay $50 per semester hour plus an educational technology fee of $7.75 per semester hour, for a total of $57.75 per semester hour. For out-of-state graduate students, tuition is $407 per semester hour plus an educational technology fee of $7.75 per semester hour, for a total of $414.75 per semester hour.

FINANCIAL AID

Distance learning students who qualify for financial aid may expect assistance through a variety of sources, which may include loans or grants. Typical sources of financial aid include Federal Pell Grants, state need-based grants, Federal Perkins Loans, and Federal Direct Student Loans. Detailed information pertaining to federal and state programs may be found in the *Student Financial Aid Handbook*. For financial aid information, students may contact the Student Financial Aid Office (336-334-7973).

APPLYING

Distance learners may apply to the Office of Undergraduate Admissions for all undergraduate programs and to the School of Graduate Studies for all graduate programs. Undergraduate applicants must complete the undergraduate application, remit a $35 application fee, and have previous college and high school transcripts mailed to the undergraduate admissions office. SAT I scores (for those under age 25) also need to be submitted.

Applicants to programs within the School of Graduate Studies must complete the graduate application and remit a $35 application fee and three letters of recommendation. Required test scores from admissions examinations vary by department.

To enroll in a distance learning course, students need to contact the Center for Distance Learning for specific on-site, telephone, and online registration dates and times. No formal application process is necessary.

CONTACT

Inquiries should be directed to:
Tracie Olds or Keith McCullough
Center for Distance Learning
North Carolina Agricultural and
Technical State University
1601 East Market Street
Greensboro, North Carolina
27411-1117
Telephone: 336-334-7607
888-323-OCES (toll-free)
Fax: 336-334-7081
Web site: http://www.ncat.edu/
~distance

North Central University

The University for Distance Learning

Prescott, Arizona

North Central University (NCU) is a private distance learning institution offering bachelor's, master's, and doctoral degrees in psychology and business. Arizona state law, rule R4-39-107(B), states that "to be provisionally licensed to operate degree programs or to grant degrees, an existing private, nonaccredited, degree-granting institution shall demonstrate reasonable and timely progress toward obtaining accreditation with an accrediting agency recognized by the United States Department of Education or the Council for Higher Education Accreditation. 'Reasonable and timely' means the continuous, diligent and successful pursuit of the various stages of accreditation within the time periods established by the accrediting agency and as determined by the board." NCU's Board of Directors is committed to obtaining regional accreditation. The regional accreditation agency's site visit to determine eligibility for candidacy is scheduled for early 2000. More information is available on the school's Web site at http://www.ncu.edu.

DISTANCE LEARNING PROGRAM

North Central University provides a self-paced learning program in which faculty mentors serve as guides rather than lecturers. Enrollment is continuous so that students can arrange start dates for their convenience. Students are free to complete courses at any time within a four-month semester and are encouraged to advance to the next semester's courses ahead of schedule. Academic advisers and faculty mentors communicate one-on-one with students through voice or electronic contact. Students have access to NCU's Electronic Library Resource Center; the research librarian is available for assistance.

DELIVERY MEDIA

Learners are advised and guided through the courses through direct, individual contact with faculty mentors via phone, fax, e-mail, and other electronic media. Each program is an organized process designed to meet educational objectives in the shortest time frame possible.

Upon enrolling in a course, the learner receives a syllabus and a course outline. Learners purchase books from local bookstores or online suppliers.

The purpose of active self-learning is to encourage the learner to apply knowledge acquired in the courses to practical situations and to use faculty mentors as resources and facilitators in the process of learning. The learner demonstrates mastery of the course material and its relevance by completing required assignments.

PROGRAMS OF STUDY

NCU offers degree programs through distance learning in two recognized professional areas: business and psychology. Many specializations are available so that students can tailor course work to their specific career needs. Both professional and research doctorates are available in each field.

A bachelor's degree requires 120 semester units, with 48 units in general education. At least 40 units must be completed through NCU.

A master's degree requires 40 semester units beyond the bachelor's degree. NCU accepts up to 8 units for relevant graduate courses completed at an accredited college.

A doctoral degree requires 96 semester units beyond the bachelor's degree. NCU accepts up to 48 units for relevant graduate courses completed at an accredited college.

The professional doctorate program provides courses with breadth and depth for practicing professionals in business and psychology. The Doctor of Business Administration (D.B.A.) and the Doctor of Psychology (Psy.D.) require an 8-unit capstone project in which learners devise a way to apply their education to their discipline or career.

The Doctor of Philosophy (Ph.D.) program prepares learners for scholarship, systematic inquiry, and research. The degree requirements include the equivalent of six courses or 24 graduate units in dissertation preparation courses and the submission and defense of an acceptable dissertation. The dissertation process is demanding, but high academic recognition is the reward for rigorous effort and scholarship.

SPECIAL PROGRAMS

Specializations available for graduate programs in business administration include applied computer science, criminal justice administration, financial management, health-care administration, human resources management, international business, management, management information systems, management of engineering and technology, and public administration.

STUDENT SERVICES

NCU recognizes that the life experiences, learning needs, and learning patterns of adults differ significantly from those of the traditional college student. NCU was designed as a new kind of university, where "we put people first in distance learning." NCU provides adult learners with an education comparable to the best that can be found at traditional campus-based institutions but at an affordable cost. Students have the opportunity to learn at their own pace, at times and in places compatible with commitments of family, work, and leisure. In a supportive, collaborative learning environment, students acquire knowledge that is relevant to their lives and careers. Faculty members offer individual treatment, professional assessment, and timely feedback on performance. Modern technology enables students to access information and to confer with colleagues around the world. A learner advocate is available to help students understand the system.

CREDIT OPTIONS

Payment options allow payment for the program either in full, by semester, by course, or monthly. Service charges apply to multiple payment plans. All charges are enumerated on the enrollment agreement that is signed by both the learner and University.

FACULTY

All faculty mentors have accredited graduate degrees. Many are active in professional practice as well as academic work.

ADMISSION

Each learner at NCU must have an e-mail address with the capability to send and receive attachments and a Java-enabled browser to access the NCU Web site.

For admission to a bachelor's program, students are required to have a high school diploma or GED equivalent. A 450 TOEFL score is required for applicants for whom English is not the primary language.

For admission to a graduate program, students must have a bachelor's degree from an accredited institution. A 500 TOEFL score is required for applicants for whom English is not the primary language.

TUITION AND FEES

Tuition for the degree program is based on the number of units required at the rate of $180 per unit. Additional fees are assessed for application evaluation, dissertation, adding or dropping courses, library or identification card replacement, and other specific items.

FINANCIAL AID

NCU does not offer financial aid.

APPLYING

To apply on line, students should go to the Web site listed below and fill out the application. Admissions screening counselors contact applicants to coordinate the fee, statement of intent, transcripts, and other documentation. Students who are merely seeking information should click on the "information only" icon to receive a bulletin and other information through the mail or call the toll-free telephone number listed below.

CONTACT

North Central University
505 West Whipple Street
Prescott, Arizona 86301
Telephone: 540-541-7777
800-903-9381
(toll-free)
Fax: 520-541-7817
Web site: http://www.ncu.edu

 # Northeastern University

OnLine and TV Distance Education Programs

Boston, Massachusetts

Founded in 1898, Northeastern University's (NU) mission as a national, private, research university that is student-oriented, practice-oriented, and urban, is to provide individuals with the opportunity for upward mobility through excellence in education. For close to a century, cooperative education has been the keystone of Northeastern's uniqueness. Students are offered the opportunity to apply lessons of the classroom directly to the workplace through the co-op program.

Northeastern University's main campus is situated on 60 acres in Boston's Back Bay. The University offers seven undergraduate colleges, nine graduate and professional schools, two part-time undergraduate divisions, and a number of continuing and special education programs and institutes. Northeastern has a long history of serving the educational needs of nontraditional students.

Northeastern University is accredited by the New England Association of Schools and Colleges, Inc.

DISTANCE LEARNING PROGRAM

Network Northeastern, the distance learning unit, provides credit and noncredit programs to corporate, business and university sites, and individuals in the Commonwealth of Massachusetts and the United States through live, interactive television, videotape, and online programs. Since 1983, Network Northeastern has served thousands of students regionally and nationally as part of adult and continuing education unit at the University.

DELIVERY MEDIA

For students located outside the Boston area, Northeastern University OnLine (NUOL) makes continuing education convenient and accessible. NUOL offers undergraduate and noncredit certificate programs entirely on line. Courses are asynchronous and accessible twenty-four hours a day. Students have e-mail and phone contact with their instructors and chat/conference sections of each online course. Students complete all of their work on line and are never required to attend class on campus.

PROGRAMS OF STUDY

NUOL offers complete certificate programs. Certificates offered include technical writing, Internet technologies (with both Webmaster and Internet Commerce track), advanced Web design, and computer programming (undergraduate course credit). Webmaster technology, data communications, and Java certificates (noncredit) are also offered. (Students can take selected courses, earn an entire certificate, and also use courses toward a degree program. Undergraduate courses can be used toward a given certificate or toward an undergraduate degree at Northeastern or transferred to another institution. The noncredit certificates carry CEU (continuing education unit) credit, but cannot be used toward a degree. For most programs, students can earn a certificate in a year or less.

Once registered in the online program, students have access to their courses twenty-four hours a day, seven days a week. Students work within the term they register but can often work at their own pace within the confines of the course syllabus. Regular contact with the instructor is encouraged and posted conferences for student discussion within the class are an integral part of the course program. Courses are offered four times a year—summer, fall, winter, and spring quarters. The program operates on an open-enrollment basis.

STUDENT SERVICES

Twenty-four hour a day access to courses is provided as well as a toll-free number for assistance with advising, registration, tuition payment, or other help. All registration for online courses is completed on line. Students may also contact instructors and order books in this manner.

CREDIT OPTIONS

Students may take courses for credit or noncredit. Most certificate programs that offer undergraduate credit are designed to also be transferred into a related degree program. The number of transfer credits which can be allowed into an NU certificate varies by certificate. Students should check with Northeastern University regarding specific transfer restrictions,

FACULTY

All online instructors are industry professionals who teach for the University part-time. Ninety-five percent of the online faculty members have master's degrees or higher.

ADMISSION

Admission to the online program is on an open admissions basis. Students simply register and begin taking their courses.

TUITION AND FEES

For academic year 2000–01, undergraduate courses are $695 per three-hour course or $895 for a noncredit course.

FINANCIAL AID

Students must be admitted to a degree program to qualify for financial aid. A student must be a U.S. citizen or eligible noncitizen. All students applying for aid must submit a Free Application for Federal Student Aid (FAFSA) to the Federal Student Aid program. Northeastern University also requires that a student complete an institutional application. A student should begin the process twelve weeks before the beginning of the quarter. To obtain an application, students should call the Office of Student Financial Services at 617-373-3190.

APPLYING

Students can register for courses at the Web site listed below. There is no application fee.

CONTACT

Linda Alosso
Assistant Director
Network Northeastern
Northeastern University
360 Huntington Avenue
328 CP
Boston, MA 02115
Telephone: 877-375-6865 (toll-free)
Fax: 617-373-5625
E-mail: lalosso@nunet.neu.edu
Web site: http://www.NUOL.edu

Norwich University

Vermont College

Montpelier, Vermont

A leader in innovative education tailored to the needs of its diverse student body, Norwich University is a comprehensive university that combines a wide range of brief-residency undergraduate and graduate degree programs on its Vermont College campus in Montpelier, Vermont, with a Corps of Cadets and traditional undergraduates on its Northfield, Vermont, campus. Now offering both undergraduate and graduate online options, Vermont College is also the first campus in the United States dedicated exclusively to brief-residency distance learning programs. The College enrolls more than 1,000 students from around the world. Students may spend from two days to two weeks on campus, studying in a community of learners who share similar interests, or they participate in vibrant online learning communities. Norwich University is accredited by the New England Association of Schools and Colleges.

DISTANCE LEARNING PROGRAM

Norwich University's Vermont College programs offer brief on-campus residencies; independent, self-designed study; one-to-one mentoring; flexible schedules; and academic excellence. Vermont College is located on Norwich's Montpelier, Vermont, campus, 35 miles south of Burlington International Airport. Boston, Massachusetts, and Montreal, Canada, are both an easy 3-hour drive via interstate highways. New York City, 300 miles south, is accessible by car, plane, train, or bus.

DELIVERY MEDIA

Most programs require limited residency on the Montpelier or Brattleboro campuses. New College uses Internet technology to provide its distance learning programs, as does the graduate program's online option.

PROGRAMS OF STUDY

Every degree program is carefully designed by the student and faculty members to meet the particular needs and goals of the student. The emphasis is on interdisciplinary, multicultural studies in the humanities and social sciences through a powerful integration of theory and practical application.

The undergraduate division offers two program options. The Adult Degree Program (ADP) offers a bachelor's degree in liberal studies that working students can earn in eighteen months to four years. Like all Vermont College programs, the ADP features flexible, individualized study and mentored instruction. New College, founded in 1997, is the newest undergraduate option at Norwich University. It offers a bachelor's degree in liberal studies for traditional-aged students that utilizes Internet technology.

Vermont College offers a variety of graduate programs as well. Since 1969, the Graduate Program offers a Master of Arts (M.A.) in humanities and social sciences which can be completed in a minimum of eighteen months with individually tailored study plans.

The Master of Arts in Art Therapy program offers the M.A.A.T. degree and features clinical training in the student's geographic area of choice throughout the United States and parts of Canada.

The newest graduate offering is the Master of Education (M.Ed.) degree. It is a part-time program that features areas of study in curriculum and instruction (including a teaching licensure option), educational leadership (including an administrative licensure option), guidance (including a guidance licensure option), and issues in education.

Established in 1981, the Master of Fine Arts in writing offers a two-year terminal degree for adult students and working writers, with concentrations in poetry, prose, and creative nonfiction.

The Master of Fine Arts in writing for children program offers a two-year terminal degree for adult students and working writers, with concentrations in picture book, middle grade, and young adult.

The Master of Fine Arts in visual art is a two-year terminal degree program for working artists, with areas of study that include painting, drawing, printmaking, sculpture, photography, craft as fine art, video/film, and nontraditional media.

The graduate division also offers a Certificate of Advanced Graduate Study, a postgraduate program that offers concentrations in school psychology, guidance counseling, community psychology, educational administration, leadership studies, and integrated studies.

STUDENT SERVICES

Two comprehensive libraries, Kreitzberg Library on the Northfield campus and Gary Library on the

Montpelier campus, support research and study. Because students study where they live, the University has interlibrary loan arrangements with many schools and local libraries. The library collections are linked with automated catalogs that are accessible on campus and via personal computers from anywhere in the world.

CREDIT OPTIONS

Credit and requirements for graduation vary by program. Students can contact Vermont College for specific credit option information.

FACULTY

More than 150 scholars, artists, and writers form the faculty at Vermont College. The faculty members possess both outstanding academic and professional qualifications. Students study with faculty members during on-campus residencies, developing close working relationships and gaining insights that help them better shape their studies. Following the residency, students work one-to-one with faculty mentors throughout the ensuing term of study.

ADMISSION

Admission requirements vary by program but rely on a variety of measures. Students are asked to send transcripts from previous education, professional references, and an essay detailing life experience and education goals. Students should contact the appropriate admissions counselor for detailed information.

TUITION AND FEES

Tuition varies by program but ranges from $4525 to $6000 per semester. Comprehensive fees include room and board for on-campus residencies. Students are responsible for travel to and from the campus as well as for books and materials necessary for their study.

FINANCIAL AID

To be considered for financial aid, Vermont College requires students to complete a Free Application for Federal Student Aid (FAFSA). To request this form or to ask questions, students can contact the financial planning office (telephone: 800-336-6794 Ext. 8709). The financial aid process can take up to three months to complete.

APPLYING

Applicants should contact the University for specific application information.

CONTACT

Office of Admissions
Vermont College Campus
Norwich University
Montpelier, Vermont 05602
Telephone: 800-336-6794 (toll-free)
Fax: 802-828-8855
E-mail: vcadmis@norwich.edu
Web site: http://www.norwich.edu/vermontcollege

Nova Southeastern University

The School of Computer and Information Sciences

Fort Lauderdale, Florida

A major force in educational innovation, the School of Computer and Information Sciences (SCIS) provides educational programs of distinction to prepare students for leadership roles in computer science, information systems, information science, and computing technology in education. It is distinguished by its ability to offer on-campus, online (via the Internet and World Wide Web), and hybrid on-campus/online formats that enable professionals to pursue B.S., M.S., Ed.D., and Ph.D. degrees without career interruption. Ranked by *Forbes Magazine* as one of the nation's top 20 cyber-universities, the School pioneered online graduate education with its creation of the electronic classroom and has been offering online graduate programs and programs with an online component since 1983. SCIS has more than 1,100 students. It has been awarding graduate degrees since 1980. Through its research, the School advances knowledge, improves professional practice, and contributes to understanding in the computer and information sciences. Located on a 232-acre campus in Fort Lauderdale, Nova Southeastern University (NSU) serves approximately 23,000 students and is the largest independent institution of higher education in Florida. It ranks twenty-fifth in the size of its graduate programs among the 1,560 universities in the U.S. with graduate programs and tenth among private universities. In addition to SCIS, NSU has an undergraduate college and graduate schools of medicine, dentistry, pharmacy, allied health, optometry, law, psychology, education, business, oceanography, and social and systemic studies. To date, the institution has produced approximately 55,000 alumni. Since 1971, NSU has enjoyed full accreditation by the Commission on Colleges of the Southern Association of Colleges and Schools.

DISTANCE LEARNING PROGRAM

All of SCIS's programs of study (four master's degree programs and five doctoral degree programs) are offered in distance learning formats. Online master's programs require no on-campus classroom attendance. Doctoral programs use one of two formats: cluster or institute. Cluster students attend four cluster meetings per year, held quarterly over an extended weekend (Friday, Saturday, and half-day Sunday) at the University. Cluster terms start in March and September. Cluster weekends take place in March, June, September, and December. Institute students attend a weeklong institute twice a year at the University. Institutes are held in mid-January and mid-July at the start

of each five-month term. Doctoral programs also have an online component. Clusters and institutes bring together students and faculty members for participation in courses, workshops, and dissertation counseling. Between meetings, students complete assignments, research papers and projects, and participate in online activities.

DELIVERY MEDIA

Master's students take an orientation and courses on line. An optional on-campus master's orientation is also available. Doctoral students participate in a combination of on-campus and online activities. Online activities require the use of a computer, a modem, and an Internet service provider. Interactive learning methods,

used throughout the instructional sequence, involve World Wide Web pages to access course materials, announcements, and other information, plus a range of online activities that facilitate frequent student-faculty and student-student interaction. Faculty members and students interact via real-time electronic classrooms, online forums using threaded bulletin boards, real-time chat rooms, online submission of assignments in multimedia formats for review by faculty members, electronic mail, and the electronic library.

PROGRAMS OF STUDY

SCIS offers programs leading to the M.S. degree in computer information systems, computer science, computing technology in education, and management information systems. The M.S., which is offered on campus or on line, requires 36 credit hours (thesis optional) and may be completed in 18 months. An option for early admission into the doctoral program from the master's program is available. To earn the M.S. in 18 months, the student must enroll in two courses each term. Terms are 12 weeks long, and there are four terms each year. Master's terms start in September, January, April, and July. Doctoral-level programs include the Ph.D. in computer information systems, computer science, information systems, and information science, and the Ph.D. and Ed.D. in computing technology in education. The Ph.D. in computer science and computer information systems are offered in cluster format and require 64 credits, including eight 3-credit courses, four 4-credit projects, and the dissertation. They may be completed in three years. Doctoral programs in information systems, information science, and computing technology in education are offered in cluster and institute formats and require 64 credits, including eight 3-credit courses, four 4-credit projects, and the dissertation. They may be completed in three years. Students attend clusters or institutes during their first two years of the program while completing course work. Cluster students attend four cluster sessions per year held quarterly over an extended weekend at the University. Cluster terms start in March and September. Institute students attend one weeklong session held at the University at the start of each five-month term. Institute terms start in January and July.

SPECIAL PROGRAMS

SCIS has four special programs: (1) a graduate certificate program in information resources management for federal employees, (2) a graduate certificate program in information systems for corporations, (3) short course and workshop programs for several companies, and (4) a comprehensive series of technology-oriented courses that have been approved for teacher certification in computer science (grades K–12) by Florida's Bureau of Teacher Certification.

CREDIT OPTIONS

Master's applicants may request transfer of up to 6 graduate credits.

Courses proposed for transfer must have grades of at least "B." Credit is not awarded for life or work experience.

FACULTY

SCIS has 20 full-time and 10 part-time faculty members. All faculty members teaching at the graduate level have doctoral degrees.

ADMISSION

The master's applicant must have an undergraduate degree with a GPA of at least 2.5 and a GPA of at least 3.0 in an appropriate major. The doctoral applicant must have a master's degree with an appropriate graduate major and a graduate GPA of at least 3.25. Degrees must be from regionally accredited institutions. All applicants must submit a score report of the GRE or a comprehensive portfolio of appropriate professional experience and credentials. English proficiency is a requirement for admission.

TUITION AND FEES

Tuition is $395 per credit for master's students; for doctoral students, tuition is $4450 per five-month term, or $445 per credit. The registration fee is $30. The application fee is $50.

FINANCIAL AID

To qualify for financial aid a student must be admitted, must be a U.S. citizen or an eligible permanent resident, and must plan on registering for a minimum of 6 credit hours per term. A prospective student who requires financial assistance should apply for financial aid while a candidate for admission. For financial aid information or application forms, students should call 800-522-3243 (toll-free).

APPLYING

Applications, including transcripts and recommendations, should be submitted at least two months before the anticipated starting term. Students who wish to matriculate in a shorter amount of time must contact the SCIS admissions office by telephone to begin the process. Unofficial copies of transcripts are acceptable for early review. Applicants may be granted provisional admission status pending completion of the application process. Late applications that cannot be processed in time for the desired starting term will be considered for the next available term. Master's terms start in September, January, April, and July. Doctoral cluster terms start in September and March. Doctoral institute terms start in January and July.

CONTACT

The School of Computer and Information Sciences
Nova Southeastern University
6100 Griffin Road
Fort Lauderdale, Florida 33314-4416
Telephone: 954-262-2000
　　　　　800-986-2247 (toll-free)
E-mail: scisinfo@nova.edu
Web site: http://www.scis.nova.edu

Ohio University

Lifelong Learning Programs

Athens, Ohio

Ohio University, founded in 1804, was the first institution of higher learning in the Northwest Territory. Today it offers all the resources of a major university—diverse intellectual stimulation and an abundance of social and cultural activities—in a quiet, small-city setting. In addition to the main campus in Athens, the University has six regional centers in the southeast quadrant of Ohio.

Ohio University offers degrees in more than 325 subject areas through its colleges: Arts and Sciences, Business, Communication, Education, Engineering and Technology, Fine Arts, Health and Human Services, Honors Tutorial, Osteopathic Medicine, and University College. The University is accredited by the North Central Association of Colleges and Schools and holds membership in a number of professional organizations; in addition, many academic programs are accredited by their respective associations.

Ohio University has also been a leader in providing learning opportunities for nontraditional students, including more than seventy-five years of correspondence education, credit for college-level learning from life experience, and the external-student degree program.

DISTANCE LEARNING PROGRAM

The Independent Study Program serves students at a distance through correspondence and online courses, course credit by examination, and individual learning contracts. Credit earned through one of these options is considered residential credit and may be applied without limit to a degree program at Ohio University or transferred to another institution (subject to any conditions set by the accepting institution). Approximately 350 courses are currently available through Independent Study; the program has about 5,000 course enrollments each year.

The External Student Program (ESP), which operates under the Adult Learning Services Office, assists students at a distance who are working toward Ohio University degrees with such services as transcript evaluation, advising, degree planning, and liaison with other University offices and departments.

DELIVERY MEDIA

Correspondence between students and instructors, using the postal system or fax, is the primary delivery system for Independent Study courses. E-mail lesson service is rapidly being added as an option for many courses. Videotape supplements the printed instructional materials in some courses. A few courses (with the number steadily increasing) currently use the Internet as a medium of instructional delivery and communication among instructors and students.

PROGRAMS OF STUDY

To earn a degree, students must enroll with the External Student Program. Students are assigned an adviser to assist them in fulfilling degree requirements, including assistance in choosing courses and creating the degree proposals necessary to complete the associate and bachelor's degrees.

Three associate degrees may be earned: Associate in Arts (A.A.), Associate in Science (A.S.), and Associate in Individualized Studies (A.I.S.). All associate degrees require the completion of 96 quarter hours of credit; transfer students must earn at least 30 quarter hours of credit from Ohio University.

The A.I.S. is a self-designed degree; students are required to submit a proposal outlining their course of study and area of concentration (which must consist of a minimum of 30 quarter hours of study). At least 30 of the 96 quarter hours of credit must be completed after admission to the A.I.S. program.

The Bachelor of Specialized Studies (B.S.S.) offers students the opportunity to design an individual program to meet career or academic goals that cannot be accommodated with a degree currently offered by the University. The B.S.S. degree program is initiated in the form of a proposal that includes a statement of rationale; students must have sophomore rank and a minimum cumulative grade point average of 2.0 before submitting the proposal. The proposal includes an "area of concentration" that is titled, consists of a minimum of 45 quarter hours of related course work from two or more related subjects, and does not duplicate any existing major. Students must complete at least 192 quarter hours, with a minimum of 90 hours at the 300–400 (junior/senior) level. At least 45 hours must be earned after the B.S.S. proposal is approved. An adviser assists students with the entire B.S.S. proposal process.

SPECIAL PROGRAMS

The M.B.A. Without Boundaries is a structured two-year program offered by the College of Business. Designed for working professionals, it combines several intensive on-site seminar sessions with group and individual projects completed at the student's own location using the OUMBA Intranet to access learning modules, collaborate with other students, and communicate with faculty members. Enrollment is limited.

The Institutes for Adult Learners are held three times a year on the Ohio University campus. These programs offer degree-seeking students the opportunity to earn credit, become acquainted with the campus and faculty, and participate in a residential experience with other nontraditional students. Courses are taught in intensive, one-week classroom formats supplemented by individual work before and after the Institute. Credit for each course is generally 4 quarter hours.

CREDIT OPTIONS

Students at a distance who are interested in completing an Ohio University degree through the External Student Program can use a combination of in-classroom courses, credit for experiential learning documented through a portfolio process, transfer credit (including possible military and professional training equivalencies established by the American Council on Education), and Independent Study options. Students may apply 24 quarter hours of experiential learning credit toward an associate degree; 48 quarter hours may be applied toward a bachelor's degree.

Regularly enrolled students on any Ohio University campus may use Independent Study or experiential learning credit toward their degrees with their college's approval.

FACULTY

All Independent Study courses are taught by permanent Ohio University faculty members; more than 90 percent of the 125 faculty members teaching in the program have a doctorate or other terminal degree.

ADMISSION

Enrollment in Independent Study courses is open to anyone who can profit from the learning. Enrollment in a course does not constitute formal admission to the University. Students must have a high school diploma to be admitted to the External Student program; transfer students must have a minimum 2.0 cumulative grade point average. Admission to the External Student Program does not guarantee on-campus admission to a specific degree program at Ohio University.

TUITION AND FEES

Fees for Independent Study courses in 2000–01 are correspondence and online courses, $80 per quarter hour; course credit by examination, $42 per quarter hour; and Independent Study projects, $90 per quarter hour. Fees for the External Student Program are a $100 application fee and a $75 annual matriculation fee. In 2000–01, students seeking credit for experiential learning pay $360 for the required portfolio development course plus $150 per course assessment (paid after completion of the portfolio development course).

FINANCIAL AID

Students may use veterans' benefits and employer reimbursement to pay course and program fees. Federal and state financial aid cannot be applied to courses and fees through Independent Study or the External Student Program. Standard tuition and fees paid by on-campus students cannot be applied to Independent Study courses.

APPLYING

Students may enroll in Independent Study courses at any time; enrollment forms are provided in the Independent Study catalog and at the program's World Wide Web site. A separate application process is required for the External Student Program; forms are provided in the External Student bulletin or may be requested from the office of Adult Learning Services.

CONTACT

Independent Study Program
Dr. Richard Moffitt, Director
Independent Study Program
302 Tupper Hall
Ohio University
Athens, Ohio 45701
Telephone: 740-593-2910
Fax: 740-593-2901
WWW: http://www.ohiou.edu/independent/

External Student Program
Barbra Frye, Coordinator
External Student Program, ALS
301 Tupper Hall
Ohio University
Athens, Ohio 45701
Telephone: 740-593-2150
Fax: 740-593-0452
WWW: http://www.ohiou.edu/adultlearning/

M.B.A. Without Boundaries
Dr. Richard Milter
Copeland Hall
Ohio University
Athens, Ohio 45701
Telephone: 740-593-2072
WWW: http://mbawb.cob.ohiou.edu/

Old Dominion University

Distance Learning/TELETECHNET

Norfolk, Virginia

Old Dominion University, a state-assisted institution in Norfolk, Virginia, is part of a metropolitan and historic area with a population of approximately 1.4 million. Established in 1930, the University enrolls more than 18,000 students, including 4,000 graduate students, and operates centers in Hampton, Portsmouth, and Virginia Beach as well as TELETECHNET locations throughout the commonwealth of Virginia and several additional states.

Old Dominion University is accredited by the Commission on Colleges of the Southern Association of Colleges and Schools (1866 Southern Lane, Decatur, Georgia 30033-4097; telephone: 404-679-4501) to award baccalaureate, master's, and doctoral degrees and certificates of advanced study. The undergraduate and graduate business programs are fully accredited by AACSB–The International Association for Management Education. The graduate and undergraduate education programs are accredited by the National Council for Accreditation of Teacher Learning Education. The engineering technology programs are fully accredited by the Technology Accreditation Commission of the Accreditation Board for Engineering and Technology, Inc. (TAC/ABET). The nursing program is accredited by the National League for Nursing Accrediting Commission.

DISTANCE LEARNING PROGRAM

Old Dominion is recognized as an international leader in telecommunications with the creation of TELETECHNET, a distance learning network in partnership with community colleges, military installations, and corporations. Within TELETECHNET, Old Dominion University offers degrees through courses televised to off-campus sites across the country and has an enrollment of more than 5,000 students. Students earn baccalaureate degrees from Old Dominion by completing the first two years of course work at their local community college or other accredited institutions. Old Dominion provides the remaining course work at the site primarily through telecourses using audio and video technologies. In addition to eighteen

baccalaureate degrees, TELETECHNET also offers eight master's degrees and two certificate programs.

DELIVERY MEDIA

Old Dominion University courses are delivered by Ku-band digital satellite with one-way video and two-way audio for interaction between faculty members and students. Classes originate in Norfolk and are transmitted to receiving sites in five states, the District of Columbia, and the Bahamas. Several classes are also offered in a Web-based format, providing students greater flexibility in completion of course work. In addition, a number of classes are streamed over the Internet, where students have access to them at home or at work.

PROGRAMS OF STUDY

Old Dominion's TELETECHNET program offers baccalaureate degrees in business administration, computer science, criminal justice, engineering technology, health sciences, human services counseling, interdisciplinary studies (elementary school education, leading to a master's degree, and professional communication), medical technology, nursing (RN to B.S.N.), and occupational and technical studies.

The following master's degrees are offered: Master of Business Administration, Master of Engineering Management, Master of Science in Education (elementary school education, which is tied to the bachelor's program, and special education, which meets certification and endorsement requirements in learning disabilities, mental retardation, and emotional/behavioral disorders), Master of Science in Nursing (family nurse practitioner studies), Master of Science in Occupational and Technical Studies, and Master of Taxation.

In addition to the bachelor's and master's programs, certificate programs in public management and survey science are offered. Other programs are in the development stage for TELETECHNET.

STUDENT SERVICES

TELETECHNET students have the advantage of checking out videotapes of class presentations if they miss a session due to family responsibilities or job conflicts. Computer labs, which are connected to the main campus and have Internet access, are available at each site for the students' use.

The Old Dominion library supports the TELETECHNET students by providing library resources, services, and reference assistance that are required for successful completion of course work, research papers and projects, and independent reading and research. Services are available primarily through the library's Web site (http://www.lib.odu.edu), with telephone, e-mail, and fax requests also provided.

CREDIT OPTIONS

Students can transfer credits earned at other accredited postsecondary institutions to Old Dominion University and can receive credit through the College-Level Examination Program (CLEP) for certain courses. Returning adult students may also have the option of applying for academic credit through the Experiential Learning Program. This program evaluates college-level learning gained outside the college classroom. Examples are military and workplace training, independent study, professional certification, portfolios, and examination.

FACULTY

More than 50 percent of Old Dominion University's full-time faculty members have taught on television, and this percentage continues to grow as TELETECHNET expands its degree offerings. Specialized training for this unique teaching environment is provided to ensure high-quality instruction for students.

ADMISSION

Prospective students must submit an application accompanied by a $30 fee for degree-seeking admission and request that official transcripts from all previous colleges be sent to the Office of Distance Learning for evaluation of credits earned (transfer admission generally requires a minimum 2.2 grade point average).

TUITION AND FEES

Old Dominion's TELETECHNET program offers affordable tuition for students. Undergraduate TELETECHNET tuition for the 2000–01 school year is $120 per credit for Virginia residents (outside the Hampton Roads area of Virginia) and $300 per credit for nonresidents. Graduate tuition is $196 per credit for in-state students and $520 per credit for out-of-state students. Tuition for TELETECHNET USA sites (those outside of Virginia) is $120 per credit for undergraduates and $196 per credit for graduate students. There is a required general services fee of $8 for each semester.

FINANCIAL AID

Old Dominion University is a direct lending institution and awards financial aid from federally funded and state-funded programs as well as from privately funded sources. The University requires all students applying for need-based assistance to complete the Free Application for Federal Student Aid (FAFSA). Those applying for merit-based awards must complete the Old Dominion University Scholarship Application.

APPLYING

The deadline for admission for the fall semester for transfer students and graduate students is June 1. The deadline for nursing students is February 1. The deadline for applying for the spring semester is November 1. The summer semester deadline is April 1. Decisions are made on a rolling basis, and applicants are notified of their admission status within four weeks after receipt of all application materials.

CONTACT

Dr. Jeanie P. Kline
Director of Distance Learning
 Operations
433 Gornto TELETECHNET
 Center
Old Dominion University
Norfolk, Virginia 23529
Telephone: 800-YOU-2ODU
 (800-968-2638, toll-free)
Fax: 757-683-5492
E-mail: ttnet@odu.edu
Web site: http://www.odu.edu/~
 distance_learning/
 TELETECHNET.html

Oregon State University

Distance and Continuing Education

Corvallis, Oregon

Founded in 1868 and accredited by the Northwest Association of Schools and Colleges, Oregon State University (OSU) is one of eighty-eight schools nationwide to receive the Carnegie Foundation's highest rating for education and research. Through teaching, research, and outreach, OSU serves the state of Oregon, the nation, and the world. More than 17,000 students are pursuing their degrees in one of 220 undergraduate and graduate academic degree programs. Oregon State was recently named by the American Productivity and Quality Center as the top university in North America for providing electronic services to students.

DISTANCE LEARNING PROGRAM

During the academic year, more than 1,000 individuals throughout Oregon and the world take OSU courses off campus. Each term, students have access to more than 100 courses in more than thirty subjects in areas as diverse as education, fisheries and wildlife, math, and psychology. Courses are designed as part of bachelor's completion programs, undergraduate minors, graduate degrees, and certificate programs.

DELIVERY MEDIA

Oregon State offers the majority of its distance courses via the Internet and videotapes and through independent study with an assigned instructor. Courses often entail a combination of delivery methods, such as a video course with class interaction through an electronic listserv or Web site. Students communicate with instructors and administrative staff via e-mail, phone, fax, or regular mail. Select courses and programs are also delivered through face-to-face instruction or interactive television broadcasting (ITV) at statewide locations.

PROGRAMS OF STUDY

Oregon State is one of a handful of universities nationwide pioneering the field of online education. Although most of the 100 distance courses offered each term include some online component such as e-mail communication with faculty members, more than forty courses are scheduled to be offered entirely on the Web in 2000–01.

Bachelor's degrees can be acquired in a "2+2" program in which students typically complete their first two years of lower-division requirements through a community college or other institution. They can complete their degree from anywhere in the world by taking upper-division course work through OSU Distance and Continuing Education. Students may select from a Bachelor of Arts/Bachelor of Science (B.A./B.S.) in liberal studies (a preprofessional elementary education option is available statewide), a B.S. in environmental sciences, a B.S. in general agriculture, and a B.S. in natural resources. Most courses are offered via the Internet and videotapes and through independent study with an instructor.

A minor in natural resources is available worldwide; a communication minor is available statewide in Oregon. Minors usually include at least 27 quarter credit hours of study and can be pursued as part of a bachelor's program or added to a transcript after graduation.

A Master of Science (M.S.) degree in nutrition and food science with an area of concentration in dietetics management is delivered primarily through Web courses. The program is geared for registered dietitians and prepares them for management responsibilities. The degree may be completed in three years by taking two to three courses per term.

Graduate-level course work delivered over the Web is also available to students interested in education, exercise and sports science, and public health. These courses are part of campus-based graduate programs at Oregon State but may also be available to students off campus who meet specific course prerequisites.

SPECIAL PROGRAMS

Practicing teachers around the world may enroll in online modules based on their individual needs and professional development plans. Oregon State University's Professional Development System (PDS) is Web based and aligned with Educational Standards for the 21st Century, i.e., Educational Reform, Goals 2000, and Oregon's Certificates of Initial and Advanced Mastery. Teachers can earn Professional Development Units (PDUs) and/or graduate credits. Students can preview modules on the PDS Web site (http://pds.orst.edu).

A preservice professional technical licensure program for Oregon educators provides preparation for professional technical teachers in arts and communication, business and management, and industrial and engineering systems. The curriculum includes 46 credits, with course work organized into two blocks (Web courses and related school-based practica and student teaching).

For more information on PDS modules and the Oregon Professional Technical Licensure Program, students can contact Dr. Allan Brazier by e-mail (braziera@orst.edu).

STUDENT SERVICES

Oregon State makes it a priority to provide excellent student services to distance learners. Statewide students have the opportunity to meet with area advisers at convenient locations throughout Oregon. For students outside of Oregon, advising is available via e-mail and a toll-free number. Students also have access to extensive online library services, toll-free hotlines for computer consulting and writing assistance, and a myriad of resources accessible from the Distance and Continuing Education Web site. *OSU E-News,* a free electronic newsletter, provides timely tips to help distance students succeed.

CREDIT OPTIONS

All credits earned through distance education are recorded on an Oregon State University transcript and do not appear any differently than on-campus courses. Each course falls under the same accreditation ratings of the individual department from which it originates. Transfer students enrolled in academic programs must have previous credits evaluated by an OSU adviser to ensure that program requirements are met. Students

in bachelor's programs must accumulate a minimum of 180 quarter credits to graduate.

FACULTY

Oregon State has more than 2,100 faculty members, with 1,050 in the tenure system; approximately 1,615 are appointed on a full-time basis. Eighty-four percent of faculty members in professorial ranks have doctoral degrees. Regular OSU faculty members provide 90 percent of the instruction in distance learning programs and must adhere to the same quality standards as any faculty member teaching on campus.

ADMISSION

Students taking distance learning courses to meet OSU degree requirements must be admitted to the University through the regular admission process and must meet the requirements for admission. Nondegree enrollment requires no formal admission and no admission fees or requirements and can be obtained by contacting the registrar at 541-737-4331.

TUITION AND FEES

Tuition for undergraduate distance degree courses for 2000–01 is $125 per quarter credit hour for most courses. Graduate-level courses are generally $240–$290 per quarter

credit, depending upon the program. Additional fees may be assessed for tape rental or other course materials. Out-of-state tuition does not generally apply to distance learning courses and does not apply to nondegree students taking fewer than 9 credits per term.

FINANCIAL AID

Distance learners are eligible for financial aid programs according to the same rules as on-campus students. Generally, to be considered, a student must be fully admitted to the University and taking at least 6 quarter hours. Some scholarships are open to part-time distance learning students. Students can consult specific information on the Web (http://osu.orst.edu/admin/finaid).

APPLYING

Distance learners seeking an OSU degree should apply through the regular application process. Some of the distance programs at the graduate level are cohort based and require admission prior to fall quarter. The undergraduate distance degree programs accept students year-round. It is recommended that students seek initial advising prior to the application process. Registration for individual courses generally requires no application other than to contact the registrar for admission as a nondegree or part-time student.

CONTACT

Distance and Continuing Education
Attention: Student Services
4943 The Valley Library
Oregon State University
Corvallis, Oregon 97331-4504
Telephone: 541-737-2676
            800-235-6559 (toll-free)
Fax: 541-737-2734
E-mail: ostateu@orst.edu
Web site: http://statewide.orst.edu

Park University

School for Extended Learning

Parkville, Missouri

Park University was founded in 1875 and is accredited by the Commission on Institutions of Higher Education of the North Central Association of Colleges and Schools. Programs in liberal arts are offered through the School of Arts and Sciences, and the School for Extended Learning offers Bachelor of Science degrees. Many undergraduate courses are offered through the Internet. Graduate programs in public affairs, education, and business administration are also offered.

Park University endeavors to educate students who will be characterized by literacy, open-mindedness, and professionalism. To foster the accomplishment of this goal, Park University is committed to providing a distinctive learning environment that is characterized by accessibility, sensitivity, and excellence.

DISTANCE LEARNING PROGRAM

Park University has been involved in distance learning courses since 1996 and currently offers more than sixty distance learning courses each term, which provide the student with the option of studying where and when it is convenient.

DELIVERY MEDIA

Students in distance learning courses should have basic computer literacy skills. The necessary equipment includes a Windows-compatible computer with a 28.8 kbps or higher modem and Netscape Navigator or an equivalent. The AOL browser is not supported by Park's online courses. Courses are designed for accelerated sessions of eight weeks. Students interact with instructors and other students through classroom threads and assignments.

PROGRAM OF STUDY

Park University currently offers degree completion courses online in criminal justice administration, and management/computer information systems. Online courses are offered in adolescent psychology; adult development and aging; agency administration; the American Civil War; American foreign policy in the twentieth century; business; business communications writing; business ethics; business law; business policy; chemistry and society; compensation management; complex organizations; computers in society; computer systems and design analysis; criminal investigation; criminal justice administration; criminal justice and the community; criminal law; criminology; early American literature; expository and research writing; financial management; financial institutions and markets; human ecology; human resources development; information systems; introduction to computers; juvenile delinquency; labor relations; macroeconomics; management; modern literature; organizational behavior; organizational development and change; network/data communications; personal financial management; principles of market-ing; probation and parole; productions and operations management; professional writing; programming; public administration; Russia in the twentieth century; science, technology, and society; scientific and technical writing; small business management; social psychology; supervision; tests and measurements; world physical geography; and World War II.

Special seminars are given in journalism on the Web and management. New courses are being developed on a continuous basis.

TUITION AND FEES

The tuition for the 2000–01 academic year is $165 per credit hour. The application and evaluation fee is $25. There is a discounted rate of $123 per credit hour for students with a home of record at Park military sites where special contracts exist. All online courses require a $10 per credit hour Internet fee.

FINANCIAL AID

Financial assistance may be awarded to full- and part-time students who qualify.

APPLYING

Degree-seeking students must meet all admission standards for Park University. Students seeking Internet course work for transfer credit to another college or university must pay a one-time $25 application fee.

For more information, students should contact Park University at the telephone number below or visit the Web site.

The Pennsylvania State University

Distance Education
University Park, Pennsylvania

From agricultural college to world-class learning community, the story of the Pennsylvania State University (Penn State) is one of an expanding mission of teaching, research, and public service. Conceived in 1855, when the commonwealth of Pennsylvania chartered the school at the request of the Pennsylvania State Agricultural Society, today Penn State is one of America's ten largest universities, enrolling more than 80,000 students at twenty-four locations throughout the state.

Penn State has been a pioneer in distance education since 1892, when it founded one of the nation's first correspondence study programs. Now, with the addition of an online World Campus, the University has reaffirmed its commitment to providing educational access to learners everywhere.

DISTANCE LEARNING PROGRAM

Penn State Distance Education offers both World Campus and Independent Learning programs. The World Campus makes some of Penn State's most highly regarded undergraduate, graduate, and continuing professional education programs available anytime, anywhere through the World Wide Web, computer interfacing, CD-ROM, and other media. Penn State's Independent Learning offers more than 150 undergraduate credit courses and a variety of noncredit courses that contribute to bachelor's and associate's degree and several certificate programs.

DELIVERY MEDIA

The World Campus uses multiple technologies to present information, facilitate interaction among students and faculty members, give access to learning resources, and provide learner support. World Campus courses are technology based and delivered via the World Wide Web, and most are offered on a semester basis, with students and faculty members interacting together in a group.

Penn State's Independent Learning program assigns each student to a Penn State instructor to communicate with by mail, telephone, fax, and/or e-mail. Students can register for courses at any time throughout the year.

PROGRAMS OF STUDY

The World Campus provides signature Penn State programs to adult learners that can help them advance professionally and remain competitive in today's ever-changing marketplace. A master's degree in adult education is offered, in addition to associate degrees. Associate degrees are offered in dietetic food systems management and hotel, restaurant, and institutional management. Postbaccalaureate credit certificate programs are available in community and economic development, counselor education–chemical dependency, educational technology integration, logistics and supply-chain management, and noise control engineering. Undergraduate certificates are offered in customer relationship management, dietary manager studies, hospitality management, turfgrass management, and logistics and supply-chain management. The noncredit certificate programs available are basic supervisory leadership, geographic information systems, and

Webmaster studies. Courses are also available in advanced antenna engineering, architectural lighting design, reliability engineering, semiconductor device reliability, and fundamentals of engineering (EIT Review). For the most up-to-date information on available programs and courses, students should visit the Web site listed below.

Through Independent Learning, courses can be taken for general interest or applied toward degree programs. A bachelor's degree completion program is offered in letters, arts, and sciences. Associate degrees are offered in business administration, human development and family studies, and letters, arts, and sciences. Credit certificate programs include advanced business management; business management; children, youth, and family services; dietetics and aging; general business; human resources; marketing management; retail management; small business management; and writing social commentary. The noncredit certificate programs offered are legal issues for business professionals, legal issues for those dealing with the elderly, and paralegal studies. For more information, students should visit the Web site listed below.

SPECIAL PROGRAMS

Independent Learning provides a bachelor's degree program in partnership with the University of Iowa, called LionHawk, in which students who complete the letters, arts, and sciences associate degree are automatically accepted into the Bachelor of Liberal Arts Studies program at Iowa. No on-campus study is required for either degree.

Penn State Distance Education uses interactive videoconferencing to link faculty members with students at other Penn State locations and at work sites globally. This distributed classroom approach to distance education extends access to Penn State graduate programs. It allows spontaneous student-to-faculty member interaction as well as student-to-student interaction through real-time, two-way audio and two-way video connections. Additionally, these programs rely on Internet communications to further enhance interaction and increase students' access to resources. For more information about Distributed Learning, students should call the toll-free telephone number listed below.

CREDIT OPTIONS

Credits earned through World Campus or Independent Learning courses are equivalent to credits earned on campus at Penn State. Advanced standing credits may be awarded for college-level work taken at regionally accredited institutions, provided that the course grade earned is equivalent to a grade of A, B, or C at Penn State and that the credits are useful to the student's program of study.

FACULTY

Penn State has a distinguished faculty of 4,100 teachers and researchers. Penn State has consistently ranked among the top ten universities in the nation in the number of faculty members who win Fulbright Scholarships for study abroad, and numerous faculty members hold memberships in the National Academies of Sciences, Engineering, or Medicine.

ADMISSION

For admission into the Independent Learning degree programs, graduation from a regionally accredited high school or a passing grade on the GED test is required, as are SAT or ACT scores. For requirements for Independent Learning certificate programs, students should contact the Distance Education office. Students should visit the Web site listed below for specific World Campus admission requirements.

TUITION AND FEES

For 2000-01, the tuition for lower-level credit courses numbered 000 to 299 is $133 per semester-hour credit, while tuition for upper-level credit courses numbered 300 to 499 is $252 per semester-hour credit. Some World Campus graduate-level courses follow the University graduate tuition rate of $291 per credit. Noncredit tuition varies by course. A $30 processing fee is charged for every course enrollment. Students should contact the Department of Distance Education or visit the Web site below for the most up-to-date details on tuition and fees.

FINANCIAL AID

Independent Learning courses are not eligible for financial aid because enrollment is accepted at any time of the year and a student can take up to eight months to complete a course. This flexibility takes Independent Learning courses out of the traditional semester timeframe on which the awarding of financial aid is based. World Campus credit courses with a set start and end date may qualify for financial aid depending on a student's degree status and credit load. Students are encouraged to contact the Penn State Office of Student Aid at 814-863-0465 or studentaid@psu.edu. Additional information is also available on line: www.psu.edu/studentaid

APPLYING

To apply or register for Penn State Distance Education programs and courses, visit the Web site below for downloadable forms, or contact the department via phone, fax, or e-mail.

CONTACT

Penn State Distance Education
The Pennsylvania State University
207 Mitchell Building
University Park, Pennsylvania 16802-3602
Telephone: 814-865-5403 (local and international)
    800-252-3592 (toll-free within the United States)
Fax: 814-865-3290
E-mail: psuwd@outreach.edu (World Campus)
    psude@cde.psu.edu (Independent Learning)
Web site: http://www.worldcampus.psu.edu

Professional Development Europe Limited

Chertsey, United Kingdom

Professional Development Europe Limited (PDE) is a fully accredited institution of the Open University, United Kingdom, and offers MBA validated study programmes of that University. PDE was established by a consortium of British professional associations in 1998 in order to provide affordable, exclusively distance learning, postgraduate study options for mature professionals.

PDE's sister programme in Australia, provided by the Association of Professional Engineers, Scientists and Managers, Australia (APESMA), offers a joint M.B.A. award with Deakin University, Australia, and has done so since 1992. This joint APESMA/Deakin M.B.A. award programme now accounts for almost 1 in 4 of all M.B.A. students in Australia and has 2,200 enrolments worldwide. This was the world's first programme to confer the award of M.B.A. (technology management).

PDE operates under the guidance of a UK Academic Board, which includes representatives from major business schools in the UK, from industry, and from professional associations. Its aim is to provide its M.B.A. graduates with the skills, knowledge, and expertise needed by employers.

DISTANCE LEARNING PROGRAM

This is an M.B.A. distance learning programme designed for busy professionals. It is particularly suited to those who work in the engineering, scientific, or technological sectors of the economy, since this provides the context in which many of the study units (modules) are set.

DELIVERY MEDIA

This is a fully portable M.B.A. distance learning study programme. The study materials are designed to be entirely self-contained and include selected readings and self-assessment exercises, as well as study text. Considerable investment has been made in the instructional design of study materials to ensure that the texts are fully accessible and intelligible to programme participants.

Where appropriate, text materials are supported by CD-ROM multimedia presentations. Academic support is provided by e-mail by well-qualified

tutors from the faculties of major business schools or from experts drawn from the professions.

Assessment is by written assignment, submitted at week nine of the programme, and by final examination in week twenty of the semester. The final examination accounts for 70 percent to 80 percent of the overall assessment and is a 3-hour written examination. Final examination venues are arranged no more than 100 kilometers from the participant's preferred correspondence address.

PROGRAM OF STUDY

There are two programmes of study available, one leading to the award of M.B.A., the other leading to the specialist award of M.B.A. (technology management).

All participants must complete 12 study units, 8 of which are compulsory; a research project; and 3 elective study units. In the case of the M.B.A. (technology management), candidates must select their electives

from those designated as "technological" and complete a research project in the area of technology management.

Compulsory study units include financial management, management perspectives, economic decision making, legal studies, strategic management, marketing, contemporary people management, and information and knowledge management. Research units (1 of 2) involve a research project or an independent work-based project. Elective study units include project management, management of innovation, operations management, management of professional services, best practice in quality management, corporate finance, international business strategy, strategic management in services, Asia Pacific international marketing, management learning contract, engineering risk management, business practice in Hong Kong, research management, and international telecommunications management.

The programme is conducted over two semesters each year. The first semester begins in January and the second, in June. Each semester is twenty weeks in duration. Assignments are submitted in the ninth week, and final examinations are held in week twenty.

STUDENT SERVICES

Each student has an appointed Personal Tutor who oversees his or her progression through the programme. The tutor is contactable by telephone, fax, or e-mail. Tutors are specially selected for their ability to teach at a distance. E-mail–based student study groups are established, and international discussions groups are facilitated.

Final examinations are held in any of the 900 examination centres available worldwide. Participants rarely have to travel more than 100 kilometers to a suitable examination venue.

CREDIT OPTIONS

Credits may be granted up to a maximum of 90 credits (50 percent of the programme) in respect of prior M.B.A. or equivalent study. Applicants seeking credit transfer are required to provide full transcripts and certified copies of all qualifications that provide the basis for the credit transfer request.

FACULTY

Programme participants may be tutored by academic experts or professional consultants based in the United States, Europe, or Australia. All are employed on a consultancy basis and are engaged on annual contracts subject to renewal on the basis of performance against specified criteria.

ADMISSION

Requirements include a university degree or a professional qualification that is recognised as equivalent to a degree by the Admissions Panel. Candidates are also required to have a minimum of three years' work experience.

A small number of participants may be accepted without tertiary qualifications if significant management responsibility can be demonstrated.

TUITION AND FEES

The total study programme cost is £5750. This is a pay-as-you-study programme, and participants pay only for the study units in which they are presently engaged. The programme cost includes all fees and is all-inclusive. There is no additional billing for application, courier services, enrolment or re-enrolment, or graduation. There are no charges for any obligatory residential study periods.

APPLYING

Applications may be made online. Alternatively, candidates may write, telephone, fax, or e-mail to the address below.

CONTACT

Professional Development Europe
  Limited
Flaxman House
Gogmore Lane
Chertsey, Surrey KT16 9JS
United Kingdom
Tel: 44-0-1932-5770878
Fax: 44-0-1932-577089
E-mail: enquiries@pde.org.uk
Web site:
  http://www.MBA-degree.com

Purdue University

Distributed Learning Services

West Lafayette, Indiana

> Purdue University, founded in 1869, is a state-supported land-grant university. It is accredited by the North Central Association of Colleges and Schools. It first offered distance learning courses in 1968.

DISTANCE LEARNING PROGRAM

In 1922, WBAA at Purdue, Indiana's first radio station, began broadcasting electrical engineering courses. Currently, a wealth of distance learning resources are offered for delivering courses by audioconferencing, television, and videotape, and on the World Wide Web.

Purdue is a member of the Indiana Partnership for Statewide Education (IPSE). This affiliation provides the University the opportunity to cooperate with other higher education institutions in Indiana to bring educational opportunities to individuals wherever they are, by enhancing access to the best that Indiana's colleges and universities have to offer.

DELIVERY MEDIA

Depending on the program, courses are delivered via television, videotapes, videoconferencing, interactive television, radio broadcast, audioconference, computer software, the World Wide Web, and print. Students and teachers may meet in person or interact via audioconferencing, mail, telephone, fax, e-mail, or the World Wide Web.

Courses are delivered to the workplace and other colleges throughout Indiana, with some courses also available for delivery to the home.

PROGRAMS OF STUDY

Individual courses are offered in health professions and related sciences, hospitality services management, and veterinary technology at the undergraduate level and business administration and management, creative arts, engineering, and technology at the graduate level. Noncredit courses are offered in agriculture and engineering. A certificate program is available in digital signal processing.

In spring 1999, 43 students enrolled in the first veterinary technology distance learning classes. As of fall 1999, seven courses were offered with 60 students enrolled. The entire 70-credit-hour degree-seeking program is expected be online by fall 2003. Of the 80 Veterinary Technology Programs in North America, the Veterinary Technology Distance Learning Program at Purdue is one of only two that is within a veterinary school. Accreditation by the American Veterinary Medical Association is pending. These courses are also appropriate for graduate technicians who need to meet continuing education requirements.

Graduate degree programs are offered in the following areas: agribusiness management (E.M.B.A.), civil engineering (M.S.C.E.), electrical and computer engineering (M.S.E.E.), industrial engineering (M.S.I.E.), interdisciplinary engineering (M.S. or M.S.E.), and management (M.S.M.). The Master of Science in Technology (M.S.T.) and the Master of Science in Mechanical Engineering (M.S.M.E.) are also available. In 1998–99, 127 degrees were earned through the M.S.M. distance learning program. In fall 1999, there were 248 students enrolled in the program.

The E.M.B.A. program is targeted to mid-career managers in the food and agribusiness industries. It is a joint offering of the Krannert School of Management and the School of Agriculture. The E.M.S. program was developed specifically for high potential managers and managers-to-be and provides an innovative alternative to traditional M.B.A. programs.

SPECIAL PROGRAMS

Purdue University is approved by the American Council on Pharmaceutical Education as a provider of continuing pharmaceutical education. The mission of Pharmacy continuing education is to partner with licensed pharmacists to advance the practice of pharmacy in Indiana and the nation. Continuing education programming is available worldwide. Certificate programs and nontraditional Doctor of Pharmacy programs are available to Indiana residents and to those in surrounding states who are within driving distance of Indiana-based sites.

STUDENT SERVICES

Distance learners have access to academic advising and career placement assistance at a distance.

CREDIT OPTIONS

The veterinary technology program requires a total of 70 credit hours, of which 43 are online, Web-based, and mostly asynchronous classes. Clinical mentorships at veterinary practices or institutions make up an additional 19 credit hours, with the remaining credits being obtained through education courses or electives. The E.M.B.A., E.M.S., and M.S.M. programs are 48-credit-hour programs. Students must attend six 2-week residency sessions on campus that are spread out over two years. The maximum time for completing a program is two years. For information about the requirements for other degree options, students should contact the University.

FACULTY

Purdue faculty members affiliated with the Distributed Learning Services program are readily available to distance learning students by phone, fax, or e-mail.

ADMISSION

Students who desire admission to the veterinary technology associate degree program must be at least 18 years of age and possess a high school diploma or its equivalent. Students must submit SAT I or ACT test scores and high school transcripts and must have completed minimum high school prerequisites, which include two semesters of algebra, biology, chemistry, geometry, and history or social science and eight semesters of English (deficiencies may be made up at the college level). Students who attended nonaccredited high schools or participated in home schooling are strongly encouraged to take SAT I exams in English and math and must complete the required chemistry course work by taking two semesters of chemistry at a nearby high school, taking a college chemistry course at a local college or university, or submitting an SAT II score in chemistry.

Graduate-level programs require a baccalaureate degree, GMAT scores, college transcripts, letters of recommendation, a minimum GPA of 3.0 (on a 4.0 scale), and five years of work experience.

TUITION AND FEES

Costs vary and depend upon the program. Students should contact the Distributed Learning Services at Purdue University for tuition information.

FINANCIAL AID

Students can direct questions regarding financial aid to the contact listed below.

APPLYING

An application fee of $30 is required for all programs. Applications for the veterinary technology program can be downloaded from the Web site (http://www.vet.purdue.edu/VTDL). Students may contact Distributed Learning Services at Purdue University for further application information.

CONTACT

Joetta S. Burrous, Director
Distributed Learning Services
Purdue University
1586 Stewart Center, Room 116
West Lafayette, Indiana 47907-1586
Telephone: 765-496-3338
Fax: 765-496-6384
E-mail: jburrous@purdue.edu

Purdue University

Krannert Executive Education Programs

West Lafayette, Indiana

Purdue University, a state-supported land-grant university, was founded in 1869. The University was named after its chief benefactor John Purdue, and is known for its academic excellence and affordable education. The West Lafayette campus offers nearly 6,700 courses in the Schools of Agriculture, Management, Consumer and Family Sciences, Pharmacy, Nursing and Health Sciences, Education, Science, Engineering, Technology, Liberal Arts, and Veterinary Medicine. The goals of the University are symbolized in its emblem, the griffin, whose three-part shield represents education, research, and service. Purdue is accredited by the North Central Association of Colleges and Schools (NCA).

DISTANCE LEARNING PROGRAM

The Krannert Executive Education Programs (KEEP) began its distance learning programs in 1983. The programs were developed specifically for mid-level managers or managers-to-be who are unable to attend classes on a full-time basis. The programs have unique scheduling, which makes it possible for participants to be drawn from a wide geographical area. Six 2-week residencies spread across twenty-two months, from orientation to graduation, allow its participants to meet their educational goals while simultaneously fulfilling their job responsibilities. During the nineteen months the students are off campus, they utilize the Internet and World Wide Web, online discussion forums and chatrooms, and other electronic media to stay in touch with each other, the faculty, and Executive Education support staff. These nationally ranked programs are part of the Krannert Graduate School of Management and admit 55 students in each cohort.

DELIVERY MEDIA

KEEP supports its programs via the World Wide Web. Students need a Windows-compatible laptop computer, an Internet service provider, and Web browser software to access the KEEP Web site and communication support tools. The program is Internet based and students have access to their course Web sites, faculty members, and program support staff anywhere they can connect to the Web. Students are expected to have the current version of Microsoft Office installed on their systems for completing their group and individual assignments.

PROGRAMS OF STUDY

An M.B.A. is offered through two unique programs: the Executive Master of Science in Management Program (EMS) and the International Master in Management Program (IMM).

The EMS Program begins each July with an orientation session where the participants are introduced to the instructors, course work, and the KEEP information technology system. The courses have an applied policymaking orientation and make extensive use of case studies and other experiential material. The third module has an emphasis on international business, and the last residency in the third module is spent at an international location. Upon completion of the program, the Master of Science in Management (M.S.M.) degree is awarded by Purdue University.

The IMM Program is taught in conjunction with Tilburg University in the Netherlands and the Budapest University of Economic Sciences in Hungary. It is structured like the EMS Program, but the residencies are alternated among the campuses of the three collaborating institutions. The program is initiated during orientation each January. Graduation yields two master's degrees: a Master of Science in Management (M.S.M.) degree from Purdue and an M.B.A. from either Tilburg or BUES.

The EMS and IMM Programs are intensive and demanding, which is consistent with a graduate professional program in management. Serious preparation is expected, and academic standards are carefully maintained to ensure integrity of the earned degrees. As a result, however, the educational benefits are substantial, and the degrees earned provide significant professional credentials.

SPECIAL PROGRAMS

Both the EMS and IMM Programs are open to executive students worldwide and are accredited by AACSB–The International Association for Management Education making the programs attractive to both national and international students.

STUDENT SERVICES

Students maintain contact with faculty members, support staff, and KEEP administration on a daily basis or as needed. Other resources include online library services, tutoring, campus computer networks, e-mail services, academic advising, and online discussion forums and chatrooms.

CREDIT OPTIONS

The programs are cohort in nature: all students in each class enter together, take a common set of courses, and graduate together. There are 48 total credits, 16 per module, that participants must complete within two years.

FACULTY

Classes are taught by the senior faculty members of the Krannert Graduate School of Management at Purdue, the Tias Business School at Tilburg University, the Budapest University of Economic Sciences, and by experienced teachers from other U.S. and international programs. All faculty members have taught extensively in executive programs containing distance learning aspects, have substantial research and publication records,

and have experience as consultants to corporations and government agencies.

ADMISSION

Applicants are expected to have a GMAT score of 520 or higher, a completed baccalaureate degree with a grade point average of B or better, a minimum of five years of work experience in positions of increasing professional responsibility, a current position of significant responsibility, and three supporting letters of recommendation. Any applicant whose first language is not English must have a minimum TOEFL score of 213 on the computer-based test or 550 on the paper-based test.

TUITION AND FEES

The total cost for each program is $42,000 ($14,000 per each of the three modules). The tuition covers books and course material, instructional costs, lodging, and most meals during the residencies. Tuition is due be-

fore the first residency of each program module. The EMS Program features an international trip in its last module, for which there is an additional charge.

FINANCIAL AID

EMBA loans offered through Purdue's financial aid office are available. Applications may be completed at a distance.

APPLYING

Candidates may apply online at any time on the World Wide Web at the Web address listed below. As admission to the program is on a rolling basis throughout the year until class capacity is reached, early application is recommended. Upon receipt of all necessary documents, the application will be reviewed by the Program Admissions Committee and, upon approval, submitted to Purdue's Graduate School for the final decision. Typically, a candidate can expect notification of application status within two weeks of receipt of all application documentation.

CONTACT

Erika C. Steuterman
Director, Executive Master's Programs
Purdue University
1310 Krannert Center, Suite 206
West Lafayette, Indiana 47907-1310
Telephone: 765-494-7700
Fax: 765-494-0862
E-mail: keepinfo@mgmt.purdue.edu
Web site: http://www2.mgmt.purdue.edu

 **Quest College**

Online Technology Programs

Davenport, Iowa

Quest College was founded in 1937 to provide professional business training. Quest College has achieved this objective for over sixty years by keeping abreast of employment demands, employer needs, teaching methods, and the use of various educational resources and industry standard equipment. Quest College is an institution of higher education offering quality programs that integrate general education, professional skills, and career-focused education empowering students to develop and achieve their personal and career potential.

As an accredited academic institution of higher education, Quest College has been approved as a Microsoft Authorized Academic Training Program (AATP) institution and delivers technical training using Microsoft official curriculum and other authorized materials.

DISTANCE LEARNING PROGRAM

Quest College provides distance education that offers a learning environment for faculty members and students who are unable to meet at the same location. The College provides distance learning that is learner-centered and interactive through synchronous and asynchronous delivery.

The offering of professional and public certifications through distance education technology allows students to attain specific career certification and employment licensing requirements as established by professional associations, governmental agencies, or industry.

DELIVERY MEDIA

Quest College's distance education courses employ interactive technology that engages the student's visual, auditory, tactile, and kinesthetic learning capabilities, which allows learning to occur for a variety of learning styles. Learning retention for the student is improved considerably. Thus, it is the College's commitment to offer certification programs that employ the following media in our

courses: textbook and other print course material, Web resources (including Internet audio/text chat sessions),peer group projects and interaction, E-mail correspondence among peers and instructors, and video and audio supplements.

Quest College online programs use a virtual classroom as the teaching platform. The virtual classroom operates from a "wizard-driven" system, where prompts are given in order to add content, documents, and URL links to the Web classroom site. In addition, the site has an integrated test/audio chat system that allows for real-time discussion online, and the site has an online assessment system that allows for immediate feedback to students upon completion of a learning assessment. The audio capabilities provide an ideal environment for electronic office hours and real-time discussion. These site resources allow for the virtual classroom to offer both synchronous and asynchronous student and faculty interaction.

PROGRAMS OF STUDY

Quest College offers both degree and certificate programs online. Students can choose an Associate of Science

degree in applied management of interdisciplinary studies. Associate degrees require completion of a total of 61 semester hours. Applied management requires completion of a general education core that consists of a total of 30 semester hours in the following disciplines: social and behavioral sciences, science and mathematics, communications and language, and humanities. In addition, students must complete a management core and general requirements. Interdisciplinary studies requires completion of the general education core, general requirements and additional hours in an open concentration area.

The Online Technology Programs at Quest College offer three Microsoft certification tracks: Microsoft Certified Systems Engineering (MCSE), MCSE+Site Builder, Microsoft Certified Solution Developer (MCSD), and Microsoft Certified Database Administrator (MCDBA). The Microsoft Network Engineer 36-credit hour certificate program is designed to prepare individuals to become certified computer Microsoft Network Engineers. Upon completion of each course, students will take the corresponding Microsoft examinations in order to attain certification through Microsoft. The Microsoft Network Engineer certificate program is designed to provide the graduate with the skills necessary to install, configure, manage, and maintain a network operating system. Graduates will be prepared to work for any organization that currently has or is planning to install a network configuration for their computer system. In addition, computer support organizations that consult with clients on the installation and maintenance of computer networks will find these graduates in high demand. The MCSE+Site Builder is an enhanced program that adds training on e-commerce and Internet development.

The Microsoft Solution Developer (MSD) 36-credit certificate program is designed to prepare individuals to become certified Microsoft Solution Developers. Upon completion of each course students will take the corresponding Microsoft examinations in order to attain certification through Microsoft. The MSD program is designed to provide the graduate with the skills necessary to conduct analysis, design, coding, debugging, testing, distribution, ongoing support, project management, and research/professional development.

The Microsoft Database Administrator (MDA) 36-credit certificate program is designed to prepare individuals to become certified Microsoft Database Administrators. Upon completion of each course students will take the corresponding Microsoft examinations in order to attain certification through Microsoft. The MD certificate program is designed to prepare graduates with the skills necessary to implement and administer Microsoft SQL Server databases. These skills prepare students to become certified as Microsoft Certified Database Administrators (MCDBA). The MDA graduate possesses the skills needed to derive physical database designs, develop logical data models, create physical databases, create data services by using Transact-SQL, manage and maintain databases, configure and manage secu-rity, monitor and optimize databases, and install and configure Microsoft SQL Server.

STUDENT SERVICES

To ensure an overall quality educational experience and to improve student chance for success, several support services are provided to distance students. Admissions, financial aid, academic advising, bookstore services, scheduling and student records, registrar, and placement services are all available to distance students. These services are available through the College Web site.

In addition to the traditional student support services, technical support is also available through e-mail and through a toll-free telephone number.

CREDIT OPTIONS

Students completing any of the online Microsoft certification programs have the option of transferring those credits into an associate degree.

FACULTY

Faculty members for the degree programs hold master's or doctoral degrees and additional technology-related expertise. Faculty members in the Online Technology Programs hold at least a bachelor degree in computer science or related fields and possess Microsoft certification at the required level to teach in the program.

TUITION AND FEES

Tuition charges for the associate degree programs are $18,000. This charge includes textbooks and course materials. The Online Microsoft Technology Programs are set up on Term Charge Tuition. Students pay $3,000 per class, including Microsoft official textbooks, tuition, access to the virtual classroom, and technical support. There is an additional $25 fee for textbook shipping.

FINANCIAL AID

Individuals who have been accepted into a program may apply for financial aid through the Quest College Financial Aid Office. This office will assist in the processing of grants, loans, and veteran's benefits for qualified students.

APPLYING

Prospective students must submit the application for admission along with a $50 application fee, an official high school transcript or GED test results, official transcripts from other postsecondary institutions, a resume outlining work experience, and an essay describing how completion of the program will help in a career advancement. In addition, applicants for the Microsoft certification courses must pass a computer competencies exam to qualify for admission. They must demonstrate through the application process that they possess the understanding, interest, and vocabulary necessary to succeed in the program.

CONTACT

Sara Baker
Quest College
1801 East Kimberly Road
Davenport, Iowa 52807-2095
Telephone: 800-817-8272, (toll-free)
E-mail: sbaker@questcollege.com
Web site: http://www.questcollege.com

Regent University

Distance Learning Programs

Virginia Beach, Virginia

Regent University is one of America's fastest-growing universities, offering twenty-five graduate degrees in business, communication, law, government, psychology and counseling, education, divinity, and organizational leadership, as well as a bachelor's degree completion program. The main campus of the University is located in Virginia Beach, Virginia.

A pioneer in distance education, Regent offers seventeen graduate programs through its Worldwide Internet Campus.

Graduate programs (in education, government, counseling, divinity, and journalism) and a degree completion program (Bachelor of Science in organizational leadership and management) are offered at the Regent University Northern Virginia/D.C. Graduate Center in Alexandria, Virginia.

Regent University is accredited by the Commission on Colleges of the Southern Association of Colleges and Schools (1866 Southern Lane, Decatur, Georgia 30033-4097; telephone: 404-679-4501) to award the master's and doctoral degrees and is a candidate for accreditation to award the bachelor's degree.

The Regent University School of Law is fully accredited by the American Bar Association (ABA). All schools except Divinity are DANTES approved. The School of Divinity is also accredited by the Association of Theological Schools (ATS).

DISTANCE LEARNING PROGRAM

Regent University serves 560 full- and part-time distance education students through its Worldwide Campus. This number constitutes 27 percent of the entire student population. In the spring of 2000, 953 Regent students, nearly half of the school population, took at least one class through the Internet at Regent.

The Worldwide Campus is for any graduate student with nontraditional educational needs. Students with at least a 28.8-kbps modem and a 486 computer can be part of the Worldwide Campus.

Regent University is fully accredited, and the Worldwide Campus gives the student access to the same principled leadership education available at the main Regent University campus in Virginia Beach and the Graduate Center in Alexandria, Virginia. Judeo-Christian principles form the framework for

personal and professional success. Regent provides students with not only the knowledge to do well professionally after they graduate, but also the spiritual foundations to do good and the ability to make a positive impact on society through their leadership.

DELIVERY MEDIA

The mode of delivery varies by college or school. Most distance degrees are offered online via the Internet. Others may utilize a combination of traditional correspondence and Internet delivery.

Students receive outlines and other study materials via e-mail. Students submit papers and quizzes to instructors via e-mail. Chat rooms are used for cohort (class) interaction. Students need access to an IBM-compatible computer with Internet service and software, a cassette player, and occasional access to a videocassette player to review certain study materials. Detailed requirements are outlined in each admission packet.

PROGRAMS OF STUDY

Worldwide Campus graduate degrees offered through Internet/Distance Education include the M.A. in communication, Ph.D. in communication, M.A. in journalism (nontechnical areas), Certificate of Graduate Studies in Leadership, M.A. in organizational leadership, Ph.D. in organizational leadership, Doctor of Strategic Leadership, Executive M.B.A., Professional M.B.A., LL.M. in international taxation, Master of International Taxation, Master of Education (individualized programs, Christian School Program, and TESOL), Doctorate in Education, courses in public policy, courses in political management, courses in public administration, and courses in practical theology.

SPECIAL PROGRAMS

Regent University offers the Accelerated Scholars and Professionals Program (ASAP), which allows some students to enter their master's program without having received a bachelor's degree. Successful applicants to this program have accrued a minimum of 90 credits toward their undergraduate degree and have acquired significant life experience (determined by an admissions committee) in a professional area relevant to their chosen master's program.

Most students in the Regent Worldwide Classroom find that the University's Internet graduate classes are more supportive than their previous educational experience. Internet/Distance Education has the benefit of making sure that every student has the best seat in the class. Students have the undivided attention of professors and classmates every time they communicate. Internet/Distance Education at Regent focuses on making students' learning experiences completely relevant to their work experience.

CREDIT OPTIONS

For all distance programs, students may transfer up to 25 percent of the total credits required for their chosen degree. Credits must be taken from an approved institution (determined by each Regent school) and must reflect grades of B or better.

FACULTY

Regent distance learning courses are taught by the same full- and part-time faculty members who teach on campus. Regent has a distinguished faculty of more than 103 men and women of varying religious denominations and diverse national and ethnic origins.

ADMISSION

With the exception of ASAP students (see "Special Programs"), admission to Regent University requires a completed four-year bachelor's degree from a state and regionally accredited postsecondary institution. Applicants possessing earned degrees from nonaccredited institutions are considered on an individual basis.

While each Regent school maintains specific admissions criteria, the following are considered universal: a minimum cumulative undergraduate GPA of 2.75, with a minimum of 3.0 in the desired area; submission of test scores (MAT, GMAT, or GRE, depending on the school's requirement); maturity in spiritual and/or character qualities; and personal goals that are consistent with the mission and goals of Regent.

International admissions requirements also vary among Regent schools. Students should contact the school of their choice for specific information.

TUITION AND FEES

Semester credit-hour rates for distance learning are as follows: business, $690; communication, $425; M.Ed., $347; Ed.D., $450; government, $350; divinity, $275; and LL.M./M.I.T., $625. Organizational leadership is $350 per credit hour for the M.A., while the Ph.D. in organizational leadership is $450. The Doctor of Strategic Leadership is $450 per credit hour.

FINANCIAL AID

Students accepted for enrollment may apply for Federal Stafford Student Loans and a variety of school-specific scholarships and grants. DANTES and veterans' benefits also apply.

APPLYING

Application deadlines and processes vary among schools. Students should contact the individual school for specific information or Central Enrollment (800-373-5504, toll-free) to request a CD-ROM on the Regent University Worldwide Campus.

CONTACT

Regent University
1000 Regent University Drive
Virginia Beach, Virginia 23464-9800
Telephone: 800-373-5504 (Central Admissions, toll-free)
E-mail: admissions@regent.edu
Web site: http://www.regent.edu

To contact distance learning programs directly:
College of Communication and the Arts (telephone: 757-226-4243; e-mail: comcollege@regent.edu)
School of Business (telephone: 800-477-3642; e-mail: busschool@regent.edu)
School of Divinity (telephone: 800-723-6162; e-mail: divschool@regent.edu)
School of Education (telephone: 888-713-1595; e-mail: eduschool@regent.edu)
School of Law (telephone: 877-850-8435; e-mail: lawschool@regent.edu)
Robertson School of Government (telephone: 888-800-7735; e-mail: govschool@regent.edu)
Center for Leadership Studies (telephone: 757-226-4122; e-mail: leadercenter@regent.edu)

Rensselaer Polytechnic Institute

Professional and Distance Education

Troy, New York

Founded in 1824, Rensselaer Polytechnic Institute in Troy, New York, is America's oldest private technological university. Internationally regarded as a prominent research institute with strong ties to industry, Rensselaer offers graduate and undergraduate degrees in engineering, science, management, architecture, and humanities and social science. Since 1995, Rensselaer's highly successful curriculum-renewal efforts have been recognized with three of the most prestigious awards in higher education: the Hesburgh Award for Faculty Development to Enhance Undergraduate Teaching, the Boeing Outstanding Educator Award, and the Pew Leadership Award for the Renewal of Undergraduate Education. National rankings in U.S. News & World Report *and* Success *have provided acclaim for Rensselaer's graduate programs in engineering, management, and entrepreneurship. For the third year in a row,* Yahoo! Internet Life *magazine ranked Rensselaer among the top five "most-wired" campuses in the nation.*

DISTANCE LEARNING PROGRAM

Rensselaer's distance learning program, RSVP, provides fifteen master's degree programs and sixteen certificate programs, as well as graduate courses and noncredit seminars, to working professionals at their work sites, homes, or other convenient locations. More than 1,300 working professionals from many of this nation's leading corporations participate each semester without having to travel to the campus.

In operation since 1987, RSVP is a highly respected program in the field of distance learning. In 1993, it was named "Best Distance Learning Program—Higher Education" by the United States Distance Learning Association. In 1996, the same organization recognized it as having an "Outstanding Partnership with a Corporation" for the development and delivery of its M.S. program in the management of technology to General Motors. RSVP is known for an emphasis on high quality, customer service, excellent production values, and innovation.

DELIVERY MEDIA

RSVP delivers courses using a range of technologies that include satellite broadcasts, videoconferencing, videotapes, and the Internet. These technologies are integrated so that the same event can be transmitted to multiple locations in different delivery formats. Most programs can be received in a live, interactive mode. A growing number of classes are now being videostreamed on the Internet, making it possible for individual students, as well as those at corporate sites, to pursue Rensselaer graduate studies at a distance and at any time of the day or night. The World Wide Web also provides for e-mail or chat interaction with the instructor and staff members and provides electronic access to course materials.

PROGRAMS OF STUDY

Working professionals may complete individual courses, four-course certificate programs, or full master's degrees through RSVP. The credits and degrees received are identical to those received by campus-based students. Most content is at the graduate level. In addition, noncredit seminars and workshops are offered in a range of technical areas.

Master's degrees are available in the following areas: business administration (M.B.A.), computer science, computer and systems engineering, electrical engineering (microelectronics), electric power engineering, engineering science (manufacturing systems engineering and microelectronics manufacturing engineering), industrial and management engineering (quality engineering and service systems), information technology, management (with optional concentrations in management information systems or human-computer interaction), mechanical engineering, and technical communications.

Certificates are available in the following areas: bioinformatics, computer graphics and data visualization, computer networks, computer science, database systems design, graphical user interfaces, human-computer interaction, management and technology, manufacturing systems engineering, mechanical engineering, microelectronics manufacturing engineering, microelectronics technology and design, quality and reliability, service systems, and software engineering.

In 1999, RSVP launched a series of new information technology degree and certificate programs called IT at a Distance. Qualified students may pursue courses leading to IT-related degrees or certificates at home or office using videostreaming on the World Wide Web and through Rennsalear's new 80/20 model for interactive Web-based delivery. In addition, Rensselaer alumni may now pursue these or any RSVP programs as individual students. Students should contact the Office of Professional and Distance Education for Web delivery schedules.

RSVP delivers approximately seventy-five courses annually via distance learning technology to both individual students and employees at more than sixty sites of many of the nation's leading corporations and other organizations. Participants include AT&T, Consolidated Edison, DuPont, U.S. Department of Defense, Federal Highway Administration, Ford, General Electric, General Motors, Hyperion Solutions, IBM, J. P. Morgan, Lockheed Martin, Lotus Development Corporation, Lucent Technology, Perkin-Elmer, Pitney Bowes, Quantum Corp., United Technologies, and Xerox, among others.

In nondegree programming, Rensselaer also provides several programs per year of one to five days in length, depending on content and audience need. In recent years, programs have been offered in bioinformatics, colloid chemistry, computer and information technology, polymer chemistry, multiphase flow and heat transfer, chemical mechanical planarization, and highway capacity, among other areas. Employees from many Fortune 500 companies and other leading organizations have attended these programs.

SPECIAL PROGRAMS

RSVP frequently works with corporate, government, and military sponsors who arrange to bring Rensselaer's programs on-site for their employees. Similar arrangements can be made with regional partners (i.e., community colleges, professional organizations, and education centers). Partner sites agree to receive courses and provide all local administrative support, which often includes a library of instructional materials. Because many programs are offered in response to the needs of sponsors, it is possible to add new courses or programs based on interest and sufficient enrollments.

STUDENT SERVICES

Professional and Distance Education staff members serve as the interface to the rest of the Rensselaer campus for RSVP student services, including admission, registration, academic advising, instructional materials, transfer credits, and degree clearance. Students also have direct access to Rensselaer's Student Information System and the library via the World Wide Web.

CREDIT OPTIONS

Except for the M.B.A., all master's programs are 30-credit minimum, ten-course degrees. Students in the master's programs can transfer up to two graduate-level courses (6 credits) that have been completed at other institutions, assuming that the courses are approved as acceptable in the plan of study by an academic adviser and were completed with a grade of B or better. The M.B.A. is a 60-credit program with the possibility of waiving 3 to 12 credits based on prior knowledge and/or work experience. Certificate programs require the successful completion of a four-course sequence of graduate-level courses. No course work can be transferred into the certificate program.

FACULTY

The RSVP faculty is drawn from approximately 400 full-time Rensselaer scholars, teachers, and researchers. Their doctorates or other degrees are from the world's leading universities. The faculty members who teach in the distance learning program also teach on campus, and more than 80 full-time faculty members have taught in the program to date.

ADMISSION

Students interested in credit courses and degree programs must apply to Rensselaer in the same manner as campus-based students, and admission standards are essentially the same. Transcripts of all college-level work and two letters of recommendation must be supplied for degree admission. Transcripts are also required for certificates. There are no admission requirements for short courses and seminars.

TUITION AND FEES

Tuition for all credit courses is invoiced at the same rate as for campus-based students. For the 2000–01 academic year, that is $700 per credit hour, or $2100 per 3-credit course. The only other costs are for the application fee ($35), a transcript fee ($25), and the cost of instructional materials. Costs for noncredit seminars and workshops vary.

FINANCIAL AID

Most students currently enrolled in the program have their tuition costs paid through their employers. If desired, students enrolled in the credit courses and programs can, like their colleagues on campus, apply for state and federal bank loans.

APPLYING

Application deadlines are typically set at four to six weeks prior to the first day of class, and admission decisions are made as soon as the completed application is received. Application materials for credit courses and programs are provided to participating locations and are also available upon request. Registration forms for noncredit seminars and workshops are included in the program announcements.

CONTACT

Peter A. Miller, Associate Director for Marketing
Office of Professional and Distance Education
Rensselaer Polytechnic Institute
Center for Industrial Innovation, Suite 4011
Troy, New York 12180
Telephone: 518-276-8351
Fax: 518-276-8026
E-mail: rsvp@rpi.edu
Web site: http://www.rsvp.rpi.edu

Rio Salado College

Distance Learning Program

Tempe, Arizona

> *In 1978, the Maricopa Community College District approved an intriguing new concept: to create a nontraditional college that offered busy, working adults the highest-quality education designed for their total convenience. The result was Rio Salado College.*
>
> *From the start, Rio Salado College has been recognized for its innovative educational delivery systems. Rio takes college beyond the confines of a traditional campus and provides education wherever a group of students and an instructor can meet to share the adventure of learning. Technology brings courses directly to thousands of students via distance learning. In addition, more than 500 adjunct faculty members teach at approximately 200 existing facilities, including shopping malls, community centers, businesses, and high schools throughout Maricopa County.*
>
> *For twenty years, Rio Salado College has consistently grown and thrived and has a current enrollment of nearly 27,000 credit and 24,000 noncredit students. Rio Salado College is accredited by the North Central Association of Colleges and Schools.*

DISTANCE LEARNING PROGRAM

"Let the College come to you" is the prevailing philosophy at Rio Salado. Rio Salado College makes it possible to earn an associate degree through distance learning, a concept the College has refined over the last twenty years. Rio offers 300 distance learning courses, with 200 of those on the Internet. All distance courses encourage maximum interaction between student and instructor. Students choose their own study times and submit assignments by mail, fax, or computer. Instructors are available by phone, fax, and e-mail.

DELIVERY MEDIA

Distance courses are available through different delivery modes that include print-based, mixed media (audiocassette and/or videocassette, teleconference, computer), and the Internet.

Courses delivered on the Internet were first introduced in fall 1996 and currently attract more than 20,000 students annually. Access requires a service provider, Macintosh/Windows capability, and a minimum of 8 MB of RAM.

PROGRAMS OF STUDY

Distance learning classes are primarily academic in nature and include accounting, anthropology, art humanities, biology, business, chemistry, child/family studies, communication, computers, counseling and personal development, economics, education, English, geology, health science, history, humanities, integrated studies, management and supervision, mathematics, office automated systems, philosophy, political science, psychology, Spanish, and theater.

Students can also enroll in distance-delivered applied certificate programs such as wastewater treatment, water distribution and collection, and water treatment. Rio Salado offers the certificates in computer technology, organizational leadership, and quality customer service; A.A.S. degrees in water/wastewater management and public administration; and A.G.S. and A.A. degrees in general studies via the Internet.

Degrees offered are the Associate of Arts, the Associate of General Studies, and the Associate of Applied Science.

SPECIAL PROGRAMS

Rio Salado College provides a variety of computer courses leading to an A.A.S. degree and/or certificates of completion in computer technology, plus eight areas of specialization, including desktop publishing, networking, and computer Web development. Sample individual courses include Windows 98, Internet Explorer, and Microsoft Office 97 and 2000.

STUDENT SERVICES

All major student services are on line, including registration, career and academic counseling, tutoring, book orders, and scholarship applications. Two easy-to-follow tutorials assist first-time Internet users. In addition, a technology help desk is available seven days a week.

CREDIT OPTIONS

Because Rio Salado College is accredited by the North Central Association of Colleges and Schools, its credits are recognized nationwide. Students who plan to transfer credits outside Arizona are encouraged to confer with an adviser to obtain specific information as to how the credits will fit into their curriculum or program of study.

FACULTY

In addition to full-time residential faculty members, Rio Salado College capitalizes on the professional career experience and expertise that more than 500 adjunct faculty members bring to the learning environment. As well as being content specialists, Rio Salado faculty members are specially trained in effective teaching techniques for distance learning.

ADMISSION

With only a few exceptions, students may begin their distance classes any one of twenty-six times throughout the year—new classes start every other week. This open-entry format allows students to enroll anytime and have up to thirteen weeks to complete their courses.

For regular and distance classes, students may be admitted under any of the following classifications: college transfer, high school/GED graduate, or 18 years of age or older. Special admission requirements and forms are available for international students or students who do not qualify for any of these classifications.

TUITION AND FEES

Students pay tuition according to their residency status. Tuition for Arizona residents is $41 per credit hour, plus a $5-per-semester registration fee. Tuition for nonresidents is $125 per credit hour, plus a $5-per-semester registration fee. Tuition and fees are subject to change.

FINANCIAL AID

Whether taking regular or distance learning courses, eligible students can apply for grants, work-study, and scholarships. To be eligible for federal financial aid, students must meet application criteria and select a program of study. The application process is approximately eight weeks long, so students should plan ahead.

APPLYING

Registration can be completed by Touch-Tone phone (480-731-8255 or toll-free at 800-729-1197) or via the World Wide Web (http://www.rio. maricopa.edu/). Along with a completed application, students need to provide an official high school transcript, GED scores, or official transcripts from previously attended colleges.

CONTACT

Rio Salado College
Student Services
2323 West 14th Street
Tempe, Arizona 85281
Telephone: 480-517-8540
E-mail: more.info@riomail.maricopa.edu

Robert Morris College

Pittsburgh, Pennsylvania

Robert Morris College, an independent coeducational institution of higher education, it is accredited by the Middle States Association of Colleges and Secondary Schools. It is authorized by the Department of Education of the Commonwealth of Pennsylvania to award the Doctor of Science degree, the Master of Science degree in nine areas, the Master of Business Administration degree, the Bachelor of Science in Business Administration degree in sixteen areas, the Bachelor of Arts degree in eight areas, the Bachelor of Science degree in eleven areas, and the Associate in Arts or Sciences degree in five areas of study. With a student population of approximately 5,000, the College offers high-quality undergraduate and graduate degree programs that integrate the liberal arts with professional programs.

Robert Morris College was admitted to candidacy status for the AACSB–The International Association for Management Education in March of 1995. This accreditation process encourages the pursuit of diverse paths to high quality in business education, and the College is active in this process.

The College has two convenient campuses. The main campus is located in Moon Township, a suburb of Pittsburgh, 17 miles from downtown and 5 miles from the Pittsburgh International Airport. The Pittsburgh Campus is located in the heart of the financial and banking area of downtown Pittsburgh and is the center for the Robert Morris College Online programs.

DISTANCE LEARNING PROGRAM

The mission of the College's online programs is to offer a high-quality and affordable education to adult students in a manner that is convenient. Adults bring a variety of experiences to the educational setting, and instructional methods should enhance and use these experiences. The faculty is trained to facilitate the adult learner.

DELIVERY MEDIA

Robert Morris College's cutting-edge distance learning programs use the Internet for online instruction. The online method allows for e-mail, interactive chat, audio and video streaming, threaded discussions, instructional connections to additional Web sites, and access to the electronic library, journals, and document sharing, among other things.

Online courses require students to have access to a computer and an Internet provider as well as an e-mail account.

PROGRAMS OF STUDY

By utilizing the Internet, students are able to participate in courses online and at their convenience. This provides them with greater freedom to complete their course requirements and the flexibility to do so when their schedules permit. A Bachelor of Science in Business Administration degree (B.S.B.A) majoring in accounting, management, or information systems may be completed in as little as four years. Students with transfer credits may finish in even less time.

The program currently requires that students also attend class at the Pittsburgh Campus. The class time is minimal, only 1 hour per week per class. Therefore, students in this program can attend college "full-time," qualify for the maximum amount of financial aid, and have their day completed at 1:40 p.m. each Saturday. The remainder of their class work is completed online, via the Internet. This program allows maximum convenience while still providing students with the opportunity to interact with their professor and classmates in person each week. They only attend classes forty weeks out of each calendar year, leaving them with twelve weeks of vacation.

STUDENT SERVICES

Robert Morris College's distance students still have access to all of the student services available to the on-campus students. Such services include enrollment counseling, the Freedom Card functions, the RMC library, student financial services options, and financial aid counseling.

FACULTY

The faculty of Robert Morris College offers students the best of both worlds. Instructors include full-time faculty members as well as adjunct professors. The faculty members bring real-world experience and knowledge to the classroom as well as the theoretical background that is necessary for a well-rounded educational experience.

TUITION AND FEES

Undergraduate tuition is $282 per credit hour. A college fee of $16 per credit and a technology fee of $20 per credit is also charged.

APPLYING

To be considered for admission into any program for any term at Robert Morris College, students must complete an admissions application. Please be sure to complete the application in its entirety. An online application may be completed on the Web site at: http://www.robert-morris.edu. The application fee is waived for all applicants who complete and submit the application online.

Robert Morris College is on rolling admissions. This means that there is no official date by which a student must apply for admission. However, students are advised to send in their application as soon as they have decided to include Robert Morris College in their college search, in order to ensure prompt processing time. A $30 nonrefundable application fee is required of all hard-copy applicants.

CONTACT
For further details and information, students should contact the Office of Enrollment Services toll-free at 800-762-0097 or at http://www.robert-morris.edu or see the online campus at http://www.rmconline.org.

R·I·T Rochester Institute of Technology

Distance Learning

Rochester, New York

Rochester Institute of Technology's (RIT) distance learning programs are built around the student convenience by offering students anytime, anywhere access to quality career education. RIT has been recognized by InterEd, an independent research company, as the third-largest provider of distance education in the U.S.

DISTANCE LEARNING PROGRAM

Rochester Institute of Technology is one of the nation's leaders in distance learning education programs. The online learning program empowers the student by providing anytime, anywhere access to courses, while maintaining essential interaction between faculty members and students. RIT distance learning students have access to more than thirty full degree and certificate programs, including eight graduate degrees, four undergraduate degrees, eighteen certificate programs, and more than 300 courses. The commitment to quality education is an inherent part of RIT distance learning programs. The faculty members are world renowned and leaders in the subject matter they teach.

DELIVERY MEDIA

All course interaction takes place online. RIT provides students with online courseware to access their courses. RIT distance learning emphasizes student-instructor interaction over the Internet. Professors deliver course materials through the Internet. Many courses also use a combination of textbooks, videotapes, audiotapes, audio conferences, chats, electronic library resources, and other components that enhance that particular course experience. Students submit most assignments online, but professors may also choose to fax or mail assignments. Students may register online, by fax, and through touch-tone telephone. Students may order course materials online and have complete access to a full range of library services online.

In order to participate, students must have full access to the Internet and a personal computer. Students must have basic computer skills and some Internet experience to be successful. In addition, a VCR that is capable of playing NTSC (American standard video) and a telephone are required. For specific computer requirements, students should visit the Web page listed in the Contact section.

PROGRAMS OF STUDY

All programs offered through RIT are available to students worldwide. Applications for all programs are available online. Most students have some college experience before coming to RIT, but admission into the certificates and the bachelor's-level programs can be accommodated without previous college experience. Master's degree candidates must meet the admissions standards required by that program and must have completed a baccalaureate degree from an accredited institution. International applicants must demonstrate English proficiency, usually through the Test Of English as a Foreign Language (TOEFL). TOEFL scores vary by program, but most programs require a score of 550 or better. For graduate students, undergraduate transcripts and two professional recommendations must be submitted.

The B.S. in applied arts and science presents a flexible opportunity for a student, with the help of an academic adviser, to create a program tailored to meet his or her educational needs. It requires the completion of 180 credit hours.

The B.S. in electrical/mechanical engineering technology has broadened its scope to an anytime, anywhere program, with the exception of some lab experiences that must be completed over several weekends at RIT or by taking an alternative course from an approved institution. The undergraduate degree requires 193 credit hours. This program is accredited by ABET-TAC.

The B.S. in telecommunications engineering technology (the technical option) is currently available to both working professionals and full-time students. The academic emphasis is placed on backbone technologies that transmit, switch, and manage networks and the information they carry. Individuals who have no background or have not completed basic lab work in this field may need to come to RIT for intensified weekend labs. This program is accredited by ABET-TAC.

The B.S. in environmental management requires students to have at least three years of mathematics, including trigonometry, and a minimum of one year of chemistry or physics. Students with a two-year degree in environmental science or a related program may have fulfilled credit requirements similar to those required in the first two years of RIT's program and may be admitted with junior standing.

The M.S. in applied statistics is designed for full-time professionals who want to learn state-of-the art statistical techniques to enhance their careers and their value to their companies. Students must complete 45 credits. Admission to the degree program is granted to qualified holders of a baccalaureate degree from an accredited college or university who have acceptable mathematics credits, including one academic year of calculus.

The M.S. in software development and management consists of 48 credit hours, comprising the software engineering core foundation, the software engineering project, and electives. A minimal background is required in mathematics (discrete structures, statistics) and computing (programming in a high-level language, data structures, elementary computer architecture, and digital logic).

The M.S. in information technology consists of 48 credit hours of graduate study in core courses, with a choice of electives and concentrations in telecommunications technology, telecommunications management, and software development and management. Entering students are expected to have programming skills at an intermediate level in an appropriate language and understand the fundamentals of computer hardware.

The M.S. in health systems administration is designed to meet the needs of health professionals who desire a non-clinical degree in management and administration. Students typically enter in cohort groups, which improves the learning environment, and take two courses per quarter until completion of the 57 credit hours.

The M.S. in cross-disciplinary professional studies consists of 48 credit hours, which comprise two or three concentrations from various areas. These areas are designed to give the student a comprehensive and customized plan of graduate study tailored to meet either career or educational objectives. Students must take a course in interdisciplinary research techniques and finish a capstone project to complete this degree.

The M.S. in environmental health and safety management requires 48 credit hours drawn from core courses like environmental health and safety management system design and performance measurement, 12 credits from professional electives, and 12 credits from the graduate thesis and graduate project.

The M.S. in imaging science is being offered to working professionals and students around the world. The worldwide demand for specialists in imaging science is well documented. The program emphasizes a systems approach to the study of imaging science, and, with a background in science or engineering, this degree prepares the student for positions in research, product development, and management in the imaging industry. The program requires completion of 45 credits.

The M.S. in microelectronics manufacturing engineering is designed for students with a B.S. degree in microelectronic engineering or other related engineering areas. The degree requires the completion of nine 4-credit courses and a 9-credit thesis for a total of 45 credits.

RIT also offers nineteen certificates for those wanting to improve or obtain skills in specialized areas. Courses in the certificate programs may be applied toward a degree.

CREDIT OPTIONS

Students have a number of options available for credit, including transfer credit, credit by exam, College-Level Examination Program (CLEP), Regents College exam, credit for educational experiences in the armed forces, credit for educational experiences in noncollegiate organizations, and credit for nontraditional learning. Advisers work with students to evaluate the number of credits that can be transferred, since the number of non-RIT credits accepted varies by program.

FACULTY

RIT's faculty members are world-renowned and teach both on-campus and distance education courses. More than 200 full-time and part-time faculty members teach distance learning courses.

ADMISSION

Requirements for admission and completion of degree or certificate programs vary by academic department. Students should refer to Program of Study descriptions.

TUITION AND FEES

Graduate tuition is $565 per credit hour. Undergraduate tuition, based on program code, is $258 per credit hour for lower-division courses and $283 per credit hour for upper-division courses.

FINANCIAL AID

RIT offers a full range of traditional financial aid programs as well as a number of innovative financing plans. Scholarships and assistantships are available to matriculated students in most graduate departments. The process of applying for aid should begin during the month of January in the year the student wishes to enroll.

APPLYING

Distance learning students follow the same procedures as all other students attending RIT. Decisions for selection rest within each college. Correspondence between the student and the Institute is conducted through the Offices of Part-Time and Graduate Enrollment Services, which reviews applications as they are received.

CONTACT

Offices of Part-Time and Graduate Enrollment Services
Rochester Institute of Technology
58 Lomb Memorial Drive
Rochester, New York 14623-5604
Telephone: 716-475-2229
　　　　　800-CALL-RIT (toll-free)
Fax: 716-475-7164
E-mail: opes@rit.edu
Web Site:
　http://distancelearning.rit.edu

Rogers University

RU Online

Claremore, Oklahoma

Rogers University (RU) is a regionally accredited university that was founded in 1909. RU offers more than fifty 2-year associate's degree programs through its liberal studies, health sciences, computer science and business, and science and mathematics divisions. RU also offers upper-division courses leading toward bachelor's and master's degrees in eight areas of study with other Oklahoma universities. The main RU campus is located in Claremont, Oklahoma, with branch campuses in nearby Bartlesville and Pryor, Oklahoma. More than 3,000 students are enrolled in RU, which enables the University to offer a student-faculty ratio of 25:1. RU is a national leader in distance education, with courses and degree programs offered via the Internet, television, and independent study. RU is the only university in Oklahoma to operate a public television station (KRSC-TV).

DISTANCE LEARNING PROGRAM

RU Online was established in 1992 and is accredited by the North Central Association of Colleges and Schools. The main mission and purpose of RU Online is to provide a university in an online form, offering students traditional courses and services at their convenience, with a commitment to quality and student success. The online program served more than 1,500 students in 1998.

DELIVERY MEDIA

Rogers University delivers the bulk of RU Online courseware over the Internet, including text, hypertext, graphics, audio, and video online. In addition, students communicate with faculty members or other students using e-mail, electronic file transfer, threaded discussions, chat rooms, phone, and fax. RU Online students need the following equipment: Windows 3.1, Windows 98, or MacOS with at least a Pentium or equivalent processor, multimedia capability, a 56K modem, a full-serve Internet connection, a Java-capable Web browser, and RealPlayer 5.0 (for audio and video).

PROGRAMS OF STUDY

RU Online students may choose from associate-level degree programs in business administration, applied technology, computer science, and liberal arts as well as bachelor's degree programs in business information technology and applied technology. Sixty credit hours are required for the completion of associate degree programs and a minimum of 120 credits for bachelor's degrees. Courses offered online parallel the campus academic semester calendar.

In addition, students may choose from more than ninety individual courses in applied technology, business management, computer science, economics, English, geography, history, humanities, information technology, mathematics, physical science, political science, and psychology. There are no residency requirements for these degrees; this enables students to earn complete degrees in the convenience of their homes, offices, or other designated locations.

SPECIAL PROGRAMS

Rogers University works with both employers and the military in mak-ing arrangements for special funding for working or military students. RU also contracts with professionals and employers to design and offer specialized courses for professionals seeking to complete continuing education and job skill requirements. In addition, RU Online is reaching international learning centers abroad.

STUDENT SERVICES

Rogers University provides RU Online students with the following services via the Internet: admissions, academic advisement, technical support, bookstore, library services, tutoring, career planning and placement, financial aid processing, and a virtual student union.

CREDIT OPTIONS

Rogers University accepts transfer credits from other accredited higher education institutions. Students are required to earn a minimum of 15 credit hours at Rogers University (online or otherwise). In addition, students may receive credits for previous military service or work experience through CLEP testing. RU does not accept "life credits" but makes special course arrangements with students with certain technical skills to participate in advanced standing placement.

FACULTY

Ninety percent of Rogers University faculty members are campus based and full-time. Sixty-five percent have doctorates in their fields. RU Online's student-faculty ratio is 17:1.

ADMISSION

RU has an open admissions policy, enabling all high school graduates/

644

GED-completion students to be accepted and enrolled. Specific requirements regarding admission based on educational goals may be found at RU's Web site, listed below. It is available 24 hours a day, seven days a week, for review.

TUITION AND FEES

In-state tuition and fees for the 2000–01 school year are $103.53 per credit hour; out-of-state tuition and fees are $196.53 per credit hour. The cost of textbooks, software (CS courses), and shipping is additional and may vary.

FINANCIAL AID

RU Online students may apply for scholarships and all federal monies (such as grants and loans). Oklahoma residents may apply for OTAG or ENGA fee waivers. In addition, vocational-rehabilitation programs, such as VA and the G.I. bill and any program covered by the Job Training Placement Act, are options for RU Online students seeking financial aid.

APPLYING

Future RU Online students should visit the Web site and complete a free application for admission. This enables students to register for desired courses and complete online student orientation prior to class. Students are required to submit admission documents to confirm their application information.

CONTACT

Online Admissions
Attention: Online Advisor
Rogers University
1701 West Will Rogers Boulevard
Claremore, Oklahoma 74017
Telephone: 918-343-7548
Fax: 918-343-7595
E-mail: online@rsu.edu
Web site: http://www.rsuonline.edu

Roger Williams University
Open College
Bristol, Rhode Island

Accredited by the New England Association of Schools and Colleges, Roger Williams University (RWU) is an independent institution that was founded in 1956. Roger Williams University offers students a strong foundation in the liberal arts and sciences, combined with a variety of professional programs. The University's Core Curriculum introduces all students to a wide range of subjects—in the humanities, natural and social sciences, history, and fine arts—to broaden their horizons and help them develop the building blocks for lifelong learning and professional success. For the second consecutive year, U.S. News & World Report *named Roger Williams University a "Top-Tier" Northern Liberal Arts College.*

The University's Open College is a comprehensive external degree program designed for people interested in nontraditional education. Most of the students are working adults who are able to pursue their educational programs with little or no interference with their personal or professional commitments.

DISTANCE LEARNING PROGRAM

Since its inception in 1974, more than 3,500 students have graduated from the Open College at Roger Williams University. In the 1999–2000 academic year, 125 courses were offered via distance learning. The average distance learning enrollment is 500 students per semester.

Academic programs are divided into regular semesters of study, including fall, spring, and summer. Campus residency is not required.

DELIVERY MEDIA

The Open College emphasizes an external approach to education, and the instructional methods available to off-campus students include non-classroom courses, such as external courses, internships, online courses, and independent study courses. Some of the external courses may include guided instruction via videotapes, audiotapes, computer software, computer conferencing, World Wide Web, e-mail, and print. Students and teachers may meet in person or interact via audioconferencing, mail, telephone, fax, e-mail, and World Wide Web. The following equipment may be required: fax machine, computer, Internet access, and e-mail.

PROGRAMS OF STUDY

Distance education through the Open College at Roger Williams University offers baccalaureate degrees in business management, criminal justice, industrial technology, public administration, and social science.

The business management major provides students with "marketplace" skills such as problem solving, information gathering and processing, and project managing. The degree also prepares students to appreciate the overall challenges of a business operation and to function effectively within an integrated business environment.

The criminal justice major is designed for students who are employed, or who are seeking employment, in direct law enforcement professions or public or private criminal justice–related agencies.

The industrial technology major is designed for students with technical and/or managerial backgrounds and interests and who are employed or seeking employment in manufacturing or service industries.

The public administration major prepares students for government service on the federal, state, or local level and for employment in non-profit organizations and international administration.

The social science major is designed for students with interests in more than one social science area and whose interests cannot be accommodated by a single discipline. Typically, students select a combination of courses that reflect personal or professional interests and represent a coherent program with one or more specific focuses or themes.

To earn a baccalaureate degree, a minimum of 120 credits are required through any combination of learning experiences, including credit for previous college work, military training and experience, CLEP exams, and credit documentation. Students are required to complete a minimum of 30 credits through the Open College at Roger Williams University. Also, a minimum 2.0 grade point average is required in all courses carrying a letter grade and in all required major courses.

Each student is assigned to a faculty adviser who works with the student to develop an education and degree plan. The adviser also assists in registration, credit documentation, and enrollment procedures; identifies appropriate courses and learning experiences; and supervises student work.

SPECIAL PROGRAMS

The Open College at Roger Williams University offers internships, co-ops, and practica for employment-related learning experiences in all academic degree programs.

STUDENT SERVICES

All college services available to the traditional student are also available to distance learning students, including access to the University's library, computer support, tutoring, advising, and career placement.

CREDIT OPTIONS

Many students are able to enter the Open College with considerable advanced standing. Students may reduce the total time required for completion of studies and degree requirements with up to three years of credit from military service and training, transfer of credits obtained from other colleges, credit documentation that awards credit for life and job-related learning experiences, and College-Level Examination Program (CLEP) or other advanced credit exams.

FACULTY

The Open College at Roger Williams University has a total of 47 faculty members to provide instruction. Eighteen are full-time faculty members at RWU (38 percent), and 29 are part-time (adjunct) faculty members (62 percent). Twenty-six faculty members (55 percent) have doctoral or other terminal degrees. All faculty members have at least one graduate degree.

ADMISSION

Admissions preference is given to students who are able to enter with advanced standing, based on credits already acquired from previous college attendance, military training, employment experiences, and/or CLEP exams. Also, preference is given to students who have access to various educational and learning resources in the event such resources need to be incorporated into their academic programs. Resources may include, but are not limited to, libraries, classroom courses at local colleges, local proctors, potential sites for internship placement, and computers.

TUITION AND FEES

Open College tuition varies by program and ranges from $705 to $1200 per 3-credit course for the 2000–01 academic year. The application fee is $35; no registration fee is required.

FINANCIAL AID

Aside from various forms of military tuition assistance that might be available to service members, Open College students are eligible for all of the traditional forms of financial aid that are normally associated with adult and continuing education students. Approximately 50 percent of distance learning students receive financial assistance (excluding employer reimbursement programs).

APPLYING

Applications must be submitted with appropriate documentation, such as a resume, official high school transcripts, GED scores, or official transcripts from previous colleges or universities. Service members must submit a copy of credit recommendations for all military training and experience from Form DD295, prepared by military education officers.

CONTACT

John Stout, Dean
Open College
Roger Williams University
One Old Ferry Road
Bristol, Rhode Island 02809-2921
Telephone: 401-254-3530
           800-458-7144 Ext. 3530 (toll-free)
Fax: 401-254-3560
E-mail: jws@alpha.rwu.edu
Web site: http://www.rwu.edu

Rutgers, The State University of New Jersey

RutgersOnline

New Brunswick, New Jersey

Rutgers University, which comprises twenty-nine undergraduate colleges and graduate and professional schools, is the flagship institution of New Jersey's public higher education system. It is a vibrant and diverse community of more than 48,000 students enrolled in over 280 degree programs, 35,000 students enrolled in continuing professional development courses, 10,000 faculty and staff members, and more than 300,000 living alumni.

Founded more than 230 years ago in 1766, Rutgers is distinguished as one of the oldest institutions of higher learning in the country. At the same time, modern-day Rutgers qualifies as the youngest of America's major public research universities. In the span of the last forty years, Rutgers has risen from a disparate collection of schools, geographically dispersed and operating largely independently, into the ranks of the nation's most prestigious educational institutions. That advancement was recognized in 1989 when Rutgers was asked to join the Association of American Universities, comprising the top research universities in North America. Driving all of Rutgers' activities, whether teaching, research, or service, is the defining characteristic of a great research university: the continuous and vigorous creation of intellectual capital and the new discoveries and insights that drive the advancement of human knowledge contributing to the improvement of the human condition.

RutgersOnline extends the services and reach of the University, providing students with the opportunity to telecommute to campus from virtually anywhere. RutgersOnline students benefit from some of Rutgers most distinguished faculty members through online courses that are equivalent to traditional courses offered on campus. Graduate courses in nursing and communication and library studies were among the first offered during 1999–2000. Additional courses in budgeting, management, accountancy, and education are being developed and will be available within the next year.

DISTANCE LEARNING PROGRAM

Rutgers University seeks to use distance learning to promote the three-fold mission of teaching, research, and service, providing the same high-quality academic program that is found on campus. RutgersOnline extends access to the resources of the University through the Internet-based distance learning program, especially for nontraditional, working adult students who are off campus. The hallmarks of the distance learning program are high quality in the academic program, a high level of

interactivity for active learning, and access to a wide range of resources found only at a top research university.

DELIVERY MEDIA

Internet-based courses delivered through RutgersOnline provide asynchronous access to selected courses from anywhere in the world. Students need computer and Internet access. Full hardware and software requirements are detailed at http://www.rutgersonline.net.

RutgersOnline courses are highly interactive and use various software-

based tools to enhance student-faculty and student-student interaction, including threaded discussion, e-mail, and chat room.

PROGRAMS OF STUDY

In fall 1999, RutgersOnline began offering courses in nursing and library studies, primarily at the graduate level. Various certificate programs will be offered in the near future. Several online master's degrees are anticipated in the future, as well, beginning with a master's degree in nursing. In addition, courses are being developed in the budgeting and management areas, accounting, economics, and other selected liberal arts areas. Most courses offered by RutgersOnline will be at the graduate level. In addition, several non-credit, professional development courses have been offered, and others are being developed.

STUDENT SERVICES

Students of the RutgersOnline distance learning program have access to a wide range of student services online. Admissions, financial aid, and library and other services are available online. In addition, online students have a 24-hour-a-day, seven-day-a-week Help Desk to support the technical aspects of their online learning. The Help Desk is available by e-mail and toll-free phone number.

TUITION AND FEES

Tuition and fees are variable, depending upon the school offering the course. The average is approximately $800 for a New Jersey resident for an undergraduate 3-credit course to approximately $1600 for a nonresident for an undergraduate 3-credit course. Graduate course tuition and fees for residents are approximately $1300 for a 3-credit course and approximately $1700 for nonresidents.

FINANCIAL AID

All forms of student financial aid are available to assist matriculated students enrolling in Rutgers undergraduate or graduate degree programs and utilizing Rutgers University distance learning courses. The application process, particular undergraduate and graduate program specifications, and other key eligibility information can be accessed through the Office of Financial Aid's Web page at http://studentaid.rutgers.edu.

APPLYING

Distance learning students apply and register through the respective school offering the online course. For matriculating students, online registration is available through the main Rutgers University Web site at http://www.rutgers.edu.

CONTACT

For more information about RutgersOnline, students should contact:

Dr. Richard J. Novak, Executive Director for Continuous Education and Distance Learning

Telephone: 732-932-3491

Fax: 732-932-2588

E-mail: ce1766@rci.rutgers.edu

Saint Joseph's College

Division of Continuing and Professional Studies

Standish, Maine

Saint Joseph's College was founded in 1912 by the Sisters of Mercy and chartered by the Maine legislature in 1915. The College grants degrees in keeping with the mission of the College and the ministries of the Sisters of Mercy. Saint Joseph's is a liberal arts college that nurtures intellectual, spiritual, and social growth in students of all ages and all faiths within a value-centered environment.

In 1970, Saint Joseph's became a coeducational institution, and in 1976, the Distance Education Program was introduced to serve the needs of the nontraditional adult learner nationwide.

Saint Joseph's is located on the shores of Sebago Lake, 18 miles from Portland. More than 1,000 students attend classes on the 331-acre campus. The beautiful lakefront of the campus faces the White Mountains. The region's natural beauty and the proximity of the College to Maine's popular ski resorts appeal to the outdoor enthusiast in winter. The nearby rocky Atlantic coastline and picturesque New England countryside offer an ideal setting for the summer experience.

DISTANCE LEARNING PROGRAM

Saint Joseph's College offers the adult learner an opportunity to integrate formal education in the liberal arts tradition with professional experience. Saint Joseph's College is accredited by the New England Association of Schools and Colleges. The Distance Education Program provides academic options in a variety of disciplines leading to undergraduate and graduate certificates and to associate, baccalaureate, and graduate degrees. Each option is designed to reflect the special nature of Saint Joseph's commitment to its students. The Distance Education Program currently enrolls about 4,000 active students, and approximately 6,500 Saint Joseph's alumni earned their degrees through the distance program.

DELIVERY MEDIA

Faculty-directed independent study is a highly flexible, accessible mode of education that allows students to study where they are. Upon enroll-

ment, students receive the texts, materials, and study guides for their courses. Some courses require access to a computer or a VCR. Faculty members assist each student with their studies through a combination of written feedback on assignments and telephone consultations. An academic adviser is assigned to work with each student from the first enrollment through to graduation. Undergraduate degree programs require one 2-week summer residency, and graduate degree programs require two 2-week summer residencies at the campus in Maine. Nondegree classes are also offered.

PROGRAMS OF STUDY

The Distance Education Program offers the following degree and certificate programs: a Master of Science in Education with an emphasis in teaching and learning (33 credits), which serves two major professional arenas—K–12 school systems and adult education programs; a master's degree in health services administration (42 credits) for senior manage-

ment roles in complex organizations; a Master of Arts in pastoral studies (33 credits) for those who seek to minister to the evolving needs of church and society; the Bachelor of Science (128 credits), with majors in health-care administration and long-term-care administration; the Bachelor of Science in professional arts (128 credits), a degree-completion program for licensed health-care professionals with concentrations in education, health-care administration, human services, and psychology; the Bachelor of Science in radiologic science (128 credits), a postcertification baccalaureate degree for radiologic science professionals; the Bachelor of Science in respiratory care (128 credits), a postcertification baccalaureate degree for respiratory care professionals; the Bachelor of Arts in criminal justice (128 credits) to provide individuals currently working in law enforcement a well-rounded curriculum; the Bachelor of Arts in liberal studies (128 credits), an interdisciplinary degree program with concentrations in American studies, women's studies, and the Christian tradition; the Bachelor of Science in business administration (128 credits), with concentrations in management and banking (a joint venture with the American Institute of Banking); the Associate of Science in management (66 credits), a foundation for the Bachelor of Science in business administration; graduate certificates (18 credits) in health-care finance, designed to provide nonfinancial health-care managers with an in-depth background in health-care financial management, and medical/dental administration for physicians and dentists; and undergraduate certificate programs (18 credits) in business administration, health-care management, long-term-care administration, home schooling, secondary education teaching, Christian tradition, women's studies, American studies, and professional studies (self-designed). Students who would like to take individual courses may enroll as continuing education students.

SPECIAL PROGRAMS

The Department of Nursing offers a Master of Science with a major in nursing (48 credits) and a Bachelor of Science in Nursing with an RN to B.S.N. track (129 credits) for students at a distance.

CREDIT OPTIONS

The Distance Education Program acknowledges the value of certain formal learning and career-based experience. For most programs, the College follows the American Council on Education guidelines in granting transfer credit for courses of study from accredited colleges or universities with a grade of C or better; ACE/PONSI-approved credit; ACE-approved military training and experience credits; CEUs earned through professional seminars, workshops, internships, and in-service education classes as elective credit; and CLEP, ACT/PEP, and DANTES exams. A maximum of 30 credits can be accepted by exam.

FACULTY

More than 90 full-time and part-time faculty members serve students in the Distance Education Program. Many teach in the traditional program as well as in distance education. All excel in their fields and have experience with nontraditional students.

ADMISSION

Admission requirements vary by program of study. Prospective students should contact the Admissions Office for the Distance Education Program at 800-752-4723 (toll-free) with specific questions about admission requirements.

TUITION AND FEES

In the 2000–01 academic year, tuition is $195 per credit hour ($570 per 3-credit course) at the undergraduate level and $235 per credit hour ($690 per 3-credit course) at the graduate level. Application fees are $50 for degree programs and $25 for certificate programs and continuing education. A complete fee schedule is available in the program catalogs.

FINANCIAL AID

Students may be eligible for the Federal Pell Grant and/or Federal Stafford Student Loan. Applying for financial aid is an individualized process requiring consultation and evaluation. For more information and assistance, students should call the Financial Aid Office at 800-752-1266 (toll-free).

APPLYING

Students are accepted on a rolling admissions basis and, therefore, can apply and begin their studies at any time during the year.

CONTACT

Admissions Office
Division of Continuing and Professional Studies
Saint Joseph's College
278 Whites Bridge Road
Standish, Maine 04084-5263
Telephone: 800-752-4723 (toll-free)
Fax: 207-892-7480
E-mail: cps.admissions@sjcme.edu
Web site: http://www.sjcme.edu

Saint Mary-of-the-Woods College

Women's External Degree Program

Saint Mary-of-the-Woods, Indiana

Founded in 1840, Saint Mary-of-the-Woods College (SMWC) is the nation's oldest Catholic liberal arts college for women and is accredited by the North Central Association of Colleges and Schools. The College offers the rich traditions of academic excellence and dedication to educating women personally and professionally for responsible roles in society. The diverse student community of 1,400 includes traditional resident students, commuters, student mothers and children, and distance learners at both the undergraduate and graduate levels. A hallmark of the College is an emphasis on personalized service.

The general studies curriculum required of all undergraduates is designed to develop the communication and analytical skills needed for success in college and in the professional world.

DISTANCE LEARNING PROGRAM

Since 1973, the Women's External Degree (WED) program has provided the College curriculum to contemporary adult women who juggle multiple responsibilities yet need or want a college degree. This structured but flexible independent study program is based on five-month semesters that begin with in-person appointments with instructors and faculty advisers and leads to a degree in one of more than twenty majors.

DELIVERY MEDIA

Faculty members and students communicate by telephone, voice mail, e-mail, and postal service. All full-time faculty members, some adjuncts, and many students have access to e-mail. Computers with modems are not required, except for accounting, CIS, and digital media communication majors, but access to a computer or word processor is strongly recommended. Some courses use videotapes, audiotapes, or optional computer programs.

PROGRAMS OF STUDY

The College is chartered to grant the degrees Associate in Arts, Associate in Science, Bachelor of Arts, and Bachelor of Science to women and the Master of Arts degree to both women and men.

Undergraduates complete the general studies curriculum, courses required for their chosen major, and additional electives to total 125 semester hours for a baccalaureate degree and 65 semester hours for an associate degree; a minimum of 30 hours must be earned at the College.

Associate majors available through WED are accounting, early childhood education, general business, gerontology, humanities, and paralegal studies. Baccalaureate majors are accounting, accounting information systems, business administration, computer information systems, education (early childhood, elementary, kindergarten-primary, secondary, and special), English, gerontology, history/political science, human resource management, human services, humanities, journalism, marketing, mathematics, paralegal studies, psychology, social sciences (history concentration), and theology.

There are no geographical restrictions, except that education majors must reside within 200 miles of campus for faculty supervision of field experience and student teaching.

The Master of Arts program in pastoral theology is designed for persons who are or plan to be engaged in ministry and for those seeking personal enrichment in theological study.

The Master of Arts program in earth literacy is designed for persons who care for and advocate a sustainable and just earth community.

The Master of Arts in art therapy program is designed for persons who use or plan to use art in therapy or art as therapy. This program emphasizes understanding and applying theories to art therapy, counseling, and psychopathology.

The Master of Arts in music therapy program is designed for professional music therapists who seek an advanced understanding of the therapeutic uses of music, especially as applied to psychotherapy and medicine. Master of Arts degrees require 36 to 40 credit hours.

SPECIAL PROGRAMS

SMWC offers several learning formats: traditional campus-based study, distance learning, and a third format that combines independent study with intensive weekend seminars on campus. WED students may combine these formats in any semester of study; about 400 choose to enroll in weekend alternative format courses each year. However, all degrees offered through WED may be completed entirely through distance learning at home, with the exception of several paralegal and digital media communication courses, which must be taken via alternative format on campus on weekends.

STUDENT SERVICES

Full-time faculty members serve as academic advisers to the WED students in their departments, meeting each semester to monitor progress and plan subsequent semesters. A WED staff of 8 provides additional support, advocacy, registrarial assistance, and information, including a quarterly newsletter for distance learners. One WED staff person provides referral to other campus services, such as career development (available by phone and in person) and library materials by mail.

CREDIT OPTIONS

Students may transfer credit earned at other accredited colleges and universities, although some credits may be too dated to meet the requirements. WED encourages students to earn credit for previous college-level learning through CLEP and DANTES, ACE/PONSI awards, and portfolio applications documenting other prior learning. At least 30 semester hours of course work must be earned under the direct supervision of SMWC faculty members.

FACULTY

Fifty-seven full-time and 55 adjunct faculty members serve as instructors and academic advisers to WED students. Sixty percent of full-time faculty members have doctoral or other terminal degrees.

ADMISSION

Applicants must have earned a high school diploma or GED certificate and demonstrate potential for success in a distance learning program. SAT I scores are required for applicants who have been out of high school for less than five years. Academic history, employment and other life experience, writing skills, and stated goals are considered. Applicants for whom English is a second language must submit TOEFL scores.

TUITION AND FEES

For 2000–01, undergraduate tuition for the WED program is $287 per semester hour. Fees include a $30 application fee, a one-time fee of $80 for the initial on-campus residency (not including housing), an annual $46 general fee, and modest materials fees for laboratory courses.

FINANCIAL AID

Available financial aid includes Federal Pell grants, student loans, and, for residents only, Indiana Higher Education grants. In 1999–2000, the College processed about $2.5 million from these sources on behalf of WED students. The College awards small WED grants to eligible seniors and offers 10 percent tuition discounts through cooperating employers; this institutional aid totaled $58,000 in 1999–2000. Finally, the WED staff maintains a directory of private grants and scholarships and encourages WED students to apply for them. More than half of WED students receive some form of aid.

APPLYING

Applications are reviewed when all materials are received; the evaluation process is usually completed within a month. Two-day orientation residencies are held on campus five times each year and conclude with enrollment in the initial semester.

CONTACT

Admission:
Gwen Hagemeyer
WED Admission Director
Saint Mary-of-the-Woods College
Saint Mary-of-the-Woods, Indiana
   47876
Telephone: 812-535-5186
      800-926-SMWC
      (toll-free)
Fax: 812-535-4900
E-mail: wedadms@smwc.edu
Web site: http://www.smwc.edu

Graduate Programs:
Mary Lou Dolan, C.S.J.
Earth Literacy Director
Telephone: 812-535-5160
Fax: 812-535-5228
E-mail: mldolan@smwc.edu
     elm@smwc.edu
Kathy Gotshall
Art Therapy Program
Telephone: 812-535-5151
E-mail: kgotshal@smwc.edu

Ruth Eileen Dwyer, S.P.
Pastoral Theology Director
Telephone: 812-535-5170
Fax: 812-535-4613
E-mail: rdwyer@smwc.edu

Tracy Richardson
Music Therapy Program
Telephone: 812-535-5154
E-mail: trichardson@smwc.edu

Salve Regina University

Extension Study

Newport, Rhode Island

Salve Regina is an independent, coeducational institution of higher learning that confers degrees in the arts and sciences. It teaches in the tradition of the Catholic Church and according to the Mission of the Sisters of Mercy who continue as its sponsors. Salve Regina's Charter was amended in June 1991 to change its name to Salve Regina University.

The University serves approximately 2,200 men and women from many states and foreign countries. Alumni number more than 12,000. Its 65-acre oceanfront campus in Newport's Ochre Point historic district includes twenty-two new and adapted buildings.

The University, through teaching and research, prepares men and women for responsible lives by imparting and expanding knowledge, developing skills, and cultivating enduring values. Through liberal arts and professional programs, students develop their abilities for thinking clearly and creatively, enhance their capacity for sound judgment, and prepare for the challenge of learning throughout their lives.

The graduate programs of Salve Regina University have two broad goals: to help the individual who enrolls to realize his or her own full potential and to prepare this individual for helping others do the same. Specific objectives of each graduate program are three-fold: to create an opportunity for critical analysis and problem solving from a Judeo-Christian perspective, to stimulate growth in wisdom by integrating the knowledge and experience gained by the student both inside and outside the classroom, and to emphasize the importance of ethics in each program's curriculum.

DISTANCE LEARNING PROGRAM

The Graduate Extension Study alternative is designed to meet the needs of students whose personal and professional circumstances make regular on-campus study impossible. Courses at the graduate level as well as systematic programs leading to the completion of requirements for the master's degree are available for eligible students. Extension Study is a highly personalized alternative to the traditional classroom approach to learning. It involves a one-on-one relationship with instructors who guide students' learning and monitor their progress through the course. Detailed syllabi prepared by faculty members provide a structured, step-by-step approach to learning while allowing students the utmost flexibility in organizing their study time.

DELIVERY MEDIA

Students can register online, by mail, or in person for Extension Study courses. Once registered, students receive a detailed syllabus and their textbooks by mail, as well as contact information for their professor. Salve Regina Extension Study also has a course Web site where students can find their syllabus on line, communicate and interact with their classmates and professor, and find links to other helpful and related sites. In addition, an online information center gives students important information on everything from applying for admission to filing for degree.

PROGRAMS OF STUDY

Four distance learning master's degree programs are offered in business administration, human development, international relations, and management.

The Master of Business Administration program is designed to prepare graduates for professional careers in organizations that operate in a rapidly changing environment. It is directed towards developing managers and focuses on finance, economics, accounting, organizational behavior, strategic management, and ethics.

The Master of Arts program in human development focuses on psychological, spiritual, emotional, and intellectual development. Students discover new ways to think, to learn, and to promote self-development both for themselves and others.

The Master of Arts in international relations focuses on new ways to achieve global harmony and justice. The program, planned for those who seek a broader and deeper understanding of the contemporary world, helps to prepare students for an increasingly interdependent twenty-first century. Courses address individual needs and prepare students for enhanced careers in government, international organizations, business, finance, teaching, and research.

The Master of Science program in management offers a solid theoretical and practical management foundation and integrates information systems into the management role.

Salve Regina University is a fully accredited member of the New England Association of Schools and Colleges (NEASC). Having met the criteria of NEASC's Commission on Institutions of Higher Education for quality and integrity through periodic peer reviews, the University is considered to have the resources to pursue its stated purposes and has shown great promise that its educational programs will continue into the future. NEASC accreditation is impartial and applies to the entire institution; it does not guarantee specific courses, programs, or individual graduate competency. Accreditation provides reasonable assurances regarding quality of student opportunities. Inquiries about NEASC accreditation may be directed to the Vice President for Academic Affairs at Salve Regina or to the Commission on Institutions of Higher Education, NEASC, 209 Burlington Road, Bedford, MA 01730-1433. (Telephone: 617-271-0022, E-mail: cihe@neasc. org)

SPECIAL PROGRAMS

The certificate program in management is for students who already have a bachelor's degree, and includes 15 hours of graduate credit. It offers opportunities for those who desire a graduate education without formal pursuit of a master's degree. The certificate program in management/correctional administration does not require a bachelor's degree. Twelve credits hours are required.

Salve Regina University also participates with the Global Risk Management Institute in providing courses for the Fellow in Risk Management (FRM). The FRM is an advanced designation specifically for risk managers and others who want to further their education and improve their risk management skills. To take courses, the student must first apply and be accepted by the Global Risk Management Institute.

All students taking seven or more courses through the Extension Study program need to complete a residency requirement. The Graduate Extension Study Institute or Summer Institute is a four-day on-campus experience which is usually held the first weekend in June. The Institute enables students to interact with faculty members and other students, fulfill residency requirements, identify with the University, and experience the beauty of Salve Regina's campus. Alternatively, those students who are close enough to campus to commute,

may take a course on campus at any time to meet their residency requirement.

CREDIT OPTIONS

The master's degree programs are all twelve courses (36 credits). Students have six months to complete each course. Students normally register for up to two courses at a time. Students have up to five years to complete all of the requirements for the degree; however, at a rate of four courses per year, students are generally able to complete the degree in three years if they are able to complete two courses every six months. Up to two graduate level courses (6 credits) that have not been used towards another degree may usually be transferred into the Extension Study master's degree program. Students who have completed courses approved by the American Council of Education (ACE) at nondegree granting military or professional schools may request additional transfer credits.

FACULTY

The faculty are a valued resource; many teach full time on campus and others are adjunct faculty members who are successful professionals within their field. They come from leading doctoral, M.B.A., and law programs and represent a wide variety of backgrounds. Their superior teaching skills, academic training and research, and knowledge of practical application bring a wealth of experience to the curriculum.

ADMISSION

Men and women with bachelor's degrees from accredited institutions of higher learning, considered to have the ability to pursue graduate study, and who show a desire for personal development that are admitted following a careful evaluation of their credentials, without regard to age, race, sex, creed, national or ethnic origin, or handicap.

TUITION AND FEES

Tuition is $350 per credit hour for all Extension Study courses. All courses

are 3 credit hours. The fees charged include application ($35), commitment ($100), incomplete/delay of grade ($100), master's degree graduation ($150), transcript ($5), and prerequisite courses ($500).

FINANCIAL AID

Salve Regina University assists students in applying for loans through the Federal Family Educational Loan Programs, particularly the Federal Stafford Loans. These loans are available to all students and may be used to fund education at the University provided the student maintains continuous quantitative and qualitative progress. Benefit plans for veterans and active duty service persons and employers' tuition reimbursement plans are welcome.

APPLYING

A Graduate Extension Study catalog with application may be requested from the Graduate Admissions Office by phone or mail. The address and phone number are listed below. The following materials must be submitted to the Graduate Admissions office: application form, nonrefundable application fee, official transcripts from all accredited degree granting institutions attended, two letters of recommendation, standardized test score no more than five years old (GRE, MAT, GMAT, LSAT, or MCAT), a personal statement of intent of study, and a nonrefundable commitment deposit upon acceptance. The TOEFL or EILTS is required of international students.

CONTACT

Debra Mitchell, Associate Director
Graduate Extension Study
100 Ochre Point Avenue
Newport, Rhode Island 02840
Telephone: 800-GO-SALVE (toll-free)
Fax: 401-849-0702
E-mail: mitcheld@salve.edu
Web site: http://www.salve.edu

San Francisco State University

SFSU Online

San Francisco, California

Founded in 1899, San Francisco State University (SFSU) is part of the largest system of higher education in the country that grants bachelor's and master's degrees—the California State University (CSU) system. The twenty-three campuses served 360,254 students in fall 1998. SFSU is accredited by the Accrediting Commission for Senior Colleges and Universities of the Western Association of Schools and Colleges. SFSU's mission is to create and maintain an environment for learning that promotes respect for and appreciation of scholarship, freedom, human diversity, and the cultural mosaic of the city of San Francisco and the Bay area; to promote excellence in instruction and intellectual accomplishment; and to provide broadly accessible higher education for residents of the region and state as well as the nation and world.

DISTANCE LEARNING PROGRAM

The SFSU Virtual Campus offers a brand new Online Web Design Certificate Program. Students from around the globe learn about the Web from industry experts in San Francisco's Multimedia Gulch.

The Certificate offers a comprehensive Web curriculum, covering topics such as virtual design, interface and interaction design, HTML, production management, e-commerce, Javascript, Flash, and much more. Each student completes a professional quality portfolio piece in culmination of their studies.

DELIVERY MEDIA

All SFSU Online courses are delivered entirely via the World Wide Web. All student-teacher interactions take place through e-mail and threaded discussions. Class media include audio and video clips, illustrations, links to relevant content on the Web, readings, and required assignments.

Multimedia classes have a high online participation requirement for students; they are expected to interact with each other as well as with the instructor. All courses are offered via the eCollege.com system.

PROGRAMS OF STUDY

SFSU Online offers three 12-week classes from its Multimedia Studies Program: Designing the Interactive Experience, for writers and designers of multimedia; Understanding the Internet, an overview of the World Wide Web, its technologies, its culture and history, and how individuals can use it effectively; and the Digital World, a comprehensive look at the world of digital media and information technology and its impact on business, education, art, science, and culture. The online Web Design Certificate consists of twenty courses.

Other courses include Elementary School Health, which acquaints prospective teachers with the comprehensive school health program, including health services, healthful school environment, and the school health instruction program, and satisfies the California state requirement for the Clear Teaching Credential; Maternal-Newborn Nursing, an overview of maternal/newborn health from a nursing perspective that is relevant to the care of pregnant women, newborn infants, and their significant others during pregnancy, childbirth, and the postpartum period; and Introduction to Independent Living Services, which provides an overview of how independent living centers approach services/advocacy to and for people with disabilities. This course may be taken as a single separate course or may be taken as part of a San Francisco State University Certificate in Independent Living Center Services and Practices.

Introduction to Computer Information Systems and further nursing and counseling courses are forthcoming.

SPECIAL PROGRAMS

SFSU offers no special programs at this time.

STUDENT SERVICES

Distance education students have access to SFSU Online's help desk at all times for technical support. Students can order books, course readers, and other course materials at the SFSU bookstore and can access SFSU's J. Paul Leonard Library via modem, which may require students to make a long-distance telephone call. Students should see the SFSU Online Web site for details on setting up an online library account.

CREDIT OPTIONS

All courses in the Web Design Certificate are offered through the College of Extended Learning and are not available for academic credit, though each course qualifies for 3 continuing education units.

FACULTY

All courses are taught by San Francisco–based multimedia professionals.

ADMISSION

SFSU Online courses are part of the SFSU College of Extended Learning and have no admission requirements. Students should visit the SFSU Online Web site for relevant deadlines for registration. Class sizes are limited.

TUITION AND FEES

Courses range from $450 to $600 and are twelve weeks in length. Course fees are due upon registration.

FINANCIAL AID

Opportunities for financial aid and scholarships are being developed. Students should refer to the SFSU Online Web site for more information.

APPLYING

SFSU offers continuing education and professional development courses. No admission to SFSU is necessary at this time. Registration applications can be found on line at the SFSU Online Web site.

CONTACT

Students should visit the Web site for more information.
Web site: http://sfsuonline.org

San Joaquin Delta College

DeltaOnline

Stockton, California

eCollege.com   www.ecollege.com/scholarships

San Joaquin Delta College, one of California's 106 community colleges, was founded in 1963 and is accredited by the Western Association of Schools and Colleges. The College offers courses leading to transfer to the University of California and California State University systems and to other colleges and universities. Associate degrees in arts and science and nearly seventy certificate programs are available. San Joaquin Delta College is recognized as a leader in computer applications and program development on a statewide and national level.

San Joaquin Delta College is committed to excellence in the provision of postsecondary education throughout the college district. This commitment is reflected in the College's comprehensive instructional programs, services to students and the public, professionalism of faculty and staff, and campus beauty and utility.

DISTANCE LEARNING PROGRAM

San Joaquin Delta College is committed to providing high-quality distance learning opportunities. Some 500 students annually have enrolled in distance learning courses, which utilize telecourses, interactive television, and the Internet.

San Joaquin Delta College has launched its virtual campus, DeltaOnline (address listed below), for fall 2000; sixteen courses will be offered on line.

DELIVERY MEDIA

San Joaquin Delta College offers distance learning via a variety of media. The College offers interactive television (ITV) and online courses.

ITV students attend classes at sites located in the communities of Jackson, San Andreas, Manteca, and Tracy. ITV has two-way video and two-way audio capabilities.

Online students have access to general elective courses as well as a variety of specialized classes via DeltaOnline. DeltaOnline students can access their courses completely at a distance by using the Internet. Online students require access to a computer and an Internet service provider and communicate via a variety of online tools.

The online courses are offered via the eCollege.com system.

PROGRAMS OF STUDY

Currently, a variety of general education courses are available through the distance education program at San Joaquin Delta College. In the future, the College will offer several associate degree programs on line.

SPECIAL PROGRAMS

Several exceptional courses are currently available on line through DeltaOnline. Culinary Art 3, a restaurant sanitation and safety course that is required for California hospitality workers, and Ornamental Horticulture, Interior Landscaping and Design are two unique online class offerings.

STUDENT SERVICES

Many of the student services available on campus are also available to distance learning students via the Internet. San Joaquin Delta College students can use the Internet to access admissions and registration as well as the Delta College Bookstore and Library. In addition, DeltaOnline students may access tutoring, guidance and counseling, financial aid, disabled student programs and services, and extended opportunity programs and services.

CREDIT OPTIONS

Delta Online courses may be taken for credit and, in some cases, with a credit/no credit option. Course descriptions indicate whether the course is transferable to the California State University or University of California. Courses may also meet general education requirements for the associate degree in arts or science, California State University, or the University of California. Credits earned from accredited institutions of higher education may be transferable.

FACULTY

Ninety-nine percent of the Delta Online faculty members are full-time instructors at San Joaquin Delta College. All faculty members have master's degrees or the equivalent in their respective disciplines.

ADMISSION

New students must submit an application for admission, which is available from the Admissions Department on campus or on line through the Delta Online Web site or through the admissions information Web page (addresses listed below). Current high school students can apply for admission and take college courses concurrently with their high school programs.

TUITION AND FEES

Students who are California residents are charged $11 per unit, regardless of the number of units. For example, a 3-unit course would cost $33. Non-resident students are charged $130 per unit for tuition plus an enrollment fee of $11 per unit and a fee of $307 for Internet classes. For example, a 3-unit course would cost $730. All fees are to be paid when a student registers for classes.

Active military personnel and their dependents living within the district may have tuition fees waived for classes taken during their stay in California.

APPLYING

Students can apply on line through Delta Online or the Delta College Web site (listed below).

CONTACT

For additional information, students should contact:

Kathryn Campbell
San Joaquin Delta College
5151 Pacific Avenue
Stockton, California 95207
Telephone: 209-954-5039
E-mail: kcampbell@sjdccd.cc.ca.us
Web site: http://deltaonline.org (Delta Online)
http://www.sjdccd.cc.ca.us (admissions information)

Santa Monica College

SMC Online

Santa Monica, California

Santa Monica College (SMC), founded in 1929, is a California public community college accredited by the Western Association of Schools and Colleges. Santa Monica College was named among the top ten best community colleges in the country by *Rolling Stone* magazine. SMC is recognized around the world as number one in college transfers and career education. The College is the national leader in transfers to the University of California and the number one choice of international students. SMC is also well known for its award-winning programs and services.

The Santa Monica College vision is to change lives through excellence in education for a global community. Santa Monica College believes that individuals should develop to their full potential. Its mission is to challenge and enable students to set and achieve personal educational goals and to understand their personal relationship to the social, cultural, political, economic, technological, and natural environments. To fulfill this mission, the College provides open and affordable access to excellent programs that prepare students for successful careers, develop college-level skills, enable transfer to universities for baccalaureate and advanced graduate and professional education, and foster a personal commitment to lifelong learning. The College prepares its students to interact with and contribute to the global community.

Santa Monica College is representative of, and sensitive to, the racial and cultural diversity of its community. Creativity, collaboration, and the free exchange of ideas are promoted in an open, caring community of learners. Continual development of individual talents is encouraged and the critical importance of each person to the achievement of a common purpose is recognized.

DISTANCE LEARNING PROGRAM

The Santa Monica College distance education program, SMC Online, is committed to providing excellence in education and increasing student access to post-secondary education. All courses are developed to ensure that the classes and programs delivered sustain the quality of teaching and learning achieved in the traditional classroom.

Students must enroll in Santa Monica College to participate in the SMC Online. The College launched its virtual campus, located at http://smconline.org, in fall 1999 with an expanded number of online courses.

DELIVERY MEDIA

Santa Monica College offers videoconference courses and online courses. Students should see the Santa Monica College Schedule of Classes, located on the Web site at http://smc.edu, for application and enrollment information.

Santa Monica College uses the eCollege.com delivery system for the online courses.

PROGRAMS OF STUDY

It is the goal of the Santa Monica distance education program to offer Associate in Arts degrees and certificate programs online. While entire degree and certificate programs are not

yet online, various courses that meet transfer, degree, and certificate requirements are available through SMC Online.

STUDENT SERVICES

A variety of online student services are currently available on the Web through SMC Online, the Internet campus of Santa Monica College. SMC Online students have access to advising services, admissions, library services, and registration as well as financial aid and the Santa Monica College Bookstore.

FACULTY

The faculty members at Santa Monica College are highly qualified in their fields and dedicated to teaching and learning. All instructors at Santa Monica College either have a master's degree or Ph.D. in their subject area or hold vocational certificates. Those teaching in both the vocational and the lower-division transfer programs have had a broad range of experience in their subject areas.

ADMISSION

Any person who has graduated from high school or who is 18 years of age or older may be admitted to Santa Monica College if he or she meets the residence requirements and can profit from the program. Each person applying for admission to a California community college is classified as either a resident or nonresident. Each new student must file a college application with information that satisfies state registration requirements and initiates the educational planning process.

TUITION AND FEES

All students in graded credit courses must pay an academic enrollment fee of $11 per unit/credit. All students enrolled in credit courses pay a fee $29 per semester. Students who are both citizens and residents of another country (including F-1 visa students) must pay an additional tuition fee of $150 per unit/credit. Other nonresident students must pay a tuition fee of $130 per unit/credit. These fees are in addition to the $11 per unit/credit and the $29 per semester non-academic fee assessed to all SMC students.

FINANCIAL AID

To aid and encourage students who need financial assistance, numerous scholarships, loans, grants, and awards are available. Applications and additional information regarding financial aid and scholarships can be obtained at the SMC Financial Aid Office.

APPLYING

Students need to apply to Santa Monica College if they have never attended or if they have not attended for one or more semesters. Admissions applications are available on line through SMC Online at the Web address listed below.

Local residents may pick up an application at the Santa Monica College Admissions Office. Applications are also available by mail. Students should include a self-addressed envelope with their request to the Admissions Office at the address below.

CONTACT

Winniphred Stone
1900 Pico Boulevard
Santa Monica, California 90405
Telephone: 310-434-3761
Fax: 310-434-3769
E-mail: stone_winniphred@smc.edu
Web site: http://smconline.org

SAYBROOK GRADUATE SCHOOL

Graduate Programs in Psychology, Human Science, and Organizational Systems Inquiry

San Francisco, California

Since 1971, Saybrook has been educating mid-career professionals in humanistic values relevant to the work place and the community. Saybrook Graduate School and Research Center's graduate education prepares scholar/practitioners to take effective leadership roles, develop the consciousness to realize the immense possibilities of these times, and minimize the potential for social and individual suffering. Saybrook provides a unique learning-centered environment based in an emancipatory humanistic tradition. Advanced studies in psychology, human science, and organizational systems inquiry are offered. Programs are designed for adult, mid-career professionals seeking an opportunity to engage in serious scholarly work, and who wish to develop the necessary research skills, scope of knowledge, and intervention skills to become more effective in their chosen sphere of work.

Approximately 425 students are currently enrolled at Saybrook, ranging in age from mid-20s to 60s, and representing more than thirty-six states and several foreign countries. Saybrook is fully accredited by the Western Association of Schools and Colleges (WASC).

DISTANCE LEARNING PROGRAM

For nearly thirty years, Saybrook Graduate School's mode of education has been at-a-distance learning. Because of the unique mix of mentorship, on-site residential programs, and Internet access, the Saybrook model encourages close contact between faculty members and students, and among students. Programs are structured to meet the personal and professional needs of adult learners and persons not able or willing to travel to traditional classrooms.

DELIVERY MEDIA

Learning takes place through one-on-one mentorships with faculty members in small cohort groups, courses online, and at seminars at residential conferences. Using learning guides, students complete course work which is evaluated by faculty members who communicate by phone, letter, fax, computer, or in person at conferences.

PROGRAMS OF STUDY

Saybrook Graduate School offers programs in psychology, human science, and organizational systems inquiry. Students may pursue an M.A. or a Ph.D. in any program. Within each program, students select an area of study which includes humanistic and transpersonal clinical inquiry and health studies; consciousness and spirituality; peace, conflict resolution, and community development; and organizational systems inquiry.

Saybrook's psychology degree program prepares its graduates to be scholars and researchers in the broad domain of human experience. Saybrook is an institute providing alternative education that conscientiously challenges many of the axioms of mainstream medicalized and industrialized psychology, and offers an emancipatory alternative. While the primary focus of Saybrook's psychology program is not clinical, Saybrook offers the course work necessary to take the licensing exam.

The human science program provides an opportunity for a humanistic, action-learning approach to group, family, public and private organizations, and community and global spheres of life. The Saybrook approach combines responsible action with scholarly reflection, exploring transformative change that respects human dignity and creative possibilities. The human science program consists of a set of perspectives pertaining to the human condition in historical, contextual, cross-cultural, political, and religious terms. It employs perspectives such as feminism, post-structuralism, critical theory, existential phenomenology, and postmodernism. The human sciences are increase a collective understanding of the common condition and contribute to the ongoing story of social improvement and consciousness evolution.

The organizational systems inquiry program is designed to develop leaders, scholars, and practitioners who are capable of addressing the challenge of building organizations and communities with greater capacity to deal with the increasing turbulence, interconnection, and diverse frameworks of interpretation of the information age/knowledge era. The mission of the organizational systems inquiry program is to educate leaders to become adept at changing and designing organizations that reflect the highest human ideals.

STUDENT SERVICES

It is Saybrook's intent to be responsive to student and institutional needs, to provide programs and services in support of the mission, to assist students in achieving academic success, and to enhance the overall learning environment.

FACULTY

Saybrook Graduate School and Research Center is proud to have an internationally recognized faculty of scholars and practitioners, all of whom hold a doctoral or terminal degree in their field. In addition to teaching, faculty members have extensive experience as researchers, practitioners, consultants, authors, business people, and organizational leaders. They are committed to Saybrook's ideals and values and are supportive of the students' personal and scholarly growth.

ADMISSION

All applicants must hold a bachelor's degree from a regionally accredited institution. Applicants to the Ph.D. program must have an appropriate master's degree from a regionally accredited institution. The minimum GPA requirement is 3.0. All international students must submit recent TOEFL scores with a minimum score of 580.

APPLYING

Students are admitted in September and March. For the September start date, all application materials should be received by June 1. For the March start date, all application materials should be received by December 1. Applications completed after this deadline are considered on a space-available basis or, with the applicant's permission, held for the next enrollment period.

Applicants are evaluated on writing ability, past academic record, and professional background. They should be a good match with both the distance learning format and Saybrook's mission and values. New students attend a four-day Residential Orientation Conference (ROC) held in the San Francisco Bay area.

TUITION AND FEES

Tuition for the 2000–01 academic year is $13,125. Fees for attending two Residential Conferences (RC) per year are also required. These fees include the cost of registration, lodging, meals, conference materials, and meeting space.

FINANCIAL AID

U.S. citizens or eligible permanent residents may borrow up to $18,500 per year through the Federal Stafford Loan Program. Saybrook offers limited tuition assistance to its continuing students.

CONTACT

Mindy Myers, Vice President, Recruitment and Admissions
Saybrook Graduate School and Research Center
450 Pacific, Third Floor
San Francisco, California 94133
Telephone: 800-825-4480 Ext. 117 (toll-free)
Fax: 415-433-9271
E-mail: mmyers@saybrook.edu
Web site: http://www.saybrook.edu

Seton Hall University

SetonWorldWide

South Orange, New Jersey

Seton Hall University has been distinguished by a number of firsts. It is the first diocesan college in the United States, founded in 1856 by James Roosevelt Bayley, the first Bishop of Newark, and named for Elizabeth Ann Seton, the first American-born saint. Now, through SetonWorldWide, it is one of the first traditional universities to offer full online graduate degree programs. The University's mission, to provide an educational experience that imparts concrete knowledge and skills in the context of ethical values, is as timely today as in 1856, and as important on the Internet as in the classroom. At Seton Hall, timeless values intersect with cybertechnology to offer high-quality online graduate programs that serve the educational aspirations and professional needs of students from across the country and around the world. By utilizing the Internet and the latest teaching technologies, students benefit from the flexibility to fulfill course requirements at the time of day when they are at their best and from the place that is most convenient. For its ability to empower students with technology, Seton Hall has been recognized as one of "America's Most Wired Universities" by Yahoo! Internet Life for two consecutive years and was awarded the prestigious EDUCAUSE Award for excellence in campus networking.

DISTANCE LEARNING PROGRAM

SetonWorldWide's online graduate degree programs are designed for professionals who have demonstrated significant achievement in their respective fields, and who have the ability, desire, and dedication to accept the rigors of a fast-paced, challenging curriculum, balance the demands of myriad personal and professional commitments, and maintain high standards of integrity and productivity—both in the workplace and in academic pursuits.

As a learning team member, a student, along with his or her peers, instructional facilitators, and executive mentors, as well as noted expert practitioners, are all interrelated and interdependent. Each plays a pivotal role in the teaching and learning process. These relationships are key to a rich and dynamic online learning experience. Each participant is a vital link in the overall success of this ef-

fort, and each must acknowledge a commitment to promoting academic integrity.

A short residency at the start and middle of the program enables students to meet their classmates and instructional team members in person. During the third residencies, students are awarded their degrees. All degrees are granted by Seton Hall University, an institution fully accredited by the Middle States Association of Colleges and Schools.

DELIVERY MEDIA

SetonWorldWide online degree programs feature electronic seminar discussions, e-mail, Internet-based audio and video, electronic research, and different types of software to enhance learning. Prior to the start of the program, students receive all the course materials, including books, articles, audiotapes, videotapes, and CD-ROMs. Computer requirements include a midrange desktop or laptop computer with Internet access.

PROGRAMS OF STUDY

SetonWorldWide continues to expand its graduate degrees, which includes M.A. programs in counselor preparation, educational administration and supervision (Catholic school leadership), health-care administration, strategic communication and leadership, and a graduate certificate in work-life ministry. Additional programs are being developed in such areas as executive M.B.A., an M.S. program in diplomacy, a B.S.N./RN program in nursing, and an M.S. program in taxation.

The Master of Arts in counselor preparation (48 credits, 2 1/2 to 3 years) provides students with a necessary background and preparation in counseling, and a thorough understanding of theory, skills, and models of intervention. Two 10-day residencies are part of the degree requirements.

The Master of Educational Administration and Supervision/Catholic School Leadership (36 credits, 21 months) program is designed to enable students to broaden their knowledge and understanding of the process of education, improve their professional techniques, or prepare for leadership positions or careers in education.

The Master of Healthcare Administration (39 credits, 20 months) provides a rigorous and thorough understanding of today's challenging health-care environment, addressing real world strategies and skills that will help managers make significant contributions to their organizations.

The Master of Strategic Communication & Leadership (36 credits, 20 months) program provides executives with the essential communication and leadership skills to achieve personal and organizational success, acknowledging the demands brought about by markets, a diverse workplace, and the explosion of electronic media technology.

SPECIAL PROGRAMS

Corporations, nonprofit agencies, and other organizations may be eligible to sponsor a learning team composed of their employees for an online graduate program modified for their specific needs. If desired, SetonWorldWide will establish an action team consisting of senior faculty members, specialists in the field, and representatives from the sponsoring organization to conduct an organizational diagnosis and need assessment based on interviews, focus groups, and surveys. Course content may then be modified to include case studies from within the organization itself, a similar organization, or within an industry or profession. Employers who provide their employees with a high-quality graduate program that also addresses specific organizational issues. This is part of the SetonWorldWide "value added" approach.

STUDENT SERVICES

Students find everything they need on line, including admission informa-tion, academic guidance, financial aid assistance, career guidance, and other services. The Help Desk's technical support staff is dedicated to helping students become confident and productive in the online learning environment. They understand that online classes can be challenging at first, but they have the knowledge and experience to help make every student's transition into the virtual classroom a smooth one. The Help Desk is available 24 hours a day, seven days a week. All SetonWorldWide participants also have access to Seton Hall University library resources. During orientation, students meet the librarians and technical staff members who provide assistance throughout the program. Students can use the library's ASK ME service to request and receive assistance from a fully qualified librarian.

ADMISSION

SetonWorldWide online graduate degree programs are designed for professionals who demonstrate significant achievement in their respective fields. Specific program admission requirements can be found on SetonWorldWide's Web site. Typical admission requirements include a baccalaureate degree, significant work experience, letters of recom-mendation, a letter of intent, a resume, and standardized test scores.

TUITION AND FEES

The all-inclusive tuition includes all fees, except for the application fee, and all expenses, including books and other materials and room and meals for short residencies. Computer equipment, software, Internet access, and travel expenses to the residencies are not covered. Reduced tuition can be offered to students employed by organizations that sponsor a full learning team of students as part of a customized program. Current tuition for graduate degree programs ranges from $24,500 to $31,500. Tuition for graduate certificates is significantly less.

FINANCIAL AID

Financial aid is available in the form of subsidized and unsubsidized government loan programs. Students who want to apply for Federal Direct Loans should visit http://www.fafsa.ed.gov on the Internet. For further information and guidance, students should contact SetonWorldWide at the Web site listed below.

APPLYING

To apply, students should visit the Web site listed below and click on Apply.

CONTACT

SetonWorldWide
Seton Hall University
400 South Orange Avenue
South Orange, New Jersey 07079
Telephone: 888-SETON-WW (toll-free)
E-mail: SetonWorldWide@shu.edu
Web site: http://www.setonworldwide.net

Sinclair Community College

Distance Learning Program

Dayton, Ohio

Sinclair Community College is located on a modern, tree-lined campus in downtown Dayton, Ohio. The College has a rich history in the Dayton community, dating back to 1887. In 1966, Sinclair became a publicly funded community college, enjoying strong community support through ongoing passage of a college levy.

Sinclair offers more than 100 transfer and technical associate degree and certificate programs, as well as continuing education opportunities through a system of diverse resources and delivery alternatives. Sinclair enrolls about 20,000 credit students each quarter.

The College is fully accredited by the North Central Association of Colleges and Schools and has been authorized by the Ohio Board of Regents to grant associate degrees in arts, sciences, applied science, and individualized and technical study. The College's technical, health, and business programs are fully accredited by national and/or state-approved accrediting organizations.

Sinclair Community College is a proud member of the prestigious League for Innovation in the Community College and has been selected as one of twelve Vanguard Learning Colleges for developing and promoting learner-centered practices and curricula.

DISTANCE LEARNING PROGRAM

Over the past twenty years, the Distance Learning Program has developed into a nationally recognized, state-of-the-art entity with in-house video and online course production facilities. The program offers more than 150 distance courses, spanning all six of Sinclair's academic divisions. The program enrolled more than 3,500 credit students in fall 1999.

DELIVERY MEDIA

Courses are delivered via the World Wide Web, videotape, videoconference, interactive television, audiotape, CD-ROM, and print. Students and faculty members communicate in person or through a variety of methods, including mail, telephone, fax, e-mail, and videoconference. The following may be required: audiocassette player, television, video-

cassette player, computer, modem, Internet access, e-mail, and CD-ROM.

PROGRAMS OF STUDY

Two complete degree programs are available to students through distance learning. The courses are delivered through a variety of distance learning and independent study methods.

The Associate of Art in distance learning is comprised of 94 quarter-credit hours. Twenty-three of the thirty program courses can be taken solely through a distance format. The remaining courses must be taken either through independent study or include an on-campus lab. It is also possible to obtain credit for these courses through transfer.

The Associate of Science in business administration is comprised of 98 quarter-credit hours. Twenty-three of the thirty program courses can be

taken solely through a distance format. The remaining courses must be taken either through independent study or include an on-campus lab. It is also possible to obtain credit for these courses through transfer.

Information about these degree programs can be accessed online by visiting the Sinclair Distance Learning Web site listed in the Contact section.

SPECIAL PROGRAMS

Sinclair Community College has a partnership with Governors State University that enables Sinclair graduates to transfer to GSU to complete a Bachelor of Arts degree via distance learning. The Governors State University B.A. degree is a generalist degree that is acceptable in almost all fields of work. It is not organized around any specific discipline or major, so it offers students the freedom to take courses that meet their educational or professional goals. Courses taken from Governors State are offered in a variety of formats: videotape, correspondence, and Internet.

STUDENT SERVICES

Services available to Sinclair Community College distance learners include academic advising and online access to tutoring and library services. Testing by proctor for placement and course testing is also available.

CREDIT OPTIONS

Sinclair Community College associate degrees range from 91 to 110 quarter-credit hours. Students must take the last 30 hours at Sinclair. Students may transfer credit from regionally accredited institutions for which they receive a passing grade or a letter grade of C or higher. Alternative credit assessment options are also available (portfolio, CLEP, PONSI).

FACULTY

Sinclair Community College has more than 400 full-time and 500 part-time faculty members. More than 12 percent of the full-time faculty members hold doctoral degrees or earned advanced degrees. About 100 faculty members support the distance learning courses; most of these individuals are experienced, full-time faculty members.

ADMISSION

Sinclair has an open door admission policy. All students are welcome. Students seeking degrees or taking math and English classes are expected to take a placement test. This testing can be done by proctor.

TUITION AND FEES

Tuition and fees for distance learning students are the same as for other Sinclair Community College students. Students pay a one-time, nonrefundable $10 admission fee. Montgomery County (Ohio) residents pay $29.45 per credit hour, other Ohio residents pay $48.45 per credit hour, and out-of-state residents pay $81.45 per credit hour.

FINANCIAL AID

The Sinclair Financial Aid Office administers grants and scholarships that do not have to be repaid, low-interest loans, and student employment. A need-based financial aid package may consist of one or more of the following: Federal Pell Grant, Ohio Instructional Grant, Federal Supplemental Educational Opportunity Grant, and Federal Direct Student Loans. Information about financial aid opportunities at Sinclair may be obtained online by visiting the Sinclair College main Web site (http://www.sinclair.edu).

APPLYING

Students may apply for admission and register for classes online by visiting the Sinclair Distance Learning Web site listed below and accessing the "How Do I Get Started?" selection from the menu. An online orientation is also available to familiarize students with college policies and procedures.

CONTACT

Linda M. PaHud
Coordinator of Distance Learning Services
Sinclair Community College
444 West Third Street
Dayton, Ohio 45402
Telephone: 937-512-2694
Fax: 937-226-2891
E-mail: lpahud@sinclair.edu
Web site: http://www.sinclair.edu/distance

Skidmore College

University Without Walls

Saratoga Springs, New York

University Without Walls (UWW) is the external degree program for adults at Skidmore College. UWW was in the vanguard in establishing a program for distance learners. The program began in 1971 as an experiment in nontraditional education jointly funded by the Ford Foundation and the U.S. Department of Education. When the funding for this experiment ended in 1975, Skidmore College took over the program as its own. Over the years, UWW has evolved to serve adult students pursuing baccalaureate degrees in a variety of liberal arts, performing arts, and preprofessional fields.

The UWW program is characterized by its flexibility and the high quality of education students receive. The unique advising system at UWW guarantees that each program meets the student's individual needs and the high standards of Skidmore College.

DISTANCE LEARNING PROGRAM

UWW serves 280 full- and part-time baccalaureate students from as near as the city of Saratoga Springs and as far away as Europe, Africa, and Asia. The UWW program does not require its students to be in residence on campus. Student programs may include on-site UWW seminars, UWW online courses, independent study with Skidmore faculty members, courses at other accredited institutions, internships, and distance learning courses from major universities. Every program includes a final project in the area of the student's focus.

DELIVERY MEDIA

Independent study courses take place through phone, mail, or e-mail communication. When possible, they may involve meetings on the Skidmore campus. At the present time, UWW's online courses are Web based and require a Web browser and e-mail capability.

PROGRAMS OF STUDY

UWW offers Bachelor of Arts degrees in most traditional liberal arts fields, including American studies, anthropology, art history, biology, chemistry, classics, computer science, economics, English, French, geology, German, government, history, mathematics, philosophy, physics, political economy, psychology, religion, Russian, sociology, Spanish, and women's studies. Bachelor of Science degrees are available in art, business, dance, human services, exercise science, and theater. Students can also combine fields to create an interdisciplinary program, such as arts management, Asian studies, communications, environmental studies, health studies, human behavior, Latin American studies, management information systems, nonprofit management, organizational behavior, public administration, and religion and culture. Individually designed majors are welcomed.

All degrees are 120-credit programs. Programs are expected to include at least 12 credits in the humanities, 6 credits in history, 12 credits in the social sciences, and 9 credits in math or science, including laboratory experience. Professional programs must include at least 60 credits in the liberal arts. Courses taken prior to entry of UWW may be considered in satisfaction of these requirements.

SPECIAL PROGRAMS

UWW's flexibility allows many students to take advantage of unusual learning opportunities. Recent UWW students have studied abroad in Austria, Canada, Costa Rica, the Czech Republic, Germany, Ireland, Poland, Spain, Switzerland, and Thailand, among other locations. Business students often have the opportunity to include professional management and banking seminars in satisfaction of their degree requirements.

UWW students are often able to participate in programs sponsored by Skidmore College and the Office of Special Programs, including a summer study program in Florence, the New York State Writers Institute, the Skidmore Jazz Institute, the Summer Dance Workshop, and the Siti Summer Theater Workshop. UWW students are eligible for substantial discounts on courses offered by Skidmore Summer Academic Sessions and the Summer Six Art Program.

UWW business students are eligible to apply for 3/2 M.B.A.

programs in cooperation with Rensselaer Polytechnic Institute in Troy and Rensselaer–Hartford.

STUDENT SERVICES

UWW is a small, personal program, and the staff members are happy to assist students in any way possible. Typical services include academic advising, registration assistance, financial aid counseling, and book-order assistance. Local students also enjoy library privileges, career counseling, access to recreational facilities, access to computer labs, and an e-mail account. Some summer housing is available for special program participants.

CREDIT OPTIONS

UWW accepts transfer credit for courses completed with a grade of C or better. There is no limit to the number of credits transferred or the age of the work, provided that the course is appropriate to a liberal arts curriculum. Credit is also available for experiential learning. In addition, students may document knowledge through CLEP, ACT-PEP, DANTES, and Regents examinations. Many college-level courses offered through the military are accepted. Credit from international universities is usually accepted.

FACULTY

There are approximately 200 full- and part-time members of the Skidmore faculty. Most participate as advisers and instructors in the UWW program. Ninety-three percent of the Skidmore faculty members have a terminal degree.

ADMISSION

UWW considers any applicant able to succeed at demanding college-level work. However, the program works best for students who have had some college experience. Applicants must have a high school diploma or the equivalent.

TUITION AND FEES

Students pay an initial enrollment fee of $3600; after the first year, an annual enrollment fee of $3000 is charged. The fee for the final project is $600. All independent study courses sponsored by Skidmore are $500.

FINANCIAL AID

Students are eligible for Federal Pell Grants, New York State TAP awards, and all federal loan programs. A small amount of scholarship assistance is available.

APPLYING

Application forms are available from UWW or can be downloaded from the UWW Web site. All students are required to attend a personal admissions interview on the Skidmore campus.

CONTACT

Cornel J. Reinhart, Director
University Without Walls
Skidmore College
Saratoga Springs, New York 12866
Telephone: 518-580-5450
Fax: 518-580-5449
E-mail: uww@skidmore.edu
Web site: http://www.skidmore.edu (click on UWW)

Southern California University for Professional Studies

The University for Distance Learning

Santa Ana, California

Southern California University for Professional Studies (SCUPS) is a private distance learning institution established in 1978 that offers associate, bachelor's, master's, and doctoral degrees in business, law, management of engineering and technology, and psychology. Southern California University for Professional Studies is approved under the Education Code of the State of California to offer the degree programs and to confer the appropriate degrees. The Committee of Bar Examiners of the State of California has authorized registration of SCUPS's School of Law to enable learners in the Juris Doctor (J.D.) program to sit for the bar examination. The Board of Psychology of the State of California accepts the University's Doctor of Philosophy in psychology and the Doctor of Psychology degrees as meeting the educational requirements for licensure as a psychologist in California.

DISTANCE LEARNING PROGRAM

The distance learning program at SCUPS offers students one-on-one contact with their academic advisers and faculty mentors, active self-learning with faculty mentors as individual guides, access to the electronic Library Resource Center and research librarian, continuous enrollment to accommodate busy schedules, and the ability to complete a course in an eight-week term.

DELIVERY MEDIA

Learners are advised and individually guided through the courses by direct contact with faculty mentors via telephone, e-mail, or other electronic devices. Each course is a steady, orderly, and organized process designed to meet the educational objectives of the degree programs.

Upon enrolling, an individualized degree plan is developed in conjunction with the student's academic adviser. Course materials, including a syllabus and course outline, are sent to students. Learners purchase books from the University's online supplier (BIGWORDS.COM) or through local bookstores.

The focus is on active self-learning, which allows students to incorporate course knowledge into real-world experiences using the faculty mentors as resources and facilitators in the learning process. The learner demonstrates mastery of the relevance by completing assignments as required in the eight-week term.

PROGRAMS OF STUDY

SCUPS offers degree programs through distance learning in the following areas: business, law, liberal studies, management of engineering technology, and psychology. Both professional and research doctorates are offered.

An associate degree requires 60 semester units, with 24 units in general education. At least 16 units must be completed through SCUPS. A bachelor's degree requires 120 semester units, with 44 units in general education. At least 32 units must be completed through SCUPS. A master's degree requires 32 semester units beyond the bachelor's degree. All 32 units must be completed through SCUPS. The Juris Doctor degree requires 88 semester units of J.D. course work. A doctorate requires 72 semester units beyond the bachelor's degree.

The professional doctorates present breadth and depth in courses for practicing professionals in business, management of engineering and technology, and psychology. The Doctor of Business Administration (D.B.A.), Doctor of Psychology (Psy.D.), and Doctor of Science (Sc.D.) in management of engineering and technology degrees require a capstone project in which learners devise a way to apply their education to their discipline.

The Doctor of Philosophy degree prepares learners for scholarship, systematic inquiry, and research. A dissertation is required.

SPECIAL PROGRAMS

Specializations are available for graduate learners in business administration. They include financial management, health-care administration, international business, human resources management, and management information systems.

STUDENT SERVICES

SCUPS recognizes that adults have different life experiences, learning needs, and learning patterns that do not fit in the traditional model of college. SCUPS provides adult learners with opportunities to learn at times and places that are compatible with commitments to family, work, and leisure; knowledge that is relevant and has application to their chosen profession; a supportive and directed learning environment; professional assessment and feedback from the faculty; and individualized treatment.

CREDIT OPTIONS

SCUPS may accept up to 28 units in transfer for relevant graduate work; 44 semester units must be completed through SCUPS.

FACULTY

All faculty mentors have graduate degrees from accredited or approved universities. In addition, they are active in their professional areas of expertise.

ADMISSION

Admission to the undergraduate program requires a high school diploma or GED equivalent. A minimum TOEFL score of 450 is required for applicants for whom English is not the primary language. Admission to the graduate program requires a bachelor's degree from an institution recognized by the U.S. Department of Education. A minimum TOEFL score of 450 is required for applicants for whom English is not the primary language. Admission to the Juris Doctor program requires an earned associate degree, an equivalent number of units (60 semester units) required for an associate degree, or the passing of the college equivalency examinations specified by the California Committee of Bar Examiners.

TUITION AND FEES

Tuition for the degree program is $140 per semester unit for undergraduate studies and $155 per semester unit for graduate studies. Tuition for the Juris Doctor program is $2700 per year. Payment options allow for the program to be paid in full or in equal monthly installments throughout the program after a $500 down payment. There is no service charge for the monthly payment option.

Additional fees are assessed for application evaluation ($100), dissertation ($900), course add/drop ($50), library/identification card replacement ($25), and the Psychology Loaner Test ($50–$150 depending on the test). Other fee information is available through the admission office.

FINANCIAL AID

SCUPS does not offer financial aid.

APPLYING

Students who wish to speak with an admission counselor should contact SCUPS via telephone at 800-477-2254 (toll-free) or e-mail at enroll@scups.edu. The admission counselor personally advises students about the enrollment process.

CONTACT

Southern California University for Professional Studies
1840 East 17th Street
Santa Ana, California 92705-8605
Telephone: 714-480-0800
         800-477-2254 (toll-free)
Fax: 714-480-0834
Web site: http://www.scups.edu

Southern Christian University

Distance Learning Programs
Montgomery, Alabama

Founded in 1967, Southern Christian University (SCU) is an independent, nonsectarian, coeducational institution dedicated to the spirit of its ideals and Christian heritage. All of SCU's programs are taught from a Christian perspective. SCU is the home of one of the nation's leading universities offering distance learning programs and services to adults nationally. Adding to the prestige of this University is its recent designation as a Distance Education Demonstration Program Institution by the U.S. Department of Education. One of fifteen initial participants in the nation, SCU is partnering with the U.S. Department of Education to serve as a national model that will help chart the future of distance learning. Accredited by the Southern Association of Colleges and Schools, SCU grants bachelor's, master's, and doctoral degrees—all available via a distance learning format.

DISTANCE LEARNING PROGRAM

SCU programs are designed with the adult learner in mind. Eighty percent of SCU's students are employed while they are attending SCU. Courses can be taken anywhere there is Internet access and at anytime. SCU has enrolled thousands of students in distance learning courses throughout the United States and internationally.

DELIVERY MEDIA

Utilizing state-of-the-art technologies, SCU's distance learning programs are delivered to students over the Internet. Students participate via online discussion groups, testing, e-mail, and telephone. Some courses are streamed live over the Internet, which can be viewed as the class is being taught, or at the student's convenience. The flexibility of the programs ensures continuity for students in transit (e.g., military, clergy, salesmen who must move while still in school).

PROGRAMS OF STUDY

SCU programs are structured with the traditional program in mind. Distance education is approved by the Southern Association of Colleges and Schools and the U.S. Department of Education, ensuring that distance education students receive the same high-quality education as on-campus students. Faculty and student services for online students are available to distance learning students. SCU ensures that students have regular contact with faculty and staff members via e-mail and telephone. Residency is only required in certain programs. No residency is required for undergraduates. Undergraduate degrees include management communication, human development, liberal studies, and Bible. These degrees promote management communication skills, human development skills, knowledge in the arts, and biblical and Christian ministry skills. Graduate degrees include organizational leadership, counseling/family therapy, and religious studies. These degrees foster leadership knowledge and skills, counseling and family therapy skills, and biblical and Christian ministry skills. The counseling degrees are designed to help prepare students for licensure. Doctoral degrees include family therapy and ministry. These degrees are advanced professional degrees for community organizations and church-related vocations, with a concentration designed to prepare participants to counsel families and individuals. SCU students are fully matriculated students of Southern Christian University with full student privileges, rights, and responsibilities.

SPECIAL PROGRAMS

In response to the adult migration into institutions of higher education, SCU has developed fully accredited programs of study to help working adults obtain their bachelor's degree in a timely manner through the EXCEL program. SCU recognizes that many adult students have lifetime experiences that should be translated into college credit. SCU's EXCEL program allows undergraduates to receive credit for lifetime learning, enabling students to complete their degree at an accelerated rate. In addition, all undergraduate courses are 4 semester hours, rather than 3. This means that a student only has to take three courses (12 semester hours) to be a full-time student and eligible for maximum financial aid benefits. Also, fewer courses are required for degree completion. Undergraduate students who enroll on a full-time basis enjoy a significant savings, receiving 50 percent off the published tuition rate.

STUDENT SERVICES

SCU provides support for all aspects of the distance learning experience. ProQuest Religion Database and First Search library programs give students access to 65 online databases, including the Library of Congress. Students have access to the collections of 150 theological schools online. Personal academic advising is performed via phone or e-mail. Students also receive personal evaluations of their degree program.

CREDIT OPTIONS

Fulfillment of some degree requirements is possible by passing the CLEP/DANTES tests or Regents examinations and through credit for lifetime learning and credit for military experience. Students can register for a course designed to show them how to prepare a portfolio that demonstrates prior learning. Credit is awarded by the Office of Portfolio Development for prior learning that is demonstrated through a documented learning portfolio.

FACULTY

Instructional faculty members total 21. Sixty-seven percent of the full-time faculty members hold doctoral degrees, 100 percent hold master's degrees, and 100 percent hold terminal degrees. Faculty members are specialized in their areas and have training in distance learning delivery.

ADMISSION

There is a rolling admission plan. Admission requirements are verification of high school graduation or GED for undergraduates, at least two semesters of college, and demonstrated proficiency in computer literacy. Ninety percent of applicants are accepted.

TUITION AND FEES

Graduate tuition cost per semester hour is $375. Undergraduate tuition per semester hour is $300. Full-time undergraduates receive a 50 percent scholarship. A comprehensive fee of $375 per semester is required of all students.

FINANCIAL AID

Aid from institutionally generated funds is provided on the basis of academic merit, financial need, or other criteria. A limited number of scholarships are available. Priority is given to early applicants. Federal funding available for undergraduates and graduates includes Pell and FSEOG grants for undergraduates, Federal Work-Study, and FFEL subsidized and unsubsidized loans for undergraduates and graduates. Eighty percent of students receive financial aid.

APPLYING

Prospective students must submit a $50 nonrefundable fee along with the completed application for admission. During the first semester, students must submit letters of recommendation, transcripts, and test scores (placement exam for undergraduates and MAT or GRE for graduates).

CONTACT

Rick Johnson
Southern Christian University
1200 Taylor Road
Montgomery, Alabama 36117
Telephone: 800-351-4040 Ext. 213 (toll-free)
E-mail: rickjohnson@southernchristian.edu
Web site: http://www.southernchristian.edu

Southern Methodist University

School of Engineering and Applied Science

Dallas, Texas

Founded in 1911, SMU is a private, comprehensive university. SMU comprises six degree-granting schools: the School of Engineering and Applied Science, Dedman College of Humanities and Sciences, Meadows School of the Arts, the Edwin L. Cox School of Business, the School of Law, and Perkins School of Theology. Southern Methodist University is accredited by the Commission on Colleges of the Southern Association of Colleges and Schools.

For more than thirty years, the School of Engineering and Applied Science (SEAS) has been a national pioneer in offering distance education courses for graduate study. In 1964, SEAS established one of the first two regional closed-circuit TV distance learning networks in the nation. In 1978, SEAS instituted its own for-credit videotape program for students living outside the Dallas–Fort Worth area. Today, video-program students are enrolled nationally from coast to coast and in Europe, Asia, South America, and Canada.

DISTANCE LEARNING PROGRAM

The SEAS distance learning programs serve more than 600 graduate students. Degree programs are offered nationally via videotape or, in the north Texas area, via a closed-circuit television network. The Master of Science in Telecommunications program is available via the National Technological University satellite network. No campus attendance is required to complete the degree programs.

DELIVERY MEDIA

Distance learning students are enrolled in classes that are given on the SMU campus. The lectures are videotaped and sent once a week to the distance learning student. North Texas and satellite students may view the lectures live. Distance learning students interact with their professor via telephone, fax, e-mail, or the Internet. Many

courses make course materials available to the student via SEAS's World Wide Web home page.

PROGRAMS OF STUDY

Engineering schools have an obligation to be responsive to challenges and opportunities in a technological society. As a private university, SMU can respond quickly to engineering needs with high-quality academic programs.

SEAS offers Master of Science distance learning programs in engineering management, environmental systems management, manufacturing systems management, software engineering, systems engineering, and telecommunications. Distance learning M.S. programs are also available in the more traditional disciplines of mechanical engineering, electrical engineering, and computer science.

The Master of Science degree requires 30–36 (depending on

the program) semester credit hours for completion, with a minimum 3.0 grade point average on a 4.0 scale. Distance learning students may meet the credit requirement entirely by course work or have the option of preparing a thesis for 6 semester hours of credit.

SPECIAL PROGRAMS

SEAS offers a certificate program in telecommunications. This program is designed for students who have extensive experience but do not hold a bachelor's degree or who do not wish to pursue a master's degree. Admission to the telecommunications certificate program requires 60 semester credit hours of college study with a minimum GPA of 2.0 on a 4.0 scale, three years of related work experience, and three letters of recommendation. Certificate students must complete six courses with a minimum grade of 70 percent in each course. All courses are available to the distance learning student via videotape.

CREDIT OPTIONS

Generally speaking, up to 6 semester hours of graduate courses may be transferred from an institution approved by the SEAS Graduate Division, provided that such course work was completed in the five years prior to matriculation, that the transferred courses carried graduate credit, that those courses were not used to meet the requirements of an undergraduate degree, and that grades of B– or higher were received in the courses to be transferred.

FACULTY

Of the 485 full-time faculty members, 88 percent hold the doctorate or terminal professional degree in their fields. In addition, in the professional degree programs, the School of Engineering and Applied Science utilizes outstanding adjunct faculty members to bring into the classroom valuable experience from industry and government.

ADMISSION

Admission to a Master of Science degree program requires the bachelor's degree appropriate to the program to which the student is applying, as well as a minimum grade point average of 3.0 (on a 4.0 scale) in previous undergraduate and graduate study. Scores on the Graduate Record Examinations (GRE) are required for the M.S. programs in electrical engineering, mechanical engineering, and computer science. The GRE is not required for the professional M.S. programs.

TUITION AND FEES

Tuition for distance learning students is $733 per credit hour or $2199 for a 3-credit-hour course. Members of the military and civilian employees of the military should inquire about special tuition rates.

FINANCIAL AID

Financial aid opportunities are available to distance learning students, including Federal Stafford Student Loans. SMU's distance learning programs are approved for Veterans Administration educational benefits.

APPLYING

Distance learning students must complete an application for admission to the Graduate Division of the School of Engineering and Applied Science and submit transcripts of all previous undergraduate and graduate work. Application deadline dates are as follows: for the fall semester, July 1; for the spring semester, November 15; and for the summer term, April 15.

CONTACT

Stephanie Dye
Associate Director, Distance Education
School of Engineering and Applied Science
Southern Methodist University
P.O. Box 750335
Dallas, Texas 75275-0335
Telephone: 214-768-3232
             800-601-4040 (toll-free)
Fax: 214-768-3778
E-mail: sdye@seas.smu.edu
Web site: http://www.seas.smu.edu

SREB Southern Regional Education Board

Electronic Campus

Atlanta, Georgia

The Electronic Campus of the Southern Regional Education Board (SREB) is a marketplace of distance learning courses, programs, and services available from colleges and universities across the South.

Founded in January 1998, the Electronic Campus has grown from 104 courses to almost 2,000 courses and seventy-five degree programs. The campus includes courses and programs from all sixteen SREB member states, and participating colleges, courses, and programs are added continually. The SREB's sixteen member states are Alabama, Arkansas, Delaware, Florida, Georgia, Kentucky, Louisiana, Maryland, Mississippi, North Carolina, Oklahoma, South Carolina, Tennessee, Texas, Virginia, and West Virginia.

The Southern Regional Education Board, the nation's first interstate compact for education, was created in 1948 at the request of Southern governors. It was designed to help leaders in government and education work together to advance education and to improve the region's social and economic life.

DISTANCE LEARNING PROGRAM

The Electronic Campus provides detailed and common information about distance learning courses and programs offered by participating colleges and universities. The Electronic Campus' goal is to provide enhanced educational opportunities for traditional and nontraditional students in a method that removes many of the barriers that long have hindered access to higher education.

DELIVERY MEDIA

Courses and programs are available in a variety of delivery formats. The predominant delivery method is the World Wide Web. Courses and programs are available via the Web in both synchronous and asynchronous modes. Other delivery formats are the Internet, videotapes, satellite, CD-ROMs, compressed video, and open broadcast. Information on the delivery formats for each course and program is available on the Web site, listed below.

PROGRAMS OF STUDY

The Electronic Campus provides access to regionally accredited academic degree programs in higher education. Certificate, associate, bachelor's, master's, and doctoral programs and credit courses are offered electronically.

Courses and programs must meet the following requirements: the course or program provides for appropriate interaction between faculty members and students and among students; quality faculty members provide appropriate supervision of the program or course that is offered electronically; academic standards for all programs or courses offered electronically are the same as those for other courses or programs delivered at the institution where they originate; each course listed meets the Principles of Good Practice, the cornerstone of this electronic marketplace; and all courses and programs have been reviewed against the Principles of Good Practice.

SPECIAL PROGRAMS

The Electronic Campus offers a variety of special programs, and that number continues to grow. More information on these special programs can be found on the Web site. Students taking courses through the Electronic Campus have access to the nationally recognized GALILEO virtual library. A student easily can access a database of more than 3,800 publications, more than 1,500 of which are available in full text. The disciplines are varied and include social sciences, general sciences, business, and education. All of these publications can be searched easily and quickly using GALILEO's powerful search engines.

FACULTY

Many of the SREB region's most respected professors have courses and programs on the Electronic Campus. The faculty members respond to students' questions and often list times that they can be reached by telephone in their campus offices.

Students often say communication with the professors through the Electronic Campus is as good as or better than in a classroom setting.

ADMISSION

The offering college or university handles admission to degree programs. Students can access this information from the Electronic Campus Web site. Many institutions allow potential students to complete the application for admission on line. Students who wish to enroll in courses may be able to do so without formal application and admission. The enrollment procedures and requirements are outlined on the Electronic Campus Web site.

TUITION AND FEES

The college or university offering the courses and programs sets tuition and fees. Tuition and fees are available at the Electronic Campus Web site.

SREB is promoting the establishment of an "electronic tuition rate" by college and universities participating in the Electronic Campus. This rate would apply to in-state and out-of-state students.

Through a pilot project, residents of SREB states will have access to selected degree programs at in-state rates. This arrangement adds electronically delivered programs to SREB's 25-year-old Academic Common Market.

FINANCIAL AID

Participating colleges and universities coordinate financial aid. Specific information on financial aid is available from the colleges and universities; general information is available on the Electronic Campus Web site.

APPLYING

Anyone with Internet access may search the courses and programs available through the Electronic Campus marketplace. There is no charge for this service, and application and registration are not required.

CONTACT

Bruce Chaloux
Director, Electronic Campus
Southern Regional Education Board
592 10th Street, NW
Atlanta, Georgia 30318-5790
Telephone: 404-875-9211
Fax: 404-872-1477
E-mail: bruce.chaloux@sreb.org
Web site: http://www.electroniccampus.org

Bracey Campbell
Director of Communications
Southern Regional Education Board
E-mail: bracey.campbell@sreb.org

Spring Arbor College

School of Adult Studies

Spring Arbor, Michigan

Founded in 1873, Spring Arbor College has become a leader in the design of degree-completion programs, and the College has a network of twenty affiliate colleges that have adopted or adapted the Spring Arbor curriculum. Currently, there are more than 1,500 students enrolled in Spring Arbor College programs. Spring Arbor College is accredited by the North Central Association of Colleges and Schools. Since 1963, when the College began its four-year curricula, the Spring Arbor Concept has expressed the educational philosophy and purposes of the institution. That concept, with slight amendments, has been incorporated as the foundational statement in the new College mission statement, which was adopted in February 1996. The mission statement affirms the College's respect for tradition, heritage of innovation, and pledge to pursue excellence.

Spring Arbor College offers bachelor's degrees at thirteen sites across Michigan; some sites also offer master's degrees.

DISTANCE LEARNING PROGRAM

Spring Arbor College offers the convenience of classroom accessibility 24 hours a day, seven days a week, from anywhere in the world. Currently, the College is in the process of offering ten courses on line. Spring Arbor College also has thirteen sites across Michigan that offer three degree-completion majors. These degrees were designed with the working adult in mind and meet one night a week.

DELIVERY MEDIA

The online courses require students to have the following requirements: a PC or Power PC processor with Windows 95, 98, or NT; a 75-MHz Pentium or faster processor; 32 MB of RAM or more; a 28.8-kbps or faster modem; speakers; and a sound card. Mac users must have MacOs or later Quadra Level. Students must have Internet Explorer or Netscape and an Internet service provider that provides them with the software necessary for getting onto the Internet. Stu-

dents should contact their local Internet service provider to set up a personal account. All courses are conducted entirely on the Internet. A good resource for finding a service is http://thelist.internet.com.

The online courses are offered via the eCollege.com system.

PROGRAMS OF STUDY

Spring Arbor College has designed courses to be delivered on line. These courses typically satisfy the general education requirements of most students. Further, some courses meet elective requirements for graduate students.

At thirteen sites across Michigan, Spring Arbor College offers bachelor's degrees; some sites also offer master's degrees. The Bachelor of Science degree in management of health services focuses on the development of management and administrative skills in the delivery of health services. Course work provides a blend of specialized knowledge, skills, and attitudes essential for effective per-

formance as a leader or manager. A gerontology certificate is available.

The Bachelor of Arts degree program in management and organizational development provides expertise in human resource management and organizational development—two of the most important aspects of business and public administration. The program takes a systems approach to the problems, principles, and practices of management, incorporating conceptual and theoretical knowledge.

The Bachelor of Arts degree program in family life education offers an applied interdisciplinary approach that focuses on the study of family dynamics and the relationships between families and the larger society. This major benefits students through frequent exposure to professionals in the field, who serve as faculty members. Students who complete the program are eligible to become certified family life educators as designated by the National Council on Family Relations. In addition, the program has been endorsed by Dr. Kenneth Ogden of Focus of the Family.

A new Master of Arts program in organizational management is available at select locations.

SPECIAL PROGRAMS

Online courses offer undergraduate classes. Several courses satisfy general education requirements at most colleges and universities.

Weekend classes are offered on Fridays and Saturdays at most of the College's off-campus locations. Weekend classes are also designed to meet the general education requirements.

STUDENT SERVICES

Every online student is assigned an e-mail account through Spring Arbor College. Through this system, students can communicate with each other and their instructors. Students have access to the Spring Arbor College library, which is connected to FirstSearch (online indexes and directories), ProQuest Direct (an index to scholarly and professional business and economics articles), and Unicorn (access to the library collection).

CREDIT OPTIONS

Spring Arbor College has transfer agreements with most community colleges. The College follows the Michigan Association of Collegiate Registrars and Admissions Officers Official Policies, recognizes college-level exams (CLEP, DANTES, and TECEP), and offers portfolio opportunities.

ADMISSION

Students have open enrollment for online courses. The bachelor's completion programs require student to have 60 transferable credits and an acceptable writing sample. The graduate program requires a GPA of 3.0 of higher for the last two years (four semesters) of undergraduate study and a bachelor's degree from a regionally accredited institution.

APPLYING

Spring Arbor College starts cohort classes several times throughout the year. Students should contact the site nearest them for more details. For more information on the online classes, students should visit the Web site listed below.

CONTACT

John Nemecek
Assistant Dean
School of Adult Studies
Spring Arbor College
106 East Main Street
Spring Arbor, Michigan 49283
Telephone: 517-750-1200
Web site: http://www.arbor.edu

Stanford University

Stanford Center for Professional Development

Stanford, California

Since 1969, the Stanford Center for Professional Development (SCPD) has extended the School of Engineering's academic programs beyond the boundaries of the Stanford campus to address the career-long education needs of the best engineering, computer science, and management professionals worldwide. This important link between Stanford University and industry is designed to keep technical professionals at the leading edge of their fields by offering them the same educational opportunities as full-time Stanford students.

SCPD provides a broad range of continuing education options, including graduate engineering and computer science degree programs, individual courses for credit or audit, certificate programs, noncredit short courses, research seminars, and executive education.

DISTANCE LEARNING PROGRAM

SCPD offers more than 250 engineering courses annually, reaching more than 250 corporate sites across the nation. Industry students access courses via the Internet, television broadcast, or videotape. SCPD's delivery options bring Stanford to the student at work, at home, or while traveling.

DELIVERY MEDIA

SCPD is one of the world's largest single-university providers of televised engineering, computer science, and technology management courses, providing hundreds of programs for technology professionals and managers. SCPD offers a wide range of delivery options, including the Internet (or company Intranet), television broadcast, two-way videoconferencing, videotape, instructional modules, multimedia, and customized courseware.

SCPD's award-winning Stanford Online program is the first service to deliver complete video-based courses over the Internet (or company Intranet), offering Stanford programs in both a live and on-demand (asyn-

chronous) videostreaming environment. Recognized nationally as the "Most Significant Advancement in Distance Learning for 1997" by the U.S. Distance Learning Association, Stanford Online's technology enables fifteen-frames-per-second videostreaming and provides a table of contents from which students may instantly access specific lecture material. Students may access courses via Stanford Online directly from their desktop, on an independent viewing schedule.

PROGRAMS OF STUDY

More than 5,000 students have earned graduate degrees by participating in the Honors Cooperative Program (HCP), Stanford's only part-time graduate degree program. HCP students are fully matriculated graduate students of Stanford University with full student privileges, rights, and responsibilities. Graduate degree programs are available in a range of academic areas including aeronautics and astronautics, computer science, electrical engineering, engineering—economic systems and operations research, industrial engineering and engineering management, materials science and engineering, and mechanical engineering.

The Non-Degree Option (NDO) is for those students who wish to enroll in individual Stanford University courses and receive a grade and units for their course work. Individual course credit is available from all of the academic departments listed above, as well as in bioinformatics, medical information sciences, scientific computing and computational math, statistics, and structural biology. Though those enrolled in the NDO program are not matriculated graduate students, they may enroll in certificate programs in more than thirty topics. These programs require completion of astronautics, bioinformatics, computer science, electrical engineering, and engineering—economic systems and operations research.

The Audit Program is available for participants to access courses without the time commitment of a graded option.

SPECIAL PROGRAMS

Through SCPD, Stanford also offers a wide range of noncredit short courses and customized programs to help participants expand their professional networks and advance in their fields. Short course topics include medical informatics, ecodesign, advanced computer science, emotional intelligence in technology corporations, advanced project management, and telecommunications.

CREDIT OPTIONS

SCPD offers a range of credit options in each program. Through the Honors Cooperative Program, students may work towards a master's degree in Engineering (in selected departments) or a Ph.D. (in selected departments). Through SCPD's Non-Degree Option, students may complete a Certificate Program, earn individual course credits, or may complete up to 18 units to be transferred to HCP status. Units may also be eligible for transfer to other institutions.

FACULTY

Stanford University has a faculty of more than 1,500 members, of whom 98.8 percent hold doctorates or terminal degrees. Among these distinguished professors are 14 Nobel Laureates, 3 Pulitzer Prize winners, 19 MacArthur Fellows, a winner of the Congressional Medal of Honor, and more than 100 members of National Academies and winners of National Medals.

ADMISSION

Traditionally, students enroll on a part-time basis while maintaining employment at an SCPD member company. However, some programs do not require SCPD membership. Both member and nonmember companies may have different procedures to authorize student participation. Each student should contact their company coordinator or manager to determine what is required for company approval of their program of study. For more information on SCPD membership, interested students should refer to the Web site located at http://scpd.stanford.edu/overview/membership/membership.html.

TUITION AND FEES

For both HCP and NDO students, a one-time $55 document fee will be assessed by the Stanford University Registrar on the first quarter of registration. In addition, a minimum charge of 3 units per student is assessed for every quarter of enrollment, at $995 per unit for HCP students and $765 per unit for NDO students. Audit students pay $524 per enrollment. Prices are subject to change. Students should refer to http://scpd.stanford.edu/ce/fees.html for updated tuition and fee information.

For further details and fee information on noncredit short courses and other programs, students should refer to the SCPD Professional Education Web site at http://scpd.stanford.edu/pd/pd.html.

APPLYING

Prospective HCP students must obtain a "Guide to Graduate Admissions" booklet and application from either the Graduate Admissions Support Section of the University Registrar's Office (Telephone: 650-723-4291) or the department to which they intend to apply (a listing is available on line at http://soc.stanford.edu/programs/graduate/graduate.html). In addition, students must provide GRE test scores from within the past five years (information may be obtained at http://www.gre/org or 609-771-7670) and may be required to submit subject test scores in some departments. Completed application, statement of purpose, transcripts, and letter of recommendation should be sent to the Admissions Committee of the department to which the student intends to apply.

First-time NDO students must complete the SCPD Registration Form as well as submit transcripts from previous universities and colleges with their application.

CONTACT

Stanford Center for Professional Development
496 Lomita Mall, Durand Building, Room 401
Stanford, California 94305-4036
Telephone: 650-725-3086
650-725-3002
Fax: 650-725-2868
E-mail: scpd@forsythe.stanford.edu
World Wide Web: http://scpd.stanford.edu

Stanford Graduate Admissions Office
Telephone: 650-725-4291
Web site: http://www.stanford.edu

State University of New York Empire State College

Center for Distance Learning

Saratoga Springs, New York

Since its founding in 1971, SUNY Empire State College has become an international leader in providing innovative models for higher education at the associate, baccalaureate, and master's degree levels throughout the state of New York and beyond. The central purpose of the College is to expand access to students, primarily adults, who prefer alternatives to the fixed schedule, place, program, and structure of campus-based education due to work, family, or other responsibilities.

Empire State College was the first public, nontraditional institution to receive regional accreditation by the Middle States Association of Colleges and Schools and among the first of its kind in the United States. The College has pioneered individualized academic programs, including such innovations as one-to-one instruction, intensive mentoring, learning contracts, undergraduate credit for college-level learning gained from life experience, and distance learning technology and pedagogy.

Empire State College is a statewide institution that serves 10,000 students per year at more than forty locations in New York State, as well as across the nation and the world through distance learning options.

DISTANCE LEARNING PROGRAM

More than 6,000 students are served by the College's Center for Distance Learning, which offers courses and structured external degree programs through the telephone, mail, personal computer, and other media.

DELIVERY MEDIA

The Center for Distance Learning makes use of the latest distance learning technology, as well as standard mail and telecommunications, in working with its students. The Empire State College Network and Intranet provides computer conferencing and courses, facilitating communication and educational exchange and thereby allowing students and faculty members to share ideas and concepts at any time of the day or night. The College offers online degree programs and individual courses for students.

PROGRAMS OF STUDY

SUNY Empire State College's Center for Distance Learning offers concentrations in the liberal arts and sciences and professional and career studies leading to associate and baccalaureate degrees: Associate in Arts (A.A.), Associate in Science (A.S.), Bachelor of Arts (B.A.), Bachelor of Science (B.S.), and Bachelor of Professional Studies (B.P.S.). Undergraduate students design individualized degree programs with their adviser in eleven broad areas of study: the arts; business, management, and economics; community and human services; cultural studies; educational studies; historical studies; human development; interdisciplinary studies; labor studies; science, mathematics, and technology; and social theory, social structure, and change. The degree in business, management, and economics includes such concentrations as fire service administration, criminal justice, and management of health services. A degree in interdisciplinary studies includes concentrations

in the social sciences or the humanities. The College also offers four Master of Arts programs, with concentrations in business and policy studies, labor and policy studies, liberal studies, and social policy, in addition to an M.B.A. with online courses.

To earn an associate degree, a student must successfully complete 64 credits, with at least 24 earned through study with Empire State College. A bachelor's degree requires successful completion of 128 credits, of which at least 32 must be earned through the College.

The emphasis at Empire State College is on the individual, and the heart of the College's individualized approach to higher education is the one-to-one relationship between a faculty member and student. Each student is assigned a mentor—an Empire State College faculty member—who helps the student plan and coordinate a course of study.

SPECIAL PROGRAMS

The College offers those students interested in earning a Bachelor of Science (B.S.) degree in business, management, and economics the opportunity to earn it completely on line. Using the World Wide Web, this special program allows technologically oriented students the option of earning their entire degree via computer. Interested students should contact the Center for Distance Learning to learn about the hardware and connection requirements for this program.

CREDIT OPTIONS

Students can transfer credits earned at other regionally accredited institutions to Empire State College and can receive credit for college-level learning gained through work and life experience and through the College-Level Examination Program (CLEP) or other standardized tests. A total of 40 prior learning credits may be granted in the associate degree program; 96 credits may be applied to a baccalaureate program.

FACULTY

There are 345 full- and part-time mentors at Empire State College. Eighty-five percent of full-time faculty members and nearly half of part-time faculty members have doctoral or other terminal academic degrees. To supplement the academic expertise of its residential faculty, the College makes use of tutors and adjunct faculty.

ADMISSION

Admission to Empire State College is made without regard to race, sex, handicap, religion, or national origin of the applicant. Two principal requirements for admission are possession of a high school diploma or its equivalent and the ability of the College to meet the applicant's educational needs and objectives.

TUITION AND FEES

In 1999–2000, undergraduate tuition was $113 per credit. A per-term telecommunications development and support fee of $50 was also charged, which provided access to electronic mail, computer conferencing, the Internet, and other information sources.

FINANCIAL AID

More than $6 million in financial aid was awarded to Empire State College students in 1999–2000, with more than 40 percent of the enrolled students receiving some form of financial assistance. General financial aid programs available through Empire State College include the Federal Pell Grant, Federal Supplemental Educational Opportunity Grant, Federal Perkins Loan, and the Federal Work-Study programs. New York State financial aid programs include the Tuition Assistance Program (TAP), Aid for Part-Time Study (APTS), and the SUNY Supplemental Tuition Award. The Empire State College Foundation awards more than $30,000 in scholarships and grants annually.

APPLYING

Empire State College reviews applications in order of date received. The number of new students accepted depends on available space.

CONTACT

Dr. Margaret Craft
Assistant Director for Academic Programs and Development
Center for Distance Learning
SUNY Empire State College
3 Union Avenue
Saratoga Springs, New York 12866-4390
Telephone: 800-847-3000 Ext. 300 (toll-free)
Fax: 518-587-2660
E-mail: margaret.craft@esc.edu
Web site: http://www.esc.edu/CDL

State University of New York Institute of Technology at Utica/Rome

School of Management

Utica, New York

State University of New York (SUNY) Institute of Technology is the newest and youngest college in the sixty-four-campus SUNY system. It is a leader in technology, innovation, and excellence. It has been ranked two years in a row as one of the 100 Most Wired Colleges by Yahoo! Internet Life magazine. The Institute's School of Management is a pioneer in delivering high-quality education over the Internet.

DISTANCE LEARNING PROGRAM

The School of Management offers a Master of Science in Accountancy (M.S.A.) degree online. For students the advantages of this program are numerous. Graduate accounting students study and take classes at any time from anywhere in the world. No classroom attendance is required. Twenty-first-century technology is employed to create a virtual college on the World Wide Web. The online M.S.A. program eliminates the constraints of time and location that colleges normally place on students as well as the problems of long commutes, child care, conflicting work schedules, handicap accessibility, and absences due to illness. The online M.S.A. program combines quality education, lifestyle flexibility, and affordable tuition.

Students utilize the Internet for career advancement. The M.S.A. is an applied program for goal-oriented individuals. Students use the program to prepare for the CPA and CMA exams. The online M.S.A. fully complies with the new AICPA education requirements and is fully accredited. CPAs and CMAs satisfy Continuing Professional Education requirements while earning a graduate degree. It is a convenient and effective way for accountants to continue their education.

DELIVERY MEDIA

Students must have access to the following resources: a computer with at least 64 MB RAM, 33.6 kbps modem, and Pentium processor (Macintosh users must have System 7 or higher); an Internet connection to the World Wide Web; a Web browser that supports file attachments (Netscape Navigator 4.0 or Microsoft Internet Explorer 4.0 or higher); a valid, working Internet e-mail account that accepts redirected mail and does not block Internet mail messages; and the ability to print documents, such as the syllabus, course schedule, and assignments. Students need to be able to create and save documents in a common file format. SUNY-IT recommends that students have access to a word processor with the capability to save files in the Microsoft Word 6.0 (or higher) file format. Professors may require their students to use additional software such as Microsoft Office 2000 or a spreadsheet application.

PROGRAM OF STUDY

The degree program requires a total of 33 credit hours distributed among courses in advanced income tax research, fund accounting, advanced auditing theory, advanced financial accounting theory, managerial economics, management information systems, research seminar, financial management problems, management

science, and two electives that consist of any two graduate courses from the School of Management, including advanced management accounting, independent study, internship, international marketing and trade, health-care industry policy, human resource management, portfolio management, and strategies in national and international business. Students must attain a grade point average of 3.0 for all graduate courses included in their program. No more than three C grades, regardless of overall grade point average, are counted toward graduation.

SPECIAL PROGRAMS

The Master of Science in Accountancy offers an internship program (ACC 595, 3 credit hours). Internship placements provide students with field experience related to their academic preparation, enabling them to apply classroom instruction to the work site. Students are placed with an organization related to their major area of interest to work with experienced professionals. These opportunities cannot not be duplicated in the classroom environment and prepare students for the transition into their chosen field.

STUDENT SERVICES

Technical support, online libraries, and transfer and career advisement are available. Placements are excellent, with students being recruited by nationally recognized accounting firms, Fortune 500 companies, government organizations, and teaching institutions.

CREDIT OPTIONS

Students from undergraduate accounting programs that are registered as CPA preparation programs typically have no prerequisite foundation course work. Other students are required to complete course work in accounting, business law, finance, statistics, economics, general business, and liberal arts as appropriate to prepare for the M.S.A. degree course requirements. Students should consult with a graduate adviser to determine appropriate course selection. Prerequisite skills may be fulfilled in a variety of ways, including transfer courses, courses at the Institute of Technology, and College Level Entrance Program (CLEP) examinations.

FACULTY

The faculty members have extensive experience and meet the highest standards for quality. All the faculty members who teach in the M.S.A. program have earned a doctorate in their field of expertise.

ADMISSION

To be admitted into the program, a student's score from the GMAT (Graduate Management Admissions Test) is combined with his or her undergraduate GPA as follows:

A total of 950 points based on 200 x undergraduate GPA + GMAT score, or a total of 1,000 points based on 200 x upper division GPA + GMAT score.

SUNY Institute of Technology makes an exception to these standards in cases where the applicant has demonstrated, through exceptional performance in a management career, that his or her undergraduate grades are not indicative of his or her ability, and conditional admission may be allowed for promising candidates who do not perform well on the GMAT. Students must maintain at least a B average in the first three courses they

complete in order to remain matriculated when admitted in this category.

TUITION AND FEES

In-state students take advantage of low SUNY tuition rates, making the M.S.A. very affordable. Graduate tuition rates are $213 per credit hour for part-time New York residents, $2550 per semester for full-time New York residents, $351 per credit hour for part-time nonresidents, and $4208 per semester for full-time nonresidents. Scholarships, financial aid, and internships are available.

APPLYING

Applications are available online or by contacting the School.

CONTACT

Dr. Thomas Tribunella, Director
School of Management
P.O. Box 3050
SUNY Institute of Technology at Utica/Rome
Utica, New York 13504-3050
Telephone: 315-792-7126 (Director)
315-792-7429 (School of Management)
315-792-7500 (admissions)
E-mail: ftjt@sunyit.edu
admissions@sunyit.edu
Web site: http://www.pubm.sunyit.edu

Stephens College

School of Graduate and Continuing Education

Columbia, Missouri

Founded in 1833, Stephens College is a private college nationally known for its innovation in education. The School of Graduate and Continuing Education is built on a history of quality education and academic service to students. Located in Columbia, Missouri, Stephens College offers distance learning programs that allow men and women to complete their degrees as quickly as their schedules allow from home or work. Stephens has generous transfer credit options, credit for prior learning, one-office registration, and individual advising and degree planning.

Stephens College is nationally known for excellence in teaching and fostering lifelong associations with alumni. Since the first graduating class in 1974, more than 1,300 students have completed their degrees through the School of Graduate and Continuing Education.

Stephens College is accredited by the North Central Association of Colleges and Schools.

DISTANCE LEARNING PROGRAM

The School of Graduate and Continuing Education offers graduate, undergraduate, and nondegree programs for adult learners. Flexibility is the hallmark. External Degree and Weekend College courses are designed for bachelor's degree candidates, and the Master of Business Administration Program is designed for graduate students seeking to complete a challenging program without relocating or leaving their current jobs.

DELIVERY MEDIA

External Degree courses are delivered through a variety of methods, including the Internet, telephone, fax, and regular mail. Students are strongly encouraged to have access to a computer with an Internet connection. Internet access and an e-mail address are requirements for M.B.A. students. Certain courses require specific software programs.

PROGRAMS OF STUDY

The adult student is at the heart of Stephens' nontraditional programs.

Students are assured of a quality education designed with flexibility that allows them to meet the demands of their busy lives. Faculty members, staff members, and advisers understand the complexities of returning to college and are aware of the many responsibilities adult students must manage. They offer encouragement and support as the students progress through their course work toward graduation.

Working with Stephens College faculty members, students enrolled in External Degree courses study at home or work. This program is designed to complement the student's commitments to career, family, and community, and because courses are taken by independent study, students have some flexibility in completing their courses in less time than the six allotted months. Working with an adviser, students plan an individual program of study for their degree completion.

Majors available to students include business administration; early childhood or elementary education certification; education; English; health care and a second area; health infor-

mation administration; health science and a second area; law, philosophy, and rhetoric; and psychology. Students who wish to develop an individualized major in two disciplines may combine approved guided study courses from the list of majors.

The Stephens College Master of Business Administration Program utilizes communication technology to deliver a challenging curriculum to students around the globe. With personal attention from instructors and interaction with students from around the world, the program combines theoretical and practical approaches to provide the student with a well-rounded business education at the advanced level. Emphasis areas within the M.B.A. Program include entrepreneurial studies, management, and clinical information systems management. Undergraduate core requirements for the M.B.A. Program are offered through the Stephens College External Degree and Weekend College courses.

SPECIAL PROGRAMS

Prior learning credit is available for adult undergraduate students who have achieved college-level learning and experience outside the classroom. Evidence of prior learning is presented by the student in a written narrative; oral interview, with supporting materials; and the actual product or demonstrations, if applicable. No letter grades are given.

Dual-disciplinary majors are available for graduates of hospital diploma programs, two-year registered nursing programs, accredited associate degree programs in allied health, or accredited noncollegiate hospital-based programs in allied health. These students may build on their specialized training in health care to earn dual-disciplinary majors such as health care and psychology, health care and business administration, health care and history, health care and philosophy/religion, health science and business administration, health science and psychology, health science and history, and health science and philosophy/religion.

STUDENT SERVICES

Students receive the following services from the College: an individual academic adviser, assistance with prior learning, periodic mailings from the program, course schedules, a course catalog, a student handbook, and maintenance of student records and academic transcripts. Students also may use the College bookstore, Hugh Stephens Library, computer labs, Career Services office, and the College's recreational and other facilities.

CREDIT OPTIONS

Stephens College offers many flexible options for earning academic credit, including independent guided study courses, Internet-based courses, Weekend College courses, short-format courses, contract-study courses, transfer credit, noncollegiate professional education or training, prior learning, and credit by standard examination (CLEP tests). Stephens accepts transfer credit from regionally accredited institutions.

FACULTY

Students are taught by experienced, qualified faculty members who are dedicated to student learning. With a low student-faculty ratio, students benefit from a high level of interaction with instructors.

ADMISSION

The Stephens College School of Graduate and Continuing Education follows an open admission policy for women and men over 23 years of age who have earned a high school diploma or GED. Students must complete the Liberal Studies Seminar with a grade of C or better to matriculate into the undergraduate program. The M.B.A. Program admits students with a bachelor's degree from a regionally accredited institution who have met minimum GPA and GMAT requirements.

TUITION AND FEES

Tuition for the undergraduate program is $650 per course ($500 per course for Missouri residents). After completing the first year, students are eligible for substantial tuition discounts when enrolling in two or more courses per year. The M.B.A. Program is $690 per course. Depending on courses selected and the degree sought, other fees may apply. Students should contact the Office of Graduate and Continuing Education for more information.

FINANCIAL AID

A variety of federal, state, and private funds may be available for students who meet specific criteria. Students should call the Office of Financial Aid at 800-876-7207 (toll-free) for more information.

APPLYING

The Stephens College School of Graduate and Continuing Education accepts applications on a rolling basis. Applicants to the undergraduate program must submit an application along with documentation such as transcripts and/or GED scores. Applicants to the M.B.A. Program must submit transcripts from an accredited college or university, GMAT scores, three references, and an essay. Students for whom English is a second language must submit a minimum TOEFL score of 550. Application fees are $50 for undergraduate applicants and $25 for graduate applicants.

CONTACT

Stephens College School of Graduate and Continuing Education
1211 East Broadway
Columbia, Missouri 65215
Telephone: 573-876-7225
 800-388-7579 (toll-free)
Fax: 573-876-7248
E-mail: sce@wc.stephens.edu
grad@wc.stephens.edu
Web site: http://www.stephens.edu

Stevens Institute of Technology

The Graduate School Distance Learning Programs

Hoboken, New Jersey

Stevens Institute of Technology, one of the world's premier technical universities, offers an array of Web-based distance learning graduate programs from its WebCampus. Stevens online initiatives include telecommunications management, wireless communications, technology management, project management, elements of computer science, and technology applications in science education. Students are instructed by noted Stevens faculty members delivering the same superior courses as taught on the main campus. Other off-campus courses in a variety of fields are conveniently offered at corporate locations in six states, suiting the needs of graduate students who are working professionals. Some classes are delivered using interactive video. Stevens is accredited by the Middle States Association of Colleges and Schools (MSA) Commission on Institutions of Higher Education (CIHE). Online programs are cosponsored by the 333,000-member Institute for Electrical and Electronics Engineers (IEEE), the largest professional society in the world.

DISTANCE LEARNING PROGRAM

Graduate certificates for professionals seeking advanced knowledge in engineering, management, and teacher education are available online through WebCampus.Stevens. Master's degrees and graduate certificates in project management or wireless communications are also offered online. A wide range of off-campus graduate degree programs in engineering, management, computer science, and mathematics, among other disciplines, are taught at corporate sites.

DELIVERY MEDIA

Stevens has been at the forefront of distance learning for a number of years, offering courses that exploit the benefits of interactive video, Internet, and other advanced instructional technologies. WebCampus. Stevens online graduate students use rich Web features such as threaded discussions, chat, bulletin boards, e-mail, file sharing, whiteboards, and work groups for in-depth online participation. Students also have online library privileges, with instant search and retrieval of important databases.

PROGRAMS OF STUDY

Graduate students may now take Web-based courses that lead to graduate certificates in telecommunications management, wireless communications, technology management, project management, elements of computer science, and technology applications in science education. Graduate certificate programs offer students the opportunity to focus on a specific area of study without having to complete a master's program. Credits earned toward a graduate certificate at Stevens may also be applied to a master's degree, should students wish to continue with their studies. In addition to offering graduate certificates, the telecommunications management and wireless communications programs offer master's degrees.

Off campus, at corporate and other sites, graduate students who enroll as part of company-sponsored and other programs may enroll in a wide variety of other programs, some of which are delivered using interactive video. Employees at some of the nation's most progressive and prominent companies, including Bell Laboratories–Lucent Technologies, AT&T, Bell Atlantic, and dozens of others, may take graduate certificate courses and master's degrees at corporate locations in a number of disciplines. These include computer engineering, computer science, electrical engineering, management, mechanical engineering, project management, technology management, and telecommunications management, among others.

STUDENT SERVICES

Distance learning graduate students access the entire range of Stevens' student services, which include faculty advising, ordering books and other materials, admission, registration, and applications for financial aid, among other services, via e-mail, telephone, and by post. Graduate students also have instant online access to the School's digital library. A CyberLibrarian is available via e-mail and telephone to guide students in the use of databases and other research tools and media. Seven days per week, 24-hour technical and other help desk support services are also available online. Stevens' Student Information System allows distance learners to access course schedules, grades, account statements, and other documents entirely online.

CREDIT OPTIONS

Nearly all graduate courses are 3 credit courses. Depending upon the program, most graduate certificates are offered after students complete four courses. To earn a master's degree in engineering and science, students are required to complete ten courses. Students are required to complete ten courses for a master's degree in management.

FACULTY

An impressive graduate faculty teaches courses at Stevens in conventional settings, providing superior instruction online and off-campus. WebCampus.Stevens faculty members are required to participate in teaching and learning colloquia, held periodically during each semester, in order to share their experiences and to demonstrate the capabilities of online teaching and learning. Net faculty are also trained in how to exploit the technological and pedagogical benefits of Web-based courseware applications.

ADMISSION

To be admitted to a distance learning program at Stevens Institute of Technology, students are required to satisfy the same qualifications as those who wish to enroll in Stevens' conventional courses. Prospective graduate students need to have completed an undergraduate degree at an accredited institution. Applicants may either apply by mail or complete an application form online at the Internet address listed below. Applications should be accompanied by a nonrefundable check or money order for $50, made payable to Stevens Institute of Technology. Two letters of recommendation are required unless applying to the Technology Applications in Science Education graduate

certificate program. For this program, students must submit three letters of recommendation confirming that they are experienced teachers with basic knowledge of the Internet and mathematics or science. Applicants must also provide official transcripts, in English, for each college or university attended. Transcripts translated into English must be prepared by the school attended or prepared by an official translator with a recognized seal. Applicants must also provide official confirmation of the degree earned if it was awarded by a non-U.S. institution. Name, Social Security number, and/or date of birth must be on all submitted documents. All documents must be in English or have attested English translations.

TUITION AND FEES

Prospective students must pay a $50 application fee, which is waived for current Stevens undergraduate students, Stevens alumni, and those entering from selected corporate programs. Each semester, students are also required to pay an $80 enrollment fee. Tuition for management courses is $605 per credit hour. Tuition for engineering and science courses is $725 per credit hour. Other fees apply for late enrollment and late payment, among other services.

FINANCIAL AID

Stevens has a strong commitment to assisting and investing in talented students. The school offers a number of scholarships, many of which are

made available through generous friends and successful alumni. Many graduate students receive tuition reimbursement from their companies.

APPLYING

Before applying to either online or off-campus distance learning programs, it is recommended that students review the Graduate School Web site or the Stevens' online learning site, both listed below, where students can find information, instructions, and online application forms.

CONTACT

Online programs:
WebCampus.Stevens
Stevens Institute of Technology
Castle Point on Hudson
Hoboken, New Jersey 07030
Telephone: 201-216-0854
       800-494-4935 (toll-free)
Fax: 201-216-8044
E-mail: webcampus@stevens-tech.edu
Web site: http://www.webcampus.stevens.edu

Off-campus programs:
The Graduate School
Stevens Institute of Technology
Castle Point on Hudson
Hoboken, New Jersey 07030
Telephone: 201-216-5234
Fax: 201-216-8044
Web site:
   http://www.stevens-tech.edu

Strayer University

Strayer Online

Newington, Virginia

Strayer University, founded in 1892 in Baltimore, Maryland, has more than 100 years of experience educating working adults. Currently, more than 11,500 students are enrolled at Strayer, the majority of whom work full-time. Undergraduate and graduate degrees are offered in technology and business-oriented programs. Strayer has thirteen campuses located in Maryland, Virginia, and the District of Columbia and is accredited by the Middle States Association of Colleges and Schools (MSA). Strayer University is a subsidiary of Strayer Education, Inc., a publicly held corporation whose stock is traded on the NASDAQ market (STRA). Strayer Education was recognized by Business Week *in both 1998 and 1999 as a "hot growth company."*

DISTANCE LEARNING PROGRAM

Strayer Online classes are delivered via the Internet by live audio from professors and use real-time text-based communication between students and the professors. Classes meet at the same time each week. Students need a computer and access to the Internet. All of the software needed is provided.

DELIVERY MEDIA

The following is a list of the minimal hardware and software recommended for participation in Strayer Online classes: a 300-MHz processor (Pentium II equivalent or higher) with Windows '98, Microsoft Office '97 Professional Edition (or more recent), a 128-KB L2 Cache (laptop) or 512-KB L2 Cache (desktop), 64 MB of memory, a 4-GB hard drive, a 12.1-inch SVGA TFT display (laptop) or larger (desktop), a 1.44-MB floppy drive, 2 MBs of video memory, a 24X (laptop) or 40X (desktop) CD-ROM drive, a 56-K PCMCIA modem with fax capability, a 10/100 Ethernet network card (laptop only), and an integrated microphone and speakers.

PROGRAMS OF STUDY

Degree programs available online include the 54-credit Master of Science (M.S.) programs in business administration, communications technology, information systems, and professional accounting; Bachelor of Science (B.S.) programs (180 credits) in accounting, business administration, computer information systems, computer networking, economics, and international business; and Associate in Arts (A.A.) programs (90 credits) in accounting, acquisition and contract management, business administration, computer information systems, computer networking, economics, general studies, and marketing. There are also 54-credit Diploma programs in accounting and computer information systems.

Courses are taught on the quarter system, and each course provides 4.5 credit hours. Associate in Arts degree programs require twenty courses, or 90 hours, to complete. B.S. degrees require forty courses, or 180 hours. M.S. degrees require twelve courses, or 54 hours, to complete.

Each degree program has a business component and a major component. The undergraduate programs also have liberal arts/general studies and an elective component.

STUDENT SERVICES

Applications for federal financial aid, the Strayer Education Loan (a low-interest loan program), and scholarships are available online. Students may register for classes through the Web site or by telephone. In addition, library resources, other learning resources, and career-development services are available online.

CREDIT OPTIONS

Students who have attended other educational institutions may receive transfer credit or advanced standing in Strayer's degree and diploma programs. College credit may be awarded for CLEP and DANTES tests, certain training received in the military, or prior work/life learning demonstrated through portfolio preparation. The required number of credits taken in residence, online or on campus, is 36 for a master's degree, 54 for a bachelor's degree, 27 for an associate, and 31.5 for a diploma.

FACULTY

Strayer University has 95 full-time and 186 part-time faculty members. Of these, 2 teach full-time and 31 teach part-time for Strayer Online. Approximately 50 percent of full-time faculty members have a doctoral or terminal degree in their field.

ADMISSION

Students who apply to undergraduate degree programs must provide certification of high school graduation or the equivalent. For admission to graduate degree programs, students must have graduated from an accredited college or university with a baccalaureate degree.

TUITION AND FEES

In the 2000–01 academic year, tuition for graduate courses is $280 per credit hour. Full-time undergraduate students (3.5 credits or more) pay $210 per credit hour, and part-time undergraduate students pay $220 per credit hour.

FINANCIAL AID

Students may apply online for financial aid. The Free Application for Federal Student Aid (FAFSA) may be accessed through the Strayer University Web address listed below. Students may apply for the following grants, loans, and scholarships: Federal Pell Grant, Federal Supplemental Educational Opportunity Grant, Federal Perkins Loan, Federal Stafford Student Loan, Federal PLUS Loan, Federal Direct Loan Programs, Federal Work-Study Program, Strayer University Education Loan Program, and Strayer University Scholarships. Thirteen percent of students studying online receive federal financial assistance.

APPLYING

Applications are accepted on an ongoing basis and can be accessed online at the Web site listed below. There is a $25 application fee.

CONTACT

Strayer Online
P.O. Box 487
Newington, Virginia 22122
Telephone: 888-4-STRAYER (toll-free)
Fax: 703-339-1852
E-mail: info@strayer.edu
Web site: http://www.strayer.edu

Suffolk University

Frank Sawyer School of Management/eMBA Program

Boston, Massachusetts

Suffolk University is a dynamic urban university that enrolls more than 6,500 students in its College of Arts and Sciences, Frank Sawyer School of Management, and Law School. The University is located in the heart of Boston's business and governmental districts on Boston's historic Beacon Hill. The Sawyer School of Management was established in 1937 and enrolls more than 2,100 undergraduate and graduate students. The Sawyer School is dedicated to providing access to pragmatic management education for preprofessional and working students. Suffolk University is accredited by the New England Association of Schools and Colleges, Inc. The Sawyer School is accredited by AACSB–The International Association for Management Education and the National Association of Schools of Public Affairs and Administration (NASPAA).

DISTANCE LEARNING PROGRAM

The distance learning program through the eMBA Program at the Sawyer School of Management continues Suffolk University's ninety-three-year tradition of providing access to higher education. Designed to meet the needs of people who wish to avoid the constraints of taking courses at a fixed location or who prefer the computer as the learning tool of convenience, the eMBA Program provides students with the opportunity to earn an accredited M.B.A. in a flexible, convenient, rigorous learning environment.

DELIVERY MEDIA

eMBA instruction utilizes a variety of media as appropriate to the subject matter. Media typically include slideshows and other forms of online text and streaming audio and video to provide the student with access to course material wherever and whenever desired. These media are combined with document sharing, chat rooms, e-mail, and threaded discussions to provide interaction with faculty members and among students as needed to facilitate class discussions,

group work, case evaluations, simulations, and exercises and to provide feedback.

Students require access to the Internet and a moderate level of comfort working on the World Wide Web to participate in online courses. As a minimum configuration, the School recommends a Pentium computer, a 28.8 k-baud modem, Microsoft Windows 95, and Office 97 Professional.

Suffolk University has partnered with eCollege.com to provide the virtual campus and online courses. The online courses are offered via the eCollege.com system.

PROGRAMS OF STUDY

The Sawyer School of Management offers an M.B.A. degree in cooperation with eCollege.com. This program is accredited by AACSB–The International Association for Management Education. The eMBA Program consists of sixteen courses, or 51 credits. The curriculum includes seven required courses (a maximum of five required courses can be waived) and nine elective courses. A student with strong prior academic preparation in business or management typically completes

the M.B.A. program in eleven to thirteen courses, depending upon the waiver process.

The eMBA captures the full value of the Suffolk M.B.A. by providing an integrated core, a global perspective, and real-life business applications. The eMBA standards are the same standards that the School demands from its on-campus students.

SPECIAL PROGRAMS

eMBA students earn the same degree as students who attend Suffolk University's campuses and work with the same faculty. eMBA students have access to special programs that are available to on-campus students. eMBA students are allowed to register for courses or transfer into the on-campus M.B.A. program with the permission of the program director. The program offers optional international seminars (one to two weeks), which are hosted by one of Suffolk's international university partners and include extensive company and government visits. In the past, students have traveled to Europe, Asia, and Latin America.

STUDENT SERVICES

eMBA students have access to the same materials and services that are available to students on campus. Remote access to library services, online registration, academic advising, and other services are available.

CREDIT OPTIONS

Transfer credit is granted for core courses for graduate-level courses completed at a college or university that is accredited by AACSB–The International Association for Management Education; courses must have been taken within the last seven years, with a grade of B or better, and must not be used toward another degree. Students are required to complete a minimum of 34 credit hours of Sawyer School classes.

FACULTY

The Sawyer School faculty consists of 65 full-time and 80 part-time members. Ninety-three percent of the full-time faculty members hold doctoral degrees. The senior faculty members who teach in eMBA program have been selected for their commitment to online instruction and depth of experience.

ADMISSION

Admissions criteria include a completed application form, an application fee, a current resume, two recommendation letters, official transcripts of all prior academic work, a statement of professional goals, TOEFL scores (for international students), and official GMAT scores.

TUITION AND FEES

For the 1999–2000 academic year, the eMBA tuition is $1845 per 3-credit course. eMBA students are also assessed a $120 technology fee per 3-credit course course.

FINANCIAL AID

For information regarding financial aid options, students should contact the Financial Aid Office.

APPLYING

Applications are accepted for the fall, spring, and summer semesters. The fall 2000 semester begins September 11. Students are encouraged to submit applications well in advance of the deadlines. When all the required materials have been received in the Admissions Office, students are notified of a decision within 24 hours.

CONTACT

Dr. Mawdudur Rahman, eMBA Program Director
Frank Sawyer School of Management
Suffolk University
8 Ashburton Place
Boston, Massachusetts 02108-2770
Telephone: 617-573-8372
Fax: 617-723-0139
E-mail: mrahman@acad.suffolk.edu
Web site: http://www.SuffolkeMBA.org

Graduate Admissions Office
Suffolk University
20 Beacon Street
Boston, Massachusetts 02108-2770
Telephone: 617-573-8302
Fax: 617-523-0116
E-mail: grad.admission@admin.suffolk.edu

Syracuse University
Independent Study Degree Programs
Syracuse, New York

Founded in 1870, Syracuse University is a major private research university of 14,500 residential students and an additional 5,000 part-time adult students located in central New York State. Organized into thirteen separate schools and colleges, each offering a variety of baccalaureate, master's, and doctoral degrees, Syracuse has excellent research facilities, including sophisticated computer networks and a library containing more than 2.4 million volumes. Syracuse is ranked by *U.S. News & World Report* as one of the top sixty universities in the United States and is one of the select group of American and Canadian universities chosen for membership in the prestigious Association of American Universities.

Syracuse has a long-standing commitment to adult education. The University's innovative Independent Study Degree Programs (ISDP) are a form of nontraditional education in which Syracuse was a pioneer. Offered through nine of the University's academic units, in partnership with Syracuse's Division of Continuing Education and Summer Sessions, ISDP is one of the three oldest external degree programs in the United States. The programs have been active since 1966 and reflect the University's response to the demands for creative educational techniques and programs in a constantly changing society.

DISTANCE LEARNING PROGRAM

Syracuse's Independent Study Degree Programs (ISDP) have a limited-residency structure: they combine short periods of intensive on-site instruction with longer periods of home study, during which students and faculty members communicate at a distance by correspondence, telephone, fax, and computer. There are currently about 1,000 adults actively enrolled in twelve different degree programs through ISDP, approximately one sixth of whom are international students or Americans living abroad. Syracuse degrees earned through ISDP are the same as those earned by traditional Syracuse students in comparable campus programs and have the same accreditation.

PROGRAMS OF STUDY

ISDP offers two undergraduate and ten master's programs by means of the limited-residency, distance edu-

cation format. Undergraduate degrees include an Associate of Arts and a Bachelor of Arts in Liberal Studies. The Associate of Arts degree is 60 credits. The bachelor's degree is a 120-credit program.

The master's degrees include an M.A. in either advertising design or illustration, a Master of Library Science (M.L.S), an M.S. in communications management, an M.S. in information resources management, an M.S. in telecommunications and network management, an M.S. in nursing, a Master of Social Science (M.S.Sc.) with an international relations emphasis, an M.B.A., and an M.S. in engineering management. The M.A. and M.S. Sc. degrees are 30-credit degrees; the M.L.S., M.S. in communications management, and M.S. in engineering management are 36 credits, the M.S. in information resources management and the M.S. in telecommunications and network management are 42 credits, the M.S. in nursing is 45 credits, and the M.B.A. is 54 credits.

In addition to state and regional accreditation, several of the master's programs enjoy professional accreditation appropriate to the field of study. The advertising design and illustration programs are accredited by the National Association of Schools of Art and Design, the nursing program is accredited by the National League for Nursing, the M.B.A. program is accredited by the American Association of Collegiate Schools of Business, and the M.L.S. program is accredited by the American Library Association.

Students may initially enroll in the A.A., B.A., and M.S.Sc. degrees on a nonmatriculated basis. All other degrees require matriculation prior to participation.

SPECIAL PROGRAMS

Syracuse University Continuing Education offers a selected number of individual online credit and non-credit courses each semester. Information on these is available on the World Wide Web (http://www.suce. syr.edu/online).

STUDENT SERVICES

ISDP students are provided with free computer accounts and have access to the Syracuse University library and mainframe computer facilities. Online students have access to a help desk for technical problems.

CREDIT OPTIONS

The associate degree program accepts a maximum of 30 credits to be transferred from another postsecondary institution. The baccalaureate program accepts a maximum of 90 transfer credits, which may include 66 credits from a junior college. Transfer credit is granted for most courses in which a grade of C or better has been earned, provided courses are from an accredited college and fit the ISDP degree requirements. For credit to be accepted from an international institution of higher learning, the institution must be a recognized third-level institution.

A maximum of 30 credits gained through testing or through evaluation of extra-institutional or experiential learning may be applied toward an undergraduate degree program. DANTES, CLEP, and Syracuse advanced credit exams may be used for this purpose. However, credit awarded through testing or experiential evaluation does not count toward the minimum number of credits that must be taken at Syracuse in order to earn a degree. On the graduate level, there is no provision for experiential credit. However, 6 credits may be taken in transfer from other accredited graduate programs, with a grade of C or better. The M.B.A. program also allows students to waive certain core courses by means of testing or documentation of prior academic experience.

FACULTY

ISDP courses are taught by full-time Syracuse University faculty members, who participate in the limited-residency programs in addition to their full-time campus responsibilities. In the case of the M.A. programs in advertising design and illustration, additional visiting faculty members are drawn from among the world's most recognized designers and illustrators.

ADMISSION

Candidates for admission to the associate and baccalaureate programs should have a high school diploma or its equivalent. Transfer students must have at least a 2.0 (C) average for the liberal studies program. On the graduate level, candidates must take the GMAT for the M.B.A. program and the GRE for the communications management, information resources management, telecommunications and network management, and nursing programs. Applicants whose primary language is a language other than English must also take the TOEFL. Portfolios of related professional work must be submitted for the advertising design, illustration, and communications management programs.

Applicants for all programs must submit official transcripts of prior academic work, letters of recommendation, and a personal statement that accompanies the application form.

Applicants to the Master of Library Science, communications management, engineering management, information resources management, telecommunications and network management, and nursing programs must also have a computer with at least a 486 microprocessor, a modem, and Internet access.

TUITION AND FEES

For 2000–01, the undergraduate tuition rate is $371 per credit, and the graduate rate is $613 per credit. Additional expenses for room and board at the on-campus residences average $72–$100 per day, depending upon the choice of facility, and book charges average $100 per course. There are additional Internet line charges each semester for programs relying upon that means of communication.

FINANCIAL AID

ISDP students who are U.S. citizens are eligible for all the standard federal grants and loans available to part-time students. Selective institutional aid is available for several of the programs listed above; detailed information is available upon request. Syracuse University awards more than $100,000 to ISDP students each year. International students (non-U.S. citizens) are not eligible for financial aid.

APPLYING

Applicants should request application materials from the address below. The undergraduate programs and the M.B.A. and M.S.Sc. programs admit students on a continuous basis, and students can begin in the fall, spring, or summer terms. The other master's programs require newly admitted students to begin each summer, with the exception of the nursing program, which begins every other summer. In-person interviews are not required, although they can be arranged upon request. Portfolios may be sent to the ISDP office for evaluation.

CONTACT

Robert M. Colley
Director, Distance Education
Syracuse University Continuing Education
700 University Avenue
Syracuse, New York 13244-2530
Telephone: 315-443-4590
            800-442-0501 (toll-free)
Fax: 315-443-4174
E-mail: suisdp@uc.syr.edu
Web site:
    www.suce.syr.edu/DistanceEd

Taylor University

World Wide Campus

Fort Wayne, Indiana

Taylor University is one of America's oldest evangelical Christian institutions. In 1846, more than 150 years ago, it began as a women's college with the conviction that women as well as men should have an opportunity for higher education. In 1855, it became coeducational and, in 1938, it offered its first distance learning course.

Today, *U.S. News & World Report* repeatedly ranks Taylor as one of America's best regional liberal arts colleges. The Templeton Foundation has named it one of the nation's top colleges for building character in students, and *Barron's* has listed it as a "best buy in college education."

Taylor University's mission is to educate men and women for lifelong learning and for ministering the redemptive love of Jesus Christ. It is accredited by the North Central Association of Colleges and Schools.

DISTANCE LEARNING PROGRAM

The World Wide Campus is the virtual campus of Taylor University; it emphasizes the integration of faith and learning through distance education. It offers three Associate of Arts (A.A.) degrees, two certificate programs, and more than seventy courses from most academic disciplines. Annually, it enrolls more than 1,200 students in more than 2,000 courses.

DELIVERY MEDIA

The World Wide Campus offers courses for credit and noncredit in a variety of formats to meet various individual learning needs. These include correspondence study, online independent study, and online classroom study.

Students and instructors interact through postal mail or e-mail, and students in online classes benefit from online discussion groups and other interactive components. Online courses require a computer and Internet access.

PROGRAMS OF STUDY

The 64-credit-hour A.A. degree in biblical studies is designed for individuals preparing for vocational or lay Christian ministry. It consists of 43 credit hours of general education course work, 15 hours in the discipline, and 6 elective hours.

The 64-credit-hour A.A. degree in justice administration is designed for individuals currently serving in or seeking to enter criminal justice, courts, corrections, law enforcement, or juvenile justice. It consists of 43 credit hours of general education course work and 21 hours in the discipline. Students also select a ministry or public policy concentration.

The 64-credit-hour A.A. degree in the liberal arts (general studies) is for students who desire a breadth of knowledge. It consists of 43 credit hours of general education course work, 15 hours in the discipline, and 6 elective hours.

The two certificate programs include the 18-credit-hour Christian Worker Certificate, designed for an in-depth study of God's Word, and the 18-credit-hour Justice and Ministry Certificate, aimed at equipping individuals who work with at-risk populations and/or inmates.

SPECIAL PROGRAMS

A special program that is open to distance learners is the American Chaplaincy Training School (ACTS), a weeklong intensive school featuring nationally known experts in the justice and ministry field. ACTS equips graduates with the theoretical concepts and ministry skills to support institutional chaplaincy programs and community-based ministries that target at-risk groups. It is part of Taylor University's respected Center for Justice and Urban Leadership and is held annually in early June at Taylor University Fort Wayne in Fort Wayne, Indiana.

STUDENT SERVICES

The World Wide Campus provides a range of services to degree-seeking students. The student services staff members assist students in any way possible, and academic advisers help them accomplish career and academic goals. In addition, students have access to staff members and resources in the Career Development Office, Learning Support Center, and Taylor University libraries.

CREDIT OPTIONS

Students earn credits by completing courses. Up to 34 hours of transfer credit may be approved toward the 64-credit-hour A.A. degree programs. Only course work with a grade of C- or better is accepted.

To receive credit for work done at other accredited institutions, students should send their transcripts to the World Wide Campus for review. CLEP, AP, and DANTES credit must meet Taylor's standards to be accepted as transfer credit.

FACULTY

The faculty members of the World Wide Campus are highly credentialed, dedicated Christians with years of teaching experience. Most hold doctorates.

ADMISSION

Admission is open to all students registering for individual courses or beginning a certificate program. Degree-seeking students must meet certain minimum admission standards and complete an application, which includes a personal reference recommendation.

TUITION AND FEES

Correspondence courses are $129 per credit hour ($169 per course for auditing). Online courses are $169 per credit hour ($219 per course for auditing). Other expenses include textbooks, study guides, and supplemental materials.

FINANCIAL AID

Students seeking degrees through the World Wide Campus are eligible to apply for financial aid available under the University's Title IV agreement with the U.S. Department of Education. Students must be enrolled in a minimum of 6 credit hours per term to qualify for aid. Students who are entitled to receive veteran's educational benefits may receive assistance from the Department of Veterans Affairs, which has approved courses offered by the World Wide Campus.

APPLYING

Students may enroll at any time in courses or certificate programs offered by the World Wide Campus by simply completing an enrollment form. Those who desire an A.A. degree must apply and be accepted.

CONTACT

Kevin Mahaffy
Enrollment Manager
Taylor University World Wide Campus
1025 West Rudisill Boulevard
Fort Wayne, Indiana 46807-2197
Telephone: 219-456-2111 Ext. 32490
   800-845-3149 (toll-free)
Fax: 219-456-2118
E-mail: wwcampus@tayloru.edu
Web site: http://wwcampus.tayloru.edu

Texas Christian University

Cyberlearning

Fort Worth, Texas

Texas Christian University (TCU) is a major teaching and research university with the person-centered environment that typifies smaller colleges. The commitment that faculty members have to both effective teaching and research/scholarly work promotes learning amid an atmosphere of discovery. The University's student life programs encourage personal growth and individual achievement. TCU was founded in 1873 and today enrolls more than 7,000 students from every state and many other countries. TCU's programs lead to bachelor's, master's, and doctoral degrees. The University is accredited by the Southern Association of Colleges and Schools; many of its programs also hold separate accreditation in their area of emphasis.

DISTANCE LEARNING PROGRAM

Initially, the goal of the TCU online program was to compliment the residential undergraduate experience. This changed with the introduction of two online graduate programs, which were initiated in the spring of 2000. Currently, over 800 students are served through the online curriculum, of which approximately 250 are graduate students.

DELIVERY MEDIA

Course materials, student-student and student-faculty discussions, and exams are all accessible through the Internet. Students need access to the Internet, with a connection and equipment that meets the minimum eCollege.com specifications. Students communicate with their colleagues and professors through threaded discussions and chat rooms. Readings and assignments are listed in an outline format. Exams are completed on line and e-mailed to the professor. In keeping with the TCU tradition of individualized attention, professors are also accessible through e-mail and telephone conversations.

All online courses are offered via the eCollege.com system.

PROGRAMS OF STUDY

The Master of Liberal Arts program is a multidisciplinary curriculum designed for individuals seeking to further their education in the general liberal arts. The M.L.A. degree is awarded upon successful completion of ten courses, four of which must be designated "Perspectives on Society." All course work can be obtained on line. M.L.A. courses strive to introduce interesting diverse subjects and are taught by many of TCU's finest instructors.

The Master of Science in Nursing Program is designed to educate clinical nurse specialists in adult health/medical-surgical nursing. Emerging Internet resources will allow teaching methodology and curriculum content to change in response to developments in medical research and information technology. Five introductory courses are currently being offered. The curriculum reaches 21 online courses in Spring of 2002. This program is especially beneficial to nurses who have been unable to advance their education because of geographical location or multiple schedules.

SPECIAL PROGRAMS

Distance learning courses are available to residential TCU students and to TCU students who are away from the campus either for a summer session or for a study-abroad program.

The Master of Science in Nursing is specifically designed to allow registered nurses to complete their degree while working full-time.

STUDENT SERVICES

Because all students in TCU distance education courses are "regular" TCU students, they have access to all TCU student services. Textbooks can be purchased on line at (bookstore@tcu.edu).

CREDIT OPTIONS

Credit for distance learning courses is awarded on the same basis as residential courses for TCU students.

FACULTY

Regular TCU faculty members are utilized for online instruction. These faculty members were chosen from a larger set, all of whom volunteered. The faculty members who are involved in online instruction receive university provided professional development in teaching methodology through technology.

ADMISSION

The M.L.A. Program requires successful completion of a bachelor's degree from an accredited college or university regardless of major or date of completion. No admission examination is required.

The Master of Science in Nursing Program will admit no more than 24 individuals per year, no more than 12 with a Associate of Arts degree, and no more than 12 with a Bachelor of Science in Nursing will be admitted. Interested students should email Dr. Kathleen Baldwin, Director of Graduate Studies, Harris School of Nursing at k.baldwin@tcu.edu.

TUITION AND FEES

Tuition and fees for distance learners is the same as that charged to residential students. For the 2000-01 academic year, tuition is $390 per credit hour. In addition, the University charges $60 per hour in fees.

FINANCIAL AID

Interested students should contact the TCU Office of Scholarships and Financial Aid at (www.fam.tcu.edu). Distance learners are eligible for the same aid consideration as residential students. Students in the M.L.A. Program currently receive a grant equivalent to 25 percent of the tuition for each course taken. Graduate nursing students are also eligible for tuition grants.

APPLYING

Information regarding TCU online programs can be found at (www. tcuglobal.edu). M.L.A. information can be obtained at (http://enterprise. is.tcu.edu/~yarbrough/mlahome. htm). Students interested in obtaining information regarding the Master of Science in Nursing should contact: Dr. Kathleen M. Baldwin at k.baldwin@tcu.edu.

CONTACT

Dr. Leo Munson
Associate Vice Chancellor for Academic Support
TCU Box 297024
Forth Worth, Texas 76129
Telephone: 817-257-7104
Fax: 817-257-7484
E-mail: l.munson@tcu.edu

Texas Tech University

Division of Outreach and Extended Studies

Lubbock, Texas

Created by legislative action in 1923, Texas Tech University (TTU) is a four-year research university composed of seven colleges (Agricultural Sciences, Architecture, Arts and Sciences, Business Administration, Education, Engineering, and Human Sciences), the School of Law, and the Graduate School. Having a residential enrollment of approximately 24,000 students each year, Texas Tech University is accredited by the Southern Association of Colleges and Schools and forty other accrediting organizations.

The mission of Texas Tech University is to provide the highest standard of excellence in higher education while pursuing continuous quality improvement, fostering the intellectual and personal development of students, stimulating the greatest degree of meaningful research, and supporting faculty and staff members in satisfying those who are served by the University.

DISTANCE LEARNING PROGRAM

Since 1927, Texas Tech has offered courses at a distance, first as print-based courses and more recently as Web-based courses. The mission of distance learning at Texas Tech University is to provide high-quality educational experiences without geographic or temporal boundaries for academic credit, personal enrichment, and professional development opportunities. Each year, Texas Tech serves more than 65,000 students in its distance learning courses; students enrolled last year from each of the fifty states and sixteen other countries.

DELIVERY MEDIA

Texas Tech University offers courses at a distance as traditional print-based courses or via the World Wide Web. All course offerings are asynchronous and students use a variety of technologies, such as fax, e-mail, and the Internet, to submit their assignments and interact with professors.

PROGRAMS OF STUDY

Texas Tech University offers college courses for various academic areas of study. Credits earned are placed on the student's official Texas Tech University transcript.

The Bachelor of General Studies degree program in the College of Arts and Sciences is flexible and adaptable. The program is designed so that the three areas of concentration create a coherent program of study based on a unifying intellectual interest or professional goal.

Extended Studies at Texas Tech University offers certificate programs that are designed to recognize achievement in developing a level of proficiency in work-related skills or expertise. Successful completion of a certificate program helps students enhance skills, prepare for a promotion, or enter into a new career. Each certificate program consists of a series of courses that are designed to meet specific goals and objectives in a particular professional area of study. Courses may be taken individually or applied toward completion of the certificate. Students must indicate their intent to participate in a complete cer-

tificate program at the time of registration for a particular course.

The Effective Employee Supervision Certificate Program is designed for students who work as supervisors, individuals who have recently accepted supervisory responsibilities, and supervisors who would like to brush up on particular skills.

The Effective Human Resource Management Certificate Program provides a comprehensive and practical course of study in the major areas of human resource management and is of benefit to the experienced human resource professional as well as newcomers to the field. It helps students to prepare for the Human Resource Institute's National Certification Examination or the Professional and Senior Professional in Human Resources (PHR and SPHR) accreditation.

In the Medical Spanish for Health Care Professionals Certificate Program, students learn the basic conversational skills required for effective communication with Spanish-speaking patients. These courses have been designed for health-care professionals. Areas of study focus on learning the specialized Spanish medical vocabulary required to diagnose medical problems, obtain family history, provide medical advice, give instructions/directions, and understand the patient.

STUDENT SERVICES

Texas Tech University's Extended Studies is known for its high-quality service to students. Counselors are available by phone, fax, mail, or e-mail to assist students with course choices. Student representatives work with each student to process enrollments, track course progress, handle examination requests, and report grades. Textbooks and other materials may be purchased from the Outreach and Extended Studies Bookstore.

CREDIT OPTIONS

Texas Tech University distance learning college credit or CEU credit courses are recorded on Texas Tech University transcripts, depending on the particular course. Academic course credits are transferable to any other institution with the receiving institution's approval. Course syllabi are available on the TTU Web site (listed below) to help determine equivalency at other institutions.

FACULTY

Texas Tech University faculty members teaching distance education courses meet the same high standards as other faculty members at Texas Tech University in order to ensure that all students receive a high-quality education. Fifty-one Texas Tech University faculty members teach for Extended Studies; 65 percent of the faculty members hold terminal degrees.

ADMISSION

Students may register for most Texas Tech University courses at a distance without being admitted to the University.

Students who wish to be admitted to the Bachelor of General Studies degree program at a distance are considered for admission on the basis of graduation from an accredited high school, transfer from an accredited college, or entrance examination. The completed application, SAT or ACT test scores, and other applicable qualifying factors constitute the basis upon which eligibility is considered. The records of students who do not meet the assured admission criteria are reviewed in order to evaluate other factors that could predict success at Texas Tech University. Records are reviewed in a holistic manner by a committee of faculty members, staff members, and student representatives.

TUITION AND FEES

University credit courses offered through Extended Studies cost $80 per credit hour plus a $25 administrative charge and the cost of textbooks. Costs are the same for in-state and out-of-state students. The cost of certificate programs varies. Students should visit the TTU Web site (listed below) for a current listing of certificate programs. The costs of course materials vary by course. A $50 application fee is required for students applying to the external degree programs.

FINANCIAL AID

Financial aid opportunities are available to distance learning students for college-level courses, including Federal Stafford Student Loans. Texas Tech University's distance learning programs are approved for Veterans Administration educational benefits. For more information on financial aid, students should contact a TTU financial aid adviser at 800-MY-COURSE Ext. 230 (800-692-6877, toll-free).

APPLYING

Students may enroll in any college credit course or certificate programs for which they are qualified. The appropriate applications, processing fees, and transcripts (for degree program only) from all high schools and colleges attended should be submitted to Extended Studies, Texas Tech University, 6901 South Quaker Avenue, Lubbock, Texas 79413.

Applications are accepted at any time. Students applying for the degree program at a distance should be advised that the review process could take several weeks. Decision notifications are mailed once the review process is complete. Falsification or omission of the requested application information voids admission to Texas Tech University.

CONTACT
Ariel Fernández, Assistant Director/Advisor
Bettye Griggs, Director of Student Services
Extended Studies
Texas Tech University
6901 South Quaker Avenue
Lubbock, Texas 79413
Telephone: 800-692-6877 (toll-free)
Fax: 806-742-7277
E-mail: distlearn@ttu.edu
Web site: http://www.dce.ttu.edu

Thomas Edison State College

Trenton, New Jersey

Thomas Edison State College provides adults with access to some of the best choices in higher education. Cited as "one of the brighter stars of higher learning" by the New York Times *and identified by* Forbes Magazine *as one of the top twenty colleges and universities in the nation in the use of technology to create learning opportunities for adults, Thomas Edison State College provides quality higher education to adults wherever they live and work. Founded in 1972, Thomas Edison State College enables adult learners to complete associate, baccalaureate, and master's degrees through distance learning and the assessment of knowledge they already have.*

Accredited by the Commission on Higher Education of the Middle States Association of Colleges and Schools, Thomas Edison State College offers a distinguished academic program for the self-motivated adult learner.

DISTANCE LEARNING PROGRAM

Thomas Edison State College offers one of the most highly regarded, comprehensive distance learning programs in the United States. Adults can choose from more than 100 distance learning courses, including on-line classes. Students also take tests and submit portfolios to demonstrate and earn credit for college-level knowledge they already have and transfer credits earned at other accredited institutions.

DELIVERY MEDIA

Distance education courses are provided through several venues, including Guided Study at home or work; the On-Line Computer Classroom®; and Contract Learning, a one-on-one learning experience with individual faculty members. Interactive television classrooms with satellite downlinks and cable access are also utilized.

PROGRAMS OF STUDY

Thomas Edison State College offers fifteen associate, baccalaureate, and master's degrees in more than 100 major areas of study. Degrees offered include Associate in Applied Science; Associate in Science in Management;

Associate in Science in Applied Science and Technology; Associate in Arts; Associate in Applied Science in Radiologic Technology; Associate in Science in Natural Science and Mathematics; Associate in Science in Public and Social Services; Bachelor of Arts; Bachelor of Science in Applied Science and Technology; Bachelor of Science in Business Administration; Bachelor of Science in Health Sciences, a joint degree program with the University of Medicine and Dentistry of New Jersey (UMDNJ) School of Health Related Professions (SHRP); Bachelor of Science in Human Services; and Bachelor of Science in Nursing.

In addition, the College offers the on-line Master of Science in Management (M.S.M.) degree. The M.S.M. degree serves employed adults who have professional experience in the management field. The program integrates the theory and practice of management as it applies to diverse organizations. A specialized track in project management is also available. The College has developed a Master of Arts in Professional Studies degree. This degree, first offered in fall 2000, enables learners to study and apply the liberal arts to their professional lives.

SPECIAL PROGRAMS

Thomas Edison State College's Military Degree Completion Program (MDCP) serves military personnel worldwide. The MDCP was developed to accommodate the special needs of military personnel whose location, relocation, and time constraints make traditional college attendance difficult, if not impossible. The program allows students to engage in a degree program wherever they may be stationed. The program allows for maximum credit for military training and education.

The College has a unique program designed specifically for community college students. The Degree Pathways Program allows community college students or graduates to complete a baccalaureate degree at home, in the workplace, or at their local two-year college. Degree Pathways lets students at community colleges make a smooth transition directly into a Thomas Edison State College baccalaureate program by transferring up to 80 credits from a community college toward the 120 credits needed for a bachelor's degree.

The program coordinated support in admissions, academic programming, advisement, registration, and the sharing of technologies. Once students complete their first year at a community college or a minimum of 30 credits, they are eligible for the Degree Pathways Program. Students may continue to take classes and use technologies available at their community college as they move toward completing their associate degree and/or baccalaureate degree.

Credit-earning options for nondegree students benefit individuals who would like to earn credit through examinations, Portfolio Assessment, and Thomas Edison State College courses. Students may do so by paying the appropriate fee for these programs. An application to the College is not required to take advantage of these nondegree, credit-earning options.

Credit Banking is for students who wish to document college-level learning. Credit Banking is for individuals who wish to consolidate college-level work into a Thomas Edison State College transcript. Credits transcribed under the Credit Banking program may or may not apply to a degree program at Thomas Edison State College.

The College grants credit for current professional licenses or certificates that have been approved for credit by the College's Academic Council. Students who have earned one of the licenses or certificates approved for credit must submit notarized copies of the license or certificate and current renewal card, if appropriate, to receive credit. A list of licenses and certificates approved for credit can be found in the College's Undergraduate Prospectus.

STUDENT SERVICES

Academic advisement is provided to enrolled students by the College's Advisement Center, which assists students in integrating their learning style, background, and educational goals with the credit-earning methods and programs available. Students can access advisement through phone and in-person appointments or through the Advisement Phone Center; they also have 24-hour access through fax and e-mail.

CREDIT OPTIONS

Students have the opportunity to earn degrees through traditional and nontraditional methods. These methods take into consideration personal needs and interests while ensuring both breadth and depth of knowledge within the degree program. Thomas Edison State College offers one of the most highly regarded, comprehensive distance learning programs in the United States. Students use several convenient methods of meeting degree requirements, depending upon their individual learning styles and preferences.

Each undergraduate degree requires work in general education, major area of study, and elective subjects. Students are encouraged to work in conjunction with one of the College's knowledgeable program advisers to develop a program plan that best meets individual needs, goals, and interests.

FACULTY

There are more than 500 consulting faculty members at Thomas Edison State College. Drawn from other highly regarded colleges and universities, consulting faculty members provide many services, including assessment of prior knowledge and mentoring.

ADMISSION

Adults seeking an associate, baccalaureate, or master's degree who are high school graduates are eligible to become a student. There are no tests required for admission. There are no on-campus requirements. A computer is not required to complete an undergraduate degree. A computer is only required to take On-Line Computer Classroom® courses. Once a student is enrolled in a specific degree program, an evaluator determines the number of credits the student has already earned and fits those into the degree program requirements. Orientation is not required.

TUITION AND FEES

Because the College uses efficient distance learning technologies, Thomas Edison State College's tuition and fees are among the most affordable in the nation. Undergraduate students may choose one of two payment plans: a comprehensive fee paid annually, which includes enrollment, technology services, courses, testing, and portfolio assessment; or the per-service fee, which enables students to pay for services as they use them. A complete listing of tuition and fees is included in the College's information packet.

FINANCIAL AID

Thomas Edison State College participates in a number of federal and state aid programs. Eligible students may receive Pell Grants or Federal Education Loans, such as the Subsidized Stafford Loan and the Unsubsidized Stafford Loan, for courses offered by the College. Eligible New Jersey residents may also tap a variety of state grant and loan programs. Students may use state aid to meet all or part of their college costs, provided they are taking at least 12 credits per semester.

Thomas Edison State College Financing Plans through First Union Bank offer students the option of spreading payment of fees over a number of years, if necessary. Students may borrow as little as $1000 or as much as $15,000.

Detailed information about the financial aid process can be found in the financial aid packet, which is available from the Office of Financial Aid and Veterans' Services. To receive this information, students should contact the office (E-mail: finaid@ tesc.edu or phone number listed below).

APPLYING

Students may apply to Thomas Edison State College any day of the year by mail or fax or through the College's Web site. The Office of Admissions assists potential applicants in determining whether Thomas Edison State College suits their particular academic goals.

CONTACT

Director of Admissions
Thomas Edison State College
101 West State Street
Trenton, New Jersey 08608-1176
Telephone: 609-984-1150
Fax: 609-984-8447
E-mail: admissions@tesc.edu
Web site: http://www.tesc.edu

Tompkins Cortland Community College

Distance Learning

Dryden, New York

Tompkins Cortland Community College (TC3) is a fully accredited public institution with a long tradition of serving the educational needs of a diverse population. Tompkins Cortland Community College was founded in 1968 by the governing bodies of Cortland and Tompkins Counties. It is accredited by the Middle States Association of Colleges and Schools and is one of thirty 2-year community colleges in the sixty-four-campus State University of New York (SUNY) system.

Tompkins Cortland Community College continues to expand its online course offerings to serve its student body, which is composed of working people who wish to add to their knowledge and students seeking a two-year degree or looking to build a foundation before transferring to a four-year college. Many of the 2,700 students have full-time jobs and families, so distance learning is crucial. Most courses are offered through the SUNY Learning Network, and the rest are offered by TC3 itself.

DISTANCE LEARNING PROGRAM

Committed to innovative instruction for a wide range of students, TC3 has been offering courses for many years at its main campus in Dryden and its extension centers in Cortland and Ithaca. That commitment has grown to include online (asynchronous) courses: the College has more than fifty scheduled for the fall 2000 semester, a number that continues to increase. TC3 also offers several synchronous courses. The online courses span several disciplines, including English, hospitality, paralegal studies, and psychology. Most recent course offerings include several in ESOL, with live audio. Three degree programs, paralegal studies, hotel and restaurant management, and chemical dependency studies–counseling can be obtained completely on line. All online courses may be taken by themselves or in conjunction with classroom-based courses.

DELIVERY MEDIA

Online courses are designed to offer close interaction with instructors who ask students to read equivalent course materials and write papers or do research as students do in a classroom. Students use personal computers connected to the Internet via the World Wide Web to receive course content and interact with the instructor and fellow students. They must have access to a graphic browser such as Netscape or Microsoft Internet Explorer.

Synchronous courses connect students in geographically separate classrooms with an instructor and some students at the "near" site (often the Dryden campus) by using high-speed digital phone lines, live video, and enhanced audio.

PROGRAMS OF STUDY

Three of TC3's Associate in Applied Science (A.A.S.) degrees can be obtained completely on line through the SUNY Learning Network: the paralegal studies program, the hotel and restaurant management program, and the chemical dependency studies–counseling program.

The paralegal studies program can be completed in either two or three semesters if students have previous college credit. It involves 10 credits of English, 20–22 credits of paralegal studies (subjects include law, ethics, estate planning, and litigation procedure), 7 credits of business, and an internship and seminar of 2 to 4 credits. Students may transfer to bachelor's degree programs.

The hotel and restaurant management program involves 13 credits in business and economics, 24 credits in management studies such as food services and marketing, 7 credits of English, and a 3-credit summer cooperative work experience. This program is designed for students who wish to seek employment after earning their associate degree. Students may also transfer to a four-year degree program.

The chemical dependency studies–counseling program includes 120 hours of field work and provides the clock hours needed by the New York State Office of Alcoholism and Substance Abuse for certified counselors.

SPECIAL PROGRAMS

TC3's Business Development and Training Center offers a selection of services for business and staff development needs, with hands-on experience in training programs for industry, government, small businesses, and nonprofit agencies. One of its features is Education To Go, which offers workshops designed to be accessed from home or office. Education To Go offerings include such topics as computer skills on either Macintosh or PC, the design of Web sites, and JavaScript. Students must enroll through Education To Go's Web site (http://www.ed2go.com/

TC3), which describes course syllabi, procedures, and contact information.

STUDENT SERVICES

Distance learners have access to academic advising, career advising, financial aid information, and TC3's online service, IQ Student, which allows students to check their bills, grades, and course schedules and descriptions.

CREDIT OPTIONS

Transfer credit is granted for course work completed with a minimum grade of 2.0 (C) at accredited colleges. Credit is accepted only for those courses applicable to the program in which a student is enrolled. TC3 accepts advanced placement credit for tests taken through the College Entrance Examination Board. The College also awards credit for tests from the College Level Examination Program (CLEP).

FACULTY

There are 65 full-time faculty members and a varying number of part-time faculty members at TC3. Fifteen percent have doctorates or other terminal academic degrees.

ADMISSION

The principal requirement for admission is a high school transcript and/or copies of the General Equivalency Diploma (GED) test scores. Transfer students need to provide an additional transcript from colleges attended. Students who plan to mix distance courses with on-campus courses must be immunized against measles, mumps, and rubella, by state law. Students who do not have a high school diploma or GED must meet additional criteria.

TUITION AND FEES

For 2000–01, part-time tuition is approximately $100 per credit hour for New York State residents and $200 for out-of-state residents. Full-time tuition is approximately $1300 per semester for state residents and $2600 for out-of-state residents. Out-of-state residents pay the lower in-state tuition rate for Web courses. All tuition and fees are subject to change.

FINANCIAL AID

Distance learners are eligible for federal financial aid such as the Pell Grant, the Supplemental Educational Opportunity Grant, and Subsidized and Unsubsidized Stafford Loans.

New York State residents enrolled full-time are eligible for the Tuition Assistance Program (TAP). State residents also qualify for the Vietnam Veterans Tuition Award program. The College offers aid and loans through the TC3 Foundation and the Service Tradition program, which honors students who are active community volunteers.

TC3 awards $8 million in aid each year through its own resources and state and federal sources. Seventy-five percent of its degree-seeking students receive financial aid.

APPLYING

TC3 has a rolling admissions procedure. Applications are accepted in person at the main campus or extension centers by mail or by fax. An application form can be obtained by calling the Office of Admission at 607-844-6580. A course registration form can be obtained from the registrar at 607-844-6562 and submitted in person by mail or by fax. If the course is offered through SUNY Learning Network, the registration form can also be found on line at the SUNY Learning Network (http://sln.suny.edu/sln).

CONTACT

Bob Yavits
Tompkins Cortland Community College
170 North Street
P.O. Box 139
Dryden, New York 13053-0139
Telephone: 607-844-8211 Ext. 4357
Fax: 607-844-6541
E-mail: yavitsr@suny.tccc.edu
Web site: http://www.TC3.edu

Touro University International

Distance Learning Program

Los Alamitos, California

Touro University International (TUI) is a newly developed campus branch of Touro College, New York, which was founded in 1971. TUI is accredited by the Commission on Institutions of Higher Education (CHE) of the Middle States Association of Colleges and Schools(MSA), as part of the scope of accreditation of Touro College.

TUI offers all of its programs via the Internet, employing the latest technology and innovative live interactive delivery methodology.

TUI is committed to the high quality of its pedagogical model, its family, and its support services in all programs. It is a worldwide university that is open 24 hours a day, 365 days a year. No matter where in the world students are, they can learn conveniently without disrupting work or personal life.

DISTANCE LEARNING PROGRAM

All TUI classes are taught via the Internet with no residency requirements. The student-centered teaching model has two major elements: modular case-based learning and the cyber classroom. These essential elements are part of every module of every course.

DELIVERY MEDIA

The cyber classroom approach includes the use of multimedia for academic transactions and interactive collaboration (live exchange with the professor and with peers). The multimedia approach includes audio and video-on-demand, Internet links, Power Point presentations, and live conferences among students and between the professors and the students. This allows students to work as a team with fellow students from around the world. The case-based learning provides real-world application to each topic.

PROGRAM OF STUDY

TUI currently has two colleges. They are the College of Business Administration and the College of Health Sciences. The College of Business Administration offers three degrees including the Bachelor of Science in Business Administration (120 semester credits), with concentrations in international finance, Internet auditing, general management, e-commerce, information technology, health care management, hospitality and tourism, and degree completion specially designed for students with an A.A. or A.S. degree. Also offered is the Masters of Science in Business Administration (32 semester credits for students with business-related undergraduate degree) with concentrations in international finance, general management, information technology, and e-commerce. There is also the Doctor of Philosophy degree in Business Administration (40 semester credits of course work plus a research dissertation). The concentration depends on the candidate's specific research interests.

The College of Health Sciences offers three degrees. There is the Bachelor of Science in Health Sciences (124 semester credits) with concentrations in health education, health care management, and professional degree completion; the Master of Science in Health Sciences (40 semester credits) with concentrations in international health, health care management, and forensic examination. The Doctor of Philosophy in Health Sciences (40 semester credits) is offered with specializations in international health educator/researcher/practitioner, occupational therapy educator/researcher/practitioner, forensic educator/researcher, and physical therapy educator/researcher/practitioner.

STUDENT SERVICES

Touro University International maintains five specific student services. Pre-admission advising assists potential students with preparatory academic advisement, enrollment in the best combination of classes, and addressing any other concerns of the student prior to entering Touro University International. Pre-admission English competency evaluation is provided for students whose first language is not English, who do not meet the TUI's English competency requirements, or feel that they do not possess adequate English skills. Post-admission advising assists students with selection of courses, sequencing of courses, assists with developing study habits and academic progress, and addressing any other concerns of the student. Information technology assistance provides students with any assistance necessary to insure that students will have access to all of the information technology features of Touro University International courses. The Information Technology department will also provide any installation and configuration assistance necessary for any student. Library resource assistance is provided by staff of Touro University International via e-mail, to assist all students in the use of all library facilities—especially those on the Internet.

TUI provides financial assistance under three Federal programs that are available to citizens and eligible non-citizens of the United States.

FACULTY

All TUI faculty members hold doctoral degrees and have experience in their respective fields in addition to having sound academic teaching, research, and dissertation advisement records. These exceptional full-time faculty members teach nearly all TUI classes. TUI also has access to the highest level of faculty expertise in each field through guest lecturers and visiting faculty via the cyber classroom delivery mode.

ADMISSION

Students enroll throughout the year at TUI. TUI offers four sessions per year with each session lasting 12 weeks. Sessions begin in March, June, September, and December. All TUI classes are four semester credits. A full courseload consists of two courses per session, which is 32 semester credits per year, enabling students to continue with family and work life.

The Office of Admissions assists potential students with determining their fit to the program on the basis of past academic performance and educational goals. For specific details on each degree program students may visit the Web site at the Internet address listed below.

TUITION AND FEES

TUI's tuition is one of the most affordable in the nation for the educational value. Tuition is $200 per semester credit for B.S. degrees, $300 per semester credit for M.S. degrees, and $500 per semester credit for Ph.D. degrees. Scholarships, graduate assistantships, and financial aid are available. Students should contact TUI registration for details.

Active-duty military, retired military, military dependents, and civilian military employees receive special tuition rates through TUI's DANTES agreement. Students should contact their base or post educational officer for contact TUI for details.

APPLYING

Applications are available online at the Internet address listed below. Applications are accepted year round. A complete application package is required two weeks prior to the start of the semester. TUI responds to applications within twenty-four business hours of receiving completed materials.

CONTACT

College of Business Administration
10542 Calle Lee, Suite 102
Los Alamitos, California 90720
Telephone: 714-816-0366
Fax: 714-816-0367
E-mail: info@tourou.edu
Web site: http://www.tourou.edu
College of Health Sciences
4332 Cerritos Avenue, Suite 207
Los Alamitos, California 90720
Telephone: 714-226-9480
Fax: 714-226-9844
E-mail: info@tourou.edu
Web site: http://www.tourou.edu

The Tri-State Community College Training Consortium Online

TriStateOnline.org

Quincy, Illinois

TristateOnline.org courses are delivered and administered by the Distance Education offices of Moberly Area Community College (MACC), Southeastern Community College (SCC), and John Wood Community College (JWCC).

Based on the philosophy that every individual deserves the chance to succeed in education, three community colleges with common boundaries along the Mississippi River are pooling their expertise to provide vital information-age training and distance education opportunities. This multistate cooperative online degree program is the area's first. Beyond their geographic proximity, the three colleges share a common focus on education that speaks to the practical needs of individuals and community. Each institution brings a proven track record in higher education: JWCC was founded in 1974, MACC in 1927, and SCC in 1920. As each school continues to serve its community with traditional on-site activities, community is redefined as technology-enhanced distance learning opportunities gain an increasing share of services available. All three institutions are fully accredited by the North Central Association of Colleges and Schools.

DISTANCE LEARNING PROGRAM

Each college provides varied interactive distance education and Web-based learning opportunities. Together, the colleges address the need for an integrated curriculum that builds on the strengths of each college's faculty to provide an online degree curriculum that none of the individual institutions would be able to offer alone.

DELIVERY MEDIA

Courses for the consortium's online degree require minimal Internet hardware, and are compatible with current browsers and RealAudio/RealVideo plug-ins. Each of the colleges makes extensive use of classrooms with compressed and full-motion interactive television capabilities. Some classes are also available as broadcast telecourses, college by cassette, and independent study.

PROGRAMS OF STUDY

Currently, TriStateOnline offers the Associate of Applied Science degree in computer information systems (CIS) business decision support. Additional degrees will be available as the programs grow.

SPECIAL PROGRAMS

In addition to the CIS online degree, the consortium is planning additional online degree programs to include Associate of Arts and Associate of Science degrees. Further occupational programs such as radio frequency communications, fire science and agricultural science are expected soon. TriStateOnline is committed to timely response to specialized training and education needs of its community and actively reviews market demand for new programs. As each school has demonstrated in the past, active teaching and rich interactions with students are highly valued and can be counted on in the online experience.

STUDENT SERVICES

As part of the consortial effort, each TriStateOnline college is committed to providing student advising, computer access, library access, technical assistance, test proctoring, and providing news and information of distance education opportunities. Regardless of the origin of the course, the community college district in which the student live is his or her home college where all student services should be provided.

CREDIT OPTIONS

Sixty-four credit hours are required for the CIS applied science degree. Students draw from the TriStateOnline course list to satisfy the requirements of their own home college degree program. Within the tristate consortium, all courses are considered to have originated by the home college, so no transfer is required. As more courses are added, more degree choices will become available.

FACULTY

One third of the combined 155 full-time faculty members are personally involved in delivering distance learning instruction. More than 80 percent of the TriStateOnline colleges' faculty possess a master's degree or higher.

ADMISSION

Students are admitted to one of these colleges and follow their home college guidelines for admission and entry assessment. The home college for residents of the tristate region is the college in the state in which the residents live. Students outside Illinois, Iowa, or Missouri may choose any one of the three schools as their home college.

TUITION AND FEES

Online courses offered by the tristateonline.org colleges in partnership with eCollege.com are available at $80 per credit hour. No supplemental fees are currently assessed beyond the cost of textbooks or course-specific materials.

FINANCIAL AID

TriStateOnline students may be eligible for Federal Pell Grants, Supplemental Educational Opportunity Grants, Federal Work-Study, and Stafford Loans. State programs vary by state and may be found listed at these Web links: http://www.jwcc. edu/students/financial_aid/default. htm, http://www.macc.cc.mo.us/~ finaid/, or http://www.secc.cc.ia.us/ financial/finindex.html. Combined, the three schools awarded almost $10 million in financial aid in the 1998–99 school year to more than one half of their students. (MACC $2,916,302 to 72.5 percent; JWCC $3,418,212 to 39 percent; and SCC $3,487,138 to 52 percent.)

APPLYING

Students should complete the "Is online learning for me?" self-assessment at the Web site http:/www. tristateonline.org. Each college has its own application process that requires an admissions information form (online or paper), a high school diploma or GED score, and an orientation. Degree-bound students may be required to complete an on-site assessment test.

CONTACT

Mark McNett
John Wood Community College
150 S. 48th Street
Quincy, Illinois 62301
Telephone: 217-224-6500 (collect)
Fax: 217-224-4208
E-mail: help@tristateonline.org
Web sites: http://www.tristateonline.org
http://www.jwcc.edu

Moberly Area Community College
101 College Avenue
Moberly, Missouri 65270-1304
Telephone: 660-263-4110
800-622-2070 (toll-free)
E-mail: info@macc.cc.mo.us
Web site: http://www.macc.cc.mo.us

Southeastern Community College
Distance Learning Department
1015 South Gear Avenue
West Burlington, Iowa 52655-0605
Telephone: 319-752-2731
800-828-7322 (toll-free)
Fax: 319-752-4957
Web site: http://www.secc.cc.ia.us

Troy State University

Distance Learning Center

Troy, Alabama

Since its founding in 1887, Troy State University has been recognized for the quality of its academic programs and its focus on the individual student. The University is dedicated to the preparation of students in a variety of fields in the arts and sciences, fine arts, business, communication, applied science, nursing, and allied health sciences, as well as to its historic role in the preparation of teachers. The administrators, faculty, staff, and students of the university, through a system of shared governance, are committed to excellence in education. A major commitment exists to provide undergraduate and graduate education for the national and international community, especially for mature students, not only by traditional means of delivery, but also by technological means. Additional information about the University may be found at its Web site: http://www.troyst.edu.

DISTANCE LEARNING PROGRAM

The distance learning program at Troy State University is an important and growing part of the mission of the University. A variety of different courses are offered including four complete graduate degrees that may be completed online. Along with personalized attention from faculty members, the TSU distance learning program is supported by the Distance Learning Center in Troy, Alabama.

DELIVERY MEDIA

Distance Learning Center course offerings are mostly Web-interactive. Students may complete course work on an anytime/anyplace basis throughout the world. Additional distance learning courses of Troy State University are also provided using Internet, satellite, cable TV, videotape, and microwave delivery systems.

PROGRAMS OF STUDY

There are currently four master's degree programs and a variety of individual courses offered by the Distance Learning Center. Complete details can be found by visiting the

Center's Web site listed in the Contact section. Degree programs are briefly described below.

The Masters of Public Administration degree at Troy State University is delivered via the Internet. The degree consists of seven core and three electives in the ten course program with comprehensive examinations, and within the twelve course option without comprehensive examinations but a final practicum course. A number of three course concentrations are available.

The Master of Science in International Relations degree program is designed to offer the graduates of diversified undergraduate programs an opportunity to obtain proficiency in international relations. Topics include: foreign policy analysis, defense and security policy, comparative politics, regional and state specific studies, international economics, and specific instruments of international affairs such as international organizations and international law.

The Master of Science in Human Resources Management (MSHRM) is a professional degree designed to offer graduates of diversified undergraduate programs an opportunity to obtain a proficiency in human re-

sources management skills. This degree program stresses fundamental problem-solving, technical, and decision-making skills, communication and interpersonal competencies, and knowledge critical for success in today's and tomorrow's, entrepreneurial and business organizations.

The Master of Science in Criminal Justice is designed to provide qualified students with an interdisciplinary graduate level education in criminal justice. It provides the student with knowledge for professional entry, advancement, or enhancement in the Criminal Justice career field, or entry into advanced studies.

SPECIAL PROGRAMS

The Troy State Distance Learning Center is a part of University College. The University College component of TSU is unique to Alabama universities, as it provides a global focus to TSU's routine operations. University College sites span from Guam to Guantanamo Bay, Cuba, giving meaning to the phrase "the sun never sets on TSU." Additional information about the University's programs may be found at its Web site listed in the Contact section.

STUDENT SERVICES

TSU is committed to providing a wide range of learning opportunities for a diverse student population. Students come to TSU with hopes and high expectations. Faculty can make a difference in the lives of students and help them to meet their expectations and expand their understanding of themselves and their world.

CREDIT OPTIONS

The Distance Learning Center offers credits through distance learning that are recorded on a Troy State University transcript in the same manner as credits earned in on-campus courses. Most students will enroll as degree seeking students, but there is the opportunity for students to take individual courses that may apply to degrees at other institutions. Students should contact the Distance Learning Center student services group to learn more about transient authorizations or other credit opportunities.

FACULTY

All distance learning faculty meet the standards set forth by the Southern Association of Colleges and Schools, the State of Alabama, and the review agencies of the various TSU Colleges. Faculty members are full-time or adjunct members of the department granting the course credit.

ADMISSION

Admission to TSU distance learning programs is the same as the criteria for any on-campus student. Interested students should access the Web site listed below for more information.

TUITION AND FEES

Current tuition and fees are subject to change and are published on the Web site liated below. For the 2000–01 academic year, undergraduate credit is $110 per credit hour, plus a distance learning fee of $50 per distance education course. Graduate credit is $250 per credit hour, with no additional fees, offered only through the main campus in Troy, Alabama. There is no difference between in-state and out-of-state tu-

ition for the Center's basic graduate programs, but students should access the Web site for differential pricing for undergraduate and some graduate special programs.

FINANCIAL AID

Troy State University offers a comprehensive program of financial assistance for students pursuing degrees. The Financial Aid Office at Troy State University helps students secure the necessary funds for education.

APPLYING

Students apply for admission and register for course via the Distance Learning Center Web site listed below. The site provides complete details regarding application and registration requirements.

CONTACT

Student Services
Distance Learning Center
Troy State University
Troy, Alabama 36082
Telephone: 334-670-3976
Fax: 334-670-5679
E-mail: tsulearn@trojan.troyst.edu
Web site: http://tsulearn.net

Tufts University

The Fletcher School of Law and Diplomacy

Medford, Massachusetts

Established by Tufts University with the cooperation of Harvard University in 1933, the Fletcher School was conceived in the midst of the Great Depression to serve as an act of hope in a time of despair and to give a boost to internationalism in a time of isolationism. Today, as the senior graduate school of international affairs in the United States, the School continues to adapt to meet the demands of a world in which the only constant is change. The primary aim of the Fletcher School is the same as it was when conceived by its founders: to offer a broad program of professional education in international affairs to a select group of graduate students committed to maintaining the stability and prosperity of a complex, challenging, and increasingly global society.

DISTANCE LEARNING PROGRAM

The Fletcher School launched a one-year combined residential and Internet-mediated master's degree program in international affairs in July 2000. Like Fletcher's traditional degree programs, the Global Master of Arts Program (GMAP) is offered to international affairs professionals employed in a wide variety of fields, including ministries and departments of national governments, the United Nations and other international organizations, nongovernmental organizations, international business, and the media. GMAP was specifically designed for mid- to high-level professionals who, for professional or personal reasons, are unable to take a full year off for a traditional residence-based program. Students in GMAP receive the hallmarks of a Fletcher education. The program provides the highest-quality professional education in international affairs and foster close student-faculty interaction while integrating participants into the Fletcher community. GMAP represents an enhanced learning experience by bringing students together via three 2-week intensive residency periods and by utilizing the extensive communication innovations provided by today's Internet-based technologies. Instruction is provided by Fletcher faculty members, and the class size is limited to 35.

DELIVERY MEDIA

GMAP provides students with a state-of-the-art IBM laptop computer that is preprogrammed with electronic seminars, lectures, and simulation exercises. Through the use of the Internet, the program fosters close contact between students and faculty members. Students also are able to connect via the Internet to the library resources and staff of the School. The Internet itself provides electronic research capabilities to enhance the learning experience. Course materials are mailed prior to the beginning of each session, including books, articles, CD-ROMs, and other research materials.

PROGRAM OF STUDY

GMAP is the only combined distance learning and Internet-mediated learning program at the Fletcher School. The program was specifically designed for a small cohort of midcareer professionals who do not have the opportunity to take time off for educational pursuits, as well as to further the mission of the School to provide quality education in international affairs to professionals in the field. GMAP is a thirteen-month program beginning in early July and ending a year later in late July. The program is taught in three sessions, with three courses taught in the first two sessions and two courses are taught in the third session. GMAP requires completion of the eight required courses, proof of oral and reading proficiency in a second-language, submission of a satisfactory M.A. thesis, and an oral examination in the subject area of the thesis. The thesis represents work of a higher standard than would be expected of a term paper. The thesis project is determined in consultation with a supervising professor. The curriculum includes the following courses: international finance, international business and economic law, international technology: the Internet as a global innovation engine, crisis management in complex emergencies, international trade and investment, transnational social issues, international negotiations, and leadership and management. Besides the three 2-week residencies, the program requires thirty-one weeks of Internet-mediated learning, with an expected weekly commitment of 15 to 20 hours.

STUDENT SERVICES

The Fletcher School strives to promote a strong sense of community for all students and the Global Master of Arts Program is not an exception. GMAP is an interactive program between all participants, including faculty members, students and staff members. The School's technical staff is be available throughout the program. GMAP participants have access to online Fletcher School library resources and, while on campus, to all Tufts libraries. As graduates of the program, students have all of the privileges of alumni, including access to the career services job listings and alumni clubs worldwide. Alumni of the Fletcher School are provided with a permanent e-mail address.

CREDIT OPTIONS

The eight-course program is required to be taken through GMAP for a letter grade. There are no credit options.

FACULTY

The GMAP faculty has been selected from among the highly qualified faculty members of the Fletcher School. Because of the nature of the field of international affairs, GMAP faculty members not only have excellent teaching credentials but also have substantial practical experience in their field of expertise. The residential sessions foster a close hands-on

relationship with the GMAP faculty and, utilizing the technologies of the Internet, faculty members are able to maintain this close contact with GMAP students during the computer-mediated portion of the program.

ADMISSION

Applicants must have a minimum of seven years of professional experience and a bachelor's degree or its equivalent. All international applicants whose native language is not English must demonstrate strong language proficiency in English or submit the Test of English as a Foreign Language (TOEFL). All other degree candidates at the Fletcher School must pass an oral and written proficiency examination in a second language; therefore, it is important for applicants to have a minimum proficiency in a language other than English or a plan to obtain this skill prior to graduation.

TUITION AND FEES

The GMAP fee is a comprehensive fee that covers tuition, computer and

other equipment if deemed necessary, books and other research materials, and room and board at the required residencies. The program fee is $42,500. There is a $65 fee for the application.

FINANCIAL AID

The Fletcher School has a limited number of fellowships available. Applicants who would like to be considered for fellowships must submit a written request. Permanent residents or U.S. citizens may be eligible to apply for up to $18,500 under the Federal Stafford Loan Program. Eligibility for all federal loan programs is determined by the Tufts University Financial Aid Office after a review of the FAFSA (SAR) report.

APPLYING

The GMAP application requires submission of two statements, a resume, a letter of sponsorship, and a recommendation letter. The application can be downloaded from the Fletcher School Web site or may be obtained by contacting the GMAP office for hard copy materials.

CONTACT

Manager of Admissions
Global Master of Arts Program
The Fletcher School
Tufts University
160 Packard Avenue
Medford, Massachusetts 02155
Telephone: 617-627-2429
Fax: 617-627-3005
E-mail: fletcher-gmap@tufts.edu
Web site: fletcher.tufts.edu/gmap

Ulster County Community College

Online Associate in Science in Individual Studies (OASIS)

Stone Ridge, New York

Ulster County Community College is a comprehensive, two-year college sponsored by the county of Ulster and operated under the program of the State University of New York (SUNY). Its curricula and course offerings are registered with the New York State Department of Education, Office of Higher Education and the Profession, Cultural Education Center, Room 5815, Albany, New York 12330 (telephone: 518-474-5851).

The College is authorized by the Board of Regents of the University of the State of New York to confer the Associate in Arts, the Associate in Science, and the Associate in Applied Science degrees. In addition, the College offers career diploma and certificate programs. Within these programs, Ulster students have almost forty choices of major. More than 60 percent of Ulster's graduates transfer, while approximately 30 percent enter the world of work immediately upon graduation. Delivery of its academic programs is achieved through the efforts of an outstanding and dedicated faculty and staff.

Ulster is accredited by the Commission on Institutions of Higher Education of the Middle States Association of Colleges and Schools, 3624 Market Street, Philadelphia, Pennsylvania 19104 (telephone: 215-662-5606). The Commission on Institutions of Higher Education is an institutional accrediting agency recognized by the U.S. Department of Education and the Council for Higher Education Accreditation.

DISTANCE LEARNING PROGRAM

Ulster offers the Associate in Science in individual studies (OASIS) through the SUNY Learning Network. The SUNY Learning Network is composed of more than forty SUNY college and university campuses that offer hundreds of courses on line. Ulster and the SUNY Learning Network began to offer online courses in 1995. Since then, more than 5,000 students have enrolled in courses.

DELIVERY MEDIA

The SUNY Learning Network technology infrastructure is based on open systems and industry standards. Multiple Intel-based servers that are connected to the Internet are utilized. The servers run Microsoft Windows NT (version 4.0) and Lotus Domino (version 4.5.6.) The SUNY Learning Network also leverages SUNYNet—the award-winning SUNY-wide telecommunications network infrastructure. The instructional delivery method is asynchronous and utilizes e-mail and electronic bulletin boards to facilitate communication.

To participate in the program, students must have graphical access to the World Wide Web and must use Netscape Navigator 3.0 or higher or Internet Explorer 4.0 as their Web browser. A working knowledge of the Internet is necessary.

PROGRAMS OF STUDY

Ulster is the degree-granting institution with the SUNY Learning Network. The courses to complete the program are available on line through the various campuses that comprise the network. Students who complete the program are awarded an Associate in Science (A.S.) degree in individual studies. This multipurpose liberal arts and science degree program enables students to plan a sequence of courses according to their individual needs and interests. The program allows students to combine career, professional, or technical courses with liberal arts courses or, if they wish, to concentrate in a particular area of liberal arts. The program has two components: the Liberal Arts Distribution and the Individual Studies Distribution. Academic advisers help students to plan their programs, and students may select courses from any of the more than forty campuses that make up the SUNY Learning Network. Course selections must be approved by the students' online academic advisers and be applicable to their programs. Specific criteria for completion of the degree is listed at the College's Web site (listed below).

SPECIAL PROGRAMS

In fall 1999, Ulster adopted a Student Success Model. Professional staff members serve as student success managers for first-year students. Student success managers guide students through the first two semesters of college to identify success skills that will help them achieve their educational goals. Ulster recognizes many nontraditional modes of learning, including credit for life experience and proficiency examinations. Students in the online program (OASIS) must meet a course requirement: a minimum of 30 credit-bearing semester hours of academic course work must be taken on line through the SUNY Learning Network, 6 credits of which must be selected from Ulster's course offerings.

STUDENT SERVICES

Distance learning students are able to complete the application and registration processes on line. Students matriculated in the online degree program are assigned an academic adviser, who works closely with each student to develop an individual educational plan. Career and transfer counseling are available on line as well as preenrollment screening for distance learners, which is accessible on Ulster's Web site.

CREDIT OPTIONS

Transfer students who wish to obtain a degree through distance learning may transfer up to 30 credits completed at an accredited institution. This may include applicable credits earned both in traditional college courses or in alternate modes, including CLEP exams. Ulster grants credit in accordance with the recommendations of the American Council on Education for certain courses listed in the national Program on Noncollegiate Sponsored Instruction (PONSI) and educational experiences in the armed forces. The cumulative GPA of all courses must be 2.0 or higher.

FACULTY

Faculty members who teach distance learning courses are considered experts in their fields and are dedicated leaders in distance education. Most faculty members have been responsible for developing and/or adapting their courses for online instruction.

ADMISSION

Applicants for admission must have earned a high school diploma or its equivalent to matriculate in programs of study at the College. Candidates for admission to OASIS follow the same admission criteria as those in traditional programs on campus. An admission checklist and information about the admission process is available on Ulster's Web site (under Getting Started at Ulster).

TUITION AND FEES

Students enrolling in the online program are charged a one-time matriculation/enrollment fee of $250 and a semester evaluation fee of $25. These fees are in addition to the per-credit or per-semester tuition and fees.

Students enrolled in the online program may select courses from the forty participating campuses. Tuition and fees are paid to the individual college or university each semester. Tuition for SUNY colleges and universities vary, and students should consult each campus to determine the proper tuition and fees for their courses. The tuition for full-time study at Ulster for residents of the county and New York State residents who provide a certificate of residence from their county is $1235 per semester.

All other full-time students pay $2470 per semester. Part-time residents (taking fewer than 12 credit hours) pay $89 per credit; this also applies to residents of other New York counties who provide a certificate of residence. All other part-time students pay $178 per credit hour.

FINANCIAL AID

Financial aid and student loans are available for the online program for students who meet the eligibility requirements. It is possible to take courses from several different colleges in one semester, thus making determination for aid eligibility more complex. Students are encouraged to work closely with Ulster's online financial aid adviser (e-mail: brownm@sunyulster.edu).

APPLYING

Candidates for admission to the online degree program should complete the SUNY application, listing Ulster as their choice of campus and indicating the academic major code 0688. The application is free if mailed to the Office of Admission, Ulster County Community College Online Degree Program at the address listed below. The application may be completed on the Internet for a $30 fee (Web site: http://infostu.suny.edu). Freshman and transfer applicants must submit official high school and college transcripts or GED scores.

CONTACT

Susan Weatherly
Office of Admission
Ulster County Community College
Stone Ridge, New York 12484
Telephone: 800-443-5331 Ext. 5018 (toll-free)
E-mail: admissions@sunyulster.edu
Web site: http://www.sunyulster.edu

The Union Institute

Distance Learning Program Opportunities

Cincinnati, Ohio

The Union Institute's distinctive educational system is designed for adults who have the desire and ability to assume a significant measure of personal responsibility for planning and executing their degree programs. Degree programs are individualized, build upon previous learning, and employ the creative engagement of knowledge through a wide variety of learning resources, under the close guidance and evaluation of the university's highly qualified faculty.

The Union Institute's undergraduate program includes the Center for Distance Learning, administered from the university's headquarters in Cincinnati, Ohio; as well as undergraduate learning centers in Miami, Florida; and San Diego, Sacramento, and Los Angeles, California. The Graduate College functions nationally and internationally and is administered from Cincinnati, Ohio. The university's Washington, D.C., research units include the Office for Social Responsibility, the Center for Public Policy, and the Center for Women.

The Union Institute was founded in 1964 by 10 college presidents as a vehicle for educational research and experimentation and was accredited by the Commission on Higher Education of the North Central Association of Colleges and Schools in 1985. It is a recognized leader in the development and implementation of programs of higher education for strongly motivated adult learners. The Union Institute's individualized programs adhere to the highest intellectual and academic standards. For more than three decades, the Union Institute's programs have met the career and educational needs of men and women from all segments of society, including government, industry, business, education, service, and the health professions.

DISTANCE LEARNING PROGRAM

The College of Undergraduate Studies' Center for Distance Learning, founded in 1993, offers courses and complete baccalaureate degree programs accessible by personal computer and other media. Graduate College learners throughout the United States and in a number of other countries work in individually designed doctoral programs of interdisciplinary research and study. Both of the Union Institute's programs include a requirement for brief face-to-face meetings and seminars, held in locations throughout the United States.

DELIVERY MEDIA

The primary instructional delivery mode for distance learners is online and faculty-guided independent study, involving a high degree of learner–faculty member interaction supported by computer conferencing. Learners enrolled in the undergraduate Center for Distance Learning are required to have access to and know how to operate a modem-equipped personal computer that is able to access the World Wide Web and e-mail.

PROGRAMS OF STUDY

The Union Institute offers concentrations in liberal arts and sciences fields leading to the Bachelor of Arts (B.A.), Bachelor of Science (B.S.), and Doc-

tor of Philosophy (Ph.D.) degrees. Doctoral programs are required to be interdisciplinary. Undergraduate learners' individualized degree programs include a specific concentration in one area (major) as well as a general education requirement ensuring breadth of knowledge. Common areas of concentration include business and management, communications, criminal justice studies, education, psychology, social sciences, and a wide variety of arts and humanities. Other liberal arts and sciences concentrations may also be available.

The baccalaureate degree requires the successful completion of 128 semester credits, of which at least 32 credits must be from sponsored learning at the Union Institute. The doctoral program is not credit-hour based, requiring a minimum of twenty-four months' enrollment for graduation.

SPECIAL PROGRAMS

The Union Institute also provides educational programs designed specifically to meet the needs of particular populations of adult learners, such as programs for substance abuse counselors and criminal justice professionals. Corporate on-site programs are also possible. The Union Institute's mission is to provide innovative yet rigorous educational opportunities to traditionally underserved adult populations; specifically designed programs are one way in which the university fulfills that mission.

CREDIT OPTIONS

The College of Undergraduate Studies accepts academic course credit (grade C or better) earned at regionally accredited postsecondary institutions, when appropriate to the learner's degree plan. The College may also accept credit recommendations from the American Council on Education (ACE) and the College-Level Examination Program (CLEP). Matriculating learners earn credit toward the remaining degree requirements through sponsored learning or the assessment of prior experiential learning. The Graduate College does not accept transfer credits, nor does it grant credit for prior experiential learning.

FACULTY

The Union Institute employs 110 full- and part-time faculty members to work as advisers, mentors, and guides to its learners. Ninety-nine percent of the full-time faculty members and 92 percent of the part-time faculty members have a Ph.D. or the terminal degree in their field.

ADMISSION

Applicants to the College of Undergraduate Studies program are required to have a high school diploma or equivalent. Graduate College applicants are required to hold a master's degree from a regionally accredited college or university. Applicants are not required to submit standardized test scores, but all are required to submit narrative essays as part of the application process. Official college transcripts and three letters of recommendation are also required.

TUITION AND FEES

For academic year 1999–2000 (July 1, 1999, through June 30, 2000), undergraduate tuition was $262 per semester credit hour. Graduate tuition was $4300 per semester. Tuition rates are the same for all learners, regardless of state of residence. A one-time, nonrefundable application fee of $50 is required.

FINANCIAL AID

General financial aid programs available through the Union Institute include the Federal Pell Grant, Federal Perkins and Stafford Student Loans, and Federal Work Study programs. Learners may also be eligible for state-based financial aid programs. The Union Institute awards a limited number of scholarships to its learners each year. More than half of all learners received some form of financial assistance in 1998–99.

APPLYING

The Union Institute accepts and reviews applications for admission on a rolling basis; admitted learners may begin the program in any semester.

The Center for Distance Learning schedules brief (three-day) orientation seminars for new learners three times a year, in October, February, and June. Graduate College learners matriculate at ten-day entry colloquia that are scheduled monthly. Orientation seminars and entry colloquia are held at locations throughout the United States.

CONTACT

College of Undergraduate Studies
Timothy Mott
Director, Center for Distance
   Learning
The Union Institute
440 East McMillan Street
Cincinnati, Ohio 45206-1925
Telephone: 513-861-6400
               800-486-3116
Fax: 513-861-9026
E-mail: dean-cdl@tui.edu
Web site: http://www.tui.edu

Graduate College
Admissions
440 East McMillan Street
Cincinnati, Ohio 45206-1925
Telephone: 513-861-6400
               800-486-3116
Fax: 513-861-0779
E-mail: admissions@tui.edu
Web site: http://www.tui.edu/

United States International University

Department of Education

San Diego, California

United States International University (USIU) is a multicampus system with campuses in San Diego, California; Nairobi, Kenya; and Mexico City, Mexico, and a graduate center in Irvine, California. USIU was founded in 1952 as California Western University. In 1967, the focus of the University changed when an international emphasis was incorporated into the mission, and the name was changed to United States International University.

The multicultural/multinational character of the University is reflected in the academic programs and student body. While the distance education program originates from the San Diego campus, it is anticipated that students on the other campuses and students from around the world will also enroll.

United States International University is accredited by the Western Association of Schools and Colleges. This accreditation applies to both traditional and online programs.

DISTANCE LEARNING PROGRAM

The online Master of Arts in Technology and Learning program provides the same high level of personal attention, support, and service that on-campus students receive at USIU. The online program is primarily tailored to teachers and professionals, so they can progress in their field while maintaining busy schedules.

DELIVERY MEDIA

Faculty members provide feedback and support to students on a continual basis. Instructors utilize threaded discussions, audio and video clips, group projects, and an integration of Web-based resources. USIU Online students need the following minimum equipment: Windows 95 or later on a 90-MHz Pentium PC or MacOS 8.1 or later on a 604 PowerPC processor (Macintosh); 32 MB RAM; 28.8 modem; sound card; and speakers. Technical support is provided by eCollege.com through their 24-hour, seven-day-a-week HelpDesk.

PROGRAM OF STUDY

The Master of Arts in Technology and Learning program is composed of eleven courses (45 units) and may be completed in as little as fifteen months. Students may complete the courses conveniently from their homes, schools, or office computers. The frequency and duration of classes are the same as those of equivalent on-campus courses; the teaching methods and learning environment have been modified to make them effective for delivering the program at a distance. The method of delivery in many ways models appropriate usage of technology in education. Thus, the main objective of the program, "to provide students with the skills and understanding necessary to utilize technology to facilitate learning," is enhanced by the online delivery mode.

STUDENT SERVICES

United States International University provides USIU Online students with the following services via the Internet: admissions, registration, financial aid application and process-ing, academic advisement, and bookstore and library services.

CREDIT OPTIONS

For the master's program, United States International University may accept up to 8 units of transfer credit from other accredited higher education institutions. Course work being considered for transfer must be equivalent to USIU course work for which it is being applied. Students are required to submit transcripts, course descriptions, and other documents for faculty review.

FACULTY

The entire program's faculty participates in the planning and development of online courses. In addition, there are two online-dedicated USIU Technology and Learning professors and a number of adjunct instructors. USIU Online's student-faculty ratio is 15:1.

ADMISSION

Applicants must meet the general requirements for admission to the University, which include a bachelor's degree, a minimum GPA of 2.5, two letters of recommendation, official transcripts, and a personal essay.

TUITION AND FEES

Tuition and fees for the 2000–01 academic year are $280 per unit and a $250 per course distance education fee. The cost of textbooks and materials is additional and varies.

FINANCIAL AID

USIU Online students may apply for scholarships and all federal, state, and institutional programs (such as grants and loans), as appropriate. In addition, new applicants to the online master's program may qualify for a $500 tuition credit.

APPLYING

Prospective USIU Online students should go to the Web site below to begin the admissions process. At this Web site, students may complete the application process, apply for financial aid, pay their tuition and fees, consult their academic advisers, register for classes, and attend classes 100 percent online.

CONTACT
Students should visit the Web site for more information.
Web site: http://www.usiuonline.net

United States Sports Academy

Continuing Education and Distance Learning

Daphne, Alabama

The United States Sports Academy (USSA) is a nonprofit, private graduate school designed to serve the nation and the world as a sport education resource, with programs of instruction, research, and service. Since 1972, the Academy has been addressing the need to provide high-quality, sport-specific programs. The Academy is accredited by the Commission on Colleges of the Southern Association of Colleges and Schools to award the Master of Sport Science degree (Level III) and the Doctor of Sport Management degree (Level V).

DISTANCE LEARNING PROGRAM

Learning experiences and student requirements in distance learning are similar to and equivalent with courses offered in the traditional on-campus setting. Courses are instructed by an Academy faculty member, who is responsible for advising and facilitating the learning experience during the structured offering of distance learning. Approximately 93 percent of the Academy's students are in the distance learning program.

DELIVERY MEDIA

Distance learning students at USSA receive study materials via the USSA Web site, a computer disk, or workbook-style study guides. Other required materials include audiotapes and textbooks, which are mailed directly to the student. The USSA library and its extensive reference database can be accessed through the USSA Web site. All students are required to have an e-mail address by the end of his or her first course of study or upon completion of fifteen weeks.

PROGRAMS OF STUDY

Distance learning offers the student an opportunity to earn a master's degree through a combination of independent and practical study. The Master of Sport Science degree is offered in the following majors: sport coaching, sport management, and sports medicine. Each major requires 33 semester hours of course work. The following courses are core curriculum and are required for each major: sport administration and finance, sport marketing, professional writing and applied research, and contemporary issues in sport.

The program in sport coaching is designed to prepare a student for leadership in the career of sport coaching. The curriculum in sport management is designed to prepare students for a number of career and leadership opportunities in sport and recreational management. The general curriculum in sports medicine is designed to prepare students for opportunities, including athletic training at high school, collegiate, clinical, and professional levels.

Each course requires the student to complete four to five enabling activities, a final examination, and a class paper. Grades are using the following percentiles: enabling activities, 30 percent; class paper, 35 percent; and final examination, 35 percent. Courses are available in the areas of sport behavior, sport medicine and fitness, sport management, sport research, and sport coaching.

All degree-seeking students must pass a written comprehensive examination in order to graduate. To be eligible to register for the comprehensive examination, a student must be in good academic standing and have completed all degree requirements.

SPECIAL PROGRAMS

Students at the Academy have the option of completing a mentorship. Also, certification programs are offered in several areas. These include sport management, sport coaching, sport coaching for figure skaters, bodybuilding, exercise physiology, strength and conditioning, sport medicine, personal training, and others.

CREDIT OPTIONS

A student may transfer up to 12 semester hours from a regionally accredited graduate school provided: such courses are equivalent to courses offered in the Academy's graduate program, credit was earned in the past four calendar years, the student received a grade of B or better in the course(s), and the academic committee approves the transfer credit.

For more information, contact the Office of Student Services.

FACULTY

The Academy has more than 30 faculty members. They are located both on-site and at various locations around the country.

ADMISSION

For full standing admission to the graduate program, an applicant must be a graduate of a four-year regionally accredited undergraduate institution, obtain either a GRE score of 800 (combined verbal and quantitative scores), an MAT raw score of 27, or a GMAT score of 400 and must have maintained a cumulative grade point average of 2.75 or better (on a 4.0 scale) in all undergraduate work. A student who has a conferred master's degree from a regionally accredited institution may waive the GRE, MAT, or GMAT requirement with an official transcript stating the date of completion of the master's degree.

TUITION AND FEES

Tuition is $350 per semester hour. Study guide prices are as follows: $15.95 (hard copy), $10 (disk) and $5 (Internet). The study guide prices are per course. The *Guidelines Manual for Writing Class Papers, Theses and Dissertations* (required) is $9.95. Shipping and handling is $4.50 in the continental U.S. Internationally, the shipping rates are $25 for the course only and $35 for the course and textbook. If available, audiotapes are required for the courses and start at $14.95 for one course tape.

FINANCIAL AID

The United States Sports Academy has a wide variety of financial aid programs available to qualified students. The financial assistance programs are divided into four categories: Federal Family Education Loan Programs, Campus-Based Programs, Institutional Assistance Programs, and the Veterans Administration Programs. These programs are administered through the Office of Student Services.

APPLYING

A student applying for general admission to the graduate program is required to submit the following to the Office of Student Services: a completed application form accompanied by a $50 nonrefundable fee; an official copy of all college transcripts; three letters of recommendation or the names, addresses, and telephone numbers of three references which can be contacted; official Graduate Record Examination (GRE), Miller Analogies Test (MAT), or Graduate Management Aptitude Test (GMAT) results taken within the last five years; a written personal statement; and a resume or vita.

A student applying for international student admission must submit the following to the Office of Student Services: a completed application form accompanied by a $125 nonrefundable fee; an official, certified copy (English transcripts) of all college transcripts; three letters of recommendation; Test of English as a Foreign Language (TOEFL) scores; a written personal statement; a resume or vita; and an evaluation of foreign education credentials (ECE report) by an Academy-approved evaluator. The evaluation must state that the student has the equivalent of a bachelor's degree from a regionally accredited institution. This service normally costs approximately $75. Contact the Office of Student Services for further information.

CONTACT

United States Sports Academy
One Academy Drive
Daphne, Alabama 36526-7055
Fax: 334-626-3303
World Wide Web: http://www.sport.ussa.edu

Dr. Gordon Strong, Director of Continuing Education and Distance Learning
Telephone: 334-626-3303 Ext. 154
E-mail: Gstrong.USSA@ussa-sport.ussa.edu

Becky Cochran, Coordinator of Continuing Education and Distance Learning
Telephone: 334-626-3303 Ext. 153
E-mail: Bcochran.USSA@ussa-sport.ussa.edu

Mark McKnight, Coordinator of Non-Resident Programs
Telephone: 334-626-3303 Ext. 155
E-mail: Mcknight.USSA@ussa-sport.ussa.edu

Jan Byrd, Secretary of Continued Education and Program Auditor
Telephone: 334-626-3303 Ext. 152
E-mail: Jbyrd.USSA@ussa-sport.ussa.edu

The University Alliance

Distance Learning Program

Tampa, Florida

Through the power of the Internet, the University Alliance, a Bisk Education Network, makes available to students worldwide master's and bachelor's degrees via distance programs from regionally accredited, nationally known universities. Students can earn their bachelor's or M.B.A. degree from accredited Top Tier Universities, as ranked by U.S. News & World Report, with no classroom attendance required.

Universities offering accredited degree programs through the University Alliance include Regis University, which currently offers the largest multimedia, Internet-based M.B.A. program in the nation, and Saint Leo University, one of the largest Catholic institutions of higher education in the United States and one of the largest providers of education to active military service members.

Saint Leo University, founded in 1889, is regionally accredited by the Southern Association of Colleges and Schools. Regis University, founded in 1877, is regionally accredited by the North Central Association of Colleges and Schools.

DISTANCE LEARNING PROGRAM

The programs are based on multimedia and Internet technology, with state-of-the-art streaming video and audio, up-to-date textbooks, and other supplements.

Students enroll in a program through the University Alliance and then receive credit from the university offering the course and/or degree. Online students are taught the same curriculum as the university's on-campus students and receive the same degree, yet have the flexibility to set their own weekly study schedules. The student is never required to log on at a specific time. Sessions are asynchronous; that is, the student can sign on and participate whenever it is convenient. The student never has to work his or her schedule around a specific time. Studying can occur at 3 a.m. or 6 p.m.—whenever and wherever it suits the student.

DELIVERY MEDIA

A major benefit of the external degree programs offered through the University Alliance is that no classroom attendance is ever required. Students' study sessions can take place in the comfort of their home or office or when they travel.

Online students are led step-by-step through the learning process and course work, with practical student guides and weekly assignments that help keep them focused, motivated, and on track. Also, students are able to communicate with faculty members and fellow students through lively chat rooms, online message boards, and convenient e-mail.

The grade for a course is based on assignments that are evaluated by the instructor. All tests and quizzes are taken online. It is not necessary to travel to a testing location or make arrangements for private proctoring of any exams. An accredited degree is the same as one earned on the university's main campus. Due to the convenience of communication methods, many students actually find themselves interacting and participating more in their online external degree program than they would if they were in a traditional classroom.

PROGRAMS OF STUDY

Saint Leo University currently offers five external degree programs through the University Alliance: a Bachelor of Arts in accounting; a Bachelor of Arts in business administration, specializing in management, MIS, or accounting; and a Bachelor of Science in computer information systems (CIS). All five degree programs are designed for working professionals to help them become more competitive and effective in today's increasingly complex business environment. All courses are 3 credit hours each, with 120 total credits required.

Regis University offers a Master of Business Administration (M.B.A.) through the University Alliance. Supplemented with videos, audio, and textbooks, the Regis M.B.A. program consists of 10 eight-week courses worth 3 credit hours each.

Students may enroll in a Saint Leo University External Bachelor's Degree Program or the Regis University External M.B.A. Program at any time and begin studies at six convenient times during the year. All courses are presented in eight-week sessions and are worth 3 credit hours each.

STUDENT SERVICES

Students can interact closely with the University Alliance student service representative, who offers administrative support throughout the degree program.

CREDIT OPTIONS

Saint Leo University accepts college credits transferred from accredited colleges and universities as well as military, nursing, and police academy training. Regis University honors up to 6 transfer credit hours from regionally accredited schools.

FACULTY

Regis and Saint Leo University's faculty include some of the country's foremost academic experts and distinguished "real-world" practicing professionals. These instructors carefully adapt their curriculums for use on the Internet to ensure that online students are taught the same subject matter as is covered in the traditional classroom.

ADMISSION

Saint Leo University candidates must submit an application for admission, any official transcripts from regionally accredited colleges or universities, and a letter of intent. All five external bachelor's degree programs require the completion of 120 academic credit hours, which must include 30 hours with Saint Leo University and 15 hours in the program major.

Admission into the Regis University External M.B.A. Program is based upon a total applicant profile. The type and length of management experiences that the individual has had throughout his or her career are important in the decision-making process. The applicant's purpose for seeking an M.B.A. degree is also considered, as are two letters of recommendation. Among other things, students must have a bachelor's degree from a regionally accredited university and two full years of significant work experience. No GMAT score or thesis is required.

TUITION AND FEES

Undergraduate tuition is $310 per credit and graduate tuition is $396 per credit. Application fees for the undergraduate programs are $35 and for the graduate program are $75. The entire ten-course Regis M.B.A. is less than $13,000. The Saint Leo bachelor's degree cost varies depending on how many credits are required for completion. Textbook costs vary by course.

FINANCIAL AID

The University Alliance offers several flexible payment plans and accepts tuition reimbursement, VA benefits, and Military Tuition Assistance in addition to financial aid through the Federal Stafford Student Loan Program and others. Students should visit http://www.universityalliance.com and look under financial aid for other options.

APPLYING

Students can download an application from http://www.universityalliance. com or contact a program representative by phone at the toll-free number listed below.

CONTACT

Admissions
The University Alliance—A Bisk Education Network
9417 Princess Palm Avenue
Tampa, Florida 33619
Telephone: 888-622-7344 (toll-free in the U.S.)
Fax: 888-879-3255 (toll-free)
E-mail: info@universityalliance.com
Web site: http://www.universityalliance.com/petersons

The University of Alabama

College of Continuing Studies/Division of Distance Education
Tuscaloosa, Alabama

The College of Continuing Studies' Division of Distance Education upholds the tradition of educational quality with world-class excellence through programs that overcome the obstacles of geography, individual schedules, and limited class sizes. By recognizing that lifelong learning and technological development are increasingly essential to the lives of individuals and organizations, the following distance learning programs have been developed.

DISTANCE LEARNING PROGRAM

The Division of Distance Education offers various educational formats to students limited by personal circumstances or distance who are seeking high school–, college-, or graduate-level credit. These programs include Independent Study, Quality University Extended Site Telecourses (QUEST), Intercampus Interactive Telecommunications System (IITS), National Technological University (NTU), and Global Online Academic Learning System (GOALS).

DELIVERY MEDIA

Independent Study offers high school and undergraduate college credit through written correspondence. QUEST offers undergraduate and graduate courses, five master's degrees in engineering, and a master's degree in nursing case management, all via videotape. IITS is a network of videoconferencing rooms equipped for full student and teacher live interaction. NTU offers master's degrees in engineering through satellite instruction in ten engineering or engineering-related fields. GOALS features online high school, undergraduate, and graduate-level courses delivered over the World Wide Web directly to the student's home or corporate desktop.

PROGRAMS OF STUDY

Through QUEST, a student may complete undergraduate- or graduate-level course work or obtain a Master of Science degree in aerospace engineering, electrical engineering, engineering, engineering with a concentration in engineering management, mechanical engineering, and nursing case management. Tapes are made of actual classes and then sent to various QUEST sites the following day to be viewed by students who complete the same requirements as students on campus. QUEST open or corporate sites are easy to establish. There is no fee to become a site. Establishing a site does require a person to serve as site coordinator and be responsible for receiving and returning tapes. Equipment needed at the site includes a television and VCR. Requirements for each degree vary. Normally, students must complete their chosen programs in six years. The following colleges offer courses through QUEST: Engineering, Commerce and Business Administration, Nursing, Human Environmental Sciences, and Education.

Master's degrees are available via IITS in health studies, rehabilitation counseling, and taxation law. Students choose one of several sites located in the state of Alabama, where they see and hear the instructor and students at all sites in real time. Courses are offered in business, communica-tions, education, engineering, foreign language, law, library studies, material science, math, and nursing, as well as in other disciplines.

Members from the College of Engineering contribute, via satellite, master's-level course work to non-profit NTU for business and government agency employees seeking advanced degrees. More than 1,200 courses are available from participating universities in the ten master's programs in engineering. Also available are undergraduate "bridging" courses in computer engineering, computer science, electrical engineering, and software engineering for students wishing to enter the master's programs.

SPECIAL PROGRAMS

Independent Study, the University's oldest distance learning program, offers high school and college credit through written correspondence. Approximately 150 college-level and sixty high school–level courses are available. Courses may be completed in as little as six weeks and as long as one year. Independent Study is DANTES approved. Students may enroll at any time.

GOALS offers high school, undergraduate, and graduate courses on line over the World Wide Web directly to the student's home computer or corporate desktop. GOALS has been developed through today's most advanced technology to offer a simple format of study for those in pursuit of academic excellence. Electronic communication reinvents and enhances the student's learning experience. New courses are currently being developed, and these updates can be accessed on the Division of Distance Education Web site.

CREDIT OPTIONS

Applicability of credit toward an undergraduate degree refers to the prerogative of the respective academic divisions to count specific credit toward a student's degree requirements. A maximum of 64 semester hours of two-year college credit may be applied toward graduation requirements.

At the graduate level, a maximum of 12 semester hours of work taken as a nondegree student may be applied to the credit-hour requirements for a degree.

Responsibility rests with the student to observe the limitations imposed on credit hours, course work, and transfer of credit. Procedures and forms for this type of admission will be furnished upon request.

FACULTY

There are approximately 180 full-time and 10 part-time faculty members involved in these programs. Of this faculty group, 99 percent of the full-time faculty members and 90 percent of the part-time faculty members have doctoral or other terminal academic degrees.

ADMISSION

All undergraduate students enrolling in the QUEST or IITS program must be admitted to the University. Admission to any undergraduate college or division of the University requires acceptable evidence of previous academic performance and scores on a recognized admission test. All graduate students enrolling in QUEST, IITS, or GOALS must also satisfy the University's Graduate School admission criteria. Formal admission is not required of students who enroll in Independent Study or undergraduate GOALS courses.

TUITION AND FEES

Independent Study tuition is $75–$90 for a high school course, $185 for a 2-hour college course, $270 for a 3-hour college course, and $355 for a 4-hour college course. QUEST tuition is $175 per credit hour plus a $25 registration fee each term. There is an $80 technology fee for engineering courses. IITS tuition is the same as on-campus tuition. NTU tuition is $585 per credit hour. GOALS tuition is $350 per 3-hour undergraduate course. Engineering GOALS courses are $600 per 3-hour course. Students should contact the Distance Education Office for more information. Tuition is payable in full by check or by VISA, MasterCard, or Discover credit card. Normally, tuition increases, when applicable, occur during the fall semester. Students should contact the Division of Distance Education for current tuition rates.

FINANCIAL AID

Loans and work-study are administered through the Office of Student Financial Services. In addition, most academic departments of the Graduate School have teaching or research assistantships that carry a stipend. Teaching and research assistants who are assigned duties of .5 FTE or more may receive a grant equal to their tuition.

APPLYING

Information can be obtained or registration completed by contacting the Division of Distance Education at the address below.

CONTACT

Division of Distance Education
College of Continuing Studies
The University of Alabama
Box 870388
Tuscaloosa, Alabama 35487-0388
Telephone: 205-348-9278
        800-452-5971 (toll-free)
Fax: 205-348-0249
E-mail: disted@ccs.ua.edu
Web site: http://bama.disted.ua.edu

University of Alaska Fairbanks

Center for Distance Education Independent Learning Program

Fairbanks, Alaska

In 1917, just fifteen years after the discovery of gold in the heart of the Alaskan wilderness, the Alaska Agricultural College and School of Mines was created by a special act of the Alaska Territorial Legislature. In 1922, the college opened with 6 faculty members and 6 students. Today, the University of Alaska Fairbanks (UAF), whose name was changed in 1931, continues to grow, both in size and stature. In addition to the main campus in Fairbanks, UAF has branch campuses in Bethel, Dillingham, Kotzebue, Nome, and the Interior/Aleutians. UAF is the state's land-, sea-, and space-grant institution. Its College of Rural Alaska has the primary responsibility for Alaska Native education and study, and UAF remains the only university in Alaska that offers doctoral degrees. UAF's colleges and schools offer more than seventy fields of study and a wide variety of technical and vocational programs. All courses are approved and meet the accreditation standards of the Northwest Association of Schools and Colleges Commission on Colleges.

DISTANCE LEARNING PROGRAM

UAF developed a Correspondence Study Program in the late 1950s, but the current Center for Distance Education and Independent Learning (CDE) was created in 1987. It supports close to 200 distance-delivered courses for several certificate and degree programs through the master's level within Alaska each academic year. The Independent Learning Program serves approximately 3,000 students throughout the world each year.

Courses that fulfill teacher certification and recertification requirements for the State of Alaska Department of Education are available. Students may choose among several courses that satisfy the Alaska studies and multicultural requirement. Students have up to one year from the date of enrollment to finish course work. Extensions may be available, depending on circumstances. Students are encouraged to use e-mail to submit lessons to circumvent delays in the standard mailing process.

DELIVERY MEDIA

Independent learning courses utilize a wide range of media, including basic written materials, audiotapes, videotapes, CD-ROMs, electronic mail, and the World Wide Web. Not all modes of delivery are available for every course, and students must have access to the appropriate equipment as specified in individual course descriptions. Most interaction between students and instructors is asynchronous in nature.

PROGRAM OF STUDY

The Center for Distance Education and Independent Learning is not a degree-granting organization; however, its approximately 100 independent learning courses can be used to fulfill degree program requirements within the University of Alaska's statewide system or at any other university that accepts the credits.

SPECIAL PROGRAMS

The Center for Distance Education and Independent Learning participates in the Defense Activity for Non-Traditional Education Support (DANTES) programs; information is available from base personnel or education officers. Veterans' educational benefits are also applicable for independent learning courses. DANTES students must complete a UAF enrollment form as well as the DANTES form.

STUDENT SERVICES

Students have access to the state library system and the UAF Rasmuson Library directly or through the Statewide Library Electronic Doorway (SLED). All students can obtain accounts on the University of Alaska Computer Network, which also gives access to the wider Internet and the World Wide Web. The UAF Writing Center offers free tele-fax tutoring for student use. Papers are faxed to the center, and a telephone appointment is made between tutor and student. Students may not schedule more than one appointment per day.

CREDIT OPTIONS

Since the Center for Distance Education and Independent Learning is not a degree-granting organization, there is no transfer of credit or credit for prior learning available.

FACULTY

The Independent Learning Program includes approximately 60 faculty members, about half of whom are also full-time members of the UAF faculty and who have terminal academic degrees. Adjunct faculty members and discipline professionals are hired to supplement the University's full-time faculty.

ADMISSION

Since the Center for Distance Education and Independent Learning is not a degree-granting organization, there are no admissions requirements or procedures. Students may enroll in individual courses any time during the year and have one year to complete the course. An extension of six additional months is available if sufficient progress has been made.

TUITION AND FEES

All students enrolled in UAF independent learning courses are charged the same tuition whether they are Alaska residents or not. Tuition for 100–200-level courses is $77 per credit, 300–400-level courses are $87 per credit, 500-level (professional graduate) courses are $100 per credit, and 600-level (academic graduate) courses are $172 per credit. The only other costs for independent learning courses are materials fees that vary by course and a $20 service fee per course. Students outside the U.S. must submit payment in U.S. dollars and are charged an extra $30 per course for additional postage charges. Students who wish to receive graded lessons via fax should submit the fax number and an additional $50 per course ($100 for international students) with the enrollment form.

FINANCIAL AID

Alaska students who are full-time (enrolled in at least 12 credits per semester) and are taking independent learning courses on a semester basis are eligible for all the types of financial aid available to other students, including Federal Pell Grants, Federal Supplemental Educational Opportunity Grants, State Educational Incentive grants, Bureau of Indian Affairs grants, Federal Stafford Student Loans, and Alaska student loans. Students enrolled in regular yearlong courses are not eligible to receive financial aid.

APPLYING

Since the Center for Distance Education and Independent Learning is not a degree-granting organization, no application is required to take independent learning courses. Completion of a UAF enrollment form and payment of fees are all that is required of students to take courses.

CONTACT

Carone Sturm, Director
Center for Distance Education and Independent Learning
P.O. Box 756700
University of Alaska Fairbanks
Fairbanks, Alaska 99775-6700
Telephone: 907-474-5353
Fax: 907-474-5402
E-mail: distance@uaf.edu
Web site: http://www.dist-ed.uaf.edu/

University of Baltimore

Robert G. Merrick School of Business

Baltimore, Maryland

The University of Baltimore was founded in 1925 as a private, coeducational institution and is now the state's only upper-division university. It offers the sophomore, junior, and senior years of baccalaureate study and graduate programs in business, liberal arts, and law. The mission of the University is to offer an outstanding educational program that provides students with a broad foundation of knowledge and the latest skills and techniques to support productive careers in the public and private sectors.

The University is accredited by the Middle States Association of Colleges and Schools and the Maryland State Board of Education. The Merrick School of Business is accredited by AACSB–The International Association for Management Education.

DISTANCE LEARNING PROGRAM

The webMBA program provides the opportunity to complete an M.B.A. in two years entirely via the Internet. The curriculum is designed for optimum use of the Internet as a teaching methodology and a learning tool.

DELIVERY MEDIA

To participate in the webMBA program, the student needs a computer with the following capabilities: an Internet provider (ISP), a Web browser (Netscape 3.02 or better or Internet Explorer 4.0 or better), an e-mail system that supports attachments, and Office 97 Suite. Students should enjoy Internet use and be enthusiastic about the opportunities for global interaction, research, and study that are offered by Web-based learning. Students interact on line with professors, classmates, and business and professional leaders.

PROGRAMS OF STUDY

The Merrick School of Business offers an M.B.A. in information-leveraged management via the Internet. The curriculum is designed to help students develop broad managerial skills and advanced technological understanding through a series of core courses, cross-functional courses, and electives. Not bound by geography, the webMBA offers a truly global context within which students can explore business issues and solutions. The program relies heavily on case studies, Internet research, and communication among the cohort and the faculty. The webMBA is a 48-credit-hour program and is appropriate for students who hold undergraduate degrees in any discipline.

Foundation and core courses include Statistical Resources and the Web, Financial Accounting, Financial Management, Leveraging Economic Principles, Managing People in Organizations, Leveraged Marketing, and Product and Service Operations. Two of these courses may be waived if the student has earned a grade of B or above in an equivalent course. Cross-functional courses include Information Systems and Technology, Applied Management Science, Accounting for Managerial Decisions: Global/Domestic Business Environment, Organization Creation and Growth, and Strategic Innovation and Renewal. None of these courses may be waived. Elective areas include Electronic Investment Solutions, Global e-Commerce, and Information-Based Management Solutions. Electives are subject to change, and no electives may be waived.

WebMBA students may access most student service areas through the University of Baltimore home page at http://www.ubalt.edu. Enrolled students gain access to the University of Baltimore Langsdale Library and the University Bookstore.

CREDIT OPTIONS

The webMBA is a 48-credit-hour program that consists of sixteen 3-credit courses. Courses at the 500 level may be waived, provided the student has earned a B or better in an equivalent course within the past five years.

FACULTY

WebMBA faculty members are all full-time; 92 percent have a Ph.D. or other terminal degree. Most have used Internet technology in their courses, and all are enthusiastic about the advantages of Web-based learning.

ADMISSION

Students should submit completed application materials and GMAT scores to the admissions office. Classes begin in January, April, July, and October.

TUITION AND FEES

Tuition and fees for each 3-credit course are as follows: $282 per credit for in-state students; $420 per credit for out-of-state students. Fees vary but average $22 per credit. Students must purchase textbooks and other learning aids.

FINANCIAL AID

Financial Aid is available for the webMBA program. Scholarships are not available for this program.

APPLYING

Students should submit a completed application, two letters of reference, GMAT test scores, official transcripts from all colleges or universities attended, a letter of intent, and the name of an individual to serve as a proctor for timed examinations to the University of Baltimore. Acceptance notifications are mailed. For more information, students should visit the Web site at http://UBonline.edu or call the admissions office at 877-APPLYUB (toll-free).

CONTACT

For specific questions about the program, students should contact:

Mr. Ray Frederick
Academic Programs Coordinator
Merrick School of Business
University of Baltimore
1420 North Charles Street
Baltimore, Maryland 21201
Telephone: 410-837-4953
Fax: 410-837-5652
E-mail: rfrederick@ubmail.ubalt.edu

University of Bridgeport

Distance Education Program

Bridgeport, Connecticut

The University of Bridgeport is a private, nonsectarian comprehensive university, founded in 1927, offering a wide variety of undergraduate, graduate, and professional degree programs through its several colleges and schools. The University's mission is to teach and search for new knowledge and new solutions to the problems of its social and natural environments. To this end, it offers a central liberal arts experience; high-quality accredited scientific, technical, business, legal, professional, and liberal arts programs; and lifelong learning opportunities. The University is accredited by the New England Association of Schools and Colleges (NEASC).

DISTANCE LEARNING PROGRAM

The University of Bridgeport's distance learning programs are committed to the larger social mission of education throughout the world. Learning is a lifelong process involving the development of a range of skills for a diversity of learners, which the University provides through advancements in technology. The distance learning program was initiated in 1997 with eight courses offered as part of the Master of Science in human nutrition program.

DELIVERY MEDIA

The online program offers a learning environment that is both convenient and instructive. With a computer, modem, and access to the Internet, a student communicates with instructors and classmates from the convenience of the home or office. The student has access to an array of online tools for use in the program, such as e-mail, newsgroups, class conferences, informal chat rooms, textbooks, and specially produced software.

PROGRAM OF STUDY

The distance education program provides students with technical and professional training in the health sciences, beginning with the Master of Science in human nutrition. The goal of the human nutrition program is to provide a biochemical and physiological understanding of human nutrition and its role in health and disease. The curriculum, highly relevant to health care, is designed to provide up-to-date graduate-level information, which enables students to acquire an understanding of nutritional issues as applied to their areas of specialization.

SPECIAL PROGRAMS

University of Bridgeport online courses and programs are fully equivalent to on-campus programs. They follow the same curriculum, have the same entrance and graduation requirements, and charge the same tuition and fees. All students receive a University login name and password, allowing access to library services, extensive databases, registration, and academic advising.

STUDENT SERVICES

Distance learning students have access to the student resources of a traditional campus, the library, counselors, registration, and financial aid, through the University of Bridgeport's Virtual Campus. Library resources, including books, journals, and other publications within the University library system, are accessible to the students. The University's full-time reference librarians assist students in using resources such as Internet search databases and scholarly indexes, reports, and articles, including special nutrition and medical databases, MedLine, the National Library of Medicine, and the Canadian Science Technical Institute. The reference librarians, academic advisers, and career placement counselors are available to the student through e-mail, fax, or telephone.

CREDIT OPTIONS

Students can transfer undergraduate credits earned at other postsecondary institutions to the University of Bridgeport and can receive undergraduate credit by taking the College-Level Examination Program or other standardized tests. A maximum of

90 credits may be transferred toward a bachelor's degree, and a maximum of 6 semester hours may be transferred into any of the graduate degree programs.

FACULTY

The faculty-student ratio in distance education is 1:15. All instructors hold doctoral or terminal degrees in their field.

ADMISSION

Admission to the graduate programs requires a bachelor's degree from an accredited institution with a minimum GPA of 3.0.

TUITION AND FEES

The tuition for the M.S. in human nutrition degree program is $385 per credit hour. There are 31 credit hours in the complete program. Other general expenses include registration fees and required textbooks, and some courses require specific software packages.

FINANCIAL AID

Students accepted for enrollment are eligible for Federal Stafford Student Loans. For further information, students should contact the Office of Financial Aid (telephone: 203-576-4568).

APPLYING

Distance education students may obtain an application form and other program descriptions from the Office of Distance Education. Applicants must submit a completed application for admission, two letters of recommendation, and official transcripts of all previous college work.

CONTACT

Michael Giampaoli
Office of Distance Education
University of Bridgeport
303 University Avenue
Bridgeport, Connecticut 06601
Telephone: 203-576-4851
　　　　　800-470-7307 (toll-free)
Fax: 203-576-4852
E-mail: ubonline@bridgeport.edu
Web site: http://www.bridgeport.edu

University of California

University of California Extension
Center for Media and Independent Learning

Berkeley, California

The University of California (UC), one of the largest and most acclaimed institutions of higher education in the world, is dedicated to excellence in teaching, research, and public service. Chartered in 1868 as California's only land-grant institution, UC began classes in Oakland, with 10 faculty members and 38 students. Today, UC has nine campuses, five medical schools and teaching hospitals, three law schools, and a statewide Division of Agriculture and Natural Resources.

The UC faculty is internationally respected for its scholarly and scientific achievements. Since 1939, faculty members have won 40 Nobel Prizes.

Academic study areas at UC span more than 150 disciplines from agriculture to zoology, giving UC one of the broadest ranges of study of any institute of higher learning in the world.

Eight of the nine UC campuses have Extension programs. UC's systemwide distance learning program is administered by UC Berkeley Extension through the UC Berkeley campus, which is accredited by the Western Association of Schools and Colleges (WASC).

DISTANCE LEARNING PROGRAM

The Center for Media and Independent Learning (CMIL) is the distance learning division of UC Extension, the continuing education arm of the University of California. CMIL's independent learning program does not require classroom attendance, and students anywhere in the world may enroll in courses. CMIL was established more than eighty years ago to expand the resources of the University throughout the community, the state, and the nation. More than 4,000 students are served each year.

DELIVERY MEDIA

CMIL offers online and independent learning (e-mail/mail) courses. Online courses feature an online syllabus and lecture notes, electronic libraries containing files for downloading, links to other online sites to aid with studies, and message boards for regular communication with the instructor and

other students in the class. Independent learning courses are print-based; students send and receive written assignments by e-mail or regular mail, working one-on-one with their instructors.

PROGRAMS OF STUDY

CMIL offers more than 200 college-and professional-level courses, as well as twenty-one core-curriculum high school courses. In addition, CMIL and UC Berkeley Extension have developed several joint certificates and professional sequences that can be earned at a distance.

The core courses for the Certificate in e-Commerce lead students to an understanding of the business and technical issues that drive e-commerce.

A Certificate in Computer Information Systems: Analysis and Design enables students to define, manage, and execute a systems approach to business. The Certificate in Marketing is a seven-course program emphasizing professional practices and real-world

applications of marketing concepts. The curriculum for a Certificate in Project Management consists of five required courses and one elective, all of which can be taken at a distance. The Certificate in Business Administration is a seven-course program offering comprehensive coverage of the fundamentals of managing a business. Finally, the Certificate in Hazardous Materials Management is an eight-course program that covers the foundations, principles, regulations, and technologies of the field.

Professional sequences in direct marketing methods, telecommunications fundamentals, and integrated marketing communications are also available at a distance.

SPECIAL PROGRAMS

UC Extension Online is an online program that is a collaboration between CMIL and UC Berkeley Extension, combining Berkeley Extension's extensive program offerings with CMIL's long experience in developing distance learning courses and supporting students at a distance. Course features include message boards, e-mail, online resources, chat rooms, and course materials that are posted on line. In 1998, UC Extension Online received a Significant Achievement Award from the University Continuing Education Association for its high-quality curriculum and its innovative approach to providing student and instructor services on line. CMIL courses are approved for the Defense Activity for Non-Traditional Education Support (DANTES) program. Members of the military who wish to continue their education should consult the DANTES Independent Study Catalog.

STUDENT SERVICES

CMIL maintains a tech-help line for students who experience technical problems with online courses. In addition, students can order textbooks for courses through an online bookstore.

CREDIT OPTIONS

Although CMIL does not offer degrees, credit earned for college-level CMIL courses may be accepted at the University of California and at other accredited institutions.

FACULTY

CMIL's approximately 170 instructors include University of California faculty members, UC Extension instructors, and faculty members from other colleges and universities. Nearly half of the instructors have doctorates; the rest have an appropriate combination of higher education and professional experience in their field.

ADMISSION

Enrollment in lower-division courses is open to students who have satisfied any specific prerequisites shown in the course description. Two years of college-level work or the equivalent is required for enrollment in upper-division courses.

TUITION AND FEES

In 2000–01, enrollment fees vary from $225 to $795 per course, with many courses ranging from $395 to $425, depending on the number and type of credit units and course materials supplied. Fees are the same for all students, regardless of their location.

FINANCIAL AID

Many businesses encourage their employees to continue their education by paying part of their tuition; students should check with their employer regarding tuition reimbursement programs. Credit courses offered by CMIL are approved for use by veterans who are concurrently enrolled in college or university degree programs. Students should contact the Veteran's Administration to determine what benefits they are eligible for. CMIL students are not eligible for funds originating through grants or loan programs, nor does enrollment in CMIL courses meet federal requirements for loan deferment.

APPLYING

Most courses are offered on a rolling basis; students may apply at any time. Some online courses do have specific start and end dates, usually a semester's length apart. Students may apply by mail, fax, telephone, e-mail, or in person. There are no orientation requirements.

CONTACT

Customer Service
University of California Extension
Center for Media and Independent Learning
2000 Center Street, Suite 400
Berkeley, California 94704
Telephone: 510-642-4124
Fax: 510-643-9271
E-mail: askcmil@uclink4.berkeley.edu
Web site: http://learn.berkeley.edu/

University of California, Los Angeles

Distance Learning Program

Los Angeles, California

OnlineLearning.net is the leading online supplier of continuing education, providing busy professionals with the tools needed to pursue their lifelong learning objectives. Combining technological innovation with extraordinary customer service, OnlineLearning.net is committed to helping adult learners around the world access the best in educational resources—anytime, anywhere, at any stage in life. Since September of 1996, OnlineLearning.net has offered more than 1,100 online courses to more than 13,500 students in all fifty states and sixty-eight countries. Founded in 1994, OnlineLearning. net delivers online instructor-led courses from leading accredited universities and established partners, including UCLA Extension, the nation's largest single-campus continuing education program; the University of San Diego; Houghton Mifflin Company, the leading publisher of textbooks and reference manuals; the California CPA Education Foundation, providing education and information to CPAs and related professionals; and computer certification courses from OnlineLearning.net.

DISTANCE LEARNING PROGRAM

OnlineLearning.net offers more than 850 online classes each quarter to fit students' educational needs. Instructor-led online courses mirror traditional classroom-style courses in that they are interactive, feature specific start and end dates, require textbooks, and provide the same levels of academic/professional credit. Online self-paced courses and online/on-site courses are also offered through OnlineLearning.net.

DELIVERY MEDIA

Access to an IBM-compatible or Macintosh system, modem, phone line, and Internet access is required. During instructor-led courses, world-class instructors deliver lectures, assignments, and feedback—all online. The interaction is asynchronous. Prior to the start of the course, students participate in an interactive online orientation designed to maximize their comfort level with the online format. Course managers are assigned to each course to assist students in their online experience.

PROGRAMS OF STUDY

OnlineLearning.net offers more than 250 online instructor-led courses, as well as more than 600 online self-paced courses each quarter. OnlineLearning.net delivers certificate programs and professional sequences in the following communities: computers, business, writing, general education, and teacher education.

In the computer community, UCLA Extension offers Web technology and production, Microsoft Office, and applications programming, specializing in C++, Java, or Visual Basic. OnlineLearning.net offers instructor-led computer certification programs in Microsoft (MCSE, MCSD, MCP), certified Novell engineer (CNE), A+ certification, Linux, or Cisco (CCNA).

In the business community, UCLA Extension offers online instructor-led courses in accounting, human resources, investing, e-commerce, and more. The Wharton School of Business (University of Pennsylvania) offers executive education courses. The Marshall School of Business (University of Southern California) teaches vital e-business skills in the Fundamentals of eBusiness.

In the writing community, UCLA Extension's online writing courses (the nation's largest online writing program) help students achieve goals in creative writing, screenwriting, public relations, and journalism.

In the general education community, students can enrich their knowledge in history, political science, writing, philosophy, and more. Students can also polish math skills to prepare for a college entrance exam. These courses and others can be found in OnlineLearning.net's online instructor-led general education community from UCLA Extension.

In the teacher education community, students can earn professional development credits online. Students can choose credential clearing, online teaching, instructional technology, CLAD, TESOL, TEFL courses, a certificate in college counseling, or the online teaching program.

SPECIAL PROGRAMS

OnlineLearning.net offers the following special programs:

Professional designation in applications programming includes specialization in Visual Basic, C/C++, or Java programming.

Computer certification programs include Microsoft certified systems engineer (MCSE), Microsoft certified solution developer (MCSD), certified Novell engineer (CNE), A+ certification, Linux, and Cisco certified network associate (CCNA).

The estate planning certificate (California CPA Education Foundation) consists of two 8-week courses delivered entirely online.

Through the award in general business studies students can choose to concentrate their studies in technical communication, accounting, human resources, or personal financial planning.

The professional designation in personal financial planning program satisfies the Certified Financial Planner Board of Standards for pursuing the CFP designation.

The certificate program in college counseling includes six courses online and a 65-hour practicum completed at a convenient school venue.

The online teaching program is the most comprehensive program of its type in the country.

CLAD/TEFL programs satisfy the state-issued CLAD certificate.

Credential-clearing courses for educators fulfill the professional clear credential requirements.

CREDIT OPTIONS

The transfer of course work is evaluated on a case-by-case basis by each university. UCLA Extension offers transferable degree credit courses

online. Courses numbered X 1 to X 199 carry undergraduate-level credit; Courses numbered X 300 to X 499 are professional credit courses. Minimum Continuing Legal Education (MCLE) is available for some UCLA Extension online courses. Educators are advised to gain prior approval from their school district, college, or university for credit acceptability.

FACULTY

The online instructors are world-class professionals or highly acclaimed experts in their field. All instructors participate in a six-week instructor development training session prior to teaching online.

ADMISSION

A college degree is not required to enroll in an online instructor-led course presented by OnlineLearning.net. Some courses have prerequisites, but most only require the desire to learn.

TUITION AND FEES

Costs vary depending on the number of credit units and course materials.

An early-bird discount and returning student discount are available, as specific association discounts. For additional information, students should visit the OnlineLearning.net Web site (http://www.OnlineLearning.net/specialoffers).

FINANCIAL AID

Financial aid may be available through the appropriate university for the program desired. Students should visit the OnlineLearning.net Web site listed below for additional information.

APPLYING

Class size is limited in all online instructor-led courses. Orientation is mandatory for new students. Students may enroll either on line or by phone. To enroll online, students should visit the Web site http://www.OnlineLearning.net/Enroll/. Students can complete the online enrollment form and submit it electronically. Enrollment by phone is available Monday through Friday from 8 a.m. to 6 p.m. Pacific time at the toll-free number listed below.

CONTACT

OnlineLearning.net
555 South Flower Street
Suite 2850
Los Angeles, California 90071
Telephone: 213-689-4656
            800-784-8436 (toll-free)
Fax: 213-689-4657
E-mail: info@OnlineLearning.net
Web site: http://www.OnlineLearning.net

University of Central Arkansas

Division of Continuing Education

Conway, Arkansas

The University of Central Arkansas (UCA) was established in 1907 by the General Assembly as the Arkansas State Normal School and was charged with the responsibility of training teachers. As a statewide, comprehensive university, it sought to deliver the best undergraduate education in Arkansas as well as excellent graduate programs in selected disciplines. The University became UCA to reflect its status as a modern, comprehensive college that offers a variety of undergraduate and graduate programs in liberal and fine arts, basic sciences, and technical and professional fields in addition to its historical emphasis in the field of education.

The University is accredited by the North Central Association of Colleges and Schools and the National Council for the Accreditation of Teacher Education as a bachelor's, master's, and specialist's degree–granting institution. Today more than 9,000 students attend classes taught by 350 faculty members. The University's mission is expressed in its commitment to the personal, social, and intellectual growth of its students; its support for the advancement of knowledge; and its service to the community as a public institution.

DISTANCE LEARNING PROGRAM

The Division of Continuing Education was formed in 1975 as a special administrative unit to respond to the University's public service. The Division's mission is to provide high-quality, lifelong learning opportunities through credit courses, noncredit programs, and support services that address market needs. Its vision, as a team of innovative people dedicated to customer satisfaction, is to unite faculty members, state-of-the-art technology, and facilities to deliver comprehensive lifelong learning programs through a worldwide educational network.

DELIVERY MEDIA

Students have the opportunity to enroll in distance education courses and guided-study courses. The distance education courses include graduate and some undergraduate-level courses offered via compressed video and Internet. Compressed video courses are open to students in Arkansas. Internet courses are open to any student with access to the Internet.

The guided-study courses are open to any student and are all undergraduate-level courses. Students who enroll in guided-study courses come from all over the world. The syllabus and lessons are mailed to students after they register for a course.

Books can be rented from Continuing Education, or the student may opt to purchase the book somewhere else. Lessons are sent to Continuing Education via regular mail. Students send in a test request form once they have completed all of their lessons. Tests are sent to an approved testing center to be administered, and the test administrator then returns the completed test to UCA's Division of Continuing Education.

PROGRAMS OF STUDY

While the distance education and guided-study programs do not award diplomas or degrees, students may use the credit earned through these programs to achieve their specific educational goals.

UCA offers more than sixty undergraduate-level courses through guided study in a wide range of subject areas, including business, education, English language and literature, geography, German language and literature, history, family and consumer sciences, marketing, mathematics, political science, psychology, social sciences, curriculum and instruction, special education, and creative writing.

UCA also offers various graduate classes and workshops in distance education, including administration of secondary education, academic technologies and educational leadership, business and marketing education, curriculum and instruction, educational media library science, family and consumer sciences, foreign language, physical therapy, occupational therapy, nursing, mathematics, management, health education, political science, and others.

STUDENT SERVICES

Students in distance learning courses have access to the UCA library, academic advising, and career placement options. However, because guided-study students are not admitted into the University solely by acceptance into this program, they do not have access to the UCA library, academic advising, career placement options, computing services, tutoring, or other such services. Students may call 501-450-5276 for information concerning any continuing education courses. Course listings can be found on the Web site listed below.

CREDIT OPTIONS

Students can earn graduate or undergraduate credit through the distance education program and undergraduate credit through guided study. While the distance education and guided-study programs do not award degrees, University credit earned through these courses may be applied toward a degree or used to achieve any other educational goal a student may have. Students should see an adviser concerning the use of course work for degree credit.

FACULTY

The Division of Continuing Education employs approximately 60 instructors to grade the guided-study course work. The distance education area employs 62 instructors. Of these 62 faculty members, 60 percent have a doctoral degree.

ADMISSION

Students must complete an application and be admitted into the graduate program to take graduate-level courses in the distance education program.

To be eligible for enrollment in a guided-study course, adult students must have a high school diploma or GED and satisfy course prerequisites. High school students who obtain written approval by the appropriate administrative official at their high school may enroll concurrently in guided-study courses. Students may enroll at any time of the year and take up to one year to complete each course.

TUITION AND FEES

Tuition for distance education courses is $148.50 per credit hour for graduate courses and $115 per credit hour for undergraduate courses. Students must also pay a distance education fee of $40 per hour for compressed video and Internet courses.

Tuition for guided-study is $70 per semester hour. There is a postage fee of $10, and books can be rented for a fee of $20 per book.

FINANCIAL AID

Scholarships and other forms of financial aid are not accepted for guided-study courses. Distance education classes may be included in a student's course load for determining financial aid eligibility.

APPLYING

Students may enroll in a continuing education course by submitting a completed application form by mail or fax or in person for guided-study courses. Students may call for an enrollment package for distance education course work. The enrollment materials, along with payment, should be returned by mail or in person. Payment for these courses can be made by credit card, check, or money order.

Applications are accepted at any time. Students are notified by mail once the review process is complete and they have been enrolled in their course(s). Falsification or omission of the requested application information voids enrollment.

CONTACT

Division of Continuing Education
McCastlain Hall, Suite 101
University of Central Arkansas
201 Donaghey
Conway, Arkansas 72035-5003
Telephone: 501-450-5276
Fax: 501-450-5277
E-mail: sondrap@ecom.uca.edu (guided-study courses)
 rebeccar@ecom.uca.edu (distance learning courses)
Web site: http://www.uca.edu/conted

University of Central Florida

Center for Distributed Learning

Orlando, Florida

The University of Central Florida (UCF) is a major metropolitan research university whose mission is to deliver a comprehensive program of teaching, research, and service. UCF was established in 1963 and opened in the fall of 1968. Its original name, Florida Technological University, was changed by the Florida Legislature on December 6, 1978.

The University's presently assigned role within the ten-campus State University System of Florida is that of a general-purpose institution offering degree programs at all levels of instruction. The University of Central Florida is accredited by the Commission on Colleges of the Southern Association of Colleges and Schools to award degrees at the associate, baccalaureate, master's, and doctoral levels.

DISTANCE LEARNING PROGRAM

UCF delivers courses and programs over the Internet and via videotape to meet the diverse needs of a growing student population and to fulfill the general University mission.

Due to its strong technological background and resources, UCF provides this delivery for those who would not otherwise be able to attend classes on one of the four UCF campuses. In the last two academic years, UCF has served more than 5,000 students with Web-based courses and more than 900 students with videotaped courses.

These courses maintain a high-quality learning environment for the nontraditional student. The course materials and methods were developed by the UCF faculty to maximize the distant learner's achievement of course objectives. All distributed learning courses provide full University credit, and are subject to standard campus tuition charges and UCF policies.

DELIVERY MEDIA

To participate in Web-based courses, students must have access to the Internet and a Pentium PC that runs Windows 95 or Windows NT or a 60 megahertz 603 CPU Macintosh with OS 7.05 or later. Video-based courses and programs require similar Internet access and students must have a VCR to view VHS tapes.

PROGRAMS OF STUDY

By statewide agreement, distance learning courses offered by Florida's public universities are limited to upper-division and graduate course work. Links to UCF's baccalaureate programs are available on line at http://distrib.ucf.edu/studentinfo/dlprograms.htm.

The Web-based Bachelor's Degree in Liberal Studies is a general studies track that leads to either the Bachelor of Arts or Bachelor of Science in liberal studies degrees. The liberal arts track is an honors-linked Bachelor of Arts degree program available to students seeking an individualized, nontraditional, interdisciplinary major.

The Web-based RN to Bachelor's Degree in Nursing curriculum is available for Florida RN's seeking a Bachelor of Science in Nursing (B.S.N). Some campus attendance is required. Students may complete course work and clinical practica in five semesters or eighteen months. The School validates registered nurses' knowledge in the areas of adult health, pediatrics, and psychiatric–mental heath (28 credits).

The Web-based Bachelor's Degree in Vocational Education and Industry Training program is for individuals with occupational course work and/or work experience who wish to teach in middle or secondary schools, correctional institutions, postsecondary technical institutes, or become technical trainers in business or industry. Courses for vocational teacher certification, curriculum development, and career and technical education are included. Once admitted, students may receive up to 30 semester credits for completed college courses in a technical or occupational area, successful completion of a national occupational competency test, or license.

The video-based Bachelor of Science in Engineering Technology (B.S.E.T.) degree program is comprised of courses that are offered via VHS videocassette, with Internet enhancement. Special arrangements are made for laboratory courses. This track provides an orientation for professional careers in technical management and operations in the manufacturing, sales, service, and construction industries. Classes are taped in a live classroom and the tapes and handouts are distributed to designated remote sites, usually within 72 hours.

The University also offers graduate study via FEEDS, the video-based Florida Engineering Education Delivery System. FEEDS is a product of the cooperative effort of the State University System (SUS) and private sector industries in Florida. FEEDS offers access to quality graduate programs and extended studies. The use of live and recorded television, telephone line–based teleconferencing, and computer-aided communication brings students and professors together.

The Web-based Master's Degree in Industrial Chemistry, Forensic Science Option program is designed for practicing professionals and full-time students who desire an advanced program of study in the forensic analysis of biological materials. The forensic science track has a strong biochemistry-DNA focus to serve the needs of supervisory (or prospective supervisory) personnel in DNA sections of crime laboratories.

Approximately 50 percent of the course work can be accessed on line and the remainder can be taken on site at UCF or other designated institutions.

The newest Web-based program is the Master's Degree in Educational Media, designed for individuals who wish to become media specialists in schools. The program develops skills in administration, production, instructional design, technologies of instruction and information management, organization, selection, evaluation, and research that relate to school library media programs. Upon completion, students qualify for Florida certification in educational media. Students must have completed basic teaching certification course work and should have successful teaching experience.

The Web-based Doctor of Education Community College Focus is a program for full-time or part-time employees of community colleges who wish to become academic leaders for this sector of higher education. Some courses are entirely Web-based, while others are Web-enhanced. Although there is a required body of course work, the plan of study is individually determined based upon a student's goals. The curriculum requires completion of a minimum of 93 graduate credits that include all facets of the comprehensive community college. A maximum of 30 semester hours of graduate credit may be transferred into the doctoral program.

FACULTY

UCF employs more than 800 full-time and 290 (FTE) part-time faculty members in the five distinct colleges that comprise the University. Eighty percent of the full-time faculty members have terminal or doctoral degrees. Nearly 200 resident faculty members have completed an eight week in-house faculty development course for Web-based instruction.

ADMISSION

Students who plan to enroll in Web-based courses must be admitted to the University and must follow the same admission procedures as other students.

TUITION AND FEES

The nonrefundable application fee is $20. The UCF Campus Card fee is $10. Summer 2000 semester registra-tion fees for residents were $73.40 per credit hour for undergraduate study and $146.22 per credit hour for graduate study; nonresident fees were $306.35 for undergraduate study and $506.95 for graduate study.

FINANCIAL AID

Information regarding financial aid is available from UCF's Office of Student Financial Assistance on line at http://pegasus.cc.ucf.edu/~finaid/.

APPLYING

Undergraduate applicants with more than 60 credit hours or who have earned an Associate of Arts degree from a Florida public community college must submit high school transcripts and transcripts from all colleges attended. Applicants with fewer than 60 credit hours must also submit SAT or ACT scores and must meet the freshmen State University System eligibility requirements. Graduate applicants must submit official GRE (or GMAT scores for selected programs) test scores and official transcripts showing a bachelor's degree earned at a regionally accredited institution. The minimum University requirements for admission into a graduate program are a 3.0 GPA on a 4.0 scale or a score of 1000 on the combined verbal-quantitative portions of the GRE or 450 on the GMAT (for programs that require it). Requirements for specific programs are in addition to or different from the minimum University requirements.

CONTACT

Dr. Steven E. Sorg
Assistant Vice President for Distributed Learning
12424 Research Parkway, Suite 256
Orlando, Florida 32826-3271
Telephone: 407-207-4910
Fax: 407-207-4911
E-mail: distrib@mail.ucf.edu
Web site: http://distrib.ucf.edu/

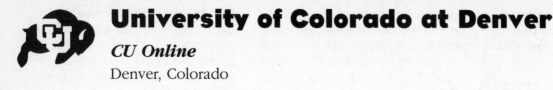

University of Colorado at Denver

CU Online

Denver, Colorado

The University of Colorado at Denver is one of four institutions in the University of Colorado system and the only public university in the Denver metropolitan area. It is an urban, nonresidential campus located in downtown Denver. The University of Colorado at Denver was founded in 1965 and is accredited by the North Central Association of Colleges and Schools.

DISTANCE LEARNING PROGRAM

CU Online is the virtual campus of the University of Colorado system, with eleven collegiate and professional development programs offering more than 125 courses via the Internet.

CU Online offers core curriculum and elective courses in a variety of disciplines, all the same high-quality courses taught throughout the University of Colorado system.

DELIVERY MEDIA

CU Online courses are not self paced. However, students enjoy a greater scheduling flexibility than in a traditional classroom by logging into class a couple of times each week at the times of their choice. Instructors delivering their courses through CU Online make use of cutting-edge technology, such as streaming audio, video, and multimedia slide shows for presenting course content. A number of technologies allow students to interact with the instructor and their peers: threaded discussions in a bulletin board–type area, live discussions in an online classroom, e-mail, and collaborative workspaces.

The online courses are offered via the eCollege.com system.

PROGRAMS OF STUDY

CU Online offers courses in liberal arts and sciences, arts and media, business, engineering, public affairs, and architecture and planning. As of September 2000, complete online degree programs, including a Bachelor of Arts in sociology, and master's degrees in business administration, engineering management, geographic information systems, and public administration, with more programs under development (check the Web site for the latest developments). All of the courses may be applied to a degree program at the University of Colorado at Denver or may be transferred to a student's home institution, pending approval.

SPECIAL PROGRAMS

CU Online offers a certificate in music industry studies through the College of Arts and Media and certificates in business writing, project management, and instructional design: developing training materials through the Professional Development Office in the College of Business.

STUDENT SERVICES

CU Online offers a vast range of student services. Students can search catalogs, register for courses, order text books and other course materials, get academic advising, and apply for financial aid, all on line.

CREDIT OPTIONS

Students may take credit and noncredit courses through CU Online and, for some courses, CEUs. The methods of evaluation are letter grades or pass/fail.

FACULTY

Online courses follow the same faculty governance policies as the established on-campus courses. All CU Online faculty members are approved by the department and, often, also instruct the on-campus courses. Many of the instructors are experts who are working in the field in which they teach and bring to the online experience vast knowledge and resources from their industry.

ADMISSION

Students living in the state of Colorado must be accepted to the University either as degree-seeking or non–degree-seeking students. Students living outside of the state of Colorado do not need to be admitted to take CU Online courses; however, if students wish to complete their degree through CU Online, formal admission must be made. Students may visit the CU Online Web site (listed below) and click on the register button for more information regarding admissions and to register for courses.

TUITION AND FEES

Tuition rates vary between colleges and depending on residency status.

Most undergraduate courses cost approximately $126–$183 per credit hour. There is a $100 course fee that is added to each online course, a $10 fee for technology resources, and a $5 fee for the student information system. For specific information regarding tuition for online courses, students should visit the CU Online Web site.

FINANCIAL AID

To be eligible for financial aid, students must be enrolled as degree-seeking students at the University of Colorado at Denver. Students may contact the financial aid office for more information (telephone: 303-556-2886; e-mail: finaid@carbon.cudenver.edu).

APPLYING

Admission requirements vary by college and school. To find specific information about applying to the University of Colorado at Denver, students may visit the home page.

CONTACT

For more information about CU Online, students should contact:

University of Colorado at Denver
Campus Box 198
P.O. Box 173364
Denver, Colorado 80217-3364
Telephone: 303-556-6505
Fax: 303-556-6530
E-mail: inquiry@cuonline.edu
Web site: http://www.cuonline.edu

University of Dallas

Graduate School of Management
Center for Distance Learning

Irving, Texas

The University of Dallas, located in Irving, Texas, was founded in 1956 as an independent Catholic university dedicated to excellence in its educational programs.

The Graduate School of Management (GSM) is the largest M.B.A.-granting institution in the Southwest. GSM was founded in 1966 with a distinctive mission: to create a professionally sound M.B.A. program accessible to individuals who are already employed in business. More than 75 percent of GSM students work full-time. The student body is made up of Americans and international students representing more than sixty countries.

GSM prepares master's-level students for leadership roles in business and industry and is accredited to award M.B.A. and Master of Management degrees by the Commission on Colleges of the Southern Association of Colleges and Schools (SACS).

DISTANCE LEARNING PROGRAM

The Graduate School of Management Distance Learning Program offers the convenience of Internet-based courses accessible 24 hours a day, seven days a week from anywhere in the world. The distance learning programs serve more than 250 graduate students. All programs are credit bearing and lead to an M.B.A. degree, Master of Management degree, or a graduate certificate.

DELIVERY MEDIA

The graduate degrees and graduate certificate programs are offered through the Internet and are accessible via any Web browser. The self-guided asynchronous method of teaching is instructor-led. There is no residency requirement.

Students from all over the globe communicate and exchange information with their instructor and each other electronically via the Internet, e-mail, facsimile, and telephone. This method of course-delivery provides flexibility for students to study on their own time anywhere in the world.

PROGRAMS OF STUDY

The Graduate School of Management offers M.B.A., Master of Management, and graduate certificate programs through distance learning in information technology, telecommunications, e-commerce, and sport management. These programs are designed with a specific focus on management. The M.B.A. degree requires the completion of sixteen courses with a one-hour lecture series requirement. The Master of Management requires the completion of ten courses, and the graduate certificate program requires the completion of five courses.

GSM is seeking corporate clients who are interested in hosting a full M.B.A. or graduate certificate program in telecommunications, health services, information technology, e-commerce, or general business for their employees.

SPECIAL PROGRAMS

Distance education students are able to take on-campus courses as part of their overall degree or certificate program.

STUDENT SERVICES

An academic adviser is available for assistance in course advising and registration. Professors are available for course curriculum advising and career counseling. The Graduate School of Management prides itself on providing exceptional customer service to its students. Students taking courses over the Internet may need additional advising, encouragement, and support. Therefore, GSM makes every effort to foster a strong relationship with the student.

CREDIT OPTIONS

For the M.B.A. program, a maximum of 4 courses or 12 hours of transfer credits may be applied. A transfer course must be a 3-semester-hour (5-quarter-hour) graduate-level course from an accredited school. The transfer course must not be more than six years old. A grade of at least a B (3.0) is required. Course content must be substantially similar to that of a course required in a student's degree plan. For further information, students can contact the GSM Admissions Department at the address below.

FACULTY

GSM's faculty provides a rare mix of competence in both the theoretical aspects of management and the applied working knowledge of its practical aspects. The faculty is organized into a relatively small resident group and a larger adjunct group. The resident faculty members are full-time instructors with extensive backgrounds in business, teaching, applied research, and consulting. The adjunct faculty consists of practicing managers, attorneys, accountants, consultants, and other professionals who teach part-time. GSM students enjoy the best of both worlds—academic and business.

ADMISSION

Applicants for the M.B.A. program must have a bachelor's degree from an accredited university and must satisfy any two of the following criteria: an overall GPA of at least 3.0 on a 4.0 scale, a satisfactory score on the Graduate Management Admission Test (GMAT), or five years or more of effective managerial or professional work experience.

For the Master of Management degree program, a student must have an M.B.A. degree from an accredited university.

For the graduate certificate program, a student must have a bachelor's degree from an accredited university and have at least three years of professional and/or managerial experience. International students must submit a TOEFL score of at least 520. Students who complete the graduate certificate program can apply course work towards the M.B.A. or Master of Management program.

TUITION AND FEES

Graduate tuition was $391 per credit hour ($1173 per course) in the 1999–2000 academic year for residents and nonresidents.

FINANCIAL AID

U.S. graduate students may obtain financial assistance through various loan programs. The University of Dallas Financial Aid Office (telephone: 972-721-5266) has information and application forms for loans. Student loan applications must be processed through the Financial Aid Office.

APPLYING

Students are encouraged to contact the GSM Admissions Department at the address below or visit the Web site to receive additional information. Students can apply from anywhere in the world.

CONTACT

Director of Admissions
Graduate School of Management
University of Dallas
1845 East Northgate Drive
Irving, Texas 75062-4736
Telephone: 972-721-5174
        800-UDAL-MBA
        (832-5622, toll-free)
Fax: 972-721-4009
E-mail: admiss@gsm.udallas.edu
Web site: http://gsm.udallas.edu

University of Delaware

UD Online/Distance Learning

Newark, Delaware

A private university with public support, the University of Delaware is a land-grant, sea-grant, space-grant, and urban-grant institution with a rich 250-year history. Its main campus is located in Newark, Delaware, a suburban community situated between Philadelphia and Baltimore. The University offers more than 100 undergraduate majors. Six of the University's colleges offer both graduate and undergraduate degrees; one college offers only graduate degrees. The University has been fully accredited by the Middle States Association of Colleges and Schools since 1921. There are more than 21,000 students enrolled at the University as undergraduate, graduate, or continuing education students.

DISTANCE LEARNING PROGRAM

The University's UD Online/Distance Learning system supports more than 2,300 registrations a year in a variety of undergraduate and graduate courses involving twenty-eight academic departments and two degree programs. In 1996, the United States Distance Learning Association gave the University the Most Outstanding Achievement in Higher Education rating for "extraordinary achievements through distance education."

DELIVERY MEDIA

More than one hundred University of Delaware courses are available in videotape or Internet formats. Student-faculty interaction is maintained through special telephone office hours and/or e-mail. The University also offers live, interactive courses through a two-way audio, two-way video system to sites in Delaware. A limited number of print-based courses are also available through UD Online/Distance Learning. In addition, selected graduate engineering courses are available through National Technological University (NTU).

PROGRAMS OF STUDY

Students can use distance learning to pursue the following degree programs:

Bachelor of Science in Nursing: Baccalaureate for the Registered Nurse major (BRN): Ten of thirteen required nursing courses are offered in a video format, and most of the prerequisites are also offered in a video format. Students are required to enroll in three 1-credit weekend courses held on the Newark, Delaware, campus. The BRN major offers a way for busy professionals to continue their education on a schedule tailored to their particular needs. The BRN major requires 125 credits for program completion.

Master of Science in Nursing (MSN) with a concentration in nursing administration: The nursing administration concentration focuses on preparing nurses to function as managers in health-care facilities. The curriculum incorporates the broad concepts of nursing and administration while providing the knowledge essential for managers to improve the productivity of the agencies they work for, assuring that quality health care is maintained or improved.

Bachelor of Science with a major in hotel, restaurant and institutional management (HRIM): Most of the specialized HRIM core courses as well as the required liberal arts and business courses are available in a distance learning format. Students may pursue a degree or take courses for professional development. Degree-seeking students complete a one-week resident management institute at the University's Newark campus. This intensive institute provides hands-on experience in the state-of-the-art food service laboratory as well as networking with faculty members, other students, and industry mentors. Students must successfully complete 120 credits, with at least 18 credits in University of Delaware HRIM courses.

SPECIAL PROGRAMS

An increasing number of engineering courses are available through distance learning, particularly at the graduate level. Engineering professionals may enroll in individual courses for professional development or may combine distance learning courses with campus courses to pursue a master's degree in a variety of engineering disciplines.

In addition to credit courses, the University offers a variety of noncredit courses through distance learning in topics ranging from art conservation to criminal justice, engineering, nursing, and technical writing.

Beginning this year, the e-commerce short courses, seminars, and certificate programs are offered. This noncredit track provides the basic knowledge needed to work on an e-commerce project or to manage a business that is making an entry into the e-commerce arena.

The University is offering Internet Literacy, a course that uses the Internet to deliver a course *about* the Internet and enables students to acquire the conceptual background and the online skills to become Internet literate. The course is offered in an eight-week, noncredit format or as a semester-long, for-credit course. Hands-on tutorials help students create a personal presence on the Web. For more information, call 1-800-597-1444 (toll-free) or 302-831-0153 or visit the Web site (http://www.udel.edu/ContEd/internet_literacy.html).

CREDIT OPTIONS

In order to be eligible for a University of Delaware degree, students must complete either the first 90 or the last 30 credits of the degree program with the University of Delaware.

A credit-by-examination system allows students to demonstrate competence obtained through professional experience. Each University academic department determines the specific courses that may be eligible for credit by examination and the specific requirements for receiving credit.

FACULTY

Eighty percent of the more than 900 faculty members hold the doctoral or terminal degree in their field. In fall and spring semesters, about 10 percent of the faculty participate in distance learning or instructional television activities.

ADMISSION

The Admissions Committee considers all academic credentials, including all previous college work and high school preparation. Students transferring from other schools are normally required to have at least a 2.5 grade point average to be considered for admission.

TUITION AND FEES

Students registering at official UD Online/Distance Learning work sites may register as site participants and pay $211 per credit hour (undergraduate) or $605 per credit hour (graduate). Students may also register as individual/nonsite participants and pay resident (undergraduate, $183 per credit hour; graduate, $243 per credit hour) or nonresident (undergraduate, $531 per credit hour; graduate, $708 per credit hour) tuition plus a handling fee of $90 per videotaped course. Tuition and fees are subject to change. For current information on fees and tuition, stu-

dents should visit the Web site (http://www.udel.edu/ce/online.html).

FINANCIAL AID

The Financial Aid Office administers grants and scholarships, which do not have to be repaid; low-interest loans; and student employment. A need-based financial aid package may consist of one or more of the following: Federal Pell Grant, Federal Supplemental Educational Opportunity Grant, Federal Perkins Loan, and Federal Direct Loan. The Federal Direct Parents Loan Program is also available. Delaware residents also may be eligible for need-based funding through General Fund Scholarships and Delaware Right to Education Scholarships. Students must be matriculated and carry at least 6 credit hours per semester.

APPLYING

A completed application consists of the Distance Learning Application for Admission, application fee, and official college and high school transcripts. Due dates for applications are no later than August 1 for fall and no later than December 1 for spring admission. On-campus orientation is not required for distance learners.

CONTACT

Mary Pritchard
Director
UD Online/Distance Learning
211 John M. Clayton Hall
University of Delaware
Newark, Delaware 19716
Telephone: 800-597-1444 (toll-free)
Fax: 1-302-831-3292
E-mail: continuing.ed@udel.edu
Web site: http://www.udel.edu/ce/online.html

The University of Findlay

Global Campus

Findlay, Ohio

The Churches of God, General Conference, and the citizens of the city of Findlay, Ohio founded the University of Findlay as Findlay College in 1882. It is accredited by the North Central Association of Colleges and Schools and the Ohio State Board of Education and has approval from a number of accrediting bodies for specific program areas. It is authorized to offer A.A., B.A., B.S., M.A., M.S., M.P.T., and M.B.A. degree programs by the Ohio Board of Regents. The institution's mission is to equip students for meaningful lives and productive careers. It creates and delivers high-quality and innovative programs for undergraduate, graduate, and continuing education for a diverse student body. Information technology has been integrated into instructional support, program enhancement, and distance learning through a separate Global Campus.

DISTANCE LEARNING PROGRAM

The mission of distance learning at the University of Findlay is to provide high-quality, innovative learning experiences through technological means to reach students unable to take courses through traditional instructional formats. A separate online Global Campus (Web site listed below) is the vehicle for both credit and noncredit Web courses and programs as well as for all needed student support services. For the academic year 1999–2000, the University served nearly 500 students via distance learning.

DELIVERY MEDIA

The Global Campus uses Internet technologies to deliver graduate, undergraduate, and noncredit workforce development courses anywhere in the world. These courses make use of synchronous online sessions once a week, as well as e-mail, fax, and phone. Some classes use threaded discussions and group projects. Supplementary videotapes or CD-ROMs are often included. Videoconferencing is also used to deliver business and education courses to several off-campus locations in Ohio.

PROGRAMS OF STUDY

The University had seventy-six graduate and undergraduate courses available on the Web during 1999–2000. These included two master's programs, the M.B.A. and the M.S. in Environmental Management (M.S.E.M.), and two degree completion programs, the B.S. in Business Management (B.S.B.M.) and the B.S. in Environmental Management (B.S.E.M.). Students in these programs can combine on-site traditional instruction with Web courses or complete their programs entirely online. Most courses range from eight to twelve weeks in length. Entry to the M.B.A. program requires the GMAT, and a TOEFL score of 525 (if appropriate) is required for admission to the M.B.A. and M.S.E.M. programs. The B.S.B.M. and B.S.E.M. degree completion programs require the applicant to have completed 62 transferable semester hours of college-level work. All four programs require some prerequisite courses, some of which can be completed by proficiency testing. In addition to these programs, several courses, each from the Master of Arts in Education and the undergraduate technology management program, are available online. The number of online courses in the general education area also continues to grow. Descriptions of all online courses may be accessed through the University's Global Campus Web site.

SPECIAL PROGRAMS

The University of Findlay offers a variety of special programs open to distance learners. These include a partnership with Solomon Software in programs for preparing technology managers and programs designed for international students. In addition, the Community Education and Technology Center provides support for on-site as well as online workforce courses available to students across the nation.

Internships are also available with a variety of local and regional companies, including Whirlpool, Cooper Tire, Solomon Software, and others. Arrangements can be made through the Office of Career Services.

Other nationally recognized programs include the master's degree in environmental, safety, and health management offered through the National Center for Environmental Management, as well as certificate courses.

STUDENT SERVICES

The University of Findlay's Global Campus was designed with the student in mind. This portal provides online students with all of the same services on-campus students have. Students can find information about financial aid, admission, registration, advising, tuition and fees, and much more. Also available is a library with an extensive list of resources and searchable full-text databases.

CREDIT OPTIONS

The Office of the Registrar evaluates all transfer credits, including those earned in the military, from official transcripts. Graduate students may transfer a maximum of 9 graduate semester hours. Undergraduate degree completion students must have 62 transferable semester hours of college-level work, some of which may be earned by portfolio assessment or CLEP tests. Proficiency tests may be used for required prerequisites. All degree completion program courses must be taken online or on-site from the University of Findlay.

FACULTY

Twenty-two full-time and 4 part-time faculty members taught in the distance learning programs in 1999–2000. Of these, 50 percent had doctoral degrees. The emphasis on full-time faculty members provides for continuity and quality control of courses.

ADMISSION

The University of Findlay's general policy for admission can be found at http://www.gcampus.org/Admissions/GradPolicy.asp and includes information on credit transfer, transient credit work, nondegree credit, loans, grants, assistantships, and the refund policy.

TUITION AND FEES

Depending on the program, graduate tuition and fees range from $265 to $340 per credit hour, and undergraduate from $203 to $345 per credit hour. Students should check with the appropriate program director for the most current fees.

FINANCIAL AID

Each year more than 90 percent of students attending the University of Findlay receive some form of financial assistance. Just as there are a variety of programs, there are a variety of forms, procedures, and dates to consider. The Global Campus provides an abundance of information, from how to apply and what is considered in the admission process, to FAQs and a wide range of financial aid sources and programs.

APPLYING

The application process for online courses is the same as it is for on-campus students. A downloadable transcript request form and other specific information about applying to the University can be found at http://www.gcampus.org/Admissions/.

CONTACT

Dr. Doris Salis
Dean of Adult and Continuing Education
The University of Findlay
1000 North Main Street
Findlay, Ohio 45840
Telephone: 800-558-9060 (toll-free)
Fax: 419-424-4822
E-mail: salis@mail.findlay.edu
Web site: http://www.gcampus.org

University of Houston

Division of Distance and Continuing Education

Houston, Texas

The University of Houston (UH) is the premier urban teaching and research institution in Texas. Founded in 1927, its activities include a broad range of academic programs encompassing undergraduate, graduate, and professional education; basic and applied research; and public service programs. Its professional schools include law, optometry, pharmacy, hotel, business, engineering, architecture, education, and social work. It is the doctoral degree granting and research-oriented component of the University of Houston System.

Serving 31,000 students, University of Houston educational programs include full-time programs for traditional students and part-time and evening programs for employed individuals. Research laboratories and institutes work directly with area corporations and governments, while public service programs contribute to and enhance the cultural and social climate of the community. UH has placed special emphasis on outreach and access for students, both locally and internationally.

DISTANCE LEARNING PROGRAM

Serving more than 4,500 students annually, UH Distance Education offers junior, senior, and graduate-level credit courses each semester. UH has the highest number of upper-level and graduate enrollments in distance education courses of any university in the state of Texas. Students may complete degrees through a combination of television, videotape, online classes, or face-to-face courses at four off-campus sites in the greater Houston area. All courses include ongoing interaction with instructors. Corporate and public sites participate in the UH Professional Training Network for continuing professional education.

DELIVERY MEDIA

UH Distance Education courses are delivered face-to-face at off-campus sites and either live/interactive (compressed video, microwave, or satellite) or asynchronously (tape, cable, or public broadcast, or on line). For online classes, students must be able to access the Internet. Students in asynchronous classes participate in scheduled, real-time sessions with the instructor and/or other class members. Special arrangements must be made for lab requirements in some degree programs. Proctored exams are arranged as needed.

PROGRAMS OF STUDY

UH Distance Education students may complete degrees in thirteen fields of study. All degree program requirements, course work, and prerequisites are the same as for on-campus students. Courses generally carry 3 credits; the number of credits needed for degree completion varies by program. Students can obtain more detailed information through the UH Distance Education Web site.

Undergraduate Distance Education program areas include computer drafting design, English, hotel and restaurant management, industrial supervision, and psychology. Undergraduate courses are available at the junior and senior level. Freshman- and sophomore-level courses may be taken on the UH campus or transferred in from other institutions.

Graduate degree program areas available through Distance Education include computer science, education (reading and language arts), electrical engineering (computers and electronics), engineering management, hospitality management, and training and development. Most of these programs are 36-hour, nonthesis options.

Students not seeking a degree may enroll in a limited number of selected credit courses.

Additional credit courses outside of these program areas are available each semester, as are noncredit training classes in a variety of subject areas such as computers, environmental safety, food and sanitation services, health-care management, personal enrichment, professional development, and technical field updates.

SPECIAL PROGRAMS

Corporate sites, schools, and libraries may join the University of Houston Professional Training Network to become a receive site for credit and noncredit classes delivered live/interactive. Membership includes special orientations and partnership opportunities with the University of Houston.

STUDENT SERVICES

University of Houston's award-winning Distance Education program provides students access to excellent academic support services. Library support is provided for enrolled students through access to the UH Online Catalog, borrowing privileges, reference services, remote access to electronic databases, guides to research, mail delivery of journal articles on request, and cooperative arrangements with other libraries.

Computer support services available to all enrolled students include a (Houston-area) computer account, e-mail, and World Wide Web browser. Documentation, training, and software are also available.

Student support services for Distance Education students include admission by mail or on line; phone registration; fee payment by mail and by phone; book and videotape orders by mail, phone, fax, or on line; remote-site proctored exams; paper exchange by fax, mail, or courier (corporate and public sites); 24-hour telephone InfoLine; and online advising.

University of Houston is an equal opportunity institution. Accommodations on the basis of disability are available.

CREDIT OPTIONS

Upon application for admission, students must submit transcripts from work completed at other post-secondary institutions. The amount and types of credit transferable to the University of Houston depend on the degree program.

FACULTY

The University of Houston has 1,960 full- and part-time faculty members. All UH faculty members teaching Distance Education courses participate in special training programs and ongoing assessment.

ADMISSION

Undergraduate admission is based on graduation from an accredited high school, college transfer, or entrance examination or through a combination of these criteria. Graduate applicants must have an earned bachelor's degree from an accredited institution. Individual programs have additional specific requirements.

TUITION AND FEES

In 2000–01, resident tuition and fees for one 3-credit-hour undergraduate course are $388 (nonresident, $1030); for a graduate course, the resident cost is $484 (nonresident, $1090). For two courses (6 credit hours), the undergraduate cost is $676 (nonresident, $1972); the graduate cost is $880 (nonresident, $2092). Students enrolling in Distance Education courses are charged a $140 per course off-campus and electronic course fee. Students are only assessed fees for the

first two off-campus courses in which they enroll each semester. Students enrolled exclusively in off-campus courses may qualify for up to $50 in fee waivers. Rates are subject to change.

FINANCIAL AID

General financial aid programs through the University of Houston include the Texas Public Education Grant, Texas Public Educational State Student Incentive Grant, Federal Pell Grant, Federal Supplemental Educational Opportunity Grant, Federal Perkins Student Loan, Hinson-Hazlewood College Student Loan, Federal Stafford Student Loan, Federal Parent Loan Program, and other loan and scholarship opportunities based on merit or need. In 1998–99, approximately 50 percent of all University of Houston students received some form of financial assistance.

APPLYING

To enroll in any UH credit course, students must first be admitted to the University of Houston. Complete admission information is available through the UH Distance Education InfoLine or through the UH Distance Education Web site. An undergraduate Texas Common Application is available on the Web at http://www.applytexas.org.

CONTACT

Distance Education Advisor
Distance Education
University of Houston
4242 South Mason Road
Katy, Texas 77450
Distance Education InfoLine: 281-395-2810
              800-687-8488 (toll-free)
Fax: 281-395-2629
E-mail: DEadvisor@uh.edu
Web site: http://www.uh.edu/uhdistance

University of Idaho

Engineering Outreach

Moscow, Idaho

The University of Idaho, established in 1889, is the land-grant institution for the state of Idaho. The University has a student population of more than 13,000 and offers degree programs in the liberal arts, sciences, agriculture, architecture, engineering, natural resources, mining and metallurgy, and law. Extended program delivery and outreach activities are central to the University's mission. The University of Idaho is a member of the National Association of State Universities and Land-Grant Colleges and the National Commission on Accrediting. The University is accredited by the Northwest Association of Schools and Colleges. The University of Idaho's College of Engineering undergraduate programs are accredited by the Engineering Accreditation Commission of the Accreditation Board for Engineering Technology (EAC/ABET). The computer science program is accredited by the Computer Science Accreditation Commission of the Computing Sciences.

DISTANCE LEARNING PROGRAM

The Engineering Outreach program offers complete distance-delivered degree programs in twelve disciplines. The program has grown from its establishment in 1975 into one of the top providers of graduate off-campus engineering degree programs, delivering more than 100 courses per semester to more than 400 students in locations around the country and around the world. More than 200 students have received graduate degrees through Engineering Outreach.

DELIVERY MEDIA

The Engineering Outreach program uses videotape, video conferencing, Internet, microwave, and satellite technology to deliver graduate-level courses to distant students. Courses do not require attendance at the University of Idaho campus. Courses are taught by University of Idaho faculty members and simultaneously video-taped in specially equipped studio classrooms. VHS videotapes are sent to students; each tape covers one 50-minute lecture. Additional course materials are provided on the World

Wide Web for immediate access by students. Both live-taped and previously taped courses are typically offered during a semester.

PROGRAMS OF STUDY

Engineering Outreach courses carry regular University of Idaho resident credit and may be used toward a degree program at the University of Idaho or transferred to other institutions that accept distance-delivered credit from the University of Idaho. By taking courses through Engineering Outreach, a student can obtain a graduate degree from the University of Idaho in biological and agricultural engineering with an emphasis in water resources and management (M.S. and M.Engr.), civil engineering (M.S. and M.Engr.), computer engineering (M.S. and M.Engr.), computer science (M.S. and Ph.D.), electrical engineering (M.S., M.Engr., and Ph.D.), engineering management (M.Engr.), geological engineering (M.S. and M.Engr.), mathematics (Master of Arts in Teaching), mechanical engineering (M.Engr.), metallurgical engineering (M.S.), mining engineering (M.S.), and psychology with an emphasis in human factors (M.S.).

SPECIAL PROGRAMS

The senior faculty members in the College of Engineering at the University of Idaho usually offer a jointly taught course in engineering fundamentals (Civil Engineering 411) through Engineering Outreach each semester. This course is a review of basic engineering and science material covered in the Fundamentals of Engineering exam that each engineering graduate must take to be registered as an engineer-in-training and work toward attainment of professional registration. Another special offering in the Engineering Outreach curriculum is a self-paced short course in the Java programming language.

Engineering Outreach now provides students with the opportunity to receive certificates of completion in the following five areas: power systems protection and relaying, secure and dependable computing systems, communication systems, and character education, with more to come. Certificates of completion draw on selected courses within larger programs and are ideal for students who want to learn more about a specific subject area but are not ready to pursue a complete degree program. Students must normally complete 12 to 18 credits, some required, others elective, depending on each topic area, to receive the certificate of completion. Students are strongly urged to apply for graduate school as they begin a certificate of completion study plan to ease into a graduate program at a later date. However, students may also petition to have up to 12 credits earned toward a certificate of completion transferred into their graduate study plan. Students should contact Engineering Outreach for complete details and an updated list of currently available certificates of completion.

STUDENT SERVICES

Communication with faculty members is facilitated by e-mail and by use of the program's toll-free telephone number. Current information about the program and courses is available on the World Wide Web. Students may enroll via fax, phone, or mail. All students have access to the University of Idaho Library via the World Wide Web or telephone.

CREDIT OPTIONS

All master's degree programs require a minimum of 30 to 36 credits. A combined total of 12 transfer, correspondence, nondegree, or approved over-aged (more than 8 years old) credits may be used toward the degree. Credits can be transferred to the University of Idaho, with the consent of the student's committee and the Vice President for Research and Graduate Studies, only from other institutions that grant similar graduate degrees.

FACULTY

Up to 100 University of Idaho faculty members teach in the program each semester. With few exceptions, these faculty members hold advanced degrees in their fields of expertise; more than 90 percent hold doctorates.

ADMISSION

Requirements for admission vary by department but generally include a bachelor's degree from an accredited college or university, a minimum undergraduate grade point average of 2.8, and a minimum grade point average of 2.8 in subsequent academic work.

TUITION AND FEES

Tuition and fees are $351 per credit hour for students enrolled in a graduate program and for all graduate-level courses and $324 per credit hour for non-degree-seeking students in undergraduate courses. There are no additional fees for nonresidents.

Fees are adjusted yearly by the State of Idaho Board of Regents. Students should contact Engineering Outreach for updated fees for the 2000–01 academic year.

FINANCIAL AID

Engineering Outreach students may be eligible for federal financial aid. Determination of eligibility is made by the University of Idaho Student Financial Aid Office. Financial aid may include scholarships, Federal Pell Grants, and Federal Perkins Loans. Last year, more than $40,000 in financial aid was awarded to Engineering Outreach students. Approximately 5 percent of all students received this aid.

APPLYING

Courses may be taken by non-degree-seeking students or for credit toward a graduate degree. Applications can be completed on the World Wide Web or with forms provided in Engineering Outreach brochures. There is a $35 application fee for graduate admissions. Students should contact the University of Idaho Graduate Admissions Office at http://www.uidaho.edu/cogs/ or call Engineering Outreach for assistance.

CONTACT

Diane Bancke
Engineering Outreach
University of Idaho
P.O. Box 441014
Moscow, Idaho 83844-1014
Telephone: 800-824-2889 (toll-free)
Fax: 208-885-6165
E-mail: outreach@uidaho.edu
Web site: http://www.uidaho.edu/evo/

University of Illinois at Springfield

UIS-Online
Springield, Illinois

The University of Illinois at Springfield (UIS) is the newest of the University of Illinois (U of I) campuses. Formerly known as Sangamon State University, the campus joined the University of Illinois as part of a statewide reorganization of public higher education in 1995. Throughout its twenty-nine-year history, the University has consistently stressed excellent teaching, practical experience, and professional development as the most effective means to enlighten students' minds and give them the skills to prepare them for the next century. UIS is committed to addressing the needs of both traditional and nontraditional learners. UIS is fully accredited by the Commission of Institutions of Higher Education of the North Central Association of Colleges and Schools (NCA).

DISTANCE LEARNING PROGRAM

UIS Online is a part of the University of Illinois Online initiative, which provides leadership, coordination, and financial support in the areas of Internet-based education and public service. U of I Online offers online learning opportunities and complete degree and certificate programs to place-bound and time-restricted students in Illinois, the U.S., and around the world. U of I Online currently offers 150 classes with an enrollment of over 5,000 students.

DELIVERY MEDIA

UIS Online courses and programs are delivered through a wide range of technologies via the World Wide Web, on a sixteen-week or eight-week basis. Technologies utilized include synchronous and asynchronous Web delivery, CD-ROM, videotape, and streaming media. Students communicate with their instructors through e-mail, conferencing tools, telephone, mail, or fax. Access to an Internet-capable computer is essential.

PROGRAMS OF STUDY

The Liberal Studies Online Bachelor of Arts degree at the University of Il-linois at Springfield is a 60-hour, upper-division program offering classes at the junior and senior level. It is built on twenty-five years of experience in assisting learners in designing individualized academic experiences. Learners from throughout the country attend virtual classes and design individualized degree programs that meet their unique educational goals.

The program emphasizes the integration of eight topical learning categories with a variety of media-based instructional methods to form a well-rounded and individualized educational experience. Through this integrative process, Liberal Studies Online helps learners to acquire an understanding of the values, meaning, concerns, choices, and commitments that serve as foundations for the quality of life. Unique features of this degree program include the development of customized degree programs, working with multidisciplinary faculty members as advisers, and utilizing the latest networked information technologies. Liberal Studies Online is designed with the learners' priorities, interests, and experiences as the central focus of their degree program.

The Educational Leadership M.A. degree with a concentration in master leadership (MTL) is a new online offering beginning in fall 2000. MTL provides practicing teachers with the opportunity to earn a high quality master's degree that can be used as a step towards Illinois or National Board Certification. The program works to meet the needs of place-bound teachers, both in Illinois and nationally, who wish to take positions of leadership within their school or district. The program is an innovative collaboration between the Education Leadership and Teacher Education programs of UIS. The courses incorporate online interactive participation and an emphasis on independent project work that links the students' coursework to their professional growth needs.

The M.S. degree program in the Management Information Systems (MIS) Department at the University of Illinois at Springfield is specifically focused on providing a balance between technical skills and knowledge of business functions and processes. The MIS Online program showcases faculty members who bring real-world experience to a curriculum designed to integrate business and management concepts with information technology.

Today's organizations require a variety of new experts, such as information systems managers, systems analysts, applications programmers, data base administrators, telecommunication analysts, and systems librarians. The MIS Online curriculum is designed to prepare students to fit these diverse organizational roles.

SPECIAL PROGRAMS

UIS strives to provide a number of additional courses online to meet the needs of its off campus students. The Departments of Chemistry, Biology, Communication, Human Development, English, Women's Studies, History, Art, Philosophy, Sociology/Anthropology, Computer Science, Public Affairs, and Business offer online classes as part of their programs.

STUDENT SERVICES

Distance learners have access to UIS library services, the campus computer network, e-mail services, academic advising, career placement assistance, and bookstore and auditorium discounts. Individual departments may have additional special services which they offer to their online students. Students should contact individual departments for details. Technical assistance is provided through the UIS online help desk, the Office of Technology Enhanced Learning (OTEL), and the Illinois Virtual Campus's (IVC) 41 support centers.

CREDIT OPTIONS

Students may transfer credits from another institution. In addition, credit for prior learning (CPL) enables qualified UIS students to receive academic credit for college-level learning acquired outside the classroom. A campus-wide faculty committee monitors the entire CPL process. For more information, students should contact CPL (217-206-7545).

FACULTY

One third of UIS faculty members teach online. Distance learning faculty members are full-time or adjunct members within the department granting the course credit. They are the same professionals who teach the course on campus and are available to answer questions via telephone, online conferencing, fax, e-mail, or regular mail. In addition, most online professors maintain regular online office hours through conferencing tools.

ADMISSION

Applicants with 45 or more semester hours and a cumulative grade point average of 2.00 or higher (on a 4.00 scale) from any regionally accredited institution of higher education may be admitted as an undergraduate. Applicants must have completed 3 semester hours of English Composition as a minimum for admission. Individuals with bachelor's degrees from regionally accredited colleges and universities are eligible to apply for admission to graduate study at UIS. A minimum undergraduate GPA of 2.50 and/or specific programs requirements must be met. Individual departments may require higher GPAs, GRE's or other qualifications before admittance to a program. Enrollment in degreed programs requires formal admission to the University. Students should contact Enrollment Services (http://www.uis.edu/~enroll/) for additional information.

TUITION AND FEES

Costs may vary depending upon program of study, number of credits taken, and course delivery. Tuition for fall 2000 is $107.75 per credit hour for graduate students and $95.75 for undergraduates. Tuition for out-of-state residents is higher. Online students pay a reduced student fee of $18.50 per credit hour. Additional fees vary by course.

FINANCIAL AID

The Office of Financial Assistance coordinates financial aid in the form of scholarships, grants, or loans. Online students may apply for this assistance. Applications and additional information can be obtained by contacting the UIS Financial Assistance Department 217-206-6724 or by visiting the Web site (http://www.uis.edu/~enroll/faid.html).

APPLYING

Students may register by mail, fax, World Wide Web, or in person. Students should visit or contact the UIS Registration Office (World Wide Web: http://www.uis.edu/~enroll/reg1.html; telephone 217-206-6174 or 800-252-6174, toll-free).

CONTACT

For further information about the University of Illinois at Springfield Online program, students should visit UIS Online (http://online.uis.edu), the U of I Online Inquiry page (http://www.vpaa.uillinois.edu/uionline/), or contact:

Ray Schroeder, Director
Office of Technology Enhanced Learning
University of Illinois at Springfield
Springfield, Illinois 62794-9243
Telephone: 217-206-7317
Fax: 217-206-6162
E-mail: Schroeder.Ray@uis.edu

The University of Iowa

Center for Credit Programs

Iowa City, Iowa

> *Established in 1847, the University of Iowa is a major national research university with a solid liberal arts foundation. Iowa was the first U.S. public university to admit men and women on an equal basis. It has won international recognition for its wealth of achievements in the arts, sciences, and humanities. A member of the select Association of American Universities, the University of Iowa maintains a balance between scholarly research and teaching. It places a strong emphasis on undergraduate, international, and interdisciplinary education. The University is accredited by the North Central Association of Colleges and Schools and other accrediting agencies.*

DISTANCE LEARNING PROGRAM

In cooperation with University of Iowa academic colleges and departments, the Center for Credit Programs (CCP) of the University of Iowa's Division of Continuing Education delivers University credit courses, both in Iowa City and off campus, to nontraditional and other part-time students who seek a college degree, career advancement, or self-improvement. The CCP supports some 19,000 enrollments annually, including some 4,500 Guided Correspondence Study (GCS) registrations. Distance education courses may use interactive and broadcast television (available only within Iowa) or correspondence study and Web courses (available worldwide to English-speaking students). Approximately 160 GCS or Web-supported courses are available both at the undergraduate and graduate levels.

DELIVERY MEDIA

University of Iowa distance education courses employ a variety of delivery media. Correspondence courses are offered in traditional print-based formats. In many cases, courses are available as Web or Web-assisted courses. Videos or CD-ROMs supplement some courses. Students interact with instructors via correspondence, fax, e-mail, or toll-free telephone. Within Iowa, degree program and other courses are offered via interactive video through the Iowa Communications Network (ICN), an advanced fiber-optic telecommunications network linking educational sites across the state.

PROGRAMS OF STUDY

The Bachelor of Liberal Studies (B.L.S.) external degree program provides an opportunity for students to complete a bachelor's degree from the University of Iowa without attending classes on campus or without ever visiting the campus. The B.L.S. degree has no specific major. Instead, students concentrate course work in three of five distribution areas (humanities, communications and arts, natural science and math, social sciences, or professional fields).

The B.L.S. degree is a flexible degree program offering convenient, self-paced work; advisers who work with students to create an individual plan of study; the diverse preparation a liberal arts degree provides; the flexibility to match education efforts with career goals; and an undergraduate degree awarded by a nationally recognized institution. More than 600 students have graduated from the program since it was established in 1977 by the Iowa Board of Regents, and hundreds of students are currently active. For more specific information, see the CCP Web site or call the toll-free number below.

SPECIAL PROGRAMS

The LionHawk program represents a formal partnership between Pennsylvania State University and the University of Iowa that allows students to earn both two- and four-year degrees without on-campus study. Students who complete Penn State's Extended Letters, Arts, and Sciences (ELAS) associate degree are ensured admission to the B.L.S. program. Upon admission to the B.L.S. program, all General Education Program requirements are considered satisfied except for the foreign language requirement.

STUDENT SERVICES

Degree-seeking students receive ongoing registration, educational advising, library access, and other services. Entry into the program provides access to a listserv that connects B.L.S. students everywhere. The CCP provides extended office hours (Monday–Thursday, 8 a.m. to 7 p.m.; Friday 8 a.m. to 5 p.m., Central Time) to better accommodate nontraditional students.

CREDIT OPTIONS

Credit for B.L.S. degree requirements may be met in several ways, including University of Iowa campus, off-campus, or evening classes (available only in Iowa); transfer credit from other institutions (a minimum number of credits from the University of Iowa are required); and other methods. B.L.S. students primarily take the GCS courses, which are available anywhere, are available for enrollment continuously, and allow for self-paced learning. GCS courses provide semester-hour credit. There is no limit on the number of GCS courses that may be applied toward the B.L.S. degree.

FACULTY

All courses and instructors are approved by appropriate departmental and collegiate officers. Courses are taught by regular or adjunct faculty members and some advanced graduate students.

ADMISSION

Students applying for admission to the B.L.S. degree program may request an information packet by calling the CCP toll-free number. No special admission requirements are necessary to enroll in GCS courses. Enrollment in GCS courses does not constitute admission to the University of Iowa.

TUITION AND FEES

For 2000–01 (effective July 1, 2000, through June 30, 2001), GCS tuition is $92 per semester hour plus a $15 per course enrollment fee. GCS tuition is the same for in-state, out-of-state, undergraduate, or graduate students. Tuition for semester-based distance learning courses is the same as University of Iowa residential tuition, or $122 per semester hour for undergraduates and $192 per semester hour for graduates for 2000–01.

FINANCIAL AID

Registration in semester-based courses (generally available only in Iowa) may qualify students for Pell Grants or Stafford Loans. These programs are not accepted to fund GCS courses. The CCP provides limited funds for per-course tuition scholarships for qualifying students. Priority for scholarships is given to B.L.S. students. A private loan program is available to degree-seeking students enrolled in GCS courses.

APPLYING

Students may enroll in GCS courses at any time. Enrollment forms may be found in the GCS catalog or on the CCP Web site. Students paying by credit card may enroll by phone. For information or enrollment in other CCP courses, call the toll-free number.

CONTACT

Center for Credit Programs
116 International Center
The University of Iowa
Iowa City, Iowa 52242-1802
Telephone: 800-272-6430 (toll-free)
Fax: 319-335-2740
E-mail: credit-programs@uiowa.edu
Web site: http://www.uiowa.edu/~ccp

University of Leicester

Centre for Labour Market Studies

Leicester, United Kingdom

In 1991, the Centre for Labour Market Studies launched a unique Master of Science degree for trainers, the first postgraduate course in the United Kingdom to focus exclusively on training. The Centre now offers a wide range of distance learning courses at the M.Sc., diploma, and certificate levels. Programs available to students in North America and the surrounding region include the M.Sc. in Training and Human Resources Management, the M.Sc. in Training and Performance Management, and related diploma programs. These developments have led to rapid expansion, with approximately 30 staff members dedicated exclusively to the global community of distance learning students. U.S. students will appreciate the benefit of DETC accreditation and DANTES approval.

DISTANCE LEARNING PROGRAM

The Centre for Labour Market Studies (CLMS) offers its unique Master of Science degrees in training and human resources management and training and performance management to students in the U.S., Canada, and surrounding regions. These programs are unique in the amount of participation by academic staff members and the number of options available to students to experience discussion and feedback. Students also have the option of netconferencing to Web-based seminars (software is provided to the student free of charge). Annual teaching visits in North America by University staff members provide the opportunity for students to meet instructors and each other face-to-face in workshops and individual student-instructor conferences.

DELIVERY MEDIA

The Centre for Labour Market Studies is a leading-edge centre and is committed to using technology combined with instructor-led sessions in distance learning. Media includes instructional modules, videotapes, CD-ROMs, Web-delivered seminars, instructor-led workshops, and tutorial sessions that are held twice a year. Students have full access to the CLMS library to help them complete their program, as well as research topics that are relevant to the workplace. Students can access the Web site to check their grades, search for information, and download relevant study materials.

PROGRAMS OF STUDY

The CLMS master's degree program is a two-year program. The Master of Science in Training and Human Resource Management examines issues relating to management within the context of training and development. The Master of Science in Training and Performance Management examines the transformation of training in the context of organizational changes and the demands associated with the role of the trainer as a performance manager and a learning consultant.

Diploma programs take one year to complete. Students are provided with a personal tutor for the duration of their studies. The Diploma in Training and Development examines the theory and practice of training and development and the learning pro-cess. The Diploma in Human Resources Management examines organizational behavior, human resources management, employee relations, and employee development.

SPECIAL PROGRAMS

The Centre for Labour Market Studies holds teaching visits in North America twice a year. During each teaching visit, students have access to professors for a private tutorial and have the opportunity to participate in workshops.

The Centre also sponsors annual conferences where human resources professionals learn and implement best practices. Using the experience of some of the global pioneers in work practices and case studies, practitioners are given the knowledge to implement training to improve performance.

CREDIT OPTIONS

Credits from other master's programs are not transferable. Because the courses are interrelated, it is not academically beneficial to waive any part of a unit.

FACULTY

The Centre for Labour Market Studies has been conducting research into aspects of training and development for more than twenty years. The Centre has established a national and international reputation for carrying out high-quality labour market and training research for a wide range of clients, including the Department for Education and Employment, the European Commission, the World Bank, the Economic and Social Research

Council, and many other professional institutions. Twelve full-time academic staff members hold Ph.D.'s and master's degrees.

ADMISSION

Entry into the master's degree program is open to students who hold a B.A. or first- or second-class honors degree with at least a 3.0 grade average or an acceptable professional qualification with suitable practical experience. Enrollment takes place in the spring and fall of each year. The application deadline for the spring enrollment period is March 15; for the fall enrollment period the deadline is September 15.

TUITION AND FEES

Annual tuition is $4950. The tuition includes netconferences and the residential teaching visits; students are responsible for travel and hotel expenses. Prices are subject to change at the discretion of the University.

APPLYING

Prospective students must obtain a prospectus and application package from the University of Leicester. Students must provide transcripts from previous universities and colleges, two references, a statement of purpose, and a resume. All documents should be sent to the University of Leicester at the address below.

CONTACT

Centre for Labour Market Studies
University of Leicester
7-9 Salisbury Road
Leicester LE1 7QR
United Kingdom
Telephone: 011-44-116-252-5951
Fax: 011-44-116-252-5953
E-mail: clmsl@leicester.ac.uk
Web site: http://www.clms.le.ac.uk

University of Maryland University College

Undergraduate and Graduate Distance Degree Programs

Adelphi, Maryland

Founded in 1947, University of Maryland University College (UMUC) is one of eleven degree-granting institutions in the University System of Maryland; its Graduate School was founded in 1978. UMUC's principal mission is to serve adult, part-time students by providing high-quality educational opportunities in Maryland and around the world.

Through its distance learning programs, UMUC offers bachelor's degrees in fifteen areas of specialization, thirteen undergraduate certificates, nine master's degrees, twenty-eight graduate certificates, and a Doctor of Management. In 1999, UMUC's online course enrollment reached 21,187.

UMUC is accredited by the Commission on Higher Education of the Middle States Association of Colleges and Schools, 3624 Market Street, Philadelphia, Pennsylvania 19104 (telephone: 215-662-5606).

DISTANCE LEARNING PROGRAM

UMUC's distance courses provide the same rigor, requirements, assignments, and tests as are available in a classroom environment. However, students are free to participate at times and from locations that are convenient to them. Online and voice-mail courses are highly structured and require students to log in several times a week and to participate actively in asynchronous, full-class, and small-group discussions.

DELIVERY MEDIA

UMUC provides undergraduate and graduate online degree programs via WebTycho, its proprietary virtual campus interface, via the World Wide Web. Students taking online classes via WebTycho require a computer running a Web browser, such as Netscape Navigator or Microsoft Internet Explorer versions 4.0 or higher, connection to the Internet, and an e-mail account.

Some undergraduate courses are delivered via voice-mail technologies that link the faculty members and students by telephone. The only equip-ment required is a standard touch-tone telephone or a dial telephone with a tone-generating device.

PROGRAMS OF STUDY

Undergraduate Programs offers online Bachelor of Arts (B.A.) and Bachelor of Science (B.S.) degree programs in fifteen areas of specialization, three of which are new. Specializations include accounting, behavioral and social sciences, business and management, communication studies, computer and information science, computer studies, English (B.A. only), fire science, history (B.A. only), humanities, management studies, paralegal studies, environmental management, information systems management, and psychology. In addition, UMUC now offers thirteen undergraduate certificate programs through distance education.

The Graduate School offers nine online degree programs, with nineteen specialty tracks. The degree programs include the Master of Science in Management, the Master of Science in Computer Systems Management, the Master of Science in Technology Management, the Master of International Management, the Mas-ter of Business Administration, the Master of Science in Environmental Management, the Master of Science in Telecommunications Management, and the Master of Software Engineering. The Graduate School also offers three dual degree programs, a Doctor of Management, and twenty-eight graduate certificate programs that can be completed online.

STUDENT SERVICES

UMUC offers a complete range of support services on line that allow students to apply for admission, obtain pre-entry advising, register, order books and materials, search for scholarships, apply for financial aid, and obtain ongoing academic advising. Once students have been admitted, they also have access to UMUC's Interactive Student Information System (ISIS), which allows them to check their course schedules and grade reports from past and current semesters, statements of account, and unofficial transcripts; to update their personal information; and to access UMUC's career resources. Students also have access to extensive library resources on line.

CREDIT OPTIONS

UMUC offers undergraduate students a number of innovative options for earning credit, all of which are available at a distance. Through Experiential Learning (EXCEL), students can earn up to 30 credits toward a first undergraduate degree (15 credits toward a second degree) by having previous work or life experience evaluated. Through Cooperative Education (Co-op), undergraduate students can earn academic credit in the workplace for new on-the-job learning.

Graduate students can transfer up to 6 semester hours of graduate credit (3 semester hours for the Master of Business Administration) to UMUC if the credit was earned at a regionally accredited institution and is relevant to the student's area of study, subject to approval by the Graduate School.

FACULTY

Before teaching on line, UMUC faculty members must complete a five-week intensive training course and be certified. Of the more than 800 Undergraduate Programs faculty members, 35 percent have taught UMUC courses in distance formats. The undergraduate faculty is composed of full-time academic directors and adjunct faculty members who work actively in the fields in which they teach. The Graduate School's 35 full-time faculty members have terminal degrees that are relevant to the online degrees. They teach, are responsible for the design of the online curriculum, and provide leadership for the school's approximately 300 adjunct faculty members. More than 85 percent of those adjunct faculty members hold terminal degrees in their disciplines; all have years of practical experience in their fields.

ADMISSION

Students who are applying for undergraduate admission must have graduated from a regionally accredited high school or have completed the General Educational Development (GED) exams with a total score of at least 225 and no individual score less than 40 and have a cumulative grade point average (GPA) of at least 2.0 on all college-level work attempted at other colleges and universities.

Applicants to the Graduate School must have a bachelor's degree from a regionally accredited college or university and an overall undergraduate GPA of at least 3.0 to be accepted as a degree-seeking student. Students with at least a 2.5 GPA in their major area of study can apply for provisional status. Applicants for the Master of Science in Technology Management must have a bachelor's degree in a social, biological, or physical science; business administration; or engineering from a regionally accredited college or university. Students applying for the Master of Science in Environmental Management program are required to have at least 3 undergraduate credits each in basic biology and chemistry.

TUITION AND FEES

Undergraduate tuition per semester hour is $191 for Maryland residents and $252 for nonresidents. Graduate tuition for Maryland residents is $292 per semester hour; it is $397 per semester hour for nonresidents, except for the Master of Business Administration program, which is $3000 per 6-credit seminar. Books, certain course materials, and some fees are additional. Active-duty military personnel are eligible for a reduced undergraduate tuition rate of $138 per semester hour and for in-state graduate tuition rates. Spouses of active-duty military are eligible for in-state tuition for undergraduate and graduate courses. The undergraduate application fee is $30. The graduate application fee is $50. For both undergraduate and graduate students, schedule adjustments are $15, the late fee for withdrawal is $15, and the late registration fee is $30.

FINANCIAL AID

UMUC offers a variety of financial aid programs to suit the needs of both undergraduate and graduate students. Students are eligible to apply for low-interest loans, state scholarship program funds, the Federal Work-Study Program, and UMUC grants and scholarships. Federal Direct Loans are available to students regardless of income. While UMUC handles most of the processes involved in delivering federal, state, and institutional funds, students are responsible for completing the Free Application for Federal Student Aid (FAFSA) and the UMUC Student Data Form and for adhering to deadlines. For more information and deadlines, students should contact UMUC via e-mail at umucinfo@info.umuc.edu.

APPLYING

Students interested in applying to any of UMUC's distance education programs can find information from the points of contact or at the Web addresses listed below. UMUC accepts and processes applications throughout the year. Test scores such as SAT, GMAT, or GRE are not required for any UMUC programs, except the Doctor of Management.

CONTACT

University of Maryland University College
3501 University Boulevard East
Adelphi, Maryland 20783
Telephone: 800-581-UMUC (toll-free) or 301-985-7000
E-mail: umucinfo@umuc.edu
Web site: http://www.umuc.edu

University of Massachusetts Amherst

Division of Continuing Education

Amherst, Massachusetts

The University of Massachusetts Amherst (UMass Amherst), the flagship campus of the University of Massachusetts system, was founded in 1863 under the Land-Grant College Act of 1862. Within its ten schools, colleges, and faculties, UMass Amherst offers associate degrees in six areas, bachelor's degrees in nearly ninety, master's degrees in more than seventy, and doctorates in more than fifty. The University serves approximately 34,000 students: 18,000 undergraduates and 6,000 graduates, plus 300 students at the Stockbridge School and nearly 10,000 Continuing Education students. The UMass Amherst Division of Continuing Education, founded in 1971, provides access to the academic resources of the University to part-time students, working professionals, local and national business firms, and the general community. The Division of Continuing Education administers the University's summer and winter sessions, as well as providing evening, weekend, and distance education courses. The University of Massachusetts is accredited by the New England Association of Schools and Colleges.

DISTANCE LEARNING PROGRAM

The Division of Continuing Education, in partnership with the University's schools and colleges, began offering distance education courses in 1995. Using the World Wide Web, students may interact with each other and the instructors from remote locations. Online courses have the same rigorous academic requirements as on-campus courses. The faculty members who develop the courses teach the courses. The University of Massachusetts Amherst is accredited by the New England Association of Schools and Colleges.

DELIVERY MEDIA

The UMass Division of Continuing Education utilizes the Internet to deliver courses throughout New England, the nation, and the globe. Web-based courses are available twenty-four hours a day but must be completed within the standard semester. Students interact with the instructor via e-mail, chat rooms, telephone, fax, and mail. Courses include exercises, readings, projects, online

discussions, chat rooms, live chat, illustrations, and video.

PROGRAMS OF STUDY

In addition to online undergraduate courses in accounting; marketing; hotel, restaurant, and travel administration; psychology; and wildlife and fisheries conservation, three online graduate degree programs are offered. The Master of Science (Nursing) in community/school health prepares advanced practice nurses as expert clinicians in the care of children, adolescents, and their families in diverse community and school health settings. The master's degree program consists of 42 credits and includes courses and clinical practica in nursing theory, nursing research, community/school health assessment, program planning, advanced health assessment, advanced pathophysiology and pharmacology, primary health care needs of children and adolescents, special and chronic health care needs of children, psychoeducational strategies for advanced practice, and community/school health management. Clinical practica involving diverse clinical ac-

tivities are tailored to meet individual learning needs and can be completed in settings identified by the student.

The Master of Public Health (M.P.H.) provides graduate education for practicing professionals. This program offers experienced health workers an opportunity to complete a course of study that leads to a terminal professional degree. Working health professionals may expand their knowledge base in public health, extend and sharpen their professional skills, broaden their perspective of public health problems, and prepare to assume greater professional responsibility. The M.P.H. curriculum is designed to enable health care professionals to earn this advanced degree while engaged in professional activities. Students must complete the 39-credit program in three years.

The Professional M.B.A. program is fully accredited by AACSB–The American Assembly of Collegiate Schools of Business. It is an accelerated program for professionals who want to continue their education in the management field but cannot attend traditional classes because of full-time career commitments. Those individuals without an undergraduate business degree or extensive managerial experience are required to enroll in an additional introductory foundations of business course. The 37-credit program must be completed in three years.

SPECIAL PROGRAMS

The certificate of individual study in arts management, a six-course series, can be earned entirely online. The certificate is a valuable professional development opportunity for arts managers as well as people employed by nonprofit organizations or agencies. The six courses teach strategic planning, board development, fundraising, marketing, basic financial management, and arts programming. The courses feature written and audio lectures, job-related field assignments, references, bulletin board, links to online resources, and chat rooms. Students communicate with each other and faculty members through e-mail, fax, mail, and telephone. The courses may also be taken for University of Massachusetts undergraduate credit.

STUDENT SERVICES

Academic advisers are available by phone, e-mail, fax, and in person to assist students in course selection, transfer credit evaluation, and academic matters. Continuing Education has its own registration and business offices which can provide assistance with registration, transcripts, financial aid, and billings.

CREDIT OPTIONS

Students may request a transcript evaluation and, upon approval, transfer credits earned at other accredited postsecondary schools to UMass. Credits may also be earned through the College Level Examination Program (CLEP) or through independent study. Credits earned through distance education are University of Massachusetts credits and, upon acceptance, may be transferred to other colleges and universities.

FACULTY

The distance education faculty for graduate programs comprises UMass faculty members who hold doctorates or terminal degrees in their respective fields. Undergraduate and noncredit courses may be taught by doctorate-holding faculty members, graduate teaching assistants, or qualified adjunct faculty members.

ADMISSION

The UMass Amherst Division of Continuing Education allows any person with a high school diploma or its equivalent to register for noncredit or undergraduate courses. Students must have a bachelor's degree to be admitted to a graduate degree program. It is possible to enroll in graduate-level courses and receive credit toward a bachelor's degree. Some courses may require prerequisite college-level work. Students may enroll in courses before being formally admitted to a degree program. Up to 6 credits may be taken as a nondegree graduate student and transferred to a degree program later. Enrollment does not imply acceptance into a degree program. For graduate degree programs, admission to the University's Graduate School is required.

TUITION AND FEES

Fees vary depending on whether the course offered is noncredit or for credit and whether the level of that credit is undergraduate or graduate. Generally, a noncredit course costs $300, while an undergraduate course costs $175 per credit; graduate-level courses vary in cost from $200 to $600 per credit. All students, regardless of residency, pay the same tuition.

FINANCIAL AID

Availability of financial aid varies depending on course status and matriculation. Financial assistance is available from employers, TERI Continuing Education loans, and for eligible military personnel under the G.I. Bill.

APPLYING

Students can find information on application and registration procedures for degree programs and individual courses on the UMass Amherst virtual campus Web site listed below.

CONTACT

Kevin Aiken, Director
Division of Continuing Education
University of Massachusetts
Box 31650
Amherst, Massachusetts 01003-1650
Telephone: 413-545-2111
Fax: 413-545-3351
E-mail: kaiken@admin.umass.edu
Web site: http://www.umass.edu/contined
http://UMAmherstOnline.Org

University of Massachusetts Lowell

Distance Learning Opportunities

Lowell, Massachusetts

The University of Massachusetts Lowell (UMass Lowell) is a comprehensive university committed to providing students with the education and skills they need for continued success throughout their lives. Specializing in applied science and technology, the University conducts research and outreach activities that add great value to the entire region. The second largest of the University of Massachusetts campuses, Lowell currently offers its 13,000 undergraduate and graduate students more than 100 different degree programs in the Colleges of Arts and Sciences, Education, Engineering, Health Professions, and Management. The UMass Lowell Continuing Studies and Corporate Education (CSCE), which includes the evening and summer schools of the University, is one of the largest continuing education programs in New England. Credit courses lead to twenty associate and baccalaureate degrees and thirty certificate programs in specialized technical or professional areas.

DISTANCE LEARNING PROGRAM

The University of Massachusetts Lowell utilizes a variety of interactive distance learning technologies to provide both undergraduate and graduate students with unique opportunities to pursue lifelong learning. The CyberEd program, offered through the University's Continuing Studies and Corporate Education Division, is one of New England's largest accredited online providers of undergraduate courses, degrees, and certificates to students from around the world. By accessing course materials and interacting with faculty members and classmates via the Internet and the World Wide Web, CyberEd students are able to learn at a time and location convenient to them.

The UMass Lowell Instructional Network offers a variety of programming to K–12 school districts, Massachusetts community colleges, and other universities within the UMass system. Students at remote locations can interact with the originating site instructor and students via bidirectional communications. The University is equipped with multiple state-of-the-art distance learning classrooms that can accommodate numerous teaching techniques, such as computer-generated presentations, laser discs, the Internet and World Wide Web, and CD-ROMs.

DELIVERY MEDIA

The CyberEd program uses the World Wide Web, e-mail, chat, and other Internet resources to provide a meaningful learning experience for students and faculty members. Students access class lectures via a Web site, participate in online chats and discussion forums, and work collaboratively to fulfill course requirements.

The UML Instructional Network utilizes an array of transmission technologies to deliver programming to remote audiences, including satellite uplink, line of sight microwave, dedicated fiber-optic analog video, compressed video via ATM, ISDN, and consumer cable connections via public and educational access channels. The delivery method is dependent on the intended audience's capability and the course content.

The University is currently developing mixed-media classes, which incorporate a blend of interactive video classrooms with Internet-based chat, e-mail, and Web resources. These new courses provide opportunities for face-to-face interaction in addition to the benefits of asynchronous communication.

PROGRAMS OF STUDY

Students who are enrolled in the CyberEd program can pursue an associate or bachelor's degree in information systems or choose from four online certificate programs in Intranet Development, UNIX, Fundamentals of Information Technology, and Multimedia Applications. Many of the courses taken toward these certificates can also be applied toward the online degree programs. Courses are offered during the fall, spring, and summer semesters.

Graduate-level courses in education, civil engineering, and plastics engineering are currently offered across the UML Instructional Network. A collaborative effort between UMass Lowell and UMass Boston now provides students on both campuses with a wider selection when choosing philosophy or communication electives to fulfill their program requirements. High school students also have the opportunity to begin accumulating college credits while fulfilling their requirements for graduation in biology, chemistry, computer science, and math.

SPECIAL PROGRAMS

In collaboration with Nortel Networks, Continuing Studies and Corporate Education offers a customized Certificate in Data Telecommunications. Students complete the certificate by taking some courses via CyberEd and additional courses through authorized Nortel Networks global training operations. The University is also actively exploring additional corporate partnerships that will greatly increase student access to state-of-the-art programs. Corporate students in particular find that online courses offer them the convenience to complete the courses from work or home.

The UML Instructional Network is engaged in several special programs that support the development of K–12 teachers and their students. Professional development opportunities are broadcast for K–12 teachers, who are then able to attend graduate-level courses and PDP workshops from the convenience of their own school. A FIPSE Pre-service Teachers grant, Looking Into Classrooms, supports the group observation of mentor teachers via two-way television. The biannual Nuclear Reactor Irradiation Experiment allows area high school students to participate in a series of experiments, including those at the University's research reactor, from the safety of their classrooms.

STUDENT SERVICES

Students can enroll in distance learning courses by telephone, fax, mail, or in person. The Advising Center provides online, telephone, and on-campus counseling regarding course selection, choice of majors, and other academic questions. Online library resources are available to students via the University's proxy server. All students are eligible for e-mail accounts on the University mail server, and students enrolled in programming courses are provided with additional remote access to University computing resources. The UMass Lowell bookstore provides telephone and

online book ordering, and all CyberEd students have access to password-protected Web sites, chat rooms, bulletin boards, and other applicable collaborative environments.

Course descriptions, curriculum worksheets, certificate and degree programs, application forms, and a schedule of courses are all available on the UMass Lowell CSCE Web site.

CREDIT OPTIONS

In general, the University of Massachusetts Lowell accepts semester credits with grades of C- (1.7 on a 4.0 scale) or better as shown on official transcripts on an hour-for-hour basis. In addition, other options for students include transfer credit, credit by exam, and independent study.

FACULTY

All distance learning courses offered by the University are taught by full or adjunct faculty members from the University's colleges or Continuing Studies and Corporate Education. All of the distance learning faculty members are required to attend training that instructs them how to best modify their course materials and facilitate communication and interaction among their students. Faculty biographies, contact information, and course syllabi are available for all CyberEd students at the CyberEd Web site.

ADMISSION

Admission requirements for UMass Lowell's various programs can be found at UMass Lowell's CSCE Web site.

TUITION AND FEES

Current information on tuition and fees for the graduate and undergraduate courses for in-state and out-of-state students can be found at UMass Lowell's CSCE Web site.

FINANCIAL AID

Availability of financial aid depends upon the matriculated status of the students. Further information is available at UMass Lowell's CSCE Web site.

APPLYING

Students can find information on application and registration procedures for individual courses on UMass Lowell's CSCE Web site.

CONTACT

Steve Tello, Associate Director of Distance Education
Continuing Studies and Corporate Education
University of Massachusetts Lowell
Lowell, Massachusetts 01854
Telephone: 978-934-4240
E-mail: Steven_Tello@uml.edu
UMass Lowell CSCE Web site: http://continuinged.uml.edu/

Mike Lucas, Coordinator of Distance Learning
UMass Lowell Instructional Network
College of Education
University of Massachusetts Lowell
255 Princeton Street
North Chelmsford, Massachusetts 01863
Telephone: 978-934-4681
E-mail: Michael_Lucas@uml.edu

For CyberEd:
Telephone: 800-480-3190 (toll-free)
E-mail: cybered@uml.edu
Web site: http://cybered.uml.edu

University of Minnesota, Twin Cities Campus

Independent and Distance Learning, University College

Minneapolis, Minnesota

The University, with its four campuses, is one of the most comprehensive universities in the country and ranks among the top twenty universities in the United States. It is both a land-grant university with a strong tradition of education and public service and a major research institution. It was founded as a preparatory school in 1851 and was reorganized as a university in 1869, benefiting from the Morrill (or Land-Grant) Act of 1862.

The University of Minnesota has campuses in the Twin Cities (Minneapolis and St. Paul), Duluth, Morris, and Crookston, Minnesota. The Twin Cities campus is made up of nineteen colleges and offers 172 bachelor's degrees, 198 master's degrees, 116 doctoral degrees, and five professional degrees.

DISTANCE LEARNING PROGRAM

Independent and Distance Learning (IDL) offers outstanding university credit courses using mail and electronic technologies. In a recent year, the department received approximately 6,500 registrations from students throughout the United States and abroad. The 150 courses are fully accredited each year by approximately fifty different academic departments of the University. IDL is part of the College of Continuing Education (CCE), the division of the University of Minnesota that serves adult and part-time learners.

DELIVERY MEDIA

Most courses are available by mail for home study and mail lesson exchange with faculty members. Many faculty members provide the option of e-mail for lesson exchange. A growing number of online courses are fully interactive. Many courses make use of audiocassettes and videos. All students who register for college credit with Independent and Distance Learning receive an e-mail and Internet account.

PROGRAMS OF STUDY

Approximately 150 credit courses are offered in a wide range of academic departments, including such varied subjects as applied business, child psychology, ecology, English literature and writing courses, management, math, and theater. Two science courses come with home lab kits: general biology and elementary physics. Independent and distance learning courses are known for their high academic quality and variety of topics. There are no degree or certificate programs available during the 2000–01 academic year.

STUDENT SERVICES

UC Student Support Services offers academic, financial aid, and career counseling. Academic advising can help students determine prerequisites and academic standing, evaluate transcripts, choose courses, and evaluate the applicability of IDL credits to University of Minnesota specific degree and certificate programs.

If students have a disability, Independent and Distance Learning coordinates efforts to provide accommodations that remove academic and physical barriers to earning credits. Such accommodations may include more time to complete exams or an alternate format for an exam, a separate testing room, audiotaping required materials, and taped rather than written comments from an instructor. Requests for such accommodations should be made well in advance of when they are needed so that necessary documentation may be obtained and accommodations facilitated.

FACULTY

IDL has approximately 80 faculty members. Approximately 40 percent are University of Minnesota professors, 30 percent are graduate student teaching assistants, and 30 percent are adjunct faculty members, lecturers, or others. All professors and many adjunct faculty members hold doctorates or other terminal degrees.

ADMISSION

There are no admission requirements to register in individual courses through Independent and Distance Learning.

TUITION AND FEES

All registrants, regardless of location, qualify for in-state tuition rates. Tuition for 2000–01 is $163 per semester credit. A materials/services fee of $52 per course enrollment is assessed. Course study guides are included in the fee. Texts and other materials may be purchased from the Minnesota Book Center at the University of Minnesota.

FINANCIAL AID

Financial aid is limited. Eligibility requirements may vary, but most aid programs place restrictions on some types of IDL enrollment and require admission to a University of Minnesota, Twin Cities degree program or eligible certificate program. Non-admitted students who reside in Minnesota may be eligible for College of Continuing Education grants or scholarships, which have more flexible eligibility criteria. Employer assistance may also be an option for some students.

APPLYING

No application is needed to register in individual courses.

CONTACT

Student Support Services, University College
150 Wesbrook Hall
University of Minnesota
77 Pleasant Street, SE
Minneapolis, Minnesota 55455
Telephone: 612-624-4000
        800-234-6564 (toll-free)
Fax: 612-625-1511
E-mail: adv@mail.cce.umn.edu
Web site: http://www.CCE.umn.edu

University of Missouri–Columbia

Center for Distance and Independent Study

Columbia, Missouri

Established in 1839 as the first public university west of the Mississippi River, the University of Missouri (UM) has a rich history of benefiting the state, the nation, and the world through its land-grant mission of teaching, research, and service. With a comprehensive array of majors and programs, including undergraduate, graduate, and professional degrees, many of the University's departments and schools rank among the nation's foremost. Among its four campuses in Columbia, Kansas City, Rolla, and St. Louis, the University enrolls more than 55,000 students, a growing number of whom learn at a distance. Often cited as one of the nation's best higher education values, the University is accredited by the North Central Association of Colleges and Schools as well as other leading accrediting organizations.

DISTANCE LEARNING PROGRAM

Since 1911, the Center for Distance and Independent Study (CDIS), a unit of the University of Missouri–Columbia Extension, has demonstrated its commitment to lifelong learning by providing individually-paced correspondence courses to those students who cannot or choose not to enroll in traditional classes. Today, with nearly 16,000 enrollments annually, the Center is one of the largest and most respected education programs in the nation.

In addition to its graduate and undergraduate University courses, the center operates the University of Missouri–Columbia High School. The school offers approximately 150 high school courses, including a college preparatory curriculum with challenging courses for gifted students. CDIS also provides a curriculum, which covers grades three through eight, for families who desire to home school or enroll their children in supplemental course work.

DELIVERY MEDIA

Students who enroll in a CDIS course receive a study guide containing lessons and instructions necessary to complete the course. CDIS courses may utilize written materials (either printed or online), audiotapes, videotapes, and/or computer disks. All required course materials, which are listed on the course description, are available through the Center's bookstore.

Lessons for most CDIS courses are computer evaluated. Students may submit lessons by mail or via the Internet for immediate response. Faculty-evaluated courses may be submitted by mail, e-mail, fax, or online, depending on the nature of the assignment.

A growing number of Web courses allow students to access their study guides online. All lessons and instructions needed to complete these courses are accessible on the World Wide Web; if supplementary materials are required, they can be purchased through the Center's bookstore.

PROGRAMS OF STUDY

Students may earn graduate or undergraduate credit, ranging from 2 to 5 hours, for each independent study course they complete. The Center for Distance and Independent Study awards the high school diploma, but

does not award degrees. Other University of Missouri programs offer degrees via online study and interactive television. Students may use credit earned through independent study to achieve their specific educational goals in these and other programs.

Independent study courses have been approved by faculty members from the appropriate academic department at one of the four University of Missouri campuses. The Center offers more than 160 University courses, graduate and undergraduate level, in a wide range of subject areas, including accountancy; animal sciences; anthropology; astronomy; atmospheric science; biological and agricultural engineering; biological sciences; black studies; classical studies; communication; computer science; consumer and family economics; criminology and criminal justice; economics; education; engineering; English; entomology; geography; geology; German and Russian studies; health services management; history; human development and family studies; management; marketing; mathematics; military science; parks, recreation, and tourism; pest management; philosophy; physical education; physics; astronomy; plant pathology; plant science; political science; psychology; Romance languages; rural sociology; sociology; statistics; and women's studies.

SPECIAL PROGRAMS

The Center for Distance and Independent Study offers approximately thirty graduate and undergraduate education courses designed to provide specialized learning to teachers, counselors, and administrators. Teachers can generally use graduate-level courses for certification and salary improvement without being admitted to graduate school. Twelve education courses are special-topics courses that incorporate textbook materials and videotapes. In order to successfully complete these courses, students must attend a weekend seminar conducted by the course instructor.

CDIS continues to add online courses in addition to taught courses. Nineteen online courses are currently available at the university level and 16 at the high school level. One popular course, CS100: Computer Survival: Applications, teaches students to use the personal computer and various software to enhance productivity and gain greater understanding of the potential of computer technology. Before enrolling, interested students should check the course home page at http://vu.umkc.edu/cs100.

The Center has been providing courses to military personnel through the Defense Activity for Non-Traditional Education Support (DANTES) program for nearly twenty years. Members of the U.S. Armed Forces, on active duty or in a reserve component, who desire to continue their education on a part-time basis outside of the traditional classroom environment are eligible to enroll in independent study. Information concerning enrollment is available in the DANTES Independent Study Catalog.

STUDENT SERVICES

The Center maintains a student services office with a toll-free number (800-858-6413) for students needing distance education curriculum information. Students may access information, request a catalog, enroll, submit lessons, request a course exam, and send questions or comments via the World Wide Web at http://cdis.missouri.edu.

CREDIT OPTIONS

It is possible for students to earn graduate or undergraduate credit, ranging from 2 to 5 hours, for each independent study course they complete. While the Center for Distance and Independent Study does not award degrees, University credit earned through independent study can be applied toward a degree or used to achieve any other educational goal a student may have.

FACULTY

More than 3,500 faculty members are employed on the University of Missouri's four campuses. Each university-level distance education course is created by a faculty member or by an author who has been approved by the appropriate UM academic department. The Center employs approximately 70 instructors to grade its University courses; most of these instructors have doctoral or other terminal degrees.

ADMISSION

There are no admission requirements for students enrolling in a CDIS course. Students may enroll at any time of the year and take up to nine months to complete each course. A three-month extension is available upon request.

TUITION AND FEES

During 2000–01, tuition at the Center is $136.80 per credit hour for undergraduate credit and $173.20 per credit hour for graduate credit. Every enrollment requires payment of tuition and a nonrefundable $10 handling fee. Textbooks and audiovisual materials rental/deposit fees, sales tax, and other fees may also be included.

FINANCIAL AID

Scholarships and other forms of financial aid are not available through the Center for Distance and Independent Study; however, some business firms and organizations encourage employees to continue their education by paying part or all of their tuition and fees. Individuals should consult their employer to see if funding for distance education is available.

CDIS University courses are approved for veterans and other persons eligible under the provisions of the GI Bill. The Veterans Administration reimburses independent study fees to students after it receives a certificate of enrollment from the Center.

APPLYING

Students may enroll in a Center for Distance and Independent Study course by submitting the completed application and textbook order form by mail, in person, by phone, fax, or via the World Wide Web. Payment for CDIS courses must accompany course enrollment and can be made by credit card, check, or money order.

CONTACT

Terrie Nagel
Student Services Adviser
Center for Distance and
    Independent Study
136 Clark Hall
University of Missouri
Columbia, Missouri 65211-4200
Telephone: 800-858-6413 (toll-free)
Fax: 573-882-6808
E-mail: cdis@missouri.edu
Web site: http://cdis.missouri.edu

University of Nevada, Reno

College of Extended Studies
Independent Learning Program

Reno, Nevada

Established in 1864, the University of Nevada first offered classes in 1874 in Elko, Nevada. In 1885, the campus was moved to Reno with 2 faculty members and 50 students. Today, the University of Nevada, Reno is the oldest of seven institutions in the University and Community College System of Nevada.

A land-grant university with an enrollment of approximately 12,500 students in ten schools and colleges, the University of Nevada, Reno offers a wide range of undergraduate and graduate programs, including selected doctoral and professional studies. The University emphasizes programs and activities that best serve the needs of the state, region, and nation. More than one fourth of students enrolled are pursuing advanced degrees. The University encourages and supports faculty research and its application to state and national problems and conducts more than $70 million in research grants and contracts each year.

The 255-acre campus is located just north of Interstate 80 near the majestic Sierra Nevada range and Lake Tahoe. The University of Nevada, Reno is an integral part of the thriving Reno-Sparks metropolitan area, home to about 311,000 people. With its blend of ivy-covered buildings, sweeping lawns, and functional, progressive architecture, the University's academic atmosphere is filled with rich surroundings for the cultural and intellectual development of students.

The University of Nevada, Reno is an Equal Opportunity/Affirmative Action, ADA institution. The University of Nevada, Reno is accredited by the Northwest Association of Schools and Colleges Commission on Colleges and recognized by the Council on Postsecondary Accreditation and the U.S. Department of Education.

DISTANCE LEARNING PROGRAM

The Independent Learning Program at the University of Nevada, Reno offers an individualized method of learning and a flexible way to earn University credit. Students who are unable to attend on-campus courses due to location, scheduling conflicts, work, or other commitments can choose from more than 100 academic credit courses in twenty-nine subject areas, as well as high school and noncredit offerings. Students may enroll any day of the year and take up to one year to complete a course. Enrollment is accepted via the Web; by mail, phone, or fax; or in person.

PROGRAM OF STUDY

The University of Nevada, Reno is the sole provider of university credit through independent study in the state of Nevada. Academic credit courses are offered from the University of Nevada, Reno and the University of Nevada, Las Vegas. Courses for high school credit, continuing education units, and noncredit are also available. Undergraduate credit courses are offered in twenty-nine subject areas, which include accounting, anthropology, Basque studies, criminal justice, curriculum and instruction, economics, educational leadership, English, environment, French, gaming management, geography, German, health science,

health-care administration, history, hotel administration, human development/family studies, Italian, journalism, managerial sciences, mathematics, nutrition, political science, psychology, sociology, Spanish, Western traditions, and women's studies. Graduate credit is available in educational leadership and human development/family studies. All credit courses have been approved by departments and colleges of the University of Nevada, Reno and the University of Nevada, Las Vegas. High School credit courses meet Nevada State Department of Education approval.

DELIVERY MEDIA

Instruction is given by means of a course syllabus, textbooks, video and audio cassettes (where appropriate), and additional reference and instructional materials. Lessons are accepted via mail, fax, and e-mail. After review by the course instructor, work is returned to students. A number of online correspondence courses are available. No classroom attendance is necessary for correspondence study courses. All courses have a final examination, which must be taken in a proctored setting; many courses have two or three progress examinations. Students who reside away from campus may take examinations using an approved proctor in their area.

SPECIAL PROGRAMS

New online courses are a convenient way to study at home and communicate with instructors via the Internet. Some classes also include a listserv feature, so students can join a mail group, ask questions of fellow online students, and discuss course topics.

STUDENT SERVICES

All textbooks, videotapes, and course materials are mailed directly to students anywhere in the world. Returning lessons for grading uses convenient e-mail or fax services or traditional mail and air mail. Independent Learning students who live in the Reno area can take full advantage of the many student services available on the University of Nevada, Reno campus; these services include tutoring, math centers, academic counseling, and support group information for nontraditional students. Local students can also receive library and computer lab privileges and use the library's video loan service. Each correspondence study student receives a student handbook upon enrollment with useful information, study tips, and guidelines. The Independent Learning staff is available to answer questions via phone, fax, or e-mail. Information about courses and programs is also included on the Independent Learning Web site, listed below.

CREDIT OPTIONS

A maximum of 60 credits earned through Independent Learning may be applied toward a University of Nevada, Reno bachelor's degree. The University of Nevada, Las Vegas awards up to a maximum of 15 semester hours of credit through Independent Learning toward a degree. Students interested in transfer credit may contact the University's Transfer Center office (telephone: 775-784-6230) for more information. Grades for all completed credit courses are recorded on a University transcript, which may be ordered from the University.

FACULTY

All instructors for Independent Learning have been approved by departments and colleges of the University of Nevada, Reno and the University of Nevada, Las Vegas. High school faculty members are certified high school teachers in Nevada high schools or are faculty members at the university or community college level.

ADMISSION

Formal admission to the University of Nevada, Reno or the University of Nevada, Las Vegas is not required to enroll in Independent Learning courses. Likewise, enrollment in Independent Learning does not constitute admission to either of these universities. Students who wish to apply may contact the University of Nevada, Reno Office of Admissions and Records (telephone: 775-784-6865).

TUITION AND FEES

The standard course fee for all undergraduate correspondence study courses is $81 per credit. Graduate tuition is $103 per credit. High school courses are $80 per one-half unit course. Textbook costs are not included in the course fee. Additional fees are charged for handling, stationery, syllabus, and special materials, as well as for air mail, international mail, and Internet courses.

FINANCIAL AID

Some financial aid may be available to certain qualified individuals through the University of Nevada, Reno Financial Aid Office (telephone: 775-784-4666), where students can call for application deadlines and forms. Independent Learning courses at the University of Nevada, Reno are approved for veterans benefits and for military personnel (DANTES) within or outside the United States.

APPLYING

Students can enroll any time and take up to one year to complete each course. Instruction by Independent Learning affords students the convenience of studying when and where they choose. Students may enroll in a maximum of 11 credits concurrently and must meet any prerequisites. Enrollment is accepted via the Web; by mail, phone, or fax; or in person.

CONTACT

Independent Learning Staff
College of Extended Studies/050
University of Nevada, Reno
Reno, Nevada 89557
Telephone: 775-784-4652
　　　　　800-233-8928 Ext.
　　　　　4652 (toll-free)
Fax: 775-784-1280
E-mail: lstudy@scs.unr.edu
Web site:
　http://www.dce.unr.edu/istudy

University of New England

Certificate of Advanced Graduate Study in Educational Leadership

Portland, Maine

The University of New England (UNE) is an independent university whose mission it is to educate men and women to advance the quality of human life and the environment. The University was created in 1978 in Biddeford, Maine, by combining St. Francis College and the New England College of Osteopathic Medicine. In 1996 the University merged with Westbrook College, a small liberal arts college in Portland, Maine, giving UNE two distinctive campuses. The University now recognizes Westbrook College's 1831 charter date as the University of New England's founding date.

The University is accredited by the New England Association of Schools and Colleges. The Certificate of Advanced Graduate Study in Educational Leadership is approved by the Maine Board of Education to be offered in Maine and elsewhere.

DISTANCE LEARNING PROGRAM

Designed and developed for working professionals who aspire to administrative and leadership roles in an educational environment, the Certificate of Advanced Graduate Study in Educational Leadership provides an innovative and convenient program of study, leading to a post-master's professional credential. The part-time online program offers the self-directed, motivated adult learner the needed flexibility to accommodate a busy lifestyle while pursuing career goals.

Degree candidates in educational leadership join other graduate students at the University continuing their professional education in osteopathic medicine, human services, health and life sciences, management, and education. The online educational leadership program builds on a successful distance learning model—the master's degree in education for experienced teachers has hundreds of students enrolled throughout the country.

DELIVERY MEDIA

Courses in educational leadership are offered online, so study is conve-

nient and accessible. Students may opt to study at home or in their school environment, wherever they have access to the Internet. With technical support from the University's instructional technology partner, eCollege.com, students quickly become adept with the technology, which is simple and easy to use. There are many opportunities for interaction with faculty mentors and other students, using Internet tools developed and adapted specifically for online learners, including threaded discussions, online class sessions, and an electronic bulletin board designed for communication from a faculty mentor to the students. Highlighting the program is the one-week residential Integration Seminar, which brings together all of the students in the program for an intensive session offered each summer.

PROGRAM OF STUDY

The University of New England currently offers the Certificate of Advanced Graduate Study in Educational Leadership in an online format. The curriculum consists of nine 3-credit online courses and a one-week residential summer seminar. Five courses, including the seminar,

are required; the additional five are available as electives. A minimum of eight 3-credit courses must be taken to be awarded the Advanced Degree. The particular program of study chosen (eight or ten courses) depends upon the existing requirements in the state where students work or seek certification as educational administrators.

The curriculum is designed to apply as broadly as possible to requirements throughout the country; however, it is the responsibility of the candidate to confirm what course content is needed in the state in which certification is sought.

STUDENT SERVICES

As a part of the University of New England's online campus, students are just a mouse click away from the services and support they need. The certificate program staff and faculty members are ready to advise on course work and program procedures; the graduate student affairs staff assists with student services and institutional policies; the library staff helps in locating and accessing learning materials; and eCollege.com staff members are available 24 hours a day on a helpline for technology-related assistance.

CREDIT OPTIONS

Upon acceptance, up to two 3-credit graduate-level courses may be transferred into the program, provided that a transcript, course description, syllabus, and a student statement justifying course equivalency is presented. The Summer Seminar and Applied Research Project cannot be satisfied through transfer credit, and no credit for experiential learning is given in lieu of courses.

FACULTY

The faculty mentors for the program are University professors as well as practicing professionals. All are certified administrators, and the majority have earned an Ed.D. Faculty mentors include talented educators with extensive backgrounds as principals, superintendents, specialists in curriculum development and special services, educational consultants, and guidance supervisors.

ADMISSION

Admissions into the educational leadership program are considered as they are received, with a new cohort accepted each term.

Criteria for admission for Advanced Degree candidacy are a master's degree from an accredited institution, a minimum of three years' teaching and/or administrative experience, current employment in an educational setting or ready access to such employment, the ability to pursue rigorous online graduate study, interest in continuing professional development and a role in educational leadership, and potential to improve practice through application of new knowledge and skills.

TUITION AND FEES

Tuition is $855 for a 3-credit course. There is a one-time $150 program fee.

FINANCIAL AID

There is currently a variety of private loan programs available to educational leadership students.

APPLYING

The application process consists of six steps: completing the application forms (available in paper or online) no later than forty-five days prior to the start of a term (i.e., August 15, December 15, and April 15); submitting the nonrefundable application fee of $40 ($25 for graduates of the University of New England's master's in education program); submitting official transcripts of all graduate work; sending in two letters of recommendation (one must be from a supervisor); writing a personal goal statement; and demonstrating evidence of teaching or administrative experience.

CONTACT

Certificate of Advanced Graduate Study in Educational
  Leadership Program
University of New England
716 Stevens Avenue
Portland, Maine 04103
Telephone: 207-797-7261 Ext. 4360
Fax: 207-878-2434
E-mail: cags@mailbox.une.edu
Web site: http://www.uneonline.org
http://www.une.edu

The University of Oklahoma

College of Continuing Education
Norman, Oklahoma

The University of Oklahoma's (OU) College of Continuing Education (CCE) is a lifelong learning organization dedicated to helping individuals, businesses, groups, and communities transform themselves through knowledge. Formally organized in 1913, CCE is the outreach arm of the University of Oklahoma. Nationally recognized for its pioneering efforts in continuing education, CCE extends the educational resources of the University through more than thirty different program formats, including graduate and undergraduate degree programs, correspondence and other distance programs, on- and off-campus courses, and a wide variety of programs conducted under the auspices of federal and state grants and contracts. On the Norman campus, adult and other learners attend programs at the Oklahoma Center for Continuing Education, one of thirteen W. K. Kellogg Foundation–funded, University-based residential conference centers in the world. Annually, CCE offers some 2,000 courses and activities to more than 150,000 nontraditional learners in Oklahoma and in locations all over the world.

DISTANCE LEARNING PROGRAM

In carrying out its mission to help nontraditional learners transform themselves through knowledge, CCE offers a variety of credit and non-credit distance learning courses and programs within the state of Oklahoma and beyond. In academic year 1998–99, more than 21,000 students enrolled in CCE's 350 distance learning courses and programs.

DELIVERY MEDIA

Courses are delivered via television, videotapes, videoconferencing, interactive television, audiotapes, audioconferencing, computer software, CD-ROM, computer conferencing, World Wide Web, e-mail, and print. Students and faculty members may meet in person or interact via videoconferencing, audioconferencing, mail, telephone, fax, e-mail, interactive television, or World Wide Web. The following equipment may be required: audiocassette player, fax machine, television, cable television, videocas-

sette player, computer, modem, Internet access, e-mail, and CD-ROM.

PROGRAMS OF STUDY

A variety of programs are available in various distance formats. Independent study courses (credit and non-credit)—some of which are offered online—are available in the following subjects: anthropology, astronomy, business administration, business communication, chemistry, Chinese, classical culture, drama, economics, education, engineering, English, finance, French, geography, geology, German, Greek, health and sport sciences, history, journalism and mass communication, Latin, library and information studies, management, marketing, mathematics, modern languages, music, philosophy, political science, psychology, Russian, and sociology. Master's degree programs in the following areas are presented on-site at military and civilian locations around the world: communication, economics, human relations (including a human resource development emphasis), education

(administration, curriculum, and supervision; adult and higher education; instructional psychology and technology; and teacher education), public administration, and social work. In addition, a Ph.D. in organizational leadership is available at some overseas sites. (These programs combine on-site course delivery with online and correspondence study.) In addition, students in Oklahoma have access to telecourses and OneNet courses.

SPECIAL PROGRAMS

CCE offers a number of distance learning special programs. Among these are the DHS/SATTRN (Satellite Training Network) programs held for Oklahoma Department of Human Services and other state employees. CCE's Independent Study Department works closely with the DANTES program and the Navy College PACE program. In addition, this department offers a number of noncredit writing courses and more than seventy-five high school courses, many of them available online.

STUDENT SERVICES

Students enrolled in CCE's Advanced Programs have access to the facilities and resources of OU's Norman-based library. Advanced Programs students order all their textbooks online through Follett, and Independent Study offers students a complete array of bookstore services.

CREDIT OPTIONS

CCE's Independent Study Department provides students various options to earn credit through testing. Among these are the College-Level

Examination Program (CLEP), DANTES, and institutionally developed advanced-standing examinations.

FACULTY

The faculty for OU distance programs includes regular University of Oklahoma faculty members, adjunct faculty members, and instructors with special appointments. All are experienced and highly qualified instructional professionals who are knowledgeable about the needs, concerns, and capabilities of distance education students.

ADMISSION

Admission to the University of Oklahoma is necessary for credit courses other than those offered through Independent Study. Independent Study students need not be first admitted to OU. To participate in graduate programs, admission to OU's Graduate College is required. For more information, prospective students should use the contact information below.

TUITION AND FEES

Tuition and fees vary based on the chosen program. Prospective students are encouraged to inquire about the costs associated with the program in which they are interested. Expenses relating to continuing education courses taken to maintain and improve professional skills may be tax deductible (Treas. Reg. 1.162-5, Coughlin v. Commissioner, 203f.2d 307). A tax adviser can make this determination based on the particular facts relating to one's professional situation. All tuition and fees at the University of Oklahoma are subject to changes made by the State Regents for Higher Education.

FINANCIAL AID

Financial aid is available for many of the semester-based programs offered through CCE. Financial aid is not available to Independent Study students. Each program has different eligibility requirements. Interested students are encouraged to use the contact information below. They will then be put in touch with the appropriate CCE department that can fully answer their financial aid questions.

APPLYING

Distance learners interested in noncredit programs may enroll by telephone (800-522-0772 Ext. 2248) or by fax (405-325-7164). For many credit programs, distance learners may also enroll by telephone. Prospective students should use the contact information below to determine the appropriate telephone number.

CONTACT

Larry Hayes
College of Continuing Education
The University of Oklahoma
1700 Asp Avenue
Norman, Oklahoma 73072-6400
Telephone: 405-325-4414
Fax: 405-325-7196
E-mail: lhayes@ou.edu
Web site: http://www.occe.ou.edu

University of Pennsylvania

School of Arts and Sciences, College of General Studies

Philadephia, Pennsylvania

The College of General Studies began its life as Penn's evening division in 1892, when it first opened its doors at the University of Pennsylvania (Penn) to Philadelphia-area teachers. Today, the College of General Studies administers outreach and continuing education programs within the School of Arts and Sciences at Penn, including undergraduate and graduate degree programs for adults, postbaccalaureate programs, noncredit enrichment courses, University-wide Summer Sessions, and service programs for high school students, senior citizens, and international students.

DISTANCE LEARNING PROGRAM

As a natural extension of outreach and nontraditional education, the College of General Studies offers a wide range of courses in the arts and sciences to students outside the Philadelphia region via distance learning programs. The College currently serves approximately 400 distance students per year.

DELIVERY MEDIA

Delivery media include online, Internet-based systems with lectures, faculty office hours, discussions, academic resources, and more on the course Web page. Minimum equipment requirements for all students include a computer with Internet access, Netscape Navigator or Internet Explorer 5.0 or higher, a Real Player, a 28.8-KB or faster modem, and at least 32 MB of RAM. Students must have Windows 95, Windows 98, or Windows NT with a 120-MHz processor or higher or Mac OS 7.5.5 or later with a 120-MHz processor.

The online courses are offered via the eCollege.com system.

PROGRAMS OF STUDY

The College of General Studies offers a variety of credit-bearing courses

in the arts and sciences for students of all ages, ranging from high school juniors and seniors to adult students. No degrees or certificates are available entirely at a distance. Prospective students must apply.

SPECIAL PROGRAMS

In the 1998–99 academic year, Penn launched PennAdvance (http://www. advance.upenn.edu), a distributed learning program for academically talented high school students. During the 1999–2000 academic year, PennAdvance was expanded to include all students who have access to the Internet. Now, adult students and current Penn students can take classes from their home computers. Penn's distance programs are all delivered in an online environment.

STUDENT SERVICES

All students have full access to the Penn Library System's online resources. In addition, the University Bookstore provides a "virtual bookstore" service as well as toll-free phone and fax numbers. Academic support and advising services are available for selected courses.

CREDIT OPTIONS

Students who successfully complete an arts and sciences PennAdvance

course or electronic seminar earn a grade and credit from the University of Pennsylvania. Credit for Penn liberal arts courses is generally transferable to other colleges and universities.

FACULTY

Each year, approximately 8 full-time faculty members and 4 part-time faculty members teach distance courses. Approximately 90 percent of all distance instructors have a doctoral degree.

ADMISSION

Prospective students must apply to the College of General Studies as nondegree students. Applications include transcripts of previous work at the high school or college level and an essay.

TUITION AND FEES

Fall 2000 and spring 2001 tuition for one PennAdvance course is $1010. Tuition and fees for fall 2000 and spring 2001 are approximately $1100. Students should contact the College of General Studies for more information on tuition and fees.

FINANCIAL AID

Financial aid is not available to PennAdvance students.

APPLYING

Applications are processed on a rolling basis until the deadlines for the fall, spring, and summer terms are reached.

CONTACT
Colleen Gasiorowski
3440 Market Street, Suite 100
Philadelphia, Pennsylvania 19104-3335
Telephone: 215-898-1684
Fax: 215-573-2053
E-mail: advance@sas.upenn.edu
Web site: http://www.advance.upenn.edu
　　　　　http://www.sas.upenn.edu/CGS

University of Phoenix

Online Campus
Phoenix, Arizona

Since its founding in 1976, the University of Phoenix has been dedicated exclusively to meeting the needs of working professionals. The University is accredited by the North Central Association of Colleges and Schools. The commitment to the adult learner is unequivocal; the University has awarded bachelor's and master's degrees to more than 42,000 graduates.

High academic standards, commitment to quality, and intensely focused programs have earned the University a reputation for leadership in both the academic and business communities. A distinguishing blend of proven academic practices and innovative instructional delivery systems has helped to build the largest private university in the country, with a growing network of campuses and learning centers throughout the United States. The goal is to provide all students with the means to be more effective at their jobs so that they may reap the rewards that follow.

DISTANCE LEARNING PROGRAM

The Online program relies on computer communications to link faculty members and students from around the world into interactive learning groups. Class size is limited to 13 for maximum interaction. Degrees are completed entirely on line for the convenience of working adults who find it difficult or impossible to attend classes at fixed times and places.

Of the 12,000 students attending class part-time from all over the world, 20 percent are executives or owners of their own businesses, 30 percent are middle managers in business and industry, and 44 percent are technical or licensed professionals. Roughly 54 percent are female, and the average student is 38 years old.

DELIVERY MEDIA

Once enrolled in an Online degree program, students log on to the computer conferencing system five out of seven days each week to participate in class discussions focused on the topics they are studying. Students communicate and work off line and only go on line to send and re-ceive material to and from class groups. This is called asynchronous communication.

PROGRAMS OF STUDY

The M.B.A. program is a classic seventeen-course program covering the complete spectrum of management science, including marketing, business law, finance, economics, and international trade. The Master of Arts in organizational management is a two-year, fourteen-course program emphasizing the skills and knowledge it takes to manage both people and projects at an advanced level. The M.B.A. in global management is a two-year, fourteen-course program designed to ingrain the abilities to identify business opportunities and threats and to develop effective courses of action within the parameters of the international environment. The M.B.A. in technology management is a highly specialized seventeen-course program that focuses on proven methods and techniques for anticipating, managing, and marketing technology. The M.B.A. in accounting is an 18-course program designed to develop or enhance the financial management skills necessary to function effectively within private businesses, nonprofit organizations, and public agencies. The M.A.Ed. program, with an emphasis on curriculum and technology, requires the completion of 37 credits and is designed to meet the specific needs of educators. The M.S.N. program, consisting of 39 credits, is designed to develop and enhance the knowledge and skills of registered nurses. The Master of Science in computer information systems program is made up of fifteen courses that provide the tools not only to understand technology but also to keep current in its many kinds of development. The Doctor of Management (D. M.) in organizational leadership provides those students with a professional master's degree a means of exploring their personal readiness to become leaders in their professions or their current organizations.

Bachelor of Science degree programs require 120 credits each. The business administration program is suited ideally to men and women who need to be familiar with every aspect of running a business. The business information systems program has been designed for individuals whose careers involve managing information systems, software, hardware, and people. The business management program focuses on the areas necessary to manage both people and projects effectively. The business marketing program provides a foundation from which to build creative, analytical, and leadership abilities in individuals and workgroups. The accounting program promotes identification with andorientation to the accounting profession and is designed to provide the knowledge, skills, and abilities necessary to pursue a successful accounting career. The project management program focuses on the professional success of its students, emphasizing real-world project management application with assignments designed to apply new-found skills and knowledge to a variety of workplace settings. The information technology program provides fundamental knowledge and practice in both the information technology function and in system development. Students in this program can specialize in one of five areas: database management, networks and telecommunications, programming and operating systems analysis, and Web management. The e-business program provides fundamental knowledge and practice in business management and information technology. The nursing program (B.S.N.) is designed to develop the professional knowledge and skills of working registered nurses. A program in project management also will be available soon. In addition, students may study toward the Associate of Arts degree, a 2-year program providing solid academic training, and apply those credits toward the Bachelor of Science in business majors.

CREDIT OPTIONS

Graduate students are permitted to waive up to 6 credits by transferring comparable graduate-level course work taken at other accredited colleges or universities.

For undergraduate study, no more than 69 credits of lower-division courses (60 credits in the case of the information systems program) may be applied toward the degree requirement. At least 39 of the 120 total credits must satisfy the University's general education requirement. Students can apply for credit by examination and portfolio.

FACULTY

The Online Campus has more than 700 faculty members. All faculty members have extensive academic credentials (more than one third hold doctoral degrees), and all work in the fields they teach, bringing practical, "real-world" experience to bear on the needs of students who are working professionals.

ADMISSION

Graduate students must have an undergraduate degree from a regionally accredited college or university, with a cumulative GPA of 2.5 or better (3.0 for prior graduate work). Students must also be currently employed; have a minimum of three years of full-time, post–high school work experience providing exposure to organizational systems and management processes; or have access to an organizational environ-

ment appropriate for the application of theoretical concepts learned in the classroom. Students must complete the University-proctored Comprehensive Cognitive Assessment; non-native speakers of English must have a minimum score of 550 on the TOEFL.

Undergraduate students must have a high school diploma or its equivalent. Students must be at least 23 years old and currently employed. Students must complete the University-proctored Comprehensive Cognitive Assessment, and non-native speakers of English must have a minimum score of 550 on the TOEFL.

TUITION AND FEES

Graduate tuition is $485 per credit and undergraduate tuition is $390 per credit. There are an application fee of $58 and a graduation fee of $50. Textbook costs vary by course.

APPLYING

Unless students are relying on foreign transcripts for admission, all that is needed to begin the first course is to complete an application, enrollment agreement, and disclosure form. While students are in their first three classes, academic counselors work with them to complete transcript requests, the Comprehensive Cognitive Assessment, and any other items necessary for formal registration.

CONTACT
Enrollment Department
University of Phoenix Online
3157 East Elwood Street
Phoenix, Arizona 85034
Telephone: 877-611-3390 (toll-free in U.S.)
Fax: 602-387-6440
Web site: http://online.uophx.edu

University of South Alabama

USA Online

Mobile, Alabama

The University of South Alabama (USA), created in 1963, is a major public university located on the upper Gulf Coast in Mobile, Alabama. The University's mission actively embraces the functions of teaching, research, public service, and health care and vigorously pursues the preservation, discovery, communication, and application of knowledge. Degrees are available in the Colleges of Allied Health Professions, Arts and Sciences, Business, Education, Engineering, and Nursing; the Schools of Computer and Information Sciences and Continuing Education and Special Programs; and the Graduate School. USA also has an outstanding College of Medicine and clinical facilities, in addition to the USA Medical Center, USA Knollwood Park Hospital, and USA Children's and Women's Hospital. Fully accredited by the Southern Association of Colleges and Schools, USA enrolls some 11,000 students at the beautiful suburban campus in west Mobile.

DISTANCE LEARNING PROGRAM

The fall semester of 1999 is the beginning term for USA Online, the University's online campus. USA Online is designed to deliver courses and programs via the Internet to those who cannot attend school in the traditional manner due to family, career, and location requirements.

DELIVERY MEDIA

USA Online offers Web-based course instruction on the Internet. The courses currently offered are designated in the course offerings list with section numbers 85–89. These courses require additional technology fees. A computer with an Internet connection and e-mail is required. For specific requirements, course information, and additional registration requirements, students may visit the University's Web site (http://usaonline.southalabama.edu).

The online courses are offered via the eCollege.com system.

PROGRAMS OF STUDY

The College of Business offers the M.B.A. degree on line. At the end of the program, the student completes the capstone course on campus through a series of Saturday class sessions.

The College of Education offers the M.S. degree in instructional design and development and M.Ed. degrees in education administration, education media (library media), and special education (gifted education and collaborative teacher).

The College of Nursing offers several online courses for students who are enrolled in the RN-to-B.S.N. track and the M.S.N. program. All nursing courses in the RN-to-B.S.N. track are offered on line and through distant education strategies. Several of the core courses in the M.S.N. program are offered on line, and Web technology augments many other courses.

In addition, online courses are offered by the Colleges of Allied Health and Arts and Sciences, the Schools of Computer and Information Sciences and Continuing Education and Special Programs, and the College of Engineering.

STUDENT SERVICES

Many student services that are available to on-campus students are available to online students. The libraries, the bookstore, the student newspaper, admissions, registration, financial aid information, academic information, and advising are available at USA Online.

CREDIT OPTIONS

For the master's degree, a minimum of 30 semester hours of credit in an approved program is required. Students should see each program for the specific number of hours and other requirements. A maximum of 9 semester hours of graduate credit obtained at another accredited institution may be approved for transfer to the University of South Alabama. Only grades of A or B may be accepted.

FACULTY

For the fall semester of 1999, approximately 20 full-time faculty members are involved with USA Online. Approximately 90 percent have a doctoral degree.

ADMISSION

Applicants to USA Online courses, whether they are undergraduate or graduate students, must meet the same admission requirements as all University students. Students should contact the Office of Admissions at the address listed below or visit the Web site for information about the requirements for admission.

TUITION AND FEES

The cost for a 3-semester-hour course is $470 for undergraduates and $548 for graduate students. The total tuition charges include tuition, a registration fee, and a technology service fee.

FINANCIAL AID

Students should see the University online bulletin for financial aid information (http://www.southalabama.edu/bulletin/financial.htm).

APPLYING

Deadlines for the application for admission, the nonrefundable processing fee, and the official required documents (transcripts and test scores, as appropriate) are August 10 for the fall semester (August 1 for Graduate School), December 15 for the spring semester, and May 20 for the summer semester. Students should request applications and admissions material through e-mail (admiss@usamail.usouthal.edu) or visit the University's Web site at http://www.southalabama.edu (the application form and instructions are available on the Web).

CONTACT

Dr. Thomas L. Chilton, Associate Dean
Fax: 334-380-2748
E-mail: tchilton@usamail.usouthal.edu
Web site: http://usaonline.southalabama.edu

University of Southern Colorado

Continuing Education

Pueblo, Colorado

The University of Southern Colorado (USC) has served the changing needs of students for more than sixty years. USC's campus, spanning more than 275 acres, crowns the north end of Pueblo, a historically and culturally rich city of 100,000 located near the Greenhorn Mountains in the colorful Pikes Peak region of southern Colorado. Enrollment exceeds 4,000 students from throughout Colorado, the nation, and several other countries. The University of Southern Colorado is accredited at the bachelor's and master's levels by the Commission on Institutions of Higher Education of the North Central Association of Colleges and Schools.

DISTANCE LEARNING PROGRAM

USC offers a Bachelor of Science in Social Science External Degree completion program. The area of concentration can be tailored to meet the student's needs, such as teaching, business, criminology, law, public and program administration, and evaluation and research. Off-campus credits are nondistinguishable from those earned on campus.

DELIVERY MEDIA

After USC receives the course registration form, a syllabus explaining course requirements is mailed to the student. Completed course work is mailed directly to the instructor. Some courses may require proctored examinations, while others have examinations sent directly to the student. A variety of online and traditional tools are available for courses, such as e-mail, textbooks, and videotapes. Instructors are available by telephone, fax, e-mail, and correspondence.

PROGRAM OF STUDY

Requirements for the social science degree are as follows: skills requirements (14 semester hours), knowledge component (13 semester hours),

social science core (24 semester hours), specialty core (24 semester hours), area of concentration (20 semester hours), and electives (33 semester hours). A minimum of 128 semester hours are required for graduation, 40 of which must be junior- or senior-level (300–400) credits. Thirty-two semester hours must be completed with USC in order to receive this degree. Sixteen of the last 32 credit hours must be completed with USC. A maximum of 96 semester credits can be transferred. Of those credits, a maximum of 64 semester credits may be from junior/community colleges. Active student enrollment is maintained by enrolling in at least one USC course per year.

Credit is accepted from accredited institutions recommended by the American Association of Collegiate Registrars and Admissions Officers. Credits from a nonaccredited institution may be accepted for transfer after the student has completed at least 24 semester hours at USC with a C (2.0 GPA) average or better. A petition is required. Courses that are not accepted in the transfer process are petitioned by the Continuing Education staff.

SPECIAL PROGRAMS

Legal certificate programs are offered without credit, including legal investigation, victim advocacy, and legal secretary studies. Noncredit enrollment cannot be applied toward academic degree programs. However, a 6-credit-hour paralegal certificate program that can be applied toward the degree program is offered.

STUDENT SERVICES

At the student's request, a preliminary, unofficial evaluation is available. Submittal of unofficial transcripts is reviewed by the Continuing Education staff in an attempt to show the placement of previous college credits against the USC requirements. The unofficial evaluation is subject to change based on the final evaluation and the official acceptance of transfer course work by the Office of Admissions.

CREDIT OPTIONS

A student may earn a maximum of 30 semester hours through the College Level Examination Program (CLEP). A maximum of 6 semester hours may be applied toward credit for life experience. A maximum of 20 semester hours of military service credit is accepted when military service credit is processed and official copies of certificates are received. Twelve credit hours of field experience can also be used to fulfill degree requirements.

FACULTY

Approximately 60 percent of the faculty members in the External Degree Program have a Ph.D. and are full-time professors on campus at USC. The remaining 40 percent are part-time professors. All professors have experience working with distance learners.

ADMISSION

Students should submit the program enrollment fee, applications for External Degree Program and undergraduate admission to Colorado collegiate institutions, and high school transcripts with ACT or SAT scores. Students with at least 30 college credits are not required to submit ACT or SAT scores.

TUITION AND FEES

Tuition, $75 per semester hour for undergraduate credit and $85 per semester hour for graduate credit, must be submitted with the registration for the course. Some courses require videotape fees of $75.

FINANCIAL AID

At the present time, students enrolled in the External Degree Program are not eligible for state or federal financial aid. Company-sponsored tuition and military tuition assistance programs may be used for USC courses. Students are encouraged to seek scholarship aid from local civic groups that may sponsor such study.

USC courses are approved for the Defense Activity for Non-Traditional Educational Support (DANTES) program. Eligible military personnel should process DANTES applications through their education office.

APPLYING

A $135 enrollment fee should be submitted with the applications for admission. Upon acceptance, students receive an acceptance letter followed by an official transfer statement of credits. Shortly thereafter, an official evaluation is issued to the student.

CONTACT

Lara Van Buskirk, Assistant Program Manager
Don Spano, Advisor
Continuing Education Program
University of Southern Colorado
2200 Bonforte Boulevard
Pueblo, Colorado 81001-4901
Telephone: 877-872-9653, press 2 (toll-free)
Fax: 719-549-2438
E-mail: coned@uscolo.edu
        spano@rmi.net
Web site: http://www.uscolo.edu/coned/

USF University of South Florida

University of South Florida

Educational Outreach

Tampa, Florida

The University of South Florida (USF), founded in 1956, has a student population of more than 35,000. Nearly 200 degree programs are offered by USF's nine colleges at four campuses and numerous off-campus instructional sites and through distance learning. USF's student body is as diverse as the academic offerings, representing every state in the U.S. and more than 100 nations. USF's fast-growing reputation as a superior academic institution was formally acknowledged in 1998 by the Florida Board of Regents' designation as a Research I University, consistent with a record of success in securing grants and contracts which totaled more than $161 million in 1998–99.

USF is accredited by the Commission on Colleges of the Southern Association of Colleges and Schools to award degrees at the baccalaureate, master's, specialty, and doctoral levels, including the Doctor of Medicine.

DISTANCE LEARNING PROGRAM

USF has historically claimed the largest distance learning program among Florida's public universities, with annual enrollments of approximately 11,000 in more than 275 courses. All distance learning courses provide full University credit, are taught by USF faculty members, and are subject to standard curricular review and academic policies.

DELIVERY MEDIA

Asynchronous learning opportunities include Web-based learning, telecourses, videotapes, audiotapes, and combinations of these "anytime, anyplace" technologies. Access to a computer, Internet access, and an active e-mail account are required for Web courses. Capability to view VHS tapes is sufficient for video-based options. Group-based courses include fully interactive videoconferencing, one-way video/two-way audio, and mixed modes of delivery. These require specially equipped classrooms, receivers, and/or IP-based videoconferencing systems and Internet access.

PROGRAMS OF STUDY

Florida's thirty-eight public higher education institutions enroll more than 60,000 distance learners annually, with the community colleges providing lower-division courses and the universities providing upper-division and graduate distance courses. The Florida Virtual Campus, a statewide support unit located at USF, maintains course listings at the Web site http://www.flcampus.org. The University of South Florida offers more than 275 courses annually, with descriptions available at the Web site listed in the Contact section.

USF, with the only accredited school of public health in Florida, offers a master's program using one-way video/two-way audio courses at a statewide network of public health agency partner sites, complemented by Web-based components.

More than 635 engineering professionals are graduates of USF through the Florida Engineering Education Delivery System (FEEDS), a statewide system providing access to graduate engineering courses at industrial and public sites or via video-

tape and Web courses. Graduate certificate and undergraduate programs are also available.

The Bachelor of Science in nursing program is a limited-access program using fully interactive videoconferencing at regional sites, with some Web-based courses. Clinical and practicum experiences are required.

The Master of Education degree (M.Ed.), with an emphasis in instructional technology, is a twelve-course program largely available online, with on-campus requirements for selected courses.

One of only forty-eight master's programs in the U.S. accredited by the American Library Association, USF's graduate program in library and information science is a statewide, site-based degree, with Web-based courses providing additional flexibility. Teachers seeking media certification can use Web-based LIS classes to meet requirements.

SPECIAL PROGRAMS

The Bachelor of Independent Studies (B.I.S.) program, an interdisciplinary, individualized program geared to adult learners, is now available online with special accommodations for distance students to meet two-week resident study requirements.

The online master's degree in gifted education includes all gifted endorsement classes for teacher certification and selected foundations courses. The 36-hour master's degree features an individualized practicum in the student's district, a flexible schedule, and a portfolio in lieu of comprehensive examinations. Two weeks of resident study are required.

All courses required for the English for speakers of other languages (ESOL) endorsement for Florida teacher certification are available online.

The Virtual Master's Degree in Varying Exceptionalities program is a statewide collaborative providing graduate courses in special education using Web-based and one-way video/two-way audio delivery. Teachers may enroll in both the virtual program and classroom courses at participating universities.

STUDENT SERVICES

USF's Virtual Library provides access to an extensive collection of electronic reserves, more than 100 databases, full-text scholarly journals, and other digital documents to support distance learners. The Florida Distance Learning Reference and Referral Center provides individual research advice and assistance for students statewide. Student services available online include admission forms and procedures, registration, grade reports, and textbook orders for distance learners.

CREDIT OPTIONS

All distance learning courses receive full USF academic credit and are subject to standard procedures and policies. Approved transfer credit can be applied toward degree requirements, in consultation with program advisers. Florida uses a common course numbering system to facilitate transfer of credit from community colleges or universities statewide.

FACULTY

USF has a faculty of more than 2,000. During fall 1999, approximately 78 percent of the distance learning courses were taught by full-time USF faculty members, with the remainder led by adjunct faculty members and graduate assistants.

ADMISSION

Students enrolled in distance learning courses must meet the same admission requirements as all students at USF. Students can register for up to 14 semester hours (undergraduates) or 12 hours (graduates) prior to formal admission to USF in most degree programs.

TUITION AND FEES

Tuition and fees for the 1999–2000 academic year for Florida residents per semester hour were $70.15 (undergraduate) and $142.97 (graduate). Nonresident tuition and fees per semester hour were $303.10 (undergraduate) and $503.70 (graduate).

FINANCIAL AID

Information regarding financial aid is available online at http://usfweb.usf.edu/finaid/. Distance learners follow the same procedures to apply for financial aid as any student at USF and are subject to the same eligibility guidelines and policies. Approximately $120.6 million was disbursed to USF students receiving some form of financial aid during 1998–99, with no separate statistics available for distance learners.

APPLYING

Distance learners are subject to standard USF admission criteria and processes. Admission policies, applications and procedures, and enrollment application forms are available online at http://usfweb.usf.edu.

CONTACT

Barbara Emil, Ph.D.
Dean, Educational Outreach
University of South Florida
4202 E. Fowler Avenue
Tampa, Florida 33620
Telephone: 813-974-7984
Fax: 813-974-7272
E-mail: distance@outreach.usf.edu
Web site: http://www.outreach.usf.edu.

University of Tennessee

Distance Education and Independent Study

Knoxville, Tennessee

The University of Tennessee, is a state-supported university, which first offered distance learning courses in 1923. It is accredited by the Southern Association of Colleges and Schools (SACS). Distance Education and Independent Study courses are delivered to the student's home, workplace, military base, hospital, the University of Tennessee at Chattanooga (Chattanooga) campus, the University of Tennessee at Martin (Martin) campus, and off-campus centers in Kingsport and Nashville.

Media Courses are delivered via videotapes, videoconferencing, interactive television, audiotapes, computer software, computer conferencing, World Wide Web, and print. Students and teachers may meet in person or interact via videoconferencing, audio conferencing, mail, telephone, fax, e-mail, interactive television, and World Wide Web. The following equipment may be required: television, videocassette player, computer, modem, Internet access, and e-mail. Geographic Service Area/Restrictions Correspondence programs are available nationwide, though some offerings are limited to in state. Courses, other than correspondence courses, may have caps on enrollment.

Degrees and certificate programs offered are graduate degrees, business administration (PEMBA), an M.S. in industrial engineering, and an M.S. in information sciences. There is a graduate certificate in applied statistical strategies.

DISTANCE LEARNING PROGRAM

Through the Department of Distance Education and Independent Study, the University of Tennessee, (UT), offers a variety of flexibly delivered programs for students who are distance learners. The goal is to extend to off-campus students the unique resources of the University. State-of-the-art live and real-time Internet-based courses are being introduced at the upper level undergraduate and graduate level, allowing both click-to-learn self study and voice–data interactive collaboration learning situations. Interactive (two-way) video and videotapes are used to deliver graduate degrees at six designated off-campus locations. UT has more than 1,000 students enrolled in video distance learning courses.

DELIVERY MEDIA

The University of Tennessee operates a bank of web servers and high-speed digital connections for its growing enrollment of online, distance-learning students. Selected courses and degree programs are offered via advanced voice and data interactive cyberclass technology over the Internet and are available to individuals. Students meet electronically on a regular basis, using multimedia computers and the Internet.

A digital interactive video network links group video interactive classrooms in Tennessee and is capable of connecting to similar sites throughout the country. Groups of students participate in graduate courses at these sites. UT also offers individuals a program of graduate engineering courses on videotape. A VCR is the only equipment needed for the videotaped courses.

Correspondence courses are offered for undergraduate credit to individuals anywhere at anytime via postal mail, e-mail, and click-to-learn web-delivery methods. Additional courses are being revised and will be delivered interactively and online.

PROGRAMS OF STUDY

The University offers the following degrees: an M.S. in industrial engineering/engineering management, an M.S. in information sciences, and several flexibly delivered M.B.A. programs.

The M.S. in industrial engineering/engineering management is available to students via videotape and at selected sites in Tennessee via interactive video. Students must have a bachelor's degree in engineering or a related scientific or technical field.

The M.S. in information sciences is accredited by the American Library Association. This program is available to students via the Internet. The program requires 43 semester hours of graduate courses; the core curriculum consists of six courses. The focus of this program is on electronic and traditional print media.

An Executive M.B.A. program for physicians is also offered through the UT College of Business Administration.

SPECIAL PROGRAMS

UT brings students a new graduate sequence of courses in practical, useful statistical methods. Knowledge delivered, when and where a student chooses, by the accredited knowledge experts at UT.

UT's Graduate Certificate in applied statistical strategies focuses on nuts-and-bolts application of advanced statistical tools students will find useful in their professional careers.

Students choose three courses that best meet their needs. They design their own course track that focuses on manufacturing and engineering data or choose a service industry and business track. Students may combine courses from both tracks for experience in both real worlds.

Students learn via the latest Internet delivery technology delivered through desktop computers or in intensive short courses on the beautiful University of Tennessee, Knoxville campus. In either option, students are in the company of working adults who are focused on gaining practical answers to tough data analysis questions. More information about this certificate program can be found on the World Wide Web at http://www.outreach.utk.edu/cyberstats/.

Student Services Students registered in UT distance education master's degree programs have access to University computer resources. A distance education librarian assists off-campus students with reference searches and in obtaining materials through interlibrary loan. Academic advising is provided by telephone and e-mail as well as in group sessions to students in interactive video programs.

CREDIT OPTIONS

Students may transfer up to 6 hours of credit from an accredited university to a UT master's degree program. In the information sciences program, some elective hours may be earned through directed independent-study projects. All credits earned in independent study courses are generally transferable to other colleges and universities toward the completion of a degree.

ADMISSION

Application to the UT Graduate School is required for credit or audit of distance education courses. The application fee is $35. Admission to the Graduate School requires a bachelor's degree with a satisfactory grade point average from an accredited college or university. The Graduate School requires a minimum grade point average of 2.7 (on a 4.0 scale) or a 3.0 during the senior year of undergraduate study. Applicants with previous graduate work must have a grade point average of at least 3.0 or the equivalent on all graduate work. The various degree programs may also have additional requirements. Admission is not required to take undergraduate correspondence courses. Enrollees are encouraged to obtain an adviser's signature in support of taking courses via independent study enrollment.

TUITION AND FEES

In 1999-2000, for in-state students there was a maintenance fee of $109 per undergraduate semester hour with a maximum of $1552 (12 hours) and $184 for graduate courses per semester hour with a maximum of $1903 (12 hours).

Out-of-state undergraduate students paid tuition of $362 per semester hour with a maximum of $4586 (12 hours). Out-of-state graduate students paid tuition of $522 per semester hour with a maximum of $4937 (9 hours). A $12 per semester hour technology fee may apply to registrations. UT participates in the Southern Regional Education Board's (SREB) Academic Common Market. Among other benefits, Academic Common Market allows students in Georgia, Arkansas, West Virginia, and Virginia to register for the Masters in Information Science at in-state rates. Undergraduate correspondence/independent study courses cost $106 per semester hour, including postage and handling.

FINANCIAL AID

Financial aid is generally not available to part-time distance education students, although students enrolled at least half-time in a graduate degree program may qualify. For the undergraduate program, many students are able to secure assistance from their current employer, the Veterans Administration, vocational rehabilitation services, or other agencies. Courses in the independent study program are covered by the Defense Activity for Non-Traditional Educational Support (DANTES). Students should contact their education officer for information and forms.

APPLYING

Students interested in enrolling in distance education or independent study programs should contact the Distance Education Call Center at either the e-mail address or the toll free number below. Additional information about programs can be obtained by visiting the Distance Education and Independent Study Web site at the address below.

CONTACT

Distance Education and
   Independent Study
1534 White Avenue
University of Tennessee
Knoxville, Tennessee 37996-1525
Telephone: 865-974-5134
            800-325-8657 (toll-
            free)
Fax: 423-974-4684
Email: disteducation@utk.edu
World Wide Web:
   http://www.outreach.utk.edu/deis

The University of Tennessee

Distance Learning Program

Chattanooga and Martin, Tennessee

The University of Tennessee at Chattanooga (UTC) and The University of Tennessee Martin (UT Martin) are two of three institutions that make up The University of Tennessee System. The main campus is in Knoxville. Both UTC and UT Martin are dedicated to excellence in undergraduate and graduate studies and committed to serving students both on campus and at a distance.

DISTANCE LEARNING PROGRAM

Through the Division of Continuing Education, the University of Tennessee at Chattanooga offers degree programs and courses via distance education. Two types of course delivery at UTC are termed as distance education. These include live off-site instruction and two-way interactive compressed video classes. Both utilize existing UTC courses and programs that are being offered in formats other than the traditional on-campus delivery. The UTC Division of Continuing Education, in cooperation with academic departments, schools, and colleges, provides support for a number of such courses.

The Office of Extended Campus and Continuing Education at the University of Tennessee at Martin provides a variety of distance learning opportunities to its constituents in Tennessee. In addition to correspondence opportunities offered through the University of Tennessee Department of Independent Study, UT Martin offers select graduate programs via interactive (two-way) video at selected off-site locations. Plans are being finalized to implement a Bachelor of University Studies Degree, a flexible degree program geared towards adult learners. The target date for the degree program is fall 2000.

DELIVERY MEDIA

The University of Tennessee at Martin is a member of the University of Tennessee video network. This network allows UT Martin to deliver courses and programs throughout the State of Tennessee. Faculty members make use of bulletin boards, e-mail and course Web sites to deliver material and communicate with students.

PROGRAMS OF STUDY

UTC offers the M.S. in Criminal Justice and the M.B.A. via interactive video to the Knoxville campus of the University of Tennessee system. UTC also offers undergraduate criminal justice courses to students on the Harriman, Tennessee campus of Roane State Community College.

The M.S. in Criminal Justice is a professional degree which prepares graduates for leadership in management positions in criminal justice and social service agencies, or entry into doctoral study. To graduate, students must earn a minimum of 36 credit hours, receive candidacy status, and successfully complete a comprehensive examination.

The M.B.A. is designed for students with an undergraduate degree in either business or an unrelated field. The M.B.A. Program requires students to complete a minimum of 31 semester credit hours in graduate course work.

Several programs are available at off-campus locations. The University of Tennessee at Martin offers the Master of Business Administration, Master of Accountancy, and Master of Science in Education at the Jackson, Tennessee location. The Oak Ridge, Tennessee location offers the Master of Business Administration, and the Master of Accountancy.

The University of Tennessee at Martin also offers general education courses at extended sites in Camden, Paris, and at a full-service center in Selmer, Tennessee.

The Jackson Center offers the RN to B.S.N. degree for nurses who already have the RN.

SPECIAL PROGRAMS

The Office of Extended Campus and Continuing Education at UT Martin offers noncredit courses in a variety of fields in Martin and Selmer, Tennessee, as well as other west Tennessee locations.

STUDENT SERVICES

Registered UTC students who attend classes at off-campus locations are served by the Office of Continuing Education regarding student services. The Office of Continuing Education provides library access and computer lab access. Continuing Education staff members also arranges for books to be available either at the classroom sites or at a bookstore on the campus where the students are attending class. Registration can be handled through the department directly, or through the Office of Continuing Education.

Students registered in any of UT Martin's programs have full access to campus resources, including library and computer labs. Both one-on-one and group advising is available on site in Jackson and Oak Ridge. Students in all locations may also take advantage of e-mail and telephone advising.

CREDIT OPTIONS

Students may transfer up to 6 hours of credit from an accredited university to a UT Martin master's degree program.

FACULTY

UTC faculty members who teach using the distance learning medium are determined by the department housing the program(s). UT Martin courses are taught by the same full-time and part-time faculty members that teach classes on campus.

ADMISSION

UT Chattanooga admissions requirements are set by the undergraduate and graduate departments on the UTC campus. Application, admission, and acceptance to UTC are handled through either the undergraduate or graduate office depending on the intended degree.

UT Martin admissions requirements for both undergraduate and graduate programs vary by curriculum. Students should contact a program representative for details.

TUITION AND FEES

For the 1999–2000 academic year at UTC, in-state students paid no tuition, but the mandatory fee for 1 semester hour of undergraduate credit was $115 and for 1 hour of graduate credit was $183. Out-of-state undergraduate students paid $204 in tuition for 1 semester hour of credit, plus fees of $115. Out-of-state graduate students paid $251 in tuition and fees of $183. To date, there are no additional fees for distance education students.

For the 1999–2000 academic year at UT Martin, undergraduate in-state tuition was $112 per credit hour. Graduate in-state tuition was $187 per credit hour.

FINANCIAL AID

Financial aid at UTC is handled directly through the Financial Aid Office.

Generally, there are fewer financial aid opportunities available to part-time students at UT Martin. Students enrolled at least half-time in graduate or undergraduate degree programs may qualify for financial aid.

APPLYING

Students should contact the Office of Undergraduate Admissions or the Graduate Office, depending upon the type of degree desired. Students are required to submit official copies of transcripts from all high schools and colleges attended (two copies for graduate students). Prospective freshmen students under the age of 21 must submit ACT or SAT scores. Graduate student should contact the Graduate Division for information about admission test requirements and other supplemental materials that may be required for admission to specific programs.

CONTACT

The University of Tennessee at Chattanooga
Beth Dodd, Director Continuing Education or
Tonya Pace, Distance Learning Manager Continuing Education
The University of Tennessee at Chattanooga
119 Race Hall
615 McCalllie Avenue
Chattanooga, Tennessee 37403
Telehone: 423-755-4344
Fax: 423-266-5549
E-mail: Beth-Dodd@utc.edu or Tonya-Pace@utc.edu
Web site: http://www.utc.edu/~conteduc/

The University of Tennessee at Martin
Office of Extended Campus and Continuing Education
110 Gooch Hall
Martin, Tennessee 38238
Telehone: 901-587-7080
E-mail: ecce@utm.edu

The University of Texas at Austin

Continuing and Extended Education
Distance Education Center

Austin, Texas

The University of Texas at Austin (UT Austin) was founded in 1883 on 40 acres near the state capitol. As the academic flagship of the UT system's fifteen component institutions, UT Austin is home to students from every county in Texas, all 50 states, and approximately 120 countries. There is an annual enrollment of approximately 49,000 students. UT Austin has the distinction of awarding the greatest number of doctorate degrees of any university in the nation. The University of Texas at Austin is accredited by the Commission on Colleges of the Southern Association of Colleges and Schools.

The mission of the University is to achieve excellence in the interrelated areas of undergraduate education, graduate education, research, and public service; to provide superior and comprehensive educational opportunities at the baccalaureate through doctoral and special professional educational levels; to contribute to the advancement of society through research, creative activity, scholarly inquiry, and the development of new knowledge; to preserve and promote the arts, to benefit the state's economy, to serve the citizens through public programs, and to provide other public service.

DISTANCE LEARNING PROGRAM

For ninety years, Continuing and Extended Education has been extending UT Austin resources to the citizens of Texas. In 1909, the first offerings through the Distance Education Center (DEC) were college courses, but today the offerings also include programs for professional and personal development. In 1999, the DEC served more than 5,000 students from across the nation and the world.

DELIVERY MEDIA

The Distance Education Center offers synchronous and asynchronous courses in traditional print-based media as well as in a blend of delivery methods including print-based materials, Internet components, audioconferencing, CD-ROMs, diskette, videoconferencing, audiotape, and videotape. Students submit lessons through U.S. mail, e-mail, the Internet, telephone, and fax. Interaction with instructors is available by phone, e-mail, U.S. mail, listserve, and through chat rooms.

PROGRAMS OF STUDY

The DEC college curriculum, which covers 30 fields of study, is aligned with on-campus curriculum. All courses are developed and taught by instructors who are approved by UT Austin department chairs. Specific content areas include anthropology, art history, curriculum and instruction, economics, educational psychology, English, government, history, kinesiology and health education, philosophy, psychology, radio, television and film production, social work, sociology, visual arts studies, and women's studies. Science and language courses include astronomy, geography, mathematics, nursing, nutrition, physics, zoology, Czech, French, German, Latin, and Spanish.

Several professional development courses of study are also offered through the DEC. In collaboration with the University of Texas at San Antonio, the Center offers a self-paced, eight-module purchasing management certificate program that trains participants in procurement, purchasing economics, and specification writing. In cooperation with the Texas Commission on Law Enforcement Officers Standards and Education, the DEC offers continuing education courses for Texas law enforcement officers. Also offered are a number of Apple ALI online computer courses. The DEC also makes available to professionals all DEC college credit courses, in which many professionals enroll on a noncredit basis for professional development.

STUDENT SERVICES

Students may enroll online, by mail, by telephone, by fax, or in person. The DEC strongly recommends that students talk to a DEC student services representative before enrolling in more than two DEC courses concurrently. Student services representatives can also provide information about learning at a distance and can answer questions about courses and materials.

CREDIT OPTIONS

If a student is taking a DEC course to satisfy a requirement for a degree or diploma, he or she should contact a university advisor or school advisor to confirm that credit acquired through the DEC will transfer as the appropriate course. Earned college credit is recorded on a UT Austin transcript.

FACULTY

More than 50 UT Austin faculty members teach for the DEC.

ADMISSION

Enrollment in DEC courses does not constitute admission to UT Austin. Any student can enroll in any of program at any time.

TUITION AND FEES

Tuition fees vary depending on the course. In most cases, tuition for a college course is $83 per credit hour. There is an additional nonrefundable enrollment fee of $20. Other fees may be applicable if the course includes additional resources, such as Internet components, faxed lesson options, tapes, proctoring, re-examination, and supplemental study materials.

FINANCIAL AID

In general, financial aid is administered through governmental agencies to military personnel, veterans, and persons with specific, identified disabilities. Federal financial programs usually require that students be enrolled in programs leading to a degree, a certificate, or some other educational credential in order to considered for assistance.

APPLYING

Students can apply over the Web, by fax, by mail, and in person. As soon as the application and payment have been processed, a receipt and study materials are mailed to the student. Applications are accepted at any time.

CONTACT

Olga Garza
Manager of Student Services
The University of Texas at Austin
Continuing and Extended Education
Distance Education Center
P.O. Box 7700
Austin, Texas 78713-7700
Telephone: 888-BE-A-GRAD (toll-free)
Fax: 512-475-7933
E-mail: dec@utexas.edu
Web site: http://www.utexas.edu/cee/dec

The University of Texas at Dallas

Global M.B.A. Online Program

Richardson, Texas

The University of Texas at Dallas (UTD) was created in September 1969. The mission of the University is to provide Texas and the nation with the benefits of educational and research programs of the highest quality. The School of Management was established in 1975. The School's mission is to meet the challenges of a rapidly changing, technology-driven, global society by partnering with the business community to deliver high-quality management education to a diverse group of undergraduate and graduate students and practicing executives, to develop and continuously improve programs advancing management education and practice, and to conduct research enhancing management knowledge. The University of Texas at Dallas is accredited by the Commission on Colleges of the Southern Association of Colleges and Schools.

DISTANCE LEARNING PROGRAM

The Global M.B.A. Online extends delivery of UTD's part-time M.B.A. Program to students who cannot commit to regularly scheduled classes on campus. The online M.B.A. is 48 credit hours, anchored by the same 27 hours of core courses as delivered in the classroom. Electives (21 hours) emphasize international management and information technology, two of UTD's strongest academic areas. Students are not organized in distinct classes (cohort groups) but select course loads consistent with their own part-time pace.

DELIVERY MEDIA

Faculty members engage online students using instructional resources and techniques that retain many of the classroom's dynamics, including audio streaming lectures supported by downloadable presentations, online text-based conferences, bulletin board and e-mail exchanges, and teleconferences. In addition to a confident level of computer literacy, technical requirements include a Pentium II or equivalent processor; a 28.8K or faster modem (56K recom.); 32 M system RAM; 200 MB free hard disk space memory; Internet access with Netscape 4.06 or better or MS Explorer 4.0 or better; and CD-ROM capabilities. Software requirements include Microsoft Office 97 or better and virus detection/protection software such as McAfee. "Plug-ins" may be required for specific courses.

PROGRAM OF STUDY

A Master of Business Administration (M.B.A.) is awarded. The online M.B.A. is anchored by the 27-hour basic core consisting of eleven courses. Electives (21 hours) emphasize international management and information technology. Core courses include accounting for managers, social and political environment of business, strategic planning, financial management, global economy, business economics, introduction to marketing management, introduction to organizational behavior, introduction to operations research, operations management, and applied statistics for management science. Electives in international management include multinational firm, international corporate finance, international marketing, and cross-cultural management. Breadth electives include Management Accounting: Plan-ning and Control Systems and Corporate Finance & Policy. Electives in information technology include the information age enterprise, economics of information goods, and Internet business models.

CREDIT OPTIONS

Some of UTD's core course equivalents are offered through the UT-System TeleCampus M.B.A. Online, and 18 hours are transferable to the Global M.B.A. Online. Transfer credit requests are initiated by students after admission. Prospective transfers from other UT-System components participating in the TeleCampus M.B.A. will be pre-approved if identified on degree plan.

FACULTY

The University of Texas at Dallas School of Management has strong, committed faculty members who teach all of the master's programs. All faculty members have extensive experience in master's education, consulting, and/or practical experience both domestically and internationally. Some are leading scholars. Many serve as editors of professional journals. Others have received awards for teaching excellence. At times, faculty members join together to team teach selected courses.

ADMISSION

Admission requirements and tuition are the same as those for the traditional M.B.A. Prospective students use the online graduate application form and submit a GMAT score and undergraduate degree transcript(s). Prerequisites for the Global M.B.A. Online include the knowledge of calculus (equivalent to UTD's Math 5304, Applied Mathematical Analysis for Non-Majors, with grade of B or better) and competence in personal computing (equivalent to UTD's BA 3351). Deficiencies must be remedied within the first 12 hours of graduate work. Currently, these prerequisite courses are not offered online.

TUITION AND FEES

Tuition and fees are approximately $679 for a 3-credit-hour course for Texas residents and $1336 for non-residents. Included are UTD fees associated with distance learning delivery and School of Management fees. Excluded are some fees associated with campus programs (e.g., student union, physical instruction facility, etc.).

FINANCIAL AID

Students may access the University of Texas at Dallas financial aid department for information and applications via http://www.utdallas.edu.

APPLYING

Like the campus-based program, courses are offered during the three regular semesters starting in August/ September, January, and May. Application deadlines for each semester are the same as for the regular M.B.A. program.

CONTACT

Mr. George Barnes, Director
Global M.B.A. Online
School of Management
The University of Texas at Dallas
P. O. Box 830688, JO51
Richardson, Texas 75083-0688
Telephone: 972-883-2783
Fax: 972-883-2799
E-mail: gbarnes@utdallas.edu
Web site: http://cyclops.utdallas.edu/som/globalmba

The University of Texas at Dallas

School of Management
M.I.M.S. Global Leadership Executive Programs

Richardson, Texas

The University of Texas at Dallas was created in September 1969. The mission of the University is to provide Texas and the nation with the benefits of educational and research programs of the highest quality. The School of Management was established in 1975. The School's mission is to meet the challenges of a rapidly changing, technology-driven, global society by partnering with the business community to deliver high quality management education to a diverse group of undergraduate and graduate students and practicing executives; to develop and continuously improve programs advancing management education and practice; and to conduct research enhancing management knowledge. The University of Texas at Dallas is accredited by the Commission on Colleges of the Southern Association of Colleges and Schools.

DISTANCE LEARNING PROGRAM

The Master's in International Management Studies Program (M.I.M.S.) at the University of Texas at Dallas (UTD) School of Management offers two degree programs via distance education: a Global Leadership M.B.A. and a Master of Arts degree in international management. The degree programs are designed for experienced midcareer managers and senior professionals who wish to develop global leadership knowledge and skills and who require a flexible, convenient learning environment.

DELIVERY MEDIA

M.I.M.S. distance learning design combines a variety of learning and delivery methods. Curriculum is delivered sequentially over the Internet through a variety of technologies including text, audio, teleconference, and groupware. Students join a cohort group and study both independently and in virtual teams. Students are required to participate in a ten-day foreign study tour and in quarterly weekend retreats on the UTD campus in Dallas.

PROGRAMS OF STUDY

The Global Leadership Executive M.B.A. (GLEMBA) is a 49-credit-hour program that can be completed in thirty months; the Master of Arts degree in international management can be completed in twenty-eight months. Students already holding an M.B.A. may, under some circumstances, complete the M.A. in fifteen months.

The comprehensive, integrated curriculum is focused on developing global leaders and designed to build knowledge, competencies, and skills required by contemporary multinational companies. Key areas of learning encompass environmental intelligence, international business best practices, systems and interfunctional thinking, and global mindset and intercultural savvy.

Curriculum is organized into three tracks: basic core (12 credit hours) global leadership (24 credit hours) and advanced core (13 credit hours). Candidates for the M.A. program, which typically includes those who already have an M.B.A. degree, complete the basic and global leadership tracks. Candidates pursuing the M.B.A. complete the basic, global leadership, and advanced tracks.

STUDENT SERVICES

Students join a cohort class and receive benefit from group interaction and support throughout the program. Class sizes are limited to allow for frequent communication and feedback among students and faculty members.

M.I.M.S. uses a groupware system to post all administrative information and course materials. Faculty members and students use e-mail and group conferencing. Students access electronic libraries for search and document retrieval. M.I.M.S. administration arranges all course registration, billing services, and UTD administrative matters.

CREDIT OPTIONS

Students who have successfully completed graduate work at an accredited institution within the past six years may petition for transfer of credits into the M.I.M.S. program. All petitions for transfer of credit must be accompanied by an official transcript and an official explanation of the course numbering at the school where the credit was earned. To qualify for transfer of credit, the grade earned in the course must be a B or better from an accredited college or university, and the course must not be a correspondence or extension course. Also, the transfer credit is not awarded for experiential learning, performance, or experience that occurs prior to enrollment. The total number of credit transfers toward the completion of a master's degree cannot exceed twelve hours toward the M.A. and fifteen towards the M.B.A. degree.

FACULTY

The M.I.M.S. faculty is composed of professors who teach in the University of Texas at Dallas School of Management, as well as distinguished faculty and experts from national and international universities.

ADMISSION

Applicants into the M.I.M.S. Global Leadership Executive Programs must have a bachelor's degree from an accredited university with a grade point average of 3.0 or better on a 4.0 scale, work experience of at least seven years in a managerial or professional position, proficient computer and Internet skills, and fluency in written and spoken English.

TUITION AND FEES

Program fees of $28,500 for the M.A. and $37,150 for the M.B.A. are inclusive of tuition, texts, specialized software, retreats, and travel and hotel costs for the international study tour. Students may incur additional costs for travel and living accommodations during the weekend retreats.

FINANCIAL AID

Students may access the University of Texas at Dallas financial aid department for information and applications via the University's Web site at www.utdallas.edu.

APPLYING

The M.I.M.S. program accepts and reviews applications for admission on a rolling basis. Enrollments in the basic core track are throughout the year; the global leadership track begins each January. Completion of the basic core marketing and finance course (or the equivalent through approved course transfer) are required prior to joining the global leadership track.

CONTACT

Dr. Stephen Guisinger, Director
M.I.M.S. Global Leadership Executive Programs
School of Management
University of Texas at Dallas
P.O. Box 830688
Richardson, Texas 75083-0688
Telephone: 972-883-MIMS
Fax: 972-883-6164
E-mail: glemba@utdallas.edu
Web site: www.utdallas.edu/mims

The University of Texas System

UT TeleCampus, Online Degrees, Courses, and Support

Austin, Texas

"Taking the Distance Out of Education," the University of Texas (UT) TeleCampus provides students, faculty, and staff of the University of Texas System with a central support unit for distance education programs and online degrees. Distance learners can find the services and links they need online, from admissions criteria, transcripts, financial aid, and course schedules to extensive digital libraries and virtual classrooms. The UT TeleCampus does not confer degrees but supports the University of Texas campuses that do. The UT TeleCampus was launched in May 1998 to serve as a central portal for collaborative online delivery programs and support services, giving students one convenient location for all Web-based learning opportunities. Complete information regarding online programs can be found at the World Wide Web address listed below. Access is free and open to the public (excluding courses and some library services).

DISTANCE LEARNING PROGRAM

UT TeleCampus–based programs and courses are comprised of the same rigorous content found on-site at its nine campuses. From application to graduation processes, students face the same general expectations and receive the same high-quality courses on-site or online. Online courses run semester to semester, allowing flexibility during the week for study and participation in group Web-based discussions. An online syllabus identifies when tests and projects are due.

An academic advisory committee oversees each online master's program. These committees are composed of deans and faculty members from participating schools, and together they ensure accreditation standards and the integrity of courses as they transfer from classroom to the Internet. Students receive the same academic credit for the courses listed with online degree programs as they would for similar courses offered on-site.

DELIVERY MEDIA

The TeleCampus uses Internet technologies for course delivery and student support via the World Wide Web.

Courses may also utilize additional distance education tools, including CDs, audiotapes and videotapes, streaming video and audio, e-mail, and chat rooms. Faculty members maintain interaction with students in a variety of ways, including timely responses to individual e-mail inquiries.

PROGRAMS OF STUDY

The University of Texas System offers eight online master's degrees in six areas of study. In addition, certification programs and general curriculum courses are available online. Most programs are collaborative in nature, which allows students to select a campus from several choices. The campus to which the student applies and is admitted is the campus that confers the degree upon successful completion of studies.

The M.B.A. Online in General Management is a 48-hour program designed for clear understanding of a marketplace that has become increasingly complex due to the addition of new technologies and communication tools. This degree offers a collaboration of eight campuses, pooling considerable faculty expertise for the benefit of the student.

The M.Ed. degree in educational technology is designed for K–12 teachers, administrators, and technology coordinators. The 36-hour curriculum prepares a new group of leaders who coordinate, plan, and direct technology in the educational arena.

The 36-hour master's in reading program offers several options, including creating a degree plan to include an English as a Second Language Endorsement and/or a Reading Specialist Certificate.

The master's in kinesiology program enables physical educators and coaches to pursue a master's degree entirely online. Graduates in this program can select the Master of Science in kinesiology or the Master of Education in health and kinesiology. A degree plan ranges from 30 to 36 hours. Four UT campuses offer this degree and an additional two campuses provide courses to this innovative collaboration.

The 33- to 36-hour master's degree in electrical engineering combines talents from and recognition of UT Dallas and UT Arlington, preparing engineers for the dynamic change facing their industry. This master's degree is conferred with the Graduate Certificate in Telecommunications Engineering.

Based on the baccalaureate area of study, students choose between the master's degree in computer science or computer science and engineering. Both degrees are integral to meeting the lifelong learning required of telecommunications professionals. Both degrees range from 33 to 36 hours and are conferred with the Graduate Certificate in Telecommunications Engineering.

The First Year Online Program provides many options in the entry-level undergraduate curriculum, ranging from art appreciation to political science. Courses are designed to transfer easily within the state of Texas. Visit the World Wide Web address listed below for available course offerings and schedules.

The English as a Second Language Program is a four-course endorsement that can be taken as part of a master's degree or as a sole credential.

SPECIAL PROGRAMS

Faculty members from within University of Texas institutions develop all academic courses within the TeleCampus. Students receive the same academic credit from distance learning courses as they do for traditional, on-site instruction. In addition, students who are enrolled in courses from the TeleCampus receive identification that allows them to utilize the digital library and other password protected campus services. The TeleCampus has worked closely with registrars from each component in the UT System so that students enrolled in TeleCampus courses need only be admitted to one UT component to take courses across the system, rather than following traditional admissions procedures at every campus offering TeleCampus courses.

STUDENT SERVICES

The UT TeleCampus was designed with the student in mind, providing all of the services students expect to find on a traditional campus, including admission, registrar, financial aid, bookstores, transcripts, veterans' resources, and student centers. In addition, important services for online students include extensive digital libraries, searchable databases for use in research projects, chat rooms, academic computing, media, various resource links, and more.

CREDIT OPTIONS

Transfer credit toward online courses and programs is generally the same as comparable on-site programs. Students should contact the program advisers listed inside the TeleCampus for specifics.

FACULTY

The same nationally recognized faculty that teaches on-campus courses at the University of Texas campuses teaches online courses offered through the UT TeleCampus. Courses are designed and developed by these faculty members with production support and faculty development provided by the UT TeleCampus.

ADMISSION

Admission criteria and processes for online offerings are approximately the same as on-site courses. It is advisable to start the initial application process 90 days prior to the beginning of a semester. Applications may be downloaded from links within the Telecampus. Students may use e-mail, fax, and phone to facilitate the process in most cases.

TUITION AND FEES

Tuition and fees vary slightly from program to program. Generally, graduate-level courses within the TeleCampus are approximately $200 per credit hour and $600 per 3-hour course for in-state tuition. Undergraduate courses average $100 per credit hour and $300 per 3-hour course. Students should access the UT TeleCampus Web site for specific details or call the Telecampus office at the toll-free number listed below.

FINANCIAL AID

Financial aid opportunities are available for students enrolled in TeleCampus courses. Links to financial aid offices are found by clicking on Student Services from within the TeleCampus. Students apply for financial aid via their home campus.

APPLYING

Application processes for online courses are the same for on-site courses, although they can be completed without going to the campus. Calendars can be referenced from within the TeleCampus. Registration can also be completed from a distance, and the Telecampus has detailed instructions. For collaborative online programs, a special form allows easy cross-campus registration when desired.

CONTACT

Darcy W. Hardy, Director
UT TeleCampus
The University of Texas System
201 West Seventh Street, Ashbel Smith Hall
Austin, Texas 78701
Telephone: 512-499-4323
    888-TEXAS-16 (toll-free)
Fax: 512-499-4715
E-mail: telecampus@utsystem.edu
Web site: http://www.telecampus.utsystem.edu

The University of the Incarnate Word

Universe Online

San Antonio, Texas

The University of the Incarnate Word (UIW) was founded in 1881 as an outgrowth of the original mission of the Sisters of Charity of the Incarnate Word who settled in San Antonio, Texas in 1869. The school maintains the mission of the founders by providing quality educational opportunities to all students, developing graduates who are concerned, and enlightening citizens. UIW is accredited by a variety of regional and national associations, but most notably by the regional accrediting body of the Commission on Colleges of the Southern Association of Colleges and Schools. Through its College of Professional Studies, UIW is nationally accredited by the Association of Collegiate Business Schools and Programs.

DISTANCE LEARNING PROGRAM

Universe Online is a natural extension of the mission and the entrepreneurial nature of UIW. By utilizing personal computers and asynchronous instruction, the program addresses the changing needs of adult learners. Maintaining the quality for which it is known, UIW allows students to complete a degree program totally online.

DELIVERY MEDIA

Students accepted in the program use computer-conferencing software that allows for asynchronous interaction in an eight-week term format. Students will interact five out of seven days each week in both private and group discussion. Students, while they are required to have an Internet Service Provider (ISP) to connect and upload/download assignments, will find that most of their work will be done offline.

PROGRAMS OF STUDY

Universe Online offers a variety of undergraduate degree programs and will offer courses in specific graduate programs.

The Bachelor of Business Administration prepares the student for to-day's changing business climate. The required core and choice of specialization prepare students for positions of leadership in the business world. Areas of specialization include accounting, marketing, management, international business, and information systems.

The Bachelor of Arts in psychology of organizations and development is an interdisciplinary major that combines the findings and methods of psychology with business and specialized human resources courses.

The Bachelor of Science in computer sciences is a traditional program, steeped in the mathematics and theory that a true computer scientist needs to function in today's changing field. A student will be well grounded in the fundamentals and pick from a variety of elective courses that allows for specialization in database, networking, and programming or advanced computer science applications.

Students must complete both course work in their major field of study and the University's general studies core as required in all courses. A minimum of 128 credits of course work is required to graduate in all programs. All classes are 3 credits (semester hours).

STUDENT SERVICES

All students at UIW, including Universe Online students, have a wide variety of student service options. Online students have access to academic and financial aid advising, library and bookstore services, and online admission application and registration. In addition, students have access to career planning services.

CREDIT OPTIONS

Universe Online welcomes transfer students. UIW accepts a maximum of 66 transferable hours from accredited two-year schools. These courses will be used to fulfill only lower-level division requirements. UIW will accept a total of 92 semester hours from senior colleges (or a combination of colleges).

Upon acceptance as a degree-seeking student at the University, a student must obtain prior written approval to transfer any additional credits from other institutions.

FACULTY

Given the stringent requirements of national/regional accreditation, faculty members must meet a very exacting set of requirements; this has led to a quality educational program delivered by a highly credentialed and dedicated faculty.

ADMISSION

Undergraduate students must possess a high school diploma or its equivalent. Students having previous college work must have a 2.5 GPA or better. Students must have worked for three years prior to application, in or outside of the home. Students who have not completed English composition I and II and college algebra, must take these courses and may be tested for level.

Nonnative speakers of English must have a minimum score of 560 on the TOEFL. International student transcripts and course descriptions must be translated.

TUITION AND FEES

Undergraduate tuition is $390 per credit and graduate tuition is $420 per credit. There is an application fee of $20 and a one-time transcript fee of $30.

FINANCIAL AID

Financial aid and payment plans are available for all qualified students. Military benefits, as well as employer reimbursement benefits, may be used for online courses.

APPLYING

To apply for admission, students can fill out an application for admission through the Web site listed below. In order to be considered for admission, students must fill out an application, remit a $20 nonrefundable application fee, and submit official high school or postsecondary school transcripts from all institutions attended. Students will be notified of application decisions via e-mail and U.S. mail.

CONTACT

University Online
University of the Incarnate Word
CPO #324
4301 Broadway
San Antonio, Texas 78209
Telephone: 877-827-2702 (toll-free)
Fax: 210-829-2756
E-mail: virtual@universe.uiwtx.edu
Web site: http://www.uiw.edu/online

University of Utah

Academic Outreach and Continuing Education
Distance Education

Salt Lake City, Utah

Founded in 1850, the University of Utah is the premier research and teaching institution in the Intermountain West. Located just east of downtown Salt Lake City, the University is an urban campus serving more than 20,000 undergraduate and 5,000 graduate students. Students can choose from seventy-three majors at the undergraduate level and more than ninety-four major fields of study at the graduate level, as well as more than fifty teaching majors and minors.

Utah offers students a huge array of outdoor activities to complement their academic studies on campus, which is minutes from the Wasatch Mountains and some of the best skiing in the world. The University will host athletes and serve as a venue for the opening and closing ceremonies of the 2002 Winter Olympic Games.

The University of Utah is a member of the Northwest Association of Schools and Colleges.

DISTANCE LEARNING PROGRAM

The University of Utah's extension program, now called Academic Outreach and Continuing Education (AOCE), was established in 1913. The mission of today's AOCE is to extend the University's educational resources beyond its campus boundaries. This requires creative, flexible delivery routes, and U-Online and Independent Study are two of these. U-Online courses communicate via e-mail, chat rooms, and news groups and use the Internet and World Wide Web as resources. The more traditional Independent Study program is currently serving more than 2,800 students and offers courses using textbooks, detailed course manuals, and, in some cases, video tapes, audio cassettes, and computer disks. Both programs offer a high level of communication with faculty members and make undergraduate credit courses available to students throughout the world.

DELIVERY MEDIA

Assignments can be submitted by e-mail, fax, or postal mail for either Independent Study or U-Online courses. Most U-Online courses have auto-submit options with each assignment. To take online courses, students need a computer (system requirements differ for each course and are listed in the course descriptions on the U-Online Web site), an Internet connection, a browser (preferably 4.0 or higher; newer browsers work with plug-ins or media enhancements), and an e-mail address. For Independent Study courses, postal mail is still the most common form of delivery, although a rapidly growing number of students fax or submit lessons via e-mail.

Exams for both U-Online and Independent Study courses must be proctored. This can take place at a university or college testing center; many distance education programs have testing facilities. Students who cannot locate such a facility can take exams under the supervision of an approved proctor, such as a school district superintendent, the head librarian at a city or county library, a high school principal, or the town sheriff.

PROGRAMS OF STUDY

U-Online currently offers courses from sixteen academic departments, with many more courses in development. Independent Study has seventy-three courses from twenty-one departments. Fifteen Educational Studies courses are offered, many of which can be applied toward the continuing education requirements of state education boards all over the United States. U-Online and Independent Study both offer general education courses in behavioral science, fine arts, science, humanities, and American history. These courses meet many of the graduation requirements for the University of Utah's general education program and may meet similar requirements at other institutions.

CREDIT OPTIONS

The University of Utah does not currently offer an external degree. Online courses earn regular college credit. There is no limit on credit hours that can be applied to a baccalaureate degree from U-Online. Independent Study credits may transfer to other schools; however, limits on the number of independent study credit hours that may be applied toward a degree vary from one institution to another. University of Utah students may apply up to 30 semester units toward a bachelor's degree. Before enrolling in any distance education course, students are encouraged to contact their academic adviser to confirm that distance education credit hours will be accepted. Independent Study courses may also be audited (students submit assignments for instructor's comments but take no exams; fees remain the same) or courses may be taken credit/non-credit.

Military personnel should consult with their education officer, and teachers seeking endorsements and lane-change credit should speak with their school district or state board of education recertification specialist regarding independent study credit prior to enrolling in any distance education course.

FACULTY

Both U-Online and Independent Study courses are developed and taught by faculty members approved by the appropriate academic department at the University of Utah.

ADMISSION

There are no admission requirements for U-Online courses unless you are a matriculated (degree-seeking) University of Utah student. However, there are different registration procedures for matriculated and nonmatriculated students. The enrollment period options for each online course are listed in the course description on the University's Web site. All U-Online courses begin and end at the same time as a traditional semester. All Independent Study courses have an open enrollment policy and have nine month terms. There are no admission requirements. Enrollment in a U-Online or Independent Study course does not constitute admission to the University of Utah.

TUITION AND FEES

Students taking semester-long online courses pay regular campus tuition (see the University's Web site, listed below, for current costs). Students taking Independent Study courses (nine-month term) pay $85 per semester unit of credit. This same tuition structure applies to courses taken credit/non-credit or audited. Required and optional textbooks and supplemental materials for U-Online courses are listed in each course description. U-Online textbooks can be purchased through neighborhood bookstores or through an online bookstore, including the University of Utah Bookstore. Independent Study course manuals cost approximately $15. All textbooks and any supplemental course materials, such as video tapes, audio cassettes, and computer disks for Independent Study courses, are purchased through Specialty Books and their costs vary. All fees are subject to change without notice, and payment for all fees and materials is due at the time of enrollment.

FINANCIAL AID

Students should contact the financial aid office for details on distance education financial aid issues. Some companies pay all or part of tuition, fees, and books for employees. Students should consult their employers to see if funding for continuing education is available.

APPLYING

A complete list of available U-Online and Independent Study courses is located on the University's Web sites (see below). To request a catalog of Independent Study courses, students should contact the University via any of the methods listed below. Once students have selected a course, they can enroll by mail, e-mail, fax, or phone.

CONTACT

Academic Outreach and Continuing Education
Distance Education
University of Utah
1901 East South Campus Drive, Room 1215
Salt Lake City, Utah 84112-9364
Telephone: 801-581-8801
800-INSTUDY (toll-free)
Fax: 801-581-6267
For Independent Study:
E-mail: Instudy@aoce.utah.edu
Web site: http://www.instudy.utah.edu
For U-Online:
E-mail: Ulearn@aoce.utah.edu
Web site: http://www.ulearn.utah.edu

University of Washington

Distance Learning Program

Seattle, Washington

Founded in 1861, the University of Washington (UW) is one of the nation's leading research institutions, with sixteen schools and colleges situated on the main campus in Seattle. Approximately 26,000 undergraduates and more than 9,000 graduate and professional students are enrolled at the University of Washington.

DISTANCE LEARNING PROGRAM

UW Distance Learning began offering fully accredited courses by correspondence in 1915 and today offers more than 120 credit courses as well as nineteen credit and noncredit certificate programs. Campus departments approve all courses and faculty members. Courses are both self-paced (students can enroll at any time, and courses are designed to be completed in three to six months) and group start (students begin as a group and meet specific deadlines). UW Distance Learning serves about 3,500 students annually. UW Distance Learning is a UW Educational Outreach program.

DELIVERY MEDIA

While delivery for most courses centers on a printed or online course guide, additional technologies such as use of e-mail, the World Wide Web, videotapes, audiotapes, telephone conferencing, online discussion groups, and television enhance the learning in many courses. All UW Distance Learning faculty members may be reached by electronic mail and voice mail, as well as by correspondence.

PROGRAMS OF STUDY

UW Distance Learning currently offers more than 130 different courses in areas of computers and engineering, education, health sciences, humanities, natural science, and social sciences. Courses include technical communication, rehabilitation medicine, gerontology, environmental science, philosophy, C programming, English, psychology, and American Indian studies.

SPECIAL PROGRAMS

UW Distance Learning currently offers courses leading to both credit and noncredit certificates. Credit certificate programs include school library media, gerontology, construction management, facilities management, and teaching, learning, and technology. Noncredit certificate programs include C programming, C++ programming, Java 2 programming, project management, fiction writing, nonfiction writing, data communications, data resource management, distance learning design, basic Internet programming, and small business Webmaster.

UW offers six master's degrees in engineering as part of the Education at a Distance for Growth and Excellence (EDGE) program: aeronautics and astronautics, aerospace engineering, electrical engineering, manufacturing engineering, materials science and engineering, and mechanical engineering. For more information, students should visit the Web site (http://www.engr.washington.edu/edge).

Also available through distance learning is the External Doctor of Pharmacy (Pharm.D.) degree, which was jointly developed by the University of Washington and Washington State University for pharmacists in the Pacific Northwest. Regional pharmacists may continue their employment during the program. Weekend workshops in locations in both western and eastern Washington are required to complete the program, as well as at least three 160-hour clerkships (twelve weeks of full-time advance professional training) at University-supervised clerkship sites. For more information, students should visit the Web site (http://www.depts.washington.edu/expharmd).

STUDENT SERVICES

UW Distance Learning registrants receive student numbers and have library check-out privileges at UW libraries. Students living outside the Seattle area may request specific library materials by mail. The Language Learning Center is open to students studying foreign languages, and the Media Center is open to students in courses that require viewing videotapes. To communicate with an adviser about distance learning opportunities at UW, students should send e-mail to advisers@ese.washington.edu.

CREDIT OPTIONS

Offerings consist primarily of credit courses scheduled regularly by the UW and approved by the faculty curriculum committee. They parallel undergraduate courses taken on campus and are comparable in content and rigor. Credit is awarded on a quarterly basis, and each credit is equivalent to two thirds of a semester credit.

FACULTY

Most UW Distance Learning courses are designed by the faculty members who teach the same course on the University of Washington campus. Gerald Baldasty, instructor for History and Development of Communication and Journalism, comments, "When I first started a distance learning class, I thought I'd miss the in-person contact with students. I've found that the assignments and notes I get from my students seem to bridge that gap. Distance Learning students ask questions that go well beyond the assignments; I find that interchange to be interesting and enjoyable."

The instructors are familiar with the questions and needs of students and, with the help of instructional designers, have developed the appropriate methods to help students achieve the course objectives in the distance learning format. Students can interact with instructors through voice mail and e-mail, receiving prompt, personal instruction and answers to questions. Approximately 80 percent of the faculty members have a Ph.D., and 20 percent have earned a master's degree or higher.

ADMISSION

For most courses, students may enroll without having matriculated into a university degree program. A registration form is included in the UW Extension catalog. For most certificate programs, students must submit application materials. Application instructions can be found in the catalog, in brochures, or on the Web site. To request a catalog or brochure, students should call 206-543-2320 or 800-543-2320 (toll-free) or use the e-mail address at requests@u.washington. edu. Students may also view the catalog on the World Wide Web at (http://www.extension.washington.edu).

Prospective students may wish to contact an adviser prior to registering. If the student has questions, he or she should call UW Distance Learning Advising at 206-543-6160 or Arts and Sciences Central Advising at 206-543-2551. Enrollment in UW Distance Learning classes does not constitute admission to the University of Washington.

TUITION AND FEES

All students must pay a nonrefundable quarterly $20 registration fee at the time of registration. Course fees are $109 per undergraduate quarter credit and $252 per graduate quarter credit. Fees for noncredit and certificate courses vary and are listed in the UW Extension catalog, both the printed and online versions. Supplementary materials also vary.

FINANCIAL AID

In general, financial aid is not available for UW Distance Learning courses. Enrollment in distance learning courses does not meet federal requirements for loan deferment. Students should explore exceptions with their financial aid office.

APPLYING

Students may register by telephone if VISA or MasterCard is used for fee payment. In the Seattle area, students should call 206-543-2350; outside Seattle, 800-543-2320 (toll-free). To enroll by mail or fax, the student should fill out the registration form found in the UW Extension catalog. To request a catalog, students should call 206-543-2320 or 800-543-2320 (toll-free). Registration is also possible on the World Wide Web at the site listed below.

CONTACT

UW Distance Learning
University of Washington Educational Outreach
5001 25th Avenue, NE
Seattle, Washington 98105-4190
Telephone: 206-543-2320
        800-543-2320 (toll-free)
        206-543-6452 (TTY)
Fax: 206-685-9359
E-mail: extinfo@u.washington.edu
Web site: http://www.extension.washington.edu

University of Wisconsin-Stout

Department of Hospitality and Tourism

Menomonie, Wisconsin

UW–Stout is a special-mission institution that is characterized by a distinctive array of programs leading to professional careers focused on the needs of society. It was founded in 1891 as a private institution but is now one of thirteen publicly supported universities in the University of Wisconsin System. It is accredited by the North Central Association of Colleges and Schools.

UW–Stout, a respected innovator in higher education, educates students to be lifelong learners and responsible citizens in a diverse and changing world through experiences inside and outside the classroom that join the general and the specialized, the theoretical and the practical, in applied programs leading to successful careers in industry, commerce, education, and human services.

UW–Stout has a reputation for putting graduates on a rewarding career path. This can be seen through its outstanding employment rate.

DISTANCE LEARNING PROGRAM

The goal of the totally online Master of Science degree is to deliver premier education to the global hospitality adult learner. It consists of twelve 3-credit courses. The degree is designed in an active learning format that applies theory from the courses to actual situations in the workplace.

DELIVERY MEDIA

Lotus LearningSpace (Lspace) is the robust delivery platform that is designed for frequent interaction among students and faculty members. The platform assists the students in progressing through the course in a sequential manner. Lspace supports a rich learning environment whereby the student is connected to a wide array of learning resources. Students need a Pentium-level computer with a CD-ROM drive and 32M of RAM. Access to the Internet is also needed.

PROGRAM OF STUDY

Students join a global network of learners. Classmates represent hospitality professionals around the world. They become part of an action learning environment that is not limited by time or space. They see the many benefits—a fully accredited program, virtual classroom flexibility, global experience, collaborative learning, and enhanced career advancement. The program remains accessible as students' jobs move and is designed for adult learners.

Students progress through the program as a cohort group. Courses run in six-week modules. Most students complete the program over a two- or three-year period. The program has a strong business management core, with application within the hospitality industry. Core courses include Issues in Hospitality and Tourism, Strategic Management in Hospitality, Managing Finance, Managing Technology in Hospitality, Leadership and Management in Hospitality, Quality Assurance and Customer Service, Research Applications, and Hospitality Operational Systems. Students also complete an applied research project near the end of their studies.

The Global Hospitality Management online concentration is the result of collaborative efforts of institutions across the globe. Oxford-Brookes, U.K.; Nottingham Trent University, U.K.; University of Paderborn, Germany; and UW–Whitewater and UW–Stout were the founding partners. Southern Cross University in Lismore, Australia, has recently joined the partnership. The collaboration ensures a global perspective for both curriculum development and delivery. UW–Stout is the degree-granting institution, and the partners are involved in team teaching and joint marketing and research. Students can view the partner information to find out more about each of the partners and their individual degree programs, campuses, and services.

STUDENT SERVICES

Students can consult the Web for specific services information at http://www.uwstout.edu/programs/msht/ghm/student_services.html.

CREDIT OPTIONS

The M.S. is a 36-credit degree program. Nine of the 36 credits can be selected from the participating global partner institutions.

FACULTY

Team teaching is utilized to provide a global perspective. Currently, 18 faculty members are involved in the online offerings from the partner institutions. Most of the faculty members hold doctoral degrees and have industry experience.

ADMISSION

Students must possess a bachelor's degree from an accredited university; have a minimum of three years of full-time, hospitality-related work experience (three years of experience at the supervisory or management level is preferred); demonstrate proficiency (or the willingness to acquire proficiency) in accounting and finance; complete a Global Concentration Application; and submit three recommendations and a resume. International students must submit a minimum Test of English as a Foreign Language (TOEFL) score of 550.

As part of the admission process, there is a mandatory in-person meeting that is held before online courses begin. This session is held in August and January and at other times, with the meeting sites determined by the geographic location of the new concentration students. This important session is designed to develop a sense of community and build collaborative online skills while introducing students to online software and course design.

TUITION AND FEES

Resident and nonresident students are charged $425 per graduate credit (subject to change). Each course is 3 credits. Students are also required to pay for their instructional materials.

FINANCIAL AID

The financial aid Web site explains what types of financial aid are available and outlines the qualifications for financial aid. Currently, financial aid for online students is limited to student loans.

APPLYING

Students must submit a complete application form, three recommendations, a resume, two copies of official transcripts from previous studies, and a $45 application fee to the Graduate College, P.O. Box 790, University of Wisconsin–Stout, Menomonie, Wisconsin 54751.

CONTACT

Dr. Christine Clements, Department Chair
429 Home Economics Building
University of Wisconsin–Stout
Menomonie, Wisconsin 54751-0790
Telephone: 715-232-2567
Fax: 715-232-2588
E-mail: clementsc@uwstout.edu
Web site: http://www.uwstout.edu/programs/
    msht/ghm/index.html

The University of Wyoming

The Outreach School

Laramie, Wyoming

The University of Wyoming (UW), a land-grant university founded in 1886, is accredited by the North Central Association of Colleges and Schools. The University of Wyoming was the first university west of the Missouri River to offer correspondence courses. In its outreach mission, the University of Wyoming is guided by the following vision: the state of Wyoming is the campus of the University of Wyoming. The University has one faculty and staff, one student body, and one set of academic programs. Teaching, research, and service are the mission of the University regardless of location. The University recognizes that its "one student body" is composed of a wide variety of students whose needs differ.

DISTANCE LEARNING PROGRAM

The Outreach School delivers the University's distance learning programs. The mission of the Outreach School is to extend the University of Wyoming's educational programs and services to the state of Wyoming and beyond. The School delivers more than 300 courses and fifteen complete degree programs to approximately 3,000 students per semester, or 6,000 each year.

DELIVERY MEDIA

In addition to delivering programs via Flexible Enrollment (correspondence study), audio-teleconference, and compressed video, the School launched the Online UW campus in 1998–99 in cooperation with eCollege.com. Currently, the bachelor's degree in business administration, the RN/B.S.N. completion degree in nursing, the master's degree for nurse educators, a real estate certification, and an M.A. in instructional technology are available completely through Online UW via http://online.uwyo.edu. All Flexible Enrollment courses, a limited number of audio-teleconference courses, and all Online UW courses are available to students outside the state of

Wyoming. More than 1,000 students completed the Online UW courses in 1999–2000.

PROGRAMS OF STUDY

Degrees and certificates are available to students outside Wyoming. Certificate programs include land surveying (offered nationwide through video and audio-teleconference) and real estate appraisal (available online). Graduate programs include an M.S. in speech-language pathology (available nationwide through audio-teleconference) and an M.A. in education with specialization in instructional technology (available online). Other distance degrees available are B.A. degrees in business administration, administration of justice, psychology, and social science; an RN/B.S.N. completion program (available online); an M.S. in nursing (online); an M.B.A. (available statewide via compressed video); and an M.P.A. (available through audio and compressed video).

SPECIAL PROGRAMS

The University of Wyoming's virtual university, Online UW, currently offers more than fifty courses and four degrees completely online. Courses are available worldwide via http://

online.uwyo.edu. Online courses are available in the areas of adult learning, astronomy, biochemistry, business administration, child development, directing preschool and day-care programs, economics, educational administration, family and consumer sciences, human resources management, instructional technology, nutrition, physics, psychology, real estate, religion, statistics, and Western integrated resource education.

STUDENT SERVICES

All student services (such as admission, enrollment, tuition payment, grade reporting, financial aid, and bookstore and library services) are available through the Outreach School.

CREDIT OPTIONS

Students may transfer courses from accredited institutions of higher education. Credit is also available through AP, CLEP, portfolio assessment, and departmental examinations. Degrees require a minimum of 48 hours of upper-division credit, with a minimum of 30 credits from the University of Wyoming. Most degree programs require 120–124 credits for graduation.

FACULTY

The majority of those who teach in the Outreach School are full-time faculty members at the University of Wyoming. A limited number of adjunct faculty members, who are approved by the academic departments, offer distance learning courses. The programs offered via distance learning are the same programs offered on the main University campus in Laramie, Wyoming. In any given semester, approximately 75 regular full-time faculty members and 15 part-time adjunct faculty members teach distance learning courses for the Outreach School.

ADMISSION

Students not seeking a University of Wyoming degree may enroll in distance learning courses without being admitted to the University. Degree-seeking students should apply to the Office of Admissions. Undergraduate admission generally requires completion of at least 13 high school units in a precollege curriculum, a cumulative high school grade point average of at least 2.75, an ACT score of at least 20, or an SAT score of at least 960. Conditional admission is available for adult learners who do not meet these criteria. Graduate programs require a GRE combined verbal and quantitative score of at least 900.

TUITION AND FEES

Generally, undergraduate resident tuition is $93.75 per credit hour, and nonresident tuition is $267.50 per credit hour. Graduate tuition is $154.90 per credit hour for residents, and nonresident tuition is $274.50 per credit hour. Nonresident fees are lower for the nursing, speech pathology, and land surveying programs ($129.50 per credit hour). Online UW courses are offered for in-state tuition rates and have an additional $40-per-credit-hour technology delivery fee.

FINANCIAL AID

All forms of federal financial aid and other scholarship aid are available to Outreach students. The Outreach School also has a number of $1000 scholarships available to Outreach students. Information describing available aid and award criteria is available from the Office of Student Financial Aid, P.O. Box 3335, University of Wyoming, Laramie, Wyoming 82071.

APPLYING

Non-degree-seeking students may apply through the Office of Outreach Credit Programs. Degree-seeking students should apply through the Office of Undergraduate Admissions (telephone: 307-766-2287) or Graduate Admissions (telephone: 307-766-2118).

CONTACT

Judith A. Powell, Associate Vice President and Dean of the Outreach School
Judith Atencio, Office of Outreach Credit Courses
The Outreach School
University of Wyoming
Box 3106
Laramie, Wyoming 82071
Telephone: 307-766-3152
　　　　　800-448-7801 Ext. 15 (toll-free)
Fax: 307-766-3445
E-mail: jatencio@uwyo.edu
Web site: http://online.uwyo.edu

University System of Georgia Independent Study

University of Georgia Center for Continuing Education

Athens, Georgia

> *University System of Georgia Independent Study (USGIS) is an academic department of the University of Georgia Center for Continuing Education. The mission of University System of Georgia Independent Study is to offer University System academic credit courses to University System students and individuals who are interested in earning academic credit through distance learning methods and technologies.*

DISTANCE LEARNING PROGRAM

University System of Georgia Independent Study offers undergraduate academic credit courses through senior institutions of the University System of Georgia, including Armstrong Atlantic State University, Georgia College and State University, Georgia Southern University, North Georgia College and State University, the University of Georgia, and Valdosta State University. USGIS allows flexibility of registration, permitting students to register at any time and to take several courses simultaneously, with up to one year to complete each course (students may purchase a three-month extension). Academic credit is recorded on the student's permanent record in the University of Georgia Registrar's Office and may be used for degree requirements according to the regulations of the institution from which the student plans to graduate. Approximately 5,000 students enroll in 6,000 USGIS courses annually. USGIS recommends that students enrolled in degree programs consult with their academic adviser prior to enrollment in a USGIS course. USGIS is developing an electronic campus for the learning and teaching community it serves. The electronic campus includes links to a vast array of resources that are useful to the distance education student and faculty member.

When students enroll in an Independent Study course, they receive a course guide and packet with materials necessary for course completion. Students must purchase required textbooks and materials. Each course consists of readings, written lesson assignments, and a final examination (some courses have midterm examinations). Students complete the lessons and submit assignments at their own pace. Midterm and final examinations must be taken under the supervision of an approved test site (such as an accredited college or university). Students must pass the final examination to pass the course. Technology enrollment options (described below) are available for selected courses.

DELIVERY MEDIA

All USGIS courses are available in the traditional print version of the course guide, allowing submission of lessons via the U.S. Postal Service. Technology enrollment options are described below. Students may choose these technology enrollment options for selected courses on the registration form.

Web courses are taken completely on line, with the exception of the course midterm and/or final examinations (all USGIS examinations must be taken at an approved test site). Web courses offer a variety of online features, such as course guides, lesson submission, World Wide Web resources, and e-mail links to Independent Study. Selected courses may offer self-assessments with immediate feedback, bulletin boards, chat areas, and interaction with faculty members and other students. Many of the Web courses use the free Adobe Acrobat Reader software (available from http://www.adobe.com) for viewing the online course guide. This software includes printing and keyword search capabilities as well as a hyperlinked table of contents and text magnification tools. In most cases, the textbook for the course is not in electronic format and must be purchased by the student.

An e-mail lesson submission course has the same requirements and follows the same process as the traditional print-based version, with one exception: lessons are delivered to Independent Study via e-mail rather than through the U.S. Postal Service. Students receive a print-based course guide or Electronic Course Guide (E-Guide) on diskette containing the same information. All e-mail lessons are submitted to Independent Study for forwarding to the instructor for grading. Once graded, lessons are returned via e-mail to students.

Many University System of Georgia Independent Study courses are available as E-Guides. This version offers the course guide and written assignments for the course in electronic format on diskette. E-Guides are created using Adobe Portable Document Format (PDF) technology. PDF files are universally readable by both IBM and Macintosh computers through the use of the Adobe Acrobat Reader, which is available free through Independent Study.

Lesson submission via fax is available for all courses, except those lessons requiring audiotape or project submissions. There is no charge for submission of ungraded lessons by fax. There is a fee to have graded lessons returned to the student via fax.

PROGRAMS OF STUDY

Approximately 120 courses are offered in the areas of agricultural and environmental sciences, arts and sciences, business, education, family and consumer sciences, forestry, and journalism and mass communication.

TUITION AND FEES

USGIS nonresident credit tuition is $104 per semester hour ($312 for a 3-semester-hour course). Tuition is payable in full by check, money orders drawn on United States banks or international banks with affiliate branches in the U.S., international money order, or credit card (MasterCard, Visa, and Discover). USGIS accepts authorization invoices to bill from an outside agency. Special fees such as drop/add, extension, special airmail/handling, and return of graded lessons via fax are described in the catalog. USGIS

does not provide financial aid or scholarship services.

APPLYING

Students must submit a completed registration form, which may be obtained from an Independent Study Bulletin, with appropriate fees. Students have the option of enrolling on line from the USGIS Web site with credit card payment. Registration for a USGIS course does not require admission tests, transcripts of previous high school or college work, or enrollment in a college or university. High school and home school students enrolled in a college early admission or joint-enrollment program may enroll in USGIS courses. Enrollment is effective for one year and may be extended for an additional three months if the extension fee is received prior to the course expiration date. Students should contact USGIS for more information.

CONTACT

Melissa Pettigrew or a Student Representative
University System of Georgia Independent Study
University of Georgia Center for Continuing Education
Athens, Georgia 30602-3603
Telephone: 706-542-3243
          800-877-3243 (toll-free)
Fax: 706-542-6635
E-mail: usgis@arches.uga.edu
Web site: http://www.gactr.uga.edu/usgis/

Upper Iowa University

Extended University

Fayette, Iowa

> *Upper Iowa University (UIU) was established in 1857 and has since become the second-largest private university in the state of Iowa. Unlike some of the newer schools offering distance learning programs, UIU has a beautiful residential campus on 90 acres with seven academic buildings and three residence halls. Upper Iowa also has seventeen sports teams, known as the Peacocks, who compete in the NCAA Division III. As a nonprofit, rapidly growing, four-year liberal arts institution of higher learning, UIU offers a wide range of high-quality degree programs to more than 4,500 students worldwide. Its vision is to become a distinctively entrepreneurial university that meets the educational needs of learners worldwide. Upper Iowa University is accredited by the Commission on Institutions of Higher Education of the North Central Association of Colleges and Schools.*

DISTANCE LEARNING PROGRAM

The Extended University's distance learning programs are offered through two primary modes of delivery. Its external degree program offers Associate of Arts and Bachelor of Science degree programs through independent study/correspondence and its online program currently offers a Master of Arts in Business Leadership and undergraduate business management core courses. Courses offered through both external degree and online formats meet the same standards as courses offered through the residential University in Fayette, Iowa. The external degree program, which began in 1972, has been successfully delivered to more than 10,000 learners. The University has an 80 percent course completion rate within the external degree program. Upper Iowa's external degree program was one of the first and most successful in the United States and continues to be a vital component in serving both civilian and military learners worldwide.

DELIVERY MEDIA

Students communicate with instructors via e-mail, fax, and regular mail. Classes are self-paced with no minimum completion time. Upper Iowa's online program is noted for its e-mail–like feel. Students log on (via the Internet) just long enough to send and receive materials, anytime, anywhere, day or night. Most work is accomplished off-line, or through asynchronous communication.

PROGRAMS OF STUDY

Upper Iowa University has a long history of offering high-quality degree programs through distance learning. Associate and bachelor's degree programs are available in a wide range of academic areas including accounting, business, human resources management, human services, management, marketing, psychology, public administration (general, law enforcement, or fire science), social science, and technology and information management. Upper Iowa's online program offers a Master of Arts in Business Leadership with areas of emphasis in accounting, human resources management, quality management, and organizational development. The course work focuses on the theories and skills that will be the foundation for tomorrow's organizations, including organizational de-sign, total quality management, self-managed teams, employee empowerment, change management, facilitation skills, high-performance work systems, and more.

SPECIAL PROGRAMS

Each summer the external degree program sponsors the Institute for Experiential Learning (IEXL) for undergraduate students. During an intensive week-long session held on the Fayette campus, students have the opportunity to earn 3 semester hours of undergraduate credit while visiting the residential campus and networking with other learners from around the world.

STUDENT SERVICES

External degree and online students are provided with one-on-one academic advising via U.S. mail, e-mail, telephone, fax communication, and through use of a special software/courseware package (for online program students). In addition to local university libraries, undergraduate and graduate students and faculty members have access to the Henderson Wilder Library holdings through Upper Iowa University's Web site (listed below).

CREDIT OPTIONS

Full credit is given for college-level courses completed at regionally accredited colleges and universities. Students can transfer a maximum of 45 semester hours for an associate degree, 90 semester hours for a bachelor's degree, and 12 semester hours for a master's degree. Other sources of credit include the American Council on Education (ACE), the College-Level Examination Program (CLEP), Defense Activity for Nontraditional Education support (DANTES) subject exams, and experiential learning.

FACULTY

Upper Iowa University has more than 100 faculty members, all of whom have doctorates or terminal degrees. Nearly 70 percent are adjunct faculty members who are involved in distance learning programs.

ADMISSION

The minimum undergraduate requirement is graduation from an accredited public or private high school or completion of a GED equivalent. An undergraduate degree from a regionally accredited college or university is the minimum requirement for prospective graduate students.

TUITION AND FEES

Associate- and baccalaureate-level tuition for courses taken through external degree (independent study/correspondence) or at off-campus learning centers (classroom) is $465 per 3 semester hours. Undergraduate and graduate online (Internet-based) courses are $600 and $800 respectively per 3 semester hours.

FINANCIAL AID

Financial aid in the form of Federal Stafford Loan or PELL Grants, Iowa Tuition Grants (Iowa residents only), Veterans Assistance, and Military Tuition Assistance is available. Last year, a total of $273,420 in financial aid was disbursed to 21 percent of Upper Iowa University's distance learning students.

APPLYING

Students may enroll in UIU's external degree program at any time. Students should send official transcripts (including CLEP, DANTES, or DD-214), GRE/GMAT score reports (if required), and a completed Application for Admission form (available online or by contacting the school via telephone or e-mail) directly to Upper Iowa University at the address below.

CONTACT

Extended University
Upper Iowa University
605 Washington Street, P.O. Box 1857
Fayette, Iowa 52142-1857
Telephone: 877-366-0581
Fax: 319-425-5771
E-mail: moreinfo@uiu.edu
Web site: http://www.uiu.edu

Utah State University

Independent and Distance Education

Logan, Utah

The academic advantages of a large university together with the friendliness of a small college are offered at Utah State University (USU). With a student body of more than 20,000, USU recognizes that the needs of individuals are of major importance, and many programs have been established to give students optimum individual attention.

USU, founded in 1888, is a member of the National Association of State Universities and Land-Grant Colleges. USU integrates teaching, research, extension, and service to meet its unique role as Utah's land-grant university. Students are the focus of the University as they seek intellectual, personal, and cultural development.

The mission of USU is to provide high-quality undergraduate and graduate instruction, excellent general education, and specialized academic and professional degree programs. USU is committed to preparing students to serve the people of Utah, the nation, and the world.

DISTANCE LEARNING PROGRAM

Outreach to Utah's citizens through extension and service programs is central to the University's mission. The University's outreach programs provide services to individuals, communities, institutions, and industries throughout the state that help improve technology, the environment, and quality of life. USU currently serves 11,000 students through distance education programs.

DELIVERY MEDIA

USU distance education employs several medias for delivery of courses and degrees. Courses offered over the digital satellite system are taught at specific times, originate at USU, and are broadcast over the satellite system to USU Education Centers in Utah. (These classes are only available in Utah.)

Print-based independent study courses are yearlong correspondence courses. Students receive a course outline at registration, hand assignments in by mail, and take proctored examinations.

Online independent study courses are yearlong courses offered over the Internet. Students are authorized to access classes online at registration, hand assignments in by e-mail, and take proctored, print-based exams or online exams.

PROGRAMS OF STUDY

The Master of Science in English (Technical Writing Online) degree is designed for students who already have some training and/or experience as practitioners of technical writing. The program's mission is to prepare students to enter or reenter nonacademic workplaces not just as practitioners but as developers and managers of technical documents. When they finish the program, students are qualified to determine and defend writing policy and practices in their workplaces. Students may take several semesters to complete the program, but courses are offered at least once during a two-year cycle so that students can complete the program in four or five semesters. Students should see the Web site for complete details (http://english.usu. edu/dept/instruction/online/

TechWriting/) or contact Keith Grant-Davie (telephone: 435-797-3547).

Students can complete general education requirements online as well as the entry-level classes for business, family and human development, and sociology majors. Graduate-level classes in theory and practice of writing are also available. Students should see the Special Programs section below for information on additional classes available.

SPECIAL PROGRAMS

Utah State University (USU) now offers a complete suite of online independent study linguistics courses. These courses are fully accredited and offer USU undergraduate credit that can be transferred to another institution or used in fulfillment of a USU undergraduate degree.

For a list of all classes available online, students should visit the Web site (http://online.usu.edu).

Print-based independent study classes are also available for out-of-state students. A list of these classes can be found online (http://www.ext.usu. edu/distance/is/index.htm).

Several master's, bachelor's, and certificate programs are offered over the digital satellite system. These programs are only available in Utah. Classes are taught at a specific time from the Logan campus and broadcast over the satellite system to USU Education Centers around the state. A listing of degrees can be found online (http://www.ext.usu.edu/ distance/distance/index.htm).

STUDENT SERVICES

There are several student services available to Independent and Distance Education students, including USU Libraries Online, writing and research resources, the bookstore, the online book exchange, and other miscellaneous student services. For more information, students should visit the Web site (http://online.usu.edu/student_resources/index.html).

CREDIT OPTIONS

Credit earned through USU distance education is measured in semester units and is transferable to most other colleges and universities in the U.S. Students who plan to transfer credit earned through USU distance education are advised to make arrangements with the transfer institution prior to registration. Students may take as many courses through distance education as desired and may apply all approved credits toward the requirements for a bachelor's degree.

FACULTY

Ninety percent of distance education faculty members are full time em-ployees of Utah State University; the remaining 10 percent are adjunct professors or graduate students.

ADMISSION

Admission to Utah State University is not required for enrollment in distance education courses. However, those who are working toward a degree at USU must apply for admission. Students should contact the admissions office for more information (telephone: 435-797-1079; Web site: http://www.usu.edu/~registra/admrec/main.html#ADMISSIONS).

TUITION AND FEES

Tuition for online independent study is $90 per credit for undergraduate courses and $176 for graduate courses, plus any extra fees for individual courses. Tuition payments can be made on USU's secured registration site, by mail, or by credit card over the phone.

FINANCIAL AID

Financial aid is available for distance education students. However, if fi-nancial aid is used, the class must be completed in one semester, not the normal one year. Some aid is only available for full-time students. Utah State University participates in the following financial aid programs: Federal Pell Grants, Federal Supplemental Educational Opportunity Grants (FSEOG), LEAP Grants, Federal Perkins Loans, Federal Work-Study, Federal Stafford Loans, Plus Loans, scholarships, and emergency loans. For more information, students should contact the financial aid office (telephone: 435-797-0173; Web site: http://www.usu.edu/~finaid/).

APPLYING

Applicants must have a high school diploma or its equivalent to register for classes. High school students may enroll in independent study online courses with written permission from their principal or counselor. To register, students can complete the online registration form at http://online.usu.edu/register or call the toll-free number listed below.

CONTACT

Independent and Distance Education
3080 Old Main Hill
Utah State University
Logan, Utah 84322-3080
Telephone: 800-233-2137 (toll-free)
Fax: 435-797-1399
E-mail: de-info@ext.usu.edu
Web site: http://online.usu.edu
http://www.ext.usu.edu/distance

Utica College of Syracuse University

Graduate Studies and Continuing Education

Utica, New York

> Utica College of Syracuse University is a comprehensive college that offers the wide range of academic programs, excellent faculty members, and diversity of a large university while providing students with the low faculty-to-student ratio and individual attention of a small college. A combination of liberal arts and professional studies gives students opportunities to gain broad-based exposure to major areas of knowledge while developing career-specific skills designed to ensure success in the workforce.
>
> Utica College was established by Syracuse University in 1946. Graduates of Utica College's undergraduate programs receive the Syracuse University baccalaureate degree, while graduates of its master's degree programs receive a Utica College degree. Utica College is accredited by the Commission of Higher Education of the Middle States Association of Colleges and Schools.

DISTANCE LEARNING PROGRAM

Utica College offers two programs on line: the Economic Crime Management (ECM) master's degree program and the undergraduate Studies in Gerontology certificate program. The 36-credit-hour ECM program requires three 1-week residencies. The 15-credit-hour gerontology program does not require a campus residency.

DELIVERY MEDIA

ECM students must have access to a Pentium computer, modem (minimum 28.800 baud), e-mail, and the Internet. Gerontology students must have access to an IBM-compatible 486/66 (Pentium preferred), Windows 3.1 or higher (95 or NT preferred), 8 MB RAM (16 or 32 preferred), minimum 28k modem, Netscape Navigator 3.0 or higher, e-mail, and Internet. Macintosh users have the same requirements as above with Mac OS 7.1 or higher.

PROGRAMS OF STUDY

The 36-credit-hour economic crime management master's degree pro-

gram combines the areas of management, technology, analytical skills, and a knowledge and understanding of economic crime from a global perspective. The program is designed for members of private corporations, government agencies, and professional associations who desire to advance their competencies in managing corporate and advanced technological resources devoted to combating economic crime. The master's program can be completed in two years. Students spend 3 one-week sessions per year in residency. Each residency provides opportunities for students to achieve hands-on technology-related skill learning through labs and demonstrations.

The Studies in Gerontology certificate program is designed for those interested in acquiring basic knowledge about gerontology and geriatrics. This five-course, 15-credit-hour online program was developed in response to the Bureau of Labor Statistics predictions that the geriatrics and gerontological fields are expected to grow by more than 35 percent through 2006, ranking these fields among the most rapidly growing employment areas.

SPECIAL PROGRAMS

The ECM master's degree program is the only graduate-level program of its kind in the United States. The program was developed with the support of Utica College's prestigious Economic Crime Investigation Institute (ECII) board of directors. Support and participation by major corporate sponsors allows this new master's degree program to provide the specialized technological, managerial, analytical, and economic crime skills needed to prevail against sophisticated information-age fraud.

The Studies in Gerontology program is also a unique program. Those seeking to increase awareness in issues related to aging, knowledge of the aging process, or skills that facilitate working with the older adult should enroll in the gerontology online program. This program would be valuable for health professionals, therapists, social workers, counselors, dietitians, administrators, and direct health and social service staff members.

STUDENT SERVICES

Courses are offered through JonesKnowledge.com and accessed through e-education.com. Each student is assigned a user name and password. A link connects them to the virtual bookstore and faculty information. Technical support is available 24 hours a day, 7 days a week, via toll-free telephone or e-mail.

CREDIT OPTIONS

A credit-by-examination system allows students to demonstrate competence obtained through professional experience. Each academic department determines the specific courses that may be eligible for credit.

FACULTY

Biographies on all ECM and Studies in Gerontology faculty members are available on Utica College's Web site listed below. All faculty members are experts in their field.

ADMISSION

ECM admission requirements include a completed application, undergraduate transcripts, GRE or GMAT scores, two letters of recommendation, work experience, letter of employer support, and a $50 application fee. Gerontology studies students are admitted into the program upon registration.

TUITION AND FEES

ECM tuition is $612 per credit hour plus a $75 technology fee per semester. The gerontology program tuition is $368 per credit hour plus a $60 per course distance-learning fee. Tuition discounts are offered to groups of three or more.

FINANCIAL AID

Utica College offers an individual deferred payment plan and an employer deferred tuition payment plan. Yearly graduate loan limits are $8500 for subsidized student loans and $10,000 for unsubsidized loans. As a Direct Lending Institution, all loans must be processed through Utica College. Students should call Utica College at 315-792-3178 for more information.

APPLYING

Students interested in the ECM program should follow admission requirements. Students interested in the gerontology program need no application. Students may enroll in the program by telephone, fax, or mail.

CONTACT

For information on the gerontology program:
Ms. Evelyn Fazekas
Director of Credit Programs
Division of Graduate and Continuing Education
Utica College of Syracuse University
1600 Burrstone Road
Utica, New York 13502
Telephone: 315-792-3001
Fax: 315-792-3002
E-mail: contedu@utica.ucsu.edu
For information on the ECM program:
Economic Crime Management
Ms. Kate M. Cominsky
Associate Director of Graduate Admissions
Utica College of Syracuse University
1600 Burrstone Road
Utica, New York 13502
Telephone 315-792-3244
Fax 315-792-3002
E-mail: gradstudies@utica.ucsu.edu
Web site: http://www.utica.edu

Virginia Tech

Virginia Polytechnic Institute and State University

Institute for Distance and Distributed Learning

Blacksburg, Virginia

For more than a century, Virginia Tech has been a leader in providing high-quality undergraduate, graduate, and continuing education and an innovator in instructional methods and delivery modes. Founded in 1872 as the state's land-grant university, Virginia Tech is dedicated to instruction, research, and outreach. The University offers more than 200 degree programs and, with an enrollment of approximately 25,000 students, is the largest university in Virginia. A comprehensive land-grant university with seven undergraduate colleges, a graduate school, and a veterinary college, Virginia Tech is also one of the nation's leading research institutions. Virginia Tech is committed to the creation of new knowledge and the transfer and dissemination of that knowledge to serve Virginia, the nation, and the international community. The University has a long and successful history of providing distance learning programming and opportunities. In recent years, the University has gained national recognition for its creative initiatives in faculty development, instructional technology, and networking. The University continues to break the barriers of time and space by providing quality learning opportunities anywhere and anytime. Using advanced technologies, Virginia Tech is creating more responsive teaching and learning environments while meeting the changing needs, resources, and expectations of its students. Through Virginia Tech's open and extended campus environment, the University is meeting the changing needs of undergraduate and graduate students, assisting in the training efforts of employers, and supporting lifelong learning. Virginia Tech is accredited by the Commission on Colleges of the Southern Association of Colleges and Schools.

DISTANCE LEARNING PROGRAM

The Institute for Distance and Distributed Learning provides leadership, coordination, and support to the growing distance and distributed learning activities of Virginia Tech. The Institute takes a holistic approach to distance learning where all aspects of a student's educational experience are considered. Through distance and distributed learning, Virginia Tech extends its campus to communities throughout the commonwealth and provides an open campus environment that allows individuals to engage in learning anytime, anywhere. In addition, Virginia Tech shares the practical application of the University's knowledge and expertise in support of economic development, increases the University's access to the world and the world's access to the University, and researches new teaching and learning environments through the application of technology. More than 6,000 enrollments were accounted for in the 166 different courses and eleven master's degrees and one certificate program. Virginia Tech actively participates in the Electronic Campus of Virginia and the Southern Region Electronic Campus and collaboratively delivers courses and degree programs at a distance with other Virginia colleges and universities through the Commonwealth Graduate Engineering Program and the Virginia Consortium of Engineering and Science Universities.

DELIVERY MEDIA

Faculty members utilize multiple methods of instructional delivery and student interaction to provide an engaging, high-quality learning environment. Virginia Tech delivers distance learning courses via the Internet, videoconferencing, satellite, archived video, and desktop computer audio-graphics. Net.Work.Virginia is a statewide, high-speed, broadband ATM network that uses cutting-edge technology. The network is used to support different types of teaching and learning activities and allows faculty members to customize their courses to meet the needs of their students. Through Net.Work.Virginia, Virginia Tech provides electronically delivered two-way interactive video courses to its four extended campuses (Northern Virginia Center, Roanoke Graduate Center, Southwest Virginia Higher Education Center, and Hampton Roads Graduate Center) and numerous other higher education, government, business, and industry sites located in Virginia and several other states. The University uses the Internet to provide a variety of learning opportunities through online assignments, chat rooms, threaded discussions, e-mail, and audio and computer conferencing.

PROGRAMS OF STUDY

Virginia Tech provides working professionals with the opportunity to obtain a master's degree in eleven different programs through distance and distributed learning. These programs include a Master of Business Administration; Master of Science degrees in Aerospace Engineering, Civil Engineering, Electrical and Computer Engineering, Industrial and Systems Engineering, Instructional Technology, Materials Science and Engineering, Ocean Engineering, Physical Education, and Systems Engineering; and a Master of Arts in Political Science. Virginia Tech also offers a certificate program in administration of community-based services for older adults.

A wide variety of credit and non-credit courses is also offered through distance learning in the areas of accounting, architecture, art, biology, black studies, building construction, communications, computer science, economics, education, engineering, English, entomology, finance, geography, hotel management, information science, landscape architecture, management, marketing, math, philosophy, physics, psychology, science and technology, sociology, Spanish, statistics, and women's studies.

STUDENT SERVICES

Virginia Tech distance learners have the ability to register on line and to access student information and services. The Virginia Tech Online Writing Lab (VT OWL) offers an electronic tutoring environment. Online tutoring sessions are individually scheduled between tutor and client, so there are no fixed hours. The OWL also includes a self-help area and a grammar hotline. The self-help area contains handouts and exercises to provide any person with 24-hour access to writing assistance. The grammar hotline (gram@vt.edu) is an e-mail-based service available to students and nonstudents alike; its main purpose is to provide assistance to students with writing questions that can be answered immediately.

Virginia Tech also provides extensive access to library services. Addison, the online library catalog, is available as a Web or telnet interface. Electronic reference assistance is easily accessed through the library's AskUs request form. Students may also contact the University's distance education librarian. Distance learners have access to Virginia Tech's full-text electronic resources and databases plus document delivery services.

CREDIT OPTIONS

Distance learners can transfer credits earned at other accredited postsecondary institutions to Virginia Tech following the established University policies. Students admitted to the University who have been certified by the Virginia Community College System or Richard Bland College as completing the transfer module will be deemed to have completed the University core curriculum components and will receive 35 total credits for the module.

FACULTY

The faculty is the foundation of Virginia Tech's distance learning programs and assures its academic excellence. Virginia Tech has 1,425 full-time instructional faculty members, more than 100 of whom taught distance learning courses in 1999–2000.

ADMISSION

To become undergraduate or graduate degree candidates at Virginia Tech, students must apply formally for admission. Students' records at Virginia Tech and all other colleges and universities attended are reviewed within the context of current admission policies.

As a member of the Electronic Campus of Virginia, Virginia Tech allows qualified students at other Virginia universities and colleges to enroll in its courses as transient students. For more information on undergraduate admissions, students should refer to the Admissions Web site at http://www.admiss.vt.edu; those interested in graduate programs should see Graduate Admission's Web site at http://www.rgs.vt.edu.

TUITION AND FEES

Tuition for undergraduate courses for in-state residents is $458.25 for one 3-credit-hour course and $1518.75 for one 3-credit-hour course for out-of-state residents. Tuition for graduate courses for in-state residents is

$812.25 for one 3-credit-hour course and $1292.25 for one 3-credit-hour course for out-of-state residents. Tuition for noncredit courses varies. Complete information on tuition and fees can be found on the World Wide Web at http://www.bursar.vt.edu/fees0001.asp.

FINANCIAL AID

Virginia Tech is a direct lending institution and awards financial aid from federally funded and state-funded programs as well as privately funded sources. Financial aid sources include the Federal Direct Stafford Loan, Federal Perkins Loan, Federal Direct PLUS Loan, Federal Pell Grant, Federal Work-Study, Virginia Guaranteed Assistance program, Commonwealth Award, and the College Scholarship Assistance Program.

APPLYING

Students applying for undergraduate admission can access current information at http://www.admiss.vt.edu. Students applying for graduate admission can access current information at http://www.rgs.vt.edu. Students can register for Internet-based courses at http://www.vto.vt.edu. There is a nonrefundable $20 processing fee for non-Virginia Tech students.

CONTACT

Cate Mowrey
Institute for Distance and
    Distributed Learning
Virginia Polytechnic Institute and
    State University
Blacksburg, Virginia 24061-0445
Telephone: 540-231-9584
Fax: 540-231-2079
E-mail: vtwebreg@vt.edu
Web site: http://www.iddl.vt.edu
            http://www.vto.vt.edu
            (online catalog)

Academic programs at Walden University combine high-quality curriculum and innovative distance delivery models. The result is a collection of highly applied, rigorous programs that are flexible without compromising academic integrity. These programs are ideally suited to adult learners who wish to pursue an advanced degree without the professional and personal sacrifices associated with traditional, campus-based programs.

Four academic divisions make up Walden University: the Management Division, the Education Division, the Health and Human Services Division, and the Psychology Division. Walden students complete much of their work on line. Both doctoral and master's degrees are offered.

A pioneer in distance delivery, Walden has been serving the needs of adult learners since the University's founding in 1970. Walden University is accredited by the North Central Association of Colleges and Schools.

DISTANCE LEARNING PROGRAM

Walden University enrolls more than 1,400 students from all fifty states and twenty-eight other countries. One third of the University's students are members of minority groups. The University offers programs that allow busy adults to complete a master's or Ph.D. degree from home or work on their own schedules.

DELIVERY MEDIA

Depending on the program in which they are enrolled, Walden students complete much of their degree requirements through online interaction, instruction, and submission of work. Individual mentoring, online courses, and progress based on demonstrations of knowledge are among the ingredients found in Walden's delivery system. Students enrolling in a Walden program should be comfortable using a personal computer, a word processor, and e-mail.

PROGRAMS OF STUDY

Ph.D. programs are offered in applied management and decision sciences, education, health services, human services, and psychology. Master of Science degrees are offered in education and psychology.

The Ph.D. in applied management and decision sciences program comprises 128 quarter credit hours. Students may elect a broad program or a self-designed specialization or specialize in engineering management, finance, leadership and organizational change, or operations research.

The Ph.D. in education program comprises 128 quarter credit hours. Enrollment options include a general program, an educational technology specialization, a higher education specialization, a K–12 educational leadership specialization, an early childhood specialization, an adult education leadership specialization offered in collaboration with Indiana University, and a self-designed specialization.

The Ph.D. in health services program comprises 128 quarter credit hours. General study is available, as are a self-designed specialization and specializations in community health, health administration, and health and human behavior.

The Ph.D. in human services program comprises 128 quarter credit hours. Students may design a specialization or specialize in clinical social work, counseling, criminal justice, family and intervention strategies, or social policy analysis and planning.

The course-based Ph.D. in professional psychology program comprises 127 quarter credit hours. Specializations offered include academic psychology, clinical psychology, counseling psychology, health psychology, and organizational psychology.

The course-based, online M.S. in psychology program comprises 45 quarter credit hours.

The M.S. in education program comprises 45 quarter credit hours and has specializations in classroom education, educational change and innovation, and educational technology.

SPECIAL PROGRAMS

Walden University offers a limited number of National Service Fellowships to enrolled doctoral students. These fellowships are available to students who have dedicated their careers to public service. National Service Fellowships are competitive among enrolled students who have completed at least one full academic quarter. Each fellowship includes an annual (twelve-month) remission of tuition and fees of $1500 per academic year, renewable up to three years.

Through its Higher Education Professional Development Fellowship program, Walden University offers other educational institutions a way to help faculty and staff members upgrade academic credentials. A minimum of

2 participants from an institution is required for participation in this fellowship, which provides waiver of the application, orientation materials, and commencement fees and reduces tuition by 10 percent.

School- and school district–based cohort groups in education are welcome and receive a tuition discount and learner support groups.

STUDENT SERVICES

Student services include academic counseling, financial aid services, an information technology help desk, orientation programming, and dissertation editing.

Walden University's partnership with the Indiana University library provides students with access to a collection of more than 4 million journals. Walden's full-time staff at the Indiana University–Bloomington graduate library provides reference, search, catalog, and distribution services.

CREDIT OPTIONS

For the M.S. programs in education and psychology, up to 10 quarter credit hours are accepted in transfer. Up to 36 quarter credit hours may be transferred into the Ph.D. in psychology program. For the Ph.D. in education program, up to 42 quarter credit hours are transferable. The Ph.D. in applied management and decision sciences allows for the transfer of up to 20 quarter credit hours into the finance, leadership and organizational change, and operations research specializations.

FACULTY

Walden University has more than 160 faculty members. Risky students have a faculty mentor who provides individualized attention as they pursue their degree.

ADMISSION

For Ph.D. admission, a master's degree from a regionally accredited institution and three years of professional experience are required. For M.S. admission, a bachelor's degree from a regionally accredited institution is required.

TUITION AND FEES

Tuition for doctoral programs is $3245 per quarter. For psychology (Ph.D. and M.S.) students, tuition is $310 per credit hour. For the M.S. in education, tuition is $235 per credit hour.

FINANCIAL AID

Walden University offers prospective students a variety of options to assist in funding their educational expenses. Approximately 67 percent of Walden students receive some form of financial assistance. Many receive 100 percent assistance in the payment of tuition and fees. Options available include federal financial assistance programs, veterans' education benefits, and institutional fellowships. Discounts are also available for group/spousal enrollment. In addition, Walden can assist students in securing private scholarships, employer tuition benefits, and loans from private lenders.

APPLYING

Submission of a completed and signed application, a $50 application fee, and a personal/professional statement of purpose is required. Applicants must also send a resume, official transcripts (from the institution that conferred the bachelor's or master's degree), and two required recommendation forms. Students can also apply on the Web at the address listed below.

CONTACT

Walden University
155 Fifth Avenue South
Minneapolis, Minnesota 55401
Telephone: 800-444-6795 Ext. 500 (toll-free)
Fax: 941-498-4266
E-mail: request@waldenu.edu
Web site: http://www.waldenu.edu

Washington State University

Extended Degree Programs

Pullman, Washington

Washington State University (WSU), the state's land-grant institution, is dedicated to the preparation of students for productive lives and professional careers, to basic and applied research, and to the dissemination of knowledge. Founded in 1890, the University is a statewide institution with a main campus in Pullman, three branch campuses, eleven community learning centers, and numerous Cooperative Extension and research facilities throughout the state. WSU is accredited by the Northwest Association of Schools and Colleges.

In addition, the University is an acknowledged leader in developing and delivering distance education programs. Since 1992, WSU's Office of Extended Degree Programs (EDP) has been serving students in Washington and across the nation. The University's undergraduate core curriculum, including world civilization courses and expanded writing requirements, is nationally recognized. Money magazine has called WSU a "public ivy" and rated the honors program as one of the nation's best, and in 1998, Yahoo! Internet Life magazine rated WSU as the top most wired college in the nation.

DISTANCE LEARNING PROGRAM

WSU's Office of Extended Degree Programs offers degree-completion programs leading to a Bachelor of Arts in social sciences, business administration, criminal justice, or human development and a Bachelor of Science in agriculture. These programs are designed primarily for students who have completed the equivalent of the first two years of college. They are delivered directly to students' homes through a variety of distance learning technologies. They are the same degrees offered on three WSU campuses; requirements are the same as those for completing degrees on campus; however, students can complete their degrees without coming to a WSU campus.

For more information about the degrees WSU has to offer, visit the Web site or call the toll-free number (listed on the next page).

DELIVERY MEDIA

Courses are delivered by the Internet, videotape (available for rent), satellite, cable television, and print materials. As computers become more common, most courses will have World Wide Web requirements.

PROGRAMS OF STUDY

WSU's Bachelor of Arts in social sciences is a liberal arts degree that offers students multiple options and emphases in the social sciences and provides a broad background applicable to a variety of careers. It emphasizes an interdisciplinary approach with possible major and/or minor course concentrations in anthropology, criminal justice, history, human development, political science, psychology, sociology, and women's studies. A formal minor in business administration is also available.

A Bachelor of Arts in human development is also available with an asynchronous distance format from WSU. The human development degree is especially effective for individuals who work in child- or elder-care programs or in direct service roles with a variety of special-needs clients. The degree program includes an internship component supervised by a WSU faculty member.

The Bachelor of Arts in Business Administration is designed to provide a broad foundation for employment in the world of business, either at a large corporation or in a small private company. A set curriculum, fully accredited by AACSB–The International Association for Management Education, leads students through courses in finance, management, information systems, marketing, international business, business law, and economics.

WSU's Bachelor of Arts in Criminal Justice degree prepares students for positions in the criminal justice system, other government agencies, and the private sector. A completion degree, the distance B.A. in Criminal Justice offers a policy-focused curriculum which provides students with broad exposure in the social sciences preferred by governmental and private agencies. The curriculum is based on 12 credit hours of criminal justice core courses, 12 credit hours of criminal justice electives, and 24 or 25 credit hours of collateral electives in sociology and psychology; most courses are available through distance learning options.

The Tri-State Agricultural Distance Delivery Alliance (TADDA) is a cooperative distance delivery program developed by the land-grant universities of the University of Idaho (UI), Oregon State University (OSU), and Washington State University (WSU). Combining resources from all three universities, TADDA enables students throughout the world to obtain a variety of bachelor's degrees in general agriculture. Courses from a variety of agricultural disciplines are offered through participating community colleges and learning centers.

To earn a bachelor's degree, WSU generally requires the completion of at least 120 semester credits, 40 at the upper-division level. At least 30 of the 120 credits must be taken through WSU. The 120 credits must include courses that meet WSU General Education Requirements (GER). To learn about requirements for each degree, students should speak to an EDP adviser.

More than eighty video courses and nearly 100 correspondence courses are available to students. Courses are also available from the National Universities Degree Consortium (NUDC), a group of nine land-grant and state universities formed to address the needs of adult and part-time learners.

STUDENT SERVICES

Academic advising is available to all prospective and currently enrolled degree-seeking students through toll-free telephone or electronic mail. The WSU Office of Admissions prepares an official evaluation of a student's transcript when he or she is admitted to the University. An EDP adviser assists EDP students in developing a study plan based on the program options and University requirements. A student services coordinator is available to help students with logistical details.

Students may register on line via toll-free telephone, fax, or e-mail. Videotapes, lab kits, and other supplementary materials are available through the EDP office. Students may order textbooks and course guides from the WSU Students Book Corporation on line via toll-free telephone.

All EDP students have access to the WSU libraries. The EDP librarian is available via toll-free telephone to assist students with database searches, in checking out materials, and in copying articles.

CREDIT OPTIONS

Students may transfer to WSU a maximum of 60 semester credits of lower-division credit and up to 30 more credits from other four-year institutions. The exact number of transfer credits accepted by WSU may vary depending upon an individual's choice of degree.

WSU recognizes there are alternative ways students may gain knowledge and credit. The University has developed a method of accepting credit by examination, including Advanced Placement (AP), College-Level Examination Program (CLEP), DANTES, and American Council on Education (ACE). Interested students should check with their advisers for details.

FACULTY

There are 1,206 full-time and 187 part-time faculty members in the Washington State University system. Ninety-three percent of the faculty members have terminal academic degrees.

ADMISSION

Admission to the Extended Degree Program requires at least 27 semester or 40 quarter credits of transferable college course work from an accredited community or four-year college, with at least a 2.0 cumulative GPA.

TUITION AND FEES

In 2000–01, undergraduate tuition (semester-based) is $183 per video credit for Washington residents and $275 per video credit for nonresidents. Videotape rental averages $60 per course. Correspondence (flexible enrollment) course tuition is $130 per credit.

Payment options for full-time students are available as well.

FINANCIAL AID

A financial aid adviser is available to all EDP students. Washington State University students receive aid from all federal programs, such as the Federal Pell Grants and Federal Supplemental Educational Opportunity Grants (FSEOG) and the Federal Perkins, Federal Stafford Student, and Federal PLUS Loans. Washington residents are eligible for institutional and state need grants. In 1999–2000, WSU awarded more than $70 million in financial aid. Approximately 50 percent of all WSU students and 52 percent of extended degree students receive financial aid.

APPLYING

WSU degree-seeking students must be admitted to the University. Admission requires that a student submit an admissions form, have official copies of his or her transcript(s) sent directly from the postsecondary institution(s) attended to the EDP office, and pay the $35 application fee.

CONTACT

Cheri Curtis
Program Coordinator
Extended Degree Programs
Van Doren 204
Washington State University
P.O. Box 645220
Pullman, Washington 99164-5220
Telephone: 509-335-3557
          800-222-4978 (toll-free)
Fax: 509-335-4850
E-mail: edp@wsu.edu
Web site:
   http://www.eus.wsu.edu/edp/

Weber State University

Distance Learning

Ogden, Utah

Weber State University (WSU) provides lifelong opportunities for diverse learners on and off campus. It offers degrees through seven colleges and forty departments via distance learning. Students may receive specialized training in health professions, criminal justice, and manufacturing. WSU's academic programs prepare students for immediate employment or further study and equip them with liberal education concepts and skills to support their lifelong learning.

WSU serves as Utah's premier public undergraduate university. The institution was founded in 1889, became a state junior college in 1933, and added upper-division courses and began bachelor's degree programs in 1959. On January 1, 1991, Weber State further expanded its offerings and was granted university status.

WSU is accredited by the Northwest Association of Schools and Colleges. In addition, applicable professional agencies accredit or approve specific departments and programs.

DISTANCE LEARNING PROGRAM

The WSU Distance Learning Program serves students who cannot attend college classes in person. During the 1999–2000 academic year, more than 5,000 students enrolled in print- and Internet-based courses. Students use distance learning to earn general education credits, as well as degrees and professional credentials in manufacturing, criminal justice, and health science areas.

DELIVERY MEDIA

Students follow study guides, read textbooks, view videotapes, hear cassettes, and/or participate in online courses. They interact with other students, instructors, and advisers by using mail, telephone, or e-mail and online discussion groups. Exams are delivered on line or through the mail and are administered by approved proctors. Access to a videocassette player, audiocassette player, word processor, or a computer with browser software and an Internet service provider may be required.

PROGRAMS OF STUDY

The WSU Distance Learning degree program evolved from a commitment to providing education for health-care professionals and other working adults regardless of location. Combining independent study with Internet courses, a bachelor's degree requires 120 semester hours (40 upper-division, 30 through WSU) with a minimum GPA of at least a 2.0 (or C).

Bachelor's degrees are available in clinical laboratory science and health sciences, with emphases in radiological sciences (advanced radiography, MRI/CT, mammography, cardiovascular–interventional technology, diagnostic medical sonography, radiation therapy, and nuclear medicine), health information management, health promotion, and health service administration.

Associate of Applied Science and Associate of Science degrees in respiratory therapy require 20 credits taken in residence at WSU, completion of the requirements for a major in respiratory therapy, and an overall GPA of at least 2.0.

The Weber State University Distance Learning associate degree program in criminal justice and the professional certificate programs in production and inventory management are designed for professionals whose work and travel schedules and far-flung locations make it difficult for them to participate in campus classwork.

Law enforcement and security professionals register on line with Weber State University or one of its six collaborating institutions: Salt Lake Community College, College of Eastern Utah, Dixie College, Southern Utah University, Snow College, or Utah Valley State College, and take their training on their home or work computers.

Weber State University works in partnership with APICS, the 70,000-member Educational Society for Resource Management, to offer its certification program through WSU Online for people who work in production and resource management.

WSU certificate programs include production inventory management radiologic sciences and respiratory therapy (entry-level respiratory care practitioner or registered respiratory therapist). Radiologic sciences classes can be used toward continuing education units (CEU).

Professional agencies such as the Commission on Accreditation for Allied Health Education Programs and the Association of University Programs in Health Administration accredit specific disciplines.

SPECIAL PROGRAMS

WSU Online, the award-winning extension of the University on the Internet, allows students to take online courses, use online support services, and participate in online discussions and activities with faculty and staff members and other students. WSU Online makes it possible for students with busy schedules and/or long commutes to take advantage of the convenience of online courses with support services and interpersonal experiences that are essential to their success. For current course listings and additional information, students can visit the WSU Web site at http://wsuonline.weber.edu.

Courses from a wide range of academic disciplines are available through Weber State University's independent study program, allowing students to complete their course work at their convenience. Each year, more than 2,000 students enroll in these "paper and pencil" courses and take advantage of this self-paced, individualized mode of study.

STUDENT SERVICES

WSU recognizes that most of its students have work, family, and other personal responsibilities that limit their participation in traditional-classroom college courses; therefore, convenience is a major factor in the design of the Distance Learning Program.

Students receive guidance from distance learning staff and faculty members. Degree-seeking students are assigned academic advisers who review transcripts and past learning experiences. This information is used to design individualized programs of study.

Students may access Stewart Library's catalog, interlibrary loan, reference help, document delivery, and other services electronically at http://library.weber.edu. Textbooks can be purchased directly from the WSU bookstore, by mail, or on line for a small handling charge (telephone: 800-848-7770 Ext. 6352).

CREDIT OPTIONS

WSU may grant credit for active military, National Guard, or reserve experience; 38 or more credits to registered radiographers; a maximum of 45 credits to diploma nursing school graduates; and varying credits to registered respiratory therapy technicians and graduates of accredited therapy/specialty programs. Official transcripts should be sent directly from universities and colleges attended. WSU also recognizes College-Level Examination Program (CLEP) credits.

FACULTY

WSU Distance Learning currently employs 111 full-time university faculty members and 14 adjunct faculty members. Nearly all faculty members hold terminal degrees in their respective fields.

ADMISSION

Degree-seeking Distance Learning applicants must meet WSU admission requirements. The programs in health professions require separate applications and information specific to their academic areas. Students not seeking to complete a degree at WSU may be eligible for simplified, nonmatriculated admission.

TUITION AND FEES

Distance Learning tuition averages $95 per semester hour. Additional materials may include course study guides ($3–$40) and audiotape or videotape deposits of $60, with a $40 refund upon their return.
All fees are subject to change. Students can consult the current catalog or visit the Web site at http://www.weber.edu/ce/dl/ for more information.

FINANCIAL AID

Eligible students may apply for federal financial aid such as Pell Grants, Supplemental Educational Opportunity Grants (SEOG), Perkins Loans, and Stafford Loans. Students can contact the office of financial aid toll-free at 800-848-7770 Ext. 7569.

Veterans may also be considered for VA educational benefits (office of Veteran Affairs telephone: 800-848-7770 Ext. 6039, toll-free). Health professions degree programs are approved by DANTES.

APPLYING

Students should send an application; an individual program application, if required; official transcripts from previous colleges; and an application fee of $30 to the contact address listed below. Students may also apply at http://www.weber.edu/admissions/. Distance Learning students need not attend an orientation.

CONTACT

Office of Distance Learning
Weber State University
4005 University Circle
Ogden, Utah 84408-4005
Telephone: 801-626-6785
   800-848-7770 Ext. 6785 (toll-free)
Fax: 801-626-8035
E-mail: dist-learn@weber.edu
Web site: http://wsuonline.weber.edu
   http://www.weber.edu/ce/dl/

Western Governors University

Distance Learning Program

Salt Lake City, Utah

WGU is a degree-granting, competency-based, online, distance education institution. By visiting the University's Web site at www.wgu.edu, a student can find everything that is needed to advance his or her educational goals, including competency-based degree programs, an online catalog of high-quality distance learning courses, an online library, bookstore, and one-on-one access to a personal WGU mentor, who guides the student through his or her customized degree program from beginning to end. As one of the most ambitious higher education initiatives of its time, WGU was founded and is supported by nineteen states and governors and is a leader in the movement to increase access to educational opportunities for today's adult, lifelong learner and to provide students with recognition for the skills and knowledge they already possess. With candidacy for accreditation status, WGU is using technology to provide accessibility, flexibility, and the opportunity for every type of student to achieve his or her educational goals.

DISTANCE LEARNING PROGRAM

Every course and program offered through or by WGU is distance delivered. WGU's campus is its Web site, which provides access to high-quality, distance-delivered educational opportunities to students no matter where they are. Currently, WGU has more than 950 courses in its online catalog from more than forty-five education providers.

DELIVERY MEDIA

The courses available through WGU from its affiliated education providers are delivered via a wide variety of methods—everything from postal correspondence to desktop video and e-mail. Interaction between faculty members and students is also conducted via many different methods. A description of the delivery methods for each course and any equipment students will need is included in WGU's online catalog as well as the syllabi for each course selected.

PROGRAMS OF STUDY

WGU currently offers three certificates and six degrees in various areas of study, with additional programs scheduled for fall 2000. The general education Associate of Arts provides students with a broad academic background in the major disciplines. The Master of Arts degree in learning and technology is awarded to individuals who can demonstrate their ability to improve education and training results by effectively using technology to support teaching. The Associate of Science in network administration is awarded to individuals who demonstrate their competence in occupations directly related to conceiving, building, monitoring, and managing network architecture. The Associate of Applied Science in software applications analysis and integration (SAAI) is awarded to individuals who demonstrate that they are capable of serving as applications experts in their organization. The Associate of Applied Science in electronics manufacturing technology certifies that individuals are prepared for occupations directly related to the production and assembly of complex electronic devices. WGU's newest degree is an Associate of Science in information technology with a Certified Netware Engineer (CNE)

emphasis. Students who already possess their CNE are recognized for the skills already obtained.

Starting in fall 2000 is WGU's first bachelor's degree program—a Bachelor of Science in business with an information technology management emphasis.

To earn a WGU degree or certificate, students must successfully complete a series of assessments that demonstrate mastery of WGU competencies. Most degree programs also include a portfolio requirement.

SPECIAL PROGRAMS

All of WGU's programs of study are entirely competency-based and distance-delivered, and they are designed with the working adult in mind. Each program is made up of a number of domains. Each domain covers roughly a subject area, such as mathematics and quantitative skills. The student, in close consultation with his or her mentor—an expert in the student's field of study—prepares for each domain assessment battery via whatever means appropriate; that may include taking distance-delivered classes or conducting self-study activities. The student who is well prepared for the domain assessment due to his or her life or work experience is not required to take any classes prior to the assessment. This system allows a student to capitalize on his or her strengths and receive recognition for prior learning, thus decreasing the overall time it takes to complete the degree program.

STUDENT SERVICES

WGU's goal is to provide distance learning students with all the student services they need to succeed. WGU offers an online bookstore, an online library, and one-on-one advising with a mentor. Every student enrolled in a WGU degree or certificate program is assigned a mentor who helps the student develop an Academic Action Plan (AAP) and select appropriate courses and generally advises the student throughout his or her academic program.

CREDIT OPTIONS

As a competency-based institution, WGU does not issue or accumulate credits. There are no required classes for a WGU degree. Instead, a student earns a WGU degree or certificate by successfully demonstrating his or her competency through a series of WGU assessments. Though WGU does not accept transfer credits, students with previous college experience may transfer their previous learning by proceeding on a fast track through their WGU degree and moving directly to the appropriate assessments.

FACULTY

Teaching faculty members associated with WGU students are located at WGU-affiliated institutions that offer courses through the WGU online catalog. WGU faculty members include council members who develop WGU competencies and identify and approve assessments, as well as WGU mentors.

ADMISSION

Applicants must be at least 16 years old and must demonstrate an ability to benefit from WGU learning opportunities. A high school diploma or its equivalent is required for entry into all college-level degree programs. A bachelor's degree is required for admission to the master's degree program.

TUITION AND FEES

WGU makes no distinction between in-state and out-of-state students. Tuition for an associate degree is $3250,

and master's degree tuition is $3850. Optional classes are extra. (Students should see the online catalog for course tuition.)

FINANCIAL AID

WGU was one of the first institutions to make federal financial aid available to distance education students. Aid available through WGU includes Federal Pell Grants and Federal Direct Loans (both subsidized and unsubsidized).

APPLYING

Students may apply to WGU via an online application form that is available at the WGU Web site. There is a $100 application fee. Applicants are contacted within a few business days regarding the status of their application and information regarding next steps for their academic progress.

CONTACT

WGU Student Information Center
Western Governors University
2040 East Murray Holladay Road, Suite 106
Salt Lake City, Utah 84117
Telephone: 877-HELP-WGU (toll-free)
Fax: 801-274-3305
E-mail: info@wgu.edu
Web site: http://www.wgu.edu

Western Illinois University

School of Extended and Continuing Education

Macomb, Illinois

Western Illinois University (WIU) is a residential, state-supported institution located in Macomb, Illinois. The University is committed to providing the premier undergraduate education among all public universities in Illinois, and, in selected disciplines, far beyond Illinois borders. The University offers forty-six undergraduate degree programs and thirty-five graduate degree programs for more than 12,600 students. WIU offers several innovative programs to help students toward timely completion of their degrees. Students choosing to participate in a GRADTRAC contract can earn a bachelor's degree in four years in most majors. Undergraduates can lock in the per-year cost for tuition, fees, and room and board for the entire four years they attend. In addition, dual admission agreements with numerous community colleges enable students to gain admission to both institutions at the same time, making the transition to Western easier. Western Illinois–Quad Cities, a branch campus in Moline, Illinois, provides ten disciplines, master's degree programs in fifteen areas, and an education specialist degree.

Western Illinois University is governed by a Board of Trustees and is accredited by the Commission on Institutions of Higher Education of the North Central Association of Colleges and Schools.

DISTANCE LEARNING PROGRAM

Each semester the Extended Learning office offers approximately forty courses, most of which are junior and senior level. Independent study courses for students seeking the Board of Trustees/Bachelor of Arts (B.O.T./B.A.) degree are available through mail and World Wide Web. Full-time WIU professors from many academic departments develop and teach these courses.

DELIVERY MEDIA

WIU distance learning options are available via independent study, e-mail, video, the World Wide Web, interactive satellite, telecourses, and compressed video. Students and faculty members correspond by telephone, mail, fax, and e-mail.

PROGRAMS OF STUDY

Western Illinois University's B.O.T./ B.A. program is designed to provide nontraditional students an opportunity to earn a regionally accredited undergraduate degree in a manner compatible with their educational needs and lifestyles. This highly individualized and flexible program recognizes that adults may have attended a variety of educational institutions and accepts transfer of passing course work taken at other regionally accredited colleges and universities.

Since its inception in 1972, the program has had more than 4,500 graduates. It includes courses by mail and telecourses and features in-state tuition rates, student-designed learning, evaluation of prior learning through a portfolio or standardized proficiency exams, professional advising services for each student, acceptance of ACE Guide-evaluated military training, and the program's potential to follow students who change locations. There is no prescribed time limit to complete the degree program and no major is required. Ninety-five percent of off-campus and independent study courses are taught by regular WIU faculty.

A Master of Business Administration (M.B.A.) is available locally. To apply, students must have a baccalaureate degree and must have taken the GMAT and submitted all college transcripts. A minimum of thirty-three semester hours are required (with a maximum of six years for degree completion). For more information, interested students should contact Dr. David Bloomberg, M.B.A. Director, Western Illinois University, College of Business and Technology, Stipes Hall 101, Macomb, Illinois 61455 (Telephone: 309-298-2442, Fax: 309-298-1039, E-mail: dj-bloomberg@wiu.edu).

A Master of Science (M.S.) in instructional technology and telecommunications is available worldwide. To apply, students must have a baccalaureate degree and must submit all college transcripts, a GRE score, and an essay or personal statement. Thirty-two to thirty-five semester hours are required (with a maximum of five years for degree completion). Students must complete a thesis, a project, or a portfolio. For more information, interested students should contact Dr. M. H. Hassan, Chair, Western Illinois University, Horrabin Hall 37, Macomb, Illinois 61455 (Telephone: 309-298-1296, Fax: 309-298-2978, E-mail: it-telecommunications@wiu.edu, World Wide Web: http://www.wiu.edu/itt/).

CREDIT OPTIONS

The B.O.T./B.A. degree program offers students the option of applying for academic credit by preparing a prior learning portfolio, successfully completing proficiency exams, and combining prior college credit with individually selected courses to create a personalized program of study.

FACULTY

Providing excellent instruction is the highest priority of the 672 WIU faculty members. The on-campus ratio of students to faculty members is 15:1 and the average class size is 25. Seventy-eight percent of the full-time faculty members hold doctorates or terminal degrees.

ADMISSION

Students seeking admission to WIU's B.O.T./B.A. degree program must submit an application to the Non-Traditional Programs office. For more information, students should contact Dr. R. W. Carter, Director, Western Illinois University, Non-Traditional Programs, Horrabin Hall 5, Macomb, Illinois 61455 (Telephone: 309-298-1929, Fax: 309-298-2226, E-mail: np-bot@wiu.edu).

TUITION AND FEES

All students enrolling in independent study courses pay in-state tuition rates. There are no fees for application, maintenance, or graduation. Advance payment for new semester charges is not required of students who are in good financial standing with WIU.

FINANCIAL AID

Students receiving any form of financial assistance are advised to check with the Financial Aid Office to determine the extent of coverage available for independent study.

CONTACT

Western Illinois University
School of Extended and Continuing Education
Distance Learning Program
Joyce E. Nielsen
1 University Circle
Macomb, Illinois 61455
Telephone: 309-298-2182
Fax: 309-298-2133
E-mail: Joyce_Nielsen@ccmail.wiu.edu

Wheaton College Graduate School

Distance Learning
Wheaton, Illinois

The Wheaton College Graduate School was established in 1937 as part of Wheaton College (founded in 1860). Its mission is to provide academic and professional preparation that will enable the committed Christian student to formulate and articulate a biblical and global understanding of life and ministry and apply it to service for Christ and His Kingdom. The emphasis of the Graduate School throughout its history has been on practical scholarship—scholarship totally rooted in the final authority of the Scriptures but practical so that educated and trained Christian leaders are equipped to relate to the real needs of people today. Wheaton College is accredited by the North Central Association of Colleges and Schools.

DISTANCE LEARNING PROGRAM

As part of the Graduate School, Distance Learning shares in its mission of scholarship committed to servanthood. The program is also committed to making this education accessible to those who are unable to relocate. Distance Learning courses enable students to pursue graduate study without leaving their place of ministry or employment.

DELIVERY MEDIA

Distance Learning courses employ a variety of media. Traditional independent study courses consist of audiocassettes, instruction manuals, and textbooks. Most Web-based courses include streaming audio and video and interactive asynchronous discussion with faculty members and other students. These courses require a PC or a Mac with a standard Internet connection (with a minimum modem speed of 28.8 KB per second), an e-mail account, and a Java-capable browser.

Wheaton College has partnered with eCollege.com to provide its Web-based courses.

PROGRAMS OF STUDY

The Certificate of Advanced Biblical Studies–Distance Learning Option may be taken entirely at a distance. It is designed for people who desire advanced training in biblical and theological studies to better equip them for personal Christian living and service in the church. The certificate program provides professional development opportunities for pastors, teachers in Christian schools, missionaries, and other Christian workers. It also provides a way for those working in other vocations and disciplines to attain a theological and biblical foundation necessary for the integration of faith, learning, and living.

Students who are interested in this 24-hour program must meet the general requirements for admission to Wheaton College Graduate School, including the biblical and theological proficiency requirements (which can also be fulfilled through noncredit distance learning courses). Required courses include Principles of Interpretation, Christian Theology, and a research course introducing standard research principles, methods, and tools as well as online resources. Additional hours are worked out in consultation with a faculty adviser. Students may choose to combine on-campus study with courses offered at a distance.

Wheaton College Graduate School also offers two special Master of Arts degree programs that combine Distance Learning courses with short intensive courses and one semester of residential study.

SPECIAL PROGRAMS

Wheaton College Graduate School offers two special Master's Programs for People in Ministry or the Marketplace (MPPM). These flexible programs combine Distance Learning courses with on-campus intensive courses and a final semester in residence. They lead to an M.A. degree in Biblical and Theological Studies (36 hours) or Missions and Intercultural Studies (40 hours). Up to 16 hours may be taken through distance learning for these programs.

Prospective students should contact the School for additional information about abbreviated summer school courses and the Institute for Cross-Cultural Training.

CREDIT OPTIONS

No transfer credit can be accepted in the MPPM programs or in the Certificate of Advanced Biblical Studies–Distance Learning Option. Students who are prematriculated in other programs may apply up to 8 to 10 semester hours of Distance Learning courses or transfer credit to a degree program, provided the courses meet degree requirements.

FACULTY

Four full-time faculty members and 1 part-time faculty member currently teach distance learning courses. All have earned doctorates. Additional support is provided by course development staff in Media Resources, Library Services, and Distance Learning.

ADMISSION

Applicants must have a bachelor's degree from a regionally accredited college or university at a level indicative of high-quality scholarship (a 2.75 minimum grade point average on a 4.0 scale). Each academic department maintains additional requirements. Prospective students should see the course catalog for a full list of requirements and recommendations for optimal preparation.

TUITION AND FEES

Tuition for Web-based and self-paced audiocassette/print courses is $260 per semester hour in 2000–01. The cost of textbooks is variable.

FINANCIAL AID

No financial aid is available for distance learning students at this time. Veterans with educational benefits who plan to complete a degree on campus should contact the program before enrolling in distance learning courses.

APPLYING

While no application fee is required to enroll in an individual distance learning course, an official undergraduate transcript must be submitted. A one-time $30 nonrefundable application fee is required for admission to the Certificate of Advanced Biblical Studies–Distance Learning Option or the MPPM programs. Students admitted to either the certificate or MPPM programs are given priority in registering for a course.

CONTACT

Doug Milford, Director
Distance Learning
501 College Avenue
Wheaton, Illinois 60187-5593
Telephone: 630-752-5944
        800-888-0141 (toll-free)
Fax: 630-752-5935
E-mail: distance.learning@wheaton.edu
Web site: http://www.wheaton.edu/distancelearning/

Worcester Polytechnic Institute

Advanced Distance Learning Network

Worcester, Massachusetts

Founded in 1865, Worcester Polytechnic Institute (WPI) has long been a pioneer in technological higher education. Three decades after it was created, the university's distinctive outcomes-oriented approach to education is being viewed as a model for reform at the national level, and WPI is recognized as the leader in global technological education. WPI is fully accredited by the New England Association of Schools and Colleges.

WPI awarded its first advanced degree in 1893. Today, most of its academic departments offer master's and doctoral programs and support leading-edge research in a broad range of fields. Through the years, WPI has earned a reputation for its academic excellence, its responsiveness to the needs of the marketplace, and for its faculty of renowned academicians and industry experts who are practitioners in their fields.

DISTANCE LEARNING PROGRAM

In 1979, WPI's commitment to active, lifelong learning prompted the creation of the Advanced Distance Learning Network (ADLN), a partnership between several academic departments and WPI's Instructional Media Center. ADLN programs empower working professionals to continue to grow within their chosen field without having to make repeated trips to the WPI campus.

DELIVERY MEDIA

ADLN courses consist of the same content and materials as on-campus class meetings. Courses originate in one of WPI's studio classrooms and are delivered to ADLN students via interactive compressed video, expressed-mail videotapes, or the World Wide Web, depending on the facilities available to the student. Materials such as books, handouts, and supplemental readings are sent by express mail, fax, or e-mail or are posted on the World Wide Web. An e-mail account and access to the World Wide Web are required for participation in an ADLN course.

PROGRAMS OF STUDY

ADLN offers a Master of Business Administration (M.B.A.), a Master of Science (M.S.) in fire protection engineering, and a Master of Science (M.S.) in civil and environmental engineering. In addition to these degree options, WPI's ADLN also offers numerous graduate certificate programs in these areas.

The M.B.A. program focuses on the management of technology and features a highly integrative curriculum that emphasizes leadership, ethics, communication, and a global perspective. Concentration areas include MIS, technology marketing, technological innovation, entrepreneurship, operations management, and management of technology. This 49-credit M.B.A. program may be reduced to as few as 31 credits with an appropriate academic background. A customized 15-credit graduate certificate program in management is also available.

The Fire Protection Engineering (FPE) program is oriented toward developing a well-rounded professional who can be successful in a competitive career environment. The curriculum is designed to teach students current standards of practice and expose them to state-of-the-art research literature that will support future practices. In addition to the ten-course (30-credit) M.S. option, professionals with a B.S. degree in an engineering, engineering technology, or science field who complete four thematically related FPE courses can receive a graduate certificate in FPE. Master's degree holders may instead opt to complete five thematically related courses for an advanced certificate in FPE.

The Civil and Environmental Engineering programs are arranged to meet the interests and objectives of individual students and their employers. The curriculum focuses on today's environmental issues and their relationship to engineering, business, and law. The 33-credit Master of Science degree is a professional practice–oriented degree designed to meet the continuing challenges faced by practicing environmental engineers. A four-course graduate certificate is also available through ADLN.

Credits earned in any WPI certificate program can later be applied toward an advanced degree, contingent upon formal admission to graduate study. A maximum of two courses taken at WPI as a nondegree-seeking student may be applied for credit to the M.B.A. program; a maximum of four courses taken at WPI as a nondegree-seeking student may be applied for credit to an M.S. in fire protection engineering or an M.S. in civil and environmental engineering.

SPECIAL PROGRAMS

ADLN and appropriate academic personnel are always willing to consider the addition of new programs for which there is sufficient interest.

STUDENT SERVICES

Academic advisers are assigned upon admission. Online library services are free, and reference services are available by phone or e-mail. Dial-up UNIX accounts (for e-mail, etc.) and career placement and counseling are available for matriculated students. Books can be ordered toll-free from the WPI bookstore (888-WPI-BOOKS) and are typically delivered one to three days after ordering.

CREDIT OPTIONS

The M.B.A. program allows 18 foundation-level credits to be waived for those with appropriate academic backgrounds, either via straight waivers for those with appropriate course work completed within the past six years with a grade of B or better

or via waiver exams. The M.B.A. program, the M.S. in fire protection engineering, and the M.S. in civil and environmental engineering allow students to transfer up to 9 credits from graduate-level course work at other schools. Graduate and Advanced Certificate programs require all credits to come from WPI.

FACULTY

Management has 26 faculty members (20 full-time members and 6 part-time members), 24 of whom have Ph.D. degrees. Fire protection engineering has 5 full-time faculty members, all with Ph.D. degrees, and 2 part-time professors. Civil and environmental engineering has 13 full-time faculty members, all with Ph.D. degrees, and 8 part-time professors.

ADMISSION

To be considered for admission to the M.B.A. program or a graduate certificate in management, an applicant must hold a B.S. degree and possess the analytic aptitude necessary to complete a technology-oriented program. Admission to WPI's M.S. programs or graduate certificate options in fire protection engineering or civil and environmental engineering require an applicant to hold a B.S. degree in an appropriate field of engineering, engineering technology, or science and meet department-specific admission standards. Conditional admission is available if all requirements are not met at the time of application.

TUITION AND FEES

Tuition is $703 per credit hour ($2109 per 3-credit course) for all programs in the 2000–01 academic year. Students wishing to earn Continuing Education Units (CEU) instead of graduate credit may opt to audit courses at half tuition.

FINANCIAL AID

Loan-based aid is available only through special arrangements. Students must be registered on at least a half-time basis (two courses per semester).

APPLYING

All departments require standard forms, official transcripts, and a $50 application fee. Management degree programs also require three letters of recommendation and GMAT scores. All international applicants must submit TOEFL scores. GRE scores are not required but may be substituted for the GMAT scores when applying for a graduate certificate in management.

CONTACT

Pennie S. Turgeon, Director
Advanced Distance Learning
  Network
Worcester Polytechnic Institute
100 Institute Road
Worcester, Massachusetts 01609-
  2280
Telephone: 508-831-5810
Fax: 508-831-5881
E-mail: adln@wpi.edu
Web site: http://www.wpi.edu/
  Academics/ADLN

INDEXES

INDEX OF INSTITUTIONS OFFERING DEGREE AND CERTIFICATE PROGRAMS

UC=Undergraduate Certificate; GC=Graduate Certificate; A=Associate; B=Bachelor's; M=Master's; D=Doctorate

Accounting
Alaska Pacific University (B)
Athabasca University (UC)
Caldwell College (B)
Central Community College–Grand Island Campus (UC, A)
Central Washington University (B)
Champlain College (UC, A)
City University (UC, B)
Cleary College (A, B)
Coastline Community College (A)
College of West Virginia (A, B)
Elizabethtown College (UC)
Golden Gate University (GC)
Graceland College (B)
Harcourt Learning Direct (A)
Herkimer County Community College (A)
Ivy Tech State College–North Central (UC)
Ivy Tech State College–Wabash Valley (A)
Lakeland College (B)
Lake Superior State University (B)
Madison Area Technical College (A)
Marywood University (B)
New Hampshire College (UC)
Northcentral Technical College (A)
Northwestern College (A)
Northwest Missouri State University (B)
Northwest Technical College (A)
Regents College (B)
Robert Morris College (B)
Saint Mary-of-the-Woods College (B)
State University of New York Institute of Technology at Utica/Rome (M)
Strayer University (A, B, M)
University Alliance (B)
University of Sarasota (D)
University of the Incarnate Word (B)
Upper Iowa University (B)
Utah State University (B)

Administrative and Secretarial Services, Other
Northwestern College (A)
University of Alaska Southeast, Sitka Campus (UC)

Administrative Assistant/Secretarial Science, General
Chippewa Valley Technical College (UC)
College of West Virginia (UC, A)
George Washington University (UC)
Marywood University (UC)
Memorial University of Newfoundland (UC)
North Country Community College (UC, A)
Northwestern College (A)
Southwestern Adventist University (A, B)
Southwest Missouri State University (M)

Adult and Continuing Teacher Education
Drake University (M)
Indiana University System (M)
newGraduate Schools (UC)

North Carolina Agricultural and Technical State University (M)
Pennsylvania State University University Park Campus (M)
University of Calgary (M)
University of New Brunswick (UC, B, M)
University of Saskatchewan (UC)

Advertising
Syracuse University (M)

Aerospace, Aeronautical and Astronautical Engineering
Auburn University (M)
Embry-Riddle Aeronautical University (M)
Embry-Riddle Aeronautical University, Extended Campus (M)
Illinois Institute of Technology (M)
Stanford University (M)
State University of New York at Buffalo (M, GC)
University of Alabama (M)
University of Colorado at Boulder (M)
University of Texas at Arlington (M)
University of Washington (B, M)
Virginia Polytechnic Institute and State University (M)

Agricultural Business and Management, General
Iowa State University of Science and Technology (B)

Agricultural Business/Agribusiness Operations
Utah State University (B)

Agricultural Economics
University of Florida (M)

Agricultural Engineering
Central Missouri State University (D)
University of Idaho (M)

Agriculture/Agricultural Sciences, General
Colorado State University (M)
Iowa State University of Science and Technology (M)
Oregon State University (B)
University of Saskatchewan (UC)
Washington State University (B)

Agronomy and Crop Science
Iowa State University of Science and Technology (M)

Air Transportation Workers, Other
Indiana State University (A)

Alcohol/Drug Abuse Counseling
Bethany College of the Assemblies of God (B)
Central Washington University (B)
Pennsylvania State University University Park Campus (M)
Tompkins Cortland Community College (A)
University of Great Falls (A)

American Indian/Native American Studies
University of Denver (GC)

American Studies/Civilization
Saint Joseph's College (UC, B)

Animal Sciences, General
Kansas State University (B, M)
Northwestern College (A)
Purdue University (M)

Architecture
Atlantic International University (B, D)
Instituto Tecnológico y de Estudios Superiores de Monterrey, Campus Monterrey (M)
newGraduate Schools (M)

Art Therapy
Norwich University (M)
Saint Mary-of-the-Woods College (M)

Art, General
Atlantic Union College (B)
Mary Baldwin College (B)
Rochester College (A)

Arts Management
Golden Gate University (GC)
Goucher College (M)
University of Massachusetts Amherst (UC)

Astronomy
Atlantic International University (M)

Athletic Training and Sports Medicine
United States Sports Academy (M)

Atmospheric Sciences and Meteorology
Mississippi State University (B)

Audiology/Hearing Sciences
Central Michigan University (D)
University of Florida (D)
University of New Mexico (B)

Aviation and Airway Science
Embry-Riddle Aeronautical University (B)
Embry-Riddle Aeronautical University, Extended Campus (A, B)
Everglades College (A, B)
Providence College and Theological Seminary (B)
Regents College (A)

Aviation Management
College of West Virginia (UC, A)
Embry-Riddle Aeronautical University (B)
Embry-Riddle Aeronautical University, Extended Campus (A, B)
University of Tennessee Space Institute (M)

Aviation Systems and Avionics Maintenance Technologist/Technician
College of Aeronautics (A, B)

Index of Institutions Offering Degree and Certificate Programs

Banking and Financial Support Services
City University (M)
Mercy College (M)

Bible/Biblical Studies
Arlington Baptist College (B)
Bethany College of the Assemblies of God (B)
Briercrest Bible College (UC)
Columbia International University (M, GC)
Eugene Bible College (UC, B)
Florida Baptist Theological College (B)
Global University of the Assemblies of God (A, B, M)
Hillsdale Free Will Baptist College (UC)
Hobe Sound Bible College (A)
Johnson Bible College (M)
LIFE Bible College (A)
Moody Bible Institute (UC, A, B)
New Orleans Baptist Theological Seminary (A)
Northwestern College (UC)
Prairie Bible College (UC, A, B, GC)
Reformed Theological Seminary (GC)
Shasta Bible College (UC, A, B)
Southern Christian University (B, M)
Taylor University, World Wide Campus (A)
Temple Baptist Seminary (UC, M)
Tennessee Temple University (A, B)
Wheaton College (GC)

Bioengineering and Biomedical Engineering
Oklahoma State University (M)

Biological and Physical Sciences
Loma Linda University (A)

Biological Sciences/Life Sciences, Other
Rensselaer Polytechnic Institute (GC)

Biology
Atlantic International University (B, M, D)
Cleveland State University (GC)
Mary Baldwin College (B)

Biology, General
Ohio University (A)

Broadcast Journalism
Mississippi State University (UC)
Southwestern Adventist University (B)

Business
Bellevue Community College (A)
Bethany College of the Assemblies of God (B)
California College for Health Sciences (M)
California State University, Dominguez Hills (UC)
Cerro Coso Community College (A)
College of West Virginia (A, B)
Colorado Electronic Community College (A)
Everglades College (B)
Florence-Darlington Technical College (A)
Instituto Tecnológico y de Estudios Superiores de Monterrey, Campus Monterrey (M)
Maysville Community College (A)
National University (M)
newGraduate Schools (UC, M)
Southern California University for Professional Studies (D)
Temple University (M)
Touro International University (UC, B, M)
United States Open University (B, M)
University of California Extension (GC)
University of California, Los Angeles (UC)
University of Houston–Victoria (M)
University of Sarasota (UC)
University of Wisconsin–Platteville (UC)

Business Administration and Management
Alaska Pacific University (B)
Bergen Community College (A)
Concordia University Wisconsin (M)
David N. Myers College (B)
Forsyth Technical Community College (A)
Mary Baldwin College (B)
National University (B)
Regent University (M)
University Alliance (B)

Business Administration and Management, General
Acadia University (UC)
Adelphi University (B, M)
Alaska Pacific University (M)
American College (GC)
American Military University (B, M)
Anne Arundel Community College (A)
Athabasca University (UC, B, M, GC)
Atlantic Cape Community College (A)
Atlantic Union College (B)
Auburn University (M)
Baker College-Center for Graduate Studies (A, B, M)
Ball State University (A, M)
Barton County Community College (UC)
Bellevue University (B, M)
Bergen Community College (A)
Berkeley College (A)
Brenau University (M)
Brookdale Community College (A)
Bucks County Community College (A)
Burlington County College (A)
Caldwell College (B)
California College for Health Sciences (M)
California National University for Advanced Studies (B, M)
California State University, Dominguez Hills (M)
California State University, Los Angeles (UC)
Capella University (M, D)
Cardinal Stritch University (P)
Catawba Valley Community College (UC)
Cayuga County Community College (A)
Central Community College–Grand Island Campus (UC, A)
Central Michigan University (B, M)
Central Washington University (B, M)
Cerro Coso Community College (A)
Chadron State College (M)
Champlain College (UC, A)
Christopher Newport University (M)
City University (A, B, M, GC)
Clarkson College (B)
Cleary College (A, B)
College of West Virginia (UC, A, B)
Colorado State University (M)
Columbus State Community College (A)
Community College of Baltimore County (A)
Dallas Baptist University (B)
Dawson Community College (A)
De Anza College (UC)
Drake University (M)
Drexel University (M)
Duke University (M)
Duquesne University (M)
Eastern Oregon University (B)
East Tennessee State University (M)
Eckerd College (B)
Elizabethtown College (B)
Everglades College (B)
Fayetteville Technical Community College (A)
Fielding Institute (M)
Florida Gulf Coast University (M)
Georgia Southern University (B, M)
Graceland College (B)
Grand View College (B)
Hamilton College (A)

Harcourt Learning Direct (A)
Hawkeye Community College (A)
Heriot-Watt University (M)
Herkimer County Community College (A)
Hill College of the Hill Junior College District (UC)
Indiana Institute of Technology (A, B)
Indiana State University (B)
Indiana University System (M)
Indiana Wesleyan University (M)
Instituto Tecnológico y de Estudios Superiores de Monterrey, Campus Monterrey (M)
ISIM University (M)
Jones International University (M)
Judson College (B)
Keller Graduate School of Management (M)
Kent State University (B)
Lakeland College (B)
Lake Superior State University (B)
Lehigh Carbon Community College (A)
Lehigh University (M)
Liberty University (M)
Madonna University (B, M)
Maharishi University of Management (M)
Marist College (M)
Marylhurst University (B)
Marywood University (B)
Memorial University of Newfoundland (UC, B)
Mercy College (B, M)
Morehead State University (B, M)
Mountain Empire Community College (A)
Mount Saint Vincent University (UC, B)
Mount Wachusett Community College (A)
National American University (B)
National Technological University (M)
National University (M)
New Hampshire College (UC, M)
New York University (M)
Northampton County Area Community College (A)
North Central Texas College (A)
North Central University (B, M, D)
North Country Community College (A)
North Dakota State University (M)
Northeastern State University (B)
Northern Michigan University (B)
Northern Virginia Community College (A)
North Harris College (A)
Northwestern College (A)
Northwest Missouri State University (B)
Northwood University (B)
Oklahoma State University (M)
Old Dominion University (B, M)
Open Learning Agency (B)
Parkland College (A)
Park University (B)
Peirce College (A, B)
Pennsylvania State University University Park Campus (UC, A)
Pitt Community College (A)
Portland State University (M)
Prince George's Community College (UC, A)
Professional Development Europe Limited (M)
Providence College and Theological Seminary (B)
Purdue University (M)
Regents College (A)
Regent University (M)
Regis University (B, M)
Rensselaer Polytechnic Institute (M, GC)
Robert Morris College (UC, B)
Rochester College (B)
Rogers State University (A)
Roger Williams University (B)
Royal Roads University (M)
Saint Joseph's College (UC, A, B)
Saint Leo University (B)
Saint Mary-of-the-Woods College (B)
St. Mary's University of San Antonio (M)

Salve Regina University (UC, M)
Scottsdale Community College (A)
Sinclair Community College (A)
Southeast Community College, Beatrice Campus (A)
Southern California University for Professional Studies (A, B, M, D)
Southern Oregon University (M)
Southern Utah University (B)
Southwestern Adventist University (B)
Southwest Missouri State University (M)
State University of New York Empire State College (A, B)
Stephens College (B, M)
Stevens Institute of Technology (M)
Strayer University (A, B, M)
Suffolk University (M)
Syracuse University (M)
Temple University (B)
Texas A&M University–Commerce (M)
Texas Tech University (B)
Thomas Edison State College (A, B, M)
Tiffin University (M)
Touro International University (D)
Troy State University (M)
Troy State University Montgomery (A, B)
Université Laval (UC)
University Alliance (B)
University of Alaska Southeast (B)
University of Baltimore (M)
University of California, Berkeley (GC)
University of California Extension (GC)
University of Colorado at Colorado Springs (M)
University of Colorado at Denver (M)
University of Denver (GC)
University of Findlay (B, M)
University of Florida (M)
University of Great Falls (A, B)
University of Management and Technology (M, D)
University of Maryland University College (B, M)
University of Massachusetts Amherst (M)
University of Missouri–St. Louis (M)
University of Montana–Missoula (M)
University of Nebraska–Lincoln (M)
University of North Alabama (M)
University of North Carolina at Pembroke (M)
University of Notre Dame (UC, M)
University of Phoenix (B, M)
University of Pittsburgh (M)
University of Richmond (UC)
University of Sarasota (B, M, D)
University of South Carolina (M)
University of Tennessee (M)
University of Tennessee at Chattanooga (M)
University of Tennessee at Martin (M)
University of Texas at Dallas (M)
University of Texas at El Paso (M)
University of Texas of the Permian Basin (M)
University of Texas–Pan American (M)
University of Texas System (M)
University of the Incarnate Word (B)
University of Vermont (M)
University of Waterloo (M)
University of Wisconsin–Platteville (B)
University of Wisconsin–Whitewater (M)
University of Wyoming (B, M)
Upper Iowa University (B)
Utah State University (B)
Valdosta State University (B)
Vincennes University (A)
Virginia Polytechnic Institute and State University (M)
Walden University (D)
Washington State University (B)
Western Baptist College (B)
Western Illinois University (M)
Western Piedmont Community College (A)

Westmoreland County Community College (A)
West Virginia University (M)
Worcester Polytechnic Institute (M, GC)

Business Administration and Management, Other

City University (M, GC)
Cleary College (A, B)
George Washington University (UC, M)
Griggs University (B)
Instituto Tecnológico y de Estudios Superiores de Monterrey, Campus Monterrey (M)
Keller Graduate School of Management (M)
Madison Area Technical College (UC)
Mississippi State University (M)
New Jersey Institute of Technology (GC)
North Country Community College (A)
Northwestern College (A)
Pennsylvania State University University Park Campus (UC)
Regis University (M)
Rochester Institute of Technology (UC)
Southern Christian University (B)
Stevens Institute of Technology (M, GC)
Syracuse University (M)
University of California Extension (GC)
University of Dallas (M, GC)
University of Washington (UC)
University of Wisconsin–Platteville (UC, M)
Western Carolina University (M)

Business Communications

Jones International University (B, M)
Marywood University (UC)
Old Dominion University (B)
Rochester College (B)
Seton Hall University (M)
Southwestern Adventist University (B)
University of Baltimore (B)

Business Computer Facilities Operator

Vincennes University (UC)

Business Computer Programming/Programmer

Bellevue Community College (UC)
Northwestern College (A)

Business Management and Administrative Services, Other

American College (UC, GC)
Capitol College (B, M)
Cleary College (A, B)
Instituto Tecnológico y de Estudios Superiores de Monterrey, Campus Monterrey (UC)
Newman University (B)
Pennsylvania State University University Park Campus (UC)
University of North Texas (M)

Business Marketing and Marketing Management

American Military University (B)
Bucks County Community College (A)
Caldwell College (B)
City University (B, M, GC)
Cleary College (A, B)
College of DuPage (UC)
Harcourt Learning Direct (A)
Instituto Tecnológico y de Estudios Superiores de Monterrey, Campus Monterrey (M)
Lakeland College (B)
Mary Baldwin College (B)
McDowell Technical Community College (A)
Mercy College (M)
Northwestern College (A)
Pennsylvania State University University Park Campus (UC)
Regents College (B)

St. Cloud State University (B)
Saint Mary-of-the-Woods College (B)
Strayer University (A)
Thomas Edison State College (A, B)
University of California, Berkeley (GC)
University of California Extension (GC)
University of California, Riverside (GC)
University of Phoenix (B)
University of Sarasota (D)
University of the Incarnate Word (B)
University of Wisconsin–Whitewater (M)
University System of Georgia (UC)
Upper Iowa University (B)
Walsh College of Accountancy and Business Administration (UC)
Xavier University of Louisiana (UC)

Business Systems Analysis and Design

Saybrook Graduate School (M, D)

Business, General

Athabasca University (B)
Bryant and Stratton Business Institute (A)
Bucks County Community College (UC)
Buena Vista University (B)
Caldwell College (B)
Central Washington University (B)
Champlain College (UC, A, B)
Charles Stewart Mott Community College (A)
City University (UC)
Cleary College (A)
Coastline Community College (A)
College of West Virginia (A, B)
Eastern Oregon University (B)
Judson College (B)
Kansas State University (B)
Lansing Community College (A)
Liberty University (B)
Marywood University (UC)
Memorial University of Newfoundland (B)
New Mexico State University (B)
New York Institute of Technology (B, M)
Ohio University–Southern Campus (M)
Oklahoma City University (B)
Parkland College (A)
Pennsylvania State University University Park Campus (UC)
Purdue University (M)
Red Rocks Community College (A)
Regents College (A, B)
Saint Mary-of-the-Woods College (A)
Salt Lake Community College (A)
Salve Regina University (B)
Seton Hall University (M)
Southwestern Assemblies of God University (B)
Troy State University (A)
University of California, Berkeley (GC)
University of Dallas (M, GC)
University of Management and Technology (M)
University of St. Francis (M)
University of Toronto (UC)
University of Wisconsin Extension (UC)
Upper Iowa University (A, B)
Utah State University (B)
Vincennes University (A)
Wayne County Community College District (A)
West Virginia Wesleyan College (UC)

Business/Managerial Economics

Cayuga County Community College (B)

Canadian Studies

Memorial University of Newfoundland (UC)
University of Waterloo (B)

Chemical Engineering

Atlantic International University (B, M, D)
Auburn University (M)
Colorado State University (M)

Chemical Engineering (continued)
Illinois Institute of Technology (M)
Kansas State University (M)
Lehigh University (M)
Mississippi State University (M, D)
National Technological University (M, GC)
University of South Carolina (M, D)

Chemistry, General
Atlantic International University (B, M, D)
Illinois Institute of Technology (M, GC)
Lehigh University (M)
Mary Baldwin College (B)
University of Central Florida (M)

Child Care Provider/Assistant
Lakeshore Technical College (UC)

Child Growth, Care and Development Studies
Concordia University at St. Paul (B, M)
Ivy Tech State College–Central Indiana (UC, A)
Ivy Tech State College–Columbus (UC, A)
Ivy Tech State College–Eastcentral (UC, A)
Ivy Tech State College–Kokomo (UC, A)
Ivy Tech State College–North Central (UC, A)
Ivy Tech State College–Northwest (UC, A)
Ivy Tech State College–Southcentral (UC, A)
Ivy Tech State College–Southeast (UC, A)
Ivy Tech State College–Southwest (UC, A)
Ivy Tech State College–Whitewater (UC, A)
Lakeshore Technical College (UC)

Chinese Language and Literature
University of Toronto (UC)

Chiropractic (D.C., D.C.M.)
Keiser College (A)

Civil Engineering, General
Atlantic International University (B, M, D)
Auburn University (M)
Colorado State University (M)
Kansas State University (M)
Mississippi State University (M, D)
Purdue University (M)
State University of New York at Buffalo (UC, M)
University of Alabama (M)
University of Idaho (M)
University of South Carolina (M)
Worcester Polytechnic Institute (M, GC)

Civil Engineering, Other
Worcester Polytechnic Institute (M, GC)

Civil Engineering/Civil Technology/Technician
Harcourt Learning Direct (A)
Old Dominion University (B)

Classics and Classical Languages and Literatures
University of Waterloo (B)

Clinical Psychology
Fielding Institute (D)

Clothing/Apparel and Textile Studies
North Carolina State University (M, GC)
University of Nebraska–Lincoln (M)

College/Postsecondary Student Counseling and Personnel Services
Athabasca University (UC)
Memorial University of Newfoundland (UC)
University of California, Los Angeles (UC)

Communication Disorders, General
California State University, Northridge (M)
West Chester University of Pennsylvania (M)

Communications
St. Cloud State University (B)
University of California, Berkeley (GC)

Communications, General
Athabasca University (B)
Atlantic International University (B, M, D)
Atlantic Union College (B)
Caldwell College (B)
Elizabethtown College (B)
Mary Baldwin College (B)
Montana State University–Billings (B)
Regent University (M, D)
Thomas Edison State College (B)
University of Florida (M)
University of Maryland University College (B)
University of Southern Indiana (A)

Communications, Other
New Jersey Institute of Technology (UC)
Southern Polytechnic State University (M)

Community Health Liaison
California College for Health Sciences (M)
Central Washington University (B)
University of Alaska Fairbanks (UC, A)

Community Organization, Resources and Services
Cayuga County Community College (B)
North Country Community College (UC)
State University of New York Empire State College (A, B)
University College of Cape Breton (B)
University of Calgary (B)
Vincennes University (UC)

Community Psychology
New York Institute of Technology (B)
North Country Community College (A)
Trinity College of Vermont (M, GC)

Comparative Literature
Cerro Coso Community College (A)

Computer and Information Sciences
Bucks County Community College (UC)
CTS University, Inc. (UC, A)
East Carolina University (GC)
Macon Technical Institute (UC)
Northwestern Technical Institute (UC)
Palomar College (UC)
University of Hawaii at Manoa (B, M)

Computer and Information Sciences, General
Athabasca University (B)
Borough of Manhattan Community College of the City University of New York (UC)
Bryant and Stratton Business Institute (A)
Caldwell College (B)
Capella University (B)
Capitol College (B)
Central Community College–Grand Island Campus (B)
Champlain College (UC, A)
City University (UC, B, GC)
College of West Virginia (A, B)
Columbia University (M, P, GC)
Columbus State University (M)
CTS University, Inc. (UC, A)
East Carolina University (B)
Everglades College (B)
Florida State University (B)
Graceland College (B)
Harcourt Learning Direct (A)
Harvard University (M)
Illinois Institute of Technology (GC)
Indiana University System (UC)

Instituto Tecnológico y de Estudios Superiores de Monterrey, Campus Monterrey (M)
Judson College (B)
Keiser College (A)
Lakeland College (B)
Macon Technical Institute (UC)
Michigan State University (UC)
Mississippi State University (UC)
Montana State University–Billings (M)
Mount Saint Vincent University (UC)
New Hampshire College (UC)
New York University (GC)
Northcentral Technical College (A)
Northern Virginia Community College (A)
Nova Southeastern University (M, D)
Peirce College (A, B)
Pennsylvania State University University Park Campus (UC)
Quest College (UC)
Regents College (A, B)
Rensselaer Polytechnic Institute (M, GC)
Rochester Community and Technical College (UC)
Rochester Institute of Technology (M)
Rogers State University (B)
Saint Mary-of-the-Woods College (B)
Southwestern Adventist University (A, B)
Southwest Missouri State University (M)
Southwest Missouri State University–West Plains (M)
Southwest Virginia Community College (UC)
Stanford University (M)
Strayer University (UC, A, B)
Touro International University (B, M)
United States Open University (B)
University Alliance (B)
University of Alaska Fairbanks (UC, A)
University of Alaska Southeast, Sitka Campus (UC, A, GC)
University of California, Berkeley (GC)
University of California Extension (GC)
University of California, Santa Cruz (UC)
University of Colorado at Denver (M)
University of Dallas (M, GC)
University of Denver (M, GC)
University of Hawaii at Manoa (UC)
University of Houston–Victoria (B)
University of Illinois at Urbana–Champaign (M)
University of Maryland University College (B)
University of Massachusetts Lowell (UC)
University of New Hampshire (M)
University of Phoenix (M)
University of the Incarnate Word (B)
University of Washington (UC)
Utah State University (B, M)
Western Governors University (UC, A)
Wytheville Community College (UC)

Computer Engineering
Auburn University (M)
Carnegie Mellon University (UC, M)
Elizabethtown College (B)
Florida International University (M)
Illinois Institute of Technology (GC)
Iowa State University of Science and Technology (M)
Kansas State University (M)
National Technological University (M, GC)
Northwestern Business College (UC)
Quest College (UC)
Rensselaer Polytechnic Institute (M, GC)
Rochester Institute of Technology (M)
Southern Methodist University (M)
University of California, Santa Cruz (M)
University of Houston–Clear Lake (M)
University of Idaho (M)
University of South Carolina (M, D)
University of Southern California (M)

University of Texas at Arlington (M)
University of Texas System (M)
University of Wisconsin–Madison (M)
Virginia Polytechnic Institute and State University (M)
Western Governors University (UC, A)
Western Washington University (UC)
West Virginia University (M)

Computer Programming
Champlain College (UC, A)
City University (UC)
Cochise College (UC)
CTS University, Inc. (UC, A)
Kent State University (UC)
Loyola University Chicago (UC)
McDowell Technical Community College (UC)
New Jersey Institute of Technology (UC, GC)
Northeastern University (UC)
University of California, Los Angeles (GC)
University of Massachusetts Lowell (UC)
University of Washington (UC)

Computer Science
Acadia University (UC)
American Institute for Computer Sciences (B, M)
Atlantic International University (B, M, D)
Atlantic Union College (B)
Ball State University (M)
California National University for Advanced Studies (B)
California State University, Chico (M)
Colorado State University (M)
Grantham College of Engineering (A, B)
Illinois Institute of Technology (M)
Instituto Tecnológico y de Estudios Superiores de Monterrey, Campus Monterrey (M)
Mercy College (B)
National Technological University (M, GC)
New Jersey Institute of Technology (B)
Nova Southeastern University (M, D)
Oklahoma State University (M)
Old Dominion University (M)
Rensselaer Polytechnic Institute (M)
Rogers State University (A)
Southern Methodist University (M)
Southern Polytechnic State University (M)
Southwestern Adventist University (B)
Stevens Institute of Technology (M, GC)
Thomas Edison State College (A)
Université Laval (UC)
University of Colorado at Boulder (M)
University of Great Falls (B)
University of Houston (M)
University of Idaho (UC, M, D)
University of Iowa (M)
University of Massachusetts Amherst (M)
University of Southern California (M)
University of Texas System (M)

Computer Systems Analysis
University of Maryland University College (M)

Construction and Building Finishers and Managers, Other
California State University, San Marcos (UC)
Florida International University (M)
Illinois Institute of Technology (GC)
University of Washington (UC)

Construction/Building Technology
Clemson University (M)

Construction/Building Technology/ Technician
Macon Technical Institute (UC)

Corrections/Correctional Administration
Northeast Wisconsin Technical College (A)
Salve Regina University (UC)

Counseling Psychology
Providence College and Theological Seminary (M)
Rochester College (B)
Ryerson Polytechnic University (GC)
Seton Hall University (M)
University of Great Falls (B)
University of Sarasota (D)

Counselor Education Counseling and Guidance Services
Buena Vista University (M)
City University (M)
Columbia International University (M)
Concordia University Wisconsin (M)
Liberty University (M)
Mississippi State University (M)
St. Mary's University of San Antonio (M)
Southern Christian University (M, D)
University College of Cape Breton (GC)

Court Reporter
Lakeshore Technical College (A)
Lenoir Community College (A)

Criminal Justice and Corrections
Cerro Coso Community College (A)
Indiana State University (UC)
Loyola University New Orleans (B)
Taylor University, World Wide Campus (A)
University of Wyoming (B)

Criminal Justice Studies
American Military University (B)
Athabasca University (B)
Atlantic International University (B, M, D)
Bellevue University (B)
Caldwell College (B)
Central Community College–Grand Island Campus (UC)
Central Missouri State University (M)
Central Washington University (B)
City University (M, GC)
College of West Virginia (B)
Concordia University at St. Paul (B)
Elizabethtown College (B)
Florence-Darlington Technical College (A)
Florida Gulf Coast University (B)
Herkimer County Community College (A)
Judson College (B)
Kaplan College (B)
Lake Superior State University (B)
Mansfield University of Pennsylvania (A)
Michigan State University (M)
Mount Wachusett Community College (A)
National University (B)
New York Institute of Technology (B)
Northcentral Technical College (A)
North Central Texas College (A)
North Country Community College (A)
Northern Michigan University (B)
Old Dominion University (B)
Park University (B)
Rochester College (B)
Roger Williams University (B)
Saint Joseph's College (B)
Sauk Valley Community College (A)
Southern California University for Professional Studies (A, B, M)
Southwestern Adventist University (B)
Troy State University (M)
University of Baltimore (B)
University of Great Falls (A, B)
University of Tennessee at Chattanooga (M)
University of Texas of the Permian Basin (M)
University of Wisconsin–Platteville (M, GC)

Washburn University of Topeka (B)
Washington State University (B)
Weber State University (A)

Criminal Justice/Law Enforcement Administration
City University (B)

Criminology
Florida State University (M)
Indiana State University (B, M)
Memorial University of Newfoundland (UC)
Snow College (A)

Culinary Arts/Chef Training
Central Arizona College (A)
Keiser College (A)

Curriculum and Instruction
City University (M)
College of St. Scholastica (M)
College of the Southwest (M)
Concordia University Wisconsin (M)
Coppin State College (M)
Florida Gulf Coast University (M)
University College of Cape Breton (GC)
University of Nebraska–Lincoln (D)
University of Washington (UC)

Data Processing Technology/Technician
Charles Stewart Mott Community College (A)
Northwest Technical College (A)
Regents College (B)
Rio Salado College (A)
Thomas Edison State College (A)
University of Washington (UC)

Dental Hygienist
Armstrong Atlantic State University (B)
Northcentral Technical College (A)
Northern Arizona University (B)
Pennsylvania College of Technology (B)

Design and Applied Arts, Other
Syracuse University (M)

Design and Visual Communications
Open Learning Agency (B)

Diagnostic Medical Sonography
College of West Virginia (UC)

Dietetics/Human Nutritional Services
Auburn University (UC)
Barton County Community College (UC)
Central Arizona College (UC, A)
Kansas State University (M)
Pennsylvania State University University Park Campus (UC)

Divinity/Ministry (B.D., M.Div.)
Assemblies of God Theological Seminary (M)
Atlantic Union College (B)
Bethel Seminary (M)
Columbia International University (M, D)
Crown College (B)
Grand Rapids Baptist Seminary (M)
Griggs University (A)
Judson College (B)
Liberty University (M)
Mid-America Bible College (A, B)
New Orleans Baptist Theological Seminary (B, M)
Prairie Bible College (B)
Providence College and Theological Seminary (M, D)
Rochester College (B)
St. Francis Xavier University (GC)
St. Mary's University of San Antonio (M)
Southern Christian University (B, D)
Southwestern Assemblies of God University (B)

National Technological University (M, GC)
Northeastern University (M)
Oklahoma State University (M)
Purdue University (M)
Rensselaer Polytechnic Institute (M, GC)
Southern Illinois University Carbondale (B)
Southern Methodist University (M)
Stanford University (M)
State University of New York at Buffalo (M, GC)
University of Alabama (M)
University of Colorado at Boulder (M)
University of Florida (M)
University of Houston (M)
University of Idaho (M)
University of Illinois at Urbana–Champaign (M)
University of Maine (UC)
University of Massachusetts Amherst (M)
University of South Carolina (M, D)
University of Southern California (M)
University of Texas at Arlington (M)
University of Wisconsin–Madison (M)
Virginia Polytechnic Institute and State University (M)

Electrical, Electronics and Communications Engineering
Illinois Institute of Technology (GC)

Electrician
Colorado Electronic Community College (A)

Electroencephalograph Technology/Technician
California College for Health Sciences (A)

Elementary Particle Physics
Illinois Institute of Technology (GC)

Elementary Teacher Education
Atlantic Union College (B)
Ball State University (M)
Central Washington University (B)
College of West Virginia (A)
Fitchburg State College (M)
Fort Hays State University (B)
Graceland College (B)
Northern Michigan University (B)
Saint Mary-of-the-Woods College (B)
South Florida Community College (B)
Southwestern Adventist University (B)
Southwest Missouri State University (B, M)
University of Alaska Southeast (GC)
University of Alaska Southeast, Sitka Campus (GC)
University of Pittsburgh (M)
University of Tennessee at Chattanooga (M)
Utah State University (M)

Emergency Medical Technology/Technician
American College of Prehospital Medicine (A, B)
Chattanooga State Technical Community College (A)
Dalhousie University (UC)
George Washington University (B)
University of Maryland, Baltimore County (M)

Engineering
Illinois Institute of Technology (M)
Wright State University (M)

Engineering Science
Broome Community College (A)
Colorado State University (M)
Rensselaer Polytechnic Institute (M)

Engineering, General
Arizona State University (M)
California National University for Advanced Studies (B, M)
Columbia University (M, P, GC)

Kettering University (M)
Michigan Technological University (B)
New Mexico State University (M)
North Carolina Agricultural and Technical State University (M)
North Carolina State University (B, M)
Northern Arizona University (M)
Northern Virginia Community College (A)
Purdue University (M)
University of Alabama (M)
University of Arizona (M)
University of Illinois at Chicago (M)
University of Illinois at Urbana–Champaign (M)
University of New Hampshire (M)
University of South Florida (M)
University of Texas at Arlington (M)
University of Virginia (M, D)
University of Wisconsin–Madison (M, P)
University of Wisconsin–Platteville (M)
Virginia Polytechnic Institute and State University (M)

Engineering, Other
Illinois Institute of Technology (M, GC)
Pennsylvania College of Technology (B)
Pennsylvania State University University Park Campus (UC, M)
Stevens Institute of Technology (M, GC)
University of California, Santa Cruz (UC)
University of Michigan (M)
University of Texas System (GC)

Engineering-Related Technologies
Chattanooga State Technical Community College (A)
University of Central Florida (B)
University of North Carolina at Charlotte (B)

Engineering-Related Technologies/Technicians, Other
California State University, Dominguez Hills (UC)
Chattanooga State Technical Community College (A)
Everett Community College (A)
Kent State University (M)
Kingwood College (UC)
Memorial University of Newfoundland (B)
Regents College (A, B)
University of Massachusetts Lowell (UC)
University of North Texas (M)
University of Wisconsin–Stevens Point (UC)
Vincennes University (A)

Engineering/Industrial Management
California State University, Northridge (B)
Carnegie Mellon University (M)
Central Missouri State University (M)
Drexel University (M)
East Carolina University (M)
Golden Gate University (UC)
Indiana State University (M, D)
Kansas State University (M)
Lake Superior State University (B)
National Technological University (M, GC)
Oklahoma City University (B)
Oklahoma State University (M)
Old Dominion University (M)
Pennsylvania College of Technology (B)
Professional Development Europe Limited (M)
Rensselaer Polytechnic Institute (M, GC)
St. Mary's University of San Antonio (M)
Southern California University for Professional Studies (M, D)
Southern Methodist University (M)
Stanford University (M)
Stevens Institute of Technology (GC)
Syracuse University (M)
University of Alabama (M)

University of Colorado at Boulder (M)
University of Colorado at Denver (M)
University of Houston (M)
University of Idaho (M)
University of Maryland University College (B, M)
University of Massachusetts Amherst (M)
University of Missouri–Rolla (M)
University of Montana–Missoula (M)
University of Phoenix (M)
University of Texas at San Antonio (M)
Washburn University of Topeka (B)

English
Atlantic International University (B, M, D)

English as a Second Language
Fairleigh Dickinson University, The New College of General and Continuing Studies (GC)
University of Calgary (M)
University of Texas System (GC)

English Composition
Pennsylvania State University University Park Campus (UC)

English Creative Writing
Goddard College (M)
Goucher College (M)
Norwich University (M)
University of Washington (UC)

English Language and Literature, General
Athabasca University (GC)
Atlantic International University (B, M, D)
Atlantic Union College (B)
Bethany College of the Assemblies of God (B)
Caldwell College (B)
Cerro Coso Community College (A)
Judson College (B)
Mary Baldwin College (B)
Mount Allison University (B)
Queen's University at Kingston (B)
Saint Mary-of-the-Woods College (B)
Southwestern Adventist University (B)
Stephens College (B)
Troy State University Montgomery (B)
United States Open University (B)
University of Houston (B)
University of Waterloo (B)

English Language and Literature/Letters
Burlington College (B)
Saint Mary-of-the-Woods College (B)

English Language and Literature/Letters, Other
Florida Gulf Coast University (GC)
University of Washington (UC)

English Technical and Business Writing
Judson College (B)
Rensselaer Polytechnic Institute (M)
Rochester Institute of Technology (GC)
Utah State University (M)

Enterprise Management and Operation, General
Michigan State University (GC)
University of Washington (UC)

Entomology
University of Nebraska–Lincoln (M)

Entrepreneurship
Instituto Tecnológico y de Estudios Superiores de Monterrey, Campus Monterrey (UC)
Stephens College (M)

Index of Institutions Offering Degree and Certificate Programs

Environmental and Pollution Control Technology/Technician
Barton County Community College (UC)
Illinois Institute of Technology (GC)
Michigan State University (UC)
Mountain Empire Community College (A)
National Technological University (M, GC)
New Mexico Institute of Mining and Technology (B, M)
Rio Salado College (A)
Southern Methodist University (M)
University of California, Berkeley (GC)
University of California Extension (GC)
University of Denver (GC)

Environmental Control Technologies
University of Alaska Southeast, Sitka Campus (UC, A)

Environmental Control Technologies/ Technicians, Other
New York Institute of Technology (M)

Environmental/Environmental Health Engineering
Colorado State University (M)
Georgia Institute of Technology (M)
Illinois Institute of Technology (M)
Lehigh University (M)
Old Dominion University (M)
State University of New York at Buffalo (UC, M)
University of Alabama (M)
Worcester Polytechnic Institute (M, GC)

Environmental Health
Rochester Institute of Technology (M)
University of Denver (GC)

Environmental Science/Studies
College of West Virginia (A, B)
Illinois Institute of Technology (GC)
Instituto Tecnológico y de Estudios Superiores de Monterrey, Campus Monterrey (M)
Lakehead University (UC)
Oregon State University (B)
Royal Roads University (M)
University College of Cape Breton (B)
University of Denver (GC)
University of Maryland University College (M)

Ethnic and Cultural Studies
Columbia International University (M)
State University of New York Empire State College (A, B)
University of California, Los Angeles (UC)

Exercise Sciences/Physiology and Movement Studies
Atlantic Union College (B)
University of Texas System (M)

Family and Community Studies
Central Michigan University (B)
University of Southern Maine (GC)

Family and Individual Development Studies
Pennsylvania State University University Park Campus (UC, A)
Providence College and Theological Seminary (M)

Family Life and Relations Studies
Western Baptist College (B)

Fashion Merchandising
Fashion Institute of Technology (A)

Film/Cinema Studies
Burlington College (B)

Finance, General
City University (GC)
Golden Gate University (UC, M, GC)
Harcourt Learning Direct (A)
Instituto Tecnológico y de Estudios Superiores de Monterrey, Campus Monterrey (M)
Keller Graduate School of Management (M)
Regents College (B)
Thomas Edison State College (A)
Touro International University (B)
University of Notre Dame (UC)
University of Wisconsin–Whitewater (M)

Financial Management and Services
American College (M)
City University (M)
Dalhousie University (M)
Nipissing University (UC, B)

Financial Management and Services, Other
American College (GC)

Financial Planning
American College (UC, M)
City University (M, GC)
College for Financial Planning (M)
Golden Gate University (GC)
Indiana State University (B)
Macon Technical Institute (UC)
Université Laval (UC)
University of California, Los Angeles (GC)

Fine Arts and Art Studies
Atlantic International University (B, M, D)
Sandhills Community College (A)

Fine Arts and Art Studies, Other
Coastline Community College (A)
Everett Community College (A)

Fine/Studio Arts
Open Learning Agency (B)

Fire Protection and Safety Technology/ Technician
Chattanooga State Technical Community College (A)
Hinds Community College (A)

Fire Science/Firefighting
Pikes Peak Community College (A)
University of Maryland University College (B)
University of North Carolina at Charlotte (B)
Vincennes University (A)

Fire Services Administration
Colorado State University (B)
Eastern Oregon University (B)
University of Cincinnati (B)
Western Oregon University (UC)

Foods and Nutrition Science
Kansas State University (UC, B)
Université Laval (UC)

Foods and Nutrition Studies
Pennsylvania State University University Park Campus (UC, A)

Foods and Nutrition Studies, General
American Academy of Nutrition, College of Nutrition (A)
East Carolina University (M)
Oregon State University (M)
University of Bridgeport (M)

Foods and Nutrition Studies, Other
Central Arizona College (UC)
Université Laval (UC)

Foreign Languages and Literatures, General
Atlantic Union College (B)
Caldwell College (B)

Forensic Pathology Residency
Touro International University (M)

Forensic Technology/Technician
University of Florida (GC)

Forestry, General
Chattanooga State Technical Community College (UC)
Lakehead University (M)

French Language and Literature
Athabasca University (UC)
Mount Saint Vincent University (UC)
University of Toronto (UC)
University of Waterloo (B)

Funeral Services and Mortuary Science
Fayetteville Technical Community College (A)

General Studies
Anne Arundel Community College (A)
Athabasca University (B)
Atlantic Cape Community College (A)
Atlantic Union College (B)
Barton County Community College (A)
Bellevue Community College (A)
Bergen Community College (A)
Brevard Community College (A)
Burlington College (B)
Central Community College–Grand Island Campus (A)
Central Texas College (A)
Charles Stewart Mott Community College (A)
Charter Oak State College (A, B)
City University (A, B, M)
College of Southern Maryland (A)
College of West Virginia (A)
Columbia International University (B)
Columbus State Community College (A)
Community College of Baltimore County (A)
Cossatot Technical College (A)
Dallas County Community College District (A)
Delta College (A)
EduKan (A)
Everett Community College (A)
Foothill College (A)
Fort Hays State University (B)
Goddard College (B, M)
Governors State University (B)
Green River Community College (A)
Herkimer County Community College (A)
Howard Community College (A)
Indiana University System (A, B)
Indian River Community College (A)
Iowa Western Community College (A)
Johnson County Community College (A)
Lakehead University (B)
Lakeshore Technical College (A)
Liberty University (A)
Longview Community College (A)
Los Angeles Mission College (UC)
Luzerne County Community College (A)
Madonna University (B)
McGregor School of Antioch University (M)
Mercer University (UC)
Missouri Southern State College (A)
Mountain Empire Community College (A)
Northampton County Area Community College (A)
North Central Texas College (A)
Northern Virginia Community College (A)
Norwich University (GC)
Ohio University (A)

Oklahoma City Community College (A)
Open Learning Agency (A, B)
Parkland College (A)
Peralta Community College District (A)
Pierce College (A)
Portland Community College (A)
Prince George's Community College (A)
Reformed Theological Seminary (UC)
Regis University (B, M)
Rio Salado College (A)
Salt Lake Community College (A)
Skidmore College (B)
Southeast Community College, Lincoln Campus (A)
Southwest Virginia Community College (A)
Strayer University (A)
Tarrant County College District (A)
Taylor University, World Wide Campus (A)
Texas Tech University (B)
Troy State University Montgomery (A)
University of Alaska Fairbanks (A)
University of Manitoba (B)
University of Pennsylvania (UC)
Université of South Dakota (A)
Vincennes University (UC, A)
Walla Walla Community College (A)
Waubonsee Community College (UC)
Wayne County Community College District (A)
Weber State University (A)
Western Illinois University (B)
Western Oklahoma State College (A)

General Teacher Education, Other
Central Washington University (UC, B)
City University (M)
Colorado State University (GC)
Columbia International University (M)
Grand Canyon University (M)
Marygrove College (M)
National University (M)
New Mexico Institute of Mining and Technology (M)
University of Calgary (M)

Geography
Atlantic International University (B, M, D)
University of North Alabama (GC)
University of Waterloo (B)
Wilfrid Laurier University (B)

Geological and Related Sciences, Other
Mississippi State University (B, M)

Geological Engineering
University of Idaho (M)

Geology
Atlantic International University (B, M, D)

Geotechnical Engineering
Illinois Institute of Technology (M)

German Language and Literature
Queen's University at Kingston (B)
University of Toronto (UC)

Gerontology
Colorado Electronic Community College (A)
Colorado State University (UC)
Florida International University (UC)
Mount Saint Vincent University (UC)
Ryerson Polytechnic University (UC)
Saint Mary-of-the-Woods College (UC, A, B)
Université de Montréal (UC)
University of North Texas (M, GC)
University of Southern California (M)
University of Vermont (UC)
University of Washington (UC)
Utica College of Syracuse University (UC)

Graphic and Printing Equipment Operators, Other
University of Alaska Southeast, Sitka Campus (UC)

Graphic Design, Commercial Art and Illustration
Mohawk Valley Community College (A)

Health and Medical Administrative Services
Central Community College–Grand Island Campus (UC)
University of Illinois at Chicago (UC)
University of Southern Maine (M, GC)
Vincennes University (A)
Weber State University (B)

Health and Medical Administrative Services, Other
Catawba Valley Community College (UC)
Northwestern Technical Institute (UC)
Regents College (UC)
Stephens College (B)

Health and Medical Laboratory Technologies/Technicians, Other
Blue Ridge Community College (A)
Central Virginia Community College (A)
City University (A)
Purdue University (A)
St. Petersburg Junior College (A)
Weber State University (B)

Health and Physical Education, General
Eastern Oregon University (B)
Emporia State University (M)
Mississippi State University (M)
North Carolina Agricultural and Technical State University (M)
Virginia Polytechnic Institute and State University (M)

Health Occupations Teacher Education (Vocational)
Florida Gulf Coast University (M)
University of Illinois at Chicago (M)

Health Physics/Radiologic Health
Georgia Institute of Technology (M)
Illinois Institute of Technology (M)
Lakeshore Technical College (A)
National Technological University (M, GC)

Health Professions and Related Sciences
University of Illinois at Chicago (UC)

Health Professions and Related Sciences, Other
Athabasca University (UC)
Atlantic International University (B, M, D)
California College for Health Sciences (A, B)
Cleary College (A, B)
Cleveland State University (M)
George Washington University (B, M)
Goddard College (B, M)
Johns Hopkins University (M)
Keiser College (A)
Loma Linda University (A)
Medical College of Wisconsin (M)
Mercy College (M)
Nebraska Methodist College of Nursing and Allied Health (A)
Northern Arizona University (B)
Old Dominion University (B)
Pennsylvania College of Technology (B)
Saint Francis College (M)
Touro International University (B, D)
University of Minnesota, Crookston (B)

University of St. Augustine for Health Sciences (M)
University of St. Francis (B)
University of St. Thomas (M)
University of Southern Indiana (B)
University of Texas System (M)
Virginia Commonwealth University (D)
Virginia Polytechnic Institute and State University (M)
Walden University (D)

Health System/Health Services Administration
Armstrong Atlantic State University (M)
Athabasca University (B)
California College for Health Sciences (M)
Central Michigan University (B)
College of West Virginia (B)
Dalhousie University (UC)
Florida Gulf Coast University (B, M)
Golden Gate University (M, GC)
Graceland College (M)
Johns Hopkins University (GC)
Kirksville College of Osteopathic Medicine (M)
Madonna University (M)
Mary Baldwin College (B)
Medical College of Wisconsin (M)
New Hampshire College (UC)
Northcentral Technical College (A)
Ottawa University (B)
Rochester Institute of Technology (UC, M, GC)
Saint Joseph's College (UC, B, M, GC)
State University of New York College of Technology at Alfred (UC)
Stephens College (M)
Touro International University (B, M)
University of Dallas (M, GC)
University of Florida (M)
University of Great Falls (B)
University of Missouri-Columbia (M)
Virginia Commonwealth University (M)

Higher Education Administration
University of Nebraska–Lincoln (D)
University of Sarasota (D)

Historic Preservation, Conservation and Architectural History
Goucher College (M)

History, General
Arizona State University (B)
Atlantic Cape Community College (A)
Atlantic Union College (B)
Caldwell College (B)
Cerro Coso Community College (A)
Judson College (B)
Mary Baldwin College (B)
Mount Allison University (B)
Queen's University at Kingston (B)
Saint Mary-of-the-Woods College (B)
Southwestern Adventist University (B)
State University of New York Empire State College (A, B)
Thomas Edison State College (B)
Troy State University Montgomery (A, B)
University of Houston (B)
University of Waterloo (B)

History, Other
Indiana University System (A)
Reformed Theological Seminary (GC)

Horticulture Science
University of Saskatchewan (UC)

Hospital/Health Facilities Administration
Saint Joseph's College (UC, B)

Index of Institutions Offering Degree and Certificate Programs

Hospitality/Administration Management
East Carolina University (B)
Harcourt Learning Direct (A)
Ivy Tech State College–Wabash Valley (A)
New York Institute of Technology (B)
University of Houston (M)

Hospitality Services Management, Other
Northeast Wisconsin Technical College (A)
University of Wisconsin–Stout (M)

Hotel/Motel and Restaurant Management
Auburn University (M)
Champlain College (UC, A)
Northern Arizona University (B)
Pennsylvania State University University Park Campus (A)
Tompkins Cortland Community College (A)
University of Delaware (B)
University of Houston (B)
University of Minnesota, Crookston (UC)

Humanities/Humanistic Studies
Athabasca University (UC, B)
Atlantic Union College (B)
Burlington College (B)
California Institute of Integral Studies (D)
California State University, Dominguez Hills (M)
Cerro Coso Community College (A)
City University (B)
Coastline Community College (A)
County College of Morris (A)
Johnson County Community College (A)
Loma Linda University (A)
Ohio University (A)
Providence College and Theological Seminary (B)
Saint Mary-of-the-Woods College (A, B)
Thomas Edison State College (B)
United States Open University (B)
University of Maryland University College (B)
University of Pittsburgh (B)
University of Waterloo (B)

Human Resources Management
Bellevue University (B)
California National University for Advanced Studies (UC, A)
Cleary College (A, B)
Clemson University (M)
David N. Myers College (UC, B)
Indiana State University (B, M)
Judson College (B)
Keller Graduate School of Management (M)
New Hampshire College (UC)
Ottawa University (M)
Pennsylvania State University University Park Campus (UC)
Regents College (B)
Royal Roads University (M)
Saint Mary-of-the-Woods College (B)
Thomas Edison State College (A, B)
Troy State University (M)
University of Arkansas (B)
University of Nebraska–Lincoln (M)
University of Wisconsin–Whitewater (M)
Upper Iowa University (B)
Utah State University (M)

Human Resources Management, Other
American College (UC)
North Carolina State University (GC)
University of Houston (M)
University of Leicester (M, GC)
University of Wisconsin–Stout (M)

Human Services
Alaska Pacific University (B)
Burlington College (B)
California Institute of Integral Studies (M)

Capella University (M, D)
Concordia University at St. Paul (B)
Dawson Community College (A)
Elizabethtown College (B)
Judson College (B)
Old Dominion University (B)
Saint Mary-of-the-Woods College (B)
University of Alaska Fairbanks (A)
University of Alaska Southeast, Sitka Campus (A)
University of Great Falls (A, B)
Upper Iowa University (B)
Walden University (D)
Washburn University of Topeka (B)
Western Washington University (B)

Individual and Family Development Studies, General
Eckerd College (B)
Pacific Oaks College (B, M, D)
Salve Regina University (M)
Saybrook Graduate School (M, D)
Southern Christian University (B)
State University of New York Empire State College (A, B)
Washington State University (B)

Individual and Family Development Studies, Other
Pennsylvania State University University Park Campus (UC)

Industrial and Organizational Psychology
Fielding Institute (D)

Industrial/Manufacturing Engineering
Atlantic International University (B, M, D)
Auburn University (M)
Boston University (M)
California National University for Advanced Studies (B)
California State University, Dominguez Hills (UC, M)
Colorado State University (M, D)
East Carolina University (M)
Elizabethtown College (B)
Georgia Institute of Technology (M)
Illinois Institute of Technology (M)
Kettering University (M)
Lehigh University (M)
Mississippi State University (M, D)
National Technological University (M, GC)
Purdue University (M)
Rensselaer Polytechnic Institute (M, GC)
Rochester Institute of Technology (M, GC)
Southern Methodist University (M)
Southern Polytechnic State University (M)
State University of New York at Buffalo (M)
University of Arizona (GC)
University of Maryland, Baltimore County (UC)
University of Michigan (M)
University of Nebraska–Lincoln (M)
University of Tennessee (M)
University of Tennessee Space Institute (M)
University of Texas at Arlington (M)
University of Washington (M)
Virginia Polytechnic Institute and State University (M)

Industrial/Manufacturing Technology/Technician
Central Community College–Grand Island Campus (UC)
East Carolina University (B)
Harcourt Learning Direct (A)
Indiana State University (B)
Roger Williams University (B)

Information Sciences and Systems
American Institute for Computer Sciences (B)
American River College (UC)
Athabasca University (UC, B)
Atlantic International University (B, M, D)
Capitol College (M)
Carnegie Mellon University (UC)
Central Community College–Grand Island Campus (UC)
Cerro Coso Community College (A)
Champlain College (B)
City University (M, GC)
CTS University, Inc. (UC, A)
Drexel University (M)
Fairleigh Dickinson University, The New College of General and Continuing Studies (GC)
Florida State University (B)
Keller Graduate School of Management (A)
Mercy College (B)
National American University (B)
New Jersey Institute of Technology (B, M)
Northcentral Technical College (A)
Northeastern University (M)
Nova Southeastern University (D)
Pennsylvania State University University Park Campus (UC)
Pitt Community College (A)
Regents College (B)
Regis University (M)
Robert Morris College (B)
St. Mary's University of San Antonio (M)
Strayer University (M)
Syracuse University (M)
University of Alaska Southeast, Sitka Campus (A)
University of Massachusetts Lowell (A, B)
University of North Texas (M)
University of Sarasota (M)
University of Tennessee (M)
University of the Incarnate Word (B)

Insurance and Risk Management
American College (UC)

Interior Design
Atlantic Union College (B)

International Business
Bellevue University (B)
Caldwell College (B)
City University (A)
Cochise College (UC)
Instituto Tecnológico y de Estudios Superiores de Monterrey, Campus Monterrey (M)
Regents College (B)
Strayer University (B)
Touro International University (B, M)
University of Maryland University College (M)
University of Phoenix (M)
University of Sarasota (D)
University of Texas at Dallas (M)
University of the Incarnate Word (B)
University of Wisconsin–Whitewater (M)

International Relations and Affairs
Atlantic International University (B, M, D)
National University (M)
St. Mary's University of San Antonio (M)
Salve Regina University (M)
Southwestern Adventist University (B)
Troy State University (M)
Tufts University (M)

Internet
Illinois Institute of Technology (GC)
University of Tennessee (GC)

Islamic Studies
Columbia International University (M)

Italian Language and Literature
University of Toronto (UC)

Japanese Language and Literature
National Technological University (GC)
University of Wisconsin–Madison (M)

Jewish/Judaic Studies
California State University, Chico (B)
Cleveland College of Jewish Studies (M)
Hebrew College (UC)
Spertus Institute of Jewish Studies (M, D)

Journalism
City University (B)
Parkland College (A)
Saint Mary-of-the-Woods College (B)
Southwestern Adventist University (B)
University of Memphis (M)
University of Nebraska–Lincoln (M)

Junior High/Intermediate/Middle School Teacher Education
College of West Virginia (A)
Utah State University (UC)

Labor/Personnel Relations and Studies
Athabasca University (UC)
Indiana University System (UC, A, B)
State University of New York Empire State College (A, B)
University of Missouri-Columbia (UC)

Law (L.L.B., J.D.)
Pennsylvania State University University Park Campus (UC)
Southern California University for Professional Studies (P)

Law and Legal Studies
Atlantic International University (B, M, D)
Brevard Community College (A)
College of West Virginia (B)
Pennsylvania State University University Park Campus (UC)
Sussex County Community College (UC)

Law and Legal Studies, Other
Franklin Pierce Law Center (M, GC)

Law Enforcement/Police Science
Indiana State University (UC)
Vincennes University (A)

Liberal Art and Sciences, General Studies and Humanities, Other
Abilene Christian University (UC)
Athabasca University (B)
Atlantic Union College (B)
Ball State University (A)
Bergen Community College (A)
Charles Stewart Mott Community College (A)
Chestnut Hill College (M)
City University (B)
Ohio University (B)
Rochester Institute of Technology (B)
Rogers State University (A, B)
St. Cloud State University (A, B)
Sandhills Community College (A)
Thomas Edison State College (B)
University of Maine (B)
University of Waterloo (B)
Walla Walla Community College (A)

Liberal Arts and Sciences, General Studies and Humanities
New Hampshire Community Technical College, Nashua/Claremont (A)
Thomas Edison State College (A)

Liberal Arts and Sciences/Liberal Studies
Andrews University (A, B)
Athabasca University (UC, B)
Atlantic Cape Community College (A)
Brookdale Community College (A)
Bucks County Community College (A)
Burlington County College (A)
California State University, Chico (B)
California State University, Fresno (B)
Cayuga County Community College (A)
Central Oregon Community College (A)
Central Piedmont Community College (A)
Cerro Coso Community College (A)
Charles Stewart Mott Community College (A)
Citrus College (A)
College of DuPage (A)
Colorado Electronic Community College (A)
Cuyahoga Community College, Metropolitan Campus (A)
Dallas County Community College District (A)
De Anza College (A)
Duquesne University (M)
Eastern Illinois University (B)
Eastern Oregon University (B)
Edison Community College (A)
Everett Community College (A)
Fayetteville Technical Community College (A)
Florence-Darlington Technical College (A)
Fort Hays State University (M)
Front Range Community College (A)
Garland County Community College (A)
Goddard College (B)
Greenville Technical College (A)
Hawkeye Community College (A)
Honolulu Community College (A)
Kingwood College (A)
Longview Community College (A)
Los Angeles Mission College (A)
Mercy College (A)
Metropolitan Community College (A)
Miami-Dade Community College (A)
Minnesota West Community and Technical College (A)
Montana State University–Billings (B)
Montgomery County Community College (A)
Mountain Empire Community College (A)
Mount Saint Vincent University (B)
Neumann College (A)
New School University (B)
North Country Community College (A)
Northern Arizona University (B)
Northern Virginia Community College (A)
North Harris College (A)
Norwich University (B, M)
Oklahoma City University (B)
Oregon State University (B)
Pennsylvania State University University Park Campus (A, B)
Piedmont Technical College (A)
Rappahannock Community College (A)
Regents College (A, B, M)
Regis University (GC)
Rockland Community College (A)
Rogers State University (A, B)
St. Cloud State University (B)
Salve Regina University (B)
Sandhills Community College (A)
Seattle Central Community College (A)
Sinclair Community College (A)
Sonoma State University (B)
Southern California University for Professional Studies (A, B)
Southern Christian University (B)
Syracuse University (A, B)
Taylor University, World Wide Campus (A)
Texas Christian University (M)
Thomas Edison State College (B)
Tulsa Community College (A)

Ulster County Community College (A)
Union Institute (B)
United States Open University (B)
University of Alaska Southeast (B)
University of Central Florida (B)
University of Hawaii at Manoa (B)
University of Illinois at Springfield (B)
University of Iowa (B)
University of Maryland University College (B)
University of Northern Iowa (B)
University of Wisconsin Colleges (A)
Upper Iowa University (A)
Western Wyoming Community College (A)

Library Assistant
Northampton County Area Community College (UC)

Library Science/Librarianship
Connecticut State University System (M)
East Carolina University (M)
Instituto Tecnológico y de Estudios Superiores de Monterrey, Campus Monterrey (UC, M)
Louisiana State University and Agricultural and Mechanical College (M)
Louisiana State University System (M)
Mansfield University of Pennsylvania (M)
Memorial University of Newfoundland (UC)
Miami-Dade Community College (A)
San Jose State University (M, GC)
Southern Connecticut State University (M)
Syracuse University (UC)
University of Illinois at Urbana–Champaign (M)
University of Montana–Missoula (GC)
University of North Carolina at Greensboro (M)
University of North Texas (UC, M)
University of South Carolina (M)
University of Washington (UC)
Utah State University (UC)

Logistics and Materials Management
Pennsylvania State University University Park Campus (UC)
Southern Polytechnic State University (B)

Management Information Systems and Business Data Processing, General
Bellevue University (B)
ISIM University (M)
Nova Southeastern University (M)
Park University (B)
Regents College (B)
Southwestern Adventist University (B)
University of Great Falls (A, B)
University of Illinois at Springfield (M)
University of Oregon (M)
University of Phoenix (B)
Utah State University (B, M)

Marine/Aquatic Biology
North Carolina State University (D)

Marketing Management and Research, Other
University of California Extension (GC)

Mass Communications
Parkland College (A)

Massage
North Country Community College (A)

Materials Engineering
Auburn University (M)
National Technological University (M, GC)
Stanford University (M)
University of Texas at Arlington (M)
University of Washington (M)
Virginia Polytechnic Institute and State University (M)

Mathematical Statistics
Colorado State University (M)
Iowa State University of Science and Technology (M)

Mathematics
Atlantic International University (B, M, D)
Mary Baldwin College (B)
Middle Tennessee State University (M)
Montana State University–Bozeman (M)
Ohio University (A)
Saint Mary-of-the-Woods College (B)
Southwestern Adventist University (B)
State University of New York Empire State College (A, B)
University of Houston–Victoria (B)

Mathematics Teacher Education
University of Idaho (M)

Mechanical Engineering
Atlantic International University (B, M, D)
Auburn University (M)
Bradley University (M)
Colorado State University (M, D)
Florida State University (M)
Georgia Institute of Technology (M)
Iowa State University of Science and Technology (M)
Michigan Technological University (M, D)
Mississippi State University (M, D)
Purdue University (M)
Rensselaer Polytechnic Institute (M)
Southern Methodist University (M)
Stanford University (M)
State University of New York at Buffalo (M)
University of Alabama (M)
University of Colorado at Boulder (M)
University of Idaho (M)
University of Illinois at Urbana–Champaign (M)
University of South Carolina (M, D)
University of Texas at Arlington (M)
University of Washington (M)
University of Wisconsin–Madison (M)

Mechanical Engineering/Mechanical Technology/Technician
Harcourt Learning Direct (A)
Old Dominion University (B)

Medical Assistant
Kapiolani Community College (UC)
Lakeshore Technical College (UC)
Portland Community College (UC)

Medical Clinical Sciences (M.S., Ph.D.)
George Washington University (B)

Medical Illustrating
Clarkson College (B)

Medical Laboratory Technician
City University (A)

Medical Office Management
Northwestern College (A)
University of Alaska Southeast, Sitka Campus (UC)

Medical Radiologic Technology/Technician
North Country Community College (A)
Saint Joseph's College (B)
Southeast Community College, Lincoln Campus (A)
University of Missouri-Columbia (UC, B)
Weber State University (UC, B)

Medical Records Technology/Technician
Dakota State University (B)
Loma Linda University (B)

Northern Virginia Community College (UC)
Pitt Community College (A)
Santa Barbara City College (UC, A)
Stephens College (B, GC)
University of Alaska Southeast, Sitka Campus (A)

Medical Transcription
California College for Health Sciences (A)
Chattanooga State Technical Community College (UC)
Hamilton College (UC)
Northwest Technical College (UC)

Medicinal/Pharmaceutical Chemistry
Illinois Institute of Technology (GC)
Lehigh University (M)

Mental Health Services, Other
Thomas Edison State College (B)

Metallurgical Engineering
Illinois Institute of Technology (M)
University of Idaho (M)

Microbiology/Bacteriology
Iowa State University of Science and Technology (M)

Military Studies
American Military University (A, B, M)
Royal Military College of Canada (B, M)

Mining and Mineral Engineering
University of Idaho (M)

Miscellaneous Health Professions
Kirksville College of Osteopathic Medicine (M)

Missions/Missionary Studies and Missiology
Crown College (M)
Eugene Bible College (B)
Global University of the Assemblies of God (A, B, M)
Grand Rapids Baptist Seminary (M)
Reformed Theological Seminary (GC)

Molecular Biology
Lehigh University (M)

Multi/Interdisciplinary Studies, Other
Clayton College & State University (A, B)
College of West Virginia (B)
Emporia State University (B)
Goddard College (M)
Hamilton College (A)
Liberty University (B)
New York Institute of Technology (B)
Old Dominion University (B)
Rochester Institute of Technology (M)
State University of New York Empire State College (A, B)
Union Institute (D)
Washburn University of Topeka (B)

Music
Mary Baldwin College (B)

Music, General
Judson College (B)
Open Learning Agency (B)
Providence College and Theological Seminary (B)

Musicology and Ethnomusicology
Crown College (M)

Music Therapy
Saint Mary-of-the-Woods College (M)

Natural Resources Management and Policy
Colorado State University (UC)
Oklahoma State University (M)

Oregon State University (B)
Rochester Institute of Technology (UC, B)
Saint Mary-of-the-Woods College (M)
Troy State University (B)
University of Denver (M, GC)
University of Findlay (B, M)

Non-Profit and Public Management
Ryerson Polytechnic University (UC)
University of Southern Maine (GC)

Nuclear Medical Technology/Technician
Weber State University (UC)

Nuclear/Nuclear Power Technology/Technician
Regents College (A, B)

Nurse Assistant/Aide
Lakeshore Technical College (UC)

Nursing
Allen College (B)
Armstrong Atlantic State University (B)
Athabasca University (B)
Ball State University (B, M)
Brenau University (B)
California State University, Chico (B)
California State University, Dominguez Hills (B, M)
California State University, Fullerton (B)
Clarkson College (B, M)
Clemson University (B, M)
Concordia University Wisconsin (M)
Dalhousie University (B, M)
Duquesne University (B, D)
Fort Hays State University (B)
Gonzaga University (B, M)
Grand View College (B)
Husson College (B)
Indiana State University (B, M)
Indiana University System (M)
Kent State University (B)
Lakehead University (B)
Lake Superior State University (B)
Loyola University New Orleans (B)
Memorial University of Newfoundland (B)
Michigan State University (UC, M)
Montana State University–Bozeman (M)
National University (B, M)
Northcentral Technical College (A)
North Central Texas College (A)
North Country Community College (UC, A)
Northeastern State University (B)
Northern Arizona University (B)
Northern Michigan University (M)
Northwest Technical College (A)
Old Dominion University (B)
Open Learning Agency (B)
Oregon Health Sciences University (B)
Plattsburgh State University of New York (B)
Prairie View A&M University (B)
Regents College (A, B, M)
Regis University (B)
Sacred Heart University (B)
St. Francis Xavier University (B)
Saint Joseph's College (B, M)
Saint Louis University (B, M, GC)
Samuel Merritt College (M)
San Jose State University (M)
Shawnee State University (B)
Southern Illinois University Edwardsville (B)
Southwestern Adventist University (B)
Syracuse University (M)
Texas Christian University (M)
University of Akron (M)
University of Calgary (B)
University of Central Florida (B)
University of Delaware (B)

University of Guam (B)
University of Iowa (B, M)
University of Maine at Fort Kent (B)
University of Manitoba (B)
University of Massachusetts Amherst (M)
University of Missouri-Columbia (B, M)
University of Missouri–St. Louis (B, M)
University of Nebraska Medical Center (B, M, D)
University of New Brunswick (B, M)
University of New Mexico (B)
University of Phoenix (B, M)
University of South Alabama (B)
University of Southern Indiana (B)
University of South Florida (B)
University of Texas at Arlington (B)
University of Texas at Tyler (B)
University of Wisconsin–Madison (B)
University of Wyoming (B, M)
Western Wyoming Community College (UC)
West Virginia Wesleyan College (B)
Wright State University (B)
York College of Pennsylvania (B)

Nursing (R.N. Training)
Austin Community College (UC)
Carlow College (UC)
Florida State University (B)
Graceland College (B)
University of Southern Maine (B, M)

Nursing, Family Practice (Post-R.N.)
Clarkson College (GC)
Graceland College (M)
Old Dominion University (M)

Nursing Midwifery (Post-R.N.)
University of Missouri-Columbia (M)
University of Pennsylvania (M, GC)

Nursing, Other
Athabasca University (UC)
Carlow College (M, GC)
College of West Virginia (B)
MCP Hahnemann University (M)
Northcentral Technical College (UC)
Saint Mary-of-the-Woods College (GC)
Santa Barbara City College (UC)
University of Illinois at Chicago (UC, GC)
University of North Dakota (M)

Nursing, Psychiatric/Mental Health (Post-R.N.)
Open Learning Agency (B)

Nursing Science (Post-R.N.)
Carlow College (M)
Holy Names College (B)

Occupational Health and Industrial Hygiene
McGill University (M)
Ryerson Polytechnic University (UC)

Occupational Safety and Health Technology/Technician
Indiana University of Pennsylvania (UC)

Occupational Therapy Assistant
Saint Mary-of-the-Woods College (B)
San Jose State University (M)

Ocean Engineering
Virginia Polytechnic Institute and State University (M)

Office Supervision and Management
College of West Virginia (A, B)
Northcentral Technical College (A)
Owens Community College (UC)

Pennsylvania State University University Park Campus (UC)
Texas A&M University–Kingsville (M)

Operations Management and Supervision
Indiana State University (B)
Kettering University (M)
North Central Texas College (A)
Regents College (B)
University of Houston (B)
University of Wisconsin–Stout (B)

Organizational Behavior Studies
Gonzaga University (M)
Regent University (M, D)
Southern Christian University (M)

Paralegal/Legal Assistant
American Institute for Paralegal Studies, Inc. (UC)
California State University, San Marcos (UC)
Central Community College–Grand Island Campus (UC)
City University (UC, A)
College of Mount St. Joseph (UC)
Ivy Tech State College–North Central (UC)
Kaplan College (B)
Lakeshore Technical College (A)
Northwestern College (A)
Pennsylvania State University University Park Campus (UC)
Saint Mary-of-the-Woods College (UC, A, B)
Southern California University for Professional Studies (A)
Tompkins Cortland Community College (A)
University of Great Falls (A, B)
University of Maryland University College (B)
University of Southern Colorado (UC)
Western Piedmont Community College (A)

Parks, Recreation and Leisure Facilities Management
North Country Community College (A)
Vincennes University (A)

Pastoral Counseling and Specialized Ministries
Eugene Bible College (B)
University of Sarasota (D)

Pharmacy
Duquesne University (D)
Ohio Northern University (D)
Purdue University (UC)
Shenandoah University (D)
University of Florida (D)
University of Iowa (D)
University of Montana–Missoula (D)
University of Washington (D)
University of Wisconsin–Madison (D)

Pharmacy (B.Pharm., Pharm.D.)
University of Illinois at Chicago (D)

Pharmacy Technician/Assistant
Ivy Tech State College–North Central (UC)
Lakeshore Technical College (UC)
Ohio Northern University (UC)

Philosophy
Atlantic International University (B, M, D)
Bergen Community College (A)
Christopher Newport University (B)
City University (B)
Stephens College (B)
University of Waterloo (B)

Philosophy and Religion
Mary Baldwin College (B)

Physical Sciences, Other
Illinois Institute of Technology (GC)
Lehigh University (B)
University of North Dakota (M)

Physical Therapy
Open Learning Agency (B)
University of St. Augustine for Health Sciences (M)

Physics
Atlantic International University (B, M, D)

Physics, Other
Michigan State University (M, D)

Physiological Psychology/Psychobiology
Fielding Institute (GC)

Plastics Technology/Technician
University of Massachusetts Lowell (UC)

Political Science and Government, Other
Christopher Newport University (B)

Political Science, General
Atlantic International University (B, M, D)
Caldwell College (B)
California State University, Chico (B)
City University (B)
Mary Baldwin College (B)
Queen's University at Kingston (B)
Troy State University Montgomery (A, B)
University of Colorado at Denver (B)
University of Great Falls (B)
Virginia Polytechnic Institute and State University (M)

Practical Nurse (L.P.N. Training)
North Dakota State College of Science (A)

Pre-Elementary/Early Childhood/Kindergarten Teacher Education
Atlantic Union College (B)
California College for Health Sciences (A)
Central Arizona College (UC, A)
Central Washington University (B)
College of West Virginia (A)
Elizabethtown College (B)
Northampton County Area Community College (UC)
Pacific Oaks College (D)
Rochester College (B)
Saint Mary-of-the-Woods College (A, B)
Southern Oregon University (M, GC)
University of Alaska Southeast (GC)
University of Alaska Southeast, Sitka Campus (A)

Professional Studies
Bethany College of the Assemblies of God (B)
Champlain College (B)
Lynn University (B)
Metropolitan Community College (A)
Saint Joseph's College (UC, B)
Southwestern Assemblies of God University (B)
Touro International University (B)
Troy State University Montgomery (B)
University of St. Francis (B)

Protective Services
Seton Hall University (M)

Psychology
St. Cloud State University (B)

Psychology, General
Atlantic International University (B, M, D)
Atlantic Union College (B)
Bethany College of the Assemblies of God (B)
Burlington College (B)
Caldwell College (B)

Psychology, General (continued)
California State University, Chico (M)
Capella University (M, D)
City University (B)
Goddard College (M)
Judson College (B)
Kansas State University (M)
Liberty University (B)
Mercy College (B)
New York Institute of Technology (B)
North Central University (B, M, D)
Pacific Graduate School of Psychology (M)
Parkland College (A)
Queen's University at Kingston (B)
Saint Mary-of-the-Woods College (B)
Saybrook Graduate School (M, D)
Southern California University for Professional
   Studies (B, M, D)
Southwestern Adventist University (B)
Stephens College (B)
Thomas Edison State College (B)
Troy State University Montgomery (A, B)
University of Houston (B)
University of Idaho (M)
University of Maine at Fort Kent (B)
University of Maine at Machias (B)
University of Waterloo (B)
University of Wyoming (B)
Utah State University (B)
Vincennes University (A)
Walden University (M, D)

Psychology, Other
Atlantic University (M)
Burlington College (B)
California College for Health Sciences (M)
Institute of Transpersonal Psychology (M, GC)

Public Administration
Athabasca University (UC)
Atlantic International University (B, M, D)
City University (M, GC)
Colorado Electronic Community College (A)
Elizabethtown College (B)
Florida Gulf Coast University (M)
Golden Gate University (B, M)
Marist College (M)
Memorial University of Newfoundland (UC)
Northern Michigan University (M)
Northern Virginia Community College (A)
Regent University (M)
Roger Williams University (B)
Ryerson Polytechnic University (UC)
St. Mary's University of San Antonio (M)
Troy State University (M)
University of Alaska Southeast (M)
University of New Mexico (M)
University of Southern Maine (M)
University of Wyoming (M)
Upper Iowa University (B)

Public Administration and Services
Georgia Southern University (M)
Indiana State University (GC)
University College of Cape Breton (UC)

Public Administration and Services, Other
Chattanooga State Technical Community College
   (A)
Jacksonville State University (M)
McGregor School of Antioch University (M)
Memorial University of Newfoundland (UC)
Oklahoma State University (M)
Providence College and Theological Seminary (B)
Rochester Institute of Technology (UC)
University of Alaska Fairbanks (B)

Public Health, General
California College for Health Sciences (M)
Johns Hopkins University (M)
Kirksville College of Osteopathic Medicine (M)
University of Massachusetts Amherst (M)
University of South Florida (M)
University of Washington (GC)

Public Health, Other
George Washington University (UC)
Touro International University (M)

Public Relations and Organizational Communications
Royal Roads University (M)

Radio and Television Broadcasting
New School University (M)
State University of West Georgia (M)

Reading
University of Texas System (UC, M)

Reading, Literacy and Communication Skills
City University (M)

Reading Teacher Education
Concordia University Wisconsin (M)
Indiana University System (M)
University of Colorado at Colorado Springs (UC)

Real Estate
St. Francis Xavier University (GC)

Recreational Therapy
Indiana University System (M)

Rehabilitation/Therapeutic Services, Other
San Diego State University (M)
University of Southern Maine (M)
Utah State University (M)
Wright State University (M)

Religion/Religious Studies
Atlantic Union College (B)
Caldwell College (B)
Concordia University at St. Paul (M)
Fuller Theological Seminary (UC)
Global University of the Assemblies of God (A, B,
   M)
Griggs University (P)
Judson College (B)
Reformed Theological Seminary (M)
St. Mary's University of San Antonio (M, GC)
Southwestern Adventist University (B)
University of Great Falls (B)
University of Waterloo (B)

Religious Education
Columbia International University (M)
Defiance College (UC, B)
Eugene Bible College (B)
Grand Rapids Baptist Seminary (M)
Griggs University (B)
Southwestern Baptist Theological Seminary (M)
Temple Baptist Seminary (M)

Religious/Sacred Music
Eugene Bible College (B)

Religious Studies
Liberty University (A, B, M)

Respiratory Therapy Technician
California College for Health Sciences (A, B)
Open Learning Agency (B)
Saint Joseph's College (B)
University of Missouri-Columbia (B)
Weber State University (A, B)

School Psychology
National University (GC)
University of Montana–Missoula (M)

Science Teacher Education, General
Montana State University–Bozeman (M)
Stevens Institute of Technology (GC)

Secondary Teacher Education
Fitchburg State College (M)
Saint Joseph's College (GC)
Southern Oregon University (M)
University of Wyoming (M)
Utah State University (M)

Security and Loss Prevention Services
Indiana State University (UC)

Social Sciences
Atlantic Cape Community College (A)
Bethany College of the Assemblies of God (B)
Northern Michigan University (B)
Providence College and Theological Seminary (B)
Thomas Edison State College (B)

Social Sciences and History
Cerro Coso Community College (A)
University of Wyoming (B)

Social Sciences and History, Other
Goddard College (M)
Regent University (M)
University of Waterloo (B)
Utah State University (M)

Social Sciences, General
Athabasca University (UC, B)
Atlantic Union College (B)
Brookdale Community College (A)
Buena Vista University (B)
California State University, Chico (B)
Eastern Oregon University (B)
Florida State University (B)
Kansas State University (B)
North Harris College (A)
Ohio University (A)
Southwestern Adventist University (B)
State University of New York Empire State
   College (A, B)
Syracuse University (M)
Troy State University Montgomery (A, B)
United States Open University (B)
University of Maryland University College (B)
University of Pittsburgh (B)
University of Southern Colorado (B)
University of Waterloo (B)
University of Wyoming (B)
Upper Iowa University (B)
Washington State University (B)

Social Work
California State University, Dominguez Hills (M)
California State University, Long Beach (M)
Cleveland State University (M)
Dalhousie University (M)
Lakehead University (B)
Madonna University (B)
McGregor School of Antioch University (M)
Memorial University of Newfoundland (B)
Michigan State University (UC)
Northern Michigan University (B)
Royal Roads University (M)
University of Akron (M)
University of Alaska Fairbanks (B)
University of Manitoba (B)

Sociology
Atlantic International University (B, M, D)
Bergen Community College (A)
Caldwell College (B)

California State University, Chico (B)
City University (B)
Goddard College (B)
Graceland College (B)
Mary Baldwin College (B)
New York Institute of Technology (B)
University of Great Falls (B)
University of Waterloo (B)
Wilfrid Laurier University (B)

Spanish Language and Literature
University of Toronto (UC)

Special Education
National University (GC)
University of South Alabama (M)
University of Wyoming (M)
Valdosta State University (B)

Special Education, General
Ball State University (M)
Central Washington University (B)
City University (M, GC)
Coppin State College (B, M)
Old Dominion University (M)
Saint Mary-of-the-Woods College (B)
Southern Oregon University (A, M)
University of Louisville (M)
West Virginia University (M)

Special Education, Other
Bethany College of the Assemblies of God (B)
Illinois State University (UC)
Northcentral Technical College (A)
University of Louisville (M)
Utah State University (UC)

Speech-Language Pathology
University of Wyoming (M)

Speech-Language Pathology and Audiology
East Carolina University (M)
University of North Carolina at Greensboro (M)

Sport and Fitness Administration/Management
United States Sports Academy (M)

Statistics
University of Tennessee (GC)

Structural Engineering
Illinois Institute of Technology (M)
State University of New York at Buffalo (UC, M)

Surgical/Operating Room Technician
Vincennes University (A)

Surveying
Michigan Technological University (B)
University of Wyoming (UC)

Systems Engineering
Colorado State University (M, D)
Illinois Institute of Technology (GC)
Iowa State University of Science and Technology (M)
Oklahoma State University (M)
Southern Methodist University (M)
University of California, Santa Cruz (UC)
University of Missouri–Rolla (M)
Virginia Polytechnic Institute and State University (M)

Taxation
Bentley College (M, GC)
Golden Gate University (M, GC)
Old Dominion University (M)
Regent University (M)

Southern California University for Professional Studies (M)

Teacher Assistant/Aide
University of Calgary (UC)

Teacher Education
Alaska Pacific University (B)
Goddard College (M)
Lehigh Carbon Community College (A)

Teacher Education, Specific Academic and Vocational Programs, Other
California State University, Long Beach (B)
Mississippi State University (GC)

Teaching English as a Second Language/ Foreign Language
City University (M)
Columbia International University (M)
McGill University (GC)
Providence College and Theological Seminary (M)
Seattle Central Community College (UC)
University of California, Los Angeles (UC, GC)
University of Saskatchewan (UC)

Technology Teacher Education/Industrial Arts Teacher Education
North Carolina Agricultural and Technical State University (M)
Old Dominion University (B, M)

Telecommunications
Atlantic International University (B, M, D)
California State University, Chico (M)
Capitol College (M)
Champlain College (UC, A)
City University (UC)
East Carolina University (M)
Golden Gate University (M)
Illinois Institute of Technology (GC)
Instituto Tecnológico y de Estudios Superiores de Monterrey, Campus Monterrey (M)
Keller Graduate School of Management (M)
New Jersey Institute of Technology (GC)
New York Institute of Technology (B)
Oklahoma State University (M)
Purdue University (UC)
Rochester Institute of Technology (UC, B)
Royal Roads University (M)
Saint Mary-of-the-Woods College (B)
Southern Methodist University (M)
State University of New York at Buffalo (UC)
Stevens Institute of Technology (M, GC)
Strayer University (B)
Syracuse University (M)
United States Open University (B, M)
University of Alaska Southeast, Sitka Campus (UC)
University of California, Berkeley (GC)
University of California Extension (GC)
University of Colorado at Boulder (M)
University of Dallas (M, GC)
University of Denver (M, GC)
University of Washington (UC)

Theological and Ministerial Studies
Taylor University, World Wide Campus (UC)

Theological and Ministerial Studies, Other
Northwestern College (B)
Saint Mary-of-the-Woods College (UC, M)
Taylor University, World Wide Campus (UC)

Theological Studies and Religious Vocations, Other
Bethany College of the Assemblies of God (B)
Bethel Seminary (M)
Columbia International University (M)

Crown College (M)
Global University of the Assemblies of God (M)

Theology/Theological Studies
Andrews University (B)
Atlantic International University (B, M, D)
Atlantic Union College (B)
Briercrest Bible College (A, B)
Central Baptist Theological Seminary (UC, M)
Columbia International University (M)
Covenant Theological Seminary (M, GC)
Eastern Mennonite University (UC)
Eugene Bible College (B)
Franciscan University of Steubenville (M)
Griggs University (P)
Lincoln Christian College (UC)
Providence College and Theological Seminary (B, M)
Reformed Theological Seminary (GC)
Saint Joseph's College (UC, B, M)
Saint Mary-of-the-Woods College (UC, B)
St. Mary's University of San Antonio (M, GC)
Seton Hall University (GC)
Southwestern Adventist University (B)

Trade and Industrial Teacher Education (Vocational)
Indiana State University (B)

Transportation and Highway Engineering
Illinois Institute of Technology (M)
National Technological University (M, GC)
North Dakota State University (M)

Transportation and Materials Moving Workers, Other
Salt Lake Community College (UC)
San Jose State University (M, GC)

Travel-Tourism Management
College of West Virginia (UC, A)
Herkimer County Community College (A)
Keiser College (A)
Mount Saint Vincent University (B)
Northwestern College (A)
Touro International University (B)
University of Denver (GC)

Turf Management
Pennsylvania State University University Park Campus (UC)
University System of Georgia (UC)
Walla Walla Community College (A)

Vehicle and Equipment Operators, Other
University System of Georgia (UC)

Visual and Performing Arts
Norwich University (M)
Providence College and Theological Seminary (B)
State University of New York Empire State College (A, B)

Visual and Performing Arts, Other
Institute of Transpersonal Psychology (GC)

Web Page Design
Bellevue Community College (UC, A)
East Carolina University (GC)
Maryland Institute, College of Art (UC)
University of Alaska Southeast, Sitka Campus (UC)

Women's Studies
Atlantic Union College (B)
Goucher College (M)
Queen's University at Kingston (B)

INDIVIDUAL COURSES INDEX

Index of individual courses offered by institutions, arranged by subject. U=Undergraduate; G=Graduate; NC=noncredit

Abnormal psychology

Anne Arundel Community College (U)
Bellevue Community College (U)
Bossier Parish Community College (U)
Brigham Young University (U)
Bristol Community College (U)
Bucks County Community College (U)
Capella University (G)
Carleton University (U)
Central Piedmont Community College (U)
Central Texas College (U)
Chaminade University of Honolulu (U)
Clark State Community College (U)
College of St. Scholastica (U)
College of Southern Maryland (U)
College of West Virginia (U)
Colorado Mountain College District (U)
Colorado State University (U)
Columbia Basin College (U)
Concordia University Wisconsin (U)
Cumberland County College (U)
De Anza College (U)
Delaware Technical & Community College, Stanton/Wilmington Campus (U)
Delta College (U)
D'Youville College (U)
Genesee Community College (U)
Goddard College (U, G)
Husson College (U)
Hutchinson Community College and Area Vocational School (U)
Indiana Institute of Technology (U)
Indiana State University (U)
John Wood Community College (U)
Lakehead University (U)
McDowell Technical Community College (U)
Mercy College (U)
Montgomery College (U)
Montgomery County Community College (U)
Moraine Valley Community College (U)
Mount Wachusett Community College (U)
Nassau Community College (U)
New Hampshire College (U)
Northeast Wisconsin Technical College (U)
Northern Virginia Community College (U)
Okaloosa-Walton Community College (U)
Open Learning Agency (U)
Oregon State University (U)
Palomar College (U)
Parkland College (U)
Piedmont Technical College (U)
Pierce College (U)
Portland Community College (U)
Providence College and Theological Seminary (G, NC)
Regents College (U)
Roane State Community College (U)
Rockland Community College (U)
San Antonio College (U)
Saybrook Graduate School (G)
Seattle Central Community College (U)
Shawnee Community College (U)
Sinclair Community College (U)
Stanly Community College (U)
State University of New York at Oswego (G)
State University of New York College at Oneonta (U, NC)

State University of New York Empire State College (U)
Stephens College (U)
Suffolk County Community College (U)
Tacoma Community College (U)
Taylor University, World Wide Campus (U)
Triton College (U)
University of Alaska Fairbanks (U)
University of Arizona (U)
University of Arkansas (U)
University of Houston–Clear Lake (G)
University of Houston–Downtown (U)
University of Illinois at Urbana–Champaign (U)
University of Manitoba (U)
University of Minnesota, Twin Cities Campus (U)
University of Missouri–Columbia (U)
University of Nevada, Reno (U)
University of South Dakota (U)
University of Southern Indiana (U)
University of Southern Maine (U)
University of Tennessee (U)
University of Texas at Austin (U)
University of Utah (U)
University of Waterloo (U)
University of West Florida (G)
University of Wisconsin Extension (U)
University System of Georgia (U)
Upper Iowa University (U, NC)
Virginia Western Community College (U)
Weber State University (U)
Western Washington University (U)
Westmoreland County Community College (U)
Wilfrid Laurier University (U)

Accounting

Adams State College (U)
Adelphi University (U, G)
Alaska Pacific University (U)
Allegany College of Maryland (U)
Anne Arundel Community College (U)
Arizona State University (U)
Arizona Western College (G)
Athabasca University (U, G)
Athens Area Technical Institute (U)
Atlantic Cape Community College (U)
Austin Community College (U)
Baker College-Center for Graduate Studies (U, G)
Bakersfield College (U)
Ball State University (U, G)
Barton County Community College (U)
Beaufort County Community College (U)
Bellevue Community College (U)
Bergen Community College (U)
Black Hills State University (U)
Blinn College (U)
Boise State University (U)
Brenau University (U, G)
Brevard Community College (U)
Brigham Young University (U)
Broward Community College (U)
Bucks County Community College (U)
Buena Vista University (U)
Cabrillo College (U)
California College for Health Sciences (U, G)
California National University for Advanced Studies (U, G)
California State University, Fullerton (G)

California State University, Los Angeles (G)
Capella University (G)
Carleton University (U)
Central Community College–Grand Island Campus (U)
Centralia College (U)
Central Michigan University (U)
Central Piedmont Community College (U)
Central Texas College (U)
Century Community and Technical College (NC)
Cerro Coso Community College (U)
Chadron State College (U, G)
Champlain College (U)
Chattanooga State Technical Community College (U)
Chippewa Valley Technical College (U)
City Colleges of Chicago, Harold Washington College (U)
City University (U)
Clarkson College (U)
Clayton College & State University (U)
Cleveland State Community College (U)
Cochise College (U)
College for Financial Planning (G)
College of Albemarle (U)
College of DuPage (U)
College of Southern Maryland (U)
College of the Southwest (U)
College of West Virginia (U)
Colorado Christian University (G)
Colorado Mountain College District (U)
Colorado State University (G)
Columbia Basin College (U)
Columbia State Community College (U)
Columbus State Community College (U)
Connecticut State University System (U, G)
Corning Community College (U)
Cuyahoga Community College, Metropolitan Campus (U)
Dalhousie University (G)
Dallas County Community College District (U)
Danville Area Community College (U)
Danville Community College (U)
Davenport College of Business, Kalamazoo Campus (U)
David N. Myers College (U)
De Anza College (U)
Des Moines Area Community College (U)
Drake University (G)
Duke University (G)
Eastern Connecticut State University (U)
Eastern Oregon University (U)
Edison State Community College (U)
El Paso Community College (U)
Embry-Riddle Aeronautical University, Extended Campus (U)
Evergreen Valley College (U)
Fairleigh Dickinson University, The New College of General and Continuing Studies (G)
Fayetteville Technical Community College (U)
Florida Community College at Jacksonville (U)
Florida International University (U, G)
Forsyth Technical Community College (U)
Fort Hays State University (U)
Franklin University (U)
Frostburg State University (U, G)
Garland County Community College (U)

Genesee Community College (U)
Georgia Southern University (U, G)
Georgia Southwestern State University (G)
Gogebic Community College (U)
Golden Gate University (U, G)
Graceland College (U)
Grand Valley State University (U, G)
Greenville Technical College (U)
Harcourt Learning Direct (U)
Heriot-Watt University (G)
Herkimer County Community College (U)
Highland Community College (U)
Houston Community College System (U)
Howard Community College (U)
Indiana Institute of Technology (U)
Indiana University System (U)
Indian River Community College (U)
Iowa Western Community College (U)
ISIM University (G)
Ivy Tech State College–Columbus (U)
Ivy Tech State College–Kokomo (U)
Ivy Tech State College–North Central (U)
Ivy Tech State College–Northwest (U)
Ivy Tech State College–Southwest (U)
Ivy Tech State College–Wabash Valley (U)
Ivy Tech State College–Whitewater (U)
Jamestown Community College (U)
Johnson County Community College (U)
Kansas State University (U, NC)
Keller Graduate School of Management (G)
Kellogg Community College (U)
Kent State University (U)
Kentucky State University (U)
Kettering University (G)
Kingwood College (U)
Lake Land College (U)
Lakeland College (U)
Lake Superior State University (U)
Lansing Community College (U)
Lawson State Community College (U)
Lehigh Carbon Community College (U)
Lewis and Clark Community College (U)
Liberty University (U)
Lorain County Community College (U)
Los Angeles Harbor College (U)
Louisiana State University System (U)
Macon State College (U)
Madison Area Technical College (U)
Maharishi University of Management (G, NC)
Manatee Community College (U)
Marshall University (U, G)
Marywood University (U)
Medical College of Wisconsin (G)
Memorial University of Newfoundland (U)
Mercer University (NC)
Mercy College (U)
Metropolitan Community College (U)
Metropolitan Community Colleges (U)
Metropolitan State University (U)
Middle Tennessee State University (U)
Midland College (U)
Milwaukee School of Engineering (G, NC)
Minot State University (U)
Missouri Southern State College (U)
Modesto Junior College (U)
Mohawk Valley Community College (U)
Montana State University–Billings (U)
Montgomery College (U)
Montgomery County Community College (U)
Morehead State University (U, G)
Mountain Empire Community College (U)
Mount Saint Vincent University (U)
Mt. San Antonio College (U)
Nassau Community College (U)
National Technological University (G)
New Hampshire College (U, G)
New Jersey City University (G)
New Mexico State University (U, G)

New School University (U, NC)
New York Institute of Technology (U)
New York University (U)
North Carolina State University (U)
Northcentral Technical College (U)
North Dakota State University (U, G)
Northeast Wisconsin Technical College (U)
Northern Arizona University (U)
Northern Illinois University (G)
Northern Michigan University (U)
Northern Virginia Community College (U)
North Harris College (U)
North Seattle Community College (U)
Northwestern College (U)
Northwestern Michigan College (U)
Northwest Missouri State University (U)
Northwest Technical College (U)
Ohio University (U)
Ohio University–Southern Campus (U)
Okaloosa-Walton Community College (U)
Oklahoma State University (U)
Old Dominion University (U, G)
Open Learning Agency (U)
Owens Community College (U)
Palomar College (U)
Parkland College (U)
Pellissippi State Technical Community College (U)
Pennsylvania College of Technology (U)
Pennsylvania State University University Park Campus (U)
Pikes Peak Community College (U, NC)
Pitt Community College (U)
Portland Community College (U)
Portland State University (U)
Prairie State College (U)
Prince George's Community College (U)
Pueblo Community College (U)
Randolph Community College (U)
Rappahannock Community College (U)
Red Rocks Community College (U)
Regis University (U, G)
Rensselaer Polytechnic Institute (G, NC)
Richland Community College (U)
Rio Salado College (U)
Robert Morris College (U)
Robert Morris College (U)
Rochester Community and Technical College (U)
Rochester Institute of Technology (U)
Roger Williams University (U)
Roosevelt University (U)
Royal Military College of Canada (U)
Saddleback College (U)
Saint Joseph's College (U, G)
Saint Leo University (U)
St. Louis Community College System (U)
St. Petersburg Junior College (U)
Salt Lake Community College (U)
Salve Regina University (G, NC)
Sam Houston State University (U)
San Jacinto College District (U)
San Joaquin Delta College (U)
Santa Monica College (U)
Sauk Valley Community College (U)
Seattle Central Community College (U)
Seton Hall University (G)
Shawnee Community College (U)
Sinclair Community College (U)
Skidmore College (U)
Snow College (U)
Southeast Community College, Beatrice Campus (U)
Southeast Community College, Lincoln Campus (U)
Southern Connecticut State University (U)
Southern Vermont College (U)
Southwestern Assemblies of God University (U)
Southwestern Community College (U)

Southwestern Michigan College (U)
Southwest Missouri State University (U, G)
Stanly Community College (U)
State University of New York College of Agriculture and Technology at Morrisville (U)
State University of New York College of Technology at Delhi (U)
State University of New York Empire State College (U)
State University of New York Institute of Technology at Utica/Rome (U, G)
State University of West Georgia (U, G)
Stephens College (U, G)
Strayer University (U, G)
Suffolk County Community College (U)
Suffolk University (G)
Syracuse University (U, G)
Tarrant County College District (U)
Temple University (G)
Tennessee Technological University (U, G)
Terra State Community College (U)
Texas A&M University–Commerce (G)
Texas Tech University (U)
Thomas Edison State College (U)
Tidewater Community College (U)
Tompkins Cortland Community College (U)
Touro International University (U, G)
Triton College (U)
Troy State University (U)
Troy State University Montgomery (U)
Tulsa Community College (U)
Tyler Junior College (U)
Université Laval (U)
University College of Cape Breton (U)
University of Alabama (G)
University of Alaska Fairbanks (U)
University of Alaska Southeast, Ketchikan Campus (U)
University of Alaska Southeast, Sitka Campus (U)
University of Arizona (U)
University of Baltimore (G)
University of California, Berkeley (U)
University of California Extension (U)
University of Dallas (G)
University of Findlay (U, G)
University of Great Falls (U)
University of Houston–Downtown (U)
University of Illinois at Springfield (U, G)
University of Illinois at Urbana–Champaign (U)
University of Maine (U)
University of Maine at Fort Kent (U)
University of Management and Technology (G, NC)
University of Maryland University College (U)
University of Massachusetts Amherst (U, G)
University of Minnesota, Twin Cities Campus (U)
University of Missouri–Columbia (U)
University of Missouri–Kansas City (U)
University of Missouri–Rolla (G)
University of Montana–Missoula (G)
University of Nebraska–Lincoln (U, G)
University of Nevada, Reno (U)
University of New Brunswick (U)
University of North Carolina at Chapel Hill (U)
University of North Dakota (U)
University of Northern Iowa (U)
University of Notre Dame (G)
University of Oklahoma (G)
University of Phoenix (U, G)
University of St. Thomas (U)
University of South Carolina (U, G)
University of South Dakota (G)
University of Southern Mississippi (U)
University of Tennessee (U)
University of Tennessee at Martin (U, G)
University of Texas at San Antonio (U)
University of Texas at Tyler (U, G)
University of Texas–Pan American (U)

Individual Courses Index

Iowa State University of Science and Technology
(G)
National Technological University (G, NC)
North Carolina State University (G)
North Dakota State University (U)
Old Dominion University (G)
Shenandoah University (G)
Stanford University (G, NC)
State University of New York at Buffalo (G)
University of Alabama (G)
University of Arizona (G)
University of Colorado at Boulder (G, NC)
University of Delaware (G)
University of Southern California (G, NC)
University of Tennessee Space Institute (G)
University of Texas at Arlington (G)
University of Virginia (G)
Virginia Polytechnic Institute and State University
(G)

African-American studies

Cuyahoga Community College, Metropolitan
Campus (U)
De Anza College (U)
Delaware Technical & Community College,
Stanton/Wilmington Campus (U)
Eastern Michigan University (U, G)
Highland Community College (U)
Indiana University System (U)
Madison Area Technical College (U)
Modesto Junior College (U)
Northern Arizona University (U)
Thomas Edison State College (U)
University of Arizona (U)
University of Iowa (U, G)
University of Michigan–Flint (U, G)
University of Missouri–Columbia (U)
University of North Carolina at Chapel Hill (U)
University of Wisconsin Extension (U)
University of Wyoming (U)
Virginia Polytechnic Institute and State University
(U)
Western Michigan University (U)
West Virginia Wesleyan College (U)

Agricultural economics

Connors State College (U)
Iowa State University of Science and Technology
(U, G)
Michigan State University (U)
Northwestern College (U)
Oklahoma State University (U)
Oregon State University (U, G)
Pennsylvania State University University Park
Campus (NC)
Southern Illinois University Carbondale (U)
Texas Tech University (U, NC)
University of British Columbia (U)
University of Illinois at Urbana–Champaign (U)
University of Nebraska–Lincoln (U)
University of Tennessee (U)
University of Wisconsin Extension (U, NC)

Agriculture

Arkansas State University (U, G)
Butte College (U)
Central Community College–Grand Island
Campus (U)
Chadron State College (U)
Colorado Electronic Community College (U)
Colorado State University (U, G)
Dawson Community College (U, NC)
Eastern Oregon University (U)
Hawkeye Community College (U)
Iowa State University of Science and Technology
(U, G)
Kansas State University (U, G, NC)
Louisiana State University and Agricultural and
Mechanical College (G)

Michigan State University (U)
Mississippi State University (G)
Modesto Junior College (U)
North Carolina State University (U)
Northcentral Technical College (U)
North Dakota State University (U)
Northeast Wisconsin Technical College (U)
Oklahoma State University (U, G)
Oregon State University (U, G)
Purdue University (NC)
Redlands Community College (U)
Sam Houston State University (U)
South Dakota State University (U)
Southeast Community College, Lincoln Campus
(U)
Southwest Missouri State University (U)
Texas Tech University (U)
University of Arizona (U)
University of British Columbia (U)
University of Delaware (U)
University of Florida (U)
University of Idaho (U, G)
University of Minnesota, Crookston (U)
University of Missouri–Columbia (U, G)
University of Missouri-Columbia (U, G)
University of Nebraska–Lincoln (U, NC)
University of Wisconsin–Madison (U)
University of Wisconsin–River Falls (U, NC)
University of Wyoming (U)
University System of Georgia (U)
Utah State University (U)
Virginia Polytechnic Institute and State University
(U)
Walla Walla Community College (U)
Western Illinois University (U)

Algebra

American Institute for Computer Sciences (U)
Andrews University (U)
Anne Arundel Community College (U)
Arizona State University (U)
Arizona Western College (G)
Atlantic Cape Community College (U)
Bellevue Community College (U)
Blinn College (U)
Bossier Parish Community College (U)
Brigham Young University (U)
Bristol Community College (U)
Broward Community College (U)
Bucks County Community College (U)
California National University for Advanced
Studies (U)
Central Arizona College (U)
Centralia College (U)
Central Methodist College (U)
Central Oregon Community College (U)
Central Piedmont Community College (U)
Central Texas College (U)
Citrus College (U)
City Colleges of Chicago, Harold Washington
College (U)
Clatsop Community College (U)
Clayton College & State University (U)
Coastline Community College (U, NC)
Cochise College (U)
College of Albemarle (U)
College of the Redwoods (U)
College of West Virginia (U)
Colorado Electronic Community College (U)
Colorado Mountain College District (U)
Columbia Basin College (U)
Copiah-Lincoln Community College (U)
Cossatot Technical College (U)
Dallas Baptist University (U)
Dallas County Community College District (U)
De Anza College (U)
Delaware Technical & Community College,
Stanton/Wilmington Campus (U)

Delta College (U)
Drake University (U)
Dutchess Community College (U)
Eastern Kentucky University (U)
Eastern Oklahoma State College (U)
Florida Community College at Jacksonville (U)
Floyd College (U)
Forsyth Technical Community College (NC)
Frank Phillips College (U)
Genesee Community College (U)
Grantham College of Engineering (U)
Great Basin College (U)
Highland Community College (U)
Hill College of the Hill Junior College District
(U)
Horry-Georgetown Technical College (U)
Houston Community College System (U)
Hutchinson Community College and Area
Vocational School (U)
Illinois Eastern Community Colleges, Wabash
Valley College (U)
Indiana State University (U)
Indiana University System (U)
Indian River Community College (U)
Judson College (U)
Kansas City Kansas Community College (U)
Kent State University (U)
Kentucky State University (U)
Lake Land College (U)
Lansing Community College (U)
Louisiana State University System (U)
Macon Technical Institute (U)
Madison Area Technical College (U)
Manatee Community College (U)
Marylhurst University (U)
Marywood University (U)
Mayville State University (U)
Mercy College (U)
Metropolitan Community Colleges (U)
Miami-Dade Community College (U)
Middlesex County College (U)
Midland College (U)
Mississippi County Community College (U)
Mount Wachusett Community College (U)
Nassau Community College (U)
Northeastern University (U)
Northern State University (U)
Northern Virginia Community College (U)
North Seattle Community College (U)
NorthWest Arkansas Community College (NC)
Northwestern College (U)
Northwestern College (U)
Oklahoma State University (U)
Oregon State University (U)
Parkland College (U)
Pennsylvania State University University Park
Campus (U)
Piedmont Technical College (U)
Portland Community College (U)
Portland State University (U)
Presentation College (U)
Richland Community College (U)
Rio Salado College (U)
Roane State Community College (U)
Saint Charles County Community College (U, G)
St. Petersburg Junior College (U)
Sam Houston State University (U)
San Jacinto College District (U)
San Joaquin Delta College (U)
San Juan College (U)
Seattle Central Community College (U)
Sierra College (U)
Sinclair Community College (U)
Southern Arkansas University Tech (U)
Southwestern Community College (U)
State University of New York Empire State
College (U)
State University of West Georgia (U)

Western Governors University (U)
Western Illinois University (U)
Western Washington University (U)
West Hills Community College (U)
West Valley College (U)
West Virginia Northern Community College (U)
West Virginia Wesleyan College (U)
William Paterson University of New Jersey (U)
Wytheville Community College (U)

American literature

Andrews University (U)
Austin Community College (U)
Bellevue Community College (U)
Bergen Community College (U)
Blue Ridge Community College (U)
Brenau University (U)
Brigham Young University (U)
Bucks County Community College (U)
California National University for Advanced
    Studies (U)
Central Arizona College (U)
Centralia College (U)
Central Piedmont Community College (U)
Cerritos College (U)
Cerro Coso Community College (U)
Charles Stewart Mott Community College (U)
Cochise College (U)
Colorado Mountain College District (U)
Columbus State Community College (U)
Connecticut State University System (U, G)
Delaware Technical & Community College,
    Stanton/Wilmington Campus (U)
Del Mar College (U)
Delta College (U)
Drake University (U)
D'Youville College (U)
Eastern Michigan University (U)
Floyd College (U)
Forsyth Technical Community College (U)
Halifax Community College (U)
Illinois State University (U, G)
James Sprunt Community College (U)
Johnson State College (U)
John Wood Community College (U)
Kellogg Community College (U)
Kentucky State University (U)
Lake Land College (U)
Linn-Benton Community College (U)
Louisiana State University System (U)
Madison Area Technical College (U)
Marylhurst University (U)
Marywood University (U)
Midland College (U)
Mount Allison University (U)
Northeast State Technical Community College
    (U)
Northern Essex Community College (U)
Northern Virginia Community College (U)
Okaloosa-Walton Community College (U)
Oregon State University (U)
Owens Community College (U)
Piedmont Technical College (U)
Pitt Community College (U)
Portland Community College (U)
Rappahannock Community College (U)
Rio Salado College (U)
Roane State Community College (U)
Rochester College (U)
St. Petersburg Junior College (U)
Salve Regina University (U, NC)
Sam Houston State University (U)
San Juan College (U)
Seattle Central Community College (U)
Shawnee Community College (U)
Southwestern Community College (U)
Spoon River College (U)
State University of West Georgia (U, G)

Stephens College (U)
Taylor University, World Wide Campus (U)
Texas Tech University (U, NC)
Tyler Junior College (U)
University of Baltimore (U)
University of California, Berkeley (U)
University of California Extension (U)
University of Colorado at Denver (U)
University of Houston (U)
University of Illinois at Urbana–Champaign (U)
University of Maine (U)
University of Minnesota, Twin Cities Campus (U)
University of Nebraska–Lincoln (U)
University of North Carolina at Chapel Hill (U)
University of South Dakota (U)
University of Southern Indiana (U)
University of South Florida (U)
University of Tennessee (U)
University of Texas at Austin (U)
University of Texas System (U)
University of the Incarnate Word (U)
University of Utah (U)
University of Waterloo (U)
University of Wisconsin Colleges (U)
University of Wisconsin Extension (U)
University System of Georgia (U)
Vincennes University (U)
Virginia Polytechnic Institute and State University
    (U)
Virginia Western Community College (U)
Walters State Community College (U)
Washington State University (U)
Western Illinois University (U)
Western Washington University (U)

American studies

Andrews University (U)
Bellevue Community College (U)
Centralia College (U)
Drake University (U)
Indiana University System (U)
Laramie County Community College (U)
Marylhurst University (U)
Seattle Central Community College (U)
Southwestern Community College (U)
Stephens College (U)
Temple University (U)
University of Arizona (U)
University of California, Berkeley (U)
University of California Extension (U)
University of Denver (U, G)
University of Iowa (U)
University of Minnesota, Twin Cities Campus (U)
University of Nebraska–Lincoln (U)
University of Nevada, Reno (U)
University of North Alabama (U, G)
University of North Carolina at Chapel Hill (U)
University of North Carolina at Pembroke (U)
University of South Florida (U)
Washington State University (U)

Anatomy

Alamance Community College (U)
American Academy of Nutrition, College of
    Nutrition (U)
Central Arizona College (U)
Central Methodist College (U)
Century Community and Technical College (NC)
Coastline Community College (U, NC)
College of West Virginia (U)
Community Hospital of Roanoke Valley–College
    of Health Sciences (U)
Dalhousie University (U)
Florida Community College at Jacksonville (U)
Floyd College (U)
Forsyth Technical Community College (NC)
Indiana University System (U)
Ivy Tech State College–Southeast (U)

John Wood Community College (U)
Louisiana State University System (U)
Manatee Community College (U)
Mansfield University of Pennsylvania (U)
Northeast Wisconsin Technical College (U)
Northwestern Technical Institute (U)
Okaloosa-Walton Community College (U)
Parkland College (U)
Piedmont Technical College (U)
Roane State Community College (U)
St. Petersburg Junior College (U)
Southern Illinois University Carbondale (U)
Southwestern Community College (U)
Stephens College (U)
Texas State Technical College–Harlingen (U)
Tyler Junior College (U)
University of Arizona (U)
University of South Dakota (U)
University of Wyoming (U)
West Virginia Wesleyan College (U)

Animal sciences

Bergen Community College (U)
Blue Ridge Community College (U)
Brigham Young University (U)
Colorado State University (U)
Connors State College (U)
Iowa State University of Science and Technology
    (U, G)
James Sprunt Community College (U)
Kansas State University (U, G, NC)
Los Angeles Pierce College (U)
Louisiana State University at Eunice (U)
Louisiana State University System (U)
Manor College (U)
Northeast Wisconsin Technical College (U)
Oklahoma State University (U)
Pennsylvania State University University Park
    Campus (U, NC)
State University of New York College of
    Technology at Canton (U)
State University of New York College of
    Technology at Delhi (U)
University of Arkansas (U)
University of British Columbia (U)
University of Connecticut (U)
University of Maine (U)
University of Missouri–Columbia (U, G)
Yuba College (U)

Anthropology

Anne Arundel Community College (U)
Arizona Western College (G)
Atlantic Cape Community College (U)
Atlantic University (G, NC)
Austin Community College (U)
Bellevue Community College (U)
Bethany College of the Assemblies of God (U)
Blinn College (U)
Bridgewater State College (U)
Brigham Young University (U)
Brookdale Community College (U)
Broward Community College (U)
Burlington County College (U)
Cabrillo College (U)
California Institute of Integral Studies (G, NC)
Carleton University (U)
Central Arizona College (U)
Centralia College (U)
Central Piedmont Community College (U)
Central Texas College (U)
Central Washington University (U)
Cerritos College (U)
Chaminade University of Honolulu (U)
Charles Stewart Mott Community College (U)
Charter Oak State College (U)
Citrus College (U)
City College of San Francisco (U)
Clackamas Community College (U)

Art history and criticism

Asian languages and literatures

Individual Courses Index

Biology

Erie Community College, North Campus (U)
Everett Community College (U)
Fairleigh Dickinson University, The New College of General and Continuing Studies (G)
Fashion Institute of Technology (U)
Fayetteville Technical Community College (U)
Florence-Darlington Technical College (U)
Florida Community College at Jacksonville (U)
Florida Gulf Coast University (G)
Foothill College (U)
Frank Phillips College (U)
Fullerton College (U)
Garland County Community College (U)
Genesee Community College (U)
George Washington University (G, NC)
Georgia Southern University (U, G)
Georgia Southwestern State University (G)
Georgia State University (U, G)
Governors State University (U)
Grand Valley State University (U, G)
Grayson County College (U)
Great Basin College (U)
Green River Community College (U)
Griggs University (U)
Harrisburg Area Community College (U)
Heriot-Watt University (G)
Hibbing Community College (U)
Hillsborough Community College (U)
Horry-Georgetown Technical College (U)
Houston Community College System (U)
Howard Community College (NC)
Indiana Institute of Technology (U)
Indiana University System (U)
ISIM University (G)
Ivy Tech State College–Wabash Valley (U)
Johnson County Community College (U)
Judson College (U)
Kansas City Kansas Community College (U)
Kellogg Community College (U)
Lake Land College (U)
Lakeshore Technical College (U)
Lamar University (U)
Laramie County Community College (U)
Lehigh University (G, NC)
Lenoir Community College (U)
LeTourneau University (U)
Louisiana State University System (U)
Madison Area Technical College (U)
Madonna University (U, G)
Marshall University (U, G)
Martin Community College (U)
Massachusetts Institute of Technology (NC)
Mayland Community College (U)
Mayville State University (U)
McDowell Technical Community College (U)
Memorial University of Newfoundland (U)
Mercer University (NC)
Mercy College (U, G)
Metropolitan Community Colleges (U)
Michigan Technological University (U, NC)
Mid-America Bible College (U)
Middle Tennessee State University (U, G)
Midland College (U)
Mid-Plains Community College Area (U)
Minot State University (U, G)
Missouri Southern State College (U)
Montana State University–Billings (U)
Moraine Valley Community College (U)
Morehead State University (U, G)
Mountain Empire Community College (U)
Mount Saint Vincent University (U)
Nassau Community College (U)
National American University (U)
National Technological University (NC)
National University (U, G)
New Hampshire College (U, G)
New Jersey Institute of Technology (G)
New Mexico State University (U, G)

New School University (U, NC)
New York Institute of Technology (U)
New York University (G)
North Carolina State University (U)
North Central State College (U)
Northcentral Technical College (U)
North Central University (U, G)
North Dakota State College of Science (U)
Northeast Wisconsin Technical College (U)
Northern Arizona University (U)
Northern Essex Community College (U)
Northern Michigan University (U)
Northern Virginia Community College (U)
North Iowa Area Community College (U)
North Seattle Community College (U)
Northwestern College (U)
Northwestern Michigan College (U)
Norwich University (U, G)
Nyack College (U)
Ohio University (U)
Ohio University–Southern Campus (U)
Oklahoma City Community College (U)
Oklahoma State University (G)
Old Dominion University (U, G)
Owens Community College (U)
Palomar College (U)
Parkland College (U)
Pensacola Junior College (U)
Peralta Community College District (U)
Pikes Peak Community College (U, NC)
Pitt Community College (U, NC)
Portland Community College (U)
Portland State University (U, G)
Prince George's Community College (NC)
Quincy College (U)
Redlands Community College (U)
Red Rocks Community College (U)
Regents College (U)
Regent University (G)
Regis University (U, G)
Richard Stockton College of New Jersey (U, NC)
Rio Salado College (U)
Roane State Community College (U)
Rochester Institute of Technology (U, G)
Rockland Community College (U)
Rogers State University (U)
Roosevelt University (U)
Royal Roads University (G)
Ryerson Polytechnic University (U, NC)
Sacramento City College (U)
Saint Charles County Community College (U, G)
St. Johns River Community College (U)
Saint Joseph's College (U)
St. Louis Community College System (U)
St. Petersburg Junior College (U)
Salt Lake Community College (U)
Salve Regina University (U, G, NC)
Sam Houston State University (U)
San Antonio College (U)
San Diego City College (U)
San Joaquin Delta College (U)
San Juan College (U)
Santa Monica College (U)
Sauk Valley Community College (U)
Scottsdale Community College (U)
Seton Hall University (G)
Sinclair Community College (U)
Skidmore College (U)
South Dakota State University (U, G)
Southeastern Community College, North Campus (NC)
Southeastern Illinois College (U)
Southern Oregon University (U, G)
Southern Utah University (U)
Southwestern Assemblies of God University (U)
Southwestern Michigan College (U)
Southwest Virginia Community College (U)
Spring Arbor College (U, G)

Springfield Technical Community College (U)
State University of New York at Farmingdale (U)
State University of New York College of Agriculture and Technology at Morrisville (U)
State University of New York College of Technology at Alfred (U)
State University of New York Empire State College (U)
State University of New York Institute of Technology at Utica/Rome (G)
Stephens College (U, G)
Stevens Institute of Technology (G)
Suffolk County Community College (U)
Syracuse University (U, G)
Tarrant County College District (U)
Texas A&M University–Commerce (G)
Texas Christian University (U)
Texas Tech University (NC)
Thomas Edison State College (U)
Touro International University (U, G, NC)
Troy State University Dothan (U)
Troy State University Montgomery (U)
Tulsa Community College (U)
Tyler Junior College (U)
Ulster County Community College (U)
Umpqua Community College (U)
Union Institute (U)
United States Open University (U, G)
United States Sports Academy (G, NC)
University College of the Fraser Valley (U)
University of Alabama (U)
University of Alaska Fairbanks (U)
University of Alaska Southeast, Sitka Campus (U)
University of Baltimore (G)
University of California, Berkeley (U)
University of California Extension (U)
University of California, Los Angeles (G)
University of Central Arkansas (U)
University of Charleston (U, NC)
University of Cincinnati (U)
University of Cincinnati Raymond Walters College (U)
University of Colorado at Denver (G)
University of Dallas (G)
University of Great Falls (U)
University of Houston (G)
University of Houston–Victoria (U, G)
University of Iowa (U, G)
University of Maine (U)
University of Maine at Fort Kent (U)
University of Management and Technology (G, NC)
University of Maryland University College (U)
University of Minnesota, Crookston (U)
University of Minnesota, Twin Cities Campus (U)
University of Missouri–Columbia (U, G)
University of Missouri–Kansas City (U)
University of Nebraska–Lincoln (U)
University of Nevada, Reno (U)
University of New Brunswick (U)
University of New Hampshire (NC)
University of North Alabama (U, G)
University of North Dakota (U)
University of Notre Dame (G)
University of Phoenix (U, G)
University of St. Thomas (G)
University of South Carolina (U, G)
University of South Dakota (G)
University of Southern Indiana (U)
University of South Florida (G)
University of Tennessee at Martin (U, G)
University of Texas at Austin (U)
University of Texas at San Antonio (U)
University of Texas of the Permian Basin (U, G)
University of Texas System (U)
University of Toronto (NC)
University of Washington (U)
University of Waterloo (G)

Jacksonville State University (U)
Jamestown Community College (U)
Jefferson Community College (U)
Johns Hopkins University (G)
John Wood Community College (U)
Jones International University (G)
Kansas State University (U, G, NC)
Keller Graduate School of Management (G)
Kellogg Community College (U)
Kent State University (U)
Kettering University (G)
Lackawanna Junior College (U)
Lake Land College (U)
Lakeland College (U, G)
Lakeland Community College (U)
Lakeshore Technical College (U)
Lake Superior State University (U)
Lamar State College–Port Arthur (U)
Lansing Community College (U)
Laramie County Community College (U)
Lawson State Community College (U)
Lehigh Carbon Community College (U)
Lesley College (G)
Lewis and Clark Community College (U)
Liberty University (U, G)
Linn-Benton Community College (U)
Lorain County Community College (U)
Los Angeles Mission College (U)
Louisiana State University and Agricultural and
    Mechanical College (U, G)
Louisiana State University at Alexandria (U)
Louisiana State University System (U)
Luzerne County Community College (U)
Lynn University (U, G)
Madison Area Technical College (U, NC)
Madisonville Community College (U)
Maharishi University of Management (G, NC)
Malone College (U)
Manatee Community College (U)
Manor College (U)
Mansfield University of Pennsylvania (U)
Marshall University (U, G)
Martin Community College (U)
Marylhurst University (U, G)
Marywood University (U)
Massachusetts Institute of Technology (G)
Mayland Community College (U)
McDowell Technical Community College (U)
Medical College of Wisconsin (G)
Memorial University of Newfoundland (U)
Mercy College (U, G)
Metropolitan Community College (U)
Metropolitan Community Colleges (U)
Metropolitan State University (U, G)
Michigan Technological University (U, NC)
Middle Tennessee State University (U, G)
Midland College (U)
Midwestern State University (U, G)
Milwaukee School of Engineering (G, NC)
Minot State University (U)
Mississippi State University (G)
Missouri Southern State College (U)
Mitchell Community College (U)
Modesto Junior College (U)
Montana State University–Billings (U)
Montana State University—Great Falls College of
    Technology (U)
Montgomery College (U)
Montgomery County Community College (U)
Morehead State University (U, G)
Motlow State Community College (U, NC)
Mount Saint Vincent University (U)
Mt. San Antonio College (U)
Nassau Community College (U)
National Technological University (NC)
newGraduate Schools (G)
New Hampshire College (U, G)
New Jersey City University (G)

New Jersey Institute of Technology (U, G)
New Mexico State University (U, G)
New School University (U, NC)
New York Institute of Technology (U, G)
New York University (NC)
Northampton County Area Community College
    (U)
North Central State College (U)
North Country Community College (U)
North Dakota State University (G)
Northeastern State University (U)
Northeast State Technical Community College
    (U)
Northeast Wisconsin Technical College (U)
Northern Arizona University (U, G)
Northern Essex Community College (U)
Northern Illinois University (G)
Northern Kentucky University (U, G)
Northern Michigan University (U)
Northern State University (U)
Northern Virginia Community College (U)
North Harris College (U)
North Iowa Area Community College (U)
North Seattle Community College (U)
Northwestern College (U)
Northwestern Michigan College (U)
Northwest Missouri State University (U)
Northwood University (U)
Oakland Community College (U)
Ohio University (U)
Ohio University–Southern Campus (U, G)
Ohlone College (U)
Oklahoma City Community College (U)
Oklahoma State University (G)
Old Dominion University (U, G)
Owens Community College (U)
Palomar College (U)
Parkland College (U)
Park University (U)
Peirce College (U)
Pellissippi State Technical Community College
    (U)
Pennsylvania College of Technology (U)
Pennsylvania State University University Park
    Campus (U, NC)
Pensacola Junior College (U)
Peralta Community College District (U)
Piedmont Technical College (U)
Pikes Peak Community College (U, NC)
Pitt Community College (U, NC)
Portland Community College (U, NC)
Portland State University (U)
Prairie Bible College (G)
Prairie State College (U)
Prince George's Community College (U, NC)
Pueblo Community College (U)
Purdue University (G)
Quincy College (U)
Randolph Community College (U)
Rappahannock Community College (U)
Redlands Community College (U)
Red Rocks Community College (U)
Regents College (U)
Regent University (G)
Regis University (U, G)
Rensselaer Polytechnic Institute (G)
Richard Stockton College of New Jersey (U)
Rio Salado College (U)
Riverland Community College (NC)
Riverside Community College (U)
Roane State Community College (U)
Robert Morris College (U)
Robert Morris College (U)
Rochester Institute of Technology (U, G)
Rockland Community College (U)
Roger Williams University (U)
Roosevelt University (U)
Royal Military College of Canada (U, G)

Royal Roads University (G)
Ryerson Polytechnic University (U, NC)
Sacramento City College (U)
Sacred Heart University (U)
Saddleback College (U)
St. Ambrose University (U, G)
St. Johns River Community College (U)
St. John's University (U, G)
Saint Joseph's College (U)
Saint Leo University (U)
St. Louis Community College System (U)
St. Mary's University of San Antonio (G)
St. Petersburg Junior College (U)
Saint Peter's College (G)
Salt Lake Community College (U)
Salve Regina University (U, G, NC)
Sam Houston State University (U)
San Antonio College (U)
San Diego City College (U)
San Jacinto College District (U)
San Joaquin Delta College (U)
Santa Ana College (U)
Seattle Central Community College (U)
Seminole Community College (U)
Shawnee Community College (U)
Sheridan College (U)
Sierra College (U)
Simpson College (U)
Sinclair Community College (U)
Skidmore College (U)
Snow College (U)
Southeast Community College, Beatrice Campus
    (U)
Southeast Community College, Lincoln Campus
    (U)
Southeastern Community College, North Campus
    (U, NC)
Southeastern Louisiana University (U)
Southeastern Oklahoma State University (G)
Southern Arkansas University Tech (U)
Southern California University for Professional
    Studies (U, G)
South Florida Community College (U)
Southwestern Assemblies of God University (U)
Southwestern Community College (U)
Southwestern Michigan College (U)
Southwest Missouri State University (U, G)
Southwest Virginia Community College (U)
Stanly Community College (U)
State University of New York at Oswego (G)
State University of New York College at Fredonia
    (U)
State University of New York College at Oneonta
    (U, NC)
State University of New York College of
    Technology at Canton (U)
State University of New York College of
    Technology at Delhi (U)
State University of New York Empire State
    College (U)
State University of West Georgia (U, G)
Stephens College (U, G)
Stevens Institute of Technology (G)
Strayer University (U, G)
Suffolk County Community College (U)
Suffolk University (G)
Surry Community College (U)
Sussex County Community College (U)
Syracuse University (U)
Tarrant County College District (U)
Technical College of the Lowcountry (U)
Terra State Community College (U)
Texas A&M University–Texarkana (U)
Texas Tech University (U)
Thomas Edison State College (G)
Tompkins Cortland Community College (U)
Touro International University (U, G)
Triton College (U)

Business administration and management (continued)

Troy State University (G)
Troy State University Dothan (U)
Troy State University Montgomery (U)
Tulsa Community College (U)
Tyler Junior College (U)
Umpqua Community College (U)
United States International University (G)
United States Sports Academy (G, NC)
Université Laval (U, G)
University of Akron (U, G)
University of Alabama (U, G)
University of Alaska Fairbanks (U)
University of Alaska Southeast (U)
University of Alaska Southeast, Sitka Campus (U)
University of Arkansas (U)
University of Baltimore (G)
University of California, Berkeley (U)
University of California, Davis (U)
University of California Extension (U)
University of California, Los Angeles (G)
University of Central Florida (U)
University of Cincinnati (U)
University of Colorado at Colorado Springs (G)
University of Colorado at Denver (G)
University of Dallas (G)
University of Delaware (U)
University of Great Falls (U)
University of Houston (G)
University of Houston–Downtown (U)
University of Illinois at Springfield (G)
University of Illinois at Urbana–Champaign (U)
University of La Verne (U)
University of Maine at Fort Kent (U)
University of Management and Technology (G, NC)
University of Maryland University College (U, G)
University of Massachusetts Amherst (G)
University of Massachusetts Lowell (U)
University of Michigan–Flint (U, G)
University of Minnesota, Crookston (U)
University of Minnesota, Twin Cities Campus (U)
University of Missouri–Columbia (U, G)
University of Missouri–Rolla (G)
University of Missouri–St. Louis (G)
University of Montana–Missoula (G)
University of Nebraska–Lincoln (U, G)
University of Nevada, Reno (U)
University of New Brunswick (U)
University of New Hampshire (U)
University of North Carolina at Greensboro (U)
University of North Carolina at Pembroke (U, G)
University of North Carolina at Wilmington (U)
University of North Dakota (U, G)
University of Notre Dame (G)
University of Oklahoma (U)
University of Phoenix (U, G)
University of Pittsburgh (G)
University of St. Francis (U, G)
University of St. Thomas (G)
University of Sarasota (G)
University of South Alabama (U, G)
University of South Carolina (U, G)
University of South Dakota (U, G)
University of Southern California (NC)
University of Southern Colorado (U)
University of Southern Mississippi (U)
University of South Florida (U, G)
University of Tennessee (U)
University of Tennessee at Chattanooga (G)
University of Tennessee at Martin (U, G)
University of Texas at El Paso (G)
University of Texas at San Antonio (U)
University of Texas at Tyler (U, G)
University of Texas System (G)
University of the Incarnate Word (U)
University of Toledo (U)
University of Toronto (NC)

University of Waterloo (U, G)
University of West Florida (U, G)
University of Wisconsin Extension (U, NC)
University of Wisconsin–La Crosse (U, G)
University of Wisconsin–Milwaukee (U)
University of Wisconsin–Platteville (U)
University of Wisconsin–River Falls (U, NC)
University of Wisconsin–Whitewater (G)
University of Wyoming (U)
University System of Georgia (U)
Upper Iowa University (U, NC)
Utah State University (U)
Valdosta State University (U)
Vance-Granville Community College (U)
Victor Valley College (U)
Vincennes University (U)
Virginia Polytechnic Institute and State University (G)
Volunteer State Community College (U)
Wake Technical Community College (U)
Walden University (G)
Walsh College of Accountancy and Business Administration (G)
Walters State Community College (U)
Washburn University of Topeka (U)
Washington State University (U)
Wayland Baptist University (U)
Wayne County Community College District (U)
Weber State University (U)
Western Carolina University (U)
Western Illinois University (U, G)
Western Nebraska Community College (U)
Western Oklahoma State College (U)
West Hills Community College (U)
Westmoreland County Community College (U)
West Shore Community College (U)
West Valley College (U)
West Virginia Northern Community College (U)
West Virginia University (G)
West Virginia Wesleyan College (U)
Wichita State University (U, G)
Wilfrid Laurier University (U)
William Rainey Harper College (U)
Wilmington College (U, G)
Worcester Polytechnic Institute (G)
Wytheville Community College (U)
Xavier University of Louisiana (U)
York College of Pennsylvania (U)
York Technical College (U)
Yuba College (U)

Business communications

Adams State College (U)
Anne Arundel Community College (U)
Arizona State University (U)
Atlantic Cape Community College (U)
Barton County Community College (U)
Boise State University (U)
Bridgewater State College (U)
California National University for Advanced Studies (U, G)
Capella University (G)
Cerritos College (U)
Cerro Coso Community College (U)
College of Albemarle (U)
Colorado Mountain College District (U)
Columbus State Community College (U)
Concordia College (U)
Cossatot Technical College (U)
CTS University, Inc. (NC)
Dallas County Community College District (U)
Delta College (U)
Eastern Michigan University (U)
Edison State Community College (U)
El Paso Community College (U)
Finger Lakes Community College (U)
Gannon University (U)
Gogebic Community College (U)

Instituto Tecnológico y de Estudios Superiores de Monterrey, Campus Monterrey (NC)
Jones International University (U, G)
Kansas City Kansas Community College (U)
Kellogg Community College (U)
Lehigh Carbon Community College (U)
Long Island University, Brooklyn Campus (NC)
Lynn University (U)
Malone College (U)
Marylhurst University (U, G)
Marywood University (U)
Miami-Dade Community College (U)
Midland College (U)
Milwaukee School of Engineering (G, NC)
New York University (NC)
North Country Community College (U)
Northeast State Technical Community College (U)
Northern Essex Community College (U)
NorthWest Arkansas Community College (U)
Ohio State University–Mansfield Campus (U)
Oklahoma City Community College (U)
Oklahoma City University (U)
Oklahoma State University (U)
Open Learning Agency (U)
Pennsylvania State University University Park Campus (U, NC)
Pitt Community College (U, NC)
Portland Community College (U)
Rappahannock Community College (U)
Rensselaer Polytechnic Institute (G, NC)
Roane State Community College (U)
Roosevelt University (U)
Royal Roads University (G)
St. Edward's University (U)
Saint Leo University (U)
St. Petersburg Junior College (U)
Saint Peter's College (G)
Salt Lake Community College (U)
Seminole Community College (U)
Seton Hall University (U)
Sinclair Community College (U)
Spring Arbor College (U, G)
State University of New York Empire State College (U)
Strayer University (G)
Suffolk University (G)
Syracuse University (U)
Texas A&M University–Texarkana (U)
Thomas Edison State College (U)
Tompkins Cortland Community College (U)
Touro International University (U)
Tyler Junior College (U)
University of California, Berkeley (U)
University of California Extension (U)
University of California, Los Angeles (G)
University of Cincinnati Raymond Walters College (U)
University of Connecticut (U)
University of Illinois at Urbana–Champaign (U)
University of Management and Technology (G, NC)
University of Nevada, Reno (NC)
University of North Carolina at Chapel Hill (U)
University of Notre Dame (G)
University of Texas–Pan American (U)
University of Texas System (G)
University of Toronto (NC)
University of Wisconsin–Platteville (U, G)
Upper Iowa University (U, NC)
Western Oregon University (U)
West Virginia Wesleyan College (U)
Worcester Polytechnic Institute (G)
York College of Pennsylvania (U)

Business information and data processing services

Roosevelt University (U)

Business law

Adams State College (U)
American Institute for Computer Sciences (U)
Anne Arundel Community College (U)
Arizona State University (U)
Atlantic Cape Community College (U)
Austin Community College (U)
Bellevue Community College (U)
Berkshire Community College (U)
Blinn College (U)
Broward Community College (U)
Bucks County Community College (U)
Cabrillo College (U)
California National University for Advanced
    Studies (U, G)
Cape Fear Community College (U)
Central Arizona College (U)
Centralia College (U)
Central Piedmont Community College (U)
Central Texas College (U)
Cerritos College (U)
Cerro Coso Community College (U)
Christopher Newport University (U)
College of Albemarle (U)
College of Southern Maryland (U)
College of West Virginia (U)
Colorado Mountain College District (U)
Columbus State Community College (U)
Cossatot Technical College (U)
De Anza College (U)
Delaware Technical & Community College,
    Stanton/Wilmington Campus (U)
Delta College (U)
Dutchess Community College (U)
Eastern Michigan University (U, G)
Embry-Riddle Aeronautical University, Extended
    Campus (U)
Fashion Institute of Technology (U)
Florida Community College at Jacksonville (U)
Forsyth Technical Community College (U)
Greenville Technical College (U)
Houston Community College System (U)
Indiana Institute of Technology (U)
John Wood Community College (U)
Kellogg Community College (U)
Lake Land College (U)
Lansing Community College (U)
Laramie County Community College (U)
Lehigh Carbon Community College (U)
Louisiana State University System (U)
Madison Area Technical College (U)
Manor College (U)
Marywood University (U)
Mercy College (U)
Metropolitan Community Colleges (U)
Metropolitan State University (U)
Midland College (U)
Midwestern State University (G)
Montgomery College (U)
Moraine Valley Community College (U)
Mountain Empire Community College (U)
Mt. San Antonio College (U)
Nassau Community College (U)
newGraduate Schools (G)
New Hampshire College (U)
North Carolina State University (U)
Northeast State Technical Community College
    (U)
Northeast Wisconsin Technical College (U)
Northern Virginia Community College (U)
Northwestern College (U)
Okaloosa-Walton Community College (U)
Oklahoma City Community College (U)
Oklahoma State University (U)
Open Learning Agency (U)
Owens Community College (U)
Palomar College (U)
Parkland College (U)

Park University (U)
Peirce College (U)
Pennsylvania State University University Park
    Campus (U)
Piedmont Technical College (U)
Pitt Community College (U)
Portland Community College (U)
Randolph Community College (U)
Rappahannock Community College (U)
Roane State Community College (U)
Robert Morris College (U)
Roger Williams University (U)
Roosevelt University (U)
Sacred Heart University (U)
Saddleback College (U)
Salve Regina University (U, G, NC)
Sam Houston State University (U)
San Diego City College (U)
San Joaquin Delta College (U)
Shawnee Community College (U)
Sinclair Community College (U)
Southeast Community College, Lincoln Campus
    (U)
State University of New York Empire State
    College (U)
State University of West Georgia (U)
Stephens College (U, G)
Strayer University (U)
Suffolk County Community College (U)
Surry Community College (U)
Texas Tech University (U, NC)
Thomas Edison State College (U)
Tompkins Cortland Community College (U)
Triton College (U)
Troy State University Montgomery (U)
Tyler Junior College (U)
Université Laval (U)
University of Alaska Southeast (U)
University of Arkansas (U)
University of Findlay (U)
University of Houston–Downtown (U)
University of Missouri–Columbia (U)
University of Texas at San Antonio (U)
University of Texas System (G)
University of the Incarnate Word (U)
University of Toronto (NC)
University of Wisconsin Extension (U, NC)
Upper Iowa University (U, NC)
Washington State University (U)
Wayne County Community College District (U)
Western Governors University (U)
Westmoreland County Community College (U)
West Valley College (U)
Wilfrid Laurier University (U)

Calculus

Anne Arundel Community College (U)
Blinn College (U)
Brigham Young University (U)
Bristol Community College (U)
California National University for Advanced
    Studies (U)
Centralia College (U)
Central Methodist College (U)
Central Piedmont Community College (U)
Cochise College (U)
College of Southern Maryland (U)
College of the Redwoods (U)
College of West Virginia (U)
Colorado Mountain College District (U)
Delaware Technical & Community College,
    Stanton/Wilmington Campus (U)
Delta College (U)
Drake University (U)
Eastern Connecticut State University (U)
Embry-Riddle Aeronautical University, Extended
    Campus (U)
Floyd College (U)

Grantham College of Engineering (U)
Hill College of the Hill Junior College District
    (U)
Horry-Georgetown Technical College (U)
Indiana State University (U)
Jefferson Community College (U)
Judson College (U)
Kellogg Community College (U)
Laramie County Community College (U)
Linn-Benton Community College (U)
Louisiana State University at Alexandria (U)
Louisiana State University System (U)
Manatee Community College (U)
Middlesex County College (U)
Midland College (U)
Mount Allison University (U)
Mount Wachusett Community College (U)
Northeastern University (U)
Northern State University (U)
Northern Virginia Community College (U)
Northwestern Michigan College (U)
Oklahoma State University (U)
Oregon State University (U)
Parkland College (U)
Pellissippi State Technical Community College
    (U)
Pennsylvania State University University Park
    Campus (U)
Piedmont Technical College (U)
Portland State University (U)
Raritan Valley Community College (U)
Rio Salado College (U)
Roane State Community College (U)
Royal Military College of Canada (U)
Sam Houston State University (U)
Sauk Valley Community College (U)
Snow College (U)
Southwest Missouri State University (U)
Southwest Virginia Community College (U)
State University of New York Empire State
    College (U)
State University of West Georgia (U)
Strayer University (U)
Suffolk County Community College (U)
Syracuse University (U)
Texas Tech University (U, NC)
University of Alaska Fairbanks (U)
University of Arizona (U)
University of Arkansas (U)
University of Colorado at Denver (U)
University of Delaware (U)
University of Idaho (U, G)
University of Iowa (U, G)
University of Manitoba (U)
University of Minnesota, Twin Cities Campus (U)
University of Missouri–Columbia (U)
University of Nebraska–Lincoln (U)
University of North Carolina at Chapel Hill (U)
University of Pennsylvania (U, NC)
University of South Dakota (U)
University of Southern Maine (U)
University of Southern Mississippi (U)
University of Tennessee (U)
University of Texas at Austin (U)
University of Utah (U)
University of Vermont (U)
University of Waterloo (U, NC)
University of Wisconsin Extension (U)
University System of Georgia (U)
Vermont Technical College (U)
Weber State University (U)
Western Governors University (U)
Western Washington University (U)
West Virginia Northern Community College (U)
William Paterson University of New Jersey (U)
Yuba College (U)

University of Findlay (U)
University of Utah (U)
University of Waterloo (U)

Chemistry, physical
California National University for Advanced
  Studies (U)
Roane State Community College (U)
University of Waterloo (U)
William Rainey Harper College (U)

Child care and development
Arizona Western College (G)
Athens Area Technical Institute (U)
Bakersfield College (U)
Bethany College of the Assemblies of God (U)
Blinn College (U)
Brenau University (U, G)
Burlington County College (U)
Cabrillo College (U)
Central Arizona College (U)
Central Missouri State University (U)
Central Texas College (U)
Cerro Coso Community College (U)
Clackamas Community College (U)
College of DuPage (U)
Colorado Electronic Community College (U)
Colorado Mountain College District (U)
Colorado State University (U)
Concordia University at St. Paul (U)
Cossatot Technical College (U)
Delaware Technical & Community College,
  Stanton/Wilmington Campus (U)
Eastern Maine Technical College (U)
El Camino College (U)
El Paso Community College (U)
Fayetteville Technical Community College (U)
Florida State University (U, NC)
Forsyth Technical Community College (U)
Glendale Community College (U)
Harrisburg Area Community College (U)
Houston Community College System (U)
Ivy Tech State College–Eastcentral (U)
Ivy Tech State College–Whitewater (U)
Jefferson Community College (U)
John Wood Community College (U)
Kansas City Kansas Community College (U)
Kansas State University (U, G, NC)
Lake Washington Technical College (U)
Lenoir Community College (U)
Lewis and Clark Community College (U)
Manatee Community College (U)
Metropolitan Community Colleges (U)
Mountain Empire Community College (U)
Mt. San Jacinto College (U)
North Dakota State University (U, G)
Northeast State Technical Community College
  (U)
Northeast Wisconsin Technical College (U)
North Seattle Community College (U)
Northwestern Michigan College (U)
Okaloosa-Walton Community College (U)
Oregon State University (U, G)
Saddleback College (U)
St. Petersburg Junior College (U)
San Diego City College (U)
San Jacinto College District (U)
San Joaquin Delta College (U)
San Juan College (U)
Seattle Central Community College (U)
Southeast Community College, Lincoln Campus
  (U)
Southwest Missouri State University (U)
State University of New York Empire State
  College (U)
Surry Community College (U)
Troy State University Montgomery (U)
University of Alaska Fairbanks (U)

University of Delaware (U)
University of Minnesota, Twin Cities Campus (U)
University of North Carolina at Greensboro (U)
University of Tennessee (U)
University of Wisconsin Extension (U, NC)
University of Wisconsin–Madison (U)
University of Wisconsin–Stevens Point (U, G)
University of Wyoming (U)
Walters State Community College (U)
Washington State University (U)
Weber State University (U)
Western Carolina University (U)
Yuba College (U)

Chinese language and literature
Manatee Community College (U)
Oregon State University (U)
Rutgers, The State University of New Jersey, New
  Brunswick (U)
University of California, Berkeley (U)
University of California Extension (U)
University of Oklahoma (U)
University of Toronto (NC)

Civil engineering
Arizona State University (U, G)
Brigham Young University (U)
Carleton University (U)
Colorado State University (G)
Florida International University (G)
Florida State University (G)
Georgia Institute of Technology (G, NC)
Harcourt Learning Direct (U)
Illinois Institute of Technology (U, G)
Iowa State University of Science and Technology
  (G)
Kansas State University (G, NC)
Louisiana State University at Alexandria (U)
Mississippi State University (G)
Montana State University–Bozeman (G)
National Technological University (G, NC)
New Jersey Institute of Technology (G)
New Mexico State University (G)
North Carolina State University (G)
North Dakota State University (G)
Old Dominion University (G)
Oregon State University (G)
Rensselaer Polytechnic Institute (G, NC)
Shenandoah University (G)
Southern Polytechnic State University (U)
State University of New York at Buffalo (G)
University of Alabama (G)
University of Alabama at Birmingham (U, G)
University of Arizona (U, G)
University of British Columbia (U)
University of Calgary (U)
University of California, Berkeley (U)
University of California Extension (U)
University of Central Florida (G)
University of Colorado at Boulder (G, NC)
University of Colorado at Denver (U)
University of Delaware (U)
University of Idaho (U, G)
University of Maine (U, G)
University of Missouri–Kansas City (G)
University of Nebraska–Lincoln (U, G)
University of New Brunswick (U)
University of New Mexico (U, G)
University of North Dakota (U)
University of South Florida (G)
University of Tennessee (G)
University of Texas at Arlington (G)
University of Texas at San Antonio (U)
University of Virginia (G)
University of Wisconsin Extension (U, NC)
University of Wisconsin–Platteville (U, G)
University of Wyoming (U)

Virginia Polytechnic Institute and State University
  (U, G)
Worcester Polytechnic Institute (G)

Classical languages and literatures
Acadia University (U)
Assemblies of God Theological Seminary (G, NC)
City Colleges of Chicago, Harold Washington
  College (U)
Community College of Rhode Island (U)
Corning Community College (U)
Darton College (NC)
Indiana University System (U)
LIFE Bible College (U)
Moody Bible Institute (U)
New School University (U, NC)
North Carolina State University (U)
Ohio University–Southern Campus (U)
Riverside Community College (U)
San Diego City College (U)
Skidmore College (U)
Southwest Missouri State University (U)
University of Alaska Fairbanks (U)
University of Delaware (U)
University of Kansas (U, NC)
University of Minnesota, Twin Cities Campus (U)
University of Missouri–Columbia (U, G)
University of Nebraska–Lincoln (U)
University of Oklahoma (U)
University of St. Thomas (U)
University System of Georgia (U)
Yuba College (U)

Clothing/apparel and textile studies
Burlington County College (U)
Fashion Institute of Technology (U)
Sam Houston State University (U)

Cognitive psychology
Campbellsville University (G)
Capella University (G)
Carleton University (U)
Colorado State University (U)
Indiana State University (U)
Lakehead University (U)
Northeast Wisconsin Technical College (U)
Patrick Henry Community College (U)
Pennsylvania State University University Park
  Campus (U)
Randolph Community College (U)
Salve Regina University (G, NC)
Saybrook Graduate School (G)
Southeastern Oklahoma State University (U)
State University of New York at Oswego (U)
Stephens College (U)
Texas A&M University–Commerce (U, G)
Université Laval (U)
University of Arizona (U)
University of Houston–Downtown (U)
University of Illinois at Urbana–Champaign (U)
University of Tennessee (U)
University of Texas at Austin (U)
University of Utah (U)
Weber State University (U)
West Hills Community College (U)

Commercial art
Bradley University (U)
Maryland Institute, College of Art (U, NC)
Mohawk Valley Community College (U)
newGraduate Schools (G)

Communications
American Academy of Nutrition, College of
  Nutrition (U)
Andrews University (U)
Arizona State University (U)
Assemblies of God Theological Seminary (G, NC)
Athabasca University (U)

Carleton University (U)
Cedarville University (U)
Cerro Coso Community College (U)
Clark State Community College (U)
Cossatot Technical College (U)
D'Youville College (U)
Eastern Kentucky University (U)
Floyd College (U)
Kellogg Community College (U)
Laramie County Community College (U)
Linn-Benton Community College (U)
Louisiana State University System (U)
Malone College (U)
Marylhurst University (U)
Mercy College (U)
Missouri Western State College (U)
Montana State University—Great Falls College of
    Technology (U)
Mount Allison University (U)
Northern Virginia Community College (U)
Pennsylvania State University University Park
    Campus (U)
Richard Stockton College of New Jersey (U)
Royal Military College of Canada (U, G)
Sacred Heart University (U)
Saint Peter's College (U)
Salve Regina University (U, G, NC)
Syracuse University (U)
Triton College (U)
Tyler Junior College (U)
University of Illinois at Urbana–Champaign (U)
University of Missouri–Columbia (U)
University of Toledo (U)
University of Utah (U)
University of Waterloo (U)
Virginia Polytechnic Institute and State University
    (U)

Computer and information sciences

Acadia University (U)
Alabama Agricultural and Mechanical University
    (G)
Allegany College of Maryland (U, NC)
American River College (U)
Anne Arundel Community College (U)
Aquinas College (U)
Arizona State University (U, G)
Athabasca University (U)
Athens Area Technical Institute (U)
Austin Community College (U)
Azusa Pacific University (U)
Baker College-Center for Graduate Studies (U, G)
Bakersfield College (U)
Ball State University (G)
Bellevue Community College (U)
Boise State University (U)
Bossier Parish Community College (U)
Bradley University (U)
Brevard Community College (U)
Broward Community College (U)
Bryant and Stratton Business Institute (U, NC)
Bucks County Community College (U)
Buena Vista University (U)
Burlington County College (U)
Caldwell College (U)
Calhoun Community College (U)
California College for Health Sciences (U)
California State University, Chico (U, G, NC)
Cape Fear Community College (U)
Capital Community College (U)
Carnegie Mellon University (G)
Central Community College–Grand Island
    Campus (U)
Centralia College (NC)
Central Missouri State University (U)
Central Piedmont Community College (U)
Central Texas College (U)
Champlain College (U)

Charles Stewart Mott Community College (U)
Chattanooga State Technical Community College
    (U)
Chestnut Hill College (G)
Chippewa Valley Technical College (U, NC)
City University (U, G)
Clackamas Community College (U)
Clatsop Community College (U)
Clayton College & State University (U)
Cleary College (U)
Cleveland State Community College (U)
Cleveland State University (U)
Coastal Carolina Community College (U)
Coastline Community College (U, NC)
College for Lifelong Learning, University System
    of New Hampshire (U)
College of DuPage (U)
College of Southern Maryland (U)
College of the Siskiyous (U)
College of West Virginia (U)
Colorado Electronic Community College (U)
Colorado State University (G)
Columbia University (G, NC)
Columbus State Community College (U)
Concordia University at St. Paul (U)
Copiah-Lincoln Community College (U)
CTS University, Inc. (U, NC)
Cuyahoga Community College, Metropolitan
    Campus (U)
Dakota State University (U)
Dallas Baptist University (U)
De Anza College (U)
Del Mar College (U)
Des Moines Area Community College (U)
Duquesne University (U)
Eastern Maine Technical College (U)
Eastern Michigan University (U)
Eastern Oregon University (U)
Eastern Shore Community College (U)
Edison State Community College (U)
Embry-Riddle Aeronautical University, Extended
    Campus (U, G)
Everett Community College (U)
Evergreen Valley College (U)
Fairleigh Dickinson University, The New College
    of General and Continuing Studies (G)
Fayetteville Technical Community College (U)
Ferris State University (U, G)
Florida Community College at Jacksonville (U)
Florida State University (U)
Foothill College (U)
Franklin University (U)
Front Range Community College (U)
Garland County Community College (U)
Georgia Southwestern State University (U)
Glendale Community College (U)
Golden Gate University (U, G)
Graceland College (U)
Grantham College of Engineering (U)
Grayson County College (U)
Great Basin College (U)
Greenville Technical College (U)
Harrisburg Area Community College (U)
Hillsborough Community College (U)
Hinds Community College (U)
Holmes Community College (U)
Honolulu Community College (U)
Houston Community College System (U)
Howard Community College (U)
Hutchinson Community College and Area
    Vocational School (U)
Illinois Institute of Technology (U, G)
Independence Community College (U)
Indiana University System (U)
Indian River Community College (U)
ISIM University (G)
Ivy Tech State College–Columbus (U)
Ivy Tech State College–Eastcentral (U)

Ivy Tech State College–Kokomo (U)
Ivy Tech State College–Northwest (U)
Ivy Tech State College–Southwest (U)
Ivy Tech State College–Wabash Valley (U)
Ivy Tech State College–Whitewater (U)
Jacksonville State University (U)
Jamestown Community College (U)
Johns Hopkins University (G)
Johnson County Community College (U)
Judson College (U)
Judson College (U)
Kansas City Kansas Community College (U)
Kansas State University (U, G, NC)
Keiser College (U)
Lake Land College (U)
Lakeland College (U)
Lamar State College–Port Arthur (U, NC)
Lansing Community College (U)
Laramie County Community College (U)
Lenoir Community College (U)
LeTourneau University (U)
Longview Community College (U)
Loyola University Chicago (U)
Lynn University (U)
Marshall University (U)
Memorial University of Newfoundland (U)
Mercy College (U, G)
Metropolitan Community Colleges (U)
Metropolitan State University (U)
Michigan State University (U, G)
Midland College (U)
Mid-Plains Community College Area (U)
Minnesota West Community and Technical
    College (U)
Mississippi State University (G)
Missouri Southern State College (U)
Modesto Junior College (U)
Mohawk Valley Community College (U)
Montana State University–Bozeman (U)
Montgomery College (U)
Montgomery County Community College (U)
Morehead State University (U, G)
Mountain Empire Community College (U)
Mt. San Jacinto College (U)
National American University (U)
National Technological University (G, NC)
Neumann College (U)
newGraduate Schools (G)
New Hampshire College (U, G)
New Jersey City University (NC)
New Jersey Institute of Technology (U, G)
New School University (U, NC)
New York Institute of Technology (U, G)
New York University (U, G)
North Arkansas College (U)
North Carolina State University (U)
North Central Texas College (U)
North Central University (U, G)
North Country Community College (U)
North Dakota State University (U, G)
Northeastern University (G)
Northeast Texas Community College (U)
Northern Arizona University (U)
Northern Essex Community College (U)
Northern State University (U)
Northern Virginia Community College (U)
North Harris College (U)
Northwestern College (U)
Northwestern Michigan College (U)
Northwest Technical College (U)
Nova Southeastern University (G)
Ohlone College (U)
Oklahoma City Community College (U)
Oklahoma State University (G)
Old Dominion University (U, G)
Open Learning Agency (U)
Oregon State University (U, G)
Ouachita Technical College (U)

Seminole Community College (U)
Sierra College (U)
Southern Polytechnic State University (G)
State University of New York at Oswego (U)
State University of New York College of
    Agriculture and Technology at Morrisville (U)
Strayer University (U, G)
Texas State Technical College (U)
Texas Tech University (G)
Tyler Junior College (U)
Université Laval (U)
University of Bridgeport (U, G)
University of California, Berkeley (U)
University of California, Davis (U)
University of California Extension (U)
University of California, Irvine (NC)
University of California, Los Angeles (G)
University of Central Oklahoma (U)
University of Colorado at Denver (U, G)
University of Houston–Downtown (U)
University of Maine at Fort Kent (U)
University of North Texas (G)
University of Tennessee (NC)
University of the Incarnate Word (U)
University of Waterloo (U)
Vermont Technical College (U)
Wake Technical Community College (U)
West Chester University of Pennsylvania (U)
Western Governors University (U, NC)
West Hills Community College (U)
Wytheville Community College (U)
York College of Pennsylvania (U)

Conservation and natural resources

Athabasca University (U)
Bellevue Community College (U)
Black Hills State University (U)
Burlington County College (U)
College of the Southwest (U)
Colorado State University (U, G)
David Lipscomb University (U)
De Anza College (U)
Garland County Community College (U)
Goddard College (U, G)
Harrisburg Area Community College (U)
Indiana University System (U)
Keiser College (U)
Kent State University (U)
Lakehead University (U)
Los Angeles Pierce College (U)
Luzerne County Community College (U)
Madonna University (U)
Memorial University of Newfoundland (U)
Michigan State University (G)
Minnesota West Community and Technical
    College (U)
Naropa University (U, G)
New Jersey Institute of Technology (U, G)
Northern Michigan University (U)
Norwich University (U, G)
Oregon State University (U, G)
Owens Community College (U)
Pikes Peak Community College (U, NC)
Richard Stockton College of New Jersey (U)
Rochester Institute of Technology (U, G)
Rogers State University (U)
Tulsa Community College (U)
University of Arizona (U)
University of Calgary (NC)
University of California, Berkeley (U)
University of California Extension (U)
University of Denver (G)
University of Kansas (U, NC)
University of Massachusetts Amherst (U)
University of Minnesota, Twin Cities Campus (U)
University of Nebraska–Lincoln (U, NC)
University of Nevada, Las Vegas (U)
University of Southern Colorado (U)

University of Southern Maine (U)
University of Tennessee (U)
University of Wisconsin–River Falls (U)
University of Wisconsin–Stevens Point (U, G,
    NC)
University of Wyoming (U)
University System of Georgia (U)
Utah State University (U)
Washington State University (U)
Westmoreland County Community College (U)

Construction

Arizona State University (G)
California State University, San Marcos (NC)
Clemson University (G)
Illinois Institute of Technology (U, G)
Macon Technical Institute (U)
Weber State University (U)

Continuing education

Bellevue Community College (U)
Capella University (G)
Connecticut State University System (U, G)
Forsyth Technical Community College (U)
Fort Hays State University (U, G)
Illinois Eastern Community Colleges, Wabash
    Valley College (U)
Instituto Tecnológico y de Estudios Superiores de
    Monterrey, Campus Monterrey (NC)
Midland College (U)
North Dakota State University (U, G)
Northern Illinois University (G)
Oklahoma State University (NC)
Parkland College (U)
Pitt Community College (NC)
Prince George's Community College (NC)
San Diego State University (U, G)
San Francisco State University (NC)
San Jose State University (U)
Snow College (U, NC)
Southeast Community College, Lincoln Campus
    (U)
State University of New York at Stony Brook (G)
Troy State University (NC)
University of Alaska Southeast (G, NC)
University of Calgary (NC)
University of Findlay (NC)
University of La Verne (NC)
University of Massachusetts Lowell (U)
University of Minnesota, Crookston (U)
University of Saskatchewan (U)
University of Texas System (NC)
University of Toledo (NC)
Virginia Polytechnic Institute and State University
    (NC)

Corrections

Central Missouri State University (G)
Cerro Coso Community College (U)
Christopher Newport University (U)
College of West Virginia (U)
Eastern Kentucky University (U)
Floyd College (U)
John Wood Community College (U)
Northeast Wisconsin Technical College (U)
Okaloosa-Walton Community College (U)
Pitt Community College (U)
St. Petersburg Junior College (U)
Taylor University, World Wide Campus (U)
University of Arizona (U)
University of Missouri–Columbia (U)
University of South Dakota (U)
University of Waterloo (U)
Vincennes University (U)
Weber State University (U)
West Hills Community College (U)

Counseling psychology

Atlantic Cape Community College (U)
Capella University (G)
Columbus State University (G)
Denver Seminary (G, NC)
Florida Baptist Theological College (U, NC)
Goddard College (U, G)
Grace University (U, NC)
Liberty University (G)
Lincoln Christian College (G, NC)
New York Institute of Technology (U, G)
Prairie Bible College (U)
Providence College and Theological Seminary (G,
    NC)
Regis University (G)
Rio Salado College (U)
St. Mary's University of San Antonio (G)
Saybrook Graduate School
Seton Hall University (G)
Southern Christian University (U, G, NC)
Southwestern Assemblies of God University (U)
State University of New York Empire State
    College (U)
Stephens College (U)
Taylor University, World Wide Campus (U)
Temple Baptist Seminary (G, NC)
University of Baltimore (G)
University of California, Los Angeles (G)
University of Central Oklahoma (U, G)
University of Minnesota, Twin Cities Campus (U)
University of Sarasota (G)
Walden University (G)
Weber State University (U)
Western Michigan University (U)

Creative writing

Anne Arundel Community College (U)
Aquinas College (U)
Athabasca University (U)
Atlantic University (G, NC)
Bellevue Community College (U)
Brigham Young University (U)
Brookdale Community College (U)
Capital Community College (U)
Catawba Valley Community College (U)
Central Community College–Grand Island
    Campus (U)
Central Washington University (U)
Chadron State College (U, G)
Chattanooga State Technical Community College
    (U)
Chippewa Valley Technical College (U)
City Colleges of Chicago, Harold Washington
    College (U)
Clark College (U)
Clark State Community College (U)
College of Albemarle (U)
College of Southern Maryland (U)
College of the Southwest (U)
Colorado Mountain College District (U)
Columbia Basin College (U)
Community College of Baltimore County (U)
Cumberland County College (U)
Dallas County Community College District (U)
Dawson Community College (U)
Drake University (U)
Garland County Community College (U)
Genesee Community College (U)
Goucher College (G)
Hebrew College (U, G, NC)
Indiana University System (U)
Judson College (U)
Kellogg Community College (U)
King's College (U)
Lansing Community College (U)
Linn-Benton Community College (U)
Lorain County Community College (U)
Madisonville Community College (U)

Creative writing (continued)
Marylhurst University (U)
Minot State University (U)
Montgomery College (U)
Mt. San Antonio College (U)
New Hampshire College (U)
New School University (U, G, NC)
New York University (NC)
North Carolina State University (U)
Northern Virginia Community College (U)
Northwestern Michigan College (U)
Ohio University (U)
Okaloosa-Walton Community College (U)
Oklahoma State University (U)
Oregon State University (U)
Palomar College (U)
Park University (U)
Pennsylvania State University University Park
   Campus (U)
Pitt Community College (NC)
Portland Community College (U)
Portland State University (U)
Redlands Community College (U)
Richland Community College (U)
Rio Salado College (U)
Saddleback College (U)
St. Petersburg Junior College (U)
Sam Houston State University (U)
Scottsdale Community College (U)
Sheridan College (U)
Sinclair Community College (U)
Skidmore College (U)
Southern Vermont College (U)
Southwestern Assemblies of God University (U)
Southwest Virginia Community College (U)
Spring Arbor College (U)
State University of West Georgia (U)
Stephens College (U)
Suffolk County Community College (U)
Tarrant County College District (U)
Tennessee Temple University (U)
Texas A&M University–Commerce (U)
Texas Tech University (U)
Tyler Junior College (U)
University College of Cape Breton (U)
University of Alaska Fairbanks (U)
University of Alaska Southeast, Sitka Campus (U)
University of Baltimore (U)
University of California, Berkeley (U)
University of California Extension (U, NC)
University of California, Los Angeles (G)
University of Central Arkansas (U)
University of Colorado at Denver (U)
University of Denver (G)
University of Great Falls (U)
University of Houston (U)
University of Houston–Downtown (U)
University of Kansas (U, NC)
University of Maine (U)
University of Minnesota, Twin Cities Campus (U)
University of Missouri–Columbia (U)
University of Missouri–Kansas City (U)
University of Montana–Missoula (U)
University of North Carolina at Chapel Hill (U)
University of Southern Mississippi (U)
University of South Florida (U)
University of Tennessee (U, NC)
University of Texas at Austin (U)
University of Utah (U)
University of Washington (U, NC)
University of Wisconsin Extension (U, NC)
Utah State University (U)
Vincennes University (U)
Virginia Polytechnic Institute and State University
   (U)
Volunteer State Community College (U)
Walters State Community College (U)
Washington State University (U)

Waubonsee Community College (U)
Weber State University (U)
Western Governors University (U)
Western Illinois University (U, G)
Western Washington University (U)
West Los Angeles College (U)
Westmoreland County Community College (U)
West Valley College (U)
Yuba College (U)

Criminal justice
Allegany College of Maryland (U)
American Military University (U)
Atlantic Cape Community College (U)
Auburn University (U)
Blinn College (U)
Buena Vista University (U)
Central Missouri State University (U, G)
Central Oregon Community College (U)
Central Texas College (U)
Cerro Coso Community College (U)
Chippewa Valley Technical College (U)
Christopher Newport University (U)
City University (U, G)
Clackamas Community College (U)
Cochise College (U)
College for Lifelong Learning, University System
   of New Hampshire (U)
College of Albemarle (U)
College of West Virginia (U)
Colorado Mountain College District (U)
Columbia State Community College (U)
Connors State College (U)
Dutchess Community College (U)
East Carolina University (G)
Eastern Kentucky University (U)
Florence-Darlington Technical College (U)
Florida Gulf Coast University (U)
Florida State University (G)
Floyd College (U)
Fort Hays State University (U, G)
Frostburg State University (U)
Graceland College (U)
Herkimer County Community College (U)
Highland Community College (U)
Houston Community College System (U)
Indiana University of Pennsylvania (U)
Johnson County Community College (U)
John Wood Community College (U)
Kaplan College (U)
Kellogg Community College (U)
Kent State University (U)
Kentucky State University (U)
Lake Land College (U)
Lake Superior State University (U)
Lansing Community College (U)
Laramie County Community College (U)
Lewis and Clark Community College (U)
Loyola University New Orleans (U)
Lynn University (G)
Mansfield University of Pennsylvania (U)
Mercy College (U)
Michigan State University (G)
Midland College (U)
National University (U)
New York Institute of Technology (U)
North Central Texas College (U)
North Dakota State University (U, G)
Northeast Wisconsin Technical College (U)
Northern Arizona University (U)
Northern Michigan University (U)
Northern Virginia Community College (U)
Okaloosa-Walton Community College (U)
Owens Community College (U)
Palomar College (U)
Park University (U)
Pennsylvania State University University Park
   Campus (U)

Piedmont Technical College (U)
Pitt Community College (U)
Prince George's Community College (U)
Rappahannock Community College (U)
Raritan Valley Community College (U)
Sacred Heart University (U)
Saint Charles County Community College (U, G)
St. Cloud State University (U)
St. Petersburg Junior College (U)
Salt Lake Community College (U)
San Antonio College (U)
Sauk Valley Community College (U)
Seminole Community College (U)
Sierra College (U)
Simpson College (U)
Skidmore College (U)
Southeastern Oklahoma State University (U)
Southwest Texas State University (U)
Stanly Community College (U)
State University of New York College of
   Technology at Delhi (U)
State University of New York Empire State
   College (U)
Taylor University, World Wide Campus (U)
Tompkins Cortland Community College (U)
Union Institute (U)
University of Arkansas (U)
University of Central Oklahoma (U, G)
University of Cincinnati (U)
University of Houston–Downtown (U, G)
University of Maryland University College (U)
University of Missouri–Columbia (U, G)
University of Nevada, Reno (U)
University of North Texas (U, G)
University of South Dakota (U)
University of Southern Mississippi (U)
University of Tennessee (U)
University of Tennessee at Chattanooga (U, G)
University of Texas of the Permian Basin (G)
University of Wisconsin–Platteville (G)
University of Wyoming (U)
Vincennes University (U)
Virginia Commonwealth University (G)
Walden University (G)
Washington State University (U)
Waubonsee Community College (U)
Weber State University (U)
Western Carolina University (U)
Western Oklahoma State College (U)
West Hills Community College (U)

Criminal justice and corrections
National University (U)

Criminology
Atlantic Cape Community College (U)
Cerro Coso Community College (U)
Eastern Oklahoma State College (U)
Fayetteville Technical Community College (U)
Florida International University (U)
Florida State University (U)
Frostburg State University (U)
Indiana State University (U, G)
Linn-Benton Community College (U)
Louisiana State University at Alexandria (U)
Louisiana State University System (U)
Manchester Community College (U)
Mansfield University of Pennsylvania (U)
Marshall University (U)
Missouri Western State College (U)
Montgomery County Community College (U)
Mount Wachusett Community College (U)
New York Institute of Technology (U)
Northeast Wisconsin Technical College (U)
Northern Virginia Community College (U)
Open Learning Agency (U)
Redlands Community College (U)
Richard Stockton College of New Jersey (U)

Drama and theater

Montana State University–Billings (U)
Northern Arizona University (U)
Northern Virginia Community College (U)
Northwest Missouri State University (U)
Parkland College (U)
Providence College and Theological Seminary (U, NC)
Queen's University at Kingston (U)
Rio Salado College (U)
Sierra College (U)
Snow College (U)
Southern Connecticut State University (U)
State University of West Georgia (U)
Texas Christian University (U)
Triton College (U)
University of Arkansas (U)
University of Colorado at Denver (U)
University of North Carolina at Chapel Hill (U)
University of Oklahoma (U)
University of South Dakota (U)
University of South Florida (U)
University of Texas of the Permian Basin (U)
University of Utah (U)
University of Wisconsin–River Falls (U)
Weber State University (U)

Early childhood education

Central Oregon Community College (U)
College of Albemarle (U)
South Puget Sound Community College (U)
Western Nevada Community College (U)
Westmoreland County Community College (U)

Earth science

Brenau University (U)
Carleton University (U)
Centralia College (U)
College of DuPage (U)
College of West Virginia (U)
Colorado Mountain College District (U)
Concordia University Wisconsin (U)
Everett Community College (U)
Florida Community College at Jacksonville (U)
Houston Community College System (U)
Indiana Wesleyan University (U)
Kapiolani Community College (U)
Lac Courte Oreilles Ojibwa Community College (U)
Lansing Community College (U)
Marywood University (U)
Montana State University–Bozeman (G)
North Country Community College (U)
Northern Essex Community College (U)
Northwest Missouri State University (U)
Okaloosa-Walton Community College (U)
Ouachita Technical College (U)
Parkland College (U)
Pennsylvania State University University Park Campus (U)
Pierce College (U)
Portland Community College (U)
St. Louis Community College System (U)
St. Petersburg Junior College (U)
Southeast Community College, Lincoln Campus (U)
State University of New York College of Technology at Canton (U)
Stephens College (U)
Suffolk County Community College (U)
Syracuse University (U)
Thomas Edison State College (U)
University of Idaho (U)
University of Iowa (U, G)
University of Manitoba (U)
University of Nevada, Reno (U)
University of Waterloo (U)
University of Wisconsin Colleges (U)
Upper Iowa University (U)

Vincennes University (U)
Western Governors University (U)

Ecology

Burlington County College (U)
California Institute of Integral Studies (G, NC)
City College of San Francisco (U)
Coastline Community College (U, NC)
College of West Virginia (U)
Cossatot Technical College (U)
Edison State Community College (U)
Gogebic Community College (U)
Hutchinson Community College and Area Vocational School (U)
Judson College (U)
newGraduate Schools (G)
Open Learning Agency (U)
Oregon State University (U)
Portland Community College (U)
Sheridan College (U)
University of Minnesota, Twin Cities Campus (U)
University of Nebraska–Lincoln (U)
University of Waterloo (U)
University System of Georgia (U)

E-commerce

Delta College (U)
University of Tennessee (NC)

Economics

Adams State College (U)
Allegany College of Maryland (U)
Anne Arundel Community College (U)
Athabasca University (U)
Auburn University (U)
Austin Community College (U)
Ball State University (U, G)
Bellevue Community College (U)
Bergen Community College (U)
Berkshire Community College (U)
Blinn College (U)
Brevard Community College (U)
Brigham Young University (U)
Brookdale Community College (U)
Broward Community College (U)
Brunswick Community College (U)
Bucks County Community College (U)
Burlington College (U)
Burlington County College (U)
California State University, Fresno (U)
Carleton University (U)
Catawba Valley Community College (U)
Central Community College–Grand Island Campus (U)
Central Michigan University (U)
Central Piedmont Community College (U)
Central Texas College (U)
Central Virginia Community College (U)
Central Washington University (U)
Cerro Coso Community College (U)
Chadron State College (U)
Champlain College (U)
Charles Stewart Mott Community College (U)
Charter Oak State College (U)
Chattanooga State Technical Community College (U)
Chippewa Valley Technical College (U)
Christopher Newport University (U)
Citrus College (U)
City Colleges of Chicago, Harold Washington College (U)
Clark College (U)
Clarkson College (U)
Clatsop Community College (U)
Coastline Community College (U, NC)
Cochise College (U)
College of Aeronautics (U)
College of Albemarle (U)
College of DuPage (U)

College of Southern Maryland (U)
College of the Southwest (U)
College of West Virginia (U)
Colorado Mountain College District (U)
Colorado State University (U)
Columbia State Community College (U)
Columbus State Community College (U)
Community College of Rhode Island (U)
Cossatot Technical College (U)
County College of Morris (U)
Cumberland County College (U)
Cuyahoga Community College, Metropolitan Campus (U)
Cuyamaca College (U)
Dallas County Community College District (U)
Dawson Community College (U)
De Anza College (U)
Delaware Technical & Community College, Stanton/Wilmington Campus (U)
Del Mar College (U)
Delta College (U)
Des Moines Area Community College (U)
Duke University (G)
Dutchess Community College (U)
D'Youville College (U)
Eastern Kentucky University (U)
Eastern Wyoming College (U)
East Tennessee State University (U, G)
Edison Community College (U)
Edison State Community College (U)
El Paso Community College (U)
Embry-Riddle Aeronautical University, Extended Campus (U)
Fairleigh Dickinson University, The New College of General and Continuing Studies (U)
Fayetteville Technical Community College (U)
Finger Lakes Community College (U)
Fitchburg State College (U)
Florida Community College at Jacksonville (U)
Floyd College (U)
Foothill College (U)
Forsyth Technical Community College (U)
Fort Hays State University (U)
Gannon University (U)
Garland County Community College (U)
Genesee Community College (U)
Georgia Perimeter College (U)
Georgia Southern University (U, G)
Golden Gate University (G)
Governors State University (U)
Graceland College (U)
Grand Valley State University (U, G)
Grantham College of Engineering (U)
Grayson County College (U)
Great Basin College (U)
Greenville Technical College (U)
Halifax Community College (U)
Heriot-Watt University (G)
Hillsborough Community College (U)
Houston Community College System (U)
Howard Community College (U)
Illinois State University (U)
Indiana State University (U)
Indiana University System (U)
Iowa State University of Science and Technology (U)
Ivy Tech State College–North Central (U)
Ivy Tech State College–Northwest (U)
Ivy Tech State College–Wabash Valley (U)
Jefferson Community College (U)
Johnson County Community College (U)
John Wood Community College (U)
Kansas City Kansas Community College (U)
Kellogg Community College (U)
Kent State University (U)
King's College (U)
Kingwood College (U)
Lackawanna Junior College (U)

Individual Courses Index

Wytheville Community College (U)
Xavier University of Louisiana (U)

Education
Acadia University (U, G)
Andrews University (G)
Arizona Western College (G)
Arkansas State University (U, G)
Assemblies of God Theological Seminary (G, NC)
Azusa Pacific University (U)
Ball State University (G)
Bellevue University (U)
Berkshire Community College (NC)
Black Hills State University (U, G)
Bossier Parish Community College (NC)
Bradley University (G)
Brenau University (U, G)
Brigham Young University (U)
Bucks County Community College (U)
Buena Vista University (U, G)
Burlington College (U)
California State University, Fresno (U, G)
Capella University (G)
Central Arizona College (U)
Central Oregon Community College (U)
Central Washington University (U)
Chattanooga State Technical Community College (U)
City University (G)
Clemson University (G)
Cleveland State University (G)
Coastline Community College (U, NC)
College of DuPage (U)
College of St. Scholastica (G)
College of Southern Maryland (U)
Concordia University Wisconsin (G)
CTS University, Inc. (U, NC)
David Lipscomb University (U)
De Anza College (U)
Delaware Technical & Community College, Jack F. Owens Campus (U)
Drake University (G)
Duquesne University (U, G)
East Carolina University (G)
Eastern Connecticut State University (U, G)
Eastern Oregon University (U, G)
Emporia State University (U, G)
Eugene Bible College (U, NC)
Foothill College (U)
Franklin Pierce Law Center (G)
Fresno Pacific University (G)
George Washington University (G, NC)
Georgia Southwestern State University (U, G)
Georgia State University (G)
Global University of the Assemblies of God (G)
Goddard College (U, G)
Grambling State University (G)
Green River Community College (U)
Griggs University (G)
Hawkeye Community College (U)
Hebrew College (U, G, NC)
Hillsdale Free Will Baptist College (U)
Hobe Sound Bible College (U)
Indiana University System (U)
Indian River Community College (U)
Inter American University of Puerto Rico, San Germán Campus (G)
James Sprunt Community College (G)
Lesley College (G)
Louisiana State University System (U)
Lynn University (U, G)
Marian College of Fond du Lac (U)
Martin Community College (U)
McGill University (U)
Memorial University of Newfoundland (U, G)
Michigan State University (NC)
Mid-America Bible College (U)
Montana State University–Billings (U, G)

Montana State University–Bozeman (U, G)
Morehead State University (U, G)
National University (G)
Neumann College (G)
New Jersey City University (G)
Northampton County Area Community College (U)
North Carolina Agricultural and Technical State University (U, G)
North Carolina State University (G)
North Dakota State University (G)
Northern Arizona University (U, G)
Northern Michigan University (U, G)
Northern Virginia Community College (U)
Northwestern College (U)
Norwich University (U, G)
Old Dominion University (G)
Open Learning Agency (U)
Oregon State University (U, G)
Red Rocks Community College (U)
Richard Stockton College of New Jersey (NC)
Rio Salado College (U)
Roane State Community College (U)
St. Petersburg Junior College (U)
San Diego State University (U, G)
Santa Barbara City College (U)
Seton Hall University (G)
Skidmore College (U)
South Dakota State University (U, G)
Southeastern Louisiana University (G)
Southern Oregon University (G)
Southwestern Assemblies of God University (U, G)
Southwestern Michigan College (U)
Southwest Texas State University (U)
Spoon River College (U)
State University of New York at Buffalo (G, NC)
State University of New York at Stony Brook (G)
State University of New York College at Cortland (U, G)
State University of West Georgia (U, G)
Stephens College (U)
Stevens Institute of Technology (G)
Terra State Community College (U)
Texas A&M University–Commerce (U)
Texas Christian University (U)
Union Institute (U, G)
Union University (U)
United States International University (G)
University College of Cape Breton (G)
University of Akron (G)
University of Alaska Fairbanks (U)
University of Alaska Southeast, Sitka Campus (U)
University of Arkansas (U, G)
University of British Columbia (U, G)
University of Calgary (U, G, NC)
University of California, Los Angeles (G)
University of California, Riverside (U, G)
University of Central Arkansas (U, G)
University of Central Florida (U, G)
University of Central Oklahoma (U, G)
University of Great Falls (U)
University of Houston (G)
University of Houston–Victoria (U, G)
University of Idaho (U, G)
University of Iowa (U, G)
University of Maryland, Baltimore County (G)
University of Missouri–Columbia (U, G)
University of Missouri–Columbia (U, G)
University of Nebraska–Lincoln (U)
University of Nevada, Reno (U, G)
University of North Alabama (U)
University of North Carolina at Chapel Hill (U)
University of North Carolina at Pembroke (U)
University of Northern Iowa (U, G)
University of North Texas (G)
University of Oklahoma (U)
University of South Carolina (U, G)

University of Tennessee at Chattanooga (G)
University of Texas at El Paso (G)
University of Texas System (G)
University of Toledo (U, G)
University of West Florida (U, G)
University of Wisconsin Extension (U)
University of Wisconsin–Milwaukee (U)
University of Wisconsin–River Falls (U, NC)
University of Wisconsin–Stevens Point (U, G)
University of Wisconsin–Stout (U, G)
University of Wyoming (U)
University System of Georgia (U)
Walden University (G)
Washington & Jefferson College (U)
Wayne State College (G)
Western Connecticut State University (G)
Western Governors University (U, G, NC)
Western Michigan University (G)
Western Wyoming Community College (U)
Westmoreland County Community College (U)
William Paterson University of New Jersey (G)
Wilmington College (G)
Wright State University (U)
Wytheville Community College (U)
Yuba College (U)

Education administration
Arizona State University (G)
Arizona Western College (G)
Ball State University (G)
Bridgewater State College (G)
Buena Vista University (G)
Cabrini College (G)
California College for Health Sciences (U)
California State University, Fresno (U)
California State University, Fullerton (U)
Capella University (G)
Central Methodist College (U, G)
Central Missouri State University (U, G, NC)
Chadron State College (U, G)
Cleveland College of Jewish Studies (U, G, NC)
College of the Southwest (U, G)
Columbus State University (G)
Connecticut State University System (U, G)
Dallas Theological Seminary (G, NC)
Denver Seminary (G, NC)
Drake University (G)
Eastern Kentucky University (G)
Eastern Michigan University (G)
Fielding Institute (G)
Florida State University (G)
Fort Hays State University (U, G)
Frostburg State University (G)
Georgia Southern University (G)
Georgia Southwestern State University (G)
Grambling State University (G)
Grand Rapids Baptist Seminary (G)
Grand Valley State University (U, G)
Henderson State University (G, NC)
Illinois State University (U, G)
Indiana State University (G)
Indiana University System (G)
Instituto Tecnológico y de Estudios Superiores de Monterrey, Campus Monterrey (G)
Jacksonville State University (G)
John Wood Community College (U)
Lakehead University (G)
Lamar University (U, G)
Liberty University (G)
Lynn University (U, G)
Marshall University (U, G)
Memorial University of Newfoundland (U)
Michigan State University (G)
Middle Tennessee State University (U, G)
Morehead State University (U, G)
National University (G)
North Carolina State University (G)
North Dakota State University (G)

Cleveland State University (G)
College of Southern Maryland (U)
Colorado State University (G)
Columbia University (G, NC)
Fairleigh Dickinson University, The New College of General and Continuing Studies (G)
Florida International University (G)
Florida State University (G)
Georgia Institute of Technology (G, NC)
Grantham College of Engineering (U)
Harcourt Learning Direct (U)
Illinois Institute of Technology (U, G)
Indiana University System (G)
Iowa State University of Science and Technology (U, G)
Johns Hopkins University (G)
Kansas State University (G, NC)
Michigan Technological University (G)
Mississippi State University (G)
Montana State University–Bozeman (NC)
National Technological University (G, NC)
New Jersey Institute of Technology (U, G)
New Mexico State University (G)
North Carolina State University (G)
North Dakota State University (U, G)
Northeastern University (G)
Northern Illinois University (G)
Oklahoma State University (G)
Old Dominion University (G)
Oregon State University (G)
Pennsylvania State University University Park Campus (U, G)
Piedmont Technical College (U)
Rensselaer Polytechnic Institute (G)
Rochester Institute of Technology (U, G)
Rutgers, The State University of New Jersey, New Brunswick (U, G, NC)
Shenandoah University (G)
Sinclair Community College (U)
Southern Illinois University Carbondale (U, G)
Southern Methodist University (G)
Stanford University (G, NC)
State University of New York at Buffalo (G)
University of Alabama (G)
University of Arizona (G)
University of Calgary (U, G)
University of California, Berkeley (U)
University of California Extension (U)
University of Central Florida (U, G)
University of Colorado at Boulder (G, NC)
University of Delaware (U, G, NC)
University of Houston (G)
University of Idaho (U, G)
University of Illinois at Chicago (G)
University of Illinois at Urbana–Champaign (U, G)
University of Maine (U, G, NC)
University of Massachusetts Amherst (U, G, NC)
University of Missouri–Kansas City (G)
University of Nebraska–Lincoln (G)
University of New Brunswick (U)
University of New Mexico (U, G)
University of North Dakota (U)
University of South Alabama (G)
University of Southern California (G, NC)
University of Southern Mississippi (U)
University of South Florida (U, G)
University of Tennessee (G)
University of Texas at Arlington (G)
University of Texas at Tyler (G)
University of Texas System (G)
University of Vermont (U)
University of Virginia (G)
University of Wisconsin–Madison (U, G)
Virginia Polytechnic Institute and State University (U, G)
Weber State University (U)
Western Nevada Community College (U)

West Virginia University Institute of Technology (U, G)
Wright State University (U)
York Technical College (U)

Electricians technology
Eastern Maine Technical College (U)

Electronics
Arizona State University (G)
Athens Area Technical Institute (U)
Blue Ridge Community College (U)
Brookdale Community College (U)
Century Community and Technical College (NC)
Clark College (U)
Cleveland Institute of Electronics (U)
Colorado Mountain College District (U)
Dallas County Community College District (U)
Forsyth Technical Community College (U)
Grantham College of Engineering (U)
Harcourt Learning Direct (U)
Ivy Tech State College–Eastcentral (U)
Ivy Tech State College–Southcentral (U)
Kellogg Community College (U)
Martin Community College (U)
North Dakota State College of Science (U)
Oklahoma State University (U)
Palomar College (U)
Piedmont Technical College (U)
Rensselaer Polytechnic Institute (G, NC)
Thomas Edison State College (U)
Triton College (U)
University of North Carolina at Charlotte (U)
University of North Texas (U, G)
University of Oklahoma (G)
University of Southern Mississippi (U)
University of Texas System (G)
University of Waterloo (U)
Western Governors University (U)
Westmoreland County Community College (U)
Wytheville Community College (U)
Yuba College (U)

Elementary education
Mid-America Bible College (U)
University of Tennessee at Chattanooga (G)

Engineering
Anne Arundel Community College (U)
Arizona State University (U, G, NC)
Auburn University (G)
Boise State University (U)
Boston University (G)
Brigham Young University (U)
Bristol Community College (U)
Central Washington University (U)
Columbia University (G, NC)
Grantham College of Engineering (U)
Hibbing Community College (U)
Honolulu Community College (U)
Houston Community College System (U)
Howard Community College (U)
Illinois Institute of Technology (U, G)
Johns Hopkins University (G)
Lafayette College (U)
Louisiana State University and Agricultural and Mechanical College (U)
Louisiana State University System (U)
Louisiana Tech University (G)
Mercer University (NC)
Metropolitan Community Colleges (U)
Moraine Valley Community College (U)
Northampton County Area Community College (U)
North Carolina State University (G)
Northern Arizona University (G)
Northern Virginia Community College (U)
Pennsylvania State University University Park Campus (U, G, NC)

Purdue University (G, NC)
Roane State Community College (U)
Rochester Institute of Technology (U)
Sam Houston State University (U)
South Dakota State University (U, G)
Southern Methodist University (G)
Springfield Technical Community College (U)
State University of New York College of Technology at Delhi (U)
Stevens Institute of Technology (U)
Temple University (U)
Texas State Technical College (U)
Texas Tech University (U, G, NC)
University of Alabama at Birmingham (G)
University of Arizona (G)
University of Central Florida (U)
University of Colorado at Denver (U, G)
University of Dayton (U)
University of Florida (U)
University of Houston–Clear Lake (G)
University of Idaho (U, G)
University of Iowa (U)
University of Michigan (G)
University of Missouri–Columbia (U)
University of Missouri–Rolla (G)
University of Nebraska–Lincoln (U)
University of New Brunswick (U)
University of New Hampshire (G)
University of North Texas (G)
University of Oklahoma (U)
University of St. Thomas (G)
University of South Carolina (U, G)
University of Texas at San Antonio (U)
University of Texas System (U)
University of Toledo (U)
University of Wisconsin Colleges (U)
University of Wisconsin Extension (U, NC)
Waubonsee Community College (U)
Western Governors University (U)
West Virginia University Institute of Technology (U, G)
Worcester Polytechnic Institute (G)
Wright State University (G)

Engineering/industrial management
Arizona State University (U, G)
Boston University (G)
California State University, Northridge (G)
Central Missouri State University (U, G)
Colorado State University (G)
Columbia University (G, NC)
Drexel University (G)
East Carolina University (U, G)
Florida International University (G)
Grand Valley State University (U, G)
Iowa State University of Science and Technology (G)
Kansas State University (G)
Lake Superior State University (U)
Mississippi State University (G)
National Technological University (G, NC)
New Jersey Institute of Technology (G)
New Mexico State University (G)
North Carolina State University (G)
North Central University (G)
Northeastern University (G)
Ohio University–Southern Campus (NC)
Old Dominion University (G)
Rensselaer Polytechnic Institute (G)
Rochester Institute of Technology (U)
Roger Williams University (U)
St. Mary's University of San Antonio (G)
Shawnee Community College (U)
Shenandoah University (G)
Southern Methodist University (G)
Stanford University (G, NC)
State University of New York at Buffalo (G)
Syracuse University (G)

Columbia State Community College (U)
Columbus State Community College (U)
Community College of Rhode Island (U)
Concordia University at St. Paul (U)
Concordia University Wisconsin (U, G)
Connecticut State University System (U, G)
Copiah-Lincoln Community College (U)
Corning Community College (U)
Cossatot Technical College (U)
County College of Morris (U)
Cumberland County College (U)
Cuyahoga Community College, Metropolitan
   Campus (U)
Dakota State University (U)
Dallas Baptist University (U)
Dallas County Community College District (U)
Danville Area Community College (U)
Danville Community College (U)
Darton College (U)
David N. Myers College (U)
Dawson Community College (U)
De Anza College (U)
Delaware Technical & Community College,
   Stanton/Wilmington Campus (U)
Del Mar College (U)
Delta College (U)
Des Moines Area Community College (U)
Dutchess Community College (U)
Eastern Kentucky University (U)
Eastern Maine Technical College (U)
Eastern Michigan University (U)
Eastern Oklahoma State College (U)
Edison Community College (U)
Edison State Community College (U)
El Paso Community College (U)
Embry-Riddle Aeronautical University (U)
Embry-Riddle Aeronautical University, Extended
   Campus (U)
Fairleigh Dickinson University, The New College
   of General and Continuing Studies (U)
Florence-Darlington Technical College (U)
Florida Community College at Jacksonville (U)
Floyd College (U)
Forsyth Technical Community College (NC)
Frank Phillips College (U)
Front Range Community College (U)
Gannon University (U)
Garland County Community College (U)
Genesee Community College (U)
Georgia Southern University (U)
Gogebic Community College (U)
Golden Gate University (U, G)
Governors State University (U)
Graceland College (U)
Grantham College of Engineering (U)
Great Basin College (U)
Green River Community College (U)
Greenville Technical College (U)
Hawkeye Community College (U)
Hill College of the Hill Junior College District
   (U)
Hillsborough Community College (U)
Hillsdale Free Will Baptist College (U)
Hinds Community College (U)
Honolulu Community College (U)
Horry-Georgetown Technical College (U)
Houston Community College System (U)
Howard Community College (U)
Husson College (U)
Independence Community College (U)
Indiana University System (U)
Indiana Wesleyan University (U)
Ivy Tech State College–Kokomo (U)
Ivy Tech State College–North Central (U)
Ivy Tech State College–Northwest (U)
Ivy Tech State College–Wabash Valley (U)
Ivy Tech State College–Whitewater (U)
Johnson County Community College (U)

Judson College (U)
Kansas City Kansas Community College (U)
Kauai Community College (U)
Kentucky State University (U)
Kingwood College (U)
Lackawanna Junior College (U, NC)
Lake Land College (U)
Lakeshore Technical College (U)
Lake Washington Technical College (U)
Lamar State College–Orange (U)
Lamar State College–Port Arthur (U)
Lamar University (U)
Lansing Community College (U)
Laramie County Community College (U)
Lehigh Carbon Community College (U)
Linn-Benton Community College (U)
Longview Community College (U)
Lorain County Community College (U)
Los Angeles Harbor College (U)
Los Angeles Mission College (U)
Louisiana State University System (U)
Loyola University New Orleans (U)
Luzerne County Community College (U)
Macon State College (U)
Madison Area Technical College (U)
Manatee Community College (U)
Manchester Community College (U)
Manor College (U)
Marylhurst University (U)
Marywood University (U)
Mayland Community College (U)
Memorial University of Newfoundland (U)
Mercy College (U, G)
Metropolitan Community College (U)
Metropolitan Community Colleges (U)
Metropolitan State University (U)
Miami-Dade Community College (U)
Middlesex County College (U)
Midland College (U)
Minnesota West Community and Technical
   College (U)
Minot State University (U)
Missouri Western State College (U)
Modesto Junior College (U)
Montana State University–Billings (U)
Montana State University—Great Falls College of
   Technology (U)
Montgomery County Community College (U)
Morehead State University (U, G)
Mountain Empire Community College (U)
Mt. San Antonio College (U)
Mount Wachusett Community College (U)
New Hampshire College (U)
New School University (U, NC)
New York Institute of Technology (U)
North Arkansas College (U)
North Carolina State University (U)
North Country Community College (U)
North Dakota State College of Science (U)
Northeast State Technical Community College
   (U)
Northeast Texas Community College (U)
Northern Essex Community College (U)
Northern Illinois University (G)
Northern Michigan University (U)
Northern State University (U)
Northern Virginia Community College (U)
North Harris College (U)
North Seattle Community College (U)
Northwestern College (U)
Northwestern Michigan College (U)
Ohio State University–Mansfield Campus (U)
Ohio University (U)
Ohlone College (U)
Okaloosa-Walton Community College (U)
Oklahoma City Community College (U)
Oklahoma State University (U)
Oregon State University (U)

Owens Community College (U)
Parkland College (U)
Patrick Henry Community College (U)
Pellissippi State Technical Community College
   (U)
Pennsylvania State University University Park
   Campus (U, NC)
Piedmont College (U)
Piedmont Technical College (U)
Pierce College (U)
Pitt Community College (U)
Portland Community College (U)
Portland State University (U)
Prairie Bible College (U)
Prairie State College (U)
Presentation College (U)
Prince George's Community College (U, NC)
Pueblo Community College (U)
Queen's University at Kingston (U)
Randolph Community College (U)
Rappahannock Community College (U)
Redlands Community College (U)
Red Rocks Community College (U)
Regents College (U)
Richard Stockton College of New Jersey (U)
Richland Community College (U)
Rio Salado College (U)
Riverland Community College (U)
Roane State Community College (U)
Robert Morris College (U)
Rochester Community and Technical College (U)
Rochester Institute of Technology (U)
Rockland Community College (U)
Roosevelt University (U)
Sacred Heart University (U)
Saint Charles County Community College (U, G)
St. Edward's University (U)
St. Johns River Community College (U)
St. John's University (U)
Saint Joseph's College (U)
St. Louis Community College System (U)
St. Petersburg Junior College (U)
Salt Lake Community College (U)
San Antonio College (U)
Sandhills Community College (U)
San Jacinto College District (U)
San Joaquin Delta College (U)
Santa Monica College (U)
Sauk Valley Community College (U)
Seattle Central Community College (U)
Seminole Community College (U)
Shawnee Community College (U)
Sheridan College (U)
Shippensburg University of Pennsylvania (U, G)
Sierra College (U)
Sinclair Community College (U)
Skidmore College (U)
Southeast Community College, Beatrice Campus
   (U)
Southeast Community College, Lincoln Campus
   (U)
Southern Utah University (U)
Southwestern Assemblies of God University (U)
Southwestern Community College (U)
Southwest Virginia Community College (U)
Spoon River College (U)
Spring Arbor College (U)
Stanly Community College (U)
State University of New York at Buffalo (U)
State University of New York at New Paltz (U)
State University of New York Empire State
   College (U)
State University of West Georgia (U)
Strayer University (U)
Suffolk County Community College (U)
Surry Community College (U)
Sussex County Community College (U)
Syracuse University (U)

877

Kent State University (U)
King's College (U)
Lakeshore Technical College (U)
Lamar University (U)
Lenoir Community College (U)
LeTourneau University (U)
Longview Community College (U)
Lorain County Community College (U)
Louisiana State University and Agricultural and
  Mechanical College (U)
Louisiana State University System (U)
Luzerne County Community College (U)
Lynn University (U)
Madison Area Technical College (U)
Madisonville Community College (U)
Manatee Community College (U)
Mansfield University of Pennsylvania (U)
Martin Community College (U)
Marywood University (U)
Memorial University of Newfoundland (U)
Metropolitan State University (U, G)
Mid-America Bible College (U)
Middle Tennessee State University (U)
Mid-Plains Community College Area (U)
Midwestern State University (U)
Minnesota West Community and Technical
  College (U)
Minot State University (U)
Mississippi County Community College (U)
Missouri Southern State College (U)
Mohawk Valley Community College (U)
Montana State University–Bozeman (U)
Moody Bible Institute (U)
Moraine Valley Community College (U)
Morehead State University (U)
Mountain Empire Community College (U)
Mount Saint Vincent University (U)
Mount Vernon Nazarene College (U)
Naropa University (U, G)
Nassau Community College (U)
Neumann College (U)
New Hampshire College (U)
New Jersey Institute of Technology (U)
New School University (U, NC)
New York Institute of Technology (U)
New York University (U)
North Carolina State University (U)
North Central Texas College (U)
North Central University (U)
North Country Community College (U)
Northeast Wisconsin Technical College (U)
Northern Arizona University (U, G)
Northern Essex Community College (U)
Northern Michigan University (U)
Northern Virginia Community College (U)
North Harris College (U)
North Iowa Area Community College (U)
NorthWest Arkansas Community College (U)
Northwestern College (U)
Northwestern Michigan College (U)
Norwich University (U, G)
Oakland Community College (U)
Ohio University (U)
Ohio University–Southern Campus (U)
Oklahoma City Community College (U)
Old Dominion University (U)
Open Learning Agency (U)
Oregon State University (U)
Ouachita Technical College (U)
Pennsylvania State University University Park
  Campus (U)
Pierce College (U)
Portland Community College (U)
Portland State University (U)
Prairie State College (U)
Prince George's Community College (U, NC)
Pueblo Community College (U)
Queen's University at Kingston (U)

Raritan Valley Community College (U)
Redlands Community College (U)
Red Rocks Community College (U)
Rend Lake College (U)
Richard Stockton College of New Jersey (U)
Richland Community College (U)
Rio Salado College (U)
Rochester Institute of Technology (U)
Rockland Community College (U)
Rogers State University (U)
Roger Williams University (U)
Ryerson Polytechnic University (U)
Sacramento City College (U)
St. Cloud State University (U)
St. Johns River Community College (U)
Saint Joseph's College (U)
Salve Regina University (U, G, NC)
Sam Houston State University (U)
Santa Monica College (U)
Seattle Central Community College (U)
Shippensburg University of Pennsylvania (U, G)
Sierra College (U)
Skidmore College (U)
South Dakota State University (U)
Southeast Community College, Lincoln Campus
  (U)
Southeastern Illinois College (U)
Southeastern Louisiana University (U)
Southern Arkansas University Tech (U)
Southern Utah University (U)
South Florida Community College (U)
Southwestern Assemblies of God University (U)
Southwest Missouri State University (U)
Southwest Texas State University (U)
Springfield Technical Community College (U)
State University of New York College at Cortland
  (U)
State University of New York College of
  Agriculture and Technology at Morrisville (U)
State University of New York College of
  Technology at Delhi (U)
State University of New York Empire State
  College (U)
State University of West Georgia (U, G)
Stephens College (U)
Suffolk County Community College (U)
Syracuse University (U)
Tacoma Community College (U)
Tarrant County College District (U)
Technical College of the Lowcountry (U)
Temple University (U, G)
Tennessee Technological University (U, G)
Tennessee Temple University (U)
Texas Christian University (U)
Texas Tech University (U)
Thomas Edison State College (U)
Triton College (U)
Troy State University Montgomery (U)
Tulsa Community College (U)
Tyler Junior College (U)
Umpqua Community College (U)
United States Open University (U)
University of Alaska Fairbanks (U)
University of Alaska Southeast, Sitka Campus (U)
University of British Columbia (U)
University of California, Berkeley (U)
University of California Extension (U, NC)
University of Central Arkansas (U)
University of Central Florida (U)
University of Charleston (U, NC)
University of Cincinnati Raymond Walters
  College (U)
University of Delaware (U)
University of Great Falls (U)
University of Houston (U)
University of Illinois at Springfield (U)
University of Iowa (U, G)
University of Kansas (U, NC)

University of Maine (U, G)
University of Maine at Fort Kent (U)
University of Maine at Machias (U)
University of Maryland University College (U)
University of Memphis (U, G)
University of Minnesota, Twin Cities Campus (U)
University of Missouri–Columbia (U, G)
University of Missouri–Kansas City (U)
University of Nebraska–Lincoln (U)
University of Nevada, Reno (U)
University of New Brunswick (U)
University of New Orleans (U)
University of North Alabama (U, G)
University of Northern Iowa (U, G)
University of Oklahoma (U, G, NC)
University of Oregon (U)
University of Saskatchewan (U)
University of South Carolina (U, G)
University of South Dakota (U)
University of Southern Colorado (U)
University of Southern Mississippi (U)
University of South Florida (U)
University of Tennessee (U)
University of Texas at San Antonio (U)
University of Texas at Tyler (U, G)
University of Texas of the Permian Basin (U)
University of Texas System (G)
University of Utah (U)
University of Vermont (U)
University of Washington (U)
University of West Florida (U)
University of Wisconsin Colleges (U)
University of Wisconsin Extension (U, NC)
University of Wyoming (U)
University System of Georgia (U)
Upper Iowa University (U, NC)
Utah State University (U)
Volunteer State Community College (U)
Walla Walla Community College (U)
Washburn University of Topeka (U)
Washington State University (U)
Waubonsee Community College (U)
Wayne County Community College District (U)
Weber State University (U)
West Chester University of Pennsylvania (G)
Western Governors University (U)
Western Illinois University (U)
Western Michigan University (U)
Western Nebraska Community College (U)
Western Nevada Community College (U)
Western Oklahoma State College (U)
Western Washington University (U)
Western Wyoming Community College (U)
Westmoreland County Community College (U)
West Virginia University (U)
West Virginia Wesleyan College (U)
Whatcom Community College (U)
Wichita State University (U)
Wilfrid Laurier University (U)
Wright State University (U)
Yuba College (U)

English literature

Anne Arundel Community College (U)
Bellevue Community College (U)
Briercrest Bible College (U)
Brigham Young University (U)
Bucks County Community College (U)
Carleton University (U)
Cerritos College (U)
Cerro Coso Community College (U)
Chaminade University of Honolulu (U)
Christopher Newport University (U)
College of West Virginia (U)
Columbus State Community College (U)
Community College of Baltimore County (U)
Dallas Baptist University (U)
Drake University (U, G)

Individual Courses Index

Delta College (U)
Denver Seminary (G, NC)
Duquesne University (U, G)
East Carolina University (U)
Eastern Connecticut State University (U)
Eastern Kentucky University (U)
Edison State Community College (U)
El Camino College (U)
Finger Lakes Community College (U)
Gonzaga University (U, G)
Husson College (U)
Hutchinson Community College and Area
    Vocational School (U)
Indiana University System (U)
Indiana Wesleyan University (U)
John Wood Community College (U)
Kellogg Community College (U)
Lake Land College (U)
LIFE Bible College (U)
Manatee Community College (U)
Marylhurst University (U, G)
Marywood University (U)
MCP Hahnemann University (U)
Midland College (U)
Modesto Junior College (U)
Mohawk Valley Community College (U)
newGraduate Schools (G)
New York Institute of Technology (U)
North Central University (G)
Northern Virginia Community College (U)
Northwestern College (U)
Open Learning Agency (U)
Oregon State University (U)
Park University (U)
Pennsylvania College of Technology (U)
Pennsylvania State University University Park
    Campus (U)
Piedmont Technical College (U)
Pierce College (U)
Prairie Bible College (U)
Randolph Community College (U)
Regis University (U, G)
Roane State Community College (U)
Robert Morris College (U)
Rochester College (U)
Royal Military College of Canada (U, G)
St. Edward's University (U)
St. Petersburg Junior College (U)
Salve Regina University (U, G, NC)
San Jose State University (U)
Saybrook Graduate School (G)
Seattle Central Community College (U)
Sierra College (U)
Snow College (U)
Southeast Community College, Lincoln Campus
    (U)
Southwestern Community College (U)
Stephens College (U)
Strayer University (U)
Suffolk County Community College (U)
Syracuse University (U)
Temple Baptist Seminary (G, NC)
Texas Tech University (U, NC)
Thomas Edison State College (U)
Triton College (U)
Troy State University Dothan (U)
University College of the Fraser Valley (U)
University of Alaska Fairbanks (U)
University of Arkansas (U)
University of California, Los Angeles (G)
University of Cincinnati (U)
University of Colorado at Denver (U)
University of Delaware (U)
University of Idaho (G)
University of La Verne (U)
University of Manitoba (U)
University of Minnesota, Twin Cities Campus (U)
University of Missouri–Columbia (U)

University of North Carolina at Chapel Hill (U)
University of Oklahoma (U)
University of Southern Mississippi (U)
University of South Florida (U)
University of Tennessee (U)
University of Texas at Austin (U)
University of Toledo (U)
University of Waterloo (U)
University of Wisconsin Extension (U)
University System of Georgia (U)
Western Governors University (U)

European history
Bellevue Community College (U)
Bergen Community College (U)
Bossier Parish Community College (U)
Brigham Young University (U)
Bristol Community College (U)
Broward Community College (U)
Bucks County Community College (U)
Burlington County College (U)
Centralia College (U)
Clackamas Community College (U)
Cleveland State University (U)
College of Albemarle (U)
College of Southern Maryland (U)
College of West Virginia (U)
Concordia University Wisconsin (U)
Cossatot Technical College (U)
Elizabethtown Community College (U)
Florida Community College at Jacksonville (U)
Floyd College (U)
Genesee Community College (U)
Hinds Community College (U)
Houston Community College System (U)
Indian River Community College (U)
Johnson State College (U)
Kellogg Community College (U)
Louisiana State University System (U)
Maysville Community College (U)
Mercy College (U, G)
Mohawk Valley Community College (U)
Mount Allison University (U)
Mount Wachusett Community College (U)
Northwestern Michigan College (U)
Oregon State University (U)
Piedmont Technical College (U)
Prairie Bible College (U)
Randolph Community College (U)
Richland Community College (U)
Roane State Community College (U)
St. Edward's University (U)
St. Petersburg Junior College (U)
Seton Hill College (U)
Southeast Community College, Lincoln Campus
    (U)
Southeastern Oklahoma State University (U)
State University of New York at Oswego (U)
State University of West Georgia (U, G)
Suffolk County Community College (U)
Texas Tech University (U, NC)
University of Alaska Southeast, Ketchikan
    Campus (U)
University of Arizona (U)
University of Illinois at Urbana–Champaign (U)
University of Iowa (U, G)
University of Minnesota, Twin Cities Campus (U)
University of Nebraska–Lincoln (U)
University of Nevada, Reno (U)
University of North Carolina at Chapel Hill (U)
University of Tennessee (U, NC)
University of Texas at Austin (U)
University of Waterloo (U)
University of Wisconsin Colleges (U)
University System of Georgia (U)
Vance-Granville Community College (U)
Virginia Western Community College (U)
Walters State Community College (U)

Washington State University (U)
Weber State University (U)
Western Washington University (U)
West Virginia Wesleyan College (U)
William Paterson University of New Jersey (U)

European languages and literatures
Acadia University (U)
Anne Arundel Community College (U)
Athabasca University (U)
Atlantic Cape Community College (U)
Austin Community College (U)
Brigham Young University (U)
Brookdale Community College (U)
Butte College (U)
Caldwell College (U)
Calhoun Community College (U)
California State University, Fresno (U)
City Colleges of Chicago, Harold Washington
    College (U)
Clark College (U)
Cleveland State University (U, G)
Coastline Community College (U, NC)
College of DuPage (U)
College of Southern Maryland (U)
Colorado Christian University (U)
Community College of Baltimore County (U)
Concordia University Wisconsin (U, G)
Cuyahoga Community College, Metropolitan
    Campus (U)
Dallas County Community College District (U)
Darton College (U)
Edison Community College (U)
Evergreen Valley College (U)
Florida Community College at Jacksonville (U)
Foothill College (U)
Garland County Community College (U)
Georgia Perimeter College (U)
Georgia Southern University (U, NC)
Griggs University (U)
Howard Community College (U)
Indiana University System (U, NC)
John Wood Community College (U)
King's College (U)
Lenoir Community College (U)
Louisiana State University at Eunice (U)
Louisiana State University System (U)
Luzerne County Community College (U)
Madison Area Technical College (U)
Memorial University of Newfoundland (NC)
Minnesota West Community and Technical
    College (U)
Mount Saint Vincent University (U)
Nassau Community College (U)
New School University (U, NC)
North Carolina State University (U)
North Harris College (U)
North Seattle Community College (U)
Northwestern Michigan College (U)
Ohio University (U)
Ohlone College (U)
Oklahoma State University (U)
Open Learning Agency (U)
Owens Community College (U)
Pennsylvania State University University Park
    Campus (U)
Peralta Community College District (U)
Piedmont College (U)
Portland State University (U)
Pueblo Community College (U)
Richland Community College (NC)
Riverland Community College (U)
Rogers State University (U)
Sacramento City College (U)
St. Louis Community College System (U)
St. Petersburg Junior College (U)
San Antonio College (U)
Skidmore College (U)

University of Central Arkansas (U)
University of Dallas (G)
University of Houston–Downtown (U)
University of Management and Technology (G, NC)
University of Maryland University College (G)
University of Minnesota, Twin Cities Campus (U)
University of Missouri–Columbia (U)
University of Missouri–Rolla (G)
University of Montana–Missoula (G)
University of Nebraska–Lincoln (U)
University of New Orleans (U)
University of Notre Dame (G)
University of Oklahoma (U, G, NC)
University of Pennsylvania (NC)
University of Sarasota (G)
University of South Alabama (G)
University of Southern Maine (U)
University of Texas at Arlington (G)
University of Texas System (G)
University of Toronto (NC)
University of Wisconsin Extension (U, NC)
University of Wisconsin–La Crosse (G)
University of Wisconsin–Milwaukee (U)
University of Wisconsin–Platteville (U)
Virginia Polytechnic Institute and State University (U)
Walden University (G)
Washington State University (U)
Wayne County Community College District (U)
Weber State University (U)
Western Governors University (U)
Western Illinois University (U, G)
Worcester Polytechnic Institute (G)
York College of Pennsylvania (U)

Financial management and services
Roane State Community College (U)

Fine arts
Anne Arundel Community College (U)
Arizona State University (U)
Atlantic University (G, NC)
Austin Community College (U)
Brigham Young University (U)
Brunswick Community College (U)
Burlington College (U)
Butte College (U)
Calhoun Community College (U)
Cape Cod Community College (U)
Cape Fear Community College (U)
Central Texas College (U)
Chattanooga State Technical Community College (U)
City Colleges of Chicago, Harold Washington College (U)
Clarkson College (U)
College of Southern Maryland (U)
College of the Southwest (U)
College of West Virginia (U)
Colorado Mountain College District (U)
Concordia University at St. Paul (U)
Cossatot Technical College (U)
Darton College (U)
Dawson Community College (U)
De Anza College (U)
Duquesne University (U)
East Carolina University (U, G)
Eastern Wyoming College (U)
Garland County Community College (U)
Goddard College (U, G)
Graceland College (U)
Griggs University (U)
Indiana State University (U)
Indiana University System (U, G)
Iowa Wesleyan College (U)
Iowa Western Community College (U)
Jamestown Community College (U)

Judson College (U)
Lamar University (U)
Loyola University New Orleans (U)
Luzerne County Community College (U)
Malone College (U)
Marshall University (U)
Maryland Institute, College of Art (U, NC)
Minnesota West Community and Technical College (U)
Missouri Southern State College (U)
Nassau Community College (U)
New School University (U, NC)
Northern Arizona University (U)
Northern Virginia Community College (U)
NorthWest Arkansas Community College (U)
Northwestern Technical Institute (U)
Ohlone College (U)
Okaloosa-Walton Community College (U)
Parkland College (U)
Pennsylvania State University University Park Campus (U)
Portland Community College (U)
Portland State University (U)
Prairie Bible College (U)
Rend Lake College (U)
Richard Stockton College of New Jersey (U)
Rockland Community College (U)
St. Cloud State University (U)
Saint Joseph's College (U)
St. Louis Community College System (U)
Salt Lake Community College (U)
San Antonio College (U)
Sandhills Community College (U)
Sierra College (U)
Sinclair Community College (U)
Skidmore College (U)
Southern Utah University (U)
Southwestern Assemblies of God University (U)
Southwest Texas State University (U)
Spring Arbor College (U)
Syracuse University (U)
Tarrant County College District (U)
Taylor University, World Wide Campus (U)
University of Arkansas (U)
University of California, Berkeley (U)
University of California Extension (U)
University of Colorado at Denver (U)
University of Delaware (NC)
University of Findlay (U)
University of Missouri–St. Louis (U)
University of Oklahoma (U, NC)
University of Southern Indiana (U)
University of South Florida (U, G)
University of Tennessee at Martin (U)
University of Texas of the Permian Basin (U)
University of Utah (U)
University of Wisconsin Extension (U, NC)
University System of Georgia (U)
Utah State University (U, NC)
Volunteer State Community College (U)
Washington State University (U)
Waubonsee Community College (U)
Western Oklahoma State College (U)
West Virginia Wesleyan College (U)
Wichita State University (U, G)
Wilfrid Laurier University (U)
Wytheville Community College (U)
Yuba College (U)

Fire protection
Minnesota West Community and Technical College (U)

Fire science
Bakersfield College (U)
Berkshire Community College (U)
Bossier Parish Community College (U)

Chattanooga State Technical Community College (U)
Elizabethtown Community College (U)
El Paso Community College (U)
Honolulu Community College (U)
Ivy Tech State College–Central Indiana (U)
Ivy Tech State College–Northwest (U)
Kansas City Kansas Community College (U)
Louisiana State University at Eunice (U)
Louisiana State University System (U)
Metropolitan Community Colleges (U)
Missouri Western State College (U)
Northeast Wisconsin Technical College (U)
Oklahoma State University (U, G)
Owens Community College (U)
Portland Community College (U)
St. Petersburg Junior College (U)
Seminole Community College (U)
University of Cincinnati (U)
University of Maryland University College (U)
University of North Carolina at Charlotte (U)
Vincennes University (U)
Western Illinois University (U)
Worcester Polytechnic Institute (G)

Fire services administration
Coastal Carolina Community College (U, NC)
St. Louis Community College System (U, NC)
St. Petersburg Junior College (U)
State University of New York Empire State College (U)
University of Maryland, Baltimore County (G)
University of Memphis (U)
Western Illinois University (U)

Food products operations
Culinary Institute of America (NC)

Food service
Central Oregon Community College (U)

Foods and nutrition studies
American Academy of Nutrition, College of Nutrition (U)
Andrews University (U)
Auburn University (U)
Barton County Community College (U)
Boise State University (U)
Bucks County Community College (U)
Central Arizona College (U)
Centralia College (U)
Central Michigan University (U)
Central Missouri State University (U)
City Colleges of Chicago, Harold Washington College (U)
Colorado Mountain College District (U)
Colorado State University (U)
Cossatot Technical College (U)
Culinary Institute of America (NC)
Cuyahoga Community College, Metropolitan Campus (U)
Dallas County Community College District (U)
De Anza College (U)
Drake University (U)
East Carolina University (G)
Eastern Kentucky University (U)
Floyd College (U)
Fullerton College (U)
Goddard College (U, G)
Griggs University (U)
Honolulu Community College (U)
Hopkinsville Community College (U)
Hutchinson Community College and Area Vocational School (U)
Indiana University of Pennsylvania (U)
Indian River Community College (U)
Kansas City Kansas Community College (U)
Kansas State University (U, G, NC)
Lamar State College–Port Arthur (U)

Pennsylvania State University University Park
  Campus (U)
Portland Community College (U)
Portland State University (U)
Queen's University at Kingston (U)
Red Rocks Community College (U)
Rio Salado College (U)
Riverside Community College (U)
Rockland Community College (U)
Roosevelt University (U)
Sacramento City College (U)
St. Edward's University (U)
Sam Houston State University (U)
San Antonio College (U)
San Diego City College (U)
San Jose State University (U)
Seattle Central Community College (U)
Sierra College (U)
Skidmore College (U)
Snow College (U)
Southeast Community College, Lincoln Campus
  (U)
South Florida Community College (U)
Southwestern Community College (U)
Southwest Texas State University (U, G)
Tacoma Community College (U)
Taylor University, World Wide Campus (U)
Université Laval (U)
University of Akron (U)
University of Alaska Fairbanks (U)
University of Arizona (U)
University of Arkansas (U)
University of Central Arkansas (U, G)
University of Idaho (U)
University of Illinois at Urbana–Champaign (U)
University of Iowa (U, G)
University of Maine at Machias (U)
University of Manitoba (U)
University of Minnesota, Twin Cities Campus (U)
University of Missouri–Columbia (U)
University of Nebraska–Lincoln (U)
University of Nevada, Reno (U)
University of North Alabama (U)
University of North Carolina at Chapel Hill (U)
University of Northern Colorado (U)
University of Oklahoma (U)
University of Regina (U)
University of Saskatchewan (U)
University of South Dakota (U)
University of Southern Colorado (U)
University of Southern Mississippi (U)
University of South Florida (U)
University of Tennessee (U)
University of Texas at Austin (U)
University of Utah (U)
University of Washington (U)
University of Waterloo (U)
University of Wisconsin Colleges (U)
University of Wisconsin Extension (U)
University of Wisconsin–Platteville (U)
University System of Georgia (U)
Virginia Polytechnic Institute and State University
  (U)
Wayne County Community College District (U)
Weber State University (U)
Western Illinois University (U)
Western Michigan University (U)
Western Nevada Community College (U)
West Hills Community College (U)
Wilfrid Laurier University (U)
William Rainey Harper College (U)

Geology
Athabasca University (U)
Austin Community College (U)
Bakersfield College (U)
Bellevue Community College (U)
Boise State University (U)

Brevard Community College (U)
Broward Community College (U)
Burlington County College (U)
Carleton University (U)
Central Community College–Grand Island
  Campus (U)
Centralia College (U)
Central Oregon Community College (U)
Charles Stewart Mott Community College (U)
City Colleges of Chicago, Harold Washington
  College (U)
Cleveland State University (U)
Coastline Community College (U, NC)
College of DuPage (U)
College of Southern Maryland (U)
College of the Redwoods (U)
College of West Virginia (U)
Colorado Electronic Community College (U)
Community College of Baltimore County (U)
Cuyamaca College (U)
East Tennessee State University (U)
Edison Community College (U)
El Camino College (U)
El Paso Community College (U)
Emporia State University (U, G)
Fitchburg State College (U)
Florida Community College at Jacksonville (U)
Florida International University (U)
Florida State University (U)
Floyd College (U)
Fort Hays State University (U)
Front Range Community College (U)
Fullerton College (U)
Garland County Community College (U)
Georgia Southern University (U, G)
Glendale Community College (U)
Grayson County College (U)
Hibbing Community College (U)
Hillsborough Community College (U)
Honolulu Community College (U)
Houston Community College System (U)
Indiana University of Pennsylvania (U)
Indiana University System (U)
Iowa Western Community College (U)
Jacksonville State University (U)
Johnson County Community College (U)
Kansas State University (U, NC)
Laramie County Community College (U)
Lehigh Carbon Community College (U)
Louisiana State University System (U)
Luzerne County Community College (U)
Mansfield University of Pennsylvania (U, G)
Marshall University (U)
Michigan Technological University (U, NC)
Missouri Southern State College (U)
Modesto Junior College (U)
Montana State University–Bozeman (G)
Montgomery County Community College (U)
Mt. San Jacinto College (U)
New School University (U, NC)
North Central University (U)
Northeast Texas Community College (U)
North Seattle Community College (U)
Oklahoma City Community College (U)
Oklahoma State University (U)
Open Learning Agency (U)
Oregon State University (U)
Park University (U)
Pennsylvania State University University Park
  Campus (U)
Pensacola Junior College (U)
Pierce College (U)
Pikes Peak Community College (U, NC)
Portland State University (U)
Prince George's Community College (U)
Pueblo Community College (U)
Red Rocks Community College (U)
Rio Salado College (U)

Roane State Community College (U)
Rochester Institute of Technology (U)
St. Petersburg Junior College (U)
San Antonio College (U)
San Diego City College (U)
San Jose State University (U)
Santa Ana College (U)
Seminole Community College (U)
Shawnee Community College (U)
Skidmore College (U)
Southeast Community College, Lincoln Campus
  (U)
South Florida Community College (U)
State University of New York at Oswego (U)
Suffolk County Community College (U)
Syracuse University (U)
Tacoma Community College (U)
Tarrant County College District (U)
Temple University (U)
Texas Christian University (U)
Thomas Edison State College (U)
Troy State University Dothan (U)
Tulsa Community College (U)
Umpqua Community College (U)
Université Laval (U)
University of Alaska Fairbanks (U)
University of Alaska Southeast, Sitka Campus (U)
University of Arkansas (U)
University of British Columbia (U)
University of California, Berkeley (U)
University of California Extension (U)
University of Great Falls (U)
University of Houston (U)
University of Idaho (U, G)
University of Iowa (U, G)
University of Kansas (U, NC)
University of Memphis (U)
University of Minnesota, Twin Cities Campus (U)
University of Missouri–Columbia (U, G)
University of Nebraska–Lincoln (U)
University of New Orleans (U)
University of Oklahoma (U)
University of Oregon (U)
University of Pennsylvania (U, NC)
University of Saskatchewan (U)
University of Southern Colorado (U)
University of South Florida (U, G)
University of Texas at Arlington (U)
University of Washington (U)
University of Waterloo (U)
University of Wisconsin Extension (U)
University of Wisconsin–Madison (U)
University of Wisconsin–River Falls (U)
University System of Georgia (U)
Utah State University (U)
Vincennes University (U)
Volunteer State Community College (U)
Walters State Community College (U)
Washington State University (U)
Wayne County Community College District (U)
Weber State University (U)
Western Governors University (U)
Western Illinois University (U)
Western Michigan University (U)
Western Oklahoma State College (U)
Westmoreland County Community College (U)
West Valley College (U)
West Virginia University (G)
West Virginia Wesleyan College (U)
Whatcom Community College (U)
Wichita State University (U)
Wilfrid Laurier University (U)
Wright State University (G)

German language and literature
Brigham Young University (U)
Clarion University of Pennsylvania (U, G)
Eastern Kentucky University (U)

Individual Courses Index

Health professions and related sciences

Georgia Southern University (U)
Glendale Community College (U)
Goddard College (U, G)
Gogebic Community College (U)
Goucher College (G)
Governors State University (U, G)
Graceland College (U)
Grace University (U, NC)
Grand Valley State University (U, G)
Green River Community College (U)
Greenville Technical College (U)
Harrisburg Area Community College (U)
Hebrew College (U, G, NC)
Hillsborough Community College (U)
Holmes Community College (U)
Honolulu Community College (U)
Hope International University (U)
Howard Community College (U)
Indiana State University (U)
Indiana University System (U)
Iowa Western Community College (U)
Jacksonville State University (U)
James Sprunt Community College (U)
Judson College (U)
Kansas State University (U, NC)
Kellogg Community College (U)
Lackawanna Junior College (U)
Lafayette College (U)
Lakehead University (U)
Lake Land College (U)
Lamar University (U)
Lawson State Community College (U)
Lehigh Carbon Community College (U)
Lenoir Community College (U)
LeTourneau University (U)
LIFE Bible College (U)
Longview Community College (U)
Lorain County Community College (U)
Louisiana State University and Agricultural and
    Mechanical College (U)
Louisiana Tech University (G)
Luzerne County Community College (U)
Madisonville Community College (U)
Manatee Community College (U)
Marshall University (U, G)
Mayland Community College (U)
McDowell Technical Community College (U)
Memorial University of Newfoundland (U)
Mercer University (NC)
Mercy College (U)
Metropolitan State University (U)
Mid-America Bible College (U)
Midland College (U)
Mid-Plains Community College Area (U)
Midwestern State University (U)
Minnesota West Community and Technical
    College (U)
Minot State University (U)
Missouri Southern State College (U)
Modesto Junior College (U)
Montana State University–Billings (U)
Montgomery County Community College (U)
Moody Bible Institute (U)
Moraine Valley Community College (U)
Mount Allison University (U)
Mount Saint Vincent University (U)
Nassau Community College (U)
New Hampshire College (U)
New Hampshire Community Technical College,
    Nashua/Claremont (U)
New School University (U, G, NC)
New York Institute of Technology (U)
North Arkansas College (U)
North Carolina State University (U)
North Central Texas College (U)
North Central University (U)
Northern Arizona University (U)
Northern Kentucky University (U)

Northern State University (U)
Northern Virginia Community College (U)
North Harris College (U)
North Iowa Area Community College (U)
Northwestern College (U)
Northwestern College (U)
Northwestern Michigan College (U)
Norwich University (U, G)
Nyack College (U)
Oakland Community College (U)
Ohio University (U)
Ohio University–Southern Campus (U)
Oklahoma City Community College (U)
Oklahoma State University (U)
Old Dominion University (U)
Open Learning Agency (U)
Parkland College (U)
Pennsylvania State University University Park
    Campus (U)
Pensacola Junior College (U)
Peralta Community College District (U)
Piedmont College (U)
Pikes Peak Community College (U, NC)
Portland Community College (U)
Portland State University (U)
Prairie Bible College (U, G)
Prairie State College (U)
Prince George's Community College (U, NC)
Queen's University at Kingston (U)
Rappahannock Community College (U)
Redlands Community College (U)
Red Rocks Community College (U)
Regents College (U)
Regis University (G)
Richland Community College (U)
Rio Salado College (U)
Riverside Community College (U)
Rochester Institute of Technology (U)
Rockland Community College (U)
Rogers State University (U)
Roosevelt University (U)
Royal Military College of Canada (U, G)
Rutgers, The State University of New Jersey, New
    Brunswick (U)
Ryerson Polytechnic University (U)
Sacramento City College (U)
St. Cloud State University (U)
St. Johns River Community College (U)
Saint Joseph's College (U)
St. Petersburg Junior College (U)
Sam Houston State University (U)
San Antonio College (U)
Sandhills Community College (U)
San Diego City College (U)
Sierra College (U)
Sinclair Community College (U)
Skidmore College (U)
Snow College (U)
South Dakota State University (U)
Southeastern Illinois College (U)
Southeastern Louisiana University (U)
Southern Arkansas University Tech (U)
Southern Utah University (U)
South Florida Community College (U)
South Puget Sound Community College (U)
Southwestern Assemblies of God University (U)
Southwestern Community College (U)
Southwest Texas State University (U)
Stanly Community College (U)
State University of New York Empire State
    College (U)
State University of West Georgia (U, G)
Stephens College (U)
Surry Community College (U)
Sussex County Community College (U)
Syracuse University (U, G)
Tacoma Community College (U)
Tarrant County College District (U)

Taylor University, World Wide Campus (U)
Technical College of the Lowcountry (U)
Temple University (U)
Tennessee Temple University (U)
Texas A&M University–Commerce (U)
Texas Tech University (U)
Thomas Edison State College (U)
Thomas Nelson Community College (U)
Tidewater Community College (U)
Troy State University Dothan (U)
Troy State University Montgomery (U)
Tyler Junior College (U)
Union Institute (U)
University of Alabama (U, G)
University of Alaska Fairbanks (U)
University of Alaska Southeast, Sitka Campus (U)
University of Baltimore (U)
University of British Columbia (U)
University of Calgary (U)
University of California, Berkeley (U)
University of California Extension (U)
University of California, Santa Cruz (U, G)
University of Central Arkansas (U)
University of Cincinnati (U)
University of Colorado at Denver (U)
University of Great Falls (U)
University of Guam (U, NC)
University of Houston (U)
University of Houston–Victoria (U, G)
University of Illinois at Springfield (U, G)
University of Kansas (U, G, NC)
University of La Verne (U)
University of Maine (U)
University of Maine at Fort Kent (U)
University of Maine at Machias (U)
University of Manitoba (U)
University of Maryland University College (U)
University of Massachusetts Lowell (U)
University of Minnesota, Twin Cities Campus (U)
University of Missouri–Columbia (U, G)
University of Missouri–Kansas City (U)
University of Missouri–St. Louis (U)
University of Nebraska–Lincoln (U)
University of Nevada, Reno (U)
University of New Brunswick (U)
University of New Orleans (U)
University of North Alabama (U)
University of North Carolina at Chapel Hill (U)
University of Northern Iowa (U, G)
University of Oklahoma (U)
University of Pittsburgh (U)
University of Saskatchewan (U)
University of South Carolina (U, G)
University of South Dakota (U)
University of Southern Colorado (U)
University of Southern Mississippi (U)
University of South Florida (U)
University of Tennessee (U)
University of Texas at Tyler (U, G)
University of Texas System (U)
University of the Incarnate Word (U)
University of Toledo (U, G)
University of Utah (U)
University of Washington (U)
University of Waterloo (U)
University of Wisconsin Colleges (U)
University of Wisconsin–Milwaukee (U)
University of Wyoming (U)
University System of Georgia (U)
Upper Iowa University (U, NC)
Utah State University (U)
Vermont Technical College (U)
Victor Valley College (U)
Vincennes University (U)
Volunteer State Community College (U)
Wake Technical Community College (U)
Walla Walla Community College (U)
Walters State Community College (U)

Individual and family development studies

Industrial engineering

Industrial psychology

Liberal arts, general studies, and humanities

Tacoma Community College (U)
Tarrant County College District (U)
Technical College of the Lowcountry (U)
Tennessee Temple University (U)
Terra State Community College (U)
Texas Tech University (U)
Thomas Edison State College (U)
Tidewater Community College (U)
Troy State University Montgomery (U)
Tulsa Community College (U)
Tyler Junior College (U)
Umpqua Community College (U)
Union Institute (U)
United States Open University (U)
University of Alabama (U, G)
University of Alaska Fairbanks (U)
University of Alaska Southeast, Sitka Campus (U)
University of Calgary (U)
University of California, Los Angeles (G)
University of California, Santa Cruz (U, G)
University of Colorado at Colorado Springs (U)
University of Colorado at Denver (U, G)
University of Connecticut (U, G)
University of Delaware (U)
University of Great Falls (U)
University of Houston (U)
University of Houston–Downtown (U)
University of Kansas (U, G, NC)
University of La Verne (U)
University of Maine (U, G)
University of Maine at Fort Kent (U)
University of Maryland University College (U)
University of Massachusetts Lowell (U)
University of Minnesota, Twin Cities Campus (U)
University of Missouri–Columbia (U)
University of Missouri–Kansas City (U)
University of Nebraska–Lincoln (U)
University of Nevada, Reno (U)
University of New Orleans (U)
University of North Carolina at Chapel Hill (U)
University of North Carolina at Greensboro (U, G)
University of North Dakota (U)
University of Northern Iowa (U)
University of Oregon (U)
University of Pittsburgh (U)
University of Saskatchewan (U)
University of South Carolina (U)
University of South Dakota (U)
University of Southern Indiana (U)
University of South Florida (U)
University of Texas at Tyler (U, G)
University of Wisconsin–River Falls (U)
University of Wyoming (U)
University System of Georgia (U)
Utah State University (U)
Vincennes University (U)
Volunteer State Community College (U)
Walla Walla Community College (U)
Walters State Community College (U)
Washington State University (U)
Waubonsee Community College (U)
Wayne County Community College District (U)
Western Illinois University (U)
Western Nebraska Community College (U)
Western Oklahoma State College (U)
West Los Angeles College (U)
Westmoreland County Community College (U)
West Shore Community College (U)
West Virginia University (U)
West Virginia Wesleyan College (U)
Wichita State University (U)
York Technical College (U)
Yuba College (U)

Library and information studies
Allegany College of Maryland (U)
American River College (U)
Arizona State University (U)
California State University, Fullerton (U)
Centralia College (U)
Central Missouri State University (U)
Central Oregon Community College (U)
Clarion University of Pennsylvania (G)
Connecticut State University System (U, G)
Cuyahoga Community College, Metropolitan Campus (U)
De Anza College (U)
East Carolina University (G)
Eastern Connecticut State University (U, G)
Eastern Kentucky University (G)
Emporia State University (U, G)
Everett Community College (U)
Florida Keys Community College (U)
Florida State University (G)
Foothill College (U)
Fort Hays State University (U, G)
Front Range Community College (U)
Indiana University System (G)
Instituto Tecnológico y de Estudios Superiores de Monterrey, Campus Monterrey (G)
Inter American University of Puerto Rico, San Germán Campus (G)
Johnson County Community College (U)
Kent State University (G)
Lewis and Clark Community College (U)
Louisiana State University and Agricultural and Mechanical College (G)
Louisiana State University at Eunice (G)
Louisiana State University System (U)
Mansfield University of Pennsylvania (G)
Marylhurst University (U)
Mayville State University (U)
Memorial University of Newfoundland (U)
Metropolitan State University (U)
New Jersey Institute of Technology (G)
Northampton County Area Community College (U)
North Central University (U)
Northern State University (U)
North Seattle Community College (U)
Northwest Technical College (U)
Norwich University (U, G)
Ohlone College (U)
Okaloosa-Walton Community College (U)
Pikes Peak Community College (U, NC)
Rutgers, The State University of New Jersey, New Brunswick (U, G)
Salt Lake Community College (U)
San Jose State University (G)
Seminole Community College (U)
Southeastern Louisiana University (U)
Southern Connecticut State University (G)
Southern Utah University (U)
Southwest Virginia Community College (U)
State University of New York at Buffalo (G)
Texas A&M University–Commerce (U, G, NC)
Ulster County Community College (U)
Umpqua Community College (U)
University College of the Fraser Valley (U)
University of Alabama (U)
University of Alaska Fairbanks (U)
University of Arizona (G)
University of California, Berkeley (U)
University of California Extension (U)
University of Illinois at Urbana–Champaign (G)
University of Missouri-Columbia (G)
University of New Orleans (G)
University of North Carolina at Chapel Hill (U)
University of North Carolina at Greensboro (G)
University of North Texas (U)
University of Oklahoma (U, G, NC)
University of South Carolina (G)

University of South Dakota (U)
University of South Florida (G)
University of Tennessee (G)
University of Utah (U)
University of Washington (U)
University of Wisconsin–Milwaukee (G)
Volunteer State Community College (U)
West Los Angeles College (U)
West Valley College (U)
Whatcom Community College (U)

Logic
Brigham Young University (U)
Chaminade University of Honolulu (U)
Coastline Community College (U, NC)
College of Southern Maryland (U)
College of West Virginia (U)
El Camino College (U)
Fairleigh Dickinson University, The New College of General and Continuing Studies (U)
Gonzaga University (U, G)
Indiana University System (U)
Lake Land College (U)
Louisiana State University System (U)
Manatee Community College (U)
Marylhurst University (U)
North Carolina State University (U)
Northern Virginia Community College (U)
Open Learning Agency (U)
Palomar College (U)
Pitt Community College (U)
Roger Williams University (U)
Seattle Central Community College (U)
Stephens College (U)
Strayer University (U)
Syracuse University (U)
Taylor University, World Wide Campus (U)
University of Arkansas (U)
University of Cincinnati (U)
University of Colorado at Denver (U)
University of Manitoba (U)
University of Minnesota, Twin Cities Campus (U)
University of Missouri–Columbia (U)
University of Nebraska–Lincoln (U)
University of North Carolina at Chapel Hill (U)
University of Pittsburgh (U)
University of Southern Mississippi (U)
University of Texas at Austin (U)
University of Texas of the Permian Basin (U)
University of Toledo (U)
University of Waterloo (U)
University of Wisconsin Colleges (U)
University of Wisconsin Extension (U)
University System of Georgia (U)

Management
Alamance Community College (U)
Cape Fear Community College (U)
Culinary Institute of America (NC)
Mississippi County Community College (U)
Regis University (G)
Stevens Institute of Technology (G)
University of Oklahoma (U)
University of Wisconsin–Platteville (G)
University of Wisconsin–Stout (G)
Western Nevada Community College (U)

Management information systems
Adams State College (U)
American Institute for Computer Sciences (U)
Barton County Community College (U)
Bellevue Community College (U)
Buena Vista University (U)
California National University for Advanced Studies (U, G)
Capitol College (G)
Cerritos College (U)
Cerro Coso Community College (U)
City University (U, G)

College for Lifelong Learning, University System
of New Hampshire (U)
College of West Virginia (U)
Connecticut State University System (U, G)
Cossatot Technical College (U)
CTS University, Inc. (U, NC)
Drake University (U)
Embry-Riddle Aeronautical University, Extended
Campus (G)
Fashion Institute of Technology (U)
Forsyth Technical Community College (NC)
Franklin University (U)
Fresno Pacific University (G)
Golden Gate University (U, G)
Heriot-Watt University (U)
Houston Community College System (U)
Indiana Institute of Technology (U)
Kansas State University (U, NC)
Kettering University (G)
Lincoln Christian College (U, NC)
Louisiana State University System (U)
Lynn University (U)
Maharishi University of Management (G, NC)
Manatee Community College (U)
Marshall University (U)
Marywood University (U)
Mercy College (U, G)
Metropolitan State University (U, G)
Mount Vernon Nazarene College (U)
National Technological University (NC)
newGraduate Schools (G)
New York University (G)
Northern Illinois University (G)
Northern Virginia Community College (U)
Oklahoma State University (U)
Old Dominion University (U, G)
Open Learning Agency (U)
Pennsylvania State University University Park
Campus (U)
Regis University (G)
Rensselaer Polytechnic Institute (G, NC)
Robert Morris College (U)
Robert Morris College (U)
Royal Military College of Canada (G)
Royal Roads University (G)
Salve Regina University (G, NC)
Saybrook Graduate School (G)
Southeastern Oklahoma State University (U, G)
State University of New York Empire State
College (U)
State University of West Georgia (U)
Stevens Institute of Technology (G)
Strayer University (U)
Suffolk University (G)
University of Alaska Southeast (U)
University of California, Berkeley (U)
University of California Extension (U)
University of California, Los Angeles (G)
University of Central Oklahoma (U)
University of Colorado at Denver (G)
University of Connecticut (U, G)
University of Dallas (G)
University of Houston–Downtown (U)
University of Illinois at Springfield (G)
University of Management and Technology (G,
NC)
University of Maryland University College (U, G)
University of Minnesota, Crookston (U)
University of Minnesota, Twin Cities Campus (U)
University of Notre Dame (G)
University of Oklahoma (G, NC)
University of Oregon (G)
University of Pennsylvania (NC)
University of Phoenix (G)
University of Sarasota (G)
University of Southern Mississippi (U)
University of Texas at El Paso (G)
University of Texas at San Antonio (U)

University of Texas System (G)
University of Waterloo (G)
Upper Iowa University (U, NC)
Virginia Polytechnic Institute and State University
(G)
Walden University (G)
Wayland Baptist University (U, G)
Weber State University (U)
Western Illinois University (U, G)
West Virginia Northern Community College (U)
West Virginia University Institute of Technology
(U)
Worcester Polytechnic Institute (G)

Marketing

Adelphi University (U, G)
American Academy of Nutrition, College of
Nutrition (U)
American Institute for Computer Sciences (U)
American Military University (U)
American River College (U)
Anne Arundel Community College (U)
Arizona State University (U)
Arizona Western College (G)
Athens Area Technical Institute (U)
Atlantic Cape Community College (U)
Austin Community College (U)
Baker College-Center for Graduate Studies (G)
Bloomfield College (U)
Boise State University (U)
Brenau University (G)
Brigham Young University (U)
Brookdale Community College (U)
Broward Community College (U)
Bucks County Community College (U)
Burlington County College (U)
California College for Health Sciences (U)
California National University for Advanced
Studies (U, G)
California State University, Los Angeles (G)
Cape Fear Community College (U)
Capella University (G)
Central Michigan University (U, G)
Central Oregon Community College (U)
Central Virginia Community College (U)
Central Washington University (U)
Cerro Coso Community College (U)
Champlain College (U)
City University (U)
Clark College (U)
College of Albemarle (U)
College of Southern Maryland (U)
College of West Virginia (U)
Colorado Christian University (G)
Colorado Mountain College District (U)
Colorado State University (G)
Columbus State Community College (U)
Community College of Baltimore County (U)
Connecticut State University System (U, G)
Cossatot Technical College (U)
Cuyahoga Community College, Metropolitan
Campus (U)
Dalhousie University (G)
Dallas County Community College District (U)
Danville Community College (U)
De Anza College (U)
Delaware Technical & Community College, Jack
F. Owens Campus (U)
Delaware Technical & Community College,
Stanton/Wilmington Campus (U)
Del Mar College (U)
Delta College (U)
Drake University (U)
Duke University (G)
Eastern Kentucky University (U)
Edison State Community College (U)
El Paso Community College (U)
Embry-Riddle Aeronautical University, Extended
Campus (U)

Fairleigh Dickinson University, The New College
of General and Continuing Studies (U)
Fashion Institute of Technology (U)
Fayetteville Technical Community College (U)
Finger Lakes Community College (U)
Florida Community College at Jacksonville (U)
Florida Keys Community College (U)
Forsyth Technical Community College (U)
Frank Phillips College (U)
Frostburg State University (G)
Gannon University (U)
Genesee Community College (U)
Georgia Southwestern State University (G)
Golden Gate University (U)
Governors State University (U)
Graceland College (U)
Harcourt Learning Direct (U)
Heriot-Watt University (U)
Hill College of the Hill Junior College District
(U)
Hillsborough Community College (U)
Houston Community College System (U)
Indiana Institute of Technology (U)
Instituto Tecnológico y de Estudios Superiores de
Monterrey, Campus Monterrey (U)
Ivy Tech State College–Eastcentral (U)
Ivy Tech State College–Northwest (U)
Johnson County Community College (U)
Johnson State College (U)
Kansas City Kansas Community College (U)
Kansas State University (U, NC)
Keller Graduate School of Management (G)
Kellogg Community College (U)
Kent State University (U)
Kettering University (G)
Lake Land College (U)
Lakeland College (U)
Lakeland Community College (U)
Lehigh Carbon Community College (U)
Lewis and Clark Community College (U)
Liberty University (U)
Linn-Benton Community College (U)
Louisiana State University System (U)
Madison Area Technical College (U)
Maharishi University of Management (G, NC)
Manatee Community College (U)
Manor College (U)
Marshall University (U)
Marylhurst University (U, G)
Marywood University (U)
Mercy College (U, G)
Metropolitan Community Colleges (U)
Metropolitan State University (U, G)
Miami-Dade Community College (U)
Midwestern State University (U, G)
Milwaukee School of Engineering (G, NC)
Montana State University–Billings (U)
Mountain Empire Community College (U)
Mount Wachusett Community College (U)
Nassau Community College (U)
Neumann College (U)
newGraduate Schools (G)
New Hampshire College (U, G)
New York Institute of Technology (U, G)
North Country Community College (U)
Northeast State Technical Community College
(U)
Northeast Wisconsin Technical College (U)
Northern Arizona University (U)
Northern Illinois University (G)
Northern Michigan University (U)
Northern Virginia Community College (U)
Northwestern College (U)
Okaloosa-Walton Community College (U)
Oklahoma State University (U)
Old Dominion University (U, G)
Open Learning Agency (U)
Owens Community College (U)

Marketing (continued)
Parkland College (U)
Park University (U)
Peirce College (U)
Pellissippi State Technical Community College (U)
Pennsylvania College of Technology (U)
Pennsylvania State University University Park Campus (U)
Pitt Community College (U)
Portland Community College (U)
Prince George's Community College (U, NC)
Randolph Community College (U)
Raritan Valley Community College (U)
Regent University (G)
Regis University (U, G)
Rensselaer Polytechnic Institute (G, NC)
Richard Stockton College of New Jersey (U)
Rio Salado College (U)
Roane State Community College (U)
Robert Morris College (U)
Robert Morris College (U)
Roger Williams University (U)
Royal Military College of Canada (U)
Sacred Heart University (U)
Saddleback College (U)
St. Louis Community College System (U)
St. Petersburg Junior College (U)
Salve Regina University (U, G, NC)
Sam Houston State University (U)
San Jacinto College District (U)
San Joaquin Delta College (U)
San Juan College (U)
Santa Ana College (U)
Sheridan College (U)
Sinclair Community College (U)
Southeastern Louisiana University (U)
Southwest Missouri State University (U, G)
Spring Arbor College (U, G)
Stanly Community College (U)
State University of West Georgia (U)
Stephens College (U, G)
Strayer University (U, G)
Suffolk County Community College (U)
Suffolk University (U)
Temple University (G)
Texas A&M University–Commerce (G)
Texas A&M University–Texarkana (U)
Texas Tech University (U, NC)
Thomas Edison State College (U)
Tompkins Cortland Community College (U)
Touro International University (U, G)
Triton College (U)
Troy State University Montgomery (U)
Université Laval (U, G)
University College of Cape Breton (U)
University of Alaska Southeast (U)
University of Baltimore (G)
University of California, Berkeley (U)
University of California Extension (U)
University of California, Los Angeles (G)
University of Central Arkansas (U)
University of Central Oklahoma (U)
University of Dallas (G)
University of Delaware (U)
University of Findlay (U, G)
University of Houston–Downtown (U)
University of Illinois at Urbana–Champaign (U)
University of Management and Technology (G, NC)
University of Maryland University College (G)
University of Massachusetts Amherst (U)
University of Michigan–Flint (U)
University of Minnesota, Crookston (U)
University of Minnesota, Twin Cities Campus (U)
University of Missouri–Columbia (U, G)
University of Missouri–Rolla (G)
University of Nebraska–Lincoln (U)

University of Nevada, Reno (U)
University of North Alabama (U)
University of Northern Iowa (U)
University of North Texas (U, G)
University of Notre Dame (U)
University of Oklahoma (U, G, NC)
University of Pennsylvania (NC)
University of Phoenix (U, G)
University of Sarasota (G)
University of Southern Colorado (U)
University of Southern Mississippi (U)
University of Tennessee (NC)
University of Texas at San Antonio (U)
University of Texas System (G)
University of the Incarnate Word (U)
University of Toronto (NC)
University of Washington (U)
University of Wisconsin–Milwaukee (U)
University of Wisconsin–Platteville (U)
University System of Georgia (U)
Upper Iowa University (U, NC)
Vance-Granville Community College (U)
Vincennes University (U)
Virginia Polytechnic Institute and State University (U)
Virginia Western Community College (U)
Volunteer State Community College (U)
Walsh College of Accountancy and Business Administration (U, G, NC)
Walters State Community College (U)
Washington State University (U)
Wayne County Community College District (U)
Weber State University (U)
Western Connecticut State University (U)
Western Governors University (U, NC)
Western Illinois University (U, G)
West Shore Community College (U)
West Valley College (U)
West Virginia Wesleyan College (U)
William Paterson University of New Jersey (U)
Worcester Polytechnic Institute (G)
Wytheville Community College (U)

Mass media
Arizona State University (U)
Bellevue Community College (U)
Bergen Community College (U)
Brigham Young University (U)
Central Missouri State University (U, G)
Charter Oak State College (U)
Coastline Community College (U, NC)
Colorado Electronic Community College (U)
Cumberland County College (U)
De Anza College (U)
Eastern Kentucky University (U)
El Paso Community College (U)
Genesee Community College (U)
Kellogg Community College (U)
Linn-Benton Community College (U)
Metropolitan State University (U)
Missouri Southern State College (U)
Mount Wachusett Community College (U)
Nassau Community College (U)
North Seattle Community College (U)
Ohlone College (U)
Palomar College (U)
Parkland College (U)
Richard Stockton College of New Jersey (U)
Roane State Community College (U)
St. Ambrose University (U)
St. Cloud State University (G)
Seattle Central Community College (U)
State University of New York at Oswego (U)
State University of West Georgia (U)
Temple University (U, G)
Université de Montréal (G)
University College of the Fraser Valley (U)
University of Connecticut (U)

University of South Dakota (U)
University of Southern Indiana (U)
University of Toledo (U)
Weber State University (U)
West Chester University of Pennsylvania (U)
Western Governors University (U)
Yuba College (U)

Mathematics
Acadia University (U)
Adams State College (U)
Alamance Community College (U)
Allegany College of Maryland (U)
American College of Prehospital Medicine (U)
Anne Arundel Community College (U)
Arizona State University (G)
Arizona Western College (G)
Athabasca University (U)
Auburn University (U)
Bakersfield College (U)
Ball State University (U)
Barton County Community College (U)
Beaufort County Community College (U)
Bellevue Community College (U)
Bergen Community College (U)
Blackhawk Technical College (U)
Boise State University (U)
Bossier Parish Community College (NC)
Bradley University (U)
Brevard Community College (U)
Brigham Young University (U)
Brunswick Community College (U)
Bryant and Stratton Business Institute (U, NC)
Bucks County Community College (U)
Butte College (U)
Caldwell College (U)
Calhoun Community College (U)
California College for Health Sciences (U)
California National University for Advanced Studies (U, G)
Cape Cod Community College (U)
Catawba Valley Community College (U)
Central Arizona College (U)
Central Community College–Grand Island Campus (U)
Centralia College (U)
Central Michigan University (U)
Central Missouri State University (U)
Central Virginia Community College (U)
Chadron State College (U)
Champlain College (U)
Charles Stewart Mott Community College (U)
Charter Oak State College (U)
Chattanooga State Technical Community College (U)
Chippewa Valley Technical College (U)
Citrus College (U)
Clackamas Community College (U)
Clark College (U)
Clarkson College (U, G)
Cleveland State Community College (U)
Coastline Community College (U, NC)
College of Aeronautics (U)
College of DuPage (U)
College of Southern Maryland (U)
College of the Southwest (U)
College of West Virginia (U)
Colorado Christian University (U)
Colorado Mountain College District (U)
Colorado State University (G)
Columbia State Community College (U)
Columbus State Community College (U)
Community College of Rhode Island (U)
Connors State College (U)
Corning Community College (U)
Cumberland County College (U)
Cuyahoga Community College, Metropolitan Campus (U)

Dakota State University (U)
Dallas County Community College District (U)
Danville Area Community College (U)
Danville Community College (U)
Darton College (U)
Dawson Community College (U)
De Anza College (U)
Delaware Technical & Community College, Stanton/Wilmington Campus (U)
Des Moines Area Community College (U)
Drake University (U)
Eastern Connecticut State University (U)
Eastern Michigan University (U)
Eastern Oregon University (U)
Eastern Shore Community College (U)
East Tennessee State University (U)
Edison Community College (U)
EduKan (U)
Embry-Riddle Aeronautical University (U)
Embry-Riddle Aeronautical University, Extended Campus (U)
Erie Community College, North Campus (U)
Fayetteville Technical Community College (U)
Florence-Darlington Technical College (U)
Florida Community College at Jacksonville (U)
Foothill College (U)
Fort Hays State University (U, G)
Franklin University (U)
Frank Phillips College (U)
Front Range Community College (U)
Garland County Community College (U)
Georgia Institute of Technology (G, NC)
Georgia Southern University (U, G, NC)
Golden Gate University (U)
Graceland College (U)
Grand Valley State University (U, G)
Grantham College of Engineering (U)
Green River Community College (U)
Greenville Technical College (U)
Griggs University (U)
Harrisburg Area Community College (U)
Hawkeye Community College (U)
Heriot-Watt University (G)
Hillsborough Community College (U)
Hobe Sound Bible College (U)
Holmes Community College (U)
Horry-Georgetown Technical College (U)
Howard Community College (U)
Illinois Institute of Technology (U, G)
Indiana Institute of Technology (U)
Indiana University of Pennsylvania (U)
Indiana University System (U, NC)
Iowa Wesleyan College (U)
Iowa Western Community College (U)
Ivy Tech State College–Columbus (U)
Ivy Tech State College–Eastcentral (U)
Ivy Tech State College–Northwest (U)
Ivy Tech State College–Southwest (U)
Ivy Tech State College–Wabash Valley (U)
Ivy Tech State College–Whitewater (U)
Jacksonville State University (U)
Johnson County Community College (U)
John Wood Community College (U)
Judson College (U)
Kansas City Kansas Community College (U)
Keiser College (U)
Kellogg Community College (U)
Lackawanna Junior College (U, NC)
Lakehead University (U)
Lakeshore Technical College (U)
Lake Washington Technical College (U)
Lansing Community College (U)
Lehigh Carbon Community College (U)
Longview Community College (U)
Lorain County Community College (U)
Louisiana State University System (U)
Luzerne County Community College (U)
Lynn University (U)

Marshall University (U)
Memorial University of Newfoundland (U)
Mercy College (U)
Metropolitan Community College (U)
Metropolitan State University (U, G)
Michigan State University (NC)
Mid-America Bible College (U)
Middle Tennessee State University (U, G)
Midland College (U)
Mid-Plains Community College Area (U)
Midwestern State University (G)
Minnesota West Community and Technical College (U)
Minot State University (U)
Mississippi State University (G)
Modesto Junior College (U)
Mohawk Valley Community College (U)
Montana State University–Billings (U)
Montana State University–Bozeman (G)
Morehead State University (U)
Motlow State Community College (U, NC)
Mountain Empire Community College (U)
Mount Allison University (U)
Mount Saint Vincent University (U)
Mount Vernon Nazarene College (U)
Mount Wachusett Community College (U)
Nassau Community College (U, NC)
National Technological University (G, NC)
New Hampshire College (U)
New Jersey Institute of Technology (U)
New School University (U, NC)
New York Institute of Technology (U)
North Arkansas College (U)
North Carolina State University (U)
Northcentral Technical College (U)
North Central University (U)
North Dakota State University (U)
Northeast State Technical Community College (U)
Northeast Wisconsin Technical College (U)
Northern Michigan University (U)
Northern Virginia Community College (U)
North Harris College (U)
North Iowa Area Community College (U)
Northwestern College (U)
Northwestern College (U)
Northwestern Technical Institute (U)
Ohio University (U)
Ohio University–Southern Campus (U)
Oklahoma City Community College (U)
Oklahoma State University (U)
Old Dominion University (U)
Open Learning Agency (U)
Oregon State University (U)
Owens Community College (U)
Parkland College (U)
Peirce College (U)
Pennsylvania State University University Park Campus (U)
Pensacola Junior College (U)
Piedmont College (U)
Pikes Peak Community College (U, NC)
Portland Community College (U)
Portland State University (U)
Prince George's Community College (U, NC)
Pueblo Community College (U)
Rappahannock Community College (U)
Redlands Community College (U)
Red Rocks Community College (U)
Richard Stockton College of New Jersey (U)
Rio Salado College (U)
Riverside Community College (U)
Roane State Community College (U)
Rochester Institute of Technology (U, G)
Rockland Community College (U)
Rogers State University (U)
Rutgers, The State University of New Jersey, New Brunswick (U)

Sacred Heart University (U)
Saint Charles County Community College (U, G)
St. Cloud State University (G)
St. Johns River Community College (U)
Saint Joseph's College (U)
St. Louis Community College System (U)
St. Petersburg Junior College (U)
Salt Lake Community College (U)
Sam Houston State University (U)
San Juan College (U)
Shawnee Community College (U)
Shenandoah University (G)
Shippensburg University of Pennsylvania (U, G)
Sierra College (U)
Sinclair Community College (U)
Skidmore College (U)
South Dakota State University (U, G)
Southeast Community College, Lincoln Campus (U)
Southeastern Illinois College (U)
Southeastern Louisiana University (U)
Southeastern Oklahoma State University (U)
South Puget Sound Community College (U)
Southwestern Assemblies of God University (U)
Southwestern Michigan College (U)
Southwest Texas State University (U, G)
Springfield Technical Community College (U)
Stanly Community College (U)
State University of New York College of Agriculture and Technology at Morrisville (U)
State University of New York Empire State College (U)
State University of West Georgia (U)
Syracuse University (U)
Tarrant County College District (U)
Taylor University, World Wide Campus (U)
Technical College of the Lowcountry (U)
Temple University (U)
Tennessee Temple University (U)
Terra State Community College (U)
Texas Christian University (U)
Texas State Technical College (U)
Texas Tech University (U)
Thomas Nelson Community College (U)
Triton College (U)
Troy State University Montgomery (U)
Tulsa Community College (U)
Ulster County Community College (U)
Umpqua Community College (U)
Union Institute (U)
University of Akron (U, G)
University of Alabama (U, G)
University of Alaska Fairbanks (U)
University of Alaska Southeast, Sitka Campus (U)
University of Arizona (U)
University of California, Berkeley (U)
University of California Extension (U)
University of California, Los Angeles (G)
University of Central Arkansas (U)
University of Central Florida (G)
University of Colorado at Denver (U)
University of Delaware (U)
University of Findlay (U)
University of Great Falls (U)
University of Houston (U)
University of Houston–Victoria (U)
University of Idaho (U, G)
University of Illinois at Springfield (U)
University of Illinois at Urbana–Champaign (U, G)
University of Kansas (U, NC)
University of Maine (U)
University of Maine at Fort Kent (U)
University of Maryland University College (U)
University of Massachusetts Amherst (U, G, NC)
University of Massachusetts Lowell (U)
University of Memphis (U)
University of Minnesota, Crookston (U)

Central Arizona College (U)
Central Michigan University (U)
Cerro Coso Community College (U)
Charles Stewart Mott Community College (U)
Chattanooga State Technical Community College (U)
Citrus College (U)
City College of San Francisco (U)
Coastline Community College (U, NC)
College of DuPage (U)
College of West Virginia (U)
Colorado Electronic Community College (U)
Copiah-Lincoln Community College (U)
Cossatot Technical College (U)
County College of Morris (U)
Cumberland County College (U)
Dakota State University (U)
Dallas County Community College District (U)
Danville Community College (U)
Darton College (U)
De Anza College (U)
Del Mar College (U)
Des Moines Area Community College (U)
Duquesne University (U, G)
Eastern Kentucky University (U)
Eastern Michigan University (U)
Eastern Shore Community College (U)
El Camino College (U)
El Paso Community College (U)
Everett Community College (U)
Fayetteville Technical Community College (U)
Florida State University (U)
Foothill College (U)
Gannon University (U)
Garland County Community College (U)
Genesee Community College (U)
Goddard College (U, G)
Governors State University (U, G)
Graceland College (U)
Howard Community College (U)
Indiana University System (U)
Jamestown Community College (U)
John Wood Community College (U)
Judson College (U)
Kansas State University (U, NC)
Lorain County Community College (U)
Louisiana State University System (U)
Loyola University New Orleans (U)
Mercy College (U)
Metropolitan Community College (U)
Metropolitan State University (U)
Miami-Dade Community College (U)
Mid-America Bible College (U)
Midland College (U)
Minnesota West Community and Technical College (U)
Missouri Western State College (U)
Mountain Empire Community College (U)
Mount Wachusett Community College (U)
Nassau Community College (U)
New School University (U, NC)
North Carolina State University (U)
Northeast Texas Community College (U)
Northern Arizona University (U)
Northern Kentucky University (U)
North Iowa Area Community College (U)
Northwest Missouri State University (U)
Ohio University (U)
Ohio University–Southern Campus (U)
Old Dominion University (U)
Open Learning Agency (U)
Palomar College (U)
Parkland College (U)
Pennsylvania State University University Park Campus (U)
Peralta Community College District (U)
Portland Community College (U)
Prairie Bible College (U)

Providence College and Theological Seminary (U, NC)
Randolph Community College (U)
Red Rocks Community College (U)
Roane State Community College (U)
Sacramento City College (U)
Saddleback College (U)
Saint Charles County Community College (U, G)
Saint Joseph's College (U)
Salve Regina University (U, NC)
San Diego State University (U)
San Juan College (U)
Santa Monica College (U)
Scottsdale Community College (U)
Seattle Central Community College (U)
Seminole Community College (U)
Sierra College (U)
Sinclair Community College (U)
Southern Utah University (U)
Southwestern Assemblies of God University (U)
Southwestern Community College (U)
Southwest Missouri State University (U)
State University of New York College at Cortland (U)
State University of West Georgia (U)
Tarrant County College District (U)
Taylor University, World Wide Campus (U)
Texas Tech University (U)
Triton College (U)
Tyler Junior College (U)
Umpqua Community College (U)
University of Alaska Fairbanks (U)
University of British Columbia (U)
University of California, Berkeley (U)
University of California Extension (U)
University of Colorado at Denver (U)
University of Houston–Downtown (U)
University of Kansas (U, NC)
University of Maine (U)
University of Maine at Machias (U)
University of Minnesota, Twin Cities Campus (U)
University of Nebraska–Lincoln (G)
University of Nevada, Reno (U)
University of North Carolina at Chapel Hill (U)
University of North Dakota (U)
University of Northern Iowa (U)
University of North Texas (U)
University of Oklahoma (U)
University of Saskatchewan (U)
University of South Florida (U)
University of Texas at Austin (U)
University of Texas–Pan American (U)
University of Texas System (U)
University of Utah (U)
University of Washington (U)
University of Wisconsin Colleges (U)
University of Wisconsin Extension (U, NC)
University of Wisconsin–Stevens Point (U)
Virginia Western Community College (U)
Volunteer State Community College (U)
Walters State Community College (U)
Waubonsee Community College (U)
Weber State University (U)
Western Governors University (U)
Western Michigan University (U)
Western Nevada Community College (U)
Western Oklahoma State College (U)
Western Washington University (U)
West Virginia University (U)
West Virginia Wesleyan College (U)
Whatcom Community College (U)
Wichita State University (U)
William Rainey Harper College (U)

Nursing
Andrews University (G)
Arizona State University (U, G)
Athabasca University (U, G)

Athens Area Technical Institute (U)
Atlantic Cape Community College (U)
Austin Community College (U)
Ball State University (U, G)
Blue Ridge Community College (U)
Boise State University (U)
Bradley University (G)
Brenau University (U)
Broward Community College (U)
California State University, Chico (U)
California State University, Dominguez Hills (U, G)
California State University, Fresno (U)
California State University, Fullerton (U)
Cape Cod Community College (U)
Carlow College (G)
Central Community College–Grand Island Campus (U)
Central Methodist College (U)
Central Missouri State University (U)
Chippewa Valley Technical College (U)
Citrus College (U)
Clarion University of Pennsylvania (U, G)
Clarke College (U)
Clarkson College (U, G)
Clark State Community College (U)
Clemson University (U, G)
College of St. Scholastica (NC)
College of Southern Maryland (U)
College of West Virginia (U)
Columbia State Community College (U)
Concordia University Wisconsin (G)
Connecticut State University System (U, G)
Dalhousie University (U, G)
De Anza College (U)
Del Mar College (U)
Des Moines Area Community College (U)
Duquesne University (U, G)
East Carolina University (U, G)
Eastern Connecticut State University (U)
Eastern Kentucky University (G)
Eastern Michigan University (U)
Eastern Oklahoma State College (U)
Eastern Oregon University (U)
East Tennessee State University (U)
Edison State Community College (U)
Elizabethtown Community College (U)
Florida State University (U)
Floyd College (U)
Fort Hays State University (U, G)
Garland County Community College (U)
Georgia Southern University (U, G)
Gonzaga University (U, G)
Graceland College (U, G)
Grand Valley State University (U, G)
Grand View College (U)
Highland Community College (U)
Husson College (U)
Indiana State University (U, G)
Indiana University System (U, G)
Iowa Western Community College (U)
Ivy Tech State College–North Central (U)
Ivy Tech State College–Northwest (U)
James Sprunt Community College (U)
Kauai Community College (U)
Kent State University (U, G)
Lakehead University (U)
Lake Superior State University (U)
Lamar State College–Orange (U)
Lehigh Carbon Community College (U)
Loyola University New Orleans (U)
Madison Area Technical College (U)
Mansfield University of Pennsylvania (U)
Marshall University (U, G)
MCP Hahnemann University (U, G)
Memorial University of Newfoundland (U)
Metropolitan State University (G)
Miami-Dade Community College (U)

Nursing (continued)

Michigan State University (U, G)
Midwestern State University (U)
Millersville University of Pennsylvania (U)
Missouri Southern State College (U)
Missouri Western State College (U)
Montana State University–Bozeman (G)
Montgomery County Community College (U)
Morehead State University (U, G)
Motlow State Community College (U, NC)
National University (U, G)
Neumann College (G)
Northcentral Technical College (U)
North Dakota State College of Science (U)
Northeastern State University (U)
Northern Arizona University (U, G)
Northern Illinois University (G)
Northern Kentucky University (U, G)
Northern Michigan University (U, G)
North Georgia College & State University (U)
Northwestern Michigan College (U)
Northwest Technical College (U)
Ohio University–Southern Campus (U)
Old Dominion University (U, G)
Oregon Health Sciences University (U, G)
Parkland College (U)
Passaic County Community College (U)
Patrick Henry Community College (U)
Plattsburgh State University of New York (U)
Regents College (U, G)
Regis University (G)
Rutgers, The State University of New Jersey, New
  Brunswick (U, G, NC)
Sacred Heart University (U)
Saint Joseph's College (U, G)
Saint Louis University (U, G)
Salve Regina University (U, NC)
San Antonio College (U)
Sandhills Community College (U)
San Joaquin Delta College (U)
San Jose State University (U)
San Juan College (U)
Santa Barbara City College (U)
Seminole Community College (U)
Shawnee Community College (U)
Shawnee State University (U)
Southeast Community College, Beatrice Campus
  (U)
Southeastern Louisiana University (U)
Southern Connecticut State University (U, G)
Southern University and Agricultural and
  Mechanical College (U)
Southern Vermont College (U)
Southwest Missouri State University (U)
State University of New York at Buffalo (U, G,
  NC)
State University of New York Institute of
  Technology at Utica/Rome (U, G)
State University of West Georgia (U)
Temple University (U)
Texas A&M University–Commerce (NC)
Texas Christian University (U)
Texas State Technical College (U)
Troy State University (U, G)
University of Akron (G)
University of Alabama (U)
University of Alabama at Birmingham (G)
University of British Columbia (U)
University of Calgary (U)
University of Central Florida (U)
University of Cincinnati (U, G)
University of Delaware (U, G, NC)
University of Florida (U)
University of Guam (U)
University of Illinois at Chicago (U, G)
University of Illinois at Springfield (U)
University of Iowa (U, G)
University of Maine (U)

University of Maine at Fort Kent (U)
University of Manitoba (U)
University of Massachusetts Amherst (G)
University of Memphis (U)
University of Michigan–Flint (U, G)
University of Minnesota, Twin Cities Campus (U)
University of Missouri–Columbia (U, G)
University of Missouri–Kansas City (U, G)
University of Missouri–St. Louis (U, G)
University of Nebraska–Lincoln (U)
University of Nebraska Medical Center (U, G)
University of Nevada, Las Vegas (U)
University of New Brunswick (U, G)
University of New Mexico (U)
University of North Alabama (U)
University of North Carolina at Chapel Hill (NC)
University of North Carolina at Greensboro (U,
  G)
University of North Carolina at Pembroke (U)
University of North Carolina at Wilmington (U)
University of North Dakota (U, G)
University of Northern Colorado (U)
University of Phoenix (U, G)
University of Pittsburgh (G)
University of St. Francis (U)
University of Saskatchewan (U)
University of South Alabama (U, G)
University of South Carolina (U, G)
University of South Dakota (U)
University of Southern Colorado (U)
University of Southern Indiana (U, G)
University of South Florida (U, G)
University of Texas at Arlington (U)
University of Texas at Austin (U)
University of Texas at Tyler (U, G)
University of Vermont (U, G)
University of Wisconsin–Milwaukee (U)
University of Wyoming (U, G)
Valdosta State University (U)
Villanova University (U)
Virginia Commonwealth University (U, G)
Weber State University (U)
Western Connecticut State University (U)
Western Nebraska Community College (U)
Western Nevada Community College (U)
West Virginia Northern Community College (U)
West Virginia University (U, G)
West Virginia University Institute of Technology
  (U)
West Virginia Wesleyan College (U)
Wichita State University (U, G)
William Paterson University of New Jersey (U)
Wright State University (U, G)
York College of Pennsylvania (U)
Yuba College (U)

Occupational therapy
Dalhousie University (U)
Manchester Community College (U)
St. Ambrose University (G)
St. Louis Community College System (U)
Temple University (G)
Touro International University (U, G)
University of Central Arkansas (G)
University of Minnesota, Twin Cities Campus (U)
University of Missouri–Columbia (U)
University of St. Augustine for Health Sciences
  (G)
University of Wisconsin–Milwaukee (U)
Western Michigan University (U)

Oceanography
Anne Arundel Community College (U)
Atlantic Cape Community College (U)
Bellevue Community College (U)
Centralia College (U)
Coastline Community College (U, NC)
College of Southern Maryland (U)

Community College of Baltimore County (U)
Florida International University (U)
Fort Hays State University (U, G)
Fullerton College (U)
Indian River Community College (U)
Johnson County Community College (U)
Miami-Dade Community College (U)
North Carolina State University (U)
Open Learning Agency (U)
Oregon State University (U)
Portland Community College (U)
Riverside Community College (U)
Saddleback College (U)
St. Petersburg Junior College (U)
Seattle Central Community College (U)
Seminole Community College (U)
Umpqua Community College (U)
University of British Columbia (U)
University of North Carolina at Chapel Hill (U)
University of Oregon (U)
University of South Florida (U)
University of Washington (U)
West Valley College (U)

Organizational behavior studies
Brenau University (U, G)
Brigham Young University (U)
California Institute of Integral Studies (G, NC)
California National University for Advanced
  Studies (U, G)
Capella University (G)
Central Michigan University (U, G)
Cerro Coso Community College (U)
City University (G)
College of Aeronautics (U)
College of West Virginia (U)
Columbus State Community College (U)
Connecticut State University System (U, G)
Drake University (U)
Duke University (G)
Embry-Riddle Aeronautical University, Extended
  Campus (U)
Fielding Institute (G)
Gonzaga University (G)
Heriot-Watt University (G)
Indiana Institute of Technology (U)
Instituto Tecnológico y de Estudios Superiores de
  Monterrey, Campus Monterrey (NC)
Kansas State University (U, NC)
Louisiana State University System (U)
Medical College of Wisconsin (G)
Mercer University (NC)
Michigan State University (G)
Milwaukee School of Engineering (G, NC)
Montana State University–Billings (U)
newGraduate Schools (G)
New Hampshire College (U, G)
New York University (U)
Northern Virginia Community College (U)
Okaloosa-Walton Community College (U)
Oklahoma State University (U)
Open Learning Agency (U)
Owens Community College (U)
Park University (U)
Pennsylvania College of Technology (U)
Pennsylvania State University University Park
  Campus (U)
Regent University (G)
Regis University (U, G)
Rensselaer Polytechnic Institute (G, NC)
Roane State Community College (U)
Robert Morris College (U)
Royal Military College of Canada (U)
Rutgers, The State University of New Jersey, New
  Brunswick (U, G, NC)
Sacred Heart University (U)
Salve Regina University (U, G, NC)
Saybrook Graduate School (G)

902

Philosophy and religion (continued)

Pikes Peak Community College (U, NC)
Portland Community College (U)
Portland State University (U)
Prairie Bible College (U)
Prince George's Community College (U, NC)
Queen's University at Kingston (U)
Quincy College (U)
Redlands Community College (U)
Red Rocks Community College (U)
Regents College (U)
Regis University (U)
Rend Lake College (U)
Richard Stockton College of New Jersey (U)
Rio Salado College (U)
Roane State Community College (U)
Rochester Institute of Technology (U)
Rockland Community College (U)
Rogers State University (U)
Rutgers, The State University of New Jersey, New Brunswick (U)
Sacramento City College (U)
St. Cloud State University (U)
Saint Joseph's College (U)
Saint Leo University (U)
Salve Regina University (U, G, NC)
Sam Houston State University (U)
San Jose State University (U)
Santa Ana College (U)
Santa Monica College (U)
Shippensburg University of Pennsylvania (U, G)
Sinclair Community College (U)
Skidmore College (U)
Southeastern Illinois College (U)
Southern Arkansas University Tech (U)
Southern Christian University (U, G, NC)
Southwestern Assemblies of God University (U)
Southwestern Baptist Theological Seminary (U, G, NC)
Southwest Missouri State University (U, G)
Southwest Texas State University (U)
Southwest Virginia Community College (U)
Spoon River College (U)
Spring Arbor College (U)
Stanly Community College (U)
State University of New York College at Cortland (U)
State University of New York Empire State College (U)
State University of West Georgia (U)
Stephens College (U)
Strayer University (U)
Syracuse University (U)
Tacoma Community College (U)
Tarrant County College District (U)
Taylor University, World Wide Campus (U)
Temple Baptist Seminary (G, NC)
Tennessee Technological University (U)
Tennessee Temple University (U)
Texas Tech University (U)
Thomas Edison State College (U)
Triton College (U)
Troy State University Montgomery (U)
Université Laval (U)
University College of Cape Breton (U)
University College of the Fraser Valley (U)
University of Alaska Fairbanks (U)
University of Alaska Southeast, Sitka Campus (U)
University of British Columbia (U)
University of Calgary (U)
University of California, Berkeley (U)
University of California Extension (U)
University of California, Los Angeles (G)
University of Central Arkansas (U)
University of Central Florida (U)
University of Colorado at Denver (U)
University of Dayton (U, NC)
University of Delaware (U)

University of Great Falls (U)
University of Houston–Downtown (U)
University of Illinois at Springfield (U)
University of Kansas (U, NC)
University of Maine (U)
University of Manitoba (U)
University of Minnesota, Twin Cities Campus (U)
University of Missouri–Columbia (U)
University of Missouri-Columbia (U, G)
University of Missouri–Kansas City (U)
University of Missouri–St. Louis (U)
University of Nebraska–Lincoln (U)
University of North Carolina at Chapel Hill (U)
University of North Dakota (U)
University of Northern Iowa (U, G)
University of Pittsburgh (U)
University of Saskatchewan (U)
University of South Dakota (U, G)
University of Southern Mississippi (U)
University of the Incarnate Word (U)
University of Toledo (U, G)
University of Utah (U)
University of Washington (U)
University of Waterloo (U)
University System of Georgia (U)
Utah State University (U)
Vance-Granville Community College (U)
Victor Valley College (U)
Villanova University (U)
Virginia Commonwealth University (U)
Virginia Polytechnic Institute and State University (U)
Volunteer State Community College (U)
Washington State University (U)
Waubonsee Community College (U)
Wayne County Community College District (U)
Weber State University (U)
Western Illinois University (U)
Western Michigan University (U)
Western Oklahoma State College (U)
Western Wyoming Community College (U)
Westmoreland County Community College (U)
West Virginia Wesleyan College (U)
Wilfrid Laurier University (U)
William Rainey Harper College (U)
Wright State University (U)
Wytheville Community College (U)
Yuba College (U)

Photography

City College of San Francisco (U)
Fashion Institute of Technology (U)
Goddard College (U, G)
Highland Community College (U)
Houston Community College System (U)
Mohawk Valley Community College (U)
Ohlone College (U)
Richard Stockton College of New Jersey (U)
Sam Houston State University (U)
San Diego City College (U)
Sinclair Community College (U)
Thomas Edison State College (U)
West Valley College (U)

Physical sciences

Acadia University (U)
Anne Arundel Community College (U)
Arizona State University (G)
Athabasca University (U)
Ball State University (U)
Barclay College (U)
Barton County Community College (U)
Bethany College of the Assemblies of God (U)
Boise State University (U)
Brigham Young University (U)
Bucks County Community College (U)
City University (U)
Clayton College & State University (U)

Coastline Community College (U, NC)
College of DuPage (U)
College of West Virginia (U)
Connors State College (U)
Cossatot Technical College (U)
Dutchess Community College (U)
Eastern Illinois University (U)
Eastern Oregon University (U)
EduKan (U)
Erie Community College, North Campus (U)
Foothill College (U)
Franklin University (U)
Georgia State University (U)
Harrisburg Area Community College (U)
Honolulu Community College (U)
Indiana University System (U, NC)
Ivy Tech State College–Northwest (U)
Ivy Tech State College–Whitewater (U)
Keiser College (U)
LIFE Bible College (U)
Longview Community College (U)
Louisiana State University at Eunice (U)
Metropolitan Community College (U)
Mid-America Bible College (U)
Missouri Southern State College (U)
Montana State University—Great Falls College of Technology (U)
New York Institute of Technology (U)
North Carolina State University (U)
Northwestern College (U)
Oklahoma City Community College (U)
Oregon State University (U)
Pennsylvania State University University Park Campus (U)
Redlands Community College (U)
Richard Stockton College of New Jersey (U)
Rochester Institute of Technology (U)
Rogers State University (U)
Roosevelt University (U)
Skidmore College (U)
South Dakota State University (U)
Southern Arkansas University Tech (U)
South Florida Community College (U)
Southwestern Assemblies of God University (U)
Tarrant County College District (U)
Taylor University, World Wide Campus (U)
Union Institute (U)
Union University (U)
University of Alaska Fairbanks (U)
University of Alaska Southeast, Sitka Campus (U)
University of British Columbia (U)
University of Central Arkansas (U)
University of Denver (G)
University of Great Falls (U)
University of Maine at Machias (U)
University of Maryland University College (U)
University of Missouri–Columbia (U)
University of Nebraska–Lincoln (U)
University of North Dakota (U, G)
University of Waterloo (U)
Upper Iowa University (U, NC)
Victor Valley College (U)
Walla Walla Community College (U)
Waubonsee Community College (U)
Wayne County Community College District (U)
Western Wyoming Community College (U)
Westmoreland County Community College (U)
West Virginia Northern Community College (U)
West Virginia Wesleyan College (U)
Wilfrid Laurier University (U)
Yuba College (U)

Physical therapy

Athens Area Technical Institute (U)
College of Southern Maryland (U)
Metropolitan Community Colleges (U)
Neumann College (G)
Northern Arizona University (G)

Ohlone College (U)
St. Ambrose University (G)
St. Louis Community College System (U)
Temple University (G)
Touro International University (G)
University of Central Arkansas (G)
University of St. Augustine for Health Sciences
(G)
Walters State Community College (U)

Physics

Arizona State University (G)
Athabasca University (U)
Brigham Young University (U)
Bucks County Community College (U)
California College for Health Sciences (U)
California National University for Advanced
Studies (U)
Carleton University (U)
Central Michigan University (U)
Christopher Newport University (U)
City College of San Francisco (U)
City Colleges of Chicago, Harold Washington
College (U)
College of Aeronautics (U)
College of DuPage (U)
College of West Virginia (U)
Colorado Electronic Community College (U)
Colorado Mountain College District (U)
Embry-Riddle Aeronautical University, Extended
Campus (U)
Erie Community College, North Campus (U)
Finger Lakes Community College (U)
Fort Hays State University (U, G)
Frank Phillips College (U)
Front Range Community College (U)
Garland County Community College (U)
Georgia Institute of Technology (G, NC)
Georgia Southern University (U)
Grantham College of Engineering (U)
Hibbing Community College (U)
Holmes Community College (U)
Illinois Institute of Technology (U, G)
Indiana University of Pennsylvania (G)
Indiana University System (U)
Ivy Tech State College–Wabash Valley (U)
Jamestown Community College (U)
Kent State University (U)
Linn-Benton Community College (U)
Lorain County Community College (U)
Louisiana State University at Eunice (U)
Louisiana State University System (U)
Maysville Community College (U)
Metropolitan State University (U)
Michigan State University (U, G)
Midwestern State University (G)
Minnesota West Community and Technical
College (U)
Missouri Western State College (U)
Montana State University–Bozeman (G)
Moraine Valley Community College (U)
National Technological University (G, NC)
New Jersey Institute of Technology (U, G)
New School University (U, NC)
North Carolina State University (U)
Northern Virginia Community College (U)
Nyack College (U)
Ohio University (U)
Oklahoma City Community College (U)
Open Learning Agency (U)
Royal Military College of Canada (U)
St. Louis Community College System (U)
Salt Lake Community College (U)
Shippensburg University of Pennsylvania (U, G)
Sinclair Community College (U)
Skidmore College (U)
Southwest Missouri State University (U, G)
State University of New York at Farmingdale (U)

Syracuse University (U)
Temple University (U)
Texas A&M University–Commerce (U, G)
Thomas Edison State College (U)
Troy State University (U)
University of Alaska Fairbanks (U)
University of Arizona (U, G)
University of Calgary (U)
University of California, Berkeley (U)
University of California Extension (U)
University of Colorado at Denver (U)
University of Great Falls (U)
University of Minnesota, Twin Cities Campus (U)
University of Missouri–Columbia (U, G)
University of Missouri–Kansas City (U)
University of Nebraska–Lincoln (U)
University of North Carolina at Chapel Hill (U)
University of North Dakota (U)
University of Oregon (U)
University of Pennsylvania (U, NC)
University of South Carolina (U, G)
University of Tennessee (U)
University of Texas at Austin (U)
University of Toledo (U)
University of Utah (U)
University of Waterloo (U, NC)
University of West Florida (U)
University of Wisconsin–Stout (U)
Utah State University (U)
Volunteer State Community College (U)
Western Nevada Community College (U)
Westmoreland County Community College (U)
West Shore Community College (U)
Wichita State University (U)

Physiology

American Academy of Nutrition, College of
Nutrition (U)
Arizona State University (U)
Central Methodist College (U)
College of West Virginia (U)
Dalhousie University (U)
Floyd College (U)
Husson College (U)
Louisiana State University System (U)
Pennsylvania State University University Park
Campus (U)
Regents College (U)
St. Louis Community College System (U)
San Diego State University (U)
Stephens College (U)
Texas State Technical College–Harlingen (U)
University of Kansas (U, NC)
University of Texas System (G)
University of Utah (U)
University of Waterloo (U)
Wayne County Community College District (U)
West Virginia Wesleyan College (U)

Plant sciences

Arizona State University (U)
Clark State Community College (U)
Colorado State University (U)
Kansas State University (U, G)
Montana State University–Bozeman (U, G)
Pennsylvania State University University Park
Campus (NC)
Southwest Missouri State University (G)
Texas Tech University (U, NC)
University of Arizona (U)
University of British Columbia (U)
University of California, Riverside (U, G)
University of Florida (U)
University of Minnesota, Twin Cities Campus (U)
University of Missouri–Columbia (G)
University of Nebraska–Lincoln (U)
University of Waterloo (U)
University System of Georgia (U)

Political science

Allegany College of Maryland (U)
Andrews University (U)
Anne Arundel Community College (U)
Arizona State University (U)
Athabasca University (U)
Auburn University (U)
Austin Community College (U)
Beaufort County Community College (U)
Bellevue Community College (U)
Bergen Community College (U)
Blinn College (U)
Boise State University (U)
Brenau University (U)
Brevard Community College (U)
Brigham Young University (U)
Broward Community College (U)
Bucks County Community College (U)
Buena Vista University (U)
Burlington County College (U)
Butte College (U)
Cabrillo College (U)
California State University, Chico (U)
Capella University (G)
Carleton University (U)
Centralia College (U)
Central Michigan University (U)
Central Piedmont Community College (U)
Central Texas College (U)
Cerritos College (U)
Cerro Coso Community College (U)
Chadron State College (U)
Champlain College (U)
Charles Stewart Mott Community College (U)
Chattanooga State Technical Community College
(U)
Christopher Newport University (U)
Citrus College (U)
City Colleges of Chicago, Harold Washington
College (U)
City University (U)
Clarkson College (U)
Clayton College & State University (U)
Clemson University (G)
Coastline Community College (U, NC)
Cochise College (U)
College of DuPage (U)
College of Southern Maryland (U)
College of the Mainland (U)
College of the Southwest (U)
College of West Virginia (U)
Colorado Mountain College District (U)
Community College of Baltimore County (U)
Community College of Rhode Island (U)
Connors State College (U)
County College of Morris (U)
Cuyamaca College (U)
Dallas County Community College District (U)
Danville Area Community College (U)
Darton College (U)
De Anza College (U)
Delaware Technical & Community College,
Stanton/Wilmington Campus (U)
Del Mar College (U)
Delta College (U)
Des Moines Area Community College (U)
Drake University (U)
D'Youville College (U)
Eastern Kentucky University (U)
Eastern Oklahoma State College (U)
Eastern Wyoming College (U)
Edison Community College (U)
El Camino College (U)
El Paso Community College (U)
Evergreen Valley College (U)
Fayetteville Technical Community College (U)
Florida Community College at Jacksonville (U)
Floyd College (U)

Psychology (continued)

Laramie County Community College (U)
Lehigh Carbon Community College (U)
Lenoir Community College (U)
LeTourneau University (U)
Liberty University (U)
Longview Community College (U)
Lorain County Community College (U)
Louisiana State University and Agricultural and
    Mechanical College (U)
Louisiana State University at Eunice (U)
Louisiana State University System (U)
Lynn University (U)
Madison Area Technical College (U)
Madisonville Community College (U)
Manatee Community College (U)
Mansfield University of Pennsylvania (U, G)
Marshall University (U)
Martin Community College (U)
Marylhurst University (U)
Memorial University of Newfoundland (U)
Mercy College (U, G)
Metropolitan Community College (U)
Metropolitan Community Colleges (U)
Metropolitan State University (U)
Miami-Dade Community College (U)
Mid-America Bible College (U)
Midland College (U)
Mid-Plains Community College Area (U)
Minnesota West Community and Technical
    College (U)
Missouri Southern State College (U)
Mitchell Community College (U)
Modesto Junior College (U)
Montana State University—Great Falls College of
    Technology (U)
Montgomery College (U)
Montgomery County Community College (U)
Moraine Valley Community College (U)
Mountain Empire Community College (U)
Mount Allison University (U)
Mount Saint Vincent University (U)
Mt. San Antonio College (U)
Mt. San Jacinto College (U)
Mount Wachusett Community College (U)
Naropa University (U, G)
Nassau Community College (U)
Neumann College (U)
Newberry College (U)
New Hampshire College (U)
New Hampshire Community Technical College,
    Nashua/Claremont (U)
New York Institute of Technology (U)
New York University (U)
North Arkansas College (U)
North Carolina State University (U)
North Central Texas College (U)
North Central University (U, G)
Northeast State Technical Community College
    (U)
Northeast Texas Community College (U)
Northeast Wisconsin Technical College (U)
Northern Arizona University (U)
Northern Essex Community College (U)
Northern Kentucky University (U)
Northern Virginia Community College (U)
North Seattle Community College (U)
NorthWest Arkansas Community College (U)
Northwestern College (U)
Northwestern College (U)
Northwestern Michigan College (U)
Northwestern Technical Institute (U)
Norwich University (U, G)
Oakland Community College (U)
Oklahoma City Community College (U)
Oklahoma State University (U)
Oregon State University (U)
Ouachita Technical College (U)

Owens Community College (U)
Palomar College (U)
Parkland College (U)
Park University (U)
Peirce College (U)
Pennsylvania State University University Park
    Campus (U)
Peralta Community College District (U)
Piedmont Technical College (U)
Pierce College (U)
Portland Community College (U)
Prairie State College (U)
Presentation College (U)
Pueblo Community College (U)
Queen's University at Kingston (U)
Quincy College (U)
Rappahannock Community College (U)
Red Rocks Community College (U)
Regents College (U)
Regis University (U, G)
Rend Lake College (U)
Richard Stockton College of New Jersey (U)
Rio Salado College (U)
Roane State Community College (U)
Robert Morris College (U)
Robert Morris College (U)
Rochester College (U)
Rochester Institute of Technology (U)
Rogers State University (U)
Roger Williams University (U)
Royal Military College of Canada (U, G)
Ryerson Polytechnic University (U)
Sacramento City College (U)
Saddleback College (U)
Saint Charles County Community College (U, G)
St. Cloud State University (U)
St. Louis Community College System (U)
Salve Regina University (U, NC)
Sam Houston State University (U)
San Antonio College (U)
Sandhills Community College (U)
San Diego City College (U)
San Joaquin Delta College (U)
San Juan College (U)
Santa Ana College (U)
Santa Barbara City College (U)
Sauk Valley Community College (U)
Saybrook Graduate School (G)
Seattle Central Community College (U)
Seminole Community College (U)
Shippensburg University of Pennsylvania (U, G)
Sinclair Community College (U)
Skidmore College (U)
South Dakota State University (U)
Southeast Community College, Lincoln Campus
    (U)
Southeastern Community College, North Campus
    (U)
Southeastern Illinois College (U)
Southeastern Louisiana University (U)
Southern Arkansas University Tech (U)
Southern California University for Professional
    Studies (U, G)
Southwestern Assemblies of God University (U)
Southwestern Community College (U)
Southwestern Michigan College (U)
Southwest Missouri State University (U, G)
Southwest Texas State University (U)
Spoon River College (U)
Spring Arbor College (U)
Springfield Technical Community College (U)
Stanly Community College (U)
State University of New York at Buffalo (U)
State University of New York at New Paltz (U)
State University of New York College at Cortland
    (U)
State University of New York College of
    Technology at Delhi (U)

State University of West Georgia (U, G)
Stephens College (U)
Strayer University (U)
Surry Community College (U)
Tacoma Community College (U)
Taylor University, World Wide Campus (U)
Technical College of the Lowcountry (U)
Temple University (U)
Tennessee Temple University (U)
Terra State Community College (U)
Texas Christian University (U)
Texas State Technical College (U)
Tidewater Community College (U)
Tompkins Cortland Community College (U)
Triton College (U)
Troy State University Dothan (U)
Troy State University Montgomery (U)
Tyler Junior College (U)
Union Institute (U, G)
Union University (U)
Université Laval (U)
University of Alaska Fairbanks (U)
University of Alaska Southeast, Sitka Campus (U)
University of Arizona (U)
University of British Columbia (U)
University of California, Berkeley (U)
University of California Extension (U)
University of California, Los Angeles (G)
University of Central Arkansas (U)
University of Central Florida (U, G)
University of Colorado at Denver (U)
University of Great Falls (U)
University of Houston (U)
University of Idaho (U)
University of Iowa (U, G)
University of Maine (U)
University of Maine at Machias (U)
University of Manitoba (U)
University of Maryland University College (U)
University of Massachusetts Amherst (U)
University of Massachusetts Lowell (U)
University of Minnesota, Crookston (U)
University of Minnesota, Twin Cities Campus (U)
University of Missouri–Columbia (U, G)
University of Nebraska–Lincoln (U)
University of Nevada, Reno (U)
University of New Brunswick (U)
University of North Carolina at Chapel Hill (U)
University of North Dakota (U)
University of Northern Iowa (U)
University of North Texas (U, G)
University of Oklahoma (U)
University of Pennsylvania (U, NC)
University of Pittsburgh (U)
University of Saskatchewan (U)
University of Southern Indiana (U)
University of Southern Maine (U)
University of Tennessee (U)
University of Texas of the Permian Basin (U)
University of Texas System (U)
University of Toledo (U, G)
University of Utah (U)
University of Washington (U)
University of Waterloo (U)
University of Wisconsin–Stout (U, G)
University of Wyoming (U)
University System of Georgia (U)
Upper Iowa University (U, NC)
Vance-Granville Community College (U)
Victor Valley College (U)
Villanova University (U)
Vincennes University (U)
Virginia Western Community College (U)
Wake Technical Community College (U)
Walden University (G)
Walla Walla Community College (U)
Washburn University of Topeka (U)
Washington State University (U)

Park University (U)
Pensacola Junior College (U)
Pikes Peak Community College (U, NC)
Prince George's Community College (U, NC)
Quincy College (U)
Red Rocks Community College (U)
Richland Community College (U)
Riverland Community College (U)
Riverside Community College (U)
Roosevelt University (U)
Saint Joseph's College (U)
St. Petersburg Junior College (U)
Salve Regina University (U, G, NC)
Saybrook Graduate School (G)
Sierra College (U)
Snow College (U)
Southeast Community College, Beatrice Campus (U)
Southwestern Assemblies of God University (U)
Southwestern Michigan College (U)
State University of New York Empire State College (U)
Stephens College (U)
Sussex County Community College (U)
Syracuse University (U)
Tacoma Community College (U)
Tarrant County College District (U)
Texas Tech University (U)
Thomas Edison State College (U)
Thomas Nelson Community College (U)
Tompkins Cortland Community College (U)
Triton College (U)
Tulsa Community College (U)
United States Sports Academy (G, NC)
University College of Cape Breton (U)
University of Alaska Southeast, Sitka Campus (U)
University of Arizona (U)
University of California, Berkeley (U)
University of California Extension (U)
University of Colorado at Denver (U)
University of Great Falls (U)
University of Houston (U)
University of Illinois at Urbana–Champaign (U)
University of Kansas (U, NC)
University of Maine (U)
University of Maine at Fort Kent (U)
University of Manitoba (U)
University of Missouri–Columbia (U)
University of Missouri–Kansas City (U)
University of Nebraska–Lincoln (U)
University of Northern Iowa (U)
University of Oklahoma (U, G, NC)
University of Southern Colorado (U)
University of Tennessee (U)
University of Texas at Austin (U)
University of Utah (U)
University of Washington (U)
University of Waterloo (U)
University of Wyoming (U)
University System of Georgia (U)
Utah State University (U, G)
Volunteer State Community College (U)
Wake Technical Community College (U)
Walden University (G)
Walters State Community College (U)
Washington State University (U)
Waubonsee Community College (U)
Weber State University (U)
Western Oregon University (U)
West Virginia University (U)
West Virginia Wesleyan College (U)
Whatcom Community College (U)
Yuba College (U)

Social sciences
Acadia University (U)
Arizona Western College (G)
Athabasca University (U)

Auburn University (U)
Barton County Community College (U)
Bellevue University (U)
Bethany College of the Assemblies of God (U)
Boise State University (U)
Brigham Young University (U)
Bristol Community College (U)
Buena Vista University (U)
Burlington College (U)
Butte College (U)
Caldwell College (U)
Calhoun Community College (U)
California State University, Chico (U)
California State University, Fresno (U)
Carleton University (U)
Central Piedmont Community College (U)
City University (U)
Coastline Community College (U, NC)
College for Lifelong Learning, University System of New Hampshire (U)
College of DuPage (U)
College of West Virginia (U)
Connecticut State University System (U, G)
Corning Community College (U)
Danville Area Community College (U)
De Anza College (U)
Eastern Oregon University (U)
Edison State Community College (U)
EduKan (U)
Erie Community College, North Campus (U)
Florida State University (U)
Foothill College (U)
Fullerton College (U)
Goddard College (U, G)
Grayson County College (U)
Great Basin College (U)
Green River Community College (U)
Harrisburg Area Community College (U)
Hawkeye Community College (U)
Hibbing Community College (U)
Hobe Sound Bible College (U)
Houston Community College System (U)
Howard Community College (U)
Indiana University System (U)
Indian River Community College (U)
John Wood Community College (U)
Kansas City Kansas Community College (U)
Keiser College (U)
Kellogg Community College (U)
Lafayette College (U)
Lakeshore Technical College (U)
Madonna University (U)
Marian College of Fond du Lac (U)
Memorial University of Newfoundland (U)
Metropolitan State University (U)
Miami-Dade Community College (U)
Michigan State University (U)
Mid-Plains Community College Area (U)
Midwestern State University (U)
Missouri Southern State College (U)
Montgomery County Community College (U)
Mount Saint Vincent University (U)
New School University (U, NC)
New York University (U)
Northampton County Area Community College (U)
North Carolina State University (U)
Northeast State Technical Community College (U)
Northern Arizona University (U, G)
Northern Essex Community College (U)
Northern Michigan University (U)
Norwich University (U, G)
Oakland Community College (U)
Oklahoma City Community College (U)
Quincy College (U)
Raritan Valley Community College (U)
Red Rocks Community College (U)

Regis University (U, G)
Richard Stockton College of New Jersey (U)
Roane State Community College (U)
Rochester Institute of Technology (U)
Rogers State University (U)
Roosevelt University (U)
St. Cloud State University (U)
St. Louis Community College System (U)
San Juan College (U)
Sinclair Community College (U)
Skidmore College (U)
South Dakota State University (U, G)
Southwestern Assemblies of God University (U)
Southwestern Michigan College (U)
Springfield Technical Community College (U)
State University of New York Empire State College (U)
State University of West Georgia (U)
Stephens College (U)
Syracuse University (G)
Taylor University, World Wide Campus (U)
Tennessee Temple University (U)
Tompkins Cortland Community College (U)
Troy State University Montgomery (U)
Ulster County Community College (U)
Umpqua Community College (U)
Union Institute (U)
United States Open University (U)
United States Sports Academy (G, NC)
University of Alaska Fairbanks (U)
University of Alaska Southeast, Sitka Campus (U)
University of British Columbia (U)
University of California, Los Angeles (G)
University of Central Arkansas (U)
University of Central Florida (U)
University of Colorado at Denver (U, G)
University of Findlay (U)
University of Great Falls (U)
University of Maine at Machias (U)
University of Maryland University College (U)
University of Memphis (U)
University of Minnesota, Twin Cities Campus (NC)
University of Nebraska–Lincoln (U)
University of North Dakota (U)
University of Northern Iowa (U)
University of Pittsburgh (U)
University of Waterloo (U)
University of Wisconsin Extension (U)
University of Wyoming (U)
Upper Iowa University (U, NC)
Wake Technical Community College (U)
Walden University (U)
Walla Walla Community College (U)
Washburn University of Topeka (U)
Washington State University (U)
Western Connecticut State University (U)
Western Oregon University (U, G)
Western Wyoming Community College (U)
West Virginia Northern Community College (U)
Whatcom Community College (U)
Wilfrid Laurier University (U)
Wilmington College (U)
Wytheville Community College (U)

Social work
Alaska Pacific University (U)
Austin Community College (U)
California State University, Long Beach (G)
Capella University (G)
Carleton University (U)
Chadron State College (U)
Chattanooga State Technical Community College (U)
City Colleges of Chicago, Harold Washington College (U)
Cleveland State University (U, G)
College of West Virginia (U)

Individual Courses Index

Social work (continued)

Dalhousie University (U, G)
East Carolina University (G)
Eastern Connecticut State University (G)
Florida State University (G)
Fort Hays State University (U, G)
Frostburg State University (U, G)
Gallaudet University (G)
Governors State University (U, G)
Grand Valley State University (U, G)
Iowa Western Community College (U)
Lawson State Community College (U)
Loma Linda University (U)
Long Island University, Brooklyn Campus (NC)
Longview Community College (U)
Madonna University (U)
Marshall University (U, G)
Memorial University of Newfoundland (U)
Michigan State University (G)
Mohawk Valley Community College (U)
New York Institute of Technology (U)
Northern Arizona University (U)
Northern Kentucky University (U, G)
Northwestern Michigan College (U)
Ohio State University–Mansfield Campus (U, G)
Redlands Community College (U)
Skidmore College (U)
Southeastern Community College, North Campus (U)
Southern Illinois University Carbondale (G)
Southwest Missouri State University (U, G)
State University of New York at Buffalo (G)
Taylor University, World Wide Campus (U)
Texas A&M University–Commerce (U)
University College of the Fraser Valley (U)
University of Akron (G)
University of Alaska Fairbanks (U)
University of Arkansas (U)
University of Calgary (G)
University of Great Falls (U)
University of Houston (G)
University of Iowa (U, G)
University of Kansas (U, NC)
University of Louisville (G)
University of Manitoba (U)
University of Michigan–Flint (U, G)
University of Minnesota, Twin Cities Campus (U)
University of Missouri–Kansas City (U)
University of North Dakota (U, G)
University of Northern Iowa (U, G)
University of Pennsylvania (NC)
University of St. Thomas (G)
University of South Carolina (U, G)
University of Southern Colorado (U)
University of South Florida (G)
University of Vermont (U, G)
University of Washington (G)
University of Waterloo (U)
University of Wisconsin–Milwaukee (U, G)
Utah State University (U)
Vincennes University (U)
Virginia Commonwealth University (G)
Volunteer State Community College (U)
Walden University (G)
Walters State Community College (U)
Waubonsee Community College (U)
Weber State University (U)
Western Michigan University (U)
West Virginia University (G)
Wilfrid Laurier University (U)

Sociology

Adams State College (U)
Allegany College of Maryland (U)
Andrews University (U)
Anne Arundel Community College (U)
Aquinas College (U)
Athabasca University (U)

Atlantic Cape Community College (U)
Austin Community College (U)
Barclay College (U)
Beaufort County Community College (U)
Bellevue Community College (U)
Bergen Community College (U)
Berkshire Community College (U)
Blinn College (U)
Boise State University (U)
Bossier Parish Community College (U)
Brevard Community College (U)
Bridgewater State College (U)
Brigham Young University (U)
Bristol Community College (U)
Brookdale Community College (U)
Broward Community College (U)
Bucks County Community College (U)
Buena Vista University (U)
Burlington County College (U)
Calhoun Community College (U)
California Institute of Integral Studies (G, NC)
California State University, Chico (U)
California State University, San Marcos (U)
Cape Cod Community College (U)
Capella University (G)
Carleton University (U)
Catawba Valley Community College (U)
Central Arizona College (U)
Central Community College–Grand Island Campus (U)
Centralia College (U)
Central Michigan University (U)
Central Piedmont Community College (U)
Central Texas College (U)
Central Virginia Community College (U)
Cerritos College (U)
Cerro Coso Community College (U)
Chadron State College (U)
Champlain College (U)
Charles Stewart Mott Community College (U)
Charter Oak State College (U)
Chattanooga State Technical Community College (U)
Chippewa Valley Technical College (U)
Christopher Newport University (U)
Citrus College (U)
City Colleges of Chicago, Harold Washington College (U)
City University (U)
Clackamas Community College (U)
Clarion University of Pennsylvania (U)
Clarkson College (U)
Clatsop Community College (U)
Coastline Community College (U, NC)
Cochise College (U)
College of Albemarle (U)
College of DuPage (U)
College of St. Scholastica (U)
College of Southern Maryland (U)
College of the Southwest (U)
College of West Virginia (U)
Colorado Electronic Community College (U)
Colorado Mountain College District (U)
Colorado State University (U)
Columbia Basin College (U)
Community College of Baltimore County (U)
Community College of Rhode Island (U)
Community Hospital of Roanoke Valley–College of Health Sciences (U)
Concordia University at St. Paul (U)
Connecticut State University System (U, G)
Connors State College (U)
Cossatot Technical College (U)
County College of Morris (U)
Cumberland County College (U)
Cuyahoga Community College, Metropolitan Campus (U)
Cuyamaca College (U)

Dallas Baptist University (U)
Dallas County Community College District (U)
Dawson Community College (U)
De Anza College (U)
Delaware Technical & Community College, Jack F. Owens Campus (U)
Delaware Technical & Community College, Stanton/Wilmington Campus (U)
Del Mar College (U)
Delta College (U)
Des Moines Area Community College (U)
Eastern Kentucky University (U)
Eastern Michigan University (U)
Eastern Wyoming College (U)
Edison Community College (U)
Edison State Community College (U)
El Camino College (U)
Elizabethtown Community College (U)
El Paso Community College (U)
Everett Community College (U)
Evergreen Valley College (U)
Fayetteville Technical Community College (U)
Finger Lakes Community College (U)
Fitchburg State College (U)
Florence-Darlington Technical College (U)
Florida Community College at Jacksonville (U)
Florida Keys Community College (U)
Floyd College (U)
Foothill College (U)
Forsyth Technical Community College (U)
Fort Hays State University (U, G)
Front Range Community College (U)
Frostburg State University (U)
Garland County Community College (U)
Genesee Community College (U)
Georgia Perimeter College (U)
Georgia Southern University (U, G)
Glendale Community College (U)
Gogebic Community College (U)
Governors State University (U, G)
Graceland College (U)
Grand Valley State University (U, G)
Grayson County College (U)
Great Basin College (U)
Greenville Technical College (U)
Griggs University (U)
Hibbing Community College (U)
Hillsborough Community College (U)
Hinds Community College (U)
Holmes Community College (U)
Hopkinsville Community College (U)
Houston Community College System (U)
Hutchinson Community College and Area Vocational School (U)
Indiana Institute of Technology (U)
Indiana State University (U)
Indiana University System (U)
Indian River Community College (U)
Iowa Wesleyan College (U)
Iowa Western Community College (U)
Ivy Tech State College–North Central (U)
Ivy Tech State College–Northwest (U)
Ivy Tech State College–Wabash Valley (U)
Jacksonville State University (U)
Jamestown Community College (U)
Jefferson Community College (U)
Johnson County Community College (U)
John Wood Community College (U)
Judson College (U)
Kansas City Kansas Community College (U)
Kansas State University (U, G, NC)
Kellogg Community College (U)
Kent State University (U)
King's College (U)
Lackawanna Junior College (U)
Lafayette College (U)
Lakehead University (U)
Lake Land College (U)

Lakeland Community College (U)
Lakeshore Technical College (U)
Lamar State College–Port Arthur (U)
Lamar University (U)
Lansing Community College (U)
Lawson State Community College (U)
Lehigh Carbon Community College (U)
Longview Community College (U)
Lorain County Community College (U)
Louisiana State University and Agricultural and Mechanical College (U)
Louisiana State University at Alexandria (U)
Louisiana State University at Eunice (U)
Louisiana State University System (U)
Loyola University New Orleans (U)
Luzerne County Community College (U)
Madison Area Technical College (U)
Madisonville Community College (U)
Manatee Community College (U)
Marshall University (U, G)
Martin Community College (U)
Marywood University (U)
Maysville Community College (U)
McDowell Technical Community College (U)
Memorial University of Newfoundland (U)
Mercy College (U)
Metropolitan Community College (U)
Metropolitan Community Colleges (U)
Metropolitan State University (U)
Mid-America Bible College (U)
Midland College (U)
Mid-Plains Community College Area (U)
Midwestern State University (U)
Minnesota West Community and Technical College (U)
Minot State University (U)
Missouri Southern State College (U)
Missouri Western State College (U)
Mitchell Community College (U)
Modesto Junior College (U)
Mohawk Valley Community College (U)
Montana State University—Great Falls College of Technology (U)
Montgomery College (U)
Montgomery County Community College (U)
Moraine Valley Community College (U)
Mountain Empire Community College (U)
Mount Saint Vincent University (U)
Mt. San Antonio College (U)
Mt. San Jacinto College (U)
Mount Vernon Nazarene College (U)
Mount Wachusett Community College (U)
Nassau Community College (U)
Neumann College (U)
New Hampshire College (U)
New Hampshire Community Technical College, Nashua/Claremont (U)
New School University (U, NC)
New York Institute of Technology (U)
New York University (U)
North Carolina State University (U)
Northcentral Technical College (U)
North Central Texas College (U)
North Dakota State College of Science (U)
Northeast Wisconsin Technical College (U)
Northern Arizona University (U)
Northern Kentucky University (U)
Northern Michigan University (U)
Northern State University (U)
Northern Virginia Community College (U)
North Harris College (U)
North Iowa Area Community College (U)
North Seattle Community College (U)
NorthWest Arkansas Community College (U)
Northwestern College (U)
Northwestern Michigan College (U)
Ohio University (U)
Okaloosa-Walton Community College (U)

Oklahoma City Community College (U)
Oklahoma State University (U)
Old Dominion University (U)
Open Learning Agency (U)
Oregon State University (U)
Ouachita Technical College (U)
Owens Community College (U)
Palomar College (U)
Parkland College (U)
Patrick Henry Community College (U)
Peirce College (U)
Pensacola Junior College (U)
Peralta Community College District (U)
Piedmont College (U)
Piedmont Technical College (U)
Pikes Peak Community College (U, NC)
Pitt Community College (U)
Portland Community College (U)
Portland State University (U)
Prairie State College (U)
Presentation College (U)
Prince George's Community College (U, NC)
Pueblo Community College (U)
Queen's University at Kingston (U)
Quincy College (U)
Randolph Community College (U)
Rappahannock Community College (U)
Redlands Community College (U)
Red Rocks Community College (U)
Regents College (U)
Regis University (U)
Richard Stockton College of New Jersey (U)
Richland Community College (U)
Rio Salado College (U)
Riverland Community College (U)
Riverside Community College (U)
Roane State Community College (U)
Rochester Institute of Technology (U)
Rockland Community College (U)
Roger Williams University (U)
Rutgers, The State University of New Jersey, New Brunswick (U)
Ryerson Polytechnic University (U)
Sacramento City College (U)
Saddleback College (U)
Saint Charles County Community College (U, G)
St. Cloud State University (U)
St. Johns River Community College (U)
Saint Joseph's College (U)
St. Louis Community College System (U)
St. Petersburg Junior College (U)
Saint Peter's College (U)
Salt Lake Community College (U)
Sam Houston State University (U)
San Antonio College (U)
Sandhills Community College (U)
San Jacinto College District (U)
San Joaquin Delta College (U)
San Jose State University (U)
Santa Ana College (U)
Santa Monica College (U)
Sauk Valley Community College (U)
Seattle Central Community College (U)
Seminole Community College (U)
Shawnee Community College (U)
Sierra College (U)
Sinclair Community College (U)
Skidmore College (U)
Snow College (U)
Southeast Community College, Lincoln Campus (U)
Southeastern Louisiana University (U)
South Florida Community College (U)
Southwestern Assemblies of God University (U)
Southwestern Community College (U)
Southwestern Michigan College (U)
Southwest Missouri State University (U)
Southwest Texas State University (U)

Southwest Virginia Community College (U)
Spoon River College (U)
Spring Arbor College (U)
Stanly Community College (U)
State University of New York at New Paltz (U)
State University of New York College at Cortland (U)
State University of New York College at Oneonta (U, NC)
State University of New York Empire State College (U)
State University of West Georgia (U)
Strayer University (U)
Suffolk County Community College (U)
Surry Community College (U)
Syracuse University (U)
Tacoma Community College (U)
Tarrant County College District (U)
Tennessee Technological University (U)
Tennessee Temple University (U)
Terra State Community College (U)
Texas A&M University–Commerce (U)
Texas State Technical College–Harlingen (U)
Texas Tech University (U)
Thomas Edison State College (U)
Thomas Nelson Community College (U)
Tidewater Community College (U)
Tompkins Cortland Community College (U)
Triton College (U)
Troy State University Dothan (U)
Troy State University Montgomery (U)
Tulsa Community College (U)
Tyler Junior College (U)
Umpqua Community College (U)
Union University (U)
Université Laval (U)
University of Akron (U)
University of Alaska Fairbanks (U)
University of Alaska Southeast, Sitka Campus (U)
University of Arizona (U)
University of Arkansas (U)
University of Calgary (U)
University of California, Berkeley (U)
University of California Extension (U)
University of Central Florida (U)
University of Cincinnati (U)
University of Cincinnati Raymond Walters College (U)
University of Colorado at Denver (U, G)
University of Connecticut (U)
University of Delaware (U)
University of Great Falls (U)
University of Hawaii at Manoa (U)
University of Houston (U)
University of Houston–Downtown (U)
University of Illinois at Urbana–Champaign (U)
University of Iowa (U, G)
University of Kansas (U, NC)
University of Maine (U)
University of Maine at Fort Kent (U)
University of Manitoba (U)
University of Maryland University College (U)
University of Massachusetts Lowell (U)
University of Missouri–Columbia (U, G)
University of Missouri-Columbia (U)
University of Missouri–Kansas City (U, G)
University of Nebraska–Lincoln (U)
University of Nevada, Reno (U)
University of New Brunswick (U)
University of North Alabama (U)
University of North Carolina at Chapel Hill (U)
University of North Carolina at Wilmington (U)
University of Northern Iowa (U, G)
University of Oklahoma (U)
University of Pennsylvania (U, NC)
University of St. Thomas (U)
University of South Dakota (U, G)
University of Southern Colorado (U)

Individual Courses Index

Student counseling
Buena Vista University (G)
Capella University (G)
City University (G)
Concordia University Wisconsin (G)
Eastern Kentucky University (G)
Indiana State University (G)
Liberty University (G)
Long Island University, Brooklyn Campus (NC)
Northern Arizona University (G)
Palomar College (U)
Riverside Community College (U)
Shippensburg University of Pennsylvania (G)
State University of West Georgia (U, G)
Stephens College (U)
University of California, Los Angeles (G)
University of Central Oklahoma (U, G)
University of Montana–Missoula (G)
University of Sarasota (G)
Virginia Polytechnic Institute and State University (G)

Substance abuse counseling
Bethany College of the Assemblies of God (U)
Central Michigan University (U, G)
Central Texas College (U)
Kansas City Kansas Community College (U)
Lake Land College (U)
Madonna University (U)
Pennsylvania State University University Park Campus (U, G)
Pitt Community College (U)
Prince George's Community College (NC)
St. Louis Community College System (U)
Southwest Missouri State University (U, NC)
Tompkins Cortland Community College (U)
Trinity College of Vermont (G)
University of Cincinnati (U)
University of Findlay (U, G)
University of Southern Colorado (U)
Washburn University of Topeka (U)
Western Governors University (U)

Surveying
Michigan Technological University (U)
University of Maine (U)
University of Wyoming (U)

Teacher education
Adams State College (G)
Alaska Pacific University (U)
Anne Arundel Community College (U)
Arizona State University (G)
Azusa Pacific University (G)
Ball State University (G)
Bergen Community College (U)
Black Hills State University (U, G)
Boise State University (U, G)
Bucks County Community College (U)
Buena Vista University (U)
California College for Health Sciences (U)
California State University, Dominguez Hills (U, G)
California State University, Fresno (U, G)
California State University, Los Angeles (U)
California State University, San Marcos (U, G)
Catawba Valley Community College (U)
Cedarville University (U)
Centralia College (U)
Central Methodist College (U, G)
Central Missouri State University (U, G, NC)
Central Washington University (U)
Cerritos College (U)
Cerro Coso Community College (U)
Chadron State College (U, G)
Chattanooga State Technical Community College (U)
Chestnut Hill College (G)
Cochise College (U)

College of DuPage (U)
College of Southern Maryland (U)
College of the Southwest (U)
Colorado Mountain College District (U)
Colorado State University (G)
Columbus State University (U, G)
Concordia College (U)
Connecticut State University System (U, G)
CTS University, Inc. (U, NC)
Cumberland University (G)
Dakota State University (U, G)
David Lipscomb University (U)
Dawson Community College (U)
Delta College (U)
Des Moines Area Community College (U)
Drake University (G)
Dutchess Community College (U)
D'Youville College (U)
East Carolina University (G)
Eastern Illinois University (G)
Eastern Kentucky University (U)
Eastern Michigan University (G)
Eastern Oregon University (U)
East Tennessee State University (G)
Fairleigh Dickinson University, The New College of General and Continuing Studies (G)
Fitchburg State College (G)
Florence-Darlington Technical College (U)
Florida State University (G)
Fort Hays State University (U, G)
Front Range Community College (U)
Frostburg State University (G)
Gallaudet University (G)
Garland County Community College (U)
Georgia Southern University (G)
Goddard College (U, G)
Governors State University (U)
Grand Canyon University (G)
Grand Valley State University (U, G)
Great Basin College (U)
Highland Community College (U)
Indiana University System (U)
Indiana Wesleyan University (G)
Indian River Community College (U)
Instituto Tecnológico y de Estudios Superiores de Monterrey, Campus Monterrey (NC)
Jacksonville State University (G)
John Wood Community College (U)
Kellogg Community College (U)
Lakehead University (U)
Lamar University (U, G)
Laramie County Community College (U)
Lehigh Carbon Community College (U)
Liberty University (G)
Lorain County Community College (U)
Los Angeles Harbor College (U)
Louisiana State University and Agricultural and Mechanical College (G)
Louisiana State University System (U)
Lynn University (U, G)
Manatee Community College (U)
Marshall University (U, G)
Marygrove College (G)
McGill University (U)
Memorial University of Newfoundland (U)
Michigan State University (NC)
Middle Tennessee State University (U, G)
Midwestern State University (G)
Millersville University of Pennsylvania (G)
Minot State University (U, G)
Mississippi State University (G)
Mohawk Valley Community College (U)
Montana State University–Billings (U, G)
Montana State University–Bozeman (G)
Morehead State University (U, G)
Mount Saint Vincent University (U, G)
National University (G)

New Mexico Institute of Mining and Technology (G)
New School University (U, G, NC)
New York Institute of Technology (U, G)
North Carolina State University (G)
Northeast State Technical Community College (U)
Northern Arizona University (U, G)
Northern Kentucky University (U, G)
Northern Michigan University (G)
North Georgia College & State University (U)
Northwest Christian College (U)
Nyack College (U)
Ohio State University–Mansfield Campus (U, G)
Ohio University–Southern Campus (U)
Oklahoma State University (U)
Old Dominion University (G)
Oregon State University (U, G)
Pennsylvania State University University Park Campus (G)
Prairie Bible College (U)
Prince George's Community College (NC)
Red Rocks Community College (U)
Regents College (U)
Regis University (U, G)
Richard Stockton College of New Jersey (NC)
Rio Salado College (U)
Riverside Community College (U)
Rutgers, The State University of New Jersey, New Brunswick (U, G, NC)
Sacred Heart University (G, NC)
St. Ambrose University (U)
St. Petersburg Junior College (U)
Saint Peter's College (G)
San Diego State University (U, G)
San Jose State University (U, G)
Seminole Community College (U)
Seton Hall University (G)
Shasta Bible College (U, NC)
Shenandoah University (G)
Shippensburg University of Pennsylvania (G)
Southeast Community College, Beatrice Campus (U)
Southern Oregon University (G)
Southern Utah University (U, G)
Southwestern Assemblies of God University (U)
Southwest Missouri State University (U, G)
State University of New York at Buffalo (G, NC)
State University of New York at New Paltz (G)
State University of New York at Oswego (U)
State University of New York at Stony Brook (G)
State University of West Georgia (U, G)
Stephens College (U)
Temple Baptist Seminary (G, NC)
Tennessee Technological University (U, G)
Texas A&M University–Commerce (U, G, NC)
Texas A&M University–Texarkana (U)
Texas Tech University (U, NC)
University of Alaska Fairbanks (U, G)
University of Alaska Southeast (U)
University of Alaska Southeast, Sitka Campus (U)
University of Calgary (U, G)
University of California, Berkeley (U)
University of California Extension (U)
University of Central Oklahoma (U)
University of Colorado at Colorado Springs (G)
University of Delaware (U, G)
University of Findlay (G, NC)
University of Florida (U)
University of Great Falls (U)
University of Guam (U)
University of Houston–Clear Lake (G)
University of Houston–Downtown (U)
University of Idaho (U, G)
University of Illinois at Springfield (U, G)
University of Kansas (U, G, NC)
University of Maine (U, G)
University of Minnesota, Morris (U)

University of Missouri–Columbia (G)
University of Missouri–St. Louis (U)
University of Montana–Missoula (G)
University of Nebraska–Lincoln (U, G)
University of Nevada, Las Vegas (U, G)
University of Nevada, Reno (U, G)
University of New Brunswick (U, G)
University of New England (G)
University of New Hampshire (NC)
University of New Orleans (U, G)
University of North Carolina at Wilmington (U)
University of North Dakota (U, G)
University of Northern Colorado (G)
University of Northern Iowa (U, G)
University of North Texas (U)
University of Pittsburgh (G)
University of Saskatchewan (U)
University of South Alabama (G)
University of South Carolina (G)
University of South Dakota (G)
University of Southern Colorado (U, G)
University of Southern Indiana (G)
University of South Florida (U, G)
University of Tennessee (U)
University of Tennessee at Martin (U, G)
University of Texas at El Paso (U, G)
University of Texas at Tyler (U, G)
University of Texas System (G)
University of the Pacific (G)
University of Utah (U)
University of Vermont (U)
University of Virginia (G, NC)
University of Washington (U)
University of West Florida (U, G)
University of Wisconsin–La Crosse (U, G)
University of Wisconsin–Platteville (G)
University of Wisconsin–River Falls (U, G, NC)
University of Wisconsin–Stevens Point (U, G)
University of Wisconsin–Whitewater (U, G)
University of Wyoming (G)
University System of Georgia (U)
Utah State University (U, G)
Valdosta State University (U, G)
Virginia Polytechnic Institute and State University
(G)
Walden University (G)
Western Carolina University (U, G)
Western Illinois University (U, G)
Western Montana College of University of
Montana (U, NC)
Western Oregon University (U, G)

Technical writing

Alamance Community College (U)
American Institute for Computer Sciences (U)
Arizona State University (U)
Austin Community College (U)
Bellevue Community College (U)
Blinn College (U)
Brigham Young University (U)
Bristol Community College (U)
Cedarville University (U)
Cerro Coso Community College (U)
Charles Stewart Mott Community College (U)
Citrus College (U)
Clark College (U)
Cochise College (U)
College of Aeronautics (U)
College of Albemarle (U)
College of Southern Maryland (U)
College of West Virginia (U)
Columbia Basin College (U)
Columbus State Community College (U)
De Anza College (U)
Delaware Technical & Community College,
Stanton/Wilmington Campus (U)
Del Mar College (U)
Delta College (U)

Drake University (U)
East Carolina University (G)
Edison State Community College (U)
Embry-Riddle Aeronautical University (U)
Embry-Riddle Aeronautical University, Extended
Campus (U)
Finger Lakes Community College (U)
Florida International University (U)
Frostburg State University (U)
Genesee Community College (U)
Grantham College of Engineering (U)
Houston Community College System (U)
Independence Community College (U)
Judson College (U)
Judson College (U)
Lamar State College–Port Arthur (U)
Lansing Community College (U)
Linn-Benton Community College (U)
Louisiana State University at Alexandria (U)
Louisiana State University System (U)
Louisiana Tech University (U)
Mayland Community College (U)
Montana State University—Great Falls College of
Technology (U)
Montgomery College (U)
New York Institute of Technology (U)
North Arkansas College (U)
Northeastern University (U)
Northeast State Technical Community College
(U)
Northern Virginia Community College (U)
Northwestern Technical Institute (U)
Ohio State University–Mansfield Campus (U)
Oklahoma City Community College (U)
Oklahoma State University (U)
Oregon State University (U, G)
Park University (U)
Pitt Community College (U)
Redlands Community College (U)
Regis University (U)
Rensselaer Polytechnic Institute (G, NC)
Roane State Community College (U)
St. Petersburg Junior College (U)
Salt Lake Community College (U)
Sam Houston State University (U)
San Jacinto College District (U)
Seminole Community College (U)
South Puget Sound Community College (U)
Stanly Community College (U)
Stephens College (U)
Strayer University (U)
Terra State Community College (U)
Texas A&M University–Texarkana (U)
Texas State Technical College (U)
Texas Tech University (U, NC)
Tompkins Cortland Community College (U)
University of Alaska Fairbanks (U)
University of California, Berkeley (U)
University of California Extension (U)
University of California, Los Angeles (G)
University of Colorado at Denver (U)
University of Denver (G)
University of Findlay (U)
University of Illinois at Urbana–Champaign (U)
University of Kansas (U, NC)
University of Maine (U)
University of Massachusetts Lowell (U)
University of Minnesota, Crookston (U)
University of Minnesota, Twin Cities Campus (U)
University of Missouri–Columbia (U)
University of Nebraska–Lincoln (U)
University of New Mexico (U, G)
University of North Texas (U)
University of South Dakota (U)
University of Southern Mississippi (U)
University of Tennessee (U)
University of Texas at Austin (U)
University of Washington (U)

University of Wisconsin Extension (U)
University System of Georgia (U)
Vermont Technical College (U)
Virginia Polytechnic Institute and State Univers.
(U)
Washington State University (U)
Western Illinois University (U)
William Paterson University of New Jersey (NC)

Telecommunications

Bellevue Community College (U)
Bossier Parish Community College (U)
California State University, Chico (G)
Central Missouri State University (U, G, NC)
Cerritos College (U)
Cerro Coso Community College (U)
Champlain College (U)
Chestnut Hill College (G)
City University (U)
De Anza College (U)
East Carolina University (U, G)
Fort Hays State University (U)
Golden Gate University (U)
Instituto Tecnológico y de Estudios Superiores de
Monterrey, Campus Monterrey (U)
Keller Graduate School of Management (G)
Lenoir Community College (U)
Michigan State University (U, G)
National Technological University (G, NC)
New York Institute of Technology (U)
Oklahoma State University (G)
Rensselaer Polytechnic Institute (G, NC)
Rochester Institute of Technology (U, G)
Salt Lake Community College (U)
Southern Methodist University (G)
State University of New York Empire State
College (U)
Stevens Institute of Technology (G)
Temple University (U, G)
Texas Tech University (U, NC)
University of California, Berkeley (U)
University of California Extension (U)
University of Colorado at Boulder (G, NC)
University of Dallas (G)
University of Denver (G)
University of Maryland University College (G)
University of New Mexico (U, G)
University of San Francisco (U)
University of Southern Mississippi (G)
University of Texas at El Paso (U, G, NC)
University of Texas System (G)
Western Governors University (U, NC)
Western Illinois University (G)
Westmoreland County Community College (U)

Theological studies

Anderson University (G)
Andrews University (U, G)
Assemblies of God Theological Seminary (G, NC)
Atlantic University (G, NC)
Azusa Pacific University (U, G)
Barclay College (U)
Bethany College of the Assemblies of God (U)
Calvary Bible College and Theological Seminary
(U)
Central Baptist Theological Seminary (G, NC)
Cincinnati Bible College and Seminary (U)
Clackamas Community College (U)
Columbia International University (U, G, NC)
Covenant Theological Seminary (G, NC)
Crown College (U, G)
Dallas Theological Seminary (G, NC)
David Lipscomb University (G)
Denver Seminary (G, NC)
Duquesne University (G)
Eastern Mennonite University (G)
Eugene Bible College (U, NC)
Florida Baptist Theological College (U, NC)

GEOGRAPHIC INDEX